The **Rough Guide** to

WITHDRAWN

Greece

written and researched by

Andrew Benson, Lance Chilton, Marc Dubin, Nick Edwards, Mark Ellingham, John Fisher, Geoff Garvey and Natania Jansz

with additional contributions by
Sarah Gear, Michael Haag, Sandy MacGillivray, George Pissalides and Miranda Rashidian

ROUGH
GUIDES

NEW YORK · LONDON · DELHI

www.roughguides.com

Contents

An Orthodox Nation
insert following p.312

Greek Cuisine insert
following p.616

Wild Greece insert
following p.1016

◄◄ Mountain village, Crete ◄ Roussanou Monastery, Meteora

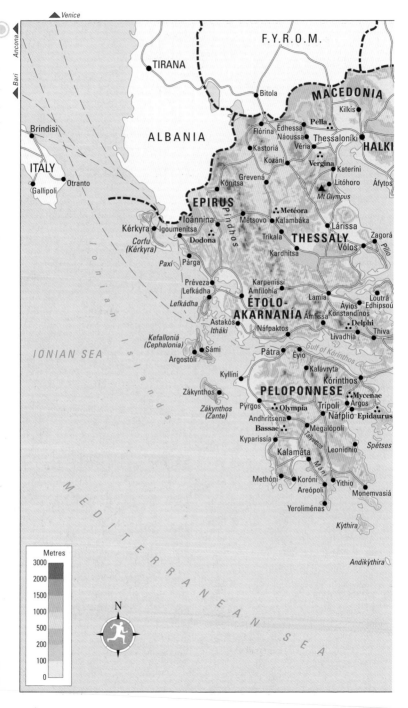

Venice
Ancona
Bari

F.Y.R.O.M.

TIRANA

Bitola

MACEDONIA

Kilkís

Pella

Brindisi

ALBANIA

Flórina Édhessa
Náoussa Thessaloníki
Kastoriá Véria

HALKI

Kozáni

Vergina Katerini

ITALY

Otranto

Grevená

Litóhoro Áfytos

Gallipoli

Kónitsa

Mt Olympus

EPIRUS

Métsovo Kalambáka

Metéora

Ioánnina

Lárissa

Zagorá

Kérkyra Igoumenítsa
Corfu
(Kérkyra)

Dodona

Trikala THESSALY

Pindhos

Kardhítsa

Vólos

Pílio

Paxí Párga

Préveza
Lefkádha

Karpeníssi
Amfilohía

Lamia

Loutrá
Edhipsoú

Lefkádha

ÉTOLO-
AKARNANÍA

Áyios
Amfissa Konstandínos

Astakós
Itháki

Náfpaktos

Delphi

Kefalloniá
(Cephalonia)

Livadhiá

Thiva

IONIAN SEA

Sámi

Pátra Éyio

Gulf of Kórinthos

Argostóli

Kalávryta

Kyllíni

Kórinthos

Zákynthos

PELOPONNESE

Mycenae

Náfplio Epidaurus

Zákynthos
(Zante)

Pýrgos Olympia

Tripoli Argos

Andhritsena

Bassae

Megalópoli

Spétses

Kyparissía

Leonidhio

Taïgetos

Kalamáta

Methóni Koróni
Areópoli

Yíthio

Mani

Monemvasiá

Yeroliménas

Kýthira

Ionian Islands

MEDITERRANEAN SEA

Andikýthira

Metres	
3000	
2000	
1500	
1000	
500	
200	
100	
0	

N

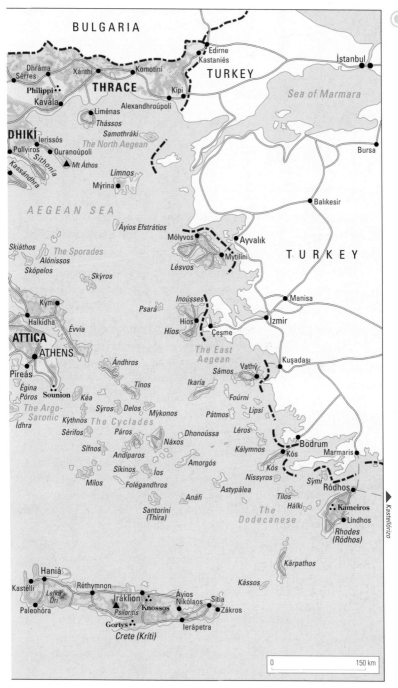

BULGARIA

Dhráma
Sérres
Philippi
Kavála
Xánthi
THRACE
Komotiní
Edirne
Kastaniés
İstanbul
TURKEY
Sea of Marmara
Kipi
Alexandhroúpoli
Liménas
Thássos
Samothráki
The North Aegean
DHIKÍ
Ierissós
Políyiros
Kassándhra
Sithonia
Ouranoúpoli
Mt Áthos
Bursa
Límnos
Mýrina

AEGEAN SEA
Áyios Efstrátios
Mólyvos
Ayvalık
Skiáthos
The Sporades
Alónissos
Skópelos
Skýros
Lésvos
Mytilíni
TURKEY
Balıkesir

Kými
Halkidha
Évvia
Psará
Inoússes
Híos
Híos
Çeşme
İzmir
Manisa
ATTICA
ATHENS
Ándhros
The East Aegean
Sámos
Vathý
Kuşadası
Pireás
Égina
Póros
Sounion
Kéa
Tínos
Ikaría
Idhra
The Argo-Saronic
Kýthnos
Sýros
Delos
Mýkonos
The Cyclades
Sérifos
Páros
Sífnos
Andíparos
Náxos
Síkinos
Íos
Mílos
Folégandhros
Santoríni
(Thíra)
Anáfi
Pátmos
Lipsí
Léros
Dhonoússa
Kálymnos
Kós
Amorgós
Kós
Astypálea
Nissyros
Tilos
Hálki
Sými
Ródhos
The Dodecanese
Bodrum
Marmaris
Kameiros
Lindhos
Rhodes
(Ródhos)
Kastellórizo

Kárpathos
Kássos
Haniá
Kastélli
Lefká Óri
Réthymnon
Iráklion
Knossos
Áyios Nikólaos
Sitía
Zákros
Paleohóra
Psiloritis
Gortys
Ierápetra
Crete (Kríti)

0   150 km

5

Introduction to

Greece

With over sixty inhabited islands and a territory that stretches from the south Aegean Sea to the Balkan countries, Greece offers enough to fill months of travel. The historic sites span four millennia, encompassing both the legendary and the obscure, where a visit can still seem like a personal discovery. Beaches are parcelled out along a convoluted coastline equal to France's in length, and islands range from backwaters where the boat calls twice a week to resorts as cosmopolitan as any in the Mediterranean.

Modern Greece is the result of extraordinarily diverse **influences**. Romans, Arabs, Latin Crusaders, Venetians, Slavs, Albanians, Turks, Italians, not to mention the Byzantine Empire, have been and gone since the time of Alexander the Great. All have left their mark: the Byzantines in countless churches and monasteries; the Venetians in impregnable fortifications in the Peloponnese; and other Latin powers, such as the Knights of Saint John and the Genoese, in imposing castles across the northern and eastern Aegean. Equally obvious is the heritage of four centuries of Ottoman Turkish rule which, while universally derided, contributed substantially to Greek music, cuisine, language and the way of life. Significant, and still-existing, minorities – Vlachs, Muslims, Catholics, Jews, Gypsies – have also helped to forge the hard-to-define but resilient **Hellenic identity**, which has kept alive the people's sense of themselves throughout their turbulent history. With no indigenous ruling class or formal Renaissance period to impose superior models of taste or patronize the arts, medieval Greek peasants, fishermen and shepherds created a vigorous and truly popular culture, which found expression in the songs and dances, costumes, embroidery, carved furniture and the white cubist houses of popular imagination. During the last few decades much of this has disappeared under the impact of Western consumer values, relegated to museums at best, but recently the country's architectural and musical heritage in particular have undergone a renaissance, with buildings rescued from dereliction and performers reviving, to varying degrees, half-forgotten musical traditions.

Of course there are also formal cultural activities: **museums** that shouldn't be missed, magnificent medieval mansions and **castles**, as well as the great **ancient sites** dating from the Neolithic, Bronze Age, Minoan, Classical, Hellenistic, Roman and Byzantine eras. Greece

▶ The Parthenon, Athens

Fact file

• Greece is, after Cyprus, the easternmost member of the EU, with a **surface area** of 131,957 square kilometres (50,949 square miles) divided into 51 provinces. No other country, with the exceptions of Indonesia and the Philippines, has so much of its territory in the form of islands. The **population** is overwhelmingly **Greek-speaking** and 96 percent are **Greek Orthodox** in religious affiliation, though there are noticeable Catholic, Sunni Muslim, Jewish, Armenian and evangelical Christian minorities, plus pockets of Turkish-, Romany- and Macedonian-speakers. Well over half the population live in urban areas.

• Per "native" population of 10.4 million, Greece has the highest proportion of **immigrants** in Europe – officially 800,000, but potentially 1.2 million, two-thirds of these Albanian.

• Since 1974 Greece has been a **parliamentary republic**, with the president as head of state, and a 300-seat, single-chamber parliament led by the prime minister. PASOK, the (approximately) social-democratic party, governed for 19 of the 23 years after 1981, finally being ousted in March 2004 by the centre-right Néa Dhimokratía party. There are also two small communist parties which between them typically pick up 8–10% of the vote.

• **Tourism** is the country's main foreign-currency earner. **Shipping**, which once occupied second place, is in crisis, replaced by **agricultural products** such as olive oil and olives, citrus, wine and raisins.

hosts some excellent summer **festivals** too, bringing international theatre, dance and musical groups to perform at ancient theatres, as well as castle courtyards and more contemporary venues in coastal and island resorts.

But the call to cultural duty will never be too overwhelming on a Greek holiday. The **hedonistic pleasures** of languor and warmth – going lightly dressed, swimming in balmy seas at dusk, talking and drinking under the stars – are just as appealing. Despite recent improvements to the tourism "product", Greece is still essentially a land

> **Not to be missed are Greece's great ancient sites and medieval castles**

for good-humoured sybarites, not for those who crave orthopedic mattresses, faultless plumbing, Cordon Bleu cuisine and obsequious service. Except at the growing number of luxury facilities in new or restored buildings, hotel and pension rooms can be box-like; Greek food at its best is fresh, abundant and uncomplicated.

The Greek people

To attempt an understanding of the Greek people, it's useful to realize just how recent and traumatic were the events that created the modern state and **national character** – the latter a complex blend of extroversion and pessimism, which cannot be accounted for merely by Greece's position as a natural bridge between Europe and

▼ Olive grove

The Evil Eye

Belief in the Evil Eye (in Greek, simply *to máti* or "the Eye") is pan-Mediterranean and goes at least as far back as Roman times, but nowhere has it hung on so tenaciously as in Greece (and neighbouring coastal Turkey). In a nutshell, whenever something attractive, valuable or unusual – an infant, a new car, a prized animal – becomes suddenly, inexplicably indisposed, it is assumed to be *matiasméno* or "eyed". Blue-eyed individuals are thought most capable of casting this spell, always unintentionally or at least unconsciously

(unlike *máyia* or wilful black magic). The diagnosis is confirmed by discreet referral to a "wise woman", who is also versed in the proper counter-spell. But prevention is always better than cure, and this involves two main strategies. When admiring something or someone, the admirer – blue-eyed or otherwise – must mock-spit (*"phtoo, phtoo, phtoo!"*) to counteract any stirrings of envy which, according to anthropologists, are the root-cause of the Eye. And the proud owners or parents will protect the object of admiration in advance with a blue amulet, hung about the baby's/animal's neck or the car's rear-view mirror, or even painted directly onto a boat-bow.

the Middle East. Until the early decades of the twentieth century many parts of Greece were under Ottoman (or in the case of the Dodecanese, Italian) rule. Meanwhile, numerous Greek Orthodox lived in Asia Minor, Egypt, western Europe and in the northern Balkans. The Balkan Wars of 1912–13, Greece's 1917–18 World War I involvement fighting Bulgaria, the Greco–Turkish war of 1919–22 and the organized **population exchanges** – essentially regulated ethnic cleansing – which followed each of these conflicts had sudden, profound effects. Worse was to come during World War II, and its aftermath of civil war between the Communists and the UK- and US-backed Nationalist government forces. The viciousness of this period found a later echo in nearly seven years of military dictatorship under the colonels' junta between 1967 and 1974.

Such memories of misrule, diaspora and catastrophe (including frequent, devastating earthquakes) remain uncomfortably close for many Greeks, despite three decades of democratic stability and the country's absorption into the EU. The poverty of, and enduring paucity of opportunity in, their homeland long frustrated talented and resourceful Greeks, many of whom **emigrated**. Those who stayed were lulled, until the late 1980s, by a civil-service-driven full-employment policy which resulted in the lowest jobless rate in western Europe. The downside of this was a staggering lack of worker initiative and a burgeoning public deficit, but official attempts to impose a more austere economic line are still often met by strikes. Since the early 1990s, Greece has become fully integrated into the Western economy, privatization and competition have demolished state monopolies, and inevitably growing disparities in wealth have appeared.

Outside the public sector, the meticulousness of Greek craft-workers is legendary, even if their values and skills took a back seat to the demands of crisis and profiteering when the evacuation of Asia Minor and the rapid 1950s depopulation

▼ Church overlooking the sea, Kefalloniá

of rural villages prompted the graceless **urbanization** of Athens and other cities. Amidst the often superficial sophistication that resulted, it's easy to forget the nearness of the village past and stubbornly lingering Third World attributes. You may find, for example, that buses operate with Germanic efficiency, but ferries sail with an unpredictability little changed since the time of Odysseus.

Social attitudes, too, have undergone a sea-change as Greece adapted to mass tourism and the modern world. The encounter was painful and at times destructive, as the values of a rural, conservative society have been irrevocably lost. Though younger Greeks are flexible as they rake the proceeds into the till, at least in tourist areas, visitors still need to be sensitive in their behaviour towards the older generation. The mind boggles imagining the reaction of black-clad elders to nudism, or even scanty clothing, in a country where the Orthodox church was, until the 1990s, an all-but-established faith and the self-appointed guardian of national identity. Although senior clerics have since the millennium almost completely depleted a huge reservoir of respect with regressive stances on a number of social issues, and a string of literally ungodly scandals throughout 2004–05, even the most cynical, worldly young Greeks – who never otherwise set foot in a church – are still likely to be married, buried and have their children baptized with Orthodox rites.

Where to go

Sprawling, polluted **Athens** is an obligatory, almost unavoidable introduction to Greece: home to over a third of the population, on first acquaintance a nightmare for many, but also – as Greeks themselves often joke – *tó megálo horió*: the largest "village" in the country. It also offers the widest range of cultural diversions, from museums to concerts; the best-stocked shops; some of the most accomplished restaurants and – due to its hosting of the 2004 summer Olympics – a noticeably improved infrastructure. **Thessaloníki**, the metropolis of the North, after years of playing provincial second fiddle to the capital, has emerged in its own right as a stimulating, cutting-edge place with restaurants and nightlife to match Athens', Byzantine monuments compensating for a lack of "ancient" ones, and – among the inhabitants – a tremendous capacity for enjoying life. In all honesty, there are no other "world class" cities in Greece. The mainland shows its best side in the well-preserved ruins of **Corinth**, **Olympia** and **Delphi** (plus the Athenian **Parthenon**), the frescoed and mosaiced Byzantine churches and monasteries at **Mount**

Wayside shrines

Throughout Greece you'll see, by the side of the road, small shrines or *proskynitária* which usually hold a saint's icon, an oil lamp, a few floatable wicks and a box of matches. Unlike in Latin America, they don't necessarily mark the spot where someone met their end in a motoring accident (though just occasionally they do); typically they were erected by a family or even one individual in fulfilment of a vow or *támma* to a specific saint to reciprocate for any favours granted, in particular being spared death in a road mishap. *Proskynitária* come in various sizes and designs, from spindly, derrick-like metal constructions to sumptuous, gaily painted models of small cathedrals in marble and plaster which you can practically walk into. Often they indicate the presence of a larger but less convenient (and often locked) church off in the countryside nearby, dedicated to the same saint, and act as a substitute shrine where the devout wayfarer can pay reverence to the icon it contains.

Áthos, **Metéora**, **Ósios Loukás**, **Kastoriá** and **Mystra**, the massive fortified towns of **Monemvasiá**, **Náfplio**, **Koróni** and **Methóni**, the distinctive architecture of **Zagóri**, **Pílio** and the **Máni**, and the long, sandy **beaches** on the Peloponnesian and Epirot west coast. Perhaps more surprisingly, the mainland mountains offer some of the best and least-exploited hiking, rafting, canyoning and skiing in southeastern Europe.

Out in the Aegean or Ionian seas, you're even more spoilt for choice. Perhaps the best strategy for initial visits is to sample assorted islands from contiguous archipelagos – Crete, the Dodecanese, the Cyclades and the northeast Aegean are all reasonably well connected with each other, though the Sporades, Argo-Saronic and Ionian groups offer limited (or no) possibilities for island-hopping. If time and money are short, the best place to head for is well-preserved **Ídhra** in the Argo-Saronic Gulf, just a short ride from Pireás (the main port of Athens), but an utterly different place once the day-cruises have gone. Among the Cyclades, cataclysmically volcanic **Santoríni (Thíra)** and **Mýkonos** with its perfectly preserved harbour-town rank as must-see spectacles, but fertile, mountainous **Náxos**, dramatically cliff-girt **Amorgós** or gently rolling **Sífnos** have life more independent of cruise-ship tourism and seem more amenable to long stays. **Crete** could (and does) fill an entire Rough Guide to itself, but the highlights have to be **Knossos** and the nearby **archeological museum** in Iráklion, the other Minoan palaces at **Phaestos** and **Ayía Triádha**, and the west in general – the proud city of **Haniá**, with its hinterland extending to the relatively unspoilt southwest coast, reachable via the fabled **Samarian gorge**. **Rhodes**, with its unique old town, is capital of the Dodecanese, but picturesque, Neoclassical **Sými** opposite, and

▼ Greengrocer's shop, Corfu

austere **Pátmos**, the island of Revelations, are far more manageable. It's easy to continue north via **Híos**, with its striking medieval architecture, to balmy, olive-cloaked **Lésvos**, perhaps the most traditional of all islands in way of life. The Ionian islands are – probably more than any other spot except Crete, Kós and Rhodes – package-holiday territory, but if you're exiting Greece towards Italy by all means stop off at **Corfu** to at least savour the Venetian-style main town, which along with neighbouring **Paxí** islet survived severe 1953 earthquake damage.

When to go

Most places and people are far more agreeable, and resolutely Greek, outside the **peak period** of early July to the end of August, when soaring temperatures, plus crowds of foreigners and locals alike, can be overpowering. You won't miss out on **warm weather** if you come in **June or September**, excellent times almost everywhere but particularly in the islands. An exception to this pattern, however, is the north-mainland coast – notably the Halkidhikí peninsula – and the islands of Samothráki and Thássos, which only really cater to visitors during **July and August**. In **October** you will almost certainly hit a stormy spell, especially in western Greece or in the mountains, but for most of

> **The mainland mountains offer some of the best hiking, rafting and skiing in southeastern Europe**

that month the "little summer of Áyios Dhimítrios" (the Greek equivalent of **Indian summer**) prevails, and the southerly Dodecanese and Crete are extremely pleasant. Autumn in general is beautiful; the light is softer, the sea often balmier than the air and the colours subtler.

December to March are the coldest and least reliably sunny months, though even then there are many crystal-clear, fine days, and the glorious lowland flowers begin to bloom very early in spring. The more northerly latitudes and high altitudes of course endure far colder and wetter conditions, with the mountains themselves under snow from November to May. The **mildest winter** climate is found on Rhodes, or in the southeastern parts of Crete. As spring slowly warms up, **April** is still uncertain, though superb for wild flowers, green landscapes and photography; by **May** the weather is more generally predictable, and Crete, the Peloponnese, the Ionian islands and the Cyclades are perhaps at their best, even if the sea is still a little cool for swimming. Note, however, that these are the

The períptero

The *períptero* or pavement kiosk is a quintessentially Greek institution. They originally began as a government-sponsored employment scheme for wounded veterans of the Balkan Wars and World War I; the concessions are jealously guarded by their descendants or sold on for tidy sums. Positioned on platíes and strategic

thoroughfares all over Greece, they keep long hours and contribute considerably to the air of public street-safety after dark. If you are lost, the *períptero* is typically the first place to go for directions, and they usually know what you're looking for. Their stock in trade is predictable: sweets, bagged nuts, tissues, newspapers, magazines, bus tickets, shaving needs, key-rings with football-team logos, cigarettes, pens and pencils, (often heat-damaged) photo film, plus cold drinks and yoghurts. Most of them used to have at least one telephone, with a queue of customers waiting their turn to shout down a crackly line, either across town or across the globe. Now, few kiosks sport even a card-phone, but they're still one of the best places to buy a top-up card for your Greek pay-as-you-go mobile.

historical patterns as observed until the late 1990s; thanks to global warming, recent years have seen erratic climate, with unusually cold Mays, warm Octobers, very wet (though not always cold) winters, plus much earlier spring flowering.

Other factors that affect ideal timing for Greek travels have to do with the level of tourism and the amenities provided. Late May, especially half-term week in the UK, can be surprisingly busy. Service standards, particularly in tavernas, slip under peak-season pressure, and room rates top out from mid-July to August 23 (as well as during Easter or Christmas

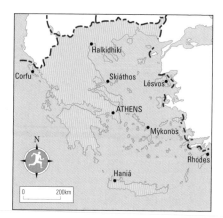

week). If you can only visit during midsummer, reserve a package well in advance, or plan your itinerary off the beaten track: you might for example explore the less obvious parts of the Peloponnese and the northern mainland, or island-hop with an eye for the remoter places.

Out of season, especially between late October and late April, you have to contend with reduced ferry and plane services (and nonexistent hydrofoil or catamaran departures), plus fairly skeletal facilities when you arrive. You will, however, find reasonable service on main routes and at least one hotel and taverna open in the port or main town of all but the tiniest isles. On the mainland, winter travel poses no special difficulties except, of course, in mountain villages either cut off by snow or (at weekends especially) monopolized by avid Greek skiers.

Average temperatures (°F) and rainfall

	Jan °F Rain			Mar °F Rain			May °F Rain			July °F Rain			Sept °F Rain			Nov °F Rain		
	Max	Min	Days	Max	Min	Days	Max	Min	Days	Max	Min	Days	Max	Min	Days	Max	Min	Days
Athens																		
	54	44	13	60	46	10	76	60	9	90	72	2	84	66	4	65	52	12
Crete (Haniá)																		
	60	46	17	64	48	11	76	56	5	86	68	0	82	64	3	70	54	10
Cyclades (Mýkonos)																		
	58	50	14	62	52	8	72	62	5	82	72	0.5	78	68	1	66	58	9
North Greece (Halkidhikí)																		
	50	36	7	59	44	9	77	58	10	90	70	4	83	64	5	60	47	9
Ionians (Corfu)																		
	56	44	13	62	46	10	74	58	6	88	70	2	82	64	5	66	52	12
Dodecanese (Rhodes)																		
	58	50	15	62	48	7	74	58	2	86	70	0	82	72	1	68	60	7
Sporades (Skiáthos)																		
	55	45	12	58	47	10	71	58	3	82	71	0	75	64	8	62	53	12
East Aegean (Lésvos)																		
	54	42	11	60	46	7	76	60	6	88	70	2	82	66	2	64	50	9

34

things not to miss

It's not possible to see everything that Greece has to offer in one trip – and we don't suggest you try. What follows is a selective taste of the country's highlights: outstanding buildings and ancient sites, natural wonders and colourful festivals. They're arranged in five colour-coded categories, which you can browse through to find the very best things to see and experience. All highlights have a page reference to take you straight into the guide, where you can find out more.

01 **Sámos** Page **883** • Despite recent fires, Sámos remains arguably the most verdant and beautiful of the east Aegean islands.

02 Metéora Page **399** • The exquisite Byzantine monasteries of Metéora, perched atop pinnacles of rock, are arguably mainland Greece's most extraordinary sight.

03 Loggerhead sea turtle Page **1051** • The Ionian islands harbour one of the Mediterranean's main concentrations of the endangered loggerhead sea turtle.

04 Ósios Loukás mosaics Page **336** • Decorated with vivid mosaics, Ósios Loukás ranks as one of Greece's finest Byzantine buildings.

06 Víkos gorge Page **434** • A hike through or around the Víkos gorge is likely to be one of the highlights of a visit to the Zagóri region.

05 Ídhra Page **594** • Ídhra's perfect horseshoe-shaped harbour is surrounded by grand eighteenth-century mansions.

08 **Lion Gate, Mycenae** Page **212** • Imposing relief lions guard the main entrance to the Citadel of Mycenae.

07 **Nightlife** Page **70** • The after-dark scene in the most popular island resorts is lively, varied and long.

09 **Mount Pílio** Page **371** • Mount Pílio peninsula has it all: lush countryside, excellent beaches, characterful villages and some superb hiking trails.

10 Tower houses in the Máni Page 252 •
Designed for pitched battles at close quarters, these medieval tower houses are a relic of internecine warfare in Greece's far south.

12 Knossos palace, Crete
Page **721** • The most restored, vividly coloured and ultimately the most exciting of Crete's Minoan palaces.

14 Temple of Poseidon, Cape Soúnio Page 184 •
Dramatically set on a cliff above the cape, the evocative Temple of Poseidon is a familiar landmark to boats at sea.

11 Volcano floor, Níssyros
Page **837** • No stay on Níssyros would be complete without a visit to the island's dormant volcano. Shown is the Stéfanos crater.

13 Windsurfing off Vassilikí, Lefkádha Page
1028 • Located in a vast, cliff-flanked bay, Vassilikí is one of Europe's biggest windsurfing centres.

15 Fortifications of Acrocorinth Page 205 •
Acrocorinth is a huge, barren rock crowned by a great medieval fortress.

16 Monastery of Ayíou Ioánnou Theológou, Pátmos

Page **871** • Built in honour of St John the Divine, this huge monastery is a warren of interconnecting courtyards, chapels, stairways, arcades, galleries and roof terraces.

17 Samarian Gorge, Crete

Page **776** • The magnificent Samarian Gorge is the longest in Europe.

19 Monemvasiá

Page **236** • The heavily fortified medieval town of Monemvasiá shelters on the flank of its island-like rock.

18 Mount Olympus

Page **507** • Believed by the ancient Greeks to be the home of the gods, Mount Olympus is Greece's highest and most magical mountain.

20 **Préspa lakes** Page **524** • The eerily beautiful Préspa lakes are a haven for birds and other wildlife.

21 **Kérkyra (Corfu) old town** Page **1004** • With its elegant Venetian architecture and fine museums, Corfu's capital is the cultural heart of the Ionians.

22 **Lindos acropolis, Rhodes** Page **809** • From the Hellenistic acropolis of Lindos, high above the modern village, you look north along the length of Rhodes island.

21

24 Delphi: the Tholos Page 339 • Delphi, site of the famous oracle, was believed by the ancient Greeks to be the centre of the earth.

23 Haniá Old Town waterfront, Crete Page 765 • Haniá displays haunting vestiges of its Venetian and Ottoman past.

25 Beaches and watersports Page 81 • Greece's extensive coast provides a multitude of opportunities for getting into the water, or just lying next to it.

26 Herodes Atticus Theatre Page 125 • The ancient Roman Herodes Atticus Theatre is a major venue for music and dance concerts during the summer Hellenic Festival.

27 Koróni town and port

Page **292** • Beautiful Koróni town commands sweeping views across the Messenian Gulf.

28 View over

Firá Page **693** • The island capital of Firá is one of several villages that teeter at the edge of Thíra's caldera cliff.

29 Mystra

Page **268** • The Byzantine town of Mystra is the most exciting and dramatic site in the Peloponnese.

30 Váï Beach,

Crete Page **749** • A superb beach, fringed by a wild date-palm grove.

31 Harbour, Sými Page **823** • The mansions of Sými's picturesque harbour, built with wealth from the sponge trade, are part of an architecturally protected area.

32 Náfplio Page **217** •
Elegant, Venetian-flavoured Náfplio covers a peninsula in the Argolid Gulf, culminating in the massive Palamídhi fortress.

34 Osíou Grigoríou monastery, Mount Áthos Page **556** • Dramatically set Osíou Grigoríou is one of twenty monasteries in the "monks' republic" of Mount Áthos.

33 Acropolis Page **117** • Dominating Athens, the Acropolis is as fascinating as it is famous.

Basics

Basics

Getting there

It's two thousand miles or so from the UK and Ireland to Athens, so for most visitors flying is the only viable option. There are direct flights to a variety of Greek destinations from all major British airports; journey time is three-and-a-half to four-and-a-half hours. Road or rail alternatives from the UK take a minimum of three days, and are only worth considering if you plan to visit Greece as part of an extended trip through Europe.

Only two carriers currently fly direct to Greece from North America, so most North Americans travel via a European hub for the onward connecting flight. You may discover that it's cheaper to arrange the final leg of the journey yourself; such onward flights from the UK are detailed on pp.28-29. It's fairly easy to track down flights from Australia to Athens, less so from New Zealand.

Airfares to Greece from Europe and North America depend on the **season**, with the highest applicable from June to early September (plus Easter week); fares drop during the "shoulder" seasons – April/May and late September/October – and you'll get the best prices during the low season, November to March (excluding Christmas and New Year weeks which count as peak season). Australian and New Zealand fares have their low season from mid-January to the end of February and October/November; high season is mid-May to August, plus December to mid-January; and shoulder season the rest of the year.

You can often cut costs by going through a **specialist/discount flight agent**, who may also offer a range of other travel-related services such as travel insurance, rail passes, car rentals, tours and the like. From the UK, you may find it more cost-effective to pick up a **package deal**, with accommodation included, from one of the tour operators listed on pp.30–32.

Booking flights online

Even if you don't end up actually buying your ticket online, a web search will clue you up on what the prevailing published economy fares are. However, the airlines' websites themselves tend to give you a choice of only nonchangeable/nonrefundable and full economy fares – for the numerous options in between, you'll have to ring them, or consult a general discount travel site. The cheapest fares require a minimum stay of three days away, and over a Saturday night, with a typical maximum period of thirty or sixty days. They also make you liable to penalties (including total loss of ticket value) if you miss your outbound departure or change your return date. Sometimes student/youth tickets are available to those under 26, as are "Senior" or "Golden" fares for those over 60.

Some general travel sites like Expedia or Travelocity offer "special bargain" fares – the problem with some of these is you don't get to see the scheduling, or the airlines used, until after you've bought the ticket, and there have also been reported instances of so-called "fare loading" – instances in which you irrevocably pay for a promised fare only to be told "no longer available" and end up with a more expensive ticket.

Online booking agents and general travel sites

Ⓦ **www.cheapflights.co.uk** (UK & Ireland), Ⓦ **www.cheapflights.com** (US), Ⓦ **www.cheapflights.ca** (Canada) or Ⓦ **www.cheapflights.com.au** (Australia & New Zealand) Not a booking site itself, but maintains links to the travel agents offering the deals.

Ⓦ **www.cheaptickets.com** Discount flight specialists (US only).

Ⓦ **www.etn.nl/discount.htm** A hub of consolidator and discount agent web links, maintained by the nonprofit European Travel Network.

Ⓦ **www.expedia.co.uk** (UK & Ireland), Ⓦ **www.expedia.com** (US) or Ⓦ **www.expedia.ca** (Canada)

Discount airfares, all-airline search engine and daily deals.

Ⓦ **www.geocities.com/thavery2000** An extensive list of airline websites and US toll-free numbers.

Ⓦ **www.kelkoo.co.uk** Useful UK-only price-comparison site, checking several sources of low-cost flights (and other goods and services) according to specific criteria.

Ⓦ **www.lastminute.com** (UK & Ireland), Ⓦ www .lastminute.com.au (Australia) or Ⓦ www .lastminute.co.nz (New Zealand) Good holiday-package and flight-only deals available at very short notice.

Ⓦ **www.opodo.co.uk** Popular and reliable source of cheap UK airfares. Owned by, and run in conjunction with, nine major European airlines.

Ⓦ **www.orbitz.com** (US only) Comprehensive web travel source, with the usual flight, car hire and hotel deals but also great follow-up customer service.

Ⓦ **www.priceline.co.uk** or Ⓦ **www.priceline .com** Bookings from the UK/US only. Name-your-own-price auction website that can knock around forty percent off standard website fares. You can't choose the airline or flight times (although you do specify dates) and the tickets are nonrefundable, nontransferable and nonchangeable.

Ⓦ **www.skyauction.com** Bookings from the US only. Auctions tickets and travel packages using a "second bid" scheme. The best strategy is to bid the maximum you're willing to pay, since if you win you'll pay just enough to beat the runner-up regardless of your maximum bid.

Ⓦ **www.travelocity.co.uk** (UK & Ireland), Ⓦ www .travelocity.com (US) or Ⓦ www.travelocity.ca (Canada) Destination guides, hot web fares and deals for car rental, accommodation and lodging as well as fares.

Ⓦ **www.travelselect.com** A subsidiary of lastminute.com (see above) that is useful and fairly easy to use, but without most of the guff and banner adverts of the better-known sites.

Ⓦ **www.travelshop.com.au** Australian website offering discounted flights, packages, insurance and online bookings.

Ⓦ **www.travel.co.nz** Comprehensive online travel company, with discounted fares.

Ⓦ **www.zuji.com.au** Destination guides, hot fares and great deals for car rental, accommodation and lodging.

Connections at Athens airport

Missing connections at Athens airport is a distinct possibility, due to the airport's enormous size (though a few well-concealed lifts for luggage trolleys between arrival and departure levels help reduce stress). Airport rules stipulate a **minimum of 55 minutes** between your incoming flight's arrival and onward flight's departure, but some airlines insist on a minimum leeway of **90 minutes**. Given late arrivals (especially on Olympic) and lengthy security checks, try to observe this rule when buying tickets. Some, but not all, ticketing systems won't let you book an itinerary if the layover is too short.

Check your luggage through to your final Greek destination. Even if your inbound international flight is hideously late, you then stand a good chance of getting yourself to the end of your itinerary that day, even if your checked baggage only shows up the next day.

From the UK and Ireland

Increasingly, there is little difference between charter and scheduled flights to Greece in terms of penalties and prices; the main suriviving distinctions are that it's difficult to get more than a four-week travel period for charters, and in winter only scheduled flights are available. So far, the only no-frills airlines serving Greece are easyJet and Air Scotland; the main advantage in using them is the ability to secure economical one-way fares.

Although **Athens** remains the prime destination for cheap fares, there are also direct flights from Britain to **Thessaloníki**, **Kalamáta**, **Kavála** (for Thássos), **Vólos** (for Mount Pílio) and **Préveza (Áktio)** on the Greek mainland, and to the islands of **Crete**, **Rhodes**, **Kós**, **Corfu**, **Mýkonos**, **Zákynthos**, **Kefalloniá**, **Skiáthos**, **Sámos**, **Santoríni**, **Lésvos** and **Límnos**. And with any flight to Athens, you can buy a **domestic connecting flight** on Olympic or Aegean to one of almost three dozen additional Greek mainland and island airports.

The **charter flight season** for Greece operates from early May to late October. The main charter airlines which offer flight-only to Greece are Excel, Thomas Cook and TUI, though flight-only deals are rare at peak season.

You can pay dearly for direct services to the island of your choice, and for many destinations you may well find two-stop scheduled services via Athens are much cheaper.

Sample return fares at high season range from a reasonable £160–210 (Gatwick to Rhodes, Skiáthos or Corfu) up to a hefty £300 (Manchester to Kefalloniá, Gatwick to Lésvos).

The greatest variety of **flight destinations** tends to be from London Gatwick and Manchester, from where you should have a choice of most of the Greek regional airports listed above. Flying from elsewhere in Britain, or looking for last-minute discounts, you'll find options more limited, most commonly to Athens, Corfu, Rhodes, Kós and Crete.

Summer charters operate **from Dublin** to Rhodes, Crete, Corfu and often Zákynthos. A high-season flight-only charter from Dublin to an island costs upwards of €320 return.

The main advantages of **scheduled flights** are that they can usually be issued as e-tickets and can be valid for up to a year. The Greek national carrier Olympic Airlines, notorious as the least punctual airline in the skies and threatened with drastic restructuring as of writing, plus British Airways, currently constitute a duopoly in terms of direct "full service" to Greece from Britain. From Ireland, there's just Malev, which offers direct service to Athens from Dublin during summer only; otherwise you have to juggle various combinations from Belfast or Dublin via London on the likes of Aerlingus, bmibaby or Ryanair.

Specimen **return fares** between the UK and Athens range from £130 or so in the pit of winter to as much as £350 in August or at Easter (add £60 for Manchester departures) – and this range will only drift upward as fuel costs rise, with easyJet fares being as high as or higher than those on the "real" airlines in peak season. From the Irish Republic, fares range from €100 to €500 depending on time of year. If cost is an overriding factor, at peak travel seasons you may have little choice but to **go indirectly to Athens**, via intervening European cities. Travel websites will pick the cheapest routes and carriers on the day, but experience has shown that Alitalia, Lufthansa, Maersk Air and Air France have the most congenial schedules from the UK. All should get you to Athens in time for the last onward flight of the day to the largest islands.

Don't overlook the possibility of using **Frequent Flyer miles** to reach Athens. From the UK, direct flights on Olympic or

BA require 25,000 points, while many indirect carriers (such as Swiss/Lufthansa) only need in the region of 20,000 miles. From North America, most airlines require 70,000–80,000 miles. You'll still have to pay all taxes and charges (around £55 from Britain), but a major advantage is that these types of tickets are usually date-changeable for a small fee.

Scheduled airlines and routes

Aer Lingus UK ℡ 0845/ 084 4444, Republic of Ireland ℡ 0818/ 365 000, ⓦ www.aerlingus.com. Connecting service to major UK airports.

Air Scotland (Grecian Airways) ℡ 0141/222 2363, ⓦ www.air-scotland.com. Two flights weekly from Glasgow to Athens, March–Oct.

bmi ℡ 0870/ 607 0555, ⓦ www.flybmi.com. Code-share service with Olympic from Scotland and north of England to major UK airports.

bmibaby Republic of Ireland ℡ 01/435 0011, ⓦ www.bmibaby.com. Connecting service from Ireland to major UK airports.

British Airways UK ℡ 0870/850 9850, Republic of Ireland ℡ 1800 626 747, ⓦ www.ba.com. Up to three flights daily Heathrow to Athens; four weekly from Gatwick to Thessaloníki, and two weekly year-round from Gatwick to Iráklion.

easyJet ℡ 0870/ 000 000, ⓦ www.easyjet.com. One flight daily from both Luton and Gatwick to Athens.

Malev Republic of Ireland ⓦ www.malev.com. Three weekly to Athens from Dublin, May–Sept only.

Olympic Airlines ℡ 0870/606 0460, ⓦ www .olympic-airways.gr. Three daily from Heathrow to Athens, six weekly (morning) from Gatwick to Athens; five evenings weekly Gatwick to Thessaloníki; one to two weekly Manchester to Athens.

Ryanair Republic of Ireland ℡ 0818/303 030, ⓦ www.ryanair.com. Connecting service to London Stansted.

Flight and travel agents in the UK and Republic of Ireland

Avro ℡ 0870/ 458 2841, ⓦ www.avro.co.uk. Seat-only sales on flights to major holiday islands from most UK airports, on Monarch Airlines; easy-to-use website.

Excel Airways ℡ 0870/998 9898, ⓦ www.xl.com. Flights to almost every major charter-served airport in Greece, mostly from Gatwick and Manchester but often Glasgow, Birmingham and East Midlands; competitive fares, easy-to-use site.

Greece & Cyprus Travel Centre ☎0121/355 6955, 🖰www.greece-cyprus.co.uk. Competent flight consolidator for Olympic in particular; myriad fares to suit every need, including one-ways.

Joe Walsh Tours Dublin ☎01/676 0991, 🖰www .joewalshtours.ie. General budget fares and holidays agent.

McCarthys Travel Republic of Ireland ☎021/427 0127, 🖰www.mccarthystravel.ie. Established Irish travel agent now part of the Worldchoice chain of travel shops.

North South Travel ☎01245/608291, 🖰www .northsouthtravel.co.uk. Friendly, competitive flight agency, offering discounted fares worldwide – profits are used to support projects in the developing world, especially the promotion of sustainable tourism.

Rosetta Travel Belfast ☎028/9064 4996, 🖰www.rosettatravel.com. Flight and holiday agent, specializing in deals direct from Belfast.

STA Travel ☎0870/ 160 0599, 🖰www.statravel .co.uk. Worldwide specialists in low-cost flights and tours for students and under-26s.

Thomas Cook ☎0870/ 750 5711, 🖰www .thomascook.com. Good selection of flight-onlys to the biggest holiday islands from a half-dozen UK airports, though difficult to find in this dense site.

Thomson Flights ☎0800/000 747, 🖰www .thomsonflights.com. Limited flight-only deals to major holiday centres on TUI, its parent-company airline.

Trailfinders UK ☎020/7938 3939, 🖰www .trailfinders.com, Republic of Ireland ☎01/677 7888, 🖰www.trailfinders.ie. One of the best-informed and most efficient agents for independent travellers; branches in all the UK's largest cities, plus Dublin.

Packages and tours

Virtually every British mainstream **tour operator** includes Greece in its programme, though with many of the larger, cheap-and-cheerful outfits you'll find choices limited to the established resorts – notably the islands of Rhodes, Kós, Lésvos, Crete, Skiáthos, Zákynthos and Corfu, plus Tólo, Párga, Messinía province and the Halkidhikí peninsula on the mainland. If you buy one of these at a last-minute discount, especially in spring or autumn, you may find it costs little more than a flight – and you can use the accommodation included as much or as little as you want.

For a more low-key and genuinely Greek resort, however, book your holiday through

Greece
Let Manos
take you
there

visit **manos.co.uk**
call **08707 530 530** (quoting RG)
pop in to your
local ABTA travel agent

manos
H O L I D A Y S

one of the **specialist agencies** listed opposite. Most of these are fairly small-scale operations, providing competitively priced packages with flights (unless otherwise stated) and often more traditional village-based accommodation. They also make an effort to offer islands and corners of the mainland without overdeveloped tourist resorts. Such agencies tend to divide into two types: those which, like the major chains, contract a block of accommodation and flight seats (or even their own plane) for a full season; and an increasing number of bespoke agencies who tailor holidays at your request, making all transport and accommodation arrangements on the spot. These can work out somewhat more expensive, but the quality of flights and lodging is often correspondingly higher.

The **walking** holiday operators listed either run treks of ten to fifteen people plus guide, or provide customers with a printed, self-guiding itinerary, and arranged accommodation each day. Of late there are outfits organizing **other physical activities**, most notably swimming between the islands.

Sailing holidays involve small flotillas of four-to-eight-berth yachts, with changing anchorages each night, or are shore-based schools. Prices start at around £415 per person, flights included, in a group of four on a thirty-foot boat for a one-week flotilla. Alternatively, confident sailors can arrange to charter a "bare boat".

Villa or village accommodation holidays

Cachet Travel ☏ 020/8847 8700, ⓦ www
.cachet-travel.co.uk. Attractive range of villas and apartments, in the more unspoilt south and west of Crete, plus remote corners of Sámos.
CV Travel ☏ 0870/606 0013, ⓦ www.cvtravel
.co.uk. Quality villas, mostly on Corfu and Paxí but also Spétses, Lefkádha and Crete.
Direct Greece ☏ 0870/191 9244, ⓦ www
.direct-greece.co.uk. Moderately priced villas, apartments and restored houses on Rhodes, Hálki, Zákynthos, Kefalloniá, Lésvos, Corfu, Lefkádha and Crete, plus (on the mainland) Párga and the outer Máni.
Filoxenia ☏ 01653/617755, ⓦ www.filoxenia
.co.uk. Tailor-made itineraries and fly-drives to unspoilt areas of the mainland such as the Peloponnese and Macedonia; also special-interest holidays (such as scuba on Crete) and a few islands offered; flight arrangements on scheduled or charter airlines.
Greek Islands Club ☏ 020/8232 9780, ⓦ www
.greekislandsclub.com. Extremely high-quality villas throughout the Ionian and Sporades islands; also Pátmos, Thíra and Crete.
Greek Sun Holidays ☏ 01732/740317, ⓦ www
.greeksun.co.uk. Good-value package holidays in the Dodecanese, northeast Aegean and Cyclades; also tailor-made island-hopping itineraries.
Hidden Greece ☏ 020/7839 2553, ⓦ www
.hidden-greece.co.uk. Two bespoke agencies, each running for forty-plus years, have joined forces, arranging accommodation on and transport to 32 less-visited islands in the Cyclades, northeast Aegean and Dodecanese, as well as the Argolid and much of Crete.
Houses of Pelion ☏ 0870/199 9191, ⓦ www
.pelion.co.uk. Longest-running operator for the area, offering an excellent collection of inland cottages, houses and apartments on the Pagasitic Gulf coast from Lefókastro to Milína inclusive.
Island Wandering ☏ 0870/777 9944, ⓦ www
.islandwandering.com. Tailor-made island-hopping itineraries between most Greek archipelagos; deals range from prebooked accommodation only (this tends to be on the basic side) to mini-tours, with local ferry or air transfers arranged.
Laskarina Holidays ☏ 01444/880380, ⓦ www
.laskarina.co.uk. Top-end villas, quality hotels and restored houses on Skópelos, Alónissos, Hálki, Sými,

Tílos, Kálymnos, Télendhos, Léros, Lipsí, Pátmos, Ikaría and Sámos; excellent customer service.
Pure Crete ☏ 020/8760 0879, ⓦ www
.pure-crete.com. Characterful, converted cottages and farmhouses in western Crete.
Simpson Travel ☏ 020/8392 5852, ⓦ www
.simpson-travel.com. Villas, upmarket hotels and village "hideaways" on Crete, Corfu, Paxí and Meganíssi.
Sunvil Holidays ☏ 020/8568 4499, ⓦ www
.sunvil.co.uk/greece. Durable and consistently high-quality outfit specializing in upmarket hotels and villas in the Ionian islands, the Sporades, western Crete, Lésvos, Límnos, Sámos, Ikaría, Pátmos, the Peloponnese, the Pílio, Párga and Sývota. Also mainland fly-drives and walking holidays on Amorgós.
Tapestry Holidays ☏ 020/8235 7788, ⓦ www
.tapestryholidays.com. Quality villas, hotels and restoration inns on Kefalloniá, Corfu, Paxí, Skópelos, Itháki and Pílio.
Travel à la Carte ☏ 01635/201250, ⓦ www
.travelalacarte.co.uk. Established Corfu specialist, now diversified into beach and rural villas on Skiáthos, Hálki, Paxí and Sými as well.

Walking and swimming holidays

ATG Oxford ☏ 01865/315678, ⓦ www.atg-oxford
.co.uk. Somewhat pricey but high-standard guided walks on Crete and select Cyclades, the Máni and Zagóri on the mainland.
Exodus ☏ 0870/240 5550, ⓦ www.exodus.co.uk.
One-week treks on Évvia or the White Mountains of Crete; also sail-walk two-week tours through the Cyclades and one week multi-activity trips.
Explore Worldwide ☏ 01252/760 000, ⓦ www
.exploreworldwide.com. Treks on Crete and Kefalloniá; also island-wanderer trips, mostly in the Cyclades, mixing kaïki-sailing with light walking ashore.
Jonathan's Tours ☏ 00 33/561046447, ⓦ www
.jonathanstours.com. Family-run walking holidays on Crete (where Jonathan has 17 years' experience), Lésvos, Lefkádha and Zagóri; spring and autumn departures.
Ramblers Holidays ☏ 01707/331133, ⓦ www
.ramblersholidays.co.uk. Spring in Crete, Easter on Sámos, plus "Classical" (mainland) Greece.
Sherpa Expeditions ☏ 020/8577 2717, ⓦ www
.sherpa-walking-holidays.co.uk. Self-guiding and escorted 8- or 15-day outings on Crete, in Zagóri, and up Mount Olympus.
Swim Trek ☏ 020/8696 6220, ⓦ www.swimtrek
.com. 6-day swimming tours between and around Náxos, Páros and the minor Cyclades, the brainchild of Aussie cross-channel swimmer Simon Murie; May–Oct except Aug.

Walking Plus ☏ 020/8835 8303, ⊛ www
.walkingplus.co.uk. Enthusiastic Gilly and Robin
Cameron Cooper offer guided and self-guided off-
season walks on Náxos, Tínos and around Athens.
Walks Worldwide ☏ 01524/242000, ⊛ www
.walksworldwide.com. Escorted and self-guided
treks on Corfu, Mount Pílio, Náxos, the Máni plus
unusual routes on Mt Olympus.

Nature and wildlife holidays

Marengo Guided Walks ☏ 01485/532710,
⊛ www.marengowalks.com. Annually changing
programme of easy walks guided by ace botanist
Lance Chilton; typical one-week offerings may
include Sámos, Sými, central Pílio, northern Lésvos,
Crete, the Párga area, southern Peloponnese and
Thássos.
Naturetrek ☏ 01962/733051, ⊛ www.naturetrek
.co.uk. Fairly pricey but expertly led one- or two-week
natural history tours; past offerings include butterflies
of the southern mainland, springtime birds and flora
on Sámos, or wildlife of the Víkos Gorge, Mt Gamíla
and Mt Smólikas.

Sailing holidays

Nautilus Yachting ☏ 01732/867445, ⊛ www
.nautilus-yachting.co.uk Bareboat yacht charter out
of just about every marina in the country, including
some unusual choices like Sámos and Kalamáta.
Seafarer Cruising & Sailing ☏ 0870/442 2447,
⊛ www.seafarercruises.com. Argo-Saronic flotilla
specialists, also a Póros-based school.
Setsail Holidays ☏ 01787/310445, ⊛ www
.setsail.co.uk. Bareboat charters across the country,
flotillas from Skiáthos, and a sail-and-stay programme
based on Póros.
Sportif ☏ 01273/844919, ⊛ www.sportif-uk.com.
Windsurfing packages on Kós, Rhodes and Kárpathos.
Instruction clinics in conjunction with nearby
accommodation.
Sunsail ☏ 0870/777 0313, ⊛ www.sunsail.com.
Resort-based tuition in dinghy sailing, yachting and
windsurfing at three locations in Greece, mostly the
Ionians but including southern Pílio; also one- or two-
week flotilla sailings in the Ionians and Sporades and
good facilities for nonsailing children.
Templecraft ☏ 01732/867445, ⊛ www
.templecraft.com. Bareboat charters and flotilla
holidays in the Ionian archipelago.

Special-interest holidays

Good Practice ☏ 020/7928 7527, ⊛ www
.yogapractice.net. Rigorous *ashtanga* yoga
workshops, one or two weeks, early and late summer
at a remote hotel in the Peloponnese.

Peligoni Club ☏ 01243/511499, ⊛ www.peligoni
.com. Painting, yoga, Pilates and photography
workshops based in a scattered cluster of villas and
cottages in northern Zákynthos.
Saga Holidays ☏ 0800 096 0074, ⊛ www.saga
.co.uk. The UK's biggest and most established
specialist in tours and holidays aimed at older people.
Skyros Holidays ☏ 020/7267 4424, ⊛ www
.skyros.co.uk. Holistic health, fitness, crafts and
"personal growth" holidays at two centres on the
island of Skýros, as well as prestigious writers'
workshops tutored by big names.

By rail

Travelling **by train** from Britain or Ireland to
Greece takes two-and-a-half to three-and-
a-half days and fares work out vastly more
expensive than flights. It is not even possible
to buy a through rail ticket; however, with an
InterRail or Eurail Pass you can take in Greece
as part of a wider train trip around Europe.

The most practical route from Britain
crosses France and Italy before embarking
on the ferry from Bari or Brindisi to Pátra
(Patras). Book seats well in advance, especially in summer (for ferry information, see
the box on p.34).

Rail passes

An **InterRail pass** offers unlimited travel
(except for express-train supplements and
reservation fees) on a zonal basis with 28
European rail networks. These passes are
only available to **European residents**, and
come in over-26 and (cheaper) under-26
versions; you can save £5 by booking via the
InterRail website ⊛ www.inter-rail.co.uk.

To reach Greece from the UK you'll need a
one-month pass valid for at least two zones;
Greece falls in Zone G, together with Italy,
Turkey and Slovenia, plus many of the Italy–
Greece ferries (though not out of Venice).

For **North Americans, Australians and
New Zealanders**, a Eurail Pass (which
must be purchased before arrival in Europe)
will not pay for itself if you're planning to
stick to Greece. You stand a better chance
of getting your money's worth out of a Eurail
Flexipass, good for ten or fifteen days' travel
within a two-month period. Like the normal
pass, this comes in first-class, under-26/
second-class (Eurorail Youth Flexipass) and
group (Eurail Saver Flexipass) versions.

Rail contacts

UK and Ireland

The Man in Seat 61 ⓦ www.seat61.com. Named after British rail buff Mark Smith's favourite seat on the Eurostar, this noncommercial site expertly offers practical advice for planning a train journey from the UK to just about anywhere in Eurasia. You can't buy tickets here, but all the necessary links are provided.

Rail Europe UK ☎ 0870 584 8848, ⓦ www .raileurope.co.uk. Discounted rail fares for under-26s on a variety of European routes; also agents for InterRail and Eurostar.

North America

DER Travel ☎ 1-888 337-7350, ⓦ www.dertravel .com/rail. Eurail and many individual country passes.

European Rail Services Canada ☎ 1-800 205-5800 or 416/695-1211, ⓦ www.europeanrail services.com. Eurail and many individual country passes.

Rail Europe US ☎ 1-877 257-2887, Canada ☎ 1-800 361-RAIL, ⓦ www.raileurope.com. Official North American Eurail Pass agent; also sells most single-country passes.

Australia and New Zealand

CIT World Travel Australia ☎ 02/9267 1255 or 03/9650 5510, ⓦ www.cittravel.com.au. Eurail passes.

Rail Plus Australia ☎ 1300 555 003 or 03/9642 8644, ⓦ www.railplus.com.au. Sells Eurail passes.

Trailfinders Australia ☎ 02/9247 7666, ⓦ www .trailfinder.com.au. All European passes.

By car

If you have the time and inclination, **driving to Greece** can be a pleasant proposition. The most popular **route** is down through France and Italy to catch one of the Adriatic ferries; alternatives via Hungary, Romania and Bulgaria are to be avoided.

The fastest way to get across **to the Continent** is the **Eurotunnel** service via the Channel Tunnel; the alternative is one of the time-honoured **ferry** crossings. Eurotunnel operates shuttle trains 24 hours a day, for cars, motorcycles, buses and their passengers. **Rates** depend on the time of year, time of day and length of stay; it's cheaper to travel between 10pm and 6am, while the highest fares are reserved for weekend departures and returns in July and August. For current information, contact the **Euro-tunnel Customer Services Centre** at ☎ 0870 535 3535, ⓦ www.eurotunnel.com.

The traditional cross-Channel options for most travellers are the **ferry or hovercraft** links between Dover and Calais or Boulogne (the quickest and cheapest routes), Ramsgate and Dunkerque, or Newhaven and Dieppe. Irish drivers will prefer routes bypassing Britain, direct to Roscoff or Cherbourg, or from the southwest of England to St-Malo or Caen.

Ferry **prices** vary according to the time of year and, for motorists, the size of your car. The Dover–Calais/Boulogne runs, for example, start at about £245–340 open return for a car with up to five passengers, though prices can nearly double in peak season.

Via Italy

For motorists heading for western Greece or the Ionian islands, it has always made most sense to drive **via Italy** – and whatever your final destination, taking a ferry on the final leg makes for a more relaxed journey. Initial routes down to Italy through **France** and **Switzerland** are a question of personal taste. One of the most direct is Calais–Reims–Geneva–Milan and then down the Adriatic coast to one of the four Italian ports available. Even on the quickest autoroutes the journey will involve two overnight stops.

Most departures from Italy sail via the island of **Corfu**; you can stop over at no extra charge if you get this specified on your ticket. Generally, ferries run year-round, but with reduced frequencies from December to April. For more details see the box on p.34.

From any Italian port, a crossing to Pátra costs the same as to Igoumenítsa or Corfu; the **cheapest** of all the crossings is from Brindisi to Igoumenítsa. Drivers will discover that the extra cost in Italian motorway tolls and fuel exactly offsets the Brindisi or Bari route's savings over those from Ancona or Venice.

In summer, it is essential to **book tickets** a few weeks ahead. During the winter you can just turn up at the main ports (Brindisi and Ancona have the most reliable departures then), but it's still wise to book a few days in advance if you want a cabin. A few phone calls or Internet searches before leaving home are, in any case, advisable, as the range of fares is considerable.

Italy–Greece ferries

From Ancona ANEK to Pátra (21hr) usually via Igoumenítsa (15hr), 6 weekly most of year with; Minoan to Pátra (20hr 30min) via Igoumenítsa (14hr 30min), 5–6 weekly year-round; Superfast daily year-round to Igoumenítsa (15hr) and Pátra (21hr), or direct to Pátra (19hr 30min). All sailings afternoon/early evening.

From Bari Superfast daily year-round to Igoumenítsa (9hr 30min) and Pátra (15hr 30min), also Corfu direct June–Aug (8hr); Ventouris to Igoumenítsa (11hr 30min) via Corfu (10hr), almost daily most of year; Agoudimos daily July–Aug only to Igoumenítsa (9hr) and Pátra (15hr 30min). Most sailings early evening.

From Brindisi Agoudimos to Corfu/Igoumenítsa, 6 weekly July–Aug (5hr 30min/6hr 30min); Fragline to Corfu/Igoumenítsa (8–9hr) almost daily April–Sept; Maritime Way to Igoumenítsa/Pátra (7hr/13hr), daily except Jan. Most departures in evening, except Agoudimos usually about noon.

From Venice ANEK to Igoumenítsa (24hr 30min), Corfu (26hr 30min) and Pátra (34hr), 6 weekly March–Oct, Igoumenítsa and Pátra only Oct–March 4 weekly; Minoan to Igoumenítsa (20hr), Corfu (21hr 30min) and Pátra (28hr 30min), daily March–Oct, 4 weekly Oct–March. Departures vary from noon to early evening.

Sample fares

Seasonal/company price ranges below are one way, port taxes included; fares to Pátra are the same as those to Corfu/Igoumenítsa. Substantial reductions apply on many lines for both InterRail and Eurail pass-holders, and for those under 26. Discounts of 20–35 percent are usually available on return tickets, even in peak season. A few companies allow you to sleep in your van on board; ask about reduced "camping" fares.

Igoumenítsa from Bari or Brindisi: pullman seat €36–73; car €25–70.

Pátra from Ancona: pullman seat €75–103; car €68–118.

Pátra from Bári: pullman seat €67–81; car €49–79.

Pátra from Venice: pullman seat €72–106; car €71–121.

Italian agents

The dialling code for Italy is ☎39; when ringing from overseas you must include the initial "0" of the local area code.

Agoudimos ⓦwww.agoudimos-lines.com. Brindisi: c/o Hellas Ferry Lines, ☎0831/550180. Bari: c/o Morfimare, ☎080/5789815l.

ANEK ⓦwww.anek.gr. Ancona: Anek Italia, ☎071/207 2346; Venice: Anek Italia, ☎041/5286522.

Fragline ⓦwww.fragline.gr. Brindisi: ☎0831/548 318.

Maritime Way ⓦwww.maritimeway.com. Brindisi: c/o Euromare ☎0831/573800.

Minoan Lines ⓦwww.minoan.gr. Ancona: ☎071/201 708; Venice: ☎041/2407177.

Superfast ⓦwww.superfast.com. Ancona: ☎071/202 033; Bari: ☎080/521 1416.

Ventouris ⓦwww.ventouris.gr. Bari: c/o P. Lorusso & Co ☎080/5217609; Brindisi: c/o Adriatico ☎0831 548340.

NB Viamare Travel Ltd (☎020/7431 4560, ⓦwww.viamare.com) is the UK agent for most of these companies.

From North America

The Greek national airline, Olympic Airways, flies direct to Athens out of New York (JFK; 3–7 weekly), Montréal and Toronto. Olympic – and its domestic competitor Aegean – offers reasonably priced add-on flights within Greece, especially to the Greek islands. Delta is the only North American carrier currently offering any direct service to Athens (daily from New York-JFK), though through fares with code-sharing airlines are quoted from Atlanta, Boston, Calgary, Chicago, Dallas/Fort Worth, Los Angeles, Miami, San Francisco, Vancouver, Winnipeg and Washington DC (National).

Nonstop flights **to Athens out of New York-JFK** cost US$600–1200 depending on season for a thirty-day ticket; one-stop flights via other European hubs can yield significant savings, especially in peak season. Common-rating (ie price-fixing) agreements between airlines means that fares to **Athens** from the **Midwest, Deep South or the West Coast** don't vary much: US$650–750 low season, US$1100–1300 high season. Such tickets typically involve the use of American Airlines, BA, United, Air France, Alitalia, Iberia, KLM and Swiss, via their European gateway cities. With little to distinguish itineraries price-wise, you might examine the stopover time at their respective European hubs, as these often differ by several hours. You may be better off getting a domestic add-on to New York and heading directly to Athens from there.

As with the US, airfares **from Canada** vary depending on where you start your journey, and whether you take a direct service. Olympic flies out of Toronto, with a stop in Montréal, three to four times weekly **to Athens**; they're rarely the cheapest option, though. Most of the time you'll have to choose among one- or two-stop itineraries on a variety of European carriers or perhaps Delta via New York; costs run from CDN$1300 in low season from Toronto to over CDN$3000 from Vancouver in high season.

Airlines

Air Canada ☎1-888/247–2262, ⊛www .aircanada.com.
Air France ☎1-800/237-2747, Canada ☎1-800/667-2747, ⊛www.airfrance.com.
Alitalia ☎1-800/223-5730, Canada ☎1-800/361-8336, ⊛www.alitalia.com.
American Airlines ☎1-800/433-7300, ⊛www .aa.com.
British Airways ☎1-800/AIRWAYS, ⊛www .ba.com.

Continental Airlines domestic ☎1-800/523-FARE, international ☎1-800/231-0856, ⊛www .continental.com.
Delta Air Lines domestic ☎1-800/221-1212, international ☎1-800/241-4141, ⊛www.delta .com.
Iberia ☎1-800/772-4642, ⊛www.iberia.com.
Lufthansa US ☎1-800/645-3880, Canada ☎1-800/563-5954, ⊛www.lufthansa.com.
Northwest/KLM US domestic ☎1-800/225-2525, international ☎1-800/447-4747, ⊛www.nwa.com, ⊛www.klm.com.
Olympic Airways ☎1-800/223-1226 or 718/896-7393, ⊛www.olympicairlines.com.
Swiss ☎1-877/FLY-SWISS, ⊛www.swiss.com.
United Airlines Domestic ☎1-800/241-6522, international ☎1-800/538-2929, ⊛www.united .com.
Virgin Atlantic ☎1-800/862-8621, ⊛www .virgin-atlantic.com.

Travel agents

Air Brokers International ☎1-800/883-3273 or 415/397-1383, ⊛www.airbrokers.com. Consolidator and specialist in RTW tickets.
Airtech ☎212/219-7000, ⊛www.airtech.com. Standby seat broker; also deals in consolidator fares.
Educational Travel Center ☎1-800/747-5551 or 608/256-5551, ⊛www.edtrav.com. Low-cost fares worldwide, student/youth discount offers, Eurail passes.
Flightcentre US ☎1-866/WORLD-51, ⊛www .flightcentre.us, Canada ☎1-888/WORLD-55, ⊛www.flightcentre.ca. Rock-bottom fares worldwide.
New Frontiers US ☎1-800/677-0720 or 212/986-6006, ⊛www.newfrontiers.com. Discount firm, specializing in travel from the US to Europe.
STA Travel US ☎1-800/329-9537, Canada ☎1-888/427-5639, ⊛www.statravel.com. Worldwide specialists in independent travel; also student IDs, travel insurance, car rental, rail passes, etc.
Student Flights ☎1-800/255-8000 or 480/951-1177, ⊛www.isecard.com/studentflights. Student/youth fares, plus student IDs and European rail and bus passes.
TFI Tours ☎1-800/745-8000 or 212/736-1140, ⊛www.lowestairprice.com. Consolidator with global fares.
Travel Avenue ☎1-800/333-3335, ⊛www .travelavenue.com. Full-service travel agent that offers discounts in the form of rebates.
Travel Cuts US ☎1-800/592-CUTS, Canada ☎1-888 246-9762, ⊛www.travelcuts.com. Popular, long-established student-travel organization, with worldwide offers.

Travelers Advantage ☎ 1-877/259-2691, ⓦ www.travelersadvantage.com. Discount travel club, with cashback deals and discounted car rental. Membership required ($1 for 3-month trial).

Travelosophy US ☎ 1-800/332-2687, ⓦ www.itravelosophy.com. Good range of discounted and student fares worldwide.

Tour operators

Astra ☎ 303/321-5403, ⓦ www.astragreece.com. Very personal, idiosyncratic, two-week tours led by veteran Hellenophile Thordis Simonsen, during spring and autumn. Itineraries take in Crete, Epirus and Thessaly, the Peloponnese and the immediate environs of her adopted Lakonian village.

Classic Adventures ☎ 1-800/777-8090, ⓦ www.classicadventures.com. Two good offerings: spring or autumn rural cycling tours of "classical Greece", crossing the north Peloponnese to Zákynthos in eleven days, or a pedal through the archeological sites and medieval towns of Crete, in twelve days.

Hellenic Adventures ☎ 1-800/851-6349 or 612/827-0937, ⓦ www.hellenicadventures.com. Small-group (14 max), customized tours (generally 3 per season), led by enthusiastic expert guides. Good info on the website for independent travellers too.

Saga Holidays ☎ 1-800/343-0273, ⓦ www.sagaholidays.com. Specializes in worldwide group travel for seniors.

Valef Yachts ☎ 1-800/223-3845, ⓦ www.valefyachts.com. North American reps for Zeus Cruises, offering a choice of fixed, seven-day motor-yacht cruises around the Dodecanese, the Sporades plus Halkidhikí, the Cyclades, the Argo-Saronics plus the Argolid, or the Ionian islands; a bit rushed, but affordable at $850–1500 per person. Also very expensive bareboat charter (yachts, mostly over 60ft); pick your craft from the online brochure.

Vantage Travel ☎ 1-800/322-6677, ⓦ www.vantagetravel.com. Specializes in worldwide group travel for seniors.

From Australia and New Zealand

As of writing, there are no direct flights from Australia or New Zealand to Greece; you'll have to get yourself to Southeast Asia of North America for onward travel. Tickets purchased direct from the airlines tend to be expensive; travel agents or Australia-based websites offer much better deals on fares and have the latest information on limited specials and stopovers.

For a **simple return fare**, you may have to buy an add-on internal flight to reach the international gateways of Sydney or Melbourne. Tickets are generally **valid for one year**; high-season departures can typically be had for A$2300–2500 for multi-stop itineraries via Southeast Asia, the Middle East and a European hub. An 180-day, two-stop ticket might cost A$2300, while for about the same price you could fly eastbound via North America. Low-season fares cost A$1600–1800.

From New Zealand, the usual routes to Athens are either westbound several times weekly via Bangkok, Sydney or Singapore, or eastbound almost daily via Los Angeles with Air New Zealand on the first leg. In **high season** count on paying NZ$2500–2800 in either direction; **low season** prices aren't much different at NZ$2200–2500.

Airlines

Aeroflot ☎ 02/9262 2233, ⓦ www.aeroflot.com.au.

Air New Zealand Australia ☎ 13 24 76, ⓦ www.airnz.com.au, New Zealand ☎ 0800/737 000, ⓦ www.airnz.co.nz.

Alitalia Australia ☎ 02/9244 2445, New Zealand ☎ 09/308 3357, ⓦ www.alitalia.com.

British Airways Australia ☎ 1300/767 177, New Zealand ☎ 0800/274 847, ⓦ www.ba.com.

Egyptair Australia ☎ 02/9241 5696, ⓦ www.egyptair.com.eg.

Emirates Australia ☎ 1300/303 777 or 02/9290 9700, New Zealand ☎ 09/377 6004, ⓦ www.emirates.com.

Gulf Air Australia ☎ 02/9244 2199, New Zealand ☎ 09/308 3366, ⓦ www.gulfairco.com.

Lufthansa Australia ☎ 1300/655 727, New Zealand ☎ 0800 945 220, ⓦ www.lufthansa.com.

Qantas Australia ☎ 13 13 13, New Zealand ☎ 0800 808 767 or 09/357 8900, ⓦ www.qantas.com.

Royal Jordanian Australia ☎ 02/9244 2701, New Zealand ☎ 03/365 3910, ⓦ www.rja.com.jo.

Singapore Airlines Australia ☎ 13 10 11, New Zealand ☎ 0800/808 909, ⓦ www.singaporeair.com.

Thai Airways Australia ☎ 1300/651 960, New Zealand ☎ 09/377 3886, ⓦ www.thaiair.com.

Travel agents

Flight Centre Australia ☎ 13 31 33, ⓦ www.flightcentre.com.au, New Zealand ☎ 0800/243 544, ⓦ www.flightcentre.co.nz.

STA Travel Australia ☎ 1300/733 035, New Zealand ☎ 0508/782 872, Ⓦ www.statravel.com. Student Uni Travel Australia ☎ 02/9232 8444, Ⓦ www.sut.com.au, New Zealand ☎ 09/379 4224, Ⓦ www.sut.co.nz. Trailfinders Australia ☎ 02/9247 7666, Ⓦ www .trailfinders.com.au.

Tour operators

Australians Studying Abroad ☎ 03/9509 1955 or 1800/645 755, Ⓦ www.asatravinfo.com.au.

This organization's fairly pricey "Hellenic Heritage" study tour – not offered every year – takes a relatively leisurely 23 days to cover most of the major ancient/medieval sites on the mainland and Crete, with Istanbul thrown in. Sun Island Tours Australia ☎ 02/9283 3840, Ⓦ www.sunislandtours.com.au. An assortment of island-hopping, fly-drives, cruises and guided land-tour options, as well as upscale accommodation on big-name islands such as Rhodes, Kós and Sámos.

Visas and red tape

UK and all other EU nationals need only a valid passport to enter Greece, and are no longer stamped in on arrival or out upon departure. US, Australian, New Zealand, Canadian and most non-EU Europeans receive mandatory entry and exit stamps in their passports and can stay, as tourists, for ninety days (cumulative) in any six-month period. Such nationals arriving by flight or boat from another EU state not party to the Schengen Agreement may not be stamped in routinely at minor Greek ports, so make sure this is done in order to avoid unpleasantness on exit. Your passport must be valid for three months after your arrival date.

Unless of Greek descent, or married to an EU national, visitors from **non-EU** countries are currently not, in practice, being given extensions to tourist visas by the various Aliens' Bureaux in Greece. You must leave not just Greece but the entire Schengen Group – essentially the entire EU as it was before May 2004, minus Britain and Eire, plus Norway and Iceland – and stay out until the maximum-90-days-in-180 rule as set forth above is satisfied. If you **overstay** your time and then leave under your own power – ie are not deported – you'll be hit with a huge fine upon departure, ranging from €587 to €1174, and possibly be banned from re-entering for a period of time; no excuses will be entertained except (just maybe) a doctor's certificate stating you were immobilized in hospital. It cannot be overemphasized just how exigent Greek immigration officials have become on this issue.

Greek embassies abroad

Australia 9 Turrana St, Yarralumla, Canberra, ACT 2600 ☎ 02/6273 3011.
Britain 1A Holland Park, London W11 3TP ☎ 020/7221 6467, Ⓦ www.greekembassy.org.uk.
Canada 80 Maclaren St, Ottawa, ON K2P 0K6 ☎ 613/238-6271.
Ireland 1 Upper Pembroke St, Dublin 2 ☎ 01/676 7254.
New Zealand 5–7 Willeston St, Wellington ☎ 04/473 7775.
USA 2221 Massachusetts Ave NW, Washington, DC 20008 ☎ 202/939-5800, Ⓦ www.greekembassy .org.

Information, maps and websites

The National Tourist Organization of Greece (Ellinikós Organismós Tourismoú, or EOT; GNTO abroad, ⓦwww.gnto.gr) maintains offices in most European capitals, plus major cities in North America and Australia (see below for addresses). It publishes an array of free, glossy, regional pamphlets, invariably five to ten years out of date, which are okay for getting an idea of where you want to go, even if the actual text should be taken with a spoonful of salt. Also available from the EOT are a reasonable foldout map of the country and a number of (equally outdated) brochures on special interests and festivals.

Tourist offices

In Greece, you will find official **EOT offices** in many of the larger towns and resorts where, in addition to the usual leaflets, you can find weekly **schedules** for the inter-island **ferries** – hardly one-hundred-percent reliable, but useful as a guideline. EOT staff should be able to advise on **bus** and **train** departures as well as current opening hours for local sites and museums, and occasionally can give assistance with accommodation.

Where there is no EOT office, you can get information (and often a range of leaflets) from **municipally run** tourist offices, for example those in Kós and Rhodes – these can be highly motivated and better than the EOT branches. In the absence of any of these, you can visit the **Tourist Police**, essentially a division (often just a single room) of the local police. They can sometimes provide you with lists of rooms to let, which they regulate, but they're really where you go if you have a **serious complaint** about a taxi, accommodation or an eating establishment.

Greek national tourist offices abroad

Australia 51 Pitt St, Sydney, NSW 2000 ☎02/9241 1663, Ⓔhto@tpg.com.au.
Canada 91 Scollard St, 2nd Floor, Toronto, ON M5R 1GR ☎416/968-2220, Ⓔgrnto.tor@sympatico.ca.
UK 4 Conduit St, London W1R 0DJ ☎020/7495 4300, ⒺEOT-greektouristoffice@btinternet.com.
USA 645 5th Ave, New York, NY 10022 ☎212/421-5777.

Maps

Maps in Greece are an endless source of confusion and often outright misinformation. Each cartographic company seems to have its own peculiar system of transcribing Greek letters into the Roman alphabet – and these, as often as not, do not match the semi-official transliterations on the road signs, which again may not match, even in the same region.

The most reliable **general touring maps** of Greece are those published by Athens-based Road Editions (ⓦwww.road.gr) and Emvelia Editions (ⓦwww.emvelia.gr). Road Editions products are widely available in Greece at selected bookstores, including their own retail outlets in Athens (Ippokrátous 39), Thessaloníki (Proxénou Koromilá 41), Pátra (Zaïmi 20) and Iráklion (Hándhakos 29), as well as at petrol stations and general tourist shops country-wide. In Britain they are found at Stanfords (see opposite) and the Hellenic Book Service (see p.40); in the US, they're sold exclusively through Omni Resources (☎910/227-8300, ⓦwww.omnimap.com). Emvelia currently has just one retail outlet in Athens – Ellinoekdhotiki, at Navarínou 12 – and very sporadic sales points overseas – notably the Hellenic Book Service in London.

Both Road Editions and Emvelia products tend to be obsolete in the matter of current road surfaces, though Road does a better job of issuing updates. Neither series is anywhere near perfect, but, based on large-scale military maps, they're the best you'll find, and where they duplicate coverage you may want to buy both.

Road Editions covers the mainland in five 1:250,000 folding sheets, as well as a 1:500,000 map encompassing the whole country. Their 1:50,000 hiking map of Mount Pílio doubles as a road map. Emvelia has the mainland on six sheets at 1:250,000. They also do a double-sided folding map of the whole country at 1:550,000 scale, with a useful index and fair accuracy.

Where Road or Emvelia products are unavailable, good second choices are the *Rough Guide Map: Greece,* GeoCenter maps *Greece and the Islands* and *Greek Islands/Aegean Sea,* which together cover the country at a scale of 1:300,000. The single-sided foldup Freytag-Berndt 1:650,000, with an index, is very nearly as good, and easier to use when driving. All of these are widely available in Britain and North America (see the list of map outlets below), though not in Greece.

Touring maps of **individual islands** are more easily available on the spot, and while most are wildly inaccurate or obsolete, a rare few are passably reliable and up to date. These include the Road Editions and Emvelia Editions products for **Crete**, plus nearly forty more Road titles for other islands at scales of 1:25,000–1:70,000, including the Ionians, east Aegean, Sporades and most Cyclades and Dodecanese. Anavasi (see below) also cover the Cyclades and Sporades well at scales of 1:25,000–1:40,000.

The most useful foreign-produced map of **Athens** is the *Rough Guide City Map*; it is full-colour, non-tearable, weatherproof and pocket-sized, detailing attractions, places to shop, eat, drink and sleep as well as the city streets. If you can read Greek, and plan to stay for some time in the city, the *Athina-Pireás Proastia Hartis-Odhigos* street atlas, published by the Fotis brothers, is invaluable, though pricey. It has a complete index, down to the tiniest alley, and also shows cinemas and most hotels, as well as all the metro stations. The only comparable product for **Thessaloníki** is Emvelia's offering, which also includes Halkidhikí and the immediate surroundings of the city; they also do a folding map of Thessaloníki if you don't want the indexed atlas.

Hiking/topographical maps

Hiking/topographical maps are gradually improving in quality and availability. **Road Editions**, in addition to their touring maps, have produced a dozen 1:50,000, GPS-compatible topographical maps for mainland mountain ranges, including Áthos, Pílio, Parnassós, Ólymbos, Taïyettos, Ágrafa and Íti, usually with rudimentary route directions in English.

Rival publisher **Anavasi** is based in Athens (℡ 210 72 93 541, ⊛ www.mountains.gr /anavasi). Their GPS-compatible, CD-ROM-available series is strongest on the mountains of central Greece and Epirus, with a dozen folding maps at 1:50,000–1:55,000 covering most ranges from Parnassós up to the Píndhos, as well as a few select massifs on the Peloponnese. The latter is better represented on their 1:25,000 series, which also includes Mount Dhýrfis on Évvia, Párnitha and central Ólymbos. Anavasi products use the same military source maps as Road, but frequently have better corrections and verifications of the road and path networks. They are sold in better Athens bookstores, as well as their own shopfront at Stoá Arsakíou 6A in central Athens, but do not have much international distribution.

A German company, **Harms**, has five maps at 1:80,000 scale which cover Crete from west to east and show, with about fifty percent accuracy, many hiking routes. Finally, for hiking in particular areas of Crete, Corfu, Kálymnos, Sámos, Rhodes, Sými, Párga, Pílio, Thássos and Lésvos, map-and-guide booklets published by **Marengo Publications** in England also prove very useful. Stanfords keeps a good stock of these, or order from Marengo direct on ℡ 01485/532710, ⊛ www.marengowalks.com.

Map outlets

In the UK and Ireland

Stanfords 12–14 Long Acre, London WC2 ℡ 020/7836 1321, ⊛ www.stanfords.co.uk. Also at 39 Spring Gardens, Manchester ℡ 0161/831 0250, and 29 Corn St, Bristol ℡ 0117/929 9966.
Blackwell's Map Centre 53 Broad St, Oxford OX1 3BQ ℡ 01865/792792, ⊛ www.maps.blackwell. co.uk. Branches in Bristol, Cambridge, Cardiff, Leeds, Liverpool, Newcastle, Reading and Sheffield.

The Map Shop 30A Belvoir St, Leicester LE1 6QH ☎0116/247 1400, ⊛www.mapshopleicester.co.uk.

National Map Centre 22–24 Caxton St, London SW1H 0QU ☎020/7222 2466, ⊛www.mapsnmc .co.uk.

National Map Centre Ireland 34 Aungier St, Dublin ☎01/476 0471, ⊛www.mapcentre.ie.

Newcastle Map Centre 55 Grey St, Newcastle upon Tyne NE1 6EF ☎0191/261 5622, ⊛www .traveller.ltd.uk.

The Travel Bookshop 13–15 Blenheim Crescent, London W11 2EE ☎020/7229 5260, ⊛www .thetravelbookshop.co.uk.

Traveller 55 Grey St, Newcastle upon Tyne ☎0191/261 5622, ⊛www.newtraveller.com.

In the US and Canada

110 North Latitude US ☎336/369-4171, ⊛www.110nlatitude.com.

Book Passage 51 Tamal Vista Blvd, Corte Madera, CA 94925, plus in the San Francisco Ferry Building ☎1-800/999-7909 or 1-415/927-0960, ⊛www .bookpassage.com.

Distant Lands 56 S Raymond Ave, Pasadena, CA 91105 ☎1-800/310-3220, ⊛www.distantlands.com.

Globe Corner Bookstore 28 Church St, Cambridge, MA 02138 ☎1-800/358-6013, ⊛www.globecorner.com.

Longitude Books 115 W 30th St #1206, New York, NY 10001 ☎1-800/342-2164, ⊛www .longitudebooks.com.

Map Town 400 5 Ave SW #100, Calgary, AB, T2P 0L6 ☎1-877/921-6277, ⊛www.maptown.com.

Travel Bug Bookstore 3065 W Broadway, Vancouver, BC, V6K 2G9 ☎604/737-1122, ⊛www .travelbugbooks.ca.

World of Maps 1235 Wellington St, Ottawa, ON, K1Y 3A3 ☎1-800/214-8524, ⊛www.worldofmaps .com.

In Australia and New Zealand

Map Centre ⊛www.mapcentre.co.nz.

Mapland 372 Little Bourke St, Melbourne ☎03/9670 4383, ⊛www.mapland.com.au.

Map Shop 6–10 Peel St, Adelaide ☎08/8231 2033, ⊛www.mapshop.net.au.

Map World 371 Pitt St, Sydney ☎02/9261 3601, ⊛www.mapworld.net.au. Also in Perth, Canberra and Brisbane.

Map World 173 Gloucester St, Christchurch ☎0800/627 967, ⊛www.mapworld.co.nz.

...e on the Internet

...strongly represented on the **Inter-**
...gh some websites are little more

than propaganda and/or polemics – anything to do with Macedonia, for example. Almost every heavily visited island will have its own site, often in bizarre, barely readable "Gringlish", though others – mastered by expatriate residents – are fluent but either obsolete or vague on specifics. Country-wide and regional sites recommended below are reasonably balanced, current and literate.

News, views and printed matter

⊛aegeantimes.net A good digest of current Greece-, Turkey- and Cyprus-related news stories from around the world.

⊛www.athensnews.gr The online edition of the *Athens* News, Greece's longest-running quality English-language newspaper, with the day's top stories.

⊛www.ekathimerini.com The online edition of the abridged English-translation of *Kathimerini*, one of Greece's most respected dailies. It's fully archived for years back, and has an excellent search facility.

⊛www.hellenicbooks.com The website of the UK's premier Greek bookstore. It posts full, opinionated reviews of its stock, offers the possibility of buying online, and has witty descriptions of every island.

Greek culture

⊛www.culture.gr The Greek Ministry of Culture's website. Good alphabetical gazetteer to monuments, archeological sites and museums; lots of info about the more obscure sites.

⊛www.geocities.com/rebetology Basically the site of an annual *rebétika*-related conference and festive gathering on Ídhra, but also posts interesting papers and snippets in its archive.

⊛www.kemo.gr The last word on Greece's minority communities, without the usual ranting polemics – many academic but readable papers posted for free download.

Travel in Greece

⊛www.gtp.gr The website of *Greek Travel Pages*, the fat (and expensive) printed manual on every Greek travel agent's desk. Mostly used for its ferry schedules (also kept on a separate site, ⊛www.gtpweb .com), this has improved no end but is still not one-hundred-percent reliable or complete, omitting some minor local ferries and hydrofoils.

⊛www.ktel.org Bilingual website of the KTEL, or national bus syndicate, which posts fairly reliable schedules. Coverage includes the entire mainland and larger (but not smaller) islands.

ⓦ **www.ose.gr** The train network online, currently in Greek only.

Greek destinations

ⓦ **www.foi.org.uk** The site of Friends of the Ionian, which encourages sustainable, off-the-beach tourism; lots on the environment, natural history and local walks.

ⓦ **www.ionian-islands.com** A good if rather commercial site with lots of links to accommodation, travel and eating establishments.

ⓦ **www.island-ikaria.com** Literate, interesting, well-organized and fairly current, covering everything from hot springs to festivals.

ⓦ **www.kalymnos-isl.gr** The island's official website, last updated early 2004.

ⓦ **www.leros.org** A bit of "Gringlish" to contend with, but clearly devised with love, giving a fun, thorough flavour of the island's landscapes, people and traditional architecture.

ⓦ **www.parosweb.com** Good all-purpose site for the island, with plenty of news on and for visitors and expats, an events calendar and the usual accommodation, property and dining info.

ⓦ **www.pelionet.gr** Profiles of selected villages, walks, skiing and selected accommodation on this popular bit of the mainland.

ⓦ **www.saronicnet.com** Accommodation (hotels and villas) and activities (diving, donkey-trekking) on Ídhra, Spétses and Póros – three separate sites best accessed through this portal.

ⓦ **www.skiathosinfo.com** Excellent info on getting to Skiáthos and what you'll find on arrival, as well as literally hundreds of useful links to sites on the Sporades specifically and Greece in general.

ⓦ **stigmes.gr/br** An English-summary online edition of what's claimed to be Crete's leading monthly magazine, plus lots of links to other Crete-related sites.

ⓦ **www.symivisitor.com** Current news for aficionados; a range of accommodation, restaurant and beach profiles, presented by the publishers of the monthly island newspaper.

ⓦ **www.west-crete.com** Cretophiles' favourite site, with all travel/cultural topics (including trekking and naturist beaches) and links to helpful businesses; not restricted to the west of the island.

Greek weather

ⓦ **forecast.uoa.gr** A good one-stop site, maintained by the University of Athens physics faculty. A limited selection of reporting stations, however; for much of Greece you click on a thumbnail image of the entire country, which must be enlarged to read conditions at specific places.

ⓦ **www.poseidon.ncmr.gr** Greek oceanographers' site maintained by the National Centre for Marine Research which profiles Aegean weather meticulously, including graphics of sea currents and surface winds, based on satellite imaging. It's slowish but sophisticated, good for yachties, and reports one topic (rain, temperature, wind speed, etc) at a time.

Insurance

Even though EU healthcare privileges apply in Greece (see p.43 for details), you should consider taking out an insurance policy before travelling to cover against theft, loss, illness or injury. Before paying for a whole new policy, however, it's worth checking whether you are already covered: some all-risks homeowners' or renters' insurance policies may cover your possessions when overseas, and many private medical schemes (such as BUPA or WPA in the UK) offer coverage extensions for abroad.

In Canada, provincial health plans usually provide partial cover for medical mishaps overseas, while holders of official student/ teacher/youth cards in Canada and the US are entitled to meagre accident coverage and hospital inpatient benefits. **Students** will often find that their student health coverage extends during the vacations and for one term beyond the date of last enrolment. Most **credit-card issuers** also offer some

Rough Guides travel insurance

Rough Guides has teamed up with Columbus Direct to offer you travel insurance that can be tailored to suit your needs.

Readers can choose from many different travel insurance products, including a low-cost backpacker option for long stays; a short break option for city getaways; a typical holiday package option; and many others. There are also annual multi-trip policies for those who travel regularly, with variable levels of cover available. Different sports and activities (trekking, skiing, etc) can be covered if required on most policies.

Rough Guides travel insurance is available to the residents of 36 different countries with different language options to choose from via our website – ⓦwww .roughguidesinsurance.com – where you can also purchase the insurance.

Alternatively, UK residents should call 0800 083 9507; US citizens should call 1-800 749-4922; Australians should call 1 300 669 999. All other nationalities should call +44 870 890 2843.

sort of vacation insurance, which is often automatic if you pay for the holiday with their card. However, it's vital to check just what these policies cover – frequently only death or dismemberment in the UK.

After exhausting the possibilities above, you might want to contact a **specialist travel insurance** company, or consider the travel insurance deal we offer (see box above). A typical travel insurance policy usually provides cover for the **loss** of baggage, tickets and – up to a certain limit – cash, cards or cheques, as well as **cancellation** or curtailment of your journey. Most of them exclude so-called **dangerous sports** unless an extra premium is paid: in the Greek islands this means motorbiking, windsurfing and possibly sailing, and on the mainland this could mean rafting, skiing or trekking, with many visitors engaging in one or the other at some point. Many policies can be chopped and changed to exclude coverage you don't need – for example, sickness and accident benefits can often be excluded or included at will. They do not pay out for medical treatment necessary for injuries incurred whilst under the influence of alcohol or drugs. If you do take medical coverage, ascertain whether benefits will be paid as treatment proceeds or only after return home, whether there is a **24-hour medical emergency number**, and how much the deductible excess is (sometimes negotiable). When securing baggage cover, make sure that the **per-article limit** – typically under £500 in the UK – will cover your most valuable possession. Travel agents and tour operators in the UK are likely to **require travel insurance** when you book a package holiday, though they can no longer insist that you buy their own – however, you will be required to sign a declaration saying that you have a policy with a particular company.

If you need to make a **medical claim**, you should keep all receipts for medicines and treatment, and in the event you have anything stolen or lost, you must obtain an **official statement** from the police or the airline which lost your bags. With a rise in the number of fraudulent claims, most insurers won't even consider one unless you have a police report. There is usually also a **time limit** for submitting claims after the end of your journey.

Health

British and other EU nationals are officially entitled to free medical care in Greece upon presentation of an E111 form, available from most post offices. By the start of 2006, this and most other E-forms are set to be replaced by a Europe-wide benefits "European Health Insurance Card". "Free", however, means admittance only to the lowest grade of state hospital (known as a yenikó nosokomío), and does not include nursing care, special tests or the cost of medication. If you need prolonged medical care, you should make use of private treatment, which is slightly less expensive than elsewhere in western Europe – this is where your travel insurance policy (see p.41) comes in handy. The US, Canada, Australia and New Zealand have no formal healthcare agreements with Greece (other than allowing for free emergency trauma treatment).

There are no required **inoculations** for Greece, though it's wise to ensure that you are up to date on tetanus and polio. The **drinking water** is safe pretty much everywhere, though you will come across shortages or brackish supplies on some of the drier and more remote islands, and nitrate levels exceed the advised limits in some agricultural areas, in particular Thessalía and Argolídha. Bottled water is widely available if you're feeling cautious.

Specific hazards

The main health problems experienced by visitors – including many blamed on the food – have to do with **overexposure to the sun**. To avoid these, don't spend too long in the sun, cover up, wear a hat, and drink plenty of fluids in the hot months to avoid any danger of **sunstroke**; remember that even hazy sun can burn. To avoid hazards by the sea, goggles or a dive mask for swimming and footwear for walking over wet or rough rocks are useful.

Hazards of the deep

In the sea, you may have the bad luck to meet an armada of **jellyfish** (tsoúkhtres), especially in late summer; they come in various colours and sizes ranging from purple "pizzas" to invisible, minute creatures. Various over-the-counter remedies for jellyfish stings are sold in resort pharmacies; baking soda or diluted ammonia (including urine)

also help to lessen the sting. The welts and burning usually subside of their own accord within a few hours; there are no deadly man-of-war species in Greek waters.

Less vicious but more common are black, spiky **sea urchins** (ahini), which infest rocky shorelines year-round; if you step on or graze one, a sewing needle (you can crudely sterilize it by heat from a cigarette lighter) and olive oil or toothpaste are effective for removing spines; if you don't extract them they'll fester.

Stingrays and skates (Greek names include platý, seláhi, vátos or trígona) can injure with their barbed tails: they mainly frequent bays with sandy bottoms where they can camouflage themselves.

When snorkelling in deeper water, especially around Crete, the Dodecanese, or the east Aegean, you may happen upon a brightly coloured **moray eel** (smérna) sliding back and forth out of its rocky lair. Keep a respectful distance – their slightly comical air and clown-colours belie an irritable temper and the ability to inflict nasty bites or even sever fingers.

Sandflies, dogs, mosquitoes, wasps and ticks

If you are sleeping on or near a **beach**, it's wise to use insect repellent, either lotion or wrist/ankle bands, and/or a tent with a screen to guard against **sandflies**. Their bites are potentially dangerous, as these insects spread two forms of leishmaniasis, parasitic infections characterized in one form by ulcerated skin and scarring, in the other by chronic fever, anaemia, weight loss, and death if untreated. These can be difficult to diagnose, and may require long courses of medication.

In Greece, the main reservoirs for leishmaniasis are **dogs**. Transmission of the disease to humans by fleas has not been proven, but it's wisest not to befriend strays as they also carry echinococcosis, a debilitating liver fluke transmitted by stroking their fur. In humans these form nodules and cysts requiring surgical removal. If bitten by a dog (or any other mammal) you should seek medical advice – **rabies** still occurs in Greece.

Mosquitoes (*kounoúpia*) in Greece carry nothing worse than a vicious bite, but they can be infuriating. The most widespread solution are the small plug-in electrical devices that vaporize a semi-odourless insecticide tablet; many accommodation proprietors supply them routinely, and if you see them supplied on your night-table it's a good bet they'll be needed. Insect repellents such as Autan are available from most general stores and kiosks. Small electronic ultrasound generators are available that supposedly repel mosquitoes, but scientific tests have shown them to be ineffective. Some modern accommodation rooms have pull-down mosquito nets fitted to the external doors and windows.

Wasps and **hornets** (*sfigónes*, *sfíkes*) are common, particularly during the winemaking season (Aug–Oct) when they're attracted by all the fermenting grape-mess. Some mind their own business, others are very aggressive, even dive-bombing swimmers some distance out to sea. One of the best repellent measures (used by tavernas) is coffee grounds set alight. Domestic **bees** (*mélisses*) can be aggressive when near their hives – particularly if you are wearing denim or wool – and individuals that decide to attack are suicidally persistent; scrape the detached, embedded sting from your skin with a finger nail to prevent the injection of more venom.

Ticks mostly feed on sheep, but wait on vegetation for new hosts, including passing dogs and humans. Check your legs after walking through long grass near flocks. If one finds you and has started to feed, you should detach it carefully by rocking or twisting, rather than pulling it off; do not use traditional methods such as oil or a lighted match. Ticks can spread Lyme disease or typhus, and any tick bite that results in a rash or other symptoms should always be examined medically.

Creepy crawlies

Adders (*ohiés*) and **scorpions** (*skorpii*) are found throughout Greece; both creatures are shy – scorpions in particular are nocturnal – but take care when climbing over dry-stone walls where snakes like to sun themselves, and don't put hands or feet in places, like shoes, where you haven't looked first. Wiggly, fast-moving, six-inch **centipedes** which look like a rubber toy should also be treated with respect, as they pack a nasty bite.

The number of annual deaths from **snakebite** in Europe is very small. Many snakes will bite if threatened, whether they are venomous or not – shock is a likely result of any bite. If a bite injects venom, then swelling will normally occur within thirty minutes. If this happens, get medical attention, keep the bitten part still, and make sure all body movements are as gentle as possible. If medical attention is not nearby then bind the limb firmly to slow the blood circulation, but not so tightly as to stop the blood flow.

In addition to munching its way through a fair fraction of Greece's surviving pine forests, the **pine processionary caterpillar** – taking this name from the long, nose-to-tail convoys which individuals form at certain points in their life cycle – sports highly irritating hairs, with a poison worse than a scorpion's. If you touch one, or even a tree trunk they've been on recently, you'll know all about it for a week, and the welts may require antihistamine lotion or pills to heal.

Plants

If you snap a **wild-fig** shoot while walking into the countryside, take care not to come into contact with the highly irritant **sap**. The immediate antidote to this alkaloid is a mild acid – lemon juice or vinegar; left unneutralized, fig "milk" raises welts which take a month to heal. Severe allergic reactions have to be treated with strong steroids, either topical cream (available from pharmacies) or intravenously in hospital casualty wards. Other plants, such as euphorbia, sumac and rue, may have similar effects on sensitive skins.

Pharmacies, drugs and contraception

For **minor complaints** it's enough to go to the local **farmakío**. Greek pharmacists are highly trained and dispense a number of medicines which elsewhere could only be prescribed by a doctor. In the larger towns and resorts there'll usually be one who speaks good English. Pharmacies are usually closed evenings and Saturday mornings, but all should have a monthly schedule (in both English and Greek) on their door showing the complete roster of night and weekend duty pharmacists in town.

Greeks are famously hypochondriac, so pharmacies are veritable Aladdin's caves of **arcane drugs and sundry formulas** – just about everything available in North America and northern Europe is here, and then some. **Homeopathic** and **herbal** remedies are quite widely available, too, now sold in most larger pharmacies alongside more conventional products.

If you regularly use any form of **prescription drug**, you should bring along a copy of the prescription, together with the generic name of the drug; this will help should you need to replace it, and also avoids possible problems with customs officials. In this regard, you should be aware that **codeine is banned** in Greece. If you import any you might find yourself in serious trouble, so check labels carefully; it's the core ingredient of Panadeine, Veganin, Solpadeine, Codis and Nurofen Plus, to name just a few common compounds.

Hayfever sufferers should be prepared for the early Greek pollen season, at its height from April to June. Pollen from Aleppo and Calabrian pine in April/May can be particularly noxious. If you are taken by surprise, you'll be able to get tablets at a pharmacy, but best to come prepared.

Contraceptive pills are more readily available every year, but don't count on getting these – or spermicidal jelly/foam – outside of a few large island towns, over-the-counter at the larger pharmacies; Greek women tend not to use any sort of birth control systematically, and have an average of four abortions during their adult life. **Condoms**, however, are inexpensive and ubiquitous at supermarkets – or just ask for *profylaktiká* (the slangy terms *plastiká* or *kapótes* are even better understood) at any pharmacy or corner *períptero* (kiosk). **Women's hygienic supplies** are sold sometimes in pharmacies, much more often in supermarkets. Napkins ("Always" brand) are ubiquitous; tampons can be trickier to find in remoter spots, especially on the smaller islands.

Doctors and hospitals

You'll find English-speaking **doctors** in any of the bigger towns or resorts. For an **ambulance**, phone ☎166. In **emergencies**, treatment is given free – apart from a €3 appointment fee – in **state hospitals** (ask for the *epígonda peristatiká* – casualty ward). You will only get the most basic nursing care, and food and changes of bedding are not provided. Somewhat better are the ordinary state-run **outpatient clinics** (*yiatría*) attached to most public hospitals and also found in rural locales. These operate on a first-come, first-served basis, so go early; usual hours are 8am to noon, though it's sometimes possible to get seen by someone between 1 and 5pm.

Travellers with disabilities

Unfortunately, many of the wonders of Greece such as stepped alleys and ancient monuments are potential hazards for anyone who has difficulty in walking, is wheelchair-bound or suffers from other **disabilities**. Access to all but the newest public buildings and hotels can also be problematical. It is possible, however, to enjoy an inexpensive and trauma-free holiday in Greece with a little forward planning. The Greek National Tourist Office is a help as long as you have specific questions to put to them; they publish a useful questionnaire that you could send to hotels or owners of apartment and villa accommodation.

Before purchasing **travel insurance**, ensure that people with a pre-existing medical condition are not excluded. A **medical certificate** of your fitness to travel, provided by your doctor, is also extremely useful; some airlines or insurance companies may insist on it.

You should also carry extra supplies of any required **drugs** and a prescription including the generic name in case of emergency. It's probably best to assume that any special equipment, drugs or clothing you may require is unavailable in Greece and will need to be brought with you.

Costs, money and banks

The cost of living in Greece has increased astronomically since it joined the EU, subsequently adopted the euro, and raised its VAT rate in early 2005. Food prices in shops, or the tariff for a coffee, now match or exceed those of many other EU member countries (including the UK). However, outside the established resorts, travel remains affordable, with the aggregate cost of restaurant meals, short-term accommodation and public transport falling somewhere in between that of cheaper Spain or France and pricier Italy.

Prices depend on where and when you go. Mainland cities, larger tourist resorts and the trendier small islands (such as Sými, Sífnos, Ídhra, Paxí and Pátmos) are more expensive, and costs everywhere increase sharply during July, August, Christmas, New Year and Easter.

Some basic costs

On most islands a **daily per-person budget** of £32/US$58/€46 will get you basic accommodation, breakfast, picnic lunch, a short ferry or bus ride and a simple evening meal, as one of a couple. Camping would cut costs marginally. On £56/US$101/€81 a day you could be living quite well, plus sharing the cost of renting a large motorbike or small car.

Inter-island **ferry fares**, a main unavoidable expense, are subsidized by the government (until 2007, anyway) in an effort to preserve remote island communities. To give you some idea of prices, the cheapest cabin for the overnight journey from Athens to Sámos, a twelve-hour trip, costs about €45, while a deck-class ticket for the four-hour trip from Rhodes to Kós costs about €13. For €7–14 you can catch a conventional ferry or high-speed craft to numerous small islands that

lie closer to Rhodes, Kós and Sámos, the most likely touchdown points if you're flying to the Dodecanese or east Aegean on a direct charter; a cheap cabin from Pireás to Rhodes, one of the longest single ferry journeys in Greece, will set you back about €60. Local ferries in the Cyclades are a bit pricier for the sea miles travelled; Páros or Náxos to Thíra costs about €11.

The simplest double **room** generally costs €30–35 a night, depending on the location and the plumbing arrangements. Bona-fide single rooms are rare, and cost about seventy percent of double rates. Organized **campsites** are little more than €5 per person, with similar charges per tent and perhaps 25 percent more for a camper van. With discretion you can camp for free in the remotest rural areas.

A basic taverna **meal** with bulk wine or a beer can be had for around €11–15 per person. Add a better bottle of wine, seafood or more careful cooking, and it could be up to €18–24 a head; you'll rarely pay more than that. Sharing seafood, Greek salads and dips is a good way to keep costs down in the better restaurants, and even in the most developed of resorts, with inflated "international" menus, you'll often be able to find a more earthy but decent taverna where the locals eat.

Youth and student discounts

Various official and quasi-official **youth, student and teacher ID cards** soon pay for themselves in savings; they all cost US$22 or local equivalent for a year. Full-time students are eligible for the **International Student ID Card** (ISIC; ⊛www.isiccard.com), which entitles the bearer to special air, rail and ferry fares and discounts at museums, theatres and other attractions. For Americans there's also a health benefit, providing token medical coverage and a per-day stipend for hospital stays up to two months. You only have to be 26 or younger to qualify for the **International Youth Travel Card**, which provides much the same benefits as the ISIC. Teachers qualify for the **International Teacher Identity Card (ITIC)**, offering similar insurance benefits but more limited travel discounts. Consult the website of the International Student Travel Confederation (⊛www.istc.org) for the nearest retail outlet for any of these cards. A university photo ID might open some doors, but is not as easily recognizable as the ISIC cards, although the latter are often not accepted as valid proof of age.

Senior discounts

Seniors are entitled to discounts at state-run attractions of 25 to 30 percent; long-term bus passes in the major cities are similarly discounted; and, without making much effort to publicize the fact, Olympic Airways (and quite possibly its new private competitors) also offer discounts on full fares on domestic flights. Keep proof of age to hand for all these benefits.

Currency

Greece is one of twelve EU countries that changed over to a single currency, the **euro** (€), in February 2002. The fixed conversion rate used was 340.75 drachmas (*dhrakhmés*) to one euro; people still commonly quote prices in dhrachmas, and many till receipts continue to show the value in both currencies. Greek shopkeepers do not bother much with shortfalls of 10 cents or

less, whether in their favour (especially) or yours. You will be able to exchange any leftover drachma paper notes until March 2012, at branches of the Bank of Greece.

For the most up-to-date **exchange rates** of the US dollar or the pound sterling against the euro, consult the very useful currency speculators' website, ⊛www.oanda.com.

Euro notes exist in denominations of 5, 10, 20, 50, 100, 200 and 500 euros, and coins in denominations of 1, 2, 5, 10, 20 and 50 cents and 1 and 2 euros. Each country in the euro-zone strikes its own coins (just one face is distinctive), but the other side – and all notes – are uniform throughout Europe. Avoid getting stuck with **counterfeit euro notes** (€100 and €200 ones abound). The best tests are done by the naked eye: genuine notes all have a hologram strip or (if over €50) patch at one end, there's a watermark at the other, plus a security thread embedded in the middle. If you end up being given such a note, you'll have to lump it – if you unwittingly try to pass it on, or report it in good faith to the police, you'll still be assumed party to the scam, and face a session of interrogation at the very least.

Banks and exchange

Greek **banks** are normally open Monday to Thursday 8.30am–2.30pm and Friday 8.30am–2pm. Always take your passport with you as proof of identity and allow time for at least one long queue. Outside these hours, the largest hotels and travel agencies provide an exchange service, albeit with hefty commissions. On small islands with no full-service bank, "authorized" bank agents will charge yet another extra fee to cover the cost of posting a travellers' cheque to a proper branch.

A number of authorized brokers for exchanging foreign cash have emerged in Athens and other major tourist centres. When changing small amounts, choose those bureaux that charge a flat percentage commission (usually one percent) rather than a high minimum. There's also a small number of 24-hour automatic **foreign-note-changing machines** in a few resorts, but a high minimum commission tends to be deducted. There is no need to **purchase euros** beforehand unless you're arriving at some ungodly hour to one of the remoter frontier posts. All major airports have an ATM or banking booth for incoming international flights.

Travellers' cheques

The safest, though most fiddly, way to carry money is as **travellers' cheques**. You can cash the cheques at most banks, though rarely elsewhere. Each travellers' cheque encashment in Greece will incur a minimum commission charge of €1.20–2.40 depending on the bank, so you won't want to make too many small-value transactions. For larger amounts, a set percentage will apply.

Credit cards and ATMs

Major **credit cards** are not usually accepted by cheaper tavernas or hotels, but they're almost essential for renting cars or buying airline tickets. Major travel agents may also accept them, though a **three-percent surcharge** is often levied on the purchase of ferry (as opposed to air) tickets.

Credit/debit cards are also likely to be your main source of funds while travelling, by withdrawing money (using your usual PIN) from the vast network of Greek **ATMs**. Larger airports have at least one ATM in the arrivals hall, and any town or island with a population larger than a few thousand (or a substantial tourist traffic) also has them. The best distributed are those of the National Bank/Ethniki Trapeza, the Trapeza Pireos/Bank of Piraeus, the Commercial Bank/Emboriki Trapeza and the Alpha Bank, which happily and interchangeably accept Visa, MasterCard, Visa Electron, Plus and Cirrus cards; American Express holders are restricted to the ATMs of Alpha and National Bank.

ATM transactions with **debit cards** linked to a current (checking) account attract **charges** of 2.25 percent on the sterling/dollar transaction value, plus a commission fee of 2.65 percent; the tourist rate rather than the more favourable interbank rate will be applied. A few banks or building societies waive some or all of these fees. Using **credit cards** at an ATM costs roughly the same – 2

percent plus a 2.75-percent "overseas transaction fee", moreover with typically inflated "cash advance" interest accruing from the minute the funds are drawn down.

Wiring money

In an emergency you can arrange to have substantial amounts of **money wired** from your home bank to a bank in Greece. Receiving funds by SWIFT transfer takes anywhere from two to ten working days. From the UK, a bank charge of 0.03 percent, with a minimum of £17, maximum £35, is typically levied for two-day service; some building societies charge a £20 flat fee irrespective of the amount. If you choose this method, your home bank will need the IBAN (international bank account number) for the account to which funds are being sent or, failing that, the bank name and branch code. It's unwise to transfer more than the equivalent of €10,000; above that limit, as part of measures to combat money-laundering, the receiving Greek bank will begin asking awkward questions and imposing punitive commissions.

Having money wired from home using one of the **companies** listed below is less convenient and even more expensive than using a bank; local affiliate offices are thin on the ground in Greece, although you may find that main post offices are the designated receiving points for Western Union. However, the funds should be available for collection at Amex's or Western Union's local representative office within hours – sometimes minutes – of being sent.

Money-wiring companies

Travelers Express MoneyGram US ☎1-800/444-3010, Canada ☎1-800/933-3278, UK, Republic of Ireland and New Zealand ☎00800/6663 9472, Australia ☎001 1800/230 100, ⊛www.moneygram.com.
Western Union US and Canada ☎1-800/CALL-CASH, Australia ☎1800 501 500, New Zealand ☎0800 005 253, UK ☎0800/833 833, Republic of Ireland ☎66/947 5603, ⊛www.westernunion.com (those in the US or Canada can send money online).

Getting around

The standard overland public transport in Greece is the bus. Train networks are limited and usually slow, though service on the Athens–Pátra and Athens–Thessaloníki lines is reasonable. Buses, however, cover most routes on the mainland – albeit infrequently on minor roads – and provide basic connections on the islands. The best way to supplement buses is to rent a scooter, full-sized motorbike or car, especially on the islands where, in any substantial town or resort, you will find at least one rental outlet.

Inter-island travel, of course, means taking ferries. These again are extensive, and will eventually get you to any of the sixty-plus inhabited isles. Planes are relatively expensive, at three to four times the cost of a deck-class ferry ticket and almost twice as much as the cheapest cabin berth.

Buses

Bus services on the **major routes**, both on the mainland and islands, are highly efficient and frequent. On **secondary roads** they're less regular, with long gaps, but even the remotest villages will be connected a few days weekly by a school or market bus to the provincial capital. These often depart shortly before dawn, returning to the village between 1.30 and 3pm. On the islands there are often, but not always, buses to connect the port and main town for ferry arrivals or departures.

The network is nationally run by a single syndicate known as the **KTEL** (Kratikó Tamío Ellinikón Leoforíon). However, even in medium-sized towns there can be several scattered terminals for services in different directions, so make sure you have the right station for your departure.

Buses are traditionally two-toned cream-and-green, being slowly replaced by hi-tech, navy-and-green models. They are amazingly **prompt** as a rule, so be there in plenty of time for scheduled departures. For the major intercity lines such as Athens–Pátra, **ticketing** is computerized, with assigned seating, and such buses often get fully booked. On smaller rural/island routes, it's generally first-come, first-served, with some standing allowed, and tickets dispensed on the spot

by an *ispráktoros* or conductor. However, these tickets tend to be issued only up to the next major town, where you'll have to alight briefly and purchase an onward fare (there is always enough time for this).

Trains

The Greek railway network, run by **OSE** (Organismós Sidherodhrómon Elládhos), is limited to the mainland and, with a few exceptions, trains are slower than the equivalent buses. However, they can be much cheaper – fifty percent less on non-express services (but much the same on express), even more if you buy a return ticket – and some of the lines are enjoyable in themselves. The best is the rack-and-pinion line between Dhiakoftó and Kalávryta in the **Peloponnese** (see p.319).

Timetables are available each spring as small, Greek-only booklets; the best places to obtain them are the OSE offices in Athens at Sína 6, or in Thessaloníki at Aristotélous 18, or the main train stations in these cities. Always check the station schedule boards, or at information counters for photocopied addenda sheets, which are more current than the booklet. Trains leave promptly at the outset, though on the more circuitous lines they're invariably late by the end of the journey.

If you're starting a journey at the initial station of a run you can (at no extra cost) **reserve a seat**; a carriage and seat number will be written on the back of your ticket. At most intermediate points, it's first-come, first-served.

There are two basic classes: first and second. **First class** may be worth the extra

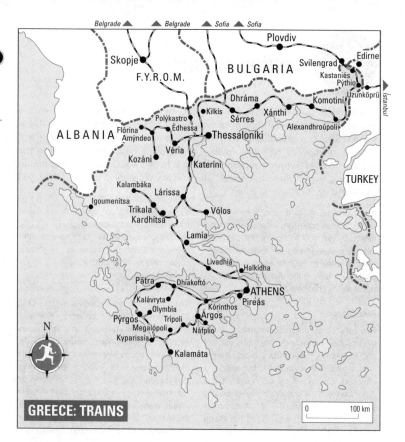

GREECE: TRAINS

0 ——— 100 km

money, insomuch as the wagons may be emptier and the seats more comfortable. A premium category, the **Intercity** (IC or ICE on timetables), exists on certain routes between Alexandhroúpoli, Thessaloníki, Vólos, Kalambáka, Athens, Pátra and Kalamáta. German-made rolling stock is relatively sleek, and much faster than the bus if the timetable is adhered to; accordingly, stiff supplements are charged depending on the distance travelled. There is also one nightly **sleeper** in each direction between Athens and Thessaloníki, with first-class compartments costing the same as a daytime IC departure. Note that any kind of ticket issued on board a train carries a fifty-percent penalty charge.

Credit cards are theoretically accepted as payment at the midtown OSE offices of Athens, Lárissa, Vólos and Thessaloníki,

as well as at the stations in Athens, Vólos, Thessaloníki, Alexandhroúpoli and Pátra; however, some readers have experienced difficulty in this respect, so check first.

InterRail and **Eurail** Pass holders (see p.32) can use their pass in Greece but must secure reservations like everyone else, and may need to pay express supplements.

Sea transport

There are several different varieties of vessel for sea travel: **roll-on-roll-off** (ro-ro) barge short-haul ferries, nicknamed *pondófles* or "slippers" in Greek, designed to shuttle mostly vehicles short distances; medium-sized-to-large **ordinary ferries**, which, stretching the definition, include a new generation of **"high-speed"** boats (*tahyplóö*), about thirty percent faster than conventional ferries; **catamarans**, also medium-sized to large, which match hydrofoils in speed but carry a certain number of cars; **hydrofoils**, which carry only passengers; and local **kaïkia**, small boats which do short hops and excursions in season. Costs are very reasonable on the longer journeys, though proportionately more expensive for shorter, inter-island connections, or baldly overpriced for monopoly crossings (eg Alexandhroúpoli–Samothráki).

We've indicated most of the **ferry, catamaran and hydrofoil connections**, both on the map (see p.52 for a general pattern) and in the "Travel details" at the end of each chapter. Don't take our listings as gospel, however, as schedules are notoriously erratic, and must be verified each year; details given are for departures between late June and mid-September. **Out-of-season** departure frequencies are severely reduced, with many islands connected only once or twice a week.

The most reliable, up-to-date information is available from the local **port police** (*limenarhío*), which on the Attic peninsula maintains offices at Pireás (☎210 45 11 310), Rafína (☎22940 28888) and Lávrio (☎22920 25249), as well as at the harbours of all fair-sized islands. Smaller places may only have a *limenikós stathmós* (marine station), often just a single room with a VHF radio. Their officers keep complete schedules posted – and, meteorological report in hand, are the final arbiters of whether a ship will sail or not in stormy weather conditions.

Many companies produce regular **schedule** booklets, which may not be adhered to as the season wears on – check websites (if any) for current information. The only attempt at an all-inclusive ferry guide is the Greek travel agents' monthly manual *Greek Travel Pages*, often outdated by the time it's printed; again you're better off referring to their website (see p.40).

Regular ferries

On most **ferry** routes, your only consideration will be getting a boat that leaves on the day, and for the island, that you want. However, when sailing from **Pireás**, the main port of Athens, to the Cyclades or Dodecanese islands, you should have a choice of at least two, often three, sailings and may want to bear in mind a few of the factors below.

Spanking-new **boats** are still a rarity; you will more often than not encounter a former English Channel or Scandinavian fjord ferry, rechristened and enjoying a new lease of life in the Aegean. **Routes** and the speed of the boats can vary enormously. A journey from Pireás to Santoríni, for instance, can take anything from five (high-speed boat) to ten ("milk-run" conventional ferry) hours. Prior to buying a ticket, establish how many stops there will be, and the estimated time of arrival.

Regular ferry **tickets** are, in general, best bought a day before departure, unless you need to reserve a cabin berth or space for a car. (If a boat fails to sail for mechanical or bad-weather reasons, the ticket price is refunded.) There are only three periods of the year – March 23–25, the week before and after Easter, and late July to early September – when ferries need to be booked at least a week in advance.

You cannot buy your ticket on board; in many cases there may not even be a last-minute sales booth at the quayside. Staff at the gangway will bar you from embarking if you don't have a ticket (the only furtive exceptions may be the short-haul, roll-on-roll-off services, for example from Igoumenítsa to Corfu, or the central mainland to Évvia). All ticket sales are now computerized, and supposedly have accurate seat/berth allocations that preclude **overbookings**. The only company that has provision for phone or Internet sales is Hellenic Seaways, which controls over half the Aegean ferry traffic; tickets must be picked up at the port at least thirty minutes before departure. **Fares** for each route are currently set by the transport ministry and should not differ among ships or agencies (though they're minutely more *towards* Pireás as opposed to *from*.

The cheapest class of ticket, which you'll probably automatically be sold, is **deck class**, variously called *tríti* or *ikonomikí thési*. This gives you the run of most boats except for the upper-class restaurant and bar.

Newly acquired boats seem, with their glaring overhead lights and plastic bucket seats, expressly designed to frustrate summertime travellers attempting to sleep on deck.

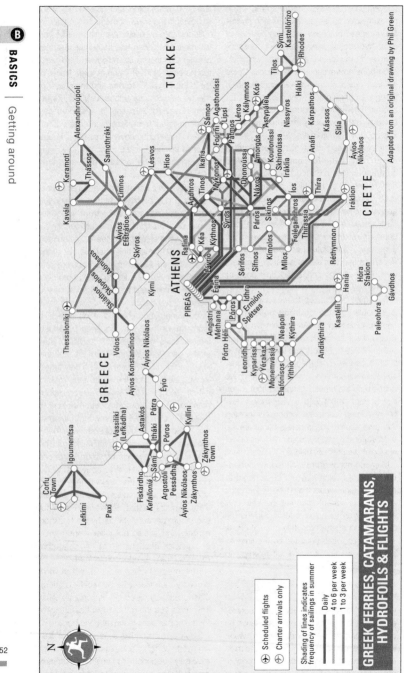

N

Scheduled flights
Charter arrivals only

Shading of lines indicates
frequency of sailings in summer

Daily
4 to 6 per week
1 to 3 per week

**GREEK FERRIES, CATAMARANS,
HYDROFOILS & FLIGHTS**

Adapted from an original drawing by Phil Green

In such cases it's worth the few extra euros for a **cabin bunk** (second-class cabins are usually quadruple, occasionally triple or double). **First-class** cabins usually cost scarcely less than a plane flight; the main difference between first and second being the presence of a bathroom in the cabin, and a better location. Most cabins are overheated or overchilled, and pretty airless; ask for an *exoteriki* (outer) cabin if you want a porthole (though these are always bolted shut).

Motorbikes and cars get issued extra tickets, in the latter case four to five times the passenger deck-class fare, depending on size. Car fees are roughly proportionate to distance: for example Sámos–Ikaría costs €26–30 depending on port and direction, while Sámos–Pireás is about €80. This limits the number of islands you'll want to drag a car to – it's really only worth it for the larger ones like Crete, Rhodes, Híos, Lésvos, Sámos, Corfu or Kefalloniá, and even then for a stay of more than four days. Elsewhere, you may find it cheaper to leave your car on the mainland and rent another on arrival. Technically, written permission is required to take rental motorbikes and cars on ferries, though in practice few crew will quiz you on this.

Ferries sell a limited range (biscuits, greasy pizzas) of overpriced, mediocre **food on board**; honourable exceptions are the meals served on overnight sailings to Crete. On the short daytime hops between the various islands of the Argo-Saronic, Cyclades and Sporades, stock up beforehand with your own snacks.

Hydrofoils and catamarans

Hydrofoils – commonly known as *dhelfínia* or "Flying Dolphins" – are roughly twice as fast (and at least twice as expensive) as ordinary ferries. On the plus side, their network neatly fills gaps in ferry scheduling, with more convenient departure times. Their main drawback (aside from frequent engine breakdowns) is that they were originally designed for cruising on placid Russian or Polish rivers, and are quite literally out of their depth on the open sea; thus they are extremely sensitive to bad weather, and even in moderate seas are not for the seasick-prone. Most of these services don't operate – or are heavily

reduced – from October to June. Hydrofoils are not allowed to carry scooters or bicycles.

At present, hydrofoils operate among the **Argo-Saronic** islands close to Athens, between Kavála and **Thássos**, between Alexandhroúpoli and **Samothráki**, and in the **Dodecanese** and east Aegean among Rhodes, Sými, Tílos, Níssyros, Kós, Kálymnos, Léros, Lipsí and Pátmos, with regular forays up to Sámos, Agathoníssi, Ikaría and Foúrni. The principal mainland ports are Aktí Tselépi in Pireás, Vólos and Áyios Konstandínos, as well as Igoumenítsa, Kavála and (some years) Alexandhroúpoli. Services in the Argo-Saronic are run by Hellenic Seaways and Vasilopoulos Flying Dolphins, and in the Dodecanese by Aegean Flying Dolphins and Samos Flying Dolphins. You may see craft with other livery, but we have excluded them from "Travel details", as they are chartered by tour agencies and do not offer scheduled services.

Catamarans attempt to combine the speed of hydrofoils with the (relative) reliability and vehicle-carrying capacity of larger ferries. The fact that they are new and sleek, purpose-built in France or Scandinavia, has not prevented numerous breakdowns, since they are constantly playing catch-up to fill in weather-cancelled itineraries and thus miss necessary maintenance. **Inside** they are rather soulless: ruthlessly air-conditioned, with no deck seating and with Greek TV blaring at you from numerous screens – paying a few euros extra for *dhiakikriméni thési* (upper class) gets you a better view and less crowding, but there's no escaping the TV. Cabins are nonexistent and food facilities even more unappetizing than on conventional ferries – bring snacks. Car fares are normal, though passenger **tickets** are at least double a comparable ferry journey, ie similar to hydrofoil rates. Their stratospheric fuel costs mean that they haven't become as ubiquitous as anticipated, but they're still found serving the Pireás–Híos–Lésvos–Límnos–north mainland line, routes to Crete, the Argo-Saronics, the Sporades, and the most popular Cyclades.

Small ferries, kaïkia and taxi boats

In season, **kaïkia** and **small ferries** sail between adjacent islands and to a few of the more obscure ones. These can be extremely useful and often very pleasant, but are no cheaper than mainline services – in fact, more expensive if classified as a tour-ist-agency charter rather than a scheduled service. The more consistent kaïki links are summarized in the "Travel details" section of each chapter, though the only firm infor-mation is to be had on the quayside. Kaïkia and small ferries, despite appearances, have a good safety record. Swarms of **taxi boats** are a feature of Sými, Rhodes, Hálki and Itháki, among other spots; these exist to shuttle clients on set routes to remote beaches or ports which can only be reached arduously, if at all, overland. Costs on these can be pretty stiff, usually per person but occasionally per boat.

Motorbikes, scooters and bicycles

The cult of the **motorcycle** is highly devel-oped in Greece, presided over by a jealous deity apparently requiring regular human sacrifice; accidents among both foreign and local bikers are routine occurrences, with annual fatalities edging into two figures on the busier islands. But with caution and common sense – and an eye to increasingly enforced regulations – riding a two-wheeler through a resort should be a lot safer than piloting one through London or New York.

Many tourists come to grief on rutted dirt tracks or astride mechanically dodgy machines. In other cases **accidents** are due to attempts to cut corners, in all senses, or by riding two to an under-powered scooter simply not designed to propel such a load. Don't be tempted by this apparent economy – you won't regret getting two separate automatic scooters, or one powerful manual bike to share – and remember that you're likely to be charged an exorbitant sum for any repairs if you do have a wipeout. Also, verify that your travel insurance policy covers motorcycle acci-dents.

One worthwhile precaution is to wear a **crash helmet** (*krános*); many rental outfits will offer you (an admittedly ill-fitting) one, and some will make you sign a waiver of liability if you refuse it. Helmet-wearing is in fact required by law, with a €78 fine levied

for failure to do so; on some smaller islands (Léros) the rule is laxly enforced, on others (Sámos and Corfu) random police road-blocks do a brisk commerce in citations, and foreign renters are most definitely not exempt.

Reputable establishments demand a full motorcycle driving licence for any engine over 80cc (Greek law actually stipulates "over 50cc"), and you will usually have to leave your passport as security. For smaller models, any driving licence will do. Failure to carry the correct license on your person attracts an €86 fine.

Fines of any sort are to be paid within ten working days at the municipal cashier's (*dhimotikó tamío*); proof of payment then needs to be taken to the police station to have the citation cancelled. Non-payment will be followed by a court date being set, and the Greek authorities – so dilatory in other respects – are amazingly efficient at trans-lating summons into foreign languages and forwarding them to your overseas address. No-shows are automatically convicted, and a conviction will make re-entry to Greece awkward at best.

Small **motor scooters** with automatic transmission, known in Greek as *papá-kia* (little ducks) after their characteristic noise, are good transport for all but the hilliest islands. They're available for rent on many islands and in a few of the popu-lar mainland resorts for €10–18 per day. Prices can be bargained down out of peak season, or if you negotiate for a longer period of rental.

Before riding off, make sure you check the bike's **mechanical state**, since many are only cosmetically maintained. Bad brakes, non-functioning electrics and worn or oil-fouled spark plugs are the most common defects; dealers often keep the front brakes far too loose, with the commendable inten-tion of preventing you going over the handle-bars. If you break down it's your responsibil-ity to return the machine; better outlets offer a free retrieval service.

The latest models of **scooters**, generally Honda, Piaggio, Vespa or Peugeot, are prac-tical enough, but thirsty on fuel; make sure there's a kick-start as backups to the battery, since ignition switches commonly fail. The new Haojin 125cc automatic scooter is the only model really powerful enough for two riders. Bungee cords (a *khtapódi*, or "octopus", in slang) for tying down bundles are supplied on request, while capacious baskets are also often a feature. The ultra-trendy, low-slung models with fat, small-radius tyres, however, are unstable on anything other than the smoothest, flattest island roads. Especially if you intend to go off-road, always choose traditionally designed bikes with large-radius, nobbly, narrow tyres, if available. Again, if you're going to spend every day of your vacation astride a scooter, consider bringing or buying cyclists' or motorcyclists' **gloves**; they may look stupid during summer, but if you lose all the skin off your hands when you go for a spill, the wounds can take months to heal, and leave huge scars.

In the family of true **motorbikes** with manual transmissions (*mihanákia*), and safer tyres (as described above), the favourites, in descending order of reliability, are the Honda 50, Yamaha Townmate and Suzuki FB Birdie; gears are shifted with an easy-to-learn left-foot pedal action, and (very important) these can all be push-started in second gear if the starting crank fails. For two riders, the least powerful safe model at nominal extra cost is the Honda Cub 90cc or Yamaha 80 Townmate. Best of all is the attractive Honda Astrea 100 and its rival-brand clones (eg Kawasaki Kaze), very powerful but scarcely bigger than older models. With the proper licence and off-road experience, dirt-bikes of 125cc and up can also be found in most resorts. **Quads** are also increasingly offered in many resorts – silly-looking, and a nuisance on beaches, but undoubtedly safer for two riders.

Cycling

Cycling in Greece is not such hard going as you might imagine (except in midsummer), especially on one of the mountain bikes that are now the rule at rental outfits; they rarely cost more than €7 a day. You do, however, need steady nerves, as roads are generally narrow with no verges or bike lanes (except on Kós and in Tríkala, Édhessa and Mesolóngi), and many Greek drivers consider cyclists a lower form of life, on a par with the snakes regularly found run over.

If you have your own mountain or touring bike (the latter not rented in Greece), you might consider taking it along by **train** or **plane** (it's free if within your 20–23kg international air allowance, but always arrange it in writing with the airline beforehand to avoid huge charges at check-in). Once in Greece you should be able to take a bike for free on most of the ferries, in the guard's van on most trains (for a small fee – it goes on a later goods train otherwise), and with a little persuasion in the luggage bays of buses. Any small spare parts you might need, however, are best brought along, since specialist bike shops are only found in the provincial capitals and main cities.

Driving and car rental

Automobiles have obvious advantages for getting to the more inaccessible parts of mainland Greece, but this is not an especially cheap Mediterranean country in which to **rent a car**. If you intend to drive **your own vehicle** to and through Greece, it's worth knowing that insurance contracted in any EU member state is valid in any other, but in many cases this is only third-party cover – the statutory legal minimum. Competition in the industry is so intense, however, that many UK insurers will throw in full, pan-European cover for free or for a nominal sum, up to sixty days; shop around if necessary.

EU citizens bringing their own cars are, in theory, free to circulate in the country for six months, or until their home-based road tax or insurance expires, whichever happens first; see remarks on p.84 for keeping a car in Greece for longer. Other nationalities will get a **non-EU car** entered in their passport; the carnet normally allows you to keep a vehicle ·in Greece for up to six months, exempt from road tax.

Car rental

Car rental within Greece starts at around €300 a week in high season for the smallest, A-group vehicle from a one-off outlet or local chain, including unlimited mileage, tax and insurance. Overseas tour operators' and international chains' brochures threaten alarming rates of nearly €400 for the same period but, except in August, no rental company expects to fetch that price for a car. Outside peak season, at the smaller local outfits, you can often get terms of €30–35 per day, all inclusive, with even better rates for three days or more. **Comparison shopping** among agencies in the larger resorts can yield a variation in quotes of up to twenty percent for the same conditions over a four-to-seven-day period; the most negotiable variable is whether or not kilometres in excess of one hundred per day (a common hidden catch) are free. Open **jeeps**, which are increasingly popular, begin at about €65 per day, rising to as much as €100 at busy times and places.

Brochure prices in Greece almost never include VAT at 19 percent, **collision damage waiver** (CDW) and personal insurance. The CDW typically has a deductible of €400–600, some or all of which can be levied for even the tiniest scratch or missing mudguard. To avoid this, it is strongly recommended that you pay the €5–7 extra per day for Super Collision Damage Waiver, Franchise Waiver or Liability Waiver Surcharge, as it is variously called. Even better, frequent travellers should take out **annual excess insurance** through Insurance 4 Car Hire (☎020/7012 6300, ⓦwww .insurance4carhire.com), which will cover all UK- and North America-based drivers.

All agencies will want a blank **credit card** slip as a deposit up front (destroyed when you return the vehicle safely); minimum age requirements vary from 21 to 23. **Driving licences** issued by any EU state are honoured, but an International Driving Permit is required by all other drivers, including Australians, New Zealanders and North Americans. This must be arranged before departure in your home country. Some unscrupulous agencies still rent to these nationals on production of just a home licence, but you can be arrested and charged if caught by the traffic police without an IDP if you require one.

In peak season, you may get a better price through one of the **overseas booking companies** that deal with local firms than if you negotiate for rental in Greece itself. One of the most competitive companies in Britain is Transhire; the website ⓦwww .rentacar-uk.com also comes recommended.

Autorent, Budget, Payless, EuroHire, European, Kosmos, National/Alamo, Reliable, Eurodollar and Just are dependable Greek, or smaller international, chains with branches in many towns; all are considerably cheaper than the biggest international operators such as Hertz or Avis, but it is always worthwhile visiting all the international chains' websites for a quote, and with a Frequent Flyer discount code you may well match prices of the discount booking companies noted above. Specific local recommendations are given in the guide.

In terms of **models**, the more reputable companies tend to offer the Citroën Saxo, Kia Pikanto, Chevrolet Matiz or Fiat Cinquecento or Seisento as A-group cars, and Opel (Vauxhall) Corsa 1.2, Fiat Uno or Punto, Peugeot 106, Hyundai Atos or Getz, Renault Clio or Twingo, or Nissan Micra in the B group. Any more than two adults, with luggage, will generally require B category, in which the Atos and the Clio are the most robust models. In the C or D categories, suitable for two adults and two kids, Renault Mègane or Peugeot 307 are preferable to the Seat Cordoba/Ibiza. The standard four-wheel-drive option is a Suzuki jeep (1.3- or 1.6-litre), mostly open – great for bashing down steep, rutted tracks to remote beaches.

Car-rental agencies

Britain

Avis ☎0870/606 0100, ⓦwww.avis.com.
Budget ☎0800/181 181,
ⓦwww.budget.com.
Hertz ☎0870/844 8844, ⓦwww.hertz.com.
National ☎0870/536 5365, ⓦwww.nationalcar .co.uk.
Sixt ⓦwww.e-sixt.com.
Thrifty ☎01494/751 600, ⓦwww.thrifty.com.
Transhire ☎0870/789 8000, ⓦwww.transhire. com.

Ireland

Avis Northern Ireland ☎028/9024 0404, Republic of Ireland ☎01/605 7500, ⓦwww.avis.ie.
Budget Republic of Ireland ☎0903/277 11, ⓦwww.budget.ie.
Cosmo Thrifty Northern Ireland ☎028/9445 2565, ⓦwww.thrifty.com.
Hertz Republic of Ireland ☎01/676 7476, ⓦwww .hertz.ie.

Sixt Republic of Ireland ☎1850/206 088, ⓦwww
.irishcarrentals.ie.
Thrifty Republic of Ireland ☎1800/515 800,
ⓦwww.thrifty.ie.

North America

Alamo ☎1-800/462-5266, ⓦwww.alamo.com.
Auto Europe ☎1-800/223-555, ⓦwww
.autoeurope.com.
Avis US ☎1-800/230-4898, Canada ☎1-800/272-
5871, ⓦwww.avis.com.
Budget ☎1-800/527-0700, ⓦwww
.budgetrentacar.com.
Dollar US ☎1-800/800-3665, ⓦwww.dollar.com.
Europe by Car ☎1-800/ 223-1516, ⓦwww
.europebycar.com.
Hertz US ☎1-800/654-3131, Canada
☎1-800/263-0600, ⓦwww.hertz.com.
National ☎1-800/962-7070, ⓦwww.nationalcar
.com.
Thrifty ☎1-800/847-4389, ⓦwww.thrifty.com.

Australia

Avis ☎13 63 33 or 02/9353 9000, ⓦwww.avis
.com.au.
Budget ☎1300/362 848, ⓦwww.budget.com.au.
Hertz ☎13 30 39 or 03/9698 2555, ⓦwww.hertz
.com.au.
National ☎13 10 45, ⓦwww.nationalcar.com.au.
Thrifty ☎1300/367 227, ⓦwww.thrifty.com.au.

New Zealand

Apex ☎0800 93 95 97 or 03/379 6897, ⓦwww
.apexrentals.co.nz.
Avis ☎09/526 2847 or 0800 655 111, ⓦwww
.avis.co.nz.
Budget ☎080/652 227, ⓦwww.budget.co.nz.
Hertz ☎0800/654 321, ⓦwww.hertz.co.nz.
National ☎0800/800 115, ⓦwww.nationalcar
.co.nz.
Thrifty ☎09/309 0111, ⓦwww.thrifty.co.nz.

Driving in Greece

As in all of continental Europe, you drive **on
the right** in Greece. The country has one of
the highest (fatal) **accident rates** in Europe,
and on mainland motorways or the larger
tourist islands it's easy to see why. Driving
habits amongst locals can be atrocious;
overtaking is erratic, tailgating and barging
out from side roads are preferred pastimes,
lane lines go unheeded, turn signals go
unused and motorbikes hog the road or
weave from side to side. **Drunk driving** is

also a major problem; Sunday afternoons in
rural areas are particularly bad, and for the
same reason you should be extra vigilant
driving late at night at weekends or on holidays. Well-publicized police campaigns are
addressing the problem, with radar guns
being deployed against speeders as well.

Matters are made worse by poor **road
conditions**: signposting is absent or badly
placed, pavement markings are faded,
curves are invariably banked the wrong way
and slick with olive-blossom drop in May,
asphalt can turn into a one-lane surface or
a dirt track without warning on secondary
routes, railway crossings are rarely guarded,
and you're heavily dependent on magnifying
mirrors at blind intersections in congested
villages. Uphill drivers insist on their **right of
way**, as do those first to approach a one-
lane bridge; **flashed headlights** usually
mean the opposite of what they do in the
UK or North America, here signifying that
the other driver insists on coming through
or overtaking. However, this gesture rapidly
repeated from someone approaching means
they're warning you of a police control-
point ahead. **Parking** in almost every mainland town, plus the biggest island towns, is
uniformly a nightmare owing to congestion
and demand. **Pay-and-display** systems
(plus residents-only schemes) as in the UK
are the rule, and it's not always clear where
you obtain tickets (sometimes from a kiosk,
sometimes from a machine).

There are a limited number of **express
highways** between Pátra, Athens and Thessaloníki, on which tolls are levied – currently
€2–2.50 for ordinary cars at each sporadically placed gate. They're nearly twice as
quick as the old roads, and good for novices
to Greek conditions. But even on these so-
called motorways, there may be no proper
far-right lane for slower traffic, which is
expected to straddle the solid white line at
the verge and allow rapid traffic to pass.

Wearing a **seatbelt** is compulsory – you
will be fined for non-observance at the many
checkpoints – as is keeping a first-aid kit in
the boot (many rental companies skimp on
this), and children under the age of 10 are
not allowed to sit in the front seats. It's illegal
to drive away from any kind of **accident** – or
to move the vehicles before the police appear

– and in cases where serious injury has resulted you can be held at a police station for up to 24 hours. For any substantial property damage, you wait for the police to arrive; they will take down the details of all drivers, note the time and place of the incident, give copies of the statement to all involved for insurance purposes (or forward one to the rental company if your car is rented), and then give you permission to go on your way if the car hasn't been crippled. Though forensics aren't their long suit, they're generally a lot more civil and calm than the Greek drivers actually involved in the accident.

Tourists with proof of AA/RAC/AAA membership are given free road assistance from ELPA, the Greek equivalent, which runs **breakdown services** on several of the larger islands; in an emergency ring their road assistance service on ☏ 10400. Many car rental companies have an agreement with ELPA's equally widespread competitors Hellas Service (☏ 1057), Interamerican (☏ 1168) and Express Service (☏ 1154). However, you will always get a faster response if you dial the local number for the province you're stranded in (ask for these in advance).

Running a vehicle

Fuel, whether regular unleaded (*amólyvdhi*), super unleaded, super lead-replacement or diesel, is currently cresting the one-euro-per-litre barrier in most of the country, and could well have reached €1.25 by the time you read this. Lead-replacement fuel for older cars without catalytic converters is called "Neo Super" or "Super LRP". Most scooters and motorbikes run better on super, even if they nominally take regular.

It is easy to run short of fuel **after dark or at weekends** in both rural and urban Greece; most stations close at 7 or 8pm, and nearly as many are shut all day Sunday. One pump per district will always remain open, but interpreting the Greek-only pharmacy-type-rota lists posted at shut stations is another matter. This is not so much of a problem on the major highways, but it is a factor everywhere else. So always fill up, or insist on full rental vehicles at the outset, and if you've brought your own car, keep a full petrol can at all times.

Some stations, which claim to be open around the clock, are in fact **automated-only at night** – you have to use bill-taking machines, which don't give change. If you fill your tank without having exhausted your credit, punch the button for a receipt and get change the next day during attended hours (assuming you're still in the area). Petrol stations run by multinational companies (BP, Shell) usually take **credit cards**; Greek chains like Aegean, EKO, Elda, Eteka, Jetoil, Revoil and Elinoil usually don't (except in tourist areas or along main highways). The tiny, generic-petrol stations of the EP (Ele`fthero Pratirio) chain are always the cheapest around.

In terms of **maintenance**, the easiest car models to have serviced and buy parts for in Greece are VWs (including old microbuses and Transporter vans), Mercedes, BMWs, Audis, Opels, Ladas, Skodas and virtually all French, Italian, Korean and Japanese makes. British models are a bit more difficult, but you should be fine as long as you haven't brought anything too esoteric like a Hillman Minx – the Mini is, for example, still a cult vehicle in Greece, Fords are present (though not common), and the Opel is of course the continental brand of Vauxhall.

Taxis

Greek **taxis** are among the cheapest in western Europe – so long as you get an honest driver who switches the meter on (see the caveats about Athens on p.110) and doesn't use high-tech devices to doctor the reading. Use of the meter is mandatory within city or town limits, where Tariff 1 applies, while in rural areas or between midnight and 5am Tariff 2 is in effect. On certain islands, set rates apply on specific fixed routes for collective taxis – these only depart when full. Otherwise, throughout Greece the meter starts at €0.75, though the minimum fare is €1.50; any baggage not actually on your lap is charged at €0.30 a piece. Additionally, there are surcharges of €2 for leaving or entering an airport (€3 for Athens), and €0.80 for leaving a harbour area. If you summon a taxi by phone on spec, there's a €1.50 charge, while a prearranged rendezvous is €2.10 extra; in either case the meter starts running from the moment the driver begins heading towards you. All categories of supplemental charges must be set out on a laminated card affixed to the dashboard. For a week or so before and after Orthodox Easter, and Christmas, a *filodhórima* or gratuity of about ten percent is levied. Any or all of these extras will legitimately bump up the basic rate of about €8 per ten rural kilometres.

Domestic flights

State-run Olympic Airlines and its subsidiary Olympic Aviation at present operate most of the **domestic flights** within Greece, though they were teetering on the brink of closure as of writing. They (or any successor) cover a fairly wide network of islands and larger mainland towns, though most routes are to and from Athens or Thessaloníki. Privately run Aegean Airlines has cherry-picked the high-volume, high-profit routes from Athens and Thessaloniki to Crete (Haniá and Iráklion), Thíra, Mytilíni, Mýkonos, Rhodes, Kós, Híos, Corfu, Kavála, Ioánnina and Alexandhroúpoli. **Tickets** for both airlines are most easily obtained from travel agents (their own high-street outlets are thin on the ground). Aegean often undercuts Olympic with price specials, and surpasses it service-wise, though flight frequencies tend to be sparse.

Olympic **schedules** can be picked up at their offices abroad (see "Getting there" for contact details in the relevant countries) or through their branch offices and representatives in Greece, which are maintained in almost every town or island of any size. Aegean's are easiest to get from their desks at major airports. Both airlines publish English-language schedules at least twice yearly (spring and autumn).

Fares for flights to and between the islands, including the domestic airport tax,

work out around three to four times the cost of a ferry journey, but on certain inter-island hauls poorly served by boat (Rhodes–Kárpathos or Corfu–Kefalloniá, for example), you should consider this time well bought, and indeed some of these subsidized peripheral routes cost less than a hydrofoil/catamaran journey would.

Island flights are often full in peak season; if they're an essential part of your plans, it is worth trying to make a **reservation** at least two weeks in advance. If a flight you've set your heart on is full, **waiting lists** exist – and are worth signing on to; experience has shown that there are almost always one or two booking cancellations. Domestic air tickets are nonrefundable, but you can change your flight, space permitting, without penalty as late as 24 hours before your original departure.

Like ferries, flights are subject to **cancellation** in very bad weather, since many services are on small 46- or 74-seat ATR turboprop planes, smaller "Dash 8" (De Havilland 37-seaters), or the tiny Dornier 18-seaters, none of which will fly in strong winds or (depending on the destination airport) after dark. Size restrictions also mean that the 15-kilo baggage weight limit can be fairly strictly enforced, especially on the Dorniers; if, however, you've just arrived from overseas or purchased your ticket outside Greece, you are allowed the standard international limit (20–23 kilos depending on carrier). All services operated on the domestic network are **non-smoking**.

Contacts for Greek domestic airlines

Aegean Countrywide ☎801 11 20 000, ⓦwww
.aegeanair.com.
Olympic Airlines/Aviation Countrywide ☎801
11 44 444, ⓦwww.olympicairlines.com.

Accommodation

There are huge numbers of beds for tourists in Greece, so most of the season you can rely on turning up pretty much anywhere and finding a room – if not in a hotel, then in a private house or block of rooms (the standard island accommodation). Only from late July to early September, and around Easter, the country's high season, are you likely to experience problems. At these times, if you don't have accommodation reserved well in advance, you'd be wise to keep well off the main tourist trails, turning up at each new place early in the day and taking whatever is available – you may be able to exchange it for something better later on.

Out of season, you face a slightly different problem: most private rooms and campsites operate only from late April or early May to October, leaving hotels as your only option. During winter you may have no choice but to stay in the main towns or ports. There will often be very little life outside these places anyway, with all the seasonal beach bars and restaurants closed. On many smaller islands, you will often find just one hotel – and perhaps one taverna – staying open year-round. Be warned also that any resort or harbour hotels which do operate through the winter are likely to have a certain number of **prostitutes** as long-term guests; licensed prostitution is legal in Greece, and the management at many places consider this the most painless way to keep the bills paid.

Hotels

Hotels and self-catering complexes in the larger resorts are often contracted out on a seasonal basis by foreign package-holiday companies, though there are often vacancies available (especially in spring or autumn) for walk-in trade. The tourist police set official **categories** for hotels, which range from L (Luxury) down to the rarely encountered E class; all except the top category have to keep within set price limits. The letter system is supposed to be replaced with a star grading system as in other countries, but the process, while begun, is being resisted; L is five-star, E is no-star, etc. While they last, letter ratings are supposed to correspond to **facilities** available, though in practice categorization often depends on location within a resort, number of rooms and influence with the tourism authorities – there are so-called E-class hotels with under nine rooms which are plusher than nearby C-class outfits. It is mandatory for D-class hotels to have all rooms with attached baths; C-class must additionally have a bar or designated breakfast area. The presence of a pool or tennis court will attract a B-class rating, while A-category hotels should have a restaurant, bar, business facilities and extensive common areas. Often these, and the L outfits (essentially self-contained complexes), back onto a quasi-private beach.

Mainland town hotels are almost invariably poor value for money, used as they are to a business clientele, and thus charging the same inflated rates all year. In ski resorts and other places with significant October-to-April leisure tourism, such as Galaxídhi, Náfplio, Pílion and Mt Ménalo, rates can be markedly higher at weekends and holidays, and generally so during winter when heating bills must be accounted for. The only exceptions to this are lowland Peloponnese (which has enough foreign tourism to generate some healthy competition), and to a certain extent Athens.

In terms of **food**, C-class hotels are only required to provide the most rudimentary of continental breakfasts – you may often choose not to take, or pay for, it – while B-class and above will usually offer some sort of buffet breakfast including cheese, cold cuts, sausages, eggs and so on. With some exceptions, hotel restaurants are rarely memorable.

Private rooms

The most common island and mainland-resort accommodation is **privately let rooms** (*dhomátia*). Like hotels, these are regulated and officially divided into three classes (A to C), according to facilities. These days the bulk of them are in new, purpose-built, low-rise buildings, but a few are still actually in people's homes, where you may be treated to disarming hospitality.

Licensed rooms are mostly scrupulously clean, however limited their other amenities. At their (now all-but-vanished) **simplest**, you'll be a bare, concrete-floored room, with a hook on the back of the door and toilet facilities outside in the courtyard. At the **fancier** end of the scale, they are modern, fully furnished places with en-suite bathroom, TV, air conditioning, and a fridge, if not a fully equipped kitchen shared by guests. Between these extremes there will be a choice of rooms at various prices – owners will usually show you the most expensive first. Some of the cheap places will also have more expensive rooms with en-suite facilities – and vice versa, with rare singles often tucked under stairways or other less desirable corners of the building. Price and quality are not necessarily directly linked, so always ask to see the room before agreeing to take it.

Areas to **look for rooms**, along with recommendations of the best places, are included in the Guide. However, the rooms may find you: owners descend on ferry or bus arrivals to fill any space they have, sometimes waving photos of the premises. Many island municipalities are acting, to outlaw this practice, owing to widespread bait-and-switch tactics and the pitching of unlicensed rooms. Rooms can often be a longer journey from the initial meeting than you had expected. In smaller places you'll often see rooms advertised, sometimes in German (*Zimmer*); the Greek signs to look out for are "ENIKIAZÓMENA DHOMÁTIA" or "ENIKIÁZONTEH DHOMÁTIA". In the more developed island resorts, where package holiday-makers predominate, *dhomátia* owners will often require you to stay for at least three days, or even a week.

It has become standard practice for rooms proprietors, like hotel staff, to ask to keep your **passport** – ostensibly for the tourist police, who require customer particulars – but in reality to prevent you skipping out with an unpaid bill. Some owners may be satisfied with just taking down your details, as is done in most hotels, and they'll almost always return the documents once you get to know them, or if you need them for another purpose.

If you are **stranded**, or arrive very late in a remote mountain or island village, you may very well find that there is someone with an unlicensed room prepared to earn extra money by putting you up. This should not be counted on, but things work out more often than not.

Old-fashioned, 1970s-vintage rooms on the remoter islets, occasionally still without

---

Accommodation price codes

Throughout the book we've categorized accommodation according to the following **price codes**, which denote the **cheapest available double room in high season**. All prices are for the room only, except where otherwise indicated in accounts. Many hotels, especially those in category ❹ and over, include breakfast in the price; we indicate this by including "B&B" in the listing, but you should check when booking. During low season, rates can drop by more than fifty percent, especially if you are staying for three or more nights. Exceptions are during the Christmas and Easter weeks when you'll pay high-season prices. Single rooms, where available, cost around seventy percent of the price of a double.

❶ Up to €25	❺ €71–90
❷ €26–35	❻ €91–120
❸ €36–50	❼ €121–170
❹ €51–70	❽ € 171 plus and upwards

Youth hostels and **mountain refuges** typically charge €7–9 for a dormitory bed.

private bath, tend to fall into the **❶** price category. Basic en-suite rooms without cooking facilities weigh in at **❷**; newer, well-amenitied rooms, self-catering studios, and modest C-class hotels occupy the top end of the **❸** niche, the better among these edging into **❹**. Category **❺** corresponds fairly well to the better-value B-class hotels and the humbler designer inns in popular centres like Zagória, Pílio and the trendier Cyclades, while **❻** tallies with most of B-class and the state-of-the-art restoration projects. **❼–❽** means A- and L-class, and the sky's the limit here – €300 is by no means unheard of these days.

Prices and supplements in any establishment should by law be displayed on the back of the door of your room, or over the reception desk. If you feel you're being overcharged at a place that is officially registered, threaten to report it to the tourist office or police, who will generally adopt your side in such cases. A hotelier is free to offer a room at any amount under the official rate, but it's an offence to charge one euro-cent over the permitted price for the **current season**. Depending on location, there are up to three of these: typically October to May (low), June to mid-July, and September (mid) and mid-July through August (high). Small amounts over the posted price may be legitimately explained by municipal tax or out-of-date forms, but usually you will pay less than the maximum.

In **winter**, officially from November 1 until early April, private rooms – except in Ródhos Old Town and the biggest towns of Crete – are closed pretty much across the board to keep the few open hotels in business. There's no point in traipsing about hoping to find exceptions; most owners obey the system very strictly. If they don't, the room-owners will find you themselves and, watching out for hotel rivals, guide you back to their place.

A fair number of hotels, and rather fewer apartments and rooms, have **websites** – but often these are run by agencies rather than the owner, and have little useful information. Be warned that some proprietors only check their email at infrequent intervals, if at all, and phoning may be essential for advance booking.

Villas and long-term rentals

The easiest – and usually most economical – way to arrange a **villa rental** is through one of the package-holiday companies detailed on p.31. They represent some superb places, from fairly simple to luxurious, and costs can be very reasonable, especially if shared between a few people. Several of the companies we list will arrange **twin-centre** stays on two islands over two weeks.

On the islands, a few local travel agents arrange villa rentals, though they are often places the overseas companies gave a miss on or could not fill. **Out of season**, you can sometimes get a good deal on villa or apartment rental for a month or more by asking around locally, though in these days of EU convergence and the increasing desirability of the islands as year-round residences, "good deal" means anything under €180 per month for a large studio (*garsoniéra*) or €250 for a small one-bedroom flat.

Youth hostels

Greece is not exactly packed with **youth hostels**, and those that do exist tend, with few exceptions, to be pretty run-down and filthy, and thus a far cry from similar north European institutions. Competition from inexpensive rooms and unofficial "student hostels", open to all, means they are simply not as cost-effective as elsewhere in Europe. It's best to have a valid IYHF card, but you can often buy one on the spot, or maybe just pay a little extra for your bed. Extra payment for sheets, towels and the like can bump up the price. Dorms tend to have four to six beds; most hostels have a curfew of 11pm or midnight, and many places only open in spring and summer.

The only surviving hostels on the **mainland** are in Athens, Olympía, Pátra and Thessaloníki. On the **islands** you'll find them on Thíra, Corfu, Rhodes and Crete. Few of these are officially recognized by the IYHF.

Monasteries

Greek **monasteries** and **convents** have a tradition of putting up travellers (of the appropriate sex). On the mainland, this is still a customary – if steadily decreasing – practice, used mostly by villagers on pilgrimage; on the islands, monastic hospitality is not common, so you should always ask locally before heading out to a monastery or convent for the night. Also, dress modestly – no shorts or short skirts – and try to arrive early in the evening, not later than 8pm or sunset (whichever is earlier).

For men, the most exciting monastic experience is a visit to the "Monks' Republic" of Mount Athos (see p.545), on the Halkidhikí peninsula, near Thessaloníki. This is, however, a far from casual travel option, involving a fair amount of advance planning and the securing of a permit.

Camping

Officially recognized campsites range from ramshackle compounds on the islands to highly organized and rather soulless complexes, formerly run by EOT prior to privatization. Most places cost about €5–7 a night per person, slightly less per tent and €6–8 per camper van, but at the fanciest sites rates for two people plus a tent can almost equal the price of a basic room. The Panhellenic Camping Association regularly (but not annually) publishes a booklet covering most officially recognized Greek campsites and the facilities they offer; it's available from many EOT offices.

Freelance camping, as the EOT calls it, was forbidden under a law originally enacted to harass gypsies, but regulations are increasingly enforced against tourists. Another drawback is the increased prevalence of theft in rural areas. You will feel less vulnerable inside a tent, camper van or even a rock-cave – not that rain is likely during the long Greek summer, but some protection is essential from wind, sun, insects and stray animals raiding your food. You will always need at least a light sleeping bag, since even summer nights can get cool and damp; a foam pad is also recommended for pitching on harder ground.

If you do camp rough, it's vital to exercise sensitivity and discretion. Police will crack down on people camping (and especially littering) around popular tourist beaches, particularly when a large community of campers develops. Off the beaten track, however, nobody is very bothered, though it is always best to ask permission locally in the village taverna or café. During high season, when everything – even the authorized campsites – may be full, attitudes towards freelance camping are more relaxed, even in the most touristed places. At such times the best strategy is to find a sympathetic taverna, which in exchange for regular patronage will probably be willing to guard small valuables and let you use their facilities.

Eating and drinking

Greeks spend a lot of time socializing outside their homes, and sharing a meal is one of the chief ways of doing it. The atmosphere is always relaxed and informal, with pretensions rare outside of the more chi-chi parts of Athens and certain major resorts. Greeks are not prodigious drinkers – tippling is traditionally meant to accompany food – though since the mid-1990s a range of bars and clubs has sprung up.

Breakfast

Greeks don't generally eat **breakfast**, something reflected in the abysmal quality of most hotel "continental" offerings; the choice of

juice tends to be orange, orange and orange, with fresh fruit rare, at any place below "B" category. *Méli me voútyro* is syrupy, commercial honey and prepacked pats of butter (or margarine) to slather on bread or *friganiés* (melba-toast slivers). Confusingly, jam is called *marmeládha* in Greek; ask for *portokáli* – orange – if you want proper marmalade. Tea means obscure Sri Lankan or Madagascan brands of bag, often left to stew in a metal pot. The only egg-and-bacon kinds of places are in resorts where foreigners congregate, or where there are returned North American- or Australian-Greeks. Such spots can sometimes be good value (€5.50–8 for the works, including "French" filter coffee or a cappuccino), especially if there's competition.

Picnics and snacks

Picnic fare is easily available at bakeries and *manávika* (fruit-and-veg stalls). **Bread**, alas, is often of minimal nutritional value and inedible within a day of purchase. It's worth paying extra at the bakery (*foúrnos* or *psomádhiko*) for *olikís* (wholemeal), *sikalísio* (rye bread), *oktásporo* (eight-grain) or even *enneásporo* (nine-grain), the latter types most commonly baked where large numbers of Germans or Scandinavians are about. When buying **olives**, go for the fat Kalamáta or Ámfissa ones; they're more expensive, but tastier. However, locally gathered olives – especially the slightly shrivelled *hamádhes* or fully ripened, ground-gathered olives – often have a distinctive nutty taste, compensating for large kernels. The best **honey** is reckoned to be the pure-thyme variety from the more barren islands (such as Límnos, Náxos, Kálymnos and Astypálea) or areas of the mainland.

Honey is an ideal topping for the famous local **yoghurt**. All larger towns have at least one dairy shop where locally produced yoghurts are sold in plastic or (better) clay containers of various sizes. Sheep-milk yoghurt is richer and sweeter, scarcely requiring honey; cow's-milk yoghurt is tarter but more widely available. Side by side with these will be *krémes* (custards) and *ryzógala* (rice puddings) in one-serving plastic containers. **Feta** cheese is ubiquitous, often with up to a dozen varieties to choose from, made from goat-, sheep- or cow-milk, or varying proportions thereof. You're encouraged to taste before buying; this sampling advice goes for other indigenous cheeses

as well, the most palatable of which are the expensive gruyère-type *graviéra*.

Despite EU membership, growing personal incomes and exotic tastes, Greece imports very little garden produce from abroad, aside from bananas, the odd pineapple and a few mangoes. **Fruit** in particular is relatively expensive and available only by season, though in the more cosmopolitan spots it is possible to find such things as avocados (the light-green Fuerte variety from Crete is excellent) for much of the year. Reliable picnic fruits include several types of cherries (June–July); *yiarmádhes*, a variety of giant peach available from August to mid-September (after which they go mealy and should be avoided; *krystália*, tiny, hard green pears that ripen a month or two later and are heavenly; *vaniliés*, orange- or red-fleshed plums whose season lasts from late August through October; and the *himoniátiko* melon (called casava in North America) which appears in September, in its yellow, puckered skin with green flecks. Greece also has a burgeoning kiwi industry, and while the first crop in October coincides with the end of the tourist season, availability continues into the following May. Less portable, but succulent, are figs; there's a crop of small fruits in May, followed by larger ones in August and September. Salad **vegetables** are more reasonably priced; besides the famous, enormous tomatoes (June–Sept), there is a bewildering variety of springtime greens, including rocket, dill, enormous spring onions and lettuces. Useful expressions for shopping are *éna tétarto* (250g) and *misó kiló* (500g).

Traditional **snacks** can be one of the distinctive pleasures of Greek eating, though they are being increasingly edged out by an obsession with Western fast food at nationwide chains such as *Goody's* (above-average burgers, pasta and salad bar), *Everest* and *Grigoris Mikroyevmata* (assorted turnovers), *Roma Pizza* and *Theios Vanias* (baked pastries) – somewhat less insipid for being home-grown. However, independently produced kebabs (*souvlákia*) are widely available, and in most larger resorts and towns you'll find *yíros* – doner kebab with garnish in thick, doughy *píta* bread.

Other common snacks include *tyrópites* (cheese pies – the best are the *striftés* or *kouroú* if available) and *spanokópites* (spinach pies), which can usually be found at the baker's, as can *voutímata* (dark biscuits heavy on the molasses, cinnamon and butter). Pizza can be very good as well, sold *al metro* (by the piece).

Restaurants

Greek cuisine and **restaurants** are usually simple and straightforward, with no snobbery attached to eating out; most people do it regularly, and it's still affordable – typically €11–16 per person for a substantial (non-seafood) meal with a measure of house wine. But even if preparation is basic, you should expect it to be wholesome – Greeks are fussy about freshness and provenance, shunning pre-fried chips and frozen New Zealand chops. That said, there's a lot of **lazy cooking** in resorts, where menus are dominated by bad pizza, spaghetti bolognese, chops and "tourist moussaká": a dish heavy with cheap potato slices, and nary a crumb of mince. There are, moreover, growing numbers of what the Greeks call "**koultouriárika**" restaurants, often pretentious attempts at Greek nouvelle cuisine with speciality wine lists, which tend to be long on airs and graces, and (at €20–30 a head) short on value. The exceptions which succeed have been singled out in the text.

In the absence of recommendations, a good strategy is to go where the Greeks go. And, despite increasing EU labour regulations limiting staff hours, they go late: 2 to 3.30pm for **lunch**, 9 to 11pm for **supper**. You can eat earlier, but you're likely to get indifferent service and doctored cuisine if you frequent establishments catering to the tourist schedule. One good omen is the waiter bringing a carafe of refrigerated water, unbidden, rather than pushing you to order bottled stuff.

Waiters are generally inclined to urge you into ordering more than you want, then bring things you haven't ordered. Although cash-register receipts are required in all establishments, these are often only for the grand total, and itemized **bills** will be in Greek script. With hard times for many popular destinations, bill-padding has become endemic, as a few unwarranted euros extra per party adds up by month's end; even without reading Greek, make sure that the number and cost of items tally with what you ordered. Though printed menu prices are supposedly inclusive of all taxes and service, a small extra tip of 7–10 percent directly to the waiter is hugely appreciated.

Bread is generally assessed as part of the "cover" charge (€0.40–0.90 per person), so you have to pay for it even if (as so often) it's barely edible. Good bread is so remarkable as to warrant mention in the restaurant accounts. **Children** are always welcome, day or night, at family tavernas, and they are quickly socialized into the Greek routine of late hours. Kids are expected to be kids – playing tag around the tables – but at the same time they are not allowed to cramp adults' style.

Estiatória

The two basic types of restaurant are the **estiatório** and the taverna. Distinctions are slight, though the former is more commonly found in large towns and tends to have the more complicated, oven-baked casserole dishes termed **mayireftá** (literally, "cooked"). With their long hours, old-fashioned-tradesmen's clientele and tiny profit margins, *estiatória* (sometimes known as *inomayiría*, "wine-and-cook-houses") are, alas, something of a vanishing breed. An *estiatório* will generally feature a variety of *mayireftá* as moussakas, macaroni pie, meat or game stews, stuffed tomatoes or peppers, the oily vegetable casseroles called *ladherá*, and oven-baked meat and fish. Usually you go into the kitchen and point at the desired steam trays to choose these dishes.

Batches are cooked in the morning and then left to stand, which is why *mayireftá* food is often **lukewarm**. Greeks don't mind this (most actually believe that hot food is bad for you), and most such dishes are actually enhanced by being allowed to steep in their own juice. Similarly, you have to specify if you want your food with little or no oil (*horís ládhi*), but you will be considered a little strange since Greeks regard olive oil as essential to digestion. **Desserts** (*epidhórpia* in formal Greek) of the pudding-and-pie variety don't exist at *estiatória*, though yoghurt is occasionally served. Fruit, however, is always available in season; watermelon (often on the house), melon and grapes are the summer standards. Autumn treats worth asking after include *kydhóni* or *akhládhi stó foúrno*, baked quince or pear with some sort of syrup or nut topping. At tavernas in the northern mainland – especially in Thessaloníki – you may be offered a complementary slice of sweet semolina halva (*smigdhalísios halvás*).

Tavernas and psistariés

Tavernas range from the glitzy and fashionable to rough-and-ready ones with seating under a reed canopy, behind a beach. Really primitive ones have a very limited (often unwritten) menu, but the more established will offer some of the main *mayireftá* dishes mentioned above, as well as standard taverna fare. This essentially means **mezéd-hes** (hors d'oeuvres) or **orektiká** (appetizers) and **tís óras** (meat and fish, fried or grilled to order). In the mountains of the mainland where there are rivers, trout, frog-legs, eel and freshwater crayfish are to be found in some eating places. **Psistariés** or grill-houses serve spit-roasted lamb, pork or goat (generically termed *kondosoúvli*), grilled chicken or *kokorétsi* (grilled offal roulade). They will usually have a limited selection of *mezédhes* and salads (*salátes*), but no *mayireftá* at all.

Since the idea of courses is foreign to Greek cuisine, starters, main dishes and salads often arrive together unless you request otherwise. The best thing is to order a selection of *mezédhes* and salads to share, in true Greek fashion. Waiters encourage you to take the *horiátiki saláta* – the so-called Greek **salad**, including *feta* cheese – because it is the most expensive. If you only want tomato, or tomato and cucumber, ask for *domatosaláta* or *angourodomáta*. *Láhano-karóto* (cabbage-carrot) and *maroúli* (lettuce) are the typical winter and spring salads respectively.

The most common **mezédhes** are *tzatzíki* (yoghurt, garlic and cucumber dip), *melit-zanosaláta* (aubergine/eggplant dip), fried courgette/zucchini or aubergine/eggplant slices, *yígandes* (white haricot beans in vinaigrette or hot tomato sauce), *tyropitákia*

or *spanakópites* (small cheese and spinach pies), *revythókeftedhes* or *pittaroúdhia* (chickpea patties similar to falafel), octopus salad and *mavromátika* (black-eyed peas).

Among **meats**, *souvláki* and chops are reliable choices, often locally produced. In both cases, pork is usually better and cheaper than veal. The best *souvláki*, though not always available, is lamb; more commonly encountered are rib chops called *païdhákia*, while roast lamb (*arní psitó*) is considered *estiatório* fare. *Keftédhes* (breadcrumbed meatballs), *biftékia* (similar, but meatier) and the spicy, coarse-grain sausages called *loukánika* are cheap and good. Chicken, especially grilled, is widely available but typically battery-farmed in Ípiros or on Évvia. Other dishes worth trying are stewed goat (*gídha vrastí*) or baked goat (*katsíki stó foúrno*) – goat in general is a wonderfully healthy meat, typically free-range and undosed with antibiotics or hormones.

Fish and seafood

Seaside *psarotavérnes* offer **fish**, though for the inexperienced, ordering can be fraught with peril. Summer visitors get a relatively poor choice of fish, most of it frozen, farmed or imported from Egypt and North Africa. Drag-net trawling is prohibited from the end of May until the beginning of October, when only lamp-lure, trident, "doughnut" trap and multihook line methods are allowed. During these warmer months, such few fish as are caught tend to be smaller and dry-textured, and are served with *ladholémono* (oil and lemon juice) sauce. Taverna owners often comply only minimally with the requirement to indicate when seafood is **frozen** (look for the abbreviation "kat", "k" or just an asterisk on the Greek-language side of the menu).

Given these considerations, it's often best to set your sights on the **humbler**, seasonally migrating or perennially local species. The cheapest consistently available fish are *gópes* (bogue), *atherína* (sand smelts) and *marídhes* (picarel), the latter two eaten head and all. In the Dodecanese, *yermanós* (same as Australian leatherback) is a good frying fish which appears in spring; a more universal, inexpensive May–June treat is fresh, grilled or fried *bakaliáros* (hake), the classic UK fish-and-chip shop species. *Gávros* (anchovy) and *sardhélles* (sardines) are late-summer fixtures, at their best in the north-east Aegean. In the north Aegean or around Pílio, *pandelís* or *sykiós* (in French, *corb*) is caught in early summer, and highly esteemed since it's a rock-dweller, not a bottom feeder – and therefore a bit pricier. *Koliós* (mackerel) is excellent either grilled or baked in sauce. In autumn especially you may encounter *psarósoupa* (fish broth) or *kakaviá* (a bouillabaisse-like stew).

Less esteemed species tend to **cost** about €20–30 per kilo; choicer varieties of fish, such as red mullet, *tsipoúra* (gilthead bream), seabass or *fangrí* (common bream), will be expensive if wild – €40–50 per kilo, depending on what the market will bear. If the price seems too good to be true, it's almost certainly **farmed**. Prices are usually quoted by the kilo (less often by the portion; standard procedure is to go to the glass-fronted cooler and pick your specimen, then have it weighed (uncleaned) in your presence. If you are concerned that you may later be overcharged, which sometimes happens, have the amount confirmed orally or on a slip of paper.

Cheaper **seafood** (*thalassiná*) such as fried baby squid (usually frozen) and octopus are a summer staple of most seaside tavernas, and often mussels, cockles and small prawns will be on offer at reasonable prices.

Wines

All sorts of eateries will offer you a choice of bottled **wines**, and many still have their own house variety: kept in barrels, sold in bulk by the quarter-, half- or full litre, and served either in glass flagons or the brightly coloured tin "monkey-cups" called *kantária*. You should ask whether they have wine *varelísio* (barrelled) or *hýma* (in bulk). Per-litre prices depend on locale and quality, ranging from €4 (Thessaly) to €8 or even €9 (Corfu, Rhodes), with smaller measures priced (more or less) proportionately. Non-resinated wine is almost always more than decent; if in doubt, order a bottle or can of soda water, which can render even the sourest wine drinkable when used to dilute it. **Retsina** – pine-resinated wine, a slightly acquired taste – is also available straight from the barrel, though the bottled brands Yeoryiadhi from Thessaloníki, Liokri from Aháïa, Malamatina from central Greece, and Cambas from near Athens, are all quaffable and likely to be more consistent in quality.

Among the **bottled wines** available **nationwide**, Cambas Attikos, Zítsa and the Rhodian CAIR products (especially the Moulin and 2400 range) are good, inexpensive whites, while Boutari Naoussa and Kourtakis Apelia are decent, mid-range reds. If you want a better but still moderately priced red, go for the Merlot of either Boutari and Tsantali, or Averof Katoï from Epirus.

If you're travelling around **wine-producing islands**, however, you may as well choose **local bottlings**; the best available guides to the emerging Greek domaines and vintners are Nico Manessis' *The Illustrated Greek Wine Book* or Konstantinos Lazarakis' *The Wines of Greece*. Almost anything produced on Límnos is decent; the Alexandrine muscat is now used for whites, the local *límnio* grape for reds and rosés. Thíra, another volcanic island, has a number of premium white products such as Ktima Arghyrou and Boutari Nykhteri, and the Gentilini Robola white of Kefalloniá is justly esteemed. Páros (Moraïtis), Náxos and Ikaria (Ktima Karimali Ikariotikos) all have acceptable local vintages, while Crete is now beginning to have labels superior to the bog-standard Logado, such as Economou (Sitía) and Lyrarakis (Iráklion). On Rhodes, Alexandhris products from Émbonas are well thought of, as is the Emery label with its Villaré white, and products of the Triandafyllou winery near Ialyssós.

Vegetarians

If you are **vegetarian**, you may be in for a hard time, and will often have to assemble a meal from various *mezédes*. Even the excellent standbys of yoghurt with honey, tzatziki and Greek salad begin to pall after a while, and many of the supposed "vegetable" dishes on menus are cooked in stock or have pieces of meat added to liven them up. Wholly or largely vegetarian restaurants, however, are slowly on the increase in touristy areas; they are highlighted through the Guide where appropriate.

Curiously, island red wines are almost uniformly mediocre, except for Hatzemmanouil from Kós; in this respect you're better off choosing **reds from the mainland**. Carras from Halkidhikí does the excellent Porto Carras, while Ktima Tselepou offers a very palatable Cabernet-Merlot blend. Andonopoulou (Pátra, including an organic line), Ktima Papaïoannou Nemea (Peloponnese), and Tsantali Rapsani (Thessaly) are all superb, velvety reds – and likely to be found only in the better *koultouriárika* tavernas or *káves* (bottle shops). Antonopoulos, Tselepos (Mantinía domaine), Spyropoulos (again Mantinía) and Papaïoannou also do excellent **mainland whites**, especially the Spyropoulos Orino Mantinia, sometimes found organically produced.

Other **premium microwineries** on the mainland whose products have long been fashionable, in both red and white, include the vastly overrated Hatzimihali (Atalánti, central Greece), the outstanding Dhiamandákou (near Náoussa, red and white), Athanasiadhi (central Greece), Skouras (Argolid) and the two rival Lazaridhi vintners (Dhráma, east Macedonia), especially their superb Merlots. For any of these you can expect to pay €8–11 per bottle in a shop, double that at a taverna.

Last but not least, CAIR on Rhodes makes its very own **"champagne"** ("naturally sparkling wine fermented en boteille", says the label), in both brut and demi-sec versions. It's not Moët & Chandon quality by any means, but at less than €6 per bottle, who's complaining?

Cafés, cake shops and bars

A venerable Greek institution, likely to survive the onslaught of mass global culture, is the **kafenío**, found in every town, village and hamlet in the country. In addition, you'll come across **ouzerís**, **zaharoplastía** (Greek patisseries) and **barákia**.

The kafenío

The **kafenío** (plural *kafenía*) is the traditional Greek coffee-house or café. Although its main business is "Greek" (Middle Eastern) coffee – prepared *skéto* or *pikró* (unsweetened), *métrio*

(medium) or *glykó* (sweet) – it also serves spirits such as ouzo (see below), brandy (usually Metaxa or Botrys brand, in three grades), beer, the sage-based tea known variously as *alisfakiá* (isles) or *tsáï vounoú* (mainland), soft drinks and juices. Another refreshing drink sold in cafés is *kafés frappé*, iced instant coffee with or without milk and sugar – uniquely Greek despite its French-sounding name. Like Greek coffee, it is always accompanied by a welcome glass of cold water. One quality fizzy soft drink to single out is the Vólos-based Epsa, with its Orangina-like bottles and high juice content. A refreshing curiosity – confined to Corfu and Paxí – is *tsitsibýra* (ginger beer), a holdover from the nineteenth-century British occupation of the Ionian islands; cloudy, greyish-white and fizzy, it tastes vaguely of lemon and the sour beginnings of fermentation.

Usually the only **edibles** available at *kafenia* are "spoon sweets" or *glyká koutalioú* (sticky, syrupy preserves of quince, grape, fig, citrus fruit or cherry) and the traditional, now-vanishing, *ipovrýhio*, a piece of mastic submerged in a glass of water like a submarine – which is what the word means in Greek.

Like tavernas, *kafenía* range from the plastic, chrome and sophisticated to the old-fashioned, spit-on-the-floor or mock-retro variety, with marble or brightly painted metal tables and straw-bottomed chairs. They still form the pivot of life in remoter villages, and you get the impression that many men spend most of their waking hours there. Greek women are rarely to be seen in the more traditional places; even in holiday resorts, you will find that there is at least one coffee house that the local men have reserved for themselves.

Some *kafenía* close at siesta time, but many remain open from early in the morning until late at night. The chief summer socializing time is 6–8pm, immediately after the afternoon nap. This is the time to take your pre-dinner ouzo, as the sun begins to sink and the air cools down.

Ouzo, tsípouro, mezédhes, ouzerís and mezedhopolía

Ouzo and the similar *tsípouro* (north mainland) and *tsikoudhiá* (Crete) are simple spirits of up to 48 percent alcohol, distilled from grape-mash residue left over from wine-making, and then usually flavoured with herbs such as anise or fennel. There are nearly thirty name brands of ouzo or *tsípouro*, with the best reckoned to be from Lésvos and Sámos islands, or Zítsa and Týrnavos on the mainland.

When you order, you will be served two glasses: one with the ouzo, and one full of water to be tipped into your ouzo until it turns a milky white. You can drink it straight, but the strong, burning taste is hardly refreshing if you do. It is also the norm to add **ice cubes**, a bowl of which will be provided upon request. The next measure up from a glass is a *karafáki* – a deceptively small 200-millilitre vial, and the favourite means of delivery for *tsípouro* – which will very rapidly render you legless if you don't alternate tippling with snacks. A much smoother, unflavoured variant of ouzo is **soúma**, found chiefly on Rhodes and Sámos, but in theory anywhere grapes are grown. The smoothness is deceptive – as with *tsípouro*, two or three glasses of it and you had better not have any other firm plans for the afternoon.

Formerly every ouzo you ordered was automatically accompanied by a small plate of **mezédhes** on the house: bits of cheese, cucumber, tomato, a few olives, sometimes octopus or even a couple of small fish. Nowadays "ouzomezés" is a separate, more expensive option on the price list. Often, however, they are not featured on any formal menu, but if you order a *karafáki* you will automatically be offered a small selection of snacks.

One kind of drinking establishment, found in the better resorts and select neighbourhoods of the larger islands and towns, specializes in ouzo and *mezédhes*. These are called **ouzerí** (same in the Greek plural, but we've added 's' through the Guide) or *tsipourádhika* (plural) in Vólos, Thessaloníki and other major centres of the north mainland. In some towns you may also come across *mezedhopolía*, basically a bigger, more upmarket kind of *ouzerí*. *Ouzerís* and *mezedhopolía* are well worth trying for the marvellous variety of *mezédhes* they serve (though some mediocre tavernas have counterfeited the name). At the genuine article, several plates of *mezédhes* plus drinks

will effectively substitute for a more involved meal at a taverna (though it usually works out more expensive if you have a healthy appetite). Faced with an often bewilderingly varied menu, you might opt for the *pikilía* (medley, assortment) available in several sizes, the largest and most expensive one usually heavy on the seafood. At other *ouzerís* or *tsipourádhika* the language barrier may be overcome by the waiter wielding an enormous tray laden with all the current cold offerings – you pick the ones you like the look of.

Sweets and coffee

The **zaharoplastío**, a cross between café and patisserie, serves coffee, a limited range of alcohol, yoghurt with honey and sticky cakes. The better establishments offer an amazing variety of pastries, cream-and-chocolate confections, honey-soaked Greco–Turkish sweets like *baklavás*, *kataïfi* (honey-drenched "shredded wheat"), *loukoumádhes* (deep-fried batter puffs dusted with cinnamon and dipped in syrup), *galaktoboúreko* (custard pie) and so on. If you want a stronger slant towards the dairy products and away from the pure sugar, seek out a **galaktopolío**, where you'll often find *ryzógalo* (rice pudding), *kréma* (custard) and locally made *yiaoúrti* (yoghurt), best if it's *próvio* (from sheep's milk). Both *zaharoplastía* and *galaktopolía* are more family-oriented places than a *kafenío*.

Ice cream, sold principally at the *gelaterie*, which have swept across Greece of late (*Dhodhoni* is the posh home-grown chain, Haägen-Dazs is the competition), can be very good and almost indistinguishable from Italian prototypes. A scoop (*baláki*) costs €1.10–1.50; you'll be asked if you want it in a cup (*kypelláki*) or a cone (*konáki*), and whether you want toppings like *santí* (whipped cream) or nuts. By contrast, the mass-produced brands like Delta or Evga are pretty unremarkable, with the exception of Skandalo and Nirvana labels.

"Nes"(café) has become the generic term for all instant **coffee**, regardless of brand; it's generally pretty vile, and since the mid-1990s there's been a nationwide reaction against it. Even in the smallest provincial capital or resort there will be at least one trendy café that does a range of foreign-style coffees – filter, dubbed *fíltros* or *gallikós* (French); cappuccino; and espresso – at overseas prices. A more enticing, recent innovation is *freddoccino*, a cappuccino-based alternative to the traditional cold frappé. Outside of the largest towns, properly made versions of these drinks will be harder to find – and may come from instant packets.

Bars, beer and water

Bars (*barákia* in the plural) are found all over Greece. They range from clones of Parisian cafés or Spanish bodegas to seaside cocktail bars, with music or TV running all day. At their most sophisticated, however, they are well-executed theme venues in ex-industrial premises or Neoclassical houses, with Western (currently techno, dub or ambient) soundtracks. Although we give recommendations in the Guide, most Greek bars have a half-life of about one year; the best way to find the current hot spots, especially if they're more club than bar, is to watch for fly-posters in the neighbourhood, advertising bar-hosted events.

Bar drinks are invariably more expensive than in a café – count on €5–8. Bars are, however, most likely to stock a range of **beers**, mostly foreign labels made locally under licence at just a handful of breweries on the central mainland. **Local brews** include Alfa, a hoppy lager brewed in Athens that's the best and most consistent of the mainstream labels; Mythos, a mild lager in a green bottle, put out by the Boutari vintners; Veryina, brewed in Komotiní and common in the northeastern mainland and isles; Pils Hellas, a sharp pilsner; and last but not least, the resurrected Fix, for years until its demise in 1980 Greece's only beer. Greece also has a **microbrewery**, the Athens-based Craft: they make a tasty pilsner and an amber lager, but distribution is not wide.

Kronenberg 1664 and Kaiser are two of the more common quality **foreign-licence** varieties, with the latter available in both light and dark. Bland, inoffensive Amstel is the standard cheapie, claimed by some Dutch to be better than the one available in Holland; Amstel also makes a very palatable, strong (seven percent) **bock**. Heineken, still referred to as a "*prássini*" by bar and taverna staff after its green bottle, despite the advent of Mythos, is too sharp for many. Genuinely imported German beers, such as Bitburger, Fisher and Warsteiner (plus a few British ones), are on offer in the fancier resorts.

Mineral water, mostly still, typically comes in half-litre and one-and-a-half-litre plastic bottles. The ubiquitous Loutraki brand is not esteemed by the Greeks themselves, who prefer various brands from Crete and Epirus. In the better tavernas there has been a backlash against plastic bottles – which constitute a tremendous litter problem – and you can now get it in one-litre glass bottles. Souroti is the principal brand of sparkling (*aerioúho* in Greek) water, in small bottles, though Tuborg club soda is ubiquitous.

Communications

Greece's postal system is adequate, especially for outgoing mail. Service provided by OTE (Organismós Tiliepikinoníon tís Elládhos, the telecoms entity) is improving drastically under the twin threats of privatization and competition from thriving local mobile networks. All land-line exchanges are digital, and you should have few problems reaching any number from either overseas or within Greece. Mobile phone users are well looked after, with a signal even in the Athens metro. At least one Internet facility is found in all major towns and resorts, while most business-class hotels will have Internet access from the room, and many resort-class hotels have a phone socket for plugging in your laptop.

Postal services

Post offices, recognizable by their stylized Hermes-head on a blue background, are open Monday to Friday from 7.30am to 2pm, though certain main branches have hours until the evening and on Saturday morning. **Airmail letters** take three to seven days to reach the rest of Europe, five to twelve days to get to North America, and a bit longer for Australia and New Zealand. Generally, the larger the island (and the planes serving its airport), the quicker the service. Postal rates for up to 20g are a uniform €0.65 to all overseas destinations. For a modest fee (about €3) you can shave a day or two off delivery time to any destination by using the **express service** (*katepígonda*). **Registered** (*systiméno*) delivery is also available for a similar amount, but proves quite slow unless coupled with express service. For a simple letter or card, a stamp (*grammatósimo*) can also be purchased at an authorized postal agency (usually a stationery store).

Parcels should (and often can) only be handled in the main provincial or county capitals; this way, your bundle will be in Athens, and on an international flight, within a day or so. For non-EU/EEA destinations, always present your box open for inspection, and come prepared with tape and scissors – most post offices will sell cardboard boxes, but nothing to actually close the package. An array of services is available: air parcel (fast and expensive), surface-air lift (a couple of weeks slower but much cheaper), insured, and proof of delivery among others.

Ordinary **post boxes** are bright yellow, express boxes dark red, but it's best to use only those by the door of an actual post office, since days may pass between collections at other street-corner or wall-mounted boxes. If you are confronted by two slots, "ESOTERIKÓ" is for domestic mail, "EXOTERIKÓ" for overseas. Often there are more: one box or slot for mail into Athens and suburbs, one for your local province, one for "other" parts of Greece, and one for overseas; if in doubt, ask someone.

The **poste restante** system is reasonably efficient, especially at the post offices of larger towns. Mail should be clearly addressed and marked "poste restante", with your surname underlined, to the main post office of whichever town you choose. It will be held for a month and you'll need your passport to collect it.

Phones

During 2002, all Greek phone numbers changed to a system resembling the French one, in which you are obliged to dial all ten numbers of a subscriber, including the former area code, wherever you may be. All land lines begin with 2, all mobiles begin with 6.

Call boxes, poorly maintained and invariably sited at the noisiest street corners, work only with phonecards (*tilekártes*); these come in various denominations starting at €4, available from kiosks and newsagents. Despite numbers hopefully scribbled on the appropriate tabs, call boxes cannot be rung back; however, green, **countertop card-phones** kept by many hotels can be rung. Other options for local calls include **counter coin-op phones** in bars, *kafenía* and hotel lobbies; these take small euro coins and also can be rung back as a rule. Most of them are made in northern Europe and bear instructions in English.

Local or intercity calls to land lines are cheap on OTE *tilekártes*, but if you plan on making lots of international calls, you'll want a **calling card**, all of which involve calling a free access number from either a phone box or fixed line (not a mobile) and then entering a twelve-digit code. OTE has its own scheme, Khronokarta, but competitors generally prove cheaper. Always tell the card vendor where you intend to call, to get the card best suited for you (Ya!-Q for the UK). Avoid making calls **from hotel rooms**, as a minimum one-hundred-percent surcharge will be slapped on.

Mobile phones

Mobile phones are an essential fashion accessory in Greece – in a population of roughly 11 million, there are claimed to be nearly 7 million mobile handsets in use. Four **networks** operate at present: Vodafone, TIM, Cosmote and Q-Telecom. Calling any of their numbers from Britain, you will find that costs are exactly the same as calling a fixed phone, though of course such numbers are pricey when rung locally. **Coverage** countrywide is good, though there are a few "dead" zones in the mountains, or on really remote islets. Contract-free plans are heavily promoted in Greece, and if you're here for more than a week or so, buying a Greek **pay-as-you-go** SIM card (for €15–20) from any of the numerous mobile phone outlets will pay for itself very quickly, and you can reuse the same number on your next visit. Top-up calling cards – starting from €8–10 depending on the network – are available at all *períptera*. UK providers may tell you that another SIM can't be fitted without a hefty surcharge to unlock your phone, but you are legally entitled to the unblock code from the manufacturer after (usually) six months of use. Otherwise, have a mobile shop in Greece unblock the phone for a small charge with a simple computer procedure. North American users will only be able to use tri-band phones in Greece. Roaming with your home provider will land you with outrageous charges of over €1 equivalent per minute minimum (UK providers – far more for North American ones), no matter where you're calling, plus almost as much to have incoming calls forwarded to you. Text messaging is a far cheaper alternative if you choose not to get a Greek SIM.

Email and Internet

Internet cafés are the easiest places to check web-based email accounts; locations are noted throughout the Guide. Rates tend to be about €6 per hour maximum, often less, with shorter increments

Useful phone codes and numbers

Phoning abroad from Greece
Dial the country code (given below) + area code (minus any initial 0) + number

Australia	☎0061	UK	☎0044
New Zealand	☎0064	Ireland	☎00353
Canada	☎001	USA	☎001

Speciality Greek phone prefixes

Local call rate	☎0801	Toll-free/Freefone	☎0800

Useful Greek telephone numbers

Ambulance	☎166	Police/Emergency	☎100
Fire brigade, urban	☎199	Speaking clock	☎141
Forest fire reporting	☎191	Tourist police	☎171 (Athens);
Operator	☎132 (Domestic)		☎210 171 (elsewhere)
Operator ☎139 (International)			

always available. Few are smoke-free – ones that host many young computer gamers are particularly bad – so check the environment and the speed of the machines before you settle down to an hour or so of email-checking.

If you are travelling with your own **laptop**, you may well be able to roam in Greece depending on what agreement your home ISP has with any Greek partners. Check with your ISP, and get the local dial-up number, before you leave. **Piggybacking charges** tend to be fairly high, but for a modest number of minutes per day, still work out much less than patronizing an Internet café. Alternatively, you can take out a **temporary Internet account** with one of the half-dozen Greek ISPs (minimum period one month, cost €10–14/month plus very modest hourly charges).

The media

Although the Greek press and airwaves have ostensibly been free since the fall of the colonels' dictatorship in 1974, nobody would ever propose the Greek media as a paradigm of responsible or objective journalism. Many papers are sensational, state-run radio and TV often biased in favour of the ruling party, and private channels imitative of the worst American programming.

British **newspapers** are fairly widely available in Greece at a cost of €1.75–2.50 for dailies, or €4 for Sunday editions. You'll find one-to-two-day-old copies (same day by noon in Athens) of *The Times*, *The Daily Telegraph*, *The Independent* and *The Guardian*'s European edition, plus a few of the tabloids, in all the resorts as well as in major towns and airports. American and international alternatives include the turgid *USA Today* and the more readable *International Herald Tribune*, the latter including as a major bonus a free though abridged English translation of the respected Greek daily *Kathimerini* (online at ⓦwww .ekathimerini.com; also see p.40). Among foreign **magazines**, *Time* and *Newsweek* are widely available.

There are few surviving **locally produced** English-language magazines or papers. Glossy *Odyssey* (€5) is produced every other month by and for wealthy diaspora Greeks; it has excellent book reviews in particular. The main English-language newspaper is the *Athens News* (weekly every Friday, online at ⓦwww.athensnews.gr; €2), in colour with good features and Balkan news, plus entertainment and arts listings, available in most resorts.

Greek publications

Many papers have ties (including funding) with specific **political groups**, with only a bare handful of quality dailies. Among these, the **centrist** *Kathimerini* – whose former proprietress Helen Vlahos attained heroic status for her defiance of the junta – approaches the standards of France's *Le Monde*, while *Eleftherotypia*, especially its Sunday edition, is the local equivalent of *The Guardian/The Observer*. *Avriani* and *To Vima* (with its excellent *Vimagazino* supplement) stake out pro-PASOK territory, whilst *Ta Nea* is a popular, MOR tabloid, much loved for its extensive small ads and its Saturday magazine, *Takhydromos*. On the far **Left**, *Avyi* is the Eurocommunist/Synaspismós forum with literary leanings, while *Rizospastis* acts as the organ of the KKE (unreconstructed Communists). *Ethnos* became notorious some years back for receiving covert funding from the KGB to act as a disinformation bulletin. At the other

73

end of the political spectrum, *Apoyevmatini* generally supports the **centre-right** Néa Dhimokratía party, while *Estia's* no-photo format and reactionary politics are both stuck somewhere at the beginning of the twentieth century.

Among **magazines** that are not merely translations of overseas titles, *To Pondíki* (The Mouse) is a satirical weekly revue in the same vein as Britain's *Private Eye*; its famous covers are spot-on and accessible to anyone with minimal Greek. More specialized niches are occupied by low-circulation titles such as *Adhesmeftos Typos* (a slightly rightist, muck-raking journal) and *Andi*, an intelligent analytical fortnightly going since 1974 (its first issue confiscated by the junta), with reviews and cultural critiques, somewhat in the mould of Britain's *New Statesman*.

Radio

Greek **radio** music programmes are always accessible (if variable in quality), and since abolition of the government's monopoly of wavelengths, regional stations have mushroomed; indeed the airwaves are positively cluttered as every island town sets up its own studio and transmitter. The two state-run channels are ER1 (a mix of news, talk and popular music) and ER2 (strictly popular music).

On heavily touristed islands like Rhodes, Corfu and Crete, there will usually be at least one station on the FM band trying its luck at English-moderated programming by and for foreigners. The Turkish state radio's Third Channel is also widely (if unpatriotically) listened to on east Aegean islands for its classical, jazz and blues programmes. The **BBC World Service** broadcasts on short wave throughout Greece; 6.18, 9.41, 15.07 and 12.09 MHz are the most common frequencies. However, short-wave services are being phased out in many parts of the world, so consult ⓦ www.bbc.co.uk /worldservice for current frequencies.

Television

Greece's state-funded **TV stations**, ET1, NET and (from Thessaloníki) ET3, nowadays lag behind private channels – Antenna, Star, Alpha, Alter and Makedonia TV – in the ratings, though not necessarily in quality of offerings. Programming tends to be a mix of soaps (especially Italian, Spanish and Latin American), game shows, movies and sports, with lately a leavening of natural history documentaries, costume dramas and today-in-history features. All foreign films and serials are broadcast in their original language, with Greek subtitles. Most private channels operate around the clock; public stations broadcast from around 5.30am until 3am. Numerous **cable and satellite** channels are received, including CNN, MTV, Filmnet, BBC World, French TV5 and Italian Rai Due. The range available depends on the area (and hotel) you're in.

Opening hours and public holidays

It's difficult to generalize about Greek opening hours, especially museum and site schedules, which change constantly. The traditional timetable starts with shops opening between 8.30 and 9am, then runs through until lunchtime, when there is a long break for the hottest part of the day. Most places, except banks and government offices, may then reopen in the mid- to late afternoon. Tourist areas tend to adopt a more northern European timetable, with shops, travel agencies and offices, as well as the most important archeological sites and museums, usually open throughout the day.

Business and shopping hours

Private businesses, or anyone providing a service, frequently operate a straight 9am to 5 or 6pm schedule. If someone is actually selling something, then they are more likely to follow a split shift as detailed below.

Shopping hours during the hottest months are theoretically Monday, Wednesday and Saturday from approximately 9am to 2.30pm, and Tuesday, Thursday and Friday from 8.30am to 2pm and 6 to 9pm. During the cooler months the morning schedule shifts slightly forward, the evening session a half or even a full hour back. In Athens many enterprises keep a continuous schedule (*synehés orário*) during the winter, but this is not yet universally observed, even with pressure being brought to bear by the EU, and the threat of its legal enforcement. There are so many exceptions to rules by virtue of holidays and professional idiosyncrasy that you can't count on getting anything done except from Monday to Friday, 9.30am and 1pm. **Delis** and **butchers** are not allowed to sell fresh meat during summer afternoons (though some flout this rule); similarly, **fishmongers** are only open in the morning until they sell out (usually by noon), as are **pharmacies**, which additionally are shut on Saturday (except for the duty pharmacist). **Travel agencies** at the busiest resorts are open continuously from about 9am to 10pm Monday to Saturday, with some Sunday hours as well.

Most **government agencies** are open to the public on weekdays from 8am to 2pm. In general, however, you'd be optimistic to show up after 1pm expecting to be served the same day, as queues can be long, and many services cease at that hour.

All of the above will be regularly thrown out of sync by the numerous public holidays and festivals – or the equally numerous strikes, which can be general or profession-specific. The most important holidays, when almost everything will be closed, are listed on p.76.

Ancient sites and monasteries

All the major **ancient sites** are fenced off and, like most **museums**, charge **admission fees** ranging from €2 to €12, with an average fee of around €3. Entrance to all state-run sites and museums is **free** on Sundays and public holidays from November to March, although they will be shut on the dates of public holidays shown on p.76.

Opening hours vary between the major **ancient sites**. As far as possible, individual times are quoted in the text, but bear in mind that these change with exasperating frequency, and at smaller sites may be subject to the whim of a local site guard. Unless specified, the times quoted are generally summer hours, in effect from around late May to the end of September. Reckon on similar days but later opening and earlier closing in winter. Usually, the **last admission ticket** is sold fifteen to twenty minutes before the cited closing time.

Along with your ticket most sites and museums will provide a little colour **folding pamphlet** prepared by the Tamío

Public holidays

January 1
January 6
March 25
First Monday of Lent (48 days before
  Easter; see below)
Good Friday (variable April/May; see
  below)
Easter Sunday (variable April/May;
  see below)
May 1
Pentecost or Whit Monday (50 days
  after Easter; see below)
August 15
October 28
December 25 and 26

Variable religious feasts
Lenten Monday
2006 March 6
2007 February 19
2008 March 10

Easter Sunday
2006 April 23
2007 April 8
2008 April 27

Whit Monday
2006 June 12
2007 May 28
2008 June 16

Arheoloyikón Porón (Archeological Receipts Fund); they usually include an accurate if potted history and site or gallery plan, and we've found them to be uniformly excellent, in stark contrast to the often miserable labelling of the sites or galleries themselves. Serious students will therefore want to invest in **site guides** or **museum catalogues**, which have often been expertly compiled by the excavating archeologists or curators.

Monasteries are generally open from approximately 9am to 1pm and 5 to 8pm (3.30 to 6.30pm in winter) for limited visits. Most impose a fairly strict **dress code** for visitors: no shorts on either sex, with women expected to cover their arms and wear skirts; the necessary wraps are sometimes provided on the spot.

It's free to take **photos** of open-air sites, though museum photography and the use of videos or tripods anywhere requires an extra fee and written permit. This usually has to be arranged in writing from the nearest Department of Antiquities (Eforía Arheotíton). It's also worth knowing that Classical studies students can get a free annual pass to all Greek museums and sites by presenting themselves at the office on the rear corner (Tossítsa/Bouboulínas) of the National Archeological Museum in Athens – take documentation and two passport-sized photographs.

Festivals and cultural events

Many of the big Greek popular festivals have a religious basis, so they're observed in accordance with the Orthodox calendar. Give or take a few saints, this is similar to the regular Catholic liturgical year, except for Easter, which can fall as many as four (but usually one or two) weeks to either side of the Western festival – though in 2001 and again in 2004 the two coincided (usually a rare occurrence). Summer cultural festivals are tied firmly to the weather and tourist traffic, with most resorts laying on events at atmospheric outdoor venues from July to September.

Easter

Easter is by far the most important festival of the Greek year – infinitely more so than Christmas – and taken much more seriously than

it is anywhere in western Europe, aside from Spain. From Palm Sunday until the following Monday, the state radio and TV networks are given over primarily to religious programmes.

The **festival** is an excellent time to be in Greece, both for its beautiful religious ceremonies and for the days of feasting and celebration that follow, though you'll need to book accommodation months in advance. The mountainous island of **Ídhra** with its alleged 360 churches and monasteries is the prime Easter resort; other famous Easter celebrations are held at Corfu, Pyrgí on Híos, Ólymbos on Kárpathos and St John's monastery on Pátmos, where on Holy Thursday the abbot washes the feet of twelve monks in the village square, in imitation of Christ doing the same for his disciples.

The first great public ceremony takes place on **Good Friday** evening as the Deposition from the Cross is lamented in church. At dusk the Epitáfios, Christ's funeral bier (in large villages there will be more than one, from each church), lavishly decorated by the women of the parish, leaves the sanctuary and is paraded solemnly through the streets. On Ídhra, the Epitáfios of Ayíou Ioánni (the fishermen's parish) is taken into the water at Kamíni to bless the boats and calm the sea; on Sámos, the various biers are taken to the village cemeteries to bless the dead. In Kérkyra Town, the Epitáfios procession takes place on Saturday morning, while special crockery rains down from upper storeys of houses to banish the evil. In many places, Crete especially, this is accompanied by the burning of effigies of Judas Iscariot.

Late **Saturday** evening sees the climax in a majestic *Anástasis* mass to celebrate Christ's triumphant return. At the stroke of midnight all the lights in every crowded church are extinguished, and the congregation plunged into the darkness which envelops Christ as He passes through the underworld. Then there's a faint glimmer of light behind the altar screen before the priest appears, holding aloft a lighted taper and chanting *Avtó to Fós* . . . ("This is the Light of the World"). Stepping down to the level of the parishioners, he touches his flame to the unlit candles of the nearest worshippers, intoning *Dévte, lévete Fós* ("Come, take the Light"). Those at the front of the congregation and on the aisles do the same for their neighbours until the entire church – and the outer courtyard, standing room

only for latecomers – is ablaze with burning candles and the miracle reaffirmed.

The traditional greeting, as dynamite explodes all around you in the street, is *Khristós Anésti* ("Christ is risen"), to which the response is *Alithós Anésti* ("Truly He is risen"). In the week up to Easter Sunday you should wish people *Kaló Páskha* ("Happy Easter"); on or after the day, you say *Khrónia Pollá* ("Many happy returns").

If you have the inclination to listen, the chanting from midnight to 2am in the half-empty churches is actually the most beautiful part of the Resurrection liturgy, unmarred by high explosives. Most worshippers, however, have long since taken the burning **candles** home through the streets; they are said to bring good fortune to the house if they arrive still burning. On reaching the front door it is common practice to make the sign of the cross on the lintel with the flame, leaving a black smudge visible for the rest of the year. The forty-day **Lenten fast** from all animal products – still observed by the devout and in rural areas – is traditionally broken early on Sunday morning with a meal of *mayerítsa*, a soup made from lamb tripe, rice, dill and lemon. The rest of the lamb will be roasted on a spit for Sunday lunch, and festivities often take place through the rest of the day.

The Greek equivalent of **Easter eggs** are hard-boiled eggs (painted red on Holy Thursday), which are baked into twisted, sweet bread-loaves (*tsourékia*) or distributed on Easter Sunday. People rap their eggs against their friends' eggs, and the owner of the last uncracked egg is considered lucky. In many remote locales, the most revered local icons spend the week after Easter in a slow procession around the district or icon, "visiting" each church (and sometimes each house) to bring luck.

The festival calendar

Most of the other Greek festivals are celebrations of one or other of a multitude of **saints**; the most important are detailed below, though there are literally scores of **local festivals**, or *paniyíria*, celebrating the patron saint of every parish church. With hundreds of possible name-saints' days (calendars list two or three, often obscure, for each day) you're unlikely to travel around

Greece for long without stumbling on some sort of observance – sometimes right across the town or island, otherwise quiet, local and consisting of little more than a special liturgy and banners adorning the chapel in question. Saints' days are also celebrated as **name days**; if you learn that it's an acquaintance's name day, you wish them *Khrónia Pollá* ("Many years", as in "Many happy returns"). Also listed are a few more pagan or secular holidays, most enjoyable of which are the pre-Lenten carnivals.

It is important to remember the concept of the *paramoní*, or **eve of the festival**. Most of the events listed below are celebrated on the night before, so if you show up on the morning of the date given you will very probably have missed any music, dancing or drinking.

January 1
New Year's Day (*Protokhroniá*) in Greece is the feast day of Áyios Vassílios (St Basil). The traditional New Year greeting is "Kalí Khroniá".

January 6
Epiphany (*Theofánia*, or *Tón Fóton*), when the *kalikántzari* (hobgoblins) who run riot on earth during the twelve days of Christmas are rebanished to the netherworld by various rites of the Church. The most important of these is the blessing of baptismal fonts and all outdoor bodies of water. At lakeside, seaside or riverside locations, the priest traditionally casts a crucifix into the deep, with local youths competing for the privilege of recovering it.

Pre-Lenten carnivals
These – known in Greek as **Apokriátika** – span three weeks, climaxing during the seventh weekend before Easter. *Katharí Dheftéra* (Lenten Monday) of the first carnival week is always 48 days before Easter Sunday. **Pátra Carnival**, with a chariot parade and costume parties, is one of the largest and most outrageous in the Mediterranean; on the last Sunday before Lent there's a grand parade, with the city's large gay population in conspicuous participation. Interesting, too, are the *boúles* or **masked revels** which take place around Macedonia (particularly at Náoussa), Thrace (Xánthi), and the outrageous **Goat Dance** on Skýros in the Sporades. The Ionian islands, especially Kefalloniá, are also good for carnival, as is Ayiássos on Lésvos, while Athenians celebrate by going around hitting each other on the head with plastic hammers. In

Thíva, a mock shepherd wedding occurs, while most places celebrate with colourful pageants reflecting local traditions.

March 25
Independence Day and the feast of the **Annunciation** (*Evangelismós* in Greek) is both a religious and a national holiday, with, on the one hand, military parades and dancing to celebrate the beginning of the revolt against Ottoman rule in 1821, and, on the other, church services to honour the news given to Mary that she was to become the Mother of Christ. There are major festivities on Tínos, Ídhra (Hydra) and any locality with a monastery or church named Evangelístria or Evangelismós.

April 23
The feast of **Áyios Yeóryios** (St George), the patron of shepherds, is a big rural celebration, with much feasting and dancing at associated shrines and towns. If April 23 falls before Easter, ie during Lent, the festivities are postponed until the Monday after Easter.

May 1
May Day (*Protomayiá*) is the great urban holiday when townspeople traditionally make for the countryside to picnic, returning with bunches of wild flowers. Wreaths are hung on their doorways or balconies until they are burnt in bonfires on St John's eve (June 23). There are also large demonstrations by the Left, claiming the *Ergatikí Protomayiá* (Working-Class First of May) as their own.

May 21
The feast of **Áyios Konstandínos** (St Constantine) and his mother, **Ayía Eléni** (St Helen), the first pro-Orthodox Byzantine rulers. There are firewalking ceremonies in certain Macedonian villages; elsewhere celebrated rather more conventionally as the name day for two of the more popular Christian names in Greece.

May–June
The Monday of **Áyio Pnévma** (the Holy Spirit, Whit Monday in UK) marks the descent of same to the assembled disciples, fifty days after Easter. Usually a modest liturgy is celebrated at rural chapels of the Holy Spirit, gaily decked out with pennants; at Pagóndas village on Sámos, there's a musical festival.

June 29–30
The joint feast of **Áyios Pétros** and **Áyios**

Pávlos (SS Peter and Paul), two of the more widely celebrated name days, is on the 29th. Celebrations often run together with that for the Gathering of (all) the **Holy Apostles** (Áyii Apóstoli), on the 30th.

July 17
The feast of **Ayía Marína**: a big event in rural areas, as she's an important protector of crops. Ayía Marína village on Kássos will be *en fête*, as will countless small mainland villages. Between mid-July and mid-September there are religious holidays every few days, especially in the rural areas, and what with these, the summer heat and a mass exodus from the big cities, ordinary business slows or even halts.

July 20
The feast of **Profítis Ilías** (the Prophet Elijah) is widely celebrated at the countless hill- or mountaintop shrines of Profítis Ilías. The most famous is on Mount Taïyettos, near Spárti, with an overnight vigil.

July 26
Ayía Paraskeví is celebrated in parishes or villages bearing that name, especially in Epirus.

August 6
Metamórfosis toú Sotíros (Transfiguration of the Saviour) provides another excuse for celebrations, particularly at Khristós Ráhon village on Ikaría, and at Plátanos on Léros. On Hálki the date is marked by messy food fights with flour, eggs and squid ink.

August 15
Apokímisis tís Panayías (Assumption or Dormition of the Blessed Virgin Mary). This is the day when people traditionally return to their home village, and in most places there will be no accommodation available on any terms. Even some Greeks will resort to sleeping in the streets at the great pilgrimage to Tínos; also major festivities at Páros, at Ayiássos on Lésvos, and at Ólymbos on Kárpathos.

August 29
Apokefálisis toú Prodhrómou (Beheading of John the Baptist). Popular pilgrimages and celebrations at Vrykoúnda on Kárpathos.

September 8
Yénnisis tís Panayías (Birth of the Virgin Mary) sees special services in churches dedicated to the event, and a double cause for rejoicing on Spétses where they also celebrate the anniversary of the

battle of the straits of Spétses, which took place on September 8, 1822. A re-enactment of the battle takes place in the harbour, followed by fireworks and feasting well into the night. Elsewhere, there's a pilgrimage of childless women to the monastery at Tsambíka, Rhodes.

September 14
A last major summer festival, the **Ípsosis toú Stavroú** (Exaltation of the Cross), keenly observed on Hálki.

September 24
The feast of **Áyios Ioánnis Theológos** (St John the Divine), observed on Níssyros and Pátmos, where at the saint's monastery there are solemn, beautiful liturgies the night before and early in the morning.

October 26
The feast of **Áyios Dhimítrios** (St Demetrios), another popular name day, particularly celebrated in Thessaloníki, of which he is the patron saint. In rural areas the new wine is traditionally broached on this day, a good excuse for general inebriation.

October 28
Óhi Day, the year's major patriotic shindig, is a national holiday with parades, folk-dancing and speeches to commemorate Metaxas's apocryphal one-word reply to Mussolini's 1940 ultimatum: *Ohi!* ("No!").

November 8
Another popular name day, the feast of the **Archangels Michael** and **Gabriel** (Mihaíl and Gavríil, or *tón Taxiárhon*), marked by rites at the numerous churches named after them, particularly at the rural monastery of Taxiárhis on Sými, and the big monastery of Mandamádhos, Lésvos.

December 6
The feast of **Áyios Nikólaos** (St Nicholas), the patron of seafarers, who has many chapels dedicated to him.

December 25
If less all-encompassing than Greek Easter, **Christmas** (*Khristoúyenna*) is still an important religious feast celebrating the birth of Christ; since the early 1990s it has taken on all the usual commercial trappings, with decorations, gifts and alarming outbreaks of plastic Santas on house-eaves. December 26 is *Sýnaxis tis Panayías*, or Gathering of the Virgin's Entourage, *not* Boxing Day as in Britain.

December 31

New Year's Eve (*Paramoní Protohroniá*), when, as on the other twelve days of Christmas, a few children still go door-to-door singing the traditional *kálanda* (carols), receiving money in return. Adults tend to sit around playing cards, often for money. A special baked loaf, the *vassilópitta*, in which a coin is concealed to bring its finder good luck throughout the year, is cut at midnight.

Cultural festivals

The granddaddy of all Greek summer festivals since 1955, the **Athens Festival** (late May to late Sept) encompasses a wide range of performances including modern and ancient theatre, ballet, opera, jazz and classical music, held mostly at the open-air Herodes Atticus Theatre. The Athens International Jazz and Blues Festival (June) puts on big-name acts at the modern open-air theatre on Lykavitós Hill. Details and tickets for events can be obtained from the Athens Festival box office (Panepistimíou 39, ☏210 32 21 459, ⊛www.greekfestival.gr), or at the Herodes Atticus box office on the day from 6 until 9pm (☏210 32 32 771), when most performances start. It's worth calling in very soon after you arrive in Greece, since the more prestigious events sell out.

The **Epidaurus Festival** (July & Aug) hosts strictly open-air performances of Classical drama in the ancient theatre. In **Pátra**, the **International Festival** (July–Sept) sees ancient drama, theatre and classical music up in the castle, as well as in the ancient *odeion*.

Thessaloníki hosts the **Dhimitría Cultural Festival** (Oct) and a prestigious film festival (Nov).

Minor festivals

Astypálea Municipal Festival (July–Aug).
Itháki Music Festival (July).
Ippokrateia Festival Kós (July–Aug).
Kalamáta Dance Festival (July–Aug).
Kassándhra Festival Síviri and Áfytos (July–Aug).
Manolis Kalomiris Festival Sámos (mid-July–early Sept).
Réthymnon Renaissance Festival (July–Aug).
Sými Festival (late June–early Sept).
Philippi/Thássos Festival Mostly at Kavála castle (early July–early Sept).
Sáni Festival Kassándhra, Halkidhikí (early July–early Sept).
Ólymbos Festival Platamónas castle/ancient Dion (mid-July–early Sept).
Lefkádha Arts Jamboree (Aug).
Vólos Festival (Aug).
Ioánnina Folk Festival (mid-July–mid-Aug).
Iráklion Festival (early Aug).
Thíra Music Festival (Aug–Sept).
Rhodes Festival (Aug–Oct).

Cinema

Greek **cinemas** show a large number of American and British movies, always in the original soundtrack with Greek subtitles, though fly-posters tend to be Greek-only. **Indoor** screenings are affordable, currently €6–8 depending on location and plushness of facilities; cinemas shut from mid-May to late September unless they have air conditioning or a roll-back roof. Accordingly, in summer, vast numbers of **outdoor** cinemas operate; an outdoor movie (same prices) is worth catching at least once for the experience alone; there are usually two screenings, at about 9pm and 11pm, with the sound at the latter turned down slightly to avoid complaints of noise from adjacent residences.

Sports and outdoor pursuits

The Greek seashore offers endless scope for watersports, with windsurfing-boards for rent in most resorts and, increasingly, waterskiing and parasailing facilities. On land, the greatest attraction lies in hiking, through what is one of Europe's more impressive mountain terrains. Winter also sees possibilities for skiing at one of a dozen underrated centres.

In terms of spectating, the twin Greek obsessions are **football** (soccer) and **basketball**, with **volleyball** a close third in popularity. Many facilities, mostly in or near the capital, were improved for the **2004 Athens Olympics**, which has undoubtedly left its mark on the national sports scene for years to come.

Watersports

Windsurfing is massively popular around Greece, with Greek gold or silver medalists at the last two Olympics. The country's bays and coves are ideal for beginners, and boards can be rented in literally hundreds of resorts. Particularly good areas, with established schools, include Vassilikí on Lefkádha island, Kéfalos on Kós, Zákynthos, western Náxos, Kokkári on Sámos, several spots on Lésvos, Corfu's west coast, numerous locales on Crete and Methóni in the Peloponnese. Board rental rates are very reasonable – about €10–15 an hour, with good discounts for longer periods – and instruction is generally also available.

Waterskiing is available at a number of the larger resorts, and a fair few of the smaller ones too. By the crippling rental standards of the ritzier parts of the Mediterranean it is a bargain, with twenty minutes' instruction often available for around €25–30. At many resorts, **parasailing** (*parapént* in Greek) is also possible; rates start at €30 a go.

A combination of steady winds, appealing seascapes and numerous natural harbours has long made Greece a tremendous place for **sailing**. Holiday companies offer all sorts of packaged and tailor-made cruises (see p.32 in "Getting there"). In Greece, small boats and motorized dinghies are rented out by the day at many resorts. Spring and autumn are the most pleasant and least expensive seasons; *meltémi* winds make for pretty nauseous sailing between late June and early September, and summer rates for the same craft can be three times as high as shoulder-season prices.

Because of the potential for pilfering submerged antiquities, **scuba diving** is still fairly restricted, though the government has relaxed its controls of late and there are now over one hundred dive centres spread throughout parts of the mainland, the Dodecanese, the Ionians, the Cyclades and Crete. Single dives start around €40 and various courses are available. For more information and an update on new, approved sites, contact the Union of Greek Diving Centres (☎210 92 29 532 or 210 41 18 909) or the Hellenic Federation of Underwater Activities (☎210 98 19 961).

Greece also has lots of white water, especially in the Peloponnese, central mainland and Epirus, so if you're into **rafting** or **kayaking** there is much potential. Any worthwhile stretch of river will have at least one outfitter who's set up shop on the banks – keep an eye peeled locally.

Skiing

Skiing is a comparative newcomer to Greece; the first centre, on Mount Parnassós, began life in the 1950s as an R&R facility for the local bauxite miners. Especially with global warming, snow conditions have become unpredictable at the southernmost resorts, and runs remain generally short. However, there are now more than a dozen ski centres scattered about the mountains, and what they may lack in professionalism is often made up for by an easy-going and unpretentious après-ski scene. Costs are, however, on a par with those of northern

Europe, at around €25 a day for rental of skis and boots, plus €15–25 a day for a lift pass. The season generally lasts from the beginning of January to the beginning of April, with a few extra weeks possible at either end, depending on snow conditions. No foreign package operators currently feature Greece among their offerings – it's very much a local, weekender scene.

The most developed of the resorts is Keláa-Fterólakkas on **Parnassós**, the legendary mountain near Delphi. The main problem here is that the lifts are often closed owing to high winds. Other major ski centres include **Vórras** (Mount Kaïmaktsalán), near Édhessa; **Veloúhi** (Mount Tymfristós), near Karpeníssi in central Greece; **Helmós**, near Kalávryta on the Peloponnese; and **Vérmion**, near Náoussa in Macedonia.

Walking

If you have the time and stamina, **walking** is probably the single best way to see the remoter backcountry. This guide includes descriptions of a number of the more accessible mountain hikes, as well as suggestions for more casual walking on the mainland and islands.

In addition, you may want to acquire one or more of the countrywide or regional **hiking guidebooks**; see p.1148 in

"Contexts". See also p.39 for details of hiking maps available, and p.31 for details of companies offering walking holidays in the mountains.

Football and basketball

Football (soccer) is far and away the most popular sport in Greece – both in terms of participating and watching, its status strengthened still further by Greece's heroic and unlikely emergence as champions of Euro 2004 in Portugal. The most important teams are Panathanaïkós and AEK of Athens, Olympiakós of Pireás and PAOK of Thessaloníki. Other major teams in the provinces include Xánthi and the Cretan Ofí. If you're interested, matches (usually played on Wed nights and Sun afternoons) are easy enough to coincide with from September to May. In mid-autumn you could catch one of the Greek teams playing European competition – their performances in the Champions League of late have been very creditable.

The nation's **basketball** team is one of the continent's strongest and won the European Championship in 1987 – cheered all the way with enormous enthusiasm. At club level, many of the football teams maintain basketball squads – Panathanaïkós were European champions in 1996, 2000 and 2002, and Olympiakós back in 1997.

 # Living in Greece

Many habitual visitors fall in love with Greece to the extent that they take up part- or full-time residence there, more likely buying property than renting it, and most probably retired or self-employed rather than working at relatively low Greek wage scales for employees or casual labour. Beyond the first hurdle of obtaining a residence permit, there are a number of other issues to consider: working, keeping a vehicle, Internet connection and animal welfare. For the full scoop on real estate, consult *Buying a Property: Greece* (Navigator Guides, UK).

Residence permits and voting

EU (and EEA) nationals are allowed to stay indefinitely in any EU state, but to ensure

avoidance of any problems – eg, in setting up a bank account – (and to be entitled to vote locally in Euro and municipal elections), get a five-year **residence permit** (ádhia dhiamonís). If you're not employed (self- or otherwise), you may be required to prove that you have sufficient resources to support yourself. If you are not contributing to one of the Greek social insurance schemes, you will require a letter (translated into Greek) from the Department of Works and Pensions in the UK stating that your home contributions are current. In the largest towns, you apply for a residence permit at the Alien's Bureau (Ypiresía Allodhapón) or, in its absence, the central police station. You will need to bring your passport, several photographs, revenue stamps (hartósima, available from the local tax office or some kiosks) and a stable address (not a hotel). Permits are given for terms of five years.

You should allow four to six weeks for all the formalities to be completed; the bottleneck is usually a required **health examination** at the nearest public hospital. Once you've assembled all the results, you trot these over yourself to the local public health office, where its administrative council will vet and endorse these, and issue you with a certificate of approval. Finally you take this to the local police or Aliens' Bureau, which should have your permit ready, free of charge, within three working days. Renewals are much more straightforward; there's no health examination, you just leave your old permit with the police who apply an update stamp within a few weeks.

EU nationals with a residence permit become eligible to **vote** in municipal elections (every four years, in October, next in 2006 and 2010) and Euro elections, though in the latter case they must choose a country – you can't vote in both the UK and Greece. Bring your passport and residence permit to the nearest town hall and you will be entered onto the computerized voter registration rolls in a matter of minutes.

Residence/work permits for **non-EU/non-EEA nationals** can only be obtained on application to a Greek embassy or consulate outside of Greece; you have a much better chance of securing one if you are married to a Greek, are of Greek background by birth (an *omoyenís*), or have permanent-resident status in another EU state, but even then expect wrangles and delays.

Many non-EU nationals working illegally in Greece still resort to the pre-Schengen ploy of heading off to Bulgaria or Turkey for a few days every three months and re-entering at a different border post for a new passport stamp; this usually works, but if not, penalties as described on p.37 potentially apply.

Working

EU membership notwithstanding, **short-term unskilled work** in Greece is often badly paid and undocumented, with employers skimping on the requirement to pay IKA (social insurance contributions) for their employees. The influx, since 1990, of over a million immigrants from various countries – chiefly Albania and central Europe – has resulted in a surplus of unskilled labour and severely depressed wages. Undocumented, **non-EU/non-EEA nationals** who wish to work in Greece do so surreptitiously, with the ever-present risk of denunciation to the police and instant deportation. In a climate of rising unemployment, Greek immigration authorities are cracking down hard on any suitable targets, be they Albanian, African, South African or North American. That old foreigners' standby, teaching English, is now available only to TEFL certificate-holders – preferably Greeks, non-EU nationals of Greek descent and EU/EEA nationals in that order. If you are a non-EU/EEA foreign national of Greek descent you are termed *omoyenís* (returned Greek diaspora member) and in fact have tremendous employment, taxation and residence rights and privileges. Similarly, that other long-standing fallback of long-haul backpackers, picking fruit or greenhouse vegetables, is now the exclusive province of semi-permanent immigrants.

Greek-language courses

The longest established outlet is The Athens Centre, Arhimídhous 48, 116 36 Athens (☏210 70 12 268, ⊛www .athenscentre.gr). One to try on Crete is Lexis, 48 Dhaskaloyiánni, 73100 Haniá (☏28210 55673, ⊛lexis.edu .gr). There are always adverts in the *Athens News* for other schools, which come and go.

You may prefer to engage in **tourism-related work**, where your language skills or specialist training put you at some advantage. Most women working casually in Greece find waiting jobs in **bars** or **restaurants** around the main resorts; men, unless they are trained chefs, will probably find it much harder to secure any position, even washing up. Corfu, with its big British slant, is an obvious choice for bar work; Rhodes, Kós, Crete, Skiáthos, Páros, Íos and Santoríni are also promising. Start looking, if you can, around April or May; you'll get better rates at this time if you're taken on for a season. If you've the expertise, you might staff one of the **windsurfing** schools or **scuba** operations that have sprung up on several islands.

Perhaps the best tourism-related work, however, is being a **rep for a package holiday company**. All you need is EU nationality and language proficiency compatible with the clientele, though knowledge of Greek is a big plus. English-only speakers are pretty well restricted to places with a big British package trade, namely Crete, Rhodes, Skiáthos, Sámos, Lésvos and the Ionian islands – or English-speaking hotels and complexes elsewhere. Many such staff are recruited from Britain, but it's also common to be hired on the spot through local affiliates in April or May. A big plus, however you're taken on, is that you're guaranteed about six months of steady work, often with use of a car thrown in.

Keeping a car or motorcycle

Both tourist visitors and residents, of any nationality, are only allowed to **keep a vehicle in Greece** with foreign number plates for a maximum of six months, or until the current road-tax sticker and/or insurance from your home country expires, whichever comes first. After that you face a number of inconvenient choices: mandatorily re-exporting the car, storing it for six months, or obtaining local registration. Many holiday home-owners long used the six-on, six-off system, storing their EU-plated car off-road under customs seal, but this has become difficult now that one must pay a full year's insurance locally anyway, and most Greek

companies will no longer insure a foreign car. Especially on isolated islands, many foreigners just drive along for years on foreign plates with no road tax, but if you're caught – either by ordinary traffic police or plainclothes customs inspectors, especially vigilant at busy ferry docks – these personnel are empowered to impound the vehicle concerned immediately, and the "ransom" (basically a fine plus arbitrary import duty) is prohibitive. If a car is circulating with foreign plates, you must always be able to prove that the car has been in Greece for less than six months (the dated ticket for any ferry you may have arrived on from Turkey or Italy is considered sufficient evidence).

Should you decide to import your beloved buggy, **import duties** run anywhere from 30 to 120 percent of the value of the car, depending on its age and engine displacement; the nearest Greek embassy overseas will provide you with a current table of fees charged. You take your car or motorcycle to the nearest customs compound, where personnel will go over it and make a written application to headquarters in Pireás; within ten working days you (or rather your designated *ektelonistís* or customs agent) will receive an assessment of duty, against which there is no appeal, and which must be paid immediately. For EU-plated cars at least this is blatantly illegal – their drivers should get Greek plates at little or no cost on demand – but despite being referred to the European Court several times on this (and always losing), the Greek state shows no sign of stopping this practice. The only way out is to make a declaration at your nearest Greek embassy or consulate that you intend to take up full-time residence in Greece (ie are not just a holiday-home owner); apparently such an official document should satisfy the most exigent Greek official and get you a pair of Greek plates in a few weeks. In any case, you will immediately begin to save massive amounts of money by paying insurance at local rates rather than the inflated Athens-equivalent rates levied on all foreign-registered cars.

If this all sounds too much hassle, remember that the **cost of cars** has plunged in Greece and for many models is much less than Britain – a Korean-made compact runabout starts at around €6000, plus tax. A nice new scooter can be had for €1000–1500, but remember that there are stiff fines for being caught driving even an 80cc scooter on a car licence (for which the limit is 50cc); budget €450 for a licence course, and enough facility in reading Greek to pass the written test.

Internet connection

Along with most other utilties, Greek telecoms are in the process of being deregulated; there are now two fixed-telephony providers (set to grow) and a myriad of Internet packages and providers. Many rural exchanges still won't support broadband (or ADSL as it's universally referred to in Greece); **dial-up** subscriptions cost from €9 per month if you pre-pay for a year, plus modest hourly charges for online time. The Yermanos chain of electronic widgets is one of the most impartial outlets for all the providers, or visit ⓦ www.otenet.gr – but not OTE premises themselves, whose poorly trained personnel disavow all knowledge of advantageous offers on their subsidiary's website. **ADSL** is vastly overpriced by north European standards – getting on for €50 a month at the lowest speeds – but there is pressure from the EU to push these rates down; watch out for specials (ie free connection and router box).

Pets and animal welfare

No single issue potentially pits foreign residents (especially English ones) in Greece against their locally born neighbours more than the status of pets and animal welfare in general. Abuse, especially in the rural areas, is rife: many islands have a remote valley where it was customary to set old donkeys loose to starve; hunting dogs are kept chained to outdoor stakes in all weathers, without enough water or food; and surplus kittens are routinely drowned in a weighted sack. Strychnine poisoning of "extra" or annoying animals is the rule (especially in winter when there are no longer soft-hearted foreigners around to leave food out for strays) – so never let your dog run loose. There is also a stubborn resistance at all social levels to neutering, or to spending money on an animal beyond a handful of cat food. Most Greek animal-lovers and pet-owners are urban and/or foreign-educated, as are veterinary practices and pet-supply shops, and they have thus far made little headway against deeply ingrained attitudes. Beasts are seen as part of the rural economy, with a job of work to do; when their usefulness is over, they are disposed of without sentimentality. It is also deeply offensive to many Greeks (especially taverna owners) for foreigners to feed scraps to the under-table cats running in mendicant packs, as signs often warn you.

Under both European and Greek law it's an offence to poison, torture, abandon or otherwise mistreat an animal, but in the deep country you are just wasting your breath, and raising the blood pressure of everyone concerned, by proselytizing to change opinions. If you feel strongly about the foregoing, support an animal welfare organization, which will be found anywhere large numbers of expats are resident – Rhodes, Corfu, Ídhra and Sámos are prime examples. Two useful UK-run organizations are the Greek Animal Welfare Fund (☎0207 828 9736) and Greek Animal Rescue (☎0208 203 1956). These groups organize mass neuterings by visiting vets, maintain feeding stations and organize the adoption of strays by overseas families. In the latter instance, they are always looking for air passengers returning to northern Europe willing to accompany a caged animal to the destination airport, where it will be met by representatives of the eventual owner.

Crime and personal safety

Greece is one of Europe's safest countries, with a low crime rate and a deserved reputation for honesty. If you leave a bag or wallet at a café, you'll probably find it scrupulously looked after, pending your return. Similarly, Greeks are relatively relaxed about leaving possessions unattended on the beach or on campsites. The biggest hazards on beaches, oddly, are free-ranging goats – who will eat just about anything left accessible – and the wake of passing cruise ships or ferries, which can wash all your possessions out to sea with little or no warning.

Recent years, however, have seen a large increase in **theft** and **crimes against persons** at archeological sites, in towns, remote villages and resorts, so it's wise to lock rooms and cars securely, treating Greece like any other European destination. In particular, there has been a huge rise in pickpocketing on the old section of the **Athens metro** (not the new extension, which is heavily policed). See p.72 for **emergency phone numbers**.

Thousands of **women** travel independently in Greece without being **harassed** or feeling intimidated. With the sea change in local mores since the 1980s – specifically, a vast increase in the "availability" of young Greek women to young local men, up to and including living together before marriage – almost all of the traditional Mediterranean macho impetus for trying one's luck with foreign girls has faded. Any hassle you do get is from a nearly extinct species of professionally single Greek men, known as *kamákia* (fish harpoons), who haunt beach bars and dance clubs. Sadly, foreign women stand more chance of being **sexually assaulted** at certain notorious resorts (Kávos, Corfu; Laganás, Zákynthos; Faliráki, Rhodes) by northern European men than they do by ill-intentioned locals. With too many people seemingly checking their common sense

in at the departing airport along with their luggage, the UK Foreign Office has been obliged to remind them in print not to go out bar-crawling alone, to go home alone, or to accept late-night rides from strangers (indeed **hitching** at any time of the day is not advisable for lone female travellers). In the more remote mountains and islands women may feel slightly uncomfortable travelling **alone**. The intensely traditional villagers may have trouble understanding why you are unaccompanied, and might not welcome your presence in their exclusively male *kafenía* – often the only place where you can get a drink. Travelling with a man, you're more likely to be treated as a *xéni*, a word meaning both (female) stranger and guest.

Lone men need to be wary of one long-established racket in the largest mainland towns and island ports. Near Sýndagma in Athens, in particular, you may be approached by dubious gents asking the time, or your origins, and then offering to take you for a drink in a nearby bar. This is invariably staffed with hostesses (who may also be prostitutes), whose main job is to convince you to treat them to drinks. At the end of the night you'll be landed with an outrageous bill, some of which goes towards the hostess's commission; physical threats are brought to bear on reluctant payers.

Cultural hints and etiquette

It's more likely that you'll (inadvertently or otherwise) give offence than receive it; accordingly, a summary of the most common misdemeanors is provided, along with some positive cultural etiquette to observe. Attitudes towards the disabled, the elderly, gays and children will also be different to what you're used to at home.

Police and potential offences

There is a single, nationwide **police force**, the Elliniki Astynomia, rather than the division into urban corps and rural gendarmerie normal in most of Europe. Greek cops can be gruff at the best of times, and many have little regard for foreigners. Police practice often falls short of northern European norms, and fit-ups or beatings in custody are not unknown.

You are required to **carry suitable ID** on you at all times (except when in bathing costume) – either a passport or a driving licence. Otherwise, the most common causes of a brush with authority are nude bathing or sunbathing, camping outside an authorized site, public inebriation or lewd behaviour, and taking photos in forbidden areas.

Nude bathing is explicitly legal on only a very few beaches (most famously on Mýkonos), and is deeply offensive to the more traditional Greeks – exercise considerable sensitivity to local feeling and the kind of place you're in. It is, for example, very bad etiquette to swim or sunbathe nude within sight of a church, of which there are many along the Greek coast. Generally, if a beach has become fairly well established as naturist, or is well secluded, laws go unenforced. Police will only be summoned if nudity is getting too overt on mainstream tourist stretches. Most of the time, the only action will be a warning, but you can officially be arrested straight off – facing up to three days in jail and a stiff fine. **Topless (sun)bathing** for women is technically legal nationwide, but specific locales often opt out of the "liberation" by posting signs, which should be heeded.

Very similar guidelines apply to **camping rough**, which has ostensibly been illegal nationwide since 1977. Even for this you're still unlikely to incur anything more than a warning to move on. The only real risk of arrest is if you are told to clear off and fail to do so. In either of the above cases, even if the police do take any action against you, it's more likely to be a brief spell in their cells than any official prosecution.

The **hours between 3 and 5pm**, the midday *mikró ípno* (siesta), are sacrosanct – one does not make phone calls to strangers or any sort of noise (especially with motorcycles) at this time. **Quiet** is also mandated by law **between midnight and 8am** in residential areas, though Greek construction crews frequently violate this by starting up at 7.30am or so.

The well-publicized ordeal of twelve British plane-spotters who processed slowly through Greek jails and courts in 2001–02 on espionage charges (they had, however, received warnings on prior occasions) should be ample incentive to **take no pictures** at all in and **around airports or military installations**. The latter are usually well festooned with signs of a bellows camera with a red "x" through it. "No pictures at all" includes farewell snaps on the runway; most civilian airports double as air-force bases.

Any sort of **disrespect** towards the Greek state or Orthodox Church in general, or Greek civil servants in particular, may be construed as actionable, so it's best to keep your comments on how things are working (or not) to yourself. Every year a few foreign louts find themselves in deep trouble over a drunken indiscretion. This is a society where verbal injuries count, with a backlog of court cases dealing with the alleged public utterance of *malákas* (wanker).

In the non-verbal field, ripped or soiled clothes and untucked-in shirts are considered nearly as insulting. Don't expect a uniformly civil reception if dressed in **grunge attire**, since Greeks will interpret this in one of two possible ways, neither reflecting well on you. Poverty is an uncomfortably close memory for many, and they may consider that you're making light of hard times. More to the point, fashion victim-hood is developed to near-Italian levels in Greece; if you clearly have so little self-respect as to appear slovenly and dishevelled in public, why should any Greek respect you?

Public drunkenness of the sort which fuelled the much-publicized crimes at Faliráki in 2003 (see p.808) has always been held in contempt in Greece, where the inability to hold one's liquor is considered unmanly and shameful. Inebriation will be considered an aggravating factor if you're busted for something else, not an excuse.

Drug offences are treated as major crimes, particularly since there's a mushrooming local use and addiction problem. The maximum penalty for "causing the use of drugs by someone under 18", for example, is life imprisonment and an astronomical fine. Theory is by no means practice, but foreigners caught in possession of even small amounts of marijuana do get long jail sentences if there's evidence that they've been supplying the drug to others. Moreover, you could be inside on remand for well over a year awaiting a trial date, with little or no chance of bail being granted.

If you get arrested for any offence, you have a right to contact your **consulate**, which will arrange a lawyer for your defence. Beyond this, there is little they can, or in most cases will, do. Details of full-ranking consulates in Athens and Thessaloníki appear in their respective "Listings" sections. There are honorary British consulates on Rhodes, Crete and Corfu as well.

Disabled and senior travellers

The **disabled**, except notably on Kós, are not especially well catered to in Greece. Few street-corners have wheelchair ramps,

beeps for the sight-impaired are rare at pedestrian crossings, and Athens buses are not generally of the "kneeling" type. Only Athens airport, and airline staff in general (who are used to handling wheelchairs), are disabled-friendly. However, as EU-wide legislation on the subject is implemented, the situation should improve.

Senior travellers by contrast fare well in Greece, which has a deeply ingrained tradition of respect for one's elders; you are, for example, rather less likely to be grumbled or shouted at by Athens bus drivers or harbour officials.

Travelling with children

Children are worshipped and indulged, demonstrably to excess, and present few problems when travelling. As elsewhere in the Mediterranean, they are not segregated from adults at meal times, and early on in life are inducted into the typical late-night routine. Thus you'll see plenty of kids at tavernas, expected to eat (and up to their capabilities, talk) like adults. Outside of certain all-inclusive resorts, however, there are very few amusements specifically for kids – certainly nothing like Disney World Paris – though luxury hotels are more likely to offer some kind of **babysitting or crèche service** than mid-range, C-class hotels.

Most ferry-boat lines and airlines in Greece offer some sort of **discount** for children, ranging from fifty to one hundred percent depending on their age; hotels and rooms won't charge extra for infants, and levy a modest supplement for "third" beds which the child occupies by him/herself.

Gay and lesbian travellers

Greece is deeply ambivalent about **homosexuality**: ghettoized as "to be expected" in the arts, theatre and music scenes, but apt to be closeted elsewhere – though the rampant 2004–05 sex scandals amongst the Orthodox clergy have blown the door wide open on the prevalent hypocrisy. Homosexuality is legal over the age of 17, and (male) bisexual behaviour common but rarely admitted; the legal code itself, however, still contains perjoative references to passive partners. Greek men are terrible flirts, but cruising them is a semiotic minefield and definitely at your own risk – references in (often obsolete) gay guides to "known" male cruising grounds should be treated sceptically. "Out" gay Greeks are rare, and "out" local lesbians rarer still; foreign same-sex couples will be regarded in the provinces with some bemusement but accorded the standard courtesy as foreigners – as long as they refrain from indulging in displays of affection in public, which remains taboo in rural areas. There is, however, a sizeable gay contingent in Athens, Thessaloníki and Pátra, plus a fairly obvious scene at resorts like Ídhra, Rhodes and Mýkonos. Skála Eressoü on Lésvos, the birthplace of Sappho, is (appropriately) an international mecca for lesbians. Even in Athens, however, most gay nightlife is underground (often literally so in the siting of clubs), with no visible signage for nondescript, heavily soundproofed premises.

Directory

Addresses In Greece, streets are cited in the genitive case, usually with no tag like "Street" or "Avenue"; the number always follows. Thus 36 Venizelos Avenue is written as Venizélou 36, and it's this convention which we've adopted throughout the book. The practice is different with **platía** (square) and **leofóros** (avenue), which always appear before the name. Postcodes are five-digit and precede the municipality concerned, for example 240 22 Kardhamýli, in the Peloponnese.

Bargaining This isn't a regular feature of touristic life, though you'll find it possible with private rooms and certain hotels out of season. Similarly, you should be able to negotiate discounted rates for vehicle rental, especially for longer periods. Services such as shoe, watch and camera repair don't have iron-clad rates, so use common sense when assessing charges (advance written estimates are not routine practice).

Departure tax This is levied on all international ferries – currently €10 per person and per car or motorbike, usually (but not always) included within the quoted price of the ticket. To non-EU states it's €19 per person, sometimes arbitrarily levied twice (on entry and exit). There's also an airport departure tax of €12 for all EU and EEA destinations, €22 for all non-EU destinations plus a security tax of €3.20, but these are always included in the price of the ticket. Some small regional flights (such as Léros–Astypálea) are exempt from the departure tax. Additionally, a special tax, nicknamed the *spatósima*, is included in the ticket price of all flights leaving Athens (€7.79 for Greek destinations, €10.30 for non-Greek ones).

Electricity Voltage is 220 volt AC throughout the country. Wall outlets – rarely abundant enough – take double round-pin plugs as in the rest of continental Europe. Three-to-two-pin adapters should be purchased beforehand in the UK, as they can be difficult to find locally; standard 5-, 6- or 7.5-amp models permit operation of a hair dryer or travel iron. Unless they're dual voltage, North American appliances will require both a step-down transformer and a plug adapter (the latter easy to find in Greece).

Photography Fuji and Kodak print films are reasonably priced and easy to have processed. APS film is also widely sold and processed. Kodak and Fuji slide films can be purchased, again at UK prices or better, in larger centres, but often cannot be processed there. Memory media for digital cameras are widely available.

Laundries *Plindíria*, as they're known in Greek, are prominent in the main resort towns; sometimes an attended service wash is available for little or no extra charge over the basic cost of €8–10 per wash and dry. Self-catering villas will usually be furnished with a drying line and a selection of plastic wash-tubs or a bucket. In hotels, laundering should be done in a more circumspect manner; management can object if you use bathroom washbasins, Greek wall-mounting being what it is, or do more than a few socks and undies. It's best to use a shower for both washing and hanging to dry.

Time Greek summer time begins at 2am on the last Sunday in March, when the clocks go forward one hour, and ends at 2am the last Sunday in October when they go back. Be alert to this, as the change is not well publicized, leading scores of visitors to miss planes and ferries every year. Greek time is thus always two hours ahead of Britain. For North America, the difference is seven hours for Eastern Standard Time, ten hours

for Pacific Standard Time, with an extra hour plus or minus for those few weeks in April when one place is on daylight saving and the other isn't.

Tipping Restaurant bills incorporate a service charge. With the increasing cost of food, drink and services in Greece, generous tipping has decreased; if you are going to tip, rounding up the bill is usually sufficient. If you receive particular hospitality, avoid trying to reciprocate with excessive cash as this could cause offence.

Toilets Public toilets are usually in parks or squares, often subterranean; otherwise try a bus station. Except in areas frequented by tourists, public toilets tend to be pretty filthy – it's best to use those in restaurants and bars. Remember that throughout Greece, you drop paper in the adjacent wastebins, not in the toilet bowl.

Guide

Guide

Athens and around

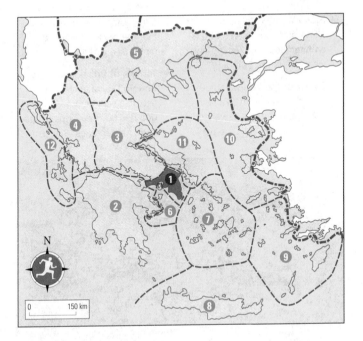

CHAPTER 1

Highlights

* **The Acropolis** Rising above the city, the great rock of the Acropolis symbolizes not just Athens, but the birth of European civilization. See p.117

* **Herodes Atticus Theatre** Marvellously atmospheric venue for classical music concerts during the Hellenic summer music festival. See p.125

* **Pláka** Wander the narrow alleys and steep steps of this architecturally interesting and vibrant quarter. See p.127

* **Tower of the Winds** Intriguing and elegant, this Roman addition to Athens is well worth seeking out. See p.132

* **The bazaar** Athens' raucous and colourful street market, extending from the Monastiráki district up to the nineteenth-century covered food hall. See p.138

* **National Archeological Museum** The world's finest collection of ancient Greek art and sculpture. See p.140

* **Psyrrí** The heart of Athens' new nightlife, packed with bars, cafés and restaurants that are buzzing til late at night. See p.162

* **Temple of Poseidon, Cape Soúnio** Dramatic and evocative, this sanctuary to the sea god has been a shipping landmark for centuries. See p.184

△ Tower of the winds

Athens and around

For all too many people, **ATHENS** is a city that happened two-and-a-half thousand years ago. It's true that even now a glorious past looms large – literally, in the shape of the mighty Acropolis that dominates almost every view, as well as every visitor's itinerary. Yet the modern conurbation is home to over four million people – more than a third of the Greek nation's population – and has undergone a transformation in the twenty-first century, partly thanks to the stimulus of the 2004 Olympics, that has made it far more than a repository of antiquities and lifted it beyond the clichés of pollution and impossible traffic that blighted its reputation in recent years.

Even now, however, it is far from a beautiful city – the scramble for growth in the decades after World War II, when the population grew from around 700,000 to close to its present level, was an architectural disaster. But for the first time, the city is starting to make the most of what it has, while massive investment in new roads, rail and metro, along with extensive pedestrianization in the centre, has resolved some of the worst traffic and smog problems. The views for which Athens was once famous are reappearing and, despite inevitable globalization and the appearance of all the usual high-street and fast-food chains, the city retains its character to a remarkable degree. Even today chickens peck around the wheels of the gleaming new Mercedes in city-centre backyards, while Eastern-style bazaars vie for space with outlets for Armani and Benetton. And hectic modernity is always tempered with an air of intimacy and hominess; as any Greek will tell you, Athens is merely the largest village in the country.

However often you've visited, the vestiges of the ancient Classical Greek city, most famously represented by the **Parthenon** and other remains that top the **Acropolis**, are an inevitable focus; along with the refurbished **National Archeological Museum**, the finest collection of Greek antiquities anywhere in the world, they should certainly be a priority. The majority of the several million visitors who pass through each year do no more, perhaps managing an evening or two dining in the romantic, touristy tavernas of Pláka. In so doing, they never manage to escape the crowds and so see little of the Athens Athenians know. Even on a brief visit, it does not do Athens justice to see it purely as a collection of ancient sites and museum pieces. It's worth taking the time to explore some of the city's neighbourhoods. For all its tourists, the nineteenth-century quarter of **Pláka**, with its mix of Turkish, Neoclassical and Greek-island architecture, and its intriguing little museums devoted to traditional arts, from ceramics to music, is perhaps the most easily appreciated. Just to its north, the **bazaar** area retains an almost Middle Eastern atmosphere in its life and trade, with the added bonus of some of the centre's best nightlife in neighbouring **Psyrrí** and up-and-coming **Gázi**. More traditional Athenian escapes are also nearby, in the form of the shady **National Gardens** and the elegant, upmarket quarter of **Kolonáki**. There are also startling **views** to be enjoyed from the many hills – Lykavitós and Filopáppou above all – while in summer, the **beach** is just a tram ride away.

The biggest surprise in Athens for most people, however, is the vibrant life of the city itself. **Cafés** are packed day and night and the streets stay lively until 3 or 4am, with some of the best **bars and clubs** in the country. **Eating out** is great, with establishments ranging from traditional tavernas to the finest gourmet restaurants. In summer, much of the action takes place outdoors, from dining on the street, to clubbing on the beach, to **open-air cinema**, **concerts** and **classical drama**. There's a diverse **shopping** scene, ranging from colourful bazaars and lively street markets to chic suburban malls crammed with the latest designer goods. And with a good-value, extensive public transportation system allied to inexpensive cabs, you'll have no difficulty getting around.

Outside Athens in the rest of the state of Attica, covered at the end of this chapter, the emphasis shifts more exclusively to ancient sites. The Temple of Poseidon at **Soúnio** is the most popular trip, and rightly so, with its dramatic

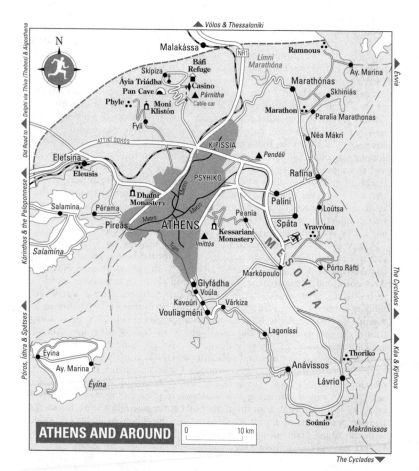

The Cyclades ▼

The Olympic legacy

The **2004 Olympics** can take much of the credit for getting Athens back on the map and regenerating the city's infrastructure, with a greatly enhanced metro and an entirely new tram above all, and an extensive network of pedestrian streets in the city centre. Successful as they were in many ways, however, the legacy of the Games is not an entirely happy one. In the rush to be ready on time many of the works went disastrously over budget – a price that Athenians will be paying for decades to come – while inadequate planning means that very few of the costly stadia have found any purpose in life since the Games finished. Even the magnificent main stadium itself, in the north of the city, has been used just a handful of times since the closing ceremony: mostly it sits forlorn behind locked fences, not even accessible for those who just want to take a look. Many of the smaller venues are already starting to deteriorate, and seem likely eventually to be demolished, to be replaced by yet more shopping malls.

clifftop position above the cape. Lesser known and less visited are the sanctuaries at **Ramnous**, **Eleusis** (Elefsína) and **Brauron** (Vravróna), or the burial mound from the great victory at **Marathon**. Walkers may want to head for the **mountains – Párnitha**, most compellingly – that ring the city, where springtime hikes reveal some of the astonishing range of Greek wild flowers. There are also **beaches** all around the coast, though if you're heading on to the islands these may not be a priority. Moving on is quick and easy, with scores of **ferries** and hydrofoils leaving daily from the port at **Pireás** (Piraeus) and, somewhat less frequently, from the two other Attic ferry terminals at **Rafína** and **Lávrio**.

Some history

Athens has been inhabited continuously for over seven thousand years. Its acropolis, supplied with spring water, commanding views of all seaward approaches and encircled by protective mountains on its landward side, was a natural choice for prehistoric settlement and for the **Mycenaeans**, who established a palace-fortress on the rock. Unlike other Mycenaean centres, Athens was not sacked and abandoned during the Doric invasion of about 1200 BC, and so the Athenians always maintained that they were "pure" Ionians with no Doric element. Gradually, Athens emerged as a city-state that dominated the region, ruled by kings who stood at the head of a land-owning aristocracy known as the Eupatridae (the "well-born"), who governed through a Council which met on the Areopagus – the Hill of Ares. Though significant, Athens at this stage was overshadowed by larger, more powerful city-states such as Corinth and Sparta.

The wealth of Athens grew during this period and spurred an explosion in the arts, particularly pottery. However, in the political arena this led to unrest, with a large class of farmers and the like excluded from political life but forced to pay rent or taxes to the nobility. Among the reforms aimed at addressing this were new, fairer laws drawn up by **Draco** (whose "draconian" lawcode was published in 621 BC), and the appointment of **Solon** as ruler (594 BC), with a mandate to introduce sweeping economic and political reform and reduce the power of the *Eupatridae*. Although his reforms greatly increased the franchise, and indeed laid the foundations of what eventually became Athenian democracy, they failed to stop internal unrest, and eventually **Peisistratus**, a cousin of Solon, seized power in the middle of the sixth century BC. Peisistratos is usually called a tyrant, but this simply means he seized power by force: thanks to his populist

The rise and fall of Classical Athens

Perhaps the most startling aspect of ancient, Classical Athens is how suddenly it emerged to the glory for which we remember it – and how short its heyday proved to be. In the middle of the **fifth century BC**, Athens was little more than a country town in its street layout and buildings. The latter comprised a scattered jumble of single-storey houses or wattle huts, intersected by narrow lanes. Sanitary conditions were notoriously lax: human waste and rubbish were dumped outside the town with an almost suicidal disregard for plague and disease. And on the rock of the Acropolis, a site reserved for the city's most sacred monuments, stood blackened ruins – temples and sanctuaries razed by the Persians in 480 BC.

There was little to suggest that the city was entering a unique phase of its history in terms of power, prestige and creativity. But following the victory over the Persians at Salamis, Athens stood unchallenged for a generation. It grew rich on the export of olive oil and of silver from the mines of Attica, but above all it benefited from its control of the **Delian League**, an alliance of Greek city-states formed as insurance against Persian resurgence. The Athenians relocated the League's treasury from the island of Delos to their own acropolis, ostensibly on the grounds of safety, and with its revenues their leader **Pericles** (see p.1074) was able to create the so-called **golden age** of the city. Great endowments were made for monumental construction, arts in all spheres were promoted, and – most significantly – it was all achieved under stable, **democratic rule**.

The Delian League's wealth enabled office-holders to be properly paid, thereby making it possible for the poor to play a part in government. Pericles's constitution ensured that all policies of the state were to be decided by a general assembly of Athenian male citizens – six thousand constituted a quorum. The assembly, which met outside at either the **Agora** or the **Pnyx**, elected a council of five hundred members to carry out the everyday administration of the city and a board of ten *strategoi* or generals to guide it. Pericles, one of the best-known and most influential of the *strategoi*, was as vulnerable as any other to the electoral process: if sufficient numbers had cast their lot (*ostrakon*) against him, his citizenship would be forfeited (he would be literally ostracized); as it was, he managed to stave off such a fate and died with his popularity intact.

In line with this system of democratic participation, a new and exalted notion of the Athenian citizen emerged. This was a man who could shoulder political responsibility, take public office and play a part in the **cultural** and **religious events** of the time. The latter assumed ever-increasing importance. The city's Panathenaic festival, honouring its protectress deity Athena, was upgraded along the lines of the Olympic Games to include drama, music and athletic contests. Athenians rose easily to the challenge. The next five decades were to witness the great dramatic works of **Aeschylus**, **Sophocles** and **Euripides**, and the comedies of **Aristophanes**. Foreigners such as **Herodotus**, considered the inventor of history, and **Anaxagoras**, the philosopher, were drawn to live in the city. And they, in turn, were surpassed by native Athenians. **Thucydides** wrote *The Peloponnesian War*, a pioneering work of documentation and analysis, while **Socrates** posed the problems of philosophy that were to exercise his follower **Plato** and to shape the discipline to the present day.

But it was the great civic **building programme** that became the most visible and powerful symbol of the age. Under the patronage of Pericles and with vast public

policies he was in fact a well-liked and successful ruler who greatly expanded Athens' power, wealth and influence.

His sons **Hippias and Hipparchus** were less successful: Hipparchus was assassinated in 514 BC, after which Hippias attempted to establish a genuine dictatorship. Deeply unpopular, he was overthrown, with the help of an army

funds made available from the Delian treasury, the architects **Iktinos**, **Mnesikles** and **Kallikrates**, and the sculptor **Pheidias**, transformed the city. Their buildings, justified in part as a comprehensive job-creation scheme, included the Parthenon and Erechtheion on the Acropolis; the Hephaisteion and several *stoas* (arcades) around the Agora; a new *odeion* (theatre) on the south slope of the Acropolis hill; and, outside the city, the temples at Soúnio and Ramnous.

Athenian culture flourished under democracy, but the system was not without its contradictions and failures. Only one in seven inhabitants of the city was an actual citizen; the political status and civil rights that they enjoyed were denied to the many thousands of women, foreigners and slaves. While the lives of men became increasingly public and sociable, with meetings at the Agora or Pnyx and visits to the gymnasiums and theatres, **women**, other than *hetaera* (the educated and entertaining courtesans) and streetwalking prostitutes, were secluded in small and insanitary homes. Their subordination was reinforced by a decree in 451 BC, which restricted their property rights, placing them under the control of fathers, husbands or guardians. At any one time, only forty women could be appointed priestesses – one of the few positions of female power. Aeschylus summed up the prevailing attitude when he declared that the mother does no more than foster the father's seed.

The city's democracy was also sullied by its **imperialist** designs and actions, which could be brutal and exploitative, although acts of mercy against rebellious allies were also documented. Atrocities included the wholesale massacre of the male population of Melos. Even within the *polis* of Athens the achievements of democracy were at times overshadowed by attacks on the very talents it had nurtured and celebrated: Aristophanes was impeached, Pheidias and Thucydides were exiled and Socrates was tried and executed.

But, historically, the fatal mistake of the Athenian democracy was allowing itself to be drawn into the **Peloponnesian War** against Sparta, its persistent rival, in 431 BC. Pericles, having roused the assembly to a pitch of patriotic fervour, died of the plague two years after war began, leaving Athens at the mercy of a series of far less capable leaders. In 415 BC a disastrous campaign in Sicily saw a third of the navy lost; in 405 BC defeat was finally accepted after the rest of the fleet was destroyed by Sparta in the Dardanelles. Demoralized, Athens succumbed to a brief period of oligarchy.

Through succeeding decades Athens was overshadowed by Thebes, though it recovered sufficiently to enter a new phase of democracy, the **age of Plato**. However, in 338 BC, nearly one-and-a-half centuries after the original defeat of the Persians, Athens was again called to defend the Greek city-states, this time against the incursions of **Philip of Macedon**. Demosthenes, said to be as powerful an orator as Pericles, spurred the Athenians to fight, in alliance with the Thebans, at Chaironeia. There they were routed, in large part by the cavalry commanded by Philip's son, Alexander (later to become known as Alexander the Great), and Athens fell under the control of the Macedonian empire.

The city continued to be favoured, particularly by **Alexander the Great**, a former pupil of Aristotle, who respected both Athenian culture and its democratic institutions. Following his death, however, came a more uncertain era, which saw periods of independence and Macedonian rule, until 146 BC when the **Romans** swept through southern Greece and it was incorporated into the Roman province of Macedonia.

from Sparta, in 510 BC. A new leader, **Kleisthenes**, took the opportunity for more radical change: he introduced ten classes or tribes based on place of residence, each of which elected fifty members to the *Boule* or Council of State, an administrative body which decided on issues to be discussed by the full Assembly. The Assembly was open to all citizens and was both a legislature and a supreme court. This system was the basis of **Athenian democracy** and remained in place, little changed, right through to Roman times.

Around 500 BC Athens sent troops to aid the Ionian Greeks of Asia Minor, who were rebelling against the Persian Empire; this in turn provoked a Persian invasion of Greece. In 490 BC the Athenians and their allies defeated a far larger Persian force at the **Battle of Marathon**. In 480 BC the Persians returned, capturing and sacking Athens, and leaving much of the city burned to the ground. That same year, however, a naval victory at **Salamis** sealed victory over the Persians, and also secured Athens' position as Greece's leading city-state, enabling it to bring much of the Aegean and central Greece together in the **Delian League** (see p.1071). This was the birth of the **Classical period** (see box), when the Athenians celebrated their success and the triumph of democracy with a flourish of art, architecture, literature and philosophy that has influenced Western culture ever since. When the **Romans** took control of the city in the second century BC, they revered it as the source of much of their own heritage but did relatively little to add to its architectural splendour. (Athens' Roman history is outlined in the box on p.132.)

Christians and Turks

The emergence of **Christianity** was perhaps the most significant step in Athens' long decline from the glories of its Classical heyday. Having survived with little change through years of Roman rule, the city lost its pivotal role in the Roman-Greek world after the division of the Roman Empire into Eastern and Western halves, and the establishment of Byzantium (Constantinople) as capital of the Eastern – **Byzantine** – empire. There, a new Christian sensibility soon outshone the prevailing ethic of Athens, where schools of philosophy continued to teach a pagan Neoplatonism. In 529 AD these schools were finally closed by Justinian I, and the city's temples, including the Parthenon, were reconsecrated as churches.

Athens rarely featured in the chronicles of the time, though it enjoyed a brief revival under foreign powers in the Middle Ages: in the aftermath of the piratical Fourth Crusade, Athens – together with the Peloponnese and much of central Greece – passed into the hands of the **Franks**. At the Acropolis they established a ducal court (of some magnificence, according to contemporary accounts) and for a century Athens was back in the mainstream of Europe. Frankish control, however, was based on little more than a provincial aristocracy. In 1311 their forces battled **Catalan** mercenaries, who had a stronghold in Thebes, and were driven to oblivion in a swamp. The Catalans, having set up their own duchy, in turn gave way to **Florentines** and, briefly, Venetians, before the arrival in 1456 of **Sultan Mehmet II**, the Turkish conqueror of Constantinople.

Turkish Athens was never much more than a garrison town, occasionally (and much to the detriment of its Classical buildings) on the front line of battles with the Venetians and other Western powers. The links with the West, which had preserved a sense of continuity with the Classical and Roman city, were severed, and the flood of visitors was reduced to a trickle of French and Italian ambassadors to the Turkish court, and the occasional traveller or painter. The city does not seem to have been oppressed by Ottoman rule, however: the Greeks enjoyed some autonomy, and both Jesuit and Capuchin monasteries continued to thrive. Although the Acropolis became the home of the Turkish governor and the Parthenon was used as a mosque, life in the village-like quarters around the Acropolis drifted back to a semi-rural existence. Similarly, the great port of **Pireás**, still partially enclosed within its ancient walls, was left to serve just a few dozen fishing boats.

Four centuries of Ottoman occupation followed until, in 1821, together with the inhabitants of a score of other towns across the country, the Greeks of Athens rose in **rebellion**. They occupied the Turkish quarters of the lower town – the current Pláka – and laid siege to the Acropolis. The Turks withdrew, but five years later were back to reoccupy the Acropolis fortifications, while the Greeks evacuated to the countryside. When the Ottoman garrison finally left in 1834, and the Bavarian architects of the new German-born monarchy moved in, Athens, with a population of only 5000, was at its nadir.

Modern Athens

For all the claims of its ancient past, and despite the city's natural advantages, Athens was not the first-choice capital of modern Greece. That honour went instead to Náfplio in the Peloponnese, where the **War of Independence** was masterminded by Kapodhistrias and where the first Greek National Assembly met in 1828. Had Kapodhistrias not been assassinated, in 1831, the capital would most likely have remained in the Peloponnese, if not at Náfplio, then at Trípoli, Corinth or Pátra, all much more established and sizeable towns. But following Kapodhistrias's death, the "Great Powers" of Western Europe intervened, inflicting on the Greeks a king of their own choosing – **Otto**, son of Ludwig I of Bavaria – and, in 1834, transferred the capital and court to Athens. The reasoning was almost purely symbolic and sentimental: Athens was not only insignificant in terms of population and physical extent but was then at the edge of the territories of the new Greek state, which had yet to include northern Thessaly, Epirus, Macedonia, or any of the islands beyond the Cyclades or Sporades.

The **nineteenth-century development** of Athens was a gradual and fairly controlled process. While the archeologists stripped away all the Turkish and Frankish embellishments from the Acropolis, a city began to take shape: the grand, German-inspired Neoclassical plan was for processional avenues radiating out from great squares, a plan that can still be made out on maps but has long ago been subverted by the realities of daily life. **Pireás**, meanwhile, grew into a port again, though until the nineteenth century its activities continued to be dwarfed by the main Greek shipping centres on the islands of Sýros and Ídhra (Hydra).

The first mass expansion of both municipalities came suddenly, in 1923, as the result of the tragic Greek-Turkish war in **Asia Minor**. The peace treaty that resolved the war entailed the exchange of Greek and Turkish ethnic populations, their identity being determined solely on the basis of religion. A million and a half "Greek" Christians, mostly from the age-old settlements along the Asia Minor coast, but also many Turkish-speaking peoples from the communities of inland Anatolia, arrived in Greece as refugees. Over half of them settled in Athens, Pireás and the neighbouring villages, changing at a stroke the whole make-up of the capital. Their integration and survival is one of the great events of the city's history, and has left its mark on modern-day Athens. The web of suburbs that straddles the metro line from Pireás to the north bears nostalgic names of the refugees' origins – Néa Smýrni (New Smyrna), Néa Ionía, Néa Filadhélfia – as do many streets. Originally, these neighbourhoods were little more than refugee camps, with populations primarily from one or another Anatolian town, often with a single water source for two-dozen families. The merging of these shanty-suburbs and their populations with the established communities of Athens and Pireás dominated the years leading up to **World War II**. With the war, however, new concerns emerged.

Athens was hit hard by German occupation: during the winter of 1941–2 there were an estimated two thousand deaths from starvation each day. In late 1944, when the Germans finally left, the capital saw the first skirmishes of **civil war**, with the British forces being ordered to fight against their former Greek allies in the Communist-dominated resistance army, ELAS. From 1946 to 1949 Athens was a virtual island in the civil war, with road approaches to the Peloponnese and the north only tenuously kept open.

During the 1950s, with the civil war over, Athens again started to expand rapidly. A massive **industrial investment** programme – financed largely by the Americans, who had won Greece for their sphere of influence – took place, and the capital saw huge **immigration** from the war-torn, impoverished countryside. The open spaces between the old refugee suburbs began to fill and, by the late 1960s, Greater Athens covered a continuous area from the slopes of mounts Pendéli and Párnitha down to Pireás and Elefsína. Much of this development is unremittingly ugly, since old buildings were demolished wholesale in the name of a quick buck, particularly during the colonels' junta of 1967–74 (see p.1099). Financial incentives encouraged homeowners to demolish their houses and replace them with apartment blocks up to six storeys high; almost everyone took advantage, and as a result most central streets seem like narrow canyons between these ugly, concrete blocks. Unrestrained industrial development on the outskirts was equally rampant, and the combined result was an appallingly polluted city, frequently choking under a noxious brown cloud known as the *nefós*.

Growth in recent decades has been much slower, but it's only since the 1990s – and more recently with a huge boost from the Olympics – that much effort has gone in to improving the city's environment. Although Athens still lags far behind Paris or London in terms of open space, the evidence of recent efforts is apparent. What's left of the city's architectural heritage has been extensively restored; there's clean public transportation; new building is controlled and there's some interesting, radical modern architecture (some of the Olympic facilities or the new Acropolis Museum under construction, for example); and pollution is far less severe than it once was. Hopefully, it is a trend that will continue.

Arrival

There are numerous ways that you could find yourself **arriving** in Athens.

By plane

Athens' **Eleftheríos Venizélos** airport (Ⓦ www.aia.gr) at Spáta, 33km southeast of the city, opened in 2001. It's a slick operation, with excellent access to Athens and to major roads bypassing the city. Facilities include **ATMs** and banks with **money-changing** facilities on all levels and **luggage-storage** with Pacific (☎210 35 30 160) on the Arrivals level. There's also the usual array of travel agencies and car-rental places, plus a very handy official **EOT tourist office** (Mon–Sat 9am–7pm, Sun 10am–4pm; ☎210 35 30 445) on the Arrivals level. Finally there's a one-room **museum** displaying artefacts discovered in the area – mainly during construction of the airport – which is much more interesting than you might expect.

Public transportation from the airport is excellent. The metro and suburban trains share a station. The **Metro** (line 3; €6 single, €10 return, discounts for multiple tickets) is usually more convenient, taking you straight into the heart of the city where you can change to the other metro lines at either Monastiráki or Sýndagma: trains run every half-hour from 6.30am to 11.30pm, and take around thirty minutes. The **suburban train** runs to Laríssis station (see below), not quite so handy for the centre of town; it is, though, more comfortable and runs longer hours (5.50am–1.20am) for identical fares. For most of the day it runs every half-hour, at 20 and 50 minutes past the hour, with a journey time of around forty minutes.

Buses are much slower, especially at rush hours, but they're also much cheaper, run all night and offer direct links to other parts of the city including Pireás. The most useful are the #X95 to Sýndagma square, via Ethnikí Ámyna metro and the *Hilton* (at least three an hour, day and night), and #X96 to the port at Pireás via Glyfádha and the beach suburbs (at least two an hour, day and night); others include the #X93 to the bus stations and #X92 to the northern suburb of Kifissiá. **Tickets** cost €2.90, and are valid for a single trip from the airport to any point in the centre; you can buy them from a booth beside the stops or on the bus – make sure you have small change. Monthly passes are also valid. There are also limited **regional bus services** to the ports of Rafina (7 daily, 5.45am–3.20pm; €3) and Lávrio (10 daily, 6.30am–10pm; €4), useful for those wishing to head straight for a ferry from either place.

Taxis are subject to the vagaries of traffic and can take anything from forty minutes (at night) to an hour and forty minutes (at rush hour) to reach the centre; the fare should be roughly €18–25 to central Athens or Pireás. See p.110 for more on taxi charges and rip-offs.

By train

Athens has two **train stations**, almost adjacent to each other and connected by a footbridge, just northwest of Platía Omonías, off Dheliyánni street. The Laríssis station handles the main lines coming from the north (Lárissa, Thessaloníki, the Balkans, Western Europe and Turkey), as well as suburban trains from the airport. Three blocks south, the Peloponníssou train station is the terminal for the line circling the Peloponnese, including the stretch to Pátra (the main port for ferries from Italy and Corfu).

From either station you are five to fifteen minutes' walk away from the concentration of hotels around Platía Viktorías and Exárhia, both handy for the National Archeological Museum and excellent restaurants. For hotels elsewhere, the Stathmós Laríssis **metro station**, outside the Laríssis train station, is by far the most convenient way to get into central Athens, or to anywhere on the metro system including the port of Pireás. Alternatively, the **#1 trolley bus** and #M2 bus pass along Sámou, one block east of Laríssis station, heading for Omónia, Sýndagma and on past Akrópoli metro station (close to the Acropolis) into Koukáki. **Bus #057** from the Peloponníssou terminal also passes through Omónia and Sýndagma. And of course there are **taxis**.

By bus

Again, there are two principal terminals: Kifissoú 100 and Liossíon 260. Coming into Athens from northern Greece or the Peloponnese, you'll find yourself at **Kifissoú 100** (Terminal A), northwest of the centre. Bus #051 runs very frequently from here to the corner of Zínonos and Menándrou, just off Omónia square. Routes from central Greece generally arrive at **Liossíon 260** (Terminal B), slightly further out to the north. From here, bus #024 runs right through the centre to Omónia, Sýndagma and on past metro Akrópoli.

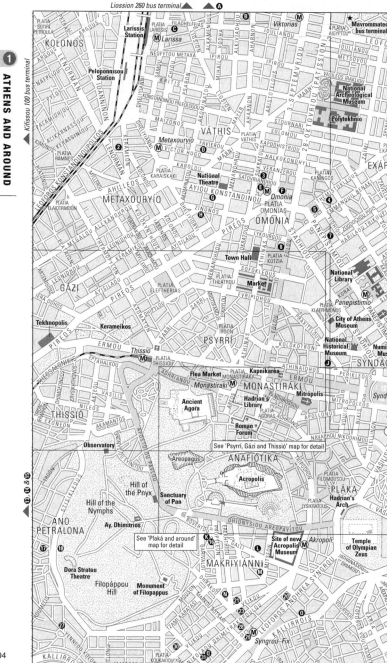

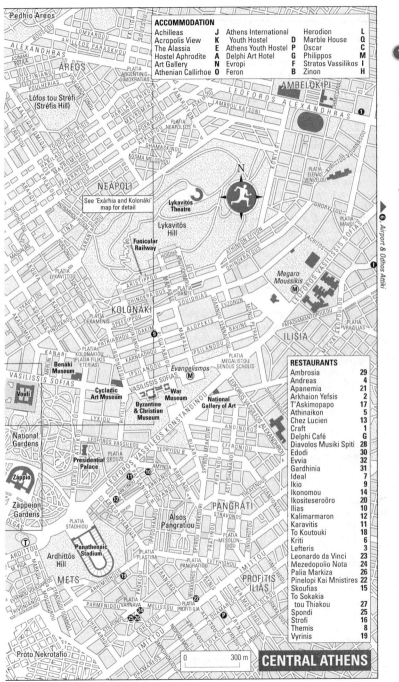

ACCOMMODATION

Achilleas	**J**	Athens International		Herodion	**L**
Acropolis View	**K**	Youth Hostel	**D**	Marble House	**Q**
The Alassia	**E**	Athens Youth Hostel	**P**	Oscar	**C**
Hostel Aphrodite	**A**	Delphi Art Hotel	**G**	Philippos	**M**
Art Gallery	**N**	Evropi	**F**	Stratos Vassilikos	**I**
Athenian Callirhoe	**O**	Feron	**B**	Zinon	**H**

RESTAURANTS

Ambrosia	29
Andreas	4
Apanemia	21
Arkhaion Yefsis	2
T'Askimopapo	17
Athinaikon	5
Chez Lucien	13
Craft	1
Delphi Café	G
Diavolos Musiki Spiti	28
Edodi	30
Evvia	32
Gardhinia	31
Ideal	7
Ikio	9
Ikonomou	14
Ikositseroöro	20
Ilias	10
Kalimarmaron	12
Karavitis	11
To Koutouki	18
Kriti	6
Lefteris	3
Leonardo da Vinci	23
Mezedopolio Nota	24
Palia Markiza	26
Pinelopi Kai Mnistires	22
Skoufias	15
To Sokakia tou Thiakou	27
Spondi	25
Strofi	16
Themis	8
Vyrinis	19

0   300 m

CENTRAL ATHENS

▶ **⑥** *Airport & Odhos Attiki*

Moving on from Athens

Not surprisingly, routes out of the city mirror the arrival points. There are **internal flights** with Olympic (ⓦwww.olympicairlines.com) and Aegean (ⓦwww.aegeanair.com) from Eleftheríos Venizélos to every significant regional airport in Greece and the islands, though island services are heavily reduced out of season. Metro trains to the airport depart from Monastiráki every half hour from 5.51am to 10.51pm, while suburban trains run from Laríssis from 4.38am to 12.06am, normally at 06 and 36 minutes past the hour. There's a separate ticket office for these trains, so don't join the inevitable queue at the main ticket desk. Buses to the airport run all night: the #X95 departs from the southeastern corner of Platía Sýndagma; the #X96 from Platía Karaïskáki in Pireás. Both make regular stops along the way, and the tourist office or your hotel should be able to point out the nearest stop. If you are taking the airport bus it's worth buying your ticket (a standard day pass) from any city metro station 24 hours before departure to have free use of the transport system for a day, as well as your journey to the airport.

On the **train**, most long-distance routes offer a choice of regular or intercity services. Intercity trains are considerably faster and more reliable but there is a hefty extra charge (also levied on rail passes). There are often huge queues for tickets at the stations so it's advisable to book in advance at the ticket office at Sína 6 (off Panepistimíou), or call central reservations on ☎1110.

Buses leave from one of three termini: for northern and western Greece most depart from Kifissoú 100; central Greece from Liossíon 260; and for most destinations in Attica from the Mavrommatéon terminal. See *Travel details* (p.193) for details of individual destinations.

So many **ferries** sail from Pireás and the other Attic ports to so many islands, with schedules that change so much throughout the year, that it's impossible to give details. You'll find the main destinations listed in *Travel details* (p.193) and more specific information in the relevant island chapters. The Tourist Office produces lists of daily sailings from Pireás for the next week, and the *Athens News* also publishes schedules.

The priority for **drivers** should be to get on to the motorway – the Attikí Odhós for the Peloponnese or the E75 Athens-Lamia road for central and northern Greece – as quickly as possible. At least to escape the city, it is well worth paying the toll. There are dozens of routes, but perhaps the easiest is to head west from the centre on Leofóros Athinón or Ierá Odhós to join the E75, and head north from there to its junction with the Attikí Odhós; for the Peloponnese you can alternatively continue on either of these roads towards Elefsína and join the motorway there.

International buses use a variety of stops. Those run by OSE, the railway company, terminate at the Peloponníssou train station, while other private companies may take you right to the city centre: most, though, use Kifissoú 100 or the train station. If you're travelling from within the state of Attica – for example from the ports at Lávrio or Rafina – you'll arrive at the **Mavrommatéon** terminus at the southwest corner of the Pedhíon Áreos Park. This is very close to metro Viktorías, or there are dozens of buses heading down 28 Oktovríou (aka Patissíon) past the National Archeological Museum towards the centre; trolley bus #5, for example, goes to Omónia and Sýndagma and on past metro Akrópoli into Koukáki.

By ferry

The simplest way to get to central Athens from the port at **Pireás** is by **metro** on line 1. Trains run from 5am to 12.30am, and a ticket to the centre of town costs €0.60 (€0.70 if you want to change to another line or continue beyond the centre up to the northern suburbs). **Buses** are much slower but run all night: #040 (about every 10min 5am–midnight; hourly 1am–5am) runs to Sýndagma, while #049 (about every 15min 5am–midnight; hourly 1am–5am) runs to Omónia. For the airport, take express bus #X96. **Taxis** between Pireás and central Athens should cost around €8, including baggage, although rates per kilometre double at night. There's a full account of Pireás, together with a map of the central area, showing the harbours, metro station and bus stops, on p.154. Ferries arriving at **Rafína** and **Lávrio** are served by KTEL buses to the Mavrommatéon terminal (see p.106).

Information and tours

The **Greek National Tourist Office** has a central information office at Amalías 26, just off Sýndagma (Mon–Fri 9am–7pm, Sat & Sun 10am–4pm; ☏210 33 10 392; ⓦ www.gnto.gr). This is a useful first stop and they have a good free map as well as information sheets on current museum and site opening hours, bus and ferry schedules, and so on. If you are arriving by plane, you can save time by calling in at the similarly well-stocked airport branch.

To complement the plans in this book and the free EOT **map**, the *Rough Guide City Map* of Athens is full-colour, non-tearable, weatherproof and pocket-sized, detailing attractions, places to shop, eat, drink and sleep as well as the city streets; the large-scale, street-indexed *Falkplan* is also good (available from the shops listed on p.181). If you are planning a long stay, it's worth getting an A-Z style **street atlas**. The red *Athina-Pireás Proastia Hartis-Odhigos* atlas and the yellow *Emvelia* version are widely available from kiosks and bookshops at €20: though both are in Greek only, they do show absolutely everything, including cinemas and concert venues. A smaller-scale version of the *Emvelia* atlas is available in English (€12), but to find it you may have to go to a specialist map shop (see p.38). *Road Editions* also produce good city plans.

Most local travel agencies offer a half-day tour of classical Athens including a bus drive around the highlights of the city and a guided tour of the Acropolis and Archeological Museum for around €40 (prices depend to some extent on whether food and drink are included), or walking tours of Pláka for half that. Also offered are Athens by night (€50), day-trips to Soúnio (€30) and Delphi (1-day €80, 2-day tour with hotel room €100–120), day cruises around the nearby islands of Égina, Póros and Ídhra (€85), and a variety of longer tours

---

The sites: opening hours and fees

Opening hours for the **sites** and **museums** in Athens are included with some trepidation; they are notorious for changing without notice, from one season to another, or even from one week to the next. To be sure of admission, it's best to visit in the morning, and to be wary of Monday – when many museums and sites close for the whole day.

Most government-run sites are free on Sundays during the off-season (Oct–March), and on some public holidays. During the summer months most sites and museums let students in for half-price (EU students free) and there may be a reduced price if you are over 65; there are usually reduced or free child and youth (under 18 or under 25) rates too.

around the Classical sites. You'll find brochures in most hotels, and any of the travel agencies listed on p.183 can help; major operators include GO Tours, Dhiakoú 20, cnr Syngroú, Makriyiánni ⓣ210 92 19 555 and Key Tours, Kallirois 4, Makriyiánni ⓣ210 92 33 166. For kids especially the Little Train, a thirty-minute trip around Pláka and the centre (€5 adults, €3 children), can be fun: it leaves from Eólou on the Platía Paliás Agorás, near the Roman Forum in Monastiráki. Trekking Hellas (see p.183) provide some interesting local tours including a foodie tour of the city and a day-trip visiting the islands by small speedboat.

City transport

Athens is served by slow but ubiquitous **buses**, a fast, mostly modern **metro** system, and a **tram** service that runs from the centre to the beach suburbs. **Taxis** are also plentiful and, for short journeys in town, exceptionally cheap. Most public transportation operates from around 5am to midnight, with just a few buses – including those to the airport – continuing all night. **Driving** is a traffic-crazed nightmare, and parking far worse. If you do have a car, you're strongly advised to find somewhere to park it for the duration of your stay and not attempt to use it to get around the city centre.

The metro

The expanded **metro** system is much the easiest way to get around central Athens; it's fast, quiet and user-friendly. It consists of three lines: **Line 1** (green; Pireás to Kifissiá) is the original section, with useful stops in the centre at Thissío, Monastiráki, Omónia and Viktorías; **Line 2** (red; Áyios Antónios to Áyios Dhimítrios) has central stops at Omónia, Sýndagma and Akrópoli at the foot of the Acropolis; and **Line 3** (blue; Monastiráki to the airport) passes through Sýndagma. Further extensions to lines 2 and 3 are underway, and likely to open in stages over the next few years. Some of the new stations are attractions in their own right, displaying artefacts discovered in their excavation (numerous important discoveries were made) and other items of local interest – Sýndagma and Akrópoli are particularly interesting central ones.

Trains run from roughly 5.30am to midnight. When travelling on the metro you need to know the final stop in the direction you're heading, as that is how the platforms are identified ("To Pireás" for example); there are plenty of maps in the stations.

Buses

The **bus network** is extensive and cheap, but pretty confusing. Buses are very crowded at peak times, unbearably hot in summer and chronically plagued by strikes and slow-downs; walking is often a better option. Express services run to and from the airport – see p.102. Other routes, where relevant, are detailed in the text. The most straightforward are the **trolleybuses**: #1 connects the Laríssis train station with Omónia, Sýndagma and Koukáki; #2, #4, #5, #9, #11 and #15 all link Sýndagma with Omónia and the National Archeological Museum on 28 Oktovríou (Patissíon). There are also scores of **city buses**, designated by three-digit numbers and serving countless routes out into the straggling suburbs and beyond: at most of the major stops there are helpful information booths.

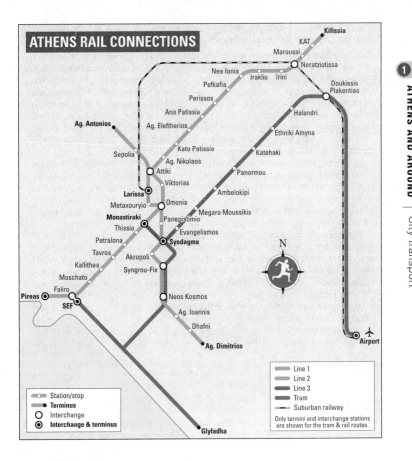

ATHENS RAIL CONNECTIONS

Kifissia
KAT
Maroussi
Neratziotissa
Nea Ionia
Iraklio Irini
Pefkafia
Doukissis Plakentias
Perissos
Ano Patissia
Halandri
Ag. Antonios
Ag. Eleftherios
Ethniki Amyna
Kato Patissia
Sepolia
Katehaki
Ag. Nikolaos
Attiki
Panormou
Viktorias
Larissa
Ambelokipi
Metaxouryio
Omonia
Monastiraki
Megaro Moussikis
Panepistimio
Thissio
Petralona
Evangelismos
Tavros
Syndagma
Akropoli
Kallithea
Syngrou-Fix
Moschato
Faliro
Pireas
Neos Kosmos
SEF
Ag. Ioannis
Dhafni
Ag. Dimitrios

N

Glyfadha

Station/stop
Terminus
Interchange
Interchange & terminus

Line 1
Line 2
Line 3
Tram
Suburban railway

Only termini and interchange stations
are shown for the tram & rail routes.

The tram

Athens' new **tram** network was finished in a hurry for the 2004 Olympics – sometimes you can tell as it sways over lines that don't seem entirely straight. Nonetheless it's a great way to the get to coastal suburbs and the beach. The tram runs from Leofóros Amalías just off Sýndagma to the coast, where it branches. To the right it heads northwest towards Pireás, terminating at SEF (the Stádhio Eirínis ké Filías or Peace and Friendship Stadium), an interchange with metro line 1 at Néo Fáliro, and within walking distance of Pireás's leisure harbours. Left, the tram lines run southwest along the coast to Glyfádha. There are effectively three lines – #1, from Sýndagma to SEF; #2, from Sýndagma to Glyfádha; and #3, from SEF to Glyfádha. These numbers are displayed on the front of the tram and are worth checking, as the electronic boards at the stations are erratic. The tram doesn't automatically stop at every station, so push the bell if you're on board, or wave it down if you're on the platform.

Bus, metro and tram tickets

The easiest and least stressful way to travel is with a **pass**. A **one-day imerísio** costs €3 and can be used on buses, trolleybuses, trams and the metro in central Athens. You validate it once, on starting your first journey, and it is good for 24 hours from then. A **weekly pass** for all the above – but not valid for trips to the airport – costs €10; again it must be validated on first use. Monthly passes cost €17.50 for buses only, €35 for bus and metro, or €38 for bus, metro and tram – these are all valid on airport buses. Passes can be bought from any metro ticket office and many places where bus tickets are sold (see below) – you can buy several daily passes at once and then cancel them as necessary.

Otherwise, normal **metro tickets** cost €0.60 on Line 1 for journeys of no more than two of its three zones (this will get you from the centre to either end of the line), €0.70 for any other journey (valid for 90min from validation, for travel in one direction – for example you can change lines, but you can't go somewhere and come back). They're available from machines and ticket offices in any metro station, and must be validated before you start your journey, in the machines at the top of the stairs.

Bus tickets cost €0.45 and must be bought in advance from kiosks, certain shops and newsagents, or from the limited number of booths run by bus personnel near major stops – look for the brown, red and white logo proclaiming *Isitíria edhó* ("tickets here"). They're sold individually or in bundles of ten, and must be validated in the machine on board the bus. Validated tickets apply only to a particular journey and vehicle; there are no transfers.

Tram tickets are sold at machines on the stations. They cost €0.60, or €0.40 if your journey is less than five stops or you're transferring from another form of transport within 90 minutes. Tickets can be validated at machines on the platform or on board.

Fare-dodgers on any of the above risk an on-the-spot **fine** of forty times the single fare.

Taxis

Athenian **taxis** can seem astonishingly cheap – trips around the city centre will rarely run above €3, which means for a group of three or four they cost little more than the metro. Longer trips are also reasonable value: the airport only costing €18–25 and Pireás €7–10 from the centre – the exact amount determined by traffic and amount of luggage. All officially licensed cars are yellow and have a red-on-white numberplate. You can wave them down on the street, pick them up at ranks in most of the major travel termini and central squares, or phone one (or get your hotel to do it).

The meter starts at €0.85, with a minimum fare of €1.75: legitimate **surcharges** that will increase the cost include those for baggage; airport, seaport or station trips; night-time journeys (midnight to 5am); ordering by phone and so on. Every taxi should display the rates and extra charges in English and Greek.

Make sure the **meter** is switched on when you get in. If it's "not working", find another taxi. Attempts at **overcharging** tourists are particularly common with small-hours arrivals at the airport and Pireás. One legitimate way that taxi-drivers increase their income is to pick up **other passengers** along the way. There is no fare-sharing: each passenger (or group of passengers) pays the full fare for their journey. So if you're picked up by an already-occupied taxi, memorize the meter reading at once; you'll pay from that point on, plus the €0.85 initial tariff. When hailing an occupied taxi, call out your destination, so the driver can decide whether you suit him or not.

Accommodation

Hotels and **hostels** can be packed to the gills in midsummer – August especially – but for most of the year you'll have no problem finding a bed. Having said that, many of the more popular hotels are busy all year round, so it makes sense to **book in advance**; almost every place listed here will have an English-speaking receptionist. If you do just set out and do the rounds, try to start as early as possible in the day. Once you locate a vacancy, ask to see the room before booking in – standards vary greatly even within the same building, and you can avoid occasional overcharging by checking the government-regulated room prices displayed by law on the back of the door in each room. Hotels throughout the city were refurbished for the Olympics, and some of these newly done-up places are very good value (at least by Athenian standards).

Our listings are grouped into half a dozen main areas. The quarters of **Pláka** and **Sýndagma**, despite their commercialization, are highly atmospheric and within easy walking distance of the Acropolis and all the main sites; many places here have Acropolis views from their roofs or upper storeys. Formerly gritty and sleazy but being rapidly gentrified, **Monastiráki** and the **bazaar area** see the city at its most colourful, while nearby **Thissío** is rather smarter and airier, with up-and-coming nightlife and wonderful Acropolis views. These central hotels, though, can be noisy thanks to narrow streets and unsilenced motorbikes, and none could be described as cheap. For better value, and in some cases more peace and quiet, head for one of the neighbourhoods a little further out. To the south **Makriyiánni**, a very upmarket residential neighbourhood on the far side of the Acropolis, easily reached via the metro at Akrópoli, merges into more earthy **Koukáki** – close to the metro at Sýngrou-Fix, or on the #1 or #5 trolleybus routes from Sýndagma. East of the centre, the ritzy shopping district of **Kolonáki** doesn't have much in the way of accommodation, but there are plenty of big, modern, business hotels slightly further out in **Ilísia** (metro Evangelismós or Mégaro Moussikís). Nearby **Pangráti**, on the route of #2, #4 or #11 trolleys all of which pass through Sýndagma, is a residential neighbourhood with a wealth of good eating places and a youth hostel. In the north, **Platía Omonías** is still very much the city centre, with lots of large hotels on busy streets. In the marginally quieter neighbourhoods – **Metaxouryío**, **Exárhia** and **Platía Viktorías** – you are again out of the tourist mainstream (though close to the archeological museum), but benefit from good-value local restaurants and the proximity of cinemas, clubs and bars. These areas now have clusters of very good-value, mid-range hotels, just a short walk away from the train stations (and metros Omónia, Metaxouryío or Viktorías). Much further out, hotels in **Pireás** offer reasonably easy access to the centre of Athens, but you're only really likely to stay here if you're taking a ferry. Along the **coast**, many beach hotels are served by the new tram, and are also convenient for all-night bus routes to the airport.

The city's **campsites** are out in the suburbs, not especially cheap and only worth using if you have a camper van; phone ahead to book space in season. There are more pleasant campsites further out on the coast – see p.188 and p.185. Camping rough in Athens is not a good idea. Police patrol many of the parks, especially those by the train stations, and muggings are commonplace. Even the train stations are no real refuge; they close when services stop and are cleared of stragglers.

Pláka and Sýndagma

Achilleas Lékka 21 ☎210 32 33 197, ⓦwww
.achilleashotel.gr. Metro Sýndagma. Comfortable
modern hotel, pleasantly refurbished pre-Olym-
pics, and reasonably quiet (especially at the back)
given a position right at the heart of the main
shopping area. All facilities including a/c, TV,
fridge, hairdryers etc. Some suite-style quads and
triples. B&B ❻

Acropolis House Kódhrou 6 ☎210 32
22 344, ⓔhtlacrhs@otenet.gr. Metro
Sýndagma. A rambling, slightly dilapidated 150-
year-old mansion much loved by its regulars
– mostly students and academics. Furnishings
are individual and some rooms have baths across
the hall; not all are a/c, though most are naturally
cool. Rates include use of fridge, shared books and
other useful items left behind by previous guests.
Discounts for longer stays. B&B ❹

Adonis Kódhrou 3 ☎210 32 49 737, ⓕ210 32 31
602. Metro Sýndagma. A 1960s low-rise *pension*
across the street from *Acropolis House*, with some
suites. Rather old-fashioned, but none the worse
for it – rooms are comfortable with a/c and TV. The
rooftop café has a stunning view of the Acropolis
and central Athens. B&B ❺

Arethusa Mitropóleos 6–8 and Níkis 12 ☎210 32
29 431, ⓦwww.arethusahotel.gr. Metro Sýndagma.
This low-key, comfortable high-rise caters to
independent travellers and small groups. Friendly
staff and well soundproofed, a/c rooms with TV at
decent value considering the position. B&B ❻

Athos Patróou 3 ☎210 32 21 977,
ⓦwww.athoshotel.gr. Metro Sýndagma.
Small hotel pleasantly refurbished in 2004, with
comfortable, carpeted en-suite rooms (some a
little cramped) with TV, a/c, mini-bar and all the
usual facilities. Also a rooftop bar with Acropolis
views. B&B ❺

Ava Apartments & Suites Lysikrátous 9–11
☎210 32 59 000, ⓦwww.avahotel.gr. Metro
Akrópoli. Between the Temple of Zeus and the
Acropolis, *Ava* offers luxurious two-room suites and
apartments accommodating up to five people and
ideal for families. All have balconies – some very
large – with sideways Acropolis views, as well as
small kitchens. ❼

Byron Výronos 19 ☎210 32 53 554, ⓕ210 32
20 276. Metro Akrópoli. Excellent location within
walking distance of the Acropolis and Pláka
museums, the *Byron* has a/c and TV in every
room, plus a few upper rooms with balconies
and impressive Acropolis views. Not great value
though. ❺

Central Apóllonos 21 ☎210 32 34 357,
ⓦwww.centralhotel.gr. Metro Sýndagma.

Completely refurbished in designer style, with
seagrass or wooden floors, marble bathrooms and
excellent soundproofing. Family and interconnecting rooms also available; all with a/c, TV, fridge and
everything you'd expect. Large roof terrace with
Acropolis views and hot tub. B&B ❻

Electra Palace Nikodhímou 18 ☎210 33 70
000, ⓦwww.electrahotels.gr. Metro Sýndagma.
Luxury hotel right in the heart of Pláka with every
facility including both indoor and rooftop pools,
small gym and sauna. Stunning if you have an
upper-floor suite, whose large balconies have
great Acropolis views, but standard rooms are
rather dull. ❽

Grande Bretagne Vassíléos Yioryíou 1, Platía Sýndagma ☎210 33 30 000, ⓦwww.grandebretagne
.gr. Metro Sýndagma. If someone else is paying, try
to get them to put you up at the *Grande Bretagne*,
the grandest of all Athens' hotels with the finest
location in town. Recently refurbished, it really is
magnificent, with every conceivable facility. Treatments in the spa cost more than a night at many
hotels; rooms are well over €300 even for an off-
season special offer. ❽

Hermes Apóllonos 19 ☎210 32 35 514, ⓦwww
.hermeshotel.gr. Metro Sýndagma. Very classily
renovated for the Olympics, with marble bathrooms, polished wood floors and designer touches
in every room (plus TV, a/c, fridge and hairdryer)
– some rooms are rather small; others have big
balconies. There's also a roof terrace with Acropolis
views. B&B ❼

Kouros Kódhrou 11, Pláka ☎210 32 27 431.
Metro Sýndagma. Faded but friendly and atmospheric *pension*, with fairly basic facilities: shared
baths and sinks in rooms. Some rooms have balconies overlooking the pedestrianized street. ❸

Phaedra Herefóndos 16, corner Adhrianoú
☎210 32 38 461, ⓕ210 32 27 795. Metro
Akrópoli. Simple, newly renovated and quiet at
night, thanks to its location at the junction of two
pedestrian alleys. Polite welcoming management;
simple rooms with bare tile floors, TV and a/c, not
all en suite (but you get a private bathroom). One of
the best deals in Pláka. ❹

Student & Traveller's Inn Kydhathinéon
16 ☎210 32 44 808, ⓦwww
.studenttravellersinn.com. Metro Akrópolí/Sýnd-
agma. Very friendly, perennially popular travellers' meeting place; a mixture of hotel and hostel.
Dorm beds from €16 to €26, depending on
room size and facilities; private quads, triples
and doubles, en suite or shared bath, are clean
and comfortable, though not always the quietest. Small courtyard breakfast area/bar, Internet
facilities, luggage storage and travel agency. ❹

Monastiráki, the bazaar area and Thissío

Attalos Athinás 29 ⓣ 210 32 12 801, ⓦ www.attalos.gr. Metro Monastiráki. Modern from the outside but traditional within, the *Attalos* has bright, comfortable rooms, well insulated from the noisy street, all with a/c and TV. Some balcony rooms on the upper floors have great views – there's also a roof-terrace bar in the evenings – but rooms facing the internal courtyard at the back are generally larger and quieter. Some triples. Buffet breakfast available. ❺

Cecil Athinás 39 ⓣ 210 32 18 005, ⓦ www.cecil .gr. Metro Monastiráki. Loving restoration of a run-down 150-year-old *pension*; attractively decorated, good-sized rooms have polished wooden floors, a/c and TV. Helpful management; roof garden; B&B ❻

Fivos Athinás 23 ⓣ 210 32 26 657, ⓦ www .consolas.gr. Metro Monastiráki. Simple travellers' place in great if rather noisy location, with some dorm beds (€18). Rooms, including lots of singles, have bare wooden floors and basic wooden furniture with a/c at extra cost, and there's a communal area with TV and Internet. B&B ❹

Fresh Hotel Sofokléous 26, ⓣ 210 52 48 511, ⓦ www.freshhotel.gr. Metro Omónia. Glossy, high-end "designer" hotel in the heart of the market area. Lavish use of colour, designer furnishings and great lighting and bathrooms, though you do wonder how long it will stay looking fresh. All facilities including wireless Internet access throughout and an elegant rooftop pool, bar and restaurant. ❼

Metropolis Mitropóleos 46 ⓣ 210 32 17 469, ⓦ www.hotelmetropolis.gr. Metro Sýndagma/ Monastiráki. Right by the cathedral, the friendly Metropolis has simple, plainly furnished rooms with vinyl floors, each with a good-size balcony, a/c and TV, plus Acropolis views from the upper floors. ❹

Phidias Apostólou Pávlou 39 ⓣ 210 34 59 511, ⓦ www.phidias.gr. Metro Thissío. With an enviable position just down from the *Thission*, the *Phidias* shares similar views, though here only the front rooms have balconies. A little smarter than the *Thission*, with a/c and TV throughout, but still overdue for a makeover. ❺

➔ ◆**Tempi** Eólou 29 ⓣ 210 32 13 175, ⓦ www .travelling.gr/tempihotel. Metro Monastiráki. A long-time favourite with budget travellers: book exchange, drinks and shared kitchen, plus handy affiliated travel agency. Rooms are simple and tiny and most have shared facilities, but the view of the flower market at Ayía Iríni across the quiet pedestrian walkway is enchanting, and it's within walking distance of most central sights. ❸–❹

Thission Apostólou Pávlou 25 ⓣ 210 34 67 634, ⓦ www.hotel-thission.gr. Metro Thissío. Virtually every room in the *Thission* has a balcony with a view of the Acropolis as good as any in Athens, and it lies at the heart of a newly fashionable area crammed with designer cafés. Which makes it even more amazing that nobody has got round to refurbishing the place; rooms are comfortable enough, with a/c and TV, but distinctly threadbare, and service can be slapdash. Great setting, though, and a pleasant roof-terrace café. ❹

Omónia, Exárhia and around

The Alassia Sokrátou 50 ⓣ 210 52 74 000, ⓦ www.thealassia.com.gr. Metro Omónia. Refurbished for the Olympics in minimalist style with lots of dark wood veneers. Rooms are small but well soundproofed (you're just off Platía Omonías here) and with every comfort including designer bathrooms. ❻

Hostel Aphrodite Inárdhou 12, between Alakmenous and Mikhaïl Vódha ⓣ 210 88 39 249, ⓦ www .hostelaphrodite.com. Metro Viktorías. Friendly, clean, IYHA-recognized hostel with some private en-suite double and triple rooms, in a quiet residential neighbourhood. A/c available at extra charge, and other facilities including breakfast room/bar, luggage storage and Internet access. Dorms €14, bed in two-bed dorm €22, discounts for YHA card-holders. ❸

Athens International Youth Hostel Víktoros Ougó 16 ⓣ & ⓕ 210 52 32 540. Metro Metaxouryío. The old official hostel (it's still official, but no longer the only one) is a huge affair, with 140 beds over 7 floors in 2- and 4-bed rooms. Frayed at the edges and badly in need of a coat of paint, it is cheap and always busy. To be sure of a bed it's best to book in advance and this is essential if you want a private room – do it online at the hostel association website ⓦ www.hihostels.com. Dorm €8.15, plus €2.50 per day for non-members.

Delphi Art Hotel Ayíou Konstandínou 27 ⓣ 210 52 44 004, ⓦ www.delphiarthotel .com. Metro Omónia. Right by the National Theatre and Áyios Konstantínos church, this 1930s mansion has been lavishly restored with Art Nouveau touches and eclectic, individual furnishings. Facilities include Internet access throughout, and Jacuzzi baths in some rooms. B&B ❼

Evropi Satovriándhou 7 ⓣ 210 52 23 081. Metro Omónia. Very basic but great value old-fashioned hotel with spacious rooms occupied only by bed, bedside table and ceiling fan, along with a concrete enclosure for en-suite shower. Reasonably quiet, despite being only a block from Platía Omonías; inexpensive single rooms available. ❷

Exarchion Themistokléous 55, Platía Exarhíon ☏210 38 01 256, ⍊www.exarchion.com. Metro Omónia. Big 1960s high-rise hotel that's a great deal less fancy inside than you might imagine. Vinyl-floored rooms, all with TV, a/c and fridge, are simply furnished and due for refurbishment. But that's reflected in the price, and it's good value if you want to be at the heart of Exarhía's nightlife. Upper-floor rooms are quieter, with better views. ❹
Feron Férron 43 at Ahárnon ☏210 82 32 083. Metro Viktorías. As cheap a hotel as any in Athens, and if you expect what you pay for you won't be disappointed. Large, simple, en-suite rooms with ceiling fans. ❷

🏃 **Museum** Bouboulínas 16 ☏210 38 05 611, ⍊www.hotelsofathens.com. Metro Viktorías/Omónia. Very pleasant, international-style hotel (part of the Best Western chain) right behind the National Archeological Museum and the Polytekhnío. Rooms in the new wing, which has triples, quads and small suites ideal for families, are better but slightly more expensive. ❻

🏃 **Orion and Dryades** Emmanouíl Benáki 5 ☏210 36 27 362, ⍊orion-dryades@mail.com. Metro Viktorías/Omónia. Quiet, inexpensive well-run twin hotels across from the Lófos Stréfi park – a steep uphill walk from almost anywhere. Reception is in the cheaper *Orion*, which has shared bathrooms, a kitchen, and communal area on the roof with an amazing view of central Athens. All rooms in the *Dryades* are en suite with a/c and TV. ❷–❹
Oscar Filadhelfías 25 ☏210 88 34 215, ⍊www.oscar.gr. Metro Laríssis. Big, modern high-rise right in front of the station, so handy for late-night and early departures including suburban trains to the airport. This is its main recommendation, along with a rooftop pool and all the facilities of a large, comfortable hotel. ❻
Zinon Keramikoú 3 and Zínonos ☏210 52 45 711, ⍊www.hotelsofathens.com. Metro Omónia. Sister hotel of the *Museum*, the 3-star *Zinon* doesn't look much, but inside has been well refurbished with wireless Internet and flat-screen TVs throughout, and some reasonably priced suites. Substantial discounts sometimes on offer. ❻

Makriyiánni and Koukáki

Acropolis View Webster 10 and Robérto Gálli ☏210 92 17 303, ⍊www.acropolisview.gr. Metro Akrópoli. Small but well-furnished rooms with a/c, TV, fridge and tiny marble bathrooms in what looks like a 1970s apartment block. The roof garden has an amazing close-up view of the Acropolis as do some of the rooms if you lean off the balcony. B&B ❹

Art Gallery Erekhthíou 5 ☏210 92 38 376, ⍊ecotec@otenet.gr. Metro Syngroú-Fix. A family-owned converted apartment block, this popular, slightly old-fashioned *pension* with many repeat customers is named for the original artworks that adorn every room. Knowledgeable and helpful staff, convenient location just a short walk from the metro and a bountiful breakfast (costing extra) served on sunny terrace with Acropolis view. ❻
Athenian Callirhoe Kalliróis 32, cnr Petmeza ☏210 92 15 353, ⍊www.tac.gr. Metro Syngroú-Fix. Between Koukáki and the centre, the *Callirhoe* was one of Athens' first "designer" hotels. It's already starting to look slightly faded, but central location and good facilities – including TV and Internet in the rooms and a small gym – make it popular with business and leisure travellers alike. It's worth checking for offers. ❽

🏃 **Herodion** Robérto Gálli 4 ☏210 92 36 832, ⍊www.herodion.gr. Metro Akrópoli. Lovely hotel, recently done up to very high standards, in an enviable position right behind the Acropolis. Comfortable rooms with all facilities and a roof terrace looking almost straight down to the south slope of the Acropolis. ❽
Marble House Cul-de-sac off A. Zínni 35A ☏210 92 34 058, ⍊www.marblehouse.gr. Metro Syngroú-Fix. The best value in Koukáki, family run and friendly. Simple rooms with and without private bath, eight of which have a/c (for extra charge); also two self-catering studios for long stays. Often full, so call ahead. ❸
Philippos Mitséon 3 ☏210 92 23 611, ⍊www.philipposhotel.gr. Metro Akrópoli. Sister hotel to the *Herodion*, the *Philippos* was also completely renovated for the Olympics though the interior is much less dramatic than the new facade. Very comfortable, well-appointed rooms with TV, a/c, minibar and hairdryer. ❼

Kolonáki, Pangráti, Ilísia

Athens Youth Hostel Dhamáreos 75, Pangráti ☏210 75 19 530, ⍊www.athens-yhostel.com. Trolleys #2 and #11 from Omónia via Sýntagma; bus #203 or #204 (or 15-20 min walk) from Metro Evangelismós. A bit out of the way but friendly, with no curfew and in a decent, quiet neighbourhood with plenty of local restaurants. Free use of kitchen and communal area with TV; charge for washing machine and hot water. There's no sign on the door, so look for the green gate. Basic 5/6 bed dorms ❶
St George Lycabettus Kleoménous 75, Kolonáki ☏210 72 90 711, ⍊www.sglycabettus.gr. A luxury boutique hotel and an Athenian classic, with a position high on Lykavitós hill in ritzy Kolonáki overlooking the city. Abundant marble and leather in the

public areas plus a welcome rooftop pool, and bars and restaurant popular with wealthy young Athenians. Some of the rooms are rather small, however, and there's no point staying here if you don't pay extra for the view. **8**

Stratos Vassilikos Michalakópoulou 114, Ilísia ☎210 77 06 611, ⌨210 77 08 137. Metro Mégaro Moussikís. Predominantly a business hotel, but very comfortable, newly renovated and with all facilities, including TV and Internet in the rooms, and even a tiny gym. Good metro and bus connections from location near the US embassy. **8**

Pireás and the coast

Acropole Goúnari 7, Pireás ☎210 41 73 313, ⓦwww.acropole-hotel.gr. Metro Pireás. Perhaps the pick of the hotels in Pireás is this newly renovated place with a variety of rooms including triples; some with Jacuzzi. Breakfast room (breakfast extra) and bar downstairs. **4**

Astir Palace Appólonos 40, Vougliaméni ☎210 89 02 000, ⓦwww.astir-palace.gr. The *Astir Palace* resort complex occupies some 75 acres of a private, pine-covered peninsula, 25km from downtown. There are three separate hotels (least expensive the *Aphrodite*, best probably the designer-style *Nafsika*), plus private villas, pools, watersports, tennis courts and no fewer than six restaurants, with a spa under construction. A shuttle bus runs twice daily to central Athens, just in case the weather prevents you using the helipad. Can at times be dominated by groups attending conferences hosted here. **8**

Delfini Leohárous 7, Pireás ☎210 41 73 110 ⓦwww.hotel-delfini.com. Metro Pireás. Tiny rooms, but each is nicely done up with fridge and balcony; there are also some multi-bed rooms available. **3** if you show this book, otherwise **4**

Mistral Al. Papanastásiou 105, Kastella, Pireás ☎210 41 17 150, ⓦwww.mistral.gr. Metro Néo Fáliro/tram SEF. Rather a bland, upscale hotel overlooking Mikrolímano and the more elegant parts of Pireás. Not especially handy for ferries, but comfortable and with great sea views. **6**

Palmyra Beach Possídhonos 70, Glyfádha ☎210 89 81 183, ⓦwww.palmyra.gr. Tram Páleo Dimarhío. Well-run, mid-scale tourist hotel with a small pool. The beach of the name isn't up to much, but the hotel is in walking distance of the centre of Glyfádha, handy for the tram, and has plenty of other beaches nearby. There's a free shuttle from the airport during the day, plus the #X96 airport express bus stops nearby. B&B **6**

Plaza Hotel Alkiónidhon 17, Voúla ☎210 89 91 079, ⓦwww.plazahotelgreece.com. Modern, budget hotel with a/c, TV and mini-bar in every room. Right on the busy main coast road and beyond the reach of the tram, but almost directly opposite Voula A beach (which means lots of buses stop here, including the #X96 airport express) and just about in walking distance of the centre of Glyfádha. **3**

Airport

Holiday Inn Attica Avenue, Peánia, at exit 18 of the motorway ☎210 66 89 000, ⓦwww.hiathens .com/attica. It's only about 40min by train or metro to the centre of Athens, less by bus to hotels at Glyfádha (see coast above), but if you really need to stay at the airport then choose this brand-new hotel (a short ride on a free shuttle bus) rather than the outrageously expensive *Sofitel* right in the airport complex. **7**

Campsites

Athens Camping Leofóros Athinón 198–200 ☎210 58 14 114, ⓦwww.campingathens.com.gr. The closest campsite to the centre of Athens, just off the busy main road towards the Peloponnese. It has a minimarket, snack-bar and hot water. The Elefsína bus #A16 passes by.

Camping Nea Kifissia Potamoú and Dhimitsánis, Néa Kifissiá ☎210 80 75 579. Located in the leafy suburb of Kifissiá, with a swimming pool, bar and the usual facilities. Take bus #A7 from Platía Kánin-gos or metro to Kifissiá and then bus #528 to the terminal close to the campsite.

The City

As a visitor, you're likely to spend most of your time in the central grid of Athens, a compact, walkable area well served by the metro. Only on arrival at, or departure from, the various far-flung stations and terminals do you have to confront the confused sprawl that surrounds the centre.

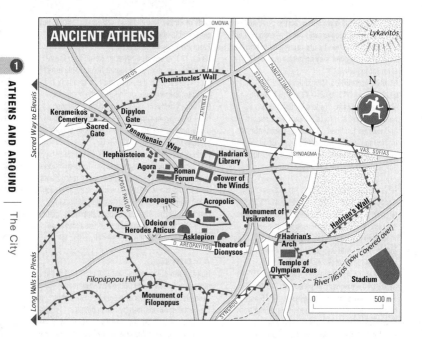

Finding your bearings is generally pretty easy: the **Acropolis** dominates most tourist itineraries and it's visible, around a corner, from almost any part of the city centre. Beneath the Acropolis on the east lies **Pláka**, the attractive old quarter where many tourists spend much of their time, with adjoining **Monastiráki** curling around to the north. **Sýndagma** (Platía Syndágmatos), the traditional centre of the city and home to the Greek Parliament, lies to the northeast of these two, midway between the Acropolis and the hill of **Lykavitós**. The ritzy **Kolonáki** quarter curls up the hill's slopes above Sýndagma, with a funicular to save you the final climb to the summit. Below Kolonáki many of the city's major museums can be found along the broad avenue of Leofóros Vassilísis Sofias, one of the main approaches to the city from the north and east. On the other side of the avenue, behind the Parliament, lie the jungly **National Gardens**.

To the north, more broad avenues lead from both Monastiráki and Sýndagma to **Omónia** (in full, Platía Omonías), the heart of commercial and business Athens. The **market and bazaar** area lies en route, while beyond to the north are the **National Archeological Museum** and the slightly alternative, studenty neighbourhoods of **Exárhia** and **Neápoli**, with a concentration of lively tavernas and bars. Close to the market you'll find the thriving nightlife of resurgent **Psyrrí**, whose modernizing influence spreads to the west in **Keramikós**, **Gázi** and **Metaxouryío**.

West and south of the Acropolis, newly pedestrianized streets open up the residential areas of **Thissío**, **Áno Petrálona**, **Makriyiánni** and **Koukáki** – all with excellent cafés and restaurants – as well as the wooded slopes of **Filopáppou Hill**. Adjoining these, and also accessible from Sýndagma via the National Gardens, the quiet, residential neighbourhoods of **Pangráti** and **Mets** are home to more local restaurants and bars. South beyond these districts, the traffic-laden axis of Leofóros Syngroú heads towards **Pireás and the coast**.

Metro and other **public transportation** information is given in the text where relevant, but it's worth knowing the main stops in the centre: **Sýndagma**, for Sýndagma and Pláka; **Monastiráki**, for Monastiráki, Psyrrí, the market area, the Ancient Agora and the northern approach to the Acropolis; **Akrópoli**, for the southern approach to the Acropolis; and **Omónia**, for Platía Omonías, the market area and the National Archeological Museum. A word of warning, too, on **pedestrian streets**: while these are generally free of cars, they are by no means traffic-free – mopeds and motorbikes see them as their property too.

The Acropolis and ancient Agora

The **rock of the Acropolis**, crowned by the dramatic ruins of the Parthenon, is one of the archetypal images of Western culture. The first time you see it, rising above the traffic or from a distant hill, is extraordinary: foreign, and yet utterly familiar. The **Parthenon** temple was always intended to be a spectacular landmark and a symbol of the city's imperial confidence, and it was famous throughout the ancient world. But even in its creators' wildest dreams they could hardly have imagined that the ruins would come to symbolize the emergence of Western civilization – nor that, two-and-a-half millennia on, it would attract some two million tourists a year.

The Acropolis itself is simply the rock on which the monuments are built; almost every ancient Greek city had its acropolis (which means the summit or highest point of the city), but the acropolis of Athens is The Acropolis, the one that needs no further introduction. Its **natural setting**, a steep-sided, flat-topped crag of limestone rising abruptly 100m from its surroundings, has made it the focus of the city during every phase of its development. Easily defensible and with plentiful water, its initial attractions are obvious. Even now, with no function apart from tourism, it is the undeniable heart of the city, around which everything else clusters, glimpsed at almost every turn.

On top of the Acropolis stands the Parthenon, along with the Erechtheion, the Temple of Athena Nike and the Propylaia or gates to the Acropolis, as well as lesser remains of many other ancient structures and a museum. All of these are included in a single, fenced site. The South Slope of the Acropolis, with two great theatres and several smaller temples, has separate entrances and ticketing.

Acropolis £12 8am–7:30pm

Opening hours and tickets

The summit of the Acropolis is **open** daily April–Sept 8am–7.30pm; Oct–March 8am–4.30pm; entry costs €12 (free on public hols and Sun Nov–March). The ticket also includes entry to the Theatre of Dionysos, Ancient Agora, Roman Forum, Kerameikos and Temple of Zeus, so if you visit any of them before the Acropolis, be sure to buy this multiple ticket rather than an individual entry; it can be used over four days, although there doesn't seem to be any way of indicating when it was issued. Backpacks and large bags are not allowed in to the site – there's a cloakroom near the main ticket office.

Crowds at the Acropolis can be horrendous – to avoid the worst come very early in the day, or late. The peak rush comes in late morning, when coach tours congregate before moving on to lunch elsewhere.

A brief history of the Acropolis

The rocky Acropolis was home to one of the earliest known settlements in Greece, its slopes inhabited by a **Neolithic** community around 5000 BC. In **Mycenaean** times – around 1500 BC – it was fortified with Cyclopean walls (parts of which can still be seen), enclosing a royal palace and temples, which fostered the cult of Athena. By the ninth century BC, the Acropolis had become the heart of Athens, the first Greek city-state, sheltering its principal public buildings. In 510 BC, the Oracle at Delphi ordered that the Acropolis should remain forever the **province of the gods**, unoccupied by humans.

It was in this context that the monuments visible today were built. Most of the substantial remains date from the **fifth century BC** or later; there are outlines of earlier temples and sanctuaries but these are hardly impressive, for they were burned to the ground when the Persians sacked Athens in 480 BC. For some decades the temples were left in their ruined state as a reminder of the Persian action. But with that threat removed, in the wake of Athenian military supremacy and a peace treaty with the Persians in 449 BC, the walls were rebuilt and architects drew up plans for a reconstruction worthy of the city's cultural and political position.

Pericles' rebuilding plan was both magnificent and enormously expensive but it won the backing of the democracy, for many of whose citizens it must have created both wealth and work – and Athens could afford it thanks to its control of the Delian League of city-states and the wealth of the silver mines around Lávrio. The work was under the general direction of the architect and sculptor **Pheidias** (Fidias) and it was completed in an incredibly short time. The Parthenon itself took only ten years to finish: "every architect," wrote Plutarch, "striving to surpass the magnificence of the design with the elegance of the execution".

The monuments survived unaltered – save for some modest Roman tinkering – for close to a thousand years, until in the reign of Emperor Justinian the temples were converted to **Christian** worship. Over the following centuries the uses became secular as well as religious, and embellishments increased, gradually obscuring the Classical designs. Fifteenth-century Italian princes held court in the Propylaia, the entrance hall to the complex, and the same quarters were later used by the **Turks** as their commander's headquarters and as a powder magazine. The Parthenon underwent similar changes from Greek to Roman temple, from Byzantine church to Frankish cathedral, before several centuries of use as a Turkish mosque. The Erechtheion, with its graceful female figures, saw service as a harem. A Venetian diplomat, Hugo Favoli, described the Acropolis in 1563 as "looming beneath a swarm of glittering golden crescents", with a minaret rising from the Parthenon. For all their changes in use, however, the buildings would still have resembled – very much more than today's bare ruins – the bustling and ornate ancient Acropolis, covered in sculpture and painted in bright colours.

Sadly, such images remain only in the prints and sketches of that period: the Acropolis buildings finally fell victim to the ravages of war, blown up during successive attempts by the Venetians to oust the Turks. In 1684 the Turks demolished the Temple of Athena Nike to gain a brief tactical advantage. Three years later the Venetians, laying siege to the garrison, ignited a Turkish gunpowder magazine in the Parthenon, and in the process blasted off its roof and set a **fire** that raged within its precincts for two days and nights. The process of stripping down to the bare ruins seen today was completed by souvenir hunters and the efforts of the first archeologists – see *The Elgin Marbles* on p.124.

You can walk an entire circuit of the Acropolis and ancient Agora on **pedestrianized streets**, allowing them to be appreciated from almost every angle: in particular, the pedestrianization has provided spectacular new terraces for cafés to

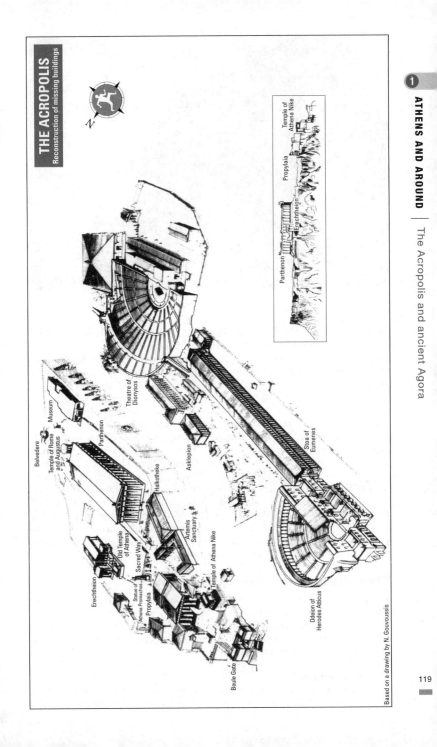

THE ACROPOLIS
Reconstruction of missing buildings

N

Temple of Athena Nike
Propylaia
Erechtheion
Parthenon

Belvedere
Museum
Temple of Rome and Augustus
Parthenon
Theatre of Dionysos
Halkotheke
Asklepion
Old Temple of Athena
Sacred Way
Artemis Sanctuary
Stoa of Eumenes
Erechtheion
Statue of Athena Promachos
Propylaia
Temple of Athena Nike
Beule Gate
Odeion of Herodes Atticus

Based on a drawing by N. Gouvoussis

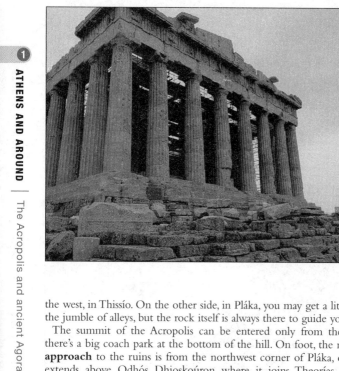

△ The Parthenon

the west, in Thissío. On the other side, in Pláka, you may get a little lost among the jumble of alleys, but the rock itself is always there to guide you.

The summit of the Acropolis can be entered only from the west, where there's a big coach park at the bottom of the hill. On foot, the most common **approach** to the ruins is from the northwest corner of Pláka, on a path that extends above Odhós Dhioskoúron where it joins Theorías. You can also approach from the south, along pedestrianized Dhionysíou Areopayítou (Metro Akrópoli), past the Theatre of Dionysos and Herodes Atticus Theatre; from the north via the Ancient Agora (entrance on Adhrianoú; Metro Monastiráki); or, slightly further but repaid with excellent views of both Agora and Acropolis, from Thissío along traffic-free Apostólou Pávlou (Metro Thissío).

There are no **shops or restaurants** within the Acropolis area, although you can buy water and sandwiches, as well as guidebooks, postcards and so on, from a couple of stands near the main ticket office. There's also a handy branch of *Everest* right opposite Akrópoli metro station (at the corner of Makriyiánni and Dhiakoú) and plenty of similar places around Monastiráki metro. If you want to sit down to eat, there are cafés and tavernas nearby in almost every direction: Pláka (p.162), Monastiráki (p.162), Makriyiánni (p.167) and Thissío (p.165).

The Summit of the Acropolis

Today, as throughout its history, there's just one way up to the top of the Acropolis. In Classical times the Sacred Way extended along a steep ramp to a massive monumental double-gatehouse, the **Propylaia**; the modern path makes a more gradual, zigzagging ascent, passing first through an arched Roman entrance, the **Beule Gate**, added in the third century AD.

The Propylaia

The **Propylaia**, gateway to the Acropolis, were constructed by Mnesikles from 437–432 BC, and their axis and proportions aligned to balance the recently completed Parthenon. They – the name is the plural of propylon, gateway, referring to the fact that there are two wings – were built from the same Pentelic marble (from Mount Pendéli, northeast of the city) as the temple, and in grandeur and architectural achievement are almost as impressive. In order to offset the difficulties of a sloping site, Mnesikles combined for the first time standard Doric columns with the taller and more delicate Ionic order. The ancient Athenians, awed by the fact that such wealth and craftsmanship should be used for a purely secular building, ranked this as their most prestigious monument.

Walking through the gateway, which would originally have had great wooden doors, is your only chance to enter any of the ancient buildings atop the Acropolis; the rest have been closed for over thirty years to protect them from the hordes of visitors. To the left of the central hall (which before Venetian bombardment supported a great coffered roof, painted blue and gilded with stars), the **Pinakotheke** was an early art gallery, exhibiting paintings of Homeric subjects by Polygnotus. Executed in the mid-fifth century BC, these pictures were described six hundred years later by Pausanias in his Roman-era *Guide to Greece*. The wing to the right is much smaller, as Mnesikles's original design trespassed on ground sacred to the Goddess of Victory and the premises had to be adapted as a waiting room for her shrine – the Temple of Athena Nike.

Beyond the gate can be seen one of the best-preserved sections of the Sacred or **Panathenaic Way**, the route along which the great procession for ancient Athens' Panathenaic festival passed every four years (as depicted on the Parthenon frieze). The procession, in honour of the city's patroness, the goddess Athena, wound right through the city from the gates now in the Kerameikos site (see p.145) via the Propylaia to the Parthenon and, finally, the Erectheion. The route was, of course, used for other processions and as a road between festivals: here you can make out grooves cut for footholds in the rock and, to either side, niches for innumerable statues and offerings. In Classical times the route would have continued past a ten-metre-high bronze statue of *Athena Promachos* (Athena the Champion), whose base can just about be made out. Created by Pheidias as a symbol of the Athenians' defiance of Persia, the statue's spear and helmet were said to be visible to approaching sailors from as far away as Soumío. She was moved to Constantinople in Byzantine times and there destroyed by a mob who believed that the beckoning hand had directed the Crusaders to the city in 1204.

The Temple of Athena Nike

Simple and elegant, the **Temple of Athena Nike** stands on a precipitous platform overlooking the port of Pireás and the Saronic Gulf. Or at least it did. At the time of writing the entire structure was missing, having been dismantled, its pieces taken away for restoration and cleaning. It should have been rebuilt by the time you read this. Amazingly, this is not the first time this has happened: the Turks demolished the building in the seventeenth century, using it as material for a gun emplacement. Two hundred years later the temple was reconstructed from its original blocks. Recovered in this same feat of jigsaw-puzzle archeology were the reliefs from its parapet – among them Victory Adjusting her Sandal, one of the most beautiful exhibits in the Acropolis Museum. The temple's frieze, realistic rather than triumphal, depicts the Athenians' victory over the Persians at Plateia.

Pausanias recounts that it was from the platform beside the temple that King Aegeus maintained a vigil for the tell-tale white sails that would indicate the safe return of his son Theseus from his mission to slay the Minotaur on Crete.

Theseus, flushed with success, forgot his promise to swap the boat's black sails for white. On seeing the black sails, Aegeus assumed his son had perished and, racked with grief, threw himself to his death.

Some of the best views of the temple (when it's there) are from inside the Acropolis, to the right after passing through the Propylaia. Here also are the scant remains of a **Sanctuary of Brauronian Artemis**. Although its function remains obscure, it is known that the precinct once housed a colossal bronze representation of the Wooden Horse of Troy. More noticeable is a nearby stretch of **Mycenaean wall** (running parallel to the Propylaia) that was incorporated into the Classical design.

The Parthenon

The **Parthenon** was the first great building in Pericles' scheme, intended as a new sanctuary for Athena and a home for her cult image – a colossal wooden statue of Athena Polias (Athena of the City) overlaid with ivory and gold plating, with precious gems as eyes and sporting an ivory gorgon death's-head on her breast. Designed by Pheidias, the statue was installed in the semi-darkness of the *cella* (cult chamber), where it remained an object of prestige and wealth, if not veneration, until at least the fifth century AD. The sculpture has been lost since ancient times but its characteristics are known through numerous later copies (including a fine Roman one in the National Archeological Museum). However, the temple never rivalled the Erechtheion in sanctity, and its role tended to remain that of treasury and artistic showcase, devoted rather more to the new god of the polis than to Athena herself. The name "Parthenon" means

---

Forty years of scaffolding

If you see a photo of a pristine Parthenon standing against a clear sky, it is almost certainly an old one. For most of the twenty-first century the Acropolis buildings have been swathed in **scaffolding** and surrounded by **cranes** – at times some structures have even been removed altogether, to be cleaned and later replaced. Though originally intended to be complete in time for the 2004 Olympics, the work is now set to continue for the foreseeable future – some claim that it will be forty years before the job is complete.

The monuments have suffered significant deterioration in modern times and as such there is little doubt that restoration was needed. Almost as soon as the War of Independence was over, Greek archeologists began clearing the Turkish village that had developed around the Parthenon-mosque; at the time a Greek regent lamented in vain that they "would destroy all the picturesque additions of the Middle Ages in their zeal to lay bare the ancient monuments". Much of this early work was indeed destructive: the iron clamps and supports used to reinforce the marble structures, for example, were not sheathed in lead, contrary to ancient example, so they have since rusted and warped, causing the stones to crack. Meanwhile, earthquakes have dislodged the foundations, generations of feet have slowly worn down surfaces and, more recently, sulphur dioxide deposits, caused by pollution, have been turning the marble to dust.

In 1975 the imminent collapse of the Parthenon was predicted and visitors have been barred from its actual precinct – as well as the interiors of other structures on the Acropolis – ever since. The restoration process includes – among many other things – replacing the iron clamps with titanium ones and removing many of the original friezes to the safety of museums, to be replaced by moulds. This work is aimed at ensuring that the Parthenon and its neighbours will continue to stand for another millennium or two, but, in the meantime, it's not improving the view.

"virgins' chamber", and initially referred only to a room at the west end of the temple occupied by the priestesses of Athena.

To achieve the Parthenon's extraordinary and unequalled harmony of design, its architect, Iktinos, used every trick known to the Doric order of architecture. The building's proportions maintain a universal 9:4 ratio, not only in the calculations of length to width, or width to height, but in such relationships as the distances between the columns and their diameter. Additionally, any possible appearance of disproportion is corrected by meticulous mathematics and craftsmanship. All seemingly straight lines are in fact slightly curved, an optical illusion known as *entasis* (intensification). The columns (their profile bowed slightly to avoid seeming concave) are slanted inwards by 6cm, while each of the steps along the sides of the temple was made to incline just 12cm over a length of 70m.

Originally the Parthenon's columns were brightly painted and it was decorated with the finest frieze and pedimental sculpture of the Classsical age, depicting the Panathenaic procession, the birth of Athena and the struggles of Greeks to overcome giants, Amazons and centaurs – also brightly coloured. One recent theory holds that the horsemen depicted represent the Athenians who died in the great victory at Marathon. The greater part of the pediments, along with the central columns and the *cella*, were destroyed by the Venetian bombardment in 1687. The best surviving examples are in the British Museum in London where they are known as the Elgin Marbles (see box overleaf); the Acropolis Museum also has a few original pieces, as well as reconstructions of the whole thing, and there are good reproductions in Akrópoli metro station.

The Erechtheion

To the north of the Parthenon, beyond the foundations of the Old Temple of Athena, stands the **Erechtheion**, the last of the great works of Pericles to be completed. Both Athena and the city's old patron of Poseidon-Erechtheus were worshipped here, in the most revered of the ancient temples, built over ancient sanctuaries, which in turn were predated by a Mycenaean palace. The site, according to myth, was that on which Athena and Poseidon held a contest, judged by their fellow Olympian gods, to determine who would possess Athens. At the touch of Athena's spear, the first ever olive tree sprang from the ground, while Poseidon summoned forth a fountain of sea water. Athena won, and became patron of the city. Pausanias wrote of seeing both olive tree and sea water in the temple, adding that "the extraordinary thing about this well is that when the wind blows south a sound of waves comes from it". The stunted olive tree now growing in the precinct was planted by an American archeologist in 1917, in honour of Athena's miracle.

Today, the many sacred objects within are long gone, but the series of elegant Ionic porticoes is worth close attention, particularly the north one with its fine, decorated doorway and frieze of blue Eleusinian marble. By far the most striking feature, however, is the famous **Porch of the Caryatids**, whose columns are transformed into the tunics of six tall maidens. The statues were long supposed to have been modelled on the widows of Karyai, a small city in the Peloponnese that was punished for its alliance with the Persians by the slaughter of its menfolk and the enslavement of the women. There is, though, little suggestion of grieving or humbled captives in the serene poses of the Caryatid women. Some authorities believe that they instead represent the Arrephoroi, young, high-born girls in the service of Athena. The ones *in situ* are replacements: five of the originals are in the Acropolis Museum, while a sixth was looted by Elgin, who also removed a column and other purely architectural features and which are replaced here by casts in a different colour marble.

The Acropolis Museum

Placed discreetly on a level below that of the main monuments, the **Acropolis Museum** (daily: April–Sept 8am–7pm; Oct–March 8am–4pm; included in Acropolis ticket) contains all of the more important portable objects removed from the site since 1834. Over recent years, as increasing amounts of stone and sculptures have been uncovered by excavation or replaced by copies, the collection has grown considerably, certainly well beyond what can be exhibited in this relatively small space. The whole collection should be moved soon to a dramatic new building below the Acropolis (see p.147). If you want more detail, museum guides are on sale, though it's also easy to eavesdrop on the many tour guides passing through – indeed usually it's impossible to avoid doing so.

In the first rooms, to the left as you enter, are fragments of pedimental sculptures from the **old Temple of Athena** (seventh to sixth century BC), whose traces of paint give a good impression of the vivid colours that were used in temple decoration. Further on is the **Moschophoros**, a painted marble statue of a young man carrying a sacrificial calf, dated 570 BC and one of the earliest examples of Greek art in marble. Room 4 displays one of the chief treasures of the building, a unique collection of **Korai**, or maidens, dedicated as votive offerings to Athena at some point in the sixth century BC. Between them they represent a shift in art and fashion, from the simply contoured Doric clothing to the more elegant and voluminous Ionic designs; the figures' smiles also change subtly, becoming increasingly loose and natural. Here too are some fine equestrian statues and a wonderfully expressive dog.

Room 5 has more impressive statuary from the Old Temple of Athena, while in Room 8 are pieces of the **Parthenon frieze** that were blown from the temple by the Venetian explosion and subsequently buried, thereby escaping the clutches of Lord Elgin. They portray scenes of Athenian citizens in the Panathenaic procession; the fact that mortals featured so prominently in the decoration of the temple indicates the immense collective self-pride of the Athenians at the height of their golden age. This room also contains a graceful and fluid sculpture, known as **Iy Sandalízoussa**, which depicts **Athena Nike** adjusting her sandal. Finally, in the last room are four authentic and semi-eroded **caryatids** from the Erechtheion, displayed behind a glass screen in a carefully rarefied atmosphere.

The "Elgin" Marbles

The controversy over the so-called Elgin Marbles has its origin in the activities of Western looters at the start of the nineteenth century: above all the French ambassador Fauvel, gathering antiquities for the Louvre, and **Lord Elgin** levering away sculptures from the Parthenon. As British Ambassador, Elgin obtained permission from the Turks to erect scaffolding, excavate and remove stones with inscriptions. He interpreted this concession as a licence to make off with almost all of the bas-reliefs from the Parthenon's frieze, most of its pedimental structures and a caryatid from the Erechtheion – all of which he later sold to the British Museum. While there were perhaps justifications for Elgin's action at the time – not least the Turks' tendency to use Parthenon stones in their lime kilns – his pilfering was controversial even then. Byron, for example, who visited in 1810–11 just in time to see the last of Elgin's ships loaded with the marbles, roundly disparaged all this activity.

Today, the British Museum's retention of the Parthenon frieze and other items rests on legal rather than moral claims. The Greeks believe that the long-awaited completion of the new Acropolis Museum (p.147), currently under construction on the site of the former Makriyiánni barracks just south of the Acropolis, would be a perfect opportunity for the British Museum to back down.

The south slope of the Acropolis

Entrance to the **south slope of the Acropolis** (daily: summer 8am–7pm; winter 8.30am–3pm; €2 or joint Acropolis ticket) is either by a path tracking around the side of the Acropolis from the area of the main ticket office, or from below, via pedestrianized Leofóros Dhionysíou Areopayítou close to metro Akrópoli. The dominant structure here is the second-century Roman **Herodes Atticus Theatre** (Odeion of Herodes Atticus), which has been restored for performances of music and Classical drama during the summer festival (see p.175). Unfortunately it's open only for shows; at other times you'll have to be content with spying over the wall.

The main reasons to visit, then, are the earlier Greek sites to the east. Pre-eminent among these is the **Theatre of Dionysos**, beside the lower site entrance. One of the most evocative locations in the city, it was here that the masterpieces of Aeschylus, Sophocles, Euripides and Aristophanes were first performed. It was also the venue for the annual festival of tragic drama, where each Greek citizen would take his turn as member of the chorus. Rebuilt in the fourth century BC, the theatre could hold some 17,000 spectators – considerably more than Herodes Atticus's 5000–6000 seats; twenty of the theatre's 64 tiers of seats survive. Most notable are the great marble thrones in the front row, each inscribed with the name of an official of the festival or of an important priest; in the middle sat the priest of Dionysos and on his right the representative of the Delphic Oracle. At the rear of the stage, along the rostrum, are reliefs of episodes in the life of Dionysos flanked by two squatting Sileni, devotees of the satyrs. Sadly, all this is roped off to protect the stage-floor **mosaic** – a magnificent diamond of multicoloured marble best seen from above.

All around the theatre a great deal of restoration and excavation work is ongoing, including the opening up of a new area on the eastern edge of the rock, above Pláka. It is all in something of a state of flux, but there are fine Byzantine cisterns to look out for, as well as numerous covered areas where groups of statues have been gathered together. More or less directly above the theatre, currently roped off, looms a vast grotto, converted perhaps a millennium ago into the chapel of **Panayía Khryssospiliótissa**. To the west of the theatre extend the ruins of the **Asklepion**, a sanctuary devoted to the healing god Asklepios and built around a sacred spring. Much of the curative centre, which is currently being extensively explored, was probably incorporated into the Byzantine church of the doctor-saints Kosmas and Damian, of which there are prominent remains. Nearer to the road lie the foundations of the Roman **Stoa of Eumenes**, a colonnade of stalls that stretched to the Herodes Atticus Theatre.

The Areopagus

Slippery, rock-hewn stairs and a rickety, rusting ladder ascend the low, unfenced hill of the **Areopagus** immediately below the entrance to the Acropolis. The "Hill of Ares" was the site of the Council of Nobles and the Judicial Court under the aristocratic rule of ancient Athens. During the Classical period the court lost its powers of government to the Assembly (held on the Pnyx) but it remained the court of criminal justice, dealing primarily with cases of homicide. In myth, it was also the site where Ares, God of War, was tried for the murder of one of Poseidon's sons; Aeschylus used the setting in *The Eumenides* for the trial of Orestes, who, pursued by the Furies' demand of "a life for a life", stood accused of murdering his mother Clytemnestra. The Persians camped here during their siege of the Acropolis in 480 BC, and in the Roman era Saint Paul preached the "Sermon on an Unknown God" on the hill, winning amongst his converts Dionysius "the Areopagite", who became the city's patron saint.

Today, there's little evidence of ancient grandeur, and the hill is littered with cigarette butts and empty beer cans left by the crowds who come to rest after their exertions on the Acropolis and to enjoy the views. These, at least, are good – down over the Agora and towards the ancient cemetery of Kerameikos.

The ancient Agora

The **Agora** or market (daily: summer 8am–7pm; winter 8.30am–3pm; €4 or joint Acropolis ticket) was the heart of ancient Athenian city life from as early as 3000 BC. Approached either from the Acropolis, down the path skirting the Areopagus, or through the northern entrance on Adhrianoú near metro Monastiráki, it is an extensive and highly confusing jumble of ruins, dating from various stages of building between the sixth century BC and the fifth century AD. As well as the marketplace, the Agora was the chief meeting place of the city, where orators held forth, business was discussed and gossip exchanged – St Paul, for example, took the opportunity to meet and talk to Athenians here. It was also the first home of the democratic assembly before that shifted location to the Pnyx, and continued to be its meeting place when cases of ostracism were discussed for most of the Classical period. Eubolus, a fourth-century poet, observed that "you will find everything sold together in the same place at Athens: figs, witnesses to summonses, bunches of grapes, turnips, pears, apples, givers of evidence, roses, medlars . . . water clocks, laws, indictments". Women, however, were not in evidence; secluded by custom, they would delegate any business in the Agora to slaves.

Originally the Agora was a rectangle, divided diagonally by the Panathenaic Way and enclosed by temples, administrative buildings, and long porticoed *stoas* (arcades of shops) where idlers and philosophers gathered to exchange views and listen to the orators. In the centre was an open space, defined by boundary stones at the beginning of the fifth century BC.

The best overview of the site is from the exceptionally well-preserved **Hephaisteion**, or Temple of Hephaistos, which overlooks the rest of the site from the west. An observation point in front of it has a plan showing the buildings as they were in 150 AD, and the various remains laid out in front of you make a great deal more sense with this to help (there are similar plans at the entrances). The temple itself was originally thought to be dedicated to Theseus, because his exploits are depicted on the frieze (hence Thissíon, which has given its name to the area); more recently it has been accepted that it actually honoured Hephaistos, patron of blacksmiths and metalworkers. This was one of the first buildings of Pericles' programme, but also one of the least known – perhaps because it lacks the curvature and "lightness" of the Parthenon's design; the barrel-vaulted roof dates from a Byzantine conversion into the church of Saint George.

The other church on the site – that of **Áyii Apóstoli** (the Holy Apostles), by the south entrance – is worth a glance inside for its fresco fragments, exposed during a 1950s restoration of the eleventh-century shrine.

The Stoa of Attalos

For some background to the Agora, head for the **Museum**, housed in the **Stoa of Attalos**, reconstructed by the American School of Archeology in Athens between 1953 and 1956. It is, in every respect bar colour, an entirely faithful reconstruction of the original; lacking its original bright red and blue paint or no, it is undeniably spectacular. Unfortunately it doesn't deliver inside – the display is small and old-fashioned, with labels that look as if they've been here since it opened in 1957. The bulk of what you see is pottery and coins from the sixth to the fourth century BC, plus some early Geometric grave offerings including red-figure dishes depicting athletes, musicians and minor deities, together with an oil flask in the form of a kneeling boy. Look out for the ostraka, or shards of pottery with names written on them. At annual assemblies of the citizens these ostraka would be handed in, and the individual with most votes banished, or "ostracized", from Athens for ten years; this was considered a fate worse than death.

Pláka and Monastiráki

The largely pedestrianized area of **Pláka**, with its narrow lanes and stepped alleys climbing towards the Acropolis, is, along with neighbouring **Monastiráki**, arguably the most attractive part of Athens, and certainly the most popular with visitors. Roughly delineated by Sýndagma and the National Gardens to the east, Odhós Ermoú in the north and the Acropolis to the west, this district was basically the extent of nineteenth-century, pre-independence Athens. In addition to a scattering of ancient sites and various offbeat and enjoyable museums, it offers glimpses of an older Athens, refreshingly at odds with the concrete blocks of the metropolis.

Although surrounded by huge, traffic-choked avenues, the area provides a welcome escape, its narrow streets offering no through-routes for traffic even where you are allowed to drive. Nineteenth-century houses, some grand, some humble, can be seen everywhere, their gateways opening onto verdant courtyards overlooked by wooden verandahs. Poor and working-class for most of the twentieth century, the private homes are now mostly thoroughly gentrified. With scores of **cafés and restaurants** to fill the time between museums and sites, and streets lined with touristy **shops**, it's an enjoyable place to wander. The main disadvantage is price – things are noticeably more expensive in Pláka than in much of the rest of the city.

Kydhathinéon and Adhrianoú streets

An attractive approach to Pláka is to follow **Odhós Kydhathinéon**, a pedestrian walkway that starts near the **Anglican and Russian churches** on Odhós Filellínon, south of Sýndagma. It leads gently downhill, past the Museum of Greek Folk Art, through café-crowded Platía Filomoússou Eterías, to Hadrian's street, **Odhós Adhrianoú**, which runs nearly the whole length of Pláka from Hadrian's Arch past the ancient Agora. These two are the main commercial and tourist streets of the district, with Adhrianoú increasingly tacky and downmarket as it approaches Platía Monastirakíou and the Monastiráki Flea Market.

The Museum of Greek Folk Art

The **Folk Art Museum** (Tues–Sun 10am–2pm; €2), at Kydhathinéon 17, has a fine collection let down somewhat by poor lighting and labelling. Its five floors are devoted to displays of weaving, pottery, regional costumes and embroidery along with other traditional Greek arts and crafts. On the mezzanine floor, the carnival tradition of northern Greece and the all-but-vanished shadow-puppet theatre are featured. The second floor features exhibits of gold

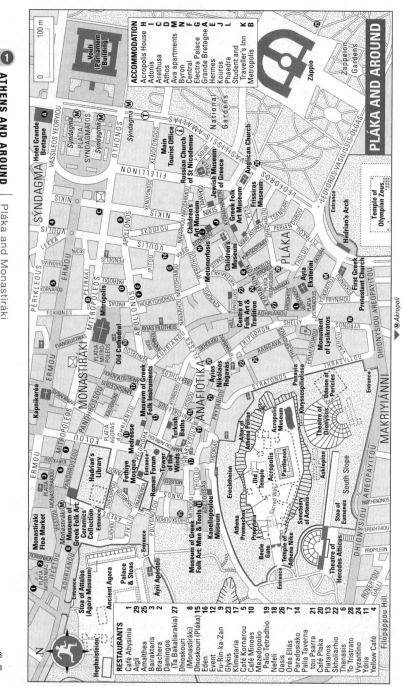

and silver jewellery and weaponry, much of it from the era of the War of Independence. The highlight, though, is on the first floor: the reconstructed room from a house on the island of Lesvós with a series of murals by the primitive artist **Theophilos** (1868–1934). These naive scenes from Greek folklore and history, especially the independence struggle, are wonderful, and typical of an artist who was barely recognized in his lifetime. Most of his career was spent painting tavernas and cafés on and around his native island, often paid only with food and board.

More nearby museums

Nearby are half a dozen additional small, quirky museums. One of the most enjoyable is the small **Centre of Popular Art and Tradition** (Tues–Fri 9am–1pm & 5–9pm, Sat & Sun 9am–1pm; free), a collection of costumes, embroidery, lace and weaving, along with musical instruments, ceramics, icons and religious artefacts. This occupies the former home of **Angelikís Hatzimi-háli**, whose championing of traditional Greek arts and crafts was one of the chief catalysts for their revival in the early twentieth century. The house itself – designed for her in the 1920s in a Greek Art Nouveau or Arts & Crafts style – is a large part of the attraction, with its cool, high rooms and finely carved wooden doors, windows and staircase. At the back, narrow stairs descend to the kitchen with its original range, while upstairs there's a library and rooms where classes are held to pass on the traditions of crafts like embroidery and weaving.

The **Frissiras Museum**, housed in two beautifully renovated, Neoclassical buildings at Monís Asteríou 3 and 7 (Wed–Fri 10am–5pm, Sat & Sun 11am–5pm; €6; ⓦ www.frissirasmuseum.com), is billed as Greece's only museum of contemporary European art – and until the new National Museum opens near Syngrou-Fix metro, it is the only significant permanent modern art collection in Athens. The museum has over three thousand works – mostly figurative painting plus a few sculptures, a regular programme of exhibitions, a fine shop and an elegant café. The space at no. 7 houses the permanent exhibition, which includes plenty of names familiar to English-speakers – David Hockney, Peter Blake and Paula Rego among them – as well as many less obvious Greek and European artists. Temporary exhibitions, along with the shop and café, are at no. 3 a block away.

The **Jewish Museum of Greece** (Mon–Fri 9am–2.30pm, Sun 10am–2pm; €5), at Níkis 39, tells the history of Jews in Greece, elegantly presented in a series of dimly lit rooms, with plenty of explanation in English. Downstairs are art and religious paraphernalia, many of the pieces centuries old. The centrepiece is the reconstructed synagogue of Pátra, dating from the 1920s, whose furnishings have been moved here *en bloc* and remounted. Upstairs more recent history includes World War II and the German occupation, when Greece's Jewish population was reduced from almost 80,000 to less than 10,000. There are features, too, on the part played by Jews in the Greek resistance, and many stories of survival.

Finally, and not to be confused with each other, there's the Children's Museum and the Museum of Greek Children's Art. The **Children's Museum** (Tues–Fri 10am–2pm, Sat & Sun 10am–3pm; free), at Kydhathinéon 14, is as much a play area as a museum, aimed at the under-12s. Labelling is entirely in Greek, and the place is primarily geared to school groups, who take part in activities such as chocolate-making. In spite of this, it should keep young kids amused for a while. Permanent exhibits include features on the Athens metro, how computers work, and the human body. The **Museum of Greek Children's Art** (Tues–Sat 10am–2pm, Sun 11am–2pm, closed Aug; €2; ⓦ www .childrensartmuseum.gr) at Kódhrou 9, meanwhile, does exactly what it says on the label – displays art by Greek children. There are a few permanent exhibits, but mainly the works are the winning entries to an annual nationwide art contest open to children up to the age of 14. On the whole, it is wonderfully uplifting.

The Monument of Lysikratos and around

In the southeastern corner of Pláka, the **Monument of Lysikratos**, a graceful stone and marble structure from 335 BC, rises from a small, triangular open area overlooked by a quiet café/taverna. It's near the end of Odhós Tripódhon, a relic of the ancient Street of the Tripods, where winners of drama competitions erected monuments to dedicate their trophies (in the form of tripod cauldrons) to Dionysos; the Monument of Lysikratos is the only survivor of these triumphal memorials. A four-metre-high stone base supports six Corinthian columns rising up to a marble dome on which, in a flourish of acanthus-leaf carvings, the winning tripod was placed. The inscription tells us that "Lysikratos of Kikyna, son of Lysitheides, was sponsor; the tribe of Akamantis won the victory with a chorus of boys; Theon played the flute; Lysiades of Athens trained the chorus; Evainetos was magistrate."

In the seventeenth century the monument became part of a Capuchin convent, which provided regular lodgings for European travellers – Byron is said to have written part of *Childe Harold* here, and the street beyond, Výronos, is named after him. The old Street of the Tripods would have continued in this direction, and many important ancient Athenian buildings are thought to lie undiscovered in the vicinity.

The church of **Ayía Ekateríni** – St Catherine's – (Mon–Fri 7.30am–12.30pm & 5–6.30pm, Sat & Sun 5–10pm; free) on Platía Ayía Ekateríni just round the corner from the monument, is one of the few in Pláka that's routinely open. At its heart is an eleventh-century Byzantine original, although this has been pretty well hidden by later additions. You can see it most clearly from the back of the church, while in the courtyard in front are foundations of a Roman building. Inside, the over-restored frescoes look brand new, and there are plenty of glittering icons.

Hadrian's Arch and the Temple of Olympian Zeus

Odhós Lysikrátous continues past Ayía Ekateríni to emerge at the edge of Pláka near one of the busiest road junctions in Athens, the meeting of Amalías and Syngroú. Across the way **Hadrian's Arch** stands in splendid isolation. With the traffic roaring by, this is not somewhere you are tempted to linger, but it's definitely worth a look on your way to the Temple of Olympian Zeus. The arch, 18m high, was erected by the emperor himself to mark the edge of the Classical city and the beginning of his own. On the west side its frieze is inscribed "This is Athens, the ancient city of Theseus", and on the other "This is the City of Hadrian and not of Theseus". With so little that's ancient remaining around it, this doesn't make immediate sense, but you can look up, westwards, to the Acropolis and in the other direction see the columns of the great temple completed by Hadrian.

Directly behind the arch, the colossal pillars of the **Temple of Olympian Zeus** (entrance on Vasilíssis Ólgas; daily 8am–3pm; €2 or joint Acropolis ticket) – also known as the Olympieion – stand in the middle of a huge, dusty clearing with excellent views of the Acropolis and constant traffic noise. One of the largest temples in the ancient world, and according to Livy, "the only temple on earth to do justice to the god", it was dedicated by Hadrian in 131 AD, almost 700 years after the tyrant Peisistratos had begun work on it. Hadrian marked the occasion by contributing a statue of Zeus and a suitably monumental one of himself, although both have since been lost. Just fifteen of the temple's original 104 marble pillars remain erect, though the column drums of another, which fell in 1852, litter the ground, giving a startling idea of the project's size. To the north of the temple enclosure, by the site entrance, are various excavated remains including an impressive Roman bath complex and a gateway from the wall of the Classical city. The south side of the enclosure overlooks a futher area of excavation (not open to the public) where both Roman and much earlier buildings have been revealed.

From the temple, a shady route up to Sýndagma or Kolonáki leads through the Záppio and the **National Gardens** (see p.136), while the Panathenaic Stadium is a short walk along Vasilíssis Ólgas.

Anafiótika

Heading northwest along **Adhrianoú** you enter the depressingly touristy home of the Manchester United beach towel and "Sex in Ancient Greece" playing cards. For a break, climb up into the jumble of streets and alleys that cling to the lower slopes of the Acropolis. Here, the whitewashed, island-style houses and ancient churches of the **Anafiótika** quarter proclaim a cheerfully architect-free zone. There's still the odd shop, and taverna tables are set out wherever a bit of flat ground can be found, but there are also plenty of hidden corners redolent of a quieter era.

Two museums: the Kanellopoulou and Man and Tools

Follow the streets round as high as you can under the looming Acropolis walls and you'll eventually emerge by the eclectic **Kanellopoulou Museum** (Tues–Sun 8am–3pm; €2), Theorías 12, cnr Panós. Though there's nothing here that you won't see examples of in the bigger museums, the collection, exhibited in the topmost house under the Acropolis, is well worth a visit. On the lower floors the many gorgeous **gilded icons** first grab your attention, but there's also Byzantine jewellery, bronze oil lamps and crosses and Roman funerary ornaments; some of the smaller items are exquisite. Upstairs is ancient pottery and bronze, including items from Minoan Crete and Egypt, as well as Stone Age tools. The top floor is perhaps the best of all, with **pottery** and **gold jewellery** from the Geometric, Classical, Hellenistic and Roman periods. Items here range from some astonishingly well-preserved large water jars and kraters to the bronze ram from the prow of a battleship, shaped like a dog's snout.

Just below the Kanellopoulou, at Panós 22, the **Museum of Greek Folk Art: Man and Tools** (Tues–Sat 9am–2.30pm; free) is a new branch of the Greek Folk Art museum, set in another fine mansion and devoted to the world of work. Tiny but fascinating and with good English labelling, its exhibits of tools and antiquated machinery concentrate on the pre-industrial world: there's a wooden grape-press as well as tools used in traditional trades including agriculture, barrel-making, cobbling and metalwork.

The Roman Forum and Tower of the Winds

The **Roman Forum** (daily: April–Sept 8.30am–7.30pm; Oct–March 8.30am–3pm; €2 or joint Acropolis ticket; entrance on Pelopídha, at the corner of Eólou) was built during the reign of Julius Caesar and his successor Augustus

Roman Athens

In 146 BC, the **Romans** ousted Athens' Macedonian rulers and incorporated the city into their vast new province of Achaia, whose capital was established at Corinth. Though something of a backwater, Athens' status as a renowned seat of learning (Cicero and Horace were educated here) and great artistic centre ensured that it was treated with respect. However, few imperial Roman monuments were built during this time, Hadrian's Arch being one of the exceptions. Even in Roman times, most building tended to follow classical Greek patterns – indeed Athenian artists and architects were much in demand in Rome.

The city's Roman **history** was shaped pre-eminently by its alliances, which often proved unfortunate. In 86 BC, for example, Sulla punished Athens for its allegiance to his rival Mithridates by burning its fortifications and looting its treasures. His successors were more lenient. Julius Caesar offered a free pardon after Athens had sided with Pompey; and Octavian (Augustus) showed similar clemency when Athens harboured Brutus following the Ides of March. The most frequent visitor was the **Emperor Hadrian**, who used the occasions to bestow grandiose monuments, including his eponymous arch, a magnificent and immense library and (though it had been begun centuries before) the Temple of Olympian Zeus. A generation later **Herodes Atticus**, a Roman senator who owned extensive lands in Marathon, became the city's last major benefactor of ancient times.

as an extension of the older ancient Greek agora. Its main entrance was on the west side, through the **Gate of Athena Archegetis**, which is still among the most prominent remains on the site. This gate marked the end of a street leading up from the Greek agora, and its four surviving columns give a vivid impression of the grandeur of the original portal. On the side facing the Acropolis you can still make out an engraved edict of Hadrian announcing the rules and taxes on the sale of oil. On the opposite side of the Forum, a second gateway is also easily made out and, between the two, is the marketplace itself, surrounded by colonnades and shops, some of which have been excavated. Inside the fenced site, but just outside the market area to the east, are the foundations of public latrines dating from the first century AD.

The best preserved and easily the most intriguing of the ruins inside the Forum site, however, is the graceful octagonal structure known as the **Tower of the Winds**. This actually predates the Forum, and stands just outside the main market area. Designed in the first century BC by Andronikos of Kyrrhos, a Syrian astronomer, it served as a compass, sundial, weather vane and water clock – the latter powered by a stream from one of the Acropolis springs. Each face of the tower is adorned with a relief of a figure floating through the air, personifying the eight winds. On the **north** side (facing Eólou) is Boreas blowing into a conch shell; **northwest**, Skiron holding a vessel of charcoal; **west**, Zephyros tossing flowers from his lap; **southwest**, Lips speeding the voyage of a ship; **south**, Notos upturning an urn to make a shower; **southeast**, Euros with his arm hidden in his mantle summoning a hurricane; **east**, Apiliotis carrying fruits and wheat; and **northeast**, Kaikias emptying a shield full of hailstones. Beneath each of these, it is still possible to make out the markings of eight sundials.

The semicircular tower attached to the south face was the reservoir from which water was channelled into a cylinder in the main tower; the time was read by the water level viewed through the open northwest door. On the top of the building a bronze Triton revolved with the winds. In Ottoman times, dervishes used the tower as a ceremonial hall, terrifying their superstitious Orthodox neighbours with their chanting, music and whirling meditation.

Turkish remains

It's not just Roman survivals that can be found in this corner of Monastiráki: around the Roman Forum are also some of the few visible reminders of the Ottoman city. The oldest mosque in Athens, the **Fethiye Tzami**, built in 1458, actually occupies a corner of the Forum site. It was dedicated by Sultan Mehmet II, who conquered Constantinople in 1453 (fethiye means "conquest" in Turkish). Sadly, you can't see inside, as it's now used as an archeological warehouse. Across Eólou, more or less opposite the Forum entrance, the gateway and single dome of a **medresse**, an Islamic school, survive. During the last years of Ottoman rule and the early years of Greek independence the building was used as a prison and was notorious for its harsh conditions; a plane tree in the courtyard was used for hangings. The prison was closed in the 1900s and the bulk of it torn down.

One local Ottoman survival you can visit is the site of the **Turkish Baths** (Mon & Wed–Sun 9am–2.30pm; free) nearby at Kirístou 8. Constructed originally in the 1450s, the baths were in use, with many later additions, right up to 1965. Newly restored, they now offer an insight into a part of Athens' past that is rarely glimpsed and well worth a look. Traditionally, the baths would have been used in shifts by men and women, although expansion in the nineteenth century provided the separate facilities you see today. The *tepidarium* and *caldarium*, fitted out in marble with domed roofs and rooflights, are particularly beautiful. The underfloor and wall heating systems have been exposed in places, while upstairs there are photos and pictures of old Athens. Labelling throughout is in Greek only, so it may be worth using the audio tour on offer (€1, plus a deposit).

For more on Ottoman Athens you could also check out the nearby Ceramic Collection of the Folk Art Museum (see overleaf) and the Benáki Museum of Islamic Art (p.143).

The Museum of Greek Folk Instruments

Also just around the corner from the Roman Forum, at Dhioyénous 1–3, the **Museum of Greek Folk Instruments** (Tues & Thurs–Sun 10am–2pm, Wed noon–6pm; free) traces the history and distribution of virtually every type of musical instrument that has ever been played in Greece. It's all attractively displayed in a fine mansion, with drums and wind instruments of all sorts (from crude bagpipes to clarinets) on the ground floor, lyras, fiddles, lutes and a profusion of stringed instruments upstairs. In the basement there are more percussion and toy instruments including some not-so-obvious festival and liturgical items such as triangles, strikers, livestock bells along with carnival outfits. Reproductions of frescoes show the Byzantine antecedents of many instruments, and headphone sets are provided for sampling the music made by the various exhibits.

The museum shop has an excellent selection of CDs for sale.

Hadrian's Library

Bordering the north end of the Forum site, and stretching right through from Eólou to Áreos, stand the surviving walls of **Hadrian's Library** (daily 8am–3pm; free; entry on Áreos), an enormous building that once enclosed a cloistered court of a hundred columns. The site has only recently opened to the public and is still being excavated: for the moment remains are sparse and poorly labelled. Much of the library, which dated from 132 AD, has been built over many times, and a lot of what you can see today consists of the foundations and mosaic floors of later Byzantine churches. However, some of the original columns survive, and above all you get an excellent sense of the sheer scale of the original building, especially when you realize that the Tetraconch Church, whose remains lie at the centre of the site, was built entirely within the library's internal courtyard.

The Folk Art Ceramic Collection

Directly opposite Monastiráki metro station, squeezed between the walls of Hadrian's library and the shacks of Pandhróssou, the **Museum of Greek Folk Art: Ceramics Collection** (Mon & Wed–Sun 9am–2.30pm; €2) is housed in the former Mosque of Tzisdarákis at Áreos 1. Built in 1759, the building has had a chequered life – converted to a barracks and then jail after Greek independence, before becoming the original home of the Greek Folk Art Museum in 1918. Today, as a branch of that museum, it houses the **Kyriazópoulos collection** of ceramics – the legacy of a Thessaloníki professor. Good as it is, the collection is, in all honesty, likely to excite you only if you have a particular interest in pottery; most people will probably find the mosque itself, the only one in Athens open to the public, at least as big an attraction.

Though missing its minaret, and with a balcony added inside for the museum, plenty of original features remain. In the airy, domed space, look out for the striped *mihrab* (the niche indicating the direction of Mecca), a calligraphic inscription above the entrance recording the mosque's founder and date, and a series of niches used as extra *mihrabs* for occasions when worshippers could not fit into the main hall.

△ Shopping in Pláka

Platía Monastirakíou and around

Platía Monastirakíou marks a return to the traffic and bustle of commercial Athens. Full of fruit stalls, nut sellers, lottery vendors and kiosks, the square gets its name from the little monastery church (monastiráki) at its centre, possibly seventeenth century in origin and badly restored in the early twentieth century. The area around has been a marketplace since Ottoman times, and it still preserves, in places, a bazaar atmosphere. The main city market (see p.138) lies straight up Athinás from here, towards Omónia, but nearer at hand you'll see signs in either direction that proclaim you're entering the famous **Monastiráki Flea Market**. These days this is a bit of a misnomer – there's plenty of shopping, but mostly of a very conventional nature. **Odhós Pandhróssou**, to the east, is almost entirely geared to tourists, an extension (though not quite literally) of Adhrianoú. West of the square the flea market has more of its old character, and among the tourist tat you'll find shops full of handmade musical instruments, or nothing but chess and *tavlí* boards, as well as places geared to locals selling bikes, skateboards or camping gear. An alley off Iféstou is jammed with record and CD shops, with a huge basement second-hand bookshop. Around **Platía Avyssinías** shops specialize in furniture and junky antiques: from here to Adhrianoú, the relics of a real flea market survive in hopeless jumble-sale rejects, touted by a cast of eccentrics (especially on Sundays). Odhós Adhrianoú is at its most appealing at this end, with a couple of interesting antique shops, and some shady cafés overlooking the metro lines, Agora and Acropolis.

The stretch of **Odhós Ermoú** fringing the flea market as it heads west from Platía Monastirakíou is the southern edge of fashionable Psyrrí, and among the workaday old-fashioned furniture stores here are some interesting new designer and retro shops; in the other direction, as it heads up towards Sýndagma, the street is much more staid. In the pedestrianized upper section are familiar high-street chains and department stores: if you're after Zara or Marks & Spencer, Mothercare or Benetton, this is the place to head.

Kapnikaréa and surrounding churches

The pretty Byzantine church of **Kapnikaréa** marks more or less the beginning of this upmarket shopping area and looks tiny, almost shrunken, in its high-rise, urban surroundings. Originally eleventh century, but with later additions, it has a lovely little dome and a gloomy interior in which you can just about make out the modern frescoes. The church is allegedly named after its founder, a tax collector: *kapnós* means smoke, and in the Byzantine era there was a tax on houses, known as the smoke tax.

Nearby, **Platía Mitropóleos** – Cathedral Square – is home to not just one but two cathedrals, though even between the pair of them they don't amount to much. The modern **Mitrópolis** is a large, clumsy nineteenth-century cannibal of dozens of older buildings; the **old cathedral** alongside it is dwarfed by comparison, but infinitely more attractive. There is said to have been a church on this site since the very earliest days of Christianity in Athens. What you see now dates from the twelfth century, a beautiful little structure cobbled together with plain and carved blocks from earlier incarnations; some almost certainly from that original church. The Platía itself is a welcome spot of calm among the busy shopping streets that surround it. There are several other small churches nearby: look out especially for the dusty, tiny chapel of **Ayía Dhynámis** crouching surreally below the concrete piers of the Ministry of Education and Religion on Odhós Mitropóleos.

Sýndagma and the National Gardens

All roads lead to **Sýndagma** – you'll almost inevitably find yourself here sooner or later for the metro and bus connections. Platía Syndágmatos, Constitution Square, to give it its full name, lies roughly midway between the Acropolis and Lykavitós hill. With the Greek Parliament building (the Voulí) on its uphill side, and banks, offices and embassies clustered around, it's the political and geographic heart of Athens. The square's name derives from the fact that Greece's first constitution was proclaimed (reluctantly under popular pressure) by King Otto from a palace balcony here in 1843. It's still the principal venue for mass demonstrations and, in the run-up to elections, the major political parties stage their final campaign rallies here.

Vital hub as it is, the traffic and the crush ensure it's not an attractive place to hang around. Escape comes in the form of the National Gardens, a welcome area of greenery stretching out south from the parliament building and offering a traffic-free route down past the Záppio to Hadrian's Arch and the Temple of Olympian Zeus (see p.130) or across to the Panathenaic Stadium (see p.148). In other directions, Odhós Ermoú prime shopping territory, heads west towards Monastiráki; Stadhíou and Panepistimíou stretch to the northwest towards Omónia; while to the north and east lies Kolonáki (see p.149) and the embassy quarter.

The square

With the exception of the Voulí, the Greek National Parliament, the vast **Hotel Grande Bretagne** – Athens' most impressive – is just about the only building on Sýndagma to have survived postwar development. Past the impressive facade and uniformed doormen, the interior is magnificently opulent, as befits a grand hotel established in the late nineteenth century. It's worth taking a look inside or having a drink at one of the bars: renovation in 2003 included a new rooftop pool, bar and restaurant with great views across the city. The hotel has long been at the centre of Greek political intrigue: in one notorious episode, Winston Churchill narrowly avoided being blown up here on Christmas Day, 1944, when saboteurs from the Communist-led ELAS movement placed an enormous explosive charge in the drains. According to whom you believe, the bomb was either discovered in time by a kitchen employee, or removed by ELAS themselves when they realized that Churchill was one of their potential targets.

The **Voulí** presides over Platía Syndágmatos from its uphill (east) side. A vast, ochre-and-white Neoclassical structure, it was built as the royal palace for Greece's first monarch, the Bavarian King Otto, who moved in in 1842. In front of it, goose-stepping **evzónes** in tasselled caps, kilt and woolly leggings – a prettified version of traditional mountain costume – change their guard at regular intervals before the **Tomb of the Unknown Soldier**. On Sundays, just before 11am, a full band and the entire corps parade from the tomb to their barracks at the back of the National Gardens to the rhythm of camera shutters.

The National Gardens

The **National Gardens** (sunrise–sunset; free; entrances on Amalías, Vasilíssis Sofías and Iródhou Attikoú), spreading out to the south and east of the Voulí, are the most refreshing acres in the city – not so much a flower garden as a luxuriant tangle of trees, whose shade and duck ponds provide palpable relief from the heat of summer. They were originally the private palace gardens – a pet project of Queen Amalia in the 1840s; supposedly the main duty of the minuscule Greek navy in its early days was the fetching of rare plants, often the gifts of other royal houses, from remote corners of the globe. Despite a major pre-Olympic clear-out there's still something of an air of benign neglect here, with rampant undergrowth and signs that seem to take you round in circles. It's a great place for a picnic, though, or just a shady respite from the city streets. There are benches everywhere, ducks being fed in the ponds, and other attractions including a small zoo, a children's playground (on the Záppio side) and a botanical museum. The tiny **zoo** (signed Irattikou) has ostriches and some exotic fowl, but most of the cages these days are occupied by chickens, rabbits and domestic cats. The **Botanical Museum** occupies an elegant little pavilion nearby; closed for refurbishment at the time of writing.

To the south, the graceful crescent-shaped grounds of the Záppio are open 24 hours. Popular with evening and weekend strollers, they're formally laid out and characterized by open spaces. The **Záppio** itself, an imposing Neoclassical edifice originally built as an exhibition hall, is not open to the public. Although it has no permanent function, the building has taken on prestigious roles such as headquarters of the Greek presidency of the European Union and of the 2004 Olympic bid. On the eastern side of the National Gardens, across Iródhou Attikoú, stands the **Presidential Palace**, the royal residence until King Constantine's exile in 1967, where more sentries stand on duty.

Towards Omónia

Northwest from Sýndagma, the broad and busy avenues of **Stadhíou, Panepistimíou** (officially called Venizélou, though the name is rarely used) and **Akadhimías** head towards Platía Omonías, lined with grandiose mansions and with mainstream retailers, many of them tucked into cavernous, often opulent arcades that would have gained the approval of the original Bavarian planners. The Sýndagma end is noticeably more upmarket, and here too are a number of small museums.

First of these, in the glorious former home of German archeologist Heinrich Schliemann at Panepistimíou 12, just off Sýndagma, is the **Numismatic Museum** (Tues–Sun 8.30am–3pm; €3), with a collection of over 600,000 coins and related artefacts dating from Mycenaean times through Classical, Macedonian and Roman to Byzantine and the modern era. The nearby **National Historical Museum** (Tues–Sun 9am–2pm; €3), on Platía Kolokotróni, occupies a building that housed the parliament from 1874 until 1935. Its exhibits cover Greek history from the fall of Constantinople to the reign of King Otto, with particular emphasis on the Byzantine era. There's also a strong section on the War of Independence that includes Byron's sword and helmet. Unfortunately, minimal labelling leaves the visitor a little short on the historical context of the valuable pieces on display. Finally, the **City of Athens Museum** (Mon, Wed & Fri 9am–4pm, Thurs noon–8pm, Sat & Sun 10am–3pm; €5) is at Paparigopoúlou 7, on Platía Klafthmónos. This was the residence of King Otto in the 1830s before his new palace was completed, and its exhibits cover Athens' history from Otto's time onwards. Some of the rooms have been restored to their state when the royals lived here, with exquisite period furnishings, and there are many artworks featuring the city as well as an interesting model of Athens in 1842, with just three hundred houses. A section of the ancient city walls can be seen in a basement.

Much cosmetic work was done in this area prior to the Olympics, and there's now a wonderful view up from Platía Klafthmónos towards three grand

Neoclassical buildings on Panepistimíou. Here the planners' conceptualization of the capital of newly independent Greece can for once be seen more or less as they envisaged it, blending the nation's Classical heritage with modern, Western values. As you look up you see, from the left, the sober grey marble of the **National Library**, the rather racier **Akadhimía (University)**, enlivened by frescoes depicting King Otto surrounded by ancient Greek gods and heroes, and the frankly over-the-top **Academy of Science** with its pediment friezes and giant statues of Athena and Apollo. The garish decoration gives an alarming impression of what the Classical monuments might have looked like when their paintwork was intact. Behind these buildings, on Akadhimías, is a major terminus for **city buses**, from where you can get a connection to almost anywhere in the city or its suburbs.

The bazaar, Platía Omonías and north

While Pláka and Sýndagma are resolutely geared to tourists and the Athenian well-heeled, Platía Omonías (Omónia Square) and its surroundings represent a much more gritty city, revolving around everyday commerce and trade. Here the grand avenues imagined by the nineteenth-century planners have been subverted by time and the realities of Athens' status as a commercial capital. Heading up from Monastiráki, the **bazaar area** around Odhós Athinás is home to a bustling series of markets and small shops spilling into the streets and offering some of urban Athens' most compelling sights and sounds, as well as an ethnic mix that is a rare reminder of Greece's traditional role as a meeting place of East and West. From here to Omónia was once the city's red-light district and, though now much cleaned up, the square itself retains a distinct grittiness. **Psyrrí**, southwest of the market area, is a formerly working-class district that is now home to Athens' busiest nightlife as well as some quirky shops; its gentrifying influence is rapidly spreading to surrounding neighbourhoods. North of Omónia the **National Archeological Museum** is an essential visit: behind it the perennially "alternative" quarter of **Exárhia** has plenty more nightlife and eating options.

The bazaar: from Ermoú to Omónia

The city's bazaar area is concentrated on **Athinás** and **Eólou streets**. Here the stores, though stocked mainly with imported manufactured goods, still reflect their origins in the Oriental souk system: their unaffected decor, unsophisticated packaging and, most strikingly, their specialization. Though it's a tradition that's gradually dying, each street still has a concentration of particular stores and wares. Hence the Monastiráki end of Athinás is dedicated to tools; food stores are gathered around the central market in the middle, especially along Evripídhou; there's glass to the west; paint and brasswork to the east; and clothes in Eólou and Ayíou Márkou. Always raucous and teeming with shoppers, kouloúri (bread-ring) sellers, gypsies and other vendors, the whole area is great free entertainment.

The lively heart of the neighbourhood is the central **meat and seafood market**, occupying almost an entire block bordered by Athinás, Evripídhou, Eólou and Sofokléous. The building itself is a grand nineteenth-century relic, with fretted iron awnings sheltering forests of carcasses and mounds of hearts, livers and ears – no place for the squeamish. In the middle section of the hall is the fish market, with all manner of bounty from the sea squirming and glistening on the marble slabs. Across Athinás is the colourful **fruit** and **vegetable** bazaar, surrounded by streets where grocers pile their stalls high with sacks of pulses, salt cod, barrels of olives and wheels of cheese. A clear sign of Athens' increasing **multi-ethnicity** is to be seen in the streets around Evripídhou just west of here, where a growing community from South Asia, predominantly Bengalis, gather in hordes around the spice-rich minimarkets and cheap and cheerful curry houses.

Odhós Eólou: The flower market and Platía Kótzia

Odhós Eólou seems far less frantic than parallel Athinás, partly because it is pedestrianized. Local businesses have taken advantage of this so that there are now café tables in the street, and benches to rest on. Its gentler nature must also reflect the goods sold here: where Athinás has power tools and raw meat, Eólou offers clothes and the **flower market**. The latter, gathered around the church of Ayía Iríni at the southern end of the street, has stalls through the week but really comes alive with the crowds on a Sunday morning.

At the northern end of the street, **Platía Kótzia** is a far more formal enclave, and one of the city's more impressive examples of Olympic refurbishment. Surrounded by the town hall and the weighty Neoclassical buildings of the National Bank, it's a rare glimpse of elegant old Athens, spoilt only by the crumbling modern blocks above the post office. In the middle of the square a large section of **ancient road** has been uncovered and can be seen in a fenced-off site – numerous tombs and small buildings lie alongside it. This road, just outside the walls, once led to one of the main **gates** of ancient Athens and this too has recently been excavated, during building work for a new Stock Exchange. You can see this gate and some of the adjoining city wall underneath the new building, between Platía Kótzia and Sofokléous; nearby more sections of the ancient road and a drainage system are visible under glass pyramids in the middle of Eólou. The sight of the Acropolis from this street as you approached Athens in ancient times must have been awe-inspiring, and Eólou still has impressive views today, with the Erechtheion's slender columns and pediment peeking over the edge of the crag straight ahead.

Around Platía Omonías

Platía Omonías itself has little to offer in terms of aesthetics, but it is the heart of Athens for a good portion of the population. A continuous turmoil of people and cars, it is Athens at its earthiest and most urban. Cleaning-up and remodelling for the Olympics has removed much of the area's character – no bad thing, some would say, as that character derived from druggies, prostitutes and homeless Albanian refugees – and the new look is ugly, brutal and shadeless. Even sanitized, though, Omónia seems to retain a generally seedy atmosphere, the perimeter of the square dominated by kiosks whose chief trade seems to be in porn, clustered in front of a mishmash of fast-food outlets and discount stores.

The streets surrounding the square are full of offices, high-rise hotels and functional shopping. To the west towards the rail stations, Metaxouryío is an area undergoing something of a revival as development spills over from fashionable neighbouring Psyrrí and Gázi; north and east lie Exárhia and the National Archeological Museum.

The Polytekhnío

Heading north, the **Polytekhnío**, a Neoclassical building housing the university's school of engineering and science, is on 28 Oktovríou (also known as

Patissíon) just beside the National Archeological Museum. In November 1973 students here launched a protest against the repressive regime of the colonels' junta, occupying the building and courtyards, and broadcasting calls for mass resistance from a pirate radio transmitter. Large numbers came down to demonstrate support and hand in food and medicines. The colonels' regime was determined to smash the protest and, on the night of November 17, snipers were positioned in neighbouring houses and ordered to fire into the courtyards while a tank broke down the entrance gate and the buildings were stormed. Even today nobody knows how many of the unarmed students were killed – estimates range from twenty to three hundred.

Though a failure at the time, the protest arguably marked the beginning of the end for the colonels; its anniversary is still commemorated by marches and sombre remembrance ceremonies, and inside the main gates of the Polytechnic you can still view the original entrance gates, mangled by the invading tank.

The National Archeological Museum

The **National Archeological Museum** (summer Mon 1–7.30pm, Tues–Sun 8.30am–7.30pm; winter Mon 10.30am–5pm, Tues–Sun 8.30am–3pm; €7), at 28 Oktovríou 44, is an unrivalled treasure trove of ancient Greek art – and an essential Athens experience. However high your expectations, the museum seems effortlessly to surpass them, full of objects that seem familiar, so often have you seen them in pictures or reproductions. The interior is surprisingly plain – there's nothing flashy at all about the new displays, but the minimalist approach is admirably clear and well labelled. You could easily spend an entire morning or afternoon here, but it's equally possible to scoot round the highlights in an hour or two; arriving early in the morning or late in the afternoon should mean you won't be competing with the tour groups for space. The nearest **metro** stations are at Viktorías or Omónia, but the museum is also very easy to get to by bus, with a local terminus outside on Vassiléos Iraklíou – look for Mousseio.

Downstairs in the museum is a small shop selling high-quality, high-priced copies of museum artifacts as well as a small collection of classy souvenirs. There are also toilets down here and a small café by a shady inner courtyard. Upstairs is an extensive Egyptian collection, though few visitors seem to get that far.

Mycenaean and Cycladic art

Directly ahead of you as you enter, the **Mycenaean halls** have always been the biggest crowd pullers. Mycenaean culture flourished in the fifteenth and fourteenth centuries BC. The gold **Mask of Agamemnon**, arguably the museum's most famous piece, is almost the first thing you see. Modern dating techniques offer convincing proof that the funerary mask actually belonged to some more ancient Achaian king, but crowds are still drawn by its correspondence with the Homeric myth and compelling expression. Schliemann's other finds from Mycenae (see p.211) are all around, along with the fruits of more recent explorations there and at other Mycenaean sites including Tiryns (p.216) and Pylos (p.295). It's a truly exceptional display, the gold shining as if it were in the window of a jeweller's shop.

Among the highlights are a golden-horned **Bull's Head** displayed alongside a gold **Lion's Head**; gold jewellery including a diadem and a gold-foil cover for the body of an infant from Grave III (the "Grave of the Women"); the **Acropolis Treasure** of gold goblets, signet rings and jewellery; and dozens of examples of the Mycenaeans' consummate art, intricate, small-scale decoration of rings, cups, seals and inlaid daggers. There's work in silver, ivory, bronze and boars' tusks as well; there are baked tablets of Linear B, the earliest Greek writing (mainly accounting records) and Cretan-style frescoes depicting chariot-borne women watching spotted hounds in pursuit of boar and bull-vaulting. Other delights are the gold **Vafio** cups, with their scenes of wild bulls and long-tressed, narrow-waisted men as well as an eye-catching cup decorated with twining octopuses and dolphins. Further references to Homer abound: bronze daggers from Pylos inlaid with gold nautilus shells; a silver bowl with a gold bull's head inlaid; two magnificent boars' tusk helmets; and an ivory lyre with sphinxes adorning the soundboard.

Still earlier Greece is represented in the adjoining rooms. Room 5 covers Neolithic pottery and stone tools from Attica and elsewhere and runs through to the early Bronze Age. The pottery shows sophisticated decoration from as early as 5000 BC, and there are many figurines, probably fertility symbols judging by their phallic or pregnant nature, as well as simple gold ornaments. Room 6 is home to a large collection of **Cycladic art** from the Aegean islands. Many of these idols suggest the abstract forms of modern Cubist art – most strikingly in the much-reproduced **Man Playing a Lyre**. Another unusual piece is a sixteenth-century BC cylindrical vase depicting a ring of fishermen carrying fish by their tails, and there are dozens of so-called "frying pan" vessels with incised decoration, use unknown.

Sculpture

Sculpture makes up a large part of the museum's most important exhibits, following a broadly chronological arrangement in a clockwise direction around the main halls of the museum. This shows the gradual development from the stiff, stylized representations of the seventh century BC towards ever freer and looser naturalism in the following centuries.

Early highlights include a statue of a **kore** (maiden) from Merenda (Myrrhinous) in Attica, in room 11. Her elegantly pleated, belted *chiton* (dress) bears traces of the original paint and decoration of swastikas, flowers and geometric patterns. Nearby is a wonderful grave stele of a young *doryphoros* (spear-bearer) standing against a red background. Room 13 has the **Stele of a Young Warrior**, with delicately carved beard, hair and tunic-folds, a funerary tribute to one Aristion, signed by the artist Aristokles, and the **Kroisus kouros** (statue of an idealized youth), who looks as if he's been working out; both are from the late sixth century BC. Other delightful pieces here include a statueless plinth carved with reliefs showing, on one side, young men exercising in the gymnasium, on the other a group of amused friends setting a dog and cat to fight each other, and a statue of Aristodikos, whose sense of movement presages the development of early Classical art.

△ National Archeological Museum

Just a few highlights of the massive **Classical art** collection can be mentioned. Room 15 boasts a mid-fifth-century BC bronze **Statue of Poseidon**, dredged from the sea off Évvia in the 1920s. The god stands poised to throw his trident – weight on the front foot, athlete's body perfectly balanced, the model of idealized male beauty. A less dramatic, though no less important, piece in the same room is the **Eleusinian Relief**. Highly deliberate in its composition, the relief shows the goddess of fertility, accompanied by her daughter Persephone, giving to mankind an ear of corn – symbol of the knowledge of agriculture and associated with the Mysteries of Eleusis (p.192). In Room 20 is a small marble statue of Athena, a copy of the great cult statue that once stood in the Parthenon. With shield and snake in her left hand, a winged, angel-like figure in her right and a triple crest of winged horses and sphinxes on her head it's a scary figure: the vast original, covered in gold and ivory, must have been extraordinary. The **Little Jockey of Artemission**, a delicate bronze figure seeming too small for his galloping horse, was found in the same shipwreck as the *Poseidon*; near it in room 21 is the **Atalante Hermes**, a wonderful funerary statue of a youth. Room 28 has some fine, fourth-century BC bronzes including the **Antikythira Youth**, thought to depict either Perseus or Paris, from yet another shipwreck, off Antikithira, and the bronze head of a *Boxer*, burly and battered. Still more naturalistic, in room 29, is the third-century BC bronze head of a *Philosopher*, with furrowed brow and unkempt hair. Too numerous to list, but offering fascinating glimpses of everyday life and also changing styles of craftsmanship and perception of the human form, are the many **stelae** and other grave monuments: rooms 16, 18, 23 and 24 are particularly rich in these.

The most reproduced of all the **later sculptures** is a first-century AD statue of a naked and indulgent *Aphrodite* (room 30) about to rap Pan's knuckles for getting too fresh – a far cry (a long fall, some would say) from the reverent, idealizing portrayals of the gods in Classical times. There is also an extraordinary bronze equestrian portrait statue (missing the horse) of the Roman *Emperor Augustus*. Room 31A has a fascinating collection of portrait heads from the second and third centuries AD; probably officials of a *Gymnasium*, these offer a uniqe look at the ordinary citizens of Roman Athens.

Exárhia and Lófos Stréfi

Exárhia, fifty-odd blocks squeezed between the National Archeological Museum and Lófos Stréfi, is one of the city's liveliest neighbourhoods, especially at night. Traditionally the home of anarchists, revolutionaries, artists, students and anyone seeking an anti-establishment lifestyle in a conformist city, Exárhia is pretty tame these days, but it's still the closest thing in central Athens to an "alternative" neighbourhood. This means a concentration of ouzerís, nightclubs and genuine music tavernas by night, and during the day some interesting, offbeat clothing and music stores. The tiny, triangular, café-lined Platía Exarhíon is at the heart of it all; or if you are around on a Saturday, check out the colourful street market on Kallidhromíou where locals flock from early morning till lunchtime.

Just above this, the little-visited **Stréfis Hill** (Lófos toú Stréfi) provides a welcome break from the densely packed streets and dull apartment blocks surrounding it. A labyrinth of paths leads up to the low summit, from where there are unexpectedly wonderful views – above all of the Acropolis with the Saronic Gulf and islands behind, but also across to nearby Lykavitós. Watch out for unguarded drops near the top and stick to the main paths as you walk up, in order to avoid one of the more obvious signs of the area's alternative lifestyle, discarded hypodermics.

From Thissío to Makriyiánni

Some of the most interesting up-and-coming areas of Athens – **Thissío**, **Gázi** and **Roúf** – lie to the west of the centre, where a new extension to Metro line 3, beyond Monastiráki, can only accelerate the pace of change. Nightlife and restaurants are the chief attractions here, but there's also a cluster of new museums and galleries, above all the Tekhnópolis centre and two annexes of the Benáki Museum, devoted to Islamic and modern art respectively. Here too is **Kerameikos**, site of the cemetery of ancient Athens and a substantial section of its walls. South of Thissío, things are rather more traditional. Pedestrianized Apostólou Pávlou leads around the edge of the Agora and Acropolis sites, under the flanks of the hills of the Pnyx and Filopáppou, and offers a pleasant, green escape from the city as well as fine views. On the west side of the hills, the residential zone of **Áno Petrálona** is a real delight, entirely untouristy, with some excellent tavernas (see p.165) and a great open-air cinema, though absolutely nothing in the way of sights. On the east side of the hills, immediately south of the Acropolis, **Makriyiánni** is a far more upmarket residential neighbourhood, merging into rather earthier **Koukáki**. Again there are good, local restaurants here and not much in the way of sights, though that will change with the opening of the new Acropolis Museum in Makriyiánni and the Contemporary Art Museum at Syngroú-Fix, on the fringes of Koukáki.

Platía Thissíou to Gázi

From Monastiráki, Odhós Adhrianoú follows the edge of the ancient Agora site alongside the metro lines (here above ground) towards Platía Thissíou, in front of Thissío metro station. From here you can head south for Thissío proper and the traffic-free route round the Acropolis, west along a pedestrianized section of Ermoú past the Kerameikos site towards Gázi, or north towards a couple of interesting new museums.

The Islamic Art and Pottery Museums

Two small new museums are just a short walk up Áyion Asomáton from Platía Thissíou. First, on the left in Melidhóni, is the **Museum of Traditional Pottery** (Mon, Thurs & Fri 9am–3pm, Wed 9am–8pm, Sat 10am–3pm, Sun 10am–2pm; €6). A tiny place, it has a series of small rooms with exhibits of traditional pottery-making methods, complete with regular hands-on demonstrations. A couple of further galleries have temporary exhibits, usually on a particular style or era of pottery. Completing the ensemble is a small café and a shop selling quality ceramics.

The **Benáki Museum of Islamic Art** (Tues, Thurs & Fri–Sun 9am–3pm, Wed 9am–9pm; €6, free Wed; ⓦwww.benaki.gr) is at Áyion Asomáton 22, corner Dhípylou. Antonis Benakis, founder of the Benáki Museum (p.151), spent much of his life in Egypt, and this new museum, taking up four floors of a Neoclassical mansion, was created to house the more than 8000 works of art that he collected. The exhibits cover not just Egypt but almost every part of the Islamic world, including India, Persia, Arabia, Egypt, North Africa, Turkey and even Spain and Sicily, and date from the emergence of Islam right up until the nineteenth century. Almost every type of art is included: textiles, jewellery, ceramics, metalwork, glass and armour as well as the reconstructed reception room of a seventeenth-century Egyptian mansion. Highlights include the early ceramics on the first floor, two eighth-century carved wooden memorial door-leaves from Mesopotamia, a unique tenth-century Tiberius reed mat, two

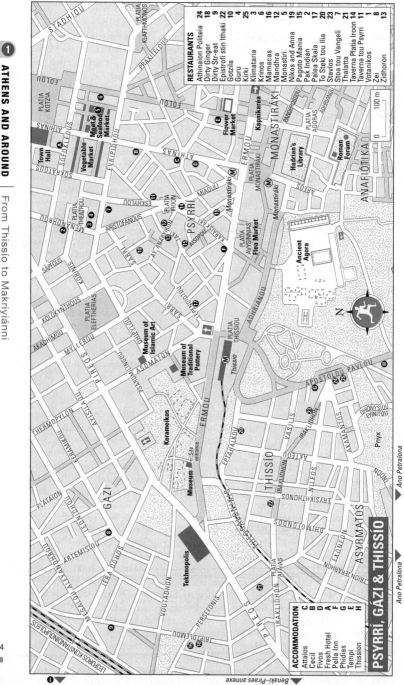

PSYRRÍ, GÁZI & THISSÍO

RESTAURANTS
Athinaion Politeia	24
Dirty Ginger	18
Dirty Str-eat	9
Epistrofi stin Ithaki	22
Gotzila	10
Guru	4
Kirki	25
Klimataria	3
Krinos	6
Mamacas	16
Mandhra	12
Monastiri	5
Nikos and Anna	19
Pagoto Mania	15
Pak Indian	2
Palea Skala	17
To Steki tou Ilia	20
Stavlos	23
Stoa tou Vangeli	7
Thalatta	21
Taverna Platia Iroon	14
Taverna tou Psyrri	11
Votanikos	1
Zei	8
Zidhoron	13

ACCOMMODATION
Attalos	C
Cecil	B
Fivos	D
Fresh Hotel	A
Pella Inn	F
Phidias	G
Tempi	E
Thission	H

Ano Petralona ▶

Ano Petralona ▶

Benaki–Pireos annexe ▶

beautiful chessboards with ivory and bone pawns, and an impressive inlaid writing desk. It's all beautifully done, a world-class collection small enough to see in under an hour, and especially exciting to find in Athens whose Islamic heritage is often ignored or denied. There's a top-floor café with views of the Acropolis and Kerameikos, and a small shop with a limited selection of English-language books. On the lower ground floor a section of the ancient city wall and a tomb found during restoration work can be seen.

Kerameikos

The **Kerameikos** (or Keramikós) site (daily 8.30am–3pm; €2 or joint Acropolis ticket; entrance on Ermoú), encompassing the principal cemetery of ancient Athens and a hefty section of the ancient wall, provides a fascinating and quiet retreat. Little visited, it has something of an oasis feel, with the lush Iridhanós channel, speckled with water lilies, flowing across the site from east to west.

To the right of the entrance is the stream and the double line of the **city wall**. The inner wall was hastily cobbled together by the men, women and children of Athens in 479 BC while Themistocles was pretending to negotiate a mutual disarmament treaty with Sparta. Two roads pierced the wall here, and the gates that marked their entrance to the city have been excavated: the great **Dipylon Gate** was the busiest in the ancient city, where the road from Pireás, Eleusis and the north arrived; the **Sacred Gate** was a ceremonial entrance where the Ierá Odhós or Sacred Way entered the city – it was used for the Eleusinian and Panathenaic processions (see p.121). Between the two gates are the foundations of the **Pompeion**, a spacious building with a peristyle courtyard, where preparations for the processions were made and where the main vehicles were stored.

Branching off to the left from the Sacred Way the **Street of the Tombs**, which is actually the old road to Pireás, heads through the **cemetery**. The plots alongside the road were reserved for wealthy or distinguished Athenians. Some twenty, each containing numerous commemorative monuments, have been excavated, and their original stones reinstated or replaced by replicas. The flat vertical stelae were the main funerary monuments of the Classical world; the sarcophagi that you see are later, from Hellenistic or Roman times. The large tomb with the massive semicircular base to the left of the path is the *Memorial of Dexileos*, the 20-year-old son of Lysanias of Thorikos, who was killed in action at Corinth in 394 BC. The adjacent plot contains the *Monument of Dionysios of Kollytos*, in the shape of a pillar stele supporting a bull carved from Pentelic marble. From the terrace overlooking the tombs, Pericles delivered his famous funeral oration dedicated to those who died in the first years of the Peloponnesian War. His propaganda coup inspired thousands more to enlist in a campaign during which one-third of the Athenian force was wiped out.

The new **site museum** is a lovely, cool, marble-floored space displaying finds from the site and related material, above all stelae and grave markers. There are also many poignant funerary offerings – toys from child burials, gold jewellery and beautiful small objects of all sorts. The ceramics are particularly fine, including lovely dishes with horses on their lids (*pyxides*) from the early eighth century BC and some stunning fifth-century BC black-and-red figure pottery.

Gázi, Tekhnópolis and around

Gázi, to the west and north of Kerameikos, is a former industrial area where the reinvention of the old gasworks as the Tekhnópolis cultural centre has helped spark a rush of hip bars and restaurants. By day the streets tend to be deserted, and by night, with so many derelict buildings, they can feel threatening. In practice it's safe enough, but you may want to take a taxi down here; Gázi really comes into its own late on Friday night and over the weekend.

The former gasworks from which the Gázi district takes its name has been converted into a stunning series of spaces for concerts and exhibitions known as **Tekhnópolis** (☏210 34 60 981). This, at least, is easy enough to reach – simply continue along Ermoú past the Kerameikos site and you'll emerge on Odhós Pireós more or less opposite the entrance; there are also lots of buses on Pireós. Two round gas-holders have become circular glass offices – one for Athens 98.4FM, the other for Tekhnópolis administration – while in the various pumping stations and boiler rooms surrounding them, galleries and exhibition halls of varying sizes have been created, many with parts of the original machinery preserved. There's also a café. The only permanent display here is a small **Maria Callas Museum** (Mon–Fri 10am–5pm; free), whose collection of personal letters and photos, plus a pair of gloves and a fur coat, is really for fans only. All sorts of temporary exhibitions and concerts take place, though, so it's well worth taking a look – or check the website or local listings magazines for details.

Numerous other galleries and cultural spaces have sprung up in the surrounding area, and two of particular note. The **Benáki Museum Piraeus St Annexe** (Wed & Thurs 9am–5pm, Fri–Sun 10am–10pm; €4; ☏210 34 53 111, ⓦwww .benaki.gr) at Pireós 138, corner Andhrónikou, is about six blocks down from Tekhnópolis (Metro Petrálona, or many buses along Pireós including #049, #B18 and trolley #021). There's no permanent collection here, but the prestige of the Benáki Museum can attract exceptional temporary shows so it's always worth checking out what's on. Apart from the exhibition space, the building also has a 400-seat amphitheatre, interesting shop with jewellery and design objects from prominent contemporary Greek designers and an airy indoor restaurant/café. Further north, Ierá Odhós (following the line of the ancient Sacred Way) heads off from behind the Kerameikos site towards the **Athinaïs**, at Kastoriás 34–36 (☏210 34 80 000; ⓦwww.athinais.com.gr). A magnificent restoration of an early twentieth-century silk factory, the Athinaïs complex contains a theatre, music space, movie screen, two restaurants, a bar and café, exhibition halls, a museum and, the real object of the place, a sizeable conference centre. The **Pierídhes Museum of Ancient Cypriot Art** (daily 9.30am–1pm; €3) is beautifully presented in four small galleries, with some top-class exhibits including ceramics and very early glassware. It does seem strange to be admiring these Cypriot objects in Athens, however. The museum shop is full of lavish (and lavishly priced) arty gifts, while upstairs are art galleries with temporary exhibitions. Again, details of what's on for both of the above can be found on their websites or in the local press.

Thissío and views of the Acropolis

Head south from metro Thissío and you can follow pedestrianized Apóstolou Pávlou right around the edge of the Ancient Agora and Acropolis sites to metro Akrópoli on the fringes of Pláka. It's a rewarding walk especially in the early evening, when the setting sun illuminates this side of the rock and the cafés of Thissío start to fill with an anticipatory buzz. As you follow the street round there are a number of small excavations at the base of the hills on your right. Perhaps the most interesting is the **Sanctuary of Pan**, on the lower slopes of the Pnyx just beyond the Thission open-air cinema. The cult of Pan was associated with caves, and in this fenced-off site you can see the opening to an underground chamber cut into the rock. Inside were found reliefs of Pan, a naked nymph and a dog. There's also a mosaic floor and, nearby, remains of an ancient road and two rock-cut, Classical-era houses. Just above the sanctuary is the so-called **Fountain of Pnyx**. Under Peisistratos a water system was engineered, with subterranean pipes bringing water from springs to rock-cut cisterns that supplied the city. This is believed to be one of those: behind a locked entrance is a chamber with a Roman mosaic floor where the water was collected. You can also see traces of the concrete used to seal the chamber during World War II, when valuable antiquities were stored inside.

Apóstolou Pávlou leads into Leofóros Dhionysíou Areopayítou, which heads along the south side of the Acropolis, past the Herodes Atticus Theatre. At the far end is the site where the **new Acropolis Museum** is finally taking shape. A new museum has been on the agenda for decades, but even when finally approved (and due to open prior to the Olympics), there were years more delays, with arguments over the design and the excavation of the site where it was to be built. The end result, however, is set to be stunning. There will be room to show far more, in a far better fashion than the current cramped Acropolis Museum can manage, while downstairs there's a raised, part-glass floor, added to the design to preserve and display remains of early Christian Athens, discovered during building work. The highlight, though, will be the top storey, an all-glass affair with a direct view up to the Parthenon. Here, it is hoped, the Parthenon Marbles (those already in the Acropolis Museum, plus the restored Elgin Marbles, see p.124) will finally be reunited in a fitting setting. To help bring this about, the Greeks have proposed that the Elgin Marbles come on loan, or that part of the museum be designated the "British Museum in Athens" so that ownership doesn't change. So far, all offers have been turned down by London, though some locals continue to believe that completion of the new museum will shame the British Museum into action.

Filopáppou Hill, the Hill of the Pnyx and the Hill of the Nymphs

From around the junction of Apóstolou Pávlou and Dhionysíou Areopayítou, a network of paths leads up **Filopáppou Hill**, also known in antiquity as the Hill of the Muses. Its pine- and cypress-clad slopes provide fabulous views of the Acropolis and the city beyond, especially at sunset (although night-time muggings have occurred here, so take care). This strategic height has played an important, if generally sorry, role in the city's history; in 1687 it was from here that the shell that destroyed the roof of the Parthenon was lobbed; more recently, the colonels placed tanks on the slopes during their coup of 1967. The hill's summit is capped by a grandiose monument to a Roman senator and consul, Filopappus, who is depicted driving his chariot on its frieze. To the west is the Dora Stratou Theatre (see p.175). On the way up the hill, the main path follows a line of truncated ancient walls, past the attractive sixteenth-century church of **Áyios Dhimítrios**, inside which are some original Byzantine frescoes. Further down, in the rock face near the base of the hill, you can make out a kind of cave dwelling, known (more from imagination than evidence) as the **prison of Socrates**.

North of Filopáppou, above the church, rises the **Hill of the Pnyx**, an area used in Classical Athens as the meeting place for the democratic assembly, which gathered more than forty times a year. All except the most serious political issues were aired here on the north side of the hill, providing a convenient, semicircular terrace from which to address the crowd. All male citizens could vote and, at least in theory, all could voice their opinions, though the assembly was harsh on inarticulate or foolish speakers. There are some impressive remains of the original walls, used to form the theatre-like court, and of *stoas* for the assembly's refreshment. This atmospheric setting provides commanding

Acropolis views, while benches on the west side allow you to contemplate the vista across Pireás and out to sea. On the northern slope, above Thissío, stands the impressive Neoclassical bulk of the **National Observatory of Athens** (Ⓦ www.noa.gr; open first Fri of every month).

Over to the west a third hill rises – the **Hill of the Nymphs** (Lófos Nymfón). Nymphs were associated with the dusty whirlwinds to which this hill is particularly prone and it is said to be the location of the fairy sequences in Shakespeare's *A Midsummer Night's Dream*. Slightly lower and quieter than its better-known neighbours, this is a peaceful place with good views across to the western suburbs of Athens and beyond, as well as pleasant shaded walks.

Mets and Pangráti

For a taste of old Athens, head south and east of the National Gardens where **Mets** and **Pangráti** are just about the only central neighbourhoods outside Pláka to have retained something of their traditional flavour. In Mets especially, a steep hillside quarter on the southwest side of the Panathenaic Stadium, streets of pre-World War II houses survive almost intact. With their tiled roofs, shuttered windows and courtyards with spiral metal staircases and potted plants, they offer an intimate glimpse of the more traditional side of the city. There are few sights here – just the stadium and the city's most prestigious cemetery – but plenty of authentic tavernas and bars, particularly in and around Platía Varnáva in Pangráti.

The Panathenaic Stadium

The old Olympic Stadium, or the **Panathenaic Stadium** (Kalimármaron), is a nineteenth-century reconstruction on Roman foundations, slotted tightly between the pine-covered spurs of Ardhittós hill. You can't normally go inside, but you can go right up to the open end of its horseshoe shape, from where you get a very good view. An easy walk from the centre via the Záppio gardens, the stadium can also be reached by tram (Záppio stop).

This site was originally marked out in the fourth century BC for the Panathenaic athletic contests, but, in Roman times, as a grand gesture to mark the reign of Emperor Hadrian, it was adapted for an orgy of blood sports, with thousands of wild beasts baited and slaughtered in the arena. The Roman senator Herodes Atticus later undertook to refurbish the 60,000 seats of the entire stadium; the white marble from these was to provide the city with a convenient quarry through the ensuing seventeen centuries.

The stadium's reconstruction dates from the modern revival of the Olympic Games in 1896 and bears witness to the efforts of another wealthy benefactor, the Alexandrian Greek Yiorgos Averoff. Its appearance – pristine whiteness and meticulous symmetry – must be very much as it was when first restored and reopened under the Roman senator. Though the bends are too tight for major modern events, it's still used by local athletes, is the finishing point of the annual Athens Marathon and lay at the end of the 2004 Olympic marathon. Above the stadium to the south, on the secluded Hill of Ardhittós, are a few scant remnants of a Temple of Fortune, again constructed by Herodes Atticus.

The Próto Nekrotafío

The **Próto Nekrotafío** (First Cemetery), just a short walk from the stadium or Záppio tram stop, shelters the tombs of just about everybody who was anybody in nineteenth- and twentieth-century Greece, from Heinrich Schliemann to Melina Mercouri and former prime minister Andreas Papandreou. The humbler tombs of musicians, artists and writers are interspersed with the ornate mausoleums of soldiers, statesmen and "good" families, whose descendants come to picnic, stroll and tend the graves. The graveside statuary occasionally attains the status of high art, most notably in the works of Ianoulis Halepas, a *belle époque* sculptor from Tínos generally acknowledged to be the greatest of a school of fellow islanders. Halepas battled with mental illness for most of his life and died in extreme poverty in 1943; his masterpiece is the idealized *Kimiméni* (Sleeping Girl), on the right about 300m in.

Kolonáki, Lykavitós and the museum quarter

If you have money to spend, **Kolonáki** is the place to do it, catering as it does to every Western taste from fast food to high fashion. It's also from here that a funicular hauls you up **Lykavitós Hill**, where some of the best views of the city can be enjoyed. Close at hand, too, is a clutch of major museums. The **Museum of Cycladic Art**, the eclectic **Benáki** collection and the **Byzantine and Christian Museum** are particularly worthwhile, the **War Museum** and **National Gallery of Art** of more specialist interest. Near the latter, what are believed to be the fourth-century BC foundations of **Aristotle's Lyceum** – where he taught for thirteen years and to which Socrates was a frequent visitor – were recently unearthed, during excavation work for a new extension. Surrounded by museums, this seems an appropriate place for it, but important as the discovery is for scholars, there's nothing actually to see.

Kolonáki

Kolonáki is the city's most chic central address and shopping area. Walk up from Sýndagma, past the jewellery stores on Voukouretsíou, and you can almost smell the money. The neighbourhood's lower limits are defined by Akadhimías and Vassilísis Sofías streets, where grand Neoclassical palaces house embassies and museums. The middle stretches of the quarter are taken up with shops, while the highest, wonderfully located on the southwest-facing slopes of Lykavitós, looking out over the Acropolis and National Gardens, are purely residential.

The heart of it all is a square officially called Platía Filikís Eterías, but known to all as **Platía Kolonakíou**, after the ancient "little column" that hides in the trees on the southwest side. Dotted

△ Museum of Cycladic Art

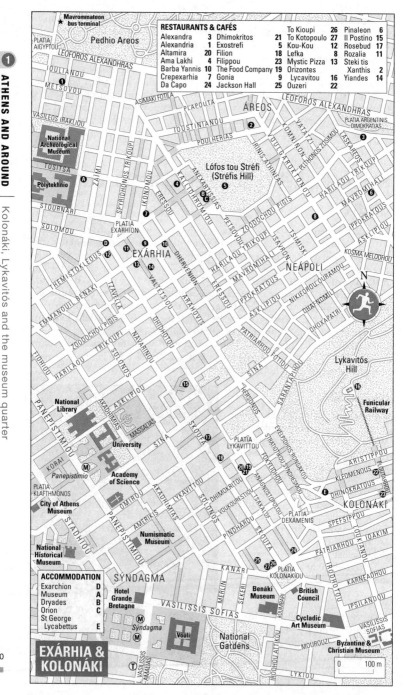

RESTAURANTS & CAFÉS

Alexandra	3	Dhimokritos	21	To Kioupi	26	Pinaleon	6
Alexandria	1	Exostrefi	5	To Kotopoulo	27	Il Postino	15
Altamira	20	Filion	18	Kou-Kou	12	Rosebud	17
Ama Lakhi	4	Filippou	23	Lefka	8	Rozalia	11
Barba Yannis	10	The Food Company	19	Mystic Pizza	13	Steki tis
Crepexarhia	7	Gonia	9	Orizontes		Xanthis	2
Da Capo	24	Jackson Hall	25	Lycavitou	16	Yiandes	14
				Ouzeri	22

ACCOMMODATION

Exarchion	D
Museum	A
Dryades	B
Orion	C
St George Lycabettus	E

EXÁRHIA & KOLONÁKI

0   100 m

around the square are kiosks with stocks of foreign papers and magazines, or in the library of the **British Council** you can check out the British press for free. The surrounding cafés are almost invariably packed with Gucci-clad shoppers – you'll find better value if you move away from the square a little. In the dozens of small, upmarket **shops** the accent is firmly on fashion and designer gear, and a half-hour stroll around the neighbourhood will garner the whole gamut of consumer style.

Lykavitós Hill

Lykavitós Hill offers tremendous views, particularly from late afternoon onwards – on a clear day you can see the mountains of the Peloponnese. After dark, the shimmering lights of Athens spread right across the Attica basin. To get to the summit you can take the **funicular** (daily 9am–3am; every 30min, more frequent at busy times; €4.50 return) or you can walk. The funicular begins its ascent from Odhós Aristípou, near the top of Ploutárhou. To get here is in itself is something of a climb – though it doesn't look far from Kolonáki square, it's a steep ascent through the stepped residential streets. To do the whole journey the lazy way take bus #060 to the base of the funicular – this starts its journey at the terminus beside the National Archeological Museum and has handy stops on Akadhimías. The principal path up the hill begins from the western end of Aristípou above Platía Dhexamenís, rambling through woods to the top. It's not as long or as hard a walk as it looks – easily done in twenty minutes – though the top half offers little shade.

On the summit, the brilliantly white chapel of **Áyios Yeóryios** dominates – a spectacular place to celebrate the saint's name-day if you're in Athens at the time. Just below it, *Orizontes* (p.168) is a very expensive restaurant with an equally expensive café, both of which enjoy spectacular views. Over to the east a second, slightly lower-peak is dominated by the open-air **Lykavitós Theatre**, which is used mainly for concerts from May to October. There's a road up to the theatre, and if you head down in this direction you emerge in Kolonáki near the lovely little enclave that the British and American archeological schools have created for themselves on Odhós Souidhías.

The Benáki Museum

The often overlooked but fascinating **Benáki Museum** (Mon, Wed, Fri & Sat 9am–5pm, Thurs 9am–midnight, Sun 9am–3pm; €6, temporary exhibitions €3–5; Ⓦwww.benaki.gr; metro Evangelismós), at Koumbári 1/cnr Vassilísis Sofías, should not be missed. Housing a private collection donated to the state in the 1950s by **Antonis Benakis**, a wealthy cotton merchant, its exhibits range from Mycenaean jewellery, Greek costumes and folk artefacts to memorabilia of Byron and the Greek War of Independence, as well as jewellery from the Hélène Stathatos collection.

More than twenty thousand items are exhibited chronologically; ancient finds are on the lower floors and more modern Greek artefacts on the upper floors. Among the most unusual items are collections of early Greek Gospels, liturgical vestments and church ornaments rescued by Greek refugees from Asia Minor in 1922. There are also some dazzling embroideries and body ornaments and unique historical material on the Cretan statesman Eleftherios Venizelos, Asia Minor and the Cretan Revolution. A couple of galleries consist entirely of reconstructed rooms from Ottoman-era homes.

An additional attraction, especially if you've been dodging traffic all day, is the pricey **rooftop café**, with views from the verandah over the nearby

National Gardens. The museum **shop** stocks a fine selection of books on Greek folk art, CDs of regional music and some of the best posters and postcards in the city.

The Goulandhrís Museum of Cycladic Art

The small, private **Goulandhrís Museum of Cycladic Art** (Mon & Wed–Fri 10am–4pm, Sat 10am–3pm; €5; Ⓦ www.cycladic-m.gr; metro Evangelismós), on Neofýtou Dhouká, is a beautifully presented collection that includes objects from the Cycladic civilization (third millennium BC, from the islands of the Cyclades group), pre-Minoan Bronze Age (second millennium BC) and the period from the fall of Mycenae to around 700 BC, plus a selection of Archaic, Classical and Hellenistic pottery.

The **Cycladic** objects are on the first floor – above all, distinctive marble bowls and folded-arm figurines (mostly female) with sloping wedge heads whose style influenced twentieth-century artists like Moore, Picasso and Brancusi. The exact purpose of the effigies is unknown but, given their frequent discovery in grave-barrows, it's possible that they were spirit-world guides for the deceased, substitutes for the sacrifice of servants and attendants, or representations of the Earth Goddess. Their clean, white simplicity is in fact misleading, for they would originally have been painted. Look closely, and you can see that many still bear traces.

Of the ancient Greek art on the upper floors, the highlight is the superb black-figure pottery, especially a collection of painted **Classical-era** bowls, often showing two unrelated scenes on opposite sides – for example one of the star exhibits depicts revellers on one face and three men in cloaks conversing on the other. Others include, on the second floor, a depiction of Hephaistos' return to Olympus, with Hephaistos and Dionysos riding donkeys, and, on the top floor, a lovely *pyxis* with a lid of four horses.

On the ground floor and basement there's a tiny children's area and a good **shop**, as well as a pleasant **café** (with good vegetarian choices) in an internal courtyard. From here a covered walkway connects to the nineteenth-century **Stathatos House**, magnificently restored as an extension for temporary exhibitions.

The Byzantine and Christian Museum

The **Byzantine and Christian Museum** (Tues–Sun 8.30am–3pm; €4; metro Evangelismós), at Vassilísis Sofías 22, was completely refurbished in 2004, and they did a wonderful job. Excellently displayed in a beautiful building, its collection is far more wide-ranging than you might expect fom the name. The setting is a peaceful, courtyarded villa that once belonged to the Duchesse de Plaisance, an extravagantly eccentric French-American philhellene and widow of a Napoleonic general who helped fund the War of Independence.

The exhibits start with art from the very earliest days of Christianity, whose fish and dove motifs can't disguise their extremely close parallels with Classical Greek objects. There are displays on everyday Byzantine life; reconstructions of parts of early churches (mosaic floors and chunks of masonry, some even from the Christian Parthenon); a Coptic section with antique clothing such as leather shoes decorated with gold leaf; and tombs in some of which offerings were left, again a reminder of a pagan heritage. But the highlights are the icons, with the earliest being from the thirteenth and fourteenth centuries. There are dozens of lovely examples, many of them double-sided, some mounted to be carried in procession, and you can follow the development of their style from the simplicity of the earliest icons to the Renaissance-influenced selections from the sixteenth century. Alongside the icons are some fine frescoes, including an entire dome reconstructed inside the museum.

The War Museum

The only "cultural" endowment of the 1967–74 junta, the **War Museum** (Tues–Sat 9am–2pm, Sun 9.30am–2pm; free; metro Evangelismós; limited English labelling), at Vassilísis Sofías 24, becomes predictably militaristic and right-wing as it approaches modern events: the Asia Minor campaign, Greek forces in Korea, and so on. One room devoted to Cyprus, in particular, has a virulently anti-Turkish message that seems extraordinary given current relations between the countries (it is also full of Cypriot antiquities, presumably to demonstrate the island's Greek heritage). However, the bulk of the collection consists of weaponry and uniforms, with a large collection of eighteenth- and nineteenth-century swords and handguns, and a particular concentration on the World War II era. Earlier times are also covered with displays on changing warfare from Mycenae through to the Byzantines and Turks, and an array of models of the acropolises and castles of Greece, both Classical and medieval. Outside are artillery pieces and planes, including a full-scale model of the Daedalus, one of the first-ever military aircraft, which dropped bombs on Turkish positions in December 1912 during the Balkan Wars.

The National Gallery of Art

The **National Gallery and Alexándros Soútsos Museum** (Mon & Wed–Sat 9am–3pm, Sun 10am–2pm; €6.50; metro Evangelismós; at Vassiléos Konstandínou 50, is a bit of a disappointment. Its core collection is of Greek art from the sixteenth century to the present, and of the artists shown here only El Greco is well known outside Greece. One of the few modern painters to stand out is Nikos Hatzikyriakos-Ghikas (Ghika), well represented on the ground floor. On the mezzanine is a small group of canvases by the primitive painter Theophilos (more of whose work can be seen at the Museum of Greek Folk Art in Pláka – see p.127). Perhaps more interesting is the large temporary exhibition space, often hosting major travelling exhibitions; keep an eye out for posters or check in the *Athens News*.

The coast: Pireás to Glyfádha

Athens' coastline is often overlooked by visitors, who are here for their Classical fix and off to the islands for beaches. For Athenians, though, it's an essential summertime safety valve and they head down here in droves: not just for beaches, but for cafés, restaurants, nightlife and shops. Technically, **Pireás** and the "Apollo Coast" around **Glyfádha** are not part of Athens – indeed, Pireás is a proud municipality in its own right. In practice, though, they form part of a single, continuous conurbation, connected by excellent public transport and an unbroken ribbon of development. Thanks to the new tram it's easy to head down to the beach for a quick swim and be back in the centre just a couple of hours later; astonishingly, the water almost everywhere is clean and crystal clear. Pireás, meanwhile, has ferries to the islands, an excellent museum and some of the best seafood in town.

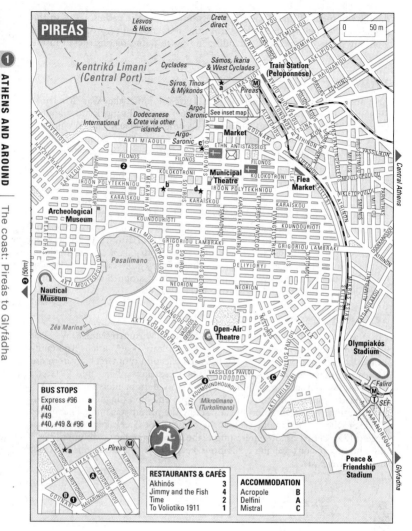

PIREÁS

Lésvos & Híos

Crete direct

Kentrikó Limani (Central Port)

Cyclades

Sámos, Íkaria & West Cyclades

Train Station (Pelopónnese)

Sýros, Tínos & Mýkonos

See inset map

Dodecanese & Crete via other islands

Argo-Saronic

International

Argo-Saronic

Market

ETHN. ANTISTASSEOS

Municipal Theatre

Flea Market

Archeological Museum

Nautical Museum

Zéa Marina

Pasalímano

Open-Air Theatre

Olympiakós Stadium

Faliro

Mikrolímano (Turkolímano)

SEF

BUS STOPS
Express #96   a
#40   b
#49   c
#40, #49 & #96   d

Pireás

RESTAURANTS & CAFÉS
Akhinós	3
Jimmy and the Fish	4
Time	2
To Voliotiko 1911	1

ACCOMMODATION
Acropole	B
Delfini	A
Mistral	C

Peace & Friendship Stadium

Central Athens

Glyfádha

Pireás

PIREÁS (Piraeus) has been the port of Athens since Classical times, when the so-called Long Walls, scattered remnants of which can still be seen, were built to connect it to the city. Today it's a substantial metropolis in its own right. The port, whose **island ferries** (see p.193) are the reason most people come here, has a gritty fascination of its own, typified by the huge Sunday-morning **flea market**, concentrated around Odhós Skylítsi parallel to the rail tracks behind the metro station. It's not really a place to shop – the goods are mostly cheap clothing and pirated CDs, plus a few junky antiques – but it is quite an experience. The real attractions of the place, though, are around the

Pireás transport and practicalities

The easiest way to get to Pireás from Athens is on **metro** line 1; the journey takes about twenty minutes from Omónia. You can also take the **tram** to SEF (the Stádhio Eirínis ké Fílias, or Peace and Friendship Stadium), the interchange with the metro at Néo Fáliro, which is in walking distance of Mikrolímano. Alternatively, there are **buses**: #40 (about every 10min from 5am–midnight; hourly 1–5am) runs to and from Sýndagma, while #49 from Omónia (roughly every 15min from 5am–midnight; hourly 1–5am) will drop you slightly closer to the ferries. Both are very slow, however – allow an hour to be safe. From the **airport**, you can take express bus #E96 (around 1hr 20min). **Taxis** cost about €8 at day tariff from the centre of Athens – worth considering, especially if you're heading over to Zéa Marina or Mikrolímano, which are a fair walk from the metro (although they are served by bus #904 and trolley bus #20 respectively). It can be hard to get a taxi amid the throng disgorging from a ferry.

Hotels and restaurants in Pireás are included with the main Athens listings: if you're simply looking for **food to take on board**, or breakfast, you'll find numerous places around the market area and near the metro station, as well as all along the waterfront. There are plenty of bakeries and *souvláki* joints here, including a handy branch of *Everest* on the corner of Aktí Kalimasióti by the metro.

small-boat harbours of Zéa Marina and Mikrolímano on the opposite side of the small peninsula. Here, the upscale residential areas are alive with attractive waterfront cafés, bars and restaurants and there's an excellent archeological museum.

Some history
The port at Pireás was founded at the beginning of the fifth century BC by **Themistocles**, who realized the potential of its three natural harbours. His

△ Ferry at Pireas

Ferries from Pireás

The tourist office publishes a **schedule of ferry departures** for the current week as well as a price list giving approximate journey times and costs to all the most popular island destinations. Though these are far from complete, they do give a good indication of what boats are leaving, when and for where. If you're staying in the city it's well worth picking one of these up. A similar schedule appears in the weekly *Athens News*.

The majority of the ships – for the Argo-Saronic, Ikaría or Sámos, and the popular Cyclades – leave between 7 and 9am. There is then another burst of activity between noon and 3pm towards the Cyclades and Dodecanese, and a final battery of departures in the evening, bound for a wide variety of ports, but especially night sailings to Crete, the northeast Aegean, the western Cyclades and Dodecanese.

There's no need to **buy tickets** for conventional ferries before you get here, unless you want a berth in a cabin or are taking a car on board; at Greek holiday times (Aug and Easter especially) these can be hard to get and it's worth booking in advance – the big companies all have Internet booking. Flying Dolphin hydrofoil reservations are also a good idea at busy times. In general, though, the best plan is simply to turn up at Pireás early and check with some of the dozens of **shipping agents** around the metro station and along the quayside Platía Karaïskáki. Bear in mind that most of these act only for particular lines, so for a full picture you will need to ask at three or four outlets. Prices for domestic boat journeys vary little, but the quality of the craft and circuitousness of routes can be vastly different. If you are heading for Thíra (Santoríni) or Rhodes, for example, try to get a boat that stops at only three or four islands en route; for Crete settle for direct ferries only.

Boats for different destinations leave from a variety of points around the main harbour, some of them a significant distance away (some of the big ferries have airport-style buses to get you there). The main **departure points** are marked on our map, but always check with the ticket agent as the port is being reorganized, and on any given day a ferry may dock in an unexpected spot. They all display signs showing their destination and departure time; you can't buy tickets on the boat, but there's often a ticket hut on the quayside nearby.

work was consolidated by Pericles with the building of the **Long Walls** to protect the corridor to Athens, and the port remained active under Roman and Macedonian rulers. Subsequently, under Turkish control, the place declined to the extent that there was just one building here, a monastery, by the end of the War of Independence. From the 1830s on, though, Pireás grew by leaps and bounds. The original influx into the port was a group of immigrants from Híos, whose island had been devastated by the Turks; later came populations from Ídhra, Crete and the Peloponnese. By World War I, Pireás had outstripped the island of Sýros as the nation's predominant port, its strategic position enhanced by the opening of the Suez and Corinth canals in 1862 and 1893 respectively. Like Athens itself, the port's great period of expansion began in 1923, with the exchange of populations with Turkey. Over 100,000 Asia Minor Greeks decided to settle in Pireás, doubling the population almost overnight – and giving a boost to a pre-existing semi-underworld culture, whose enduring legacy was rebétika (see p.1123), outcasts' music played in hashish dens along the waterfront.

The Archeological Museum and around

The **Archeological Museum of Pireás** (Tues–Sun 8.30am–3pm; €3), at Hariláou Trikoúpi 31, is an excellent collection, and for Classical enthusiasts merits a special trip. The displays begin upstairs, where one of the star exhibits is a bronze *kouros* (idealized male statue) of Apollo. Dating from 520–530 BC, this is the earliest known life-size bronze, here displayed with two similar but slightly later figures of Artemis and Athena. They were all found in 1959, in a store-room, where they had supposedly been hidden in 86 BC, when the Roman general Sulla besieged Pireás.

Many other items in the museum were dragged from shipwrecks at the bottom of the harbour, including, in the last room on the ground floor, second-century AD stone reliefs of battles between Greeks and Amazons, apparently mass-produced for export to Rome (note the identical pieces). Other highlights include some very ancient musical instruments, and many funeral stelae and statues. One huge grave monument, from Istros on the Black Sea, is more like a miniature temple. Outside in the back yard, a small theatre has been excavated, though this is usually locked.

The route to the museum from the port takes you from one side of the peninsula to the other, over a hill. At the top are Pireás's main shopping and administrative streets, and at the bottom the very different atmosphere of the residential districts. Beyond the museum you can descend to **Zéa Marina** (aka Pasalimáni) to admire some of the monstrous gin palaces moored there. Nearby, on Aktí Themistokléous, the **Naval Museum** (Tues–Fri 9am–2pm, Sat 9am–1.30pm; €3) traces Greece's maritime heritage with models and actual sections of ancient triremes and modern warships. The museum is mainly of interest to specialists and small boys; anyone else might find their time better spent wandering around the harbours. The boats at **Mikrolímano** (known to many locals as Turkolímano) are more modest than those at Zéa, but the harbour itself is prettier, and there are more cafés to sit and enjoy it.

Glyfádha and Vouliagméni

Athens' southern suburbs form an almost unbroken line along the coast all the way from Pireás to Vouliagméni, some 20km away. This coast is Athens' summer playground and the centre of it – for shopping, clubbing, dining or posing on the beach – is **Glyfádha**, a bizarre mix of glitz and suburbia. At weekends, half of Athens seems to decamp down here. The epicentre is around the crescent of Leofóros Angélou Metáxa, lined with shops and malls, with the tram running down the centre and streets of cafés and restaurants heading off on either side. Glyfádha merges almost indistinguishably into its neighbour **Voúla**, and then into quieter, more upmarket **Kavoúri** and **Vouliagméni**. The latter is one of the city's posher suburbs, and its beautiful cove beaches are a traditional hang-out of Athens' rich and famous. Last stop for the local buses is **Várkiza**, more of a seaside resort pure and simple.

If you are prepared to walk a bit, or are driving and happy to battle the locals for parking space, then some of the best beaches can be found around the **Vouliagméni peninsula**, off the main road. Immediately after Voúla B pay beach, a road turns off to Kavoúri, past the *Divani Palace Hotel* and some packed free beaches with excellent tavernas. Further along on this Kavoúri side of the peninsula are some still better, less crowded, free beaches: the #114 bus runs a little way inland, not far from these. Carrying on round, you get to Vouliagméni itself, with beautiful little coves, a few of which remain free, and eventually rejoin the main road by Vouliagméni A beach. Beyond Vouliag-méni the road runs high above the coast en route to Várkiza; the rocky shore a steep climb below, known as **Limanákia**, is largely nudist and has a large gay attendance.

People swim from the rocks or seawall almost anywhere on the coast southeast of Pireás – especially the older generation (the youth tend to head down towards the fleshpots and pay beaches of Glyfádha) – but the closest pleasant beach to the centre is **Edem**, reached by tram to the Edem or Váthis stops. A small patch of sand with cafés and tavernas, this is busy and urban but fine for a quick swim and sunbathe, and remarkably has Blue Flag status. There are other small, free beaches near the Váthis and Flisvós tram stops. Almost all of the really good beaches within easy reach of Athens, however, demand **payment** for entry. For your money you'll get clean sand, lifeguards, somewhere to buy food and drink, a lounger (usually at extra cost) and a variety of other facilities including beach volleyball, massage, fun parks and all sorts of watersports. Some of the fanciest, in Glyfádha and Vouliagméni, charge upwards of €10 per person at weekends (the *Astir Palace* hotel charges an exorbitant €45); more basic places cost €3–5. There are plenty of places to **swim for free**, but this may mean from the rocks, or a long hike from the road. The best sandy beach with free access is at Skhiniás (p.187), but that's a long way out on the northeast Attic coast. On summer weekends, every beach – and the roads to them – will be packed.

Among the better **pay beaches** are Áyios Kósmas (summer daily 9am–8.30pm; €5, children €2), a relatively quiet choice at Ag. Kosmas 2 tram stop; Asteria (summer daily 8am–8pm; €5, €10 weekends, children half-price), a slightly glam and busy choice right in the heart of Glyfádha; Voúla A & B (summer daily 7am–9pm; €4), large twin beaches in Voúla between Glyfádha and Vouliagméni, cheap and cheerful with decent facilities; and Vouliagméni A (summer daily 8am–8pm; €5), on the main road in Vouliagméni, with few facilities but a lovely setting. For beaches further down the coast, see p.184.

As far as Glyfádha the easiest transport option is the **tram**, and at most stops you'll be able to find somewhere to swim. For the better beaches beyond Glyfádha, though, you'll have to transfer to the **bus**. The main routes from central Athens to Glyfádha are the #A2 or #E2 express (which go as far as Voúla), #A3 or #B3, all of which leave from Akadhimías. The #A1 or #E1 or the #X96 airport bus (with fewer stops) run from Pireás all the way along the coast to Voúla. For beaches further out, transfer onto local services #114 (Glyfádha–Kavoúri–Vouliagméni) or #115/6 (Glyfádha–Vouliagméni–Várkiza). If you **drive**, be warned that parking is a nightmare, especially in Glyfádha and Vouliagméni; the pay beaches all have parking, though some charge extra.

Inland suburbs: Kessarianí and Kifissiá

Athens pushes its suburbs higher and wider with each passing year and **Kessarianí**, once well outside the city limits, is now approached through more or less continuous cityscape. The great attraction here is the **monastery**, still remarkably remote in feel, whose Byzantine architecture and mountainside setting offer peace and opportunities for walking. The northern suburb of **Kifissiá**, meanwhile, populated with expensive villas, provides an insight into wealthy Athenian life. Its relaxed combination of upmarket shopping and café society, especially busy on Saturdays, can be combined with a visit to the Goulandhrís Natural History Museum and Gaia Centre.

Kessarianí

East of the centre on the lower slopes of Mount Imittós, **Kessarianí** grew up after the 1922 exchange of populations, thrown together by refugees who'd left everything behind in Turkey. You can still see traces of that early history in some of the ramshackle streets and tiny houses around you, but these days it's a prosperous place, enjoying its fine position high above the central pollution yet only 5km out. There are some excellent tavernas here too.

The real reason to come, though, is **Kessarianí monastery** (Tues–Sun 8.30am–2.30pm; €2.50), some thirty to forty minutes, walk beyond the houses, on a path that follows the main road. Here you're starting to climb the mountain and, despite the proximity of the new Imittós ring road, it is extraordinarily peaceful. The sources of the River Ilissos provide for extensive gardens hereabouts, as they have since ancient times: Athenians still come to collect water from the local fountains, though these days you're strongly advised not to drink it. The monastery buildings date from the eleventh century, though the frescoes in the chapel (a classic, cross-in-square design) are much later – executed during the sixteenth and seventeenth centuries. It's a small place, and doesn't take long to see; don't miss the ram's head spouting spring water at the back of the church. The monastery gardens and the pine-forested slopes are popular **picnic** and **hiking** spots for Athenians. Follow the paths above the monastery and you'll find a number of chapels and ruined buildings, many of them signposted. From the top – follow signs to Lófos Taxiarchoú – there are wonderful **views** across Athens to Pireás and the sea beyond, with the Acropolis in the foreground. To the north are the uniform blocks of Panepistimioúpoli, the university campus.

To get here, take **bus** #223 or #224 from Akadhimías to the terminus by Kessarianí municipal stadium, and then walk straight on for the monastery.

Kifissiá

Set on the leafy lower slopes of Mount Pendéli, about 10km north of the city centre at the end of metro line 1, **Kifissiá** is one of Athens' swishest suburbs. In the nineteenth-century the area began to develop as a bourgeois summer residence, cooler and healthier than the city centre. The original villas – Neoclassical, Swiss or simply vulgar – still hold their own amid the newer concrete models. The metro and downtown pollution helped accelerate development, but Kifissiá is still distinctly "old money", despite the fact that these days it has a thoroughly suburban atmosphere, and the local branches of Gucci and Chanel are housed in upmarket malls.

Still, it's a fascinating place to see how the other half lives, full of pricey cafés and bars where young locals preen themselves and chat on their mobiles. Shopping and drinking aside, the **Goulandhrís Natural History Museum** (Mon–Thurs & Sat 9am–2.30pm, Sun 10am–2.30pm; €3), at Levídhou 13, offers a more cultural excuse to visit. Set in a fine old mansion, the collection has especially good coverage of Greek birds, butterflies and endangered species like the monk seal and loggerhead sea turtle, plus a 250,000-specimen herbarium. Perhaps more interesting, especially for kids, the **Gaia Centre** (same hours; €5), part of the same complex but with its own entrance round the corner at Óthonos 100, offers a mildly interactive trip through the natural cycle of the earth and ecological issues; labelling is in Greek only, but audio guides are available in English. The museum has a café and a shop selling superb illustrated books, postcards, posters and prints.

Eating and drinking

As you'd expect in a city that houses almost half the Greek population, Athens has the best and the most varied **restaurants** and **tavernas** in the country – and many places are sources not just of good food but of a good night out too.

Fast-food and takeaway places are also plentiful – the usual international chains are all here but keep a relatively low profile, and there are plenty of more authentic alternatives. Handy bakeries include *Artokopos*, in the heart of Pláka on Khrisóstomou, just off Kydhathinéon close to the Folk Art Museum, *Ariston* at Voulís 10 near Sýndagma, a traditional zaharoplastío, and three in Koukáki – *Nestoras Tzatsos* at Veïkoú 45, *Khristina* at Veïkoú 75 and *To Paradosiako* at Olymbíou 13. The *Everest* chain, which does a nice line in sandwiches and pastries, is ubiquitous, with convenient branches at Platía Omonías 18, corner Athinás; Tsakálof 14 in Kolonáki; Heyden and 3 Septemvríou, Platía Viktorías (handy for the Archeological Museum) and Makriyiánni and Dhiakoú by metro Akrópoli (for the Acropolis). Many branches stay open late. The *Grigoris* chain serves similar fare and is also reliable.

Restaurants and a few of the better **cafés** are listed below by area. Most tourists never stray beyond the obvious central choices, but while Pláka's hills and narrow lanes can provide a pleasant, romantic evening setting, they also tend to be marred by aggressive touts and general tourist hype. For better value and better food, it's well worth striking out into the ring of **neighbourhoods** around: Mets, Pangráti, Exárhia, Neápoli, Koukáki, Áno Petrálona, Thissío or the more upmarket Kolonáki. None of these is more than a half-hour's walk, or a quick taxi or bus ride, from the centre – effort well repaid by more authentic menus and often a livelier atmosphere. Reservations are rarely necessary in ordinary Greek tavernas – indeed the simpler places probably won't have a reservation system (they can usually squeeze in an extra table if necessary) – but it is worth calling ahead at the fancier places, or if you're planning a special trip across town.

Pláka, Monastiráki and Sýndagma

Pláka has scores of places to eat and most are average at best, and virtually all charge more than similar places in other parts of the city. Many employ touts to lure you to their tables – usually a bad sign. The better places tend to be on the periphery rather than the more travelled squares and stairways, perhaps because there they have to try harder to attract custom. Heading over towards **Monastiráki** things are rather more earthy, with some of the city's best and busiest *souvláki* places around Platía Monastiráki; also here are some quieter cafés around the Cathedral and along pedestrianized Adhrianoú, and a few more adventurous restaurants that reflect the proximity of Psyrrí's nightlife. The area around Sýndagma, meanwhile, has plenty of functional places for office workers and shoppers, plus a few smart restaurants for business lunches or dinners.

Restaurants, tavernas and ouzerís

Aigli Záppio Gardens, on the east side of the Záppio ☎ 210 33 69 300, ⓦ www.aeglizappiou. gr. Pricey, smart restaurant with a fabulous setting, allegedly the haunt of the rich and famous and certainly popular with politicians and diplomats. "Modern Mediterranean" food, which here means Greek with French and Italian influences. A bar, open-air cinema and nightclub are part of the same complex.

Baïraktaris Mitropóleos 88, cnr Platía Monastirakiou ☎ 210 32 13 036. Over a century old, this lively restaurant occupies two buildings whose walls are lined with wine barrels and photos of local celebrities. Some tables are set on the bustling pedestrian street, but for a cosier atmosphere, eat inside with the Greek regulars where there's often some impromptu live traditional music. The straightforward, inexpensive menu includes *souvláki*, *yíros* and oven dishes such as *tsoutsoukákia* (meatballs in tomato sauce), which can be inspected in pots in front of the kitchen.

Brachera Platía Avysinnías 3, Monastiráki ☎ 210 32 17 202. Upmarket, modern Greek and Mediterranean café-bar-restaurant in a restored mansion overlooking the flea market. In summer, the roof garden offers views of the Acropolis. Evenings (from 9pm till the early hours) and Sunday lunch only. Closed Mon.

Café Abysinia Kynétou 7, Platía Avysinnías, Monastiráki ☎210 32 17 047, ⊛www .avissinia.gr. With dining on two floors and a delicious, modern take on traditional Greek cooking (moussaka with spinach, for example, or mussel pilaf), *Café Abysinia* is always busy, popular with a local alternative crowd. More expensive than many, but good value for what you get, and live music most weekday evenings and weekend lunchtimes. Tues–Fri 10.30am–1am, Sat & Sun 10.30am–7pm.

Damingos (Ta Bakaliarakia) Kydhathinéon 41, Pláka ☎210 32 35 084. Open since 1865 and tucked away in the basement, this place has dour service, but the old-fashioned operation and the excellent *bakaliáro skordhaliá* (cod with garlic sauce) for which it is famed (and named) make up for it. Eves only; closed mid-July to end Aug.

Dhioskouri Adhrianoú 37, Monastiráki ☎210 32 53 333. A very popular café-*mezedhopolío* with tables spreading across both sides of the pedestrianized street, some overlooking the metro lines. *Pikilía* – mixed *meze* plates – are good value at €10–15.

Eden Lissíou 12, off Mnisikléous, Pláka ☎210 32 48 858. Vegetarian restaurant in an old mansion with a strangely old-fashioned atmosphere. Seating is indoors only and there have been some complaints of small portions and high prices; the food is good, though, with plenty of things you won't often see in Greece such as mushroom pie, chilli and soya lasagne. Mon & Wed–Sun noon to midnight.

Event Mnisikléous 7, off Adhrianoú, Pláka ☎210 33 15 209. Not at all the typical Pláka establishment, serving pricey modern Greek dishes in a cool designer space.

Fu-Rin-Ka-Zan Apóllonos 2, Sýndagma ☎210 32 29 170. Busy Japanese restaurant – popular at lunchtimes – with sushi, sashimi, yakisoba and the like at reasonable prices. Mon–Sat.

Klimataria Klepsýdhras 5, Pláka ☎210 32 11 215. Over a hundred years old, this unpretentious, pleasant taverna serves simple food – mainly grilled meat and fish. In winter, you're likely to be treated to live music, which inspires singalongs by the mostly Greek clientele. In summer, tables spill onto the vine-shaded alley outside. Evenings only.

Mezedopolio Palio Tetradhio Mnisikléous 26, cnr Thrassívoulou, Pláka ☎210 32 11 903. One of the touristy tavernas with tables set out on the stepped streets beneath the Acropolis. The food is a cut above that of most of its neighbours, though

you pay for the romantic setting. Live music some evenings.

Nefeli Panós 24 Cnr Aretoúsas, Pláka ☎210 32 12 475. Delightful setting on a peaceful side street, outdoors under a secluded grapevine arbour or inside an old mansion with a panoramic view. Serves a small but interesting selection of mid-priced classic Greek dishes such as veal and lamb *stamna* (casserole baked in a clay pot). Live Greek music (and a small dance floor) on Friday, Saturday and Sunday nights. Dinner only but drinks and snacks served during the day.

Palia Taverna tou Psarrá Erekhthéos 16 at Erotókritou, Pláka ☎210 32 18 733. Large, classic Greek taverna around a restored old mansion with plenty of tables outside, on a tree-shaded and bougainvillea-draped pedestrian crossroads. You're best making a meal of the *mezédhes*, which include humble standards as well as seafood and fish concoctions.

Paradosiako Voulís 44a, Pláka ☎210 32 14 121. Small place on a busy street serving unpretentious, reasonably priced, fresh Greek food.

Platanos Dhioyénous 4, Pláka ☎210 32 20 666. A long-established taverna, with outdoor summer seating in a quiet square under the plane tree from which it takes its name. Reasonably priced traditional dishes such as chops and roast lamb with artichokes or spinach and potatoes, and good house wine from vast barrels.

Skholiarhio Tripódhon 14, Pláka ☎210 32 47 605, ⊛www.sholarhio.gr. Attractive split-level taverna, known as *Kouklis* by the Greeks, with a perennially popular summer terrace, sheltered from the street. It has a great selection of *mezédhes* (all €2–4) brought out on long trays so that you can point to the ones that you fancy. Especially good are the flaming sausages, *bouréki* (thin pastry filled with ham and cheese) and grilled aubergine. The house red wine is also palatable and cheap. All-inclusive deals for larger groups at around €10 a head. Daily 11am–2am.

Thanasis Mitropóleos 69, Monastiráki. Rivals *Baïraktaris* for the title of best *souvláki* and *yíros* place in central Athens. Always packed with locals at lunch time. There's no booking so you may have to fight for a table, though there are plenty of them, especially in summer when they practically block the street.

Vyzantino Kydhathinéon 18 on Platía Filomoússou Eterías, Pláka ☎210 32 27 368. Reliable, traditional taverna that still attracts locals on this busy, touristy square. Take a look in the kitchen at the moderately priced daily specials such as stuffed tomatoes or *youvétsi*.

Cafés

Amalthea Tripódhon 16, Pláka. Tasteful if pricey café-patisserie, serving mostly crêpes, as well as non-alcoholic drinks.

Café Kornarou Kornárou 4, Sýndagma. A good place to break your shopping trip for coffee and a sandwich, just off the bustle of the main Ermoú shopping strip. Similar cafés can be found in many of the side streets north of Ermoú.

Café Minoas Platía Mitropóleos cnr Venizélou, Monastiráki. A peaceful café on a pedestrianized square serving sandwiches, salads and ice cream.

Café Pláka Tripódhon 1, Pláka. Touristy but convenient – offers crêpes, sandwiches, ice cream and a roof terrace on which to enjoy them

Dhioskouri Dhioskoúron, cnr Mitröon, Pláka. Popular café right on the edge of Pláka with great views over the ancient Agora. Simple food – salads and omelettes – as well as the inevitable frappés and cappucinos.

Glykis Angélou Yéronda 2, Pláka. A secluded corner under shaded trees just off busy Kydhathinéon in Plaká, with a mouthwatering array of sweets. Frequented by a young Greek crowd.

Oasis West side of the National Gardens, opposite cnr of Amalías and Filellínon, Pláka. An unexpected shady haven just off the main avenue, offering light meals – sandwiches, pizza, pasta – ice cream and drinks.

Oréa Ellás Mitropóleos 59 or Pandhróssou 36, Monastiráki. Tucked away on the upper floor of the Kendro Ellinikis Paradosis store, this consciously old-fashioned *kafenío* offers a welcome escape from the crowded Flea Market. There's also a great view of the rooftops of Pláka on the slope towards the Acropolis. Open 9am–6pm.

To Tristrato Dedhálou 34, cnr Angélou Yéronda, Pláka. Lovely little traditional-style café just off the madness of Platía Filomoússou Eterías: coffee, juices, sandwiches, desserts and cakes.

Ydria Adhrianoú 68 cnr Eólou, Monastiráki. Platía Paliás Agorás, just round the corner from the Roman Forum, is packed with the tables of competing cafés: this is one of the best. A lovely place to sit outside for a quiet coffee or breakfast (they also serve more substantial meals), though, like its neighbours, very expensive.

Yellow Café Karayeóryi Servías 9, corner Voúlis, Sýndagma. Handy for Sýndagma and the local shopping, the Yellow Café serves excellent coffee, sandwiches and salads by day and morphs into a quiet cocktail bar at night.

Psyrrí and the bazaar

The focus of the city's nightlife, **Psyrrí** is home to a throng of ever-changing, fashionable *mezedhopolí* and bars that spread out from the crossroads of Ayíon Anaryíron and Táki. Though relatively recently developed, Psyrrí's influence is already spreading to the surrounding neighbourhoods like **Gázi** (covered in the following section) and the area around the **bazaar**. Here there's a fascinating meeting of the capital's high and low life, as traditional, functional restaurants for market workers and visitors (such as the trio of places within the **meat market**, open, for those with strong stomachs, through the night) rub shoulders with trendy newcomers and the cuisine of Athens' immigrant communities.

Restaurants, tavernas and ouzerís

Gotzila Ríga Palamídhou 5 ☏210 32 21 086. Small sushi bar in this über-trendy little street off Platía Ayíon Anaryíron. Reasonably priced and mostly a late-night joint.

Guru Platía Theátrou 10 ☏210 32 46 350. High-fashion Thai restaurant plus late-night bar/club, whose artistically rusty iron facade is utterly out of keeping with the ugly concrete office blocks round about. Given the setting, the food is surprisingly authentic and not too pricey.

Klimataria Platía Theátrou 2 ☏210 32 16 629. Just west of the central market, the *Klima-taria* serves good, basic taverna fare in ample portions, including some interesting *mezédhes* at reasonable prices. Barrels of wine are just about the only decoration, but there's open courtyard seating in summer and live music at weekends. Mon–Sat eves plus Fri & Sat lunch.

Mandhra Ayíon Anaryíron 8 cnr Táki ☏210 32 13 765. Popular place right at the heart of Psyrrí's restaurant quarter, with live music most evenings and standard taverna fare.

To Monastiri Central meat market (entrance from Eólou). The best of the three restaurants here; the raw ingredients are certainly fresh, and there's *patsás* (tripe and trotter soup) if you're in desperate need of a hangover cure. Daily 24hr.

Nikos & Anna Ayías Théklas 7, Psyrrí ☎210 32 21 119. Excellent fresh seafood, though can be short on atmosphere. The fish, sold by the kilo, is predictably pricey (€70 for lobster spaghetti), but you can eat for far less by sticking to plainer dishes like octopus or seafood pasta. Good wine list.

Pak Indian Menándhrou 13, Platía Theátrou ☎210 321 9412. Handsomely decorated Indian restaurant, somewhat at odds with its grungey surroundings. The food is excellent – fresh and delicately spiced – and there's interesting taped music as well as the occasional live performance.

Palea Skala Lependiótou 25 near Leokoríou ☎210 32 12 677. Reasonably priced ouzerí with seating inside an old house and on a terrace in summer. Excellent *mezédhes* and wine to accompany the acoustic house band; generally packed and lots of fun. Tues–Sun eves only till late.

Stoa tou Vangeli Evripídhou 63, on the edge of Psyrrí near the central bazaar ☎210 32 51 513. Congenial taverna, liveliest at late lunchtime, with an authentic local atmosphere and frequented by workers from the nearby market and offices. The decor includes songbirds in a huge cage and a large butcher block in the corner where your meats are cut to order. The food is simple, inexpensive fare: soups, grills and abundant Greek salads. Mon–Sat market hours (approx 6am–9pm), closed Aug.

Taverna Platía Iróon Platía Iróon 1 ☎210 32 11 915. With tables set out on the square, this is a great place for people-watching; inside, there's often live music in the evening. The food includes excellent *fáva* (hummus-like bean purée) and taverna standards. Tues–Sun.

Taverna tou Psyrri Eskhýlou 12 ☎210 32 14 923. Some of the lowest prices and tastiest food in Psyrrí, so unsurprisingly popular. The menu is an unusual take on Greek classics, and is written in deliberately obscure Greek, so it may be easier to choose from the kitchen. Garden courtyard seating at the back is accessed via an alleyway alongside the next-door restaurant.

Zidhoron Táki 10, ☎210 32 15 368. A typical Psyrrí upscale *mezhedopolío*, painted bright yellow and in a great location offering a vantage point over the goings-on of the area. It serves tasty Middle Eastern-influenced foods like *pastourmás*, *haloúmi* and hummus, as well as Greek favourites such as baked feta, grilled peppers and baked aubergine. Closed Aug.

Cafés

Krinos Eólou 87, behind the central market. Operating since 1922, though thanks to recent refurbishment the only signs of that are the old photos adorning the walls. Still popular for old-fashioned treats like *loukoumádhes* (pastry puffs soaked in honey-citrus syrup and dusted in cinnamon) and *bougátsa* as well as sandwiches and ice creams.

Pagoto Manía Eisópou 21 cnr Táki, Psyrrí. Dozens of flavours of superb ice cream – an eight-year-old's heaven – as well as cakes, coffee and tea.

Omónia and north: Platía Viktorías, Exárhia and Neápoli

Around **Omónia** and heading up towards the National Archeological Museum and the train stations there are plenty of good, functional places to eat, many frequented by office workers, but few that are very interesting – though one exception is a new restaurant serving "ancient Greek" food. In **Exárhia** and neighbouring **Neápoli** there's much more choice. Neither is convenient for the Metro, though you can walk up to Exarhía from the Archeological Museum, so you might consider a taxi. These places are surprisingly untrodden by tourists, considering their proximity to the centre, and the mildly alternative, student atmosphere means plenty of good, inexpensive food.

Restaurants, tavernas and ouzerís

Alexandra Zonára 21, Neápoli, off Leofóros Alexandhrás, Neápoli ☎210 64 20 874. Not a great location, but this modernized mansion has smart decor, a verandah in summer and occasional accordian music. The food is imaginative and not too pricey: aubergine croquettes, beetroot salad with walnuts, and meat in various sauces. Mon–Sat.

Alexandria Metsóvou 13 cnr Rethýmnou, near Archeological Museum ☎210 82 10 004. Middle Eastern food with an Egyptian theme – palms and ceiling fans – and a pleasant courtyard garden. Booking advised. Mon–Sat, eves only; closed Aug.

Ama Lakhi Kallidhromíou 69 or Methónis 66, Exárhia ☎210 38 45 978. A fine old mansion with a huge courtyard where tables are set out in summer: entry to the house from Kallidhromíou, to the courtyard from Methónis. The food is good-value traditional taverna fare.

Arkhaion Yefsis Kodhrátou 22, Metax-ouryío ℡210 52 39 661, ⓦwww.arxaion.gr. The name means "ancient tastes" and this highly original restaurant claims to serve ancient Greek food, based on evidence from contemporary writings. It certainly makes for an enjoyable evening, in a lovely if slightly tacky setting with bare stone walls, statues, flaming torches and a courtyard. Dishes include wild boar cutlets and goat leg with mashed vegetables, cheese, garlic and honey (at €27 for two), as well as plenty of less meaty options.

Andreas Themistokléous 18, Omónia ℡210 38 21 522. Like the *Athinaïkon* (below) a traditional ouzerí that's popular for long weekday lunches. Mon–Sat.

Athinaïkon Themistokléous 2, cnr Panepistimíou, Omónia ℡210 38 38 485. Long-established, old-fashioned ouzerí with a huge variety of good-sized, mid-priced *mezédes*: seafood – such as shrimp croquettes and mussels *saganáki* simmered with cheese and peppers – is a speciality. Mon–Sat; closed Aug.

Barba Yannis Emmanouíl Benáki 94, Exárhia ℡210 33 00 185. Popular neighbourhood treasure with a varied menu of home-style oven food (changes daily and displayed in large pots near entrance) in a relaxed atmosphere, aided and abetted by barrelled wine. Tables outside on pedestrianized street in summer. Very popular with students. Open all day until the small hours.

Exostrefi Lófos Stréfi. Halfway up the Stréfi hill beside a basketball court, *Exostrefi* is most easily approached via the steps opposite the *Orion* hotel, though if you stick to the main paths you'll find it eventually wherever you start. A breezy ouzerí set amidst the pines offering substantial portions of tasty food and a range of ouzo, as well as wine.

Gonia Arahóvis 59, Exárhia. Mushroom *saganáki*, meatballs, spicy sausages and octopus are among the delights at this little ouzerí near Platía Exarhíon.

Ideal Panepistimíou 46, Omónia. A staunch, city-centre establishment favoured by middle-class Greeks – especially at lunchtime – for its clubby, Art Nouveau atmosphere. Swish and slightly old-fashioned – schnitzel and chops – but the mid-priced menu also includes twenty or more fresh daily specials. Mon–Sat.

Kou-Kou Cooked Food Themistokléous 66, Exárhia ℡210 38 31 955. Just off Platía Exarhíon, this inexpensive, modern, café-style place serves traditional dishes like *tsoutsoukákia* (meatballs in tomato sauce) as well as more modern Greek food. Menu in Greek only. Mon–Sat; closed mid-Aug.

Lefka Mavromiháli 121, Neápoli ℡210 36 14 038. Beloved old taverna with great *fáva* (hummus-like bean purée), black-eyed beans and baked and grilled meat with barrelled retsina. Summer seating in a huge garden enclosed by barrels. Mon–Sat.

Lefteris Satovriándhou 20, Omónia ℡210 52 25 676. Hole-in-the-wall *souvláki* place that also serves simple grills – good for a quick lunch.

Mystic Pizza Emmanouíl Benáki 76, Exárhia ℡210 38 39 500. Tiny, unpretentious place serving pasta and salads as well as excellent, inexpensive pizzas. Takeaway and delivery service too.

Pinaleon Mavromiháli 152, Neápoli ℡210 64 40 945. A classic ouzerí-style establishment, serving rich *mezédhes* (choose from tray brought to table) and meaty main courses, washed down with home-made wine, lovingly brewed by the chef/owner from Híos. Advance booking recommended. Open winter only, mid-Oct to early May.

Rozalia Valtetsíou 58, Exárhia ℡210 33 02 933. Ever popular, excellent-value *mezédhes*-plus-grill taverna, with renowned chicken and highly palatable barrelled wine. You order *mezédhes* from the tray as the waiters thread their way through the throng; also a regular menu of grilled fish and meat. Garden opposite in summer.

Steki tis Xanthis Irínis Athinéas 5, Neápoli ℡210 88 20 780. A delightful old mansion at the base of Lófos Stréfi with a roof garden that offers fine views: approach from the hill, or up steep steps from Leofóros Alexandhrás. House specialities from a traditional menu include rabbit stew and schnitzel. Mon–Sat.

Yiandes Valtetsíou 44, Exárhia ℡210 33 01 369. Modern and, for Exárhia, upmarket restaurant serving a range of unusual dishes from cold cuts to stuffed mushrooms and a number of meat and fish recipes from Asia Minor.

Cafés

Crepexarhia Platía Exarhíon, cnr Themistokléous and Ikonómou, Exárhia. Simple crêperie in a busy corner of the square, also serving coffee, sandwiches and ice cream.

Delphi Café Ayíou Konstandínou 27 below the *Delphi Art Hotel*, Omónia. A peaceful escape just a short way from Platía Omonías, with excellent coffee as well as hamburgers, omelettes, salads and sandwiches.

Themis Platía Kótzia, cnr Apollo, opposite the Post Office, Omónia. A truly old-fashioned *kafenío* – an almost forgotten institution in Athens – peopled almost exclusively by old men drinking traditional Greek coffee.

Thissío, Gázi and around

Thissío and Gázi are among the most interesting up-and-coming areas in central Athens. **Thissío**, easily accessible by metro, is the place to head in the early evening. Revitalized by the pedestrianization of Apóstolou Pávlou, where the terraces of competing cafés overlook the Agora and Acropolis, it's a buzzy mix of new cafés/bars and a few long-established restaurants serving this predominantly residential area. **Gázi**, by contrast, gets going later, and the industrial wasteland feel of its streets can be a little intimidating. Though safe enough in practice, you may feel more secure getting to the restaurants and nightclubs here by taxi – at least until the new metro station at Votanikos opens.

Restaurants, tavernas and ouzerís

Dirty Ginger Triptolémou 46, Gázi ☎210 34 23 809. Attracting a young crowd, *Dirty Ginger* is as much bar as restaurant, serving cocktails plus a tasty mixture of Greek and foreign food at moderate prices in a buzzy garden setting. Open every eve and weekend lunchtimes, summer only.

Dirty Str-eat Triptolémou 12, Gázi ☎210 34 74 763. Popular bar-restaurant with a garden courtyard at the back – originally specialized in fish, which is still a good choice, but now has a broader, simpler menu. Mon–Sat, eves only.

Epistrofi stin Ithaki Iraklidhón 56, Thissío ☎210 34 72 964. Tiny, unpretentious place attached to an equally small organic food and craft shop, serving inexpensive organic *mezes*, including plenty of vegetarian choices. Mon–Sat 9am–9pm, Sun 1–9pm.

🏃 **Mamacas** Persefónis 41, Gázi ☎210 34 64 984. One of the restaurants that made Gázi fashionable, and still a favourite with the young, stylish and well-heeled. The white decor spreads through a house and across several terraces. Service can be slow, but the food – traditional Greek, *mezédhes*-style, with a modern twist – is reliably good. It's fairly pricey and, like everywhere here, doesn't get lively till late – some time after midnight, the DJs take over. Booking advised.

🏃 **To Steki tou Ilia** Eptahálkou 5, Thissío ☎210 34 58 052. Simple, inexpensive place on a pedestrianized street above the metro tracks that's so popular the owners have opened a second branch 200m further down (at Thessaloníkis 7). Renowned for some of the finest lamb chops in the city. Tables out on the street in summer.

Stavlos Iraklidhón 10, Thissío ☎210 34 67 206, ⓦ www.stavlos.gr. Originally used as royal stables during the nineteenth century, Stavos is now one of the more popular meeting points in the area. A bar, gallery and club as well as a slightly upmarket restaurant; the food is modern Mediterranean – Italian meets updated Greek. Mon–Thurs eves only, Fri–Sun from midday.

Thalatta Vítonos 5, Gazi ☎210 34 64 204. A lovely, upmarket seafood restaurant (*Thalatta* means "sea" in Ancient Greek), with a marine theme and an internal courtyard in summer, in a thoroughly unprepossessing location. Mon–Sat, evenings only.

Votanikos Kastoriás 34–36, Votanikós ☎210 34 80 000. A big, brasserie-style place in the Athinaïs complex, serving modern Greek food as well as salads and the like.

Zei Artemisíou 4, Keramikós ☎210 34 60 076. Charming old house serving imaginative Anatolian and Greek *mezédhes* in an enclosed courtyard. Live rebétika and laïká music. Wed–Sun.

Cafés

Athinaion Politeia Akamántos 1 cnr Apóstolou Pávlou, Thissío. An enviable position in an old mansion, with great views from the terrace towards the Acropolis, make this a popular meeting place and a great spot to relax over a frappé. Light meals also served.

Kirki Apóstolou Pávlou 31, Thissío. Another café with a fabulous Acropolis view from its outdoor tables, serving good *mezédhes* as well as drinks and ice creams. Popular with the clientele of the late-night gay club (*Lizard*) upstairs.

Áno Petrálona

Áno Petrálona, an old refugee neighbourhood on the west flank of Filopáppou Hill, is the least touristy district of central Athens, despite being a relatively short walk from the buzzing area of Thissío. Why this should be is a mystery: the range of tavernas is excellent, the #15 trolleybus appears regularly, there's a nearby metro station (Petrálona) and it's a natural choice for eating after an evening at the Dora Stratou Theatre. There's a trolley stop on the Platía Amalías Merkoúri, from where Tróon and Dhimifóndos are a short downhill stroll; Petrálona metro station is at the bottom of Odhós Dhríopon, which crosses Tróon and Dhimifóndos. A taxi won't cost much either. The stretch of Odhós Tróon around the Zefyros open-air cinema is particularly lively, and an absolutely authentic Athens neighbourhood experience.

Restaurants, tavernas and ouzerís

T'Askimopapo Iónon 61 ☎210 34 63 282. A wonderful winter-only taverna with *mezédhes* and unusual main dishes like meat in creamy sauces. Occasional live music. Mon–Sat; closed summer.

Chez Lucien Tróon 32 ☎210 34 64 236. Excellent French bistro with a short menu of authentic, well prepared dishes at reasonable prices; you may have to share a table. No booking and very popular, so turn up early or very late. Tues–Sat 8.30pm–1am.

Ikonomou Tróon 41, cnr Kydhantidhón ☎210 34 67 555. Wonderful traditional taverna with home-cooked food served to packed pavement tables in summer. No menu, just a dozen or so inexpensive daily specials: check out what others are eating as the waiters may not know the names of some of the dishes in English. Mon–Sat.

To Koutouki Lakíou 9 (reached from Filopáppou hill, or by a tunnel under the main road) ☎210 34 53 655. Inexpensive traditional taverna with good *fáva* and grilled meat. Pleasantly rural atmosphere despite the proximity of the flyover, with no houses nearby and roof seating overlooking Filopáppou Hill. Mon–Sat.

Ta Sokakia tou Thiakou Gen. Kolokotroni 58, Platía Filopáppou. Large taverna just down the road from Dora Stratou Theatre. Known for its pasta with lobster, lamb chops and mixed salads. Outdoor tables on a small square, friendly management and service and live Greek music on weekends.

Skoufias Tróon 63 ☎210 34 12 210. Winter-only place with hearty, meat-based seasonal dishes – the honeyed roast pork is the house speciality.

Koukáki and Makriyiánni

South of the Acropolis, **Makriyiánni** and **Koukáki** are among the most pleasant parts of the city in which to while away the middle of a day or round off an evening. It's very much middle-class, residential Athens – uneventful and a bit early-to-bed, except for lively pedestrianized Odhós Dhrákou, teeming with bars, cafés and eateries, and to a lesser extent Olymbíou, off the central platía in Koukáki. Makriyiánni is immediately beneath the Acropolis and handy for the metro at Akrópoli, while Koukáki is easily reached by #1 or #5 trolleybus, or from the metro at Syngroú-Fix, which is right by the bottom of Dhrákou.

Restaurants, tavernas and ouzerís

Ambrosia Dhrákou 3–5 ☎210 92 20 281. A friendly *psistaría* packed with neighbourhood residents, especially on summer nights when the tables spill out into the pedestrian walkway. Food is simple but delicious – succulent grilled chicken, pork chops, kebabs and Greek salads – and service friendly and attentive.

Apanemia Erekthíou 2 and Veïkoú ☎210 92 28 766. Basic, inexpensive *mezedhopolío* with a wide selection of authentic *mezédhes* as well as good menu of Greek standards.

Edodi Veïkoú 80 ☎210 92 13 013. Some say this is the finest restaurant in Athens, and if you want to splurge on exquisitely elaborate creations, this is the place to choose. Starters such as lobster-tail with spinach or carpaccio of smoked goose go for €15–20, mains like sea bass with lavender or duck with cherries around €25; fancy desserts too. Before you choose, the waiter will display everything to you, raw. Booking is essential. Mon–Sat; closed all summer.

Evvia Olymbíou 8. Simple place serving hearty food and drink at tables outside on the pedestrian way. Very reasonable and informal, and the best of the cluster of eateries on this street.

Gardhinia Zínni 29. Extremely basic place with inexpensive but tasty casserole food and barrel wine in a cool, cavernous setting. Lunchtime only in summer.

Ikositeroöro Syngroú 42/44. The name means "24 hours", and that's its main virtue. Fair, if rather overpriced, portions of anti-hangover food such as lamb tongues and *patsás* at any time of day or night, in brightly lit, fast-food ambience. At its liveliest after midnight in summer.

Strofi Robérto Gálli 25 ☎ 210 92 14 130. A comfortable, old-fashioned taverna serving classic Greek dishes like *stifado*, lamb with aubergine, or chops. Higher than average prices, but worth it for the roof terrace with great Acropolis views.

Cafés

Diavlos Musiki Spiti Dhrákou 9. Music club by night, but by day a really welcoming café with Greek sweets and snacks.

Dionysos Zonar's Robérto Gálli 43 ☎ 210 92 33 182. Traditional upmarket patisserie relocated to a modern building. The unbeatable position opposite the Herodes Atticus Theatre is somewhat spoilt by being right above the main Acropolis coach park, and by the eye-watering prices. The complex also houses a pricey restaurant.

Leonardo da Vinci Dhimitrakopoúlou 42, cnr Dhrákou. A reliable, all-purpose café; breakfast, frappé, ice cream, light meals, beer and wine. Seating indoors and out.

Pangráti and Mets

Pangráti and **Mets** feature yet more exceptionally fine neighbourhood restaurants – indeed Platía Varnáva in Pangráti may have as many good eating places in a small space as anywhere in Athens, from basic ouzerís to haute cuisine. Taxi is probably the easiest way to get here, but you can also walk across the National Gardens, past the Záppio, to the Panathenaic Stadium and Mets (and from there continue uphill into Pangráti), or trolleybuses #2, #4 and #11 head from the centre to Pangráti.

Ilias Cnr Stasínou and Telesílis, Pangráti. A very good, popular taverna with a standard menu and barrel wine. Tables outside in summer. Eves only.

Kalimarmaron Evforíonos 13 & Eratosthénous, near the Panatheniac Stadium ☎ 210 70 19 727. Old-fashioned, smart taverna with a regularly changing menu featuring unusual old-fashioned dishes including some based on island recipes from Crete and Híos. Tues–Sat.

Karavitis Arktínou 33, cnr Pafsaníou (off Leofóros Vassiléos Konstandínou), Pangráti ☎ 210 75 15 155. Old-style taverna with barrel wine, *mezédhes* and clay-cooked main courses. In summer there's outdoor seating in an enclosed garden. Eves only.

🏃 **Mezedopolio Nota** Platía Varnáva 9, Pangráti, ☎ 210 70 15 169. Small neighbourhood *mezedhopolío*, with tables out on the square in summer and live music most Friday and Saturday evenings. Excellent *meze*, including some unusual varieties, and grilled meats.

Palia Markiza Empedhokléous 26 (off Platía Varnáva), Pangráti ☎ 210 75 22 540. Barn-like place with rustic decor and live music plus tasty, traditional *mezédhes*-type fare. Closed late May to late Sept.

Pinelopi kai Mnistires Ymittoú 130 on Platía Profíti Ilía, Pangráti ☎ 210 75 68 555. Lively and bustling, "Penelope and her Suitors" is a friendly, elegant place with no-nonsense Greek food and regular live music.

Spondi Pýrronos 5, just off Platía Varnáva, Pangráti ☎ 210 75 20 658, ⓦ www.spondi.gr. Long-time contender for the title of Athens' best restaurant, *Spondi* serves superb French-influenced cuisine, with fish a speciality. With starters – crab soup with ravioli scented with coriander, for example – from €25 and mains such as sea bass in fennel, olive oil and vanilla sauce or rabbit Provençal starting at €30 it's not cheap, but for a special occasion it's worth it. Eves only; booking essential.

Vyrinis Arhimídhous 11 (off Platía Plastíra), Pangráti ☎ 210 70 12 153. Classy taverna, recently redecorated in a modern style (prices increased to match, so slightly above average), with its own house wine and a wide variety of interesting *mezédhes*. Tables in a garden courtyard in summer. Mon–Sat.

Kolonáki, Ilísia and Ambelókipi

Kolonáki has a ritzy, upmarket reputation and some swanky eateries, but also boasts some surprising cheaper options. It's also one of the main centres of Athenian café culture. There are cafés everywhere, particularly around Platía

Kolonakíou and the streets leading off it, and among the shops along Skoufá; they tend to be pricey, especially those on the square itself, which attract an older, moneyed crowd. Among the **museums** along Vassilísis Sofías, both the Benáki and the Cycladic Art museum have excellent lunchtime café-restaurants. Following the avenue north leads you through **Ilísia**, a diplomatic quarter with several upmarket eating options, to **Ambelókipi**, where numerous big, new youth-oriented restaurants and clubs have opened up in recent years.

Restaurants, tavernas and ouzerís

Altamira Tsákalof 36A, Kolonáki ☏210 36 14 695. Multi-ethnic menu with Mexican, Indian, Asian and Arabic dishes – on the whole well done, and an interesting change from the usual Greek fare. The setting is lovely too, upstairs in an old mansion.

Craft Leofóros Alexándras 205, Ambelókipi (right by metro Ambelókipi) ☏210 64 62 350. Upstairs restaurant in industrial-style space in a micro-brewery (see p.70), with Tex-Mex and Asian-themed menu, plus good beer, of course.

Dhimokritos Dhimokrítou 23, Kolonáki ☏210 36 13 588. Posh and perhaps a bit snooty – lots of suits at lunchtime – but a beautiful building and well-prepared, reasonably priced food from a vast menu, much of which is displayed in glass counters near the entrance. Mon–Sat; closed late summer.

Filippou Xenokratous 19, Kolonáki ☏210 72 16 390. This old-time taverna, a favourite of local office workers and residents, is liveliest at lunchtime. Fresh food, moderately priced for the area, includes grills, stews and casseroles. Mon–Fri, Sat lunchtime only; closed Sun.

The Food Company Anagnostópoulo 47, Kolonáki ☏210 36 30 373. Wonderful healthy salads and pasta dishes plus daily specials from around the world, from meatballs to won-tons. Small, café-like interior for eating in, or take away and enjoy a picnic on Lykavitós hill.

Ikio Ploútarhou 15, Kolonáki ☏210 72 59 216. The name means "homely", and that seems to be how the locals find it – a very busy, reasonably priced neighbourhood restaurant with a slightly modern take on Greek classics and a short menu of daily specials plus pasta and salads.

Jackson Hall Milióni 4, Kolonáki ☏210 36 16 098. A very Kolonáki type of place; a big, busy, expensive American-themed diner with a music bar upstairs. Burgers, pasta, salads and the like.

To Kioupi Platía Kolonakíou 4, Kolonáki ☏210 36 14 033. Budget subterranean taverna with good, standard Greek fare such as moussaka and stuffed vine leaves. Mon–Sat; closed Aug.

To Kotopoulo Platía Kolonakíou, north side. As the name indicates, this tiny hole-in-the-wall is the place for chicken – juicy, crispy, rotis-serie-stye chicken, the best in Athens. It's strictly no-frills, lit by fluorescent lights and packed with people at all hours. A few tables on the pavement too, or take it away to eat in the nearby National Gardens or on the slopes of Lykavitós. Mon–Sat.

Kriti Ayíou Thomá 18, off Michalakópoulou, Ambelókipi ☏210 77 58 258. Very popular, simple ouzerí serving inexpensive Cretan-style food, often with live music. Tues–Sun.

Orizontes Lycavitou summit of Lykavitós hill ☏210 72 10 701. Fabulous views from this glassed-in eyrie, or from its sheltered terrace. The prices are just as elevated, however, and the complex dishes (sea bass with green tagliatelle and moschato wine sauce with peanuts, for example, at around €30) don't always live up to their promise.

Ouzeri Kleoménous 22, cnr Ploútarhou, just below the funicular, Kolonáki. Nameless, simply furnished and very inexpensive ouzerí with salads and sandwiches as well as good, plain *mezédhes*.

Il Postino Grivéon 3, in alleyway off Skoufá, Kolonáki ☏210 36 41 414. Good-value modern Italian trattoria, serving freshly made pasta and simple Italian dishes in a friendly, bustling room.

Cafés

Filion Skoufá 34, Kolonáki. A local institution for coffee, cakes, omelettes, salads and breakfast: busy at all times of day with a more sober crowd than the average Kolonáki café.

Rosebud People's Café Bar Skoufá 40, Kolonáki. One of a crowd of youth-oriented café-bars around the junction of Omírou: iced coffee by day; chilled sounds and DJs at night.

Da Capo Tsákalof 1, Kolonáki. One of the most popular of the many establishments on this pedes-trianized street, just north of Kolonáki square. Da Capo is very chic but, unusually, self-service.

Pireás, Glyfádha and the coast

Not surprisingly, the big attraction along the coast is fish. The pleasure harbours of **Pireás**, especially, are a favourite Sunday lunchtime destination; over on the port side of town, food is more functional. **Glyfádha** is geared to crowds of shoppers and bar-hoppers, with busy, crowded "fun" restaurants, fast-food outlets and cafés, along the coast thereabouts, though there are plenty of excellent, upmarket psarotavernas.

Restaurants, tavernas and ouzerís

🏃 **Akhinos** Themistokléous 51, Pireás ☏ 210 45 26 944. Wonderful seafood and traditional Greek specialities served on a covered terrace overlooking a small beach just round the corner from the Naval Museum. Pricey if you go for the fish, but less so than harbourfront alternatives. Book at weekends.

Akti Possidhónos 6, Vouliagméni ☏ 210 89 60 448. On the main road just beyond the Vouliagméni peninsula, with waterfront tables and great views, this is a top-class fish taverna. Fish is expensive and so is Vouliagméni; by those standards €50–60 for a fish or lobster main course is reasonable value. Waterfront tables are very heavily in demand; booking essential.

Buffalo Bill's Kýprou 13, Glyfádha ☏ 210 89 43 128. Get into the Glyfádha mood at this lively, atmospheric Tex-Mex joint. As you'd expect, tacos, steaks, chilli, and margaritas by the jugful. Eves only plus Sunday lunchtime.

George's Steak House Konstantinoupóleos 4, Glyfádha ☏ 210 894 6020. Despite the name this is a fairly traditional Greek grill-house, large, reasonably priced and very popular. Located on a side street crowded with restaurants close to the main Platía Katráki tram stop. Excellent lamb chops and meatballs.

🏃 **Island** Limanakia Vouliagménis; km27 on Athens–Soúnio road between Vouliagméni and Várkiza ☏ 210 96 53 563. Beautiful bar/restaurant/ club with a breathtaking clifftop setting which, as the name suggests, evokes island life; very chic and not as expensive as you might expect at €15–25 for a main course. Modern Mediterranean food and tapas lounge. Summer eves only 9.30pm–late (club from 11pm); booking is essential, especially at weekends.

Jimmy and the Fish Aktí Koumoundhoúrou 46, Mikrolímano, Pireás ☏ 210 41 24 417. Excellent, glamorous and inevitably expensive fish taverna occupying the prime position among the harbourside places on Mikrolímano. Booking essential at weekends.

Time Skouzé 14, Pireás ☏ 210 42 85 937. The cosmopolitan nature of Pireás is very much in evidence here: this authentic Indo-Pakistani restaurant caters largely to locals, in the midst of a small ethnic and red-light quarter.

Vincenzo Yiannitsopoúlou 1, Platía Espéridhon, Glyfádha ☏ 210 89 41 310. Good, reasonably priced Italian fare, including excellent pizzas from a wood oven.

To Voliótiko 1911 Goúnari 9, Pireás ☏ 210 42 25 905. Traditional Greek taverna right in the heart of the port area. Gastronomy isn't this area's forte, but this is a good option if you're waiting for a ferry.

Yevsis En Elladhi Marángou 4, Glyfádha ☏ 210 89 44 580. Simple, inexpensive but very good plain Greek food – *souvláki*, stuffed tomatoes and the like.

Cafés

Ego Mio Zissimopoúlo 10, Glyfádha. One of a crowd of glam, upmarket café-bars on this street just off the main shopping drag in the heart of Glyfádha.

Filoxenia Aktí Tsélegi 4, Pireás. Less manic than most around the port, with tables outside on a pedestrianized part of the waterfront just off Platía Karaïskáki, this café serves breakfast and light meals throughout the day.

Pagoto Manía Konstantinoupoléos 5, Glyfádha. As with the Psyrrí branch, wonderful ice cream in a huge variety of flavours, plus all the usual café fare.

Kifissiá and Kessarianí

The northern suburb of **Kifissiá** is a popular excursion with Athenians, for shopping and to meet up afterwards: there are plenty of cafés and restaurants, all of them relatively pricey, catering both to the more traditional locals and the younger visitors. **Kessarianí** is less of a destination, but has a number of excellent, local places to eat.

Restaurants, tavernas and ouzerís

Dos Hermanos, Kyriazí 24, Kifissiá ☎ 210 80 87 906. Decent Mexican food – tacos, burritos, fajitas – and tasty margaritas in a lively, late-leaping bar-restaurant. Tues–Sun.

Masa Ethnikís Andístasis 240, Kessarianí ☎ 210 72 36 177. A straightforward Greek taverna with good simple food and barrel wines. Tues–Sun.

Monippo Dhrosíni 12, Kifissiá ☎ 210 62 31 440. Wide range of *mezédhes* from all over Greece and smart, modern decor make this a typical Kifissiá hangout. Better value than most, though, and often has music on Friday and Saturday nights.

Tesseres Epohes Platía Ayíou Dhimitríou 13, Kifissiá ☎ 210 80 18 233. The "Four Seasons" is an attractive café-*mezedhopolío* where you can enjoy *mezédhes*, drinks, snacks and, on Thursday to Saturday evenings, excellent, unamplified live Greek music.

Trata Platía Anayeníseos 7–9, Kessarianí ☎ 210 72 91 533. Well-known fish restaurant on a square with several tavernas, just off the main Ethnikís Andístasis. Fish is always pricey in Athens, but this is good value. Closed Aug.

Cafés

Várson Kassavéti 5, Kifissiá. Huge old-fashioned café/patisserie that's an Athens institution. Home-made yoghurts, jams and sticky cakes to take away or to enjoy with a coffee in the cavernous interior or in a quiet courtyard out back.

Entertainment, music and nightlife

When it comes to entertainment and nightlife, Athens is a very different place in winter than in summer. Perhaps surprisingly, to see the best live traditional **Greek music** you have to visit during the winter months, as in summer many musicians head off to tour the countryside and islands. This winter period – from around May to October – is also when the major **classical music**, **ballet** and **drama** performances are staged, and the **sporting** calendar is at its busiest. On the other hand, summer is the **festival** season. Most significant is the June-to-September **Hellenic Festival** of dance, music and ancient drama, but there are also annual rock, jazz and blues events, while you may see big international bands at one of the major outdoor venues.

More everyday nightlife in the form of **bars and clubs** shows a similar divide as, in summer, venues move out of the city centre to escape the heat and into temporary homes in the coastal suburbs.

Traditional music

For an introduction to Greek **traditional** and **folk music** see Contexts, p.1121. In Athens, the various styles often coexist or can be heard on alternate evenings

---

Listings information

Sources of information on **what's on** in English are somewhat limited. There are some listings in a number of free monthly or weekly publications distributed to hotels, but these are partial and not always accurate; better are the weekly *Athens News* (published Friday; ⊛www.athensnews.gr), with full movie lisitings and coverage of most major events, or the daily local edition of the *International Herald Tribune*. Much more exhaustive listings including music, clubs, restaurants and bars, but in Greek only, can be found in local weeklies *Athinorama, Exodos* or *Time Out Athens*. All of the above can be bought at kiosks anywhere in the city: look out too for the free weekly *Athens Voice* (again, Greek only), copies of which can be picked up in galleries, record shops and the like. Specialist record shops (see p.181) are also good sources of information in themselves, frequently displaying posters and selling tickets for rock, jazz or festival concerts.

at the same club. Traditionally, these music venues are places where people go to dance, or to celebrate weddings and other occasions. Most gigs start pretty late – there's little point in arriving much before 10.30pm – and continue until 3 or 4am. After midnight (and a few drinks) people tend to loosen up and start dancing; at around 1am there's generally an interval, when patrons may move to other clubs

△ Traditional music, Athens

down the street or across town. Prices tend to be pretty stiff, with expensive drinks (and sometimes food), plus an admission fee or a minimum consumption per set.

Sto Baraki Tou Vassili Dhidhótou 3, Exárhia ☎210 36 23 625; ⓦwww.tobaraki.gr. Daily acoustic performances: a showcase for up-and-coming rebétika acts and popular singer-songwriters. Entry around €15, includes first drink.

Boemissa Solomoú 19, Exárhia ☎210 38 43 836. Rebétika and laïká. Extremely popular with university students, who jam the dance floor and aisles, and inevitably end up writhing on the tabletops as well. Good company of musicians play music from all regions of Greece, but avoid sitting on the second floor where the speakers blast out the music. Drinks €7: two drink minimum; *mezédhes* served. Tues–Sun 11pm–4am, reservations advised. Open all summer.

Diavlos Musiki Spiti Dhrákou 9, Koukáki ☎210 92 39 588. Owned by popular singer Yiannis Glezos, who sometimes appears. Music ranges from rebétika to popular, with well-known singers often on the bill. Cover charge includes one drink. Thursday-night tango lessons are followed by open dancing. Wed–Sun; closed May–Sept.

Elatos Trítis Septemvríou 16, Omónia ☎210 52 34 262. An eclectic assortment of *dhimotiká* in this traditional, downtown basement club. Mon, Tues Thurs–Sun.

Enallax Mavromiháli 139, Neápoli ☎210 64 37 416. Lively, recently refurbished venue which hosts acts of various folk styles. Live gigs mostly Thurs–Sat. No cover charge but reservation needed. Drinks from €8.

Gazi Ierofándos 9 at Pireós, Roúf ☎210 34 74 477. Big *bouzoúkia* club in an up-and-coming

industrial area just down from Gázi – as a result attracts a younger crowd than some.

Laba Víktoros Ougó 22, cnr Akominátou, Metaxouryío ☎210 52 28 188. Big, central rebétika place that can attract big names. Drinks €10.

Pangratiotissa Zinodhótou 2, cnr Ippitoú, Pangráti ☎210 75 19 475. Traditional neighbourhood place with nightly performances of rebétika and laïká: good *mezédhes* to enjoy while you listen.

Perivoli T'Ouranou Lysikrátous 19, Pláka ☎210 32 25 558. Traditional rebétika club on the edge of Pláka (so used to tourists) with regular appearances by classy performer Babis Tsertsos. Mon, Tues & Thurs–Sun.

Rebetiki Istoría Ippokrátous 181, Neápoli ☎210 64 24 937. A lovely old house with traditional rebétika sounds from a good company. Drinks from €6 and some tasty cold and hot plates. Mon, Tues Thurs–Sun; closed July–Aug.

Romeo Kalliróis 4, Koukáki ☎210 92 24 885. Central *bouzoúkia* with a poppy atmosphere.

Stoa Athanaton Sofokléous 19 (in the old meat market) ☎210 32 14 362. Fronted by *bouzoúki* veterans Hondronakos and company. Good taverna food at reasonable prices but expensive drinks. Mon–Sat 3–6pm & midnight–6am; closed May–Aug.

Taximi Isávron 29B, off Hariláou Trikoúpi, Exárhia ☎210 36 39 919. This large, crowded rebétika salon on the third floor of a Neoclassical building seems to have been around for ever. It attracts a crowd of all ages; no cover, but drinks from €7 and pricey *mezédhes* available. Mon–Sat; closed July–Aug.

Jazz, Latin and world music

Jazz has only a small following in Greece, but there are still some good clubs that can attract touring bands of international repute. The major events take place as part of the **Jazz and Blues Festival** at the end of June; information and tickets are available from the Hellenic Festival box office (see p.176) and some record stores. **Latin** and other **world music** styles are also low-profile, but increasing in popularity.

Alabastron Dhamaréos 78, Pangráti, near Platía Profitis Ilías ☎210 75 60 102. Excellent atmosphere and live performances of a wide variety of music, from trad jazz to African and Latin. Closed Summer.

Half-Note Trivonianoú 17, Mets ☎210 92 13 310. Athens' premier jazz club, with live jazz most nights and frequent big-name touring performers. Mon & Wed–Sun; closed for much of the summer.

Palenque Farandáton 41, near Platía Ay. Thomá,

Ambelókipi ☎210 64 87 748, ⓦwww.palenque.gr. Live Latin music by South American groups, salsa parties, flamenco music and dance lessons.

Parafono Asklipíou 130A, Neápoli ☎210 64 46 512 ⓦwww.parafono.gr. Excellent jazz and blues – mainly local groups – in a congenial small, cabaret-style club.

Take Five Patriárkhou Ioakím 37, Kolonáki ☎210 72 40 736. Supper club with live jazz bands. Reservations suggested. Tues–Wed & Fri–Sun.

Rock: live venues and music bars

The indigenous Greek **rock scene** is small but manages to support a number of local bands, while Athenian rock enthusiasts tend to be knowledgeable to the point of obsession. Major international bands generally appear in the summer to play open-air venues, either as part of the official Athens Festival or for other events that rarely seem to survive from year to year. For rock bars, clubs and record shops, Exárhia is the place to be.

An Club Solomoú 13–15, Exárhia ☎210 33 05 056. Basement club featuring live performances by local and lesser-known foreign rock bands.

Gagarin 205 Liossíon 205, near metro Attikís ☎210 85 47 601 ⊛www.gagarin205.gr. Probably the finest venue for live rock in Athens, where some 2000 fans can crowd in to see the best touring indie bands as well as local talent and club nights. In summer, the action moves down to Fáliro, on the coast, and *Gagarin on the Beach*.

Kyttaro Live Club Ipírou 48, near Aharnón, Viktorías ☎210 82 24 134. Features live bands, usually playing solid Seventies-style rock. Thurs–Sun.

Memphis Vendíri 5, Ilísia, behind *Hilton Hotel*. Indie rock bar with cool interior plus garden, and good sound system pumping out rock and dance. Closed Tues–Sat.

Mo Better Kolétti 32, Exárhia. Cramped but fun bar on the first floor of a Neoclassical building. Hip-hop, garage, punk and indie rock with resident DJ.

Revenge of Rock Leofóros Alexandhrás 34, opposite Pedhíon Áreos Park, ☎210 88 30 695. Large club with classic and hard rock sounds and occasional live performances.

Stavros tou Notou Tharípou 37, Néos Kósmos ☎210 92 26 975. One of the liveliest rock clubs in town; live shows mostly feature Greek artists, but plenty of touring foreigners too.

Temple of the King Agathárkhou 5, Psyrrí 210 33 18 311. One of a couple of chilled music clubs in this alley in the heart of Psyrrí; all kinds of sounds but primarily rock.

Bars and clubs

Athens has a huge array of **clubs**, few of which really start to warm up much before midnight, though some operate as quieter bars in the earlier evening. There's every variety of music from trance to hip-hop (though little that's too far from the mainstream), but it pays to expect the unexpected: don't be surprised if the sound shifts to Greek or belly-dancing music towards the end of the night. In the city centre, the most vibrant nightlife is in and around Psyrrí, Gázi and Thissío, though there are clubs almost everywhere. As in any big city, venues come and go quickly, so it's worth asking around – especially at specialist record stores – or checking the listings magazines; look out, too, for posters advertising rave events and the like. Some central Athens air-conditioned clubs remain open year round, but in **summer** the scene really moves out to the long stretch of coast from Fáliro to Várkiza, where huge temporary clubs operate on and around the beaches. If you head out, bear in mind that the taxi fare will be just one of several hefty bills, although admission prices usually include a free drink. With drinks available at any café, and many cafés effectively becoming bars in the evenings, there aren't many simple **bars** as such in Athens. You can have a drink at almost any of the places in these music or club listings, but we've also included a few bars that are simply good places to meet, or to catch a football game on a big screen.

Bars

Bee Miaoúli 6, Psyrrí ☎210 32 12 624. Thanks to a location right by an exit from Monastiráki metro station on the way up to Psyrrí, this cool, modern, moodily lit bar is a popular meeting place; partly, but by no means exclusively, gay. Food is served during the day.

Brettos Kydhathinéon 41 ☎210 32 32 110. By day a liquor store, selling mainly the products of their own family distillery, at night Brettos is one of the few bars in Pláka. It's a small and simple but wonderful-looking place, with giant barrels along one wall and a huge range of bottles, dramatically backlit at night, along another.

Craft Leofóros Alexándhras 205, Ambelókipi (right by metro Ambelókipi) ℡210 64 62 350. Vast, modern microbrewery bar with half a dozen styles of in-house draught beer available in jugs, and giant-screen TVs for entertainment.

Hammam Platía Ayíon Anaryíron, Psyrrí ℡210 32 18 285. Hammam-themed bar with *nargilehs* (hubble-bubble pipes) and floor cushions, as well as tables out on the square. Later on there's ambient music, often with an Eastern tinge.

Mike's Irish Bar Sinópis 6, Ambelókipi ℡210 77 76 797. In the shadow of the Athens Tower, a huge American-style basement bar with a young crowd and big screens for sporting events. Karaoke on Mondays and Tuesdays, live music most weekends.

Wunderbar Themistokléous 80, Platía Exarhíon, Exárhia ℡210 38 18 577. Handy Exárhia meeting place that's open all day – first café, then bar, and finally club with electro and techno-pop sounds.

Clubs

45° Mires Iákhou 18, cnr Voutádhon, Gázi ℡210 34 72 729. A big, lively, rock-music based bar-club with a rooftop terrace in summer.

Astron Táki 3, Psyrrí ℡697 74 69 356. One of Psyrrí's busiest bars – partly perhaps because it's so small – which gets really packed when the guest DJs crank it up later on; electric techno and minimal sounds.

Baila Háritos 43, Kolonáki ℡210 72 33 019. "Freestyle" sounds in this busy Kolonáki club, where an adjoining café-bar (*City*) offers a quieter alternative and outdoor tables.

Balthazar Tsóha 27, Ambelókipi ℡210 64 12 300. Late-night meeting place of more mature, well-heeled clubbers, Balthazar has a wonderfully glamorous setting in an elegant mansion and its garden: restaurant earlier; cocktail bar with restrained sounds later.

Bios Pireós 84, Gázi ℡210 34 25 335. Arty club (set among studios, with frequent exhibitions of its own) with late-night avant-garde sounds. Open as a café by day.

Blaze-T Aristofánous 30, Psyrrí ℡210 32 34 823. Freestyle disco, long-established by Psyrrí standards, with sounds ranging from hip-hop to techno.

Cubanita Karaïskáki 28, Psyrrí ℡210 33 14 605. Enjoyable Cuban-themed bar, with plenty of rum-based drinks, Cuban food and Latin music, occasionally live. Party atmosphere till the early hours.

Envy Paralía Ayíou Kosmá, right by Áyios Kósmas beach ℡210 98 52 994. Huge complex right on the shore with café, restaurant and palm trees to complement the party-atmosphere club. Regular sunset parties, Greek nights and the like make this typical of the slicker summer-only beach clubs.

Island km27 on Athens-Soúnio road between Vouliagméni and Várkiza ℡210 96 53 563. Stunning clifftop setting attracts a chic, stylish crowd. One way to be sure of making it past the queue and the bouncers is to book into the restaurant (see p.169).

Micraasia Konstantinoupóleos 70, Gázi ℡210 34 64 851. Elegant Asian-themed bar with chilled music to match.

Mommy Dhelfón 4A, in an alley off Skoúfa, Kolonáki ℡210 36 19 682. Fashionable watering-hole for thirty-somethings, where soulful house is pumped out by resident DJs.

Soul Evripídhou 65, Psyrrí ℡210 33 10 907. Laid-back, popular upstairs cocktail bar (also serving Thai-influenced food), alternative sounds.

Venue km30 on Athens-Soúnio road, Várkiza ℡210 89 70 333. Lush setting and eclectic selection of dance music, including some Greek, attracts a young crowd.

Vibe Aristofánous 1, Psyrrí ℡210 32 44 794. Freestyle bar with minimal Japanese decor and frequent "happenings", featuring guest DJs playing everything from trance to house.

Gay and lesbian venues

The **gay scene** is mostly very discreet, but Athens has its share of established clubs. Gázi is the hot new area for bars and clubs, and some of the older places have moved down here: the area of Makriyiánni and Koukáki off Syngroú is home to some longer-established alternatives. For further information, check the gay sections in the listings magazines, buy the annual *Greek Gay Guide* (€16 from many kiosks), or check out the excellent website ⓦ www.gaygreece.gr.

Alekos Island Sarrí 41, Psyrrí. Alekos is one of Athens' more colourful bartenders, and his long-established, easy-going bar has recently moved down from Kolonáki to this more lively location near metro Thissío. Low-key atmosphere and rocky/poppy music. Open nightly, year-round.

Blue Train Konstantinoupóleos 84, Gázi ☎210 34 60 677. Open from early evening, this is a popular gay meeting place before going on to the clubs, with a courtyard in summer. Upstairs, *Kazarma* (same phone) is one of the better clubs you could go on to, with dance music, laser shows and giant screens.

Fairy Tale Kolétti 25, Exárhia ☎210 33 01 763 ⓦwww.fairytale.gr. Predominantly lesbian bar with loud Greek music. Also open Sunday afternoon for coffee and cake. Daily 10pm–3am.

Granazi Lembési 20, Makriyiánni ☎21092 13 054 ⓦwww.granazi.gr. Handy for metro Akrópoli, a chilled bar with videos and quiet music early on, getting louder as the night progresses. Mostly Greek music, shows at weekends.

The Guys Lembési 8, Makriyiánni ☎210 92 14 244. Greek and foreign music in a cool lounge with a more mature crowd. Wed–Mon 10pm–3am.

Koukles Zan Moreás 3, just off Syngroú, Koukáki ☎210 92 48 989. The name means "dolls" and the drag acts are said to be the best in Athens. Wed–Sun.

Sodade Triptolémou 10, Gázi ☎210 34 68 657 ⓦwww.sodade.gr. Both lesbian- and gay-friendly, with a stylish crowd and great music – one room plays Greek and mainstream, the other quality dance music. Daily 11pm–3.30am.

Troll Alikarnassoú 7, Kolonós (across the railway lines from Metaxouryío) ☎210 51 58 920. Late-night lesbian club. Daily from 11.30pm.

Theatre, dance and classical music

Unless your Greek is fluent, the contemporary **Greek theatre** scene is likely to be inaccessible. As with Greek music, it is essentially a winter pursuit; in summer, the only theatre tends to be satirical and (to outsiders) totally incomprehensible revues. **Dance** is easier to get to grips with and includes a fine show of traditional Greek dance by the **Dora Stratou Ethnic Dance Company** in their own open-air theatre at Arakínthou and Voutié on Filopáppou Hill (☎210 32 44 395 or 32 46 188; ⓦwww.grdance.org). They combine traditional music, fine choreography and gorgeous costumes for an experience you'd be hard put to encounter in many years' travelling around Greece. Performances are held Tuesday to Saturday at 10.15pm plus Wednesday and Sunday at 8.15pm from late May to late September. To reach the theatre, follow Dhionysíou Areopayítou along the south flank of the Acropolis, until you see the signs. Tickets (€13) can almost always be picked up at the door. Somewhat pricey snacks are on offer.

In the winter months, you may also be able to catch **opera** from the Greek National Opera Lyrikí Skiní, in the Olympia Theatre at Akadhimías 59 and also **classical events** either in the Mégaro Mousikís concert hall on Leofóros Vassilísis Sofías next to the US embassy (metro Mégaro Mousikís), or at the Filippos Nakas Concert Hall, at Ippokrátous 41.

The Hellenic Festival

The annual **Hellenic Festival** encompasses a broad spectrum of cultural events: most famously **ancient Greek theatre** (performed, in modern Greek, at the Herodes Atticus Theatre on the south slope of the Acropolis), but also modern theatre, traditional and contemporary dance, classical music, jazz, traditional Greek music and even a smattering of rock shows. The **Herodes Atticus Theatre** (p.125) is a memorable place to watch a performance on a warm summer's evening – although you should avoid the cheapest seats, unless you bring along a pair of binoculars and a cushion. Other festival venues include the open-air Lykavitós Theatre on **Lykavitós Hill**, and the two ancient theatres at **Epidaurus** (see p.224). For the latter, you can buy inclusive trips from Athens from the festival box office, either by coach or boat – the two-hour boat trip includes dinner on board on the way home.

Performances are scheduled from late May right through to early October, although the exact dates vary each year. If you can, it's worth **booking** in advance

Greek football: Euro 2004 and all that

When the Greek national football side won the **Euro 2004** European championship under German coach Otto Reinhagel, there were delirious celebrations across the country, especially as the victory came in the immediate run-up to the Athens Olympics. Sadly, since that glorious moment of overachievement, the team has reverted to form, failing to qualify for the 2006 World Cup. Nonetheless, Greeks are fanatical about **football**, both their own brand and the big European leagues. They have a particular affinity for the English game and Greek commentaries are sprinkled with English terms like "offside", "foul" and "hat trick".

Most Greeks support one of the big three teams of greater Athens: Panathinaïkós, AEK or Olympiakós. These three dominate the domestic league to such an extent that the last time any other club won it was in 1987–88, a glorious season for little Lárissa. Of late, the Pireás team Olympiakós has been in the ascendancy, winning a record seven consecutive championships from 1996–2003, and again in 2005: Panathinaïkós took the missing year.

Thanks to the Olympics, all three Athenian teams have magnificent new stadia (or at least, two between the three of them), but even so most fans stick to their armchairs or *kafenío* seats throughout the game and, aside from local Derbies and big European games, matches are surprisingly poorly attended. This makes it easy for the casual visitor to gain **admission** on the day and even the big matches are not too difficult to obtain tickets for. With Greek sides currently performing well in the Champions League, the chances of catching a famous English, Italian, Spanish or German side in town remain good, especially in the autumn months. Look out for kiosks in the centre of town selling advance tickets or for details in the press.

The big three also support teams in various **other sports**: basketball, volleyball, even water polo.

The teams: where to watch

Panathinaïkós (founded 1908; colours green and white; ⓦ www.pao.gr) play at the vast Olympic Stadium at Maroúsi in the north of the city, home of the 2004 Olympics. Take the metro to Iríni, and you can't miss it.

AEK (founded 1924; colours yellow and black; ⓦ www.aekfc.gr, Greek only) share the Olympic stadium with Panathinaïkós.

Olympiakós (founded 1925; colours red and white; ⓦ www.olympiacos.org) play at Karaïskáki stadium in Néo Fáliro, on the edge of Pireás. Both Néo Fáliro metro station and SEF tram terminal are directly connected to the stadium by bridge.

Others If you've a liking for the underdog, there are plenty of less famous sides in Athens, at least one of which qualifies for a European competition most years, though they rarely go far. Others currently in the top division are Paniónios in Néa Smýrni, Ioníkós in Níkea, and Egaléo, in the western suburb of Egaléo. A division below you'll find Apóllon in Perissós, Ethnikós (who share Karaïskáki with Olympiakós), and the redoubtable Atrómitos (Intrepid) Athinón out in Peristéri, known for their small but diehard support.

(credit card bookings on ☎ 210 92 82 900 and at ⓦ www.hellenicfestival.gr); tickets go on sale three weeks before the event at the box office, one day later than that for telephone bookings. As well as online, **programmes** are available from tourist offices or from the **festival box office** in the arcade at Panepistimíou 39, downtown (Mon–Fri 8.30am–4pm, Sat 9am–2.30pm). There are also box offices at the Herodes Atticus Theatre (daily 9am–2pm and 6–9pm) and Epidaurus (Mon–Thurs 9am–2pm and 5–8pm, Fri & Sat 9.30am–9.30pm) for events at those venues only.

Film

Athens is a great place to catch a movie. In summer **outdoor** screens seem to spring up in every neighbourhood of the city – literally dozens of them – for a quintessentially Greek film-going experience. There are also plenty of regular indoor cinemas, including a good number in the centre, though a significant proportion of these, with no air-conditioning, close from mid-May to October. There's a good choice of first-run pictures (which usually arrive here before they make it to the UK) and also plenty of art, second-run and cult and alternative choices. **Admission**, whether at indoor or outdoor venues, is reasonable: count on €6–7 for outdoor screenings, €7–8 for first-run fare at a midtown theatre. Films are almost always shown in the original language with Greek **subtitles** (a good way to increase your vocabulary, though remember that the original language may not be English). There are good listings in the *Athens News*, as well as all the Greek listings magazines.

The summer **outdoor screens** tend not to show brand-new films, or at least not mainstream ones, but they do have repeats of recent hits, new art-house and alternative offerings and classics, such as Hitchcock thrillers, as well as festivals featuring prominent European and American directors. To attend simply for the film is to miss much of the point. You may in any case never hear the soundtrack above the din of Greeks cracking *passatémpo* (pumpkin seeds), drinking and chatting (sit near a speaker if you want to hear). Snack-bars serve sandwiches, popcorn, pizza, beer and wine; an intermission gives you a chance to stretch your legs and order refreshments. The first screening is usually at around 9pm early in the summer and 8.30pm later in the summer; at late screenings (usually 11pm), the sound is turned right down, so as not to disturb local residents. Among the most central and reliable **outdoor venues** are Cine Pari, Kydhathinéon 22, Pláka (☎210 32 22 071), a rooftop setting with a side view of the Acropolis; Thission, Apostólou Pávlou 7 in Thissío (☎210 34 70 980), another with an Acropolis view; Psyrrí, Sarrí 40-44, Psyrrí (☎210 32 12 476); Zefyros, Tróon 36 in Áno Petrálona (☎210 34 62 677), newly done up and a particular favourite; and Vox Themistokléous 82, Platía Exarhíon (☎210 33 01 020), and Riviera at Valtetsíou 46 (☎210 38 37 716), both in Exárhia. There are also a few places, such as the Alfavil, Mavromiháli 168, Neápoli (a good alternative venue; ☎210 64 60 521), with roofs that are opened in summer and closed in winter.

Markets and shops

Shopping in Athens is decidedly schizophrenic. On the one hand the **bazaar area** is an extraordinary jumble of little specialist shops and stalls, while almost every neighbourhood still hosts a weekly **street market**. On the other, the upmarket shopping areas of the city centre, and the **malls** and fashion emporia of the ritzier suburbs, are as glossy and expensive as any in Europe. Somewhere between the extremes, in the city centre you'll find endless *stoas*, covered arcades off the main streets full of little shops. Some have been expensively refurbished and house cafés and designer-label stores; most, though, are a little dilapidated, and many still specialize in a single product – books here, computer equipment there, spectacles in another.

Even on a purely visual level, the **central bazaar** and nearby flower market (p.138) are well worth a visit, while the surrounding streets, especially Evripídhou, are full of wonderfully aromatic little shops selling herbs and nuts, and others concentrating on supplies for a peasant way of life that seems entirely at odds with modern Athens – rope, corks, bottles and preserving jars. The so-called **Monastiráki flea market** is, most of the time, no such thing – simply a continuation of the touristy shops you'll find lining Adhrianoú in Pláka. However, between Monastiráki and Thissío metro stations there are a few interesting, alternative stalls, while on Sunday mornings, from around 6am until 2pm, you will find authentic Greek junk (used phone cards and the like) spread out on the pavements, especially along the metro lines towards the Thissío end of Adhrianoú. The **Pireás flea market** – at similar times on Sunday mornings (see p.154) – has fewer tourists and more goods, though in this case mostly cheap clothing and luggage. There are a few interesting antique stores in the streets nearby, though rarely anything in the market itself.

Among the best and most central **street markets** are: Mondays, Hánsen in Patissíon (metro Áyios Eleftheríos); Tuesdays, Lésvou in Kypséli (metro Viktorías) and Láskou in Pangráti (trolley #2 or #11); Fridays Xenokrátous in Kolonáki, Dhragoúmi in Ilísia (metro Evangelismós/Mégaro Mousikís), Tsámi Karatássou in Koukáki (metro Akrópoli) and Arhimídhous in Mets, behind the Panathenaic stadium; and on Saturdays Plakendías in Ambelókipi (metro Ambelókipi) and Kallidhromíou in Exárhia. Usually running from 7am to 2pm, these are inexpensive and enjoyable, selling household items and dry goods, as well as fresh fruit and vegetables, dried herbs and nuts.

Handicrafts, antiques and gifts

Greek **handicrafts** are not particularly cheap but the standard of workmanship is usually very high. In addition to the stores listed below, several **museums** have excellent shops, including the National Archeological Museum, Benáki Museum and Cycladic Art Museum, which sell original designs as well as reproduction artworks. Monastiráki, Pláka and Kolonáki all have their fair share of **antique** and handicraft shops too. For more touristy items Monastiráki and Pláka, especially along Pandhróssou and Adhrianoú, are the places to look: in the alleys between Monastiráki and Thissío metro stations there are some fascinating places. Platía Avyssinías, for example, is packed with little antique and furniture stores as well as jumbled junk and people selling stuff off the back of carts, and there's more quirky shopping in the adjoining section of Ermoú (for furniture especially) and along Karaïskáki (for antiques), heading off towards Psyrrí.

Amorgos Kódhrou 3, Pláka (across from the *Acropolis House Hotel*). A small shop filled with an eclectic collection of tasteful woodcarvings, needlework, lamps, lace, shadow puppets and other handicrafts.

Annita Patrikiadhou Pandhróssou 58, Monastiráki. Short on atmosphere, but genuine antiquities – pottery and coins mainly, some of them made into jewellery – are sold here, with official export licences to guarantee authenticity and legality. Prices are steep, but then many of the items are over 2000 years old.

Dharousos Thoetokis Normánou 7, Monastiráki. Wonderful old posters, maps, advertisements and etchings: if you are looking for something specific it's amazing what they can find among their stock.

Elliniko Spiti Kekropós 14, just off Adhrianoú, Pláka. Amazing artworks and pieces of furniture created from found materials, especially driftwood but also metal and marble. Probably too big to take home (for your wallet as well as your suitcase), but well worth a look.

Kendro Ellinikis Paradosis entrances at Mitropóleos 59 and Pandhróssou 36, Monastiráki. As the name, "Centre of Hellenic Tradition", suggests, this pleasant upstairs emporium has a wide selection of traditional arts and crafts, especially ceramics and woodcarving, with mercifully little of the hard sell often encountered in the nearby flea market.

Paleopoleion Iródhotou 15, Kolonáki. A lovely little shop, specializing in Greek as well as other European antiques.

Pelikanos Adhrianoú 115, Pláka. Tiny shop specializing in copper and brassware, a mix of old pieces as well as new ones that George Pelikanos makes himself.

Studio Kostas Sokaras Adhrianoú 25, Monastiráki. Overlooking the Stoa of Attalos, this place is packed with a wonderful jumble of antiques and curiosities, including old shadow puppets, brass doorknobs, musical instruments, pistols and more.

Vitallis Pandhróssou 75, Monastiráki. Antiquities, icons, old coins, glasswork and jewellery as well

pieces of folk art. All in an environment that makes you feel as if you are discovering them for the first time.

Yiannis Samouelian Iféstou 36, Monastiráki. Long-established musical instrument shop in the heart of the Monastiráki flea market, selling hand-made guitars, *lyra* and the like.

Zoumboulakis Galleries Háritos 26, Kolonáki. Small, pricey antique artefacts and furniture, old and new.

Fashion

Greeks love to shop, for **clothes** above all. On the whole it's familiar international labels you'll find here, in the main shopping area of **Ermoú** below Sýndagma, and in the dozens of malls in the suburbs. For high fashion, however, there's only one place to be, and that's **Kolonáki**, where wandering the narrow streets around the Platía will reward you with dozens of small boutiques. For something a little more alternative, wander over into adjoining **Exárhia**. If you do want to sample the suburban malls, which is probably the most authentic Athens shopping experience of all, then head for **Kifissiá**, where the upmarket residents mean you'll find branches of Chanel and Gucci between the High Street labels, or the younger atmosphere of beachside **Glyfádha**.

Attica Panepistimíou 9, Sýndagma. Athens' only fashion department store, with the finest window displays in the city. Convenient if you want to do everything under one roof, especially in the summer when it's hot, though the designer labels include nothing you wouldn't find at home.

Crop Circle Themistokléous 52 & 66, Exárhia. Reasonably priced vintage clothing and ethnic jewellery. The branch higher up the hill sells new stock, the lower one vintage.

Enny di Monaco Iródhotou 15, Kolonáki. Eccentric selection of designer clothing and shoes: labels include Diane Von Furstenberg, Luella, Roland Mouret and Lacroix. Also check out their stock shop opposite.

Free Shop Háritos 8 and Voukourestíou 50, Kolonáki. Own-label clothes, designed in Athens, including unisex tracksuits and T-shirts. These are sold mainly at the Háritos branch, while the Voukourestíou shop concentrates on international designers like Balenciaga.

Hondos Center Ermoú 39, Sýndagma, and branches throughout Athens. Standard department store, especially good for toiletries of all sorts, from designer perfumes to cotton buds.

Ice Cube Tsakálof 28, Kolonáki. Beautiful designer boutique whose avant-garde designs are a welcome breath of fresh air. Attracts a young but deep-pocketed crowd. Also in Glyfádha.

Lemisios Lykavitoú 6, Kolonáki. Lemisios has been around since 1912. They mainly make leather sandals and ballet flats of a much better quality than the tourist versions on sale in Pláka and Monastiráki. They even do custom-made if you can wait two weeks: take material along with you and they will make shoes up with it.

Lily Panayítsas 3, Kifissiá. Home to Lily's incredibly creative clothes made from gauze – timeless pieces that were celebrated all over Europe in the 1970s. A treasure trove.

Remember Adhrianoú 79, Pláka. Dimitris Tsouanato's shop has been around for 25 years but never seems to run out of inspiration: if there is one piece of clothing you should buy in Athens it's one of his hand-painted T-shirts. Also stocks rock memorabilia and has some amazing sculptures in the courtyard.

Solo Sole Perikléous 37d, off Ermoú, Sýndagma. A small, friendly sunglasses outlet right downtown, with an excellent selection of cut-price designer shades.

Stavros Melissinos/Athena's Sandals Ayías Théklas 2, Psyrrí. Stavros, the "poet sandal-maker", was an Athens institution, numbering The Beatles, Anthony Quinn and Sophia Loren amongst his hundreds of celebrity clients. Evicted prior to the Olympics after over fifty years in the Monastiráki Flea Market, he has relocated to Psyrrí, where his daughter now carries on the tradition.

Le Streghe son Tornate Háritos 9, Kolonáki. One of the few vintage-clothes shops in Athens: mainly designer and top-end clothing, though, so few bargains.

Yes Shop Pindhárou 38, Kolonáki. A great little boutique with clothes by Greek designer Yioryios Eleftheriades, whose designs manage to be original and classic at the same time.

2morrow Kynéttou 3, Monastiráki, in the Flea Market. Yota Kayaba sells her designs on the first floor of the building where she also creates them. A small collection of interesting vintage and ethnic clothes too.

Food and drink

These listings are not so much for food you'll need to survive (there are plenty of mini-markets and fruit stalls in the city centre, and supermarkets further out) as to find presents – **cakes** or sweets are a traditional gift if you're invited into a Greek home – and souvenirs. Also included are a couple of places that sell **health foods** that are otherwise hard to find, especially if you're heading on from Athens to the islands. **Herbs** and herb teas are sold dry and fresh at most street markets and in stalls around the central market.

Aristokratikon Karayeóryi Servías 9, Sýndagma. An old Athenian favourite for traditional Greek chocolates; try the chocolate-covered prunes. Also much-coveted pistachios and sour cherry jam. A token from here is always welcome when visiting someone's home.

Ariston Voulís 10, Sýndagma. Traditional zaharoplastío with the best cheese pies in town.

Bachar Evripídhou 31, central bazaar. Aromatic bags of teas, herbs and medicinal remedies in large sacks.

Biologicos Kyklos Skoufá 52, Kolonáki. A small store that specializes in organic produce and caters for people with food allergies. Supplements, health foods and herbal teas.

Brettos Kydhathinéon 41, Pláka. A liquor store by day, bar by night. Sells mainly traditional products from the family distillery.

Cake Iródhotou 13, Kolonáki. Specializes, surprise, surprise, in cakes. Not traditional, rich, syrupy Greek cakes though, just a great selection of home-baked goodies. The best in town.

Eteria Hatzidhimia Evripídhou 32, central bazaar. Wonderfully old-fashioned liquor store with dozens of types of ouzo, brandies and wines.

Ikologi Elladas Panepistimíou 57, Omónia. A tremendously well-stocked health-food store and vegetarian snack-bar with a pleasant loft where afternoon treats are served.

Lesvos Athinás 33, central bazaar. Very different from the traditional shops around the nearby market, this glossy and somewhat touristy deli sells high-quality wine, honey, preserves and olive oil as well as bread, cheese and deli meats.

Misseyannis Levéndi 7, Kolonáki. Selling freshly ground coffee and all sorts of coffee drinkers' accessories since 1914; also stocks nuts (especially pistachios) and dried fruits. Worth a visit if only for the old-world charm.

Jewellery

There is a long tradition of **jewellery** making in Greece, and Greeks seem to love it almost as much as eating and drinking. High-priced traditional items can be found above all on Voukourestíou, which leads from Sýndagma up to Kolonáki. The shops below represent younger Greek talent plus a couple of classics.

Elena Votsi Xanthoú 7, Kolonáki. An amazing little shop that's home to Elena's internationally acclaimed innovative designs, which incorporate precious and semi-precious stones as well as materials such as shells.

Eleni Marneri Agathoupóleos 3, Kypséli (off 28 Oktovríou, north of metro Viktorías). A beautiful contemporary jewellery shop whose decor reflects the innovative style of the various designers. A great selection and occasional exhibitions.

Fanourakis Patriárkhou Ioakím 23, Kolonáki. High-quality work, in gold especially, that sells around the world. Prices are high, but lower here than when sold internationally. Branches in Sýndagma and Kifissiá.

Lalaounis Panepistimíou 6, Sýndagma. The best-known Greek jewellery designer of all takes its inspiration from ancient pieces. Heavy to wear and heavy on the pocket.

Mariana Petridi Háritos 34, Kolonáki. A showcase for Greek designers with varying styles, as well as work by Mariana Petridi herself.

Books

To Biblio Ippo Tap Panepistimíou 57, Omónia, in the arcade. High-quality outlet for official archeological service publications – including guides to many obscure sites – that also sells first-rate museum reproductions.

Compendium Nikodhímou 5, cnr Iperídhou, Pláka. Long-established English-language bookshop in a corner location: small second-hand section, noticeboards for travellers and residents, and regular poetry readings and other events.

Eleftheroudhakis Panepistimíou 17, Sýndagma. Five floors of books provide space for an extensive stock, and there's plenty in English; there's also an Internet café and an excellent cafeteria with a large selection of vegetarian dishes and sweets.

A smaller branch at Níkis 20, Pláka, is also very well stocked.

Iy Folia tou Vivliou (The Book Nest) Panepistimíou 25, Omónia, occupying a couple of separate units in the recently renovated arcade. Eclectic selection of English-language fiction, with a good collection of recent academic work on Greece, and back issues of the *Korfes* hiking magazine. There's also a good travel shop, with *Rough Guides* and *Anavasi* maps.

Reymondos Voukourestíou 18. Good for foreign periodicals in particular.

Road Editions Ippokrátous 39, Exárhia. A good mix of English and Greek travel guides, plus their own and other companies' maps.

Records and CDs

Outlets for mainstream music in Athens are generally poor, though we've included a couple below. However, if you want to explore Greek sounds there's obviously plenty of choice (see the discographies on p.1132 for help) and there are also a surprising number of places selling classic vinyl as well as tiny specialist stores with a very narrow focus, especially in Exárhia.

7+7 Iféstou 7, Monastiráki. A choice selection of old and new rock and Greek music on vinyl and CD. This alley in the Flea Market has several other record and second-hand bookstores.

Art Nouveau Solomoú 23, Exárhia. Amazing collection of classic vinyl, new and second-hand. Mostly traditional rock – Led Zeppelin, The Mighty Groundhogs, The Grateful Dead – but also 1960s soul and all sorts of other gems.

Capp Stournári 18, Exárhia ⓦwww.capp.gr. Indie label that runs its own bizarre store specializing in independent ambient/electronic sounds plus a selection of independently published books (almost all in Greek).

Metropolis Panepistimíou 64, Omónia. City-centre branch of a Greek chain; strictly mainstream.

Music Wave Iféstou 29, Monastiráki. Another excellent place to rummage in the Flea Market.

Sound Core Themistokléous 48, Exárhia. Dance music of every kind – techno, electronica, industrial, chill-out and more.

Virgin Megastore Stadhíou 7–9, Sýndagma. Not terribly inspired, but does exactly what you'd expect – a wide variety of regulation hits and Greek pop.

Xylouris Panepistimíou 39, Omónia, in the arcade. Run by the widow of the late, great Cretan singer Nikos Xylouris, this is currently one of the best places for finding Greek popular, folk and Cretan music.

Film and outdoor supplies

For more practical goods, Athens is still a city where the old bazaar system applies. If you want to buy a bike, for example, head for 28 Oktovríou (Patissíon), or 3 Septemvríou just south of the Polytekhnío, and you'll find half a dozen outlets. There are several outdoor and camping supply stores in the same area. For anything to do with cameras, look in the arcades around Omónia or, to a lesser extent, Sýndagma.

Fuji Film Photo Express Níkis 18, Sýndagma.
Fast, efficient, helfpul and good-quality development, including slides and digital.
Klaoudatos 28 Oktovríou 52, near the Archeological Museum. Extensive state-of-the-art hiking/
climbing gear – Lowe packs, ice axes, stoves,

water containers, parkas, foam pads – as well as
designer-label surf gear.
Nazca Eólou 89, central bazaar. Five floors of
outdoor gear, from high-fashion T-shirts to ropes
and crampons.

Listings

Airlines Aegean, Óthonos 10 ☏ 210 33 15 515,
reservations ☏ 801 11 20 000; Air France, Vouliagménis 18, Glyfádha ☏ 210 96 01 100; Alitalia,
Vouliagménis 577 ☏ 210 99 88 900; American
Airlines c/o Goldair, Panepistimíou 15 ☏ 210 33 11
045; British Airways, Themistokléous 1, Glyfádha
☏ 210 89 06 666; Delta, Óthonos 4 ☏ 00800 44
12 9506; easyJet, airport only ☏ 210 35 30 300;
Lufthansa, Zirídhi 10, Maroúsi ☏ 210 61 75 200;
Olympic, ticket office at Fillelínon 15 ☏ 210 92 67
500, main office at Syngroú 96 ☏ 210 92 69 111,
reservations ☏ 801 11 44 444; Singapore Airlines,
Xenofóndos 9 ☏ 210 37 28 000; Swiss Airlines, at
the airport ☏ 210 35 37 400; Thai, E. Venizélou 32,
Glyfádha ☏ 210 96 92 012.

Airport enquiries For flight arrivals and departures,
and all other airport information ☏ 210 35 30 000.

Banks and currency exchange Normal banking
hours are Mon–Thurs 8am–2.30pm and Fri 8am–
2pm and just about all banks can do exchange
during those hours; several banks with longer
hours can be found around Sýndagma, plus there
are numerous currency exchange places (generally
with worse rates) in Pláka and around Sýndagma,
and hotels will change money at a worse rate still.
Almost every bank in the centre has an ATM.

Buses For arrival points, see p.103. For information
on buses out of Athens (and the respective terminals),
see "Travel details" at the end of this chapter. There's
excellent city bus information at ⊛ www.oasa.gr.

Car rental The vast majority of downtown car
rental offices are on Leofóros Syngroú, mostly in
the first section close to the Temple of Olympian
Zeus. They include Antena at no. 36–38 ☏ 210
92 24 000, ⊛ www.antena.gr; Avance, no. 40–42
☏ 210 92 40 107; no. 43 ☏ 210 92 48 810; Hertz,
no. 12 ☏ 210 92 20 102; Holiday Autos, no. 8
☏ 210 92 23 088; and Thrifty, no. 25 ☏ 210 92 43
304. Ilios are at Sólonos 138, between Omónia and
Exárhia ☏ 210 38 31 124. The local companies
are generally cheaper; if you turn up in person and
compare prices, you can often haggle a better rate.

Doctors and hospitals For emergencies, see below.
You'll find a list of hospitals, and a few adverts for
English-speaking doctors, in the weekly *Athens*

News, or the US embassy website at ⊛ www
.usembassy.gr has hospital addresses and a long list
of practitioners (look under Consular Services). Most
doctors speak at least some English, and medical
care is generally very good, though nursing and after-
care tend to rely on the help of family. The largest
central hospital is Evangelismós at Ipsilándhou 45,
Kolonáki ☏ 210 72 01 000 (metro Evangelismós).

Embassies and consulates Most major embas-
sies are in Kolonáki or Ambelókipi, on or not far
from Leofóros Vassilísis Sofías. They include:
Australia, Dhimitríou Soútsou 37 ☏ 210 87 04 000,
⊛ www.ausemb.gr (metro Ambelókipi); Canada,
Ioánnou Yennadhíou 4 ☏ 210 72 73 480, ⊛ www
.athens.gc.ca (metro Evangelismós); Ireland,
Vassiléos Konstandínou 7 ☏ 210 72 32 771, in
Pangráti near the Panathenaic Stadium; New
Zealand (consul-general), Kifissiás 76, Maroúsi
☏ 210 69 24 136; South Africa, Kifissiás 60,
Maroúsi ☏ 210 610 6645, ⊛ www.southafrica
.gr; UK, Ploutárhou 1, Kolonáki ☏ 210 72 72 600,
⊛ www.british-embassy.gr (metro Evangelismós);
US, Vassilísis Sofías 91 ☏ 210 72 12 951, ⊛ www
.usembassy.gr (metro Mégaro Mousikís).

Emergencies For immediate police assistance,
dial ☏ 100, or ☏ 112 from a mobile. ☏ 166
summons an ambulance, ☏ 1434 for emergency
hospitals and duty doctors. In a medical emergency, care is free, but don't wait for an ambulance
if you can travel safely – get a taxi straight to the
hospital address that the tourist police give you.
Also see doctors and hospitals, above.

Greek-language courses Reliable schools include
the long-established Athens Centre, Arhimídhous 48,
Mets ☏ 210 70 12 268, ⊛ www.athenscentre
.gr; and the Hellenic American Union, Massalías 22
☏ 210 36 80 900, ⊛ www.hau.gr, though this is
more geared to the needs of Greeks learning English.

Internet cafés Some of the more central and reliable Internet cafés are: Bits & Bytes, Kapnikaréas
19, off Adhrianoú, Pláka; Café 4U, Ippokrátous 44,
Exárhia (24hr); Easy Internet Café, west side of
Platía Syndágmatos above *Everest* (also in Kiffisiá,
again above *Everest*, at Levídhou cnr Kassavéti);
Futura, Víktoros Ougó 15, opposite the Youth Hostel

(cheap; serves breakfast all day; Mon–Sat 24hr); Internet World, 5th floor, Pandhróssou 29, Pláka; Museum Internet Café, 28 Oktovríou 46 by the Archeological Museum; QuickNet, Gladhstónos 4, Omónia (inexpensive and open 24hrs); and Xplorer, just off Platía Katráki, Glyfádha, behind Marks & Spencer. Charges vary from €1.50–4 per hour – the cheapest rates are often at night.

Laundry Most hotels will do laundry but charge a fortune. Locations of laundromats that do service washes include: Angélou Yéronda 10, Pláka (Mon–Sat 8am–7pm, Sun 8am–1pm, €9 per load); National, Apóllonos 17, Pláka (€4.50 per kilo, also offers dry cleaning); and Psárron 9, just off Platía Karaïskáki, Metaxouryío (Mon–Fri 8am–8pm, Sat 8am–5pm, Sun 8am–noon; €10).

Luggage storage Best arranged with your hotel; many places will keep the bulk of your luggage for free or for a nominal amount while you head off to the islands. Pacific Ltd, Níkis 26, Sýndagma ☎210 32 41 007, charges €2 per day for the first week, €1 thereafter for each item. It also has a storage area at the airport.

Motorbike rental Motorent, Robérto Gálli 1, cnr Kavalóti, Makriyiánni ☎210 92 34 939, ⌨www .motorent.gr; and Avance, Syngroú 40–42 ☎210 92 40 107.

Pharmacies There are a number of large general pharmacies (*farmakía*) around Omónia, especially on 28 Oktovríou (Patission) and Panepistimíou; many also sell homeopathic remedies. Bakakos, at Ayíou Konstandínou 3 just off Platía Omonías, is the largest general pharmacy in Athens and stocks just about anything. Standard hours are Mon & Wed 8am–2.30pm, Tues, Thurs & Fri 8am–2pm & 5.30–8.30pm. The weekly *Athens News* has full listings of pharmacies open out-of-hours every day: a list of these is also on display at many pharmacies, or call ☎107.

Phones Phonecard booths are ubiquitous, and calling cards for cheap overseas calls are sold at many kiosks, especially around Omónia.

Police Dial ☎100 for emergency help (☎112 from a mobile) or ☎171 for the Tourist Police; for thefts, problems with hotel overcharging, etc, it's the latter you should contact.

Post offices (*tahydhromía*) For ordinary letters and parcels up to 2kg, the branch on Sýndagma (cnr Mitropóleos) is open Mon–Fri 7.30am–8pm, Sat 7.30am–2pm, Sun 9am–1pm. There are machines selling stamps and phonecards. To send heavier parcels, use the post office at Mitropóleos 60, near the Cathedral (Mon–Fri 7.30am–8pm) or at Koumoundhoúrou 29 by the National Theatre, Omónia. There are also major branches near Omónia at Eólou 100 (the central office for poste restante) and on Platía Kótzia. Queues can be enormous, so be sure you're at the right counter – there are often separate ones (with shorter lines) for stamps and parcels.

Travel agencies There are dozens of travel agencies, including many budget and youth or student-oriented ones, in the streets of Pláka just off Sýndagma, especially on and around Filellínon and Níkis. As well as ferry and plane tickets, many of these will offer island packages or tours of Greece. Among them are Magic Travel, Níkis 33 ☎210 32 37 471, ⌨www.magic.gr; Pacific, Níkis 26 ☎210 32 41 007, ⌨www.pacifictravel.gr; and STA, Voúlis 43 ☎210 32 11 188. Closer to Omónia, try City of Athens, Efpólidhos 2, Platía Kótzia ☎210 32 47 557. Trekking Hellas, Filellínon 7, on the 3rd floor of the arcade ☎210 33 10 323, ⌨www.trekking .gr, arrange particularly adventurous and well-run tours throughout Greece, including trekking, sea kayaking and sailing as well as more regular island-hopping.

Western Union The easiest way to wire money to Athens is with Western Union, as they have an agreement with the Greek Post Office which means you can pick up your money from any branch.

Around Athens: Attica

Attica (Attikí), the region encompassing the capital, is not much explored by tourists – only the great romantic ruin of the **Temple of Poseidon** at Soúnio is well known. The rest, if seen at all, tends to be en route to somewhere else – the airport or the Peloponnese (both unrelentingly ugly motorway drives) or the islands from the ports of **Rafína** or **Lávrio**, a fast and cheap route to many of the Cyclades.

At first sight the neglect is not surprising; the mountains of **Imittós**, **Pendéli** and **Párnitha**, which surround Athens on three sides, are progressively less successful in confining the urban sprawl, and the routes out of the city are unenticing to say the least. Yet a day-trip or two or a brief circuit by car can make a pleasant and rewarding break, with much of Greece to be seen in microcosm within an hour or two of the capital. There's mountainside at **Párnitha**, rewarding archeological sites at **Eleusis** and **Ramnous** as well as Soúnio, and **beaches** almost everywhere you turn, though none remote enough to avoid the Athenian hordes. Combine a couple of these with a meal at one of the scores of seaside *psarotavernas* (fish restaurants), always packed out on summer weekends, and you've got a more than worthwhile day out.

Cape Soúnio and Lávrio

Beyond the beaches at Várkiza (p.158) and beyond the reach of urban transport, the coast road south of Athens rapidly becomes much emptier, the countryside more barren. **Anávissos**, roughly halfway from Várkiza to Soúnio, has a large sandy beach with a gently shelving bottom, very popular with windsurfers, and a row of *psarotavernas* along its more sheltered southern beach. Beyond here the coast starts to get rockier, the road more winding, looking out on small islands offshore, until finally you begin to catch glimpses of the Temple of Poseidon ahead.

Access to this part of southern Attica is straightforward. Orange KTEL Attikis **buses** leave from the terminal on Mavrommatéon at the southwest corner of the Pedhíon Áreos Park. For Soúnio via the coast (€4.60, roughly 2hr) they leave every hour on the half hour from 6.30am to 5.30pm; there's also a more central (but in summer, very full) stop ten minutes later on Filellínon, south of Sýndagma (corner of Xenofóndos). Returns are hourly from 9.30am to 7.30pm, plus a couple of extra early morning departures and a final one at 8pm. On the less attractive but marginally cheaper inland route to Lávrio and Soúnio there are half-hourly departures from 5.45am to 6.45pm, slightly less frequently to Lávrio from then until 10.30pm (only a few of these continue to Soúnio). There are also direct buses to Lávrio from the airport. Drivers can take either route or complete a circuit, but there's little to see in the interior, where the road takes you via the airport and the toll motorway; and unless you're based in the northern suburbs it will probably be slower.

Cape Soúnio

Aktí Souníou – **Cape Soúnio** – on the southern tip of Attica some 70km from the city centre, is one of the most imposing spots in Greece, for centuries a landmark for boats sailing between Pireás and the islands, and an equally dramatic vantage point from which to look out over the Aegean. On its tip stands the fifth-century BC Temple of Poseidon, built in the time of Pericles as part of a major sanctuary to the sea god.

Below the promontory are several **coves** – the most sheltered a five-minute walk east from the car park and site entrance. The main Soúnio beach, a short distance to the north, is more crowded, but has a couple of tavernas at the far end.

The Temple of Poseidon

The **Temple of Poseidon** (Tues–Sun 10am–sunset; €4) owes much of its fame to Lord Byron, who visited in 1810, carved his name on the nearest pillar (an unfortunate and much-copied precedent) and immortalized the place in verse:

Place me on Sunium's marbled steep,
Where nothing, save the waves and I,
May hear our mutual murmurs sweep;
There, swan-like, let me sing and die:
A land of slaves shall ne'er be mine –
Dash down yon cup of Samian wine!

from *Don Juan*

In summer, at least, there is faint hope of silent solitude, unless you slip into the site before the tour groups arrive or after they've left. But the setting is still wonderful – on a clear day, the view takes in the islands of Kéa, Kýthnos and Sérifos to the southeast, Égina and the Peloponnese to the west – and the temple as evocative a ruin as any in Greece. Doric in style, it was probably built by the architect of the Hephaisteion in the Athens Agora. That it is so admired and visited is in part due to its site, but also perhaps to its picturesque state of ruin – preserving, as if by design, sixteen of its original thirty-four columns.

The rest of the site is of more academic interest. There are remains of a fortification wall around the sanctuary; a **propylaion** (entrance hall) and **stoa**; and cuttings for two shipsheds. To the north are the foundations of a small **Temple of Athena**.

Practicalities

Places to stay are few, which means it's wise to book. The *Hotel Aegeon* (☎22920 39200, ⓦwww.aegeon-hotel.com; B&B; ❼), on Soúnio beach itself, had a stunning Olympic makeover that has left it looking brand new, with warm, earthy tones, wood finishes and effective designer touches. There are often deals available, making this place very good value. The *Hotel Saron* (☎22920 39144, ⓦwww.saronhotel.com; ❺), about 4km round the coast road towards Lávrio, is substantially cheaper, with an attractive pool, but its rather basic rooms are not great value. Just beyond is Camping Bacchus (☎22920 39572), a pleasantly old-fashioned site among pine trees, where they have tents or permanent caravans that can be rented (❷).

The better of the **tavernas** on Soúnio beach is the simple *Akroyiali* (☎22920 39107), right down by the water, with seafood at reasonable prices (as ever, the fish is priced by weight). A good alternative is *Syrtaki* (☎22920 39125), on the road towards the *Hotel Saron*, with a more varied taverna menu and, again, seafood at fair prices.

Lávrio

Ten kilometres north of Soúnio, around the cape, is the port of **LÁVRIO**. With upgraded facilities, and fast roads to the new airport (and from there to Athens), Lávrio has been earmarked for major development as an alternative to Pireás. So far, though, there's not a great deal to show for it: just the two or three daily ferries to Kéa and Kýthnos that always ran from here, plus summer services to the Cyclades and twice-weekly to Límnos and Samothráki.

The port's ancient predecessor, Laurion, was famous for its silver mines, worked almost exclusively by slaves, which were a mainstay of the classical Athenian economy (1.6 million kilos were extracted in the fifth century BC). Today, Lávrio remains an industrial and mining town, nowadays for less precious minerals (cadmium and manganese), but there's a busy and attractive cluster of restaurants and cafés around the seafront where the yachts moor – a sizeable yacht-rental fleet is based here and at the nearby marina. The island offshore, **Makrónissos**, now uninhabited, has a sinister past, for it was here that hundreds of ELAS members and other leftists were imprisoned in "re-education" labour camps during and after the civil war.

If you have time to kill, the one-room **Archeological Museum** (Mon & Wed–Sun 10am–3pm), signed just north of the centre, is worth a look. The centrepiece is part of the frieze from the temple at Soúnio, so worn as to be almost impossible to make out, and there's also the mosaic floor of an early church and a fascinating little display on silver mining in the Classical era. If this interests you, there's a map which picks out various mining sites in the hills around that can be visited, though there's rarely much to see when you get there. For **food**, the *Ouzeri-Psarotaverna Karahalios* (☎22920 60841), on the waterfront, serves excellent fish straight from the boats, though it's not cheap.

The east coast

Central Attica has been blighted by the new airport and its associated motorways, and though there are still villages with Byzantine churches and countryside where wine is made, there's little incentive, when heading east, to stop anywhere before you reach the coast. This, as ever, is popular with weekending Athenians and the site of many of their second homes. Almost due east of Athens lies the port of **Rafína**, and to the north of here are **Marathon** and the isolated site of ancient **Ramnous**, as well as some relatively uncrowded beaches. South of Rafína, the coast towards **Pórto Ráfti** is much more developed; the beautiful site of **ancient Brauron** is worth seeking out here.

KTEL **buses** to the east coast again leave from the Mavrommatéon terminal. Main services include those to Rafína every half hour from 6.45am to 5.15pm, and almost as frequently outside those hours from 5.30am to 10.30pm; to Pórto Ráfti and Avláki hourly from 5.45am to 7.45pm; and to Marathon half-hourly from 5.30am to 10.30pm – roughly half of these go via the local beaches. The main route for **drivers** is straight out on Messoyíon (following airport signs) onto the eastbound Leofóros Marathónos, which heads straight for Rafína and Marathon. For destinations further south head via the airport to Markópoulo, and from there to Pórto Ráfti; there are also some attractive, winding routes from the northern suburbs through the mountains towards Marathon (see opposite).

Rafína

The port of **RAFÍNA** has **ferries** and **catamarans** to a wide assortment of the Cyclades, the Dodecanese and the northeast Aegean, as well as to nearby Évvia. Many Athenians have summer homes overlooking the attractive, rocky coast, but the beaches are tricky to reach even with a car, so for visitors the chief attraction, ferries aside, is gastronomic. Overlooking the harbour is a line of excellent **seafood restaurants**, many with roof terraces and a ringside view of the comings and goings at the harbour. They're interspersed with cafés and fishmongers, and the pick of them is *Ta Kavoúria tou Asimáki* (☎22940 24551), the first as you descend towards the harbour from the square. The pedestrianized square above the harbour is also a lively place, ringed with cafés and rather cheaper eating options: particularly good here is the *Ouzeri Limeni*, at Platía

Plastíra 17 (☎22940 24750). A lunchtime outing is an easy operation, given the frequency of the bus service. Evenings, when it's more lively, you need to arrange your own transport back, or stay. There are three very central **hotels**: cheapest and simplest, but still very comfortable, is the *Hotel Corali* (☎22940 22477; **❹**), on the square at Platía Plastíra 11; the *Hotel Akti* (☎22940 29370, **ⓦ**www.aktihotel.gr; **❺**), towards the harbour at Arafinídhon Alon and Vithiniás, has sea views from many of its rooms, along with mini-bars and satellite TV; while the designer-refurbished *Avra* (☎22940 22780, **ⓦ**www.smartotel.gr; **❼**) occupies a prime position on the opposite side of Arafinídhon Alon, perched high above the harbour, with luxury rooms and suites. There's also a beachside **campsite** at nearby Kókkino Limanáki (☎22940 31604; **❷**), where permanent tents and huts are available.

If you want a **swim**, the pleasant little bay of **Blé Limanáki** is just ten minutes' walk north over the headland above the harbour and avoids the pollution of the longer town beach. There is nothing to eat or drink here, though. Alternatively, you can walk the extra fifteen minutes to **Kókkino Limanáki**, which has a good shady beach and some restaurants and shops.

Marathon and around

The site of the **battle of Marathon**, the most famous and arguably most important military victory in Athenian history, is not far from the village of **Marathónas**, 42km from Athens. Here, in 490 BC, a force of 9000 Athenians and 1000 of their Plataian allies defeated a Persian army 25,000 strong. After the victory a runner was sent to Athens to declare the news: having run the first marathon, he delivered his message and dropped dead. Just 192 Athenians died in the battle (compared to some 6,000 Persians), and the burial mound where they were laid, the **Týmfos Marathóna** (Tues–Sun 8.30am–3pm; €3), can still be seen, off the main road between Rafina and Marathónas. It is a quietly impressive monument, though surrounded now by one-way roads installed for the Olympic marathon race, which followed the route of the original marathon, over the hills from here to central Athens. The **Mound of the Plataians**, where the eleven Plataians (including a 10-year-old boy) who died were laid to rest, is about 5km away, near the edge of the mountain; there's also an **archeological museum** (Tues–Sun 8.30am–3pm; €3) here, with a sparse collection of artefacts mainly from the local Cave of Pan, a deity felt to have aided the victory.

MARATHÓNAS village itself is a dull place, though plentifully endowed with cafés and restaurants for the passing trade, and with now-neglected Olympic facilities (the rowing lake was also nearby).

Paralía Marathónas and Skhiniás

The coast around Marathon has some great stretches of sand. **ÁYIOS PANDELÍMONAS**, also known as Paralía Marathónas, is straight on past the burial mound. There's only a small beach here, but a string of waterfront fish tavernas and an open-air movie theatre ensure plenty of local visitors in summer. Of the places to eat, the pick is *Tria Adhelfia* (☎22940 56461), a simple seafood taverna with a stunning waterfront position 300m or so from the village centre – follow the coast road round and you'll see signs. The *Marathon Hotel* (☎22940 55222; **❸**), still with its original 1960s decor, is very basic, but great value if you get one of the rooms with sea views.

There's a far better **beach** to the north at **SKHINIÁS**, a long, pine-backed strand with shallow water, big enough to allow some chance of escaping the crowds. Marathon buses run along the road behind the beach, where there are a number of stops. At the southern end there's a **campsite**, *Camping Ramnous* (☎22940 55855), and a number of cordoned-off pay-beach sections offering cafés, showers, loungers and watersports; the central section of the beach, beyond the Olympic rowing and kayaking centre, is the least developed, with numerous tracks leading through the pines from the road to the sand. At the northern end there's some low-key development, mainly in the form of cafés and scattered **tavernas** on the sand – try *Glaros*. Towards Rafina, the coast around **Néa Mákri** is much more developed.

Límni Marathóna

Heading west from Marathónas, a road climbs into the mountains towards the scenic **Límni Marathóna** – Marathon Lake, 6km away – with its huge marble dam. This provided Athens' entire water supply until the 1950s and is still used as a storage facility for water from the giant Mórnos project in central Greece. A single-track road takes you across the top of the dam: there's an upmarket café-restaurant, *Fragma* (☎210 81 43 415; café daily, restaurant eves & weekends only) on the east side, while on the west there are numerous vantage points as the road switchbacks its way up pine-clothed slopes. Carry on past the lake and you'll wind your way into Athens' northern suburbs, eventually reaching Kifissiá.

Ramnous

Further to the north, the little-visited ruins of **RAMNOUS** (summer daily 7am–5pm; winter Tues–Sun 8.30am–3pm; €2) occupy an isolated, atmospheric site above the sea, with magnificent views across the strait to Évvia. The site was an Athenian lookout point from the earliest times, and remains can be clearly seen continuing way below the fenced site, all the way down to the rocky shore. Within the site, the principal ruin is a Doric **Temple of Nemesis**, goddess of divine retribution. Pausanias records that the invading Persians incurred her wrath by their presumption in bringing with them a giant marble block upon which they intended to commemorate their victory. They met their nemesis, however, at the battle of Marathon, and the Athenians used the marble to create a statue instead. There are also the remains of a smaller temple dedicated to Themis, goddess of justice, and a section of ancient road.

Ramnous is not realistically accessible by public transport, though you might get a lift for the final few kilometres if you take a bus to **AYÍA MARÍNA** and hitch from the junction, some 5km from the site. There are frequent buses to Ayía Marína, largely because from here eight ferries a day – more at weekends – make the short crossing to Néa Stýra on Évvia. There's a snack-bar on the quay, a rocky beach to swim from, and the attractive *Taverna Panorama* overlooking it all from the hillside.

From Rafína to Pórto Ráfti

South of Rafína, the coast is largely unattractive, with continuous development all the way down through **Loútsa** (aka Artemis) to **Vravróna**. A local bus plies up and down the coast road here, as far as the site of Brauron (see opposite). There are plenty of free beaches should you find yourself in the area, and hundreds of restaurants and cafés, but planes from the new airport constantly take off overhead and there's no particular reason to visit, nor anywhere much to stay since development is mainly apartments for weekenders.

There's a brief break in development before **PÓRTO RÁFTI**, whose bay, protected by islets, forms an almost perfect natural harbour. On the small island in the harbour is a large Roman statue of a woman whose now missing arm held the "first fruits" of crops that were sent each year to the sacred island of Delos. During the sixteenth century the statue was thought to hold scissors, and the port came to be known as the tailor's port, Pórto Ráfti. More intrinsically attractive than much that has gone before, Pórto Ráfti is no less developed; there are plenty of waterfront restaurants, and in summer a thriving nightlife scene. There are, however, very few **places to stay**: the *Kiani Akti*, Ayías Marínas 40 (☎22990 86400, ℉22990 86050; ❹), is a smart, modern hotel on the road to Avláki. Some of the best **restaurants** are in the port section of town (many of the signs read Limín Mesoyía), a pretty little harbour with leisure boats; the better beaches are on the whole to the south, towards Avláki (often signed Luláki) – this road ends at a popular pay beach (€5 at weekends).

Vravróna

On the hill between the village of Vravróna and Pórto Ráfti lies ancient **Vravróna**, or Brauron (site closed for restoration at time of writing). The attractive remains here, centred on a vast *stoa*, are of a **Sanctuary of Artemis**, goddess of hunting and childbirth, and protector of new-born children. Vravróna was the chief site of the Artemis cult, which staged an important festival every four years. This featured a procession from Athens and other rites, now shrouded in mystery, in which young girls dressed as bears to enact a ritual connected with the goddess and childbirth. The **Stoa of the Bears**, where these initiates stayed, has been substantially reconstructed, along with a stone bridge; both are fifth century BC. Somewhat scantier are the ruins of the temple itself, whose stepped foundations can be made out; immediately adjacent, the sacred spring still wells up, squirming with tadpoles in spring. Nearby, steps lead up to a chapel that contains some damaged frescoes.

The site overlooks a marshy bay, which comes alive early in the morning and late at night with birdsong and the croaking of frogs. The site **museum** (Tues–Sun 8.30am–3pm; €3) lies down here, not far as the crow flies but a good 2km by road (towards Pórto Ráfti, then left). It's a charming little collection, well labelled in English, with finds from the sanctuary as well as nearby sites such as the Necropolis of Myrrhinos (Merenda), a burial ground used from the ninth century BC through to Roman times. Highlights include marble heads of children (some with bear masks), red-figure pottery, bronze mirrors and some lovely marble reliefs of children coming to make sacrifices.

Local **bus** #340 stops right outside the site (look for the Club Med, directly opposite) and terminates just beyond, so from Athens the simple approach is to get to Loútsa and then change to this service. Drivers could detour along the dead-end coast road beyond Vravróna to the south; there are rocky coves to which you can clamber down all along this road, and a café-bar, *Hamolia*, with a great view of Évvia and the island-studded sea.

Mount Párnitha and Phyle

Mount Párnitha is an unexpectedly vast and virgin tract of forest, rock and ravine, just an hour-and-a-half's bus ride from the centre of Athens. It will give you a taste of what Greek mountains are all about, including a good selection of mountain flowers. The trip is especially worthwhile in March or April, when snow lies surprisingly late on the north side and, in its wake, carpets of crocus, alpine squills and mountain windflowers spring from the mossy ground, while lower down you'll find aubretia, tulips, dwarf iris and a whole range of orchids. The Olympic mountain-biking events were held on Mount Párnitha, and the Olympic Village was built up against the eastern side of the mountain.

Much of Párnitha is now protected in a National Park, and there are numerous **waymarked paths** (look for red discs and multicoloured paint splodges on the trees). The easiest access and some of the best walking is off the circular drive that starts by the chapel of Ayía Triádha: a map showing local landmarks (labelled in Greek), superimposed on a topographical map, is posted just behind the church. There's also a bus stop here and a few seasonal cafés and restaurants. Among the most attractive destinations are the **Skípiza spring** (around two hours), the **Cave of Pan**, an evocative spot for lovers of Classical ghosts which Menander used as the setting for one of his plays, and the slightly more challenging approach to the **Báfi refuge**.

Over to the west of the main Párnitha trails, another route up the mountain will take you to the ruined but still impressive fourth-century BC Athenian fort of **Phyle**, about an hour and three-quarters on foot beyond the village of Fylí (known locally as Hasiá). It's signposted for the first part of the trip; the fort is 300m to the left after the marked side road leading up towards the Párnitha National Park. On the way up to the fort you pass the unattractively restored fourteenth-century monastery of Klistón, situated at the mouth of the Goúra ravine that splits through the middle of the Párnitha range. The walking, unfortunately, is all on asphalt. Fylí itself is a popular culinary outing for Athenians of the northern suburbs and is equipped with a disproportionate number of rustic family-style tavernas and restaurants.

Practicalities

Mount Párnitha is approached through the northern suburb of Ahárnes, which can be reached on the motorway, or from central Athens via Liossíon and Dhimokratías. This route is followed twice a day (6.30am and 2.30pm, more often on Sunday) by **bus** #714, which departs from Platía Váthis, near Omónia, and winds all the way up the mountain-top casino and Ayía Triádha. For Fylí, bus #A12 leaves Platía Váthis every half-hour or so throughout the day, daily. The casino is also the terminus of the **funicular** (9am–7pm, €3; currently being extended all the way down to Ahárnes from its base halfway up the mountain); this is a pleasant ride and avoids a winding and sometimes scary drive, but the **casino** is not the most attractive place from which to start your walks. Operating day and night, it's always packed and smoky – if you want to play on the thousands of slot machines or the blackjack tables, you'll need a passport or driver's licence to register. The entry fee depends on time of day; weekdays during the day it's free. The casino also operates free buses from the centre of town, leaving the Hilton Hotel at 2.30pm (return departs at 10pm, by which time presumably your wallet should be empty) and from Platía Lavríou, just off Omónia, at 6.15pm (returning 1.15am). At the Báfi refuge the warden normally provides **board and lodging**, particularly on weekends, but it would be wise to check in advance with the Aharnés EOS (☎210 24 69 777) or the Alpine Club of Athens (☎210 32 12 355); there are also restaurants and bars at the casino. In Fylí, one of the better places to eat is *Farangi* (☎210 24 11 475), a hearty grill on the main street.

Eleusis and west to the Peloponnese

The coastal highway from Athens **towards Kórinthos** (Corinth) follows the ancient Ierá Odhós – the Sacred Way – as far as Elefsína, ancient Eleusis. There's nothing sacred about it these days, though: this is as ugly a road as any in Greece, traversing a grotesque industrial wasteland. For the first thirty or so kilometres you have little sense of leaving Athens, whose western suburbs merge into Elefsína and then Mégara. Offshore, almost closing off the bay, is **Salamína** (ancient Salamis), not a dream island in anyone's book but a nicer escape than it looks, and accessible by ferries from the mainland here at Lákki Kaloyírou (and at Pérama, near Pireás).

If the Peloponnese is your destination, there are only a couple of places you might break your journey on the way: at **ancient Eleusis** or the **monastery of Dhafní**. The latter, a beautiful example of Byzantine architecture at its best, is decorated with mosaics that are considered among the artistic masterpieces of the Middle Ages. Unfortunately, it was damaged by earthquake in 1999 and has missed several deadlines to reopen since, so check with the tourist office before visiting; it is easily accessible, right next to the main road or on the route of the #A16 bus (see Eleusis). **Drivers** should note that the Athens–Kórinthos non-toll road is notoriously dangerous, switching from four-lane highway to a rutted two-laner without warning; the toll for the motorway is well worth paying. The Attikí Odhós motorway from the airport joins this road just outside Elefsína.

Eleusis

The **Sanctuary of Demeter** at **Eleusis** (Tues–Sun 8.30am–3pm; €3) was one of the most important in the ancient Greek world. For two millennia, the ritual ceremonies known as the Mysteries (see box) were performed here. Today, the extensive **ruins** of the sanctuary occupy a low hill on the coast right in the heart of modern Elefsína's industrial blight. The site offers something of an

△ Temple, Eleusis

escape from its surroundings: from outside the museum, at one of the highest points, the gulf and its rusty shipping even manage to look attractive.

The best plan on arrival is to head straight for the **museum**, which features models of the sanctuary at various stages in its history: Eleusis is impressively large, with huge walls and gates, some of which date back to Mycenaean times, but the numerous eras of building can also be confusing, especially as signage is poor and mainly in Greek. As well as the models and maps, the museum has some excellent finds from the site, especially Roman statuary (though also some much older objects). Exploring outside, the most important structure of ancient Eleusis was the **Telesterion**. This windowless Hall of Initiation lay at the heart of the cult, and it was here that the priests of Demeter would exhibit the **Sacred Objects** and speak "the Unutterable Words".

Practicalities

The main road out of Athens towards Eleusis is the busy Leofóros Athinón, though it's also possible to follow the Ierá Odhós (Sacred Way) from the centre of town, which may have less traffic and certainly seems more appropriate. To get there by **bus**, take #A16, #B16 or express #E16 from Platía Eleftherías (aka Platía Koumoundhoúrou), on Pireós. Between them they run several times an hour every day; the #E16 doesn't stop at Dhafní. In Elefsína the buses head straight down the main street, Ierá Odhós: get off where you see the sign, and the sanctuary is a short walk down towards the sea. This is also the route to drive, ignoring confusing signs on the outskirts of Elefsína. There are plenty of small cafés and places to eat in Elefsína, including a good, nameless café almost directly opposite the site entrance.

The Mysteries of Eleusis

The ancient **Mysteries** had an effect on their initiates that was easily the equal of any modern cult. According to Pindar, who experienced the rites in Classical times and, like all others, was bound on pain of death not to reveal their content, anyone who has "seen the holy things [at Eleusis] and goes in death beneath the earth is happy, for he knows life's end and he knows the new divine beginning."

Established in Mycenaean times, perhaps as early as 1500 BC, the cult centred around the figure of **Demeter**, the goddess of corn, and the myth of her daughter Persephone's annual descent into and resurrection from the underworld, which came to symbolize the rebirth of the crops and the miracle of fertility. By the fifth century BC the cult had developed into a sophisticated annual festival, attracting up to 30,000 people every autumn from all over the Greek world. The ceremonies lasted nine days: the **Sacred Objects** (identity unknown, but probably sheaves of fungus-infected grain, or vessels containing the magic potion) were taken to Athens, where they were stored in the Ancient Agora for four days. Various rituals took place in the city, many on the Acropolis but also mass bathing and purification in the sea at Fáliro. Finally a vast procession brought the objects back, following the Sacred Way to the sanctuary at Eleusis. Here over the final days initiates took part in the final rituals of *legomena* (things said), *dhromena* (things done) and *dheiknumena* (things shown). One theory suggests that these rituals involved drinking a potion containing grain-ergot fungus, producing similar effects to those of modern **psychedelic drugs**. The Mysteries survived well into the Christian era, but eventually fell victim to the new orthodoxy.

Demeter is said to have threatened to render the land permanently barren if her worship at Eleusis ever ceased. Looking at the ecological havoc wreaked by the area's industry, it would seem that the curse has been fulfilled.

On from Elefsína

Northwest from Elefsína, the **old road to Thebes and Delphi** heads into the hills. This route is described in Chapter Three (p.332), and is highly worthwhile, with its detours to **ancient Aegosthena** and the tiny resort of **Pórto Yermenó**. At Mégara another, more minor, road heads north to reach the sea at the village of Alepohóri, where it continues as a good road past Psátha Pórto Yermenó.

Heading directly west, on towards the Peloponnese, there are shingle beaches – more or less clear of pollution – along the old coastal road at Kinéta and Áyii Theódhori. This highway, with the Yeránia mountains to the north and those of the Peloponnese across the water, has a small place in pre-Homeric myth, as the route where Theseus slew the bandit Skiron and threw him off the cliffs to be eaten by a giant sea turtle. Thus, Skiron met the same fate as the generations of travellers he had preyed upon.

You leave Attica at Isthmía, a village beside the **Corinth Canal** (see p.207), where buses tend to break the journey for a drink at the café by the bridge. To the north of the canal, Loutráki and Perahóra are technically part of Attica but, as they are more easily reached from Kórinthos, are covered in the Peloponnese chapter.

Travel details

Trains

For details of stations see p.103. Journey times are approximate.

Stathmós Peloponníssou to: Árgos (5 daily; 3hr); Kalamáta (3 daily; 6hr); Kórinthos (13 daily, 5 of which intercity; 1hr 50min); Náfplio (2 daily; 3hrs 30 min); Pátra (8 daily; 4hr); Pýrgos (7 daily; 6hr 50min).

Stathmós Laríssis to: Alexandhroúpoli (5 daily, 3 of which intercity; 14hr/10hr); Halkídha (19 daily; 1hr 30min); Livadhiá (11 daily, 3 intercity; 1hr 30min); Thessaloníki via Lárissa (11 daily, 6 intercity; 5/7hr, intercity 4/5hr); Vólos (1 direct daily; 5hr).

Buses

For details of termini see p.103. Journey times are approximate.

Mavrommatéon terminal Buses for most destinations in Attica including: Lávrio (half hourly 5.45am–6.45pm, less frequent until 10.30pm; 1hr 30min); Marathon (every 30min; 1hr 20min); Pórto Ráfti (hourly; 1hr 30min); Rafína (every 30min; 1hr); Soúnio via the coast (hourly on the half-hour; 2hr) or inland route (see Lávrio; 1hr 45min).

Kifissoú 100 Destinations in Peloponnese and western/northern Greece include: Árgos (hourly; 2hr); Árta (8 daily; 5hr 30min); Corfu (3 daily; 8hr 30min); Igoumenítsa (4 daily; 7hr 30min); Ioánnina (9 daily;

6hr 30min); Kalamáta (8 daily; 4hr 30min); Kefallonía (3–4 daily; 8hr); Kórinthos (every 30min; 1hr 15min); Lefkádha (4 daily; 5hr 30min); Mycenae/Náfplio (hourly; 2hr 30min); Olympia (2 daily; 5hr 30min); Pátra (every 30min; 3hr); Pýlos (2 daily; 5hr 30min); Pýrgos (9 daily; 5hr); Spárti (11 daily; 3hr 30min); Thessaloníki (12 daily; 6hr 30min); Trípoli (16 daily; 2hr 30min); Zákynthos (4 daily; 6hr).

Liossíon 260 Buses for most other destinations in central Greece including: Áyios Konstandínos (hourly; 2hr); Delphi (6–8 daily; 3hr); Halkídha (every 30min; 1hr); Karpeníssi (3 daily; 4hr 30min); Kými, for Skýros ferries (2–4 daily; 3hr 30min); Ósios Loukás (8 daily; 2hr 30min); Thiva/Thebes (hourly; 1hr 30min); Tríkala (8 daily; 4hr 30min); Vólos (10–12 daily; 4hr 30min).

Island ferries, catamarans and hydrofoils

See also Moving On (p.106) and the relevant island chapters.

Pireás Ferries and hydrofoils to the Argo-Saronic, Crete, the Cyclades, Dodecanese and northeast Aegean islands. Port authority ☏ 210 42 26 000; hydrofoils ☏ 210 41 99 200.

Lávrio Ferries daily to Kéa, Kýthnos and many of the Cycladic islands, twice or more a week to Tínos, Híos, Lésvos, Límnos, Áyios Efstrátios and Samothráki. Port authority ☏ 22940 22300.

Rafína Ferries and hydrofoils daily to Évvia as well as Ándhros, Tínos, Páros, Mýkonos, Ikaría and Sámos; most days also to Náxos and Amorgós. Port authority ☎22920 25249.

Domestic flights

Eleftheríos Venizélos airport (p.102) Olympic (⊛ www.olympicairlines.com) and Aegean (⊛ www .aegeanair.com) operate daily flights in summer to the following domestic destinations.

Alexandhroúpoli, Astypálea, Haniá (Crete), Híos, Ikaría, Iráklion (Crete), Ioánnina, Kalamáta, Kárpathos, Kastoriá, Kavála, Kefalloniá, Kérkyra (Corfu), Kós, Kozáni, Kýthira, Léros, Límnos, Mílos, Mýkonos, Mytilíni (Lésvos), Náxos, Páros, Préveza, Ródhos (Rhodes), Sámos, Sitía (Crete), Skiáthos, Skýros, Sýros, Thessaloníki, Thíra (Santoríni) and Zákynthos.

The Peloponnese

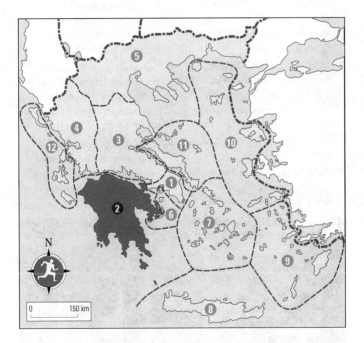

CHAPTER 2 # Highlights

✳ Acrocorinth A huge, barren rock arising from and dominating the plains of Kórinthos, crowned by a great medieval fortress. See p.205

✳ Mycenae Agamemnon's legendary palace and possible site of his murder upon his return from the Trojan War. See p.211

✳ Náfplio Genteel and cultured (if slightly faded) nineteenth-century elegance, it makes a picturesque and lively base from which to explore the Argolid. See p.217

✳ Monemvasiá The Byzantines' impregnable rock and stronghold now offers both a stylishly rejuvenated island of traffic-free relaxation, and insights into its historic past. See p.236

✳ Paleohóra, Kýthira The ruined medieval island capital; a fortified town, hidden between ravines. See p.245

✳ Máni Towers Anachronistic medieval architecture; high-rise internecine warfare in the deep south. See pp.258–260

✳ Mystra A visually stunning medieval city that once had a population of 20,000; a superb collection of frescoed Byzantine churches remains. See p.268

✳ Loúsios Gorge Green and luxuriant gorge with extraordinary monasteries clinging to the cliffs. See pp.282–283

✳ Olympia It's worth braving the crowds to see 1400 years of the Olympic Games laid bare along the green valley of the Alfiós. See p.303

✳ Vouraïkós Gorge Greece's most remarkable and scenic railway line, winding through the northern mountains. See p.319

△ The palaestra at Olympia

The Peloponnese

The appeal of the Peloponnese (Pelopónnisos in Greek) is hard to over-state. This southern peninsula, technically an island since the cutting of the Corinth Canal, seems to have the best of almost everything Greek. Its ancient sites include the Homeric palaces of Agamemnon at **Mycenae** and of Nestor at **Pýlos**, the best preserved of all Greek theatres at **Epidaurus**, and the lush sanctuary of **Olympia**, host for a millennium to the Olympic Games. The medieval remains are scarcely less rich, with the fabulous Venetian, Frankish and Turkish castles of **Náfplio**, **Methóni** and **Kórinthos**; the strange battle towers and frescoed churches of the **Máni**; and the extraordinarily well preserved Byzantine shells of **Mystra** and **Monemvasiá**.

Beyond this incredible profusion of cultural monuments, the Peloponnese is also a superb place to relax and wander. Its **beaches**, especially along the west coast, are among the finest and least developed in the country, and the **landscape** inland is superb – dominated by range after range of forested mountains, and cut by some of the lushest valleys and gorges to be imagined. Not for nothing did its heartland province of **Arcadia** give its name to the concept of a classical rural idyll.

The Peloponnese is at its most enjoyable and intriguing when you venture off the beaten track: to the old hill towns of Arcadia like **Karítena**, **Stemnítsa** and **Dhimitsána**; the Maniot tower villages such as **Kítta** or **Váthia**; at **Voïdhokiliá** and **Elafónissos** beaches in the south; or the trip along the astonishing **rack-and-pinion railway** leading inland from the north coast at **Dhiakoftó** to **Kalávryta**.

Anciently known as the **Moreas**, from the resemblance of the outline to the leaf of a mulberry tree (*mouriá*), rounded at the top, with three long fingers below (from west to east, Messinía, the Máni and Maléas), plus the thumb of the Argolid, it will amply repay any amount of time that you devote to it. The **Argolid**, the area richest in ancient history, is just a couple of hours from Athens, and if pushed you could complete a circuit of the main sights here – **Corinth**, **Mycenae** and **Epidaurus** – in a couple of days, making your base by the sea in Náfplio. Given a week, you could take in the two large sites of Mystra and Olympia at a more leisurely pace. To get to grips with all this, however, plus the wonderful southern peninsulas of the Máni and Messinía, and the hill towns of Arcadia, you'll need at least a couple of weeks.

If you were planning on a combination of Peloponnese-plus-islands, the **Argo-Saronic** or **Ionian islands** are the most convenient, although you would be better off limiting yourself to the mainland on a short trip. The Argo-Saronic islands (see p.581) are linked by hydrofoil with the Argolid and Pireás. Of the Ionian islands, isolated **Kýthira** is covered in this chapter since closest

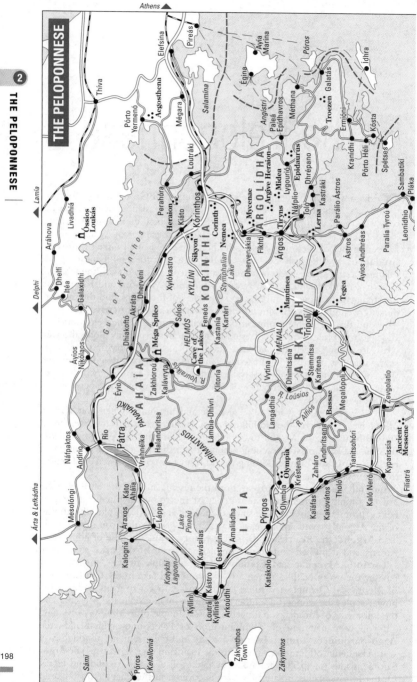

THE PELOPONNESE

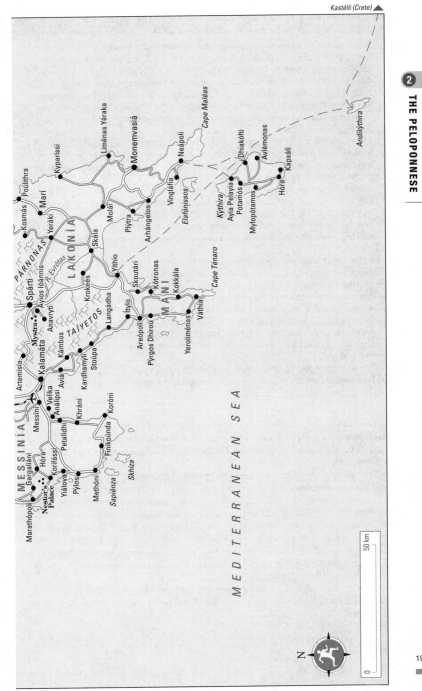

Andikýthira

Cape Maléas

Liménas Yéraka
Kyparíssi
Monemvasiá
Neápoli
Vingláfia
Elafónissos
Arhángelos
Pírtra
Molái
Skála
Yeráki
Marí
Kosmás
Poúlithra

Dhiakófti
Avlémonas
Kapsáli
Hóra
Mylopótamos
Potamós
Ayía Pelayía
Kýthira

PÁRNONAS
LAKONÍA
R. Evrótas
Spárti
Ayíos Ioánnis
Anavrytí
Mystrá
Kámbos
TAÏYETOS
Artemisía
Messíni
Gargaliáni
Hóra
Korifássi
Nestor's Palace
Yiálova
Pýlos
Methóni
Sapiénza
Skhíza
Finikoúnda
Koróni
Khráni
Petalídhi
Análipsi
Avía
Velíka
Kardhamýli
Stoúpa
Langádha
Kámbos

MESSINÍA
Marathópoli

Krokeés
Ýthio
Skoutári
Kótronas
Kokkála
Areópoli
Pýrgos Dhiroú
Yeroliménas
Váthia
Cape Ténaro
MÁNI
Ítylo

MEDITERRANEAN SEA

N

50 km
0

199

The **ancient history** of the Peloponnese is very much that of the Greek mainstream. During the **Mycenaean period** (around 2000–1100 BC), the peninsula hosted the semi-legendary kingdoms of Agamemnon at Mycenae, Nestor at Pýlos and Menelaus at Sparta. In the **Dorian** and **Classical** eras, the region's principal city-state was Sparta, which, with its allies, brought down Athens in the ruinous Peloponnesian War. Under **Roman** rule, Corinth was the capital of the southern Greek province. For more on all these periods, see "A History of Greece" on p.1059, and the individual accounts in this chapter.

From the decline of the Roman Empire, to the Ottoman conquest, the Peloponnese pursued a more complex and individual course. A succession of occupations and conquests, with attendant outposts and castles, left an extraordinary legacy of medieval remains throughout the region.

The Peloponnese retained a nominally Roman civilization, well after the colonial rule had dissipated, with Corinth at the fore until the city was destroyed by two major earthquakes in the fourth and sixth centuries. Around this time, too, came attacks from barbarian tribes of Avars and Slavs, who were to pose sporadic problems for the new rulers, the **Byzantines**, the eastern emperors of the now divided Roman Empire.

The Byzantines established their courts, castles and towns from the ninth century onward; their control, however, was only partial, as large swathes of the Moreás fell under the control of the Franks and Venetians. The **Venetians** settled along the coast, founding trading ports at Monemvasiá, Pýlos and Koróni, which endured, for the most part, into the fifteenth century. The **Franks**, led by the Champlitte and Villehardouin clans, arrived in 1204, bloodied and eager from the sacking of Constantinople in the piratical Fourth Crusade. They swiftly conquered large tracts of the peninsula, and divided it into feudal baronies under a prince of the Moreas.

Towards the middle of the thirteenth century, there was a remarkable **Byzantine revival**, which spread from the court at Mystra to reassert control over the

access is from the southern Peloponnese ports, but **Zákynthos** (see p.1045) or **Kefaloniá** (see p.1031) can also be reached from the western port of Kyllíni, and Greece's second port city of **Pátra** serves as a gateway to Corfu and to eastern Italy.

Travelling about the peninsula by **public transport**, you'll be dependent mostly on **buses**. These are fast and regular on the main routes between the seven provincial capitals, and from these towns go to most other places at least once a day; travelling between smaller towns in different provinces is considerably more complicated. The Peloponnese **train line** is gradually being upgraded, in particular with the Athens–Pátra section being converted to a high-speed track by 2008. The highly scenic southern loop still runs to a leisurely timetable but it does provide some direct connections and landscape views unavailable on buses.

Renting a **car** is worthwhile – even for just a few days – to explore the south from Kalamáta, Yíthio or Spárti, or coastal and heartland Arcadia from Náfplio or Trípoli.

peninsula. A last flicker of "Greek" rule, it was eventually extinguished by the **Turkish conquest** between 1458 and 1460, and was to lie dormant, save for sporadic rebellions in the perennially intransigent Máni, until the nineteenth-century **War of Greek Independence**.

In this, the Peloponnese played a major part. The banner of rebellion was raised near Kalávryta on March 25, 1821, by Yermanos, Archbishop of Pátra, and the Greek forces' two most successful leaders – the great, flawed heroes Petros Mavromihalis and Theodhoros Kolokotronis – were natives of, and carried out most of their actions in, the Peloponnese; as you journey around with all the benefits of a present-day transport infrastructure, you will be in the footsteps of Kolokotronis almost everywhere you go. The international naval battle that accidentally decided the war, Navarino Bay, was fought off the west coast at Pýlos; and the first Greek parliament was convened at Náfplio. After independence, however, power swiftly drained away from the Peloponnese to Athens, where it was to stay. The peninsula's contribution to the early Greek state became a disaffected one, highlighted by the assassination of Kapodhistrías, the first Greek president, by Maniots in Náfplio.

Throughout the **nineteenth** and **early twentieth centuries**, the region developed important ports at Pátra, Kórinthos and Kalamáta, but its interior reverted to backwater status, starting a population decline that continues today. It was little disturbed until **World War II**, during which the area saw some of the worst German atrocities; there was much brave resistance in the mountains, but also some of the most shameful collaboration. The **civil war** that followed left many of the towns polarized and physically in ruins. In its wake there was substantial **emigration** from both towns and countryside, to North America and Australia in particular, as well as to Athens and other Greek cities. Earthquakes still cause considerable disruption, as at Kórinthos in 1981, Kalamáta in 1986, and Éyio in 1995.

Today, the southern Peloponnese has a reputation for being one of the most traditional and politically **conservative** regions of Greece. The people are held in rather poor regard by other Greeks, though to outsiders they seem unfailingly hospitable.

Corinth and the Argolid

The usual approach from Athens to the Peloponnese is along the highway through Elefsína and across the Corinth Canal to modern-day **Kórinthos** (Corinth); buses and trains come this way almost every hour, the former halting at the canal (see p.207). A fast train link now connects Athens with Kórinthos. Another, more attractive, approach to the peninsula is by ferry or hydrofoil, via the **Argo–Saronic** islands (see p.581); routes run from Pireás through those islands, with brief hops over to the Argolid ports of Ermióni and Pórto Héli.

The region that you enter, to the south and southeast of Kórinthos, was known as the **Argolid** (Argolídha in modern Greek), after the city of Árgos, which held sway in Classical times. The greatest concentration of ancient sites in Greece is found in this compact peninsula, its western boundary delineated by the main road south from Kórinthos. Within an hour or so's journey of each other are Agamemnon's fortress at **Mycenae**, the great theatre of **Epidaurus**, and lesser sites at **Tiryns**, **Árgos**, **Lerna**, **Midea** and **Argive Heraion**.

Inevitably, these, along with the great Roman site at **Ancient Corinth**, draw the crowds, and in peak season you may want to see the sites early or late in the day to realize their magic. When ruin-hopping palls, there are the small-town pleasures of elegant **Náfplio**, and a handful of pleasant **coastal resorts**.

Drivers heading from the north towards the Argolid (Mycenae, Tiryns, Náfplio and Epidaurus) should join the broad new road, south of Dhervenákia, which bypasses the chaotic streets of Árgos. The funding ran out before the road was finished, so at the southern end you must follow farm roads to emerge near Tiryns.

Kórinthos

Like its ancient predecessor, the city of **KÓRINTHOS** (modern Corinth) has been levelled on several occasions by earthquakes – most recently in 1981, when a serious quake left thousands in tented homes for most of the following year. Repaired and reconstructed, with buildings of prudent but characterless concrete, the modern city has little to offer the outsider; it is largely an industrial and agricultural centre, its economy bolstered by the drying and shipping of currants, for centuries one of Greece's few successful exports (the word "currant" itself derives from Corinth). As a first stop in the Peloponnese, it gives a poor impression: noisy, chaotic with traffic in the rush hour, and providing a fragmented and inconvenient transport system. In summer, it is the hottest, driest part of the peninsula. If you want to base yourself here for a night or two, you are unlikely to escape from the continuous traffic noise anywhere in the centre of town, so it is worth considering the small village of **Arhéa Kórinthos**; 7km to the southwest, it is a quieter, slightly cooler alternative, with magnificent views at night, and close to the remains of ancient and medieval Corinth. Kórinthos itself provides access to Perahóra and a couple of other minor sites.

The only specific sight in the modern city is the **folklore museum** (Tues–Sun 8.30am–1.30pm; €2), overlooking the marina and containing the usual array of peasant costumes, old engravings and dioramas of traditional crafts.

Practicalities

Orientation is straightforward. The centre of Kórinthos is its **park**, bordered on the longer side by Ermoú street and bisected by the parallel Ethnikís Andístasis (formerly Konstandínou). The **train station** is a few blocks to the east, opposite the KTEL **bus station** for Athens, Léheo, Kiáto and the campsites. Changing trains at Kórinthos is easy; changing buses can be a nightmare. Most buses between Athens and the Peloponnese avoid going in to the centre and either pass by on the New National Road (Néa Ethnikí Odhós) with a stop at Isthmós, or along the nearer Old National Road (Paleá Ethnikí Odhós). On the latter route, locals alight at "Yefira" – a bridge under which you can access the town via a long walk along Ethnikís Andístasis. **Buses** to Ancient Corinth (Arhéa Kórinthos), Dhervéni, Kiáto, Léheo and Xylókastro go from outside the well-stocked Erataino zaharoplastío on Koliátsou, west of the park. Some **long-distance buses** to Argolídha (Mycenae, Árgos and Náfplio), plus those to Isthmia, Loutráki, Loutró Elénis (for Kekhriés) and Nemea, use a café near the *Ephira* hotel, at the corner of Ethnikís Andístasis and Arátou. Unlike others, this station – much used by tourists – has no signboard for destinations and times. Information and tickets are grudgingly provided by the café staff. You'll find various **banks** along Ethnikís Andístasis, and the main **post office** on

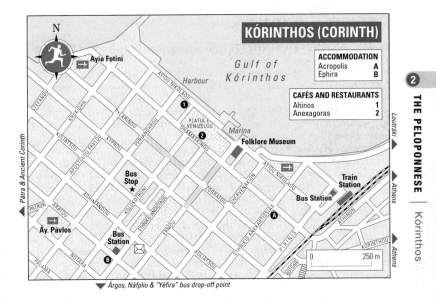

Árgos, Náfplio & "Yéfira" bus drop-off point

Adhimandoú, on the south side of the park. There's a **tourist police** post at Ermoú 51 (☎27410 23282), and **taxis** wait along the Ethnikís Andístasis side of the park. If you want to rent your own **car**, try Vasilopoulos at Adhimandoú 30 (☎27410 28437), near the post office.

Accommodation

At most times of year, **hotel rooms** are reasonably easy to find, though almost all suffer from road noise: the *Acropolis*, Ethnikís Anexartissías 25 (☎27410 22430, ⓔacropoli@otenet.gr; B&B ❹), is on the way into town from the train station; nearer the centre, the modern *Ephira*, Ethnikís Andístasis 52 (☎27434 24021; B&B ❸), is one block from the park and nearest to the long-distance bus station – the interior rooms are quietest.

There are a couple of **campsites** along the gulf to the west: *Corinth Beach* (☎27410 27967; April–Oct) is 3km out at Dhiavakíta, opposite the Lechaion site – to reach the beach, such as it is, you must cross the coastal road and the train line. *Blue Dolphin* (☎ 27410 25766, ⓦwww.camping-blue-dolphin.gr; April–Oct) is a bit further away at Léheo, but it is on the seaward side of the tracks, and for that alone it's preferable. For both sites, take the bus to Léheo (part of Ancient Corinth) from Koliátsou – or opposite the train station – in modern Kórinthos.

Eating and drinking

Kórinthos has many fast-food places along the waterfront, mostly reasonably priced, and only a few **tavernas**: *Anexagoras*, in a car park at Ayíou Nikoláou 31, west of the marina, has a good range of *mezédhes* and grilled meats, while *Ahinos*, by the marina, serves tasty, well-prepared seafood. Other than in the marina area, eating places tend to be in uncomfortable proximity to relentless traffic. On the coast road near the *Corinth Beach* campsite, the *Arhontiko* (☎27410 27968) is very popular with the locals, so phone first before heading off.

Ancient Corinth

Buses to **ANCIENT CORINTH** (Arhéa Kórinthos) leave modern Kórinthos ten past every hour from 8am to 9pm and return on the half-hour (20 mins; €1). The ruins of the **ancient city**, which displaced Athens as capital of the Greek province in Roman times, occupy a rambling sequence of sites, the main enclosure of which is given a sense of scale by the majestic ruin of the Temple of Apollo. Most compelling, though, are the ruins of the medieval city, which occupy the stunning acropolis site of **Acrocorinth**, towering 565m above the ancient city.

The ruins of Ancient Corinth spread over a vast area, and include sections of ancient walls (the Roman city had a fifteen-kilometre circuit), outlying stadiums, gymnasiums and necropolises. Only the central area, around the Roman forum and the Classical Temple of Apollo, is preserved in an excavated state; you come across the rest – odd patches of semi-enclosed and often overgrown ruin – unexpectedly while walking about the village and up to Acrocorinth.

The overall effect is impressive, but it only begins to suggest the majesty of this once extremely wealthy city. Ancient Corinth was a key centre of the Greek and Roman worlds, whose possession meant the control of trade between northern Greece and the Peloponnese. In addition, the twin ports of **Lechaion**, on the Gulf of Kórinthos, and **Kenchreai**, on the Saronic Gulf, provided a trade link between the Ionian and Aegean seas – the western and eastern Mediterranean. Not surprisingly, therefore, the area's ancient and medieval history was one of invasions and power struggles that, in Classical times, was dominated by Corinth's rivalry with Athens, against whom it sided with Sparta in the Peloponnesian War.

Despite this, Corinth suffered only one major setback, in 146 BC, when the Romans, having defeated the Greek city-states of the Achaean League, razed the site. For a century the city lay in ruins before being rebuilt, on a majestic scale, by Julius Caesar in 44 BC; initially intended as a colony for veterans, it was later made the provincial capital. Once again Corinth grew rich on trade – with Rome to the west, and Syria and Egypt to the east.

Roman Corinth's reputation for wealth, fuelled by its trading access to luxury goods, was soon equalled by its appetite for earthly pleasures – including sex. Corinthian women were renowned for their beauty and much sought after as *hetairai* (courtesans); over a thousand sacred prostitutes served a temple to Aphrodite/Venus, on the acropolis of Acrocorinth. **St Paul** stayed in Corinth for eighteen months in 51–52 AD, though his attempts to reform the citizens' ways were met only with rioting – tribulations recorded in his two letters to the Corinthians. The city endured until rocked by two major earthquakes, in 375 and 521, which brought down the Roman buildings, and again depopulated the site until a brief Byzantine revival in the eleventh century.

The excavations

Inevitably, given successive waves of earthquakes and destruction, the **main excavated site** (daily: summer 8am–7.30pm; winter 8am–5pm; €6) is dominated by the remains of the Roman city. Entering from the north side, you'll find yourself in the Roman agora, an enormous marketplace flanked by the substantial foundations of a huge *stoa*, once a structure of several storeys, with 33 shops on the ground floor. Opposite the *stoa* is a *bema*, a marble platform used for public announcements. At the far end are remains of a **basilica**, while the area behind the *bema* is strewn with the remnants of numerous Roman administrative buildings. Back across the agora, hidden in a swirl of broken marble and shattered architecture, there's a fascinating trace of the Greek city – a **sacred spring**, covered over by a grille at the base of a narrow flight of steps.

More substantial is the elaborate Roman **Fountain of Peirene**, which stands below the level of the agora, to the side of a wide, excavated stretch of the marble-paved **Lechaion Way** – the main approach to the city. Taking the form of a colonnaded and frescoed recess, the fountain occupies the site of one of two natural springs in Corinth – the other is up on the acropolis – and its cool waters were channelled into a magnificent fountain and pool in the courtyard. The fountain house was, like many of Athens' Roman public buildings, the gift of the wealthy Athenian and friend of Emperor Hadrian, Herodes Atticus. The waters still flow through the underground cisterns and supply the modern village.

The real focus of the ancient site, though, is a rare survival from the Classical Greek era, the fifth-century BC **Temple of Apollo**, whose seven austere Doric columns stand slightly above the level of the forum and are flanked by foundations of another marketplace and baths. Over to the west is the site **museum** (same hours as site; included in site admission), housing a large collection of domestic pieces, some good Greek and Roman mosaics from nearby and a frieze depicting some of the labours of Hercules, several of which were performed nearby at Nemea, Stymfalía and Lerna. The city's other claim to mythic fame, incidentally, is as the home of the infant Oedipus and his stepparents, prior to his travels of discovery to Thebes.

A number of miscellaneous smaller excavations surround the main site. To the west, just across the road from the enclosing wire, there are outlines of two **theatres**: a Roman **odeion** (once again endowed by Herodes Atticus) and a larger Greek theatre, adapted by the Romans for gladiatorial sea battles. To the north are the inaccessible but visible remains of an **Asklepion** (dedicated to the god of healing).

Acrocorinth

Rising almost sheer above the lower town, **Acrocorinth** (summer daily 8am–7pm; winter Tues–Sun 8.30am–3pm; free) is sited on an amazing mass of rock, still largely encircled by 2km of wall. The ancient acropolis of Corinth, it became one of Greece's most powerful fortresses during the Middle Ages, besieged by successive waves of invaders, who considered it the key to the Moreas.

Despite the long, four-kilometre climb to the entrance gate (nearly an hour's walk) – or a taxi ride from Ancient Corinth – a visit to the summit is unreservedly recommended. Looking down over the Saronic Gulf and the Gulf of Kórinthos, you get a real sense of the strategic importance of the fortress's position. Amid the extensive remains is a jumble of chapels, mosques, houses and battlements, erected in turn by Greeks, Romans, Byzantines, Frankish crusaders, Venetians and Turks.

The Turkish remains are unusually substantial. Elsewhere in Greece evidence of the Ottoman occupation has been physically removed or defaced, but here, at the start of the climb to the entrance, you can see a midway point in the process – the still-used **fountain of Hatzi Mustafa**, which has been Christianized by the addition of great carved crosses. The outer of the citadel's **triple gates** is also largely Turkish; the middle is a combination of Venetian and Frankish; the inner, Byzantine, incorporating fourth-century BC towers. Within the citadel, the first summit (to the right) is enclosed by a **Frankish keep** – as striking as they come – which last saw action in 1828 during the War of Independence.

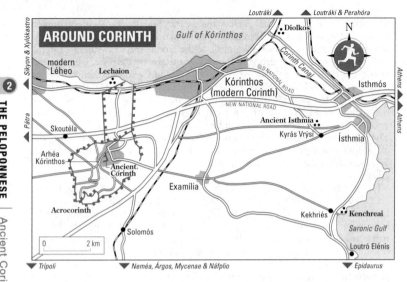

Keeping along the track to the left, you pass some interesting (if perilous) cisterns, the remains of a Turkish bathhouse, and crumbling Byzantine chapels.

In the southeast corner of the citadel, hidden away in the lower ground, is the **upper Peirene spring**. This is not easy to find: look out for a narrow, overgrown entrance, from which a flight of iron stairs leads down some 5m to a metal screen. Here, broad stone steps descend into the dark depths, where a fourth-century BC arch stands guard over a pool of (nonpotable) water that has never been known to dry up. To the north of the fountain, on the second and higher summit, is the site of the **Temple of Aphrodite**; after its days as a brothel, it saw use as a church, mosque and belvedere.

Practicalities: Arhéa Kórinthos

To explore both ancient and medieval Corinth you need a full day, or, better still, to stay here overnight. The modern **village** of **ARHÉA KÓRINTHOS** spreads around the edge of the main ancient site; the church has a memorial with, appropriately enough, a quotation from St Paul to the Corinthians. There is a scattering of **rooms** to rent – follow the signs or ask at the cafés. A good option, just after the cemetery on the road in from Kórinthos, is the hospitable *Hotel Shadow* (☎27410 31481; B&B ❹), with great views from the rear rooms; a restaurant downstairs includes an extensive and labelled collection of minerals, fossils, petrified wood and local relics. In the centre, the *Tasos* serves good, traditional Greek *psistariá* **food** at reasonable prices. The solitary modern building up on Acrocorinth is the *Acrocorinthos* café, which serves food until early evening during summer months.

Around Corinth

As well as the **Corinth Canal**, which you can't help but cross en route between Kórinthos and Athens, a number of minor sites are accessible by bus (at least most of the way) from Kórinthos, both on the Peloponnese and the western Attic peninsula of Yeránia. Just south of the canal is ancient **Isthmia**, site of the Panhellenic Isthmian Games. To the northwest are the spa of **Loutráki** and the classical **sanctuary of Hera** at **Perahóra** on Cape Melangávi. If you have a car, there's a grand and rather wild route east from the cape, around the Alkyonidhón Gulf to Pórto Yermenó (see p.332). There are beaches along the way, though little settlement or development, and the final stretch of road beyond Káto Alepohóri is scarcely better than a jeep track.

Back in the Peloponnese proper, **Nemea** – home to the Lion of Hercules' labour – is a brief detour southwest of Kórinthos, off the road to Mycenae and Árgos. **Sikyon** is a bit more remote, 25km up the coast towards Pátra, but again accessible by bus.

The Corinth Canal

The idea for a **Corinth Canal**, providing a short cut and safe passage between the Aegean and Ionian seas, dates back at least to Roman times, when Emperor Nero performed initial excavations with a silver shovel and Jewish slave labour. It was only in the 1890s, however, that the technology became available to cut right across the six-kilometre isthmus. Opened in July 1893, the canal, along with its near-contemporary Suez, helped establish Pireás as a major Mediterranean port and shipping centre, although the projected toll revenues were never realized. Today supertankers have made it something of an anachronism and the canal has fallen into disrepair, but it remains a memorable sight nonetheless.

Approaching on the Athens road, you cross the canal near its southeastern end, often referred to as Isthmós. From Kórinthos you can use the Loutráki buses to get there and back. At both ends of the **bridge** there's a line of **cafés**, where buses from Athens usually stop if they're going beyond Kórinthos – rather than into Kórinthos itself. At the Athens end of the bridge is a KTEL office and bus stop for buses to Athens and the Peloponnese, although getting onto buses here can be a hit-or-miss affair, depending on seat availability and drivers who can be reluctant to pick up tourists with luggage. To get into Kórinthos, a taxi may be more practical. Peering over from the bridge, the canal appears a tiny strip of water until some huge freighter assumes toy-like dimensions as it passes nearly 80m below. If you were to take one of the cruise ships from Pireás to the Ionian islands, you would actually sail through the canal – a trip almost worthwhile for its own sake. At the northwestern end of the canal, by the old Kórinthos–Loutráki ferry dock, there are remains of the **diolkos** (summer Mon noon–7pm, Tues–Sun 8am–7pm; winter Tues–Sun 8.30am–3pm; free), a paved way along which a wheeled platform used to carry boats across the isthmus. In use from Roman times until the twelfth century, the boats were strapped onto the platform after being relieved temporarily of their cargo.

Ancient Isthmia

Modern Ísthmia (also pronounced Isthmía) lies either side of the southern, Saronic Gulf entrance to the canal, and is served by regular buses from Kórinthos. To the west of the modern settlement, on a hillock alongside the present-day village of Kyrás Vrýsi, is the site of ancient **ISTHMIA** (Tues–Sun 8.30am–3pm, but both site and museum are closed for restoration; free).

There is nothing very notable to see at the site, though the ancient settlement was an important one, because of its **sanctuary of Poseidon** – of which just the foundations remain, much having been incorporated into the seven-kilometre Byzantine Hexamilion Wall – and the Panhellenic **Isthmian Games**. The latter ranked with those of Delphi, Nemea and Olympia, though they have left scant evidence in the form of a **stadium** and **theatre**, together with a few curiosities – including starting blocks used for foot races – in the small adjacent **museum** (same times as site; €2), which also houses some of the finds from Kenchreai. There are decent swimming spots and some accommodation at Kekhriés and Loutró Elénis on the coast heading south towards Paleá Epídhavros. The *Isthmia Beach* campsite (☎27410 37447, ⓦwww.isthmiacamping.gr; April–Oct) is about 1km north of the Kenchreai site, and provides a free shuttle bus to modern Ísthmia.

Loutráki

Six kilometres north of the canal is the spa resort of **LOUTRÁKI**. The epicentre of the 1981 Corinth earthquake, today it has straight lines of unmemorable concrete buildings. The resort is, nonetheless, immensely popular, with a larger concentration of hotels than anywhere else in the Peloponnese. The visitors are mostly Greek or Italian, coming here since 1847 for the "cure" at the **hot springs**, and to sample Loutráki mineral water – the country's best-selling bottled brand. The thermal baths are at Lékka 24 (summer daily 6am–2pm; winter Mon–Fri 9am–noon & 4–6pm; ☎27440 61990). A sign of the times is the Pepsi-Cola bottling plant on the outskirts of Loutráki. Others come for Greece's oldest **casino** at Posidhónos 48 (daily, open 24hr; ☎27440 65501) on the southwest seafront. Near the train station, there is a helpful **tourist kiosk** on E. Venizélou, the main road through town, four blocks south of the bus station, and a second near the baths. The local council has a choice range of well-produced brochures and a town map (ⓦwww.loutraki.gr), available at the kiosks.

Loutráki is connected by bus and special summer trains with Athens, and by bus (every 30min) with Kórinthos. **Car hire** is available from Hertz, Lékka 12b (☎27440 66655) or Alamo, 25-Martíou 8 (☎27440 64919, ☏27440 26150). **Hotels** include the *Pappas*, to the left of the Perahóra road (☎27440 23026, Ⓔpappasae@otener.gr; B&B ❻), with good facilities and fine views across the gulf, and the friendly, family-run *Acropole*, Tsaldhári 11 (☎27440 22265, ☏27440 61171; ❸), with comfortable rooms. To **eat**, the *Harama psistariá* at the corner of Kanári and Ethnikís Andístasis has good grills at decent rates.

Perahóra

The road to **Cape Melangávi** is enjoyable in itself, running above the sea in the shadow of the Yeránia mountains, whose pine forests are slowly recovering from fire devastation in 1986. En route the road loops through the modern village of **PERAHÓRA** (11km) before heading out to the cape along the shore of **Lake Vouliagméni**, a beautiful two-kilometre-wide lagoon with sheltered swimming. Perahóra is connected by hourly bus with Loutráki; one daily bus makes the journey between Loutráki and Lake Vouliagméni, but runs in high summer only.

Ancient Perahóra (summer daily 8am–7pm; winter Tues–Sun 8.30am–3pm; free) – also known as Peréa or the Heraion Melangávi – stands just 1km from the western tip of the peninsula, commanding a marvellous, sweeping view of the coastline and mountains along both sides of the gulf. The site's position is its chief attraction, though there are the identifiable ruins of a sanctuary in two parts, the **Hera Akraia** (*akron* is the extremity of the peninsula) and **Hera Limenia** ("of the port"), as well as the *stoa* of the ancient harbour, which has great snorkelling opportunities.

The initial excavation of Perahóra, between 1930 and 1933, is described by Dilys Powell in *An Affair of the Heart*. Humfry Payne, her husband, directed the work until his death in 1936; he was then buried at Mycenae. The site also features in myth, for it was here that Medea, having been spurned by her husband Jason at Corinth, killed their two children.

Nemea

Ancient **NEMEA**, the location for Hercules' (Herakles) slaying of its namesake lion (his first labour), lies 6km off the road from Kórinthos to Árgos. To get there by public transport, take the bus to modern Neméa and ask to be dropped at Arhéa Neméa, also the name of a village just 300m west of the ruins.

Like Olympia and Isthmia, Nemea held athletic games for the Greek world from the sixth century BC, until these were transferred to Árgos in 270 BC. A sanctuary rather than a town, the principal remains at the **site** (summer daily 8am–7pm; winter Mon noon–7pm, Tues–Sun 8.30am–3pm; €3 for site and museum, €4 for site, stadium and museum) are of the **Temple of Nemean Zeus**, currently three slender Doric columns surrounded by other fallen and broken drums, but slowly being reassembled by a team of University of California archeologists. Nearby are a **palaestra** with **baths** and a Christian **basilica**, built with blocks from the temple. There is also an excellent **museum** (same hours, except summer Mon noon–7pm; included in ticket price), with contextual models, displays relating to the biennial games and items from the area. Outside the site, 500m east, is the **stadium** (same hours as site; €2), which once seated 40,000 spectators. The vaulted entrance tunnel, now reconstructed, and complete with the graffiti of ancient athletes, is the oldest known. There is a guide available, written by archeologist Stephen Miller, who organized the (now quadrennial) **New Nemean Games** in 1996 as a non-commercial alternative to the Olympics; anyone can enter if they run barefoot and wear traditional tunics.

Signs locally indicate the Wine Road of Neméa, marking the notable **vineyards** of the area.

Xylókastro and the coast westward

A string of resorts, popular with Greeks despite the mountain backdrop being damaged by serious fires in 2000, runs westwards along the Korinthian coast, accessible by bus or train from Kórinthos. There are hotels in Vraháti, Kokkóni, **Kiáto**, Melíssi and Sykiá, but **XYLÓKASTRO** is of more interest, with good beaches and accommodation and a new marina, all in a pleasant setting backed by Mount Kyllíni. The main beach, Pefkiás, is lined by a strip of pine woodland. Cheapest of its dozen **hotels** is the basic but very hospitable *Hermes*, Ioánnou 95, near Pefkiás (☏27430 22250, @nikapos@panafonet.gr; B&B ❸). Other hotels include the *Kyani Akti*, near the sea at Tsaldhári 68 (☏27430 22225, ⓕ27430 28930; ❸), and the *Apollon*, housed in a fine old building at Ioánnou 119 (☏27430 22239, @apollonx@otenet.gr; ❹). The long seafront boasts a number of restaurants, of which *Zesti Gonia* is friendly and serves good fish, while *Palea Exedhra* has more variety. It is only possible to connect westwards with Pátra and Ahaïa by train, not by local buses, since the latter only run to and from Kórinthos.

The Stymphalian Lake

If you have transport, it's possible to cut across the hills from Nemea towards Arcadia, detouring into another Herculean locale, the **Stymphalian Lake** (around 35km from ancient Nemea). In myth, this was the nesting ground of man-eating birds who preyed upon travellers, suffocating them with their wings, and poisoned local crops with their excrement. Hercules roused them from the water with a rattle, then shot them down – one of the more straightforward of his labours.

The lake is known in modern Greek as **Límni Stymfalías**, though it is really more of a swamp: an enormous depression with seasonal waters, ringed by reed beds, woods and the dark peaks of Mount Olíyirtos to the south. Between Stymfalía village and the lake are the ruins of the thirteenth-century Frankish Cistercian **Abbey of Zaráka**, one of the few Gothic buildings in Greece, and the extensive site of **ancient Stymfalos**. Signs around the lake mark suggested hiking routes.

If you don't have your own transport, the most promising approach to the lake is from Kiáto on the Gulf of Kórinthos, where there are several hotels and rooms to rent; the road, much better than that from Nemea, has the occasional bus. The nearest place to stay is the pleasant – though very busy at weekends – *Hotel Karteri* (T27470 31203; B&B ❸), behind the *Taverna Leonidas* in **Kartéri** village, 3km west of the lake. Some of the rustic-style rooms have their own working fireplaces. Alternatively, head northwest, up 8km of winding road through **Kastaniá**, then up to the pass overlooking Fenéos (one of the great viewpoints of the northeast Peloponnese); a side road brings you to the *Xenia Hotel* (T27470 61283, F27470; B&B ❹, weekends ❺), beautifully situated overlooking the fir and cherry trees at 1170m.

The main road continues into the spectacular, windy, Fenéos plateau – once a vast lake – which is covered with walnut trees, then continues up over a second pass and through Lykouriá to join the Trípoli-Pátra road.

Ancient Sikyon

Six kilometres inland from Kiáto, ancient **SIKYON** (Sikyóna; summer daily 8.30am–3pm; winter Tues–Sun 8.30am–3pm; free) is a fairly accessible if little-known site, which deserves more than the handful of visitors it attracts each year. Six buses a day run from Kiáto (on the bus and train routes from Kórinthos) to the village of Vasilikó, on the edge of a broad escarpment running parallel to the sea, from where it's a kilometre's walk to the site.

In ancient history, Sikyon's principal claim to fame came early in the sixth century BC, when the tyrant Kleisthenes purportedly kept a court of sufficient wealth and influence to entertain suitors for his daughter's hand for a full year. After his death the place was rarely heard of politically, except as a consistent ally of the Spartans, but a mild renaissance ensued at the end of the fourth century when Demetrios Polyorketes moved Sikyon to its present location from the plain below. The town became renowned for sculptors, painters and metallurgic artisans, and flourished well into Roman times; it was the birthplace of Alexander the Great's chief sculptor, Lysippos, and, allegedly, of the art of sculptural relief.

The road from Vasilikó cuts through the site, which is fenced off into a number of enclosures. To the right is the **Roman baths museum**, which shelters mosaics of griffins from the second to third centuries AD. To the left are the majority of the public buildings, with a theatre and stadium on the hillside above. As you enter the **main site** (unrestricted access), opposite the Roman baths, the foundations of the **Temple of Artemis** are visible to your left. Beyond it are traces of a **bouleuterion** (senate house) dating from the first half of the third century BC. The most important remains in this section are of the **Gymnasium of Kleinias** in the far right-hand corner, at the base of the hill; this is on two levels, the lower dating from around 300 BC, the upper from Roman times.

Although only the first ten rows of seats have been excavated, the impressive outline of the **theatre** – larger than that of Epidaurus – is easy to distinguish. From the upper half there is a marvellous view encompassing the rest of the site, the village of Vasilikó, the lemon and olive groves around Kiáto, plus the Gulf of Kórinthos and distant mountains.

Mycenae (Mykínes) and around

Tucked into a fold of the hills just east of the road from Kórinthos to Árgos, Agamemnon's citadel at **MYCENAE** fits the legend better than any other place in Greece. It was uncovered in 1874 by the German archeologist Heinrich Schliemann (who also excavated the site of Troy), impelled by his single-minded belief that there was a factual basis to Homer's epics. Schliemann's finds of brilliantly crafted gold and sophisticated tomb architecture bore out the accuracy of Homer's epithets of "well-built Mycenae, rich in gold".

Mycenaean history and legend

The Mycenae-Árgos region is one of the longest occupied in Greece, with evidence of Neolithic settlements from around 3000 BC. But it is to a period of three centuries at the end of the second millennium BC – from around 1550 to 1200 BC – that the citadel of Mycenae and its associated drama belong. This period is known as **Mycenaean**, a term that covers not just the Mycenae region but a whole Bronze Age civilization that flourished in southern Greece at the time.

According to the **legend** related in Homer's *Iliad* and *Odyssey* and Aeschylus' *Oresteia*, the city of Mycenae was founded by Perseus, the slayer of Medusa the gorgon, before it fell into the bloodied hands of the **House of Atreus**. In an act of vengeance for his brother Thyestes' seduction of his wife, Atreus murdered Thyestes' sons, and fed them to their own father. Not surprisingly, this incurred the wrath of the gods. Thyestes' own daughter, Pelopia, subsequently bore her father a son, Aegisthus, who later murdered Atreus and restored Thyestes to the throne.

The next generation saw the gods' curse fall upon Atreus' son **Agamemnon**. On his return to Mycenae after commanding the Greek forces in the Trojan War – a role in which he had earlier consented to the sacrifice of his own daughter, Iphigeneia – he was killed in his bath by his wife Klytemnestra and her lover, the very same Aegisthus who had killed his father. The tragic cycle was completed by Agamemnon's son, Orestes, who, egged on by his sister Elektra, took revenge by murdering his mother, Klytemnestra, and was pursued by the Furies until Athena finally lifted the curse on the dynasty.

The **archeological remains** of Mycenae fit remarkably easily with the tale, at least if it is taken as a poetic rendering of dynastic struggles, or, as most scholars now believe it to be, a merging of stories from various periods. The buildings unearthed by Schliemann show signs of occupation from around 1950 BC, as well as two periods of intense disruption, around 1200 BC and again in 1100 BC – at which stage the town, though still prosperous, was abandoned.

No coherent explanation has been put forward for these events, since the traditional "Dorian invasions" theory (see p.1064) has fallen from favour; but it seems that war among the rival kingdoms was a major factor in the Mycenaean decline. These struggles appear to have escalated as the civilization developed in the thirteenth century BC, and excavations at Troy have revealed the sacking of that city, quite possibly by forces led by a king from Mycenae, in 1240 BC. The citadel of Mycenae seems to have been replanned, and heavily fortified, during this period.

The Citadel

The **Citadel of Mycenae** (daily: summer 8am–7.30pm; winter 8.30am–5pm; €8) is entered through the famous **Lion Gate**, whose huge sloping gateposts bolster walls which were termed "Cyclopean" by later Greeks in bewildered attribution to the only beings deemed capable of their construction. Above them a graceful carved relief stands out in confident assertion: Mycenae at its height led a confederation of Argolid towns (Tiryns, Árgos, Assine, Hermione – present-day Ermióni), dominated the Peloponnese and exerted influence throughout the Aegean. The motif of a pillar supported by two muscular lions was probably the symbol of the Mycenaean royal house, for a seal found on the site bears a similar device. Inside the walls to the right is **Grave Circle A**, the royal cemetery excavated by Schliemann and believed by him to contain the bodies of Agamemnon and his followers, murdered on their triumphant return from Troy. Opening one of the graves, he found a tightly fitting and magnificent gold mask that had somehow preserved the flesh of a Mycenaean noble; "I have gazed upon the face of Agamemnon," he exclaimed in an excited cable to the king of Greece. For a time it seemed that this provided irrefutable evidence of the truth of Homer's tale. In fact, the burials date from about three centuries before the Trojan War, though given Homer's possible accumulation of different and earlier sagas, there's no reason why they should not have been connected with a Mycenaean king Agamemnon. They were certainly royal graves, for the finds (now in the National Archeological Museum in Athens) are among the richest that archeology has yet unearthed.

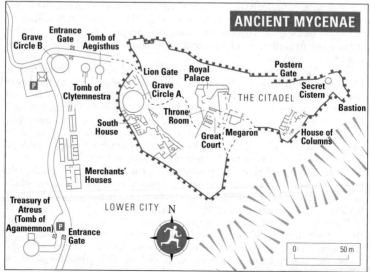

ANCIENT MYCENAE

Grave Circle B
Entrance Gate
Tomb of Aegisthus
Lion Gate
Royal Palace
Postern Gate
Tomb of Clytemnestra
Grave Circle A
THE CITADEL
Secret Cistern
Bastion
Throne Room
South House
Megaron
House of Columns
Great Court
Merchants' Houses
Treasury of Atreus (Tomb of Agamemnon)
Entrance Gate
LOWER CITY
N
0   50 m

▼ Modern village of Mykínes (2 km)

Schliemann took the extensive **South House**, beyond the grave circle, to be the Palace of Agamemnon. However, a building much grander and more likely to be the **Royal Palace** was later discovered near the summit of the acropolis. Rebuilt in the thirteenth century BC, this is an impressively elaborate and evocative building complex; although the ruins are only at ground level, the different rooms are easily discernible. Like all Mycenaean palaces, it is centred around a **great court**: on the south side, a staircase would have led via an anteroom to the big rectangular **throne room**; on the east, a double porch gave access to the **megaron**, the grand reception hall with its traditional circular hearth. The small rooms to the north are believed to have been **royal apartments**, and in one of them the remains of a red stuccoed bath have led to its fanciful identification as the scene of Agamemnon's murder.

With the accompaniment of the sound of bells drifting down from goats grazing on the hillsides, a stroll around the ramparts is evocative of earlier times. A more salutary reminder of the nature of life in Mycenaean times is the **secret cistern** at the eastern end of the ramparts, created around 1225 BC. Whether it was designed to enable the citadel's occupants to withstand siege from outsiders, rival Mycenaeans or even an increasingly alienated peasantry is not known. Steps lead down to a deep underground spring; it's still possible to descend the whole way, though you'll need to have a torch and be sure-footed, since there's a drop to the water at the final turn of the twisting passageways. Nearby is the **House of Columns**, a large and stately building with the base of a stairway that once led to an upper storey.

Only the ruling Mycenaean elite could live within the citadel itself. Hence the main part of town lay outside the walls and, in fact, extensive remains of **merchants' houses** have been uncovered near to the road. Their contents included Linear B tablets recording the spices used to scent oils, along with large amounts of pottery, the quantity suggesting that the early Mycenaeans may have dabbled in the perfume trade. The discovery of the tablets has also prompted a reassessment of the sophistication of Mycenaean civilization, for they show that, here at least, writing was not limited to government scribes working in the royal palaces as had previously been thought, and that around the citadel there may have been a commercial city of some size and wealth.

Alongside the merchants' houses are the remains of **Grave Circle B**, dating from around 1650 BC and possibly representing an earlier, rival dynasty to the kings buried in Grave Circle A, and two **tholos** (circular chamber-type) tombs, speculatively identified by Schliemann as the **tombs of Aegisthus** and **Klytemnestra**. The former, closer to the Lion Gate, dates from around 1500 BC and has now collapsed, so is roped off; the latter dates from some two centuries later – thus corresponding with the Trojan timescale – and can still be entered.

The Treasury of Atreus

Four hundred metres down the road from the Citadel site is another, infinitely more startling, tholos, known as the **Treasury of Atreus** or – the currently preferred official name – "Tomb of Agamemnon" (same hours as the Citadel; admission included in Citadel entrance fee). This was certainly a royal burial vault at a late stage in Mycenae's history, contemporary with the "Tomb of Klytemnestra", so the attribution to Agamemnon or his father is as good as any – if the king was indeed the historic leader of the Trojan expedition. Whoever it might have belonged to, this beehive-like structure, built without the use of mortar, is an impressive monument to Mycenaean building skills. Entering the tomb through a majestic fifteen-metre corridor, you come face

to face with the chamber doorway, above which is a great lintel formed by two immense slabs of stone – one of which, a staggering 9m long, is estimated to weigh 118 tonnes.

Practicalities: Mykínes

The modern village of **MYKÍNES** is 2km from the main Kórinthos–Árgos road and the small train station at Fíkhti. Buses from Athens to Árgos or Náfplio usually drop passengers at Fíkhti (where the café sells bus tickets), rather than in Mykínes village; crowded local buses from Náfplio via Árgos serve the village and site. The site is a further two-kilometre walk uphill from Mykínes centre, and in season has a couple of canteens and a **post office** caravan.

△ The Treasury of Atreus, Mycenae

Accommodation and eating

Unless you have your own transport, you might want to stay at Mykínes, which can be heavily touristy by day, but is quiet once the site has closed and the tour buses depart. Along the village's single street, there is quite an array of hotels – most of their names taken from characters in the House of Atreus saga – as well as a number of signs for rooms. Mycenae's two **campsites** are both centrally located, on the way into the village. Both open all year and there's not a great deal to choose between them, though *Camping Mykines* (☎27510 76121, ℱ27510 76247) is smaller and a little closer to the site than *Camping Atreus* (☎27510 76221, ℱ27510 76760).

All the hotels listed below have **restaurants** catering for the lunchtime tour-group trade, therefore don't raise your expectations too high. Eating places worth trying are the *Electra*, the *King Menelaos* and the *Menelaos*, all along the main street.

Belle Helene ☎27510 76225, ℱ27510 76179. The village's most characterful hotel, with a good restaurant, converted from the house used by Schliemann during his excavations. Signatures in its visitors' book include Virginia Woolf, Henry Moore, Sartre and Debussy. B&B ❷

Klytemnestra ☎27510 76451, ℱ27510 76731. Clean, pleasant, modern rooms run by friendly Greek-Australians. B&B ❸
Le Petite Planète ☎27510 76240, ℱ27510 76610. At the top end of the village, so the nearest hotel to the site, with great views and a swimming pool. Open April–Oct. B&B ❹

Rooms Dassis ☎ 27510 76123, ℗ 27510 76124. A pleasant, well-organized setup, run – along with a useful travel agency below – by Canadian Marion Dassis, who married into the local dynasty. Good for groups, students or families. Mention you are using the Rough Guide. B&B ❸

The Argive Heraion and Ancient Midea

The little-visited **Argive Heraion** (daily 8.30am–3pm; free) is an important sanctuary from Mycenaean to Roman times and the site where Agamemnon is said to have been chosen as leader of the Greek expedition to Troy. It lies 7km south of Mycenae, off the new highway that continues to Tiryns, and with sweeping views out over the plain to Árgos. There are various Mycenaean tombs near the isolated site, but the principal remains of a temple complex, built over three interconnnecting terraces, date from the seventh to fifth centuries BC. There are also Roman baths and a *palaestra* (wrestling and athletics gym). The central temple base is of a similar size to that of the Parthenon in Athens.

The Heraion makes a pleasant diversion for anyone driving between Mycenae and Náfplio, or an enjoyable afternoon's walk from Mykínes – it takes a little over an hour if you can find the old track southeast from the village, running parallel to the new road towards Ayía Triádha. Hónikas (Néo Iréo), 2.5km from the site, has the occasional bus to Árgos; Ayía Triádha, 5km on, has more frequent connections to Náfplio.

Ancient Midea (daily; free), in gorgeous countryside between the villages of Midhéa and Dhéndhra, was the third fortified Mycenaean palace of the area, after Mycenae and Tiryns. Excavations have uncovered a fortified hilltop area of some six acres, the remains of a young girl – an earthquake victim in the thirteenth century BC – and numerous workshop items. However, the most famous find, from the ancient cemetery site at nearby Dhendhrá, is the remarkable Dendra cuirass, bronze body armour now in the archeological museum in Náfplio.

Árgos

ÁRGOS, 12km south of the Mykínes junction, is said to be the oldest continuously inhabited town in Greece (ca. 5000 years), although you wouldn't guess it from first impressions. However, this busy trading centre has some pleasant squares and Neoclassical buildings, and a brief stop is worthwhile for the excellent museum and mainly Roman ruins. Try to time your visit to coincide with the regular Wednesday and Saturday **market**, which draws locals from all the surrounding hill villages; the market square is between the Kapodhistría barracks' three-sided courtyard and the Neoclassical market building, and is unofficially though invariably referred to as the Laïkí Agorá.

The modern **archeological museum** (Tues–Sun 8.30am–3pm; €2, or €3 for the museum and theatre) is just off the pedestrianized Elgás street between the market square and the main church square, Platía Ayíou Pétrou. It makes an interesting detour after Mycenae, with a good collection of Mycenaean tomb objects and armour as well as extensive pottery finds. The region's Roman occupation is well represented here, in sculpture and mosaics, and there are also finds from Lerna on display.

Before you leave Árgos, visit the town's ancient remains which are ten minutes' walk down the Trípoli road – initially Fidhónos, then Theátrou – from the market square. The **site** (Tues–Sun 8.30am–3pm; €2) is surprisingly extensive and excavations continue. The **theatre**, built by Classical Greeks and adapted by the Romans, looks oddly narrow from the road, but climb up to the top and it feels immense. Estimated to have held 20,000 spectators – six thousand more than Epidaurus – it is matched on the Greek mainland only by the theatres at Megalopolis and Dodóna. Alongside are the remains of an **odeion** and **Roman baths**.

Above the site looms the ancient **acropolis**, on a conical hill capped by the largely Frankish **medieval castle** of Lárissa (Tues–Sun 8.30am–3pm; free), built on sixth-century BC foundations and later augmented by the Venetians and Turks. Massively walled, cisterned and guttered, the sprawling ruins offer wonderful views – the reward for a long, steep haul up, either on indistinct trails beyond the theatre, or a very roundabout road.

Practicalities

You may well need to change **buses** in Árgos since some of its connections are better than those of Náfplio. There are local bus stops and a ticket kiosk on Kalléryi, at the southeast corner of the market square near the Dhikastikó Katástima building, for Mykínes and Nemea. Just around the corner, on Kapodhistría, is a KTEL office for buses back towards Athens, and for Trípoli, Spárti and down the coast towards Leonídhio. **Taxis** go from Fidhónos, the central street on market square, as do buses to Kefalári and Kivéri (get off at Mýli for Lerna).

For a good meal between buses, try the *Retro* restaurant on the central square, although there are cheaper options in the backstreets. Staying overnight shouldn't prove necessary, unless you find Náfplio full – a possibility in high season. **Hotels** on the Ayíou Pétrou main square include the comfortable, air-conditioned *Morfeas* (℡27510 68317, ⓦwww.hotel-morfeas.gr; B&B ❸) with balconies overlooking the square, and *Mycenae* (℡27510 68332, Ⓕ27510 68754; B&B ❸), though the latter prefers longer-stay guests, groups, families or archeologists.

Tiryns (Tírynthos)

In Mycenaean times **TIRYNS** stood by the sea, commanding the coastal approaches to Árgos and Mycenae. The Aegean shore gradually receded, leaving the fortress stranded on a low hillock in today's plains, surrounded by citrus groves, and alongside the Argolid's principal modern prison. It's not the most enchanting of settings, which in part explains why this highly accessible, substantial site is undeservedly neglected and relatively empty of visitors. After the crowds at Mycenae, however, the opportunity to wander about Homer's "wall-girt Tiryns" in near-solitude is worth taking. The site lies just to the east of the main Árgos–Náfplio road, and half-hourly local buses drop off and pick up passengers outside. There is also a small halt for infrequent trains.

The Citadel

As at Mycenae, Homer's epigrams correspond remarkably well to what you can see on the ground at Tiryns. The fortress, now over three thousand years old, is undeniably impressive, and the site itself had been occupied for four thousand years before that. The walls, 750m long and up to 7m thick, formed of huge

Cyclopean stones, dominate the site; the Roman guidebook writer Pausanias, happening on the site in the second century AD, found them "more amazing than the Pyramids" – a claim that seems a little exaggerated, even considering that the walls then stood twice their present height.

The entrance to the site (daily: summer 8am–7pm; winter 8.30am–3pm; €3) is on the far side of the fortress from the road, and visitors are restricted to exploring certain passages, staircases and the palace. Despite this, the sophistication and defensive function of the citadel's layout are evident as soon as you climb up the **entrance ramp**. Wide enough to allow access to chariots, the ramp is angled so as to leave the right-hand, unshielded side of any invading force exposed for the entire ascent, before forcing a sharp turn at the top – surveyed by defenders from within. The **gateways**, too, constitute a formidable barrier; the outer one would have been similar in design to Mycenae's Lion Gate, though unfortunately its lintel is missing, so there is no heraldic motif that might confirm a dynastic link between the sites.

Of the **palace** itself only the limestone foundations survive, but the fact that they occupy a level site makes them generally more legible than the ruins of hilly and boulder-strewn Mycenae, and you can gain a clearer idea of its structure. The walls themselves would have been of sun-dried brick, covered in stucco and decorated with frescoes. Fragments of the latter were found on the site: one depicting a boar hunt, the other a life-sized frieze of courtly women, both now in the Náfplio museum. From the forecourt you enter a spacious **colonnaded court** with a round sacrificial altar in the middle. A typically Mycenaean double porch leads directly ahead to the **megaron** (great hall), where the base of a throne was found – it's now in the Archeological Museum in Athens, with miscellaneous finds and frescoes from the site. The massive round clay hearth that is characteristic of these Mycenaean halls – there's a perfect example at Nestor's Palace (see p.299) – is no longer to be seen at Tiryns, because some time in the sixth century BC this part of the palace became the site of a temple to Hera, a structure whose column bases now pepper the ground. **Royal apartments** lead off on either side; the women's quarters are thought to have been to the right, while to the left is the bathroom, its floor – a huge, single flat stone – still intact. The **lower acropolis**, north of the megaron, is currently out of bounds due to the excavation of two underground cisterns discovered at its far end in the late 1980s.

A tower further off to the left of the megaron gives access to a **secret staircase**, as at Mycenae, which winds down to an inconspicuous **postern gate**, although currently both are closed off. The site beyond the megaron is separated by an enormous inner wall and can only be viewed from a distance.

Náfplio and around

NÁFPLIO (also sometimes known as Nauplia or Navplion) is a rarity amongst Greek towns. A lively, beautifully sited place, it exudes a grand, occasionally slightly faded elegance, inherited from the days when it was the fledgling capital of modern Greece. The seat of government was here from 1829 to 1834 and it was in Náfplio that the first president, Kapodhistrias, was assassinated by vengeful Maniot clansmen. It was here too that the young Bavarian Prince Otho, put forward by the European powers to be (briefly) the first king of Greece, had his initial royal residence from 1833 to 1834; he is commemorated by a new but locally unpopular statue. Since the 1980s the town has increasingly served as a popular year-round weekend retreat, with the result that hotel rooms and meals have crept up to Athens rates and above, but it remains by far the most attractive base for exploring the Argolid and resting for a while by the sea. The nearest good **beach** is at Karathónas, with others further afield at Toló, Kastráki, Dhrépano and Íria.

Arrival and information

Wedged between the sea and a doubly fortressed headland, the old part of Náfplio is an easy town to find your way around. Arriving by bus, you are set down at the **bus station** (☎27520 27323) on Syngroú, just south of the interlocking squares, **Platía Trión Navárhon** and **Platía Kapodhistría**. The **train** will deposit you near the junction of Polyzoïdhou and Irakléous, where a new station has been built, with two old carriages serving as ticket office and waiting room.

The **tourist office** is at 25-Martíou 2 (daily 9am–1pm & 4–8pm; ☎27520 24444), but hours are unpredictable and the information provided is not always accurate.

Accommodation

Accommodation in Náfplio is generally overpriced for what you get, particularly in the old town, though out of season during the week most **hotels** drop their prices significantly. There are a number of private **rooms** advertised, mostly clustered on the slope above the main squares. A few other hotels and rooms, generally the last to fill but often more reasonably priced, are located out in the modern town on the Árgos road (known locally as "stoús Argoús"). If you come by car, bear in mind that its popularity with Athenians makes finding a parking place in or near the old town very difficult in summer – your best chance may be on the harbourfront. There is nowhere to **camp** in Náfplio itself, but southeast on the stretch of coast from Toló (11km from Náfplio) to Íria (26km away), there are a dozen or so campsites – see p.224.

Amymone Othonos 39 ☎27520 99477, ⓦwww
.amymone.gr. New, high-quality pension in a restored small mansion in the heart of the town.
B&B ④–⑥
Byron Plátonos 2 ☎27520 22351, ⓦwww
.byronhotel.gr. A beautifully restored old mansion just above Áyios Spyrídhon church. ④
Dioscouri Zygomála and Výronos 6 ☎27520 28550, ⒡27520 21202. A friendly hotel, reached via a steep flight of steps. Rooms at the front overlook the old town and the port. ④
Economou Argonaftón 22 ☎27520 23955. To the northeast of town, near the Dia supermarket on the Árgos road. Recently refurbished, hospitable and excellent value – worth the 15min walk from the centre. Some dorm beds available (€15). ③
Kapodistrias Kokinou 20 ☎27520 29366, ⓦwww.hotelkapodistrias.gr. Beautifully decorated rooms, each one different, in a 200-year-old house

just 50m away from where Kapodhistrías was murdered. ③
King Othon 1 Farmakopoúlou 4 ☎27520 27585, ⒡27520 27595. Popular, well-placed hotel, beautifully refurbished with an impressive staircase. There is a second, pricier, *King Othon 11* around the corner at Spiliádhou 5. April–Oct. ④–⑥
Leto Zygomála 28 ☎27520 28093, ⓦwww
.leto-hotel.com. A friendly, recently refurbished hotel, with fridges in the rooms, located at the base of the Akronafplía fortress. March–Oct. ④
🏃 **Marianna** Potamiánou 9, ☎27520 24256, ⓦwww.pensionmarianna.gr. Very comfortable, restored house by the Akronafplía fortress walls, with some of the best views in town from the breakfast terrace. B&B ⑤
Park Dhervenakíon 1, off Platía Kapodhistría ☎27520 27428, ⒡27520 27045. Large, well-run 1960s hotel which may have space when the smaller old-town places are full. ③

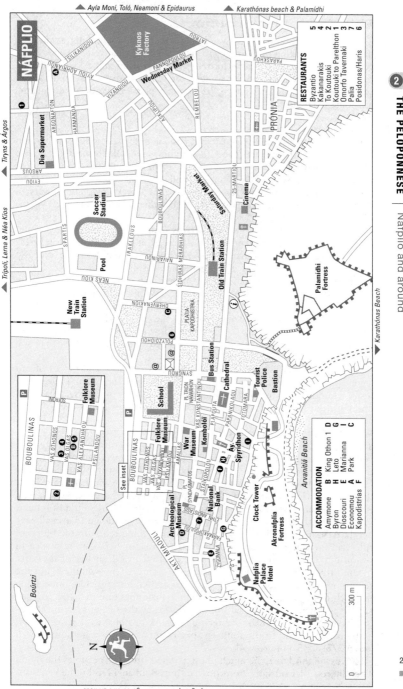

NÁFPLIO

▲ Ayía Moní, Toló, Neamoní & Epidaurus   ▲ Karathónas beach & Palamídhi

Kyknos Factory

Wednesday Market

Dia Supermarket

▲ Tíryns & Árgos

▲ Trípoli, Lérna & Néa Kíos

Soccer Stadium

Pool

New Train Station

Old Train Station

Saturday Market

Cinema

PRÓNIA

Palamídhi Fortress

▼ Karathónas Beach

See inset

Folklore Museum

BOUBOULINAS

School

Bus Station

Cathedral

Tourist Police

Bastion

Arvanitiá Beach

Folklore Museum

War Museum

Komboloï

Áy. Spyridhon

Archeological Museum

National Bank

Clock Tower

Akronafplía Fortress

Nafplia Palace Hotel

AKTÍ MIAOÚLI

▲ Boúrtzi

N

0   300 m

▼ Flying Dolphins to the Argo-Saronic & Pireás

THE PELOPONNESE | Náfplio and around

2

RESTAURANTS
Byzantio	5
Kakanarakis	4
To Koutouki	2
Koutouki to Pareíthon	1
Omorfo Tavernáki	3
Palia	7
Posidonas/Harís	6

ACCOMMODATION
Amymone	B	King Othon 1	D
Byron	H	Leto	G
Dioscouri	E	Marianna	I
Economou	A	Park	C
Kapodistrias	F		

219

The Town and around

There's ample pleasure in just wandering about Náfplio: looking around the harbourfront, walking to the rocky town beach and, when you're feeling energetic, exploring the great twin fortresses of **Palamídhi** and **Akronafplía** on the headland. Náfplio also offers some of the best **restaurants** and most varied and modern shops in the eastern Peloponnese, plus a range of useful facilities including car rental.

Palamídhi

The **Palamídhi**, Náfplio's principal fort, was one of the key military flash points of the War of Independence. The Greek commander Kolokotronis – of whom there's a majestically bewhiskered statue at Platía Kapodhistría – laid siege to the castle for over a year before finally gaining control. After independence, he was imprisoned in the same fortress by the new Greek government; wary of their attempts to curtail his powers, he had kidnapped four members of the parliament.

The most direct approach to the **fortress** (daily: summer 8am–7pm; winter 8am–6.30pm; €4) is by a stairway from the end of Polyzoïdhou street, beside a Venetian bastion, though there is also a circuitous road up from the southeast end of town. On foot, it's a very steep climb up 890-plus stone-hewn steps (in shade early morning) and, when you near the 216-metre summit, you're confronted with a bewilderingly vast complex. Within the outer walls there are three self-contained castles, all of them built by the Venetians between 1711 and 1714, which accounts for the appearance of the city's symbol – the Lion of St Mark – above the various gateways. The middle fort, San Niccolo (Miltiádhes), was the one where Kolokotronis was incarcerated; it became a notorious prison during the 1947–51 civil war.

The fortress takes its name from Náfplio's most famous and most brilliant legendary son, **Palamedes** – the inventor of dice, lighthouses and measuring scales. He was killed by the Greeks at Troy, on charges of treachery trumped up by Odysseus, who regarded himself as the cleverest of the Greeks.

Akronafplía and Boúrtzi

The **Akronafplía** (Íts Kalé – "Three Castles" – in Turkish), to the west of the Palamídhi, occupies the ancient acropolis, whose walls were adapted by three successive medieval restorers – hence the name. The fortifications are today far less complete than those of the Palamídhi, and the most intact section, the lower Torrione castle, was adapted to house the *Xenia Hotel* (to the west is the newer and very expensive *Nafplia Palace Hotel*). There's little of interest in the fortress, but a fork in the access road brings you down to a small pay-beach, **Arvanitiá** (said to be so named from running red with the blood of Albanian mercenaries slaughtered by Hasan Pasha in 1779), overcrowded in season but an enjoyable enough spot to cool off in the shelter of the forts. In the early evening it's more pleasant, with only a few swimmers, but the refreshment kiosks shut outside peak hours and high season. Continue along the path from just past the beach entrance for a few minutes, and you can take steps down to some small stone platforms by the sea, or take the attractive paved path around the western end of Akronafplía, to the main town harbour. A dirt road to the southeast of Arvanitiá leads to Karathónas beach (see p.222), a 45-minute walk.

The town's third fort, the much photographed **Boúrtzi**, occupies the Ayíou Theodhórou islet offshore from the harbour. Built in 1473 by the Venetians to control the shipping lane to the town and to much of Árgos bay, the castle has seen various uses in modern times – from the nineteenth-century home of the town's public executioner to a luxury hotel in the earlier twentieth century. In her autobiography *I Was Born Greek*, the late actress and politician Melina Mercouri claimed to have consummated her first marriage there.

Mosques and museums

In the town itself there are a few minor sights, mainly part of its Turkish heritage, and two excellent museums. **Platía Syndágmatos**, the main square of the old town, is the focus of most interest. In the vicinity, three converted **Ottoman mosques** survive: one, the Trianón, in the southeast corner of the square, is an occasional theatre and cinema; another, the Vouleftikón, just off the southwest corner, was the modern Greek state's original **Voulí** (parliament building). A third, fronting nearby Plapoúta, was reconsecrated as the cathedral of **Áyios Yeóryios**, having started life as a Venetian Catholic church. In the same area are a pair of handsome **Turkish fountains** – one abutting the south wall of the theatre-mosque, the other on Kapodhistría, opposite the church of Áyios Spyrídhon. On the steps of the latter, president Ioannis Kapodhistrías was assassinated by two of the Mavromihalis clan from the Máni in September 1831; there is a scar left in the stone by one of the bullets. The Catholic church, which has also been a mosque, on Potamiánou, has a monument to foreigners who died in the War of Independence, including Byron.

The **archeological museum** (Tues–Sun 8.30am–3pm, closed for refurbishment, due to reopen in 2006; €2) occupies a dignified Venetian mansion at the western end of Syndágmatos. It has some good collections, as you'd expect in a town near the Argolid sites, including a unique and more or less complete suit of Mycenaean armour, the Dendra cuirass from around 1400 BC, and reconstructed frescoes from Tiryns.

The fine **Peloponnesian Folklore Foundation Museum** (Mon, Wed–Sun 9am–3pm,

△ Palamídhi fort, Náfplio

closed Feb; €3) at Vassiléos Alexándhrou won a European "Museum of the Year" award when it opened in 1981 and features gorgeous embroideries, costumes and traditional household items from all over Greece. At Staïko-poúlou 25 is possibly the world's only **Kombolóï (worry-beads) Museum** (daily 9.30am–8.30pm; €3), while a little further down at no. 40 you can see shadow puppets being made by Ilias Moros at To Enotion. The **War Museum** (Tues–Sun 9am–2pm; free) at Amalías 22 has weaponry, uniforms, illustrations and other military memorabilia from the War of Independence to the civil war, including a series of portraits of the heroes of the War of Independence, enabling you to put faces to all those familiar Greek street names.

Ayía Moní

More handicrafts are on sale at the convent of **Ayía Moní**, 4km east of Náfplio on the Epidaurus road, just south of the suburb of Ária. The monastic church, one of the most accomplished Byzantine buildings in the Peloponnese, dates back to the twelfth century. From the outer wall bubbles a nineteenth-century fountain, identified with the ancient spring of Kanthanos, in whose waters the goddess Hera bathed each year to restore her virginity. Modern Greeks similarly esteem the water, though presumably with less specific miracles in mind.

Karathónas beach

The closest proper beach to Náfplio is at **Karathónas**, a fishing hamlet just over the headland beyond the Palamídhi fortress, which can be reached by a short spur off the drive going up to the ramparts. A more direct dirt road, theoretically closed to traffic, around the base of the intervening cliffs, can make a pleasant 45-minute walk; however, women alone are occasionally pestered by local scooter drivers. There are four morning bus services from Náfplio in season.

The narrow **sandy beach** stretches for a couple of kilometres, with a summer taverna at its far end. Karathónas attracts plenty of Greek day-trippers in season, along with windsurfing foreigners in camper vans; in summer, cafés compete to provide the loudest music. There are some organized **rock climbing** routes between Náfplio and Karathónas (inquire at tourist office for information).

Eating, drinking and nightlife

Waterside **Bouboulínas**, where the locals take their early-evening *vólta*, is lined with luxurious cafés where the beautiful people meet; tourists not wearing designer clothes and gold jewellery may feel a little out of place here. A cosier place to start restaurant menu-gazing in Náfplio is **Staïkopoúlou**, off which are many enjoyable if touristy **tavernas**. For **breakfast** or coffee, it's hard to beat the *Propylaion* right beside the bus station; assorted bakeries, gelateria and juice bars around Platía Syndágmatos are also worth investigating. Eating out is oriented towards evening rather than lunchtime meals, and **nightlife** is mainly along Bouboulínas and Syngroú. A quieter drink can be had at the **cafés** on Platía Syndágmatos, which stay open late. The real night-out haunts are the numerous huge discos and expensive nightclubs on the coast road out towards Néo Kíos.

Byzantio Vassiléos Aléxandrou 15. Excellent and friendly taverna, on a quiet corner of a beautiful street, with a varied menu and large portions. Specialities include home-made sausages.

Kakanarakis Vassilísis Ólgas 18 ☎27520 25371. A lively place serving a variety of dependably good *mezédhes*, plus dishes such as braised cockerel (*kókoras*) with noodles, and *kokkinistó* (meat simmered in tomato sauce). Open evenings only; popular with Greeks so arrive early or book ahead.

To Koutouki Vassilísis Ólgas. Stylish new taverna on square by Ágios Nikólaos church with good *mezédhes* and *mayireftá*.

Koutouki to Parelthon Profítis Ilías 12. The place to come for excellent *mezédhes* at very reasonable prices. Near the Árgos road and the *Economou* hotel.

Omorfo Tavernaki Vassilísis Ólgas 16. Local specialities include *kolokotroneïko* (pork in a rich wine and basil sauce). Very dependable, with prompt service.

Palia Staïkopoúlou 6. A *mayireftá* taverna since 1810. Friendly, with good food and reasonable prices.

Posidonas/Haris Sidhirás Merarhías. Eating out in the park, with tasty, well-prepared *mezédhes*, at good prices.

Listings

Banks These are concentrated around Platía Syndágmatos and along Amalías; most have ATMs.

Bookshops Odyssey, on Platía Syndágmatos, has a good stock of English-language books, newspapers, cassettes, CDs and videos.

Car rental Safeway, Eyíou 2 ☎27520 22155; Avis, Bouboulínas 51 ☎27520 24160, ℱ27520 24164; or Staïkos Travel, Bouboulínas 50 ☎27520 27950, ⓦwww.argolida.com/staikos. They are also agents for train tickets and can also book ferries and flights.

Cinema On Kyrinéas, near the junction of 25-Martíou and the Árgos road, showing English-language films with Greek subtitles.

Internet Posto, Sidhirás Merarhías, three doors from the post office – and many others.

Laundries 25-Martíou 28; Bubbles, Asklipíou 61 (the Toló road).

Post office The main branch (Mon–Fri 7.30am–2pm) is on the northwest corner of Platía Kapodhistría.

Scooter, motorbike and bicycle rental Nikopoulos, Bouboulínas 49; MotorTraffic, Sidhirás Merarhías 15 ☎27520 22702.

Taxis There's a rank on Syngroú, opposite the bus station.

Tourist police Koundourióti ☎27520 28131. Helpful and open daily 7.30am–9pm.

Beaches around Náfplio: Toló, Kastráki and beyond

Southeast from Náfplio are the ever-expanding resorts of **Toló** and **Kastráki** – popular and established enough to feature in some British package-holiday brochures. Inevitably, this means that they are busy at the height of the season, although they're still more tranquil than the big island resorts; you can always seek refuge at the low-key places further along the coast.

Toló (Tolon)

TOLÓ, 11km from Náfplio (hourly buses in season; last back at 10pm), is frankly overdeveloped, with a line of thirty or more hotels and campsites swamping its limited sands. Out of season it can still be quite a pleasant resort and the new bypass has, to some extent, improved traffic in the central area, but in summer it is about as un-Greek an experience as you'll find in the Peloponnese. Redeeming features include views of the nearby islets of Platía and Romví, and in summer a good range of watersports (windsurfing, waterskiing, paragliding) from operators such as *Poseidon* (☎ & ℱ 27520 59843), near the harbour, but the local mosquitoes can be a problem.

Hotels in Toló tend to be block-booked through the summer but you could try some of the smaller places, like the *Artemis*, Bouboulínas 7A

(☎27520 59458, ℻27520 59125; ⓺), with a seafront taverna, or the nearby, modern-style *Tolo*, Bouboulínas 15 (☎27520 59248, ⓦwww.hoteltolo.gr; B&B ⓹), with fridges in the rooms. If they're full or beyond your budget, it's usually possible to find **rooms** by asking around or following the signs, but be prepared for inflated summer prices. The **campsites** charge similar rates to the rooms: try *Sunset* (☎27520 59556; March–Oct) first; failing that, there's the quieter *Lido II* (☎27520 59396). The taverna, *Chez-Gilles*, at Bouboulínas 14, is highly rated, with well-prepared **food**, pricey but with large portions.

Kastráki and ancient Assine

A pleasant alternative to Toló, especially if you're looking for an inexpensive campsite, is the longer beach at **KASTRÁKI**, 2km to the east. Coming from Náfplio by bus, ask to be let off where the road reaches the sea – it forks right to Toló and left (500m) to Kastráki, marked on some maps as Paralía Asínis. Here, too, development is under way, but it's a fair bit behind that of Toló, with only a scattering of small-scale hotels and campsites. *Camping Kastraki* (☎27520 59386, ℻27520 59572; April–Oct) is on the beach, and has windsurfing equipment, pedaloes and canoes for hire.

If you get tired of the water, wander along the beach to the scrub-covered rock by the Náfplio road junction. This is, or was, **ancient Assine** (daily 8.30am–3pm; free), an important Mycenaean and Classical city destroyed by the jealous and more powerful Árgos in retribution for the Assinians having sided with the Spartans against them. There's little to see other than a 200-metre length of ancient wall, but it's an oddly atmospheric spot.

East to Íria

Further around the coast, to the east of Kastráki, the road runs on to **DHRÉPANO**, a sizeable village with four **campsites** and a very expensive hotel. The best campsite is *Triton* (☎27520 92128; March–Nov); it's 1.2km from the main square of Dhrépano – follow signs to the beach. The ✲ *Yefiraki* taverna behind the beach is popular with the locals both for its excellent fresh fish and seafood. Beyond Dhrépano, the **Vivári lagoon** has a couple of excellent **tavernas** on its shore, including the *Mermaid* with good seafood and a wonderful view along the bay. If you continue this way for another 13km, you reach a turning to the beach and the *Poseidon* campsite (☎27520 94341; May–Oct) at **Paralía Iríon**, below Íria village.

For the coast southeast of here towards Pórto Héli, Ermióni, Galatás and Méthana (each a local port for the Argo-Saronic islands) see pp.229–230.

Epidaurus (Epídhavros) and around

EPIDAURUS is a major Greek site (daily: summer 8am–7pm; winter 8am–5pm; €6), visited for its stunning **ancient theatre**, built around 330–320 BC. With its extraordinary acoustics, this has become a very popular venue for the annual Athens Festival productions of **Classical drama**, which are staged on Friday and Saturday nights from June through until the last weekend in August. The works are principally those of Sophocles, Euripides and Aeschylus; given the spectacular setting, they are worth arranging your plans around, whether or not you understand the modern Greek in which they're performed. Should you wish to have a better grasp of what you are watching, English translations of the plays are available at the Odyssey bookshop in Náfplio. Note that for festival performances the theatre is open late, after the rest of the site is closed.

The theatre, however, is just one component of what was one of the most important sanctuaries in the ancient world, dedicated to Asklepios (god of healing) and a site of pilgrimage for half a millennium, from the sixth century BC into Roman times, and now a World Heritage site.

The ancient theatre and Asklepian sanctuary

The dedication of the sanctuary at Epidaurus to **Asklepios**, the legendary son of Apollo, probably owes its origin to an early healer from northern Greece who settled in the area. There were Asklepian sanctuaries throughout Greece and they were sited, rationally enough, alongside natural springs. Epidaurus, along with the island of Kós, was the most famous and inspirational of them all,

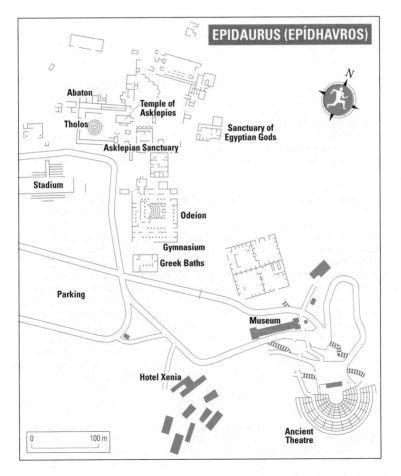

and probably the richest. The sanctuary was much endowed by wealthy visitors and hosted a quadrennial festival, including drama in the ancient theatre, which followed the Isthmian Games. Its heyday was in the fourth and third centuries BC, after which Rome, having been ravaged by an epidemic in 293 BC, sent for the serpent that was kept in the sanctuary.

This aspect of the site, however, along with much of the associated Asklepian ruins, is incidental for most visitors since it is Epidaurus's **ancient theatre** that is the primary sight. With its backdrop of rolling hills, this 14,000-seat arena merges perfectly into the landscape, so well in fact that it was redis-covered and unearthed only in the nineteenth century. Constructed with mathematical precision, it has an extraordinary equilibrium and, as guides on the stage are forever demonstrating, near-perfect natural acoustics – such that you can hear coins, or even matches, dropped in the circular orchestra from the highest of the 54 tiers of seats. Constructed in white limestone (red for the dignitaries in the front rows), the tiered seats have been repaired, but otherwise restoration has been minimal, with the beaten earth stage being retained, as in ancient times.

The museum

Close by the theatre is a small **museum** (summer Mon noon–7pm, Tues–Sun 8am–7pm; winter closes 5pm; entrance fee included in site ticket price), which is best visited before you explore the sanctuary. The finds displayed show the progression of medical skills and cures used at the Asklepian sanctuary; there are tablets recording miraculous and outrageous cures – like the man cured from paralysis after being ordered to heave the biggest boulder he could find into the sea – alongside quite advanced surgical instruments.

In 86 BC, by which time Epidaurus's reputation was in decline, the Roman consul Sulla, leader of the forces invading the Peloponnese, looted the sanctuary and destroyed its buildings. Hence, most of the ruins visible today are just foun-dations and a visit to the museum helps identify some of the former buildings.

The sanctuary

The **Asklepian sanctuary**, as large a site as Olympia or Delphi, holds consid-erable fascination, for the ruins are all of buildings with identifiable functions: hospitals for the sick, dwellings for the priest-physicians, and hotels and amuse-ments for the fashionable visitors to the spa. Their setting, a wooded valley thick with the scent of thyme and pine, is clearly that of a health farm.

The reasonably well-labelled **site** begins just past the museum, where there are remains of **Greek baths** and a huge **gymnasium** with scores of rooms leading off a great colonnaded court; in its centre the Romans built an **odeion**. To the southwest is the outline of the **stadium** used for the ancient games, while to the northeast, a small **sanctuary of Egyptian gods** reveals a strong presumed influence on the medicine used at the site.

North of the stadium are the foundations of the **Temple of Asklepios** and beside it a rectangular building known as the **Abaton** or **Kimitirion**. Patients would sleep here to await a visitation from the healing god, commonly believed to assume the form of a serpent. He probably appeared in a more physical manifestation than expected; harmless snakes are believed to have been kept in the building and released at night to bestow a curative lick.

The deep significance of the serpent at Epidaurus is elaborated in the circular **Tholos**, one of the best-preserved buildings on the site. Its inner foundation walls form a labyrinth which is thought to have been used as a snakepit and,

Tickets

Theatre tickets cost €17–35. In recent years there have been chaotic scenes with overselling and ticket-holders being turned away at the gates, so turn up early. Tickets for the plays are available in advance in Athens (at the festival box office), or sometimes at the site (☎27530 22009) on the day of performance, but definitely *not* at Náfplio bus station. Advance information is usually unavailable until just before the festival. In Athens (festival box office; ☎210 92 82 900) you can buy all-inclusive tickets for performances and return bus travel. There are also special evening buses from the site to Náfplio after the show; check at Náfplio bus station. English translations of the plays are available at the site and at the Odyssey bookshop in Náfplio.

according to one theory, to administer a primitive form of shock therapy to the mentally ill. The afflicted would crawl in darkness through the outer circuit of the maze, guided by a crack of light towards the middle, where they would find themselves surrounded by writhing snakes. Another theory is that the labyrinth was used as an initiation chamber for the priests of Asklepios, who underwent a symbolic death and rebirth in it.

Practicalities

Most people take in Epidaurus as a day-trip; there are four buses daily from Náfplio to the site. They are marked "Theatre", "Asklipion" or "Epidhavros" and shouldn't be confused with those to the modern villages of Néa or Arhéa (Paleá) Epídhavros. Alternatively, there are modestly priced hotels in nearby **LYGOURIÓ** village, 25km from Náfplio and 5km northwest of the site. Possibilities include the *Alkion*, Asklipíou 195 (☎27530 22002, ☏27530 22552; ❸), at the turning off the main road to the village, or the *Koronis*, Asklipíou 82 (☎27530 22267, ✉lassaris@otenet.gr; ❸), in the village itself; both are open all year but fully booked long in advance for the festival period. Alternatively, it's possible to **camp** in the grass car park on days of performances, though you must wait until an hour after the play's end before setting up a tent. Pleasant beachside accommodation is available at Paleá Epídhavros, 15km to the northeast (see below).

Lygourió itself has a few tavernas and cafés, but little of interest other than the Byzantine church of Áyios Ioánnis Elémonos and a Mycenaean pyramid on the northeast road.

For meals, the nearest **restaurant** is the *Oasis* on the Lygourió road, although there is a café at the *Xenia*, the unattractive and expensive hotel at the site. Much better than either is *Taverna Leonidas* (☎27520 22115), in the village proper, a friendly spot with a garden out the back; you'd be wise to book ahead if your visit coincides with a performance at the ancient theatre. Actors eat here after shows, and photos on the wall testify to the patronage of Melina Mercouri, the Papandreous, François Mitterrand and Sir Peter Hall.

Paleá Epídhavros

The closest beach resort to Epidaurus is **Paleá Epídhavros** (officially Arhéa Epídhavros; ⊛www.epidavros.gr), which has expanded since the improvement of the direct coast road from Kórinthos, but remains pleasantly small-scale. The recent discovery of ancient remains here means that some road signs for the beach now indicate "Ancient Epidavros", while the main inland site is referred to as "Ancient Theatre of Epidavros". As far as the remains are concerned, excavations are still in progress but they are worth a quick visit. A smaller classical theatre (Tues–Sun 8.30am–3pm; €6) on the headland, past the small town beach, is a festival venue for weekend musical shows in July and August, for which advance information is available at the hotel *Christina* or from Athens (☎210 92 82 900, ⓦwww.hellenicfestival.gr). You can find some small, open, Mycenaean tholos (tombs) behind the main street through town; turn inland up Odhós Ippokrátous by the BP petrol station, then left just above it.

Facing the harbour and town beach, there are a number of **hotels** and purpose-built **rooms**, with more, plus campsites, on the 2km of road south to Yialási beach. All are full with festival patrons in season. Two friendly hotels to try are the ⚓ *Christina* on the waterfront square (☎27530 41451, ⓦwww .christinahotel.gr; ❹), with large rooms and excellent home-made breakfasts, and the *Paola Beach*, the last hotel northwards beyond the church at Vayioniá beach (☎27530 41397, ℻27530 41697; closed in winter; ❹). Three **campsites** are on Yialási beach: *Verdelis* (☎27530 41425; March–Oct), *Bekas* (☎27530 41524, ⓦwww.bekas.gr; April–Oct) and *Nicholas II* (☎27530 41218, ℻27530 41492; April–Oct). **Buses** from Náfplio are scheduled to run late morning and return mid-afternoon, some via Epidaurus, though they can be unreliable; the central bus stop is at the *Platanos* café. **Taxis** can be summoned on ☎27530 41723.

The Saronic ports: Méthana to Pórto Héli

The roads across and around the southern tip of the Argolid are sensational scenic rides, but the handful of resorts here lack character, have disappointing beaches and are generally overdeveloped. With a car, you can pick your route and take a leisurely drive back to Náfplio, perhaps exploring the site of **ancient Troezen** and the **Lemonódhasos** lemon groves. Otherwise, you'll probably travel this way only if heading for one of the **Argo-Saronic islands**: **Méthana** has local connections to Égina (Aegina) and Póros; **Galatás** to Póros; **Ermióni** to Ídhra (Hydra) and Spétses; and **Kósta** and **Pórto Héli** to Spétses. Geographically part of the Peloponnese, Galatás, Trizína and Méthana are, like the Argo-Saronic islands, administratively in the province of Pireás, and sometimes prices are inflated to match those on the islands.

Méthana and ancient Troezen

It's a sixty-kilometre drive from Epidaurus to **MÉTHANA**, the last section along a cliff-hugging corniche road. Set on its own peninsula – the most volcanically active area in the Peloponnese – Méthana is a disappointing spa-town, whose devotees are attracted by foul-smelling sulphur springs. Of the half-dozen hotels, the most pleasant is the seafront *Avra* (☎22980 92382; B&B ❸). The agent for the **hydrofoil** is Palli at Aktí Saronikoú 34 (☎22980 92460). The sixty-metre-deep **volcanic crater of Hephaistos** at Kaïméni Hóra ("Burnt Village"), on the northwest side of the peninsula, is semi-dormant; Strabo recorded an eruption in the area 2200 years ago, probably of the nearby undersea volcano Pausanias, 2km northwest of Méthana.

South and inland of the turning to the Méthana peninsula is the village of Trizína, and the nearby ruins of ancient **TROEZEN**, legendary birthplace of

Theseus and location of his complicated domestic dramas. Aphrodite, having been rejected by Theseus's virgin son Hippolytos, contrived to make Phaedra – Theseus's then wife – fall in love with the boy (her stepson). Phaedra, too, was rejected and responded by accusing Hippolytos of attempted rape. Hippolytos fled, but was killed when his horses took fright at a sea monster. Phaedra confessed her guilt and committed suicide. Originally told by Euripides (later reworked by Racine), a full account of the tragedy, together with a map of the ruins' remains, is on sale in the modern village.

The **remains** of the ancient town are spread over a wide site. Most conspicuous are three ruined Byzantine chapels, constructed of ancient blocks, and a structure known as the Pýrgos Dhiatihísmatos or **Tower of Theseus**, whose lower half is third century BC and top half is medieval. This stands near the lower end of a gorge, the course of an ancient **aqueduct**, which you can follow in fifteen minutes' walk up a dirt road; a short, signed path leads to the **Dhiavoloyéfyro** ("Devil's Bridge"), natural rock formations spanning the chasm. On the far side, a short path to the right leads down to the lower bridge; a path to the left continues upstream past attractive rockpools.

Galatás and Lemonódhasos

Workaday **GALATÁS** lies only 350m across the water from the touristy island of Póros, with which it is connected by a five-minute skiff ride; these cross almost continuously in the summer months (5min). The town has a cluster of **hotels** on seafront 25-Martíou, of which the best value are the *Saronis* (☎22980 42356, ⓦwww.poros-island.co.uk/saronis; ❸), and the friendly *Papasotiriou* (☎22980 22841, ⓕ22980 25558; ❸), with a taverna; there are also **rooms** for rent around the waterfront, a **bike rental** place and **taxis**. The town is connected by daily buses with Epidaurus and Náfplio, and has local services to Trizína and Méthana.

On the coast road to the south is the small, unattractive **Pláka** beach (2km); two left turns shortly after bring you to the slightly better **Alykí** beach (4km), backed by a small salt lake. From a church on the main paved road behind Alykí, a route, signposted "Taverna Kardassi", leads into the **Lemonódhassos** – a vast, irrigated lemon grove. Paths meander through 30,000 lemon trees, heading upwards (20min) to an inspiringly positioned **taverna** serving fresh lemonade on its shady terrace. Henry Miller recounts a visit here in *The Colossus of Maroussi*, hyperbolizing that "in the spring young and old go mad from the fragrance of sap and blossom". There is also a café and a good seafront taverna at Alykí beach, both seasonal. Further along the main road is the longer, cleaner Lemonódhasos beach (5km).

Ermióni, Kósta and Pórto Héli

Continuing clockwise around the coast from Galatás, you follow a narrow, modern road, cut from the mountainside to open up additional resorts close to Athens. **Plépi**, part of Aktí Ídhras ("Hydra Beach"), is a villa-urbanization, visited by boats from beachless Ídhra opposite. **ERMIÓNI** (ancient Hermione) is better: a small town, on a rocky peninsula, overlooking Dhokós and Ídhra, and perhaps saved from development by lack of a sandy beach. The wooded tip of the peninsula has pleasant walks. Ermióni has **accommodation**, including the *Ganossis Philoxenia* apartments in the centre and on the seafront (☎27540 31218, ⓕ27540 32177; ❹). The agent for the **hydrofoil** is Fun in the Sun Travel (☎27540 31514, ⓦwww.ermionifuninthesun.gr). To the east, **rock-climbing** is possible at several sites: between Iliókastro and Thermisía; Thermisía castle; Katafygi gorge; and Frágkhthi cave (@www .oreivatein.com; grades 3–7).

Further round, **KÓSTA**, facing Spétses, and much larger **PÓRTO HÉLI**, squeezed between two enclosed bays, are purpose-built resorts that have swallowed up their original hamlets. Beyond the pretty waterfront views, both feature a rather soulless mix of package-tour hotels and facilities for yachters exploring the Argo-Saronic islands. The **campsite** in Kósta, *Camping Costa*, is 1km to the west (T 27540 51113, @www.costacamping.com; May–Oct) – as well as some fairly upmarket **hotels**, including the comfortable, family-run, beachfront *Lido* (T 27540 57393, F 27540 57364; B&B ➎). There are more reasonable options near the harbourfront in Pórto Héli, such as *Limani* on the war-memorial square (also called *Porto* T 27540 51140; ➌). On the same square is Hellenic Vision Travel (T 27540 51543, E evlassi@otenet.gr), which books **hydrofoils** and can find accommodation. There are numerous restaurants and cafés, one of the best of which is the sea-view *Kavouraki*, near the harbour, serving fresh fish since 1945, as well as car and bike rental. Kósta connects four times a day by **ferry** to Spétses (tickets available on the boat). About 2km east of Kósta is the excellent *Limanaki* taverna, at the attractive small beach at **Áyios Emilianós**. With your own transport, you can go further to the very long, part-sand, part-pebble beach of Kranídhi bay, east across the peninsula from Pórto Héli.

The circuitous route back to Náfplio from Pórto Héli runs inland, via attractive Kranídhi (7km) village, then scrambling its way up through the mountains past the 1121-metre viewpoint peak of Mount Dhídhymo. It is covered three to four times daily by a bus, which usually dovetails in Pórto Héli and Kósta with ferries and hydrofoils to and from Spétses and elsewhere; in low season, however, you may have to change buses in Kranídhi. Dhídhymo summit has **rock-climbing** routes (grades 4b–7c), as does Mount Ortholíthi. For this and other climbs in the area, see @www.oreivatein.com/climb/rock/e_argolis.htm or Jim Titt & Inge Zaczek's book *Climb Argolis*.

The east coast: Náfplio to Leonídhio

The **coastline** between Náfplio and Leonídhio is mountainous terrain. Considering its proximity to Náfplio – and Athens – the whole stretch is enjoyably low key and remarkably unexploited, remaining more popular with Greek holiday-makers than with foreign tourists; the accommodation at resorts before Leonídhio may be fully booked well in advance for the mid-June to mid-August Greek school holidays.

Getting to the **beaches** – Parálio Ástros, Áyios Andhréas, Paralía Tyroú and Pláka – is perhaps best done by car, though there are also **buses** two to three times daily, Monday to Friday, from Árgos to Leonídhio. Change money in advance, as there are few **banks** between Náfplio and Leonídhio.

At the beginning of the route, around the coast from Náfplio, the minor site of **ancient Lerna** makes an interesting halt. If you are travelling by train from Árgos to Trípoli, you could stop off at the station of Mýli, only 500m from the site.

Ancient Lerna

The site of ancient **LERNA** (daily 8.30am–3pm; €2) lies 10km south of Árgos and 12km from Náfplio by the minor road around the coast via Néa Kíos. On the way in from Árgos there is an interesting detour possible to the cave-lake church of **Panayía Kefalariótissa** at Kefalári, where even today some locals still wash their carpets in the nearby freshwater springs, although these springs are drying up as farmers extract increasing volumes of ground water upstream. The numerous tavernas here are very popular with locals. A further 4km inland is the remarkable fourth-century BC "**pyramid**" (Tues–Sun 8.30am–3pm; free) at Ellinikó village, actually a small fortress with inward-leaning walls, standing nearly at full height, on the ancient road from Árgos to Arcadia.

Ancient Lerna is at Mýli, on the bus and train routes from Árgos to Trípoli; there is a small **taverna** on the southeast side of the T-junction that is considered by Náfplians to make the best *souvláki* in the area. Just south of the straggle of the village a narrow lane leads to the small prehistoric site, which lies between the main road and the railway. This is one of Greece's most important Bronze Age sites, but most of it is now under a hideous concrete roof. American excavations carried out in the 1950s unearthed ruins of an early **Neolithic house** and a well-preserved **fortification wall**, revealing it as one of the most ancient of Greek settlements, inhabited from as early as 5500 BC.

Another large house at the north end of the site is thought to have been an early palace, but was superseded by a larger and more important structure known as the **House of Tiles**. Measuring approximately 24m by 9m, this dwelling, labelled as another palace, takes its name from the numerous terracotta roof tiles found inside, where they are thought to have fallen in approximately 2200 BC when either lightning or enemy raiders set the building ablaze. The house is the earliest known instance of the use of terracotta as a building material, and is the most impressive pre-Helladic structure so far unearthed on the Greek mainland. A symmetrical ground plan of small rooms surrounding larger interior ones has stairs mounting to a now-vanished second storey. The substantial walls, made of sun-dried brick on stone foundations, were originally covered with plaster. Even after its destruction, this palace may have retained some ritual significance, since two Mycenaean **shaft graves** were sunk into the ruins in around 1600 BC, and the site was not completely abandoned until around 1250 BC at the end of the Mycenaean period. Further excavations are taking place in Mýli itself, and an archeological park has been proposed, to connect the two sites.

As implied by the chronology, the founders and early inhabitants of Lerna were not Greeks. Certain similarities in sculpture and architecture with contemporary Anatolia suggest Asiatic origins, but this has yet to be proved conclusively. Excavated finds, however, demonstrate that the Lerneans traded across the Aegean and well up into the Balkan peninsula, cultivated all the staple crops still found in the Argolid, and raised livestock, as much for wool and hides as for food. Elegant terracotta sauce tureens and "teaspoons" (now in the Árgos archeological museum) hint at a sophisticated cuisine.

According to myth, Hercules performed his second labour, the slaying of the nine-headed serpent-like monster, Hydra, at Lerna. As if in corroboration of the legend, the nearby swamps still swarm with eels.

Coastal Arcadia: Parálio Ástros, Ástros, Paralía Tyroú and Sambatikí

The initial section of coast from Lerna to Ástros is low-lying and less spectacular than the sections further south. The first resort of any size is **PARÁLIO ÁSTROS**, whose older houses are tiered against a headland shared by a medieval **fort** (Tues–Sun 8.30am–3pm; free) and the ruins of a thirteenth-century BC acropolis. Back from the northern end of the sand-and-gravel beach, which extends 6km south of the fishing harbour, there are a few tavernas, more cafés, numerous rooms to let and some **hotels**: just south and inland of the main seafront square is the *Crystal* (T27550 51313, Ehotelcrystal@hotmail.com; ❹), with fridges in the rooms – family apartments are also available. The *Alexandros* (T27550 21743; ❸) is nearer the castle, and has well-appointed studio rooms; both have parking. The beautiful *Il Gusto* (also called *Maglis*) apartments (T27550 52733; ❺–❻) have large balconies directly overlooking the beach near the square. The nearest **campsite** is *Thirea*, 3km south at Meligoú Beach (T27550 51002, F27550 29206; May–Sept).

To the west and south, a trio of surprisingly neat and compact villages – **ÁSTROS** (site of the second National Assembly in 1823), Korakavoúni and Áyios Andhréas – perch at the foothills of **Mount Párnonas** as it drops to meet the lush, olive-green plain. The **Kynouria archeological museum** (Tues–Sun 8.30am–3pm; €2) in a traditional building (the Karytsióti School) in Ástros contains local items – including a collection from the Roman villa of Herodes Atticus at Éva Dholianón, 5km inland on the road to Trípoli. At **Áyios Andhréas** (10km from Ástros), Paralía Áyiou Andhréou is a small fishing harbour with a fish taverna; nearby are fragments of the cyclopean walls of Ancient Athini.

Heading further south, the busy road curls towards the coast and reaches the first in a series of pebbled swimming coves, crammed between the spurs of Párnonas. There are seasonal roadside **rooms** at Kryonéri, Tsérfo, Zarítsi and Tigáni beaches, plus **tavernas** at all except Tsérfo. On the main road opposite an unattractive new development, Arkadikó Horió, there is the *Repontina* **campsite** (T27550 31282; May–Oct), popular with middle-aged Greeks; *Tserfos Camping* (T27570 41083, April–Oct) and *Zaritsi Camping* (T27570 41429, F27570 41074; April–Oct) are at the eponymous beaches. With accommodation and campsites very much aimed at holidaying Greeks, few concessions are made to tourists along this stretch of coast; out of season, you'll definitely need your own supplies.

PARALÍA TYROÚ is a fair-sized town, with banks and a post office, and is a popular resort, mostly with older Greeks; younger Greeks tend to go further south along the coast, to Poulíthra. The place feels sedate, with comfortable, mid-range hotels and cafés spread back from its long, narrow pebble beach. **Hotel** accommodation options at the southern end of the beach include the *Apollon* (T27570 41393; B&B ❷) with fridges in the rooms, which has apartments for longer stays, and the more upmarket *Kamvyssis* (T27570 41424, F27570 41685; ❹). It also has cheaper rooms.

Twelve kilometres south, en route to Leonídhio, there is a good fish taverna, the *Klimataria*, above very pretty **SAMBATIKÍ** fishing beach. A circuitous road leads down to the beach itself and **accommodation**: the *Porto Sambatiki* (T27570 61316, Etasoslys@forthnet.gr; ❷), which has a taverna underneath, and the *Armenaki* (T27570 61274, F27570 61040; ❸), with comfortable studios.

Leonídhio, Pláka and Poúlithra

Gigantic ochre cliffs that wouldn't look out of place in deserts of the American Southwest or the Canary Islands confine red-roofed **LEONÍDHIO** (Leonídhion in formal Greek). Set inland, with rich agricultural land spreading down to the sea, this prosperous and traditional market town sees little need to pander to tourists, most of whom head for the coast at Leonídhio's diminutive port, Pláka. The **Tsakonic dialect** – a form of ancient Doric – is still used locally, notably for the Easter Sunday Mass. Also unique is the streaky, pale purple, sweet-tasting Tsakonikí aubergine, celebrated in a Pláka festival each August. There are some enjoyable, small-town **tavernas**, such as the *Mouria* near the small square.

PLÁKA, 4km away, is a delightful place consisting of a harbour and some **eateries**. It also has a fine pebble beach, which in recent years has become popular with Greek and European tourists, plus a sporadic influx of yachters. The Bekarou family have run the *Michael & Margaret* taverna here since 1830.

Accommodation is much easier to find 3km south of Pláka in the attractive small resort of **POÚLITHRA**, from where the coast road heads inland to small, isolated, mountain villages. With little development to distract you, this makes a relaxing staging post. There are tavernas close by the narrow strip of beach, although prices can be high; a **hotel**, the friendly, family-run ☆ *Akroyiali* (☏27570 29106, Ⓕ27570 51262; ❹), has spacious studio rooms by the sea, and rooms are available at *Spanoudakis* (☏27570 51325; ❸) and *Kyma* (☏27570 51250; ❸).

Inland from Leonídhio

The route inland from **Leonídhio** is worth taking for its own sake, climbing through the huge **Dhafnón gorge**, past the **monastery of Élonas** – although the views are even better if this route is covered in the reverse direction, descending through the gorge to Leonídhio. The road peaks at the high mountain village of **Kosmás**, providing a temperature shock in the height of summer, but a great place to stop and enjoy the fresh mountain air over a drink in the shady square. The whole route is a decent road for cars, and brings you out near the Byzantine site of **Yeráki** (see p.235); from there, you have a choice of roads – to Spárti or Yíthio (Gythion) via Skála, or to Monemvasiá and Neápoli via Molái. An alternative route south, to Monemvasiá or Neápoli, is the now surfaced road from Leonídhio via Poúlithra, Marí and Apidhiá. Without a car, you'll have to plan very carefully: a weekly bus runs from Leonídhio to Yeráki, with a few onward connections to Spárti – but check with the Náfplio bus station (☏27520 27323) first.

Moní Panayía tís Elónis

The **Panayía tís Elónis** (Élonas) monastery stands out as a white slash in the mountainside – though as you twist around and up the ravine, it drops away from view. The turn-off to the monastery (visitors permitted from sunrise to sunset) comes 16km from Leonídhio, via a short approach road which ends at a gateway and parking area. A cliff path leads you on to the main building, where you can wander down to a small church (closed during siesta) crammed with icons and lanterns, and to an *ayíasma* (spring), where water dribbling from the cliff has supposedly curative powers. Most of the monastery, originally founded in medieval times following the appearance of a miraculous and inaccessible icon by St Luke, was rebuilt following the War of Independence, becoming a nunnery in 1972. Today, it is maintained by three nuns who sell a classic little history (in Greek only) of the monastery's legends and vicissitudes.

Kosmás

Continuing south, 15km past the Élonis turning, you reach **KOSMÁS**, a handsome alpine village set about a grand platía and giant plane tree, with several **tavernas**. Straddling the most important pass of Párnonas, at 1150m, it can be a chilly place during the spring or winter, but very beautiful, too, with its streams, cherries and walnut trees, and would make a pleasant base for mountain walking.

△ Panayía tis Elónis monastery

The *Xenonas Maleatis Apollo* (☎27570 31494; ❸) has rooms with kitchens, sleeping two to four, in a refurbished eighteenth-century building. Just at the edge of the village, on the Leonídhio side, and with countryside views, are the *Kosmas studios* (☎27570 31483; ❸), also with kitchens. The taverna *O Navarhos* on the platía has good food and prices. The village's folklore museum appears to be permanently closed. Beyond Kosmás the road runs through a pass, then sweeps down the valley through fir forests to the village and Byzantine ruins of Yeráki.

The southeast: Lakonía

Lakonía, the ancient territory of the Spartans, covers the area between the high ridges of Mount Taïyetos and Mount Párnonas and everywhere to the south. Apart from the lush Evrótas valley, with Spárti itself and Mystra, it is a dramatic and underpopulated landscape of harsh mountains and poor, dry, rocky soil. Landforms apart, the highlights here are the extraordinarily preserved Byzantine town of **Monemvasiá** – an essential visit for any tour of the southern Peloponnese – and the aridly remote **Máni** peninsula, with its bizarre history of violence, piety and feuds, and its unique tower-houses and frescoed churches with barrel roofs. **Kýthira** and **Elafónissos**, historically Ionian islands but now under the administration of Pireás and Lakónia respectively, are reached from the Peloponnese, so are covered in this chapter.

Yeráki

If you choose the southeastern route over Mount Párnonas from Leonídhio then it is well worth making the effort to visit the **Byzantine antiquities** at **YERÁKI**. With its **Frankish castle** and fifteen **chapels** spread over a spur of the mountain, Yeráki stands a creditable third to the sites of Mystra and Monemvasiá. The "modern" village of Yeráki has no regular **accommodation**, though rooms may be negotiable through the **cafés** in the square. If you're dependent on public transport, you'll need to take in Yeráki as a day-trip from Spárti: **buses** run several times daily, but only once a week along the splendid route over Mount Párnonas to Leonídhio.

Medieval Yeráki

Yeráki (Tues–Sun 8.30am–3pm; free) was one of the original twelve **Frankish baronies** set up in the wake of the Fourth Crusade, and remained an important Byzantine town through the fourteenth century, straddling the road between Mystra and its port at Monemvasiá. The site is spectacular, with sweeping vistas over the olive-covered Evrótas plain and across to Taïyetos. It stands 4km outside and overlooking the current village of Yeráki.

All the main churches – many incorporating material from Yeráki's ancient predecessor, Geronthrai – are kept locked, and to visit them you should, theoretically, enquire at the caretaker's office (red door) near the rural doctor by the town square, and you may be given a tour (tip expected), clambering around the rocks to the best-preserved **chapels**, including **Zoödhóhos Piyí** and **Ayía Paraskeví**, both of which have restored fifteenth-century frescoes. However, they may only open for organized excursions from the larger resorts, or Athens.

The most substantial remains of the medieval town are of its fortress, the **Kástro**, built in 1256 by the local Frankish baron, Jean de Nivelet, who had inherited Yeráki, with six other lordships, from his father. Its heavily fortified design is based on that of the Villehardouin fortress at Mystra, for this was one of the most vulnerable Frankish castles of the Moreas, intended to control the wild and only partially conquered territories of Taïyetos and the Máni. In the event, Jean retained his castle for less than a decade, surrendering to the Byzantines in 1262 and buying an estate near Kórinthos on the proceeds. In the late seventeenth century it became Venetian, then Turkish in 1715 until being abandoned in the late eighteenth century. Within the fortress are huge **cisterns** for withstanding sieges, and the largest of Yeráki's churches: the thirteenth-century **Mitrópolis**, also known as **Áyios Yeóryios**, which features Byzantine frescoes, a Frankish iconostasis and the Villehardouin arms.

Poulíthra to Monemvasiá

The Lakonía coastline between Poulíthra and Monemvasiá is wild and sparsely inhabited, with just a couple of isolated coastal settlements – Kyparíssi and Limáni Yéraka – cut into the cliffs. By road, it's a roundabout route to Kyparíssi: 45km from Molái on the Spárti–Monemvasiá road, via a 900-metre col; 51km from Yeráki via Ágios Dimítrios; or 53km from Monemvasiá via Rikhiá. All routes take in a final, spectacular, precipitous corniche beyond Hárakas.

KYPARÍSSI is a verdant Shangri-La, sandwiched between huge cliffs and the sea, and divided into three settlements: inland Kyparíssi, Mitrópoli and Paralía. **Mitrópoli** at the northern end of the bay has the *Tiris* and *Poulaki* tavernas, both with good seafood at reasonable prices. Behind them is a small supermarket; at the far end is a petrol station. The jetty is at **Paralía** at the southern end, where there is studio **accommodation**, including the sea-view *Helioti* (☎27320 55238; ➎) – the same family have a taverna next door with more basic rooms (➊) – and the *Myrtoo* (☎27320 55327, ⓦwww.myrtoo.gr; ➎); both are well-placed for the sea, between the harbour and Megáli Ámmos beach on the coast road to Mitrópoli. On the inland road to Mitrópoli are the attractively refurbished *Kyfanta* studios (☎27320 55356 ⓦwww.kyfantahotel .gr; ➎), set in their own large olive garden. Accommodation prices drop considerably outside July and August.

Limáni Yéraka, not to be confused with its inland settlement Yérakas (also called Iérakas), or the previously mentioned Yeráki, is a rocky, elongated, fjord-like harbour – though without any accommodation.

Monemvasiá

MONEMVASIÁ, standing impregnable on a great island-like irruption of rock, was the medieval seaport and commercial centre of the Byzantine Peloponnese, the secular counterpart of Mystra. Nowadays the lower town is a fascinating mixture of atmospheric heritage, careful restoration and sympathetic redevelopment in matching stone and style – and an experience that should not be missed.

The town's name, an elision of Moni Emvasis, "single entrance", is a reference to its approach from the mainland, across a kilometre of causeway and a small bridge built in the twentieth century to replace earlier wooden bridges. Such a defensible and strategic position gave it control of the sea lanes from Italy and the West, to Constantinople and the Levant. Fortified on all approaches, it was invariably the last outpost of the Peloponnese to fall to invaders, and was only ever taken through siege. Even today, it differs deeply in character from the nearby mainland.

Some history

Founded by the **Byzantines** in the sixth century, Monemvasiá soon became an important port. It remained in Byzantine possession for almost seven hundred years, passing only very briefly to the Franks – who took it in 1249 after a three-year siege but had to ransom it back for the captured Guillaume de Ville-hardouin. Subsequently, it served as the chief commercial port of the Despotate of Mystra and was for all practical purposes the Greek Byzantine capital. Mystra, despite the presence of the court, was never much more than a large village; Monemvasiá at its peak had a population of almost 60,000.

Like Mystra, Monemvasiá had something of a golden age in the thirteenth century, when it was populated by a number of noble Byzantine families, and reaped considerable wealth from estates inland, from the export of wine (the famed Malmsey – *Malvasia* – mentioned in Shakespeare's *Richard III* and now being replanted locally) and from roving corsairs who preyed on Latin shipping heading for the East. When the rest of the Moreas fell to the Turks in 1460, Monemvasiá was able to seal itself off, placing itself first under the control of the papacy, later under the **Venetians**. Only in 1540 did the **Turks** gain control, the Venetians having abandoned their garrison after the defeat of their navy at Préveza.

Turkish occupation precipitated a steady decline, both in prestige and popula-tion, though the town experienced something of a revival during the period

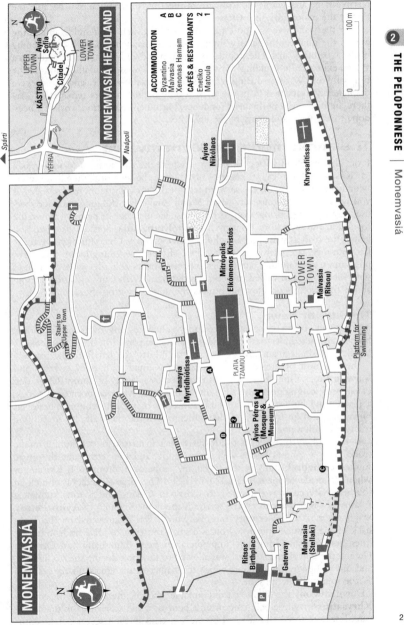

MONEMVASIÁ

N

Stairs to
Upper Town

Panayía
Myrtidhiótissa

Mitrópolis
Elkómenos Khristós

PLATIA
TZAMIOU

Áyios Pétros
(Mosque &
Museum)

LOWER
TOWN

Áyios Nikólaos

Khrysafítissa

Malvasia
(Ritsou)

Platform for
Swimming

Ritsos'
Birthplace

Gateway

Malvasia
(Stellaki)

P

ACCOMMODATION
Byzantino   A
Malvasia   B
Xenonas Hamam   C

CAFÉS & RESTAURANTS
Enetiko   2
Matoula   1

0   100 m

N

Spárti ◄

YÉFIRA

Neápoli ▼

KÁSTRO

UPPER
TOWN

Ayía
Sofía

Citadel

LOWER
TOWN

MONEMVASIÁ HEADLAND

of Venetian control of the Peloponnese (1690–1715). Monemvasiá was again thrust to the fore in the **War of Independence**, when, in July 1821, after a terrible siege and wholesale massacre of the Turkish inhabitants, it became the first of the major Turkish fortresses to fall.

After the war, there was no longer the need for such strongholds, and, at the end of the nineteenth century, shipping routes changed too, with the opening of the Corinth Canal. The population plummeted and the town drifted into a village existence, its buildings for the most part allowed to fall into ruin. By the time of World War II – during which four thousand New Zealand troops were dramatically evacuated from the rock – only eighty families remained. Today there are just ten in permanent residence, but much restoration work has been done to the walls and many of the churches.

The rock: medieval Monemvasiá

From the mainland village of **Yéfira** – where the causeway to **Monemvasiá** (or **Kástro**, as locals call it) begins – nothing can be seen of the medieval town, which is built purely on the seaward face of the rock. Little more is revealed as you walk across the causeway, past a Mobil garage, but the long entrance road, used for **parking**, brings you to huge castellated walls. In peaceful times, the town was supplied from the tiny harbour, **Kourkoúla**, outside the town and below the road as you approach the entrance gateway. Once through the fortified entrance gate, narrow and tactically z-shaped, everything looms into view: piled upon one another, amid narrow stone streets and alleyways, are houses with tiled roofs and walled gardens, and distinctively Byzantine churches. High above, the extensive castle walls protect the upper town on the summit.

The Lower Town

The **Lower Town** once numbered forty churches and over eight hundred homes, an incredible mass of building, which explains the intricate network of alleys. A single main street – up and slightly to the left from the gateway – shelters most of the restored houses, and is lined with cafés, tavernas and souvenir shops. One of the tavernas is owned by relatives of Yannis Ritsos, one of Greece's leading poets and a lifelong communist, who was born on the rock; a plaque and bust statue at a house above the main gate commemorate his birthplace, and he is buried in the cemetery outside the walls, his gravestone inscribed with a poem.

At the end of this street is the lower town's main square, a beautiful public space, with a cannon and a well in its centre, and the setting for the great, vaulted **cathedral**, built by the Byzantine emperor Andronikos II Komnenos when he made Monemvasiá a see in 1293. The largest medieval church in southern Greece, it is dedicated to Christ in Chains, and is thus known as Elkómenos Khristós. Across the square is the domed church of **Áyios Pétros**, originally a sixteenth-century mosque, which was reconverted by the Turks back into a mosque and now houses a small museum of local finds (officially Tues–Sun 8.30am–3pm, but unpredictable; free). Unusually for Ottoman Greece, the Christian cathedral was allowed to function during the occupation, and did so beside this mosque, hence the name of this square, Platía Tzamíou – "the square of the mosque".

Down towards the sea is a third notable church, the seventeenth-century **Khrysafítissa**, whose bell hangs from a bent-over old acacia tree in the court-yard. It was restored and adapted by the Venetians in their second, eighteenth-century, occupation. The **Portello** is a small gate in the sea wall, due south of

Platía Tzamíou; you can **swim** safely off the rocks here. There are two minor churches just off the main street. **Panayía Myrtidhiótissa**, to the north of the cathedral, is a small, single-aisled basilica with a single dome; inside there is a beautifully carved iconostasis – ask around for the priest if the basilica is locked. The big grey church built alongside the main street, above the Khrysafitissa, is **Áyios Nikólaos**; it dates from the early eighteenth century, and was used for many years as a school.

The Upper Town

The climb to the **Upper Town** is highly worthwhile – not least for the solitude, since most day-trippers stay down below – and it is less strenuous than it initially looks. To get the most from the vast site, it's a good idea to bring some food and drink (from Yéfira – Monemvasiá has no proper supermarket), so you can explore at leisure. There are sheer drops from the rockface, and unguarded cisterns, so descend before dusk, and if you have young children keep them close by.

The fortifications, like those of the lower town, are substantially intact, with even the **entrance gate** retaining its iron slats. Within, the site is a ruin, unrestored and deserted – the last resident moved out in 1911 – though many structures are still recognizable. The only building that is relatively complete, even though its outbuildings have long since crumbled to foundations, is the beautiful thirteenth-century **Ayía Sofía** (usually locked), a short distance up from the gateway. It was founded on the northern rim of the rock as a monastery by Andronikos II, along a plan similar to that of Dhafní.

Beyond the church extend acres of ruins; in medieval times the population here was much greater than that of the lower town. Among the remains are the stumpy bases of Byzantine houses and public buildings, and, perhaps most striking, a vast **cistern** to ensure a water supply in time of siege. Monemvasiá must have been more or less self-sufficient in this respect, but its weak point was its food supply, which had to be entirely imported from the mainland. In the last siege, by Mavromihalis's Maniot army in the War of Independence, the Turks were reduced to eating rats and, so the propagandists claimed, Greek children.

Practicalities

Direct **buses** connect with Spárti three times daily – although they are not timed to allow a day visit from the latter – and occasionally with Yíthio; the change of bus at Moláï can involve a lengthy wait. Buses arrive in the modern mainland village of Yéfira (see below). This is little more than a straggle of hotels, rooms and restaurants for the rock's tourist trade, with a pebble beach; for a **beach** day-trip, it's best to head 3–4km north along the coast to Porí beach.

Accommodation on the rock is expensive – in season and out – and from June to September you'll need to book ahead. Within the walls, the choice includes some very upmarket **hotels**, with attractively restored and traditionally furnished rooms. The most renowned is the *Malvasia* (℡27320 61323, ✉malvasia@otenet.gr; ❹), which occupies three separate locations between the main street and the sea; call first at the hotel reception, well signposted from just inside the main gateway. The similarly characterful *Byzantino* (℡27320 61254, ℻27320 61351; ❹–❻), further along the main street, is more expensive; they also own the *Enetiko* café and the *Xenonas Hamam* (❻–❼) with beautiful, eclectic suites in the restored baths: ask at the *Byzantino* café or office. The *Xenonas Goulas* has rooms and studios (℡27320 61223, ✉gialos@gialos.gr; ❺–❼). There are other **furnished apartments** and **traditional hotels** on the rock:

ask around at the shops and tavernas on the main street. Or you could seek the help of Malvasia Travel in Yéfira (see below). **Eating out** in the old village is enjoyable, as much for the location as for its food. Of the several restaurants, the best all-round place is *Matoula*, going since the 1960s, which has a leafy garden overlooking the sea.

Yéfira

There's more accommodation in **YÉFIRA**, along with various other useful tourist services including a **bank**, **post office** and a **travel agent**, Malvasia Travel (☎27320 61752, ✉malvtrvl@otenet.gr), which can help with rooms and **scooter** rental. There are several **hotels** near or just north of the causeway. The cheapest is the refurbished but basic *Akroyiali* (☎27320 61360; ❸) on the main street near the causeway. North of the road are the upmarket *Filoxenia* (☎27320 61716, ⓦwww.web-greece.gr/hotels/filoxenia; ❺) and the friendly *Pramataris* (☎27320 61833, ⓦwww.pramatarishotel.gr; ❸), which is good value, with some balconies overlooking the sea; just inland of the road is the *Flower of Monemvasia* (☎27320 61395, ⓦwww.flower-hotel.gr; B&B ❹) with rooms with fridges. There are good **rooms** for rent such as the hospitable, stone-clad ⚭ *Petrino* (☎ & ☎27320 61136; B&B ❹) on the southern seafront. The nearest **campsite** is 3km to the south, along the coast road; *(Kapsis) Paradise* (☎27320 61123, ⓦwww.camping-monemvasia.com) is open year-round, and has water-skis and scooters for rent.

Back in Yéfira, on the south side, good, cheap food with a sea view is available at *Skorpios*; if you have transport, you could also try the *Pipinelis* (☎27320 61044; May–Oct), about 2km out on the road south to the campsite, but call first to be sure it's open and to make a reservation if the weather's cool, as indoor seating is limited. Even closer to the campsite is the pleasant *Kamares* taverna with good grilled and oven food. For nightlife in Yéfira, try the popular *Rock Café* bar.

South to Neápoli and Elafónissos

The isolated southeastern most "finger" of the Peloponnese below Monemvasiá, locally known as Vátika, is little visited by tourists, except for the area around **Neápoli**, the southernmost town in mainland Greece, which offers access to the islet of **Elafónissos**, just offshore, and to the larger islands of Kýthira and Andikýthira, midway to Crete. Beyond Neápoli, the Peloponnese ends at Akrotíri (Cape) Maléas, a cluster of tiny monasteries known as "Mikró Áyion Óros", and a petrified forest. From Monemvasiá the southerly route high over the central ridge via Ellinikó village is the slower but more attractive of the two roads to Neápoli; the other, longer route is being extensively widened and straightened.

Neápoli

NEÁPOLI (full name Neápoli Vión) is a mix of old buildings and modern Greek concrete behind a grey-sand beach with views of Kýthira and Elafónissos islands – and mainly of interest for its ferry connections. For such an out-of-the-way place, it is surprisingly developed, catering mostly to Greek holiday-makers. Besides rooms, there are three modest **hotels**: older-style *Aïvali* (☎27340 22287, ☎27340 22777; ❸) and more upmarket *Arsenakos* (☎27340

22991, ⓦwww.geocities.com/arsenakos; ❹) on the seafront and, more quietly situated, the newer, friendly *Vergina* (☎27340 23443, ⓕ27340 23445; ❹) with fridges in the rooms; all may need to be booked ahead in summer. If you are waiting for the early ferry, you can have a breakfast snack of tasty, freshly cooked octopus at an ouzerí by the jetty. The agency for the Kýthira **ferry** is Vatika Bay at Agías Triádhas 3, a side street near the jetty (☎27340 24004, ⓕ27340 22660). Neápoli has several **banks**; **taxis** can be ordered on ☎27340 22590; and the KTEL **bus** office is on Dhimokratías, opposite the bus park. A signboard here has a map detailing hiking routes in Vátika.

Neápoli **beach** extends northwest to the village of Vingláfia and the recently upgraded harbour of **Poúnda**, which has between five and 26 daily ferry crossings over the short strait to Elafónissos (10min; ☎27340 61117, ⓦwww .elafonisos.net/dromolo.htm; pay on the boat, €2). The short hop makes a day-trip to the island practical, even with a car. Nearby Lake Strongylí, south of Áyios Yeóryios, is a nature reserve.

Elafónissos island

Part of the mainland until 375 AD, when an earthquake separated it, **Elafónis-sos** is very busy in the short summer season, when its 700-odd resident population is vastly outnumbered by visitors, mainly Greek. The island's eponymous town is largely modern, but has plenty of rooms, mostly in the narrow back-streets, plus some good fish tavernas. **Hotels** include the *Asteri*, one row back from the western seafront (☎27340 61271, ⓕ27340 61077; ❹), with fridges in the rooms. Places with sea views include the *Exantas* (☎27340 61024; ❸), conveniently positioned for the tavernas on the northern seafront near the ferry dock, and the *Iliovasilema* studios (☎27340 61212; ❺) on the western side. Details of other accommodation are available at ⓦwww.elafonisos.net. Those on the western shoreline can have wonderful sunset views.

Near the main church on its tiny peninsula, the *Spyros & Spyroula* taverna has well-prepared traditional food.

△ Símos beach, Elafónissos

One of the island's two surfaced roads leads to **Símos**, 5km southeast of the town, one of the best **beaches** in this part of Greece, a large double bay with fine pale sand heaped into dunes and views to Kýthira; the *kaïki* (boat) leaves from the town to Símos every morning in summer. There's a seasonal café at the eastern end of the beach, and the well-equipped *Simos Camping* and bungalows (☎27340 22672, ⓦwww.hotels-in-Greece.com/lakonia/simoscamping-e.htm; June–Sept; ❹) at the western end. To the southwest of town is the small, scattered settlement of Káto Nisí, and **Panayítsa** beach, quieter than Símos but almost as beautiful, with views to the Máni peninsula. There is a petrol station on the Panayítsa road.

Arhángelos

Further up the coast from Neápoli, just off the more northerly route from Monemvasiá, **ARHÁNGELOS** is a pleasant little resort at the southern end of a quiet sandy and deserted bay. The smart, apricot-coloured ⚲ *Hotel Palazzo* (☎27320 54111, ⓦwww.palazzo.gr; ❺), with a seafront café and restaurant, is open all year. The rooms are luxurious, and the owners hospitable and knowledgeable. The *Anokato* **bar** is a popular hangout for the whole peninsula, especially in winter. By a quaint twist the village, whose name means "archangel", is the harbour for Dhemonía ("devilry") several kilometres up the coast, which has tavernas, cafés and a big empty beach.

Continue north, from Dhemonía, in the direction of Moláï, and you pass Pahiámmos beach and laid-back **Plýtra**, which is becoming increasingly popular, with a large harbour, scattered houses, tavernas and some high-season rooms to rent.

Kýthira and Andikýthira islands

Isolated at the foot of the Peloponnese, the island of **Kýthira** traditionally belongs to the Ionian islands, and shares their history of Venetian and, later, British rule; under the former it was known as Cerigo. Administratively it is part of Pireás in mainland Attica – like the Argo-Saronic islands. For the most part, similarities end there. The island architecture of whitewashed houses and flat-roofs looks more like that of the Cyclades, albeit with an ever stronger **Venetian** influence. The landscape is different, too: wild scrub- and gorse-covered hills, or moorland sliced by deep valleys and ravines.

Depopulation has left the land underfarmed and the abandoned fields overgrown, for, since World War II, most of the islanders have left for Athens or Australia, giving Kýthira a reputation for being the classic emigrant island; it is known locally as "Australian Colony" or "Kangaroo Island", and Australia is referred to as "Big Kýthira". Many of the villages are deserted, their platíes empty and the schools and *kafenía* closed. Kýthira was never a rich island, but, along with Monemvasiá, it did once have a military and economic significance – which it likewise lost with Greek independence and the opening of the Corinth Canal. These days, tourism has brought prosperity (and a few luxury hotels), but most summer visitors are Greeks and especially Greek Australians. For the few foreigners who reach Kýthira, it remains something of a refuge, with its undeveloped **beaches** a principal attraction. However, Theo Angelopoulos' film *Taxidhi sta Kýthira* ("Journey to Kýthira"), and, to a much greater extent, a 1998 popular Greek television serial filmed on the island, have attracted a huge amount of domestic attention and, consequently, holiday-makers from the mainland. Much of the accommodation is now fully booked by Christmas for the entire Greek school summer holiday period; outside of this period some accommodation does not open until June and closes early in September. The Association of Rental Room Owners (T & F 27360 31855) has a list of places to stay: in addition to the following, there is accommodation in the villages of Aroniádhika, Dhókana, Dhrymónas, Frátsia, Frilingiánika, Goudhiánika, Kálamos, Kalokerinés, Karvounádhes, Káto Livádhi, Kondoliánika, Mitáta, Mylopótamos, Strapódhi and Travasariánika.

Arrival and getting around

Most large ferries dock at the huge all-weather **harbour** at Dhiakófti, although some Neápoli ferries (W www.atlas-marine.gr) may go into Ayía Pelayía. The airport is deep in the interior, 8km southeast of Potamós, although there are not many flights. The few Olympic Airways flights are met by taxis, as are most high-season boats. The island's **buses** are mostly used for school runs, but a single service runs Ayía Pelayía–Kapsáli–Dhiakófti, starting at 9am Mondays to Saturdays, returning Dhiakófti–Kapsáli–Ayía Pelayía late mornings or mid-afternoon, depending on the ferry times. The only alternative to taxis that often overcharge is to hitch or, more advisedly, hire a **car** or **scooter**. The roads are now well surfaced all over the island and there are reliable petrol stations on the central road at Potamós, Kondoliánika and Livádhi.

Dhiakófti

DHIAKÓFTI, towards the bottom of the northeast coast, was a relatively inaccessible backwater before the opening of the harbour, constructed by joining the islet of Makrónissi to the shore by a causeway. Perched on nearby Prasónissi island – and slightly disconcerting when arriving by sea – is a Greek container ship that went aground in 1999. Dhiakófti has a nice sandy beach, and exploitation of the tourist potential is currently fairly low-key and seasonal; there are just a few **eating places**, including the fish taverna *Manolis*, and **apartments** and rooms such as the *Porto Diakofti* (T 27360 33041, F 27360 33760; April–Oct; ❹–❻). Active (T 27360 33207, F 27360 33911) have an office for **car rental**.

Ayía Pelayía and northern Kýthira

There's a reasonable choice of **rooms** and **tavernas** in **AYÍA PELAYÍA**; best value of the upmarket hotels is *Venardos* (T 27360 34205, W www.kythira.com/ greek/venardos.htm; B&B ❻), which is open all year and can offer very good deals off season. The clean and comfortable *Hotel Kytherea* (T 27360 33321; ❺) is more luxurious, as are the *Filoxenia Apartments* (T 27360 33100, F 27360 33610, W www.filoxenia-apartments.gr; April–Oct; B&B ❻), with a pool and an imaginative layout around small courtyards. The *Moustakias* taverna, amongst the seafront eating places north of the jetty, has good, fresh food, including fish, while the *Paleo* ouzeri is also recommended. The main beaches are small, rather scruffy and disappointing, despite the provision of blue-and-white-striped changing huts; the beach at Kalamitsa, a two-kilometre dirt track away to the south, is better.

Potamós and around

From Ayía Pelayía, the main road winds up the mountainside towards **POTAMÓS**, Kýthira's largest village – a pleasant and unspoilt place which, if you have a rented vehicle, makes a good base for exploring the island. It has a few **rooms** with kitchens, such as those at the ≯ *Xenonas Porfyra* (T 27360 33329,

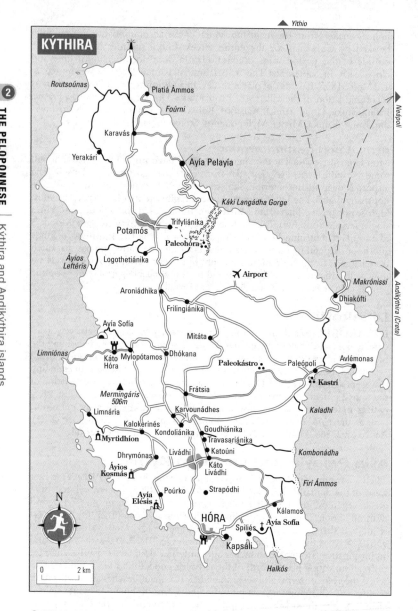

KÝTHIRA

Yíthio

Routsoúnas

Platiá Ámmos

Foúrni

Neápoli

Karavás

Yerakári

Ayía Pelayía

Káki Langádha Gorge

Trifyliánika

Potamós

Paleohóra

 Áyios
Leftéris

Logothetiánika

✈ Airport

Makrónissi

Aroniádhika

Dhiakófti

Frilingiánika

Ayía Sofía

Mitáta

Andikýthira (Crete)

Limniónas

Káto
Hóra

Mylopótamos

Dhókana

Paleokástro

Paleópoli

Avlémonas

Kastrí

Mermingáris
506m

Frátsia

Kaladhí

Limnária

Karvounádhes

Kalokerinés

Kombonádha

Myrtidhíon

Kondoliánika

Goudhiánika

Travasariánika

Dhrymónas

Livádhi

Katoúni

Firí Ámmos

Áyios
Kosmás

Káto
Livádhi

Ayía
Elésis

Poúrko

Strapódhi

Kálamos

HÓRA

Ayía Sofía

Spiliés

Kapsáli

Halkós

N

0   2 km

ⓕ27360 33924; ❹), which has a pretty terrace and courtyard, and the *Alevi-
zopoulos* (☎27360 33245, ⓦwww.greek-tourism.gr/kythira/alevizopoulos/
index.htm; ❹) with air conditioning. In addition to **tavernas**, a **bank**, a **post
office** and **petrol stations**, facilities include an Olympic Airways office
(☎27360 33362). Most of the shops on the island are here, too, as is the
Sunday market, Kýthira's liveliest regular event. The *Selana* café has **Internet**
facilities.

From **Logothetiánika**, just south of Potamós, an unpaved road leads down to Áyios Leftéris beach, where you can **swim** from rocks on the west coast, backed by high cliffs. At Logothetiánika itself, there is a popular taverna, *Karydies* (℡27360 33664), with live music Thursday to Saturday, when booking is advisable.

Paleohóra

The main reason for visiting Potamós is to get to **PALEOHÓRA**, the ruined **medieval capital** (then called Áyios Dhimítrios) of Kýthira, 3km to the east of the town. Few people seem to know about or visit these remains, though they constitute one of the best Byzantine sites around. The most obvious comparison is with Mystra, and although Paleohóra is much smaller – a fortified village rather than a town – its natural setting is perhaps even more spectacular. Set on a hilltop at the head of the **Káki Langádha Gorge**, it is surrounded by a sheer hundred-metre drop on three sides.

The site is lower than the surrounding hills and invisible from the sea and most of the island, something which served to protect it from the pirates that plagued Paleohóra through much of its history. The town was built in the thirteenth century by Byzantine nobles from Monemvasiá, and when Mystra fell to the Turks, many of its noble families also sought refuge here. Despite its seemingly impregnable and perfectly concealed position, the site was discovered and sacked in 1537 by Barbarossa, commander of the Turkish fleet, and the island's seven thousand inhabitants were killed or sold into slavery.

The town was never rebuilt, and tradition maintains that it is a place of ill fortune, which perhaps explains the emptiness of the surrounding countryside, little of which is farmed today. The hills are dotted with Byzantine **chapels**, which suggests that, in its heyday, the area must have been the centre of medieval Kýthira; it is rumoured to have once had eight hundred inhabitants and 72 churches. Now the principal remains are of the surviving churches, some still with traces of frescoes (but kept firmly locked), and the castle. The site is unenclosed and has never been seriously investigated.

The road to Paleohóra is signposted off the main road from Potamós just north of Aroniádhika: the first 2.4km is asphalt, the remainder driveable gravel. By foot, it's more interesting to take the path from the tiny village of Trifyliánika, just outside Potamós – look out for a rusting sign to the right as you enter the village. The path is overgrown in parts and not easy to follow; the ruins only become visible when you join the road above the gorge.

Karavás

KARAVÁS, 6km north of Potamós, has architecture and a setting – above a deep, partly wooded valley with a stream – which are more reminiscent of the Ionian islands. There is nowhere to stay, but there is a popular **café-bar**, *Amir Ali*, providing a large range of *mezédhes* (and sometimes live music) in a shady, streamside setting at the northern end of the village, off the road to Platiá Ámmos.

Platiá Ámmos, at the end of the valley, and en route to the lighthouse at the island's northern tip, is a sandy beach with a seasonal fish **taverna**. There is also an ouzerí, café, the *Modeas* restaurant and several establishments with **rooms**, of which the best is the *Akrotiri* (℡27360 33216; ❸). The little pebble beach at **Foúrni**, 2km south by dirt road, is more attractive.

Kapsáli

KAPSÁLI, on the south coast, in addition to its harbour function, is the one place on Kýthira largely devoted to tourism, although much of it closes down from September to June. Most foreign visitors to Kýthira in summer stay here, and it's a popular port of call for yachts heading from the Aegean to the Ionian islands and Italy, particularly since it is sheltered from the strong north winds of summer. Set behind double pebble-and-sand bays, overlooked by Hóra castle, and backed by high grey cliffs on which the tiny white monastery of Áyios Ioánnis Éngremmos perches, it is certainly picturesque. The larger of its two bays has a line of **tavernas**: *Vlastos* is one of the earliest to open in the season, with fish, local dishes and its speciality, cockerel (*kókoras*) in wine; *Venetsianiko*, halfway along the front, has good food at reasonable prices, but the best is *Idragogio* at the Hóra end of the beach which serves up good veggie options.

The best **accommodation** is in high demand and expensive. Top of the tree is the *Porto Delfino* (☎27360 31940; April–Oct; ⑥); a few hundred metres above the bay are *Kalokerines Katikies* (☎ & ℱ27360 31265; May–Oct; ⑥) and *Hotel Raikos* (☎27360 31629, ℱ27360 31801, ✉raikosho@otenet.gr; May–Sept; ⑥). The *Afroditi Apartments* (☎27360 31328; ④) have more reasonable rates. A basic **campsite** (☎27360 31580; June–Sept) nestles in the pine trees behind the village.

There's a mobile **post office** in summer, and Panayiotis (☎27360 31600, ✉panayoti@otenet.gr) rents **cars**, **motorbikes** and **scooters**, as well as canoes and pedalboats; you can call off season (☎29442 63757) and get wheels when most places are closed.

Hóra

HÓRA (or Kýthira Town), a steep two-kilometre haul above Kapsáli, has an equally dramatic site, its Cycladic-style houses tiered on the ridge leading to the Venetian **castle**. Access to the fortress is up a modern pathway, but, to the right of this, the original narrow tunnel entrance is still usable. Within the walls, most of the buildings are in ruins, except the paired churches of Panayía Myrtidhiótissa and the smaller Panayía Orfáni (these were Catholic and Orthodox respectively, under the Venetian occupation), and the office of the archives of Kýthira opposite. There are spectacular views down to Kapsáli and out to sea to the striking chunk of inaccessible islet known as Avgó (Egg), legendary birthplace of Aphrodite. On the cliffs grow the yellow-flowered everlasting (*sempreviva*), used locally for making small dried flower arrangements. Below the castle are both the remains of older Byzantine walls and, in Mésa Vouryó, numerous well-signed but securely locked Byzantine churches. A small **museum** (Tues–Sun 8.30am–2.30pm; free), at the junction of the Hóra–Kapsáli road, houses modest remnants (labelled only in Greek) of the island's numerous occupiers, in particular Minoan finds from excavations at Paleópoli and an Archaic stone lion, as well as a telling selection of gravestones from the English cemetery. The Stavros bookshop, almost opposite, sells a book of walks (mainly in the southern half of the island).

Compared with Kapsáli, Hóra stays quiet and many places are closed out of season. Facilities include a couple of **banks**, a **post office**, a branch of Panayiotis vehicle rental (☎27360 31004) and the office of Kýthira Travel (☎27360 31390, ✉kkmk@otenet.gr), the island's agent for the Neápoli ferry. A few **tavernas** open in summer, of which *Zorba* is by far the best, but the climb from Kapsáli discourages the crowds. A popular café-bar is *Mercato*, which stays open in the winter and also has exhibitions of local art. **Accommodation** is slightly easier to find than in Kapsáli. Options include the *Castello* rooms and studios (℡27360 31069, ⓦwww.castelloapts-kythera.gr; ④), and the *Hotel Margarita* (℡27360 31711, ⓦwww.hotel-margarita.com; B&B ⑤) in a beautiful 1840s house, with air conditioning in the rooms. The *Xenonas Keiti/Keti/Kaiti* (℡27360 31318, ⓕ27360 31558; April–Oct; ④) has non-smoking rooms in a large 240-year-old characterful house that has seen General Metaxas and George Papandreou as visitors. At **Manitohóri**, 2km further inland, is the more basic pension *Ta Kythera* (℡27360 31563; June–Aug; ③).

The southeast coast

The beach at Kapsáli is decent but not large and gets very crowded in July and August. For quieter, undeveloped beaches, it's better to head out to the southeast coast, towards Avlémonas.

Firí Ámmos, Kombonádha and Halkós beaches, and Spiliés cave

Firí Ámmos, the nearest good sand beach to Kapsáli, is popular but not overcrowded, even in summer. To get there, you can follow paved roads from Kapsáli or Livádhi as far as the *Filio* taverna with good traditional food and local specialities (June–Sept) in the scattered settlement of Kálamos; the onward road becomes a four-kilometre dirt track to the beach. Firí Ámmos can also be reached by a second dirt track off the Livádhi–Kálamos road, while another, longer, dirt track, off the Káto Livádhi–Frátsia road, leads to **Kombonádha**, the next beach north. There are summer canteens at both beaches. Much smaller, but prettier, pebbly **Halkós** beach near the southeast corner of the island is signposted from the crossroads at the entrance to Kálamos. Between Kálamos and Kapsáli, a short surfaced road leads south to **Spiliés** village; immediately before the village a signed earth road leads down to a small gorge and a large stalagmite cave with an open-roofed church dedicated to Ayía Sofía (not to be confused with the sea cave near Mylopótamos).

Paleópoli and Avlémonas

PALEÓPOLI, a hamlet of a few scattered houses, is accessible by asphalt roads from Aroniádhika, Frátsia and Kondoliánika. The area is the site of the ancient city of **Skandia**, and excavations on the headland of **Kastrí** have revealed remains of an important Minoan colony. There's little visible evidence, apart from shards of pottery in the low crumbling cliffs, but, happily, tourist development in the area has been barred because of its archeological significance. Consequently, there's just one solitary **taverna**, the *Skandia* (June–Oct), on the two-kilometre sand-and-pebble **beach** that stretches to either side of the headland. This taverna has a great atmosphere, with home cooking and some spontaneous musical evenings.

Paleokástro, the mountain to the west, is the site of ancient Kýthira where there was a sanctuary of Aphrodite, but again, there's little to be seen today. Heading west from Paleópoli, and crossing the river bridge onto the Kondoliánika road, an unpaved road off to the left leads up to a tiny, whitewashed church. From there, a rougher track leads down to **Kaladhí**, a beautiful cliff-backed pebble beach with caves, and rocks jutting out to sea.

AVLÉMONAS, on a rocky shoreline 2km east of Paleópoli beach, is a small fishing port with a bleak end-of-the-world feel as you approach from a distance. It becomes much more attractive once reached, and has a remarkable coordination of colour schemes throughout the village. There is a small, unimpressive

Venetian fortress, and two **tavernas**, of which *Sotiris* is particularly recommended for a wide selection of fresh, well-prepared and reasonably priced fish dishes. A number of **rooms**, including the newer apartments of *Popi Kastrisiou* (℡27360 33735; ❹), and the older, air-conditioned *Schina* studios (℡27360 33060;❹), are available. The Petrohilos family has a number of rooms or studios, including those of *Evdokhia* (℡27360 34069;❸) opposite the *Sotiris*.

North and west of Hóra

LIVÁDHI, a pleasant but unexciting small town 4km north of Hóra, makes a good base for the southern half of the island if you have transport. It has **accommodation**, including, on the main road, the *Hotel Aposperides* (℡27360 31656, ✉aposperides@freemail.gr; B&B ❹), which makes a good base. Livádhi is also home to one of the most efficient travel agencies on the island, Porfyra Travel, which is the main ANEK/ANEN and Olympic Airways agent (℡27360 31888, 🌐www.kythira.info), with exchange and car rental; they can also arrange accommodation or transfers. Doufexis Travel (℡27360 34371, ✉douftvl@hellasnet.gr) has recently opened an office and can help with accommodation and car rental for Kýthira and mainland Peloponnese.

At **Káto Livádhi**, 1km to the east of Livádhi, there is a small **museum** of Byzantine and post-Byzantine art (July–Oct Tues–Sun 8am–3pm; Nov–June Mon–Fri 8.30am–2pm; free) next to the large central church. It contains (labelled in Greek only) frescoes, painstakingly removed from island churches, dating from the twelfth to the eighteenth centuries, a seventh-century mosaic floor and some portable icons. Not far away there is also a cooperative pottery workshop (open mornings and evenings, with a 2–4pm break) and, on the road to Katoúni, a multiple-arched bridge, said to be the longest stone bridge in Greece and a legacy of the nineteenth century when all the Ionian islands were a British protectorate; like others on the island it was built by a Scottish engineer called McPhail. The best view of it is from beside *Rena's zaharoplastío* in Livádhi. A popular **taverna** nearby is the *Theofilos*.

From Livádhi, a side road heads west to Kalokerinés, and continues 3.6km further to the island's principal monastery, **Myrtidhíon**, set above the wild and windswept west coast, among a dead forest of pines burned in June 2000. The monastery's main icon is said to date from 1160. Beyond the monastery, a track leads down to a small anchorage at **Limnária**; there are few beaches along this rocky, forbidding shore.

An early left fork off the Myrtidhíon road out of Livádhi brings you through the hamlet of Poúrko and past the unusual Byzantine church of Áyios Dimítrios. From Poúrko, an increasingly steep road leads up to the **Ayía Elésis**, a nineteenth-century monastery marking the martyrdom of the saint on the hilltop in 375 AD, an event depicted in recent wall-paintings inside the church. For many visitors, however, the breathtaking view from the western side of the courtyard is the main reason to visit.

Mylopótamos, Káto Hóra and the Ayía Sofía cave

North of Livádhi, just beyond Dhókana, it is worth making a detour off the main road for **MYLOPÓTAMOS**, a lovely traditional village and an oasis in summer, set in a wooded valley with a small stream. The shady *Platanos kafenío* makes a pleasant stop for a drink above the village's springs, and the music bar *To Kamari*, in an old restored building, serves snacks and drinks on a lower waterside terrace. Follow the signs for "Katarráktis Neráïdha" to find a waterfall, hidden from view by lush vegetation, next to a long-closed café. The valley below the falls is overgrown but contains the remains of the watermill that gave the village its name.

Káto Hóra (also called Kástro Mylopotamoú), 500m down the road, was Mylopótamos's predecessor, and remains half-enclosed within the walls of a Venetian fortress. The fortress is small, full of locked, well-labelled churches, and has a rather domestic appearance: unlike the castle at Hóra, it was built as a place of refuge for the villagers in case of attack, rather than as a base for a Venetian garrison. All the houses within the walls are abandoned – as are many outside – but are open and accessible. Beyond here, a surfaced but briefly precipitous road continues 5km through spectacular cliffscapes to **Limniónas**, a rocky inlet with a small sand beach, but a fire in June 2000 has left the surrounding countryside exposed and barren.

Most visitors come to Mylopótamos to see the **cave of Ayía Sofía**, the largest and most impressive of a number of caverns on the island. A half-hour signposted walk from the village, or a short drive by a new dirt road being constructed off the Limniónas road, the cave is open regularly from mid-June to mid-September (Mon–Fri 3–8pm, Sat & Sun 11am–5pm; €3). When the cave is closed, you can probably find a guide in Mylopótamos; ask at the village, giving a day's notice if possible. The cave is worth the effort to see: the entrance has been used as a church and has an iconostasis carved from the rock, with important Byzantine frescoes on it. Beyond, the cave system comprises a series of chambers, which reach 250m into the mountain, although the thirty-minute guided tour (in Greek and English) only takes in the more interesting outer chambers. These include some startling formations such as the "shark's teeth", but you have to ask to be shown "Aphrodite's chambers". A minute new species of disc-shaped insect has been discovered there.

Andikýthira island

Thirteen kilometres to the south of Kýthira, the tiny, wind-blown 22-square-kilometre island of **ANDIKÝTHIRA** has, theoretically, a twice-weekly connection with Crete on the Kýthira–Kastélli–Kýthira run (Ⓦ www.anen.gr), but landings are often impossible due to adverse weather. There are attempts to organize a ferry from Kýthira for the festival of Áyios Mýron on August 17 at Galalaniá - an annual reunion jamboree for the Andikytheran diaspora - returning the following day, but these are often thwarted by the wind. Rocky and poor, and a site of political exile until 1964, the island only received electricity in 1984. Attractions include good birdlife (a bird observatory has been built in the old school at Lazianá) and flora, but it's not the place if you want company: with only 45 residents divided among a scattering of settlements – mainly in **Potamós**, the harbour, and **Sohória**, the village – people are rather thin on the ground. The only official accommodation is the set of **rooms** run by the local community (Ⓣ 27360 31390, Ⓔ info@antikythera.gr) at Potamós, which also has a couple of **tavernas**, but you'd be wise to bring plenty of supplies with you. In Sohória the only provisions available are basic foodstuffs at the village shop.

Recent excavation work above Xeropotamos has revealed the site of ancient **Aigila**, a 75-acre fortress city of the Hellenistic period. At the harbour below are the remains of one of ancient Greece's best-preserved warship slipways, a *neosoikos*, carved out of the rock.

The island has one remarkable claim to fame, the **Antikythera Mechanism**, an ancient bronze clockwork "calendar computer" discovered in 1902 in a nearby shipwreck and dated to around 87 BC. It is thought to have been used for calculating the motion and positions of the earth, moon and five other planets, and is the earliest known mechanism with a differential gear by about 1600 years. It is now kept in the National Archeological Museum, Athens.

Yíthio (Gythion)

YÍTHIO, Sparta's ancient port, is the gateway to the dramatic Máni peninsula, and one of the south's most attractive seaside towns in its own right. Its somewhat low-key harbour, with occasional ferries to Pireás and Kýthira, gives onto a graceful nineteenth-century waterside of tiled-roof houses – some of them now showing their age. There are beaches within walking distance, and rooms are relatively easy to find. In the bay, tethered by a long narrow mole, is the islet of **Marathoníssi**, ancient Kranae, where Paris of Troy, having abducted Helen from Menelaus's palace at Sparta, dropped anchor, and where the lovers spent their first night.

Arrival and information

The **bus station** is close to the centre of town, with the main waterfront street, **Vassiléos Pávlou**, ahead of you, and several **banks** nearby. Rozaki Shipping and Travel Agency on the waterfront (℡27330 22650, @rosakigy@otnet.gr) can provide **ferry** sailing times and **car rental** and will also change money. There is a small EOT office at Vassiléos Yeoryíou 20.

A trip of at least three days is worth considering for the Máni; the extensive Hasanakos **bookstore** is worth scouring for books on the Máni, and food supplies can be bought from the large supermarket behind the bus station. **Internet** facilities are available at the *Mystery* café just beyond the supermarket.

Accommodation

Finding **accommodation** shouldn't be hard, with a fair range in town – most hotels are along the waterfront. Despite double-glazing in a number of the waterfront rooms on Vassiléos Pávlou, there is late-night noise from the many bars. Numerous cheaper rooms are signposted up the steps behind the waterfront, or facing Marathoníssi islet.

Out along **Mavrovoúni** beach, which begins 3km south of the town off the Areópoli road, there are numerous hotels and three **campsites**, the nearest and best of which is the *Meltemi* (℡27330 23260, @www.campingmeltemi .gr; April–Oct); a couple of kilometres further are the *Gythion Bay* (℡27330 22522, @www.campinggythio.gr) and *Mani Beach* (℡27330 23450, @www .manibeach.gr; April–Oct).

Demesticas Mavrovoúni beach ℡27330 22775, @www.demestihas.gr. Immediately behind the beach, in a large garden, with a good variety of rooms. ❹

Githion Vassiléos Pávlou 33 ℡27330 23452, @www.campinggythio.gr. A fine old (1864) hotel with period decorated rooms on the waterfront, and above a Dodoni ice-cream parlour. ❹

Kalypso ℡27330 24449, ℻27330 22265. Just off the main road in Mavrovoúni village, opposite the *Milton Hotel*. Very good-value, spacious rooms with kitchens and magnificent sea views north over Yíthio Bay. ❸

Kranai Vassiléos Pávlou 17 ℡ & ℻27330 24394, @kranai@ath.forthnet.gr. On the waterfront, near *Matina*; ask for a room at the front with a balcony. The restaurant below is very popular. ❹

Matina Vassiléos Pávlou 19 ℡27330 22518. A small, friendly pension (formerly *Kondogiannis*), up steep steps alongside the management's jewellery shop, and next to the police station. Back rooms without balconies may be cheaper. ❸

Saga Tzanetáki ☎ 27330 23220, ⓕ 27330 24370. Comfortable seafront pension run by a friendly, knowledgeable French-Greek family, with an excellent restaurant on the ground floor, overlooking the Marathoníssi islet. ❸

The Town and around

Marathoníssi islet is the town's main attraction, with swimming possible off the rocks towards the lighthouse. Amid the island's trees and scrub stands the restored Tzanetákis tower-fortress, built around 1810 by the Turkish-appointed Bey of the Máni, to guard the harbour against his lawless countrymen. It now houses a **Museum of the Máni** (officially Tues–Sun 9.30am–3pm, though often closed; €2), which deals with the exploration of the Máni from Ciriaco de Pizzicoli (1447) to Henri Belle (1861), with captions in Greek and English.

For an aerial view of the islet and town, climb up through Yíthio's stepped streets on to the hill behind – the town's ancient acropolis. The settlement around it, known as **Laryssion**, was quite substantial in Roman times, enjoying wealth from the export of murex, the purple-pigmented mollusc used to dye imperial togas.

Much of the ancient site now lies submerged, but there are some impressive remains of a **Roman theatre** at the northeast end of the town. Follow the road past the post office for about 300m, until you reach the army barracks – the site stands just to the left, inside the outer gate. With most of its stone seats intact, and 50m in diameter, the theatre illustrates perfectly how buildings in Greece take on different guises through the ages: built to one side is a Byzantine church (now ruined) which, in turn, has been pressed into service as the outer wall of the barracks. The archeological museum is currently under restoration, but possesses items from Yíthio and the Lakonian Máni. For some more recent history, visit poet Kostas Vrettos' antiquities shop, Paliatzoures, at Vassiléos Pávlou 25.

Beaches near Yíthio

For swimming, there are a number of places within reach of Yíthio. The small, pebbly Selinítza beach 2km north of the town can be very busy in July and August, as can the five-kilometre beach to the southwest at **Mavrovoúni**, near the campsites detailed opposite; head to the far western end to get away from the crowds and find better sand. The *Ocean's Pub* (☎ 27330 24392, ⓦ www .oceancafe.gr), near *Meltemi Camping*, has windsurfing equipment for hire – May to June is the best season. Some of the buses serving Yíthio from Spárti continue to Mavrovoúni, but ask on board to be sure. Alternatively, if you've got your own transport, there are the superb beaches in Vathý Bay, further south-west, off the Areópoli road. To the north (7km) the little beach of Trínisa ("three islands") is kept clean by the *Afroditi* café. In the village of Áyii Taxiárhes, 4km southeast of Skála, there is an **environmental centre** (☎ & ⓕ 27350 23666, ⓔ lakonikos@archelon.gr): the coastline eastwards from Trínisa to Kokkiniá has nesting turtles; the Evrótas delta, Astéri marsh and Dhivári lagoon are significant migratory bird sites, while the extensive dune areas around the Evrótas are botanically important refuges. At Kyaní Aktí beach, 10km southeast of Skála (via Vlahiótis), there are two nature trails of 600m and 1200m, laid out next to the illegal canteens and motorhome camping.

Eating and drinking

For **meals**, the waterside is the obvious location – though choose carefully from among the tavernas since most have inflated prices for fish and seafood. At the inner end of the harbour, near the jetty, the unpretentious but popular ✈ *Iy Nautilia* ouzerí has water's-edge tables, excellent seafood and tasty *mezédhes*, and fine views of the waterfront, sunsets and Mount Profitis Ilías.

The Máni

The southernmost peninsula of Greece, **the Máni**, stretches from Yíthio in the east to Kardhamýli in the west and terminates at Cape Ténaro, the mythical entrance to the underworld. Its spine, negotiated by road at just a few points, is the vast grey mass of Mount Taïyetos and its southern extension, Sangiás. It is a wild landscape, an arid Mediterranean counterpart to Cornwall or the Scottish highlands, with an idiosyncratic culture and history to match. Nowhere in Greece does a region seem so close to its violent medieval past – which continued largely unaltered until the end of the nineteenth century. Despite, or perhaps because of this, the sense of hospitality is, like nearby Crete, as strong as anywhere in Greece.

The peninsula has two distinct regions: the Éxo (Outer) Máni and the Mésa (Inner or Deep) Máni. The **Mésa Máni** – that part of the peninsula south of a line drawn between Ítylo and Vathý bays – is classic Máni territory, its jagged coast relieved only by the occasional cove, and its land a mass of rocks. It has one major nonhistorical sight, the remarkable caves at **Pýrgos Dhiroú**, which are now very much on the tourist circuit. Beyond this point visitor numbers thin out fast. Attractions include the coastal villages, like **Yeroliménas** on the west coast, or **Kótronas** on the east, but the pleasure is mainly in exploring the **tower-houses** and **churches**, and the solitude. A fair number of the towers survive, their groupings most dramatic at **Kítta**, **Váthia** and **Flomohóri**. The churches are subtler and harder to find, often hidden away from actual villages, but worth the effort to locate them. Many were built during the tenth and

---

Practicalities in the Máni

Getting around can be time-consuming unless you have your own transport, and you may want to consider renting a motorbike from Yíthio or Kalamáta, or a car from Stoúpa or Kalamáta. Without a vehicle, you will need to walk or hitch to supplement the buses. In Mésa Máni, there are just two services: Areópoli–Yeroliménas–Álika–Váthia, although the Váthia section is unreliable (daily in summer; three weekly out of season), and Areópoli–Kótronas–Láyia (daily). An alternative is to make use of the handful of taxis, generally negotiable, at Areópoli, Yeroliménas, Kótronas and Yíthio. Currently, for example, a taxi from Areópoli to Váthia would cost €30.

There is a **bank** at Areópoli. You can sometimes change cash at the **post offices** (Mon–Fri 7.30am–2pm) in Yeroliménas or Areópoli, but it's wiser to bring as much as you think you'll need. **Opening hours** of shops, tavernas, petrol stations and almost anything else can be idiosyncratic in the Mésa Máni, so it may also prove wise to bring some general supplies with you – there are well-stocked **supermarkets** in Yíthio, Stoúpa and Kalamáta, and smaller ones in Areópoli. Always try and arrange in advance for any **accommodation** that is not a hotel – owners can be very hard to locate.

A good, large-scale map is invaluable for navigating among the innumerable tiny settlements of the Mésa Máni: both Road Editions and Anavasi have a 1:50 000 scale map of the area, while Anavasi also produce a 1:25 000 map of the southernmost half.

twelfth centuries, when the Maniots enthusiastically embraced Christianity; almost all retain at least traces of frescoes, though most are kept locked, with elusive wardens. The remarkable and well-illustrated website of John Chapman (Ⓦ www.zorbas.de/maniguide) is a comprehensive information source on the Máni, in particular its history, churches and frescoes.

The **Éxo Máni** – the coast up from Areópoli to Kalamáta, much of it in Messinía province – sees the emphasis shift much more to walking and beaches. **Stoúpa** and **Kardhamýli** are both beautiful resorts, developing but far from spoilt. The road itself is an experience, threading up into the foothills of Taïyetos before looping back down to the sea.

Some Maniot history

The **mountains** offer the key to Maniot history. Formidable natural barriers, they provided a refuge from, and bastion of resistance to, every occupying force of the last two millennia. The Dorians never reached this far south in the wake of the Mycenaeans. Roman occupation was perfunctory and Christianity did not take root in the interior until the ninth century (some five hundred years after the establishment of Byzantium). Throughout the years of Venetian and Turkish control of the Peloponnese there were constant rebellions, climaxing in the Maniot uprising on March 17, 1821, a week before Archbishop Yermanos raised the Greek flag at Kalávryta to officially launch the War of Independence.

Alongside this national assertiveness was an equally intense and violent internal tribalism, seen at its most extreme in the elaborate tradition of **blood feuds** (see box overleaf), probably prolonged, and certainly exploited, by the **Turks**. The first Maniot uprising against them had taken place in 1571, a year after the Ottoman occupation. There were to be renewed attempts through the succeeding centuries, with plots involving the Venetians, French and Russians. But the Turks, wisely, opted to control the Máni by granting a level of local autonomy, investing power in one or other clan whose leader they designated "bey" of the region. The position provided a focus for the obsession with arms and war and worked well until the nineteenth-century appointment of **Petrobey Mavromihalis**. With a power base at Liméni he united the clans in revolution, and his Maniot army was to prove vital to the success of the War of Independence.

Unsurprisingly, the end of the war and the formation of an **independent Greece** did not mark the end of Maniot rebellion. Mavromihalis swiftly fell out with the first president of the nation, Kapodhistrías and, with other members of the clan, was imprisoned by him at Náfplio – an act which led to the president's assassination at the hands of Petrobey's brothers. The monarchy fared little better until one of the king's German officers was sent to the Máni to enlist soldiers in a special Maniot militia. The idea was adopted with enthusiasm, and was the start of an enduring tradition of Maniot service in the modern Greek military.

In the twentieth century, the area slipped into decline, with persistent **depopulation** of the villages. In places like Váthia and Kítta, which once held populations in the hundreds, the numbers are now down to single figures, predominantly the old. Socially and politically the region is notorious as the most conservative in Greece. The Maniots reputedly enjoyed an influence during the colonels' junta, when the region first acquired roads, mains electricity and running water. They voted almost unanimously for the monarchy in the 1974 plebiscite, and this is one of the very few parts of Greece where you may still see visible support for the ex-king or the far-right National Party. Recently, there has been an influx of money, and considerable refurbishment: many postwar concrete houses have now acquired "traditional" stone facings.

Maniot blood feuds

Blood feuds were the result of an intricate feudal society that seems to have developed across the peninsula in the fourteenth century. After the arrival of refugee Byzantine families, an aristocracy known as Nyklians arose, and the various clans gradually developed strongholds in the tightly clustered villages. The poor, rocky soil was totally inadequate for the population and over the next five centuries the clans clashed frequently and bloodily for land, power and prestige.

The feuds became ever more complex and gave rise to the building of **strongholds**: marble-roofed battle towers that, in the elaborate mores of the peninsula, could be raised only by those of Nyklian descent. From these local forts the clans – often based in the same village – conducted vendettas according to strict rules and aims. The object was to annihilate both the tower and the male members of the opposing clan. The favoured method of attack was to smash the prestigious tower roofs; the forts consequently rose to four and five storeys.

Feuds would customarily be signalled by the ringing of **church bells** and from this moment the adversaries would confine themselves to their towers, firing at each other with all available weaponry. The battles could last for years, even decades, with women (who were safe from attack) shuttling in food, ammunition and supplies. During the really prolonged feuds, temporary truces were declared at harvest times; then with business completed the battle would recommence. Ordinary villagers – the non-Nyklian peasantry – would, meanwhile, evacuate for the duration of the worst conflict. The feuds would end in one of two ways: destruction of a family in battle, or total surrender of a whole clan in a gesture of *psyhikó* ("a thing of the soul"), when they would file out to kiss the hands of enemy parents who had lost "guns" (the Maniot term for male children) in the feud; the victors would then dictate strict terms by which the vanquished could remain in the village.

The last full-scale feud took place as late as 1870, in the village of Kítta, and required a full detachment of the regular army to put it down.

Into the Máni: Yíthio to Areópoli

The road from Yíthio into the Máni begins amid a fertile and gentle wooded landscape, running slightly inland of the coast and Mavrovoúni beach, through tracts of citrus and olive groves and between hilltop towers. About 12km beyond Yíthio, the Máni suddenly asserts itself as the road enters a valley below the **castle of Passavá**. The castle is one of a pair (with Kelefá to the west) guarding the Máni or perhaps, more accurately, guarding against the Máni. Signed from a house just west of the 3rd Avin petrol station, it is a scramble up, but the site is ample reward, with views out across two bays and for some miles along the defile from Areópoli. There has been a fortress on Passavá since Mycenaean times; the present version is an eighteenth-century Turkish rebuilding of a Frankish fort (1210) that the Venetians destroyed on their flight from the Peloponnese in 1684. It was abandoned by the Turks in 1780 following the massacre of its garrison and their civilian dependants by the Maniot Grigorakis clan – their vengeance for the arrest and execution by the Turks of the clan chief.

Shortly after Passavá, a turning to the left leads down to an attractive long sandy beach at **Vathý Bay** (Vathý Ayéranou), which is mostly used by German tourists. At the southern end of the beach is the *Hotel Belle Helene* (☎27330 93001, ⓕ27330 98006; April–Oct; ❻), often block-booked by German groups; towards the north end, behind the reasonable *Gorgona* restaurant, the *Kronos* campsite (☎27330 93320; April–Oct) is well suited to families.

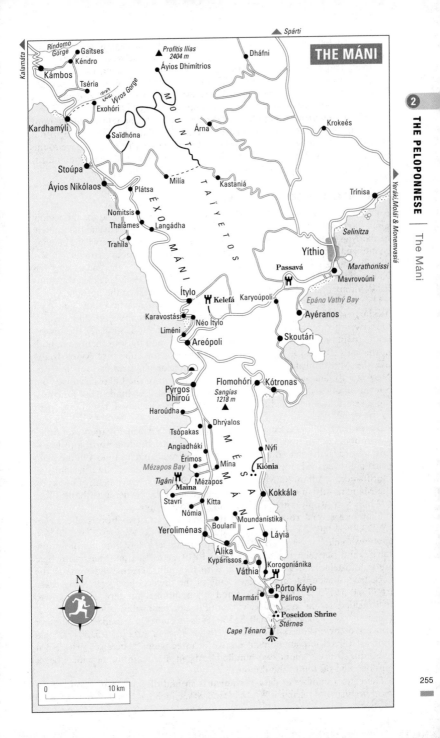

The road beyond the beach deteriorates rapidly, though it is possible to continue through woods to the village of **Ayéranos**, with a tower-house complex, and from there – if you can find your way among the numerous rough tracks – to Skoutári, below which is another reasonable beach with some Roman remains. A better road to Skoutári leaves the main Yíthio–Areópoli road near Karyoúpoli, itself dominated by an imposing tower-house.

Continuing towards Areópoli from Passavá, the landscape remains fertile until the wild, scrubby mass of Mount Kouskoúni signals the final approach to the Mésa Máni. You enter another pass, with **Kelefá castle** (see p.262) above to the north, and beyond it several southerly peaks of the Taïyetos ridge. Areópoli, as you curl down from the hills, radiates a real sense of arrival.

Areópoli and around

An austere-looking town, **AREÓPOLI** sets an immediate mood for the region. Until the nineteenth century it was secondary to Ítylo, 6km north and the gateway to the Mésa Máni, but the modern road has made it, to all intents, the region's centre, and many of the stone buildings are now undergoing tasteful renovation. Formerly Tsímova, its present name ("Town of Ares" – the god of war) was bestowed for its efforts during the War of Independence. It was here that Mavromihalis (commemorated by a statue in the main platía) declared the uprising.

The town's sights are archetypally Maniot in their anachronisms. The **Áyii Taxiárhes** cathedral, for example, has primitive reliefs above its doors which look twelfth century until you notice their date of 1798. Similarly, the tower-houses could readily be described as medieval, though most of them were built in the early 1800s. On its own, in a little platía, is the church of **Áyios Ioán-nis**, the Mavromihalis' family church; the interior has strip-cartoon frescoes. Nearby, a Byzantine museum is under construction in the Nikolakis tower, but remains unopened, even after eight years' work. Also EU-funded, but function-ing successfully, a new traditional bakery produces a variety of tasty breads next to the cathedral.

Buses leave Areópoli from the main square, Platía Athánatos; the ticket office is two doors down from the *Europa Grill*. If you are heading north into Mess-inía, towards Kalamáta, you will probably need to change in Ítylo. On the main platía are several zaharoplastía, a useful **supermarket** (especially if heading on south) and the Adhou oti Mani **bookshop**, with an extensive stock of books on the Máni, mostly in Greek, and maps; just around the corner are a **bank** (Tues & Thurs 9am–1pm) with an ATM, and the **post office**.

There are several **rooms** around the cathedral and two **hotels**: the *Kouris* (T27330 51340; ❹) on the main square, and the ⚔ *Mani* (T27330 51190, Wwww.hotelmani.gr; B&B ❺) in a quiet street a few minutes from the square, and between the bank and the EKO petrol station. The rooms here are comfortable and well equipped, with mosquito screens, and some at the back have wonderful sunset views. One of the towers, the *Pyrgos Kapetanakou* (T27330 51479; ❹), has been restored as a traditional guesthouse; the two- to five-bedded rooms are austerely beautiful and reasonably priced. Nearby is the upmarket *Londas* (T27330 51360, Wusers.otenet.gr/~londas; ❺), another converted tower-house. The cheaper *Pyrgos Tsimova* (T27330 51301; ❹) has more of a lived-in feel; rooms sleep two or three people. There is a private war museum, covering about two hundred years, in the living room, with a Lewis gun perched on top of the dresser.

There are a number of **café-restaurants** around the main square; one of the most popular and reliable is ⚔ *Nicola's Corner*, which has a large variety of good *mezédhes*. The *inomayirio O Barba Petros* has a little courtyard off a pedestrian street towards Áyii Taxiárhes.

The Pýrgos Dhiroú caves

Eight kilometres south of Areópoli, at the village of **PÝRGOS DHIROÚ**, the road forks off to the underground caves – the Máni's major tourist attraction. The village itself has an isolated 21-metre tower-house, but is otherwise geared to the cave trade, with numerous tavernas and cafés, and a number of **rooms** for rent. The closest to the caves, and the sea, are at the *Panorama* restaurant (☎27330 52280; ❸); the rooms have impressive sea views. A little higher up the hill is a new and stylishly minimalist hotel, *Sole e Mare* (☎27330 52240, ✉soleemare91@in.gr; ❼). *Xenonas Katafygi* at Hariá, just northeast of the village, is a restored eighteenth-century castle with apartments (☎27330 52331; ❺).

The **Pýrgos Dhiroú caves** (daily: June–Sept 8.30am–5.30pm; Oct–May 8.30am–3pm; €12), often referred to simply as "Spílea", are 4km beyond the main village, set beside the sea and a separate beach (accessed from a higher fork in the road). They are very much a packaged attraction but, unless caves leave you cold, they are worth a visit, especially on weekday afternoons when the wait is shorter. A visit consists of a thirty-minute punt around the underground waterways of the **Glyfádha (Vlyhádha) caves**, well lit and crammed with stalactites, whose reflections are a remarkable sight in the two- to twenty-metre depth of water. You are then permitted a brief tour on foot of the **Alepótrypa caves** – huge chambers (one of them 100m by 60m) in which excavation has unearthed evidence of prehistoric occupation. Unfortunately there is no foreign-language commentary.

You should buy a ticket as soon as you arrive at the caves: this gives you a priority number for the tours. At a mid-season weekend you can wait for an hour or more, so it's best to arrive as early as possible in the day with gear to make the most of the adjacent beach. If time is short, taxis from Areópoli will take you to the caves, then wait and take you back; prices, especially if split four ways, are reasonable.

The nearby **museum** (theoretically Tues–Sun 8.30am–3pm but unreliable; €3), on a bend of the road, contains interesting Neolithic finds from the caves; the few captions are in Greek.

South towards Yeroliménas

The narrow, raised coastal plain between Pýrgos Dhiroú and Yeroliménas is one of the more fertile parts of the Mésa Máni with a uniform sprinkling of dwarf olive trees. This seventeen-kilometre stretch of the so-called "shadow coast" supported, until the twentieth century, an extraordinary number of small villages. The main road carefully avoids most of them, but many are sited just a kilometre or so to the east or west of it. Few villages have shops, or facilities such as public phones, so you should carry sufficient water if walking. Drivers will find the road surfaces patchy, new in places, potholed elsewhere. There are numerous road signs, although a number are used for firearms target practice.

The area retains a major concentration of **churches**, many of them Byzantine, dating from the ninth to the fourteenth centuries. Though many are now signposted, they can still be hard to find, but are well detailed in Peter Greenhalgh's *Deep Into Mani* (see p.1149). The main feature to look for is a barrel roof. Almost all are kept locked, though a key can sometimes be found by asking around. Among Greenhalgh's favourites on the seaward side are the eleventh-century **church of the Taxiárhis** at Haroúdha (3km south of Pýrgos Dhiroú), the semi-ruined **Trissákia church** west of Tsópakas (5km south of Pýrgos Dhiroú) and the twelfth-century **Ayía Varvára** at Érimos (8km south of Pýrgos Dhiroú).

At **Angiadháki**, the hospitable, stone-built *Villa Koulis* (also called *Xenonas Strilakou*) (☎27330 52350; ❸) has rooms and apartments (❹) set in a pleasant garden and orchard. A shared kitchen is available for guests.

Mézapos and the Castle of the Maina

An easy excursion from the main road is to the small village of **MÉZAPOS**, whose deep-water harbour made it one of the chief settlements of Máni, until the road was built in the twentieth century. From the main road, take the side road to Áyios Yeóryios and then to Mézapos, where there are a few rooms. The best of some fine coastal walks leads to the twelfth-century **church of Vlahérna**, which has a few fresco fragments, including a memorable John the Baptist. If you ask at one of the cafés in Mézapos, it's sometimes possible to negotiate a boat trip out to Tigáni, or even around the cape to Yeroliménas.

The nearby village of **STAVRÍ** (3km from the main road) offers traditional **tower-house accommodation** in the converted *Tsitsiris Castle* complex (☎27330 56297, ⊛www.holidayshop.gr/tsitsiriscastle; B&B ❺), similarly priced to the tower hotels in Areópoli, though much bigger and in a more remote, exciting setting – and well placed for local hiking. The broad plateau here has a confusing network of small, unsigned roads, and many maps are hopelessly inadequate. To the northeast of Stavrí, but within walking distance, is the twelfth-century **Episkopí church**, in Katayióryis hamlet; the roof has been restored, while inside there are some fine but faded frescoes, and columns crowned by Ionic capitals, with a surprising marble arch at the entry to the iconostasis. Head from Stavrí to the deserted hamlet of **Ayía Kyriakí** for good views, and access to the castle (2.5km) on the bare **Tigáni** ("Frying Pan") **peninsula**. The fortress, by general consensus, seems to have been the **Castle of the Maina**, constructed like those of Mystra and Monemvasiá by the Frankish baron, Guillaume de Villehardouin, and ceded with them to the Byzantines in 1261. Tigáni is as arid a site as any in Greece – a dry Monemvasiá in effect – whose fortress seems scarcely man-made, blending as it does into the terrain. It's a jagged walk out to the castle across rocks fashioned into pans for salt-gathering; within the walls are ruins of a huge Byzantine church and numerous cisterns.

Kítta and Boularíï

Continuing along the main road, **KÍTTA**, once the largest and most powerful village in the region, boasts the crumbling remains of more than twenty tower-houses. It was here in 1870 that the last feudal war took place, only being suppressed by a full battalion of four hundred regular soldiers. Over to the west, visible from the village, is another eruption of tower-houses at Kítta's traditional rival, Nómia.

Two kilometres south of Kítta and east of the main road, **BOULARÍÏ** is one of the most interesting and accessible villages in the Mésa Máni. It is clearly divided into "upper" and "lower" quarters, both of which retain well-preserved tower-houses and, in varying states of decay, some twenty churches. The two most impressive are tenth-century **Áyios Pandelímon** to the northwest (enclosed and locked, with two frescoes that are the earliest in the Máni) and eleventh-century **Áyios Stratigós**, which is just over the brow of the hill at the top of the village. This second church is also kept locked, but there are possibly keys at the Yeroliménas post office. Entry is well rewarded as the church possesses a spectacular series of frescoes from the twelfth to the eighteenth centuries (torch necessary).

Yeroliménas and Cape Ténaro

After the journey from Areópoli, **YEROLIMÉNAS** (Yerolimín) feels like a village in limbo, of uncertain purpose, but it does make a good base for exploring the southern extremities of the Máni. Despite appearances, the village was only developed in the 1870s – around a jetty and warehouses built by a local (a non-Nyklian migrant) who had made good on the island of Sýros. There are a few shops, a **post office**, a couple of **cafés** and several **hotels**, including the long-established *Akroyiali* (T 27330 54204, W www.gerolimenas-hotels .com; B&B ❸–❺), with air-conditioned rooms, apartments and a traditional stone-built hotel. There are several **eating options** nearby, but the baked fish in lemon juice and olive oil served at the *Akroyiali* takes some beating.

At the dock, occasional boat trips are offered – when the local owners feel like it – around Cape Ténaro, formerly known as Cape Mátapan (see overleaf). The petrol station just beyond Yeroliménas is currently the southernmost of the peninsula.

Álika to Pórto Káyio and Marmári

South from Yeroliménas, the scenery becomes browner and more arid; a good road (and the bus) continues to **Álika**, where it divides. One fork leads east through the mountains to Láyia (see p.261), and the other continues to Váthia

△ Váthia village, the Máni

and across the Marmári isthmus towards Ténaro. Between Álika and Váthia there are good coves for swimming. One of the best is **Kypárissos**, reached by following a dry riverbed about midway to Váthia. On the headland above are scattered Roman remains of ancient Kaenipolis, including (amid the walled fields) the excavated ruins of a sixth-century basilica.

VÁTHIA, a photogenic group of tower-houses set uncompromisingly on a high hillside outcrop, is one of the most dramatic villages in the Mésa Máni. It features in Colonel Leake's account of his travels, one of the best sources on Greece in the early nineteenth century. He was warned to avoid going through the village in 1805 as a feud had been running between two families for the previous forty years. Today it has the feel of a ghost town. The EOT-restored inn, occupying a dozen tower-houses, has been bankrupt and inactive for some years now, though there is a seasonal café.

From Váthia the road south to the cape edges around the mountain, before slowly descending to a couple of junctions. Left at the second brings you down to the beach and laid-back hamlet of **PÓRTO KÁYIO** ("Bay of Quails", 6km from Váthia). There are comfortable **rooms** at the *Akrotiri* (☎27330 52013, Ⓦwww.porto-kagio.com; ❹) and the *Porto* (☎27330 52033; ❹), both of which have popular **fish tavernas**; the latter also has an art gallery. A pleasant half-hour walk goes out to the Ágios Nikólaos chapel on the southeastern headland of the bay, while across the bay on the north side are the spectacular ruins of a Turkish fortress contemporary with Kelefá and the monastery of Korogoniánika.

Above Pórto Káyio, the right branch of the road goes south along the headland, capped by the Grigorákis tower, to pleasant sandy **beaches** at the double bay of **Marmári**. A variety of rooms is available above the beach at *To Marmari* (☎27330 52101; Easter–Oct; ❹–❺), which has sea views and serves good food.

On to Cape Ténaro

Starting from the left fork before Marmári, follow the surfaced road and signs for the fish taverna, passing a turning for Páliros and making your way along the final barren peninsula, to Stérnes (Kokkinóyia). The road ends at a knoll crowned with the squat **chapel of Asómati**, constructed largely of materials from an ancient temple of Poseidon. The nearby taverna *Akron Tainaro* (☎27330 53064; ❸) has good, locally caught fish, and rooms.

To the left (east) as you face the chapel is the little pebbly **bay of Asómati**; on the shore is a small **cave**, another addition to the list of mythical entrances to the underworld. Patrick Leigh Fermor, in *Mani* (see p.1136), writes of yet another "Gates of Hades" cave, which he swam into on the western side of the point, just below Marmári. To the right (west) of Asómati, the marked main path continues along the edge of another cove and through the metre-high foundations of a **Roman town** that grew up around the Poseidon shrine; there is even a mosaic in one structure. From here the old trail, which existed before the road was bulldozed, reappears as a walled path, allowing 180-degree views of the sea on its twenty-five-minute course to the lighthouse on **Cape Ténaro**.

The east coast

The east coast of the Mésa Máni is most easily approached from **Areópoli**, where there's a daily **bus** through Kótronas to Láyia. However, if you have transport, or you're prepared to walk and hitch, there's satisfaction in doing a full loop of the peninsula, crossing over to Láyia from Yeroliménas or Pórto Káyio.

The landscape of the eastern side, the "sunward coast", is different to the west, the "shadow coast". There are few beaches, and less coastal plain, with larger, more scattered villages hanging on the hillsides. Road signs are fewer than in the west.

Láyia to Kokkála

From the fork at Álika (see p.259), it's 10km to **LÁYIA**, one of the highest villages (400m) in the Mésa Máni. A turning off the road, not far above Álika, to Moundanístika, the Máni's highest village, is recommended for spectacular views. Coming from Pórto Káyio on foot, it takes around three hours; the route, at times on narrow tracks, is dramatic, passing the semi-deserted hilltop village of **Korogoniánika**. Láyia itself is a multi-towered village that perfectly exemplifies the feudal setup of the old Máni. Four Nyklian families lived here, and their four independently sited settlements, each with its own church, survive. One of the taller towers, so the locals claim, was built overnight by four hundred men of one clan, hoping to gain an advantage at sunrise. During the eighteenth century the village was home to a Maniot doctor – a strategic base from which to attend profitably to the war-wounded all across the peninsula. Today, a council-owned café faces the main church and the village shows healthy signs of revival, with the ongoing refurbishment of a number of houses.

Leaving Láyia northwards, the spectacularly descending road has possibly the best view in the Máni – of most of the northeast coast. Seven kilometres on is **KOKKÁLA**, a larger, though visually unexciting, village, with a small harbour and scruffy beach, a longer beach to the north and walking possibilities. The village boasts several café-restaurants, and rooms for rent above the *Taverna Marathos* (☎27330 21118; summer only; ❸) on the beach. More central is the friendly *Hotel Soloteri* (☎27330 21126; ❸), which may be the only place open out of high season. Three kilometres to the northwest, on the mountainside above Nýfi, is one of the area's few ancient sites, a spot known as Kiónia (columns), with the foundations of two Doric temples.

Flomohóri and Kótronas

Kokkála is the first of a string of undistinguished villages until Dhrymós appears on the hillside high above. After 22km northwards you reach **FLOMOHÓRI**; the land below is relatively fertile, and the village has maintained a reasonable population as well as a last imposing group of tower-houses. **KÓTRONAS**, a few kilometres downhill, feels less harsh than the rest of the Máni. It is still a fishing village, and its pebble beach (there are sandy strips further around the bay) and causeway-islet make it a good last stop in the region. The village is frequented by a fair number of tourists (mainly Germans) each summer, and has a trio of pensions. The most pleasant is the well-priced *Kali Kardia* (also known as *4-Asteria*; ☎27330 21246; ❷) above a seafront café. The attractive *Kotronas Bay* studios (☎27330 21340, ⓦ www.kotronasbay.gr; April–Nov; ❻) are set in a large garden overlooking the sea. The coastal road from here to Skoutári, and hence Yíthio, has been (mostly, though not entirely) widened and paved, and offers an alternative to the inland route from Flomohóri to Areópoli – although the latter passes through the lovely, oak-wooded Himára valley.

The Éxo Máni: Areópoli north to Kalamáta

The forty kilometres of road into Messinía, between Areópoli and Kalamáta, are as dramatic and beautiful as any in Greece, almost a corniche route between the **Taïyetos** ridge and the **Gulf of Messinía**. The first few settlements en route are classic Maniot villages, their towers packed against the hillside. As you move north, with the road dropping to near sea level, there are three or four small resorts, which are becoming increasingly popular but are as yet relatively unspoilt. For walkers, there is a reasonably well-preserved *kalderími* (footpath) paralleling (or short-cutting) much of the paved route, with a superb **gorge hike** just north of Kardhamýli. The beach resort of **Stoúpa** makes a good base for local exploration and touring.

North to Liméni

Areópoli stands back a kilometre or so from the sea. **LIMÉNI**, the town's tiny traditional port, lies 3km to the north: a scattering of houses dominated by the restored tower-house of Petrobey Mavromihalis, which resembles nothing so much as an English country parish church. On one of the bends on the road down to Liméni is the newish *Limeni Village* (T27330 51111, F27330 51182; ⑥), a re-creation of Maniot houses, high above the rocky shore and with its own swimming pool. Further round the bay, on the waterside, there are a few tavernas, including *Tò Limeni*, and some basic rooms.

Ítylo and around

ÍTYLO (Oítylo), 11km from Areópoli, is the transport hub for the region. If you are heading into Messinía province towards Kalamáta, either from Yíthio or Areópoli, you will probably need to change here, at the *Petrini Gonia* café. While waiting for the bus, walk a short distance down to the main church – perched on a balcony overlooking the bay and with a pointed memorial to civil-war dead. The village is currently experiencing a resurgence in fortunes, with many of the old houses, until recently falling into disrepair, now being restored. In earlier days, Ítylo was the capital of the Máni, and from the sixteenth to the eighteenth century it was the region's most notorious base for piracy and slave trading. The Maniots traded amorally and efficiently in slaves, selling Turks to Venetians, Venetians to Turks, and, at times of feud, the women of each other's clans to both. Irritated by the piracy and hoping to control the important pass to the north, the Turks built the sprawling **castle of Kelefá** in 1670. This is just 1km's walk from Ítylo across a gorge, and its walls and bastions, built for a garrison of five hundred, are substantially intact. Also worth exploring is the **monastery of Dhekoúlou**, down towards the coast; its setting is beautiful and there are some fine eighteenth-century frescoes in the chapel.

There are a few **rooms** to rent in Ítylo, and a smart guesthouse with a pool just south of town: the *Pyrgos Alevras* (T27330 59388, W www.alevrastower.gr; ④), with self-catering studios and views – well positioned if you have your own transport. Another option is to look for accommodation by the beach in **NÉO ÍTYLO**, which is just round the bay from Ítylo's ancient and modern seaport, Karavostási. Néo Ítylo is a tiny hamlet, but as well as rooms for rent it boasts the comfortable *Hotel Ítylo* (T27330 59222; ⑤), which also runs the slightly cheaper *Alevras* (④) guesthouse. The *Faros* taverna in Karavostási makes good fish dishes, and also has en-suite rooms (T27330 59204; ③).

Langádha, Nomitsís, Thalámes and Plátsa

If you want to walk for a stretch of the onward route, you can pick up the *kalderími* just below the main road out of Ítylo. As it continues north, the track occasionally crosses the modern road, but it is distinct at least as far as Kotróni or Rínglia. The most interesting of the villages along the way are **LANGÁDHA**, for its setting that bristles with towers, and **NOMITSÍS**, for its trio of frescoed Byzantine churches strung out along the main street. A couple more churches are off the road just to the north, including the **Metamórfosis**, which has delightful sculpted animal capitals. Just before Nomitsís, you pass the hamlet of **THALÁMES**, where a local enthusiast has set up a widely advertised **Museum of Maniot Folklore and History** (April–Sept daily 9am–4pm; €2.50). The tag "museum" is perhaps a bit inflated for what is really an unlabelled collection of junkshop items, but it's a nice stop nonetheless and it also sells local honey and olive oil. **PLÁTSA**, the last village before the road descends, has no less than four Byzantine churches: Áyios Dimítrios, Áyios Ioánnis, Áyios Nikólaos and Ayía Paraskeví.

Áyios Nikólaos and Stoúpa

The beaches of the Éxo Máni begin south of **ÁYIOS NIKÓLAOS** (Selenítsa), at the pleasant, tree-shaded Pantazí beach. The village's delightful little harbour is flanked by old stone houses, cafés and tavernas overlooking the fishing boats. The *Limeni* taverna at the southern end of the harbour, with a small shaded extension over the water, does excellent fresh fish. There is a scattering of **rooms** and apartments; one of the best is the *Skafidakia* (☎27210 77698; ❹) in a stone building near the OTE mast, and near a hidden swimming jetty known as Gnospí; the owner can suggest local walks. The coastal road continues south, through Áyios Dimítrios and then past spectacular cliffs and the Katafiyi cave, one of several, to the end of the road at pretty **Trahíla**. Enquire there at the tower behind the harbour for the spacious and well-priced *Kosta* apartments (☎27210 98058; ❸).

Just to the north of Áyios Nikólaos, **STOÚPA** is much more developed, and justifiably so. It has possibly the best sands along this coast, with two glorious **beaches** (Stoúpa and the smaller, deeper Kalogriá) separated by a headland, each sloping into the sea and superb for children. Submarine freshwater springs gush into the bay, keeping it unusually clean, if also a bit cold. Ten minutes to the north of Kalogriá beach is the delightful and often deserted cove of Dhelfíni. A further 600m brings you to the pebble beach of Fonéa, wrapped around a rock outcrop and tucked into a corner of the hillside. Stoúpa was home in 1917–18 to the wandering Cretan writer, Nikos Kazantzakis, who is said to have based the title character in *Zorba the Greek* on a worker at the lignite mine in nearby Pástrova, though the book itself was written later on Égina island in the Saronic Gulf. Just inland of Stoúpa, in 371 BC, the dominance of the Spartans was finally broken, by the Thebans, at the battle of Leuctra (modern Léfktro).

Out of peak season, Stoúpa is certainly recommended, though in July and August, and any summer weekend, you may find the crowds a bit overwhelming and space at a premium. The area is an excellent base for walkers, with interesting villages and a network of paths that includes some magnificently engineered *kalderímia*. A popular walking-guide booklet and large-scale map are available: ask at the helpfully efficient Doufexis Travel (☎27210 77677, ✉douftvl@hellasnet.gr) who can also find accommodation, provide exchange and organize car hire (including car hire and accommodation for the southern Peloponnese during the winter). Accommodation in the resort includes numerous **rooms** and apartments, and several **hotels**. The *Lefktron* (☎27210 77322, ⓦwww.lefktron-hotel.gr; ❹) and the *Stoupa* (☎27210 77308, ☏27210 77568; ❹) are upmarket but very friendly and reasonably priced. Over the road from Kalogriá beach is *Kalogria Camping* (☎27210 77319; May–Oct). Towards Kard-hamýli, above Dhelfíni beach, there is another, livelier, **campsite**, *Ta Delfinia*

(☎27210 77318; April–Sept). There are plenty of **tavernas**, but *Akroyiali* at the southern end of the main beach not only has well-prepared food, including fresh fish, but also has views after dark of the lights of the mountain village Saïdhóna which look remarkably like an extra constellation of stars. The *Gelateria* home-made ice-cream place at the other end of the beach is justifiably famous. Bus services can be unreliable on the Kalamáta–Ítylo route, and **taxis** are in short supply locally; the Stoúpa taxi is on ☎27210 77477 and the nearest to Áyios Nikólaos is at Plátsa on ☎27210 74226.

Kardhamýli

KARDHAMÝLI, 8km north of Stoúpa, is also a major resort, by Peloponnese standards at least, with ranks of self-catering apartments and pensions, block-booked by the package trade in season, and suffering from the busy main road that splits it. But once again the **beach** is good, though not sandy – a long pebble strip north of the village and backed by acres of olive trees.

Inland from the platía, it's a nice walk up to "Old Kardhamýli"; a partly restored citadel of abandoned tower-houses is gathered about the eighteenth-century church of **Áyios Spyrídhon** with its unusual multistorey bell tower, and the courtyard where the Maniot chieftains Kolokotronis and Mavromihalis played human chess with their troops during the War of Independence. Further back, on the *kalderími* up to Ayía Sofía, is a pair of ancient tombs, said to be of the **Dioskoúri** (the Gemini twins).

On the main road near the platía is a branch of the Agricultural Bank (Mon–Thurs; summer only) and a **post office**. **Hotels** include the upmarket and comfortable *Cardamili Beach* (☎27210 73180, ✉axem@kal.forthnet.gr; ❺) to the north. Down a narrow street at the southern end of town is *Kyria Lela's* (☎27210 73541; ❹), an excellent traditional taverna with fine sea-view **rooms**, which should be booked well ahead in summer. The **campsite**, *Melitsina* (☎27210 73461; May–Sept), is 2km from the village. Among Kardhamýli's **tavernas**, try *Kiki's* on the square, as well as the aforementioned *Kyria Lela's*.

Inland to the Výros gorge

North of Kardhamýli the road leaves the coast, which rises to cliffs around a cape, before finally dropping back to the sea in the bay near Kalamáta. But before moving on, a day or two spent exploring Kardhamýli's immediate environs on foot is time well spent.

The giant **Výros gorge** plunges down from the very summit ridge of Taïyetos to meet the sea just north of the resort, and tracks penetrate the gorge from various directions. From Kardhamýli, the *kalderími* from the citadel continues to the church and village of Ayía Sofía, and then proceeds on a mixture of tracks and lanes either across the plateau up to the hamlet of Exohóri, or down into the gorge, where two **monasteries** nestle deep at the base of dramatic cliffs. An hour or so inland along the canyon, more cobbled ways lead up to either Tséria on the north bank (there's a taverna, but no accommodation) or back towards Exohóri on the south flank, which has a **hotel**, *To Farangi* (☎27210 73372, ℱ27210 73392; ❹), and is well placed for starting walks, or simply for magnificent views. Linking any or all of these points is a reasonable day's hiking at most; forays further upstream require full hiking gear and detailed topographical maps.

Spárti, Mystra and Taïyetos

The central core of the Peloponnese is the luxuriantly spreading Mount Ménalo; but due south, in the Lakonian Evrótas valley, are **Spárti** and its Byzantine companion, **Mystra**, both overlooked and sheltered from the west by the massive and astonishing wall of the **Taïyetos** mountain ridge. Spárti is inextricably entwined with the development of ancient Greece, while Mystra, arrayed in splendour on its own hillside, is one of the country's most compelling historical sites of the last two millennia.

Spárti (Sparta)

Thucydides predicted that if the ancient city of **Sparta** were deserted, "distant ages would be very unwilling to believe its power at all equal to its fame". The city had no great temples or public buildings and throughout its period of greatness it remained unfortified: Lykurgos, architect of the Spartan constitution, declared that "it is men not walls that make a city". Consequently, modern **SPÁRTI**, laid out on a generous grid in 1834, has few ancient ruins, and is today the pleasant organizational centre of a huge agricultural plain. Spárti's appeal is its ordinariness – its pedestrianized side streets, café-lined squares, orange trees and evening *vólta*. The reason for coming here is basically to see **Mystra**, the Byzantine town, 5km to the west, which once controlled great swaths of the medieval world.

Arrival and information

If it is Mystra that brings you here, and you arrive early in the day, you may well decide to move straight on. Getting out of Spárti is straightforward. The **main bus terminal** (for Trípoli, Athens, Monemvasiá, Kalamáta and the Máni) is on the eastern edge of town at the far end of Lykoúrgou, but for the centre the locals alight earlier on Lykoúrgou, near the archeological museum. Buses for **Mystra** leave (hourly Mon–Sat, less frequently at lunchtime and on Sun) from the main terminal.

Most of the **banks** are on Paleológou. There is a good **map and bookshop** near the corner of Paleológou and Lykoúrgou, and **Internet** facilities at the Cosmos video shop at Paleológou 34.

Accommodation

There are usually enough **hotels** to go around, many of them on the main avenue, Paleológou. **Camping** is available at two sites out along the Mystra road; both can be reached via the Mystra bus, which will stop by the sites on request. The nearest, 2.5km from Spárti, is *Paleologio Mystra* (☎27310 22724) and is open year-round. Two kilometres closer to Mystra is the *Castle View* (☎27310 83303, ⓦwww.castleview.gr; April–Oct), a very clean, well-managed site, with a pool, and a bus stop outside.

Apollo Thermopýlon 84, cnr Tripoléos ☎27310 22491, ⓕ27310 23936. A pleasant hotel, though overlooking a busy street; it has a parking area and restaurant; open all year. ❸

Cecil Paleológou 125, cnr Thermopýlon ☎27310 24980, ⓕ27310 81318. Small, recently renovated hotel, with very friendly and knowledgeable owners. It's nearest to the sites. ❸

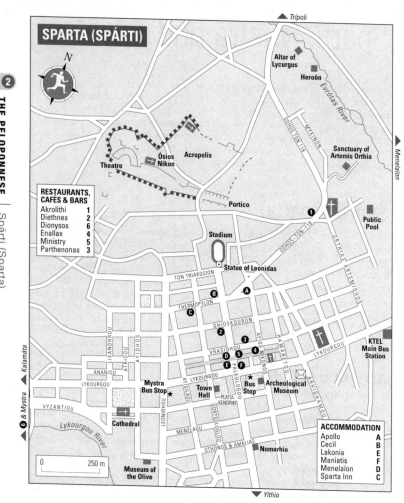

Lakonia Paleológou 61 ☎27310 28951, ℻27310
82257. Well-priced hotel on the main street. ❷
Maniatis Paleológou 72–76, cnr Lykoúrgou
☎27310 22665, ⓦwww.maniatishotel.gr. Modern,
with good facilities. The in-house *Zeus* restaurant,
unusually for a hotel, is recommended for its excellent Greek cuisine. ❺

Menelaïon Paleológou 91 ☎27310 22161,
ⓦwww.menelaion.com. A modernized hotel, with a
pool. Rooms at the front are best avoided as there's
an all-night taxi rank outside. B&B ❻
Sparta Inn Thermopýlon 105, cnr Gortsológiou
☎27310 21021, ℻27310 24855. Huge and modern,
with a roof garden and two swimming pools. ❸

Ancient Sparta

Descending from the mountains that ring Spárti on three sides, you get a
sense of how strategic the location of the ancient city-state of **SPARTA**
was. The ancient "capital" occupied more or less the site of today's town,
though it was in fact less a city than a grouping of villages, commanding the

Lakonian plain and fertile Evrótas valley from a series of low hills just west of the river.

The Greek city was at the height of its power from the eighth to the fourth century BC, a period when Sparta structured its society according to the laws of **Lykurgos**, defeated Athens in the Peloponnesian War, established colonies around the Greek world, and eventually lost hegemony through defeat to Thebes. A second period of prosperity came under the Romans – for whom this was an outpost in the south of Greece, with the Máni never properly subdued. However, from the third century AD, Sparta declined as nearby Mystra became the focus of Byzantine interest.

The sites

Traces of ancient Spartan glory are in short supply, but there are some ruins to be seen to the north of the city (daily 8.30am–3pm; free): from the bold **Statue of Leonidas**, hero of Thermopylae, at the top of Paleológou, follow the track around and behind the modern stadium towards the old **Acropolis**, tallest of the Spartan hills. An immense **theatre** here, built into the side of the hill, can be quite clearly traced, even though today most of its masonry has gone – hurriedly adapted for fortification when the Spartans' power declined and, later still, recycled for the building of Byzantine Mystra. Above the theatre a sign marks a fragment of the **Temple of Athina Halkiakou**, while at the top of the acropolis sit the knee-high ruins of the tenth-century Byzantine church and monastery of **Ósios Níkon**.

Out on the Trípoli road (Odhós-ton-118, just past the junction with Orthias Artémidhos), a track leads to the remains of the **sanctuary of Artemis Orthia**, where Spartan boys underwent endurance tests by flogging. The Roman geographer and travel writer Pausanias records that young men often expired under the lash, adding that the altar had to be splashed with blood before the goddess was satisfied. Perhaps it was the audience potential of such a gory spectacle that led the Romans to revive the custom – the main ruins here are of the spectators' grandstand they built. They also added shops to supply the audiences at performances.

Further out is the **Menelaïon** (Tues–Sun 8.30am–3pm; free), a late Mycenaean settlement and a sanctuary of Menelaus and Helen, about 5km to the southeast of town, on the far side of the river. At the modern village of Amýkles, 7km south of Spárti on the road to Yíthio, is the Amyklaïon acropolis and **sanctuary of Apollo Amyklaïos** (same hours), which until the Roman period was the most important Spartan site after the city itself and location for the Hyacinthia festival which celebrated the reconciliation of the Dorians and the Achaians.

The Archeological Museum and the Museum of the Olive

All moveable artefacts and mosaics have been transferred to the town's small **Archeological Museum** (Mon–Sat 8.30am–3pm, Sun 9.30am–2.30pm; €2) on Áyios Níkonos. Among its more interesting exhibits are a number of votive offerings found on the sanctuary site – sickles set in stone that were presented as prizes to the Spartan youths and solemnly rededicated to the goddess – and a fifth-century BC marble bust of a running Spartan hoplite, found on the acropolis and said to be Leonidas. There is a dramatic late sixth-century BC stele, with relief carvings on both sides, possibly of Menelaos with Helen and Agamemnon with Klytemnestra; the ends have carved snakes. There are fragments of Hellenistic and Roman mosaics, and numerous small lead figurines, clay masks and bronze idols from the Artemis Orthia site.

At the southwest corner of town is the **Museum of the Olive and Greek Olive Oil** (Mon & Wed–Sun: summer 10am–2pm & 5–7pm; winter 10am–4pm; €2), at Óthonos & Amalías 129. Displays cover the history, uses and production technology of the olive.

Eating and drinking

There is a wide choice for meals, with most **restaurants** and **tavernas** concentrated on the main street, Paleológou. The most popular music **bars** are *Enallax* by the OTE and *Ministry* opposite the *Menelaïon* hotel.

Akrolithi Odhós-ton-118, 75. Highly rated by the locals, with a wide range of *mezédhes*, outdoor tables in summer and live music in winter.
Diethnes Paleológou 105. Another local favourite, with an extensive menu of traditional dishes. The interior lacks atmosphere, but a delightful garden behind with orange and lemon trees compensates.

Dionysos 1500 metres out on the road towards Mystra. Expensive dishes, but served with style outdoors on a summer's evening.
Parthenonas Vrasídhou, next to the cinema. *Psistariá* serving well-priced traditional Greek food, and takeaways.

Mystra (Mystrás)

A glorious, airy place, hugging a steep, 280-metre-high foothill of Taïyetos, **MYSTRA** is one of the most exciting and dramatic sites that the Peloponnese can offer. Winding up the lushly vegetated hillside is a remarkably intact Byzantine town that once sheltered a population of some 20,000, and through which you can now wander. Winding alleys lead through monumental gates, past medieval houses and palaces and above all into the churches, several of which yield superb and radiant frescoes. The overall effect is of straying into a massive museum of architecture, painting and sculpture – and into a different age.

There are no facilities at the site itself, so you'll need to base yourself at either the nearby modern settlement of Néos Mystrás (see p. 000) or at Spárti. In addition to the local bus from Spárti, you can walk a reconstructed stone path to the site. Head westwards on Lykoúrgou, turn left at the end and follow the road (no pavement), then join the start of the path opposite the *Dionysos* taverna. The path and some dirt tracks bring you up to the entrance of the site in about one hour.

Some history

Mystra was basically a Frankish creation. In 1249, Guillaume II de Villehardouin, fourth Frankish prince of the Moreas, built a castle here – one of a trio of fortresses (the others were at Monemvasiá and in the Máni) designed to garrison his domain. The Franks, however, were driven out of Mystra by the Byzantines in 1262, and by the mid-fourteenth century this isolated triangle of land in the southeastern Peloponnese, encompassing the old Spartan territories, became the **Despotate of Mystra**. This was the last province of the Greek Byzantine empire and for years, with Constantinople in terminal decay, was its virtual capital.

During the next two centuries, Mystra was the focus of a defiant rebirth of Byzantine power. The despotate's rulers – usually the son or brother of the eastern emperor, often the heir apparent – recaptured and controlled much of the Peloponnese, which became the largest of the ever-shrinking Byzantine provinces. They and their province were to endure for two centuries before eventual subjugation by the Turks. The end came in 1460, seven years after the fall of Constantinople, when the last despot Demetrios Paleologos, feuding with his brothers, handed the city over to the Sultan Mehmet II.

Mystra's political significance, though, was in any case overshadowed by its **artistic achievements**. Throughout the fourteenth and the first decades of the fifteenth centuries it was the principal cultural and intellectual centre of the Byzantine world, sponsoring, in highly uncertain times, a renaissance in the arts and attracting the finest Byzantine scholars and theologians – among them a number of members of the imperial families, the Cantacuzenes and Paleologues. Most notable of the court scholars was the humanist philosopher **Gemisthus Plethon**, who revived and reinterpreted Plato's ideas, using them to support his own brand of revolutionary teachings, which included the assertions that land should be redistributed among labourers and that reason should be placed on a par with religion. Although his beliefs had limited impact in Mystra itself – whose monks excommunicated him – his followers, who taught in Italy after the fall of Mystra, exercised wide influence in Renaissance Florence and Rome.

More tangibly, Mystra also saw a last flourish of **Byzantine architecture**, with the building of a magnificent palace for the despots and a perfect sequence of churches, multi-domed and brilliantly frescoed. It is these, remarkably preserved and sensitively restored, that provide the focus of this extraordinary site. In the frescoes, it is not hard to see something of the creativity and spirit of Plethon's court circle, as the stock Byzantine figures turn to more naturalistic forms and settings.

The town's **post-Byzantine history** follows a familiar Peloponnesian pattern. It remained in Turkish hands from the mid-fifteenth to late seventeenth centuries, then in 1687 was captured briefly by the Venetians under Francesco Morosini, under whom the town prospered once more, attaining a population of 40,000. Decline set in with a second stage of Turkish control, from 1715 onwards, culminating in the destruction that accompanied the War of Independence, the site being evacuated after fires in 1770 and 1825. Restoration begun in the first decades of the twentieth century was interrupted by the civil war – during which it was, for a while, a battle site, with the ruins of the Pandánassa convent sheltering children from the lower town – and renewed in earnest in the 1950s when the last inhabitants were relocated.

The Byzantine city

The site of the Byzantine city (daily: summer 8am–8pm; winter 8am–2pm; €5) comprises three main parts: the **Káto Hóra** (lower town), with the city's most important churches; the **Áno Hóra** (upper town), grouped around the vast shell of a royal palace; and the **Kástro** (castle). There are two entrances to the site, at the base of the lower town and up near the Kástro; once inside, the site is well signposted. A road loops up from the modern village of Néos Mystrás to Trýpi, passing near both upper and lower entrances. Buses from Spárti always stop at the lower entrance, and usually go up to the top as well (which saves a considerable climb). It's a good idea to stock up on refreshments before setting out: there's a mobile snack-bar at the lower gate, serving freshly pressed orange or lemon juices, but nothing in the site itself. This lack of commercialism within the site contrasts distinctly with Monemvasiá and contributes to the powerfully historic atmosphere at Mystra.

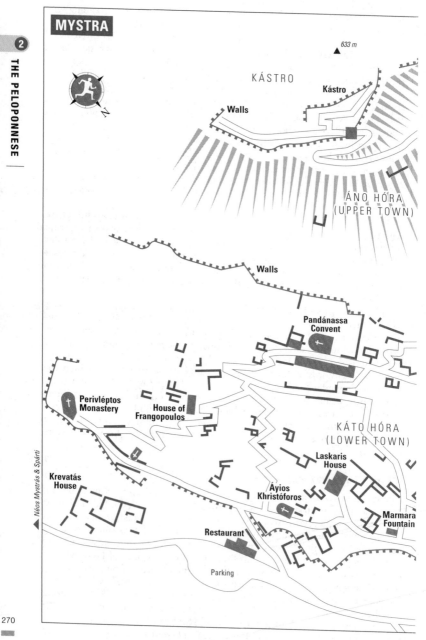

MYSTRA

633 m ▲

KÁSTRO

Kástro

Walls

ÁNO HÓRA
(UPPER TOWN)

Walls

Pandánassa
Convent

Perivléptos
Monastery

House of
Frangopoulos

KÁTO HÓRA
(LOWER TOWN)

Laskaris
House

Áyios
Khristóforos

Krevatás
House

Marmara
Fountain

Restaurant

Parking

◀ Néos Mystrás & Spárti

Trýpi & Kalamáta ▲

Parking

Walls

Upper Entrance

Ayia Sofía

Náfplio Gate

Palatáki

Despots' Palace

Áyios Nikólaos

Monemvasiá Gate

Mosque

Refectory

Odhiyítria

Vrondohión Monastery

Evangelístria

Ayii Theódorii

Walls

Mitrópolis

Toilet

Lower Entrance

Canteen

Museum

0   100 m

▼ Path to Spárti

The Upper Town and Kástro

The **Kástro**, reached by a path direct from the upper gate, maintains the Frankish design of its original thirteenth-century construction, though it was repaired and modified by all successive occupants. There is a walkway around most of the keep, with views of an intricate panorama of the town below. The castle itself was the court of Guillaume II de Villehardouin but in later years was used primarily as a citadel.

Following a course downhill from the upper entrance, the first identifiable building you come to is the church of **Ayía Sofía** (1350), which served as the chapel for the Despots' Palace – the enormous structure below. The chapel's finest feature is its floor, made from polychrome marble. Its frescoes, notably a *Pandokrátor* (Christ in Majesty) and *Nativity of the Virgin*, have survived reasonably well, protected until recent years by coatings of whitewash applied by the Turks, who adapted the building as a mosque. Recognizable parts of the refectory and cells of its attached monastery also remain.

Heading down from Ayía Sofía, there is a choice of routes. The right fork winds past ruins of a Byzantine mansion, one of the oldest houses on the site, the **Palatáki** ("Small Palace"; 1250–1300), and **Áyios Nikólaos**, a large seventeenth-century building decorated with unsophisticated paintings. The left fork is more interesting, passing the fortified **Náfplio Gate**, which was the principal entrance to the upper town, and the vast, multistoreyed, Gothic-looking complex of the **Despots' Palace** (1249–1400; currently undergoing extensive rebuilding and restoration that looks set to continue for a number of years).

Parts of the palace probably date back to the Franks. Most prominent among its numerous rooms is a great vaulted audience hall, built at right angles to the line of the building, with ostentatious windows regally dominating the skyline; this was once heated by eight great chimneys and sported a painted facade. Behind it were various official public buildings, while to the right of the lower wing, flanking one side of a square used by the Turks as a marketplace, are the remains of a **mosque**.

The Lower Town

At the **Monemvasiá Gate**, which links the upper and lower towns, there is a further choice of routes: right to the Pandánassa and Perivléptos monasteries or left to the Vrondohión monastery and cathedral. If time is running out, it is easier to head right first, then double back down to the Vrondohión.

When excavations were resumed in 1952, the last thirty or so families who still lived in the lower town were moved out to Néos Mystrás. Only the nuns of the **Pandánassa** ("Queen of the World") **convent** have remained; currently, there are seven in residence and they have a reception room where they sell their own handicrafts and sometimes offer a cooling *vyssinádha* (cherryade) to visitors. The convent's church, built in 1428, is perhaps the finest surviving in Mystra, perfectly proportioned in its blend of Byzantine and Gothic. The **frescoes** date from various centuries, with some superb fifteenth-century work, including one in the gallery that depicts scenes from the life of Christ. David Talbot Rice, in his classic study, *Byzantine Art*, wrote of these frescoes that "Only El Greco in the west, and later Gauguin, would have used their colours in just this way." Other frescoes were painted between 1687 and 1715, when Mystra was held by the Venetians.

Further down on this side of the lower town is a balconied Byzantine mansion, the **House of Frangopoulos**, once the home of the Despotate's chief minister – who was also the founder of the Pandánassa.

Beyond it is the diminutive **Perivléptos monastery** (1310), whose single-domed church, partially carved out of the rock, contains Mystra's most complete cycle of frescoes, almost all of which date from the fourteenth century. They are in some ways finer than those of the Pandánassa, blending an easy humanism with the spirituality of the Byzantine icon traditions, and demonstrating the structured iconography of a Byzantine church. The position of each figure depended upon its sanctity, and so upon the dome the image of heaven is the *Pandokrátor* (the all-powerful Christ in glory after the Ascension); on the apse is the Virgin; and the higher expanses of wall portray scenes from the life of Christ. Prophets and saints could only appear on the lower walls, decreasing in importance according to their distance from the sanctuary.

△ Pandánassa convent, Mystra

Along the path leading from Perivléptos to the lower gate are a couple of minor, much-restored churches, and, just above them, the **Laskaris House**, a mansion thought to have belonged to relatives of the emperors. Like the House of Frangopoulos, it is balconied; its ground floor probably served as stables. Close by, beside the path, is the old Marmara Turkish Fountain.

The **Mitrópolis** or cathedral, immediately beyond the gateway, is the oldest of Mystra's churches, built between 1270 and 1292 under the first Paleologue ruler. A marble slab set in its floor is carved with the double-headed eagle of Byzantium, commemorating the 1448 coronation of Constantine XI Paleologos, the last Eastern emperor (also celebrated in a statue in Néos Mystrás); he was soon to perish, with his empire, in the Turkish sacking of Constantinople in 1453. A stone with red stains is said to mark where Bishop Ananias Lambadheris was murdered in 1760. Of the church's frescoes, the earliest, in the northeast aisle, depict the torture and burial of Áyios Dhimítrios, the saint to whom the church is dedicated. The comparative stiffness of their figures contrasts with the later works opposite. These, illustrating the miracles of Christ and the life of the Virgin, are more intimate and lighter of touch; they date from the last great years before Mystra's fall. Adjacent to the cathedral, a small **museum** (included in main admission charge) contains various fragments of sculpture and pottery.

Finally, a short way uphill, is the **Vrondohión monastery**. This was the centre of cultural and intellectual life in the fifteenth-century town – the cells of the monastery can still be discerned – and was also the burial place of the despots. Of the two attached churches, the further one, **Odhiyítria** (Afendikó; 1310), has been beautifully restored, revealing early fourteenth-century frescoes similar to those of Perivléptos, with startlingly bold juxtapositions of colour.

Practicalities: Néos Mystrás

Buses run through the day from Spárti to the lower Mystra site entrance, stopping en route at the modern village of **NÉOS MYSTRÁS**. This small roadside community has a small square with several often pricey tavernas, crowded with tour buses by day but low-key at night, except at the end of August when the place buzzes with live music and a gypsy market during the week-long annual *paniyíri* (fête).

In general, staying in Néos Mystrás is worth the bit extra over Spárti, for the setting and easy access to the site, though you will need to book ahead, or arrive early in the day, to find a place. **Accommodation** is limited to two hotels, the refurbished and very pleasant *Byzantion* (⊕27310 83309, ⊜byzanhtl@otenet .gr; April–Oct; B&B ❸), which can be oversubscribed for much of the year, and the new *Pyrgos Mystra* (⊕27310 83309; B&B ❽), in a beautifully restored and luxurious mansion near the start of the road to Taïyéti. There are also a small number of private rooms along the main street. There are **campsites** along the Mystrás–Spárti road: see under accommodation details for Spárti on p.265.

Walks from Mystra

There are a number of marked paths heading into the Taïyetos foothills behind Mystra, with signs at the start of each detailing the options; a good circular route of about 12km goes up through the narrow valley immediately south of the site, via the hamlets of Taïyéti and semi-deserted Pergandéïka, then down, past the monastery of Faneroméni and the cliff-hung monastery of Panayía Zayoúna (Zoyéni), to Paróri village. From there it's just a couple of kilometres back to Néos Mystrás, with a short detour into a gorge to visit the cave-church of Panayía Langadhiótissa.

A second option is to set off from Paróri, on the spectacular cliff path up through the Langadhiótissa gorge, then join the E4 footpath to Faneroméni (4km). Take the surfaced road towards Anavrytí, but about 700m along join an old path to enter **ANAVRYTÍ**, which boasts superb vistas, and a **hotel** – the *Antamoma* (℡27310 81595, ⓦwww.antamoma.com; ❷–❸). **Buses** run from Spárti to Anavrytí three times a week, early morning and early afternoon (Mon, Wed & Sat). From Anavrytí, take the road to Spárti, but follow signs off left at the edge of the village to join a remarkable *kalderími* through the Marousó valley (3km). Rejoin the road at the Ágios Geórgios church, from where it is 3.5km downhill to Áyios Ioánnis village (6 weekday buses to Spárti, 5km away).

Mount Taïyetos and the Langádha pass

Moving on from Spárti there is a tough choice of routes: west over the Taïyetos ridge, either on foot or by road through the dramatic **Langádha pass** to Kalamáta; east to the Byzantine towns of Yeráki and Monemvasiá; or south, skirting the mountain's foothills, to Yíthio and the Máni. For anyone wanting to get to grips with the Greek mountains, there is **Mount Taïyetos** itself. Although the range is one of the most beautiful, dramatic and hazardous in Greece, with vast grey boulders and scree along much of its length, it has one reasonably straightforward path to the highest peak, Profítis Ilías. Three areas, covering different and specialized ecological habitats, in the higher mountains and the gorges of Langádha and Nédhondas, were included for conservation under the EU's NATURA 2000 programme.

Spárti to Kalamáta: the Langádha pass

The **Langádha pass**, the sixty-kilometre route over the Taïyetos from **Spárti to Kalamáta**, was the second ancient crossing after the Kakí Skála (see box p.277) and is still the only fully paved road across the mountain. Remote and wild, with long uninhabited sections, it unveils a constant drama of peaks, magnificent at all times but startling at sunrise; sadly the pine forests suffered extensive damage in the fires of 1998. This route was taken by Telemachus in the *Odyssey* on his way from Nestor's palace near Pýlos to that of Menelaus at Sparta. It took him a day by chariot – good going by any standards, since today's buses take four hours.

Heading from Spárti, the last settlement is **TRÝPI**, 9km out, where there is one of the best **tavernas** in the Spárti area, *Barba Vozola*, and a basic small **hotel**, the *Keadas* (℡27310 98222; ❷), open Easter to late autumn. Just beyond the village, the road climbs steeply into the mountains and enters the **gorge of Langádha**, a wild sequence of hairpins. At the rock of Keádhas, high above the southern side of the road a short distance from the village, the Spartans used to leave their sick or puny babies to die from exposure. Above Keádhas is a **climbing park** (grades 5–8b+; guidebook *Rock Climbing in Langada* is available locally) with marked routes for rock-climbers. Beyond the gorge, just before the summit of the pass, 22km from Spárti and 37km from Kalamáta, the *Canadas* **guesthouse** (℡27210 99281; ❶), built in the style of an alpine chalet, is excellent value, with a restaurant that serves good *bakaliáros* (cod or hake), *loukániko* (sausage), smoked pork, and (in winter) bean soup. It's also a good place to sample mountain tea, made from the local herb *sidherítis*. At the **pass**, Selibovés, 3km further on and 125m higher at 1375m, is the *Touristiko Taïyetou* (℡27210 99236, Ⓕ27210 98198; ❷) hotel, also open all year. This has a very good ✼**restaurant**, with tasty home cooking and panoramic alpine views. From here

Hiking in the Taïyetos range

Most **hikes** beyond Anavrytí need experience and proper equipment, including the relevant Anavasi Editions maps, and should definitely not be undertaken alone – a sprained ankle could be fatal up here. The area is prone to flash floods, so seek advice locally. If you are confident, however, there are various routes to the Profítis Ilías summit and beyond. The EOS at Gortosológlou 97 in Spárti can give advice.

The only straightforward route is to follow the **E4 long-distance footpath**, marked variously by yellow diamonds or red-and-white stripes, for five hours south to the **alpine refuge** at Ayía Varvára (see below).

The classic approach to the 2404-metre **Profítis Ilías summit** entails a ten-kilometre road-walk – or taxi – up from the village of Paleopanayía (a short bus ride south of Spárti off the Yíthio road) to the spring at Bóliana (Kryonéri), where there's a single ramshackle hut that serves drinks and sometimes meals in summer. Proceed past Bóliana towards Anavrytí on the E4 track for about thirty minutes, then bear left near a picnic ground and spring (the last reliable water on the mountain). Another half-hour above this, following E4 signs, what's left of the old trail appears on the right, signposted "EOS Spárti Katafíyio". This short-cuts a new road except for the very last 50m to the Ayía Varvára refuge.

A more challenging option, requiring mountaineering skills and camping equipment, is to adopt the red-dotted trail veering off the E4 early on, and follow it to a point just below a 1700-metre saddle, where you must choose between dropping over the pass to the far side of the range or precarious ridge-walking to the Profítis Ilías summit. Crossing the pass takes you to the head of the **Ríndomo gorge**, where you can camp at the deserted chapel-monastery of Panayía Kapsodhematoúsa before descending the next day to either Gaïtsés or Pigádhia, towards the Messinian coast. It is seven tough hours to the peak even in optimum conditions and with a light load, involving exposed rock pinnacles, sheer drops and difficult surfaces – not a hike to be undertaken lightly.

Ayía Varvára to the summit

The **Ayía Varvára refuge** (unstaffed, but open sporadically – more likely at weekends), above Bóliana, sits on a beautiful grassy knoll shaded by tremendous

tracks and paths head north and south along the mountain ridge – peaks up to 1900m are accessible in a day's outing.

The first actual village on the Kalamáta side is **Artemisía**, where the buses from one side meet those from the other, and from where you enter the **Nédhondas** gorge for the final zigzagging descent to Kalamáta. There is basic accommodation here, in rooms above one of the cafés, but the *Canadas* and *Touristiko Taïyetou* are far better value for little more cost.

Arcadia

Arcadia (Arkadhía in modern Greek), the heartland province of the Peloponnese, lives up to its name. It contains some of the most beautiful and verdant

storm-blasted black pines. The conical peak of Profítis Ilías rises directly above; if you can get your climb to coincide with a full moon you won't regret it. There is plenty of room for camping, and the hut has a porch to provide shelter in bad weather.

The path to the **summit** starts at the rear left corner of the refuge and swings right on a long reach. Level and stony at first, it leaves the tree line and loops up a steep bank to a sloping meadow, where it is ineffectually marked by twisted, rusting signs with their lettering long obliterated. Keep heading right across the slope towards a distinct secondary peak until, once around a steep bend, the path begins to veer left in the direction of the summit. It slants steadily upward following a natural ledge until, at a very clear nick in the ridge above you, it turns right and crosses to the far side, from where you look down on the Gulf of Messinía (total time from the refuge around 2.5hr).

There is a squat stone chapel and outbuildings on the **summit**, used during the celebrations of the feast of the Prophet Elijah (Profítis Ilías) between July 18 and 20. The views, as you would expect, are breathtaking, encompassing the sea to east and west.

Summit to the coast

The ridge terrain **beyond the peak** is probably beyond the ambitions of casual hikers. The easiest and safest way off the mountain towards the Messinian coast is to follow the E4 from Ayía Varvára to the gushing springs at Pendávli, and then over a low saddle to the summer hamlet of **Áyios Dhimítrios**. This takes just a couple of hours and you can camp in the beautiful surroundings. In the morning you're well poised, at the head of the **Výros gorge**, to handle the all-day descent to Kardhamýli through the other great Taïyetan canyon. At one point you negotiate stretches of the **Kakí Skála**, one of the oldest paths in Greece, built to link ancient Sparta and Messene. Dirt roads now also link Áyios Dhimítrios with Saïdhóna (24km), above Stoúpa and Kardhamýli in the west, and via Kastaniá with Yíthio in the southeast.

landscapes in Greece, though fire damage in summer 2000 has taken its toll on the fir forests (ironically, the first woodlands in Greece to receive international certification for sustainable management). Dramatic hills are crowned by a string of medieval towns, and the occasional Classical antiquity. The best area of all is around **Andhrítsena**, **Stemnítsa** and **Karítena**, where walkers are rewarded with the luxuriant (and rarely visited) **Loúsios gorge**, and archeology buffs with the remote, though permanently covered, **Temple of Bassae** (Apollo Epikourios). En route, if approaching from **Trípoli**, you may also be tempted by the ancient theatre at **Megalópoli**. Drivers should be aware that Arcadia's highways, some of the broadest and emptiest in the Peloponnese, are shared with sheep- and goat-herds moving their flocks.

Trípoli

Trípoli is a major crossroads of the Peloponnese, from where most travellers either head **northwest** through Arcadia towards Olympia or Pátra, or **south** to Spárti and Mystra or Kalamáta. To the **east**, a decent road, looping around

Mount Kteniás, connects Trípoli with Árgos and Náfplio, via Lerna. A second road runs southeast across the Tegean plain, then east down to Ástros. To the **southwest**, a winding road over the intervening ridge leads to Megalópoli – and its evocative, scattered ruins – from where a faster road reaches the coast near Kyparissía. To the **northeast**, a fast highway starting near Megalópoli links Trípoli, via the Artemisíon Tunnel, with Kórinthos and Athens.

The Peloponnese **railway** also passes through Trípoli, continuing its meandering course from Kórinthos and Árgos to Kyparissía or Kalamáta. Those with passes might be tempted to use the train to Trípoli and then take a bus to Spárti, but it's not a good idea, as Árgos–Spárti buses are not scheduled to meet trains in Trípoli and furthermore they often pass through full; it's better to take a direct bus (7–9 daily from Athens to Spárti, via Árgos and Trípoli).

The Town

Set in a huge upland plain, and surrounded by spectacular mountains, the Arcadian capital doesn't live up to expectations: **TRÍPOLI** is a large, modern town, and home to one of the country's biggest army barracks. It doesn't pander to tourism and has few obvious attractions, although the **Panarcadic Archeological Museum**, Evangelistriás 6 (Tues–Sun 8.30am–3pm; €2), signposted off Vassiléos Yeoryíou (which leads off the central square, Platía Kolokotróni) and housed in a Neoclassical building with a beautiful rose garden, makes a pleasant diversion; the collection includes finds from much of Arcadia, from Neolithic to Roman. The town's altitude of 665m means an often markedly cooler summer climate and harsh winters. Traffic can be chaotic and you may wish to escape to the quiet greenery of Platía Áreos. Medieval Tripolitsa was destroyed by retreating Turkish forces during the War of Independence, when the Greek forces, led by Kolokotronis in one of their worst atrocities, had earlier massacred the town's Turkish population. Tripolitsa's ancient predecessors, the rival towns of Mantinea to the north and Tegea to the south, are the main points of archeological interest to the tourist.

Practicalities

Getting in and out of the town can be fairly complicated. The new, major **bus terminal**, serving all destinations in Arcadia and the northern Peloponnese, is 1.25km from the centre on the Akhladókambos road, to the southeast of town. Services to Messinía, Kalamáta, Pýlos, the Máni and Spárti leave from the corner café on Lagopáti, directly opposite the train station, 1.5km away at the southeastern edge of town. There are a number of reliable **hotels**, including the good-value *Alex*, Vassiléos Yeoryíou 26 (℡27102 23465; ❹); and the very friendly *Anactoricon*, Ethnikís Andístasis 48 (℡27102 22545, Ⓔroinioti@compulink.gr; ❹. Eating establishments are mostly of the functional variety, but for decent food in more pleasant surroundings there are a couple of **tavernas**, *Neos Dionysos* and the more homely *Klimataria*, almost adjacent to one another on Kalavrýton, beyond the Aello cinema and about 100m past the far end of Platía Áreos.

Ancient Mantinea and Tegea

ANCIENT MANTINEA (Tues–Sun 8.30am–3pm; free), known to Homer as "pleasant Mantinea", was throughout its history a bitter rival of nearby Tegea, invariably forming an alliance with Athens when Tegea stood with Sparta, then switching allegiance to Sparta when Tegea allied with Thebes. It stands 15km north of Trípoli, between the road to Pátra and the Trípoli–Kórinthos highway, and is served by hourly buses from Platía Kolokotróni in Trípoli. The principal remains are a circuit of the 4km of fourth-century BC **walls**, still more or less intact, though much reduced in height – originally they had around ten gates and 120 towers – and a few tiers of its ancient theatre.

Alongside the site, however, is one of the most bizarre sights in Greece: the modern **church of Ayía Fotiní** constructed in an eclectic pastiche of Byzantine and Egyptian styles. Put together in the 1970s, from ancient building stones, by a Greek-American architect, it is dedicated to "The Virgin, the Muses and Beethoven".

ANCIENT TEGEA, 8km south of Trípoli, was the main city of the central Peloponnese in Classical and Roman times, and, refounded in the tenth century, was an important town under the Byzantines. The diffuse and partially excavated site (Tues–Sun 8.30am–3pm; free) lies just outside the village of Aléa (modern Tegea), on the Spárti road. Local buses from Platía Kolokotróni in Trípoli stop in the village beside a small **museum** (Tues–Sun 11am–3pm; €2), which is well stocked with sculptures from the site. Take the road to the left as you leave, and it is 100m to the main remains, the **Temple of Athena Alea**, in whose sanctuary two kings of Sparta once took refuge. Keeping on the road past the site, it's a twenty-minute walk to the village of Paleá Episkopí, whose church – a huge modern pilgrim shrine – incorporates part of ancient Tegea's theatre and a number of Byzantine mosaics.

Megalópoli

Modern **MEGALÓPOLI** (Megalopolis) is an important road and bus junction, and your first thoughts on arrival may be directed towards getting out. It's a rather characterless place, with a military presence and two vast power stations; there are few visitor diversions. The adoption of its ancient name, "Great City", was an altogether empty joke. However, the impulse to move on should be resisted, because just outside the city to the northwest is one of the most extensive and least touristy sites in the Peloponnese: **ancient Megalopolis**.

Practicalities

Megalópoli has regular **bus connections** with Trípoli (and on to Árgos and Athens) and Kalamáta. Moving north or west into Arcadia is slightly more problematic, with just two buses daily to Karítena and Andhrítsena (currently at noon and 7pm). However, hitching is a viable proposition along this route, as local drivers are aware of the paucity of transport, and it's also possible to negotiate a **taxi** to Karítena. Facilities such as **banks** and a **post office** are around the central Platía Gortynías.

There are several **hotels** in Megalópoli, catering mostly to local business travellers rather than tourists. Most are in the vicinity of the central platía, of which the best is *Paris*, Ayíou Nikoláou 5 (℡27910 22410; ❸). The *Leontara* **restaurant** on the main square is good for baked dishes.

Ancient Megalopolis

Ancient Megalopolis (Tues–Sun 8.30am–3pm; free) was one of the most ambitious building projects of the Classical age, a city intended by the Theban leader Epaminondas, who oversaw construction from 371 to 368 BC, to be the finest of a chain of Arcadian settlements designed to hold back the Spartans. However, although no expense was spared on its construction, nor on its extent – 9km of walls alone – the city never took root. It suffered from sporadic Spartan aggression, and the citizens, transplanted from forty local villages, preferred, and returned to, their old homes. Within two centuries it had been broken up, abandoned and ruined.

As you approach the site, along a 250-metre tree-lined track off the Andhrítsena road (signposted "Ancient Theatre"), the countryside is beautiful enough; a fertile valley whose steaming cooling towers seem to give it added grandeur; beyond the river bed is just a low hill, and no sign of any ruins. Suddenly, you round the corner of the rise and its function is revealed: carved into its side is the largest **theatre** built in ancient Greece. Only the first few rows are excavated, but the earthen mounds and ridges of the rest are clearly visible as stepped tiers to the summit where, from the back rows, trees look on like immense spectators. Restoration work is planned.

The theatre was built to a scale similar to those at Árgos and Dodona, and could seat 20,000; the **Thersileion** (Assembly Hall) at its base could hold 16,000. Today you're likely to be alone at the site, save perhaps for the custodian (who has plans of the ruins). Out beyond the enclosed part of the site you can wander over a vast area, and with a little imagination make out the foundations of walls and towers, temples, gymnasiums and markets. "The Great City", wrote Kazantzakis in *Journey to the Morea*, "has become a great wasteland". But it's the richest of wastelands, gently and resolutely reclaimed by nature.

Megalópoli to Vytína

North of Megalópoli the best of Arcadia lies before you: minor roads that curl through a series of lush valleys and below the province's most exquisite medieval hill towns. The obvious first stop is **Karítena**. Moving on from Karítena, there is a choice of roads. The "main" route loops west through Andhrítsena to Créstena, from where irregular buses run to Olympia. An alternative route to the northwest winds up around the edge of the Ménalo mountains to the delightful towns of **Stemnítsa** and **Dhimitsána**, meeting the main Trípoli–Langádhia–Olympia–Pýrgos road at Karkaloú. From either of these you can visit the dramatic and remote site of **ancient Gortys** and explore the **Loúsios gorge**, above which, outrageously sited on 300-metre-high cliffs, is the eleventh-century **Ayíou Ioánnou Prodhrómou monastery** (commonly abbreviated to Prodhrómou). North of Dhimitsána is modern **Vytína**, a ski-centre with more extensive tourist facilities – snow-chains may be necessary if driving around the Ménalo villages in the winter. If you have time on your hands, perhaps the most attractive option is to explore the region as far north as Dhimitsána or Vytína, then backtrack through meadows and woodland on Ménalo lanes to Stemnítsa and Karítena, finally proceeding on to Olympia via Andhrítsena.

Karítena

Picturesquely set, high above and guarding the strategic Megalópoli–Andhrítsena road, **KARÍTENA** may look familiar to Greece aficionados; with its medieval bridge over the River Alfiós (Alpheus), it used to grace the 5000-drachma note. Like many of the Arcadian hill towns hereabouts, its history has

Frankish, Byzantine and Turkish contributions, the Venetians having passed over much of the northern interior. It was founded by the Byzantines in the seventh century and had attained a population of some 20,000 when the Franks took it in 1209. Under their century-long rule, Karítena was the capital of a large barony under Geoffroy de Bruyères, the paragon of chivalry in the medieval ballad *The Chronicle of the Morea*, and probably the only well-liked Frankish overlord.

These days the attractive village has a population of just a couple of hundred, but as recently as the beginning of the nineteenth century there were at least ten times that figure. Stop on the south side of the modern bridge over the Alfiós and follow a short track down to the **medieval bridge**, almost underneath the new. It is missing the central section, but is an intriguing structure nonetheless, with a small Byzantine chapel built into one of the central pillars.

From the main road, there's a winding three-kilometre road up to the village, in the upper part of which is a small central platía with a *kafenío*. Off the platía are signposted two Byzantine churches: the fourteenth-century **Zoödhóhos Piyí** (with a Romanesque bell tower) and the late seventeenth-century **Áyios Nikólaos** (with crumbling frescoes) to the west, down towards the river; ask at the *kafenío* for the keys. Also off the platía is the **Froúrio**, the castle built in 1245 by the Franks, with added Turkish towers. It was repaired by Theodhoros Kolokotronis and it was here that he held out against Ibrahim Pasha in 1826 and turned the tide of the War of Independence – hence the view of Karítena on the old 5000-drachma note and a portrait of Kolokotronis on the reverse.

The best choice for **rooms** is the *Vrenthi* (☎27910 31650; ❷, weekends ❸) on the right just before the main square: ask at the *Vrenthi* café on the left just beyond. **River rafting** is organized by the Alpin Club (🌐www.alpinclub.gr), near the bridge.

Stemnítsa

Fifteen kilometres north of Karítena and at an altitude of 1050m, **STEM-NÍTSA** (or Ipsoúnda in its official Hellenicized form – Ipsoús on many maps) was for centuries one of the premier metal-smithing and goldworking centres of the Balkans. Although much depopulated, it remains a fascinating town, with a small folklore museum, an artisan school and a handful of quietly magnificent medieval churches.

The town is divided by ravines into three distinct quarters: the Kástro (the ancient acropolis hill), Ayía Paraskeví (east of the stream) and Áyios Ioánnis (west of the stream). The **folklore museum** (summer Mon & Wed–Fri 6–8pm, Sat 11am–1pm & 6–8pm, Sun 11am–1pm; winter Mon 4–6pm, Wed, Thurs, Sat & Sun 11am–1pm & 6–8pm, Sun 11am–1pm; closed Feb; free) is just off the main road in the Ayía Paraskeví quarter, and repays the trip out in itself. The ground floor is devoted to mock-ups of the workshops of indigenous crafts such as candle-making, bell-casting, shoe-making and jewellery. The next floor up features re-creations of the salon of a well-to-do family and a humbler cottage. The top storey is taken up by the rather random collections of the Savopoulos family: plates by Avramides (a refugee from Asia Minor and ceramics master), textiles and costumes from all over Greece, weapons, copperware and eighteenth- and nineteenth-century icons. Across the way is the seventeenth-century **basilica of Tríon Ierarhón**, the most accessible of the town's Byzantine churches; its caretaker lives in the low white house west of the main door.

To visit the other churches, all of which are frescoed and locked, requires more determined enquiries to find a key. The *katholikón* of the seventeenth-century

monastery of Zoödhóhos Piyí has perhaps the finest setting, on the hillside above Ayía Paraskeví, but the tiny windows do not permit much of an interior view. The little adjoining monastery hosted the first *yerousía* (convention) of guerrilla captains in the War of Independence, giving rise to the local claim that Stemnítsa was Greece's first capital.

Near the viewpoint summit of the Kástro hill, overlooking a small gorge, are two adjacent chapels: the tenth-century **Profítis Ilías** (with a convenient window for fresco-viewing) and the twelfth-century **Panayía Vaferón** (with an unusual colonnade). The last of the town's five churches, **Áyios Pandelímon**, is located at the western edge of the town, to the left of the paved road to Dhimitsána.

Accommodation options include the hospitable and homely *Xenonas Stemnitsa* (℡27950 81349 or 27950 29504; ❸, winter ❹) off the northern end of the main square. You can eat in town at the simple *Klinitsa* on the square or pleasant *Kastro* near the hill; vegetarians, however, may find suitable dishes limited both here and at Dhimitsána. There is one bus a day linking Stemnítsa with Trípoli via Dhimitsána.

Ancient Gortys and the Loúsios River valley

The site of **ancient Gortys** can be approached either from Karítena or from Stemnítsa (8km northwest of the site). **From Karítena** the most direct route to the valley runs up and through the town to Astíholos (11km), a village 3km southwest of the site. The last section is no more than a jeep track, but is well used. If you don't have your own transport, bus or hitch to Ellinikó, 6km up the Stemnítsa road. From the edge of Ellinikó, a six-kilometre side road descends northwest to the bank of the Loúsios river. Here, across an old bridge, is the site of ancient Gortys. It is possible to camp overnight near Gortys, or to stay at the nearby monastery of Prodhrómou. The towns of Stemnítsa or Dhimitsána (see opposite), the latter with more choice of accommodation, make the best bases for exploring the area, and walkers may want to follow the Stemnítsa–Gortys–Prodhrómou–Filosófou–Dhimitsána route.

If walking **from Stemnítsa**, head out of town on the paved road to Dhimitsána and, 500m after the town-limits sign, bear down and left onto the obvious beginning of an old *kalderími*. The shrub-lined path with fine views takes you down, in around 75 minutes, to near a surfaced road T-junction at the Prodhrómou parking area. Turn left and down towards Gortys (3.5km), but before doing so it is worth going to the parking area and the church viewpoint beyond, perched over the rim of the gorge.

Ancient Gortys

Ancient Gortys is one of the most stirring of all Greek sites, set beside the rushing river known in ancient times as the Gortynios. The remains are widely strewn over the hillside on the west bank of the stream, but the main attraction, below contemporary ground level and not at all obvious until well to the west of the little chapel of Áyios Andhréas (by the old bridge), is the huge excavation containing the remains of a **temple to Asklepios** and an adjoining **bath**, both dating from the fourth century BC.

The most curious feature of the site is a circular **portico** enclosing round-backed seats, which most certainly would have been part of the therapeutic centre. It's an extraordinary place, especially if you camp with the roar of the Loúsios to lull you to sleep. The only drawbacks are mosquitoes and the climate: temperatures up here plummet at night, no matter what the season, and heavy mists, wet as a soaking rain, can envelop the mountains from midnight to mid-morning.

The Loúsios gorge and monastery of Prodhrómou

The farmland surrounding ancient Gortys belongs to the monks of the nearby **Prodhrómou monastery**, who have carved a donkey path along the **gorge of the Loúsios** between Áyios Andhréas and the monastery. It's about forty minutes' walk upstream, with an initially gradual and later steady ascent up a well-graded, switchbacked trail. If you look up through the trees above the path, the monastery, stuck on to the cliff like a swallow's nest, is plainly visible a couple of hundred metres above. A set of park benches by a formal gate indicates the entrance.

The interior of the monastery does not disappoint; the local villagers accurately describe it as *politisméno* (cultured) as opposed to *ágrio* (wild). Once inside, it is surprisingly small; there were never more than fifteen tenants, and currently there are twelve monks, many of them very young and committed. Visitors are received in the *arhondaríki* (guest lounge and adjoining quarters), and then shown the tiny frescoed *katholikón*, and possibly invited to evening services there. The strictest rules of dress apply, but the monks welcome visitors who wish to stay the night. The only problem, especially at weekends, is that there are only a dozen or so beds, and people from Trípoli and even Athens make pilgrimages and retreats here, arriving by the car-load along an asphalt lane that makes a circuitous seven-kilometre descent from the Stemnítsa road. Be prepared for this possibility, and arrive in time to get back to level ground to camp.

Prodhrómou to Dhimitsána

Beyond Prodhrómou the path continues clearly to the outlying monasteries of **Paleá** and **Néa Filosófou** on the opposite side of the valley. The older dates from the tenth century but, virtually ruined, is easy to miss since it blends into the cliff against which it is flattened. The newer (seventeenth-century) monastery has been restored and recently expanded considerably, but retains frescoes from 1663 inside; there is a permanent caretaker monk. Accommodation is sometimes possible, but here too mosquitoes can be a hazard. From here, paths follow the west then east banks of the river, to reach Dhimitsána via Paleohóri in under two hours.

Dhimitsána

Like Stemnítsa, **DHIMITSÁNA** has an immediately seductive appearance, its cobbled streets and tottering houses straddling a twin hillside overlooking the Loúsios River. Views from the village are stunning: it stands at the head of the gorge, and looking downriver you can just see the cooling towers of the Megalópoli power plant and the bluff that supports Karítena. To the east are the folds of the Ménalo mountains, most visible if you climb up to the local **kástro**, whose stretch of polygonal walls attests to its ancient use.

In the town, a half-dozen churches with tall, squarish belfries recall the extended Frankish, and especially Norman, tenure in this part of the Moreas during the thirteenth century. Yet no one should dispute the deep-dyed Greekness of Dhimitsána. It was the birthplace of Archbishop Yermanos, who first raised the flag of rebellion at Kalávryta in 1821, and of the hapless patriarch, Grigoris V, hanged in Constantinople upon the sultan's receiving news of the insurrection mounted by the patriarch's coreligionist, and of the massacre at

Tripolitsa. Grigoris's house is now an **Ecclesiastical Art Museum** (daily except Wed & Fri 10am–1pm & 4–6pm; free). During the hostilities the ubiquitous Kolokotronis maintained a lair and a powder mill in the then almost inaccessible town. Before the War of Independence, the nunnery of **Emyalón** (daylight hours except 2–5pm), 3km south towards Stemnítsa, was used by the Kolokotronis clan as a hideout. About 2km south of Dhimitsána, the excellent **Open-Air Water Power Museum** (summer daily 10am–2pm & 5–7pm; winter Mon & Wed–Sun 10am–4pm; €2; Ⓦwww.piop.gr) has a reconstructed watermill, tannery and powder mill, with restored equipment, and exhibitions on the processes involved.

Accommodation

Though quite a small resort, there is now a selection of very good accommodation, making Dhimitsána a prime base for exploring the centre of the Peloponnese.

Dimitsana ☎27950 31518, ℻27950 31040. Completely refurbished and popular hotel, 1km out on the road to Stemnítsa – easiest for parking with your own transport. ❹, winter ❺

Pyrgos Xeniou ☎27950 31750, Ⓦwww.pyrgos-xenioy.gr. Luxurious, restored five-storey tower, said to be the tallest building constructed in Greece in the mid-nineteenth century. ❺–❼, winter ❻–❽

Tefthys ☎27950 32604. Hospitable, beautifully constructed hotel below the village, most rooms with gorgeous views down the Lousios valley. B&B ❹, winter ❹–❺

Velissaropoulos ☎27950 31617. Good-value studios and apartments next to Pýrgos Xeniou in the northwest corner of town. ❷–❸, winter ❸–❹

Xenonas Kazakou ☎27950 31660, Ⓦwww.xenonaskazakou.gr. Old restored mansion, in the higher part of town, near the school and Agía Kyriakí church. ❸, winter ❹

Eating

The **taverna** *Kali Thea*, just across the road from the *Dimitsana*, is good and reasonably priced. At the southern entrance to town, the cosy *Drymonas* has a large variety of *mezédhes* and local dishes. In nearby **Zátouna** village, 4km

△ Dhimitsána

southwest, the *Kaffenio tou Kentron* of Barba Nikita is a picture-crammed café, preserved as it was in the 1930s.

Vytína

Continuing the clockwise circuit around the Ménalo mountains for a further 19km brings you to the small town of **VYTÍNA**. The local accommodation is intended mainly for winter use during the skiing season, but the town makes a good base for self-drive exploration of the northern mountains and is on the E4 walking route; the roads out and facilities are considerably better here than at the other, more traditional, villages in this area, and there are up to six buses a day to and from Trípoli. **Hotels** include the *Aegli* (☎27950 22216; ❹) and *Villa Valos* (☎27950 22210 or 27950 22047; ❺) towards the bypass. Hidden in the fir forest, above the nearby village of **Elati**, at 1220m, is the luxurious *Salé (Chalet) Elati* (☎27950 22906, ⓦwww.sale-elati.gr; B&B ❻, winter ❼). In Vytína, the **taverna** ♨ *Ta Kokkina Pytharia* offers a wide choice of well-prepared local dishes, including a reasonable choice for vegetarians and local wild boar or venison for the carnivores.

Heading south, deep into Ménalo, on the small road from Vytína to Khrysovítsi, but turning off left to **Limbovísi** (signed in Greek only), brings you to the isolated house, now a small **museum** (summer daily, 10am–2pm; free), in the forest glade where Kolokotronis spent his childhood.

Moving on to Olympia

Through buses from Stemnítsa and Dhimitsána are scarce, and you may well need to hitch or take a taxi to Karkalоú junction (or to Vytína), on the main Trípoli–Pýrgos road, where you can pick up buses more easily. Once on the road to Olympia, the most enjoyable halt is **LANGÁDHIA** (18km from Dhimitsána), whose tiers of houses and bubbling sluices tumble downhill to the river far below the road. Often you can stop on a late-morning bus, eat lunch and pick up the next through service with little lost time. There is the central *Kentrikon Hotel* (☎ & ⓕ27950 43221; ❹), with good-sized rooms and mountain views. Above the village are the *Agnantio* studios (☎27950 43671, ⓦwww.hit360.com/agnantio; ❺, winter ❻), with even better views.

You may find that you have fewer changes and stops if you backtrack south to join the Karítena–Andhrítsena route and travel on to Olympia from there. Alternatively, if you're approaching Olympia from the north, through Arcadia from Pátra, then a pleasant staging post is the twin village of **LÁMBIA-DHÍVRI**, exactly halfway (78km) between Vytína and Pátra. There are a couple of tavernas, the *Balkonia* and the *Platanos*, as well as the *Xenonas Kosmopoulou* (☎26240 81205; ❸) and the *Mountains* (also known as *Orí*) hotel (☎ & ⓕ26240 81323; ❹).

Andhrítsena and the Temple of Bassae

Moving west from Karítena towards Andhrítsena, the Alfiós River falls away to the north and the hills become mountains – sacred Lýkeo to the south and Mínthi to the west. The route, only slightly less remote than the twists of road around Dhimitsána, is a superb one for its own sake, with the added attractions of **Andhrítsena**, a traditional mountain town, and the **Temple of Apollo Epikourios** at **Bassae** up on the flanks of Mount Lýkeo.

Andhrítsena

ANDHRÍTSENA, 28km west of Karítena, is a beautiful stop, and the traditional base from which to visit the Temple of Apollo at Bassae up in the mountains to the south. Though very much a roadside settlement today, it was a major hill town through the years of Turkish occupation and the first century of independent Greece. It remains remarkably untouched, with wooden houses spilling down to a stream, whose clear ice-cold headwaters are channelled into a fountain set within a plane tree in the central platía.

Hotel accommodation is available only at the *Theoxenia* (☎26260 22219; March–Oct; B&B ❹) on the Karítena side of town. For **meals**, try the small *Tsigouri* taverna, for local specialities.

The Temple of Apollo Epikourios at Bassae

Fourteen kilometres into the mountains south of Andhrítsena, the **Temple of Apollo** at **BASSAE** (Vásses) (summer daily 8.30am–3pm; €3) is the most remote, one of the highest, and arguably the most spectacular site in Greece. In addition, it is, after the Thiseion in Athens, the best-preserved Classical monument in the country, and for many years was considered to have been designed by Iktinos, architect of the Parthenon – though this theory has fallen from favour.

There the superlatives must cease. Romantic though the temple was in the past, it is now swathed in a gigantic grey marquee supported on metal girders and set in concrete with wire stays; its entablature and frieze lie dissected in neat rows on the ground to one side. No doubt the **restoration** is badly needed for its preservation – and the marquee is quite a sight in itself – but visitors are likely to be a bit disappointed. If you are not put off, take the Kréstena road out of town and then, almost immediately, turn off to the left and you begin the climb to the temple. Without transport, the simplest approach is to share a taxi, which should charge around €35 for the round trip, waiting an hour at the site. On foot it's a tiring ascent, with little likelihood of a lift. The site has a full-time guardian who lives alongside, but it's a lonely place, and must have felt even more isolated in ancient times.

The temple was erected in dedication to **Apollo Epikourios** ("the Succourer") by the Phigalians. It's known that they built it in gratitude for being spared from plague, but beyond this it is something of a puzzle. It is oddly aligned on a north-south axis and, being 1130m up in the mountains, is only visible when you are comparatively near. There are also oddities in the architecture: the columns on its north side are strangely thicker than in the rest of the building, and incorporated into its *cella* was a single Corinthian column, the first known in Greece (though now vanished save for its base). Unusually again, the cult statue, probably a four-metre-high bronze, would have stood in front of this pillar. Many of the frieze marbles are now in London's British Museum (Ⓦwww.thebritishmuseum.ac.uk/compass).

Moving on from Bassae or Andhrítsena

Leaving the Bassae-Andhrítsena area, there are a number of choices: from Andhrítsena two daily **buses** head back up towards Karítena and Megalópoli and two go down to Pýrgos (for **Olympia**).

A well-surfaced road winds through the mountains from Bassae down to the coast at **Tholó**. It takes quite a while to cover the 46km, but for the unhurried there's an opportunity to stop at **Perivólia** (10km), which is a surprisingly lively little place with a couple of restaurants, cafés and even a bar. This mountain hamlet has a short road connecting it with the similarly diminutive Figália, close by the ruins of the enormous Classical walls of **ancient Phigalia** and remarkable viewpoints over the Nédha gorge.

Messinía: Kalamáta to Kyparissía

The province of **Messinía** stretches from the western flank of the Taïyetos ridge across the plain of **Kalamáta** to the hilly southwesternmost finger of the Peloponnese. Green, fertile and luxuriant for the most part, it is ringed with a series of well-preserved castles overlooking some of the area's most expansive beaches. The pale curve of fine sand at the bay of **Voïdhokiliá**, near Yiálova, sandwiched between sea, rock and lagoon, is one of the most beautiful in Greece. Smaller beaches at **Koróni, Methóni** and **Finikoúnda** draw the crowds, but Messinía's important archeological sites, such as **Nestor's Palace** near Hóra, rarely see visitors in the quantity of the Argolid sites.

Kalamáta and around

KALAMÁTA is by far the largest city in the southern Peloponnese, spreading for some 4km back from the sea, and into the hills. It's quite a metropolitan shock after the small-town life of the rest of the region. The city has a long-established export trade in olives and figs from the Messinian plain, flourishing as a commercial centre during the Turkish period and as one of the first independent Greek towns in 1821, with the first newspaper to be printed on Greek soil five months later. In 1986, however, Kalamáta was near the epicentre of a severe **earthquake** that killed twenty people and left 12,000 families homeless. But for the fact that the quake struck in the early evening, when many people were outside, the death toll would have been much higher. As it was, large numbers of buildings were levelled throughout the town. The intensity of the damage was in part due to the city's position over several subterranean streams, but mostly it was, it seems, the legacy of poor 1960s construction. The result was an economic depression across the whole area, from which the town has only recently recovered fully.

Arrival and information

If you're looking to get transport straight through, arrive early to make connections. The **bus station** (℡27320 23145) is nearly 1km north of the centre; follow the river Nédhondos, partly covered with car parks. The most regular buses run north to Megalópoli, Trípoli and Athens, and west to Messíni, Koróni or Pýlos; the magnificent route over the Taïyetos ridge to Spárti is covered twice daily, and the one to Kardhamýli, Stoúpa and Ítylo (connection to Areópoli) four times daily.

The **train station** is on Frantzí, 200m to the west of the central Platía Konstandínou Dhiadhókhnou. Kalamáta is the railhead for trains chugging along the pretty, but slow and at times uncomfortable, route to Kyparissía (and ultimately to Pátra, with a possible detour to Olympia), or inland even more scenically to Trípoli and Árgos.

The **airport** (☎27210 69442) is 10km west of Kalamáta on the highway to Messíni, Pýlos and Koróni, and buses to these destinations pass the entrance. In season there are four charters a week from the UK, all on Sundays. The small terminal has an automatic **exchange** machine, and a helpful (when open) tourist office that will book accommodation.

There is an **EOT tourist office** in the city, upstairs at Polyvríou 6 (☎27210 86868), near the top of Aristoménous.

Drivers going through Kalamáta between the Máni and Arcadia or the west should follow the signed southern route through the city, along Kritís, Lykourgoú and Artémidhos, and then on the western bypass (which partly follows the train line); drivers to or from Spárti must brave the narrow crowded streets of the northern part of town.

Accommodation

In the city centre, there are very few mid-range **hotels**, so you'll do better down by the waterfront, where there are many more hotels, some of them expensive, though they seem to spend more on the reception areas than the bedrooms. However, they are often full by mid-afternoon and if you have not booked ahead, particularly at weekends, you may have to look around.

The nearest **campsites** are along the eastern end of the beach, at Vérga. The first, about 3km along the waterfront, is the *Elite* (☎27210 80365; April–Oct), behind the pricey *Hotel Elite*, Navarínou 2 (☎27210 22434, Ⓦwww.elite.com .gr; ❻), where campers can eat, and swim in the pool; *Maria* (also known as *Sea and Sun*, ☎27210 41060) is a popular and friendly campsite 1km down the road at Ayía Sión, which fronts onto the beach. However, unless you are stuck, you'd do better heading west towards Petalídhi (see p.292), or southeast to Kardhamýli and Stoúpa (see pp.263–264).

Flisvos Navarínou 135 ☎27210 82177, Ⓕ27210 226 179. Quiet, comfortable rooms, on the waterfront next to the church of Ayía Anástasi. ❹

George Frantzí 5 ☎27210 27225, Ⓕ27210 226 179. Under the same management as the larger *Vyzantio*, both are good value, very close to the train station, and not too far from the buses – but street noise can be a problem. ❷

Haïkos Navarínou 115 ☎27210 88902, Ⓕ27210 226 179. A modern hotel with pleasant rooms, air conditioning and helpful staff. ❹

Nevada Just off Fáron on Santaróza 9 ☎27210 82429. Cosy budget establishment, with shared bathrooms and a number of house rules. If full, try the *Avra* opposite. ❶

Vyzantio Sidhiroú Stathmoú 13 ☎27210 86824, Ⓕ27210 226 179. See above, under the *George*. ❷

The City

Few visitors plan to linger here, but if you are travelling for a while it's a good place to get things done, and there are other simple pleasures such as eating at tavernas among the Neoclassical houses on the waterfront or around the centre, which comprises the broad avenue formed by the long Platía Konstandínou Dhiadhókhnou.

KALAMÁTA

ACCOMMODATION
Flisvos	D
George	B
Haïkos	E
Nevada	C
Vyzantio	A

CAFÉS AND RESTAURANTS
Kannas	2
Karamanos	3
Katofli	5
Kioupi	1
Krini	4
Petrino	6
Pyrofani	8
Tambaki	7

KALAMÁTA WATERFRONT

A twenty-minute walk north of the centre will bring you to the area around the **Kástro**. Built by the Franks and destroyed and adapted in turn by the Turks and Venetians, the Kástro survived the quake with little damage; an **amphitheatre** at its base hosts summer concerts. A short way south of the Kástro is Polyzóglou 6 is the excellent **Benakion Archeological Museum** (Tues–Sun 8.30am–3pm; €2), which houses a modest but well-labelled collection of tomb reliefs, sculptures and smaller artefacts from the surrounding areas, as well as a colourful Roman mosaic from Desylla.

Kalamáta's **beach**, along Navarínou, a ten-minute bus ride (#1) south of the centre, is always crowded along the central section. The gritty sands are functional but improve continuously eastwards until the popular gay area at Vérga, beyond the *Filoxenia Beach Hotel*. If you prefer to walk to the harbour from the centre, it's a thirty-minute walk down Aristoménous, and en route you can wander in the park alongside the narrow bottom end of the street and admire the old steam engines, rolling stock and mechanical paraphernalia at the open-air **Railway Museum** (free). Graffiti artists may have taken their toll, but you can, like the local children, climb freely into the exhibits. There is an international dance festival hosted by the city every summer (information Kessári 6, ☏27210 20352, ⓦwww.kalamatadancefestival.gr).

Eating and drinking

The best **restaurants** in the summer months are down by the western **harbour**, which has been set up as a yacht marina – unfortunately all are accessed through a somewhat insalubrious area of abandoned warehouses and grain silos. Only in winter does the older **centre** of town get into its culinary stride.

There are a couple of well-priced **cafés** directly opposite the bus station, and a plethora of cafés, bars, gelateria and eating places along waterfront Navarínou. For afternoon or evening drinks, the cafés along the central broad Platía Konstandínou Dhiadhókhnou are very pleasant, and less noisy with traffic. Round the corner, the pace heats up in the **bars** along Frantzí and by the train station, of which *Stathmos* is one of the most popular.

Kannas Lakonikís 18. An atmospheric place serving traditional dishes. To the east of the centre, it featured in Sheelagh Kanelli's memoir, *Earth and Water* (see p.1136). Occasional live music.

Karamanos Psaron 146. Ouzerí west of the waterfront branch of the post office that does nice fish *mezédhes*. More expensive than the local average, but high quality.

Katofli Salamínos 20. Near the marina; outdoor summer seating and a huge menu.

Kioupi Alexíki 52 (off the Areópoli road). Idiosyncratically decorated and with clay-pot cooking

(as the name implies). Fish, *mezédhes* and *mayireftá*.

Krini Evangelistrías 40. Near the marina; a neighbourhood fish-and-wine taverna open most of the year.

Petrino Navarínou 93. A good selection of *mezédhes*; also open for seafront breakfasts.

Pyrofani At a corner on the waterfront with views of the marina and the lights of the eastern villages. A large selection of meat and vegetarian dishes and good local wine.

Tambaki Navarínou 91. A wide menu, tasty food and cheerful service by the sea.

Listings

Airlines Olympic, Yiatrákou 3 ☏27210 86410.
Banks and ATMs Most are on Aristoménous or adjacent Platía Konstandínou Dhiadhókhnou and Sidhiroú Stathmoú.

Bike & scooter rental Bastakos (also mountain bikes), Fáron 190 ☏27210 26638.
Car rental Maniatis, Iatropoúlou 1 ☏27210 27694, ⓔmaniatis@kal.forthnet.gr; Agni Travel,

Kessári 2 ⊕ 27210 20352, ⓕ 27210 22428; Stavri-
anos, Nédhondos 89 ⊕ 27210 23041, ⓕ 27210
25370.

Cinemas There are several cinemas near Platía
Konstandínou Dhiadhókhnou, some with family
entertainment; English-language films are shown
with Greek subtitles.

Ferry agent Maniatis, Psaron 148 ⊕ 27210
20704, ⓔ mantrv@acn.gr. Agent for ANEN.

Market The Wednesday and Saturday produce

market, one of the region's most colourful, is
across the bridge from the bus station, below the
castle.

Post office Near the railway station on Iatropoúlou,
with a second near the customs house beyond the
park at the seaward end of Aristoménous.

Taxis Ranks on Aristoménous, Nédhondos and
Navarínou.

Tourist police Miaouli, near the harbour ⊕ 27210
95555.

Ancient Messene

The ruins of **ancient Messene** (Ithómi) lie 30km northwest of Kalamáta and
22km north of modern Messíni. The ancient city was the fortified capital of the
Messenians, and achieved some fame in the ancient world as a showcase of military architecture. The highlights of the widely dispersed site are the outcrops of
its giant walls, towers and gates.

The ruins share the lower slopes of Mount Ithómi (800m) with the pretty
village of **MAVROMÁTI**. An hour's climb to the summit is rewarded with
spectacular views of the region of Messinía and the southern Peloponnese. If
you wish to stay and see the sunset from the site of the temple of Zeus which
crowns this peak, there are some **rooms** in the village.

The site is a tricky place to get to, unless you're driving. Buses run only twice
a day from Kalamáta (very early morning and early afternoon). With a car it's a
fairly easy detour en route to either western Messinía or Arcadia.

The site

Messene's fortifications were designed as the southernmost link in a defensive
chain of **walled cities** (which included Megalopolis and Árgos) masterminded by the Theban leader Epaminondas to keep the Spartans at bay. Having
managed to halt them at the battle of Leuctra (near Stoúpa) in 371 BC, he set
about building an astonishing nine-kilometre circuit of ten-metre-high walls
(which lasted almost undamaged for 750 years) and restoring the Messenians
to their native acropolis. The Messenians, who had resisted Spartan oppression
from the eighth century BC onwards, wasted no time in re-establishing their
capital; the city, so chronicles say, was built in 85 days.

The most interesting of the remains (summer Tues–Fri 8am–7pm, Sat
& Sun 8.30am–5pm; winter Tues–Sun 8.30am–3pm; free) is the **Arcadia
gate** at the north end of the site, through which the nine-kilometre side
road to the village of Meligalás still runs. It consisted of an outer and inner
portal separated by a circular courtyard made up of massive chunks of stone
precisely cut to fit together without mortar. The outer gate, the foundations
of which are fairly evident, was flanked by two square towers from where
volleys of javelins and arrows would rain down on attackers. The inner gate,
a similarly impregnable barrier, comprised a huge monolithic doorpost, half
of which remains. In paved stretches within the gateway you can still trace
the ruts of chariot wheels.

Further south, and signposted "Ithomi: Archeological site" on the road
running northwest from Mavromáti, is a recently excavated **sanctuary of
Asklepios**. This site, at first mistakenly believed to be the agora, consisted of a
temple surrounded by a porticoed courtyard; the bases of some of the colonnades and traces of benches have been unearthed. Next to it is the site of a

theatre or meeting place. Excavations continue in the summer with archeologists digging in the shade of semi-permanent canopies.

There are other remains up Mount Ithómi, an hour's hike along a steep path forking north from the track at the Laconia gate, which is to the southeast of the site. Along the way you pass remains of an Ionic **temple of Artemis**. At the top, on the site of a temple of Zeus, are the thirteenth-century ruins of the original **monastery of Voulkanós**, founded in the eighth century. Spread below are the lush and fertile valleys of Messinía.

Around the coast to Koróni

Beaches stretch for virtually the entire distance west from Kalamáta then south to Koróni, along what is steadily developing as a major resort coast. At present, however, it is more popular with Greeks than foreigners, and the resorts, tucked away in the pines, consist primarily of campsites and the odd room for rent. The beach at Boúka, 5km south of modern Messíni, is a fine stretch of sand with views of the Máni. It is popular with the locals, especially as a place to go for Sunday lunch. The nearest **campsite** is *Golden Sands* at Análipsi (℡27220 24020).

There are more beaches around **PETALÍDHI**, 25km west around the coast from Kalamáta. There are several **campsites** along this coast: *Petalidi Beach* (℡27220 31154, ℱ27220 31690; April–Sept), 3km north of the village, is well established and reasonably priced. There are ample **tavernas** and cafés around the spacious sea-facing square and some cheap **rooms**. Moving south (you'll need your own transport), there are numerous restaurants, rooms and some hotels along the stretch of coast – and busy road – to Koróni. The *Aphrodites* **taverna** at **KHRÁNI** is recommended for its fresh fish and traditional Greek dishes, and the *Sunrise Village* at **KALAMAKÍ** has an unusually good restaurant for a hotel (the rooms themselves are booked up by package holidays).

Koróni, Finikoúnda and Methóni

The twin **fortresses** at Koróni and Methóni were the Venetians' oldest and longest-held possessions in the Peloponnese: strategic outposts on the route to Crete and known through the Middle Ages as "The Eyes of the Serene Republic", when Koróni was also noted for the manufacture of siege-engines. Today they encompass three of the more attractive small resorts in the south, Koróni, Finikoúnda and Methóni.

Public **transport** around the Messinian peninsula has improved of late and there are good bus connections between Kalamáta and Koróni, or Pýlos, plus several buses a day from Pýlos to Methóni and Finikoúnda. Direct connections between Methóni and Koróni are still elusive, although a new fast road has been built connecting the two. In season, one or two buses a day (usually early morning and mid-afternoon) on the Kalamáta–Koróni route continue to Finikoúnda. If moving on from Koróni to Pýlos, you can change from the Koróni–Kalamáta bus to the Kalamáta–Pýlos bus at the café at Rizómylos junction.

Koróni

KORÓNI has one of the more picturesque locations in Greece, stacked against a fortified bluff and commanding grand views across the Messenian gulf to the Taïyetos peaks. The town is rustically beautiful in itself, with tiled and pastel-washed houses arrayed in a maze of stair-and-ramp streets that can have changed little since the medieval Venetian occupation (1206–1500) when it was a fleet supply base. Buses terminate in the square below the main church, outside a café and excellent zaharoplastío and one row back from the waterfront. Koróni's **citadel** is one of the least militaristic-looking in Greece, crowning rather than dwarfing the town. Part of the interior is given over to private houses and garden plots, but the greater part is occupied by the flower-strewn nunnery of **Timíou Prodhrómou**, whose chapels, outbuildings and gardens occupy nearly every bastion.

From the southwest gate of the fortress, stairs descend to the park-like grounds of **Panayía Elestrías**, a church erected at the end of the nineteenth century to house a miraculous icon – unearthed with the assistance of the vision of one Maria Stathaki (buried close by). The whole arrangement, with fountains, shrubbery and benches for watching the sunset, seems more like the Adriatic than the Aegean.

Continuing downhill, you reach **Zánga beach** which runs into **Mémi beach**, making a two-kilometre stretch of sand and preternaturally clear water that sets the seal on Koróni as a place to relax, drink wine and amble about a countryside lush with vineyards and olive groves. The beach is about the only place to go during the afternoon, when Koróni strictly observes siesta. Turtles nest in the Mémi area.

Practicalities

To be sure of a room in summer, it's worth trying to phone ahead. The only large hotel, the *Auberge de la Plage* (☎27250 22401; ❹), is way out on the road towards Mémi beach. Looking for **private rooms** on arrival, try the places to the right of the fishing port as you face the water, and don't leave it too late in the day; there are also cheaper, quieter rooms in the Panórama district, up behind Zánga beach. Several of the town **tavernas** rent rooms, including the *Parthenon* (☎27250 22146; ❷) on a seafront corner below the square, and the *Pension Koroni* (☎27250 22385; ❸) above the *Symposion* restaurant on the main street. An attractive and only slightly more expensive option, with a leafy setting and views of the bay and castle, is *Marinos Bungalows* (☎ & ℗27250 22522; April–Oct; ❸) on the road north just out of town. There are two **campsites**: *Memi Beach* (☎27250 22130, ⓦwww.memibeachcamping.gr; June–Sept), which is 2km south of Koróni on the Vasilítsi road, and *Koroni* (☎27250 22884, ℗27250 22119; April–Oct) on the main road into town; both have sandy beaches, though from *Memi Beach* you have to cross the road.

There is a reasonable selection of **restaurants** on the waterfront, and some authentic **tavernas** (barrel-wine and oven-food places) along the main shopping street. The *Flisvos* has good seafood at reasonable prices, and the *Symposion* serves moussaka, grills and seafood.

Many people make wine or raki in their basement and the heady local tipple figures prominently in the **nightlife**. The main venue is the sprawling *Astra Club* out towards Mémi beach. There are two or three tavernas on the beach and by night a solitary disco, though all of these close down by mid-September. Koróni has two **banks** (one with an ATM) and a **post office**.

Finikoúnda

FINIKOÚNDA, 18km west of Koróni, is a small fishing village with a superb cove-beach plus another to the east, and a gigantic strand to the west. Over recent years it has gained a reputation as a backpackers' – and especially windsurfers' – resort, with half the summer intake staying at a trio of campsites on either side of the village, the others housed in a variety of rooms including some taken by British package companies. It can be a fun, relaxed place.

To book **rooms** in advance, try the central, laid-back hotel *Finikounda* (℡ & 🅕 27230 71208; B&B ❹), the beach-front *Porto Finissia* (℡27230 71358, 🅕27230 71458; summer only; B&B ❹), or the nearby *Korakakis Beach* (℡27230 71221, 🅕27230 71232; B&B ❸), which also has self-catering apartments at similar prices. The local **campsites** are the well-equipped *Anemomylos* (℡27230 71120, 🅕27230 71121; open all year), 500m west of town; *Ammos* (℡27230 71262, 🅕27230 71124; May–Oct), 3km west of the village; and the *Loutsa* (℡27230 71169, 🅕27230 71445; June–Sept), 2km to the east. Among the **tavernas**, *Elena* is recommended for good traditional fare and for a drink with a harbour view, while *Psychos* has tasty food, including pasta and pizzas, at good prices. *Theasis* **bar** features a mixture of old and new rock **music**.

Methóni

In contrast to the almost domestic citadel at Koróni, the huge fortress at **METHÓNI** is as imposing as they come – massively bastioned, washed on three sides by the sea, and cut off altogether from the land by a great moat. It was maintained by the Venetians in part for its military function, in part as a staging post for pilgrims en route, via Crete and Cyprus, to the Holy Land, and from the thirteenth to the nineteenth centuries it sheltered a substantial town. It was from here, in 1825, that Ibrahim Pasha launched his destructive reinvasion of the Peloponnese that was only finally stopped by the events at Navaríno in 1827 (see box on p.297).

Within the **fortress** (Mon 8.30am–3pm, Tues–Sun 8am–7pm; closes 3pm in winter; free), entered across the moat along a stone bridge, are the remains of a Venetian cathedral (the Venetians' Lion of St Mark emblem is ubiquitous), along with a Turkish bath, the foundations of dozens of houses and some awesome, but mostly cordoned-off, underground passages. Walk around the walls and a sea gate at the southern end leads out across a causeway to the **Boúrtzi**, a small fortified island that served as a prison and place of execution. The octagonal tower was built by the Turks in the sixteenth century to replace an earlier Venetian fortification. Unusually, and for no obvious reason, photography is forbidden inside the site – probably because of archeological excavations; it seems unlikely that the Greek military regard it as still of strategic significance.

Practicalities

The **bus** from Pýlos stops at the first forked junction in town, near the **bank** and ATM, but if planning a day-trip check return times with the driver. The rather scruffy beach runs eastwards from the castle, although the small Paralías square has been recently paved and revamped. In high season, there may be boat trips out to the southern islands of Skhíza and Sapiénza.

Methóni is geared more conspicuously to tourism than Koróni and gets very crowded in season, when **accommodation** can be expensive and often over-subscribed. Out of season, the hotels are cheaper and a number stay open all year. The well-priced *Castello* (℡27230 31300, 🅔castellohotel@mailcity; ❸) is near the entrance to the fortress, with beautiful gardens, balconies and a stunning view; the friendly *Aris* (℡27230 31125, 🅕27230 31336; ❸) is on the small platía Syngroú behind *Castello*. The renovated *Anna* (℡27230 31332, 🅕27230 31277; B&B ❸) is also very friendly, nearer to the town centre, and has a good restaurant. In addition, there is the usual collection of cheaper **rooms** at the

△ The Boúrtzi, Methóni

fortress end of town. At the east end of the beach is a municipal **campsite**, the *Methoni* (☎27230 31228; May–Oct); it's popular and gets crowded, but the facilities are good and the beach tolerable.

Methóni has several **restaurants**, including the pricey *Klimataria* (☎27230 31544, reservations suggested; May–Oct, evenings only), which serves a well-prepared selection of dishes (including good veggie choices) in a courtyard garden opposite the *Castello*. Among the dozen or so other eateries, *Sapienza*, set back from the seafront on the Finikounda road, is recommended for fresh fish.

Pýlos and around

PÝLOS is a compact but quite stylish town for rural Messinía; guarded by a pair of medieval castles, it occupies a superb position on one of the finest natural harbours in Greece, the almost landlocked **Navarino Bay**. Given the town's associations with the Battle of Navarino, and, more anciently, with Homer's "sandy Pýlos", the domain of "wise King Nestor" whose palace (see p.299) has been identified 16km to the north, it makes a good base for exploring this part of the Peloponnese, particularly if equipped with a car. Relying on public transport, you'll find the long afternoon gaps in services make complex day-trips impractical.

The Town

The main pleasures of Pýlos are exploring the hillside alleys, waterside streets and fortress. Getting your bearings is easy as it's not a large town, and the main square facing the port is very much the heart of the town.

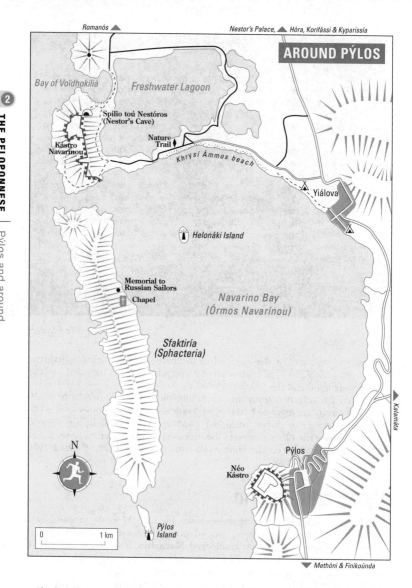

AROUND PÝLOS

Bay of Voïdhokiliá   Freshwater Lagoon

Spílio toú Nestóros
(Nestor's Cave)

Kástro
Navarínou

Nature
Trail

Khrysí Ámmos beach

Yiálova

Helonáki Island

Memorial to
Russian Sailors
Chapel

Navarino Bay
(Órmos Navarínou)

Sfaktiría
(Sphacteria)

Kalamáta ▲

N

Pýlos

Néo
Kástro

0   1 km

Pýlos
Island

Methóni & Finikoúnda ▼

Shaded by a large plane tree and several of its offspring, **Platía Trión Navárhon** is a beautiful public space, encircled by cafés and colonnaded shops. At its head is a **war memorial** commemorating the admirals Codrington, de Rigny and von Heyden, who commanded the British, French and Russian forces in the Battle of Navarino (see box opposite). Nearby, just uphill on the Methóni road, the little **Antonopouleion Museum** (Tues–Sun 8.30am–3pm; €2) boasts remains from the battle, along with archeological finds from the region.

The battles of Navarino Bay

Arriving at Pýlos your gaze is inevitably drawn to the bay, almost landlocked by the long offshore island of Sfaktiría (Sphacteria). Its name, Órmos Navarínou – Navarino Bay – marks the **battle** that effectively sealed implementation of Greek independence from the Turks on the night of October 20, 1827, though the battle itself seems to have been accidental. The Great Powers of Britain, France and Russia, having established diplomatic relations with the Greek insurgent leaders, were attempting to force an armistice on the Turks. To this end they sent a fleet of 27 warships to Navarino, where Ibrahim Pasha had gathered his forces – 16,000 men in 89 ships. The declared intention was to coerce Ibrahim into leaving Messinía, which he had been raiding ruthlessly.

In the confusion of the night an Egyptian frigate, part of the Turks' supporting force, fired its cannons, and full-scale battle broke out. Without intending to take up arms for the Greeks, the "allies" responded to the attack and, extraordinarily, sank and destroyed 53 of the Turkish fleet without a single loss. There was considerable international embarrassment when news filtered through to the "victors", but the action had nevertheless effectively ended Turkish control of Greek waters and within a year Greek independence was secured and recognized.

Navarino Bay also features in one of the most famous battles of **Classical times**, described in great detail by Thucydides. In 425 BC, during the Peloponnesian War, an Athenian force encamped at Kástro Navarínou (the old castle of Pýlos) laid siege to a group of Spartans on the island of **Sfaktiría**, just across the straits. In a complete break with tradition, which decreed fighting to the death, the Spartans surrendered. "Nothing that happened in the war surprised the Hellenes as much as this," commented Thucydides.

Further memories of the Navarino battles can be evoked by a visit to the **island of Sfaktiría**, across the bay, where there are various tombs of Philhellenes, a chapel and a memorial to Russian sailors. You can hire a **boat** from the port and also snorkel to see the remains of the Turkish fleet lying on the sea bed; ask at the harbour office or cafés by the port.

The principal sight in town, however, is the **Néo Kástro** (Tues–Sun 8.30am–3pm; €3), further up the Methóni road from the museum. The huge "new castle" was built by the Turks in 1572, and you can walk around much of the 1500m of arcaded battlements. For much of the eighteenth and nineteenth centuries, it served as a prison and its inner courtyard was divided into a warren of narrow yards separated by high walls, a design completely at odds with most Greek prisons, which were fairly open on the inside. This peculiar feature was necessitated by the garrison's proximity to the Máni. So frequently was it filled with Maniots imprisoned for vendettas, and so great was the crop of internal murders, that these pens had to be built to keep the imprisoned clansmen apart. The pens and walls have been pulled down as part of an ongoing programme to restore and convert the castle into a planned **museum** for underwater archeology. So far, the only attraction is René Puaux's extensive collection of historical pictures and cartoons.

Practicalities

The National Bank is on the central platía, and the **post office** on Niléos, just west from the **bus station** (℡27230 22230). **Car rental** (also from Kalamáta airport) is available through AutoUnion (℡27230 22393, @autounionkalamata @mailbox.gr) on the Kalamáta road, and from the *Miramare* (see overleaf).

Pýlos has somewhat limited accommodation and in the summer months you should definitely try to phone ahead. Among the **hotels** are the *Galaxy*, on the platía (☎27230 22780, ℱ27230 22208; B&B ❸) and the posher *Karalis*, Kalamátas 26 (☎27230 22960, ℯhotel_karalis@yahoo.gr; B&B ❺), an attractive sea-view hotel. The *Miramare*, Myrtidhiotíssis 35 (☎27230 22751, ℯmmpylos@otenet.gr; April–Sept; B&B ❹), near the port, has fine views. There are many **rooms** around the winding main road on the hill out towards Kalamáta and Kyparissía, and a few near the castle and *Miramare*. A more relaxed alternative to staying in Pýlos is the beachfront part of Yiálova (see below).

For **drinks**, the Platía Trión Navárhon cafés are the obvious choice, although they can be pricey. Among **tavernas**, try *Lykourgos* for *mayireftá* on the small street northeast from the platía, or *Gregory's*, at the T-junction at the top of the same street. Nightlife revolves around bars on the square, and the larger, summer-only **clubs** *Gigi's* and *Zoglo Summer Matter*, both a little out of town. There is also an outdoor summer **cinema**, south of the square.

The northern rim of Navarino Bay

YIÁLOVA, 6km north out of Pýlos, has tamarisk trees shading its sandy beach, and makes a delightful base for walkers, naturalists or beach-lovers. The *Navarino* **campsite** (☎27230 22761, ℱ27230 23512) has good facilities including a recommended restaurant, and is popular with windsurfers. A second campsite, *Erodios* (☎27230 28240, Ⓦwww.camping.gr/erodios; March–Nov), is on the Golden Beach road and also has watersports facilities. Nearer the central jetty there is a **hotel**, the *Zoe* (☎27230 22025, Ⓦwww.hotelzoe.com; ❹), where the owner has an interest in the wildlife that inhabits the local lagoons and can suggest walks; the cheaper *Helonaki* (☎27230 23080; ❷) has a variety of rooms and apartments. Both have good tavernas underneath, and great views, though for eating, you can't beat the excellent home cooking at *To Spitiko* or *Farmakio*, just south of the corner of the pier. There is a small **shop** for picnic supplies between the pier and the main road; northwards along the main road is more, though less well-positioned, accommodation.

Pýlos's northern castle, and ancient acropolis, **Kástro Navarínou** (Paleó Kástro), stands on a hill ridge almost touching the island of Sfaktiría, at the end of the bay 5km west of Yiálova. It has substantial walls and identifiable courtyards and cisterns within fortifications, which are a mix of Frankish and Venetian, set upon ancient foundations. The panoramic outlook over one of the best beaches in the Peloponnese – a gorgeous crescent of fine sand curling around the spectacular **Bay of Voïdhokiliá** – is tremendous, but the interior is a jungle of shrubs and other vegetation that makes progress through it difficult. It's a ten-to twelve-kilometre trip from Pýlos, for which you'll need some transport. Go north through Yiálova, turn left at the sign to Voïdhokiliá and Golden Beach (the Pýlos–Hóra bus will bring you this far); at the end of the surfaced road, go left until the dirt road ends below the castle hill. From here, proceed left up to the castle, or head right along the footpath between the lagoon and the hill until you reach the Voïdhokiliá dunes and beach. With your own transport, follow the main road north towards Hóra, and when the road swings right to Korifássi, go left on a side road signed to Romanós and Navarino castle. Continue on the increasingly badly surfaced roads and you will end up at Voïdhokiliá.

The **lagoon** behind the beach is an important bird conservation area, and vehicles are not allowed on the earth road around its eastern rim. Near the end of the Golden Beach asphalt, a signed nature trail has been laid out. Turtles still breed at Voïdhokiliá (and at the beaches of Romanoú and Máti, further north), but a tiny population – the only one in mainland Europe – of slow-moving chameleons amongst the dune shrubs is endangered by illegal drivers, camper vans and reptile collectors. A large golf resort, one of three for the Navarino area, is planned for the area immediately behind Romanós beach.

A path from the southern Voïdhokiliá dunes ascends to the **Spílio toú Nestóros** (Nestor's Cave), and then (head right, up steep rocky steps) to the castle. This impressive bat-cave with a hole in the roof is fancifully identified as the grotto in which, according to the *Odyssey*, Nestor and Neleus kept their cows, and in which Hermes hid Apollo's cattle. It is not impossible that the cave sparked Homer's imagination, for this area is reckoned by archeologists to have been the Mycenaean-era harbour of King Nestor, and later of the Classical town of Korifasio.

North to Nestor's Palace

Nestor's Palace (also known as the Palace of Áno Englianós, after the hill on which it stands) was discovered in 1939, but left virtually undisturbed until after World War II; thus its excavation – unlike Mycenae, or most of the other major Greek sites – was conducted in accordance with modern archeological techniques. In consequence, its remains are the best preserved of all the Mycenaean royal palaces, though they shelter rather prosaically beneath a giant metal roof. The site guide by excavators Carl Blegen and Marion Rawson is an excellent buy.

The palace is located some 17km from modern Pýlos, a half-hour drive. Using public transport, take any of the **buses** from Pýlos towards Hóra (3–6 daily); these follow the main road inland past Korifássi to the site and its museum at Hóra (4km to the east).

The palace site

Flanked by deep, fertile valleys, the **palace site** (summer Tues–Fri 8am–7pm, Sat & Sun 8.30am–3pm; winter daily 8.30am–3pm; €3) looks out towards Navarino Bay – a location perfectly suiting the wise, measured and peaceful king described in Homer's *Odyssey*. The scene from the epic that is set here is the visit of Telemachus, son of Odysseus, who had journeyed from Ithaca to seek news of his father from King Nestor. As Telemachus arrives at the beach, accompanied by the disguised goddess Pallas Athena, he comes upon Nestor with his sons and court sacrificing to Poseidon. The visitors are welcomed and feasted, "sitting on downy fleeces on the sand", and although the king has no news of Odysseus he promises Telemachus a chariot so he can enquire from Menelaus at Sparta. First, however, the guests are taken back to the palace, where Telemachus is given a bath by Nestor's "youngest grown daughter, beautiful Polycaste", and emerges, anointed with oil, "with the body of an immortal".

By some harmonious twist of fate, a bathtub was unearthed on the site, and the palace ruins as a whole are potent ground for Homeric imaginings. The walls stand a metre high, enabling you to make out a very full plan. Originally, they were half-timbered (like Tudor houses), with upper sections of sun-baked brick held together by vertical and horizontal beams, and brilliant frescoes within. Even in their diminished state they suggest a building of considerable prestige. No less should be expected, for Nestor sent the second largest contingent to Troy – a fleet of "ninety black ships". The remains of the massive complex are in three principal groups: the **main palace** in the middle, on the left an earlier and **smaller palace**, and on the right either **guardhouses** or **workshops**.

The basic design will be familiar if you've been to Mycenae or Tiryns: an internal court, guarded by a sentry box, gives access to the main sections of the principal palace. This contained some 45 rooms and halls. The **megaron** (throne room), with its characteristic open hearth, lies directly ahead of the entrance, through a double porch. The finest of the frescoes was discovered here, depicting a griffin (perhaps the royal emblem) standing guard over the throne; this is now in the museum at Hóra. Arranged around are domestic quarters and **storerooms**, which yielded thousands of pots and cups during excavations; the rooms may have served as a distribution centre for the produce of the palace workshops. Further back, the famous **bathroom**, with its terra-cotta tub *in situ*, adjoins a smaller complex of rooms, centred on another, smaller, megaron, identified as the **queen's quarters**. Finally, on the other side of the car park there is a tholos tomb, a smaller version of the famous ones at Mycenae.

Archeologically, the most important find at the site was a group of several hundred tablets inscribed in **Linear B**. These were discovered on the first day of digging, in the two small rooms to the left of the entrance courtyard. They were the first such inscriptions to be discovered on the Greek mainland and proved conclusively a link between the Mycenaean and Minoan civilizations; like those found by Sir Arthur Evans at Knossos on Crete, the language was unmistakeably Greek. The tablets were baked hard in the fire which destroyed the palace at the time of the Dorian invasion around 1200 BC, perhaps as little as one generation after the fall of Troy.

The museum at Hóra

At **Hóra** (Hóra Trifylías), a small town despite the name "village", the **museum** (officially Tues–Sun 8.30am–3pm, but can be erratic; €2) on Marinátou, signed above the main square (with Friday-morning produce market), adds significantly to a visit to the site. If you've no transport, it might be better to take a bus here first, to the central bus station stop, and then walk the 45 minutes to the site after viewing the exhibits. In hot weather, or if pressed for time, you might be able to hitch, or get a taxi.

Pride of place in the display goes to the **palace frescoes**, one of which, bearing out Homer's descriptions, shows a warrior in a boar-tusk helmet. Lesser finds include much pottery, some beautiful gold cups and other objects gathered both from the site and from various Mycenaean tombs in the region.

The coast north of Pýlos

The stretch of **coast** between Pýlos and Pýrgos is defined by its **beaches**, which are on a different scale to those elsewhere in the Peloponnese, or indeed anywhere else in Greece – fine sands, long enough (and undeveloped enough) to satisfy the most jaded Australian or Californian. Their relative anonymity is something of a mystery, though one accounted for in part by poor communications. For those without transport this entails slow and patient progress along the main "coast" road, which for much of the way runs 2 to 5km inland, and a walk from road junction to beach.

Heading north from the Bay of Voïdhokiliá, near the turning inland to Korifássi and Nestor's Palace, you can take a paved road, flanked by orange and olive orchards. This keeps close to the sea for most of the way to Kyparissía, allowing access to isolated beaches and villages.

If you're travelling to Olympia by **train** from this coast, you can save the detour to Pýrgos (not an exhilarating town – see p.310) by getting a connection at Alfiós, a tiny station at the junction of the Olympia line and as bucolic a halt as any on the network (but not to be confused with next stop Alfioúsa station). Alfiós is seven minutes down the line from Pýrgos, and thirteen from Olympia.

Marathópoli and Filiatrá

If you are looking for little more than accommodation and a village café, then **MARATHÓPOLI**, the harbour of Gargaliáni, holds most promise. It has a long beach, rockier than most along this coast, and faces the islet of Próti, shaped like a long-tailed turtle and once a pirate refuge. The better hotel is the popular beachfront *Artina* (℡27230 61400, ℻27230 61402; ➍), with fridges in the rooms; it should be booked in advance. There are some **rooms** for rent; a **campsite**, *Proti* (℡27230 61211, ℻27230 29806; May–Oct), with a swimming pool; and two or three summer **tavernas** by the sea. A small taxi boat makes the short crossing to the islet of Próti, with its sandy beach and monastery, but can be expensive – ask at the supermarket.

Further on, the road passes through Ayía Kyriakí, a fishing village with a sweet little harbour and a few rooms, before reaching **FILIATRÁ**, which is on the bus route between Pýlos and Kyparissía. By a curious pattern of emigration, just as Kýthira is home to Greek-Australians, the villages along the Kyparissía coast have a concentration of returned Greek-Americans, virtually all of them having done a stint of work in New York or New Jersey. Disgraced American ex-Vice President (1968–73) Spiro Agnew was perhaps the most infamous local boy. However, the Greek-American who has left most mark on his home domain is one Haris Fournarakis, also known as **Harry Fournier**, a doctor from Chicago who came back in the 1960s and started building his fantasies. At the northern entrance to Filiatrá, Fournier constructed a garden-furniture version of the **Eiffel Tower** (illuminated at night by fairy lights) and a mini-replica of the globe from the 1964 New York Expo. His most ambitious project, however, was his **Kástro tón Paramythíon** ("Castle of the Fairytales"), a truly loopy folly with white concrete battlements and outcrops of towers, plus ten to thirteen-metre statues of Poseidon's horse (flanked by vases of flowers) and the goddess Athena. The castle is located right on the sea, 6km north of Filiatrá. Apart from Fournier's castle, the only feature of the town is the pleasant central square with a large, functioning fountain, the bus station and numerous cafés. There is no good beach.

Kyparissía

KYPARISSÍA is a small, congenial agricultural and market town, positioned in the shadow of the eponymous peak, part of the spectacular Egáleo mountain ridge. On a lower outcrop of the range is a Byzantine-Frankish **castle** (free), around which spreads the **old town**. Its ochre-hued mansions suffered heavy damage during the civil war, but there are some **tavernas** here.

Below the hill, the modern town is a functional but pleasant place. A few tourist boutiques and a nightclub or two have sprung up recently, and it is possibly preferable to a night in Kalamáta if you're on your way to Olympia by bus or train (Kyparissía is the junction of the Kalamáta and Pýrgos lines). Within walking distance of town are long, near-deserted sands – turtle breeding-grounds – and rocky cliff paths.

Practicalities

The centre of the modern town, just south of the adjacent **bus** (T27610 22260) and **train stations** (T27610 22283), is Platía Kalantzákou, where you'll find several **banks**, the **post office** and a remarkable number of cafés. There's pricey **Internet** access at Heaven's Net, at E. Venizélou 76. Accommodation consists of a half-dozen **hotels**, divided between the town and the beach. The cheapest place to stay in town is the *Trifolia*, 25-Martíou 40 (T27610 22066; ❶), a down-to-earth and welcoming pension, just east of the square and round the corner from the bus station. Other hotels include the comfortable and friendly *Ionion* (T27610 22511, F27610 22512; ❸), facing the train station; by the beach is the well-equipped **campsite**, *Kyparissia* (T27610 23491, F27610 24519; April–Oct). Beyond this beach, over a small rocky headland there's a better beach used by naturists, though it has strong currents at times. There are a handful of no-nonsense **restaurants** and pizzerias in the streets around Platía Kalantzákou; one of the best is *Stars*, at the southwest corner of the main square. For atmosphere it's better to eat down at the beach, where the taverna *Ta Porakia*, towards the campsite, is a fine choice, or up at the old town, where the liveliest place to dine is the *psistariá Arcadia*.

Beaches north from Kyparissía

Between Kyparissía and Lake Kaïáfas, the road and rail lines continue, 1km or so back from the coast. All of the hamlets on this coast have long stretches of sandy beach, often edged with olive groves, reed beds or pinewoods – their lack of development seems almost miraculous. Behind the beach pine forest at **Eliá** there's a good shady taverna, *O Mythos*. Nearby, 2km south, in the old train station at Ayianákis, is an environmental centre (T27610 91181, Wwww .archelon.gr) with information about the turtles along this coast; they also have an organized 1.5-kilometre forest trail through the Eliá pine woodland.

Among the occasional **campsites** advertising their particular stretch of beach are the *Apollon Village* (T26250 61200; May–Sept) at **Yianitsohóri** (18km along), which also has the *Panorama Apartments* (T26250 34930; ❷), near the BP garage. A few kilometres further on, there is a better campsite at **Tholó** – the *Tholo Beach* (T26250 61345; March–Oct). There are also a few **rooms** to rent at **Neohóri**, just past Tholó.

One of the more accessible of the beaches (5min from the train station and 25 from the main highway) is 5km beyond Tholó at **KAKÓVATOS**, which combines breakers with incredibly shallow, slowly shelving waters – though lacking any shade. The area is slightly more commercialized now with the *To Kohyli* (*Grigoris*) taverna and the *Baywatch* café (complete with watchtower) on the beach, while the village has a number of pensions, including *Kallifidhas* (T26250 31167; ❷) and *Timoleon* (T26250 32253; ❷).

Just north, at **ZAHÁRO**, the largest town between Kyparissía and Pýrgos, and a train stop, there are numerous shops and four **hotels**, though a shortage of tavernas. Near the main crossroads, on the railway station side, is the *Nestor* (T26250 31206; ❸) with clean rooms and old-fashioned hospitality, while the *Sugar Town* opposite, above a café (T26250 31985; ❸), is newer. The train station is just under 1km from the crossroads, on the road to the sea; midway from the station to the excellent beach is the *Banana Place* (T26250 34400; ❺; April–Oct), which offers chalet-type accommodation with cooking facilities – booking is advisable. Afternoon buses through the Zaháro **bus station** – east of the crossroads and right – are few and far between; **taxis** in Zaháro are on T26250 31357.

Another enormous strand, backed by sand dunes and pine groves, is at **Kaïáfas** just before the roads loop inland. At the beach there's just a rather uninspired taverna and the train station, both on the main road, opposite the entrance to the spa. On a side road a couple of kilometres inland, however, the village of **LOUTRÁ KAÏÁFAS** assumes the atmosphere of a spa. Strung out alongside the reed-screened lagoon is a scattering of hotels and pensions, frequented mainly by Greeks seeking hydrotherapy cures. Each morning a small shuttle-boat takes the visitors from their hotels to the sulphurous and often foul-smelling hot springs of Mount Lapíthas across the lake. The best deals for accommodation are probably at the friendly *Hotel Jenny* (☎26250 32234; ❸), which has a decent restaurant, as does the clean and comfortable *Archaea Sami* (☎26250 32257, ℗26250 34639; spring–Oct; ❷), which is the nearest accommodation (1.5km) to the main highway; the latter has cheaper rooms with shared bathrooms, intended for its Greek summer clientele. Two kilometres north of the lake, as the national road loops around a spur in the hills, you can just make out the walls of ancient Samikon on the hillside.

Ilía and Ahaïa: the northwest

Dominated economically by the sprawling city of **Pátra**, the large province of **Ahaïa** combines high mountains and a narrow, densely populated coastal strip. From **Dhiakoftó** in the north, one of Greece's most remarkable railway lines follows the dramatic **Vouraikós gorge**, up to Kalávryta. To the southwest of Ahaïa, the flat coastal plains of **Ilía** support a series of undistinguished market towns and are bordered on the west by long, narrow, often underused beaches. The **Olympia** archeological site is the jewel of the fertile Alfiós valley and this area's main tourist attraction.

Olympia (Olymbía)

The historic associations and resonance of **OLYMPIA**, which for over a millennium hosted the most important **Panhellenic games**, are rivalled only by Delphi or Mycenae. It is one of the largest and most beautiful sites in Greece, and the setting is as perfect as could be imagined: a luxuriant valley of oak, pear and plane trees, spread beside the twin rivers of Alfiós (Alpheus) – the largest in the Peloponnese – and Kládhios, and overlooked by the pine-covered Hill of Krónos. The site itself is picturesque and shaded, perfect ground for picnics, but the sheer quantity of ruined structures can give a confusing impression of their ancient grandeur and function. However, on walking through from the sanctuary to the first glimpse of the stadium it is hard not to feel in awe of the Olympian history. Despite the crowds, the tour buses, the

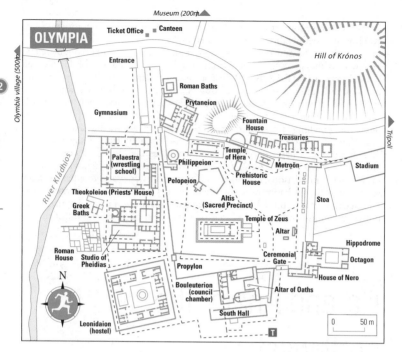

Museum (200m)
Olympia village (500m)
Tripoli

OLYMPIA
Ticket Office — Canteen
Entrance
Hill of Krónos
Roman Baths
Prytaneion
Gymnasium
Fountain House
Treasuries
Palaestra (wrestling school)
Philippeion
Temple of Hera
Metroön
Stadium
Prehistoric House
Pelopeion
Theokoleion (Priests' House)
Altis (Sacred Precinct)
Stoa
Greek Baths
Temple of Zeus
Altar
Hippodrome
Roman House
Studio of Pheidias
Ceremonial Gate
Octagon
Propylon
House of Nero
Bouleuterion (council chamber)
Altar of Oaths
South Hall
Leonidaion (hostel)
River Kládhios
N
0   50 m

souvenir shops and other trappings of mass tourism, it demands and deserves a lengthy visit.

The modern village of Olympía acts as a service centre for the site, and has little in the way of other distractions, save for three somewhat dutiful minor museums. The **Museum of the Modern Olympic Games** (Mon–Sat 8am–3.30pm, Sun 9am–4.30pm; €2), on the street above the *Hotel Phedias*, has commemorative postage stamps and the odd memento from the modern games, including the box that conveyed the heart of Pierre de Coubertin (reviver of the modern games) from Paris to its burial at Olympia. The **Museum of the History of the Olympic Games in Antiquity** and the **Museum of the History of Excavations in Olympia** (both: summer daily 8am–7.30pm, winter Tues–Sat 8.30am–3pm; free) lie above the coach-park at the eastern end of the village, en route to the main site.

The site

From its beginnings the **site** (May–Oct daily 8am–7pm; Nov–April Mon–Fri 8am–5pm, Sat & Sun 8.30am–3pm; €6, or €9 for combined site and archeological museum) was a sanctuary, with a permanent population limited to the temple priests. At first the games took place within the sacred precinct, the walled, rectangular **Altis**, but as events became more sophisticated a new **stadium** was built to adjoin it. The whole sanctuary was, throughout its history, a treasure trove of public and religious statuary. Victors were allowed to erect a statue in the Altis (in their likeness if they won three events) and numerous city-states installed treasuries. Pausanias, writing in the second century AD, after the Romans had already looted the sanctuary several times, fills almost a whole volume of his *Guide to Greece* with descriptions.

The entrance to the site leads along the west side of the **Altis wall**, past a group of public and official buildings. On the left, beyond some Roman baths, is the **Prytaneion**, the administrators' residence, where athletes were lodged and feasted at official expense. On the right are the ruins of a **gymnasium** and a **palaestra** (wrestling school), used by the competitors during their obligatory month of pre-games training.

Beyond these stood the Priests' House, the **Theokoleion**, a substantial colonnaded building in whose southeast corner is a structure adapted as a Byzantine church. This was originally the **studio of Pheidias**, the fifth-century BC sculptor responsible for the great chryselephantine (gold and ivory) cult statue in Olympia's Temple of Zeus. It was identified by following a description by Pausanias, and through the discovery of tools, moulds for the statue and a cup engraved with the sculptor's name. The studio's dimensions and orientation are exactly those of the *cella* in which the statue was to be placed, in order that the final effect and lighting matched the sculptor's intentions.

To the south of the studio lie further administrative buildings, including the **Leonidaion**, a large and doubtless luxurious hostel endowed for the most important of the festival guests. It was the first building visitors would reach along the original approach road to the site.

The Altis

In the earlier centuries of the games, admission to the **Altis** was limited to freeborn Greeks – whether spectators or competitors. Throughout its history it was a male-only preserve, save for the sanctuary's priestess. An Olympian anecdote records how a woman from Rhodes disguised herself as her son's trainer to gain admission, but revealed her identity in joy at his victory. She was spared the legislated death penalty, though subsequently all trainers had to appear naked.

The main focus of the precinct, today as in ancient times, is provided by the great Doric **Temple of Zeus**. Built between 470 and 456 BC, it was as large as the almost contemporary Parthenon, a fact quietly substantiated by the vast column drums littering the ground. The temple's decoration, too, rivalled the finest in Athens; partially recovered, its sculptures of Pelops in a chariot race, of Lapiths and Centaurs, and the Labours of Hercules, are now in the museum. In the *cella* was exhibited the (lost) cult statue of Zeus by Pheidias, one of the seven wonders of the ancient world. Here, too, the Olympian flame was kept alight, from the time of the games until the following spring – a tradition continued at an altar for the modern games.

The smaller **Temple of Hera**, behind, was the first built in the Altis; prior to its completion in the seventh century BC, the sanctuary had only open-air altars, dedicated to Zeus and a variety of other cult gods. The temple, rebuilt in the Doric style in the sixth century BC, is the most complete building on the site, with some thirty of its columns surviving in part, along with a section of the inner wall. The levels above this wall were composed only of sun-baked brick, and the lightness of this building material must have helped to preserve the sculptures – most notably the *Hermes of Praxiteles* – found amid the earthquake ruins.

Between the temples of Hera and Zeus is a grove described by Pausanias, and identified as the **Pelopeion**. In addition to a cult altar to the Olympian hero, this enclosed a small mound formed by sacrificial ashes, among which excavations unearthed many of the terracotta finds in the museum. The sanctuary's principal altar, dedicated to Zeus, probably stood just to the east.

The Olympic games: some history

The origins of the games at Olympia are rooted in **legends** – the most predominant relating to the god Pelops, revered in the region before his eclipse by Zeus, and to Hercules (Herakles), one of the earliest victors. Historically, the contests probably began around the eleventh century BC, growing over the next two centuries from a local festival to the quadrennial celebration attended by states from throughout the Greek world.

The impetus for this change seems to have come from the Oracle of Delphi, which, with the local ruler of Elis, Iphitos, and the Spartan ruler Lykurgos, helped to codify the Olympic rules in the ninth century BC. Among their most important introductions was a sacred truce, the Ekeheiria, announced by heralds prior to the celebrations and enforced for their duration. It was virtually unbroken throughout the games' history (Sparta, ironically, was fined at one point) and as host of the games, Elis, a comparatively weak state, was able to keep itself away from political disputes, meanwhile growing rich on the associated trade and kudos.

From the beginning, the main Olympic events were athletic. The earliest was a race over the course of the stadium – roughly 200m. Later came the introduction of two-lap (400m) and 24-lap (5000m) races, along with the most revered of the Olympiad events, the pentathlon. This encompassed running, jumping, discus and javelin events, the competitors gradually reduced to a final pair for a wrestling-and-boxing combat. It was, like much of these early Olympiads, a fairly brutal contest. More brutal still was the *pancratium*, introduced in 680 BC and one of the most prestigious events. *Pancratium* contestants fought each other, naked and unarmed, using any means except biting or gouging each other's eyes; the olive wreath had on one occasion to be awarded posthumously, the victor having expired at the moment of his opponent's submission. Similarly, the chariot races, introduced in the same year, were extreme tests of strength and control, only one team in twenty completing the seven-kilometre course without mishap.

The great gathering of people and nations at the festival extended the games' importance and purpose well beyond the winning of olive wreaths; assembled under the temporary truce, nobles and ambassadors negotiated treaties, while merchants chased contacts and foreign markets. Sculptors and poets, too, would

West of the Temple of Hera, and bordering the wall of the Altis, are remains of the circular **Philippeion**, the first monument in the sanctuary to be built to secular glory. It was begun by Philip II after the Battle of Chaironea gave him control over the Greek mainland, and may have been completed by his son, Alexander the Great. To the east of the Hera temple is a small, second-century-AD **fountain house**, the gift of the ubiquitous Herodes Atticus. Beyond, lining a terrace at the base of the Hill of Krónos, are the **state treasuries**. All except two of these were constructed by cities outside of Greece proper, as they functioned principally as storage chambers for sacrificial items and sporting equipment used in the games. They are built in the form of temples, as at Delphi; the oldest and grandest, at the east end, belonged to Gela in Sicily. In front of the treasuries are the foundations of the **Metroön**, a fourth-century BC Doric temple dedicated to the mother of the gods.

The ancient ceremonial entrance to the **Altis** was on the south side, below a long **stoa** taking up almost the entire east side of the precinct. At the corner was a house built by the Roman emperor Nero for his stay during the games. He also had the entrance remodelled as a triumphal arch, fit for his anticipated victories. Through the arch, just outside the precinct, stood the **Bouleuterion** or council chamber, where before a great statue of Zeus the competitors took their oaths to observe the Olympian rules. As they approached the stadium,

seek commissions for their work. Herodotus read aloud the first books of his history at an Olympian festival to an audience that included Thucydides – who was to date events in his own work by reference to the winners of the *pancratium*.

In the early Olympiads, the rules of competition were strict. Only free-born male Greeks could take part, and the rewards of victory were entirely honorary: a palm, given to the victor immediately after the contest, and an olive branch, presented in a ceremony closing the games. As the games developed, however, the rules were loosened to allow participation by athletes from all parts of the Greek and Roman world, and nationalism and professionalism gradually crept in. By the fourth century BC, when the games were at their peak, the athletes were virtually all professionals, heavily sponsored by their home states and, if they won at Olympia, commanding huge appearance money at games elsewhere. Bribery became an all too common feature, despite the solemn religious oaths sworn in front of the sanctuary priests prior to the contests.

Under the Romans, predictably, the commercializing process was accelerated. The palms and olive branches were replaced by rich monetary prizes, and a sequence of new events was introduced. The nadir was reached in 67 AD when Emperor Nero advanced the games by two years so that he could compete in (and win) special singing and lyre-playing events – in addition to the chariot race in which he was tactfully declared victor despite falling twice and failing to finish.

Notwithstanding all this abuse, the Olympian tradition was popular enough to be maintained for another three centuries, and the games' eventual closure happened as a result of religious dogma rather than lack of support. In 393 AD Emperor Theodosius, recently converted to Christianity, suspended the games as part of a general crackdown on public pagan festivities. This suspension proved final, for Theodosius's successor ordered the destruction of the temples, a process completed by barbarian invasion, earthquakes and, lastly, by the Alfiós River changing its course to cover the sanctuary site. There it remained, covered by 7m of silt and sand, until the first excavation by German archeologists in the 1870s.

the gravity of this would be impressed upon them: lining the way were bronze statues paid for with the fines exacted for foul play, bearing the name of the disgraced athlete, his father and city.

The stadium

In the final analysis, it is neither foundations nor columns that make sense of Olympia, but the two-hundred-metre track of the **stadium** itself, entered by way of a long arched tunnel. The starting and finishing lines are still there, with the judges' thrones in the middle and seating ridges banked to either side.

Originally unstructured, the stadium developed with the games' popularity, forming a model for others throughout the Greek and Roman world. The tiers here eventually accommodated up to 20,000 spectators, with a smaller number on the southern slope overlooking the **hippodrome** where the chariot races were held. Even so, the seats were reserved for the wealthier strata of society. The ordinary populace – along with slaves and all women spectators – watched the events from the Hill of Krónos to the north, then a natural, treeless grandstand.

The stadium was unearthed only in World War II, during a second phase of German excavations between 1941 and 1944, allegedly on the direct orders of Hitler.

The Archeological Museum

Olympia's site **museum** (May–Oct Mon noon–7.30pm, Tues–Sun 8am–7.30pm; Nov–April Mon 10.30am–5pm, Tues–Sun 8.30am–5pm; €6) lies a couple of hundred metres north of the sanctuary. It contains some of the finest Classical and Roman sculptures in the country, all superbly displayed.

The most famous of the individual sculptures are the **head of Hera** and the **Hermes of Praxiteles**, both dating from the fourth century BC and discovered in the Temple of Hera. The Hermes is one of the best preserved of all Classical sculptures, and remarkable in the easy informality of its pose; it retains traces of its original paint. On a grander scale is the **Nike of Paionios**, which was originally 10m high. Though no longer complete (it's well displayed in a special area), it hints at how the sanctuary must once have appeared, crowded with statuary.

The best of the smaller objects include several fine bronze items, among them a **Persian helmet**, captured by the Athenians at the Battle of Marathon, and (displayed alongside) the **helmet of Miltiades**, the victorious Athenian general; both were found with votive objects dedicated in the stadium. There is also a superb terracotta group of **Zeus abducting Ganymede** and a group of finds from the workshop of **Pheidias**, including the cup with his name inscribed.

In the main hall of the museum is the centrepiece of the Olympia finds: statuary and sculpture reassembled from the **Temple of Zeus**. This includes three groups, all of which were once painted. From the *cella* is a frieze of the **Twelve Labours of Hercules**, delicately moulded and for the most part identifiably preserved. The other groups are from the east and west pediments. The east, reflecting Olympian pursuits, depicts Zeus presiding over a **chariot race** between Pelops and Oinamaos. The story has several versions. King Oinamaos, warned that he would be killed by his son-in-law, challenged each of his daughter Hippomadeia's suitors to a chariot race. After allowing them a start he would catch up and kill them from behind. The king (depicted on the left of the frieze) was eventually defeated by Pelops (on the right with Hippomadeia), after – depending on the version – assistance from Zeus (depicted at the centre), magic steeds from Poseidon or, most un-Olympian, bribing Oinamaos's charioteer to tamper with the wheels.

The west pediment, less controversially mythological, illustrates the **Battle of the Lapiths and Centaurs** at the wedding of the Lapith king, Peirithous. This time, Apollo presides over the scene while Theseus helps the Lapiths defeat the drunken centaurs, depicted attacking the women and boy guests. Many of the metope fragments are today in the Louvre in Paris, and some of what you see here are plaster-cast copies.

In the last rooms of the museum is a collection of objects relating to the games – including *halteres* (jumping weights), discuses, weightlifters' stones and other sporting bits and pieces. Also displayed are a number of **funerary inscriptions**, including that of a boxer, Camelos of Alexandria, who died in the stadium after praying to Zeus for victory or death.

Practicalities: Olymbía

Modern **OLYMBÍA** is a village that has grown up simply to serve the excavations and tourist trade. It's essentially one long main avenue, **Praxitéles Kondhýli**, lined with gold shops, and with a few short side streets. Nevertheless, Olymbía is quite a pleasant place to stay, and is probably preferable to Pýrgos (see p. 310), with the prospect of good countryside walks along the Alfiós River and around the Hill of Krónos.

Most people arrive at Olympía **via Pýrgos**, which is on the main Peloponnese rail line and has frequent bus connections with Pátra and four daily with Kyparissía. The refurbished **train** link from Pýrgos to Olympía has five daily services. **Buses** leave hourly between Pýrgos and Olympía, from 5.15am to 9.45pm, some signed to "Vasiláki" beyond Olympía. The only other direct buses to Olympía are **from Trípoli**, via Langádhia. These run twice daily in either direction. If you are approaching **from Andhrítsena**, take the bus to Pýrgos and change.

There is a **tourist office** (Mon–Sat: May–Oct 9am–3pm; Nov–April 11am–5pm; ☎26240 23100), on the right of Praxitéles Kondhýli, as you come into town from Pýrgos. Olympía has three **banks** on the main avenue, and a **post office** just uphill. **English-language books** are to be found in a couple of shops near the site end of town.

Accommodation

Accommodation is fairly easy to come by, with a swift turnaround of clientele and a range of hotels and private rooms whose prices are kept modest by competition. A few **rooms** are signposted on Stefanopoúlou, a side street behind the National Bank, or on Spiliópoulou, parallel to and above Kondhýli. As elsewhere, rates can drop substantially out of season (never precisely defined), though many of the smaller and cheaper places close; it's best to check in advance. The centre of town can be very noisy at night.

There are three **campsites**, closest of which is *Diana* (☎26240 22314, ⓕ26240 22425; March–Nov), 1km from the site, with a pool and good facilities. The others are *Alphios* (☎26240 22951, ⓕ26240 22950; April–Oct), 1km out on the Créstena road (from where there are good views of the area), and *Olympia* (☎26240 22738), 2km out on the Pýrgos road.

Achilles Stefanopoúlou 4 ☎26240 22562. A pension on a side street behind the National Bank; large and comfortable if somewhat noisy rooms above a snack bar. ❷

Europa Dhroúva 1 ☎26240 22650, ⓦwww.hoteleuropa.gr. A popular, well-run and comfortable hotel, part of the Best Western group, situated near the top of the hill to the southwest. ❼

Hercules Tsoúreka ☎26240 22696. A congenial small hotel by the church and school on a side street off Praxitéles Kondhýli. ❸

Pelops Varélas 2 ☎26240 22543, ⓔhotel-pelops@hotmail.gr. On a square by the church and school; a hotel run by a Greek-Australian couple and recently extensively refurbished. March–Oct. B&B ❻

Youth Hostel Kondhýli 18 ☎26240 22580, ⓕ26240 23125. Average facilities, but warm water in the showers; good value. Dorms €9

Eating and drinking

The main avenue is lined with **tavernas**, which offer standard tourist meals at notably inflated high-season prices – some cafés charging at Athenian levels – but there is a growing number of fast-food kerbside cafés which are often far better value. The *Kladhios* taverna, 2km northwest out of the village beyond the rail station on the banks of the Kládhios River, serves good food in a pleasant setting. The *Klimataria Taverna* in **Kokkinés** village, a few kilometres northeast, is also recommended.

The northwest coast to Pátra

Despite the proximity of Olympia and Pátra, the northwest corner of the Peloponnese is not much explored by foreign visitors. Admittedly, it's not the most glamorous of coasts, although there are some very attractive beaches including the glorious one at **Kalogriá**, but a visit to the old port of **Katákolo** or around **Loutrá Kyllínis/Arkoúdhi** can provide a pleasant enough diversion.

From Kyllíni there are regular crossings to Zákynthos, and in summer to Kefalloniá, while Katákolo has occasional (summer-only) *kaïkia* to Zákynthos.

Pýrgos

PÝRGOS has a grim recent history. When the Germans withdrew at the end of World War II, it remained under the control of Greek Nazi collaborators. These negotiated surrender with the Resistance, who were met by gunfire as they entered the town. Full-scale battle erupted and for five days the town burned. Today, it's a large, friendly and modern town with a pleasantly pedestrianized centre. The town also proudly hosts the Currant Institute of the Autonomous Currant Organization. Serious diversions are nonexistent for the tourist, except for the avid clothes shopper (clothes shops here are abundant, well stocked and well priced), although there are plans to convert the Neoclassical Central Market building into an archeological museum. For an overnight **stay**, a convenient hotel is the *Pantheon*, Themistokléous 7 (T 26210 29748, F 26210 36791; ❹).

The main escape routes are by **train** or **bus** to Pátra, Olympia or Kyparissía – though services to the last are not well timed for onward connections; the new bus station is to the west of town, and the train station fifteen minutes away at the bottom on Ipsilándou, so allow time for interchange. Drivers should be aware that the main road from Pýrgos to Pátra, though level and comparatively straight, is a scary mix of very fast and very slow traffic, bad driving and numerous stray dogs.

Katákolo and around

Thirteen kilometres west of Pýrgos, **KATÁKOLO** is somewhat more enticing: a decayed, ramshackle old port with good beaches close by. Until the last few decades, when new roads improved connections with Pátra, it controlled the trade for Ilía province. Today only a few tramp steamers rust at anchor, though the navy calls occasionally and, oddly, the port remains a stop for Italian summer-cruise ships. Consequently, the town has become aware of a potentially lucrative tourist trade, and most of the old warehouses have been converted into boutiques and trinket shops. The main drag can be noisy at night, belying the town's torpid daytime appearance, but arriving from Pýrgos it feels relaxed.

There are a few small **room** establishments, with cabins fronted by peach and apricot trees (ask around for these on arrival), and the small hotel *Zefyros* (T 26210 41170; ❸). For **meals**, there is a handful of good tavernas on the quay.

Beaches

Katákolo's beach, the **Spiándza**, stretches away for miles to the southeast, a popular spot with Greeks, many of whom own shuttered little cottages set just back from the sea. Though it is sandy, it is hard-packed and more of a spot for football or jogging, with the sea too shallow for real swimming. However, a thirty-minute walk north, past the overgrown Byzantine-Frankish **castle of Pondikón** (Pondikókastro, Beauvoir), will take you to much better swimming at **Áyios Andhréas** beach, the port of Ancient Pheia: 200m of sloping, outcrop-studded sand, with views over a few attendant islets and out to Zákynthos. There are summer **tavernas** here, the comfortable **hotel** *Vriniotis*

(☎ 26210 41294, ⓦ www.vriniotis.gr; B&B ❻), plus a few rooms to let. An even better beach is to be found at **Skafidhiá**, 3km north of Katákolo and accessible by road via Korakohóri. There are several large all-inclusive resort hotels here, but smaller **accommodation** is available 2km inland at **MYRTIÁ**, at *Zorbas* (☎ 26210 54238; ❹). Further northwest is the long sandy beach at **Kouroúta**, with several campsites, including *Camping Kouroutas* (☎ 26220 28543, ⓕ 26220 25169; May–Sept).

The cape north of Pýrgos

North from Pýrgos, road and rail meander through a series of uneventful market towns, but there are two forks west to a sandy cape and the coast. The first is at Gastoúni and heads for the spa of **Loutrá Kyllínis** (1–3 daily buses from Pýrgos and Pátra) and beaches to the south; the second is at Kavásilas, where a side road heads down to **Kyllíni** port proper (3–4 daily buses from Pýrgos and Pátra). Take care not to confuse the two.

LOUTRÁ KYLLÍNIS has a long beach, and a crop of upmarket **hotels** catering for the resort's spa trade. It's better to continue south to Arkoúdhi or Paralía Glýfa for places to stay.

Only a few kilometres south, near the point where this most westerly coast of the Peloponnese bends back east into the long bay that curves towards Katákolo, is **ARKOÚDHI**, a compact village resort that has something of an island feel to it and a fine sandy bay enclosed by a rocky promontory. As well as a **campsite**, there is a surprising number of **hotels** and **rooms**. On the edge of the village is the posh but good-value hotel *Arkoudi* (☎ 26230 96480; April–Oct; B&B ❺), which has a pool. In the village centre, apartments with kitchen and fridge are available at *Soulis* (☎ 26230 96379, ⓦ www.soulis-hotel.com; ❹). For meals try the central *Spyros psistariá*, or the *Akrogiali*, which offers a sea view and a wide selection of dishes.

At **PARALÍA GLÝFA**, 3.5km from Arkoúdhi, there are two **campsites** – the *Anginara Beach* (☎ 26230 96211, ⓕ 26230 96157) and the *Ionian Beach* (☎ 26230 96395, ⓦ www.ionianbeach.gr), both bordered by trees and beaches of fine shingle and sand and best approached via Lygiá on the road from Gastoúni.

Cheerless little **KYLLÍNI** (accessible by taxi from Loutrá Kyllínis) has little more to offer than its **ferry connections** (ⓦ www.ionianferries.gr). It is the principal port for **Zákynthos** (6–7 daily; cars €27.30, passengers €5.80; ☎ 26230 92100) and **Kefaloniá** (to Argostoli: summer 1 daily, winter 1–2 daily; to Póros: summer 5–6 daily, winter 1–2 daily; cars €34.70, passengers €7.40; ☎ 26230 92013). Buses coming off the ferry, to Pátra and Athens, are often full and will not take extra passengers. If you're stuck overnight in Kyllíni, **places to stay** are limited: the choice is between the *Hotel Ionian* (☎ 26230 92318; ❹) on the main street where some rooms have private facilities, rooms (also on the main street) – or sleeping on the beach. The *Taverna Anna*, beyond the harbour, serves a wide range of traditional dishes and is particularly popular with locals at Sunday lunchtimes.

Using Loutrá Kyllínis, Arkoúdhi or Kyllíni as a base, it's worth taking time to hitch or walk to the village of **KÁSTRO**, at the centre of the cape. Looming above the village and visible from miles around is the Frankish **castle of Khlemoútsi** (Castel Tornese; summer daily 8am–7pm; winter Tues–Sun 8.30am–3pm; €3), a vast hexagonal structure built in 1220 by Geoffrey de Villehardouin. Its function was principally to control the province of Aháïa, though it served also as a strategic fortress on the Adriatic. Haze permitting, there are sweeping views across the straits to Zákynthos, and even to Kefalloniá and Itháki, from the well-preserved and restored ramparts. Kástro has the welcoming *Katerina Lepidas* (aka *Chryssi Avgi*) rooms with kitchen facilities, at Loutrópoleos 9 (℡26230 95224; May–Oct; ❹). You can **dine** well at the nearby *Apollon* taverna.

Kalogriá and Niforéïka Patrón

Midway between Kyllíni and Pátra, **KALOGRIÁ** (locally Kalógria) is a seven-kilometre strand of beach, partly naturist, bordered by a swathe of **umbrella pine forests**. A fair proportion of Pátra, including the gay community, descends here at the weekend as it's the nearest good **beach** to the city. The whole area is protected as part of the Strofyliá Forest-Kotýkhi Wetland National Park, which covers beach dunes, the forest, and lagoons with their rare birdlife, and permanent development remains low-key. There is an enthusiastic information and environmental monitoring centre (Mon–Fri, 8am–2pm; ℻26930 31651, Ⓔciks@otenet.gr) for the park at nearby Láppa, in a building opposite the train station. Kalogriá is not actually a village – the nearest bona fide town is Metóhi – but rather a small cluster of tavernas and stores. At the far north end of the beach there's the *Kalogria Beach* (℡26930 31276, Ⓔkalogria@otenet.gr; ❹), a large, French-oriented **hotel complex** with many sports facilities. For a quieter stay there's the ⚘*Amalia Hotel* studios (℡26930 31762, Ⓦwww.amaliahotel.gr; ❹), hidden in a large garden behind their own good taverna. Behind the hotels, the 200-metre outcrop MávraVoúna has a number of organized climbing routes (Ⓦwww.geocities.com/patrasclimbing).

Around the northwest coast towards Pátra, 3km west of Káto Aháïa, lies another busy little resort, **NIFORÉÏKA PATRÓN**, where hotels include the

△ Umbrella pines at Kalogriá

An Orthodox nation

The rituals of the Greek Orthodox church permeate every aspect of Greek society and, with over ninety-five percent of the population describing themselves as Orthodox, Greece is, in this sense, an extraordinarily homogeneous nation. For most, religion is a constant but almost unnoticed part of everyday life – taxi drivers cross themselves as they pass a church, not pausing for a moment in their animated discussion of last night's match; shoppers pop into the church to rest their feet and light a candle before continuing with the errands; and lamps are lit daily in front of icons in most homes

▲ Easter procession, Corfu

Orthodox Easter

Religious ceremonies punctuate the Greek year. They are celebrated with gusto and always with respect to local tradition: a major wedding or baptism will bring out a vast extended family, all of whom will expect lavish hospitality. No major event, in fact, is allowed to go by without some kind of party to mark it – and especially in smaller villages and islands away from the tourist trail, visitors will invariably be invited to join in.

Orthodox Easter, not usually on the same date as that celebrated by western churches, is the biggest and holiest of the festivals. Many Greeks still fast in the week leading up to Easter weekend, when restaurants serve special fasting dishes known collectively as *nistísima* which avoid meat, dairy, fish and even olive oil and wine at the most extreme. On Good Friday images of Christ are taken from churches throughout the country and paraded through the local town or village in a flower-strewn casket, symbolizing Christ's tomb. The highlight is on the evening of Easter Saturday, when everyone attends church carrying an unlit candle. At midnight the congregation is plunged into darkness, just as Christ's life was extinguished, until the light is resurrected in a single candle, lit from the holy flame behind the altar. From here light spreads again throughout the church and out into the street as candles are lit from candles and the cry of "*Christos Anesti*" ("Christ is Risen") spreads, along with a wilder celebration of fireworks and food to break the fast, traditionally *mayerítsa*, a soup made from the instestines of the sheep that are to be roasted the following day.

▲ Monk with Mount Athos in the background

The black-clad Papas or priest is an everyday sight, not just in the island villages – where as often as not he'll be a fixture in the kafenío – but also in the cities, astride a moped or out shopping.

Island celebrations

Throughout Greece, Easter celebrations follow the same broad pattern, but there are plenty of local twists. In **Crete**, for example, home-made effigies of Judas are burned on Holy Saturday. On **Pátmos**, at the great Monastery of St John the Divine, the Father Superior washes the feet of twelve monks on Easter Thursday, re-enacting Jesus washing the feet of his disciples. Easter Saturday on **Corfu** sees locals throwing great ceramic pots (often filled with water to increase the dramatic impact) out of their windows to smash on the ground – an old Venetian custom, according to some, or a symbolic throwing out of the old year. On **Híos**, a very un-Christian war breaks out every Easter, when two rival churches in the town of Vrondádhos fire thousands of home-made fireworks at each other, in an attempt to hit the other's bell during the service.

▲ Church illustration, Crete

▼ Lighting Easter candles

The holy flame

The flame from which all the Easter candles are lit has its source at Christ's Tomb in the Church of the Holy Sepulchre in Jerusalem; here the Patriarch of the Greek Orthodox church celebrates the ceremony of the Holy Fire each Holy Saturday. From here it is transported every year on a special flight to Athens, and distributed within hours by land, sea and air to churches throughout the country.

Name days

In Greece, everyone gets to celebrate their birthday twice a year. More important, in fact, than your actual birthday, is the feast day of the saint whose moniker you share – their name day. Greek ingenuity has stretched the saints' names (or invented new saints) to cover almost every single forename, so even pagan Dionysos or Socrates get to celebrate. If yours isn't covered, no problem – your party is on All Saints' Day, eight weeks after Easter.

The big name day celebrations (such as for Iannis and Ianna on January 7, and Yioryios on April 23) can involve thousands of people, and tradition guarantees that families get to celebrate together. In most families, for example, the eldest boy is still named after his paternal grandfather, and the eldest girl after her grandmother, so that all the eldest cousins will share the same name, and the same name day. Any church or chapel bearing the saint's name will mark the event – some smaller chapels will open just for this one day of the year – while if an entire village is dubbed after the saint, you can almost guarantee a festival.

▼ Icon of Ayía Katerina (St. Katherine), Crete

well-appointed *White Castle* (☎26930 23390, ℉26930 22274; B&B ❺) with attractive, spacious, sea-view rooms, in addition to *Alikes* camping (☎26930 22730). There is a choice of several average restaurants.

Pátra

PÁTRA (Patras) is the largest city in the Peloponnese and, after Pireás, the major port of Greece; from here you can go to Italy as well as to certain Ionian islands. The city is also a hub of the Greek-mainland transport network, with connections throughout the Peloponnese and, via the ferry at Río, across the straits to Delphi or western Greece.

Unless you arrive late in the day from Italy, you shouldn't need to spend more than a few hours in the city. A conurbation of close to a quarter of a million souls, it's not the ideal holiday retreat: there are no beaches and no major sights. Traffic noise goes on well into the night and starts earlier than you'd want to get up. However, it is an opportunity to experience a vibrant and reasonably civilized city life, unrelated to tourism. There is a **summer festival** which sponsors events from late June to mid-September. These include Classical plays and the occasional rock concert in the Roman **odeion**, and art and photographic exhibitions that bring a bit of life to the warehouses by the harbour (details from the tourist office or the Apóllon theatre on Platía Yeoryíou). The three-week **carnival** (🌐www.carnivalpatras.gr), ending on the Sunday before Lent Monday (Katharí Dheftéra), is one of the biggest in the country, with a grand parade through the city centre on the final day.

Arrival and information

If you are driving in or through Pátra, you will find the traffic and one-way system no less frustrating than in Athens; a map showing the direction of traffic, if not vital, will at least save time and probably maintain sanity. If going beyond Pátra, then there is a fast bypass to the east. The **train station** is on Óthonos & Amalías. Trains travel south (changes at Alfiós or Pýrgos for Olympia) to Kaló Neró (for Kyparissía) then on to Kalamáta; north and east to Dhiakoftó, Kórinthos (change for Árgos, Náfplio or Trípoli), Athens and Pireás.

For **tourist information**, the city has opened the helpful large Info Center Patras in an old raisin-processing factory at Óthonos & Amalías 6 (daily 8am–10pm; ☎2610 461 740, 🌐www.infocenterpatras.gr), with a good photographic gallery of the province's attractions. They also have a kiosk on Platía Trión Symáhon (daily 9am–1pm & 5–8pm). The **tourist police** (daily 7am–11pm; ☎2610 452 512) are at the western end of Nórman near the new Italy ferry terminal, where the **EOT** office also is (Mon–Fri 7am–9pm; ☎2610 430 915).

Accommodation

Most of Pátra's **hotels** are on Ayíou Andhréou, one block back from Óthonos & Amalías, or on Ayíou Nikoláou, which runs back from the sea, near the train station and Platía Trión Symáhon. Don't expect too much in the way of standards, value for money or quiet nights; most of the places cater for a very passing trade and don't make great efforts. Many of the older hotels nearer the waterfront have closed, or indeed collapsed. Of those still standing, choices include the following:

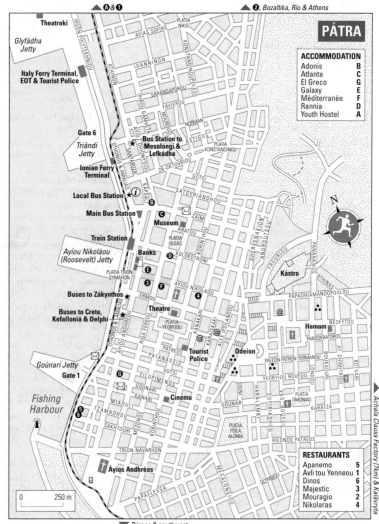

Accommodation map labels:

Theatraki

Glyfádha Jetty

Italy Ferry Terminal, EOT & Tourist Police

Gate 6
Triándi Jetty

Ionian Ferry Terminal

Local Bus Station

Main Bus Station

Train Station

Ayíou Nikoláou (Roosevelt) Jetty

Banks

Buses to Zákynthos

Buses to Crete, Kefalloniá & Delphi

Goúnari Jetty
Gate 1

Fishing Harbour

Áyios Andhréas

Bus Station to Mesolóngi & Lefkádha

Museum

Theatre

Kástro

Hamam

Tourist Police

Odeion

Cinema

PÁTRA

ACCOMMODATION

Adonis	B
Atlanta	C
El Greco	G
Galaxy	F
Méditerranée	E
Rannia	D
Youth Hostel	A

RESTAURANTS

Apanemo	5
Avli tou Yenneou	1
Dinos	6
Majestic	3
Mouragio	2
Nikolaras	4

▲ **❹&❶**   ▲ **❷**, Bozaïtika, Río & Athens

▼ Pýrgos & southwest

► Achaïa Clauss Factory (7km) & Kaláyryta

Adonis Kapsáli 9, cnr Záïmi ☎ 2610 224 213, ⓕ 2610 226 971. On the junction with Kapsáli opposite the bus station. It's well furnished and maintained; good value. **❹**

Atlanta Záïmi 10 ☎ 2610 220 098, ⓕ 2610 220 019. Central hotel, but still good value; out of season you should get a competitive price. **❹**

El Greco Ayíou Andhréou 145 ☎ 2610 272 931, ⓕ 2610 272 932. A good bargain hotel and top of its class with refurbished rooms. **❸**

Galaxy Ayíou Nikoláou 9 ☎ 2610 275 981, ⓕ 2610 278 815. A well-placed hotel, if a touch pretentious; serves a good breakfast. B&B **❹**

Méditerranée Ayíou Nikólaou 18 ☎ 2610 279 602, ⓔ mediterran@otenet.gr. Modern and adequate hotel, with helpful staff. Both the *Galaxy* and the *Méditerranée* are on a pedestrian street packed with popular bars and cafés. B&B **❺**

Rannia Platía Ólgas & Ríga Feréou ☎ 2610 220 114, ⓕ 2610 220 537. Very friendly, clean and well placed on the square, with a café and snack bar. **❸**

Youth Hostel Iróon Polytekhníou 62 ☎ 2610 427 278. Cheap and set in a pleasant tree-filled garden opposite the marina, but a 1.5km walk from the centre. Dorms €9.

The City

For relaxation, the best places to make for are the café-table-studded **Platía Psilá Alónia** with its monument to Bishop Yermanos, or the **Kástro** (daily 8am–7pm; free), a mainly Frankish-Byzantine citadel a fifteen-minute walk up from the water. This partly restored fortress is not particularly exciting, but it is away from the city bustle, surrounded by a small park and with woodland beyond. Nearby, at Boukaoúri 29, is the **hamam** (Turkish bath; ☎2610 274 267), still functioning after six hundred years, while the Roman **odeion** (Tues–Sun 8.30am–3pm; free) is on Sotiriádhou, near the castle. Like many a Greek metropolis in summer, Pátra is perhaps at its best after dark, when the heat is less oppressive, the concrete structures less overpowering, and the city life and lights rather brighter; a stroll down to the huge jetty at the foot of Ayíou Nikoláou can bring you to cool sea breezes – and takeaway refreshments, at the port kiosk just over the railway lines. Join the evening *vólta* here, or watch the sunset and departing ferries, with the spectacular mountains of Étolo-Akarnanía to the northwest and the 1924-metre backdrop of Mount Panahaïkó to the east. The pedestrianized bottom end of Ayíou Nikoláou is a very lively area at night, with busy cafés spread across the street. To the north, just beyond the Glyfádha jetty, is the Theatráki ("little theatre"; contact the Info Center for details) and marina cafés.

Opened in 1979, the huge neo-Byzantine **church of Áyios Andhréas** lies at the southwest end of the waterfront on a spot where St Andrew, whose relics the church houses, is said to have been martyred in 69 AD. It is a massive confection of yellow-and-cream walls, blue-tiled domes and an excess of marble pillars and arches. The nearby seafront area has been converted into a pleasant grassed area. In the centre, on the corner of Mézonos and Arátou, a small **archeological museum** (Tues–Sun 8.30am–3pm; free) contains a number of exquisite objects from the province of Ahaïa dating from the Mycenaean to the Roman eras.

Swimming near Pátra isn't advisable with the sea polluted for some kilometres to the southwest. Locals go to the **beaches** around Río (7km northeast; bus #6 goes frequently from the stop on Yerokostópoulou, near the Zákynthos bus station) or to Kalogriá (46km southwest; 3 daily buses in high season from the KTEL station).

The Achaïa Clauss factory

The **Achaïa Clauss** factory (daily tours 9am–5pm), founded in 1854, is 8km southeast of Pátra; those with an interest in modern wine-making should take the #7 bus (half-hourly) from the local bus station near the Info Center. Tours show you around the wine-making process, and feature some treasured, century-old barrels of Mavrodhafni – a dark dessert wine named after the woman Clauss wanted to marry. You're given a glass of white wine to sample on reaching the factory's rather Teutonic bar, an echo of its founder's nationality. Along the walls are signed letters from celebrity recipients of Mavrodhafni. A shop sells all the factory's products, if you want a bottle for yourself.

Eating and drinking

Pátra's **restaurants** are sometimes uninspiring, with countless fast-food places – many of which offer discounts to ISIC card-holders – around Platía Trión Symáhon, and along Ayíou Andhréou and Ayíou Nikoláou. But even here there are some reliable restaurants with character, and some mouth-watering

Ferry routes and companies

Innumerable ticket agents along or near the waterfront each sell different permutations of **ferry crossings** to Italy on one or more of the lines detailed below. It is worth spending an hour or so researching these, especially if you're taking a car, since costs, journey times and routes all differ from one company to another. Glossy ferry company **brochures** quoting times and prices are freely available from the agents. En route to Italy, it is possible to make stopovers on Kefalloniá or, more commonly, Corfu (Kérkyra). Domestic tickets to Kefalloniá and Itháki are also available from Pátra.

Routes

Pátra–Ancona has become the standard route. At one time this entailed two nights on board, but high-speed ferries operated by ANEK, Maritime Way (My Way) Ferries, Minoan Lines and Superfast Ferries can now complete the crossing in 18–21 hours. Other routes include Pátra–Brindisi, Pátra–Bari, Pátra–Trieste and Pátra–Venice.

High season

All frequencies of ferry crossings detailed opposite are for the high season, the definition of which varies slightly from company to company. Broadly, for crossings from Italy to Greece, high season is between early July and mid-August; from Greece to Italy, it is between early August and early September. Check with company agents for exact dates. Out of season, all services are reduced.

Fares

All companies offer a variety of fares for cabin, airline-type seats and deck passage, with reductions according to age and student or railcard status. High-speed ferries cost only fractionally more than the normal ones. All ferry companies offer a substantial discount (normally 30 percent) on return trips if booked together with the outward journey. Travellers with camper vans may be allowed to sleep in them, thus saving the cost of a cabin.

---

patisserie-bakeries. For fish, the best places are a couple of tavernas down by the fishing harbour, home to a somewhat half-hearted fleet.

If you're stuck for the night and feel the urge to escape to a quieter stretch of sea, hop on any #5 blue bus labelled "Tsoukaleíka" or "Vrahneika" and alight at either **Monodhéndhri** or **Vrahnéïka**, 10km southwest of the city. There is now a practically unbroken chain of tavernas stretching 2km between these resorts. They vary in price, range and quality, but all share the seaside and sunset view. Choices in Pátra include the following:

Apanemo Óthonos & Amalías 107. Seafood taverna, with good fresh fish and noted for its *galaktoboúreko* dessert, opposite the fishing harbour.

Avli tou Yenneou (also called *Nirika*) Paraskhoú ☎ 2610 429 521. Hidden behind waterfront apartments in Terpsithéa, not far north of the youth hostel. Recommended for seafood.

Dinos Óthonos & Amalías 102. Long-established taverna, providing tasty seafood and salads, almost next door to *Apanemo*.

Majestic Ayíou Nikoláou 2–4. Old-style restaurant where you can choose from the day's hot dishes, which are tasty but can be expensive.

Mouragio Kastellókambos, Boznitika. 6km north of Pátra, towards the university; take the Río bus. Specialities include artichoke soufflé and seafood pasta served in a conch shell; the prices are mid-range.

Nikolaras Ayíou Nikoláou 50. Another old-style restaurant serving good, traditional food on a self-serve basis.

Embarkation tax
All international departures carry a levy of €5–7 per person and per car.

Checking in
If you have bought tickets in advance, or from a travel agent other than the official agent listed opposite, you must check in (to the appropriate agent's office, or at their booth in the departure hall) at least two hours before departure.

Stopovers
Free if you specify them when booking, though you may have to pay re-embarkation taxes.

Companies, agents and destinations
ANEK
United Ferries, Óthonos & Amalías 25 ☎2610 226 053, ⊛www.anek.gr.
Ancona: daily via Igoumenítsa (20hr).
Venice: six times a week (33hr).
Maritime Way (My Way) Ferries
Nostos Travel, Iróön Polytekhníou 40 ☎2610 420 639, ⊛www.maritimeway.com.
Brindisi: daily, some via Igoumenítsa and/or Kefalloniá (14hr).
Minoan Lines
Fotopoulos–Sotiropoulos, Athinón 2–6 ☎2610 455 622, ⊛www.minoan.gr.
Ancona: daily via Igoumenítsa (20hr).
Igoumenítsa: daily via Corfu (9hr).
Venice: daily via Corfu and Igoumenítsa (31hr).
Superfast Ferries
Filopoulos–Parthenopoulos, Óthonos & Amalías 12 ☎2610 622 500, ⊛www.super-fast.com.
Ancona: daily direct (20hr) or via Igoumenítsa (21hr).
Bari: daily via Igoumenítsa (16hr).

Listings

Airlines Olympic, Arátou 8 ☎2610 222 901.
Banks and money exchange National Bank of Greece, Platía Trión Symáhon (normal banking hours plus 6–8pm); several banks in the area have ATMs. Kapa foreign exchange bureau, Ayíou Andhréou 97.
Books and newspapers Book's Corner, Ayíou Nikoláou 32, stocks useful maps and English-language newspapers. Lexis, Mézonos 38 and Patréos 90, stocks maps and a selection of Penguins. English-language papers are available from kiosks on the waterfront. The Ermis bookshop at Zaïmi stocks Road's map of Ahaïa.
Buses The KTEL bus terminal, cnr Óthonos & Amalías and Zaïmi for towns in the Peloponnese, Athens, Ioánnina, Thessaloníki and Vólos ☎2610 623 886; local buses leave from Óthonos & Amalías a couple of minutes to the north; buses for Mesolóngi and Agrínio leave from Norman 5

☎2610 421 205; buses for Crete, Kefalloniá and Itéa (for Delphi) leave from Óthonos & Amalías 58 ☎2610 277 854; and buses for Zákynthos leave from Óthonos & Amalías 47 ☎2610 438 592.
Car rental Alamo/National, Ayíou Andhréou 1 ☎2610 273 667, ⒻConsulate 2610 277 864; AutoUnion/ Thrifty, Ayíou Dhionysíou 2 ☎2610 623 200, Ⓕ2610 622 201; Avis, 28-Oktovríou 16 ☎2610 275 547; Delta, Óthonos & Amalías 44 ☎2610 272 764; Euro-dollar, Albatros Travel, Óthonos & Amalías 48 ☎2610 220 993; Hertz, 28-Oktovríou 2 ☎2610 220 990; InterRent-EuropCar, Ayíou Andhréou 6 ☎2610 621 360; Sixt, Ayíou Andhréou 10 ☎2610 275 677.
Consulate Britain, Vótsi 2 ☎2610 277 079, Ⓕ2610 225 334.
Ferry agents Mostly on Óthonos & Amalías (see box above).
Internet Netrino, Karaïskaki 133; others in nearby Yerokostopoúlou. Most are very well priced.

Post office Cnr Mézonos and Záïmi (Mon–Fri 7.30am–8pm); also near cnr Gounári and Ayíou Andhréou (Mon–Fri 7.30am–2pm).

Travel agents Most are on Óthonos & Amalías; also Marine Tours, Vassiléos Yeoryíou 3 ☏ 2610 621 166.

The north coast and the Kalávryta railway

From Pátra you can reach Kórinthos in two hours by **train** or **bus** along the national highway; the onward journey to Athens takes another ninety minutes. The resorts and villages lining the Gulf of Kórinthos are nothing very special, though none of them is overdeveloped. At most of them you find little more than a narrow strip of beach, a campsite, a few rooms for rent and a couple of seasonal tavernas. At **Río** you can cross the gulf to the mainland by the **new bridge** across the Gulf of Kórinthos to Andírio, or by ferry, and at **Éyio** by ferry. Beyond **Dhiakoftó**, if you're unhurried, it's worth taking the old **coast road** along the Gulf of Kórinthos; this runs below the national highway, often right by the sea.

However, to travel from Pátra to Kórinthos without taking the time to detour along the **Kalávryta railway** from Dhiakoftó would be to miss one of the best treats the Peloponnese has to offer – and certainly the finest train journey in Greece. Even if you have a car, this trip should still be part of your plans.

Río and Éyio

RÍO (Ríon), connected by local bus #6 to Pátra in thirty minutes (or by train in ten, though with a long walk from the station to the harbour), signals the beginning of swimmable water, though most travellers pass through for the suspension bridge across the gulf to Andírio (5 min; €10 car toll). Surprisingly, the ferry (every 30 min; ☏ 29320 74717; €6 including driver, passengers €0.50) that functioned before the opening of the bridge in autumn 2004 continues to flourish, with many drivers preferring the cheaper fares and short break from driving.

Testimony to the long-established crossing here are the squat Turkish **forts** paired on either side of the gulf; the opening times of the Río fortress, with its marine moat, are unreliable (officially Tues–Fri 8am–7pm, Sat & Sun 8.30am–3pm).

If you are crossing into the Peloponnese via Andírio, you might be tempted to stop by the sea here, rather than at Pátra. In town towards the train station are several **hotels**, including the inland *Georgios*, Ionías 9 (☏ 2610 991 134; ❸), or, both on the seafront south of the jetty, the *Rion Beach* (☏ 2610 991 421, ⓕ 2610 991 390; ❸) and the ultra-swish *Hotel Porto Rio* and casino (☏ 2610 992 102, ⓦ www.portoriohotel.gr; B&B ❻). There are two **campsites**: the *Rio Mare* (☏ 2610 992 263; May–Oct), just east of the jetty and fortress, and the *Rion* (☏ 2610 991 585, ⓕ 2610 993 388), south of the jetty but closer to the beach, which is poor just here but improves a little as you go south. The best of the **restaurants** is the *Tesseres Epohes* ("Four Seasons"), with bargain prices in a romantic setting by the train station. Río seafront also boasts some of the liveliest bars in the Pátra area – *Mojo* is particularly popular.

Moving east, there are better beaches, and a **campsite**, the *Tsolis* (☏ 26910 31469), at **ÉYIO**. Although away from the sea and not a place many people would choose to stay, there are a few hotels and rooms in the centre of the town.

It's more likely you might want to **eat** there, though, and the main town, inland and uphill, has several decent *psistariés*, while just east of the harbour around Dhódheka Vrýsses square are more eating establishments; the *Plessas Inomayirio* taverna, at Zoödhóhou Piyís 89, is authentic and well priced – nearby stands an ancient plane tree supposedly from 200 AD and dedicated to the theoretically near-contemporaneous historian Pausanias. Local cliffs cut sharply into the hillside near the impressive Panayía Trypití church, marking the spot where resident hero Miralis escaped from the Turks in 1821 by jumping over with his horse. A **ferry** crosses the gulf four times daily (7.30am–5pm; €10 cars including driver, €1.60 passengers; ☎26910 22792) to Áyios Nikólaos, well placed for Delphi. Buses from Pátra stop at the bus station on the inland side of town, a considerable and inconvenient distance from the harbour or the train station.

The best sands are at the village of **RODHODHÁFNI**, 2km northwest of Éyio; the *Corali Beach* (☎26910 71546; May–Sept) and the *Aeoli Beach* (☎26910 71317; April–Oct) **campsites** are close to the beach.

Dhiakoftó and around

It is from **DHIAKOFTÓ** (officially Dhiakoptó) that the rack-and-pinion railway heads south up into the Vouraïkós gorge for Kalávryta (see below). If you arrive late in the day, it's worth spending the night here and making the train journey in daylight; the town can, in any case, be an attractive alternative to staying overnight in Pátra. The climate is very pleasant, less humid than Pátra and less furnace-like than Korinthía province to the east. There are several **hotels**, including the central, upmarket *Chris-Paul* (☎26910 41715, ⓦwww .chrispaul-hotel.gr; ❹), which has a pool, and the small, friendly ⚥ *Lemonies* (☎26910 41229, ⑤26910 43710; ❸), with comfortably refurbished rooms, opposite the school on the road to the beach so well positioned for both sea and train. The seafront *Kohyli* **taverna** on the corner of the beach road has excellent seafood. A few minutes inland of the station, on the road out to the main highways, there is a map and bookshop, Epi Hartou, carrying a comprehensive stock of Anavasi and Road maps.

Travelling 5km east beyond Dhiakoftó there is a better beach at **Paralía Trápezas**. **AKRÁTA**, the final minor resort in Aháïa, before the coastal strip of Korinthía province, is a small town with a beach annexe, but is a little crowded, with three hotels and three campsites set along a drab, exposed stretch of beach.

Dhiakoftó to Kalávryta: the rack-and-pinion railway

Even if you have no interest in trains, the **rack-and-pinion railway** from Dhiakoftó to Kalávryta is a must. The journey can be hot, crowded and uncomfortable, but the track is a crazy feat of Italian engineering, rising at gradients of up to one in seven as it cuts inland through the **Vouraïkós gorge**. The route is a toy-train fantasy of tunnels, bridges and precipitous overhangs.

The railway was built between 1889 and 1896 to bring minerals from the mountains to the sea. Its 1896 steam locomotives were replaced some years ago – one (*O Moutzouris*) remains by the line at Dhiakoftó station (☎26910 43206) with other relics, and another at Kalávryta – but the track itself retains all the charm of its period. The tunnels, for example, have delicately carved window openings, and the narrow bridges zigzagging across the Vouraïkós seem engineered for sheer virtuosity.

△ The Río–Andírio bridge

With lines relaid in 2004, it takes around 45 minutes to get from Dhiakoftó to Zakhloroú (confusingly listed on timetables as Méga Spiléo), and about another twenty minutes from there to Kalávryta. The best part of the trip is the stretch to **Zakhloroú** (see below), along which the gorge narrows to a few feet at points, only to open out into brilliant, open shafts of light beside the Vouraïkós, clear and fast-running even in midsummer. In peak season the ride is very popular (there are just four to six trains a day), so you'll probably need to buy tickets in advance of your preferred departure (including the return journey). Inflated ticket prices reflect the popularity. Despite only covering some 22km, trains on this line can be subject to the same lengthy delays (or cancellations) as their grown-up counterparts on the main line below.

Zakhloroú and Méga Spiléou

ZAKHLOROÚ is as perfect a train stop as could be imagined: a tiny hamlet echoing with the sound of the Vouraïkós River, which splits it into two neighbourhoods. It's a lovely, peaceful place with an old hotel, the *Romantzo* (☎26920 22758; ③), with en-suite rooms, which has a taverna opposite. The adjacent *Messina* restaurant has basic rooms: coming down to the station it could be mistaken for the *Romantzo*.

The eight-storey **Monastery of Méga Spiléou** ("Great Cave"; open mornings and evenings), built at a sixty-metre cave entrance under a 120-metre cliff, is a 45-minute walk from the village, up a rough donkey track along the hillside; this joins a road, then an access drive along the final stretch, which is often chock-a-block with tour buses. The monastery is reputedly the oldest in Greece, but it has been burned down and rebuilt so many times that you'd hardly guess at its antiquity – from a distance it looks like a misplaced hotel. The last major fire took place in 1934, after a keg of gunpowder left behind from the War of Independence exploded. In 1943, the Nazis killed many of the residents and looted seventy lorryloads of furniture and relics, much of it later recovered. Dress conduct for visitors is strict: skirts for women, and long sleeves and trousers for men. Only men are allowed to stay overnight, at the precipitous *xenónas*, and the monks like visitors to arrive before 8pm, serving up a rough repast before closing the gates.

The view of the gorge valley from the monastery is for many the principal attraction. However, the cloister once had 450 monks and was among the richest in the Greek world, owning properties throughout the Peloponnese, in Macedonia, Constantinople and Asia Minor; in consequence, its treasury, arranged as a small **museum** (€1), is outstanding. In the main church, among its icons is a charred black wax and mastic image of the Virgin, one of three in Greece said to be by the hand of St Luke (but more probably from the tenth century); a smaller chapel houses a remarkable collection of body parts from various saints. The monastery was founded by Saints Theodoros and Simeon, after a vision by the shepherdess Euphrosyne in 362 AD led to the discovery of the icon in the cave (Ayíazma) behind the site of the later church; cardboard cutouts now model the story, including flames leaping from the icon to destroy a serpent.

If returning to Dhiakoftó from Zakhloroú, it is possible to walk alongside the 12km of railway line down through the gorge – part of the E4 walk route – in about two hours. You should of course be aware of the times that trains are due on that section of line – the most photogenic points are around the 5.8-kilometre mark above Dhiakoftó. The walk may not be easy for vertigo sufferers, since it involves crossing some rather precipitous bridges. The southward E4 continues through Kalávryta, Vytína, Trípoli, Spárti, Mystra and Taïyétos to Yíthio.

Kalávryta and around

From Méga Spiléou a scenic road has been constructed 28km down to coastal Trápeza, and another has been hacked 10km through to **KALÁVRYTA**. The train line is more in harmony with the surroundings, but coming from Zakhloroú the drama of the route is diminished as the gorge opens out. Kalávryta itself is beautifully positioned, with Mount Helmós as a backdrop, but has a melancholy atmosphere. During World War II, on December 13, 1943, the German occupiers carried out one of their most brutal reprisal massacres because of partisan activity in the area, killing the entire male population – 1436 men and boys – and leaving the town in flames. Rebuilt, it is both depressing and poignant. The first and last sight is a mural, opposite the station, that reads: "Kalávryta, founder member of the Union of Martyred Towns, appeals to all to fight for world peace." The left clocktower on the central church stands fixed at 2.34pm – the hour of the massacre. In the old primary school is the **Museum of the Sacrifice of the People of Kalávryta** (daily, 9am–4pm), while out in the countryside behind the town is a shrine to those massacred, with the single word "Peace" (*Iríni*).

The Nazis also burned the tenth-century **monastery of Ayías Lávras** (open mornings and evenings), 6km out of Kalávryta. As the site where Yermanos, Archbishop of Pátra, raised the flag to signal the War of Independence, the monastery is one of the great Greek national shrines. It, too, has been rebuilt, along with a small historical museum.

Staying at Kalávryta has a sense of pilgrimage about it for Greeks; it's crowded with school parties during the week and with families at weekends. The general attitude to foreigners – perhaps understandably – is business-like rather than overtly friendly, and the town will probably not have the same appeal for the casual visitor. If you miss the last train back to Zakhloroú (currently at 3.50pm, but check upon arrival) there are several pleasant **hotels** whose rates drop outside of winter weekends. Among them are the hospitable *Polyxeni*, Lohagón Vassiléos Kapóta 13 (☎26920 22141; ❷) and the friendly, good-value (in summer) and luxurious *Filoxenia*, Ethnikís Andístasis 20 (☎26920 22422, ⓦwww.hotelfiloxenia.gr; B&B ❸, winter ❻). The Info Center in Pátra has an extensive list of **rooms** in Kalávryta. There are several adequate **restaurants** around the square – *To Tzaki* has a nice atmosphere and good, mostly grilled, food. Kalávryta is also the main base for the **Helmos Ski Centre** (☎26920 24451, ⓦwww.kalavrita-ski.gr; Dec–April, daily 9am–4pm), which is rapidly growing in popularity; their website also carries contact details for accommodation in nearby villages. There are a number of shops that rent out equipment, give information about the state of the slopes and can sometimes help with transport up to the centre.

A thirty-minute drive southeast of Kalávryta, and 1.5km north of Kastriá, is the **Spílio tón Limnón** or Cave of the Lakes (summer daily 9am–6pm; winter Mon–Fri 9.30am–4.30pm, Sat & Sun 9.30am–6.30pm; €8; ☎26920 31633, ⓦwww.kastriacave.gr). Mineral-saturated water trickling through a two-kilometre cavern system from the Apanókambos plateau has precipitated natural dams, trapping a series of small underground lakes. As yet, only the first 300m or so are open to the public, and the guided tour can be short and hurried. The cave is on the same **bus** line from Kalávryta as the villages of Káto Loussí, Kastriá and Planitéro, and is 2km north of Kastriá. Buses also run from Kalávryta to Pátra four times daily.

Mount Helmós

The highest peaks of the imposing Helmós (Aroánia) range rear up a dozen or so kilometres to the southeast of Kalávryta. **Mount Helmós** itself, at 2355m, is only 50m short of the summit of Taïyetos to the south. The walk from Kalávryta is not an interesting approach, the trail having vanished under a paved road and the ski centre (1900m) approached by it. To get the most from hiking on the mountain you need to climb up from the village of **Sólos**, on the west side – a five-hour-plus walk which takes you to the **Mavronéri waterfall**, source of the legendary Styx (Stýga, Stygós), the river which souls of the dead had to cross in order to enter Hades.

The hike from Sólos

To reach the path opening at Sólos, start at **Akráta** on the Pátra–Kórinthos road. From here it's a slow but beautiful 35-kilometre haul up a winding paved road. Buses run only three times a week, but hitching may be possible in high summer.

SÓLOS is a tiny place, a cluster of stone cottages on a steep hillside just below the fir trees, inhabited only in summer. Facing it across the valley is the larger but more scattered village of Peristéra, past which runs the easiest of the routes to Mavronéri.

Follow the **track** through Sólos, past the combined inn (ten beds) and *magazí* (café-store), where you can get a simple meal. Beyond the last houses the track curves around the head of a gully. On the right, going down its wooded flank, is a good path to a bridge over the river at the bottom. Just beyond (15min; this and all subsequent times are from Sólos), you reach another track. There is a **chapel** on the left, and a path to the left which leads past a **church** on a prominent knoll to rejoin the jeep track again. After 75 minutes, turn left to the half-ruined hamlet of **Gounariánika**, then continue steadily upwards along the west (right) flank of the valley through abandoned fields until you come to a stream-gully coming in from your right. Beyond the stream the fir forest begins: it's an ideal camping place (2hr 30min; 1hr 30min going back down).

Once into the **woods**, the path is very clear. After about an hour (3hr 30min), descend to a boulder-strewn **stream bed** with a rocky ravine to the right leading up to the foot of a huge bare crag, the east side of the Neraïdhórahi peak (2238m) visible from Kalávryta. Cross the stream and continue leftwards up the opposite bank. In June there are good displays of wild flowers, all the way up from here.

After fifteen minutes' climb above the bank, you reach the top of a **grassy knoll**, then dip back into the trees again. At the four-hour mark, turn a corner into the mouth of the **Styx ravine** where another five minutes' walk brings you to a **deep gully** where enormous banks of snow lie late into the spring. A few paces across a dividing rib of rock there is a second gully, where the path has been eroded and you must cross some slippery scree.

Arriving at a wooded spur running down from the crag on the right, the trail winds up to a shoulder (4hr 20min), descends into another gully, then winds up to a second shoulder of level rocky ground by some large black pines (4hr 30min), known as *Tò Dhiáselo toú Kynigoú* ("Hunter's Saddle"). From there you can look into the Styx ravine. Continue down the path towards the right until it dwindles at the foot of a vast crag (4hr 45min). You can now see the **Mavronéri waterfall**, a two-hundred-metre-long, wavering plume of water pouring off the red cliffs up ahead.

To get to it, angle across the scree bank without losing altitude – the track is obliterated soon after the saddle – until you reach the base of the falls (5hr). It is possible to continue up the valley, past some turf next to a seasonal pond where people camp, but the summit area proper is a bit of a letdown after the majesty of the Styx valley. Fairly clear and easy trails lead down from the south side of the watershed to join the E4 trail between the villages of Káto Loussí (12km above Kalávryta) or Planitéro (8km from Klitoría). The appropriate Korfes, YIS or Anavasi maps have more details on these routes.

Travel details

Trains

There are two main Peloponnesian lines:
Athens–Kórinthos–Dhiakoftó–Éyio–Pátra–Pýrgos–Kyparissía; two trains daily cover the full route.

Kórinthos to: Dhiakoftó (3 daily; 1hr–1hr 30min); Pátra (3 daily; 45min–1hr 25min); Pýrgos (3 daily; 1hr 30min–2hr 15min); Kyparissía (2 daily; 1hr–1hr 35min).

Pátra to: Pýrgos (4 daily; 1hr 30min–2hr); Kyparissía (4 daily; 3hr); Kalamáta (1 daily; 4hr 45min).

Pýrgos to: Kyparissía (6 daily; 1hr 20min); Kalamáta (2 daily; 3hr).

Kyparissía to: Kalamáta (4 daily; 1hr 30min).

Athens (starts in Pireás)–Kórinthos–Mykínes (Mycenae)–Árgos–Trípoli–Diavolítsi–Kalamáta; three trains daily cover the full route.

Kórinthos to: Mykínes (50min); Árgos (10min); Trípoli (1hr 20min–1hr 35min); Kalamáta (2hr–2hr 20min).

In addition, there are the following branch lines and extra seasonal services on the main lines:

Árgos–Náfplio 2–3 daily (18min) – this section has a large supplementary fare.

Dhiakoftó–Zakhloroú–Kalávryta 4–6 daily (Dhiakoftó–Zakhloroú 46min; Zakhloroú–Kalávryta 21min).

Isthmós–Loutráki 3 daily in summer (13min).

Kalamáta–Diavolítsi 5 daily (45min) Kalamáta–
TEI (Technical Education Institute at Andikálamos)
7 daily (9min).
Pátra–Éyio–Dhiakoftó (3 daily in summer
Mon–Sat; 45min–1hr).
Pýrgos–Olymbía 5 trains daily (27min).

Buses

Buses detailed usually have similar frequency in
each direction, so entries are given just once; for
reference check under both starting point and
destination. Bus station timetables rarely indicate
when there is a change of bus en route – this can
involve a long wait. Long-distance buses from
Athens often have a break at Isthmós, by the
Corinth Canal.

Connections with Athens: Árgos (hourly; 2hr
15min); Hóra (4 daily; 5hr 30min); Kalamáta
(12–13 daily; 4hr 30min); Kalávryta (1–2 daily; 3hr
30min); Kórinthos (hourly; 1hr–1hr 30min); Koróni
(1 daily; 7hr); Kyparissía (4 daily; 5hr 30min);
Loutráki (9 daily; 1hr 30min); Monemvasiá (2 daily;
6hr); Mykínes–Fíkhti (for Mycenae; hourly; 2hr);
Náfplio (hourly; 3hr); Olymbía (4 daily; 5hr 30min);
Pátra (28 daily, 2.30am–9.30pm; 3hr); Poulíthra (1
daily via Leonídhio; 4hr 30min); Pýlos (2 daily; 5hr
30min–7hr); Pýrgos (8 daily; 5hr); Spárti (9 daily;
4hr); Tiryns (hourly; 2hr 45min); Trípoli (14 daily;
2hr 30min–3hr); Yeroliménas (2 daily in season
only; 7hr); Yíthio (4–6 daily; 5hr).

Areópoli to: Ítylo (4 daily, 20min); Kalamáta (4
daily changing at Ítylo; 1hr 30min–2hr 30min);
Láyia (daily; 1hr); Spárti (2 daily; 2hr); Váthia (daily
in season; 1hr 30min); Yeroliménas (2 daily in
season; 1hr); Yíthio (4 daily; 35–50min).

Árgos to: Andhrítsena (1 daily; 3hr); Ástros (3
daily Mon–Fri; 1hr); Ayía Triádha (8 daily; 20min);
Kórinthos (15 daily; 1hr); Leonídhio (3 daily Mon–
Fri; 3hr); Midhéa (3 daily; 40min); Mykínes (Mycenae; 5 daily; 30min); Mýli (for Lerna; 5–10 daily;
25min); Náfplio (15–32 daily; every 30min; 30min);
Nemea (2 daily; 1hr); Néo Kíos (11 daily; 20min);
Olymbía (3 daily on weekdays; 4hr 30min); Spárti
(8 daily; 3hr); Tíryns (every 30min; 15min); Trípoli
(4 daily Mon–Fri, 3 daily Sat–Sun; 1hr 20min).

Galatás to: Méthana (2–4 daily; 45min); Náfplio (3
daily; 2hr); Trizína (2 daily; 15min).

Kalamáta to: Exohóri (2 daily; 1hr 30min);
Finikoúnda (4 daily, changing at Pýlos, 2 daily
via Koróni; 2hr 15min); Hóra (4 daily, changing at
Pýlos, plus 4 direct; 3hr); Kardhamýli (4 daily; 50–
75min); Kórinthos (7 daily; 3hr 15min–4hr); Koróni
(8 daily; 1hr 20min–2hr); Kyparissía (5 daily; 2hr);
Megalópoli (8 daily; 1hr 15min); Messíni (frequent
except Sun; 25min); Methóni (4 daily, via Pýlos;
2hr); Pátra (2 daily, via Pýrgos; 4hr–4hr 30min);

Petrálona (for Ancient Messini, 2 daily); Pýlos (5–9
daily; 1hr 20min); Pýrgos (2 daily; 2hr); Saïdhóna
(2 daily; 90–120min); Spárti (2 daily, changing
at Artemisia; 2hr–2hr 30min); Stoúpa (4 daily;
60–90min); Trípoli (8 daily; 1hr 45min–2hr).

Kórinthos to: Loutráki (every 30min; 20min);
Mykínes (Mycenae; hourly; 30min); Náfplio (7 daily;
1hr 20min); Nemea (5 daily; 45min); Spárti (8 daily;
4hr); Tíryns (hourly; 1hr 15min); Trípoli (9 daily; 1hr
30min); Xylókastro (every 30–60min; 45min).

Kyparissía to: Filiatrá (7 daily; 20min); Pýlos (5
daily changing at Hóra; 2hr); Pýrgos (2–4 daily;
1hr); Trípoli (2 daily; 1hr 30min–2hr); Zaháro (4
daily; 25min).

Megalópoli to: Andhrítsena (2 daily; 1hr 15min);
Pýrgos (2 daily; 4hr).

Náfplio to: Dhrépano (6–8 daily, except Sun;
20min); Epidaurus ("Asklipio", 4–5 daily; 45min);
Ermióni (3–4 daily; 2hr 15min); Galatás for Póros
(1–3 daily; 2hr); Íria (2 daily; 1hr); Isthmós (14
daily; 1hr 20min); Karathónas beach (4 daily;
20min); Kósta (3–4 daily; 2hr 15min); Kranídhi
(3–4 daily; 1hr 50min); Lygourió (7 daily; 40min);
Méthana (2 daily; 2hr); Midhéa (5 daily; 40min);
Mykínes (Mycenae; 3–4 daily; 1hr); Néo Kíos (11
daily; 20min); Paleá Epídhavros (3 daily; 1hr); Pórto
Héli (3–4 daily; 2hr); Tíryns (every 30min; 15min);
Toló (14 daily; 25min); Trípoli (2–4 daily; 2hr).

Pátra to: Ahaïa (26 daily; 40min); Éyio (12–18
daily; 1hr); Itéa (for Delphi; 2 daily, Mon–Sat;
3–4hr); Ioánnina (4 daily; 5hr); Kalamáta (2 daily;
4hr); Kalávryta (4 daily; 2hr 15min); Kalogriá (3
daily in high season; 1hr 15min); Lápas/Metóhi
(for Kalogriá; 6–10 daily; 50–60min); Pýrgos (6–11
daily; 2hr); Thessaloníki (3 daily; 9–10hr); Trípoli
(1–2 daily, via Lámbia; 3–4hr); Vólos (1 daily; 6hr);
Zákynthos (4 daily; 2hr 30min including ferry from
Kyllíni).

Pýlos to: Finikoúnda (3–5 daily; 45min); Filiátra
(2–6 daily, usually changing at Hóra; 1hr 30min)
Hóra (2–6 daily; 40min); Kyparissía (1–5 daily,
usually changing at Hóra; 2hr); Methóni (3–6 daily;
20min); Yiálova (2–8 daily; 20min).

Pýrgos to: Andhrítsena (2 daily; 2hr); Katákolo (9
daily; 30min); Kyllíni (3 daily; 1hr); Olymbía (hourly,
but none 12.30–3.30pm; 45–60min); Trípoli (3
daily; 3hr).

Spárti to: Moláï (6 daily; 1hr 40min–2hr);
Monemvasiá (3 daily, 2 on Sun, changing at Moláï;
2hr 30min–3hr); Mystra (11 daily, 4 on Sun;
15–30min); Neápoli (3–4 daily; 4hr); Pýrgos Dhiroú
(1 daily; 2hr 30min); Trípoli (9–10 daily; 1hr–1hr
20min); Yeroliménas (2 daily; 3hr); Yíthio (5–6
daily; 1hr).

Trípoli to: Andhrítsena (2 daily; 1hr 30min); Ástros
2 daily Mon–Sat; 1hr 30min); Dhimitsána

(1 daily; 1hr 30min); Kalávryta (1 daily; 2hr 30min); Karítena (2 daily; 1hr); Klitoría (1–2 daily; 2hr); Leonídhio (1–2 daily; 3hr 30min); Megalópoli (9 daily Mon–Fri, 6 daily Sat–Sun; 40min); Neápoli (2 daily; 5hr 30min); Olymbía (2 daily Mon–Fri, 1–3 Sat–Sun; 5hr); Pýlos (3 daily; 3hr); Stemnítsa (1 daily; 1hr 15min); Tegéa (hourly; 20min); Vytína (6 daily; Mon–Fri, 4 Sat–Sun; 1hr 15min); Yíthio (3 daily; 2hr 30min).

Yíthio to: Láyia (daily; 1hr); Mavrouvoúni ("Kamping"; 4 daily; 15–20min); Monemvasiá (2 daily in high season; 2hr 30min); Pýrgos Dhiroú ("Spílea"; 1 daily; 1hr 10min); Váthia (1 daily, Mon, Wed, Fri; 2hr); Yeroliménas (2–3 daily; 2hr).

Ferries

Across the Gulf of Kórinthos: Andírio–Río (every 15min, every 30min between 11pm and 7am; 10–20min); Éyio–Áyios Nikólaos (4 daily; 7.30am–5pm; 4 daily; 35–50min).

Galatás to: Póros (every 15min from dawn till past midnight; 5min).

Kalamáta to: Kastélli, Crete (1 weekly in season; 8hr 30min); Kýthira (1 weekly in season; 5hr 30min).

Kósta to: Spétses (4 daily; 20min).

Kyllíni to: Zákynthos (4–5 daily; 1hr 30min); Kefalloniá (daily 6–7 summer, 2–4 winter; 1hr 15min–2hr 15min).

Kýthira to: Andikýthira (2 weekly in season); Kastélli, Crete (4–6 weekly in season; 2hr 15min; 5hr via Andikýthira); Pireás (2 weekly in season).

Neápoli to: Kýthira (2–3 daily mid-season, 3–4 daily late July–Aug; 1hr).

Neápoli (Poúnda) to: Elafónissos (5–15 daily; 10min);

Pátra to: Igoumenítsa and Corfu (2–3 daily; 6–11hr/8–11hr); Kefalloniá and Itháki (1–2 daily; 2hr 30min/3hr 45min); also to Brindisi, Ancona, Bari, Trieste and Venice (Italy).

Yíthio to: Kýthira (1–5 weekly in season; 2hr 30min); contact Rozaki (☏27330 22650) for current information.

Hydrofoils

For details and frequencies of services, which vary drastically with season, contact local agents or the Minoan Flying Dolphins' main office in Pireás (Aktí Themistokléous 8 ☏210 41 28 001).

Flying Dolphin hydrofoils run between the following ports: **Ermióni** to: Spétses, Pórto Héli, Ídhra, Póros, Méthana and Pireás.

Méthana to: Póros, Ídhra, Ermióni, Égina and Pireás.

Summer-only excursion boats

Kósta and Pórto Héli: Water-taxis to Spétses according to demand (10–20min).

Flights

To/from **Athens–Kýthira** (1–2 daily; 50min); Olympic Airways no longer flies to Kalamáta airport; several German charter airlines fly to Pátra–Áraxos airport.

Thessaly and central Greece

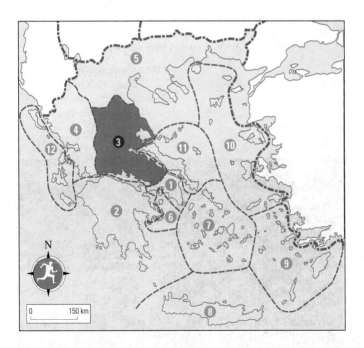

N

0   150 km

CHAPTER 3

Highlights

✳ **Ósios Loukás** A remote Byzantine monastery decorated with vivid mosaics from the eleventh century. See p.336

✳ **Delphi** Spectacularly set ruins of an oracle believed in ancient times to be the centre of the earth. See p.339

✳ **Galaxídhi** The most perfectly preserved settlement on the Gulf of Kórinthos, this was one of Greece's major ports in the nineteenth century. See p.350

✳ **Náfpaktos** A lively market town with a stage-set old harbour and swooping castle walls. See p.353

✳ **Karpenisiótis valley** This alpine valley, known as the "Greek Switzerland", is an all-year recreation paradise. See p.361

✳ **Mount Pílio** Hiking trails link mansion-filled villages clinging to wooded hillsides; the mythical home of the centaurs. See p.371

✳ **The northeast Pílio coast** Superb, pale-sand beaches provide respite after arduous hiking. See p.376

✳ **The Metéora** Meaning "rocks in the air"; bizarre, stunning scenery and exquisite Byzantine monasteries. See p.399

△ Ósios Loukás mosaic

Thessaly and central Greece

Central Greece is a region of scattered highlights, above all, the site of the ancient oracle at **Delphi** (modern Dhelfí), and, further north, the other-worldly rock monasteries of the **Metéora**. The area as a whole, dominated by the vast agricultural plain of Thessaly, is less exciting, with rather drab market and industrial towns. The southern part of this region, below Thessaly proper, is known as **Stereá Elládha** – literally "Greek Continent", a name that reflects its mid-nineteenth-century past as the only independent Greek mainland territory, along with Attica and the quasi-island of the Peloponnese. It corresponds to the ancient divisions of Boeotia and Phokis, the domains respectively of Thebes (modern Thíva) and Delphi. Most visitors head straight through these territories to Delphi, but if you have time, the most rewarding detour is to the monastery of **Ósios Loukás** – containing the finest Byzantine mosaics in the country. For hikers there is also the opportunity of climbing **Mount Parnassós**, the Muses' mountain.

The basin of **Thessaly** (Thessalía in Greek) formed the bed of an ancient inland sea – rich agricultural land that was ceded reluctantly to the modern nation by the Turks in 1881. This region's attractions lie at its periphery, hemmed in by the mountain ranges of Ólymbos (Olympus), Píndhos (Pindus), Óssa and Pílio (Pelion). East from the major port city of Vólos extends the hilly peninsula of **Mount Pílio**, whose luxuriant woods and idyllic beaches are easily combined with island-hopping to the Sporades. Less visited **Mount Óssa** is most easily accessed en route to northern Greece, lying between the sea and the major motorway to Thessaloníki. To the west, **Kalambáka** gives access to the Metéora (not to be missed) and across the dramatic **Katára pass** over the Píndhos to Epirus. To the north, the horizon is dominated by **Mount Olympus** (covered in Chapter Five), home of the ancient gods.

Looming across a narrow gulf from Stereá Elládha, and joined by a bridge at Halkídha, is the island of **Évvia** (Euboea). Though this feels – especially in summer – like an extension of the mainland (from where there are many ferry crossings), it is nonetheless a bona-fide island, detailed in Chapter Eleven.

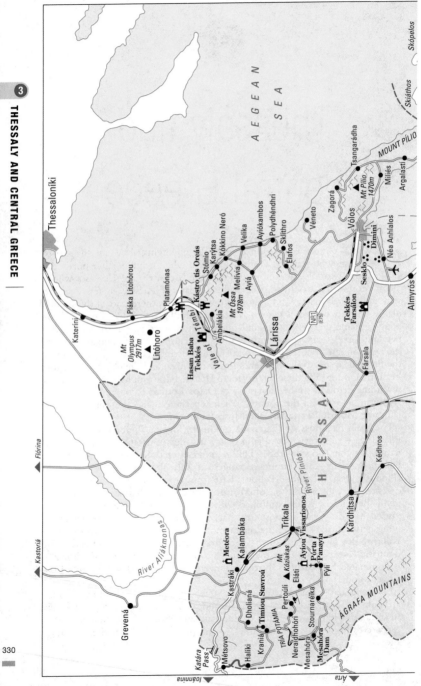

AEGEAN SEA

Skópelos

Skiáthos

MOUNT PILIO

Tsangarádha

Mt Pílio
1470m

Milíes

Argalastí

Zagorá

Vólos

Véneto

Polydhéndhri

Néa Anhíalos

Skíthro

Ayiókambos

Dimíni

Elafos

Almyrós

Velíka

Sesklo

Avía

Melívia

Tekkés
Farsálion

Kókkino Neró

Karýtsa

Kástro tis Oreás

Stómio

Mt Óssa
1978m

NR1
(E75)

Ambelákia

Fársala

Thessaloníki

Pláka Litohórou

Platamónas

Katerini

Litóhoro

Mt
Olympus
2917m

Hasan Baba
Tekkés

Témbi

Vale of

Lárissa

T H E S S A L Y

River Piniós

Kédhros

Kardhítsa

Flórina

Kastoriá

River Aliákmonas

Grevená

Metéora

Kalambáka

Kastráki

Dholianá

Trikala

Ayíou Yissaríonos

Pórta
Panayía

Pýli

Mt
Kóziakas

Eláti

Pertoúli

Timíou Stavroú

TRÍA POTÁMIA

Neraidhohóri

Stournaréika

Mesohóra

Mesohóra
Dam

AGRAFA MOUNTAINS

Kraniá

Halíki

Métsovo

Katára
Pass

Ioánnina

Arta

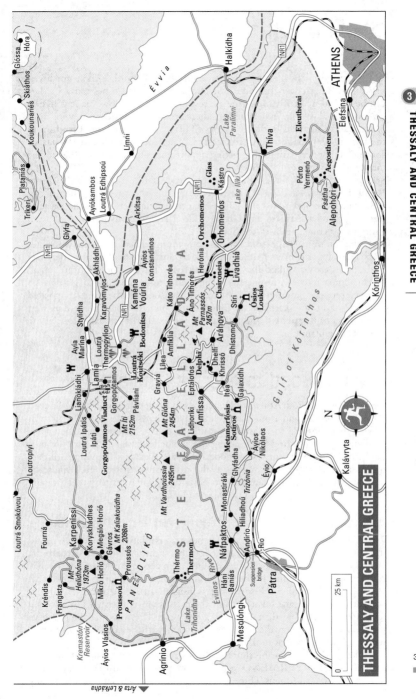

THESSALY AND CENTRAL GREECE

▲ Arta & Lefkádha

ATHENS

NR1

Eleftherai
Elefsína
Aegosthena
Pórto
Yermenó
Psátha
Alepohóri
Thíva
Kórinthos
Lake
Paralímni
Lake Ilíki
Halkídha
Limni
Évvia
Glóssa
Hóra
Koukounariés
Skíathos
Plataniás
Trikéri

Gulf of Kórinthos

Kalávryta

N

Orhomenós
Orchomenos
Glas
Kástro
Herónia
Chaironeia
Livadhiá
Káto Tithoréa
Áno Tithoréa
Stíri
Osios
Loukás
Dhístomo
Aráhova
Mt Parnassós
2457m
Delphí
Dhelfí
Khríssó
Galaxídhi
Itéa
Ámfissa
Eptálofos
Lílea
Graviá
Amfíklia
Ayíos
Konstandínos
Kaména
Voúrla
Arkítsa
Loutrá
Edhipsoú
Ayiókambos
Akhládhi
Glýfa
NR1

Metamorfósis
Soúros
Ayios Nikólaos
Glyfádha
Trizónia
Hiliadhoú
Andírio
Río
Náfpaktos
Andírio
Suspension
bridge
Pátra

Lidhoríki
Monastiráki

Mt Gióna
2454m

S T E R E Á   E L L Á DHA

Mt Vardhoússia
2495m

Mt Íti
2152m
Pávliani

Gorgopótamos Viaduct
Gorgopótamos
Lianokládhi
Loutrá Ipáti
Ipáti

Lamía
Loutrá
Ayía
Marína
Stylídha
Thermopýlon
Karavómylos
Loutrá
Koutséki
Bodonitsa
Ayios
Konstandínos

Loutropiyí
Loutrá Smokóvou

Karpeníssi
Koryskhádhes
Megálo Horió
Gávros
Fourná
Mt Kaliakoúdha
2098m

Mt
Helidhóna
1973m
Mikró Horió
Proussós
Proussós

Kréndis
Frangísta

Ayíos Vlásios
Kremastón
Reservoir

P A N E T O L I K Ó

Thérmo
Thermón

Háni
Baniás
Évinos River

Lake
Trihonídha

Agrínio

Mesolóngi

THESSALY AND CENTRAL GREECE

0   25 km

Stereá Elládha

The inevitable focus of a visit to Stereá Elládha is **Delphi**, 175km northwest of Athens. Buses cover the route from the capital several times a day, or they can be picked up at **Livadhiá**, the nearest rail terminus. However, if you're in no hurry or have your own transport, there are ample rewards in slowing your progress: take the Old Road to Thebes (**Thíva**), or detour from **Livadhiá** to the Byzantine monastery of **Ósios Loukás**. The legendary **Mount Parnassós** above Delphi offers skiing and walking opportunities by season, and shelters the mostly winter resort of **Aráhova**.

To the northeast of the Athens–Delphi road, traffic roars along **National Road 1** towards Lárissa and Thessaloníki, skirting the coast for much of the way, with Évvia just across the gulf. Along this route there are ferries over to this long island at **Arkítsa** and **Glýfa**, while at **Áyios Konstandínos** you can also pick up connections to the Sporades.

Moving on from Delphi and Lamía, the town immediately north, two routes cross Thessaly: northwest to the Metéora, or northeast to Pílio. Another road leads southwest via **Galaxídhi** and **Náfpaktos** to the Gulf of Kórinthos, offering an approach to – or from – the Peloponnese, using the Andírio–Río bridge or ferry services between Áyios Nikólaos and Éyio, or the thinly populated province of Étolo-Akarnanía. A fourth, more remote, route leads due west from Lamía to **Karpeníssi** and then across the southernmost extensions of the Píndhos mountains.

The Old Road to Thebes (Thíva)

The ancient road from Athens to Delphi began at the Parthenon as the **Sacred Way to Eleusis**, and from there climbed northwest into the hills towards Thebes. It is possible to follow this route, its course almost unchanged since Oedipus supposedly trod it, by taking the minor road, signposted for "Mándhra", north off the motorway at modern Elefsína. Leaving the polluted industrial port, matters improve quickly, as the road winds up through a landscape of pines and stony hills. There are two buses daily along this road to Thíva and connections from there on to Livadhiá and Delphi.

Aegosthena, Pórto Yermenó and Psátha

The first thing to tempt you off the Thebes road is a look at the best-preserved stretch of ancient walls in Greece – the fourth-century BC fort of **Aegosthena** – 23km from the Elefsína–Thíva road (no bus), above the mouth of a valley running between mounts Kytherónas and Patéras, overlooking a secluded arm of the Gulf of Kórinthos. Historically it is insignificant, being merely an outpost of Sparta's ally Megara, but the ruins themselves are impressive, the two end towers rising up more than 12m above the walls. The seaward ramparts have mostly vanished; up on the acropolis, a church with frescoes survives from a medieval monastery that took root here.

A kilometre below on the shore at this extreme eastern corner of the Gulf sprawls **PÓRTO YERMENÓ**, a little resort popular with the working-class districts of western Athens. Three gravel-sand beaches here are divided by tiny, low headlands, with pine- and olive-draped hills as a backdrop, and are certainly the cleanest near Athens. If you avoid high summer and shoulder-season weekends, when the place gets packed out, Pórto Yermenó makes an excellent first-night halt by the sea, especially if you've started late out of Athens. Give the overpriced inland *Hotel Egosthenion* a miss in favour of the 1980s-vintage **rooms and apartments** just above the northerly beach: *Vassiliki Mastroyianni* (☎22630 41394; ❸) is representative of such. At peak season, up to a dozen **tavernas**, pizzerias and fast-food takeaways operate, but the *Psarotaverna To Kaïki tou Mihali* (daily May–Oct, weekends only Nov–April), out behind the southerly beach of Áyios Nikólaos, is hard to better for its meat and fish grills, salads and home-made retsina. In town, the *Psaropoula*, first of several seafood tavernas in a row on the pedestrianized lane behind the north beach, is reliably open daily from early to late in the season, but their quality comes at a price – allow €25 each for a fish meal.

From a junction just uphill from Pórto Yermenó, a steep, winding road through the pines leads 8km to the bay of **Psátha**, with a longer (2km) and trendier beach than its neighbour – there are two beach bar/nightclubs at mid-strand. Otherwise, it's surprisingly undeveloped – there's no short-term accommodation – but plenty of fish **tavernas** are concentrated at the north end of the sand; *Limanaki* and *Lagoudhera* are most likely to be open at lunch outside of summer.

Eleutherai and Thíva (Thebes)

Back on the Thebes road, 1km north of the Pórto Yermenó turning, you pass another fortress defending a critical pass: fourth-century BC **Eleutherai** (unlimited access). Signposted from the road, 400m east of it, the fort is well preserved, with its northeast side almost intact and six of its circuit of towers surviving to varying degrees.

The modern town of **THÍVA** lies 20km north of Eleutherai, built right on the site of its mighty predecessor, birthplace of Pindar and Epaminondas. For this very reason, there are almost no traces of the past: archeologists have had little success in excavating the crucial central areas, and the most interesting visit is to the excellent **archeological museum** (summer Mon 12.30–7pm, Tues–Sun 8am–7pm; winter Mon 10.30am–5pm, Tues–Sun 8.30am–3pm; €2). This is at the north (downhill) end of Pindhárou, the main street; look out for the enormous Frankish tower in its forecourt, where archeologists can often be seen at work in their labs. The collection is strongest on Bronze Age to Classical Boeotia, in particular votive offerings from religious centres, though as so often labelling is spotty and tends to be by group rather than by item. Room A features funerary *stelae*, in particular one from the sixth century BC depicting a youth holding a cockerel and sniffing a lotus; from the same era are two *kouroi* (idealized Archaic male figures) from an Apollo shrine at Ptóön, reminiscent of the larger one found on Sámos (see p.887). Room D is devoted to a unique collection of painted *larnakes* (sarcophagi) from Mycenaean Tanagra, dating to 1350–1250 BC. Bold expressionistic strokes display heavy Cretan influence; along with floral and abstract patterns there are well-observed hunting scenes, and women lamenting their dead.

There are no direct **buses** from Thíva to Delphi, but services run frequently to Livadhiá (where there are better connections) and a couple of times a day (with a change at Skhimatári) to Halkídha, gateway to Évvia. There are two central, overpriced **hotels** opposite each other on Epaminónda; the *Niobe* at no. 63 (☎22620 27949; ❹) is preferable. The main **taverna** district is the pedestrianized section of Epaminónda, where *Dionysos* is a good choice for traditional *mayireftá*.

Livadhiá and around

Livadhiá lies at the edge of a great agricultural plain, much of it reclaimed lake bed scattered with a few minor archeological sites such as ancient **Orchomenos**, **Glas** and **Chaironeia** with its stone lion. It's a part of Greece that sees few tourists, most of whom are in a hurry to reach the glories of the Parnassós country just to the west, and will mainly interest veteran travellers to Greece with their own transport.

Livadhiá

LIVADHIÁ is a pleasant cotton-milling town on the banks of the Érkyna, a river of legendary fame, which emerges from a dark gorge at the base of a fortress. Paired ancient and medieval sights, along with landscaping and gentrification in the vicinity of the river springs, make it an enjoyable daytime pause before, or after, Delphi. But if you're without transport, and on a budget, keep in mind the last bus or train connection out, since there are no cheap places to stay.

The older curiosity is the site of the **Oracle of Trophonios**, a ten-minute walk from the main square, beside an Ottoman-era bridge. Here the waters of the Érkyna rise from a series of springs, now channelled beside the *Xenia Café-Piano Bar*. Above the springs, cut into the rock, are niches for votive offerings – in one of which, in a large chamber with a bench, the local Ottoman governor would sit for a quiet smoke. In antiquity, all who sought to consult the Oracle of Trophonios first had to bathe in the Springs of Memory and Forgetfulness. The oracle, a circular structure which gave entrance to caves deep in the gorge, has been tentatively identified at the top of the hill, near the remains of an unfinished temple of Zeus. It was visited by the Greek traveller-scholar Pausanias, who wrote that it left him "possessed with terror and hardly knowing himself or anything around him".

The **kástro**, or castle, which overlooks the springs, provides the medieval interest; its entrance lies just around the corner up the hill to the west. An impressive and well-bastioned square structure, it was built in the fourteenth century and was a key early conquest in the War of Independence. But its early history is more compelling. The castle was the stronghold of a small group of Catalan mercenaries, the Grand Company, who took control of central Greece in 1311 and – appointing a Sicilian prince as their ruler – held it for sixty years. They were a tiny, brutal band who had arrived in Greece from Spain in the wake of the Fourth Crusade. They wrested control from the Franks, who were then established in Athens and Thebes, in a cunning deviation from traditional rules of engagement. As the Frankish nobility approached Livadhiá, the vastly outnumbered Catalans diverted the river to flood the surrounding fields. The Frankish cavalry advanced into the unexpected marsh and were cut down to a man.

Practicalities

Arriving by **bus**, you'll be dropped near the central square, **Platía Lámbrou Katsóni**; in season buses towards Delphi often arrive and leave full. The **train station** is 6km out, but arrivals should be met by an OSE shuttle bus into town.

Staying overnight, your choice is limited to *Livadhia* on Platía Lámbrou Katsóni at the main junction (✆22610 23611; ●), or the plusher *Philippos*, a modern pile at the eastern outskirts (✆22610 24931; ●). **Eating out** here is a better proposition; in the pedestrianized zones surrounding the riverside park are a number of grills, *mezedhopolía* and cafés, some only active by night and two housed in converted water mills. *Neromylos*, one of the mill restorations on the pedestrianized riverbank, is a conventional suppertime taverna, not too overpriced, with the old sluice running through its premises; for lunch, *Iy Krya*, officially at Trofoníou 13 (the first establishment on the right, facing upriver), is acceptable as a simple grill. Between the two, you can sample good coffees and desserts at *Kafe Erkyna*.

Orchomenos, Glas and Chaironeia

Just 10km northeast of Livadhiá (hourly buses) is the site of **ancient ORCHOMENOS**, inhabited from Neolithic to Classical times. As the capital of the Minyans, a native Thessalian dynasty, it was one of the wealthiest Mycenaean cities. Near the edge of the rather drab modern village of Orhomenós, along the road signposted for Dhiónysos village, is the **"Treasury" of Minyas** (Tues–Sun 8.30am–3pm; €2), a stone tholos-type tomb similar to the tomb of Atreus at Mycenae, and also excavated by Heinrich Schliemann in 1880. The roof has collapsed but it is otherwise complete, and its inner chamber, hewn from the rock, has an intricately carved marble ceiling. Closer to the road are the remains of a fourth-century BC **theatre** (locked), and behind, way up on the rocky hilltop, a tiny fortified acropolis from the same period. Across the road is the ninth-century Byzantine **church of Panayía tís Skripoús**, built entirely of blocks from the theatre and column drums from a Classical temple. The larger triple-apsed church has some fine reliefs, including a sundial on the south transept, with the remains of monastic cells just to the south.

Continuing east, it's a further 16km to the village of **Kástro**, right next to the motorway towards Lárissa (use "Kástro" exit from this). A minor road leads, 2km from Kástro village or 1500m from the motorway, to the well-signposted Mycenaean citadel of **GLAS**. An enormous if ultimately disappointing site, Glas (unrestricted entrance) is nominally a far larger citadel than either Tiryns or Mycenae. Almost nothing, however, is known about Glas, save that it was once an island in Lake Kopaïs (drained late in the nineteenth century) and that it may have been an outpost of the Minyans. The **walls**, with their Cyclopean blocks and **city gates**, still stand to 4m in places, despite having been damaged when the city fell, and are almost 3km in circumference – the lazy can drive around them on a dirt track. The easiest entry is on the west side, along an ancient path starting from two abandoned guard-booths; once inside, there is almost nothing to see, as excavations have long been suspended and remains of a palace and agora are scarcely two masonry-courses high.

Directly north of Livadhiá, on the main road to Lamía, lies **Chaironeia**, once the home of the writer Plutarch, but more famous for one of the most **decisive battles** of ancient Greece. Here, in 338 BC, Philip of Macedon won a resounding victory over an alliance of Athenians, Thebans and Peloponnesians assembled by Demosthenes. This defeat marked the death of the old city-states, from whom control passed forever into foreign hands: first Macedonian, later Roman.

Set beside the road, at modern **Herónia**, is a six-metre-high **stone lion**, originally part of the funerary monument to the Thebans (or, some say, to the Macedonians) killed in the battle. Adjacent is a small **museum** of local finds;

like Glas, it might be a potential stop with your own transport, but not worth alighting a bus for.

The Oedipus crossroads, Ósios Loukás, Dhístomo and Aráhova

West from Livadhiá, the landscape becomes ever more striking as Mount Parnassós and its attendant peaks loom high above the road. After 22km, about halfway to Delphi, you reach the so-called **Schist** (Split) or **Triodos** (Triple Way) **crossroads**, which was the intersection of the ancient roads from Delphi, Daulis (today Dávlia), Thebes (Thíva) and Ambrossos (modern Dhístomo). The old road actually lay in the gorge, below the modern one.

Pausanias identified this crossroads as the site of Oedipus's murder of his father, King Laius of Thebes, and all but one of his retainers (who later, unwillingly, identifies Oedipus). According to myth, Oedipus was returning on foot from Delphi while Laius and his entourage were speeding towards him from the opposite direction on a chariot. Neither would give way, and in the altercation that followed Oedipus killed them, ignorant of who they were. It was to be, in the supreme understatement of Pausanias, "the beginning of his troubles". Continuing to Thebes, Oedipus solved the riddle of the Sphinx, which had been ravaging the area, and was given the hand of widowed Queen Iokaste in marriage – unaware that he was marrying his own mother.

Dhístomo

With your own transport, turn south at the crossroads and follow the minor road to **Dhístomo**, which has a couple of small, badly kept, unwelcoming **hotels** on the town square facing the church. Despite valiant attempts at beautification in its centre, Dhístomo remains a drab place, distinguished historically by one of the worst World War II **atrocities** in Greece: German occupying forces shot 232 of the inhabitants on June 10, 1944, looting and burning part of the village for good measure. The event is immortalized in a bleak grey-and-white **memorial**, erected in 1996 on a nearby hilltop – follow the signs to the marble-clad "mausoleum". On one plaque are the names of the victims; on two others apologetic sentiments from a German citizens' group and then-president, Roman Herzog. All this has not mollified the survivors a bit, who have pursued the current German government through court cases in Greece and Strasbourg for more monetary compensation than was paid by West Germany in the 1960s; in 2003, German assets in Athens (including the Goethe Institute) came within a whisker of being seized in lieu of blood money, and the case is still rumbling along, pending final adjudication.

Ósios Loukás monastery

Eight kilometres east of Dhístomo is the **monastery of Ósios Loukás**. Travelling by bus, you may need to take a more roundabout route: first from Livadhiá to Dhístomo, then another bus on from there towards Stíri and Kyriáki – getting off at the fork to Ósios Loukás, leaving just a 2.5-kilometre walk; alternatively, it's possible to hare a taxi in Dhístomo. The **monastery of Ósios Loukás** (daily: May to mid–Sept 8am–2pm & 4–7pm; mid–Sept to April 8am–5pm; €3) was a precursor of that last defiant flourish of **Byzantine art** that produced the great churches at Mystra in the Peloponnese. Although modest in scale, from an architectural or decorative point of view it ranks as one of the great buildings of medieval Greece. The setting, too, is exquisite – as beautiful as it is remote, especially in February when the many local almond trees are in bloom. As one approaches from Dhístomo, the monastery suddenly appears on its shady terrace, overlooking a spectacular sweep of the Elikónas mountain range and an intervening valley.

The main structure comprises two domed churches, the larger **katholikón** of Ósios Loukás and the adjacent chapel of **Theotókos**. They are joined by a common foundation wall but otherwise share few architectural features. Ten monks still live in the monastic buildings around the courtyard, but the monastery is essentially maintained as a museum, with snack and souvenir stalls in the grounds.

The katholikón

The **katholikón** (main church), built around 1040, is dedicated to a local beatified hermit, Luke of Stiri (not the Evangelist). Its design formed the basis of later churches at Dhafní and at Mystra. Externally it is modest, with rough brick-and-stone walls surmounted by a well-proportioned octagonal dome. The interior, however, is startling. Built to a conventional cross-in-square plan, its atmosphere switches from austere to exultant as the eye moves along walls lined in red, grey and green marble to the gold-backed mosaics on the high ceiling. Light filtering through marble-encrusted windows reflects across the curved surfaces of the mosaics in the nave and bounces onto the marble walls, bringing out the subtlety of their shades.

The **mosaics** were damaged by an earthquake in 1659, and in the dome and elsewhere have been replaced by unremarkable frescoes, but surviving examples testify to their glory. On the right as you enter the narthex are a majestic *Resurrection*, rivalled only by the version at Néa Moní on Híos (see p.914), and *Thomas Probing Christ's Wound*. The mosaic of the *Niptir* (*Washing of the Apostles' Feet*) on the far left (north side) of the narthex is one of the finest here; its theme is an especially human one, the expressions of the Apostles ranging between diffidence and surprise. This dynamic and richly humanized approach is again illustrated by the *Baptism*, high up in the naos, on the northwest squinch (the curved surface supporting the dome). Here the naked Jesus reaches for the cross amidst a swirling mass of water, an illusion of depth created by the angle and curvature of the wall. On other squinches, the Christ Child reaches out to the High Priest Simeon in *The Presentation*, while in *The Nativity*, angels predominate rather than the usual shepherds. The church's original **frescoes** are confined to the vaulted chambers at the corners of the cross plan and, though less imposing than the mosaics, employ subtle colours and shades, notably in *Christ Walking towards the Baptism*.

The Theotókos chapel and crypt

The chapel of **Theotókos** (literally "God-Bearing", meaning the Virgin Mary), built shortly after Luke's death, is thus nearly a century older than the *katholikón*. From the outside it overshadows the main church with its elaborate brick decoration culminating in a highly Eastern-influenced, marble-panelled drum. The interior seems gloomy and cramped by comparison, highlighted only by a couple of fine Corinthian capitals and an original floor mosaic, now dimmed by the passage of time.

Finally, do not miss the vivid frescoes in the **crypt** of the *katholikón*, entered on the lower right-hand (south) side of the building. It's a good idea to bring a torch, since illumination is limited to three spotlights to preserve the colours of the post-Byzantine frescoes.

Aráhova

Arriving at **ARÁHOVA**, the last town east of Delphi (just 11km further), you are well and truly in Parnassós country. The peaks stand tiered above, sullied somewhat by the wide asphalt road cut to a ski-resort – the winter-weekend haunt of well-heeled Athenians. Also of note is the local **festival of Áyios Yeóryios** (April 23, or the Mon after Easter if this date falls within Lent), centred on the church at the top of the hill, and one of the best opportunities to catch genuine folk dancing during almost two days of continuous partying.

Arrival and information

Buses use a stop on the platía at the west end of town (still dubbed "Xenías" after the eponymous, vanished, hotel) for both directions. A few paces away is a municipal **tourist office** (variable hours; ☎22670 29170, ⓦarachova.tripod.com), which can help on a number of matters including bus schedules. For more involved information, there's a small, central **bookshop/newsagent** with some foreign-language material. There are also four **bank** ATMs (two freestanding) in town.

Accommodation

In the summer, most people just stop for a meal and to souvenir-shop, so finding **accommodation** is easy, even though several establishments close down. In winter, particularly at weekends, rooms are at a premium in all senses, with prices bumped up at least two categories.

Apollon Main road, Livadhiá end of town ☎22670 31427. Acceptable budget hotel; rooms have views over the canyon and shared bathrooms. ❶
Apollon Inn Delphi end of town ☎22670 31057, ⓔapolloninn-arahova@united-hellas.com. Owned by the same people as *Apollon*, its pine-and-white tile en-suite rooms are plain but spacious. ❷
Lykoreia West edge of town ☎22670 32132. Good-sized rooms with standard hotel decor, common lounge with fireplace, "American style" buffet breakfast, easy (for Aráhova) parking. Summer ❺, winter ❼
Paradhosiakos Xenonas Maria Village centre, just up a pedestrian lane from through road ☎22670 31803, ⓕ22670 31069. One of Aráhova's two restoration inns, occupying a pair of lovely old buildings with an array of rustic-decor doubles, triples and quads. B&B summer ❸, winter ❺; family quads €75–150 by season.

🏃 **Xenonas Generali** Down stair-path at eastern outskirts, below the clocktower and

church ☎22670 31529, ⓦwww.generalis-xenon.com. Aráhova's "other" restoration inn, offering the best standard in town: nine very different, named rooms, most with fireplace; the decor in some can be too cute, but the welcome's warm and the breakfasts are unusually interesting. An indoor pool, spa, hamam and sauna are all popular with the après-ski set. B&B summer ❹, winter ❺ (midweek) ❼ (weekends)
Xenonas Petrino Village centre, south of the through road ☎22670 31384, ⓕ22670 32663. Small inn, built in 1999, with a basement breakfast salon; upstairs galleried rooms (sleeping four) are more exciting than the conventional ground-floor doubles. B&B summer ❸, winter ❺
Xenonas Ro Platía Xenías ☎22670 29180 or 697 76 18 994. Wood-floored rooms on the small side (except for the family suites), but tastefully appointed and some with balconies and views to the mountain. Summer ❸, winter ❺

The Town

Skiing aside, the town is appealing (if fairly desolate in summer), despite being split in two by the Livadhiá–Delphi road, and fairly comprehensive après-ski commercialization. If you're not making for any other mountain areas, Aráhova

3

Skiing on Parnassós

There are two main **skiing** areas developed on the northwest flank of Mount Para-nassós: Keláría (23km from Aráhova) and Fterólakka (29km). The top point for each is about 2200m, descending to 1600–1700m when conditions permit; the twenty or so runs are predominantly red-rated, making this a good intermediate resort, and served by fourteen lifts, of which about half are bubble-chair type as opposed to drag-lift. The preponderance of facilities (and the biggest car park) are at Keláría, but Fterólakka has longer, more challenging runs.

Equipment is rented on a daily basis at the resort, or for longer term in Aráhova (which teems with sports equipment shops). The resort's main problem is high winds, which often lead to lift closure, so check the forecast before you set off. The skiing season is generally from mid-December to April, though the pistes have operated into May several times in recent years.

---

is worth an afternoon's pause before continuing to Delphi; those with their own transport may prefer staying here, as opposed to modern Dhelfi village. A dwindling number of houses in Aráhova retain their vernacular architecture, flanking narrow lanes twisting north up the slope or poised to the south on the edge of the olive-tree-choked Plistós gorge. The area is renowned for its strong purplish wines, honey, candied fruits and nuts, cheese (especially cylindrical *formaélla*), the novelty noodles called *hilopíttes*, *tsípouro* and woollen weavings; all are much in evidence in the roadside shops, though most of the woven goods are now imported from northern Greece and/or machine-loomed.

Eating and drinking

During summer, a good fifty percent of Aráhova's eateries close down, but numerous state-of-the-art bars, music clubs (especially around the taxi square) and sweet shops continue to serve the trendy local youth as well as visiting Athenians. As testimony to the village's dual personality, the *kafenío* and ouzerí tables on the main fountain-square attract an older crowd, remaining packed until late. Reliably good and usually open **tavernas** include meat-strong *Dhasaryiris* (closed Aug), on the through road; *To Kalderimi*, downhill from *Dhasaryiris*, with high-quality traditional cuisine; and *Panayiota* (closed May–July), way up the steps by Áyios Yeóryios church, offering more upmarket takes on local recipes. For milk-based sweets, there's *Galaktopolio En Arahovi*, up the steps from the main fountain-plátia, with indoor and outdoor seating.

Delphi (Dhelfí)

With its site raised on the slopes of a high mountain terrace and dwarfed on either side by the ominous crags of Parnassós, it's easy to see why the ancients believed **DELPHI** to be the centre of the earth. But more than the natural setting or even the occasional earthquake and avalanche were needed to confirm a divine presence. This, according to Plutarch, was achieved through the discovery of a rock chasm that exuded strange vapours and reduced all comers to frenzied, incoherent and undoubtedly **prophetic** mutterings.

The oracle: some history

The **first oracle** established on this spot was dedicated to Gaia ("Mother Earth")

△ The Tholos, Delphi

and to Poseidon ("the Earth Shaker"). The serpent Python, son of Gaia, was installed in a nearby cave, and communication made through the Pythian priestess. Python was subsequently slain by Apollo, whose cult had been imported from Crete (legend stated that he arrived in the form of a dolphin – hence the name Delphoi). The **Pythian Games** were established on an eight-year cycle to commemorate the feat, and perhaps also to placate the deposed deities.

The place was known to the **Mycenaeans**, whose votive offerings (tiny striped statues of goddesses and worshipping women) have been discovered near the site of Apollo's temple. Following the arrival of the **Dorians** in Greece at the beginning of the twelfth century BC, the sanctuary became the centre of the loose-knit association of Greek city-states known as the **Amphyctionic League**. The territory still belonged, however, to the nearby city of Krissa, which, as the oracle gained in popularity, began to extort heavy dues from the pilgrims arriving at the port of Kirrha (near modern Itéa). In the sixth century BC the League was called on to intervene, and the first of a series of **Sacred Wars** broke out. The League wrested Delphi from the Krissaeans and made it an autonomous state. From then on Delphi experienced a rapid ascent to fame and respect, becoming within a few decades one of the major sanctuaries of Greece, with its tried and tested oracle generally thought to be the arbiter of truth.

For over a thousand years thereafter, a steady stream of **pilgrims** made its way up the dangerous mountain paths to seek divine direction in matters of war, worship, love or business. On arrival they would sacrifice a sheep or a goat and, depending on the omens, wait to submit questions inscribed on lead tablets. The Pythian priestess, a simple and devout village woman of fifty or more years in age, would chant her prophecies from a tripod positioned over the oracular chasm. Crucially, an attendant priest would then "interpret" her utterings and relay them to the enquirer in hexameter verse.

Many of the **oracular answers** were studiously ambiguous: Croesus, for example, was told that if he embarked on war against neighbouring Persia he would destroy a mighty empire; he did – his own. But it's hard to imagine that the oracle would have retained its popularity and influence for so long without offering predominantly sound advice. Indeed, Strabo wrote that "of all oracles in the world, it had the reputation of being the most truthful." One explanation is that the Delphic priests were simply better informed than any other corporate body around at the time. Positioned at the centre of the Amphyctionic League, which became a kind of "United Nations" of the Greek city-states, they were in a position to amass a wealth of political, economic and social information and, from the seventh century BC onwards, Delphi had its own network of agents throughout the Greek world.

The **influence** of the oracle spread abroad with the Classical age of colonization and its patronage grew, reaching a peak in the sixth century BC, with powerful benefactors such as Amasis, King of Egypt, and the unfortunate King Croesus of Lydia; many of the Greek city-states also dedicated treasuries at this time. Privileged position and enormous wealth, however, made Delphi vulnerable to Greek rivalries; the first Sacred Wars left it autonomous, but in the fifth century BC the oracle began to be too closely identified with individual states. Worse, it maintained a defeatist, almost treacherous, attitude towards the Persian invasions – only partially mitigated when a Persian force, sent by Xerxes to raid Delphi, was crushed at the entrance to the sanctuary by a well-timed earthquake.

It never quite regained the same level of trust – and consequently of power – after these instances of bias and corruption. However, real **decline** did not set in until the fourth century BC, with the resumption of the Sacred Wars and the emergence of Macedonian control. Following prolonged squabbling among the Greek city-states, the sanctuary was seized by the Phokians in 355 BC, leading to Philip of Macedon's intervention to restore the Amphyctionic League to power. Seven years later, when the League again invited Philip to settle a dispute, this time provoked by the Amphissans, he responded by invading southern Greece. The independence of the city-states was brought to an end at the Battle of Chaironeia, and Delphi's political intriguing was effectively over.

Under **Macedonian** and later **Roman** control, the oracle's role became increasingly domestic and insignificant, dispensing advice on marriages, loans, voyages and the like. The Romans thought little of its utterances, rather more of its treasure: Sulla plundered the sanctuary in 86 BC and Nero, outraged when the oracle denounced him for the murder of his mother, carted away some five hundred bronze statues. Finally, with the proscription of paganism by Theodosius late in the fourth century AD, the oracle became defunct.

In modern times, the sanctuary site was rediscovered towards the end of the seventeenth century and explored haphazardly from the 1840s onwards. Real **excavation** of the site began only in 1892 when the French School of Archeology leased the land, in exchange for a French government agreement to buy the Greek currant crop. There was initially little to be seen other than the outline of a stadium and theatre, but the land was expropriated with a sizeable loan from the French parliament, and the villagers living on it were persuaded (with the help of an army detachment) to move to a new town 1km west, and digging commenced. Over the next decade or so, most of the excavations and reconstruction visible today were completed.

The most interesting development in Delphi's recent history came through the efforts of the poet Angelos Sikelianos and his (first) American wife Eva Palmer to set up a "University of the World" in the 1920s. The project eventually failed, though it inspired an annual **Delphic Festival**, held now in July of each year, with performances of contemporary drama and music in the ancient theatre.

The sites

Split by the road from Aráhova, the ancient site divides essentially into three parts: the **Sacred Precinct**, the **Marmaria** and the **Castalian spring**. In addition there is a worthwhile **museum**, which reopened in 2004 after a complete refurbishment. All in all, Delphi is a large and complex ruin, best taken in two stages, with the sanctuary ideally at the beginning or end of the day, or (in winter) at lunchtime, to escape the coached-in crowds. Make sure you have sturdy footwear as there's a lot of clambering up rough stone steps and paths, and take food and drink if you're planning a full day's visit; good **picnicking** spots are the theatre with its panorama of the sanctuary (its seats, alas, off limits), or try the stadium for fewer interruptions.

The Sacred Precinct

The **Sacred Precinct** (daily: summer 8.30am–6.45pm; winter 8am–5pm; €9 joint ticket with museum), or Temenos (Sanctuary) of Apollo, is entered, as in ancient times, by way of a small **agora** enclosed by ruins of Roman porticoes and shops for the sale of votive offerings. The paved **Sacred Way** begins after a few stairs, and zigzags uphill between the foundations of memorials and treasuries to the Temple of Apollo. Along each edge is a jumble of statue bases where gold, bronze and painted-marble figures once stood; Pliny counted more than three thousand on his visit, and that was after Nero's infamous raid.

The choice and position of these **memorials** were dictated by more than religious zeal; many were used as a deliberate show of strength or as a direct insult against a rival Greek state. For instance, the **Offering of the Arcadians** on the right of the entrance (a line of bases that supported nine bronzes) was erected to commemorate their invasion of Laconia in 369 BC, and pointedly placed in front of the Lacedaemonians' own monument. Besides this, and following the same logic, the Spartans celebrated their victory over Athens by erecting their **Monument of the Admirals** – a large recessed structure, which once held 37 bronze statues of gods and generals – directly opposite the Athenians' **Offering of Marathon**.

Further up the path, past the Doric remains of the **Sikyonian Treasury** on the left, stretch the expansive foundations of the **Siphnian Treasury**, a

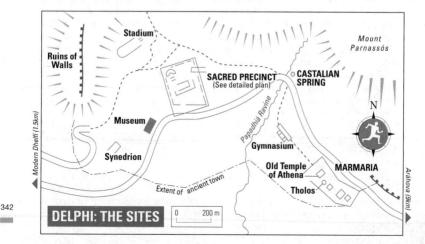

DELPHI: THE SITES — 0 — 200 m

grandiose Ionic temple erected in 525 BC. Ancient Siphnos had rich gold mines and intended the building to be an unrivalled show of opulence. Fragments of the caryatids that supported its west entrance, and the fine Parian marble frieze that adorned all four sides, are now in the museum. Above this is the **Treasury of the Athenians**, built, like the city's "offering", after Marathon (490 BC). It was reconstructed in 1904–1906 by matching the inscriptions that completely cover its blocks. These include honorific decrees in favour of Athens, lists of Athenian ambassadors to the Pythian Festival and a hymn to Apollo with its musical notation in Greek letters above the text.

Next to the Treasury are the foundations of the **Bouleuterion**, or council house, a reminder that Delphi needed administrators, and above sprawls the remarkable **Polygonal Wall** whose irregular interlocking blocks have withstood, intact, all earthquakes. It, too, is covered with inscriptions, but these almost universally refer to the emancipation of slaves; Delphi was one of the few places where such freedom could be made official and public by an inscribed register. An incongruous outcrop of rock between the wall and the treasuries marks the original **Sanctuary of Gaia**. It was here, or more precisely on the recently built-up rock, that the Sibyl, an early itinerant priestess, was reputed to have uttered her prophecies.

Finally, the Sacred Way leads past the **Athenian Stoa** (which housed trophies from an Athenian naval victory of 506 BC) to the temple terrace where you are confronted with a large altar, erected by the island of Chios (Híos). Of the main body of the **Temple of Apollo**, only the foundations stood when it was uncovered by the French. Six Doric columns have since been re-erected, giving a vertical line to the ruins and providing some idea of the temple's former dominance over the whole of the sanctuary. In the innermost part of the temple was the *adyton*, a dark cell at the mouth of the oracular chasm where the Pythian priestess would officiate. No sign of cave or chasm has been found, nor any vapours that might have induced a trance, but it is likely that such a chasm did exist and was simply opened and closed by successive earthquakes. On the architrave of the temple – probably on the interior – were inscribed the maxims "Know Thyself" and "Moderation in All Things".

The theatre and stadium used for the main events of the Pythian Festival lie on terraces above the temple. The **theatre**, built in the fourth century BC with a capacity of five thousand, was closely connected with Dionysos, the god of ecstasy, the arts and wine, who reigned in Delphi over the winter months when the oracle was silent. A path leads up through cool pine groves to the **stadium**, a steep and longish walk which discourages some people. Its site was artificially levelled in the fifth century BC, though it was banked with stone seats (giving a capacity of seven thousand) only in Roman times – the gift, like so many other public buildings in Greece, of Herodes Atticus. For even greater solitude, climb up above to the pine trees that have engulfed the remains of the fourth-century BC walls.

The museum

Delphi's **museum** (daily: summer 8am–6.45pm; winter 8.30am–2.45pm; included in site ticket) contains a rare and exquisite collection of sculpture spanning the Archaic to the Roman eras, matched only by finds on Athens' Acropolis. It features pottery, bronze articles and friezes from the various treasuries and temple pediments, which, grouped together, give a good picture of the sanctuary's riches. Following its refit, the museum's lighting and labelling is exemplary throughout.

The most famous exhibit, with a room to itself at the south end of the galleries, is the **Charioteer**, one of the few surviving bronzes of the fifth century BC, unearthed in 1896 as part of the "Offering of Polyzalos", which probably

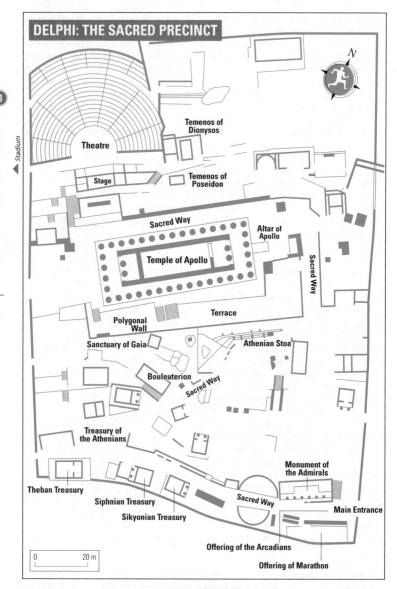

DELPHI: THE SACRED PRECINCT

N

◀ *Stadium*

Temenos of Dionysos

Theatre

Stage

Temenos of Poseidon

Sacred Way

Altar of Apollo

Temple of Apollo

Sacred Way

Terrace

Polygonal Wall

Sanctuary of Gaia

Athenian Stoa

Bouleuterion

Sacred Way

Treasury of the Athenians

Monument of the Admirals

Theban Treasury

Siphnian Treasury

Sikyonian Treasury

Sacred Way

Main Entrance

Offering of the Arcadians

Offering of Marathon

0   20 m

toppled during the earthquake of 373 BC. The charioteer's eyes, made of onyx and set slightly askew, lend it a startling realism, while the demure expression suggests a victory lap. It is thought that the odd proportions of the body – the torso seems far too abbreviated when seen straight on – were designed by the sculptor with perspective in mind; they would be "corrected" when the figure was viewed, as intended, from below.

Other major pieces include two huge **kouroi** from the sixth century BC, betraying – like so many of this genre – clear Asiatic/Egyptian stylistic traits; a life-size, sixth-century BC votive **bull** fashioned from hammered silver and copper sheeting; and an elegant Ionic winged **Sphinx of the Naxians**, dating from 565 BC. Other notable works of the same period include two lion-spouted marble rain gutters from the Temple of Apollo, as well as bronze *protomes* or **griffin heads**, used extensively during Archaic times on the edge of cauldrons. Large chunks of the beautiful and meticulously carved **Siphnian frieze**, in the same northernmost gallery as the Naxian sphinx, depict Zeus and other gods looking on as the Homeric heroes fight over the body of Patroclus, as well as Hercules (Herakles) and Apollo engaged in a tug-of-war over an oracular tripod. Another portion of this frieze shows a battle between gods and giants, including a lion graphically mauling a warrior.

The **Athenian Treasury** (490 BC) is represented by fragments of the metopes (frieze) which depict the labours of Hercules, the adventures of Theseus and a battle with Amazons. A group of three colossal if badly damaged **dancing women**, carved from Pentelic marble around an acanthus-topped column, probably a tripod-stand, dates from the fourth century BC and is now thought to represent the daughters of Kekrops. Among later works is an exquisite second-century AD figure of **Antinoös**, favourite of Roman emperor Hadrian.

The Castalian spring

Following the road east of the sanctuary, towards Aráhova, you reach a sharp bend. To the left, marked by niches for votive offerings and by the remains of an Archaic fountain house, the celebrated **Castalian spring** still flows from a cleft in the Phaedriades cliffs.

Visitors to Delphi (only men were allowed during the early centuries) were obliged to purify themselves in its waters, usually by washing their hair, though murderers had to take the full plunge. **Lord Byron**, impressed by the legend that it nurtured poetic inspiration, also jumped in. This is no longer possible, since the spring is fenced off owing to sporadic rock falls from the Phaedriades cliffs.

The Marmaria

Across and below the road from the spring is the **Marmaria** (same hours as main sanctuary; free), or Sanctuary of Athena, whom the Delphians worshipped as Athena Pronaia ("Guardian of the Temple"); *marmariá* means "marble quarry" and derives from the medieval practice of filching the ancient blocks for private use.

The most conspicuous building in the precinct, and the first visible from the road, is the **Tholos**, a fourth-century BC rotunda. Three of its dome-columns and their entablature have been set up, but while these amply demonstrate the original beauty of the building (which is *the* postcard image of Delphi), its purpose remains a mystery.

At the entrance to the sanctuary stood the **Old Temple of Athena**, destroyed by the Persians and rebuilt in the Doric order during the fourth century BC; foundations of both structures can be traced. Outside the precinct on the northwest side (above the Marmaria) is a **gymnasium**, again built in the fourth century BC, but later enlarged by the Romans who added a running track on the now collapsed terrace; prominent among the ruins is a circular plunge-bath which, filled with cold water, served to refresh the athletes after their exertions.

Modern Dhelfí

Modern Dhelfí is as inconsequential as its ancient namesake, 1500m to the east, is impressive. Entirely geared to tourism (including Greek skiers), its attraction lies in its mountain setting, proximity to the ruins and access to Mount Parnassós (see opposite).

There is a single **bus terminal**, located at the Itéa (west) end of town, where the upper and lower commercial streets link up. Westbound buses go to Ámfissa (from where you can pick up connections north), Itéa and (usually with a change) Náfpaktos, while eastbound services go to Aráhova, Livadhiá or Athens. The main difficulty, since all coaches originate elsewhere, is that seats allocated for the Dhelfí ticket booth are limited and they sell out some hours in advance. If you're going to be stuck standing all the way to Athens, it's better to get off at Livadhiá and continue by train. Bus timetables are available from the helpful **tourist office** (Mon–Fri 8am–2.30pm; ☎22650 82900) in the town hall on the lower main thoroughfare. Other amenities, again along the lower main street, include several **banks** (with ATMs), a **post office**, and a number of bar-cafés, at least one of which will be offering **Internet access**.

Accommodation

Accommodation is plentiful if not always especially good value, with the fancier hotels often block-booked by coach tours; like most Greek site villages, Dhelfí has a quick turnaround of visitors and, with over twenty hotels and pensions, finding an actual vacancy should present few problems. However, there is no set peak season – indeed winter weekends can see top rates charged, courtesy of the ski-trade spillover from Aráhova (see p.338) – so scope for bargaining depends on current traffic. As an alternative to Dhelfí or Aráhova, you might consider **KHRISSÓ** village, 13km downhill towards the gulf; it's far less touristy, with considerable character in its centre where there's at least one **inn** (☎22650 83220; ❸) and a couple of **tavernas** under the plane trees, the more popular being *Fourla* (eves only except summer).

There are three **campsites** in the immediate area. Closest is *Camping Apollon* (☎22650 82762; May–Sept), alongside the road to Ámfissa/Itéa and less than 1km west of Dhelfí, with a pool, restaurant and more caravan space than tenting turf; out of season you'll have to continue to *Camping Delphi* (☎22650 82475; March to mid-Nov), 3km further along the same road, just above Khrissó. The third option is *Camping Chrissa* (☎22650 82050; all year), 12km from Dhelfí at the west edge of Khrissó.

Acropole Fillellínon 13 ☎22650 82675, ☎22650 83 171. On the quietest, lowest street of the village, this hotel's no architectural marvel but the rooms are adequate, with unbeatable views from the rear ones over the Plistós gorge. ❹

Athina Pávlou ké Fredheríkis 55 ☎22650 82239 or 697 38 81 509, ☎22650 82239. Near the bus station at the Itéa (west) end of town, this hotel has wood decor, well-kept if smallish rooms, mostly en suite, and views of the gulf from rear units. Closed Nov–Christmas and weekdays Christmas–end March. B&B ❷

Odysseus Pension Iséa 1, cnr Fillellínon, the street below and parallel to Pávlou ké Fredheríkis ☎22650 82235. Spartan 1970s rooms with shared bathrooms, but this is perhaps the quietest spot in town, with a flowered terrace for unobstructed views. ❶

Orfeas Ifiyenías Syngroú 35 ☎22650 82077. Rooms are all spacious and well maintained, the top floor redone in 2003, with superb views and air conditioning. Better-than-average parking chances, fifteen percent discount to Rough Guide readers. B&B ❸

Pan Pávlou ké Fredheríkis 53 ☎22650 82294, ☎22650 83244. Adequate and comfortable with fine views of the gulf; the best, newest rooms, sleeping four, are in the attic. Immediately opposite is their annexe, the 2002-built *Artemis*, whose doubles equal the standard of the family quads

(including tubs in the bathrooms), but you sacrifice views. ❸–❹
Sivylla Pávlou ké Fredheríkis 9 ☎ 22650 82335, ✉ sibydel@otenet.gr. Slightly distressed fittings in the small-to-medium-sized en-suite rooms, but they do have fans and balconies overlooking the gorge. ❷

Sun View Pension Apóllonos 84, far west end of upper commercial street, near *Amalia Hotel* ☎ 22650 82349, ✉ dkalentzis@internet.gr. Fair-sized rooms in pastel colours with wall art; rear-facing ones are a bit dark. Pleasant, four-table breakfast area on the ground floor; easy parking adjacent. B&B ❸

Eating and drinking

Eating out is not a Dhelfí strong point, despite the winter Athenian-skier custom; the three much-promoted "traditional" tavernas are far too uneven to merit consideration. Better choices include *Iy Skala*, up steps from nearby hotel Sivylla, for cheap and honest fare, or *Garganduas* at the west end of town by the BP petrol station, moved to new premises and gone more upmarket in 2004, but still affordable. Another good-value carnivorous option – though open September to June only – is *Hasapotaverna Panagakos*, opposite the *Athina* hotel.

Mount Parnassós

For a taste of the Greek alpine scene, **Parnassós** is probably the most convenient peak in the land, though its heights no longer rank as unspoilt wilderness, having been disfigured by the ski-station above Aráhova and its accompanying parapher-nalia of lifts, snack-bars and access roads. The best routes for walkers are those up from Dhelfí to the **Corycian cave** (practicable from April to Nov, but not in midsummer without a dawn start), or the more strenuous **Liákoura summit ascent** (May to Oct only). Those with their own transport can take advantage of a ride along surfaced roads up the mountain from Aráhova on the south, or Lílea, Polýdhrosos or Amfíklia on the north slope, any of which could easily be combined with a walk. For extended explorations, Road Editions' 1:50,000 **map** no. 42, *Parnassos*, or Anavasi Editions' 1:55,000 map no. 1, also entitled *Parnassos*, are wise investments, though neither is infallible; an attached booklet in the Road Editions' map summarizes a slightly alternative route to the Corycian cave.

Dhelfí to the Corycian cave

You'll need to allow a full day for the outing – the ascent to the cave takes four hours, descending to Dhelfí takes slightly less time – and take ample food. To reach the **trailhead** for this walk – and the initial path up the mountain – take the right-hand (approaching from Athens), uphill street through Dhelfí village, officially Apóllonos. At the top of the slope, by the church, turn right onto a road that doubles back to the **museum-house** (daily except Tues 9am–3pm; €2) where the poet **Angelos Sikelianos** once lived – look for the bust of him outside, and the grave of his first wife, Eva Palmer. The exhibits mostly concern the revived Delphic Festivals the couple organized in 1927–30.

Continue climbing from here, with more zigzags along a gravel surface, until you reach the highest point of the fence enclosing the sanctuary ruins. Where the track ends at a gate, don't go into the site, but adopt a trail on your left, initially marked by a black-and-yellow rectangle on a white background. From the top of the hill the trail continues, well marked by more black-on-yellow metal diamonds: it's part of the **E4 European long-distance trail**. Initially steep, the way soon flattens out on a grassy knoll overlooking the stadium, and continues along a ridge next to a line of burned cypresses.

Soon after, you join up with an ancient cobbled trail coming from inside the fenced precinct, the **Kakí Skála**, which zigzags up the slope above you in broad arcs. The view from here is fantastic, stretching back over the Gulf of Kórinthos to the mountains of the Peloponnese. The cobbles end near two concrete inspection covers in Dhelfi's water supply, an hour-plus above the village, at the top of the Phaedriades cliffs. Nearby stand some rock pinnacles, from one of which those guilty of sacrilege in ancient times were thrown to their deaths – a custom perhaps giving rise to the name Kakí Skála or "Evil Stairway".

E4 markers remain visible in the valley that opens out ahead of you. You can get simultaneous views south, and northeast towards the Parnassan summits, by detouring a little to the left to a wooden hut and a barn, then to a slight rise perhaps 150m further. The principal route becomes a gravel track bearing northeast and still marked by E4 diamonds; forsake this and follow instead a metal sign pointing toward the cave, by taking the right fork near the Krokí spring and watering troughs, with a fenced-in complex of summer cottages on your right. This track passes a picnic ground and a chapel of Ayía Paraskeví within the next fifteen minutes, and acquires intermittent paved surface. Continue along this track for some forty minutes beyond the chapel, heading gently downhill and passing another sign for the cave, until you emerge from the fir woods (a bit over 2hr 30min from Dhelfi) with a view east and ahead to the rounded mass of the Yerondóvrahos peak (2367m) of the Parnassós massif.

The Corycian cave (Korýkio Ándro)

Another fifteen minutes bring you to a spring, followed by another chapel (of Ayía Triádha) on the left, with a spring and picnic ground. To the left rises a steep ridge, on whose flank lies the ancient **Corycian cave**, in Greek the Korýkio Ándro. Ignore the Greek-only sign just behind the chapel, which indicates a dangerous and disused old trail, and persevere along the road for about five more minutes to where a white bilingual sign points to a newer path, marked by orange paint splodges and red-triangle signs. After a forty-minute scramble up the slope, you meet another dirt road; turn left and follow it five minutes more to the end, about 10m below the conspicuous cave mouth at an altitude of 1370m.

The cave was sacred to Pan and the nymphs in ancient times, the presiding deities of Delphi during the winter months when Apollo was said to desert the oracle. Orgiastic rites were celebrated in November at the cave by women acting as the nymphs, who made the long hike up from Delphi on the Kakí Skála by torchlight. The cavern itself is chilly and forbidding, but if you look carefully with a torch you can find ancient inscriptions near the entrance; without artificial light you can't see more than 100m inside. By the entrance you'll notice a rock with a man-made circular indentation – possibly an ancient altar to hold libations.

The marked E4 route, on the other hand, continues almost due north – more on track than on path, it must be said – to the large village of **EPTÁLOFOS**, a full day's walk from Dhelfi on the Aráhova–Lílea–Graviá paved road. This, just below the forest with sweeping views north, is a popular Greek "hill station" and a prominent staging point on the E4; accordingly, there are a half-dozen **places to stay**, including the hotel *Panorama* (T 22340 61302; ❸) or the *Mavrodhimos* rooms (T 22340 61309; ❸), plus lots of **psistariés** around the plane-shaded platía.

Liákoura summit

Liákoura is Parnassós's highest and finest peak (2457m) and can be approached either from the Delphi/Aráhova side or from the northeastern foothills of the mountain. The latter is the best walk, starting from **Tithoréa**, but it involves taking a bus or train and then local taxi to the trailhead – plus probably camping out on the mountain. If you want a more casual look at Parnassós, it's probably better to walk up from the **Dhelfí side**, as a continuation of the Corycian cave outing, staying overnight at the hamlet of **Kalývia** on the Livádhi plateau, some 45 minutes' walk beyond the cave. Here there are numerous chalet-hotels for skiers and a number of tavernas, some of them shut during summer.

For the energetic, it's possible to traverse the whole massif in a single long day's walk, with a dawn start from **ZEMENÓ**, between Aráhova and the Trio-dos of Oedipus, and descending to Áno Tithoréa, or vice versa. From Zemenó, which has two affordable roadside **hotel-restaurants**, a trail marked initially as part of local path 22 ascends 1200m to Baïtanórahi and then the pass known as Sidheróporta before joining the route up from Tithoréa (see below). It is wisest, however, to take a day's food, two litres of water per person and basic bivouacking supplies, as bad weather can descend without warning, springs are poorly spaced, and the alpine shelters near the summit are either locked unless prearranged, or very primitive.

Tithoréa to Liákoura via the Velítsa ravine

The principal surviving wilderness route up Parnassós to Liákoura involves starting with a trip by train or bus as far as Káto Tithoréa, which is on the Livadhiá–Amfiklia road and the Athens–Thessaloníki railway. You then need to get to the higher village of **TITHORÉA**, a six-kilometre haul easiest accomplished by taxi. You should allow at least six hours for the ascent with a day-pack, and around four and a half hours for the descent, so it's best to set out early in the day (all times given are from Tithoréa). The village itself is a beauty, with stone houses interspersed with patches of **ancient wall** (including an elaborate tower) and the little chapel of Áyios Ioánnis Theológos, containing an exquisite **Paleochristian mosaic** under glass (illuminated on entry). There are plenty of **tavernas** off the scenic platía, though only one confirmed **rooms** establishment, the *Tithorea* at the outskirts approaching from downhill (☎22340 71021; ❸).

From Tithoréa's main platía, head southwest past a church with a few graves adjacent, and the secondary Platía Andhroútsou (with a bust of the Greek Revolutionary figure it is named after, who had a hideout nearby). Continue up a flagstoned lane, past the last houses, towards the first red-on-white painted-diamond waymark, beyond which is a flagstoned, half-circular platía with a plane tree, fountain and cement *proskynitário*, overlooking the giant **Velítsa ravine**. The flagstoned path continues perhaps 20m, but then hairpins up and right; you – and the waymarks – adopt a now-dirt path descending briefly towards the bed of the canyon. Cross the remains of a cement aqueduct to the far side, and less than an hour along you'll reach the isolated chapel of Áyios Ioánnis.

Past the chapel, a fine alpine path heads off through the firs in front of you. The way is obvious for the next ninety minutes, with tremendous views of the crags filing up to the Liákoura summit on your right across the valley. You emerge onto a narrow neck of land, the ridge of Askí, with a brief glimpse over the Ayía Marína valley and a monastery of Kímisis Theotókou to the east (left) – as well as a dirt track which nearly meets your route. The path, faint for an interval, heads slightly downhill and to the right to meet the floor of the Velítsa at the Tsáres spring (3hr 30min) – it's the last reliable water supply.

On the far bank of the river, head up a steep, scree-laden slope through the last of the trees to some sheep pens (4hr), then climb up to another pastoral hut (4hr 30min) at the base of the defile leading down from the main summit ridge. Beyond this point the going is gentler for much of the final ascent to the northwest (top right-hand) corner of this valley. A brief scramble up a rockfall to a gap in the ridge and you are at the base of Liákoura (5hr 30min). Orange paint-splashes – primarily oriented for those descending – stake out most of the approach from the Tsáres spring.

The **final ascent** is an easy twenty-minute scramble more or less up to the ridge line. On a clear day, especially after rain, you're supposed to be able to see Mount Olympus in the north, the Aegean to the east, the Ionian to the west and way down into the Peloponnese to the south.

Along the gulf: Itéa to Náfpaktos

The train-less, almost beach-less north shore of the **Gulf of Kórinthos** is far less frequented than the south coast. The arid landscape, with harsh mountains inland, can be initially off-putting, but there are patches of cultivated valley and coastal plain, and attractive, low-key resorts in **Galaxídhi** and **Náfpaktos**, both well connected by bus. This coast also offers convenient access south to the Peloponnese, via car-ferries at Áyios Nikólaos–Éyio and Andírio–Río, the latter straits also spanned by a futuristic bridge completed in 2004. At either Éyio and Río, you are on the main rail and road routes between Kórinthos and Pátra.

All buses heading southwest of Delphi towards the Gulf of Kórinthos stop first at Itéa, where you may have to change buses for the next leg of the journey. **ITÉA** is more pleasant than the purplish-red bauxite tailings piled at the outskirts would suggest, with two **hotels** and a half-dozen **tavernas** on the seafront; the adjacent *Park* or *Skala* at mid-front are both perfectly acceptable for an inexpensive seafood meal.

Galaxídhi

GALAXÍDHI, a quiet port rearing mirage-like out of an otherwise lifeless shore 17km southwest of Itéa, is the first place you'd probably choose to break a journey. Amazingly, Galaxídhi was once one of Greece's major harbours, with a fleet of over four hundred two- and three-masted *kaïkia* and schooners, built alongside **Hirólakkas** anchorage, north of the headland, which traded as far afield as the UK. But shipowners failed to convert to steam power after 1890, and the town's prosperity vanished. Clusters of nineteenth-century shipowners' mansions, reminders of those heady days, don't match the rest of Fokídha province architecturally, but reflect borrowings from Venice, testament to the sea-captains' far-flung travels. Lately they've become the haunt of Athenian second-homers, but despite their restorations and a bit of a marina ethos down at the main southeasterly harbour, the town still remains just the right side of tweeness, with an animated commercial high street and a good range of places to eat and drink.

Arrival, information and accommodation

Buses call at the landscaped, central Platía Iróön, with KTEL offices inside the *Kourdhisto Portokali* café; Galaxídhi is large enough to support a **post office** and a **bank** (ATM).

Accommodation is on the pricey side and hard to find in summer, or at weekends year-round, though all of it is en suite and usually air conditioned. Most of the recommendable outfits are housed in converted seafarers' mansions.

Arhondiko ℗22650 42292. Newly built complex in a secluded spot beyond Hirólakkas with easy parking, partial sea-views, themed mock-traditional rooms (including one with a mirrored ceiling) and self-catering breakfast facilities. ⑤

Galaxa ℗22650 41620, ℗22650 42053. Somewhat casually run hillside hotel on the west shore of Hirólakkas with private parking; most of the rooms have some sort of water view, all have blue-and-white decor and small baths. Manolis, your genial host, presides over the popular garden-bar where breakfast is served. B&B ⑥

Ganimede/Ganymidis Southwest market street ℗22650 41328 ⓦwww.ganimede.gr. Under the energetic management of the Papalexis family since 2004, who have thoroughly overhauled the units, this remains the clear winner amongst local top-flight outfits. There are six doubles in the old house (best is no. 1) and a family suite with loft and fireplace across the courtyard-garden where a copious breakfast is served, still featuring founder Bruno's exquisite recipes for pâtés and jams. B&B ⑤

Hirolakas ℗22650 41170, ℗ 22650 41371. A mix of standard doubles, studios and family suites, with fridge, air conditioning and TV, at this pension set just back from the water. Fairly easy street parking. ❸

Poseidon Two blocks uphill from harbour ℗22650 41426. Dead-central and thus potentially noisy budget hotel; wood-floored rooms are en suite but a bit creaky. ❸

Votsalo Pension ℗22650 41788 or 697 79 94 227. Just three en-suite rooms on the east shore of Hirólakkas, with air conditioning/heating, in a refurbished 1861 house; minimal breakfast arrangements in the common room. ❸

The Town

The old town stands on a raised headland, crowned by the eighteenth-century church of Ayía Paraskeví (the old, basilica-like one, not the more obvious belfried Áyios Nikólaos, patron saint of sailors). With its protected double harbour, the place proved irresistible to early settlers, and thus you see stretches of Pelasgian walls – all that's left of **ancient Chaleion** and its successor **Oianthe** – between the two churches and the water on the headland dividing the two anchorages. What you see dates from 1830–70, as the town was largely destroyed during the War of Independence.

Just uphill from the main harbour is the 2005-opened **Nautical and Historical Museum** (daily: July–Sept 10.10am–1.30pm & 5.30–8.30pm; Oct–May 10.10am–4.15pm; €5), whose galleries do a well-labelled, clockwise gallop

△ Galaxídhi

(including a trip to the basement) of this citadel-settlement in all eras. Ancient Chaleion is represented by engaging painted pottery and a bronze folding mirror, then it's on to the chronicles of Galaxídhi – as the place was known from Byzantine times onwards – at its peak supporting a half-dozen shipyards, mostly alongside the northerly Hirólakkas anchorage. The local two- and three-masters are followed from their birth – primitive, fascinating ship-building and sail-making tools – to their all-too-often sudden violent death. Along the way are propeller-operated "harpoon" logs, wooden rattles to signal the change of watches, a *bouroú* or large shell used as a foghorn and – best of all – superb polychrome figureheads.

If you stroll or drive around the pine-covered headland flanking the southeastern harbour, you'll find tiny pebbly **coves** where most people swim (accessed by steps from the narrow road), with chapel-crowned islets offshore. The closest "real" beaches are at the end of this road, or at **Kalafátis** just north of town, though neither is brilliant – harsh shingle underfoot and occasionally turbid water.

Eating and drinking

Tavernas, mostly on the southeasterly quay (Iánthi), are generally adequate, though an obvious cluster at the head of the port are overpriced and worth avoiding. An exception to this rule here, one block inland, is the very good and inexpensive seafood ouzerí *To Maïstrali*, with all the usual (fried) standards. The only other budget choice is friendly 🎋 *Albatross*, inland on the street between the two churches, which has well-executed *mayireftá* from a short daily menu which might stretch to octopus, spinach/cheese pie, rabbit stew, pale taramosaláta and the house speciality *samári* (pancetta in savoury sauce). On the water, *Anamniseis ap' ta Limania* is the best attended mid-range taverna, while *Barko Maritsa* (weekends only in winter, daily otherwise) near the far northeastern end of the esplanade features savoury, non-greasy *píttes* and an approximation of seafood risotto – allow €20 a head with bulk wine. For those with a sweet tooth, there are an improbable number of oriental pastry shops on the street linking Platía Iróön with the main harbour.

As for **nightlife**, a half-dozen bars along the quay cater to sophisticated Athenian forty- and fifty-somethings. Beyond traces of the ancient walls, *Ocean Drive* incorporates a sand-strewn lido, while *Oianthe* nestles below the pines across the harbour. The only establishment at Hirólakkas is *Paleo Liovtrivi*, ideal for a snack, a home-made dessert or a nightcap at the water's edge, watching spotlights play on the fish.

West of Galaxídhi

West of Galaxídhi lies some of the sparsest scenery along the Greek shoreline; there are just a handful of villages with scrappy beaches, few of them warranting a stop. At **Áyios Nikólaos**, however, there's a year-round, roll-on-roll-off **ferry** (around €2 per passenger, €10 per small car) across the gulf to the Peloponnese – an alternative to the straits at Andírio–Río, 60km further west (see p.354). Westbound bus timings are perversely (some say deliberately) designed to just miss coinciding with ferry departures; if you don't catch the last sailing, **accommodation** is restricted to Theodore Katharakis's rooms (☎22660 31177; ❸), just east of the pebble beach.

Trizónia and Monastiráki

The Gulf of Kórinthos has about a dozen islets, but **TRIZÓNIA** – roughly halfway between Áyios Nikólaos and Náfpaktos, just across a narrow strait – is the largest and only inhabited one (permanent population around 55). Green with vegetation and blissfully vehicle-free (except for a handful of service trucks), it has long been a favourite stopover for yachties, and makes an idyllic retreat for conventional travellers despite a lack of good beaches. To reach the island, follow signs from the main highway down to the settlement of Hánia (only its neighbour Glyfádha is shown on most maps), where a little boat shuttles across eleven times daily until about 9pm (about €1 per person; more frequent service in midsummer). This calls at the appealing fishing harbour with its three fish **tavernas**, among which *Ta Dhyo Limania* and *Porto Trizonia* both prove reasonable and friendly. **Accommodation** includes the *Roni Apartments* (☎22660 71297; ❸) and the modern but well-designed *Hotel Drymna* (☎22660 71204, ☏22660 71304; ❹), most of whose peaceful rooms overlook the yacht anchorage – and *Lizzie's Yacht Club* on the hillside opposite, a revered institution amongst the boating fraternity but open to all, constituting the island's main **nightlife**. The access track to it continues towards Trizónia's southeast tip, where the small, red-sand beach at **Poúnda**, a half-hour in total from the village, is the best of several swimming coves on the far side of the island.

Beyond Trizónia, the most pleasant spot along the approach to Náfpaktos is **MONASTIRÁKI**, some 11km shy of the former. Monastiráki retains plenty of old stone houses, along a serpentining, tree-studded quay; there are no short-term places to stay but there is a handful of **seafood tavernas**, much the best being ✻ *Iliopoulos* around the easterly headland. This has a superb selection of wild-caught fish, plus a few seafood appetizers and home-made *píttes*; reckon on €15–23 each for fish, two appetizers and a beer. For a pre- or post-prandial swim, there's a pebble **beach** just below the *Iliopoulos* terrace, or the much larger, less windy but shadeless one of **Parathálassa** west of the main port, backed by a lagoon and a few seasonal beach-bars. There's a sandier, longer and more developed beach 3km further west at **Hiliadhoú**, with accommodation and tavernas.

Náfpaktos

The other place that stands out west of Galaxídhi, and indeed the largest settlement on the gulf's north shore, is **NÁFPAKTOS**, a lively market town and resort which straggles for some distance along a plane-tree-shaded seafront, below its rambling Venetian castle. The planes are nurtured by numerous running springs, which attest to water-rich, deceptively gaunt mountains just inland. Some two hours' drive from Dhelfí, or an hour by road and ferry from Pátra, it makes a convenient and attractive stopover, though relentlessly heavy traffic through town somewhat dents its charm.

Arrival, information and accommodation

Despite the town's size, it's not a major transport hub: through KTEL **buses** only run to and from Itéa and Ámfissa (for connections north into Thessaly). Local blue-and-white city bus #1 goes west frequently to Andírio, where you can intercept buses north from Pátra to Ípiros, or catch a ferry across to the Peloponnese.

Despite ten hotels and a similar number of rooms or apartments, **accommodation** can be in short supply or overpriced in summer, and noisy at mid-town locales. The cleaner, more popular westerly beach of **Psáni**, with Navmahías as its frontage road (and hub of café society), is both central and relatively quiet; if your finances stretch to it, go for the spotless *Plaza*, Navmahías 37 (☎26340 22226, ⓦwww.plaza-hotel.gr; ❹), or the slightly noisier apartments *Regina* at the east end of the esplanade near the old port (☎26340 21555, ℱ26340 21556; ❹). About 250m inland, in the old town at the base of the kástro, the simple but adequate *Ilion* (☎26340 21222; ❹) has the best views in town from both its rooms and its terrace bar, and more charm, though it's best not to be too laden as there's a fair climb up and no easy parking nearby.

For even more tranquillity and comfort (and easier parking), head for the easterly beach of **Grímbovo** (Paralía Grimbóvou), just 1km east of the old port – though swimming here is emphatically not recommended, as foul-smelling culverts drain straight into the sea. Here the best-value choice, right beside the creek-fountain flowing to the sea, is the ⚓ *Akti* (☎26340 28464, ℮akti@otenet.gr; ❹), with partial gulf views from about half the rooms and an airy, cheerful breakfast salon for a good start on the day; standard doubles (B&B ❹) were enlarged and refurbished to state-of-the-art appointment in 2005, while the rooftop suites (sleeping two to three) are palatial, and just about worth the splurge (❺). There's a good **campsite**, *Platanitis Beach* (☎26340 31555; mid-May to Sept), 5km west of the town towards Andírio, served by the aforementioned urban bus #1 – the last one leaves at 10pm.

The Town

The vast, pine-tufted **kástro** provides a picturesque backdrop; most of what's on view dates from the fifteenth-century era of Venetian rule. A complete tour is only really possible by driving the well-marked 2.5km to the car park at the highest citadel, passing en route a clutch of cafés taking advantage of the superb view. At the very summit are the adjacent remains of a Byzantine baths and Ottoman mosque, both of which have been converted into chapels. The curtain walls plunge down to the sea, enclosing the highest town neighbourhoods and oval-shaped old harbour in crab-claw fashion (you can climb each rampart for free), with one of the original gates giving access to one end of the westerly town beach.

The castle formed a formidable part of the Venetian defences, and the **Battle of Lepanto** (Náfpaktos's medieval name) was fought just offshore from here on October 7, 1571. An allied Christian armada commanded by John of Austria devastated an Ottoman fleet – the first European naval victory over the Turks since the death of the dreaded pirate-admiral Barbarossa. Cervantes, author of *Don Quixote*, lost his left arm to a cannonball during the conflict; there is a Spanish-erected statue honouring him at the old harbour. But Western supremacy on the high seas proved fleeting, since the Ottomans quickly replaced their navy and had already wrested Cyprus from the Venetians that same year.

Andírio and the Andírio–Río suspension bridge

The roll-on-roll-off ferries that for decades crossed the straits between Andírio and Río, on the opposite side of the Gulf of Kórinthos, were in August 2004 almost eclipsed by a futuristic antiseismic suspension bridge completed by a French consortium. Spanning a three-kilometre channel, it's the longest in the world, and plainly visible to approaching airline passengers from 30,000 feet (as pilots never tire of pointing out). The ferries have survived largely because their fares for a car and driver cost about half of the stiff bridge toll – €10 for ordinary passenger cars and rising. The #1 bus from Náfpaktos deposits you at Andírio's east quay, the only one now used by the ferries, where you can either cross to Río and its train station as a foot passenger, or refer to the handy KTEL booth here for all passing services between northwestern Greece, Pátra and Athens.

Eating and drinking

Most of Náfpaktos's full-service **tavernas** and ouzerís line the plane-tree esplanade at Grímbovo, some half-dozen strong and all fairly comparable in quality; *Stavros*, near the west end, is reasonable value. The only eateries near the old port are the traditional *Tsaras* (Wed–Sun only), dedicated to a limited range of daily-changing *mayireftá*, and the popular *Papoulis Ouzeri* on the pedestrian zone near the mosque missing its minaret, with a good mix of not overly fried meat and seafood, local wine, and seating both indoors and out. Otherwise, the medieval harbour is ringed by cafés and bars which provide a fair proportion of the town's **nightlife** (and at least one in any season will have **Internet** facilities).

North to Lamía

Lamía is a half-day's journey north from Dhelfí by bus (but under three hours with your own car), with a connection at Ámfissa: a pleasant route skirting mounts Parnassós, Gióna and (to the northwest) Íti. Just west of the historic pass of **Thermopylae**, at the open-air hot springs of **Loutrá Koutséki**, 12km shy of Lamía, the road joins the **coastal highway** from Athens.

Inland: Ámfissa to Gorgopótamos

The inland road west from Dhelfí climbs slowly through a sea of groves, source of the acclaimed local green olives, to **ÁMFISSA**, a small town in the foothills of Mount Gióna. Its medieval name of Sálona is still used conversationally; like Livadhiá, this strategic military location was a base for the Catalan Grand Company, who left their mark on the originally thirteenth-century **castle**. If you have time to kill between buses (the **KTEL** station is on the main square), its ruins, which incorporate remnants of an ancient acropolis, make for a pleasant walk, if only to enjoy the shade of the pine trees and examine a few stretches of Classical polygonal masonry. Otherwise, an enforced halt in Ámfissa is to be avoided; there is just one overpriced hotel functioning, and (unusually for a market town) no full-service tavernas in the centre.

Most travellers continue north along the scenic **Lamía road**, dividing mounts Parnassós and Gióna; some 20km north of Ámfissa, at the pass linking the two massifs, is the region's major tourist attraction, the **Vagonetto** or **Fokis Mining Park** (daily 9am–3.45pm; €13; ⓦ www.vagonetto.gr). This gives visitors a taste of Fokídha province's long-standing mining tradition, specifically Gallery 850, worked out in the 1970s; hour-plus tours in six languages begin on the "*vagonetto*" or underground train used by the miners.

Other than this, the area is thinly populated and has few amenities; the only reliable **meal** stop between Itéa and Lamía is at attractively set **GRAVIÁ**, 10.5km below the Vagonetto, where either of two grills – *Ble Gonia*, on the through road, or *O Lefteris*, a few paces away and quieter – are both popular, salubrious and inexpensive.

Just beyond Graviá, you cross the **rail line** between Livadhiá and Lamía. This is one of the most dramatic stretches of railway in Greece, with a history to match; it runs through the foothills of mounts Parnassós, Kallídhromo and Íti, and over the precipitous defile of the **Gorgopótamos River**, where in late November 1942 the Greek Resistance – all factions united for the first and last time, under the command of British intelligence officer Brigadier Eddie Meyers – blew up a critical **railway viaduct**, cutting one of the Germans' vital supply lines to their army in North Africa for three months. You can pay your respects to the intrepid guerrillas at the commemorative plaque by the new viaduct, and then retire to **GORGOPÓTAMOS** village where *Pardhalis* is an excellent **grill**, open 9pm till late.

The coastal highway

The **Athens–Lamía** coastal motorway is fast, efficient and dully flat, with EU-funded improvement completed during the years either side of the millennium. It initially runs a fair distance inland, skirting the Ilíki reservoir north of Thíva, before reaching the coast just before Atalándi, home to many of Greece's breweries.

There are also various links with the island of **Évvia** (see p.985): first at Halkídha (where there's a causeway), then by ferry at **Arkítsa** to Loutrá Edhipsoú (passengers €1.65, cars €10.60).

Áyios Konstandínos and Kaména Voúrla

ÁYIOS KONSTANDÍNOS is the closest port to Athens if you're heading for the islands of the Sporades, with daily catamaran or car-ferry departures to Skiáthos, Skópelos and Alónissos. For current information ask the Bilalis (☎22350 31614) or Alkyon (☎22350 31920) agencies, on the main square.

There should be no reason to stay here, but if you're stranded you can choose from among eight **hotels** – try the D-class *Hotel Poulia* just off the platía (☎22350 31663; ❷) for spartan en-suite rooms, or the more pleasant *Amfitryon* (☎22350 31702; ❸) on the waterfront. **KAMÉNA VOÚRLA**, 9km west, has a better beach; this is, however, very much a resort, used mainly by Greeks attracted by the spas here and at nearby Loutrá Thermopylíon (see below). Seafood aficionados are well looked after at the long line of decent fish **tavernas** along the promenade here, particularly at *Falaraïka* in Áyios Pandelímon district, and there are scores of acceptable **hotels** and rooms on the main street and shady backstreets.

Thermopylae, its spa and Bodonítsa castle

Just before joining the road descending north from the mountains, the motorway enters the **Pass of Thermopylae** (modern Thermopýles), where **Leonidas**, king of Sparta, and his entourage made a last stand against Xerxes' thirty-thousand-strong Persian army in 480 BC. The pass was much more defined in ancient times: a narrow defile with Mount Kallídhromo to the south and the sea, now 4km distant across a silted-up plain, just to the north. The tale of Spartan bravery is described at length by Herodotus. Leonidas stood guard over the pass with a mixed force of seven thousand Greeks, confident that it was the only approach an army could take to enter Greece from Thessaly. By night, however, Xerxes – tipped off by the traitor Ephialtes – sent an advance party of his forces along a little-used mountain trail and skirted around the pass to attack the Greeks from behind. Leonidas ordered a retreat of the main army, but remained in the pass himself, with a rearguard consisting of about three hundred Spartans, Thespians and Thebans, to delay the Persians' progress. He and all but two of the guard fought to their deaths.

Loutrá Thermopylíon, midway through the pass, is named for the hot springs present here since antiquity. The grave mound of the fallen rearguard lies 500m away, opposite a gloriously heroic statue of Leonidas. The **spa** and restaurant facilities are intimidatingly built up and the surroundings generally tatty, but off to one side are a few hot cascades and drainage sluices where you can bathe undisturbed in the open air.

From just east of the spa, a paved road leads southeast 14km to the village of Mendhenítsa on the flank of Mount Kallídhromo, overlooked by the fine **castle of Bodonítsa**. This is reached by a short, sharp climb, rewarded by the sweeping view north and substantial remains of the citadel. Built in 1205 by a clan from Parma, it soon passed to the Venetians, who held it until a successful Ottoman siege in 1410.

Loutrá Koutséki

For an even better outdoor **spa** experience, leave the motorway heading southwest on the minor road to Dhamásta, and after 750m bear left onto a paved, unmarked road; you'll see a few streetlights ahead, seemingly in the middle of nowhere. Road's end is a car park beside a long, narrow pond, reaching to over a metre's depth; this is **Loutrá Koutséki** (free, unenclosed). The water, quite clean considering there's a natural bottom here, ranges from 30–33°C, so proves tolerable for long dips even in summer. The place is popular with Lamians, so there are always plenty of people bobbing about in the shadow of the hillside greenery or applying face-packs from muddy patches. It's an idyllic spot, perhaps more so at night when the high-voltage lines overhead are less obvious (though noise from the motorway always intrudes).

Lamía and around

LAMÍA, with a population of around 50,000, is the busy capital of Fthiotídha province, and an important transport junction for travellers. It sees few overnight visitors, but has a worthwhile sight in its Catalan castle, and abounds in excellent restaurants and ouzerís.

The town centre is arranged around four main squares: Platía Párkou, Platía Eleftherías, Platía Laoú and Platía Dhiákou. **Platía Eleftherías** is the town's traditional social hub and scene of the evening *vólta*, with a few outdoor café tables and a little bandstand-gazebo. The cathedral and Neoclassical provincial government building flank the square on the north, with the Galaxias three-screen **cinema** tucked into the southwest corner. Just east and downhill from Eleftherías is the atmospheric **Platía Laoú**, shaded by plane trees crowded in autumn with migratory birds and site of a statue of controversial wartime Resistance leader Aris Velouhiotis, a native of the town.

Looking down on the city from the north is the fourteenth-century Catalan **castle** ("El Cito" to its medieval garrison), which boasts superb views and also houses an **archeological museum** (both Tues–Sun 8.30am–3pm; €2 for museum) exhibiting a variety of finds – Neolithic, Mycenaean, Classical, Hellenistic and Roman – in a Neoclassical former barracks dating from the 1850s; the displays, mostly from nearby ancient tombs, are well arranged, but many items are labelled in Greek only.

Leaving town there's a choice of three routes: northwest to Tríkala and Kalambáka, north to Lárissa, or northeast to Vólos, but none is especially memorable in itself. Fársala and Kardhítsa, on the routes to Lárissa and Tríkala respectively, are small, nondescript country towns. The **Vólos road**, however, leading initially east along the coast of the Maliakós Gulf, has a little more to delay your progress.

Practicalities

Buses, including a local service from Lianokládhi **train** station (6km out, but in-town OSE office at Avérof 28, southwest of Platía Párkou), arrive at several terminals scattered throughout the town, though none is much further than ten minutes' walk away from Platía Párkou. Karpeníssi services, and those for western Fthiotídha in general, use a terminal at Márkou Bótsari 3, near the little-used, in-town train station for the minor line to Stylídha; buses for Dhelfí, Pátra and Tríkala stop out on Thermopýlon near the corner of Nikopóleos, southeast of the centre just past the train tracks; those for Vólos use a more central stop at the corner of Livadhítou and Rozáki-Ángeli; while buses for Athens and Thessaloníki go from the corner of Papakyriazí and Satovriándou, near the Karpeníssi station. The most convenient **taxi** rank is at the top end of Andhroútsou, behind the cathedral. **Drivers** should be aware that the town centre is blanketed by a particularly strict parking control scheme (2hr limit); pay-and-display card outlets are elusive, spaces are rare in any case, and you're best off **parking** remotely and walking to the attractions.

Heart of the shopping district is **Platía Párkou**, with several **banks** (ATMs) grouped around it, and the blue city-bus terminus, while west and uphill from here is diminutive **Platía Dhiákou**, with a few more cafés and the **post office**. Just north of Eleftherías, past the cathedral at Ipsilándi 6, is Lamía's most central **Internet café**.

Accommodation

Accommodation prospects in Lamía are noisily sited, but (for the most part) well placed and well maintained. On Rozáki-Angelí, near the wholesale meat-and-fish market, are two budget choices opposite each other: the *Thermopyles* at no. 36 (℡22310 21366, ℱ22310 26645; ❸), in a mosaic-floored, 1960s building, its rooms with baths and air conditioning, or the similarly recently redone *Athina* at no. 41 (℡22310 20700; ❸), which has the additional bonus of an underground car park. Moving up a notch, the *Apollonio* at one corner of Párkou (entrance on Hatzopoúlou 25; ℡22310 22668, ℱ22310 23032; ❸) has medium-sized, double-glazed rooms.

Eating, drinking and nightlife

You're spoilt for choice in the matter of **food and drink**, making Lamía a good lunch-hour halt. On or just off Platía Laoú, you'll find three options, all open at midday: *Fytilis* at no. 6, a good all-rounder specializing in bacon-and-cheese-stuffed *biftéki*, with big portions; the *Ilysia* at Kalyvá Bakoyiánni 10, offering a variety of reasonably priced *mayireftá*; and (best of all) *Ouzou Melathron*, in an old house up some steps at Aristotélous 3, with fair-sized, reasonably priced portions of rich Middle Eastern and Macedonian recipes washed down by Límnos bulk wine, followed by complimentary dessert crêpes, and served in a lovely courtyard in summer or stunning interior. Nearby, Odhysséa Andhroútsou, a pedestrianized lane threading south-to-north between Laoú and Eleftherías, ending in a tiny square of its own, is crammed full of more attractive ouzerís; *Aman Aman*, *Allo Skedhio* (both evenings only) and *Alaloum* (lunch too, opposite *Aman Aman*) are the best. Of late, the focus for the trendiest **nightlife** and **cafés** has shifted away from Platía Eleftherías to a cluster of establishments on contiguous Athanasíou Dhiákou, leading towards Platía Dhiákou.

East of Lamía

The first temptation on the coast road to Vólos is **AYÍA MARÍNA**, 12km east of Lamía, where the seafood tavernas – a popular weekend jaunt for Lamian families – are much better than the rather pathetic beach.

A couple of kilometres further, **STYLÍDHA** was once one of the major ports of the Aegean but now has just two local trains daily from Lamía. At the opera house here, Maria Callas's grandfather out-sang a visiting Italian star and began a family tradition; today the unsightly town is chiefly concerned with olive-oil bottling and cement manufacture. At Karavómylos and Akhládhi, 8km and 19km east of Stylídha respectively, the fish **tavernas** are again more inviting than the beaches; *Andonopoulos* at Karavómylos is right on the water and thus popular.

The best beaches along this route are near **GLÝFA** 30km further east, actually 11km off the motorway and served by just one afternoon bus from Lamía. It has the mainland's northernmost ferry crossing to **Évvia**; if you miss the last departure (check first on ☎22380 61288), **rooms** are on offer, plus there are several **hotels**, the cheapest being the *Oasis* (☎22380 61353; ❷).

West of Lamía

The road west from Lamía traces the preternaturally lush Sperhiós valley, with more pistachio orchards than Égina island, and glimpses of mounts Íti, Gióna and Vardhoússia, 10km to the south. If you want to do some **hiking**, there are satisfying routes on Mount Íti (the Classical Oeta), easiest approached from the village of Ipáti. The **Karpeníssi valley** also lends itself to treks amid a countryside of dark fir forest – ravaged of late by either acid rain or some mysterious disease – and snow-fringed mountains, which the EOT promotes (with some justice) as "the Greek Switzerland". Besides walking, skiing on Mount Tymfristós and summertime rafting or canyoning on the local rivers are the main outdoor activities.

Summer and winter tourism, mostly domestic, has really taken off here, such that accommodation prices in the Karpeníssi area are also authentically Swiss, ratcheted up by a clientele of wealthy Athenians and Thessalonians, although reality has bitten to some extent, with local tourism stagnating and thus freezing rates. Backpackers and budget travellers don't really get a look-in unless they are part of an organized group.

Ipáti and Mount Íti

Mount Íti is one of the most beautiful of Greek mountains – its green northeast slopes constituting a national park – and also unusually accessible by Greek standards. There are buses almost hourly from Lamía to Ipáti, the usual trailhead; if you arrive by train, these can be picked up en route at the main Lianokládhi station. Be sure not to get off the bus at the sulphurous spa of Loutrá Ipátis, 5km northeast of and below Ipáti proper.

IPÁTI is a medium-sized village, clustered below a much-ruined Byzantine/Catalan castle. Two modest **hotels** cater mainly for Greek families: the courteous, slightly dated *Panorama* (☎22310 98222; ❷), just above the square and open most of the year, or the more basic and noisy *Panhellinion* (☎22310 98340; ❷) right on the platía, open in high summer only. There are a few reasonable **tavernas** and **ouzerís**, both on the platía and on the road into town.

Route-finding on Mount Íti has been eased by the availability of two decent, rival topographic maps, published respectively by Road Editions (no. 43, 1:50,000, with route summaries in English) and Anavasi (no. 10, 1:50,000), also with a useful booklet in bilingual text. The classic full traverse of the range from Ipáti to Pávliani, taking in the 2150-metre summit of Pýrgos, is an ambitious undertaking of between ten and eleven hours, best spread over two days; a limited day outing, however, should be feasible if you've reasonable orientation skills. The way out of Ipáti, starting from the square, is marked with red paint splodges or square placards; the actual path starting at the top of the village leads in around four hours to an EOS refuge known as **Trápeza** (usually locked, but with a spring and camping space nearby). This is a steep but rewarding walk, giving a good idea of Iti's sheer rock ramparts and lush meadows. From there you could return on a different path via Zapandólakka to Ipáti for a full-day looped hike, overnighting twice in the village. Otherwise, continue more or less due south to the flat-topped peak of Pyrá ("the pyre"), where in legend Hercules immolated himself to escape the agony of the poisoned tunic which his wife Deinaneira had given him. From there, proceed southwest via the Piyés and Katavóthra plateaus, on a mixture of track, path and cross-country surface, to the villages of **Áno and Káto Pávliani** where there are patchy (if any) bus connections back to Lamía, but more reliable **accommodation** in the lower village at the *Xenonas Petrino* (☏ 22310 83111; ❹).

Karpeníssi and around

The main road west from Lamía and Ipáti, after scaling a spur of Mount Tymfristós, drops down to the town of **KARPENÍSSI**. A 1400-metre tunnel below the snow line guarantees year-round access and spares drivers at least twice that distance of curvy road over the pass. Karpeníssi's site is spectacular – huddled at the base of the peak and head of the Karpenisiótis valley, which extends south all the way to wall-like Mount Panetolikó – but the town itself is entirely nondescript, having been destroyed in World War II by the Germans and again in the civil war. During the latter, it was captured and held for two weeks by Communist guerrillas in January–February 1949. During the fighting, an American pilot was shot down, thereby gaining, as C.M. Woodhouse observed in *The Struggle for Greece* (see "Books" p.1142), "the unenviable distinction of being the first American serviceman to be killed in action by Communist arms".

Practicalities

Arriving **by bus** is a bit of a nonstarter, since the KTEL terminal has been exiled 3km out to the remote suburb of Xiriá, though buses occasionally do a run into town, along main drag Zinopoúlou, to the leafy, café-table-crowded central square and its **taxi** rank. **Parking** in the centre is difficult and heavily controlled, so we've indicated lodging where this is less of a problem. Except on summer weekends or during the skiing season, **accommodation** is easily found, if not that appealing; many of the half-dozen hotels are noisy or over-priced, though bargaining at midweek year-round is always productive. Best value and quietest are **rooms** kept by Kostas Koutsikos, up some steps opposite the town hall (☏ 22370 21400; ❷), or the *Hotel Galini* (☏ 22370 22914, ℻ 22370 25623; ❸) on Ríga Feréou 3, a lane (parking feasible) in the bazaar downhill from the main thoroughfare, 250m southeast of the *Panorama* restaurant (see opposite). For more comfort, try the externally unprepossessing *Hotel Elvetia*, Zinopoúlou 17 (☏ 22370 22465, ⓦ www.elvetiahotel.gr; doubles ❺, suites ❼), where superb communal areas (including an arcaded stone-and-wood bar) and helpful management make up for somewhat small rooms, or the recently refurbished *Anesis*, Zinopoúlou 50 (☏ 22370 80700, ⓦ www.anesis.gr; ❺), mainly worth it if you get one of the rooms with stunning valley views.

Eating options are surprisingly limited, with downtown overrun by a plethora of fast-food outlets and après-ski bars. The only real full-service tavernas are the *Panorama* (lunch and dinner) at Ríga Feréou 18, just below an unmissable unfinished hotel, which offers well-executed *mayireftá* and grills in a tranquil garden, and the more upmarket ouzerí *Esy Oti Pis*, in Langádhia district at the junction of Kafandári and Karaïskáki, with reservations suggested (T22370 24080) at peak seasons.

The more reliable of two locally based **activity outfitters** is Ev Zein, beyond the *Anesis* at Zinopoúlou 61 (T22370 80150), with a full programme of mountain-biking and river sports; April to early June is the main rafting season.

South of Karpeníssi

Your first conceivable halt in the Karpenisiótis valley, 5km by road south of town, is the rather embalmed village of **KORYSKHÁDES**, whose stone houses are famous for their ornate wooden balconies with views across the valley to Mount Kaliakoúdha. All but ten of the permanent population have decamped, selling up to an enterprise which has meticulously restored a growing number of mansions as premier **accommodation** – rooms, suites and family apartments (T22370 25102, Wwww.koryschades.com.gr; summer ❹–❺, winter weekends ❼). The only place to **eat** or **drink** is the combination *kafenío*-restaurant-breakfast salon, also the scheme's contact office, on the platía by the church.

For villages with a more lived-in feel to them, deeper into the stunning countryside, return to the valley floor and head a kilometre or two downriver to the respective signposted turnings to Klafsí (east) and Voutýro (west). At the church-platía in **KLAFSÍ**, there are superb views, three **tavernas** and **rooms** offered by the Mathes brothers (T22370 22397; ❸). Up its own side-valley, **VOUTÝRO** has two **tavernas**, *O Avstralos* and *O Spithas*, on its square, plus a superior **inn**, 🍴 *Amadryades* (T22370 80909, Wwww.amadryades.gr; rooms ❺, suites ❻), arrayed over two restored buildings dwarfed by a lawn-terrace, where the large units have fireplaces or balconies (or both), and a reasonable café operates on-site (3pm onwards Mon–Fri, all day Sat & Sun).

Megálo Horió and Gávros

From Karpeníssi it's 16km down the valley to Megálo Horió and Mikró Horió ("Big Village" and "Little Village"); buses make the trip from Karpeníssi twice daily. **MEGÁLO HORIÓ**, on the east side of the valley, is a pleasant if architecturally heterogeneous place set right under Mount Kaliakoúdha. There are several places to stay and eat, but again no lodging bargains. The friendliest, best sited and least expensive **accommodation** is the *Agnandi* (T22370 41303; summer ❸, winter ❻), to your left on the approach road, which has modern but tasteful rooms with knockout views across the village to the mountains, and a communal ground-floor kitchen providing self-service breakfast; the proprietor is helpful and knowledgeable about the area. Otherwise try, right in the heart of things, the high-rise *Antigone Hotel* (T22370 41395, F22370 41450; summer ❸, winter ❹), which doubles as the main bar-restaurant; rooms feature carpeting for winter and pastel-coloured bedding and drapery. There are a few other tentative eateries in the village centre, but for the best meals head down to **GÁVROS**, a little suburb of Megálo Horió on the valley floor (the name means "hornbeam", which once abounded here). Several **tavernas** lining the through road are all better than anything up the hill, but *To Spiti tou Psara* gets top marks for grilled trout, *píttes*, dips and local bulk wine, with seating on

△ Megálo Horio and Mount Kaliakoúdha

the rear terrace overlooking the riverside trees. There's also **accommodation** here worth considering, by the bridge: the *Pension Agrambeli* (☎22370 41148; summer ③, winter ⑤), which has cool, cave-like rooms in a variety of formats, but all with balconies or verandahs, and an indoor bar and breakfast area and medium-size swimming pool sharing space on a riverside lawn.

Mikró Horió

MIKRÓ HORIÓ, visible opposite Megálo at the foot of Mount Helidhóna, has a turbulent history as it was a major centre for the leftist ELAS resistance during World War II, with a clandestine printing press. On Sunday, January 13, 1963, after two weeks of uninterrupted rain, an avalanche wiped out the western two-thirds of the village, killing thirteen (the death toll would have been far higher except that many locals were in church). The place was already in bad official odour because of its wartime stance, and every government since the disaster has exerted pressure in various ways to move the survivors 4km downhill to the replacement community of **Néo** (New) **Mikró Horió**. Here "Swiss" pricing policies apply at the *Hellas Country Club* (☎22370 41570, ⓦwww .countryclub.gr; summer ⑥, winter ⑧), where you can spend €320 a night in peak season on a luxury suite if you're so inclined; the best rooms have balconies facing the garden and Mount Kaliakoúdha, while common facilities include a gym, conference hall and lawn-café. There are a few other, considerably more reasonable, **room** options scattered along the grid of streets in the purpose-built village, its stone-built houses not so wretched as many such disaster responses are. Two of the best, both well-signposted from the bottom of the village, are *Iy Gonia* near the top of the hill (☎22370 41393; summer ③, winter ⑤), which has modern rooms with mountain views from their verandahs, or (200m downhill on the same street) the very friendly *Fotini Zara's* units (☎22370 41236; summer ③, winter ⑤), a mixture of standard doubles and wood-panelled suites with fireplaces. Much the best **taverna** in the area is ⋏ *To Horiatiko* down on what passes for the platía, with a broad mix of well-priced grills and *mayireftá*; booking is advisable at peak times (☏22370 41257).

You might prefer to continue to road's end at **Paleó** (Old) **Mikró Horió**, where the municipally run, en-suite *Helidhona Hotel* (☏22370 41221; summer ❸, winter ❹; open weekends only off season) by the fountain and plane tree is about the most reasonable lodging in the valley, with knockout views out back towards Mount Tymfristós. The ground-floor restaurant, *Iy Kyra María*, puts tables out under the tree in fair weather. Your only alternative, by the church, is the new *Studio Merses* complex (☏22370 41444, ⓦwww.merses.gr; summer ❺, winter ❼), rustic-style suites with fireplaces, fitting four, enjoying the same views from the on-site bar-café. There are no shops in the moribund village, so come equipped for the three-hour hike west up Mount Helidhóna (1973m), indicated by blue or yellow waymarks. The first half of this is along forestry track, rather than path, with a potential detour early on to visit a small **natural lake** near the village entrance. This is signed in Greek ("Límni, 200m") and proves pleasant and clean if shallow, but just swimmable in July or August.

Mount Kaliakoúdha

The full-day **hike** up and down **Mount Kaliakoúdha** (2098m), the peak which dominates Megálo Hório, is one of the most popular outings in the Karpenisiótis valley. There's a good, waymarked path much of the way, but a certain amount of shadeless track-tramping near the top, and the final ascent conquers one of the sharpest grades in the Greek mountains – advanced peak-bagging skills are essential. The route, and geographical features, are shown more or less correctly on Anavasi Editions 1:50,000 map no. 13, *Karpenisi Prousos*. You'll want an early start, to polish off most of the 1250-metre altitude difference before the sun catches you.

From the village square near the *Hotel Antigoni*, leave Megálo Horió heading southeast, following painted red or yellow waymarks. Adopt a corniche path for just under half an hour, which briefly becomes an old and not too onerous bulldozer track ending by a cement cistern with an overflow valve – fill up, this is the last water for some time. The proper trail resumes, climbing steadily through fir forest; you'll notice that about one in twenty trees is dead or dying, but the survivors provide welcome shade. There's also substantial deadfall and litter obscuring parts of the path, making you dependent on the frequent waymarks, especially at the half-dozen crossings of the modern dirt track heading up the mountain.

About two hours from the village, the path ends for now just below tree line, at a sharp bend in the track with a culvert; just to the left, in a clump of firs, is **Malakássa**, the only other reliable spring this side of the mountain. After topping up again, you're forced to adopt the track for about 45 minutes, with shortcuts only possible once beyond a fenced-in "base camp" belonging to a trekking company. Between the spring and this, you'll pass a small chapel with an unreliable fountain, two crude *stánes* or pastoral huts, and a memorial to an 1823 battle here during the War of Independence. With or without shortcuts through a couloir, three hours' hike from Megálo Horió should see you up on the saddle at the northeast flank of the peak.

The track over the saddle continues down and south into the signposted territory of Dhomnísta municipality; for Kaliakoúdha, however, head west and relentlessly up, following red-paint waymarks. The trail is poor to nonexistent, well strewn with scree midway along, but there's little danger of getting lost and on a fine summer's day you'll have plenty of company. Just under an hour (roughly 4hr in total from the village) is required to reach the **summit** and trig point (missing its "2098" disc); the staggering **views** over much of central Greece are your reward. The Vardhoússia and Íti ranges loom to the east; the Ágrafa region unfolds beyond Mount Tymfristós to the north-northeast; while Mount Panetolikó approximates the provincial border south-southwest. Due south, you see Stournára village in the Krikellopótamos valley, poised just above **Pandavréhi**, a popular beauty spot and trekkers' destination where waterfalls pour year-round from a rock wall. Many hikers elect to continue there, rather than return to Megálo Horió; there's no confirmed lodging in Stournára, so you should plan to camp out. Return to the saddle takes about an hour owing to the scree and the sharp gradient, and from there the descent back to Megálo Horió requires three-and-a-half hours, for a nearly eight-hour walking day.

Proussós village and Proussoú monastery

Beyond Gávros, the valley narrows to a spectacular **gorge** with two narrows at Klidhí and Patímata tís Panayías before emerging at Dhípotama, the mingling of the Karpenisiótis and Krikellopótamos rivers to form the Trikeriótis, a favourite put-in and take-out point of rafting outfitters. A paved if steep road through the canyon makes a visit to the monastery and village of **PROUS-SÓS** (33km out of Karpeníssi) straightforward, though only two dawn and two afternoon buses a week do the trip from Karpeníssi. The **monastery**, set amazingly on a cliff in a bend of a tributary to the Krikellopótamos, opposite two rock pinnacles, is flanked by two eighteenth-century defensive towers associated with Yiorgos Karaïskakis, the revolutionary war figure who used the place as a stronghold. Massive and much rebuilt after a succession of fires started by candles, **Proussoú** (the official nomenclature) is presently inhabited by just two monks plus some layworkers. Coachloads of pilgrims revere the icon of the Panayía Proussiótissa in the ninth-century *katholikón*. Here, or in the treasury (signed as the *skevofylakíon*), you can see curiosities such as paper made from the skin of a goat embryo and an icon of the Panayía with its eyes gouged out. (According to the locals, the Communist rebels of the 1940s were responsible for this, though Muslim Turks were wont to perform the same sacrilege, and credulous villagers attributed magical powers to the dust thus obtained.)

The **village's** houses, 1km further on, are dispersed across incredibly steep slopes, plagued by the sort of earth movements that did for Mikró Horió. The central neighbourhood has a drab, fitfully operating community **hotel**, the *Agathidis* (T22370 91248; ❸), and several meat-oriented, evening-only tavernas around the central square.

Proussós to Náfpaktos

The road south of Proussós creeps over the **Panetolikó** range, which separates the Evrytanía province (which encompasses the Karpenisiótis valley) from Étolo-Akarnanía, en route **to Náfpaktos**, a three-hour drive. This scenic route is entirely paved but there's no public transport, and the first 35km is mostly extremely narrow and slow-going. Landslides are nibbling away at the pavement up to the pass in Panetolikó giving a last, vast panorama of Evrytanía, before it drops down to Lambíri, the first village in Étolo-Akarnanía. This and succeeding communities up to Kallithéa have a wild, God-forsaken aspect; there's little evidence on this side of the watershed of the prosperity introduced by alpine tourism to the Karpenisiótis valley. At livelier Kallithéa you have your first, sweeping views of **Lake Trihonídha**, the largest body of fresh water in

Greece; it's of irrigational rather than recreational use, the shore by turns sheer or reedy, but apparently in pretty good ecological shape, with three native fish species caught for food.

About ninety minutes out of Proussós you reach **THÉRMO**, a surprisingly large place – almost a small town – dominating a fertile upland just invisible from the lake; it has a pleasant, plane-shaded square, petrol, **banks** (ATMs), shops, **tavernas** and regular **buses** to Agrínio if needed. Of potentially more interest is its predecessor, **ancient Thermon** (Tues–Sun 8.30am–3pm; free, photography forbidden), well signposted 1.5km southeast of the centre. This, being excavated since 1994, was the walled political capital and main religious shrine of the Aetolians, built against the base of a hill. The main temple, oddly orientated north-to-south rather than the usual west-to-east, was dedicated to Apollo Thermios; just east lies an older, smaller shrine to Apollo Lyseios, while to the northwest are foundations of an Artemis temple. South of the main temple – which is off limits like much of the site – the sacred spring still flows, full of frogs. Beyond the spring extend two long *stoas* (with the occasional exedra), terminating at a presumed bouleuterion. The keeper will unlock the small, one-room museum, crammed with unlabelled finds from the excavations.

Beyond Thérmo the way drops to the lush, intensely cultivated southeast shore of the lake before climbing again over surprisingly green hills into the valley of the **Évinos River**, the last undammed one in this part of Greece. Accordingly, there are a handful of **rafting outfitters** at or near **Háni Baniás** at the river bridge, as well as a restaurant and *xenónas*, but these tend to work only at high-water season (March–May), with most clients coming for the day from Náfpaktos, just 15km further. If you are reversing these directions, take the road out from Platía Liménos in Náfpaktos labelled "Kástro", but keep going straight rather than up and right.

Routes west and north from Karpeníssi

Roads west or north from Karpeníssi climb high into the **Ágrafa** mountains, the southernmost extension of the Píndhos. As with the saddle of Panetoilikó above Proussós, critical passes are generally closed in winter, but through the summer they're open. Either of these routes is intrinsically enjoyable, and much the quickest way out in the directions indicated.

West to Agrínio

The road west from Karpeníssi, then southwest to Agrínio, is well paved and fairly broad, but extremely sinuous, so it still takes the one daily bus from Karpeníssi a good three-and-a-half hours to cover the 114km (cars will easily make it in 3hr). The beauty of the first three-quarters of the journey up to Áyios Vlásios village cannot be overemphasized; it's largely empty country, with the only place of any size being the double village of **FRANGÍSTA**, which straddles a compact valley – Anatolikí Frangísta, 39km from Karpeníssi, with three simple inns, and Dhytikí Frangísta, 3km further, offering another **inn**, a filling station and four **psistariés**, of which the most reliable two are *To Steki* and *Trikorfo*. Beyond Frangísta, the road uses a causeway to cross the giant, surprisingly scenic **Kremastón reservoir** on the Tavropós, Trikeriótis and Ahelóös rivers, with a clutch of fish tavernas (exactly halfway to Agrínio) on the far side. Next, the route climbs again, skirting Panetolikó, until the fir trees stop at Áyios Vlásios and the still-narrow road winds down through tobacco-planted hills to Agrínio.

North to Kardhítsa

Again with your own transport, one of the best options – giving direct access to the Metéora (see p.399) – is the **route north to Kardhítsa**, which takes off from the top of the pass on the old road east of Karpeníssi, directly above the tunnel. Except for stretches damaged by rain and landslip, the way is paved and wide, a beautiful drive where sweeping vistas over central Greece alternate with fir forest. It's 28km around Mount Tymfristós to the turning for **FOURNÁ** village, where there is a hotel, *Wild Beauty* (℡22370 51223; ❸), if needed. Kardhítsa is 64km further, with little in-between other than **Loutropiyí**, where you may pause to munch on *souvláki*; **Loutrá Smokóvou**, where you can drown any sorrows in the little spa; and Kédhros, with the first fuel since Karpeníssi, and where the road straightens out for the final flat, straight approach to Kardhítsa. Allow just over two hours of driving from Karpeníssi.

Thessaly

The highlights of travelling through **Thessaly** are easily summarized. Over to the east, curling down from the port-city of **Vólos**, is the mountainous **Pílio** (Pelion) peninsula. The villages on its lush, orchard-covered slopes are among the most beautiful in the country – a long-established resort area for Greeks and numerous foreign tourists, though still with many unspoilt corners. To the west is a sight not to be missed on any mainland exploration: the extraordinary "monasteries in the air" of the **Metéora**.

The **central plains** are something to be passed through, rather than visited. That said, **Tríkala**, capital of the province of the same name, has transformed itself into a relatively pleasant city, besides providing efficient connections by bus to nearby **Kalambáka**, gateway to the Metéora, and to Vólos (via dreary **Lárissa**).

Heading north or west from Lárissa, you'll find yourself in one mountain range or another. One dramatic route over the Píndhos, from Kalambáka to Ioánnina, is covered in the following chapter, though the less-travelled but equally scenic passage from Pýli towards Árta is detailed below on p.397. North from Kalambáka there are reasonable roads, though few buses, into western Macedonia, with the lakeside town of Kastoriá an obvious focus. Most travellers, however, head north from Lárissa towards Thessaloníki, an attractive route in the shadow of Mount Olympus; with your own transport it's well worth detouring via the hill villages of **Mount Óssa**, or its underrated coast.

Vólos and around

Arriving at the resolutely industrial outskirts of **VÓLOS** gives little hint of Pílio's promise. It's hard to imagine the mythological past of this busy modern port, but just 4km west is purportedly the site of ancient Iolkos, from where Jason and the Argonauts legendarily embarked on their quest for the Golden

Fleece. With a population approaching 150,000, Vólos ranks as the fifth-largest Greek town, rebuilt in utilitarian style after a series of devastating earthquakes between 1947 and 1957, and now edging to its natural limits against the Pílio foothills behind. It's a lively place with a large student population, beginning to revel in recently acquired prosperity, and you could do worse than spend a few hours or even a night here while waiting for a bus up the mountain or a boat to the Sporades (see Chapter Eleven), for which Vólos is the **main port**.

Along with Lárissa, Halkídha and Ioánnina, Vólos was historically home to one of the larger **Jewish communities** of central Greece. Local Jews were well integrated into the social and political life of the town, such that during World War II only 155 out of the thousand-strong community were caught and murdered by the Nazis; the rest joined the resistance or were otherwise hidden on Mount Pílio. The unlucky victims have a prominent, sculpted memorial in one corner of Platía Ríga Feréou, donated by one of the survivors, just a few paces from the modern, post-earthquake synagogue.

Arrival and information

The nearest **airport**, receiving infrequent overseas charters (but not domestic flights), is 26km southwest, beyond Néa Anhíalos. Ferries and hydrofoils call at the port's **main quay**, and most other services are found within a couple of blocks. An exception is the **KTEL station** with its adjacent **taxi rank** and **city bus terminal** on Sekéri, just off Grigoríou Lambráki, ten minutes' walk southwest of the main square, **Platía Ríga Feréou**, with the **train station** just off the latter.

Vólos has a helpful, state-of-the-art **tourist information office** opposite the KTEL (April–Oct daily 8am–10pm, Nov–March Mon–Sat 8am–8pm, Sun 8am–3.30pm; ⓦwww.volos-city.gr), with copious leaflets on every conceivable local topic, plus free Internet access. Commercial **maps** and **guides**, plus a selection of foreign-language **books** and **periodicals**, can be found at Papasotiriou, on Dhimitriádhos, corner of Koumoundoúrou; Newsstand, Iássonos 80; and (maps only) Tsekouras, Venizélou 1, just by the quay.

If you want to **rent a car** to explore Mount Pílio, try one of the following agencies: Avis, Argonaftón 41 (☎24210 28880); European, Iássonos 79 (☎24210 36238); or helpful and efficient Hertz, Iássonos 90 (☎24210 22544) and at the airport.

Accommodation

Hotels are fairly plentiful if not for the most part great value, with a concentration of acceptable ones in the grid of streets behind the port. Budget options (relatively speaking) include the double-glazed, air-conditioned *Iasson* (☎24210 26075; ❸), partly facing the port at Pávlou Melá 1 or, further out at Iatroú Tzánou 1, corner of Plastíra 16, the en-suite *Roussas* (☎24210 21732, ⓕ24210 22987; ❷), easily the best value, and best reserved in advance, with relatively easy parking, convenience to many ouzerís, and helpful staff offsetting no breakfast facilities. Mid-range places include the slightly noisier but comfortable, air-conditioned *Avra*, Sólonos 3 (☎24210 25370; ❹); the *Aigli*, Argonaftón 24–26 (☎24210 24471, ⓕ24210 33006; ❺), a restored Art Deco complex on the quayside, only worth the price if you get a sea-view room; or, best placed of all, the *Park*, just inland from Platía Yeoryíou at Dheliyióryi 2 (☎24210 36510, ⓔamhotels@otenet.gr; ❺), a classic businesspeople's hotel whose rooms are on the small side, but well-equipped, and with state-of-the-art baths.

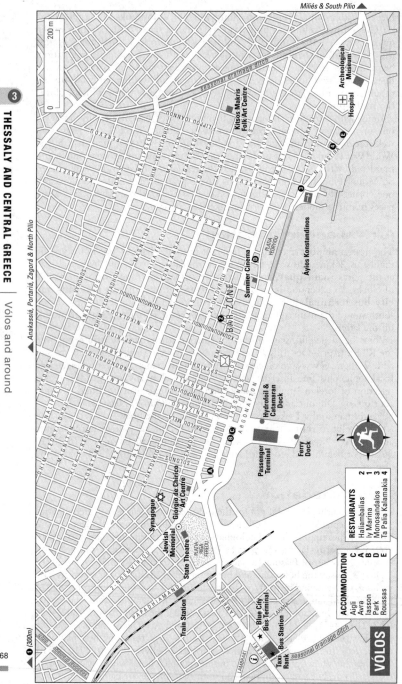

Miliés & South Pílio ▲

◀ Anakassiá, Portariá, Zagorá & North Pílio

▲ Airport, Athens, Lárissa, Sesklo & Dimíni

VÓLOS

Archeological Museum

Hospital

Kitsos Makris Folk Art Centre

PLATIA YEORYIOU

Áyios Konstandinos

Summer Cinema

BAR ZONE

Hydrofoil & Catamaran Dock

Passenger Terminal

Ferry Dock

Synagogue

Jewish Memorial

Giorgio de Chirico Art Centre

State Theatre

PLATIA RIGA FEREOU

Train Station

Blue City Bus Terminal

Bus Station

Taxi Rank

ACCOMMODATION	
Aigli	C
Avra	A
Iasson	B
Park	D
Roussas	E

RESTAURANTS	
Haliambalias	2
Iy Marina	1
Monosandalos	3
Ta Palia Kalamakia	4

200 m

0

N

The Town

Art buffs might want to drop in at one of two free local museums: the **Giorgio de Chirico Art Centre**, at Metamorfoséos 3 (Mon–Fri 10am–1pm & 6–9pm, Sat 10am–1pm), with an upstairs wing devoted to the locally born Surrealist artist (see p.383) plus changing exhibits, and the **Kitsos Makris Folk Art Centre**, out at Kítsou Makrí 38 (Mon–Fri 8.30am–12.30pm, Sun 10.30am–2pm), containing a score of paintings by naïve artist Theophilos (see p.374).

The most attractive place to linger is along the eastern waterfront esplanade, between the landscaped **Platía Yeoryíou** and the **archeological museum** (Tues–Sun 8.30am–3pm; €2). A lengthy overhaul has resulted in exemplary labelling and well-lit galleries, one reserved for annually changing exhibits. Highlights of the permanent collection include one of the best European assemblages of Neolithic (6500–3500 BC) figurines from various surrounding sites; faint but expressive painted grave stelae from Hellenistic Dimitrias depicting everyday scenarios of fifth-century BC life, with some inscriptions helpfully translated; and a massive quantity of items, including superb stone and gold jewellery, from tombs of all eras across Thessaly, some of it (in Hall 2) uncovered as a result of ongoing public-works projects such as road-widening.

Eating and drinking

Vólos specializes in one of Greece's most endearing and enduring institutions – the authentic **ouzerí**, serving a huge variety of *mezédhes* washed down not necessarily with ouzo but with *tsípouro*, the favoured spirit of the northern mainland. The western third of Argonaftón is lined with half-a-dozen of them, all adequate but pricey; the Voliots themselves go elsewhere, for example to *Iy Marina* out in Néa Ionía at Magnisías 13. To reach it, pass the drainage ditch on the map, bear right at the stoplights just after, then take the third left. Service can be stretched, as it's just Marina herself at the grill and her son serving at tables outside, but each *tsípouro* comes with random titbits which might be *kténia* (scallops), grilled octopus or fish of the day. There are a few more such establishments at the start of Nikifórou Plastíra, near the enormous Áyios Konstandínos church, interspersed with cafés and bars. Of these, the poshest and most durable is *Monosandalos*, most reliably open evenings and all day weekends, with waterside seating; meals feature the house-special *garidhokrokétes* (shrimp patties). Continuing a few steps east to *Ta Palia Kalamakia* will save you a few euros, sacrificing the direct sea view (but not quality) for grilled fresh squid or scaly fish in the cooler drawer. If seafood and ouzerís are not your thing, look no further than air-conditioned *Haliambalias* (aka *Zafiris*; closed Sun), inland at pedestrianized Kondarátou 8, corner Skýrou; it's a lodestar of *mayireftá* (the vegetarian *tourloú* or baked *pérka* fish in particular), where a meal with good bulk wine shouldn't top €15 each. The daytime **café** nucleus, with eight or nine contenders, is predictably by the main university building, towards the pediestrianized east end of Argonaftón.

Entertainment and nightlife

Concerts and plays are frequently performed in the open-air **theatre** or the covered one both on Platía Ríga Feréou; there's also a **summer cinema** off Platía Yeoryíou. The newest nightlife zone, comprising intimate **live-music venues** and café-bars where conversation is possible, is in the grid of pedestrianized lanes east of Koumoundoúrou; a few barn-like indoor **clubs** survive at the west edge of town, particularly on Lahaná, though the big summer thing is seasonal outdoor clubs in the southerly beach suburb of Alykés.

Around Vólos: Dimini, Sesklo and Tekkés Farsálon

Since the 1990s, **ancient Dimini** (Tues–Sun 8.30am–7.30pm, closes 3pm winter; €2), west of Vólos, has emerged as something of a local attraction, with the circuit of Neolithic walls cleaned and labelled, plus two fairly intact Mycenaean tholos-type tombs. Adjacent to the site, and still closed for excavations, is a Mycenaean palace complex, three times larger than Dimini, which is now thought to be ancient Iolkos. Vólos city bus #8 covers the 3km to modern Dhimíni village, 400m away.

You'll need your own transport to reach **ancient Sesklo** (Tues–Sun 8.30am–7.30pm, closes 3pm winter; €2), 15km from Vólos. The acropolis, inhabited from about 7000 to 3000 BC, occupies a slight protuberance (Kastráki hill) at the top of a secluded valley, near the modern village of Sésklo. The vividly coloured pottery found here, on view at the Vólos museum, was the distinguishing feature of the local culture.

At **Néa Anhíalos**, southwest of Vólos, are several **early Christian basilicas** uncovered next to the road. However, their mosaics are sanded over, and the two excavation sites and small site museum are off limits until at least 2008.

Tekkés Farsálon (Turbali Tekke)

Heading west from Néa Anhíalos will bring you to the largest surviving rural Muslim monument in Greece, the **Tekkés Farsálon (Turbali Tekke)**, a "monastery" (more properly, lodge or *tekkés*) of the Bektashi dervishes, the dominant Islamic mystical order in the Balkan peninsula from the time of the Ottoman conquest. To reach it, leave the E1/E75 motorway at the Aerinó exit and follow signs for Perívleptos. Drive through the village, and climb northwest towards the border with Lárissa province; just past the pass marking it, some 12km from the motorway, a fading signpost points south to "Moní Tekké Farsálon". Ascend the steep, sometimes muddy, track indicated and park after 400m under the plane trees of the spring-fed oasis here; the *tekkés*, studded by prominent cypresses, is a short walk uphill.

On the downhill side, the large lath-and-plaster building which housed the Bektashi dervishes is in an advanced state of dereliction, though it was reportedly inhabited by Albanian-speaking Muslim Tsamídhes until 1964. Of primary interest are the two sixteenth-to-seventeenth-century, octagonal dome-on-square structures on your left, arcaded on their east side, both with schist-slab roofs. The northernmost building, built of brick and rubble in the Byzantine manner, was probably the *semahane* or ceremonial hall; though bare inside, its portal has gaily painted stalactite vaulting and floral decoration. Below the portico is a small graveyard, with calligraphic headstones of perhaps twenty dervishes; their *şeyhs* or spiritual leaders are entombed in the southerly, stone-built *türbe* (marabou), joined to the *semahane* by a more contemporary building containing graves of three warriors (Turbali Sultan, Jafer and Mustafa) from Ottoman times. All these are still venerated with floral offerings and a bizarre assortment of Disney-character towels over the sarcophagi – most likely by the inhabitants of nearby Lefkóyia village, said to be the Christianized descendants of the dervishes. Throughout the territory of the Ottoman empire, it was (and still is) common for the closest tomb or shrine to be reverenced, by locals of whatever creed, as a form of spiritual insurance and petitioning for favours.

The Mount Pílio (Pelion) peninsula

The **Mount Pílio peninsula**, with its lush orchards of apple, pear and nut trees and dense forests of beech and oak, seems designed to confound stereotypical images of Greece. Scarcely a rock is visible along the slopes, and the sound of water comes gurgling up from fountains or aqueducts beside every track; summer temperatures here can be a good 5°C cooler than on the baking Thessalian plains. Pílio is reputed to be the land of the mythical centaurs – thus the name *Kentavros* (Centaur) for various hotels and bars – and the site of revelries by ancient gods.

Pílio **villages** are equally idiosyncratic, often spread out over wide areas due to easy availability of water, their various quarters linked by winding cobbled paths. They formed a semi-autonomous district throughout the Ottoman occupation, and during the eighteenth century became something of a nursery for Greek nationalism and culture, fostered by church-sponsored education and a revival of **folk art** and **traditional architecture**. There is also a strong regional **cuisine**, with specialities such as *spedzofáï* (sausage and pepper casserole), *kounéli kokkinistó* (rabbit stew) and *gídha lemonáti* (goat stew with lemon sauce); seafood is often garnished with *krítamo* (pickled rock samphire) or *tsitsíravli* (pickled terebinth shoots). To wash it down, surprisingly palatable wine bottled by the Dhimitra Co-op at Néa Anhíalos is widely available. In the far south, the gastronomic pattern changes a bit: obvious touristic tavernas are confined to the coast, while unassuming-looking *kafenía* on most village squares function, after dark, as *tsipourádhika* producing *tís óres* titbits plus a few ready dishes. Herbs, a wide range of fruit, home-made preserves and honey are important local products and souvenirs, pitched at the roadside; the only significant non-touristic enterprises are timber-cutting, the quarrying of the famous local schist stone, and nurseries propagating every sort of shade-loving plant.

Many of the communities have changed little in appearance over the centuries, and their ornate mansions, churches and sprawling *platíes* – invariably shaded by several vast plane trees, and flanked by the local cafés – make for rewarding visits. Stone-roofed **churches** are highly distinctive, built low and wide, often with a detached bell tower, marble reliefs on the apse and always ornamented inside with carved wood. Two villages, **Makrynítsa** and **Vyzítsa**, have been designated as protected showpieces of the region, but almost every place offers its own unique attractions.

Add the delights of numerous excellent **beaches**, plus a growing number of recognized **hiking** routes (see box p.374), and you have a recipe for an instant holiday idyll – or disaster, if you time it wrong. Lying conveniently between Athens and Thessaloníki, Pílio is a long-established favourite with Greek holiday-makers, who inundate the place at Eastertime or Christmas week, from mid-July to mid-August and during any three-day weekend year-round. At such times you'd really be pushing your luck to show up without a reservation, when, in any case, prices are among the highest on the mainland. Additionally, many of the mansions restored as accommodation are typically unattended, their owners absent in Vólos unless they know they'll have customers; thus it's essential to reserve such lodging in advance year-round.

Arriving fairly directly in Pílio **from overseas** is now possible, thanks to summer-only charter flights to either Skiáthos (frequent) or Almyrós airport, near Vólos (once weekly only), followed by a short transfer. UK package companies have the lion's share of seats on such flights, thus tickets for flight-only or fly-drive packages are in short supply.

Getting around the Pílio peninsula

The peninsula is divided into three regions, the best concentration of distinctive communities lying just **north and east** of Vólos and along the **northeast coast**. The **southwest coast** is less scenically interesting, with concentrated development along the Pagasitic Gulf, despite its lack of decent beaches. The far **south**, relatively low-lying and sparsely populated, has just two major resorts – Plataniá and Milína – plus a few scattered inland villages.

Travelling between the villages can be tricky without your own transport. **Buses** to the east cover two main routes: Vólos–Hánia–Zagorá and Vólos–Tsangarádha–Áyios Ioánnis, with just one daily service linking Zagorá and Tsangarádha to complete the loop. The far south is equally infrequently served, with

△ Taverna tables at Vyzítsa, Pílio

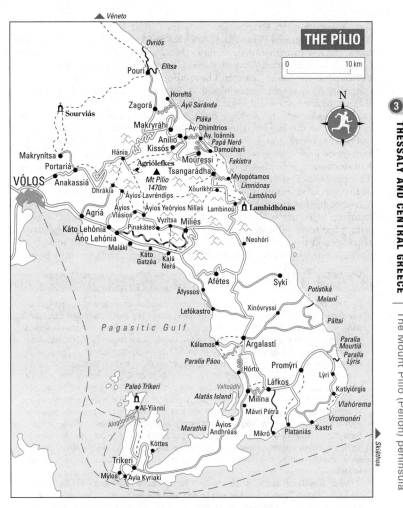

just a few daily departures to Milína, Tríkeri, Plataniá and Katiyiórgis, though the respective northern and western highlights of Makrynítsa and Vyzítsa both have far more frequent connections.

Alternatives include **renting a car** in Vólos (essential if you're pushed for time) or walking. Any mode of transport means slow progress, since gradients are sharp, and perilously narrow roads snake around ravine contours, seemingly never getting closer to villages just across the way.

Northern Pílio

Before crossing over to the popular east coast on the main Vólos–Zagorá route, consider pausing at either **Portariá** or **Makrynítsa**. Both villages have intrinsic attractions and make good first or last stops on any touring circuit.

Anakassiá and Portariá

The first encountered Pílio village, **ANAKASSIÁ** (Iolkós), is just 4km out of town, and few casual visitors give more than a passing glance to what is essentially a suburb of Vólos. What they miss is a small but very beautiful museum dedicated to the "naive" painter **Theophilos** (1873–1934). A prize eccentric, originally from Lésvos, Theophilos lived for long periods in both Athens and Vólos, where he wandered around, often dressed in traditional costumes, painting frescoes for anyone prepared either to pay or feed him. In Pílio you find his murals in the most unlikely places, mostly unheralded, including village tavernas, bakeries and *kafenía*. The badly signposted **museum** (Tues–Sun 8am–3pm; free) – turn off at the roadside platía – occupies the **Arhondikó Kondoú**, an eighteenth-century mansion whose first floor preserves much of Theophilos' earliest (1912–27) work, with unusually vivid colours, the result of two specialist cleanings in recent decades. The Greek War of Independence – one of his favourite themes – features often, including such scenes as the dumping of Patriarch Gregory's body into the Bosphorus, Admiral Tombazis setting fire to the Turkish flagship from a rowboat, the capture of Athanasiso Dhiakos, and the taking of Tripoli, with the notorious attendant massacre of Turk civilians graphically depicted. Nearer floor level, there's an entire bestiary,

---

Walking on Mount Pílio

Until the mid-twentieth century, the Pílio villages were linked exclusively by an unusually dense network of **kalderímia** (old cobbled paths). The automobile age saw many either bulldozed or consigned to disuse, and in the local hothouse climate neglected trails were blocked by vegetation within a few years. Since the early 1990s, however, committed local residents and village councils have mounted various campaigns to clean, restore, mark and document these superb walking routes, so that now, along with Zagóri (see p.433), the Pílio is the only region of Greece where the number of hiking opportunities is at least stable rather than dwindling. Even if you are not a hard-core trekker, the refurbished paths provide essential **short-cuts** between villages or down to the beaches. You'll see lots of yellow metal directional placards with a black walking-man logo – occasionally helpful, more often vaguely useless, though indication of trail-starts has improved of late. Frequently only the first 50m or so of the trail in question have been cleaned and refurbished, and the new *kalderími* construction – unlike the deeply rooted originals – has been done too superficially to last.

The best **walking seasons** are late April through early June, and early September through October; summer is hot and humid, and the winter mist- and snow line in the north can dip well below the villages. If you're serious about hiking here, you may want to equip yourself with some or all of the following: Road Editions' 1:50,000 map no. 33 *Pílio*, which is also by far the best touring map, and sold locally; Anavasi's 1:25,000 Topo 25 map *Pílio* (which, however, only covers the centre of the peninsula) and Nikos Haratsis' *A Hiker's Guide to Mount Pelion* (Epikinonia Editions, Vólos). These each have their virtues and defects, and do not solve all problems. Despite Haratsis' participation, and the use of Ordnance Survey-type contours, the Road Editions' map does not trace walking routes or some minor roads at all accurately. The Haratsis' book itself has non-scale, hand-drawn maps, and imprecise or obsolete text directions were not corrected or updated when translating from the older Greek original. Lance Chilton's *Walks in The Pilion* (with a detailed map; see "Books", p.1148) is generally excellent, but does not estimate elapsed times, and covers only the east-coast villages from Anílio to Tsangarádha. In the accounts in this chapter, we have indicated the best and most useful routes, with elapsed times, start points and brief summaries.

featuring a hunting scene with a bear-headed hippo (a common quirk of the painter's animals, who never saw most of his subjects in the flesh). Near the stairway are the ancient gods and goddesses Hermes, Aphrodite, Athena and Ares – the last being a depiction of Theophilos himself; opposite is a portrait of his patron Kondos on a horse.

PORTARIÁ, 14km east of Vólos, has a more mountainous feel with a soundtrack of running streams. Regrettably, the areas closest to the busy road have become tacky and commercialized (including a convenient **ATM** next to the main car park), but the backstreets are still rewarding. The chief glory, as so often in Pílio, is the main square, shaded by tremendous plane trees, one planted in 1220; to one side are the vast, ghostly ruins of the belle époque Hotel Theoxenia, once the grandest hotel in the Balkans, where Venizelos stayed during its prime. Extant **accommodation** runs to more than a dozen traditional mansions and conventional hotels; the most economical among the former are *Tis Marios* (T24280 99535; ❺), below the road south, and the dead-central but plainer *Arhondiko Klitsa* (T24280 99418, F24280 27551; ❹). Among hotels, the clear winner is *Kritsa* on the platía (T24280 99121, Wwww .hotel-kritsa.gr; summer ❸, winter ❺), a previously indifferent interwar building tastefully refurbished into an eight-room hotel (with two suites) of top standard; the hearty €8 breakfasts, with their array of breads, cheese, eggs, turnovers and savoury titbits, are a model of what hotel breakfasts should be. If you can't get in, try for the *Alkistis* (T24280 99175, F24280 99630; ❺), deeper into the village, a 1970s-built mock-traditional pile with its own parking, ample common areas and views over greenery, compensating for rather plain rooms. **Eating** out, the congenial dining room of the ✄ *Kritsa* again stands head and shoulders above the rest, with large portions, professional service, proper table linen and specialities such as parsley-purée dip, Skópelos olive biscuits and a hearty rendition of *spetzofáï*, accompanied by excellent local bulk wine.

Makrynítsa

From Portariá you can detour 2km northwest to **MAKRYNÍTSA**, 17km from Vólos, where stone houses straggle picturesquely down the mountainside. Founded in 1204 by refugees from the Fourth Crusade's sacking of Constantinople, it offers six outstanding churches plus a monastery, and numbers of **traditional mansions** – many restored as accommodation. Inevitably, there is blight on the main lane into the centre from tatty souvenir shops, and plenty of (Greek) day-trippers, but both are easy to escape, and the views over the Pagasitic Gulf are splendid.

There's a 200-metre altitude difference between the upper and lower quarters of Makrynítsa, so it takes a half-day's rambling to get a full sense of the village. Most impressive of the churches are **Áyios Ioánnis**, next to the fountain on the shady main platía, and the beautiful eighteenth-century **monastery of Panayía Makrynítissa**, right under the clocktower. The marble relief work on Áyios Ioánnis' apse, plus that on the fountain right opposite, are among the best of its type in Greece. A few paces above the Áyios Ioánnis square there's a **Theophilos fresco** (see opposite) in the right-hand café, showing revolutionary chieftain Kastsandonis and his men merry-making.

If you are looking for a **challenging walk** in Pílio, the village is also the starting point for the five-hour trek to the deserted, frescoed **monastery of Sourviás**. This begins at the little plaza known as Bránis, and sticks largely to *kalderími* and path surface. There is another route via the chapel of Panayía Leskhianí which takes only three-and-a-half hours one way, and which also starts at Platía Bránis, but in this case you begin on a steep cement track west past the monastery of Ayíou Yerasímou, though trail resumes for most of the way once Makrynítsa is out of sight.

Accommodation in Makrynítsa is abundant but, as usual on Pílio, not cheap. Among more affordable options, all just above the lane in from the car park, are the *Theophilos* (☎24280 99435; summer ❸, winter ❺), with bright, salubrious if rather kitschly decorated units; the cosy, en-suite *Arhondiko Routsou* (☎24280 99090; summer ❸, winter ❹); and the *Arhondiko Repana* (☎24280 99067, ☻24280 99548; ❹), its rooms a bit over-restored but the best value here. There are a few rather commercialized **tavernas** right on the platía, but it's best to continue beyond and uphill to the **ouzerí** *Alfa Vita*.

Hánia and Agriólefkes

Travelling on over the mountain, beyond Portariá, the road hairpins up to the **Hánia pass**, and the cheerless "village" of the same name, a string of modern houses and a smattering of hotels which see little use except in winter. Its **tavernas**, however, may come in handy as a lunch stop for hikers **trekking** between Portariá or Dhrákia and Zagorá, five-to-six-hour undertakings, much of the way on path. A minor road leads 4km southeast to the **Agriólefkes ski resort** (all of five lifts and six runs plus a nordic piste; top point 1473m); it's open January to March as a rule, though recent harsh winters helped the place work into late April.

Once past Hánia, the view suddenly opens to take in the whole northeast coast of the peninsula as you spiral down to a fork: the left turning leads to Zagorá, the right towards Tsangarádha. The old *kalderími* between Hánia and Zagorá has been cleaned and repaired, but the main problem with this three-hour walk is that you're never far from the busy road, and the final approach to Zagorá is entirely on asphalt.

The northeast Pílio coast

Pílio's best (and most popular) beaches, plus its lushest scenery, are found on the Aegean-facing **northeast coast**, which bears the brunt of winter storms. A relatively humid climate and shady dells nurture exotic flowers such as hydrangeas, gardenias and camellias, locally bred and sold at the roadside. The "county town" of the region and major producer and packer of fruit is **Zagorá**, self-proclaimed apple capital of Greece.

Zagorá and Pourí

The largest Pílio village, **ZAGORÁ** has a life more independent of tourism than its neighbours, though government studies give the fruit orchards only until the year 2020 to survive, owing to depleted soil and overuse of pesticides. After kiwis were tried and found wanting, raspberries are being proposed as a potential breakaway from apple monoculture; most of the residents wish to continue somehow as farmers rather than in the tourism sector.

Visitors often jump to unfavourable conclusions from the workaday, concrete main street where the bus calls; in fact, there are four well-preserved and architecturally more varied areas, with many handsome Neoclassical mansions, based around the squares of **Ayía Paraskeví**, **Ayía Kyriakí**, **Áyios Yeóryios** and **Metamórfosis (Sotíra)**, strung out over 5km. Coming from Vólos, turn left at the first petrol station to find Ayía Paraskeví (Perahóra) up the hillside, with its pleasant, unvisited platía. Ayía Kyriakí is effectively the centre of Zagorá. Bearing left away from the turning for Horeftó will bring you to the broad platía of Áyios Yeóryios, in the shadow of its lovely plane tree and beautiful eighteenth-century church, while Sotíra lies beyond this, above the road to Pourí.

The prime **accommodation** choice in Zagorá is the impeccably restored ☥ *Arhondiko Gayanni* (☎24260 23391, ⊕www.villagayannis.gr; B&B summer ❹, winter ❺), a gorgeous three-storey mansion dating from 1770, with a beautiful garden, ample parking, a genial host and copious breakfasts. Families should head for the *Xenonas Stefania* on the road to Horeftó (☎24260 23233, ⊕www .pelion.com.gr/stefania.htm; summer ❸, winter ❹), whose air-conditioned studios with fireplaces and terraces sleep up to four. Other lodging in Zagorá is often more reasonably priced than elsewhere in the region. Two places with rooms which underwent thorough refits relatively recently are *Marika Vlahou* (☎24260 22153;❷), above a metalworking shop in Ayía Kyriakí, or the warmly welcoming *Yiannis Halkias* (☎24260 22159;❸), in Áyios Yeóryios by the turning for Horeftó. All four parishes host grill-**tavernas**, though best-in-show are *Tsipouradhiko Tò Meïdani* by the roadside in Sotíra, where you fight for one of the few seats on the flower-lined balcony, and ☥ *O Petros* (also called *Fani's*; open all day every day), off the *kalderími* above Áyios Yeóryios square, where the quality of the cooking and views over the church and squat belfry to the Sporades offset somewhat small portions. There's also a **post office** in Áyios Yeóryios and a **bank** (ATM) in Ayía Kyriakí – the latter one of just two in the remoter villages of the peninsula.

The road beyond Zagorá continues to **POURÍ**, one of the remotest – and most spectacularly sited – communities on Pílio. Theoharis Hiotis rents **rooms** (☎24260 23168;❸) in his modern pension 250m beyond the square; the only **taverna** is *Tò Balkoni*, below the square. The nearest beach is **Elítsa**, 4km below by paved, then dirt, road; it's tiny, functional and shady early in the afternoon, though a welcoming **taverna**, *Plymari*, straddles the final approach. Better **Ovriós** beach is reached by a different track taking off from the Elítsa road just below the village. Pourí is also a major trailhead for ambitious **treks** such as the five-and-a-half-hour hike to Sourviás monastery, initially track but then trail, or the eight-hour expedition to Véneto, the northernmost village in Pílio, via the abandoned hamlet of Paleá Mintzéla. Either requires more stamina, planning and orientation skills than the usual Pílio outing.

Horeftó

Eight twisting kilometres down the mountain, **HOREFTÓ** (infrequent bus from Zagorá) makes an excellent coastal base. There is ample choice of **beaches**: a long, decent one in front of this former fishing village; secluded Áyii Saránda 2km south (see below); and two coves at Análipsi, to the north – a brief hike from the end of the frontage road brings you to the first cove, a little paradise popular with nudists and rough campers taking advantage of a spring behind the sand. Determined explorers can follow a coastal path for twenty minutes more to the northerly cove, road-accessible and rockier. There are also two hour-plus *kalderímia* up to Zagorá, which can be combined to make an enjoyable loop.

Horeftó supports half-a-dozen hotels and an equal number of studio apartments for rent. The best-value and best-located **hotels** are – near the quieter south end of the coast road – the high-standard *Hayiati* (☎24260 23540, ⓕ24260 22405; ❹), with off-street parking, spacious garden bar, wheelchair access and fridges in the mostly sea-view rooms, heated in winter; the simpler *Erato* (☎24260 22445; ❸), more of a *dhomátia* since breakfast isn't available, a 1970s block with partial sea views and fridges; and, above the final curve on the road in from Zagorá, the simple, homey *Aegeus* (☎24260 22778, ⓕ24260

22784; ❸), making an attempt to soften the communal areas with textiles. If you show up without booking during midsummer you're likely to end up at the basic municipal **campsite** (no phone), at the extreme south end of the main beach. You can continue past the campsite to the unmarked but paved and very useful shortcut up to Makryráhi, saving the long way around back through Zagóra. This passes the steep, one-kilometre driveway down to **Áyii Saránda** beach, with its lone taverna-rooms, *In Front of the Sea* (❷), with four non-en-suite rooms and equally basic food; the sand itself extends for 700m, punctuated by rock outcrops (one with a whimsical statue on top), halting just below one of the liveliest all-day-and-all-night **clubs** in the region.

Eating options in Horeftó are decent, with both of the following recommendations open much of the year. *O Petros* (a branch of the one in Zagóra) is an excellent all-rounder – *hortópitta*, salad and wild sea bass might well figure on the menu – while *Ta Dhelfínia* proves a competent ouzerí, with dishes such as fried fish and starters like stuffed olives.

Kissós

The easterly turning at the junction below Hánia leads through, resolutely untouristy Makryráhi, a perennial traffic bottleneck, north-facing Anílio (meaning "without sun"); and the upper edge of Áyios Dhimítrios before reaching the side road for **KISSÓS**. This unspoilt corner of Pílio lies 1km off the main road, virtually buried in foliage, with sleepy residential quarters ascending in terraces either side of eighteenth-century **Ayía Marína**, one of the finest churches on the peninsula. It's protected (and usually kept locked) by the archeological service, but you can always admire fine frescoes above the south door. The interior of this three-aisled basilica contains an extravagantly ornate *témblon* and rather dark ceiling frescoes.

Accommodation here tends to be simple but good value, for example the modern, bland *Rooms Sofia Gloumi-Hanou* (☎24260 31267 or 697 28 21 841; ❸), uphill from the multilevel platía – the largest on the mountain – with limited parking and an evening-only *psistariá* on the ground floor. The smallish rooms at *Xenonas Kissos* (☎24260 31214 or 697 42 04 652; ❹, also triples and quads), opposite the church, have wood trim, bright curtains and fridges, with a new wing added in 2003. Its ground-floor **taverna** (*Iy Klimataria*) has a fine terrace, but the more prosaically set *Makis* across the street pips it for value with *mayireftá* (such as rabbit stew, broccoli, potato croquettes, beans) all year, plus grills in high season. If you're based here, the hike up to Hánia is a good two-hour jaunt, mostly on path.

Áyios Dhimítrios and Áyios Ioánnis

Heading for the coast instead, you tackle 6km of twisting paved road via **ÁYIOS DHIMÍTRIOS**, whose main bright spot is a **taverna** on the lowermost Platía Xyróvrysi, *Ta Pende Platania* (weekends only late May & June; daily July–Sept), named for the five plane trees which grace the square and a reliable source of eminently reasonable, simple and salubrious grills and vegetable *mezédhes*.

ÁYIOS IOÁNNIS, 2km below, was once the port and boat-building yards for Áyios Dhimítrios but is now eastern Pílio's major resort. Densely packed hotels and private rooms were thrown up during the mid-1980s in a manner that would no longer be allowed, but despite this, finding a bed here in peak season is as problematic as anywhere on the peninsula. Budget **accommodation** options include the *Hotel Marina* (☎24260 31239 or 24260 31097; ❷), in a peaceful cul-de-sac at the south end of the strip, or the kitschly furnished *Zephyros* (☎24260 31335; ❸) nearby. With a bit more

to spend, try the tasteful *Anesis* (☎24260 31123, ⓦwww.hotelanesis.gr; ❹),
with a slightly alternative ambience and pastel-coloured rooms; the *Sofoklis*
(☎24260 31230, ⓦsofokleshotel.pelionet.gr; ❹), towards the northern end
of the front, completely refurbished in 2003, with a century-old stone-walled
lounge, oblique or direct sea views from most of the rooms, and an attractive
terrace-pool; or the somewhat impersonal but comfortable *Aloe* (☎24260
31240; ❺), sprawling just inland behind its lawn-garden.

Restaurants along the front at first seem to be similar and touristy, but on
trial, ⌁ *Poseidhonas* proves to be an excellent, reasonably priced, all-year seafood
taverna kept by a fishing family who only purvey their own fresh catch. For
something more unusual, the *Ostria* up the hill (well-signed) acquits itself as a
koultouriárika taverna, with rich, generic-Mediterranean recipes making good
use of herbs and other strong flavourings; proprietress Hariklia spent years in
Florence, so pasta dishes are emphasized. It's worth the cost of about €25 a
head, but seating is limited so reserve (☎24260 32132).

The **beach** at Áyios Ioánnis, though of average quality, is popular and
commercialized with windsurfing boards for rent. For more ambitious activities, such as sea-kayaking, mountain-biking and horse-riding, contact local
travel and accommodation agency Les Hirondelles (☎24260 31181, ⓦwww
.les-hirondelles.gr), which also represents most of the ocean-view studios in the
area. For a quieter time and finer sand, walk either ten minutes north to **Pláka**
beach, with its mostly young, Greek clientele and popular beach bar-taverna,
or fifteen minutes south (past the **campsite** – ☎24260 31319; June–Sept) to
Papá Neró beach, the best tanning spot in the vicinity, and accordingly cluttered with sunbeds. At sea level, cars are banned all day in summer, and there are
just a few **rooms** for rent – for example *Iy Orea Ammoudhia* (☎24260 31219,
ⓔpapanero@internet.gr; Easter–Oct; ❹), light-pine-and-tile-bedecked units
with sea view. Downstairs is the better of two **tavernas** here, known locally as
Papoutsis after the founder; the fare's a mix of humbler fish species and *mayireftá*,
with nice touches like *toursí* (pickled vegetables) mix and samphire on the salads,
plus real table linen.

Damoúhari

South from the Áyios Ioánnis campsite, a narrow paved road leads up, over a
low ridge and down to **DAMOÚHARI**, a hamlet set amid olive trees and
bordering a postcard-perfect port. The construction of another road down from
Moúressi put an end to its seclusion, and villas have sprung up mushroom-like
amongst the olive trees. However, cars are excluded from the shoreline area,
which offers a large pebble beach, the overgrown ruins of a Venetian castle, and
several **tavernas**, best of which by some way is *Kafezythestiatorio Barba Stergios*,
where you can dine on excellent wild fish, two starters and bulk wine for about
€24 each, or assorted meat grills and *mayireftá* for rather less. Top **accommodation** choice here is the attractive, unobtrusive *Hotel Damouhari* (☎24260 49840,
ⓕ24260 49841; ❺), a mock-traditional "village" of stone-built studio cottages
and rooms arrayed below a small infinity pool, with antiques and wood trim in
the units and *objet-trouvé* decor in the bar which is better known as *Kleopatra
Miramare*. The place is block-booked much of the year by tour companies, but
there's an excellent waterside annexe of five state-of-the-art rooms (❹). Failing
the annexe, adjacent alternatives are the comparatively modest *Rooms Kastro*
(☎24260 49475; ❸) and *Rooms Viktoria* (☎24260 49872; ❸).

From Damoúhari, it's possible to **walk to Tsangarádha** in 75 minutes, a
popular and rewarding trip (though most folk do it downhill in something
under an hour). At the mouth of the ravine draining to the larger bay, a

spectacular *kalderími* begins its steep ascent, allowing glimpses of up to six villages simultaneously, plus the Sporades on a clear day, from points along the way. Subsequently there is deep shade, and a potable spring approaching Ayía Kyriakí; the path emerges in the Ayía Paraskeví quarter of Tsangarádha, just downhill from the post office.

Tsangarádha

TSANGARÁDHA is the largest northeastern village after Zagorá, though it may not seem so at first, since like Zagorá, it's divided into four distinct quarters – **Taxiárhes**, **Ayía Paraskeví**, **Ayía Kyriakí** and **Áyios Stéfanos** – strung along several kilometres of road. Each of these lies scattered around a namesake church and platía, the finest of which is **Ayía Paraskeví**, shaded by reputedly the heftiest plane tree in Greece – pushing a thousand years in age, and requiring eighteen men to encircle. More local botanical prodigies are found in Taxiárhes at the private **Serpentin Garden** (visits by appointment only, ☎24260 49060, ⓦwww.serpentin-garden.com), a lovingly nurtured hillside Eden featuring many heirloom roses and other rare plants.

Most **accommodation** in this area is pricey, and on the noisy main road. Exceptions in one respect or another include the friendly, en-suite *Villa ton Rodhon* (☎24260 49340; ❹), right by the top of the cobbled path to Damoúhari, a 1970s construction where most plain rooms have sea views and balconies; the *Arhondiko Hatzakou* (☎24260 49911; ❹), a somewhat over-modernized mansion well below the highway in Taxiárhes quarter; or the slightly more expensive but good-value *Konaki Hotel* (☎24260 49481; ❹), just south of the Ayía Paraskeví square but set back from the road. All rooms have fridges and views, some also have balconies, and there's a pleasant basement breakfast area. You can splurge at Ioannis and Margarita's *Kastanies* (☎24260 49135, ⓦwww.kastanies.com; ❻), the last building on the left in Áyios Stéfanos heading northwest; this is a sympathetic restoration inn, with tasteful rooms, tubs in the designer bathrooms and limited private parking. Down on Ayía Paraskeví's platía, *The Lost Unicorn* (☎24260 49930; ❻), under the sympathetic new management of Claire and Christos Martzos since 2004, scores as much for its common areas – kitted out like a British gentlemen's club – and champagne breakfasts as for the eight antique-furnished rooms. Tsangarádha's **eating** options are mostly less than brilliant; the lone exception is *Apostolis*, under the old police station on the approach to the same square, which is the area's only genuine *tsipourádhiko*, serving in season until 1am. A **post office** and stand-alone **bank** ATM round out the list of amenities.

Moúressi

In general, better meals are to be had at any of the **tavernas** in **MOÚRESSI**, 3km northwest of Áyios Stéfanos. Both *To Tavernaki* and *Iy Dhrosia* up on the main highway are famously dour, but you can get specialities like *fasólies hándres* (delicately flavoured pinto beans) and assorted offal on a spit. Good food at *To Kentriko* by Moúressi's linden-shaded platía offsets a clinical atmosphere and service worthy of *Fawlty Towers*, while *O Vangelis*, 300m down the road to Damoúhari, is an inexpensive, friendly grill with good bulk wine (but pre-fried chips). Approaching the village centre on the access road, there's also a prime en-suite **accommodation** choice: ⚥ *The Old Silk Store* (☎24260 49086 or 693 71 56 780, ⓦwww.pelionet.gr/oldsilkstore; closed Feb; B&B ❹), a lightly restored nineteenth-century mansion with a lush garden, barbecue area and high-ceilinged, wood-floored rooms (plus a studio cottage ❺). Breakfasts change daily but always include excellent bread and home-made preserves.

The proprietress also runs Mulberry Travel (☎24260 48864), which helps with incoming travel arrangements, acts as the local Hertz **car rental** rep and leads regular walking tours. An excellent short stroll, very useful for reaching the beach or completing a loop via Áyios Ioánnis, is the 45-minute descent to Damoúhari; look for the signposted start of the trail on the bend in the road about 100m past *O Vangelis*.

Fakístra to Lambinoú

From Tsangarádha, ninety-minute paths from both Taxiárhes and Ayía Paraskeví districts, or a seven-kilometre hairpin road, snake down to **Mylopótamos**, a collection of attractive pebble coves. The two largest are separated by a naturally tunnelled rock wall, with a pair of musical beach bars just above. They attract mostly Greek summer crowds, who pack into **accommodation** lining the approach road; one of the nearest is *Diakoumis* (☎24260 49203; ❸), with popular, mock-traditional rooms spread over two rambling buildings, and spectacular views from wooden terraces. Another bend uphill stands the blindingly white rooms of *Dhimitris Angelikas* (☎24260 49588 or 697 40 44 364; ❸) – the same family manages the kindly, efficient *Angelika* **taverna** (daily Easter–Oct, weekends otherwise), just above the Mylopótamos parking area; the fish is a bit expensive but the *mayireftá* is tasty and reasonably priced.

If you want more solitude, try **Fakístra beach**, the next swimmable cove north of Mylopótamos. It's most satisfyingly reached on foot from Damoúhari, via a coastal corniche trail which takes off between two prominent stakes, fifteen minutes uphill from the latter beach. Just beyond, there's been some disruption from an illegal road threatening the *kalderími*, but persevere – the way goes through. Green-dot waymarks lead you down towards sea level through olive groves. After about half an hour, you cross Makrolítharo bay with its rocky shore and striking promontory; the path, unmarked now, continues from the far side, climbing gradually through more olives to a spectacular viewpoint taking in a cliff-cave which was purportedly a "secret school" in bygone times. Some thirty minutes past Makrolítharo, you pass the marked side-trail accessing the school, and then almost immediately the end of the road down from Ayía Kyriakí; that's unpaved the last 3km, with a tiny parking area, from which it's a few minutes more (total 80min from Damoúhari) to the cliff-girt, pea-gravel-and-sand bay with a shattered castle atop the southerly palisade.

Southeast of Mylopótamos lie two more attractive **beaches**: Limniónas and Lambinoú. You can get there on foot from Mylopótamos, but most people arrive via the inland village of Lambinoú (no facilities except during peak season), from where a paved road leads 3km down past the abandoned **monastery of Lambidhónas**, its *katholikón* locked but sporting fine frescoes over the doors. **Lambinoú** cove, with a seasonal snack-bar, is a narrow, deep square of sand where four parties would constitute a crowd; you can continue to much larger, more scenic Limniónas within 35 minutes' walk, mostly on path, along the coast, or by a separate track system from Lambinoú village. **Limniónas** has a fresh-water shower but no other reliable amenities.

Hikes from Xouríkhti

Just above the main road en route from Tsangarádha to Lambinoú, the comparatively workaday village of Xouríkhti, accessed by path from Tsangarádha, is also the start point for more **walks**. Near the lower end of the village, a yellow walking-man sign points down a weedy **path towards Lambinoú**; within twenty minutes you're spilled out onto the asphalt highway, along which you must walk south 2km or so until the resumption of the path (signed), near a circular wooden gazebo just below the road. The route, now somewhat maintained, reaches more characterful Lambinoú village and then descends sharply to the monastery of the same name, nicely short-cutting the road in; then it's briefly road to Lambinoú cove, mostly path to Limniónas, and then coastal track to Mylopótamos, the final ten minutes or so on path and steps emerging at the recommended *Angelika* taverna (see p.381). Total walking time from Xouríkhti is just over two hours; if you're wise, you'll arrange a taxi out of Mylopótamos, instead of completing a loop back to Xouríkhti (encouraged by both the Road and Anavasi maps) – the direct path up from Mylopótamos has mostly been destroyed by bulldozing and quarrying, and the final surviving stretch is very overgrown.

More rewardingly, Xouríkthi is also the eastern trailhead for an enjoyable three-hour **hike to Miliés**, one of the most popular Pílio treks. The path proper, which wends its way through a mix of open hillside and shady dell, starts about fifteen minutes southwest of the platía (follow signs to Áyios Dhimítrios), branching left off the track system; from here on the route is obvious and well-marked, with stretches of restored *kalderími*. Before the road around the hill via Lambinoú and Kalamáki was opened in 1938, this was the principal thoroughfare between the railhead at Miliés and the Tsangarádha area. It is feasible to do this walk one-way and then, with an eye to bus schedules, take the afternoon KTEL back to your starting point.

Western Pílio

Lying in the "rain shadow" of the mountain, the western Pílio slopes and coast have a drier, more Mediterranean climate, with olives and arbutus shrubs predominating except in shady, well-watered ravines. The beaches, at least until you get past Kalá Nerá, are far more developed than their natural endowments merit and lack the character of those on the east side. Inland it is a different story, with pleasant foothill villages and – for a change – decent bus services. **Vyzítsa** and **Pinakátes** in particular both make good bases for car-touring or hiking.

Miliés

Like Tsangarádha, the sizeable village of **MILIÉS** (sometimes Miléës or Mileai) was an important centre of culture during the eighteenth century. It retains a number of imposing mansions and Pílio's most interesting church, **Taxiárhis** (unpredictable hours; most likely open at 6pm). Its narthex frescoes are the oldest (eighteenth-century) and most unusual, including scenes from Noah's Flood (with two elephants boarding the Ark) and, in one corner, a mandala of three concentric rings showing the seasons, the zodiac and the cycle of human existence. With five wells under the floor and 48 clay urns secreted in the walls, the church's acoustics are superb, so it's occasionally used for concerts of sacred music.

Accommodation is somewhat limited, since most people stay nearby at Vyzítsa; the choice boils down to either a couple of pricey co-managed mansions – the *Filippidi* and *Evangelinaki* (T 24230 86714, F 24230 90151, ⓸) – or *O Paleos Stathmos* (T 24230 86425, F 24230 86736; ⓸), down by the train line and accessible by *kalderími* from the main square, whose very plain rooms are only worth it if you get a balconied front unit. Quality **eating and drinking** options are also limited; the simple grill, *Panorama*, occupying a wedge-shaped building just above the platía (with terrace seating opposite), is about the most consistent. The most distinctive food in town emerges from the Korbas bakery down near the Vólos road junction by the bus stop, purveying every kind of Pílio bread, pie, turnover and cake imaginable.

Vyzítsa

VYZÍTSA, 3km further up the mountain from Miliés and alive with water in streams and aqueducts, has been officially designated a "traditional settlement". It has a more open and less lived-in feel than either Makrynítsa or Miliés, though it draws crowds of day-trippers in summer. Nonetheless it's an excellent base, with several **accommodation** options in converted mansions. Pick of these from the standpoint of decor and quiet is the *Arhondiko Karayianopoulou* (☎24230 86717, ℱ24230 86878; B&B ❺), 200m uphill from the village through-road, with well-restored rooms and breakfast served out in the courtyard; it's also worth trying the slightly plainer but airy *Arhondiko Kondou* (☎24230 86793, ✉vikonto@otenet.gr; ❹), also a five-minute walk uphill from the car-park platía. About the best value and most consistently attended here, if not the most inspired restoration job, is the *Thetis* (☎24230 86111; summer ❷, winter ❸), conveniently just west of the central car park but calm enough, with good breakfasts at the adjacent stone-built café included. The approach road from Miliés to the village is lined with more prosaically located inns; best of these are the *Xenonas Dimou* (☎24230 86718, ℱ24210 21222; summer ❹, winter ❺), small and set back a bit from the road, with a breakfast salon; or the *Hotel Stoïkos* (☎24230 86406, ℱ24230 86061; ❹), most of whose well-executed modern rooms appointed in mock-traditional style have views. The tiered upper platía with its fountains and three plane trees, each larger than the last, offers three **tavernas**, acceptable though nothing extraordinary;

The Pílio trenáki

A prime attraction in the western Pílio is the old *trenáki*, or **narrow-gauge railway**, which originally ran between Vólos and Miliés. The sixty-kilometre line, in normal service until 1971, was laid out between 1894 and 1903 by an Italian consortium under the supervision of engineer Evaristo de Chirico, father of the famous artist Giorgio de Chirico. The boy, born in Vólos in 1888, spent his formative years with his father on the job-site, which accounts for the little trains which chug across several of his paintings (such as *The Hour of Silence* and *The Seer's Reward*, both from 1913). To conquer the maximum 2.8-percent gradient and numerous ravines between Áno Lehónia and Miliés, the elder de Chirico designed six multiple-span stone viaducts, buttressing with blind arches, tunnels and a riveted iron trestle bridge, all justly considered masterpieces of form and function. The bridge, some 700m west of the terminus below Miliés, spans a particularly deep gorge and can be crossed on a **pedestrian catwalk**; indeed, following the entire route down to Áno Lehónia is a popular 5.5-hour walk, with occasional springs and picnic spots en route.

An **excursion service**, using one of the original Belgian steam locomotives (since, alas, converted to diesel), is now a tourist attraction during weekends and holidays Easter–October, and several of the *belle époque* stations have been restored. The train leaves Áno Lehónia (city bus #5 from Vólos) on the coast at 11am, taking ninety minutes to reach Miliés, from where it returns at 4pm. Tickets are currently €13 adults, €8.50 kids, whether you travel one-way or round trip, and go on sale at 10.30am (best to start queuing at 10am), at either Vólos or Áno Lehónia. However, groups often book out the handful of carriages, so you're well advised to make enquiries at Vólos station a few days in advance. There is talk of extending the run from Lehónia to Vólos, but this would involve expensive rerouting of the track or at least prising it free from the asphalt road in which it's embedded from Káto Lehónia to Vólos.

the best eating is available at *O Yiorgaras*, out on the main road next to *Hotel Stoïkos*.

Hikes around Vyzítsa

Vyzítsa sits at the nexus of a number of trails down to the coast at Kalá Nerá, which can be combined into **loop-hikes** of a half-day's duration. From the chapel of Zoödhóhou Piyís, just below Vyzítsa's platía, a sporadically marked route takes you around a vast landslip zone, and then across two ravines (bridges provided) and a brief stretch of farm track until dropping to Kalá Nerá, via Aryireïka hamlet, just under two hours later (if you're going in the other direction, the opening to this path is conspicuously signposted at Kalá Nerá). Once down on the main highway in Kalá Nerá, you can bear left (east) and adopt the oblique cemetery track (actually signposted for two monasteries and Aryiraïka) which begins the ninety-minute hike up to Miliés. There is a signposted *kalderími* from Miliés to Vyzítsa, which takes less than an hour.

Alternatively, and preferably perhaps, turn right (west) at Kalá Nerá and complete a circuit by turning onto the well-indicated *kalderími* taking off just before the petrol station, opposite the telecoms circuit building. This climbs, in just over ninety minutes, to Pinakátes, almost entirely along a cleaned and meticulously restored *kalderími*, with superb views over the ravine separating Olgá hamlet from Aryireïka, and de Chirico's five-arched rail bridge there. Once on Pinakátes, the final link back to Vyzítsa can be problematic; the path from the edge of Pinakátes to Vyzítsa's upper square, shown promisingly in the Haratsis guide and on the recommended maps, has been damaged by a landslide halfway along, plus subsequent treefall, so it's impassable at present and you'll have to take a taxi or walk along the road back to Vyzítsa.

Pinakátes

PINAKÁTES, tucked at the top of a densely forested ravine, was once among the least visited and most desolate of the west Pílio villages, despite being the terminus of a bus line from Vólos. No longer: the surfacing of the road in from Vyzítsa, and trendy Greeks buying up crumbling mansions for restoration, have seen to that. For the moment it remains a superbly atmospheric spot, with just enough food and lodging to make it a practical base. In the village centre there are two mansion-**inns**: the *Alatinou*, a few steps below the square (☎24230 86995 or 697 28 38 282; ❹), with simple en-suite rooms with dark-wood decor and a basement breakfast salon; and the much grander *Xiradhakis* (☎ & ☞24230 86375; summer ❺, winter ❻), a bit further down the same lane. The shaded platía offers a single **taverna**, but the best eating for some distance around – and where the villagers themselves prefer to hang out – is at ⚔ *Iy Dhrosia* (alias *Taverna tou Papa*), at the far western edge of Pinakátes. The food – including *dolmádhes* and *gídha lemonáti* (goat stew with lemon sauce) – uses local, free-range meat and poultry. There are also excellent *mezédhes* available (off-menu) to accompany a *karafáki* of *tsípouro* – or a jug of their deceptively potent red bulk wine.

Áyios Yeóryios Nilías to Dhrákia — and more walks

The next village on the road (and bus route) west to Vólos, **ÁYIOS YEÓRYIOS NILÍAS**, should be a major walkers' mecca – except that **accommodation** is limited to two traditional mansion-inns: the eighteenth-century *Arhondiko Dereli* (☎24280 93163 or 697 76 12 287; ❻), a courtyard house with an attached bar and restaurant, just below the through road; and the nineteenth-century *Arhondiko Tzortzis* (☎24280 94923, ☞24280 94252;

summer ❺, winter ❼), at the start of the path up the mountain, both of them likely to be unattended without prior notice. Of three **tavernas** on the platía, *O Tsakitzis* is the most consistently open, with reliable meat from its own butcher's downstairs.

The two long **hikes** from here, however, are superb; both initially use the same path, but 25 minutes above the village square, at a cement aqueduct, there's a division, with a left turn taking you up to the Agriólefkes ski centre within three-and-a-half hours, mostly through beech woods with long stretches of path underfoot.

Continuing straight rather than left, following profuse red or blue paint dots or arrows (as well as the occasional sign), brings you to **Taxiárhes of Tsangarádha** within five hours from Áyios Yeóryios Nilías. This scenic, trans-Pelion traverse goes at a much higher contour than the Xouríkhti–Miliés one (see p.382), attaining an elevation of 1057m at Kourvéndelis ridge, just over two hours along. The changes in landscape – from apple orchards to dense beech forest – are marvellous, drinking water abundant, and the views southeast from the heights magnificent; the main drawback is that just under half the distance is along track rather than trail, with a dreary final-hour descent from the Mylopótamos springs to the main highway.

Another, much briefer, *kalderími* links Áyios Yeóryios with Áyios Vlásios, the next village downhill – no accommodation, just a taverna-café – before continuing ninety minutes north on foot over a *kalderími* to **ÁYIOS LAVRÉNDIOS**, an unspoilt if architecturally hotch-potch village with another lovely platía, which only comes alive in summer, if at all. **Accommodation** is limited, the most affordable being the spacious, wood-floored *Rooms Thalpori* (☎24280 96310; ❸). The village is connected with Káto Lehónia by a well-marked *kalderími* (90min). **DHRÁKIA**, just across the top of the valley from here and an hour away on foot (mostly by dirt track), has no public transport along its eleven-kilometre access road from Agriá, and is thus one of the least visited and most primitive villages on the mountain: lots of barnyard animals, wrecked cars and derelict houses. There are a few **rooms** – like those of *Stamatis Zisis* (☎24280 91233; ❸), in a mock-traditional building above the upper platía with its *psistariá* – but you're unlikely to stay at Dhrákia unless you are a fanatical walker.

Southern Pílio

Once **south** of the road linking Kalá Nerá, Miliés and Tsangarádha, Pílio becomes drier, lower and more stereotypically Mediterranean. The region was hit hard by wildfires during the mid-1990s, such that the only undamaged pine forests are found around Neohóri, southeast of Miliés; the terrain overall is less dramatic, the villages more scattered. There are, however, some interesting pockets, and considerably less tourism inland, though a number of busy coastal resorts attract a mixed clientele of foreigners and locals.

The area can be reached a little tortuously by bus or car from Vólos, and somewhat more comfortably by sea, via a few weekly hydrofoils to Ayía Kyriakí (Tríkeri) and Tríkeri island from Vólos or the Sporades.

Argalastí and around

AFÉTES is the first village encountered by land, and worth the brief detour for its vast platía with five plane trees, ornate church, dinner-only taverna and single-arch bridge below the car park. A few kilometres downhill lies **Áfyssos**, a busy but surprisingly pleasant resort with a shady waterfront square, its development courtesy of the town beach of Ambovós, more scenic Kalliftéri to the north, and other secluded ones along the 3km of road south to Lefókastro.

ARGALASTÍ, 12km southeast of Afétes, is much the biggest place in the south, with a **post office**, stand-alone **bank** ATM by the church, petrol stations and shops (including two bakeries). You can **stay** a bit west of the main through road at the high-standard ⚲ *Agamemnon* (☎ & ℱ 24230 54557, ⓦ www.agamemnon.gr; ❹), a well-restored, eighteenth-century mansion-hotel with a swimming pool, antiques throughout the common areas and on-site bar-restaurant; rooms, some with fireplaces, have stone or wood floors. On the platía, admittedly not as attractive as some others on the mountain but authentically workaday, *Sfindio* is the most reliable of two **grill-ouzerís**, quick-serving and reasonable, with *mezédhes* at night, while *O Kaloyeros (Tis Nikolettas)* across the way does fuller meals.

Argalastí is close to the Pagasitic Gulf, just a brief walk or drive west; a half-day loop takes in Kálamos resort (1hr west by path), Paralía Páou (fine coastal trail south) and the walled monastery of Páou (locked), just uphill. The beach at **Kálamos** is long and one of the sandiest on the Pagasitic side, but the fairly busy road runs just behind it; there are literally dozens of rooms (mostly ❹) and several tavernas, plus a discernible package-holiday presence. Secluded **Paralía Paoú**, reached by a different, dead-end road if you don't walk over from Kálamos, is by contrast fine gravel, one of the best on the Pagasitic, but devoid of amenities other than a few private villas.

Potistiká to Páltsi: the east coast

Better, less developed beaches are found on the east coast, with fine views across to the islands of Skiáthos, Skópelos and Alónissos, though fire damage has made their hinterlands decidedly unscenic. Closest to Argalastí, reached along a paved road (10km) via the village of Xinóvryssi, lies **Potistiká**. This is stunning, and just out of the burn zone, if a little windy; huge rock formations at the south end separate it from more secluded Melaní (walkable; see below for road access). Potistiká is a potential base, given the presence of a welcoming **hotel**, *Elytis* (☎ & ℱ 24230 54482 or 697 77 35 775; ❸), all of whose bland, white-tiled rooms face the sea, with heating for year-round operation and the only full-service **taverna** here. For other meals, you're best off heading back to the platía of **Xinóvryssi**, where the *Aigli* is the more accomplished of two eateries.

The beach at **Páltsi** lies 13km from Argalastí via a paved turning from the Xinóvryssi road (it's officially, and confusingly, signposted at points as "Áyios Konstandínos"). The sandy beach is marred somewhat by a reef in the middle, but the edges are fine, with islets and outcrops to dive off or swim towards. **Melaní** beach (no facilities) can be reached by a mostly paved road (2.5km) from the inland side of Páltsi hamlet.

Páltsi facilities comprise three **tavernas** – including *Levendis* by the chapel which serves cheap, sustaining *mayireftá* – and a number of **rooms**, the best placed of these being *Olga* (☎ 24230 55300; ❷), right behind the beach, with broad sea-view balconies.

Hórto to Marathiá via Láfkos: the west coast

Continuing due south from Argalastí, you reach the sea again after 7km at **HÓRTO**, a quiet little resort largely protected from exploitation by its mediocre beaches. **Accommodation** is mostly self-catering, and handled by tour companies; three **tavernas** intersperse themselves among a like number of coves here. Of these, *Flisvos*, to the left of the creek mouth as you face the sea, is the cheap-and-cheerful option favoured by locals.

Just 3km further, **MILÍNA** seems far more commercialized, attended mostly by folk from Vólos; the beach is the scanty Pagasitic norm, making it mostly a place to watch magnificent sunsets over the offshore islets and distant mainland ridges from one of the waterside **bar-cafés**. A dozen or so **accommodation** establishments also overlook the water or line the inland street grid; plain but serviceable *Xenon Athina* (℡24230 65473, ⓦwww.athina-pelion.com; ❸) on the front is worth it only if you get a sea-view room. For more comfort, refer to the local trading office of the recommended Houses of Pelion agency (see p.31), run by Tim and Aphroula Smart (℡24230 65471, ℉24230 65910), who can fix you up on-spec with one of their premises in the area, though they're mostly geared to packages based on Friday charter arrivals and departures. The agency also gives self-guiding walk instructions and changes money (there's no bank here). Among half-a-dozen fully fledged **tavernas**, *O Sakis* is far and away the best and most Greek-feeling, where you can assemble a tasty meal of seafood, two or three *mezédhes* and bulk wine for €11–16 – a fairly amazing feat for such a resort. There are plenty of shops and bakeries for self-catering, plus well-priced **cars and scooters** from Pelion Rent (℡24230 65762) at the north end of the quay, also with branches in Argalastí and Áfyssos.

Milína is one terminus of a pair of hour-long *kalderímia* linking the coast with the inland village of Láfkos, which can be combined for an enjoyable circuit. Beginning from the church on the shore road in Milína, head ten minutes inland along the side road until you see the *kalderími* erupting in an olive grove; from Láfkos, the return route starts at the far end of its platía, exiting the village from its lowest houses.

LÁFKOS itself is a handsome, ridgetop village in the throes of restoration by outsiders, graced by another respectable, car-free platía with a record number of plane trees and a cluster of **tavernas**, best of these being *Pigasos*, where the good food is complemented by the eccentric managing couple; equally interesting perhaps, on the lane in from the south edge of the village, is one of the last wood-fired bakeries in the region. Just off the start of the path down to Milína are two high-standard restoration **inns**, the better of which is sumptuous *Arhondiko Parissi* (℡24230 65856, ℉24230 66098; ❺), with iron beds in the rooms, a pool terrace and a full breakfast on offer.

Beyond Milína, there are no more proper shoreline villages and the landscape becomes increasingly bleak, with only the occasional weekend villa or moored boat to vary the horizon. Some 2km along, at nearly landlocked **Valtoúdhi Bay**, yachts anchored in the lee of Alatás islet (Sunsail has an anchorage and office here) outnumber fishing boats. About 4km past Milína, a side road on the right leads to the little anchorage of **Áyios Andhréas**, where the fishermen sit about talking shop and *O Pingouínos* is another good bet for somewhat pricey fish (allow over €25 each for a meal), in particular the bass-like, much-esteemed *sykiós*. All along this coast, people tend to play on the water rather than in it, as the gulf here is apt to be unpalatably warm, with flotsam and garbage washed down from Vólos. About the best swimming beach hereabouts is at **Marathiá** (also signposted as Marathiás), 7km further, with two rival tavernas and a *kantína* with sunbed concession.

The lower southeast coast: Paralía Mourtiá to Kastrí

Heading east from Láfkos, you'll again find better beaches on the east-facing coast. About halfway to the Aegean you pass through **PROMÝRI**, spilling down the slope where it's been hidden, out of sight from the sea and prying pirate eyes; there's a grill-ouzerí in the centre, and the start of an excellent three-hour **walk** to Plataniás, shown more or less correctly on the Road Editions' map. If necessary, get up the hill from Plataniás with a taxi or morning bus, and be prepared for catastrophic damage to the *kalderími* from rubble-dumping just ten minutes' walk south of Promýri – you have to worm your way through undergrowth for five minutes, but thereafter it's plain sailing to the ridge and asphalt road down to Plataniá. Cross this for a brief stretch on track, then descend a shady canyon (one old working fountain en route), sticking to path and *kalderími* until the last moments where you're in the stream bed, emerging on the asphalt at Plataniás about 700m inland.

After climbing northeast out of the ravine beyond the village, the onward road from Promýri dips to the sea again at **Paralía Mourtiá**, a tiny but fairly attractive beach with a single place with rooms for rent. Most will continue one bay south to **Paralía Lýris**, bigger and sandier than its neighbour although less secluded, with a reliably open **taverna** and more **rooms**. Like most of the little coves on the coast south of Potistiká, these spots are hugely popular with German and Austrian caravanners.

The main road passes through inland Lýri (no facilities) before arriving at the little port of **KATIYIÓRGIS**, the only sizeable coastal settlement in these parts, and the terminus of a regular bus line from Vólos, 66km away. The minuscule sandy bay here isn't great for swimming, owing to the numbers of fishing boats and yachts at anchor, but Katiyiórgis makes a good lunch stop, with terrace seating opposite Skiáthos, just three nautical miles distant. The more venerable of two **tavernas** is ⚲ *Flisvos* (April–Oct), with *mayireftá* and famously fresh fish served at tables on the sand, at only slightly bumped up prices considering the number of excursion boats which call here from Skiáthos; if you ask nicely, dishes will be garnished with *ftéri* (fried fern) and *tsitsíravla* (marinated terebinth shoots). They also have self-catering **rooms** upstairs (☎24230 71071, ⓕ24230 71072; ❷) – basic but perfectly adequate, even better if you get one with a sea-view balcony. There's lots more comfortable accommodation on the hillside to the south (❸–❹), with a significant UK package-holiday presence; the tour clients support a little waterside breakfast café/sweetshop, *Iy Avra*. For better, more secluded, beaches, take the well-defined path beginning below the last private villa, which leads within fifteen minutes to the secluded sandy covelet of **Vlahórema**, and then continues for another fifteen minutes over a ridge to larger **Vromonéri**, which also has track access from the west and a summer drinks *kantína*.

From 500m north of the Katiyiórgis quay, a paved road heads southwest through as-yet-unburnt olives and pines, with big eyefuls of Skiáthos and Évvia across the straits. After 7km it emerges off the paved road linking Promýri and Láfkos with Plataniá and **KASTRÍ**. Bearing left leads to the latter, a large, slightly exposed, sandy bay with a small **campsite** (☎24230 54248; June–Sept), which also manages the beachfront **taverna**, plus two **studio-room** outfits: *Kastri* (☎24230 71201; ❸) and *Ktena* (☎24230 71345; ❸).

Plataniás and Mikró

Turning down and right from the above-cited junction brings you shortly to **PLATANIÁS** (sometimes spelled "Plataniá"), on the south coast of Pílio, 10km in total from Láfkos. Taking its name from the robust plane trees in the stream valley which meets the sea here, this is the biggest resort in the south after Milína, with a regular bus service from Vólos, and excursion *kaïkia* – on which you might be able to arrange passage – calling most days from Skiáthos. The small beach is fine, but always oversubscribed by a mix of local and foreign holiday-makers; from the olive grove just inland an obvious path, threading spectacularly above the coast with some patches of cobbles, leads twelve minutes west to the much bigger and better strand of **Mikró**, with naturist covelets in-between. Plataniás is also the destination of the excellent three-hour **walk** in from Promýri (see opposite), but the walk to Láfkos via Sykiá, shown on the Road Editions map, is no longer followable and should not be attempted.

One of the first Pílio beach resorts to be developed, Plataniás is essentially a collection of junta-era low-rises, but innocuous enough outside of high season. Among six licensed **hotels**, much the best and quietest is the *Platania*, east of the river mouth, on the waterfront (☎24230 71266; ❸; open all year). At this rambling complex, all rooms have a fridge and balcony, and mostly mountain rather than sea views; there are also family units suitable for four, and a respectable **taverna** (*To Steki*) with good seafood, on the ground floor. Accommodation alternatives include many *dhomátia* establishments to the west (right) of the seaside bridge; remotest of these is the old-fashioned, secluded *Helena Apartments* in the olive grove behind the beach (☎24230 71012; ❷), accessible by path or roundabout road, with all units en suite and some with kitchen. On the road into Plataniás there's also a large **campsite**, the *Louisa* (☎24230 71260), some 600m before the sea.

MIKRÓ is arguably more attractive as a base, and served by an 8.5-kilometre dirt road from the Láfkos–Promýri asphalt. There are **tavernas** at each end of the sand, and a handful of **rooms** outfits, the ever-expanding *Mikro* (☎24230 71212; ❸) halfway along being the most established.

Tríkeri and Kóttes

At the extreme southwest end of Pílio, the crab-claw-shaped semi-peninsula of **Tríkeri** still feels very remote. During the Greek War of Independence, the Trikeriots put their considerable fleets at the disposal of the insurrection, and later the local sponge fleet rivalled the more renowned ones of the Argo-Saronics and Dodecanese. More recently, the area was used after the 1946–49 civil war as a place of exile for political prisoners (along with the island of Paleó Tríkeri, which housed a detention camp for women leftists), and until 1974 there was no road connecting it with the rest of Pílio. It now boasts the best highway in Pílio, connecting it with Milína in less than 45 minutes.

The hilltop village of **TRÍKERI** (called simply "Horió" in local parlance) has few amenities for outsiders other than one place with rooms (☎24230 91660; ❷) and some simple *kafenía* and grills on the little square, shaded in this arid climate by pea-family trees rather than the usual planes. The road has prompted a spate of cement construction and re-roofing, though a few *arhondiká* with views to the straits with Évvia survive in the back lanes. Donkeys and mules as a mode of transport are on the wane, but the 1500-metre *kalderími* down to the port of **AYÍA KYRIAKÍ** is still well used (drivers face a winding, six-kilometre road). This is principally a working fishing village, something of a rarity in modern Greece, and much the most attractive spot on this coast. In the boatyard, a variety of craft are still built in much the same way they have been for the last century or so, continuing the strong local seafaring tradition. There are a few **rooms** to rent at Mýlos cove, 1km west (*O Lambis* ☎24230 91587; ❸), but otherwise minimal concessions to tourism, perhaps because there's no good beach close by. However, multicoloured fishing boats, views across to Évvia and the chance for a seafood meal combine to make the trip worthwhile. Facing east from the car park and bus turnaround area, you see two **tavernas**, *Manolas* and *Mouragio*, of which the former is dearer but has more selection and patronage. Both, however, are surprisingly expensive considering their remoteness from Vólos; Greeks in the know repair instead to Tríkeri's traditional winter port, **KÓTTES**, on the other side of the isthmus, where *O Khristos* is the most reliable of three less expensive **tavernas** purveying fresh, unfarmed fish.

Paleó Tríkeri islet

Balanced just north of the tip of the "crab claw" is **Paleó Tríkeri** (also called Nisí Tríkeri – Tríkeri Island – or Nisí Panayías, after its main monastery of Evangelistrías, the Annunciation of the Virgin). The only inhabited islet in the Pagasitic Gulf was the original site of Tríkeri, settled from prehistoric times until sixteenth-century piracy compelled its abandonment and the move to "Horió". Today there's a permanent population of under fifty, a few places to stay, a couple of tavernas, burgeoning real-estate sales (as everywhere on Pílio) and clean sea. Little more than 2.5km from end to end, the blessedly car- and road-free islet consists of a few olive-covered hills and a fringe of small, rocky beaches.

The port and lone village of **AÏ-YIÁNNI** is tiny, with a single shop patronized by the many yachts calling here; a ten-minute path leads up to the nineteenth-century **monastery** in the middle of the islet. At the waterside are two **tavernas**: *Skala* (℡24230 55240) and *Dhiavlos* (℡24230 55210 or 697 34 10 908), the latter with a few **rooms** (❷).

If you don't coincide with one of the very rare hydrofoils calling at Paleó Tríkeri, the only way to reach the islet besides a yacht is by following the 6.2-kilometre the paved road from just north of "Horió" to **Alogóporos** ("Ford of the Horse"), the traditional crossing point. A large car park is provided for your (and the islanders') convenience; whip out your mobile and dial one of the two tavernas listed above to summon a "free" shuttle boat – though you'll be obliged to eat at the sponsoring taverna.

Lárissa

LÁRISSA stands at the heart of the Thessalian plain: a large market centre approached across a prosperous but dull landscape of wheat and corn fields. It is also a major garrison: army camps surround it, the airport remains reserved for use by the Greek Air Force, and the southwestern part of the city – for such it is now, with nearly 130,000 inhabitants – is still dominated by ranks of military housing.

Despite such unpromising impressions, modern and unremarkable Lárissa retains a few old streets that hint at its distant past as ancient and Byzantine Larissa, and later the Ottoman provincial capital of Yenişehir. The highest point of the town – the ancient acropolis of Áyios Ahíllios – is dominated by the remains of a medieval **froúrio**, home to an Ottoman **bezesténi** (lockable bazaar), a popular café and the foundations of an ancient **Athena temple**. Just south and below are the excavated and fairly impressive remains of the **ancient theatre** (closed). Further south in the flatlands, the city centre consists of a pair of landscaped squares (Sapká and Makaríou), connected by pedestrianized streets lined with the usual upmarket boutiques. Save a few minutes for the **archeological museum** in the old mosque at 31-Avgoústou 2 (Tues–Sun 8.30am–3pm; €2), with its fascinating collection of Neolithic finds and grave stelae. Otherwise, the **Alkazar** park beside the Piniós, Thessaly's major river, remains relatively cool throughout the summer, when Lárissa as a whole bakes.

Practicalities

As a major **road and rail junction**, the town has efficient connections with most places you'd want to reach. The main **KTEL** is on Yeoryiádhou at the far north end of Olýmbou, about 200m east of the acropolis, but all buses towards Tríkala leave from a substation on Iróön Polytekhníou southwest of the centre, near the military housing, and a few other random services use a third stop on Ptoleméou, opposite the **train station**, 1km southeast of the central plazas. Drivers will find **parking** easiest and relatively unrestricted in the streets east of the acropolis.

You probably won't need or choose to stay in Lárissa, but if you do there are numerous, often pricey, **hotels**. Among a trio in the square by the train station, the *Dhiethnes* (℡ 2410 234 210; ❸) is the most appealing. More central options include the moderately comfortable *Adonis* on Panagoúli 8A (℡ 2410 534 648; ❹), its underground garage a blessing in a town with difficult parking, or the plusher *Asteras*, a block southwest on pedestrianized Asklipíou on the corner with Koumá (℡ 2410 534 772, 🌐 www.asterashotel.gr; ❺), also with a garage.

It's more likely that you'll just stop for **lunch**. There's a reliable ouzerí (*To Ayioklima*) near the museum-mosque at Olýmbou 9, flanking currently dug-up Platía Laoú, while *To Syndrivani* at Protopapadháki 8, on the south side of Platía Makaríou, purveys a wide range of *mayireftá*, including baked fish, with tables outside in summer. Makaríou itself, with flowerbeds and fountains, is also the hub of **daytime café** life, but **after dark** the focus shifts to the gentrified, pedestrianized, old-bazaar lanes around the *froúrio*, in particular Filellínon and Papafléssa. Most organized events take place in the restored *Mylos* complex on Yeoryiádhou by the KTEL, a frank imitation of Thessaloníki's namesake complex, with a summer cinema, indoor theatre, bar, exhibition space and concert venue.

North of Lárissa: Témbi and the Óssa coast

Travelling north from Lárissa, the motorway heads towards Thessaloníki, a highly scenic route through the **Vale of Témbi**, between mounts Olympus and Óssa, before emerging on the coast. Accounts of the valley and the best of the **beaches** east of **Mount Óssa** follow; for details of Mount Olympus, see p.510.

Ambelákia

If you have time, or your own transport, a worthwhile first stop in the Témbi region is **AMBELÁKIA**, a large village in the foothills of Mount Óssa. You can walk up to Ambelákia from the Témbi train station in about an hour along a cobbled way, part of the **O2 long-distance trail**, which continues within three hours to Spília village, high up on Mount Óssa, and from there over the top to Stómio or Karítsa.

During the eighteenth century, this community supported the world's first **industrial cooperative**, producing, dyeing and exporting textiles, and maintaining branch offices as far afield as London. The cooperative fostered a rare and enlightened eighteenth-century prosperity. At a time when much of Greece lay stagnant under Ottoman rule, Ambelákia was largely autonomous; it held democratic assemblies, offered free education and medical care and even subsidized weekly performances of ancient drama. This brave experiment lasted over a hundred years, eventually succumbing to the triple ravages of war, economics and the industrial revolution. In 1811 Ali Pasha raided Ambelákia, and a decade later any chance of recovery was lost with the collapse of the Viennese bank in which the town's wealth was deposited.

Until World War II, however, over six hundred mansions survived in Ambelákia. Today there are just 36, many in poor condition but some finally benefiting from renovation. You can still get some idea of the former prosperity by visiting the **Mansion of George Schwarz** (Tues–Sat 8am–3pm, Sun 9am–2pm; €2). The home of the cooperative's last president, this *arhondikó* is built in grand, old-Constantinople style. The exterior has been admirably restored, as has the charming Ottoman-Rococo interior. Schwarz, incidentally, was a Greek, despite the German-sounding name, which was merely the Austrian bank's translation of his real surname, Mavros (Black).

Without being twee, Ambelákia is an attractive, unselfconscious place, with a cobbled high street, a couple of old-fashioned bakeries and three *pistariés* on the plane-and-mulberry-shaded square. Simple **rooms** are available through the Women's Agrotourism Cooperative (℡24950 93314; ❷), visitable in person at their café, *To Rodi*. There's also a mock-traditional **hotel**, the *Ennea Mousses* (℡24950 93405; ❹), on the left entering town just before the square, with somewhat dark and dated wood-trimmed rooms but its own parking (which is a problem here).

The Vale of Témbi

At the edge of **TÉMBI** village, visible from the north-bound toll post and road turning to Ambelákia, is Thessaly's other surviving (if scaffolded) Bektashi **tekkés** (see p.370), that of **Hasan Baba**. It's accessible by crossing an almond grove, and well worth the effort for the sake of a fine dome with stalactite vaulting and three bands of Arabic calligraphy.

△ George Schwarz Mansion, Ambelákia

Two kilometres beyond the Ambelákia turn-off, you enter the actual **Vale of Témbi**, a valley cut over the eons by the Piniós, which runs for nearly 10km between the steep cliffs of the Olympus (Ólymbos) and Óssa ranges. In antiquity it was sacred to Apollo and constituted one of the few possible approaches into central Greece – being the path taken by both Xerxes and Alexander the Great – and it remained an important passage during the Middle Ages. The river here is popular with rafters – the main outing organizer is Olympos Trek, based in Lárissa (℡2410 921244 or 693 25 45 001, ✉oltrek@otenet.gr) – but both motorway and railway forge through Témbi, impinging considerably on its beauties. Halfway through the vale (on the southeast flank) are the ruins of the **Kástro tís Oreás** ("Castle of the Beautiful Maiden"), one of four Frankish guardposts here, while marking the northern end of the pass – and the border with Macedonia – is a **medieval fortress** at Platamónas (summer Tues–Fri 8am–7pm; winter Tues–Fri 8.30am–5pm; all year Sat & Sun 8.30am–3pm), also Crusader-built. An impressive citadel, it's been restored for use in the Olympos Festival (July–Aug) (see p.80), while a new rail tunnel has been bored right under it, so that the train no longer stops here, but 4km before at Néi Póri. A steep dirt track leads to the fort from the busy main highway, for the expected views.

The Óssa coast: Stómio to Polydhéndhri

A side road, close by the Kástro tís Oreás, takes you the 12km to **STÓMIO**, an unexceptional seaside village near the mouth of the River Piniós. The beach here is a relatively new phenomenon – a 1950s flood changed the river's course, creating a vast sandspit behind the abandoned riverbed. The dense beech and linden forest of Óssa marches down almost to the shore, masking some of Stómio's more uninspired recent construction, mixed in with old stone houses; the place is cheerfully downmarket and resolutely Greek working-class, though EU funding has resulted in cosmetic improvements. The marshes flanking the old river-branch make the beach a fine spot for bird-watchers, while the five-star-quality sand merges seamlessly with **Stríntzo** beach, which runs northeast to the current river-delta near Kouloúra.

Outside July and August – when Stómio draws big crowds from the hinterland – you shouldn't have any trouble finding **accommodation**, though rooms closest to the waterfront are apt to be noisy. Good choices include the *Hotel Alexiou* (℡24950 91210, ⓦwww.hotel-alexiou.gr; ❸), in a calm uphill setting, with somewhat small rooms but ample parking and a roof-restaurant, or the *Vlassis* right above the harbour (℡24950 91301; ❹), again with its own restaurant. A municipal beachside **campsite** is well equipped with hot showers and power hook-ups for caravans. Of the four **tavernas** on the seafront road leading to the fishing port, the two best are *Tò Tsayezi* ("river-mouth" in Turkish) and *Iy Gorgona*, though prices for seafood are surprisingly high.

Much the highest-standard **accommodation** in the region is 6km south and uphill at **KARÝTSA**, where Yiorgos and Stella's ✤ *Dohos Katalymata* (℡24950 92001; ❺) takes in a view extending from Káto Ólymbos to the Sithonía peninsula, from a perch amidst Greece's only true cloud-forest environment. You've a choice of huge wood-floored rooms or suites, all with sea-facing balconies and music systems, as well as a free-standing circular wigwam; in winter when the snow falls you'll appreciate the fireplaces. The stone-floored common areas, crammed with a museum's worth of antiques, include a concert hall – hosting special events all summer – a pool, and a bar and breakfast salon; a sauna and hamam are planned for 2006, while mountain bikes are available for exploration. If it's full, continue another 6km to the Platánia district of **KÓKKINO NERÓ**, where the *Hotel Hlidhi* (☎24950 92111, ℉24950 92112; ❹) has plush rooms with fridges, large baths and sea or mountain views; you'll be encouraged to patronize the affiliated *Akrotiri* fish **taverna**, one of a group on the shore and not too bad.

Between Stómio and Cape Dhermáti, the steep shoreline is broken up by secluded little light-sand coves like Platýs Ámmos, often with rough access tracks; the construction of a new direct Kókkino Neró–Stómio bypass makes them easier to reach. Between Kókkino Neró and the cape are larger, congenial beaches at **Koutsoupiá** and **Paliouriá**, but further south the coast settles down into long, continuous but comparatively featureless and exposed beaches at Velíka, Sotirítsa and Ayiókambos. Except for a few Czech and Polish tourists, the area – especially Ayiókambos – is effectively the summer-weekend annexe of Lárissa, with no short-term accommodation amongst the villas. You're better off continuing straight through to **POLYDHÉNDHRI** village 3km south, with one **rooms**, three **tavernas**, and a lovely small beach just south popular with campers; from here the paved road veers scenically inland via the mountain villages of Sklíthro and Élafos on its way back to the Thessalian plain.

West from Lárissa: Trikala, the Pýli region and routes to Epirus

West from Lárissa, the road trails the River Piniós to **Trikala**, an enjoyable provincial capital with a scattering of Byzantine monuments nearby. For most travellers, it's simply a staging post en route to Kalambáka and the Metéora; frequent buses join it with Lárissa, and there are connections north and west as well. The rail line linking Lárissa, Trikala and Kalambáka was refitted with standard-gauge track in the year 2000, but a projected high-speed train link from Vólos to Igoumenítsa through the Píndhos mountains has been deferred to the remote future.

Trikala

TRÍKALA is quite an attractive and manageable metropolis compared to most Thessalian towns, with a population of 50,000; it's evenly divided by the Lethéos, a tributary of the Piniós – clean enough to harbour trout – and backed by the mountains of the Kóziakas range rising abruptly to the west. Almost uniquely in Greece, it's **bicycle-friendly** if not actually bicycle-besotted; people of all ages pedal about and there are even municipally provided racks for locking up.

Trikala was the capital of a nineteenth-century Ottoman province and retains quite a few lanes full of variably restored houses from that era, in the **Varoúsi** district below the fortress clocktower at the north end of town. Downriver from the bus station on the same bank, the **Koursoún Tzamí**, a very stately restored sixteenth-century mosque, also survives, a graceful accompaniment to the town's numerous stone churches; it's locked at present but you may peer in the windows, as you can with the octagonal *tekkés* or dervish ceremonial hall just southeast, purportedly built by Ali Pasha of Ioánnina (see p.426).

The town's inner **fortress**, a Turkish and Byzantine adaptation of a claimed fourth-century BC citadel around an Artemis temple, is closed to the public except for special events (including summer film showings), but the outer walls host attractive gardens and a pleasantly shaded terrace café. Down in the flat-lands, on busy Saráfi, lie the meagre, half-excavated remains of a **sanctuary of Asklepios**; according to some accounts, the cult of the healing god originated here in ancient Trikke. The liveliest part of town, encompassing what's left of the old **bazaar**, are the streets around the central Platía Iróön Polytekhníou on the riverside, with a statue of local hero Stefanos Sarafis, commander of ELAS from 1943 to 1945. Rebétika great Vassilis Tsitsanis (see p.1127 in Contexts) also hailed from here, and he too is honoured by the street bearing his name, heading east from the platía.

Practicalities

The **post office** is situated off Platía Iróön Polytekhníou, as are several **banks** with ATMs. The **bus station** is on the southwest bank of the river, 300m southeast of the square; the main **taxi** ranks are on Iróön Polytekhníou and its continuation across the river (via an 1886-built iron bridge), Platía Ríga Feréou. As ever, drivers should be mindful of the prevailing pay-and-display **parking** scheme, easily enough avoided by parking slightly out of the centre – or follow-ing signs to attended fee car parks.

Accommodation is problematic; the cheapest hotel, the *Palladion* (☎24310 28091; ❸), vastly overpriced, lies within sight of the two squares at Výronos 4 and has shared bathrooms. Three mid-range alternatives are pretty comparable in price, so you may as well plump for the most distinctive and historic of them: the Neoclassical *Panellinion* at one corner of Platía Ríga Feréou (☎24310 73545; ❹), away from traffic noise. Dating from 1914, it hosted leading Greek politicians and artists of the era, and served as the Italian and German HQ during World War II. En-suite rooms are parquet-floored and air conditioned, some with balconies and small tubs; there's a mezzanine bar and a decent ground-floor restaurant, the *Aigli*.

Other **tavernas** are scattered throughout the town, on either bank of the river. *Psistariés* abound, as Thessaly in general and Tríkala specifically is renowned for its fine meat. A salubrious *mayireftá* lunch amidst updated decor can be had between bus connections at *Selemekos*, Óthonos 10, near the KTEL; another west-bank possibility is *Pliatsikas* on Iouliéttas Adhám 8, between Karnasíou and Platía Makaríou. Pedestrianized Asklipíou, forging southwest from Ríga Feréou towards the train station, is the mecca of **daytime café** society, but **after dark** the action moves to the partly pedestrianized **Manávika**, especially on and just off Ipsilándou. Gentrification of the area isn't quite complete, as ouzerís and **clubs** continue to coexist with cobblers and tinsmiths; most clubs change constantly, but from October to May Tríkala honours its heritage down the river at the durable *Orfeas*, Amalías 8, where surviving rebétika stars perform. Consistently working eateries in Manávika – open lunchtime as well – include cavernous, brick-interior *Ta Mezedhokomomata* at Ipsilándou 16–18, the first established here in 1997, offering good value for slightly heavy food; or the superior *Palia Istoria* at no. 3 with a lighter touch and fair prices for sardines, grilled mushrooms and hot peppers.

Pýli and around

It takes some exercise of will to delay immediate progress from Tríkala to Kalambáka and the Metéora. Byzantine aficionados, however, may be tempted by a detour to **PÝLI**, 19km southwest, for the thirteenth-century church of **Pórta Panayía**, one of the unsung beauties of Thessaly, in a superb setting at the mouth of a gorge. Nearby, there is an outstanding cycle of frescoes at the monastery of **Ayíou Vissaríonos Dousíkou** (men only admitted), which would be a major tourist attraction were it not overshadowed by its spectacular neighbour, the Metéora.

Buses run to Pýli from Trikala almost hourly during the day. Near Pórta Panayía and beside a fountain-fed oasis on the north bank there are two simple **psistariés**; one of these, the *Porta Panayia*, has some rooms for rent (℡24310 22691; ❷), but the best accommodation here is the *Hotel Pyli* a bit further upstream on the same bank (℡24310 23510; ❹), its wood-floored rooms enjoying superb views from their balconies (a new wing has colder tile floors).

Pórta Panayía

The church of **Pórta Panayía** (daily: summer 8am–noon & 4–8pm; winter 9am–noon & 3–5pm; €1.50) is a ten-minute walk uphill from the bus stop in Pýli village. Cross the Portaïkós River on the footbridge, then bear left on the far bank until you see its dome in a clump of trees below the north-bank frontage road; cars must use a slightly longer route via a one-lane vehicle bridge. The caretaker lives in a white house below the nearby tavernas, and may offer to admit you outside of the stated hours.

Much of the church was completed in 1283 by one Ioannis Doukas, a prince of the Despotate of Epirus. Its architecture is somewhat bizarre, in that the current narthex is probably a fourteenth-century Serbian remodelling of the original dome and transept. The original nave on its west side collapsed in an earthquake, and its replacement to the east gives the church a "backwards" orientation compared to the norm. In the Doukas section, perpendicular barrel vaults over a narrow transept and more generous nave lend antiseismic properties, with further support from six columns. The highlights of the interior are a pair of **mosaic icons** depicting the adult Christ plus Mary and the Child, and a marble iconostasis. The **frescoes** have fared less well, with many of the figures blackened by fire and barely discernible. The most interesting image is next to the tiny font, over Ioannis Doukas's tomb, where a lunette shows the Archangel Michael leading a realistically portrayed Doukas by the hand to the enthroned Virgin with Child; there's also an interesting, late-medieval Holy Trinity over the apse, showing the influence of the Renaissance.

A kilometre upstream, easiest reached along the Pýli bank of the river, a graceful if scaffolded **medieval bridge** spans the Portaïkós at the point where it exits a narrow mountain gorge. A couple of cafés and bars take advantage of the setting; the whole area being a very popular weekend outing venue for the locals, so that its tranquil beauty is best appreciated on a weekday. You can cross the bridge to follow paths some distance along the gorge on the opposite side.

Ayíou Vissaríonos Dhousíkou

The monastery of **Ayíou Vissaríonos Dhousíkou** – known locally as Aï-Vissáris – has a stunning setting, 500m up a flank of Mount Kóziakas, looking out over most of Thessaly. The small community of monks seems keen to maintain its isolation, excluding women from visits and admitting foreign men with occasional reluctance. In theory, visits are allowed from 8am to noon and 3.30pm to 7pm (3–6.30pm in winter), with preference given to Orthodox visitors and Greek speakers. To reach the monastery, cross the single-lane road bridge over the Portaïkós as if heading for Pórta Panayía, but turn right instead, then left almost instantly onto a signed paved road which leads up for 4.5km.

The monastery was founded in 1530 by Vissarionos (Bessarion), a native of Pýli, and contains a perfect cycle of **frescoes** by Tzortzis – one of the major painters of Mount Athos – executed between 1550 and 1558 and restored to brilliance during the early 1990s. These, and the institution as a whole, miraculously escaped damage in 1940, when two Italian bombs fell in the courtyard but failed to explode.

Originally, the monastery perched on a cliff as steep as any at the Metéora, but in 1962 the abyss was largely filled in with kitchen gardens, and a new road and gate opened. This rendered ornamental the pulleys and ladder on the east wall, which, like much of the place, had survived intact since its foundation. In its heyday, nearly three hundred monks lived at the monastery; currently there are around ten.

Routes to Epirus and alpine resorts

West of Tríkala and Pýli lies a wild, impressively scenic alpine region that has long been known to Greek holiday-makers, and is beginning to pitch itself to foreigners. Villages and attractions line a reasonable road network, which (with a few remaining unmade patches) can also be followed southwest all the way to Árta, via Vourgarélli (see p.450). During summer, with a bit of nerve and a sturdy, high-clearance vehicle, you can also cross northwest over a Píndhos ridge in considerably less time, emerging at Métsovo (see p.398).

The Mesahóra dam

Just 4km west of Pýli, signs indicate the turning left for the most direct way to Árta, via Stournareïka. It's 142km to Árta from Pýli, all but 10km of it paved, with some massive tunnels (including a 5km one near Lafína) to be finished by late 2007. Unless bicycles are banned in the tunnels, this road is much the best (and most scenic) choice for cyclists as the gradients are easier and traffic lighter than on the usual Kalambáka–Métsovo route. There is, however, no food or petrol between Stournareïka and Athamánio – pretty much half the distance – and the curves and lingering rough patches mean that drivers should allow well over three hours for the traverse.

En route, over an hour from Pýli, you'll pass the completed, but thus-far empty, **Mesahóra dam**, Greece's most controversial **hydroelectric project**. It was approved by ex-prime minister Constantine Mitsotakis in 1993, despite strenuous opposition. Although the European Union pulled the financial plug on the project, construction proceeded. As a compromise, the scaled-down result is only for generating power, omitting a scheme to divert vast quantities of water for agricultural use. The dam remains empty while the inhabitants of three upstream villages that would be flooded resist being moved through court action.

Eláti, Pertoúli and Neraïdhohóri

Most people will continue from the junction after Pýli another 10km on the wider road to **ELÁTI**, a "hill station" for Trikalans and nestled in fir trees as the place name implies. There are numerous places to stay and eat, though **accommodation** (except off season when the place is dead) is apt to be noisy – on the upper, through highway from traffic noise, on the lower *agorá* from late-night revelling. The *Lingeri* on the upper road (☎24340 71196, ⓦwww .ligerihotel.gr; B&B summer ❹, winter ❻), a modern but stone-clad structure with fireplaces in some rooms, represents the highest standard here; more affordable is the *Koziakas* down on the commercial street (☎24340 71270, ⓕ24340 71106; ❹), whose ground-floor **restaurant** *Kalamaras* runs to such exotica as ostrich steak in plum sauce, venison, wild-boar chop and an eighty-label-strong wine cellar.

Another 10km takes you past the **Pertoúli ski resort** at 1200m – all of one downhill run, plus some nordic pistes – to a junction with the side road north marked "Kalambáka 38km". The distance is grossly underestimated – it's more like 51km – but it's still a quicker way to the Metéora region than retracing your tyre treads, and allows a satisfying circuit of mounts Kóziakas and Kerkétio via Khryssomiliá. The uplands here – the so-called Pertouliótika Livádhia – form part of the Píndhos watershed; behind you all rivers drain eventually into the Aegean, while from all points west streams find their way into the Aheloös and eventually the Ionian Sea near Pátras.

PERTOÚLI village itself lies 4km west of this intersection in some of the densest stands of local fir, even more attractive and upmarket than Eláti, and with facilities priced accordingly. Among several places to **stay** and **eat**, none could be classed as budget; the stone-built *Arhondiko Dhivani* (☎24340 91252, ℱ24340 91111; ❻), with a respected restaurant, is typical of offerings here, while the *Arhondiko Louka* (☎24340 91465, ℱ24340 91518; ❺) is another conversion inn. The cost-conscious might continue another 3km to **NERAÏDHOHÓRI**, the last place of any size and the end of the bus line. A collection of scattered buildings, more extensive than Pertoúli, with views southwest to 2148-metre Avgó, includes roadside businesses like the *Hotel Niavis* (☎24340 91201; ❹) and a **taverna**, *Margaritis*, specializing in game. In summer both Pertoúli and Neraïdhohóri are start-points for day-long walks up the peaks immediately north.

Tría Potámia to Métsovo

Just 2km west of Neraïdhohóri, the medieval roadside church of **Ayía Paraskeví** (always open) – with its high hexagonal cupola, fine masonry and slate roof – is the last trace of civilization for some time. Beyond, the valley opens up dramatically to twice the breadth of the Karpenisiótis, with bony ridges rising everywhere above the fir forest. Most villages are tucked away up side valleys, though not remotely enough to have saved them from the pyromaniac vengeance of the German army in late 1943; it's lonely country, with only the occasional goatherd and his flock for human scale.

At **Tría Potámia**, the Aspropótamos and the Komnaïtikos you've been following unite to form the Aheloös – thus the "Three Rivers" of the name. It's a popular **kayaking and rafting venue**, as numerous "put-in" signs indicate, but for how much longer is a moot point, as the Mesahóra dam waters will back up as far as the nearby Alexíou bridge. Until then, Trekking Hellas in Tríkala (☎24310 87964) are the people to contact about arranging an outing.

If you bear right (north), away from the turnings for Gardhíki and Mesohóra, and follow the Aspropótamos upstream to another fork (67km from Pýli) and then veer right again, you reach the ⚔ *Pyrgos Mantania* (☎24320 87351, ⓦwww.mantania-ae.gr), the region's most interesting and best-value **accommodation**. Units in this stone-built hotel vary from large, tasteful designer doubles (summer ❹, winter ❺) to even bigger top-floor family suites with fireplaces (summer ❹, winter ❻); rates drop a category for longer says, and there's a pleasant **bar-restaurant** in a separate building, specializing in wild trout.

Veering left instead at this last fork takes you up another stream valley for 16km to **Halíki** village, the end of the asphalt and last settlement in the province. Beyond Halíki, a dirt road – kept open from mid-May to October – continues some 25km to Anílio, by Métsovo in Epirus. There may be some rutted, muddy patches for the first 7km to a saddle (the provincial border) in the Lákmos range, but from there on it's a pretty easy descent through forest. Allow an hour from Halíki to Métsovo, and don't try this in a Group A or B rental car.

The Metéora and around

The **monasteries of the Metéora** are indisputably one of the great sights of mainland Greece. These extraordinary buildings, perched on seemingly inaccessible pinnacles of rock, occupy a valley just to the north of **Kalambáka**; the name *metéora* means "rocks in the air", and *kalabak* is an Ottoman Turkish word meaning roughly the same thing. Arriving at the town, your eye is drawn inexorably towards the outermost of these weird grey cylinders. Overhead to the right you can make out the closest of the monasteries, Ayíou Stefánou, firmly ensconced on a massive pedestal; beyond stretches a chaos of pinnacles, cones and stubbier, rounded cliffs. These are remnants of river sediment which flowed into a prehistoric sea that covered the plain of Thessaly around 25 million years ago, subsequently moulded into bizarre shapes by the combined action of fissuring from tectonic-plate pressures and erosion by the infant River Piniós.

Some history

The Meteoran monasteries are as enigmatic as they are spectacular. Legend has it that **St Athanasios**, who founded Megálou Meteórou ("the Great Meteoron") – the earliest of the buildings – flew up to the rocks on the back of an eagle. A more prosaic version suggests that the villagers of Stáyi, the medieval precursor of Kalambáka, may have become adept at climbing, and helped the original monks up. The difficulties of access and building are hard to overstate; a German guide published for rock climbers grades almost all Metéora routes as "advanced", even with modern high-tech climbing gear.

The earliest religious communities here appeared in the late tenth century, when groups of **hermits** made their homes in the caves that score many of the rocks. In 1336 they were joined by two monks from Mount Athos: **Gregorios** and his disciple **Athanasios**. Gregorios returned shortly to Athos but he left Athanasios behind, ordering him to establish a monastery. This Athanasios did shortly after 1344, whether supernaturally assisted or not, imposing a particularly austere and ascetic rule. He was quickly joined by many brothers, including, in 1381, **John Uroş Paleologos**, who renounced the throne of Serbia to become the monk Ioasaph.

The royal presence was an important aid to the **endowment** of the monasteries, which followed swiftly on all the accessible, and many of the all-but-inaccessible, rocks. They reached their zenith during the reign of the Ottoman sultan Süleyman the Magnificent (1520–66), by which time 24 of the rocks were surmounted by monasteries and hermitages. The major establishments accumulated great wealth, flourishing on revenues of estates granted them in distant Wallachia and Moldavia, as well as in Thessaly itself. They retained these estates, more or less intact, until the eighteenth century, at which time monasticism here, as elsewhere in Greece, began to decline.

During the intervening centuries, numerous disputes had arisen over power and precedence among the monasteries. However, the principal factors in the Metéora's fall from glory were physical and economic. Many of the buildings, especially the smaller hermitages, were simply not built to withstand centuries of use and, perhaps neglected or unoccupied, gradually disintegrated. The grander monasteries suffered **depopulation**, conspicuously so in the nineteenth century as a modern Greek state was established to the south – with Thessaly itself initially excluded – and monasticism lost its exclusive identification with Greek nationalism and resistance to Turkish rule.

During the twentieth century the crisis accelerated after the monastic lands and revenues, already much reduced from their heyday, were expropriated by the state for use by Greek refugees from Asia Minor, after the Greco-Turkish war of 1919–22. By the late 1950s, there were just four active monasteries, struggling along with barely a dozen monks between them – an era superbly chronicled in Patrick Leigh Fermor's *Roumeli*. Ironically, before being overtaken by **tourism** in the 1970s, the monasteries had begun to revive a little, attracting a number of young and intellectually rigorous brothers. Today, put firmly on the map by appearances in such films as James Bond's *For Your Eyes Only*, the four most accessible monasteries and convents are essentially showcase monuments. Only the two easterly foundations, **Ayías Triádhos** (the "Holy Trinity") and **Ayíou Stefánou**, continue to function with a primarily religious purpose.

Practicalities: Kalambáka and Kastráki

Visiting the Metéora demands a full day, which means staying at least one night in **Kalambáka** or, preferably, at the village of **Kastráki**, 2km to the northwest, which wins hands down on atmosphere and its situation right in the shadow of the rocks. The older upper quarters of the village, with their stone-paved lanes, make for pleasant strolls. Kastráki also offers much better value for money lodging-wise, and has two of the best local campsites.

Kalambáka

KALAMBÁKA has no particular allure, save for its position near the rocks. The town has tried valiantly to make itself more attractive, with fountains in every square, but the effort founders on the fact that Kalambáka was burned by the Germans during World War II and very few prewar buildings remain. Among these are the **Mitrópolis** or old cathedral, dedicated to the Kímisis tís Theotókou ("Dormition of the Virgin"; daily 8am–1pm & 4–6pm; €1.50), standing a couple of streets above its modern successor, at the top end of the town. It was founded in the sixth century on the site of a temple to Apollo and incorporates various classical drums and fragments in its erratically designed walls. The interior is overarched by a unique coffered-wood ceiling and dominated, equally unusually for a Greek church, by a great double marble pulpit in the central aisle, itself staked out by marble columns. The thirteenth- and fourteenth-century Byzantine frescoes are best preserved in the narthex, stressing the miracles of Christ's ministry (*Healing the Paralytic, The Storm on Galilee, Raising Lazarus, The Wedding at Cana*), though there's also a vivid portrayal of Hell on the south wall.

Practicalities

The **train station** is on the ring road at the south edge of town; incoming **buses** stop at the central Platía Dhimarhíou, but the KTEL is actually just downhill towards the train station. Kalambáka hasn't a tourist information office; the only local documentation is found at the **bookshop–newsagent**, with maps, foreign-language guides, papers and magazines, on the west side of the same plaza, at the corner of Ioannínon and Patriárhou Dhimitríou. Those arriving by bus or train are apt to be met by **accommodation** touts. You are advised to avoid them and stick with our listings, following various complaints about substandard rooms and price-fiddling. You also don't get much value out of the undistinguished hotels lining the main street, most of them filled with coach tours and plagued by traffic noise despite double glazing.

One good **budget** choice is the welcoming *Hotel Meteora* (℡24320 22367, ⓦ www.meteorahotels.com; B&B ❸) at Ploutárhou 13, a quiet side street up to the right as you leave Kalambáka for Kastráki, at the foot of the extraordinary rocks. This has a wide variety of rooms, with air conditioning and heating, as well as adequate parking; breakfasts are enhanced with home-made cakes and cheese, while proprietors Nikos and Kostas Gekas are a fount of information on the area. In the upper, most village-like, part of town, some 700m uphill from either of the two main squares, near the Mitrópolis and start/end of the trail to Ayías Triádhos, are two more options. The more comfortable is 充 *Alsos House* at Kanári 5 (☎24320 24097, ⓦwww.kalampaka.com/alsoshouse; ❸), where top-floor units comprise doubles, triples and a family suite, with a well-appointed communal kitchen; owner Yiannis Karakantas speaks good English. *Koka Roka Rooms* at Kanári 21 (☎24320 24554, ⓔkokaroka@yahoo.com; ❷), are a mix of en suite and not, a classic backpackers' hangout, if a fairly salubrious one. Service at the ground-floor grill (cheap and cheerful meals from €10) can be decidedly leisurely; there's also **Internet** access for all comers.

Mid-range choices include the *Odyssion* (☎24320 22320, Ⓕ24320 75307; ❹) on the main through road at the Kastráki end of things, but fairly quiet since set back; rooms were mostly redone in 2004, with a mix of tile or parquet floors, and showers or tubs. There's a bright new salon for the buffet breakfast, but plans for a rear garden and pool have been stalled by the archeological authorities In the same price bracket, back in the old quarter, *Xenonas Elena* at Kanári 3 (☎24320 77789; ❹) offers just four large, quiet rooms with superior furnishings.

As with hotels, so with **restaurants** – there are lots of mediocre ones, used to a quick turnover of a captive audience. A sterling exception, in a decidedly unscenic location some 400m from the edge of town on the road to Tríkala, is *O Houtos*. Not many tourists find it, but the locals certainly know all about the superb and reasonably priced lamb kebab, chops, *biftéki* and *kokorétsi* made from local lamb and pork. At peak seasons it's wise to book (☎24320 24754). In the centre, *Panellinion* on Platía Dhimarhíou has over-the-top rustic-kitsch decor and high prices, but the latter are justified by high-quality ingredients, good brown bread, fresh-cut chips and generally good fare, making it a popular spot.

Kastráki

KASTRÁKI is twenty minutes' walk out of Kalambáka along the busy and somewhat dangerous road; work has stalled on a proper pedestrian route from the vicinity of the Mitrópolis. In season (May 15–Sept 15) there are regular buses throughout the day to Kastráki.

Entering the downhill end of the village, you pass the first of two **campsites** here, *Camping Vrachos* (☎24320 22293), where in season a resident outfitter offers adventure sports across the region. The other, *Camping Boufidhis/The Cave* (☎ & ⒻP24320 24802; May–Oct) at the top end of the through road, is a bit more cramped but wonderfully grassy (except in a dry year) and shady for tents, incomparably set on the far side of the village with the monasteries of Ayíou Nikoláou and Roussánou soaring above. Both have swimming pools, as do the other more distant sites out on the Tríkala and Ioánnina roads.

The village has scores of **rooms** for rent, mostly of a very high standard, as well as five hotels. It's vital, however, to get off the main through road up to the monasteries, which has coaches rumbling through much of the day (and scooters buzzing along by night). Meeting this criterion admirably is 充 *Doupiani House* (☎24320 77555, ⓔdoupiani-house@kmp.forthnet.gr; ❸), well signposted left of the road near *The Cave*, with superb views from the front-facing air-conditioned rooms; proprietors Thanassis and Toula serve breakfast in the finest hotel garden of Kastráki, and can point walkers to the start of various hikes. Reservations are mandatory year-round, and demand is such that

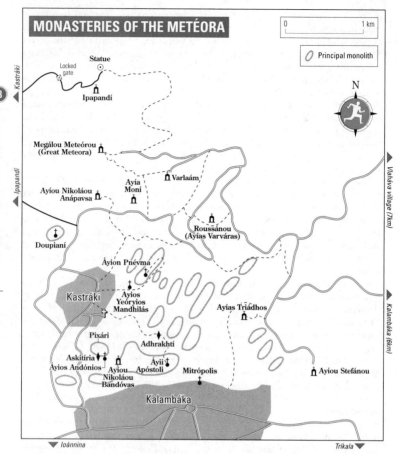

MONASTERIES OF THE METÉORA

0   1 km

⟡ Principal monolith

N

Kastráki

Locked gate

Statue ⊙

Ipapandí

Ipapandí

Megálou Meteórou
(Great Meteora) ⛪

⛪ Varlaám

Ayíou Nikoláou
Anápavsa ⛪

Ayía
Moní ⛪

Roussánou
(Ayías Varváras) ⛪

Vlaháva village (7km)

Doupianí ⊕

Áyion Pnévma ⛪

Kastráki

Ayios
Yeóryios
Mandhilás ⛪

Ayías Triádhos ⛪

Kalambáka (6km)

Pixári

Adhrakhtí

Askitíria
Áyios Andónios

Ayíou
Nikoláou
Bandóvas ⛪

Áyii
Apóstoli ⛪

Mitrópolis ⛪

⛪ Ayíou Stefánou

Kalambáka

▼ *Ioánnina*   *Tríkala* ▼

an annexe is to be built in 2006–7. *Ziogas Rooms* (☎24320 24037; ❸), further downhill and again set well back from the road, offers large, balconied units, most with superb views and heating for winter; there's also a huge breakfast salon/taverna on the ground floor. Closer to the road, but still peaceful if you get one of the predominantly rear-facing pine-and-white-tile units, is the friendly, spotless *Hotel Tsikelli* (☎24320 22438, ⓦwww.tsikeli.com; ❸), with ample parking and a pleasant front-lawn café. *The Cave* campsite also offers the remote *Villa San Giorgio* (❸), in a calm lane at the top of the village, plus noisier rooms (❷) by the campsite, with swimming-pool privileges for both.

Among nearly a dozen **places to eat** (overwhelmingly *psistariés*), the best all-rounder is probably *Paradhisos* on the through road; a meal of a kebab, with a red-bean salad, red peppers and a beer served on the popular view terrace, won't much top €14. On summer nights, an atmospheric choice is *Bakalarakia*, with terrace seating behind the church and below the central platía; this little *koutoúki* (joint) is much favoured by locals in winter for its grills, salads, *bakaliáros* (of course) and house wine. The quality isn't astoundingly high, but prices are astoundingly low, at about €15 for two. If you have transport, though, don't miss well-signed 🜚 *Neromylos* at the far end of **DHIÁVA** village, 4km south-west. The high-ceilinged interior with fireplace was the owner's grandfather's watermill; the summer terrace seating near the trout-tanks is equally attractive. Besides trout, very high-calibre ingredients include their own meat and *galotýri* as well as vegetarian *mezédhes*, served in huge portions and washed down by a light, quaffable bulk wine.

Ayíou Nikoláou Anápavsa and around

North of Kastráki the road threads between the huge rock outcrops of Áyion Pnévma and Doupianí, the latter named for a just-visible chapel-hermitage, among the first monastic settlements. To avoid having to walk along the road, follow instead the street, which becomes a track, that takes off from the north-west corner of Kastráki's village square. This passes right under the curious cave-shrine of **Áyios Yeóryios Mandhilás**, low down on the side of the Áyion Pnévma monolith, its cavity marked by what looks like a lot of colourful washing hung up to dry. These are votive kerchiefs or *mandhília* (hence the shrine's

---

Visiting the monasteries

There are six major Metéora monasteries, each open to visits at slightly different hours and days. To see them all in a day, start early to take in Ayíou Nikoláou Anápavsa Varlaám and Megálou Meteórou before 1pm, leaving the afternoon for Roussánou, Ayías Triádhos and Ayíou Stefánou.

The road from **Kastráki to Ayíou Stefánou** is just under 10km long, often narrow and dangerous with speeding cars; if you're on foot, we recommend you follow the hiking directions given below to spare you the tarmac as much as possible – by using the trails and dirt tracks available you can avoid most of the asphalt. Ayíou Stefánou is in a cul-de-sac for both drivers and hikers; the through road signposted Kalambáka just before Ayías Triádhos is a fairly indirect 6km. In season there are a number of daily **buses** (most reliably at 8.20 or 9am and 1.20pm) from Kalambáka up the road as far as Megálou Meteórou/Varlaám; even taken just part of the way, they will give you the necessary head start to make a hiking day manageable.

You may want a local **map** in addition to that provided opposite, especially if you intend to leave the beaten track. A lot of dross is sold in Kalambáka, but the only two products worth having are stocked at the newsagent on the upper platía. The *Panoramic Map with Geology* (co-produced by Karto Atelier, Switzerland and Trekking Hellas) is aerial-view art format, but fairly accurate and good enough to follow the main routes. Andonis Kaloyirou's Greek-only text booklet, with topographic map in back (Road Editions), is superior, and many will find the map alone worth the investment.

Before setting out, it is worth buying **food and drink** to last the day; there are only a couple of drinks and fruit stands on the circuit, by Varlaám and Megálou Meteórou. And finally, don't forget to carry money with you: each monastery levies an admission charge – currently €2, with student discounts generally not given. All monasteries enforce a strict **dress code**. For women this means wearing a skirt – not trousers; for men, long trousers. Both sexes must cover their shoulders. Skirts or simple wraps are often lent to female visitors, but it's best not to count on this. Finally, it's worth noting that **photography** and **videoing** are strictly forbidden in all of the monasteries.

Metéora is really at its best visited out of season, when the leaves turn and snow blankets the pinnacles. In **midsummer**, you may be depressed by the commercialization and crowds (and the shocking amount of roadside litter), which together detract from the wild, spiritual romance of the valley. At such times you're better off heading for the less visited monasteries such as Ipapandí or Ayías Triádhos.

name), changed once a year on April 23 by a hundred or so of the ablest local youths (plus a similar number from all over Greece), who climb or abseil up and bring back down last year's kerchiefs for luck. The rite is always televised nationally, sometimes with a grisly conclusion; the rock overhang is exceptionally challenging, and many have quite literally fallen from the saint's favour.

The track deposits you, after twenty minutes, at the base of the stair-path up to **Ayíou Nikoláou Anápavsa** (Mon–Thurs, Sat & Sun 9am–3.30pm; closes 3pm Nov–March). A small monastery restored during the 1980s, this has some superb early sixteenth-century frescoes in its *katholikón* (main chapel) by the Cretan painter Theophanes. Oddly, the tiny *katholikón* faces almost due north rather than east because of the rock's shape. On the east wall of the naos, a

△ Roussánou convent, Metéora

shocked disciple topples over in a back somersault at the *Transfiguration*, an ingenious use of the cramped space; in the *Denial of Peter* on the door arch, the protagonists warm their hands over a fire in the pre-dawn. On the west wall of the narthex, a stylite (column-dwelling hermit) perches in a wilderness populated by wild beasts, while an acolyte prepares a basket of supplies to be hoisted up – as would have been done in real life just outside when the fresco was new. Other Desert Fathers rush to attend the funeral of St Ephraim of Syria: some riding beasts, others – crippled or infirm – on litters or piggyback on the strong. As well as the Theophanes paintings there are later, naïve images, such as one of Adam naming the animals, including a basilisk – the legendary lizard-like beast that could kill by a breath or glance.

Next to Ayíou Nikoláou, on a needle-thin shaft, sit the shattered wall fragments of **Ayía Moní**, abandoned after an earthquake in 1858.

Megálou Meteórou (Great Meteoron)

Beyond the ruins of Ayía Moní, some 250m past the parking area and steps for Ayíou Nikoláou, a cobbled and partly shaded path (signposted only for Varlaám) leads northwest from the road; fifteen minutes up this path bear right at an unsigned T-junction to reach Varlaám monastery in ten minutes, or turn left for Megálou Meteórou within ten slightly steeper minutes. There is no other direct route between the two (other than the unpleasantly cluttered access roads serving both); if you visit Megálou Meteórou first, re-descend the path to pick up the Varlaám turning.

The **Megálou Meteórou** (summer Mon & Wed–Sun 9am–5pm; winter Mon & Thurs–Sun 9am–4pm) is the grandest and highest of the monasteries, built on the Platýs Líthos ("Broad Rock") 615m above sea level. It had extensive privileges and dominated the area for several centuries: in an eighteenth-century engraving (displayed in the museum) it is depicted towering above the others. How Athanasios got onto this rock remains a mystery.

The monastery's **katholikón**, dedicated to the Metamórfosis (Transfiguration), is the most magnificent in Metéora, a beautiful cross-in-square church, its columns and beams supporting a lofty dome with a *Pandokrátor* (Christ in Majesty). It was enlarged in the fifteenth and sixteenth centuries, with the original chapel, constructed by the royal Serbian Ioasaph in 1383, forming just the *ierón*, the sanctuary behind the intricately carved *témblon*, or altar screen. Frescoes, however, are much later (mid-sixteenth century) than those of most other monasteries and not as significant artistically; those in the narthex concentrate almost exclusively on grisly martyrdoms.

The other monastery rooms comprise a vast, arcaded cluster of buildings. The *kellári*, or storage cellar, holds an exhibit of rural impedimenta; in the domed and vaulted refectory, still set with the traditional silver/pewter table service for monastic meals, is a **museum**, featuring a number of exquisite carved-wood crosses and rare icons. You can also visit the ancient domed and smoke-blackened kitchen adjacent, with its bread oven and soup-hearth.

Ipapandí

For a real escape, you can take a short walk north from near Megálou Meteórou to its dependency, the tiny hermitage of **Ipapandí**. From the car park for Megálou Meteórou, head northeast along multiple trail tracings visible beside a downed metal fence; after about five minutes, you'll reach a prominent pass in the ridge where several trails cross and the main, wide path begins descending, still northeast, through oak woods. The path arcs twice around the tops of ravines, until some thirty minutes along you hit the rough service track leading ten more minutes westwards towards Ipapandí, now visible wedged into its cliff-face. Its lengthy restoration was completed in late 2000, but there are not yet any resident monks to receive visitors who come to admire the fine frescoes in the fourteenth-century chapel here. Until and unless this happens, the best view is from the next round-topped monolith along, with a statue of a heroic monk, a crucifix and a circular area with a flagpole. It's possible to follow the dirt service track about 3km southwest, then southeast as it loops around the rock formations to emerge on the main paved road between Áyiou Nikoláou and Doupianí; ordinary cars can approach in the opposite direction, up to a locked gate about 500m before Ipapandí.

Varlaám (Barlaam)

Varlaám (summer Mon–Wed & Fri–Sun 9am–2pm & 3.20–5pm; winter Mon–Wed, Sat & Sun 9am–3pm) is one of the earliest established monasteries, standing on the site of a hermitage established by St Varlaam – a key figure in Meteorite history – shortly after Athanasios' arrival. The present building was founded by the two Apsaras brothers from Ioánnina in 1540–44 and is one of the most beautiful in the valley.

The monastery's *katholikón*, dedicated to Ayíon Pándon (All Saints), is small but glorious, supported by painted beams and with walls and pillars totally covered by frescoes. A dominant theme, appropriate to the Metéora, are the desert ascetics, and there are many scenes of martyrdom. The highly vivid *Last Judgement* (1566) has a gaping Leviathan swallowing the damned, and, dominating the hierarchy of paintings, a great *Pandokrátor* in the inner of two domes (1544) – the outer dome has an equally fine *Ascension*. In the refectory is a small museum of icons, inlaid furniture and textiles; elsewhere the monks' original water barrel is displayed.

Varlaám also retains intact its old **ascent tower**, with a precipitous reception platform and dubious, now inactive, windlass mechanism (replaced by an electric winch), though the original rope and "basket" are still used. Until the 1920s the only way of reaching most of the Meteorite monasteries was by being hauled up in a net drawn by rope and windlass, or by the equally perilous retractable ladders. Patrick Leigh Fermor relates a macabre anecdote about a former abbot: asked how often the rope was changed, he replied, "When it breaks."

Steps were eventually cut to all of the monasteries on the orders of the Bishop of Tríkala, doubtless unnerved by the vulnerability of his authority on visits. Today rope-baskets are used only for carrying up supplies and building materials, often supplemented by aerial cable cars bridging chasms from the nearest car park.

Roussánou

To hike from Varlaám to Roussánou, the most efficient path, with the least unnecessary altitude change and amount of road-tramping, is as follows. Proceed down the access road for Varlaám to a point about 150m past where the access drive for Megálou Meteórou joins up. Leave the road by the guard rail, keeping an eye out for blue-paint waymarks, and adopt paths with (except initially) decent surface underfoot; you thread around (and briefly over) some minor, rounded monoliths, the Plákes Kelaraká, until you reach the bed of a ravine, with a few puddles even in July, just above a sharp bend in the road. Cross the streambed and head briefly up the canyon on the far bank, then bear right into the trees on another path after about 50m. You'll emerge on the ascending road, right below Roussánou, some 35 minutes after leaving Varlaám, with only a final twenty-metre scramble where the path has been ruined by rubble-dumping.

More or less opposite, a well-signed and cobbled path ascends to the compact sixteenth-century convent of **Roussánou** (summer daily 9am–6pm; winter Mon, Tues & Thurs–Sun 9am–2pm), also known as Ayías Varváras; there's another descending trail off a still higher loop of road, but in either case the final approach is across a dizzying bridge from an adjacent rock. Roussánou has perhaps the most extraordinary site of all the monasteries, its walls edging right up to sheer drops all around. Inside, the narthex of its main chapel has particularly gruesome seventeenth-century frescoes of martyrdom and judgement, the only respite from sundry beheadings, spearings, crushings, roastings and mutilations being the lions licking Daniel's feet in his imprisonment (left of the window); diagonally across the room, two not-so-friendly lions are engaged in devouring the saint Ignatios Theoforos. On the east wall – normally it's on the west – is an exceptionaly vivid Apocalypse.

If you need to return to Kastráki directly from Roussánou, there's an excellent trail shortcut. From the lower access path, walk downhill some thirteen minutes, through the first hairpin bend, to the point by the roadside with another sharp-bend warning sign and a transformer pole. Take the path which drops from here south to the course of the Paleokraniés stream, and then follow this until you emerge at a small pumping station on the Kastráki–Ayíou Nikoláou farm track noted above. This takes about twenty minutes on foot, and saves nearly as much compared to using the road.

Ayías Triádhos

Alternatively, from the base of Roussánou's lower access path, descend the main road for just seven minutes until the first curve and then adopt the path signposted for Ayías Triádhos. After about ten minutes' climb you reach a ridge, beyond which lies the rugged canyon called Houní Ayías Triádhos. There is no way straight across this; instead bear left, following red paint-dots on the rocks, to climb more gently to a point on the circuit road about 600m shy of your goal – this won't save a huge amount of time compared to the half-hour road walk from Roussánou, but is far more pleasurable. The final approach from the end of the lane down from the parking area of **Ayías Triádhos** (daily except Thurs: summer 9am–5pm; winter 9am–12.30pm & 3–5pm) consists of 130 steps carved into a tunnel in the rock. You emerge into a light and airy compound, renovated during the 1980s and 1990s. There are small displays of weavings and kitchen/farm implements, but in lieu of labelling there are maxims from Corinthians 1:13 emblazoned everywhere: "Love is Patient", "Love Does not Criticize", etc.

The frescoes in the *katholikón* have been completely cleaned and restored to their former glory, and fully justify a visit. On the southwest wall, the *Dormition* is flanked by the *Judgement of Pilate* and the *Transaction of Judas*, complete with the thirty pieces of silver and subsequent self-hanging. Like others at the Metéora, this church was clearly built in two phases, as evidenced by two domes, each with a *Pandokrátor* (the one by the *témblon* is very fine), and two complete sets of Evangelists on the squinches. In the south arch is a rare portrait of a beardless Christ Emmanuel, borne aloft by four cherubs. Relatively few tour buses stop here, and the life of the place remains essentially monastic, even if there are only four brothers to maintain it – including the voluble senior monk Ioannis, who has been here since 1975 and who, he will proudly tell you, was cured of blindness in one eye by the Virgin (though he lost the other).

Although Ayías Triádhos teeters above a deep ravine and the little garden ends in a precipitous drop, there is an obvious, well-signposted **path** from the bottom of the monastery's access steps which leads back to the upper quarter of **Kalambáka**. This is about a 45-minute descent, saving a long trudge back around the circuit; it's a partly cobbled, all-weather surface in decent shape.

Ayíou Stefánou

Ayíou Stefánou (Tues–Sun: summer 9am–2pm & 3.30–6pm; winter 9am–1pm & 3–5pm), the last and easternmost of the monasteries, is fifteen minutes' walk beyond here (no path short-cut possible), appearing suddenly at a bend in the road. Again it is active, occupied this time by nuns (who are keen to peddle trinkets), but the buildings are a little disappointing, having been bombed during World War II and then raided by the Communists during the civil war, and it's the obvious one to miss if you're short of time. That said, the fifteenth-century refectory contains an apsidal fresco of the Virgin, beyond the museum graced by a fine *Epitáfios* covering embroidered in gold thread. The old trail towards Kalambáka from Ayíou Stefánou is disused and dangerous – return to Ayías Triádhos to use the descending path as described above.

Other local walks

Once they've toured the monasteries, many visitors – especially during low season – are seduced into staying an extra day by the otherworldly scenery. There are a number of other hikes to hidden attractions on and around some of the lesser monoliths, where you're virtually assured solitude.

One of the easier walks is to the **cave-chapel of Áyion Pnévma**. From the Kastráki platía, get onto the fieldstoned lane just above and north, heading northeast towards the last house on this side of the ravine dividing the village. Behind it a clear but unmarked path heads off into the wilds. Once through the last abandoned fruit and nut groves, this route enters scrub and boulder falls, with the wall-like Áyion Pnévma monolith to your left. Roussánou pops into sight as the path executes a hairpin and begins scaling a ravine, essentially a fissure in the side of the rock. Some 35 minutes out of town you'll reach a level spot overhung by the monolith on two sides; to the right (west) the cave-chapel of Áyion Pnévma has been dug out of the rock strata. This was once a hermit's quarters, and inside – otherwise all whitewash and modern icons – you'll see a sarcophagus for his (vanished) bones, again carved from the rock. To the left of the chapel door is the rain cistern which supplied the hermit; the adept can scramble a few minutes further, onto the rock surface with the metal belfry, for superb views.

A more advanced stroll – though still not quite up to abseiling standard – is the steep scramble from the edge of Kastráki up to the partly frescoed **cave-church of Áyii Apóstoli**, the highest sacred monument of the Metéora atop its 630-metre namesake monolith. From beside the prominent village cemetery, a good path leads steeply up for fifteen minutes to the obvious "finger" of Adhrakhtí; the easy going is over now, and you must find the hard-to-spot continuation of the route up the steep gully to the right, keeping to the left side. After five minutes on all fours, you reach the proper onward path. There's a ladder at the trickiest point near the top, but overall this isn't an outing for the acrophobic.

Those intent on solitude should head for the area around the cave-chapel of Áyios Andónios. On the southeastern outskirts of Kastráki, opposite *Taverna*

To Harama, turn onto the narrow road signposted towards "Old Habitation of Kastráki" in English. Drive or walk a short distance up this, then bear right onto a one-lane cement drive which soon becomes dirt, then stops at a modern but attractive chapel built in traditional style. (You can also get here by road from the top of old Kastráki.) Overhead to the east, wedged into the cliff face, is the restored monastery of **Ayíou Nikoláou Bandóvas** (visits forbidden), a dependency of Ayías Triádhos, now used as a hermitage. But the real reason you've come here, ideally at sunset, is bang in front of you, on the side of the Pixári monolith: the **cave-chapel of Áyios Andónios** (restored in 2005–6; may be visitable) and a series of rickety wooden platforms jammed into natural cavities in the cliff face, with half-rotten ladders dangling from them. These **askitíria** or extreme hermitages are now home only to rock doves, but they were inhabited well into the twentieth century, and on their patron saint's day a monk used to be levered up to conduct a liturgy until the 1960s. Here then in the raw, without souvenirs, multilingual guides and tour buses, are the origins and impulse of Metéora contemplative life.

Timíou Stavroú

With your own transport, the flamboyant medieval **church of Timíou Stavroú**, 42km west of Kalambáka, between the villages of Kranía (Kranéa on some maps) and Dholianá, is well worth a visit. The church itself, originally eighteenth century but seeming far older, is a masterpiece of whimsy, matched in concept only by two specimens in Romania and Russia. It sports no fewer than twelve turret-like cupolas, higher than they are wide: three are over the nave, one over each of the three apses, and six over the ends of the triple transept. The church is in excellent external repair, despite some hasty postwar restoration (it was burnt by the Germans in 1943 as a reprisal for local resistance activity) and bulldozing around it; a terrace below with a wooden table (and a water tap nearby) makes an ideal picnic spot. Should you gain admission (it's usually locked), a stone *sýnthrono* or bishop's bench stands in the apse, which survived the fire.

Practicalities

To reach the church, head 10km north of Kalambáka and instead of taking the Métsovo/Ioánnina-bound highway, bear left into a narrower road at Mourgáni, the junction festooned with multiple signposts for high villages. Climb steadily over a pass on the shoulder of Mount Tringía and then drop sharply into the densely forested valley of the upper Aspropótamos River, one of the loveliest in the Píndhos. From the *Aspropotamos* taverna continue 1.5km further south to a tiny bridge and a track on the left, signposted in Greek as "Prós Ierán Monín Timíou Stavroú Dholianón". This leads after 700m to the church, at a height of 1150m. There's a bus from Tríkala to nearby **Kraniá** most days in the summer; on the village platía there's a small **hotel-taverna**, the *Aspropotamos* (☎24320 87235; late June–Aug; ❸).

From the church or Kraniá it's an easy matter to continue 7km down the valley to *Pyrgos Mantania* (see p.398), or 17km further to Tría Potámia, where you can carry on east through Pertoúli and Eláti for a loop back to Tríkala.

If you are heading north from Kalambáka, the **Grevená-bound road** is scenic, well graded and little travelled; its only drawback is that there is just one daily bus to ghastly Grevená itself, and not a lot of other transport.

Travel details

Trains

Athens–Thíva–Livadhiá–Lianokládhi (Lamía)–Lárissa
12 trains daily in each direction: 9 of these are fast or express, which may skip Thíva or Livadhiá, and take a maximum of four hours to reach Lárissa. Approximate non-express journey times:
Athens–Thíva (1hr).
Thíva–Livadhiá (20min).
Livadhiá–Lianokládhi (1hr–1hr 15min).
Lianokládhi–Lárissa (1hr 20min–1hr 40min).

Lárissa–Kateríni–Thessaloníki
11 daily in each direction, 8 of these fast or express.
Approximate journey times:
Lárissa–Kateríni (40–50min).
Kateríni–Thessaloníki (40–55min).
Lárissa–Thessaloníki (1hr 10min–1hr 50min).

Vólos–Athens
1 daily through express train in each direction via Lárissa; otherwise you must change trains there (4hr 45min).

Vólos–Lárissa
15 daily stopping trains in each direction (55min).

Kalambáka–Athens
Two express trains daily in each direction (4hr 30min); through service without changing.

Buses

Buses detailed have similar frequency in each direction, so entries are given just once; for reference check under both starting point and destination.
Ámfissa to: Lamía (3 daily; 2hr 30min); Náfpaktos (5 daily; 2hr).
Andírio to: Agrínio (12 daily; 80min); Mesolóngi (12 daily; 40min).
Athens to: Dhelfí (6 daily; 3hr); Karpeníssi (2 daily; 4hr 30min); Lamía (hourly; 3hr); Lárissa (6 daily; 4hr 15min); Livadhiá (hourly, less on Sun; 2hr 10min); Thíva (hourly; 1hr 30min); Tríkala (7 daily; 5hr); Vólos (10 daily; 4hr 30min).
Dhelfí to: Ámfissa (6 daily; 30min); Itéa (5–6 daily; 30min); Pátra (3 daily, 1 direct; 3hr).
Elefsína to: Thíva (Thebes; 2 daily; 1hr 30min).
Galaxídhi to: Itéa (5 daily Mon–Fri, 4 Sat & Sun; 30min); Náfpaktos (5 daily Mon–Fri, 3 Sat, 2 Sun to Áyios Nikólaos ferry only; 1hr 15min).

Kalambáka to: Grevená (1 daily; 1hr 30min); Ioánnina (2 daily; 3hr 30min); Métsovo (2 daily; 1hr 30min); Vólos (4 daily; 3hr).
Karpeníssi to: Agrínio (1 at 9am most days, extra at 1.30pm Fri; 3hr 30min); Megálo/Mikró Horió (2 daily; 15min); Proussós (Mon & Fri at 5.30am & 1pm; 1hr).
Lamía to: Karpeníssi (4–5 daily; 1hr 30min); Lárissa (3 daily; 2hr 15min); Thessaloníki (2 daily; 4hr); Tríkala (6 daily; 2hr 30min); Vólos (2 daily; 2hr).
Lárissa to: Ambelákia (Mon–Sat 2 daily, Sun 1; 30min); Kalambáka (hourly; 1hr 15min); Litóhoro junction (almost hourly; 1hr); Stómio (2 daily; 40min); Tríkala (hourly; 1hr); Vólos (almost hourly; 1hr).
Livadhiá to: Aráhova (6 daily; 45min); Dhelfí (6 daily; 1hr); Dhístomo, for Ósios Loukás (10 daily; 45min); Ósios Loukás, direct (daily at 12.45pm; 1hr).
Náfpaktos: frequent blue city bus #1 to Andírio for most connections.
Thíva to: Halkídha (2 daily; 1hr 20min); Livadhiá (hourly; 1hr).
Tríkala to: Grevená (1 daily; 1hr 45min); Ioánnina (2 daily; 4hr); Kalambáka (at least hourly 6am–10pm; 15min); Métsovo (2 daily; 2hr); Pertoúli, via Eláti (3 daily Mon–Fri, 1 Sat & Sun at 3.45pm; 1hr 15min); Pýli (14 daily Mon–Fri, 12 Sat & Sun; 20min).
Vólos to: Áyios Ioánnis (2 daily except 1 Sun; 2hr 30min); Makrynítsa (9 daily Mon–Fri, 7 Sat & Sun; 50min); Miliés (6 daily Mon–Fri, 4 Sat & Sun; 1hr); Milína via Hórto (3 daily Mon–Sat, 2 Sun; 1hr 40min); Plataniá (4 daily Mon–Fri, 2 Sat & Sun; 2hr); Portariá (9 daily Mon–Fri, 7 Sat & Sun; 40min); Thessaloníki (8–9 daily; 3hr); Tríkala (4 daily; 2hr 30min); Tríkeri (2 daily; 2hr 30min); Tsangarádha (2 daily; 2hr); Vyzítsa (6 daily Mon–Fri, 2 Sat & Sun; 1hr 10min); Zagorá (4 daily Mon–Fri, 2 Sat & Sun; 2hr–2hr 30min).
Zagorá to: Horeftó (2 daily Mon–Fri, 1 daily Sat & Sun; 15min).

Ferries and catamarans

"In season" means mid-June to mid-September; "otherwise" means mid-April to mid-June and mid-September to end October.
Áyios Konstandínos to: Alónissos (5–6 weekly in season; 2hr 45min); Skiáthos (at least daily in season; 2hr); Skópelos (at least daily in season; 3hr).
Vólos to: Alónissos (1 daily July–Aug, 2–3 weekly

otherwise; 4hr 30min); Skiáthos (2 daily in season, 1 daily otherwise; 2hr 15min); Skópelos (2 daily in season, 1 daily otherwise; 3hr 30min).

Also one weekly service in season on GA Ferries to Límnos, Lésvos and Sámos via Skiáthos and Skópelos.

For current details, ring ℡ 24210 20336 for Sporades services, ℡ 24210 31059 for long-haul services.

To Évvia Arkítsa–Loutrá Edhípsou (at least hourly July–Sept 15, every 2hr otherwise, last sailing at 11pm/10pm; 45min); Glýfa–Ayiókambos (10 daily summer, 8 in winter; last sailing at 8.30pm/6.30pm; 30min).

Hánia–Trizónia (11 daily spring/autumn 7am–9pm, more in summer; 5min journey; no cars taken).

Across the Gulf of Kórinthos Andírio–Río (every 15min, much less often after midnight; 15min);

Áyios Nikólaos–Éyio (4 daily year-round, well-spaced 8.30am–6pm; 45min journey; ℡ 22660 31854 or 26910 28888 for current info).

Hydrofoils

Hellas Flying Dolphins (℡ 24210 21626) run as follows:

Vólos 2 daily in season to Skiáthos (1hr 15min), Skópelos (2hr) and Alónissos (2hr 30min).

Vospo Flying Dolphins (℡ 24210 31400) run as follows:

Vólos 2 daily May–Sept to Skiáthos (1hr 20min), Skópelos (2hr 5min) and Alónissos (2hr 30min); 1 weekly to Péfki, Évvia (1hr); 2 weekly to Paleó Trikeri (30min); 1 weekly to Ayía Kyriakí (1hr 40min).

Epirus and the west

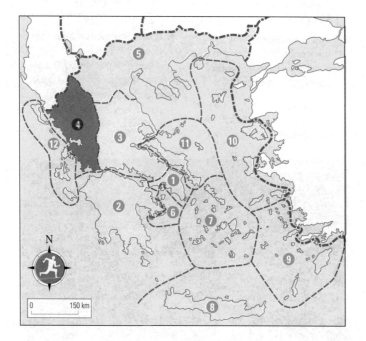

CHAPTER 4   # Highlights

* **Ioánnina** The Ottoman citadel, lakefront and island associated with locally infamous
hero/villain Ali Pasha. **See
p.422**

* **Dodona** Remote and ancient
theatre and ruins of the
Oracle of Zeus. **See p.431**

* **Zagóri** Old stone arhondiká
(mansions) and villages set
in rugged mountain scenery.
See p.433

* **The Víkos Gorge** One of
the longest in Europe and
a worthy rival to its Cretan
counterpart. **See p.434**

* **Karavostási** Perhaps the best
of many excellent beaches on
the Thesprotian coast from

Igoumenítsa to Préveza. **See
p.455**

* **The Ahérondas River** A
delight, from the gorge at its
wild upper reaches to the sea
at the pleasant beach resort
of Ammoudhiá. **See pp.460–
463**

* **Ancient Kassope** Underrated, atmospheric remains
of a former city-state, abandoned in 31 BC. **See p.464**

* **Byzantine monuments** These
abound in and around Árta,
a former autonomous Byzantine despotate; the monastic
church of Panayía Vlahernón
particularly stands out. **See
p.468**

△ Ancient Kassope

4

Epirus and the west

pirus (Ípiros in modern Greek) has the strongest regional identity in mainland Greece. It owes this character to an unrelentingly mountainous terrain: the rugged peaks, forested ravines and turbulent rivers of the **Píndhos** (Pindus) **range**. The **climate** is **wet** almost everywhere, with thundery squalls occurring even during warmer months, bouncing off the coastal ranges to dissipate a short distance offshore. The mountains have always protected and isolated Epirus from outside interference, securing it a large measure of autonomy even under Ottoman rule.

Because of this remoteness, the region's role in Greek affairs was peripheral in ancient times. There are just four archeological sites of importance, two of them isolated oracles. At **Dodona**, the sanctuary includes a spectacular Classical theatre; at **Ephyra**, the weird remains of a Nekromanteion (Oracle of the Dead) was touted by the ancients as the gateway to Hades. **Kassope** and **Nikopolis**, both near Préveza, are more conventional ancient cities. During more recent centuries, **Lord Byron** was the region's greatest publicist. He passed through in 1809 when tyrannical local ruler Ali Pasha was at the height of his power, and the poet's tales of passionate intrigue and fierce-eyed brigandage sent a shiver down romantic Western spines. Byron went on to distinguish himself in the southern province of **Étolo-Akarnanía** by supplying and training troops for the Greek War of Independence, and of course by dying during it at **Mesolóngi**.

A disputed frontier territory throughout the nineteenth century, the Ottomans were not finally ousted from Epirus until March 1913, and the region never recovered its late-medieval prosperity. After 1923, **refugees** from Asia Minor were resettled on extensive ex-Muslim holdings around Ioánnina, Préveza and across Thesprotía, the westernmost county of Epirus. When the Italians invaded in 1940, followed by the Germans in 1941, the Píndhos mountains became first a stronghold of the **Resistance**, then a battleground for rival political factions and finally, after 1946, the chief bastion of the Communist "Democratic Army" in the **civil war**. The events of this period (see the box on p.416) are among the saddest of modern Greek history, and still reverberate today, not least in Epirus's consistent ranking in European Union studies as one of the poorest parts of Western Europe.

However, for visitors it is the remoteness and the **mountains** that provide much of the attraction of Epirus. The physical beauty is stunning, with limestone peaks and dense forest providing a backdrop to traditional stone-built villages and arched packhorse bridges. The most easily accessible and rewarding area for walking is **Zagóri**, in particular its magnificent **Víkos** and **Aóös gorges**, while **mounts Gamíla** and **Smólikas** provide several days of serious trekking for the committed. Beyond the Píndhos villages, a dwindling number of Latinate-speaking Vlach (see Contexts p.1094) and Grecophone Sarakatsan transhumant shepherds bring their flocks to the high mountain pastures in summer, though owing to changed EU subsidy policies, unattended cattle rather than sheep are now more common. The wild fauna is even more impressive: there's good bird-watching, increasing numbers of wolves keep a hungry eye out for stray livestock, while brown bears – protected by law – overturn beehives and leave footprints in riverside mud.

Certain road itineraries offer less strenuous travelling, though many two-lane highways will soon be superseded by motorways. The route from Mesolóngi to Ioánnina via Árta will be covered by the so-called "**Ionian Highway**" as of 2010 – Árta to Filipiádha is now open. The old Kalambáka–Ioánnina highway via Métsovo is being eclipsed by the showcase **Via Egnatia**, which will, by 2007 or so, seamlessly link Igoumenítsa and Ioánnina with Métsovo, Grevená

World War II and the civil war in Epirus

In **November 1940**, the **Italians** invaded Epirus, pushing down from Albania as far as Kalpáki, just south of Kónitsa; the Greeks repulsed the attack and humiliated Mussolini. However, the euphoria was short-lived, since the following April German armoured divisions rapidly overran Greece.

When parcelling out various portions of the country to their allies for administration, the Germans initially assigned Epirus to the Italians, who trod lightly in the province where they had recently been so soundly beaten. After Mussolini's capitulation in September 1943, the Germans assumed direct responsibility for Epirus, and conditions worsened. Together with the mountains of central Greece to the southeast, the Epirot Píndhos was the main staging point for various **partisan bands**, foremost among them the Communist-dominated **ELAS**. Resistance, harassment and ambush of the occupying forces incurred harsh reprisals, including the burning in early 1944 of almost every village along the Aóös River.

The wartime flight to the cities from the mountains dates more or less from these atrocities, and the vicissitudes of the subsequent **civil war** (1946–49) dashed any lingering hope of a reasonable existence in the mountains. Victims of reprisals by either the Communists or the Royalist/Nationalist central government, villagers fled to safety in the cities, or abroad, and many never returned.

Since 1975, many men (and a few women) who fought in ELAS or the Communist Democratic Army, either as volunteers or conscripts, have returned to their villages – some of them after nearly four decades of exile in what was the USSR and other East Bloc countries. Numerous others had been carried off as children to Albania, and made to work in labour camps before being distributed to various East European states. The political Right claims that this *pedhomázema* – the roundup of children – was a cynical and merciless ploy to indoctrinate an army of dedicated revolutionaries for the future. The Left retorts that it was a prudent evacuation of noncombatants from a war zone.

One thing, however, is certain. The Right won, with the backing of the British and – after 1947 – the Americans, and they used that victory to maintain an undemocratic and vengeful regime for the best part of the following quarter-century. Many Epirot villagers, regardless of political conviction, believe that the poverty and backwardness in which many of their communities still remain is a deliberate punishment for being part of Communist-held territory during the civil war. For decades they were constantly harassed by the police, who controlled the issue of all sorts of licences and certificates needed to find public-sector work, to travel, to put children in better schools, to run one's own business and so forth. Only since 1981, and the election of Greece's first PASOK government, have things really changed, and the past finally treated as another, separate, age.

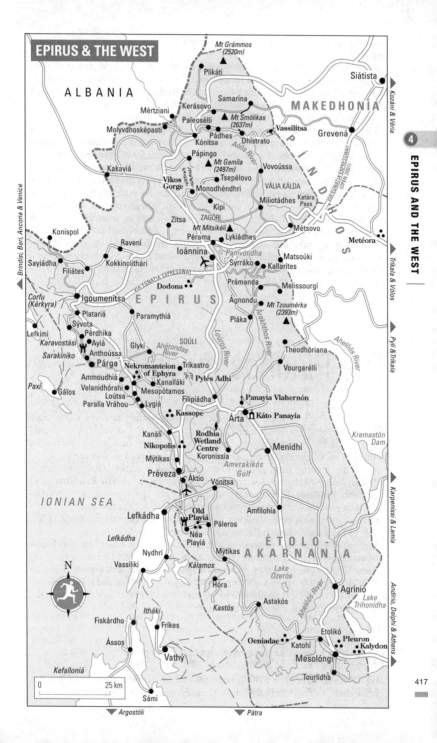

and Macedonia as a whole (the Igoumenítsa–Ioánnina section is already operating).

Roughly halfway between Ioánnina and the Metéora stands **Métsovo**, perhaps the easiest location for a taste of mountain life, albeit with a fair dose of commercialization. The main urban attractions are **Ioánnina**, Ali Pasha's capital, which retains ample character with its fortress, island and lake, and **Árta**, prettily set and blessed with a fine group of Byzantine churches and monasteries.

The coast, in both Epirus and the southerly province of Étolo-Akarnanía, is generally low-key, with a series of sandy and not unduly developed **beaches** between **Igoumenítsa** – a useful ferry terminal for Corfu and Italy, but otherwise unmemorable – and sleepy **Préveza**, boosted by proximity to those beaches, and by a recently expanded airport. In-between lies photogenic **Párga**, the only significant Epirot resort, but one that has been developed beyond its capacity. Inland, however, the eminently scenic **gorge of the Ahérondas River** beckons, several degrees cooler than the coast in midsummer. South of Préveza, you enter a low, marshy landscape of lakes and landlocked gulfs hemmed in by bare hills – of interest mainly to the bird-watcher and fish-dinner enthusiast. For better beach escapes around Étolo-Akarnanía you need islands, fortunately close at hand in the Ionian group; **Lefkádha** (see p.1024) is actually connected to the mainland by a moveable bridge.

The Píndhos mountains

Even if you don't plan on hiking, the **Píndhos range** deserves a few days' detour. The remoteness, traditional architecture, the air and scenery, all constitute a very different Greece to the popular tourist image and, despite increasing popularity as a trekking destination, the area remains relatively unspoilt.

If you are coming from central Greece, the easiest of the transalpine routes is **Kalambáka–Métsovo–Ioánnina**, which divides the **north Píndhos** from the **south Píndhos**. If you are arriving by ferry at Igoumenítsa, getting up to **Ioánnina** enables you to reverse this itinerary, which is the most attractive route into the central mainland. **Walkers** will want to make directly for the **Zagóri**, north of Ioánnina, where trekking opportunities abound.

A number of **hiking routes** are detailed in the text; others can be found in specialist guides (see "Books" in Contexts, p.1148). Most of the routes are arduous and lonesome, rather than downright dangerous. But nonetheless, this is high-mountain country, with unpredictable microclimates, and it's inadvisable to set off on the longer, more ambitious itineraries without any previous trekking experience and at least the basic gear.

The Katára Pass to Ioánnina

West of Kalambáka (see p.400), the 1694-metre **Katára Pass** breaches the central chain of the Píndhos to link Thessaly and Epirus. This route, the only motor road across these mountains kept open in winter (except during blizzards), is one of the most spectacular in the country and worth taking for the journey alone. Though nominally the shortest east–west crossing over the Píndhos, distances here are deceptive. The road switchbacks and zigzags through folds in the enormous peaks, which rise to more than 2300m around **Métsovo**, and from November to April the snow line must be crossed. All this, however, will soon be optional, as sixty enormous tunnels (28km in total, over the 129-kilometre route) linked by long viaducts have been bored through the ridges here as part of the pharaonically ambitious **Vía Egnatía** expressway, designed to spare drivers (especially of lorries) the dangerously curvy and narrow existing highway.

Just two buses daily cover the entire existing route across the mountains, running between Tríkala and Ioánnina, with stops at Kalambáka and Métsovo. If you're driving, allow half a day for the journey from Kalambáka to Ioánnina (114km), and in winter check on conditions before setting out; aside from Métsovo, there's nothing but forest in-between, except for a few small villages without significant facilities.

Métsovo and around

MÉTSOVO stands just west of the Katára pass, right below the Kalambáka–Ioánnina highway (and just above the Vía Egnatía expressway). It's a small, often rainy, alpine town, built on two sides of a ravine and guarded by a forbidding range of peaks to the south and east. Immediately below the highway begin tiers of eighteenth- and nineteenth-century stone houses with wooden balconies. These dwellings spill down the slope to and past the main platía, where a few old men still loiter, especially after Sunday Mass, magnificent in their traditional festive dress, from flat black caps to pompommed shoes, and chatting in Vlach (or Arouman, to give the language its proper name). The women, enveloped in rich blue weave and a headscarf over a pair of braids, have a more subdued appearance but are more regularly seen in such garb.

If you arrive outside of the two high seasons (midsummer and Christmas week), stay overnight and take the time to walk in the valley below, the place can seem magical. In season, Métsovo has become a favourite target for tour-buses full of Greeks, and its beauty veers perilously close to the artificially quaint, with souvenir shops selling kitsch wooden artefacts and "traditional" weavings (all too often mass-produced these days). Even the garish pantiles on the mansion roofs are replacements for the stone originals, which apparently required too much maintenance.

Nonetheless, it would be a shame to pass through Métsovo too speedily, for its history and status as the Vlach "capital" are unique. Positioned astride the only commercially and militarily viable route across the Píndhos, it won a measure of independence, both political and economic, in the earliest days of Ottoman rule. These privileges were elaborated in 1659 by a grateful Turkish vizier who, returned to the sultan's favour, wanted to say a proper "thank you" to the Metsovot shepherd who had protected him during his disgrace and exile. Métsovo's continued prosperity, and the preservation of some of its traditions, are largely due to Baron Mihaïl Tositsas (1888–1950), banker offspring of a Metsovot family living in Switzerland, who left his colossal fortune to an endowment that benefits industries and crafts in and around the town.

The Métsovo **museum** occupies the eighteenth-century **Arhondikó Tosítsa** (daily except Thurs: summer 9.30am–1.30pm & 4–6pm; winter 3–5pm; group tours only every 30min; €3), the old Tositsa mansion just off the main thoroughfare. This has been restored to its full glory, and with its panelled rooms, rugs and fine collection of Epirot crafts and costumes, gives a real sense of the town's wealth and grandeur in that era.

Practicalities

The **bus stop** is on the main platía, the **post office** is on the main street 200m uphill, while five **banks** with ATMs are scattered between the two.

Meals are overwhelmingly meat-oriented, as befits a pastoral centre. Four of the simpler grills are *Kryfi Folia* on the main platía, *To Tzaki* next door, *To Kout-ouki tou Nikola* (also with some non-meat dishes), directly below and behind the post office, and *To Arhondiko* opposite; all function principally in the evening. The main vegetarian and lunchtime options are the ground-floor restaurant at *Hotel Athinai/Athens* (due to reopen in 2007) just below the main square, and the less distinguished one at the nearby *Hotel Galaxias*, where you can sit out on the lawn under giant trees.

Wine buffs may want to try the fabled Katóyi, available in some of these restaurants and in local shops (and fairly widely across Greece). It's a moderately expensive limited bottling from tiny vineyards down on the Árakhthos River, though the quality of the main label – Averoff – is variable (the Ktima line is best). This, and other **local specialities** such as *trahanádhes* (a porridge base of milled wheat and soured sheep's milk, either sweet or savoury), the smoked *metsovóne* cheese and *hilópites* (like tagliatelle, long or chopped into cubes, with added egg), can be obtained at local shops such as Iy Piyi or O Vlahos, just downhill from the *Hotel Bitounis*. For genuine **hand-loom items**, the Zouvias and Tsiroyiannis storefronts at the very top of town are reliable.

Nightlife takes the form of a few noisy music bars and cafés uphill from the post office on the main street; their identity, though not their location, tends to change yearly.

Accommodation

Métsovo has a wide range of **accommodation**, with thirteen hotels plus quite a few rooms for rent, nearly all of it en suite. Outside Christmas week, the town's festival (July 26) or late August, you should have little trouble in getting a bed or bargaining posted rates down a category.

Andonis Just above the main square ☎ 26560 42300, ⓦ www.metsovo.com/apollon. Quietly sited and with the largest, most plushly appointed rooms in town; if they're full, you'll be sent to their affiliate, the *Hotel Apollon* (❹), below the main square. B&B peak season ❺, rest of year (room only) ❹

Bitounis At the top of the main street ☎ 26560 41217, ⓔ bitounis@met.forthnet.gr. The affable proprietor of this welcoming place speaks fluent English, the result of eight years' residence in London. Over two-thirds of the rooms have balconies with valley views; there are attic suites suitable for four, plus a sauna. ❹

Filoxenia Just behind the grassy hillock of the central park ☎ 26560 41021, ⓕ 26560 42009. Officially *dhomátia* (rooms), these en-suite units are excellent value, with valley views out of the rear rooms and some pricier luxury units (❸). ❷

Flokas On the street leading south from the square ☎ 26560 41309, ⓕ 26560 41547. Rustic-style, with views from the top-floor rooms. Winter ❹, summer ❷

Kassaros On the street leading south from the square ☎ 26560 41800, ⓕ 26560 41262. All rooms at this large hotel have views over to Anílio, and the management can organize summer or winter activities in the nearby mountains. ❹

Around Métsovo

Outside Métsovo, the main attraction is the monastery of **Áyios Nikólaos**, signposted from the main platía but in fact fifteen minutes' walk below town; it is reached just off the half-cemented *kalderími* (path) bound for Anílio, the village across the ravine. The monastery's *katholikón*, topped by a simple barrel vault, was built in the fourteenth century to an unconventional plan; what might once have been the narthex became over time a *yinaikonítis* or women's gallery, rarely seen elsewhere in Greece. The brilliant, unconventional **frescoes** date from 1702, and were cleaned and illuminated during the 1960s, courtesy of the Tosítsa Foundation. Since there is no dome, the Four Evangelists are painted on four partly recessed columns; between them are scenes from the life of Christ, and assorted martyrdoms. The barrel vault features four medallions – the Virgin and Child, the Holy Trinity, an Archangel and a *Pandokrátor* (Christ in Majesty) – forming an unusual sequence. Otherwise the iconography is the norm for post-Byzantine churches: a *Crucifixion* on the west wall, and a *Virgin Enthroned* in the conch of the apse, flanked by the *Communion of the Apostles* (six to each side). A warden family lives on the premises and receives visitors until 7.30pm. You'll be shown the monks' former cells, with insulating walls of mud and straw, and the abbot's more sumptuous quarters; a purchase of postcards or souvenirs is expected.

In winter, weather permitting, a small **ski centre** operates between Anílio and the Katára Pass. It's hardly Greece's premier winter-sports venue, with three drag lifts serving just six runs, mostly green- and blue-rated; a hopefully more reliable piste on a north-facing slope is being prepared across the valley.

Eastern Zagóri: Vovoússa and the Vália Kálda

For a taste of lonelier scenery, and a truer picture of contemporary mountain life, follow the paved road into the **eastern Zagóri** district from just west of the Baldhoúma bridge on the Métsovo–Ioánnina highway. This precipitous route snakes its way north along the valley of the Várdhas River, through a lush landscape of broad-leafed trees and scrub. At Greveníti, 21km along and the first of a series of predominantly Vlach villages, a mixed black-pine-and-beech forest takes over, cloaking the Píndhos most of the way to Albania. Beyond Flambourári – like all its neighbours badly depopulated, and wrecked by the Germans in reprisal for Resistance activities, with only fine stone churches spared – the road becomes ever more twisty. Hazardous driving conditions are aggravated by lumber trucks hauling logs out daily from the sawmill at **VOVOÚSSA**, which, 51km from the main highway, straddles the Aóös River, its milky-green waters spanned by a high-arched, eighteenth-century **bridge**; there's a smaller one just upstream, by the jeeps-only road to central Zagóri. On either side, wooded ridges rise steeply to the skyline, culminating in the 2177-metre Avgó peak, which presides over the **Vália Kálda**, heart of a small national park, traversed by the E6 long-distance trail and home to numbers of bears, who have lent their name to the Arkoudhórema (Bear Stream) that threads through the valley.

Like its southerly neighbours, Vovoússa (except for bridge and church) was burnt by the Germans; the village, the last one before the border with Grevená province in Macedonia, now serves as closest gateway to the national park. **Accommodation** includes a few summer-only rooms, as well as the rambling, very basic *Xenon Perdhiki* (℡26560 22850; ❶) at the riverside, or, 500m upstream in the small west-bank quarter, the all-year *Xenonas Dhrouyia* (℡26560 22555 or 697 70 27 207, ⓦwww.zagori.biz/vovousaappartments; ❸), with sparsely furnished but good-standard doubles, triples and quads, as well as an on-site taverna. The main independent **eating** option is the *Psistaria Angelos* back on the east-bank main street, with terrace seating overlooking the river.

For visiting the Vália Kálda, the 2002-built *Kataflyio Valia Kalda* (☎26510 29445, ⓦ www.katafigiovaliacalda.com; bunks €10), 3.5km south of Vovoússa near the edge of the park, is possibly a better base. There are multi-bed dorms as well as five-person family rooms, a lounge, and cheapish meals on offer. Kostas, the full-time warden, is a mine of information on the area and can advise on excursions into the Vália Kálda ("Warm Valley" in Vlach, named ironically, given it has one of the coldest climates in Greece). The twin **tarns of Flénga**, just below the eponymous 2159-metre peak of the lightning-blasted Mavrovoúni ridge bounding the park on the south, are a favourite destination, just feasible as a day-trip with an early start.

Bus services to or from Vovoússa are limited to twice weekly, so chances are you've either driven your own car or walked here. If walking, you may have no choice but to follow a marked long-distance route down the Aóös River valley to the village of Dhístrato (see p.447); the trek, partly along trail and partly on forestry track, keeps to the east bank of the Aóös, and takes a full day.

Ioánnina and around

Moving west from Métsovo, you drop first into the Árakhthos River valley, then climb again over a shoulder of Mount Mitsikéli before the final descent to the north margin of the great, reed-fringed **lake of Pamvótidha** (or Pamvótis). On its south shore, the old town of **IOÁNNINA** (often spelled Yiánnena) covers a rocky promontory jutting out into the water, its fortifications punctuated by bastions and minarets. From this base, Ali Pasha carved out – at the expense of the sultan's authority – a fiefdom that encompassed much of western Greece and present-day Albania: an act of contemptuous rebellion that portended wider defiance in the Greeks' own War of Independence.

Although much of the city is modern and undistinguished – a testimony not so much to Ali (although he did raze much of it to the ground while under siege in 1820) as to developers in the 1960s – the old town remains one of the more characterful in Greece. There's a pair of stone-built **mosques** (and a synagogue) to evoke the Ottoman era, two worthwhile **museums**, and the fortifications of Ali Pasha's citadel, the **Kástro**, surviving more or less intact; you can also explore **Nissí island** with its car-free if overly prettified village. Ioánnina is also the jump-off point for visits to the **caves of Pérama**, among the country's largest, on the western shore of the lake, and the longer excursion to the mysterious and remote Oracle of Zeus at **Dodona**, as well as to Epirus's most rewarding corner, **Zagóri** (see p.433).

Modern Ioánnina, incidentally, is one of Greece's fastest-growing provincial capitals, with the city and suburbs' **population** doubling since the 1970s to a current 130,000. Much of this has been sucked inward from moribund villages in the remoter reaches of the province, but it also includes some 25,000 students at the major university here, plus military personnel and their dependants; Ioánnina has served as a strategic garrison town since its incorporation into Greece.

Arrival, information and town transport

Ioánnina **airport** is on the road out to the Pérama caves, 5km from the centre (city bus #7 goes to and from town); currently, it has only domestic flights with Olympic (Platía Pýrrou; ☎26510 23120) and Aegean (airport only; ☎26510 65200). If you're driving, be careful where you park; the city's pay-and-display

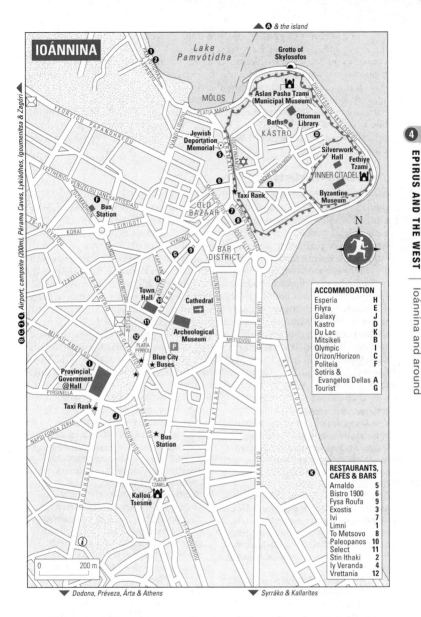

IOÁNNINA

Lake Pamvótidha

Grotto of Skylosofos

Aslan Pasha Tzami (Municipal Museum)

MÓLOS

PLATIA MAVILI

Baths

Ottoman Library

KÁSTRO

Jewish Deportation Memorial

Silverwork Hall · Fethiye Tzami

INNER CITADEL

Taxi Rank

OLD BAZAAR

Byzantine Museum

N

Bus Station

BAR DISTRICT

Town Hall

Cathedral

Archeological Museum

Blue City Buses

Provincial Government @Hall

PYRSINELLA

Taxi Rank

Bus Station

PLATIA TZAVELA

Kalloú Tsesmé

ACCOMMODATION

Esperia	H
Filyra	E
Galaxy	J
Kastro	D
Du Lac	K
Mitsikeli	B
Olympic	I
Orizon/Horizon	C
Politeia	F
Sotiris &	
Evangelos Dellas	A
Tourist	G

RESTAURANTS, CAFÉS & BARS

Arnaldo	5
Bistro 1900	6
Fysa Roufa	9
Exostis	3
Ivi	7
Limni	1
To Metsovo	8
Paleopanos	10
Select	11
Stin Ithaki	2
Iy Veranda	4
Vrettania	12

0   200 m

Dodona, Préveza, Árta & Athens   Syrráko & Kallarítes

Airport, campsite (200m), Pérama Caves, Lykiádhes, Igoumenítsa & Zagóri

& the island

EPIRUS AND THE WEST | Ioánnina and around

4

parking scheme is pretty comprehensive, with punch-out cards permitting only two hours at a time – it's easiest to use the central car park shown on the map (€2/24hr).

    KTEL buses arrive at one of three terminals. One station is at Zozimádhon 4, north of Platía Pýrrou; this serves most points north and west, including Métsovo, Kalambáka, Igoumenítsa, Kónitsa and the Zagóri villages. Another terminal at Bizaníou 19 connects Árta, Préveza, Dodona and all villages in the

423

south or east parts of Epirus, though this shuts at weekends when all services use the Zozimádhon terminal. Kastoriá services use a separate terminal at Yeoryíou Papandhréou 58. It's advisable, especially on summer weekends, to buy tickets for both coast and mountains the day before. Local blue-and-white **city buses** leave from a cluster of stops below the central Platía Pýrrou; buy tickets from adjacent booths beforehand, and cancel them when boarding. Information on current bus timetables is most easily obtained from the friendly **EOT** at Dhodhónis 39 (Sept–June Mon–Fri 7.30am–2.30pm), though they keep very little printed literature in English. The local **taxis** are dark green; central ranks are marked on our map.

Accommodation

Most Ioánnina **hotels** are noisy, badly placed and expensive for what's on offer, though at slow times prices may drop a category. High season tends to be Christmas and Easter more than summer, and weekends year-round can see the better places packed out. In view of the town's congestion, hotels with unrestricted street parking or their own garages are indicated.

If you are willing to sacrifice midtown convenience for better value, you will also find more than twenty licensed **rooms** outfits in Pérama village (see p.431), between the main highway and the caves. If you can afford the better mid-range Ioánnina hotels, you could pay about the same (or less) for quality lodgings 12km away in the stunningly set nearby village of Lykiádhes, halfway up the slopes of Mount Mitsikéli, which closes off the lake to the north.

Camping, unusually for a town, is an attractive option, and lakeside *Camping Limnopoula* (☎26510 25265), 2km out of town on the Pérama road (city bus #2 or 20min walk from Platía Mavíli), is a pleasant, well-equipped, mosquito-free site, though a bit cramped and more geared towards campervans than tents.

Midtown Ioánnina

Esperia Kapláni 3 ☎26510 24111, ☎26510 77498. About the only savoury, quiet cheapie in town, with large, balconied, en-suite rooms (though decor is distressed 1970s vintage, right down to the peeling lino) and private parking out back. ❷

Du Lac cnr Miaoúli and Íkkou, 700m south of Kástro ☎26510 59100, ⓦwww.dulac.gr. The city's A-class convention-and-businessperson's hotel, with a suburban setting, some lake views from the large standard doubles, and sizeable balconies. Hopefully your company's paying the bumped-up rates. ❼

Filyra Alley off Andhroníkou Paleológou 18, Kástro ☎26510 83560 or 693 22 57 290. Just four appealing studios (some triple) in a restored old building, with full kitchens (though breakfast is offered) and a young, trendy clientele. B&B ❹

Galaxy Platía Pýrrou, south corner ☎26510 25056, ☎26510 30724. Comfortable and quiet rooms with spectacular mountain/lake views from the balconies, air conditioning and small tubs in the bathrooms. You don't get much more central; limited street parking. ❹

Kastro Andhroníkou Paleológou 57, Kástro ☎26510 22866, ⓦwww.epirus.com /hotel-kastro. A tastefully restored inn on the way to the Fethiye Tzamí, whose seven unique rooms are mostly equipped with double beds. Cooler downstairs units (fans but no air conditioning are cheaper. Limited street parking. B&B ❺

Olympic Melanídhis 2 ☎26510 25888, ⓦwww .hotelolymp.gr. The highest-standard hotel in the city centre, in a fairly quiet spot. Well-appointed rooms (plus a few suites) have music systems, a safe, small but well-executed designer bathrooms with tubs, and balconies or large terraces. Full-service restaurant on-site, private parking. ❻

Politeia Anexartissías 109 ☎26510 22235, ⓦwww.etip.gr. Built on the site of an old tradesmen's hall, this hotel retains some period details (stone walls) and its arrangement around a courtyard. Handy for the bus station, but an oasis of quiet calm in the bazaar; choose between standard units at the back or the palatial upstairs suites which can sleep four. Some off-street parking; breakfast available in the bar-café flanking the courtyard. Rooms B&B ❺, suites ❼

Tourist Kolétti 18, cnr Krystálli ℡ 26510 25070, ℻ 26510 20002. Around the corner from the inadvisable *Metropolis*, this is quieter and much more comfortable. Rooms have all been converted to en suite, but some bathrooms are still basic, and it's somewhat overpriced. ❸–❹

Lykiádhes and Nissí

Mitsikeli Lykiádhes village ℡ 26510 81964. Simple but serviceable en-suite rooms, heated but with no balconies, above an eponymous taverna. Easy access and parking. ❸

Orizon/Horizon Lykiádhes village ℡ 26510 86180 or 697 60 06 756, ⓦ www.epirus .com/horizon. The name says it all – knockout

views over the entire lake basin from this well-designed modern hotel. The en-suite, double-glazed, wood-floored rooms are huge, all with balconies and some with tubs in the bathrooms; an ample breakfast is served out on the terrace or in the large lounge, and own-label wine is on offer. Adequate parking, but a steep, hairpin drive to reach it. ❺

Sotiris & Evangelos Dellas Nissí island ℡ 26510 81494, ℻ 26510 79380. A good if simple *pension* with six rooms sharing bathrooms; you'll find the proprietors at the house right next to the school, or in the ground-floor bar of the inn-building (thus some potential nocturnal noise). ❶

The Town

Once through its extensive modern suburbs, **orientation** in Ioánnina is fairly straightforward. Main drag Avéroff leads from the gate of the lakeside Kástro, past the dense grid of lanes in the old bazaar area, to central Platía Pýrrou, before continuing south as Dhodhónis.

The Kástro

The **Kástro** is an obvious point to begin your explorations. In its heyday the walls dropped abruptly to the lake, and were moated on their landward (south-west) side. The moat has been filled in, and a quay-esplanade now extends below the lakeside ramparts, but there is still the feel of a citadel; inside nestles a quiet residential district with narrow alleys and its own shops.

Signs inside direct you to the **Municipal Ethnographic Museum** (daily: summer 8am–8.30pm; winter 9am–4pm; €3), an elegantly arranged collection of Epirot costumes, guns and jewellery. More poignant is a section devoted to synagogue rugs and tapestries donated in the early 1990s by the dwindling Jewish community of about fifty; their *hávra* or **synagogue** at Ioustinianoú 16 can be visited on application (8am–2pm) to the community office at Ioséf Eliyiá 18B (the unmarked, ground-floor storefront – only Greek or Hebrew spoken – where there's a good, brief display on the community's history). Some 150m west of the clocktower over the *kástro* gate, a municipally erected, trilingual **memorial** honours the 1850 local Jews deported on March 25, 1944 to their deaths at Auschwitz.

The museum's so-called Muslim wing features a walnut and mother-of-pearl suite, complete with the pipe of Esat Pasha, last Ottoman governor here. The museum is housed in the well-preserved, floodlit **Aslan Pasha Tzamí**, allowing a rare glimpse of the interior of an intact Greek mosque; it retains painted decoration in its dome and *mihrab* (niche indicating direction of Mecca), as well as the recesses in the vestibule for worshippers' shoes. The mosque dates from 1618, built on the site of an Orthodox cathedral pulled down in reprisal for a failed local revolt of 1611. Its instigator, Skylosofos ("The Dog-Sage"), was a charismatic religious hermit who lived in a dank cave directly underneath the cathedral and its replacement; the grotto is now signposted from the lake esplanade.

In the adjacent, arcaded *medresse* or Muslim seminary, tradition places Ali's attempted rape in 1801 of Kyra Frosyni, the mistress of his eldest son. In return

Ali Pasha, a highly ambivalent "heroic rebel", is the major figure in recent Ioanninan and Epirot history. The so-called "Lion of Yiannena", on balance a highly talented sociopath, pursued a policy that was consistent only in its ambition and self-interest. His attacks on the Ottoman imperial government were matched by acts of appalling and vindictive **savagery** against his largely Orthodox Christian subjects. Despite all this, he is still held in some regard by locals, the justifications apparently being "a son of a bitch, but at least *our* son of a bitch", and his perceived role as a defier of Istanbul, the common enemy – a platía in the citadel is even named after him.

Ali was born in 1741 in Tepelene, now in modern Albania, and rose to power under imperial patronage, being made pasha of Tríkala in 1787 as reward for his efforts in the sultan's war against Austria. His ambitions, however, were of a grander order, and the following year he **seized Ioánnina**, an important town since the thirteenth century, with a population of 30,000 – probably the largest in Greece at the time. Paying sporadic tribute to the sultan, he operated from this power base for the next 33 years, allying himself in turn, as the moment suited him, with the Ottomans, the French or the British.

In 1809, when his dependence upon the sultan was nominal, Ali was visited by the young **Lord Byron**, whom he overwhelmed with hospitality and attention. (The tyrant's sexual tastes were famously omnivorous, and it is recorded that he was particularly taken with the poet's "small ears", a purported mark of good breeding.) Byron, impressed for his part with Ali's daring and stature, and the lively **revival of Greek culture** in Ioánnina (which, he wrote, was "superior in wealth, refinement and learning" to any other town in Greece), commemorated the meeting in *Childe Harold*. The portrait that he drew, however, was an ambiguous one, since he was well aware that beneath Ali's splendid court and deceptively mild countenance there were "deeds that lurk" and "stain him with disgrace". When writing to his mother he was more explicit, concluding that "His highness is a remorseless tyrant, guilty of the most horrible cruelties, very brave, so good a general that they call him the Mahometan Buonaparte . . . but as barbarous as he is successful, roasting rebels, etc, etc".

Of those who rebelled against Ali, the most illustrious was Lambros Katsandonis who, wracked by smallpox, was captured by Ali in a cave in the Ágrafa mountains. He imprisoned the unfortunate wretch in a waterlogged lakeside dungeon and finally executed him in public by smashing his bones with a sledgehammer. Ali himself met nearly as grisly an end: in 1821, resolved to eliminate the Epirot threat to his authority before tackling the Greek revolutionary insurgents, the Ottoman sultan sent an army of 50,000 to Ioánnina to besiege and capture Ali. He was lured from the security of his citadel to a monastery on the lake island of Nissí with false promises of lenient surrender terms, but was shot and decapitated instead in an ambush. His severed head was displayed in all the provinces he had terrorized, to assure folk that the monster was dead – and that the sultan's writ ran once again – before being sent off to Istanbul. The rest of Ali is believed to lie in the northeast corner of the citadel.

for refusing the 60-year-old tyrant's sexual advances, she was bound, weighted and thrown alive into Lake Pamvótidha, together with seventeen of her companions. The incident gave rise to several folk songs (and not a few kitsch postcards); her ghost is still said to hover over the water on moonlit nights. The *medresse* is currently home to the **Fotis Rapakousis Museum** (same hours as museum; free, but items labelled only in Greek), a huge collection of medieval weaponry and jewellery.

The inner citadel

To the east of the Aslan Pasha Tzamí lies the "Its Kale" or **inner citadel** of the fortress (daily 7am–10pm; free); the grounds are often used for concerts after-hours, and there's a pleasant, reasonably priced café near the entrance, occupying the garrison's former canteen. The citadel was used for some years by the Ottoman, then Greek, military, and most of its buildings – including Ali's palace where Byron was entertained – have unfortunately been adapted or restored in a way that few can be recognized any longer as eighteenth-century structures. One of two Ottoman graves in front of the old **Fethiye Tzamí** ("Victory Mosque"), surmounted by an elegant wrought-iron cage, is probably that of Ali Pasha, while the other contains his wife and one son. The tyrant's former palace has been pressed into service as the **Byzantine Museum** (summer Mon 12.30–7pm, Tues–Sun 8am–7pm; winter Tues–Sun 8am–5pm; €3), a rather thin and largely post-Byzantine collection that can be skipped if time is short or if you're heading towards Kastoriá. The displays mostly comprise masonry, coins, pottery, icons and colour prints of frescoes from various ages, few of them Byzantine; the only Byzantine painting is a fresco fragment of *The Betrayal*, from a church near Vourgarélli (see p.450). A few paces away, in the purported treasury of Ali Pasha's seraglio, is a more interesting auxiliary exhibit, labelled as the **Silverwork Hall**, devoted to Ioánnina's long-running silver industry.

The rest of the town

Apart from the Kástro, the town's most enjoyable quarter is that of the **old bazaar**, a roughly semicircular area focused on the citadel's main gate. This retains a cluster of Ottoman-era buildings (including some imposing houses with ornate window grilles), as well as a scattering of copper- and tinsmiths, plus the silversmiths who were for centuries a mainstay of the town's economy.

Just off the central Platía Dhimokratías (recently renamed Andhréa Papandhréou), set beside a small park behind the National Bank, is the **archeological**

△ Ioánnina

museum (closed indefinitely for works). When it reopens, a fascinating collection of lead tablets inscribed with questions to the oracle at Dodona should return to view, along with some exceptionally well-crafted bronze seals. There are also numerous bronze statuettes, including two Hellenistic children, one throwing a ball and one holding a dove; Roman artefacts including ornate relief-carved sarcophagi from Paramythiá and Igoumenítsa; and earlier funerary and votive bronze and ceramic items from Ambrakia (Árta), Akheron (the Nekromanteíon of Ephyra) and Vítsa.

The oldest item, part of a small exhibit on prehistoric Epirus, is a crudely hewn hand-axe, dated to 200,000 BC, the earliest such tool known in Greece. There is also a wealth of finds from a Molossian cemetery near Kónitsa, almost all of it from ancient Corinth, the city-state which colonized much of Epirus.

Nissí island

The island of **Nissí** in Lake Pamvótidha is connected by water-buses (half-hourly in summer, hourly otherwise; 8am–11pm, return journey 6.30am–10.45pm; €1.30 each way) from the Mólos quay northwest of the Kástro on Platía Mavíli. Only cars belonging to islanders are allowed, hauled across on a chain-barge to the mainland opposite. The beautiful island village, founded during the sixteenth century by refugees from the Máni in the Peloponnese, is flanked by several **monasteries**, providing a focus for an afternoon's visit. By day the main lane leading up from the boat dock is crammed with stalls selling jewellery and kitsch souvenirs. Except at three overpriced restaurants on the waterfront and another cluster by Pandelímonos (including a popular *kafenío*), quiet descends with the sun as it sets superbly over the reed beds that fringe the island.

The **monastery of Pandelímonos**, just to the east of the village, is perhaps the most dramatic of Ioánnina's Ali Pasha sites, though it is in fact a complete reconstruction, as the original building was smashed some years ago by a falling tree. In January 1822 Ali was assassinated here after being lured to the island by spurious promises of imperial pardon; trapped in his rooms on the upper storey, he was shot from the floor below, then decapitated (supposedly on the second step from the top). The fateful bullet holes in the floorboards form the centrepiece of a small **museum** (daily: summer reasonable daylight hours; winter hours vary; €0.75) devoted to Ali, along with numerous wonderful period prints and knick-knacks like a splendid hubble-bubble on the fireplace.

Three other **monasteries** – **Filanthropinón**, **Ayíou Nikólaou Stratigopoúlou** or **Dilíou**, and **Eleoússas** (closed to the public) – lie south of the village in the order cited. They are quite clearly signposted and stand within a few hundred yards of one another along a lovely tree-lined lane; the first two are maintained by resident families, who allow brief visits except during siesta hours (knock for admission if doors are shut). Both monasteries are attractively situated, with pleasant courtyards, though visits essentially consist of being shown their main chapel, or *katholikón*. These feature late- and post-Byzantine **frescoes**, in various states of preservation.

The finest are those of Filanthropinón, a simple barrel-vaulted structure with a blind narthex and two *pareklísia* (side chapels). A complete cycle of Christ's life dates from just after the monastery's foundation in 1292; there are plenty of episodes on boats in the Sea of Galilee, as befits a lake-island church. Lower down, throughout the building, are the saints, including (just east of the door to the south *pareklísion*) Khristóforos (Christopher). Higher up, in the outer nave and north *pareklísion*, graphic martyrdoms predominate:

Lake Pamvótidha and its ecology

Murkily green and visibly polluted, **Lake Pamvótidha** is in desperate straits. The springs that historically fed it along its north shore dried up in the early 1980s (though they have resumed again in the past few years), leaving runoff as its main replenishment. This – from Ioánnina and surrounding farmland – is heavily **contaminated** with rubber tyre particles, pesticides and fertilizers. The lake only drains toward the Ionian Sea in winter, via a ditch near Pérama linking it to the Kalamás River; in dry years Pamvótidha may fail to drain at all, with water levels falling up to 2m in a lake that's at best 15m deep. Swimming is forbidden, though few would want to under present circumstances; amazingly, the lake – and a variable-width zone along most of the shore – has been officially protected since 2003, though results are hardly evident yet.

In the face of all this, the inhabitants of the island struggle to continue **fishing**. The lake was stocked with three species from Hungary in 1986, though all but one of these, the hardy, carp-like *kyprínos*, have been fished out as they failed to reproduce. Another Hungarian bass-like fish was later introduced, and did thrive – it attains two kilos in weight within two years, and a monstrous fifteen kilos by four years of age. But Ioánnina inhabitants generally refuse to eat anything caught in the lake, so the islanders are forced to sell their catch at a pittance for shipment to Thessaloníki, where it retails for ten times the price. Given such dire economics, fishing continues mainly to pass the time and supplement islanders' diets. The only lake items on Nissí restaurant menus are the legs of frogs caught in the surrounding reed beds, some of the eels, the *kyprínos*, and those leviathans at two kilos and up.

sundry beheadings, draggings, impalings and boilings. At the east end of the north chapel, Adam names the beasts in the Garden of Eden, while the ceiling of the narthex holds a fine *Transfiguration*. In the south chapel, just west of the door, ancient Greek sages (Solon, Aristotle, Plutarch) make a rare appearance, indicating that this may have been a school for Hellenic culture during the Turkish period.

The frescoes in Ayíou Nikólaou Stratigopoúlou are being slowly cleaned, and should eventually equal Filanthropinón's in interest. Currently the narthex offers, from the Life of the Virgin, a fine *Adoration of the Magi* and a *Flight into Egypt* on the west wall, plus a typically surreal *Apocalypse* over the door to the naos. There's a fine touch to the *Nativity*, where an angel sternly awakens Joseph with a wagging finger.

Beyond these three monasteries the track loops anticlockwise around the island until you emerge by a fourth monastery, **Ioánnou Prodhrómou**, right behind Pandelímonos, which holds the keys. However, the interior is of far less interest than the exterior's three-windowed gables and brickwork.

Eating and drinking

Ioánnina offers a decent range of **restaurants** both in town and across the lake. The most obvious concentration of eateries, with both meat and seafood prominent, is on part-pedestrianized Odhós Pamvótidhas northwest of the Mólos quay (though addresses are cited as Stratigoú Papágou, the parallel back alley). Just outside the Kástro gate are a number of *koultouriárika* tavernas occupying former Jewish mansions, in particular specializing in Italian or generic Mediterranean food, as well as traditional Greek tavernas and *psistariés*. Over on Nissí island, the obvious dockside tavernas are atmospheric but overpriced and mediocre venues for a meal, based on freshwater specialities such as eel (*héli*), crayfish (*karavídhes*), carp (*kyprínos*) and frogs crammed rather off-puttingly into glass tanks outside. Most Ioanninots, if they want a meal out of town, head instead for the villages of Amfithéa or Lykiádhes, the latter directly above the island on Mount Mitsikéli and always several degrees cooler year-round.

Restaurants

Arnaldo Soútsou 9 ☏ 26510 30900. Slightly tired tart's-boudoir decor inside at this Italian specialist, but there's superb garden seating out back, and visiting Italians rate this as authentically home-style. Dinner only, book on weekends. Closed Mon.

Bistro 1900 Neoptolémou 9 ☏ 26510 33131. This makes a good fist of generic Italian/Mediterranean dishes such as *psaronéfri* (pork medallions) in plum sauce and risotto, served upstairs under a painted ceiling; budget €18 per person plus wine. Dinner only; booking advisable. Closed Mon.

Fysa Roufa Avéroff 55. Upmarket *mayireftá* such as baked fish, suckling pig and *spet-zofáï*, whose slightly bumped-up prices are amply justified by the calibre of the cooking, the service and large portions; unusually, there's a full line of desserts too at this busy place. Cosy loft seating for winter, and a decor of archival photos from Parga, the proprietor's birthplace. Open 24hr.

Exostis far end of Lykiádhes village. The most reliable of three tavernas here, providing good-value, locally sourced grills and *mezédhes*; on an airy terrace. Dinner only except summer.

Ivi base of Avéroff. Basic but sustaining, inexpensive *mayireftá* at Ioánnina's last surviving old-style working man's canteen.

Iy Veranda Amfithéa, 7km out of Ioánnina, on the highway. Worth the trip out for well-executed *mezédhes* and grills, with views over the island and lake. Closed Mon, also lunch except summer.

Limni Stratigoú Papágou 26. More likely than its neighbours to have seafood, and slightly elevated prices are compensated for with large, salubrious portions.

To Metsovo Ethnikís Andístasis 6. Very popular with the locals at night, serving all manner of roast beast washed down with bulk wine. Dinner only.

Stin Ithaki Stratigoú Papágou 20A. The most ambitious menu on the lakefront, encompassing Turkish-style kebabs, Cypriot specialities, Smyrna recipes and curries as well as Epirot standards such as trout, frogs' legs, turnovers, cheeses and mushrooms in various guises. With such a broad brush, some duff platters are inevitable, but the kitchen succeeds more often than not. Don't over-order starters; they're huge.

Snacks and cafés

In terms of **snacks**, Ioánnina is the original home of the *bougátsa* (custard-tart; always served with a salty *kouloúra* or ring biscuit), fresh at breakfast time with sweet or savoury fillings from *Select* at Platía Dhimokratías (aka Andhréa Papandhréou) 2, whose decor of mosaic floors and marble tables has remained unchanged for thirty years. An alternative, with a more updated design sense, is *Paleopanos* at Avéroff 3. In a mock-belle-époque environment, the patisserie *Vrettania*, under the eponymous hotel at Platía Dhimokratías 11A, has excellent own-brand ice cream as well as all imaginable sticky cakes.

Nightlife and entertainment

The large local student population keeps Ioánnina lively after dark. **Nightlife** and **coffee society** oscillates between the calmer **cafés** around Platía Pýrrou and along nearby Leofóros Dhodhónis, and the more nocturnal café-bars, patisseries and ice-cream parlours on Platía Mavíli, heart of the **Mólos** or lakefront. At night, a gas-lantern-lit carnival atmosphere prevails at Mólos, enlivened by sellers of Fársala *halvás* (sweetmeat) and roast corn. There are more wine bars, crêperies and the odd "pub" scattered across the approaches to the castle, along Karamanlí.

After-hours **bars** concentrate at the far end of Ethnikís Andístasis, at the southern corner of the citadel, and in the little platía behind a former crafts-men's bazaar; premises all merge together into what seems like one giant seating area. During summer posters announce ephemeral, hangar-like **dance venues** out in industrial premises on the western lakeshore.

Back up around Platía Pýrrou, there are also three **cinemas**, which usually host quite a decent programme of first-run films, as does the Odeon five-screen at the Paralimnio Centre, out in Votanikós district. From mid-July to mid-August, there are formal music/theatre events of various sorts, usually kicking off with a folk festival featuring various international groups. Most performances take place in the hillside EHM (or Fróntzos) **theatre** just outside the town, with fine views down to the town and lake. Information and tickets for all latter events are available from the EOT office.

Listings

Banks Several near Platía Pýrrou (all with ATMs).

Books, maps and newspapers For quality maps and a respectable stock of books in English (including a few Rough Guides), head for Papasotiriou bookstore at Mihaïl Angélou 6, just off Platía Pýrrou; Newsstand at Pyrsinélla 14 has foreign newspapers.

Car rental Most rental offices are on Dhodhónis: Avis, no. 71 ☎26510 46333; Budget, no. 109 ☎26510 43901; Tomaso, no. 42 ☎26510 66900; National/Alamo, no. 10 corner Kaliáfa 3G ☎26510 47444; and Hertz, no. 105 ☎693 70 96 377. Hertz and Avis also have booths at the airport.

Internet access On-Line, on Pyrsinélla, behind the provincial government hall, is open 24hr and with very cheap rates.

Post office Central post office is on 28-Oktovríou (Mon–Fri 7.30am–8pm). There's a second post office closer to the lake on Yeoryíou Papandhréou.

The Pérama caves

Five kilometres north of Ioánnina, the village of **PÉRAMA** claims to have Greece's largest system of **caves** (daily 8am–8pm; €6), which extend and echo for kilometres beneath a low hill. They were discovered during late 1940 by locals attempting to find shelter from Italian bombing raids. The 45-minute mandatory tours of the complex are Greek-only, save a brief printed summary in English, and are a little perfunctory (consisting of a student reeling off the names of various suggestively shaped formations, including a dead ringer for Santa Claus), but not enough to spoil the experience.

To reach the caves on public transport, take a #8 blue city bus from the terminal below Platía Pýrrou to Pérama village; the caves are a ten-minute walk inland from the bus stop, past tacky souvenir shops. If you are driving, you can make a circuit of it. The road splits shortly after Pérama, at Amfithéa: one fork leads up towards Métsovo, with superb views down over Ioánnina and Pamvótidha, while the other runs around the lake, passing – just shy of halfway – the **monastery of Dhouraháni**, now run as a vocational school for disadvantaged children. The odd name stems from its founder, Durahan Pasha, an Ottoman general who founded it in 1434 as thanks for being miraculously saved by the Virgin while unwittingly crossing the frozen lake.

Dodona: the Oracle of Zeus

At **DODONA**, 22km southwest of Ioánnina, in a mountainous and once-isolated region, lie the ruins of the ancient **Oracle of Zeus** (daily 8am–5pm, may close 7pm mid-summer; €3), dominated by a vast and elegant theatre. "Wintry Dodona" was mentioned by Homer, and the worship here of a sacred oak tree seems to have been connected with the first Hellenic tribes who arrived in Epirus around 1900 BC.

The origins of the oracle – the oldest in Greece – are shadowy. Herodotus relates an enigmatic story about the arrival of a *peleiae* or dove from Egyptian Thebes which settled in an oak tree and ordered a place of divination to be made. In ancient Greek, *peleiae* could mean both dove and old woman, so it's possible that the legend refers to an original priestess – perhaps captured from the Middle East and having some knowledge of Asiatic cults and divination. The **oak tree**, stamped on the ancient coins of the area, was central to the cult. Herodotus also recorded that the oracle spoke through the rustling of the oak's leaves in sounds amplified by copper vessels suspended from its branches. These would then be interpreted by frenzied priestesses and strange priests who slept on the ground and never washed their feet. Legend also asserts that the Argonauts used timber from this oak to build their ship, with the presumably charmed properties of the wood enabling them to get out of numerous tight spots.

Dodona occasionally hosts **ancient drama and music performances** on summer weekends, though unfortunately they now take place on a temporary stage, rather than in the ancient theatre.

The site

Entering the site past a few tiers of a third-century BC **stadium**, you are immediately confronted by the massive western retaining wall of the **theatre**. Built during the time of King Pyrrhus (297–272 BC), this was one of the largest on the Greek mainland, rivalled only by those at Árgos and Megalopolis. Later, the Romans made adaptations necessary for their blood sports, adding a protective wall over the lower seating and also a drainage channel, cut in a horseshoe shape around the orchestra. What you see today is a meticulous late nineteenth-century reconstruction, since until then the theatre had been an almost incomprehensible jumble of stones; the seating rows are alas now roped off, though you can follow a path around and up to the top of the *cavea*, or seating curve. It is worth the climb to fully savour the glorious setting, facing out across a green, silent valley to the slopes of Mount Tómaros. At the top of the *cavea*, a grand entrance gate leads into the **acropolis**, an overgrown and largely unexcavated area. The foundations of its walls, mostly Hellenistic, are a remarkable 4 to 5m wide.

Beside the theatre, and tiered uncharacteristically against the same slope, are the foundations of a *bouleuterion*, beyond which lie the complex ruins of the **Sanctuary of Zeus**, site of the oracle itself. There was no temple as such until the end of the fifth century BC; until then, worship had centred upon the sacred oak, which stood alone within a circle of votive tripods and cauldrons. Building began modestly with a small stone temple-precinct, and in the time of Pyrrhus the precinct was enclosed with Ionic colonnades. In 219 BC the sacred house was sacked by the Aetolians and a larger temple was built with a monumental *propylaion*. This survived until the fourth century AD, when the oak tree was hacked down by Christian zealots. It is the remains of the later precinct that can be seen today, with a modern **oak tree** planted at the centre by a helpfully reverent archeologist. Ruins of an early Christian **basilica**, constructed on a sanctuary of Hercules (Herakles), are also prominent nearby – distinguished by rounded column stumps. Excavations on the site have resumed, which should result in greater comprehensibility when completed.

Many **oracular inscriptions** were found scattered around the site when it was first systematically excavated in 1952. Long displayed in Ioánnina's archeological museum, they give a good idea of the oracle's lingering influence even after it had been eclipsed by Delphi. More interestingly, they also afford a glimpse of the fears and inadequacies that motivated the pilgrims of the age to journey here, asking such domestic questions as: "Am I her children's father?" and, memorably, "Has Peistos stolen the wool from the mattress?"

Practicalities

Relatively few people make the detour to Dodona, so the site and **DHOD-HÓNI** – the little village to the west of it – are completely unspoilt. **Public transport** is accordingly sparse, with buses direct from Ioánnina only two days a week (Mon & Fri 6.30am & 3.30pm) to Melingí village, via the site. Alternatively, buses for the village of Zotikó (Mon & Fri at 2.15pm) pass within 2km of the site; the bus conductor will point out the *kafenío* where you should alight for the final, downhill walk, and the dedicated Dhodhóni village return bus calls at the site car park at about 4.40pm, giving you over two hours to look around. Hitching to the site from the junction 7km south of Ioánnina should be feasible in summer, or a round trip by taxi from Ioánnina with an hour at the site can be negotiated for a reasonable amount – about €22 per car load.

Alternatively, you could always stay the night here. There are some lovely spots to **camp**, a friendly if basic **taverna** in the village, and a small **hotel** close to the site, the basic but clean *Andromachi* (☎26510 82296; ❸), which fills (and charges peak rates) only when performances are on – it also has its own, rather good, restaurant.

Zagóri

Few parts of Greece are more surprising or more beguiling than **Zagóri**. A wild, thinly populated region, it lies to the north of Ioánnina, bounded by the roads to Kónitsa and Métsovo on the west and south, and the Aóös River valley to the northeast. The beauty of its landscape is unquestionable: miles of forest, barren limestone and Flysch wastes, rugged mountains deeply furrowed by foaming rivers and partly subterranean streams. But there is hardly an arable inch anywhere, and scarcely a job for any of its few remaining inhabitants other than herding livestock or cutting timber. The last place, in fact, that one would expect to find some of the most imposing architecture in Greece.

Yet the **Zagorohória**, as the 46 villages of Zagóri are called, are full of grand stone *arhondiká* (mansions) enclosed by semi-fortified walls, with deep-eaved gateways opening onto immaculately cobbled streets. Though they look older, the *arhondiká* date mostly from the late eighteenth or early nineteenth century. By the 1960s, many had fallen into disrepair or been insensitively restored, but the government now ensures (in several listed villages, anyway) that repairs are carried out in the proper materials, rather than cheap brick and sheet metal; new structures are required to have local stone cladding.

Inside, the living quarters are upstairs, arranged on an **Ottoman** model. Instead of moveable furniture, low platforms line the rooms on either side of an often elaborately hooded fireplace; strewn with rugs and cushions, they serve as couches for sitting during the day and sleeping at night. The wall facing the fire is usually lined with panelled and sometimes painted storage cupboards called *misándres*; in the grander houses the intricately fretted wooden ceilings are often painted as well. Additionally, most houses have a *bímtsa* (secret, fireproof bunker) for hiding the family gold and perhaps a wife and child or two whenever Albanian or other Muslim marauders threatened; even if the house was torched, the survivors could dig out their wealth and start over again.

As for the countryside, much the best way of savouring it is on foot, **hiking** numerous paths which, gliding through forest and pasture or slipping over passes and hogbacks, connect the outlying villages. The most popular outing – now very much part of trekking-company programmes – is along the awesome

Víkos Gorge and then up over the Astráka pass to an alpine lake. It's not to be missed, though for more of a backcountry feel, you may want to continue northeast, over **Mount Gamíla** towards the remoter Vlach villages at the base of **Mount Smólikas** (see p.446). Lately, however, other more organized activities in the area – canyoning, paragliding, kayaking and rafting – are beginning to take precedence, and a number of local outfitters (cited in the text) will kit you out.

The Víkos Gorge and western Zagóri

The walls of the **Víkos Gorge** are nearly 1000m high in places, cutting right through the limestone tablelands of Mount Gamíla, and separating the villages of the western and central Zagóri. It is quite the equal of the famous Samarian gorge in Crete, and a **hike** through or around it – depending on your abilities and time available – is likely to be the highlight of a visit to the Zagóri. Since 1975 a national park has encompassed both Víkos and the equally gorgeous Aóös River canyon to the north, and thus far various plans for ski centres, cable cars and dams have been fended off.

Touristic development, however, has burgeoned apace since the early 1980s, when foreign trekking companies first began coming here, and today almost every hamlet within spitting distance of the canyon (and indeed any sizeable village in western Zagóri) has some form of accommodation, usually open

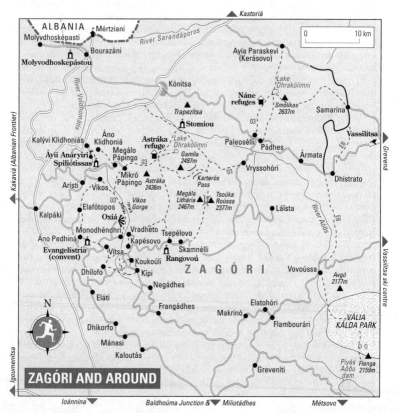

ZAGÓRI AND AROUND

all year, and tavernas. Be warned, though, that the area's popularity is such that you won't get a room without prior booking from mid-July through late August, when a tent provides an essential fallback. During the rest of the year, weekends and bank holidays are also unwise times to show up without advance reservations. You may have to settle for staying in some of the outlying villages, away from the immediate environs of the gorge – though this can work out slightly less expensive, and some of these villages have a more genuine community feel. Pre-Metaxas-dictatorship place names, mostly Slavic

Hiking warnings: Zagóri and the Píndhos

Despite the **Víkos Gorge**'s popularity, and periodic bouts of trail maintenance and waymarking, it's worth emphasizing that its traverse is not a Sunday stroll, and there is still ample scope for getting lost or worse. During April and early May, snowmelt often makes the Monodhéndhri end impassable due to high run-off, and in a rainstorm the sides of the gorge can become an oozing mass of mud, tree trunks and scree.

At the best of times it's not a hike to be undertaken in trainers and with PVC water bottles, as so many do. You need proper, over-the-ankle boots and a leak-proof water container; a stout stick for warding off snakes, guard dogs and belligerent livestock, and for stability when traversing bald or scree-laden slopes, would not go amiss either. Owing partly to the decrease in grazing and the gradual reforestation of the area, the local **bear population** is on the increase; sightings of tracks and actual individuals are becoming commonplace, especially around Kípi and the Pápingo villages, though they are timid and (except for females with cubs) flee humans who stumble upon them.

In 1995, the EU-funded **Life programme** signposted some thirty "Z"-prefixed trails and tracks in western and central Zagóri, but the walking times given on the various signposts are often unreliable, waymarking en route – often vandalized by hunters and other interested parties – can be haphazard at best, and trail maintenance since then has been almost nonexistent. If you intend to follow any of these routes in earnest, a fold-up pruning saw – available for about €5 from any gardening or agricultural shop – is a wise investment for cutting through brambles, gorse and broom blocking the less-used paths.

Currently the **best topographical map** for the region is Anavasi Editions' 1:50,000, GPS-compatible folding sheet *Pindus Zagori*, available in Athens, Ioánnina or map specialists abroad (€7 in Greece). This is hard-wearing, waterproof and largely accurate, but the chosen coverage excludes most of the Smólikas range. For further guidance, you really need access to a specialist guide and some trekking nous if you plan to venture off the most trodden routes.

Treks over the **high ridges of Gamíla or Smólikas** are in a different category altogether – you must be a hardy, experienced hill-walker used to carrying fifteen-to-twenty-kilo loads. Optimal seasons for walking are late May to late June and mid-September to mid-October; hike in July (let alone August) and you'll be cooked to death by the sun at all altitudes, and eaten alive by the fierce *davánia* (deer-flies). You should also be self-sufficient in all respects (including at least two days' supply of food in your pack); few villages have any sort of shop at all, and where they exist, stocks are limited to the odd carton of juice, eggs and tins of sardines. Given the region's severe depopulation, buses do not run every day (or at all) to or from critical trailhead villages, so you will probably have to use taxis or do a lot of extra road-trudging before or after your trek. Last but not least, there is little help available should you get into difficulties: no formal alpine rescue service exists, and the approaching end of the traditional pastoral life means that shepherds – traditionally an excellent source of information, emergency shelter and food – do not reliably occupy the high meadows.

or Vlach plus a few Albanian, are now creeping back into use as part of an assertion of local pride.

Monodhéndhri is the most popular starting point for a traverse of the gorge, but by no means the only one; local explorations lend themselves to linear or loop trips of some days' length, rather than basing yourself somewhere for a week.

Monodhéndhri

Near the south end of the gorge, perched right on the rim at 1150-metre elevation, stands the handsome village of **MONODHÉNDHRI**. It is one of the best preserved of the western Zagóri communities, all of which escaped the wartime devastation suffered by their eastern cousins. Just before the flag-stoned platía with its giant tree, the early-seventeenth-century church of **Áyios Minás** is usually locked, but the narthex, with fine eighteenth-century frescoes, is always open to admire. The wide, rather artless modern *kalderími* leading off from the far end of the platía reaches, after 900m (not "500m" as signed) the eagle's-nest monastery of **Ayía Paraskeví**, teetering on the very brink of the gorge and now uninhabited, though left open. If you have a good head for heights, continue on around the adjacent cliff face and the path eventually comes to a dead end near **Megáli Spiliá**, a well-concealed cave where the villagers used to barricade themselves in times of danger. In all, count on just under an hour for visiting these sites. For an even more spectacular view of the gorge, follow signs towards **Oxiá** (7km by car, slightly shorter by the Z8 path), where a short *kalderími* leads out from the road's end onto a natural balcony with all of Víkos spread vertiginously at your feet.

There are **buses** to Monodhéndhri from Ioánnina only three days weekly; those with their own transport should leave vehicles at the car park by the lower, cobbled platía (marked only as Víkos Gorge) If you take an afternoon bus, be advised that the handful of **inns** along the upper, asphalted road-curve where the bus calls are relatively pricey – all accept credit cards. Among these, quiet and well-placed *Arhondiko Kalderimi* (℡26530 71510 or 694 52 11 241; summer ❸, winter ❹) is, with its wood-floored rooms, some with balconies, and snug breakfast bar, the best value. The only real budget option is the *Monodendri Pension* (aka *Katerina's*; ℡26530 71300; ❷), with plain but adequate rooms both en suite and not. For **meals**, the best and most reliably open options, both under new management in 2005, are *Iy Pyli tou Viko*, offering salads, dips and grills opposite Áyios Minás church, or *Pitta tis Kikitsas* on the platía, specializing in *alevrópitta* (a heavy dish made from dough, egg and cheese). There is no shop, so bring supplies for trekking in the gorge.

Vítsa and the Skála Vítsas

During busy times of the year, you may choose – or be forced – to stay in other villages near the south end of the gorge. At **VÍTSA** (also called **Vezítsa**), 2km below Monodhéndhri, slightly kitsch but homey, old-fashioned en-suite accommodation, approached through a long vegetable patch, is available at *Eleni Kondou* (℡26530 71464; ❸), in the lower of two ridgeline neighbour-hoods; the owner lives on-site, with breakfast available on request. To some tastes Vítsa is a less claustrophobic, more attractive village than Monodhéndhri, with a few **tavernas**, a fine platía (below which is a restored-mansion inn, the *Troada*, ℡26530 71468; ❹) and alternative access to the gorge. This is via the signposted **Skála Vítsas**, a half-hour's gentle descent along the **Z9** path, partly on engineered stair-path, to the handsome single-arched Mísiou bridge; from there it's possible to continue upstream to Kípi village via the O3 path, or veer downstream along the heart of the gorge.

Dhílofo, Eláti and the Kaloutás bridge

From either Vítsa or the Misíou bridge, the **Z15** trail leads south to Dhílofo; the start of the path in Vítsa is trickier to find than the branch leading from the bridge, but once accomplished it's a twenty-minute descent to a stream bed (ford, no bridge), where the Misíou branch joins it, then there's a climb along a crumbled *kaldérimi* which peters out in Flysch badlands. After another stream crossing with just a few painted waymarks to help, the path resumes before becoming a track system leaving you at the outskirts of **DHÍLOFO**, just over an hour along.

One of the most handsome of the Zagorian villages, formerly called **Sopotséli**, it also has road access (though cars must be left at the outskirts) and has been "discovered" since the mid-1990s. You may **stay** at the *Aithrio Inn* (☎26530 22600, ⓦwww.epirus.com/lithos; ❹), on the plane-tree platía, which has five rooms (three en suite) run by the *Lithos Bar Restaurant* at the village entrance. The *Lithos* (closed Tues & other random times) hosts special events on summer weekends.

From Dhílofo, walkers can continue down to the chapel of Áyios Minás on the main valley-floor road. From this point, the **Z24** path gives access to Eláti village, but nearly half of the one-hour course is along asphalt or bulldozer track, with path (and an old watermill) only near the end, so you may as well visit **ELÁTI** by car. You're rather distant here from the gorge country, but there are fine views north to the peaks of Gamíla, plus a good **hotel**, the *Elati* (☎ & ⓕ26530 71181; B&B ❹), run by Alex Yiannakopoulos, an engaging Canadian-Greek – reserve in summer when walking groups pile in. Meals are only served to guests, but fortunately there's an excellent independent **restaurant** down the street, ⌁ *Sta Riza* (closed Tues), doing local *píttes* and cooked dishes at fair prices.

These are pretty much the last reliable facilities on this side of the valley; the next village, **Dhíkorfo**, is a beauty with grand houses and an unusual minaret-like church belfry, but the platía café only opens sporadically. Beyond here the chief attraction is the **triple-arched bridge** below **Kaloutás**, about 250m off the paved road by dirt track. All villages past Kaloutás were burnt by the Germans, but the road continues paved to Miliotádhes and thence the old Ioánnina–Métsovo highway – a very useful short-cut.

Áno Pedhiná and Elafótopos

ÁNO PEDHINÁ (formerly **Soudhená**), 4km west of Vítsa and Monodhéndhri and sharing the same bus service, offers a few rooms establishments and two superior **hotels**. Longest-running of the latter is Dutch co-managed *Spiti tou Oresti* (☎26530 71202 or 26510 32686; ❺) near the very top of the village, its double-glazed rooms warmly furnished, and with an adequate attached restaurant. Your alternative is the *Ameliko* (☎26530 71501 or 694 47 72 638, ⓦwww.epirus.com/ameliko; B&B ❹), done out in traditional style, with an alarmingly bright colour scheme in the comfortable double and quad en-suite rooms, set to multiply to 16 in 2006. At the lower entrance to the village is a more affordable option, *Pension Akhnoula* (☎26530 71216 or 26530 71291; ❸), with a good attached *psistariá*. Also at the base of the village, to your right as you approach, stands the old **convent of Evangelístra**, restored in 1997 though currently untenanted, and locked. Should you gain admission, you'll see the *katholikón's* magnificent carved *témblon* and vivid, cleaned frescoes from 1793, though the structure is much older.

From Áno Pedhiná, the **Z5** (densely overgrown immediately above the village) and **Z4** (much clearer) routes, via Elafótopos, take you around most of the Víkos

Gorge when that is impassable in early spring, ending up at Víkos village (see p. 000) after three-and-a-half hours. **ELAFÓTOPOS** itself (**Tservári** before the Metaxas-mandated renaming), on a bare hillside, has an attractive stone-built **hotel/restaurant**, the *Paradhosiako Katalyma Elafotopos* (℡26530 71001 or 697 74 17 537; July–Sept, by request otherwise; ❸), run by the volubly welcoming Eleni Dinalexi.

Through the gorge: Monodhéndhri to the Pápingo villages

The most-used **path down to the gorge** begins beside the arcaded church of Áyios Athanásios in Monodhéndhri's main platía; a sign promises relatively accurate times of four-and-a-half hours to Víkos village, six hours to either of the Pápingos. Having first passed Monodhéndhri's municipal amphitheatre, the path is cobbled for most of the forty minutes down to the riverbed, whose stony course you can follow for another few minutes before shifting up the west (true left) bank, reaching the best viewpoint at a saddle ninety minutes from the village.

The entire route along the gorge is waymarked, in parts a bit faintly, by red-paint dots and white-on-red stencilled metal diamonds with the legend "O3". This refers to a long-distance path, which begins south of Kípi at Lykiádhes on Mount Mitsikéli and can be followed across Mount Gamíla all the way to Mount Smólikas. However, the surface underfoot is arduous, with a certain amount of boulder-hopping in the gorge bed, and metal or felled-branch ladders getting you over tricky bits on the bank, as well as slippery, land-slid patches.

About two hours out of Monodhéndhri you draw even with the mouth of the **Mégas Lákkos ravine**, the only major breach in the eastern wall of the gorge; a spring here has been improved with piping to make it more reliable later in the summer. Another thirty minutes' level tramping brings you past the small, white shrine of **Ayía Triádha** with a recessed well (not potable) opposite; a further half-hour (around 3hr from Monodhéndhri) sees the gorge begin to open out and the sheer walls recede.

Víkos village and the Voïdhomátis springs

As the gorge widens you are faced with a choice. Continuing straight, on the best-defined path, takes you past the fifteen-minute side trail to the beautifully set eighteenth-century chapel of the **Panayía** (unlocked, excellent frescoes). Beyond here, the route becomes a well-paved, well-maintained *kalderími*, climbing up and left to the village of **VÍKOS** (alias **Vitsikó**; 870m elevation, four-plus hours from Monodhéndhri; also accessible by a five-kilometre paved road from Arísti). This underrated village has two **inns**, of which the one kept by Ioannis Dinoulis (℡26530 42112; ❹), right where the gorge trail arrives, is preferable, with modern but comfortable rooms and an on-site restaurant-bar. Up on the square, with its exceptionally handsome church of **Áyios Trýfon**, there's an independent **restaurant** and another, larger, inn, impersonally managed and with drab rooms.

Most walkers, however, prefer to follow the marked O3 route to the two **Pápingo villages**, crossing the gorge bed at the **Voïdhomátis springs**, some three-and-a-half hours from Monodhéndhri. It's about two hours' walk from the springs up to Mikró Pápingo, slightly less to Megálo, with the divide in the trail nearly ninety minutes above the riverbed crossing. Midway, after an initial steep climb, there's a fine view down into the north end of the gorge in the vicinity of some weathered, tooth-like pinnacles, before the trail traverses a stable rock slide to the fork. Should you be taking the same route, but in reverse, the start of the path in Mikró Pápingo village is signposted bilingually, and marked by a fancy stone archway in Megálo Pápingo.

The Pápingo villages

MEGÁLO PÁPINGO, as its name suggests, is the larger of these paired villages and comprises two distinct quarters of fifty or so houses in total along a tributary of the River Voïdhomátis, which served as the location for the film *Signs and Wonders*, starring Charlotte Rampling, in 1999. Even before this, it had long been a haunt of wealthy, trendy Greeks, making it a poor choice of base in peak season, though it is still delightful at other times. The fact that large coaches simply can't make it up the hairpin road from the Voïdhomátis river-bridge has made all the difference between here and Monodhéndhri.

Accommodation is abundant if not exactly budget-priced. Behind the central café is the refurbished *Xenonas tou Kouli* (T26530 41115 or 693 28 47 752; ❸) in the historic original inn, with en-suite rooms. It is run by the Khristodhoulou family, who are also the local booking agency (T26530 41138) for the mountain refuge on Astráka col (see p. 000); managers Nikos and Vangelis speak English, and their father Mr Koulis keeps a tiny shop with basic tinned/dried trekking staples and camera film. Above the second shop, just across the way, the rooms kept by Lakis Kotsoridhis (T26530 41087; ❸) are more modern but also excellent value. Just across the street, between the two churches and arranged around a narrow courtyard, are the eight, variable-sized, traditional rooms (T26530 41893 or 697 36 82 252; ❹) of *Nikos and Ioulia Tsoumani* attached to their ✴ **restaurant**, much the best of several in the village, with tasty soufflés, lamb and regional dishes, an understatedly classy dining room for winter, plus an unimproveable view of the Pýrgi of Astráka from the summer terrace. On the south side of the village, another affordable inn, *Xenonas Kalliopi* (T & F26530 41081, Wwww.epirus.com/kalliopi; ❸), offers en-suite rooms with views and good home-style meals at their year-round taverna. A more sumptuous choice, way off at the far north end of the village, is the ✴ *Xenonas Papaevangelou* (T26530 41135 or 694 60 44 260, F26530 41988; ❻), with large, variable rooms, a self-catering studio amidst well-tended gardens, inviting common areas and a genial, multilingual manager, Yiorgos.

Megálo Pápingo is linked to its smaller namesake by a three-kilometre surfaced road, which takes 45 minutes to walk; it's better to take the marked, short-cutting, restored *kalderími* off the road, via a historic bridge, which reduces the journey time to half an hour. If you do take the road, just before the bend – at an obvious spot adorned by low masoned walls – you can detour to the **kolymvitíria** or natural swimming pools, a few paces up the stream bed of the Rongovós canyon.

MIKRÓ PÁPINGO, around half the size of its neighbour, crouches below an outcrop of grey-limestone rocks known as the Pýrgi (Towers). Just below the church the WWF maintains an **information centre**, with worthwhile exhibits on the human and natural history of Pápingo and environs (Mon, Tues, Thurs & Sun 10.30am–5.30pm; Fri, Sat & hols 11am–6pm; free). The village has one main restoration **inn**, ✴ *Xenon O Dhias* (T26530 41257, Wwww .zagori.biz/dias; ❹; discount for trekkers), its rooms distributed over two buildings bracketing a serviceable, sometimes lively, bar-restaurant. The only other year-round accommodation is that of Yiorgos Ioannidhes (T26530 41894; ❸), the last house at the top of the village.

Bus departures from the two Pápingos back to Ioánnina are erratic at best, just two days weekly year-round (with an additional day in summer only). If you fail to coincide, the best strategy is to walk to the village of Kalývi Klidhoniás on the Kónitsa–Ioánnina highway, which has regular services. It's around a two-and-a-half-hour hike west from Megálo Pápingo, via the nearly abandoned hamlet of **Áno Klidhoniá** (**Goúliari** in the old Slavic nomenclature), on a better-than-average marked path, most of it unbulldozed, and far quicker and easier than the dreary 23-kilometre haul to the highway along the paved road which passes through Arísti. There's one snack bar/café in Áno Klidhoniá to pause at en route.

Packhorse bridges

A perennial pleasure as you stumble down boulder-strewn ravine beds, bone-dry an hour after a thunderstorm, is coming upon one of the many fine stone "**packhorse**" bridges that abound in Zagóri. One-, two- or even three-arched, these bridges, and the old cobbled paths serving them, were the only link with the outside world for these remote communities until motor roads were opened up in the mid-1950s. They were erected mainly in the nineteenth century by gangs of itinerant craftsmen and financed by local worthies.

These wandering construction gangs or *bouloúkia* were away from home between the feasts of Áyios Yeóryios (St George's Day) in late April and Áyios Dhimítrios (St Demetrius) in late October. As in other mountainous regions of Europe, they came from remote and poor communities: Pyrsóyianni and Voúrbiani in the Kónitsa area in particular, and Ágnanda, Prámanda and Houliarádhes southeast of Ioánnina. Closely guarding the secrets of their trade with their own argot, they travelled the length and breadth of Greece and the Balkans, right up to World War II.

While you're in the Zagóri region, a good side-trip, easiest done from Vítsa, Dhílofo, Kípi or Koukoúli, is to take a look at the half-dozen fantastic bridges in the vicinity, all named after their major sponsors. One, the Misíou, lies below Vítsa; the Kokorós stands right beside the main valley road; the Kondodhímou nestles between Kípi and Koukoúli; and most of the remainder are scattered to either side of Kípi – one spectacular triple span (the Plakídha) downstream, three more upstream from the village. Remoter, but equally spectacular, are the triple span below Kaloutás, and the high-arched one 4.5km north of Miliotádhes in eastern Zagóri. These bridges mostly span the upper reaches of the Víkos gorge and its tributaries, and constitute the most representative and accessible examples of the vanished craft of pack-horse-bridge building.

△ Bridge over Vikákis ravine, Kípi

The lower Voïdhomátis River valley

If you're up for a walk through the lower **Voïdhomátis river gorge**, start (or continue) from Kalývi Klidhoniás, where a track system brings you to an exceptionally graceful, single-arch, nineteenth-century bridge – the national park boundary – within twenty minutes. On the south (left) bank stands *Exohiko Kendro O Voïdhomatis*, fair priced and popular, and the main base of the No Limits activity outfitter (☎26550 23777, ⓦwww.nolimits.com.gr). The first bit of the onward walk, on the true right (north) bank, follows a fake *kalderími* laid in garishly inappropriate white fieldstone, but this ends quickly, a more rugged trail bringing you within forty minutes alongside the brief detour up to tiny but vividly frescoed **Áyii Anáryiri** church. The route, which often follows the banks, gives you a close look at the river environment (otters have been reported here); you emerge on a curve of the Arísti–Pápingo road, with the best views possible over the restored, cliff-clinging **monastery of Spiliótissas** (always locked).

Just below this point, a graceful **modern bridge** (built 1923) carries the Pápingo-Arísti road across the Voïdhomátis as it flows out of the Víkos Gorge. The immediate environs of the bridge are a popular picnic area in summer (no camping allowed), but riverbank trails allow you to hike to more peaceful, tree-shaded spots upstream before the gorge blocks further progress. **Kayaking** and **rafting** are the only ways to visit these narrows; swimming in the Voïdhomátis is done only by the (not-to-be-fished) trout, though anyone ignoring the ban would probably perish anyway in the icy waters.

With persistence, you can find the old path up from near the river bridge to a point on the Arísti–Víkos asphalt, just under 2km from the latter, making possible an all-day loop taking in Pápingo, the Klidhoniá villages, the lower gorge, Víkos village, the Voïdhomátis springs and back to Pápingo.

Should you need them, there are almost always **accommodation** vacancies in relatively unglamorous, 1944-damaged **ARÍSTI** (ex-**Artsísta**), southwest of the Voïdhomátis River, where pleasant cafés surround the central plane tree. Best value of several inns here is the *Zissis* (☎26530 41147, ⓕ26530 41088; ❹), with small but appealing rooms, and a good attached restaurant; it's near the bottom of the village en route to the river bridge.

Hikes across the Gamíla range

For walkers keen on further, fairly arduous hiking, there are a number of itineraries beyond the Pápingo villages, over and across the **Gamíla** range into the central Zagóri. These are served by the aforementioned O3 long-distance trail, and several of the more ambitious "Z" routes.

Pápingo to Astráka col

All onward hikes east into Gamíla begin with the steep but straightforward ascent to **Astráka col**. Though the refuge on the col is clearly visible from Megálo Pápingo, the trail essentially starts at Mikró Pápingo (see p.439).

At the top of Mikró Pápingo, the well-signposted and maintained O3 trail resumes, having climbed out of the Víkos Gorge. Ten minutes out, you pass a chapel of Áyios Pandelímon, then head through forest to the Antálki spring (about 40min from Mikró Pápingo). From here the forest thins as you climb towards the Tráfos spring (1hr 40min from Mikró). Twenty minutes beyond Tráfos, a signposted trail branches right towards the **Astráka summit** (2436m), which is a three-hour round trip from this point. If you ignore this trail, and keep straight with the O3 markers, in around 35 minutes you will reach the **EOS refuge**, perched on the saddle joining Astráka with Mount Lápatos (2hr

45min from Mikró Pápingo). The hut (70 bunks; €10) is open and staffed from Easter to late October; for reservations it's best to contact the warden, Yiorgos, on ☎697 32 23 100.

East of Astráka

Northeast of the refuge, on the far side of the boggy Lákka Tsoumáni valley below, the gleaming **lake of Dhrakólimni**, alive with newts, is tucked away on the very edge of the Gamíla range. This lies about an hour from the refuge, along a well-grooved and waymarked path.

East of the refuge, the O3 route takes you on a strenuous eight-hour hike to the village of Vryssohóri via the nastily steep **Karterós pass**. Despite waymarking, this should only be attempted if you're a very experienced trekker and equipped with the appropriate maps. A more casual and accessible outing is to the **summit of Mount Gamíla** (2497m), an easy two-hour-plus climb from the refuge, with superb wildflowers en route and unbeatable views into the Aóös valley from up top.

South to central Zagóri: Tsepélovo and around

The most popular onward trek from Astráka col is the five-hour route on an often faint trail south across the Gamíla uplands, via Mirioúli with its free-range cattle and the head of the Mégas Lákkos gorge, to the villages of central Zagóri. Besides water at Mirioúli, there are only two other springs en route, and for the most part the scenery consists of forbidding if often impressive limestone-dell-scape, but **TSEPÉLOVO**, the main destination, is among the finest of the Zagorohória. With a sawmill at the outskirts, and 180 permanent inhabitants, it has a lived-in feel compared to west-Zagóri villages. The major local attraction is the **monastery of Rangovoú**, about 1km southwest of the village, just off (and below) the main road. Dedicated to Áyios Ioánnis Pródhromos (St John the Baptist), it was founded in the eleventh century; its partly cleaned frescoes are much later but still well worth a look. The *katholikón* is most likely to be open on summer Sundays, when it's a popular venue for weddings and baptisms. From the perimeter wall of the grounds, two recently opened trails (one cobbled) dead-end at different points in the bed of the Vikákis ravine; it is *not* possible for ordinarily equipped walkers to continue downstream to Kípi, though local adventure outfitters will organize canyoning expeditions in late summer, with some swimming involved.

Tsepélovo is the biggest tourist centre in Zagóri after the Pápingo villages. The oldest, least expensive and friendliest **accommodation** is the ☪ *Hotel Gouris* (☎26530 81214 or 26530 81288, ⓦwww.epirus.com/hotelgouris; B&B ❸), run by Anthoula Gouri, who can be found at the traditional Kafeníou Gouri on the platía (where breakfast is served), and daughter Maria; rooms are en suite, with wood floors and restrained decor. A good second choice is *To Arhondiko* (☎26530 81216, ⓦwww.tsavalia.gr; ❹), an unmissable, gaily painted, arcaded mansion 70m below the platía, with well-kept rooms around an upstairs salon and an attractive courtyard below. On the platía are two self-catering options: the well-appointed *Deligiannis Rooms* (☎26530 81232; ❸) have a small area for making breakfast; and *Iy Mikrí Arktos* (☎26530 81128 or 697 70 79 871; summer ❹, winter ❺), above *Edhesma* restaurant, comprises three comfortable apartments. Also on the square, and the lane leading up to it from the main road, are most of Tsepélovo's **tavernas**; most popular of these is *Edhesma*, with simple fare and tables out under the plane tree in summer. There's a bus service three days weekly to and from Ioánnina, with Skamnélli (the next village) the end of the run.

Descending 12km by road from Tsepélovo towards Ioánnina brings you to the celebrated cluster of **old bridges** (see box on p.440) around Kípi, passing en route the amazing coiled-spring *kalderími* linking Kapésovo and Vradhéto. The bridges span the very upper reaches of the Víkos Gorge, which you can access nearly as easily from here as you can from Monodhéndhri or Vítsa. If you haven't a vehicle, by far the best way of heading down-valley is via a faint path due west out of Tsepélovo, across the ravine and then up the palisade, which links up with the paved road heading for Vradhéto. From Vradhéto, use the marvellous "*skála*" (see p.462) to reach the edge of Kapésovo, from where an older track can be used to short-cut the asphalt road to Koukoúli. From Koukoúli, proceed on the Z31 path to Kípi.

Kapésovo, Koukoúli and Kípi

Of the three villages closest to the bridges, **KAPÉSOVO** is the highest – an attractive place, mostly invisible from the road. The gigantic former school-house, dating from 1861, is now home to an informal ethnographic collection, including wolf-traps, and also hosts special events. The local **inn**, *To Kapesovo* (☎26530 71724 or 694 55 29 357; ❹), though well appointed and featuring historic wall paintings, is neurotically managed, with more rules than a Victorian orphanage; there is no consistently operating place to eat or drink. Besides the famous *kalderími* up to Vradhéto, signposted at the village edge as "Skála Vradhé-tou", there's a brief corniche route (the "Katafi") to an overlook of the Mezariá ravine. The conventional trail down to Víkos, though alluringly marked at the outset, is overgrown and ultimately impassable owing to landslips.

Some 4km downhill from Kapésovo, **KOUKOÚLI** is another scarcely commercialized, atmospheric village, with cars banned from the village proper and nightingales audible by day until June. There are two **accommodation** options here. *Xenon Koukouli* (☎26530 71070, ⊛www.epirus.com/koukouli; ❹; open only on demand) occupies three separate buildings – the best units are in the old monastery, and breakfast is served in the old school; it's co-managed with the *Hotel Ameliko* in Áno Pedhiná and rooms share the same rustic wood-and-shaggy-rug decor. An English couple run ♨ *Roy and Effi's Place* (☎26530 71743 or 694 64 73 276; ❹, discounts for longer stays), consisting of three large pine-trim, white-stucco rooms, and (in the future) a two-room apartment, overlooking a spacious garden (a rarity in Zagóri) where breakfast is currently served. For other **meals**, there's only the fitfully operating *Ta Panta Rei*, under the plane tree by the church. Koukoúli has relatively direct access to the Víkos Gorge: an unmarked but still useable path leads from the southwest entrance of the village down to the O3 threading between Kípi and the Misíou bridge. Alternatively, the well-marked **Z31** path heads southeast from a point on the paved, easterly access road near the park bench, with a brief *kalderími* descent to the Kondodhímou bridge, reaching Kípi within 45 minutes.

KÍPI, by road 2km up a side turning 6km below Kapésovo, is another hand-some village, which until the 1930s was known as **Báya**, and served as the administrative centre for the whole area. There's **accommodation** at Vangelis Vlahopoulos' en-suite *Spiti stou Artemi* (☎26530 71644, ⊛www.epirus.com /spititouartemi; ❸), a wonderfully restored nineteenth-century mansion where several of the seven rooms have fireplaces; the rooms of Evangelia Dherva (☎26530 71658; ❸) are an alternative. Down on the main road stands the best **taverna** in the area, ♨ *Stou Mihali*, emphasizing local ingredients (beans, greens) and recipes (various *píttes*) at fair prices, washed down by a lovely purple wine – though service can be uneven. On the same road, at the east edge of town, is the **Tolis Agapios Folklore Museum** (daily, any reasonable hour – knock next door). These days every Zagorian village claims to have such a display, but this one, with some 50,000 articles crammed in, is the real deal. **Bus** services to Ioánnina are shared with that of Tsepélovo. Other amenities include a small **shop** and **bakery**, and a small **activity centre**, Robinson Expeditions (☎ 26530 71517, ⓦ www.robinson.gr).

North to the Aóös valley and the north Píndhos

Beyond Skamnélli, forest appears, extending north to the **Aóös valley**. Fourteen kilometres or so out of the village, the road branches north towards Vryssohóri, which has two buses a week from Ioánnina. Rather than follow this relatively dull route on foot, you can get there in seven hours from Skamnélli by walking over a pass between the peaks of **Megála Lithária** (2467m) and **Tsoúka Roússa** (2377m). This is a rather easier hike than that through the Karterós pass previously described, and covered by some organized trekking groups. An added bonus is the unrivalled display of mountain wild flowers in the **Goúra valley**, directly below Tsoúka Roússa.

After the approach, **VRYSSOHÓRI** is a little anticlimactic, being almost swallowed by the dense woods at the base of Tsoúka Roússa peak. Tiny and ramshackle (this was one of the settlements burned by the Germans in the war), the village has a couple of **inns**. The four-room one of the Tsoumani family (☎ 26530 22687 or 697 45 89 930; April–Oct, otherwise on request; ❸) has a communal balcony to hang laundry and from which you can admire the mountains; there's the slightly larger one of Marianna Tsiomidhou (☎ 26530 22785 or 697 30 82 870; ❸). If necessary, you can **camp** at the edge of town by one of two springs on either side of the O3 coming down from Karterós. Otherwise, Vryssohóri can offer only a basic *kafenío* **taverna** dishing out simple country fare (sausages, salad, *galotýri* – a yoghurt-like dish).

The O3 across the Aóös from Vryssohóri to **Paleosélli** in the north Píndhos has been either bulldozed or paved over, with nothing remaining of the old trail; engage a taxi in Vryssohóri for the shuttle across the river to Paliosélli, main southerly trailhead for Mount Smólikas (see p.446).

The north Píndhos

The region **north of the Aóös River** is far less visited than Zagóri. Its landscape is just as scenic but its villages are very poor relatives – almost all those within sight of the river were burned by the Germans during early 1944, accounting for their present thrown-together appearance. The villagers claim that before this disaster their houses exceeded in splendour those of Zagóri, since they had ample timber to span huge widths and for carved interiors.

Mounts **Smólikas** and **Grámmos**, two of the highest peaks in Greece, dominate the area. The former can be approached from **Mount Gamíla** (see p. 000) or by vehicle from **Kónitsa**, the largest settlement in these parts, just off the Ioánnina–Kastoriá highway.

Kónitsa and around

KÓNITSA is a sleepy little town whose most memorable features are a famous bridge and a view. The **bridge**, over the Aóös, is a giant, built around 1870 (and repaired after the retreating Ottoman army tried to destroy it in 1913) but looking far older. The **view** comes from the town's amphitheatrical setting on the slopes of Mount Trapezítsa, above a broad flood plain where the Aóös and Voïdhomátis rivers mingle with the Sarandáporos before flowing through Albania to the sea as the Vijöse.

The town was besieged by the Communist "Democratic Army" in the week after Christmas 1947, in their first, unsuccessful, bid to establish a provisional capital. Much was destroyed in the fighting, though parts of the old bazaar and a tiny Ottoman neighbourhood near the river survive, as well as (near the top of town) a very dilapidated mansion which was apparently the birthplace of Hamko Hanim, mother of Ali Pasha (see p.426).

The **bus terminal** (buses daily to Ioánnina and less regular connections to most villages in this section) is on the central platía, and two **banks** (with ATMs) and the **post office** lie just to the south. Kónitsa is now a recognized **adventure-sports** centre, albeit in something of a slump lately; outfits with stations down by the modern bridge over the main highway include Alpiki Zoni/Alpine Zone (☏ 26550 24822, ⓦ www.alpinezone.gr) and En Fysei (☏ 694 73 33 113, ⓦ www.enfisi.gr); the going rate for a river-rafting trip is €35 per person. Longest established, and one of the best **rooms** establishments, is *Xenonas To Dhendro* on the hairpin bend of the main access road (☏ 26550 23982, ⓦ www.epirus.com/todendro; ❷), whose English-speaking proprietor Yiannis Mourehidhes, one of the characters of Epirus, is a mine of local information. Cooking at the attached 🍴 **restaurant** is good too, featuring baked goat (*gástra*) or lamb, Yiannis's (in)famous *fétta psití*, baked feta cheese spiked with hot green chillies, and Zítsa bulk wine. Amongst other options, calmest is *Yerakofolia* (☏ 26550 22168; ❷), 300m along the road to Pádhes, housed in a pair of contiguous buildings with great views. As for **hotels**, a mid-range choice is *Gefyri*, down by the old bridge (☏ 26550 23780, ⓦ www .gefyri.konitsa.net.gr; standard room ❹, suite ❻); the rooms, one or two with river views, are decent enough, and there's now a large pool. Noise from the on-site bar – much the biggest nightspot in Kónitsa – may be a problem. Much the best standard in the area is the Mourehidhes family's 2004-built *Grand Hotel Dhendro* (☏ 26550 29365, ⓦ www.grandhoteldentro.gr) down the road from their *xenónas*; the standard rooms (❹) have good bathrooms and some balconies, whilst the attic suites (❻–❼) feature fireplaces and hydromassage in the baths.

The Aóös gorge

Kónitsa can serve as a base for a fine afternoon's walking, or even longer treks. Beginning at the old bridge over the Aóös, either of two interweaving paths on the south bank leads within ninety minutes to the eighteenth-century **monastery of Stomíou**, perched on a bluff overlooking the narrowest part of the Aóös gorge. The *katholikón* here (usually locked) is of minimal interest, and the premises have been rather brutally restored, but the setting is sublime. There are two springs to drink from, and many visitors camp in the surroundings, after bathing in the river below.

Beyond Stomíou the slopes are shaggy with vegetation constituting one of the last pristine habitats for lynx, roe deer and birds of prey. A minimally waymarked path climbs from the monastery gate up to the **Astráka area** (see p.441). This is a five-hour-plus uphill walk, rather less in reverse, and a very useful trekkers' link between the Gamíla and the Smólikas regions, provided you have a good map. Do not, incidentally, be tempted by red-on-yellow diamonds for a supposed direct, riverside trail to Vryssohóri; this has had its middle section destroyed by landslides. The only way to Vryssohóri from here goes via the Kátsanos meadow below the Karterós pass, on a safe but faintly marked path.

Molyvdhosképasti village and Molyvdhoskepástou monastery

The tiny hillside village of **MOLYVDHOSKÉPASTI** (ex-**Dhipalítsa**) hugs the Albanian border 23km west of Kónitsa, in an appropriately end-of-the-world setting. The place was once a haunt of the seventh-century Emperor Constantine IV Pogonatos, though only a few of his monuments survive intact, and most of the half-dozen assiduously signposted churches scattered across the slopes are post-Byzantine. Finest of these is the sixteenth-century parish church (locked) of **Áyii Apóstoli**, right on the frontier. The view from its terrace – into Albania beyond the riverside Mértziani border post, over the Aóös valley, and east to Smólikas and Gamíla – is among the best in Epirus. On June 29, the village comes to life for the **festival** of its patron saints, Peter and Paul, with music and feasting until dawn; during summer a single *tsipourádhiko* works in the village centre.

Few **buses** call from Kónitsa, so you really need your own transport to get here. The only nearby **accommodation** is the *Hotel Bourazani* (T26550 61283, Wwww.bourazani.gr; rooms ❹, suites ❼), set in its own enormous "environmental (game) park" by the Bourazáni bridge 9km before Molyvdhosképasti and 3km from the Mértziani border post. Wood-and-stone common areas include a pricey restaurant, the menu featuring game culled from the park herds; there's also a swimming pool and tennis courts. Standard doubles are large, if a bit dated (especially the baths); two giant suites are wood-floored.

Five kilometres below the village stands the **monastery of Molyvd-hoskepástou**, the most important of the emperor's surviving monuments. Repopulated in the early 1990s and attractively restored by its half-dozen monks, it enjoys a bucolic setting on the bank of the Aóös. The curiously long and narrow church, with a precariously high Serbian-type dome, is thirteenth century; its frescoes are in a poor state. This is a working monastery, so don't visit between 3 and 5pm; as with all such monastic revivals, the monks are also quite fanatical, peddling lots of ecclesiastical literature (in Greek). Prominent, too, is the **exomoloyitírio** or confessional chapel, where (unlike in the Catholic tradition) the penitent sits at right angles to the priest at his desk, facing the altar where an icon of Christ presumably gazes into their very soul.

East of Kónitsa: Mount Smólikas

Mount Smólikas (2637m) is the second-highest peak in Greece. It dominates a beautiful and very extensive range, covering a hundred square kilometres of mountain territory above 1700m in elevation, and including another mountain lake, **Dhrakólimni** (not to be confused with its namesake on Mount Gamíla). The region also retains some of the last vestiges of traditional shepherd life, best witnessed in summer at the Vlach village of **Samarína**, though many of the sheepfolds on the Epirot side of the mountain now lie abandoned. Unlike Mount Gamíla, Smólikas saw very heavy fighting between the Greeks and the Italians in November 1940, and some of the higher ridges still have a rather shell-blasted look.

Kónitsa–Dhístrato **buses** (3 afternoons weekly) roll through the mountains, stopping en route at Paleosélli, the best trailhead on the mountain's southern flank. **PALEOSÉLLI** (1100m elevation) has a pair of *kafenía* and a not particularly friendly **inn-taverna** (T26550 24760; ❶), on the square, with a single shared bathroom. You might prefer the better-value inn of Dhimitris Grentziou just behind (T26550 24626; ❶). Pádhes, 3km further along, has even less to offer: a single, stone-built building in the centre, once the former school, serving as the shop and **taverna** (July–Aug only).

The paved road continues for 20km from Pádhes to **DHÍSTRATO**, end of the bus line. This large, relatively thriving village has four licensed conventional **rooms** establishments, thanks in part to the ski centre nearby just over the provincial border (see overleaf), though few are attended outside peak winter or summer seasons; those of Elias Svarnas (☎26650 24841; ❹) on the platía are the plushest. Two **psistariés** (one on the platía, one on the uphill lane north) work fitfully, and the single taxi driver (phone numbers posted on the platía) can prove elusive to find – and uncooperative once you do locate him. From just before Dhístrato it's possible to drive north to Samarína (see overleaf), but it's nineteen badly rutted kilometres, passable only from May until the first snows, and requiring a jeep or high-clearance vehicle even then.

Hiking from Paleosélli to Ayía Paraskeví

There is a fine trail from Paleosélli up to **Dhrakólimni** (a little over 3.5hr), and from there you can make an ascent of **Mount Smólikas** (another hour). You may read in some sources that a newer variant of the O3 ascends to the lake from Pádhes, but this is largely scissored apart and/or bulldozed under by a forestry track – it's emphatically not worth following.

The Paleosélli–Dhrakólimni route is haphazardly waymarked (with red or green paint dots or arrows in addition to the standard diamonds) as part of the original O3; a new track briefly disrupts the path 35 minutes along, but the old trail resumes just over an hour out of the village, bringing you to a pair of **refuges** one hour and forty minutes out at the idyllic locale known as **Náne** (1650m). There's spring water and camping space, but both shelters – an older log cabin, and a newer structure (24 bunks) just beyond at 1700m – are firmly locked and unstaffed; if you're determined to stay here, ask around for the keys in Paliosélli before setting off.

Beyond the refuge, the trail becomes less distinct but waymarks lead you up onto a ridge aiming for the summit of Mount Smólikas; the best path keeps just to the right (east) side of the ridge. Just under two walking hours from the newer refuge you should emerge into the little depression containing the heart-shaped, fairly shallow **lake** at 2200m. You can camp here, but space is at a premium – three or four parties will fit at a pinch – and you'll need a tent to protect against cold and damp. Owing in part to global warming, this alpine tarn has become a murky brown pond, with a reed patch sheltering noisy frogs who croak all night.

The classic ascent to the **summit of Smólikas** begins from the base of the knoll just east of the lake. There's a proper path at first, up to the 2400-metre level, staked out by red-on-yellow "lollipop" markers; after a brief interval on stepped turf, the trail resumes to a point just below the summit, with a short scramble taking you to the top just under an hour from Dhrakólimni (provided you're not carrying much). Besides the expected views, you'll find a trig point, a solar-power unit of uncertain function, and a memorial plaque in black granite to a young Hungarian climber-biologist who fell to his death here in 1997.

The easiest way down from Smólikas is a scenic and well-trodden two-and-a-half-hour path, leading off from an abandoned sheepfold in the vale between the lake and the summit, to the hamlet of **AYÍA PARASKEVÍ** (alias **Kerásovo**). There are a couple of basic **tavernas** in the village, including one on the ground floor of the central *Kerassovo* **hotel** (☎26550 41215; ❸); if it's full, camping near the village is tolerated. There are just two weekly morning **bus** links to Kónitsa.

Hiking from Dhrakólimni to Samarína

If you have a good head for heights, and you're not carrying too heavy a pack, the best hiking route from **Dhrakólimni to Samarína** involves tracing the ridge east from the summit, the start of a seven-hour walking day. After an hour-plus of cross-country progress, you'll reach a small, bleak pass in the watershed, where you link up with a "real" path, marked by faint yellow paint splodges, coming up from a sheepfold at the top of the stream valley draining to Pádhes. Once through this gap (called Lemós), you descend into the lunar, northwest-facing cirque which eventually drains down to Ayía Paraskeví.

Next you traverse the base of one of Smólikas's secondary peaks as a prelude to creeping up a scree-laden rock "stair". Here waymarks change colour to yellow-and-red blazes, plus metal "lollipops" in the same scheme; a line of cairns guides you across a broad, flat-topped ridge. The path soon levels out on another neck of land. To the left yawns a dry gully (to be avoided) and way off to the right (south) can be glimpsed the other of Smólikas's tarns, as large as Dhrakólimni but difficult to reach. The path eventually becomes more distinct as it snakes its way down through gullies in badly weathered rock.

Beyond, you encounter the leading edge of the black-pine forest, at the foot of a peak capped by a wooden altimeter. The trail threads between this knoll and another, at the foot of which lies Samarína. Twenty minutes or so beyond this pass, a spring oozes from the rock strata, some six hours from the Smólikas summit. There follows a sharper descent through thick forest, with a second spring (Sopotíra) gurgling into a log trough set in a beautiful mountain clearing. Below this, the woods end abruptly and you'll emerge on a bare slope directly above Samarína's fenced-in football pitch and its largest hotel.

Samarína and the Vassilítsa ski centre

At 1450m, just over the border in Macedonia's Grevená province, **SAMARÍNA** claims to be the highest village in Greece. It's principally inhabited in the summer by Vlachs from the plains of Thessaly, and their sheep – their odour alive or cooked permeating the air (and everything else). The village was burned during both World War II and the civil war, and rebuilt in Brutalist, cheap-and-easy style, with no concessions to "olde worlde" town planning. Thus, while Samarína may seem like the Bright Lights after several days' trekking, it's not somewhere you'd go out of your way to visit. This acknowledged, it's a thriving and friendly place, very proud of its Vlach traditions. The high point of the year is the August 15 festival, when there is music and merry-making and the place is swamped by nostalgic Vlachs from all over the country. Yet appearances are deceptive – pastoral life is vigorous only in comparison to the Epirot side of the mountain, with flocks down from the tens of thousands to barely a few hundred.

The interior of the main church of the **Panayía** is superb, with frescoes and painted ceilings and an intricately carved *témblon*, where the angels, soldiers and biblical figures are dressed in mustachios and *fustanélles* (the Greek kilt). Though it looks a lot older, like many other churches in the region it dates from around 1800. Its special hallmark is an adult black pine growing out of the roof of the apse, there as long as anyone can remember. The keys are with the priest, who lives opposite the main gate.

Samarína used to be deserted (save for a guard) in winter, but this is emphatically no longer true since the late-1990s inauguration of the **Mount Vassilítsa ski centre** (2247m), which with 24km of mostly north-facing pistes is by far the biggest in northwestern Greece. Some 20km from Samarína, the slopes are also a similar distance from Dhístrato and Vovoússa, guaranteeing all these villages winter tourist trade. The ski school is run by Alpine Zone (see p.445), with runs for all ability levels and two chair lifts to get you to the top point of about 2100m (though 5 others are drag lifts).

Practicalities

The improbably large stone building that greets you at the top of the village is the barracks-like municipal **hotel** (☎24620 95216; open most of year; ❹), whose wood-trimmed interior and east-facing terrace are more inviting than first impressions suggest. There are less pricey en-suite **rooms** on or just off the stone-paved platía; best are those of Ioannis Parlitsis (☎24620 95279), spread over two premises – older ones, with small kitchens, above the fruit stall (❶), and superior units on a quiet lane towards the church, with fireplaces, balconies and central heating (❷). Otherwise, *Avellas* (☎24620 95278; ❶) has a few poky if quiet rooms, facing away from the platía, which springs to life by night with a half-dozen **grills**, of which the one run by the Parlitsis family is okay. A single **shop**, its stock not terribly practical for trekkers, offers canned fish, dried pulses, rice, noodles, cheese and eggs.

Leaving Samarína, you have two choices if you don't have a car. There is a bus along the paved road to **Grevená**, 40km away on the Kalambáka–Kastoriá highway, from June to September, but not every day, though a lift is not too hard to get if you ask around. If you are committed to staying in Epirus, follow the E6 route four-and-a-half hours to **Dhístrato** (see p.447) – which has lodging and where you might coincide with an early-morning bus back to Kónitsa – or keep going to Vovoússa on the east bank of the Aóös, with even less frequent buses to Ioánnina. The E6 is very good wilderness in parts, but the first hour out of Samarína and the final hour-plus descent to Dhístrato are dirt and asphalt road-trudging respectively.

The south Píndhos

Most hikers arriving at Ioánnina have their sights firmly set northwards, especially on the Víkos Gorge and the Zagóri villages. If you're feeling adventurous, however, and tolerant of a limited range of places to eat and sleep, the **remote villages** of the south Píndhos provide an interesting, and less touristy, alternative. They perch on the beetling flanks of **mounts Tzoumérka** and **Kakardhítsa**, two overlapping ridges of bare mountains linked by a high plateau, plainly visible from Ioánnina. There are few special sights, but you'll get a solid, undiluted experience of Epirot life.

Buses depart Ioánnina's southern station for Ágnanda and Prámanda daily; there is also regular frequent service from Árta. Buses run a couple of times daily in either direction along the secondary road between Árta and Ioánnina, stopping at **Pláka**, which has, amid stunning scenery, a huge eighteenth-century bridge over the Árakhthos – a favourite takeout point for **rafting trips** which start upstream at Harokópi. Here you can flag down one of the aforementioned buses further up the mountain.

Ágnanda to Melissourgí

The first village of any size, 12km above Pláka, is **ÁGNANDA**, heavily damaged in World War II and not particularly attractive in itself, though nearby – closer to the higher village of Katarráktis and the slopes of Mount Tzoumérka

– is the *Dhasiko Horio Kedhros* (℡26850 31791, ⓦ www.guesthousekedros.com; ❺), a self-contained resort of nineteen wooden chalets, run by an adventure activity company. Most will press on to **PRÁMANDA**, no more distinguished architecturally than Ágnanda, but enjoying a wonderful setting strewn across several ridges overlooking the Kallaritikós valley. Just 2km south is the area's major signposted attraction, the **Anemótrypa** (daily dawn to dusk, €5), a cavern discovered in 1960; the first 300m or so, with pools and the usual strange formations, are open to visits. The enormous church of **Ayía Paraskeví** almost uniquely escaped wartime devastation, and as an example of nineteenth-century kitsch it is hard to beat. The village has a **post office**, a rather primitive central **inn**, plus a handful of **tavernas** and *psistariés*, while there's a more comfortable **hotel**, the *Tzoumerka* (℡26590 61590, ⓕ 26590 61336; ❹), in the tiny hamlet of Tsópelas, 2km towards Melissourgí.

MELISSOURGÍ, 5km to the southeast of Prámanda, is more rewarding. The village escaped destruction during the war, though most buildings – including the historic church – have lost their slate roofs in favour of ugly pantiles. There is a **taverna** and one large **inn** (℡26590 61357; ❸), run by a Mr Karadhimas, though in midsummer all accommodation is likely to be booked by holidaying relatives from the cities. There are sparse bus connections from Árta to Melissourgí.

Melissourgí to Vourgarélli

Melissourgí is a good base for rambles on the **Kostelláta plateau**, the upland separating Mount Kakardhítsa (2429m), which looms sheer above the village, from the more pyramidal Mount Tzoumérka (2393m). Heading south, you can cross these high pastures in a day and a half. The initial stretch of path from Melissourgí is very faintly waymarked with red-paint arrows, and there are intermittent *stánes* (summer sheepfolds) if you need water. You descend to the villages of Theodhóriana and thence **VOURGARÉLLI**, at the edge of the Ahelóös river basin, 57km from Árta, with which there are bus links just two days weekly. Both have **accommodation**, though Vourgarélli – as the administrative centre for the region – is far more equipped to deal with visitors. There, the most congenial of three inns is the well-signed *Hotel Galini* (℡26850 22135; ❷), an attractive chalet with large common areas and easy parking 100m downhill; the rooms are plain but quiet, with fridges and balconies. The platía, ringed by several gushing springs, is home to a handful of **tavernas**. Some 5km below, by the roadside, stands the Byzantine **Kókkini Eklissía**, contemporary with Parigorítissa in Árta (see p.468), a cross-in-square structure with exceptionally fine exterior brickwork, and fragmentary frescoes in the later narthex – under which a presumably monastic burial ground with six graves was discovered in 2004.

Prámanda to Syrráko

With your own transport, you can continue from Prámanda up the Kallaritikós valley to Kallarítes or Syrráko, a pair of handsome villages untouched by the ravages of war. Relying on public transport, however, there's only an occasional minibus to remoter Matsoúki from Prámanda, from which it's a substantial hike to the preceding two; the bus for Syrráko approaches from Ioánnina by the most direct route, a scenic but twisty 52km via Harokópi and Paleohóri, a ninety-minute drive minimum with your own car.

The separate turn-off for Kallarítes is at the hamlet of **KIPÍNA** (seasonal taverna). A famous namesake **monastery**, founded in 1212 but uninhabited today, hangs like a martin's nest from the cliff face 1.5km beyond the hamlet. The premises are locked, though the view from its terrace is superb; immediately beneath, at the roadside, an icy underground river emerges from a cave.

A right-hand turning off the road towards Kipína leads within 16km to the working pastoral village of **MATSOÚKI**, approached in the final moments by a Bailey bridge under which all the snowmelt of Kakardhítsa seems to cascade. Before this was built, access was mainly from Kallarítes by path (2hr), which still exists, taking in the eighteenth-century **monastery of Vylíza** en route (about 30min from Matsoúki). The village itself, redolent of sheep, was again burnt by the Germans and has little to offer other than a few basic **rooms** for mountaineers, and an unrivalled back-of-beyond feel.

Kallarítes

Beyond Kipína monastery, the road continues about 2km upstream, through a tunnel and over a bridge, to give access to the remnant of a wonderful *kalderími* climbing to the village of **KALLARÍTES**, perched superbly above the head-waters of the Kallaritikós river (you can continue driving if you don't wish to walk). This Vlach village was a veritable El Dorado until the close of the nineteenth century. Fame and fortune were based on its specialization in gold- and silversmithing, and even today the craftsmen of Ioánnina are mostly of Kallaritiot descent – as are those of Bulgari, one of the world's most exclusive contemporary jewellers. Though the village is nearly deserted except during summer holidays, the grand houses of the departed rich are kept in excellent repair by their descendants. The flagstoned platía has probably remained unchanged since 1881 (when the village was sacked and rebuilt), with its old-fashioned stores and stele commemorating local émigré Kallaritiots, who helped finance the War of Independence. There are two **kafenío–grills** on the platía, and the same number of small **inns**: that of Pavlos Patounis (☎26590 62235; ❷) and the one kept by Napoleon Zanglis (☎26590 61518; ❷), which has four simple but serviceable rooms above one of the *kafenía*.

Khroússias gorge and Syrráko

Just beyond Kallarítes, the awesome **Khroússias gorge** separates the village from its neighbour Syrráko, visible high up on the west bank but a good hour's walk away. The trail is spectacular, including a near-vertical "ladder" hewn out of the rock face. Down on the bridge over the river you can peer upstream at a pair of abandoned water mills. The canyon walls are steep and the sun shines down here for only a few hours a day, even in summer.

SYRRÁKO (1120m), hugging a steep-sloped ravine with views towards Kakardhítsa, is even more strikingly set than Kallarítes, with well-preserved stone mansions, archways and churches reminiscent of those in the Zagóri, only built on a far grander scale, right down to the stage-like platía with its huge plane trees. The village is a car-free zone; you leave vehicles at the lower car park and make the final approach on a *kalderími* with two little bridges. Despite this problematic access, the paving of the direct road west to Ioánnina has made Syrráko trendy as a weekend retreat, and the place is in the throes of a restoration boom. Not to be outdone by Kallarítes, the village has also erected a number of monuments to various national figures including the poet Kostas Krystallis, who hailed from here. There are two **tavernas** on the platía (*Galani* and *Stavraetos*) and at least two **inns**, the *Xenonas Galani* off the platía (☎26510 53569; B&B ❹) and the *Kasa Kalda* (☎26510 66210 or 697 70 34 517; ❸).

The Epirot coast and Étolo-Akarnanía

The **Epirot coast** has some very attractive **beaches** between Igoumenítsa and Préveza, among the best on the mainland outside of Mount Pílio. **Igoumenítsa** itself, the capital of Thesprotía province, is a purely functional ferry port, while the first beaches you'd detour for are at **Sývota**, 23km south. **Párga**, the most historic resort on the way to Préveza, has become overdeveloped and is best left for June or September visits. Inland near Párga, there are plenty of interesting detours from the main coastal route south: the intriguing **Nekromanteíon of Ephyra** was the legendary gate of Hades; the **gorge of the Ahérondas River** offers fine hiking; and the imposing ruins of **Kassope** and **Nikopolis** break the journey to **Préveza**, a fairly low-key provincial capital at the mouth of the Amvrakikós gulf. **Árta** is another interesting town surrounded by Byzantine churches, approached either around the gulf from Préveza, past the **Rodhiá** wetland reserve, or more impressively along the plane-shaded Loúros River gorge from Ioánnina.

Moving south into **Étolo–Akarnanía**, the landscape becomes increasingly desolate, with little to delay your progress to the island of Lefkádha or to Andírio and the crossing to the Peloponnese. The port of **Páleros** is the one place with any maritime feel, or much foreign-tourist trade. Committed hermits might hole up on **Kálamos** island, south of castle-topped **Vónitsa** and reached from the enjoyable little coastal settlement of **Mýtikas**. Lord Byron's heart is buried at walled **Mesolóngi**; it's otherwise an unglamorous town, though enjoyable enough for a few hours.

Igoumenítsa and around

IGOUMENÍTSA is Greece's third passenger port, after Pireás and Pátra, with frequent ferries to Corfu and several daily to Italy. As land travel through most of ex-Yugoslavia remains a dodgy option, sea traffic between Greece and Italy

---

Heading to the coast

For most travellers, the first stage of the journey to the coast – even with the new Via Egnatia – will be the old **main highway from Ioánnina to Igoumenítsa**, which mostly follows the valley of the Thiámis (Kálamos) River. This is a dangerous "slaughter alley", especially the curves west of Vrosína village, and for the moment infested by long-distance lorries. If you're in your own car or on a bike, a far better (and safer) alternative involves bearing right (north) some 500m east of Vrosína at a disused sentry post, then crossing the river bridge and veering immediately left towards Ravení, and then through Keramítsa and Dháfni. This route – shown rather disparagingly and erroneously as a secondary road on the Road Editions *Epirus/Thessaly* map – is far more scenic, less stressful, and actually 3km shorter by the time you emerge on the "main" highway between Parapótamos and Mavroúdhi.

has increased significantly. With the impending completion of the Via Egnatia expressway sector from Grevená to here, this unloved provincial capital will soon become the country's leading cargo port; a mega-terminal has been built at the harbour to service lorries exiting the motorway, and all shipping agencies have opened branches close to the new terminal, plus embarcation booths inside it.

These seagoing functions and its waterfront apart, the town is pretty unappealing; Igoumenítsa was levelled during World War II and rebuilt in a sprawling, utilitarian style. If you can arrange it, try to get a ferry out straight away; every day in season there are sailings to Italy in the morning, and throughout the evening. To take a vehicle, or get a cabin berth on evening sailings (see box on p. 000) during high season, it's best to make reservations in advance. If you find yourself stuck for the day, you are better off taking one of the limited range of excursions from Igoumenítsa than hanging around the town.

Practicalities

International **ferries** now depart from the new terminal at the far south end of town, and the quay here is extensive enough that you should ascertain exactly where your boat is berthed to avoid last-minute dashes. Local ferries to Corfu or Paxí operate from just north of the new port; tickets for these services are purchased only at little booths on this domestic ferry quay. Close to the central part of the quay, you'll still find the **tourist information office** (daily 8am–2.30pm; ☎26650 22227). The **bus station** is five minutes away at Kýprou 47. Driving your own car, beware of Igoumenítsa's **fee-parking** scheme, nominally in effect 8am–10pm (though enforcement on recent visits was lax); most will prefer the free car park at the north end of the waterfront.

The town is not large but **hotels** are plentiful, if rather lugubrious and overpriced; most are either along or just back from the waterfront. The nearest budget hotel to the port is the *Acropolis* at Ethnikís Andístasis 58A (☎26650 22342; ❷), which has shared bathrooms and some sea views. More comfortable is the *Oscar* at Ayíon Apostólon 149 (☎26650 23338; ❹), also on the seafront opposite the Corfu/Paxí dock. Inland, at the southeast corner of the main platía, stands the comfortable, air-conditioned *Egnatia* at Eleftherías 1 (☎26650 23648; ❸); ask for a rear room facing the pine grove, and take advantage of unrestricted street parking. Perhaps the best budget choice is the *Stavrodhromi*, Soulíou 14, the street leading diagonally uphill and northeast from the square (☎26650 22343; ❷); this has en-suite rooms with air conditioning, as well as an in-house restaurant. The closest **campsite** is the *Drepano* (☎26650 24442; April–Oct), out at Dhrépano beach, 5km west.

Not surprisingly, **restaurants** and **cafés** are generally uninspiring if plentiful on the pedestrian zone one block inland; for lunch, try *Nikolaos Martinis*, inland at pedestrianized Grigoríou Lambráki 32, for *mayireftá*, or *Ouzeri Tò Kohyli* at the south end of Lambráki, near Venizélou, for seafood. After dark, several fish tavernas and ouzerís at the very north end of the front, near the Dhrépano turning, come to life. Several **banks** with ATMs are scattered along the south end of the front; at the north end, just inland on Evangelistrías, is the **post office**.

Around Igoumenítsa

The best brief escapes are along the coast north of town. The closest beach lies 5km west at **Dhrépano**, a two-kilometre-long, crescent-shaped sand spit (the name means "sickle") shaded by eucalypts and closing off a lagoon. Near the campsite is an adequate and popular municipally run **restaurant**, the *Kendriko*, with a seaside terrace from where you watch the ferries bound for Corfu.

With more time at your disposal, make for **SAYIÁDHA**, the last coastal settlement before Albania. It's reached by a direct, twenty-one-kilometre road (not shown on some maps) from the north end of Igoumenítsa, passing the hilltop Byzantine **monastery of Ráyio**, which has some blurred frescoes. Next you cross the Kálamos River weir and wind through citrus groves to this little fishing and yacht port with exceptionally wide horizons. On the flagstoned quay are a half-dozen bars and **tavernas**, the most popular of the latter being *Alekos* – the sort of place yachters come to because they know the seafood will be

International ferry companies in Igoumenítsa

There's a healthy spread of **departure times** across the day for Italy-bound ferries. You can expect boats to leave for various Italian destinations between 7.30am and 10.30am, with a larger cluster of evening departures between 7pm and 1am (most commonly 11–11.30pm). "High season" prices for the Greece–Italy trip apply between early August and early September. Services to all destinations remain frequent over most of the year; even Venice, the remotest port, is called at three or four times weekly in winter.

Companies offer a variety of **fares** for cabin and dormitory berths, or "airplane" seats and deck passage, as well as occasional reductions for student-card holders and discounts on return tickets. Brindisi tickets tend to be marginally less expensive than those for Bari, Ancona rather more; Venice is vastly more costly. Fares and conditions vary significantly from company to company, according to boat quality and speed; the new generation of high-speed craft has cut optimum travel times by a third and forced many slower boats out of business. Cars, motorcycles and bicycles (the last free to transport) are carried on all ferries. ANEK and Minoan Lines allow you to sleep in your camper or van on deck, sparing you the cost of a cabin.

If you have bought tickets in advance, or from a travel agent other than the local authorized agent – and all waterfront agencies cheerfully and promiscuously sell for several companies – you must **check in** (with the appropriate *official* agent as listed below, or at their embarcation booth in the new port) at least two hours before departure, three hours if you want to stay in your camper van. Unlike sailings from Pátra, ferries from Igoumenítsa to Italy are **not allowed** to sell tickets with a **stopover** on Corfu. You can, however, take the domestic Corfu ferry and then pick up many routes on from there, though the fare will be the same as from Igoumenítsa.

International ferry companies, main agents and destinations

Agoudimos Nikos Zois, Ayíon Apostólon 147 ☎26650 25682. Bari, daily Aug–Sept (9hr); Brindisi, daily Aug–Sept (7hr 30min).

ANEK Revis Tours, Ayíon Apostólon 145 ☎26650 22104. Ancona, 6–7 weekly all year (15hr 30min); Venice, 4–6 weekly all year (25hr).

Fragline Revis Tours, Ayíon Apostólon 145 ☎26650 22104. Brindisi, 5–7 weekly April–Sept (9hr 45min).

Maritime Way Ayíon Apostólon 149 ☎26650 26410. Brindisi, daily all year except Jan when 3 weekly (8hr).

Minoan Lines Ethnikís Andístasis 58A ☎26650 26715. Ancona, 4–7 weekly all year (15hr); Venice, 4–6 weekly all year (22hr).

Superfast Ayíon Apostólon 7–9 ☎26650 29200. Bari, daily all year (9hr 30min); Ancona, daily all year (15hr 30min).

Ventouris Milano Travel, New Harbour ☎26650 23565. Bari, daily except Jan (11hr 30min).

better and cheaper than at Corfu and Sývota. The only proper beaches nearby are the tiny one at **Keramídhi** (2.5km north), where there is a snack bar, and and larger **Strovíli** (4.5km north; no facilities), both along the broad road heading for the Albanian **border crossing** towards Konispol.

South along the coast, other beaches flank Kalámi (9km) and Platariá (12km), but the beaches at Sývota (23km), and Karavostási and Sarakíniko further south, are more attractive options.

Sývota

The sleepy resort of **SÝVOTA**, surrounded by olive groves, drapes itself over some evocative coastal topography gazing out to Corfu and Paxí. It hosts a couple of British holiday operators (and a small resort), but also serves as a popular summer destination for Greeks and Italians. The village centre, such as it is, lies several hundred metres inland, while the pedestrianized little port, a popular berthing for yachts despite fierce afternoon winds, fronts a line of restaurants and cafés.

Sývota has a small **town beach**, just to the north, while to the west there are a couple of sandy patches on the goat-inhabited islet of **Mávro Óros**, joined to the mainland by the sandspit of **Bélla Vráka**. This is a de facto private beach for *The Retreat*, an attractive watersports-oriented resort, though the beach and island are accessible to all via a track veering off the main drive into the resort. If you have transport, you can reach a sequence of rather better beaches off the road to the south (leading to Pérdhika and eventually Párga), in order, small, shady **Zaviá**; bigger, sunnier **Méga Ámmos**; **Mikrí Ámmos** (also known as "BB Beach"); **Méga Tráfos** with its two secluded coves (foot or boat access only); **Ayía Paraskeví**, with an islet to swim to; and **Sofás**. Almost all these beaches have grills or simple snack-bars in season.

Much of Sývota's accommodation is pre-booked by tour companies, but a smattering of **hotels** and **rooms** takes walk-in trade. These include the tree-shrouded *Hellas* (T26650 93227; ❸) in the village centre, with a restaurant; the *Hotel Fylakas* (T26650 93345, F26650 93166; Easter & May–Oct; ❺), with pleasant common areas and fair-sized rooms overlooking the harbour; and the well-maintained *Studios Anneta* gallery apartments sleeping up to four (T26650 93457 or 694 25 57 584; ❹), set in a peaceful olive grove 200m back from the harbour. You'll get more for your money out at the beaches: at Méga Ámmos, 3km from town, try the *Mikros Paradisos* (T26650 93281; ❹), scattered across lovely grounds and with a tennis court. There's also a **campsite** (T26650 93275; May–Sept) north of the harbour, near the town beach.

Around the harbour, a dozen **tavernas**, **pizzerias**, **snack-cafés** and **bars** vie for your custom. *Tzimas* (also called *O Faros*) is a reliable all-rounder; *Parasole* does authentic wood-fired, thin-crust pizzas; and *Ostria*, just inland from the *Parasol* under a vine-shaded pergola, does a nice range of *mezédhes*.

You can **rent cars** or **scooters**, or book an excursion, at Isabella Tours (T26650 93317) **travel agency**, which also sells foreign **newspapers**. A couple of outlets on the quay rent out **dinghies**, and run **boat-taxis** to the local beaches and islets. Near the harbour there's also a freestanding **bank** ATM and a **pharmacy**.

Karavostási, Pérdhika, Sarakíniko and Ayiá

About 11km south of Sývota, you reach the edge of Pérdhika village and the poorly marked but well-paved side road (5km) down to **Karavostási** beach – its hotels are better signposted. The 500-metre beach itself – generally thought the best on the Thesprotian coast – usually has a light surf, but the water is clean and brisk, with just a few sunbeds, and camper vans at the south end, above which (on the headland) are the scanty remains of **ancient Elina** (under excavation). At the river mouth (a protected environment) there are two snack and drink bars, and another bar-restaurant above the south end of the beach, but no other facilities independent of the three **hotels** here. Of these, the B-class ☀ *Karavostasi Beach* is your best-value option (☎26650 91104, ⓦwww.hotel -karavostasi.gr; B&B ❺). Some of the minimalist, marble-clad rooms have sea views, while the well-designed and landscaped pool-bar area makes an attractive breakfast venue. **Arílla**, the next bay north and reached from a split in the road 1500m above Karavostási, doesn't have nearly as good a beach, but does offer a couple of summer-only **restaurants** and a yachting and fishing anchorage.

For more reliable eating options, you're best advised to backtrack uphill and across the highway to **PÉRDHIKA**, the closest "real" village; like many spots in Thesprotía province, it was substantially Muslim before 1923, and subsequently resettled in a grid plan by Corfiots, Paxiots and Asia Minor refugees. Pérdhika has a lively after-dark scene centred on a score of restaurants and cafés around its pedestrianized platía; they're all used to foreigners but geared up as much to the needs of the sociable locals – it's standing room only in July or August. The most characterful **restaurant**, with fare as good as any served here and great taste in Greek music, is *Ta Kavouria*.

Beyond Karavostási, you cross the provincial border into Préveza and just before Ayiá meet the paved, five-kilometre road down to scenic **Sarakíniko**, a short (about 150m) if broad cove of sand and pebbles, with currents making for a cool sea year-round, and a certain amount of day-trip patronage from Párga. Descending from the highway, take the left fork on each of two occasions to reach one of the region's best **tavernas**, ☀ *Christos*, where it's advisable to book and preorder during peak season (☎26840 35207 or 697 79 82 207). Only a few select vegetable dishes are cooked daily, but quality is high, prices fair and seafood is served fresh or not at all. Excellent microwinery products and an eclectic soundtrack are also featured. A garden with swimming pool has been prepared in anticipation of luxury rooms (ready 2008). Among a handful of existing places to **stay**, try for the peaceful, friendly rooms of Periklis and Simela Nanos, 300m south (☎26840 35292; ❸), run as a sideline to their vast farm; it too must be prebooked from July through mid-August.

AYIÁ village, 10km south of Pérdhika, is a more attractive village, its houses amphitheatrically draped over slopes looking towards the Ionian; near the summit of the village, the church of **Áyios Yeóryios** has engaging naive frescoes on its ceiling-vault. Among a handful of **tavernas** along the commercial street – which still shows signs of traditional life – *Oasis* (all year, dinner only) is far and away the favourite, its interior a veritable museum of Greek adverts from the 1920s to the 1960s and an old jukebox; the fare, principally grilled meat, salads, starters and bulk wine, is fair-priced, with locals predominating at the terrace seating except in peak season.

Párga and around

PÁRGA, approximately 50km south of Igoumenítsa, is the main Epirot seaside resort, thanks to its alluring setting on a stretch of riotously lush coastline with a string of rocky islets offshore. The town itself is less photogenic, as concrete construction has completely swamped the outskirts and spread west to the village of Anthoússa; the old centre, however, an arc of tiered houses set below a Norman-Venetian **kástro** with some fine old mansions and mysterious archways in the lower quarter, retains considerable charm. What saves Párga is the fact that Epirots (and other Greeks) love it for their own holidays – and that amidst the holiday activity normal life (just) continues, exemplified by numbers of older ladies in the traditional garb of black veil, braids and dark blue kerchiefs. Still, in midsummer there are just too many people for comfort in such a compact place, and you'll have a better time in June or September.

Some history

Párga has an idiosyncratic history, being linked with the Ionian islands as much as with mainland Epirus. From the fourteenth to the eighteenth centuries the port was a lone **Venetian** toehold in Epirus, complementing the Serene Republic's island possessions. Under Venetian rule, a small community of Jews prospered here from the export of citrons to western Europe for liturgical use; they, and the citrons, are long gone, but lemon groves remain at Anthoússa, and the Lion of St Mark – symbol of Venice – is still visible on the *kástro* keep.

Later, the Napoleonic **French** took Párga for a brief period, leaving additional fortifications on the largest islet guarding the harbour. At the start of the nineteenth century, the town enjoyed a stint of autonomy under **Russian** protection, and was self-sufficient through the export of olives, before being acquired by the **British**, who sold it on to **Ali Pasha**. Ali Pasha rebuilt all the local castles, while the townspeople, knowing his reputation, decamped to the Ionian islands on Good Friday 1819 (though some returned a half-century later to inhabit the lower quarter of town). The area was subsequently resettled by **Muslims**, who remained until the exchange of populations in 1923, when they were replaced in part by **Orthodox Greek** refugees from the area around Constantinople. The Muslim quarter lined the upper ridge still known as Tourkopázaro, and a magnificent mosque and minaret stood there until razed in the 1950s to make way for a car park.

△ Váltos beach, Párga

The Town, beaches and castles

The town is dominated by the blufftop Venetian **kástro** (8am–midnight; free), a haven from Párga's bustle. A long stair-street leads up to the ruined, cypress-tufted ramparts, which offer excellent views of the town, its waterfront and a mountainous backdrop. A restored barracks inside the castle boundary houses a recommended café (see opposite); you can continue up a cobbled way to one of Ali Pasha's summer palaces on the summit, a warren of vaulted rooms and cisterns, with the remains of a domed bath at the very top.

Párga's fine **beaches** – which get very crowded in midsummer – line several consecutive bays, split by various headlands. The small bay of **Kryonéri** lies opposite the islet studded with a monastery and Napoleonic fortifications, a 200-metre swim or pedalo from the south end of the town quay. Tiny but scenic **Gólfo** beach, the next cove southeast, is reached by a narrow lane signposted for its eponymous taverna. Immediately northwest beyond the *kástro* (on foot easiest reached by the long ramp from the *kástro* gate, otherwise frequent water-taxis in season from the town dock) lies **Váltos beach**, more than 1km in length as it arcs around to the hamlet of the same name. **Lýkhnos**, 3km in the opposite (southeast) direction, is a similarly huge beach; a shaded path through the olive groves, starting beyond the supermarket and bakery behind Kyronéri, short-cuts the winding road in, or again taxi-boats spare you the walk.

A short, five-kilometre excursion leads to the diminutive, hatbox **castle of Ayiá** (actually between Anthoússa and Ayiá), nocturnally illuminated in season. Head west on the main road through and beyond Anthoússa, then turn off at the well-marked side road passing Tríkorfo hamlet. The castle is more elaborate and intact than it seems from a distance, having been rebuilt in 1814 by Ali Pasha, using Italian engineers. You have unrestricted access to the dungeons, the upper U-shaped gallery and the roof with its two rusty cannons and superb views encompassing Paxí, Váltos beach, Ammoudhiá and Lefkádha.

Practicalities

Buses link Párga with Ioánnina, Igoumenítsa and Préveza several times daily on weekdays, less at weekends; the stop is up on the bypass road, near the start of Spýrou Livadhá (the way to Váltos) and Avis (T 26840 26632) **car rental**; there's also Eurohire inside the premises of efficient travel agency ITS (T 26840 32584) at Spýrou Livadhá 4. This is one of a handful of travel agencies, mostly on the waterfront, which **rent scooters** and arrange **excursions** up the Ahérondas River to the Nekromanteion of Ephyra, allowing good views of the delta birdlife en route (though this is more easily and cheaply arranged in Ammoudhiá, see p.463). There is no longer a scheduled summer ferry to Paxí; you can only visit that island on a relatively expensive day-excursion. The **post office** is on Alexándhrou Bánga, start of the main market street, which also has four **banks** with ATMs; a small **bookshop**, Sotiris Deskas at Spýrou Livadhá 3, has a limited stock of English-language material and maps.

Accommodation

Various tour operators and repeat clients booking in advance monopolize most of Párga's **hotels** and quality **apartments** between mid-June and the end of September. Outside of these times, however, those showing up on spec will have a fair choice – though parking most places is a nightmare, and avoiding scooter and bar noise is paramount. Areas to look for **rooms** on your own include the lanes beyond Kryonéri and the ridge of Tourkopázaro (officially Odhós

Patatoúka), where many premises have unbeatable views over Váltos beach. There are **campsites** just behind Kryonéri beach at *Parga Camping* (℡26840 31161), and a newer, unobtrusive site, *Valtos* (℡26840 31287; May–Sept), at the far end of Váltos beach by the yacht harbour; the enormous *Enjoy Lyhnos Camping* (℡26840 31171) straddles the road access to Lýkhnos beach, and also has bungalows (❹).

Achilleas Kryonéri ℡26840 31600, ℻26840 31879. Well-furnished hotel, though the pricier sea-view rooms are usually booked by holiday firms. ❹
Galini edge of town below Váltos road ℡26840 31581, ℻26840 32221. Hotel set in an orchard and as quiet as the name ("Serenity") implies, with enormous rooms. ❸
Golfo Beach Kryonéri ℡26840 32336, ℻26840 31347. A choice of basic but spotless 1970s rooms, en suite and not, facing a pleasant garden or the sea. ❸
Kostas and Martha Christou Tourkopázaro, near *kástro* ℡26840 31942 or 693 77 96 209. Spartan but en-suite rooms in a calm environment, with terrace garden and self-catering kitchen. Kostas does boat excursions, and Martha will do laundry, on request. Rates include breakfast in low season. ❸
Lichnos Beach on Lýkhnos beach ℡26840 31257, ⓦwww.lichnosbeach.com. A good-value choice for the car-bound or families, with a mix of standard rooms and bungalows set in lush grounds, big enough that tours don't completely monopolize it. Tennis court, pool and "private" beach with water-sport facility. ❺

Magda's Apartments Váltos road just before lane to *kástro* ℡26840 31228, ⓦwww.magdas-apartments.parga.com. A mix of studios redone in 2004 (❺ but usually taken by holiday companies), and six superior 2005-built apartments (❻, but let by the week) direct-bookable only, in a hillside garden environment with mountain and partial sea views, plus a terrace pool with separate spa. Good breakfasts extra, easy parking. English-speaking hosts Kostas and Spyros will do anything for their clients; not surprisingly, three-month advance booking is usually necessary. Greek Easter to late Oct.
Villa Koralli Kryonéri main beach ℡26840 31069, ℻26840 32469. Anodyne white-pine-and-tile *dhomátia*, some sea-view, and limited parking. ❺

Eating and drinking

For **meals**, there are upwards of two dozen tavernas around town, though the quality of cooking varies and most menus are aimed squarely at the package trade. Mussels are fresh, despite what menus might say, only at weekends when the shipments from the farms arrive. Incidentally, most Párga tavernas offer local wine from the barrel; the red is generally excellent. For more extended drinking, **nightlife** centres around a half-dozen semi-open-air bars on the main quay and along the steps to the *kástro*, pumping out 1960s and 1970s sounds to match the largely thirty-to-fifty-something crowd; Párga isn't really a youth mecca. The most durable indoor **clubs** are *Camares* and *Factory*, both at or just in from mid-quay, and *Blue Bar* up towards the castle.

Apangio Up stair-lane inland from mid-quay. Párga's only ouzerí, with Greeks in attendance, though the platters tend towards taverna mains rather than *mezédhes*. Open all year, dinner only.
Café Castle/Kastro Restored barracks, *kástro*. The most civilized chill-out place in Párga; a full bar, but the real speciality is forty different kinds of novelty hot and cold chocolate. Live music (Greek folk/contemporary) two nights weekly in season. Open 9.30am to midnight.
Eden/Edem Platía Ayíou Dhimitríou, market. Long-running, good-value crêperie and breakfast venue that's diversified to pasta dishes, salads, fresh juices, professionally made coffees and a full bar. Open 8am–1am.

Filomela Patatoúka. Upmarket Italian eatery that makes a decent fist of Italian pasta dishes, and was the first in town to use fresh mussels.
Golfo Beach Kyronéri. Evangelia is heart and soul of one of the oldest tavernas in town, with a cult following for her sustaining *mayireftá*; three courses and a beer won't much exceed €15; live music some nights. Open 8am–11pm.
Oskar North side of waterfront. Friendly and tiny – thus seasonally packed – Italian/generic Mediterranean place with assorted pizzas and pastas, as well as baked *plevrótous* mushrooms and substantial house salad with prosciutto, sun-dried tomatoes, etc. Open all year; does takeaway.

Sakis Turkopázaro, next to fountain and plane trees. The place for a cheap-and-cheerful, village-style feed. Good grills and a few *mayireftá* per day; no seafood.

To Souli Southeast quay. Oldest taverna in town, and still about the most reliable of several here,

offering all the *mayireftá* standards plus a few grills.

Stefanos Lane between the castle and Váltos. Touting can be off-putting but the fish is very good, said to be the best in town – and the view from the terrace is fabulous.

The Nekromanteion of Ephyra

The **Nekromanteion of Ephyra** (or Sanctuary of Persephone and Hades, Nekrómándio in modern Greek) stands just above the village of Mesopótamos, 22km southeast of Párga. Compared with Greece's other ancient remains, the site has few visitors, and this, coupled with its evocative location, makes it a worthwhile and slightly unusual excursion. The sanctuary is sited on a low, rocky hill, above which, in ancient times, the Acheron (Ahérondas in modern Greek), associated with the mythical Styx, river of the underworld, the Kokytos, "River of Lamentation", and the Pyriphlegethon, "River of Flaming Fire", all flowed into the marshy lake of Acherousia. According to mythology, this was the spot from which Charon rowed departed souls across the lake to the gates of Hades, and from Mycenaean to Roman times it maintained an elaborate oracle of the dead. Ephyra never achieved the stature of Delphi or Dodona, but its fame was sufficient for Homer, writing (one assumes) in the ninth century BC, to use it as the setting for Odysseus's visit to Hades. Circe describes it explicitly, when advising Odysseus:

You will come to a wild coast and to Persephone's grove, where the hill poplars grow and the willows that so quickly lose their seeds. Beach your boat there by Ocean's swirling stream and march on into Hades' Kingdom of Decay. There the River of Flaming Fire and the River of Lamentation, which is a branch of the Waters of the Styx, unite around a pinnacle of rock to pour their thundering streams into Acheron. This is the spot, my lord, that I bid you seek out . . . then the souls of the dead and departed will come up in their multitudes.

The sanctuary

Trees still mark the sanctuary's site (daily 9am–2pm, later summer closing if staffing permits; €2, site booklet €5), though today they are primarily cypresses, emblems of the dead throughout the Mediterranean. The ancient Lake Acherousia, which once enclosed the island-oracle, has receded to the vague line of the Ahérondas skirting the modern, marshy plain of Fanári, which still floods in winter; from the sanctuary you can pick out its course from a fringe of Homer's willows. All the mythological rivers still exist, though the Pyriphlegethon is the modern Vovós.

As for the sanctuary itself, its **ruins**, flanked by an early **Christian basilica**, offer a fascinating exposé of the confidence tricks pulled by its priestly initiates. According to contemporary accounts, **pilgrims** arriving on the oracle-island were accommodated for a night in windowless rooms. Impressed by the atmosphere, and by their mission to consult with the souls of the dead, they would then be relieved of their votive offerings while awaiting their "day-trip" to the underworld. When their turn came, they would be sent groping along labyrinthine corridors into the heart of the sanctuary, where, further disoriented by having ingested psychoactive lupin seeds, they would be lowered into the antechamber of "Hades" itself to witness whatever spectral visitation the priests might have devised.

The remains of the sanctuary – walls of polygonal masonry standing up to head height – allowed excavators to identify the function of each room, and there is a rudimentary plan at the entrance. At the very top, visible from a considerable distance, sits a **medieval chapel** of Ayíou Ioánnou Prodhrómou, retaining eighteenth-century fresco fragments; just below, *pithária*, **giant storage urns**, have been left *in situ*. At the centre of the site is a long room with high walls, flanked by chambers used for votive offerings. From here metal steps lead to the damp, vaulted **underground chamber** where the necromantic audiences took place. Originally this descent was by means of a precarious windlass mechanism, which was found on the site.

Practicalities

The Nekromanteion is most easily reached by boat **tour** from Párga or Ammoudhiá (see p.463), or by motorbike. Puny scooters will *not* cope well with the gradients and speeds of the improved main highway between the two points – you'll need at least a 90cc bike. **Buses** from Párga stop at Kastrí, 5km from the site, but they do not call at Mesopótamos or Ammoudhiá, which are on the direct coast road to Préveza, and a different bus line. Buses from Párga and Préveza also pass through the county town of Kanalláki, which has banks (ATMs), petrol, shops and a few *psistariés*, but Ammoudhiá (5km) is a far more amenable base, and slightly closer to the Nekromanteion in any case.

East of Párga: Soúli

The highland region four valleys east of Párga was the traditional heartland of the **Souliots**, an independent-spirited tribe of Albanian Orthodox Christians, who inhabited eleven separate villages here. From 1787 until their initial defeat and dispersal in 1803, these 12,000 doughty mountain warriors conducted a perennial rebellion against Ali Pasha and his Muslim Albanians from their strongholds above the **Ahérondas gorge** and in the mountains to the south. In 1820 they allied themselves with Ali Pasha and were allowed to return to their homes, but following the sultan's final victory over Ali, the Souliots were exiled permanently as punishment. Today the region remains impoverished and deserted, though celebrated as a linchpin of resistance against Ottoman rule.

Although it seems hard to think now of the placid Ahérondas near the Nekromanteion of Ephyra as the way to Hell, just a few kilometres inland its waters cut deep into rock strata and swirl in unnavigable eddies as the river saws a course through its gorge at the so-called "Gates of Hades", which begins its downstream course between the remote villages of Tríkastro and Seriziana. While not in quite the same league as the Víkos Gorge (see p.438), it is certainly a respectable wilderness, and if you're looking for a solitary adventure inland from Párga you won't find better (although it's busy at summer weekends and all of August, when locals will be out in force).

Glykí – and the Ahérondas Gorge

Excursions up the Ahérondas gorge start at **GLYKÍ**, 12km from Kanalláki on the inland road between Préveza and Paramythiá (1 daily bus), or 18km from Mórfi junction (above Párga) by car or bike. The river, still relatively calm here, is flanked by several rather mediocre eateries near the main road. A side road on the north (true right) bank, signed as "Piyés Ahéronda", soon dead-ends after passing a few rooms and a handful of **rafting outfitters** (20min trips, good fun for kids). Alternatively, in summer, join the literally hundreds of Greeks **wading upriver** through the deeply shady gorge, attended by clouds of butterflies and rivulets tumbling in from the side. You can wander for a kilometre or so through knee-high water, with occasional deeper patches where you may want to clamber briefly along the shore, plus a few swimmable if icy **pools** where you can leap in.

On the other (south or true left) riverbank, a sign reading "Skála Tzavélenas" points up a paved road. Following this, you can bear left after 800m towards the signposted *Piyes Aheronda* **taverna** (1400m in total from the main road), calmer than its rivals, with simple grilled fare served on tree-shaded tables set up in the river sand.

Hiking into Soúliot country

Beyond the *Piyes Aheronda* taverna, there are a number of more serious **walking trails**, part waymarked, into the hills. Continue along the main road parallel to the river, and bear left towards a modern chapel, about 1km from the bridge; some 300m further on is a flagstoned car park and picnic benches. Here the way deteriorates to a track which ends 1.9km from Glykí at a laboriously wrought tunnel which often has cars parked inside, as well as beside it.

The **Skála Tzavélenas** ("Tzavélena's Stairway") begins just to the tunnel's left; in Souliot days it was a vertiginous corniche path several hundred metres long, named in honour of a local woman who managed to traverse it on a donkey when her menfolk declined to do so. This now has a retaining wall, and the formerly washed-out course of the *skála* down and to the left has been rehabilitated. Below, the canyon walls squeeze together, and upstream a carpet of greenery covers a wilderness, rolling up to the plainly visible castle of Kiáfa.

Beyond the *skála*, the main trail into Soúli, waymarked sporadically with blue arrows, yellow rectangles and newer red squares, descends towards the Ahérondas. About twenty minutes along, there's a junction right for the path to the **Pylés Ádhi** ("Gates of Hell") **narrows** via the Póros Pyrás spring, suppos-edly five hours' hike one-way upstream, waymarked with red diamonds. Even though it's more like three hours one way, much of the walk is in deep forest – giving you scant views – and the roller-coaster trail is somewhat neglected; most people visit the "Gates" by road from the Préveza side, via the villages of Loúros and Vrysoúla.

Most walkers, therefore, will continue on the main path, crossing a damaged modern bridge over the Ahérondas and reaching (half an hour from the tunnel) the tributary Tsangariótiko stream, known locally as the **Piyés Soulíou** (Souliot Springs); the historic Dála bridge over it was swept away in record storms of March 2004 and hasn't been rebuilt. Beyond here the marked route climbs up through the oaks out of the Ahérondas valley, arriving at another path junction (1hr from tunnel) below a circular, roofed gazebo. This, waymarked with green triangles, leads steadily up within another 35 minutes to a pass (*kiáfa* in Albanian) just below **Kiáfa castle**, with goat pens, robust plane trees and a few wells on the col. The south gate of the castle, more of a fortified manor built by Ali Pasha to overawe the Souliots, lies another quarter-hour's scramble up a scree slope with a poor path. The interior is ruins, patrolled by cows, but the climb is justified by fine views west to Paxí and north to the conical hill where the **fortified monastery of Koúngi** used to sit until Souliot rebels under the monk Samuel blew it, and themselves, up rather than surrender – a newer chapel marks the spot.

At the base of the Koúngi hill, reached by a rough descending track from the col (another 35min), is impoverished **Samoníva** (Samonídha), the only one of the eleven Souliot villages still inhabited after a fashion – though there are no reliable facilities, so bring any snacks and water along. At a little church below Samoníva's scattered houses, you can pick up the red-rectangle path for the return journey to the tunnel and car park; allow just over an hour for this, for a generous half-day outing.

The coast to Préveza

Approaches to Préveza from the Nekromanteion and Ahérondas area feature a few more minor sites and resorts before edging out onto the landlocked **Amvrakikós (Ambracian) Gulf**, where in 31 BC Octavian defeated Antony and Cleopatra at the Battle of Actium. Suitably enough, the most substantial of the ruins is Octavian's "Victory City" of **Nikopolis**, just south of the point where the Igoumenítsa–Préveza and the Árta–Préveza highways meet.

Ammoudhiá and the coast road

Two daily local **buses** cover the coastal route to Préveza from **AMMOUDHIÁ**, a surprisingly unspoilt little beach-resort 5km due west of the Nekromanteion at the mouth of the Ahérondas. By the roundabout at the entrance to the village is a worthwhile **visitor information centre** (summer daily 8.30am–3.30pm; free), whose intelligent, non-jingoistic exhibits highlight the unique ecology of the river and its marshes, as well as the history and ethnology of Soúli. There are various informative booklets, offered both free and for sale, though these only partially offset bouts of Greek-only labelling of the displays.

As with most of the spots along this coast, tourists equipped with camper vans or caravans occupy the eucalyptus grove separating the rather scrappy village, only founded after the 1950s draining of the Fanári marsh, from the 700-metre sandy **beach**. There's usually washed-up flotsam, and the water can be chilly, but it's clear and scenic, with more coastal mountains visible beyond the headland closing off the funnel-shaped bay.

Bounding the village on the south, the Ahérondas River meets (and cools) the sea here; the quay is packed with fishing boats and excursion boats for the jaunt upriver to the Nekromanteion, and lined with most of Ammoudhiá's **tavernas** and cafés. Easternmost in the series is *Iy Roxani* (also known as *Thanasis Babos*), considered best for fish, but rather overpriced; cheap-and-cheerful *O Pateras*, closest to the river mouth, also gets lots of custom. If you want to stay, there are various rooms and apartments, as well as several bona-fide **hotels**, among which the simple but air-conditioned, en-suite *Glaros* (T 26840 41300, F 26840 41118; ❷), right behind the river esplanade 200m back from the beach, is the most convenient and quiet enough.

There are more sandy coves a short distance south, across the river, which can only be reached via the village of Velanidhórahi. The largest is **Keréntza** (3.2km from the village), created by a stagnant arm of the Ahérondas, with showers, a *kantína* and views out to Paxí and Andípaxi. Postcard-perfect **Alonáki**, 2.8km distant by a different road, is a miniature pine-and-cliff-grit cove opening to the south, again with a shower and seasonal *kantína*. There's a rough dirt track between the two, off which a third beach, **Amóni**, can be reached.

Other places to break your journey south of Ammoudhiá – especially if you take this route with your own vehicle – are at **LYGIÁ**, unmarked on some maps, or **Loútsa** and **Paralía Vráhou** immediately north (shared exit from the newish main highway). At Lygiá an enormous if boulder-strewn beach is overlooked by a crumbling castle in the distance; there are **rooms** to rent (rather than the mega-hotels found further south at Kanáli), an impromptu **campsite** (*Akroyiali*; ☎26820 56382) and several **tavernas**, best of these – with cheaper and better seafood than at Ammoudhiá – being *Skaloma* (alias *O Yios tou Fotí*) at the little harbour. The run-together beach of Loútsa and Paralía Vráhou is longer and sandier, with a similar range of amenities behind. The long-distance buses to and from Párga or Igoumenítsa don't pass this way, but head inland at Mórfi junction, before rejoining the coast road near Nikopolis.

Inland: Zálongo and ancient Kassope

Some 28km from Mesopótamos on the inland route, you pass a turning east to the village of **Kamarína** (3km), overlooked by the monastery and monument of Zálongo and the ruins of ancient Kassope. These are a steep, shadeless six-kilometre climb from the main highway, so a taxi or your own transport is a good idea. There's also access (unsignposted) through the village of Kryopiyí, also 3km off the main road, somewhat quicker if you're approaching from the north.

Zálongo monastery is a staple of Greek schoolbook history, immortalized by the defiant mass suicide of a group of Souliot women. In 1803, Ali Pasha's troops, commanded by his son Veli, cornered in the monastery a large band of Souliots who were fleeing the destruction of Koúngi. As this refuge was overrun, about sixty Souliot women and children fled to the top of the cliff above and, to the amazement of the approaching Albanian Muslims, the mothers danced one by one, with their children in their arms, over the edge of the precipice. This act is commemorated by a truly hideous modern cement-and-stone **sculpture**, accessible by several hundred steps. The monastery, just below and of no intrinsic interest, and the monument attract regular coach tours of Greek schoolchildren and (at weekends) adults.

Slightly to the west of the monastery, on a natural balcony just below the summit of a similar bluff, are the remains of **ancient Kassope** (Tues–Sun 8.30am–3pm, may close later in summer; €3 if warden present), a minor Thesprotian city-state today approached via a long path through a pine grove. The ruins date mainly from the fourth century BC, with extensive second-century rebuilding after the city was sacked by the Romans; the place was definitively abandoned in 31 BC when its citizens were commanded to inhabit Nikopolis (see below). An excellent site plan affixed to the warden's hut helps to locate highlights, including the central agora, a tiny, eroded *odeion* and (most impressive) a *katagoyeion*, or hostelry, for representatives of the Kassopean federation. Principally, though, Kassope is memorable for its superb location – some 600m above sea level, with the Ionian Sea's coastline and Lefkádha laid at your feet.

Nikopolis

The "Victory City" of **NIKOPOLIS** was founded by Octavian on the site where his army had camped prior to the Battle of Actium. An arrogant and ill-considered gesture, it made little geographical sense. The settlement was on unstable ground, water had to be transported by aqueduct from the distant springs of the Loúros, and a population had to be forcibly imported from towns as far afield as the Gulf of Kórinthos. However, such a *folie de grandeur* was perhaps understandable. At **Actium**, Octavian had first blockaded and then largely annihilated the combined fleets of Antony and Cleopatra, gathered there for the invasion of Italy. The rewards were sweet, subsequently transforming Octavian from military commander to emperor of Rome, under the title of Augustus.

The subsequent history of Nikopolis is undistinguished, with much of its original population drifting back to their homes. As the Roman Empire declined, the city suffered sacking by Vandals and Goths. Later, in the sixth century AD, it was restored by Justinian and flourished for a while as a Byzantine city, but within four centuries it had sunk again into the earth, devastated by the combined effect of earthquakes and Bulgar raids.

The site and museum

The far-flung and overgrown monuments begin 7km north of Préveza, on either side of the main road. The site is really too scattered to tour by foot or KTEL bus; hire a taxi in Préveza for a couple of hours, or visit with a rental car.

The ruins (access generally unrestricted, certain items fenced) look impressive from the road. A great **theatre** stands to the east and as you approach the site museum, past remnants of the **baths**, there is a formidable stretch of sixth-century Byzantine **fortified walls**. But as you walk around, the promise of this enormous site is unfulfilled; few other monuments reward close inspection, though they're home to snakes, butterflies, the odd tortoise and, in spring, numerous wild flowers.

From the scant foundations of the sixth-century **basilica of Alkysonos**, it's 2km to the main **theatre**, whose arches stand amidst dangerously crumbling masonry. To the left of this you can just make out the sunken outline of the **stadium**, below the modern village of Smyrtoúna. Octavian's own tent was pitched upon the hill above the village, and a massive **podium** remains from the commemorative monument that he erected. On a terrace alongside, excavations have revealed the remains of ramming protuberances of some of the captured warships, which he dedicated to the gods.

The dull **museum** (Tues–Sun 8.30am–2.30pm, may close 5pm summer; €3) consists of two rooms containing a rather uninspiring collection of Roman sarcophagi and coins. Its caretaker's main function used to be wardenship of the Roman and Byzantine mosaics unearthed amidst the foundations of the sixth-century **basilica of Doumetios** nearby, but these are now covered by a protective layer of sand and polythene. The caretaker may escort you to the Roman **odeion**, for which he has the keys. This dates from the original construction of the city and has been well restored for use in the local summer festival.

Préveza

Modern **PRÉVEZA**, at the mouth of the Amvrakikós Gulf, is a relatively insignificant successor to Nikopolis, but not without appeal. Numerous **cafés** line the east waterfront, facing Actium (modern Áktio) where the forces of Antony and Cleopatra were defeated. Since the advent of international flights to nearby Áktio airport, this provincial capital has had a facelift, and more character remains in the pedestrianized old quarter than at Párga. Préveza merits a brief stopover, not only for Nikopolis, but also for its enjoyable evenings at the **tavernas** in its commercial quarter, offering the most reasonably priced and varied fare for some way around.

Practicalities

Charter flights arriving at nearby Áktio airport generally have transport laid on to Lefkádha or Párga; otherwise there are only taxis for the seven-kilometre trip to town. The **airport** itself is a cheerless shed at the edge of an air-force base, with two car-rental booths, snacks at the bar, and no banking facilities or anywhere to sit. The **bus station** in Préveza is on Leofóros Irínis, 1km south-west of the ferry dock (for trucks only) at the north end of the quay, with the massive castle of Ayíou Andhréou interposed between the two; there are **taxi** ranks both near the KTEL and on the waterfront. A high-tech **tunnel** under the straits links Préveza and Áktio (3min; €3 car toll, €5 camper vans), though it is badly signposted on the Préveza side. Arriving on the highway from Párga, this isn't such a problem, but coming from Árta, you must wend through town to Pandokrátoras district in the south of Préveza, following very sporadic signs for "Áktio", to find the "rabbit hole" entrance.

The **post office** is on Spiliádhou, near the castle. Several **banks** with ATMs are found at the north end of the waterfront, as is a municipal **tourist office** (Mon–Fri 8am–2.30pm). Olympic Airways, for **flights** to Athens, Thessaloníki, Crete and various Ionian islands, is out near the bus station at Irínis 37 (☎26820 28343); a good source of one-way and return charter seats back to Britain is Karyatis Travel, just in from the waterfront at Navarínou 10 (☎26820 60745).

Accommodation

None of the four in-town **hotels** is especially inviting or great value; most tourists will be staying at beachfront resort hotels or apartments to the north, and only coming to town after dark for the lively nightlife. The best two are the *Dioni* on Platía Papayeoryíou, a quiet pedestrian zone (☎26820 27381, ⓕ26820 27384; ❹), or the only seafront establishment, the *Avra* at Venizélou 19 (☎26820 21230, ⓕ26820 26454; ❸). Failing these, there are several **rooms** on the shore road towards the far side of the peninsula; follow this south out of town about 2km, curling around the Venetian **Pandokrátoras** castle (a shell, though used as a venue for the summer festival) at the peninsula tip.

The nearest **campsite** is *Kalamitsi* (☎26820 22368), around 4km north of town on the broad highway which skims along a few hundred metres back from the coast. Any bus running towards Kanáli (15km out, not to be confused with Kanalláki) will pass the summer-only sites of *Monolithi* (☎26820 51755) and *Kanali* (☎26820 22741), on either side of the road at **Monolíthi** beach, a fine stretch of sand beginning 11km from Préveza.

Eating, drinking and nightlife

There are at least a dozen **tavernas** (many closed at lunchtime) scattered around the inland market lanes in central Préveza, with cafés and bars on the pedestrianized portion of waterfront esplanade Venizélou. Good inland choices include *Psatha*, Dhardhanellíon 4–6 (one block south of the Venetian clocktower along the main shopping thoroughfare, then west), for standard oven fare, and the long-running *Amvrosios*, specializing in grilled sardines and barrel wine at budget prices, on the lane – officially Grigoríou toú Pémptou – leading seaward (east) from the clocktower. If this is shut for any reason, try its adjacent competitors *Tou Stavraka* or *Iy Trata*, or the *Ouzeri Kaixis* at Parthenogoyíou 7, three lanes south. Just up from *Kaixis* at Nilabá 5, *Dinos* is one of the few establishments reliably open at midday, while *Saïtan Pazar*, on the tiny eponymous square (official Kóndou), is perhaps the most celebrated ouzerí in the old bazaar. By **night**, these pedestrianized alleys, particularly within a 100-metre radius of the fish-market building and the clocktower, come alive with an assortment of **bars**, **cafés** (including **Internet café** *Ascot* at Vasilíou Bálkou 6–8) and shops, patronized by a mixture of locals, guests from the surrounding resorts and denizens of the yachts moored at the esplanade. In terms of organized culture, July and August see a range of musical and theatrical events as part of the **Nikopolia festival**, held at various local outdoor venues, plus there's a summer outdoor **cinema** south of town on the road to Pandokrátoras; the winter one's in the centre on Ethnikís Andístasis.

Árta and around

Fifty kilometres northeast of Préveza lies **ÁRTA**, well situated in a loop of the broad Árakhthos River as it meanders towards the **Amvrakikós Gulf**, 20km to the south. One of the more pleasant mainland towns, it's a low-key place, very much the provincial capital, which retains much of its Ottoman-bazaar aspect (including a covered market on Vassíléos Pýrrou, and some celebrated medieval monuments, in the centre).

From the west, you enter town within sight of the restored packhorse **bridge**, subject of song and poetry throughout the mainland. A grisly legend – found elsewhere in the Balkans – maintains that the bridge-builder, continually thwarted by the current washing his foundations away, took the advice of a talking bird and sealed up his wife in the central pier; the bridge finally held but the woman's voice haunted the place thereafter.

Arrival and accommodation

Arriving by **bus**, you'll be dropped at the KTEL station on the riverbank, on the northeastern outskirts of town, though there is a discretional stop on the ring road east of both the modern and the Byzantine bridges. From the KTEL it's a ten-minute walk southwest along **Odhós Skoufá**, the main commercial street and thoroughfare, to the central **Platía Ethnikís Andístasis**. Skoufá, pedestrianized along much of its length (as are most of its narrower perpendiculars), and its parallel streets, Vassíléos Pýrrou and Konstandínou, wind through the oldest part of town. The main **taxi rank** is on Platía Kilkís, at the southwest end of Skoufá. If you travel by car, beware of the city-centre **fee-parking scheme** in effect during business hours: a red strip on the sign means parking of one to two hours – get a pay-and-display ticket from kerbside machines – while a green strip denotes long-term parking for residents only.

There are just two **hotels**, though neither constitutes great value. The *Amvrakia*, Priovólou 13 (☎26810 28311; ❸, en suite ❹), is the quieter choice, with a good position on a pedestrian way, just off Platía Ethnikís Andístasis. The *Cronos* (☎26810 22211; ❹), on Platía Kilkís, is air conditioned.

The Town

Árta was known anciently as Ambracia and had a brief period of fame under Pyrrhus, fourth-century BC king of Epirus; it was his capital, and base for the king's hard-won campaigns ("Another such victory and I am lost") in Italy – the original Pyrrhic victories. The foundations of a **temple of Apollo** and an **odeion** lie to either side of Vassíléos Pýrrou, but otherwise are scant remains from this period. At the northeast end of the street looms the **Froúrio**, the ancient acropolis and the citadel in every subsequent era; regrettably, it is now locked, except for performances at its open-air theatre.

More substantial monuments date from Árta's second burst of glory, following the 1204 fall of Constantinople, when the town was the centre of the

Despotate of Epirus, an autonomous Byzantine state. The despotate, which stretched from Corfu to Thessaloníki, was governed by the Angelos dynasty (the imperial family expelled from Constantinople) and survived until 1449, when the garrison surrendered to the Turks.

Most striking and certainly the most bizarre of the Byzantine monuments is the **Panayía Parigorítissa** (sometimes rendered Parigorítria; Tues–Sun 8.30am–3pm; €2), a grandiose, five-domed cube that rears above Platía Skoufá, at the southwest end of Skoufá. The interior is almost Gothic in appearance, with the main dome supported by an extraordinary cantilevered-pilaster system that looks unwieldy and unsafe. Up top, this insecurity is accentuated by a looming *Pandokrátor* (Christ in Majesty) mosaic in excellent condition, overshadowing the sixteenth- and seventeenth-century frescoes in the sanctuary and nave. The church, flanked by two side chapels, was built between 1283 and 1296 by Despot Nikiforos I as part of a monastic complex; of this, sixteen cells and the refectory remain east and south of the church, along with the excavated foundations of an early shrine.

Two smaller Byzantine churches from the same period also survive in the town. Both have a more conventional structure but are enlivened by highly elaborate brick-and-tile decorations on the outside walls. They're usually locked, but this is no tragedy since the exteriors present the main interest. **Ayía Theódora**, containing the fine marble tomb of the wife of Epirot ruler Michael II, stands in its own courtyard halfway down Pýrrou. A little further north, opposite the produce market, is thirteenth-century **Áyios Vassílios**, ornamented with glazed polychrome tiles and bas-reliefs.

Eating and drinking

Árta **restaurants**, what few there are, cater for locals rather than tourists. A classic working-man's canteen, with all the usual *mayireftá*, is *Papadhakos* at Skoufá 31. Most visitors, however, will gravitate towards the old bridge, where you can admire the structure at leisure over a coffee or a meal. *O Protomastoras* and the adjacent *Yéfira* offer adequate, inexpensive fare to a young crowd under shady trees, though both are really more geared up for drinks than food. In the evenings, people perform their *vólta* around Platía Ethnikís Andístasis or congregate in its **cafés**; a slightly less central, pleasant one, within sight of Panayía Paregorítissa, is *En Arti*, with seating by a fountain and plane tree.

Monasteries and churches around Árta

Amid the orange groves surrounding Árta, a number of **monasteries and churches** were built during the despotate, many of them by members of the imperial Angelos dynasty; all are well signposted with yellow-on-brown placards.

Within easy walking distance (2km south along Odhós Komménou, past the hospital turning) stands the **monastery of Káto Panayía** (daily: May–Sept 7am–1pm & 4.30–7.30pm; Oct–April 8am–1pm & 3–6pm; ring for admission), erected by Michael II between 1231 and 1271. This is now a working convent occupied by a dozen nuns and, in one corner of the garden, several caged peacocks. The *katholikón* in a shaded courtyard has extravagant exterior decoration, and frescoes inside showing Christ in three guises. Many of the frescoes are badly smudged, but the highlight is an undamaged version of Christ as Emmanuel in the front vault. The west outer wall sports a graphic *Last Judgement*, but this is one case where the interior is more compelling than the exterior.

Further out of Árta, 6km north by a circuitous route (11–12 buses daily from the ring-road stop), the monastic church of **Panayía Vlahernón** in Vlahérna village is engaging both inside and out. To the basic three-aisled twelfth-century plan, Michael II added the trio of domes in the following century, as well as the narthex; one of the two tombs inside is thought to be his. Having found the key custodian at the nearby *kafenío*, you enter the south narthex door under a fine **relief** of the Archangel Michael. Dissimilar columns support the added cupolas, but the church is more remarkable for what is normally hidden from view. The warden will lift a section of carpet to reveal a magnificent **mosaic**, just one portion of a vast marble floor punctuated with such tessellations. Only a few of numerous **frescoes** thought to be under plaster are exposed. This is the most beautiful of Árta's churches, worth contemplating at length from the *kafenío*.

If you get hooked, there are three more churches within easy reach of Árta, all signposted after a fashion; these have apparently never been associated with a monastery, and today serve as the graveyard chapels for the nearest village. **Panayía tís Bryónis** lies 800m up the side road towards Megárhi, the turning 6km out of Árta en route to Amfilohía; dating from 1232, it has fine exterior brickwork. By taking the road for Kostáki and Anéza from the historic bridge, and then turning west towards Plisí, you reach **Áyios Dhimítrios Katsoúris** after 5km, partly eleventh-century, with a freestanding belfry. If the priest is in at the neighbouring cottage, you'll get to see a frescoed interior. Some 2km further north, at the edge of Kirkizátes village, stands **Áyios Nikólaos tís Rodhiás**, a thirteenth-century, single-apsed chapel with contemporary frescoes in fair condition.

△ Panayía Parigorítissa in Árta

Around the Amvrakikós Gulf

Aside from Árta, the Rodhiá wetland reserve is the exceptional bright spot close to the **Amvrakikós Gulf**; moving clockwise around it, there is little else to prompt a stop. Eighteen kilometres west of Árta, you reach the six-kilometre side-turning for the **Rodhiá Wetland Centre**, in the village of Strongylí. This protected environment at the mouth of the Loúros River is home to a wide variety of fauna, from water buffalo to eels by way of an assortment of wading birds. The Centre conducts a set tour (daily by arrangement, ☎26830 41219) on motorized punts, which includes a stop at the medieval monastery of Panayías Rodhiás (also accessible by trail) and a meal of local dishes at a pavilion in mid-marsh.

At weekends, locals from Árta head for **seafood meals** at nearby coastal villages, and you should imitate them if passing through. The final approach to **KORONISSÍA** (25km southwest of Árta), more or less in the middle of the gulf, lies along a wave-lashed causeway flanked by a seaweed-caked beach popular with **windsurfers**. Today the village, once an island, offers a few fish **tavernas**, of which – last in the row – the most notable and consistently open (all year) is *Myrtaria* (*tou Patenda*), with more gulf-sourced, fair-priced seafood, and some pleasant **apartments** to rent next door (☎26810 24021; ❸). Up on the hill, yet another Byzantine church, the rather lopsided, tenth-century **Yénnisis tís Theotókou**, surveys the gulf and lagoons below.

Heading clockwise towards the open sea, **MENÍDHI**, 21km southeast from Árta, lies slightly off the main road, with three **hotels**, the best being the *Sorokos* at mid-quay (☎26810 88213; ❸), and plenty of fish **tavernas**. Of these, *Vouliagmeni* (*Pandioras*), the first on the left as you drop down from the highway, is famous for its fresh shrimps from the gulf, but has seen prices climb with fame – budget €22 minimum per person.

Amfilohía is promisingly situated at the head of the gulf, but proves to be a dull, small town fronted by rather stagnant water. If you need to stay the night on this coastline, **VÓNITSA**, 35km further west, is a more convenient and pleasant choice. Again, it's not a wildly exciting place, and frustratingly distant from real sea, but represents a definite improvement, with its lively waterside, tree-lined squares and a substantial Byzantine **castle** above. Among three surviving **hotels**, pick of the litter is the comfortable enough *Bel Mare* (☎26430 22394, ☎26430 22564; ❹) on the castle end of the seafront. As at Préveza across the gulf, sardines figure prominently on the menus of a half-dozen waterfront **tavernas**; bars and cafés are found by the water, or the little platía just inland. Infrequent **buses** cover the 17km to Préveza via the gulf-mouth tunnel, passing Áktio airport.

The Etolo-Akarnanian coast

Heading south for Mesolóngi and the Gulf of Kórinthos, there is not much of interest, at least on the more direct **inland route**. Beyond Amfilohía, you pass a few swampy lakes like Amvráki and Ozerós, pumped for irrigating the local tobacco. Halfway along the Amfilohía–Mesolóngi road, in-your-face ugly **Agrínio** – also the hottest town in Greece during summer – is of scant note except as the public transport link for this area, with buses northwest to Árta/Ioánnina, northeast to Karpeníssi and south to Andírio, from where there are local buses to Náfpaktos, and Pátra in the Peloponnese.

The **coast south from Vónitsa** is bleakly impressive, linked by a quiet stretch of road that skirts the shoreline, with nothing but parched wilderness inland. By default as much as anything else, the little resorts of **Páleros** and **Mýtikas** are the highlights, approachable also by a more roundabout route taking in the castle and ghost village of **Playiá**.

Páleros and Playiá

Some 18km south of Vónitsa on the direct road, the port-resort of **PÁLEROS** is almost a small town. Traditionally, local men sought their fortunes as captains and crew, staying away for years; today this is echoed only in yacht-based tourism, with UK package companies Sunsail and Mark Warner monopolizing the two local hotels. The district nearest the shore has some charm, with its smattering of old houses, yacht anchorages and a decent in-town **beach**; another grittily sandy one, shadeless but popular, extends 2km west of town. A **post office**, one stand-alone **ATM** and a clutch of **tavernas** around the harbour platía constitute the main amenities. The most obvious waterfront tavernas push bland, multilingual menus, so best forego the sea view in favour of *Platanos*, at the back of the square under the namesake plane tree, which dishes up a variety of grills and fresh fish, washed down by microbrewery beer, at fair prices (budget €18 per head). They can arrange **rooms**, too (☎26430 41664; ❸), more or less for the asking except in July or August.

If approaching Páleros from Lefkádha or Préveza, take the route via Néa Playía, which is slightly quicker and more scenic. Once on the east side of the channel and its pontoon bridge serving Lefkádha, follow signs towards Peratiá (and take special care at the hazardous turn above Kástro Peratiás). Carry on to **Néa Playía**, a modern, post-1953-earthquake village enlivened by an enormous **castle** guarding the straits with Lefkádha; like its neighbour Sánta Mávra it probably dates from the fourteenth century. The onward road curls under this, then continues 4km east and uphill to **old Playiá**, abandoned after the quake and inhabited now by just a few pastoralists; it's a surprisingly large place, looking northwest to the island and the Ionian, with lovely old tiled houses of a type no longer seen locally. From here it's 11km further through a pass to Stenó hamlet, then 7km to Páleros, paved the entire way.

Mýtikas

Beyond Páleros, you can find tiny deserted pebble beaches along the ten-kilometre stretch south to the next settlement, sleepy but pleasant **MÝTIKAS**; here, rows of old-fashioned houses strung along a pebbly shore look out onto the island of Kálamos, with a backdrop inland of sheer, amphitheatric mountainside. Behind the long but decidedly average shingle beach sprawls a steadily expanding, grid-plan modern annexe. There's nowhere as inviting to stay going southeast until you reach Náfpaktos (see p.353), and if you're coming northwest from Andírio, it's the first place that prompts thoughts of an overnight stay.

You'll probably need to stay here to catch the boat across to the island of Kálamos (see overleaf); among three central **hotels**, best is the *Kymata* (☎26460 81258 or 26460 81311; ❸) above a well-attended sweet shop, its rooms all with air conditioning, bug screens and fridges. Among **rooms**, most atmospheric are those above O *Glaros* **taverna** (☎26460 81240; ❶) – utterly spartan, with baths down the hall but unbeatable views on the gulf side. Fish meals downstairs are inexpensive and well-grilled; the only other alternative, *Taverna stou Thoma* at the far end of the village, is more elaborate but still very reasonable. Two **banks** with ATMs, plus a **post office**, complete the list of facilities.

Kálamos island

The island of **Kálamos**, the largest of a mini-archipelago southwest of Mýtikas, is essentially a partly wooded mountain rising abruptly from the sea. Though administratively a dependency of Lefkádha in the Ionian group, all public utility and transport links are to the mainland opposite. In summer there are usually a few yachts moored in the small harbour below the main village, Hóra, and at Pórto Leóne in the south, but otherwise the island, with a permanent population of about three hundred, sees few visitors and is ill equipped to host them. The only regular connection is a daily *kaïki* from Mýtikas, which leaves the mainland at about noon and returns from the island at 7.30am the next day; in summer the same craft may do scheduled day-trips, but otherwise you must charter the entire boat for €30 (one way). There is just one **place to stay** in Hóra – rooms kept by the Lezentinos family (☎26460 91238; ❶) – but it only operates during July and August, when it will probably be full anyway, so come with camping gear if you intend to stay overnight (though even this is difficult, given the lack of flat ground).

HÓRA, spread out among gardens and olive groves on the south coast, largely survived the 1953 earthquake which devastated many of the Ionian islands, though there's been no lack of insensitive building since. There are two basic *kafenía*/tavernas and a "supermarket" by the harbour, plus a bakery and sweet shop higher up, next to a **post office**. The gravelly village **beach** fifteen minutes southwest has no reliable facilities; the much better beach of **Merithiá** lies twenty minutes northeast of the port, via a rough scramble along the shore. Your reward will be 500m of sand and fine gravel which could easily host all the tourists Kálamos is ever likely to get, and is one of the better places to camp, though there's no shade or fresh water.

Kástro, an old fortified settlement at the north tip of the island facing Mýtikas, is linked to the port by a seven-kilometre asphalt road; the ninety-minute walk is drudgery, despite pine-shade and views, so try and hitch the sparse traffic. The small, five-bastioned castle here may possibly be Byzantine, and surveys the straits between here and Mýtikas, as suggested by the name of the road's-end hamlet 2km beyond, Episkopí ("Overlook"; no facilities). Small, exquisite beaches dot the coast between Hóra and Kástro, though they can only be seen and reached by sea.

Southwest of Hóra, a broad mule-and-tractor track leads across scrub-covered mountainside to **Kefáli (Pórto Leóne)**, its deep bay protected in all weathers and thus beloved of yacht flotillas. The lower village of a dozen buildings has been deserted since the 1953 earthquake, except for a single **taverna**, *Panos*. A higher, pirate-proof settlement of the same size, nearly invisible now, was abandoned after World War II when the local olive-oil shipping fleet was destroyed. It's a shadeless, two-hour walk from Hóra, with views across to the neighbouring island of Kastós to compensate; as ever in this region, you're best off going by boat.

Astakós, Oeniadae and Etolikó

South of Mýtikas, the coast road offers stunning views west over Kálamos, Kastós, Itháki, Kefalloniá and the Ehinádhes islets – one of the most dramatic seascapes in Greece. After 31km you reach **ASTAKÓS**, which means "lobster". You are, however, most unlikely to get lobster at any of the decidedly mediocre tavernas which line its quay on the north flank of the all-but-beachless gulf. Like Amfilohía, the location of the village is its most attractive attribute, though yacht flotillas call to take on water; Astakós was once a port of some importance, however, judging from the two parallel streets of the marketplace, where many Neoclassical buildings from the 1870s preserve their period details.

Arriving by land, the KTEL is at one end of the quay, while the single, vastly overpriced hotel, *Stratos* (☎26460 41911; ❾), sprawls at the other, overlooking the tiny, gravelly town beach; in peak season numbers of cheaper **rooms** are on offer elsewhere. There's just one daily summer **ferry** to Itháki and Kefalloniá at around midday; ring ☎26460 38020 for current departure time.

Beyond here the scenery becomes greener as the road winds for 26km over hills covered by the protected **Lesíni ash forest** – last remnant of a once-vast ecosystem – and then down onto the fertile floodplain of the Ahelóös River. At Katohí, by the river, there's a turning for the five-kilometre, well-signposted detour west to **ancient Oeniadae**, also known by its medieval name Trikard-hókastro. In ancient times, when the river delta was not so far advanced as today, Oeniadae was the most prominent port of western Greece, and irresistible to any conqueror; accordingly a section of the 7km of still-extant Hellenistic **walls and gates** loops around to defend it. The American School first excavated it in 1901, after which the city became overgrown again; recently the under-growth has been cleared to re-expose a number of monuments. From the site gate (usually open, free) you can with care drive most of the way up an access drive to the small **theatre**, backed into an ash-shaded hill with views west over the delta to the Ionian Sea. Closer to the main entrance, a stoutly fenced zone – unhappily locked – contains ancient **shipyards**, a fortification **tower** and an arched **gateway**.

East of the Ahelóös delta stands **ETOLIKÓ**, built on an island in the rather stagnant lagoon of the same name and reached by two causeways. The town was apparently founded in Byzantine times as a refuge from assorted raiders, but is today visibly less prosperous than Mesolóngi (see below), of which it seems a miniature version – there's an obvious Roma shanty-town west of the centre. Yet it could make an adequate emergency halt, with an acceptable en-suite **hotel** on the west-facing quay: the *Alexandra* (☎26320 23019; ❷). Next door is the town's fanciest **restaurant**, *To Stafnokari*, open at lunch and featuring local seafood (including eel), though the fare's not quite as good value as in Mesolóngi. There's the usual complement of bars and *kafenía* in the centre, plus a **bank** and **post office**. Blue-and-white urban buses ply to Mesolóngi, just 10km southeast, past the salt factories that are today the area's mainstay.

Mesolóngi and around

Mesolóngi (Missolongi), for most visitors, is irrevocably associated with **Lord Byron**, who died in the town, to dramatic effect, while organizing the local Greek forces during the War of Independence (see box overleaf). Mesolóngi can claim some attention for this literary past but, as in Byron's time, it's a fairly shabby and rather unromantic place: rainy from autumn to spring, and comprised largely of drab, modern buildings between which the locals enthu-siastically bicycle along a flat grid plan. Amazingly, it, rather than larger Agrínio, is the capital of Étolo-Akarnanía, a decision surely taken more on sentimental than practical grounds. To be fair, the town has been spruced up since the 1990s, especially around the centre, but if you come here on a pilgrimage, it's still best to move on the same day. If you have your own transport, you can get more out of the region by stopping at two underrated nearby archeological sites, **Pleuron** and **Kalydon**, major towns of the ancient Aetolians.

The Town

You enter the town from the northeast through the **Gate of the Exodus (Sortie)**, whose name recalls an attempt by nine thousand men, women and children to break out on April 12, 1826, culminating the Ottomans' year-long siege. In one desperate dash the Greeks managed to get free of Mesolóngi, leaving a group of defenders to destroy it – and some three thousand civilians not capable of leaving – by firing the powder magazines. But those fleeing were betrayed, ambushed on nearby Mount Zygós; less than two thousand evaded massacre or capture and enslavement by a large Albanian mercenary force.

Just inside this gate, on the right, partly bounded by the remains of the fortifications, is the **Kípos Iróön**, or "Garden of Heroes" (daily: summer 9am–1.30pm & 5–7pm; winter 9am–1.30pm & 4–7pm; free) – though signposted in English as "Heroes' Tombs" – where a tumulus covers the bodies of the town's unnamed defenders. Beside the tomb of the Souliot commander, Markos Botsaris, is a **statue of Byron**, erected in 1881, under which is buried the poet's heart (some sources claim it's his lungs). The rest of Byron's remains were taken back to his

O Lórdhos Výronos: Byron in Mesolóngi

Lord Byron arrived at Mesolóngi, a squalid, inhospitable place surrounded by marshland, in January 1824. The town, with its small port allowing access to the Ionian islands, was the western centre of **resistance** against the Ottomans. The poet, who had contributed much of his personal fortune to the war effort, as well as his own fame, was enthusiastically greeted with a 21-gun salute.

On landing, he was made **commander-in-chief** of the five-thousand-strong garrison, a role that was as much political as military. The Greek forces, led by brigand-chieftains, were divided into factions, and each one separately and persistently petitioned him for money. He had already wasted months on the island of Kefalloniá adjudicating their claims and quarrels before finalizing his own military plan – to march on Náfpaktos and from there take control of the Gulf of Kórinthos – but in Mesolóngi he was again delayed.

Occasionally Byron despaired: "Here we sit in this realm of mud and discord", he wrote at one juncture in his journal. But while other Philhellenes were returning home, disillusioned by the squabbles and larceny of the Greeks, or appalled by the conditions in this quasi-tropical town, he stayed, campaigning eloquently for the cause. Outside his house, he drilled soldiers; in the lagoon he rowed, and shot, and caught a fever. On April 19, 1824, Byron died, pronouncing a few days earlier, in a moment of resignation, "My wealth, my abilities, I devoted to the cause of Greece – well, here is my life to her!" It was, in fact, the most important contribution he could have made to the struggle.

The news of the poet's death reverberated across northern Europe, swelled to heroic proportions by his admirers. Arguably it changed the course of the war in Greece. When Mesolóngi fell again to the Ottomans, in spring 1826, there was outcry in the European press, and the French and English forces were finally galvanized into action, sending a joint naval force for protection. It was this force that unintentionally engaged an Egyptian fleet at Navarino Bay (see p.297), striking a fatal blow against the Ottoman navy.

Ever since independence, Byron has been a Greek national hero. Almost every town in the country has a street – Výronos – named after him; not a few men still answer to "Vyron" as a first name; and there was once an eponymous brand of cigarettes (perhaps the ultimate Greek tribute). Most importantly, the respect he inspired was for many years generalized to his fellow countrymen – before being dissipated after 1943 by British interference in the Resistance and bungling in Cyprus.

family home, Newstead Abbey, despite his dying request: "Here let my bones moulder; lay me in the first corner without pomp or nonsense." There had been speculation that Byron would have been offered the throne of an independent Greece; thus the touch of pomp in the carving of Byron's coat of arms with a royal crown above. Among the palm trees and rusty cannons there are other monuments – busts, obelisks, cenotaphs – to an astonishing range of American, German and French Philhellenes.

Elsewhere in the town, traces of Byron are sparse. The **house** in which he lived and died was destroyed during World War II, its site marked by a clumsy memorial garden on Levídhou, reached from the central platía by walking down to the end of Hariláou Trikoúpi and turning left.

Back in the central Platía Bótsari, the mock-Neoclassical town hall houses a small **museum** devoted to the revolution (Mon–Fri 9am–1.30pm & 4–7pm, Sat & Sun 9am–1pm & 4–7pm, closes 6pm winter; free), with some emotive paintings of the independence struggle on the upper floor (including a copy of Delacroix's *Gate of the Sortie*), reproductions of period lithographs and a rather disparate collection of Byronia on the ground floor, padded out with a brass souvenir plaque of Newstead Abbey. Pride of place, by the entrance, goes to an original edition of Solomos's poem *Hymn to Liberty*, now the words to the national anthem.

Practicalities

Long-distance **buses** arrive at the KTEL on Mavrokordhátou 5, next to Platía Bótsari, while the local blue-and-white ones park just a few paces away. Several banks with ATMs surround the square; the **post office** stands just a block east on Spyrídhona Moustaklí, opposite a supermarket.

Hotels in Mesolóngi are a bit cheerless, overpriced and often block-booked by Greek tour groups. If you need or want to stay in the town, a good option is the air-conditioned *Avra*, Hariláou Trikoúpi 5 (℡26310 22284; ❸); it's adjacent to the central platía and close to the best of Mesolóngi's eating and drinking venues. More upmarket and impersonal choices include the massive *Liberty*, Iróön Poly-tekhníou 41 (℡26310 28050; ❹), with park views from most rooms, one block from the Garden of Heroes, or the *Theoxenia* (℡26310 22493; ❺), a small complex amidst landscaping just south of town on the lagoon shore – the best choice if you're driving, though the 1970s-vintage rooms are ripe for an overhaul.

The prevailing Greek craze for cutting-edge **ouzerís** and **bars** has swept through Mesolóngi, resulting in a vastly improved eating and drinking scene, making a lunch stop at least something to plan on. The place is especially noted for its eels, hunted with tridents in the lagoon and then smoked or grilled fresh; also famous is the local *avgotáraho* or *haviára*, caviar made from grey mullet roe. The main concentration of **tavernas**, interspersed with a few bars, is along and around Athanasíou Razikótsika, a pedestrianized street one block south of similarly car-free Hariláou Trikoúpi. The most durable establishment is *Stin Agora* (*tou Panou*) at no. 7, with an upmarket interior and grilled eels as standard; also noteworthy are *Iy Rena* at no. 5 and *O Aris* at no. 23. In the narrow alleys – especially K. Metaxá – linking these two broader streets are far too many **bars**, kafenía **and ouzerís** to list – you'll find something to suit.

Around Mesolóngi: Tourlídha, Pleuron and Kalydon

Perhaps more interesting and enjoyable than any sight in town is a walk across the **Klísova lagoon**, past two **forts** which were vital defences against the Turkish navy. The lagoon, with its salt-evaporation ponds and fish farms, attracts a variety of coastal wading birds, especially in spring. A causeway extends for about 5km to reach the open sea at **TOURLÍDHA**, a hamlet of wood-plank and prefab summer cottages on stilts, plus a few **tavernas**, the most reliable of these (with rooms upstairs) being the *Toúrlidha*. If you can stomach the stench from the nearby salt-ponds, there's a packed-sand **beach** flanking the open sea to swim from, with showers and a few café-bars.

Some 4km northwest of town, on the major road to Etolikó, lies **ancient Pleuron** (signed also as Plévro; variable hours; enclosed but free), which reached its zenith during Hellenistic times. The access road has been paved and excavations have resumed. The most obvious remains are the massive **perimeter wall** of polygonal masonry, a small **theatre** whose stage is built against one of the towers, and an ingenious **reservoir**; equally impressive are sweeping views over the local salt pans and the lagoon.

About 10km east of Mesolóngi, a hazardous turn off the highway deposits you at the tiny car park and warden's shed of **ancient Kalydon** (enclosed but unlocked; free), being excavated by a Danish team each summer. Next to the entrance they've uncovered a curious rectangular structure, most likely a **bouleuterion**. Follow the signed track first to the massive foundations of a **Heroön**, with an intact subterranean tomb (locked), and then continue west through olive groves to the equally imposing plinths of a joint **temple to Apollo, Artemis and Laphrias**, atop a fortified and artificially augmented hill. Despite the hum of the motorway below, it's well worth the short detour, and the views are equal to Pleuron's.

Travel details

Buses

Buses detailed have similar frequency in each direction, so entries are given just once; for reference check under both starting point and destination.

Agrínio to: Corfu (bus/ferry, 2 daily in season; 4hr); Ioánnina (6 daily; 2hr 20min); Karpeníssi (1 daily, 2 Fri; 3hr 30min); Lefkádha (5 daily; 1hr 20min); Mesolóngi–Andírio (12 daily; 40min–1hr 15min).

Árta to: Ioánnina (10 daily Mon–Fri, 6 Sat & Sun; 1hr 30min); Prámanda and Ágnanda (1 daily 2pm; 1hr 30min); Melissourgí (Mon & Fri 2pm; 1hr 40min); Préveza (5 daily Mon–Fri, 2 Sat & Sun; 1hr); Theodhóriana (1 daily Tues & Thurs; 1hr 15min); Vourgarélli (1 daily Sat & Sun; 1hr).

Igoumenítsa to: Athens (5 daily; 8hr); Párga (4 daily Mon–Fri, 3 Sat, 1 Sun; 1hr); Préveza (2 daily; 2hr); Sývota (bus marked Pérdhika; 3 daily, 2 Sat; 30min); Thessaloníki (1 daily; 8hr 30min).

Ioánnina to: Athens (11 daily; 6hr 30min); Dodona (Mon & Fri 6.30am & 3.30pm; 40min); Igoumenítsa (8 daily, 7 Sat & Sun; 2hr); Kastoriá, via Kónitsa (2 daily, change at Neápoli; 5hr); Kónitsa (7 daily, 4 Sat & Sun; 1hr); Métsovo (4 daily Mon–Fri, 2 Sat & Sun; 1hr 30min); Monodhéndhri (Mon, Wed & Fri 6.15am & 3.15pm; 45min); Pápingo (Tues & Fri 5.30am/2.30pm; 1hr 15min); Párga (4 daily; 2hr 30min); Pátra via Agrínio (4 daily; 3hr 30min); Prámanda (2 daily Mon–Fri 5.45am & 3pm, Sat & Sun 3pm only; 2hr); Préveza (10 daily Mon–Fri, 8 Sat & Sun; 2hr); Thessaloníki (6 daily; 7hr); Tríkala, via Métsovo and Kalambáka (2 daily, 3 Fri & Sun; 3hr); Tsepélovo (2 daily Mon, Wed & Fri 6.15am & 3pm; 1hr 15min); Vovoússa (Fri 2pm, Sun 7.30am; 2hr 30min).

Kónitsa to: Dhístrato (Mon & Wed 1.45pm, Fri 2.30pm; 1hr 15min); Kerásovo (Mon & Fri 2pm; 45min); Molydhosképastos (2–3 weekly; 30min).

Mesolóngi to: Astakós (2 daily; 45min); Athens (8 daily; 4hr); Ioánnina (6 daily; 2hr 50min); Náfpaktos (3 daily; 45min); Pátra (8 daily; 1hr).

Préveza to: Glykí (1 daily; 1hr); Lefkádha (5 daily; 25min); Párga (5 daily Mon–Fri, 3 Sat & Sun; 1hr 30min).

Vónitsa to: Áktio (3 daily; 15min); Lefkádha (5 daily; 20min).

Ferries

Astakós to: Itháki and Kefalloniá (Sámi), 1 daily around mid-day, early May to mid-Sept only; 3hr 30min for full journey.

Igoumenítsa to: Corfu Town (almost hourly in season, 4am–10pm; 1hr for "fast" ferry, 1hr 30min for "slow"); Lefkími in southern Corfu (6 daily in summer, 7.30am–8.45pm, 4 daily in winter, 8.45am–6.30pm); 1hr; current info on ☎ 26650 26796); Paxí (Gáïos; 1 daily ferry Mon–Fri at 1pm, 2 Sat at 10.30am & 4pm, 1 Sun at 10.30am; 1hr 20min). Also large boats to Bari, Brindisi, Ancona and Venice (Italy). See box on p.454 for details.

Flights

All are on Olympic Airways/Aviation unless otherwise specified.

Ioánnina to: Athens (3–4 daily, plus 1 daily on Aegean; 1hr); Thessaloníki (5 weekly; 50min).

Préveza to: Athens (1 daily; 55min); Corfu (3 weekly; 25min); Kefalloniá (3 weekly; 25min); Sitía, Crete (3 weekly; 1hr 40min); Thessaloníki (2 weekly via Corfu; 1hr 45min); Zákynthos (3 weekly; 1hr 10min).

Macedonia and Thrace

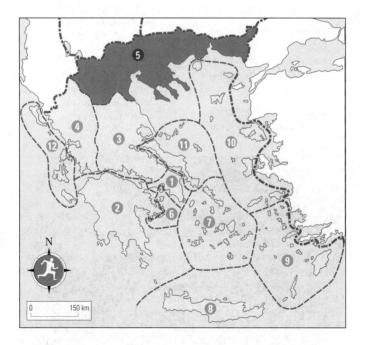

CHAPTER 5 # Highlights

✳ **Thessaloníki** Balkan in atmosphere, Greece's second city offers historic monuments and a vibrant nightlife. See p.484

✳ **Mount Olympus** The mythical home of the gods; a three-day hike to the summit offers pristine scenery and riots of wild flowers. See p.507

✳ **Vergina** Beguiling treasures unearthed in the poignant burial chambers of Macedonia's royal dynasty. See p.517

✳ **Édhessa** Clifftop wooden houses and impeccably restored water mills make this one of Greece's most inviting towns. See p.520

✳ **The Préspa lakes** Forming the leading ornithological reserve in the region, the reed-fringed shores are a haven for nature lovers. See p.524

✳ **Kastoriá** Situated on a wooded headland jutting into the pewter-coloured Lake Orestiádha, this unusual resort is the country's fur capital. See p.528

✳ **Mount Athos** Timeless Orthodox monasteries set among unspoilt landscapes in a semi-independent republic run by monks. See p.545

✳ **Dhadhiá** Oak and pine forests draped over volcanic ridges, home to black vultures and other rare raptors. See p.575

△ The Préspa lakes

5

Macedonia and Thrace

he two northern regions of **Macedonia** and **Thrace** have been part of the Greek state for less than a century. Macedonia (Makedhonía) was surrendered by the Turks after the Balkan wars in 1913; Greek sovereignty over western Thrace (Thráki) was not confirmed until 1923. As such, they stand slightly apart from the rest of Greece, an impression reinforced for visitors by architecture and scenery, customs and climate that seem more Balkan than typically Mediterranean. The two regions even have their own government ministry, in recognition of their specific nature and needs. In physical terms, they are characterized by densely forested mountains and a clutch of picturesque lakes to the west, and in the east by heavily cultivated flood plains and bird-rich river deltas. Essentially continental in nature, the climate is harsher than in the rest of the country, with steamy summers and bitterly cold winters, especially up in the Rodhópi mountain range that forms the border with Bulgaria. These factors, along with a dearth of good beaches and fewer direct charter flights from abroad, plus often poor-value accommodation, may explain why northern Greece is relatively little known to outsiders.

Only Halkidhikí, a beach-fringed sub-region trailing to the southeast of Thessaloníki, and lofty Mount Olympus, to the southwest, draw large numbers of visitors. While two of **Halkidhikí**'s three mountainous peninsulas serve as a playground for the inhabitants of Greece's second city, more hard-won pleasures – including stunning views – are available on the slopes of **Mount Olympus**, the mythical abode of the gods. If you are male, over 18 and interested enough in monasticism – or Byzantine art, music and architecture – to obtain a pilgrimage permit, **Mount Athos** may prove to be a highlight of a visit to Greece. This "Monks' Republic" occupies most of the spectacular third prong of Halkidhikí, and maintains control over twenty monasteries and numerous dependencies and hermitages. **Women** (and most female domesticated animals) have been **excluded** from the peninsula since a decree of 1060, although it is possible for both sexes to view the monasteries from the sea by taking a boat tour from the resorts of Ierissós and Ouranoúpoli in the secular part of Athos.

Part of northern Greece's charm lies in its non-touristy insouciance. Both the sybaritic capital of Macedonia, **Thessaloníki** (Salonica), and the region's

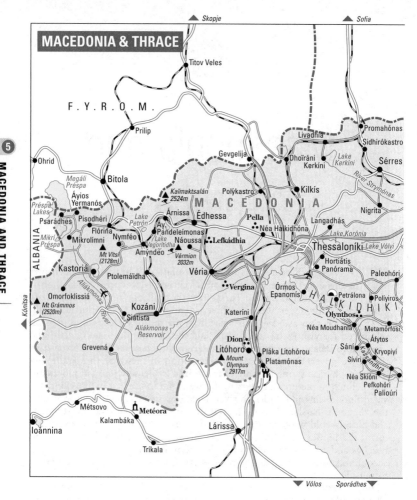

other main city, **Kavála**, just seem to get on with their vigorous day-to-day lives. Nonetheless, the region has some outstandingly beautiful spots, especially the **Préspa national park** in rugged western Macedonia and the bird-watchers' heaven of the **Kerkíni wetlands** to the east. The lakeside city of **Kastoriá** and the clifftop town of **Édhessa** are among Greece's most beguiling urban centres, thanks to a belated but determined attempt to restore some fine old buildings. Admittedly, the region's ancient sites are relatively modest, though there is one notable exception: the awe-inspiring Macedonian tombs discovered at **Vergina** in the 1970s. Not so well known are the Macedonian and Roman sites at **Pella**, with its fabulous mosaics, and at **Philippi**, St Paul's first stop in Greece, as well as an up-and-coming trio of archeological digs along the Thracian seaboard: **Abdera**, **Maroneia** and **Mesembria**. Few travellers on their way to Bulgaria or Turkey stray from the dull trunk road through eastern Thrace, but the well-preserved town of **Xánthi**, the waterfowl reserves

▲ *Plovdiv*

BULGARIA

River Néstos

RODHÓPI

Falakró (2230m) ▲ Paranésti Oréo
Dhráma Smínthi Ehínos
Alistráti Stavroúpoli Xánthi T H R A C E Komotiní
  •• Philippi Pórto Marónia
Kavála Khryssoúpoli Fanári Lágos Maroneía
Eléftheroúpoli Néa Abdera Platanítis Mesimvría
• Amphipolis Karváli Keramotí Ay. Harálambos Mesembria Alexandhroúpoli
Néa Péramos Thássos (Liménas) *Évros Delta*
Asproválta Loutrá Skála *Thássos*
Stavrós Eleftherón Prínou
Olymbiádha
• Stageira Limenária
Stratóni
Ierissós Kamariótissa
Ouranoúpoli Hóra (Samothráki)
Pyrgadhíkia Karyés *Samothráki*
Vourvouroú *Mount Athos*
Parthenónas Sárti
Toróni Kalamítsi *Límnos*
Pórto Koufó Mýrina

Svilengrad Edirne
  Kastaniés
  Orestiádha
Metaxádhes Pýthio
  Dhidhymótiho
  Soufí
  Dhadhiá
  DHADHIÁ FOREST RESERVE
  Kípi Ipsala
  Keşan
  TURKEY

İstanbul
İstanbul
İstanbul

TURKEY

N

0 ——— 50 km

▼ *Lávrio, Lésvos & Híos*

of the **Évros delta** and the **Dhadhiá Forest**, with its black vultures, deserve more than just a meal stop. **Alexandhroúpoli** rewards the curious with one of the best ethnological museums in the whole of Greece. Other attractions are two islands just off the coast – popular **Thássos** and introverted **Samothráki**, covered in Chapter Ten.

Public **transport** in the north is somewhat limited. A few trains link some of the urban centres, but the railway line east from Thessaloníki curls unhelpfully inland, bypassing Kavála altogether and leaving buses or your own transport as the only alternatives for travelling along the coast. The road system has improved beyond recognition in recent years, however, and the "Via Egnatia" highway – sections of which are already operational – will by 2010 provide an uninterrupted link between the west coast and the Bulgarian and Turkish borders. The Athens–Thessaloníki motorway should also be finally completed by around the same date.

Thessaloníki and western Macedonia

Thessaloníki is the focal point for travellers in northern Greece, with its international airport, major rail and bus hub, motorway links, its fine churches and museums, and a range of facilities, including a couple of top-rate hotels – plus plenty of good food, culture, nightlife and entertainments. The train ride west from here to Flórina via the appealing hilltop town of **Édhessa** is one of the most scenic in the country. More remote **Kastoriá**, speckled with Byzantine monuments, is also highly rewarding. Way up in the northwestern corner, the secluded **Préspa lakes**, straddling the frontiers of three countries, constitute one of the finest wildlife refuges in the Balkans, but are virtually inaccessible unless you have your own transport. The biggest natural attraction in this part of Macedonia, however, has to be **Mount Olympus** (Óros Ólymbos); the fabled home of the gods soars high above the town of **Litóhoro**, easily approached from the highway or rail line between Thessaloníki and Lárissa. Near the town of **Véria**, another transport hub, lie the region's most fascinating ancient finds, the tombs of Philip II of Macedonia and other members of his dynasty at **Vergina**. Macedonia's southwestern reaches, around **Kozáni**, are not as compelling but do boast some fine views towards the natural barrier of the Píndhos mountains.

Thessaloníki (Salonica)

The administrative capital of Macedonia and Thrace, **THESSALONÍKI** – or Salonica, as it is sometimes known to English-speakers – has a distinctly Balkan feel that sets it apart from other Greek cities. Situated at the head of the Gulf of Thessaloníki, a horseshoe-shaped inner recess of the Thermaic Bight, it seems open to the rest of the world, with a wide ethnic mix and an air of general prosperity, stimulated by a major university, an international trade fair and a famously avant-garde live music and entertainment scene. The food is generally better than in the rest of the country, too: there are some very sophisticated restaurants, but also flavoursome traditional fare on offer in a great number of old-fashioned ouzerís and undeniably Turkish-influenced tavernas.

Athenians have always delighted in disparaging their rival city as "Bulgaria", especially at football matches. In fact Thessaloníki is the main metropolis for 1923 refugees from Asia Minor, a presence most obvious in the preponderance of Turkish surnames (such as Dereli, Mumtzi and Aslanoglu) and the spicy Anatolian food seldom seen anywhere else in Greece.

A commercial and industrial centre, rather than a tourist resort, the city has enough to offer the visitor for two or three days, at least. Its many **churches** (see box, p.500) constitute a showcase of Orthodox architecture through the ages, while you can catch glimpses of the Turkish city both in the walled Upper City and in the modern grid of streets on the flatlands below: isolated pockets of **Ottoman buildings**, many of them Islamic monuments, which miraculously survived the 1917 fire (see below). Modern Greek architecture is exemplified by Art Deco piles dating from the city's twentieth-century heyday, put up in time for the first International Trade Fair in 1926. Much of the city was restored when it was European Capital of Culture in 1997, while the Byzantine and other buildings that suffered damage in the severe 1978 earthquake are still undergoing painstaking repairs. Thessaloníki's many and often excellent **museums** cover subjects as varied as Byzantine culture, the city's Jewish heritage, folklife, musical instruments, Atatürk (who was born here) and, more recently, modern art and photography. For most visitors, however, the one that stands out is the **Archeological Museum**, albeit depleted since the transfer of most Philip II-related exhibits back to the burial sites at Vergina.

Some history

When King Cassander of Macedonia founded the city in 315 BC, on the site of the ancient Greek settlement of Thermae, he named it after his wife, half-sister of **Alexander the Great**: in turn she had received her name, Thessalonike, after the Macedons' decisive victory (*nike*) over the Thessalians under her father, Philip II. It soon became the region's cultural and trading centre, issuing its own coins.

Macedonia became a **Roman province** in 146 BC, and **Salonica**, with its strategic position allowing both land and sea access, was the natural and immediate choice of capital. Its fortunes and significance were boosted by the building of the Via Egnatia, the great road linking Rome (via Brindisi) with Byzantium and the East, along whose course Amphipolis, Philippi and Neapolis (now Kavála) were also to develop.

Christianity had slow beginnings in the city. Saint Paul visited twice, being driven out on the first occasion after provoking the local Jewish community. On the second, in the year 56 AD, he stayed long enough to found a church, later writing the two Epistles to the Thessalonians, his congregation there. It was another three centuries, however, before the new religion took full root. **Galerius**, who acceded as eastern emperor upon Byzantium's break with Rome, provided the city with virtually all its surviving late Roman monuments, including the **Rotónda** and the **Arch** named after him – and its patron saint, Demetrius (Dhimítrios), whom he martyred. The first resident Christian emperor was **Theodosius** (reigned 379–95), who after his conversion issued the Edict of Salonica, officially ending paganism.

Under Justinian's rule (527–65) Salonica became the second city of **Byzantium** after Constantinople, which it remained – under constant pressure from Goths and Slavs – until its sacking by Saracens in 904; today the city's Byzantine monuments undoubtedly surpass the Roman ones. The storming and sacking continued under the Normans of Sicily (1185) and with the Fourth Crusade (1204), when the city became for a time capital of the Latin Kingdom of Salonica. It was, however, restored to the Byzantine Empire of Nicea in 1246, reaching a cultural "**golden age**" amidst the theological conflict and political rebellion of the next two centuries, until Turkish conquest and occupation in 1430.

Thessaloníki was the premier **Ottoman Balkan city** when Athens was still a backwater. Its population was as varied as any in the region, with Greek Orthodox Christians in a distinct minority. Besides Ottoman Muslims, who had called the city "Selanik" since their arrival in 1430, a generation before the conquest of Constantinople, there were Slavs (who knew and still know it as "Solun"), Albanians, Armenians and, following the Iberian expulsions after 1492, the largest European **Jewish community** of the age (see box on p.497).

The modern quality of Thessaloníki is due largely to a disastrous **fire** in 1917 which levelled most of the old plaster houses along a labyrinth of Ottoman lanes, including the entire Jewish quarter with its 32 synagogues, rendering 70,000 – nearly half the city's population – homeless. The city was rebuilt, often in a special form of Art Deco style, over the following eight years on a grid plan prepared under the supervision of French architect and archeologist Ernest Hébrard, with long central avenues running parallel to the seafront, and cross-streets densely planted with shade trees. Hébrard's prohibition of high-rises was blithely disregarded, however, within two decades.

The city's opulence has traditionally been epitomized by the locals' sartorial elegance, but since the 1990s an upsurge in **prosperity**, owing to a stable economy and, undoubtedly in part, EU subsidies, has resulted in an upwardly mobile class, whose lifestyles offer a sharp contrast with those of a permanent floating underclass living in shantytowns near the port. There, Pontic or Black Sea Greeks flog substandard goods at the street markets, while unemployed Albanians and eastern European refugees eke out a meagre living by selling contraband cigarettes or cleaning car windscreens. Since around 2000, they have been joined by Africans peddling bootleg CDs. Visitors and residents alike face a

The Macedonian controversy

Since the early 1990s **Macedonia** has been the subject of much controversy in Greece. While inter-ethnic strife is nothing new in the Balkans, what sets this specific disagreement apart is the **ancient historical dimension**. The name Macedonia is a geographical term of long standing, applied to an area that has always been populated by a variety of races and cultures. It is today divided unequally between Greece (the lion's share), Bulgaria and the Former Yugoslav Republic of Macedonia (FYROM), with a tiny fraction in Albania.

The original Kingdom of Macedonia, which gained pre-eminence under **Philip II** and his son **Alexander the Great**, was part of the Greek cosmos; **Aristotle**, born at Stageira, Halkidhikí, tutored Alexander. The capital, first established at **Vergina**, was transferred around 400 BC to **Pella**, which shortly afterwards became the capital of Greece. The **empire** lasted for little more than two centuries, exhausted by its galloping expansion: under Alexander's dynamic and despotic leadership Macedonia spread as far as Egypt and India. The lands were then controlled successively by the Romans, Saracens and Bulgars, while pockets were settled by Albanians and Serbs; it was part of the cosmopolitan Byzantine empire before eventual subjugation under Ottoman Turkish rule.

In the late nineteenth century, when the disintegration of the **Ottoman empire** began to raise the issue of future national territories, the name Macedonia denoted simply the geographical region. Its highly heterogeneous population included Greeks, Jews, Vlachs, Albanians, Turks and various Slavs. The first nationalist struggles for the territory began in the 1890s, when small armies of Greek *andartes*, Serbian *chetniks* and Bulgarian *comitadjis* took root in the mountains, battling each other ferociously before uniting briefly against the Ottomans in the first Balkan War (1912).

Following Turkish defeat, the **Bulgarians**, traditionally Greece's second foe, laid sole claim to Macedonia in the second Balkan War (1912–13), but were defeated by a Greco–Serb alliance; a 1913 agreement between the victors divided much of Macedonian territory between them, roughly along linguistic/ethnic lines. During World War I the Bulgarians occupied much of Greek Macedonia, before capitulating in 1917. After Versailles, a small part of Slav-speaking Macedonia remained in Bulgaria, and Greek-speakers living in Bulgaria were "exchanged" for Bulgarian-

complex of **nuisances** all too reminiscent of those experienced in many other large Mediterranean cities: the discharge of untreated industrial and household waste into the Gulf (with slight improvements in the early part of the twenty-first century), and traffic jams on the main avenues, despite a comprehensive one-way system and a ring road.

Arrival, information and city transport

Arriving in Thessaloníki is fairly straightforward. The **train station** on the west side of town, with convenient bus links and a reliable taxi rank, is just a short walk from both the central grid of streets and the harbour. **Buses** arrive at the main terminal (predictably called "Makedonia"), located some way to the west of the city centre at Yiannitsón 194 (⊕2310 500 111), from where buses #1 and #78 take you to the train station (and in the latter case on to the airport), while #31 heads along Egnatía.

"Makedonia" **airport** is located 15km south of the city centre. Facilities include a tourist booth of sorts, operating restricted hours, and ATMs, located near the first-floor café, on departures level. City bus #78 (€0.70) shuttles back and forth from the airport to the KTEL bus terminal once or twice hourly

speakers in Greece, under the 1919 Treaty of Neuilly. Then, under the terms of the Treaty of Lausanne in 1923, hundreds of thousands of ethnic Greek refugees from Asia Minor were settled throughout Greece (what would now be called ethnic cleansing). In the north they swamped the remaining Slavophones.

The position of Yugoslavia, however, under Tito, was more ambiguous. Yugoslavia had established the **Socialist Republic of Macedonia** in its share of the historical territory, and from time to time Belgrade issued thinly veiled irredentist threats. When the Yugoslav federation fell apart chaotically and violently in mid-1991, and the population of Yugoslav Macedonia voted overwhelmingly for an independent state, with Skopje as its capital, many Greeks predicted that the tiny resourceless country would not survive, especially given its "ethnic heterogeneity". But under wily autocrat President Gligorov the population rallied together. Both officially and at grassroots level, Greek reaction was vitriolic, especially when the fledgling nation provocatively adopted the sixteen-pointed star of Vergina (the symbol of the ancient Macedonian dynasty) on its flag and coinage (later abandoned). Greece implored its allies not to recognize the new state and, increasingly rebuffed by the international community, the PASOK government instigated a unilateral **economic boycott** of the new republic, eventually lifted in 1995.

After negotiations, the country was officially recognized by the international community as the Former Yugoslav Republic of Macedonia (**FYROM**). Greeks grudgingly accepted this *fait accompli*, but virtually all still refuse to use the name. The media refer to it as *Ta Skópia* and its people as *Skopianí*; Greek tabloids tend to use the phrase "pseudo-statelet of Skopje" and the press is not allowed to refer in print to Yugoslav "Macedonia" – the Greek rendition of the official acronym is "PYDM" (Próin Yougoslavikí Dhimokratía tis Makedhonías). Icons of ancient Macedonian culture, such as the sixteen-pointed star of Vergina (albeit sometimes missing four rays) and images of the heroic figure of Alexander the Great, are ubiquitous in northern Greece. At the height of the crisis, official posters and stickers throughout Greece proclaimed that Macedonia had always been part of Greece and exhorted visitors to "read history". Even now, although the brouhaha has dropped from the fever pitch that it reached back in the 1990s, the Macedonian question remains the subject of fiery arguments in Greece and is best avoided in conversation.

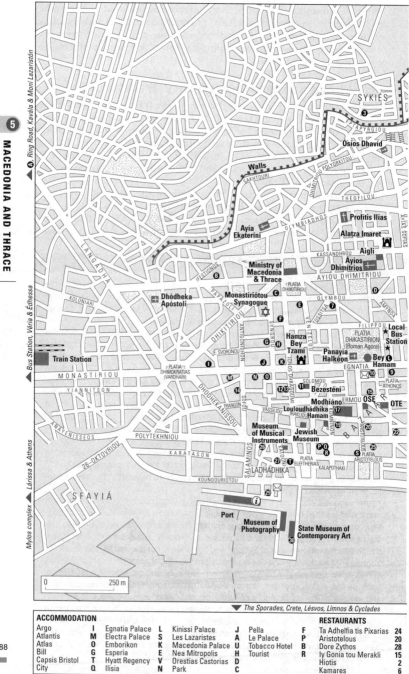

SYKIÉS

Osios Dhavid

Walls

Profitis Ilias

Alatza Imaret

Ayía
Ekateríni

Aigli

Ayios
Dhimitrios

Ministry of
Macedonia
& Thrace

Dhódheka
Apóstoli

Monastiriótou
Synagogue

Local
Bus
Station

PLATIA
DHIKASTIRION
(Roman Agora)

Hamza
Bey
Tzamí

Panayía
Halkéon

Bey
Hamam

Train Station

PLATIA
DHIMOKRATIAS
(VARDHARI)

Bezesténi

Modhiáno

OSE

OTE

Louloudhádhika
Hamam

Museum
of Musical
Instruments

Jewish
Museum

PLATIA
ELEFTHERIAS

PLATIA
ARISTOTELOUS

LADHÁDHIKA

SFAYIÁ

Port

Museum of
Photography

State Museum of
Contemporary Art

The Sporades, Crete, Lésvos, Límnos & Cyclades

| 0 | 250 m |

ACCOMMODATION						RESTAURANTS	
Argo	I	Egnatia Palace	L	Kinissi Palace	J	Pella	F	Ta Adhelfia tis Pixarias	24
Atlantis	M	Electra Palace	S	Les Lazaristes	P	Le Palace	P	Aristotelous	20
Atlas	O	Emborikon	K	Macedonia Palace	U	Tobacco Hotel	B	Dore Zythos	28
Bill	G	Esperia	E	Nea Mitropolis	H	Tourist	R	Iy Gonia tou Merakli	15
Capsis Bristol	T	Hyatt Regency	V	Orestias Castorias	D			Hiotis	2
City	Q	Ilisia	N	Park	C			Kamares	6

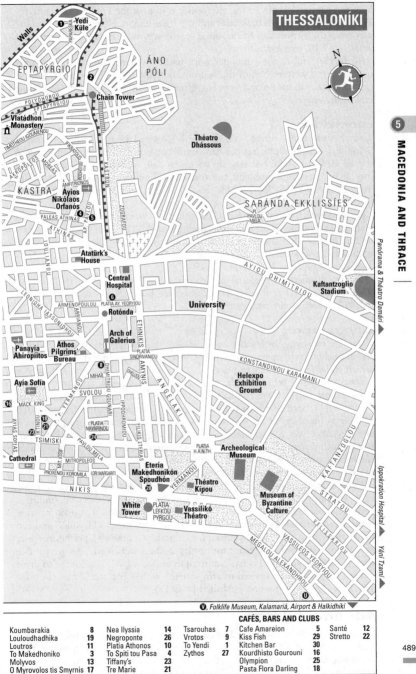

THESSALONÍKI

Walls
Yedi Küle ❶
PAPARESKA
EPTAPÝRGIO ❷
ÁNO PÓLI
POLYDHOROU
EPTAPÝRGIOU
Chain Tower
Vlatádhon Monastery ⛪
TIMOTHEOU IGOUMENOU
IPPOKRATOUS OLYMBIADHOS
Théatro Dhássous
AKROPOLEOS
MOREAS
AFXENTIOU
KÁSTRA
AMFITRIONOS
Áyios Nikólaos Orfanós ❹ ❺
PALEAS ATHINAS
KASTRON
ZOGRATOU
SARÁNDA EKKLISSÍES
PAVLOU MELA
IOULIANOU
ATHINAS
AP. PAVLOU
Atatürk's House
AYIOU DHIMITRIOU
Central Hospital ❻
ARMENOPOULOU
PLATIA AY. YEORYIOU
Rotónda ●
University
LEONIDHA IASSONIDHOU
ARRIANOU
ETHNIKIS AMÍNIS
Kaftantzoglio Stadium
Arch of Galerius
Panayía Ahiropíitos 🕇
Athos Pilgrims' Bureau
PLATIA SINDRIVANIOU
DHELFON
KONSTANDINOU KARAMANLI
❽ MIHAÍL
DHIMITRIOU GOUNARI
IPPODHROMIOU
Helexpo Exhibition Ground
Ayia Sofia 🕇
SVOLOU
YERMANOU
MACK. KING ⓰
PLATIA NAVARINOU
FILIKIS ETERIAS
ANGELAKI
⓲ ⓴ⓩ ❷❹
PLATIA H.A.N.TH.
IONOS
AVIAS SOFIAS
ⓩ TSIMISKI
PAVLOU MELA
Archeological Museum
Cathedral 🕇
MITROPOLEOS
PROXENOU KOROMILA LORI MARGARITI
MIT. IOSIF
Eteria Makedhonikón Spoudhón ❷❽
YERMANOU
KAFTANZOGLOU
N I K I S
Théatro Kípou
STRATOU
White Tower
PLATIA LEFKOU PYRGOU
Vassilikó Théatro
Museum of Byzantine Culture
VELISSARIOU
MEGALOU ALEXANDHROU
VASSILEOS YEORYIOU
Ⓥ
ⓤ

Ⓥ, *Folklife Museum, Kalamariá, Airport & Halkidhíki* ▼

					CAFÉS, BARS AND CLUBS	
Koumbarakia	**8**	Nea Ilyssia	**14**	Tsarouhas	**7**	Cafe Amareion	**5**	Santé	**12**
Louloudhadhika	**19**	Negroponte	**26**	Vrotos	**9**	Kiss Fish	**29**	Stretto	**22**
Loutros	**11**	Platia Athonos	**10**	To Yendi	**1**	Kitchen Bar	**30**		
To Makedhoniko	**3**	To Spiti tou Pasa	**4**	Zythos	**27**	Kourdhisto Gourouni	**16**		
Molyvos	**13**	Tiffany's	**23**			Olympion	**25**		
O Myrovolos tis Smyrnis	**17**	Tre Marie	**21**			Pasta Flora Darling	**18**		

between 6am and 11pm; in the city centre it stops at the Folklife Museum, the White Tower, Platía Dhimokratías and the train station, plying Tsimiskí on the way from the airport and Mitropóleos on the way back. A **taxi** ride into town comes to €10, plus extras.

All **ferries** call at the passenger port, within walking distance of the train station, at the western end of the seafront. For all ferry agencies, see "Listings" on p.505; Aegean routes and frequencies are given in the "Travel details" at the end of the chapter.

Information

The abysmal **EOT** office is "temporarily" located in the harbour terminal (Mon–Fri 7.30am–3pm, Sat 8.30am–3pm) but is not worth making a special trip to. A fairly useful but not always up-to-date **website** is ⓦ www.saloniki .org. If you have any problems, the **tourist police** post (daily 8am–2pm; plus Tues, Thurs & Fri 5–9pm; ☎2310 554 870/871) is at Dhodhekaníssou 4, off Platía Dhimokratías.

For detailed city **maps**, the one published by Emvelia, which also includes Halkidhikí and the immediate surroundings of the city, is best; they also do a folding map of Thessaloníki if you don't want the indexed atlas. A useful **book**, with a large-scale folding map, is the recently reprinted *Monuments of Thessaloníki* by Apostolos Papayiannopoulos (€8.30), available at many bookshops. Other recommended regional archeological guides, *Wandering in Byzantine Thessaloniki* and *Monuments of Thessaloniki* (see box, p.501), are easier to find locally but have rudimentary street plans.

City transport

There are two types of **local buses** (€0.70): the orange articulated "caterpillar" models which operate within the city, and the deep-red or blue buses which travel further afield, to places such as Panórama. In most cases there's an automatic ticket machine on the bus (correct money only), but there are still a few where you pay the conductor at the rear entrance. Useful lines include #10 and #11, both of which ply the length of Egnatía/Karamanlí. From Platía Eleftherías (just behind the seafront), buses initially run east along Mitropóleos; line #5 takes you to the archeological and folklore museums, and #22/28 heads north through Kástra to the highest quarter, known as Eptapýrgio. **Taxis** (dark-blue and white livery) are plentiful and reliable, but drivers refuse to go to destinations they find inconvenient.

If you bring your own car, it's best to use the attended fee-**parking** area that occupies all of Platía Eleftherías, where you pay on exit. Otherwise, finding a kerbside space is a fairly hopeless task, even in the suburbs; if you do manage to find a space you then usually have to go to a *períptero* to buy blue-and-red strip cards which you cancel yourself for an hour at a time (€1 per hour) – buy as many as you need in advance for display in the windscreen. Fees are payable 8am to 8pm Monday to Friday, 8am to 3pm on Saturday. If you intend to drive around the city, you're advised to arm yourself with a map that shows the one-way system (such as the one published by EOT).

Accommodation

From after Easter until the end of August, reasonably priced **hotel** rooms are fairly easy to find, albeit not always attractively situated. You will, however, find accommodation more expensive than elsewhere in Greece, even Athens, for equivalent facilities; a couple of **luxury** establishments seem to come on the scene every year and some of these are of the highest international standard. During the **International Trade Fair** (Sept) and the autumn festival season (Oct and Nov) hotels are allowed to add a **twenty-percent surcharge** to the standard rate. Low season runs from June to August, this being a business-oriented city rather than a tourist resort; in the heat of summer air conditioning is more than a luxury.

At the lower end of the price range, none of the city hotels charging less than €25 can be recommended, while most of the modest to comfortable hotels cluster around the southwestern end of Egnatía – although many of the establishments here are plagued by street noise. Others are concentrated on or around quieter Syngroú and in the more agreeable zone between Eleftherías and Aristotélous squares.

The closest **campsites** are at the small resorts of Ayía Triádha and Órmos Epanomís, 24km and 33km away respectively. Both are EOT sites and, of the two, the further is the better – as is the beach there. Take bus #73 from Platía Dhikastiríon for Ayía Triádha, bus #69 for Órmos Epanomís.

Lower Egnatía

Argo Egnatía 11 ☎2310 519 770. An old affair with basic but acceptable rooms, some of which have private facilities. ❷

Atlantis Egnatía 14 ☎2310 540 131. Mostly with shared bathrooms, with the better rooms facing a side street. ❷

Atlas Egnatía 40 ☎2310 537 046. A very friendly hotel, centrally located and the furthest of the Lower Egnatía hotels from the train station. Some rooms are en suite. Those at the front are noisy. ❷

Ilisia Egnatía 24 ☎2310 528 492. A good deal, this hotel has purpose-built en-suite facilities. ❸

Syngróu and around

Bill Syngroú 29, cnr Amvrossíou ☎2310 537 666. In a quiet, tree-lined side street, this is a good find, if getting a bit well worn; rooms have balconies, and original bathrooms in en-suite units (avoid the bathless rooms, they're in dire need of refurbishment). ❷

Emborikon Syngroú 14, cnr Egnatía ☎2310 514 431. Good value, despite the shared bathrooms, and with helpful staff. ❷

Esperia Olýmbou 58 ☎2310 269 321, ℱ2310 269 457. Slightly overpriced rooms, with views north to the hills. ❹

🏃 **Kinissi Palace** Egnatía 41 and Syngroú ☎2310 508 081, ℯinfo@kinissi-palace. gr. By far the smartest in the area, this hotel is good value for money. Its comfortable rooms all have mod cons, but they are marred by cramped bathrooms and noisy air con. The hotel boasts a sauna, *hamam* and massage service. There is an appealing bar and a decent restaurant, the *Averof.* ❼

Nea Mitropolis Syngroú 22 ☎2310 525 540, ℱ2310 539 910. Clean, good value and well maintained; not too noisy despite its proximity to Egnatía. ❸

Park Íonos Dhragoúmi 81 ☎2310 524 121, ℱ2310 524 193. Modern and sterile, but comfortable, spotless, double-glazed rooms with limited sea views. ❹

Pella Íonos Dhragoúmi 63 ☎2310 524 221 or 2310 555 550, ℱ2310 524 223. A tall, narrow, modern hotel on a moderately quiet street; pleasant, impeccably clean rooms and modern bathrooms. ❸

Rest of the city

🏃 **Capsis Bristol** Oplopíou 2 and Katoúni ☎2310 506 500, ⓦwww.capsisbristol .gr. Thessaloníki's only boutique hotel to date, with twenty period-furnished rooms in an impeccably restored 1870 building; the *Dhipnosofistis* restaurant and *Medusa* bistro are further attractions. ❽

City Komninón 11 ☎2310 269 421–9, ⓦwww .cityhotel.gr. One of the newest establishments in the city, its smart spacious rooms with state-of-the-art bathrooms are obviously aimed at business travellers. Some have balconies offering views of the Upper Town. Attractive breakfast bar where a bountiful American-style buffet can be sampled. ❻

Egnatia Palace Egnatía 61 ☎2310 222 900, ⓦwww.egnatia-hotel.gr. A smart hotel in a modern building with some Art Deco flourishes, it has spacious rooms whose modish decor ranges from kitsch to stylish; the *Wellness Paradise* spa presumably takes its inspiration from the disused Turkish baths across the road, but that's where the comparison ends. ❻

Electra Palace Platía Aristotélous 9/A ☎2310 294 000, ℱ2310 235 947. In one of the town's most prestigious positions – but it can get noisy when there are events in the square. That said, it is as palatial inside as out, with large rooms and a good dining room, albeit with a slightly dated air. **❼**

Hyatt Regency Near the airport, on Halkidhikí road ☎2310 401 234, ⓦwww.hyatt.com. Offering world-class service and comfort, this large, opulent hotel lives up to the chain's high standards, but is really aimed at the business traveller. Excellent restaurant, spacious rooms and a casino. **❽**

Les Lazaristes (Domotel) Kolokotróni 16, Stavroúpoli ☎2310 647 400, ⓕ2310 647 484, ⓦwww.domotel.gr. Opposite the Moní Lazaristón arts complex (see p.504), this handsome new hotel, in a converted tobacco factory, is a long way from the centre but has convenient access for people with a car (free parking). Beautiful magazine interiors, with a lot of attention to detail, and a gorgeous pool; the *Fred and Ginger* restaurant draws locals with its gourmet cuisine. **❼**

Macedonia Palace Megálou Aléxandhrou 2 ☎2310 897 197, ⓔmpalace@mkp.grecotel.gr. The smart, elegant and spacious rooms and suites in this city establishment hotel come with the best seafront views and an excellent restaurant, the *Porphyra*, famous for its Sunday brunch. **❽**

Orestias Castorias Agnóstou Stratiótou 14, cnr Olymbou ☎2310 276 517, ⓕ2310 276 572.

With most rooms in this 1920s building recently converted to en suite, this is a prime, friendly choice and one of the quieter hotels in the city; reservations advised. **❷**

Le Palace Tsimiskí 12 ☎2310 257 400, ⓦwww.lepalace.gr. This Art Deco hotel is extremely good value: spacious rooms with modern baths and double glazing (but it's still best to ask for a room away from the street). Characterful common areas comprise a mezzanine lounge, a ground-floor café and a restaurant. An outstanding buffet breakfast is included. B&B **❻**

The Tobacco Hotel (Davitel) Ayíou Dhimitríou 25 ☎2310 515 002, ⓕ2310 530 711, ⓦwww.davitel.gr. Sleek double-glazed rooms with contemporary decor verging on the spartan but comfortable; efficient air con, polite staff and healthy breakfasts served in a designer-rustic mezzanine salon. Although it takes its name from the converted 1922 tobacco warehouse in which it is housed, you can ask for non-smoking rooms. **❼**

Tourist Mitropóleos 21 ☎2310 270 501, ⓕ2310 226 865. A friendly, rambling *belle époque* palace with parquet-floored lounges and breakfast salon and a 1920s Swiss lift; 1990s-refurbished rooms all en suite; just two singles. You'll need to book in advance. **❹**

The City

Once you're within the central grid of streets, **orientation** is made relatively straightforward by frequent sightings of the bay and a series of main commercial avenues: Ayíou Dhimitríou, **Egnatía** (the city's busiest main street), Tsimiskí and Mitropóleos. All run parallel to the quay, but confusingly change their names repeatedly as they head east into the city's post-medieval annexe. Most of central Thessaloníki's principal sights are within easy walking distance of each other, many located on either side of Egnatía. Perpendicular to the avenues, **Aristotélous** is a partly pedestrianized street with Italianate porticos on either side and lined with freshly painted, pale ochre buildings, housing offices, shops and facilities such as the post office and the national railways bureau. It slopes down from Egnatía and opens out at the seaside end into completely pedestrianized **Platía Aristotélous**, where you can enjoy views across to Mount Olympus on clear days. The divide between the older and newer parts of town is marked by the exhibition grounds and the start of the seaside park strip, known locally as Zoo Park and dominated by the **White Tower** (Lefkós Pýrgos).

In the city's best museum, the remarkable **Archeological Museum**, you can admire some of the splendid Vergina treasures, the pride of Macedonia, while minor museums dotted around the centre deal with Byzantine culture, musical instruments, modern art and photography. **Ayía Sofía**, one of the city's most outstanding churches (and there are many ancient Byzantine centres of worship still standing here), houses some superb mosaics, as does the converted Roman mausoleum still known by its Latin name, the **Rotónda**. Further highlights include the Turkish **bazaars**, along with other Ottoman monuments – and what remains of the **Jewish city**, now also represented by an interesting museum.

Venture into the city's eastern districts and you'll find some fine early-twentieth-century mansions, one of which houses an interesting **Folklore Museum**, together with the **Yéni Tzamí**, a beautiful Art Nouveau mosque, now an art gallery.

The archeological museum

Although some of its star exhibits have been returned to the original site at Vergina (see p.517), the **archeological museum** at Platía H.A.N.TH. (summer Mon 12.30–7pm, Tues–Sun 8am–7pm; winter Mon 10.30am–5pm, Tues–Sun 8.30am–3pm; €4), beautifully refurbished and fully reopened in 2004, is undoubtedly the city's leading museum. The central gallery, opposite as you enter, is devoted to rich grave finds from ancient Sindos, a few kilometres north of the modern city, while the left-hand wing is taken up by Hellenistic and Roman art, in particular some exquisite blown-glass birds, found in the tumuli or *toúmbes* which stud the plain around Thessaloníki. Downstairs is an exhibition of prehistoric finds from the city and region, of limited interest.

But these are all just appetizers for – or anticlimaxes after – the marvellous **Gold of Macedon exhibition** in the south hall, which displays – and clearly labels in both English and Greek – many of the finds from the royal tombs of Philip II of Macedon (father of Alexander the Great) and others at the ancient Macedonian capital of Aegae, at modern Veryína. They include startling amounts of gold and silver – masks, crowns, necklaces, earrings and bracelets – all of extraordinarily imaginative craftsmanship, both beautiful and practical, as well as pieces in ivory and bronze. Examples include a silver wine strainer with goose-head handles, a perforated bronze lampshade and an enormous bronze *krater* (wine-mixing bowl), which, in its richly ornate rendition of the life of the god Dionysos, prefigures Baroque art. However, the long-running star attractions – the *larnax* or gold ossuary casket of Philip II, plus that of a consort of his, and assorted gold wreaths – have been transferred back to Veryína itself. Philip II's bones are also no longer on view: they have been given a symbolic reburial at Vergina.

The Museum of Byzantine Culture

The prize-winning **Museum of Byzantine Culture**, in a handsome brick structure at Stratoú 2, just east of the archeological museum (summer Mon 12.30–7pm, Tues–Sun 8am–7pm; winter Mon 10.30am–5pm, Tues–Sun 8.30am–3pm; €4), does a fine job of displaying the early Christian tombs and graves excavated in the city, featuring rescued wall paintings depicting, among others, *Susannah and the Elders*, and a naked rower surrounded by sea creatures. Despite this and the faultless lighting and display techniques, most of the displays will appeal more to specialists than to lay visitors.

The White Tower

Close by, at the eastern end of the seafront promenade, Leofóros Níkis, the **White Tower (Lefkós Pýrgos)** is the city's graceful symbol – for years it has appeared as the background logo on the evening TV news. Originally known as the Lions' Tower and the Fortress of Kalamariá, it formed a corner of the city's Byzantine and Ottoman defences before most of the walls were demolished, late in the nineteenth century. Prior to this, it was the Bloody Tower, a place of imprisonment and, in 1826, execution of the janissaries. In 1890 a Jewish prisoner was given the task of whitewashing the tower, in exchange for his freedom, hence the new name, which stuck, even though it has since been stripped of the white pigment. It was restored in 1985 for the city's 2300th birthday celebrations, and is still undergoing restoration work and refurbishment as the City Museum; it currently houses a small exhibition about its own history (Tues–Sun 8.30am–3pm; €2), but the main reason for visiting is for the **views** from the top.

The Arch of Galerius and the Rotónda

The **Arch of Galerius**, another symbolic city monument, Roman this time, dominates a pedestrianized square just off the eastern end of Egnatía. Along with the nearby Rotónda (see below), it originally formed part of a larger Roman complex which included palaces and a hippodrome. The mighty arch is the surviving span of a dome-surmounted arcade that once led towards the palaces. Built to commemorate the emperor's victories over the Persians in 297 AD, its piers contain rather weathered reliefs of the battle scenes interspersed with glorified poses of Galerius himself. The well-displayed remains of **Galerius's palace** can be viewed, below the modern street level, along pedestrianized Dhimitríou Goúnari and into its extension, Platía Navarínou.

A short way up in the opposite direction, across the pedestrianized square dominated by the Arch, the **Rotónda**, later converted into the church of **Áyios Yeóryios**, is the most striking single Roman monument in the city. It was designed, but never used, as an imperial mausoleum, possibly for Galerius, hence the name. Consecrated for Christian use in the late fourth century, by the addition of a sanctuary, an apse, a narthex and rich mosaics, it later became one of the city's major mosques, from which period the minaret remains. Áyios Yeóryios is open to the public (Tues–Sun 8am–5pm; free), though interior restoration work is scheduled to last at least until 2006. It ranks as a must-see for the sake of its superb mosaics, the finest of their era outside Constantinople or Ravenna. Ones already visible include a miscellaneous aviary of birds in the south vault; ducks, partridge and woodcock in the southeast vault; while up in the damaged dome the head of a mythical phoenix is visible with angels just outside a circular rainbow. Unfortunately hidden by scaffolding, just down from

△ The Rotónda, Thessaloníki

the dome, are fifteen naturalistically portrayed saints, many Roman soldier-martyrs, all sheltering under a fantastic structure where peacocks and birds of paradise perch, meant to symbolize the City of Heaven.

Atatürk's house

As you head up towards the **Kástra**, as the lower fringes of the Upper Town are known, you will pass the **Turkish consulate** at the corner of Ayíou Dhimitríou and Apostólou Pávlou. In the pink nineteenth-century building immediately behind it, at Apostólou Pávlou 17, **Kemal Atatürk**, creator and first president of the modern secular state of Turkey, was born in 1881 (his exact birth date is unknown). The consulate maintains the house as a small **museum** (daily 10am–5pm; free), with its original fixtures and some Atatürk memorabilia. Security is tight, so to visit you must apply for admission at the consulate itself, with your passport (☎2310 248 452; Mon–Fri 9.30am–12.30pm; ring the bell).

Ayía Sofía

Located between Egnatía and Platía Navarínou, in the lower city, to the west of the Arch of Galerius, the heavily restored eighth-century church of **Ayía Sofía** is the finest of its kind in the city. Modelled on its more illustrious namesake in Constantinople, it replaced an older basilica, the only trace of which remains a few paces south: the below-street-level holy well of John the Baptist, originally a Roman *nymphaeum* (sacred fountain). Ayía Sofía's dome, 10m in diameter, bears a splendid **mosaic** of the *Ascension*, for which you'll need opera glasses or binoculars. Christ, borne up to the heavens by two angels, sits resplendent on a rainbow throne, right hand extended in blessing; below, a wry inscription quotes Acts 1:11: "Ye men of galilee, why stand ye gazing up into heaven?" The

---

Ottoman Thessaloníki

Despite years of neglect, the 1917 fire and the 1978 quake, Thessaloníki has quite a number of vestiges of **Ottoman architecture** to show, mostly within walking distance of Platía Dhikastiríon. At the eastern corner of the square itself stands the disused but well-preserved **Bey Hamam** or Parádhisos Baths (Mon–Fri 9am–9pm, Sat & Sun 8.30am–3pm; free), the oldest Turkish bathhouse in the city (1444) and in use until 1968. The doorway is surmounted by elaborate ornamentation, while inside art exhibitions – often paradoxically with Byzantine themes – are held from time to time.

To the south of Platía Dhikastiríon lies the **main Turkish bazaar** area, bounded roughly by Egnatía, Dhragoúmi, Ayías Sofías and Tsimiskí. Much the most interesting bit, and a quiet midtown oasis, is a grid of lanes between Ayías Sofías and Aristotélous, devoted to selling animals, crafts and cane furniture. Nearby Ottoman monuments include the six-domed **Bezestén** or covered valuables market at the corner of Venizélou and Egnatía, now housing jewellery and other shops. Directly opposite, on the north side of Egnatía, rather more modest stores occupy a prominent mosque, the fifteenth-century purpose-built **Hamza Bey Tzamí** (most mosques in Ottoman Thessaloníki were converted churches), now looking decidedly ramshackle.

Well to the north of Platía Dhikastiríon, beyond Áyios Dhimítrios basilica, is the seventeenth-century Yeni Hamam, now a summer cinema and music venue serving basic food, and better known as the **Aigli** (see p.503); the fifteenth-century **Altaza Imaret**, tucked away in a quiet square diagonally opposite, sports a handsome portico and multiple domes.

whole is ringed by fifteen figures: the Virgin attended by two angels, and the twelve Apostles reacting to the miracle. The dome was restored late in the 1980s; the rest of the interior decoration was plastered over after the 1917 fire. Another fine mosaic of the *Virgin Enthroned* in the apse apparently replaced a cross, of which traces are visible, dating from the Iconoclast period.

Áyios Dhimítrios

Up at Ayíou Dhimitríou is the massive yet simple church that gives the street its name, **Áyios Dhimítrios** (Mon 1.30–7.30pm, Tues–Sun 8am–7.30pm; free), conceived in the fifth century but heavily restored since. Far more impressive than the official cathedral down at Mitropóleos, it is the de facto cathedral of the city, with pride of place in Thessalonian hearts, and was almost entirely rebuilt after the 1917 fire, which destroyed all but the apse and colonnades. The church is dedicated to the city's patron saint and stands on the site of his martyrdom, and even if you know beforehand that it is the largest basilica in Greece, its immense interior comes as a surprise.

Amid the multicoloured marble columns and vast extents of off-white plaster, six small surviving **mosaics**, mostly on the columns flanking the altar, make an easy focal point; of these, four date back to the church's second reconstruction after the fire of 620. The astonishing seventh-century mosaic of *Áyios Dhimítrios Flanked by the Church's Two Founders*, on the inside of the south (right-hand) pier beside the steps to the crypt, and the adjacent mosaics of *Áyios Sérgios* and *Áyios Dhimítrios with a Deacon*, contrast well with their contemporary on the north column, a warm and humane mosaic of the saint with two young children. The other two mosaics date back to the fifth century. The one on the north pier is a *Deisis* with the Virgin and Áyios Theódhoros, while the other, high on the west wall of the inner south aisle, depicts a child being presented or dedicated to the saint.

The **crypt** (Mon 1.30–7.30pm, Tues–Sat 8am–7.30pm, Sun 10.30am–7.30pm; free) contains the *martyrion* of the saint – probably an adaptation of the Roman baths in which he was imprisoned – and a whole exhibit of beautifully carved column-capitals, labelled in Greek only and arrayed around a seven-columned fountain and collecting basin.

Áno Póli (Upper Town)

Above Odhós Kassándhrou, the street parallel to Ayíou Dhimitríou, rises the Upper Town or **Áno Póli**, the main surviving quarter of Ottoman Thessaloníki. Although the streets here are gradually becoming swamped by new apartment buildings, they remain ramshackle and atmospheric, a labyrinth of timber-framed houses and winding steps. In the past few years the stigma of the district's "Turkishness" has been overcome as the older houses have been bought up and restored – indeed it has become one of its draws – and it is justifiably one of the city's favourite after-dark destinations. Sections of the fourteenth-century **Byzantine ramparts**, constructed with brick and rubble on top of old Roman foundations, crop up all around the northern part of town.

The best-preserved portion begins at a large circular keep, the Trigónion or **Chain Tower** (so called for its encircling ornamental moulding), in the northeast angle where the easterly city walls change direction. A much smaller circuit of walls rambles around the district of **Eptapýrgio** (Seven Towers), enclosing the old eponymous acropolis at the top end. Undergoing painstaking restoration, for centuries it served as the city's **prison** until abandoned as too inhumane in 1989; it is described as a sort of Greek Devil's Island in a number of plaintive old songs entitled *Yedi Küle*, the Turkish name for Eptapýrgio. On its south side, the wall is followed by Odhós Eptapyrgíou and edged by a small strip of park – a good place to sit and scan Thessaloníki.

The Jewish Museum

Way down in the Bazaar quarter, an early-twentieth-century house, once belonging to a Jewish family, has been beautifully renovated to accommodate the impressive **Jewish Museum**, or Museo Djudio de Salonik to give it its Judeo-Spanish name (Tues, Fri & Sun 11am–2pm, Wed & Thurs 5–8pm; free), at Ayíou Miná 13. On the ground floor are a few precious remains (and some moving photographic documentation) of the city's Jewish cemetery, which contained half a million graves until it was vandalized by the Nazis. Outstanding is a marble Roman stele from the third century, recycled as a Jewish tombstone for a member of the post-1492 Sephardic community from Iberia. In the middle of the courtyard is a finely sculpted fountain that once stood in a city synagogue. Upstairs, a well-presented exhibition, clearly labelled in Greek and English, traces the history of the Jewish presence from around 140 BC to the present day, and displays some of the few religious and secular items that miraculously survived the 1917 fire and the Holocaust.

Museum of Greek Musical Instruments

Nearby in the Ladhádhika district across Tsimiskí, at Katoúni 12–14, is the heavily promoted, privately run **Museum of Greek Musical Instruments** (Mon & Wed–Sun: April–Sept 10am–2pm & 5–7pm; Oct–March 10am–4pm; free) occupying three floors of a purpose-built block. Unfortunately, this is a triumph of style over substance – you're paying to see reproductions of artistic presentations of ancient instruments on walls, vases, drinking cups and so forth. Though each type of instrument (such as bagpipes or harps) is given a wing to itself, there's nothing in the way of interpretation or context, nor any musical accompaniment. On the ground floor worthwhile photography and art exhibitions are regularly staged.

Thessaloníki, a former Jewish metropolis

In the early sixteenth century, after virtually all the Jews were expelled from Spain and Portugal, nearly half of the inhabitants of Thessaloníki, over 80,000 people, were Jewish. For them **"Salonik"** or "Salonicco" ranked as a "Mother of Israel" and the community dominated the city's commercial, social and cultural life for some four hundred years, mostly tolerated by the Ottoman authorities but often resented by the Greeks. The first waves of **Jewish emigration** to Palestine, western Europe and the United States began after World War I. Numbers had dropped to fewer than 60,000 at the onset of World War II, when all but a tiny fraction were deported from Platía Eleftherías to the concentration camps and immediate gassing. The vast Jewish cemeteries east of the city centre, among the world's largest, were desecrated in 1944; to add insult to injury, the area was later covered over by the new university and expanded trade-fair grounds in 1948. At last, however, the role of the Jewish community in making the city what it is has received some recognition in the form of a new **museum**, inaugurated in 2001, and a **memorial** to the victims of the 1943 deportations. Thessaloníki's only surviving pre-Holocaust **synagogue** is the Monastiriótou at Syngroú 35, with an imposing, if austere, facade; it's usually open for Friday-evening and Saturday-morning worship. At the very heart of the former Jewish district (until 1942 Thessaloníki had no ghetto) sprawls the **Modhiáno**, the central meat, fish and produce market, named after the wealthy Jewish **Modiano family** which long owned it. The market has suffered steady decline, with many stalls vacant, but still makes an atmospheric and authentic destination for a meal.

The portside museums

If you cross busy Koundouriótou, the harbour-end extension of Níkis, to the city's **port**, through Gate A you'll find a set of dockside warehouses that have been converted into the city's latest arts complex, complete with bars and, perhaps bizarrely, a kindergarten. Sharing the same warehouse as the hermetic Cinema Museum, only of interest to Greek film buffs, the outstanding **Museum of Photography** (Tues–Fri 11am–7pm, Sat & Sun 11am–9pm; free) stages exhibitions by Greek and international photographers. Across the road in an unprepossessing breeze-block bunker, the **State Museum of Contemporary Art** (Mon–Fri 10am–6pm, Sat & Sun 11am–7pm; free) hosts exhibitions of paintings, often related to the city and its history.

The Yéni Tzamí and the Folklife (Ethnological) Museum of Macedonia

The most enduring civic contribution made to the city by the **Dönme** or **Ma'min** (see box, below) is the orientalized Art Nouveau **Yéni Tzamí** out to the south of the city, at Arheoloyikoú Mousíou 30; dating from 1904, it was the last mosque ever built in the city. Designed by an Italian architect, this engaging folly long served as Thessaloníki's archeological museum from 1923 until the new purpose-built building opened. The interior is nothing other than an Iberian synagogue in disguise, and its elegant decor is likely to overshadow the occasional art exhibitions it houses. It's easy to find, about 0.5km south of the Museum of Byzantine Culture, well signposted off Vasilíssis Ólgas, the southern extension of Vassiléos Yeoryíou.

Still farther out, the **folklife (or Ethnological) museum** (Fri–Tues 9am–3pm, Wed 10am–10pm) is housed in the elegant early twentieth-century mansion of the **Modiano** family (they of the meat market) – one of several Jewish-built villas in the district – at Vasilíssis Ólgas 68. It is one of the best of its kind in Greece, with well-written commentaries (English and Greek) accompanying temporary exhibitions on housing, costumes, day-to-day work and crafts. The museum is just a half-hour walk (or short bus ride) from the White Tower; catch the #5 bus as it runs east along (Mitropóleos and) Meghálou Aléxandhrou.

Eating

First impressions are that the city centre is dominated by fast-food outlets, but there has been an explosion of interesting **places to eat** in Thessaloníki, paralleling the increasing prosperity of the city. The downtown area listings are all within walking distance of Platía Aristotélous; for the others we've given the

---

The Dönme, followers of a False Messiah

The **Dönme** or **Ma'min** were followers of Sabbatai Zvi, the seventeenth-century False Messiah, as he was known; outwardly they embraced Islam after Sabbatai Zvi's forced conversion, and were counted as part of the Ottoman Muslim population, but secretly continued certain aspects of Jewish worship and married only among themselves. Numbering about 15,000 of the city's wealthiest citizens, they were disproportionately important in the commerce of pre-fire Salonica, and later – following their voluntary emigration or **1923 expulsion** – that of republican Turkey. Concentrated in the wealthy southeastern annexe, they were also responsible for numerous sumptuous villas, many still standing and mostly transformed into businesses, and the **Yéni Tzamí** mosque.

appropriate transport connections. Many establishments close from mid-July to mid-August – the time when Thessalonians typically take their summer holidays, a bit earlier than the Athenians. Traditionally, the city's ouzerís will provide some sort of sweet on the house, often semolina *halvás* or watermelon.

There are several recommended places scattered across town where you can get a **breakfast** or quick **snack**. Perhaps the best all-rounder is *Hotpot* at Komninón 15, open 24 hours, with full omelette-based breakfasts, pizzas, salads and pasta dishes. *Terkenlís*, at the corner of Mitropóleos and Ayías Sofías (plus other central branches), offers pastries, turnovers, sandwiches and good coffee or juice for breakfast, plus pizzas and pasta after midday. There's cheaper self-service at the window stools, or pay extra to be waited on at the sidewalk tables. *Vavel/Babel*, at Komninón 20, has crêpes, plus a salad bar, fresh juices and coffee in a pleasant indoor/outdoor environment. Lovers of quality biscuits will be in heaven at either *Armenaki*, Venizélou 10, or *Cookie Man*, Mackenzie King 8 (by Ayía Sofía church), both purveying myriad varieties of fresh-baked cookies by weight.

Downtown: between the sea and Odhós Ayíou Dhimitríou

The city's central oblong is where you're most likely to be staying, so eating here will save you a taxi fare or a long detour. Mostly clustered in the bazaar area, plus the trendy Ladhádhika district (see p.503), the downtown eateries tend to be no-nonsense ouzerís with the odd taverna dotted here and there.

Ta Adhelfia tis Pixarias Platía Navarínou 7. The best of the good-value places on this archeological site/square, with delicacies such as *tzigerosarmás* (lamb's liver in cabbage) and *mýdhia saganáki* (mussels with cheese), plus real tablecloths – though the service tends to be haphazard and the portions are on the small side. It's often packed, so arrive early.

Aristotelous Aristotélous 8. Tucked discreetly into a courtyard off Odhós Aristotélous (enter next to Blow Up Records), this stylish, mid-range ouzerí with its fine, arcaded interior and courtyard gets crowded due to its standard but well-executed *mezédhes*. Excellent *tsípouro* is available. Closed mid-July to mid-Aug & Sun afternoon.

Dore Zythos Tsiroyiánni 7, opposite the White Tower ☏ 2310 279 010. Younger branch of the original *Zythos*, with food regarded as good as or even better than its parent's, served in stylishly retro decor and accompanied by mellow music. Reservations recommended at weekends.

Iy Gonia tou Merakli Avyerinoú, alley off Platía Áthonos. Inexpensive seafood and bulk wine make this about the best of several ouzerís in these atmospheric lanes between Platía Áthonos and Aristotélous.

Kamares Platía Ayíou Yeoryíou 11, by the Rotónda. Excellent, keenly priced seafood, salads and grilled meat at this year-round place, washed down by bulk wine from Límnos. Summer outdoor seating beside the park.

Koumbarakia Egnatía 140. Tucked behind the little Byzantine chapel of the Transfiguration, the outdoor tables of this durable, budget ouzerí groan with Macedonian-style grills, seafood and salads, including *túrsi* (pickled vegetables). Closed Sun and midsummer.

Louloudhadhika Komninón 20. An upmarket eatery, with yellow walls and smart tablecloths, serving extremely good food, especially the fresh fish, and the barrel retsina is wonderfully refreshing. Try and get an outside table in front of the old Jewish baths.

Loutros M. Koundoúra 5. Good fried seafood, simple *orektiká* and excellent retsina, at reasonable prices, next to the Bezesténi. Closed mid-July to mid-Aug.

Molyvos Kapodhistríou 1. Cretan rusks with cheese and salad are among the regional specialities served at this charmingly rustic, moderately priced taverna-ouzerí, with quiet street seating and an Aladdin's cave of a shop selling non-industrial ouzo and olive oils.

O Myrovolos tis Smyrnis In arcade in the Modhiáno off Komninón 32 ☏ 2310 274 170. Friendly, crowded ouzerí, also known as *Tou Thanassi* and reckoned the best of several clustered here. Typical fare includes cheese-stuffed squid, Smyrna-style meatballs, stuffed potatoes and grilled baby fish. Open all year, air conditioned in summer; despite ample seating, reservations are recommended.

The most prominent of Roman public buildings, the **basilica** – a large wooden-roofed hall, with aisles split by rows of columns – was ideally suited for conversion to Christian congregational worship, a process achieved by simply placing an altar at what became the apse, and dividing it from the main body of the church (the nave) by a screen (a forerunner to the iconostasis). The upper reaches of wall were usually adorned with mosaics illustrating Christ's incarnation and man's redemption, while at eye level stood a blank lining of marble. Frescoes did not become fashionable until much later – during the thirteenth and fourteenth centuries – when their scope for expression and movement was fully realized. By the sixth century, architects had set about improving their basilicas with the addition of a **dome**. For inspiration (in **Ayía Sofía**, for example – see p.495) they turned to the highly effective St Sophia in Constantinople. Aesthetic effect, however, was not the only accomplishment, for the structure lent itself perfectly to the prevailing representational art. The mosaics and frescoes adorning its surfaces became physically interrelated, creating a powerful spiritual aid. The eye would be uplifted at once to meet the gaze of the *Pandokrátor* (Christ in Majesty) in the dome, illuminated by the surrounding windows. Between these windows the prophets and Apostles would be depicted, and as the lower levels were scanned the liturgy would unfold amid a hierarchy of saints.

The most successful shape to emerge during experiments with the dome was the **"Greek cross-in-square"** – four equal arms that efficiently absorb the weight of the dome. Architecturally it was a perfect solution; a square ground plan was produced inside the church with an aesthetically pleasing and religiously significant cruciform shape evident in the superstructure. Best of all, it was entirely self-supporting. By the mid-tenth century it had become the conventional form.

Almost all the **Byzantine churches** in Thessaloníki are located in the central districts or on the slopes heading up towards the Upper Town. Under the Turks most of the buildings were converted for use as mosques, a process that obscured many of their original features and destroyed (by whitewashing) the majority of their frescoes and mosaics. Further damage came with the 1917 fire and, more recently, with the 1978 earthquake. Restoration seems a glacially slow process, guaranteeing that many of the sanctuaries are locked, or shrouded in scaffolding. Nevertheless, the churches of Thessaloníki remain an impressive group.The main ones are described below, apart from the two most important churches, **Ayía Sofía** and **Áyios Dhimí-trios**, given their place in the main city account.

One of the most central is the eleventh-century **Panayía Halkéon** church (daily 7.30–11.30am), a classic though rather unimaginative example of the "cross-in-square" form, nestling on Egnatía at the southwestern corner of Platía Dhikastiríon, amid luxuriant palms, cypress and pines. It is worth popping inside to see the frag-mentary frescoes in the cupola and some fine icons. As the Greek name indicates, it served during the Ottoman occupation as the copperworkers' guild mosque; the only remnant of this tradition is the handful of kitsch-copper souvenir shops just across the street.

Nea Ilyssia Sófou 17. Opposite the *Averof* hotel, this popular travellers' restaurant maintains long hours (8.30am–2am) and serves highly regarded *mayireftá*.

Negroponte Just off Polytechníou, Ladhádhika. One of the few authentic tavernas in an otherwise gentrified zone – witness the strings of garlic, traditional seating and barrelled wine. Delicious taverna fare and low prices compared with most places in this district.

Platia Athonos Dhragoúmi, an alley off Platía Athónos. Another good choice in this popular area, and one that's open for lunch offering fish, seafood and a variety of *mezédhes*.

Tiffany's Iktínou 3. A well-established favourite with locals, specializing in meat dishes, such as veal with okra, and offering delicious appetizers like aubergine *bourekákia*.

Tre Marie P.P. Yermanoú 13. If any restaurant epitomizes Thessalonian sybaritism then it is

Several blocks east, and tucked away just out of sight north of the boulevard, the restored, fifth-century, three-aisled basilica of **Panayía Ahiropíitos** is the oldest in the city, featuring arcades, monolithic columns and often highly elaborate capitals – a popular development begun under Theodosius. Only the mosaics inside the arches survive, depicting birds, fruits and vegetation in a rich Alexandrian style.

Around Áyios Dhimítrios (see p.496) are several more churches, utterly different in feel. To the west along Ayíou Dhimitríou is the church of **Dhódheka Apóstoli** (daily 7.30am–noon & 4.30–6.30pm), built with seven more centuries of experience and the bold Renaissance influence of Mystra. Its five domes rise in perfect symmetry above walls of fine brickwork, while inside are glorious fourteenth-century mosaics, among the last executed in the Byzantine empire. High up in the arches to the south, west and north of the dome respectively are a *Nativity*, an *Entry into Jerusalem*, a *Resurrection* and a *Transfiguration*.

A short climb up Ayías Sofías is **Ósios Dhavíd** (Mon–Sat 8am–noon & 6–7.30pm, Sun 8–10.30am), a tiny fifth-century church on Odhós Timothéou. It doesn't really fit into any architectural progression, since the Ottomans demolished much of the building when converting it to a mosque. However, it has arguably the finest mosaic in the city, depicting a clean-shaven Christ Emmanuel appearing in a vision, surrounded by the Tetramorphs or symbols of the four Gospels. The four Rivers of Paradise, replete with fish, flow from beneath Christ, lapping the feet of the prophets Ezekiel and Habakkuk, who respectively cringe in terror and ponder at the revelation. Ask the curator to switch on the floodlights for a better view; a small donation for a candle will be appreciated.

Farther east in Kástra, to the north of Atatürk's house, fourteenth-century **Áyios Nikólaos Orfanós** (Tues–Sun 8.45am–2.45pm; entrance from Irodhótou, warden at no. 17) is a diminutive, much-altered basilica; the imaginative and well-preserved frescoes inside are the most accessible and expressive in the city. In the south aisle, Áyios Yerásimos of Jordan is seen with anthropomorphic lions, while Christ's miracles are set forth in a row above. The naos is devoted to episodes from the Passion, in particular the rarely depicted *Christ Mounting the Cross* and *Pilate Seated in Judgement* at a wooden desk. Above the Virgin Platytera in the apse conch looms the equally unusual *Áyion Mandílion*, an image of Christ's head superimposed on a legendary Turin-style veil sent to an ancient king of Anatolian Edessa. Around the apse is a wonderful *Niptir* (Christ Washing the Disciple's Feet), in which it is thought the painter inserted (in lieu of a signature) an image of himself at the top right above the conch, riding a horse and wearing a white turban.

If you're keen to find out more about the subject it's worth trying to get hold of two locally available stone-by-stone **guides**: the succinct *Monuments of Thessaloniki* (Molho Editions), with coverage only of Roman and Christian sites but better site plans, or the more comprehensive but pricier and rather densely written *Wandering in Byzantine Thessaloniki* (Kapon Editions), which includes Ottoman monuments and has better reproductions. Another thing you might consider is arming yourself with a pair of **opera glasses** or **binoculars**, as many of the mosaics are high up and difficult to see.

this expensive trattoria where the sophisticated menu includes delicacies such as zucchini blooms stuffed with cheese and spearmint in a truffle honey sauce. White-aproned waiters scurry efficiently through a sumptuous decor of marble and dark wood beneath stained-glass ceiling panels and sparkling chandeliers. Small summer terrace in the street.

Tsarouhas Olýmbou 78, near Platía Dhikastiríon. Reputedly the best, and certainly the most famous (and therefore one of the priciest), of the city's *patsatzídhika* – kitchens devoted to tripe-and-trotter soup. Lots of other *mayireftá*, and Anatolian puddings such as *kazandibí* (baked pudding). Closed mid-July to mid-Aug; otherwise open all hours.

Vrotos Mitropolítou Yennadhíou 6, Platía Áthonos ☎2310 223 958. The most imaginative and currently one of the most popular (despite higher prices) of the half-dozen ouzerís in this area, with something for all tastes: elaborate vegetable dishes with or without cheese, meats and seafood recipes. Seating from long, narrow premises spills out onto the pavement, but space is still limited and so it's wise to book ahead. Open daily for lunch and supper except perhaps late July.

 Zythos Platía Katoúni 5 ☏ 2310 540 284. One of the best places in the Ladhádhika

district. Very decent, moderately priced food is served at midday and in the evening, along with an excellent selection of wine and several brews of draught and bottled Greek and foreign beers. Reservations recommended at weekends.

Áno Póli (Kástra and Eptapýrgio)

The **Áno Póli** (Upper Town) is home to a variety of eateries, mostly reasonably priced and full of atmosphere; buses #22 or #28 from Platía Eleftherías spare you the climb. Incidentally, the garish, neon-lit joints on either side of the Chain Tower are perfectly fine for a terrace-with-a-view drink, but are not noted for their cuisine.

Hiotis Graviás 2. Just inside the second (eastern) castle gate, near the Chain Tower. Mussels, kebabs and *kokorétsi* served on the terrace under the ramparts, weather permitting. Dinner only in summer, lunch and dinner rest of the year.

To Makedhoniko Sykiés district. To get here, from the main Portára gate, head west, keeping to the walls as much as practicable, passing a second gate, until you reach the west end of the walls, near a third minor gate. You can also get a bus: #28 goes right through this gateway. A limited menu of *tís óras*, dips, salad and retsina is on offer, but it's cheap and popular with the trendy set as well as locals.

To Spiti tou Pasa Apostólou Pávlou 35. As the name (*The Pasha's house*) suggests, this elegant, two-storey house, stylishly but discreetly decorated, lays emphasis on creature comforts – they include tip-top Límnos wine from the barrel and fresh grilled fish and meats, plus impeccable service, with prices to match.

To Yendi Paparéska 13, at the very top of Kástra, opposite the Yedi Küle citadel. An ouzerí-type menu that changes daily, dished up in largish portions, and accompanied by *tsípouro*, ouzo or house wine. Ample indoor or terrace seating under trees opposite the gate of Yedi Küle, but service can get overstretched owing to popularity. Evenings only.

The eastern suburbs

The **eastern suburbs** are one of the city's more affluent areas and the restaurants tend to be correspondingly more expensive than elsewhere; you may need to factor in taxi fares too.

Archipelagos Kanári 1, cnr Platía Eleftherías, Néa Kríni. A fancy seafood place and one of the best in the area. Take bus #5 or a taxi. Open daily 1pm–midnight.

Batis Platía Eleftherías 2, Néa Kríni, opposite the *Archipelagos*, but much more homely and economical. Grilled octopus and other fish dishes served on the open-air sea-view terrace.

Ellinisti Filelínon 11 and Alexandhrias. Ouzo and *tsípouro* accompany excellent *mezédhes*, followed by some of the best fish in the city, all served in quaintly attractive surroundings.

Krikelas Ethnikís Andistásis 32, in the Vyzándio district, on the way to the airport. A somewhat touristy venue marooned in a desert of private medical clinics and car showrooms, but the chef here is one of the best in Greece, drawing on half a century of experience. Indoor seating only; closed July–Sept.

Vosporos Krítis 60, just east of 25-Martíou and 600m beyond the Folklife Museum. Delicious Constantinopolitan-Greek food served in a pleasant three-level designer building; you select from proffered trays of hot and cold *mezédhes*. Open all year; closed Sun eve and all day Mon.

Drinking, nightlife, entertainment and shopping

Thessaloníki is a city where you can easily get the impression that the entire population spends most of its time gathering at the multitude of cafés and bars, showing off designer gear, sipping an iced coffee and chain-smoking.

Downtown, the most fashionable nightlife is to be found in **Ladhádhika**, a still partly ramshackle district near the harbour. Pedestrianized Katoúni, Eyíptou and Platía Morihóvou and surrounding streets are lined with a bewildering mix of cafés, *gelaterie*, numerous ouzerís, salsatecas and even a few full-on tavernas. Most establishments have a high turnover rate, so singling them out is fairly pointless: just stroll by and choose according to crowd and noise level. Two, *Sodade* and *Banal*, are currently the city's main **gay** venues.

Another profitable hunting ground for drinking places is **Leofóros Níkis**, the seafront esplanade that is a perennial *vólta* (promenade) favourite owing to its endless row of bar terraces; similar bars can also be found around the more fashionable **Platía Aristotélous**, and along into **Proxénou Koromilá**. A couple of trendy designer bars on the square opposite the **White Tower** are certainly worth checking out, while bustling **Platía Navarínou** and the nearby pedestrianized streets, **Iktínou** and **Zefxídhou**, are lined with some of the trendiest establishments in the city. During the warmer months, action mostly shifts to various glitzy, barn-like establishments lining the coast road out to **Kalamariá**, for which you'll need to take taxis.

Bars, cafés and clubs

Aigli Cnr Ayíou Nikoláou and Kassándhrou, behind Áyios Dhimítrios church. A classy bar-ouzerí, with Anatolian decor, occupies part of this dependency of the nearby Alatza Imaret. A small events hall takes up the double-domed main chamber of the baths, with bar seating outside in summer, when the garden becomes an outdoor cinema.

Cafe Amareion Apostólou Pávlou ☎ 2310 248 812. This relative newcomer with excellent acoustics puts on good music gigs at weekends.

Kiss Fish Averof and Fokéas. One of a clutch of trendy bars tucked away in these narrow lanes near the up-and-coming portside zone; definitely a place to be seen.

Kitchen Bar Port, next to State Museum of Contemporary Art. A huge harbour warehouse, converted into one of the city's most fashionable hangouts. Head upstairs in the cooler months and out to the seafront terrace in the summer to enjoy sweeping city views as you sip a cocktail, eat a full-blown meal or just tuck into breakfast or an afternoon cheesecake and coffee.

Kourdhisto Gourouni Ayías Sofías 31. Several foreign brews on tap, and a bewildering range of bottled varieties, at this stylish bar with indoor and outdoor seating; expensive food menu also.

Olympion Platía Aristotélous 10. Coffees, beers and cocktails are all on offer here – at outrageously inflated prices – but this is a place primarily for showing off designer kit.

Pasta Flora Darling Zefxídhou 6. Garden gnomes and flowery wallpaper, jazzy tables and psychedelic lighting suggest the decor is every bit as eclectic as the clientele at this typical Iktínou-Zefxídhou bar; good for cocktails and vegetarian snacks.

Santé Kapodhistríou 3. Fabulously eccentric bar in a converted Neoclassical silk-factory showroom, with intriguing papier mâché Amerindians and other exotica. There's a Latin flavour to the music, mostly tango, Cuban and Brazilian; the decor is partly inspired by the mind-boggling Santé cigarette pack that gives the place its name.

Stretto Karólou Diehl 18. Small, gay-friendly café-bar, frequented by arty types and intellectuals and dispensing some of the best coffee in town, in a gallery-like interior or at an equally tiny street terrace.

Events

In **winter**, cultural events, often of high quality, mostly take place in one of the State Theatre of Northern Greece (Kratikó Théatro Voríou Elládhos) venues. Downtown this means either the Etería Makedhonikón Spoudhón or the ultramodern Vassilikó Théatro, within sight of each other behind the White Tower. In **summer**, things move to one of a number of outdoor venues: the Théatro Kípou, near the archeological museum; well up the hill at the Théatro Dhássous, in the pines east of the upper town, with events from late June to mid-September; or the Théatro Damári, above the Kaftantzoglio Stadium in

△ Café, Thessaloníki

Triandhría district, which hosts big Greek or international stars. In the absence of a reliable listings magazine, apart from the free weekly *City* (in Greek only), watch for **posters** in the windows of the usual ticket vendors: the record stores Blow Up (Aristotélous 8), Albandis (Mitropóleos 14–16), Patsis (Tsimiskí 41) and Virgin (shopping mall at Tsimiskí 43), as well as at *Zythos* or *Doré Zythos* (see p.502).

More cutting-edge events are held at Mylos, at Andhréou Yeoryíou 56 (Ⓦwww.mylos.gr), a multifunctional cultural complex housed in an old flour mill some way west of the centre. Here you'll find a couple of bars, a live jazz café, a popular *tsipourádhiko* (open for lunch), a summer cinema, concert halls and exhibition galleries of various sizes, plus a theatre. Another venue of note is the very active Moní Lazaristón in Stavroúpoli at Kolokotróni 25 (Ⓣ2310 652 020; Ⓦwww.monilazariston.gr), a deconsecrated Catholic monastery 2km north of the centre along Langadhá. Officially part of the State Theatre of Northern Greece project (Ⓦwww.ntng.gr), its main and smaller theatres host regular concerts, operas and plays, by top Greek performers and visiting foreign troupes, plus art exhibitions. Buses #34 and #38 go there from Platía Dhikastiríon.

Cinema

Indoor cinemas, closed in summer unless otherwise indicated, tend to cluster between the White Tower and the Arch of Galerius; those known to concentrate on quality first-run material include Alexandhros, Ethnikís Amanis 1 (open in summer); Egnatia, Patriárhou Ioakím 1, corner Keramopoúlou, by Ayía Sofía; Esperos, Svólou 22 (open in summer); Makedhonikon, Filikís Eterías, corner Dhimitríou Margaríti; Navarinon, on the namesake plaza; and Vakoura, Ioánnou Mihaïl 10. **Open-air cinemas** have all but vanished from downtown Thessaloníki, owing to spiralling property values; the only ones left are the Alex, at Olambou 106; the nearby Aigli outside the Yeni Hamam; Ellinis, the summer branch of the Egnatia, on Platía H.A.N.TH.; and Natali, at the start of Megálou Alexándhrou, by the *Macedonia Palace* hotel. Listings are given in the daily Greek papers.

Shopping

Thessaloníki is not really a mecca for consumer therapy but, in addition to its smart clothing and shoe emporia, mostly concentrated along or just off Tsimiskí, you can find some fine shops around the city. Three main possibilities for souvenir hunters would be books, records and a decent bottle of local wine.

Books and newspapers Molho, Tsimiskí 10, is far and away the best shop in the city, with an excellent stock of English-language books (in particular related to Thessaloníki), magazines and newspapers. Promitheus, at Ermoú 75 and Isávron 1, near Platía Navarínou, and Konstandinidhis, at Egnatía 125, are good alternatives.

Music Best of Thessaloníki's various record stores for Greek music are Studio 52, Dhimitríou Goúnari 46, basement, with lots of out-of-print vinyl and cassettes plus well-sorted CDs; and En Chordais,

Ippodhromíou 3–4, a traditional music school and instrument shop, which also has a well-selected stock of folk and innovative CDs.

Wine Northern Greece nurtures some fine vineyards, and accordingly Thessaloníki has some excellent bottle-shops affordably selling vintages superior to your average taverna plonk: ly Tsaritsani, Avyerinoú 9, off Platía Áthonos; Anereto, Dhimitríou Goúnari 42; and Reklos, Ayíou Dhimitríou 118, cnr Ayías Sofías.

Listings

Airlines Aegean, Venizélou 2 ☏ 2310 280 050; Alitalia, Níkis 9A ☏ 2310 257 707; Olympic, Koundouriótou 3 ☏ 2310 344 444. Most other airlines have offices at the airport.

Airport ☏ 2310 411 977 for flight information.

Camping gear Petridhis, Vas. Iraklíou 43; or World Jamboree, at Íonos Dhelíou 6, off Ethnikís Amknis.

Car rental Many agencies are clustered near the fairgrounds and archeological museum on Angeláki, which is a good place to compare prices. The leading agencies have kiosks at the airport, too. Specific outfits include Avis, Níkis 3 ☏ 2310 227 126; Budget, Angeláki 15 ☏ 2310 274 272; Eurodollar, Ethnikís Andistásis 157 ☏ 2310 456 630; Europcar/Inter Rent, Papandhréou 5 ☏ 2310 826 333; European, Angeláki 15 ☏ 2310 281 603; Eurorent, Angeláki 3 ☏ 2310 286 327; Hertz, Venizélou 5 ☏ 2310 224 906; Thrifty, Angeláki 5 ☏ 2310 241 241.

Consulates Canada, Tsimiskí 17 ☏ 2310 256 350; UK/Commonwealth: honorary consul is at Aristotélous 21 (Mon–Fri 8am–1pm; ☏ 2310 278 006); US, Níkis 59 (Mon–Fri 9am–noon; ☏ 2310 242 905).

Cultural institutes British Council, Ethnikís Amynis 9, cnr Tsimiskí; free library and reading room, plus various events in the winter months.

Exchange For changing notes, use the 24hr automatic exchange machine at the National Bank on Platía Aristotélous 6. Thessaloníki has plenty of reliable ATMs accepting a variety of foreign plastic.

Ferry tickets The main agent for the DANE ferry to Sámos and the Dodecanese, plus GA sailings to the Dodecanese, is Omikron Travel, Salamínos 4 ☏ 2310 555 995. Minoan Line or GA sailings to the Sporádhes, Cyclades and Crete are best obtained from Kriti/Crete Air Travel, Íonos Dhragoúmi 1, cnr Koundouriótou ☏ 2310 534 376. Karacharisis at Koundouriótou 8 ☏ 2310 524 544 is the main NEL agent, and also deals in all GA sailings and Minoan Lines.

Football Thessaloníki's main team is PAOK, whose stadium is in the east of the city at Toúmba.

Hospitals For minor trauma, use the Yeniko Kendriko at Ethnikís Amynis 41; otherwise, head for Ippokraton at Konstantinopóleos 49, in the eastern part of town.

Internet café There are dozens, but two of the least noisy are *Enterprisse* at Dhimitríou Goúnari 52 and *Planet* at Svólou 55.

Laundries Bianca, Antoniádhou 3, near the Arch of Galerius (quick service and long hours); Freskadha, Filíppou 105, beside the Rotónda; Ion, Karaóli Dhimitríou 52 (good dry cleaning).

Post office Main branch (for poste restante and complicated parcel services) is at Aristotélous 26 (Mon–Fri 7.30am–8pm, Sat 7.30am–2pm, Sun 9am–1.30pm). There are other post offices around the city: the most useful ones are at Koundouriótou (by the port), Ethnikís Amynis 9A and Ayíou Dhimitríou 98.

Train tickets All services depart from the antiquated station down on Monastiríou, the southwestern

continuation of Egnatía, well served by buses. If you want to buy tickets or make reservations in advance, the OSE office at Aristotélous 18 (Mon & Sat 8am–3pm, Tues–Fri 8am–9pm) is far more central and helpful than the station ticket-windows.
Travel agents Most general sales agents and consolidators cluster around Platía Eleftherías, especially on Kalapotháki, Komninón, Níkis and Mitropóleos. Students and under-27s should try Nouvelles Frontières at Kalapotháki 8 (☎2310 237 700) or Sunflight at Tsimiskí 114 (☎2310 280 500). For cheap buses to Turkey, try Bus and Atlantic Tours, Aristotélous 10, 4th Floor ☎2310 226 036. Mountain trekking and other outdoor expeditions are offered by Trekking Hellas, Mitropóleos 60 (☎2310 264 082).

❺ Around Thessaloníki

The main **weekend escape** from Thessaloníki is to the Halkidhikí peninsula, but to get to its better beaches requires more than a day-trip. If you just want a respite from the city, or a walk in the hills, consider instead Thessaloníki's own local villages and suburbs. Further out, drivers en route to Néa Moudhaniá can take in the extraordinary cave near Petrálona – though half-day trips with a local tour operator make this a possibility for those without their own transport, too.

The anastenáridhes: the fire-walkers of Langadhás

On May 21, the feast day of Saints Constantine and Helen, villagers at **LANGADHÁS**, 20km north of Thessaloníki, perform a ritual barefoot **dance** across a bed of burning coals known as the *anastenária*. The festival rites are of unknown and strongly disputed origin. It has been suggested that they are remnants of a Dionysiac cult, though devotees assert a purely Christian tradition. This seems to relate to a fire, around 1250, in the Thracian village of Kostí (now in Bulgaria), from where many of the inhabitants of Langadhás originate. Holy icons were heard groaning from the flames and were rescued by villagers, who emerged miraculously unburnt from the blazing church. The icons, passed down by their families, are believed to ensure protection during the fire walking. Equally important is piety and purity of heart: it is said that no one with any harboured grudges or unconfessed sins can pass through the coals unscathed. The Greek church authorities, however, refuse to sanction any service on the day of the ritual; it has even been accused of planting glass among the coals to try and discredit this "devil's gift".

Whatever the origin, the rite is still performed most years – lately as something of a tourist attraction, with an admission charge and repeat performances over the next two days. It is nevertheless eerie and impressive, beginning around 7pm with the lighting of a cone of hardwood logs. A couple of hours later their embers are raked into a circle and, just before complete darkness, a traditional Macedonian *daoúli* **drummer** and two **lyra players** precede a group of about sixteen women and men into the arena. These *anastenáridhes* (literally "groaners"), in partial trance, then shuffle across the coals for about a quarter of an hour.

During the 1980s participants in the ritual were subjected to various **scientific tests**. The only established clues were that the dancers' brain waves indicated some altered state – when brain activity returned to normal they instinctively left the embers – and that their rhythmical steps maintained minimum skin contact with the fires. There was no suggestion of fraud, however. In 1981 an Englishman jumped into the arena, was badly burnt and had to be rescued by the police from irate devotees and dancers. If you decide to go, arrive early at Langadhás – by 5.30pm at the latest – in order to get a good seat. Frequent buses leave from Odhós Langadhá in Thessaloníki. Be prepared, too, for the circus-like commercialism, though this in itself can be quite fun.

Panórama and Hortiátis

On the hillside 11km southeast of town, **PANÓRAMA**, the closest escape from the city, is exactly what its name suggests: a hillside viewpoint looking down over Thessaloníki and the gulf. Rebuilt after World War II, it is mainly composed of smart villas, coffee shops and a large, modern shopping mall. Of more appeal are a number of traditional cafés, tavernas and *zaharoplastía*, these last selling the premier local speciality, *trígona* (very sweet custard-filled triangular confections) and wonderful *dondurma* (Turkish-style ice cream flavoured with mastic). The village can be reached by #58 bus from Platía Dhikastiríon, or by taxi (around €4 one way).

Still more of a retreat is **HORTIÁTIS**, 11km away due east (or 16km direct from Thessaloníki), set in a mountainous area known as Hília Dhéndhra (Thousand Trees), which since ancient times has supplied Thessaloníki with water – you can still see the ruined aqueduct to one side of the road. To get there from Thessaloníki, take the #61 bus, which meets passengers alighting the #58 at the crossroads where those buses head up to Panórama. Attractions include sweeping views over the city, good walking among the pines and some popular places to eat; the *Tsakis* **taverna** (℡2310 349 874) has a well-deserved reputation, so in summer you should reserve tables in advance to avoid disappointment.

Petrálona

Fifty kilometres southeast of Thessaloníki, and set among handsome mountain scenery, is the cave of **Kókkines Pétres** (Red Stones), discovered in 1959 by villagers from nearby **PETRÁLONA** looking for water. Besides an impressive display of stalagmites and stalactites, the villagers – and, later, academics – found the fossilized remains of prehistoric animals and, most dramatic of all, a Neanderthal skull, all of which are displayed in a decent museum near the cave entrance.

The cave, kitted out with dioramas of prehistoric activities and well worth a visit, makes an interesting diversion on the way to or from the Kassándhra peninsula; you'll find the village of Petrálona itself roughly 4km north of Eleohória, on the old road running from Thessaloníki to Néa Moudhaniá at the neck of the peninsula. The cave and museum are open daily (9am to sunset; €5; guided tours only, photography forbidden) and there's a small café on site. Doucas Tours in Thessaloníki (Venizélou 8), and other outfits, operate a half-day trip.

Litóhoro and Mount Olympus (Óros Ólymbos)

The highest, most magical and most dramatic of all Greek mountains, **Mount Olympus** – Ólymbos in Greek – rears straight up to 2917m from the shores of the Thermaic Bight and, when pollution allows, is visible from downtown Thessaloníki, some 100km away to the northeast. Its summit was believed by the ancient Greeks to be the home of the gods and it seems that quite a few locals still follow the old religion. Dense forests cover its lower slopes, and its **wild flowers** are without parallel even by Greek standards.

By far the best base for a walk up the mountain, if only part of the way for the views, is the small town of **LITÓHORO** on the eastern side. An intrinsically dull, rough-and-ready garrison town with two huge army camps on the approach road, its setting, in good weather, affords intoxicating vistas into the heart of the range.

Litóhoro practicalities

Reaching Litóhoro is fairly easy: it has its own motorway turn-off, and buses to the central platía **KTEL** from Thessaloníki or the market town of Kateríni are frequent. The **train station** is 5km away, down by the motorway, but taxis do not always await arrivals – you might have to call your hotel to ask them to send you one.

Information sources in Litóhoro are virtually nonexistent, but with this guide you can find your way up the mountain in summer without the need for any other information. If you do want further advice, there are two specialized mountaineering organizations with representation in the town: the SEO has an office tucked away just 50m along the road to the national park. It opens only in the evenings; ask around for EOS staff, some of whom speak English but who no longer have a proper office in town, or call ☏ 23520 81800. The **post office** is at 28-Oktovríou 11, and a couple of **banks** in Litóhoro have ATMs.

At the budget end of accommodation in Litóhoro, you're best off looking for **rooms** (❶–❷) by asking in the cafés and tavernas around the main square. The best, those in the hospitable *Xenonas Papanikolaou* (☏ 23520 81236, Ⓔ xenpap@otenet.gr; ❷), are particularly good value, despite being slightly more expensive than the others, and hidden away in a quiet part of town (signposted). Otherwise there is a handful of hotels, listed below, some of them very good value.

Accommodation

Enipefs/Enipeas located beyond the main square near the National Bank ☏ 23520 81328 or 23520 84328. Newer than most, and spotless, its upper rear rooms have fine views, while attic rooms with skylight only are cheaper. ❷–❸

Markesia Dhionýsou 5 ☏ 23520 81831. Basic but passable place off 28-Oktovríou, some way from the central platía – if it's unattended, enquire at the novelty shop nearby. ❶

Myrto Ayíou Nikoláou, just off the main square ☏ 23520 81398, Ⓕ 23520 82298. Comfortable, extremely clean hotel, but gets noise from the street and the square. ❸

Villa Drossos Arheláou 18 ☏ 23520 84561, Ⓔ grigoris@kat.forthnet.gr. The finest accommodation in town, if not the best located (it is tucked away two or three streets back from Ayíou Nikoláou), the *Villa* boasts smart rooms, an enticing swimming pool and an open fire in winter, plus parking space. English spoken. ❹

Xenios Dias On the main square ☏ 23520 81234. With views to equal those of the Enipefs/Enipeas, this place has smarter rooms and a cosy bar. ❸

Eating

You'll find a rash of fast-food places in the square and on Ayíou Nikoláou but, on the uphill side streets near the central platía, there are more attractive possibilities, such as the *Ouzeri Manos* at 28-Oktovríou 3, with a limited menu of seafood titbits. Even better is the *Ouzeri Pazari* nearby on Platía 3-Martíou, serving locally caught octopus and squid. Best of all, both for its central-platía location and commendable culinary endeavours, is the pricey ⚒ *Gastrodromio en Olympo*; rabbit and suckling pig stand out from the usual fare, and there's a decent wine list. If you're keen to stock up on carbohydrates before a climb, try the pasta at the *Fournos*, on the roundabout at the bottom of Ayíou Nikoláou. At the start of the road towards the mountain (signposted "Olympos"), just above the SEO office, are a couple of cheap-and-cheerful, sit-down *psistariés* – the *Zeus* in particular passes muster.

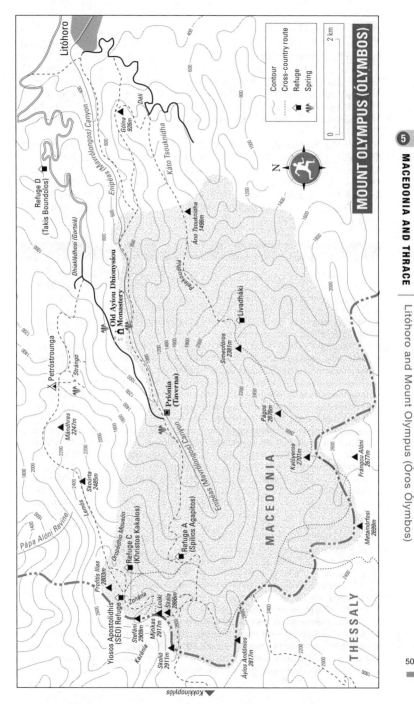

MOUNT OLYMPUS (ÓLYMBOS)

Litóhoro

Refuge D
(Takis Boundolos)

Dhiakládhos (Gortsiá)

Enipéas (Mavrólongos) Canyon

Góina
926m

Déli

Káto Tsoukídha

Áno Tsouknídha
1498m

Petróstrounga

Stráŋgo

Old Áyiou Dhionysíou
Monastery

Priónia
(Taverna)

Paleŋkyoudhiá

Livadháki

Simeóforos
2381m

Mándhres
2247m

Skoúrta
2485m

Lémos

Pápa Alóni Ravine

Oropédhio Mousón

Profítis Ilías
2803m

Refuge C
(Khrístos Kákalos)

Zonária

Refuge A
(Spílios Agapitós)

Enipéas (Mavrólongos) Canyon

Pagós
2676m

Kalóyeros
2701m

Frángou Alóni
2677m

Metamórfosi
2699m

Yíosos Apostolídhis
(SEO) Refuge

Stefáni
2909m

Mýrikas
2917m

Loúki

Skála
2866m

Skólió
2911m

Áyios Andónios
2817m

Kazánia

THESSALY

MACEDONIA

Kokkinoplós

N

~~	Contour
·······	Cross-country route
◆	Refuge
♦	Spring

0   2 km

509

The mountain

To reach alpine Olympus, you've a choice of road or foot routes. With your own vehicle, you can **drive** deep into the mountain along a fairly decent road, the first 11km of which is paved. There is an information booth at km3, where (in high season, anyway) your nationality is recorded and you're given some literature advising you of the park rules, but so far there's no admission charge. It is much better, however, to **walk** in from Litóhoro, as far as the monastery of **Ayíou Dhionysíou**, and beyond to the two trailheads following.

As for the final **ascent routes**, there are two main paths: one beginning at **Priónia** – just under 18km up the mountain at the road's end and a €20 taxi ride from Litóhoro – where there's a spring, toilets and a primitive taverna (May–Oct); the other at a spot called **Dhiakládhosi/Gortsiá** (13km along), marked by a signboard displaying a map of the range. The Priónia path is more frequented and more convenient, the Dhiakládhosi trail longer but more beautiful.

Climbing Mount Olympus

The best and most easily available commercial **trekking map** is Road Editions' no. 31 *Olymbos* at 1:50,000, available from specialist map shops abroad (see pp.39–40 for some recommended outlets) or in Athens or Thessaloníki; a good alternative is one of the same scale that is co-produced by *Korfes* magazine and EOS. One or other is sometimes available at a shop on Ayíou Nikoláou opposite the start of the Ólymbos road, but they often run out.

To make the most of the mountain, you need to allow two to three days' hiking. You should go **equipped** with decent boots and warm clothing. No special expertise is necessary to get to the top in summer (mid-June to Oct), but it's a long hard pull, requiring a good deal of stamina; winter climbs, of course, are another matter, with heavy snowfall quite low down adding to the challenge. At any time of year Olympus is a mountain to be treated with respect: its weather is notoriously fickle, with sudden fogs or storms, and it regularly claims lives.

Accommodation on Mount Olympus itself is better organized than on any other mountain in Greece. There are two staffed refuges: the EOS-run *Spilios Agapitos* at 2100m (☎23520 81800; May 15–Oct 15, reservations recommended in summer), commonly known as Refuge A, and the SEO-managed *Yiosos Apostolidhis* hut at 2700m (July–Sept, though its glassed-in porch is always available for climbers in need). There is no set phone number for this refuge, since the wardenship is often in a state of flux; contact the SEO information office in Litóhoro on ☎23520 82300 (evenings only). Both charge around €10 for a bunk (you can **camp** at Refuge A for €5, and have use of their bathroom), with lights-out and outer door locked at 10pm, so bring a torch. It's best to stay overnight at Refuge A, as you should make an early start (certainly pre-8am) for the three-hour ascent to Mýtikas, the highest peak at 2917m. The peaks frequently cloud up by midday and you lose the view, to say nothing of the danger of catching one of Zeus's thunderbolts, for this was the mythical seat of the gods. Besides, nights at the refuge are fantastic: a log fire blazes, you watch the sun set on the peaks and dawn break over the Aegean, and you can usually see a multitude of stars.

Meals at either shelter are relatively expensive, and mandatory since no cooking is allowed inside; bring more money than you think you'll require, as bad weather can ground you a day or two longer than planned. For sustenance while walking, you'll need to buy food at the well-stocked grocery **stores** in Litóhoro, though water can wait until you're in the vicinity of either of two trailheads (see p.511 and p.512).

The Enipéas (Mavrólongos) canyon and Ayíou Dhionysíou monastery

Rehabilitated old paths in the superlatively beautiful **Enipéas** (**Mavrólongos**) river canyon form a fine section of the **E4 overland trail**. Black-on-yellow diamond markers begin near Litóhoro's central platía; follow road signs for Mýli and bear down and right at the cemetery. Once out of town, waymarks lead you along a roller-coaster course by the river for four hours to Ayíou Dhionysíou. It's a delightful route, but you'll need basic hiking skills, as there are some scrambles over steep terrain, and a few water crossings. The **monastery** itself was burned by the Germans in 1943 and the surviving monks, rather than rebuilding, relocated to new premises nearer Litóhoro. After years of dereliction and vandalism, Ayíou Dhionysíou is undergoing a snail's-pace restoration.

From Ayíou Dhionysíou it's just under an hour more upstream along the riverside E4 to Priónia, or slightly less if you go up the driveway and then east to the Dhiakládhosi trailhead.

The ascent from Priónia

The E4 carries on just uphill by a signpost giving the time to Refuge A as two hours thirty minutes, though it actually takes more like three hours, even at a brisk pace. You cross a stream (last water before Refuge A; purification advisable) and start to climb steeply up through woods of beech and black pine. This path, the continuation of the E4, is well trodden and marked, so there is no danger of getting lost. As you gain height there are majestic views across the Enipéas (Mavrólongos) ravine to your left and to the peaks towering above you. **Refuge A** (see opposite) perches on the edge of an abrupt spur, surrounded by huge storm-beaten trees.

The summit area

The E4 path continues behind the refuge (your last **water source** on the ascent), climbing to the left up a steep spur among the last of the trees. Having ignored an initial right fork towards the usually unstaffed *Khristos Kakalos* hut (Refuge C), within about an hour you reach a signposted **fork** above the tree line. Continuing straight on takes you across the range to Kokkinopylós village with the E4 waymarks, or with a slight deviation right to Mýtikas, via the ridge known as Kakí Skála (1hr 30min–2hr). An immediate right turn leads to the *Yiosos Apostolidhis* hut in one hour along the so-called Zonária trail, with the option after 45 minutes of taking the very steep Loúki couloir left up to Mýtikas; if you do this, be wary of rockfalls.

For the safer **Kakí Skála route**, continue up the right flank of the stony, featureless valley in front of you, with the Áyios Andónios peak up to your left. An hour's dull climb brings you to the summit ridge between the peaks of Skolió on the left and Skála on the right. You know you're there when one more step would tip you over a five-hundred-metre sheer drop into the Kazánia chasm; take great care. The Kakí Skála ("Evil Stairway") begins in a narrow cleft on the right just short of the ridge; paint splashes mark the way. The route keeps just below the ridge, so you are protected from the drop into Kazánia. Even so, those who don't like heights are likely to be reduced to a whimpering crouch.

You start with a slightly descending rightward traverse to a narrow nick in the ridge revealing the drop to Kazánia – easily negotiated. Continue traversing right, skirting the base of the Skála peak, then climb leftwards up a steepish gully made a little awkward by loose rock on sloping footholds. Bear right at the top over steep but reassuringly solid rock, and across a narrow neck. Step left around an awkward corner and there in front of you, scarcely 100m away, is **Mýtikas summit**, an airy, boulder-strewn platform with a trigonometric point, tin Greek flag and visitors' book. In reasonable conditions it's about forty minutes to the summit from the start of Kakí Skála; three hours from the refuge; five and a half hours from Priónia.

A stone's throw to the north of Mýtikas is the **Stefáni peak**, also known as the Throne of Zeus, a bristling hog's back of rock with a couple of nastily exposed moves to scale the last few feet.

Descending from Mýtikas, you can either go back the way you came, with the option of turning left at the signpost for the *Yíosos Apostolídhis* hut (2hr 30min from Mýtikas by this route), or you can step out, apparently into space, in the direction of Stefáni and turn immediately down to the right into the mouth of the Loúki couloir. It takes about forty minutes of downward scrambling to reach the main path where you turn left for the hut, skirting the impressive northeast face of Stefáni (1hr), or go right, back to the familiar signpost and down the E4 to *Spílios Agapitós* (2hr altogether).

The ascent from Dhiakládhosi (Gortsiá)

Starting from the small parking area beyond the information placard, take the narrow path going up and left via faint steps – with a wood railing and wooden awning – not the forest track heading down and right. An hour along, you reach the meadow of **Bárba**, and two hours out you'll arrive at a messy junction with a modern water tank and various placards – take left forks en route when given the choice. The signs point hard left to the spring at **Strángo**; right for

△ Mount Olympus

the direct path to Petróstrounga; and straight on for the old, more scenic way to **Petróstrounga**, passed some two-and-a-half hours along.

Beyond **Petróstrounga**, there's an indicated right, then the trail wanders up to the base of **Skoúrta** knoll (4hr 15min), above the tree line. After crossing the Lemós (Neck) ridge dividing the Papá Alóni and Enipéas (Mavrólongos) ravines, with spectacular views into both, five-and-a-quarter hours should see you up on the Oropédhio Musón ("Plateau of the Muses"), five-and-a-half hours to the *Apostolidhis* refuge, visible the last fifteen minutes. But you should count on seven hours, including rests, for this route; going down takes about four and a half hours, a highly recommended descent if you've come up from Priónia.

It takes about an hour, losing altitude, to traverse the onward Zonária path linking *Apostolidhis* and the E4, skimming the base of the peaks – about the same time as coming the other way as described above.

Dion

Ancient **DION**, in the foothills of Mount Olympus, was the Macedonians' sacred city. At this site – a harbour before the river mouth silted up – the kingdom maintained its principal sanctuaries: to Zeus (from which the name Dion, or Dios, is derived) above all, but also to Demeter, Artemis, Asklepios and, later, to foreign gods such as the Egyptians Isis and Serapis. Philip II and Alexander both came to sacrifice to Zeus here before their expeditions and battles. Inscriptions found at the sanctuaries referring to boundary disputes, treaties and other affairs of state suggest that the political and social importance of the city's festivals exceeded a purely Macedonian domain.

Most exciting for visitors, however, are the finds of mosaics, temples and baths that have been excavated since 1990 – work that remains in progress whenever funds allow. These are not quite on a par with the Vergina tombs (see p.517), but still rank among the major discoveries of ancient Macedonian history and culture. If you're near Mount Olympus, they are certainly worth a detour, and the abundance of water and vegetation makes it cooler and more pleasing on the eye than many sites. The frog ponds and grazing geese in a lush landscape littered with voluptuous statuary lend the place the air of a decadent Roman villa and its gardens.

At the village of **DHÍON** (Malathiriá until the archeological discovery), 7km inland from Litóhoro beach or reached by #14 bus from Kateríni, take a side road 400m east from the *Hotel Dion*, past the remains of a **theatre**, put to good use during the summer Olympus Festival. The main **site** or "park" lies ahead (daily: summer 8am–7pm; winter closes 5pm; €6, including admission to museum). A direct, signposted, paved road links Dion to Litóhoro (see p.507), crossing a formerly out-of-bounds army firing range; coming from Litóhoro, take the Olympus road and keep going ahead instead of turning left up the mountain. Recommended for an **overnight** stay is the decent *Hotel Dion*, which stands at the crossroads by the bus stop (☎03510 53682; ❹), 100m below the museum; on the pedestrian street linking the two are a few tavernas firmly pitched at the tourist trade. The nearest campsites are on the beach at Varikó, 11km away: *Stani* (☎23520 61277) and *Niteas* (☎23520 61290), both open all year round.

The integrity of the site and its finds is due to the nature of the city's demise. At some point in the fifth century AD, a series of earthquakes prompted an evacuation of Dion, which was then swallowed up by a mudslide from the mountain. The place is still quite waterlogged, and constant pumping against the local aquifer is necessary. The main visible excavations are of the vast **public baths** complex and, outside the city walls, the **sanctuaries** of Demeter and Aphrodite-Isis. In the latter, a small temple has been unearthed, along with its cult statue – a copy of which remains *in situ*. Two Christian **basilicas** attest to the town's later years as a Byzantine bishopric in the fourth and fifth centuries AD. An observation platform allows you to view the layout of the site more clearly.

In the village, a large but poorly labelled **museum** (same hours as site but sometimes closed Mon morning) houses most of the finds. The sculptures, perfectly preserved by the mud, are impressive, and accompanied by various tombstones and altars. In the basement sprawls a mosaic of Medusa, along with the finest **mosaics** yet discovered at the site: they would have paved the banquet room and depict the god Dionysos on a chariot. Upstairs, along with extensive displays of pottery and coinage, is a collection of everyday items, including surgical and dental tools perhaps connected with the sanctuary of Asklepios, the healing god. Pride of place, however, goes to the remains of a first-century BC **pipe organ**, discovered in 1992 and exhibited on the upper storey.

Véria and Vergina

The broad agricultural plain extending due west from Thessaloníki eventually collides with an abrupt, wooded escarpment, at the panoramic edge of which is a series of towns including Édhessa (see p.520). The largest of these, **VÉRIA** (ancient Berrhoea or Berea, and Karaferiye for Turkish-speakers), has few outstanding sites or monuments, with the exception of its excellent new Byzantine museum. That said, it is one of the more interesting northern Greek communities, thanks to its mixed Jewish, Muslim and Christian heritage: in the nineteenth century the town became an important industrial centre, and many of the townsfolk grew prosperous from flour and sesame milling as well as hide tanning. Perhaps most importantly, Véria lies within twenty minutes' drive of the history-changing excavations of ancient Aegae at **Vergina**.

Véria

Arrival and information

If you don't have your own transport the best way to get here is by regular bus, as the train station is very inconvenient, a good 3km from the centre. The **KTEL** at the northern end of central Véria handles the regular services to and from all regional destinations. **Taxis** are lemon-yellow with white roofs. At central Platía Eliás, known locally as the Belvedere, there is an all-but-useless **EOT** information booth, in the summer. Just off one-way Mitropóleos, towards the hub-like Platía Konstandínou Raktiván – universally called Platía Oroloyíou, after a long-vanished clock tower – are the **post office** (on side-street Dhionysíou Solomoú) and various banks (with **ATMs**), plus lots of shops and fast-food joints. The best (quietest) **Internet** café is along Eliás.

Accommodation

Of the bare handful of **hotels** in Véria, the least expensive is the adequate and clean en-suite *Veroi* at Kendrikís 4, just off Platía Oroloyíou (☎23310 22866; ❸).

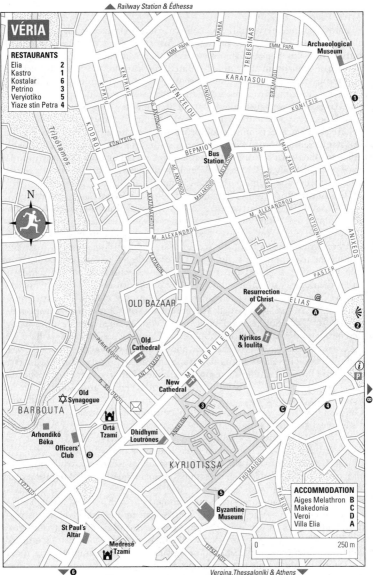

VÉRIA

RESTAURANTS
Elia	2
Kastro	1
Kostalar	6
Petrino	3
Veryiotiko	5
Yiaze stin Petra	4

N

Archaeological
Museum

Bus
Station

OLD BAZAAR

Resurrection
of Christ

Old
Cathedral

Kýrikos
& Ioulíta

New
Cathedral

Old
Synagogue

BARBOUTA

Ortá
Tzamí

Dhídhymi
Loutrónes

Arhondikó
Béka

Officers'
Club

KYRIOTISSA

Byzantine
Museum

ACCOMMODATION
Aiges Melathron	B
Makedonia	C
Veroi	D
Villa Elia	A

St Paul's
Altar

Medresé
Tzamí

0   250 m

A slightly smarter, better-value choice is the *Villa Elia*, Elías 16 (☏ 23310 26800, ℻ 23310 21880; ❸), but prone to street noise. Much quieter, albeit with rather functional rooms, is the *Makedonia*, Kondoyeorgáki 50 (☏ & ℻ 23310 66902, ⓦ www.hotelmakedonia.gr; ❹), with a roof garden and substantial breakfasts. Down on the ring road is the pricey and new *Aiges Melathron* (☏ 23310 77777, ⓦ www.aigesmelathron.gr; ❼), really aimed at business travellers, with bright rooms, a good restaurant and a swimming pool.

The Town

Towards the northern end of Leofóros Aníxeos, which snakes along the cliff edge past Véria's most prestigious district, is the town's **archeological museum** (Tues–Sun 8.30am–3pm; €2); it contains mostly Hellenistic and Roman remains from the immediate area, but some of the artefacts piled up in the outside courtyard are also worth a viewing, even if you don't or cannot enter the museum. Far more impressive is the town's outstanding new **Byzantine museum**, well signposted along Thomaídhou (Tues–Sun 8.30am–3pm; €2). Housed in a beautifully restored nineteenth-century flour mill, with an austere stone facade, it mostly comprises an exquisite display of icons – Véria was renowned for its painting workshops in the late Middle Ages – along with other treasures mostly from the Byzantine era, including coins. On the ground floor, a highly moving video, with English subtitles, records the history of the mill, its demise and its exemplary refurbishment.

Christianity has a venerable and long history in Véria: Saint Paul preached here (Acts 17:10–14) on two occasions, between 50 and 60 AD, and a gaudy alcove shrine or **"altar"** of modern mosaics at the base of Mavromiháli marks the supposed spot of his sermons. Four dozen or so small **churches**, some medieval but mostly dating from the sixteenth to eighteenth century, are scattered around the town, earning it the moniker of Little Jerusalem. Under Ottoman rule, many were disguised as barns or warehouses, with little dormer windows rather than domes to admit light; but today, often surrounded by cleared spaces and well labelled, they're not hard to find. The only church regularly open, however, is the well-signposted **Resurrection of Christ, or Anastásseos Christoú** (Tues–Sun 8.30am–3pm; free), with cleaned fourteenth-century frescoes, near the fork end of Mitropóleos. The most striking images here are a *Dormition/Assumption* over the west door; a *Transfiguration* on the south wall, with one disciple somersaulting backwards in fear; and on the north wall a rare image of Christ mounting the cross on a ladder. The key-keeper may offer to show you the nearby tenth-century chapel of **Kýrikos and Ioulíta**, but its frescoes are alas uncleaned and likely to remain so for the foreseeable future. On Kendrikís, the ramshackle **twelfth-century cathedral** stands opposite a gnarled plane tree from which the conquering Turks hanged Archbishop Arsenios in 1430; with its chimney-like truncated minaret, added when it was converted to a mosque, the church looks like some disused factory.

Nearby what remains of the old **bazaar** straddles Kendrikís, while downhill and to the west tumbles the riverside Ottoman quarter of **Barboúta** (aka Barboúti). Largely **Jewish** before the 1944 deportations annihilated the one-thousand-strong community, it is today more or less abandoned, though EU-funded restoration of the crumbling houses – many bearing Hebrew inscriptions and ornate frescoes – is now proceeding apace. The disused **synagogue** can be reached via Odhós Dhekátis Merarhías, past the conspicuous officers' club near Platía Oroloyíou. Situated on a plaza with a small amphitheatre, it is a long stone building with an awning over the door, which is sometimes left ajar, allowing you to look at the rambling, arcaded interior. Of the many handsome nineteenth-century mansions hereabouts, the impeccably restored **Arhondikó Béka** currently houses the International Institute of Traditional Architecture.

Survivals of the **Muslim** presence in Véria are more numerous and conspicuous, but less well restored. It is worth hunting down the twin *hamam* complex, **Dhídhymi Loutrónes**, at the end of Loutroú, the small **Ortá Tzamí** mosque just off Kendrikís, and the splendid **Medresé Tzamí** mosque on Márkou Bótsari, but do not expect to enter them or be impressed by their state of conservation.

Eating and drinking

Along pedestrianized Patriárhou Ioakeím, a lane lined with old Ottoman houses, many of them housing trendy **café-bars**, is a gastro-taverna, *Petrino*, serving the usual fare with a twist. An enduring favourite for supper is *Kostalar* in the Papákia district at Afrodhítis 2/D, reached by following Mavromiháli uphill from the Saint Paul shrine to a plane-tree-shaded square with rivulets; this place has been going strong for decades, offering clay-pot oven dishes and grills. Another popular spot is the *Ouzeri Yiaze stin Petra*, on the corner of Aníxeos and Koundourióti; although not in the most inspired location, it serves up consistently good grills and appetizers. Just along from the Byzantine Museum at Thomaídhou 2, the respectable *Veryiotiko* serves predictable cuisine, though in winter it comes up with the likes of wild boar with quinces; the summer terrace suffers from road noise but the taverna has the virtue of opening on Mondays when nearly everywhere else seems to shut.

In the daytime, by far the most pleasant place for a **coffee or a beer** is *Elia*, at the edge of the Belvedere, with its shady terrace overlooking the plain. The very sweet-toothed should not leave Véria without trying the local speciality, **revaní**, a syrup-soaked sponge cake. The trendy **bars** along Eliás and around the Belvedere heave with locals sporting tight shirts, bare midriffs and the very latest in mobile phones; for slightly less showing off try the well-located *Kastro*, along towards the archeological museum. For the best ice cream in town head for *Prapas* at Mitropóleos 51. If you crave more action after dark, the pedestrianized area around Patriárhou Ioakeím crammed full with noisy bars comes into its own.

Vergina: ancient Aegae

The site of **VERGINA**, 16km southeast of Véria, undoubtedly qualifies as one of the most memorable experiences that Greece has to offer. The main finds consist of a series of **chamber tombs** unearthed by Professor Manolis Andronikos in 1977 – the culmination of decades of work on the site – and unequivocally accepted as those of Philip II, the father of Alexander the Great, and other members of the Macedonian royal family. This means that the site itself must be that of **Aegae**, the original Macedonian royal capital before the shift to Pella, and later the sanctuary and royal burial place of the Macedonian kings. It was here that Philip II was assassinated, cremated and buried – and tradition maintained that the dynasty would be destroyed if any king were buried elsewhere, as indeed happened after the death of Alexander the Great in Asia. Until Andronikos's finds, Aegae had long been assumed to be lost beneath modern Édhessa.

Finds from the site and tombs, the richest Greek trove since the discovery of Mycenae, are exhibited in the complex. Some are also on display at Thessaloníki's Archeological Museum (see p.493), though recently many have been returned to Vergina. The main tombs remain *in situ*, while the magnificent treasures found inside are shown off in remarkably well-lit cases, along with erudite texts in Greek and English. Visitors walk down narrow underground passages into a climate-controlled bunker, which allows them to see the ornamental facades and the empty chambers beyond; overhead, the earth of the tumulus has been replaced. It's best to try and get here very early or visit at siesta time (it's refreshingly cool inside during the fierce summer heat) in order to avoid crowds and the increasing number of Greek school groups.

The modern village of **Veryína** right next door has limited facilities, with a slew of tourist-trap **tavernas**, an **ATM** and a foreign-note changer. For somewhere to **stay** try the decent *Pension Vergina* (☎23310 92510 or 23310 25703; B&B; ❷), conveniently located near the stop for Véria-bound buses; it offers en-suite rooms with fans and balconies, and breakfast is copious.

The Royal Tombs

Under a tumulus just outside modern Veryína, Andronikos discovered several large Macedonian chamber tombs, known simply as the **Royal Tombs** (summer: Mon 12.30–7pm, Tues–Sun 8am–7pm; until 5pm in winter; €8; photography forbidden). From outside, all that's visible is a low hillock with skylights and long ramps leading inside, but once underground you can admire the facades and doorways of the tombs, which are well illuminated and behind glass.

A clockwise tour takes you round the tombs in the order IV-I-II-III. Tomb IV, the so-called Doric, was looted in antiquity; so too was **Tomb I**, or the **Persephone tomb**, but it retained a delicate and exquisitely crafted **mural** of the rape of Persephone by Hades, the only complete example of an ancient Greek painting that has yet been found. **Tomb II**, that of **Philip II**, is a much grander vaulted tomb with a Doric facade adorned by a sumptuous painted **frieze** of Philip, Alexander and their retinue on a lion hunt. This – incredibly – was discovered intact, having been deliberately disguised with rubble from later tomb pillagings. Among the treasures to emerge – now displayed in the dimly lit but well-labelled hall here – were a marble sarcophagus containing a **gold ossuary** (*larnax*), its cover embossed with the exploding, sixteen-pointed star symbol of the royal line. Still more significantly, five small **ivory heads** were found, among them representations of both Philip II and Alexander. It was this clue, as well as the fact that the skull bore marks of a disfiguring facial wound Philip was known to have sustained, that led to the identification of the tomb as his. Also on view are a fabulous **gold oak-leaf wreath** – so delicate it quivers – and a more modest companion *larnax* found in the antechamber, presumed to contain the carefully wrapped bones and ashes of a legitimate queen or concubine, quite probably a Thracian aristocrat, married for political reasons, and who, according to some sources, stepped into the dead king's pyre of her own accord.

Tomb III is thought to be that of Alexander IV, "the Great's" son, murdered in adolescence – thus the moniker **Prince's Tomb**. His bones were discovered in a silver vase. From the tomb frieze, a superb **miniature of Dionysos and his consort** is highlighted. You should also spare a moment or two to view the excellent **video**, subtitled in English, which brings the archeological finds to life.

Macedonian Tomb

The so-called **Macedonian Tomb**, actually five adjacent tombs, can also be visited after a fashion (same times as Royal; same admission ticket). They are about 500m uphill and south of the village and, like the Royal Tombs, lie well below ground level, protected by a vast tin roof. When he's around, the guard will let you into the dig, though not into the tombs themselves. Excavated by the French in 1861, the most prominent one, thought to be that of Philip's mother Eurydike, is in the form of a temple, with an Ionic facade of half-columns breached by two successive marble portals opening onto ante- and main chambers. Inside you can just make out an imposing marble throne with sphinxes carved on the sides, armrests and footstool. The neighbouring two pairs of tombs, still undergoing snail-paced excavation, are said to be similar in design.

Palace of Palatítsia

The ruins of the **Palace of Palatítsia** (Mon 12.30–7pm, Tues–Sun 8am–7pm; closes 5pm in winter; included in Royal Tombs ticket) occupy a low hill 1km southeast of the village. It is reached by crossing a ravine and continuing past the main village crossroads to a vast new car park, where the entrance is located. The palace complex was probably built during the third century BC as a summer residence for the last great Macedonian king, Antigonus Gonatas. Little more than the foundations remain, but amidst the confusing litter of column drums and capitals you can make out a triple *propylaion* (entrance gate) opening onto a central courtyard. This is framed by broad porticoes and colonnades which, on the south side, preserve a well-executed mosaic now invisible under protective sand and gravel following frost damage. Despite its lack of substance, Palatítsia is an attractive site, dominated by a grand old oak tree looking out across the plains, scattered with Iron Age (tenth- to seventh-century BC) tumuli among other things. The only substantial items dug up to date are the first two tiers of the **theatre** just below, where Philip II was assassinated in 336 BC, some say at the wedding of his daughter.

Pella

PELLA was the capital of Macedonia throughout its greatest period, and the first capital of Greece after Philip II forcibly unified the country around 338 BC. It was founded some sixty years earlier by King Archelaos, who transferred the royal Macedonian court here from Aegae (see p.517); from its beginnings it was a major centre of culture. The royal palace was decorated by the painter **Zeuxis** and was said to be the greatest artistic showplace since the time of Classical Athens. **Euripides** wrote and produced his last plays at the court, and here, too, **Aristotle** was to tutor the young Alexander the Great – born, like his father Philip II, in the city.

The site today is a worthwhile stopover en route to Édhessa and western Macedonia. Its main treasures are a series of pebble mosaics, some in the museum, others *in situ*. For an understanding of the context, it is best to visit after looking around the archeological museum at Thessaloníki, from where the site can also be visited comfortably on a rewarding day-trip.

The site

When Archelaos founded Pella, it lay at the head of a broad lake, connected to the Thermaïkós gulf by a navigable river. By the second century BC the river had begun to silt up and the city fell into decline. It was sacked by the Romans in 146 BC and never rebuilt; an earthquake caused further damage around two centuries later. Today its **ruins** (April–Oct Mon noon–7pm, Tues–Sun 8am–7pm; closes 3pm Nov–March; €6 combined ticket with museum) stand in the middle of a broad expanse of plain, 40km from Thessaloníki and the sea.

Pella was located by chance finds in 1957; preliminary digs have revealed a vast site covering over 485 hectares. As yet, only a few blocks of the city have been fully excavated but they have proved exciting, and investigations are continuing. The **acropolis** at Pella is a low hill to the west of the modern village of Pélla. Work is in progress on a sizeable building, probably a palace, but at present it's illuminating mainly for the idea it gives you of the size and scope of the site. To the north of the road, at the main site, stand the low remains of a grand official building, probably a government office; it is divided into three large open courts, each enclosed by a *peristyle*, or portico (the columns of the central one have been re-erected), and bordered by wide streets with a sophisticated drainage system.

The three main rooms of the first court have patterned geometric floors, in the centre of which were found intricate **pebble mosaics** depicting scenes of a lion hunt, a griffin attacking a deer and Dionysos riding a panther. These are now in the excellent **museum** across the road (same hours as site), next to the car park. But in the third court three late fourth-century BC mosaics have been left *in situ* under sheltering canopies; one, a stag hunt, is complete, and astounding in its dynamism and use of perspective. The others represent, respectively, the rape of Helen by Paris and his friends Phorbas and Theseus, and a fight between a Greek and an Amazon.

It is the graceful and fluid quality of these compositions that sets them apart from later Roman and Byzantine mosaics, and which more than justifies a visit. The uncut pebbles, carefully chosen for their soft shades, blend so naturally that the shapes and movements of the subjects seem gradated rather than fixed, especially in the action of the hunting scenes and the rippling movement of the leopard with Dionysos. Strips of lead or clay are used to outline special features; the eyes, now missing, were probably semi-precious stones.

The mosaics are inevitably a hard act to follow, but the museum merits another half-hour of perusal of its other well-presented exhibits. Highlights include rich grave finds from the two local necropolises, delicately worked terracotta figurines from a sanctuary of Aphrodite and Cybele, a large horde of late Classical/early Hellenistic coins, and – on the rarely seen domestic level – metal door fittings: pivots, knocker plates and crude keys.

Practicalities

The nearest **hotels** to the site are at Néa Halkidhóna, a major junction 8km east. Opposite each other on the Véria road, 1km from the junction with the Thessaloníki road, are the decent *Kornelios* (☎23910 23888; ❷) and the slightly more appealing *Filippos* (☎23910 22125, ℉23910 22198; ❷). **Buses** from Véria and Veryína to Thessaloníki stop right in front of the *Hotel Kornelios*. The site of Pella lies on the main Thessaloníki–Édhessa road and is served by half-hourly buses, stopping in **Néa Halkidhóna**, in either direction.

Édhessa and around

The main gateway to the intriguing northwest corner of Macedonia – a land of lofty peaks and mirror-like lakes – **Édhessa**, teeters atop the same escarpment as Véria. Since the late 1990s, it has been resolutely turning itself into a regional centre for tourism. The authorities also began overseeing the stylish renovation of the town's old buildings, including some handsome water mills. A wide range of activities is now on offer both within the town and in the nearby mountains. Édhessa makes a good base from which to visit the unspoilt archeological site of **Lefkádhia**.

Édhessa

ÉDHESSA, like Véria, is a delightful place for a stopover but with rather better accommodation. Its modest fame is attributed to the waters that flow through the town; descending from the mountains to the north, these waters flow swiftly through the middle of town in several courses and then, just to the east, cascade down a dramatic ravine, luxuriant with vegetation, to the plain below. Most of the town's architecture is humdrum, but the various stream-side parks and wide pedestrian pavements are a rare pleasure in a country where the car is tyrant – indeed, Édhessa was the pioneering town in Greece for pedestrianization.

Arrival and Information

Édhessa's **train and bus stations** are both well placed: the main KTEL is on the corner of Filíppou (the main road into the town centre) and Pávlou Melá; there's a second, smaller terminal for Flórina/Kastoriá services only, nearby at the corner of Egnatía and Pávlou Melá. The train station is in the north of town. The town's excellent new **tourist information office** is in the park at Garéfi and Pérdhika (daily 10am–8pm; ☎23810 20300 or 23810 23101, Ⓦ www.edessacity.gr) and is far and away the best in the region. English-speaking staff can provide exquisitely produced bilingual leaflets and all manner of information about activities, such as trekking, rafting, kayaking and skiing in the surrounding region. You'll find the **post office** on Dhimokratías, while several **banks** sport ATMs.

Accommodation

Accommodation at the lower end of the scale is available at the modest but decent *Alfa*, Egnatía 36 (☎23810 22221; ❸), whose rooms are functional but noise-prone. Far more upmarket, the *Xenia* (☎23810 21898; ❺), signposted off Filíppou, is the town's most expensive hotel, yet its comfortable rooms and deluxe facilities make it good value. For some real old-fashioned hospitality, however, try the delightful and popular ⚒ *Varossi*, in the eponymous district at Arh. Meletíou 45–47 (☎23810 21865, Ⓕ23810 28872; ❹), run by charming owners and with open fire, cosy en-suite rooms decorated in a vernacular style, and delicious breakfasts. The shiny *Aigai* hotel (☎23810 23810, Ⓔ aigaihotel@otenet.gr; ❹), with all mod cons and fashionably decorated airy rooms, is located off the main road, some 4km out of the city centre, convenient only if you have your own transport.

The Town

The most interesting neighbourhood in the town is the **Varóssi**, tottering atop the cliffs just west of the waterfalls. Its mills and old Balkan-style houses, some decorously decaying, others tastefully renovated, reward aimless wanderings – though everything is well signposted. Some of the **water mills** have been renovated as part of a scheme to create a so-called open-air water museum, which also includes an unusual freshwater **aquarium** (Mon & Wed–Sun 10am–6pm; €1.50). Several churches and chapels, new and restored, are proudly signposted, but the only real sight as such is a delightful little **folklore museum** (Tues–Sun 10am–6pm; €1.50), on Megálou Alexándhrou, near Ayía Paraskeví church; it displays various household objects and other traditional items of the kind that would once have graced every home in the district.

Eating and drinking

The range of **restaurants** is more limited. *Paeti* at 18-Oktovríou 20 is the undisputed top choice in town, offering a small but flavoursome range of *mayireftá* and *tis óras*, and specializing in roast suckling pig and delicious barrelled wine. Apart from the municipal restaurant in the *Katarraktes* complex by the tourist office, you'll also find a couple of decent tavernas and a pizzeria at the eastern or park end of Tsimiskí, plus various standard eateries, including a rash of fast-food outlets, around town. Superbly sited among the woods, 2km out of town on the road to Aridhéa, the *Fysiolatrikos Omilos Edhessas*, or *FOE*, puts more effort into its decor than its food, but the latter is appetizingly presented and, with some adventurous Gallic touches, is a welcome change from the norm.

Café and **bar** life is concentrated in the pedestrian zones flanking the rivulets, especially on Angelí Gátsou. Away from here, the municipal café-bar *Psilos Vrahos*, perched atop its namesake vantage point, is worth a visit for a beer or fruit juice. However, Édhessa's – and possibly the whole country's – most unusual entertainment venue is the dramatically sited *Tò Kanavouryio*, a recently converted hemp factory (complete with intact machinery dating from the early twentieth century) that doubles up as a café-bar-cum-restaurant and **live music** locale (jazz, rock and folk). Located at the foot of the cliffs, it can be reached by two giddying glass lifts accessible from a platform near Áyios Vassílis chapel at the edge of the Varóssi district (signposted). Anyone whose nerves aren't up to it, or who doesn't quite trust the engineering, can get there the long way (3km), via a signposted road off the main route towards Pélla, down in the valley.

Lefkádhia

Thirty kilometres south of Édhessa on the road to Véria, **LEFKÁDHIA** has not been positively identified with any Macedonian city, but it is possible that it was Mieza, where Aristotle taught. The modern village lies just west of the main road, but for the ancient site you should turn off east at a sign reading "To the Macedonian Tombs". There are, in fact, four subterranean tombs in all – though only one has a guard, who keeps the keys to the other three.

The staffed one, the so-called **Great Tomb** or **Tomb of Judgement** (currently closed for restoration), east of the main road just past the train tracks, is the largest Macedonian temple-tomb yet discovered. Despite extensive cement protection, it has been badly damaged by creeping damp from the very high local water table; consolidation work is currently underway, and will probably involve its complete dismantling and reconstruction. It dates from the third century BC, and was probably built for a general, who is depicted in one of the barely surviving frescoes, on the left, being led by Hermes in his role as conductor of souls. Other faded frescoes on the right represent the judges of Hades – hence the tomb's alias. A once-elaborate double-storeyed facade, half-Doric and half-Ionic, has almost completely crumbled away; on the entablature frieze you can just make out a battle between Persians and Macedonians.

The **Anthimíon Tomb**, 150m further along the same country road, is more impressive, with its four Ionic facade columns, two marble interior sarcophagi with inscribed lids, and well-preserved frescoes. The tympanum bears portraits of a couple, presumably the tomb occupants, though the man's face has been rubbed out. Ornamental designs and three giant cornice ornaments complete the pediment decoration. Between the double set of portals, the ceiling frescoes are perhaps stylized representations of octopuses and other water creatures.

West from Édhessa: Nymféo, Flórina and the Préspa Lakes

The highlights of the area immediately to the west of Édhessa are the bird-rich **Préspa** lakes, both of which nestle in a strategic spot where Greece, Albania and the FYROM meet; and a handsome mountain village, **Nymféo**, where some of the attractive stone houses have been converted into classy accommodation.

Immediately west of Édhessa lies Lake Vegorítidha, far less appealing than the Préspa pair; its northwest shore is traced by the scenic rail line between Édhessa and **Flórina** – the area's main urban centre but a rather charmless place, whose one attraction is its archeological museum. An equally scenic road skirts the northern side of the lake, passing through one or two picturesque villages and rocky sheep pasture, and offering panoramic views of the water.

To the north rises **Mount Kaïmaktsalán**, whose 2524-metre summit marks the FYROM frontier, the scene of one of the bloodiest and most important battles of World War I. The area has recently been developed as the **Vórras ski resort** (☎23810 82169 or 23810 20300), one of the highest and best in northern Greece.

Although there are infrequent trains to Flórina and the odd bus service, visiting this northwestern nook of the region is really best tackled only if you have your own transport – one option might be to rent a car in Kastoriá.

Whatever you do, don't get stuck in the dire rail/road junction town of **Amýndeo** – where there is no reputable accommodation – from where paved roads lead north, west and south to Flórina (see below), Kastoriá (see p.528) and Kozáni respectively.

Nymféo

Perched at 1300m on the eastern flank of Mount Vítsi, some 25km west of Amýndeo and 60km northeast of Kastoriá, lies the well-groomed mountain village of **NYMFÉO**, popular of late with prosperous young Greek professionals looking for alternative recreational activities in retreats far from the city. To get there take the poorly marked turn-off at the village of Aetós; you then climb up an incredibly steep side road with hairpin bends.

Facilities fall within the higher budget range. The least expensive **accommodation** is also the least attractive: central *Xenonas Neveska* (☎23860 31442; ❸). You can also find **rooms** at the *Ederne* which has self-catering facilities (☎23860 31230 or 23860 31351; ❹), or at *La Galba* (☎23860 22818; ❸), for a little more atmosphere. The professionally run **inn** at the entrance to the village, *Ta Linouria* (☎23860 31030 or 2310 300 050, ℗23860 31133; ❻), offers attractively decorated suites and is also a reliable source of decent, if pricey, food; otherwise try one of the cheaper **tavernas** in the village centre. For a special occasion you might consider a night at one of Greece's most exclusive hotels, ⚲ *La Moara* (☎2310 287 626, ℗2310 287 401; closed July; ❽), a luxurious mansion a short way uphill. Run by nationally renowned wine-makers, the Boutari family, it offers refined cuisine, to match the cellar, while the rooms are tastefully appointed, with state-of-the-art bathrooms and top-quality linens and accessories.

Flórina

Surrounded by steep hills carpeted with beech woods, **FLÓRINA** is the last Greek town before the FYROM border, 13km to the north. Flórina's only attraction is the **Archeological Museum** (Tues–Fri 8.30am–3pm; €2), which is just up from the train station and houses, among other things, a collection of enchanting votive reliefs, including a couple of gems from the Hellenistic site of Petres, near Amýndeo (see above), and some artefacts rescued from the shores of the Préspa lakes, including fine icons – in a rather pathetic upstairs display.

Hotel prices are exorbitant for what you get; you're much better off staying in Édhessa, Kastoriá or by the lakes. If you do end up spending a night here, you'll find the cheapest decent place is the *Hellinis* at Pávlou Melá 31 (☎23850 22671; ❹), beyond the museum.

Although it has numerous cafés, bars and fast-food places – mostly on Pávlou Melá – Flórina doesn't score highly on **restaurants**. The best, notwithstanding its location on the grim Soviet-style square beneath the KTEL, is the *To Koutouki*, open daily for lunch and dinner and serving decent barrelled wine with the usual array of dishes. Another option is *Iy Prespa* (closed Tues) on Tyrnávou, a side street off Pávlou Melá, but its half-dozen indoor tables fill up quickly.

There are two daily buses (early morning and late afternoon) to **Áyios Yermanós** in the **Préspa** basin.

The road out of Flórina snakes up the valley to the 1600-metre Pisodhéri saddle, site of one of the livelier villages en route and the **Vígla** ski lift. **PISODHÉRI** village offers the **hotel** *Modestios* (☎23850 45566, ☎23850 45928; ❹), a restored traditional inn that's far better value than anything in Flórina, but is closed during the week outside the winter holiday season. Open all year and a cosy alternative is *Eleni* (☎23850 46415; ❸), up on the other side of the main road, with comfortable rooms and a **restaurant**. From here the road follows the headwaters of the Aliákmonas River – the longest and one of the most beautiful in Greece – most of the way to Kastoriá.

The Préspa lakes

Climbing west out of the Aliákmonas valley on the serpentine paved side road towards **Préspa**, you have little hint of what's ahead until suddenly you top a pass, and a shimmering expanse of water riven by islets and ridges appears. It is not, at first glance, postcard-pretty, but the basin has an eerie beauty and a back-of-beyond quality that grows on you with further acquaintance. It also has a turbulent recent history that belies its current role as one of the Balkans' most important wildlife sanctuaries.

△ Nymféo village

During the Byzantine era, Préspa became a prominent place of exile for troublesome noblemen, thus accounting for the surprising number of **ecclesiastical monuments** in this backwater. In the tenth century it briefly hosted the court of the Bulgarian Tsar Samuel before his defeat by Byzantine emperor Basil II. Under the Ottomans the area again lapsed into obscurity, only to regain the dubious benefits of strategic importance in just about every European war of the last century, culminating in vicious local battles during the 1947–49 Greek civil war. In 1988, a forest fire on the eastern ridge treated observers to a dangerous fireworks display, as dozens of unexploded artillery shells were touched off by the heat. After World War II Préspa lay desolate and largely depopulated, as locals fled abroad to either Eastern Europe or North America and Australia, depending on which side they had fought on. It is only since the late 1970s that the villages, still comparatively primitive and neglected, have begun to refill during the summer, when beans and hay are grown as close to the two lakes as the national park authorities allow. A common sight everywhere is that of lake-reeds, cut and stacked for use as beanpoles.

Mikrí Préspa, the southerly lake, is mostly shallow (9m maximum depth) and reedy, with a narrow fjord curling west and just penetrating Albanian territory. The borders of Greece, Albania and the FYROM meet in the middle of deeper **Megáli Préspa** and, since the early 1990s, Albanian refugees have used the basin as an exit corridor into Greece. Their presence as illegal agricultural workers is now tolerated, as farms in the area are perennially short-handed. The border here is extremely porous – though unofficial forays into Albania are emphatically not recommended – and a considerable amount of smuggling in duty-free goods goes on.

The core of the **national park**, established in 1971, barely encompasses Mikrí Préspa and its shores, but the peripheral zone extends well into the surrounding mountains, affording protection of sorts to a variety of land mammals. You'll almost certainly see foxes crossing the road, though the wolves and bears up on the ridges are considerably shyer. The lakes have a dozen resident fish species, including *tsiróni* – a sort of freshwater sardine – and *grivádhi*, a kind of carp. But it's **birdlife** for which the Préspa basin, particularly the smaller lake, is most famous. There are few birds of prey, but you should see a fair number of egrets, cormorants, crested grebes and pelicans (this being one of the few breeding sites of both the white and Dalmatian pelican), which nest in the spring, with the chicks out and about by summer. They feed partly on the large numbers of snakes, which include vipers, whip snakes and harmless water snakes which you may encounter while swimming. Observation towers are available at Vromolímni and near Áyios Ahíllios, but dawn spent anywhere at the edge of the reedbeds with a pair of binoculars will be immensely rewarding (though bear in mind that you are not allowed to boat or wade into the reeds). There are **park information centres** in the villages of **Áyios Yermanós** and **Psarádhes** (see p.526 and p.527).

While you may arrive from Flórina by bus, you really can't hope to tour the area without some means of **transport** – either a mountain bike or a car. Similarly, in view of the area's past underdevelopment, don't expect much in the way of **facilities**: food is adequate and inexpensive, but exceedingly simple; the same might be said of local accommodation, though this has improved in recent years. Préspa is becoming increasingly popular, and you'd be wise to reserve at one of the few accommodations listed during midsummer, especially at weekends.

Mikrolímni

MIKROLÍMNI, 5km up a side road off the main route into the valley, would be your first conceivable stop. The small shop and fish taverna owned by Yiorgos Hassou, on the shoreside square, has a few **rooms** to let (℡23850 61221 or 23850 45931; ❶). In the evening, you can look towards sunsets over reedbeds and the snake-infested Vidhronísi (or Vitrinítsi) islet, though swimming isn't good here, or anywhere else on Mikrí Préspa for that matter. At the far end of the hamlet is a sporadically used biological observation station, literally the last house in Greece, and beyond that the lake narrows between sheer hillsides on its way to Albania.

Return to the main road, which reaches a T-junction 16km from the main Flórina–Kastoriá highway, on the spit which separates the larger and smaller lakes. It's probable that at one time there was just one lake here, but now there's a four-metre elevation difference. Bearing right at the junction leads within 4km to Áyios Yermanós; the left option splits again at the west end of the spit, bearing south towards the islet of Áyios Ahillíos or northwest towards the hamlet of Psarádhes.

Áyios Yermanós

ÁYIOS YERMANÓS is a large village of tile-roofed houses, overlooking a patch of Megáli Préspa in the distance. It's worth making the trip up just to see two tiny late-Byzantine churches, whose frescoes, dating from the time when the place belonged to the bishopric of Ohrid, display a marked Macedonian influence. Inside the lower church, **Áyios Athanásios**, seldom open, you can glimpse a dog-faced *St Christopher* among a line of saints opposite the door.

Far more impressive, however, is the tiny, eleventh-century parish church of **Áyios Yermanós** up on the square, hidden behind a new monster awkwardly tacked onto it in 1882. The Byzantine structure has its own entrance, and the frescoes, skilfully retouched in 1743, can be lit; the switch is hidden in the narthex. There are more hagiographies and martyrdoms than possible to list here, but there's a complete catalogue of them (in Greek and English) by the door. Among the best are the dome's *Pandokrátor*; a *Nativity* and *Baptism* right of the dome; a *Crucifixion* and *Resurrection* to the left; plus the saints *Peter and Paul, Kosmas and Damian, Tryphon and Pandelimon* by the door. Less conventional scenes include the *Entry into Jerusalem* and *Simon Helping Christ with the Cross*, opposite the door, and the *Apocalypse*, with the *Succouring of Mary the Beatified by Zosimas*, in the narthex. Mary was an Alexandrine courtesan who, repenting of her ways, retired to the desert for forty years. She was found, a withered crone on the point of death, by Zosimas, abbot of a desert monastery, and is traditionally shown being spoon-fed like an infant.

In the village is the helpful **Préspa information centre** (daily 9.30am–2.30pm; ℡23850 51211, ✉spp@line.gr), focusing on the wildlife of the national park; given sufficient warning, the centre can arrange guides for bird-watching trips into the park. It also sells locally farmed organic products. The village has a **post office** – the only one in the Préspa basin – and a few places to **stay**: *Xenonas Iy Paradossi*, opposite the church (℡23850 51266; ❸), and, in the upper part of the village, the slightly better run *To Petrino* (℡23850 51344; ❸). The best **taverna** is *Lefteris*, nearby; when it is closed you can fall back on *To Tzaki*, along from the church.

Koúla beach and Psarádhes

At the far end of the wide causeway dividing the two lakes, 4km from the T-junction, is **Koúla beach**, and a cluster of what passes for tourist development hereabouts: a patch of reed-free sand from where you can swim in Megáli Préspa; a free but basic camping area, now bereft of its water tap; plus an army post. Tents are also pitched near the run-of-the-mill taverna *Plaz Prespon*; *Iy Koula*, up by the army post, is the only (not very good, and overpriced) alternative. Just below it, you can see where the waters of Mikrí Préspa trickle into Megáli Préspa.

If you don't intend to camp, it's best to bear right just above the army post, reaching after 6km of panoramic corniche the rickety village of **PSARÁDHES** (Nivitsa in Slav dialect), whose lanes make for a pleasant stroll. Unfortunately, the wonderful old houses lining them are increasingly derelict, with nothing being done either to preserve them, or check the spread of unsightly modern construction. Two **hotels** offer relative comfort: *To Arhontiko* (T23850 46260; ❷) and *To Hayiati* (T23850 46611; ❸), both back from the lakeside. There are some **rooms** for rent, such as the spartanly furnished ones above the *Taverna Syndrofia* (T23850 46107; ❸), a good spot to sample *fassoládha* (bean soup), lake fish and the proprietor's wine. You won't find the fish fried here anywhere else in Greece; similarly, the cows ambling through the lakeside meadows are a locally adapted dwarf variety. Of the other **tavernas**, *Paradhosi* is the best of the bunch and the most reliably open. The inland-platía *kafenío* has been refurbished as a bar-café, *Mythos*, which does creditable coffees; similarly, the waterfront has been paved and landscaped, with parking provided for tour coaches.

If the boatmen are granted permits (once safety measures have been complied with) you will once again be able to go on a **boat excursion** to or past various medieval shrines and hermitages tucked into the shore leading around the promontory to Albania. The ride alone is well worth it, as cormorants, gulls and pelicans skim the limpid waters of Megáli Préspa, in which the mountains of Albania are reflected. Your guide will point out a fifteenth-century icon of the Virgin painted onto the rock opposite the village, and (on the far side of the peninsula) the thirteenth-century hermitage of Metamórfosis, whose icons have either been stolen or taken to the safety of the Flórina museum (see p.523). Usually, your only landfall is the spectacular fifteenth-century rock-church of **Panayía Eleoússas**, concealed at the top of a deep chasm some 500m before the frontier. From the top of the long stairway up, you've a fantastic framed view of the lake and the Albanian shore; the deceptively simple vaulted chapel contains a plethora of expressive, naive frescoes. They commemorate critical episodes from the life of Christ: to the right of the door, Mary Magdalene washes Christ's feet, with the *Transfiguration* just above, while opposite are a moving *Lamentation*, the two Marys at the sepulchre and an unusual *Resurrection* showing only Adam.

Áyios Ahíllios

If you keep straight at the end of the causeway, instead of turning right, the road soon brings you to a floating footbridge, 1500m in length, which leads across to the islet of **Áyios Ahíllios** and its impoverished hamlet. Five families totalling under thirty members still live on the islet, outnumbered by their cattle. A five-minute walk from the footbridge is the ruined Byzantine basilica of **Áyios Ahíllios**, while another ruin, a sixteenth-century monastery, Panayía Porfaras, lies at the southern end of the islet. For unrivalled views of Mikrí Préspa climb up to the summit of the islet's hill. Should you want to **stay** the night or get some refreshment, you'll find **rooms**, a café and decent **taverna** at *Xenonas* (T23850 46601, F23850 46931; ❸), outwardly rather unprepossessing, but pleasant inside.

Kastoriá and around

Set on a hilly, wooded peninsula extending deep into a slate-coloured lake, **KASTORIÁ** is one of the most interesting and attractive towns of mainland Greece. It's also wealthy and has been so for centuries as the centre of south-eastern Europe's fur trade; although the local beavers (*kastóri* in Greek) had been trapped to extinction by the nineteenth century, Kastoriá still supports a considerable industry of furriers who make up coats, gloves and other items from fur scraps imported from Canada and Scandinavia and, increasingly, from the pelts of locally farmed beavers. Animal-rights activists will find the place heavy going as the industry is well-nigh ubiquitous: you'll see scraps drying on racks, and megastores with profuse Russian signposting line all the approach highways. **Siátista** is also worth a visit for its impressive eighteenth-century mansions, but you really need your own vehicle to get there.

For most visitors, however, Kastoriá's main appeal lies in traces of its former prosperity: dozens of splendid *arhondiká* – **mansions** of the old fur families – dating from the seventeenth to nineteenth centuries, plus some fifty Byzantine and medieval **churches**, though only a handful is visitable and of compelling interest. About the only reminder of Muslim settlement is the minaret-less Koursoún Tzamí, marooned in a ridgetop car park; there's also a patch of an originally Byzantine-fortification wall down on the neck of the peninsula.

Kastoriá suffered heavy damage during both **World War II** and the **civil war** that followed it. Platía Van Fleet, by the lakeside at the neck of the promontory, commemorates the US general who supervised the Greek Nationalist Army's operations against the Communist Democratic Army in the final campaigns of 1948–49. The town was nearly captured by the Communists in 1948, and Mount Vítsi (2128m), the mountain dominating the northeastern shore of the lake, was, together with Mount Grámmos (2520m) to the west, the scene of their last stand in August 1949. However, most of the destruction of Kastoriá's architectural heritage is not due so much to 1940s munitions as to 1950s neglect, 1960s development and 1970s "renovation". It is miraculous that so many isolated specimens of Balkan vernacular and Neoclassical townhouses survive, mostly higher up on the peninsula where the steep gradients have frustrated cement mixers.

The town has a strong tradition of **rowing**, and rowers can be seen out daily on the lake opposite Odhós Megálou Alexándhrou. Even the Oxford and Cambridge Blues have been known to practise their strokes here. The less energetic might prefer to take one of the regular **boat trips** on the lake during the spring and summer months; they leave from the jetty near the fish market on the northern side of town (℡24670 26777 or 24670 22312; noon &, sometimes, 7pm; €5).

Arrival

The **airport** is 10km south of town, and the Olympic Airways office, where airport buses also drop off, is at Megálou Alexándhrou 15. Arriving at the **bus station**, you'll find yourself at the western edge of the peninsula. Coming by **car**, beware of the fee-parking scheme in effect across much of the city centre, operated by ticket machines; only a couple of central hotels have free or off-street parking, and they are the more expensive ones. Kastoriá has a locally based **car-rental** outfit, *Tómaso*, at Grámou 147 (℡24670 84000).

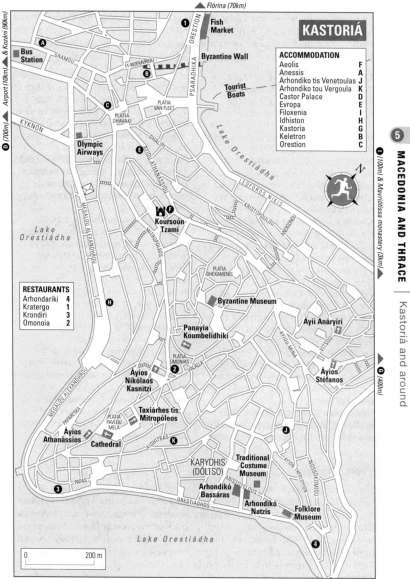

Flórina (70km)

Fish Market

Bus Station

Byzantine Wall

Airport (10km) ▲ & Kozáni (90km)

(700m)

Tourist Boats

KASTORIÁ

Lake Orestiádha

GRAMOU

11-NOEMVRIOU

PSARADHIKA

ORESTION

PLATIA VAN FLEET

PLATIA DHAVAKI

KYKNON

Olympic Airways

DHALIPI

AYIOU ATHANASSIOU

LEOFOROS NIKIS

KRISTOPOULOU

DHOMOKOU

Lake Orestiádha

MEGALOU ALEXANDHROU

MITROPOLEOS

Koursoún Tzamí

PLATIA DHEXAMENIS

5

MACEDONIA AND THRACE | Kastoriá and around

(100m) & Mavriótissa monastery (3km) ▲

(400m)

Byzantine Museum

Panayía Koumbelidhikí

Áyii Anáryiri

PLATIA OMONIAS

VALALA

AYIOU MINA

MITSIOU

Áyios Nikólaos Kasnitzi

Áyios Stéfanos

Taxiárhes tis Mitropóleos

AIDHITRAS

MEGALOU ALEXANDHROU

PAPARESKA

PLATIA PAVLOU MELA

Áyios Athanássios

Cathedral

PAPAS

KARYDHIS (DÓLTSO)

Traditional Costume Museum

AYATON IHEOLOTON

NOSSOKOMIOU

(400m)

Arhondikó Bassáras

ARISTOTELOUS

ORESTIADHOS

Arhondikó Natzís

Folklore Museum

Lake Orestiádha

0   200 m

Mavriótissa monastery (1.3km) ▼

Accommodation

Many of Kastoriá's **hotels**, especially those within easy walking distance of the bus station, are rather noisy with prices above average; despite this, they tend to be full pretty much year-round, so it's worth phoning ahead to book. All addresses given below are fairly central; along the lakeside road towards the airport and Kozáni you'll find more, mostly sizeable, establishments, which could be useful overflows if no central accommodation is going; these all lie on the bus route.

Aeolis Ayíou Athanassíou 30 ☎ 24670 21 070 or 24670 21080, ℻ 24670 21086. Designer-magazine interiors, tip-top service and every comfort – minibar, hairdryer, hydro-massage – make this 1930s villa one of the town's leading hotels. A full breakfast is served in your room or in the smart dining room. B&B ❺

Anessis Grámou 10 ☎ 24670 83908 or 24670 83909, ℻ 24670 83768. A modern, clean and eminently appealing hotel, with charmingly decorated rooms and all mod cons, spoiled only by a noisy location. ❸

Arhondiko tis Venetoulas Ayíon Theolóyion 6 ☎ & ℻ 24670 22446. A mansion conversion oozing charm. Great location and friendly, attentive service though the rooms are tiny. B&B ❹

Arhondiko tou Vergoula Aïdhítras 14 ☎ 24670 23415 or 24670 23416, ✉ sfinas@otenet.gr. Kastoriá's leading boutique hotel, housed in a handsome mid-nineteenth-century mansion, is in a particularly quiet part of the Dóltso. Rooms with a view are heftily surcharged, but all are faultlessly done out in traditional yet comfortable style, albeit with midget bathrooms. The ground-floor wine bar, serving Greek vintages, is open for patrons and non-residents every Friday and Saturday evening. ❻

Castor Palace Grámou 237 ☎ 24670 82160, ℻ 24670 82161. The nearest palace hotel to the town centre, bizarrely located near the lakefront overlooking a military camp. Impeccable rooms and extremely comfortable throughout. B&B ❺

Evropa Ayíou Athanassíou 12 ☎ 24670 23826, ℻ 24670 25154. With the town's fur-inflated hotel rates, this is the least expensive hotel that can be unreservedly recommended. Clean, decent rooms and a relatively quiet location. ❸

Filoxenia Nr Profítis Elías church ☎ 24670 22162. Kastoriá's nearest thing to budget accommodation, this hostel is well located. Some of its modest rooms enjoy lake views and cost more accordingly. Clean and simple. ❷

Idhiston Megálou Alexándhrou 91 ☎ 24670 22250. Self-catering apartments in a prime location over one of the town's trendy bars, with lake views. Run by a returnee from Canada whose passion for his native town is contagious. Book well ahead. ❺

Kastoria Leofóros Níkis 122 ☎ 24670 29453, ℻ 24670 29608. At the far end of the northern waterfront, this smart, traditional establishment offers lake views from its balconied, air-conditioned front rooms, plus free parking. ❺

Keletron 11-Noemvríou 52 ☎ 24670 22676. Rather shabby but passable hotel with its entrance on a side street and some rooms overlooking leafy Platía Van Fleet. ❹

Orestion Platía Dhaváki 1 ☎ 24670 22257 or 24670 22258. Clean, well-run, modern hotel with small but decent rooms, all en suite. Helpful reception but fairly noisy location. B&B ❸

The Town

For a sense of what Kastoriá must once have been during its heyday, head for the former lakeside quarter officially called **Karýdhis** but better known as Dóltso. At Kapetán Lázou 10, the splendidly opulent seventeenth-century Aïvazís family mansion has been turned into a **folklore museum** (daily 10am–noon & 4–7pm; €1). The house was inhabited until 1972 and its furnishings and most of its ceilings are in excellent repair, having miraculously survived German shelling; the Ottoman-style kiosk sports a set of stained-glass windows, three of them original, the others (blown out during bombardments) replaced by a local craftsman. Other features are an oriental fireplace in the master bedroom and the kitchen with all the original pots and pans. The caretaker, on request, will show you some of the other nearby mansions. The most notable are **Bassáras** and **Natzís**, close together on Vyzandíon; the latter was admirably restored in the 1990s. A third, also close by, on Platía Dóltso, now houses the **Traditional Costume Museum** (open by appointment; free; ☎ 24670 22697), a magical display of traditional clothing from western Macedonia and a chance to see another magnificent interior.

The **Byzantine museum** (Tues–Sun 8.30am–3pm; free) up on Platía Dhexamenís, opposite the derelict *Xenia Limnis* hotel, is rather more rewarding than Ioánnina's, wisely going for quality over quantity in this well-lit if unimaginatively displayed collection spanning the twelfth to the sixteenth centuries. Highlights include an unusually expressive thirteenth-century icon of Áyios Nikólaos and a fourteenth-century Ayii Anaryiri, plus a later one depicting the life of St George. There are also a few double-sided icons, including a rare *Deposition*, intended for use in religious processions. Captions are in Greek only.

Kastoriá's churches

The excellent frescoes of the twelfth-century church of **Áyios Nikólaos Kasnítzi** were returned to their former glory during the late 1980s. The unusual epithet stems from the donor, who is shown with his wife on the narthex wall presenting a model of the church to Christ. Lower down are ranks of exclusively female saints, to console the women congregated in the narthex which long served as a women's gallery. High up on the west wall of the nave, the *Dormition* and the *Transfiguration* are in good condition, the former inexplicably backwards (the Virgin's head is usually to the left). **Taxiárhes tís Mitropóleos**, the oldest (ninth-century) church, was built on the foundations of an earlier pagan temple, of which recycled columns and capitals are visible. Its most prominent frescoes, such as that of the *Virgin Platytera and Adoring Archangels* in the conch of the apse, and a conventional *Dormition* on the west wall, are fourteenth century. In the north aisle is the tomb of Greek nationalist Pavlos Melas, assassinated by Bulgarians at a nearby village in 1906, and commemorated by street names across northern Greece; his widow, who survived to the age of 101 (she died in 1974), is interred with him. Lastly, the **Panayía Koumbelidhikí**, so named because of its unusual dome (*kübe* in Turkish), retains one startling and well-illuminated fresco: a portrayal – almost unique in Greece – of God the Father in a ceiling mural of the *Holy Trinity*. The building was constructed in stages, with the apse completed in the tenth century and the narthex in the fifteenth. The cylindrical dome was meticulously restored after being destroyed by Italian bombing in 1940.

If tracking down churches seems too much like hard work, one of the most pleasant things to do in Kastoriá is to follow the narrow road along the tree-lined water's edge all around the **peninsula** to the east of town; at the tip vehicles must circulate anticlockwise, but the route is mainly used by joggers and the odd walker. Although the lake itself is visibly polluted, wildlife still abounds – pelicans, swans, frogs, tortoises and water snakes especially, and on a spring day numerous fish break water. Near the southeastern tip of the peninsula, some 3km along from the *Hotel Kastoria*, stands the **Mavriótissa monastery**, flanked by peacocks and a fair-value restaurant. Two churches are all that remains of the monastery: a smaller fourteenth-century chapel, with fine frescoes of scenes from Christ's life, abutting the larger, wood-roofed eleventh-century *katholikón* on whose outer wall looms a well-preserved *Tree of Jesse*, showing the genealogy of the Saviour.

Eating and drinking

For traditional **restaurants**, head for Platía Omonías: the *Omonoia*, for example, is excellent for *mayireftá*, and has outdoor tables in good weather. Lakeside dining is popular: *Kratergo*, at Orestíon 19, is a trendy ouzerí featuring specialities such as aubergines stuffed with bacon and cheese. A couple of stylish tavernas are located on Orestiádhos: the *Krondiri* at no. 13, which serves the town's best food, specializes in fancy *mezédhes*, gratins and "soufflés" in attractive clay pots, and has tables on the lake bank. Further along at no. 87, *Arhondariki* is somewhat less sophisticated, but the barrelled wine accompanying fish and other delicacies is very good indeed. **Cafés and bars** are mostly to be found at the water's edge: there are some near the fish market and more stylish ones on the western side of the promontory.

Around Kastoriá

If you have your own transport, you might make a trip to **SIÁTISTA**, draped along a single ridge in a forbiddingly bare landscape 70km south of Kastoriá. Located just above the point where the road splits for Kozáni or Grevená (and the Metéora beyond), it too was an important fur centre, and also boasts a handful of eighteenth-century mansions which you can visit. The eighteenth-century house of **Hatzimihaïl Kanatsoúli** at Mitropóleos 1, near the police station, is still lived in but you can ring to be shown around. The first two floors are occupied; upstairs, a corner room has naive murals of mythological scenes (including Kronos's castration of Ouranos). The warden of the dilapidated **Nerantzópoulos mansion** (Mon–Sat 8.30am–3pm, Sun 9.30am–2.30pm), on the upper square, has the keys for several other houses, of which the largest and most elaborate is the **Manoússi mansion**, dating from 1763, in a vale below the Kanatsoúli, along with various other surviving mansions. The church of **Ayía Paraskeví**, on the lowest platía, behind a tall belfry, has soot-blackened seventeenth-century frescoes inside. You can view them by calling the warden on ☎04650 21353, but until the scheduled cleaning takes place you're probably better off just looking at the exterior frescoes.

Most of what you'll need in Siátista – **banks** with ATMs and the **post office** – can be found on the single, long main street, Megálou Alexándhrou. This is also the location of the large and comfortable *Archontikon* **hotel** (☎04650 21298, ℗04650 22835; ❹), which has a reasonable restaurant and café on the ground floor, despite the TV; rooms often fill with tours, so check for space in advance. Other options for **eating** out tend to have rather boozy male-dominated environments, such as the *Psistaria Ouzeri O Platanos*, just below Ayía Paraskeví, or the slightly more appealing *To Xani*, nearby. The most frequent **bus** connections are with Kozáni, 28km to the southeast, which has good onward connections to Thessaloníki.

Eastern Macedonia and Halkidhikí

The northeastern part of Macedonia is mostly an inland plain, fringed to the north by mountains, with a scattering of lakes and small market towns serving a population that – as in neighbouring Thrace – produces the main Greek tobacco crop. Nevertheless, the bird-rich wetlands around **Lake Kerkíni**, the formation-filled caves at **Alistráti** and the site of a major Roman battle, at **Philippi**, are worth the detour.

By way of contrast, the forked peninsula of **Halkidhikí**, easily reached by road from Thessaloníki, is the main tourist destination in Macedonia's eastern half, indeed in the whole region. Its two westernmost sub-peninsulas, Kassándhra and Sithonía, shelter the north's main concentration of beaches; the third, **Athos**, harbours the country's finest, though most secretive, monasteries.

Further east, there are a few more good beaches en route to **Kavála**, a bustling harbour town with a couple of important vestiges of Ottoman rule, an interesting archeology museum and an airport that mostly serves the nearby island of **Thássos**.

Northeastern Macedonia

Few people ever venture into the arable plains northeast of Thessaloníki, where few attractions await the traveller apart from golden fields of corn and tobacco and incredible numbers of storks' nests. Up near the craggy mountains that form the frontier with Bulgaria, artificial **Lake Kerkíni** is home to masses of birds, some of them extremely rare in Europe, making it as interesting to ornithologists as the Préspa Lakes much farther west. It can be reached by train, or by the road that heads due north from the northern capital past Kilkís, before winding up to the Bulgarian border or, like the railway, curling back down to the prosperous but not terribly interesting town of **Sérres**.

An alternative way of reaching Kavála (rather than the dull toll motorway) and/or Xánthi is the busy but scenic route that climbs northeast out of Thessaloníki, first taking you via Sérres before passing **Alistráti**, worth visiting for its memorable caves, and then heading towards Dhráma and ancient **Philippi** along a quieter road that offers majestic panoramas of Mount Meníkio (1963m), Mount Pangéo (1956m) and Mount Falakró (2230m). Regular **buses** from Thessaloníki and between Sérres and Dhráma ply this road.

The Kerkíni Wetlands

Artificial, marsh-fringed **Lake Kerkíni**, tucked up near the mountainous Bulgarian border, enjoys international protected status, thanks to the three-hundred-plus species of **birds** that spend at least part of the year here, some of them on the endangered species list. Huge expanses of water lilies stretch across the large anvil-shaped lake, out of which the River Strymónas flows to the northern Aegean near ancient Amphipolis, while a herd of water buffalo wallows and grazes the eastern banks, and local fishermen compete for eels and roach with every type of heron known to inhabit Europe. Other birds breeding in the Kerkíni wetlands include various species of grebes, terns, egrets, ducks, geese, ibis, spoonbills, avocets and pelicans, plus raptors such as the black kite, the short-toed eagle and the Levant sparrowhawk.

The small town of **Livadhiá**, some 80km north of Thessaloníki on the Kilkís-to-Promahónas road, can also be reached by train. From here it is just 7km south to the lake's northern shore and the village of **KERKÍNI**, where you will find the **Kerkíni Wetlands Information Centre**, a few **tavernas** serving fish from the lake and a couple of **hotels**, including the *Oicoperiigitis* (☎23270 41450; ❹); in addition to comfortable rooms, a decent restaurant and **camping** facilities, this offers local tours by boat, canoe, bike, jeep or on horseback. You can also negotiate **bird–watching** trips in a *pláva*, a traditional punt-like fishing

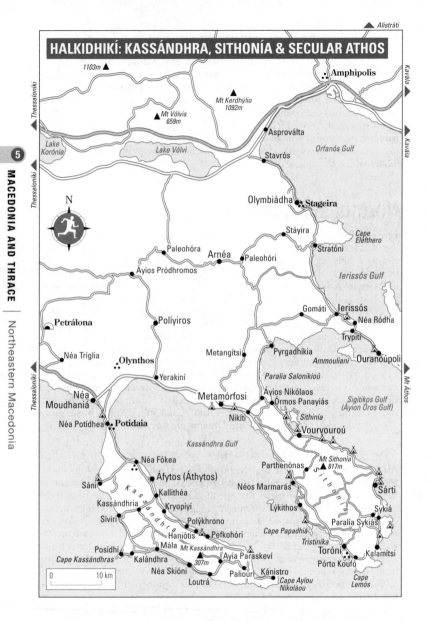

HALKIDHIKÍ: KASSÁNDHRA, SITHONÍA & SECULAR ATHOS

boat. The surroundings reward exploration with their abundance of flora and fauna, with huge numbers of wildflowers in the spring and early summer.

Alistráti

Just over 20km before you reach the dull market town Dhráma, on the road from Sérres, you come to the village of **ALISTRÁTI**, a pleasant cluster of houses with one or two decent **tavernas**. The only **hotel** is a delightfully restored mansion, 🍴 *Arhondiko Voziki* (☎03234 20400, ⓕ03234 20408; ❹), with beautifully furnished rooms and a swimming pool. The village is well placed for exploring the nearby mountains. The main reason for coming here, though, is to visit the impressive **caves** (daily: Easter–Sept 30 9am–9pm; rest of year 9am–5pm; guided tours only, 1hr; €6, with reductions; ⓦwww.alistraticave.gr), reached down a scenic side road 6km southeast of the village. First explored in the mid-1970s, these caves easily rival those at Pérama (see p.431), and are claimed to be the most extensive of their kind in Europe not requiring special equipment or training to visit. Dating from the Quaternary period, these gigantic limestone cavities are over two million years old, and bristle with a variety of wonderful formations, including the relatively rare eccentrites and helictites, respectively stalactites sticking out at angles, rather than hanging vertically, and twisted forms resembling sticks of barley sugar. The entrance, a long tunnel bored into the hillside, takes you right into the caverns, and a winding path weaves its way through masses of stalagmites, many of them outstandingly beautiful, and some exceeding 15m in length.

Philippi

Some 42km from Alistráti, set a short way back from the busy Dhráma-Kavála road, you come to the major site of **PHILIPPI** (Filippoi on some maps and signs). Not surprisingly, the town was named after Philip II of Macedon, who wrested it from the Thracians in 356 BC for the sake of nearby gold mines on Mount Pangéo. However, it owed its later importance and prosperity to the Roman construction of the Via Egnatia. With Kavála/Neapolis as its port, Philippi was essentially the easternmost town of Roman-occupied Europe.

Here, as at Actium, the fate of the Roman empire was decided at the **Battle of Philippi** in 42 BC. After assassinating Julius Caesar, Brutus and Cassius had fled east of the Adriatic and, against their better judgement, were forced into confrontation on the Philippi plains with the pursuing armies of Antony and Octavian. The "honourable conspirators", who could have successfully exhausted the enemy by avoiding action, were decimated by Octavian in two successive battles. As defeat became imminent, first Cassius, then Brutus killed himself – the latter running on his comrade's sword with the purported Shakespearean sentiment, "Caesar now be still, I killed thee not with half so good a will."

Saint Paul landed at Kavála and visited Philippi in 49 AD and so began his religious mission in Europe. Despite being cast into prison, he retained a special affection for the Philippians, his first converts, and the congregation that he established was one of the earliest to flourish in Greece. It has furnished the principal remains of the site: several impressive, although ruined, basilican churches.

Philippi is also easily reached from Kavála, just 14km distant; Kavála-Dhráma **buses** leave every half-hour, and drop you by the road that now splits the site.

The site

The most conspicuous of the churches at the site (Tues–Sun: summer 8am–7pm; winter 8am–3pm; €3) is the **Direkler** (Turkish for "columns" or "piers"), to the south of the modern road which here follows the line of the Via Egnatia. Also known as Basilica B, this was an unsuccessful attempt by its sixth-century architect to improve the basilica design by adding a dome. In this instance the entire east wall collapsed under the weight, leaving only the narthex convertible for worship during the tenth century. The central arch of its west wall and a few pillars of reused antique drums stand amid remains of the Roman **forum**. A line of second-century porticoes spreads outwards in front of the church, and on their east side are the foundations of a colonnaded octagonal church which was approached from the Via Egnatia by a great gate. Behind the Direkler and, perversely, the most interesting and best-preserved building of the site, is a huge monumental **public latrine** with nearly fifty of its original marble seats still intact.

Across the road on the northern side, stone steps climb up to a terrace, passing on the right a Roman crypt, reputed to have been the **prison of Saint Paul** and appropriately frescoed. The terrace flattens out onto a huge paved atrium that extends to the foundations of another extremely large basilica, the so-called Basilica A. Continuing in the same direction around the base of a hill you emerge above a **theatre** cut into its side. Though dating from the original town, it was heavily remodelled as an amphitheatre by the Romans – the bas-reliefs of Nemesis, Mars and Victory (on the left of the stage) all belong to this period. It is now used for performances during the annual summer Philippi-Thássos Festival. The best general impression of the site – which is extensive despite a lack of obviously notable buildings – and of the battlefield behind it can be gained from the **acropolis**, a steep climb along a path from the museum. Its own remains are predominantly medieval.

Kassándhra, Sithonía and secular Athos

Halkidhikí (ⓦ www.halkidiki.com) begins at a perforated edge of shallow lakes east of Thessaloníki, then extends into three prongs of land – Kassándhra, Sithonía and Athos – trailing like tentacles into the Aegean Sea. **Mount Athos**, the easternmost peninsula, is in all ways separate, a "Holy Mountain", whose monastic population, semi-autonomous within the Greek state, **excludes all females** – even as visitors. The most that women can do is to glimpse the buildings from offshore cruise *kaïkia* sailing from the two small resorts on the periphery of the peninsula – Ierissós and Ouranoúpoli – on the "secular" part of the Athos peninsula.

Kassándhra and **Sithonía**, by contrast, host some of the busiest holiday resorts in Greece. Large signs at the entrance to both peninsulas remind you that camping outside authorized sites is strictly prohibited. You should have no trouble getting accommodation outside the busy midsummer period (mid-July to mid-August). The beaches themselves consist of white sand, ranging in consistency from powder to coarse-grained; less appealing are the fortunately stingless jellyfish that drift about nearly everywhere.

Both Kassándhra and Sithonía are connected to Thessaloníki by a four-lane expressway which ends at **NÉA MOUDHANIÁ**, a dull town and minor passenger port, from where a network of fast two-lane roads extends around their coastlines. Buses run frequently to all the larger resorts. In spite of this, neither peninsula is that easy to travel around if you are dependent on **public transport**. You really have to pick a place and stay there, perhaps renting a **motorbike** or **car** for excursions.

Kassándhra

Vaguely boot-shaped **Kassándhra**, the nearest of Halkidhikí's three peninsulas to Thessaloníki, is also by far the most developed, though beyond the grain fields around Kallithéa, extensive forest survives unscathed along the hilly spine of the peninsula. Its population took part in the independence uprising of 1821, but was defeated and massacred; the handful of attractive villages, mostly inland and lower down, essentially date from the mid-nineteenth century, often built atop ancient or medieval foundations. On the coast, there were only a few small fishing hamlets here until after 1923, when the peninsula was resettled by refugees from around the Sea of Marmara – these have since burgeoned into holiday venues. Unless very pushed for time, most travellers choose to bypass Kassándhra and keep going to Sithonía or the top end of Athos.

Néa Potídhea, Néa Fókea and Sáni

NÉA POTÍDHEA, some 6km beyond Néa Moudhaniá and across the ancient canal, which severs the narrow neck of Kassándhra, is an eyesore with its mechanical animals, and fast-food joints alternating with bars. That said, the front is pedestrianized and well landscaped, and the beach itself broad, sandy and reef-free. Greek families rent summer apartments here long-term, making it a poor bet for a quick overnight, while an otherwise fairly young crowd lends the place a laid-back feel. The way to the fishing port at the west end of the canal is flanked by the ruined fortifications of ancient Potidaia; at the end you'll find two worthy **fish tavernas**, *Kastro* (perched amidst bits of wall) and *Marina*, overlooking the sea and another, half-submerged, bit of antiquity.

The next resort, **NÉA FÓKEA** (again mostly apartments), is by comparison a modest place, rendered picturesque by a Byzantine watchtower on a grassy headland. There are several fish **tavernas** in the delightful little harbour, right by the main road, from where a long beach heads north under cliffs, improving as you distance yourself from the tower.

Just north of Néa Fókea, an eight-kilometre paved side road takes you westwards through bucolic countryside to **SÁNI** on the west coast, where you'll find the municipally run *Blue Dream* **campsite** (☎23740 31435; May–Sept), plus several luxury megacomplexes. Sáni is noted for its summer **festival**, which boasts a cosmopolitan billing of world music, salsa, jazz and cutting-edge Greek stars.

Áfytos

Some 5km south of Néa Fókea, you reach the turning east for **ÁFYTOS** (or Áthytos), by far the most attractive spot on Kassándhra. This large village of tile-roofed traditional houses spreads over a series of ravines furrowing the bluff here, which ends in a sharp drop to the sea. Near the cliff bottom, a series of springs bubbles from a rock overhang, nurturing a little oasis – doubtless a spur in the founding of Aphytis, the village's ancient predecessor. The beach is marred by rock sills with lots of sea urchins. On the square, the focus of a mesh of slightly twee cobbled lanes closed to traffic for the nightly promenade, stands a handsome church in post-Byzantine style, dating only from 1850 but seeming much older.

Independent travellers have a choice of **rooms**, best sited for sea views at the cliff edge (though you'll get mosquitoes from the oasis) and priced at ❹, often with some sort of self-catering facility. For a bona-fide **hotel**, try the charming *Stamos* (☎23740 91520, ⓕ23740 91234; ❻) on the minor road leading to the cliff edge; it has a flowery courtyard and pool, and its studios for three or four make it good for families. Down on the shore, the medium-sized *Blue Bay* (☎23740 91644, ⓕ23740 91646; ❺) dominates one of the most usable patches of beach, but tends to fill in peak season with tour groups.

Eating out is best at no-nonsense *Tò Perasma*, with reliable fare and excellent wines, or, in season, the upmarket *Soussouradha*, next to the bakery. By

△ Village church, Áfytos

the church is an anonymous ouzerí, the old boys' hangout, serving copious drink, salads and one dish of the day only. For full **buffet breakfast** at a fair price, look no further than *Gastronomia*, near the *Stamos* (no relation to the namesake in the centre) – it's worth trying their Italian fare by night as well. **Nightlife** is fairly lively, with Greek musicians often playing the bars at summer weekends, sometimes under the aegis of the **Kassándhra Festival** which Áfytos shares with Síviri (see opposite): performances include blues, soul, classical and traditional Greek music.

From Kallithéa to Palioúri

Bypass **KALLITHÉA**, 4km to the south and a complete contrast to Áfytos with only **banks** (ATMs) and **car, motorbike and windsurfer rental** to its credit. At **KRYOPIYÍ**, just under 6km further, most of the development is concentrated along the steep roads that cascade down to the water, where there's a beach, but Kryopiyí has managed to preserve its old village core up the hill, on the land side of the main road. By the somewhat gentrified platía are a couple of **tavernas**: the *Platia* has a slight edge over the *Anoyi*. A regular **shuttle bus** from the beach area stops by the church in the summer.

Beyond Kryopiyí, you head towards the "toe" of the Kassandhrian boot via a trio of tacky coastal resorts – Polakhrono, Haniótis and Pefkohóri. At **HANIÓTIS** in particular, you have to wend your way through some fairly downmarket development to reach the long, narrow and crowded beach. Just southeast of **PEFKOHÓRI**, which has an official **campsite**, a lagoon enclosed by a pine-tufted spit is just about the only spot on the peninsula where rough camping seems to be winked at. At the bay of **Khroussoú**, there are two more recognized **campsites** and rather more low-key development than at the preceding. From here, rather than continuing to the disappointing "toe"-cape at Kánistro, you're better off heading west and inland along the main road to the rambling ridge-top village of **PALIOÚRI**, also full of lodging.

Kassándhra's southern shore

The southern shore of Kassándhra is, in general, developed more for Greek weekenders. Some 6km beyond hilltop Palioúri you emerge at **AYÍA PARASKEVÍ**, a delightful village with sea views, a pair of simple **tavernas** and a fancy-paved central roundabout. **NÉA SKIÓNI**, 6km northwest, can be a decent base, with its good clean beach and appealing seafront. The string of tavernas is supplied by a tiny fleet in the fishing port, and the best, open for lunch and all year, is *Yiorgos*, opposite the jetty entrance. Amongst the apartments are some **rooms** (❺). **Mála**, nominally 8km northwest, is not really a village so much as a string of weekend real estate that blocks access to most of the coast from just outside Néa Skióni. Hidden away up on the cape is the picturesque village of **KALÁNDHRA**, just off the route to **Posídhi beach**, which itself isn't wonderful, though beyond the lively beach bar, at the lighthouse cape, the rock reef abates and you can skinny-dip.

Kassándhra's west coast

Some 9km north of Kalándhra, **SÍVIRI** is a larger, busier version of Néa Skióni. It has a lovely **beach**, good **tavernas** (*Dhiamandis* has the prime position) and lively summer nightlife. It's also one of the best spots on the peninsula for sunset views across the gulf to Mount Olympus. There's just the one **hotel**, the 1999-vintage *Samel* (☏ 23740 23400, ✉ samel@otenet.gr; ❹; late April to Sept), with very smart rooms, a pool and a stylish bar.

Sithonía

As you move east across Halkidhikí and away from the frontline of tourism, the landscape becomes increasingly green and hilly, culminating in the isolated and spectacular scenery of the Holy Mountain, looming across the gulf. The **Sithonía** peninsula is more rugged but better cultivated than Kassándhra, though here there are even fewer true villages, and those that do exist mostly date from the 1920s resettlement era. Pine forests cover many of the slopes, particularly in the south, giving way to olive groves on the coast. Small sandy inlets with relatively discreet pockets of campsites and tavernas make a welcome change.

If you're travelling under your own steam, some 6km past the last motorway exit at Néa Moudhaniá en route to Sithonía it's worth making the slight detour to splendidly located **ancient Olynthos** (Tues–Sun 8am–2.30pm; €3), atop a hill offering mountain and sea views. This is a rare example of an unmodified Classical town laid out to the geometric grid plan of Hippodamus – the fifth-century BC architect who designed Piraeus and Rhodes. There's an initially off-putting walk of 700m, partly up a slope, from the ticket booth, but well-excavated streets, houses and even some mosaics to see once you arrive. Like the new, informative museum near the entrance, everything is clearly labelled in Greek and English. The modern village of **ÓLYNTHOS**, 1km west across the riverbed here, has **food** and a **hotel**, the central *Olynthos* (☏ 23790 91666; ❷).

Metamórfosi

Suitably enough, **METAMÓRFOSI** ("Transfiguration"), at the western base of Sithonía, signals the transformation. Its beach is only adequate, but there's good swimming, and the village, while relentlessly modern, has an easy-going air. In addition to the friendly *Hotel Golden Beach* (☏ 23750 22063; ❺; May–Sept), with its cool courtyard and café backing onto the village square, there are two **campsites**: *Sithon*, 5km west (☏ 23750 22414; May–Sept), and the preferable *Mylos*, 3km east, on the beach side of the road. In high season, both campsites and village can be a little crowded, but there's a fair number of **tavernas** clustered in and around the village square which seem to soak up business.

Moving on to Sithonía proper, it's best to follow the loop road clockwise around the east coast, so that the peak of Athos is always before you. **Bus services** are sparse: there are up to five daily around the west coast to Sárti, and up to three a day direct to Vourvouroú, but there's no KTEL connection between these two endpoints. A complete circuit is only really possible with your own transport.

Órmos Panayiás and Vourvouroú

ÓRMOS PANAYIÁS, first of the east-coast resorts, is well developed; ranks of villas dwarf the picturesque hamlet and tiny harbour, and the nearest decent beaches lie 4km north en route to Pyrgadhíkia, below the inland village of Áyios Nikólaos. The only conceivable reason to stop at Órmos would be to catch the excursion boats that sail around Athos from here, but these are expensive and often reserved for tourists bused in from the big Halkidhikí resorts (for better alternatives see Ouranoúpoli, p.544).

VOURVOUROÚ, 8km down the coast from Órmos, is not a typical resort, since it's essentially a vacation-villa project for Thessaloníki professors, established in the late 1950s on land expropriated from Vatopedhíou monastery on Athos. Even so, there is a fair amount of short-term **accommodation**: along with a number of rooms, there's the seafront hotel *Diaporos* (℡23750 91313; ❺, half-board may be obligatory), with its rooftop restaurant, and the plain but en-suite *Vourvourou* (℡23750 91261; ❹; June–Sept), plus the ecologically minded, high-luxury *Ekies Manor House* (℡2810 300330; ❼), well located on the sea-edge, with its designer rooms, gourmet restaurant and enticing pool. The strange feel of the place is accentuated by those plot owners who haven't bothered to build villas (so far very scattered) and merely tent down, making it hard to tell which are the real campsites. Islets astride the mouth of the bay make for a fine setting, but the beach, while sandy, is extremely narrow, and Vourvouroú is really more of a yachters' haven. **Tavernas** are relatively inexpensive; the *Itamos*, inland from the road, is the best; the *Gorgona/Pullman*, while the nicest positioned – on the waterfront – gets coach tours as the alias implies. There are two **campsites**: *Dionysos* (℡23750 91214; April–Oct), simple but adequate, part of which faces the beach, and *Glaros* (no phone; mostly caravans), facing Karadhi beach at the eastern end of things.

Some of Sithonía's best **beaches** lie off the 30km of corniche road between Vourvouroú and Sárti: five signposted sandy coves, each with a **campsite** and little else. The names of the bays, such as Koutloumousíou or Zográfou, reflect the fact that most of the land here belonged to various Athonite monasteries until confiscated by the Greek government to resettle Anatolian refugees.

Sárti

Popular, concrete-grid **SÁRTI**, rising to a ridge on the north, is set slightly back from its broad, two-kilometre-long beach. There are hundreds of **rooms** (though often not enough to go around), the choicest being in the southerly part of town, and not all of these block-booked by foreign companies. At the far south end of the beach is another cluster of development, including some **hotels**, among them the *Sarti Beach* (℡23750 94250; ❹), and a **campsite**, the shady *Camping Sarti Beach* (℡23750 94629; May–Sept), laid out between the road and the hotel grounds. *Iy Neraïda* and *O Stavros* are two of the less expensive **tavernas** lining the landscaped shore esplanade, but the perennial (if pricey) favourite amongst Greeks, *Ta Vrahakia*, stands at the far north end of the beach, overlooking the "little rocks" of the name, and dishing up rich *mayireftá*. Inland you'll find a short-hours **bank** and a rather tattily commercialized square ringed by forgettable fast-food joints – plus the big local travel agency, Sithon Travel (℡23750 94066, @sithon@otenet.gr), which does **car rental**.

Paralía Sykiás and Kalamítsi

PARALÍA SYKIÁS, 8km further along, has beach in a fine setting, with just a few tavernas well back from the sea along 2km of coastal highway. At the north end of the beach a **campsite**, *Melissi* (☎23750 41631), shelters in some trees. The best strategy here is to follow the side road at the south end of the beach towards the more scenic coves at **Linaráki**, where *Pende Vimata stin Ammo* is the most noteworthy of several **tavernas** along here, or beyond to Pigadháki. For a **post office** and shops head for **SYKIÁ**, 2km inland, hemmed in by a bowl of rocky hills.

KALAMÍTSI, another 8km south of Paralía Sykiás, consists of a beautiful double bay, with relatively little commercialization. At the sheltered north bay of Pórto, there's a basic **campsite** (☎23750 41346) with a **taverna**, *O Yiorgakis*, next door, serving varied, reasonably priced food, and good **rooms** behind (☎23750 41338; ❸). The small beach just out front can get cramped in summer, at which time you can easily swim out to the main islet for less company. The equally sandy south bay is rather monopolized by the fancier *Camping Kalamitsi* (☎23750 41411; May–Sept).

Pórto Koufó, Toróni and Tristiníka

The forest cover gets progressively thinner the further south you go from Sárti, and as you round the tip of the peninsula it vanishes completely, with bare hills spilling into the sea to create a handful of deep bays. **PÓRTO KOUFÓ**, just northwest of the cape, is the most dramatic of these, almost completely cut off from the open sea by high cliffs. The name Koufó ("deaf" in Greek) is said to come from one's inability to hear the sea within the confines of this inlet, which served as an Axis submarine shelter during World War II. There's a decent beach near where the road drops down from the east, as well as a small, stark, pricey **hotel** and a few **rooms**. The north end of the inlet, 1km from the beach area, is a yacht and fishing harbour with a string of somewhat expensive seafood **tavernas**.

TORÓNI, 3km north, is the antithesis of this, an exposed, two-kilometre-long crescent of sand with wooded hills behind. It's probably your best Sithonian bet as a base if you just want to flop on a beach for a few days; for more stimulation there is a minimal **archeological site** on the southern cape, sporting the remains of an ancient fortress, while nearby is an early Christian basilica. There are lots of apartments here for Greek weekenders, but the Sykiá municipality has banned beachfront building. Half a dozen combination **taverna-studio rooms** are scattered the length of the beach, among them *Haus Sakis* (☎23750 51261; ❹), at the northernmost end, with comfortable rooms upstairs and good food plus German beer on tap at street level.

Just 2km north is the turning for less-developed **Tristiníka**, with another outstanding two-kilometre beach, reached by a bumpy, 1800-metre sand-and-dirt track. On the way you pass a taverna-and-rooms outfit, with a tiny hamlet 1km off the main road. At the south end of the sand, served by its own access drive, is *Camping Isa* (☎23750 51235; May–Sept).

Some 5km further north along the main road, there's a turning for the recommended, friendly *Camping Areti* (☎23750 71430, ℻23750 71573), nestled between Cape Papadhiá and Lakithos hamlet, with views of three islets over its private beach. Besides tent space in well-landscaped olive groves, there are also wood chalets with all amenities at ❸ rates.

Pórto Carrás to Parthenónas

Beyond Tristiníka, you edge back into high-tech-resort territory, epitomized by Greece's largest planned holiday complex, **Pórto Carrás**. Established by the Carras wine and shipping dynasty, it features an in-house shopping centre, golf course and vineyards, while from the ten-kilometre private beach in front, you can indulge in every imaginable watersport. The complex comprises three futuristic luxury hotels (₩ www.portocarras.com): *Meliton Beach*, *Village Inn* and *Sithonia Beach*. However, both more affordable and desirable is the *Kelyfos* **hotel** (☏ 23750 72833, ℱ 23750 72247, ₩ www.kelyfos.gr; ➐), 1km north of the Pórto Carrás turn-off and impressively located on a hilltop; the smart, new rooms have sea views and all mod cons.

The nearest proper town to all this, with **banks** (ATMs), **tavernas** and a **post office**, is **NÉOS MARMARÁS**, a little fishing port with a small beach. Nowadays, it's popular with Greeks who stay in a score of modest hotels and apartments. Some 3km to the north, there is a decent **campsite**, the *Castello* (☏ 23750 71095; May–Sept) – at which point the beach is sandy, and there's tennis, volleyball and a restaurant. Exceptionally good kebabs are carved at *Fast Food O Dhimitris*, between the church and the bus stop.

A visit to **PARTHENÓNAS**, the lone traditional village on Sithonía, will give you some idea of what Sithonía must have looked like before the developers moved in. Crouched at the base of 808-metre Mount Ítamos, it's 5km up from Néos Marmarás and reached via a good road lined with pine and olive groves. Parthenónas was abandoned in the 1960s in favour of the shore, and never even provided with mains electricity; its dilapidated but appealing houses are now being restored. The *Pension Parthenon* (➍) in a fine stone house on high ground offers some of the peninsula's most charming accommodation. *To Steki tou Meniou* serves very basic fare in a pleasant hut, but don't go out of your way.

East to secular Athos

From Órmos Panayiás a road winds around the coast and up over a ridge to the head of the Athos peninsula. The principal place you'd think to stop is **PYRGADHÍKIA**, a ravine-set fishing village jutting out into the Sigitikós gulf. It can offer no more than a few basic, unenticingly placed **hotels**, but you still might lunch here at one of the waterfront tavernas. There's little beach to speak of, although there are some good ones dotted along the stretch between here and **PARALÍA SALONIKIOÚ**, located 6km to the southwest and offering studio rooms and more tavernas.

Inland Halkidhikí

From Pyrgadhíkia the road heads inland towards Paleohóri and Arnéa, while a turn-off via Gomáti takes you to Ierissós through unspoilt moors. No buses cover these routes, however, and if you're dependent on public transport you'll have to backtrack as far as Yerakiní and then inland to Halkidhikí's capital, **POLÍYIROS**. At Áyios Pródhromos, 20km north, you can pick up one of the frequent buses heading for Athos via **ARNÉA**. This small, quaint town has some fine old quarters with attractive Balkan-style houses – one of which, Tó Yiatrádhiko, has been turned into a **historical and folklore museum** (erratic opening; free) – and a reputation for carpets and other colourful hand-woven goods, along with delicious honey. Although it has a dearth of good places to eat – you'll be forced to fall back on pizzerias – Arnéa does have some high-quality **accommodation**. In particular there is the ⚜ *Alexandrou* traditional inn (☏ 23102 22721, ₩ www.oikia-alexandrou.gr; ➏), opposite the main church at Platía Patriárhou Vartholoméou A', with a top-rate **restaurant** serving local specialities and a wine cellar stocked with Macedonian vintages. The atmospheric rooms in this early-nineteenth-century hostelry – which served as a family residence for decades – are all furnished with antiques and some have open fireplaces. Less luxurious but equally charming is *Archontiko Mitsiou*, a restored old mansion just off the central platía (☏03720 22744, ℱ03720 22988; ❹), which has large, wood-decor rooms and is run by the town council. More accommodation can be found at **PALEOHÓRI**, 5km further east towards Stáyira (and not to be confused with Paleohóra, 16km to the west of Arnéa), where the genial *Park Hotel Tassos* (☏03720 41722, ℱ03720 41858; ❸), on the westerly outskirts, has exceptionally quiet, if 1970s-vintage, rooms. The ground-floor lounge is a veritable museum of Macedoniana or good-natured kitsch; none of the several tavernas on the road through town is up to much, so if the hotel restaurant is open, take advantage. From the high, partly forested plateau here, the road drops down to the sea again at Stratóni, then veers south to Ierissós, taking you through some fine scenery reminiscent of Mount Athos itself.

Ierissós and Néa Ródha

With its good, long beach and a vast, promontory-flanked gulf, **IERISSÓS** is the most Greek-patronized of the secular Athos resorts, although the sizeable town itself, built well back from the shore and with room to expand, is a sterile concrete grid dating from after a devastating 1932 earthquake. The only hint of pre-touristic life is the vast boat-building dry dock to the south.

There's an inexpensive **hotel** – the en-suite, friendly if sometimes noisy *Marcos* (☏23770 22518; ❷), overlooking its own garden and car park at the south end of town, as well as numerous **rooms for rent**, such as pleasant *Aliki* (☏23770 22363; ❶), on the water's edge to the far north of the town. One of the two basic **campsites** is situated at the northern edge of town, while the other, *Delfini* (☏23770 22208), lies en route to Néa Ródha. The beach is surprisingly uncluttered with just a handful of **bars** behind the landscaped promenade. The best of several mediocre **tavernas** is *O Iosif*, just inland on the main drag, with decent *mezédhes*, but establish prices before ordering. Rounding off the list of amenities, there's a **post office**, two **banks** and a summer **cinema** by the campsite. Ierissós is also the main **port** for the northeast shore of Athos; see p.549 for details.

The road beyond Ierissós passes through the resort of **NÉA RÓDHA**, with a small beach and no more claim to architectural distinction than its neighbour, but worth knowing about as an alternative point for picking up the morning boat from Ierissós. Just beyond here your route veers inland to follow a boggy depression that's the remaining stretch of **Xerxes' canal**, cut by the Persian invader in 480 BC to spare his fleet the shipwreck at the tip of Athos that had befallen the previous expedition eleven years before.

Ammoulianí

You emerge on the southwest-facing coast at **Trypití**, not a settlement but merely the western exit of Xerxes' canal and now also the ferry jetty for the small island of **AMMOULIANÍ** (15min; 7 daily crossings in summer, fewer off season and more on busy days to meet demand; €0.60, car €7.40). This is Macedonia's only inhabited Aegean island apart from Thássos, and after decades of eking out an existence from fishing, the island's population, originally refugees from the Sea of Marmara, has in recent years had to adjust to an influx of holiday-makers. Like anywhere else in Halkidhikí, it's impossibly oversubscribed in July and August, but in spring or autumn this low-lying, scrub- and olive-covered islet can make an idyllic hideaway.

The only town, where the ferries dock, is another unprepossessing grid of concrete slung over a ridge, with few pre-1960s buildings remaining; it is, however, chock-a-block with **rooms**, many self-catering, and there are two **hotels** plainly visible on the left as you sail in. The better of these is the *Sunrise* (☎23770 51273, ⓕ23770 51174; ❸), with its own swimming jetty. Of the village's half-dozen **tavernas**, *Glaros* (on the front), *Iy Klimataria* (on the road out) and *Janis* (facing the rear Limanáki port) get high marks for hygiene and good value. There are a few shops for self-caterers, but no bank or post office. As for **nightlife**, you've got two bars (one, *Barko*, does breakfasts) and two discos a few hundred metres out of town on the main island road.

Two kilometres southwest of the town is **Alykés**, the islet's most famous beach, with a namesake salt-marsh inland, a taverna and separate café behind the sand, and a rather parched campsite. Ammouliani's best beaches however, lie in the far southeast, facing the straits with the Athos peninsula. To reach them, bear left off the pavement 1500m out of town where the *Agionissi* luxury resort is signposted, onto a smooth, sand-dirt track. Some 2km along this, you pass the tiny chapel and cistern of **Áyios Yeóryios** overlooking the excellent eponymous beach. Just beyond stands the popular lunchtime-only *Sarandis*, but it's pricier than the exceedingly simple fare warrants, and you might prefer to continue to the far end of the beach to the better-value *Gripos Ouzeri* – so popular it has been extended, with the meals now served in a modern construction that's a bit of an eyesore. This also offers a few rooms ⚲ of considerable charm (☎23770 51049; ❸), with copper antiques, beam ceilings, terracotta floor tiles and large balconies, with a swimming pool in the garden. The affable owner keeps pheasants and other exotic fowl, whose squawkings vie with those of the gulls nesting on the rock islets of the Dhrénia archipelago just offshore. You can continue a final 500m to the even more enticing **Megáli Ámmos** beach, where there's a café with seats in the sand and blaring music, a seasonal taverna and a pleasant, olive-shaded campsite. Still other, less accessible, beaches beckon in the northwest of the island, served in season by excursion boats from the town; a popular map-postcard on sale will give necessary hints on how to reach them on foot or by bicycle.

Ouranoúpoli

Fifteen kilometres beyond Ierissós, **OURANOÚPOLI** is the last community before the restricted monastic domains, with a centre that's downright tatty, showing the effects of too much tourism. Somewhat mysteriously, it has become a major resort aside from its function as the main gateway to Mount Athos; local beaches, stretching intermittently for several kilometres to the north, are sandy enough but narrow and cramped – certainly not the best Halkidhikí has to offer. If you're compelled to stay the night while waiting for passage to Athos, the best temporary escape would be either to take a cruise, or to **rent a motor boat**, to the mini-archipelago of **Dhrénia** just opposite, with almost tropical sandy bays and tavernas on the larger islets.

Ferries call along the southwest shore of Athos and they're probably the main reason you're here. Throughout the year there's just one daily departure, at around 9.45am; tickets, the price of which depends on destination, should be purchased before boarding, from the agency along the seafront alley near the Phosphori tower. Modern craft also offer three-hour **cruises** in season (€15 a head; departs 10.30am, sometimes 1pm), which skim along the Athonite coast, keeping their contaminating female presence 500m offshore as required by the monastic authorities.

If you need to **stay** – and proprietors are fairly used to one-night stays, en route to or from Athos – there are a fair number of rooms and a similar quantity of hotels, virtually all of them en suite. Less expensive ones include the *Diana* (☎23770 71052; ②) on the road leading down from the pilgrims' office. On the southerly seafront there's the *Akroyali* (☎23770 71201, ⓕ23770 71395; ②), which shares management with the *Makedonia*, slightly uphill and inland (☎23770 71085, ⓕ23770 71395; ②), a pleasantly quiet spot with a small package presence. The closest high-grade hotel to town that isn't utterly dominated by packages is the *Xenia*, on the beach (☎23770 71412, ⓔxenia@papcorp .gr; ⑥, half-board), with bargains outside peak season. A **campsite**, better appointed than those in Ierissós, lies 2km north of the village, amidst a crop of luxury hotel complexes. The half-dozen waterfront **tavernas** all tout identical rip-off menus, though you're unlikely to care much about value for money before (or especially after) several lean days on Athos eating at the monasteries. On the south waterfront, respectively just before and after the town limits sign, are two more appealing alternatives: *Mantho*, a traditional-format *estiatório* with plenty of *mayireftá*, and the fancier *Athos*, next to the hotel *Avra*, with a huge menu featuring grilled vegetables, soups and sweets. Ouranoúpoli has a **post office**, but no bank.

Mount Athos: the monks' republic

The population of the **Mount Athos** peninsula has been exclusively male – farm animals included – since the *ávaton* edict banning females permanent or transient was promulgated by the Byzantine emperor Constantine Monomachos in 1060. Known in Greek as the **Áyion Óros** (Holy Mountain), it is an administratively autonomous province of the country – a "monks' republic" – on whose slopes are gathered twenty monasteries, plus a number of smaller dependencies and hermitages.

Most of the **monasteries** were founded in the tenth and eleventh centuries; today, all survive in a state of comparative decline but they remain unsurpassed in their general and architectural interest, and for the art treasures they contain. If you are male, over 18 years old and have a genuine interest in monasticism or Greek Orthodoxy, sacred music or simply in Byzantine and medieval architecture, a visit is strongly recommended. It can be easily arranged in Thessaloníki (see p.548 for details), but for much of the year you'll need to plan your visit well in advance. In addition to the religious and architectural aspects of Athos, it should be added that the peninsula remains one of the most beautiful parts of Greece. With only the occasional service vehicle, two buses and sporadic coastal boats, a visit involves walking between settlements – on paths through dense woods, up the main peak or above what is perhaps the Mediterranean's last undeveloped coastline. For many visitors, this – as much as the experience of monasticism – is the highlight of time spent on the Holy Mountain.

Some history

By a legislative decree of 1926, Athos has the status of **Theocratic Republic**. It is governed from the small town and capital of Karyés by the Ayía Epistasía (Holy Superintendency), a council of twenty representatives elected for one-year terms by each of the monasteries. At the same time Athos remains a part of Greece; all foreign monks must adopt Greek citizenship and the Greek civil government is represented by an appointed governor and a small police force.

Each monastery has a distinct place in the **Athonite hierarchy**: Meyístis Lávras holds the prestigious first place, Konstamonítou ranks twentieth. All

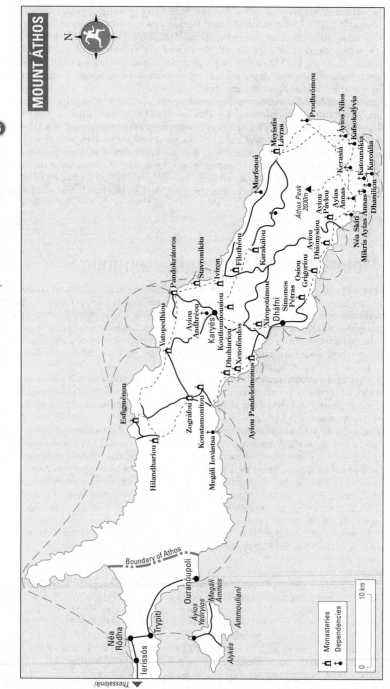

MOUNT ÁTHOS

Prodhrómou

Meyístis Lávras

Morfonoú

Áyios Nílos
Kafsokalývia
Kerasiá
Katounákia
Ayías Ánnas
Karoúlia
Dhaníilon
Néa Skíti
Mikrís Ayías Ánnas

Áthos Peak 2030m

Ayíou Pávlou

Ayíou Dhionysíou

Karakálou

Filothéou

Ayíou Grígoriou

Osíou

Simonos Pétras

Xiropotámou

Stavronikíta

Íviron

Pandokrátoros

Vatopedhíou

Ayíou Andhréou

Koutloumousíou

Karyés

Dhohiaríou

Xenofóndos

Dháfni

Ayíou Pandeleímonos

Esfigménou

Zográfou

Konstamonítou

Megáli Iovántsa

Hilandharíou

Boundary of Athos

Ouranóupoli

 Áyios Yeóryios

Megáli Ámmos

Ammoulianí

Alykés

Trypiti

Néa Ródha

Ierissós

◄ *Thessaloníki*

Monasteries

Dependencies

0 — 10 km

other settlements are attached to one or other of the twenty "ruling" monasteries; the dependencies range from a *skíti*, or minor monastic community (either a group of houses, or a cloister-like compound scarcely distinguishable from a monastery), through a *kellí* (a sort of farmhouse) to an *isihastírio* (a solitary hermitage, often a cave). Numerous laymen – including many Muslim Albanians of late – also live on Athos, mostly employed as agricultural or manual labourers by the monasteries.

The **development of monasticism** on Athos is a matter of some controversy, and foundation legends abound. The most popular asserts that the Virgin Mary was blown ashore here on her way to Cyprus; she was overcome by the great beauty of the mountain and a celestial voice consecrated the place in her name. Another tradition relates that Constantine the Great founded the first monastery in the fourth century, but this is certainly far too early as the earliest historical reference to Athonite monks is to their attendance at a council of the Empress Theodora in 843; probably there were some monks here by the end of the seventh century. Athos was particularly appropriate for early Christian monasticism, its deserted and isolated slopes providing a natural refuge from the outside world – especially from the Arab conquests in the east, and during the Iconoclastic phase of the Byzantine empire (eighth to ninth centuries). Moreover, its awesome beauty facilitated communion with God.

The most famous of the **early monks** were Peter the Athonite and Saint Euthymios of Salonica, both of whom lived in cave-hermitages on the slopes during the mid-ninth century. In 885 an edict of Emperor Basil I recognized Athos as the sole preserve of monks, and gradually hermits came together to form communities known in church Greek as *koinobia* (literally "life in common"). The year 963 is the traditional date for the **foundation of the first monastery**, Meyístis Lávras, by Athanasios the Athonite; Emperor Nikiforos Fokas provided considerable financial assistance. Over the next two centuries, with the protection of other Byzantine emperors, foundations were frequent, the monasteries reaching forty in number (reputedly with a thousand monks in each), alongside many smaller communities.

Troubles for Athos began at the end of the eleventh century. The monasteries suffered sporadically from pirate raids and from the settlement of three hundred Vlach shepherd families on the mountain. After a reputedly scandalous episode between the monks and the shepherdesses, the Vlachs were ejected and a new imperial *chryssobull* (golden edict) was issued, confirming that no female mammal, human or animal, be allowed to set foot on Athos. This edict, called the *ávaton*, remains in force today, excepting various cats to control rodents.

During the twelfth century, the monasteries gained an international – or at least, a **pan-Orthodox** – aspect, as Romanian, Russian and Serbian monks flocked to the mountain in retreat from the turbulence of the age. Athos itself was subjected to Frankish raids during the Latin occupation of Constantinople (1204–61) and, even after this, faced great pressure from the Unionists of Latin Salonica to unite with western Catholics; in the courtyard of Zográfou there is still a monument to the monks who were martyred at this time while attempting to preserve the independence of Orthodox Christianity. In the early fourteenth century the monasteries suffered two disastrous years of pillage by Catalan mercenaries, but they recovered, primarily through Serbian benefactors, to enjoy a period of great prosperity in the fifteenth and sixteenth centuries.

After the fall of the Byzantine empire to the Ottomans, the fathers wisely declined to resist, maintaining good relations with the early sultans, one of whom paid a state visit. The later Middle Ages brought **economic problems**, with heavy taxes and confiscations, and as a defence many of the monasteries dissolved their common holdings and reverted to an idiorrhythmic system, a self-regulating form of monasticism where monks live and worship in a loosely bound community but work and eat individually. However, Athos remained the spiritual centre of Orthodoxy, and during the seventeenth and eighteenth centuries even built and maintained its own schools.

The mountain's real decline came after the early nineteenth-century **War of Independence**, in which many of the monks fought alongside the Greek revolutionary forces. In Macedonia the insurrectionists were easily subdued, the region remaining under Ottoman control, and the monks paid the price. A permanent Turkish garrison was established on the mountain and monastery populations fell sharply as, in the wake of independence for southern Greece, monasticism became less of a focus for Greek Orthodox Christianity.

At the end of the nineteenth century and beginning of the twentieth, **foreign Orthodox** monks, particularly Russian ones, tried to step in and fill the vacuum. But the Athonite fathers have always resisted any move that might dilute the Greek character of the Holy Mountain, even – until recently – at the expense of its material prosperity. During the early 1960s, numbers were at their lowest ever, barely a thousand, compared to 20,000 in Athos's heyday. Today, however, the monastic population has climbed to about two thousand, its average age has dropped significantly and the number of well-educated monks has increased markedly.

While welcoming the revival, some monks and observers feel there are too many outward signs of worldliness on the Mountain, such as faxes and mobile phones, and parts of the peninsula resemble a building site, with extensive, ongoing restoration or new building works underway at several monasteries.

To reach Athos from Thessaloníki, first take a Halkidhikí KTEL bus from its terminal at Karakássi 68 to Ouranoúpoli or Ierissós (see "East to secular Athos", p.542). From **Ouranoúpoli** two **boats** sail daily for most of the year the year: most people take the one that sails at 9.45am as far as **Dháfni** (ninety minutes), the main port on the southwestern coast of Athos, stopping at each harbour or coastal monastery en route; from Dháfni, there's a connecting service onward

Permits and entry

The first step in acquiring the necessary **dhiamonitírion** (permit) for visiting and staying on Athos is to telephone the **Mount Athos Pilgrims' Bureau** (Grafío Proskynitón Ayíou Órous) in Thessaloníki (☎2310 252 578, ℱ2310 222 424). It is located in a fine Neoclassical building at Egnatía 109 (Mon–Fri 9am–2pm, Sat 10am–noon, closed Sun and major holy days; postcode 54635); there is also a bookshop selling icons, along with tomes on Athos art, history and flora and the monasteries themselves. Staff members speak English. They frown on walk-in visits for reservations or even enquiries, so call first. Once you have your booking you must post them a copy of the relevant pages of your passport or national ID, and reconfirm the reservation closer to the intended date, up to the day before. Ten permits per day are issued to non-Orthodox, one hundred daily to baptized Greek Orthodox of whatever nationality. You will then be issued with a reservation confirmation valid for residence on Athos for up to three nights (four days), specifying a date for initial entry to the monastic republic; this may not be the date of your choice, especially from May to September. To visit at Orthodox Easter time, and increasingly at any time of year, you'll need to apply for permission months in advance; note that reservations can be made up to a maximum of six months ahead. At this stage you will not be issued with the permit proper but with a slip, to be exchanged for a permit in Ouranoúpoli (see opposite). You can have the slip posted or faxed to you or you can drop by the office in person.

Arhondáris Guestmaster of a monastery or minor monastic community, responsible for all visitors; similarly, *arhondaríki*, the guest quarters themselves.

Arsanás Harbour annexe of each monastery or *minor monastic community*, where roll-on-roll-off ferries or *kaḯkia* anchor; they can be a considerable distance from the institution in question.

Cenobitic/Idiorrythmic Historically, this is (increasingly, was) the major distinction between religious foundations on the mountain. At cenobite establishments the monks eat all meals together, hold all property in common and have rigidly scheduled days. Those remaining foundations that are idiorrhythmic are more individualistic: the monks eat in their own quarters and study or worship when and as they wish. Beginning in the mid-1980s, all of the remaining idiorrhythmic monasteries reverted to cenobitic status, with Pandokrátoros the last holdout until 1992. Currently monks wishing to follow a more independent path must take up residence in an idiorrhythmic *skíti* (most of them are) or a *kellí*.

Dhíkeos The "righteous one" – head of an idiorrhythmic foundation.

Dhókimos A novice monk.

Fiáli The covered font for holy water in some monastery courtyards; often very ornate.

Igoúmenos Abbot, the head of a monastery.

Isihastírio A solitary hermitage, often a cave.

Katholikón Main church of a monastery.

Kellí A sort of farmhouse.

Kyriakón Central chapel of a *skíti*, where the residents worship together once weekly.

Skíti Minor monastic community usually dependent on a monastery.

Trápeza Refectory, or dining room.

Yérondas A novice's spiritual elder and supervisor, not necessarily the abbot; akin to the *staretz* of the Russian Orthodox tradition.

to the minor monastic community of Ayías Ánnas. If you're setting out on the day your permit starts, you'll have to take the earliest (6am) KTEL departure to connect with this boat. There is also an earlier, faster and more expensive boat (6.30am) that sails direct to Dháfni (you would have to stay overnight in Ouranópoli, of course).

From **Ierissós**, the boat leaves at 8.30am (July–Sept 12 daily in summer; Sept 13–June Mon & Thurs–Sun), but will usually wait for the first bus to arrive; an overnight stop here reduces the risk of missing the boat. This service, along the northeast shore, goes as far as the monastery of **Ivíron** (more than two hours), but it may not stop at every harbour on the way.

Boats turn around for the return trip more or less immediately upon arrival. **Fares** are about €4 from Ouranoúpoli to Dháfni, or €1 from one of the southwest coastal monasteries back to Dháfni. The faster boats cost around €10.

If you are sailing from **Ouranoúpoli**, you must call at the **Grafío Proskynitón** (Pilgrims' Office; daily 8.10am–2pm), at the entry to the town, behind the filling station. If you've stayed overnight, it's suggested that you arrive well before opening time, as the little office is mobbed once the 6am bus from Thessaloníki arrives. This is where you exchange your reservation confirmation slip from the Thessaloníki office for your **permit** proper and pay for it (€30, or €15 for card-carrying students under 27); this entitles you to stay at any of the main or minor monasteries. Armed with it, you may get off the boat at the harbour of any of the southwest coastal monasteries. Starting from **Ierissós**, passengers will be granted this permit from a police post at the harbour of **Hilandharíou**, the first monastery on the northeast coast; they are then free to disembark or continue with the boat to a dock of another monastery of their choice.

At the time of writing, fifteen of the twenty main and two minor monasteries required **advance reservations** (two months ahead, officially) by phone or fax throughout the year, if you want to stay the night; those showing up on spec will, in theory, be turned away, though experience suggests that most of the guestmasters are not consistently strict on this point. All seventeen institutions are identified in the text, and **telephone and fax numbers** given for all of them. If the phone isn't answered at once, be persistent, and only call during the specified time slot, Monday to Saturday, and don't expect an answer on major holy days.

Many visitors wish to arrange for an **extension** of the basic four-day period. This can theoretically be done at the Ayía Epistasía (Holy Superintendancy) in Karyés, though you should have a good reason; two or three extra days are normally granted, and your chances are much better out of season. If you and a particular monastery are particularly taken with each other, and you intend to become a novice, the *idhikó dhiamonitírio* (special sojourning permit) can be arranged. Most guestmasters ask to see your permit, and if you strike the monks as behaving presumptuously or inappropriately, no amount of time remaining on your permit will persuade them to host you. As signs on walls repeatedly remind you, "Hospitality is not obligatory."

Visiting the monasteries

With permit in hand, you will be admitted to stay and eat in the main monasteries – and certain minor ones – free of charge. If you offer money it will be refused, though all pilgrims are encouraged to buy candles, incense, CDs of liturgical music and icon reproductions of varying quality. **Accommodation** is typically in dormitories, and fairly spartan, but there's usually a shower down the hall (sometimes hot) and you're always given sheets and blankets, so you don't need to lug a sleeping bag around. Athos grows much of its own **food**, and the monastic diet is based on tomatoes, beans, olives, green vegetables, coarse bread, cheese and pasta, with occasional treats like *halvás* and fruit included. After Sunday-morning service, wine often accompanies fish (fresh or tinned) in the heartiest meal of the week. Normally only two daily meals are served, the first at mid-morning, the latter about an hour and a half to two hours before sunset. You will probably need to be partly self-sufficient in provisions – dried fruits, nuts and other energy-rich food are a good idea – both for the times when you fail to coincide with meals and for the long walks between monasteries. (If you arrive after the morning or evening meal you will generally be served leftovers set aside for latecomers.) There are a few shops in Karyés, but for a better selection and to save valuable time you should stock up before coming to Athos.

If you're planning to **walk between monasteries**, you should get hold of one of two **maps**: the first simply entitled *Athos*, produced in Austria at a scale of 1:50,000 by Reinhold Zwerger (Wohlmutstr 8, A 1020 Wien; ☎43/222/262205 or 43/2641/67212), is no longer available in Greece but may still be stocked by specialist map shops like Stanford's in London (see p.39). The other, a simple sketch map of all the roads and trails on Mount Athos, was prepared by Theodhoros Tsiropoulos of Thessaloníki (☎2310 430 196), who has marked most of the surviving Athonite trails with white-lettering-on-red-field wooden signposts. The map provided by *Korfes* magazine is obsolete and contains potentially dangerous errors, but it's still more useful than any of the fanciful tourist productions sold in Ouranoúpoli. Even equipped with the better maps, you'll still need to be pointed to the start of trails at each monastery, and confirm walking times and path conditions. New roads are constantly being built, and trails accordingly abandoned, and in the humid local climate they become completely overgrown within two years if not used.

If need be, you can supplement walking with the regular **boat** service provided by the little *Ayia Anna* on the southwest coast only. This departs from Kafsokalývia, near the southern tip of the peninsula, via all intervening harbours, to Dháfni at about 9.15am in summer, with onward connections towards the "border" just after noon. Sleek Landrover minibuses are scheduled (in theory) to coincide with the arrival times of the larger ferries; they can be expensive and, if they're driven by lay-workers, you should establish a price beforehand.

However you move around, you must reach your destination **before dark**, since all monasteries and many minor communities lock their front gates at sunset – which would leave you outside with the wild boars. Upon arrival you should ask for the **guestmaster**, who will proffer the traditional welcome of a *tsípouro* (distilled spirits) and *loukoúmi* (Turkish delight) before showing you to your bed. Many guestmasters speak good English.

You will find the monastic **daily schedule** somewhat disorienting, too, as it is reckoned according to the time of sunrise or sunset in the traditional Byzantine manner. On the northeast side of the peninsula "12 o'clock", or in other words the time when clocktowers show both the hour and the minute hands pointing upwards, corresponds neither to noon nor midnight but to sunrise, whereas on the opposite side of Athos it coincides with sunset. Yet Vatopedhíou keeps "worldly" time, as do most monks' wristwatches, and in the majority of monasteries two wall-clocks are mounted side-by-side: one showing secular time, including the same daylight savings adjustments made in the rest of Greece, the other displaying "Byzantine" time. However, the **Julian calendar**, a fortnight behind the outside world, is observed throughout Athos, in particular for the frequent holy days. Most monasteries have electric power from generators – though this may be switched on for just a few hours at dusk, powering feeble bulbs – and all now have phones, sometimes faxes as well. But these have affected the round of life very little; both you and the monks will go to bed early, shortly after sunset. Sometimes in the small hours your hosts will awake for solitary meditation and study, followed by *órthros*, or matins. Around sunrise there is another quiet period, just before the *akolouthía*, or main liturgy. Next comes the morning meal, anywhere from 9.30am to 11.30am depending on the time of year and day of week. The afternoon is devoted to manual labour until the *esperinós*, or vespers, often announced by a carillon "concert" of some musicality, and actually almost three hours before sunset in summer (much less in winter). This is followed immediately by the evening meal and the short *apódhipno*, or compline service.

A few words about **attitudes and behaviour** towards your hosts (and vice versa) are in order, as many misunderstandings arise from mutual perceptions of disrespect, real or imagined. For your part, you should be fully clad at all times, even when going from dormitory to bathroom; this in effect means no shorts, no hats inside monasteries and sleeves that cover all or nearly all the arm. If you swim, do so where nobody can see you, and certainly don't do it naked. Smoking in most foundations is forbidden, though a few allow you to indulge out on the balconies. It would be criminal to smoke on the trail, given the chronic fire danger; you could give it up as a penance for the duration of your stay. Singing, whistling and raised voices are taboo; so is standing with your hands behind your back or in your pockets or crossing your legs when seated, both considered overbearing stances. If you want to photograph monks you should always ask permission, though photography is forbidden altogether in many monasteries, and video cameras are completely banned from the mountain. It's best not to go poking around corners of the buildings where you're not specifically invited, even if they seem open to the public.

Monasteries, and their tenants, tend to vary a good deal in their handling of visitors, and their reputations, deserved or otherwise, tend to precede them as a favourite subject of trail gossip among foreigners. You will find that as a non-Orthodox you may be politely ignored; signs at some institutions specifically forbid you from attending services or sharing meals with the monks. Other monasteries put themselves at the disposal of visitors of whatever creed; it is possible to be treated to ferocious bigotry and disarming gentility at the same place within the space of ten minutes, making it tricky to draw conclusions about Athos in general and given monasteries in particular. If you are non-Orthodox, and seem to understand enough Greek to get the message, you'll probably be told at some point, subtly or less so, that you ought to convert to the True Faith. It's worth remembering that the monks are expecting religious pilgrims, not tourists, and that their role is to be committed, rather than tolerant. Generally speaking, you can expect those monks with some level of education or smattering of foreign languages to be benignly interested in you, and to pursue a very soft-sell in the form of a reading library of pamphlets and books put at your disposal. Incidentally, minor idiorrhythmic communities (see box on p.549) tend to provide exceedingly basic accommodation and food, even by austere monastic standards, and *kelliá* are not bound by the monastic rule of hospitality, so you really need to know someone at a *kellí* in order to stay the night in one.

The monasteries

Obviously you can't hope to visit all twenty monasteries during a short stay, though if you're able to extend the basic four-day period for a few days you can fairly easily see the peninsula's most prominent foundations. The dirt road linking the southwestern port of Dháfni with the northeastern coastal monastery of Ivíron by way of Karyés, the capital, not only cuts the peninsula roughly in two but also separates the monasteries into equal southeastern and northwestern groups; the division is not so arbitrary as it seems, since the remaining path system seems to reflect it and the feel of the two halves is very different.

The southeastern group

Dominated metaphorically by two of the biggest institutions on Athos, and physically by the Holy Mountain itself, this group includes some of the most visually dramatic monasteries of all, those that seem to hang in mid-air above the Aegean.

Ivíron

The vast **IVÍRON** monastery (☎23770 23643, ℗23770 23248; booking required noon–2pm) is not a bad introduction to Athos, and is well poised for walks or rides in various directions. Although founded late in the tenth century by Iberian (Georgian) monks, the last Georgian died in the 1950s and today it is a cenobitic house of forty monks. Many of them moved here from nearby

△ Fresco, Hilandharíou Monastery

Stavronikíta, under the tutelage of the abbot Vasilios, one of the luminaries of the monastic revival, who to his credit has also spoken out on occasion against the unseemly modernization of life on the mountain. The focus of pilgrimage is the miraculous **icon** of the *Portaítissa*, the Virgin Guarding the Gate, housed in a special chapel to the left of the entrance. It is believed that if this protecting image ever leaves Athos, then great misfortune will befall the monks. The **main church** is among the largest on the mountain, with an elaborate mosaic floor dating from 1030. There are various pagan touches such as the Persian-influenced gold crown around the chandelier, and two Hellenistic columns with ram's-head capitals from a temple of Poseidon which once stood here. Because of the Georgian connection, Russians were lavish donors to this monastery and one of their most notable gifts is a silver-leaf lemon tree crafted in Moscow. The bare-white refectory is, unusually, unadorned except for a pulpit on the south wall, formerly used to deliver the mealtime homily. The monastery is also endowed with an immensely rich library and treasury-museum, presided over by the kindly Father Iakovos, who speaks excellent French and English, and sells copies of the abbot's monographs.

Karyés and around: minor monasteries

Visits are compulsory only for anyone wishing to extend their permit, but a look around **KARYÉS** is certainly rewarding: the main church of the Protáton, dating from 965, contains exceptional fourteenth-century **frescoes** of the Macedonian school. Karyés also has a few **restaurants**, where you may be able to get heartier fare than is typical in the monasteries, and a simple inn. At the northern edge of "town" sprawls the enormous cloister-like building of the **Ayíou Andhréou skíti**, a former Russian dependency of the great Vatopedhíou monastery, erected in the nineteenth century and today virtually deserted.

A signposted trail leads up and west within an hour to small but tidy **KOUTLOUMOUSÍOU** (☎23770 23226, ⓕ23770 23731; booking required noon–3pm), at the very edge of Karyés. Much the most interesting thing about it is its name, which appears to be that of a Seljuk chieftain who converted to Christianity. From Ivíron another path stumbles south uphill, tangling with roads, to reach **FILOTHÉOU** (☎ 23770 23256, ℱ 23770 23674; booking required noon–3pm), which was at the forefront of the monastic revival in the early 1980s, courtesy of its abbot Ephraim, and hence one of the more vital monasteries. It is not, however, one of the more impressive foundations from an architectural or artistic point of view – though the lawn surfacing the entire courtyard is an interesting touch – and it's one of those houses where the non-Orthodox are forbidden from attending church or eating with the monks.

The same is true at **KARAKÁLOU** (☎ 23770 23225, ℱ 23770 23746; booking required noon–2pm), forty-five minutes' walk (mostly on paths) below Filothéou and also accessible via a short trail up from its harbour. The lofty keep is typical of the fortress-monasteries built close enough to the shore to be victimized by pirates. Between here and Meyístis Lávras the trail system has been destroyed and replaced by a road that makes for six hours of dreary tramping, so it's advisable to arrange a lift with a service vehicle. Fairly regular transfers are provided by Landrover minibus from the boat jetty at Ivíron; such vehicles tend to show up between 12.30 and 1pm, and you should pay no more than €6 to get to Meyístis Lávras or Prodhrómou just beyond. If a monk is driving, you may just get a lift for free; the drive takes just over an hour to Meyístis Lávras, nearly ninety minutes to Prodhrómou.

Meyístis Lávras and the Athonite wilderness

MEYÍSTIS LÁVRAS (Great Lavra; ☎ 23770 23754, ℱ 23770 23013) is the oldest and foremost of the ruling monasteries, and physically the most imposing establishment on Athos, with no fewer than fifteen chapels within its walls. Although there are a fair number of additions from the nineteenth century, it has (uniquely among the twenty) never suffered from fire. The treasury and library are both predictably rich, the latter containing over two thousand precious manuscripts, though the ordinary traveller is unlikely to be allowed to view them; as is usual, several monks (out of the 25 here) have complementary keys which must be operated together to gain entrance. At mealtimes you can enjoy the superior **frescoes** in the **refectory**, executed by Theophanes the Cretan in 1535. Hagiographies and grisly martyrdoms line the apse, while there's a *Tree of Jesse* (the genealogy of Jesus) in the south transept, the *Death of Athanasios* (the founder) opposite and an *Apocalypse* to the left of the main entry. In the western apse is a *Last Supper*, not surprisingly a popular theme in refectories. Just outside the door stands a huge **covered font**, largest on the mountain, with recycled columns from a pagan temple supporting the canopy. The **church**, near the rear of the large but cluttered courtyard, contains more frescoes by Theophanes.

Beyond Meyístis Lávras lies some of the most beautiful and deserted wilderness on the peninsula – the so-called Athonite "desert", beloved of ascetics – now partly compromised by a track bulldozed over the most direct path south to one of Meyístis Lávras's many dependencies, the large **Skíti** of **Prodhrómou**. Under the aegis of the saintly elder Petronios, it is now full of young Romanian monks who keep the place immaculate. Just ten minutes away by marked path there's the **hermitage–cave of St Athanasios**, watched over by five skulls.

Most first-time visitors will, however, proceed without delay from Meyístis Lávras on a traverse of up to six hours across the tip of Athos, through incomparably rugged territory along paths unlikely to be destroyed in the future – the local monks intend to keep it this way, and this is currently one of the few places on Athos where trails are at all maintained. A few minutes past the point where the ascending paths from Meyístis Lávras and Prodhrómou link up, there's a turning down and left towards the *kellí* of **Áyios Nílos**, reached by crossing an intimidating but stabilized rockfall. There's a welcome **spring** here – many on Athos are neglected and dried up – and you can visit the cave of the medieval hermit Nilos on the far side of the prominent crag here. Otherwise, it's plainly visible after you descend through a fearsome ravine and climb up the far side; Nilos's tomb, towards the base of the same cliff, is difficult to reach.

About an hour past Áyios Nílos, or nearly three from Meyístis Lávras, you come to **Kafsokalývia (Ayías Triádhas)**, where donkeys are much in evidence toiling up between the tiered cottages. This minor community took root around the tombs of the saints Maximios and Akakios, and there's a surprisingly large and comprehensively frescoed chapel beside the small and rather plain guest quarters; overnight stays are not normally allowed.

To rejoin the main trail from here involves a punishing climb over a five-hundred-metre altitude difference, which can be avoided by taking the daily morning boat from Kafsokalývia's harbour, a half-hour below. Disembark at the next port for the hermitages of Karoúlia and Katounákia, where you face a much more manageable climb of 200m (45min) up to the **Dhanilíon** academy, where monks and laymen perfect their technique of Byzantine chanting. From here it's an hour-plus walking on a gentle contour path to the Ayías Ánnas, via incongruously modernized Mikrís Ayías Ánnas, whose helipad and solar-powered villas would not disgrace a trendy Greek island.

However, the commonest strategy involves heading directly west from Prodhrómou, via the only water at the Krýa Nerá stream, to the large **Skíti** of **Ayías Ánnas** (☎23770 23320; booking required – no specific booking times), whose buildings tumble downhill to a perennial-summer patch of coast capable of ripening lemons. This, with its renovated guest quarters, is the usual "base camp" for the climb of **Athos peak** itself (2030m) – best left for the next morning, and the months May–June and September.

With a (pre-)dawn start, you gain the necessary mercy of a little shade and can expect to be up top in just over four walking hours from Ayías Ánnas, with the combination refuge-church of **Panayía** passed a little over an hour before reaching the summit. Some hikers plan an overnight stop at this shelter, to watch the sunrise from the peak, but for this you must be self-sufficient in **food**. There's no spring **water** en route – you drink from cisterns at Panayía or at **Metamórfosis**, the tiny chapel atop the peak.

Returning from the peak before noon, you'll still have time to reach one of the monasteries north of Ayías Ánnas; the scenic path continues past **Néa Skíti** (☎23770 23656; booking required for visits 8am–1.30pm; no overnight stays) and affords a sudden, breathtaking view of **AYÍOU PÁVLOU** (☎23770 23741, 🖷23770 23355; booking required 10am–12.30pm) as you round a bend. Except for the ugly scar of the new access road off to the left, which continues down to its harbour, little can have changed in the perspective since Edward Lear painted it in the 1850s. Up close, the monastery, about ninety minutes from Ayías Ánnas, does not fulfil the promise of first sight; the courtyard lacks charm, as does the echoing, hospital-like guest area. Traditionally home to monks from the island of Kefalloniá, Ayíou Pávlou now has far more Cypriot brothers.

The "hanging" monasteries

From Ayíou Pávlou it's another hour to **AYÍOU DHIONYSÍOU** (☎23770 23687, 🖷23770 23686), a fortified structure perched spectacularly on a coastal cliff, and among the most richly endowed monasteries. It is one of those houses where the non-Orthodox must eat separately from the monks, though there are neat and airy guest quarters that come as a relief after so many claustrophobic facilities. Sadly, it is difficult to make out the sixteenth-century **frescoes** by the Cretan Tzortzis in the hopelessly dim church, likewise an icon attributed to the Evangelist Luke; however, those of Theophanes on the inside and out of the **refectory** are another story. The interior features *The Entry of the Saints into Paradise* and *The Ladder to Heaven*; the exterior wall bears a version of the *Apocalypse*, complete with what looks suspiciously like a nuclear mushroom cloud. Unusually, the Cypriot warden may offer a tour of the **library** with its illuminated gospels on silk-fortified paper, wooden carved miniature of the Passion Week and ivory crucifixes. You've little chance, however, of seeing Dhionysíou's great treasure, the three-metre-long **chryssobull** of the Trapezuntine emperor Alexios III Komnenos. Extensive modernization has been carried out here, with mixed results: clean electric power is supplied by a water turbine up-canyon, but the old half-timbered facade has been replaced with a rather brutal concrete-stucco one.

The onward path to **OSÍOU GRIGORÍOU** (℡23770 23668, ℻23770 23671; booking required 11am–1pm) is a bit neglected but spectacular and still usable, depositing you at the front door within an hour and a quarter of leaving Dhionysíou. Of all the monasteries this one has the most intimate relation with the sea. Owing to yet another charismatic abbot, some forty monks live here, usually vastly outnumbered by Greek pilgrims attracted by the place's reputation and quality of chanting. In the old guest quarters there's an attractive common room/library with literature on Orthodoxy; the guest overflow stays in a wood-trimmed hostel outside the gate, by the boat dock.

The southwest coastal trail system ends ninety minutes later at **SÍMONOS PÉTRAS** (abbreviated **Simópetra**; ℡23770 23254, ℻23770 23707; reservations required 1–3pm) or the Rock of Simon, after the foundation legend asserting that the hermit Simon was directed to build a monastery here by a mysterious light hovering over the sheer pinnacle. Though entirely rebuilt in the wake of a fire at the beginning of the twentieth century, Simópetra is perhaps the most visually striking monastery on Athos. With its multiple storeys, ringed by wooden balconies overhanging sheer three-hundred-metre drops, it resembles a Tibetan lamasery. The monastery rivals Filothéou in vigour, with sixty monks from a dozen countries around the world, and the choir is generally acknowledged to be the best on Athos. Unfortunately, because of the spectacle it presents, and its feasibility as an easy first stop out of Dháfni, Simópetra is always crowded with visitors, and might be better admired from a distance, especially during summer.

Further walking is inadvisable and it's best to arrange a lift northwest up the peninsula, or catch the morning boat in the same direction.

The northwestern monasteries

Since they are closer to the secular mainland and Karyés, the only real town on Athos, you might expect these monasteries to feel less isolated, yet their relative poverty – with the exception of magnificent Vatopedhíou – and the distance between them seem to lend this half of Athos a feeling of heightened remoteness. This exclusion reaches its apogee at the infamously conservative monastery of Esfigménou.

Dháfni port and the Russian monastery

At some point you'll make the acquaintance of **DHÁFNI**, if only to change boats, since the service on this coast is not continuous. There's a **post office**, some rather tacky souvenir shops and a **customs** post – much more vigilant when you leave than upon entry; all passengers' baggage is inspected to check traffic in smuggled-out treasures. A number of eagle-brooch-capped Athonite police skulk about, ever ready to pounce on real or imagined violations of the Athonite dress and behaviour codes. There's a **taverna** where you can get a beer and the dish of the day (usually frugal), but no shops adequate for restocking on food and drink.

The boat usually has an hour's layover here before heading back towards Ayías Ánnas, during which time the captain can often be persuaded (for a reasonable fee) to take groups as far as the Russian monastery of **AYÍOU PANDELÍMONOS** (alias **Roussikó**; ☎&ℱ23770 23252; booking required 10am–noon), sparing you a dull forty-minute walk from the port. Many of the monks are Russian, an ethnic predominance strongly reflected in onion-shaped **domes** and the softer faces of the frescoes. The majority of the buildings were erected at speed just after the mid-1800s, as part of Tsarist Russia's campaign for eminence on the Mountain, and have a utilitarian, barracks-like quality. The sole unique features are the corrosion-green lead roofs and the enormous **bell** over the refectory, the second largest in the world, which always prompts speculation as to how it got there. Otherwise, the small population fairly rattles around the echoing halls, the effect of desolation increased by the remains of outer dormitories gutted by a 1960s fire. If you're an architecture buff, Roussikó can probably be omitted without a twinge of conscience; students of early twentieth-century kitsch will be delighted, however, with mass-produced saints' calendars, gaudy reliquaries and a torrent of gold (or at least gilt) fixtures in the seldom-used main church. It's worth trying to get into a service in the top-storey chapel north of the belfry for the sake of the Slavonic chanting, though it must be said that the residents don't exactly put themselves out for non-Slavs.

Actually closer to Dháfni, a bit inland on what remains of the old path towards Karyés, stands the square compound of **XIROPOTÁMOU** (☎23770 23251, ℱ23770 23733; booking required 10am–12.30pm), with most of its construction and church frescoes dating from the eighteenth century, except for two wings that were fire-damaged in 1952. Like Filothéou, this monastery was at the forefront of the 1980s "renaissance"; here again non-Orthodox are kept segregated from the faithful at meal times.

Greek coastal monasteries

From the vicinity of Dháfni or Roussikó, most pilgrims continue along the coast, reaching **XENOFÓNDOS** (☎23770 23633, ℱ23770 23631; booking required noon–2pm) along a mix of trail and tractor-track an hour after quitting the Russian monastery. Approached from this direction, Xenofóndos's busy sawmill gives it a vaguely industrial air. The enormous, sloping, irregularly shaped court, expanded upwards in the nineteenth century, is unique in possessing two main churches. The small, older one, decorated with exterior frescoes of the Cretan school, was outgrown and replaced during the 1830s by the huge upper one. Among its many icons are two fine **mosaics** of saints George and Demetrios. The guest quarters occupy a modern wing overlooking the sea at the extreme south end of the perimeter.

A half-hour's walk separates Xenofóndos from **DHOHIARÍOU** (☎23770 23245; call ahead to visit), one of the more picturesque monasteries on this coast but not conspicuously friendly to the non-Orthodox (no overnight stays). Early 1990s renovations left untouched the spare but clean guest quarters, which see few foreigners. An exceptionally lofty, large **church** nearly fills the court, though its Cretan-school frescoes, possibly by Tzortzis, were clumsily retouched in 1855. Much better are the late seventeenth-century ones in the long, narrow **refectory**, with its sea views – some of the nicest on Athos. Even Orthodox pilgrims have trouble getting to see the wonder-working icon of *Gorgoipikóöu* ("She who is quick to hear"), housed in a chapel between church and refectory.

The far northern monasteries

The direct trail inland and up to **KONSTAMONÍTOU** (also known as Kastamonítou; ☎&℉ 23770 23228) has been reclaimed by the forest, so to get there you have to go in a roundabout fashion 45 minutes along the coast to its harbour, and then as much time again sharply up on a track which has regrettably buried the old cobbled way. Hidden up in a thickly wooded valley, Konstamonítou seems as humble, bare and poor as you'd expect from the last-ranking monastery; the church nearly fills the quadrangular court where the grass is growing up through the cracks. Non-Orthodox and believers are segregated, not that many foreigners make it this far.

From here you can continue on foot for ninety minutes to Zográfou, more usually reached directly from its harbour (second stop on the boat route from Ouranoúpoli) within an hour by a track which has obliterated eighty percent of the old path. **ZOGRÁFOU** (☎&℉ 23770 23247), the furthest inland of the monasteries, is populated by a handful of elderly Bulgarian monks whose numbers are not being replenished, owing to long-standing indifference by both the Greek and Bulgarian governments. A stroll down the empty, rambling corridors past the scarcely maintained seventeenth- and eighteenth-century cells lends an appreciation of the enormous workload that falls on so few shoulders, yet even here building materials are piled high for the imminent makeover. "Zográfou" means "of the Painter", in reference to a tenth-century legend: the Slavs who founded the monastery couldn't decide on a patron saint, so they put a wooden panel by the altar, and after lengthy prayer a painting of Saint George – henceforth the institution's protector – appeared.

From Zográfou the direct trails to Esfigménou and Vatopedhíou have been bulldozed, so the best option if you're crossing the peninsula is to follow the one surviving trail which begins as a shaded path and is only sullied by tracks for about twenty minutes near the high point. After some three hours on this high-quality route, you suddenly drop down to the enormous, irregularly shaped monastery of **HILANDHARÍOU** (**Hilandar** in Serbian; ☎ 23770 23797; call ahead to visit – no overnight stays), hidden in a shady glen and fringed by vast, mechanically tilled gardens and orchards. The mostly young monks who come in rota from Serbia are hospitable to all visitors, whatever their nationality. Hilandharíou has been Serbian since its thirteenth-century patronization by Serbian kings, and as you'd expect for a beacon of medieval Serbian culture, the library and treasury are well endowed. The **church**, at the bottom end of the sloping, triangular courtyard, dates from the fourteenth century, but its frescoes, similar in style to those in the Protáton at Karyés, have been retouched. On the south side of the church, an allegedly 800-year-old grapevine sprouted miraculously of its own accord from a holy tomb; the monks make raisins of its grapes, to which are ascribed various miraculous properties. Opposite the door of the **refectory**, there's a fresco of the *Ouranóskala* or "Stairway to Heaven", in which righteous monks are being assisted upwards by angels, while a few wicked ones are being yanked down by demons to the mouth of Hell. Last but perhaps not least, the reception area is the most sumptuous and tasteful on the mountain, more like the lobby of a Spanish parador, and the guest quarters are also among the most salubrious.

Northeast coast monasteries

From Hilandharíou a path heads east, then north, with considerable elevation change, to **ESFIGMÉNOU** monastery (☎23770 23796), though most will opt for the easier though duller hour-long track walk north, then east. Built directly at sea level in fortress style, it is the strictest foundation on Athos, and in its schismatic state has had little to do with the other nineteen monasteries for decades; the premises, lit by oil lamp, have an accordingly harsh feel despite a lush courtyard full of citrus and banana trees. Controversy turned into ugly confrontation in 2003 (see box overleaf) and you are advised to check the latest situation before even considering a visit.

Nonetheless, Esfigménou marks the start of one of the more wonderful surviving Athos treks, the three-and-a-half-hour coastal trek to Vatopedhíou (which, incidentally, tends to close an hour *before* sunset). There's track for the initial twenty minutes, then a path heads off left (seawards); shortly after the high point of the route, an hour along the path, a well-preserved cobbled path kicks in for the long descent through the thick Dhafnára laurel groves to emerge briefly on the coast, two-and-a-half hours along, before heading slightly inland again as a cobbled path on the final approach.

VATOPEDHÍOU (☎23770 23219, ⓕ23770 2381; booking required 9am–1pm) exceeds Meyístis Lávras in size, nearly matches it in importance and wealth and makes a good beginning or farewell to Athos. The cobbled, slanting court with its freestanding belfry is like a town plaza, ringed by stairways and stacks of cells for more than three hundred monks. The **katholikón**, one of the oldest on the mountain, contains a set of exceptional fourteenth-century **frescoes** of the Macedonian school and three **mosaics** flanking the door of the inner narthex: Gabriel (left) and the Virgin (right) comprising an *Annunciation*, with the *Deisis* (the Virgin, Christ and John the Baptist) above, and some more wonderful mosaics in the nave. The growing international population of eighty-plus welcoming monks, mostly young and some Cypriot or Australian in background, makes this a good place to get to grips with Orthodoxy, with plenty of English-speakers to talk to and reading material provided in the guest quarters. Even if you're not staying, it's possible to have a small snack here and retire from the heat of midday before resuming progress to other monasteries.

Continuing southeast, you can initially short-cut dust-tracks on the cobbled path for the first hour-plus up to the ridge, but the ninety-minute trail from there to Pandokrátoros was chewed up by bulldozers in 1998 and is now all but impossible to find going in this direction. Allow nearly three hours to reach **PANDOKRÁTOROS** (☎23770 23880, ⓕ23770 23685; booking required 11.30am–2pm & 7.30–9pm). Other than a hilltop setting overlooking its own picturesque fishing harbour, and the courtyard with its eight Valencia orange trees, there is little of artistic note – perhaps still less given ambitious renovations – though the thirty-odd young monks are welcoming, and the guest wing overlooks the sea. In a valley above looms its dependency of **Profítis Ilías**, a relic of the Russian expansion drive and today home to a handful of monks from several different countries.

Continuing on the now-shady, roller-coastering shoreline trail, it's under an hour door-to-door to tiny **STAVRONIKÍTA** (☎&ⓕ23770 23255; booking required 10am–noon). With some of the best views of Athos peak, this is also the most distinct example of an Athonite coastal fortress-monastery, vertically orientated on its surf-lashed promontory. Long one of the poorest houses, Stavronikíta was completely revitalized under the abbot Vasilios before his move to Ivíron; surrounded by aqueduct-fed kitchen gardens, it remains pin-neat. The narrow **church** occupies virtually all the gloomy courtyard, and the **refectory**,

Esfigménou: Athos's zealot monks

Esfigménou is traditionally one of the more militant bastions of conservative religious practice (its name appropriately means "tightly girt"), even by Athonite standards. Its monks became angered back in the 1970s, when Orthodox Patriarch Athenagoras unforgivably (as they believe) began a rapprochement with the Catholic Church in Rome. Since then they have refused to recognize the authority of the patriarchate, especially current Patriarch Bartholomew, who has continued to work for ecumenical understanding. A number of these zealot monks have even erected a sign facing the sea, reading "Orthodoxy or Death", adding black flags emblazoned with the same war cry to the monastery's fortress-like turrets.

Things came to a head in 2002 when the Patriarch declared the brotherhood schismatic and ordered them to leave Athos, as they refused to obey the governing body's instructions to mention him in their prayers. In December of that year, the peninsula's acting civil governor, Aristos Kasmiroglou, signed an eviction order, giving the monks – who have nowhere to go – until the end of January to comply. Esfigménou's 117 brothers, led by defiant *igoúmenos* **Methodius** and including one monk claiming to be 100 years old, said that they would "use their rosaries as weapons" and refused to budge, despite an eight-week blockade (by the Greek police) of all supplies and communications with the outside world.

When they first appealed to Greece's Supreme Court, the Council of State, they won a reprieve. As support mounted throughout the Greek Orthodox world, with pledges of assistance from the United States and Australia, noisy demonstrations were held by nuns, monks, priests and their supporters all across Greece. Following a new decision by the Council of State in March 2005, which simply concluded that it had no jurisdiction over Athonite monasteries, there seemed to be no solution in sight to this long dispute.

normally opposite, had to be shifted upstairs to the south wing; it's a spartan room with a single window on the water, and fresco fragments by Theophanes of the *Death of Áyios Nikólaos* (the patron) and the *Last Supper*. Many Australians, including the most recent abbot, number among the two dozen monks, who really are strict about bookings for the small, oil-lamp-lit guest quarters and who will roust all, Orthodox and infidel alike, for 3.30am matins. All non-Orthodox guests will be sent on their way an hour or so after sunrise, after coffee and biscuits. Despite (or because of) this, it is a popular monastery with young, educated city Greeks. From here an hour's walk, mostly on path, separates you from Ivíron.

The coastal road to Kavála

It is not easy to reach Kavála from Sithonía or the Mount Athos peninsula by public transport. First take the Ouranoúpoli–Thessaloníki bus, getting off at the drab coastal village of **STRATÓNI**, dominated by the local mine workings and the associated docks. From here, a scenic (but transport-less) road glides over a forested ridge north 17km to the beach resort of **OLYMBIÁDHA** (aka Olymbiás), a very low-key resort, with a more authentic atmosphere than anywhere in Halkidhikí. You can stay in **rooms** (❶), a pair of shaded, stream-side **campsites** – *Olympias* and *Corali* (☎23760 51304) – 1km north and 500km inland respectively, or a pair of co-managed **hotels**: the quieter *Liotopi* at the south edge of town, with a delicious breakfast served in a lush garden, and the central

Germany, with an atmospheric ground-floor taverna (both ℡23760 51362, ⓔhotel_liotopi@hal.forthnet.gr; ❹, half-board), the best in town. There are more **tavernas** on the southern bay, the cheapest and most characterful being the *Kapetan Manolis/Platanos* by the concrete jetty. All along this shore the local speciality is **mussels** (*mýdhia*), farmed in floating nursery beds and typically served in a spicy cheese sauce, or sold live, for cooking, at roadside stalls.

The small town **beaches** are fine, but there are other ones – such as Próti Ammoudhiá, where the water can be murky – 2km back towards Stratóni, behind the promontory containing **ancient Stageira**, birthplace of Aristotle. This covers two hilltops joined by a saddle, and is under continuous summer excavation; it's completely fenced off, but when the gates are open you're free to have a wander around. There's not much on view yet apart from the western wall and towers guarding the landward approach, a few paved streets and house foundations. It is, however, perhaps unique in ancient Greece for having been a city built of granite rather than marble or limestone.

From Olymbiádha, regular **buses** run to Thessaloníki (4 daily Mon–Fri, 3 on Sat, 2 on Sun). On the way, there is little reason to linger in **STAVRÓS**, 12km north of Olymbiádha, despite its beautiful seafront of plane trees, and a couple of relatively authentic **tavernas** such as *Iy Amalthia* or *Iy Platania*, at the far south end of town. The main E90 highway is only 4km farther north and, just east of the junction (where you catch eastbound buses for Kavála), is the first coastal resort of any size – **ASPROVÁLTA**, effectively a summer suburb of Sérres and Thessaloníki, with a frequent bus service to and from both, plus Kavála.

Fourteen kilometres east of Asproválta, the road to Kavála crosses the **River Strymónas**. If you bear onto a minor road signposted for Nigríta, rather than continuing over the river bridge, after less than 1km you'll find on your left the colossal marble **Lion of Amphipolis**. This was reconstructed in 1937 from fragments found when excavating the nearby ancient city of Amphipolis, and is thought to date from the end of the fourth century BC. **Ancient Amphipolis** itself (Tues–Sun 9am–3pm; free), some 3km further on, beyond the old iron bridge across the Strymónas, figured largely in Thucydides' *History of the Peloponnesian War*. It's worth the slight detour, preserving considerable chunks of fortification wall, foundations of a fifth-century BC river bridge and an early Christian basilica with mosaic floors.

Beyond the Strymónas, en route for Kavála, there's not a great deal along the way other than some vineyards, an occasional crumbled medieval watchtower and duney, white-sand **beaches**, easily the best in eastern Macedonia, though without any facilities.

Kavála and around

Backing onto the easterly foothills of Mount Sýmvolo, **KAVÁLA** is the second-largest city of Macedonia and the second port for northern Greece; it was an extremely wealthy place in the nineteenth century when the region's tobacco crop was shipped from its docks to the rest of the world. Although its attempt to style itself as the "Azure City", on account of its position at the head of a wide bay, is going a little overboard, it does have a characterful centre, focused on the harbour area with the few remaining tobacco warehouses. A picturesque citadel looks down from a rocky promontory to the east, and an elegant Ottoman aqueduct leaps over modern buildings into the old quarter on the bluff.

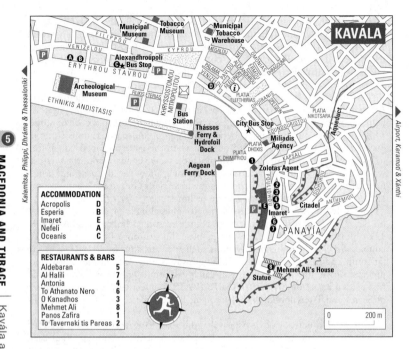

KAVÁLA

Municipal Museum

Tobacco Museum

Municipal Tobacco Warehouse

Alexandhroúpoli Bus Stop

Archeological Museum

Bus Station

Thássos Ferry & Hydrofoil Dock

City Bus Stop

Miliadis Agency

Aegean Ferry Dock

Zolotas Agent

Citadel

Imaret

PANAYÍA

Mehmet Ali's House

Statue

N

ACCOMMODATION	
Acropolis	D
Esperia	B
Imaret	E
Nefeli	A
Oceanis	C

RESTAURANTS & BARS	
Aldebaran	5
Al Halíli	7
Antonia	4
To Athanato Nero	6
O Kanadhos	3
Mehmet Ali	8
Panos Zafira	1
To Tavernaki tis Pareas	2

0   200 m

Known in ancient times as Neapolis, the town was for two centuries or more a staging post on the Via Egnatia and the first European port of call for merchants and travellers from the Middle East. It was here that Saint Paul landed en route to Philippi (see p.535), on his initial mission to Europe. In later years, the port and citadel were occupied in turn by the Byzantines, Normans, Franks, Venetians, Ottomans and (during both world wars) Bulgarians. Kavála is also one of the main departure points for Thássos (see p.949) and, to a lesser extent, Samothráki (see p.944) and Límnos (see p.937).

Arrival and information

The main **bus station** is on the corner of Mitropolítou Khryssostómou and Filikís Eterías, near the Thássos ferry and hydrofoil dock; buses to and from points east may drop you off or pick you up on Erythroú Stavroú, in front of the *Hotel Oceanis*. **Taxis** are deep tangerine in colour; if you're **driving** in, you can usually (just) find a space on the quay car park near the Thássos dock. In the main square, Platía Eleftherías, you'll find an **EOT** office, which can provide details, and sell tickets, for the summer Philippi–Thássos Festival, but little else; the square is ringed by several banks with **ATMs**. Kavála's **airport**, used by package holiday-makers en route to Thássos and providing domestic flights to and from Athens, lies 29km southeast.

Car ferries sail from Kavála to **Thássos** almost hourly from 6am to 9pm in season; virtually all run to the port of Skála Prínou (1hr 15min). There is also a regular seasonal **hydrofoil** service to and from the island (30min each way); check locally for details. Other ferry services from Kavála are fairly predictable as to basic weekly pattern, though specific days vary. From late July until late

August, there are in theory five weekly departures to **Samothráki** (typically Mon–Wed, Fri & Sat; 4hr), though these don't run every year; on the other hand, in some years they've started as early as Easter, so you'll need to check. More certain are the four boats a week to **Límnos** (usually Tues, Thurs, Sat & Sun; 5hr), dwindling to two off season. For much of the year two or three of these continue to various islands and mainland ports, among them Áyios Efstrátios, Lésvos, Híos and Lávrio. Details for all services are available from either Nikos Miliadis, behind the tavernas on Platía Dhoxís/Platía Karaolí Dhimitríou (☎2510 226 147 or 2510 223 421), or Yiorgos Zolotas (☎2510 835 671), a little further along the harbour front towards the terminal/customs house.

Accommodation

Abundant, good-value **hotel** rooms are not the order of the day in Kavála. Apart from a set of seedy dosshouses, you have a choice between one of the most luxurious hotels in the country, with rates to match, or overpriced, uninspiring establishments, though proprietors can often be bargained down a category or two in the off season. If you're arriving on an afternoon charter in summer, you might well prefer to transfer from the airport to Keramotí for a ferry to **Thássos** with its wide choice of accommodation, reserving Kavála for a day-trip; there is also an unusual hotel at **Néa Karváli**, 12km to the east (see p.565). The closest **campsite** is *Iríni* (☎2510 229 785; open all year), on the shore 3km east of the port and served by city bus #2. Rather better are the *Estella*, 9km west, while the pricier *Batis*, only 4km west, is still hedged by the city sprawl. *Camping Anatoli* (☎05940 21027; May–Sept), with a saltwater swimming pool, at the west end of Néa Péramos, a full 14km west of Kavála, can also be recommended.

Acropolis Venizélou 29 ☎2510 223 543, ℱ2510 830 752. The cheapest acceptable outfit in town, with English-speaking management and large, eccentric but not unpleasant rooms. ❹

Esperia Erythroú Stavroú 42 ☎2510 229 6215, ⓦwww.esperiakavala.gr. A decent hotel with air conditioning, good breakfasts served on a terrace – ask for the quieter side or back rooms. ❺

Imaret Poulídhou 6 ☎2510 620 151, ℱ2510 620 156, ⓦwww.imaret.gr. This expertly refurbished Ottoman monument, a gift to the city from its great benefactor Mehmet Ali but still officially the property of the Egyptian government, now functions as a deluxe resort, where every detail has been carefully selected for the discerning traveller; silence is only broken by the

sound of water running into a courtyard pool. The faultless rooms and suites, home in the nineteenth century to Islamic students, are now modern hotel accommodations, though the original building is intact. Services include a traditional *hamam* with massage, a restaurant serving Ottoman dishes and a womb-like indoor pool. ❽

Nefeli Erythroú Stavroú 50 ☎2510 227 441, ℱ2510 227 440. Just along from the *Esperia*, this nondescript hotel is much less appealing, though perfectly decent. ❹

Oceanis Erythroú Stavroú 32 ☎2510 221 981. A rather impersonal modern hotel with functional rooms, but helpful when the town is busy in season, especially during the festival. ❺

The Town

Although the remnants of Kavála's Ottoman past are mostly neglected, the wedge-shaped **Panayía** quarter to the east of the port preserves a scattering of eighteenth- and nineteenth-century buildings with atmospheric lanes wandering up towards the citadel. The most conspicuous and interesting of its buildings is the splendid **Imaret**, overlooking the harbour on Poulídhou. A long, multi-domed structure, it was originally a soup-kitchen-cum-hostel for theological students. After many decades of dereliction it was lovingly refurbished and, in

2004, opened as a luxury resort **hotel** (see "Accommodation"). Undoubtedly the best-preserved Islamic building on Greek territory, it was built in 1817 and endowed to the city by **Mehmet (or Mohammed) Ali**, pasha of Egypt and founder of the dynasty which ended with King Farouk. Farther up the promontory, near the corner of Poulídhou and Mohámet Alí, you can see the prestigious **Ottoman-style house** where Mehmet Ali was born to an Albanian family in 1769. Its wood-panelled reception rooms, ground-floor stables and first-floor harem have also been expertly restored, and now function as a high-quality **restaurant** (see "Eating and drinking"), under the same ownership as the Imaret hotel. Nearby rears an elegant equestrian bronze **statue** of the great man, one of the finest of its kind in Greece.

Wonderful views can be had from the Byzantine **citadel** (daily: summer 8am–7pm, sometimes closed for siesta; winter 8am–5pm; free), signed "castle". You can explore the ramparts, towers, dungeon and cistern, and in season it co-hosts the Philippi-Thássos Festival of drama and music in its main court. From here, sweeping down towards the middle of town, the **Kamáres aqueduct**, built on a Roman model during the reign of Süleyman the Magnificent (1520–66), spans the traffic in Platía Nikotsára.

Finally, on the other side of the harbour from the old town, there are three museums of moderate interest. The **Archeological Museum** (Tues–Sun 8.30am–3pm; €2) on Erythroú Stavroú contains a fine dolphin and lily mosaic upstairs in the Abdera room, plus painted sarcophagi in the adjacent section devoted to Thassian colonies. Downstairs in the ground-floor rear left gallery is a reconstructed Macedonian funeral chamber, with many terracotta figurines still decorated in their original paint and gold ornaments from tombs at Amphipolis. Just inland, next to some rather dilapidated former tobacco warehouses at Filíppou 4, is the **Municipal Museum** (Mon–Fri 8am–2pm, Sat 9am–1pm; free); along with various collections of stuffed birds, traditional costumes and household utensils, this has a couple of interesting rooms devoted to the Thássos-born sculptor Polygnotos Vayis (see p.954). One more street up, at Paleológou 4, the potentially interesting **Tobacco Museum** (Mon–Sat 9am–1pm; free) falls down on presentation and the lack of explanations in Greek, let alone English, though some of the exhibits, including historic photographs and antique cigarette packets, are worthwhile. The tobacco-led prosperity of nineteenth-century Kavála is perhaps better illustrated by the fabulous facade of the nearby **Municipal Tobacco Warehouse** (Dhimotikí Kapnapothíki), at Platía Kapnergáti; the building is being carefully restored for conversion to a shopping centre sometime in 2007.

Eating and drinking

Eating out in Kavála is generally a better prospect than staying the night; most places on the waterfront, however, are tourist traps, and to find a fish taverna where the locals eat you will need transport to take you along the coast to the east of town. You're far better off walking up into the Panayía district, where a row of moderately priced tavernas with outdoor seating, interspersed with café-bars, tempts you with good and reasonably priced grills and seafood. Two of the **bars** that stand out are the *Aldebaran*, which offers occasional live music in addition to draught beer, and the *mezedhopolío Al Halili*, farther up, where delicious titbits accompany the ouzo and wine. A string of trendy **café-bars** lurks on pedestrianized Palamá, parallel to Venizélou street. The city's youth head for university town Dhráma for their nightlife, however.

Antonia Poulídhou. Traditional family taverna dishing up platefuls of fried squid accompanied by good bulk wine.

To Athanato Nero Poulídhou. Consistently the best of the Poulídhou establishments, priding itself on a mean mussels *saganáki* and excellent white wine from Limnos.

O Kanadhos Poulídhou. Fish is the speciality at this homely place run by returnees from Toronto – hence the name and the English-speaking management.

Mehmet Ali House Poulídhou. Expensive gourmet restaurant housed in an eighteenth-century monument; Ottoman cuisine.

Panos Zafira Platía Karaolí Dhimitríou. The most reliable of the waterfront eateries, serving decent fish at reasonable prices.

To Tavernaki tis Pareas Poulídhou. The first taverna you come to as you climb Poulídhou – a clubby little place with good music as the name suggests.

Keramotí and Néa Karváli

Rather than negotiate the streets of Kavála, many people find it more convenient to take the bus or drive to **KERAMOTÍ**, 46km southeast, and take the car ferry from there to Thássos – especially between September and April, when services from Kavála drop to just a handful of boats daily. Keramotí is a small, rather drab village, 9km beyond the Kavála airport turn-off, with a decent enough beach backed by pines, a few rooms and a half-dozen hotels which you shouldn't have to patronize – the best of a bad bunch is the *Golden Sands* (☎05910 51509; ❷), tucked away in a quieter part of town. Alternative **accommodation** is available at the *Akontisma Hotel* (☎&☎2510 316790 – call ahead; ❹) just outside **NÉA KARVÁLI**, 34km west of Keramotí; described as a "traditional stone village", it offers very tasteful rooms with a wide range of services including a sauna and *hamam*.

Thrace

Separated from Macedonia to the west by the Néstos River and from the Turkish territory of eastern Thrace by the Évros River and its delta, western **Thrace** (Thráki) is the Greek state's most recent acquisition, under effective Greek control only since 1920. The Treaty of Lausanne (1923) confirmed Greek sovereignty but also sanctioned the forced evacuation of 390,000 Muslims, principally from Macedonia and Epirus, in exchange for more than a million ethnic Greeks from eastern Thrace and Asia Minor (both now part of the modern Turkish state). But the Muslims of western Thrace, in return for a continued Greek presence in and around Constantinople (Istanbul), were exempt from the exchanges and continue to live in the region.

In ancient times, Thrace was inhabited by a people with their own, non-Hellenic, language and religion. From the seventh century BC onwards it was **colonized** by Greeks, and after Alexander's time the area took on a strategic significance as the land route between Greece and Byzantium. It was later controlled by the Roman and Byzantine empires, and after 1361 by the Ottoman Turks. Nowadays, out of a total population of 360,000, there are officially around 120,000 Muslims, about half of them **Turkish-speakers**, while the rest are **Pomaks** (see p.568) and Roma. Although there are dozens of functioning mosques, some Turkish-language newspapers and a Turkish-language radio station in Komotiní, only graduates from a special Academy in Thessaloníki have been allowed to teach in the Turkish-language schools here – thus isolating Thracian Turks from mainstream Turkish culture. Local Turks and Pomaks claim that they are the victims of **discrimination**, but despite occasional explosions of intercommunal violence in the past, as an outsider you will probably not notice the tensions; in mixed villages Muslims and Greeks appear to coexist quite amicably. All Thracians, both Muslim and Orthodox, have a deserved reputation for hospitality.

Most travellers rush straight through to **Alexandhroúpoli** – which now has an outstanding ethnological museum – for the ferry to Samothráki, or head determinedly on to **Istanbul**. But Thrace's many rulers all left some mark on the area, and there are a few well-preserved monuments, most significantly the remains of the coastal cities of Abdera, south of **Xánthi**, Maroneia, southeast of **Komotiní**, the regional capital, and Mesembria, west of Alexandhroúpoli – Greek colonies in the seventh century BC that were abandoned in Byzantine times when the inhabitants moved inland to escape pirate raids. Otherwise, it is the landscape itself that holds most appeal, with the train line forging a circuitous but scenic route below the foothills of the Rodhópi mountains: the best stretch is the **Néstos valley** between Paranésti and Xánthi. Unfortunately, many of the towns and villages have lost their charm, owing to unattractive twentieth-century architecture, but if you make time to explore the backstreets or venture up to tiny, isolated settlements in the Rodhópi mountains, you'll find an atmosphere quite unlike any other part of Greece. In particular, the alpine-looking village of **Stavroúpoli** rewards off-the-beaten-track explorations.

Xánthi and around

Coming from Kavála, after the turning to the airport and shortly after the turning to Keramotí, you cross the Néstos River which, with the **Rodhópi mountains**, forms the border of Greek Thrace. The Greek/Turkish, Christian/Muslim demographics are almost immediately apparent in the villages: the Turkish settlements, long established, with their tiled, whitewashed houses and pencil-thin minarets; the Greek ones, often adjacent, built in drab modern style for the refugees of the 1920s. The same features are combined in the region's biggest urban centre, the attractive market town of **Xánthi**.

Xánthi

XÁNTHI (Iskeçe for Turkish-speakers), the first town of any size, is perhaps the most interesting point to break a journey. There is a busy market area, good food, and – up the hill to the north of the main café-lined square – a very attractive old quarter. The town is also home to the University of Thrace, which lends a lively air to the place, particularly in the area between the bazaar and the campus, where bars, cinemas and bistros are busy in term time. Try, if you can, to visit on Saturday, the day of Xánthi's **street fair** – a huge affair, attended equally by Greeks, Pomaks and Turks, held in an open space near the fire station on the eastern side of the town.

Arrival and information

The **train station** lies just off the Kavála road, 2km south of the centre (taxis await arrivals and are green with white tops; approximately €2), while buses draw in at the new **KTEL**, over 1km north of the centre. The main south–north thoroughfare is 28-Oktovríou, lined with fast-food outlets and sundry shops. One end is marked by the Kendrikí Platía, recognizable by its prominent, if unsightly, clocktower. Xánthi's pay-and-display **parking** scheme is pretty comprehensive, with fees payable in the centre from 8.30am to 8.30pm, Monday to Saturday. The **post office**, signposted, and Olympic Airways are both very close to the platía, on its uphill side. Several **banks** with **ATMs** line the square.

Accommodation

Downtown **hotel** choices are limited and rather overpriced, and disappointingly there's no official accommodation in the atmospheric old town. Nearest the centre is the recently refurbished *Democritus*, 28-Oktovríou 41 (T 25410 25111, F 25410 25537; ❹), where you should insist on a room away from the street. More or less around the corner at Mihaïl Karaolí 40, the 1996-vintage *Orfeas* (T 25410 20121, F 25410 20998; ❹) has spacious, bright, en-suite rooms. Smartest, quietest and least expensive, however, is the business-oriented but good-value *Xanthippion*, 28-Oktovríou 212 (T 25410 77061, F 25410 77076; ❹), a short walk from the centre and not far from the KTEL.

The Town

The narrow cobbled streets of the **old town** are home to a number of very fine mansions – some restored, some derelict – with colourful exteriors, bay windows and wrought-iron balconies; most date from the mid-nineteenth century when Xánthi's tobacco merchants made their fortunes. One of them has been turned into a **folk museum** (daily 11am–1pm; €1.50), at Odhós Antíka 7, at the bottom of the hill up into the right-bank quarter of the old town. Originally built for two tobacco magnate brothers, its home is a beautiful semi-detached pair of mansions worth seeing for their exterior alone; some years ago the interior was lovingly restored with painted wooden panels, decorated plaster and floral designs on the walls and ceilings. The interesting displays include Thracian clothes and jewellery, a postcard collection and cakes of tobacco.

Further up, the roads become increasingly narrow and steep, and the Turkish presence (about fifteen percent of the total urban population) is more noticeable: most of the women have their heads covered, and the more religious ones wear full-length cloaks. Churches and mosques hide behind whitewashed houses with tiled roofs, and orange-brown tobacco leaves are strung along drying frames. Numerous houses, no matter how modest, sport a dish for tuning in to Turkish satellite television.

Eating, drinking and entertainment

Xanthi's **restaurants** are somewhat better than its hotels. Tucked away just to the north of the Kendrikí Platía, at Yeoryíou Stavroú 18, is the eminently reasonable *Taverna Midhos* (more of an ouzerí), with a delightful summer garden in back, efficient service and a mix of *mezédhes* and *mayireftá*. At the lower reaches of cobbled Paleológou and Odhós P. Christídhi, you'll find a gaggle of taverna-cum-ouzerís, of which the best is arguably *Myrovolos* – all with identical prices and similarly predictable menus, but featuring wonderful barrel retsina. For a good-value summertime grilled supper from a limited menu but in a superb setting, look no further than the *Nissaki* on the banks of the Podhonífi River dividing the town. To find it, follow Odhós Pindhárou upstream from behind the abandoned *Xenia* hotel, to this street's end at the base of the old town.

Xánthi's buzzing **nightlife** is focused on Odhós Vasilíssis Sofías, which forks off Paleológou at the little park sporting a bust of war hero Antíkas, and on the platía itself. Doyen of the various bars on the former is the enormous *Kyverneio*, boasting a huge terrace, while a whole cluster of see-and-be-seen **café-bars** on the platía vies for your custom. For a coffee and cake, the mock-traditional zaharoplastío *Vyzandio*, also on the platía, may look fake, but the pastries, chocolates and ice cream are divine and the coffee's the best in town. There's a quality **cinema**, Olympia, at the bottom of the old town behind the municipal library, or in summer premises next to the town hall.

North of Xánthi

Much of the countryside north of Xánthi, towards the Bulgarian border, is a military controlled area, dotted with signs denoting the fact. If you venture up into the western Rodhópi range here, the main reward is some magnificent scenery; there's not much arable land amidst the wild, forested hills, and what there is – down in the river valleys – is devoted entirely to tobacco, hand-tilled by the Pomaks, who tend to keep themselves to themselves. Owing to the modest increase in material prosperity since the 1980s, the Pomak villages have mostly lost their traditional architecture to concrete multistorey apartments. **SMÍNTHI**, a large and dispersed settlement with a mosque and tall minaret, has a couple of *psistariés* on the through road, the only thing remotely resembling tourist facilities in the immediate area. **ORÉO**, 6km up a side road northwest of Smínthi, is dramatically set on a steep hillside with cloud-covered peaks behind and terraces falling away to the riverbed.

Stavroúpoli

Set among some of the region's most inviting scenery – deep gorges, fir-draped crags and high waterfalls, more like the French Jura than a typically Greek landscape – neat little **STAVROÚPOLI**, 25km west of Smínthi, is doing its very best to attract tourists, so far mainly Greeks. Having suffered a major population drain during the decades of mass emigration, the village, with its immaculate cobbled streets, shady central platía, complete with traditional café, and well-restored Thracian-style houses, is showing sure signs of a revival. Some 30km northwest of Xánthi along the scenic Dhráma road, it is conveniently placed for visiting the most spectacular stretch of the Néstos River, whose meanders and rapids lend themselves to safe rafting and canoeing. With some of the finest hiking in the whole of Greece in its surroundings, Stavroúpoli makes a credible centre for alternative tourism. The town has a delightful little **Folklore Museum** (follow signs from the town centre), a proudly displayed collection in a restored house full of local memorabilia donated by residents – everything from embroidered bodices to an ancient still-functioning record player; ask around for the curator as it has no fixed opening hours.

Stavroúpoli is potentially an excellent alternative to staying in either Xánthi or Komotiní, but for now the only **accommodation** in the town itself is the atmospheric and extremely welcoming ✻ *Xenios Zeus* (☎25420 22444; ❸), an old Thracian house with traditional decor just off the main square. Nearby is the excellent **taverna** ✻ *Oinos*, which offers not only delicious game and vegetable dishes but also information about kayaking, mountain bikes and horse riding in the region. Just a couple of kilometres south is the hotel *Nemesis* (☎25420 21005; ❹), which looks like a medieval castle and has simple but comfortable rooms and a swimming pool.

South of Xánthi

South of Xánthi, the coastal plain, bright with fields of cotton, tobacco and cereals, stretches to the sea. Heading towards modern Ávdhira, you'll pass through **YENISSÉA** (Yeniçe), an unspectacular farming village with one of the oldest **mosques** in Thrace, dating from the sixteenth century. Now derelict, it's a low whitewashed building with a tiled roof, crumbled wooden portico and truncated minaret.

Regular buses serve the village of **ÁVDHIRA**, 10km further on, and, in summer, run on to the **beach** of Paralía Avdhíron, 7km beyond, passing through the site of **ancient Abdera** (daily 8am–2pm; free), founded in the seventh century BC by Clazomenians from Asia Minor. The walls of the ancient acropolis are visible on a low headland above the sea, and there are fragmentary traces of Roman baths, a theatre and an ancient acropolis. The remains are unspectacular, and the setting not particularly attractive, but the **archeological museum** (daily 11am–2pm; free), located in the village, puts it all into context with a beautifully presented exhibition, accompanied by extensive English texts. A rich collection of ceramics, coins, oil lamps, mosaics and jewellery is dominated by a moving section devoted to burial customs, including some spectacular reconstructions of graves dating from the seventh to fifth centuries BC.

For the most part, the coast east from here is flat and dull. At the southern end of brackish Lake Vistonídha stands **PÓRTO LÁGOS**, a semi-derelict harbour partly redeemed by the nearby modern monastery of **Áyios Nikólaos** (closed 1–5pm), built on two islets in the lagoon. The surrounding marshland, a major site for birdlife including herons, spoonbills and pelicans, is more accessible, though less important, than the Évros delta (see p.574); a few observation towers have been provided along the reedy shoreline. Ornithologists might like to know that this is one of the few wintering habitats in Europe of the endangered white-headed duck.

Nearby, 7km southeast and 32km from Xánthi, the small resort of **FANÁRI** has a long, sandy beach – one of the better ones in Thrace – backed by several **places to stay**, including two co-managed hotels: the modern *Fanari Hotel* (℡ 25350 31300, ✉ fanarih@otenet.gr; ❹), set well back from the beach at the eastern edge of the village, and the smaller, potentially noisier *Villa Theodora* (℡&℻ 25350 31242; ❸), out on the village promontory by the fishing port. Given the cost and unattractiveness of accommodation in both Xánthi and Komotiní, this could be an option worth considering, and you could visit each town on day-trips. The *Fanari* has a restaurant and there are other fish **tavernas**. An EOT campsite, the *Fanari* (℡ 25350 31270; May–Oct), lies 500m east of the *Fanari Hotel*, just before the the the public beach. Fanári village is a popular gathering point in the evenings and at weekends, and its beach gets busy in the high summer, but there are less crowded spots on the coast a few kilometres east.

Komotiní and around

The fertile central plains of Thrace, with their large ethnic Turkish population, are one of the least visited areas of the country, but are not without some appeal. Though outwardly unattractive, the market town of **Komotiní** rewards a closer look, with its two well-presented museums, one devoted to folk life and history, the other to archeological finds fom the region. The contents of the latter are complemented by the delightful ancient site of **Maroneia**, on the coast, and **Mesembria**, further east.

Komotiní

Lying 48km east of Xánthi along the direct road skirting the Rodhópi foothills, **KOMOTINÍ** is larger and markedly more Turkish than Xánthi. On first impression, it's a rather charmless place, with ranks of apartment buildings and gridded suburbs to the south and west, their noisy streets clogged with traffic. It does, however, have a couple of worthwhile museums, a lively bazaar and some of the region's best food. It also has more than a dozen functioning mosques. Social mixing between the different ethnic groups, however – roughly at parity population-wise – is almost nonexistent, although Orthodox and Muslims live in the same neighbourhoods. Since the 1990s the town has become even more polyglot, with an influx of Greek, Armenian and Georgian Christians from the Caucasus.

During the thirteenth century, the city gained importance owing to its position on the Via Egnatia. When the Ottomans took the city in 1361, they changed its name to Gümülçine, and it's still known as this to its ethnic Turks. In 1912, at the outbreak of the First Balkan War, Komotiní fell to the Bulgarians; it was liberated by Greek forces in the following year, only to be taken once more by the Bulgarians during World War I. It was finally and definitively joined to Greece on May 14, 1920.

The old **bazaar**, to the north of Platía Irínis, is a little bit of Istanbul, lodged between fine mosques and an elegant Ottoman-era **clocktower**. Alongside shady cafés, tiny shops sell everything from dried apricots to iron buckets; it's especially busy on Tuesdays when the villagers from the surrounding area come into town to sell their wares. Behind this old quarter, you can see the remains of Komotiní's **Byzantine walls**.

Traditionally a city with both Greek and Turkish inhabitants, Komotiní began to be dominated by Greek influence in the waning years of the Ottoman empire, when rich Greeks funded schools in the city to develop Greek culture and ideals. Some of these educational foundations still survive: one, a handsome half-timbered building at Ayíou Yeoryíou 13, has become the **Museum of Folk Life and History** (Mon–Sat 10am–1pm; free), displaying examples of Thracian embroidery, traditional Thracian dress, silverware, copperware and a collection of religious seals, but avoiding any mention of the ethnic Turkish community. The **archeological museum** at Simeonídhi 4 (daily 9am–6pm; free) is also worth a visit, giving a lucid overview of Thracian history, by means of plans and finds from local sites, from its beginnings up to the Byzantine era.

Practicalities

The **train station** is over 1km to the southwest of the centre, but **taxis** (red or maroon, mostly with white tops) await arrivals. The **KTEL** (also with a taxi rank) is some way to the south of central Platía Irínis, via Énou. Should you need to stay, be aware that the **hotel** situation is nearly as unpromising as Xánthi's. Basic in a quaint way, and very friendly, is the *Hellas* at Dhimokrítou 31 (☎25310 22055; ❷), with shared showers and toilets, at a noisy intersection in the west of town. Marginally quieter, but overpriced, is the *Astoria*, a Neoclassical inn restoration at Platía Irínis 28 (☎25310 35054; ❺); calmer still, but a long way out, beyond the war memorial, at the east end of Platía Irínis, is the *Anatolia*, Anhiálou 53 (☎25310 36242; ❹).

By far the best **eating** is to be found at 🍴 *Inopion* at Platía Irínis 67, in the form of conventional, impeccably prepared dishes served with considerable style. Tucked away in the narrowest lanes of the bazaar just north of Orféos, two decent ouzerís, *Apolafsis* and *Yiaxis* (the better of the two), put out tables under arbours.

Marónia and Mesimvría

Just off the E90 motorway, southeast of Komotiní, lie two archeological sites that make an excellent break in the journey to Alexandhroúpoli. Clearly indicated from the Sápes turn-off is **ancient Maroneia**, a set of ancient and Byzantine ruins scattered among seaside olive groves. It's just below the modern village of **MARÓNIA**, served by six daily buses from Komotiní via the old road. Marónia has held onto a few surviving old Thracian mansions with balconies, and, on the edge of the village, there's an excellent **hotel**, 🍴 the *Roxani* (☎25330 21501, ⓦwww .ecoexplorer.gr; ❹); the spacious rooms look out on fabulous views, and breakfasts are copious, with other meals available. The enthusiastic archeologist who owns the hotel can fix you up with all manner of activities, from bird-watching and astronomy to sea-canoeing and archery, or exploring the nearby caves.

To get to the ruins of ancient Maroneia, attractively situated at the foot of Mount Ísmaros, follow the signs to Marónia's harbour of **Áyios Harálambos**, taking care not to enter the airforce camp nearby. The founder of the city is reckoned to be Maron, the son of the god of wine, Dionysos (Ísmaros is known locally as the Mountain of Dionysos), and the city became one of the most powerful in all of ancient Thrace. Mostly unexcavated, the remains can be explored at will but are badly signposted. Even so, you should be able to track down traces of a theatre, a sanctuary of Dionysos and various buildings including a house with a well-preserved mosaic floor. The land walls of the city are preserved to a height of 2m, together with a Roman tower above the harbour. Over time, the sea has done its own excavation, eroding the crumbling cliffs and revealing shards of pottery and ancient walls.

The port area, below the edge of the archeological site and 4km south of the modern village, is not a very enticing place, baking in the heat of the surrounding red cliffs, with no usable beach and two overpriced, overstretched tavernas. By contrast, **Platanítis**, 4km west of Marónia by another paved but unsigned road (just look for signs to various hotels), has a small but adequate gravel-and-sand beach – essentially a gap in the red cliffs – and a good, reasonably priced fish taverna, *O Yerasimos*.

A more worthwhile site, **ancient Mesembria**, or **MESIMVRÍA** in modern Greek (Mon 7am–2.30pm, Tues–Fri 7am–4pm, Sat & Sun 9.30am–4pm; free), is clearly signposted from the motorway and is reached via the nondescript village of Dhíkela. Thanks to its unspoilt seaside location, fruitful recent excavations and a well-thought-out display, it easily qualifies as the most appealing of the three ancient sites on the Thracian coastline. You can stay nearby at the smart, seaview **hotel** *Klio* (☎25510 71311, ⓕ25510 71411; ❹), with a decent restaurant at Ayía Paraskeví, near Mákri, a fishing village 11km west of Alexandhroúpoli along the old road.

Alexandhroúpoli

Some 120km southeast of Xánthi, the modern city of **ALEXANDHROÚPOLI** (Dedeagaç for Turkish-speakers) was designed by Russian

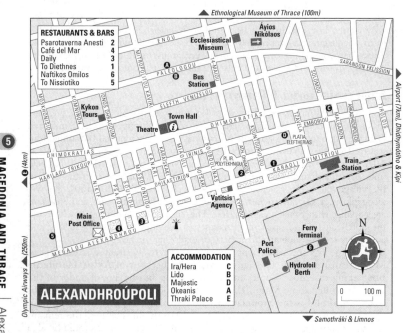

Ethnological Museum of Thrace (100m)

RESTAURANTS & BARS
Psarotaverna Anesti 2
Café del Mar 4
Daily 3
To Diethnes 1
Naftikos Omilos 6
To Nissiotiko 5

Áyios Nikólaos
Ecclesiastical Museum
Bus Station
Town Hall
Theatre
Kykon Tours
Main Post Office
Vatitsis Agency
Ferry Terminal
Port Police
Hydrofoil Berth
Train Station

ACCOMMODATION
Ira/Hera C
Lido B
Majestic D
Okeanis A
Thraki Palace E

ALEXANDHROÚPOLI

Airport (7km), Dhidhymótiho & Kípi
Olympic Airways ◄ (250m)   ◄ (4km)

0   100 m

Samothráki & Límnos

military architects during the Russo–Turkish war of 1878. It does not, on first acquaintance, have much to recommend it: a border town and military garrison, with overland travellers in transit and Greek holiday-makers competing in summer for limited space in the few hotels and the campsite. The town became Greek only in 1920, when it was renamed Alexandhroúpoli after a visit from Greece's King Alexander. There is, however, an excellent **ethnological museum** and a lively seafront promenade.

Arrival and information

Arriving by **train**, you'll be deposited next to the port; the **KTEL** is at Venizélou 36, several blocks inland. **Drivers** will find it prudent to enter town from the west along coastal Megálou Alexándhrou, signposted for the ferries and restaurants, since pedestrianization, one-way systems and fee parking effectively block movement between Dhimokratías – local name for the Via Egnatia – and the sea. There is a rudimentary, seasonal **tourist office** in the town hall building at the corner of Dhimokratías and Mitropolítou Kavíri.

Ferries and hydrofoils will take you to the island of **Samothráki** (see p.944), whose dramatic silhouette looms 50km off the coast.

Accommodation

Booking ahead is wise and the choice is not that great, ranging from some rather third-rate bathless rooms to a luxurious resort-cum-conference hotel, some way out of town; if no rooms are available receptionists are usually good at calling around to find you a room.

Ira/Hera Dhimokratías 179 ☎ 25510 23941–3, ℱ 24670 21086; ⓔ herahtl@hotmail.com. The entrance, lobby and breakfast room are shiny and modern but the rooms are still on the dowdy side, albeit functional. ❹

Lido Paleológou 15 ☎ 25510 28808, ℱ 24670 21086. A bright and cheerful place, with large en-suite rooms, not far from the bus station. ❸

Majestic Platía Eleftherías 7 ☎ 25510 26444. The closest hotel to the train station, it is a decent, old-fashioned cheapie with shared bathrooms. ❷

Okeanis Paleológou 20 ☎ 25510 28830. Smart, modern hotel with pleasantly decorated rooms, though, as at the *Lido*, street noise can be problematic. ❹

Thraki Palace Paleológou 20 ☎ 25510 89100, ⓦ www.thrakipalace.gr. Four kilometres west of town, this sleek, modern five-star establishment has a sea-view swimming pool, a swish restaurant, piano bar, fitness centre and spacious, contemporary rooms, though the surroundings give off an arid sensation. ❼

The Town

If you have an hour or so to spare it can be enjoyably spent at the excellent **Ethnological Museum of Thrace** (Tues–Sat 10am–2pm & 6–9.30pm, Sun 6am–9.30pm; €3), one of the best of its kind in the whole country, at 14-Maïoú 63, several blocks due north of the ferry terminal. Housed in a tastefully restored Neoclassical mansion constructed in 1899 as the country residence of a wealthy tradesman from Edirne, its eye-catching modern displays cover almost every aspect of traditional life in Thrace, for once mentioning every ethnic component of what has always been a multicultural region: Pomaks, Turks, Armenians, Jews and Roma as well as Greeks. Professionally produced videos, with commentaries in Greek only, complement the beautifully lit cabinets on the themes of ritual, music, costume, food, agriculture and crafts. Curiosities include stamps for communion bread, colourful ceremonial brooms, carnival masks, Pomak calendars and colanders, chickpea roasters, ice-cream-making equipment and a *yahanás*, or sesame-oil press, in use until 1967. A delightful café, serving local specialities, and a quality museum shop complete the picture.

Otherwise it's the lively seafront that best characterizes the town; dominated by a seventeen-metre-tall **lighthouse** built in 1880 (and adopted as the town's symbol), it comes alive at dusk when the locals begin their evening promenade. In summer, café tables spill out onto the road and around the lighthouse; makeshift stalls on the pavements sell pirate cassettes, pumpkin seeds and grilled sweetcorn.

Eating and drinking

For **restaurants** in town, check out the row of good tavernas with terraces, near the train station – the best is *To Diethnes* (or *Kyras Dimitras*), where a wide range of vegetable dishes accompanies fried fish. Two other commendable addresses are *To Nissiotiko*, at Zarífi 1, and *Psarotaverna Anesti* at Athanasíou Dhiákou 5; the former, with its picturesque decor, serves a delicious dill-flavoured seafood risotto (*piláfi thalássino*) along with a variety of grilled and fried fish and seafood. Good fish cuisine and an attractive location make the *Naftikos Omilos*, or *Marine Club*, next to the ferry terminal, also worth heading for. Trendy seafront **bars** with popular terraces include *Café del Mar* and *Daily*, though a string of **cafés** along Dhimokratías also attracts the crowds.

The Évros Valley and northeastern Thrace

The **Évros Valley**, extending northeast of Alexandhroúpoli, is a prosperous but dull agricultural area. Most towns are ugly, modern concrete affairs full of bored soldiers, with little to delay you; others, such as **Souflí** and **Dhidhymótiho**, retain some character and medieval monuments, and the main route through the valley as far as **Orestiádha** is well served by public transport. No village is complete without its stork's nest, dominating the landscape like a watchtower. The standout here by some way is the **Dhadhiá Forest** and wildlife reserve, also reachable by bus; you'll need your own transport to head east from Alexandhroúpoli to the **Évros delta**, one of Europe's most important wetland areas for birds – and one of Greece's most sensitive military areas.

The Évros delta

To the southeast, the **Évros delta** is home to more than 250 different species of birds, including sea eagles, pygmy cormorants and the lesser white-fronted goose. Leave Alexandhroúpoli on the main road (E90/E85) towards Turkey and Bulgaria; some 10km after the airport, you'll reach the turn-off to **Loutrá Traianópolis**, the site of an ancient Roman spa and its modern continuation Loutrós. Either of the two following hotels in the vicinity would make a good base for exploring the delta: the *Athina* (☎25510 61208; ❷) and the *Plotini* (☎25510 61106; ❷). The delta is best approached by turning right off the main road, opposite the side road to the hotels; the lane is paved only as far as the level crossing but remains good thereafter. The delta is crisscrossed with tracks along the dykes used by farmers taking advantage of the plentiful water supply for growing sweet corn and cotton. The south is the most inspiring part, well away from the army installations to the north; as you go further into the wetlands, the landscape becomes utterly desolate, with decrepit clusters of

△ Pelicans on the Évros delta

fishing huts among the sandbars and inlets. At the mouth of the delta sprawls a huge saltwater lake called **Límni Dhrakónda**. Obviously what you see depends on the time of year, but even if birdlife is a bit thin on the ground, the atmosphere of the place is worth experiencing.

Dhadhiá Forest

The **Dhadhiá Forest Reserve** consists of 35,200 hectares of protected oak and pine forest covering a succession of volcanic ridges. The diversity of landscape and vegetation and the proximity of important migration routes make for an extremely diverse flora and fauna, but raptors are the star attraction, and main impetus for this WWF-backed project. The reserve is reached by a clearly marked road off to the left, 1km after passing the second right-hand turn-off to Likófi (Likófos). After a drive of 7km through the rolling, forested hills, you reach the reserve complex (March–May & Sept–Nov daily 9am–7pm; June–Aug daily 8.30am–8.30pm; Dec–Feb Mon–Thurs 10am–4pm, Fri–Sun 9am–6pm), with its information centre and exhibition about the region's wildlife.

All cars – except for a tour van which makes sorties several times daily (€3) – are banned from core areas totalling 7200 hectares, and foot access is restricted to two marked trails: a two-hour route up to the reserve's highest point, 520-metre **Gíbrena** with its ruined Byzantine castle, and another ninety-minute loop-route to an observation hide overlooking **Mavrórema** canyon. The region is one of two remaining European homes of the majestic **black vulture**, the other being the Extremadura region of Spain. Their numbers have increased from near extinction when protection began in 1980 to some one hundred individuals, and they and griffon vultures make up the bulk of sightings from this post. In all, 36 of Europe's 38 species of diurnal birds of prey, including eagles, falcons, hawks and buzzards, can be sighted at least part of the year.

It's a good idea to stay the night, as the best raptor viewing is in the early morning or evening in summer (but virtually all day Oct–March). Next to the visitors' centre is the comfortable **ecotourism hostel** run by **Dhadhiá** village (☎25540 32263, ✉dadia@otenet.gr; ❸) 🏠, where the en-suite rooms have been given bird names instead of numbers (keys from the café across the car park, until 11pm). The café supplies breakfast, drinks and cold meals, but for hot **meals** you'll have to retire to the village where you can try the inexpensive *Psistaria Pelargos* on the platía.

Souflí

The nearest town to Dhadhiá, 7km north of the side turning and set among lush mulberry groves, is **SOUFLÍ**, renowned for a now all-but-vanished silk industry. The town's history as Greece's silk centre in Byzantine and Ottoman times, and a fascinating explanation of the whole silk-making process, are documented (with English text) in a **folk and silk museum** (Wed–Mon: Easter to mid-Oct 10am–2pm & 5–7pm; rest of year 10am–4pm; €1.50), a little way uphill and west of the main through road. It's lodged in a fine old yellow mansion, one of a number of surviving vernacular houses, including semi-ruined *bitziklíkia*, or *koukoulóspita* in Greek (cocoon-houses), which lend Souflí some distinction. Accommodation is limited to just two **hotels**, both on the noisy main highway: the basic *Egnatia* (☎25540 24124; ❷) at no. 225, with shared bathrooms, or the overpriced *Orfeas/Orpheus* (☎25540 22922; ❸), with air conditioning, almost opposite at no. 172. **Eating** and **drinking** options in town aren't great either, consisting mostly of pizzerias, *souvladzídhika* and *barákia*. If you have your own transport – or if you don't mind taking a taxi – head towards Yiannoúli (signposted) and, 4km away, you'll find the excellent *Lagotrofío* taverna which serves wild boar and other game, plus *mayireftá* standards, at a wonderful hilltop location with panoramic views, under shady trees in summer, when it opens for lunch as well as dinner.

North of Souflí

A pleasant scenic alternative to the trunk road, especially if Bulgaria is your destination, is the labyrinthine, but well-signposted, network of smaller roads that heads inland through isolated villages and beautiful countryside of rolling hills and deciduous woods. It has been a state priority to establish a Greek population in this extremely sensitive and strategic corner of Thrace, hemmed in on three sides by Bulgaria and Turkey; the many signs **forbidding photography** of bridges, rivers and dams should be heeded. Military barracks and traffic police are conspicuous throughout the hinterland and along the eastern border with Turkey.

METAXÁDHES, reached from the village of Mándhra, 5km north of Souflí, is one of the most handsome villages in the area, sited on a steep hill. Once fought over by Bulgars and Turks, Metaxádhes used to support a Turkish community, but now its population is exclusively Greek. Beyond here, you descend north into the vast, fertile **Árdhas river plain** where rich farmland supports a large number of modern villages. One of the most picturesque is hilltop **PENDÁLOFOS**. The nearby **hotel**, *To Evrothírama* (☎05560 61242; ❹), is the sole accommodation for miles around and is unusual in that it doubles up as a game reserve. The **restaurant**, open at weekends only outside high season, specializes in delicious venison, wild boar and hare dishes. Accommodation consists of plain but comfortable rooms with traditional furnishing and mod cons, and the hotel's lonely but attractive setting is definitely part of the appeal.

Dhidhymótiho and Orestiádha

DHIDHYMÓTIHO, 30km northeast of Souflí, is the last place on the trunk route into Turkey of any interest. The old part of town is still partially enclosed by the remains of double Byzantine fortifications, and some old houses and churches survive, but the area has a feeling of decay despite continuing efforts at restoration. Below the fortified hill, on the central platía, stands the most important surviving monument, a fourteenth-century **mosque**, the oldest and second largest in the Balkans. A great square box of a building with a pyramidal metal roof, its design harks back to Seljuk and other pre-Ottoman prototypes in central Anatolia, and you'll see nothing else like it between here and Divriği or Erzurum in Turkey. Unfortunately, the interior is closed indefinitely for restoration, though you can still admire the ornate west portal.

Staying presents a problem, as neither of the town's two **hotels** is wonderful; you're much better off waiting till you reach Orestiádha. If you do stay, you'll find the cheaper and more central one is the none-too-welcoming *Anessis* (☎25530 24850; ❸), 250m northwest of the mosque at Vassiléos Aléxándhrou 51. Your other choice is the *Plotini* (☎25530 23400; ❸), a rather gaudy building 1km south of town across the river, on the west side of the road. For a **meal**, try the *Zythestiatorio Kypselaki* in the central market hall just above the mosque.

The main town beyond Dhidhymótiho and the last before the border post is **ORESTIÁDHA**, a lively but far from attractive market centre with restaurants, bars and lots of cake shops around its main square. Its several banks, with ATMs, could be particularly useful when entering Greece from Bulgaria or

Turkey, though you'll get a poor rate exchanging your remaining leva or lira. **Accommodation** is better here than at Dhidhymótiho or Souflí, though fairly expensive. All within walking distance of the main platía are the smart *Alexandros* (☎25520 27000; ❹) at Vassiléos Constantínou 10, the appealing and popular *Selini* (☎25520 22636; ❹), at Skra 44, and the comfortable *Elektra* (☎25520 23540; ❹) at Pandazídhou 50. Pandazídhou also hosts a string of decent **tavernas** and ouzerís, though the best reputation is enjoyed by nearby *O Petinos*, at Lohagoú Dhiamándi 7. The **cafés** (some with Internet) in this neighbourhood are surprisingly chic and trendy.

Travel details

Domestic trains

Thessaloníki to: Kateríni/Lárissa/Athens (11 daily; 4hr 30min–7hr); Lárissa (10 daily; 2hr–2hr 30min); Litóhoro (4 daily; 1hr); Véria/Édhessa/Amýndeo/Flórina (3–4 daily; 1hr 15min to Édhessa); Sérres/Dhráma/Xánthi/Komotiní/Alexandhroúpoli (6 daily; 3hr 30min to Xánthi, 4hr 30min to Alexandhroúpoli).

International trains

Thessaloníki to: Istanbul (Turkey) (1 daily; 14hr); Gevgelija(FYROM)/Skopje/Belgrade (1 daily; 1hr 30min–2hr to Gevgelija, 3hr 30min to Skopje, 13hr to Belgrade); Promahónas/Kulata (Bulgarian frontier) (1 daily; 2hr 30min–3hr).

Alexandhroúpoli to: Dhidhymótiho–Orestiádha–Kastaniés (for Edirne) (6 daily; 2hr 45min); Svilengrad (Bulgaria) (1 daily; 3hr).

Buses

Alexandhroúpoli to: Dhadhiá (2 daily; 1hr 20min); Dhidhymótiho (17 daily Mon–Fri, 14 daily Sat–Sun; 2hr); Istanbul (daily OSE bus; 8hr); Kípi (5 daily; 45min); Komotiní (14 daily; 1hr).
Édhessa to: Flórina (4 daily; 2hr); Kastoriá (4 daily; 2hr 30min, change at Amýndeo); Véria (6 Mon–Sat, 2 Sun; 50min).
Flórina to: Préspa basin (2 daily; 1hr).
Kastoriá to: Flórina (4 daily indirect services via Amýndeo; 3hr including layover).
Kateríni to: Dhión (12 daily; 20min); Litóhoro, for Mt Olympus (18 Mon–Sat, 12 Sun; 30min).
Kavála to: Keramotí (12 daily; 1hr); Komotiní (half-hourly 6am–9pm; 2hr); Philippi (half-hourly 6am–8.30pm; 20min); Xánthi (half-hourly 6am–9pm; 1hr); Alexandhroúpoli (5 daily; 3hr).
Komotiní to: Fanári (7 daily Mon–Fri, 6 Sat, 4 Sun; 45min).

Kozáni to: Grevená (8 daily; 1hr); Siátista (4 daily; 30min).
Thessaloníki to: Alexandhroúpoli (5 daily; 6hr); Arnéa (5–7 daily; 2hr); Athens (16 daily; 7hr); Édhessa (hourly; 1hr 30min); Flórina (6 daily; 3hr 30min); Ierissós (5–7 daily; 3hr 30min); Ioánnina (5 daily; 7hr); Istanbul (almost daily with OSE, occasional privately operated; 14hr); Kalambáka (7 daily; 4hr 30min); Kastoriá (5 daily; 4hr); Kavála (hourly 6am–10pm; 2hr 15min–3hr); Litóhoro, for Mt Olympus (7 daily; 1hr 30min); Ouranoúpoli (5–7 daily; 3hr 30min); Pélla (hourly; 1hr); Sárti, via Políyiros (3 daily; 4hr 30min); Sofia (daily with OSE; 7hr 30min); Véria (half-hourly; 1hr 15min); Vólos (4 daily; 4hr); Vourvouroú, via Políyiros (3 daily; 3hr).
Véria to: Édhessa (6 daily; 1hr 15min); Kozáni (8 daily; 1hr).
Xánthi to: Kavála (half-hourly, 6am–9pm; 1hr); Komotiní (17–18 daily, via coast or inland; 50min); Thessaloníki (6–7 daily; 4hr).

Ferries

Alexandhroúpoli to: Límnos, Lésvos, Híos, Sámos, Kós or Kálymnos, Rhodes (1 weekly); Samothráki (2–3 daily, 2hr 30min).
Kavála to: Lésvos and Híos (2–3 weekly; 12hr); Límnos (5hr) and Áyios Efstrátios (2–4 weekly; 8hr); Samothráki (2–5 weekly; 5hr); Thássos (Skála Prínou) (8 daily; 1hr 15min).
Keramotí to: Thássos (Liménas) (10 daily; 40min).
Thessaloníki to: Iráklion (Crete) via Skiáthos, Tínos, Skýros, Mýkonos, Páros, Náxos and Thíra (1–4 weekly); Límnos, Lésvos and Híos (1–2 weekly); Sámos, Kós, Rhodes (1 weekly).

Flights

Alexandhroúpoli to: Athens (6 daily; 1hr); Sitía, Crete (3 weekly; 1hr 45min); Thessaloníki (3 weekly; 50min).

Kastoriá to: Athens (3–4 weekly; 1hr 15min).
Kavála to: Athens (3–4 daily; 1hr).
Kozáni to: Athens (3–4 weekly; 1hr 10min).
Thessaloníki to: Athens (9–11 daily; 50min); Corfu (2–4 weekly; 1hr); Haniá, Crete (3 weekly; 2hr); Híos (4 weekly; 1hr 50min); Ioánnina (5 weekly; 50min); Iráklion, Crete (2–4 daily; 2hr); Lésvos (2 daily; 1–2hr); Límnos (4 weekly; 50min); Mýkonos (1–2 daily; 1hr 20min); Préveza (1 weekly; 1hr 40min); Rhodes (1–3 daily; 50min); Sámos (4 weekly; 1hr 20min); Skýros (1–3 weekly; 40min); Thíra (3 weekly summer only; 1hr 30min).

Hydrofoils

Alexandhroúpoli to: Samothráki (1–2 daily April–Sept; 1hr 10min).
Kavála to: Thássos (Liménas) (8–15 daily; 40min); Thássos (west-coast resorts) (1–3 daily).

The Argo-Saronic

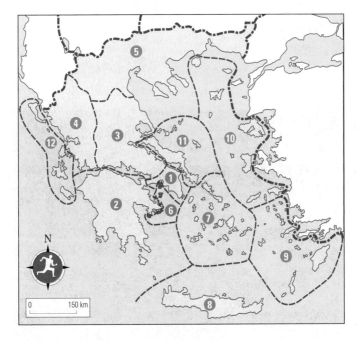

CHAPTER 6

Highlights

✳ Faneroménis Monastery, Salamína Admire the post-Byzantine frescoes at the oldest monastery in this archipelago. **See p.583**

✳ Temple of Aphaea, Égina The best-preserved Archaic temple on any island, set on a pretty pine-wooded hill. **See p.587**

✳ Póros Town Climb up the clocktower for a view over the Argo-Saronic Gulf and the Peloponnese. **See p.591**

✳ Ídhra Town A perfect horseshoe-shaped harbour surrounded by grand eighteenth-century mansions. **See p.595**

✳ Spétses Enjoy some of the most alluring beaches in the Argo-Saronics along Spétses' pine-speckled coastline. **See p.599**

△ Ídhra Town

6

The Argo-Saronic

he rocky, partly volcanic **Argo-Saronic** islands, most of them barely an olive's throw from the Argolid, differ to a surprising extent not just from that peninsula but also from one another. Less surprising – given their proximity to the mainland – is their massive popularity, with Égina (Aegina) almost becoming an Athenian suburb at weekends. Ídhra (Hydra), Póros and Spétses are scarcely different in summer, though their visitors include a higher proportion of foreign tourists. More than any other group, these islands are best out of season, when transient populations fall dramatically and the port towns return to a quieter, more provincial pace.

The northernmost island of the Argo-Saronic group, **Salamína**, is effectively a suburb of Pireás, just over 1km offshore to the east; it is as much a dormitory for those commuting to the capital as it is a weekend retreat, but sees very few foreign visitors. **Égina**, important in antiquity and more or less continually inhabited since then, is the most fertile of the group, famous for its pistachio nuts, as well as for one of the finest ancient temples in Greece. Like Salamína, it's just feasible as a commuter base, though Égina's main problem – crowds – can be avoided by visiting at midweek, advice that applies equally to its pine-cloaked satellite isle, **Angístri**.

The three southerly islands, **Spétses**, **Ídhra** and **Póros**, are piney to various degrees, comparatively infertile, and (like Égina and Angístri) have only a single natural spring between them (on Póros), all of them relying on water-tankers or pipes from the mainland. Accordingly, they were not extensively settled until medieval times, when refugees from the mainland – principally Albanian Christians – established themselves here. In response to the barrenness and dryness of their new homes the islanders adopted seagoing commerce (and piracy) as livelihoods. The seamanship and huge fleets thus acquired were placed at the disposal of the Greek insurgents during the War of Independence. Today, foreigners and Athenians have replaced locals in the depopulated harbour towns; windsurfers, water-taxis and yachts are faint echoes of the massed warships, schooners and *kaïkia* once at anchor.

Salamína

Salamína (Salamís; popularly called Kouloúri) is the quickest possible island-hop from Athens. Take the metro to Pireás and then one of the green buses to the shipyard port of Pérama, 5km west of Pireás, and a roll-on-roll-off ferry

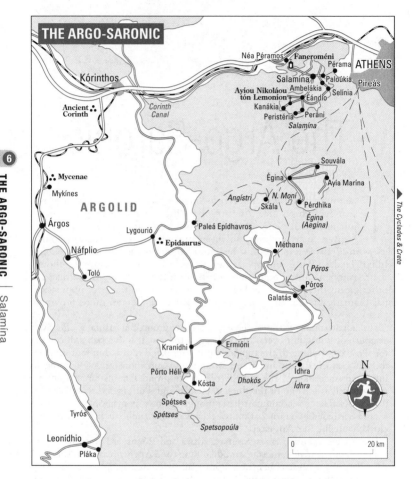

THE ARGO-SARONIC

Néa Péramos · **Faneroméni**
Kórinthos
Salamína · Péramos
Paloúkia · ATHENS
Ayíou Nikoláou · Ambelákia · Pireás
tón Lemonión · Éándio · Selínia
Ancient · Corinth · Corinth Canal · Kanákia
Peristéria · Peráni
Salamína

Souvála
Mycenae · Égina
Ayía Marína
Mykínes
Angístri · N. Moní
ARGOLID · Skála · Pérdhika
Árgos · Égina (Aegina)
Lygourió · Paleá Epídhavros
Náfplio · Epidaurus · Méthana
Toló
Póros
Póros
Galatás

Kranídhi · Ermióni
Pórto Héli · Ídhra
Kósta · Dhokós · Ídhra
Spétses
Tyrós · Spétses
Spetsopoúla
Leonídhio
Pláka

N

0   20 km

The Cyclades & Crete

will whisk you across to the little harbour of **Paloúkia** in a matter of minutes. The craft crosses the narrow strait where, in 480 BC, the Greek navy trounced the Persian fleet, despite being outnumbered three to one; this battle is said by some to be more significant than the battle of Marathon, ten years earlier.

On arrival, you won't be rewarded by unspoilt beaches or a poster-picturesque island, but you will find a slow-paced, lived-in place with some surprisingly large bays supporting rural communities, as well as distinct, *Arvanítika*-influenced folk dances and costumes at festival times. Saronic Gulf water quality has improved markedly since the 1990s and pockets of bathers splash happily about, especially on the less exposed western side of the island. Despite Athenian reticence about (or outright disparagement of) Salamína, it makes an excellent escape from the capital's pollution and frenetic pace.

Paloúkia, Selínia, Salamína Town and Faneroméni

The **bus station** by the **ferry dock** in **PALOÚKIA** has services to the nearby capital Salamína Town (3km) and beyond, though the large selection of signed destinations can be confusing. Around 6km to the south of Paloúkia (direct buses) is the popular local town of **SELÍNIA**, which supports a fairly lively tourist scene. This is the main summer resort, with a pleasant waterfront, a bank, several tavernas and two inexpensive but quite pleasant hotels, the *Akroyali* (☎210 46 73 263; ❸) and the *Votsalakia* (☎210 46 71 334; ❸).

SALAMÍNA TOWN (also known, like the island, as Kouloúri) is home to 26,000 of the island's 31,000 population. It's a busy, functional place, with a couple of banks, a fish market and a long palm-tree laced promenade facing Salamína Bay. Pretty much uniquely for an island town – and emphasizing the absence of tourists – there is no bike or scooter rental outlet, and also no hotel. However, the locals throng several decent **ouzerís** on the shore esplanade, and such full-on **tavernas** as *O Lakis* (in Katástima district near the town hall), or adjacent *O Thanasis* and the small but impressive *O Kakias* (*Nikolakakias*). **Iliaktí beach**, some 5km to the west, is innocuous enough, as is the coastal strip running through the resorts of **Áyios Ioánnis** and **Résti** to the south of Salamína Town.

Buses marked for Faneroméni run to the port at the northwest tip of the island, Stenó, from where there are frequent ferries across to Néa Péramos, near Mégara on the Athens–Kórinthos road. En route, the road passes the frescoed **monastery of Faneroméni** (6km from Salamína; daily 8.30am–12.30pm & 4pm–sunset), majestically sited above the gulf amidst pine woods and working as a convent (25 nuns) since 1944. Founded in the thirteenth century, its unusual *katholikón* was restored in 1670 by Osios Lavrendios of Mégara and subsequently decorated by Yeoryios Markos of Árgos with frescoes so vivid that their painter, stepping back to admire his finished creation, supposedly died of amazement. Near the monastery, occupying its former boathouse, is the so-called **Kellí Sikelianoú**, which the local archbishop granted to the prominent modern Greek poet Angelos Sikelianos as a retreat from 1941 until the latter's death in 1952. Sikelianos wrote some of his finest poetry here in between bouts of entertaining various literati, and plans are afoot to restore the *kellí* ("cell") as a museum.

Eándio and the south

South from Salamína Town, the road edges the coast towards Eándio (6km; regular buses). There are a few tavernas along the way and opportunities to swim, though a well-organized, fenced-off public beach lies just outside Eándio. **EÁNDIO** (also known as Moúlki) itself is quite a pleasant village, with a little pebble beach and the island's best **hotel**, the *Gabriel* (☎210 46 62 275; ❹), overlooking the bay.

Several roads continue beyond Eándio. The most interesting route heads southwest towards Kanákia (8km from Eándio; two buses daily), over the island's main pine-covered mountain, passing (at around 5km) the photogenic monastery of **Ayíou Nikoláou tón Lemoníon**. Another road runs more or less due south to **Peráni** coastal resort (4km along) before emerging at the small-scale resort of **Peristéria** (5km). This is much more attractive than the littered, exposed beach and scruffy huts of **Kanákia**, which has an end-of-the-world feel.

Égina (Aegina)

Ancient **Aegina** was a major power in Classical times, rivalling Athens. It traded to the limits of the known world, maintained a sophisticated silver coinage system (the first in Greece) and had prominent athletes and craftsmen. During the fifth century BC, however, the islanders made the political mistake of siding with their fellow Dorians, the Spartans. Athens used this as a pretext to act on long-standing jealousy; her fleets defeated those of the islanders in two separate sea battles and, after the second, the population was expelled and replaced by more tractable colonists.

Subsequent history was less distinguished, with a pattern of occupation familiar to central Greece – by Romans, Franks, Venetians, Catalans and Ottomans – before the War of Independence brought a brief period as seat of government for the fledgling Greek nation. For many decades thereafter it was a penal island, and you can still see the **enormous jail** at the top of Odhós Faneroménis (it is now being restored to house a museum); the building was originally an **orphanage**, founded by first president Kapodhistrias in 1828. Only since the 1980s has Égina shaken off its consequently dour reputation and begun to attract significant numbers of expatriate residents.

These days, the island is most famous for its **pistachio orchards**, whose thirsty trees lower the water table a foot or so annually – hence the bags of nuts for sale in the main town, and the notices warning you of the perennial water crisis. In common with other Argo-Saronics, there are also a surprising number of pine trees, especially in the north and east. Athenians regard Égina mainly as a beach/weekend annexe, being the closest place to the capital most of them would swim, though for foreign visitors an added draw is its beautiful fifth-century BC **Temple of Aphaea**. This is located on the northeast coast, close to the resort-port of **Ayía Marína**.

Hydrofoil services are more frequent than ferries, run from the same quay in Pireás as the conventional boats, and cost hardly any more. Make sure your boat docks at **Égina Town**, the island capital, rather than at **Souvála**, an Athenian bolthole on Égina's north coast and generally devoid of interest to outsiders. If you bring a car over for the weekend, reserve your Sunday return trip well in advance – spots sell out quickly year-round and you could find yourself trapped on the island until Monday midday.

Égina Town

ÉGINA TOWN, the island's capital, makes an attractive base, with some grand old buildings dating from when it served as the first capital of Greece (1826–28) during the War of Independence. The Neoclassical architecture is matched by a sophisticated ethos, with a semi-permanent yacht-dwelling contingent, special events and a well-stocked bazaar which remains lively even at weekends.

Arrival and information

The **bus station** is on the spacious Platía Ethneyersías, just north of the ferry arrival point, with excellent services to most villages; buy your tickets beforehand at the little booth. The **taxi** rank is at the base of the jetty, opposite the row of **booths** selling tickets for various catamarans, ferries and hydrofoils, including the Keravnos catamaran for Angístri (☎22970 91163); Vasilopoulos Flying Dolphins (☎22970 29027); the slow Ayios Nektarios Eginas ferry (☎22970 25625); and Hellenic Seaways (conventional ferries ☎22970 22945; hydrofoils ☎22970 24456). The **post office** is at the rear of the square, and

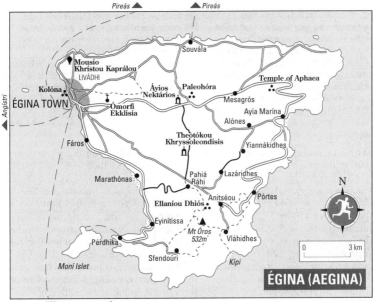

numerous **banks** have ATMs. Several premises on and behind the main water-front, touting assiduously, rent cars, scooters, motorbikes and mountain bikes – Égina is large and hilly enough to make a motor worthwhile for anything other than a pedal to the beaches towards Pérdhika. Aegina Island Holidays (℡22970 26430), on the waterfront near the church of Panayítsa, offers excursions to the Epidaurus theatre festival (see p.227). **Internet** access is available at Prestige, on Eákou at the corner of Spýrou Ródhi. **Foreign-language papers** are stocked by Kalezis, midway along the waterfront.

Accommodation

As on most of the Argo-Saronics, **accommodation** is at a premium at week-ends but, out of season, discounts apply Monday to Thursday nights. With the exceptions noted, most lodgings are subject to a certain amount of traffic noise. Bathrooms, curiously, are rudimentary just about everywhere, including our top-rated listings.

Artemis Kanári 20 ℡22970 25195, ⊛www .pipinis-travel.com. Basic 1960s hotel, but rooms (with fridges and air conditioning) are adequate and it's probably the quietest location in town; views from the front rooms over a pistachio orchard are second to none. ❸

Brown Southern waterfront, past Panayítsa church ℡22970 22271, ⊛www.hotel brown.gr. The town's top offering, this B-class/3-star hotel opposite the southerly town beach, housed in a former sponge factory dating from 1886, earns its rating from its vast common areas (terrace bar, buffet-breakfast salon). The best and

calmest units are the garden bungalows; there are also galleried family suites sleeping four. B&B ❺
Eginitiko Arhontiko Corner Thomaïdhou and Ayíou Nikólaou, by giant church ℡22970 24968, ⊛www.aeginitikoarchontiko.gr. Well-appointed rooms, all with double beds, fridges and air conditioning, at this converted ochre- and-orange Neoclassical mansion. The *pièce de résistance* is the suite (❺) with painted ceilings; breakfast is served in a coloured-glass conservatory. B&B ❹
House of Peace Corner Afrodhítis and Kanári ℡22970 23790, ⓔthehouseofpeace@can.gr. Slightly airless bungalow-studios set in a garden

studded with palm and pistachio trees; the standard rooms in the main house were recently renovated. Breakfast by arrangement. ❹

Ilektra Leonárdhou Ladhá 25, northwest of the square ☎ 22970 26715 or 693 87 26 441. Quiet *dhomátia* establishment with smallish rooms and equally small balconies. ❷

Pavlou Behind Panayítsa church at Eyinítou 21 ☎ 22970 22795. A good budget hotel with air conditioning and sometimes double beds in the mosaic-floored rooms; because it was retrofitted to en-suite status, some rooms have their baths across the hall. ❸

Plaza Seafront just south of town beach ☎ 22970 25600. Great sea views from this hotel's front rooms with mosaic floors, fridges and air conditioning, though of course they will be a bit noisy. ❸

The Town

The long harbour **waterfront** combines the workaday with the picturesque, but is nonetheless appealing: fishermen talk and tend their nets, *kaïkia* sell produce from the mainland, and there's one of the finest seascapes in Greece, comprising other Argo-Saronic isles and Peloponnesian mountains. North of the port, beyond the tiny but popular town beach, a lone column on a promontory, known logically enough as **Kolóna** (column), marks the remains of the Temple of Apollo and the ancient acropolis. Near the entrance to the ruins (Tues–Sun 8.30am–3pm; €3), a small but worthwhile **archeological museum**, houses finds from the extensive excavations that revealed 2500 years and ten layers of settlement, which dwarf the actual temple precincts. Highlights of the display, some of it labelled in Greek or German only, include a room of Middle Bronze Age pottery, rescued from a nearby building site, with renowned squid/octopus motifs and less common checkerboard patterns.

On the north flank of Kolóna hill there's an attractive bay with a small, sandy **beach** – the best swimming spot in the immediate vicinity of the town, where clean water belies an often seaweed-strewn shore. The other town beaches, south of Kolóna and south of the yacht marina respectively, are smaller and markedly less clean, if more popular.

Other sights include the restored (1802) **Pýrgos Markéllou**, seat of the first Greek government, dominating a park near the large church of Áyios Nikólaos whose landmark square belfries pierce the skyline from every vantage point. In the suburb of Livádhi, just to the north, a plaque marks **Nikos Kazantzakis'** 1940s–1950s residence, where he wrote his most celebrated book, *Zorba the Greek*. Three kilometres out of town in the same direction, admirably signposted, is the **Mousío Khrístou Kaprálou/Christos Kapralos Museum** (June–Oct Tues–Sun 10am–2pm & 6–8pm; Nov–May Fri–Sun 10am–2pm; €2), housed in several ateliers in which the prominent Greek sculptor and painter spent his summers for three decades up to his death in 1993. The influence of Henry Moore is evident in the wood, terracotta and bronze pieces on display; there's a whole wing of canvases, often startlingly elongated nudes, and a replica of his famous frieze *Monument of the Battle of the Pindus*, the original of which now adorns a hall in the Greek Parliament building.

Eating, drinking and entertainment

There are several recommendable **ouzerís** and **tavernas**, particularly at the south end of pedestrianized Panayióti Irióti behind the fish market, and at opposite ends of the waterfront – fussy Athenian patronage keeps the standards up (for the most part). By contrast, the obvious central-waterfront cafés near the ferry jetty are poor value, charging Kolonáki (Athens) prices; as well as our more moderate recommendations below, there are two normal-priced sea-view *kafenía* to either side of the fish-market entrance, where the locals go. Athenians are also partly responsible for surprisingly ample choice in **nightlife** given a town of about nine thousand souls. There are three summer **cinemas** – Anesis on Eákou towards the Pýrgos Markéllou beginning in June, joined later on by the Olympia on Faneroménis opposite the football grounds, and the Akroyiali beyond the football grounds on the Pérdhika road – all showing high-quality foreign films; the winter cinema Titina stands opposite the Pýrgos Markéllou. There are two good places for **live music**: the *En Egini*, Spýrou Ródhi 44 (℡22970 22922), and *Kyvernio*, Mitropóleos 4 (℡22970 25801); both kick off at midnight on Fridays and Saturdays and feature live Greek acts. Reservations are recommended at both places if you want to secure a table.

Avli Panayióti Irióti 17. Some of the least expensive sit-down breakfasts in town, but the place later becomes a full-service taverna and low-key bar with Latin/jazz sounds. Summer seating is in the *avlí* (courtyard), but it also has a cosy interior with fireplace for winter.

Flisvos North waterfront by town beach. The best spot for grilled fresh fish and a few meat dishes, at fair prices.

Ippokambos Faneromenis 9, south of town near the football stadium and the ex-orphanage. A *mezedhopolío* run by Lebanese George, with rich, slightly bumped-up fare (allow €18–20 each), including dishes such as pork roulade and stuffed squid. Evenings only, 7.30pm–1am.

Lekkas Kazantzáki 4, adjacent to *Flisvos*. Renowned for good vegetable platters and well-sourced meat grills, washed down by excellent bulk sherry-style wine. Very inexpensive for Égina; two can eat for about €20.

Pelaïsos Waterfront between fish market and Panayítsa. The best value of a cluster of Greek-patronized taverna-ouzerís in this area, with a good mix of platters, but limited seating. Opens 8.15am for breakfast too.

Yeladhakis (also known as *tou Steliou* or *ly Agora*) Rear of fish market. Much the best, and least expensive, of three rival seafood ouzerís here; accordingly it's usually mobbed and you may have to wait for a table. The stock-in-trade is octopus, sardines, shrimp, plus a few vegetarian starters; summer seating in the cobbled lane, winter up in the loft inside.

Áyios Nektários and Paleohóra

Áyios Nektários, a whitewashed modern convent situated around 6km east of Égina Town, was named in honour of the Greek Orthodox Church's most recent and controversial saint (born Anastasios Kefalas), a rather high-living monk who died in 1920 and was canonized in 1962. An oversized church – supposedly the largest in Greece – looms beside the convent.

A kilometre or so further east is **Paleohóra**, which was established as the island's capital in the ninth century as a refuge against piracy, but failed singularly in this capacity during Barbarossa's 1537 raid. Abandoned in 1826–27, Paleohóra is now utterly deserted, but possesses the romantic appeal of a ghost village. You can drive right up to the site (unenclosed, free): take the turning left after passing Áyios Nektários and keep going about 400m. Some thirty of Paleohóra's churches and monasteries remain in a recognizable state (there's a helpful map-placard at the north entrance to the site), but only those of Áyios Dhionýsios, Episkopí (both usually locked), Áyios Yeóryios Katholikós and Metamórfosis (on the lower of the two trails, both open) and Ayía Kyriakí/Zoödhóhou Piyís (the remotest) retain frescoes of any merit and in recognizable condition. Little remains of the town itself – when the islanders left, they simply dismantled their houses and moved the masonry to newly founded Égina Town.

The Temple of Aphaea

The Doric **Temple of Aphaea** (Tues–Sun 8am–5pm; €4) lies 12km east of Égina Town, among pines, which are tapped to flavour the local retsina, and beside a less aesthetic radio mast. It is one of the most complete and visually complex ancient buildings in Greece, its superimposed arrays of columns and lintels evocative of an Escher drawing. Built between 500 and 480 BC to replace two destroyed sixth-century predecessors, it slightly predates the Parthenon. The dedication is unusual: Aphaea was a Cretan nymph who, fleeing from the lust of King Minos, fell into the sea, was caught by some fishermen and brought to ancient Aegina, the only known locus of her cult, and one observed here since 1300 BC. As recently as two centuries ago, the temple's pediments were intact and essentially in perfect condition, depicting two battles at Troy. However, like the Elgin marbles, they were "purchased" from the Turks – this time by Ludwig I of Bavaria, and they currently reside in Munich's Glyptothek museum.

Nine daily **buses** from Égina Town to Ayía Marína stop at the temple, or you can walk up from Ayía Marína along a path.

The east: Ayía Marína to Mount Óros

The island's major beach resort **AYÍA MARÍNA**, another 3km on, sits on the east coast of the island, south of the Aphaea temple ridge. The demise of most foreign package holidays here in the past five years has sent the place into a tailspin, with one out of three commercial premises dustily vacant. The beach is still packed, though, overlooked by an abandoned, half-built hotel; the water, while now adequately clean, is rather shallow and more suited to children than adults.

Beyond the resort, the paved road continues south 8km to **PÓRTES**, a low-key shore hamlet. Among the mix of modern summer villas and old basalt cottages are scattered several tiny fish **tavernas**: *Galinopetra*, overlooking the northerly anchorage, is the most basic, *Thanasis* next up is the most ambitious, whilst *Akroyiali* to the south falls somewhere in-between, all offering fish and *mezédhes*. Beyond *Akroyiali*, towards the south anchorage, stretches a functional but partly sandy beach with decent snorkelling offshore.

The road climbs to the village of Anitséou (with a taverna), just below a major saddle on the flank of Mount Óros, and then forges west towards the scenic village of **Pahiá Ráhi**, almost entirely rebuilt in traditional style by foreign and Athenian owners. From here a rough, single-lane, winding track leads down to the main west-coast road at Marathónas (see below), passable to any scooter and – with care – a compact car, though large vehicles should stick to the longer, paved, tree-lined route back to Égina Town, and then loop back to Marathónas along the coastal road.

Mount Óros

South of the saddle between Pahiá Ráhi and Anitséou, signposted 400m off the paved road, are the foundations of the shrine of **Ellaníou Dhiós**, with the monastery of Taxiárhis squatting amid the massive masonry. The 532-metre summit cone of **Mount Óros**, an hour's walk from the highest point of the road, is capped by the modern chapel of Análipsi (Ascension) and has views across the entire island and much of the Argo-Saronic Gulf.

Gerald Thompson's *A Walking Guide to Aegina*, available locally, details a series of walks across the range of mountains and wooded valleys between Mount Óros and the Aphaea temple and down to the port of Souvála, all avoiding main roads.

The west: Marathónas to Pérdhika

The road southeast of Égina Town, along the west coast of the island, is served by regular buses (8–9 daily). Sprawling **MARATHÓNAS**, 5km from Égina, has the biggest of the west coast's rather scruffy sand beaches, and is tolerable enough, with a scattering of rooms, tavernas and cafés along the shore. The next settlement, **EYINÍTISSA**, has a popular, sheltered cove backed by eucalypts and a beach bar.

PÉRDHIKA, 9km along at the end of the coastal road, scenically set on a little bay packed with yachts, is the most picturesque village on the island; the back streets of this elongated village may be rather characterless, but its pedestrianized, southerly waterfront esplanade reveals a relaxed, seaside-holiday atmosphere. It also has the best range of non-package holiday **accommodation** outside Égina Town: there are rooms on the main road, and just off it. Immediately before the waterfront you'll find the *Hotel Hippocampus* (☎22970 61363; ❸), and nearer the harbour are the *Antzi Studios* (☎22970 61233; ❷), distinguishable in high summer by the bougainvillea draped over the blue-and-white painted facade.

On the quay, overlooking Moní islet and the Peloponnese, are a half-dozen or so **tavernas**, among which *Saronis* is a little cheaper and gets considerable local patronage; *Tò Proreon*, with its potted-plant decor, has the most attractive atmosphere; while *Andonis*, an Athenian hangout, is the most popular fish taverna of the bunch. Among several **café-bars**, mostly at the far end, *Ermis* is the main late-night spot.

The only other diversion at Pérdhika is a trip to the pale-limestone offshore islet of **Moní** (10min; several departures daily; €5 return). There are no facilities on the island, most of which is fenced off as a nature conservation area, but it's worth the trip for a swim in wonderfully clear water, since Pérdhika Bay itself is shallow and yacht-tainted.

Angístri

Angístri, fifteen minutes by catamaran from Égina, is small enough to be overlooked by most island-hoppers, though the visitors it does have are a diverse mix: Athenian and German old-timers who bought and restored property here years ago, plus British or Swedish short-termers on package trips. Beaches are cleaner and less crowded (if not hugely better) than on Égina, and out of season pine-covered Angístri lapses into a leisurely village pace, with many islanders still making a living from fishing and farming. Headscarves worn by the old women indicate the islanders' Albanian ancestry, and until the mid-1990s they still spoke *Arvanítika* – a dialect of medieval Albanian with Greek accretions – amongst themselves.

Skála, Metóhi and Mýlos

The contemporary resort of **SKÁLA**, built over vineyards during the 1970s, is dominated by modern apartment buildings and hotels with little to distinguish them, spreading west halfway along the north shore of the island. The popular town beach, Angístri's only sandy one, nestles against the protected east shore of this headland, between the landmark church of Áyii Anáryiri and the car-ferry jetty. At slow times arriving craft will probably be met by **accommodation** touts, including those affiliated with the *Aktaion Hotel* (☎22970 91222; ❹), the best option on the main strip, a few paces up the beach, with a swimming pool, restaurant and standard rooms. Continuing in the same direction, then about 200m along the street leading west from the church, you'll find the large studios of *Ilios* (☎22970 91029; ❸), above the namesake giftshop, with a pleasant managing family and partial sea views. For an unobstructed view of the water

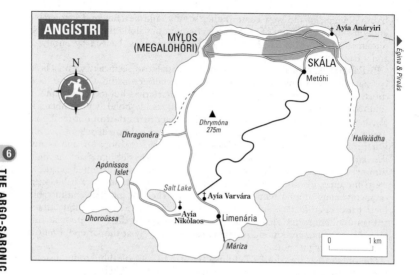

and much the best position in Skála, head ten minutes left (south) from the jetty to reach the *Alkyoni Hotel* (☏22970 91377; ❸), with large stone-floored rooms and a lovely coffee/breakfast bar. When **eating out**, choose from among *Yiorgos*, long-running seafood specialist just above the jetty; shed-like *Gionis* (no sign), the original 1970s taverna under some trees, at the north end of the beach opposite Áyii Anáryiri; and *Plori*, a few steps west by the bus stop, a decent ouzerí with locals in attendance and acoustic music some nights. Other **nightlife** takes place in the various bars along the north-shore road, for example at *Copacabana*, which also does breakfasts, coffees, waffles and desserts.

From the paved road's end just beyond the *Alkyoni Hotel*, a marked path leads within ten minutes to secluded **Halikiádha**, a pebble beach backed by crumbling cliffs and pine-covered hills; this is Angístri's best beach, and is clothing-optional.

METÓHI, the hillside hamlet just above Skála, was once the main village, but during the 1980s was completely bought up and restored by foreigners and Athenians. The only native islanders dwelling here now run the reasonably priced *Taverna Parnassos*, which offers its own cheese, a few *mayireftá* per day and good bulk wine in addition to the usual grills and *mezédhes*.

Ever-spreading Skála threatens in the future to merge with **MÝLOS** (Megalohóri), just 1.5km west along the north coast. Once you penetrate a husk of new construction, you find an attractive, traditional Argo-Saronic-style village centre with a church and platía. Although there's no decent beach nearby, it makes a good alternative base, with plenty of rented **rooms**, **studios** and a hotel or two, though the place has a more limited season (June–Aug) than Skála. **Tavernas** include *Sailor*, top for meat grills, and *Yiannis*, a cavernous spot with sea views and live music at weekends.

The rest of the island

Scooters and **mountain bikes** are available for rent from several outlets in Skála and Mýlos; it is less than 8km to Limenária, near the end of the trans-island road, so in cooler weather you can comfortably cross Angístri by pedal power, or on foot from Metóhi along a winding dirt track through the pines. In summer only, four daily departures of a box-like **minibus** connect Skála and Mýlos with Limenária. The broad, paved west-coast road takes you past the turning for **Dhragonéra**, a smallish, pine-fringed pebble beach with a dramatic panorama across to the mainland; there's a summer *kantína*, and more secluded, well-attended covelets to the right.

LIMENÁRIA, a small farming community at the edge of a fertile plateau in the southeast corner of the island, is still largely unaffected by tourism. The single, central **taverna** – *O Tasos* – is adequate and popular at weekends, but pricier than you'd expect for the location, functioning also as a *kafenío* and general store selling local farm products such as honey, retsina, pickled capers and olive oil. The closest good swimming is a few hundred metres east down a cement drive, then steps, at **Máriza**, where a cement lido gives access to deep, crystalline water. A broader paved road leads 2km west, past a shallow salt marsh, to the little anchorage of **Apónissos**, connected via a small causeway to an eponymous islet (private, off limits), with the larger island of **Dhoroússa** looming beyond. The *Aponisos Taverna* (summer only) is the single **eating** option here, but swimming opportunities (minuscule sand patches, stagnant water) are even more limited.

Póros

Separated from the mainland by a 450-metre strait, **Póros** ("the ford") barely qualifies as an island, and more than any other Argo-Saronic island it remains a (mostly Swedish) package-tour venue despite a marked slump in the trade in recent years; proximity to Pireás – and storm-proof access from the Argolid opposite – also guarantees a weekend Athenian invasion. The port town retains character, however, and the topography is interesting: Póros is in fact two islands, **Sferiá** (Póros Town) and the far larger **Kalávria**, separated from each other by a shallow engineered canal, now silting up, and spanned by a bridge.

In addition to regular ferry and hydrofoil connections with Pireás and the other Argo-Saronics, Póros has frequent, almost round-the-clock boats shuttling across from the workaday mainland port of **Galatás** in the Peloponnese (5 min; €0.50, €0.80 after midnight), plus there's a car ferry every half hour from the north end of the quay. These permit interesting excursions – locally to ancient Troezen near Trizína, and the nearby Devil's Bridge (see p.229). Further afield, day-trips to Náfplio or nocturnal ones to performances of ancient drama at the great theatre of Epidaurus (Epídhavros) are possible by car, or by taking an excursion provided by travel agents in Póros Town.

Póros Town

Ferries from other Argo-Saronics or from Galatás drop you at **PÓROS TOWN**, the only proper settlement on the island, which rises steeply on the western half of tiny volcanic Sferiá to its landmark clocktower at the summit, with great views of the tiled rooftops and straits. The cafés and waterfront lined with fishing and pleasure craft are lively until late – which means it's inadvisable to stay nearby. The only real sight is a two-room **archeological museum** about halfway along the southeast quay (Tues–Sun 8.30am–3pm; €2), with items from Troezen, Méthana, Hermione, Kalaureia and Galatás; there are no real knock-out exhibits, but the assortment of grave finds, jewellery, painted

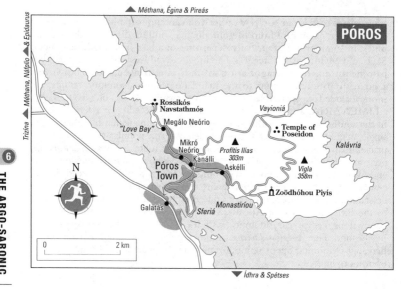

pottery, loom weights, oil lamps and grave *stelae*, from Mycenaean to Byzantine times, is well worth a half-hour perusal.

Practicalities

Drivers must use the public **car park** next to the Galatás ferry dock; the local **bus stop** is on the quay, near the foot passengers' water-taxi to Galatás. Strung along the waterfront, on either side of the separate car-ferry and hydrofoil moorings, are several **travel agents**, including Marinos Tours (℡22980 23423), main sales point for Hellenic Seaways hydrofoil tickets and with well-priced local **maps**; Askeli Travel (℡22980 24900), handling conventional ferries; and the Euroseas agent (℡22980 25902). These, and other agencies such as Family Tours (℡22980 23743) and Saronic Gulf Travel (℡22980 24555), deal in tours to the Argolid and most notably as **accommodation** bureaux for various apartments and hotels on Kalávria; touts can be persistent here and are worth avoiding.

Additional facilities around the waterfront include **scooter**, **car** and **bicycle** rental outlets (you can take all of them across to the mainland; thus scooters are surprisingly expensive at €15–20 per day), four **banks** (with ATMs) and a **post office**. **Internet** access and foreign-language newspapers are available at the Kendro Typou, opposite the long-haul ferry berthing.

Accommodation

Hotels on Sferiá are scarce, and mostly found in the area around the Galatás car-ferry dock: two options are the adequate if bland *Dimitra* (℡22980 25981 or 22980 25901; ❸) a bit inland, and the more distinguished *Dionysos* (℡22980 23511; ❹–❺), a converted mansion immediately opposite the dock, but with potential noise problems and unwelcoming management. **Rooms** or studios in the town tend to be unmarked; one conspicuous exception is *Villa Tryfon* (℡22980 25854; ❹), with 1970s rooms, mostly with bay-view balconies and cheerful blue-and-white decor. Even quieter places to stay are up on the hill behind the clocktower, although prices are high for what you get; the budget-conscious should seriously consider staying across the way in Galatás, where equivalent facilities are pitched a category lower.

Eating, drinking and nightlife

Down on the quay amongst the cafés, bars and souvenir shops facing Galatás are a few full-service **tavernas**, of which *Poseidon* on the north promenade is one of the few open at lunchtime, making a decent fist of seafood dishes in particular, though you'll have more choice and quality up the hill and on Kalávria. Beside the summer Cinema Diana above the small shopping centre, signs point up to ᚱ*Karavolos* ("snail"; dinner only), which unsurprisingly has snails on the menu along with other typical ouzerí fare; portions are large and prices (for Póros anyway) fair. On or just off of Platía Ayíou Yeoryíou (the way up is well marked from the northern promenade) is a cluster of evening-only tavernas, the most atmospheric (set under a plane tree) being *O Platanos* (dinner only), run by a local butcher and offering excellent meat grills washed down by the oddity of rosé retsina. For seafood, *Kathestos*, on the front between the town hall and the museum, is about the best.

As you head further southeast along the front, cafés serving **breakfast** or **light snacks** become quieter and better value; two to single out are *Mostra*, at the rear of Platía Dhimarhíou, and *Iy Platía*, next to the archeological museum. A cluster of noisy music-bars on the quay provides the main **nightlife** options, though the island's top venue (in all senses) is hillside day-and-night-club *Poseidonio*, 3km above town (1pm until small hours), with a pool and DJ.

Kalávria

Most of Póros' accommodation is found on Kalávria, the main body of the island, along the couple of kilometres to either side of the bridged canal beyond

△Póros Town

the Naval Cadets' Training School. Some of the hotels to the west in **Kanálli** and **Mikró Neório** are ideally situated to catch the dawn chorus – the Navy's marching band – though Mikró does have a worthwhile independent **taverna**, *Petros*. If you'd rather sleep in, head 2km beyond the bridge to **Megálo Neório**, where the pleasant *Pavlou* **hotel-taverna** (T 22980 22734, F 22980 22735; ④–⑤) fronts a larger beach and a watersports centre offering water-skiing. The paved road – and westerly **bus** service from Póros Town – continues past small, scenic but hopelessly overcrowded **"Love Bay"** before reaching the **Rossikós Navstathmós**, a crumbling Russian naval base dating from the late eighteenth century and Count Orloff's protracted but ultimately failed attempt to coordinate a Greek anti-Ottoman revolt. There's a hard-packed, mostly shadeless beach here, with lots of small craft anchored offshore; in general beaches west of the canal are more protected but the water can be stagnant.

Beach resorts east of the canal are comparatively exposed to the open sea but by the same token the water is often cleaner. **Askélli**, with its strip of hotels and villas, is long but crowded, with another motorized watersports centre; **Monastiríou**, about 4km from town, is more peaceful and fills last, with two **tavernas** – the more Greek-feeling and affordable being *Kalavria* – dividing the sunbed trade between them.

Zoödhóhou Piyís, the Temple of Poseidon and Vayioniá

The easterly bus route, and the paved road in this direction, end at the eighteenth-century **monastery of Zoödhóhou Piyís**, next to the island's only spring. The present buildings, dating from 1804, are currently inhabited by four monks; there's an expensive but pleasant snack café outside by the fountain.

Initially, Kalávria appears to be mostly pine forest, but the northern side of the island has fertile plateaus (especially Foússa, where wine is made), olive terraces and magnificent panoramic views. The loop road beyond Askélli leads you to a saddle between the island's two highest peaks and the well-signed foundations of a sixth-century BC **Temple of Poseidon** (enclosed but gate always open; free), the major item of Kalaureia, the ancient name for Póros. It was here that Demosthenes, fleeing from the Macedonians after taking part in the last-ditch resistance of the Athenians, took poison rather than surrender. Since 1997 the Swedish Institute of Archeology has reprised its nineteenth-century excavations of the surprisingly extensive site, though this means that the most interesting bits are roped off. Beyond the temple a road leads down to **Vayioniá**, port of the ancient shrine and the best of several beaches on the island's north shore, with a seasonal snack bar.

Ídhra (Hydra)

The island of **Ídhra** is treated as a preserved national monument, blessedly free of wheeled traffic and modern construction, making it one of the most peaceful and refreshing destinations in Greece. The island became established as a fashionable venue during the 1950s, when Sophia Loren appeared in *Boy on a Dolphin* (filmed here in 1957) and characters ranging from Greek painter Nikos Hatzikyriakos-Ghikas to Canadian songster Leonard Cohen bought and restored grand old houses. Since then Ídhra has experienced a predictable metamorphosis into one of the more popular resorts in Greece, despite a very limited number of good beaches. The town's busy from Easter until October, although the "three islands in one day" cruises that used to disgorge hundreds of trippers per liner have dwindled to just one or two arrivals per day. Weekends still see Ídhra packed to the gills, when the front becomes one long outdoor café and souvenir stall, though it's easy enough to leave all this behind on foot or by excursion boat.

Ídhra Town

ÍDHRA TOWN and port, with tiers of substantial grey-stone mansions and humbler white-walled, red-tiled houses climbing up from a perfect horseshoe harbour, form a beautiful spectacle. The waterfront mansions were built mostly during the eighteenth century on the accumulated wealth of a remarkable merchant fleet of 160 ships, which traded as far afield as America and – during the Napoleonic Wars – broke the British blockade to sell grain to France. Fortunes were made and the island also enjoyed a special relationship with the Ottoman Porte, governing itself and paying no tax, but providing sailors for the sultan's navy. These conditions naturally attracted Greek immigrants from the less privileged mainland, and by the 1820s the town's population was nearly 20,000 – an incredible figure when you reflect that today it is under 3000. During the War of Independence, Hydriot merchants provided many of the ships for the Greek forces and consequently many of the commanders.

Arrival and information

The town is fairly compact, but away from the waterfront, streets and alleyways are steep and labyrinthine; the best **map** is that issued by Saitis Tours next to the Alpha Bank (☎22980 52184), also agents for the Euroseas **catamaran**. Tickets for Hellenic Seaways **hydrofoils** and conventional ferries (which do not unload cars here) are sold on the eastern front, upstairs right opposite their anchorage (☎22980 54007). Several **banks** (**ATMs**) line the waterfront; the **post office** is on the market-*halle* square just inland, while a **laundry** is found on the lane opposite the telecoms building and next to the state clinic. Hydra Divers, at the entrance to the market-*halle* square (☎22980 53900, ⓦwww.divingteam.gr), offers round-the-island cruises as well as **dive trips** year-round by arrangement, PADI courses and Nitrox-Trimix tanks.

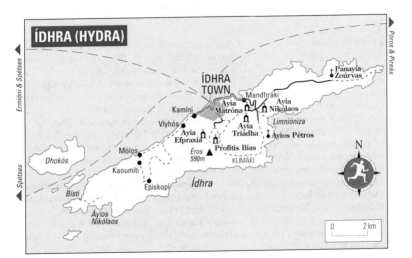

Accommodation

Because of the preservation order affecting the entire town, construction of new accommodation is banned, private balconies are rare (though air conditioning is almost universal) and the limited number of beds are in restored premises, all priced accordingly. There are no street addresses per se, and signage can be inconspicuous – ask for further directions when booking. Unless otherwise specified, establishments are open all year; high-season prices also apply to weekends in any season.

Alkionides Same lane as summer cinema ☎ 22980 54055, ⊛ www.alkionideshydra.com. Peaceful yet central pension with a pleasant courtyard and helpful management; all rooms have hot plates and fridges. ❹

Amaryllis 100m inland from the hydrofoil dock, take the right fork ☎ 22980 53611, ⨍ 22980 52249. Nondescript 1960s building that somehow evaded the preservation code, yet it proves a decent small hotel and has small balconies. ❹

🏃 **Bratsera** 150m inland from the hydrofoil dock, past the *Amaryllis* ☎ 22980 53971 ⊛ www.greekhotel.com/saronic/hydra/bratsera. Easily the best available on the island, this A-class/4-star hotel occupies a former sponge factory, and the extensive common areas (including bar, restaurant, conference room and medium-sized pool) serve as a de facto museum of the industry with photos and artefacts. Five grades of rooms, even the lowest two having flagstone floors and proper shower stalls. Open mid-March to Oct. ❼–❽

🏃 **Miranda** 200m inland along main lane from mid-quay ☎ 22980 52230, ⊛ www .mirandahotel.gr. An 1810 mansion converted into one of the most popular hotels here, with wood floors and fridges. Rooms vary; best are nos. 2 and 3, both with painted, coffered ceilings and large sea-view terraces. Large breakfasts in the shaded courtyard are another big plus; there is a basement bar for winter. B&B ❻

Nikos Botsis About 100m inland along main lane from mid-quay ☎ 22980 52395, ⊛ www .hydra-island.gr/botsis. Clean, plain white rooms in a four-storey building, most with balconies – and potentially street noise out front. Fri–Sun ❹, Mon–Thurs ❸

Orloff On largest inland square, near pharmacy ☎ 22980 52564, ⊛ www.orloff.gr. Another restored mansion hotel, with blue-curtained and -carpeted, high-ceilinged, variable rooms. High enough in town for partial sea views, with a very secluded courtyard where a superior buffet breakfast is served. B&B ❽

Pityoussa Main lane heading southeast out of town; info at Stavento shop. ☎ 22980 52810, ⊛ www.piteoussa.com. Named after the three giant pines out front, this inn has just five ground-floor, recently refurbished units, with cutting-edge facilities, including CD and DVD players and designer baths; quietest – though none is especially noisy – is no. 5 facing the garden. If full, there is co-managed, more basic *Theodoros* (❸) next door, upstairs. ❺

The Town

The **mansions** (*arhondiká*) of the eighteenth-century merchant families, designed by Venetian and Genoese architects, are still the great monuments of the town; some are labelled at the entrance with "*Oikía*" (Residence of…) followed by the family name. On the western waterfront stands the **Voulgaris** mansion, with its interesting interior, and on the hill behind it is the **Tombazis** mansion, used as a holiday hostel for arts students. Set among pines above the restored windmill on the western point, the sumptuous **Koundouriotis** mansion (Tues–Sun 10am–5pm; €4), with panelled ceilings and a collection of paintings, was the home of George Koundouriotis, a wealthy shipowner who fought in the War of Independence and whose great-grandson, Pavlos Koundouriotis, was president of republican Greece during the 1920s. On the eastern waterfront are the **Kriezis**, the **Spiliopoulos** and the **Tsamadhos** mansions – the latter now the national merchant navy college, which you can sometimes visit between lectures. The **historical archives museum** is also on the eastern waterfront (Tues–Sun 9.30am–5pm; €3), with a museum wing containing costumes, period engravings, plus ships' prows and sidearms from the independence struggle.

Ídhra also reputedly has no fewer than 365 churches – a total claimed by many a Greek island, but here with some justice. The most important is the church of **Kímisis tís Theotókou**, set in a monastic courtyard by the port, with a distinctive clocktower and an **Ecclesiastical Museum** (Tues–Sun 10am–5pm; €2).

Eating, drinking and nightlife

The obvious quayside cafés are fine for people-watching, but you pay for this – €4 coffees are the norm – and there are few bona-fide restaurants on the harbour. For better **eating** (and **drinking**) opportunities you'll have to head either inland or around the promontory just to the west.

Tavernas and ouzerís

Annita's 70m in from mid-quay, lane leading to *Miranda Hotel*. Never mind the silly numbered tourist menus and the occasional touting, the food – a mix of *mayireftá* and grills – is good and reasonably priced, with locals in attendance. Good rosé bulk wine; seating indoors or on the cobbles.

Barba Dhimas About 125m inland, on the same lane as the summer cinema. A small, well-priced taverna with decent *mezédhes*, small fish and even snail casserole.

Gitoniko (Manolis & Christina's) Inland, near Áyios Konstandínos church. Very friendly, durable taverna with excellent, well-priced *mayireftá* at lunch – which runs out early – plus grills (including succulent fish) in the evening; extensive roof-terrace seating or indoors according to time of year.

Iliovasilema (Sunset) Behind the cannons, west promontory. The place for an end-of-holiday treat or romantic tryst; upmarket, continental-style cooking that will set you back about €30 per person with (bottled) wine.

To Koutouki tis Agoras Rear of market-*halle*. Doesn't look like much with its rickety tables, but this inexpensive tradesmen's ouzerí can be inspired, with titbits ranging from *pastourmás*

(cured meat) to octopus. At its best in the early evening.

Paradhosiako 80m inland on lane leading up from the hydrofoil dock. All the standard platters at this heaving, popular ouzerí – so service often suffers; €20 per person with drink.

To Steki Inland lane between *Nikos Botsis* rooms and *Miranda Hotel*. Consistently good-value if slightly oily *mayireftá* (tempered by strong retsina) served by welcoming staff, at either the street-side terrace or a lovely shady courtyard that's an extension of the main inland square.

O Thanasis Same lane as *Annita's*, closer to the water. Ídhra's best *souvláki* stall, providing takeaways or sit-down meals at a handful of outdoor tables with water-views you'd pay twice as much for elsewhere.

Bars and cafés

Amalour 150m straight inland from the hydrofoil dock. Laid-back bar with an eclectic play list and thirty-to-forty-something crowd; sometimes hosts special events or theme nights.

Apangio 90m inland on lane leading up from the hydrofoil dock, opposite *Amaryllis* Hotel. A favourite morning spot, with some of the least expensive breakfasts in town, though

Ídhra festivals

On the second or third weekend in June, Ídhra Town celebrates the **Miaoulia**, in honour of Admiral Andreas Miaoulis whose **fire boats**, packed with explosives, were set adrift upwind of the Turkish fleet during the War of Independence. The highlight of the celebrations is the burning of a boat at sea as a tribute to the sailors who risked their lives in this dangerous enterprise.

Easter is a particularly colourful and moving experience, especially on Friday evening when the fishermen's parish of Áyios Ioánnnis at Kamíni carries its *Epitáfios* or symbolic bier of Christ into the shallows to bless the boats and ensure calm seas. On the second full weekend in October, the town hosts the annual, four-day **Rebétiko Conference**, with academic seminars by day and performances in this musical genre (see p.1123) at various venues after dark. Indeed the calendar is punctuated by conferences and seminars; if you learn of any that coincide with your travel plans, move quickly to secure hydrofoil seats and hotel beds.

coffees can taste peculiar owing to the island's water supply.

Hydronetta Tucked under the cannons on the west side of the promontory. The classic sunset-watching venue, with appropriate soundtrack, though

it carries on into the small hours. Limited seating gives it an exclusive, chill-out vibe.

Pirate Corner of waterfront by clocktower. Going since the 1970s, this is a more lively venue, with a younger crowd and Western music.

Beaches around Ídhra Town

The only sandy beach near town is at **MANDHRÁKI**, 1.5km east of the harbour along a concrete road; it's dominated by the *Miramare Hotel* (T22980 52300, W www.miramare.gr; ❻), whose garden bungalows are not quite up to the standard of some in-town digs, though the bar-restaurant occupies an imposing former shipyard of independence war hero Admiral Miaoulis. Weekday (Mon–Thurs) specials reduce the price to ❹–❺, and there are also non-motorized watersports, open to all, and frequent boat-shuttles to town for guests. At the shingly public bathing cove a few paces west, *Mandraki 1800* (also known as *tou Lazarou*; Easter–Oct) is one of the better rural **tavernas** on the island, with slightly pricey ouzerí fare.

Around the westerly harbour promontory in the opposite direction, a paved coastal path leads around to **KAMÍNI**, about a twenty-minute walk. Just as you reach Kamíni, on the right is a small pension, *Antonia* (T22980 52481; ❸); Eleni Petrolekka has a popular rival pension and apartments (T22980 52701; ❸) across the street. Arrival at Kamíni fishing anchorage proper is signalled by the *Taverna tis Kondylenias*, famous for its seafood – the grilled *thrápsalo* (giant squid) is very good – and wonderful sunset views. About 50m up the dry, paved stream bed from the anchorage there's a less expensive alternative, *Christina's*, with a more limited, daily-changing menu – again including some fish – and partial sea view.

Thirty minutes' walk beyond Kamíni, past the popular swimming cove at **Kastéllo**, brings you to **VLYHÓS**, a small hamlet with a rebuilt nineteenth-century bridge and a shingle beach; swimming in the lee of an offshore islet is decent. In peak season three taverna-cafés function – stronger at drinks than food – while there's a single rooms establishment, *Antigone* (T22980 53228, F22980 53042; ❹). **Water-buses** ferry passengers (€1.50 one way) to Ídhra port every half hour. Out of season you'll have to **charter** a craft at the port, which ranges from €9 (Kamíni) to €50 (Bísti) per boat, depending on destination.

The rest of the island

There are no motor vehicles on Ídhra, except for a few trucks to transport supplies and rubbish or do trench-works, and just one surfaced road (from the port to Mandhráki); the island is mountainous and its interior accessible only by foot or hoof. Accordingly, most tourists don't venture beyond the town, so with a little walking you can find a dramatically different kind of island – one of rural cottages, terraces of grain to feed the donkeys, hilltop monasteries and pine forest, mostly recovered from a devastating 1985 blaze.

Following the streets of the town upwards and inland behind the *Miranda*, you reach a path that winds up the mountain for about an hour's walk to either the **monastery of Profítis Ilías** or (slightly lower) the **convent of Ayía Efpraxía**, the only inhabited and open rural monasteries on Ídhra. What must be the longest stairway in Greece (or alternatively a zigzag path) constitutes the final approach to the former (closed noon–4pm, but water and *loukoúm* are hospitably left at the gate to revive you from the climb up). A trail continues left behind Profítis Ilías to a saddle overlooking the south coast, from where a path-less scramble brings you within twenty minutes to the 590-metre summit of **Mount Éros**, the Argo-Saronic islands' highest viewpoint. Otherwise, the path continues as an initially revetted *kalderími* descending the deserted back-side of Ídhra to scattered houses and locked chapels near the sea at Klimáki, before climbing again as a trail, past Áyios Pétros chapel and some spectacular coast, to a stretch of bulldozer track ending (1hr 15min from Profítis Ilías) at **Áyios Nikólaos** monastery. This is more usually reached directly from town on a well-marked (with multicoloured paint stripes) and obvious path, thread-ing between Ayía Matróna and Ayía Triádha (both locked); at Áyios Nikólaos' saddle, flanked by a namesake hamlet, the trail drops to **Limnióniza** (1hr 15min from town), the best and most scenic cove on the south coast, with a pebble beach and pines on the slopes above – though no facilities, and no water-buses out. Committed walkers can continue east of Áyios Nikólaos to **Panayía Zoúrvas**, near the eastern tip of the island (2hr each way from town).

Southwest of Vlyhós, a broad dirt donkey-track continues past a busy boat-repair yard to **Episkopí**, a high plateau planted with olives and vineyards and dotted by a scattering of homes (no facilities), and then climbs above Mólos Bay. Beyond Episkopí itself, paths towards the southwestern tip of Ídhra are overgrown and should not be attempted without local guidance. The idyl-lic coves of **Bísti** (Áyios Yeóryios) and **Áyios Nikólaos** to either side of the cape are normally reached by **water-buses** provided by Hydra Divers (hourly 11am–3pm, mid-May to early Oct; €10 return). Bísti has a pebble beach with a snack bar; Áyios Nikólaos has a fair-sized, partly sandy beach, and there are kayaks to rent at both.

Spétses

Spétses was the island where the author John Fowles lived during the early 1950s and which he used, thinly disguised as Phraxos, as the setting for *The Magus*. Since the 1890s, it has been a favourite resort for well-to-do Athenians, with foreigners following after World War II; the island seems to have risen above a bad 1980s reputation earned by cheap package tours and lager louts. The architecture of Spétses Town is distinct and distinguished, though less photogenic (and less regulated) than that of Ídhra; various concrete monsters were allowed to creep in during the 1960s, but all buildings now must be roofed with the traditional Byzantine canal-tiles rather than the hideous flanged "*Romaïká*" tiles used in much of Greece. Despite two devastating forest fires in 1990 and 2001, which together burnt over half of Spétses' area, hints of the landscape described by Fowles are still to be seen: "away from its inhabited corner [it is] truly haunted . . . its pine forests uncanny". Haunted perhaps, and certainly all but empty; even at Áyii Anáryiri, Spétses' largest of several excellent beaches, there are only scattered holiday villas on the slopes inland.

Spétses Town

SPÉTSES TOWN is the island's port – and the only proper settlement apart from a private villa estate at Ligonéri just west. It shares with Ídhra the same history of late eighteenth-century mercantile adventure and prosperity, and the same leading role in the War of Independence, which made its foremost citizens the aristocrats of the newly independent Greek state. Pebble-mosaic courtyards and pavements sprawl around 200-year-old mansions, whose

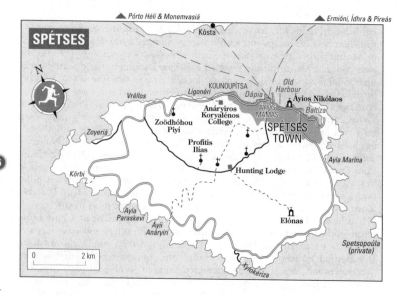

architecture is quite distinct from the Peloponnesian styles across the water. Though homeowners may bring private cars onto the island, their movement inside town limits is prohibited. A few conventional taxis supplement (expensive) horse-drawn buggies, whose bells jingle cheerfully night and day along the long waterfront. Hundreds of scooters, three-wheeled trikes and minivans are the preferred mode of transport, careering continuously through the town streets and making life almost as difficult for pedestrians as if cars had been completely unrestricted.

Arrival and information

Bus services are limited to two summer-only lines: from the *Hotel Poseidonion* to Ligonéri, and from Áyios Mámas beach to Áyii Anáryiri. A better way to get around is by rented **mountain bike** (at least 4 outlets), and despite many hills you can make the 25-kilometre paved circuit without too much exertion. Otherwise, avail yourself of up to ten **scooter-rental** outlets scattered across town – the going rate is €15 per day – and fill up at one of just two **petrol stations** (at the Dápia (main harbour) and at Ayía Marína). Spétses is also a great place to tour by sea, as many tempting coves aren't accessible overland: the Yachting Club (see opposite) rents **small boats** by the day. At the Dápia, *kaïkia* advertise set routes or round-the-island trips, while **water-taxis** are a pricey alternative (€15–60 per boatload depending on destination). The two **ticket agencies** are Bardakos (℡22980 73141), on the Dápia, for hydrofoils, and Mimoza Travel (℡22980 75170), 100m east, for the Eurofast catamaran. The **post office** is just inland from Áyios Mámas beach, while several **banks** (all with ATMs) surround the Dápia. **Internet** access is provided by Delfinia Net Café, behind Áyios Mámas beach.

Accommodation

Town **accommodation** ranges from relatively basic, 1970s-vintage rooms to jaw-droppingly expensive luxury complexes by way of self-catering studios. At slow times, proprietors meet arriving seacraft, and it might not be a bad idea to consider their (sometimes remote) offerings – anywhere central is apt to be noisy. If you don't fancy pounding the streets yourself, contact the Dápia travel agencies Alasia Travel (☎22980 74098) and the Yachting Club (☎22980 73400), which between them control bookings for a half-dozen lodgings.

Economou Mansion Kounoupítsa shoreline ☎22980 73400. Spetses' premier restored inn, occupying part of an 1851 property. The ground floor of the main house has six well-converted rooms retaining period features (€175); an outbuilding hosts two luxury sea-view suites (€235). Breakfast (included) is served by the fair-sized pool. **❽**

Klimis Waterfront 200m east of the Dápia ☎22980 72334. Not exactly bags of character here, but it's convenient, theoretically open all year and the most congenial of a few adjacent, similar 1960s box-hotels; direct or oblique sea views from all the balconied rooms. **❸**

Nissia Kounoupítsa shoreline ☎22980 75000, ⊕www.nissia.gr. Built on the grounds of an early twentieth-century factory (of which only the Art Nouveau facade remains), and arrayed around a large pool, this is Spétses' *poseur* address. Units range from two-person studios at the back (€230), through four-person maisonettes with two bedrooms, living room and kitchen (€450), to luxury four-person units with sea-view salons

(€570). Rates include breakfast, though kitchens are fully equipped. **❽**

Poseidonion Waterfront 50m west of Dápia ☎22980 72308, ⊕www.poseidonion.com. Kings and presidents once slept at this now slightly faded Edwardian period piece. Wood-floored, high-ceilinged rooms, with antique furniture and tubs in the bathrooms, and the extensive common areas, are better kept than the neglected hotel exterior suggests. Open daily June–early Sept, only weekends otherwise. **❺**

Villa Christina 200m inland from the Dapia ☎22980 72218, ⊕villachristina@hol.gr. Restored inn occupying a rambling old building with two courtyards, though no sea views. Air-conditioned rooms are basic but adequate; top-floor units are vastly preferable. **❹**

Villa Orizondes 500m inland from the Dápia, via Platía Oroloyíou ("Clocktower square") ☎22980 72509 or 697 44 69 893. Spartan hotel in a quiet spot, with variable-sized rooms with fridges, air conditioning and TVs; more than half have knock-out sea views over a bucolic orchard. **❹**

The Town

The town's sights are principally its majestic old houses and gardens, the grandest of which is the well-signposted Hatziyannis Mexis family mansion, built in 1795 and now used as the **local museum** (Tues–Sun 8.30am–2pm; €3). Exhibit highlights, well labelled in English, include magnificent polychrome-wooden ships' prows from the revolutionary fleet, as well as its flag, plus (out of sight in a plain wooden ossuary) the bones of Spetsiot admiral-heroine Laskarina Bouboulina, a wealthy widow who commanded her own ship (the *Agamemnon*), reputedly seduced her lovers at gunpoint, and was shot in 1825 by the father of a girl her son had eloped with. One of Bouboulina's homes, behind the cannon-studded main harbour known as the **Dápia**, has been made into a **museum** by her descendants and is well worth visiting. Guided tours (30min; €5) – the only admission permitted – are given in English up to ten times daily.

Just outside the town, Fowles aficionados will notice **Anáryiros Koryalénos College**, a curious Greek recreation of an English public school where the author was employed and set part of his tale; it is now vacant, save for the occasional conference or kids' holiday programme. Like the massive waterfront **Hotel Poseidonion**, the college was endowed by Sotirios Anaryiros, the island's great nineteenth-century benefactor. An enormously rich self-made man who made his fortune in America, he was also responsible for replanting the island's pine forests, depleted by generations of shipbuilders. His former **residence**, one block inland from the Dápia and signposted inconspicuously in Greek only, is a colossus of Neoclassical kitsch, complete with two sculpted sphinxes out front.

Walking east from the Dápia, after 1500m you reach the entrance to the **Palió Limáni**, still a well-protected anchorage used by overnighting water-tankers and roll-on-roll-off ferries. It's overlooked by the monastic church of **Áyios Nikólaos** with its graceful belfry and some vast pebble mosaics out front; inside, Paul-Marie Bonaparte, nephew of Napoleon and casualty of the Greek War of Independence in 1827, was embalmed for five years in a barrel of rum until his body could be repatriated to France. End of the road is **Baltíza** inlet where, among the sardine-packed yachts and excursion craft, a few boatyards continue to build *kaïkia* in the traditional manner.

Eating, drinking and nightlife

Brace yourself for the steepest **food** and **drink** prices in the Greek islands outside of Mýkonos and Rhodes – decades of Athenian patronage ensure that they're 25–30 percent higher than usual. That said, a number of fair-value, reasonable-quality spots are listed below. The perennial centres for **nightlife** are Baltíza, where over half-a-dozen clubs and bars try their luck in any given season – most durable are *Tsitsiano*, for Greek sounds, and *Baltiza*, a vaulted structure on the north shore, given to theme nights – and Áyios Mámas beach, where there are several bars, including *Rendez Vouz*. Just behind the Bouboulina mansion, *Titania* is a summer **cinema**.

Exedra (tou Siora) Palió Limáni. High-quality standard dishes like *moussakás* and *angináres ala políta*, and unbeatable waterside seating, make it worth the higher prices.

Kafeneion Dápia, by Alpha Bank. Pebble mosaics underfoot and sepia photos indicate that this was the island's first watering hole; start the day with well-priced English breakfast, and tame sparrows begging for crumbs, progressing later to a full range of *mezédhes*, or just a drink whilst waiting for a hydrofoil.

Lazaros 500m inland from the Dápia, starting from the newsagent. Cavernous interior with an old jukebox, dangling gourds and wine barrels; it serves a limited but savoury menu of grills, goat in lemon sauce, superior *taramás* and decent bulk wine – shame about the prefab oven chips. Dinner only, late March–early Oct.

Nykhthimeron (To Amoni) Baltíza. The alias means "the forge", and chef Nektarios' father and grandfather ran the local smithy out of this characterful building, which is now an eminently reasonable ouzerí. Seasonal fresh seafood titbits, vegetarian appetizers, a few grills and home-made *tyropitákia* are the simple but well-executed specialities. Despite the name ("night-and-day" in ancient Greek), open dinner only.

Patralis Kounoupítsa waterfront, 300m before the *Spetses Hotel*. The most upmarket, white-tablecloth venue on this side of town, with excellent service. Their *psári ala Spetsióta* (fish in ratatouille sauce) is made with tuna or amberjack, not low-quality *pérka* as elsewhere; there's good bulk wine if your wallet doesn't stretch to the startlingly priced wine list, and baked-apple dessert rounds off the experience.

Roussos Áyios Mámas beach. A shrine of unfussy *mayireftá* – courgettes au gratin, *yiouvétsi*, baked fish – and about the least expensive taverna in town; tellingly popular with locals.

Around the island

Some people **swim** happily enough at the **Áyios Mámas** town beach, though most will prefer to get clear of the built-up areas. The most popular beaches within twenty-minute walking distance are (east of town) the long, one with amenities at **Ligonéri**, between the *Spetses* and *Lefka Palace* hotels, and (west of town) more cramped **Ayía Marína**, with watersports, a popular bar and the first views offshore towards the tempting but off-limits islet of **Spetsopoúla**, the private property of the heirs of shipping magnate Stavros Niarchos.

Beyond these in either direction a paved road loops around the island in sinuous bends. The pine forest that survived the 1990 and 2001 blazes is mostly in

△ Ayía Paraskeví bay, Spétses

the far southwest, close to the coastline of little coves and rocky promontories. Heading anticlockwise beyond Ligonéri, the first beach you reach is **Vréllos** (no facilities), with just a single surviving copse of trees in a fire-denuded landscape. Next up is **Zoyeriá**, where forest resumes and sculpted rocks make up for the small beach. Naturists will appreciate secluded **Kórbi**, accessible only by a steep, ten-minute path starting from beside a concrete roadside water-tank, but **Ayía Paraskeví** just beyond is arguably the island's best beach, a 600-metre arc of pebbles backed by a chapel, an attractive *kantína* and a full-service taverna (May–Oct).

Áyii Anáryiri, on the south side of Spétses halfway around from town, is the island's most popular beach, a long, sheltered, mostly sandy bay. Gorgeous first thing in the morning, it fills up later with bathers, windsurfers and, at one corner, speedboats driving water-skiers. There's a good seafront taverna, *Manolis* (open all season), and another, *Tasos*, just behind (summer only). If it's all too much, carry on a bit to unheralded **Xylokériza** beach, reached by a 500-metre access drive signed merely for its snack bar (June–Sept); the protected bay itself is mixed sand and white pebbles.

Walkers might want to go directly over the top of the island to Áyii Anáryiri; the 1990 blaze ravaged most of the forest between Ayía Marína and Áyii Anáryiri, though happily new trees are now growing back. Routes out of town start from beyond the *Lazaros* taverna, and pass various rural chapels, a hunting lodge, and a forest service lookout tower – as well as the island's summit, with fine views. Scooter-riders will find the track optimistically marked ("Profítis Ilías 5") from the Áyii Anáryiri end to be in fact impassable on two wheels.

Travel details

All services to the Argo-Saronic islands from the Athens area, whether conventional ferry, catamaran or hydrofoil, depart from Aktí Tselépi in Pireás – slower craft from the Posidhónos side of Tselépi, faster conveyances from the Miaoúli side. There are always more at weekends (Fri–Sun) and fewer from October to June; hydrofoils or catamarans are twice as fast, and about twice as expensive, as conventional craft. Égina, not surprisingly, has the most frequent departures over the longest time range (hourly in season 7am–9.45pm *to* Pireás, 6am–9pm *from* Pireás). Car ferries on the Égina–Póros–Ídhra route also stop in both directions at Méthana on the Peloponnesian mainland, where it is possible to board; hydrofoils or catamarans also link Póros, Ídhra and Spétses two to four times daily with Pórto Héli or Emióni on the Argolid mainland opposite. At the time of writing there is no conventional ferry service between Spétses and Pireás, nor are there any hydrofoil or catamaran links between Égina/Angístri and the other Argo-Saronic islands.

Company contact details for Pireás (local island agencies are given in the island accounts):

Hellenic Seaways (ferries, hydrofoils and Flying Cat to all points) ☏ 210 41 99 000, ⊛ www.hellenicseaways.gr

Vasilopoulos Flying Dolphins (to Égina) ☏ 210 41 19 500

Ayios Nektarios Eginas (ferry to Égina) ☏ 210 42 25 625

Euroseas (Eurofast catamaran to Póros, Ídhra, Spétses) ☏ 210 41 13 108

Ferries

All conventional ferry services are operated by Hellenic Seaways unless otherwise stated.

Égina (Égina Town) to: Pireás (9–12 daily with Hellenic Seaways; 1hr 30min; 3 daily with Ayios Nektarios Eginas; 2hr); Angístri (2 daily Mon–Thurs, 3 daily Fri–Sun; 30min); Póros (4 daily Mon–Thurs, 5 daily Fri–Sun; 1hr 15min); Ídhra (4 weekly; 2hr 15min).

Égina (Souvála) to: Pireás (3–4 daily; 1hr 15min).

Póros to: Pireás (4 daily Mon–Thurs & Sun, 5–6 Fri & Sat; 3hr); Égina (4 daily Mon–Thurs & Sun, 5–6 daily Fri & Sat; 1hr 20min); Galatás, Argolid mainland (roll-on-roll-off barge every 30min 6am–10.40pm; 5min).

Ídhra to: Pireás (4 weekly, Fri–Sun afternoon only, calling at Póros and Égina Town; 3hr 45min for full journey).

Salamina (Paloúkia) to: Pérama (every 60min 1–5am, every 15min 5am–10pm, every 30min 10pm–1am; 15min).

Spétses to: Kósta (Almost hourly roll-on-roll-off barges; 15min).

Keravnos catamaran

Angístri (Mýlos and/or Skála) to: Égina Town (4–5 daily Mon–Fri, 2 daily Sat & Sun; 7.30am–8.30pm; 15–20min); Pireás (4–5 daily Mon–Fri, 2 daily Sat & Sun; 65–70min).

Égina to: Pireás (4–5 daily Mon–Fri, 2 daily Sat & Sun; 50min).

NB The Keravnos berth in Égina Town is at mid-quay, in front of three banks.

Eurofast catamaran

Runs twice daily between Spétses, Ídhra, Póros and Pireás in each direction, often omitting Póros on the evening run back to Pireás. Typical departures from Pireás at 9.30am and 3pm, from Spétses noon and 5.30pm.

Hydrofoils and Flying Cat

Égina to: Pireás (16 Hellenic Seaways hydrofoils and 6–7 Vasilopoulos Flying Dolphins daily; 45min).

Póros to: Pireás (5 daily Mon–Sat, 7 daily Sun; 1hr); Ídhra (6 daily Mon–Sat, 7 daily Sun; 40min); Spétses (4–5 daily; 1hr 30min).

Ídhra to: Pireás (8 daily Mon–Sat, 10 daily Sun; 1hr 40min); Póros (4 daily Mon–Sat, 6 daily Sun; 40min); Spétses (6 daily Mon–Thurs, 7–8 daily Fri–Sun; 45min).

Spétses to: Pireás (6 daily Mon–Thurs, 7–8 daily Fri–Sun; 2hr 25min); Ídhra (6 daily Mon–Thurs, 7–8 daily Fri–Sun; 45min); Póros (3 daily Mon–Sat, 5 daily Sun; 1hr 25min).

The Cyclades

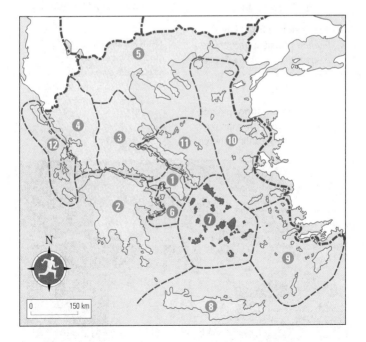

Highlights

✳ **Boat tour around Mílos**
The best way to take in the geological diversity of this volcanic island. See p.626

✳ **Mýkonos Town** Labyrinthine lanes filled with restaurants, boutiques and nightlife. See p.643

✳ **Delos** The Cyclades' sacred centre and holiest ancient site, birthplace of Apollo and Artemis. See p.649

✳ **Ermoúpoli, Sýros** Once Greece's busiest port, the elegant capital of the Cyclades is now a UNESCO heritage site. See p.651

✳ **Church of Ekatondapylianí, Parikía, Páros** An imposing and ornate Byzantine church incorporating an impressive number of architectural styles. See p.659

✳ **Tragéa, Náxos** This fertile inland plain, covered with orchards, shelters most of the villages on the Cyclades' largest island. See p.672

✳ **Hóra, Folégandhros** Free of traffic and sitting atop a spectacular cliff, this capital has a handsome old kástro. See p.690

✳ **Caldera of Santoríni** A geographical wonder, this crater left by a colossal volcanic explosion averages five miles in diameter. See p.693

△ Church of Ekatondapylianí, Parikía, Páros

The Cyclades

N amed, most probably, after the circle they form around the sacred island of Delos, the **Cyclades** (Kykládhes) is the most satisfying Greek archipelago for island-hopping. On no other group do you get quite such a strong feeling of each island as a microcosm, each with its own distinct traditions, customs and path of modern development. Most of these self-contained realms are compact enough to explore in a few days, giving you a sense of completeness and identity impossible on, say, Crete or most of the Ionian islands.

The islands do share some features, with the majority of them (Ándhros, Náxos, Sérifos and Kéa excepted) being arid and rocky; most also share the "Cycladic" style of brilliant-white Cubist architecture. The extent and impact of tourism, though, is markedly haphazard, so that although some English is spoken on most islands, a slight detour from the beaten track – from Íos to Síkinos, for example – can have you groping for your Greek phrasebook.

But whatever the level of tourist development, there are only three islands where it completely dominates their character in season: **Íos**, the original hippie-island and still a paradise for hard-drinking backpackers, **Thíra**, the major island in the volcanic cluster of **Santoríni** and a dramatic natural backdrop for luxury cruise liners, and **Mýkonos**, by far the most popular of the group, with its teeming old town, selection of nude beaches and sophisticated restaurants, clubs and hotels. After these, **Páros**, **Náxos** and **Mílos** are the most popular, with their beaches and main towns packed at the height of the season, which in the Cyclades is late July to late August. The once-tranquil **Minor Cyclades** around Náxos have become fashionable destinations for well-heeled Athenians in recent years, as have nearby **Amorgós**, and **Folégandhros** to the west, with its unspoilt hóra. To avoid the hordes altogether – except in August, when escape is impossible – the most promising islands are **Síkinos**, **Kímolos** or **Anáfi**. For a different view of the Cyclades, visit **Tínos** and its imposing pilgrimage church, a major spiritual centre of Greek Orthodoxy, or **Sýros** with its elegant townscape and (like Tínos) large Catholic minority. Due to their closeness to Athens, adjacent **Ándhros**, **Kéa**, **Kýthnos** and **Sérifos** are predictably popular – and relatively expensive – weekend havens for Greeks, while **Sífnos** remains a popular destination for upmarket tourists of all nationalities. The one major ancient site is **Delos** (Dhílos), certainly worth making time for; the commercial and religious centre of the Classical Greek world, it's visited most easily on a day-trip, by *kaïki* or jet-boat from Mýkonos. When it comes to **moving on**, many of the islands – in particular Mílos, Páros, Náxos and Thíra – are handily connected with Crete (easier in late July and August), while from Tínos, Mýkonos, Sýros, Páros, Náxos, Thíra or Amorgós, you can reach many of

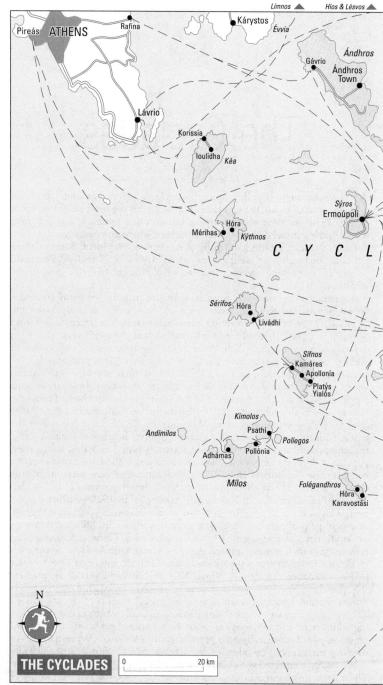

Kárystos

Pireás **ATHENS**   Rafina

Évvia

Ándhros

Gávrio

Ándhros Town

Lávrio

Korissía

Ioulídha   *Kéa*

Sýros
Ermoúpoli

Hóra
Mérihas   *Kýthnos*

C   Y   C   L

Sérifos   Hóra

Livádhi

Sífnos
Kamáres
Apollonía

Platýs
Yialos

Kímolos

Andímilos   Psathí

Pollónia   *Poliegos*

Adhámas

Mílos   *Folégandhros*
Hóra
Karavostási

N

THE CYCLADES   0 —————— 20 km

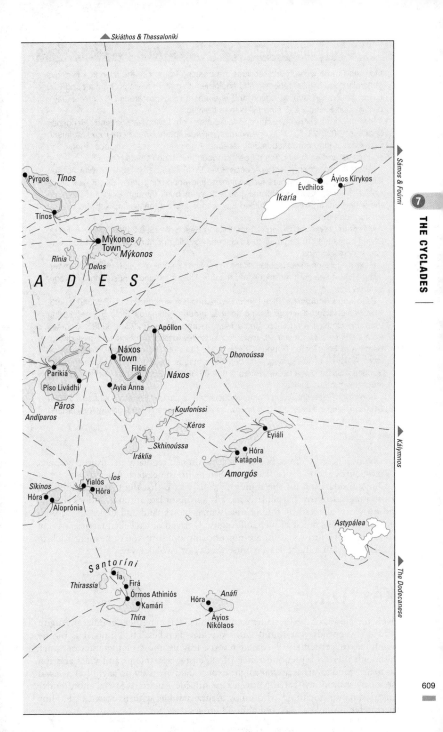

Pýrgos • Tínos

Tínos •

Évdhilos

Áyios Kírykos •

Ikaría

Mýkonos
Town •

Rínia

Mýkonos

Delos

A D E S

Apóllon •

Náxos
Town •

Dhonoússa

Filóti •

Náxos

Parikiá •

Píso Livádhi •

Ayía Ánna •

Koufoníssi

Kéros

Páros

Eyiáli •

Andíparos

Skhinoússa

Hóra •

Iráklia

Katápola

Amorgós

Yialós •

Íos

Síkinos

Hóra •

Hóra •

Astypálea

Hóra •

Aloprónia

Santoríni

Thirassía

Ía •

Firá •

Órmos Athiniós •

Hóra •

Anáfi

Kamári •

Áyios
Nikólaos •

Thíra

Watersports in the Cyclades

More and more watersports facilities are opening up across the islands, offering a generally good level of teaching and equipment to rent. Prices start from around €20 for an hour's windsurfing lesson and equipment rental, to around €70 for a day's diving course, and €250 for a full week's training.

Íos: Meltemi Extreme Watersports, outlets on Mylopótamos and Manganári beaches ☎ 693 21 53 912, ⓦ www.meltemiwatersports.com. Rental and waterskiing, windsurfing and wakeboarding lessons. Also hire canoes, pedaloes, snorkelling equipment and sailboats. Ten percent discount for Rough Guide readers.

Mílos: Apollon Diving Centre, *Apollon Hotel*, Pollónia ☎ 22870 41347, ⓦ www.apollon -diving.com. Diving courses for beginners and snorkelling trips; Sea Kayak Mílos ☎ 22870 23597, ⓦ www.seakayakgreece.com, or book through Brau Kat travel on the waterfront in Adhámas. Guided kayak trips around the island, with the chance to stop for a swim.

Mýkonos: Mykonos Diving Center, Psaroú Beach ☎ 22890 24808, ⓦ www.dive.gr. Diving courses from beginner to advanced, including night dives for certified divers and snorkelling trips.

Náxos: Flisvos Sportsclub, Áyios Yeóryios beach ☎ 22850 22935, ⓦ www .flisvos-sportclub.com. Arranges and teaches kitesurfing and windsurfing, and rents catamarans.

Páros and Andíparos: Blue Island Divers, main street, Andíparos ☎ 22840 61493, ⓦ www.blueisland-divers.gr. Diving courses around Andíparos, including snorkelling trips; Fly Under Diving Club, Sánta Maria beach, Páros ☎ 22840 52491. Courses from beginners to advanced, including kids' lessons and wreck and reef diving; Páros Kite Pro Center, Poúnda, Páros ☎ 22840 42757, ⓦ www.paroskite-procenter .com. All levels of kite surfing, from beginner courses upwards, and equipment rental; Surfistas, Sánta Maria beach, Páros ☎ 694 65 06 340. Board rental and windsurfing taught by professionals.

Santoríni: Santoríni Diving Centre, outlets on Kamári and Périssa beaches ☎ 22860 31006. Diving courses for beginners, as well as volcanic reef diving for certified divers and snorkelling trips.

the Dodecanese by direct boat. Similarly, you can regularly get from Mýkonos, Náxos, Sýros and Páros to Ikaría and Sámos (in the eastern Aegean).

One consideration for the timing of your visit is that the Cyclades often get frustratingly **stormy**, particularly in early spring or late autumn, and it's also the group worst affected by the *meltémi*, which blows sand and tables about with ease throughout much of July and August. Delayed or cancelled ferries (even in the height of tourist season) are not uncommon, so if you're heading back to Athens to catch a flight, leave yourself a day or two's leeway.

Kéa (Tziá)

Kéa, the closest of the Cyclades to the mainland, is extremely popular in August and on weekends year-round with Athenian families. Their impact is mostly confined to certain small coastal resorts, leaving most of the interior quiet, although there is a preponderance of expensive apartments and villas and not as many good tavernas as you might expect (and virtually no nightlife) because so many visitors self-cater. Midweek or outside August, Kéa is a more enticing destination for those who enjoy a rural ramble, with its rocky, forbidding perimeter and inland oak and almond groves.

As ancient Keos, the island and its strategic, well-placed harbour supported four cities – a pre-eminence that continued until the nineteenth century when Sýros became the main Greek port. Tourists account for the bulk of the sea traffic with regular (in season) **ferry/speed boat connections** to and from Lávrio on the mainland (only a ninety-minute bus ride from Athens), plus sporadic catamarans and ferries to and from Sýros and Kýthnos. Frequency of these services should improve as Lávrio port capacity is expanded, but for details you'll have to check directly with its port police as agents in Athens usually won't sell tickets to Kéa.

The northwest coast: Korissía to Otziás

The small northern ferry and hydrofoil port of **KORISSÍA** has fallen victim to uneven expansion; if you don't like its looks upon disembarking, try to get a bus to Písses (16km), Otziás (6km) or Ioulídha (6km). **Buses** usually meet the boats; during July and August there's a regular fixed schedule around the island, but at other times public transport can be very elusive. There are a few **taxis** on Kéa and several **motorbike-rental** outfits at the port, all more expensive than on neighbouring islands.

The ill-equipped seafront **tourist information** office is only sporadically open, but *To Stegadhi*, agents for any hydrofoils or catamarans operating, sell maps and guides, and can phone around in search of **accommodation**. The best year-round choices at the port are the very friendly *Nikitas* pension (☎22880 21193; ❸), with plain, comfortable en-suite rooms, *Hotel Korissia* (☎22880 21484; ❹), well inland along the stream bed with decent air-conditioned rooms, and the somewhat noisy *Karthea* (☎22880 21222; ❹) which does, however, boast single rooms. For **eating**, a series of nondescript tavernas along the waterfront serves standard Greek fare, though the only standout is *Apothiki*, a great place to splurge on hearty dishes like chicken *souvláki* wrapped in bacon. There's good swimming at **Yialiskári**, a small, eucalyptus-fringed beach between Korissía and Vourkári; along the way, at the northern edge of Korissía, cool, contemporary *Keos Katoikies* (☎22880 84002, ⓦwww.keos.gr; ❼), and the swanky, more traditional *Hotel Brillante Zoi* (☎22880 22685; ❻), offer plush amenities and a peaceful setting. The *Yialiskari* rooms (☎22880 21197; ❸), not far from the beach, are basic, but far better value. The nearby *Tastra* beach bar-café is something of a hub for nightlife on the island, having lured revellers from now more residential Korissía and Ioulídha.

VOURKÁRI, a couple of kilometres to the northeast, is more compact and arguably more attractive than Korissía, serving as the favourite hangout of the yachting set. A few expensive **tavernas**, including the nationally renowned *Giannis Maroulis* and *Konstantina Marouli*, serve up fresh seafood, and there's a very good ouzerí – *Strofi tou Mimi* – located where the road cuts inland towards Otziás. Despite a few nondescript bars, the nightlife here, as on the rest of the island, consists primarily of hanging out in tavernas long after plates have been cleared.

Another 4km on, past the picked-over ruins of the Minoan palace **Ayía Iríni** that lie virtually unnoticed on the peninsula north of the island's main harbour, **OTZIÁS** has a small beach that's a bit better than the one at Korissía, though more exposed to prevailing winds; facilities are limited to a couple of tavernas and a fair number of apartments for rent. Kéa's only functioning monastery, the eighteenth-century **Panayía Kastrianí**, is an hour's walk along a dirt road from Otziás. Although more remarkable for its fine setting on a high bluff than for any intrinsic interest, the hostel at the monastery (☎22880 24348) is the cheapest accommodation on the island, albeit rather basic, isolated and not dependably open. From here you can take the pleasant walk on to the island's capital, Ioulídha, in another two hours.

Ioulídha

IOULÍDHA (ancient Ioulis), also known as Hóra, was the birthplace of the renowned early fifth-century BC poets Simonides and Bacchylides. With its numerous red-tiled roofs, Neoclassical buildings and winding flagstoned paths, it is by no means a typical Cycladic village, but, beautifully situated in an amphitheatric fold in the hills, it is architecturally the most interesting settlement on the island, and the best base for exploring it. Accordingly Ioulídha has "arrived" in recent years, with numerous bars and bistros, much patronized in August and on weekends, but during other times it's quiet, its narrow lanes excluding vehicles. It's accessible from Korissía by paved road or on foot over the ancient stone paths that connected the towns during the island's heyday.

The **archeological museum** (Tues–Sun 8.30am–3pm; free) displays surprisingly extensive finds from the four ancient city-states of Kéa, although the best items were long ago spirited away to Athens. The lower reaches of the town stretch across a spur to the **kástro**, a tumbledown Venetian fortress incorporating stones from an ancient temple of Apollo. Fifteen minutes' walk northeast, on the path toward Panayía Kastrianí, you pass the **Lion of Kéa**, a sixth-century BC sculpture carved out of an outcrop of rock, 6m long and 3m high. There are steps right down to the lion, but the effect is most striking from a distance.

Along with a **post office** and **bank agent**, there are a couple of **pensions**, the best of which is the comfortable *Ioulís* (☏22880 22177; ❺), with its own terrace restaurant, up in the *kástro*. Choices for **eating** and **drinking** tend to be of a generally higher quality than in Korissía; however, unless you arrive during a busy season, you may find many places closed. *Iy Piatsa*, just as you enter the lower town from the car park, has a variety of tasty dishes, while up on the platía, *Rolando's* serves a full range of fish plates best enjoyed with the ubiquitous ouzo; neighbouring *To Kalofagadhon* is the best place for a full-blown meat feast. The aptly named *Panorama* serves up pastries and coffee and is a good place to watch the sun set. Once a hub of nightlife, the central town shuts down early these days, though the mayor, Antonakis Zoulos, happens to be one of the most accomplished traditional musicians in Greece, so you could stop at the town hall to ask where he'll be performing next. Full-on *bouzoúki* nights occur regularly at bars, cafés and tavernas in town or back at the port.

Southern Kéa

About 8km southwest of Ioulídha, reached via a mix of tracks and paths, or by mostly paved road, the crumbling Hellenistic watchtower of **Ayía Marína** sprouts dramatically from the grounds of a small nineteenth-century monastery. Beyond, the paved main road twists around the startling scenic head of the lovely agricultural valley at **PÍSSES**, emerging at a large and little-developed beach. There are two tavernas, plus a pleasant **campsite**, *Camping Kea*, which has good turfy ground and also runs the studios (☏22880 31302; ❸) further inland. Of the tavernas, the best is *To Akroyiali*, with a good range of dishes and some decent house wine, as well as rooms to rent upstairs (☏22880 31301 or 22880 31327; ❸).

Beyond Písses, the asphalt peters out along the five-kilometre road south to **KOÚNDOUROS**, a sheltered bay popular with yachters; there's a taverna behind the largest of several sandy coves, none cleaner or bigger than the beach at Písses. The luxury *Kea Beach* hotel (☏22880 31230; ❻) sits out on its own promontory with tennis courts, pool, and a hamlet of dummy windmills built as holiday homes. At the south end of the bay, *St George Bungalows* (☏22880 31277; ❸) has well-kept rooms at very reasonable prices, as well as its own taverna which is recommended. A further 2km south at **Kambí**, there's a nice little beach and a good taverna, *To Kambi*.

Besides the very scant ruins of ancient Poiessa near Písses, the only remains of any real significance from Kéa's past are fragments of a temple of Apollo at **ancient Karthaia**, tucked away on the southeastern edge of the island above Póles Bay, with an excellent deserted twin beach that's easiest reached by boat. Otherwise, it's a good three-hour round-trip walk from the hamlet of Stavroudháki, some way off the track road linking Koúndouros, Hávouna and Káto Meriá. Travelling by motorbike, the road between Písses and Káto Meriá is worth following along the island's summit to Ioulídha; it's paved between Ioulídha and Káto Meriá, and the entire way affords fine views over the thousands of magnificent oaks which are Kéa's most distinctive feature.

Kýthnos (Thermiá)

Though one of the duller and most barren of the Cyclades, a short stay on **Kýthnos**, which owes its alternative name, Thermiá, to its renowned hot springs, is a good antidote to the exploitation likely to be encountered elsewhere. Few foreigners bother to visit, and the island is even quieter than Kéa, particularly to the south where hikes from Dhryopídha, with its colourfully tiled roofs, to coastal coves are the primary diversion. It's a place where Athenians come to buy land for villas, go spear-fishing and sprawl on generally mediocre beaches without having to jostle for space. You could use it as a first or last island stop; in August there are several **ferry connections** a week with Kéa and Lávrio, and frequent ferry and catamaran services to and from Sérifos, Sífnos, Pireás, Mílos and Kímolos.

Mérihas and around

In good weather, boats dock on the west coast at **MÉRIHAS**, a rather functional ferry and fishing port with most of the island's facilities. This fact almost obliges you to stay here, and makes Mérihas more touristy than other spots on

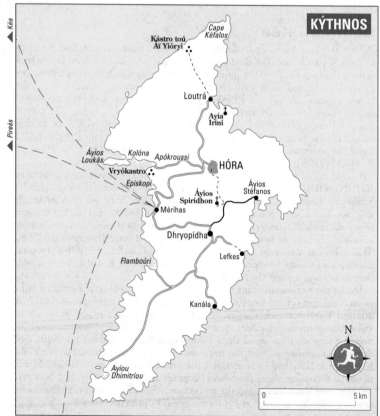

the island, but it's redeemed by proximity to the island's best beaches. The nearest is Martinákia, which has a taverna of the same name, but the closest beach of any repute is **Episkopí**, a 500-metre stretch of averagely clean grey sand with a single taverna, thirty minutes' walk north of the town; you can shorten this considerably by sticking to coast-hugging trails and tracks below the road. Far better are the adjacent beaches of **Apókroussi**, which has a canteen, and **Kolóna**, the latter essentially a sand spit joining the islet of Áyios Loukás to Kýthnos. These lie about an hour's walk northwest of Episkopí, and are easiest reached by boat trip from the harbour. Between the first two beaches lie the sparse ruins of the tenth-century fortified town of **Vryókastro**.

Owners of **accommodation** often meet the ferries in high season. There are numerous rooms to let, but they tend to be large and equipped for visiting families, so they can be on the expensive side – although with some opportunity for bargaining during the week. Out of season, owners are often not on the premises, but a contact phone number is usually posted. Few places have sea views, one exception being the rooms maintained by Yannoulis Larentzakis (☎22810 32247; ❸), near the ferry dock. A little inland, behind the small bridge on the seafront, *Panayiota* (☎22810 32268; May–Oct; ❸) and *Studios Panorama* (☎22810 32184; May–Oct; ❹) are decent choices; and there are plenty of other rooms and studios of similar price and quality along the same road. The Milos Express agency near the dock may be able to help you find a room (☎22810 32104, ⓕ22810 32291). Camping is generally tolerated, even on Martinákia beach.

The best **restaurants** are *Ostria*, a classic fish taverna on the waterfront, *Gialos*, specializing in lamb dishes, and *To Kandouni*, furthest from the ferry, a tasty grill with specialities such as *sfougáto* ("Cretan omelette"). There's also a bakery on the road to Dhryopídha.

The **bus service**, principally to Loutrá, Hóra, Dhryopídha and Kanála, is reasonably reliable, running around six times daily in season; the only motorbike rental is through the main Milos Express agency and is noticeably more expensive than on many islands. The Cava Kythnos shop doubles as the official **National Bank** outlet (exchange all day, credit cards accepted for a three-percent fee), and is the agent for hydrofoil tickets and the boat to Kéa.

Hóra and Loutrá

HÓRA lies 6km northeast of Mérihas, in the middle of the island. Tilting south off an east–west ridge, and laid out to an approximate grid plan, it's an awkward blend of Kéa-style gabled roofs, Cycladic churches with dunce-cap cupolas, and concrete monsters. There is a **post office** (open only until noon); the closest accommodation at present is at Loutrá. You can **eat** at the friendly *To Kentro* taverna near the small, central square, at the folksy *To Steki tou Detzi* grill, or at *Messaria*, whose specialities include rabbit in wine sauce.

The much-vaunted resort of **LOUTRÁ** (3km north of Hóra and named after its thermal baths) is scruffy, its nineteenth-century spa long since replaced by a sterile modern construction. The best **taverna**, *Katerini*, is a little out on a limb in the neighbouring bay to the west. Otherwise there are a few seafront bars and tavernas offering basic services, such as showers, to yachting crews. There is no shortage of places to sleep: **pensions** such as *Delfini* (☎22810 31430; ❸), *Meltemi* (☎22810 31271, ⓦwww.meltemihotel-kythnos.gr; ❸, apartments ❺), where the owners run walking trips around the island, and *Porto Klaras* (☎22810 31276, ⓦwww.porto-klaras.gr; ❹), with lovely sea views, are acceptable choices. The new *Kythnos Bay* (☎22810 31218; ❻), meanwhile, is probably the most comfortable option. You can also stay in the state-run *Xenia* baths complex (☎22810 31217; ④), where a twenty-minute bath plus basic check-up – blood pressure, heart rate and weight – costs about €5. The small bay of Ayía Iríni, just 1km east of Loutrá, and north of the church from which it takes its name, is a more pleasant place to swim and boasts the decent *Trehandiri* taverna on the hill above the bay. About a ninety-minute walk from Loutrá, on Cape Kéfalos, lie the picturesque ruins of the medieval **Kástro toú Áï Yióryi**, abandoned in the mid-seventeenth century.

Dhryopídha and southern Kýthnos

You're handily placed in Hóra to tackle the most interesting thing to do on Kýthnos: the beautiful **walk** south to Dhryopídha. It takes about ninety minutes, initially following the old cobbled way that leaves Hóra heading due south; critical junctions in the first few minutes are marked by red paint dots. The only reliable water source is a well in the valley bottom, reached after thirty minutes, just before a side trail to the triple-naved **chapel of Áyios Spyrídhon** which has recycled Byzantine columns. Just beyond this, you collide with a bulldozed track between Dhryopídha and Áyios Stéfanos, but purists can avoid it by bearing west towards some ruined ridgetop windmills and picking up secondary paths for the final forty minutes of the hike.

More appealing than Hóra by virtue of spanning a ravine, **DHRYOPÍDHA**, with its pleasing tiled roofs, is reminiscent of Spain or Tuscany. A surprisingly large place, it was once the island's capital, built around a famous cave, the Katafíki, at the head of a well-watered valley. Tucked away behind the cathedral is a tiny **folklore museum** that opens erratically in high season. Beside the cathedral is a cheap *psistariá*, *To Steki*. Some people let rooms in their houses, but the nearest official accommodation is 6km south at Kanála.

KANÁLA is a good alternative to Loutrá. There are some rooms in the older settlement up on the promontory and a good taverna, *Louloudhas*, with a huge terrace overlooking the larger western beach, **Megáli Ámmos**, which also has rooms and a combination snack-bar and taverna. Three of the nicer **pensions** in the area are *Nikos Bouritis* (☎22810 32195; ④), *Nikos Filippaios* (☎22810 32653; ④) and the *Margarita* (☎22810 32265; B&B ④), which has a home-like atmosphere. From Kanála, a succession of small coves extends up the east coast as far as **ÁYIOS STÉFANOS**, a small coastal hamlet.

Southwest of Dhryopídha, reached by a turning off the road to Kanála, **Flamboúri** is the most presentable beach on the west coast. The double bay of **Ayíou Dhimitríou** further south, although not too exciting, has a couple of tavernas and rooms to rent in high season.

Sérifos

Sérifos has long languished outside the mainstream of history and modern tourism. Little has happened here since the legendary Perseus returned with Medusa's head, in time to save his mother, Danaë, from being ravished by the local king Polydectes – turning him, his court and the green island into stone. Many would-be visitors are deterred by the apparently barren, hilly interior, which, with the stark, rocky coastline, makes Sérifos appear uninhabited until the ferry turns into Livádhi bay. Though newly paved roads have made the interior more accessible in recent years, the island is best recommended for serious **walkers**, who can head for several small villages in the under-explored

Greek **cuisine**

Although standards like kalamári and moussaka still figure strongly in taverna fare, Greek cuisine is considerably more complex and varied than the ubiquity of these well-loved dishes might suggest. In fact, modern Greeks are busy rediscovering their rich rural culinary heritage, which began as simple and functional, relying on local products, and later expanded under the influence of elaborate, Anatolian-influenced recipes in the 1920s, brought by immigrants from Asia Minor. The result is a rich and wide-ranging cuisine based on fresh, raw ingredients, subtle herbal filips and preparation by charcoal grilling or in wood-burning ovens. You'll find myriad local specialities, all proudly touted: anything from whole pickled caper sprigs to smoked eels, molluscs bottled in brine to soft sheep's cheese or thyme honey to almond syrup.

Market, Keffaloniá

Eat your greens

Wild and cultivated **vegetables** are the bedrock of Greek cuisine; until the 1950s, most people could afford to eat little else. During the cooler months of the year, street markets will be stocked with **leafy greens**: purslane and rocket to be eaten raw, or the various chicories, chards and even edible weeds known as *hórta*. These and more usual garden vegetables find their way into salads, *píttes* (baked pies), fritters and casseroles. *Briám* or *tourloú* is, for example, a ratatouille strong on courgettes, potatoes, eggplants and tomatoes; chickpeas are stewed or formed into *revythokeftédhes* (like coarse falafels) and aubergine (eggplant) has numerous uses: fried in slices, stuffed and baked, or even puréed. Greeks are also avid consumers of *toursí* or pickled vegetables – anything from baby cauliflowers, peppers or carrots to terebinth shoots or rock samphire. Finally, hand-cut chips are a staple and any restaurant with an eye to its reputation among local diners prepares them fresh, daily.

Olives and olive oil

Olive oil is a universal ingredient in Greek cuisine; traditionally every family made its own supply, if only from a handful of trees on a remote country property. As in most of the Mediterranean, **olives** are harvested between November and January depending on the locale and variety: beaten off the trees early on, or harvested ripe from the ground at later stages. There are over a dozen Greek varieties, ranging in colour from green to black to purple: some are used mainly for oil, but others – such as the famed Kalamatas and Amfissas – are reserved for eating, particularly as an integral ingredient of the ubiquitous *horiátiki* or "peasant" salad.

Olive oil mill

Goat's cheeses

Cheeses

Greeks are, perhaps surprisingly, Europe's biggest **cheese** consumers and every region of the country produces it, with feta merely the most famous. You'll find every consistency, from hard blocks of *kéfalograviéra* suitable for grating over pasta – a habit adopted from Italy – to pyramids of soft cheese, like the sweet *manoúri* or *anthótyro* and the savoury *touloumbísio*, used for spreading or stuffing. Treats to look out for include the Hiot cow's-milk cheese *mastéllo*, served grilled, or the smoked sheep's cheese known as *metsovóne*, from Epirus.

Greek wine

Quality **wine-making** is a large part of the Greek culinary renaissance, though while local vintners have a distinguished pedigree going back four thousand years, they still have a relatively small production capacity. If you think that Greek wine begins and ends with retsina, think again – top-drawer vintages, such as Porto Carras from Macedonia, Ktima Papaïoannou Nemea from the Peloponnese and the Emery label on Rhodes, are excellent – every bit as sophisticated as their French, Australian or South American counterparts. See p.67 for a summary of Greek wine domaines.

Vineyard near Kavála, Thrace

Meat dishes

In the days when the ownership of animals represented a family's wealth, eating **meat** was reserved for festivals, though it now figures almost daily in the local diet. The legendary *stó héri* (takeway) snack, **souvlaki**, is traditionally pork-based from November to April, but made from lamb the rest of the year. Besides chops and *pansétta* (spare ribs), **pork** appears everywhere as locally made *loukánika* (sausages), or in winter stewed with celery or plums. Many meat dishes are oven-baked casseroles, cooked in the morning and then left to stand and slowly cool throughout the day, a method which enhances the flavour – standards include the perennial favourites *moussaka* and *stifádho*. Another popular meat in Greece is **goat**; whether stewed, baked or grilled, it's the healthiest meat around, free-range and redolent of the herby hillside on which it grazed. Those same herbs reappear at taverna **grills**, where the proprietor bastes the order, sizzling over olive- or oak-wood coals, with a "broom" of thyme or oregano.

Moussaka

Fish and seafood

As well as familiar varieties such as bream and bass, there are many indigenous, seasonably available species to choose from. Delicacies of the eastern Aegean, the richest fishing grounds in Greece owing to the nearby Dardanelles and Turkish river mouths, include **shrimp** and **sole** in the springtime, and **anchovies**, *atherína* (silver smelt) and **sardines** in late summer; these are all best prepared flash-fried. In other regions, fried *gópes* (bogue), *soupiá* (cuttlefish) with rice and spinach, and grilled or wine-stewed octopus are good choices for seafood platters all year round. The truly acculturated will tuck into unusual **shellfish** such as *petalídhes* (limpets), *yialisterés* (smooth Venus), *kydhónia* (cockles) and *petrosolínes* (razor clams), which must be eaten alive to avoid being poisoned – if they twitch when lemon juice is dribbled on them, they're alive.

Seafood Market, Athens

Ouzo

Ouzo, the quintessential Greek apéritif, is a spirit produced by boiling, in a copper still, the fermented grape-mash residue left after wine-pressing. The resulting liquid, originally known as **rakí**, grew in popularity during the nineteenth century, when distilleries were established in Smyrna, Constantinople and Lésvos. The word ouzo probably derives from the Italian *uso Massalia*, used to label early *rakí* shipments leaving the Ottoman empire for Marseille. Nowadays it means *rakí* flavoured with various **aromatic spices**, usually star anise or fennel, both of which contain a compound called anethole. This is responsible for ouzo's harmless property of turning milky white when water is added. Bottled ouzo's alcohol content varies from 40 percent to 48 percent, never higher as the risk of the glass exploding is too great – however you may find home-made ouzo at higher strengths which is kept in barrels to avoid this problem.

Ouzo still

Greek coffee

Greek coffee (*ellinikós kafés*), despite its name, is essentially the same drink as prepared across the Middle East and Balkans, though with minor variations in each country. Indeed the term "Turkish coffee" was used in Greece until the Cyprus crises of the mid-twentieth century prompted the renaming. This speciality is made with fine-ground robusta coffee beans (rather than the arabica used to make western filter coffee), sugar to taste and water combined in a long-handled vessel known as a **bríki**. Allowing it to surge, but not boil, twice before decanting produces the froth or **kaïmaki**, highly prized and a test of properly made coffee, which is always served with a large glass of cold water.

interior, plus some isolated coves. Modern Serifots love seclusion, and here, more than anywhere else in the Cyclades, you will find farmsteads miles from anywhere, with only a donkey path to their door. Many people still keep livestock and produce their own wines, and many also cultivate the wild narcissus for export.

Few islanders speak much English; even a few select words of amateur Greek will come in handy and will be warmly received.

Livádhi and the main beaches

Most visitors stay in the port, **LIVÁDHI**, set in a wide greenery-fringed bay and handy for most of the island's beaches. The usually calm bay here is a magnet for island-hopping yachts, whose crews chug to and fro in dinghies all day and night to take on fresh water which, despite appearances, Sérifos has in abundance. It's not the most attractive place on Sérifos and mosquitoes abound, but Livádhi and the neighbouring cove of Livadhákia are certainly the easiest places to find rooms and any amenities you might need, all of which are very scarce elsewhere.

Unfortunately, the long **beach** at Livádhi is nothing to write home about; the sand is hard-packed and muddy, and the water weedy and prone to intermittent jellyfish flotillas – only the far northeastern end is at all usable. Heading away from the dock, turn left up the main business street, or climb over the southerly headland from the cemetery, to reach the neighbouring, far superior, **Livadhákia**, a golden-sand beach, shaded by tamarisk trees, with an acceptable taverna. If you prefer more seclusion, five minutes' stroll across the headland to the south brings you to the smaller **Karávi** beach, which is cleaner and almost totally naturist, but has no shade or facilities.

A 45-minute walk north of the port along a bumpy track leads to **Psilí Ámmos**, a sheltered, white-sand beach considered the best on the island. Accordingly it's popular, with two rival tavernas that tend to be full in high season. Naturists are pointed – via a ten-minute walk across the headland – towards the larger and often deserted **Áyios Ioánnis** beach, but this is rather exposed with no facilities at all, and only the far south end is inviting. Both beaches are theoretically visited by *kaïkia* from Livádhi, as are two nearby sea caves, but don't count on it. Additionally, and plainly visible from arriving ferries, two more sandy coves hide at the far eastern flank of the island opposite an islet; they are accessible on foot only, by a variation of the track to Psilí Ámmos. The more northerly of the two, **Áyios Sóstis**, has a well with fresh water and is the most commonly used beach for secluded camping.

Practicalities

The helpful Krinas Travel (☎22810 51448, ⓦwww.serifos-travel.com), near the jetty, sells **boat** tickets. The **bus stop** and posted schedule are at the base of the yacht and fishing-boat jetty; **buses** connect Livádhi with Hóra, 2km away, every half hour in season, but only manage one or two daily trips to Megálo Livádhi, Galaní and Kállitsos. You can rent a **bike** or **car** from Blue Bird (☎22810 51511), next to the filling station on the main street, or from Krinas Travel. There are a couple of **ATM**s along the seafront, and **Internet** access on a sole computer is available at the Malabar pub, inside the shopping arcade.

Accommodation

Proprietors don't always meet ferries, with the exception of the excellent *Coralli Camping* (see below), complete with pool and restaurant, by the beach in Livadhákia, which regularly sends a minibus. In high season you'll have to step lively off the boat to get a decent bed; the most rewarding hunting grounds are on the headland above the ferry dock in Livádhi itself, or the more peaceful Livadhákia, a ten-minute walk away. Unlike many other islands, most of the accommodation is open year-round.

Livádhi

Anna's Rooms On the seafront ☎22810 51263. Comfortable doubles with shared veranda. ❸

Margaritas On the beach at the other end of the bay away from the main town ☎22810 51321. Basic, family-run rooms with verandas in a peaceful spot. ❷

Naias Hotel Near the ferry dock ☎22810 51749, ⓦwww.naiasserifos.gr. Slightly dated, but comfortable, good-value hotel. All rooms come with balconies and some with sea views. Breakfast €5 extra. ❹

🏃 **Pension Cristi** On the headland overlooking the bay ☎22810 51775. Beautiful, cool modern pension in great location. Rooms are large and airy, sharing an enormous veranda with sea views. ❹

Livadhákia

Alexandros Vassilea On the beach, behind the taverna of the same name ☎22810 51119. Cluster of spotless, balconied doubles (❸) and apartments (❹). April–Oct.

Coralli Camping Bungalows On the beach ☎22810 51500, ⓦwww.coralli.gr. Excellent bungalows (❹) on the campsite, with communal pool and bar. Also run the brand-new 4–6-person *Coralli Studios* (❻) closer to town.

Helios Main road through Livádhakia ☎ & ⓕ22810 51066. Welcoming bougainvillea-draped pension with homely doubles and all mod cons. ❹

Vaso Rooms Close to the beach ☎22810 51346. Spacious doubles and triples, some with kitchens, and all with balconies. ❸

Eating and nightlife

As on most islands, **tavernas** near the quay tend to be slightly pricier; walk up the beach and meals get less expensive. The new bar-restaurant *Passaggio* does some good trans-European fare, although it's not the cheapest spot, and it is popular later in the evening, whilst a little further along the bay, the more traditional *Takis* is another good choice. Cheaper options include *Stamatis*, a local favourite, and, at the extreme northeast end of the beach, *Margarita's* with a homely feel and courtyard seating. For crêpes, ice cream, and *loukoumádhes* try *Meli*, in the commercial centre by the port police.

Nightlife is surprisingly lively, and most of it is clustered in or near a mini-mall on the seafront just up from the yacht jetty, so you should be able to quickly find something to suit your taste. As well as *Passaggio*, *Karnayio* next door is a popular night-time spot; both play excellent and varied music. One street back, *Metalleio* is a more full-on dance bar that gets into the swing after midnight. For something more Greek, try *Alter Ego* behind the shopping arcade, or the fiercely local *Edem Music Club* on the road up to Hóra.

Hóra

HÓRA is a pleasant if steep forty-minute walk up a cobbled way (if you're travelling light), with the *kalderími* leading off from a bend in the road about 300m out of Livádhi. By late September, you'll have no choice but to walk, since the bus – like nearly everything else – ceases operation for the winter.

Quiet and atmospheric, Hóra teeters precariously above the harbour and is one of the least spoilt villages of the Cyclades. The best sights are on the town's borders; tiny churches cling to the cliff-edge, and there are breathtaking views across the valleys below. At odd intervals along its alleyways, you'll find part of the old castle making up the wall of a house, or a marble statue leaning incongruously in one corner.

The central platía is home to a couple of atmospheric tavernas, which make a nice alternative to eating on the rowdier seafront down below, whilst *Aerino* bar, nearby, offers a romantic spot for an evening drink. Near the bus stop, the *Petros* and *Stavros* tavernas are also good choices. The latter, also known as the *Panorama Restaurant* for its view, can arrange **rooms** (☏22810 51303; ❷). The island's **post office** is found in the lowest quarter, and a few more expensive rooms for rent lie about 200m north of town, on the street above the track to the cemetery.

From Hóra, a pleasant diversion is the hour-long **walk** down to **Psilí Ámmos**: start from beside Hóra's cemetery and aim for the lower of two visible pigeon towers, and then keep close to the phone wires, which will guide you towards the continuation of the double-walled path descending to a bend in the road just above the beach.

Northern Sérifos

North of Hóra, the island's high water table sometimes breaks the surface to run in delightful rivulets swarming with turtles and frogs, though in recent years many of the open streams seem to have dried up. Reeds, orchards and even the occasional palm tree still take advantage of the unexpected moisture, even if it's no longer visible. This is especially true at **KÁLLITSOS** (Kéndarhos), reached by a ninety-minute path from Hóra, marked by fading red paint splodges along a donkey track above the cemetery. Once at Kállitsos (no facilities), a paved road leads west for 3km to the fifteenth- to seventeenth-century **monastery of Taxiarhón**, designed for sixty monks but presently home only to one of the island's two parish priests – part of a dying breed of farmer-fisherman monks. If he's about, the priest will show you treasures in the monastic church, such as an ivory-inlaid bishop's throne, silver lamps from Egypt (to where many Serifots emigrated during the nineteenth century) and the finely carved *témblon*.

As you loop back towards Hóra from Kállitsos on the asphalt, the fine villages of Galaní and Panayía (named after its tenth-century church) make convenient stops. In **GALANÍ** you can sometimes get simple **meals** at the central store, which also sells excellent, tawny-pink, sherry-like wine; its small-scale production in the west of the island is highly uneconomic, so you'll find it at few other places. Below the village, trails lead to the remote and often windswept beach of **Sykaminiá**, with no facilities and no camping allowed; a better bet for a local swim is the more sheltered cove of **Platýs Yialós** at the extreme northern tip of the island, reached by a partly paved track (negotiable by scooter) that branches off just east of Taxiarhón. The neighbouring beach has a taverna that may have a couple of very basic rooms available in season. The church at **Panayía** is usually locked, but comes alive on its feast day of Xilopanayía (August 16). Traditionally, the first couple to dance around the adjacent olive tree would be the first to marry that year, but this led to unseemly brawls so the priest always goes first these days.

Southwestern Sérifos

A little way south of Panayía, you reach a junction in the road. Turn left to return to Hóra, or continue straight towards **Megálo Horió** – the site of ancient Seriphos, but with little else to recommend it. A few kilometres' detour off this road, **Avéssalos** is one of the island's least explored beaches, making up for its relatively uninspiring landscape with sheer peace and quiet. **Megálo Livádhi**, further on from Megálo Horió, is a remote and quiet beach resort 8km west of Hóra, with two lovely tavernas whose tables are practically on the beach. *Iy Marditsa* taverna has some simple rooms behind the beach (T22810 51003; ❷). Iron and copper ore were once exported from here, but cheaper African deposits sent the mines into decline and today most of the idle machinery rusts away, though some gravel-crushing still goes on. At the north end of the beach, there's a monument to four workers killed during a protest against unfair conditions in 1916. An alternative turning just below Megálo Horió leads to the small mining and fishing port of **Koutalás**, a pretty sweep of bay with a church-tipped rock, and a long if narrow beach. It has become rather a ghost settlement and the workers' restaurants have all closed down, but there is one snack-bar/taverna, catering mainly to yachting crews. Above the port are the scant ruins of a medieval **kástro**. The winding track above the village leads to Livádhi, and apart from the pleasant **Gánema** beach, which has a taverna of the same name, there are no places to rest or buy refreshments on the two-hour journey back.

Sífnos

Sífnos is a more immediately appealing island than its northern neighbours since it's prettier, more cultivated and has some fine architecture. This means that it's also much more popular; be aware that in July and August, rooms are very difficult to find. Take any you can find as you arrive, or come armed with a reservation. In keeping with the island's somewhat upmarket clientele, signalled by new luxury hotels springing up across the island, camping rough is forbidden, while nudity is tolerated only in isolated coves.

The island's modest size – no bigger than Kýthnos or Sérifos – makes it eminently explorable. The **bus service** is excellent, most of the roads quite decent, and there's a network of paths that is fairly easy to follow. Sífnos has a strong tradition of pottery (as early as the third century BC) and has long been esteemed for its distinctive cuisine, intrinsically linked to the development of pottery, which allowed for the more sophisticated preparation of baked dishes. The island is perhaps best appreciated today, however, for its many beautifully situated **churches** and **monasteries**.

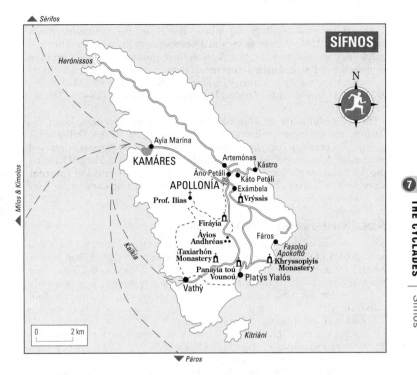

Ferry connections are more frequent to Sífnos than to the other more northerly islands. In season, the *Express Milos* and *Express Pegasus* ply a regular shuttle via Kýthnos and Sérifos, then on to Mílos and Kímolos before heading east to Folégandhros, Síkinos, Íos and Thíra, from where the course is reversed back to Pireás, whilst the new Speedrunner (operated by the family who run *Elies*; see p.625) links Sífnos with Kýthnos, Sérifos, Páros and Mílos on an almost daily basis in season. Links with the central Cyclades are far less frequent, with twice-weekly high-season ferries to Páros or Sýros, as well as a high-speed service to Thíra.

Kamáres

KAMÁRES, the island's port, is tucked away at the foot of high, bare cliffs in the west, which enclose a beach. A compact resort with concrete blocks of villas edging up to the base of the cliffs, Kamáres' seafront road is crammed with bars, travel agencies, ice-cream shops and restaurants. Proprietors tend not to meet boats; while hunting for a room, you can store luggage at the Aegean Thesaurus **travel agency** (℡22840 33151) right by the ferry dock, who also book accommodation across the island, and sell a worthwhile package consisting of an accurate topographical map, bus/boat schedules and a short text on Sífnos (€2). They can also book you on hiking tours or Greek cookery lessons.

Accommodation is relatively expensive, though bargaining can be productive outside peak season. Try the reasonable *Hotel Stavros* (℡22840 33383, Ⓦwww.sifnostravel.com; ❹), who have a decent book exchange in their reception, or, further along above the town beach, the friendly *Boulis Hotel* (℡22840

32122, Ⓦ www.hotelboulis.gr; ❺). Above the *Boulis*, the welcoming *Makis* **campsite** (☎ 22840 32366, Ⓦ www.makiscamping.gr) has good facilities and good-value air-conditioned rooms (❸). Continue past the *Makis* and turn right up from the end of the beach to find newer, quieter accommodation in a cluster of houses known as Ayía Marína, including the *Mosha Pension* (☎ 22840 31719, Ⓕ 22840 33719; ❸), and the *Delphini Hotel* (☎ 22840 33740 Ⓕ 22840 33741; ❼), which has its own pool.

The best **restaurants** are *Meropi Kambourakis*, ideal for a pre-ferry lunch; the *Boulis* on the waterfront with its collection of huge retsina barrels; *O Argyris* fish taverna; *Camaron*, serving great pastas and pizzas; the cosy *Kamares* ouzerí and good-value *Kyra Margena* at the far end of the beach in Ayía Marína. Kamáres also has a little **nightlife**; try *Yamas*, good for a sunset cocktail and **Internet** access, and *Follie-Follie*. The best place to **rent a scooter or car** is at *No.1*, on the road to Apollonía.

Apollonía and Artemónas

A steep twenty-minute bus ride (hourly service until late at night) takes you up to **APOLLONÍA**, the centre of Hóra, an amalgam of three hilltop villages which have merged over the years into one continuous community. With white buildings, flower-draped balconies, belfries and pretty squares, it is eminently scenic, though not self-consciously so. On the central platía, Iroöon, the **folk museum** (daily 9.30am–2pm & 6–10pm; €1), with its collection of textiles, lace, costumes and weaponry, is worth a visit.

Radiating out from the platía is a network of stepped marble footways and the main pedestrian street, flagstoned Odhós Stylianoú Prókou, which leads off to the south, lined with shops, restaurants, bars and churches, including the cakebox cathedral, **Áyios Spyrídhon**, and the eighteenth-century church of **Panayía Ouranoforía** (commonly transliterated as Yeraniofórou and many variations thereof), which stands in the highest quarter of town, incorporating fragments of a seventh-century BC temple of Apollo and a relief of St George over the door. Nearby, **Áyios Athanásios**, next to Platía Kleánthi Triandafýlou, has frescoes and a wooden *témblon*. Some 3km southeast, a short distance from the village of Exámbela, you'll find the active monastery of **Vrýssis** which dates from 1612 and is home to a good collection of religious artefacts and manuscripts.

ARTEMÓNAS, fifteen minutes north of Apollonía on foot and served by frequent buses, is worth a morning's exploration for its churches and elegant Venetian and Neoclassical houses. **Panayía Gourniá** (the key is kept at the house next door) has vivid frescoes; the clustered-dome church of **Kohí** was built over an ancient temple of Artemis (also the basis of the village's name); and seventeenth-century **Áyios Yeóryios** contains fine icons. Artemónas is also the point of departure for **Herónissos**, an isolated hamlet with a few tavernas and potteries behind a deeply indented, rather bleak bay at the northwestern tip of the island. The road is paved, and you may find occasional boat trips from Kamáres, though these are only worth the effort on calm days.

Practicalities

The **post office** and **bus stop** edge onto Apollonía's central platía. The **bank** and **police station** are located on the main road leading north out of town, and there's an **Internet** café on the road to Fáros. You can rent **bikes** at Moto Apollo, beside the petrol station on the road to Fáros, but the island is best explored on foot. There are **rooms** scattered all over the village, making them hard to find; *Giamaki Rooms* (☎22840 33973, ⓕ22840 33923; ❸) just off the main pedestrian street is an excellent choice. Your best bet is to look on the square for the main branch of the excellent Aegean Thesaurus travel agency (☎22840 33151, ⓦwww.thesaurus.gr), or try the nearby Room Rental Association (☎22840 31333). The very friendly *Hotel Sifnos* (☎22840 31624, ⓦwww.sifnoshotel.com; ❺), on the main pedestrian street, is the most traditional in its architecture and furnishing. A bit further along, *Patriarca* (☎22840 32400, ⓦwww.patriarca.gr; ❼) is a stunning new boutique hotel just below the cathedral. All the central hotels are sure to be noisy when the nearby clubs are open during the summer, but if you want quieter premises with a better view, be prepared to pay more: *Margarita Kouki* (☎22840 31894; ❸), above the luxurious *Petali Village* (☎22840 33024, ⓦwww.hotelpetali.gr; ❼), north of the square on the pedestrian lane, is a welcome exception.

There are a number of **restaurants** in Apollonía, including *Iy Orea Sifnos*, with good food despite its kitsch decor, on the central square. On the main pedestrian street, the charmingly decorated *Odos Oneiron* offers eclectic upscale dishes, while the more reasonably priced *Adiexodos* offers great *mezédhes* on its terrace with a view; *Cafe Sifnos* does something for nearly every taste and is open all day. There are several tavernas up in the backstreets: *To Apostoli to Koutouki* is quite good for standard Greek fare and very reasonable. Probably the best and most famous place to eat on the island, owing to its highly rated chef, is ⚷ *Liotrivi (Manganas)* (☎22840 31246) on the square up in Artemónas, where there's also an excellent bakery.

Most of the **nightlife** can be found on the main pedestrian street south of the square, where you'll find *Botsi*, *Volto* and the long-standing *Argo*. The *Camel Club*, on the road to Fáros, is another popular place for late-night action. For *rebétika* music there's the *Aloni*, just above the crossroad to Kástro.

The east coast

Most of Sífnos's coastal settlements are along the less precipitous eastern shore, within a modest distance of Apollonía and its surrounding cultivated plateau. These all have good bus services, and a certain amount of food and accommodation, **Kástro** being far more appealing than the resorts of **Platýs Yialós** and **Fáros** which can get very overcrowded in July and August.

Kástro

KÁSTRO seems the last place on Sífnos to fill up in season, and can be reached on foot from Apollonía in 45 minutes, all but the last ten on a clear path threading its way east via the hamlet of Káto Petáli. Built on a rocky outcrop with an almost sheer drop to the sea on three sides, the ancient capital of the island retains much of its medieval character. Parts of its boundary walls survive, along with a full complement of sinuous, narrow streets graced by balconied, two-storey houses and some fine sixteenth- and seventeenth-century churches with ornamental floors. Venetian coats of arms and ancient wall fragments can still be seen on some of the older dwellings; there are the remains of the ancient acropolis (including a ram's-head sarcophagus by one of the medieval gates), as well as a small **archeological museum** (Tues–Sun 8am–2.30pm; free), which does not always stick closely to the official opening hours, installed in a former Catholic church in the higher part of the village.

Among the several **rooms**, the modernized *Aris Rafeletos* apartments (☎ & ⓕ22840 31161; ❻) are open all year. More basic, but boasting gorgeous views, *Maximos* (☎22840 33692; ❸) has a couple of rooms next to his jewellery shop.

Nationally renowned, but disarmingly shabby, ☕ *To Astro* is an obvious taverna to try, as is the slightly more orderly *Leonidas*, while the *Kavos Sunrise* café-bar is laid-back and has a fantastic view. On the edge of town, the *Castello* disco-bar is a livelier hangout.

There's nothing approximating a beach in Kástro; for a swim you have to walk to the nearby rocky coves of **Serália** (to the southeast, and with more rooms) and **Paláti**. You can also hike – from the windmills on the approach road near Káto Petáli – to either the sixteenth-century monastery of **Khryssostómou** or along a track opposite the cliff face that overlooks the picture-postcard-perfect church of the **Eptá Martýres** (Seven Martyrs) which juts out into the sea; nudists sun themselves and snorkel on and around the flat rocks below.

Platýs Yialós

From Apollonía, there are almost hourly buses to the resort of **PLATÝS YIALÓS**, 12km away, near the southern tip of the island. Despite claims to be the longest beach in the Cyclades, the sand can get very crowded. Diversions include a pottery workshop, but many are put off by the continuous row of snack-bars and rooms to rent, which line the entire stretch of beach, and also the strong winds that plague it. **Rooms** are generally expensive; the welcoming *Pension Aggeliki* (☎22840 71288, ⊛www.sifnosageliki.com; ❹), near the bus stop, has reasonably priced doubles (❹) however, as well as some stunning apartments (❼); *Hotel Efrossyni* (☎22840 71353, ⊛www.hotel-efrosini.gr; B&B ❺), next door, is comfortable. The local **campsite** (☎22840 71286) is rather uninspiring – a stiff hike inland, shadeless and on sloping, stony ground. Among several fairly pricey **tavernas** are *Ariadne*, with a nicely shaded verandah, *Foni*, a friendly fish taverna that hosts live music acts some evenings, and *Kalimera*, with French-influenced Greek cuisine, whilst a five-minute walk over the headland brings you to Lazarou Beach, a tiny bay entirely occupied by a bar and restaurant stretching right the way down to the water's edge.

A more rewarding half-hour walk uphill from Platýs Yialós brings you to the convent of **Panayía toú Vounoú** (though it's easy to get lost on the way without the locally sold map); the caretaker should let you in if she's about.

Fáros and around

There are less crowded beaches just to the northeast of Platýs Yialós (though unfortunately not directly accessible along the coast). **FÁROS**, with regular bus links to Apollonía, makes an excellent fall-back base. A small and friendly resort, it has some of the cheapest **accommodation** on the island, as well as a couple of more upmarket places, including Fabrica (☎22840 71427, ⊛www.fabrica-sifnos.com; ❻), which maintains comfortable rooms in two charming properties; one a historic eighteenth-century stone structure. *To Kyma* is a pleasant seafront **taverna**, and the smart *On the Rocks*, perched on the headland at the far end of **Fasoloú beach**, serves a tasty selection of snacks as well as full meals. The chef at *Zambelis,* meanwhile, claims to have served as personal chef to Christina Onassis. The closest beaches are not up to much: the town strand itself is muddy, shadeless and crowded, and the one to the northeast past the headland is not much better. Head off in the opposite direction, however, through the older part of the village, and things improve at **Glyfó**, a longer, wider family beach about twenty minutes away.

Continuing from Glyfó, a fifteen-minute cliffside path leads to the beach of **Apokoftó**, with a couple of good tavernas, and, up an access road, to the *Hotel Flora* (☎22840 71278; ❺), which has superb views. The shore itself tends to collect seaweed, however, and a rock reef must be negotiated to get into the water. Flanking Apokoftó to the south, marooned on a sea-washed spit and featuring on every EOT poster of the island, is the disestablished, seventeenth-century **Khryssopiyís monastery**. According to legend, the cleft in the rock appeared when two village girls, fleeing to the spit to escape the attentions of menacing pirates, prayed to the Virgin to defend their virtue. The friendly nearby **taverna** bearing the name of the monastery and known locally as *Lebesis* specializes in reasonably priced lamb dishes and has a lovely, shaded terrace.

The interior and Vathý

Apollonía is a good base from which to start your explorations of more remote Sífnos. Taking the path out from Katavatí (the district south of Apollonía) you'll pass, after a few minutes, the beautiful empty **monastery of Firáyia** and – fifteen minutes along the ugly modern road – the path climbing up to **Áyios Andhréas**, where you'll be rewarded with tremendous views over the islands of Sýros, Páros, Íos, Folégandhros and Síkinos. Just below the church is an enormous Bronze Age archeological site.

Even better is the all-trail walk to Vathý, around three hours from Katavatí. Bear right at a signed junction; part way along, you can detour on a conspicuous side trail to the **monastery of Profítis Ilías**, on the very summit of the island, with a vaulted refectory and extensive views.

Vathý

A fishing village on the shore of a stunning funnel-shaped bay, **VATHÝ** is the most attractive and remote base on the island. However, with the opening of a brand-new luxury hotel, frequented by celebrities and politicians, *Elies Resorts* (T22840 34000, Wwww.eliesresorts.com), the character of this previously remote spot is certainly beginning to change. There are an increasing number of **rooms**, the best deals probably being at *Marana Rooms* (T22840 71120; ❷), at the opposite end of the bay to *Elies*, or those attached to the tiny **monastery of the Archangel Gabriel**. For **food**, *Manolis* does excellent grills and has a fascinating gyrating clay oven in the courtyard; *Okeanida* has good *mezédhes* such as chickpea balls and cheesy aubergine patties, while *To Tsikali* behind the monastery has farm-fresh cheese and rabbit dishes.

There are regular **buses** (8 daily in high season, 2 daily at other times), and *kaïkia* run daily in season from Kamáres. It is possible to walk to Platýs Yiálos in ninety minutes, but the path is not well marked.

Mílos

Volcanic **Mílos** is geologically diverse with weird rock formations, hot springs, good beaches and sensational views. Minoan settlers were attracted by obsidian, and other products of its volcanic soil made the island one of the most important of the Cyclades in the ancient world. Today, the quarrying of barite, perlite and porcelain has left deep scars on the landscape but given the island a relative prosperity and independence. With more **beaches** than any other island in the Cyclades, Mílos hasn't had to tart itself up to court tourism – in itself a good reason to stay several days.

You get a good preview of the island's **geological wonders** as your ferry enters Mílos Bay, one of the world's most striking natural harbours, shaped by a series of ancient explosions. Off the north coast, accessible only by excursion boat, the Glaroníssia (Seagull Isles) are shaped like massed organ pipes, and there

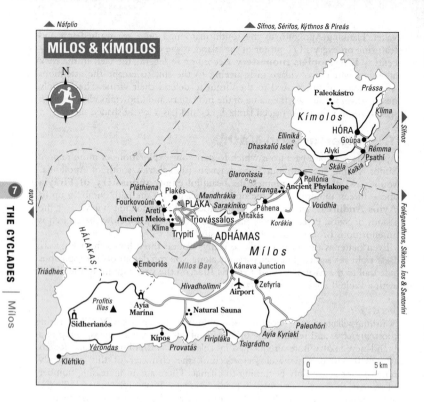

are more strange formations on the southwest coast at Kléftiko. Inland, too, you frequently come across odd, volcanic outcrops, and thermal springs burst forth.

Like most volcanic islands, Mílos is quite fertile; away from the summits of **Profítis Ilías** in the southwest and lower hills in the east, a gently undulating countryside is intensively cultivated to produce grain, hay and orchard fruits. The island's domestic architecture, with its lava-built, two-up-two-down houses, isn't as immediately impressive as its more pristine neighbours, but is charming nonetheless.

Adhámas

The main, lively port of **ADHÁMAS**, known as Adhámandas to locals, was founded by Cretan refugees fleeing a failed rebellion in 1841. With a handsome marble-paved esplanade around its natural headland, it's now among the most attractive ports in the Cyclades.

Towards the south beach, the **Mining Museum of Mílos** (summer daily 9am–2pm & 6–9pm; free) houses an extensive collection of mining tools, minerals and geological maps of Mílos. Near the quayside, the small but interesting **Ecclesiastical Museum** (sporadically open in summer; free) is housed in the century-old Áyia Triádha church. Highly recommended is one of the **boat tours** around the island, which make several stops at otherwise inaccessible swimming spots like the magnificent Kléftiko, continuing along the bizarre coastline and passing the Glaroníssia on the way to Kímolos (see p.631) where they often stop for a late lunch. Weather permitting, the boats normally leave at 9am from the quayside, and return at 6pm. Tickets cost around €30 per person, including lunch.

Practicalities

There are several **banks**, a **post office** and an **Internet café** near the Ecclesiastical Museum, as well as the hub of the island's **bus services**, which run hourly to Pláka, nine times daily in high season to Pollónia, seven times daily to Provatás and Paleohóri via Zefyría. The taxi rank is nearby – call ☎22870 22219 to book. Some visitors arrive by plane from Athens; most seats, however, are reserved by the local mining industry. Olympic Airways is located near the National Bank, near Adhámas port; the **airport** is 5km southeast of the port, close to Zefyría.

During high season, the highly organized **tourist office** opposite the ferry dock (☎22870 22445, ⓦwww.milos-island.gr) has a daily updated list of available rooms around the island and a handy brochure, while Milos Travel, also on the waterfront (☎22870 22000, ⓦwww.milostravel.gr), is another good resource for finding somewhere to stay, and also offers coastal boat trips, car rental, maps and ferry tickets; next door, the Brau Kat agency can book sea kayaking trips (see p.610).

Accommodation

Most accommodation is concentrated on the hill above the harbour and on or just off the main road to Pláka, and ranges from moderately priced addresses with shared facilities, such as the rooms of *Anna Gozadinou* (☎22870 22364; ❸), to smart rooms with TV and all mod cons, such as *Mimosa* (☎22870 21688, Ⓔmimosa@panafonet.gr; ❹), and the spacious, elegant studios of 🍴 *Villa Notos* (☎22870 21943, ⓦwww.villanotos.gr; ❺), run by a charming family, in a peaceful spot by the town beach left of the ferry landing. Some of the best hotels include the *Delfini* (☎22870 22001; ❹), one block behind the town beach; the stylish, central, double-glazed *Portiani Hotel* (☎22870 22940, Ⓔsirmalen@otenet.gr; ❻) and the luxury *Santa Maria Village* (☎22870 21949, ⓦwww.santamaria-milos .gr; ❼), 300m behind the beach. The **campsite** (☎22870 31410, ⓦwww .miloscamping.gr) at Hivadholímni beach (see p.630) on the south shore of the bay also has bungalows (❺); its minibus meets ferries.

Eating and nightlife

🍴 *Flisvos*, near the jetty, is a good place to **eat**, with a varied menu, and excellent people-watching potential. Of the three adjacent tavernas along the seafront towards the long tamarisk-lined beach south of town, *Navagio*, specializing in fish, is the best value. Just off the main street inland, *Pitsounakia* is a good, cheap *psistariá* with a pleasant courtyard. For **nightlife**, apart from the obvious string of cafés along the main seafront drag, *Akri* and *Aragosta* above the jetty are trendy **bars**, with pleasant views. *Vibera La Betina* next door, and *Malion*, behind the beach, are other current hot spots where the music ranges from loud rock or techno (usually at the former) to Greek pop or the odd live *bouzoukí* night (often at the latter).

Pláka, Trypití and Triovássalos

The main appeal of Mílos is in an area that has been the island's focus of habitation since Classical times, where a cluster of villages huddles in the lee of a crag, 4km northwest of the harbour.

PLÁKA (MÍLOS) is the largest of these communities and the official capital of the island. Behind the lower car park, at the top of the approach boulevard through the newer district, the **archeological museum** (Tues–Sun 8.30am–3pm; €3) contains numerous obsidian implements, plus a whole wing of finds from ancient Phylakope (see p.630), whose highlights include a votive lamp in the form of a bull and a rather Minoan-looking terracotta goddess. Labelling is scant, but you'll no doubt recognize the plaster-cast copy of the *Venus de Milo*, the original of which was found on the island in 1820. The statue was promptly delivered to the French consul for "safekeeping" from the Turks; her arms were knocked off in the melee surrounding her abduction. This was the last the Greeks saw of *Venus* until a copy was belatedly sent from the Louvre in Paris. Up in a mansion of the old quarter, the newly renovated **folk museum** (Tues–Sat 10am–2pm & 6–9pm, Sun 10am–2pm; €3) has a well-presented array of artefacts related to the history of arts, crafts and daily life on Mílos.

A stairway beginning near the police station leads up to the old Venetian **kástro**, its slopes clad in stone and cement to channel precious rainwater into cisterns. The enormous chapel of **Panayía Thalassítra** looms near the summit, where the ancient Melians made their last stand against the Athenians before the massacre of 416 BC. It offers one of the best views in the Aegean, particularly at sunset in clear conditions.

Pláka has a **post office** and a **motorbike-rental** outfit near the archeological museum. There are **rooms** available scattered around the village, with those on the west side offering spectacular views. Among the nicest of these are the pretty studios of Stratis Vourakis (☎22870 21702; ④). Dimitri Moraitis (☎22870 41353; ⑤) has newly refurbished rooms in the house where the *Venus de Milo* was allegedly hidden following its discovery, and *Maria's Rooms* (☎22870 21572; ③) are charming, if basic, studios close to the archeological museum. There are also three or four blocks of modern accommodation overlooking the busy approach road. A number of ouzerís make Pláka a good base for **eating**: highly recommended are *Arhondoula*, serving excellent seafood dishes, and slightly more upscale *Alisachni*, offering classic Greek dishes with a modern flair.

△ Roman amphitheatre and Milos Bay

The attractive village of **TRYPITÍ** (meaning "perforated"), which takes its name from the cliffside tombs nearby and covers a long ridge 1km south of Pláka, is another good base. There are a few modest **rooms**, two of which are just down the steep street from the tiny platía below the main church. The best places to **eat** are rustic *Glaronisia* serving up traditional taverna fare, and *Ergina*, which features oven-roasted goat and cuttlefish; for coffee and evening drinks, the stylish *Remvi Café* just past the bus stop has great views. From Trypití, it's a pleasant 45-minute walk down to Adhámas via Skinópi on the winding old *kalderími*, which begins on the saddle linking Trypití with the hamlet of Klimatovoúni.

Catacombs, Ancient Melos and the coast

From Pláka's archeological museum, signs point you towards the **early Christian catacombs** (Tues–Sun 8am–5pm; free), 1km south of Pláka and just 400m from Trypití village; steps lead down from the road to the inconspicuous entrance. Some 5000 bodies were buried in tomb-lined corridors stretching some 200m into the soft volcanic rock, making them the largest catacombs in Greece; only the first 50m is illuminated and accessible by boardwalk. Don't miss the ruins of **ancient Melos**, located just above the catacombs, which extend down from Pláka almost to the sea. There are huge Dorian walls, the usual column fragments lying around and, best of all, a well-preserved Roman **amphitheatre** (unrestricted access). Only seven rows of seats remain intact, but these look out evocatively over Klíma to the bay. En route to the theatre from the cement road is the signposted spot where the *Venus de Milo* was found in what may have been the compound's gymnasium.

At the very bottom of the vale, **KLÍMA** is the most photogenic of several fishing hamlets on the island, with its picturesque boathouses tucked underneath the principal living areas. There's no beach to speak of, and only one place to stay – the impeccably sited, if a little basic, *Panorama* (☎22870 21623, ☏22870 22112; ❹), with an acceptable balcony taverna.

Pláthiena, 45 minutes' walk northwest of Pláka, is the closest proper beach, and thus is extremely popular in summer. There are no facilities, but the beach is fairly well protected and partly shaded by tamarisks.

Southern Mílos

The main road to the south of the island splits at **Kánava junction**, a dreary place at first glance owing to the large power plant. But opposite this, indicated by a rusty sign pointing seaward, is the first of Mílos's **hot springs**, which bubble up in the shallows and are much enjoyed by the locals.

The left or easterly fork leads to **ZEFYRÍA**, hidden among olive groves below the bare hills; it was briefly the medieval capital until an eighteenth-century epidemic drove out the population. Much of the old town is still deserted, though some life has returned, and there's a magnificent seventeenth-century church.

South of here it's a further 8km down a winding road to the coarse-sand beach of **Paleohóri**. Actually a triple strand totalling 800m in length, it's indisputably the island's best; clothing's optional at the westerly cove, where steam vents heat the shallow water and the rock overhangs onshore. There are a number of **places to stay**, such as the inland *Paleochori Studios* (☎22870 31267, ✉paleochori@in.gr; ❹), the purpose-built rooms at the *Vihos Artemis* restaurant (☎22870 31222, ☏22870 23386; ❹) nearer the beach, and the rooms of Maria Tsirigotaki (☎22870 31231; ❸) and at *Panayiota Vikeli* (☎22870 31228; ❹). The best place to **eat** is *Pelagos*, which has a large raised patio.

The westerly road from Kánava junction leads past the airport gate to **Hivad-holímni**, the best beach on Mílos bay itself. Not that this is saying much: Hivadholímni is north-facing and thus garbage-prone, with shallow, grubby water offshore, although there is a taverna, a disco-bar and a sizeable community of campers during the summer. It's better to veer south to **Provatás**, a short but tidy beach, closed off by colourful cliffs to the east. Being so easy to get to, it hasn't escaped some development: there are two rooms establishments plus, closer to the shore, a newer, luxury complex, *Golden Mílos Beach* (℡22870 31307, @gmilosbe@otenet.gr; ❼). The best value for food and accommodation is the *Maïstrali* (℡22870 31420, ℗22870 31164; ❺), with private rooms and restaurant right on the beach.

Several kilometres before Provatás, a road forks east through a dusty white quarry to the trendy and popular beach of **Firipláka**. Further east, **Tsigrádho** beach is accessible by boat, or by the novel means of a rope hanging down a crevice in the cliff face. Two kilometres west of Provatás, you'll see a highway sign directing you below and to the left of the road for the village of **Kípos**, home to a small **medieval chapel** dedicated to the Kímisis (Assumption). It sits atop foundations far older – as evidenced by the early Christian reliefs stacked along the west wall and a carved, cruciform baptismal font in the *ierón* behind the altar screen. At one time a spring gushed from the low-tunnel cave beside the font – sufficiently miraculous in itself on arid Mílos. A few minutes to the west, unspoilt **Yérondas** beach is easily accessed, though seldom visited by tourists.

For the most part **Hálakas**, the southwestern peninsula centred on the wilderness of 748-metre Profítis Ilías, is uninhabited and little built upon, with the exception of the **monastery of Sidherianós**. The roads are memorable, if a little tiring, and several spots are worth making the effort to see. **Emboriós** on the east side of the peninsula has a fine little beach and a great local taverna with a few cheap rooms run by Manoulis Koliarkis (℡22870 21389; ❸). On the mostly rugged west coast, **Triádhes** is one of the finest and least spoilt beaches in the Cyclades, but you'll have to bring your own provisions. **Kléftiko** in the southwest corner is only reachable by boat (from Kípos via Yérondas or from Adhámas, see p.626), but repays the effort to get there with its stunning rock formations, semi-submerged rock tunnels and colourful coral.

The north coast

From either Adhámas or the Pláka area, good roads run roughly parallel to the **north coast** which, despite being windswept and largely uninhabited, is not devoid of interest. **Mandhrákia**, reached from Triovássalos, is another boathouse settlement, and **Sarakíniko**, to the east, is a sculpted inlet with a sandy sea bed and a summer beach café. Nearby **Mitakás** is difficult to find along an unmarked trail from the main road but worth the search for its secluded beach. A few kilometres further east, the little hamlet of **Páhena** is not shown on many maps, though it has another lovely beach. For **rooms** in the area try Terry's Travel, based in Adhámas (℡22870 22640, ⓦwww.terrysmilostravel.com; ❸). Still heading east, the remains of three superimposed Neolithic settlements crown a small knoll at **Fylakopí** (ancient Phylakope); the site was important archeologically, but hasn't been maintained and is difficult to interpret. Just before the site is another of Mílos's coastal wonders: the deep-sea inlet of **Papáfranga**, set in a ravine and accessible through a gap in the cliffs.

Pollónia

POLLÓNIA, 12km northeast of Adhámas, is immensely popular with wind-surfers, and a diving centre (see p.610) has further increased its popularity among watersports enthusiasts. Pollónia is essentially a small harbour protected by a storm-lashed spit of land on the northeast, where self-catering units are multiplying rapidly, fringed by a long, but narrow, tamarisk-lined beach to the rear, and closed off on the south by a smaller promontory on which the tiny original settlement huddles. Besides the town beach, the only other convenient, half-decent beach is at **Voúdhia**, 3km east, where you will find more of the island's hot springs, although it is effectively spoilt by its proximity to huge mining works, which lend it the desolate air of a *Mad Max* location.

On the quay are several **tavernas** and a couple of very mediocre café/snack-bars. Inland and south of here you'll find a concentration of **accommodation**, more simple rooms and apartments, most with the slight drawback of occasional noise and dust from quarry trucks. Among the highest-quality units are *Kapetan Tasos Studios* (T 22870 41287 W www.kapetantasos.gr; 6), with good views of the straits between Mílos and Kímolos, and the nearby *Kostantakis Studios* (T 22870 041357, W www.kostantakis.gr; 6), which allows children to help out on the farm. *Flora* (T 22870 41249, E roulamix@hotmail.com; 6), with a few cute rooms arranged around a courtyard, and breakfast on the beach, on the road towards the spit, is another option, as are *Efi* rooms (T 22870 41396, E milos2233@yahoo.gr; 4), above the far end of the beach. *Andreas* (T 22870 41262, E brigitte-milos@bluewin.ch; 4) has triple studios with stunning views and easy access to the quiet neighbouring bay. Pollónia has no bank or post office, but the friendly Axios Rent A Car office (T & F 22870 41234) can change money and advise you on accommodation matters. They also sell second-hand English books.

Taking the ferry to Kímolos may be the main reason you're here. The *Levkas* car ferry makes the trip about four times daily year-round, although it tends not to sail in high winds; call the port authority (T 22870 28860) to check.

Kímolos

Of the three islets off the coast of Mílos, only **Kímolos** is inhabited. Volcanic like Mílos, with the same little lava-built rural cottages, it profits from its geology and used to export chalk (kimolía in Greek) until the supply was exhausted. Fuller's earth is still extracted locally, and the fine dust of this clay is a familiar sight on the island, where mining still outstrips fishing and farming as an occupation. Rugged and barren in the interior, it has some fertile land on the southeast coast where wells provide water, and this is where the population of about eight hundred is concentrated.

Kímolos is sleepy from September to June, and even in August sees few visitors, just as well since there are fewer than a hundred beds on the whole island, and little in the way of other amenities. This, however, may be about to change as rumours spread of plans to build a geothermic spa on the island.

Psathí, Hóra and Goúpa

Whether you arrive by ferry, or by *kaïki* from Pollónia, you'll dock at the hamlet of **PSATHÍ**, which is pretty much a nonevent except for the excellent *To Kyma* ("The Wave") **taverna** midway along the beach, specializing in fried octopus.

The laissez-faire attitude towards tourism on the island is demonstrated by the fact that **ferry tickets** are only sold outside the expensive café at the end of the jetty, an hour or so before the anticipated arrival of the boat. The *Levkas* comes and goes from Pollónia on Mílos from the base of the jetty four times a day, whilst some of the larger ferries call in on their way to and from Mílos. A minibus runs from the port to the capital, which can also be reached by foot in about fifteen minutes.

Around the bay, there are a few old windmills and dazzlingly white **HÓRA** perched on the ridge above them. The magnificent, two-gated sixteenth-century **kástro** is one of the best preserved of such fortresses, built against marauding pirates in the Cyclades; the perimeter houses are intact and inhabited, though its heart is a jumble of romantic ruins. Just outside the *kástro* to the north stands the conspicuously unwhitewashed, late sixteenth-century church of **Khryssóstomos**, the oldest and most beautiful on the island. Near the church is the new **archeological museum** (irregular hours) with pottery from the Geometric to the Roman period.

There are a few adequate **rooms** near the port, most reserved through the same number (☎22870/51392; ❷–❹) at which you can also inquire about other rooms around Kímolos. Better situated **accommodation** options include Margaro Petraki's rooms (☎22870 51314; ❷), tucked away in the rather unglamorous maze of backstreets, or try those of Apostolos Ventouris (☎22870 51329; ❷) above his *kafenío* nearby. Sofia Ventouris (☎22870 51219; ❺) has a few new studios with sea views, close to the church. For **meals**, aside from a couple of basic *psistariés* and a café-bar, the aptly named *Panorama*, near the east gate of the *kástro*, is the most elaborate and consistently open taverna. *Meltemi*, to the west of the village, is another good taverna, which also has some rooms (☎22870 51360; ❸). Finally, there are a couple of boat agencies, and a **post office** in the west of the village, as well as an **ATM**.

East of Hóra, a ten-minute walk brings you to **GOÚPA**, a traditional fishing village with a few **tavernas**. At its base, **Rémma** beach remains unspoilt, as does **Klíma**, just off the main dirt road to Prássa to the north.

Around the island

During summer at least, the hamlet of **ALYKÍ** on the south coast is a better bet for staying than Psathí and Hóra; it only takes about thirty minutes to walk there on the paved road that forks left from the port. Alykí is named after the saltpan that sprawls between a rather mediocre beach offering no shade or shelter, but where you'll find the **rooms** of Sardi (☎22870 51458; ❸) and Pasamichalis (☎22870 51340; ❸), as well as a few simple **tavernas**. You can stroll west one cove to **Bonátsa** for better sand and shallow water, though you won't escape the winds. Passing another cove you come to the even more attractive beach of **Kalamítsi**, with better shade and a decent taverna. To the east, between Alykí and Psathí, the smaller, more secluded beach of **Skála** is better for camping, which is generally tolerated here.

The 700 metre coarse-sand beach of **Elliniká** is a 45-minute walk west of Alykí; starting on the road, bear left – just before two chapels on a slope – onto a narrower track which runs through the fields at the bottom of the valley. Divided by a low bluff, the beach is bracketed by two capes and looks out over Dhaskalió islet and across to harder-to-reach Kambána beach, home of nesting turtles. Elliniká tends to catch heavy weather in the afternoon, and there are no facilities here.

Another road leads northeast from Hóra to a beach and radioactive springs at **Prássa**, 7km away. The route takes in impressive views across the straits to

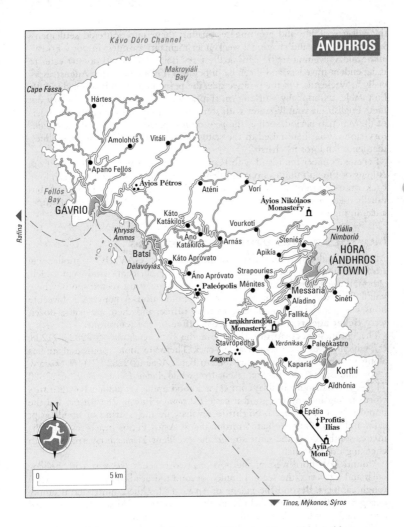

Políegos, and there are several shady peaceful coves where it's possible to camp
out. Innumerable goat tracks invite exploration of the rest of the island; in the
northwest, on Kímolos's summit, are the ruins of an imposing Venetian fortress
known as **Paleókastro**.

Ándhros

Ándhros, the second largest and northernmost of the Cyclades, is also one of
the most verdant, making it a great place for serious walkers. Thinly populated
but prosperous, its fertile, well-watered valleys and gorges have sprouted scores
of Athenian holiday villas whose red-tiled roofs and white walls stand out
among the greenery. Some of the more recent of these have robbed many of

the villages of life and atmosphere, turning them into scattered settlements with no nucleus, and creating a weekender mentality manifest in noisy Friday- and Sunday-evening traffic jams at the ferry dock. The island doesn't cater to independent travellers, and it can be difficult to find a bed during August, especially at weekends. On the positive side, the permanent population is distinctly hospitable; traditionally working on ships, they are only too happy to try out their English on you. Together with some of the more idiosyncratic reminders of the Venetian period, such as the *peristereónes* (pigeon towers) and the *frákhtes* (dry-stone walls, here raised to the status of an art form), it is this friendliness that lends Ándhros its charm.

Ferries connect the island with Rafina on the mainland, only an hour from Athens or fifteen minutes from the airport by bus, and, in season, you can loop back onto the central Cycladic routes via Mýkonos, Tínos or Sýros. A bus usually meets arriving ferries and runs to Batsí and on to Hóra at least six times a day in high season.

Northern and western Ándhros

All ferries and catamarans arrive at the main port, **GÁVRIO**, a moderately attractive holiday resort. Few venture onto the adjacent windswept beach, although there are plenty more attractive alternatives just to the south, where you'll find some of the area's better accommodation. A converted dovecote houses a sporadically functioning **tourist office**, and there are half-a-dozen ferry **ticket agents**, a **bank**, and a **post office** on the waterfront.

The cheapest **accommodation** is in the basic *Galaxias* (℡22820 71228; ❸), which serves as a late-arrival fall-back. There are more rooms and studios along and above the main coastal road to Batsí: *Aktio* (℡22820 71607, ⓦwww .aktiostudios.gr; ❹) is fairly representative, while *Andros Holiday Hotel* (℡22820 71384, ⓦwww.androsholiday.com; ❼) is a good upmarket choice. **Restaurants** worth trying include the good if basic *Estiatorio o Valmas*, *Tria Asteria*, and the popular *En Gavrio* ouzerí. **Nightlife** revolves around a string of nondescript cafés and bars along the harbourfront and at Áyios Pétros beach several kilometres south. Along the same stretch the excellent *Yiannouli* taverna is worth checking out for lunch.

Around 3km northwest of the port are two beaches, the first with holiday villas and a taverna, the second hidden beyond the headland and popular with rough campers. Beyond the village of Apáno Fellós, the countryside is empty except for a few hamlets inhabited by the descendants of Albanians who settled here and in southern Évvia some six hundred years ago.

Most visitors head 8km south down the coast, past the lively Khryssí Ámmos beach and the upmarket *Perrakis Hotel* above it (℡22820 71456, ⓦwww .hotelperrakis.gr; ❼), to **BATSÍ**, the island's main resort, with large hotels and bars around its fine natural harbour. The beautiful though often crowded beach curves round the port, and the sea is cold, calm and clean (except near the taxi park). **Hotels** range from the central, comfortable *Chryssi Akti* (℡22820 41236, Ⓕ22820 41628; ❺) to the upmarket *Aneroussa Beach Hotel* (℡22820 41044, Ⓕ22820 41045; ❼), south of town past the Stivári area towards **Ayía Marína beach** – a picturesque cove with *Yiannoulis Mastrozannes* fish taverna and studios (℡22820 41963; ❸). Besides these there are plenty of other rooms and **restaurants**: *Sirocco* (on the steps above the port) serves a range of international dishes, while *Stamatis* is an established taverna with a nice atmosphere, and *Delfinia* has a pleasant, sheltered balcony. There are several **café-bars**, such as *Capriccio* and *Nameless*, a half-a-dozen or so loud indoor bars featuring the standard foreign/Greek musical mix, and even an outdoor cinema with a different film every night in the summer. For information on walking tours, free local brochures or other travel needs, go to Greek Sun Travel (℡22820 41190, @greeksun@traveling.gr), upstairs near the taxi park. Two **banks** have ATMs.

Inland villages and Delavóyias beach

From Batsí you're within easy walking distance of some beautiful inland villages. At **KÁTO KATÁKILOS**, one hour inland, there are a couple of seasonal **tavernas**; a rough track leads after another hour to **ATÉNI**, a hamlet in a lush, remote valley. **ÁNO KATÁKILOS**, also reached from Batsí, has a couple of under-visited tavernas with fine views across the village. A right-hand turning out of Ano Katákilos heads up the mountain to **ARNÁS** after about an hour, whose lone taverna is often shrouded in mist. A long, three-hour rough hike down from Arnás to the eastern coast of the island brings you to the secluded, sheltered beach of **Vorí** with its clean, course sand and romantic landscape featuring several shipwrecks. Another rewarding trip is to a well-preserved, twenty-metre-high tower at **Áyios Pétros**, a mystery even to locals, 5km from Gávrio and 9km from Batsí.

South of Batsí along the main road are **Káto** and **Áno Apróvato**. Káto has rooms, including *Galini* (℡22820 41472; ❷), a taverna and a path to a quiet beach, while nearby is the largely unexplored archeological site of **Paleópolis**. Áno has the excellent taverna *Balkoni tou Aigaiou* (or "Aegean Balcony"). Along the shore here, though just as easily accessed on the road beginning in Batsí, **Delavóyias** beach is something of a haven for naturists. Within walking distance, the *Blue Bay Village* (℡22820 41150, ⓦwww.blue-bay.gr; ❺) has simple, comfortable rooms as well as a pool.

Hóra

A bus service links the west-coast Gávrio and Batsí with **HÓRA** (also known as **ÁNDHROS TOWN**), 35km from Gávrio. With its setting on a rocky spur cutting across a huge bay, the capital is the most attractive place on the island. Paved in marble and schist from the still-active local quarries, the buildings around the bus station are grand nineteenth-century affairs, and the squares with their ornate wall fountains and gateways are equally elegant. The hill quarters are modern and rather exclusive, while the small port on the west side of the headland has a yacht supply station and ferry landing. There are beaches on both sides of the headland, the better of which is Parapórti, to the east, though it's somewhat exposed to the *meltémi* winds in summer.

From the square right at the end of town you pass through an archway and down to windswept **Platía Ríva**, with its statue of the unknown sailor scanning the sea. Beyond lies the thirteenth-century Venetian **kástro**, precariously joined to the mainland by a narrow-arched bridge, which was damaged by German munitions in World War II. Inside the stark modern **archeological museum** (Tues–Sun 8.30am–2.30pm; €2), on the main street – are well laid out and labelled displays, with instructive models. Its prize item is the fourth-century *Hermes of Andros*, reclaimed from a prominent position in the Athens archeological museum. Behind it, the **Modern Art Museum** (Mon, Wed–Sun 8am–2.30pm, also 6–8pm in summer; €3) has a sculpture garden and a permanent collection with works by Picasso, Matisse, Kandinsky, Chagall and others, as well as temporary shows.

The few **hotels** in town are on the expensive side and tend to be busy with holidaying Greeks, although you could try the traditional *Aegli* (℡22820 22303;

❸), opposite the big church on the main walkway. Most rooms are clustered behind the long **Nimborió beach** northwest of town, and range from good clean rooms like those of *Villa Stella* (☎22820 22471; ❸) to modern apartments such as the *Alcioni Inn* (☎22820 23652, ℱ22820 24522; ❺). The *Paradise Hotel* (☎22820 22187, ⓦwww.paradiseandros.gr; ❼), with its swimming pool and tennis court, is the best upmarket choice, while the hillside *Stagira* (☎22820 23525, ℱ22820 24502; ❼), just outside of town, is the best spot for a romantic retreat. For **eating**, *Plátanos* has a generous *mezédhes* selection that can be enjoyed with an ouzo under the plane trees, and *O Stathmos*, right by the bus station, is good with reasonable prices. The nicest fish taverna is *Nona*, tucked away at the town end of Nimborió at the old Plakoura harbour, while *Cabo del Mar* is pricey but good, with an unsurpassed view.

Nimborió beach is the epicentre of the island's **nightlife**, such as it is, with a few thumping discos that start with Western music and shift into Greek pop into the wee hours of the morning. There's a **post office** and **bank** around town, a couple of **travel agents** and three **motorbike rentals** behind the beach.

Villages around Hóra

Hiking is particularly inviting south and west from Hóra, where there are lush little river valleys. One obvious destination is **MÉNITES**, a hill village 6km up a green valley choked with trees and straddled by stone walls. The church of the **Panayía** may have been the location of a temple of Dionysos, where water was turned into wine; water still flows continuously from the local rocks. Heading from here back to Hóra, you pass the medieval village of **MESSARIÁ**, with the deserted twelfth-century Byzantine church of **Taxiárhis** below, the picturesque setting for a nine-day festival of the Virgin Mary that begins on August 15. The finest monastery on the island, **Panakhrándou**, is only an hour's (steep) walk away, via the village of Falliká: reputedly tenth-century, it's still defended by massive walls but occupied these days by just three monks. It clings to an iron-stained cliff southwest of Hóra, to which you can return directly with a healthy two- to three-hour walk down the creek valley, guided by red dots.

Hidden by the ridge directly north of Hóra, the prosperous nineteenth-century village of **STENIÉS**, an hour's hike away, was built by the vanguard of today's shipping magnates; just below, at **Yialiá**, there's a small pebble beach with a taverna and *Paraskevi Tsoumezi* rooms (☎22820 23130; ❸) nearby. On the road to Strapouriés is a wonderful taverna, *Bozakis*, which boasts a view all the way down to the coast and excellent food. Beyond Steniés is **APIKÍA**, a tidy little village, which bottles Sariza-brand mineral water for a living; there are a few **tavernas**, including *O Tassos*, which has a lovely garden setting and specialities such as goat and rabbit. There are a very limited number of **rooms** here, including *Pighi Sariza Hotel*, Apikía (☎22820 23799, ℱ22820 22476; ❺). The road is now asphalted up to Vourkotí and even past this point is quite negotiable via Arnás to the west coast. There are some stunning views all along this road but bike-riders need to take care when the *meltémi* is blowing – it can get dangerously windy.

With your own transport, the sheltered cove of **Sinéti** south of Hóra is also worth a detour.

Southern Ándhros

If you're exploring the south of the island from Gávrio or Batsí, you might head first to **Zagorá**, a fortified Geometric town – unique in having never been built over – that was excavated in the early 1970s. Located on a desolate, flat-topped promontory with cliffs falling away on three sides, it's worth a visit for the view alone.

Alternatively, from Hóra, **PALEÓKASTRO** is one of the first stops, a tumbledown village with a ruined Venetian castle and a legend about an old woman who betrayed the stronghold to the Turks, then jumped off the walls in remorse, landing on a rock now known as "Old Lady's Leap". Further south, the village of **KORTHÍ** is a friendly place which is slowly waking up to its tourist potential. Set on a large sandy bay, cut off from the rest of the island by a high ridge and so relatively unspoilt, it is pleasant enough to merit spending the night at the austere-looking *Hotel Korthion* (T 22820 61218; ❸). There are also several good **tavernas**, including *Tó Vintsi tis Yitsas* at the waterfront. You could also take in the nearby convent (about half an hour's walk away) of **Zoöd-hóhou Piyís** (open to visitors before noon), with illuminated manuscripts and a disused weaving factory.

Tínos

Tínos still feels like one of the most Greek of the larger islands in the Cyclades. A few foreigners have discovered its beaches and unspoilt villages, but most visitors are Greek, here to see the church of **Panayía Evangelístria**, a grandiose shrine erected on the spot where a miraculous icon with healing powers was found in 1822. A local nun, now canonized as Ayía Pelayía, was directed in a vision to unearth the relic just as the War of Independence was getting underway, a timely coincidence that served to underscore the links between the Orthodox Church and Greek nationalism. Today, there are two major annual pilgrimages, on March 25 and August 15, when, at 11am, the icon bearing the Virgin's image is carried in state down to the harbour over the heads of the faithful.

The Ottoman tenure here was the most fleeting in the Aegean. **Exóbourgo**, the craggy mount dominating southern Tínos and surrounded by most of the island's sixty-odd villages, is studded with the ruins of a Venetian citadel that defied the Turks until 1715, long after the rest of Greece had fallen. An enduring legacy of the long Venetian rule is a persistent **Catholic minority**, which accounts for almost half the population, and a sectarian rivalry said to be responsible for the numerous graceful belfries scattered throughout the island – Orthodox and Catholic parishes vying to build the tallest. The sky is pierced, too, by distinctive and ornate **dovecotes**, even more in evidence here than on Ándhros. Aside from all this, the inland village architecture is striking and there's a flourishing folk-art tradition that finds expression in the abundant local marble. The islanders have remained open and hospitable to the relatively few foreigners and the steady stream of Greek visitors who touch down here, and any mercenary inclinations seem to be satisfied by booming sales in religious paraphernalia to the faithful.

Tínos Town

At **TÍNOS TOWN**, trafficking in devotional articles certainly dominates the streets leading up from the busy waterfront to the Neoclassical church **Panayía Evangelístria** (daily 8am–8pm) that towers above. Evangelistrías in particular overflows with holy-water vessels, votive candles and plastic icons, while parallel Megaloháris, which points a slightly more direct approach to

△ Venetian dovecotes on Tínos

the church, is relatively clear of shops, making room for the long, thick pad that has been bolted to the street in sympathy of devotees who crawl to the church uphill on their hands and knees from the harbour every day. Approached via a massive marble staircase, the famous **icon** inside the church is all but buried under a dazzling array of jewels; below is the crypt (where the icon was discovered) and a mausoleum for the sailors drowned when the Greek warship *Elli*, at anchor off Tínos during a pilgrimage, was torpedoed by an Italian submarine on August 15, 1940. Museums around the courtyard display more objects donated by the faithful (who inundate the island for the two big annual festivals), as well as icons, paintings and work by local marble sculptors.

The shrine aside – and all the attendant stalls, shops and bustle – the port is none too exciting, with just scattered inland patches of nineteenth-century buildings. You might make time for the **archeological museum** (Tues–Sun 8.30am–3pm; €2) on the way up to the church, whose collection includes a fascinating sundial from the local Roman sanctuary of Poseidon and Amphitrite (see p.640).

Practicalities

Ferries dock at any of three different **jetties**; which one depends on weather conditions. There are at least four boats a day from Pireás via Sýros going on to Mýkonos, and several from Rafína via Ándhros, as well as a useful catamaran, and less frequent ferry connections to Páros, Náxos and Thíra. When you're leaving, ask your ticket agent which jetty to head for. **Buses** leave from a small parking area in front of a cubbyhole-office on the quay, to Pánormos, Kallóní, Stení, Pórto and Kiónia (timetables available here; no buses after 7.30pm). A **motorbike** is perhaps a more reliable means of exploring – Vidalis at Zanáki Alavánou 16 is a good rental agency.

Windmills Travel (☎ & ⓕ 22830 23398, ⓦ www.windmillstravel.com), on the front towards the new jetty, can help with information as well as **tour bookings** and hotel bookings both here and on Mýkonos; they even have a book exchange. In season an excursion boat does day-trips taking in Delos (see p.649)

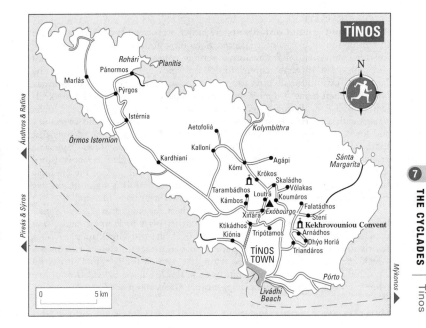

and Mýkonos (Tues–Sun; €20 round trip); this makes it possible to see Delos without the expense of staying overnight in Mýkonos, but only allows you two-and-a-half hours at the site. The **tourist police** are located on the road to the west of the new jetty.

Accommodation

To have any chance of securing a reasonably priced **room** around the pilgrimage day of March 25 (August 15 is hopeless), you must arrive several days in advance. At other times, there's plenty of choice, though you'll still be competing with out-of-season pilgrims, Athenian tourists and the ill and disabled seeking a miracle cure. The accommodation listed below is open from mid-April to October only, unless stated otherwise.

Anna's Rooms Road to Kionia ☏ 22830 22877, ⓦ www.tinos.nl. Excellent, family-run apartments set in a large garden just ten minutes' walk out of town. ❹

Avra On waterfront ☏ 22830 22242, ⓔ georgegerardis@yahoo.co.uk. Neoclassical relic with spacious rooms and attractive plant-filled communal area. B&B ❸

Eleana 200m inland from the Commercial bank ☏ 22830 22461. A good, if basic, budget option hotel, with clean rooms and breakfast included in the price. ❸

Hotel Tinion On waterfront ☏ 22830 22261, ⓦ www.tinionhotel.gr. Stylish 1920s hotel just back from the waterfront. Spacious rooms, some with balconies. Breakfast €9. ❹

Meltémi Near Megaloháris ☏ 22830 22881, ⓕ 22830 22884. Basic, dated hotel useful if you're here out of season. Open all year. ❸

Tinos Camping Ten-minute walk south of port ☏ 22830 22344. Popular, comfortable en-suite rooms with air conditioning and kitchens, set on one of the nicest campsites in the Cyclades. Follow the signs from the port. ❸

Eating and drinking

As usual, most seafront **restaurants** are rather overpriced and indifferent, with the exception of a friendly *psitopolió* right opposite the bus station, and the smarter Lymposion on Evangelistrías, serving coffees, pastas and *mezédhes*, and also with a fast **Internet** connection. About midway along the port near the *Leto Hotel*, behind the dolphin fountain, there is a cluster of excellent tavernas, one of the best being 🍴 *Epineio* with good-value, tasty Greek dishes and excellent seafood. A small vine-covered alleyway leads from here to Palládha, a public square with a farmers' **market** every morning with local fruit and vegetables, and lined with yet more good choices: *Metaxi Mas*, a pricey *mezedopólio* that has a remarkably varied menu, including delicious *hortokeftédhes* (vegetable croquettes); and *Palea Palladha*, justifiably proud of its grilled *loukániko* (spicy sausage), sharp local feta and smooth house wine. At the end of the alleyway there's a small traditional bakery, *Psomi Horiatiko*. For late-night snacks, try *Edesma* (meaning "food") just off Palládha, which stays open till 5am.

There are a few **bars**, mostly in a huddle near the new quay. Sleek *Fevgatos* has sophisticated decor, *Koursaros* on the corner plays rock music, and *Pyrsos* is pretty lively with a mixture of international hits and Greek music. *Kaktos*, meanwhile, has dancing on a terrace with ocean views, while *Sivilla* blends Greek and world music in a cosy setting. At 3am all the bars in Tínos Town close, but for those not ready to hit the sack, *Paradise* up past *Anna's Rooms* (see p.639), stays open until dawn playing mainly Greek music.

Southern beaches

Kiónia, 3km northwest of Tínos Town (hourly buses in summer), is the site of the **Sanctuary of Poseidon and Amphitrite** (Tues–Sun 8.30am–3pm; free), which was discovered in 1902; the excavations yielded principally columns (*kiónia* in Greek), but also a temple, baths, a fountain and hostels for the ancient pilgrims. The **beach** is functional enough, lined with rooms to rent and snack-bars, but it's better to walk past the large *Tinos Beach Hotel* (☎22830 22626, ⓦwww.tinosbeach.gr; ❼), the last stop for the bus, and follow an unpaved road to a series of sandy coves beyond.

The beach beyond the headland east of town starts off rocky but improves if you walk 500m further along. Further east, **Pórto** (six buses daily) boasts two good beaches, with a couple of good tavernas as well as family-friendly **apartments** with a pool at the reasonably priced restaurant *Akti Aegeou* (☎22830 24248, ⓦwww.aktiaegeou.gr; ❺), on the first beach of Áyios Pandelímon, as well as the smart studios *Porto Raphael* (☎22830 23913, ⓦwww.portoraphael .gr; ❸), above Áyios Ioánnis beach. 🍴 *Porto Tango* (☎22830 24411, ⓦwww .portotango.gr; ❼) is an excellent upmarket hotel here, with a lovely pool setting, luxurious rooms and its own spa.

Northern Tínos

A good beginning to a foray into the interior is to take the stone stairway – the continuation of Odhós Ayíou Nikoláou – that passes behind and to the left of the Evangelistrías. This climbs for ninety minutes through appealing country-side to **KTIKÁDHOS**, a fine village with a good sea-view taverna, *Drosia*. You can either flag down a bus on the main road or stay with the trail until Xinára (see opposite).

Heading northwest from the junction flanked by Ktikádhos, Tripótamos and Xinára, there's little to stop for – except the fine **dovecotes** around Tarambád-hos – until you reach **KARDHIANÍ**, 8km along, one of the most strikingly set and beautiful villages on the island, with its views across to Sýros from amid a dense oasis. The cliff-hugging *O Dinos* here serves shellfish with a prime sunset view. The *Tavsternia* taverna also commands stunning panoramic views and there are a few café-bars perched above the turning for **Órmos Isterníon**, a comparatively small but overdeveloped beach.

Five daily buses along this route finish up at **PÝRGOS**, a few kilometres further north and smack in the middle of the island's marble-quarrying district. A beautiful village, its local artisans are renowned throughout Greece for their skill in producing marble ornamentation; ornate fanlights and bas-relief plaques crafted here adorn houses throughout Tínos. Pýrgos is also home to the School of Arts, and the **museum of Tinian artists** (daily 10.30am–1.30pm & 5.30–7pm; €2, ticket also valid for Yiannoulis Halepas Museum) contains numerous representative works from some of the island's finest artists. Nearby, the **Yiannoulis Halepas Museum** (same hours and ticket) is devoted exclusively to the work of the artist who was born in this home and who is generally recognized as the most important Neoclassical Greek sculptor. There are two *kafenía* and the excellent *Ta Myronia* **taverna** on the attractive shady platía. Pýrgos is popular in summer, and if you want to stay there are some new **studios** for rent on the main road coming into the village; alternatively, ask the locals on the platía.

The marble products were once exported from **PÁNORMOS** harbour, 4km northeast, which has a tiny, commercialized beach, a few tavernas and cafés, and some good-value accommodation at *Elena* (☏22830 31694; ❸) right on the waterfront. Better is **Rohári** beach on the northwest side of the bay, accessible by foot or *kaïki*, with its deep clear waters and massive waves. The tiny island it faces is called Planítis, "the Planet".

Around Exóbourgo

The ring of villages around **Exóbourgo** mountain is another focus of interest on Tínos. The fortified pinnacle itself (570m), with ancient foundations as well as the ruins of three Venetian churches and a fountain, is reached by steep steps from **XINÁRA** (near the island's major road junction), the seat of the island's Roman Catholic bishop. Most villages in north central Tínos have mixed populations, but Xinára and its immediate neighbours are purely Catholic; the inland villages also tend to have a more sheltered position, with better farmland nearby – the Venetians' way of rewarding converts and their descendants. Yet **TRIPÓTAMOS**, just south of Xinára, is a completely Orthodox village with possibly the finest architecture in this region – and has accordingly been pounced on by foreigners keen to restore its historic properties.

At **LOUTRÁ**, the next community north of Xinára, there's an Ursuline convent and a good **folk art museum** (summer only, daily 10.30am–3.30pm; free) in the old Jesuit monastery; to visit, leave the bus at the turning for Skaládho. From Krókos, 1km northwest of Loutrá, which has a scenically situated taverna, it's a forty-minute walk via Skaládho to **VÓLAKAS** (also transliterated as Vólax), one of the most remote villages on the island, a windswept oasis surrounded by bony rocks. Here, half a dozen elderly Catholic basketweavers fashion some of the best examples in Greece. There is a small **folklore museum** (free) which you have to ask the lady living in the house opposite the entrance to open, and the charming outdoor Fontaine Theatre which in August hosts visiting theatre groups from all over Greece. Accommodation is hard to come by, but there are a couple of places to eat, including the recommended *O Rokos* and *I Volax* **tavernas**.

At Kómi, 5km beyond Krókos, you can take a detour for **KOLYMBÍTHRA**, a magnificent double beach: one part wild, huge and windswept (temporary residence to pink flamingos migrating to Africa during May), the other sheltered and with a couple of tavernas including *Kolibithra Beach* (☎22830 51213), which also has rooms (❹). The bus to Kallóni goes on to Kolymbíthra twice a day in season; out of season you'll have to get off at Kómi and walk 4km.

From either Skaládho or Vólakas you go on to Koúmaros, where another long stairway leads up to Exóbourgo, or skirt the pinnacle towards the agricultural villages of **FALATÁDHOS** and **STENÍ**, which appear as white speckles against the fertile Livádha valley. Falatádhos has a number of whitewashed churches, the most notable of which is **Áyios Ioánnis** for its marble decoration. There is also a **house of exhibitions** (changing hours; free), which shows contemporary art in summer. The village has a number of excellent restaurants including *Lefkes* taverna and *To Katoï*, specializing in grilled dishes. From Stení, which has fewer amenities but plenty of postcard-perfect whitewashed buildings to admire, you can catch the bus back to the harbour (7 daily). On the way down, try to stop off at one of the beautiful settlements just below the important twelfth-century **convent of Kekhrovouníou**, where Ayía Pelayía had her vision. Particularly worth visiting are **Triandáros** and **Dhýo Horiá**, which has a fine main square where cave-fountains burble. If you have your own transport, there are quite wide and fairly negotiable tracks down to some lovely secluded bays on the east of the island from the area of Stení. One such is **Sánta Margaríta**; given the lack of tourist development here, it's a good idea to take something to drink.

This is hardly an exhaustive list of Tiniot villages; armed with a map and good walking shoes for tackling the many old trails that still exist, you could spend days within sight of Exóbourgo and never pass through the same hamlets twice. Take warm clothing out of season, especially if you're on a scooter, since the forbidding mountains behind Vólakas and the Livadhéri plain keep things noticeably cool.

Mýkonos

Originally visited only as a stop on the way to ancient Delos, **Mýkonos** has become easily the most popular (and the most expensive) of the Cyclades. Boosted by direct air links with Britain and domestic flights from Athens, it sees more than a million tourists pass through in a good year (half of them in August alone), producing some spectacular overcrowding in high summer on Mýkonos's 75 square kilometres. But if you don't mind the crowds, or you come in the shoulder season, the prosperous capital is still one of the most beautiful of all island towns, its immaculately whitewashed houses concealing hundreds of little churches, shrines and chapels.

The sophisticated nightlife is pretty hectic, amply stimulated by Mýkonos's former reputation as *the* gay resort of the Mediterranean – a title that has been surrendered to Sitges in Spain. Today, gay tourists are well in the minority on the island until September, when the gay clientele is present in full force. The locals (more than 10,000 at last estimate, more than half of them Albanian immigrants) take it all in their stride, ever conscious of the important revenue generated by their laissez-faire attitude. When islanders first opened up to the artsy tourists who began appearing on Mýkonos in the 1960s, they assumed their eccentric visitors were sharing cigarettes due to lack of funds. Since then,

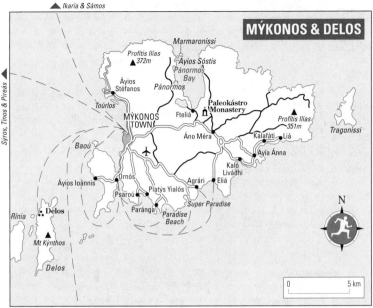

Marmaroníssi
Profítis Ilías
▲372m
Áyios Sóstis
Pánormos
Bay
Áyios
Stéfanos
Pánormos
Toúrlos
Paleokástro
Monastery
MÝKONOS
TOWN
Fteliá
Profítis Ilías
351m ▲
Tragoníssi
Áno Méra
Kalafáti Liá
Baoú
Áyia Ánna
Kaló
Livádhi
Áyios Ioánnis
Órnos
Agrári
Eliá
Psaroú
Platýs Yialós
Parángá
Super Paradise
Rínia
Délos
Paradise
Beach
Mt Kýnthos
Délos
N
0   5 km

a lot of the innocence has evaporated, and the island certainly isn't unspoilt, but Mýkonos does offer excellent (if busy) beaches, picturesque windmills and a rolling arid interior. Best of all, the well-organized local tourist industry does everything in its power to see that beaches are more cared for and that transportation runs more frequently than on most neighbouring islands. A local ban on the construction of large international chain restaurants and hotels has done much to preserve the landscape, as does the presence of the second-largest biological cleaning plant in Greece.

Mýkonos Town and around

Don't let the crowds put you off exploring **MÝKONOS TOWN**, the archetypal postcard image of the Cyclades. Its sugar-cube buildings are stacked around a cluster of seafront fishermen's dwellings, with every nook and cranny scrubbed and shown off. Most people head out to the beaches during the day, so early morning or late afternoon are the best times to wander the maze of narrow streets. The labyrinthine design was intended to confuse the pirates who plagued Mýkonos in the eighteenth and early nineteenth centuries, and it still has the desired effect.

Arrival, information and accommodation

There is some accommodation information at the recently expanded **airport** (3km southeast of town) and at the **new port** where large cruise ships dock (a few kilometres north of town in Toúrlos), but unless you know where you're going it's easier to take a bus or taxi into town, and sort things out there. The vast majority of visitors arrive by ferry at the **jetty** at the north end of town, where a veritable horde of room-owners pounces on the newly arrived. The scene is actually quite intimidating, so it is far better to go 100m further,

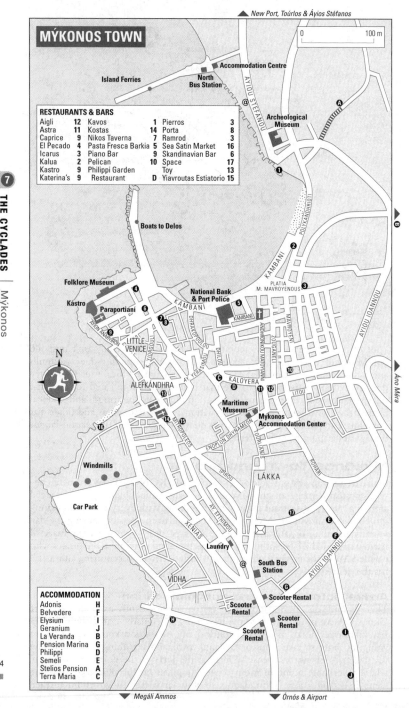

▲ New Port, Toúrlos & Áyios Stéfanos

MÝKONOS TOWN

0   100 m

Accommodation Centre

Island Ferries

North
Bus Station

AYIOU STEFANOU

Archeological
Museum

POLYKANDHRIOTI

RESTAURANTS & BARS

Aigli	12	Kavos	1	Pierros	3
Astra	11	Kostas	14	Porta	8
Caprice	9	Nikos Taverna	7	Ramrod	3
El Pecado	4	Pasta Fresca Barkia	5	Sea Satin Market	16
Icarus	3	Piano Bar	9	Skandinavian Bar	6
Kalua	2	Pelican	10	Space	17
Kastro	9	Philippi Garden		Toy	13
Katerina's	9	Restaurant	D	Yiavroutas Estiatorio	15

Boats to Delos

KAMBANI

PLATIA
M. MAVROYENOUS

Folklore Museum

Kástro

Paraportiani

National Bank
& Port Police

KAMBANI

DIRAKOPOULOU

KAMBANI

AYIOU ANARYRON

MAVROYENI

ZOUGANELI

ANDRONIKOU MATOYIANNI

AYIOU IOANNOU

Ano Méra

LITTLE
VENICE

DHLOU

AY. YERASIMOU

KALOYERA

ALEFKÁNDHRA

Maritime
Museum

Mýkonos
Accommodation Center

LITOU

IOULANIS

ENOPLON DHYNAMEON

METROPOLEOS

MITROPOLEOS

LÁKKA

RODARI

Windmills

TPIROU

Car Park

AY. EFTHIMIOU

XENIAS

Laundry

South Bus
Station

AYIOU IOANNOU

Scooter
Rental

Scooter
Rental

VÍDHA

Scooter
Rental

Scooter
Rental

ACCOMMODATION

Adonis	H
Belvedere	F
Elysium	I
Geranium	J
La Veranda	B
Pension Marina	G
Philippi	D
Semeli	E
Stelios Pension	A
Terra Maria	C

▼ Megáli Ammos   ▼ Órnós & Airport

where a row of offices deals with official hotels, rented rooms and camping information, or go into the heart of town to the extremely helpful Mykonos Accommodation Center (☎22890 23160, ⓦwww.mykonos-accommodation .com) on Énóplon Dhynaméon near the Maritime Museum.

The **north bus station** for Toúrlos, Áyios Stéfanos, Eliá and Áno Méra is located by the old ferry landing, whilst past the dull central Polikandhrioti beach, at the other end of town, the **south bus station** serves the beaches to the south. Also here is the **post office**, Olympic Airways office and several **motorbike rental** agencies, along with a host of **Internet** cafés, among the best being Internet World. Buses to all the most popular beaches and resorts run frequently until the early hours. **Taxis**, of which there are only 32 on the island, run from Platía Mavroyénous on the seafront and from the south bus station, and their rates are fixed and quite reasonable; try Mykonos Radio Taxi (☎22890 22400). Be aware that some taxi drivers may try and get you to pay the full fare per person; this is not legal, and you should refuse. There are countless advertiser-based tourist **publications** circulating throughout Mýkonos during high season, the best of which is the free *Mykonos Sky Map*, available from most agents and hotels.

Catamaran and ferry tickets are sold at several separate and uncooperative **travel agencies** on the harbour front. Check out the various possibilities, and if your boat leaves from the new port, catch the bus up from the old ferry landing across from the Eurobank.

Accommodation

Accommodation prices in Mýkonos rocket in the high season to a greater degree than almost anywhere else in Greece. For this reason, it may well be worth considering **camping** in high season – there are two campsites; both will rent out tents, or even sell them for €25, should you get stuck. *Mykonos Camping* (☎22890 24578, ⓦwww.mycamp.gr) above Paránga beach is smaller and has a more pleasant setting than nearby *Paradise Camping* on Paradise Beach (☎22890 22129, ⓦwww.paradisemykonos.com). However, the latter also has bungalows (❺). Both are packed in season, and dance music from the 24-hour bars on Paradise beach makes sleep difficult. Hourly bus services to Paránga and Paradise beaches continue into the early hours but can get overcrowded.

Adonis Near the waterfront, south of town ☎22890 22434, ⓦwww.mykonosadonis.gr. Beautiful hotel in the Vídha area, with views of the windmills from some of its nicely appointed rooms. ❼

Belvedere Off Ayíou Ioánnou ☎22890 25122, ⓦwww.belvederehotel.com. Upmarket hotel with stunning rooms, views and a pool, in a quiet area of town. It even has its very own swanky Japanese restaurant, *Matsuhisa*. ❼

Elysium On hillside south of town ☎22890 23952, ⓦwww.elysiumhotel.com. Almost exclusively gay hotel with beautiful views, boasting a poolside bar that's also a popular setting for a late-afternoon cocktail. ❼

Geranium On hillside south of town ☎22890 24620, ⓦwww.geraniumhotel.com. Very stylish gay hotel with rooms, studios and a villa. Pool and

bar with nude sunbathing area if you're beautiful enough. ❼

La Veranda On hillside east of town. ☎22890 23670, ⓔlaveranda@panafonet.gr. A laid-back, upmarket hotel with rooms set around a small pool. ❼

Pension Marina Off Ayíou Ioánnou ☎22890 24960, ⓔmarina@mykonos-web.com. Nice neat rooms arranged around courtyard in a quiet spot to the south of town. ❺

Philippi Kaloyéra 25 ☎22890 22294, ⓔchriko@otenet.gr. Clean, comfortable en-suite rooms set around a quiet garden right in the middle of the bustling old town. ❺

Semeli Off Ayíou Ioánnou ☎22890 27466, ⓦwww.semelihotel.gr. Pricey, luxurious hotel above town with pool, whirlpool and very tastefully decorated rooms. ❽

Stelios Pension Above the old port ☎ 22890 24641, ⓕ 22890 26779. Excellent-value en-suite rooms in prime location, but still away from the bustle of town. Take the steps leading up from the OTE office. ❺

Terra Maria Kaloyéra 18 ☎ 22890 24212, ⓔ tertaxma@otenet.gr. Contemporary hotel with cool, clean rooms with balconies. Central, but remains nice and peaceful. ❻

The Town

Getting lost in the convoluted streets and alleys of town is half the fun of exploring Mýkonos, although there are a few places worth seeking out. Coming from the ferry quay you'll pass the **archeological museum** (Tues–Sun 8.30am–3pm; €2) on your way into town, which displays some good Delos pottery; the town also boasts a **maritime museum** displaying various nautical artefacts, including a lighthouse re-erected in the back garden (Tues–Sun 10.30am–1pm & 6.30–9pm; €3). Next door is **Lena's House** (Mon–Sat 6–9pm, Sun 5–7pm; free), a completely restored and furnished middle-class home from the nineteenth century. At the base of the Delos jetty, the **folklore museum** (Mon–Sat 5.30–8.30pm, Sun 6.30–8.30pm; free), housed in an eighteenth-century mansion, crams in a larger-than-usual collection of bric-a-brac, including a vast four-poster bed. The museum shares the same promontory as the old Venetian *kástro*, the entrance to which is marked by Mýkonos's oldest and best-known church, **Paraportianí**, which is a fascinating asymmetrical hodgepodge of four chapels amalgamated into one.

The shore leads to the area known as **Little Venice** because of its high, arcaded Venetian houses built right up to the water's edge. Together with the adjoining **Alefkándhra** district, this is a dense area packed with art galleries, trendy bars and discos. Away from the seafront, behind Platía Alefkándhra, are Mýkonos's two **cathedrals**: Roman Catholic and Greek Orthodox. Beyond, the famous **windmills** look over the area, a little shabby but ripe for photo opportunities. South of here, sleepier **Vídha**, which runs along a tiny beach, has seen the recent arrival of accommodation spilling over from the rest of town.

Eating

Even **light meals** and **snacks** are expensive in Mýkonos, but there are several bakeries, supermarkets and fruit stalls, some concentrated near the south bus station. The area around Alefkándhra is a promising place to head for a full **meal**, whilst if you're looking for late-night coffee, try *Kavos*, open 24 hours right by the town beach.

Kostas Mitropoleos. Friendly taverna near Little Venice, with competitive prices, and a good wine list including barrelled wine (not easily found on Mýkonos).
Nikos Taverna near the port at Little Venice. One of the most famous restaurants on the island. Every inch of its terrace is packed with customers, which can have a detrimental effect on service.
Pasta Fresca Barkia near the beach. Lively pizzeria on the waterfront; a great spot for people-watching.
Pelican off Kaloyéra. Popular taverna serving Greek staples and good pasta dishes. Not the cheapest, but has one of the nicest settings on a vine-covered platía.
Philippi Garden Restaurant Kaloyéra. Exclusive restaurant in romantic setting serving home-grown vegetarian food, as well as superb seafood and traditional local dishes.
Sea Satin Market below the windmills. Expensive, beautifully located restaurant right on the water with excellent seafood and grills, and a clubby vibe after midnight.
Yiavroutas Estiatorio Mitropoleos. Small, unpretentious, family-run place serving excellent-value Greek dishes and good barrelled wine. Also open most of the night, if you're in need of fuel.

Gay nightlife

Although there are no huge gay clubs on Mýkonos, there is a good batch of excellent, comparatively laid-back bars, both for dancing and drinking, in town, and bar-hopping is definitely the way to go. The *Piano Bar*, with fun cabaret acts, is a very good place to warm up, as is nearby *Toy*, which has great drinks. *Porta*, near *Nikos Taverna*, is a lively place to head to as the evening gets going. Things inevitably end up on the other side of town on the platía where seemingly hundreds of men gather outside around dancing bars *Ramrod*, *Icarus*, and the legendary *Pierros*, that's been on the go here since the 1960s.

Nightlife

Nightlife in town is every bit as good as it's cracked up to be – and every bit as pricey. Those looking for a cheap drink should head for to the *Skandinavian Bar* which thumps out dance music and good cocktails until the early hours. For something a bit more sophisticated, try *Aigli* and *Astra*, two chic cafés by day that turn clubby by night; or head to the bars that line Andhroníkou Matoyiánni and Enóplon Dhynaméon, collectively referred to by some as "Fifth Avenue" for the nightly fashion parade along its cobblestone catwalk. A slightly more low-key vibe happens in Little Venice's *Katerina's*, *Caprice*, *Piano Bar* and *Kastro*; or you could try the stylish lounge-style clubs along the waterfront including *El Pecado* and *Kalua*.

For out-and-out dancing, *Space*, on Lákka square, is the largest club on the island. *Cavo Paradiso* (Ⓦwww.cavoparadiso.gr), near *Paradise Camping*, however, is the after-hours club where die-hard party animals of all persuasions come together, often united by world-famous DJs.

The beaches

The closest **beaches** to town are those to the north, at **Toúrlos** (only 2km away but horrid) and **Áyios Stéfanos** (3km, much better), both developed resorts and connected by a very regular bus service to Mýkonos Town. There are tavernas and rooms to let (as well as package hotels) at Áyios Stéfanos, away from the beach; *Mocambo Lido* taverna at the far end of the bay has a pleasant setting and good food.

Other nearby destinations include southwest peninsula resorts, with undistinguished beaches tucked into pretty bays. The nearest to town, 1km away, is **Megáli Ámmos**, a good beach backed by flat rocks and pricey rooms, but nearby Kórfos bay is disgusting, thanks to the town dump and machine noise. Buses serve **Ornós**, an average beach, and **Áyios Ioánnis**, a dramatic bay with the new super-deluxe *St John Hotel* (Ⓣ22890 28752, Ⓦwww.saintjohn.gr; ❽) and a tiny, stony beach, which achieved its moment of fame as a location for the film *Shirley Valentine*.

The south coast is the busiest part of the island. *Kaïkia* ply from town to all of its beaches, which are still regarded to some extent as family strands by the Greeks. You might begin with **Platýs Yialós**, 4km south of town, though you won't be alone: one of the longest-established resorts on the island, it's not remotely Greek any more, the sand is monopolized by hotels, and you won't get a room to save your life between June and September. **Psaroú**, next door to the west, is very pretty – 150m of white sand backed by foliage and calamus reeds, crowded with sunbathers. Here you'll find *N'Ammos*, an elegant fish **restaurant** on the waterfront. Other beach facilities include a diving club (see box on p.610), waterskiing and windsurfer rental, but again you'll need to reserve well in advance to secure **rooms** between mid-June and mid-September. Try *Soula Rooms* (T22890 22006, Wwww.soula-rooms.gr; ❺), a surprisingly calm property on the beach.

Just over the headland to the east of Platýs Yialós is **Paránga beach**, actually two beaches separated by a smaller headland, the first of which has a decent taverna with some basic rooms and is quieter than its noisy neighbour, which is home to a loud beach bar and *Mykonos Camping* (see p.645). A dusty footpath beyond Platýs Yialós crosses the fields and caves of the headland across the clifftops past Paránga, and drops down to **Paradise beach**, a crescent of golden sand that is packed in season. Here, as on many of Mýkonos's most popular beaches, it can be difficult to find an opening big enough to fit a towel, and what little space you manage to find clear of people is likely to be taken up by straw umbrellas, which can be rented (usually along with two accompanying loungers) for about €5. Behind the beach are shops, self-service restaurants and the noisy 24-hour beach bars of *Paradise Camping*. The next bay east contains **Super Paradise** (officially "Plindhrí") beach, accessible by footpath or by *kaïki*. One of the most fun beaches on the island, it has a decent taverna and two bars at opposite ends of the beach pumping out cheesy summer hits. One half of the beach is very mixed, getting progressively more gay as you walk away from where the *kaïkia* dock towards the beach bar perched in the hills, below which the beach is almost exclusively gay and nudist.

One of the best beaches on Mýkonos is **Eliá**, the last port of call for the *kaïkia*. A broad, sandy stretch with a verdant backdrop, it's the longest beach on the island, though split in two by a rocky area, and almost exclusively gay late in the season. To retreat from the crowds, follow the bare rock footpath over the spur (look for the white house) at the end of the beach that cuts upwards for grand views east and west and then winds down to **Kaló Livádhi** (seasonal bus service), a stunning beach adjoining an agricultural valley scattered with little farmhouses; even here there's a restaurant (a good one at that) at the far end of the beach. **Ayía Ánna**, further on, boasts a shingle beach and taverna, with the cliffs above granting some fine vistas. **Kalafáti**, still further east, is more of a tourist community, its white-sand beach supporting a few hotels, restaurants and a disco. There's a local bus service from here to Áno Méra (see below), or you can jump on an excursion boat to **Tragoníssi**, the islet just offshore, for spectacular coastal scenery, seals and wild birds. The rest of the east coast is more difficult to reach: there are some small beaches, really only worth the effort if you crave solitude, and the region is dominated by the peak of Profítis Ilías, sadly spoilt by a huge radar dome and military establishment. **Liá**, roughly 12km east of Eliá, is smaller but delightful, with bamboo windbreaks and clear water, plus another good taverna.

The **north coast** suffers persistent battering from the *meltémi*, plus tar and litter pollution, and for the most part is bare, brown and exposed. **Pánormos Bay** is the exception to this, with the lovely, relatively sheltered beaches of **Pánormos** and **Áyios Sóstis** along its western edge. Despite a good restaurant, a relaxed beach bar and the rather conspicuous *Albatros Club Hotel* (T22890 25130, Wwww.albatros-mykonos.com; ❻) on Pánormos, these beaches remain the least crowded on the island, and although they are not served by buses, they are becoming increasingly popular.

Áno Méra

From Pánormos Bay, it's an easy walk to the only other settlement of any size on the island, **ÁNO MÉRA**, where you should be able to find a **room**. The village prides itself on striving to maintain a traditional way of life, although the result is rather pseudo and wishy-washy: the so-called traditional *kafenío* has long since ditched Greek coffee for cappuccino and traditional sweets for "ice-cream special". There are, however, several acceptable **restaurants** on the platía, of which *Daniele at Basoulas* is currently the most popular for its wide range of Mediterranean dishes; you'll also find a large **hotel** here, the upmarket, if ageing, *Ano Mera* (℡22890 71215, ℻22890 71276; ❼). The red-roofed church near the square is the sixteenth-century **monastery of Panayía Tourlianí**, where a collection of Cretan icons and the unusual eighteenth-century marble baptismal font are worth seeing. It's not far, either, to the late twelfth-century **Paleokástro monastery** (also known as **Dárga**), just north of the village, in a magnificent green setting on an otherwise barren slope. To the northwest are more of the same dry and wind-buffeted landscapes, though they do provide some enjoyable, rocky walking with expansive views across to neighbouring islands.

Delos (Dhílos)

The remains of **ancient Delos**, Pindar's "unmoved marvel of the wide world", though skeletal and swarming now with lizards and tourists, give some idea of the past grandeur of this sacred isle a few sea-miles west of Mýkonos. The ancient town lies on the west coast on flat, sometimes marshy ground that rises in the south to **Mount Kýnthos**. From the summit – an easy walk – there's a magnificent view across the Cyclades.

The first excursion boats to Delos leave the small port near the west end of Mýkonos harbour daily at 8.30am (€7 round trip), except Mondays when the site is closed. You have to return on the same boat, but in season each does the trip several times and you can choose what time you leave. The last return is usually about 3pm, and you'll need to arrive early if you want to make a thorough tour of the site. In season a daily *kaïki* makes return trips from the beaches (€10) with pick-up points at Platýs Yialós and Órnos, but only allows you three hours on the island. Check ahead with operators of Delos excursion boats or look for posters advertising evening concerts and other special performances that occasionally animate the ancient site in season.

Some history

Delos's ancient fame was due to the fact that Leto gave birth to the divine twins Artemis and Apollo on the island, although its fine harbour and central position did nothing to hamper development. When the Ionians colonized the island around 1000 BC it was already a cult centre, and by the seventh century BC it had become the commercial and religious centre of the **Amphictionic League**. Unfortunately Delos also attracted the attention of Athens, which sought dominion over this prestigious island; the wealth of the Delian Confederacy, founded after the Persian Wars to protect the Aegean cities, was harnessed to Athenian ends, and for a while Athens controlled the Sanctuary of Apollo. Athenian attempts to "purify" the island began with a decree that no one could die or give birth on Delos – the sick and the pregnant were taken to the islet of Rínia – and culminated in the simple expedient of banishing the native population.

Delos reached its peak in the third and second centuries BC, after being declared a free port by its Roman overlords. In the end, though, its undefended

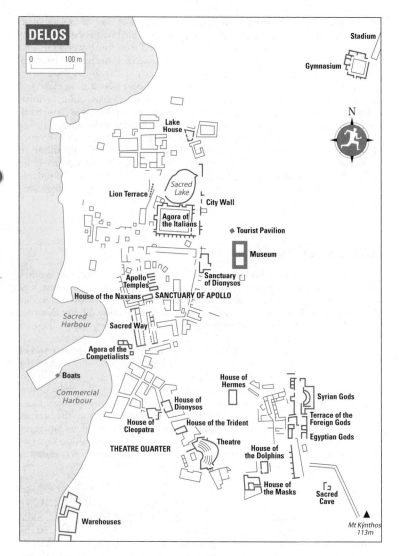

wealth brought ruin: first Mithridates (88 BC) then Athenodorus (69 BC) plundered the treasures and the island never recovered. By the third century AD, Athens could not even sell it, and for centuries every passing seafarer stopped to collect a few prizes.

The site

As you land at **the site** (Tues–Sun 8.30am–3pm; €5), the Sacred Harbour is on your left, the Commercial Harbour on your right and straight ahead lies the **Agora of the Competialists**. Competialists were Roman merchants or freed slaves who worshipped the Lares Competales, the guardian spirits of crossroads; offerings to Hermes would once have been placed in the middle of the agora, their position now marked by a round and a square base. The **Sacred Way** leads north from the far left corner; it used to be lined with statues and the grandiose monuments of rival kings. Along it you reach three marble steps leading into the **Sanctuary of Apollo**; much was lavished on the god, but the forest of offerings has been plundered over the years. On your left is the Stoa of the Naxians, while against the north wall of the House of the Naxians, to the right, a huge statue of Apollo stood in ancient times. In 417 BC the Athenian general Nikias led a procession of priests across a bridge of boats from Rínia to dedicate a bronze palm tree; when it was later blown over in a gale it took the statue with it. Three **Temples of Apollo** stand in a row to the right along the Sacred Way: the Delian Temple, that of the Athenians and the Porinos Naos, the earliest of them, dating from the sixth century BC. To the east towards the museum you pass the **Sanctuary of Dionysos**, with its marble phalluses on tall pillars.

The best finds from the site are in Athens, but the **museum** (same hours; included in the price) still justifies a visit, if only to see the famous **lions**, their lean bodies masterfully executed by Naxians in the seventh century BC to ward off intruders who would have been unfamiliar with the fearful creatures. Of the original nine, three have disappeared and one − captured by Venetians in the seventeenth century − adorns the Arsenale in Venice. To the north stands a wall that marks the site of the **Sacred Lake** where Leto gave birth, clinging to a palm tree, guarded by excellent reproductions of the lions. On the other side of the lake is the City Wall, built in 69 BC − too late to protect the treasures.

Set out in the other direction from the Agora of the Competialists and you enter the residential area, known as the **Theatre Quarter**. Many of the walls and roads remain, but there is none of the domestic detail that brings other such sites to life. Some colour is added by the mosaics: one in the House of the Trident, and better ones in the House of the Masks, most notably a vigorous portrayal of Dionysos riding on a panther's back. The theatre itself seated 5500 spectators, and, though much ravaged, offers some fine views. Behind the theatre, a steep path leads past the Sanctuaries of the Foreign Gods and up Mount Kýnthos for spectacular views back down over the ruins and out to the surrounding Cyclades.

Sýros

Don't be put off by first impressions of **Sýros**. From the ferry it can seem vaguely industrial, but away from the Neório shipyard things improve quickly. Very much a working island with only a relatively recent history of tourism, it is among the most Greek of the Cyclades and the most populous island in the group. It might also come as a refreshing change from its more touristic neighbours. Of course, outsiders do come to the island − in fact there's a thriving permanent foreign community − and the beaches are hardly undeveloped, but everywhere there's the underlying assumption that you're a guest of an inherently private people.

Ermoúpoli

The main town and port of **ERMOÚPOLI** is one of the most striking in the Cyclades. A UNESCO World Heritage Site, it possesses an elegant collection of grand town houses which rise majestically from the bustling, café-lined

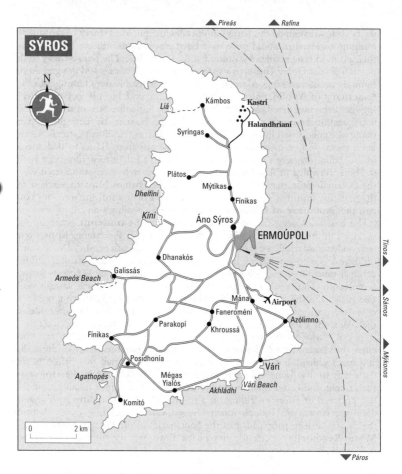

▲ Pireás   ▲ Rafína

SÝROS

Tinos ►
Sámos ►
Mýkonos ►

▼ Páros

waterfront. The town was founded during the War of Independence by refugees from Psará and Híos, and grew in importance to become Greece's chief port in the nineteenth century. Although Pireás outstripped it long ago, Ermoúpoli is still the largest town in the Cyclades, and the archipelago's capital. Medieval Sýros was largely a Catholic island, but an influx of Orthodox refugees during the War of Independence created two distinct communities; now almost equal in numbers, the two groups today still live in their respective quarters occupying two hills that rise up from the sea. They do, however, commonly celebrate each others' festivals, lending a vibrant mix of culture that gives the island its colour.

Arrival, information and accommodation

Sýros is a major crossover point on the ferry-boat routes, and most people arrive by boat to be met by the usual horde of locals offering rooms. There is no bus service from the airport, and you will have to take a taxi (☎22810 86222). On the waterfront there are several **travel agencies** that sell boat tickets, and you'll also find the **bus station**, **tourist police** and **banks** here. Of the several

motorbike-rental places, Apollon on Andipárou, one block behind the seafront, is recommended. The town's only **Internet café**, *Bizanas*, is on Platía Miaoúli in the base of the town hall.

Accommodation

TeamWork agency (☎22810 83400, ⓦ www.teamwork.gr), on the waterfront, is a useful source of information and is able to help with your accommodation needs. In the summer you might try one of the accommodation kiosks on the waterfront. The accommodation listed overleaf is open all year, unless stated otherwise.

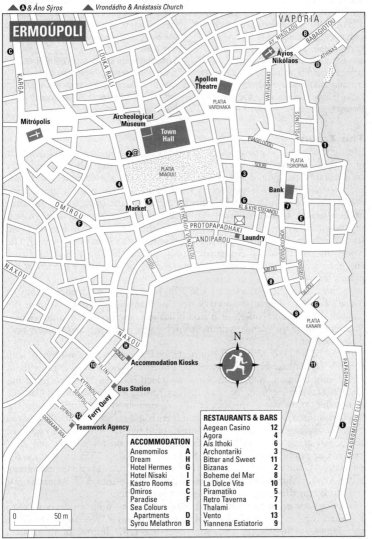

▲ ❹ & *Áno Sýros*   ▲ *Vrondádho & Anástasis Church*

ERMOÚPOLI

VAPÓRIA

Áyios Nikólaos

Apollon Theatre

Archeological Museum

Mitrópolis

Town Hall

PLATIA VARDHAKA

PLATIA MIAOÚLI

PLATIA TSIROPINA

Bank

Market

PROTOPAPADHAKI

ANDIPAROU   Laundry

PLATIA KANARI

N

Accommodation Kiosks

Bus Station

Ferry Quay

Teamwork Agency

ACCOMMODATION

Anemomilos	A
Dream	H
Hotel Hermes	G
Hotel Nisaki	I
Kastro Rooms	E
Omiros	C
Paradise	F
Sea Colours Apartments	D
Syrou Melathron	B

RESTAURANTS & BARS

Aegean Casino	12
Agora	4
Ais Ithoki	6
Archontariki	3
Bitter and Sweet	11
Bizanas	2
Boheme del Mar	8
La Dolce Vita	10
Piramatiko	5
Retro Taverna	7
Thalami	1
Vento	13
Yiannena Estiatorio	9

0   50 m

▼ ⓭, *Neório Shipyard & Southern Villages*

Anemomilos Áno Sýros ☎6944 515366. Deluxe apartment-style lodging in a renovated windmill up in Áno Sýros. **❼**

Dream Off Naxou ☎22810 84356, ⓕ22810 86452. Decent, basic rooms, some with balconies, run by a charming family and situated just back from the waterfront. **❸**

Hotel Hermes Platía Kanári ☎22810 88011, ⓦwww.hermes-syros.com. Smart hotel in a prime location, overlooking the port. All rooms have sea views, and the hotel is also home to a very popular seafront restaurant. **❻**

Hotel Nisaki Papadhám (behind the port authority) ☎22810 88200, ⓦwww.hotelnisaki.gr. Bright, airy, modern hotel with sea views. **❺**

Kastro Rooms Kalomenopóulou 12 ☎22810 88064. Spacious rooms in a beautiful old mansion house near the main square, with access to a communal kitchen. If you're lucky, you'll be treated to some traditional music from owner Markos. **❸**

Omiros Karga, past Mitropolis ☎22810 84910, ⓔomirosho@otenet.gr. One of the most romantic options on Sýros, on a quiet road in the direction of Áno Sýros. Classically styled rooms set in an elegant nineteenth-century mansion built for Tinoan sculptor Vitalis. **❺**

Paradise Omirou ☎22810 83204, ⓦwww .hotel-paradise-syros.com. Clean basic en-suite rooms in a quiet part of town. All rooms have access to a pleasant shaded courtyard, whilst rooms on the top floor have good views. **❸**

Sea Colours Apartments Athinas (book through TeamWork Agency; see p.653). Traditionally decorated apartments for 2–6 people, right next to the peaceful Áyios Nikólaos beach, 5min walk from the main platía. **❹**

Syrou Melathron Babagiotou ☎22810 86495, ⓔsyroumel@otenet.gr. Rather regal hotel set in restored nineteenth-century mansion in a quiet area of town. Has suites as well as spacious rooms, some with sea views. **❼**

The Town

Ermoúpoli itself is worth at least a night's stay, with grandiose buildings a relic of its days as a major port. The long, central **Platía Miaoúli** is named after an admiral of the War of Independence whose statue stands there, and in the evenings the population parades in front of its arcades, while children ride the mechanical animals. Up the stairs to the left of the town hall is the small **archeological museum** (Tues–Sun 8.30am–3pm; free), with three rooms of finds from Sýros, Páros and Amorgós. To the left of the clocktower more stairs climb up to **Vrondádho**, the hill that hosts the Orthodox quarter. The wonderful church of the **Anástasis** stands atop the hill, with its domed roof and great views over Tínos and Mýkonos – if it's locked, ask for the key at the priest's house.

Up from the right of the square you'll find the **Apollon Theatre**, a copy of Milan's La Scala, which occasionally hosts performances. Further on up is the handsome Orthodox church of **Áyios Nikólaos**, and beyond it to the right is **Vapória**, where the island's wealthiest shipowners, merchants and bankers built their mansions.

On the taller hill to the left is the intricate medieval quarter of **Áno Sýros**, with a clutch of Catholic churches below the cathedral of St George. It takes about 45 minutes of tough walking up Omírou, which becomes Karga, to reach this quarter (or a rare bus from the main station), passing the Orthodox and Catholic cemeteries on the way – the former full of grand shipowners' mausoleums, the latter with more modest monuments and French and Italian inscriptions (you can halve the walking time by taking a shortcut onto the stair-street named Andhréa Kárga, part of the way along). There are fine views of the town below, and, close by, the **Cappuchin monastery of St Jean**, founded in 1535 to do duty as a poorhouse. Once up here it's worth visiting the local art and church exhibitions at the Markos **Vamvakaris museum** (daily 10.30am–1pm & 7–10pm; €1.50), and the **Byzantine museum** attached to the monastery.

Heading west from Ermoúpoli, on the road leading from the ferry quay to Kíni, accessible by bus, the **industrial museum** (Mon & Wed–Sun 10am–2pm, also Thurs–Sun 6–9pm; €2.50, Wed free) traces the history of the island's

△ Áyios Nikólaos, Ermoúpoli

ship-building, mining and many other industries through a well-labelled series of artefacts and exhibitions.

Eating

As well as being home to a number of excellent restaurants, there are numerous shops along the waterfront selling *loukoúmia* (Turkish delight), *madoláta* (nougats) and *halvadhópita* (sweetmeat pie) for which the island is famed.

Ais Ithoki Kyr Stefanou. Welcoming taverna on small bougainvillea-covered street, serving traditional local dishes such as fried tomatoes, as well as a good *souvláki*.

Archontariki One block east of main platía. Very popular rustic taverna tucked away on a side street behind the port. Serves local specialities, including a special casserole of mushrooms and ham baked in cheese.

Artemision Áno Sýros. Romantically situated restaurant with some of the best views in town, and a tasty, traditional menu.

La Dolce Vita Filini. One of the best, though not the cheapest, restaurants on the island, it occupies a nice spot on steps leading up Filini near where

the ferries dock. Serves creative Greek fusion cooking; try the chicken and ouzo dish. Closed Sun.

Lilis Áno Sýros. Legendary taverna much beloved by locals, and once frequented by Markos Vamvakaris himself (see below).

Retro Taverna Vorotopoulou. Excellent-value taverna near the main platía serving Greek food with some decent vegetarian options. You'll be treated to *bouzoúki* music most nights too.

Thalami On waterfront off Apollonos. Top-notch seafood restaurant in a splendid nineteenth-century villa right on the water's edge.

Yiannena Estiatorio Platía Kanári. Popular, friendly spot by the water with a French bistro feel. Serves great seafood and other Greek standards.

Nightlife

Sýros still honours its contribution to the development of **rebétika**; *bouzoúki*-great Markos Vamvakaris hailed from here, and a platía in Áno Sýros has been named after him on which there is a tiny, sporadically open **museum** in his honour. **Taverna–clubs**, with music at weekends, now take their place beside a batch of more conventional disco–clubs, and there are several other (often expensive) *bouzoúki* bars scattered around the island, mostly strung along routes to beach resorts (see posters and local press for details). The seafront has a rash of lively **bars** in apparent competition for the title of trendiest, but with little to choose between them.

Aegean Casino Opposite ferry dock. Large casino open till 6am for those who have money to burn (and are sufficiently well dressed).

Agora Platía Miaoúli. Pleasant, relaxed bar and club with garden. Plays an eclectic, ethnic mix of music to a chilled-out crowd.

Bitter and Sweet On waterfront past Platía Kanári. Intimate little club in the old Port Authority building. Open 7 days a week in summer, when a live DJ plays a good range of music to dressed-up people.

Bizanas Platía Miaoúli. Cavernous pool hall right on the platía. Also open for Internet access during the day.

Boheme del Mar On waterfront. Trendy, laid-back bar playing everything from reggae to jazz. A great spot for coffee during the day too.

Piramatiko Platía Miaoúli. Busy, sophisticated bar, playing a loud and varied mix from indie to house.

Vento On road to the airport. Huge dance club about 3km out of town, which gets going with trance and European hits around 4am. Take a taxi or find a friend with a scooter.

Southern Sýros

Buses ply the main loop road south (to Gallissás, Fínikas, Mégas Yialós and Vári) hourly in season, and run until late. First stop, **GALISSÁS**, is fundamentally an agricultural village, but has been taken over since the mid-1980s by backpackers attracted by the island's best **campsite**, *Two Hearts* (☎22810 42052, ⓦwww .twohearts-camping.com). The site has good facilities and sends minibuses to most boats. There is also a surplus of **rooms**, which makes bargaining possible, and a few bona fide hotels, of which the cheapest are *Semíramis* (☎22810 42067, ⓕ22810 43000; ❹) and the excellent *Françoise* (☎22810 42000, ⓦwww.francoise-hotel.com; ❹), though the *Benois* (☎22810 42833, ⓦwww .benois.gr; B&B ❹) is decent value. Among the many **eating** choices, *To Iliovasilema*, next to *Benois*, is an acceptable fish taverna, and *Cavos*, part of a luxury complex, the *Dolphin Bay* Hotel (☎22810 42924, ⓕ22810 42843; ❼), has impressive views overlooking the bay. *Argo* is a great place for live Greek music. Galissás's identity crisis is exemplified by the proximity of bemused, grazing dairy cattle, a heavy-metal music **pub** and upmarket handicraft shops. Still, the locals are welcoming, and if you feel the urge to escape, you can rent a scooter, or walk ten minutes past the headland to the nudist beach of **Armeós**, where there's fresh spring water. Note that buses out can be erratically routed out of season; to be sure of making your connection you must wait at the high-road stop, not down by the beach.

A pleasant forty-minute walk or a ten-minute bus ride south from Galissás brings you to the more mainstream resort of **FÍNIKAS**, purported to have been settled originally by the Phoenicians (although an alternative derivation could be from *fínikas*, meaning "palm tree" in Greek). The **beach** is narrow and gritty, right next to the road but protected to some extent by a row of tamarisk trees; the pick of the **hotels** is the *Cyclades* (☎22810 42255, ⓦwww .hotelcyclades.com; B&B ❹), with an acceptable restaurant just in front, while the *Amaryllis* **rooms** (☎22810 42894, ⓕ22810 43681; ❹) are slightly cheaper. The fish taverna *Barbalias* on the seafront is recommended. *Maistrali Marine*, near the bus stop, has **Internet** access.

Fínikas is separated by a tiny headland from its neighbour **POSIDHONÍA** (or Delagrazzia), a nicer spot with some idiosyncratically ornate mansions and a bright-blue church right on the edge of the village. It's worth walking ten minutes further south, past the naval yacht club and its patrol boat, to **Agathopés**, with a sandy beach and a little islet just offshore. **Komitó**, at the end of the road leading south from Agathopés, is little more than a stony beach fronting an olive grove. **Accommodation** around Posidhonía ranges from the smart *Possidonion* hotel (☎22810 42100, @posidonion@syr.forthnet.gr; ❹) on the seafront to basic rooms inland. *Meltemi*, on the road to Agathopés, is a good seafood **taverna**.

From Posidhonía the road swings east to **MÉGAS YIALÓS**, a small resort below a hillside festooned with brightly painted houses. The long, narrow beach is lined with shady trees and there are pedal boats for hire. Of the **room** set-ups, *Mike and Bill's* (☎22810 43531, ⓦwww.syrosmikeandbill.gr; ❹) is clean and comfortable, whilst the nearby *Alexandra Hotel* (☎22810 42540, ⓦwww .hotelalexandra.gr; ❹), on the bay, enjoys lovely views, and includes breakfast in the price. **VÁRI** is more – though not much more – of a town, with its own small fishing fleet. Beach-goers, generally a younger crowd than on the other beaches, are in a goldfish bowl as it were, with tavernas and **rooms** looming right overhead, but it is the most sheltered of the island's bays, something to remember when the *meltémi* is up. The *Kamelo* hotel (☎22810 61217, ⓕ22810 61117; ❹) provides the best value, while the *En Plo* beach **bar** is a fun spot in season. The adjacent cove of **AKHLÁDHI** is far more pleasant and family-friendly and boasts a small good-value hotel, *Hotel Emily* (☎22810 61400; ❹), on the seafront, and one taverna.

Northen Sýros

Closest to the capital, and a few kilometres north of Galissás, and reached by bus in fifteen minutes (hourly in season), is the twin-beach coastal settlement of **KÍNI**. Good accommodation can be found at the *Sunset Hotel* (☎22810 71211, @enxensyr@otenet.gr; ❹), with the excellent *Zalounis* taverna just below. **Dhelfíni**, just to the north, is also a fine pebbly beach, dramatically accessed on a rather awkward footpath.

Elsewhere, expect potholes, especially further to the north where the land is barren and high, with few villages. The main route north from Áno Sýros is quite easily negotiable by bike, provided you don't mind the hills; en route, the village of **Mýtikas** has a decent taverna just off the road. A few kilometres further on, the road forks, with the left turn leading, after another left, to the small settlement of **Sýringas**, where there's an interesting cave to explore. Straight on leads to **Kámbos**, from where a path leads down to Liá beach; the right fork eventually descends to the northeast coast and the early-Cycladic cemetery at **Halandhrianí**. Most of the finds from the nineteenth-century excavation of the site are now in Athens, though there is still an unexcavated settlement here. On **Kastrí** hill, to the north, are the remains of one of the Cyclades' most ancient fortified habitations dating from the third millennium BC.

Páros and Andíparos

Gently and undramatically furled around the single peak of Profitis Ilías, **Páros** has a little of everything one expects from a Greek island: old villages, monasteries, fishing harbours, a labyrinthine capital, nice beaches and varied nightlife. Parikía, the hóra, is the major hub of inter-island ferry services, so that if you wait long enough you can get to just about any island in the Aegean. However, the island can be touristy and expensive, so it's touch and go when it comes to finding rooms and beach space in August, when the more attractive inland settlements, the port of **Náoussa** and the satellite island of **Andíparos** handle

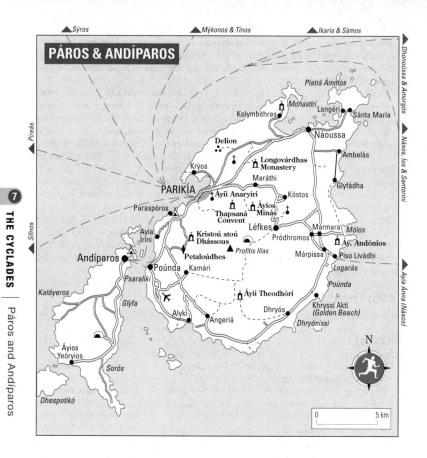

the overflow. The August 15 festival here is one of the best such observances in Greece, with a parade of flare-lit fishing boats and fireworks delighting as many Greeks as foreigners, though it's a real feat to secure accommodation around this time.

Parikía and around

Bustling **PARIKÍA** sets the tone architecturally for the rest of Páros, with its ranks of typically Cycladic white houses punctuated by the occasional Venetian-style building and church domes.

Arrival, information and accommodation

Ferries dock in Parikía by the windmill; the **bus stop** is 100m or so to the right. Bus routes extend to Náoussa in the north, Poúnda (for Andíparos) in the west, Alykí in the south and Dhryós on the island's east coast (with another very useful service between Dhryós and Náoussa). Be aware that there are two places called Poúnda on Páros, one being the west-coast port, the other a beach on the way to Dhryós on the east coast (see p.665). Buses to Náoussa carry on running hourly through the night, while other services stop around midnight.

The **airport** is around 12km south of town, close to Alykí – from where ten daily buses run to Parikía.

Most of the island is flat enough for cycling, though you'll be hard pressed to find any bicycles. **Motorbikes** are more common and are available for rent at several places in town; Forget-Me-Not, along the seafront west of the bus stop, offers a professional and friendly service. Polos Tours, left of the windmill, is one of the more together and friendly **travel agencies**, issuing air tickets when Olympic is shut, and acting as agents for virtually all the boats. Luggage can be left at various travel agents (look for the signs) along the waterfront. There is an excellent **Internet** café, *Memphis*, on the waterfront where you can also burn digital photos to CD.

Continue inland from the **windmill** past the taxi station to reach **Mavroyénous Square**, around which you'll find a maze of houses designed to thwart both the wind and pirates, and the telephone office, police station (and tourist police), banks and Olympic Airways office.

Accommodation

You'll be met off the ferry by locals offering accommodation, even at the most unlikely hours, although you'll have to be quick to grab a room in summer. Most rooms and hotels are to the left of the windmill, and some can be a long walk. Of the two **campsites** nearest to town, *Koula Camping* (℡22840 22081, ⓦwww.campingkoula.gr), along the seafront east of the bus stop, is an acceptable choice for a night or two, whilst *Krios Camping* (℡22840 21705, ⓦwww.krios-camping.gr), across the bay to the north, has a nice beach, a pool and a regular minibus into town. There is a good **hostel**, the *Young Inn*, in Alykí (see p.664).

Argonauta Back of Platía Mavroyénous near the National Bank ℡22840 21440, ⓦwww.argonauta.gr. Friendly hotel with smart, simple rooms arranged around a beautiful courtyard. One of the best deals in town. April–Oct. ❹

Dina just off the old market street ℡22840 21325, ⓦwww.hoteldina.com. Pleasant, central little hotel set in its own gardens in a quiet spot near the market. Open May–Oct. ❹

Festos West of Ekatondapyliani ℡22840 21635, ⓔconsolas@hol.gr. Excellent pension with clean doubles and communal courtyard on a quiet backstreet inland. B&B ❸

Hotel Anna Platanou 500m west of the port ℡22840 21751, ⓦwww.annaplatanou.gr. Smart, family-run property with clean, spacious rooms, on the road towards Cinema Rex. Ten-percent discount for Rough Guide readers. April–Oct. ❺

Kypreou Opposite ferry dock ℡22840 21383. Small family-run hotel with basic en-suite rooms in a prime location across from Ekatondapyliani church. ❹

Mike's Rooms Opposite ferry dock ℡22840 22856. Backpacker-friendly place near the port with clean, comfortable rooms and hospitable staff. ❹

Rena Rooms Behind ancient cemetery ℡22840 22220, ⓦwww.cycladesnet.gr/rena. Spacious doubles and family rooms on a quiet street near the post office. Sea views from the top floor. ❸

Villa Katerina 10 minutes' walk out of town towards Cinema Rex ℡22840 21864, ⓦwww.villakaterina.gr. Bright, family-friendly doubles, studios and apartments in a peaceful location. ❹

The Town

Just beyond the central clutter of the ferry port, to the left (southeast) of the windmill, Parikía has one of the most architecturally interesting churches in the Aegean – the **Ekatondapyliani**, or "The One Hundred Gated". What's visible today was designed and supervised by Isidore of Miletus in the sixth century, but construction was actually carried out by his pupil Ignatius. Legend tells that it was so beautiful on completion that the master, consumed with jealousy, grappled with his apprentice on the rooftop and both of them fell to their deaths. They are portrayed kneeling at the column bases across the courtyard, the old master tugging at his beard in repentance and his rueful pupil clutching a broken head. The church was substantially altered after a severe earthquake in the eighth century, but its essentially Byzantine aspect remains, its shape an imperfect Greek cross. Enclosed by a great wall to protect its icons from pirates, it is in fact three interlocking churches; the oldest, the chapel of Áyios Nikólaos to the left of the apse, is an adaptation of a pagan building dating from the early fourth century BC. To the right of the courtyard, the **Byzantine museum** (daily 9am–9pm; €1.50) displays a collection of icons. Behind Ekatondapyliarí, the **archeological museum** (Tues–Sun 8am–3pm; €2) has a fair collection of antique bits and pieces, its prize exhibits being a fifth-century winged Nike and a piece of the Parian Chronicle, a social and cultural history of Greece up to 264 BC engraved in marble. Nearby are the exposed, excavated ruins of an **ancient cemetery** used from the eighth century BC until the second century AD, and a few hundred metres east of town lies a smattering of **archeological sites** including the ruins of a sculpture and pottery workshop from the Hellenistic period as well as an ancient sanctuary.

These sights apart, the real attraction of Parikía is simply to wander the town itself, especially along the meandering **old market street**. Arcaded lanes lead past Venetian-influenced villas, traditional island dwellings and ornate wall-fountains. The town culminates in a seaward Venetian **kástro**, whose surviving east wall incorporates a fifth-century BC round tower and is constructed using masonry pillaged from a temple of Athena. Part of the temple's base is still visible next to the beautiful, arcaded church of Áyios Konstandínos and Ayía Eléni which crowns the highest point, from where the fortified hill drops sharply to the quay in a series of hanging gardens.

Eating

Most of the **eating** establishments in Parikía are along the waterfront to the right of the windmill. The Parian Products Farmers' Union, near the police station, is a lovely wine and cheese shop perfect for stocking up for a beach picnic, while the Ragousis Bakery, behind the National Bank, is a good place for sandwiches and pastries. For snacks, there is a cluster of fast-food outlets near the ferry dock, whilst hidden in the backstreets, and along the seafront to the west, there are plenty of small crêperies and cafés.

Apollon Off old market street. Set in a converted 1920s olive press on the tiny backstreets near the market, this is one of the island's best restaurants. Considering its popularity, its prices aren't bad.

Cavo D'Oro Livádhia. Italian restaurant with a large choice of pizza and pasta near *Koula Camping*. They also do takeaway.

Ephessus Inland past *Mike's Rooms* (see p.659). Good, bustling taverna serving excellent grills and seafood, and with good meal deals for couples.

Happy Green Cow On side street behind National Bank. Fantastically eclectic vegetarian restaurant. Not cheap, but some of the most imaginative vegetarian cooking around.

Hibiscus On waterfront south of windmill. One of the oldest restaurants on the island, it serves generous-sized, wood-oven-baked pizzas in a great spot overlooking the sea.

Ippocrates On seafront away from ancient cemetery. Great-value taverna specializing in fresh seafood.

Trata Behind ancient cemetery. Family-run taverna serving tasty seafood and grilled meats on a vine-covered patio.

Nightlife

Parikía has a wealth of **pubs**, **bars** and low-key **discos**. The most popular cocktail bars extend along the seafront, mostly to the south of the windmill, tucked into a series of open squares and offering staggered "happy hours", so that you can drink cheaply for much of the evening. There's also a thriving cultural centre, Arhilohos (near Ekatondapyliní), which caters mostly to locals, but which has occasional **film** screenings – there are also two open-air cinemas, Neo Rex and Paros, where foreign films are shown in season.

Alexandros Café Southern end of quay. One of the more grown-up choices for a sophisticated evening drink in a fabulously romantic spot around the base of a windmill.

Alga Quay south of windmill. Hip dance bar further along the bay with outdoor seating and live DJ playing anything from R&B to house to 1970s music.

Black Dog Serenade Quay south of windmill. French-owned bar on the waterfront playing quietly hip music and serving a good gin fizz.

Dubliner/Paros Rock Just off quay. Large, brash dance complex set back from the main drag, comprising four loud bars, a snack section, disco and seating area.

Pebbles Quay south of windmill. Upstairs bar playing classical and lounge music, with good sunset views.

Pirate Bar One block inland from quay. Popular, established jazz and blues bar near the town hall.

Saloon D'Or Quay south of windmill. Rowdy but fun spot on the main drag, with cheap drinks and mainstream music.

Around Parikía

If you're staying in Parikía, you'll want to get out into the surroundings at some stage, if only to the beach. The most rewarding **excursion** is the hour's walk along the road starting just past the museum up to the **Áyii Anáryiri** monastery. Perched on the bluff above town, this makes a great picnic spot, with cypress groves, a gushing fountain and some splendid views.

There are **beaches** immediately north and south of the harbour, though none is particularly attractive when compared with Páros's best. In fact, you might prefer to avoid the northern stretch altogether and head **south** along the asphalt road instead. The first unsurfaced side-track you come to leads to a small, sheltered beach; fifteen minutes further on is **PARASPÓROS**, with an attractively landscaped and relatively quiet **campsite** (T22840 21100) and beach near the remains of an ancient temple to Asklepios, the god of healing and son of Apollo. Continuing for 45 minutes (or a short hop by bus) brings you to arguably the best of the bunch, **AYÍA IRÍNI**, with good sand and a taverna next to a farm and shady olive grove.

In the same direction, but a much longer two-hour haul each way, is **PETA-LOÚDHES**, the so-called "Valley of the Butterflies", a walled-in oasis where millions of Jersey tiger moths perch on the foliage during early summer (June–Sept 9am–8pm; €2). The trip pays more dividends when combined with a visit to the eighteenth-century nunnery of **Khristoú stoú Dhássous**, at the crest of a ridge twenty minutes to the north. Only women are allowed in the sanctuary, although men can get as far as the courtyard. The succession of narrow drives and donkey paths linking both places begins just south of Parikía. Petaloúdhes can be reached from Parikía by bus (in summer), by scooter or on an overpriced excursion by mule.

Náoussa and around

The second port of Páros, **NÁOUSSA**, is a far more attractive choice than Parikía. Although a major resort town, with modern concrete hotels and attendant trappings, it's developed around a charming little port where fishermen still tenderize octopuses by thrashing them against the walls, and you can wander among winding, narrow alleys and simple Cycladic houses. The local **festivals** – an annual Fish and Wine Festival on July 2, and an August 23 shindig celebrating an old naval victory over the Turks – are still celebrated with enthusiasm; the latter tends to be brought forward to coincide with the August 15 festival of the Panayía. Most people are here for the local beaches (see opposite) and the relaxed nightlife; there's really only one attraction, a **museum** (daily 9am–1.30pm & 7–9pm; free) in the monastery of Áyios Athanásios, with an interesting collection of Byzantine and post-Byzantine icons from the churches and monasteries around Náoussa.

The town is noted for its nearby beaches and is a good place to head for as soon as you reach Páros. Because it's newer and more fashionable than Parikía, accommodation is more expensive. Nissiotissa Tours (T22840 51480), off the left side of the main square, can help you find a room, though it specializes in transport. The *Sea House* (T22840 52198; ⑤) on the rocks above Pipéri beach was the first place in Náoussa to let **rooms** and has one of the best locations. Out of season you should haggle for reduced prices at the basic but well-located *Stella* (T22840 51317, Wwww.hotelstella.gr; ③), with rooms arranged around its own garden, several blocks inland from the old harbour. If you don't mind a five-minute climb, family-run *Katerina Rooms* (T22840 51642, Wwww.katerinastudios.gr; ④) have beautiful uninterrupted sea views. Most elegant is the spotlessly cool boutique **hotel** *Heaven* (T22840 51549, Wwww.heaven-naoussa.gr; ⑦), which is also set back away from the harbour. Further along the bay is the peaceful *Captain Dounas* (T22840 52525, Wwww.dounas.com; B&B ⑦), with large family-friendly apartments and pool. There are two **campsites** in the vicinity: the relaxed and friendly *Naoussa* (T22840 51565), out of town towards Kolymbíthres (see p. 000), and the newer *Surfing Beach* complex (T22840 52491-6, Wwww.surfbeach.gr) at Sánta María, northeast of Náoussa, with bungalows as well as a popular beach bar, beach and watersports facilities (see box on p.610); both run courtesy minibuses to and from Parikía.

Most of the harbour **tavernas** are decent, specializing in fresh fish and seafood, though there are more interesting places to eat at along the main road leading inland from just beside the little bridge over the canal. *Glaros*, with good barrelled unresinated wine, and the *Vengera* opposite, stay open until the early hours. There are some excellent **bars** clustered around the old harbour, making bar-hopping easy: *Linardo* and *Agosta* play dance music, whilst *Café del Mar* has

△ Fishermen in Náoussa, Páros

one of the best settings with its busy tables stretching out to the edge of the sea. Nearby *Shark* is another recommended spot. There are several big clubs up from the bus station, including *Vareladikos,* popular with a younger, late-night crowd. Once a week in summer, hordes of people take the 3.30am bus to the Beach Bar at Sánta María Camping for a weekly beach party – keep an eye out for flyers.

Local beaches

Pipéri beach is a couple of minutes' walk west of Náoussa's harbour; there are other good-to-excellent beaches within walking distance, and a summer *kaïki* service to connect them for about €4 round trip. To the west, an hour's hike brings you to **Kolymbíthres** ("Basins"), where there are three tavernas and the wind- and sea-sculpted rock formations from which the place draws its name. A few minutes beyond, **Monastíri** beach, below the abandoned Pródhromos monastery, is similarly attractive, and partly nudist. If you go up the hill after Monastíri onto the rocky promontory, the island gradually shelves into the sea via a series of flattish rock ledges, making a fine secluded spot for diving and snorkelling, as long as the sea is calm. Go northeast and the sands are better still, the barren headland spangled with good surfing beaches. **Langéri** is backed by dunes; the best surfing is at **Sánta María,** a trendy beach connected with Náoussa by road, which also has a couple of tavernas, including the pleasant Aristofanes; and **Platiá Ámmos** perches on the northeastern tip of the island.

The northeast coast and inland

AMBELÁS hamlet marks the start of a longer trek down the **east coast**. Ambelás itself has a good beach, a small taverna and some rooms and hotels, of which the *Hotel Christiana* (☎22840 51573, ℱ22840 52503; ❸) is good value, with great fresh fish and local wine in the restaurant and extremely friendly proprietors. From here a rough track leads south, passing several undeveloped stretches on the way; after about an hour you reach **Mólos beach**, impressive and not particularly crowded. **MÁRMARA,** twenty minutes further on, has rooms to let and makes an attractive place to stay, though the marble that the village is built from and named after has largely been whitewashed over.

If Mármara doesn't appeal, then serene **MÁRPISSA,** just to the south, might – a maze of winding alleys and ageing archways overhung by floral balconies, all clinging precariously to the hillside. *Afendakis* (☎ & ℱ22840 41141; ❷) has clean and modern rooms and furnished apartments (❺), and you can while away a spare hour climbing up the conical Kéfalos hill, on whose fortified summit the last Venetian lords of Páros were overpowered by the Ottomans in 1537. Today the monastery of **Áyios Andónios** occupies the site, but the grounds are locked; to enjoy the views over eastern Páros and the straits of Náxos fully, pick up the key from the priest in Márpissa before setting out (ask in the minimarket of his whereabouts). On the shore nearby, **PÍSO LIVÁDHI** was once a quiet fishing village, but is now dominated by package-holiday facilities; the main reason to visit is to catch a (seasonal) *kaïki* to Ayía Ánna on Náxos. *Hotel Andromache* (☎22840 41387, ℱ22840 41733; ❺) is a good place behind the beach, as is the *Akteon Hotel* (☎22840 41873, ℱ22840 41733; ❺) at the tamarisk-shaded **Logarás beach** next door, or ask at the friendly Perantinos Travel Agency (☎22840 41135) near the bus stop. For a meal try *Vrochas* **taverna,** and head to the *Anchorage* café/bar for afternoon snacks or night-time cocktails. You can catch a (seasonal) *kaïki* to Ayía Ánna on Náxos from here.

Inland

The road runs west from Píso Livádhi back to the capital. A **medieval flag-stoned path** once linked both sides of the island, and parts of it survive in the east between Mármara and the villages around Léfkes. **PRÓDHROMOS**, encountered first, is an old fortified farming settlement with defensive walls girding its nearby monastery, while **LÉFKES** itself, an hour up the track, is perhaps the most beautiful and unspoilt settlement on Páros. The town, whose name means "poplars", flourished from the seventeenth century on, its population swollen by refugees fleeing from coastal piracy; indeed it was the island's hóra during most of the Ottoman period. Léfkes's marbled alleyways and amphitheatrical setting are unparalleled, and also undisturbed by motor-bikes, which are forbidden in the middle of town. The central **church** that dominates the town's landscape is made largely of local marble and contains an impressive collection of icons, though it is most often closed; the views over the hill-hugging cemetery behind it and across the interior to the sea are the most remarkable on the island. Despite the few rooms, a disco (Akrovatis), a taverna on the outskirts and the presence of two oversized hotels – the *Hotel Pantheon* (☎22840 41646, ⓕ22840 41700; ❺), a large 1970s hotel at the top of the village, and *Lefkes Village* (☎22840 41827, ⓦwww.lefkesvillage.gr; ❼), a beautiful hotel on the outskirts, with stunning views – the area around the main square has steadfastly resisted change; the central *kafenío* and bakery observe their siestas religiously, and reserved local residents seem to prefer that tourists remain along the coastal resorts.

Thirty minutes further on, through olive groves, the path reaches **KÓSTOS**, a simple village and a good place for lunch in a taverna. Any traces of path disappear at **MARÁTHI**, on the site of the ancient marble quarries which once supplied much of Europe. Considered second only to Carrara marble, the last slabs were mined here by the French in the nineteenth century for Napoleon's tomb. From Maráthi, it's easy enough to pick up the bus on to Parikía, but if you want to continue hiking, strike south for the monastery of **Áyios Minás**, twenty minutes away. Various Classical and Byzantine masonry fragments are worked into the walls of this sixteenth-century foundation, and the friendly custodians can put you on the right path up to the convent of **Thapsaná**, 4km from Parikía. From here, other paths lead either back to Parikía (two hours altogether from Áyios Minás), or on up to the island's summit for the last word in views over the Cyclades.

The south of the island

There's little to stop for south of Parikía until **POÚNDA**, 6km away, and then only to catch the ferry to Andíparos (see opposite). What used to be a sleepy hamlet is now a concrete jungle, and neighbouring **ALYKÍ** appears to be permanently under construction. The **airport** is close by, making for lots of unwelcome noise; redeeming features include a good-value **hostel**, the *Young Inn* (☎697 64 15 232, ⓦwww.young-inn.com; €8 per bed), and an excellent beachside restaurant, by the large tamarisk tree. The end of the southern bus route is at Angeriá, about 3km inland of which is the **convent of Áyii Theod-hóri**. Its nuns specialize in weaving locally commissioned articles and are further distinguished as *paleomeroloyítes*, or old-calendarites, meaning that they follow the medieval Orthodox (Julian) calendar, rather than the Gregorian one.

Working your way around the **south coast** on foot, there are two routes east to Dhryós. Either retrace your steps to Angeriá and follow the (slightly inland) coastal road, which skirts a succession of isolated coves and small beaches, or keep on across the foothills from Áyii Theodhóri – a shorter walk. Aside from an abundant water supply (including a duck pond) and surrounding orchards, **DHRYÓS** village is mostly modern and characterless, lacking even a well-defined platía. You'd do better to follow the signs to the attractive, and relatively quiet, **Dhryós** beach.

Between here and Píso Livádhi to the north are several sandy coves – Khryssí Aktí ("Golden Beach"), Tzirdhákia, Mezádha, Poúnda (not to be confused with the port of the same name on the opposite coast) and Logarás – prone to pummelling by the *meltémi*, yet all favoured to varying degrees by campers and windsurfers. **KHRYSSÍ AKTÍ** now has many tavernas, room complexes and hotels, such as the *Amaryllis Hotel* right on the beach (T22840 41410, Wwww.amaryllis-hotel-paros.com; ❺); it also offers the whole range of watersports. In addition, there are tavernas at Logarás, but other facilities are concentrated in Dhryós, which is still the focal point of this part of the island.

Andíparos

The secret is definitely out about **Andíparos**. The waterfront is lined with new hotels and apartments, and in high season it can be full, though in recent years families seem to be displacing the young, international crowd. However, the island has managed to hold on to a friendly small-island atmosphere and still has a lot going for it, including good sandy beaches and an impressive cave, and the rooms and hotels are less expensive than on Páros.

Most of the population of eight hundred live in the large low-lying northern **village**, across the narrow straits from Páros, the new development on the outskirts concealing an attractive traditional settlement around the *kástro*. A long, flagstoned pedestrian street forms its backbone, leading from the jetty to the Cycladic houses around the outer wall of the *kástro*, which was built by Leonardo Loredano in the 1440s as a fortified settlement safe from pirate raids – the Loredano coat of arms can still be seen on a house in the courtyard. The only way into the courtyard is through a pointed archway from the platía, where several cafés are shaded by a giant eucalyptus. Inside, more whitewashed houses surround two churches and a cistern built into the surviving base of the central tower.

Andíparos's **beaches** begin right outside town: **Psaralíki**, just to the south with golden sand and tamarisks for shade, is much better than Sifnéïko (aka "Sunset") on the opposite side of the island. Villa development is starting to follow the newly paved road down the east coast, but has yet to get out of hand. **Glýfa**, 4km down, is another good beach and, further south, **Sorós** has rooms and tavernas. On the west coast there are some fine small sandy coves at **Áyios Yeóryios**, the end of the road, and another long stretch of sand at **Kalóyeros**. *Kaïkia* make daily trips round the island and, less frequently, to the uninhabited islet of Dhespotikó, opposite Áyios Yeóryios.

The great **cave** (summer daily 10.45am–3.45pm; €3) in the south of the island is the chief attraction for day-trippers. In these eerie chambers the Marquis de Nointel, Louis XIV's ambassador to Constantinople, celebrated Christmas Mass in 1673 while a retinue of five hundred, including painters, pirates, Jesuits and Turks, looked on; at the exact moment of midnight explosives were detonated to emphasize the enormity of the event. Although electric light and cement steps have diminished its mystery and grandeur, the cave remains impressive. Tour buses (€3 round trip) and public buses (€1 one way) run from the port every hour in season; bus services and opening hours are reduced out of season, and in winter you'll have to fetch the key for the cave from the mayor or village council (T22840 61218).

Practicalities

To get here, you have a choice of **boats** from Parikía (hourly in season, weather permitting; 40min), arriving at the jetty opposite the main street, or the car ferry from Poúnda (every 30min; 10min), arriving 150m to the south.

There are plenty of **hotels** along the waterfront, including *Anargyros* (☎22840 61204; ❸), which has good, basic rooms. More upmarket places to the north of the jetty include *Mantalena* (☎22840 61206; ⓦwww.hotelmantalena.gr; ❹) with large rooms and balconies, and spotless, contemporary *Artemis* (☎22840 61460, ⓦwww.artemisantiparos.com; ❹), while inland there are some cheaper rooms as well as the *Hotel Galini* (☎22840 61420; ❺) to the left of the main street. The popular **campsite** (☎22840 61221) is a ten-minute walk northeast along a track, next to its own nudist beach; the water here is shallow enough for campers to wade across to the neighbouring islet of Dhipló. For peace and quiet with a degree of comfort try *Oliaros* (☎22840 25305, ⓦwww.oliaros.gr; ❹) at Áyios Yeóryios, a long stretch of beach with several tavernas, of which *Captain Pipinos* is recommended.

The best of the waterfront **tavernas** is *Anargyros*, below the hotel of the same name. The main street leads up beside it; *Klimataria*, 100m inland off to the left, has tables in a pleasant garden, though it's only open at night. *The Internet Cafe*, also on the main street, has excellent coffee, as does *Romvi's* on the waterfront. There are plenty of **bars** around the eucalyptus-filled platía, where a festive atmosphere prevails at night. *Café Margarita* is a pleasant street-side hangout on the way up to the platía, while the *Nautica* is probably the liveliest of the water-front spots. For quiet music and views of the mountains try *Yam*, an outdoor restaurant and bar near the *Klimataria*. A **bank**, a **post office**, a cinema and several **travel agents** cluster around the waterfront, and there's a launderette near the windmill. You can rent scooters and **bicycles** at Europcar near the ferry dock.

Náxos

Náxos is the largest and most fertile of the Cyclades, and, with its green and mountainous highland scenery, seems immediately distinct from many of its neighbours. The difference is accentuated by the **unique architecture** of many of the interior villages: the Venetian Duchy of the Aegean, which ruled from the thirteenth to the sixteenth century, left towers and fortified mansions scattered throughout the island, while medieval Cretan refugees bestowed a singular character upon Náxos's eastern settlements.

Today Náxos could easily support itself without tourists by relying on its production of potatoes, olives, grapes and lemons, but it has thrown in its lot with mass tourism, so that parts of the island are now almost as busy as Páros in season. The island certainly has plenty to see if you know where to look: the highest mountains in the Cyclades, intriguing central valleys, a spectacular north coast and marvellously sandy beaches in the southwest. It is also renowned for its wines, cheese – sharp *kefalotýri* and milder *graviéra* – and *kítron*, a sweet liqueur distilled from the fruit of this citrus tree.

Náxos Town

A long causeway, built to protect the harbour to the north, connects the town with the islet of Palátia – the place where, according to legend, Theseus abandoned Ariadne on his way home from Crete. The famous stone **Portára**

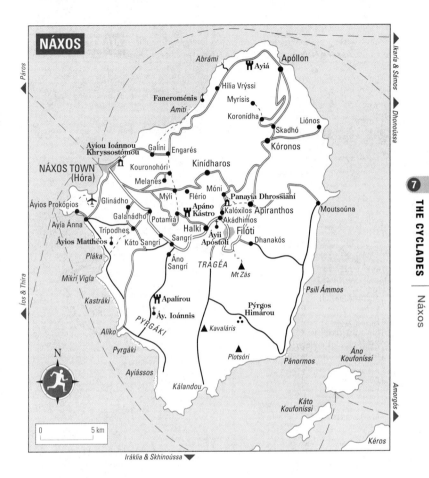

that has greeted visitors for 2500 years is the portal of a temple of Apollo, built on the orders of the tyrant Lygdamis in the sixth century BC, but never completed.

Most of the town's life goes on down by the crowded port esplanade or just behind it; backstreets and alleys lead up through low arches of the old town, Bourgos, to the fortified **kástro** from where Marco Sanudo, the thirteenth-century Venetian who established the Duchy of Archipelago, and his successors ruled over the Cyclades.

Arrival, information and accommodation

Náxos is served by a tiny **airport**, located just a few minutes' bus ride from Náxos Town. Large **ferries** dock along the northerly harbour causeway; all small boats and the very useful Express Skopelitis ferry use the jetty in the fishing harbour, not the main car-ferry dock. The **bus station** is at its landward end; buses run five times a day to Apóllon, with one of the morning services going via Engarés and Abrámi, which is much slower though not any cheaper. There are six buses a day to Apíranthos via Filóti, two of these going on to Moutsoúna

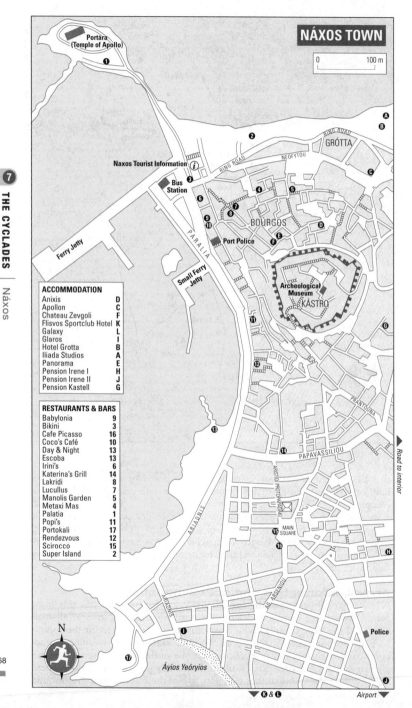

NÁXOS TOWN

0   100 m

Portára
(Temple of Apollo) ❶

ⓐ
ⓑ

❷

RING ROAD

GRÓTTA

NEOFÝTOU

Naxos Tourist Information ⓘ

RING ROAD

ⓒ

Bus
Station ❸

❹
❺

❻
❼
❽
BOÚRGOS

ⓓ

❾
❿

PARALIA

Port Police

ⓕ ⓔ

Ferry Jetty

Small Ferry
Jetty

Archeological
Museum
KÁSTRO

⓫

ⓖ

⓬

FRANTOÚNA

❿⓭

⓮

PAPAVASSILÍOU

Road to interior ▶

ACCOMMODATION

Anixis	D
Apollon	C
Chateau Zevgoli	F
Flisvos Sportclub Hotel	K
Galaxy	L
Glaros	I
Hotel Grotta	B
Iliada Studios	A
Panorama	E
Pension Irene I	H
Pension Irene II	J
Pension Kastell	G

RESTAURANTS & BARS

Babylonia	9
Bikini	3
Cafe Picasso	16
Coco's Café	10
Day & Night	13
Escoba	13
Irini's	6
Katerina's Grill	14
Lakridi	8
Lucullus	7
Manolis Garden	5
Metaxi Mas	4
Palatia	1
Popi's	11
Portokali	17
Rendezvous	12
Scirocco	15
Super Island	2

ARIADNIS

ARISTIDÍ PRÓTOPAPADÁKI

MAIN
SQUARE ⓯
⓰

AG. ARSENÍOU

ⓗ

Police

N

ARIADNIS

⓱

ⓘ

Áyios Yeóryios

ⓙ

▼ Ⓚ & Ⓛ   Airport ▼

on the east coast. Buses run (every 30min 8am–midnight) to Áyios Prokópios, Ayía Ánna and as far as the Pláka campsite on Pláka beach, and four times a day to Pyrgáki. Printed timetables are available from the bus station. More convenient are the **day-tours** of Náxos (€20) that can be booked at **Naxos Tourist Information** (ⓣ22850 25201, ⓕ22850 25200), on the seafront near the jetty, which offers a wealth of information, and somewhere to leave your bags (€1.50). It's also the best place to book special tours to the Minor Cyclades as well as accommodation, since the proprietor maintains some of the finest properties on the island. German-run **Naxos Horse Riding** (ⓣ694 88 09 142) organizes daily trips in the area for all levels for around €40 per person.

Accommodation

There's plenty of accommodation in Náxos and you should have no problem finding somewhere to stay. Once you've run the gauntlet of touts on the jetty, you would do well to head straight to Naxos Tourist Information (see above) who can book **rooms** for you. There are three basic areas to look: the old quarter near the *kástro*, where they are hard to find and relatively expensive; up to the left (north) of town in Grótta; and south of town near Áyios Yeóryios beach, where they are most abundant and less expensive, but with significant night-time noise from clubs and discos.

Anixis Bourgos ⓣ22850 22932, ⓦwww.hotel-anixis.gr. Pleasant, simply decorated rooms set around a garden near the *kástro*. March–Oct. ❸
Apollon South of Grótta ⓣ22850 22468, ⓦwww.naxostownhotels.com. Comfortable, modern doubles, all with balconies, in a good location near Grótta beach. ❻
Chateau Zevgoli Bourgos ⓣ22850 22993, ⓦwww.naxostownhotels.com. Charming, traditional hotel near the *kástro*, with nice views and antique-furnished rooms. March–Nov. ❺
Flisvos Sportclub Hotel Áyios Yeóryios ⓣ22850 24308, ⓦwww.flisvos-sportclub.com. Self-contained mini-resort with hotel and restaurant. Also home to a watersports centre (see box p.610), and can organize walking tours of the island and mountain bike rental. ❻
Galaxy Southern part of Áyios Yeóryios ⓣ22850 22422, ⓦwww.hotel-galaxy.com. Upmarket hotel with pool and large modern rooms and studios with sea views and balconies. ❼
Glaros Áyios Yeóryios ⓣ22850 23101, ⓦwww.hotelglaros.com. Comfortable, stylish hotel practically on the beach. Most rooms come

with sea views, and all have verandas. March–Oct. ❹
Hotel Grotta Grótta ⓣ22850 22215, ⓦwww.hotelgrotta.gr. Welcoming hotel in good location, only a 5min walk from the waterfront. Offers comfortable rooms, a Jacuzzi and a generous breakfast. B&B ❺
Iliada Studios Grótta ⓣ22850 23303, ⓔiliada@otenet.gr. Quiet studio complex in Grótta on the cliff beyond town, with good views out to sea. Feb–Nov. ❹
Panorama Bourgos ⓣ22850 24404, ⓔpanoramanaxos@in.gr. Spotless family-run hotel near the *kástro*, with airy rooms and sea views. May–Oct. ❸
Pension Irene I & II Both near the main square ⓣ22850 23169 or 69733 37782, ⓦwww.irenepension-naxos.com. Clean, spacious pension with two locations, one with a nice pool. The friendly proprietors will meet guests at the ferry jetty. ❸
Pension Kastell Just south of *kástro* ⓣ22850 23082, ⓦwww.kastell.gr. Friendly pension offering large rooms with balconies and a nice roof garden. €5 extra for a hearty breakfast. March–Oct. ❸

The Town

Only two of the *kástro*'s original seven towers remain, though the **north gate** (approached from Apóllon and known as the Traní Portá or "Great Gate") survives as a splendid example of a medieval fort entrance. The Venetians' Catholic descendants, now dwindled to a few old ladies, still live in the old mansions that encircle the site, many with ancient coats of arms above crumbling doorways. One of these, the **Domus Della-Rocca-Barozzi** (daily 10am–3pm & 7.30–10.30pm; €5), is open to the public and offers the best views from the *kástro*; the guided tour even includes a tasting from the family's wine cellar, and live classical concerts often animate the adjoining courtyard on summer evenings. Other brooding relics survive in the same area: a seventeenth-century Ursuline convent and the Roman Catholic cathedral, restored in questionable taste in the 1950s, though still displaying a thirteenth-century crest inside. Nearby was one of Ottoman Greece's first schools, the French School; opened in 1627 for Catholic and Orthodox students alike, its pupils included, briefly, Nikos Kazantzakis (see p.1145). The school building now houses an excellent **archeological museum** (Tues–Sun 8.30am–3pm; €3), with finds from Náxos, Koufoníssi, Kéros and Dhonoússa, including an important collection of Early Cycladic figurines. Archaic and Classical sculpture and pottery dating from Neolithic through to Roman times are also on display. On the roof terrace, a Hellenistic mosaic floor shows a nereid (sea nymph) surrounded by deer and peacocks.

Eating

The waterfront is crammed with places to eat, most of them decent. For picnics, there's a good bakery about midway along the harbour front, while for local cheese, wine, *kítron*, spices and other dried comestibles, head for Tirokomika Proionia Naxou, a delightful old store on Papavassilíou.

Bikini Opposite ferry dock. This popular crêperie also serves good breakfasts and snacks. Ideal if you're waiting for a ferry.

Cafe Picasso Main square. Excellent Mexican restaurant, with some good vegetarian options, and another branch on Pláka beach. Evenings only.

Irini's Paralia. One of the best of the simple oven-food tavernas on the waterfront.

Katerina's Grill Papavassiliou. Good choice for cheap breakfasts, grills and wood-oven baked pizzas. Also a good spot for people-watching.

Lucullus Bourgos. Romantic restaurant serving home-made local specialities in an intimate setting in the old town.

Manolis Garden Bourgos. Popular taverna with small but excellent menu both in taste and value for money. Located in a large garden in the old town.

Metaxi Mas Bourgos. No-fuss ouzerí serving excellent food on a little street heading up to the *kástro*.

Palatia Below Portára. Fish taverna, which, despite its location, is surprisingly reasonable and serves great food.

Popi's Paralia. A veritable institution, specializing in lamb raised on the proprietor's own land. Inside there's also a wine, *kítron* and cheese shop.

Portokali Overlooking Áyios Yeóryios. Perched on the headland to the south of town with good views, this is an excellent spot for watching the sunset, although the international and Greek dishes are accordingly overpriced.

Rendezvous Paralia. Busy waterfront café serving excellent cakes and coffee.

Scirocco Main square. Well-known restaurant popular with locals and tourists alike for its good-value traditional meals, hence the occasional long queue to get in.

Nightlife

Much of the evening action goes on at the south end of the waterfront, where you'll find **café-bars** and **clubs** jostling for business, luring people in with staggeringly huge menus of cheap cocktails. Should that fail to tempt, there's also an open-air **cinema**, the Cine Astra, on the road to the airport at the southern end of town; it's a fair walk out, but the Ayía Ánna bus stops here.

Babylonia Náxos's first and currently only gay bar, discreetly situated on an upper-level building on the waterfront.

Coco's Café Good little cocktail spot on the waterfront, playing South American music and serving breakfast through the day.

Day & Night Popular bar turning out European, and later on Greek, music every weekend on its packed veranda.

Escoba Just behind *Day & Night*, this place serves yet more great cocktails, and is a little larger, so less of a crush.

Lakridi A tiny jazz bar, which sometimes plays classical music, tucked away on a street behind the port police.

Super Island The town's biggest club, with dancing to European hits split over two floors.

The southwestern beaches

The **beaches** around Náxos Town are worth sampling. For some unusual swimming just to the **north** of the port, beyond the causeway, **Grótta** is easiest to reach. Besides the caves after which the place is named, the remains of submerged Cycladic buildings are visible, though only when you're out in the water. The finest spots, though, are all **south** of town, the entire southwestern coastline boasting a series of excellent **beaches** accessible by regular bus. **ÁYIOS YEÓRYIOS**, a long sandy bay fringed by the southern extension of the hotel area, is within walking distance. There's a line of cafés and tavernas at the northern end of the beach, and a windsurfing school, plus a campsite, although there are far more attractive places to camp on Pláka beach (see below).

Buses take you to **ÁYIOS PROKÓPIOS** beach, with plenty of reasonably priced hotels, rooms and basic tavernas, plus the upmarket *Hotel Lianos Village* (℡22850 26366, ⓦwww.lianosvillage.com; ⑥), with its pleasant pool setting. Two excellent, traditional restaurants are *Anessio* and *Colosseo*, while the younger, funkier *Kahlua* and *Splash* are good cafés. Rapid development along this stretch means that this resort has blended into the next one of **AYÍA ÁNNA**, further along the busy road, with accommodation of a similar price and quality. The seaview *Iria Beach Hotel* (℡22850 42600, ⓦwww.iriabeach-naxos.com; ⑤) and the nearby *Kouros Hotel* (℡t22850 29151, ⓦwww.kouros-naxos.com; ③) are comfortable options. The best food in Ayía Anna is at the *Gorgona* taverna, family run and with excellent prices. *Gorgona* also offers rooms, studios and apartments, all newly refurbished with en-suite bathrooms and air conditioning (℡ 22850 41007; ③). Moving along the coast, away from the built-up area, the beach here is nudist.

Beyond the headland, **PLÁKA** beach, a vegetation-fringed expanse of white sand, stretches for 5km. Things are not so built up here, and parts of the beach are nudist (past *Plaka* campsite). There are two suitably laid-back and friendly **campsites** here: *Maragas* (℡22850 24552, ⓦwww.maragascamping .gr), which also has double rooms (③) and studios (③), and the newer *Plaka* (℡22850 42700, ⓦwww.plakacamping.gr), a little further along, which is small and quiet with a few inexpensive bungalows (②), and a hotel (③). The *Hotel Orkos Village* (℡22850 75321, ⓦwww.orkoshotel.gr; ④) has apartments in an attractive location, on a hillside above the coast between Pláka beach and Mikrí Vígla, and the *Plaza Beach Hotel* ℡22850 29400, ⓦwww.plazabeachhotel.gr; ⑦) is a glittering new mega-resort at the southern end of the beach that is likely to push the nudists further out. Good **tavernas** in the vicinity of Pláka are the equally good *Golden Beach*, *Paradiso* and *Galini*, while *Amore Mio* is the most romantic spot for dining, with views of the coast. The nearby *Waffle House* has a tasty range of home-made ice cream.

For real isolation, go to the other side of the Mikrí Vígla headland which begins at the southern edge of Pláka beach, along a narrow footpath across the cliff-edge, to **KASTRÁKI** beach; towards the middle of the beach, *Areti* (℡22850 75292; ⑤) has apartments and a restaurant, but the fresh food at nearby *Axiotissa* **taverna** is unbeatable. A few people camp around the taverna on the small headland a little further down. In summer, this stretch – all the way from Mikrí Vígla down to Pyrgáki – attracts camper vans and windsurfers from all over Europe. On the **Alíko** promontory to the south of Kastráki there is a small nudist beach, known locally as "Hawaii Beach" for the vibrant blue colour of its waters.

From Kastráki, it's a couple of hours' walk up to the Byzantine castle of **Apalírou**, which held out for two months against the besieging Marco Sanudo.

The fortifications are relatively intact and the views magnificent. Picturesque **Pyrgáki** beach has a couple of tavernas and a few rooms; 4km further on is the slightly larger **Ayiássos** beach.

The rest of the **southern coast** – virtually the whole of the southeast of the island – is remote and mountain-studded; you'd have to be a dedicated and well-equipped camper and hiker to get much out of the region.

Central Náxos and the Tragéa

Although buses bound for Apóllon (in the north) link up the central Naxian villages, the core of the island – between Náxos Town and Apíranthos – is best explored by moped or on foot. Much of the region is well off the beaten track, and can be a rewarding excursion if you've had your fill of beaches; Christian Ucke's *Walking Tours on Naxos*, available from bookshops in Náxos Town, is a useful guide for hikers.

Once out of Náxos Town, you quickly arrive at the neighbouring villages of **GLINÁDHO** and **GALANÁDHO**, both scruffy market centres, forking right and left respectively. Glinádho is built on a rocky outcrop above the Livádhi plain, while Galanádho displays the first of Náxos's fortified mansions and an unusual double church. A combined Orthodox chapel and Catholic sanctuary separated by a double arch, the church reflects the tolerance of the Venetians during their rule, and the locals, to each other's religions. Continue beyond Glinádho to **TRÍPODHES** (ancient Biblos), 9km from Náxos Town. Noted by Homer for its wines, this old-fashioned agricultural village has no sights as such, but you can enjoy a coffee at the shaded *kafenío*. The start of a long but rewarding walk is a rough road (past the parish church) which leads down the colourful Pláka valley, past an old watchtower and the Byzantine church of **Áyios Matthéos** ("mosaic pavement"), and ends at the glorious Pláka beach (see p.671).

To the east, the twin villages of **SANGRÍ**, on a vast plateau at the head of a long valley, can be reached by continuing to follow the left-hand fork past Galanádho, a route which allows a look at the domed eighth-century church of **Áyios Mámas** (on the left), once the Byzantine cathedral of the island but neglected during the Venetian period and now a sorry sight. **Káto Sangrí** boasts the remains of a Venetian castle, while **Áno Sangrí** is an attractive little place, all cobbled streets and fragrant courtyards. Thirty minutes' stroll away, on a path leading south out of the village, are the partially reconstructed remains of a Classical temple of Demeter.

The Tragéa

From Sangrí, the road twists northeast into the **Tragéa** region, scattered with olive trees and occupying a vast highland valley. It's a good jumping-off point for all sorts of exploratory rambling, and **HALKÍ** is a fine introduction to what is to come. Set high up, 16km from Náxos Town, it's a noble and quiet town with some lovely churches, including the **Panayía Protóthronis** church, with its eleventh- to thirteenth-century frescoes; it only opens to visitors in the morning. Nearby are the romantic ruins of the seventeenth-century Venetian **Grazia-Barozzi Tower**. Tourists wanting to stay here are still something of a rarity, although you can usually get a **room** in someone's house by asking at the store. *Yiannis* **taverna** is the focal point of village activity and has a good selection of fresh *mezédhes* to enjoy with a glass of ouzo. Nearby is the distillery and shop of Vallindras Naxos Citron, whose charming proprietors explain the process of producing *kítron* followed by a little tasting session. The olive and citrus plantations surrounding Halkí are crisscrossed by paths and tracks, the groves dotted with numerous Byzantine chapels and the ruins of fortified *pýrgi* or Venetian mansions.

The road from Halkí heads 2km north to **MONÍ**. Just before the village, you pass the sixth-century monastery of **Panayía Dhrossianí**, a group of stark, grey-stone buildings with some excellent frescoes; the monks allow visits at any time, though you may have to contend with coach tours from Náxos Town. Moní itself enjoys an outstanding view of the Tragéa and surrounding mountains, and has four traditional **tavernas**, plus some **rooms** (ask at the tavernas; ❷). The main road leads on to Kinídharos, with an old marble quarry above the village; a few kilometres beyond, a signpost points you down a rough track to the left, to **FLÉRIO** (commonly called Melanés). The most interesting of the ancient marble quarries on Náxos, this is home to two famous **kouri**, dating from the sixth century BC, that were left recumbent and unfinished because of flaws in the material. Even so, they're finely detailed figures, over 5m in length. One of the statues lies in a private, irrigated orchard; the other is up a hillside some distance above, and you will need local guidance to find it.

From Flério you could retrace your steps to the road and head back to Hóra via Mýli and the ruined Venetian castle at Kouronohóri, both pretty hamlets connected by footpaths (9km). If you're feeling more adventurous, ask to be directed south to the footpath that leads over the hill to the Potamiá villages. The first of these, **ÁNO POTAMIÁ**, has a fine taverna and a rocky track back towards the Tragéa. Once past the valley, the landscape becomes craggy and barren, the forbidding Venetian fortress of **Apáno Kástro** perched on a peak just south of the path. This is believed to have been Sanudo's summer home, but the fortified site goes back further, if the Mycenaean tombs found nearby are any indication. From the fort, paths lead back to Halkí in around an hour. Alternatively, you can continue further northwest down the Potamiá valley towards Hóra, passing first the ruined **Cocco Pýrgos** – said to be haunted by one Constantine Cocco, the victim of a seventeenth-century clan feud – on the way to **MÉSO POTAMIÁ**, joined by some isolated dwellings with its twin village **KÁTO POTAMIÁ** nestling almost invisibly among the greenery flanking the creek. From here you can follow the road back to Náxos Town, about a six-kilometre trek.

At the far end of the gorgeous Tragéa valley, **FILÓTI**, the largest village in the region, lies on the slopes of Mount Zás (or Zeus) which, at 1000m, is the highest point in the Cyclades. Under the shade of the plane trees on the main platía are several pleasant *kafenía*, as well as *Babulas Grill-Restaurant* (☎22850 31426; ❷), which has the best rooms in the village. To get an idea of the old village, climb the steps up the hill starting at the platía. A turning at the southern end of the village is signposted to the **Pýrgos Himárou**, a remote twenty-metre Hellenistic watchtower, and also to **Kalándou** beach, 25km away on the south coast; beyond the turning the road is unpaved. There are no villages in this part of the island, so bring supplies if you're planning to camp. From the village, it's a round-trip walk of three to four hours on mostly unmarked trails to the summit of **Zás**, a climb which rewards you with an astounding panorama of virtually the whole of Náxos and its Cycladic neighbours. Save yourself the rather tedious walk along the main Filóti–Apóllon road by taking the bus towards Apóllon and asking the driver to let you off at the Dhánakos turning, where the waymarked final approach trail begins just beside a small chapel on your right. There is also a marked turn-off to the Zás Cave, a pleasant place for a picnic, but not the best point from which to tackle the steep ascent to the summit.

Apíranthos

APÍRANTHOS (Apérathos in local dialect), a hilly, winding 10km beyond the cave, shows the most Cretan influence of all the interior villages. It is a good quiet place to stay for a few days, and being high in the mountains is noticeably cooler and greener than the coast. There are two Venetian fortified mansions, and the square contains a miniature church with a three-tiered bell tower. Ask to be pointed to the start of the spectacular **path** up over the ridge behind; this ends either in Moní or Kalóxilos, depending on whether you fork right or left respectively at the top. Cafés and tavernas on the main street look out over a terraced valley below; the nationally renowned **taverna** *Leftheri*, here, is generally regarded as one of the best restaurants on the island, serving up carefully prepared local dishes. **Rooms** are available but are not advertised – ask in the cafés or in the embroidery shop.

Apíranthos has a beach annexe of sorts at **Moutsoúna**, 12km east. Emery mined near Apíranthos used to be transported here by means of an aerial funicular and then shipped out of the port. The industry collapsed in the 1980s, and the sandy cove beyond the dock now features a growing colony of holiday villas and the excellent *Ostria* taverna. An unpaved road heads south along the coast to a remote sandy beach at **Psilí Ámmos** – ideal for self-sufficient campers, but you must take enough water. From here a track carries on to relatively secluded **Pánormos** beach in the southeastern corner of the island.

Northern Náxos

The route through the mountains from Apíranthos to Apóllon is very scenic, and the road surface is in good condition all the way. Jagged ranges and hairpin bends confront you before reaching Kóronos, the halfway point, where a road off to the right threads through a wooded valley to **Liónas**, a tiny and very Greek port with a pebble beach. You'd do better to continue, past Skadhó, to the remote, emery-miners' village of **KORONÍDHA** which is a pleasing, vine-covered settlement – the highest village on the island and the original home of *kítron* liqueur.

Back on the main road, a series of slightly less hairy bends leads down a long valley to **APÓLLON**, a small resort with two beaches: a tiny and crowded stretch of sand backed by cafés and restaurants, and a longer and quieter stretch of shingle, popular mainly with Greek families. The only major attraction is a **kouros**, approached by a path from the main road just above the village. Lying *in situ* at a former marble quarry, this largest of Náxos's abandoned stone figures is just over 10m long, but, compared with those at Flério, disappointingly lacking in detail. Here since 600 BC, it serves as a singular reminder of the Naxians' traditional skill; the famous Delian lions (see p.651) are also made of Apollonian marble. Not surprisingly, bus tours descend upon the village during the day, and Apóllon is now quite a popular little place. The local festival, celebrated on August 28–29, is one of Náxos's best.

It's easy to make a round trip of the north coast and inland villages by bus from Náxos Town. The coastal road is spectacularly beautiful, going high above the sea for most of the way, making it more like parts of Crete or the mainland than other islands. Ten kilometres past the northern cape sprouts the beautiful **Ayiá** *pýrgos*, or tower, another foundation (in 1717) of the Cocco family. There's a tiny hamlet nearby, and, 7km further along, a track leads off to **Abrámi** beach, an idyllic spot with a highly recommended family-run **taverna** with **rooms** to let, *Pension and Restaurant Efthimios* (T 22850 63244, E abram@can .gr; ❷). Just beyond the hamlet of Hília Vrýssi is the abandoned **monastery of**

Faneroménis, built in 1606. Carrying on along the coastal road you will reach the Engarés valley, at the foot of which is another quiet beach, **Amití**, accessed via one of two dirt tracks, the most obvious being the one leading down from Galíni, only 6km from Náxos Town. Inland from Galíni, the unspoilt town of **Engarés** is home to the excellent *Haris* taverna; *Vasilis* in equally undervisited **Melanés** (reachable by road from Engarés) serves chickens and game raised on site. On the final stretch back to the port, you pass a unique eighteenth-century Turkish fountain-house and the fortified monastery of **Ayíou Ioánnou Khryssostómou**, where a couple of aged nuns are still in residence. A footpath from the monastery and the road below lead straight back to town.

Minor Cyclades

Four of the six small islands in the patch of the Aegean between Náxos and Amorgós have slid from obscurity into fashion in recent years. The group is known commonly as the Minor Cyclades and includes **Áno Koufoníssi**, **Skhinoússa**, **Iráklia** and **Dhonoússa**. The islands' new popularity is hastening the development of better facilities and higher prices, but with little room for expansion and only limited ferry service, they've managed to avoid the mass tourism of the rest of the Cyclades. You can even find peace and quiet – what the Greeks call *isykhiá* – here in August, when you should make the crossing from Áno Koufoníssi to **Kéros**, with no permanent population but an important archeological site, or **Káto Koufoníssi**, inhabited only by goatherds.

Though a Pireás-based **ferry** has been known to call at the islands – linking them with Náxos and Amorgós and (sometimes) Páros and Sýros – the small, local *Express Skopelitis* is a more frequent fixture, leaving the little ferry quay in Náxos almost daily in August to head to most of the islets. At other times of year, don't arrive unless you're in no hurry to push on.

Áno Koufoníssi, Káto Koufoníssi and Kéros

Áno Koufoníssi (usually referred to simply as Koufoníssi) is the most populous island of the group, and is reachable by ferries from Náxos several times per week in high season, outside of which you might better use the private vessel of Prasinos Excursions from Pánormos (T 22850 71438; €20–50 per person depending on size of group). With some of the least-spoilt beaches in the Cyclades, the island is attracting increasing numbers of Greek and foreign holidaymakers. Small enough to walk round in a morning, the island can actually feel overcrowded in July and August.

The old single-street village of **HÓRA**, on a low hill behind the harbour, is being engulfed by new room and hotel development, but still has a friendly, small-island atmosphere. A map by the jetty shows where to find all the island's **rooms**: the popular restaurant and pension *Melissa* (T 22850 71454, F 22850 71732; ❸) is a good, family-run choice, just inland from the beach. The most upmarket options include *Hotel Aegeon* (T 22850 74050, W www.hotel-aigaion .gr; B&B ❺), with clean, modern rooms, right by the village beach; friendly *Katerina Studios* (T 22850 71670, F 22850 71455 ; ❸), complete with kitchens, nearby; and the newer *Ermes Rooms* (T 22850 71693, F 22850 74214; ❹), all with balconies, behind the post office. The more basic *Akroyiali* (T 22850 71685; ❹), on the front just beyond the beach, is open all year. Yeoryia Kouveou has beautifully situated rooms at *Hondros Kavos* (T 22850 71707, F 22850 71441; ❹), located over an equally popular seafood taverna outside the village to the east.

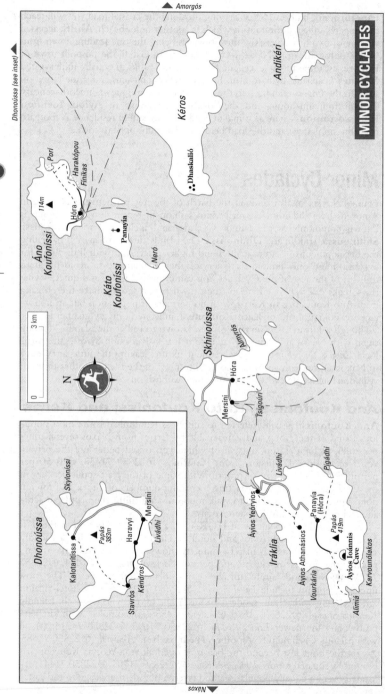

MINOR CYCLADES

Amorgós

Dhonoússa (see inset)

Áno Koufoníssi

Pori

114m ▲

Hóra

Harakópou

Finíkas

Kéros

Dhaskalió

Andikéri

Káto Koufoníssi

Panayía

Neró

N

0   3 km

Skhinoússa

Mersíni

Hóra

Alimrós

Tsigoúri

Dhonoússa

Skyloníssi

Kalotarítissa

Papás 383m ▲

Haravyí

Mersíni

Stavrós

Kéndros

Livádhi

Iráklia

Áyios Yeóryios

Livádhi

Pigádhi

Áyios Athanásios

Panayía (Hóra)

Papás 419m ▲

Vourkária

Áyios Ioánnis Cave

Alimiá

Karvounólakos

Náxos

Koufoníssi is noted for its fish **tavernas**; *Remezzo*, up in Hóra, has excellent food and a cosy atmosphere, while *Captain Nicola* at the bay is cheaper than most and has a fine array of seafood. Nearby *To Steki Tis Marias* is a good breakfast place with a few rooms (❷), and has views over the narrow channel to Káto Koufoníssi. The most popular nightspot is *Soroccos*, a lively **café–bar** on the front, while good alternatives include *Ta Kalamia*, with a quieter choice of music, and *Nikitas*, which has excellent views. *To Palio Fanari*, to the west of the village, is the club favoured by locals, playing a mix of dance and Greek music. The ticket agency is on the main street, and there is a **post office** (limited hours) just north of the town hall, with an **ATM** installed outside.

All the good beaches are in the southeast of the island, getting better as you go east along a dirt path that skirts the coastline along the edge of low cliffs. **Fínikas**, a ten-minute walk from the village, is the first of four wide coves with gently shelving golden sand, where there are rooms and a good taverna. Further east is **Harakópou**, which has a windswept **campsite** (☎22850 71683) with cane shade and rather poor facilities, on the headland before the next beach **Thános**; the owners may meet the boat to collect your luggage, but you may have to walk. Next is **Platiá Poúnda**, where caves have been hollowed out of the cliffs. Further east, the path rounds a rocky headland to **Porí**, a much longer and wilder beach, backed by dunes and set in a deep bay. It can be reached more easily from the village by following a track heading inland through the low scrub-covered hills.

Káto Koufoníssi, the practically uninhabited island to the southwest, has a seasonal taverna and some more secluded beaches; a *kaïki* shuttles people across until late in the evening. A festival is held here on August 15, at the church of the Panayía. The island of **Kéros** is harder to reach, but if there is a willing group of people keen to visit the ancient site, a boat and boatmen can be hired for around €50 for the day.

Skhinoússa

A little to the southwest, the island of **Skhinoússa** is just beginning to awaken to its tourist potential. Boats dock at the small port of Mersíni, which has one pension (☎22850 71159; ❹) and a couple of cafés; a road leads up to **HÓRA** (also called Panayía), the walk taking just over fifteen minutes. As you enter the village, the well-stocked **tourist centre**, which is also the main ferry agent, is one of the first buildings you'll come across; it has a metred phone and sells Greek and foreign press. There is also another, newer tourist office at the other end of town, which is just as helpful, and also sells locally made produce, and burns digital photos onto CDs.

Accommodation is mostly in fairly simple rooms, such as *Agnadema* (☎22850 71987, ✉agnadema@nax.forthnet.gr; ❸), with basic rooms ten minutes' walk from town, and the pleasant *Pension Galini* (☎22850 71983; ❸), set in a quiet garden, and with sea views. The rooms belonging to Anna (☎22850 71161; ❷) are quiet and comfortable, whilst nearby the *Iliovasilema Hotel* (☎22850 71948, ✉iliovasilema@schinousa.gr; ❸) enjoys stunning views of the harbour. The main concentration of **restaurants**, cafés and bars is along the main thoroughfare. Traditional *Panorama* and *Margarita* offer diners some of the best views on the island.

There are no fewer than sixteen **beaches** dotted around the island, accessible by a network of trails. **Tsigoúri** is a ten-minute walk southwest from Hóra; largely undeveloped except for *Grispos Villas* (☎22850 71930, ⊕www .grisposvillas.com; B&B ❺), which has a good taverna with great views. The only other beach with any refreshments is **Almyrós**, a half-hour southeast of Hóra, which has a simple canteen.

Iráklia

Iráklia (pronounced Iraklía by locals), the westernmost of the Minor Cyclades, has just over 100 permanent residents. As the first stop on the ferry service from Náxos, the island is hardly undiscovered by tourists, but with fewer amenities than some of its neighbours it retains the romantic, ramshackle feel of a more secluded retreat.

Ferries call at **ÁYIOS YEÓRYIOS**, a small but sprawling settlement behind a sandy tamarisk-backed beach. *Anna's Place* (T & F 22850 71145; ❸) has some excellent rooms with shared cooking facilities and great views. Nearby, friendly Alexandra Tournaki (T 22850 71482; ❷) also has decent rooms. Other accommodation options dotted around the town include; *Maïstrali* (T 22850 71807, ⓔnickmaistrali@in.gr; ❸), closer to the port, Dhimitrios Stefanidhis (T 22850 71484; ❷), *Sohoro Rooms* (T 22850 71565; ❷), and *Anthi & Angelo's* (T 22850 71486; ❷). Up on the top of the hillside, the brand-new *Aiolos* hotel (T 693 26 32 050, ⓔmroussos@hol.gr; ❻) is a sign of things to come; it currently has only two suites, but should grow over the next two years into a fully fledged upmarket hotel. For eating, *O Pefkos* is a pleasant **taverna**, with tables shaded by a large pine tree. Two agencies sell tickets for **ferries**, but there are no banks in town, nor are there bus or taxi services. The *Perigiali* taverna also has a small shop selling maps showing the mule path to a fine **cave** of Áyios Ioánnis on the west side of the island.

Livádhi, the best beach on the island, is a fifteen-minute walk southeast of town. There is shade, but bring refreshments, as the taverna, whose owner allows **campers** to pitch their tents on his land, might not be open. The village of Livádhi, deserted since 1940, stands on the hillside above, its houses ruined and overgrown; among the remains are Hellenistic walls incorporated into a later building, and fortifications from the time of Marco Sanudo. Marietta Markoyianni (T 22850 71252; ❷) has rooms on the beach; *Zografos Rooms* (T 22850 71946, F 22850 71956; ❹), above the road to Panayía, has fine views but is rather remote.

PANAYÍA or **HÓRA**, an unspoilt one-street village at the foot of Mount Papás, is another hour's walk inland along the paved road. It has a bakery and mini-market, two café-shops and an excellent ouzerí, but no rooms. A track to the east heads down to Pigádhi, a rocky beach with sea urchins, at the head of a narrow inlet. To the west, a track from the near-deserted hamlet of **Áyios Athanásios** leads back to the port.

The **cave of Áyios Ioánnis** lies behind the mountain, at the head of a valley leading to Vourkária bay. From Panayía, follow a signposted track west before zigzagging up to a saddle well to the north of the summit, with views over Skhinoússa, Koufoníssi, Kéros, Náxos and Amorgós; the path drops down to the south around the back of the mountain. A painted red arrow on the left indicates the turning to the cave, just over an hour's walk from Panayía. A church bell hangs from a cypress tree above the whitewashed entrance; inside there's a shrine, and the cave opens up into a large chamber with stalactites and stalagmites. It can be explored to a depth of 120m and is thought to be part of a much larger cave system, yet to be opened up; a festival is held here every year on August 18.

The main trail continues beyond the cave to a small sandy beach at **Alimiá** but this can be reached more easily with the beach-boat from Áyios Yeóryios.

In season, the boat sails daily to either Skhinoússa, Alimiá or the nearby pebble beach of Karvounólakos.

Dhonoússa

Dhonoússa is a little out on a limb compared with the other Minor Cyclades, and ferries call less frequently. Island life centres on the pleasant port settlement of **STAVRÓS**, spread out behind the harbour and the village beach.

Rooms, most without signs, tend to be booked up by Greek holiday-makers in August; try Maria Prasinos (℡22850 51578; ➍), with rooms along a lane behind the church; *Iliovasilema* (℡22850 51570, ℻22850 51607; ➍), which also has a decent restaurant; or *Firoa* (℡22850 51658; ➌), 150m away from the centre. There are a few **tavernas** in town, all of them reasonable and good. The **ticket agency** above the harbour changes money at astronomically high rates and has been known to be less than accommodating, so you would be wise to bring enough with you.

The hills around Stavrós are low and barren and scarred by bulldozed tracks, but a little walking is repaid with dramatic scenery and a couple of fine beaches. Campers and nudists head for **Kéndros**, a long and attractive stretch of sand fifteen minutes to the east, although shade is limited and there are no facilities. A road on the hillside above leads to the farming hamlets of Haravyí and Mersíni; these have more hens and goats in the streets than people, and there are no cafés, shops or rooms. **Mersíni** is an hour's walk from Stavrós and has a welcome spring beneath a plane tree, the island's only running water. A nearby path leads down to Livádhi, an idyllic white-sand beach with tamarisks for shade. In July and August, there's often a beach-boat from the port.

The road to **Kalotarítissa**, on the northeast coast, is paved and not an especially attractive walk. You might want to head inland from Stavrós toward Papás, the island's highest point, from where a valley drops down rapidly to the tiny village with a simple taverna that sometimes has a room to rent. There are two small pebble beaches and a path that continues above the coast to Mersíni. It takes four to five hours to walk round the island.

Amorgós

Amorgós, with its dramatic mountain scenery and laid-back atmosphere, is attracting visitors in increasing numbers; most ferries and catamarans call at both Katápola in the southwest and Aegiali (Eyiáli) in the north – with these destinations, rather than Amorgós, on schedules – and there is a regular bus service (6 daily in summer) between both ports. The island can get extremely crowded in midsummer, the numbers swollen by French people paying their respects to the film location of Luc Besson's *The Big Blue*, although few actually venture out to the wreck of the *Olympia*, at the island's west end, which figured so prominently in the movie. In general it's a low-key, escapist clientele, happy to have found a relatively large, interesting and uncommercialized island with excellent walking.

Katápola and around

KATÁPOLA, set at the head of a deep bay, is actually three separate hamlets: **Katápola** proper on the south flank, **Rahídhi** on the ridge at the head of the gulf and **Xilokeratídhi** along the north shore. There is a beach in front of

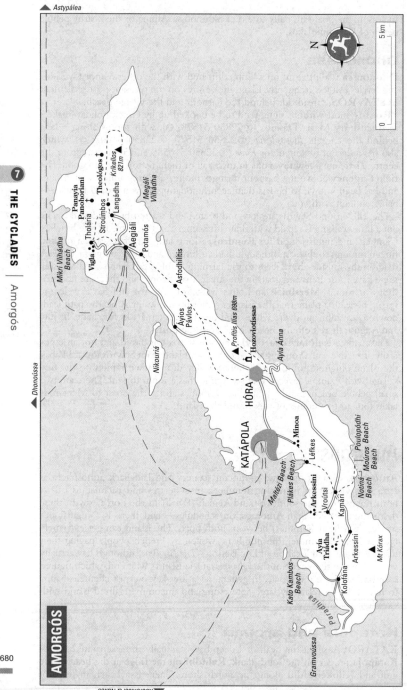

AMORGÓS

Astypálea

Dhonoússa

Koutsonísi & Naxos

Mikrí Vlihádha
Beach

Vígla
Tholária
Stroúmbos
Panayía
Panohoriani
Theológos
Kríkellos
821m
Langádha
Megáli
Vlihádha
Aegiáli
Potamós

Asfodhilítis

Nikouriá

Áyios
Pávlos
Profítis Ilías 698m
Hozoviótissa
Ayía Ánna

HÓRA

KATÁPOLA
Minoa
Leíkes
Poulopódhi
Beach
Maltézi Beach
Plákes Beach
Notiná
Beach
Moúros
Beach
Arkessíni
Vroútsi
Kamári

Ayía
Triádha
Arkessíni
Mt Kórax

Kato Kambos
Beach
Kolofána

Paradhísa

Gramvoússa

N

0   5 km

Rahídhi, but the beach to the west of Katápola is better, though not up to the standards of Aegiali in the northeast. In season there is also a regular *kaïki* to nearby beaches at **Maltézi** and **Plákes** (€3 return) and a daily *kaïki* to the islet of **Gramvoússa** off the western end of Amorgós (€6–8 return).

Prekas in Katápola, just along from the ferry dock, is the one-stop **boat-ticket agency**, and there are several **motorbike-rental** outlets – the best is Thomas Auto Moto – though the local bus service is more than adequate and the walking trails are delightful. There are walking maps on sale throughout the island, the maps published by Anavasi being the most useful. The **bus** shuttles almost hourly until 11pm between Katápola and Hóra, the island capital; several times daily it continues to Ayía Ánna via Hozoviotíssas monastery, and once a day (9.45am) out to the "Káto Meriá", made up of the hamlets of Kamári, Arkessíni and Kolofána.

There are plenty of small **hotels** and **pensions** and, except in high summer when rooms are almost impossible to find, proprietors tend to meet those boats arriving around sunset – though not necessarily those that show up in the small hours. A good clean place next to the beach at the western end of Katápola is *Eleni Rooms* (☎22850 71628, ✉roomseleni@hack-box.net; ❹); *Dimitri's Place* in Rahídhi (☎22850 71309; ❷) is a compound of interconnecting buildings in an orchard with shared cooking facilities. The smart traditional *Hotel Minoa* (☎22850 71480, ✉hotelminoalanderis@yahoo.com; ❺), on the waterfront, has clean rooms and also offers **Internet** access. South of the port you'll find *Anna Studios* (☎22850 71218, 🆎22850 71084; ❸), in a garden setting and with basic cooking facilities. There are several similarly priced pensions further east, including *Sofia* (☎22850 71493, 🆎22850 71494; ❸) in its own garden. The town **campsite** (☎ & 🆎22850 71257) is just off the beach well signed between Rahídhi and Xilokeratídhi. There's also a newer one, *Camping Kastanis* (☎22850 71277, 🌐www.kastanis.com), a ten-minute walk uphill towards Hóra.

In Katápola proper, *Mourayio* is the most popular **taverna** in town; alternatively, try the *Psaropoula* or *Minos*. There are four tavernas close to the campsite near Xilokeratídhi, of which the first is a friendly fish taverna, and of the others around the corner **Vitzentzos** is by far the best. What **nightlife** there is focuses on a handful of cafés and pubs. The bar *Le Grand Bleu* in Xilokeratídhi regularly shows *The Big Blue* on video, but there are other less obvious and less expensive places to drink, such as *The Blue Moon Bar* next door.

A signed surfaced road runs past the church in Rahídhi and south out of Katápola to the remains of **ancient Minoa**, about a half-hour's walk uphill. The site is in the process of being excavated, and is impressive for its size, and the views it commands over the bay, Hóra and ancient Arkessíni, as much as anything else. Your walk is rewarded by fragments of polygonal wall, four or five courses high, the foundations of an Apollo temple, a crumbled Roman structure and bushels of unsorted pottery shards. Beyond Minoa, the road dwindles to a jeep trail, continuing within a few hours on foot to Arkessíni (see p.683) via several hamlets – a wonderful **excursion** with the possibility of catching the bus back.

Hóra and around

HÓRA, accessible by an hour-long walk along the path beginning from behind the Rahídhi campsite, is one of the best-preserved settlements in the Cyclades, with a scattering of tourist shops, cafés, tavernas and rooms. Dominated by a volcanic rock plug, wrapped with a chapel or two, the thirteenth-century Venetian fortifications look down on countless other bulbous churches including the tiny **Áyios Fanoúrios**, and a line of decapitated windmills beyond. Of the half-dozen or so **places to stay**, the rooms belonging to Maria Theologitou (℡22850 71542; ❹) are recommended, as is the stunning ⚓ *Traditional Guest House* (℡22850 71814, ⓦ www.amorgos-studios.amorgos.net; ❹), one of the most beautiful boutique hotels in the Cyclades. Hóra is littered with atmospheric little places to **eat** and **drink**: *Liotrivi* restaurant, down the steps from the bus stop, is probably the best place for a meal, whilst *To Tsagaradiko* on the platía is another excellent choice. Of the several café-bars, *Kallisto* and *Zygos* are good, whilst *Bayoko*, by the bus stop, does a hearty breakfast. Also in the upper square is the island's main **post office**.

From the top of Hóra, near the upper telecoms tower, a wide cobbled *kalderími* drops down to two major attractions, effectively short-cutting the road and taking little longer than the bus to reach them. Bearing left at an inconspicuous fork after fifteen minutes, you'll come to the spectacular **monastery of Hozoviotíssas** (daily 8am–1pm; donation expected; modest dress required; skirts are not supplied for women – bring your own), which appears suddenly as you round a bend, its vast wall gleaming white at the base of a towering orange cliff. Only four monks occupy the fifty rooms now, but they are quite welcoming considering the number of visitors who file through; you can see the eleventh-century icon around which the monastery was founded, along with a stack of other treasures. Legend has it that during the Iconoclastic period, a precious icon of the Virgin was committed to the sea by beleaguered monks at Hózova, in the Middle East, and it washed up safely at the base of the palisade here. The view from the *katholikón's* terrace is the highlight for most visitors, and to round off the experience, you are ushered into a comfy reception room and treated to a sugary lump of *loukoúmi*, a warming shot of *rakomelo* (raki made with honey) and a cool glass of water.

The right-hand trail leads down, within forty minutes, to the pebble **beaches** at **Ayía Ánna**. Skip the first batch of tiny coves in favour of the path to the westernmost bay, where naturists cavort, almost in scandalous sight of the monastery far above. As yet there are no tavernas here, nor a spring, so bring food and water for the day.

△ Monastery of Hozoviotíssas, Amorgós

Southwestern Amorgós

For alternatives to Ayía Ánna, take the morning bus out toward modern Arkessíni, alighting at **Kamári** hamlet (where there's a single taverna) for the twenty-minute path down to the adjacent beaches of **Notiná**, **Moúros** and **Poulopódhi**. Like most of Amorgós's south-facing beaches, they're clean, with calm water, and a freshwater spring dribbles most of the year. The road is paved as far as **Kolofána**, where there is one place with **rooms**. From here unpaved roads lead to the western tip of the island, and remote beaches at Káto Kámbos and at Paradhísa, facing the islet of Gramvoússa.

Archeology buffs will want to head north from Kamári to Vroútsi, start of the overgrown hour-long route to **ancient Arkessíni**, a collection of tombs, six-metre-high walls and houses out on the cape of Kastrí. The main path from Minoa also passes through Vroútsi, ending next to the well-preserved Hellenistic fort known locally as the "Pýrgos", just outside modern **ARKESSÍNI**. The village has a single taverna with rooms, and, more importantly, an afternoon bus back to Hóra and Katápola.

Northeastern Amorgós

The energetically inclined can walk the four to five hours from Hóra to Eyiáli, continuing on the faint trail just beyond Hozoviotíssas; remember to take along water, as there is nowhere to fill up on the way. Along most of the route, you're treated to amazing views of **Nikouriá islet**, nearly joined to the main island, and in former times a leper colony. The only habitations en route are the summer hamlet of **Asfodhilítis**, and **Potamós**, a double village with a café.

EÝIALI (AEGIALI) is smaller and more picturesque than Katápola, and so tends to be more popular. For **boat tickets** and money exchange try Nautilus, just back from the water; there's also an **ATM** right by the ferry dock. **Accommodation** is scattered around the backstreets and is easy to find; friendly *Pension Christine* (☎22850 73236, ⓦwww.christina-pension.amorgos.net; ❸) has bright, cheerful rooms, whilst for something a bit more upmarket, *Filoxenia* (☎22850 73453, ⓦwww.amorgosfiloxenia.gr; ❹) has a lovely, peaceful position perched on the hillside at the edge of town. Stretching along the beach, the *Lakki Village* (☎22850 73253, ⓦwww.lakkivillage.gr; ❹) complex offers family-friendly rooms and studios, and behind this sits the flower-draped *Pension Askas* (☎22850 73333, ⓦwww.askaspension.gr; ❹); both have their own shaded tavernas. Next to *Pension Askas* is the friendly official **campsite**, *Aegiali Camping* (☎22850 73500, ⓦwww.aegialicamping.gr), usually busier than the one in Katápola. Overlooking the bay on the road up to Tholária is a luxury hotel with a swimming pool, the *Aegialis* (☎22850 73393, ⓦwww.amorgos-aegialis.com; ❼). For **eating out**, ☙ *Limani* (also called *Katina's*) is packed until midnight by virtue of its excellent food and barrel wine. Other places tend to be pricier and of inferior quality, with the exception of the tiny *12 Acropolis* restaurant. Besides a few seasonal music **bars**, nightlife is focused around the *Corte Club* at the *Egialis* hotel and the strip of bars along the beach, with evenings inevitably ending up at *The Que*.

The main Eyiáli **beach** is more than serviceable, getting less weedy and reefy as you stroll further north, the sand interrupted by the remains of a Roman building jutting into the sea. A trail here leads over various headlands to three bays: the first sandy, the second mixed sand and gravel, the last shingle, where naturism is just about tolerated. There are no facilities anywhere so bring along what you need.

There is a **bus service** up to each of the two villages visible above and east of Eyiáli, with eight departures daily up and down (a timetable is posted by the harbour bus stop), but it would be a shame to miss out on the beautiful **loop walk** linking them with the port (2hrs). A path starting at the far end of the beach heads inland and crosses the road before climbing steeply to **THOLÁRIA**, named after vaulted Roman tombs found around Vígla, the site of ancient Aegiale. Vígla is on a hill opposite the village but there is little to see beyond the bases of statues and traces of city walls incorporated into later terracing. Another path winds down behind the hill to a tiny pebble beach at Mikrí Vlihádha far below. There are a few **taverna-cafés**, including the handsome wooden-floored *Iy Kali Kardhia* near the church, and several places to stay, including some comfortable **rooms** (reserve through *Lakki Village* in Aegiali), the large and upmarket *Vigla* (☎22850 73288, ⓕ22850 73332; ❻) and the *Thalassino Oneiro* (☎22850 73345; ❸), which has a fine restaurant and an extremely friendly owner.

LANGÁDHA is another hour's walk along a path starting below Tholária; to the left of the trail is the chapel of Astrátios with an altar supported by the capital of a Corinthian column. Past here there are views down to the inlet of Megáli Vlihádha and, on a clear day, across to Ikaría in the north. The path descends through the village of Stroúmbos, abandoned apart from a few houses restored as holiday homes, and into a small gorge before climbing the steps up to Langádha. The *Artemis Pension* (☎22850 73315, ⓦwww.artemis-pension.gr; ❹) is a good place to stay here, and runs a decent taverna nearby.

Beyond Langádha, another rocky path travels around the base of the island's highest peak, the 821-metre-high **Kríkellos**, passing the fascinating church of **Theológos** on the way, with lower walls and ground plan dating to the fifth century. Somewhat easier to reach, by a slight detour off the main Tholária–Langádha trail, are the church and festival grounds of **Panayía Panohorianí** – not so architecturally distinguished but a fine spot nonetheless.

Íos

Though not terribly different – geographically or architecturally – from its immediate neighbours, no other island attracts the same vast crowds of young people as **Íos**. Attempts are being made, however, to move the island's tourism upmarket; buildings are now painted white with blue trim, instead of garish psychedelic hues, camping rough is discouraged, and Greece's early closing laws (3am except Fri & Sat) are enforced, so bars no longer stay open all night. The island is still extremely popular with the young backpacker set, who take over the island with a vengeance in the high season, although the rest of the year a large number of young families are choosing to holiday here.

The only real villages – **Yialós**, **Hóra** and **Mylopótamos** – are in one small corner of the island, and development elsewhere is somewhat restricted by poor roads. As a result there are still some very quiet beaches with just a few rooms to rent. Yialós has one of the best and safest natural harbours in the Cyclades, with a paved esplanade.

Most visitors stay along the arc delineated by the port – at Yialós, where you'll arrive (there's no airport), in Hóra above it or at the beach at Mylopótamos; it's a small area, and you soon get to know your way around. **Buses** constantly shuttle between Koumbára, Yialós, Hóra and Mylopótamos, with a daily service running roughly from 8am to midnight; you should never have to wait more than fifteen minutes during high season, but at least once try the short walk up (or down) the stepped path between Yialós and Hóra. Various travel offices run their own buses to the beaches at Manganári and Ayía Theodhóti; they sell return tickets only and are a bit expensive (€6). To rent your **own transport**, try Jacob's Car and Bike Rental (☎22860 91047) in Yialós or Vangelis Bike Rental (☎22860 91919) in Hóra; unlike most of the other islands, here you'll need a valid motorcycle licence. For a motorboat, head to Mylopótamos where Ios Boat Rental (☎22860 91301, ⓦwww.iosboat.com) requires no licence, just a credit card. For a quick escape from the party atmosphere at the height of

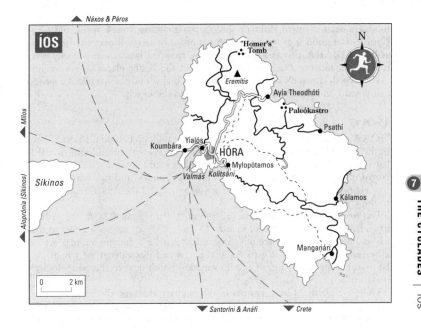

Náxos & Páros

ÍOS

N

"Homer's"
Tomb

Eremítis

Ayía Theodhóti

Paleókastro

Psathí

Koumbára   Yialós

HÓRA

Mylopótamos

Valmás   Kolitsáni

Kálamos

Manganári

0   2 km

Milos

Aloprónia (Síkinos)

Síkinos

Santoríni & Anáfi   Crete

the season, try one of the daily excursions around quiet nearby beaches on the beautiful *Leigh Browne* sailing vessel parked in the harbour (€20).

Despite its past popularity, **sleeping on the beach** on Íos is discouraged these days; given the problem of theft, it's best to stick to the official campsites.

Yialós

From **YIALÓS** quayside, **buses** turn around just to the left, while Yialós **beach** – surprisingly peaceful and uncrowded – is another five minutes' walk in the same direction. You might be tempted to grab a room in Yialós as you arrive; owners meet the ferries, hustling the town's **accommodation**, and there are also a couple of kiosks by the jetty that will book rooms for you. In shoulder season you can bargain for prices considerably lower than those listed below. *Hotel Mare Monte* (☎22860 91585, ✉maremonte@otenet.gr; ➎), about halfway down the beach, has clean spacious rooms, a small pool, and includes breakfast; *Galini Rooms* (☎22860 91115, ✉galiniios@yahoo.com; ➍), down a lane behind the beach, is a good quiet choice; whilst further down the same road, the *Brother's Hotel* (☎22860 91508, ⓦwww.brothershotel.com; ➎) is a relaxed family option with comfortable rooms and pool. One of the best choices is the family-owned *Golden Sun* (☎22860 91110, ⓦwww.goldensun. gr;➍), about 300m up the road to Hóra, which has a large pool, and the newly revamped *Yialos Beach* (☎22860 91421, ⓦwww.yialosbeach.gr; ➎) with smart doubles and studios set around yet another pool, just behind the hospital. There are more rooms on the stepped path from Yialós to Hóra, although they can be noisy at night. *Ios Camping* (☎22860 91329) is friendly and clean and has a rather luxurious swimming pool. Yialós has other essentials, including a reasonable supermarket and a few **tavernas**. The *Octopus Tree*, a small *kafenío* by the fishing boats, serves cheap fresh seafood caught by the owner, while on the front heading towards the beach, the *Waves Restaurant* does good Indian food; *Enigma* is a warm, intimate space serving cuisine from Cyprus, and *Café Cyclades* is a good spot for a snack. A twenty-minute stroll over the headland at **KOUMBÁRA**, there's a smaller and less crowded beach, with a rocky islet to explore, and the *Polydoros* taverna, one of the better places to eat on Íos – well worth the walk or bus ride; here you'll also find the excellent *Filippos* fish taverna and the lively *La Luna* café-bar on the beach.

Hóra

HÓRA (also called Íos Town), a twenty-minute walk up behind the port, is one of the most picturesque towns in the Cyclades, filled with meandering arcaded lanes and whitewashed chapels, though it's not exactly quiet when the younger crowd moves in for the high season. It divides naturally into two parts: the old town climbing the hillside to the left as you arrive, and the newer development to the right.

The **archeological museum** (Tues–Sun 8.30am–3pm; €2), in the yellow town hall, is part of an attempt to attract a more diverse range of visitors to the island. The **outdoor theatre** of Odysseus Elytis, behind the windmills, provides a beautiful setting in which to enjoy concerts and plays, details of which can be found at the **travel agent** and information booth next to the archeological museum.

There are plenty of basic **rooms** in the old part, although the bars can make it noisy. Your best strategy for a modicum of quiet is to wend your way up to the left where you find several establishments, including the excellent ✳ *Francesco's* (☎22860 91223, ⓦ www.francescos.net; ❸) which offers the best value on the island, with clean doubles, a small number of dorms (€12 per person) and spectacular views from its bar. Near the bus stop, there's the new, more grown-up, *Mediterraneo* (☎22860 91521, ⓦ www.mediterraneo-ios.com; ❻), with nice balconied rooms overlooking a pool. In the new quarter *Lofos Pension* (☎22860 91481, ⓔ lofosvillagehotel@yahoo.com; ❸), to the right up from the Rollan supermarket, is a good bet, and also runs the swanky new *Lofos Village* hotel (❸) further up the hill (contact details as above). The friendly *Four Seasons Pension* (☎22860 91308, ⓕ 22860 91136; ❹), up from Vangelis Bike Rental, is another quiet, but still central, choice.

Every evening in summer, Hóra is the centre of the island's **nightlife**, its streets throbbing with music from ranks of competing discos and clubs – mostly free, or with a nominal entrance charge, and inexpensive drinks. (Do, however, be wary of drinks that are overly cheap, as a few unscrupulous bars still resort to selling *bomba*, a cheap local drink that gets you drunk fast and makes you sick. If in doubt, ask for spirits by brand name.) Most of the smaller **bars** and pubs are tucked into the thronging narrow streets of the old village on the hill, offering something for everyone, and you'll have no trouble finding them. A welcome exception to the techno-pop dancing fodder can be found at the *Ios Club*, perched right up on the hill, which plays quieter music, has reasonable food and is a good place to watch the sunset. Evenings tend to start out in places like the *Fun Pub*, which also plays free films and has a pool table, and then progress around midnight to the bars up in the old town where *Rehab*, *Flames* and the *Red Bull Bar* are popular choices. Those looking to carry on, eventually stagger down to the main road, where the larger **dance clubs** such as *Star Club*, *Scorpion* and the somewhat kitsch *Sweet Irish Dream* are clustered near the bus stop.

Eating is a secondary consideration, but there are plenty of cheap and cheerful *psistariés* and takeaway joints: sound choices include the Italian restaurant

Pinocchio, The Nest taverna, and the *Lord Byron mezedhopolíon* in an alley up to the left in the old quarter – it's open year round and tries hard to recreate a traditional atmosphere, with old rebétika music and some good, unusual Greek food. *Ali Baba's*, meanwhile, is an excellent place to start the evening, with good food deals on a range of international choices and a free film most nights.

Around the island

The most popular stop on the island's bus routes is **MYLOPÓTAMOS** (universally abbreviated to Mylópotas), the site of a magnificent beach with watersport facilities (see box on p.610) and a mini-resort. Due to the large number of young travellers in Íos, **camping** is a popular option. *Far Out Beach Club* (T 22860 91468, W www.faroutclub.com) is the larger of the campsites, with excellent facilities, including a good-value cafeteria and bar (where you may well end up even if you're not staying). It is, however, very popular and can get noisy and crowded in August. *Purple Pig Stars* (T 22860 91302, W www .purplepigstars.com) is a friendly, laid-back complex by the road up to Hóra, with clean bungalows (❷) and good camping facilities, including its own club and poolside bar. Up the road at the far end of the beach, *Gorgona* (T & F 22860 91307; ❹), *Dracos* (T 22860 91281; ❹) and *Hotel Ios Plage* (T 22860 91301, W www.iosplage.com; ❺) have reasonable rooms, the last with an excellent restaurant on its terrace. *Hotel Katerina* (T 22860 91614, W www.ioskaterina .com; ❺), nicely situated by a pool looking over the bay, and the luxurious *Ios Palace Hotel* (T 22860 91269, W www.iospalacehotel.com; ❻), above the near end of the beach, are among the most upmarket choices besides the two expensive hotels maintained by *Far Out* (T 22860 91468, W www.faroutclub.com; ❻), the *Far Out Village Hotel*, next to the *Far Out Beach Club*, and the *Far Out Hotel* (❻), up on the hill on the road approaching Mylopótamos. On the rocks, beyond the *Ios Palace*, the *Harmony Restaurant* is one of the better places to eat, serving pizzas and Mexican food. The restaurants and self-service cafés behind the beach are uninspiring, and only the *Faros Café* rates a mention for staying open through the night to cater for the crowds returning from Hóra in the early hours. Mylopótamos itself has surprisingly little in the way of nightlife.

From Yialós, daily boats depart at around 10am (returning in the late afternoon; €12 return) to **Manganári** on the south coast, where there's a beach and a swanky hotel; you can also get there by scooter. Most people go from Yialós to Manganári by private buses run by travel agencies (€6 return), which leave Yialós about 11am, calling at Hóra and Mylopótamos and returning later in the afternoon; the condition of the road, however, makes the boat a much more pleasant option. Once predominantly nudist, shedding clothes here is now officially discouraged though still very much in practice. There's more to see, and a better atmosphere, **Ayía Theodhóti** up on the east coast. You can get there on a paved road across the island – the daily excursion bus costs €3 return. A couple of kilometres south of Ayía Theodhóti is **Paleókastro**, a ruined Venetian castle which encompasses the remains of a marble-finished town and a Byzantine church. In the unlikely event that the beach – a good one and mainly nudist – is too crowded, try the one at **Psathí**, 14km to the southeast, although you'll need your own transport. Frequented by wealthy Athenians, this small resort has a couple of average, but pricey, tavernas, although *Alonistra* fish taverna is a cheaper, excellent exception. Another decent beach is at **Kálamos**: get off the Manganári bus at the turning for Kálamos, which leaves you with a four-kilometre walk.

"Homer's" tomb can be reached by motorbike along a safe unpaved road (turning left from the paved road to Ayía Theodhóti 4.5km from Hóra). The town itself has long since slipped down the side of the cliff, but the rocky ruins of the entrance to a tomb remain, as well as some graves – one of which is claimed to be Homer's, but which in reality probably dates only to the Byzantine era.

Síkinos

Síkinos has so small a population that the mule ride or walk up from the port to the village was only replaced by a bus late in the 1980s and, until the new jetty was completed at roughly the same time, it was the last major Greek island where ferry passengers were still taken ashore in launches. With no dramatic characteristics, nor any nightlife to speak of, few foreigners make the short trip over here from neighbouring Íos and Folégandhros or from sporadically connected Páros, Náxos or Thíra. There is now a **bank** with an ATM on the island as well as a **post office** up in Kástro-Hóra, and you can sometimes change cash at the store in Aloprónia.

Aloprónia and Kástro-Hóra

Such tourist facilities as exist are concentrated in the little harbour of **ALOPRÓNIA**, with its long sandy beach and extended breakwater and jetty. More and more formal **accommodation** is being built, but it's still possible to camp or just sleep out under the tamarisks behind the beach. Try *Flora* (T 22860 51214; **3**), with comfortable rooms near the main road leading to Hóra, or the popular *The Rock* (T 22860 51186; **3**), above the *Rock Café*. Alternatively, the comfortable and traditional *Hotel Kamares* (T 22860 51234, T 22860 51281; **3**) has a nicer setting than the pricier, but luxurious, *Porto Síkinos* complex (T 22860 51220, W www.portosikinos.gr; **6**). The handful of **tavernas** and

café-bars in town are virtually all affiliated with the properties listed above and bear the same names, *Loukas* taverna being the most affordable if the most standard option.

The double village of **KÁSTRO-HÓRA** is served by the single island bus, which shuttles regularly from early morning till quite late in the evening between the harbour and here, though the route should soon be extended to Episkopí with the completion of the new road. On the ride up, the scenery turns out to be less desolate than initial impressions suggest. Draped across a ridge overlooking the sea, Kástro-Hóra makes for a charming day-trip, and the lovely oil-press **museum** (summer 5–7pm; free), run privately by a Greek-American, is highly recommended. A partly ruined monastery, **Zoödhóhou Piyís** ("Life-giving Spring", a frequent name in the Cyclades), crowns the rock above. The architectural highlight of the place, though, is the central quadrangle of **Kástro**, a series of ornate eighteenth-century houses arrayed defensively around a chapel square, their backs to the exterior of the village. There are only a few basic **rooms** in town, reserved through the Divoli family (T 22860 51263 or 22860 51212; **②**) or Antonios Margetis (T 22860 51253; **③**). A good selection of **food** is available, along with fine local wine, at *Klimataria* and *To Steki tou Garbi* next door. The *kafenía* up here are very traditional affairs and you might feel more welcome at the café-bars *Kastro* or *Platía*.

Around the island

West of Kástro-Hóra, an hour-plus walk takes you through a landscape lush with olive trees to **Episkopí**, where elements of an ancient temple-tomb have been ingeniously incorporated into a seventh-century church – the structure is known formally as the Iröön, though it's now thought to have been a Roman mausoleum rather than a temple of Hera. Ninety minutes from Kástro-Hóra, in the opposite direction, lies **Paleókastro**, the patchy remains of an ancient fortress. The beaches of **Áyios Yeóryios** and **Áyios Nikólaos** are reachable by a regular *kaïki* from Aloprónia; the former is a better option because it has the daytime *Almira* restaurant. It is possible to walk to them, but there is no real path at the later stages. A more feasible journey by foot is to the pebble beach at **Áyios Pandelímonas**: just under an hour's trail walk southwest of Aloprónia, it is the most scenic and sheltered on the island, and is also served by a *kaïki* in season.

Folégandhros

The cliffs of **Folégandhros** rise sheer over 300m from the sea in places, and until the early 1980s they were as effective a deterrent to tourists as they always were to pirates. Folégandhros was used as an island of political exile right up until 1974, but life in the high, barren interior has been eased since the junta years by the arrival of electricity and the construction of a road running lengthways from the harbour to Hóra and beyond. Development has been given further impetus by the recent increase in tourism and the mild commercialization this has brought.

A veritable explosion in accommodation for most budgets, and improvement in ferry arrival times, means there is no longer much need for – or local tolerance of – sleeping rough on the beaches. The increased wealth and trendiness of the heterogeneous clientele are reflected in fancy jewellery shops, an arty postcard gallery and a helipad. Yet away from the showcase Hóra and the beaches, the countryside remains mostly pristine, and is largely devoted to the spring and summer cultivation of barley, the mainstay of many of the Cyclades before the advent of tourism. Donkeys and donkey paths are also still very much in evidence, since the terrain on much of the island is too steep for vehicle roads.

Karavostási and around

KARAVOSTÁSI, the rather unprepossessing port whose name simply means "ferry stop", serves as a last-resort base; it has several **hotels** but little atmosphere. Best value is *Hotel Aeolos* (☎22860 41205, ⓦwww.aeolos-folegandros .gr; ❹), while *Vardia Bay* (☎22860 41277, ⓦwww.vardiabay.com; ❻, out of season ❶) has a great location and is open all year. The modern *Vrahos Hotel* (☎22860 41450, ⓦwww.hotel-vrahos.gr; ❺) has some nice rooms on the far side of the bay. *Iy Kali Kardhia* **taverna** above the harbour has an excellent traditional menu, and there are a couple of pleasant beach **bars** including the *Smyrna Ouzeri*, housed in a converted boathouse. There are many buses a day in summer to Hóra, three continuing to Áno Meriá; Jimmy's **motorbike rental** (☎22860 41448) is cheaper than its counterparts in Hóra.

The closest **beach** is the smallish, but attractive enough, sand-and-pebble **Vardhiá**, signposted just north over the headland. Some fifteen minutes' walk south lies **Livádhi**, a rather average beach with tamarisk trees and the island's official **campsite**, *Livadhi Camping* (☎ & ⓕ22860 41204), which is good and friendly, although the hot water supply can be erratic.

Easily the most scenic beach on Folégandhros, a 300-metre stretch of pea-gravel with an offshore islet, is at **Katergó**, on the southeastern tip of the island. Most people visit on a boat excursion from Karavostási or Angáli, but you can also get there on foot from the hamlet of Livádhi, a short walk inland from Loustriá. Be warned, though, that it's a rather arduous trek, with some nasty trail-less slithering in the final moments.

Hóra

The island's real character and appeal are to be found in the spectacular **HÓRA**, perched on a clifftop plateau some 45 minutes' walk from the dock; an hourly high-season **bus** service (6 daily spring & autumn) runs from morning until late at night. Locals and foreigners – hundreds of them in high season – mingle at the cafés and tavernas under the almond, flowering Judas and pepper trees of the two main platíes, passing the time undisturbed by traffic, which is banned from the village centre. Towards the cliff-edge, and entered through two arcades, the defensive core of the medieval **kástro** is marked by ranks of two-storey houses, whose repetitive, almost identical stairways and slightly recessed doors are very appealing.

From the square where the bus stops, a zigzag path with views down to both coastlines climbs to the cragtop, wedding-cake church of **Kímisis Theotókou**, nocturnally illuminated to grand effect. Beyond and below it hides the **Khryssospiliá**, a large cave with stalactites, accessible only to proficient climbers; the necessary steps and railings have crumbled away into the sea, although a minor, lower grotto can still be visited by *kaïki* from the port.

Practicalities

Accommodation in and around Hóra seems slightly weighted to favour hotels over rooms, with concentrations around the bus plaza at the eastern entrance to the village and at the western edge. Many of the tavernas and shops advertise rooms in their windows; otherwise try the basic but comfortable *Nikos Rooms* (☎22860 41055; ❹) in the centre. Of the hotels, the *Polikandia* (☎22860 41322, 🖷22860 41323; ❹), just below the bus stop, is one of the best choices. The most luxurious facilities are at the cliff-edge *Anemomilos Apartments* (☎22860 41309, 🖳www.anemomilosapartments.com; ❻), immaculately appointed, with stunning views and a romantic cocktail bar from which to watch the sunset. They also have a room specially adapted for wheelchair users. The new *Meltemi* (☎22860 41328, 🅴meltemihotel@yahoo.gr; ❹), just opposite, has clean, beautiful rooms. The only hotel actually within Hóra is the traditional *Castro* (☎22860 41230, 🖳www.hotel-castro.com; ❻), built in 1212, with three rather dramatic rooms looking directly out on an alarming drop to the sea. At the western edge of Hóra near the police station, a dense cluster of rooms tend to block each other's views. By the roadside on the way to Áno Meriá, the *Fani-Vevis* (☎22860 41237; ❹), in a Neoclassical mansion overlooking the sea, functions only in high season.

Hóra's dozen or so **restaurants** are surprisingly varied. The *Folegandhros* ouzerí in the first plaza is fun, if a bit eccentrically run. Breakfast can be enjoyed on the adjacent Platía Kondaríni at *Iy Melissa*, which does good fruit and yoghurt, omelettes and juices. *Iy Piatsa* has a nightly changing menu of well-executed Greek dishes, while their neighbour and local hangout *O Kritikos* is notable only for its grills. *Iy Pounda* near the bus stop is the most traditional place and has a small garden. Hóra is inevitably beginning to sprawl at the edges, and the burgeoning **nightlife** – a few dance bars along with a number of music pubs and ouzerís – is to the north, away from most accommodation. *Avissos* and *Patitiri* are two hip, lively bars, while *Avli* offers use of its hubbly bubbly pipes, and *Kellari* is a rustic and charming wine bar where the atmosphere is more relaxed. A **post office**, **ATM**, and **Internet** access in the travel agency by the bus station, completes the list of amenities, though the single **ferry agent** also does money exchange, as does the friendly and competent Italian-run Sottovento agency on the other side of town (☎22860 41444, 🅴sottovento94@hotmail .com), which also offers a wide range of other services.

The rest of the island

Northwest of Hóra, a narrow, paved road threads its way towards **ÁNO MERIÁ**, the other village of the island; after 4km you pass its first houses, clustered around the three churches of Áyios Pandelímonas, Áyios Yeóryios and Áyios Andhréas. The **folk museum** (daily 5–8pm; donation requested), on a nineteenth-century farm near the town's entrance, traces the history of the island's people. **Tavernas**, which operate in high season only, include the traditional *O Mimis*, *Tou Mitsaki* and *Iliovasilema*.

Up to seven times a day in high season, a **bus** trundles out here to drop people off at the footpaths down to the various sheltered beaches on the southwest shore of the island. Busiest of these is **Angáli** (also called Vathý), where there are a few simple summer-only tavernas, reached by a fifteen-minute walk along a dirt road from the bus stop. Near to Angáli are the better of the few basic **rooms** available in the northern part of the island: *Irini* (☎22860 41190; ❸) and *Panagiotis* (☎22860 41301; ❸).

Nudists should take the paths which lead twenty minutes east or west to **Firá** or **Áyios Nikólaos** beaches respectively; the latter in particular, with its many tamarisks, coarse sand and view back over the island, is Katergó's only serious rival in the best-beach stakes. At Áyios Nikólaos, a lone taverna operates up by the namesake chapel; Firá has no facilities at all. From the *Iliovasilema* taverna, a motorable track continues north to a point from where a 500-metre path takes you down to the pleasant little bay of **Ambéli**.

Santoríni (Thíra)

As the ferry manoeuvres into the great caldera of **Santoríni**, the land seems to rise up and clamp around it. Gaunt, sheer cliffs loom hundreds of metres above, nothing grows or grazes to soften the awesome view, and the only colours are the reddish-brown, black and grey pumice striations layering the cliff face of **Thíra**, the largest island in this mini-archipelago, and the location of all but the smallest of its modern settlements. The landscape tells of a history so dramatic and turbulent that legend hangs as fact upon it.

From as early as 3000 BC, the island developed as a sophisticated outpost of Minoan civilization, until sometime between 1647 and 1628 BC (according to

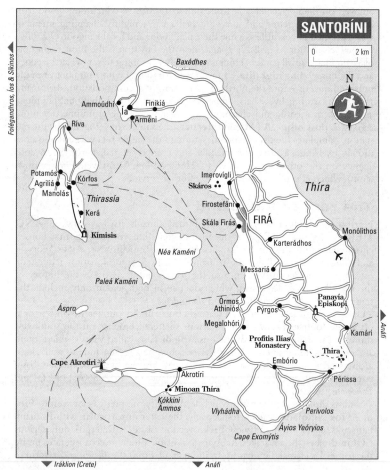

latest estimates) when catastrophe struck: the volcano-island erupted, its heart sank below the sea, leaving a crater (**caldera**) 10km in diameter, and earthquakes reverberated across the Aegean. Thíra was destroyed and the great Minoan civilization on Crete was dealt a severe blow. At this point, the island's history became linked with legends of Atlantis, the "Happy Isles Submerged by Sea". Plato insisted that the legend was true, and Solon dated the cataclysm to 9000 years before his time – if you're willing to accept a mistake and knock off the final zero, a highly plausible date.

These apocalyptic events, though, scarcely concern modern tourists, who come here to take in the spectacular views, stretch out on the island's dark-sand beaches and absorb the peculiar, infernal geographic features; as recently as a century ago, Thíra was still reckoned to be infested with vampires. The tourism industry has changed traditional island life, creating a rather expensive playground, which on the plus side makes this one of the most tourist-friendly islands in the Cyclades. There is one time-honoured local industry, however, that has benefited from all the outside attention: **wine**. Santoríni is one of Greece's most important producers, and the fresh, dry white wines it is known for (most from the *assýrtiko* grape for which the region is known) are the perfect accompaniment to the seafood served in the many restaurants and tavernas that hug the island's postcard-perfect cliffs.

Arrival

Ferries dock at the somewhat grim port of **Órmos Athiniós**; **Skála Firás** and **Ía** in the north are reserved for local ferries, excursion *kaïkia* and cruise ships. **Buses**, astonishingly crammed, connect Athiniós with the island capital Firá, and, less frequently, with Ía and the main beaches at Kamári and Périssa. Disembark quickly and take whatever bus is going, if you want to avoid a long wait or a tedious hike up. You'll be accosted at Athiniós by people offering rooms all over the island; in the summer it might be a good idea to pay attention to them, given the scramble for beds, in Firá especially. There have been reports, though, of various scams involving the promise of beds in Firá which turn out to be elsewhere; keep your wits about you, and if in doubt, ask someone else. From Skála Firás, you have the traditional route of 580 steps (about 45 minutes) up to Firá – not too difficult a walk, if you don't mind mule manure – or you can go by mule (€3.50, negotiable off-season) or cable car (summer only 6.40am–10pm, every 20min; €3), so exhilarating a ride that you may want to take it for fun. The **airport** is on the east side of the island, near Monólithos; there is a regular shuttle-bus service to the Firá bus station, which runs until 10pm.

Firá

Half-rebuilt after a devastating earthquake in 1956, **FIRÁ** (also known as Thíra or Hóra) still clings precariously to the edge of the enormous caldera. The rising and setting of the sun are especially beautiful when seen here against the whites of the Cycladic buildings clinging to the clifftop, and are even enough to make battling through the high-season crowds worthwhile.

Arrival, information and accommodation

Buses leave Firá from just south of Platía Theotokopoúlou to Périssa, Perívolos, Kamári, Monólithos, Akrotíri, Órmos Athiniós and the airport. **Taxis** go from near the bus station, within steps of the main square. If you want to see the whole island in a couple of days, a rented **motorbike** might do, though you must be very careful – especially since local drivers seem to enjoy antagonizing tourists on difficult and precipitous roads. Try Moto Chris at the top of the road that leads down to *Santorini Camping* (see below), while Ancient Thira Tours (℡ 22860 23915) on the main street in Firá, hire out **mountain bikes** and quads. The Firá branch of Nomikos Travel, opposite the OTE, is friendly and organizes **excursions** and trips to ancient Thíra and Thirassía in conjunction with Kamari Tours (℡ 22860 31390). The state-run **tourist office** (daily 9am–midnight in season; ℡ 22860 25490), on the main street near the bus station, may also be able to help you out. There are several **Internet cafés** gathered on the main square, and a number of **launderettes** dotted around town, the best being We do Laundry, just above the road to the campsite.

Accommodation

Santoríni certainly isn't cheap, and properties in Firá with a view of the caldera tend to be expensive. **Firostefáni**, between Firá and Imerovígli, has slightly less expensive rooms with equally stunning views, though as the area gets trendier by the minute, it's hardly a bargain destination. Another good location, where you don't have to pay as much for the view, is **Karterádhos**, a small village about twenty minutes' walk southeast of Firá. The official **youth hostel** was closed for renovation at the time of writing, but plans to reopen in 2006; contact the hostel in Ía (see p.696) to find out. The only other option for budget accommodation is *Santorini Camping* (℡ 22860 22944, ⓦ www.santorinicamping .gr), the nearest **campsite** to town. (The best campsite on the island is near Akrotíri village; see p.699.) Considering Santoríni's popularity, it's definitely worth phoning for accommodation in advance.

Firá

Archontiko Apartments Off Agiou Mina ℡ 22860 24376, ⓔ archontikoapartments@hotmail.com. Stunning antique-furnished apartments perched in a quiet spot over the caldera. May–Oct. ❺

Hotel New Haroula On road to the campsite ℡ 22860 24226, ⓦ www.newharoula.com. Stylish but laid-back family-run hotel with pool and smart doubles. April–Oct. ❺

Loucas Off Ypapantis ℡ 22860 22480, ⓦ www .loucashotel.com. Traditional caldera-side hotel with rooms in barrel-ceilinged caves carved into the cliffside to prevent collapse during an earth-quake, and a beautiful new pool. Feb–Oct. ❼

Pelican Hotel On road to campsite ℡ 22860 23113, ⓦ www.pelican.gr. Large hotel with spacious rooms near the centre. B&B ❻

🏃 **San Giorgio** Opposite fast-food restaurant *Goody's* on the main square ℡ 22860 23516, ⓦ www.sangiorgiovilla.gr. Excellent value, clean en-suite rooms, all with balconies (ten percent discount for Rough Guide readers). April–Oct. ❹

Theoxenia Ypapantis ℡ 22860 22740, ⓦ www .theoxenia.net. Stylish boutique hotel with large rooms right in the old town. Guests can also use the caldera-side pool at the nearby *Arisanna* hotel. ❼

Villa Rena 10 minutes' walk from town towards the folklore museum ℡ 22860 28130. Comfortable hotel with a large pool in a quiet spot near the open-air cinema (ten percent discount for Rough Guide readers). April–Oct. ❺

Firostefáni

Hotel Galini On waterfront ℡ 22860 22095, ⓦ www.hotelgalini.gr. Good-value, friendly hotel carved into the cliff face in a relatively quiet spot 10 minutes' walk from Firá. March–Nov. ❻

Hotel Mylos On main street ℡ 22860 23884. One of the cheaper options in Firostefáni; rooms come with all mod cons and balconies. April–Oct. ❺

Manos Apartments On waterfront ℡ 22860 23202, ⓦ www.manos-apartments.gr. Large, cool apartments with kitchens, huge verandas and great views. April–Oct. B&B ❼

Karterádhos

Pension George ℡ 22860 22351, ⓦ www .pensiongeorge.com. Great pension with comfort-able rooms, pool, and a good welcome, just fifteen minutes' walk from Firá. ❸

The Town

To go along with the views, Firá also has several excellent museums. The **archeological museum** (Tues–Sun 8am–3.30pm; €3 includes entrance to museum of Prehistoric Thira), near the cable car to the north of town, has a collection which includes a curious set of erotic Dionysiac figures. At the other end of town, between the cathedral and bus station, the new **museum of Prehistoric Thira** (Tues–Sun 8.30am–7.30pm; €3 includes entrance to the archeological museum), has interesting displays of fossils, Cycladic art and astonishing finds from Akrotíri. The handsome **Megaro Ghyzi** (Mon–Sat 10.30am–1.30pm & 5–8pm, Sun 10.30am–4.30pm; €3), above the archeological museum in an old mansion owned by the Catholic diocese of Santoríni, has been restored as a cultural centre, and has a good collection of old prints and maps as well as photographs of the town before and after the 1956 earthquake. Further north along the caldera, the **Thíra Foundation**, housed in galleries carved into the cliffside, contains superb life-size colour photo reproductions of the frescoes of Akrotíri (daily 10am–8pm; €3). Towards the back of the town, north of the main square, is the extensive **Lignos folklore museum** (daily 10am–2pm & 6–8pm; €3), which features a completely furnished nineteenth-century house with period winery, cavern, garden and workshops, as well as a gallery and historical archive.

Eating and nightlife

Firá's **restaurants** are primarily aimed at the tourist market, but for dependably good food with a sensational view (and prices to match) find *Aris*, below the *Loucas* hotel, or try the *Flame of the Volcano*, the last of the caldera-side restaurants north past the cable-car station (towards Firostefáni). *Mama's House*, just north of the main square on the road to Ía, is an excellent, backpacker-friendly spot with cheap, filling dishes and views from its balcony. On Erythroú Stavroú, the first street up from the main square, *Nikolas* is an old and defiantly traditional taverna, but it can be hard to get a table; the best moderately priced choice is *Naoussa*, further north on the same street, upstairs on the right. Nearby *Sphinx* offers exotic pasta dishes with a Greek twist, while *Calderimi*, near the cathedral, serves excellent Italian and Mediterranean food. Otherwise try *Vanilla*, a romantic, candlelit spot in Firostefáni. A good breakfast or afternoon snack can be found at *Corner Crêpes*, near the main square, or at the slightly trendier *Diverso* on the square itself.

△Firá, Santoríni

Most of the **nightlife** is northwest of the central square on Erythroú Stavroú: *Murphy's Bar* is an expensive but fun Irish pub with all the obligatory hilarity, while above there's the slightly cooler *Enigma* and *Koo* with chilled-out music and candles to set the scene. The best bars from which to admire the caldera are *Franco's* and *Palia Kameni*, two rather exclusive and pricey cocktail bars with unbeatable locations. More laid-back, but set back from the caldera, is the *Kira Thira* bar, which also offers a wine-tasting package. There is a new open-air **cinema** near the folklore museum.

Northern Santoríni

Once outside Firá, the rest of Thíra comes as a nice surprise. The volcanic soil is highly fertile, with every available space terraced and cultivated: wheat, tomatoes, pistachios and grapes are the main crops (see p.699 for information on Santoríni's wines), all still harvested and planted by hand.

A satisfying – if demanding – approach to **Ía**, 12km from Firá in the northwest of the island, is to walk the stretch from **IMEROVÍGLI**, 3km out of Firá, using a spectacular footpath along the lip of the caldera; the walk takes around two hours. Jutting up from the side of the cliff is the conspicuous conical rock of **Skáros**, once the site of an important settlement and Venetian fortress, the scant remains of which can still be seen; known also as Castle Rock, it can be mounted along a steep but obvious trail for unsurpassed views over the caldera and back to Thíra. Imerovígli is crowded with luxury, caldera-side **apartments** such as *Chromata* (☎22860 24850, ⓦwww.chromata-santorini.com; ❼) and *Astra* (☎22860 23641, ⓦwww.astra.gr; ❼), requiring reservations well in advance; *Katerina* (☎22860 22708, Ⓕ22860 23398; ❺) is a more moderately priced hotel, with caldera views from the large balcony/bar area only. Between the *Katerina* and *Chromata*, *Altana* is a small **café** whose position and relaxed atmosphere make for a pleasing breakfast spot. Continuing to Ía, you'll pass Toúrlos, an old Venetian citadel on Cape Skáros.

Ía and around

ÍA, the most delightful village on the island, was once a major fishing port of the Aegean, but it has declined in the wake of economic depression, wars, earthquakes and depleted fish stocks. Partly destroyed in the 1956 earthquake, the town has been sympathetically reconstructed, its pristine white houses clinging to the cliff face. Apart from the caldera and the village itself, there are a couple of things to see, including the **naval museum** (Mon & Wed–Sun 10am–2pm & 5–8pm; €3) and the very modest remains of a Venetian castle. Ía is a fine, and quieter, alternative to Firá, with a **post office** and several **bike-rental** offices (of which Motor Fun is particularly good), an **Internet** café, and a good foreign-language bookshop, Atlantis Books. There are also a couple of travel agencies – Karvounis (☎22860 71290, ⓔmkarvounis@otenet.gr), on the pedestrian street, is older and more reliable.

Much of the town's **accommodation** is in its restored old houses, including the traditional *Hotel Lauda* (☎22860 71204, Ⓕ22860 71274; ❻), the popular *Hotel Anemones* (☎22860 71220; ❺), the *Hotel Fregata* (☎22860 71221, ⓦwww .fregata.gr; ❺) with its central location and good views; and the luxurious *Perivolas Traditional Houses* (☎22860 71308, ⓦwww.perivolas.gr; ❼), which are cut into the cliff near a pool suspended at its edge. Yet another step up are the stunning *Art Maisons* (☎22860 71831, ⓦwww.artmaisons.gr; ❽), four self-contained apartments on their own promontory in the heart of the town. Near the bus terminal, and well signposted, is the excellent ⚐ *Oia Youth Hostel*

(☎22860 71465; €13 per person), with a terrace and shady courtyard, a good bar, clean dormitories and breakfast included.

Generally, the further you go along the central ridge towards the new end of Ía, the better value the **restaurants**: the *Anemomilos* and *Laokastri* are two such examples. Slightly removed from the sunset tourist stampede, the pleasant *Karma*, serving Eastern cuisine, is on the road leading down to the youth hostel, while, for a splurge, ✖ *1800* is generally regarded as the finest restaurant on the island, serving a highly refined Mediterranean cuisine. **Nightlife** revolves around sunset-gazing, for which people are coached in from all over the island, creating traffic chaos and driving up prices, though the sunset is no different seen from Ía than from Firá.

Below the town, two sets of 200-odd steps switchback hundreds of metres down to two small harbours: one to **Ammoúdhi**, for the fishermen, and the other to **Arméni**, where the excursion boats dock. Both have decent fish tavernas, the one in Arméni specializing in grilled octopus lunches. **FINIKIÁ**, 1km east of Ía, is a very quiet and traditional little village. *Lotza Rooms* (☎22860 71051; ❸) are located in an old house in the middle of the village, while *Hotel Finikia* (☎22860 71373, ⓕ22860 71118; ❺), above the village near the main road, is a smarter option. About 2km north of Ía is **Baxédhes** beach, with a few tavernas including the *Paradhisos*, which has good food and reasonable prices. It's a quiet alternative to Kamári and Périssa (see below), though it's not much of a beach until you reach a secluded cape, about 1km east, where ancient tombs have been discovered carved into the rock.

The east coast

Beaches on Thíra, to the east and south, are bizarre – long black stretches of volcanic sand which get blisteringly hot in the afternoon sun. They're no secret, and in the summer the crowds can be a bit overpowering.

Closest to Firá, **MONÓLITHOS** has a couple of tavernas including the excellent *Mario* and *Galini*. To the south is the pricier *Domata*, serving fusion cuisine that gives Italian food a Greek flair. Further south, **KAMÁRI** is popular with package-tour operators, and hence more touristy. Nonetheless it's quieter and cleaner than most, and is home to a decent diving centre (see box p.610). There's a range of beachfront **accommodation**, including *Hotel Nikolina* (☎22860 32363, ⓔnikolina-htl@hol.gr; ❸), with basic but cheap rooms towards the southern end of the beach, as well as the spacious, if ageing, *White House* (☎69970 91488; ❹) and the friendly *Sea Side Hotel* (☎22860 33403, ⓦwww.seaside.gr; ❹) further along the beach. *Rose Bay Hotel* (☎22860 33650, ⓦwww.rosebay.gr; ❼) is a much pricier option, with a pleasant pool setting, set back away from the noisy beach thoroughfare.

Psistaria O Kritikos, a taverna-grill frequented by locals, is one of the best places to **eat** on the island. It's a long way out of Kamári on the road up to Messariá, and too far to walk, but the bus stops outside. There are plenty of cafés and restaurants behind the beach, though many are expensive or uninspiring. *Saliveros*, in front of the *Hotel Nikolina*, has taverna food at reasonable prices, and *Almira*, next to *Sea Side Rooms*, is a smarter restaurant and only a little more expensive. Kamári is a family resort with little in the way of clubs and nightlife, but there is a good open-air **cinema** near the campsite, and in summer buses run until 1am, so there's no problem getting back to Firá after seeing a film. West of Kamári is **Panayía Episkopí**, the most important Byzantine monument on the island. Built in the eleventh century, it was the setting of centuries of conflict between Orthodox Greeks and Catholics, but is most notable today for its carved iconostasis of light blue marble with a white grain.

Things are scruffier at **PÉRISSA**, around the cape. Because of its attractive situation and abundance of cheap rooms, it's crowded with backpackers. *Camping Perissa Beach* (☎22860 81343) is right behind the beach and has plenty of shade but is also next to a couple of noisy late-night bars. There is also a basic youth hostel on the road into Périssa: *Anna* (☎22860 82182, ✉annayh@otenet .gr; €8 per person). There are plenty of cheap rooms in the same area and some upmarket hotels behind the beach; the modern *Meltemi Hotel* (☎22860 81325, ⓦwww.meltemivillage.gr; ❻) on the main road, and which also runs the nearby water park, is a good choice. The beach itself extends almost 7km to the west, sheltered by the occasional tamarisk tree, with beach bars dotted along at intervals. *Dichtia* and *Aquarius* are two excellent restaurants here.

Kamári and Périssa are separated by the Mésa Vounó headland, on which stood **ancient Thira** (Tues–Sun 8.30am–2.30pm; free), the post-eruption settlement dating from the ninth century BC. Excursion buses go up from Kamári (€8), staying two hours at the site (ask at Ancient Thira tours, ☎22860 31827, at the foot of the hill), but you can also ride a donkey up (€15) or walk the **cobbled path** starting from the square in Kamári by the Argo General Store. The site can also be reached by a path from Périssa; from either it's less than an hour's walk.

The path zigzags up to a whitewashed church by a **cave**, containing one of Thíra's few freshwater springs, before crossing over to meet the road and ending at a saddle between Mésa Vounó and Profítis Ilías, where a refreshments van sells expensive drinks. From here, the path to the site passes a chapel dating back to the fourth century AD before skirting round to the Temenos of Artemidoros with bas-relief carvings of a dolphin, eagle and lion representing Poseidon, Zeus and Apollo. Next, the trail follows the sacred way of the ancient city through the remains of the agora and past the theatre. Most of the ruins (dating mainly from Hellenistic and Roman times) are difficult to place, but the site is impressively large and the views are awesome.

Inland Santoríni

About 2km inland from Périssa, on the paved road west, lies **EMBÓRIO**; though virtually ignored by tourists, it's Santoríni's largest village, with a goldmine of whimsical island architecture and the important remnants of the medieval Venetian fortress that once dominated the landscape.

North of here, **PÝRGOS** is one of the oldest settlements on the island, a jumble of old houses and alleys that still bear the scars of the 1956 earthquake. It climbs to another Venetian fortress crowned by several churches, and you can clamber around the battlements for sweeping views over the entire island and its Aegean neighbours. A thirty-minute hike up the steep, winding road to the south leads to the monastery of **Profítis Ilías**, now sharing its refuge with Greek radio and TV pylons and the antennae of a NATO station. With just one monk remaining to look after the church, the place only really comes to life for the annual Profítis Ilías festival, when the whole island troops up here to celebrate. The views are still rewarding, though, and from near the entrance to the monastery an old footpath heads across the mountainous ridge in about an hour to ancient Thíra.

By way of contrast, **MESSARIÁ** – a thirty-minute stroll north – has a skyline consisting solely of massive church domes that lord it over the houses huddled in a ravine. The **Arhondikó Aryírou** (daily 9am–2pm & 4.30–7pm; €4) is a fully restored nineteenth-century mansion combining Neoclassical elements with island architecture. Southwest of here, **MEGALOHÓRI**, conveniently close to Athiniós, has a few diversions including several tavernas, the hip *Art Café*, and the exclusive *Villa Vedema Hotel* (T 22860 81796, W www.vedema .gr; ●), one of the island's finest properties. East of here are scattered a few of Santoríni's most important **wineries**, the largest of which, *Boutari* (just out of Megalohóri), and *Santo* (near Pýrgos) offer the most comprehensive tours (€2–3), complete with multi-media presentations. Slightly more hidden on the road to Kamári are smaller wineries, such as the welcoming *Canava Roussos*, *Antoniou* and *Koutsoyianopoulos* – the last is also home to the **wine museum** (daily noon–8pm; €4 includes tasting) – which offer a more intimate glimpse at the wine-making process. Whatever the scale of the tour, none is complete without a taste of Santoríni's prized dessert wine, **visánto** (remniscent of the *vin santo* of Tuscan fame), among the finest wines produced in Greece. Tour prices at the smaller wineries (€2–5) usually include tastings, while samples are available from the larger wineries for a nominal fee.

Akrotíri and the south coast

Evidence of the Minoan colony that once thrived here has been uncovered at the ancient site of Minoan Thira at **Akrotíri** (Tues–Sat 10am–3pm, but check times with the prehistoric museum in Firá, see p.695; €5), at the southwestern tip of the island. Tunnels through the volcanic ash uncovered structures, two and three storeys high, first damaged by earthquake, then buried by eruption; Professor Marinatos, the excavator and now an island hero, was killed by a collapsing wall and is also buried on the site. Only a small part of what was the largest Minoan city outside of Crete has been excavated thus far, but progress is being made; a protective roof has been installed and walkways have been constructed, allowing you to walk down an ancient Minoan street. Many of the lavish frescoes that once adorned the walls are currently exhibited in Athens, though you can see excellent reproductions at the Thíra Foundation in Firá (see p.695). Visit early to avoid crowds and heat.

Akrotíri itself can be reached by bus from Firá or Périssa. The newest and best **campsite** on the island, *Caldera View Camping* (T 22860 82010, F 22860 81889), is situated here, as is the excellent *Glaros* **taverna**, on the way to **Kókkini Ámmos** beach, which has fine food, though the equally good *Dolphins Taverna* is better situated on the water. Kókkini Ámmos is about 500m from the site and is quite spectacular, with high reddish-brown cliffs above sand of the same colour (the name means "red sand"). There's a drinks stall in a cave hollowed into the base of the cliff. It's a better beach than the one below the site, but gets crowded in season.

The south coast

More secluded black-sand beaches lie under the surreal, pockmarked pumice stone that dominates the lunar coast around **Cape Exomýtis** at the island's southern extremity. Both **Vlyhádha** to the west and **Áyios Yeóryios** to the east of the cape are accessed by decent roads branching off from the main one to Embório, though no buses run here and there are no amenities to speak of. An hour's walk west of ancient Akrotíri, a lighthouse marks the tip of **Cape Akrotíri**, which offers excellent views of the Kaméni islets and Thirassía.

The Kaméni islets and Thirassía

From either Firá or Ía, boat excursions and local ferries run to the charred volcanic islets of **Paleá Kaméni** and **Néa Kaméni**, and on to the relatively unspoilt islet of Thirassía, which was once part of Thíra until shorn off by an eruption in the third century BC. At Paleá Kaméni you can swim from the boat to hot springs with sulphurous mud, and Néa Kaméni, with its own mud-clouded hot springs, features a demanding hike to a smouldering, volcanically active crater.

To escape Thíra's tourist throngs, **Thirassía** is an excellent destination, except during the lunch-hour, tour-boat rush. At other times, the island is one of the quietest in the Cyclades, with views as dramatic as any on Thíra. The downside is that there is no sandy beach, no nightlife and nowhere to change money, though there is an ATM.

Most tour boats head for **Kórfos**, a stretch of shingle backed by fishermen's houses and high cliffs. It has a few tavernas, including *Tonio* which stays open when the day-trippers have gone, but no rooms. From Kórfos a stepped path climbs up to **MANOLÁS**, nearly 200m above. Donkeys are still used for transport, and stables can be seen in both villages. Manolás straggles along the edge of the caldera, an untidy but attractive small island village that gives an idea of what Thíra was like before tourism arrived there. It has a bakery, a couple of shops and the friendly *Panorama* and *Candouni* tavernas which both do a great octopus *souvláki*, and open for the midday rush. Dhimitrios Nomikos has **rooms** (☎22860 29102; ❷) overlooking the village from the south.

The best **excursion** from Manolás is to follow the unmade road heading south; about halfway along you pass the church of Profítis Ilías on a hilltop to the left. From here an old and overgrown trail descends through the deserted caldera-side village of **Kerá**, before running parallel with the road to the **monastery of the Kímisis** above the southern tip of the island. Minoan remains were excavated in a pumice quarry to the west of here in 1867, several years before the first discoveries at Akrotíri, but there is nothing to be seen today.

Ferries run to Thirassía from Órmos Athiniós five times a week; ask at Santo Star (☎22860 23082, ⓦwww.santostar.gr) in Firá for details. There is no problem taking a car or rental bike over, but fill up with petrol first. **Day-tours**, arranged through any of the travel companies in Firá and Ía, take in a hike up to the active crater of Néa Kaméni and a dip in the hot springs at Paleá Kaméni, then stay two or three hours on Thirassía. Prices range from €10 for transport on a large ferry to about €30 for a more intimate guided tour on a traditional *kaïki*. The glass-bottom *Calypso* makes the same excursion for €20 and hovers over the volcanic reefs at the end of each journey to allow passangers a peak at the depths of Santoríni's flooded crater.

Moving on

When it comes to **leaving**, especially for summer evening ferry departures, it's best to buy your ticket in advance. Note, too, that although the bus service stops around midnight, a taxi isn't expensive (about €6 from Firá to Athiniós). Incidentally, **ferry information** from any source is notoriously unreliable on Thíra and rival agencies don't inform you of alternatives – Nomikos Travel (☎22860 23660), with seven branches, is the largest, though Pelikan (☎22860 22220) is also recommended. In any case, it's wise to enquire about your options at several agencies and triple-check departure times before working your way back to the port. If you do get stranded in Athiniós, there's no place to stay, and the tavernas are pretty awful, though there is Internet access at @thinios.com café. With time on your hands, it's probably worth calling for a taxi (☎22860 22555) or zigzagging the 3.5km up to the closest village, **Megalohóri** (see p.699).

Anáfi

A ninety-minute boat ride to the east of Santoríni, **Anáfi** is the last stop for ferries and is something of a travellers' dead end, with no high-season ferries on to Crete or the Dodecanese, and no bank. Not that this is likely to bother most of the visitors, who come here for weeks in midsummer to enjoy the island's beaches.

Although idyllic geographically, Anáfi is a harsh place, its mixed granite and limestone core overlaid by volcanic rock spewed out by Thíra's eruptions. Apart from the few olive trees and vines grown in the valleys, the only plants that seem to thrive are prickly pears.

The harbour and Hóra

The tiny harbour hamlet of **ÁYIOS NIKÓLAOS** has a single taverna, *Akroyiali Popi's*, with a few rooms (☎22860 61218; ❸), and a travel agent selling boat tickets next door. In August there are enough Greek visitors to fill all the rooms on the island, so it's a good idea to book ahead. In season a bus runs from the harbour up to Hóra every two hours or so, 9am to 11pm, to stops at both ends of the village.

HÓRA itself, adorning a conical hill overhead, is a stiff 25-minute climb up the obvious old mule path which short-cuts the modern road. Exposed and blustery when the *meltémi* is blowing, Hóra can initially seem a rather forbidding ghost town. This impression is slowly dispelled as you discover the hospitable islanders taking their coffee in sheltered, south-facing terraces, or under the anti-earthquake barrel vaulting that features in domestic architecture here.

For accommodation, try the terraced, purpose-built **rooms** of *Villa Galini* (☎22860 61279; ❸), or the nearby *Ta Plagia* (☎22860 61308, ⓦ www.taplagia .gr; ❹), and welcoming *Panorama* (☎ & ⓕ 22860 61292; ❸) at the east edge of the village, with stunning views south to the islets of Ftená, Pahiá and Makriá, and the distinctive monolith at the southeastern corner of Anáfi. Also recommended are the rooms of *Illiovasilema* (☎22860 61280, ⓕ 22860 61238; ❸) on the other side of the village (ask at *To Steki* restaurant if you can't find them).

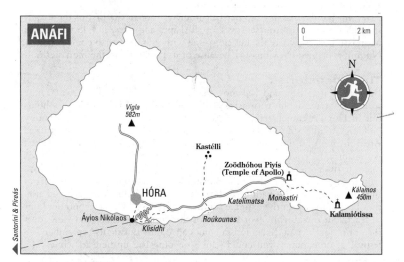

Evening **diners** seem to divide their custom between the simple, welcoming *To Steki*, with reasonable food and barrel wine served on its terrace, and the more upmarket *Alexandhra's* on the central walkway. *Armenaki* is a lively taverna-ouzerí which hosts regular *bouzoúki* nights, whilst the fisherman-owned *Liotrivi* serves up the daily catch. Otherwise, nightlife takes place in *Mylos*, in a converted windmill in the village, and *Argo*, which is also a good spot for breakfast. Anáfi's new roads are best explored by **bike**, and you can rent one at either *Panorama* (see p.613) or Rent Moto-Bikes (℡22860 61280) at the other side of the village. There is also a **travel agency**, Jeyzed Travel (℡22860 61253), who sell boat tickets and arrange excursions around the island. Several shops, a bakery and a **post office** round up the list of amenities.

⑦ East along the coast: beaches and monasteries

The glory of Anáfi is a string of south-facing beaches starting under the cliffs at Áyios Nikólaos, and accessible by road; four buses a day ply the route from Hóra, although walking is still a pleasant option. Rough campers head for **Klisídhi**, a short walk to the east of the harbour, which has 200m of tan, gently shelving sand. Above the calamus-and-tamarisk oasis backing the beach, there are two cafés and a taverna, *Margaritas*, which has decent rooms (℡22860 61237, ℇanafi1@hol.gr; ❷) and accepts credit cards, and the *Villa Apollon* (℡22860 61348; ❹) on the hillside. Klisídhi can be reached by road but it's quicker to take the clifftop path starting behind the power station at the harbour.

From a point on the paved road just east of Hóra, the **main path** skirting the south flank of the island is signposted "Kastélli – Paleá Hóra – Roúkounas – Monastíri". The primary branch of this trail roller-coasters in and out of several agricultural valleys that provide most of Anáfi's produce and fresh water. Just under an hour along, beside a well, you veer down a side trail to **Roúkounas** (also popular with campers and nudists), easily the island's best beach, with some 500m of broad sand rising to tamarisk-stabilized dunes, which provide welcome shade. A single taverna operates up by the main trail in season; the craggy hill of **Kastélli**, an hour's scramble above the taverna, is the site both of ancient Anafi and a ruined Venetian castle.

Beyond Roúkounas, it's another half-hour on foot to the first of the exquisite half-dozen **Katelímatsa** coves, of all shapes and sizes, and 45 minutes to **Monastíri** beach, where the bus stops – all without facilities, so come prepared. Nudism is banned on Monastíri, because of its proximity to the monasteries.

The monasteries

Between Katelímatsa and Kálamos, the main route keeps inland, past a rare spring, to arrive at the **monastery of Zoödhóhou Piyís**, some two hours out of Hóra. A ruined temple of Apollo is incorporated into the monastery buildings to the side of the main gate; according to legend, Apollo caused Anáfi to rise from the waves, pulling off a dramatic rescue of the storm-lashed Argonauts. The courtyard, with a welcome cistern, is the venue for the island's major festival, celebrated eleven days after Easter. A family of cheesemakers lives next door, not far from where the bus stops, and can point you up the start of the spectacular onward path to **Kalamiótissa**, a little monastery perched atop the abrupt pinnacle at the extreme southeast of the island. It takes another hour to reach, but is eminently worthwhile for the stunning scenery and views over the entire south coast. Kalamiótissa comes alive only during its September 7–8 festival; at other times, you could haul a sleeping bag up here to witness the amazing sunsets and sunrises, with your vantage point often floating in a sea of cloud. There is no water up here, so bring enough with you.

Travel details

Ferries

Most of the Cyclades are served by main-line ferries from **Pireás**. Boats for Kéa, and less often Kýthnos, depart from **Lávrio**. There are daily services from **Rafína** to Ándhros, Tínos and Mýkonos, with less frequent sailings to Sýros, Páros, Náxos and Amorgós, and the north and east Aegean. All three ports are easily reached by bus from Athens. From May to September there are also a few weekly sailings from **Thessaloníki** to the most popular islands.

The frequency of sailings given below is intended to give an idea of services from late June to early September, when most visitors tour the islands. During other months, expect departures to be at or below the minimum level listed, with some routes cancelled entirely.

All agents are required to issue computerized tickets, using a computerized booking system. This was designed to conform to EU regulations and prevent the overcrowding of ferries so common in the past. It means that, in high season (particularly August), certain popular routes may be booked up days in advance, so it is important to check availability on arrival in Greece and book your outward and final inbound pre-flight tickets well ahead (particularly those returning to Pireás from the most popular islands). That said, agents are notoriously ill-equipped with advance information on ferry schedules, and purchasing a ticket too far in advance can lead to problems with delayed or cancelled boats. There is usually more space on ferries sailing between islands than to and from Pireás.

Amorgós to: Ándhros (2–3 weekly; 8hr); Astypálea (2–3 weekly; 3hr); Dhonoússa (2–3 weekly; 1hr); Iráklia (2–3 weekly; 1hr); Koufoníssi (2–3 weekly; 1hr); Mýkonos (2–3 weekly; 6hr); Náxos (6–8 weekly; 4hr); Páros (6–8 weekly; 5hr 30min); Pireás (daily; 10hr); Rafina (1 weekly; 12hr); Skhinoússa (2–3 weekly; 1hr); Sýros (3–4 weekly; 7hr); Tínos (2–3 weekly; 7hr).

Anáfi to: Folégandhros (1 weekly; 4hr 30min); Íos (6–8 weekly; 2hr 30min); Náxos (6–8 weekly; 3hr 30min), Páros (6–8 weekly; 4hr); Síkinos (1 weekly; 4hr); Sýros (1 weekly; 10hr); Thíra (6–8 weekly; 1hr

30min & 2 weekly mail boats; 2hr).

Ándhros to: Amorgós (2 weekly; 8hr); Mýkonos (3 daily; 2hr 30min); Náxos (2 weekly; 7hr); Páros (1–4 weekly; 7hr); Sýros (4 weekly; 3hr); Tínos (3 daily; 2hr).

Dhonoússa to: Amorgós (3–4 weekly; 1hr); Iráklia (2–3 weekly; 1hr); Koufoníssi (2–3 weekly; 1hr); Mýkonos (2–3 weekly; 6hr); Náxos (2–3 weekly; 5hr); Páros (2–3 weekly; 5hr 30min); Skhinoússa (2–3 weekly; 1hr); Sýros (2–3 weekly; 7hr 30min); Tínos (2–3 weekly; 6hr 30min).

Folégandhros to: Íos (3–6 weekly; 1hr 30min); Kímolos (2 weekly; 2hr 30 min); Kýthnos (2 weekly; 8hr); Mílos (2 weekly; 2hr 30min); Náxos (3–6 weekly; 2hr 30min); Páros (3–6 weekly; 4hr); Sérifos (2 weekly; 5hr 30min); Sífnos (2 weekly; 5hr); Síkinos (6 weekly; 30min); Sýros (2 weekly; 5hr 30min).

Íos to: Anáfi (4 weekly; 4hr); Crete (1 weekly; 3hr); Folégandhros (4–5 weekly 1hr); Kímolos (1 weekly; 4hr); Mílos (1 weekly; 4hr); Mýkonos (1 daily; 2hr); Náxos (3 daily; 3hr); Páros (3 daily; 5hr); Sérifos (1 weekly; 5hr); Sífnos (1 weekly; 5hr 30min); Síkinos (4–5 weekly; 30min); Sýros (2–3 weekly; 6hr); Thíra (3 daily; 1hr).

Kéa to: Kýthnos (4 weekly; 1hr 30min); Lávrio (1–3 daily; 1hr 30min); Sýros (2 weekly; 3hr).

Kímolos to: Folégandhros (2 weekly; 1hr); Kýthnos (2–5 weekly; 3hr 30min); Mílos, Adhámas (2–5 weekly; 30min); Mílos, Pollónia (4 daily; 30min); Sérifos (2–5 weekly; 2hr 30min); Sífnos (2–5 weekly; 2hr); Síkinos (2 weekly; 1hr 30min); Thíra (2 weekly; 3hr).

Koufoníssi, Skhinoússa, Iráklia to: Amorgós (6 weekly; 2hr); Dhonoússa (6 weekly; 1hr); Mýkonos (1–2 weekly; 1hr 30min); Náxos (2–3 weekly; 1–4hr); Páros (1–2 weekly; 2hr); Sýros (1–2 weekly; 4hr 30min); Tínos (1–2 weekly; 2hr).

Kýthnos to: Folégandhros (3–4 weekly; 8hr 30min); Íos (1–2 weekly; 8hr); Kéa (1–2 weekly; 1hr 30min); Kímolos (4–8 weekly; 3hr 30min); Mílos (4–8 weekly; 4hr); Sérifos (4–8 weekly; 1hr); Sífnos (4–8 weekly; 1hr 30min); Síkinos (1–2 weekly; 8hr), Sýros (1–2 weekly; 3hr); Thíra (3–4 weekly; 10hr).

Mílos to: Crete (Áyios Nikólaos or Sitía; 2 weekly; 8hr); Folégandhros (2–3 weekly; 1hr); Hálki and

Rhodes (1 weekly; 22hr); Íos (2–3 weekly; 2hr); Kárpathos (2 weekly; 16hr); Kássos (2 weekly; 14hr); Kímolos (2–5 daily *kaïkia* & 4–6 weekly ferries; 30min); Kýthnos (1 daily; 3hr); Sérifos (1 daily; 1hr 30min); Sífnos (1 daily; 2hr); Síkinos (2–3 weekly; 1hr 30min); Sýros (2 weekly; 6hr); Thíra (2–3 weekly; 3hr).

Mýkonos to: Amorgós (2–3 weekly; 6hr); Ándhros (at least 2 daily; 2hr 30min); Crete, Iráklion (2 weekly; 9hr); Dhonoússa (1–2 weekly; 2hr); Foúrni (1 weekly; 4hr); Ikaría (3–4 weekly; 2hr); Íos (1 daily; 2hr); Koufoníssi, Skhinoússa and Iráklia (1–2 weekly; all approx. 1hr 30min); Náxos (1 daily; 1hr); Páros (daily; 1hr); Sámos (3–4 weekly; 4hr); Sýros (at least 2 daily; 2hr); Tínos (at least 2 daily; 1hr).

Náxos to: Amorgós (5–7 weekly; 2–6hr); Anáfi (3 weekly; 7hr); Ándhros (2 weekly; 4hr); Astypálea (2–3 weekly; 3hr 30min); Crete, Iráklion (3 weekly; 7hr); Dhonoússa (3–6 weekly; 5hr); Folégandhros (5 weekly; 3hr 30min); Foúrni (1 weekly; 16hr); Ikaría (4–6 weekly; 3hr 30min); Íos (at least 3 daily; 2hr); Iráklia (3–6 weekly; 3hr 30min); Kárpathos (1–2 weekly; 15hr); Kassos (1–2 weekly; 15hr); Kós (1 weekly; 16hr); Koufoníssi (3–6 weekly; 4hr); Páros (at least 3 daily; 1hr); Síkinos (5 weekly; 3hr); Sámos (4–6 weekly; 5hr); Skhinoússa (3–6 weekly; 3hr 30min); Skiáthos (2–3 weekly; 20hr); Sýros (6–8 weekly; 3hr); Thessaloníki (2–3 weekly; 24hr); Thíra (at least 3 daily; 2hr 30in); Tínos (4–5 weekly; 4hr).

Páros to: Amorgós (4–6 weekly; 4hr); Anáfi (4–6 weekly; 9hr); Ándhros (4 weekly; 5hr); Andíparos (hourly from Parikía, 40min; hourly car ferry from Poúnda, 20min); Astypálea (2–3 weekly; 4hr 40min); Crete, Iráklion (2–4 weekly; 7hr); Dhonoússa (2–4 weekly; 7hr); Folégandhros (4–6 weekly; 4hr 30min); Foúrni (1–2 weekly; 6hr); Ikaría (5–7 weekly; 5hr); Ikaría (3–6 weekly; 5hr); Íos (at least 3 daily; 3hr); Kárpathos (1–2 weekly; 16hr); Kássos (1–2 weekly; 16hr); Kós (1–2 weekly; 16hr); Koufoníssi (2–4 weekly; 6hr 30min); Mýkonos (at least 1 daily; 1hr); Náxos (at least 3 daily; 1hr); Rhodes (2–3 weekly; 17hr); Sámos (3–6 weekly; 6hr); Síkinos (4–6 weekly; 4hr); Skhinoússa (2–4 weekly; 6hr); Skiáthos (2–3 weekly; 10hr); Sýros (6–8 weekly; 2hr); Thessaloníki (2–3 weekly; 14hr); Thíra (at least 3 daily; 3hr 30min); Tínos (6–8 weekly; 1hr 30min); Vólos (1 weekly; 15hr).

Sérifos to: Folégandhros (2–3 weekly; 2hr 30min); Íos (1 weekly; 6hr 30min); Kímolos (2–5 weekly; 1hr 30min); Kýthnos (5–12 weekly; 30min); Mílos (5–10 weekly; 1hr 30min); Sífnos (5–12 weekly; 30min); Síkinos (2–3 weekly; 3hr); Sýros (2 weekly; 6hr); Thíra (2–3 weekly; 7hr 30 min).

Sífnos to: Folégandhros (2–3 weekly; 2hr); Íos (1 weekly; 6hr 30min); Kímolos (2–5 weekly; 1hr);

Kýthnos (5–12 weekly; 1hr); Mílos (5–10 weekly; 1hr); Páros (twice weekly; 5hr); Sérifos (5–12 weekly; 30min); Síkinos (2–3 weekly; 2hr 30min); Sýros (2 weekly; 6hr 30min); Thíra (2–3 weekly; 7hr).

Síkinos to: Folégandhros (6 weekly; 30min); Íos (3–6 weekly; 2hr); Kímolos (2 weekly; 2hr); Kýthnos (2 weekly; 7hr 30min); Mílos (2 weekly; 2hr); Náxos (3–6 weekly; 3hr); Páros (3–6 weekly; 4hr 30min); Sérifos (2 weekly; 5hr), Sífnos (2 weekly; 4hr 30min); Sýros (2 weekly; 5hr); Thíra (3–6 weekly; 2hr).

Sýros to: Amorgós (3 weekly; 7hr); Ándhros (at least 2 weekly; 30min); Astypálea (2–3 weekly; 5hr); Folégandhros (1 weekly; 4hr 30min); Ikaría (4–7 weekly; 4hr); Íos (2–4 weekly; 7hr); Iráklia (3 weekly; 7hr); Kéa (2 weekly; 4hr); Koufoníssi (3 weekly, 7hr 30min); Kýthnos (2 weekly; 3hr); Lipsí (1 weekly; 5hr); Mílos (2 weekly; 5hr); Kímolos (2 weekly; 5hr); Mýkonos (at least 2 daily; 2hr); Náxos (at least 2 daily; 3hr); Páros (at least 2 daily; 2hr); Pátmos (1 weekly; 5hr); Sámos (4–7 weekly; 6hr); Sérifos (2 weekly; 4hr); Sífnos (2 weekly; 3hr 30min); Síkinos (1 weekly; 6hr); Skhinoússa (3 weekly; 8hr); Skiáthos (1–3 weekly; 12hr); Thessaloníki (1–3 weekly; 15hr); Thíra (2–4 weekly; 8hr 30min); Tínos (at least 2 daily; 1hr).

Thíra to: Anáfi (4–6 weekly; 2hr, 2 weekly mail boats); Crete, Iráklion (5–6 weekly; 5hr); Folégandhros (6–8 weekly; 1hr 30min); Íos (at least 3 daily; 1hr); Kárpathos (1–2 weekly; 12hr); Kássos (1–2 weekly; 10hr); Mílos and Kímolos (2–4 weekly; 2hr); Mýkonos (daily; 2hr 30min); Náxos (at least 3 daily; 2hr); Páros (at least 3 daily; 3hr); Rhodes (2 weekly; 16hr); Sérifos (1–2 weekly; 7hr); Sífnos (1–6 weekly; 7hr); Síkinos (6–8 weekly; 2hr); Skiáthos (3–5 weekly; 14hr); Sýros (6–8 weekly; 8hr); Thessaloníki (5–6 weekly; 18hr); Thirassía (4–6 weekly; 30min); Tínos (3–5 weekly; 5hr).

Tínos to: Ándhros (at least 2 daily; 1hr); Crete, Iráklion (3 weekly; 5hr); Íos (1 weekly; 8hr); Mýkonos (at least 2 daily; 30min); Náxos (3–4 weekly; 2hr); Páros (3–4 weekly; 1hr 30min); Skiáthos (1–3 weekly; 10hr); Sýros (at least 2 daily; 1hr); Thessaloníki (1–3 weekly; 12hr); Thíra (3 weekly; 5hr).

Other services

To simplify the lists above, certain strategic **catamaran** and **small-boat services** have been omitted. Of these, the *Express Skopelitis* plies daily in season between Mýkonos and Amorgós, spending each night at the latter and threading through all of the minor isles between it and Náxos, as well as Náxos and Páros (Píso Livádhi), in the course of a week; however, it's unreliable and often overcrowded – for current info call ☎ 22850 71256. The *Seajet* catamaran – a small-capacity (and expensive) jet-boat (☎ 2210 414 1250 for details) – operates daily during summer out of Rafína and connects Sýros, Ándhros, Tínos, Mýkonos, Páros, Náxos and Thíra. The long-haul, full-sized *Blue Star* ships shave a few hours off the travel time to some of the most popular Cyclades (through the hubs of Páros and Náxos) for only slightly more than the price of standard tickets and much less than the cost of catamaran services. Cycladic routes are pretty well mapped out by the three companies – Minoan Flying Dolphins, Speed Lines and Cruises (Santorini Dolphin) and Dolphin Sea Line, with regular services from Pireás, Thíra and Rafína respectively.

Catamaran travel is expensive; however, when time is an issue, or for more regular connections to some of the less commonly serviced routes such as the minor islets around Náxos, these handy high-speed craft are a welcome addition to the conventional fleet.

Flights

There are **airports** on **Páros**, **Mýkonos**, **Thíra**, **Sýros**, **Mílos** and **Náxos**. In season, or during storms when ferries are idle, you have little chance of getting a seat on any flight at less than three days' notice, and tickets are predictably expensive. Expect off-season (Oct–April) frequencies to drop by at least eighty percent. Flights are on Olympic unless otherwise stated.

Athens to: Mílos (1–2 daily; 45min); Mýkonos (4–5 daily on Olympic; 3–4 daily on Aegean; 40min); Náxos (6 weekly; 45min); Páros (2–3 daily; 40min); Sýros (3–6 weekly; 35min); Thíra (5–6 daily on Olympic; 3–4 daily on Aegean; 50min).

Mýkonos to: Rhodes (2 weekly; 55min); Thessaloníki (2 weekly on Olympic, 1 daily on Aegean; 1hr 20min); Thíra (4 weekly; 30min).

Thíra to: Rhodes (2–5 weekly; 50min); Thessaloníki (2 weekly on Olympic, 1 daily on Aegean; 1hr 20min).

Crete

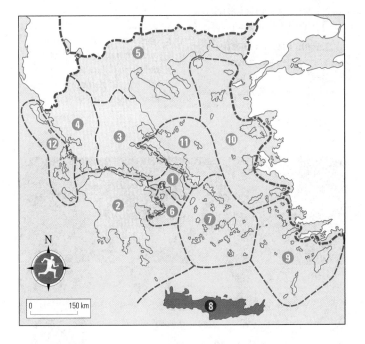

CHAPTER 8

Highlights

✳ **Archeological Museum, Iráklion** The world's foremost Minoan museum. **See p.717**

✳ **Minoan sites** Knossos is the most exciting, but Malia, Phaestos, Zakros and other archeological ruins across the island are also worth a visit. **See p.721**

✳ **Beach resorts** Mátala, Sitía and Paleohóra have bags of charm and excellent strands. **See p.728, p.747 & p.780**

✳ **Lasíthi Plateau** This green and fertile high mountain plateau has picturesque agricultural villages and unique white cloth-sailed windmills. **See p.740**

✳ **The Dhiktean cave** Mythological birthplace of Zeus, the Dhiktean cave is stunningly situated on the Lasíthi Plateau. **See p.740**

✳ **Haniá and Réthymnon old towns** These atmospheric centres display haunting vestiges of their Venetian and Turkish pasts and are a joy to wander around. **See p.756 & p.768**

✳ **Samariá Gorge** A magnificent gorge: the longest in Europe, offering a chance to see brilliant wildflowers, golden eagles and perhaps a Cretan ibex. **See p.773**

△ Minoan fresco, Knossos

8

Crete

Crete (Kríti) is a great deal more than just another Greek island. In many places, especially in the cities or along the developed north coast, it doesn't feel like an island at all, but rather a substantial land in its own right. Which of course it is – a precipitous, wealthy and at times a surprisingly cosmopolitan one with a tremendous and unique history. But when you lose yourself among the mountains, or on the lesser-known coastal reaches of the south, it has everything you could want of a Greek island and more: great beaches, remote hinterlands and hospitable people.

In history, Crete is distinguished above all as the home of Europe's earliest civilization. It was only at the beginning of the twentieth century that the legends of King Minos and of a Cretan society that ruled the Greek world in prehistory were confirmed by excavations at Knossos and Phaestos. Yet the Minoans had a remarkably advanced society, the centre of a maritime trading empire as early as 2000 BC. The artworks produced on Crete at this time are unsurpassed anywhere in the ancient world, and it seems clear that life on Crete in those days was good. This apparently peaceful culture survived at least three major natural disasters; each time the palaces were destroyed, and each time they were rebuilt on a grander scale. Only after the last destruction, probably the result of an eruption of Santoríni and subsequent tidal waves and earthquakes, do significant numbers of weapons begin to appear in the ruins. This, together with the appearance of the Greek language, has been interpreted to mean that Mycenaean Greeks had taken control of the island. Nevertheless, for nearly 500 years, by far the longest period of peace the island has seen, Crete was home to a culture well ahead of its time.

The Minoans of Crete probably originally came from Anatolia; at their height they maintained strong links with Egypt and with the people of Asia Minor, and this position as meeting point and strategic fulcrum between east and west has played a major role in Crete's subsequent history. Control of the island passed from Greeks to Romans to Saracens, through the Byzantine empire to Venice, and finally to Turkey for more than two centuries. During World War II, the island was occupied by the Germans and attained the dubious distinction of being the first place to be successfully invaded by paratroops.

Today, with a flourishing agricultural economy, Crete is one of the few Greek islands that could probably support itself without tourists. Nevertheless, tourism is heavily promoted and is making inroads everywhere. The northeast coast in particular is overdeveloped, and though there are parts of the south and west coasts that have not been spoilt, they are getting harder to find. By contrast, the high mountains of the interior are still barely touched, and one of the best things to do on Crete is to rent a vehicle and explore the remoter villages.

Every part of Crete has its loyal devotees and it's hard to pick out highlights, but generally if you want to get away from it all you should head west, towards Haniá and the smaller, less well-connected places along the south and west coasts. It is in this part of the island that the White Mountains rise, while below them yawns the famous Samariá Gorge. The far east, around Sitía, is also relatively unscathed, with a string of isolated beaches worth seeking out to the south of the over-popular Váï beach, which lures crowds attracted by its famous palm grove. However, Sitía's new international airport, opening for international flights in 2007, could change things significantly here in the next few years.

Whatever you do, your first priority will probably be to leave Iráklion (Heraklion) as quickly as possible, having paid the obligatory, and rewarding, visit to the archeological museum and nearby Knossos. The other great Minoan sites cluster around the middle of the island: Phaestos and Ayía Triádha to the south (with Roman Gortys to provide contrast), and Malia on the north coast. Almost wherever you go you'll find a reminder of the island's history, whether it's the superbly preserved Minoan town of Gourniá near the cosmopolitan resort of Áyios Nikólaos, the exquisitely sited palace of Zakros in the far east, or the lesser sites scattered around the west. Unexpected highlights include Crete's Venetian forts at Réthymnon and Frangokástello; its hundreds of frescoed Byzantine churches, most famously at Kritsá; and, at Réthymnon and Haniá, the cluttered old Venetian and Turkish quarters.

Crete has by far the longest summers in Greece, and you can get a decent tan here right into October and swim at least from May until November. The one seasonal blight is the *meltémi*, a northerly wind, which regularly blows harder here and more continuously than anywhere else in Greece – the best of several

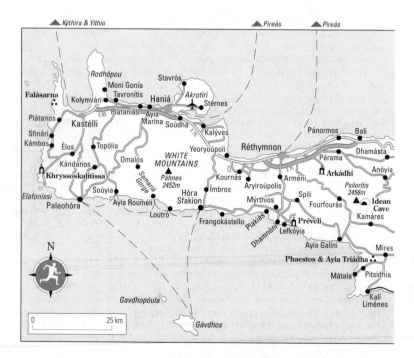

reasons for avoiding an August visit if you can. It's far from an ill wind, however, as it also lowers humidity and makes the island's higher summer temperatures more bearable.

Iráklion, Knossos and central Crete

Many visitors to Crete arrive in the island's capital, **Iráklion** (Heraklion), but it's not an outstandingly beautiful city, and its central zones are often a maelstrom of traffic-congested thoroughfares. However, it does provide a convenient base for visits to an outstanding **Archeological Museum** and nearby **Knossos**. On the positive side, the city does have quite a few plus points – superb fortifications, a fine market, atmospheric old alleys and some interesting lesser museums added to a recent makeover of central areas by the city hall that has improved things considerably.

The area immediately around the city is less touristy than you might expect, mainly because there are few decent beaches of any size on this central part of

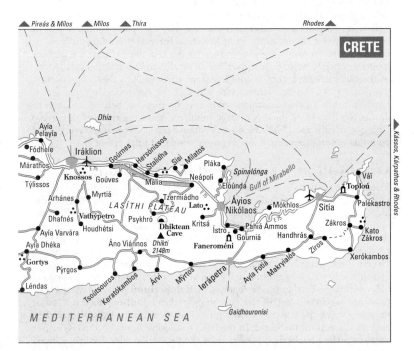

the coast. To the west, mountains drop straight into the sea virtually all the way to Réthymnon, with just two significant coastal settlements: **Ayía Pelayía**, a sizeable resort, and the more attractive **Balí**, which is gradually becoming one as well. Eastwards, the main resorts are at least 30km away, at **Hersónissos** and beyond, although there is a string of rather unattractive developments all the way there. Inland, there's agricultural country, some of the richest on the island, a cluster of Crete's better vineyards and a series of wealthy but rather dull villages. Directly behind the capital rises **Mount Ioúktas** with its characteristic profile of Zeus; to the west the Psilorítis massif spreads around the peak of **Mount Psilorítis** (Ídha) the island's highest mountain. On the south coast there are few roads and little development of any kind, except at **Ayía Galíni** in the southwest, a nominal fishing village which has grown into a popular resort, and beautiful **Mátala** which has thrown out the hippies that made it famous, and, though crowded with package-trippers in high summer, is still an appealing spring and autumn destination. Isolated **Léndas** has to some extent occupied Mátala's old niche, and has a fine beach.

Despite the lack of resorts, there seem constantly to be thousands of people trekking back and forth across the centre of the island. This is largely because of a trio of superb archeological sites in the south: **Phaestos**, second of the Minoan palaces, with its attendant villa at **Ayía Triádha**, and **Gortys**, capital of Roman Crete.

Iráklion

The best way to approach **IRÁKLION** is by sea, with Mount Ioúktas rising behind it and the Psilorítis range to the west. As you get closer, it's the city walls that first stand out, still dominating and fully encircling the oldest part of town; finally you sail in past the great **Venetian fortress** defending the harbour entrance. Unfortunately, big ships no longer dock in the old port but at great modern concrete wharves alongside, which neatly sums up Iráklion itself. Many of the old parts have been restored and are attractive, but these are offset by the bustle and noise that characterize much of the city today. In more recent times, however, Iráklion's administrators have been giving belated attention to dealing with some of the city's image problems, and large tracts of the centre – particularly the focal Platía Eleftherías – have been landscaped and refurbished with the aim of presenting a less daunting prospect to the visitor.

Orientation, arrival and information

Virtually everything you're likely to want to see in Iráklion lies within the northeastern corner of the walled city. The most vital thoroughfare, **25-Avgoústou**, links the harbour with the commercial city centre. At the bottom it is lined with shipping and travel agencies and rental outlets, but further up these give way to banks, restaurants and stores. **Platía Venizélou** (or Fountain Square), off to the right, is crowded with cafés and restaurants; behind Venizélou lies **El Greco Park** (actually a rather cramped garden), with more bars, while on the opposite side of 25-Avgoústou are some of the more interesting of Iráklion's older buildings. Further up 25-Avgoústou, **Kalokerinoú** leads down to Haniá Gate and westwards out of the city; straight ahead, **Odhós-1821** is a major shopping street, and adjacent 1866 is given over to the animated street **market**, perhaps the best on the island. To the left, Dhikeosínis heads for the city's main square, **Platía Eleftherías**, paralleled by the pedestrian alley, Dedhálou, lined with many of the city's swankier fashion stores and the direct link between the two squares. The revamped Eleftherías is very much the traditional centre of the city, both for traffic – which swirls around it constantly – and for life in general; it is ringed by more upmarket tourist cafés and restaurants and comes alive in the evening with crowds of strolling locals.

Points of arrival

Iráklion **airport** is right on the coast, 4km east of the city. **Bus** #1 leaves for Platía Eleftherías every few minutes from the car park in front of the terminal; buy your ticket (€0.70) at the booth before boarding. There are also plenty of **taxis** outside (which you'll be forced to use when the buses stop at 11pm), and prices to major destinations are posted here and in the domestic departures hall – it's about €8 to the centre of town, depending on traffic. Get an agreement on the fare before taking a cab and beware if the driver extols the virtues of a particular place to stay and offers to drop you there – he'll usually be getting a kickback from the proprietors. To avoid such hassles ask to be dropped at the central Platía Eleftherías, from where everything is in easy walking distance.

There are two main **bus stations** (often titled A and B on maps). Bus station A straddles both sides of the main road between the ferry dock and the Venetian harbour, and Station B lies just outside the Haniá Gate. Buses run from here **west** to Réthymnon and Haniá and **east** along the coastal highway to Hersónsissos, Mália, Áyios Nikólaos and Sitía, as well as **southeast** to Ierápetra and points en route. Local bus #2 to Knossos also leaves from here (south side of the main road). Buses for the **southwest** (Phaestos, Mátala and Ayía Galíni) and along the inland roads west (Týlissos, Anóyia) operate out of terminal B, a very long walk from the centre up Kalokerinoú (or jump on any bus heading down this street). From the wharves where the **ferries** dock, the city rises directly ahead in steep tiers. If you're heading for the centre, the Archeological Museum or the tourist office, cut straight up the stepped alleys behind the bus station onto Dhoúkos Bofór and to Platía Eleftherías; this will take about fifteen minutes. For accommodation, though, and to get a better idea of the layout of Iráklion's main attractions, it's simplest to follow the main roads by a rather more roundabout route. Head west along the coast, past the major eastbound bus station and on by the Venetian harbour before cutting up towards the centre on 25-Avgoústou.

Information

Iráklion's **tourist office** (June–Sept: Mon–Fri 9am–9pm; Oct–May: Mon–Fri 9am–2.30pm; ☎2810 246 299) is located just below Platía Eleftherías, opposite the Archeological Museum at Zanthoudhídhou 1. A sub-office at the **airport** (April–Sept daily 9am–9pm) is good for basic information and maps. The **tourist police** – more helpful than most – are at Dhikeosínis 10 (☎2810 283 190), halfway between Platía Eleftherías and the market.

Accommodation

Finding a **room** can be difficult in season. The best place to look for inexpensive places is in the area around Platía Venizélou, along Hándhakos and towards the harbour to the west of 25-Avgoústou. Other concentrations of affordable places are around El Greco Park and in the streets above the Venetian harbour. Better hotels mostly lie closer to Platía Eleftherías, to the south of Platía Venizélou and near the east- and westbound bus stations.

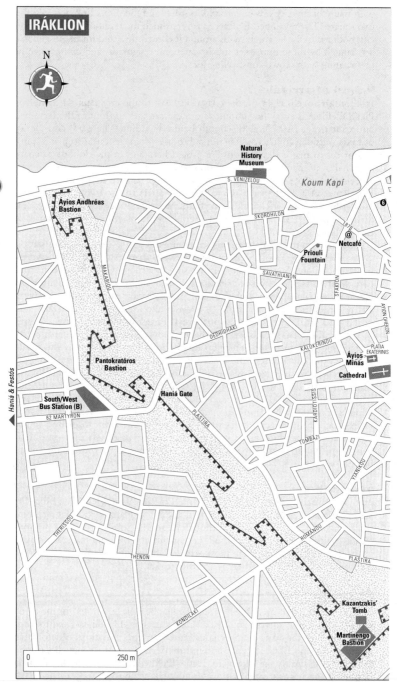

IRÁKLION

N

Natural History Museum

S. VENIZELOU

Koum Kapí

Áyios Andhréas Bastion

SKORDHILON

Netcafé

Priouli Fountain

SAVATHIANON

MAKARIOU

DEDHIDHAKI

KALOKERINDOU

AYION DHEKON

SFAKION

PLATIA EKATERINIS

Áyios Minás

Cathedral

KARDIOTISSIS

Pantokratóros Bastion

Haniá Gate

South/West Bus Station (B)

62 MARTYRON

PLASTIRA

TOMBAZI

YZARKOU

Haniá & Festós

THERISSOU

THENON

ROMANOU

PLASTIRA

KONDILAKI

Kazantzakis' Tomb

Martinéngo Bastion

0   250 m

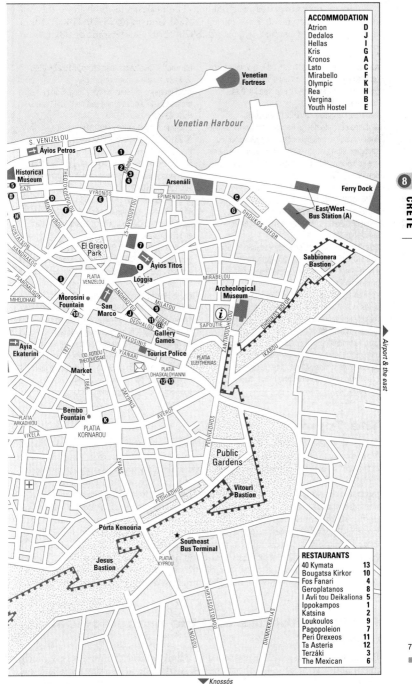

Venetian Fortress

Venetian Harbour

Áyios Petros

Historical Museum

Arsenáli

Ferry Dock

East/West Bus Station (A)

El Greco Park

Áyios Títos

Sabbionera Bastion

Lóggia

Archeological Museum

Morosini Fountain

San Marco

Ayia Ekaterini

Gallery Games

Tourist Police

Market

Bembo Fountain

PLATIA KORNAROU

Public Gardens

Vitouri Bastion

Pórta Kenoúria

Jesus Bastion

Southeast Bus Terminal

Airport & the east

Knossós

ACCOMMODATION

Atrion	D
Dedalos	J
Hellas	I
Kris	G
Kronos	A
Lato	C
Mirabello	F
Olympic	K
Rea	H
Vergina	B
Youth Hostel	E

RESTAURANTS

40 Kymata	13
Bougatsa Kirkor	10
Fos Fanari	4
Geroplatanos	8
I Avli tou Deikaliona	5
Ippokampos	1
Katsina	2
Loukoulos	9
Pagopoleion	7
Peri Orexeos	11
Ta Asteria	12
Terzáki	3
The Mexican	6

There are no **campsites** near Iráklion. The nearest sites both lie to the east of the city: first comes *Creta Camping* at Káto Goúves (☎28970 41400), 16km out, followed by *Caravan Camping* (☎28970 22901) at Hersónissos, 28km from the city.

Atrion Hronaki 9 ☎2810 246 000, ⓦwww.atrion .gr. Attractive, new central hotel with well-equipped balcony rooms, satellite TV and free Internet connection. ❻

Dedalos Dedhálou 15 ☎2810 244 812, ⓔdaedalos@internet.gr. Recently refurbished hotel with balcony rooms overlooking a pedestrianized shopping street which is tranquil at night. All rooms are en suite and equipped with TV and a/c (€7 surcharge). ❸

Hellas Hándhakos 24 ☎2810 288 851, ⓕ2810 284 442. Hostel-type place with simple doubles, and dormitory rooms (❶) favoured by younger travellers. Also has a roof garden and snack-bar. ❸

Kris Dhoúkos Bofór 2, near the Venetian harbour ☎2810 285 853. Studio rooms with kitchenette, fridge, great balcony views and friendly female proprietor. ❹

Kronos Agaráthou 2, west of 25-Avgoústou ☎2810 282 240, ⓦwww.kronoshotel.gr. Pleasant, friendly and modern hotel with en-suite, sea-view balcony rooms. ❹

Lato Epomenídhou 15 ☎2810 228 103, ⓦwww .lato.gr. Stylish and luxurious hotel where a/c rooms have minibar, TV and fine balcony views over the Venetian harbour (the higher floors have the better views). B&B ❼

Mirabello Theotokopoúlou 20 ☎2810 285 052, ⓦwww.mirabello-hotel.gr. Good-value, family-run hotel featuring en-suite balcony rooms, some with a/c and TV. In a quiet street just north of El Greco Park. ❸—❹

Olympic Platía Kornárou ☎2810 288 861, ⓕ2810 222 512. Overlooking the busy platía and the famous Bembo fountain. One of the many hotels built in the 1960s, but one of the few that has been refurbished; facilities include minibar and strongbox. B&B ❻

Rea Kalimeráki 1 ☎2810 223 638, ⓕ2810 242 189. A friendly, comfortable and clean *pension* in a quiet street. Some rooms with washbasin, others en suite. ❷—❸

Vergina Hortátson 32 ☎2810 242 739. Basic but pleasant rooms with washbasins in a quiet street and set around a courtyard with a giant banana tree. ❷

Youth Hostel Vkronos 5 ☎2810 286 281, ⓔheraklioyouthhostel@yahoo.com. Formerly Iraklión's official youth hostel, it has been stripped of its HI status. It is in fact a good place to stay, family-run and very friendly and helpful. There's plenty of space and some beds (albeit illegal) on the roof if you fancy sleeping out under the stars. Private rooms (❶) as well as dormitories (❶); hot showers, breakfast and other meals available.

The Town

A good place to start your explorations of the town is the focal **Platía Venizélou**, crowded most of the day with locals patronizing its café terraces, and with travellers who've arranged to meet in "Fountain Square". The **Morosini Fountain**, which gives the square its popular name, is not particularly spectacular at first glance, but on closer inspection is really a very beautiful work; it was built by Venetian governor Francesco Morosini in the seventeenth century, incorporating four lions which were some three hundred years old even then. From the platía you can strike up Dhedhálou, a pedestrianized street full of fashion and tourist shops, or continue on 25-Avgoústou to a major traffic junction at Platía Nikifoúrou Foka. To the right, Kalokerinoú leads west out of the city, the market lies straight ahead along Odhós-1866, and Platía Eleftherías is a short walk to the left up Dhikeosínis.

Platía Eleftherías and the archeological museum

Platía Eleftherías, with seats shaded by palms and eucalyptuses, is very much the traditional heart of the city; traffic swirls around it constantly, and on summer evenings strolling crowds come to fill its café terraces. Most of Iráklion's more expensive shops are in the streets leading off the platía.

The **Archeological Museum** (April–Sept Mon 1–7.30pm, Tues–Sun 8.30am–7.30pm; Oct–March daily 8am–5pm; €7) is nearby. Almost every important prehistoric and Minoan find on Crete is included in this fabulous, if bewilderingly large and unimaginatively presented, collection. The museum tends to be crowded, especially when a guided tour stampedes through, but it's worth taking time over. You can't hope to see everything, nor can we attempt to describe it all (several good museum guides are sold here, the best probably being the glossy ones by J.A. Sakellarakis or Andonis Vasilakis), but highlights include the "**Town Mosaic**" from Knossos in Room 2 (the galleries are arranged basically in chronological order), the famous **inscribed disc** from Phaestos in Room 3 (itself the subject of several books), most of Room 4, especially the magnificent bull's-head **rhyton** (drinking vessel), the **jewellery** in Room 6 (and elsewhere) and the engraved steatite **black vases** in Room 7. Save some of your time and energy for upstairs, where the **Hall of the Frescoes**, with intricately reconstructed fragments of the wall paintings from Knossos and other sites, is especially wonderful. A long-overdue **renovation** of the Archeological Museum is set to start in 2006. When this finally happens it should place the collection at the forefront of museum presentation in Greece. However, once work is under way there will inevitably be some frustration for visitors as rooms are closed and items moved around.

Walls and fortifications

The massive **Venetian walls**, in places up to 15m thick, are the most obvious evidence of Iráklion's later history. Though their fabric is incredibly well preserved, access is virtually nonexistent. It is possible, just, to walk along them from Áyios Andhréas Bastion over the sea in the west, as far as the Martinengo Bastion where lies the **tomb of Nikos Kazantzakis**, Cretan author of *Zorba the Greek*, whose epitaph reads: "I believe in nothing, I hope for nothing, I am free." At weekends, Iraklians gather here to pay their respects and enjoy a free view of the soccer matches played by one of the city's two teams in the stadium below. If the walls seem altogether too much effort, the **port fortifications** are much easier to see. Stroll out along the jetty (crowded with courting couples at dusk) and you can get inside the sixteenth-century **Venetian fortress** (Tues–Sun 8.30am–3pm; €2) at the harbour entrance, emblazoned with the Venetian Lion of St Mark. Standing atop this, you begin to understand how Iráklion (or Candia as both the city and the island were known to the Venetians) withstood a 22-year siege before finally falling to the Ottomans. On the landward side of the port, the Venetian **arsenáli** (arsenals) can also be seen, their arches rather lost amid the concrete road system all around.

Churches and other museums

From the harbour, 25-Avgoústou will take you up past most of the town's other highlights. The **church of Áyios Títos**, on the left as you approach Platía Venizélou, borders a pleasant little platía. Byzantine in origin but substantially rebuilt by the Venetians, it looks magnificent principally because, like most of the churches here, it was adapted by the Turks as a mosque and only reconsecrated in 1925; consequently it has been renovated on numerous occasions. On the south side of this platía, abutting 25-Avgoústou, is the Venetian **city hall** with its famous loggia, again almost entirely rebuilt. Just above this, facing Platía Venizélou, is the **church of San Marco**, its steps usually crowded with sightseers spilling over from the nearby platía. Neither of these last two buildings has found a permanent role in its refurbished state, but both are generally open to house some kind of exhibition or craft show.

Slightly away from the obvious city-centre circuit, but still within the bounds of the walls, there is a clutch of lesser museums worth seeing if you have the time. First of these are the excellent collection of **icons** in the **church of Ayía Ekateríni** (Mon–Sat 10am–1.30pm; €2), an ancient building just below the undistinguished cathedral, off Kalokerinoú. The finest here are six large scenes by Mihaïl Damaskinos (a near-contemporary of El Greco) who fused Byzantine and Renaissance influences. Supposedly both Damaskinos and El Greco studied at Ayía Ekateríni in the sixteenth century, when it functioned as a sort of monastic art school.

The **Historical Museum** (Mon–Fri 9am–4pm, Sat 9am–2pm; €3; ⓦwww.historical-museum.gr) lies some 300m north of here, on the waterfront. Its display of folk costumes and jumble of local memorabilia include the reconstructed studies of both Nikos Kazantzakis and Emanuel Tsouderos (the latter both Cretan statesman and former Greek prime minister). There's enough variety to satisfy just about anyone, including the only El Greco painting on Crete, the uncharacteristic *View of Mount Sinai and the Monastery of St Catherine*.

To the west, in a converted old power plant overlooking the bay of Koum Kapí, is the **Natural History Museum** (Sept–June Mon–Fri 9am–3pm, Sun 9am–5pm; July–Aug daily 9am–8pm; €4.50; ⓦwww.nhmc.uoc.gr), definitely worth a visit. As well as the usual flora and fauna displays, it has exhibits detailing the island's geological evolution, the arrival of man, and the environment as it would have appeared to the Minoans.

The beaches

Iráklion's **beaches** are some way out, whether east or west of town. In either direction they're easily accessible by bus: #6 heads west from the stop outside the *Astoria* hotel in Platía Eleftherías; #7 east from the stop opposite this, under the trees in the centre of the platía.

Almyrós (or Ammoudhári) to the west has been subjected to a degree of development, comprising a campsite, several medium-size hotels and one giant one (the *Zeus Beach*, in the shadow of the power station at the far end), which makes the beach hard to get to without walking through or past something built up.

Amnissós, to the east, is the better choice, with several tavernas and the added amusement of planes swooping in immediately overhead to land at the nearby airport. This is where most locals go on their afternoons off; the furthest of the beaches is the best, although new hotels are encroaching. Little remains to indicate the once-flourishing port of Knossos here, aside from a rather dull, fenced-in dig. If you're seriously into antiquities, however, you'll find a more rewarding site in the small Minoan villa, known as **Nírou Háni** (Tues–Sun 8.30am–3pm; free) at Háni Kokkíni, the first of the full-blown resort developments east of Iráklion.

Eating

Big city though it is, Iráklion disappoints when it comes to eating, and not many of the central restaurants and tavernas provide good value. The cafés and tavernas of platíes Venizélou and Eleftherías are essential places to sit and watch the world pass, but their food is expensive and mediocre. One striking exception is *Bougatsa Kirkor*, by the Morosini Fountain in Venizélou, where you can sample authentic Cretan *bougátsa* – a creamy cheese pie sprinkled with sugar and cinnamon. For **snacks** and **takeaways**, there's a group of *souvláki* and other fast-food stalls clustering around the top of 25-Avgoústou near the entrance to El Greco Park, which is handy if you need somewhere to sit and eat. For *tyrópita* and *spanakópita* (cheese or spinach pies) and other pastries, sweet or savoury, there is no shortage of zaharoplastía and places such as *Everest* – just north of the Morosini Fountain – which does takeaways of these as well as lots of other savouries. On and around Platía Dhaskaloyiánni (near the archeological museum) are some authentic and inexpensive ouzerís: try *Ta Asteria* or *40 Kymata* on the platía itself for atmosphere and tasty *mezédhes*.

I Avli tou Deikaliona Kalokairinoú 8 at the rear of the Historical Museum (☎2810 244 215). Popular taverna with a great little terrace fronting the Idomeneus fountain serving up well-prepared meat and fish dishes. In high summer you may need to book to ensure an outdoor table.

Fos Fanari Marineli 1, opposite the tiny church of Ay. Dimítrios. The first in a row of ouzerís that line this alley off Vironos, sloping down to the harbour. Good fish dishes and *mezédhes*. The similar and neighbouring *Terzáki* is also worth a try.

Geroplatanos in the leafy square fronting the church of Ay. Títos. Taking its name from the great old plane tree beneath which its tables are set out, this is one of the most tranquil lunch spots in town and provides the usual taverna staples.

Ippokampos Sófokli Venizélou, west of 25-Avgoústou, close to the *Kronos* hotel. The best and least expensive fish to be had in Iráklion, served in unpretentious surroundings. Deservedly popular with locals for lunch *mezédhes* as well as dinner, this place is often crowded late into the evening, and you may have to queue or turn up earlier than the Greeks eat. Has a pleasant shaded terrace over the road on the seafront.

Katsina Marineli 12. A simple and friendly ouzerí at the opposite (seaward) end of the alley from *Fos Fanari* (above). Tasty and economical seafood *mezédhes* served at outdoor tables.

Loukoulos on the alley Koraí, parallel to Dedhálou. With a leafy courtyard terrace and an Italian slant to its international menu, this is one of the better tavernas in Iráklion. However, the pricey food and an expensive wine list seem aimed more at luring Iráklion's smart set than the casual visitor.

The Mexican Hándhakos 71. Inexpensive Mexican tacos and beers, complemented by salads and bean dishes.

Pagopoleion Platía Áyios Títos. Iráklion's most original bar has added a mid-priced restaurant serving Cretan and international dishes to a high standard; the wine list includes interesting bottles from little-known but excellent small vineyards around the island. There's also a recommended *mezedhákia* buffet (Sat & Sun 1–4pm).

Peri Orexeos which allows you to fill a plate for €6. A pleasant terrace is also good for lazy breakfasts and snacks.

Koraí 10 almost opposite *Loukoulos* (above). This newly opened taverna is a good bet for traditional Cretan cooking at reasonable prices.

Drinking, nightlife and entertainment

Iráklion is a bit of a damp squib as far as **nightlife** goes, certainly when compared with many other towns on the island. If you're determined, however, there are a few city-centre possibilities, and plenty of options if all you want to do is sit and **drink**. Indeed there is a new breed of **kafenío** emerging in Iráklion, aimed at a younger crowd: the drinks are cocktails rather than *raki*, the music is modern Greek or Western, and there are prices to match. *Andromeda* and *Living Room*, both on Platía Venizélou, are a couple of the most popular. The city's most animated **bars** are located around **Platía Koráï** behind Dhedhálou (up from *Taverna Loukoulos* listed above) and along the alley of the same name to the west.

Bars

To Avgo Platía Koraí. Trendy little bar frequented by students, on a pleasant square just to the north of Dedhálou.

Flash Platía Koraí. This bar has outdoor tables and serves a wide variety of exotic (and expensive) beers and cocktails. Those on a tight budget can nurse a *frappé* for hours.

Jasmin Ayiostefanitón 6, tucked in an alley on the left midway down Hándhakos. Another good nighttime rendezvous, with jazz, soul and Latin music and an outdoor terrace. Also serves 45 different types of tea, including herbal.

Korais on the alley Koraí, parallel to Dedhálou. Glitzy open-air café with spacious plant-festooned terraces, overhead movie screens and music – highly popular with Iráklion's stylish set.

Mayo Milatou 11, just north of Koraí. This new extravaganza of a bar with spotlights, screens and music under a big canopy terrace is the latest place to be seen if you're part of Iráklion's student set. Its arrival has spawned a whole new set of bars and cafés along the same street.

Orionas Psaromíligon 15. Lively music and drinks bar on two floors with a stylish terrace upstairs; has a varied programme of live music at weekends in summer, with alternating jazz, blues, reggae and rock acts performing.

Pagopoleion (Ice Factory) Platía Áyios Títos. Stunningly stylish bar created by photographic artist Chryssy Karelli inside Iráklion's former ice factory. She has preserved much of the old building including a fitting for hauling the ice from the basement freezer and a fascistic call to duty in German Gothic script on one wall – a remnant of Nazi occupation of the factory in World War II. Make sure to visit the toilets, as they are in an artistic league of their own.

Rebels Perdhíkari 3. A stylish bar which has cloned numerous similar places nearby. On weekends in summer this whole zone is the trendiest place to be if you're under 30.

Clubs and discos

For **discos** and **clubs** proper, there is a large selection, playing Western music, interspersed with Greek tunes (not the type played for tourists). *Privilege* is the most popular, down towards the harbour at the bottom of Dhoúkos Bofór, below the Archeological Museum. The nearby *GDM*, *Megaron* and *Envy* provide competition. Two pleasant and popular music bars with a seafront location are *Loft* and *Caprice* overlooking the western end of Koum Kapí bay near the Natural History Museum. One of the Iráklion beach set's favourite summer venues is at Amnissós beach (see p.718). Here two beach clubs, *Akti* and *Wet Wet*, play host to an under-30 crowd who turn up in their droves to swim, drink and dance to DJ rhythms; night-time is slightly more formal when the dress is smarter and people tend not to swim.

Listings

Airlines Aegean, 25-Avgoústou 34 (☎2810 344 324, ⓦwww.aegeanair.com), and Olympic, 25-Avgoústou 27 (☎2810 244 802, ⓦwww.olympic -airways.com), are the main scheduled airlines with connecting flights to Athens and other parts of Greece. Charter airlines flying into Iráklion mostly use local travel agents as their representatives.

Airport For airport information call ☎2810 397 129. Bus #1 runs from the eastern side of Platía Eleftherías to the airport every few minutes; buy a ticket (€0.70) from a kiosk near the bus stop.

Banks There are ATMs all over town, but the main bank branches are on 25-Avgoústou.

Car and bike rental 25-Avgoústou is lined with rental companies, but you'll often find cheaper rates on the backstreets; it's always worth asking for discounts. For cars and bikes, good places to start include: Blue Sea, Kosmá Zótou 7, near the bottom of 25-Avgoústou (☎2810 241 097, ⓦwww .bluesearentals.com), which gives a twenty percent discount to Rough Guide readers, and Sun Rise, 25-Avgoústou 46 (☎2810 221 609). For cars try: Reliable, Epimenidou 8 off the east side of the same street (☎2810 344 212); Caravel,

25-Avgoústou 39 (☎2810 335 900, ⓦwww .caravel.gr); and Ritz in the Hotel Rea, Kalimeráki 1 (☎2810 223 638). All offer free delivery to hotels and airport.

Ferry tickets Available from Minoan Lines, 25-Avgoústou 78 (☎2810 229 646, ⓦwww .minoan.gr), which handles the islands and Athens; and ANEK Lines, 25-Avgoústou 33 (☎2810 222 481, ⓦwww.anek.gr), for Athens only; also try any of the travel agents listed opposite. Another source for tickets and ferry information is the long-established Paleologus Travel, 25-Avgoústou 5 (☎2810 346 185); their comprehensive websites (ⓦwww.ferries.gr, ⓦwww.greekislands.gr) are excellent.

Hospital Most central is the hospital on Apollónion, southwest of Platía Kornárou (☎2810 229 713), between Albér and Moussoúrou.

Internet Iráklion now has a number of Internet cafés located in and around the city centre. Two central places are Netcafé, Odhós-1878 4 (daily 10am–2am) and Gallery Games, Koraï 14.

Laundry Washsalon, Hándhakos 18 (Mon–Sat 8.30am–9pm), is reliable and also does service

washes (€6 for 5kg). Laundry Perfect at Malikoúti 32, north of the Archeological Museum, will do the same and has similar prices (Mon–Sat 9am–9pm).
Left luggage Offices in Station A (daily 6.30am–8pm; €1 per bag per day), but not Station B, as well as a commercial agency at Hándhakos 18 (daily 24hr; €1.50 per large locker per day). You can also leave bags at the youth hostel (even if you don't stay there) for €1.50 per bag per day. If you want to leave your bag while you go off on a bike for a day or two, the rental company should be prepared to store it.
Newspapers and books For English-language newspapers and novels, Bibliopoleio, almost opposite the Morosini Fountain on Platía Venizélou, is the most central. The excellent Planet International Bookstore, on four floors behind Platía Venizélou at the corner of Hándhakos and Kydhonías, has the island's biggest stock of English-language titles and is a great place to browse.
Pharmacies Plentiful on the main shopping streets – at least one is open 24hr on a rota basis; the others will have a sign on the door indicating which it is. There are traditional herbalists in the market.

Post office Main office in Platía Dhaskaloyiánnis, off Platía Eleftherías (Mon–Fri 7.30am–8pm).
Taxis Major taxi ranks in Platía Eleftherías and by the Morosini Fountain, or call ☎2810 210 102 or 2810 210 168. Prices displayed on boards at the taxi stands.
Toilets In Platía Kornarou (at the southern end of the market) and the public gardens near the cathedral, or at the bus stations; there's also an excellent one at the Archeological Museum (access without paying the museum entrance charge).
Travel agencies Budget operators and student specialists include the extremely helpful Blavakis Travel, Platía Kallergón 8, just off 25-Avgoústou by the entrance to El Greco Park (☎2810 282 541), and Prince Travel, 25-Avgoústou 30 (☎2810 282 706). For excursions around the island, villa rentals and so on, the bigger operators are probably easier: Creta Travel Bureau, Dhikeosínis 49 (☎2810 300 610), and Adamis Tours, 25-Avgoústou 23 (☎2810 346 202). The latter is also the local American Express agent.

Knossos

KNOSSOS, the largest of the **Minoan palaces**, reached its cultural peak more than three thousand years ago, though a town of some importance persisted here well into the Roman era. It lies on a low, largely man-made hill some 5km southeast of Iráklion; the surrounding hillsides are rich in lesser remains spanning 25 centuries, starting at the beginning of the second millennium BC.

Just over a century ago the palace existed only in mythology. Knossos was the court of the legendary King Minos, whose wife Pasiphae bore the Minotaur, half-bull, half-man. Here the labyrinth was constructed by Daedalus to contain the monster, and youths were brought from Athens as human sacrifice until Theseus arrived to slay the beast and, with Ariadne's help, escape its lair. The discovery of the palace, and the interplay of these legends with fact, is among the most amazing tales of modern archeology. Heinrich Schliemann, the German excavator of Troy, suspected that a major Minoan palace lay under the various tumuli here, but was denied the necessary permission to dig by the local Ottoman authorities at the end of the nineteenth century. It was left for Sir Arthur Evans, whose name is indelibly associated with Knossos, to excavate the site, from 1900 onwards.

The #2 and #4 local **buses** set off every ten minutes from Iráklion's city bus stands (adjacent to the eastbound bus station), proceed up 25-Avgoústou (with a stop just south of Platía Venizélou) and out of town on Odhós-1821 and Evans. This is also the route you should take if **driving** (follow the signs from Platía Eleftherías); there's a free car park downhill on the left, immediately before the site entrance, which will enable you to avoid paying for the private car parks dotting the road before this. A **taxi** from the centre will cost around €6. At Knossos, outside the fenced site, stands a partly restored Minoan caravanserai where ancient wayfarers would rest and water their animals. Head out onto the

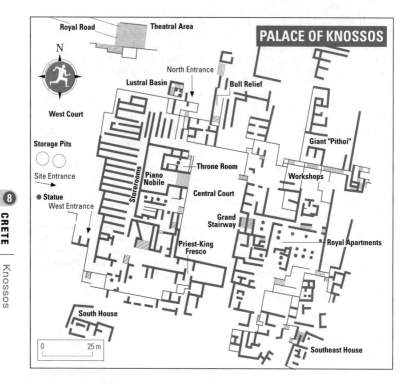

road and you'll find no lack of watering holes for modern travellers either – a string of rather pricey tavernas and tacky souvenir stands.

The British School at Athens has a useful website (Ⓦwww.bsa.gla.ac.uk /knossos/vrtour) dedicated to Knossos, with detail on the history of the site and excavations in addition to a virtual tour.

The site

As soon as you enter the **Palace of Knossos** (daily: April–Sept 8.30am–7.30pm; Oct–March 8.30am–3pm; €6) through the West Court, the ancient ceremonial entrance, it is clear how the legends of the labyrinth grew up around it. Even with a detailed plan, it's almost impossible to find your way around the complex with any success, although a series of **timber walkways** now channels visitors around the site, severely restricting the scope for independent exploration. If you're worried about missing the highlights, you can always tag along with one of the constant guided tours for a while, catching the patter and then backtracking to absorb the detail when the crowd has moved on. Outside the period December to February you won't get the place to yourself, whenever you come, but exploring on your own does give you the opportunity to appreciate individual parts of the palace in the brief lulls between groups.

Knossos was liberally "restored" by Evans, and these restorations have been the source of furious controversy among archeologists ever since. It has become clear that much of Evans's upper level – the so-called *piano nobile* – is pure conjecture. Even so, and putting archeological ethics to one side, his guess as to what the palace might have looked like is certainly as good as anyone's, and it makes the other sites infinitely more meaningful if you have seen Knossos first. Almost as controversial are Evans's designations of the various parts of the palace: he fantasized a royal family living here and in the words of one critic turned the Minoans into "second-millennium BC Victorians". Some sceptical scholars are still not convinced the structure *was* a palace and argue that the building could well have been a religious centre or shrine. Still, without the restorations, it would be almost impossible to imagine the grandeur of the multistorey palace or to see the ceremonial stairways, strange, top-heavy pillars and gaily painted walls that distinguish the site. For some idea of the size and complexity of the palace in its original state, take a look at the cutaway drawings (wholly imaginary but probably not too far off) on sale outside.

Royal Apartments

The superb **Royal Apartments** around the central staircase are not guesswork, and they are plainly the finest of the rooms at Knossos. The **Grand Stairway** itself (now closed to public access) is a masterpiece of design: not only a fitting approach to these sumptuously appointed chambers, but also an integral part of the whole plan, its large well bringing light into the lower storeys. Light wells such as these, usually with a courtyard at the bottom, are a constant feature of Knossos and a reminder of just how important creature comforts were to the Minoans, and how skilled they were at providing them.

For evidence of this luxurious lifestyle you need look no further than the **Queen's Suite** (now viewed behind glass screens), off the grand **Hall of the Colonnades** at the bottom of the staircase (reached by descending a timber walkway). Here, the main living room is decorated with the celebrated **dolphin fresco** (a reproduction; the original is now in the Iráklion Archeological Museum, see p.717) and with running friezes of flowers and abstract spirals. On two sides it opens out onto courtyards that let in light and air; the smaller one would probably have been planted with flowers. The room may have been scattered with cushions and hung with plush drapes, while doors and further curtains between the pillars would have allowed for privacy, and provided cool shade in the heat of the day. Remember, though, that all this is speculation and some of it is pure hype; the dolphin fresco, for example, was found on the courtyard floor, not in the room itself, and would have been viewed from an upper balcony as a sort of trompe l'oeil, like looking through a glass-bottomed boat. Whatever the truth, this is an impressive example of Minoan architecture, the more so when you follow the dark passage around to the queen's **bathroom** (now only partially visible behind a screen). Here is a clay tub, protected behind a low wall (and again probably screened by curtains when in use), and the famous "flushing" toilet (a hole in the ground with drains to take the waste away – it was flushed by throwing a bucket of water down).

The much-perused **drainage system** was a series of interconnecting terracotta pipes running underneath most of the palace. Guides to the site never fail to point these out as evidence of the advanced state of Minoan civilization, and they are indeed quite an achievement, in particular the system of baffles and overflows to slow down the runoff and avoid any danger of flooding. Just how much running water there would have been, however, is another matter. Although the water supply was, and is, at the bottom of the hill, the combined efforts of rainwater catchment and hauling water up to the palace can hardly have been sufficient to supply the needs of more than a small elite. The recent discovery of remnants of an aqueduct system carrying water to the palace from springs on nearby Mount Ioúktas (the same source that today provides water for the Morosini fountain in Iráklion) could mean that this was not the only water supply.

The Grand Stairway ascends to the floor above the queen's domain, and a set of rooms generally regarded as the **King's Quarters** (currently not on view). These are chambers in a considerably sterner vein; the staircase opens into a grandiose reception chamber known as the **Hall of the Royal Guard** (or Hall of the Colonnades), its walls decorated in repeated shield patterns. Immediately off here is the **Hall of the Double Axes** (or the King's Room), believed to have been the ruler's personal chamber, a double room that would allow for privacy in one portion while audiences were held in the more public section. Its name comes from the double-axe symbol carved into every block of masonry.

The Throne Room and the rest of the palace

At the top of the Grand Stairway (you will need to retrace your steps up the timber staircase), you emerge onto the broad **Central Court**, a feature of all the Minoan palaces. Open now, this would once have been enclosed by the walls of the buildings all around. On the far side, in the northwestern corner of the courtyard, is the entrance to another of Knossos's most atmospheric survivals, the **Throne Room**. Here, a worn stone throne – with its hollowed shaping for the posterior – sits against the wall of a surprisingly small chamber; along the walls around it are ranged stone benches, suggesting a king ruling in council, and behind there's a reconstructed fresco of two griffins. Just how much rebuilding took place here can be gauged from the fact that when the throne was unearthed the surrounding ruins cleared its back by only a few centimetres: the ceiling and rooms above are all the creation of Evans's "reconstitution", as he preferred to describe his imaginative reconstructions. Anyway, in all probability in Minoan times this was the seat of a priestess rather than a ruler (there's nothing like it in any other Minoan palace), and its conversion into a throne room seems to have been a late innovation wrought by the invading Mycenaeans, during their short-lived domination prior to the palace's final destruction in the fourteenth century BC. The Throne Room is now closed off with a wooden gate, but you can lean over this for a good view, and in the antechamber there's a wooden copy of the throne on which everyone used to perch to have their picture taken, but this is now also off limits.

The rest you'll see as you wander, contemplating the legends of the place which blur with reality. Try not to miss the giant *pithoi* in the northeast quadrant of the site, an area known as the palace workshops; the storage chambers which you see from behind the Throne Room, and the reproduced frescoes in the reconstructed room above it; the fresco of the Priest-King looking down on the south side of the central court, and the relief of a charging bull on its north side. This last would have greeted you if you entered the palace through its north door; you can see evidence here of some kind of gatehouse and a lustral bath, a sunken area perhaps used for ceremonial bathing and purification. Just outside this gate is the **theatral area** (another Evans designation), an open space a little like a stepped amphitheatre, which may have been used for ritual performances or dances. From here the **Royal Road**, claimed as the oldest road in Europe, sets out. At one time, this probably ran right across the island; nowadays it ends after about 100m in a brick wall beneath the modern road. Circling back around the outside of the palace, you can get an idea of its scale by looking up at it; on the south side are a couple of small reconstructed Minoan houses which are worth exploring.

Beyond Knossos

If you have transport, the drive beyond Knossos can be an attractive and enjoyable one, taking minor roads through much greener country, with vineyards draped across low hills and flourishing agricultural communities. If you want specific things to seek out, head first for **MYRTIÁ**, an attractive village with the small **Kazantzakis Museum** (March–Oct daily 9am–7pm; Nov–Feb Sun only 10am–3pm; €3) in a house where the writer's parents once lived. **ARHÁNES**, at the foot of Mount Ioúktas, is a much larger and wealthy farming town that was also quite heavily populated in Minoan times. There are plenty of places to eat on an animated central square, but no places to stay. None of the three archeological sites here is open to the public, but **Anemospiliá**, 2km northwest of the town (directions from the archeological museum cited below), can be visited and has caused huge controversy since its excavation in the 1980s: many traditional views of the Minoans, particularly that of Minoan life as peaceful and idyllic, have had to be rethought in the light of the discovery of an apparent human sacrifice. Close to Arhánes' main square, an excellent **archeological museum** (Wed–Mon 8.30am–3pm; free) displays finds from here and other nearby excavations, including the strange ceremonial dagger seemingly used for human sacrifice. From Arhánes you can also drive (or walk with a couple of hours to spare) to the summit of Mount Ioúktas to see the imposing remains of a Minoan **peak sanctuary** and enjoy spectacular panoramic **views** towards Knossos (with which it was linked) and the northern coast beyond. At **VATHÝ-PETRO**, some 4km south of the mountain, is a **Minoan villa and vineyard** (Tues–Sun 8.30am–3pm; free), which once controlled the rich farmland south of Arhánes. Inside, a remarkable collection of farming implements was found, as well as a unique **wine press**, which remains *in situ*. Substantial amounts of the farm buildings remain, and it's still surrounded by fertile vines (Arhánes is one of Crete's major wine-producing zones) three-and-a-half-thousand years later – making it probably the oldest still-functioning vineyard in Europe, if not the world. Continuing southeast for 2km soon brings you to another agricultural village, **HOUDHÉTSI**, where you'll find the remarkable **Museum of Musical Instruments of the World** (daily 9am–3pm & 5.30–8.30pm; €3; @www.labyrinthmusic.gr). Founded by Irish *lýra* player Ross Daly who is famed in Crete and lives in the village, the museum consists of a collection of mainly string and percussion instruments (many very rare) from across the globe. To locate the museum head for *Bar Paranga* at the top (or south end) of the village – the museum is opposite. Should it not be open during these times, ring the English-speaking guardian, Eleni Arvanti, from the public phone alongside the bar, and she will open it up for you (☎2810 743 634).

Southwest from Iráklion: sites and beaches

If you take a **tour** from Iráklion (or one of the resorts), you'll probably visit the **Gortys**, **Phaestos** and **Ayía Triádha** sites in a day, with a lunchtime swim at **Mátala** thrown in. Doing it by public transport, you'll be forced into a rather more leisurely pace, but there's still no reason why you shouldn't get to all three and reach Mátala within the day; if necessary, it's easy enough to hitch the final stretch. **Bus services** to the Phaestos site are excellent, with some nine a day to and from Iráklion (fewer Sun), five of which continue to or come from Mátala;

there are also services direct to Ayía Galíni. If you're arriving in the afternoon, plan to visit Ayía Triádha first, as it closes early.

The route to Áyii Dhéka

The road from Iráklion towards Phaestos is a pretty good one by the standards of Cretan mountain roads, albeit rather dull. The country you're heading towards is the richest agricultural land on the island and, right from the start, the villages en route are large and businesslike. In the biggest of them, **Ayía Varvára**, there's a great rock outcrop known as the **Omphalos** (Navel) of Crete, supposedly the very centre of the island.

Past here, you descend rapidly to the fertile fields of the Messará plain, where the road joins the main route across the south near the village of **ÁYII DHÉKA**. For religious Cretans Áyii Dhéka is something of a place of pilgrimage; its name, "The Ten Saints", refers to ten early Christians martyred here under the Romans. The old Byzantine church in the centre of the village preserves the stone block on which they are supposed to have been decapitated and in a crypt below the modern church on the village's western edge you can see the martyrs' (now empty) tombs. It's an attractive village to wander around, with several places to eat and even some **rooms** – try *Dimitris Taverna* (T 28920 31560; ●), where you can both stay and eat, which has excellent-value en-suite, air-conditioned rooms with views above the restaurant and a splendid new terrace at the rear below.

Gortys and around

Within easy walking distance of Áyii Dhéka, either through the fields or along the main road, sprawls the site of **Gortys** (daily 8am–7pm; €4), ruined capital of the Roman province that included not only Crete but also much of North Africa. After a look at the plan of the extensive site at the entrance, cutting across the fields to the south of the road will give you some idea of the scale of this city, at its zenith in approximately the third century AD. An enormous variety of remains, including an impressive **theatre**, and a couple of **temples** are strewn across your route and more spectacular discoveries are being unearthed by the archeologists who return to dig each summer. Even in Áyii Dhéka you'll see Roman pillars and statues lying around in people's yards or propping up their walls.

There had been a settlement here from the earliest times and evidence of a Minoan site has been unearthed on the acropolis, but the extant ruins date almost entirely from the Roman era. Only now is the site being systematically excavated by the Italian Archeological School. At the main entrance to the **fenced site**, to the north of the road, are the ruins of the still impressive **basilica of Áyios Títos**; the eponymous saint converted the island to Christianity and was its first bishop. Beyond this is the **odeion** which houses the most important discovery on the site, the **Law Code**. These great inscribed blocks of stone were incorporated by the Romans from a much earlier stage of the city's development; they're written in an obscure early Greek-Cretan dialect, and in a style known as *boustrophedon* (ox-ploughed), with the lines reading alternately in opposite directions like the furrows of a ploughed field. At 10m by 3m, this is reputedly the largest Greek inscription ever found. The laws set forth reflect a strictly hierarchical society: five witnesses were needed to convict a free man of a crime, only one for a slave; raping a free man or woman carried a fine of a hundred *staters*, violating a serf only five. A small **museum** in a loggia (also within the fenced area) holds a number of large and finely worked sculptures found at Gortys, more evidence of the city's importance. Next to the museum is a **café** (same hours as site).

Míres

Some 20km west of Gortys, **MÍRES** is an important market town and focal point of transport for the fertile Messará plain: if you're switching buses to get from the beaches on the south coast to the archeological sites or the west, this is where you'll do it. There are good facilities including a **bank**, a few **restaurants** and a couple of **rooms**, though there's no particular reason to stay unless you are waiting for a bus or looking for work (it's one of the better places for agricultural jobs). A useful **Internet** café, *Net Escape*, near the bus stop will allow you to send a few emails while awaiting onward connections. Heading straight for Phaestos, there's usually no need to stop.

Phaestos (Festós)

The **Palace of Phaestos** (daily 8.30am–7.30pm; €4) was excavated by the Italian Federico Halbherr (also responsible for the early work at Gortys) at almost exactly the same time as Evans was working at Knossos. The style of the excavations, however, could hardly have been more different. Here, to the approval of most traditional archeologists, reconstruction was kept to an absolute minimum – it's all bare foundations, and walls which rise at most 1m above ground level. This means that, despite a magnificent setting overlooking the plain of Messará, the palace at Phaestos is not as immediately arresting as those at Knossos or Malia, but no less fascinating.

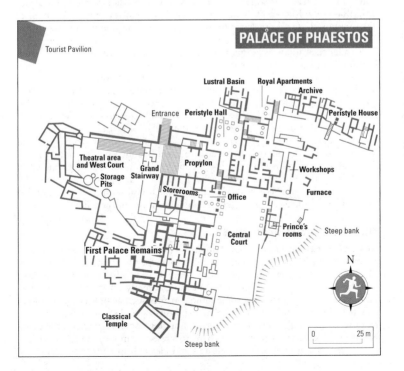

PALACE OF PHAESTOS

Tourist Pavilion

Lustral Basin   Royal Apartments
Archive
Entrance   Peristyle Hall   Peristyle House

Theatral area
and West Court   Grand   Propylon   Workshops
Storage   Stairway
Pits   Furnace
Storerooms
Office
Prince's
rooms   Steep bank
Central
Court
First Palace Remains

Classical
Temple   0   25 m

Steep bank

N

It's interesting to speculate why the palace was built halfway up a hill rather than on the plain below – certainly not for defence, for this is in no way a good defensive position. Psychological superiority over the peasants or reasons of health are both possible, but it seems quite likely that it was simply the magnificent view that finally swayed the decision. The site looks over Psilorítis to the north and the huge plain, with the Lasíthi mountains beyond it, to the east. Towards the top of Psilorítis you should be able to make out a small black smudge: the entrance to the Kamáres cave (see p.739).

On the ground closer at hand, you can hardly fail to notice the strong similarities between Phaestos and the other palaces: the same huge rows of storage jars, the great courtyard with its monumental stairway, and the theatre area. Unique to Phaestos, however, is the third courtyard, in the middle of which are the remains of a **furnace** used for metalworking. Indeed, this eastern corner of the palace seems to have been home to a number of craftsmen, including potters and carpenters. Oddly enough, Phaestos was much less ornately decorated than Knossos; there is no evidence, for example, of any of the dramatic Minoan wall-paintings.

The **tourist pavilion** near the entrance serves drinks and **food**, as well as the usual postcards, books and souvenirs. The nearby village of **ÁYIOS IOÁN-NIS**, along the road towards Mátala, has economical **rooms**, including some at *Taverna Ayios Ioannis* (☎28920 42006; ●), which is also a good place to eat charcoal-grilled *kounélli* (rabbit) and lamb on a leafy terrace.

Ayía Triádha

Some of the finest artworks in the museum at Iráklion came from **Ayía Triádha** (daily: May–Sept 10am–4pm; Oct–April 8.30am–3pm; €3), about a 45-minute walk (or short drive) from Phaestos. No one is quite sure what this site is, but the most common theory has it as some kind of royal summer villa. It's smaller than the palaces but, if anything, even more lavishly appointed and beautifully situated. In any event, it's an attractive place to visit, far less crowded than Phaestos, with a wealth of interesting little details. Look out in particular for the row of **stores** in front of what was apparently a marketplace, although recent thinking tends towards the idea that these were constructed after the villa had declined, possibly in the Mycenaean period. The remains of a **paved road** that probably led down to a harbour on the Gulf of Messará can also be seen running alongside the royal villa. The sea itself looks invitingly close, separated from the base of the hill only by Timbáki airfield (mainly used for motor racing these days), but if you try to drive down there, it's almost impossible to find your way around the unmarked dust tracks. There's a fourteenth-century **chapel** – dedicated to Áyios Yeóryios – at the site, worth visiting in its own right for the remains of ancient frescoes (key available from the ticket office).

Mátala and around

MÁTALA has by far the best-known beach in Iráklion province, widely promoted and included in tours mainly because of the famous caves cut into the cliffs above its beautiful sands. These are believed to be ancient tombs first used by Romans or early Christians, but more recently inhabited by a sizeable hippie community (including some famous names such as Bob Dylan and Joni Mitchell) in the 1960s and 1970s. You'll still meet people who will assure you that this is *the* travellers' beach on Crete, although today in high season the town is full of package tourists and tries hard to present a more respectable image. The caves have long since been cleared and cleaned up and these days are a fenced-off archeological site (April–Sept daily 10am–7pm; free) and locked up every evening.

The years since the early 1980s have seen the arrival of crowds and the development of hotels, restaurants and even a disco to service them; early afternoon, when the tour buses pull in for their swimming stop, sees the beach packed to overflowing. If you're prepared to accept Mátala for what it is – a resort of some size – you'll find the place more than bearable. The town beach is beautiful, and if the crowds get excessive, you can climb over the rocks in about twenty minutes (past more caves, many of which are inhabited through the summer) to another excellent stretch of sand, known locally as "Red Beach". In the evening,

△ Mátala beach and caves

when the day-trippers have gone, there are waterside bars and restaurants looking out over invariably spectacular sunsets. If you are arriving **by car**, park either on the road leading into the town or at the beach car park (€1 per day), on the right as you reach the town proper.

The chief problems with staying in Mátala concern prices and crowds: rooms are relatively expensive and oversubscribed, and food is good but not cheap. If you want **accommodation**, a cluster of places lies near to the *Zafiria* hotel (☎28920 45112, ✆info@zafiria-matala.com; ❸), just beyond the car park turn-off. Here rooms come with a/c but no TV, and there's a pool. For more economical options try looking in the little street to the left just beyond the *Zafiria* signed "Hotels and Rent Rooms". Here you'll find several rooms for rent, such as *Matala View* (☎28920 45114, ⓦwww.matala-apartments. com; ❷), which also rents studios and apartments sleeping two (❸) or up to four (❹). Nearby, the pleasant, modern and good-value *Fantastik* (☎28920 45362, ✆28920 45492; ❶) has airy a/c en-suites with fridge and the equally good and very friendly ⚓ *Hotel Nikos* (☎28920 45375, ⓦwww.kreta-inside .com; ❷) has pleasant a/c rooms off a plant-filled patio. If these are full, then everywhere closer in is likely to be as well, so head back out along the main road where places tend to fill up last, or try the **campsite**, *Camping of Matala* (☎28920 45720), next to the beach above the car park; *Kommos Camping*

(☎28920 45596) is a nicer site, but a few kilometres out of Mátala and reached by heading back towards Pítsidia and turning left along a signed track.

There are places to **eat and drink** all over the main part of town, and it's worth seeking out the *Skala* fish taverna on the south side of the bay for fresh seafood and a great view. Nightlife is confined to a solitary summer **disco**, *Kandari*, plus a couple of music bars on the main square. On the south side of the bay the most popular music bars are the *Marinero*, and *Tommy's Music Bar* above it, plus the nearby *JB Juke Box*. **Internet** access is available inside the stylish *Kafeneio* bar on the main square or at the *Zafiria Café* opposite (and owned by) the hotel of the same name. Impossible to miss are most other facilities, including various stores and a bookshop (with international press) next to *Kafeneio*, currency exchange, car and bike rental, travel agents, post office and a covered market where tourist tat has almost squeezed out the fruit and veg stalls.

Around Mátala: Pitsídhia and Kalamáki

One way to enjoy a bit more peace is to stay at **PITSÍDHIA**, about 5km inland. This has long been a well-used option, so it's not quite as cheap as you might expect, but there are plenty of rooms, lively places to eat and even music bars. If you decide to stay here, the beach at **KALAMÁKI** is an alternative to Mátala. Both beaches are approximately the same distance to walk, though there is a much better chance of a bus or a lift to Mátala. Kalamáki has developed somewhat, with a number of **rooms** – *Psiloritis* (☎28920 45693, ℱ28920 45249; ❷) is a good bet – and a couple of tavernas, but it's still a rather unfinished, soulless little place. The beach stretches for miles, surprisingly wild and windswept, lashed by sometimes dangerously rough surf. At the southern end (more easily reached by a path off the Pitsídhia–Mátala road) lies **Kommos**, once a Minoan port serving Phaestos and now the site of a major archeological excavation. It's not yet open to the public, but you can peer into the fenced-off area to see what's been revealed so far, which is pretty impressive: dwellings, streets, hefty stonework and even the ship sheds where repairs on the Minoan fleet were carried out.

Iráklion's south coast

South of the Messará plain are two more beach resorts, **Kalí Liménes** and **Léndas**, with numerous other little beaches along the coast in between, but nothing spectacular. **Public transport** is very limited indeed; you'll almost always have to travel via Míres (see p.727). If you have your own transport, the roads in these parts are all passable and newly sealed, but most are very slow going; the Kófinas hills, which divide the plain from the coast, are surprisingly precipitous.

Kalí Liménes

While Mátala itself was an important port under the Romans, the chief harbour for Gortys lay on the other side of Cape Líthinon at **KALÍ LIMÉNES**. Nowadays, this is once again a significant port – for oil tankers. This has rather spoilt its chances of becoming a major resort, and there are few proper facilities, but some people like Kalí Liménes: it's certainly off the beaten track and the constant procession of tankers gives you something to look at while beach lounging. There are a couple of places offering **rooms** – the best is the seafront *Taverna Panorama* (☎28920 97517; ❷; April–Nov), which has a decent **taverna** attached. The coastline is broken up by spectacular cliffs and, as long as there hasn't been a recent oil spill, the beaches are reasonably clean and totally empty.

Léndas

LÉNDAS, further east along the coast, is far more popular, with a couple of buses daily from Iráklion and a partly justified reputation for being peaceful (sullied by considerable summer crowds). Many people who arrive think they've come to the wrong place, as at first sight the village looks shabby, the beach is small, rocky and dirty, and the rooms are frequently all booked. A number of visitors leave without ever correcting that initial impression; the attraction of Léndas is not the village at all but the beach on the other (west) side of the headland. Here lies a vast, excellent sandy strand named **Dhytikós** (or Dhiskós) **beach**, part of it usually taken over by nudists, with a number of taverna/bars overlooking it from the roadside. The beach is a couple of kilometres from Léndas, along a rough track; if you're walking, you can save time by cutting across the headland. A considerably more attractive prospect than staying in Léndas itself is **camping** on the beach to the west of the village or, with luck, getting a **room** at one of the few beach tavernas – try ⚑ *Villa Tsapakis* (☎28920 95378, ⊛www .villa-tsapakis.gr; ❷), with sea-view rooms and reductions for longer stays. They will also change money on a credit card here (a useful service in this part of Crete where banks and ATMs are nonexistent) and have their own **taverna**, *Odysseas*, nearby. After you've discovered the beach, even Léndas begins to look more welcoming, and at least it has most of the facilities you'll need, including a couple of minimarkets, both of which will change money, a dual-screen **Internet** café on the main square, and numerous places to **eat and drink**: the outstanding ⚑ *Taverna El Greco* (☎28920 95322) with a leafy terrace above the beach on the east side of the village is one of the best restaurants on the whole south coast – their *oktapódhi* (octopus), *kolikythákia* (fried zucchini) or prime Messará beef pepper steak are all recommended.

Once you've come to terms with the place, you can also explore some deserted beaches eastwards, and the scrappy remains of **ancient Lebena** on a hilltop overlooking them. There was an important Asklepion (temple of the god Asklepios) here around some now-diverted warm springs, but only the odd broken column and fragments of mosaic survive in a fenced-off area on the village's northern edge.

East of Iráklion: the package-tour coast

East of Iráklion, the startling pace of **tourist development** in Crete is all too plain to see. The merest hint of a beach is an excuse to build at least one hotel, and these are outnumbered by the concrete shells of resorts-to-be. It's hard to find a room in this monument to the package-tour industry, and it can be expensive if you do. That said, there are one or two highlights amidst the dross, which are well worth a visit. Beyond the teenage-package resort of Mália a fine **Minoan palace** will transport you back three and a half millennia, or, if you're looking for splendid isolation, the twin sea hamlets of **Sísi** and **Mílatos** are refreshingly out of sync with the rest of this coast.

Goúrnes and Goúves

As a general rule, the further east you go, the better things get: when the road detours all too briefly inland, the more alluring Crete of olive groves and stark mountains asserts itself. You certainly won't see much of it at **GOÚRNES**, where an abandoned former US Air Force base still dominates much of the coastline, awaiting a plan for its redevelopment, or at nearby Káto Goúves, where there's a **campsite**, *Camping Creta* (☎28970 41400), sharing a boundary with the former base. From here, however, you can head inland to the old village of **GOÚVES**, a refreshing contrast, and just beyond to the **Skotinó cave**, one of the largest and most spectacular on the island (about an hour's walk from the coast; open all hours; free).

Hersónissos (Límin Hersoníssou)

Heading east from Goúves you'll pass the turn-off for the new E75 Hersónissos bypass (avoiding the beach resort's bottleneck), which cuts inland to rejoin the coast road just before Stalídha (see opposite). Shortly beyond this junction, there's the turning for the direct route up to the Lasíthi Plateau. Carry straight on, though, and you'll roll into the first of the really big resorts, **HERSÓNISSOS** or, more correctly, Límin Hersoníssou; Hersónissos is the village in the hills just behind, also overrun by tourists.

Hersónissos was once just a small fishing village; today it's the most popular of Crete's package resorts. If what you want is plenty of video-bars, tavernas, restaurants and Eurodisco nightlife, then this is the place to come. The resort has numerous small patches of sand beach between rocky outcrops, but a shortage of places to stay in peak season.

The focal main street, two-kilometre-long Odhós Elefthériou Venizélou, is a seemingly endless ribbon of bars, travel agents, tacky jewellery and beachwear shops, amusement arcades and – during the daytime at least – nose-to-tail traffic jams. North of here, along the modern seafront, a solid line of restaurants and bars is broken only by the occasional souvenir shop; in their midst you'll find a small pyramidal Roman **fountain** with broken mosaics of fishing scenes, the only real relic of the ancient town of Chersonesos. Around the headland above the harbour and in odd places along the seafront, you can see remains of Roman harbour installations, mostly submerged.

Beach and clubs excepted, the distractions of Hersónissos comprise **Lychnostatis Open-Air Museum** (Mon–Fri & Sun 9.30am–2pm; €4), a surprisingly rewarding "museum" of traditional Crete, on the coast at the eastern edge of the town; a small aquarium, **Aqua World** (April–Oct daily 10am–6pm; €5), just off the main road at the west end of town, up the road almost opposite the *Vibe* style bar. To cool down, there's the watersports paradise **Star Beach Water Park** (daily: April & May 10am–6pm; June–Sept 10am–7pm; free entry) near the beach at the eastern end of the resort or, a few kilometres inland, the competing and more elaborate **Aqua Splash Water Park** (€15 full day, €12.50 half day).

A short distance inland are the three **hill villages** of Koutoulafári, Piskopianó and "old" Hersónissos, which all have a good selection of tavernas, and are worth searching out for accommodation.

Practicalities

Hersónissos is well provided with all the back-up **services** you need to make a holiday go smoothly. Banks, bike and car rental and post office are all on or just off the main drag, Elefthériou Venizélou, as are the taxi ranks. There are a number of **Internet** cafés: *Cafe Neon*, Elefthériou Venizélou 40, and the central *Internet Cafe*, Elefthériou Venizélou 10, alongside the church, both have plenty of screens. **Buses** running east and west leave from the main bus stop on Venizélou every thirty minutes.

Finding somewhere to stay here can verge on the impossible in July and August. Much of the **accommodation** is allocated to package-tour operators and what remains for casual visitors is among the priciest on the island. To check for general availability of accommodation, the quickest and best option is to enquire at one of the many travel agencies along Venizélou such as KTEL Tours next to the bus stop and opposite the petrol station in the centre of town. The town's most reasonably priced central options include *Zorba's Hotel*, Beach Road (℡28970 22134, Ⓦwww.hersonissos.com/zorbas; ❸), and *Selena*, Maragáki 13 (℡ & ℻28970 25180; ❷), near the sea-front action which can be noisy at night. One place to try on the western edge as you enter the town is *Hotel Ilios* (℡28970 22500, ℻28970 22582; ❹), just back from the main road, which has a rooftop pool. There are two good **campsites**: one at the eastern end of town, *Caravan Camping* (℡28970 24718), which also has several reed-roofed bungalows, and *Camping Hersonissos* (℡28970 22902), just to the west of town.

Despite the vast number of **eating places**, there are few in Hersónissos worth recommending, and the tavernas down on the harbourfront should be avoided. One of the few Greek tavernas that stands out is *Kavouri* along Arhéou Theátrou, but it's fairly expensive; a cheaper in-town alternative for some delicious and inexpensive Cretan cooking is 🍴 *Taverna Creta Giannis*, Kaniadhakí 4, just off the south side of Venizélou slightly east of the church. Nearby, and also definitely worth a try, is 🍴 *Passage to India*, an authentic and extremely good Indian restaurant; it lies on Petrákis, another side street just off the main street near the church. Heading out of town on the Piskopianó road, near the junction to Koutoulafári, the friendly *Fegari* taverna also serves good Greek food at reasonable prices. Sitting at your table overlooking the street below you can view the steady trek of clubbers heading down the hill to the bars and nightclubs of Hersónissos. The hill villages have the greatest selection of tavernas, particularly Koutoulafári, where you can have a relaxed evening amongst the narrow streets and small platíes.

Hersónissos is renowned for its **nightlife**, and there's certainly no shortage of it. A night's partying kicks off around the **bars** ringing the harbour, which is packed with promenaders and the overspill from countless noisy music bars from 10pm through to the early hours. After midnight, the larger **disco-clubs** and **pubs** in the streets leading up to and along Eleuthériou Venizélou are the places to be seen. Currently the most popular music clubs are *Aria* (open July–Aug only), the island's largest, on the main road at the west end of town, *Cinema*, also on Venizélou, and *Camelot*, *New York* and *Status* (which opens at 4.30am), all near the harbour. Close to *Aria* on Venizélou, the *Hard Rock Café* has transmuted into *Vibe*, with a terrace where clubbers chill out between venues. If you fancy a quiet drink then you've come to the wrong resort, but you could try *Kahluai Beach Cocktail Bar* or *Haris Ouzo & Raki Place* (beneath the *Hotel Virginia*). There is an open-air **cinema** showing original-version films at the *Creta Maris* hotel at the west end of the town and close to the beach.

Stalídha

STALÍDHA is a Cinderella town, sandwiched in between its two louder, brasher and some would say uglier sisters, Mália and Hersónissos, but it is neither quiet nor undeveloped. This rapidly expanding beach resort, with more than sixty tavernas and bars and a few discos, can offer the best of both worlds, with a friendlier and more relaxed setting, a better beach (and usual array of watersports) and very easy access to its two livelier neighbours. The town essentially consists of a single, relatively traffic-free street, which rings the seafront for more than 2km, before the apartment blocks briefly become fewer and further between, until the mass development of Málía begins.

Finding a place to stay can be difficult, since **accommodation** is almost entirely in studio and apartment blocks which are booked by package companies in high season. Out of season, however, you may well be able to negotiate a very reasonable price for a studio apartment complete with swimming pool; ask in the central travel agencies first, as they will know what is available, and expect to pay around ❷–❸ for two. Finding somewhere to **eat** is less difficult as there are plenty of rather ordinary tavernas, the best and most authentic being *Maria's*, the *Hellas Taverna* and the more upmarket *Blue Sea Restaurant*, all at the western end of the seafront.

Stalídha is completely overshadowed by its neighbours when it comes to **nightlife**, though you can dance at *Rhythm*, on the beach; the music bars *Sea Wolf Cocktail Bar* and *Akti Bar* are near each other along the beach nearby.

Málía

Three kilometres east of Stalídha and similar to the other resorts along this stretch of coast, much of **MÁLÍA** is carved up by the package industry, so in peak season finding a place to stay is not always easy. The town's focus is a T-junction (where the **bus** drops you) from where the beach road – a kilometre-long strip lined with bars, clubs, games arcades, tavernas and souvenir shops – heads north to the sea and beaches. South of this junction the older village presents a slightly saner image of what Málía used to be, but even here rampant commercialism is making inroads.

Practicalities

The best **accommodation** options, especially if you want any sleep, are among the numerous **rooms** and **pensions** signposted in the old town, such as *Esperia* (☎28970 31086; ❹), up a side road slightly east of the T-junction. Backtracking from the junction, along the main Iráklion road, there are a number of reasonably priced **pensions** on the left and right, including *Hibiscus* (☎28970 31313, ℉28970 32042; ❸), which has rooms and studios with kitchenette and fridge around a pool in a garden behind. If you really want to be in the centre of things, try *Kostas* (☎28970 31101; ❷), a family-run pension incongruously located behind the mini-golf at the end of the beach road. Otherwise, on arrival visit one of the travel companies along the main road – such as the reliable SK-Travel, Venizélou 200 (☎28970 31481) – to enquire about accommodation availability. All the other things you're likely to need – **banks** with ATMs, **post office** and food shops – are strung out along the main street near the junction, but the town's best **Internet** access, *Internet Cafe*, is bang in the middle of the beach road madness (about a third of the way down on the right).

Eating in Málía is unlikely to be a problem as **restaurants** jostle for your custom at every step, especially along the beach road. None is particularly good here, and a few are diabolical. The best places for a meal are around Platía Ayíou Dhimitríou, a pleasant square beside the church in the centre of the old village to the south of the main road. Here, you could try *Kalimera* or *Petros*, or the pleasant *Kalesma* with a delightful terrace, perhaps after an aperitif at *Bar Yiannis* just north of the church or *Ouzeri Elizabeth* alongside it, where they serve local wine from the barrel. A little harder to find, and to the west of the square, *Apolafsi* is a good-quality small family taverna which is slightly less pricey than the others.

The beach road comes into its own at night, when the profusion of **bars**, **discos** and **clubs** erupts into a pulsating cacophony. The aptly named *Zoo* is one of the most frenetic, and once past midnight the internal walls part to reveal an even larger dance area. Other popular venues (many British-owned and -run) along the strip include *Cloud Nine, Malibu, Zig-Zag, Apollo* and *Camelot Castle*. There is also a clutch of "English pubs" with names like *Newcastle* and *Brit's Bar*. Unfortunately, a good night's clubbing is frequently spoilt by groups of drunken youths pouring out of these places and getting into brawls. At one point the situation got so bad that tour operators threatened to pull out of the resort if action wasn't taken to deal with the hooligans – all rather ironic as it was they who were shipping them in by the plane-load on cut-price packages. Recent years have seen a police clampdown on such activities as drinking on the street, and the situation has improved considerably.

The Palace of Malia

Much less imposing than either Knossos or Phaestos, the **Palace of Malia** (daily 8.30am–3pm; €4), 2km east of Mál

ia town, in some ways surpasses both. For a start, it's a great deal emptier and you can wander among the remains in relative peace. While no reconstruction has been attempted, the palace was never reoccupied after its second destruction in the fifteenth century BC, so the ground plan is virtually intact. It's much easier to comprehend than Knossos and, if you've seen the reconstructions there, it's easy to envisage this seaside palace in its days of glory. There's a real feeling of an ancient civilization with a taste for the good life, basking on the rich agricultural plain between the Lasíthi mountains and the sea.

From this site came the famous **gold pendant** of two bees (which can be seen in the Iráklion Archeological Museum or on any postcard stand), allegedly part of a hoard that was plundered and whose other treasures can now be found in the British Museum in London. The beautiful leopard-head axe, also in the museum at Iráklion, was another of the treasures found here. At the site, look out for the strange indented stone in the central court (which probably held ritual offerings), for the remains of ceremonial stairways and for the giant *pithoi*, which stand like sentinels around the palace. To the north and west of the main site, archeological digs are still going on as the **large town** which surrounded the palace comes slowly to light, and part of this can now be viewed via an overhead walkway.

Any passing **bus** should stop at the site, or you could even rent a **bike** for a couple of hours as it's a pleasant, flat ride from Mália town. Leaving the archeological zone and turning immediately right, you can follow the road down to a lovely stretch of clean and relatively peaceful **beach**, backed by fields, scrubland and a single makeshift taverna, which serves good fresh fish. From here you can walk back along the shore to Mália or take a bus (every 30min in either direction) from the stop on the main road.

Sísi and Mílatos

Head **east** from the Palace of Malia, and it's not long before the road leaves the coast, climbing across the hills towards Áyios Nikólaos. If you want to escape the frenetic pace of all that has gone before, try continuing to Sísi or Mílatos. These little shore villages are bypassed by the main road as it cuts inland, and are still very much in the early stages of tourist development. The larger of the two, **SÍSI**, is charmingly situated around a small harbour overlooked by balcony bars and more tavernas. The opening of the resort's first disco bar (*Faros*) and

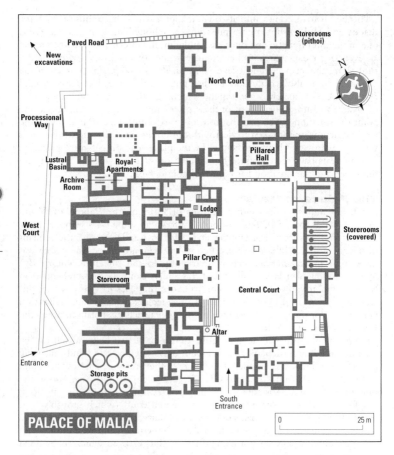

Paved Road

New
excavations

North Court

Storerooms
(pithoi)

N

Processional
Way

Pillared
Hall

Lustral
Basin

Royal
Apartments

Archive
Room

□ Lodge

West
Court

Storerooms
(covered)

Pillar Crypt

Central Court

Storeroom

○ Altar

Entrance

Storage pits

South
Entrance

PALACE OF MALIA

0   25 m

the large holiday complex (*Kalimera Krita*), a couple of kilometres to the east,
are a sure sign that more development is on its way; there's even a **post office**,
confirming the resort status. **Accommodation** is mainly in studios and apartments; it's best to ask in the travel agencies and bars for details of availability.
There's also a small pension, *Elena* (❶), just behind the harbour, and a shady
campsite with pool and taverna (℡28410 71247) signposted on the way in.
Among a cluster of seafront **tavernas** all specializing in freshly caught fish, the
Fisherman's Place is worth a try.

In quieter **MÍLATOS**, rooms can be found in the old village, 2km inland,
but the seaside settlement – despite a rather pebbly beach – is more desirable.
A number of the seafront tavernas let out rooms and, outside the peak season
when there's little chance of a bed, the friendly ⚑ *Rooms Taverna Sokrates*
(℡28410 81375;❷) is worth a try and does decent **food**, especially fish, netted
by the village boats. Despite their pebbly main **beaches**, the resorts make for a
refreshing change of pace, and there are some fine, deep aprons of sand in the
rocky coves beyond the resort centres.

West of Iráklion: around Psilorítis

Most people heading west from Iráklion speed straight out on the **E75 coastal highway**, nonstop to Réthymnon. If you're in a hurry this is not such a bad plan; the road is fast and spectacular, hacked into the sides of mountains which for the most part drop straight to the sea, though there are no more than a couple of places where you might consider stopping. By contrast, the old roads inland are agonizingly slow, but they do pass through a whole string of **attractive villages** beneath the heights of the Psilorítis range. From here you can set out to explore the **mountains** and even walk across them to emerge in villages with views of the south coast.

The coastal route towards Réthymnon

Leaving the city, the **new highway** runs behind a stretch of highly developed coast, where the hotels compete for shore space with a cement works and power station. As soon as you reach the mountains, though, all this is left behind and there's only the clash of rock and sea to contemplate. As you start to climb, look out for **Paleókastro**, hovering beside a bridge which carries the road over a small cove; the castle is so weathered as to be almost invisible against the brownish face of the cliff.

Ayía Pelayía and Fódhele

Some 3km below the highway, as it rounds the first point, lies the resort of **AYÍA PELAYÍA**. It looks extremely attractive from above but, once there, and especially in July and August, you're likely to find the narrow, taverna-lined beach packed to full capacity. This is not somewhere to roll up in high season without reserved **accommodation**, although in quieter times *Zorba's Apartments* (T & F 28102 56072, E zorbas@freemail.gr; ❹), along the nameless main street behind the beach, or, on the road above it, the excellent-value ⌁ *Danai Rooms* (T 28102 85936; ❷), with air-conditioned, en-suite rooms with kitchenette and fridge, should have space. Opposite *Zorba's Apartments*, the Pangosmio travel agency (T 28108 11402, F 28108 11424) may be able to come up with something, even at the last minute in high season. Out of season you might find a real bargain apartment and, despite the high-season crowds, the resort maintains a dignity long since lost in Mália and Hersónissos, and even a certain exclusivity; a couple of Crete's most luxurious hotels, including the enormous *Peninsula* (T 28108 11313, W www.peninsula.gr; ❼), nestle on the headlands just beyond the main town beach. There are plenty of **minimarkets** for buying picnic food, and **Internet** access is available at *Netcafé Atlas*, next door to *Zorba's Apartments*.

Not far beyond Ayía Pelayía, there's a turning inland to the village of **FÓDHELE**, allegedly El Greco's birthplace. A plaque from the University of Valladolid (in Spain) acknowledges the claim and, true or not, the community has built a small tourist industry on that basis. There are a number of craft shops and some pleasant tavernas where you can sit outside along the river. A peaceful one-kilometre walk (or drive) takes you to the spuriously titled **El Greco's House** (May–Oct Tues–Sun 9am–5pm; €1.50), exhibiting a few reprints of his works and not much more, and the more worthwhile and picturesque fourteenth-century Byzantine **church of the Panayía** (Tues–Sun 9am–3.30pm; free) with frescoes, opposite. None of this amounts to very much but it is a pleasant, relatively unspoilt village if you simply want to sit in peace for a while. A couple of **buses** a day run here from Iráklion, and there's the odd tour; if you arrive on a direct bus, the walk back down to the highway (about 3km), where you can flag down a passing service, is not too strenuous.

Balí and Pánormos

BALÍ, on the coast approximately halfway between Iráklion and Réthymnon, also used to be tranquil and undeveloped and, by the standards of the north coast, it still is in many ways. The village is built around a trio of small coves, some 2km from the highway (a hot walk from the bus), and is similar to Ayía Pelayía except that the beaches are not quite as good and there are no big hotels, just an ever-growing proliferation of studios, apartment buildings, rooms for rent and a number of smaller hotels. You'll have plenty of company here and it has to be said that Balí has become a package resort too popular for its own good. The third and best beach, known as "Paradise", no longer really deserves the name; it's a beautiful place to splash about, surrounded by mountains rising straight from the sea, but there's rarely a spare inch on the sand in high season.

Continuing along the coast, the last stop before you emerge on the flat stretch leading to Réthymnon is at **PÁNORMOS**. This makes a good stopover if you're in search of somewhere more peaceful and authentic. The small sandy beach can get crowded when boats bring day-trippers from Réthymnon, but most of the time the attractive village remains relatively unspoilt, and succeeds in clinging to its Cretan identity. There are several decent **tavernas** – try *Taverna Panorama* in the heart of the village or *Sofoklís* near the harbour – and **rooms** places, one large hotel and the very comfortable *Pension Lucy* (⊕28340 51328, ❸), which has also sprung a seafront offshoot with balcony studio rooms and apartments.

Inland towards Mount Psilorítis

Of the **inland routes**, the old main road (via Márathos and Dhamásta) is not the most interesting. This, too, was something of a bypass in its day and there are few places of any size or appeal, though it's a very scenic drive. If you want to dawdle, you're better off on the road which cuts up to **Týlissos** and then goes via **Anóyia**. It's a pleasant ride through fertile valleys filled with olive groves and vineyards, a district (the Malevísi) renowned from Venetian times for the strong, sweet Malmsey wine.

Týlissos and Anóyia

TÝLISSOS has a significant archeological site (daily 8.30am–3pm; €2) where three Minoan houses were excavated; unfortunately, its reputation is based more on what was found here (many pieces in the Iráklion Archeological Museum) and on its significance for archeologists than on anything which remains to be seen. Still, it's worth a look, if you're passing, for a glimpse of Minoan life away from the big palaces, and for the tranquillity of the pine-shaded remains.

ANÓYIA is a much more tempting place to stay, especially if the summer heat is becoming oppressive. Spilling prettily down a hillside close below the highest peaks of the mountains, it looks traditional, but closer inspection shows that most of the buildings are actually concrete; the village was destroyed during World War II and the local men rounded up and shot – one of the German reprisals for the abduction of General Kreipe by the Cretan resistance. The town has a reputation as a **handicrafts** centre (especially for woven and woollen goods), skills acquired both through bitter necessity after most of the men had been killed, and in a conscious attempt to revive the town. At any rate it worked, for the place is thriving today – thanks, it seems, to a buoyant agricultural sector made rich by stockbreeding, and the number of elderly widows keen to subject any visitor to their terrifyingly aggressive sales techniques.

Quite a few people pass through Anóyia during the day, but not many of them **stay**, even though there are some good *pensions* and rented rooms in the upper half of the town, including the flower-bedecked *Rooms Aris* (T 28340 31460, F 28430 31058; 2) and the nearby *Aristea* (T 28340 31459; B&B; 2), which has an ebullient female proprietor, en-suite rooms with spectacular views and rates that include breakfast.

The town has a very different, more traditional ambience at night, and the only problem is likely to be finding a **place to eat**: although there are plenty of snack-bars and so-called tavernas, most have extremely basic menus, more or less limited to spit-barbecued lamb, which is the tasty local speciality served up by the grill places on the lower square. If you can face it, a steep hike to the top of the village will bring you to *Taverna Skalomata* offering well-prepared taverna standards, some pretty good barbecued lamb, plus a fine view.

Mount Psilorítis and its caves

Heading for the mountains, a smooth road ascends the 21km from Anóyia to an altitude of 1400m on the **Nídha plateau** at the base of Mount Psilorítis. Here, the *Taverna Nida* (T 28340 31141; April–Sept daily; Oct–May Sat & Sun only) serves up hearty mountain dishes featuring lamb, pork and chicken, and has a couple of simple **rooms** (1), which makes it a good base for hikes in the surrounding mountains. A short path leads from the taverna to the celebrated **Idean cave** (Idhéon Ándhron), a rival of that on Mount Dhíkti (see overleaf) for the title of Zeus's birthplace, and certainly associated from the earliest of times with the cult of Zeus. The remnants of a major archeological dig carried out inside – including a miniature railway used by archeologists to remove tonnes of rock and rubble – still litter the site, giving the place a rather unattractive prospect. When you enter the cave down concrete steps into the depths, it turns out to be a rather shallow affair, devoid even of natural wonders, with little to see.

The taverna also marks the start of the way to the top of **Mount Psilorítis** (2456m), Crete's highest mountain, a climb that for experienced, properly shod hikers is not at all arduous. The route (now forming a stretch of the E4 Pan-European footpath) is well marked with the usual red dots and paint splashes, and it should be a six- to seven-hour return journey to the **chapel of Tímios Stavrós** ("Holy Cross") at the summit, although in spring, thick snow may slow you down.

If you're prepared to camp on the plateau (it's very cold, but there's plenty of available water) or find rooms at the taverna, you could continue on foot next day down to the southern slopes of the range. It's a beautiful hike and also relatively easy, four hours or so down a fairly clear path to **Vorízia** where there is no food or accommodation, although **KAMÁRES**, 4km west, has both: for **rooms**, the very cheap, very basic and unsigned (you'll need to ask for it) *Hotel Psiloritis* (T 28920 43290; 1) should have a bed, and the best **place to eat** is the *Taverna Bournelis* at the village's western end. If you're still interested in caves, there's a more rewarding one above Kamáres, a climb of some five hours on a good but aggressively steep path; if you're coming over from Nídha, the cave actually makes a rather shorter detour off the main traverse path. The start of the route is just to the left of the *Taverna Bournelis* and the proprietors here can advise on the ascent (in Greek and German only). There is at least one daily **bus** from here down to Míres and alternative (more difficult) routes to the peak of Psilorítis if you want to approach from this direction.

Eastern Crete

Eastern Crete is dominated by **Áyios Nikólaos**, and while it is a highly developed resort, by no means all of the east is like this. Far fewer people venture beyond the road south to **Ierápetra** and into the eastern isthmus, where only **Sitía** and the famous beach at **Váï** ever see anything approaching a crowd. Inland, too, there's interest, especially on the extraordinary **Lasíthi Plateau**, which is worth a night's stay if only to observe its abidingly rural life.

Inland to the Lasíthi Plateau

Leaving the palace at Malia, the highway cuts inland towards **NEÁPOLI**, soon beginning a spectacular climb into the mountains. Set in a high valley, Neápoli is a market town little touched by tourism. Just off a leafy main square there's an excellent **hotel**, ⚜ *Neapolis* (☎28410 33967, ⓦwww.neapolis-hotel.gr; ❸), with a/c rooms, some with fine views. On the main square there's a superb little **folk museum** (Mon 9am–2pm, Wed–Sun 9.30am–4.30pm; €1.50) displaying some fascinating photos, utensils and farming equipment from Neápoli's past as well as reconstructions of a bar, schoolroom, cobbler's workshop and domestic kitchen from a bygone age. On the square – and 50m from the museum entrance – *Taverna Yeúseis* is a good place for **food** and has a pleasant shady terrace. Beyond the town, it's about twenty minutes before the bus suddenly emerges high above the Gulf of Mirabéllo and Áyios Nikólaos, the island's biggest resort. If you're stopping, Neápoli also marks the second point of access to the **Lasíthi Plateau**.

Scores of bus tours drive up here daily to view the "thousands of white-cloth-sailed windmills" which irrigate the high plain ringed by mountains, and most groups will be disappointed. There are very few working windmills left, and these operate only for limited periods (mainly in June), although most roadside tavernas seem to have adopted many of those made redundant as marketing features. The drive alone is worthwhile, however, and the plain is a fine example of rural Crete at work, every inch devoted to the cultivation of potatoes, apples, pears, figs, olives and a host of other crops; stay in one of the villages for a night or two and you'll see real life return as the tourists leave. There are plenty of easy rambles around the villages as well, through orchards and past the rusting remains of derelict windmills.

You'll find **rooms** in the main village of **TZERMIÁDHO**, where the *Hotel Kourites* (☎28440 22194; ❸) is to be found on the eastern edge, in **ÁYIOS YEÓRYIOS** – where there's a **folk museum**, and the economical and friendly *Hotel Dias* (☎28440 31207; ❶) – and **PSYKHRÓ**, where the *Hotel Zeus* (☎28440 31284; ❷) lies close to the Dhiktean cave.

The Dhiktean cave

Psykhró is the most visited village on the plateau, as it's the base for visiting Lasíthi's other chief attraction: the birthplace of Zeus, the **Dhiktean cave** (daily 8am–7pm; €4; ask for the free information leaflet on the cave). In legend, Zeus's father, the Titan Kronos, was warned that he would be overthrown by a son, and accordingly ate all his offspring; however, when Rhea gave birth to

Zeus in the cave, she fed Kronos a stone and left the child concealed, protected by the Kouretes, who beat their shields outside to disguise his cries. The rest, as they say, is history (or at least myth). There's an obvious path running up to the cave from Psykhró, near the start of which (beyond the car park) the mule handlers will attempt to persuade you the ascent is better done on one of their steeds (costing a hefty €10 one way). In reality, it's hardly a particularly long or dauntingly steep hike to the cave entrance.

The cave has been made more "visitor friendly" in recent years, with the introduction of concrete steps in place of slippery stones, and electric lighting instead of flashlamps and candles. Inevitably some of the magic and mystery has been lost, and the guides, who used to make the visit much more interesting with their hilarious and preposterous tales, have now been banned, presumably in the interests of accuracy and decorum. Thus you will now have to pick out for yourself the stalactites and stalagmites formed in the image of the breasts of Rhea where the infant Zeus was suckled, as well as the baby Zeus himself – a feat verging on the impossible for someone lacking a Cretan imagination.

One of the cave guardians, Petros Zarvakis, is also a wildlife expert and leads **guided wild-flower and bird-spotting hikes** (April–Sept) into the mountains surrounding the plain, and also to the summit of Mount Dhíkti; if he is not on duty at the cave entrance or at the taverna in the car park, he can be contacted on ☎28440 31600 or 694 56 16 074. **Buses** run around the plateau to Psykhró direct from Iráklion and from Áyios Nikólaos via Neápoli. Both roads offer spectacular views, coiling through a succession of passes guarded by lines of ruined windmills.

Áyios Nikólaos and around

ÁYIOS NIKÓLAOS ("Ag Nik" to the majority of its British visitors) is set around a supposedly bottomless salt lake, now connected to the sea to form an

△ Áyios Nikólaos

inner harbour. It is supremely picturesque and has some style and charm, which it exploits to the full. There are no sights as such, but the excellent archeological museum (Tues–Sun 8.30am–3pm; €3) and an interesting folk museum (Mon–Fri & Sun 10am–4pm; €3) are both worth seeking out. The lake and port are surrounded by restaurants and bars, which charge above the odds, and whilst the resort is still very popular, some tourists are distinctly surprised to find themselves in a place with no decent beach at all.

There are swimming opportunities further north, however, where the pleasant low-key resort of **Eloúnda** is the gateway to the mysterious islet of **Spinalónga**, and some great backcountry inland – perfect to explore on a scooter. Inland from Áyios Nikólaos, **Kritsá** with its famous frescoed church and textile sellers is a tour-bus haven, but just a couple of kilometres away, the imposing ruins of **ancient Lato** are usually deserted.

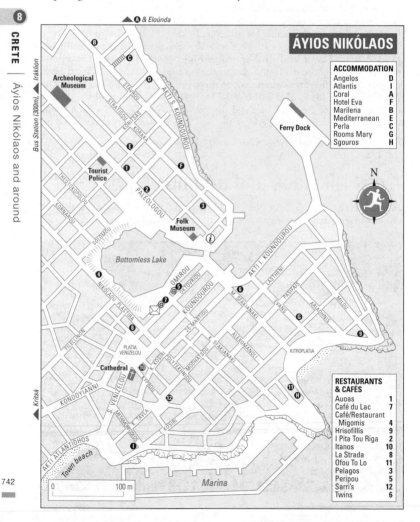

ÁYIOS NIKÓLAOS

ACCOMMODATION	
Angelos	D
Atlantis	I
Coral	A
Hotel Eva	F
Marilena	B
Mediterranean	E
Perla	C
Rooms Mary	G
Sgouros	H

RESTAURANTS & CAFÉS	
Auoas	1
Café du Lac	7
Café/Restaurant Migomis	4
Hrisofillis	9
I Pita Tou Riga	2
Itanos	10
La Strada	8
Ofou To Lo	11
Pelagos	3
Peripou	5
Sarri's	12
Twins	6

Áyios Nikólaos practicalities

The **tourist office** (daily: July–Aug 8am–10pm; Sept–June 8am–9.30pm; ℡28410 22357), situated between the lake and the port, is one of the best on the island for information about accommodation. The **bus station** is situated to the northwest end of town near the archeological museum. You'll find the greatest concentration of **stores** and **travel agents** on the hill between the bridge and Platía Venizélou (along the streets 25-Martíou, Koundoúrou and pedestrianized 28-Oktovríou), and the main **ferry agent**, Plora Travel (℡28410 25868), on the corner of 28-Oktovríou and K. Sfakianáki. The **post office** (Mon–Sat 7.30am–2pm) is halfway up 28-Oktovríou on the right. To **hire a motorbike**, **scooter** or **mountain bike** try the reliable Mike Manolis (℡28410 24940), who has a pitch along Modhátsou near the junction with K. Sfakianáki. Good **car-rental** deals are available at Club Cars, 28-Oktovríou 24 (℡28410 25868), near the post office. Various **boat trips** to points around the gulf (such as Spinalónga and Eloúnda; about €12–15 depending on company) leave from the west side of the harbour. **Internet** access is available at *Peripou*, 28-Oktovríou 25 (daily 9.30am–2am), and *Café du Lac* at no. 17 on the same street.

Accommodation

Since many of the package companies have pulled out in recent years the town is no longer jammed solid as it once was, though in the peak season you won't have so much choice. One thing in your favour is that there are literally thousands of **rooms**, scattered all around town. The tourist office normally has a couple of boards with cards and brochures about hotels and rooms, including their prices. If the prices seem very reasonable it is because many are for the low season. The nearest **campsite** is *Gournia Moon*, 17km away (see p.747).

Angelos Aktí S. Koundoúrou 16 ℡28410 23501, ℱ28410 25692. Welcoming small hotel offering excellent a/c balconied rooms with TV and fine views over the Gulf. ❸

Atlantis Aktí Atlantidhos 15, near the town beach ℡28410 28964, ✉p.mixalis@mailcity.com. Nothing special, but handy enough for the town beach, offering a/c en-suite balcony rooms with fridge. Also has a snack-bar below serving cheap breakfasts. ❷

Coral Aktí S. Koundoúrou 28363, ⓦwww.hermes-hotels.gr. One of Áyios Nikólaos's leading in-town hotels offering a/c rooms with sea view, fridge, balcony and satellite TV, plus a rooftop pool and bar. When things are slack, prices can fall by up to 25 percent. In summer you may need to ask for the room-only price as they will quote you half-board. B&B ❻

Hotel Eva Stratigoú Kóraka 20 ℡28410 22587. Decent en-suite a/c rooms with TV in a misnamed *pension* close to the centre. ❷

Marilena Érythrou Stavroú 14 ℡28410 22681, ℱ28410 24218. Not the bargain it once was, but it's still a pleasant place to stay; some rooms with sea view and balcony. ❹

Mediterranean S. Dhávaki 27 ℡28410 23611. Clean, economical en-suite rooms with fridges and fans, and close to the lake. ❷

Rooms Mary Evans 13, near the Kitroplatía ℡28410 24384. Very friendly place with a/c (€5 extra) en-suite balcony rooms (some with sea view); access to fridge and use of kitchen. Also has some apartments nearby costing only slightly more. ❶

Perla Salaminos 4, ℡28410 23379. Decent budget option close to the sea, on a hill to the north of the harbour. En-suite rooms with fans and fridge, and front rooms have sea-view balconies. ❶

Sgouros Kitroplatía ℡28410-28931, ⓦwww .sgourosgrouphotels.com. Good-value modern hotel with a/c balcony rooms overlooking one of the town's beaches, and close to plenty of tavernas. ❷

Eating

At least when it comes to eating there's no chance of missing out, even if some of the prices are fancier than the restaurants. There are tourist-oriented

tavernas all around the lake and harbour and little to choose between them, apart from the different perspectives you get on the passing fashion show. Have a drink here perhaps, or a mid-morning coffee, and choose somewhere else to eat. The places around the Kitroplatía are generally fairer value, but again you are paying for the location.

Auoas Paleológou 44. This taverna serves good, traditional Cretan dishes in a plant-covered trellised courtyard, where food and wine prices are among the lowest in town.

Hrisofillis Aktí Themistokleous. Attractive and stylish new eatery with reasonably priced fish, meat and veggie *mezédhes* served on a pleasant terrace fronting the east side of the Kitroplatía beach.

Itanos Kýprou 1, off the east side of Platía Venizélou. Popular with locals, this taverna serves Cretan food and wine and has a terrace across the road.

Café/Restaurant Migomis Nikoláou Plastíra 22 (☎28410 24353). Pleasant café high above the bottomless lake with a stunning view. Perfect (if pricey) place for breakfast, afternoon or evening drinks. Their next-door restaurant enjoys the same vista and is pricier than the norm, but perhaps worth it if you've booked a frontline table to feast on that view.

Ofou To Lo Kitroplatía. Best of the moderately priced places on the seafront here: the food is consistently good.

Pelagos Stratigoú Kóraka, just back off the lake behind the tourist office ☎28410 25737. A stylish fish taverna with the best garden terrace in town, serving excellent food reflected in the prices.

I Pita Tou Riga Paleológou 24, close to the lake. Excellent Lilliputian snack-bar/restaurant serving imaginative fare – salads, filled pitta breads and some Asian dishes; has a small terrace up steps across the road.

Sarri's Kýprou 15. Great little economical neighbourhood café-diner especially good for breakfast fare and *souvláki*, all served on a leafy terrace.

La Strada Nikoláou Plastíra 5. Authentic Italian fare in swish surroundings serving up good-value pizza and pasta (meat dishes are pricier), should you fancy a change of cuisine.

Twins Fronting the harbour. Handy pizzeria, fast-food outlet and coffee bar, open all hours. Their "small" pizzas measure a giant 40cm in diameter.

Drinking and nightlife

After you've eaten you can get into the one thing which Áyios Nikólaos undeniably does well: **bars and nightlife**. Not that you really need a guide to this – the bars are hard to avoid, and you can just follow the crowds to the most popular places centred around the harbour and 25-Martíou. For a more relaxed drink you could try *Hotel Alexandros* on Paleológou (behind the tourist office), with a rooftop cocktail bar overlooking the lake, which after dark metamorphoses into a 1960s-to-1980s period music bar. A similar pace rules at *Zygos* on the north side of the lake, which serves low-priced cocktails and ices until the small hours. One curiosity worth a look in the harbour itself is *Armida* (April–Oct), a bar inside a beautifully restored century-old wooden trading vessel, serving cocktails and simple *mezédhes*.

Quiet drinking, however, is not what it's all about in the **disco-bars**. *Allou* on the east side of the harbour is the only genuine full-blown dance club, while the nearby *Rule Club* (above the *Creta Café*) doesn't hit its stride until the small hours when the pubs and restaurants close. There are raucous music bars to try at the bottom of 25-Martíou ("Soho Street") where it heads up the hill – *Rififi*, *Royale*, *Oxygen*, *Cellar* and *Cube Club* all get going after sunset, while around the corner on M. Sfakianáki *Santa Maria* is a popular place with locals. Across the harbour *Aquarius* and *Sportz Bar* both get lively, while *Sorrento* is another "golden-oldies" music bar frequented by a north-European crowd.

The coast north of Áyios Nikólaos

North of Áyios Nikólaos, the swankier hotels are strung out along the coast road, with upmarket restaurants, discos and cocktail bars scattered between them. **ELOÚNDA**, a resort on a more acceptable scale, is about 8km out along this road. **Buses** run regularly, but if you feel like renting a **scooter** it's a spectacular ride, with impeccable views over a gulf dotted with islands and moored supertankers. Ask at the bookshop near the post office, on the central square facing the sea, about the attractive *Milos* and *Delfinia* **rooms**, studios and apartments (T 28410 41641, W www.pediaditis.gr; ❷–❹), which come with sea views and, at the *Milos*, a pool. You could also try the friendly *Pension Oasis* (T 28410 41076, W www.pensionoasis.gr; ❸), which has en-suite rooms with kitchenette and is just off the square, behind the church. There are quite a few similar places along the same road, or ask at one of the many travel agents around the main square for help finding a room or apartment; try the friendly Olous Travel (T 28410 41324, F 28410 41132), which also gives out **information** and changes money and travellers' cheques. For **eating**, *Britomares*, in a plum spot in the centre of the harbour, the nearby *Poulis* and the even pricier ultra-chic *Ferryman* (tellingly with a menu in English only) are the town's best tavernas, but more economical fish and *mezédhes* are to be had at the simple *Ouzeri Maritsa* below the church tower at the north end of the square. **Nightlife** tends to be generally low-key, and centres around café terraces and cocktail bars. The *Hellas* café, on a backroad behind the beach, has live Greek music at weekends.

Just before the centre of the village, a road (signposted) leads downhill to a natural causeway leading to the ancient "sunken city" of **Olous**. Here you'll find restored windmills, a short length of canal, Venetian salt pans and a well-preserved dolphin **mosaic**, inside a former Roman basilica, but nothing of the sunken city itself beyond a couple of walls in about 70cm of water. Swimming here is good, however – but watch out for sea urchins.

From Eloúnda, boats run half-hourly in high season (€8 return) to the fortress-rock of **Spinalónga**. As a bastion of the Venetian defence, this tiny islet withstood the Turkish invaders for 45 years after the mainland had fallen; in more recent decades and until 1957 it served as a leper colony. As you look around at the roofless shells of houses once inhabited by the unfortunate lepers, and the boat which brought you disappears to pick up another group, an unnervingly real sense of the desolation of those years descends. **PLÁKA**, back on the mainland, and 5km north of Eloúnda, used to be the colony's supply point; now it is a haven from the crowds, with a small pebble beach and a clutch of fish **tavernas**, one of which, *Taverna Spinalonga*, can arrange a boat to take you across to Spinalónga (April–Sept) for about €7 return. This taverna also rents **rooms** (❷) and good-value apartments for the same price for stays of at least two nights. There are **boat trips** daily from Áyios Nikólaos to Olous, Eloúnda and Spinalónga (costing around €12–15), usually visiting at least one other island along the way.

Inland to Kritsá and Lato

The other excursion everyone takes from Áyios Nikólaos is to **KRITSÁ**, a "traditional" village about 10km inland. Buses run at least every hour from the bus station, and despite the commercialization it's still a good trip: the local **crafts** (weaving, ceramics and embroidery basically, though they sell almost everything here) are fair value, and it's also a welcome break from living in the fast lane at "Ag Nik". In fact, if you're looking for somewhere to stay around here, Kritsá has a number of advantages: chiefly availability of **rooms**, better prices and something at least approaching a genuinely Cretan atmosphere; try *Argyro* (T & F 28410 51174; ❷), with pleasant rooms – some en suite – around a courtyard on your way into the village. The small platía at the centre of the village is the focus of life and there are a number of decent places **to eat** here, too: the central *Saridhakis* is a cool place to sit out under a plane tree, or you could head for the bakers for tempting *tyrópita* (cheese pies) or currant breads. One of the best-situated tavernas is *Castello*, also in the centre, and there are a few others near where the bus stops.

On the approach road, some 2km before Kritsá, is the lovely Byzantine **church of Panayía Kyrá** (daily 8.30am–6pm; €3), inside which survives perhaps the most complete set of Byzantine frescoes in Crete. The fourteenth- and fifteenth-century works have been much retouched, but they're still worth the visit. Excellent (and expensive) reproductions are sold from a shop alongside. Just beyond the church, a surfaced road leads off for 3km to the archeological site of **Lato** (Tues–Sun 8.30am–3pm; €2), where the substantial remains of a Doric city are coupled with a grand hilltop setting. The city itself is extensive, but largely neglected, presumably because visitors and archeologists on Crete are more concerned with the Minoan era. Ruins aside, you could come here just for the views: west over Áyios Nikólaos and beyond to the bay and Olous (which was Lato's port), and inland to the Lasíthi mountains.

The eastern isthmus

The main road south and then east from Áyios Nikólaos is not a wildly exciting one, essentially a drive through barren hills sprinkled with villas and skirting above the occasional sandy cove. The stretch of the E75 northern highway beyond Ístro is now undergoing major **engineering works** intended to by-pass the archeological site of Gourniá and the coastal town of Pahía Ámmos making the route to Ierápetra more direct. Five kilometres east of Ístro, along a newly completed stretch of the E75, an exit on the left is signed for the **monastery of Faneroméni**. The way bends around to cross the E75 on a viaduct before heading inland along a track (partly asphalted in its early stage) that climbs dizzily skywards for 6km, giving spectacular views over the Gulf of Mirabéllo along the way. The **view** from the monastery over the gulf is one of the finest in Crete. To get into the rather bleak-looking monastery buildings, knock loudly. You will be shown up to the chapel, built into a cave sanctuary, and the frescoes – although late – are quite brilliant.

Gourniá, Pahiá Ámmos and Mókhlos

Back on the coast road, it's another 2km to the site of **Gourniá** (Tues–Sun 8.30am–3pm; €2), slumped in the saddle between two low peaks. The most completely preserved **Minoan town**, its narrow alleys and stairways intersect a throng of one-roomed houses (of which only the ground-floor walls survive – they would have had at least one upper floor) centred on a main square, and the rather grand house of what may have been a local ruler or governor. Although less impressive than the great palaces, the site is strong on revelations about the lives of the ordinary people – many of the dwellings housed craftsmen (who worked with wood, metal and clay), who left behind their tools and materials to be found by the excavators. Its desolation today (you are likely to be alone save for a dozing guardian) only serves to heighten the contrast with what must have been a cramped and raucous community 3500 years ago.

It is tempting to cross the road here and take one of the paths through the wild thyme to the sea for a swim. Don't bother – the bay and others along this part of the coastline act as a magnet for every piece of floating detritus dumped off Crete's north coast. There is a larger beach (though with similar problems), and rooms to rent, in the next bay along at **PAHIÁ ÁMMOS**, about twenty minutes' walk, where there is also an excellent seafront fish taverna, *Aiolus*; all the fish (caught with their own boat) plus *kolokithokéftedes* (courgette balls) and *achinosalata* (sea urchin's eggs) are outstanding. In the other direction, there's the campsite of *Gournia Moon* (T 28420 93243; May–Sept), with its own small cove and a swimming pool.

This is the narrowest part of the island, and from here a fast road cuts across the isthmus to Ierápetra (see p.752) in the south. In the north, the route on towards Sitía is one of the most exhilarating in Crete. Carved into cliffs and mountain-sides, the road teeters above the coast before plunging inland at Kavoúsi. Of the beaches you see below, only the one at **MÓKHLOS** is at all accessible, some 5km below the main road. This sleepy seaside village has a few rooms, a hotel or two and a number of **tavernas** – *To Bogazi* is good – squatting along its tiny harbour; if you find yourself needing a **place to stay**, you could try the rooms at the clean and simple *Pension Hermes* (T 28430 94074; ❷) behind the waterfront, which are the cheapest in the village, or there's *Hotel Sofia* (T 28430 94738, F 28430 94238; ❷) on the harbour itself for a bit more en-suite luxury. Nearer Sitía the familiar olive groves are interspersed with vineyards used for creating wine and sultanas, and in late summer the grapes, spread to dry in the fields and on rooftops, make an extraordinary sight in the varying stages of their slow change from green to gold to brown.

Sitía

SITÍA is the port and main town of the relatively unexploited eastern edge of Crete. It's a pleasantly scenic if unremarkable place, offering a plethora of waterside restaurants, a long sandy beach and a lazy lifestyle little affected even by the thousands of visitors in peak season. There's an almost Latin feel to the town, reflected in (or perhaps caused by) the number of French and Italian tourists, and it's one of those places that tends to grow on you, perhaps inviting a longer stay than intended. For entertainment there's the **beach**, providing good swimming and windsurfing, and in town a mildly interesting **folklore museum** (Mon–Sat 10am–1pm; €2), a Venetian fort and Roman fish tanks to explore, plus an excellent **archeological museum** (Tues–Sun 8.30am–3pm; €2). As part of a government push to increase tourism at this end of the island, a new **international airport** (set to open to international flights in 2007) is being constructed on a plateau above the town, and will most likely have a big impact on Sitía itself as well as the surrounding area.

Arrival and information

The bus drops you at the **bus station** (actually an office on the street) on the southwest fringe of the centre and close to the town's main **supermarket**, useful for stocking up on provisions. **Internet** access is available at *Enter Café*, Venizélou 95, to the west of Platía Iroón Polytekhniou (daily 8am–midnight).

Should you have problems finding somewhere to stay, the **tourist office** (Mon–Fri 9.30am–2.30pm & 5.30–9pm, Sat 9.30am–2.30pm & 5–8.30pm; T 28430 28300), on the seafront at the start of the beach road, should be able

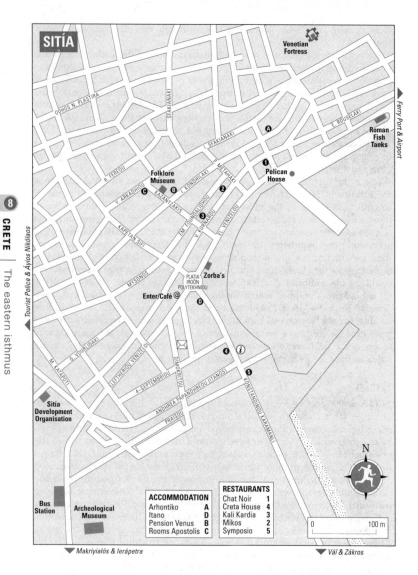

◀ *Tourist Police & Áyios Nikólaos*

▼ *Makriyialós & Ierápetra*

▼ *Váï & Zákros*

ACCOMMODATION	
Arhontiko	**A**
Itano	**D**
Pension Venus	**B**
Rooms Apostolis	**C**

RESTAURANTS	
Chat Noir	**1**
Creta House	**4**
Kali Kardia	**3**
Mikos	**2**
Symposio	**5**

to help, or there's the **tourist police** at Therisou 33 (daily 7.30am–2.30pm; ☎28430 24200), who also provide limited tourist information; both can supply a good town map. A colourful weekly **market** takes place on Tuesdays between 7am and 2pm along Odhós Itanou near the archeological museum.

Accommodation

There are plenty of cheap pensions and **rooms** within easy walking distance, especially in the streets around the folklore museum and beyond here towards the ferry port. For economical rooms, try the friendly *Pension Venus*, I.

Kondhiláki 60 (☎28430 24307; ❷) for rooms sharing bath, or *Arhontiko*, I. Kondhiláki 16 (☎28430 28172; ❷) with attractive rooms in a house with a pleasant garden terrace. En-suite accommodation is available at *Rooms Apostolis*, N. Kazantzákis 27 (☎28430 22993; ❷), where balcony rooms come with fridges and fans, or *Nora*, Rouseláki 31 (☎28430 23017, ✉norahotel@yahoo.gr; ❷), near the ferry port with excellent balcony rooms featuring harbour views. An upmarket option in the centre is *Itanos*, Platía Iróön Polytekhníou (☎28430 22146, ⓦwww.forthnet.gr/internetcity/hotels/itanos; ❹), with balconied sea-view rooms on the town's main square.

Eating, drinking and nightlife

For **food**, the waterside places are relatively expensive; the best-value choices near here are ♨ *Kali Kardia*, M. Foundalídhou 28, two blocks in from the waterfront, for tasty snail, fish and cheese *mezédhes* served on a pleasant terrace, and *Creta House*, at the start of the beach road (Konstandínou Karamanlí), serving traditional island dishes. The newly arrived *Symposio* almost next door to the latter is also good for fish and meat dishes. Just behind the seafront, the popular *Mikos*, V. Kornárou 117, serves up charcoal-grilled meat and a potent local wine and has a seafront terrace around the corner. At the north end of the seafront *Chat Noir*, Galanáki 3, does the usual standard dishes well and has a small seafront terrace.

Nightlife centres on a few bars and discos near the ferry dock and out along the beach. The town's monster disco-club, *Planitarion*, attracts crowds from all over the east. It's a couple of kilometres beyond the ferry port, and is best reached by taxi. The in-town alternative is *Oasis*, a stylish new bar near the start of the beach road with an attractive terrace, popular with a younger crowd. Sitía's main bash is the summer-long Kornaria **cultural festival** featuring concerts, dance and theatre by Greek and overseas participants (details from the tourist office).

Onward to Váï beach and Palékastro

Leaving Sitía along the beach, the Váï road climbs above a rocky, unexceptional coastline before reaching a fork to the **monastery of Toploú** (daily 9am–7pm, Oct–March closes 4pm; €2.50). The monastery's forbidding exterior reflects a history of resistance to invaders, and doesn't prepare you for the gorgeous flower-decked cloister within. The blue-robed monks keep out of the way as far as possible, but in quieter periods their cells and refectory are left discreetly on view. In the church is one of the masterpieces of Cretan art, the eighteenth-century icon *Lord Thou Art Great* by Ioánnis Kornaros. Outside you can buy enormously expensive reproductions.

Váï beach itself features alongside Knossos or the Lasíthi Plateau on almost every Cretan travel agent's list of excursions. Not surprisingly, it is now covered in sunbeds and umbrellas, though it is still a superb beach. Above all, it is famous for its palm trees, and the sudden appearance of the grove is indeed an exotic shock; lying on the fine sand in the early morning, the illusion is of a Caribbean island – a feature seized upon by countless TV-commercial makers seeking an exotic location on the cheap. As everywhere, notices warn that "camping is forbidden by law", and for once the authorities seem to mean it – most campers climb over the headlands to the south or north. If you do sleep out, watch your belongings, since this seems to be the one place on Crete with crime on any scale. There's a compulsory car park (€2.50), a café and an expensive taverna at the beach, plus toilets and showers. Because of its status as a nature reserve there is **no accommodation** here whatsoever; the nearest place offering a bed for the night is Palékastro. By day you can find a bit more solitude by climbing the rocks or swimming to one of the smaller beaches which surround Váï. **Ítanos**, twenty minutes' walk north by an obvious trail, has a couple of tiny beaches and some modest ruins from the Classical era.

PALÉKASTRO, an attractive farming village some 9km south, makes a good place to stopover. Although its beaches can't begin to compare with those at Váï, you'll find several modest places with **rooms** – among them ⚤ *Hotel Hellas* (☎28430 61240, ✉hellas_h@otenet.gr; ❷), which offers comfortable en-suite rooms with balcony, TV and fridge and reductions for longer stays; the terrace restaurant below is also excellent. The good-value *Vaï* (☎28430 61414; ❶), with rooms above a taverna at the west end of the village, on the Sitía road is another possibility. The extensive **beaches** provide plenty of space to **camp** out without the crowds, but you should respect local sensitivities, keeping away from the main strands and responsibly disposing of any rubbish. Add in a **tourist office** (April–Oct daily 9am–10pm; ☎28430 61546) on the main street, a small **folk museum** (May–Oct Tues–Sun 8.30am–1pm & 5–8.30pm; €1.50), a number of reasonable **tavernas**, a few **bars** and even a **dance-club**, *Design*, and the place begins to seem positively throbbing. The sea is a couple of kilometres down a dirt track, effortlessly reached with a **scooter** hired from Moto Kastri (☎28430 61477), on the eastern edge of the village along the Váï road. Palékastro is also the crossroads for the road south to Zákros and your own transport presents all kinds of beach and exploration possibilities.

Zákros

ÁNO ZÁKROS (Upper Zákros) lies a little under 20km from Palékastro. There are several tavernas and a simple hotel, the *Zakros* (☎ & ☎28430 93379; ❷), which has some rooms with bath and great views from its rear rooms; it also offers guests a free minibus service to the Minoan palace and beach. The Minoan palace is actually at Káto ("lower") Zákros, 8km further down towards the sea. Most buses run only to the upper village, but in summer a couple do run every day all the way to the site; it's usually not difficult to hitch if your bus does leave you in the village. Two kilometres along the road you can, if on foot, take a short cut through an impressive **gorge** (the "Valley of the Dead", named for ancient tombs in its sides). The gorge entrance is signed "Dead's Gorge" next to an information board and car-park area with a steep path leading down to the trail, which then follows a stream bed for 4km to reach the sea near the Minoan palace. It's a solitary but magnificent hike, brightened especially in spring with plenty of plant life.

The **Palace of Zakros** (Tues–Sun: July–Oct 8am–7pm, Nov–June 8am–3pm; €3) was an important find for archeologists; it had been occupied only once, between 1600 and 1450 BC, and was abandoned hurriedly and completely. Later, it was forgotten almost entirely and as a result was never plundered or even discovered by archeologists until very recently. The first major excavation began only in 1960; all sorts of everyday objects, such as tools, raw materials, food and pottery, were thus discovered intact among the ruins, and a great deal was learned from being able to apply modern techniques (and knowledge of the Minoans) to a major dig from the very beginning. None of this is especially evident when you're at the palace, except perhaps in a particularly simple ground plan, so it's as well that it is also a rewarding visit in terms of the setting. Although the site is set back from the sea, in places it is often marshy and waterlogged – partly the result of eastern

Crete's slow subsidence, partly the fault of a spring which once supplied fresh water to a cistern beside the royal apartments, and whose outflow is now silted up. In wetter periods, among the remains of narrow streets and small houses of the town outside the palace and higher up, you can keep your feet dry and get an excellent view down over the central court and royal apartments. If you want a more detailed overview of the remains, buy the guide to the site on sale at the entrance.

The delightful village of **KÁTO ZÁKROS** is little more than a collection of tavernas, some of which rent out rooms around a peaceful beach and minuscule fishing anchorage. It's a wonderfully restful place, but is often unable to cope with the volume of visitors seeking accommodation in high season, and as rooms are rarely to be had on spec you'd be wise to ring ahead. You should also be aware that villagers are far more hostile these days to wild camping after years of problems, and you should be sensitive to their concerns. Reliable rooms can be found at *Poseidon* (℡28430 26896; ❶–❷), which has fine sea views, and the friendly *George Villas* (℡ & ℱ28430 26883, ✉georgevillas@sit.forthnet.gr; ❷–❸), 600m behind the archeological site along a driveable track. Otherwise ask at the *Taverna Akrogiali* (℡28430 26893, ✉akrogiali@sit.forthnet.gr; ❷) on the seafront, which acts as an agent for many other room options.

Ierápetra and the southeast coast

The main road from Sitía to the south coast is a cross-country, roller-coaster ride between the east and west ranges of the **Sitía mountains**. One of the first places it hits on the south coast is the sprawling resort of **Makryialós** soon followed by the bustling town and resort of **Ierápetra**. More tranquil hideaways lie further west at the charming pint-sized resorts of **Mýrtos** and **Keratókambos** and the slightly less inviting **Árvi** and **Tsoútsouras**.

Makryialós

Although originally comprised of two distinct villages, the larger **MAKRYIALÓS** (Ⓦwww.makrigialos.gr) has gobbled up its neighbour Análipsi to form a single and unfocused resort, whose only real plus point is a long strand with fine sand which shelves so gently you feel you could walk the two hundred nautical miles to Africa. Unfortunately, since the early 1990s it has been heavily developed, so while still a very pleasant place to stop for a swim or a bite, it's not somewhere that's overflowing with cheap **rooms**. The first budget option is *María Tsanakalioti* (℡28430 51557, ✉dtsanakalioti@hotmail.com; ❸) on the seaward side as you enter the resort from the east; the friendly proprietor offers pleasant studio rooms – some with sea view and terrace – with kitchenette, a/c and TV. Nearby and up a track inland signed "María Apartments" lies *Stefanos Rooms* (℡28430 52062; ❷) offering decent en-suite rooms with fans. A little before these two and signed up a side road (that soon degenerates into a track) 1km inland to the more upmarket *White River Cottages* (℡28430-51120; ✉wrc@sit.forthnet.gr; ❹), where an abandoned hamlet of traditional stone dwellings (originally Áspro Pótamos or "White River") has been restored as a warren of charming a/c studios and apartments with a focal pool. At the western end of town beyond a steep hill (topped with a sign on the left for a Roman villa), *Taverna-Rooms Oasis* (℡28430 51918; ❸) fronts the sea at the end of a short track. Offering sea-view en-suite rooms with a/c and fridge, downstairs there's an outstanding 🍴 **taverna** which has based its reputation on using only fresh (never frozen) fish, meat and vegetables, and they claim with some justification that their *moussakás* is the best on the island.

From here to Ierápetra there's little reason to stop; the few beaches are rocky and the coastal plain submerged under ranks of polythene-covered greenhouses. Beside the road leading into Ierápetra are long but exposed stretches of sand, including the appropriately named "Long Beach", where you'll find a **campsite**, *Camping Koutsounari* (☎28420 61213), which offers plenty of shade and has a taverna and minimarket.

Ierápetra

IERÁPETRA itself is a bustling modern supply centre for the region's farmers. It also attracts a fair number of package tourists and the odd backpacker looking for work in the prosperous surrounding agricultural zone, especially out of season. The tavernas along the tree-lined seafront are scenic enough and the EU blue-flagged beach stretches a couple of miles east. But as a town, most people find it pretty uninspiring, despite an ongoing modernization programme, which has cleaned up the centre and revamped the seafront. Although there has been a port here since Roman times, only the **Venetian fort** guarding the harbour and a crumbling Turkish minaret remain as reminders of better days. What little else has been salvaged is in the one-room **Archeological Museum** (Tues–Sun 8.30am–3.30pm; €2) near the post office.

One way to escape the urban hubbub for a few hours is to take a boat to the **island of Gaidhouronísi** (aka Chrissi or Donkey Island) some 10km out to sea. It's a real uninhabited desert island 4km long with a cedar forest, fabulous "**Shell beach**" covered with millions of multicoloured mollusc shells, some good beaches and a couple of tavernas. **Boats** (daily 10.30am & 12.30pm out, 4pm & 7pm return; €20, under-12s €10) leave from the seafront harbour, but you'll need to buy tickets from Iris Travel (☎28420 25423) at the north end of the seafront before boarding. The voyage to the island takes 50min and the boats have an on-board bar.

Practicalities

In the absence of a tourist office the town hall on the main square, Platía Kanoupáki, or the library next door, should be able to provide a copy of the detailed town map (but not much else) which will help you find your way around. If you want to stay, head up Kazantzákis from the chaotic bus station, and you'll find a friendly welcome and good-value, apartment-style **rooms** with kitchenette at *Rooms Popy* at no. 27 (☎28420 24289, ℉28420 27772; ②), or equal comfort in the nearby ⚶ *Cretan Villa*, Lakérdha 16 (☎28420 28522, ⓦwww .cretan-villa.com; ③) where sparkling a/c rooms with TV and fridge overlook the flower-bedecked patio of a beautiful 180-year-old house. More central and economical is the *Hotel Ersi*, Platía Eleftherías 20 (☎28420 23208; ②), which will also rent you a seafront apartment nearby for not much more than the cost of a room. The cheapest seafront rooms option is *Katerina* (☎28420 28345, ℉28420 28519; ①–③) at the eastern end of the strand, offering a/c rooms with TV, fridge and seaview, which also has bargain rooms without a/c or fridge.

You'll find places to **eat** and **drink** all along the waterfront, the better of them, such as *Taverna Napoleon*, *Gorgona* and *Babi's*, being towards the Venetian fort. **Nightlife** centres on a clutch of **clubs**, **bars** and fast-food places along central Kyrba, behind the seafront promenade. The town's most central **Internet café** is *Internet Café* (daily 9am–10pm) inside the *Cosmos Hotel*, Koundoúrou 16, slightly north of Platía Eleftherías.

West from Ierápetra

Heading **west** from Ierápetra, the first stretch of coast is grey and dusty, the road jammed with trucks and lined with drab ribbon development and plastic green-houses. There are a number of small resorts along the beach, though little in the way of public transport. If travelling under your own steam, there is a scenic detour worth taking at Gría Lygiá: the road on the right for Anatolí climbs to Máles, a village clinging to the lower slopes of the **Dhíkti range**. Here would be a good starting point for **walking** through some stunning mountain terrain (the E4 Pan-European footpath which crosses the island from east to west passes just 3km north of here). Otherwise, the dirt road back down towards the coast (signposted Míthi) has spectacular views over the Libyan Sea, and eventually follows the Mýrtos river valley down to Mýrtos itself.

Mýrtos and Árvi

MÝRTOS, 18km west of Ierápetra, is the first resort that might actually tempt you to stop, and it's certainly the most accessible, just off the main road with numerous daily **buses** from Ierápetra and a couple direct to Iráklion. Although developed to a degree, it nonetheless remains a tranquil and charming white-walled village kept clean as a whistle by its house-proud inhabitants. There are plenty of **rooms** possibilities, amongst which you could try the central, friendly and good-value ⅓ *Hotel Mirtos* (℡28420 51227, ⓦ www.mirtoshotel.com; ❷) with comfortable en-suite rooms above an excellent taverna. Nearby, *Rooms Angelos* (℡28420 51091; ❶) and *Nikos House* (℡28420 51116, ⓦ www.nikoshouse.cz; ❶) are slightly cheaper options, or there's the even less expensive *Rooms Despina* (℡28420 51524; ❶) at the back of the village near the bus stop. A useful travel agent, Magic Tours (℡28420 51203, ⓦ www.welcometo-magic.com) on the central main street, is a good source of **information**, and also **changes money**, rents **cars**, sells boat and plane tickets and operates a taxi service to Iráklion and Haniá airports. Just off the road from Ierápetra a couple of kilometres east of the village (and signed) are a couple of excavated hilltop **Minoan villas** you might want to explore: Néa Mýrtos (aka Fournoú Korifí) and Mýrtos Pýrgos. Some of the finds from these sites – in addition to a folklore section with tools, kitchen and farming implements once used by the villagers – are displayed in a superb village **museum** (April–Oct Mon–Fri 9am–1pm; €1.50), located to the side of the church. A recent and highly popular addition to the museum is a wonder-fully detailed **scale model** of the Fournoú Korifí site as it would have looked in Minoan days by resident English potter, John Atkinson.

After Mýrtos the main road turns inland towards Áno Viánnos, then continues across the island towards Iráklion; several places on the coast are reached by a series of recently asphalted roads replacing the former rough tracks. **ÁRVI** is a resort of similar size to Mýrtos, although it lacks the latter's charm. The beach, flanked by a new harbour development, hardly justifies it, but it's an interesting little excursion (with at least one bus a day) if only to see the bananas and pine-apples grown here and to experience the microclimate – noticeably warmer than neighbouring zones, especially in spring or autumn – that encourages them. For **rooms** you could try the central *Pension Gorgona* (℡28950 71353; ❷) or, beyond the river at the east end of the beach, the cheaper *Taverna Kyma* (℡28950 71344; ❷).

Beyond Árvi

KERATÓKAMBOS, reached on a side road 4km from Áno Viánnos, has a rather stony beach and, although popular with Cretan day-trippers, is a great place to escape the tourist grind for a spell. It has a range of **rooms**, though they're not easy to come by in August. Try the *Morning Star* taverna (☏ 28950 51209; ❶) which has a/c rooms with and without bath, or the comparable *Taverna Kriti* (☏ 28950 51231, 🅕 28950 51456; ❷) next door; the **food** at both places is tasty, too.

TSOÚTSOUROS (🅦 www.tsoutsouros.com), 10km west as the crow flies and now linked by an eleven-kilometre-long asphalted road to the major highway further north, is similar to its neighbour with a line of tavernas, hotels and rooms places arching behind a seafront and yacht harbour, to the east and west of which are a couple of decent if pebbly, grey-sand **beaches**. **Accommodation** may be available here when the other resorts are full: *Rooms Mihalis* (☏ 28910 92250; ❷) or the good-value *San Georgio Hotel* (May–Sept ☏ 28910 92322; ❷) further east are both worth trying. There are no facilities for changing money at either place, although both have a couple of **supermarkets**, handy for gathering picnic ingredients.

If you hope to continue across the **south** of the island, be warned that there are no buses, despite completion of the road towards Míres after years of work. It's an enjoyable rural drive, but progress can be slow.

Réthymnon and around

The relatively low, narrow section of Crete which separates the Psilorítis range from the White Mountains in the west seems at first a nondescript, even dull, part of the island. Certainly in scenic terms it has few of the excitements that the west can offer; there are no major archeological sites and many of the villages seem modern and ugly. On the other hand, **Réthymnon** itself is an attractive and lively city, with some excellent beaches nearby. And on the south coast, in particular around **Plakiás**, there are beaches as fine as any Crete can offer and, as you drive towards them, the scenery and villages improve.

Réthymnon

Since the early 1980s, **RÉTHYMNON** has seen a greater influx of tourists than perhaps anywhere else on Crete, with the development of a whole series of large hotels extending almost 10km along the beach to the east. For once, though, the middle of town has been spared, so that at its heart Réthymnon remains one of the most beautiful of Crete's major cities (only Haniá is a serious rival) with an enduringly provincial air. A wide sandy beach and palm-lined promenade border a labyrinthine tangle of Venetian and Turkish houses lining streets where ancient minarets lend an exotic air to the skyline. Dominating everything from the west is the superbly preserved outline of the **fortress** built by the Venetians after a series of pirate raids had devastated the town.

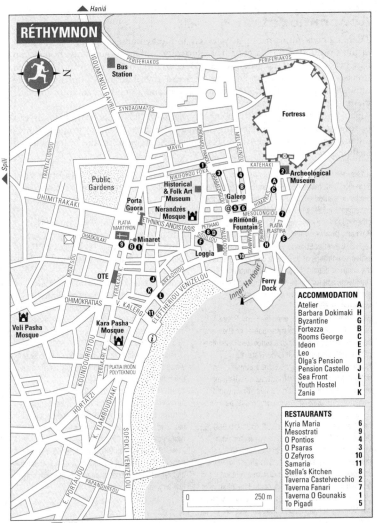

RÉTHYMNON

Haniá

Spili

Iráklion

Bus Station

PERIFERIAKÓS

PERIFERIAKÓS

Fortress

SYNDAGMATOS

IGOUMENIOU GAVRIIL

TRANTALIDHOU

DHIMITRAKAKI

Public Gardens

Porta Guora

Nerandzés Mosque

Historical & Folk Art Museum

Galero

NIKIFOROU FOKA

ARKADHIOU

Archeological Museum

KATEHAKI

MAVILI

KORNAROU ANN

MELISSINOU

ARAMPATZOGLOU

PLATIA MARTYRON

ETHNIKIS ANDISTASIS

Rimóndi Fountain

MESOLONGIOU

PETIHAKI

PLATIA PLASTIRA

NANNIS

VERNARDOU

DHASKALAKI

Minaret

PALEOLOGOU

XANTHOUDHIDOU

Loggia

MOATSOU

OTE

V. KALERGI

ARKADHIOU

VERNARDOU

Ferry Dock

Inner Harbour

DHIMOKRATIAS

Kara Pasha Mosque

ELEFTHERIOU VENIZELOU

Veli Pasha Mosque

KOUNDOURIOTOU

VERNARDOU

YIAMBOUDHAKI

PLATIA IROÖN POLYTEKNIOU

HORTATZI

K. YIAMBOUDHAKI

SOFOKLI VENIZELOU

E. PORTALIOU

PAPANDHREOU

0   250 m

8

CRETE | Réthymnon

ACCOMMODATION
Atelier	A
Barbara Dokimaki	H
Byzantine	G
Fortezza	B
Rooms George	C
Ideon	E
Leo	F
Olga's Pension	D
Pension Castello	J
Sea Front	L
Youth Hostel	I
Zania	K

RESTAURANTS
Kyria Maria	6
Mesostrati	9
O Pontios	4
O Psaras	3
O Zefyros	10
Samaria	11
Stella's Kitchen	8
Taverna Castelvecchio	2
Taverna Fanari	7
Taverna O Gounakis	1
To Pigadi	5

Arrival and information

The **bus station** in Réthymnon is by the sea to the west of the town centre just off Periferiakós, the road which skirts the waterfront around the fortress. If you arrive by **ferry**, you'll be more conveniently placed, over at the western edge of the harbour. The **tourist office** (Mon–Fri 8am–4pm; ☎28310 29148, ⊚www .rethymnon.com) backs onto the main town beach and provides maps, timetables and accommodation lists. To access the **Internet** head for the *Galero Internet Cafe* (daily 9am–midnight), beside the Rimóndi fountain in the old town.

Accommodation

There's a great number of places to stay in Réthymnon, and only at the height of the season are you likely to have difficulty finding somewhere, though you may get weary looking. The greatest concentration of **rooms** is in the tangled streets west of the inner harbour, between the Rimóndi fountain and the museums; there are also quite a few places on and around Arkadhíou and Platía Plastíra.

The nearest **campsite**, *Camping Elizabeth* (☎28310 28694), lies 4km east of town; take the bus for the hotels (marked *Scaleta/El Greco*) from the long-distance bus station to get there. It's a pleasant, large site on the beach, with all facilities.

Atelier Himáras 32 ☎28310 24440, ✉atelier@ret.forthnet.gr. Pleasant en-suite rooms run by a talented potter, who has her studio in the basement and sells her wares in a shop on the other side of the building. ❶

Barbara Dokimaki Platía Plastíra 14 ☎ & ℗28310 24581. Strange warren of rooms, with one entrance at the above address, just off the seafront behind the *Ideon*, and another on Dambérgi; ask for the newly refurbished top-floor studio rooms, which have balconies and kitchenettes. ❹

Byzantine Vospórou 26, near the Porta Guora ☎28310 55609, ⓦwww.byzantineret.gr. Pleasant en-suite rooms with fans in a renovated Byzantine palace with elegant interior courtyard. ❸

Fortezza Melissinoú 16, near the fortress ☎28310 55551, ⓦwww.fortezza.gr. Stylish, top-of-the-range hotel with almost everything you'd expect for the price, including a/c rooms, pool and restaurant. B&B ❹

Rooms George Makedhonías 32 ☎28310 50965. Decent and friendly en-suite rooms (some with fridge), near the archeological museum. ❶

Ideon Platía Plastíra 10 ☎28310 28667, ⓦwww .hotelideon.gr. High-class hotel with a brilliant position just north of the ferry dock; little chance of getting one of their balcony, en-suite rooms without pre-booking in high season, though. B&B ❺

Leo Vafé 2 ☎28310 26197. Good hotel with lots of wood and a traditional feel; en-suite rooms come with fans and some have balconies. B&B, and there's a bar. ❷

Olga's Pension Soulíou 57 ☎28310 54896, ℗28310 29851. The star attraction at this very friendly *pension* on one of Réthymnon's most touristy streets is the resplendent flower-filled roof garden. ❶–❷

Pension Castello Karaoli 10 ☎28310 23570, ✉castelo2@otenet.gr. A very pleasant small *pension* in a 300-year-old Venetian-Turkish mansion; a/c en-suite rooms with fridge and a delightful patio garden. ❸

Sea Front Arkadhíou 159 ☎28310 51981, ✉lotia@ret.forthnet.gr. En-suite rooms with sea views and balconies in an attractively refurbished mansion with ceiling fans. ❷

Youth Hostel Tombázi 41 ☎28310 22848, ⓦwww.yhrethymno.com. The cheapest beds (€8) in town. Large, clean, very friendly and popular, it has food, showers, clothes-washing facilities and a multilingual library. ❶

Zania Pávlou Vlástou 3 ☎28310 28169. *Pension* right on the corner of Arkadhíou in a well-adapted and atmospheric Venetian mansion, but with only a few airy, simple rooms. ❷

The Town

With a **beach** right in the heart of town, it's tempting not to stir at all from the sands, but Réthymnon repays at least some gentle exploration. For a start, you could try checking out the further reaches of the beach itself. The waters protected by the breakwaters in front of town have their disadvantages – notably crowds and dubious hygiene – but less sheltered sands stretch for miles to the east, crowded at first but progressively less so if you're prepared to walk a bit.

Away from the beach, you don't have far to go for the most atmospheric part of town, immediately behind the **inner harbour**. Almost anywhere here, you'll find unexpected old buildings, wall fountains, overhanging wooden balconies, heavy, carved doors and rickety shops, many still with local craftsmen sitting out front, gossiping as they ply their trades. Look out especially for the **Venetian loggia**, which houses a shop selling high-quality and expensive reproductions of Classical art; the **Rimóndi fountain**, another of the more elegant Venetian survivals; and the **Nerandzés mosque**, the best preserved in Réthymnon but currently serving as a music school and closed to the public. When (seemingly endless) repairs are completed it should again be possible to climb the spiral staircase to the top of the **minaret** for a stunning view over the town. Simply by walking past these three, you'll have seen many of the liveliest parts of Réthymnon. Ethnikís Andístasis, the street leading straight up from the fountain, is the town's **market** area.

The old city ends at the Porta Guora at the top of Ethnikís Andístasis, the only surviving remnant of the city walls. Almost opposite are the quiet and shady **public gardens**. These are a soothing place to stroll, and in the latter half of July the **Réthymnon Wine Festival** is staged here. Though touristy, it's a thoroughly enjoyable event, with spectacular local dancing as the evening progresses and the barrels empty. The entrance fee includes all the wine you can drink, though you'll need to bring your own cup or buy one of the souvenir glasses and carafes on sale outside the gardens.

The museums and fortress

A little further up the street from the Nerandzés mosque at M. Vernárdhou 28, a beautifully restored seventeenth-century Venetian mansion is the home of the small but tremendously enjoyable **Historical and Folk Art Museum** (Mon–Sat 9am–2pm & 6–8pm; €3). Gathered within four, cool, airy rooms are musical instruments, old photos, basketry, farm implements, an explanation of traditional ceramic and breadmaking techniques, smiths' tools, traditional costumes and jewellery, lace, weaving and embroidery (look out for a traditional-style tapestry made in 1941 depicting German parachutists landing at Máleme), pottery, knives and old wooden chests. It makes for a fascinating insight into a fast-disappearing rural (and urban) lifestyle, which survived virtually unchanged from Venetian times to the 1960s.

Heading in the other direction from the fountain you'll come to the fortress and **Archeological Museum** (Tues–Sun 8.30am–3pm; €3), which occupies a building almost directly opposite the entrance to the fortress. This was built by the Turks as an extra defence, and later served as a prison; it's now entirely modern inside: cool, spacious and airy. Unfortunately, the collection is not particularly exciting, and really only worth seeing if you're going to miss the bigger museums elsewhere on the island.

The massive **Venetian fortress** (Sat–Thurs 8.30am–7pm; Nov–March closes 6pm; €2.90) is a must, however. Said to be the largest Venetian castle ever built, this was a response, in the last quarter of the sixteenth century, to a series of **pirate raids** (by Barbarossa among others) that had devastated the town. Inside is now a vast open space dotted with the remains of all sorts of barracks, arsenals, officers' houses, earthworks and deep shafts, and at the centre a large domed building that was once a church and later a **mosque** (complete with a surviving but sadly defaced *mihrab*). It was designed to be large enough for the entire population to take shelter within the walls. Although much is ruined, it remains thoroughly atmospheric, and you can look out from the walls over the town and harbour, or in the other direction along the coast to the west. It's also worth walking around the outside of the fortress, preferably at sunset, to get an impression of its fearsome defences, plus great views along the coast; there's a pleasant resting point around the far side at the *Sunset* taverna.

Eating and drinking

Immediately behind the town beach are arrayed the most touristy **restaurants**, the vast majority being overpriced and of dubious quality. Around the inner **harbour** there's a second, rather more expensive, group of tavernas, specializing in fish, though as often as not the intimate atmosphere in these places is spoilt by the stench from the harbour itself.

If you want takeaway food, there are numerous **souvláki** stalls, including a couple on Arkadhíou and Paleológou and another at Petikháki 52, or you can buy your own ingredients at the **market** stalls set up daily on Ethnikís Andistásis below the Porta Guora. The **bakery** *Iy Gaspari* on Mesolongíou, just behind the Rimóndi fountain, sells the usual cheese pies, cakes and the like, and it also bakes excellent brown, black and rye bread. There's a good zaharoplastío, *N.A. Skartsilakos*, at Paleológou 36, just north of the fountain, and several more small cafés which are good for **breakfast** or a quick coffee. The *Cul de Sac* and *Galero* cafés overlooking the fountain are relatively expensive, but great for people-watching.

Taverna Castelvecchio Himáras 29. A long-established family taverna next to the fortress which has a pleasant terrace with view over the town and offers some vegetarian choices.

Taverna Fanari Makedhonías 5, slightly west of Platía Plastíra. A good-value little seafront taverna serving up tasty lamb and chicken dishes.

Taverna O Gounakis Koronéou 6. Hearty, no-frills traditional cooking by a family who leave the stove to perform *lyra* every night, and when things get really lively the dancing starts.

Kyria Maria at Moskhovítou 20, tucked down an alley behind the Rimóndi fountain. Pleasant, unassuming little taverna for good-value fish and meat dishes; after the meal, everyone gets a couple of Maria's delicious *tyropitákia* with honey on the house.

Mesostrati Yerakári 1. Tucked behind the church on Platía Martíron, this is a pleasant little neighbourhood ouzerí/taverna serving well-prepared Cretan country dishes on a small terrace.

To Pigadi Xanthoúdhidhou 31, slightly west of the Rimóndi fountain. In a street containing a cluster of upmarket restaurants with overinflated prices and pretensions, this place stands out for its excellent, reasonably priced food and efficient service; an attractive terrace's main feature – an ancient well (*pigádi*) – has also inspired its name.

O Pontios Melissinoú 34. A good lunchtime stop close to the Archeological Museum, this is a simple place with surprisingly good food, outdoor tables and an enthusiastic female proprietor.

O Psaras corner of Nikiforou Foka and Kironaiou. An economical and unpretentious fish taverna with tables on a terrace beside a church.

Samaria Venizélou, almost opposite the tourist office. One of the few seafront tavernas that maintains some integrity (and reasonable prices) and is patronized by locals.

Stella's Kitchen Great-value little diner serving healthy, home-baked food and six daily specials (at least two of which are vegetarian); there's a leafy terrace roof garden and they also do breakfasts. Closes 9pm.

O Zefyros at the inner harbour. One of the less outrageously pricey fish places here and maintains reasonable standards.

Nightlife

Nightlife is concentrated in the same general areas as the tavernas. At the west end of Venizélou, in the streets behind the inner harbour, the overflow from a small cluster of noisy music bars – *Venetsianako*, *Dimman* and *Xtreme* – begins to spill out onto the pavement as partygoers gather for the nightly opening of the *Fortezza Living Room Club* in the inner harbour itself, which is the glitziest in town, flanked by its competitors *Metropolis*, *ADO Club Rock* and the nearby *Budha Club* a little way down Salamínos. Heading up this street, a string of more subdued cocktail bars – *Ice*, *Aman* and *Aynaia* – caters for those in search of a quieter drink, as does *Notas*, at Himáras 27 near the *Fortezza* and facing the *Atelier pension*, which puts on live (acoustic) guitar and song every night. A relatively new bar scene popular with the local student community has taken root around Platía Plastíra, above the inner harbour, where music bars include *Art*, *Da Cappo*, *Coz*, *Kenzo* and *Aroma*, all with expansive terraces.

Around Réthymnon

While some of Crete's most drastic resort development spreads ever eastwards out of Réthymnon, to the west a sandy coastline, not yet greatly exploited, runs all the way to the borders of Haniá province. But of all the short trips that can be made, the best-known and still the most worthwhile is to the **monastery of Arkádhi**.

Southeast to Arkádhi

The **monastery of Arkádhi** (daily 8am–7pm; €2), some 25km southeast of the city and immaculately situated in the foothills of the Psilorítis range, is also something of a national Cretan shrine. During the 1866 rebellion against the Turks, the monastery became a rebel strongpoint in which, as the Turks gained the upper hand, hundreds of Cretan independence fighters and their families took refuge. Surrounded and on the point of defeat, the defenders ignited a powder magazine just as the Turks entered. Hundreds (some sources claim thousands) were killed, Cretan and Turk alike, and the tragedy did much to promote international sympathy for the cause of Cretan independence. Nowadays, you can peer into the roofless vault where the explosion occurred and wander about the rest of the well-restored grounds. Outside the entrance a modern monument displays the skulls of many of the victims. The sixteenth-century **church** survived, and is one of the finest Venetian structures left on Crete; other buildings house a small **museum** devoted to the exploits of the defenders of the (Orthodox) faith. The monastery is easy to visit by public bus or on a tour.

West to Aryiroúpolis, Yeoryoúpoli and beyond

Leaving Réthymnon to the west, the main road climbs for a while above a rocky coastline before descending (after some 5km) to the sea, where it runs alongside sandy **beaches** for perhaps another 7km. An occasional hotel offers accommodation, but on the whole there's nothing but a line of straggly bushes between the road and the windswept sands. If you have your own vehicle, there are plenty of places to stop for a swim, with rarely anyone else around – but beware of some very strong currents.

One worthwhile detour inland is to **ARYIROÚPOLIS**, a picturesque village perched above the Mousselás river valley and the seat of ancient Lappa, a Greek and Roman town of some repute. The village is famous for its **springs**, which gush dramatically from the hillside and provide most of the city of Réthymnon's water supply. Among a number of **places to stay** try the excellent-value ✦ *Rooms Míkedaki* (☎28310 81225; ❶) on the right at the foot of the road which climbs to the village; en-suite terrace balcony rooms here have fine views and guests have use of a kitchen. Near the springs *Rooms Argiroupolis* (☎28310 81148; ℱ28310 81149; B&B; ❷) has more en-suite rooms in a garden setting. In the upper village there's *Rooms Zografakis* (☎28310 81269; B&B; ❷), or – with great views from its air-conditioned rooms and taverna terrace – the friendly and excellent-value 🍴 *Agnantema* (☎28310 81172; ❶). For **places to eat**, you're spoilt for choice, with five tavernas at the springs (try *Vieux Moulin* with an attractive terrace) and a bar (serving tasty *mezédhes*) in the upper village, together with tavernas at *Zografakis* and *Agnantema*, the latter enjoying a spectacular terrace view down the river valley. A shop under the arch in the main square, named Lappa Avocado and selling local products of the region including olive oil and avocado-based skin products, can provide a free **map** detailing a surprising number of churches, caves and ancient remains to see in and around the village, including an outstanding third-century **Roman mosaic**. An interesting **folklore museum** (daily 10am–7pm; free) – signed from the main square – is worth a look for its collection of tapestries, farm implements, photos and ephemera collected by the Zografakis family who have lived here for countless generations. There are numerous fine **walks** in the surrounding hills, on which the proprietor of Lappa Avocado, who speaks English, will advise. Although little over 20km from Réthymnon and easy to get to with your own transport, Aryiroúpolis is also served by **buses** from Réthymnon's bus station (Mon–Fri only), currently leaving at 11.30am and 2.30pm, and in the reverse direction at 7am, 12.30pm and 3.30pm.

Back on the coastal route, if you are looking for a place to relax for a while, probably the best base is **YEORYOÚPOLI** just across the provincial border in Haniá, where the beach is cleaner, wider and further from the road. There's been a distinct acceleration in the pace of development at Yeoryoúpoli over the last few years and it's now very much a resort, packed with rooms to rent, small hotels, apartment buildings, tavernas and travel agencies. But everything remains on a small scale, and the undeniably attractive setting is untarnished, making it a very pleasant place to pass a few days, as long as you don't expect to find many vestiges of traditional Crete. Most of the new beachfront places are exclusively for package tourists, so it's best to head along the roads down towards the beach from the central platía. Here, you'll find *Andy's Rooms* (☎28250 61394; ❷), and *Cretan Cactus* (☎28250 61449, ✉cretancactusge@hotmail.com; ❷), close to the beach and both offering en-suite rooms with fans. On the far side of the bridge across the river, 🍴 *Anna* (☎28250 61376; ❶) offers some of the best-value rooms in town in a garden setting and also has a number of apartments (❹) and houses (❻), both sleeping up to five. *Taverna Paradise* (☎28250 61313; ❷), towards the river from the square, has more rooms, studios and apartments plus tasty food. Also for **food** *Taverna Babís*, in the other direction on the main street, is good for standards, as is *Sirtaki*, near the bridge. **Internet** access is on offer at the relaxing *Internet Bar Planet* (9am–midnight) on the main square.

Within walking distance inland – though it can also be visited on the tourist road train from Yeoryoúpoli – is **Kournás**, Crete's only freshwater lake, set deep in a bowl of hills and almost constantly changing colour. There are a few tavernas with rooms to rent along the shore here (bring mosquito repellent), or you could try for a bed in the nearby hill village of **MATHÉS** where the *Villa Kapasa* (☎28250 61050, 🌐www.villa-kapasas.com; ❷) has some very pleasant en-suite rooms around a garden. *Taverna Mathes*, the village taverna, has great terrace views and good food. A few kilometres uphill from the lake in **KOURNÁS** village, the *Kali Kardia* taverna on the main street is another great place to sample the local lamb and *loukánika* (sausages).

Beyond Yeoryoúpoli, the main road heads inland, away from a cluster of coastal villages beyond Vámos. It thus misses the Dhrápano peninsula, the setting for the film of *Zorba the Greek*, with some spectacular views over the sapphire Bay of Soúdha and several quiet beaches. **Kókkino Horió**, the movie location, and nearby **Pláka** are indeed postcard-picturesque (more so from a distance), but **Kefalás**, inland, outdoes both of them. On the exposed north coast there are good beaches at **Almyrídha** and **Kalýves**, and off the road between them. Both have been discovered by package operators; accommodation is mostly in apartments and rooms are scarce, although there are a few mid-range and more upmarket hotels. Almyrídha is the more pleasant, with a string of good fish tavernas (try *Dimitri's*) along the beach that make for an enjoyable lunch stop. If you want to stay here try *Marilena's Pension* (☎28250 32202; ❷), on the seafront to the east, or the more central, modern *Almira Apartments* (☎28250 61376; ❸).

South from Réthymnon

There are a couple of alternative routes south from Réthymnon, but the main one heads straight out from the centre of town, an initially featureless road due south across the middle of the island towards **Ayía Galíni**. About 23km out, a turning cuts off to the right for **Plakiás** and **Mýrthios**, following the course of the spectacular Kourtaliótiko ravine.

Plakiás and the south coast

PLAKIÁS has undergone something of a boom in recent years and is no longer the pristine village all too many people arriving here expect. That said, it's still quite low-key, with a satisfactory beach and a string of good tavernas around the dock. There are hundreds of **rooms**, but at the height of summer you'll need to arrive early if you hope to find one; the last to fill are generally those furthest inland, heading towards the youth hostel. Good places to try include *Gio-ma Taverna* (☎28320 32003, ⓦwww.gioma.gr; ❷–❸), on the seafront by the harbour with rooms and studios, or the excellent balcony rooms at *Ippokambos* (☎28320 31525, ⓔamoutsos@otenet.gr; ❶), slightly inland on the road to the enjoyably relaxed **youth hostel** (☎28320 32118, ⓦwww .yhplakias.com; dorms ❶), which is 500m inland and signed from the seafront. *Pension Afrodite* (☎28320 31266; ❸) is a quiet spot with pleasant apartments, off the road to the hostel.

Once you've found a room there's not a lot else to discover here. Every facility you're likely to need is strung out along the waterfront or on the few short streets off it, including a **post office** (Mon–Fri 7.30am–2pm), **bike rental**, ATMs and **money exchange**, several **supermarkets** and even a **laundry**. Places to eat are plentiful too. The attractive **tavernas** on the waterfront in the centre are a little expensive; the pick of them – with inviting terraces – are *Sofia* and the adjoining *Christos* and *Gio-ma* for fish. You'll eat cheaper further inland: seek out *Taverna Medousa* at the east end of town, reached up the road inland past the post office and then right. On the way here you'll pass *Nikos Souvlaki* which dishes up the least expensive meals in town – excellent *souvláki* or even fish and chips – often accompanied by live *bouzoúki* music in the evenings. Beyond the harbour at the west end of town *Psarotaverna Tassomanolis* is one of a line of waterfront places enjoying spectacular sunsets and specializes in fish caught by the proprietor from his own boat.

Mýrthios

For a stay of more than a day or two, **MÝRTHIOS**, in the hills behind Plakiás, also deserves consideration. Originally put on the map for legions of younger travellers by a legendary youth hostel (now closed), these days it's distinctly pricey, but there are some great apartments and wonderful views and you'll generally find locals still outnumbering the tourists. To **stay**, check out the classy *Anna Apartments* (☎697 33 24 775, ⓦwww.annaview.com; ❷–❹), while for food the long-established *Plateia Taverna* has had a complete makeover but still serves up excellent traditional Cretan cooking. A car is an advantage here, although the Plakiás bus will usually loop through Mýrthios (be sure to check – otherwise, it's less than five minutes' walk uphill from the junction). It takes twenty minutes to walk down to the beach at Plakiás, a little longer to Dhamnóni.

Dhamnóni and Skhinariá

Some of the most tempting **beaches** in central Crete hide just to the east of Plakiás, though unfortunately they're now a very poorly kept secret. These three splashes of yellow sand, divided by rocky promontories, are within easy walking distance and together go by the name **Dhamnóni**. At the first, Dhamnóni proper, there's a taverna with showers and a wonderfully long strip of sand, but there's also a lot of new development including a number of nearby rooms for rent and a huge and ugly Swiss-owned holiday village, which has colonized half of the main beach. At the far end, you'll generally find a few people who've dispensed with their clothes, while the little cove which shelters the middle of the three beaches (barely accessible except on foot) is entirely nudist. Beyond this, **Ammoúdhi** beach has another taverna, *Ammoudi* (☎28320 31355, ⓦwww.ammoudi.gr; ❸), with good if slightly pricey rooms for rent, and more of a family atmosphere. **Skhinariá** beach, just around the corner, is a considerable distance by road via the village of Lefkóyia. A popular diving spot, in summer it attracts Greek families, but is otherwise quiet. There's a decent (daytime) taverna here, *Lybian Star*.

Préveli and "Palm Beach"

Next in line along the coast is **PRÉVELI**, some 6km southeast of Lefkóyia, served by two daily **buses** from Réthymnon (check current times with any tourist office). It takes its name from a **monastery** (April & May daily 8am–7pm; June–Oct Mon–Sat 8am–1.30pm & 3.30–8pm, Sun 8am–8pm; in winter, knock for admission; ⓦwww.preveli.org; €2.50) set high above the sea which, like every other in Crete, has a proud history of resistance, in this case accentuated by its role in World War II as a shelter for marooned Allied soldiers awaiting evacuation. There are fine views and a new monument – to the left as you approach – commemorating the rescue operations and depicting a startling life-size, rifle-toting abbot and an allied soldier cast in bronze. The evacuations took place from "**Palm Beach**", a sandy cove with a small date-palm grove and a solitary drink stand where a stream (actually the Megapótamos river) feeds a little oasis. The beach usually attracts a summer camping community (now officially discouraged by the authorities due to litter and sanitation problems) and is also the target of day-trip boats from Plakiás and Ayía Galíni. Sadly, these groups between them deposit heaps of rubbish, often leaving this lovely place filthy, and despite an ongoing clean-up campaign it seems barely worth the effort. The easiest way to get to "Palm Beach" from the monastery is to follow a newly asphalted road that leaves the main road 1km before the monastery itself. This leads, after a further kilometre, to a **pay car park** (€1.50) where you'll need to leave any transport. From here, a marked path clambers steeply down over the rocks – about a ten-minute descent to the beach (but a sweaty twenty-minute haul back up). Should you not wish to return this way (although you'll have little option if you've brought transport), you can avoid the arduous, steep climb by taking a track on the east side of the beach which follows the river valley 2km back to a stone bridge, where there are cafés. You should be able to get one of the two daily buses to drop you at this bridge. All this said, **boat trips** from Plakiás and Ayía Galíni will get you here with a great deal less fuss.

Spíli and Ayía Galíni

Back on the main road south, the pleasant country town of **SPÍLI** lies about 30km from Réthymnon. A popular coffee break for coach tours passing this way, Spíli warrants time if you can spare it. Sheltered under a cliff are narrow alleys of ancient houses, all leading up from a platía with a famous 24-spouted **fountain** that replaced a Venetian original. If you have your own transport, it's a worthwhile place to stay, peacefully rural at night but with several good **rooms** for rent. Try the *Green Hotel* (☎28320 22225; ❶), on the main road, or the charming ⚡*Rooms Herakles* (☎28320 22411, ✉heraclespapadakis@hotmail .com; ❷, reductions for more than one night) just behind; the genial eponymous proprietor can advise on some superb **walks** in the surrounding hills and also rents out **mountain bikes**. There are two **banks** along the main street (with ATMs) and **Internet** access is possible at *Cafe Babis*, close to the fountain.

The ultimate destination for most people on this road is **AYÍA GALÍNI**. If heading here was your plan, maybe you should think again since this picturesque "fishing village" is so busy in high season that you can't see it for the tour buses, hotel billboards and British package tourists. It also has a beach that is much too small for the crowds that congregate here. Even so, there are a few saving graces – mainly some excellent restaurants and bars, a lively nightlife scene, plenty of rooms and a friendly atmosphere that survives and even thrives on all the visitors. Out of season, when the climate is mild, it can be quite enjoyable too, and from November to April, despite competition from immigrant workers, a number of long-term travellers spend the winter packing tomatoes or polishing cucumbers here. If you want somewhere to stay, start looking at the top end of town, around the main road: the economical *Hotel Minos* (☎28320 91292; ❶), with en-suite rooms with superb views, is a good place to start, with the nearby *Hotel Idi* (☎28320 91152, ⨏28320 91082; ❶) and *Hotel Hariklia* (☎ & ⨏28320 91257; ❷) as back-ups, and close to the foot of the hill leading to the harbour, *Neos Ikaros* (☎28320 91447, ⓦwww .neosikaros.gr; ❸) is a more upmarket option with superb garden pool. There are dozens of other possibilities, and usually something to be found even at the height of summer.

The coastal plain east of Ayía Galíni, hidden under acres of polythene greenhouses and burgeoning concrete sprawl, must be among the ugliest regions in Crete, and **Timbáki** the dreariest town. Since this is the way to Phaestos and back to Iráklion, you may have no choice but to grin and bear it.

The Amári Valley

An alternative route south from Réthymnon, and a far less travelled one, is the road which turns off on the eastern fringe of town to run via the **Amári Valley**. Very few buses go this way, but if you're driving it's well worth the extra time. There's little specifically to see or do (though hidden away are a number of richly frescoed Byzantine churches), but it's an impressive drive under the flanks of the mountains and a reminder of how, in places, rural Crete continues to exist regardless of visitors. The countryside here is delightfully green even in summer, with rich groves of olive and assorted fruit trees, and if you **stay** (there are rooms in Amári, Thrónos, Yerákari and Kouroutes), you'll find the nights are cool and quiet. It may seem odd that many of the villages along the way are modern: they were systematically destroyed by the German army in reprisal for the 1944 kidnapping of General Kreipe and many have poignant roadside monuments commemorating these tragic events.

Haniá and the west

The substantial attractions of Crete's westernmost quarter are enhanced by its relative lack of visitors, and despite the now-rapid spread of tourist development, the west is likely to remain one of the emptier parts of the island. This is partly because there are no big sandy beaches to accommodate resort hotels, and partly because it's so far from the great archeological sites. But for mountains and empty (if often pebbly) beaches, it's unrivalled.

Haniá itself is an excellent reason to come here, but the immediately adjacent coast, especially to the west of the city, is overdeveloped and not particularly exciting; if you want beaches head for the south coast. **Paleohóra** is the only place which could really be described as a resort, and even this is on a thoroughly human scale; others are emptier still. **Ayía Rouméli** and **Loutró** can be reached only on foot or by boat; **Hóra Sfakíon** sees hordes passing through but few who stay; **Frangokástello**, nearby, has a beautiful castle and the first stirrings of development. Behind these lie the **White Mountains** (Lefká Óri) and, above all, the famed walk through the **Samariá Gorge**.

△ Haniá harbour and Mosque of the Janissaries

Haniá

HANIÁ, as any of its residents will tell you, is spiritually the capital of Crete, even if the official title was passed back (in 1971) to Iráklion. For many, it is also by far the island's most attractive city, especially if you can catch it in spring, when the White Mountains' snowcapped peaks seem to hover above the roofs. Although it is for the most part a modern city, you might never know it as a tourist. Surrounding the small outer harbour is a wonderful jumble of half-derelict **Venetian streets** that survived the wartime bombardments, and it is here that life for the visitor is concentrated. Restoration and gentrification, consequences of the tourist boom, have made inroads of late, but it remains an atmospheric place.

Arrival, information and orientation

Large as it is, Haniá is easy to handle once you've reached the centre; you may get lost wandering among the narrow alleys of the old city but that's a relatively small area, and you're never far from the sea or from some other obvious landmark. The **bus station** is on Kydhonías, within easy walking distance from the centre – turn right out of the station, then left down the side of Platía-1866, and you'll emerge at a major road junction opposite the top of Halídhon, the main street of the old quarter leading straight down to the Venetian harbour. Arriving by **ferry**, you'll anchor about 10km east of Haniá at the port of Soúdha: there are frequent buses from here which will drop you by the **market** on the fringes of the old town, or you can take a taxi (around €8); there are also KTEL buses to Réthymnon and Kastélli meeting most ferries. From the **airport** (15km east of town on the Akrotíri peninsula) taxis (around €10) will almost certainly be your only option, though it's worth a quick check to see if any sort of bus is meeting your flight. The very helpful **tourist office** is in the *dhimarhío* (town hall) at Kydhonías 29 (Mon–Fri 8am–2.30pm ☎28210 36155, ⓦwww.chania .gr), four blocks east of the bus station.

Accommodation

There are thousands of **rooms** to rent in Haniá and, unusually, quite a few luxurious **hotels**. Though you may face a long search for a bed at the height of the season, eventually everyone does seem to find something. The nearest **campsite** within striking distance is *Camping Hania* (☎28210 31138), some 4km west of Haniá behind the beach, served by local bus. The site is rather small, and hemmed in by new development, but it has a pool and all the facilities just a short walk from some of the better beaches.

Harbour area

Perhaps the most desirable rooms of all are those overlooking the **harbour**, which are sometimes available at reasonable rates: be warned that this is often because they're very noisy at night. Most are approached not direct from the harbourside itself but from the streets behind; those further back are likely to be more peaceful. Theotokopoúlou and the alleys off it make a good starting point. The nicest of the more expensive places are here, too, equally set back but often with views from the upper storeys. In recent years the popularity of this area has led to anyone with a room near the harbour tarting it up and attempting to rent it out at a ridiculously inflated price. You'll often be touted in the street for these and it's wise not to commit yourself until you've made some comparisons.

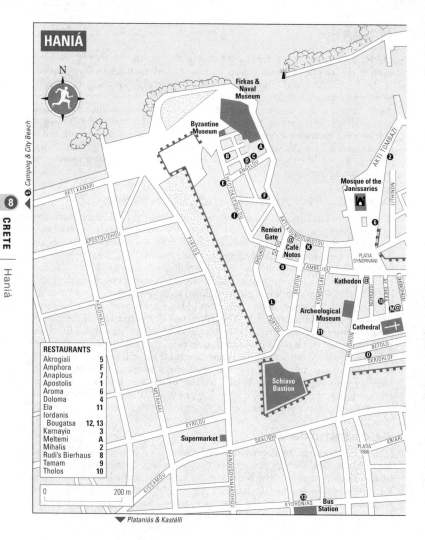

HANIÁ

N

◄ ⑤ Camping & City Beach

Firkas & Naval Museum

Byzantine Museum

Ⓐ Ⓑ Ⓒ Ⓓ

ANGELOU

THEOTOKOPOÚLOU

Ⓔ

Ⓕ

Ⓞ

AKTÍ KANARI

APOSTOLIDHOU

PARDHALI

PIRÉOS

DHOUKIS

AKTÍ TOMBÁZI

Ⓩ

LITHINON

Mosque of the Janissaries

AKTÍ KOUNDOURIÓTOU

Ⓖ

⑥

PLATÍA SYNDRIVANI

Renieri Gate

Ⓚ
Café Notos

⑨

ZAMBELÍOU

SKOUFON

KONDHILÁKI

ISODHION

AY. DHÉKA

E. DHOXIADHOU

Kathodon @

⑩

Ⓜ@

Archeological Museum

Ⓛ

PORTOU

⑪

Cathedral

✚

HÁLIDHON

BETOLO

Ⓞ

SKRIDHLOF

METAHÁKI

Schiavo Bastion

KYRILOU

KISSAMOU

MANOÚSOYANAKIDHOU

KYDHONÍAS

SKALIDHI

Supermarket ◼

MANOUSOYANAKIDHOU

PLATÍA 1866

KRIARI

Bus Station

⑬

0 —————— 200 m

▼ Plataniás & Kastélli

RESTAURANTS
Akrogiali	5
Amphora	F
Anaplous	7
Apostolis	1
Aroma	6
Doloma	4
Ela	11
Iordanis Bougatsa	12, 13
Karnayio	3
Meltemi	A
Mihalis	2
Rudi's Bierhaus	8
Tamam	9
Tholos	10

Amphora 2 Párodos Theotokopoúlou 20 ☏ 28210 93224, Ⓦ www.amphora.gr. Large, traditional hotel in a Venetian mansion, and beautifully renovated; worth the expense if you get a view, but probably not for the cheaper rooms without one. Good restaurant below; see p.770. ⑤

Casa Veneta Theotokopoúlou 57 ☏ 28210 90007, Ⓕ 28210 75931. Very well-equipped, comfortable studios and apartments with friendly owner behind a Venetian facade; good value. ④

El Greco Theotokopoúlou 47–49 ☏ 28210 94030, Ⓦ www.elgreco.gr. Comfortable hotel with nicely furnished if rather compact rooms which include fridge, a/c and TV. Some have balconies and there's a seasonal roof terrace. B&B ④

Lucia Aktí Koundouriótou ☏ 28210 90302 Ⓦ www.ellada.net/loukia. Harbourfront hotel with a/c balcony rooms; less expensive than you might expect for one of the best views in town, and – thanks to double-glazing – reasonably soundproof. ③

Maro B Párodos Porto 5 ☏ 28210 54981. Probably the cheapest en-suite rooms in the old town, hidden away in a quiet, unmarked alley off Portou not far from the Schiavo bastion. Basic but friendly and clean; a/c €2 extra. ②

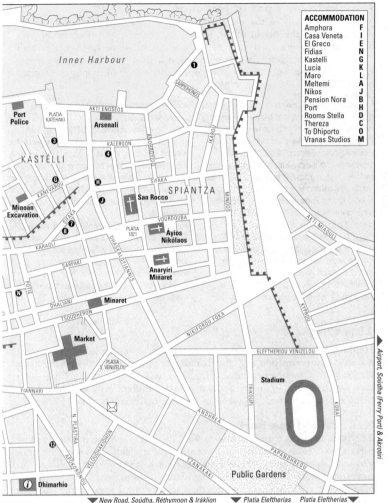

ACCOMMODATION

Amphora	F
Casa Veneta	I
El Greco	E
Fidias	N
Kastelli	G
Lucia	K
Maro	L
Meltemi	A
Nikos	J
Pension Nora	B
Port	H
Rooms Stella	D
Thereza	C
To Dhiporto	O
Vranas Studios	M

▼ *New Road, Soúdha, Réthymnon & Iráklion*   ▼ *Platía Eleftherías*   *Platía Eleftherías* ▼

Meltemi Angélou 2 ☎ 28210 92802. First of a little row of *pensions* in a great situation on the far side of the harbour near the Naval Museum; decent rooms with fans and (some) balcony are perhaps noisier than neighbours, but excellent views and a good café downstairs (see p.770). ②–③

Pension Nora Theotokopoúlou 60 ☎ 28210 72265, ℱ 28210 72265. Charming a/c en-suite rooms in an old wooden Turkish house, some with kitchenette and balcony (for the same price which you should ask for). Pleasant breakfast café below. ②

Rooms Stella Angélou 10 ☎ 28210 73756. Creaky, eccentric old house above an eclectic gift shop, with pleasant en-suite rooms equipped with a/c and fridge. ③

Thereza Angélou 8 ☎ & ℱ 28210 92798. Beautiful old house in a great position, with stunning views from roof terrace and a/c, en-suite rooms (some with TV); classy decor, too. Slightly more expensive than its neighbours but deservedly so; unlikely to have room in high season unless you book. ④

The old town: east of Halídhon

In the eastern half of the old town, rooms are far more scattered, usually cheaper, and in the height of the season your chances are much better over here. **Kastélli**, immediately east of the harbour, has some lovely places with views from the heights. Take one of the alleys leading left off Kanevárou if you want to try these, but don't be too hopeful since they are popular and often booked up.

To Dhiporto Betólo 41, one block north of Skridhlóf ☎ 28210 40570 Ⓦ www.geocities.com/to-diporto. Pleasant, good-value en-suite rooms all with a/c, TV and fridge; some triples and singles. ❸

Fidias Kalinákou Sarpáki 8 ☎ 28210 52494. Signposted from the cathedral, this favourite backpackers' meeting place has been going forever and has the real advantage of offering single rooms or fixing shares. Recently renovated to add some remarkably cheap en suites, but also has the cheapest beds in town. ❶

Kastelli Kanevárou 39 ☎ 28210 57057, Ⓦ www.kastelistudios.gr. A comfortable, modern, reasonably priced *pension* that's very quiet at the back. All rooms come with fans or a/c and anti-mosquito machines. The owner is exceptionally helpful and also has a few apartments and a beautiful house (for up to five people) to rent. ❷

Nikos Dhaskaloyiánnis 58 ☎ 28210 54783. Built on top of a Minoan ruin (visible through a basement window), this is one of several rooms places along this street near the inner harbour; good-value, relatively modern rooms, all with a/c, shower, fridge and (the more expensive ones) TV. Same owner has economical studios nearby with fully-equipped kitchens. ❶–❸

Port Sífaka 73, just off Dhaskaloyiánnis ☎ 28210 59484 Ⓔ lioliosk@chania.cci.gr. Clean, quiet modern place with good-size, en-suite rooms with a/c. ❸

Vranas Studios Ayíon Dhéka and Kalinákou Sarpáki, near the cathedral ☎ & ⒻⒻ 28210 58618, Ⓦ www.vranas.gr. Pleasant, spacious studio-style rooms with TV, a/c, fridge and kitchenette. ❹

The City

Haniá has been occupied almost continuously since Neolithic times, so it comes as a surprise that a city of such antiquity should offer little specifically to see or do. It is, however, fascinating simply to wander around, stumbling upon surviving fragments of city wall, the remains of **ancient Kydonia**, which are being excavated, and odd segments of Venetian or Turkish masonry.

Kastélli and the harbour

The **port** area is as ever the place to start, the oldest and the most interesting part of town. It's at its busiest and most attractive at night, when the lights from bars and restaurants reflect in the water and crowds of visitors and locals turn out to promenade. By day, things are quieter. Straight ahead from Platía Syndriváni (also known as Harbour Square) lies the curious domed shape of the **Mosque of the Janissaries**, built in 1645 (though heavily restored since) and the oldest Ottoman building on the island. It is occasionally open as a gallery, housing temporary exhibitions in the messy structures that adjoin the original mosque.

The little hill that rises behind the mosque is **Kastélli**, site of the earliest habitation and core of the Minoan, Venetian and Turkish towns. There's not a great deal left, but archeologists believe that they may have found the remains of a Minoan palace (logically, there must have been one at this end of the island), and the "lost" city of Kydonia, in the **excavations** being carried out – and open to view – along Kanevárou. It's also here that you'll find traces of the oldest **walls**; there were two rings, one defending Kastélli alone, a later set encompassing the whole of the medieval city. Beneath the hill, on the inner (eastern) harbour, the arches of sixteenth-century **Venetian arsenals**, a couple of them beautifully restored (and one housing a reconstructed Minoan ship), survive alongside remains of the outer walls.

Following the esplanade around in the other direction leads to a hefty bastion which now houses Crete's **Naval Museum** (daily 9am–4pm; €2). The collection consists of model ships and other naval ephemera tracing the history of Greek navigation, plus a section on the 1941 **Battle of Crete** with fascinating artefacts, and poignant photos depicting the suffering here under the Nazis. You might want to wander in through the gate beside the museum anyway for a (free) look at the seaward fortifications and the platform from which the modern Greek flag was first flown on Crete (in 1913). Walk around the back of these restored bulwarks to a street heading inland and you'll find the best-preserved stretch of the outer walls. Just behind the Naval Museum at the top of Theotokopoúlou lies the new **Byzantine Museum** (Tues–Sun 8.30am–3pm; €2, combined ticket with Archeological Museum €3), with a small but interesting collection of mosaics, icons and jewellery from the various periods of Byzantine rule. Continue up Theotokopoúlou and explore the alleys off it to discover some of the most attractive parts of the old town, with widespread restoration and plenty of fascinating small shops.

Halídhon and beyond

Behind the harbour lie the less picturesque but more lively sections of the old city. First, a short way up Halídhon on the right, is Haniá's **Archeological Museum** (Tues–Sun 8.30am–3pm; €3), housed in the Venetian-built church of San Francesco. Damaged as it is, especially from the outside, this remains a beautiful building and it contains a fine little display, covering the local area from Minoan through to Roman times. In the garden, a huge fountain and the base of a minaret survive from the period when the Ottomans converted the church into a mosque; around them are scattered various other sculptures and architectural remnants. The nearby **Folklore Museum** (Mon–Sat 9.30am–3pm & 6–9pm; €2) is worth a look as much for its setting, on a fine courtyard that is also home to Haniá's Roman Catholic church, as for its contents.

The **cathedral**, ordinary and relatively modern, is just a few steps further up Halídhon on the left. Around it are some of the more animated shopping areas, particularly **Odhós Skrídhlof** ("Leather Street"), lined with the shops of traditional leathermakers plying their trade, with streets leading up to the back of the market beyond. In the direction of the Spiántza quarter are ancient alleys with tumbledown Venetian stonework and overhanging wooden balconies; though gentrification is spreading apace, much of the quarter has yet to feel the effect of the city's modern popularity. There are a couple more **minarets** too, one on Dhaliáni, and the other in Platía-1821, which is a fine traditional square to stop for a coffee.

From the top of Halídhon, or beyond the market (well worth a visit, see p.772), spread the broad, traffic-choked streets of the **modern city**. You may venture out here for business – travel agencies and banks lie in this direction, along with the post office, bus station and shops, but few tourists stay long. And in truth there's little reason to linger. On Tzanakáki, not far from the market, you'll find the **public gardens**, a park with strolling couples, a few caged animals (including *krí-krí* or Cretan ibex) and a café under the trees; there's also an open-air auditorium which occasionally hosts live music or local festivities. Locals tend not to hang around this part of town – though they are drawn to the seafront cafés of Aktí Miaoúli, east of the old city, and to the seafood tavernas behind the beach.

The beaches

Haniá's beaches all lie to the west of the city. For the usually crowded and recently cleaned-up **city beach**, this means no more than a ten-minute walk following the shoreline from the Naval Museum, but for more extensive spaces you're better off taking the local bus (#21) out along the coast road. This leaves from the east side of Platía-1866 and runs along the coast as far as **Kalamáki beach**. Kalamáki and the previous stop, **Oásis beach**, are again pretty crowded but they're a considerable improvement over the beach in Haniá itself. In between, you'll find plenty of alternatives, though some of these are quite a walk from the bus stop. Further afield there are even finer beaches at **Ayía Marína** (see p.773) to the west, or **Stavrós** (p.773) out on the Akrotíri peninsula, either of which can be reached by KTEL buses from the main station.

Eating

You're never far from something to **eat** in Haniá: in a circle around the harbour is one restaurant, taverna or café after another. These tend to be pricey, though, and the quality at many leaves a lot to be desired. Away from the water, there are plenty of slightly cheaper possibilities on Kondhiláki, Kanevárou and most of the streets off Halídhon. For snacks or lighter meals, the cafés around the harbour generally serve cocktails and fresh juices at exorbitant prices, though breakfast (especially "English") can be good value. For more traditional places, try around the market and along Dhaskaloyiánnis (*Synganaki* here is a good traditional bakery serving *tyrópita* and the like, with a cake shop next door). Fast food is also increasingly widespread.

Akrogiali Aktí Papanikolí 19, behind the city beach ☏ 28210 73110. Worth the walk, or short taxi ride, to this excellent, reasonably priced seafront fish taverna with a summer terrace. Always packed with locals, so may be worth booking – though there are plenty of alternatives along the same street.

Amphora Aktí Koundouriótou, under the *Hotel Amphora*. One of the most reliable places on the outer harbour, with good, simple Greek food.

Anaplous Sífaka 37. A couple of blocks west of Platía-1821, *Anaplous* occupies a stylishly "restored" ruin of a Turkish mansion bombed in the war. Serves both *mezédhes* and full meals to live guitar music.

Apostolis Aktí Enóseos 6 & 10, inner harbour. The fish tavernas at the inner end of the harbour are rated much higher by locals than those further round – some locals claim *Apostolis 2*, practically the last, and just a couple of doors down from its seemingly identical sister restaurant, is the best of all. The fish is excellent, but pricey.

Aroma Aktí Tombázi 4, next to the Mosque of the Janissaries. Pleasant café with great harbour view to savour over lazy breakfasts or late drinks. *Mousses*, nearby at the corner of Kanevárou, is equally good, and open 24 hours.

Doloma Karsokalyvon 5, near the Arsenali. Excellent little taverna with a nice terrace serving well-prepared and economical Cretan dishes.

Ela Top of Kondhiláki. Standard taverna food with live Greek music accompaniment to enliven your meal in yet another roofless taverna townhouse.

Iordanis Bougatsa Kydhonías 96, opposite the bus station. This place serves little except the traditional creamy *bougátsa*, a sugar-coated cheese pie to eat in or take away. Another branch is at Apokorónou 24, between the market and the tourist office.

Karnayio Platía Kateháki 8 ☏ 28210 53366. Set back from the inner harbour near the port police. Not right on the water, but one of the best harbour restaurants nonetheless. Excellent fish, traditional Cretan cooking and a fine selection of wines – all served on an inviting terrace – make this a winner. The nearby *Faka* is also good.

Meltemi Angélou 2. Slow, relaxed terrace bar beneath the rooms place of the same name; good for breakfast, and where locals (especially expats) sit whiling the day away or playing *tavli*.

Mihalis Aktí Tombazi, on the outer harbour ☏ 28210 58330. Near the mosque, this is currently the number-one venue for *haniotes* dining out. Excellent selection of fish and meat dishes appears on a menu featuring many Cretan specialities such as *cóchli* (snails) and *hórta* (wild greens). Throw in a lively terrace, good wine list, attentive service and (very likely) a dessert on the house and you have a memorable place to dine.

Rudi's Bierhaus Sífaka 24 ☎ 28210
50824. Hania's beer shrine: Austrian – and
long-time Hania resident – Rudi Riegler's bar
stocks more than a hundred of Europe's finest
beers to accompany some outstanding *mezédhes*.
Tamam Zambelíou. Excellent, fashionable place
with adventurous Greek menu including much

vegetarian food. Unfortunately only a few cramped
tables in the alley outside, and inside it can get
very hot. Service can be slow.
Tholos Ayíon Dhéka 36. Slightly north of the
cathedral, *Tholos* is another "restaurant in a ruin",
this time Venetian/Turkish, with a wide selection of
Cretan specialities.

Bars and nightlife

Haniá's **nightlife** has more than enough venues to satisfy most night owls. The
majority of the touristy clubs and disco bars are gathered in the area around
the harbour, whilst there are plenty of terrace bars along both harbourfronts,
with more scattered throughout the old quarter. Young locals, however, tend to
start their evenings in the bars and cafés along Aktí Miaoúli, east of the harbour,
and Sarpidhónos, which leads from the inner harbour in that direction. Around
midnight, most move on to clubs, either in town or out along the coast, especially in Plataniás.

As everywhere, places go in and out of fashion, and names change frequently,
but the venues generally remain where they were – in the old town **bars**
you're occasionally reminded of the proximity of the Soúdha NATO bases by
an influx of rowdy servicemen. Reliable places around the harbour include the
Four Seasons, a very popular bar by the port police, and several bars, including
long-running *Scorpio*, in an alley starting behind the Mosque of the Janissaries.
Nearby, on upper floors, is the laid-back *Point* bar (above *Mousses* café). At the
opposite or western end of the harbour *Fagotto*, Angélou 16, is a pleasant, laid-
back jazz bar, often with live performers.

Most younger *haniotes* get their nightlife kicks by heading out along the
coast to the west where a vibrant **club scene** – based around Ayía Marina and
Plataniás – goes on all summer. Big out-of-town places here include *Destyle* in
Ayía Marina, *Mambo* on the Kató Stalós waterfront (just before Ayía Marina)
and *Utopia* in Plataniás. Current boss of the in-town **clubs** scene is *King*, down
an alley off the top of Halídhon, under the Schiavo bastion, closely followed by
its rival *Premier*, a big, bright place on Tsoudherón behind the market. The most
popular drinking locations are the numerous terraces lining **Aktí Míaouli**, the
waterfront to the east of the old quarter where dozens of music bars provide
lounging chairs and even enormous sofas for their (literally) laid-back clientele.
Of the numerous places here, you could try *Ellinikon*, *Mythologia* or *Il Nostro*,
though most seem almost interchangeable.

A venue offering more traditional entertainment is the *Café Kriti*, Kalergón 22, at
the corner of Andhroyíou, basically an old-fashioned *kafenío* where there's **Greek
music** and **dancing** virtually every night. It's also worth checking for events at
the open-air auditorium in the public gardens, and for performances in restaurants
outside the city, which are the ones the locals will go to. Look for posters, especially
in front of the market and in the little platía across the road from there.

For **films**, you should also check the hoardings in front of the market. There
are open-air screenings at Attikon, on Venizélou out towards Akrotíri, about
1km from the centre, and occasionally in the public gardens.

Listings

Airlines Olympic, with scheduled daily flights
between Haniá and Athens plus frequent flights
to Thessaloníki, has an office at Tzanakáki 88

(Mon–Fri 9am–4pm; ☎ 28210 57701–3) opposite
the public gardens. Aegean (to Athens only) is
at Venizélou 12 (☎ 28210 51100) across from

the market. For airport information call ☎28210 63264.

Banks and exchange The main branch of the National Bank of Greece is directly opposite the market with two ATMs, and there's a cluster of banks with more ATMs around the top of Halídhon. You'll also find plenty of out-of-hours exchange places on Halídhon, in the travel agencies.

Bike and car rental Possibilities everywhere, especially on Halídhon, though these are rarely the best value. For bikes, Summertime, Dhaskaloyiánnis 7, slightly northeast of the market (☎28210 45797, ⊕ www.strentals.gr) has a huge range, including mountain bikes. Bike Trekking, Karaóli 15 (☎28210 20143), has organized mountain-biking tours. For cars, look along Halídhon – two reliable local companies are Hermes, Tzanakáki 52 (☎28210 54418), or Tellus Rent a Car, Halídhon 108, opposite Platía-1866 (☎28210 91500). Good deals for *Rough Guide* readers (25 percent off normal rates) are available from El Greco Cars at the *El Greco* hotel (☎28210 60883, ⊕www .elgreco.gr; see "Accommodation").

Boat trips A number of boats make daily trips from Haniá, mainly to the nearby islands of Áyii Theódori and Lazarétta, for swimming and *krí-krí* (ibex) spotting: you're unlikely to escape the attentions of their stalls around the harbour. The *Evagelos* glass-bottomed boat, for example, makes this trip three times daily, with an all-day alternative on Saturdays to the Rodhópou peninsula (roughly €20; for information call ☎694 58 74 283); the *MS Irini* (☎28210 52001) is a more traditional vessel.

Diving Blue Adventures Diving, Arholeon 11 near the inner harbour (☎28210 40403), runs daily diving and snorkelling trips.

Ferry tickets From any travel agent, or the ANEK line office is on Venizélou, right opposite the market (☎28210 27500); Hellenic Sea Ways at Platía-1866 14 (☎28210 75444).

Internet There are plenty of Internet cafés including: Kathodon, Isodhíon 10; the more tranquil Vranas, Ayíon Dhéka beneath *Vranas Studios* (see p.768) minimum 1hr, though credit given); and

Café Notos, on the outer harbour under the *Hotel Notos*.

Laundry There are plenty to choose from, including Speedy Laundry (☎28210 88411; 9am–2pm & 6–9pm), junction of Koronéou and Korkídhi, just west of Platía-1866, who will collect and deliver your load if you call; Afrodite, Ayíon Dhéka 22 (daily 8.30am–8.30pm) in the old town, and Fidias, Kalinákou Sarpáki 6 (next to the *pension* of the same name; Mon–Sat 9am–9pm). All do service washes (5kg including drying and folding) for around €7.50.

Left luggage The bus station has a left-luggage office open 6am–8.30pm; €1–2 per item per day depending on size.

Market and supermarkets To buy food, head for the entertaining market which has fresh fruit and vegetables, meat and fish, bakers, dairy stalls and general stores for cooked meats, tins, etc; on Saturday mornings there's a wonderful line of stalls along Minóos, inside the eastern city wall, where local farmers sell their produce. Several small stores by the harbour platía sell cold drinks and food; they are expensive but open late. Small supermarkets can be found on Platía-1866, and the larger Champion supermarket is at the top of Pireos, outside the western wall, close to the Schiavo bastion.

Post office The main post office is on Tzanakáki (Mon–Fri 7.30am–8pm, Sat 9am–1pm).

Taxis The main taxi ranks are in Platía-1866. For radio taxis try ☎28210 18300, ☎28210 94300 or ☎28210 98700.

Tourist police April–Sept they man an office in the Mosque of the Janisseries on the outer harbour (☎28210 28750). Their inconveniently located main office is at Iraklíou 23 in the southern suburb of Koubés (☎28210 53333 or 28210 28708).

Travel agencies El Greco Travel, on Kydhonías near the bus station (☎28210 86015), and Tellus Travel, Halídhon 108, opposite Platía-1866 (☎28210 91500), are both good for inexpensive bus tickets, flights and standard excursions. For cheap tickets home try Bassias Travel, Halídhon 69 (☎28210 44295), very helpful for regular tickets too. They also deal in standard excursions.

Around Haniá: the Akrotíri and Rodhópou peninsulas

Just north of Haniá, the **Akrotíri peninsula** loops around to protect the Bay of Soúdha and a NATO military base and missile-testing area. In an ironic twist, the peninsula's northwestern coastline is fast developing into a luxury suburb; the beach of Kalathás, near Horafákia, long popular with jaded

Haniotes, is surrounded by villas and apartments. **STAVRÓS**, further out, has not yet suffered this fate, and its **beach** is absolutely superb if you like the calm, shallow water of an almost completely enclosed lagoon. It's not very large, so it does get crowded, but rarely overpoweringly so. There's a makeshift taverna/*souvláki* stand on the beach, and a couple of tavernas across the road, but for accommodation you need to search slightly south of here, in the area around **Blue beach**, where there are plenty of apartment buildings but no low-budget accommodation in summer whatsoever. On Blue beach you could try *Zorba's Apartments* (☎28210 52525; ❸).

Inland are the **monasteries** of **Ayía Triádha** (daily 7.30am–2pm & 5–7pm; €1.50) and **Gouvernétou** (daily 7am–2pm & 4–8pm; free). The former is much more accessible and has a beautiful seventeenth-century church inside its pink-and-ochre cloister, though ongoing renovations – the latest has turned one building into an olive-oil factory where the monks produce and bottle their own oil – on occasions make the normally peaceful enclosure more like a building site. Four kilometres north of Ayía Triádha, Gouvernétou – in a far better state of preservation and where traditional monastic life can still be observed – is a tranquil oasis with some fine frescoes in its ancient church. From just beyond the monastery you can clamber down a craggy path to the amazing and abandoned ruins of the **monastery of Katholikó**, built into a craggy ravine, and the remains of its narrow (swimmable) harbour.

West to Rodhópou

The coast to the west of Haniá was the scene of most of the fighting during the German invasion in 1941, and at Máleme there's a big German cemetery; the Allied cemetery is in the other direction, on the coast just outside Soúdha. There are also beaches and considerable tourist development along much of this shore. At **Ayía Marína** there's a fine sandy beach and an island offshore said to be a sea monster petrified by Zeus before it could swallow Crete. Seen from the west, its "mouth" still gapes open.

Between **Plataniás** and **Kolymvári** an almost unbroken strand unfurls, exposed when the wind blows and by no means all sandy, but deserted for long stretches between villages. The road here runs through mixed groves of calamus reed (Crete's bamboo) and oranges; the windbreaks fashioned from the reeds protect the ripening oranges from the *meltémi*. At Kolymvári, the road to Kastélli cuts across the base of another mountainous peninsula, **Rodhópou**. Just off the main road here is a monastery, **Goniá** (summer Mon–Fri & Sun 7am–12.30pm & 4.30–8pm, Sat 4–8pm; winter daily 3.30–5.30pm; free; respectable dress required), with a view most luxury hotels would envy. Every monk in Crete can tell tales of his proud ancestry of resistance to invaders, but here the Turkish cannon balls are still lodged in the walls to prove it, a relic of which the good fathers are far more proud than any of the icons.

South to the Samariá Gorge

From Haniá the **Samariá Gorge** (May–Oct; €5 for entry to the national park) can be visited as a day-trip or as part of a longer excursion to the south. At 16km, it is Europe's longest gorge and is startlingly beautiful. In the June to August period (ring Haniá tourist office or check at the bus station for other times) **buses** leave Haniá bus station for the top at 6.15am, 7.30am, 8.30am and 2pm (this latter service changes to 4.30pm outside school holidays), depositing

△ Samariá Gorge

you at the gorge entrance and then collecting you at the port of Hóra Sfakíon for the return trip to Haniá. You can also get the boat and bus back via Soúyia or Paleohóra, and if this is your intention you should specify when you buy your ticket: otherwise, for the three early buses, you'll normally be sold a return trip (valid from Hóra Sfakíon at any time). Should you take the last bus you will need to spend a night at Ayía Rouméli (the end of the gorge) as you will not get through the gorge in time for the last boat. It's well worth catching the earliest bus to avoid the full heat of the day while walking through the gorge, though be warned that you will not be alone – there are often as many as five coachloads setting off before dawn for the nail-biting climb into the White Mountains. There are also direct early-morning buses from Iráklion, Réthymnon, Soúyia and Paleohóra as well as bus tours from virtually everywhere on the island, adding up to a couple of thousand plus walkers on most days during high season.

Despite all the crowds, the walk *is* hard work, especially in spring when the stream is a roaring torrent. Early and late in the season, there is a danger of **flash floods**, which are not to be taken lightly: in 1993, a number of walkers perished when they were washed out to sea. For this reason the first and last three weeks of the season are entirely dependent on the weather and you will only be allowed into the gorge if the authorities deem it safe. If in doubt (and to save yourself a wasted journey), phone the Haniá Forest Service's **gorge information number** (☎28210 92287) or the gorge office (☎28210 67179). Should you arrive after 4pm you will only be allowed into the first couple of kilometres from each end of the gorge and the wardens ensure that no one remains in the gorge overnight, where camping is strictly forbidden.

Omalós

One way to avoid an early start from the north coast would be to stay at the elevated village of **OMALÓS**, in the middle of the mountain plain from which the gorge descends. The climate is cooler here all year round and a welcome bonus is the many paths into the hills surrounding the plateau where in season a profusion of wildflowers and birdlife is to be seen. There are plenty of **tavernas** and some ordinary **rooms** for rent – the friendly no-frills *Samaria pension* (☎28210 67168; ❶) is the cheapest – plus a clutch of surprisingly fancy **hotels**; the *Hotel Gigilos* (☎28210 67181; ❶) is good value and its proprietor will drive you the 5km to the top of the gorge in the morning if you stay overnight. However, since the village is some way from the start of the path, and the first buses arrive as the sun rises, it's almost impossible to get a head start on the crowds. Some people sleep out at the top (where there's a bar-restaurant in the *Tourist Lodge* and kiosks serving drinks and sandwiches), but a night under the stars here can be a bitterly cold experience. The one significant advantage to staying up here would be if you wanted to undertake some other **climbs** in the White Mountains, in which case the Kallérgi mountain hut (☎28210 33199 or ☎693 66 57 954; €12 per person including shower) is about an hour's hike (signed) from Omalós or ninety minutes from the top of the gorge; you can also drive up there from Omalós.

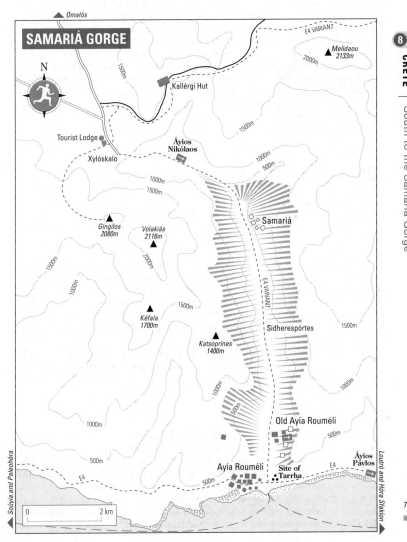

The gorge

The **gorge** itself begins at the *xylóskalo*, or "wooden staircase", a stepped path plunging steeply down from the southern lip of the Omalós plain. Here, at the head of the track, opposite the sheer rock face of Mount Gíngilos, the crowds pouring out of the buses disperse rapidly as keen walkers march purposefully down while others dally over breakfast, contemplating the sunrise. You descend at first through almost alpine scenery: pine forest, wildflowers and very un-Cretan greenery – a verdant shock in the spring, when the stream is at its liveliest. Small churches and viewpoints dot the route, and about halfway down you pass the abandoned village of **Samariá**, now home to a wardens' station, with picnic facilities and filthy toilets. Further down, the path levels out and the gorge walls close in until, at the narrowest point (the *sidherespórtes* or "iron gates"), one can practically touch both tortured rock faces at once and, looking up, see them rising sheer for almost a thousand feet.

At an average pace, with regular stops, the walk down takes five or six hours (though you can do it far quicker), and the upward trek considerably longer. It's strenuous – you'll know all about it next day – the path is rough, and walking boots or solid shoes are vital. On the way down, there is plenty of water from springs and streams (except some years in Sept and Oct), but nothing to eat. The park that surrounds the gorge is a refuge of the Cretan wild ibex, the *krí-krí*, but don't expect to see one; there are usually far too many people around.

Villages of the southwest coast

When you finally emerge from the gorge, it's not long before you reach the singularly unattractive village of **AYÍA ROUMÉLI**, which is all but abandoned until you come to the beach, a mirage of iced drinks and a cluster of tavernas with **rooms** for rent. *Livikon* (☎28250 91363; ❶) at the back of the village is one of the more tranquil places. On arrival, it's best to buy your boat tickets straightaway to be sure of getting the sailing you want (though in theory they guarantee that no one will be left behind, and that the buses will wait for the boat). If you plan to stay on the south coast, you should get going as soon as possible for the best chance of finding a room somewhere nicer than Ayía Rouméli. From May to October there are three boats daily to Loutró and Hóra Sfakíon (11.30am, 3.45pm and 6pm, plus 9am June–Sept), and a sailing to Soúyia and Paleohóra daily at 4.45pm.

If you are planning on staying down here, bring enough cash – the Visa-only ATM in Hóra Sfakíon is the only one between Paleohóra and Plakías. Drivers heading for Soúyia should also ensure their tanks are full – there's no fuel there.

Loutró

For tranquillity, it's hard to beat **LOUTRÓ**, two-thirds of the way to Hóra Sfakíon, and accessible only by boat or on foot. The chief disadvantage of Loutró is its lack of a real beach; most people swim from the rocks around its small bay. If you're prepared to walk, however, there are **deserted beaches** along the coast to the east which can also be reached by hired **canoe**. Indeed, if you're really into walking there's a **coastal trail** through Loutró which covers the entire distance between Ayía Rouméli and Hóra Sfakíon (now part of the E4 Pan-European footpath), or you could take the daunting zigzag path up the cliff behind to the mountain village of **Anópoli**. Loutró itself has a number of **tavernas** and **rooms**, though not always enough of the latter in peak season. Call the 🪑 *Blue House* (☎28250 91127, 🌐www.delftmark.nl/thebluehouse; ❷) if you want to book ahead, where there are comfortable en-suite rooms and a wonderful (slightly pricier) top-floor extension; this is also the best place to eat. Slightly more upmarket accommodation is on offer at the nearby *Hotel Porto Loutro* (☎28250 91433, 🌐www.hotelportoloutro.com; ❷–❸), which also hires out canoes and runs full-day **cruises** on its own boat to "Palm Beach" (see p.762) and the island of Gávdhos; prices should be posted outside. There's space to **camp** out on the cape by a ruined fort, but due to a long history of problems, you should be aware that campers are not very popular in the village. If you're determined to camp, head for the **beaches** and coves to the east (such as Sweetwater) and west (Mármara) of the resort which can be reached on foot, or more comfortably by canoe or daily boats from the harbour.

Hóra Sfakíon and beyond

HÓRA SFAKÍON is the more usual terminus for walkers traversing the gorge, with a regular boat service along the coast to and from Ayía Rouméli. Consequently, it's quite an expensive and not an especially welcoming place; there are plenty of **rooms** and some decent **tavernas**, but for a real beach you should jump straight on a bus (currently running at 11am and 6pm April–Sept) going toward Plakiás (see p.761). Plenty of opportunities for a dip present themselves en route, one of the most memorable at **Frangokástello**, named after a crumbling Venetian attempt to bring law and order to a district that went on to defy both Turks and Germans. The four-square, crenellated and imposing thirteenth-century **castle**, isolated a few kilometres below a chiselled wall of mountains, looks like it's been spirited out of the High Atlas or Tibet. The place is said to be haunted by ghosts of Greek rebels massacred here in 1829: every May, these *dhrossoulítes* ("dewy ones") march at dawn across the coastal plain and disappear into the sea near the fort. The rest of the time Frangokástello is peaceful enough, with a superb beach and a number of tavernas and rooms, but there's not a lot to do. The greatest concentration of rooms is immediately below the castle – try *Maria's Studios* (☎28250 92159, 🌐www.marias-studios .com; ❷) or *Kali Kardia* (☎28250 92123; ❶), for example. Slightly further east, and less influenced by tourism or modern life, are the attractive villages of **Skalotí** and **Rodhákino**, where basic lodging and food can be found in the villages proper or their seafront offshoots a couple of kilometres to the south.

Soúyia

In quite the other direction from Ayía Rouméli, less regular boats also head to **SOÚYIA** and on to Paleohóra. Soúyia, until World War II merely the anchorage for Koustoyérako inland, is a low-key resort, with a long, grey pebble beach and mostly modern buildings (except for a church with a sixth-century Byzantine mosaic as the foundation). Since the completion in 1990 of the paved road to Haniá, the village has started to expand; even so, except in the very middle of summer, it continues to make a good fall-back for finding a room or a place to camp, eating cheaply and enjoying the beach when the rest of the island is swarming with visitors.

Rooms (slightly more expensive than on the rest of this coast) are scattered around the road on the way in, and in the seafront zone where it hits the sea, although places here tend to be both pricier and noisier. One of the many places on the road as it comes into Soúyia is *Captain George* (☎28230 51133; ❸), where there are some larger apartments, or the peaceful *El Greco*, set further back (☎28230 51186; **❷**); both offer balcony rooms with fridge and (some) kitchenette. On the seafront, *Hotel Santa Irene* (☎28230 51342, **Ⓦ**www.sougia .info/hotels/santairene; **❸**) is the fanciest place in town with a/c balcony rooms with marble floors and fridges. Since the local travel agent closed, there's no one centre for **information**. Your hotel should be able to fill you in on how to walk the beautiful **Ayía Iríni gorge** or do a wonderful hour-long hike over to the nearby ancient site of **Lissós** with temples and mosaics. Otherwise, bus tickets are sold at *Snacks Roxana*, near the bottom of the main road, while the two supermarkets opposite can arrange taxi boats to local beaches (get one to bring you home from Lissós, for example). Boat tickets are sold at the *períptero* on the seafront, and the boats leave from the dock at the western end of the beach. For **food**, *Rembetiko* has a pleasant garden terrace just off the main street, while the seafront is packed with possibilities. The German-run *Omikron* taverna has a more northern-European ambience and offers some **vegetarian** choices; *Café Lotos* provides **Internet** access.

Kastélli and the western tip

Apart from being Crete's most westerly town, and the end of the main E65 coastal highway, **KASTÉLLI** (Kíssamos, or Kastélli Kissámou as it's variously known) has little obvious attraction. It's a busy town with a rocky central **beach** (although there's an excellent sandy beach to the west) visited mainly by people using the boat that runs twice weekly to the island of Kathira and the Peloponnese. The very ordinariness of Kastélli, however, can be attractive: life goes on pretty much regardless of outsiders, and there's every facility you might need. The town was important in antiquity, though sadly the recently excavated **mosaics** signed around the centre have all been buried under a layer of earth to protect them, while the new **museum** (located in the refurbished former Venetian governor's residence on the main square), planned to display finds from these digs and others nearby, has yet to open thanks to wrangling over the status of the contents – it will possibly begin operating by May 2006.

As regards **practicalities**, you'll find most of what you need around the main square, Platía Kastellíou. The bus station is here, as are a couple of cafés; banks, shops and travel agencies (for ferry tickets or car rental) lie east of the square along Skalídhi (another group can be found around Platía Venizélou, on the main road through town). The harbour itself is a good 2km west of town – a significant walk if you're heavily laden, or a €5 taxi ride. For **rooms**, *Koutsounakis* (☎28220 23416; **❷**) and the more basic but clean and friendly *Vergerakis* (aka *Jimmy's*; ☎28220 22663; **❶**) are both right by Platía Kastellíou. For more facilities and a beachside location, the excellent ✤ *Hotel Galini Beach* (☎28220 23288, **Ⓦ**www.galinibeach.com; B&B; **❸**) with sparkling balconies, a/c, sea-view rooms is well worth the extra; it lies at the pebbly, eastern end of the seafront near the sports stadium with easy parking and serves bountiful breakfasts. At the western end of the strand the friendly ✤ *Maria Beach* (☎28220 22610, **Ⓦ**www.mariabeach.gr; **❷–❹**) has a whole variety of attractive en-suite a/c balcony rooms, plus studios and apartments on the town's sandy western beach.

Heading north from the main square brings you to the beach promenade where there are a number of **tavernas** – *Papadakis* is worth a try and, for its summer *mezédhes* and winter taverna, *Dionysos* is also good. The seafront strip's late-night drinking and music **bars** are also popular with the local younger set, particularly at weekends.

Falásarna to Elafoníssi

To the west of Kastélli lies some of Crete's loneliest and, for many visitors, finest coastline. The first place of note is **Falásarna**, where the scant ruins of an ancient city are ignored by most visitors in favour of some of the best beaches on Crete, wide and sandy with clean water. There's a handful of **tavernas** and an increasing number of **rooms** for rent: *Sunset* (T 28220 41204; ❶), at the end of the paved road near the archeological site, is among the better choices for both. Plenty of people **camp** out here too; if you join them, be sure to take any litter away with you. Rubbish, occasional tar and crowds of locals on summer weekends can always be escaped if you're prepared to walk, and the beaches are worth it. The nearest real town is **Plátanos**, 5km up a paved road, serviced by a couple of daily buses; the town has supermarkets and a bank with ATM.

Further south, the western coastline is far less discovered. **SFINÁRI** is a quiet village with a number of rooms to rent on the road down to a quiet pebble beach. At the bottom are a couple of tavernas; try *Captain Fidias,* which offers free camping and sunloungers for the pebbly beach.

KÁMBOS is similar, but even less visited, its beach a considerable walk down a hill (or a very steep drive). **Accommodation** is available at the good-value *Rooms Hartzulakis* (T 28220 44445; ❶) on the edge of a long gorge which also leads down to the sea; the same place has a terrace taverna with great views, and you should be able to get information about walking locally. Beyond them both is the **monastery of Khryssoskalítissa**, increasingly visited by tours from Haniá and Paleohóra, but well worth the effort for its isolation and nearby beaches; the bus gets as far as Váthy, from where the monastery is another two hours' walk, although you could try hitching – with a fair chance of success – as many of the tourist cars are bound to be heading for the same destination.

Five kilometres beyond Khryssoskalítissa, the tiny uninhabited islet of **Elafoníssi** lies marooned on the edge of a gloriously scenic turquoise lagoon. It's all too easy to get here now, a fact reflected in the huge number of visitors who do, by car, with coach tours, or on a boat from Paleohóra. The pinky-white sand, the warm, clear lagoon and the islet to which you can easily wade still look magnificent, but you certainly won't have it to yourself. There's a single, inadequate portable toilet and a number of stalls selling cold drinks and basic food, while 1km or so up the road are a couple of taverna/rooms places

A round trip

If you have transport, a circular drive from Kastélli, via the west coast and back by the inland route through Élos and Topólia, makes for a stunningly scenic circuit. Near the sea, villages cling to the high mountainsides, apparently halted by some miracle in the midst of calamitous seaward slides. Around them, olives ripen on the terraced slopes, the sea glittering far below. Inland, especially at **ÉLOS**, the main crop is the chestnut, whose huge old trees shade the village streets.

South of **TOPÓLIA**, the chapel of Ayía Sofía is sheltered inside a cave which has been used as a shrine since Neolithic times. Cutting south just before Élos, a spectacular paved road continues through the high mountains towards Paleohóra. On a motorbike, with a sense of adventure and plenty of fuel, it's great: the bus doesn't come this way, villagers still stare at the sight of a tourist, and a host of small, seasonal streams cascades beside or under the asphalt.

– *Elafonissi* (☎28220 61274; ❷) is the better of them with its own taverna and minimarket. For a day-trip, though, it's best to bring your own supplies.

Kándanos and Paleohóra

The easiest route to the far southwest leaves the north coast at Tavronítis, 22km west of Haniá, heading for Paleohóra; several buses follow this route from Haniá every day, and although this road also has to wind through the western outriders of the White Mountains, it lacks the excitement of the alternatives to either side. **KÁNDANOS**, at the 58-kilometre mark, has been entirely rebuilt since it was destroyed by the Germans for its fierce resistance to their occupation. The original sign erected when the deed was done is preserved on the war memorial in the central square: "Here stood Kándanos, destroyed in retribution for the murder of 25 German soldiers, and never to be rebuilt again." The pleasantly easy-going and once-again substantial village had the last laugh.

When the beach at **PALEOHÓRA** finally appears below, it is a welcome sight. The little town is built across the base of a peninsula, its harbour and a beach known as "Pebble Beach" on the eastern side, the wide sands ("Sandy Beach") on the other. Above, on the outcrop, ruined Venetian ramparts stand sentinel. These days Paleohóra has developed into a significant resort, but it's still thoroughly enjoyable, with a main street filling with tables at night as diners spill out of the restaurants, and with a pleasantly chaotic social life. You'll find a helpful **tourist office** (Mon & Wed–Sun 10am–1pm & 6–9pm; ☎28230 41507) in a cabin on "Pebble Beach", close to the ferry harbour. They have full accommodation lists and provide a decent **map** which is useful for finding food and accommodation locations.

There are plenty of **places to stay** (though not always many vacancies in high season) – try the friendly *Castello Rooms* (☎28230 41143; ❷), at the southern end of Sandy beach; the alleys behind here, beneath the castle, have many more simple rooms places. Just north of here the *Sandy Beach Hotel* (☎08230 42138, ⓕ08230 42139; ❸) is the town's chicest hotel option for a/c balcony rooms with fridge, TV and sea view. *Villa Marise* (☎28230 42012, ⓔjetee@otenet.gr; ❹) enjoys one of the best locations in town, right on the sandy beach more or less opposite the post office, and has a variety of well-equipped rooms, apartments and studios for up to six people. Probably the least expensive rooms in town are at *Anonymous* (☎28230 41509; ❶), in a backstreet behind the main street (Odhós Venizélos), with shared bathrooms and kitchen, and a very friendly atmosphere. There's also a fair-sized **campsite**, *Camping Paleohora* (☎28230 41120), 2km north of "Pebble Beach". If you are tempted to sleep on the main "Sandy Beach" – one of the best on the south coast, with showers, trees and acres of sand – be prepared for trouble from police and local residents who are no longer willing to tolerate it. When you tire of beach life there are plenty of alternative entertainments from dolphin-watching trips to excursions into the hills to Azoyirés, or a five-to-six-hour hike along the coastal path to Soúyia.

For **eating** and **drinking**, tavernas, bars and cafés are to be found throughout the resort, particularly along the roads behind the two beaches. A good place to try for some imaginative **vegetarian** specials is *The Third Eye*, just out of the centre towards Sandy beach. Other decent in-town eating places include *Pizzeria Niki*, off the south side of Kondekáki (the road running from east to west at the south end of Venizélou), and *The Wave* at the south end of "Pebble Beach", serving good fish on a seaside terrace. Paleohóra's flagship seafood restaurant, however, is the outstanding 🗲 *Caravella*, with a pleasant waterfront terrace just beyond the harbour at the south end of "Sandy Beach"; the cooking and service are excellent, as is their chilled *hyma* (barrelled wine) from a vineyard in the Kastélli Kissámou area.

As Paleohóra publicizes itself as a "family" resort, there's an unwritten curfew around 11pm when the bars lower their sounds, so if you're looking for some untamed nightlife you've definitely come to the wrong place. Even *Escape Paleohora Club*, at the extreme north end of "Pebble Beach" close to the campsite, has had to close its outdoor **dance** floor, although the authorities recently allowed them a smaller one; but the action still continues till late indoors. In the other direction, just beyond the southern end of the "Sandy Beach", *Nostos* has a more chilled vibe, and opens throughout the day. A great little open-air **cinema**, Cine Attikon, is tucked away in the northern backstreets; most of their films are in English and programmes (which change daily) are posted outside the tourist office and on fliers attached to the odd tree trunk around town.

Almost everything else you're likely to need is located in the centre of town along and around Odhós Venizélos. **Banks** (with ATMs), **travel agents**, a **laundry**, **mountain-bike** and **car-rental** companies and **Internet** access (at *Er@to Cafe* or Notos Travel) are all along Venizélou, while the **post office** is on the road behind "Sandy Beach". There are three **pharmacies** on Kondekáki and there's a **health centre** in the street parallel to Venizélos to the west. When the tourist office is closed, Notos Travel (☎28230 42110), on Venizélou, is a friendly source of information on almost everything to do in Paleohóra and has lots of information on renting apartments, cars, mountain bikes and lots more. PADI-certificated courses in **scuba diving** are on offer at Aquacrete, Kontekáki 4, close to Venizélos (☎28230 41393, ⓦwww.aquacreta.gr).

Boats run from Paleohóra to Elafoníssi, to the island of Gávdhos and along the coast to Soúyia and Ayía Rouméli; Notos Travel (see above), on Venizélos, and E-Motion (☎28230 41755), on Kontekáki by the harbour, are good sources of information and tickets. They also have information about other trips – to walk the **Samariá Gorge**, for example, although you can also do that independently by catching the bus leaving daily at 6am throughout the summer, and a boat back from Ayía Rouméli.

Gávdhos

The island of **Gávdhos**, some 50km of rough sea south of Paleohóra, is the most southerly land mass in Europe. Gávdhos is small (about 10km by 7km) and barren, but it has one major attraction: the enduring **isolation** which its inaccessible position has helped preserve. This may not last much longer, as a big new port is under construction (currently stalled due to the discovery of its Minoan predecessor), together with a new electricity plant and asphalted roads. Providing you avoid the crowds in August, if all you want is a beach to yourself and a taverna to grill your fish, this remains the place for you. For the moment not too much has changed, and it is usually possible to turn up on spec and find a bed, but travel agents in Paleohóra (see above) will arrange a room if you want one and also provide current ferry information. There's a semi-permanent community of campers and would-be "Robinson Crusoes" resident on the island throughout the summer – in addition to the six indigenous families who live here all year round.

Largely because water is often difficult to obtain, most people choose to base themselves near to one of the three largest beaches; at the most popular of all, **SARAKÍNIKO**, there's a slew of beachfront tavernas in addition to a squatters' community spreading a shanty town of unsightly breezeblock summer dwellings behind the beach. For **rooms** *Taverna Gerti & Manolis* (☎ 28230 41103; ❷) is reliable, while *Sarakiniko Studios* (☎ 28230 42182, ⓦ www.gavdostudios.gr; B&B; ❸) is a step upmarket. The latter's proprietors will collect you from the harbour and they have a **campsite** for pitching tents. Good **places to eat** at Sarakíniko include *Gerti & Manolis* (see above) for fresh fish, *Karapistolas* for Middle Eastern specialities, and the friendly *Sorolop* with a nice "community" feel when people hang around to play chess or Scrabble after eating. At Áyios Ioánnis, one of the other beach settlements 2km to the northwest (where's there's a thriving "hippy" and nudist community), a solitary and unnamed taverna is also an excellent place for fresh fish. Although many people still bring as much food as they can with them on the boat, there are now well-stocked **minimarkets** at Sarakíniko and Áyios Ioánnis.

Travel details

Buses

The following are the main routes only. For the latest timetables and complete route and fare information for the west of the island, visit the website at ⓦ www.bus-service-crete-ktel.com. There are also plenty of unofficial websites with timetables for the east: the official central timetable at ⓦ www.ktel.org rarely seems to work.

Áyios Nikólaos to: Iráklion (21 daily, 6 via Iráklion Airport 6am–8.30pm; 1hr 30min); Kritsá (9 daily 6.45am–8pm; 30min); Lasíthi plateau (2 daily; 2hr); Sitía (7 daily 6.15am–8.30pm; 1hr 30min).

Haniá to: Hóra Sfakíon (3 daily 8.30am–2pm; 2hr); Omalós (Samariá Gorge; 4 daily 6.15am–2pm; 1hr 15min); Paleohóra (3 daily 8.30am–4pm; 2hr); Iráklion via Réthymnon (21 daily, 2 via old road 5.30am–10pm; 2hr 30min total).

Iráklion to: Ayía Galíni (7 daily 6.30am–4.30pm; 2hr 15min); Áyios Nikólaos (19 daily 6.30am–9.30pm; 1hr 30min); Haniá (21 daily 5.30am–9pm; 2hr 30min); Phaestos (7 daily 7.30am–4.30pm; 1hr 30min); Ierápetra (7 daily 6.30am–7.30pm; 2hr 30min).

Kastélli to: Haniá (14 daily 6.30am–9.30pm; 1hr 15min).

Réthymnon to: Ayía Galíni via Spíli (5 daily 5.30am–2.15pm; 45min–1hr 30min); Haniá (21 daily 7am–10.30pm; 1hr); Iráklion (23 daily 6.30am–10.15pm; 1hr 30min); Plakiás (3 daily 6.15am–2.15pm; 1hr 15min).

Ferries

For the latest timetables for domestic and international ferries to and from Crete visit ⓦ www .cretetravel.com, ⓦ www.ferries.gr or ⓦ www .greekislands.gr.

Áyios Nikólaos and Sitía 3–4 sailings a week to Pireás (12hr); 2–3 ferries a week to Kássos, Kárpathos, Hálki and Rhodes; 2–3 weekly to Mílos.

Haniá Daily overnight to Pireás with ANEK (9–11hr) or Blue Star (5hr 45min).

Hóra Sfakíon 5 ferries daily to Loutró/Ayía Rouméli (1hr/2hr 30min); 3–4 weekly to Gávdhos (1hr 30min) in season.

Iráklion 2 ferries daily to Pireás (12hr); 1 daily fast ferry to Pireás (6hr); 3 ferries weekly to Thessaloníki; 1 daily ferry to Thíra (4hr), also fast boats and hydrofoils (2hr 30min); daily ferries to Páros, Mýkonos, Íos and Náxos in season; twice weekly to Tínos & weekly to Skíathos.

Kastélli (Kíssamos) 2 ferries weekly to Kýthira/ Pireás (3hr 30min/12hr), one of them via Yíthio (6hr); 1 ferry weekly to Kalamáta (7hr 30min).

Paleohóra 2–3 boats a week in season to Gávdhos. Also daily sailings to Elafoníssi and Soúyia/Ayía Rouméli.

Réthymnon Daily ferries to Pireás (11hr 30min); seasonal day-trips to Thíra.

Flights

Haniá to: Athens (5 daily on Olympic; 4 daily on Aegean); Thessaloníki (3 weekly on Olympic).

Iráklion to: Athens (5–7 daily on Olympic; 7 daily on Aegean); Rhodes (4 weekly, summer only, on Olympic; 1–2 daily on Aegean); Thessaloníki (2 weekly on Olympic; 2 daily on Aegean).

Sitía to: Alexandhroúpoli in Thrace (3 weekly on Olympic); Athens (3 weekly on Olympic); Préveza in northwest Greece (3 weekly on Olympic).

The Dodecanese

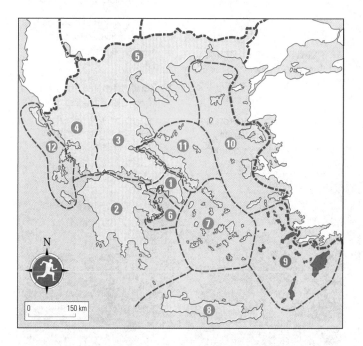

CHAPTER 9

Highlights

* **Northern Kárpathos** Old walking trails take you between traditional villages. See p.795

* **Ródhos old town** Superbly preserved medieval streets, inextricably linked with the Knights of Saint John. See p.802

* **Lindos Acropolis, Rhodes** A pleasing blend of ancient and medieval culture, with great views over the town. See p.809

* **Thárri monastery, Rhodes** Superb Byzantine frescoes in the oldest religious foundation on the island. See p.813

* **Sými** The officially protected harbour and hillside village teem with trippers during the day, but a stay overnight is rewarding. See p.822

* **Volcano of Níssyros** The craters of the dormant volcano still hiccup, with the most recent activity in 1933. See p.837

* **Brós Thermá, Kós** Relax in shoreline hot springs, which flow into the sea, protected by a boulder ring. See p.845

* **Mount Dhíkeos, Kós** The hike up is worthwhile for the views over the Dodecanese. See p.846

* **Hóra, Astypálea** The windswept island "capital" is perched dramatically above the sea and has a beautiful Venetian *kástro*. See p.852

△ Hóra of Astypálea, with Venetian castle

The Dodecanese

The furthest island group from the Greek mainland, the **Dodecanese** (Dhodhekánisos) lie close to the Turkish coast – some of them, such as Kós and Kastellórizo, almost within hailing distance of Anatolia. Because of their strategic position, these islands have had a turbulent history: they were the scene of ferocious battles between German and British forces in 1943–44, and were only finally included in the modern Greek state in 1948 after centuries of occupation by Crusaders, Ottomans and Italians. Although relations between Greece and Turkey are currently at their best ever, the Greek army and air force clearly prefer to keep their powder dry, in the form of numerous military bases and smaller watch-points which multiplied after the 1996 incident over the disputed islet-duo of Ímia.

Whatever the rigours of the various occupations, their legacy includes a wonderful blend of architectural styles and of Eastern and Western cultures. Medieval Rhodes is the most famous, but almost every island has some Classical remains, a Crusaders' castle, a clutch of traditional villages and abundant grandiose public buildings. For these last the Italians, who occupied the Dodecanese from 1912 to 1943, are mainly responsible. In their determination to beautify the islands and turn them into a showplace for Fascism they undertook public works, excavations and reconstruction on a massive scale; if historical accuracy was often sacrificed on the altar of visual propaganda, only an expert is likely to complain. A more sinister aspect of the Italian administration was the attempted forcible Latinization of the populace: spoken Greek and Orthodox observance were banned in progressively stricter increments between the mid-1920s and 1936. The most tangible reminder of this policy is the (rapidly dwindling) number of older people who can still converse – and write – as fluently in Italian as in Greek.

Aside from this bilingualism, the Dodecanese themselves display a marked topographic and economic schizophrenia. The dry limestone outcrops of **Kastellórizo**, **Sými**, **Hálki**, **Kássos** and **Kálymnos** have always been forced to rely on the sea for their livelihoods, and the wealth generated by this maritime culture – especially during the nineteenth century – fostered the growth of attractive port towns. The sprawling, relatively fertile giants **Rhodes** (Ródhos) and **Kós** have recently seen their traditional agricultural economies almost totally displaced by a tourist industry focused on good beaches and nightlife, as well as some of the most exciting historical monuments in the Aegean. **Kárpathos** lies somewhere in between, with a lightly forested north grafted on to a rocky limestone south; **Tílos**, despite its lack of trees, has ample water, though the green volcano-island of **Níssyros** does not. **Léros** shelters softer contours and more amenable terrain

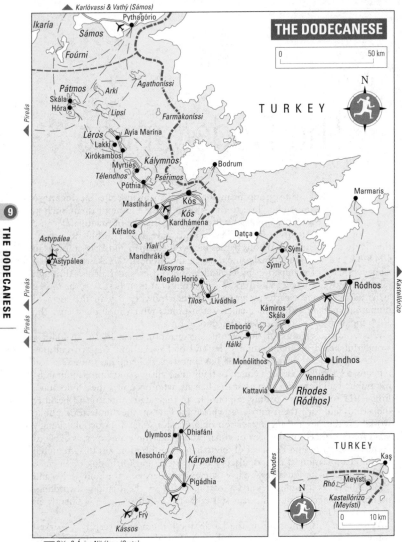

THE DODECANESE

0 — 50 km

▲ Karlóvassi & Vathý (Sámos)
Pythagório
Ikaría
Sámos
Foúrni

Pátmos / Arkí
Skála
Hóra
Lipsí

Agathoníssi

Farmakoníssi

TURKEY

N

▲ Piréas

Léros / Ayía Marína
Lakkí
Xirókambos
Myrtiés / Kálymnos
Télendhos / Psérimos
Póthia

Bodrum

Mastihári
Kós
Kardhámena

Marmaris

Astypálea
Astypálea

Yialí
Mandhráki

Datça
Sými
Sými

Nissyros
Megálo Horió

Kéfalos

Ródhos

Tílos Livádhia

Kámiros
Skála

Emborió
Hálki

Monólithos

Líndhos

Yennádhi

Kattaviá

Rhodes
(Ródhos)

▲ Piréas ▲ Piréas

Kastellórizo ▲

Ólymbos / Dhiafáni
Mesohóri
Kárpathos
Pigádhia

Frý
Kássos

▼ Sitía & Áyios Nikólaos (Crete)

TURKEY
Kaş
Meyísti
Rhó
Kastellórizo
(Meyísti)
0 — 10 km
N

▲ Rhodes

than its map outline would suggest, while **Pátmos** and **Astypálea** at the fringes of the archipelago offer architecture and landscapes more typical of the Cyclades.

The largest islands in the group are connected by regular **ferries and catamarans**, and none (except Kastellórizo, Astypálea and Tílos) is hard to reach. Rhodes is the main transport hub, with connections for Crete, the northeastern Aegean, the Cyclades and the mainland as well. Kálymnos and Kós are jointly an important secondary terminus, with a useful ferry based on Kálymnos, hydrofoil services using Kós and Kálymnos as a focus and transfer point, and two catamarans based on Rhodes and Pátmos providing a valuable supplement to larger ferries calling at uncivil hours.

Kássos

Like Psará islet in the northeast Aegean, **Kássos** contributed its large fleet to the Greek revolutionary war effort, and likewise suffered appalling consequences. In May 1824, an Ottoman army sent by Ibrahim Pasha, Governor of Egypt, besieged the island; on June 7, aided perhaps by a traitor's tip as to the weak point in Kássos's defences, the invaders descended on the populated north-coastal plain, slaughtered most of the inhabitants and put houses, farms and trees to the torch.

Barren and depopulated since then, Kássos attracts few visitors, despite regular air links with Rhodes and Kárpathos, and being a port of call on ferry lines from those isles to Crete. Numerous sheer gorges slash through lunar terrain, with fenced smallholdings of midget olive trees providing the only visual relief. Springtime grain crops briefly soften the usually empty terraces, and livestock somehow survives on a thin furze of thornbush. The remaining population occupies five villages facing Kárpathos, leaving most of the island uninhabited and uncultivated. Until the millennium, there was little sign here of the wealth brought into other islands by diaspora Greeks or – since Kássos hasn't much to offer them – tourists; amidst the occasional new concrete monster, crumbling houses and disused farmland poignantly recall better days. A long pattern of serving as roving pilots, or residence in Egypt (Kassiots were instrumental in digging the Suez Canal), has been eclipsed by subsequent **emigration to the US**. Thus American-logo T-shirts and baseball caps are *de rigueur* summer fashion, and the conversation of vacationing expatriates is spiked with Americanisms.

Kássos can be tricky to reach, despite the 2002 completion of a proper jetty at Frý (pronounced "free"); in extreme wind conditions, ferries may still not be able to dock. In such cases, you disembark at Kárpathos and fly the remaining distance in a dual-prop, 38-seater aircraft. The air ticket plus a taxi fare to Kárpathos airport isn't much more than the fare charged by Finíki (Kárpathos)-based excursion boats which can manoeuvre into Boúka in most weathers. The airport lies 1km west of Frý, an easy enough walk, otherwise a cheap ride in one of the island's three taxis. Except during summer, when a single scooter/quad rental outfit operates, a Mercedes van provides a regular bus service and boat excursions are offered, the only way of exploring the island's remoter corners is by hiking along fairly arduous, shadeless paths and roads. Place-name signposting tends to be in Greek only, and in Kassiot dialect at that – the islanders clearly aren't expecting many non-Kassiot visitors.

Frý and Emboriós

Most of the appeal of the capital, **FRÝ**, is confined to the immediate environs of the wedge-shaped fishing port of **Boúka**, protected from the sea by two crab-claws of breakwater and overlooked by the cathedral of Áyios Spyrídhon. Inland, Frý is engagingly unpretentious, even down-at-heel in spots; there are no concessions to tourism, though some attempts are now being made to prettify a little town that's quite desolate out of season. Among **accommodation**, there's just one surviving, overpriced seafront hotel, the *Anagenissis* (☎22450 41495, ⓦwww.kassos-island.gr; ❸), run by the eponymous travel agency just below (though Olympic Airways has its own premises two doors down). Better-value, quieter lodgings include the basic, seaside *Flisvos* (☎22450 41430 or 22450 41284; ❷), 150m east of the new harbour, with a shared kitchen, or the *Captain's House* (☎22450 42716, ⓔhpetros@otenet.gr; ❹), galleried trad-style studios above Kassian Travel, near the police station. There's no full-service **bank**, but there are two stand-alone **ATMs**, plus an eight-terminal **Internet** café by the police station.

Outside of peak season, Frý supports only one full-service **taverna**: *O Mylos*, overlooking the intermittent harbour works. Luckily it's excellent and reasonable, with a variety of daily-special *mayireftá* at lunch and sometimes fish grills by night. From late June to early September at least one taverna, perched above Boúka, will function, or head for the suburb of Emboriós, fifteen minute's walk east, where *Taverna Emborios* (May–Sept) usually matches *O Mylos* in quality (though exceeds it in price). Failing this, shops in Frý are fairly well stocked for self-catering. Several **bar-kafenía-ouzerí** perched above Boúka – *Zantana* and *To Apangio* being the most durable – are the focus for such nightlife as there is.

Local beaches

Frý's town **beach**, if you can call it that, is at **Ammouá** (Ammoudhiá), a thirty-minute walk beyond the airstrip along the coastal track. This sandy cove, just before the landmark chapel of Áyios Konstandínos, is often caked with seaweed and tar, but persevere five minutes more and you'll find much cleaner pea-gravel coves. The determined can swim off the little patch of sand at **Emboriós**, along with the resident ducks, and there's a more private pebble stretch off to the right. But having got this far, you may as well continue ten to fifteen minutes along the shore, first along an old track, then on a path past the last house, for a final scramble to the base of the **Pouthená** ravine, where there's another secluded pebble cove. Otherwise, it's worth patronizing high-season boat excursions to far better beaches on a pair of islets visible to the northwest, **Armathiá** and **Makrá**.

The villages and Áyios Mámas

At the edges of the agricultural plain just inland from Frý cluster a number of villages, linked to each other by road; all are worth a passing visit, and can be toured on foot in a single day.

Larger in extent and more rural than Frý, **AYÍA MARÍNA**, 1500m inland and uphill, is most attractive seen from the south, arrayed above olive groves; one of its two belfried churches is the focus of the island's liveliest festival, on July 16–17. Some fifteen minutes beyond the hamlet of Kathístres, a further 500m southwest, the cave of **Ellinokamára** is named for the late Classical, polygonal wall completely blocking the entrance; its ancient function is uncertain, perhaps a cult shrine or tomb complex. To reach it, turn south at the two restored windmills in Ayía Marína, then right (west) at the phone-box junction; carry on, straight and down (not level and left) until you see a red-dirt path going up the hillside to a crude, stone-built pastoral hut. Some modern masonry walls enclose the start of this path, but once at the hut (the cave is more or less underneath it) you're compelled to hop a fence to visit – there are no gates. From Ellinokamára another, fainter path – you'll probably need a guide, or at least detailed directions – continues for ninety minutes in the same direction to the larger, more natural cave of **Seláï**, with impressive stalactites in the rear chamber.

Generally, walking opportunities on Kássos are poor – trails are few, unmarked and in poor condition, with no shade and few reliable water sources. An exception is the forty-minute path from Arvanitohóri to Póli, which is clearly walled in and enjoyable, shortcutting the road effectively – it starts at the base of the village, where two trees occupy planter-wells. **PÓLI**, somewhat impoverished and resolutely agricultural, is the site of a badly deteriorated ancient and medieval acropolis – a few stretches of fortification remain – and marks the start of a four-kilometre paved-road system leading southeast to **Áyios Mámas**, signposted in dialect as "**Áï Mámas**", one of two important rural monasteries, perched spectacularly overlooking the sea. Alternatively, from Póli you can descend – again on walled-in path for the first twenty minutes, then dirt track – to **PANAYÍA**, famous for its now-neglected mansions (many of Kássos's wealthiest ship captains hailed from here) and for the oldest surviving church on the island, the eighteenth-century **Panayía tou Yióryi**.

Áyios Yeóryios Hadhión and Hélatros

Between Ayía Marína and Arvanitohóri, another road veers off southwest towards the rural monastery of **Áyios Yeóryios Hadhión**. The pleasure of walking this route, however, has been pretty well negated by its having been paved, so you'll want to hire a taxi, rent a scooter if available or hitch a lift in at least one direction. The start of the route skirts the narrows of a fearsome gorge, and from there on you are unlikely to see another living thing aside from goats, sheep or an occasional Eleonora's falcon. Soon the Mediterranean appears to the south, a dull expanse ruffled only by the occasional ship bound for Cyprus and the Middle East. When you finally reach a fork, adopt the upper, right-hand turning, following phone lines towards Áyios Yeóryios Hadhión (signed as "**Áï Yeóryi**"), 12km from Frý. This is busiest at its late-April festival time; there's also cistern water if you need to fill canteens.

From the monastery it's another 2.5km on a paved road to **Hélatros** ("Hélathros" on older maps), a lonely cove at the mouth of one of the larger, more forbidding Kassiot canyons. Only the right-hand 80m of this sand-and-pea-gravel beach is really usable, but the water is pristine and – except for the occasional fishing boat or yacht – you'll probably be alone. The lower, left-hand option at the fork is the direct, dirt-surface track to Hélatros; this is only 700m shorter but perfectly passable to a scooter, and makes an interesting variation of the return to town.

Kárpathos

A long, narrow island between Rhodes and Crete, wild **Kárpathos** has always been an underpopulated backwater, although it's in fact the third largest of the Dodecanese. A habitually cloud-capped **mountainous spine** rises to over 1200m, dividing the more populous, lower-lying south from an exceptionally rugged north. A magnificent, windswept coastline of cliffs and promontories attracts significant numbers of Scandinavian and German package tourists, who pretty well monopolize several resorts in the southern part of the island, pushing independent travellers up to the remote north. Thanks in part to this clientele, Kárpathos' road system has improved no end since the millennium, but food prices (in the south especially) have been pushed to beyond-Rhodes levels, which offsets reasonable room rates. Most island-hoppers come here for a glimpse of the traditional village life in the far north, and for the numerous superb, secluded beaches lapped by proverbial crystalline water.

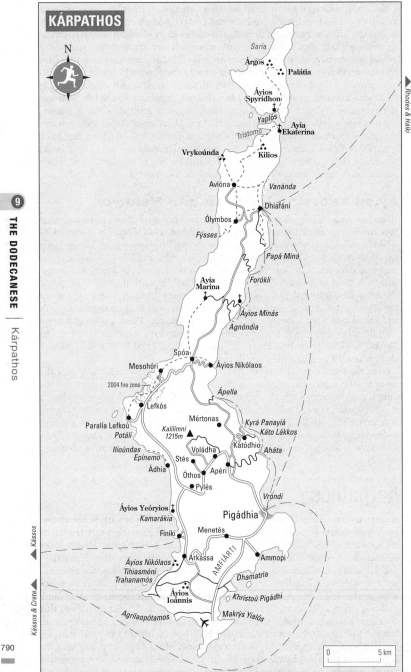

KÁRPATHOS

N

Saría

Árgos

Palátia

Áyios Spyrídhon

Yaplós

Ayía Ekaterína

Tristomo

Vrykoúnda

Kílios

Avlóna

Vanánda

Dhiafáni

Ólymbos

Fýsses

Papá Miná

Ayía Marína

Forókli

Áyios Minás

Agnóndia

Spóa

Mesohóri

Áyios Nikólaos

Ápella

2004 fire zone

Lefkós

Mértonas

Kyrá Panayiá
Káto Lákkos

Paralía Lefkoú
Potáli

Kalilímni
1215m

Katódhio

Aháta

Ilioúndas

Voládha

Epínemo

Stés

Apéri

Ádhia

Óthos

Pylés

Vróndi

Áyios Yeóryios
Kamarákia

Pigádhia

Finíki

Menetés

Ammopí

Áyios Nikólaos
Tihiasméni
Trahanamós

Arkássa

AMFIÁRTI

Dhamatría

Áyios Ioánnis

Khristoú Pigádhi

Agrilaopótamos

Makrýs Yialós

0   5 km

Rhodes & Háíki

Kássos

Kássos & Crete

Kárpathos' **interior** isn't always the most alluring: the central and northern uplands have been scorched by repeated forest fires since the 1980s, while agriculture plays a slighter role than on any other Greek island of this size. The Karpathians are too well off to bother much with farming; emigration to North America and the resulting remittance economy has transformed Kárpathos into one of the wealthiest parts of Greece.

Four local Classical **cities** figure little in ancient chronicles. Alone of the major Dodecanese, Kárpathos was held by the Genoese and Venetians after the Byzantine collapse and so has no castle of the crusading Knights of St John, nor any surviving medieval fortresses of note. The Ottomans couldn't be bothered to settle or even garrison it; instead they left a single judge or *kadi* at the main town, making the Greek population responsible for his safety during the many pirate attacks.

Pigádhia (Kárpathos Town)

The island capital of **PIGÁDHIA**, often known simply as Kárpathos, nestles at the south end of scenic **Vróndi Bay**, whose sickle of sand extends 3km northwest. The town itself, curling around the jetty and quay where ferries and excursion boats dock, is as drab as its setting is beautiful; an ever-increasing number of concrete blocks lend an air of a vast building site, making the Italian-era port police and county-government buildings heirlooms by comparison. Although there's nothing special to see, Pigádhia does offer almost every facility you might need, albeit with a definite package-tourism slant. The name of the main commercial street – Apodhímon Karpathíon (**"Karpathians Overseas"**) – speaks volumes about the pivotal role of emigrants and emigration here.

Information

Olympic Airways (book well in advance in summer – **planes** have just 38 seats) is on Platía 5-Oktovríou, corner Apodhímon Karpathíon, but has very restricted hours, so everyone buys tickets from Possi Travel (☎22450 22235) on the front. They're also principal agents for LANE, currently the only **shipping** line to serve Kárpathos. The **post office** is on Ethnikís Andístasis up from Platía 5-Oktovríou, while several **banks** have ATMs. Pigádhia's main **Internet** cafés are Café Galileo (all year), on Apodhímon Karpathíon, and Pot Pourri (summer only), diagonally across the square from Olympic; there's also a fairly useless **tourism information** bureau in a hexagonal booth on the west quay (June–Aug Mon–Fri 9am–2pm).

Accommodation

Most ferries are met by people offering **self-catering studios**, though they may be forbidden from touting on the quay itself. Unless you've arranged something in advance, you might consider such offers – the town is small enough that no location will be too inconvenient, though the best place to stay is on the hillside above the bus terminal and central car park. More luxurious places lie north, behind **Vróndi** beach to either side of the ruined fifth-century basilica of **Ayía Fotiní**, but tend to be occupied by package groups. Better hillside premises include *Amarillis Studios* (☎22450 22375, ⓔjohnvolada@in.gr; ❸), with enormous suite-sized, air-con units, and the helpful *Elias Rooms* (☎22450 22446 or 697 85 87 924, ⓦhttp://Eliasroooms.tripod.com; ❷; mid-May to Sept) just above the *Hotel Karpathos*, with variable, mostly en-suite rooms in a converted older house. Up an alley beyond Avis at the start of Vróndi, *Paradise Studios* (☎22450 22949, ⓦwww .paradisestudios.gr; ❸ room only) offers seven simple but practical, good-sized

For exploring the island as a passenger, regular **buses** serve Pylés, via Apéri, Voládha and Óthos, as well as Ammopí, Menetés, Arkássa, Finíki and (less frequently) Mesohóri via Paralía Lefkoú; the Pigádhia "station" is a car park at the western edge of town, a block past the post office. Set-rate, unmetered **taxis** have a terminal in the municipal car park two blocks inland from the fountain along Dhimokratías (table of current fares posted), and are affordable as long as you stay off what's left of the island's dirt-track network.

Upwards of ten outfits **rent cars**, though in season you may have to try every one to find an available vehicle, and rates are well over the norm. Reputable agencies include Circle (☏22450 22690) near the post office; Avis (☏22450 22702), at the north edge of town; Drive (☏22450 61249), 2km out behind Vróndi beach; Hertz, inside Possi Travel (☏22450 22235); and Trust, based in Ammopí, which will deliver and collect in Pigádhia (☏22450 81060). You can save €20 return in taxi transfers by car rental from/to the cheerless **airport** (17km distant, no snacks or diversions to hand) which must be arranged in advance with either Hertz or Avis. Moto Carpathos (☏22450 22382), 60m uphill from the town hall (*dhimarhío*), has the largest fleet of scooters for rent. Be warned that the only fuel on the island is to be found at two pairs of stations just to the north and south of town, and that tanks on smaller scooters are barely big enough to permit completing a circuit of the south, let alone head up north. In early 2006 the Spóa–Ólymbos road was finally paved, making hire of a jeep unnecessary except to access certain remote beaches.

Despite this infrastructure improvement, reaching **Northern Kárpathos by boat** is still very much on the agenda. One surviving excursion boat on the jetty, the *Chrisovalandou III*, offers all-in **day-tours** to Dhiafáni and Ólymbos for €15 maximum (pay on board); less well publicized is the fact that you can use this boat to travel **one-way** (1hr 20min journey time) between the north and the south in either direction – the standard rate is €6. Departures are typically 8.30am northbound, 4pm southbound. It's also worth knowing about the tiny **mail kaïki** *Chrisovalandou I*, which reverses this pattern: southbound from Dhiafáni on Mon, Wed and Fri at 7.30am, northbound from Pigádhia on Mon, Wed and Sun at 3pm (one-way fare again €6). Various agents also offer trips to Kássos and to isolated east-coast beaches without facilities (bring lunch if not included).

air-con studios in a quiet, aesthetic orchard setting. The only relatively comfortable hotel that caters in any way to nonpackage guests is the helpful *Atlantis*, opposite the Italian "palace" (☏22450 22777, Ⓔhtatlantis@yahoo.com; B&B; ❹).

Eating, drinking and nightlife

Many of Pigádhia's waterfront **tavernas**, where tacky photo-menus and defrosted *yíros* and chips reign supreme, are undistinguished and overpriced; quality and value improve significantly as you head east towards the ferry dock. Near the end of the strip are two worthy choices: characterful *Anna*, good for non-farmed fish with heaping salads, and the best all-rounder, *Iy Orea Karpathos*, with palatable local bulk wine, *trahanádhes* soup, spicy sausages, marinated artichokes and great spinach pie – you can, as the locals do, use it as an ouzerí and just order *mezédhes*. One block inland, the clear winner is *To Ellinikon*, a *mezedhopolío* that caters all year round to a local clientele with hot and cold *orektiká*, meat and good desserts. If *yíros* and chips it must be, then by far the best place for the fresh kind, own-sourced, is *Ovelistirio tis Erasmías*, inland on Dhimokratías opposite the taxi rank. Trendy, musical **café-bars** such as *Enigma* offer taped sounds from perches overlooking the bay, while *Oxygen* and *Amnesia* are the two most durable indoor midnight-to-dawn **dance clubs**.

Southern and western Kárpathos

The southern extremity of Kárpathos, towards the airport, is extraordinarily desolate and windswept. There are a few relatively undeveloped sandy beaches along the southeast coast in the region known as **Amfiárti**, but many are only really attractive to foreign windsurfers who come to take advantage of the prevailing northwesterlies. The most established surf school here is Pro Center Kárpathos (T 22450 91063 or 697 78 86 289, W www.windsurfen-karpathos .com), which as the web address suggests caters mostly to Germanophones, though all are welcome. They have the advantage of three separate bays near the airport, catering to different ability levels. The most comfortable hotel in the region, though sometimes full with surf packages, is the *Poseidon* (T 22450 91066, W www.hotel-poseidon.gr; B&B; ❸) above sheltered **Dhamatría** beach, also with a full-service taverna open to all.

Most people go no further than **AMMOPÍ** (sometimes transliterated as "Amoopi"), just 7km south of Pigádhia. This, together with development at Arkássa and Paralía Lefkoú, is the closest thing on Kárpathos to a purpose-built beach resort. Three sand-and-gravel, tree- or cliff-fringed coves are bordered by half a dozen tavernas and numbers of **hotels** and **studios**. Quietest of these are the highly recommended, well-designed ⳡ *Vardes Studios* (T 22450 81111 or 697 21 52 901, W www.hotelvardes.com; ❸), with distant sea views and orchard setting. Of the **tavernas**, far and away the best is ⳡ *Esperida* about halfway along the approach road, with such delicacies as local cheese, wine and sausage, roast eggplant, and pickled wild vegetables.

West out of Pigádhia the road climbs steeply 9km up to **MENETÉS**, draped in the lee of a ridge, with some handsome old houses and a spectacularly sited – if hideous – church. The best local **taverna**, east beyond the World War II resistance monument memorial, is ⳡ *Pelayía* in Kritháres district, offering local marinated "sardines" (really a larger fish, *ménoula*) cheese and wild greens; it's open all year, with live music some nights.

Arkássa, Finíki and Ádhia

Beyond Menetés, you descend to **ARKÁSSA**, on the slopes of a ravine draining to the west coast, with excellent views to Kássos en route. A few hundred metres south of where the ravine meets the sea, a signposted cement side-road leads briefly to the whitewashed chapel of **Ayía Sofía**, marooned amidst Classical and Byzantine Arkessia. Its visible remains consist of several mosaic floors with geometric patterns, the best one being inside a vaulted cistern at one corner of the area. The Paleókastro headland beyond was the site of Mycenaean Arkessia; the walk up is again signposted, but scarcely worth it for the sake of a few stretches of polygonal wall and a couple of tumbled columns.

Despite just one good nearby beach, Arkássa has been heavily developed, with hotels and restaurants sprouting along the rocky coastline. Much **accommodation** (and mediocre village-centre tavernas) are aimed squarely at the package market, but independent travellers could try various facilities inland from **Áyios Nikólaos** beach signposted just south, a 100-metre stretch of sand – rare hereabouts. These include the *Montemar Studios* (T 22450 61394; ❹), almost one-bedroom apartments; and – right behind the beach – the *Glaros* (T 22450 61015, F 22450 61016; ❹), five studios and an attached taverna run by a Karpathian-American from Virginia.

The tiny fishing port of **FINÍKI**, just 2km north, offers a minuscule beach, seasonal excursions to Kássos, several tavernas and a few rooms/studios establishments. For value and comfort, top **accommodation** is the well-designed and -built *Arhontiko Studios* up on the main bypass road (☎22450 61473, ℱ22450 61054; ❸). Skip the port **tavernas** here in favour of well-loved 🍴 *Under the Trees* (*Kostas*), 1km north under two tamarisks at Áyios Yeóryios monastery above reefy **Kamarákia** beach; it's open all day until two hours after sunset, offering such delights as expertly grilled swordfish, mountainous salads and chips made from home-grown courgettes.

Some 7km north of Finíki along the coast road, Karpathian forest resumes at **ÁDHIA** hamlet, giving rise to the name of the *Pine Tree Restaurant*, which has home-baked bread, lentil soup and octopus *makaronádha* washed down by sweet Óthos wine. There are also six **rooms** and **studios** (plus a basic, free **campsite**) off to one side, overlooking the orchard and the sea (☎697 73 69 948, ℮pinetree_adia@hotmail.com; ❷). Ádhia is becoming something of a **walkers' mecca**: easy paths lead twenty minutes west to tiny **Epínemo** beach (and 10min further to larger **Ilioúndas**), whilst a meatier, three-hour (one-way) route up Mt Kalí Límni starts from the main-road bridge.

Paralía Lefkoú and Mesohóri

Dense forest continues much of the way to the turning for the attractive resort of **PARALÍA LEFKOÚ**, shore annexe of the inland hamlet of Lefkós. Unless you **rent a car** locally – there are two agencies here now, Lefkos (☎22450 71057) and Drive (☎22450 71415) – it's not a particularly convenient touring base. But this is a delightful place for flopping on the beach, graced by a striking topography of cliffs, hills, islets and sandspits surrounding a triple bay. There are over two dozen places to stay, and perhaps half as many tavernas, but package companies tend to monopolize the better **accommodation** from June to September. About the only exception is the spartan but en-suite *Sunweek Studios* (☎22450 71025; ❷), on the seaward promontory. You'll have better luck at **Potáli**, the stonier, fourth bay just south of the access road; here go for the excellent, quiet and spacious *Akroyiali Studios* (☎22450 71263, ℱ22450 71178; ❸), with balconies overlooking the beach, or the smaller *Lefkosia Studios* close to the road (☎22450 71176 or 22450 71148; ❸). **Tavernas** at the main resort can severely disappoint: best options are *Mihalis* at the base of the point, with lots of vegetarian platters, or the kindly *Blue Sea* with its pizzas, meat-rich *mayireftá* and pancake breakfasts.

Back on the main road, you climb northeast through severely fire-damaged pine forest to **MESOHÓRI**. The village tumbles down towards the sea around narrow, stepped alleys, coming to an abrupt halt at the edge of a flat-topped bluff dotted with three tiny, ancient chapels and separated from the village proper by a vast oasis of orchards. These are nurtured by the fountain (best water on the island) underneath the church of **Panayía Vryssianí**, wedged against the mountainside just east and invisible from the end of the access road. On the stair-street leading to this church is an excellent taverna, the *Dhramoundana*, remarkably reasonably priced for Kárpathos, and featuring local capers, sausages and the local marinated "sardines". The paved main road continues over the island's watershed to Spóa, overlooking the east coast.

Central Kárpathos

The **centre** of Kárpathos supports a group of villages blessed with superb hillside settings, ample running water – and a cool climate, even in August. Nearly everyone here has "done time" in North America, then returned home with their nest eggs. New Jersey, New York and Canadian car plates tell you exactly where repatriated islanders struck it rich – often fabulously so (the area has the highest per capita income in Greece). West-facing **PYLÉS** is the most attractive, set above another spring-fed oasis, while **ÓTHOS**, noted for its sweet, tawny-amber wine, is the highest (approx 400m) and chilliest, on the flanks of 1215-metre Mount Kalilímni. On the east side of the ridge you find **VOLÁDHA** with its tiny Venetian citadel and a trio of nocturnal tavernas. From the smart track-and-footie stadium below **APÉRI**, the largest, lowest and wealthiest settlement, you can drive 5km along a dirt road to the dramatic pebble beach of **Aháta**, with a spring and reasonable taverna.

Beyond Apéri, the road up the **east coast** passes above beaches often visited by boat trips from Pigádhia. A paved but twisty side road via Katódhio hamlet leads first to a further turning (2km of rough dirt track) to **Káto Lákkos**, 150m of scenic sand and gravel favoured by naturists, and then after 4km on the main pavement to **Kyrá Panayiá**. Here there's a surprising number of villas and rooms in the ravine behind 150m of fine gravel and sheltered, turquoise water; the beach taverna is, alas, mediocre. **Ápella** is the best of the beaches you can reach by road, though there's a final short path from the single, good-value taverna-rooms (the only facility) at the road's end to the scenic 300-metre gravel strand. The end of this route is **SPÓA**, high above the shore just east of the island's spine, with a **snack-bar** and more reliably open *kafenío* at the edge of the village, which might make better meal stops than the overpriced *Votsalo* down at **Áyios Nikólaos**, 5km below, a small port with an average beach.

Northern Kárpathos

Although it's now far easier to reach **northern Kárpathos** from Spóa, sea transport will remain an attractive choice for the immediate future, as there's still no bus service and taxi fares are exorbitant. Inter-island ferries call at Dhiafáni three times a week in season, or passengers can use the above-cited smaller daily *kaïkia* from Pigádhia. The journey time on the excursion boats can be ninety minutes in rough sea, with arrivals met at Dhiafáni eight-kilometre bus transfer up to the traditional village of **Ólymbos**, the main attraction in this

△ Hiking near Ólymbos, northern Kárpathos

part of the island, along with good walking opportunities. The paving of the entire road in from Spóa will, however, pull the rug out from under the day-trip industry, and should encourage a more thoughtful type of tourism than the present commercialized circus. If you can't tear yourself away from the sea, coastal **Dhiafáni** makes a better base, with excellent **beaches** within walking distance to either side.

Ólymbos and hiking

Originally founded as a pirate-safe refuge during Byzantine times, windswept **ÓLYMBOS** straddles a long ridge below slopes studded with mostly ruined windmills. Two restored ones, beyond the main church, grind wheat and barley during late summer only, though one is kept under sail during any tourist season. The village has long attracted foreign and Greek ethnologists, who treat it as a living museum of peasant dress, crafts, dialect and music long since vanished elsewhere in Greece. It's still a very picturesque place, yet traditions are vanishing by the year. Nowadays it's only the older women and those working in the several tourist shops who wear the striking and magnificently colourful traditional dress – an instant photo opportunity in exchange for persistent sales pitches for trinkets mostly imported from China or Bulgaria.

You'll quickly notice the prominent role that the women play in daily life: tending gardens, carrying goods on their shoulders or herding goats. Nearly all Ólymbos men emigrate to Baltimore or work outside the village, sending money home and returning only on holidays. The long-isolated villagers also speak a unique dialect, said to maintain traces of its Doric and Phrygian origins – thus "Ólymbos" is pronounced "Élymbos" locally. Live vernacular music is still heard regularly and draws crowds of visitors at **festival** times, in particular Easter and August 15, when you've little hope of finding a bed.

From the village, the superb west-coast beach at **Fýsses** is a sharp 35-minute drop below, first cross-country, later by path. Most **local hikes**, however, head more gently north or east, many of them on waymarked paths, though you'll have to stay overnight in the area to enjoy them. The easiest option is the ninety-minute walk back down to Dhiafáni, beginning just below the two working windmills. The way is well marked, with water en route. It eventually drops to a ravine amidst extensive forest, though the last half-hour is mostly over bulldozed riverbed. You could also tackle the trail north to the ruins and beach at **Vrykoúnda** ("Vrougoúnda" in dialect), via sparsely inhabited **AVLÓNA**, set on a high upland devoted to grain. From Ólymbos, it's just under three hours' walk one way to Vrykoúnda, which offers traces of Hellenistic/Roman Brykous, the remote cave-shrine of John the Baptist on the promontory and good swimming. **Trístomo**, a Byzantine anchorage in the far northeast of Kárpathos, can also be reached on a magnificent cobbled way beginning above Avlóna (2hr 30min); until the direct Trístomo–Vanánda path is rehabilitated, the return is by the same way. There's also a fine ninety-minute marked path from Avlóna down to Vanánda beach (see opposite).

Among places to **stay** in Ólymbos the friendly *Rooms Restaurant Olymbos* (T 22450 51252 or 22450 51009; ❷), near the village entrance, has rooms with baths or unplumbed ones with traditional furnishings, while the *Café-Restaurant Zefiros*, near the centre and run by two young sisters, manages the eight-room, en-suite *Hotel Astro* (T 22450 51421; B&B; ❸), with breakfast given in the **restaurant**, much the best thing going along with the *Olymbos*. The father of the *Rooms Restaurant Olymbos* management has opened an annexe at Ávlona, *Restaurant Avlona*, on the through road, with four en-suite rooms (T 22450 51046; ❶) in the hamlet centre, an ideal base for committed walkers.

Dhiafáni and beaches

Rooms in **DHIAFÁNI** are inexpensive, and the pace of life slow outside of July and August. Seaonal boat trips are offered to remoter local **beaches**, as well as to the uninhabited islet of **Saría** (most reliably Thur, 10am out, 4.30pm back; €24 with lunch), with passengers hiking the trans-island path to the Byzantine site of Palátia, where a barbeque and opportunity for a swim are provided before the return trip. Among several coves within walking distance, closest is **Vanánda**, a stony beach with an eccentrically managed campsite snack-bar in the oasis behind. To get there, follow the pleasant sign-posted path north through the pines, but don't believe the signs that say "ten minutes" – it's over thirty minutes away, shortcutting the more recent road. **Papá Miná**, with a few trees and cliff-shade, lies an hour's walk distant via the cairned trail taking off from the road to the ferry dock. An ordinary car can just drive the 4.5km there – a jeep's better, with the last 300m on foot in either case; with a jeep you can also confidently reach three other superb beaches below the Spóa–Ólymbos road; the closest, also with path access from Ólymbos, is 250-metre long **Forókli** (clothing optional). Some 7km further towards Spóa, there's the turning for the even worse track down to **Áyios Minás** (seasonal taverna; bear left at fork partway along) or **Agnóndia** (bear right), equally pristine.

Dhiafáni has abundant sleeping and eating opportunities, though the most obvious, aggresively touting ones at mid-quay are well worth avoiding. There's also a small travel agency where you buy ferry tickets and can change money if the stand-alone **ATM** by the waterfront fountain is non-functional. In terms of **accommodation**, top of the heap in all senses is hospitable George and Anna Niotis' ✗ Hotel Studios Glaros (☎22450 51501 or 694 79 44 601, ⓦwww.hotel-glaros.gr; ❸) up the south slope, with some of its sixteen huge, tiered units sleeping four. Worthy alternatives, 300m along the road west more or less opposite each other, are the pleasant, ground-floor *Dolphins/Dhelfinia Studios* (☎22450 51354; ❶) under the eponymous restaurant, or the *Hotel Nikos* (☎22450 51410, ⓔorfanos-hotel@hol.gr; ❸). As for **tavernas**, *Dolphins/Dhelfinia* does good fish, and vegetables from the garden just below, while vine-shrouded *Iy Anixi* in a backstreet behind the water offers a few inexpensive, homestyle *mayireftá* daily. Behind the fountain, favourite meeting places are Italian-run ✗ *Iy Gorgona/L'Angolo*, featuring light dishes, wonderful ownmade desserts, proper coffees, and *limoncello* digestif, and ✗ *Koral* (*Mihalis & Popi's*) across the lane, which serves good grills and salads, Cretan *tsikoudhiá* and doubles as the most atmospheric **nightspot**.

Rhodes (Ródhos)

It's no accident that **Rhodes** is among the most visited of the Greek islands. Not only is its southeast coast lined with numerous sandy beaches, but the capital's nucleus is a beautiful and remarkably preserved medieval city, the legacy of the crusading Knights of St John who used the island as their main base from 1309 until 1522. Unfortunately this showpiece is jammed to capacity with over a million tourists in a good season, as against about 110,000 permanent inhabitants (including many foreigners). Of transient visitors, Germans, Brits, Swedes, Italians and Danes predominate, though they tend to arrive in different months of the year.

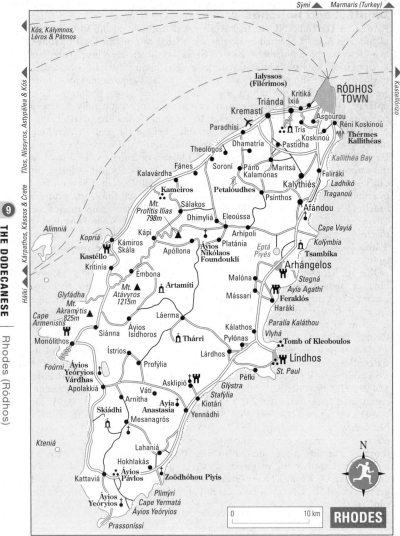

Ialyssos
(Filérimos)
Kritiká
Ixiá
RÓDHOS
TOWN
Triánda
Kremastí
Asgoúrou
Réni Koskinoú
Paradhísi
Tris
Thérmes
Koskinoú
Kallithéas
Dhamatriá
Pastídha
Theológós
Kallithéa Bay
Fánes   Soroní   Páno   Maritsá
Kalavárdha
Kalamónas
Faliráki
Kameiros   Petaloúdhes   Kalythiés   Ladhikó
Psinthos
Traganoú
Mt.   Sálakos
Profítis Ilías   Afándou
798m   Dhimyliá   Eleoússa
Cape Vayiá
Kopriá   Kápi   Arhípoli
Kámiros   Apóllona   Platánia   Eptá   Kolýmbia
Kastéllo   Skála   Áyios   Piyés   Tsambíka
Kritinía   Nikólaos
Foundouklí   Arhángelos
Émbona
Malóna   Stegná
Artamíti   Áyia Agathí
Mt.   Mássari   Feraklós
Atávyros   Haráki
1215m   Láerma
Glyfádha
Mt.   Kálathos   Paralía Kaláthou
Akramýtis   Áyios   Pylónas   Vlyhá
825m   Siánna   Isídhoros   Tómb of Kleoboulos
Cape
Armenistís   Ístrios   Thárri
Monólithos   Lárdhos
Profýlia   Líndhos
Foúrni   Áyios   St. Paul
Yeóryios   Péfki
Várdhas   Asklipió
Apolakkiá   Glýstra
Váti   Stafýlia
Arnítha   Áyia   Kiotári
Skiádhi   Anastasía   Yennádhi
Mesanagrós
Kteniá   Lahaniá
Hokhlakás
Áyios
Kattaviá   Pávlos   Zoödhóhou Piyís
Áyios   Plimýri
Yeóryios   Cape Yermatá
Áyios Yeóryios
Prassoníssi

N

0   10 km   RHODES

Ródhos Town's medieval Old Town is very much the main event, but the
rest of this sizeable island also repays exploration. **Líndhos**, with its ancient
acropolis and (occasionally) atmospheric village, ranks second place on most
people's lists. The southeastern beaches – particularly near **Afándou** and
Yennádhi – and isolated monuments of the interior, such as castles near
Monólithos and **Kritinía**, and frescoed churches at **Thárri** and **Asklipió**,
are also worth pointing a car towards. Adrenalin junkies will (literally) want to
go to extremes at the far south cape, **Prassoníssi**, one of the best windsurfing
venues in Europe.

Some history

Blessed with an equable climate and strategic position, Rhodes was important from earliest times despite a lack of good harbours. The best natural port engendered the ancient town of Lindos which, together with the other city-states Kameiros and Ialyssos, united in 408 BC to found the new capital of **Rodos** (Rhodes) at the windswept northern tip of the island. At various moments the cities allied themselves with Alexander, the Persians, Athenians or Spartans as prevailing conditions suited them, generally escaping retribution for backing the wrong side by a combination of seafaring audacity, sycophancy and burgeoning wealth as a trade centre. Following the failed siege of Demetrios Polyorketes in 305 BC, Rhodes prospered even more, displacing Athens as the major venue for rhetoric and the arts in the east Mediterranean.

Decline set in when Rhodes became involved in the Roman civil wars, and Cassius sacked the island; by late imperial times, it was a backwater, a status confirmed by numerous barbarian raids during the Byzantine period. The Byzantines were compelled to cede Rhodes to the Genoese, who in turn surrendered it to the Knights of St John. The second great siege of Rhodes, during 1522–23, saw Ottoman Sultan Süleyman the Magnificent oust the stubborn knights, who retreated to Malta; Rhodes once again lapsed into relative obscurity, though heavily colonized and garrisoned, until its seizure by the Italians in 1912.

Arrival and information

All international and inter-island **ferries** and the *Dodekanisos Express/ Dodekanisos Pride* **catamarans** dock at the middle of Rhodes' three ports, the commercial harbour of **Kolóna**; the only exceptions are local **boats** to and from Sými, all excursion craft, the small *Sea Star* catamaran and the **hydrofoils**, which use the yacht harbour of **Mandhráki**. Its entrance was supposedly once straddled by the Colossus, an ancient statue of Apollo built to celebrate the end of the 305 BC siege; today two columns surmounted by bronze deer are less overpowering replacements.

The **airport** lies 14km southwest of town, by the village of Paradhísi; public buses returning from Paradhísi, Kalavárdha, Theológos or Sálakos pass the stop (look for the perspex-and-wood kiosk) on the main road opposite the northerly car-park entrance fairly frequently between 6am and 11.30pm (fare €1.70). A taxi into town will cost €14–23, plus bags and airport supplement, depending on the time of day. **Buses** for both the west and east coasts of Rhodes – sleek air-con turquoise-and-blue models displacing the old orange-and-white ones – leave from two almost adjacent terminals on Papágou and Avérof, just outside the Italian-built **New Market** (a tourist trap, to miss without regret except for the wonderful rotunda of the old fish market inside). Between the lower eastern station and the **taxi** rank at Platía Rimínis there's a **municipal tourist office** (June–Sept Mon–Sat 8am–9.30pm, Sun 9am–3pm), while some way up Papágou on the corner of Makaríou stands the **EOT office** (Mon–Fri 8.30am–3pm); both dispense bus and ferry schedules, the latter also providing a list of standard taxi fares, complete with complaint form. Rhodes taxi drivers have a deservedly poor reputation – overcharging of new arrivals is routine, as is refusing to take you to your chosen hotel, while steering you to inconvenient accommodation that gives them kickbacks.

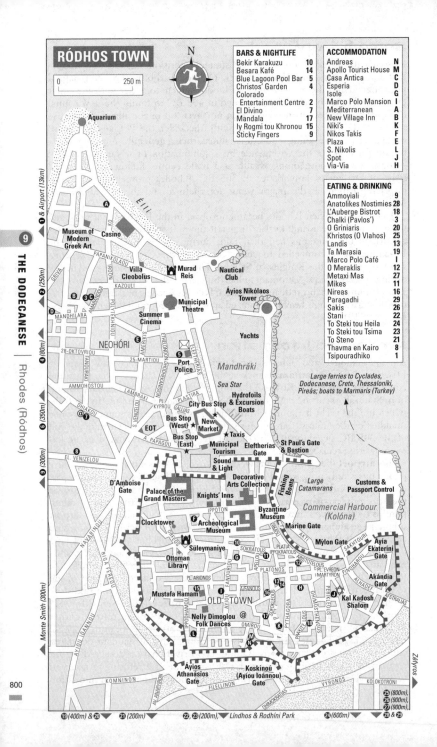

RÓDHOS TOWN

N

0   250 m

BARS & NIGHTLIFE

Bekir Karakuzu	10
Besara Kafé	14
Blue Lagoon Pool Bar	5
Christos' Garden	4
Colorado Entertainment Centre	2
El Divino	7
Mandala	17
Iy Rogmi tou Khronou	15
Sticky Fingers	9

ACCOMMODATION

Andreas	N
Apollo Tourist House	M
Casa Antica	C
Esperia	D
Isole	G
Marco Polo Mansion	I
Mediterranean	A
New Village Inn	B
Niki's	K
Nikos Takis	F
Plaza	E
S. Nikolis	L
Spot	J
Via-Via	H

EATING & DRINKING

Ammoyiali	9
Anatolikes Nostimies	28
L'Auberge Bistrot	18
Chalki (Pavlos')	3
O Griniaris	20
Khristos (O Vlahos)	25
Landis	13
Ta Marasia	19
Marco Polo Café	I
O Meraklis	12
Metaxi Mas	27
Mikes	11
Nireas	16
Paragadhi	29
Sakis	26
Stani	22
To Steki tou Heila	24
To Steki tou Tsima	23
To Steno	21
Thavma en Kairo	8
Tsipouradhiko	1

Aquarium

Museum of Modern Greek Art

Casino

Villa Cleobolus

Murad Reis

Nautical Club

Áyios Nikólaos Tower

Municipal Theatre

Summer Cinema

NEOHÓRI

Yachts

Mandhráki

Port Police

Sea Star

Hydrofoils & Excursion Boats

EOT

City Bus Stop

Bus Stop (West)

New Market

Taxis

Bus Stop (East)

Municipal Tourism

Eleftherias Gate

St Paul's Gate & Bastion

Sound & Light

D'Amboise Gate

Decorative Arts Collection

Large Catamarans

Customs & Passport Control

Palace of the Grand Masters

Knights' Inns

Byzantine Museum

Commercial Harbour (Kolóna)

Clocktower

Archeological Museum

Marine Gate

Süleymaniye

Ottoman Library

Mýlon Gate

Áyia Ekaterini Gate

Mustafa Hamam

OLD TOWN

Akándia Gate

Nelly Dimoglou Folk Dances

Kal Kadosh Shalom

Áyios Athanásios Gate

Koskinoú (Ayíou Ioánnou) Gate

Large ferries to Cyclades, Dodecanese, Crete, Thessaloníki, Pireás; boats to Marmaris (Turkey)

Monte Smith (300m)

Zéfyros

⑲ (400m) & ⑳   ㉑ (200m)   ㉒, ㉓ (200m), Líndhos & Rodhíni Park   ㉔ (600m)   ㉘ & ㉙

㉕ (800m), ㉖ (900m), ㉗ (900m),

Airport (13km)   (250m)   (80m)   (350m)   (300m)

Ródhos Town

Ancient Rodos, which lies underneath nearly all of the modern city, was laid out by Hippodamos of Miletos in the grid layout much in vogue at the time, with planned residential and commercial quarters. Its perimeter walls totalled almost 15km, enclosing nearly double the area of the present town, and the Hellenistic population was said to exceed 100,000 – a staggering figure for late antiquity, as against 50,631 at the 2001 census.

The contemporary town divides into two unequal parts: the compact **old walled city**, and the **New Town**, which sprawls around it in three directions. The latter dates from the Ottoman occupation, when Greek Orthodox residents – forbidden to dwell in the old city – founded several suburb villages or *marásia* in the environs, which have since merged. Commercialization is predictably rampant in the walled town, and in the modern district of Neohóri ("Niohóri" in dialect), west of Mandhráki yacht harbour; the few buildings that aren't hotels are souvenir shops, car-rental or travel agencies and bars – easily seventy in every category.

Accommodation

Hotels and pensions at all price levels abound in the Old Town, mostly in the quad bounded by Omírou to the south, Sokrátous to the north, Perikléous to the east and Ippodhámou to the west. There are also a few possibilities worth considering in Neohóri, especially if you're off to the airport or a ferry at an early hour. During crowded seasons, or late at night, it's prudent to reserve well in advance – only the very lowest standard of unlicensed accommodation is touted by their desperate proprietors at the ferry and catamaran quays.

Old Town

Andreas Omírou 28D ☎22410 34156, @www.hotelandreas.com. Perennially popular (reservations mandatory) and under the dynamic management of Belgian-American Constance Rivemal, this is one of the more imaginative old-Turkish-mansion restoration-*pensions*, thoroughly refurbished in 2003–05. Rooms in a variety of formats (including family-size and a spectacular "penthouse") all have baths, though a few are across a corridor. Terrace bar with views for excellent breakfasts and evening drinks; two-night minimum stay, credit cards accepted, indeed vital for advance booking. Open all year. ❹–❻
Apollo Tourist House Omírou 28C ☎22410 32003, @www.apollo-touristhouse.com. Six unique, wood-trimmed, centrally heated, en-suite rooms emerged from a thorough overhaul of this old budget standby in 2004–05 by owner Umberto; the self-catering kitchen makes it good for longer stays. Open most of the year. ❸
Isole Evdhóxou 75 ☎22410 20682, @www.hotelisole.com. Simple but salubrious rooms with Hellenic-blue decor in a converted Ottoman house, run by a welcoming, multilingual Italian couple. Pleasant breakfast area at reception, superb roof terrace. Normally open March to mid-Nov, winter by appointment. B&B ❸ standard rooms, ❹ tower suite.

Marco Polo Mansion Ayíou Fanouríou 42 ☎ & ℗22410 25562, @www.marcopolomansion.web.com. Superb conversion of another old Turkish mansion, with a *hamam* on site; all rooms are en suite and exquisitely furnished with antiques from the nearby gallery of the same name, plus cotton pillows and handmade mattresses. Large buffet breakfasts are provided by Spyros and Efi in the garden snack-bar, open to all later in the day (see p.805). One-week minimum stay, reservations and credit-card deposit mandatory. B&B Rates room-dependent ❻–❼
Niki's Sofokléous 39 ☎22410 25115, @www.nikishotel.gr. Some rooms can be on the small side, but all are en suite, most have air con, and upper-storey ones have fine views (three with private balconies). There's a washing machine, two common terraces and very friendly, helpful management to round things off. Someone will wait up for late-night arrivals; credit cards accepted. ❸
Nikos Takis Panetíou 26 ☎22410 70773, @www.nikostakishotel.com. Miniature "fashion hotel" in a restored mansion with just four, somewhat gaudily coloured units (including painted ceilings); junior suites with just CD players are ❻, "honeymoon" suites offer fridge, DVD and TV at ❽. Pebble-mosaic courtyard, with fine views over town, for breakfast and drinks.

S. Nikolis Ippodhámou 61 ☎22410 34561, ⓦwww.s-nikolis.gr. A variety of restored premises in the west of the Old Town. Hotel/honeymoon suite rates (❼) include rooftop breakfast, TV and air con. The self-catering apartments (❺–❻) interconnect to accommodate groups or families. Booking essential, and accepted only with credit-card number. Open April–Nov.

Spot Perikléous 21 ☎ & Ⓕ22410 34737, ⓦwww.spothotelrhodes.com. This modern building has cheerfully painted en-suite rooms of varying formats with textiles on the walls, fridges and air con, representing excellent value (including unlimited buffet breakfast). Internet facilities, rear patio and free luggage storage. Open March–Nov. ❹

Via-Via Lysipoú 2, alley off Pythagóra ☎ & Ⓕ22410 77027, ⓦwww.hotel-via-via.com. Efficiently but congenially run hotel; most one- to four-person rooms are en suite but two share a bath, about half have air con. All are simply but tastefully furnished, with ongoing improvements. Self-catering kitchen, roof terrace for breakfast with an eyeful of the Ibrahim Pasha mosque opposite. Three grades of breakfast offered, from continental to full brunch. Open all year. ❹–❺

Neohóri

Casa Antica Amarándou 8 ☎22410 26206. Double and quad studios in a made-over 150-year-old house, with clean, white-tile decor, courtyard and roof terrace. Near some of the better Neohóri tavernas. ❹

Esperia Yeoryíou Gríva 7 ☎22410 23941, ⓦwww.esperia-hotels.gr. Well-priced, well-run B-class hotel in a quiet location overlooking a little plaza. Small-to-medium size, though salubrious and tasteful rooms with showers. Open all year. ❹

Mediterranean Kó 35 ☎22410 24661, ⓦwww.mediterranean.gr. Beachfront hotel in a superb location; though nominally A-class, it's less expensive than you'd think, especially if booked through the recommended travel agent (see p.808). The street-level snack-bar/café is very popular around the clock with nonresidents as well. ❻ standard, ❽ suites.

New Village Inn Konstandopédhos 10 ☎22410 34937, ⓦwww.newvillageinn.gr. Whitewashed, somewhat grotto-like en-suite rooms (only upper-floor units have balconies), arrayed around a courtyard breakfast-bar; friendly Greek and American management; singles available at a good rate. Open April–Oct. ❹

Plaza Ieroú Lóhou 7, Neohóri ☎22410 22501, ⓦwww.rhodes-plaza.gr. One of the best A-class hotel within Rhodes city limits, in the heart of Neohóri. Pool, sauna, jacuzzi, buffet English breakfast, heating/air con. Open all year; substantially discounted rates Nov–April. ❻

The Old Town

Simply to catalogue the principal monuments and attractions cannot do full justice to the infinitely rewarding **medieval city**. There's ample gratification to be derived from slipping through the eleven surviving gates and strolling the streets, under flying archways built for earthquake resistance, past the warm-toned sandstone and limestone walls painted ochre or blue, and over the *votsalotó* (pebble-mosaic) pavements.

Dominating the northernmost sector of the city's fourteenth-century fortifications is the **Palace of the Grand Masters** (summer Mon 12.30–7pm, Tues–Sun 8.30am–7pm; winter Mon 12.30–3pm, Tues–Sun 8.30am–3pm; €6, or joint €10 ticket includes all museums in this section). Largely destroyed by an ammunition depot explosion set off by lightning in 1856, it was reconstructed by the Italians as a summer home for Mussolini and Vittore Emmanuele III ("King of Italy and Albania, Emperor of Ethiopia"), neither of whom ever visited Rhodes. The exterior, based on medieval engravings and accounts, is passably authentic, but inside, free rein was given to Fascist delusions of grandeur: a marble staircase leads up to rooms paved with Hellenistic mosaics from Kós, and the ponderous period furnishings rival many a northern European palace. The ground floor is home to splendid galleries entitled **Rhodes from the 4th century until the Turkish Conquest** and **Ancient Rhodes, 2400 Years** (same hours and admission ticket), together the best museums in town. The medieval collection highlights the importance of Christian Rhodes as a trade centre, with exotic merchandise placing the island in a trans-Mediterranean context. The Knights are represented with a display on their sugar-refining industry and a gravestone

of a Grand Master; precious manuscripts and books precede a wing of
post-Byzantine icons, moved here
permanently from Panayía Kástrou
(see below). Across the courtyard in
the north wing, "Ancient Rhodes"
overshadows the official archeological museum by explaining the everyday life of the ancients, arranged
topically (beauty aids, toys, cookware, worship and so on); highlights
include a Hellenistic floor mosaic
of a comedic mask and a household
idol of Hecate, goddess of the occult.
On Tuesday and Saturday afternoons,
there's supplementary self-guiding
access of the **city walls** (one hour
starting at 2.45pm; separate €6
admission), beginning from a gate
next to the palace and finishing at
the Koskinoú gate.

△ Buttressed lanes, Rhodes Old Town

The heavily restored, Gothic **Street
of the Knights** (Odhós Ippotón)
leads due east from the Platía Kleo-
voúlou in front of the palace; the
"Inns" lining it housed the Knights of St John, according to linguistic and
ethnic affiliation, until the Ottoman Turks compelled them to leave for Malta
after a six-month siege in which the defenders were outnumbered thirty to one.
Today the Inns house various government offices, foreign consulates or cultural
institutions vaguely appropriate to their past, with occasional exhibitions, but
the whole effect of the Italians' renovation is predictably sterile and stagey
(indeed, nearby streets were used in the 1987 filming of *Pascali's Island*).

At the bottom of the hill, the Knights' Hospital has been refurbished as the
Archeological Museum (summer Tues–Sun 8am–7pm; winter Tues–Sun
8.30am–3pm; €3 or joint ticket), though the arches and echoing halls of the
building somewhat overshadow contents – largely painted pottery dating from
the ninth through the fifth centuries BC. Behind the second-storey sculpture
garden, the Hellenistic statue gallery is more accessible; in a rear corner stands
Aphrodite Adioumene or the so-called "Marine Venus", beloved of Lawrence
Durrell, but lent a rather sinister aspect by her sea-dissolved face – in contrast
to the friendlier *Aphrodite Bathing*. Virtually next door is the **Decorative
Arts Collection** (Tues–Sun 8.30am–3pm; €2 or joint ticket), gleaned from
old houses across the Dodecanese; the most compelling artefacts are carved
cupboard doors and chest lids painted in naïve style with mythological or
historical episodes.

Across the way stands the **Byzantine Museum** (Tues–Sun 8.30am–3pm; €2
or joint ticket), housed in the old cathedral of the Knights, who adapted the
Byzantine shrine of Panayía toú Kástrou for their own needs. Medieval icons
and frescoes lifted from crumbling chapels on Rhodes and Hálki, as well as
photos of art still *in situ*, constitute the exhibits. The highlight of the permanent
collection is a complete fresco cycle from the domes and squinches of Thárri
monastery (see p.813) dating from 1624, removed in 1967 to reveal much older
work beneath.

Turkish and Jewish Rhodes

If instead you head south from the Palace of the Grand Masters, it's hard to miss the most conspicuous Turkish monument in Rhodes, the rust-coloured **Süleymaniye Mosque**. Rebuilt in the nineteenth century on foundations three hundred years older, it's currently closed like many local Ottoman monuments, though scheduled to emerge soon from a lengthy refit in all its candy-striped glory. The Old Town is in fact well sown with mosques and *mescids* (the Islamic equivalent of a chapel), many of them converted from Byzantine churches after the 1522 conquest, when the Christians were expelled from the medieval precinct. A couple of these, such as the **Ibrahim Pasha Mosque** on Plátonos, are still used by the sizeable **Turkish-speaking minority** here, some descended from Muslims who fled Crete between 1898 and 1913. Their most enduring civic contributions are, opposite the Süleymaniye, the **Ottoman Library** (Mon–Sat 9.30am–4pm; tip to custodian), with a rich collection of early medieval manuscripts and Korans, and the imposing, still-functioning **Mustafa Hamam**, or Turkish bath, on Platía Aríonos up in the southwest corner of the medieval city (Mon–Fri 10am–5pm, Sat 8am–5pm, last admission 3.30pm; €1.50); bring everything you need – soap, shampoo, towel, loofa – to enjoy the separate men's and women's sections. Heading downhill from the Süleymaniye Mosque, you come to **Odhós Sokrátous**, since time immemorial the main commercial thoroughfare, and now the "Via Turista", packed with fur and jewellery stores pitched at cruise-ship tourists. Beyond the tiled central fountain in Platía Ippokrátous, Odhós Aristotélous leads into the **Platía tón Evréon Martýron** ("Square of the Jewish Martyrs"), named in memory of the large local community that was almost totally annihilated during the summer of 1944; a black granite column in the centre honours them. Of the four synagogues that once graced the nearby Jewish quarter, only the ornate, arcaded **Kal Kadosh Shalom** (daily 10am–5pm; donation) on Odhós Simíou, just to the south, survives. It's maintained essentially as another memorial to the approximately 2100 Jews of Rhodes and Kós sent from here to the concentration camps; plaques in French – the language of educated Ottoman Jews across the east Aegean – commemorate the dead. At the rear of the building, a one-room **museum**, set up by a Los Angeles attorney of Jewish Rhodian descent and scheduled to be expanded, features archival photos of the community's life on Rhodes and in its far-flung diaspora in the Americas and Africa.

Neohóri

The pointy bit of **Neohóri** is surrounded by a continuous **beach**, complete with deckchairs, parasols and showers, particularly on the more sheltered east-facing section called **Élli**. At the northernmost point of the island an **Aquarium** (daily: April–Sept 9am–8.30pm; Oct–March 9am–4.30pm; €3.50), officially the "Hydrobiological Institute", offers some diversion with its subterranean maze of seawater tanks. Upstairs is a less enthralling collection of half-rotten stuffed sharks, seals and even a whale. Immediately south of this, on Ekatón Hourmadhiés ("100 Palms") Square, in the Nestorídhio Mélathro, is housed the **Museum of Modern Greek Art** (Tues–Sat 8am–2pm & 6–9pm; €3), one of the most important collections of 20th-century Greek painting and sculpture. East of "100 Palms", the Italian-built Albergo delle Rose (*Hotel Rodon*) has been converted into the **Casino of Rhodes**, Greece's third largest and, unusually, open to locals as well as visitors. Continue in the same direction to the **Murad Reis mosque** and its atmospherically neglected Muslim cemetery, just past the **Villa Cleobolus**, where Lawrence Durrell lived from

1945 to 1947, recently refurbished as home to the Dodecanesian Literature and Arts Club.

About 2km southwest of Mandhráki, the sparse, unenclosed remains of **Hellenistic Rhodes** – a restored theatre and stadium, plus a few columns of an Apollo temple – perch atop Monte Smith, the hill of Áyios Stéfanos renamed after a British admiral who used it as a watchpoint during the Napoleonic Wars.

Eating and drinking

Eating well for a reasonable price in and around Ródhos Town is a challenge, but not an insurmountable one. As a general rule, the further south towards Zéfyros you go, the better value you'll find – so touristy, alas, has the Old Town (and much of Neohóri) become. Unless otherwise stated, the following restaurants are open all year round.

Old Town

L'Auberge Bistrot Praxitélous 21 ⌖22410 34292. Genuine, popular, French-run bistro with excellent Frenchified food: allow €21 per person for a starter, meaty main course and dessert; they also feature fish or bouilllabaise, and a "light" menu for a tad less. Wine (extra) from a well-selected Greek list; jazz soundtrack included. Summer seating in the courtyard of this restored medieval inn; inside under the arches during cooler months. Open late March to late Dec for supper Tues–Sun (the place operates with distinguished guest chefs in winter); book in high season.

Landis Sofokléous 5. Hole-in-the-wall ouzerí with sought-after seating out in the lane; big platters of well-fried or -marinated seafood titbits, cheapish ouzo by the carafe.

Marco Polo Café Ayíou Fanouríou 42. What started out as the breakfast venue of the eponymous hotel (see p.801) has become, under Spyros Dedes' stewardship, the sleeper of the old town, open to all. Excellent generic Mediterranean fare – mostly vegetables, salads and seafood – with good wines (Spyros is a fanatic) and in-house desserts. April–Oct.

O Meraklis Aristotélous 30. A *patsatzídhiko* (tripe-soup kitchen) that's only open 3–8am for a motley clientele of post-club lads, Turkish stallholders, nightclub singers and travellers just stumbled off an overnight ferry. Great free entertainment, including famously rude staff, and the soup – the traditional Greek hangover cure – is good too.

Mikes (pronounced "mee-kess") Nameless alley behind Sokrátous 17. Inexpensive but salubrious hole-in-the-wall, serving only grilled fish, a few shellfish appetizers, salads and wine; outdoor tables, galley-like kitchen. April–Nov.

Nireas Sofokléous 22. A kindly proprietor, fair fish prices (for Rhodes Old Town, anyway) and atmospheric indoor/outdoor seating make this a good choice for a last-night-of-holiday treat. If for any

reason *Nireas* doesn't suit, **Sea Star** immediately next door also has its passionate devotees in the seafood sweepstakes.

Neohóri

Ammoyiali Voríou Ipírou 17, cnr Kennedy. 2005-opened, high-end bistro purveying "power breakfasts", salads, pasta dishes like tagliatelle and salmon, accomplished desserts and a decent wine list. Moderately expensive, busiest at night; by day sit outside for the sea view.

Chalki (Pavlos') Kathopoúli 30. Ancient, full bottles of who-knows-what form the eclectic decor of this little ouzerí doing good vegetarian *mezédhes* and a limited daily range of main platters (some cheap seafood), washed down by ouzo and CAIR wine. Average-sized portions, but quite cheap. Evenings only.

O Griniaris Platía Ayíou Ioánni 155. Italian-run "traditional *kafenío*" with superbly executed dishes like cumined chickpeas, grilled aubergine with basil, smoked herring, octopus salad, stewed mussels, and panna cotta for dessert. The organic red Peloponnesian house wine is pricey but worth it. March 15–Nov 15, evenings only.

Ta Marasia Platía Ayíou Ioánni 155. The most daring ouzerí in the town limits, operating out of a 1923-vintage house. The food's excellent, if not always very traditional (grilled oyster mushrooms, red cabbage, yoghurt-and-nut salad), though there are more usual seafood platters like urchins and *rengosaláta*. Don't over-order, as portions tend to be generous.

Stani Ayías Anastasías 28, cnr Paleón Patrón Yermanoú, south of the Koskinoú Gate. Most central outlet of a chain of Rhodian Turkish confectioners, scooping out two dozen flavours of the best ice cream on the island – queues at all hours (until 1am) tell you this is the spot.

To Steki tou Tsima Peloponnísou 22, around cnr from *Stani*. Reasonable seafood ouzerí, with the stress on aficionados' shellfish titbits such as *foúskes* (fresh marine invertebrates), *spiníalo* (pickled version of same) and small fish not prone to farming – always ask about off-menu specials. No airs or graces (except for proper table napery), just patently fresh materials. Daily eves only.

To Steno Ayíon Anaryíron 29, 400m southwest of Ayíou Athanasíou Gate. A small, welcoming taverna, with outdoor seating in the warmer months. The menu encompasses sausages, chickpea soup, *pitaroúdhia* or courgette croquettes, stuffed zucchini blossoms and fried little fish; "discovery" means it's oilier and pricier than it once was, but still worth the trek out.

Thavma en Kairo Eleftheriou Venizelou 16–18. ☏ 22410 39805, ⊛ www.restaurantwonder.com. Anders, the Swedish founder of the late, legendary *7.5 Wonder*, has upped sticks and chefs, and migrated to this elegant Belle Époque mansion overlooking parkland. He's repeated his fusion of Asian, Mediterranean and Scandanavian cuisine to good effect, but it – and the four-star wine list – will set you back a minimum €33 per person. Supper only.

Tsipouradhiko Aktí Miaoúli 20. All the meat and seafood ouzerí/*tsipourádhiko* standards in deceptively small but rich platters – six will feed two people – at competitive prices considering the unobstructed sea view. Run by nice folk from mainland Thessaly, who make their own *tsípouro*. Daily noon–3am or so; Tues–Sun in low season.

Zéfyros and around

Anatolikes Nostimies Klavdhíou Pépper 109, Zéfyros beach. The name means "Anatolian Delicacies", and that's what's on offer at this Rhodian-Turkish-run grill: Turkish/Middle Eastern dips and starters, plus a dozen varieties of strictly beef-based kebabs (as opposed to the usual lamb or pork). Beach-hut atmosphere, but friendly and

reasonable; post-prandial hubble-bubble provided on request. 1pm–midnight.

Khristos (O Vlahos) Klavdhíou Pépper 165, at the big bend before Zéfyros beach. Enduringly popular *estiatório* where civil servants from the nearby tax office habitually lunch at outdoor seating. Great *tzatzíki*, plus vegetable-strong *mayireftá* (cuttlefish with spinach, pork stew, fish soup, eggplant *imam*) that sell out quickly. Portions have shrunk and prices inched up over the years, but still worth the trek out.

🏃 **Metaxi Mas** Klavdhíou Pépper 113–115, Zéfyros beach. No sign in English – look for the elevated boat – at this excellent-value seafood ouzerí purveying various titbits such as marinated red mullet, a few shellfish, lobster on occasion, vegie starters and meat too for the fish-averse; three can eat well for about €45 – a fraction of Old-Town costs, and with a sea view (and winter fireplace) to boot. Mon–Sat lunch and supper, Sun lunch only.

Paragadhi corner Klavdhíou Pépper and Avstralías. 2004-opened seafood/fish restaurant (as opposed to ouzerí), with fair portions and prices. Their *risótto thalassinoú* is excellent if not puristically authentic. Closed Sun eve & Mon noon.

Sakis Kanadhá 95, corner Apostólou Papaïoánnou. An old favourite in a new location closer to the beach, with pleasant patio and indoor seating, equally popular with Rhodians and savvy expats. Known for excellent seafood (such as limpets), meat (Cypriot *seftaliés*) and starters; inexpensive by Rhodian standards. Open year round; supper daily, also Sun lunch.

To Steki tou Heila Hatziangélou, corner Episkópi Kyrinías, near Zéfyros. Very popular seafood ouzerí which probably just pips *To Steki tou Tsima* for quality at similar prices, though the street's noisy. Rocket and onion salad, Sými shrimps, squid, marinated sardines, *fáva*, shellfish (check price of last). Daily supper only.

Nightlife

In the Old Town, there's an entire alley (Miltiádhou) off Apelloú given over to around ten loud **music bars** and **clubs**, extending into Plátonos and Platía Dhamayítou, and frequented almost exclusively by Greeks; their names and proprietors change yearly, but the locations remain the same. Another, somewhat lower-decibel nucleus of activity is around Platía Aríonos. These are just appetizers for the estimated seventy or so suriviving foreigner-patronized bars and clubs in Neohóri, where theme nights and various other gimmicks predominate. They are found mostly along the streets and alleys bounded by Alexándhrou Dhiákou, Orfanídhou, Lohagoú Fanouráki and Nikifórou Mandhilará.

Sedate by comparison, Ministry of Culture-approved **folk dances** (June 15–Oct 1 Mon, Wed & Fri 9.20pm; €12) are presented with live accompaniment by the Nelly Dimoglou Company, performed in the landscaped Old

Town Theatre off Andhroníkou, near Platía Ariónos. More of a technological extravaganza is the **Sound and Light** show, spotlighting sections of the city walls, staged in a garden just off Platía Rimínis. There's English-language narration nightly except Sunday, its screening time varying from 8.15pm to 10.15pm (€6).

Thanks to a large contingent from the local university, there are year-round **cinemas** showing first-run fare indoors or open-air according to season and air-con capabilities. Choose from among the summer-only outdoor cinema by the Municipal Theatre, next to the town hall in Neohóri; the Metropol multiplex, at the corner of Venetokléon and Výronos, southeast of the old town opposite the stadium; and the nearby Pallas three-plex on Dhimokratías.

Bekir Karakuzu Sokrátous 76. Bags of atmosphere in this, the last traditional Turkish *kafenío* in the Old Town, with an ornate *votsalotó* floor for its Oriental-fantasy interior. Yoghurt, *loukoúmi*, *alisfakiá* tea and coffees on the expensive side, but you are effectively paying admission to an informal museum. 11am–midnight.

Besara Kafé Sofokléous 11–13, Old Town. Congenial breakfast café/low-key boozer run by Australian-Texan Besara Harris, with interesting mixed clientele and live Greek acoustic music some nights Oct–May.

Blue Lagoon Pool Bar 25-Martíou 2, Neohóri. One of the better theme bars, in this case a "desert island" with palm trees, waterfalls, live turtles and parrots, a shipwrecked galleon – and taped music. March–Oct 8.30am–3am.

Christos' Garden Dhilberáki 59, Neohóri. This combination art-gallery/bar/café occupies a carefully restored old house and courtyard with pebble-mosaic floors throughout. Incongruously classy for the area.

Colorado Entertainment Centre Orfanídhou 57, cnr Aktí Miaouli, Neohóri; ⓦ www.coloradoclub .gr. Triple venue: "Colorado Live" with in-house band (rock covers), "Studio Fame" with taped sounds, and club, plus chill-out "Heaven" R&B bar upstairs.

El Divino Alexándhrou Dhiákou 5, Neohóri. Upscale, Greek-frequented "music bar" with garden seating and the usual range of coffees and alcohol. June–Oct.

Mandala Sofokléous 38. Part-Swedish-run, enduringly popular snack-café/garden bar where the generic Med-lite salads and pasta dishes are overpriced and incidental to good beer, the crowd, and live Greek acoustic music Sat eve. Open all year 2pm–3am; in winter there's a cozy interior with fireplace.

Iy Rogmi tou Khronou Platía Ariónos, Old Town. Taped proper music (not house or techno) at a reasonable level and a congenial crowd make this established bar worth a look; much the same clientele spills over to **Baduz Loutra** next door, which hosts live rock or jazz one night weekly.

Sticky Fingers Anthoúla Zérvou 6, Neohóri. Long-lived music bar with reasonably priced drinks; live rock several nights weekly from 10.30pm onwards, Fri & Sat only off-season. Typical admission €12.

Listings

Airlines Olympic Airways, Iérou Lóhou 9 ☏ 22410 24555; Aegean Airlines, Ethelondón Dhodhekanisíon 20 ☏ 22410 24400.

Bookshop Newsstand at Grigoríou Lambráki 23 is the only (very limited) outlet for any quality foreign-language books.

Car rental Prices at Greek chains are fairly standard at €45–55 per day, but can be bargained down to about €25–35 a day, all-inclusive, out of peak season and/or for long periods. Especially recommended is Drive/Budget, who change their cars every 12–18 months; they have several premises across the island, including at the airport (☏ 22410 81011); their central, long-hours reservation number is ☏ 22410 68243. Other flexible outfits, all in the New Town, include Just/Ansa, Mandhilará 70 ☏ 22410 31811; Kosmos, Papaloúka 31 ☏ 22410 74374; and Orion, Yeoryíou Leóndou 36 ☏ 22410 22137. Major international chains include Alamo/National, Iraklídhon 41, Ixiá ☏ 22410 91117 and at the airport ☏ 22410 81600; Avis, Theodhoráki 3, Neohóri ☏ 22410 24990 and the airport ☏ 22410 82896; plus Hertz at Yeoryíou Gríva 16, Neohóri ☏ 22410 21819 and at the airport ☏ 22410 82902.

Exchange 8 conventional bank branches are grouped around Platía Kýprou in Neohóri, plus there are various exchange bureaux keeping long hours. In the Old Town, there are two full-service banks with ATMs near the museums, plus a pair of stand-alone ATMs on Sokrátous.

Ferry agents ANES ℡ 22410 37769, for catamaran and hydrofoil to Sými; Kydon ℡ 22419 23000, for Agoudimos Lines; Dodhekanisos Navtiliaki ℡ 22410 70590, for the *Dodekanisos Express/Dodekanisos Pride* catamarans to most Dodecanese islands; Inspiration, Aktí Sakhtoúri 4 ℡ 22410 24294 (base of main ferry dock), for most GA boats to Dodecanese and Cyclades; LANE ℡ 22410 33607, to Crete via Hálki, Kárpathos, Kássos; *Sea Star* catamaran to Tílos and Níssyros, booth at Mandhráki port or ℡ 22410 78052. Weekly tourist office departure-schedule handouts are deeply unreliable; authoritative sailing information is available at the *limenarhío* (port police), on Mandhráki esplanade near the post office.

Internet cafés The most central and competitive of several are EasyInternet, inside El Divino (address p.807), and *Mango Bar* at Platía Dhoriéos 3, Old Town.

Laundries Tornado, Apolloníou Rodhíou 28, Neohóri; Wash & Go, Plátonos 33, Old Town.

Motorbike rental Low-volume scooters will make little impact on Rhodes; sturdier Yamaha 125s, suitable for two people, start at about €25 a day. Recommended outlets in Neohóri include Margaritis, Ioánni Kazoúli 23, with a wide range of late models up to 500cc, plus mountain bikes; or Kiriakos, Apodhímon Amerikís 16, which will deliver to the old town and take you back once you've finished.

Travel agencies In Neohóri, conveniently located Triton Holidays at Plastíra 9 (℡ 22410 21690, ℮ info@tritondmc.gr) is excellent for all local travel arrangements, including car rental, domestic catamaran, ferry and air tickets for every company, plus the catamaran to Turkey or charters to the UK. They also have a network of accommodation across the Dodecanese, and can book you an entire itinerary at attractive rates. French-run Passion Sailing Cruises (℡ 22410 73006, Ⓦ www.aegeanpassion.com) offers a bespoke service for skippered cruises, as well as bareboat charter.

The east coast

Heading down the coast from the capital you have to go some way before you escape the crowds from local beach hotels, their numbers swollen by visitors using the regular buses from town or on boat tours out of Mandhráki. You should look in at the abandoned spa of **Thérmes Kallithéas**, a prize example of orientalized Art Deco dating from 1928–29, the work of a young Pietro Lombardi who, in his old age, designed the European Parliament building in Strasbourg. Located 3km south of Kallithéa resort proper, down a paved side-road through pines, the buildings are set in a palm grove, though an EU-funded restoration begun in 1999 has slowed to a snail's pace. The concrete lido beyond the domed structure is popular, as are several secluded coves south of the ex-spa, framed by rock formations which often interpose themselves between the water and the sand. These beachlets are furnished with sunbeds and (in most cases) snack-bars – best of these reckoned to be *Oasis*.

The resort of **FALIRÁKI** has acquired considerable notoriety as the "boozing and bonking" capital of the Dodecanese, a reputation reinforced by a string of rapes and, in August 2003, the fatal stabbing of one British youth and the arrest of several others on charges of public lewdness. This was all fuelled by a culture of pub-crawls organized by tour reps, many of whom were also arrested and charged for taking kickbacks from bar owners. The British press indulged in an orgy of self-flagellation about "ugly Brits", while local authorities made pious noises about cleaning up the resort, with the malefactors subject to (by the standards of any country, let alone Greece) extraordinarily speedy justice *pour encourager les autres*. The clamp-down suceeded far beyond the Rhodian authorities' expectations; since then central Faliráki has all but become a ghost town, with the party action shifted to Laganás on Zákynthos. The cape to the south, **Ladhikó** (45min path from Faliráki), shelters the more scenic bay of

"Anthony Quinn", named in honour of the late actor whom Greeks took to their hearts following his roles in *Zorba the Greek* and *The Guns of Navarone* (the latter filmed locally).

South of Ladhikó headland extends the sweeping pebble-and-sand expanse of **Afándou Bay**, the most undeveloped large beach on the east coast, with just a few stretches of sunbeds and showers (laid on by the municipality, as at most beaches). Spare a moment, heading down the main access road to mid-bay, for the atmospheric, frescoed sixteenth-century **church of Panayía Katholikí**, paved with a *votsalotó* floor throughout and incorporating fragments of a much older basilica. Immediately opposite is a very popular, cheap-and-cheerful **taverna**, doing just grills, salad and dips: *Estiatorio Katholiki* (Mon–Sat supper, Sun lunch also).

The enormous promontory of **Tsambíka**, 26km south of town – actually the very eroded flank of a once much-larger mountain – offers unrivalled views from up top along some 50km of coastline. From the main highway, a steep, 1500-metre cement drive leads to a small car park and a snack-bar, from where steps take you to the summit. The little monastery here is unremarkable except for its September 8 festival: childless women climb up – sometimes on their hands and knees – to be relieved of their barrenness, and any children born afterwards are dedicated to the Virgin with the names Tsambikos or Tsambika, which are particular to the Dodecanese. Shallow **Tsambíka Bay** on the south side of the headland (two-kilometre access road) warms up early in the spring, and the excellent beach, protected by its owners, the Orthodox Church, from permanent development – there are just seven *kantínas* – teems with people all summer. For a proper **taverna**, head for *Panorama Tsambikas*, one of a cluster on the grade of the main highway south of the beach turning.

The next beach south is gravelly **Stegná** with its mix of summer cottages for locals and accommodation for Germans, plus a couple of **tavernas** that attract a Greek clientele. Stegná is reached by a steep road east from the less rewarding village of **ARHÁNGELOS**, just inland and overlooked by a crumbling castle. The place is now firmly caught up in package tourism, with a full complement of banks, tavernas, minimarts and jewellery stores. Another overnight base on this stretch of coast, English-dominated this time, is **HARÁKI**, a pleasant if undistinguished two-street fishing port with mostly self-catering accommodation (generally ❸) overlooked by the stubby ruins of **Feraklós Castle**, the last stronghold of the Knights to fall to the Turks. You can swim off the town beach if you don't mind an audience from the handful of waterfront cafés and tavernas, but most people head west out of town, then north 800m along a marked dirt track to secluded **Ayía Agáthi beach**, or down the coast 8km to **Paralía Kaláthou**, with an attractive, and less claustrophobic, stretch of sand and fine gravel.

Líndhos

LÍNDHOS, the island's number-two tourist attraction, erupts from barren surroundings 12km south of Haráki. Like Ródhos Old Town, its charm is heavily undermined by commercialism and crowds. At midday dozens of tour coaches park nose-to-tail at the outskirts; back in the village itself, those few vernacular houses not snapped up by package operators have, since the 1960s, been bought up and refurbished by wealthy British, Germans and Italians. The old *agorá* or serpentine high street presents a mass of fairly indistinguishable bars, crêperies, mediocre restaurants and travel agents. Although high-rise hotels and all vehicular traffic have been prohibited inside the built-up area, the result is a relentlessly commercialized theme park – hot and airless from June to August, but eerily deserted in winter.

Nonetheless, if you arrive before or after peak season, when the pebble-paved streets between the immaculately whitewashed houses are relatively empty of both people and droppings from the donkeys shuttling punters up to the acropolis (see below), you can still appreciate the beautiful, atmospheric setting of Líndhos. The belfried, post-Byzantine **Panayía church** is covered inside with well-preserved eighteenth-century frescoes. The most imposing fifteenth-to-eighteenth-century **captains' residences** are built around *votsalotó* courtyards, their monumental doorways often fringed by intricate stonework, with the number of braids or cables supposedly corresponding to the number of ships owned. A few are open to the public, notably the **Papakonstandis Mansion**, the most elaborate and home to an unofficial museum (erratic hours, nominally daily 11am–2pm).

On the bluff looming above the town, the ancient acropolis with its Doric **Temple of Athena** (restorations ongoing until 2008) and imposing **Hellenistic stoa** is found inside the Knights' **castle** (summer Mon 12.30–6.40pm, Tues–Sun 8am–6.40pm; rest of year Tues–Sun 8.30am–3pm; €6) – a surprisingly felicitous blend of ancient and medieval culture. Though the ancient city of **Lindos** and its original temple dated from at least 1100 BC, the present structure was begun by local ruler Kleoboulos in the sixth century BC after a fourth-century fire.

Líndhos's north beach, once the main ancient harbour, is overcrowded and heavily commercialized; if you do base yourself here, quieter **beaches** are to be found one cove beyond at **Pállas** beach (with a nudist annexe around the headland), or 5km north at **Vlyhá Bay**. South of the acropolis huddles the small, perfectly sheltered **St Paul's harbour**, with excellent swimming; the apostle is said to have landed here in 58 AD on a mission to evangelize the island.

Practicalities

It used to be tempting fate to just turn up and hope for **accommodation** vacancies on spec, but since certain British tour companies abandoned Líndhos, it's something of a buyers' market. If you're not met at the bus stop under the giant fig tree by proprietors touting rooms, Pallas Travel (℡22440 31494) can arrange a room or even a whole villa for a small fee; just watch that you're not shoved into a windowless cell – ventilation is paramount here. The only real **hotel** in Líndhos, the most exclusive on the island, is ✻ *Melenos* (℡22440 32222, ⊛www.melenoslindos.com; April–Oct; ➌), unimprovably sited on the second lane above the north beach, by the school. No expense has been spared in laying out the twelve suites with semi-private, *votsalotó* terraces, from Kütahya tiles in the vast bathrooms to antiques and wood bed-platforms; all balconies have views, there's an equally pricey on-site garden-bar and restaurant, and by ➌ we mean €200–500 by season.

Most local **restaurants** tend to be exploitatively priced and serve bland fare, with a quick turnover in ownership. You may as well push the boat out at ✻ *Mavrikos* on the fig-tree square, founded in 1933 and in the same family ever since. *Mezédhes* such as *manoúri* cheese with basil and pine-nuts, sweet marinated sardines, or beets in goat-cheese sauce, are accomplished, as are main courses such as cuttlefish in wine sauce, raw tuna with fennel or skate terrine with pine nuts; dipping into the excellent (and expensive) Greek wine list as well will add €18 minimum a bottle to the typical food charge of €23–28 per person. For snacks and desserts, try *Il Forno*, an Italian-run bakery, and *Gelo Blu*, the most genuine of several *gelaterie* here, also offering decadent cakes. The better of two **Internet cafés** is helpful and well-equipped Lindianet; The Link is a unique combination **laundry** and secondhand **bookshop** (Mon–Sat

9am–8pm). Líndhos has one amenity that would be the envy of much larger towns: a **spa** (Mon–Sat 1pm–9pm), offering the full range of services including all-day packages. There are two proper **banks**, each with ATMs. Finally, Lindos Suntours (℡22440 31333) and Village Holidays (℡22440 31486) both may have unclaimed one-way charter seats back to Britain.

The west coast

Rhodes' **west coast** is the windward flank of the island, so it's damper, more fertile and more forested; most beaches, however, are exposed and decidedly rocky. None of this has deterred development and, as in the east, the first few kilometres of the busy main road down from the capital have been surrendered entirely to tourism. From Neohóri's aquarium down to the airport, the shore is fringed by an almost uninterrupted line of generic Mediterranean-*costa* hotels, though such places as Triánda, Kremastí and Paradhísi are still nominally villages, with real centres.

There's not much inducement to stop until you reach the important archeological site of **KAMEIROS**, which together with Lindos and Ialyssos was one of the three Dorian powers that united during the fifth century BC to found the powerful city-state of Rhodes. Soon eclipsed by the new capital, Kameiros was abandoned and only rediscovered in 1859. Thus it's a particularly well-preserved Doric townscape, doubly worth visiting for its beautiful hillside setting (summer Tues–Sun 8am–6.40pm; winter 8.30am–3pm; €4). While none of the individual remains is spectacular, you can make out the foundations of two small temples, the re-erected pillars of a Hellenistic house, a Classical fountain, and the *stoa* of the upper agora, complete with a water cistern. Because of the gentle slope of the site, there were no fortifications, nor was there an acropolis.

At the tiny anchorage of **KÁMIROS SKÁLA** (aka Skála Kamírou) 15km south, there are five rather touristy restaurants, the best being *Loukas* nearest the quay. Less heralded is the daily **kaïki** which leaves for the island of **Hálki** at 2.30pm, weather permitting, returning at 6am the next morning; on Sundays there's a single journey at 9am, returning from Hálki at 5pm. For a taverna alternative, proceed 400m southwest to off-puttingly named **Paralía Kopriá** ("Manure Beach"), where *Psarotaverna Johnny's* has good fish and *mezédhes*; it's been "discovered" and so is pricier than formerly, but still worth a stop.

A couple of kilometres south of Skála, the "Kastello", signposted as **Kástro Kritinías** is, from afar, the most impressive of the Knights' rural strongholds, and the paved access road is too narrow and steep for tour buses. Close up it proves to be no more than a shell, but a glorious shell, with fine views west to Hálki, Alimniá, Tílos and Níssyros. The castle is being restored, with a small museum in the old church, a café, and formal admission tickets foreseen; until then (and afterwards) you should not pay any "toll" to fruit-sellers accosting you illegally on the access road.

Beyond the quiet hillside village of Kritinía itself, the main road winds south through the dense forests below mounts Akramýtis and Atávyros to **SIÁNNA**, famous for its aromatic pine-and-sage honey and *soúma*, a grape-residue distillate similar to Italian *grappa* but far smoother. The tiered, flat-roofed farmhouses of **MONÓLITHOS**, 4km southwest at the end of the public bus line, don't themselves justify the long trip out here, but the view over the bay is striking and you could base yourself at the *Hotel Thomas* (℡22460 61291; ❷), whose fair-sized rooms bely a grim exterior. Best of several **tavernas** is welcoming *O Palios Monolithos*, opposite the church: not bargain-priced but tops for grilled meat and dishes of the day, accompanied by good bread and non-CAIR bulk wine. Diversions in the area include yet another **Knights' castle**, 2km west of town, photogenically perched on its own pinnacle but enclosing very little, and the sand-and-gravel beaches at **Foúrni**, five paved but curvy kilometres below the castle.

The interior

Inland Rhodes is hilly and still mostly wooded, despite the depredations of arsonists. You'll need a vehicle to see its highlights, especially as enjoyment resides in getting away from it all; no single site justifies the tremendous expense of a taxi or the inconvenience of trying to make the best of sparse bus schedules.

Ialyssos and Petaloúdhes

Starting from the west-coast highway, turn inland at the central junction in Tríanda for the five-kilometre ride up to the scanty acropolis of ancient **Ialyssos** (Mon–Sat 8am–6.40pm, Sun 8.30am–2.40pm; €3) on flat-topped, strategic Filérimos hill; from its Byzantine castle Süleyman the Magnificent directed the 1522 siege of Rhodes. Filérimos means "lover of solitude", after the tenth-century settlement here by Byzantine hermits. The existing **Filérimos monastery**, restored successively by Italians and British, is the most substantial structure here. As a concession to the Rhodian faithful, the church alone may be open to pilgrims after the stated hours. Directly in front of the church sprawl the foundations of third-century **temples to Zeus and Athena**, built atop a far older Phoenician shrine. Below this, further towards the car park, lies the partly subterranean church of **Aï-Yeórgis Hostós**, a barrel-vaulted structure with faint fourteenth- and fifteenth-century frescoes. Southwest of the monastery and archeological zone, a **Via Crucis**, with the fourteen stations marked out in copper plaques during the Italian era, leads to an enormous concrete crucifix, a 1995 replacement of an Italian-built one; you're allowed to climb out onto the cross-arms for a supplement to the already amazing view. Illuminated at night, the crucifix is clearly visible from the island of Sými and – perhaps more pertinently – "infidel" Turkey across the way.

The only highly publicized tourist "attraction" in the island's interior, **Petaloúdhes** ("Butterfly Valley") (May–Sept daily 8am–dusk; April & Oct 9am–3pm; admission €3–5 by season), is reached by a seven-kilometre side road bearing inland between Paradhísi and Theológos and is actually a rest stop for Jersey tiger moths. Only in summer do these creatures congregate here, attracted for unknown reasons by the abundant *Liquidambar orientalis* trees growing abundantly in this stream canyon. The moths roosting in droves on the tree trunks cannot eat during this final phase of their life cycle, must rest to conserve energy and die of starvation soon after mating. When sitting in the trees, the moths are a well-camouflaged black and yellow, but flash cherry-red overwings in flight.

Some 2km before Petaloúdhes, the **microwinery** (15,000–20,000 bottles annually) of Anastasia Triandafyllou is worth a stop for its nine varieties, including Athiri whites and Cabernet or Mandhilari reds (daily 8.30am–7pm). There's a popular roadside **taverna** partway up the valley, but for even better fare continue all the way to the edge of **PSÍNTHOS** village, where friendly ⚓ *Piyi Fasouli* serves excellent grills and appetizers as well as a few *mayireftá* at seating under plane trees beside the namesake spring, and is worth the bit extra for the quality.

Eptá Piyés to Profítis Ilías

Heading inland from Kolýmbia junction on the main east-coast highway, it's 4km to **Eptá Piyés** ("Seven Springs"), a lush oasis with a tiny dam created by the Italians for irrigation. A trail, or a rather claustrophobic Italian aqueduct-tunnel, both lead from the vicinity of the springs to the reservoir.

Continuing inland, you reach neglected Rationalist structures at Eleoússa (built as the planned agricultural colony of Campochiaro in 1935–36) after another 9km, in the shade of the dense forest at the east end of Profítis Ilías ridge. From the vast Art Deco pool just west of the village, keep straight on 3km further to the late Byzantine church of **Áyios Nikólaos Foundouklí** ("St Nicholas of the Hazelnuts"). The partly shaded site has a fine view north over cultivated valleys; frescoes inside, dating from the thirteenth to the fifteenth centuries, could use a good cleaning, but various scenes from the life of Christ are recognizable.

Continuing west from the church gets you finally to **Profítis Ilías**, where the Italian-vintage chalet-hotels *Elafos* and *Elafina* (now hosting childrens' summer camps) hide in deep woods just north of the 798-metre peak, Rhodes' third-highest point but out of bounds since it's a military area. However, there's good, gentle strolling below and around the summit, and a snack-bar on the through road is generally open in season. The closest facilities are in **SÁLAKOS** downslope, for example the *Hotel-Café Nymph* (℡22460 22206, ⓦwww .nymph.com.gr; ❸) at the top of the village.

Atávyros villages

All tracks and roads west across Profítis Ilías converge on the main road from Kalavárdha bound for **ÉMBONA**, a large and architecturally nondescript village backed up against the north slope of 1215-metre **Mount Atávyros**. Émbona, with a half-dozen meat-oriented **tavernas** (try *Panayiotis Bakis* on the platía, which has its own butcher's), is more geared to handling tourists than you might expect, since it's the venue for summer "folk-dance tours" from Ródhos Town. The village also lies at the heart of the island's most important wine-producing districts, and CAÏR – the Italian-founded vintners' co-operative – produces a choice of acceptable mid-range varieties. However, products of the smaller, family-run Emery **winery** (daily 9am–4.30pm) at the northern outskirts are more esteemed. To get some idea what Émbona would be like without tourists, carry on clockwise around the peak to less celebrated **ÁYIOS ISÍDHOROS**, with nearly as many vines and tavernas, a more open feel and the **trailhead** for the five-hour return ascent of Atávyros. This path, beginning at the northeast edge of the village at a wooden placard and well marked with paint splodges, is the safest and easiest way up the mountain, though you'll find the slopes sullied by a wind-power farm, an air force radar "golf ball" up top and the tracks built to install these.

Thárri monastery

The road from Áyios Isídhoros to Siánna is paved; not so the perennially rough one that curves for 12km east to Láerma, but it's worth enduring if you've any interest in Byzantine monuments. The **monastery of Thárri**, lost in pine forests 5km south, is the oldest religious foundation on the island, re-established as a living community of half a dozen monks in 1990 by the charismatic abbot Amfilohios. The striking *katholikón* (open daily, all day) consists of a long nave and short transept surmounted by barrel vaulting. Various cleanings have restored damp-smudged frescoes dating from 1300 to 1450 to their former exquisite glory. The most distinct, in the transept, depict the Evangelists Mark and Matthew, plus the Archangel Gabriel, while the nave boasts various acts of Christ, including such scenes as the *Storm on the Sea of Galilee, Meeting the Samaritan Woman at the Well* and *Healing the Cripple*. In **LÁERMA**, you can dine on the terrace of the aptly named *Psistaria Bella Vista* at the eastern outskirts.

The far south

South of a line connecting Monólithos and Lárdhos, you could easily begin to think you had strayed onto another island. Gone are most of the multi-star hotels, and with them the bulk of the crowds. Only one or two daily buses (in season) ply to the depopulated villages here (Yennádhi has much better services), approaching along the east coast; tavernas dot the village centres and the more popular beaches, but aside from the package enclaves of Lárdhos, Péfki and Kiotári, there are few places to stay.

Despite the shelving of plans for a second airport nearby, new beachfront development mushrooms to either side of **LÁRDHOS**, itself solidly on the tourist circuit despite the village's inland position between Láerma and the Líndhos peninsula. The beach 2km away is gravelly and exposed to southeasterly storms, so you might continue 3km to **Glýstra** cove, a small but delightful crescent which gets crowded in season. Four kilometres east of Lárdhos, **PÉFKI** (Péfkos on some maps) began life as the garden annexe and overflow for Líndhos, but is now a burgeoning package resort in its own right; the sea is clearer than at Lárdhos proper, with small, well-hidden beaches tucked at the base of low cliffs (biggest of these, in western Péfki, is **Lothiáriko**). Among **tavernas**, *Kavos* at the eastern edge of town has the most Greek menu and the pleasantest setting.

Asklipió

Nine kilometres beyond Lárdhos, a side road heads 3.5km inland to **ASKLI-PIÓ**, a sleepy village guarded by a crumbling Knights' castle and graced by the Byzantine church of **Kímisis Theotókou** (daily 9am–6pm, closes 5pm spring/autumn; €1). The building dates from 1060, with a pebble-floored ground plan nearly identical to Thárri's, except that two subsidiary apses were added during the eighteenth century. Frescoes inside are in better condition than those at Thárri owing to the drier local climate; they are also a bit later, though some claim that the final work at Thárri and the earliest here were executed by the same hand, a master from Híos.

The format and subject matter of the frescoes are equally rare in Greece: didactic "cartoon strips" that often extend completely around the church, featuring extensive Old Testament stories in addition to the more usual lives of Christ and the Virgin. There's a complete sequence from Genesis, from the *Creation* to the *Expulsion from Eden*; note the comically menacing octopus among the fishes in the panel of the Fifth Day, and Eve subsequently being fashioned from Adam's rib. A *Revelation of John the Divine* takes up most of the south transept, while an enormous Archangel Michael dominates the north transept, with sword in right hand and a small soul being carried to judgement in his left. Two adjacent buildings house separate museums: an ecclesiastical exhibit, and a more interesting folklore gallery in an ex-olive mill, full of unlabelled rural craft tools and antiquated, belt-driven machinery.

Kiotári, Yennádhi. Váti and Profýlia

Back on the coast road, the beachfront hamlet of **KIOTÁRI** has mushroomed as a package venue for Germans and Italians since 1995, when the Orthodox

Church elected to sell up its vast holdings here. You could stop for a **meal** in the northern sector at bistro-bar *Mourella*, or in the southerly section at more Greek-feeling *Stefanos*, and have a swim. But there's little local character remaining, so you'll most likely continue 4km to **YENNÁDHI**, the only sizeable settlement on this coast, whose rather drab outskirts mask the attractive older village core inland. Amenities include a **post office**, **car rental** and some **accommodation** – pick of this being *Effie's Dreams* at the northern end of things (T 22440 43410, W www.effiesdreams.com; ❸), overlooking a fountain-fed oasis. The serviceable studios upstairs have a loyal repeat clientele; returned Greek-Australians Effie and Phillip also keep a lively bar and **Internet** café downstairs. They can also assist in locating the key-keeper for sixth-to-fifteenth-century **Ayía Anastasía**, the village cemetery-church 300m northwest through the oasis, covered inside with naïve post-Byzantine frescoes. Most local **tavernas** (no particular recommendation) stand just behind the dark-sand-and-gravel beach extending for kilometres in either direction, clean and with the usual amenities laid on; on summer Sundays at least one "all-day **beach bar**" sets up shop, to the delight of local youth.

From Yennádhi, a good road heads 7km inland, past baby pines slowly greening up a fire-blasted landscape, to the oasis village of **VÁTI**. Here, the superior of two **tavernas** is *O Petrinos Kafenes*, also doubling as the central *kafenío*; it's pricey for the location, but the quality of country-style offerings like spicy *revíthia* soup, good bread, *hórta* and roast suckling pig is such that many Greeks attend, especially at weekends. If this doesn't suit, the nearby village of **PROFÝLIA** can offer the comparable *To Limeri tou Listi* (closed Mon low season).

The southern tip

Some 10km south of Yennádhi, then 2km inland, **LAHANIÁ** village with its smattering of private **rooms** makes another possible base. Abandoned after a postwar earthquake, since the 1980s its older houses have been mostly occupied and renovated by English and Germans on long-term lease agreements. On the main platía at the lower, eastern end of the village, the ✻ *Platanos* **taverna** has superb home-made *mezédhes* platters like hummus and *dolmadhákia*, and seating between the church and two wonderful fountains, one with an Ottoman Turkish inscription.

From Lahaniá it's also possible to head 9km northwest along a narrow road to the picturesque hilltop village of **MESANAGRÓS**. This already existed in some form by the fifth century AD, judging from foundations of a ruined basilica at the village outskirts. A smaller thirteenth-century chapel squats amidst traces of the larger, earlier church, with a *votsalotó* floor and stone barrel arches (key from the nearby *kafenío*). You can also go directly from Lahaniá to **Plimýri**, an attractive sandy bay backed by dunes, with swimming in the clean, brisk water marred only by strong afternoon winds; the sole facility is an indifferent taverna next to the **church of Zoödhóhou Piyís** (interior open May–Oct Sun only noon–5pm), which has ancient columns upholding its vaulted porch.

Beyond Plimýri the road curves inland to **KATTAVIÁ**, nearly 90km from the capital, lost amidst grain fields; the village, like so many in the far south, is seasonally occupied at best, their owners having emigrated to find work in Australia or North America. There are a few **rooms** to rent, a vital **filling station** and several **tavernas** at the junction that doubles as the platía – most interesting of these being the brightly coloured *Martine's Bakaliko/Mayeriko* (closed Thurs), run by folk from Lahaniá, which has vegetarian dishes and home-made desserts.

From Kattaviá a road continues to **Prassoníssi**, Rhodes' southernmost extremity and a mecca for European **windsurfers**. The sandspit which tethers Prassoníssi ("Leek Island") to Rhodes was breached by currents to form a channel in 1996, but enough remains to create flat water on the east side and up to two-metre waves on the west, ideal for all ability levels. Of the two **windsurfing schools** operating here, Polish-run Prasonisi Center (late April–Oct; ☎22440 91044, ⓦwww.windsurfing-rodos.com) is keener and friendlier. They're geared up for one-week packages, and lodge their clients in one of the half-dozen food and accommodation outfits further inland. One which has been recommended for walk-in service, despite a sizeable allotment to the surf schools, is *Faros/Lighthouse Taverna Rooms to Let* (☎22440 91030; ❹).

West of Kattaviá, the paved island loop road emerges onto the deserted, sandy southwest coast. Only strong swimmers should venture far offshore here, as it's exposed and tricky currents are the rule. The next village is nondescript, agricultural **APOLAKKIÁ**, equipped with **tavernas** but no accommodation. Northwest, the road leads to Monólithos, while the northeasterly bearing leads quickly and pleasantly back to Yennádhi via Váti. Due north, just below an irrigation reservoir, the tiny frescoed Byzantine chapel of **Áyios Yeóryios Várdhas** (unlocked) is well worth the four-kilometre detour if you have your own transport.

Hálki

Hálki, a tiny (20 square kilometres), waterless, limestone speck west of Rhodes, is a fully fledged member of the Dodecanese, though all but about 250 of the former population of three thousand emigrated (mostly to Rhodes or to Florida) in response to Italian restrictions on sponge-fishing in 1916. Despite a renaissance through tourism, the island is tranquil compared with its big neighbour, albeit with a rather artificial, stage-set atmosphere, owing to foreigners in their villas vastly outnumbering locals for much of the year. The big event of the day is the arrival of the regular afternoon *kaïki* from Kámiros Skála on Rhodes.

Hálki first attracted outside attention in 1983, when **UNESCO** designated it the "isle of peace and friendship" and the seat of regular international conferences. Some 150 crumbling houses were to be restored at UNESCO's expense as accommodation for delegates, but by 1987 just one hotel had been completed, and the only sign of "peace and friendship" was a stream of UNESCO and Athenian bureaucrats staging musical binges under the rubric of "ecological seminars". Confronted with an apparent scam, the islanders sent UNESCO packing and engaged two UK package operators to complete restorations and bring in paying guests. There are now in fact two more tour companies present, and most of the ruins have been refurbished to the companies' specifications.

Emborió

The skyline of **EMBORIÓ**, the island's port and only habitation, is pierced by the tallest freestanding clocktower in the Dodecanese and, a bit further north, by the belfry of Áyios Nikólaos church. Emborió's restored houses are pretty much block-booked from May to late September by the tour companies mentioned; independent travellers will be lucky to find anything on spec, even early or late in the season. Non-package **accommodation**, all requiring advance

△ Emborió quayside, Hálki

reservations, includes the delightful, en-suite ⚓ *Captain's House* (☎22460 45201; ❷), which has the feel of an old French country hotel; the house (sleeping four) of Frances Mayes, editor of the local bimonthly newspaper *Halki Visitor* (ⓕ22460 45061, ⓔfrancesm@otenet.gr); and four rather basic, terrazo–floored, sea-view rooms (☎& ⓕ22460 45295; ❸) at the Póndamos beach taverna (see overleaf). The municipally owned *Hotel Halki* (☎22460 45390; ❹) in the old sponge factory on the south side of the bay was being throughly gutted and rebuilt during 2005; contact Takis on ☎694 621 28 36 for its current status. Of the seven full-service **tavernas** along the field-stoned, pedestrianized waterfront, *Remezzo* is excellent for *mayireftá* and pizzas, *Maria* behind the post office has good grills, *Houvardas* (aka *Asia's*) near the north end of the quay has proven reliable for *mayireftá* and grills, while *Avra* is conscientiously run by Greeks from Caucasian Georgia. Amongst a similar number of quayside **bars** and **cafés**, *Theodosia's* (or "The Parrot Bar" after its resident bird), near the base of the jetty, has puddings and home-made ice cream to die for, while *Tò Stéki* is usually the most musically active, with a sculpted counter outdoors. More formal entertainment is provided through the **Halki Festival** (late June to mid-Sept), with performances by top Greek musical names. There's a **post office**, four well-stocked stores, a bakery, plus two **travel agencies** that sell boat tickets and change money (though there's also a stand-alone **ATM**); one, Zifos Travel (☎22460 45028, ⓔzifos-travel @rho.forthnet.gr) often has a few vacancies amongst studios which they hold back from the UK companies.

The rest of the island

Three kilometres west looms the old pirate-safe village of **HORIÓ**, abandoned in the 1950s but still crowned by its Knights' castle. Except during the major August 14–15 festival, the church here is kept securely locked to protect its frescoes. Across the valley, the little monastery of **Stavrós** is the venue for the other big island bash on September 14. There's little else to see or do inland, though you can cross the island on an eight-kilometre road, the extension of the cement "Tarpon Springs Boulevard" donated by the expatriate community in Florida. At the end (best arrange a ride out, and walk back) you'll reach the monastery of **Ayíou Ioánnou Prodhrómou** (festival 28–29 Aug). The terrain en route is monotonous, but compensated by views over half the Dodecanese and Turkey.

Longish but narrow **Póndamos**, fifteen minutes' walk west of Emborió, is the only sandy beach on Hálki, and even this has had to be artificially supplemented. The sole facility is the somewhat pricey *Nick's Pondamos Taverna*, serving lunch daily, plus supper two to three random evenings weekly. A few minutes' well-signposted path-walk behind the *Hotel Halki*, tiny coves of pebbles at **Ftenáya** are also heavily subscribed; a dirt track leads to a decent **taverna-bar** (*Tou Vangeli*) right above the main cove, with good seafood and *ouzomezédhes* on offer.

Small, pebbly **Yialí**, west of and considerably below Horió via jeep track, lies an hour's hike away from Póndamos. A thirty-minute walk north of Emborió is **Kánia**, with a rocky foreshore and a rather industrial ambience from both power lines and the island's only petrol pump to one side.

Since these coves are no great shakes, it's worth signing on at Emborió quay for **boat excursions** to more remote beaches. More or less at the centre of Hálki's southern shore, directly below Horió's castle, **Trahiá** consists of two coves to either side of an isthmus; you can (just) reach this overland by rough path from Yialí. North-coast beaches figuring as excursion-boat destinations include the pretty fjord of **Aréta**, **Áyios Yeóryios** just beyond and the remote double bay of **Dhýo Yialí**. Of these, Aréta is the most attractive, and the only one accessible overland (90min one way) by experienced hillwalkers equipped with the *Chalki, Island of Peace and Friendship* map based on the old Italian topographical survey sheet.

Alimniá (Alimiá) islet

The most promoted boat excursion visits **Alimniá (Alimiá) islet**, roughly halfway between Hálki and Rhodes. Despite more well-water and greenery, and a better harbour than at Hálki, the deserted village here, overlooked by a few palm trees and yet another Knights' castle, was completely abandoned by the 1960s. The locals were initially deported during World War II after they admitted to assisting British commandos sent in April 1944 to sabotage the German submarines who used the deep harbour here. The seven commandos themselves were captured on the spot by the Nazis, bundled off first to Rhodes, then to Thessaloníki, where six were summarily executed as spies rather than regular prisoners of war; future Austrian premier and UN Secretary General Kurt Waldheim allegedly countersigned their death sentences.

Interesting history acknowledged, Alimniá is probably not a place you'd want to be stuck for an entire day. Excursions on offer are overpriced (€25–30, picnic lunch included), beach space very limited, the castle a hot, 45-minute walk up (the best thing to do here) and the crumbling village behind its salt marsh unedifying. If you snorkel beyond little Áyios Minás monastery, you might glimpse outlines of the Italian-built submarine pens to one side of the deep bay. The former inhabitants only show up to graze livestock, or for the annual festival on April 23.

Kastellórizo (Meyísti)

Kastellórizo's official name, Meyísti ("Biggest") refers to its being the largest of a tiny local group of islands. It's actually the smallest of the Dodecanese, over seventy nautical miles from Rhodes but barely more than a nautical mile off the Turkish coast. At night its lights are quite outnumbered by those of the Turkish town of Kaş, which lies across the bay and with whom Kastellórizo generally has excellent relations.

During the island's **heyday** (1860–1910) almost 10,000 people lived here, supported by a schooner fleet that transported timber from the towns on the Anatolian mainland opposite. But the withdrawal of island autonomy after the 1908 "Young Turk" revolution, the Italian seizure of the other Dodecanese in 1912 and period of 1913–15 self-rule sent the island into decline. A French occupation of 1915–21 prompted destructive shelling from the Anatolia, a harbinger of worse to come. Shipowners failed to modernize their fleets, preferring to sell ships to the British for the Dardanelles campaign, and the new frontier between the island and republican Turkey, combined with the expulsion of all Anatolian Greeks in 1923, deprived any remaining vessels of their trade. During the 1930s the island enjoyed a brief renaissance as a major stopover point for French and British seaplanes, but events at the close of World War II ended any hopes of the island's continued viability.

When Italy capitulated to the Allies in September 1943, about 1500 Commonwealth commandos occupied Kastellórizo, departing in November once the German capture of the other Dodecanese made their position untenable – and leaving the island vulnerable to looters. In early July 1944, a harbour fuel dump caught (or was set on) fire and an adjacent arsenal **exploded**, taking with it more than half of the two thousand houses on Kastellórizo. Even before these events most of the population had left for Rhodes, Athens, Australia and North America. Today there are just 342 official residents here by the last census (with only about 250 actually living permanently on Kastellórizo), largely maintained by remittances from over 30,000 emigrants and by subsidies from the Greek government, which fears that the island will revert to Turkey should numbers diminish any further.

Yet Kastellórizo has a future of sorts, thanks partly to repatriating "Kassies" who have begun renovating their crumbling ancestral houses as second homes. Each summer, the population is swelled by these returnees, who occasionally celebrate traditional weddings in the Áyios Konstandínos cathedral at Horáfia, which incorporates ancient columns from Patara in Asia Minor. Access has also improved since an airport (domestic flights only) was completed, larger aircraft laid on in 2003, and the harbour dredged to accommodate larger ferries, though the island has yet to be designated an official port of entry to Greece, which causes problems for both yachties and conventional travellers crossing from Turkey.

Perhaps the biggest boost in the island's fortunes, however, was serving as the location for the Italian film **Mediterraneo**, winner of the Oscar for Best Foreign Film in 1992, which has resulted in substantial numbers of Italian midsummer visitors (though the island in fact gets a broad spectrum of tourists). You will either love Kastellórizo and stay a week, or crave escape after a day; detractors dismiss the island as a human zoo maintained by the Greek government for the edification of nationalists, while partisans celebrate an atmospheric, barely commercialized outpost of Hellenism.

Kastellórizo Town

The current population is concentrated in the northern settlements of **KASTELLÓRIZO** – supposedly the finest natural harbour between Beirut and Fethiye on the Turkish coast – and its little "suburb" of **Mandhráki**, just over the fire-blasted hill with a half-ruined Knights' castle. Most of the town's surviving mansions are ranged along the waterfront, their tiled roofs, wooden balconies and blue or green shutters on long, narrow windows having obvious counterparts in the originally Greek-built houses of Kalkan and Kaş just across the water. Just one or two streets back, however, many properties remain derelict – abandonment having succeeded where the World War I shelling, a 1926 earthquake, 1943 air-raids and the 1944 explosions failed; sepia-toned posters and black-and-white postcards on sale of the town in its prime are poignant evidence of its later decline.

The castle's outer bulwark now houses the worthwhile local **museum** (Tues–Sun 7am–2.30pm; free), with displays including plates from a Byzantine shipwreck, frescoes rescued from decaying rural churches and a reconstruction of an ancient basilica on the site of today's gaudy, crumbling Áyios Yeóryios Santrapé church at Horáfia. Just below and beyond the museum, in the cliff-face opposite Psorádhia islet, is Greece's only **Lycian house-tomb**; it's well sign-posted from the shoreline walkway, up some steps beside the first wooden lamp standard. The old **mosque**, also below the castle in waterfront Kávos district, is supposed to open as another museum in 2007.

Arrival, information and transport

A single **bank**, with handy ATM, stands on the east quay; the **post office** is on the far side of the bay. The more reliable and competent of the town's two **travel agencies** is Papoutsis (☏22410 70630), which represents all sea-craft, and sells air tickets. An eleven-seater **minibus** shuttles between town and airstrip at flight times (fare €1.50); excess passengers are accommodated in the lone **taxi**, which may have to make multiple journeys at €5 per passenger.

It is possible to arrange a ride over **to Turkey** on one of four local boats, most reliably on Monday or Friday (8am departure). The standard day-return fee is €15, plus the cost of any visa required on the Turkish side (if you stay overnight), and you have to leave your passport with the authorities the day before. Although Kastellórizo is not yet a legal port of entry to Greece – it lacks a proper Schengen database computer – police here cannot legally deny disembarkation to EU nationals arriving **from Kaş**, which is an official entry/exit point for Turkey.

Accommodation

Kastellórizo is not really geared up for large numbers of visitors, though old-house **pensions** have been upgraded, and prices have climbed sharply, since 2000. Budget options include the large-roomed if basic *Pension Caretta* (☏ & ☏22460 49028; ❷), which also has a fine restored apartment (❸) for two, and the *Pension Asimina*, wood-trimmed rooms behind the arcaded Italian market (☏22460 49361; ❷). An excellent mid-range choices is ✝ *Karnayo* off the platía at the west end of the south quay (☏22460 49225, ✉karnayo@otenet .gr); air-conditioned rooms or studios (❹) and an apartment sleeping four spread over two quiet, sensitively restored buildings, all wood and stone with furniture in matching taste. Also in this category, at the end of the northwest quay, *Pension Mediterraneo* (☏22460 49007 or 697 36 76 038, ⓦwww.mediterraneopension.org; ❹) has simple rooms, well furnished with mosquito nets and wall art, half with sea view, plus an arcaded, waterside basement suite (**⑥**) and optional breakfast with proprietress Marie's home-made marmalade.

Eating, drinking and nightlife

Apart from fish, goat meat and wild-fig preserves, plus fresh produce smuggled over from Kaş, Kastellórizo has to import foodstuffs and drinking water from Rhodes; taverna prices can thus be higher than usual, with the further pretext of the island's celebrity status. Incidentally, do *not* drink the mains water; storage cisterns have become contaminated and you will get very ill. The two most conspicuous central-waterfront **tavernas** are also not recommended – it's best to continue a few steps to *To Mikro Parisi* for affordable, and more likely fresher, seafood and meat grills. Other good quayside choices include *Iy Ipomoni* (dinner only), two doors left from the arcaded market, for simple fish grills; and the inexpensive but savoury *Akrothalassi*, purveying large grills and salads near the west end of the quay, by the church – it's popular at lunch, as they've the only shaded seating. One to dine at inland (still adorned with film posters – it served as the canteen for the *Mediterraneo* film crew) is *Ta Platania* (June to mid-Oct), opposite Áyios Konstandínos in Horáfia, good for daily-changing *mayireftá* and desserts. There are more puddings and good breakfasts at *Zaharoplastio Iy Meyisti*, back on the waterfront.

Nightlife spills out of the half-dozen *barákia* lining the quay, occasionally ending up in the water when tipplers overbalance at their tables. *Faros* near the mosque is a cool place with a roof terrace and music noise levels kept under control; friendly *Mythos* back at centre quay also does cheap snacks – good to know when all the tavernas are booked in mid-summer; and at *Kaz-Bar* (late June–Sept) to the right of the market, host Colin also purveys light snacks appropriate for summer.

The rest of the island

Kastellórizo's austere hinterland is predominantly bare rock, flecked with stunted vegetation; incredibly, three generations ago much of the countryside was carefully tended, producing wine of some quality and in quantity. A rudimentary paved road system links points between Mandhráki and the airport, plus there's an ugly dirt track opened by the army to Áyios Stéfanos, but there aren't many specific places to visit and no scooters for rent. Karstic cliffs drop sheer to the sea, offering no anchorage for boats except at the main town, Mandhráki and Návlakas fjord (see overleaf).

Rural monasteries and ruins

Heat permitting, you can hike up the obvious, zigzag stair-path from town, then south through scrub to the rural **monastery of Ayíou Yeoryíou toú Vouni-ioú**, 35 minutes away. The sixteenth-to-eighteenth-century church boasts fine rib-vaulting and a carved *témblon*, but its highlight is a crypt, with the frescoed, subterranean chapel of **Áyios Harálambos** off to one side; access is via a steep, narrow passage descending from the church floor – bring a torch and grubby clothes, and get the key first from the annually changing keeper in town. Just beyond, east of the old path (not the new track), there's a sixth-century BC **wine press** carved into the rock strata; another, even better one can be seen by varying the return to town and using a secondary path from the monastery to Horáfia via Avlónia district.

Alternatively, a fifteen-minute track-walk west of the port leads to the peaceful monastery of **Ayías Triádhas**, perched on the saddle marked by the telecom tower, and an army base – one of many strong points which have sprouted here since the Ímia crisis of 1996. The onward path arrives after twenty minutes at the ancient citadel of **Paleókastro**, where you'll find masonry from Classical to medieval times, a warren of vaulted chambers, tunnels, cisterns plus another little monastery with a *votsalotó* courtyard. From any of the heights above town there are tremendous views north over sixty kilometres of Anatolian coast.

The shoreline and Rhó

Swimming is complicated by a total absence of beaches and an abundance of sea urchins and razor-sharp limestone reefs; the safest entries near town lie beyond the graveyard at Mandhráki and the cement jetty below the power plant at road's end – or people just dive from the lidos on the northwest quay. Once away from the shore, you're rewarded by clear waters with a rich variety of marine life. From Ayíou Yeoryíou toú Vounioú, you can continue 45 minutes further on foot, first on a useless modern bulldozer track, then on the original, French-built *kalderími*, to the multi-lobed fjord of **Návlakas**, a favourite mooring spot for yachts and fishing boats. The French built this cobbled way to facilitate offloading the components of a 120-millimetre gun battery here during World War I, safe from Ottoman artillery. Uniquely on Kastellórizo, this bay is sea-urchin-free, with freshwater seeps keeping the temperature brisk; there's superb snorkelling to 25-metre depths off the south wall.

Over on the southeast coast, accessible only by a 45-minute boat ride from town, the grotto of **Perastá** (Galázio Spílio) deserves a look for its stalactites and strange blue-light effects; the low entrance, negotiable only by inflatable raft, gives little hint of the enormous chamber within, with monk seals occasionally nesting in another adjacent cave. Rubber-raft trips (€8–10 depending on passenger numbers) visit only the cave, or for about double that amount on a larger *kaïki*, you can take it in as part of a five-hour tour that includes Rhó islet.

Should you make the trip out to **Rhó**, the tomb of **Iý Kyrá tís Rhó** ("The Lady of Rhó"), aka Dhespina Akhladhiotis (ca.1898–1982) – who resolutely hoisted the Greek flag each day on that islet in defiance of the Turks on the mainland – is the first thing you see when you dock at the sandy, northwestern harbour. From here a path heads southeast for 25 minutes to the islet's southerly port, past the side trail up to the intact Hellenistic fortress on the very summit. The islet has no facilities – just a few soldiers to prevent Turkish military landings or poaching of the hundreds of goats – so bring your own food and water.

Sými

Sými's most pressing problem, lack of fresh water, is in many ways also its saving grace. As with so many dry, rocky Dodecanese islands, water must be imported at great expense from Rhodes, pending completion of a reservoir in the distant future. Consequently, the island can't hope to support more than a handful of large hotels; instead, hundreds of people are shipped in daily during the season from Rhodes, relieved of their money and sent back. This arrangement suits both the Symiots and those visitors lucky enough to stay longer; many foreigners

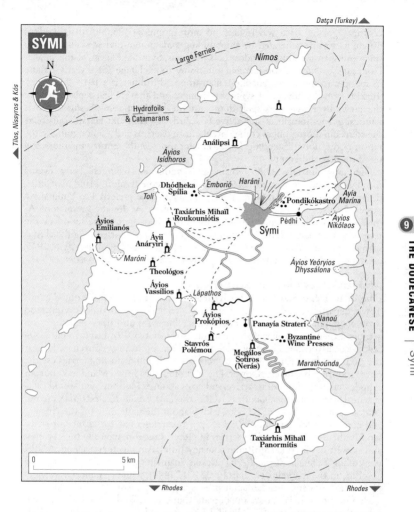

return regularly, or even own houses here. Sými, long fashionable amongst Italians in particular, has entered domestic Greek consciousness in a big way by featuring prominently in the 2005–06 Turkish TV serial, *The Frontiers of Love*.

Once beyond the inhabited areas, you'll find a surprisingly attractive island that has retained some forest cover of junipers, valonea oaks and even a few pines – ideal walking country in spring or autumn (though not midsummer, when temperatures are among the highest in Greece). Another prominent feature of the landscape are dozens of tiny monasteries, usually locked except on their patron saint's day, though their cisterns with a can on a string for fetching water are usually accessible.

Sými Town

SÝMI, the island's capital and only proper town, consists of **Yialós**, the excellent natural port, and **Horió**, on the hillside above. Incredibly, just over a century ago the place was richer and more populous (25,000) than Ródhos Town, its wealth generated by shipbuilding and sponge-diving, skills nurtured since pre-Classical times. Under the Ottomans, Sými, like most of the smaller Dodecanese, enjoyed considerable autonomy in exchange for a yearly tribute in sponges to the sultan; but the Italian-imposed frontier, the 1919–22 Greco-Turkish war, the advent of synthetic sponges and the gradual replacement of the crews by Kalymniots spelt doom for the local economy. Vestiges of past nautical glories remain in still-active boatyards at Pédhi and Haráni, but today the souvenir-shop sponges come entirely from overseas and – an ongoing restoration boom notwithstanding – magnificent nineteenth-century mansions still stand roofless and empty.

The approximately 2500 remaining Symiots are scattered fairly evenly throughout the mixture of Neoclassical and more typical island dwellings; despite the surplus of properties, many outsiders have preferred to build anew, rather than renovate derelict shells accessible only by donkey or on foot. As on Kastellórizo, a September 1944 ammunition blast – this time set off by the retreating Germans – levelled hundreds of houses up in Horió. The official Axis surrender of the Dodecanese to the Allies was signed in Yialós on May 8, 1945: a plaque marks the spot at the present-day *Restaurant Les Catherinettes*.

Arrival, information and transport

One of two **catamarans** and a **hydrofoil** run daily to Sými from Ródhos Town, departing at least morning and late afternoon – sometimes evening too – on an *epivatikó* (scheduled service) basis. There are also daily departures on a more expensive *ekdhromikó* (excursion) basis at 8.30–9am, returning 2.30–3.45pm. All ANES craft usually dock at Yialós's south quay, conveniently near the **taxi and bus stops**, while the excursion craft and main-line ferries use the north mooring by the clocktower. The hydrofoil *Aigli* leaves Mandhráki port in Rhodes, takes 55 minutes to arrive, and costs about €14. Both Sými-based catamarans (*Symi II* and *Panormitis*), as well as the *Dodekanisos Express/Pride*, use the central Kolóna harbour of Rhodes, taking about the same time for the crossing and cost rather less (around €7); the *Symi II* carries a few cars. Once or twice weekly there are also mainline ferries in either direction, typically the cheapest and slowest of all (€4, 1hr 40min journey time). Among **ferry** agents, ANES, controlling *Panormitis/Symi II/Aigli* tickets, maintains a booth on the quay and an office in the marketplace lanes (☎22460 71444), while GA and *Dodekanisos Express/Pride* catamarans are handled by Symi Tours nearby (☎22460 71307).

There's no official tourism bureau, but the island's English-language **advertiser-newspaper**, *The Symi Visitor* (free; ⓦwww.symivisitor.com), is literate and has current island topics with informative historical and ethnographic features. The **post office** in the official Italian "palace" is open standard hours; both **banks** have ATMs. During the season a small green **bus** (€0.70 flat fare) shuttles between Yialós and Pédhi via Horió on the hour (returning at the half-hour) until 11pm. There are also six **taxis** (allow €3 Yialós–Horió with baggage), and two pricey outlets for **motor-scooter** (minimum €18–24 daily, the better being Glaros on the north quay (☎22460 71926), and **car rental** (a whopping €58–70 daily). **Taxi-boat** fares climbed sharply in 2005, making a scooter – or walking – that much more attractive. A **laundry** operates next to *Pahos'* quayside *kafenío*.

Accommodation

Accommodation for independent travellers is somewhat limited and proprietors tend not to meet arriving boats, though the situation isn't nearly so bad as on Hálki. Studios, rather than simple rooms, predominate, and package operators control most of these, though curiously you may find vacancies more easily in July/August than during spring/autumn, considered the most pleasant seasons here. Despite asphyxiating summer heat, air conditioning and/or fans are not universally present – go for north-facing and/or balconied units when possible.

Albatros Marketplace ℡22460 71707, ⓦwww .albatrosymi.gr. Partial sea views from this exquisite, small hotel; pleasant second-floor breakfast salon and air con.❺

Aliki Haráni quay ℡22460 71665, ⓦwww .simi-hotelaliki.gr. A complete overhaul of an 1895 mansion, and Sými's poshest hotel: tasteful rooms with wood floors and some antique furnishings and large bathrooms, though only some have sea views.❽ standard.❼ suite.

Les Catherinettes Above eponymous restaurant, north quay ℡22460 72698, ⓔmarina-epe@rho .forthnet.gr. Creaky but spotless en-suite *pension* in a historic building with painted ceilings, fridges, fans and sea-view balconies for most rooms. They also offer three studios in Haráni, plus a family apartment.❹

Fiona At the top of the Kalí Stráta ℡22460 72088. Mock-traditional hotel building whose large airy rooms have double beds and stunning views; breakfast in mid-air on common balcony. Also 2 studios next door.❹

Jean Manship c/o *Jean & Tonic Bar* ℡ & ⓕ02460 71819 8pm–1am Greek time. Jean manages four traditional houses in Horió, suitable for two to six persons, with stunning views.❸–❹

Katerina Tsakiris Rooms Horió ℡22460 71813. Just a handful of very plain but air-con en-suite rooms with shared kitchen and grandstand view; reservations essential.❸–❹

Kokona Rear of marketplace, beyond main church ℡22460 71549, ⓕ22460 72620. Small hotel with bland if cheerful tile-and-pine, air-con rooms, some with balcony (and some package presence). Breakfast served outdoors, at base of the church belfry.❹

Niriides Apartments On Haráni–Emborió road, 2km from Yialós ℡22460 71784, ⓦwww.niriideshotel .gr. Spacious and quiet if plain units, distributed over four hillside buildings, sleep four and have phone, TV and optional air con. Friendly father-and-son management; discount for Internet bookings.❺

Symi Visitor Accommodation ℡22460 72755, ⓦwww.symivisitor.com. Managed by returned Greek-Australian Nikos Halkitis and partner Wendy Wilcox, who offer a variety of restored houses as double-occupancy studios in prime locations of Horió. Rates range from❹–❻ ; they also have pricier units suitable for four to five persons.

Villa Thalassa Far end of south quay. Contact as for Hotel Albatros. Old mansion divided into two air-con studios for couples (❻), and three larger apartments (❻) accommodating families.

The town

At the lively **port**, an architecturally protected area since the early 1970s, spice and sponge stalls plus a few jewellery shops throng with Rhodes-based trippers between 10am and 2.30pm, and the several excursion craft disgorging them envelop the quay with exhaust fumes. But just uphill, away from the water, the more peaceful pace of village life takes over, with livestock and chickens roaming free range. Two massive stair-paths, the **Kalí Stráta** and **Katarráktes**, effectively deter many of the day-trippers and are most dramatic towards sunset; large, owl-haunted ruins along the lower reaches of the Kalí Stráta are lonely and sinister after dark, though these too are now undergoing restoration one by one.

A series of blue arrows through Horió leads to the excellent local **museum** (Tues–Sun 8.30am–2.30pm; €2). Housed in a fine old mansion at the back of the village, the collection concentrates on Byzantine and medieval Sými, with exhibits on frescoes in isolated, locked churches and a gallery of medieval icons, as well as antiquarian maps and the inevitable ethnographic wing. The nearby **Hatziagapitos mansion** has been refurbished as an annexe; here, wonderful carved wooden chests are the main exhibits, along with fragmentary wall-paintings. On the way back to central Horió, the nineteenth-century pharmacy, with its apothecary jars and wooden drawers labelled for exotic herbal remedies, is worth a look.

At the very pinnacle of things, a **Knights' castle** occupies the site of Sými's ancient acropolis, and you glimpse a stretch of Classical polygonal wall on one side. A dozen churches grace Horió; that of the Assumption, inside the fortifications, is a replacement of the one blown to bits when the Germans detonated the munitions cached there. One of the bells in the new belfry is the nose-cone of a thousand-pound bomb, hung as a memorial.

Eating and drinking

You're best off avoiding most **eateries** on the north and west quays of the port, where menus, ingredients, prices and attitudes have been terminally warped by the day-trip trade. Away from these areas, you've a fair range of choice among *koultouriárika* tavernas, old-style *mayireftá* places, a few genuine ouzerís and even a traditional *kafenío* or two.

Dhimitris South quay, on the way out of town. Excellent, family-run seafood-stressing ouzerí with exotic items such as *hokhlióalo* (sea snails), *foúskes, spinóalo* and the miniature local shrimps, along with the more usual dishes and lots of vegetarian starters.

Haritomeni Northeast edge of Horió, about halfway up the hill in kink of the road above Yialós filling station ☏22460 71686. Somewhat pricey Greek-patronized ouzerí with such fare as *pastourmá* turnovers, *mydhopílafo* (mussels in rice), artichokes in egg-lemon sauce, assorted aubergine platters. Open all year: lovely terrace with views in summer, fireplace interior in winter. Reserve in peak season.

Lefteris Top of the Kalí Stráta where it levels off into a small platía, Horió. The local characters' *kafenío*, well attended by all. The place for a coffee or an ice cream at any hour.

O Meraklis Rear of the bazaar. Polite service and fair portions of moderate-priced *mayireftá*, fresh fish and *mezédhes* make this a reliable year-round bet. Sample meal: beans, beets, dips, and roast lamb with potatoes as a tender main course.

Mythos South quay between bus and taxi stops, Yialós. Supper-only ouzerí that's reckoned among the best, and best-value, cooking on the island. There is a menu, but let chef Stavros hit you with his Frenchified medley which might include salad, seafood starters (squid in

basil sauce), *poungí* (seafood parcel in fyllo), courgette-and-mushroom mould, and home-made desserts. Budget €23 a head before dipping into the decent wine list. In summer, operations move 150m down the quay to *Aktaion*, a roof-terrace annexe, and *Mythos* becomes a snack-café open at lunch too; otherwise supper only at the main premises spring and autumn. Credit cards accepted.

Pahos West quay (no sign). The old-boys' *kafenío*, in operation since World War II, and still a classic spot for a sundown ouzo and people-watching. Pahos himself has retired and can often be found sitting out front as a customer; otherwise it's unchanged.

Syllogos Just south off Horió platía. Vast but not impersonal place with indoor and outdoor seating, great for taverna standards like *skordhaliá, saganáki*, fried fresh fish and eggplant recipes. George Bush (Snr) dined here repeatedly on his visits to the island, as much for the food as for the fact that security arrangements were easy.

Yiorgos Near top of Kalí Stráta in Horió. Jolly, much-loved institution since 1977, with summer seating on a pebble-mosaic courtyard. Service can be slipshod, food quality fluctuates wildly, and prices match Yialós levels, but perennial recipes include feta-stuffed peppers, spinach-rice, chicken in mushroom-wine sauce, and grilled fish when available. Open random lunchtimes in season, supper all year (indoors in winter).

Nightlife and events

Nightlife continues into the early hours and is biased towards Yialós. Convivial *Jean & Tonic* is the heart and soul of the bar scene in Horió, catering to a mixed clientele (visitors and expats until 3am, Greek restaurateurs 3am until dawn) most of the year. Down at Yialós, the *Harani Club* offers a mix of Greek and international music depending on the crowd; in the same alley, *Vapori* was the first outsider-owned bar here (in 1983), and continues the tradition with newspapers draped over chairs, breakfasts and **Internet** access (three terminals). Elsewhere, *Katoi* on the south quay is a no-hassle bar favoured by locals. In terms of more formal **events**, there's a year-round Friday-night **filmthèque** inside the Petrideio mansion, while the July-to-September **Sými Festival** has, since its mid-1990s inception, become one of Greece's more interesting small summer bashes, with a mix of classical and Greek-popular performances.

Around the island

Sými has no big sandy beaches, but there are plenty of pebbly stretches at the heads of the deep, protected bays which indent the coastline. **PÉDHI**, a short bus ride down from Horió, retains some of its former identity as a fishing hamlet, with enough water in the plain behind – the island's largest – to support a few vegetable gardens. The beach is poor, though, and patronage from yachts and the *Pedhi Beach* hotel has bumped up prices at local **tavernas**, of which the most reasonable and authentic is fish specialist *Tolis* (no sign), tucked away by the boatyard at the north corner of the bay. Many will opt for either a taxi-boat or another twenty minutes of walking via a rough but obvious path along the south shore of the almost landlocked bay to **Áyios Nikólaos**. The only all-sand cove on Sými, this offers sheltered swimming, tamarisks for shade and an adequate taverna. Alternatively, a paint-splodge-marked path on the north side of the inlet leads in half an hour to **Ayía Marína**, where there's a minuscule beach, a shingle lido with sunbeds, a rather posh taverna-bar complete with tended lawn, and a monastery-capped islet to which you can easily swim.

Around Yialós, you'll find tiny *Symi Paradise* "beach" (still called **NOS** or Navtikós Ómilos Sýmis by most) ten minutes past the boatyards at Haráni, but there's sun here only until lunchtime – not a bad thing in high summer. You can continue along the cement-paved coast road, with steps leading down to rock slabs favoured by nudists, or cut inland from the Yialós platía past the abandoned desalination plant, to quiet **Emborió** (Nimborió) Bay, with a taverna and a coarse-shingle beach a bit beyond. Inland from this lie Byzantine mosaic fragments under a protective shelter (follow signs to "Early Christian Basilica"), and, nearby, a catacomb complex known locally as **Dhódheka Spília**.

Remoter bays

Plenty of other, more secluded coves are accessible to energetic walkers with sturdy footwear, or those prepared to pay for the taxi-boats (daily in season 10am–1pm, returning 4–6pm. These are the most popular method of reaching the southern bays of Marathoúnda and Nanoú, and the only method of getting to the spectacular fjord of **Áyios Yeóryios Dhyssálona**. Dhyssálona lacks a taverna and lies in shade after 1pm, while **Marathoúnda** is fringed by coarse, often slimy pebbles (though it has a normal-priced, tasty eponymous **taverna**, very popular at weekends), making **Nanoú** the most popular destination for day-trips. The 200-metre beach there consists of gravel, sand and small pebbles, with a scenic backdrop of pines and a reasonable **taverna** (menu of squid, chips and salad) just behind. It's also possible to reach Nanoú overland, via Panayía Strateri chapel up on the main trans-island road, descending a scenic, forested gorge for some forty minutes; most of the old path from Horió to Panayía Strateri still exists, making a marvellous traverse of about three hours in total, leaving time for a meal and swim at Nanóu before the boat trip back to Yialós.

For more hiking adventures, you can cross the island from Horió in ninety minutes to **Áyios Vassílios**, the most scenic of the gulfs with its namesake little monastery and **Lápathos** beach; in about the same time to

Tolí, a deserted, west-facing cove, also accessible from Emborió; or in three hours, partly through forest, from Yialós to **Áyios Emilianós** at the island's extreme west end, where another little monastery is tethered to the body of Sými by a causeway. On the way to the latter you'll pass near the monastery of **Taxiárhis Mihaïl Roukouniótis** (usually shut, ring current warden on posted mobile number), Sými's oldest, with naïve eighteenth-century frescoes and a peculiar ground plan: the current *katholikón* is actually superimposed on a lower, thirteenth-century structure abandoned after being burnt and pillaged by pirates during the 1400s, though a fine fresco of St Lawrence (Áyios Lavréntios) survives behind the altar screen. However, some of the best frescoes on the island, of early-eighteenth-century vintage, are found at the monastery of **Megálos Sotíros**, on the road south to Panormítis, just before the drop down the escarpment. Frescoes inside the *katholikón*, in the middle of the arcaded, pebble-paved courtyard, are devoted unsurprisingly to the life of the Saviour (*Sotír* in Greek), include a fine *Deposition*, with Joseph of Arimathaea holding a winding sheet to receive the dead Christ, and a *Resurrection* with Jesus all but doing a jig on the sepulchre. Across the road, you can follow a signposted trail to some worthwhile, reconstructed Byzantine **wine presses**.

Panormítis monastery

The Archangel is also honoured at the huge monastery of **Taxiárhis Mihaïl Panormítis** near the southern tip of the island, Sými's biggest rural attraction and the first port of call for some excursion boats from Rhodes (confirm the itinerary if you wish to proceed direct to Yialós – many craft do). These allow only a quick thirty-minute tour; if you want more time, you'll have to come by scooter from Yialós (though the road down from the central escarpment is steep, with nine hairpin bends), or stay the night (€10 minimum donation) in the *xenónas* (inn) set aside for pilgrims. They monopolize it all summer, as Mihaïl has been adopted as the patron of sailors in the Dodecanese.

Like many of Sými's monasteries, Panormítis is of recent (eighteenth-century) vintage and was thoroughly pillaged during World War II, so don't expect much of the building or its treasures. An appealing *votsalotó* courtyard surrounds the central *katholikón*, tended by the Archimandrite Gabriel and lit by an improbable number of oil lamps. It's also graced by a fine *témblon* and of course the cult icon, though the frescoes are recent and mediocre. One of the two small museums (€1.50 each) contains a strange mix of precious antiques, exotic junk (stuffed crocodiles and koalas, elephant tusks), votive offerings, models of ships and a chair piled with messages-in-bottles brought here by Aegean currents – the idea being that if the bottle or toy boat arrived, the sender got their prayer answered. There's a shop/*kafenío*, a bakery and a **taverna** (*Panormion*) popular with passengers of the many yachts calling in. Near the taverna stands a memorial commemorating three Greeks, including the monastery's abbot, executed on February 11, 1944 by the Germans for aiding British commandos.

Tílos

The small, usually quiet island of **Tílos**, with an official population of about five hundred (dwindling to 100 in winter), is one of the least frequented and worst connected of the Dodecanese, though it can (in theory) be visited on a day-trip by catamaran from Rhodes. Why anyone would want to come for

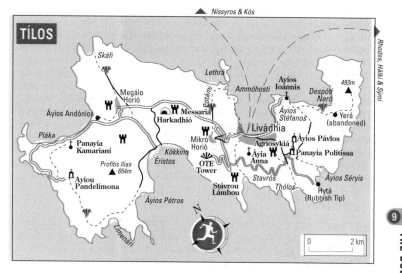

just a few hours is unclear: while it's a great place to rest on the beach or go walking, there is nothing very striking at first glance. After a few days, however, you may have stumbled on several of the seven small **castles** of the Knights of St John, which stud the crags, or found some of the inconspicuous medieval chapels clinging to the hillsides.

Tílos shares the characteristics of its closest neighbours: limestone **mountains** resembling those of Hálki, plus volcanic lowlands, pumice beds and red-lava sand as on Níssyros. Though rugged and scrubby on its heights, the island has ample water – from springs or pumped up from the agricultural plains – and clusters of oak and terebinth near the cultivated areas. From many points on the island you've startling views across to Kós, Sými, Turkey, Níssyros, Hálki, Rhodes and even (weather permitting) Kárpathos.

Since the mid-1990s, however, development on Tílos has threatened to reverse the conditions which many visitors have come to enjoy; besides the Dodge City atmosphere of Livádhia, a hyperactive bulldozing programme has scarred virtually every mountain in the east of the island. Thankfully the remotest beaches are located in too steep a terrain to be approached by road without prohibitive expense, and a project is afoot to protect much of coastal and mountain Tílos as a national park (consult ⓦ www.tilos-park.org).

Getting around and information

Tílos's main road runs 7km from Livádhia, the port village, to Megálo Horió, the capital and only other significant habitation. A public **bus** links the two, and services are theoretically scheduled to coincide with seaborne arrivals; at other times the sleek bus makes up to six runs daily along the Livádhia–Éristos stretch. There are also two **taxis**, or you can rent a **car** from outlets in Livádhia such as Drive (ⓣ 22460 44173) and Tilos Travel (number below). Stefanakis, also in Livádhia (ⓣ 22460 44310), has a monopoly on ferry and hydrofoil tickets; Tilos Travel is arguably the more helpful, however (ⓣ 22460 44294 or 694 65 59 697, ⓦ www.tilostravel.co.uk), offering an accommodation booking service, used-book swop and scooter as well as car rental. For more active sea-going jaunts with kayaks or windsurfers, contact French-run Tilos Marine at Livádhia beach. The *Sea Star* catamaran has its own office by the church (☎22460 44000). the single **filling station**, keeping odd hours, lies between Livádhia and Megálo Horió.

Many visitors come specifically to **walk**, assisted by the extremely accurate **map** prepared by Baz "Paris" Ward and sold locally – or by certified walking **guides** Iain and Lyn Fulton (☎22460 44128 or 694 60 54 593, ⓔfulton@otenet.gr), who may take you on unusual itineraries not described or mapped in existing literature. A half-dozen sections of deteriorating trail or *kalderími* have been surveyed in preparation for cleaning and consolidation, so quality walking opportunities should improve in the future.

There's a **post office** in Livádhia, a single **bank** with an ATM, **Internet** facilities at Kosmos gift shop and two well-stocked if overpriced **supermarkets**.

Livádhia

Despite an ambitious waterfront improvement programme in 2005 – flagstoned terraces, shoreline walkway, garish 2000-watt lighting – **LIVÁDHIA** with its unfinished building sites and higgledy-piggledy layout makes a poor introduction to the island. Yet it remains the best-equipped settlement to deal with tourists, and is closest to the majority of remaining path-hikes.

Accommodation

There are generally enough beds in the various **studios** and **hotels** to go around, but in peak season it's certainly worth phoning ahead or consulting the Tilos Travel website. Truly budget options are steadily vanishing in favour of newer, better-appointed, sea-view choices like the galleried ✻ *Blue Sky Apartments* above the ferry dock (apply to Tilos Travel; ❹); *Marina's Studios* (☎22460 44023; ❸), up the hillside from these, large if basic studios arrayed over three buildings; *Pavlos* (☎22460 44011; ❸), four small if well-kept rooms overlooking their own sunbeds at mid-beach; and the *Faros Hotel* (☎22460 44068; ❸) at the extreme end of Livádhia bay, well regarded for its calm atmosphere and hospitable managing family.

Inland, go for the well-appointed *Studios Irinna* (☎22410 44366; ❸), alias *Kula's*; or the *Hotel Irini* (☎22410 44293, ⓦwww.tilosholidays.gr; ❸–❹), 200m inland from mid-beach, with a popular pool, good breakfasts and pleasant gardens making up for somewhat small rooms. The same keen management has the *Studios Ilidi Rock* on the west hillside (❹ for 2, ❺ for 4-person apartments).

Eating, drinking and nightlife

Up to a dozen **tavernas** operate around Livádhia in peak season; of these barely a third merit consideration. At shoulder season, you have to book for timed seatings at the more Anglophilic eateries – unheard of on other islands. Among the more authentic spots for a no-nonsense Greek feed are much-improved *Mihalis* with its popular garden tables, good for roast goat and fish, as well as good vegetable platters and non-CAIR bulk wine; *To Armenon* (alias *Níkos'*) on the shore road, an excellent and salubrious beach-taverna-cum-ouzerí, with octopus salad, white beans and the like; and the restaurant attached to the *Marina Hotel*. French-Vietnamese-run *Calypso* (☎694 72 13 278; supper only) lost its lease at the end of 2005; if it has re-opened elsewhere, it should still excel at Creole-colonial dishes like *Martiniqueois* prawn *acras* or Vietnamese pork-and-mushroom vermicelli.

For **breakfast** (plus evening thin-crust pizzas, home-made desserts and strong cocktails), Anglo-Italian *Joanna's Café*, just inland from the bakery is accomplished but pricey and thus losing business to seaside alternatives. 🛪 *Iy Omonia* (aka *Tou Mihali*), under trees strung with light bulbs, near the post office, is the enduringly popular traditional alternative for a sundowner, breakfast or a tipple while waiting for a ferry, and also does inexpensive, tasty *mezédhes* so generous as to obviate the need for a formal meal. The jetty-café *Remezzo* also does excellent, reasonable ouzo-*mezédhes*.

Organized **nightlife** in or near Livádhia is limited to *Bozi* at the far east end of the bay (nightly in summer, weekends otherwise) and the *Café Akti* upstairs opposite the Italian "palace", with great views.

Around Livádhia

From Livádhia you can walk an hour north along the obvious trail to the pebble bay of **Lethrá**, or in about the same time south on separate itineraries to the secluded coves of **Stavrós** or **Thólos**. The track to the former begins between the *Tilos Mare Hotel* and the *Castellania Apartments*, becoming a trail at the highest new house in the village; once up to the saddle with its paved road, you've a sharp drop to the beach – ignore over-eager cairning in the bed of the descending ravine, the true path is up on the right bank, indicated by red-painted surveyor's marks. The route to Thólos begins by the cemetery and the chapel of **Áyios Pandelímon**, then curls around under the seemingly impregnable castle of **Agriosykiá**; from the saddle on the paved road overlooking the descent to Thólos (25min; also surveyed in preparation for refurbishment), a route marked with cairns leads northwest to the citadel in twenty minutes. You can use that paved road, heading a couple curves east, to reach the trailhead for **Áyios Séryis** bay, the most pristine of Tílos' beaches but the hardest to get to (30min one-way, path poor but cairned).

It's less than an hour's walk west, with some surviving path sections shortcutting the road curves, up to the ghost village of **Mikró Horió**, whose 1200 inhabitants left for Livádhia during the 1950s. The only intact structures are the church (locked except for the August 15 festival) and an old house which has been restored as a small-hours **music pub** and operates only during July and August, with a rather aggressive house/techno playlist.

Megálo Horió and Éristos

The rest of Tílos's inhabitants live in or near **MEGÁLO HORIÓ**, which enjoys an enviable perspective over the vast agricultural plain stretching down to Éristos (see overleaf), and is overlooked in turn by a prominent castle of the Knights, built on the site of ancient Tílos, whose recycled masonry remains evident. You reach it by a stiff, thirty-minute climb that begins on the lane behind the Ikonomou supermarket before threading its way through a vast jumble of cisterns, house foundations and derelict chapels – the remains of the much larger medieval Megálo Horió. Two more flanking fortresses stare out across the plain: the easterly one of **Messariá** helpfully marks the location of the **Harkadhió** cave (closed), where Pleiocene midget-elephant bones were discovered in 1971; the cave-mouth was hidden for centuries until a World War II artillery barrage exposed it. The bones themselves have been transferred to a tiny, not very compelling **museum** in Megálo Horió, on the ground floor of the town hall (Mon–Fri 8am–2.30pm on application upstairs to the warden).

Best choices for **accommodation** in the village are the central *Milios Apartments* (☎22460 44204, 🖷22460 442665; ❷–❸ size-dependent) or

Studios Ta Elefandakia (℡22460 44213;❷), set among attractive gardens by the car park. The better and friendlier of two **tavernas** is *Iy Kalia Kardhia*, on the downhill one-way street out of the village, with good grills and views. There's a traditional **kafenío** by historic Taxiárhis church, and further up, Athenian-run *Kafenio Ilakati* (late May to early Sept only; opens 7pm), with cakes and drinks.

Below Megálo Horió, signs direct you towards the three-kilometre side road to long, pink-grey-sand **Éristos** beach, allegedly the island's best, though a reefy zone must be crossed entering the water. The far south end, where the reef recedes, is also a designated nudist zone, as are the two secluded, attractive coves at **Kókkino** south beyond the headland (accessible by path only). On the secondary, parallel road down to Éristos, the *En Plo* is the best nearby venue for a snack – also affiliated with the *Nitsa Apartments* (℡694 49 89 437❷), while the *Eristos Beach Hotel* (℡22460 44025❸) offers some of the highest room standards on Tílos, with a plusher ❹) annexe attracting package clientele.

The far northwest

The main road beyond Megálo Horió hits the coast again at somewhat grim **ÁYIOS ANDÓNIOS**, whose main bright spot is a **taverna**, *Dhelfíni*, packed at weekend lunch because of its fresh seafood and frequented otherwise by the local fishermen. At low tide on the exposed, truncated beach you can find more lava-trapped skeletons strung out in a row – human this time – presumably tide-washed victims of a Nissyrian eruption in 600 BC, and discovered by the same archeologists who found the miniature pachyderms. There's better, warm-water swimming at isolated, sandy **Pláka** beach, 2km west of Áyios Andónios, where people camp rough despite a total lack of facilities.

The paved road finally ends 8km west of Megálo Horió at the fortified **monastery of Ayíou Pandelímona** (daily: May–Sept 10am–7pm, Oct–April 10am–4pm), founded in the fifteenth century for the sake of its miraculous spring, still the best water on the island. A fitfully operating drinks café hosts the island's major festival of July 25–27 – as well as several peacocks and Rhodian miniature deer. The monastery's tower-gate and oasis setting, more than two hundred forbidding metres above the west coast, are the most memorable features, though an eminently photogenic inner courtyard boasts a *votsalotói* surface, and the church a fine marble floor. On the south *katholikón* wall, an early eighteenth-century fresco shows the founder-builder holding a model of the monastery, while behind the ornate altar screen, in the conch, hides another rare fresco of the Holy Trinity.

The public bus calls here just once a week as part of a tour, so you'll need transport to get here. To vary the **return to Megálo Horió**, take a taxi out, then walk back much of the way on a signposted path; it's shown correctly on Baz Ward's recommended map, and ends at the minor monastery of Panayía Kamrianí near Áyios Andónios. Committed and experienced hill-walkers can tackle the challenging path which curls around the southwest flank of Profítis Ilías, Tílos's highest mountain, finishing three-plus hours later near Áyios Pétros cove, with a further half-hour track-walking to Éristos (allow 5hr with stops). This begins, as signposted, beside the monastery; it's a well-surveyed route, with no real exposure or sharp drops, but there's only one spring along the way, rather disheartening scree at the start, and the wild feel of a remote traverse on a much larger island.

Níssyros

Volcanic **Níssyros** is noticeably greener than its southern neighbours Tílos and Hálki, and unlike them has proven wealthy enough to retain over eight hundred of its population year-round (down, though, from 10,000 in 1900). While remittances from abroad (particularly New York) are significant, most of the island's income is derived from the offshore islet of Yialí, essentially a vast lump of **pumice** slowly being quarried away by Lava Ltd. The concession fee collected from Lava by the municipality has engendered a huge public payroll and vast per-capita sums available to spend, making Níssyros something of a mini-Kuwait. Under the circumstances, the Nissyrians bother little with agriculture other than keeping cows and pigs; the hillside terraces meticulously carved out for grain and grapes lie fallow, and wine is no longer made here.

The main island's peculiar geology is potentially a source of other benefits: DEI, the Greek power company, spent the years between 1988 and 1992 sinking exploratory **geothermal** wells and attempting to convince the islanders of the benefits of cheap electricity. In 1993, a local referendum went massively against the project, as did (by a closer margin) a 1997 poll, after which DEI and its Italian contractor took the hint and packed up. The desalination plant scarcely provides enough fresh water to spur a massive growth in package tourism; the relatively few tourists (mostly German) who stay the night, as opposed to the day-trippers from Kós, still find peaceful villages with a minimum of concrete eyesores and a friendly if rather tight-knit population.

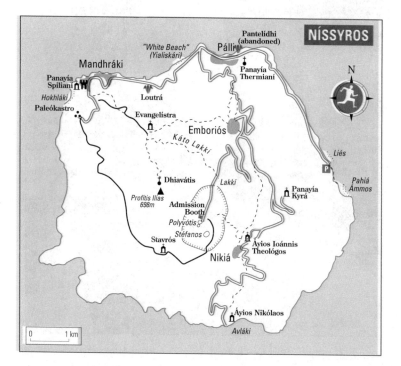

△ Langadháki district, Mandhráki, Níssyros

Níssyros also offers good **walking** opportunities through a countryside planted with oak and terebinth, on a network of trails fitfully marked and maintained; you may hear the contented grunting of pigs as they gorge themselves on acorns from the many oak trees. Autumn is a wonderful time, especially when the landscape has perked up after the first rains; the late-January almond-blossoming is much reduced owing to an early-1990s blight that devastated the trees, which are now making a slow comeback.

Mandhráki

MANDHRÁKI is the deceptively large port and island capital, with blue patches of sea visible at the end of narrow streets lined with tightly packed houses, whose brightly painted balconies and shutters are mandated by law. Except for the tattier fringes near the ferry dock, where multiple souvenir shops and bad tavernas pitched at day-trippers leave a poor first impression, the bulk of the place is cheerful and village-like, arrayed around the community orchard or *kámbos* and overlooked by two ancient fortresses.

Into a corner of the nearer citadel, the fourteenth-century Knights' castle, is wedged the little monastery of **Panayía Spilianí**, built on this spot in accordance with instructions from the Virgin, who appeared in a vision to one of the first Christian islanders. The monastery's prestige grew after raiding Saracens failed to discover the vast quantities of silver secreted here in the form of a rich collection of Byzantine icons. During 1996–97, the Langadháki area just below was rocked by a series of earthquakes, damaging a score of venerable houses (mostly repaired now); the seismic threat is ever present, quite literally cutting the ground out from under those who erroneously dub the volcano "extinct".

As a defensive bastion, the seventh-century-BC Doric **Paleókastro** (unrestricted access), twenty minutes' well-signposted walk out of Langadháki, is infinitely more impressive than the Knights' castle, and ranks as one of the more underrated ancient sites in Greece. Despite lingering scaffolding from a 2002–06 restoration, you can clamber up onto the massive, polygonal-block walls by means of a broad staircase beside the still-intact gateway.

Information and transport

The most useful of Mandhráki's four **travel agencies** are Kentris (℡22420 31227), near the town hall, handling GA and Blue Star ferries, and Dhiakomihalis (℡22240 31459), which acts as a representative for the catamarans and hydrofoils and rents cars; both sell Olympic Airways tickets. There's a **post office** at the port and **Internet** access at *Proveza* café, in Lefkandió district; get money at a single **bank** in town, or an unrelated, stand-alone **ATM** at the harbour. Also at the base of the jetty is the **bus stop**, with (theoretically) up to five daily departures to the hill villages and six to Pálli. Otherwise, there are two set-rate **taxis** and two outlets for **scooter rental**: Yannis (℡693 7234033), on the shore lane, and Manos K (℡22420 31028), by the single filling station, which also **rents cars**.

Accommodation

You'll see a handful of port **hotels** on your left as you disembark, of which the best value and most comfortable are the waterfront *Three Brothers* (℡22420 31344; ❷) and the municipally run *Xenon Polyvotis* (℡22420 31011, ℉22420 31204; ❸), whose biggish, neutral-decor rooms have fans and (mostly) knockout sea views. In the town centre is Mandhráki's best-amenitied accommodation, the *Hotel Porfyris* (℡22420 31376, ℉22420 31176; ❹), with a large swimming pool and breakfast terrace; many rooms, which have air con and fridges, overlook the sea and *kámbos*. Other than this, you're advised to splurge on two excellent restoration projects which are finally making use of Níssyros' considerable architectural heritage. On the shore lane near the windmill are the two comfortable if pricey suites of ↟ *Ta Liotridia* (☎22420 31580, ⓔliotridia@nisyrosnet.gr;❼), hosting up to four and arguably worth it for the sea views and pointed-volcanic-stone-and-wood decor, though the bar downstairs could be noisy. Near the top of the village stands *Spiliada* (☎22420 31166,❼), quieter and a tad cheaper, with the same masonry scheme but tile-floored and set up for self-catering.

Eating and nightlife

Culinary **specialities** include *pittiá* (chickpea croquettes), pickled caper greens, honey and *soumádha*, an almond-syrup drink widely sold in recycled wine bottles, which should be consumed within three months of purchase; the latter three specialties are most easily available at To Paradhosiako shop, 250m towards town from the port.

When eating out, give all of the commercialized, shoddy shoreline **tavernas** a miss in favour of more genuine haunts inland. Top of the heap is evenings-only ↟ *Ouzeri Iy Fabrika* (June–Sept Fri–Wed, Oct–May Thur–Sat), with indoor/outdoor tables by season, *rebétilka* soundtrack and well-priced, hearty fare with plenty for vegetarians. Runners-up include friendly *Irini* on lively, ficus-shaded Platía Ilikioméni, with more involved *mayireftá* unavailable elsewhere as well as fish, or little *Taverna Nissiros*, the oldest eatery in town, always busy despite predictably average grill quality.

Foci of **nightlife** are several cafés on Platía Ilikioméni, and a string of *barákia* on the shore at Lefkandió district, the most popular of these being *Enallax* and the stunning, ex-olive-press bar of the *Liotridia* inn, which also has periodic exhibits.

Pálli and around

Beaches on Níssyros are in even shorter supply than water, so much so that tour agencies here occasionally peddle excursions to a sandy cove on **Áyios Andónios** islet, opposite the Yialí mines. Closer to hand, the short, black-rock beach of **Hokhláki**, behind the Knights' castle, is unusable if the wind is up. It's best to head east along the main road, passing the refurbished spa of **Loutrá** (hot mineral water baths 8–11am; only by doctor's referral), worth a stop for its "snack-bar" at the far end of the building, really an **ouzerí** with a well-chosen soundtrack and fair portions of salads, fried appetizers, seafood and meat – though it's frankly overpriced.

A kilometre or so further, 4km in total from Mandhráki, the fishing village of **PÁLLI** makes an excellent hangout at lunchtime, when the port fills with trippers. **Tavernas** have multiplied, but the newer ones generate reader complaints of price-gouging, so best stick with the two long-term favourites: the less expensive *Ellinis*, with spit-roasted meat by night, grilled fish in season and simple rooms upstairs (☎22420 31453,❷), or the adjacent *Afroditi* (aka *Nikos & Tsambika*), with big portions of grills and *mayireftá*, Cretan bulk wine and excellent home-made desserts. A scooter-rental outlet, an excellent bakery cranking out brown bread and fine pies (branch in Mandhráki), and modest nightlife make Pálli also worth considering as a base. About the only other **accommodation** is *Frantzis Studios* by the bakery (☎22420 31240;❸), with well-kept units in slightly scruffy grounds. A tamarisk-shaded, dark-sand **beach**, kept well groomed, extends east of Pálli to the abandoned Pantelídhi spa, behind which the little grotto-chapel of **Panayía Thermianí** is tucked inside the vaulted remains of a Roman baths complex.

To reach Níssyros's best beaches, continue in this direction for an hour on foot (or twenty minutes by bike along the road), past an initially discouraging seaweed- and cowpat-littered shoreline, to the delightful cove of **Liés**, with a snack-bar, *Oasis* (July–Aug only). Just beyond here the paved road ends at a car park 5km beyond Pálli; in summer boat trips from Mandhráki call here too. Walking another fifteen minutes along a trail over the headland brings you to the idyllic, 300-metre expanse of **Pahiá Ámmos**, with grey-pink sand heaped in dunes, limited shade at the far end and a large colony of rough campers and/or naturists in summer.

The interior

Níssyros's central, dormant **volcano** gives the island its special character and fosters the growth of the abundant vegetation – and no stay would be complete without a visit. When excursion boats arrive from Kós, several agency coaches and usually one of the public buses are pressed into service to take customers into the interior. These tours tend to monopolize the crater floor between 11am and 2pm, so if you want solitude, use early-morning or late-afternoon scheduled buses to Nikiá (a few daily continue to the crater floor), a scooter or your own two feet to get there.

The road up from Pálli winds first past the virtually abandoned village of **EMBORIÓS**, where pigs and free-ranging cattle (a major driving hazard) far outnumber people, though the place is slowly being bought up and restored by Athenians and foreigners. New owners are often surprised to discover natural saunas, heated by volcano steam, in the basements of the crumbling houses; at the outskirts of the village there's a signposted public **steam bath** in a grotto, its entrance outlined in white paint. If you're descending to Pálli from here, an old cobbled way starting at the sharp bend below the sauna offers an attractive short cut of the four-kilometre road, while another *kalderími* drops from behind *To Balkoni tou Emboriou* **taverna** (May–Oct; limited, if cheap, menu) to within a quarter-hour's walk of the craters.

NIKIÁ, the large village on the east side of the volcano's caldera, is – with fifty year-round inhabitants – more of a going concern, and its spectacular situation 14km from Mandhráki offers views out to Tílos as well as across the volcanic caldera. The best place to **eat** and **drink** here is *Iy Porta* (all year, but reduced menu Oct–June), serving good salads, dips and variable *mayireftá* on the engagingly round plaza ringed by stone seating, itself called the Pórta and marked out in white paint for the steps of folk dances. By the bus turnaround area, signs point to the 45-minute **trail** descending to the crater floor; a few minutes downhill, you can detour briefly to the eyrie-like **monastery of Áyios Ioánnis Theológos**, which only comes to life at the September 25–26 evening festival. To **drive** directly to the volcanic area you must use the road that veers off just past Emboriós.

The volcano – and walks

However you approach the **volcano**, a sulphurous stench drifts out to meet you as trees and pasture, then clumps of oregano, gradually give way to lifeless, caked powder. The sunken main crater of **Stéfanos** is extraordinary, a striated moonscape of grey, white, brown and sickly yellow; there is another, less-visited double crater (dubbed **Polyvótis**) to the west, arguably more dramatic, with a clear trail leading up to it from the snack-bar. The perimeters of both are pocked with tiny blowholes from which jets of steam puff constantly and around which form little pincushions of pure sulphur crystals. Towards the eastern side of Stéfanos, boiling mud-pots have surfaced since the millennium (not for the first time, and there's a danger of falling through the crater-floor at their edges); anywhere nearby it sounds like a huge cauldron bubbling away below you. According to legend this is the groaning of Polyvotis, a titan crushed here by Poseidon under a huge rock torn from Kós. When there are tour groups around, a small, tree-shaded snack-bar operates in the centre of the wasteland, and a booth on the access road charges admission (€1.50) to the volcanic zone.

Since DEI's 1991 destruction of the old direct *kalderími* between the volcano and Mandhráki, finding pleasant options for **walking** back to town requires a bit of imagination – though paths are marked with red paint-dots and wooden signposts – and possession of Beate and Jürgen Franke's GPS-drawn topographical map (downloadable free from ⓦwww.bjfranke.privat.t-online .de/n1-e.htm). First choice involves backtracking along the main crater access road for about 1km from the admission booth to find the start of a clear, crudely marked path which passes the volcanic gulch of **Káto Lákki** and the monastery of **Evangelístra** on its two-hour-plus course back to the port. You can lengthen the trip by detouring from Evangelístra south to **Profítis Ilías**, the island's summit, a two-hour round-trip – the route is well marked with cairns or white paint. An alternative approach to Evangelístra requires returning to Emboriós and leaving from the top of the village, near the cemetery and small castle, on a 45-minute course to the monastery – an enjoyable link, despite haphazard marking and cleaning. From Evangelístra, the onward route to Mandhráki briefly follows the road down before the marked path resumes, handily shortcutting hairpin bends.

Kós

After Rhodes, **Kós** is the second largest and second most popular island in the Dodecanese, and there are superficial similarities between the two. Here also the harbour is guarded by an imposing castle of the Knights of St John; the streets are lined with grandiose Italian-built public buildings; and minarets and palm trees punctuate extensive Hellenistic and Roman remains. Although its hinterland for the most part lacks the wild beauty of Rhodes' interior, acre for acre Kós is the most fertile of the Dodecanese, blessed with rich soil and abundant ground water.

Mass **tourism** has largely displaced the old agrarian lifestyle amongst the population of just over 28,000; all-inclusive complexes totalling tens of thousands of beds are a spreading blight which contribute nothing to the local economy. Except for Kós Town and Mastihári, there aren't many independent travellers, and from early July to early September you'll be lucky to find any sort of room at all without reservations far in advance, or a prebooked package. The tourist industry is juxtaposed rather bizarrely with cows munching amid baled hay, and Greek Army tanks exercising in the volcanic badlands around the airport. All these peculiarities acknowledged, Kós is still definitely worth a few days' time while island-hopping: its handful of **mountain villages** are appealing, the tourist infrastructure excellent (including such amenities as regular city buses and cycle paths) and swimming opportunities are limitless – about half the island's perimeter is fringed by **beaches** of various sizes, colours and consistencies.

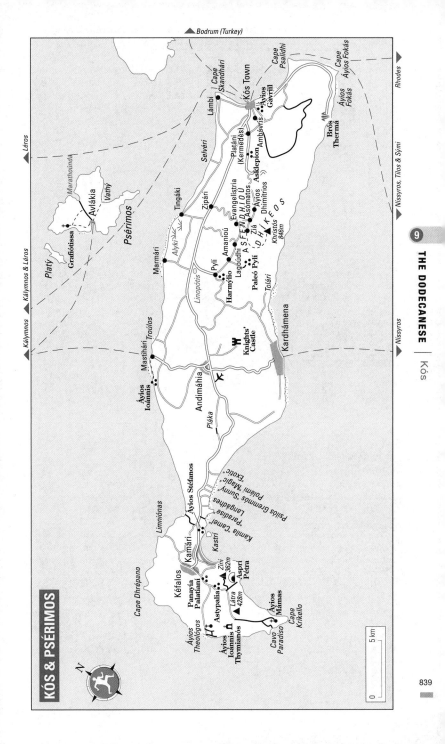

KÓS & PSÉRIMOS

Bodrum (Turkey)

Léros

Kálymnos & Léros

Kálymnos

Nissyros

Nissyros, Tílos & Sými

Rhodes

Cape Skandhári

Kós Town

Cape Psalídhi

Cape Áyios Fokás

Lámbi

Áyios Gávril

Áyios Fokás

Marathoúnda

Vathý

Avlákia

Pláti

Platáni (Kermedés)

Asklepíon

Ambávris

Brós Thermá

Grafiótissa

Psérimos

Selvéri

Tingáki

Zipári

Evangelistría

Ásómatos

Áyios Dhimítrios

Áyios

Khristós 846m

A S F E N D H I O U

Alykí

Amanioú

Pylí

Lagoúdhi

Paleó Pylí

Marmári

Harmýlio

Tolári

Linopótis

Troúlos

Masthári

Kardhámena

Áyios Ioánnis

Knights' Castle

Andimáhia

Pláka

Limniónas

 Áyios Stéfanos

Kamári

Kastrí

Psiloś Grémmos "Sunny" "Magic" "Exotic"

Langádhes "Paradise"

Kamíla "Camel"

Polémi

Cape Dhrépano

Kéfalos

Panayía Palatianí

Astypalia

Zíni 362m

Aspri Pétra

Látra 428m

Áyios Mámas

Cape Kríkello

Áyios Theológos

Áyios Ioánnis Thymianós

Cavo Paradíso

N

0   5 km

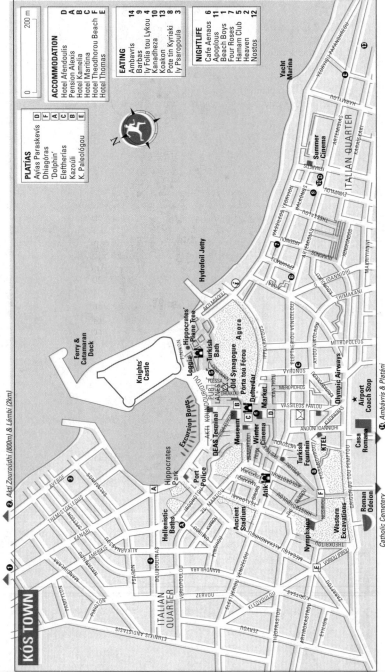

KÓS TOWN

⑪ (100m), Ⓕ (200m), ⑫ (300m), Campsite (1500m), Psalídhi, Áyios Fokás & Brós Thermá ▶

PLATÍAS
Ayías Paraskevís	D
Dhiagóras	F
'Dolphin'	A
Eleftherías	A
Kazoúli	C
K. Paleológou	B
	E

ACCOMMODATION
Hotel Afendoulis	D
Pension Alexis	A
Hotel Kamelia	B
Hotel Maritina	C
Hotel Theodhorou Beach	F
Hotel Thomas	E

EATING
Ambavris	14
Barbas	9
Iy Folia tou Lykou	4
Kanadheza	10
Koakon	13
Pote tin Kyriakí	8
Iy Psaropoula	3

NIGHTLIFE
Cafe Aenaos	6
Apoplous	11
Beach Boys	7
Four Roses	5
Hamam Club	2
Heaven	1
Nostos	12

Knights' Castle

Ferry & Catamaran Dock

Yacht Marina

Hydrofoil Jetty

ITALIAN QUARTER

Summer Cinema

Hippocrates' Plane Tree

Loggia

Turkish Bath

Old Synagogue

Agora

Pórta tou Fórou

Defterdar

Market

Hellenistic Baths

Port Police

Hippocrates Park

Excursion Boats

DEAS Terminal

Museum

Winter Cinema

Ancient Stadium

Turkish Fountain

Nymphaion

Western Excavations

Casa Romana

Roman Odeion

Olympic Airways

Airport Coach Stop

KTEL

Catholic Cemetery

ITALIAN QUARTER

◀ ② Ákti Zouroúdhi (800m) & Lámbi (2km)

◀ Villages, Airport & Asklepíon

▶ ⑩, Ambávris & Platáni

Kós Town

KÓS TOWN, home to over half of the island's population, spreads in all directions from the harbour, with most of its charm residing in scattered ancient and medieval antiquities. Apart from the Knights' castle, the first thing you see on arrival, there's a wealth of Hellenistic and Roman remains, many of which were only revealed by an earthquake in 1933, and excavated subsequently by the Italians, who also planned and laid out the "garden suburb" extending either side of the central grid. Elsewhere, vast areas of open space alternate with a hotchpotch of Ottoman monuments and later mock-medieval or Rationalist-Modernist buildings.

Arrival, transport and information

Large **ferries and catamarans** anchor just outside the harbour at a special dock by one corner of the castle; **excursion boats** to neighbouring islands sail right in and berth all along Aktí Koundouriótou. **Hydrofoils** tie up south of the castle at their own jetty, on Aktí Miaoúli. Virtually all ferry and excursion-boat agents sit within 50m of each other at the intersection of pedestrianized Vassiléos Pávlou and the waterfront. Among the more helpful and genuinely representative of ferries and hydrofoils, not just expensive excursions, are Kentriko (for Blue Star) by the DEAS terminal (℡ 22420 28914); Exas (for most everyone else) opposite the National Bank at Andóni Ioannídhi 4 (℡ 22420 29900); and Hermes at Vasiléos Pávlou 2 (℡ 22420 26607) for most hydrofoils.

The **airport** is 24km southwest of Kós Town in the centre of the island; an Olympic Airways shuttle bus (€3) meets Olympic flights for a transfer to the town terminal by the Casa Romana, but if you arrive on any other flight you'll have to either take a taxi, or head towards the giant roundabout outside the airport gate and find an orange-and-cream-coloured KTEL bus – they pass here en route to Mastihári, Kardhámena and Kéfalos as well as Kós Town. The **KTEL bus terminal** in town is a series of stops around a triangular park 400m back from the water, with an info booth adjacent at Kleopátras 7 (tickets on the bus). The municipality also runs a frequent **local bus** service, DEAS, through the beach suburbs and up to the Asklepion, with a ticket and information office at Aktí Koundouriótou 7. Push- or **mountain-bike** rental are popular options for getting around, given the island's relative flatness; if you want a **motor scooter**, try Moto Harley at Kanári 42, or Moto Service at Harmylíou 17. Budget at Vassiléos Pávlou 31 (℡ 22420 28882 or 694 4500062) and in Psalídhi suburb (℡ 22420 24853), at both the *Ramira* and *Okeanis* hotels, has a reputation for good-condition **cars**, as does AutoWay at Vassiléos Yeoryíou 22 (℡ 22420 25326). Major chains, most nearer the marina on Vassiléos Yeoryíou, include Hertz (℡ 22420 28002) and National/Alamo (℡ 22420 21722). The main **taxi** stand is at the east end of Koundouriótou.

The municipal **tourist office** at Vassiléos Yeoryíou 3 (May–Oct Mon–Fri 8am–2.30pm & 5–8pm, Sat 9am–2pm; Nov–April Mon–Fri 8am–2.30pm) keeps stocks of local maps, bus timetables and ferry schedules. For more involved information, head for the Newsstand **book shop/newsagent** just behind the archeological museum on Platía Kazoúli. No fewer than seven **banks** have ATMs, while the **post office** is at Vassiléos Pávlou 14. The most central and best-equipped **Internet café** is Cafe del Mare at Megálou Alexándhrou 4. **Laundries** include Happy Wash at Mitropóleos 20 and Laundromat Center at Alikarnassoú 124.

Accommodation

If you're just in transit, you're effectively obliged to **stay** in Kós Town, and even if you plan a few days on the island, it still makes a sensible base, as it's the public transport hub and has the greatest concentration of vehicle rental and nightlife. Be wary of touts which besiege most arriving sea-craft – their rooms are apt to be unlicensed, inconveniently remote and of dubious cleanliness. They may further claim to represent the legitimate establishments listed below, and then take you elsewhere.

Hotel Afendoulis Evrypýlou 1 ☎22420 25321, ✉afendoulishotel@kos.forthnet .gr). Large, air-con, balconied en-suite rooms include a few family quads, but what guarantees a loyal repeat clientele is the way Alexis Zikas, brother Ippokrates and wife Dionysia really look after their guests. Breakfast and mini-fridges on request. April–end Oct; credit cards accepted. ❸

Pension Alexis Irodhótou 9, cnr Omírou ☎22420 25594. Deservedly popular budget option across from the Roman agora with wood-floored rooms, which share bathrooms and a self-catering kitchen. Alexis has opted for the *Hotel Afendoulis* (see above), leaving his ebullient sister Sonia in charge here. March to early Nov. ❷

Hotel Kamelia Artemisías 3 ☎22420 28983, ⓦwww.geocities.com/kamelia.hotel. Rear-facing

rooms at this well-kept C-class have a quiet orchard view; tends to get overflow from the *Afendoulis*. May–Sept. ❸

Hotel Maritina Výronos 19 ☎22420 23511, ⓦwww.maritina.gr. Standard mid-town businessmen's hotel with conference facilities and all mod cons in the rooms. Open all year. ❹

Hotel Theodhorou Beach 1200m from the centre, towards Psalídhi ☎22420 22280, ✉22420 23526. Generous-sized units renovated in 2004, with disabled access, and now encompassing suites and a wing of self-catering studios. A green environment includes a lawn-pool in back and a small "private" beach. ❹

Hotel Thomas Manoúsi, cnr Artemisías ☎22420 24646. Small but adequate heated rooms in 1980s decor, with marble floors and a buffet-breakfast salon. Open all year. ❸

The Town

The **castle** (Tues–Sun 8.30am–2.30pm; €3), called "Nerantziás" locally, is reached via a causeway over its former moat, now filled in and planted with palms (hence the avenue's Greek name, Finíkon). The existing double citadel, built in stages between 1450 and 1514, replaced an original fourteenth-century fort deemed incapable of withstanding advances in medieval artillery. A fair proportion of ancient Koan masonry has been recycled into the walls, where the escutcheons of several Grand Masters of the Knights of St John can also be seen.

Immediately opposite the castle entrance stands the riven trunk of Hippocrates' plane tree, its branches now propped up by scaffolding instead of the ancient columns of yore; at seven hundred years of age, it's not really elderly enough to have seen the great healer, though it has a fair claim to being one of the oldest trees in Europe. Adjacent are two Ottoman fountains (a dry hexagonal one and a working one spilling into an ancient sarcophagus) and the eighteenth-century **mosque of Hassan Pasha**, also known as the Loggia Mosque after the portico on one side; its ground floor – like that of the **Defterdar mosque** on central Platía Eleftherías – is taken up by rows of shops.

Also on Platía Eleftherías stands the Italian-built **Archeological Museum** (Tues–Sun 8.30am–2.30pm; €3), with a predictable Latin bias in the choice of exhibits. Four rooms of statuary are arrayed around an atrium with a mosaic of Hippocrates welcoming Asklepios to Kós; the most famous item, purportedly a statue of Hippocrates, is indeed Hellenistic, but most of the other highly regarded works (such as Hermes seated with a lamb) are Roman.

The largest single section of ancient Kós is the **agora**, a sunken, free-access zone containing a confusing jumble of ruins, owing to repeated earthquakes between the second and sixth centuries AD. More comprehensible are the so-called western excavations, lent definition by two intersecting marble-paved streets and the **Xystos** or restored colonnade of a covered running track. In the same area lie several floor mosaics, such as Europa being carried off by Zeus in the form of a bull; gladiators; a boar being speared; plus gods and muses, all viewable under protective canopies. To the south, across Grigoríou toú Pémptou, are a Roman-era **odeion**, garishly restored both during the 1930s and again in 2000, and the **Casa Romana** (shut for works until early 2006), a third-century-AD house built around three atria with surviving patches of mosaic floors showing panthers and tigers, plus assorted sea creatures.

△ Ancient agora, Kós

Kós also retains a thoroughly commercialized **old town**, lining the pedestrianized street running from behind the Italian market hall on Platía Eleftherías as far as Platía Dhiagóras and the isolated minaret overlooking the western archeological zone. One of the few areas of town to survive the 1933 earthquake, today it's crammed with expensive tourist boutiques, cafés and snack-bars. About the only genuinely old thing remaining here is a capped **Turkish fountain** with a calligraphic inscription, found where the walkway cobbles cross Odhós Venizélou.

Eating

Despite an overwhelming first impression of Euro-stodge cuisine, it's easy to **eat** well and even reasonably in Kós Town, as long as you search inland, away from the harbour. Koan wine-making has been revived recently, and the Hatziemmanouil label is particularly worth sampling. For **breakfast**, the *Central/Kentriko Café* on Platía Ayías Paraskevís behind the market hall uniquely does American pancakes, French toast and fresh fruit juices.

Ambavris 500m south of the edge of town along the road from near Casa Romana, in eponymous suburb village. To order from their English-only à la carte menu is to miss the point of the place; take the hint about "Mezedes" and let the house bring on their best. This changes seasonally but won't much exceed €20 for six plates – typically *pinigoúri* (bulgur pilaf), *pikhtí* (brawn), little fish, spicy *loukánika*, stuffed squash flowers and *fáva* – drinks extra. May–Oct eves only.

Barbas Evrypýlou 6, opposite *Hotel Afendoulis*. Excellent grills as well as the odd seafood touch like octopus salad, at cozy outdoor seating. April–Oct.
Iy Folia tou Lykou Bouboulína 24. Very reasonable prices for taverna standards, with live *rebétika* music on some weekends. Open all year.
Kanadheza Evrypýlou, cnr Artemisías. Creditable pizzas as well as grills, served at indoor/outdoor tables. Open all year.
Koakon (aka *Andonis*) Artemisías 56. Possibly the best all-rounder in town, purveying grilled meat

and fish, *mezédhes* and a few daily *mayireftá* with equal aplomb, without the usual multinational flags and photo-menus. Open all year.

🏃 **Pote tin Kyriaki** Pissándhrou 9. Kós's sole genuine ouzerí, where the creatively drawn menu (in school copy-books) has delights such as fried mussels and *dhákos* (Cretan "monk's" salad), as well as grilled chops and *pantsétta*. Mon–Sat (winter Thurs–Sat) eves only.

Iy Psaropoula Avérof 17. Currently the town's best-value fish/seafood specialist, with many Greeks in attendance; open all year.

Drinking and nightlife

Join the largely Greek crowd at *Cafe Aenaos*, right under the Defterdar mosque, and people-watch while refilling your Greek coffee from the traditional *bríki* used to brew it up. For a convivial drink on the water in wicker chairs under a wood gazebo, try *Nostos* on Yeoryíou Papandhréou; doyenne of the beach-bars in this district, it works out of a 1930-vintage house, with occasional live music sessions.

Durable music bars with **dance floors** elsewhere include *Four Roses* on the corner of Arseníou and Vassiléos Yeoryíou, and *Beach Boys* at Kanári 57. Local and touring **live Greek acts** tend to stop at *Apoplous* (mid-June to early Sept) at the start of Psalídhi. If you prefer loud techno and house, look no further than the "**Pub Lanes**" area, officially Nafklírou and Dhiákou; bar identities tend to change each season, and it's gotten very naff. Much the classiest and most stable venue here is *Hamam Club*, installed in an ex-Turkish bath with its original oriental décor and chill-out sofas in the corner rooms; there's a mix of guest and local DJs and live sessions, with outdoor seating before a midnight "curfew" moves everyone indoors. There's a **newer, better nucleus** of nightlife out at Aktí Zouroúdhi, with a more mixed clientele, where *Heaven* (mid-June to early Sept) is the most established club. Otherwise there is one active **cinema**, the Orfeas, with summer and winter (Oct–May) premises as shown on the map; the indoor premises also hosts concerts and other special events.

The Asklepion and Platáni

Native son **Hippocrates** is justly celebrated on Kós; not only does he have a tree, a street, a park, a statue and an international medical institute named after him, but the **Asklepion** (June–Aug Tues–Sun 8am–6.30pm, Sept–May 8.30am–2.30pm; €3), 4km south of town, one of just three in Greece, is a major tourist attraction. A little fake green-and-white train shuttles up to the site regularly; otherwise take a DEAS bus up to Platáni (see opposite), from where the

---

Hippocrates

Hippocrates (ca. 460–370 BC) is generally regarded as the father of scientific medicine, though the Hippocratic oath probably has nothing to do with him and is anyway much altered from its original form. Hippocrates was certainly born on Kós, probably at Astypalia near present-day Kéfalos, but otherwise details of his life are few and disputed; what seems certain is that he was a great physician who travelled throughout the Classical Greek world, but spent at least part of his career teaching and practising at the Asklepion on his native island. A vast number of medical writings have been attributed to Hippocrates, only a few of which he could have actually written; *Airs, Waters and Places*, a treatise on the importance of environment on health, is widely thought to be his, but others were probably a compilation from a medical library kept on Kós, which later appeared in Alexandria during the second century BC. This emphasis on good air and water, and the holistic approach of ancient Greek medicine, now seems positively contemporary.

ruins are a further 15-minute walk. There's a small snack-bar at the Asklepion, or pause for lunch in Platáni en route.

The Asklepion was actually founded just after the death of Hippocrates, but it's safe to assume that the methods used and taught here were his. Both a temple to Asklepios (god of healing, son of Apollo) and a renowned curative centre, its magnificent setting on three artificial hillside terraces overlooking Anatolia reflects early recognition of the importance of the therapeutic environment. Until recently, two fountains provided the site with a constant supply of clean, fresh water, and extensive stretches of clay piping are still visible, embedded in the ground.

Today, very little remains standing above ground, owing to periodic earth-quakes and the Knights' use of the site as a quarry. The lower terrace in fact never had many buildings, being instead the venue for the observance of the Asklepieia – quadrennial celebrations and athletic/musical competitions in honour of the healing god. Sacrifices to Asklepios were conducted at an **altar**, the oldest structure on the site, whose foundations can still be seen near the middle of the second terrace. Just to its east, the Corinthian columns of a second-century-AD **Roman temple** were partially re-erected by nationalistically minded Italians. A monumental **staircase** leads from the altar to the second-century-BC Doric temple of Asklepios on the topmost terrace, the last and grandest of a succession of the deity's shrines at this site.

About halfway to the Asklepion, the village of **PLATÁNI** (also Kermedés, from the Turkish name Germe) is, along with Kós Town, the remaining place of residence for the island's dwindling community of ethnic Turks. Until 1964 there were nearly three thousand of them, but successive Cyprus crises and the worsening of relations between Greece and Turkey prompted mass emigra-tion to Anatolia, and a drop in the Muslim population to currently well under a thousand. Several excellent, Turkish-run **tavernas** are to be found at and around the main crossroads junction, with a working Ottoman fountain: *Arap* (summer only); the slightly less touristy *Asklipios* (aka *Ali's*) and *Sherif*, adjacent across the way (also summer only); and *Gin's Place* (all year), each offering Anatolian-style mezédhes (fried vegetables with yoghurt, *bourekákia*, and so on) and kebabs better than most in Kós Town. Afterwards, retire across from *Arap* to *Zaharoplastio Iy Paradhosi* for the best ice cream on the island.

Just outside Platáni on the road back to the port, the island's neglected **Jewish cemetery** lies in a dark conifer grove, 300m beyond the well-kept Muslim graveyard. Dates on the Hebrew-Italian-script headstones stop after 1940, after which none of the local Jews were allowed the luxury of a natural death prior to their deportation in summer 1944. Their former **synagogue** or *hávra*, a wonderfully orientalized Rationalist specimen from 1934, at Alexándhrou Dhiákou 4, has been refurbished as a municipal events hall but also has a plaque commemorating its former use.

Eastern Kós

If you're looking for anything resembling a deserted **beach** near the capital, you'll need to make use of the DEAS bus line connecting the various resorts to either side of town, or else rent a vehicle; push-bikes can take advantage of the cycle paths extending as far east as Cape Psalídhi.

The easterly bus line usually terminates at Áyios Fokás, 8km southeast of Kós Town, but sometimes continues an extra 4km almost to unusual and remote **Brós Thermá** (last service around 6pm); with your own transport be prepared to negotiate a dirt track for the final kilometre. Brós Thermá is known for its massively popular **hot springs** – best experienced at sunset or after – which issue from a grotto and flow through a trench into a shoreline pool protected by boulders, heating the seawater to an enjoyable temperature. Winter storms typically disperse the boulder wall, rebuilt every April, so that the pool changes from year to year. Just uphill, the long-running *Psarotaverna Therma* does affordable fish, though the rest of the menu is unmemorable. There's also a drinks-and-ice-cream café right by the pool.

Tingáki and Marmári

The two neighbouring beach resorts of Tingáki and Marmári are separated from each other by the salt marsh of **Alykí**, which retains water – and throngs of migratory birds, including flamingoes – until June after a wet winter. There's almost always a breeze along this coast, which means plenty of windsurf boards for hire at either resort; the profiles of Kálymnos, Psérimos and Turkey's Bodrum peninsula all make for spectacular offshore scenery. If you're aiming for either of these resorts from town, especially on a two-wheeler of any sort, it's safest and most pleasant to go by the **minor road** which takes off from the southwest corner of town (follow initial signage for the Vassiliadhi supermarket); the entire way to Tingáki is paved, and involves the same distance as using the main trunk road and marked turn-off. Similarly, a grid of paved rural lanes links the inland portions of Tingáki and Marmári.

TINGÁKI, a busy beachside resort popular with Brits, lies 12km west of the harbour. Oddly, there's very little **accommodation** near the beach amongst the dozen or so medium-sized hotels and more numerous studios; most of these are scattered inland through fields and cow pastures. By far the best local **taverna** here, with pleasant seating indoors and out, is ⌖ *Ambeli* (summer daily; winter Fri/Sat eve, Sun lunch), well signposted 2.5km east of the main beach-front crossroads; featured dishes include *pinigoúri* (cracked wheat), pork-based *bekrí mezé*, *pykhtí* (brawn), *yaprákia* (the local *dolmádhes*) and *arnáki ambelourgoú*, washed down with sixty kinds of wine from their cellar. Among **car-rental** outfits, Sevi (☎22420 68299) can be recommended, and will even deliver vehicles on request to Kós Town. The beach itself is white sand, long and narrow – it improves, and veers further away from the traffic of the frontage road, as you head southwest.

MARMÁRI, 15km from town, has a smaller built-up area than Tingáki, and the beach itself is broader, especially to the west where it forms little dunes (and supports a wind-surf school). Most hotels here are monopolized by German tour groups, but you might hit on an on-spec vacancy at the B-class *Esperia* on the main access road down from the island trunk road (☎22420 42010, ⓕ22420 42012; ❹), in grassy surroundings.

The Asfendhioú villages

The main interest of inland Kós resides in the villages on **Mount Dhíkeos**, a handful of settlements collectively referred to as **Asfendhioú**, nestled amidst the island's only natural forest. Together these communities give a good idea of what Kós looked like before tourism and ready-mix concrete arrived, and all are now severely depopulated by the mad rush to the coast. They are accessible via the curvy side road from Zipári, 8km from Kós Town; an inconspicuously marked minor road to Lagoúdhi; or by the shorter access road for Pylí.

The first Asfendhioú village you reach up the Zipári road is **Evangelístria**, where a major crossroads by the parish church and taverna of the same name leads to Lagoúdhi and Amanioú (west), Asómatos (east) and Ziá (uphill). **ZIÁ**'s spectacular sunsets make it the target of up to six evening tour buses daily, though the village has barely a dozen families still resident, and its daytime tattiness seems to increase each tourist season. Best of the dozen **tavernas** here is the secluded ⋇ *Kefalovrissi*, near the top of the village, great for *mezédhes* plus selected daily mains like *pantsétta* or *bakaliáros*, accompanied by Hatziemmanouil red wine; runner-up is the *Olympia*, at the start of the lane up to the church, open all year with such dishes as chickpeas, *spédzofaï* (sausage and pepper stew), dark bread and good bulk wine; there's a good *pikilía* or medley of *mezédhes* off-menu. Ziá is also the trailhead for the ascent of 846-metre **Dhíkeos peak**, a minimum two-and-a-half-hour round-trip, initially on track but mostly by path. The route is fairly obvious, and the views from the pillbox-like summit chapel of Metamórfosis are ample reward for the effort. Up top, you can also ponder the esoteric symbolism of a giant crucifix fashioned out of PVC sewer pipe and filled with concrete.

East of Ziá or Evangelístria, roads converge at **ASÓMATOS**, home to about thirty villagers and a number of outsiders restoring abandoned houses; the evening view from the church of Arhángelos with its pebble mosaic rivals that of Zía, though there's just a single *kafenío*. **ÁYIOS DHIMÍTRIOS**, 2km beyond along a paved road, is marked by its old name of Haïhoútes on some maps, and is today completely abandoned except for a single house next to the attractive church; in the narthex, a small photo display documents a much larger population during the war years, when the village was a centre of resistance to the German occupation. You can continue from here 3.5km more to the junction with the road linking Platáni with the municipal rubbish tip.

Pylí

PYLÍ can be reached via the road through Lagoúdhi and Amanioú, or from the duck-patrolled Linopótis pond on the main island trunk road, across from which *Ouzeri Iy Limni* (aka *Karamelengos*) dishes up excellent seafood *mezédhes*. In the upper of its two neighbourhoods, 100m west of the partly pedestrianized square and church, the simple *Iy Palia Piyi* taverna serves inexpensive but appetizing meat grills and fried-vegetable *mezédhes* in a superb setting, beside a giant cistern-fountain (*piyí*). Pylí's other attraction is the so-called **Harmýlio** ("Tomb of Harmylos"), signposted near the top of the village as "Heroon of Charmylos". This consists of a subterranean, niched vault (fenced off), probably a Hellenistic family tomb; immediately above, traces of an ancient temple have been incorporated into the medieval chapel of Stavrós.

Paleó (medieval) **Pylí**, roughly 3km southeast of its modern descendant, was the Byzantine capital of Kós. Head there via Amanioú, keeping straight at the junction where signs point left to Ziá and Lagoúdhi. In any case, the castle should be obvious on its rock, straight ahead; the deteriorating road ends next to a spring, opposite which a stair-path leads within fifteen minutes to the roof of the fort. En route you pass the remains of the abandoned town tumbling southwards down the slope, as well as three fourteenth-to-fifteenth-century chapels with fresco fragments within; the first church encountered, **Arhángelos**, has the best-preserved ones, mostly scenes from the Life of Christ.

Western Kós

Near the arid, desolate centre of the island, well sown with military installations, a pair of giant, adjacent roundabouts by the airport funnels traffic northwest towards **Mastihári**, northeast back towards town, southwest towards **Kéfalos**, and southeast to **Kardhámena**. Most visitors are after the south-coast **beaches**, reached from the Kéfalos-bound turning.

Mastihári and Andimáhia

The least developed, least "packaged" and least expensive of the north-shore resorts, **MASTIHÁRI** has a shortish, broad beach extending west; at its end, inside a partly fenced enclosure, lie remains of the fifth-century basilica of **Áyios Ioánnis**, one of several on the island. If you want to **stay**, try quieter digs overlooking the west beach such as the simple *Hotel Kyma* (☎ 22420 59045; ❸) or the *Hotel Fenareti* (☎ 22420 59024) further up the grade, with rooms ❷) and studios ❸) in a peaceful garden environment. *O Makis*, one street inland from the quay, and⚓ *Kali Kardia*, at the base of the jetty, are the best of a half-dozen **tavernas**, both well regarded for fresh fish, *mezédhes* and (at *Kali Kardia*) *mayireftá* and desserts. Mastihári is also the port for small roll-on-roll-off **ferries** to Kálymnos; there are three to four well-spaced daily departures in each direction most of the year (current info on ☎ 22420 59124), timed more or less to coincide with Athens-originating flight schedules – though KTEL buses to or from Kós Town don't (perhaps deliberately) always dovetail well.

The workaday village of **ANDIMÁHIA**, 5km southeast of Mastihári, straggles over several ridges; the only concession to tourism is a line of ouzerís and snack bars at the southwestern edge, easily accessible from the airport (across the road and car park) if your outbound flight is delayed. East of Andimáhia, reached via a marked, 2.8-kilometre side road, an enormous, triangular **Knights' castle** overlooks the straits to Níssyros. Once through the imposing north gateway (unrestricted access), you can follow the well-preserved west parapet, and visit two interior chapels: one with a fresco of Áyios Khristóforos (St Christopher) carrying the Christ child, the other with fine ribvaulting. Gravel walkways, illumination and a ticket booth were installed in 2001, but are never really used aside from the occasional concert held here.

Kardhámena

KARDHÁMENA, on the southeast coast 31km from Kós Town, is the island's largest package resort after the capital itself, with locals outnumbered twenty to one in a busy season by visitors (mostly young Brits) intent on getting as drunk as possible as cheaply as possible. Runaway local development has banished whatever redeeming qualities the place once had, reducing it to a seething mass of off-licences, bars, trinket shops and excursion agencies. Pubs named the *Black Swan*, *Crackers* and *Boozers* dispense imported beer, you can easily find fish and chips and there's even a *McDonalds* now – one of the very few in the islands. A beach stretches to either side of the town, sandier to the southwest, but intermittently reefy and hemmed in by a road towards the northeast as far as Tolári, home to the massive *Norida Beach* all-inclusive complex.

Kardhámena is most worth knowing about as a place to catch a **boat to Níssyros**. There are supposedly two daily sailings in season: the morning tourist excursion *kaïki* at 9–9.30am, and another, less expensive, unpublicized one – either the *Ayios Konstandinos* or the *Nissyros* – at anywhere from 2.30 to 8pm depending on the day.

South-coast beaches

The thinly populated portion of Kós southwest of the airport and Andimáhia boasts the most scenic and secluded beaches on the island, plus a number of minor ancient sites. Though given fanciful English names and shown as separate extents on tourist maps, the south-facing **beaches** form essentially one long stretch at the base of a cliff, most with sunbeds, a rudimentary snack-bar and a jet-ski franchise. "**Magic**", officially Polémi, is the longest, broadest and wildest, with a proper taverna above the car park, no jet skis and a nudist zone (dubbed "**Exotic**") at the east end. "**Sunny**", signposted as Psilós Gremmós and easily walkable from "Magic", has another taverna and jet-skis; **Langádhes** is the cleanest and most picturesque, with junipers tumbling off its dunes and more jet-skis. "**Paradise**", often dubbed "Bubble Beach" because of volcanic gas vents in the tidal zone, is small and over-subscribed, with wall-to-wall sunbeds. Jet-ski-free "**Camel**" (Kamíla) is the shortest and loneliest, protected somewhat by the steep, unpaved drive in past its hillside taverna; the shore here is pure, fine sand, with good snorkelling to either side of the cove.

Uninterrupted beach resumes past a headland at **Áyios Stéfanos**, overshadowed by a huge Club Med complex, and extends 5km west to Kamári (see below). A marked public access road leads down to the beach either side of a small peninsula, crowned with the remains of two triple-aisled, sixth-century basilicas. Though the best preserved on the island, several columns have been toppled since the 1980s, and wonderful bird mosaics languish under a permanent layer of "protective" gravel. The basilicas overlook tiny but striking **Kastrí** islet with its little chapel; in theory it's an easy swim (sometimes wading) across from the westerly beach, with some of the best snorkelling on Kós around the rock formations, but you must run a gauntlet of boats from the local watersports outfit.

The far west

Essentially the shore annexe of Kéfalos, **KAMÁRI** is a sprawling package resort of scattered breeze-blocks, pitched a few notches above Kardhámena; it's a major watersports centre and an alternative departure point for Níssyros in peak season. *Faros* is the most passably authentic, least stodgy **taverna** here, at the far (southwest) end of things near the start of the road up to **KÉFALOS**, 43km from Kós Town. Squatting on a bluff looking down the length of the island, this is the end of the line for buses: a dull village that's a staging point for expeditions into the rugged peninsula terminating dramatically at Cape Kríkello.

Main highlights of a half-day tour here, beginning along the widened ridge road south, include a Byzantine church, **Panayía Palatianí**, built amidst the ruins of a much larger ancient temple, 1km beyond the village; the late Classical theatre (unrestricted access) – with two rows of seats remaining – and Hellenistic temple of **ancient Astypalia**, 500m further at the side-path starting from an unmarked but unlocked gate; and the cave of **Asprí Pétra** (inhabited during the Neolithic period), marked rather vaguely off the ridge road and requiring a half-hour walk to reach. A paved road west from just after Astypalia leads to an often windy beach and small chapel at **Áyios Theológos**, 7km from Kéfalos; the *Ayios Theologos* **taverna** here is popular with locals at weekends especially, despite considerably bumped-up prices (though portions are also generous). Keeping to the main paved road to its end brings you to the appealing (but usually locked) monastery of **Áyios Ioánnis Thymianós**, also 7km from the village; 4km past this on dirt track leads to clothing-optional "**Cavo Paradiso**" beach, 250m of fine sand with sunbeds but no other amenities.

About 1.5km north of Kéfalos on the road tracing the island's summit ridge, a paved side road covers the 2.7km to **Lim(n)iónas**, the only north-facing beach and fishing anchorage on this part of Kós. There's just one surviving fish **taverna** here, the fair-priced *Limionas*; two compact sandy beaches sit either side of the peninsula.

Psérimos

Psérimos could be an idyllic little island were it not so close to Kós and Kálymnos. Throughout the season, both of these larger neighbours dispatch daily excursion boats in such numbers that a second jetty has been built to accommodate them at the small harbour village of **AVLÁKIA**. In midsummer, daytrippers blanket the main sandy beach which curves around the bay in front of Avlákia's thirty-odd houses and huge communal olive grove; even during May or late September you're guaranteed at least eighty outsiders daily (versus a permanent population of 25). There are three other, variably attractive beaches to hide away on during the day: clean **Vathý** (sand and gravel), a well-marked, thirty-minute path-walk east, starting from behind the *Taverna Iy Pserimos*; grubbier **Marathoúnda** (pebble), a 45-minute walk north on the main trans-island track; and best of all **Grafiótissa**, a 300-metre-long beach of near-Caribbean quality at the base of low cliffs. This lies half an hour's walk west of town, more or less following the coast; the way there is cross-country around illegally fenced hillside plots, until a proper trail kicks in at a large, solitary tree by a stone corral.

Even during high season there won't be too many other overnighters, since there's a limited number of beds available. Pick of the several small rooms establishments is *Tripolitis* (☎22430 23196; May–Oct; ❶), upstairs from English-speaking *Anna's* café/snack-bar or the rooms above *Taverna Manola* on the opposite end of the beach (☎22430 51540; ❶). Next door are the slightly higher standard *Studios Kalliston* (❸), though the management is changing and you'll have to contact them on the spot. There's just one small, limited-stock **store**, since most of the island's supplies are brought in daily from Kálymnos. Eating out however, won't break the bank, and there's often fresh fish in the handful of **tavernas**; many of these have contracts with the tour boats, but *Taverna Manola* doesn't, and despite bar-like appearances (it doubles as the main **night spot**) proves adept at ouzerí fare and seafood.

Most **boats** based on Kós and Kálymnos harbour operate triangle tours (approximately €20), which involve departure between 9.30am and 10am, followed by a stop for swimming on either Platý islet or adjacent Psérimos, lunch in Avlákia, or Póthia, the port of Kálymnos (sometimes on board), and another swimming stop at whichever islet wasn't visited in the morning. If you want to spend the entire day on Psérimos, you're much better off departing Póthia at 9.30am daily on the tiny *Nissos Pserimos*, returning at 4pm (€6 round-trip). The islanders themselves use this boat to visit Kálymnos for shopping and administrative business.

Astypálea

Geographically, historically and architecturally, **Astypálea** (alias Astropália) would be more at home among the Cyclades – on a clear day you can see Anáfi or Amorgós (to the southwest and northwest respectively) far more easily than any of the other Dodecanese. Moreover, Astypálea's inhabitants are descendants of medieval colonists from the Cyclades, and the island looks and feels more like these than its neighbours to the east.

Despite an evocative butterfly shape, Astypálea does not immediately strike you as especially beautiful. Many beaches along the bleak, heavily indented coastline have reef underfoot and suffer periodic dumpings of seaweed. The heights, which offer limited walking opportunities, are windswept and covered in thornbush or dwarf juniper. Yet the sage *alisfakiá*, brewed as a tea, flourishes too, and hundreds

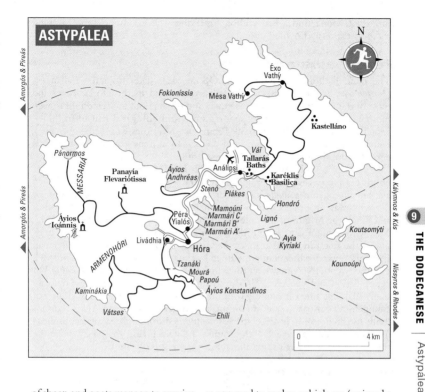

of sheep and goats manage to survive – as opposed to snakes, which are (uniquely in the Aegean) entirely absent. Lush citrus groves and vegetable patches in the valleys signal a relative abundance of water, hoarded in a reservoir.

In antiquity the island's most famous citizen was Kleomedes, a boxer disqualified from an early Olympic Games for causing the death of his opponent. He came home so enraged that he demolished the local school, killing all its pupils. Things have calmed down a bit in the intervening 2500 years, and today Astypálea is renowned mainly for its **honey**, **fish and lobster** (which finds its way into the local dish of *astakomakaronádha*); the abundant local catch has only been shipped to Athens since the late 1980s, a reflection of traditionally **poor ferry links** in every direction. Though in theory there are regular high-season links with both Pireás and Rhodes via several intervening islands, in practice arrival/departure times are grim (typically 3am) and berths or bunks are spuriously booked or otherwise not allocated to the island. Outside July or August you risk being marooned here for a day or two longer than intended; all told, you may need or want to take advantage of **flights** to Léros, Kós or Rhodes. There is no conventional package tourism here since Laskarina Holidays dropped the island in 1995, frustrated by chronically unreliable connections to Kós and its major airport.

This isolation and the logistical difficulties discourage casual trade, but motivated people do find their way to Astypálea during the short, intense **midsummer season** (mid-July to first Sept Sun before school starts), when the 1500 permanent inhabitants are vastly outnumbered by their guests. Most arrivals are Athenians, French or Italians, supplemented by large numbers of yachties and foreign owners of second homes in the understandably popular Hóra. At such times you won't find a bed without reserving well in advance, and camping rough is expressly frowned upon.

Péra Yialós and Hóra

The main harbour of **PÉRA YIALÓS** or Skála dates from the Italian era (Astypálea was the first island the Italians occupied in the Dodecanese) and most of the settlement between the quay and the line of nine windmills is even more recent. Its only real bright spot is a small **archeological museum** (June–Sept Tues–Sun 10am–1pm & 6.30–10pm; Oct–May Tues–Sun 8am–2pm; free), a single well-lit room crammed with the best local finds spanning all historical periods from the Bronze Age to medieval times.

As you climb up beyond the port towards **HÓRA**, however, the neighbourhoods get progressively older and more attractive, their steep streets enlivened by the photogenic *poúndia*, or colourful wooden balconies-with-stairways of the whitewashed houses, which owe much to the building styles of Mýkonos and Tínos, the origins of the colonists brought to repopulate the island in 1413. The whole culminates in the thirteenth-century **kástro** (always open; free), one of the finest in the Aegean, erected not by the Knights but by the Venetian Quirini clan and subsequently modified by the Ottomans after 1537. Until well into the twentieth century over three hundred people lived inside the *kástro*, but depopulation and a severe 1956 earthquake combined to leave only a desolate shell today. The fine rib vaulting over the main west gate supports the church of Evangelístria Kastrianí, one of two intact here, the other being Áyios Yeóryios (both usually locked). In 2005 the *kástro* emerged from a three-year consolidation and restoration project, with catwalks and stairs giving you pretty much the run of the place, though some unstable areas are still off-limits.

Information and transport

Two **buses** run along the paved road between Hóra, Péra Yialós, Livádhia and Analípsi, frequently in July and August from 8am until 11pm, at best four times daily out of season. The Analípsi-bound bus usually doesn't dovetail well with arriving/departing aeroplanes, so get your chosen accommodation or rental-car outfit (see below) to come fetch you. There's only one official set-rate **taxi**, incapable of coping with passenger numbers in season; fares are reasonable, for example €6 from Skála to the airport. Around five places offer **scooters**, the most reliable being Lakis and Manolis (☏22430 61263), with branches at Hóra and Skála dock; they also rent out a few pricey **cars** and jeeps, as does Vergoulis (☏22430 61351) near the museum. Also near the museum, Astypalea Tours (☏22430 61571) is the main ticket **agency**, representing GA ferries, the *Nissos Kalymnos* and Olympic Airways; Paradisos under the namesake hotel (☏22430 61224) handles Blue Star. The best island **map** is issued by Road Editions, worth snagging in advance; others sold locally are grossly inaccurate, even by lenient Greek-island standards, though in compensation rural junctions are adequately signposted. The **post office** and most shops are in Hóra, though the island's only **bank**, complete with ATM, is down in Péra Yialós by the port police.

Accommodation

Péra Yialós, and to a lesser extent Hóra, have **accommodation** ranging from spartan, 1970s-vintage rooms to new luxury studios; proprietors tend not to meet ferries unless arrangements have been made, even if they have vacancies. Owing to high-season harbour noise – particularly the sound of ferries dropping anchor at 3am – you might prefer more atmospheric restored studios or entire houses (❹ for two people peak season,❸ low) up **in Hóra** if uninter-rupted sleep is a priority; enquire at Kostas Vaïkousis' antique shop on the quay or reserve in advance on ☎22430 61430 or 697 74 77 800. Rather plusher are the⚘ *Studios Kilindra* on the quiet west slope of Hóra (☎22430 61966, Ⓔstudioskilindra@otenet.gr; open all year), offering luxury amenities including a swimming pool – units accommodate two to three people, with the smallest at❻ , the suites❽ . About halfway along the road from Hóra to Livádhia, the *Provarma Studios* (☎22430 61096; June to early Sept,❸), comprise southwest-facing galleried studios with large balconies but no air conditioning.

The better of two not wildly inspiring **hotels in Péra Yialós** is the *Astynea* (☎22430 61040;❸), though it can get nocturnal noise from bars and cafés just below. On the east shore of the bay, the en-suite *Rooms Australia* above the restaurant of the same name (☎22430 61275 or 22430 61067;❸) have fans or air con; the same family offers more comfortable studios closer to the water (school hols only;❹). The remoter *Akti Rooms* (☎22430 61114, Ⓦwww .aktirooms.gr❹) are also well equipped and maintained, with on-site car rental and a popular restaurant on the ground floor. A small, basic, July–August-only **campsite** operates amongst calamus reeds and tamarisks behind Dhéftero Marmári Bay, about 4km along the road to Análipsi, but (like much of the island) it can be mosquito-plagued any year after a wet winter.

Eating, drinking and nightlife

During August, nearly thirty **tavernas** and beach snack-bars operate across the island, few of them memorable and many concerned primarily with turn-ing a quick profit. Among the more reliable Péra Yialós options, *Akroyiali* has somewhat better than average food but fills nightly owing to fair prices and its unbeatable setting with tables on the sand. The *Astropalia* (closes end Sept) on the hillside above the street up to Hóra, does good, if somewhat pricey, fish and not much else. Best of the lot, with even better seafood, and superbly prepared home-grown vegetable dishes, is the homey⚘ *Australia* (April–Nov), just inland from the head of the bay. Behind the *Hotel Paradhisos*, you'll find more ambitious cooking, polished presentation (and much higher prices) at *Aitherio* and *Maïstrali* (both open into Oct); it's pot-luck as to which is better any given night. Under the *Hotel Astynea*, the *Dapia Café* is good for full **breakfasts**, midday crêpes and novelty teas; a few steps down, on the corner, *O Mihalis* is tops for inexpensive home-made desserts.

Except for the *Yialos* music club near the *Akroyiali*, most **nightlife** happens up in more atmospheric Hóra, where the esplanade between the windmills and the base of the *kástro* seems to be one solid café-bar. Of these, the favourites are the unsigned *Tou Nikola* (*Iy Mylí*) on the corner, with the island's characters in residence, the *Ayeri Ouzeri* diagonally opposite, and music bar *Notos* tucked in by the triple chapel, with desserts as well. These are joined in season by the long-lived *Kastro*, good for conversation-level music.

Southwestern Astypálea

A twenty-minute walk (or a short bus journey) from Hóra brings you to **LIVÁ-DHIA**, a fertile valley draining to a popular, good beach with a generally indiffer-ent collection of restaurants and cafés immediately behind. You can rent a **room or studio** just inland – for example at *Studios O Manganas* (☎22430 61468,❹), on the frontage road, representing the highest standard here (they've even tiny washing machines in the units), or *Venetos Studios* (☎22430 61490 or 694 43 01 381❸ ; May–Sept), at the base of the westerly hillside, comprising several separate buildings scattered in a pleasant orchard. Among the half-dozen **tavernas**, ✻ *To Yerani* is the most consistently open (until Oct) and renowned for its excellent *mayireftá*; they also offer equally high standard rooms adjacent, redone in 2005 with modern furnishings and marble floors (☎22430 61484; ❸).

If the busy beach here doesn't suit, continue southwest fifteen minutes on foot to three small single coves at **Tzanáki**, packed out with naturists in midsummer. The third large bay beyond Livádhia, more easily reached by motorbike, is **Áyios Konstandínos**, a partly shaded, sand-and-gravel cove with a good seasonal taverna. Around the headland, the lonely beaches of Vátses and Kaminákia are visited by excursion boat from Péra Yialós; wooden *kaïki* the *Agios Georgios* is the most characterful. By land, **Vátses** has the easier dirt road in, some twenty minutes by scooter from Livádhia; it's one of the sandier island beaches, with a basic *kantína*, but prone to wind. The track to **Kaminákia**, 8.5km from Livádhia, is rough and steep for the final 2km – best to go in a car – but the sheltered, clean and scenic cove, Astypálea's best, makes the effort worthwhile. There's a good, stone-clad **taverna** (July–Sept) here, overseeing a handful of sunbeds and offering honest rustic fare (salads, very fresh fish and a dish of the day).

Northeastern Astypálea

Northeast of the harbour are three coves known as **Próto** (First), **Dhéftero** (Second) and **Tríto** (Third) **Mármari**, and marked as **Marmári A'**, **B'** and **C'** respectively on some maps. The first is home to the power plant and boatyards; the next hosts the campsite, while the third, relatively attractive, also marks the start of the path east to the perfectly decent coves of unfortunately named **Mamoúni** ("bug" or "critter" in Greek). Beyond Tríto Marmári, the main beach at **Stenó** ("narrow", after the isthmus here), with sandy shore and shallows, a few tamarisks and a high-season *kantína*, is the best.

ANÁLIPSI, widely known as **Maltezána** after medieval Maltese pirates, is 9km from Péra Yialós. Although the second-largest settlement on Astypálea, there's surprisingly little for outsiders save a narrow, exposed, packed-sand beach (there are better ones east of the main bay, and west at **Plákes**) and a nice view south to some islets. Despite this, blocks of **rooms/studios** (most open only July & Aug) sprout in ranks well back from the sea, spurred by the proximity of the airport, less than 1km away. A more reliable exception, and the largest **hotel** complex on the island, is the 48-unit *Maltezana Beach* (☎22430 61558, ⓦwww.maltezanabeach.gr; ❺ high, ❸ low season; Easter to mid-Sept), with large, well-appointed bungalow-rooms and on-site restaurant. There are about five independent **tavernas** here, the most reliably open (Feb–Christmas) being *Analipsi* (aka *Ilias and Irini's*, after the managing couple) by the jetty, which doubles as the *kafenío* for the local fishermen and seemingly every passing worker on the island. The food – fried squid, bean soup – is simple but good; confirm prices and portion size of the often frozen seafood. For meat dishes patronize *Skhinondas* (aka *Tassos*) by the final bus stop, where the road changes to dirt surface. Behind calamus reeds and eucalyptus near the fishing jetty lie the best-preserved mosaic floors on the island: those of the Byzantine **Tallarás baths**, with somewhat crude figures of zodiacal signs, the seasons personified, and a central androgynous figure (Time or Fortune) holding the cosmic orb.

The motorable dirt track ends 23km from Hóra at **Mésa Vathý** (invariably and erroneously shown on most maps as Éxo Vathý), a sleepy fishing village with a single **taverna** (*Iy Galini*) and superb small-craft anchorage in what's an almost landlocked inlet. Frankly, though, it's not really worth the long, bumpy trip out overland, and to rub salt in the wound, the fish on the menu is usually frozen (as all too often on Astypálea).

Kálymnos

Most of the 17,000-strong population of **Kálymnos** lives in or around the large port of Póthia, a prosperous but not conventionally beautiful town, famed for its **sponge industry**. Unfortunately, almost all of the eastern Mediterranean's sponges were devastated by a mysterious disease in 1986, related to freak warm currents, and only a few of the fleet of thirty-odd boats are still in use. Warehouses behind the harbour continue to process and sell sponges, but most of these are imported from Asia and the Caribbean. There are also still numbers of elderly gentlemen about who rely on two canes, walking frames or even

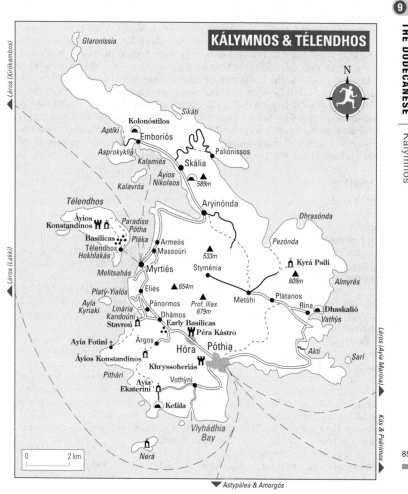

wheelchairs, stark evidence of the havoc wrought in their youth by nitrogen embolism (the "bends"), long before divers understood its crippling effects.

In response to the sponge blight (and a repeat outbreak in 1999), the island established a tourist industry – confined to one string of beach resorts – and also adapted most of its sponge boats for deep-sea fishing. But **mass tourism** proved as fickle as sponges, and has essentially **collapsed** since the millennium. The nonfunctioning, half-finished airport near Árgos village, two decades a-building, and thus the continuing need for tedious transfers from Kós, was the main excuse for a mass pull-out by most package companies. Given this crash in bucket-and-spade holidays, the island has striven to reinvent itself as an off-season hiking and rock-climbing destination – it has some of the best cliffs in Greece, and a respectable surviving path network – and more recently taken to promoting scuba-diving and sea-kayaking through a late-summer festival.

Kálymnos essentially consists of two cultivated and inhabited valleys sandwiched between three limestone ridges, harsh in the full glare of noon but magically tinted towards dusk. The climate, especially in winter, is purported to be drier and healthier than that of neighbouring Kós or Léros, since the quick-draining limestone strata, riddled with many caves, doesn't retain as much moisture. The rock does, however, admit seawater, which has tainted Póthia's wells; drinking water must be brought in by tanker truck from the Vathýs valley, and there are also potable springs at Kamári, Potamí district of Póthia and Hóra.

Since Kálymnos is the home port of the very useful local namesake ferry (see p.877), a minor hub for hydrofoils, and moreover where the long-distance ferry lines from the Cyclades and Astypálea join up with the main Dodecanesian routes, many travellers arrive unintentionally, and are initially most concerned with how to move on quickly. Yet Kálymnos has sufficient attractions to justify a stay of several days while island-hopping – or even longer, as the vestiges of the package industry at the western beaches suggest.

Póthia

PÓTHIA (sometimes pronounced Pothiá), without being obviously picturesque, is colourful and authentically Greek, its houses marching up the valley inland or arrayed in tiers along the sides of the mountains framing it. Your first and overwhelming impression will be of the phenomenal amount of noise engendered by traffic and the cranked-up sound systems of the half-dozen waterfront cafés. This is not entirely surprising, since with nearly 16,000 inhabitants, Póthia has overtaken Kós Town as the second-largest municipality in the Dodecanese after Ródhos Town. Things get even louder on **Easter Sunday** evening, when competing teams stationed on the heights either side of town engage in an organized dynamite-throwing contest, with feasting and general merriment after the inevitable casualties are carted away.

Perhaps the most rewarding way to acquaint yourself with Póthia is by wandering the **backstreets**, where elegant Neoclassical houses are surrounded by surprisingly large gardens, and craftsmen ply their trade in a genuine workaday bazaar. The Pothians particularly excel in iron-working, and all but the humblest dwellings in the eastern Evangelístria district are adorned with splendidly ornate banisters, balcony railings and fanlights. During the Italian occupation, many local houses were painted blue and white to irritate the colonial overlords, and though the custom has all but died out, the Greek national colours still appear amongst more traditional pink and ochre buildings.

Of the two local museums, priority should be given to the **Municipal Nautical and Folklore Museum** (Mon–Fri 8am–1.30pm, Sat & Sun

10am–12.30pm; €1.50), on the seaward side of Khristós cathedral. A large photo in the foyer shows Póthia as it was in the 1880s, with no quay, jetty, roads or sumptuous mansions, and with most of the population still up in Hóra, while other photos document sponge fishing and the Allied liberation of 1945. Three-dimensional exhibits include horribly primitive divers' breathing apparatuses, and "cages" designed to keep propellers from cutting air lines, a constant fear. However, in late 2006 or early 2007, a spectacular new annexe to the rather soporific existing **archeological museum** in Evangelístria (Tues–Sun 9.30am–2pm) should open, featuring a dazzling array of Roman and Byzantine finds.

△ Sponge-seller, Póthia, Kálymnos

Information and transport

All **boat** and **hydrofoil** agents, plus a municipal **tourist information** booth (sporadic Mon–Fri hours), line the waterfront as you bear right out of the pier-area gate. Useful agencies include Mangos (☎22430 28777), for Blue Star, LANE and Agoudimos; Sofia Kouremeti (☎22430 23700) for the *Dodekanisos Express/Pride*; Kalymna Yachting (☎22430 28200) for GA and the hydrofoils; plus the *Nissos Kalymnos* headquarters (☎22430 29612). Olympic Airways has a helpful representative agent at Patriárhou Maxímou 12 (☎22430 29265), 200m inland from the quay. The *Neon* Café on the northwest waterfront has a few **Internet** terminals; finally, four **banks** on or just behind the waterfront have ATMs.

Buses run as far as Emboriós in the northwest and Vathýs in the east, from two stops beside the municipal "palace", with schedules helpfully posted near many stops, and departures in season fairly frequent. Tickets must be bought beforehand from authorized kiosks, and cancelled on board. Otherwise, you can use shared **taxis** from Platía Kýprou (more than KTEL rates, less costly than a normal taxi), or rent a **scooter** from reputable Scootermania (☎22430 51780), just back from the waterfront, near where it bends south. There's plenty of **car rental** available on the quay (Spiros Kypraios, ☎2430 51470; Budget, phone as for Scootermania, or ☎697 28 34 628), though the island's compact enough that only groups would need one.

Accommodation

Accommodation is rarely a problem, with a little high-season booking office on the quay; as on Kós, beware of *dhomátia* touts as you disembark, since many of their premises are substandard, unlicensed or remote – often all three. The town's best, and quietest **hotel**, near the archeological museum, is the garden-set⚓ *Villa The-melina* (☎22430 22682, ℻22430 23920; open all year; B&B;❸), housed in an early-twentieth-century mansion, plus modern studio and apartment annexes ❹), with breakfast patio and a large swimming pool.

The high-ceiling, bug-screened, wood-floored rooms in the main house make this Kálymnos's most elegant accommodation. The only remotely comparable alternative, on the west quay but fairly quiet, is the *Arhondiko* (☏22430 24051, ℱ22430 24149; ❷), another refurbished mansion whose somewhat plain rooms have TV, fridge and air con; some also have balconies. Places in Amoudhára district (west of the harbour) include the en-suite *Pension Greek House* (☏22430 29559; ❶) with volubly friendly management, some studios and kitsch decor; and considerably above this, the well-signposted, well-kept *Hotel Panorama* (☏22430 22917, ℱ22430 23138; April–Oct; ❸), which has balconied rooms with views and a pleasant breakfast salon.

Eating and drinking

The most obvious place for **eating out** is the line of seafood tavernas northeast along the waterfront past the Italian-built municipal "palace", but standards are low and prices inflated. Much the best seafood and Kalymnian specialties are found at ✶*Kafenes*, on the esplanade opposite the county "palace", with slightly bumped-up prices justified by generous, savoury portions of salad, seafood, the odd dip and bulk wine; or at *Taverna Pandelis*, tucked inconspicuously into a cul-de-sac behind the waterfront *Olympic Hotel*; this features fresh-gathered shellfish like *foúskes* and *kalógnomes* (related to mussels) and wild scaly fish. Other alternatives include *mayireftá* and grills at *Xefteris*, under new management in 2005 inland from Khristós cathedral, or excellent wood-fired pizzas at *Pizza Imia* at mid-quay. *Dhodhoni*, past the bus stops on the shore, is the main ice-cream outlet, but fans of sticky cakes will want to attend the traditional *Zaharoplastío O Mihalaras* two steps away; they've a more modern annexe near the ferry jetty. Since the crash in tourism, the sole out-and-out **bar** is *Blue Note*, near *Pandelis*; for more ambitious seasonal venues just outside of town, watch for wall posters. A **cinema**, Cine Oasis, operates both summer and winter premises behind the traditional, column-facaded café-tearoom *Ai Musaï*, on the front.

Around Póthia

Just over 1km northwest of Póthia, in the suburb of Mýli, is a castle of the Knights of St John, **Kástro Khryssoheriás** (unrestricted access). From the whitewashed battlements there are wonderful views southeast over town to Kós, and north towards Hóra and Péra Kástro. The former Kalymnian capital of **HÓRA** (aka Horió), 1.5km further along the main road, is still a village of nearly three thousand inhabitants, and guards a critical pass in local geography, focus of settlement in every era. Steep steps lead up from its eastern edge to the nocturnally illuminated Byzantine citadel-town of **Péra Kástro** (daily 8.30am–2pm; free), appropriated by the Knights of St John and inhabited until late in the eighteenth century. Inside the gate and recently consolidated perimeter walls you'll find nine little **medieval chapels**, several – in particular Áyios Nikólaos/Pódhromos, Ayía Ánna, Timíou Stavroú and Metamórfosis – containing fifteenth-to-sixteenth-century fresco fragments. A visitors' centre and café should begin operation in the near future.

Some 200m past the turning for Árgos en route to the northwest coast from Hóra, you can detour briefly left to visit two early Byzantine basilicas which are fairly representative, and among the easiest to find, of a vast number on Kálymnos. The more impressive of the two, accessed by whitewashed steps on the left just as the highway begins to descend, is that of **Khristós tís Ierousalím**, probably dating from the late fourth century, with its apse fully preserved; the three-aisled **Limniótissa** church in an adjacent field is larger but considerably less intact.

West coast resorts

From the basilicas, the road dips into a tree-shaded valley leading to the consecutive **beach resorts** of Kandoúni, Myrtiés and Massoúri, collectively referred to as "Brostá" by islanders. **KANDOÚNI**, some 200m of brown, hard-packed sand favoured by the locals, is the shore annexe of the rich agricultural valley-villages of **Pánormos** and **Eliés**. Kandoúni **accommodation** freed up by the departure of the tour companies includes the *Kalydna Island Hotel* (℡22430 47880; ❹), but for both bathing and staying you're probably better off at **LINÁRIA**, the north end of the same bay. A smaller cove set apart from Kandoúni proper by a rock outcrop, this has better sand and the possibility of staying at *Skopellos Studios* (℡22430 47155; ❸), on the slope below the church. Of two shoreline full-service **tavernas** here, *Tò Egeo* is better value for seafood and more locally attended.

The next beach north, **PLATÝ-YIALÓS**, though again a bit shorter than Kandoúni, is arguably the best on the island: cleaner than its southern neighbours, more secluded, and placed scenically at the base of a cliff, opposite Ayía Kyriakí islet. A lone **taverna** (*Kyma/Wave*), right behind the sand at road's end, proves popular for simple, inexpensive lunches or sunset drinks (it closes shortly after). Among a handful of choices for **staying** on spec, long-time budget favourite is the Vavoulas family's *Pension Plati Gialos* (℡ & ℻22430 47029), actually overlooking Linária, with spacious balconies, mosquito nets and a terrace bar; choose between simple, fan-equipped rooms (❷) or two family apartments (❸). For more comfort, blue-and-white-decor *Mousselis Studios* (℡22430 48307, ✉mousellis_studios@yahoo.gr; ❸) just down the road towards the beach accommodate two to six people, with half board offered at its acceptable restaurant.

The main road climbs from Pánormos up to a pass, before descending in zigzags to meet the sea again 8km from Póthia at **MYRTIÉS**. Together with **MASSOÚRI** (1km north) and **ARMEÓS** (2km north and end of the line for most buses), Myrtiés has been hardest hit by the Kalymnian tourism slump, so vacant and boarded-up premises abound. Exceptions include ⌘ *Akroyiali* (℡22430 47521 or 693 89 13 210; ❸), seven two-room, beachside apartments in Massoúri sleeping two adults and two kids which require long advance booking; *Bar Babis* on the square in Myrtiés, an Anglophile institution, and jointly operated Avis/Alfa (℡22430 47430) **renting cars and bikes** respectively. No great loss in many other cases, as during their long tenure the package companies had a predictably dire effect on local **tavernas**; much the best survivor, in Armeós, is friendly meat specialist ⌘ *Tsopanakos* (open all year), which has fresh meat and cheese dishes from island-grazed goats, along with the usual grills and appetizers. Armeós is also the local mecca for **rock-climbers**, with many of the most popular cliffs overhead and a small equipment shop (Climber's Nest) catering to them. There's also some Greek-pitched **nightlife**, with live acts at *Kastelli Club*.

The beach at Myrtiés is narrow, pebbly and cramped by development, though it does improve as you approach Massoúri. The closest all-sand beach to Myrtiés lies 500m south, at **Melitsahás** cove (Melitsáhas in dialect), which also has the only locally patronized **taverna** at its fishing anchorage, *Iy Dhrossia* (aka *O Andonis*; open all year), best for oysters, lobster and shrimp as well as scaly fish at affordable rates. On-spec **accommodation** is fairly easy to find here, for example at the spacious *Maria's Studios* (℡22430 48135 or 22430 28528; ❷) up on the hillside. Possibly this coast's most appealing feature is its position opposite the evocatively shaped islet of Télendhos (see overleaf), which frames some of the most dramatic sunsets in Greece. It's also possible to go from Myrtiés directly to Xirókambos on Léros aboard the daily early-afternoon **kaïki**.

Some 5km beyond Massoúri, **ARYINÓNDA** has a clean pebble beach, two **tavernas** and sunbeds. It's also the trailhead for the spectacular two-and-a-half-hour walk inland and over two gentle passes to Metóhi in the Vathýs valley. From the bus stop and gravelled car-park area and small spring, head southeast on a path between rock walls which soon climbs the south flank of the ravine here, sporadically marked by paint dots. Don't believe sources which show the route emerging at Styménia, and be aware that the municipality is bulldozing a road to Vathýs, which will severely disrupt the trail about half an hour along. You'll need a sun hat, stout shoes and a litre or two of water, as the next source is in Plátanos hamlet, beyond Metóhi.

The end of the bus line, **EMBORIÓS**, 20km from the port, offers a gravel-and-sand beach, which gets better as you head west, **accommodation** and a number of **tavernas**, including the long-running *Harry's Paradise*, with attached, air-conditioned garden apartments (☎22430 40061;❸) in bland white-and-pine decor. If the twice-daily bus service fails you, there is a shuttle boat back to Myrtiés at 4pm (leaving the latter at 10am). There are also better, if unamenitied beaches between here and Skália, such as **Kalamiés** and **Áyios Nikólaos**.

Télendhos

The trip across the strait to the striking, volcanic-plug islet of **TÉLENDHOS** is arguably the best reason to come to Myrtiés; little boat-buses shuttle to and fro regularly (8am–midnight, half-hourly each direction; €1.50), occasionally dodging the sea-kayaks which have become a popular sporting device locally. According to local legend, Télendhos is a petrified princess, gazing out to sea after her errant lover; the woman's-head profile is most evident at dusk. The hardly less pedestrian geological explanation has the islet sundered from Kálymnos by a cataclysmic earthquake in 554 AD; traces of a submerged town are said to lie at the bottom of the straits.

Home to about fifteen permanent inhabitants, Télendhos is car-free and blissfully tranquil, even more so since certain package operators gave up allotments here. For cultural edification you'll find the ruined thirteenth-century **monastery of Áyios Vassílios** and an enormous **basilica of Ayía Triádha** up on the ridge, part way along the flagstoned, ten-minute path to **Hokhlakás** pebble beach, which is small but very scenic, with sunbeds for rent. **Pótha** and nudist "**Paradise**" on the other side of the islet are preferred by some: sandy and with calm water, but no afternoon sun.

There are about eight places to eat and a roughly equal number of **accommodation** establishments, most (but not all) linked to the tavernas. Places to stay that get uniformly positive reviews include *Pension Studios Rita* (☎22430 47914, ☎22430 47927), rooms ❶) and renovated-house studios ❷), managed by the namesake snack-bar/café; the simple but en-suite rooms above *Zorba's* (☎22430 48660;❶); *Rinio Studios* (☎22430 23851;❷), set a bit inland and built in 2003 to a high standard; or, north beyond Áyios Vassílios, the Greek-Australian-run 🍴 *On the Rocks* (☎22430 48260, ⓦwww.otr.telendos.com;❸ ; April–Nov), three superbly appointed rooms with double glazing, satellite TV, bug screens, fridges and internet access, as well as use of kayaks on the beach out front. If you want more (relative) luxury on Télendhos, it's fairly easy to secure a vacancy at the large *Hotel Porto Potha* (☎22430 47321, ⓦwww.telendoshotel .gr;❸), set at the very edge of things but with a large pool, "private" beach, some self-catering studios and friendly managing family. Endorseable **tavernas** include *Barba Stathis* (aka *Tassia's*), en route to Hokhlakás, with a few cooked dishes each day; *Zorba's*, doing slightly pricey but excellent goat in tomato sauce or fresh squid; *Plaka*, next to *On the Rocks*, good for inexpensive meat straight from grandpa's flock; and the slightly pricey, full-service taverna at *On the Rocks* itself, with lovely home-made desserts, and a bar that's the heart and soul of local **nightlife**. At one corner of the premises you can visit the chapel of Áyios Harálambos, occupying a former Byzantine bathhouse.

Vathýs and around

The first 4km east from Póthia seem vastly unpromising (power plant, rubbish tip, multiple gasworks, cement quarries, fish farms), until you round a bend and the ten-kilometre ride ends dramatically at **VATHÝS**, a long, fertile valley, carpeted with orange and tangerine groves, whose colour provides a startling contrast to the mineral greys and oranges higher up on Kálymnos. At the simple fjord port of **RÍNA**, more ruined basilicas flank the bay; near the southerly one is the best **accommodation** option, the helpful *Rooms Manolis* (☎22430 31300;❶), simple but en suite and with sweeping views, set in landscaped terraces and accessible by a lane behind *The Harbors* (see below). Some of the **tavernas** are pricier than you'd expect, owing to patronage from the numerous yachts that call here; the best choice, with shambolic service but good grilled fish, is *The Harbors*, the first place on the right at the road's end.

The steep-sided inlet has no beach to speak of, so people swim off the artificial lido on the south side; the closest pebble-coves reachable overland are **Aktí**, about 3km back towards Póthia, a functional pebble strand with sunbeds and a single snack-bar, and **Pezónda**, a little further north, reached by steep track (and then a 45-minute walk northwest) starting from Metóhi hamlet. At track's end another path heads east in fifteen minutes to the amazingly set little **monastery of Kyrá Psilí**, frequented only on August 15.

Boat excursions sometimes visit the stalactite cave of **Dhaskalió**, inhabited in Neolithic times, out towards the fjord mouth on its north flank, and the remoter, tiny beaches of **Almyrés** and **Dhrasónda**, accessible only by sea.

It's possible to **walk** back to Póthia along the old direct *kalderími* which existed before the coastal highway – a two-hour jaunt that begins in Plátanos hamlet. The route is tricky to find in this direction, however, so most people start in Póthia, at the church of Ayía Triádha behind the *Villa The-melina* hotel – the way is marked initially by red paint splodges.

The southwest

Climbing southwest out of Póthia towards Áyios Sávvas monastery, the most worthwhile halt is the privately run **Folklore Museum-Traditional House of Kalymnos** (daily 9am–9pm; €1.50), a treasure trove of old-time furnishings and costumes. Some 6km southwest of Póthia, the small bay of **Vlyhádhia** is reached through a narrow ravine draining from the nondescript village of Vothýni. The sand-and-pebble beach here isn't really worth a special trip, since the bay is apt to be stagnant and at least some of the locals (who have blotted out all Roman-alphabet road signs) are resentful of foreigners. If you're interested in **scuba diving**, the coast to either side of Vlyhádhia is one of the limited number of legal areas in Greece. A local diver has also assembled an impressive **Museum of Submarine Finds** (Mon–Sat 9am–7pm, Sun 10am–2pm; free), which in addition to masses of sponges and shells offers a reconstructed ancient wreck with amphorae and World War II debris. The best local dive operator,

Pegasus Diving Club (☎694 4180746), works out of Póthia and visits ancient wrecks *in situ*.

Póthia-based *kaïkia* also make well-publicized excursions to the cave of **Kefála** just west of Vlyhádhia, the most impressive of half a dozen caverns around the island. You have to walk thirty minutes from where the boats dock, but the vividly coloured formations repay the effort; the cave was inhabited before recorded history, and later served as a sanctuary of Zeus (who is fancifully identified with a particularly imposing stalagmite in the biggest of six chambers).

Léros

Léros is so indented with deep, sheltered anchorages that between 1928 and 1948 it harboured, in turn, much of the Italian, German and British Mediterranean fleets. Unfortunately, many of these magnificent fjords and bays seem to absorb rather than reflect light, and the island's fertility – there are orchards and vegetable gardens a-plenty – can make Léros seem scruffy when compared with the crisp lines of its more barren neighbours. These characteristics, plus the island's lack of spectacularly good beaches, meant that until the late 1980s just a few thousand foreigners (mostly Italians who grew up on Léros), and not many

more Greeks, came to visit each August. The tourist profile is now broader, with a longer season; Scandinavian, British, Dutch and German package operators alternate by season in "discovering" Léros and the company of islanders relatively unjaded by mass tourism. Foreign-visitor numbers have, however, dipped since the millennium, with matters unlikely to change until and unless the airport runway is lengthened to accommodate jets.

Until recently Léros didn't strenuously encourage mass tourism; various **prisons and sanatoriums** dominated the Lerian economy from the 1950s onwards, directly or indirectly employing about a third of the population. During the junta era, the island hosted a notorious detention centre at Parthéni, and for over four decades several mental hospitals served as warehouses for many of Greece's more intractable psychiatric cases and mentally handicapped children. The island's domestic image problem was compounded by its name, the butt of jokes by mainlanders who pounced on its similarity to the word *lerá*, connoting rascality and unsavouriness. In 1989, a major scandal emerged concerning the administration of the various asylums, with EU maintenance and development funds found to have been embezzled by staff, and inmates kept in degrading conditions; a subsequent influx of EU inspectors, foreign psychiatrists and extra funding resulted in drastic improvements. By 1995 the worst wards were closed down, and the inmates placed in sheltered housing around the island, farming and engaging in "work internships" for pocket money; the remaining seven hundred carers now haven't enough to do but legally can't be made redundant. Some of the slack was taken up by tourism, some by the 1999 opening of one of Greece's main nursing colleges, but the institutional identity is not nearly as pervasive as you'd expect.

More obvious is the legacy of the **Battle of Léros** on November 12–16, 1943, when overwhelming German forces displaced a Commonwealth division, which had landed on the island following the Italian capitulation. Bomb nose-cones and shell casings still turn up as gaily painted garden ornaments in the courtyards of churches and tavernas, or have been pressed into service as gateposts. Each year for three days following September 26, memorial services and a naval festival commemorate the sinking of the Greek battleship *Queen Olga* and the British *Intrepid* during the German attack.

Unusually for a small island, Léros has abundant ground water, channelled into cisterns at several points (only the two on the Plátanos upper bypass are potable). These, plus low-lying ground staked with the avenues of eucalyptus trees planted by the Italians, make for a horrendously active mosquito contingent, so come prepared.

Léros is sufficiently compact for the energetic to walk around, but there is a reasonably reliable bus service, plus several motor- and mountain-bike rental outlets, of which Motoland (outlets in Pandélli, ☎22470 24103, and Álinda, ☎22470 24584) has proven reliable on several occasions; Koumbaros in Álinda is by contrast worth avoiding. The island is hilly enough to make motorised wheels a better bet, though the reasonably fit could manage with just a mountain bike between Álinda and Lakkí. If you rent a scooter, take extra care – Lerian roads are particularly narrow, potholed and gravel-strewn, and the low-slung, fat-tyred bikes on offer don't cope well.

Lakkí and Xirókambos

All large **ferries**, the *Nissos Kalymnos* and the *Dodekanisos Pride* arrive at the main port of **LAKKÍ**, originally constructed in 1935–38 as a model town to house 7500 civilian dependents of an adjacent Italian naval base. Boulevards far too wide for today's paltry amount of traffic are lined with some marvellous Rationalist edifices, including the round-fronted cinema, the church, the primary school, a shopping centre with a round atrium and the derelict remains of the Leros Palace Hotel. Their architectural importance has finally been acknowledged and a phased restoration programme should see them all returned to decent condition by 2008.

Buses don't meet the ferries – instead there's a **taxi squadron** that charges set fares to standard destinations. If you arrive during business hours, consider renting a car or bike from Koumoulis (☎22470 22330), near the cinema. Few people stay willingly at any of the handful of drab hotels in Lakkí, preferring to head straight for the resorts of Pandélli, Álinda or Vromólithos (see opposite). There are just two proper **tavernas**: *Marina*, at the base of the yacht jetty, and *Tò Petrino*, inland next to the **post office**. Other amenities include three ATMs attached to as many **banks**; travel **agencies** are Leros Travel, for GA and the *Nissos Kalymnos* (☎22470 22154); and Aegean Travel a block inland (☎22470 26000), for Blue Star Ferries and the catamaran. The nearest approximation of a **beach** is at sand-and-gravel **Kouloúki**, 500m west, where there's a seasonal taverna and some pines for shade, though it's too close to the ferry jetty for most tastes. You can carry on another kilometre or so to **Merikiá**, a slight improvement, also with a taverna.

XIRÓKAMBOS, nearly 5km from Lakkí in the far south of the island, is the point of arrival for the afternoon *kaïki* from Myrtiés on Kálymnos (it returns early the following morning). Though billed as a resort, it's essentially a fishing port where folk also happen to swim – the beach is poor to mediocre, improving as you head west. Top **accommodation** here is the *Hotel Efstathia* (☎22470 24099;❸), actually studio apartments with huge, well-furnished doubles as well as family four-plexes, plus a large pool. You've a choice of three evenly spaced **tavernas**, where the road hits the shore. The island's **campsite** (☎22470 23372; May–Oct), with an in-house scuba-diving centre (☎694 42 38 490; ⓦwww .lerosdiving.com), is in an olive grove at the village of **LEPÍDHA**, 750m back up the road to Lakkí. Just north of the campsite, an access drive on the far side of the road (signposted as "Ancient Fort") leads up to a tiny acropolis with stretches of ancient masonry behind the modern chapel on the summit.

Pandélli and Vromólithos

Just under 3km north of Lakkí, Pandélli and Vromólithos together form an attractive and scenic resort, Álinda's (see p.866) only rival.

PANDÉLLI is still a working port, the cement jetty benefiting local fishermen as well as an increasing number of yachts that call here. A small but reef-free, pea-gravel beach is complemented by a relative abundance of nonpackage **accommodation**, such as the *Pension Happiness* (☎22470 23498;❸), where the road down from Plátanos meets the sea, or the newer *Pension Lavyrinthos*, directly opposite (☎22470 24165;❸). For a higher standard, try⚡ *Niki Studios* (☎22470 25600;❸) at the base of the road up to the castle – air-con double units and quad apartments, Australian-Greek-run and with partial sea views. Up on the ridge dividing Pandélli from Vromólithos in **Spília** district, the *Hotel Rodon* (☎22470 23524;❸) actually comprises 2005-refurbished studios and larger apartments downstairs, with knock-out views. On summer nights there may be a faint strain of music from *Café del Mar*, perched on a rock terrace below (it operates as a daytime beach-café; May–Oct); the other long-lived local **bar** is the civilized, English-Danish-run *Savana*, at the opposite end of Pandélli, with excellent music (you can nominate your favourite tracks). It stands beyond a row of decidedly uneven waterfront **tavernas**, the best of which are⚡ *Psaropoula* (open all year), with good, non-farmed fish and *mayireftá*, and *Tou Mihali*, a corner *kafenío* where expertly fried *gópes*, mixed salads and good wine are scoffed by a largely local crowd. Up in Spília, adjacent to the *Hotel Rodon*, *Mezedhopolio O Dimitris O Karaflas* is one of the best-sited ouzerís on the island, scoring highly for delicacies such as chunky local sausages and unusual dips like *xynógalo* and *tsitsíri*.

VROMÓLITHOS boasts the best easily accessible **beach** on the island, car-free and hemmed in by hills studded with massive oaks. The shoreline is gravel and coarse sand, and the sea here is clean, but as so often on Léros you have to cross a rock pavement at most points before reaching deeper water; there's a more secluded, sandier cove southeast at **Tourkopígadho**. Two **tavernas** behind the beach trade more on their location than their cuisine – *To Pigadhi* at the main inland junction is better – but the general standard of **accommodation** here is higher than at Pandélli. Prime choices are *Tony's Beach*, spacious studio units set in equally extensive waterside grounds (☎22470 24743, Ⓦwww.tonysbeachstudios.gr; June–Sept;❹), and the stone-floored *Glaros*, just inland in pleasant grounds (☎22470 24358, Ⓕ22470 23683; May–Oct;❹).

Plátanos and Ayía Marína

The Neoclassical and vernacular houses of **PLÁTANOS**, the island capital 1km west of Pandélli, are draped gracefully along a saddle between two hills, one of them crowned by the inevitable Knights' castle. Known locally as the **Kástro** (daily 8am–1pm, also May–Oct Wed, Sat & Sun 3–7pm; €1), this is reached either by a zigzagging road peeling off the Pandélli-bound road, or via a more scenic stair-path from the central square; the battlements, and the views from them, are dramatic, especially near sunrise or sunset. The medieval church of **Panayía tou Kástrou** inside the gate houses a small museum (additional €1), though its carved *témblon* and naïve oratory are more remarkable than the sparse exhibits, mostly icons and other liturgical items. The **archeological museum** (Tues–Sun 8am–2.30pm; free), down the road to Ayía Marína, is more interesting, compensating for a dearth of artefacts with a comprehensible gallop through Lerian history.

Plátanos is not really a place to stay or eat, although it's well sown with **shops** and **services**. The latter include Olympic Airways (☎22470 24144), south of the turning for Pandélli; a **post office**, down the road towards Ayía Marína; and a few **banks** with ATMs. The single **bus** (schedule posted at stop, opposite the island's main **taxi** rank) plies several times daily between Parthéni in the north and Xirókambos in the south.

Plátanos merges seamlessly with **AYÍA MARÍNA**, 1km north on the shore of a fine bay, still graced by a small, Italian-built public market building. If you're travelling to Léros on an excursion boat from Lipsí, the *Dodekanisos Express*, or a hydrofoil, this will be your port of entry unless high winds force a diversion to Lakkí. At the western edge of things the superior🗲 *Ouzeri Neromylos*, out by the wave-lapped windmill, indisputably has the most romantic setting on the island (mid-March–Oct; reservations mandatory July-Aug on ☎22470 24894), the best musical sound-track, and arguably the best food. Host Takis' specialties include *garidhopílafo* (shrimp-rice), superb fresh fish, edible bread and *kolokythokeftédhes* (courgette patties), expertly prepared by his wife and mother-in-law. Lively (for Léros) **nightlife** is provided by several bars near the customs house, such as *Enallaktiko*, with a few **Internet** terminals, and cavernous *Apothiki New Face* on the quay. Kastis Travel nearby (☎22470 22140) handles all ticket sales for hydrofoils and the *Dodekanisos Express*, plus there are two bank **ATMs**.

Álinda and Krithóni

ÁLINDA, 3km northwest of Ayía Marína, ranks as the longest-established resort on Léros, with development just across the road from a long, narrow strip of pea-gravel beach. It's also the first area for accommodation to open in spring, and the last to shut in autumn. Most **hotels** and **pensions** here are partly allotted to tour companies, but worthwhile establishments that keep rooms for walk-ins include *Hotel Gianna* (℡22470 23153; ❸), with fridge-equipped units plus a few studios overlooking the war cemetery, or – set back from mid-beach – the well-kept *Hotel Alinda* (*Xenonas Mavrakis*) (℡22470 23266, ⓦwww .alindahotel.gr; ❸), with the very good, affiliated *Taverna Alinda* and sunken Byzantine mosaic out front, plus well-kept rooms with air con and fridges. The other reliable beachfront **restaurant** is *Finikas*. One lodging to avoid is *Studios Diamantis*, whose thoroughly unpleasant management touts aggressively from their taxi and gift shop in Ayía Marína. At **KRITHÓNI**, 1.5km south, more comfort is available at the island's top-flight accommodation: the ⚥ *Crithoni's Paradise* (℡22470 25120, ⓦwww.crithonishotel.com; open all year; rooms ❻, suites ❽), a mock-traditional low-rise complex with decent buffet breakfast, a large pool and all mod cons in the rooms – it's worth the little extra for "superior standard" or a suite.

The **Allied War Graves Cemetery**, mostly containing casualties of the November 1943 battle, occupies a walled enclosure at the south end of the beach; immaculately maintained, with a guestbook, it serves as a moving counterpoint to the beachside life outside. The other principal sight at Álinda is the privately run **Historical and Ethnographic Museum** (May–Sept only, Tues–Sun 9am–1pm & 7–9pm; €3), housed in the unmistakable castle-like mansion of Paris Bellinis (1871–1957). Most of the top floor is devoted to the Battle of Léros: relics from the sunken *Queen Olga*, a wheel from a Junkers bomber, a stove made from a bomb casing. There's also a rather grisly mock-up clinic (mostly gynecological tools) and assorted rural impedimenta, costumes and antiques.

Alternative beaches near Álinda include **Dhýo Liskária**, a series of gravel coves at the far northeast of the bay (one taverna, two cafés), and **Goúrna**, the turning for which lies 1km or so off the trans-island road. The latter, Léros's longest sandy beach, is hard-packed and gently shelving, if wind-buffeted; a few sunbeds are provided by the single taverna.

The far north

Seven kilometres from Álinda along the main route north, a marked side-track leads left to the purported **Temple of Artemis**, on a slight rise just west of the airport runway. In ancient times, Léros was sacred to the goddess, and the temple here was supposedly inhabited by guinea fowl – the grief-stricken sisters of Meleager, metamorphosed thus by Artemis following their brother's death. All that remains now are some jumbled, knee-high walls, which are more likely to have been an ancient fortress, but the view is superb.

The tiny **airport** terminal itself has been expanded for a busier future, but it's still no place to be stuck a minute longer than necessary; if your midday flight to Astypálea or Rhodes is delayed (more likely than not), your only diversion lies across the road at vastly overpriced *Taverna To Arhondiko* – eat elsewhere before you set out, and just have a coffee here.

The onward route skims the shores of sumpy, reed-fringed Parthéni Bay, with its yacht dry dock and dreary, Italian-built army base (the 1967–74 political prison). The camp has, however, left one outstanding cultural legacy: the chapel of **Ayía Kioúra** (always open), reached by a one-kilometre marked access road. During the junta era, certain political prisoners decorated this otherwise unremarkable church with striking murals – squarely in the tradition of Diego Rivera's 1930s Leftist art – rather than conventional frescoes. The Orthodox Church has, of course, always abhorred these images – a resident monk obliterated several in the 1980s – but Ayía Kioúrá is now a protected monument. The paved road ends 11km from Álinda at **Blefoútis** and its huge, almost landlocked bay. The small beach (the rough Lerian norm) has tamarisks to shelter under and an adequate taverna, *Iy Thea Artemi*.

Pátmos

Arguably the most beautiful and certainly the best known of the smaller Dodecanese, **Pátmos** has a distinctive, immediately palpable atmosphere. It was in a cave here that St John the Divine (in Greek, O Theológos or "The Theologian"), set down the New Testament's Book of Revelation and unwittingly shaped the island's destiny. The monastery honouring him, founded here in 1088 by the Blessed Khristodhoulos (1021–93), dominates Pátmos both physically – its fortified bulk towering high above everything else – and, to a considerable extent, socially. While the monks inside no longer run the island unchallenged as they did for more than six centuries, their influence has stopped it going the way of Rhodes or Kós – though Pátmos now has no less than four nudist beaches, something unthinkable a decade or so ago.

Despite vast numbers of visitors and the island's firm presence on the cruise, hydrofoil and yacht circuits, tourism has not been allowed to take Pátmos over completely. While there are several after-hours clubs around the main port town, drunken rowdiness is virtually unknown. Package clients only equal independent visitors in certain years, and are pretty much confined to Gríkou and a handful of larger hotels at Skála and Kámbos. Day-trippers still exceed overnighters, and Pátmos seems an altogether different place once the last cruise-ship passengers have gone after sunset. Away from Skála, touristic development is appealingly subdued if not deliberately retarded, thanks to the absence of an airport. On outlying beaches, little has superficially changed since the 1980s, though "for sale" signs on every seafront field and farmhouse, plus massive villa developments at coves closer in, suggest that such days are strictly numbered.

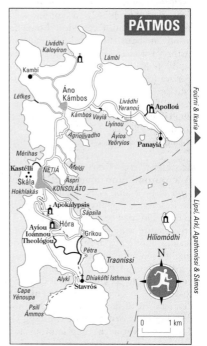

Skála and around

SKÁLA, where most of the island's three thousand people live, seems initially to contradict any solemn, otherworldly image of Pátmos. The waterside, with its ritzy cafés, arty gift boutiques and clientele, is a bit too sophisticated for such a small town, and certain service staff more than a little world-weary. During peak season, the quay and commercial district swarm by day with trippers souvenir-hunting or being shepherded onto coaches for the ride up to the monastery; after dark there's still a considerable traffic in well-dressed cliques of visitors on furlough from the huge, humming cruisers which weigh anchor around midnight. In winter (which here means by early October), Skála assumes a ghost-town air as most shops and restaurants close, their owners and staff going back to Rhodes or Athens.

Hóra, a brief bus- or taxi-ride up the mountain, would be a more attractive base, but has little accommodation. Yet given time, Skála reveals some more enticing corners in the residential fringes to the east and west, where vernacular mansions hem in pedestrian lanes creeping up the hillsides. The modern town dates only from the 1820s, when the Aegean had largely been cleared of pirates, but at the summit of the westerly rise, **Kastélli**, you can see the extensive foundations of the island's ancient acropolis.

Information and transport

Almost everything of interest can be found within, or within sight of, the Italian-built municipal "palace": all arriving sea-craft anchor opposite, the port police occupy the east end, the **post office** one of its corners, and the main **bus stop**, with a posted timetable, is right in front. There are three **banks**, each with an ATM. **Scooter rental** outfits (such as Billis ☎ 22470 32218 and Aris ☎ 22470 32542) are common, with lowish rates owing to the modest size of the island. **Excursion boats** to Psilí Ámmos and Arkí/Maráthi leave mostly at about 10am (to Léros and Lipsí, sometimes 8am) from just in front of Astoria Travel and Apollon Travel, the two **agencies** handling hydrofoil tickets; Apollon (☎22470 22470) is also the central rep for Blue Star Ferries. GA Ferries (☎22470 31217) and the *Nissos Kalymnos* (☎22470 32575) have separate agencies on, or just off, the central waterfront square; several outlets sell tickets for the *Dodekanisos Express/Pride* catamarans; try Kyriaki Liapi (☎22470 29303) in Konsoláto district to the east. Skála has two **Internet cafés**: one inside the *Blue Bay* Hotel, the other – Millennium – just behind the little park inland from the port-terminal building.

Accommodation

Accommodation touts meet all arriving seagoing craft, and their offerings tend to be a long walk distant and/or inland – not necessarily a bad thing, as no location is really remote, and anywhere near the waterfront, which doubles as the main road between Gríkou and Kámbos, will be noisy. Pátmos vernacular architecture is quite distinctive, but you wouldn't know it from most lodgings; bland if inoffensive rooms thrown up during the 1980s, with institutional (one might even say monastic) furnishings.

Establishments worth reserving in advance (they'll often send a van to fetch you) are scattered across several districts. Unless otherwise stated, assume April-to-October operation. Besides **central Skála**, you could end up in **Konsoláto** district, east of the centre near the fishing anchorage, with fairly high-quality digs, but the worst noise from fishing boats and ferries coming and going from 1 to 4am. **Netiá**, the unglamorous area northwest between the power plant and Mérihas cove, is actually not a bad choice as a base. Pebbly **Hokhlakás** Bay, just a ten-minute walk southwest starting from the central market street, is perhaps the quietest district, with wonderful sunset views. **Melóï** cove, 1.5km northwest, has a good beach and is home to island's well-run **campsite**, *Stefanos-Flowers* (T 22470 31821).

Asteri Netiá, near Mérihas cove T 22470 32465, © pasca@otenet.gr. The highest standard in this area, unimprovably set on a knoll overlooking the bay, in a well-landscaped environment; guests have own-produced honey, eggs and tomatoes at breakfast. 2003-expanded with a large sea-view lounge and variably sized rooms (including 2 with wheelchair access). B&B❺

Australis Netiá T 22470 31576, W www.patmos _web.gr/australishotel.htm. Somewhat spartan but en-suite hotel owned by a returned Greek-Australian family; full breakfast and an affiliated scooter-rental business saves you traipses into town. There's a better-standard apartment annexe, whose units accommodate 6 people – at❼ per unit. B&B❹

Blue Bay About 150m beyond Konsoláto on the Gríkou road T 22470 31165, W www .bluebay.50g.com. Probably the best-value, quietest choice for this area, with helpful Australian-Greek management, reasonably furnished air-con, fridged, sea-view rooms piled in tiers, plus Skála's most reliable Internet facilities. Credit cards accepted for stays of over 2 days❺

Captain's House Konsoláto T 22470 31793, W www.patmosisland.com/captainhouse. The newer wing of much quieter rear rooms overlooks a fair-sized pool and shady terrace. Further pluses are friendly management, above-average furnishings and on-site car rental❺

Doriza Bay Hokhlakás, south hillside T 22470 32702, W www.portoscoutari.com/doriza_bay.html. Co-managed with the *Porto Scoutari* as a more affordable annexe, this has the best sunsets in Skála, bar none. There's a wing of standard rooms with a breakfast salon, and galleried maisonettes (including some two-bedroom apartments) across the way. Off-street scooter parking❺

Effie On hillside above the municipal car park, centre T 22470 32500, W www.effiehotel.gr. Two-wing hotel with anodyne, pine-and-tile, heated/air-con rooms and private parking. Unusually, open all year❹

Galini secluded cul-de-sac in from ferry dock, centre T 22470 31240, F 22470 31705. Welcoming C-class hotel that provides excellent value, with the standard of furnishing (including fridges and air con) in the large, terra-cotta-tiled rooms, most with balconies, approaching B-class❹

Maria Hokhlakás flatlands, 150m from sea T 22470 31201, F 22470 32018. Quietly set small hotel where a pleasant front garden, air con and big sea-view balconies make up for tiny bathrooms❹

Porto Scoutari Melóï T 22470 33124, W www.portoscoutari.com. Pátmos's premier hotel, this bungalow complex overlooks the beach from a hillside setting. Both the spacious individual units, with TV, phone, plus air con, and the vast common areas are furnished with mock antiques and original art, all arrayed around a large pool. A small, on-site spa should commence operation in 2006. But what really makes the place is Elina Scoutari's dedication to her customers' welfare❼

Pension Sydney Netiá, up the hill from *Australis* T 22470 31689. Spartan but adequate balconied rooms with fridge and fan; helpful management. Purified drinking water (a necessity) included❸

Yvonni Studios Hokhlakás north hillside T 22470 32466 or 22470 33066, W www.12net.gr/yvonni. Basic but salubrious pine-and-tile, medium-sized units with fridges, air con and oblique sea views over a hillside garden. Walk-ins should call at the gift shop next to the *Nissos Kalymnos* agency❸

Eating, drinking and nightlife

Restaurant options in Skála have improved from an era of surplus *souvláki/ yíros* joints or snack stalls, and no t enough full-service, sit-down places. Easily the town's most distinctive is seafood-only *Ouzeri To Hiliomodhi* (open all year), just off the start of the Hóra road, with its vegetarian *mezédhes* and delicacies such as limpets (served live, be warned), grilled octopus and salted anchovies and summer seating in a pedestrian lane. The best all-rounder (Easter to early Sept) is reckoned to be *Vegghera*, prosaically set opposite the yacht marina, with a VIP clientele, flawless presentation for such as stuffed scorpion fish, vegetarian or seafood salads, superb desserts, and per-head bills of about €40; reservations required on T 22470 32988. Honourable mentions go to *Yiayia*

△ Mosaic outside the monastery of Ayíou Ioánnou Theológou, Pátmos

in Konsoláto (Thurs–Tues, supper only), which has expanded from several seasons of purveying Indonesian food to generic Southeast Asian fare at slightly elevated prices, and *Pandelis* (all year), one lane inland behind Astoria Travel, where a wide-ranging menu of reliably good *mayireftá* make up for famously dour – if efficient – service.

Aside from these, you're best off heading a bit out of town; this is one island where the beach tavernas excel. **Melóï** has a decent *mayireftá* taverna, *Melloi* (alias *Stefanos*), reasonably priced and open early or late in the season, best at lunch (though it gets coach tours). Just over the hill at **Áspri** cove are two more, *Aspri* and *Kyma*: the former, just inland with a wider-ranging menu, stays open later in the season, but the latter (mid-June to Aug 31 only), fish specialist down on a concrete mole by the water, scores for its romantic setting even though presentation is basic and service often sloppy. At **Sápsila** cove, 2km southeast of Skála, *Benetos* (June–early Oct Tues–Sun supper only; summer reservations mandatory on ☎22470 33089) has since 1998 established a reputation as one of the top eateries on the island due to its Mediterranean and Pacific-Rim fusion dishes, with a stress on seafood. Budget a minimum of €33 for drink and three courses, which may include roast vegetable terrine with balsamic vinegar and raisins, baked fish fillet with risotto and Hubbard squash, *barboúni* sashimi and lemon sorbet.

Back in town, the biggest and most durable **café-bar** is the wood-panelled, barn-like *Café Arion* on the waterside, where all sorts of people sit outside, dance, or prop up the long bar. Other **nightlife** venues include the pricey *Isalos*, inland from the Italian "palace", occasionally hosting live music, and *Celine*, at the opposite end of the quay, beyond the town beach. More perhaps in sync with the tone of the island is the annual **Festival of Religious Music**, held the first two weeks of September in a hillside amphitheatre and featuring performers from Russia, Turkey and the entire Balkans.

The monasteries and Hóra

Top of your sightseeing agenda is likely to be the monastery of Ayíou Ioánnou Theológou (St John), sheltered behind massive defences in the hilltop capital of Hóra. There's a regular KTEL bus up (about 8 daily), or you can do a forty-minute walk along a beautiful old cobbled path. To find its start, proceed through Skála towards Hokhlakás, and once past the telecoms building bear left onto a lane starting opposite an ironmonger's; follow this uphill to its end on the main road – immediately opposite you'll see the cobbled path. Just over halfway, you might pause at the **monastery of Apokálypsis** (daily 8am–1.30pm, also Tues, Thurs & Sun 4–6pm; free) built around the cave where St John heard the voice of God issuing from a cleft in the rock, and where he sat dictating his words to a disciple. In the cave wall, the presumed nightly resting place of the saint's head is fenced off and outlined in beaten silver.

This is merely a foretaste of the monastery of **Ayíou Ioánnou Theológou** (same hours and admission as Apokálypsis). In 1088, the soldier-cleric Ioannis "The Blessed" Khristodhoulos was granted title to Pátmos by Byzantine emperor Alexios Komnenos; within three years he and his followers had completed the essentials of the existing monastery, the threats of piracy and the Selçuk Turks dictating a heavily fortified style. A warren of interconnecting courtyards, chapels, stairways, arcades, galleries and roof terraces, it offers a rare glimpse of a Patmian interior; hidden in the walls are fragments of an ancient Artemis temple which stood here before being destroyed by Khristodhoulos. Off to one side, the **treasury** (same hours; €6) doesn't quite justify its hefty entrance fee with its admittedly magnificent array of religious treasure, mostly medieval icons of the Cretan school. Pride of place goes to an unusual mosaic icon of Áyios Nikólaos, and the eleventh-century parchment chrysobull (edict) of Emperor Alexios Komnenos, granting the island to Khristodhoulos. Coach-tour patrons can crowd out the place at midday, so wisely go early or late. The best time to show up, besides the famous Easter observances, is September 25–26 (Feast of John the Theologian) and October 20–21 (Feast of Khristodhoulos), both marked by solemn liturgies and processions of the appropriate icon.

Hóra

The promise of security afforded by St John's stout walls spurred the growth of **HÓRA** immediately outside the fortifications. It remains architecturally homogeneous, with cobbled lanes sheltering dozens of shipowners' mansions from the island's seventeenth-to-eighteenth-century heyday. High, windowless walls and imposing wooden doors betray nothing of the opulence within: painted ceilings, *votsaló* terraces, flagstone kitchens and carved furniture. Inevitably, touristic tattiness disfigures the main approaches to the monastery gate, but away from the principal thoroughfares are lanes that rarely see traffic, and by night, when the monastery ramparts are floodlit to startling effect, it's hard to think of a more beautiful Dodecanesian village. Neither should you miss the **view** from Platía Lótza (named after the remnant of an adjacent Venetian *loggia*), particularly at dawn or dusk. Landmasses to the north, going clockwise, include Ikaría, Thýmena, Foúrni, Sámos with its brooding mass of Mount Kérkis, Arkí and the double-humped Samsun Dağ (ancient Mount Mykale) in Turkey.

Hóra has several tavernas, but none are really estimable; you'll get better value at *Lotza*, just below the eponymous platía, with light meals, crêpes and desserts as well as creditable hot and alcoholic drinks. There are, however, very few places to **stay**; foreigners here are mostly long-term occupants, who have bought up and restored almost half of the crumbling mansions since the 1960s. Finding a short-term room can be a pretty thankless task, even in spring or autumn; phone well ahead for reservations at the *dhomátia* of Yeoryia Triandafyllou (T22470 31963;❸) on the south flank of the village, en suite with a communal terrace and self-catering kitchen, or for more comfort the *Epavli Apartments* at the east edge of Hóra, on the ring road (T 22470 31261, Wwww.12net.gr/epavli❸), a restored building with superb views, high-standard bathrooms and raised bed-platforms.

The rest of the island

Pátmos, as a locally published guide once memorably proclaimed, "is immense for those who know how to wander in space and time"; lesser mortals get around on foot or by bus, if not a scooter. Unfortunately, most paths have been destroyed by road-building and property development; the single **bus** offers surprisingly reliable service between Skála, Hóra, Kámbos and Gríkou.

After its extraordinary atmosphere and striking volcanic scenery, **beaches** are Patmos's principal attraction. From Konsoláto, a principal road heads east to the average beach at **Sápsila**, home not only to aforementioned *Benetos* but also to ⚚ *Studios Mathios* (T22470 32119, Wwww.mathiosapartment.gr;❹), superior rural **accommodation** with creative furnishing and décor, extensive gardens and a lovely managing family. The continuation of this road, and another from Hóra, converge at the sandiest part of rather overdeveloped and cheerless **GRÍKOU**, the main venue for Patmian package tourism – and shut tight as a drum come mid-September. The beach itself, far from the island's best, forms a narrow strip of hard-packed sand, giving way to sand and gravel, then large pebbles at **Pétra** immediately south, whose far end is colonized by nudists – and whose near side features much the best rural **taverna** on Pátmos, ⚚ *Ktima Petra* (Easter to early Oct), where owner Mihalis is likely to personally serve your brown bread, lush salads, good bulk retsina, carefully cooked *mayireftá*, plus grills after dark. Still later, it becomes a bar with a full cocktails list.

En route to Pétra, named for its peculiar volcanic monolith on the shore, you pass hillside *Flisvos* (aka *Floros*), now rather eclipsed by nearby *Ktima Petra* but going since the 1960s with a limited choice of inexpensive, savoury *mayireftá*, served on the terrace. They also have basic **rooms** (❷) and fancier apartments (❹) – reserve on ☎22470 31380, 🖷22470 32094.

From Hóra – but *not* Pétra – you can ride a scooter over as far as the car-park beyond the Dhiakoftí isthmus, beyond which a 20- to 25-minute walk south-west on the island's last surviving bona fide path leads to **Psilí Ámmos** beach. This is the only pure-sand cove on the island, with shade lent by tamarisks, nudism at the far south end and a good lunchtime **taverna** that occasionally does roast goat, freshly culled from the surrounding hills. The summer *kaïki* service to here from Skála departs by 10am and returns at 4 or 5pm.

Northern Pátmos

More good beaches are to be found in the **north of the island**, tucked into the startling eastern shoreline (west-facing bays are uniformly unusable owing to the prevailing wind and washed-up debris); most are accessible from side roads off the main route north from Skála. **Melóï** is handy and quite appealing, with tamarisks behind the slender belt of sand, and good snorkelling offshore. The first beach beyond Melóï, **Agriolívadho (Agriolivádhi)**, has mostly sand at its broad centre, kayak rental, and two tavernas, the better being fish specialist *O Glaros* on the south hillside. Hilltop Kámbos is the only other real village on Pátmos, the focus of scattered farms in little oases all around; **Kámbos** beach, 600m downhill, is popular with Greeks, and the most developed remote resort on the island, with seasonal, non-motorized watersports facilities and a durable taverna (*Ta Kavourakia*), though its appeal is diminished by the road just inland.

East of Kámbos are several less-frequented coves, including pebbly **Vayiá**, nudist, double-bay **Liyínou** and long, sand-and-gravel **Livádhi Yeranoú**, the latter with more tamarisks, an islet to swim out to and a very good eponymous **taverna** with something of a cult following, doing simple seafood dishes, chops, *keftédhes*, *hórta* and salads. From lower Kámbos you can also journey north to the bay of **Lámbi**, best for swimming when the prevailing wind is from the south, and renowned for an abundance of multicoloured volcanic stones – as well as another excellent **taverna**, 🍴 *Leonidas* (May to early Oct), up at Koumariá pass overlooking the bay, with terrace seating and massive portions of expertly grilled chops, and maybe a dessert on the house.

Lipsí

Of the various islets to the north and east of Pátmos, **LIPSÍ** is the largest, most interesting, most populated and the one that has the most significant summer tourist trade. The presence of a British package company (Laskarina), on-spec Italian and French travellers, and the island's appearance on minor ferry routes and catamaran/hydrofoil lines means that it's unwise to show up in peak season without a reservation (though rooms proprietors meet arrivals at other times).

During quieter months, however, Lipsí still provides an idyllic halt, its sleepy pace making plausible a purported link between the island's name and that of **Calypso**, the nymph who legendarily held Odysseus in thrall. Deep wells provide water for many small farms, but there is only one flowing spring, and pastoral appearances are deceptive – four times the full-time population of about six hundred live overseas (many in Hobart, Tasmania). Most of those who remain cluster around the fine harbour, as does the majority of food and lodging.

Of late, however, Lipsí has acquired a definite – and unwanted – link with **Dhekaeftá Noemvríou/17 November**, Greece's (and Europe's) longest-lived terrorist organization (see p.1104). In July 2002, the national anti-terrorist squad swooped on the island and apprehended the group's supremo, Alexandhros Yiotopoulos (alias Mihalis Ikonomou), in the act of leaving for Sámos, eventual destination exile in Turkey. He had been living quietly here for 17 years in a faded-pink hilltop villa, now abandoned and shuttered (save for occasional visits from his wife) following his December 2003 conviction on all charges and life sentencing; ironically Yiotopoulos was much liked by the islanders for his generosity, sociability and willingness to help with bureaucratic problems.

The port settlement

All **arriving** craft use the same dock at the far west end of the port settlement, the only significant habitation on Lipsí. Among **travel agents**, Laid Back (T22470 41141) sells tickets for Aegean Hydrofoils, both catamarans and *Nissos Kalymnos*, while Rena's Boats (T22470 4110) by the port police reps for Samos Hydrofoils, changes money (though there's a free-standing **ATM** nearby) and organizes popular cruises to nearby islets. The **post office** is up a stairway on the attractive cathedral platía, opposite a hilariously eclectic **ecclesiastical museum** (9am–2.30pm daily; free) featuring such "relics" as earth collected from Mount Tabor and water from the Jordan River, as well as archeological finds, medieval glazed ware and two faded letters of 1824 from Greek revolutionary hero Admiral Miaoulis.

Accommodation

A prime **accommodation** choice in all senses is Nikos' and Anna's welcoming *Apartments Galini* (T22470 41212, F22470 41012; ❸), the first building you see above the ferry jetty; Nikos may take guests for fishing trips on request. Equally sought after, though less airy, are *Studios Kalymnos* (T22470 41141, Wwww.lipsiweb.gr; ❸) in a garden on the road north out of town and run by Laid Back Holidays. Other good options not monopolized by package clients include *Rena's Rooms* (T22470 41110 or 697 9316512; ❸), overlooking Liendoú beach – ask for room nos. 3 or 4 – and the *Glaros* (T22470 41360; ❷) on the north hillside, with terrazzo-floored 1980s rooms sharing cooking facilities. Top of the heap is the *Aphrodite Hotel* (T22470 41000; ❹), a studio-bungalow complex designed to accommodate package clients, though they're not averse to walk-ins at slow times.

Eating and drinking

Among nine full-service **tavernas**, mostly on or just behind the quay, the best are indisputably *O Yiannis* (early May to early Oct), an excellent all-rounder with meat/seafood grills and *mayireftá* – the only one open at lunch out of peak season – and *Tò Pefko* nearby, with creative oven dishes and *mezédhes*, plus service that copes well with the typical crowds. On the waterfront to either side of the *Kalypso*, *kafenía* and **ouzerís** with idiosyncratic decor (especially *Asprakis*) offer drinks and *mezédhes* outdoors at twilight – an atmospheric and almost obligatory pre-supper ritual – or even a full meal; rivals *Nikos* and *Sofoklis* operate all year. Later on, *The Rock* is the clear winner amongst a handful of **bars** for a congenial crowd and good taped music; after sunrise, *To Limani* (*Stratos*) is the place for breakfast and coffees.

Around the island

The island's **beaches** are scattered, though none is more than an hour's walk distant. Closest to town, and sandiest, are **Liendoú** and **Kámbos**, but many visitors prefer the attractive duo of **Katsadhiá** and **Papandhriá**, adjacent sand-and-pebble coves 2km south of the port by paved road, with a musical taverna-café, ♣ *Dilaila* (June–Sept), which overlooks the left-most bay here and serves such delights as rosemary fish, saffron rice, *fáva* and salad with balsamic dressing. You can **stay** locally at Scottish-run, hillside *Katsadia Studios* (℡22470 41317 or 697 87 09 558; ❸), well designed and with sweeping views.

Another paved road leads 4km west from town to protected **Platýs Yialós**, a small, very shallow, sandy bay with a single taverna (mid-June to late Sept). During this period a pair of white transit vans provides a **minibus** service from the port to all the points cited above (there's also a single **taxi**); otherwise rent a **scooter** from one of two outlets and point them towards isolated east-coast beaches without facilities. Of these, **Hokhlakoúra** consists of rather coarse shingle (finer pebbles at mid-strand); nearby **Turkómnima** is much sandier and shadier, if windy, while **Xirókambos** is calmer if treeless. A final ten-minute path scramble gets you from a rough track's end to **Monodhéndhri**, on the northeast coast, notable only for its lone juniper tree and nudist practice – though there's a superior, nameless cove just to the right.

The road network, paved or otherwise, rather limits opportunities for genuine path **walks** through the undulating countryside, dotted with blue-domed churches. The most challenging route heads west, high above the coast, from the far end of Kámbos bay to the bay of **Kímisi** (3hr round-trip), where the religious **hermit Filippos**, long a cult figure amongst foreign visitors, used to dwell in a tiny monastery above the shore, next to the single island spring. A particularly steep, ugly road was bulldozed in from the north in 1999 and later paved, disturbing his solitude; Filippos moved to town and died, aged 85, in 2002, though a small memorial at the entry to the monastery grounds commemorates him.

Arkí and Maráthi

About two-thirds the size of Lipsí, **Arkí** is considerably more primitive, lacking properly stocked shops or much in the way of a distinct village. Just 45 permanent inhabitants eke out a living here, mostly engaged in fishing or goat/sheep-herding, though catering for yacht parties attracted here by the superb anchorage is increasingly important. Arkí is a frequent stop on the *Nissos Kalymnos*, which you can use to make cheap day-trips from Pátmos; post *kaïkia* (4 weekly) or excursion boats sail right into the main harbour to dock at the inner quay. Of the three **tavernas** on the round harbourside platía, the more frequented two – *Nikolas* (℡22470 32477; B&B; ❸) and *O Trypas* (aka *Tou Manoli*; ℡22470 32230; ❷) – provide **accommodation**; those of *O Trypas* – with fridges and some with stone floors – are perhaps better value. *Nikolas* has home-made puddings, while *O Trypas* doubles as the happening music pub, courtesy of the owner's enormous collection of CDs and tapes – and does very decent fish meals. But perhaps the most accomplished fish grills are to be had at ♣ *Apolavsi*, one inlet southeast at **Dhídhymi Ormí**; yachties (and land-lubbers) in the know come here for the indomitable Angeliki's garden vegetables, slow-cooked fish, octopus and other *mezédhes* at attractive prices.

You can swim at the "Blue Lagoon" of **Tiganákia** at the southeast tip of the island, but other beaches on Arkí take some resourcefulness to find. The more obvious ones are the succession of covelets at **Pateliá** by the ferry jetty, or tiny **Limnári** bay on the northeast coast which fits four or five bathers at a pinch, a 25-minute walk away via the highest house in the settlement.

The nearest large, sandy, tamarisk-shaded beach is just offshore on the islet of **Maráthi**, where more **tavernas** caters to day-trippers who come several times a week from Pátmos or Lipsí. *Marathi* (☎22470 31580; all year; ❷) is the more traditional, cosy outfit, with waterside seating and simple, adequate rooms; *Pantelis* (☎22470 32609; June–Oct; ❷) is plusher but more commercially minded – and apt to lock the compound's outer gate at 11pm if you go drinking at his rival's bar. In summer 2005, a third taverna between the two began operations.

Agathoníssi

The small, steep-sided, waterless islet of **Agathoníssi (Gaïdharo)** is too remote – much closer to Turkey than Pátmos, in fact – to be a popular target of day-excursions, though a few are half-heartedly offered on Sámos. Intrepid Greeks and Italians form its main clientele, along with a steady trickle of yachts. Even though the *Nissos Kalymnos* (and two weekly hydrofoils) appear regularly, you should count on staying for at least two days, especially if the wind's up. Despite the lack of springs (cisterns are ubiquitous, topped up by tanker shipments from Rhodes), the island is greener and more fertile than apparent from the sea; mastic, carob and scrub oak on the heights overlook two arable plains in the west. Just 146 people live here, down from several hundred before World War II, but those who've opted to stay seem determined to make a go of raising goats or fishing (more accurately fish-farming), and there are almost no abandoned or neglected dwellings.

Most of the population lives in the hamlet of **Megálo Horió**, just visible on the ridge above the harbour of **ÁYIOS YEÓRYIOS**, and eye-level with tiny **Mikró Horió**. Except for two fitfully working café-restaurants in Megálo Horió, all amenities are in the port. Among five **accommodation** choices there, most preferable are *Rooms Theoloyia Yiameou* (☎22470 29005; ❷), the vine-patioed *Hotel Maria Kamitsi* (☎22470 29003; ❷), or the *Aganandi* above the *Limanaki* taverna (☎22470 29019; ❷). Eating out, you'll almost certainly try all three full-service **tavernas**: *George's* for fish, *Seagull/Glaros* for meat dishes, *Limanaki* as the cheap-and-cheerful Greeks' hangout. There is no post office, bank or ATM; ferry and hydrofoil tickets must be bought in advance at a little booth opposite the *Café-Bar Yetoussa*, the best **bar** and also a good source of breakfast.

With no wheeled transport for rent, exploring involves **walking** along the cement- or dirt-road network, or following a limited number of tracks and paths. If you don't swim at the port, which has the largest beach, you walk ten minutes southwest along a track to shingle-gravel **Spiliás**, or continue another quarter-hour along a faint path over the ridge to **Gaïdhourávlakos**, where nudists enjoy a finer gravel cove. Bays in the east of the island, all served by the paved road system (occasionally supplemented by trails), include **Thóli** in the far southeast, with good snorkelling and some morning shade, and **Pálli** on the opposite shore of the same bay, a small but pristine fine-pebble cove reached by fifteen-minute walk down from the trans-island road. Also at **Thóli**, an hour-plus trek away, you can see an arcaded Byzantine structure, probably a combination granary and trading post, and by far the most venerable sight on Agathoníssi.

Travel details

To simplify the lists below, some companies are summarized here. Agoudimos provides a once-weekly link between Rhodes, Kós, Kálymnos, Sámos and Thessaloníki in each direction, while LANE also plies once weekly (north, then south) between Rhodes, Kós, Kálymnos, Sámos, Híos, Lésvos, Límnos and Alexandhroúpoli.

Nissos Kalymnos

The small, slow but reliable **Nissos Kalymnos** (cars carried) is the most regular lifeline of the smaller islands between Kálymnos and Sámos – it visits them all several times weekly between mid-March and mid-January. Its movements are as follows:
Mon, Wed, Fri & Sun Leaves Kálymnos 7am for Léros (Lakkí), Lipsí, Pátmos, Arkí, Agathoníssi, Sámos (Pythagório; arrives 2.30pm). Turns around more or less immediately and retraces steps through the same islands (in reverse order), arriving Kálymnos 10.30pm.
Tues, Thur & Sat Leaves Kálymnos 7am, arrives Astypálea 10am, turns around almost immediately to arrive Kálymnos at 1.30pm.

Large ferries and local services

The following frequencies are only valid for the period mid-June to mid-September.
Astypálea 2 weekly to Kálymnos, Amorgós, Náxos, Dhonoússa, Páros, Kós, Rhodes and Pireás on GA; 1–2 weekly to Kálymnos, Páros and Náxos on Blue Star; 1 weekly to Níssyros, Tílos and Sými on GA.
Hálki 3 weekly to Ródhos Town, Kárpathos (both ports), Kássos, Crete (Sitía & Áyios Nikólaos), Santoríni and Mílos on LANE. Once-daily *kaïki* (6am) to Rhodes (Kámiros Skála).
Kálymnos Similar ferry service to Kós, except no Blue Star service to Rhodes, Pátmos or Léros, plus 3 daily roll-on-roll-off ferries, well-spaced, to Masti-hári; 5 passenger-only speed-boats daily to Masti-hári; daily morning *kaïki* to Psérimos; and a daily *kaïki* (1pm) from Myrtiés to Xirókambos on Léros.
Kárpathos (both ports) and **Kássos** 3 weekly with each other, Hálki, Crete (Áyios Nikólaos & Sitía), Mílos, Santoríni and Ródhos Town, on LANE.
Kastellórizo (Méyisti) 1–2 weekly to Rhodes, then Pireás indirectly, on LANE.
Kós at least daily to Rhodes and Pireás on GA or Blue Star; 6 weekly to Léros and Pátmos on GA or Blue Star; 2 weekly to Tílos, Níssyros, Astypálea and Sými on GA; 3 weekly to Amorgós on Blue Star or GA; 1–2 weekly to Mýkonos and Sýros on Blue star or GA; 1 weekly to Náxos and Páros on GA; 5 weekly (Mon–Fri) *kaïkia* to Níssyros; daily islanders' *kaïkia* from Kardhámena to Níssyros.

Léros 6 weekly to Pireás, Pátmos, Kós and Rhodes on GA or Blue Star; 4 weekly to Kálymnos on GA or Blue Star; 2 weekly to Sýros on Blue Star or GA; 1 weekly to Mýkonos, Tílos and Níssyros on GA; seasonal daily excursion boats from Ayía Marína to Lipsí and Léros (2pm), and from Xirókambos to Myrtiés on Kálymnos (7.30am).
Níssyros and Tílos 1–2 weekly with each other, Sými, Rhodes, Kós, Kálymnos, Astypálea, Amorgós, Náxos, Páros and Pireás on GA. Excursion boats between Níssyros and Kós as follows: to Kard-hámena and Kós Town nearly daily at 3.30–4pm (these are seasonal). The islanders' less expensive "shopping" *kaïkia* the *Panayia Spiliani* leaves Mon–Fri at 7.15am for Kós Town, while the *Ayios Konstandinos* and/or Nisyros goes daily at 7am to Kardhámena. Unless you're bound for the airport it's not cheaper to use Kardhámena services when you consider the cost of a bus to Kós Town.
Pátmos Similar ferry service to Léros, with the addition of tourist *kaïkia* to Sámos (Pythagório), Lipsí and Léros on a daily basis; to Arkí and Maráthi 4 weekly.
Rhodes at least daily to Kós and Pireás on GA or Blue Star; 6 weekly to Léros and Pátmos on GA or Blue Star; 4 weekly to Kálymnos on GA; 3 weekly to Hálki, Kárpathos, Kássos, Crete (Sitía & Áyios Nikólaos), Santoríni and Mílos on LANE; 2–3 weekly to Amorgós on GA or Blue Star; 2 weekly to Astypálea on GA; 2 weekly to Sýros on Blue Star; 1 weekly to Mýkonos on Blue Star; 1–2 weekly to Sými, Tílos, Níssyros on GA; 1 weekly to Náxos, Dhonoússa and Páros on GA.
Sými 1 weekly to Rhodes, Tílos, Níssyros, Kós, Kálymnos, Léros, Pátmos, Astypálea, Amorgós, Náxos, Páros and Pireás on GA; 2–3 daily catamarans or hydrofoil run by ANES to Rhodes.

Catamarans

Three high-speed, long-distance **catamarans** ply the Dodecanese: The *Dodekanisos Express*, the co-owned *Dodekanisos Pride* and the *Sea Star*.

Dodekanisos Express

The *Dodekanisos Express*, based on Rhodes, can carry 4–5 cars and a slightly larger number of two-wheelers; it's a sleek, 2000-built, Norwegian craft, with a limited amount of aft deck space.

High-season schedules are as follows: Tues–Sun, 8.30am departure from Rhodes to Kós, Kálymnos, Léros, Lipsí and Pátmos; it returns from Pátmos at 1.30–1.45pm, arriving at Rhodes 6.30pm. On Sun & Wed it makes a stop at Sými, in each direction; on Mon it makes a single journey to Kastellórizo, arriving 11am, returning at 4pm. In spring or autumn there is no Kastellórizo service, and services to Lipsí may be infrequent.

Dodekanisos Pride

The *Express's* 2005-built sister ship, *Dodekanisos Pride*, is based on Pátmos but nearly identical in all other respects. Schedule patterns are as follows: departure from Pátmos daily at 6am, arriving at Rhodes via Lipsí, Léros, Kálymnos, Kós and Sými (Panormítis, not Yialós, on Sun), at 10.40am, leaving for Pámos via the same islands at 3.30pm.

Sea Star

The *Sea Star* does not carry vehicles and badly serves only the route Rhodes–Tílos, with occasional extensions to Níssyros or Hálki; it frequently breaks down and may in fact not see the 2006 season through. Schedules are so user-hostile that it's impossible to generalize or predict meaningfully, other than saying it serves Níssyros at best twice weekly (usually Mon and/or Wed), Hálki at weekends, and spends frequent, 24-hour spells idle on Rhodes for maintenance and/or the maximum convenience of the crew.

Hydrofoils

Two **hydrofoil** companies, Aegean Flying Dolphins and Samos Hydrofoils, serve the Dodecanese between mid-May and mid-Oct, operating out of Rhodes, Kálymnos, Kós and Sámos.

Aegean has three remaining active craft; schedules are complicated but fairly predictable. In peak season, there is a daily link from Kós to Rhodes and back, south in the morning and north in the evening; twice a week stops will be made at intervening islands (Sými, Níssyros, Tílos). Another craft leaves Kálymnos at 7.20am for Kós, Kálymnos, Léros, Lipsí, Pátmos and Pythagório on Sámos, returning via the same islands at 1.20pm; while the third craft, based in Pythagório, leaves Kós between 2.15 and 2.45pm, returning to Sámos via Kálymnos, Léros, Lipsí and Pátmos. Twice a week this craft calls at Agathoníssi in each direction as well. For current routes and schedules, phone ☏ 22420 25551 (Kós), ☏ 22410 21690 (Rhodes) or ☏ 22730 25065 (Sámos).

Samos Hydrofoils has just one active craft, which provides an 8am service out of Pythagório as far as Kós and all intervening Dodecanese 3 days weekly,

but goes no further than Lipsí or Léros most other days, owing to extensive detours to Foúrni and Ikaría.

International ferries

NB: In all cases below, the cost of Turkish visas, required by many nationals, is not included.

Kálymnos to Bodrum, Turkey (1hr 45min), departing at 7–8am; €30 day-return, though €20 "specials" 2 days weekly.

Kós 2–14 weekly to Bodrum, Turkey (45min). Greek boat leaves 9am &10am, returns 4pm & 5pm; additional out-and-back 11am/6pm on Tues & Sat, Bodrum market days; €25 return, Greek tax inclusive, no Turkish port tax. Slightly pricier Turkish boat (*Fahri Kaptan*) or hydrofoil departs Bodrum 9am or so, leaves Kós 4.30pm; this provides the only service in winter.

Kastellórizo 2 weekly (Mon & Fri) to Kaş, Turkey; €15 one way or day return; €32 maximum (bargain with boatman if necessary) if you begin travel from the Turkish side.

Rhodes Daily May–Nov to Marmaris, Turkey (1hr) by Greek catamaran at 8–9am, Turkish catamaran at 4pm; €49 day return, €35 plus €19 Greek tax plus €14 Turkish tax open return, €25 plus €19 Greek tax one way. Anka Travel at Gallías 13 in Neohóri (☏ 22410 26835) is the central agent for the Turkish craft, though most agencies (such as Triton Travel) will readily sell you passage. Also, one daily Turkish hydrofoil to Fethiye in late afternoon; June–Sept; €45 one way.

Sými Up to 3 weekly *kaïkia* (80min, €40 return plus $12 Turkish tax) and 1 hydrofoil or catamaran (40min, €30 return plus Turkish tax); Sat is the most reliable day.

Flights

NB: All are on Olympic Aviation/Olympic Airways unless stated otherwise.

Astypálea 4 weekly to Athens; 3 weekly to Léros, Kós and Rhodes on the same plane.

Kárpathos At least 2 daily to Rhodes; 9 weekly to Kássos; 5 weekly to Athens.

Kássos 9 weekly to Kárpathos and Rhodes.

Kastellórizo (Meyísti) 5 weekly to Rhodes.

Kós 3–4 daily to Athens on Olympic, 3 daily on Aegean; 3 weekly to Astypálea, Léros and Rhodes.

Léros 1 daily to Athens; 3 weekly to Astypálea, Kós and Rhodes.

Rhodes Olympic: 4–5 daily to Athens; at least daily to Iráklion; 3 weekly to Kós, Léros and Astypálea with the same plane; 2 weekly to Sámos and Híos; 5 weekly to Lésvos and Límnos; 8–9 weekly to Thessaloníki. Aegean: 6 daily to Athens; 1 daily to Thessaloníki.

The East and North Aegean

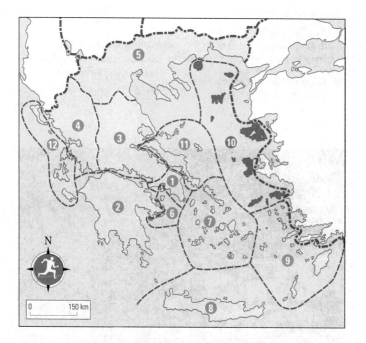

CHAPTER 10

Highlights

* **Vathý, Sámos** The two-wing archeological museum is among the best in the islands. See p.887

* **Ikaría** Western Ikaría has superb beaches and an idio-syncratic lifestyle. See p.900

* **Southern Híos** The architec-turally unique *mastihohoriá* (mastic villages) have a Middle Eastern feel. See p.911

* **Sykiás Olýmbon cave, Híos** Superb formations make this multilevelled cave one of the finest in the islands. See p.913

* **Thermal baths, Lésvos** There are four well-kept Ottoman-era spas, ideal for relaxing in. See p.925, p.928, p.935

* **Mólyvos, northern Lésvos** This castle-crowned resort village is arguably the most beautiful on the island. See p.932

* **Mýrina, Límnos** A characterful port town with a fine castle – and great wines to sample. See p.938

* **Samothráki** Remote Samoth-ráki's Sanctuary of the Great Gods is surrounded by natural grandeur. See p.946

* **Alykí, Thássos** A beautifully situated beach flanked by ancient and Byzantine archeological sites. See p.955

△ Mýrina harbour, Límnos

10

The East and North Aegean

T he seven substantial islands and four minor islets scattered between the Aegean coast of Asia Minor and northeastern Greece form a rather arbitrary archipelago. Although there are some similarities in architecture and landscape, the strong individual character of each island is far more striking. Despite their proximity to modern Turkey, members of the group bear relatively few signs of an Ottoman heritage, especially when compared with Rhodes and Kós. There's the occasional mosque, often shorn of its minaret, but by and large the enduring Greekness of these islands is testimony to the four-millennium-long Hellenic presence in Asia Minor, which ended only in 1923. This heritage has been regularly referred to by the Greek government in an intermittent propaganda war with Turkey over the sovereignty of these far-flung outposts. Tensions here have often been worse than in the Dodecanese, aggravated by potential undersea oil deposits in the straits between the islands and the Anatolian mainland. The Turks have also persistently demanded that Límnos, astride the sea lanes to and from the Dardanelles, be demilitarized, and only since the start of the new millennium has Greece shown signs of complying.

Despite the growth of tourism, large tracts of land remain off-limits as army or air force bases. But as in the Dodecanese, local tour operators do a thriving business shuttling passengers for inflated tariffs between the easternmost islands and the Turkish coast with its amazing archeological sites and busy resorts. Most of these islands' main ports and towns are not quaint, picturesque spots, but urbanized administrative, military and commercial centres; you should suppress any initial impulse to take the next boat out, and press on into the interiors. Bear in mind that the tourist season this far north is short – early July to early September – with many restaurants and lodgings shut down outside this period.

Sámos ranks as the most visited island of the group but, once you leave the crowded resorts behind, is still arguably the most verdant and beautiful, even after a devastating July 2000 fire. **Ikaría** to the west remains relatively unspoilt, if a minority choice, and nearby **Foúrni** is (except in summer) a haven for determined solitaries, as are the Híos satellites **Psará** and **Inoússes**, neither of which has any package tourism. **Híos** proper offers far more cultural interest than any neighbours to the south, but the development of tourism was, until the late 1980s, deliberately retarded. **Lésvos** may not impress initially, though once you get a feel for its old-fashioned Anatolian ambience you may find it hard to leave.

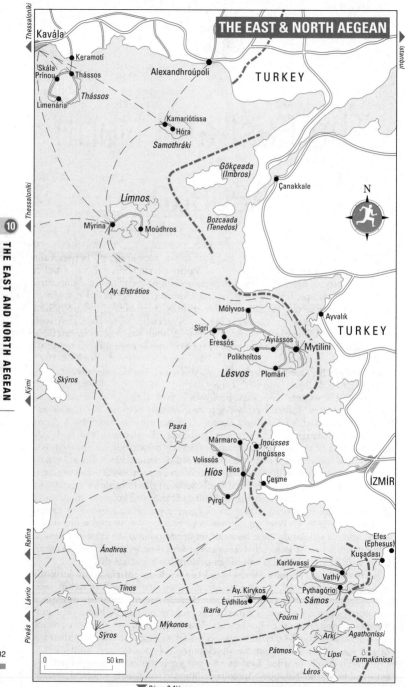

N

Kavála

Keramotí

Skála
Prínou

Thássos

Limenária

Thássos

Alexandhroúpoli

TURKEY

Istanbul

Thessaloníki

Kamariótissa

Hóra

Samothráki

*Gökçeada
(Imbros)*

Çanakkale

Thessaloníki

Límnos

Mýrina

Moúdhros

*Bozcaada
(Tenedos)*

Ay. Efstrátios

Kými

Skýros

Mólyvos

Sígri

Eressós

Ayiássos

Polikhnítos

Lésvos

Plomári

Mytilíni

Ayvalık

TURKEY

Psará

Mármaro

Volissós

Híos

Inoússes

Inoússes

Híos

Çeşme

Pyrgí

İZMİR

Rafína

Ándhros

Karlóvassi

Efes
(Ephesus)

Kuşadası

Vathý

Lávrio

Tínos

Áy. Kírykos

Évdhilos

Ikaría

Pythagório

Sámos

Foúrni

Arkí

Agathoníssi

Pireás

Mýkonos

Sýros

Pátmos

Lipsí

Farmakónissi

Léros

0   50 km

Páros & Náxos

By contrast, virtually no foreigners and few Greeks visit **Áyios Efstrátios**, and with good reason. **Límnos** to the north is much livelier, but its appeal is confined mostly to the area immediately around the attractive port town. To the north, Samothráki and Thássos are relatively isolated from the others (though the former now has ferry links with Límnos, Lésvos and Híos), and remain easier to visit from northern Greece, which administers them. **Samothráki** (officially in Thrace) has one of the most dramatic seaward approaches of any Greek island, and one of the more important ancient sites. **Thássos** (technically belonging to eastern Macedonia) is more varied, with sandy beaches, mountain villages and minor archeological sites.

Sámos

The lush and seductive island of Sámos was formerly joined to Asia Minor, until sundered from Mount Mykale opposite by Ice Age cataclysms; the resulting 2500-metre strait is now the narrowest distance between Greece and Turkey in the Aegean, except at Kastellórizo. There's little tangible evidence of it today, but Sámos was also once the **wealthiest island** in the Aegean and, under the patronage of the tyrant Polykrates, home to a thriving intellectual community: Epicurus, Pythagoras, Aristarkhos and Aesop were among the residents. Decline set in as the star of Classical Athens was in the ascendant, though Sámos's status improved in early Byzantine times when it constituted its own imperial administrative district. Towards the end of the fifteenth century, the Genoese abandoned the island to the mercies of pirates; following their attacks, Sámos remained **almost uninhabited** until 1562, when an Ottoman admiral received permission from the sultan to repopulate it with Greek Orthodox settlers recruited from various corners of the empire.

The heterogeneous descent of today's islanders largely explains an enduring identity crisis and a rather thin topsoil of indigenous culture. Most of the village names are either clan surnames, or adjectives indicating origins elsewhere – constant reminders of **refugee descent**. Consequently there is no distinctly Samian music, dance or dress, and little that's original in the way of cuisine and architecture. The Samiotes compensated somewhat for this deracination by fighting fiercely for independence during the 1820s, but despite their accomplishments in sinking a Turkish fleet in the narrow strait and annihilating a landing army, the Great Powers handed the island back to the Ottomans in 1830, with the consoling proviso that it be **semi-autonomous**, ruled by an appointed Christian prince. This period, referred to as the *Iyimonía* (Hegemony), was marked by a mild renaissance in fortunes, courtesy of the hemp and (especially) tobacco trades. However, union with Greece in 1912, the ravages of a bitter World War II occupation and mass emigration effectively reversed the recovery until tourism appeared on the horizon during the 1980s.

Today the Samian economy is dependent on **package tourism**, far too much of it in places; Kokkári, and the southeastern and southwestern coasts, have pretty much been surrendered to holiday-makers, although the more rugged northwestern part has retained some of its undeveloped grandeur. The sedate, couples-orientated clientele is overwhelmingly Scandinavian, Dutch, German and Swiss, with a growing number of Brits, Belgians and even Czechs or Slovenians; the absence of an official campsite on such a large island, tame nightlife a world away from that in the Dodecanese and Cyclades, and phalanxes of self-catering villas hint at the forty-something custom expected.

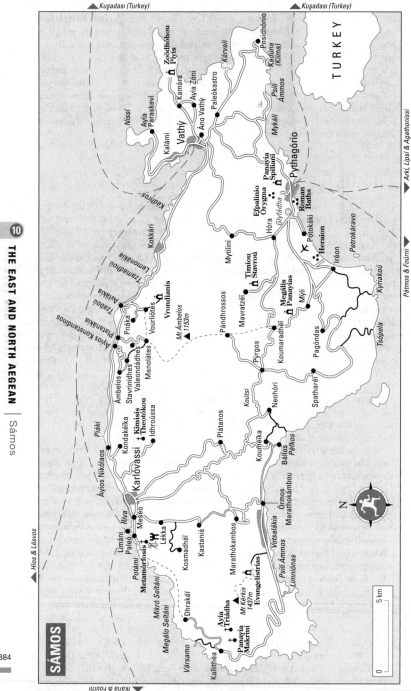

SÁMOS

▲ *Kuşadası (Turkey)*   ▲ *Kuşadası (Turkey)*

T U R K E Y

Zoödhóhou Píyis
Kamára
Ayía Zóni
Vathý
Áno Vathý
Paleókastro
Kérveli
Kadína (Klíma)
Posidhónio

Nissí
Ayía Paraskeví
Kalámi

Panayía Spilianí
Pythagório
Epáno Órygma
Mykáli
Psilí Ámmos

Kédhros

Héra
Glyfádha
Roman Baths
Potokáki
Heraíon
Iréon

Mytilíni

► *Arkí, Lípsi & Agathoníssi*

Tsamadoú
Avlákia
Kokkári
Lemonákia

Vrondianís
Mt Ámbelos ▲ *1153m*

Timíou Stavroú
Mavratzéï
Megális Panayías
Mýli
Pandhróssos

Áyios Konstandínos
Tzaboú
Platanákia
Vourliótes
Pnáka

► *Pátmos & Foúrni*

Kondakéïka
Kímisis Theotókou
Idhroússa
Ámbelos
Stavrinídhes
Valeondádhes
Manolátes

Kyriakoú

Pyrgos
Koumaradhéï
Pagóndas
Tsópela

Piáki

Áyios Nikólaos
Karlóvassi
Neohóri
Spatharéï

Plátanos
Koútsi

Riva
Meséo
Kosmadhéï
Lékka
Kastaniá
Koúmeïka
Báïlos
Pýrkos

Limáni
Paleó
Metamórfosis
Potámi

Marathókambos
Órmos Marathokámbou

► *Ikaría & Foúrni*

Mikró Seïtáni
Megálo Seïtáni

Dhrakéï
Ayía Triádha
Mt Kérkis ▲ *1437m*
Evangelístrias
Panayía Makrini
Psilí Ámmos
Votsalákia
Limniónas

Vársamo
Kallithéa

◄ *Hios & Lésvos*

N

5 km
0

894

△ Vine and olive terraces, Sámos

The heavily developed areas have unsurprisingly been the most afflicted by **repeated wildfires**, in particular one which lasted a week in July 2000, destroying twenty percent of the island's forest and orchards, and over ninety dwellings; if you take into account other areas that had been torched since 1987, Sámos is indeed about half-scorched. The trees as ever will be a half-century in returning, and the tourist market – admittedly for other reasons also – has not overcome this stigma. Volunteer fire-lookouts with pumper-trucks have now sprouted at critical points, but it does seem a case of locking the stable door after the horse has bolted.

Arrival and getting around

Sámos' 2003-enlarged **airport** (5 car rental booths, no ATM) lies 14km south-west of Vathý and 3km west of Pythagório. There is no airport bus service; **taxi** fares to various points are stipulated on prominent placards, and in high season taxis to the airport or ferry docks must be booked several hours in advance. There are no fewer than three **ferry ports**: Karlóvassi in the west, plus Vathý and Pythagório in the east, making the island a major hub for travel in every direction. All ferries between Pireás and Sámos call at both Karlóvassi and Vathý, as does the small, locally based Samos Spirit, linking the island with Foúrni and Ikaría. Vathý also receives the LANE and/or GA sailings between northern Greece and the Dodecanese, via most intervening islands, the weekly Agoudimos ferry between Thessaloníki and Rhodes, plus small boats from Kuşadasi. Pythagório sees four regular weekly ferry connections from as far south as Kálymnos in the Dodecanese, as well as hosting the **hydrofoil services** to all the Dodecanese down to Kós, and forays over to Foúrni and southern Ikaría.

The **bus terminals** in Pythagório and Vathý lie within walking distance of the ferry dock; at Karlóvassi, you must make your own way the 3km into town from the port. The weekday KTEL service itself is excellent along the Pythagório–Vathý and Vathý–Kokkári–Karlóvassi routes, but poor at weekends or for other destinations; with numerous car- and motorbike-rental outlets, it's easy to find a good deal all year round.

Vathý

Lining the steep northeastern shore of a deep bay, beachless **VATHÝ** (often confusingly referred to as "Sámos", like the island) is a busy provincial town which grew from a minor anchorage after 1830, when it replaced Hóra as the island's capital. It's an unlikely, somewhat ungraceful resort, which has seen numerous hotels gone bankrupt or converted to apartments since the late 1990s, and is minimally interesting aside from tiers of surviving Neoclassical houses and the hill suburb of **ÁNO VATHÝ**, a separate community of tottering, tile-roofed houses.

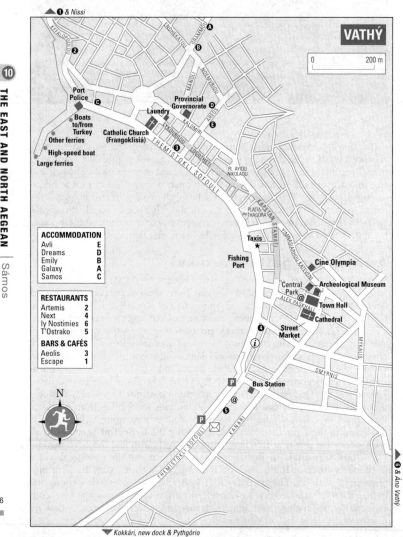

VATHÝ

0   200 m

0 & Nissi

Port
Police

Boats
to/from
Turkey
Other ferries

High-speed boat
Large ferries

Provincial
Governorate

Laundry

Catholic Church
(Frangoklisiá)

PL. AYIOU
NIKOLAOU

PLATIA
PYTHAGORA

Taxis

Fishing
Port

Cine Olympia

Central
Park

Archeological Museum

Town Hall

Cathedral

Street
Market

Bus Station

Kokkári, new dock & Pythgório

6 & Áno Vathý

ACCOMMODATION

Avli	E
Dreams	D
Emily	B
Galaxy	A
Samos	C

RESTAURANTS

Artemis	2
Next	4
Iy Nostimies	6
T'Ostrako	5

BARS & CAFÉS

Aeolis	3
Escape	1

N

The only real must is the excellent **archeological museum** (Tues–Sun 8.30am–3pm; €3), set behind the small central park beside the nineteenth-century town hall. One of the best provincial collections in Greece is housed in both the old Paskhallion building and a modern wing across the way, specially constructed to house the star exhibit: a majestic, five-metre-tall *kouros* discovered out at the Heraion sanctuary. The *kouros*, the largest free-standing effigy to survive from ancient Greece, was dedicated to Apollo, but found together with a devotional mirror to Mut (the Egyptian equivalent of Hera) from a Nile workshop, one of only two discovered in Greece to date.

In the compelling **small-objects collection** of the Paskhallion, more votive offerings of Egyptian design prove trade and pilgrimage links between Sámos and the Nile valley going back to the eighth century BC. The Mesopotamian and Anatolian origins of other artwork confirm the exotic trend, most tellingly in a case full of ivory miniatures: Perseus and Medusa in relief, a kneeling, perfectly formed mini-*kouros*, a pouncing lion and a drinking horn ending in a bull's head. The most famous local artefacts are the dozen-plus bronze griffin-heads, for which Sámos was the major centre of production in the seventh century BC; mounted on the edge of bronze cauldrons, they were believed to ward off evil spirits.

Arrival, information and transport

From the **ferry dock** the shore boulevard – Themistoklí Sofoúli – describes a 1300-metre arc around the bay. About 400m along is pedestrianized Platía Pythagóra, distinguished by its lion statue; about 800m along there's a major turning inland to the **KTEL** terminal, a chaos of buses at a perennially cluttered intersection by the ticket office. The minimally useful **tourist information** office is at 25-Martíou 4 (May–Oct Mon–Fri 9am–2pm; winter sporadic hours), only worth a stop for bus schedules and accommodation listings. If you've arrived with your own vehicle, use the free **parking lots** shown on the map – there's never any street parking to be had.

The most comprehensive waterfront **ferry/travel agent** for independent travellers is By Ship, with two branches – one at the base of the jetty (℡22730 80445), and one about 300m southeast (℡22730 25065) – selling tickets for most ferry lines, the hydrofoil and airlines. An exception is the Agoudimos ferry, represented solely by Nautica (℡22730 25133). Vathý is chock-a-block with **bike-** and **car-rental** franchises, with supply in excess of demand keeping rates reasonable. Among ten or so agenices, three to try are Aramis/Sixt (℡22730 22682) at Themistoklí Sofoúli 7, Reliable (phone as for By Ship), with branches island-wide, or Hertz (Rhenia Tours) at no. 17 (℡ 22730 24771). Other amenities include the **post office** inconveniently remote on Themistoklí Sofoúli, six waterfront **banks** with ATMs and a self-serve **laundry** on pedestrianized Lykoúrgou Logothéti. The most durable **Internet café** is Dhiavlos, on Themistoklí Sofoúli near the KTEL, though there's another in the café of the central gardens.

Accommodation

Most **accommodation** available to independent travellers is clustered in the hillside district of Katsoúni, more or less directly above the ferry dock; except in August, you'll have little trouble finding affordable vacancies. Budget choices include *Pension Dreams*, up a stair-lane at Áreos 9 (℡22730 24350; ❷), with well-kept en-suite rooms with fridges, or the superior ✱ *Pension Avli* (℡22730 22939; ❷), a wonderful period piece at Áreos 2, the former convent school of the French nuns who ran the local Catholic church until 1973; affable owner Spyros is an excellent source of information on local eating and drinking opportunities.

For more comfort, go for proper hotels such as the surprisingly affordable *Galaxy* (☎22730 22665; ❸), at Angéou 1 near the top of Katsoúni, set in garden surroundings and with a small pool, though avoid being sent to their lower-standard annexe opposite. If they're full, try the sympathetic *Emily*, just downhill at the top of Grámmou (☎22730 24691; open all year; ❹), a small outfit with a roof garden and plenty of parking out front. The *Samos Hotel* (☎22730 28377; ❹), right by the ferry dock but with double glazing against noise, also works all year, with a plunge-pool in the roof garden.

Eating, drinking and nightlife

The only **waterfront tavernas** worth a second glance, open all year, are *T'Ostrako* at Themistoklí Sofoúli 141, doing shellfish, a few scaly fish of the day and an ample selection of *orektiká*; *Next* at no. 97, reckoned the best of several local pizzerias; and *Artemis* near the dock at Kefalopoúlou 4, good for a pre-ferry lunch or a leisurely supper, though opt for *mezédhes* (especially their fáva) and grills rather than their oven dishes. Way up high in Áno Vathý, *Iy Nostimies* (aka *Tassos*; dinner all year, lunch too Oct–May) by the school and community office is well loved for its creative vegetarian dishes, seafood and the odd meat platter.

Vathý's more active **nightlife** revolves around its waterfront bars, the longest lived of these being the ground floor of the *Aeolis Hotel*, where the town's beau monde have their evening *mezédhes* and ouzo, or *Escape*, on a seaview terrace at Kefalopoúlou 9 (north of the jetty). Other, indoor clubs come and go every six months. Cine Olympia, inland on Yimnasiárhou Katevéni, is plushly fitted and operates all year with a variable programme of **films**.

Around Vathý

The immediate environs of Vathý offer some modest beaches and small hamlets, though you'll usually need your own transport to visit them. Two kilometres east and uphill spreads the vast inland plateau of **Vlamarí**, devoted to vineyards and supporting the hamlets of Ayía Zóni and Kamára (plus an increasing number of bad-taste modern villas); from Kamára you can climb up a partly cobbled path to the clifftop **monastery of Zoödhóhou Piyís** (daily except 2–5pm) for superb views across the end of the island to Turkey.

As you head southeast from Vathý along the main island loop road, the triple chapel at **Trís Ekklisíes** marks an important junction, with another fork 100m along the left-hand turning. Bearing left twice takes you through the hilltop village of Paleókastro, where the unassuming-looking *Leonidas* on the square does surprisingly competent snacks. Some 3km beyond is another junction; forking left yet again brings you after another 3km to the quiet, striking bay of **Kérveli**, with a small beach, a pair of **tavernas** by the water (the friendly *Sea and Dolphin* has good *mezédhes* and *soúma*, the local spirit, as well as mains) and another characterful favourite with simple grills only, *Iy Kryfí Folia*, about 500m uphill along the access road. Taking the right fork leads to **Posidhónio**, with an even smaller beach and another taverna, *Kerkezos*, which takes its cooking more seriously, though it's expensive. Bearing right at the junction before Paleókastro leads to the beaches of Mykáli and Psilí Ámmos. **Mykáli**, 1 km of windswept sand and gravel, has three package hotels; the best place to try on spec here is *Villa Barbara* (☎22730 25192; ④), which has apartments behind the *Sirenes Beach* hotel. **Psilí Ámmos**, further east around the headland, is a crowded, sandy cove backed by several tavernas, much the best of which are *Psili Ammos*, on the far right as you face the sea, with good seafood, salads and meat grills. If you swim to the islet, beware of strong currents which sweep through the narrow straits.

Pythagório and around

Most traffic south of Vathý heads for **PYTHAGÓRIO**, the island's premier resort, renamed in 1955 to honour native son Pythagoras, ancient mathematician, philosopher and mystic. Until then it was known as Tigáni (Frying Pan) – in midsummer you'll learn why. The sixth-century BC tyrant Polykrates had his capital here, now subject to sporadic excavations which have forced modern Pythagório to expand northeast and uphill. The village core of cobbled lanes and thick-walled mansions abuts a small **harbour**, fitting almost perfectly into the confines of Polykrates' ancient jetty, but today devoted almost entirely to pleasure craft and overpriced cocktail bars.

Sámos's most complete **castle**, the nineteenth-century *pýrgos* of local chieftain Lykourgos Logothetis, overlooks both the town and the shoreline. Logothetis, together with a certain "Kapetan Stamatis" and Admiral Kanaris of Psará, chalked up decisive victories over the Turks in the summer of 1824. The final battle was won on Transfiguration Day (August 6), and accordingly the church inside the castle precinct is dedicated to this festival. A new **archeological museum** at the start of the road to Vathý was set to open as of writing, featuring finds from the ancient city. Other antiquities include the somewhat dull **Roman baths**, signposted as "Thermai", 400m west of town (Tues–Sun 8.45am–2.30pm; free); considerably more interesting is the **Efpalínio tunnel** (Tues–Sun 8.45am–2.15pm; €4), a 1040-metre aqueduct bored through the mountain just north of Pythagório at the behest of Polykrates. To get there, take the signposted path from the shore boulevard at the west end of town, which meets the vehicle access road toward the end of a twenty-minute walk. Visits consist of traversing a hewn rock ledge used to transport the spoil from the water channel far below; there are guard-grilles over the worst drops, and lighting for the first 650m. Although the slave-labour crews started from opposite sides of the mountain, the eight-metre horizontal deviation from true, about halfway along, is remarkably slight, and the vertical error nil: a tribute to the competence of the era's surveyors.

Practicalities

The **bus** stop lies just west of the intersection of Lykoúrgou Logothéti and the road to Vathý; the taxi rank is at the harbour end of Lykoúrgou Logothéti. A few **bank** ATMs and the **post office** are also along the same street. The flattish country to the west is ideal for cycling, a popular activity, and if you want to rent a **motorbike** several outfits on Logothéti will oblige you. These are interspersed with outlets for every brand of **car rental**, though **parking** in Pythagório is impossible – use the pricey fee lot near the castle, or the free one just west behind the town beach.

Accommodation proprietors meet all arriving ferries and hydrofoils, even in peak season – some of the prices touted seem too good to be true, but it's free to look. The **tourist information booth** (June–Sept daily 8.30am–9.30pm; ☎22730 62274), on the main thoroughfare, Lykoúrgou Logothéti, can also help in finding rooms. Quietly located at the seaward end of Odhós Pythagóra, south of Lykoúrgou Logothéti, the modest *Tsambika* (☎22730 61642; ❷) or the more comfortable *Dora*, a block west (☎22730 61456; ❸–❹), are two pensions worth contacting in advance. A peaceful area is the hillside north of Platía Irínis, where *Studios Galini* (☎22730 61167 or 210 98 42 248 in winter; ❹) has high-quality self-catering units with ceiling fans, balconies and kind English-speaking management. The *Evelin* (☎22730 61124, ℱ22730 61077; ❸) 2km out by the traffic lights isn't brilliantly located – convenient only for the airport – but it's good value and friendly, and has a swimming pool, double glazing against noise and on-site motorbike rental.

Eating out can be frustrating in Pythagório, with value for money often a completely alien concept. Currently the only place the islanders themselves will be caught dead or alive in (especially at weekend afternoons) is also the most atmospherically set: *Varka*, at the base of the jetty, fine for seafood and *orektiká*. Passably authentic Chinese fare at the *Oriental Garden*, two blocks inland from the water behind the town hall, attracts yachties from as far away as Léros; the €13.50 all-you-can-eat buffet is good value. With transport, it's worth heading out 3km east of town to *Yalos* (*Paul's*), the Greek-American-managed seaside taverna of the *Glikoriza Beach Hotel*; though prices are a bit bumped up relative to portion size, the presentation and quality of the fare are also higher than usual. Pythagório's current **nightlife** focus is *Sirius Club* on Dhespóti Kyrílou, which hosts occasional live gigs, while all-year Cine Rex in Mytiliní village, 7km northwest, screens standard first-run **films**; the summer premises at the far edge of town are great fun, with free *loukoumádhes* (sweet fritters) served at intermission.

Around Pythagório

The main local beach stretches for several kilometres west of the Logothetis castle, punctuated about halfway along by the end of the airport runway, and the cluster of nondescript hotels known as **POTOKÁKI**. Just before the turn-off to the heart of the beach sprawls the luxury *Doryssa Bay* complex (☎22730 61360, ⓦwww.doryssa-bay.gr; ❻–❽), which includes a meticulously concocted fake village, guaranteed to confound archeologists of future eras. No two of the units, joined by named lanes, are alike, and there's even a platía with a (pricey) café. In early October the *Doryssa Bay's* functions hall hosts an excellent, if poorly publicized, **pan-Mediterranean documentary film festival** (free screenings). Although you'll have to contend with the hotel crowds and low-flying jets, the sand-and-pebble **beach** here is well groomed and the water clean; for more seclusion head out to the end of the road.

Under layers of alluvial mud, plus today's runway, lies the processional Sacred Way joining the ancient city with the **Heraion**, the massive shrine of the Mother Goddess (daily July–Aug 8am–7pm; Sept–June 8.30am–3pm; €3). Much touted in tourist literature, this assumes humbler dimensions – one surviving column and assorted foundations – upon approach. Yet once inside the precinct you sense the former grandeur of the temple, never completed owing to Polykrates' untimely death at the hands of the Persians. The site chosen, near the mouth of the still-active Imvrassós stream, was Hera's legendary birthplace and site of her trysts with Zeus; in the far corner of the fenced-in zone you glimpse a large, exposed patch of the paved Sacred Way.

The modern resort of **IRÉON**, nearby, is a nondescript grid-plan resort behind a coarse-shingle beach, where the water can be cold owing to the outflow of the Imvrassós; nonetheless the place has its fanatical devotees who patronize assorted rooms and small hotels, most within sight of the sea.

Tempting, too, are the handful of waterfront **tavernas,** but for the best eating here follow the locals to *Angyra,* a super-hygienic, seafood-strong ouzerí on an inland corner.

Southern Sámos

Since the circum-island bus only passes through or near the places below once or twice daily, you really need your own vehicle to explore them. Some 5km west of Hóra, a well-marked side road leads up and right to **MAVRATZÉÏ,** one of two Samian "pottery villages", which lost 49 houses to the 2000 fire. The few surviving local potteries specialize in the Koúpa toú Pythagóra or "Pythagorean cup", supposedly designed by the sage to leak over the user's lap if they are overfilled. More practical wares can be found in **KOUMARADHÉÏ,** back on the main road, another 2km along.

From here you can descend a paved road to the sixteenth-century monastery of **Megális Panayías** (theoretically daily 9am–noon & 5–7pm), containing frescoes now very smudged by damp. This route continues to **MÝLI,** submerged in citrus groves and also accessible from Iréon. Four kilometres above Mýli sprawls **PAGÓNDAS,** a large hillside community with a splendid main square (venue for a lively Pentecost Sunday-evening festival) and an unusual communal fountain house on the south hillside. From here, a scenic paved road curls 15km around the hill to **PÝRGOS,** at the head of a ravine draining southwest and the centre of Samian honey production; here the best eating is not on the through road but at *Barba Dhimtris,* in the village centre.

The rugged and beautiful coast south of the Pagóndas–Pýrgos route is largely inaccessible, glimpsed by most visitors for the first and last time from the descending plane bringing them to Sámos. **Tsópela,** a highly scenic sand-and-gravel cove at a gorge mouth, is the only beach here with marked track access and a good taverna in a surviving pine grove, with fish and a dish or two of the day; you'll need a sturdy motorcycle (not a scooter) or a car to get down there. The western reaches of this shoreline are approached via the small village of **KOUMÉÏKA,** with a massive inscribed marble fountain and a pair of *kafenía* on its square. Below extends the long, pebble bay at **BÁLLOS,** with sand, a cave and a naturist area at the far east end. Bállos itself is merely a sleepy collection of summer houses, several simple places to stay and a few tavernas, all on the shore road. The best **accommodation** for walk-ins is the *Hotel Amfilisos* (☎22730 31669; ❹), while the finest **dining** is at *Akrogiali* nearby, with an honourable mention for humbler *Iy Paralia* off to the east. Returning to Kouméïka, the dubious-looking side road just before the village marked "Velanidhiá" is in fact entirely paved – a very useful short cut if you're travelling towards the beaches beyond Órmos Marathokámbou (see p.895).

Kokkári and around

Leaving Vathý on the north coastal section of the island loop road, you've little to stop for until **KOKKÁRI,** Sámos's second major tourist centre after Pythagório. The town's profile, covering two knolls behind twin headlands, remains unaltered, and one or two families still doggedly untangle their fishing nets on the quay, but in general its identity has been altered beyond recognition, given inland expansion over vineyards and the abandoned fields of small boiling-onions that gave the place its name. Since the exposed, rocky beaches here are buffeted by near-constant winds, locals have made a virtue of necessity by developing the place as a successful windsurfing resort – just west of town a windsurf school thrives all season long.

Practicalities

Buses stop on the through road, by the church. Other amenities on the same road include a few **bank** ATMs, branches of all major Samian **travel agents**, and a **newsstand/bookstore**, Lexis; on a seaward lane stands a **post office** in a Portakabin and, next door, a long-hours, self-service **laundry**. We don't usually recommend shops, but Astrid Koumalatsos' Pinokio (opposite the church) has the best stock of olive-wood souvenirs and kitchen ware we've seen in Greece.

As in Vathý and Pythagório, a fair proportion of Kokkári's **accommodation** is block-booked by tour companies; establishments not completely devoted to such trade include *Lemos* (☎22730 92250; ❹), near the north end of the west beach. For a guaranteed view of the fishing port, try the *Pension Alkyonis* (☎22730 92225; ❸) or the *Pension Angela* (☎22730 92052; ❸). If you get stuck, seek assistance from the municipal tourist office (Mon–Fri 8.30am–1.15pm; ☎22730 92217), with premises just east of the main church. If money's no object, then it has to be the A-class *Arion* (☎22370 92020, ⓦwww.arion-hotel.gr; ❼), a well-designed bungalow-hotel complex on an unburnt patch of hillside 2km west.

Tavernas lining the north waterfront have a nice view and little else to recommend them; the area is better regarded as a nightlife venue, with **bars** ringing the little square just west of where the concreted stream meets the sea. By far the best eating is either at *Iy Bira*, opposite the church, packed every night for the sake of proprietor Artemis' mother's cooking, or at *Ammos Plaz* on the west beach, one of the oldest (1988) establishments in town, offering very good and fair-priced *mayireftá* and fish – they've a loyal repeat clientele, and you must book days in advance (☎22730 92463) for seaside conservatory tables.

West of Kokkári: the coast

The closest sheltered beaches are thirty to forty minutes' walk away to the west, all with sunbeds and permanently anchored umbrellas. The first, **Lemonákia**, is a bit close to the road, though many *Arion* patrons favour it and the taverna's not too bad; 1km beyond, the graceful crescent of **Tzamadhoú** figures in virtually every tourist-board poster of the island. With path-only access, it's marginally less spoilt, and the far east end of the beach (saucer-shaped pebbles) has become a well-established nudist zone. There's one more pebble bay, 7km west beyond Avlákia, called **Tzaboú**, again with a serviceable snack-bar, but it's not worth a special detour when the prevailing northwest wind is up.

The next spot of any interest along the coast road is **Platanákia**, essentially a handful of buildings at a bridge by the turning for Manolátes (see opposite); here *Iy Apolavsis* **taverna** has a limited choice of very good *mayireftá*. Platanákia is actually the eastern suburb of **ÁYIOS KONSTANDÍNOS**, whose surf-pounded esplanade has been prettified. However, there are no usable beaches within walking distance, so the collection of warm-toned stone buildings, with few modern intrusions, constitutes a peaceful alternative to Kokkári, only getting much trade in spring when Dutch hikers frequent the place. For **accommodation**, try the *Hotel Iro* (☎22730 94013, ⓕ22730 94610; ❸), or the *Hotel Apartments Agios Konstantinos* (☎22730 94000, ⓕ22730 94002; ❹), both on the road down to the sea. **Eating** out, you're spoilt for choice; besides *Iy Apolavsis*, there's *Tò Kyma* at the east end of the quay, with good bulk wine and *mayireftá*, or (best of all) the *Aeolos* at the far west end of the esplanade (June–Sept), with terrific fish or grilled meat and a few well-chosen baked dishes, served at tables on the jetty or by the tiny beach.

Once past "Áyios", as it's locally abbreviated, the mountains hem the road in against the sea, and the terrain doesn't relent until **Kondakéïka**; its diminutive shore annexe of **Áyios Nikólaos** has an excellent venue for fish meals in ⚒ *Iy Psaradhes* (☎ 22730 32489; Easter–Oct), with a terrace lapped by the waves – booking in season is mandatory as it's appeared (deservedly) in so many guides. There's also the reasonable beach of **Piáki**, ten minutes' walk east past the last studio units.

The next turning inland beyond Áyios Nikólaos, just at the riverbed marking the eastern boundary of Karlóvassi, leads 6km to the little-visited village of Ídhroússa, gateway to the Byzantine **church of Kímisis Theotókou**. The oldest and most artistically noteworthy on Sámos, its extensive frescoes are contemporaneous with the building (late 12th or early 13th century). Once in Idhroússa, follow "Petaloúdha" signs from the platía along a dirt-track system for about 3km. The deceptively simple interior (unlocked), a single barrel-vaulted aisle, is covered with frescoes, many still vivid except on the ceiling where damp has blurred them.

Hill villages

Inland between Kokkári and Kondakéïka, an idyllic landscape of pine, cypress and orchards is overawed by dramatic mountains; except for some streaks of damage reaching the sea between Lemonákia and Tzaboú, it miraculously escaped the July 2000 fire. Despite destructive nibblings by bulldozers, some of the trail system linking the various **hill villages** is still intact, and walkers can return to the main highway to catch a bus back to base.

The monastery of **Vrondianís** (Vrónda), directly above Kokkári, was once a popular destination, but between severe fire damage in 2000 and the army's long, hard-wearing use of it as a barracks, it's closed indefinitely for renovations. **VOURLIÓTES**, 2km west of the monastery, has beaked chimneys and brightly painted shutters sprouting from its typical tile-roofed houses. Restaurateur greed has ruined the formerly photogenic central square; it's best to pass over the **tavernas** there in favour of *Iy Pera Vrysi*, at the village entrance, or the *Piyi Pnaka* taverna, in the idyllic hamlet of the same name just off the ascending Vourliótes road.

MANOLÁTES, further uphill and an hour-plus walk away via a deep river canyon, also has several simple **tavernas** (the pick of these being *Iy Filia* near the village entrance), and is the most popular trailhead for the five-hour round-trip up Mount Ámbelos (Karvoúnis), the island's second-highest summit. From Manolátes you can no longer easily continue on foot to Stavrinídhes, the next village, but should plunge straight down, partly on a cobbled path, through the shady valley known as Aïdhónia (Nightingales), towards Platanákia. By far the most characterful base in the area is down in Aïdhónia at the ⚒ *Hotel Aidonokastro* (☎ 22730 94686, ℱ 22730 94404; ❹). Here the kindly, English-speaking Yannis Pamoukis has renovated half the abandoned hamlet of **Valeondádhes** as a unique cottage-hotel, each former house comprising a pair of two- or four-person units with traditional touches.

Karlóvassi

KARLÓVASSI, 31km west of Vathý and Sámos's second town, is decidedly sleepier and more old-fashioned than the capital, despite having roughly the same population. It's potentially useful as a base for enjoying western Sámos's excellent beaches or taking a number of rewarding walks. The name, despite a vehement denial of Ottoman legacy elsewhere on Sámos, appears to be a corruption of the Turkish for "snowy plain" – the plain in question being the conspicuous saddle of Mount Kérkis overhead. The town divides into five straggly neighbourhoods: Néo, well inland, whose growth was spurred by the influx of post-1923 refugees; Meséo, across the usually dry riverbed, tilting appealingly off a knoll and then blending with the shoreline district of Ríva; and picturesque Paleó (or Áno), above Limáni, the small harbour district.

Most tourists stay at or near **Limáni**, the part of town with most of the tourist facilities. Hotels tend to have road noise and not much view; **rooms**, all on the inland pedestrian lane behind the through road, are quieter – try those of *Vangelis Feloukatzis* (☎22730 33293; ❷). The port itself is an appealing place with a working boatyard at the west end and all the **ferry-ticket agencies** grouped at the middle. **Tavernas** and bars abound on the quay, though the only remarkable one is *Rementzo* (April–Oct), tellingly the locals' hangout, with good fish in season plus *mayireftá*. The local university contingent (a maths and computer science faculty is based here) keeps formal **nightlife** surprisingly lively; try *Popcorn* on the quay.

Immediately overhead is the partly hidden hamlet of **Paleó**, its hundred or so houses draped on either side of a leafy ravine, but with no reliable facilities. **Meséo**, just east, has three **tavernas** on the central platía, of which the most accomplished is *Dionysos* (all year), with a range of creative dishes, equally pleasant indoor/outdoor tables and a wine list aspiring to Athenian sophistication. Following the street linking the central square to **Ríva**, you pass one of the improbably huge, early twentieth-century churches, topped with twin belfries and a blue-and-white dome, which dot the coastal plain here. Just at the intersection with the shore road, you'll find the good-value, sunset-view ouzerí *Tò Kyma* (April–Oct), where Ethiopian proprietress Berhane adds a welcome Middle Eastern/East African touch (eg *alí saláta*, with sun-dried tomatoes, cashews and courgettes) to the broad variety of seafood and vegetarian dishes – most days you'll fight for a table (no reservations taken). Otherwise, Ríva has little to recommend it besides a wilderness of derelict stone-built warehouses and mansions down near the river mouth, reminders of the vanished leather industry, which flourished here during the first half of the twentieth century. As for **Néo**, you'll almost certainly visit one of several **bank** ATMs, the **post office** or the **bus stop/taxi rank** on the main lower square. The student contingent guarantees some low-key **nightlife** (eg, *Café-Bar Toxotis*) and on the same street helps keep the local **cinema** (Gorgyra) going.

Western Sámos

The closest **beach** to Karlóvassi is **Potámi**, forty minutes' walk away via the coast road from Limáni or an hour by a more scenic, high trail from Paleó. This broad arc of sand and pebbles gets crowded at summer weekends, when virtually the entire town descends on the place. Near the end of the trail from Paleó there are a very few **rooms**, though many folk camp rough along the lower reaches of the river which gives the beach its name. A streamside path leads twenty minutes inland, past the eleventh-century church of **Metamórfosis** – the oldest on Sámos – to a point where the river disappears into a small gorge (a guardrailed but still vertiginous stairway takes you up and left here). Otherwise, you must swim and wade 100m in heart-stoppingly cold water through a sequence of fern-tufted rock pools before reaching a low but vigorous waterfall; bring shoes with good tread and perhaps even rope if you want to explore above the first cascade. You probably won't be alone until you dive in, since the canyon is well known to locals and tour agencies. Just above the Metamórfosis church, a clear if precipitous path leads up to a small, contemporaneous **Byzantine fortress**. There's little to see inside other than a subterranean cistern and badly crumbled lower curtain wall, but the views out to sea and up the canyon are terrific, while in October the place is carpeted with pink autumn crocuses.

The coast beyond Potámi ranks among the most beautiful and unspoilt on Sámos; since the early 1980s it has served as a protected refuge for the rare monk seal. The dirt track at the west end of Potámi bay ends after twenty minutes on foot, from which you backtrack 100m or so to find the well-cairned side trail running parallel to the water. After twenty minutes along this you'll arrive at **Mikró Seïtáni**, a small pebble cove guarded by sculpted rock walls. A full hour's walk from the trailhead, through olive terraces, brings you to **Megálo Seïtáni**, the island's finest beach, at the mouth of the intimidating Kakopérato gorge. You'll have to bring food and water, though not necessarily a swimsuit – there's no dress code at either of the Seïtáni bays. If you don't fancy the walk in, during peak season there are a couple of daily **water-taxi** services from Karlóvassi port (€10 return).

Southwestern beach resorts

The first place you reach on the island loop road south of Karlóvassi is **MARATHÓKAMBOS**, an amphitheatrical village overlooking the gulf of the same name; there are no tourist facilities, and by taking the bypass road you'll miss out on the village's traffic bottlenecks – and save about 4km. Its port, **ÓRMOS MARATHOKÁMBOU**, 18km from Karlóvassi, has emerged as a tourist resort since the 1990s, though some character still peeks through in its backstreets. The harbour has been improved, with *kaïkia* offering day-trips to Foúrni and the nearby islet of Samiopoúla, while the pedestrianized quay has become the focus of attention, home to several **tavernas**; best by a whisker is *Lekatis*, though portions aren't huge and seafood freshness can vary. Nearby, *The Mad Pomegranate Tree* is a slightly pricey but tasteful **café-bar** with a good line in piped music. For **accommodation** not monopolized by tours, try *Studios Avra* (☎22730 37221; ❷), unimprovably perched above the jetty.

The beach immediately east from Órmos is hardly the best; for better ones continue 2km west to **VOTSALÁKIA** (officially signposted as "Kámbos"), Sámos's newest, family-pitched resort, straggling a further 2km behind the island's longest (if not its most beautiful) beach. But for most, Votsalákia is still a considerable improvement on the Pythagório area, and the mass of 1437-metre Mount Kérkis overhead rarely fails to impress (see below). For **accommodation**, try Elsa Hiou's rooms behind her sympathetic *Evoinos* taverna near mid-strand (☎22730 37791 or 694 67 92 923; ❸); Emmanuil Dhespotakis has numerous premises towards the quieter, more scenic western end of things (☎22730 31258; ❸–❹). Also in this vicinity is *Loukoullos*, an unusual *koutouriárika* **taverna** overlooking the sea where all food is prepared in a wood oven. Other facilities include branches of nearly all the main Vathý travel agencies, offering **vehicle rental** (necessary, as only two daily buses call here), and a couple of stand-alone ATMs.

If Votsalákia doesn't suit, you can continue beyond for 3km to the 600-metre beach of **Psilí Ámmos**, more aesthetic and not to be confused with its namesake beach in the southeast corner of Sámos. The sea shelves very gently here, and cliffs shelter clusters of naturists at the east end. Surprisingly, there is still little development: just three small studio complexes in the pines at mid-beach, and two tavernas back up on the approach road. Access to **Limniónas**, a smaller cove 2km further west, passes the *Limnionas Bay Hotel* (☎22730 37057; ❺), much the highest-standard accommodation locally, with its tiered units arrayed around a garden and pool. Yachts and pleasure *kaïkia* occasionally call at the protected bay, which offers decent swimming away from a rock shelf at mid-strand, especially at the east end.

Mount Kérkis and around

Gazing up from a supine seaside position, you may be inspired to climb **Mount Kérkis**. The classic route begins at the west end of the Votsalákia strip, along the bumpy jeep track leading inland towards Evangelistrías convent. After 45 minutes or so on the track system, through olive groves and past charcoal pits (a major local industry), the path begins, more or less following power lines up to the convent. A friendly nun may proffer an ouzo in welcome and point you up the paint-marked trail, continuing even more steeply up to the peak. The views are tremendous, though the climb itself is humdrum once you're out of the trees. About an hour before the top there's a chapel with an attached cottage for sheltering in emergencies, and just beyond, a welcome spring. All told, it's a seven-hour outing from Votsalákia and, back, not counting rest stops.

Less ambitious walkers might want to circle the flanks of the mountain, first by vehicle and then by foot. The road beyond Limniónas to Kallithéa and Dhrakéï, truly back-of-beyond villages with views across to Ikaría, is paved all the way to Dhrakéï, making it possible to venture out here on an ordinary motorbike. The bus service is better during the school term, when a vehicle leaves Karlóvassi (Mon–Fri 1.20pm) bound for these remote spots; during summer it only operates two days a week at best (currently Mon & Fri).

From **DHRAKÉÏ**, a lovely trail – minimally damaged by a track – descends ninety minutes through forest to Megálo Seïtáni, from where it's easy enough to continue on to Karlóvassi within another two-and-a-half hours. People attempting to reverse this itinerary often discover to their cost that the bus (if any) returns from Dhrakéï at dawn or 2.45pm, compelling them to either retrace their steps or stay at one of two unofficial **rooms** establishments (summer only) in Dhrakéi, and dine at one of four taverna-*kafenía*. In **KALLITHÉA**, there's only a simple *psistariá* on the tiny square. From Kallithéa, a newer track (from beside the cemetery) and an older trail both lead up within 45 minutes to a spring, rural chapel and plane tree on the west flank of Kérkis, with path-only continuation for another thirty minutes to a pair of faintly frescoed cave-churches. **Panayía Makriní** stands detached at the mouth of a high, wide but shallow grotto, whose balcony affords terrific views of Sámos's west tip. By contrast, **Ayía Triádha**, a ten-minute scramble overhead, has most of its structure made up of cave wall; just adjacent, another long, narrow, volcanic cavern can be explored with a torch some hundred metres into the mountain.

After these subterranean exertions, the closest spot for a swim is **Vársamo** (Válsamo) cove, 4km below Kallithéa and reached via a well-signposted dirt road. The beach here consists of multicoloured volcanic pebbles, with two caves to shelter in, and a single very friendly **taverna** just inland, run by three generations of women.

Ikaría

Ikaría, a narrow, windswept landmass between Sámos and Mýkonos, is little visited and invariably underestimated by travel writers who don't even bother to show up. The name supposedly derives from the legendary Icarus, who fell into the sea just offshore after the wax bindings on his wings melted. For years

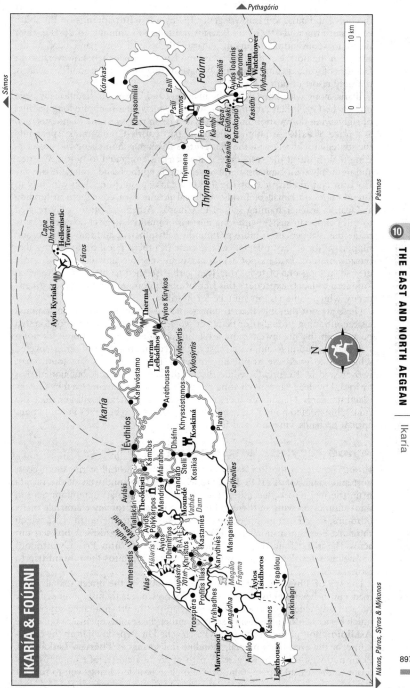

IKARÍA & FOÚRNI

0   10 km

N

Foúrni

Kórakas ▲

Khryssomiliá

Psilí
Ámmos

Balí

Vitsiliá

Ágios Ioánnis
Pródhromos

Italian
Watchtower

Foúrni

Vlyhádha

Kambí

Aspá

Kasídhi

Thýmena

Thýmena

Pelekánia & Elidháki

Petrokopió

Thermá

Cape
Dhrákano

Hellenistic
Tower

Áyia Kyriakí

Fáros

Ikaría

Kalavóstamo

Aréthoussa

Xylosýrtis

Xylosýrtis

**Thermá
Lefkádhos**

Ágios Kírykos

Évdhilos

Kámbos

Dháfni

Khryssóstomos

Koskiná

Playiá

Avláki

Meghálo

Áyios Theóktisti

Mandriá

Máratho

Frandáto

Stelí

Kosikiá

Liádhi

Polýkapos

Moundé

Vathés

Kastaniés

Seyhelles

Armenístis

Náis

Hálaris

Áyios
Dhimítrios

Vathés
Dam

Karydhiés

Manganítis

70m Khrístos

Loupástra

Profítis Ilías

Megálo
Frágma

Áyios
Isídhoros

Trapálou

Proospéra

Vráhadhes

Langádha

Kálamos

Karkinágri

Mavriánoi

Amálo

Lighthouse ✈

the only substantial tourism was generated by a few **hot springs** on the south coast; until the mid-1990s, the Ikarians resisted most attempts to develop their island for conventional tourism. Charter flights still don't land here, as the airport at the northeast tip can't accommodate jets. Since then, however, tourist facilities of some quantity and quality have sprung up in and around Armenistís, the only resort of note.

Ikaría, along with Thessaly on the mainland and Lésvos, has traditionally been one of the Greek Left's strongholds. This tendency dates from the long decades of right-wing domination in Greece, when (as in past ages) the island was used as a place of **exile** for political dissidents, particularly Communists. Apparently the strategy backfired, with the transportees favourably impressing and proselytizing their hosts; at the same time, many Ikarians emigrated to North America, and ironically their capitalist remittances help keep the island going. Of late, the Ikarians tend to embrace any vaguely Left cause; posters urge you variously to attend rallies on behalf of Turkish political prisoners or contribute to funding a Zapatista teacher-training school in Chiapas. Athens has historically reacted to this contrarian stance with long periods of punitive neglect, which has only made the islanders even more profoundly self-sufficient and idiosyncratic, and supportive (or at least tolerant) of the same in others. Local pride dictates that outside opinion matters not a bit, and until very recently Ikarians – mostly dressed in long-out-of-style American garb – seemed to have little idea what "modern tourists" expect. It's this lack of obsequiousness, and a studied eccentricity, which some visitors mistake for hostility.

These are not the only Ikarian quirks, and for many the place is an acquired taste, contrasting strongly (for better or worse) with Sámos. Except for forested portions in the northwest (now a bit fire-denuded near the shore), it's not a strikingly beautiful island, with most of the terrain consisting of scrub-covered schist put to good use as building material. The mostly desolate south coast is overawed by steep cliffs, while the north face is less sheer but nonetheless furrowed by deep canyons creating hairpin road-bends extreme even by Greek-island standards. Neither are there many postcard-picturesque villages, since the rural schist-roofed houses are generally scattered so as to be next to their famous apricot orchards, vineyards and fields.

Áyios Kírykos and around

Passing ferries on the Pireás–Páros–Náxos–Sámos line call at the south-coast port and capital of **ÁYIOS KÍRYKOS**, about 1km southwest of the island's main thermal resort. Because of the spa trade, beds are at a premium here in mid-summer; arriving in the evening from Sámos, accept any reasonable offers of rooms, or – if in a group – proposals of a taxi ride to the north coast, which shouldn't cost much more than €40 per vehicle to Armenistís. A **bus** sets out across the island from the main square (July–Sept 15 Mon–Fri only at noon) to Évdhilos, usually changing vehicles there at 1.30pm for the onward trip to Armenistís.

The spa of **Thérma**, 1km northeast of the port by the direct coastal access road, saw its heyday between the world wars; now distinctly fusty, it relies chiefly on a mostly elderly clientele on limited national-health-insurance stipends. A much better bet for a less formal soak are either the seaside, open-air pool of the **Asklipioú** hot springs in Áyios Kírykos, reached by steps down from the court-house, or the even more natural, shoreline hot springs at **Thérma Lefkádhos**, 2km southwest of Áyios Kírykos. A path opposite a cluster of eucalyptus trees drops to the sea, and then 100m over shoreline boulders brings you to the hot source, which mixes with the sea between giant volcanic boulders to a pleasant temperature.

A more conventional beach – the largest on the south coast – is found at **Fáros**, 10.5km northeast of Áyios Kírykos along a good paved road, which also serves the airport. A considerable colony of summer cottages shelters under tamarisks fringing the mixed sand-and-gravel strand, with a reefy zone to cross before deep water; this rather end-of-the-world place looks across to Foúrni and Thýmena, whose beaches (and landscape) it strongly resembles. But the best reason to make the trip out are two inexpensive **tavernas**, better than anything in Áyios Kírykos: *Leonidas* (open all year), with grilled or fried seafood plus bulk wine, and the more dour, less popular but quality-wise slightly better *O Grigoris* adjacent.

From a signposted point just inland from Fáros beach, a dirt track leads 2km to the trailhead for the round **Hellenistic watchtower** at Cape Dhrákano, much the oldest (and most impressive) ancient ruin on the island.

Practicalities

Hydrofoils, small ferries and *kaïkia* use the small east jetty; large ferries dock at the main west pier. Several **banks** with ATMs, a **post office** on the road out of town and three ferry/hydrofoil **agents** – Ikariadha (☎22750 22277) for hydrofoils, Roustas (☎22750 23691) and Lakios (☎22750 22426) for conventional boats – round up the list of essentials. You can **rent** motorbikes and cars here, too, from Dolihi Tours/Lemy (☎22750 23230) and Glaros (☎22750 23637), both near the east jetty.

There are several **hotels**, most useful (and consistently open) of which is the friendly, air-conditioned, en-suite, spotless *Akti* (☎22750 22694; ❸), on a knoll east of the hydrofoil and *kaïki* quay, with views of Foúrni from the garden. Otherwise, directly behind the base of the large-ferry jetty and two blocks inland there's the *Pension Maria-Elena* (☎22750 22835; ❸), a large modern block in a quiet setting. All in a row above the eastern quay and potentially suffering some noise from the several *kafenía* and snack-bars below are the *Pension Ikaria* (☎22750 22804; ❷), the studios above the *Taverna stou Tsouri* (☎22750 23400; ❸) and the clean *dhomátia* run by Ioannis Proestos (☎22750 23176; ❷).

Eating out, you've less choice than with lodging, with both options operating summer only: grilled dishes served up at the *Estiatorio Tzivaeri* just inland from Ioannis Proestos's rooms, or *Iy Klimataria* just around the corner for less distinguished *mayireftá*. On the front, *Casino* is the last remaining traditional *kafenío*; for further entertainment there's a **summer cinema**, the Rex, and a few summer clubs at the start of the road to Thermá Lefkádhos.

Évdhilos and around

The twisting, 37-kilometre road from Áyios Kírykos to Évdhilos is one of the most hair-raising on any Greek island (especially as a taxi passenger), and the long ridge extending the length of Ikaría often wears a streamer of cloud, even when the rest of the Aegean is clear. Although **ÉVDHILOS** is the island's second town and a regular ferry stop on the Sámos–Mýkonos–Sýros–Pireás line, it's slightly less equipped to deal with visitors than Áyios Kírykos. Évdhilos offers just two **hotels** – the *Evdoxia* on the slope southwest of the harbour (☎22750 31502; ❹) and the low-lying *Atheras* (☎22750 31434, ☻22750 31926; ❹) with a small pool – plus a few **rooms**. A **post office** up on the through road, a pair of **bank ATMs**, and two good **beaches** just to the east, are also worth knowing about, though the nearer beach has been blighted by a massive car park which will in due course become a new, much-needed harbour jetty. The **boat-ticket** trade is divided between the **agencies** Blue Nice (☏22750 31990) and Roustas (☏22750 32293); you can **rent cars** from Aventura ☏22750 31140). Among numerous harbourside sweet shops, *kafenía* and **restaurants**, the wood-signed *Coralli* on the west quay is the most reliable and reasonable option, but for more interesting fare head 1km west of the harbour to **FÝTEMA** hamlet, where just on the roadside *To Inomayerio tis Popis*, alias *Sto Fytema* (open only Easter week & school hols; ☏22750 31928), has lots of options for vegetarians, excellent local wine, low prices and pleasant terrace seating, though opening hours are erratic and it's best to call first.

KÁMBOS, 1.5km west of Fýtema, offers a small hilltop museum with finds from nearby **ancient Oinoe**; the twelfth-century church of Ayía Iríni stands adjacent, with column stumps and mosaic patches of a fourth-century Byzantine basilica defining the entry courtyard. Lower down still are the sparse ruins of a Byzantine palace (visible from the road) used to house exiled nobles, as well as a 250-metre-long sandy beach (unmarked track to it) with a musical *kantína* offering sunbeds. *Rooms Dhionysos* are available from the green-doored store immediately below the church run by Vassilis Kambouris (☏22750 31300 or 22750 31688; 2), who also acts as the unofficial and enthusiastic tourism officer for this part of Ikaría, keeping the keys for the church and museum.

From Kámbos, a twisty road leads up 4km – as does an easier road from Avláki, in 3km – to Ikaría's outstanding medieval monument, the **monastery of Theóktisti**, looking over pines to the coast from its perch under a chaos of slanted granite slabs. The *katholikón* features damaged but eminently worthwhile naïve frescoes dated to 1688; there's also a pleasant *kafenío* on site.

By following the road heading inland from the large church in Évdhilos, you can also visit the Byzantine **castle of Koskiná** (Nikariás), just over 15km south. The road signposted for Manganítis is paved through Kosíkia, 9km away, and for 2km more to the marked side-track. You can get a bike or jeep along this to within a short walk of the tenth-century castle, perched on a distinctive conical hill, with an arched gateway and a fine vaulted chapel.

Beyond this turning, the road creeps over the island watershed and drops steadily towards the south coast; it's completely paved, and with your own vehicle offers an alternative, quicker and much less curvy way back to Áyios Kírykos compared to going via Karavóstomo. The principal potential detour, 2km past the castle turning, is the road right (west) to the secluded pebble beach of **Seyhélles** ("Seychelles"), the best on this generally inhospitable coast, with the final approach by ten-minute hike.

Armenistís and around

Most visitors congregate at **ARMENISTÍS**, 51km from Áyios Kírykos via Évdhilos, and with good reason: this little resort lies below Ikaría's vastest (if slightly diminished) forest, with two enormous, sandy beaches battered by seasonal surf – **Livádhi** and **Mesaktí** – five and fifteen minutes' walk to the east respectively, the latter with no less than four reed-roofed *kantínas* in summer. The waves are complicated by strong lateral currents (as signs warn), and regular summer drownings have prompted the institution of that Greek rarity, a lifeguard service, and the placement of a line of marker buoys beyond which you should not stray. Armenistís itself is spectacularly set, facing northeast along the length of Ikaría towards sun- and moonrise, with Mount Kérkis on Sámos closing off the horizon on a clear day. A dwindling proportion of older, schist-roofed buildings, plus fishing boats hauled up in a sandy cove, lend Armenistís the air of a Cornish fishing village. Despite a 1990s mushrooming it remains a manageable place, even if gentrification (and a noticeable package presence) has definitely set in; the semi-official campsite behind Livádhi beach closed in 2001, though a few tents still sprout in the greenery behind Mesaktí by the river mouth, home to terrapins.

Accommodation

There are easily a score of rooms establishments in the Armenistís area, as well as four bona fide **hotels**. Among the latter, the *Erofíli Beach*, right at the entrance to town (☎22750 71058, ⓦwww.erofili.gr; ⓺), is considered the best on the island and has a small pool perched dramatically over Livádhi beach. Runners-up include the *Messakti Village* complex (☎22750 71331, ⓦwww .messakti-village.com; ⓺) just above Mesaktí beach, with a larger pool, its common areas and private terraces complementing large if minimally furnished self-catering units suitable for families of three to six, or – on the western edge of Armenistís – the *Daidalos* (☎22750 71390, ⓦwww.daidaloshotel.gr; ⓹), the less impersonal and less package-dominated of two adjacent hotels, with another eyrie-pool, unusually appointed rooms and a shady breakfast terrace. Among the various **rooms**, the *Kirki* by the *Erofíli Beach* (☎22750 71254 or enquire at *Dhefini* taverna; ⓷) is spartan but en suite, with large private balconies and sea views; along the shore lane, the *Paskhalia Rooms* (☎22750 71302; Easter–Oct ❷) are on the small side but en suite and good value, with great views east, while at the far end of Livádhi beach, the adjacent ✕*Atsahas Apartments* (☎ & Ⓕ22750 71226; April–Oct; ❹) and the *Valeta Apartments* (☎22750 71252; ❹) offer the best standard and setting outside of the hotels.

Eating, drinking and nightlife

Discounting the zaharoplastía and *souvláki* stalls (a pair each), there are a half-dozen full-service **tavernas** in Armenistís, of which two have a consistently good reputation. *Dhelfíni*, its terrace hovering right above the fishing cove, is an established favourite – come early or very late for a table, and a mix of grills or *mayireftá*. ✕*Paskhalia* (aka *Vlahos* after the helpful managing family) serves similar fare, more expertly prepared at its seaview terrace immediately above, and is the most reliable venue for both breakfast and off-season travellers, open until mid-October. Further afield, the *Atsahas*, attached to the namesake apartments, is acceptable as a beach taverna, with generous portions of slightly oily vegetarian fare. Just east of Mesaktí in the fishing settlement of **Yialiskári**, looking out past pines to a picturesque church on the jetty, there's another cluster of tavernas overlooking the boat-launching slips, of which *Kelaris* (aka *tis Eleftherias*) is the best value for well-executed *mayireftá* and grilled fish. Small clubs like *Casmir* and *Pleiades* operate during summer in the river reeds behind Livádhi, though for the rest of the year **nightlife** is mostly about extended sessions in the line of *kafenía* at the north end of Armenistís quay – or the cafés up in Ráhes, for reasons made clear below.

Information, transport – and getting away

The area's main **Internet café** is Internet Point, at the west edge of the resort. There are at least three **scooter/mountain-bike rental** agencies in Armenistís; among a like number of **car-rental** outlets, Aventura (☎22750 71117) and Dolihi Tours/Lemy (☎22750 71122) are the most prominent, with branches for drop-offs in Évdhilos and Áyios Kirykos respectively, which could be handy for ferry departures towards Sámos at an ungodly hour (typically 4am). Indeed, getting away when you need to is the main drawback to staying in Armenistís, since both taxis and buses can be elusive – with the exception of the fairly frequent (late June to early Sept) shuttle linking Armenistís with Yialiskári and Ráhes. Theoretically, long-distance **buses** head for Évdhilos three times daily mid-July to mid-September, fairly well spaced (though not necessarily coinciding with westbound ferry departures; Áyios Kírykos has only one through service year-round at either 8am or 11am, though this can be full with school kids in term-time. If you've a ferry to catch, it's far easier on the nerves to prebook a **taxi**: a list of all locally based drivers, with their mobile numbers, is posted at the entrance to Armenistís.

Ráhes

Armenistís is actually the shore annexe of four inland hamlets – Áyios Dhimítrios, Áyios Polýkarpos, Kastaniés and Khristós – collectively known as **RÁHES**. Despite the modern, mostly paved access roads through the pines (trails short-cut them), the settlements retain a certain Shangri-La quality, with the older residents speaking a positively Homeric dialect. On an island not short of foibles, Khristós (Khristós Rahón in full) is particularly strange inasmuch as most locals sleep until 11am or so, shop until about 4pm, then have another nap until 8pm, whereupon they rise and spend most of the night shopping, eating and drinking the excellent home-brewed **wine** which everyone west of Évdhilos makes. In fact most of the villages west of Évdhilos adhere to this schedule, defying central government efforts to bring them into line with the rest of Greece. The local festival is August 6, though better ones take place further southwest in the woods at the Langádha valley (August 14–15) or at the Áyios Isídhoros monastery (May 14).

Near the pedestrianized *agorá* of Khristós, paved in schist and studded with gateways fashioned from the same rock, there's a **post office**, plenty of café-bars (4pm–3am) and two sweet shops. In accordance with the above-cited nocturnal habits, lunchtime can offer pretty slim pickings, though two surprisingly expensive, adjacent **tavernas** commence operations at about 8pm.

Walking between Ráhes and the coastal resorts is one of the favourite activities for visitors, and locally produced, accurate if somewhat chatty map-guides are widely available. The black-and-white *Road & Hiking Map of Western Ikaría* shows most asphalt roads, tracks and trails in the west-centre of the island; the more closely focused, colour *Round of Rahes on Foot* details a loop hike taking in the best the Ráhes villages have to offer. The route sticks mostly to surviving paths, and is well marked; the authors suggest a full day for the circuit, with ample rests, though total walking time won't be more than six hours. More advanced outings involve descending the Hálaris canyon, with its historic bridge, to Nás, or crossing the island to Manganítis via Ráhes.

Nás

By tacit consent, Greek or foreign hippies and beachside naturists have been allowed to shift 3km west of Armenistís by paved road to **Nás**, a tree-clogged river canyon ending in a small but deceptively sheltered sand-and-pebble beach. This little bay is almost completely enclosed by weirdly sculpted rock formations, but for the same reasons as at Mesaktí it's unwise to swim outside the cove's natural limits – marked, as at Mesaktí, with a line of buoys. The crumbling foundations of the fifth-century temple of **Artemis Tavropoleio** (Patroness of Bulls) overlook the permanent deep pool at the mouth of the river. If you continue inland along the river past colonies of rough campers defying prohibition signs, you'll find secluded rock pools for freshwater dips. Back at the top of the stairs leading down to the beach from the road are six tavernas, most of them offering rooms. Among **accommodation**, the rambling *Artemis* (⊤22750 71485; ❷ rooms, ❸ studios) overlooks the river canyon, while ⚓ *Thea* (⊤22750 71491; ❸) faces out to sea. The latter offers much the most accomplished **cooking** in the area, working weekends October to May as well, with lots of vegetarian options like *soufikó* (the local ratatouille).

Satellite islands: Thýmena and Foúrni

The straits between Sámos and Ikaría are speckled with a mini-archipelago of three islets, of which the inhabited ones are Thýmena and Foúrni. More westerly **Thýmena** has one tiny hillside settlement; *kaïkia* call regularly at the quay below on their way between Ikaría or Sámos and Foúrni, but there are no tourist facilities or attractions to speak of, save one large beach south of "town".

FOÚRNI is home to a huge fishing fleet and one of the more thriving boat-yards in the Aegean; thanks to these, and the improvement of the jetty to receive car ferries, its population is stable, unlike so many small Greek islands. The islets were once the lair of Maltese pirates, and indeed many of the islanders have a distinctly North African appearance.

The small ferries *Samos Spirit* and *Samos Sun* are based much of the week at Foúrni, making morning shopping-and-post departures to either Ikaría or Sámos, returning in the afternoon or early evening. The larger main-line ferries which appear every few days in either direction are likewise not tourist excursion boats but exist for the benefit of the islanders. The only way to visit Foúrni on a day-trip is by using one of the few weekly morning **hydrofoils** out of Pythagório on Sámos.

Apart from the remote hamlet of **Khryssomiliá** in the north, where the island's longest (and worst) road goes, most of Foúrni's inhabitants are concentrated in the **port** and Kambí hamlet just to the south. The harbour community is larger than it seems from the sea, with a friendly ambience reminiscent of 1970s Greece.

△ View from Foúrni toward Thýmena and Ikaría

Foúrni port practicalities

The central "high street", fieldstoned and mulberry-shaded, ends well inland at a little platía with two giant plane trees; between them stands a Hellenistic sarcophagus found in a nearby field, and overhead is a conical hill, site of the ancient acropolis. Nearby there's a **post office** and stand-alone **bank** ATM, plus several surprisingly well-stocked shops.

Among several **rooms** establishments, the most popular are the various premises run by Manolis and Patra Markakis (T 22750 51268, F 22750 51355), immediately to your left as you disembark; these range from simple rooms, some with balconies (❷), to fourteen superb hilltop apartments, most sleeping up to four, in a tiered complex (❹). If they're full, try *Kosta-Reli*, just back from the little town beach (T 22750 51481; ❸).

There are three full-service waterfront **tavernas**: local favourite *Rementzo*, better known as *Nikos'*, where, if you're lucky, the local *astakós* or Aegean lobster may be on the menu (except Sept–Jan); shambolically managed *Miltos*, but with good seafood; or newer contender *Ta Dhelfinakia*, a good, hygienic all-rounder with more meat dishes. For breakfast and desserts, repair to the tamarisk terrace at the Markakis family's *To Arhondiko tis Kyras Kokonas*, under their inn. There's surprisingly lively **nightlife** at a half-dozen music bars, clubs and ouzerís, often until 5am.

Around Foúrni

A fifteen-minute trail-walk south from the primary school, skirting the cemetery and then slipping over the windmill ridge, brings you to **KAMBÍ**, a scattered community overlooking a pair of sandy, tamarisk-shaded coves which you'll share with hauled-up fishing boats. There are two cheap and sustaining **tavernas**: the *Kambi* with tables on the sand, and slightly more accomplished *O Yiorgos* clinging to the side of a valley inland. A path system continues south around the headland to other, more secluded bays of varying sizes and beach consistencies which, like Kambí cove, are favourite anchorages for passing yachts, but unlike Kambí have substantial summer communities of rough campers and naturists. One, **Elidháki**, has motorbike-track access, and (like Kambí) taxi-boat service from the port.

Foúrni's only paved road ends at the southerly hamlet and monastery of **Áyios Ioánnis Pródhromos**. Just before arrival, dirt tracks lead to the isolated coves of **Vlyhádha** and **Vitsiliá**, which like most local beaches have no facilities. Overall, southern Foúrni is the most rewarding part of the island; two beaches immediately north of the harbour have been ruined in various ways and, in the extreme north of the island, remote **KHRYSSOMILIÁ** is still easiest approached by the taxi-boat from the port or on the *Samos Spirit* rather than along the atrocious eighteen-kilometre road. The village, split into a shore district and a hillside settlement, has a decent beach flanked by better if less accessible ones. There are two **tavernas** near the jetty and a few **rooms** to be had, though the locals can be less than forthcoming with outsiders.

Híos

"Craggy Híos", as **Homer** aptly described his putative birthplace, has a turbulent history and a strong identity. This large island has always been prosperous: in medieval times through the export of mastic **resin** – a trade controlled by Genoese overlords between 1346 and 1566 – and later by

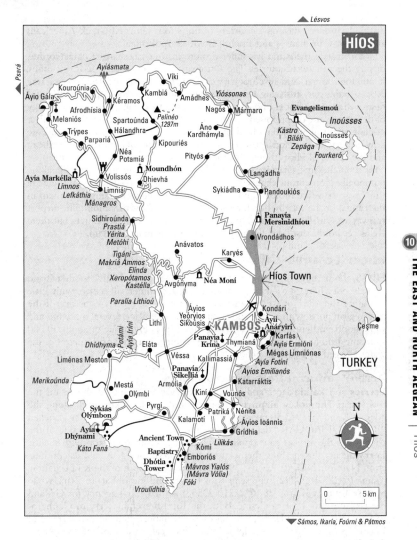

10

Ayiásmata

Víki

Kouroúnia
Kambiá
Amádhes
Yióssonas

Áyio Gála
Kéramos
Nagós
Mármaro

Afrodhísia
Pelinéo
Evangelismoú
Inoússes

Melaniós
Spartoúnda
1297m

Trýpes
Hálandhra
Áno
Kástro
B-la-li
Inoússes

Parpariá
Kardhámyla
Zepága

Néa
Kipouriés
Fourkeró

Potamiá

Pityós

Ayía Markélla
Moundhón
Langádha

Límnos
Volissós
Dhievhá

Lefkáthia
Sykiádha
Pandoukiós

Mánagros
Limniá

Sidhiroúnda
Panayía

Prastiá
Mersinidhíou

Yérita
Vrondádhos

Metóhi

Tigáni
Anávatos

Makriá Ámmos
Karyés

Elínda

Xeropótamos
Híos Town

Kastélla
Avgónyma
Néa Moní

Paralía Lithioú

Áyios
Kondári

Yeóryios
Ayii

Lithí
Sikoúsis
KÁMBOS
Anáryiri

Potámi
Panayía
Thymianá
Karfás

Dhídhyma
Krína
Ayía Ermióni

Ayía Iríni
Eláta
Véssa
Mégas Limniónas

Liménas Mestón
Kallimassiá
Ayía Fotíni

Áyios Emilianós

Merikoúnda
Panayía
Çeşme

Mestá
Sikelliá
Katarráktis

TURKEY

Olýmbi
Armólia
Kiní

Sykiás
Pyrgí
Vounós

Olýmbon
Patriká
Nénita

N

Ayía
Kalamotí
Áyios Ioánnis

Dhýnami
Grídhia

Káto Faná
Ancient Town
Lilikás

Kómi

Baptistry
Emboriós

Dhótia
Mávros Yialós

Tower
(Mávra Vólia)

Vroulídhia
Fóki

0   5 km

the Ottomans, who dubbed the place Sakız Adası ("Resin Island"). Since union with Greece in 1912, several shipping dynasties have emerged here, continuing the pattern of wealth. Participation in the maritime way of life is widespread, with someone in almost every family spending time in the merchant navy.

The more powerful ship-owning dynasts, the local government and the military authorities did not encourage tourism until the late 1980s, but the worldwide shipping crisis and the saturation of other, more obviously "marketable" islands eroded resistance. Since then, numbers of foreigners have discovered an Híos beyond its rather daunting port capital: fascinating villages, important Byzantine monuments and a respectable, if remote, complement of beaches. While unlikely ever to be dominated by tourism, the local scene has a distinctly modern flavour – courtesy of numerous returned Greek-Americans and Greek-Canadians – and English is widely spoken.

Unfortunately, the island has suffered more than its fair share of **catastrophes** during the past two centuries. The Ottomans perpetrated their most infamous, if not their worst, anti-revolutionary atrocity here in March 1822, massacring 30,000 Hiots and enslaving or exiling even more. In 1881, much of Híos was destroyed by a violent earthquake, and throughout the 1980s the natural beauty of the island was compromised by devastating forest fires, compounding the effect of generations of tree-felling by boat-builders. Over half of the majestic pines are now gone, with substantial patches of woods persisting only in the far northeast and the centre of Híos (though reafforestation is beginning to have an effect).

In 1988 the first charters from northern Europe were instituted, signalling potentially momentous changes for the island. Nearly two decades on there are still fewer than five thousand guest beds on Híos, the vast majority of them in the capital or the nearby beach resorts of Karfás and Ayía Ermióni. The airport runway was finally lengthened in 2004 to safely accommodate all jets, but there are as yet no direct flights from most countries, including Britain.

Híos Town

HÍOS, the harbour and main town, will come as a shock after modest island capitals elsewhere; it's a brash, concrete-laced commercial centre, with little predating the 1881 quake. Yet in many ways it is the most satisfactory of the east Aegean ports, with a large and fascinating marketplace, several museums and some good, authentic tavernas. Although it's a sprawling place of about 30,000 souls, most things of interest to visitors lie within a hundred or so metres of the water, fringed by Leofóros Egéou.

Arrival, information and transport

Ferries and **kaïkia** large and small dock at various points as shown on the town map. The pokey **airport** (2 car-hire booths) lies 3km south along the coast at Kondári, a €3.50 taxi-ride away; otherwise any blue urban bus labelled "JOMDAQI JAQUAR" departing from the terminal on the north side of the park passes the airport gate, opposite which is a conspicuous stop with shelter. **Ferry** agents cluster along the north end of waterfront Egéou and its continuation Neoríon: NEL (℡22710 23971) is a few paces south of the KTEL station, Traïna (℡22710 29292) represents Saos Ferries and local boats to Psará, while Sunrise Tours at Kanári 28 (℡22710 23558) is the central agency for GA and the fast morning boat to Çeşme. Both the Turkish evening ferry to Çeşme, as well as the most regular boat to Inoússes, are represented by Faros Travel at Egéou 18 (℡22710 27240). The helpful municipal **tourist office** (May–Sept daily 7am–10pm; Oct–April Mon–Fri 7am–3pm; ℡22710 44389) is at Kanári 18; quality commercial maps and a limited stock of English-language **books** are at Newsstand, at the first "kink" in Egéou near the Cine Diana. The most reliable **Internet** facilities are at Enter, just seaward of the Fedra Hotel, with upwards of ten terminals upstairs.

The standard green-and-cream **KTEL buses** leave from just behind the passenger waiting-room on Egéou. While services to the south of Híos are adequate, those to the centre and northwest of the island are almost nonexistent, and to explore there you'll need to rent a powerful **motorbike** or a car, or share a **taxi** (which are bright red here, not grey as in most of Greece). Two independent or small-chain **car-rental** agencies sit at Evyenías Handhrí 5–7, behind the eyesore *Chandris Hotel*; of these, Vassilakis/Reliable Rent a Car

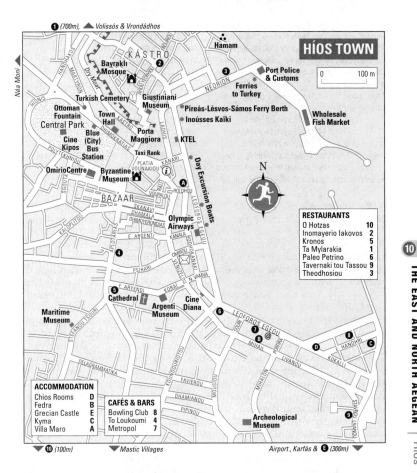

HÍOS TOWN

0   100 m

(700m), ▲ Volissós & Vrondádhos

Hamam

KÁSTRO

Bayraklı Mosque

Port Police & Customs

Ferries to Turkey

Turkish Cemetery   Giustiniani Museum

Pireás-Lésvos-Sámos Ferry Berth

Inoússes Kaïki

Wholesale Fish Market

Ottoman Fountain   Town Hall

Central Park

Blue (City) Bus Station

Cine Kipos

Porta Maggiora

KTEL

Taxi Rank

PLATIA VOUNAKIOU

OmirioCentre   Byzantine Museum

Day Excursion Boats

N

BAZAAR

Olympic Airways

RESTAURANTS

O Hotzas	10
Inomayerio Iakovos	2
Kronos	5
Ta Mylarakia	1
Paleo Petrino	6
Tavernaki tou Tassou	9
Theodhosiou	3

Maritime Museum

Cathedral

Argenti Museum

Cine Diana

LEOFOROS EGEOU

MIHAIL   PERPERA   LIVANOU   KOKALI

HANDHRI

ACCOMMODATION

Chios Rooms	D
Fedra	B
Grecian Castle	E
Kyma	C
Villa Maro	A

CAFÉS & BARS

Bowling Club	8
To Loukoumi	4
Metropol	7

Archeological Museum

(100m)   Mastic Villages   Airport, Karfás & ❺ (300m)

(☎22710 29300 or 694 43 34 898, ✉ivasila@otenet.gr), with a branch at Mégas Limniónas (☎22710 31728), is particularly recommended. The **post office** is on Omírou, while numerous **banks** all have ATMs. A final Hiot idiosyncrasy is afternoon **shopping hours** limited to Monday and Thursday in summer.

Accommodation

Híos Town has a fair quantity of affordable **accommodation**, rarely completely full. Most places line the water or the perpendicular alleys and parallel streets behind, and almost all are plagued by traffic noise to some degree – listed are the more peaceful establishments.

Chios Rooms Egéou 110, cnr Kokáli ☎22710 20198 or 697 28 33 841, ✉ chiosrooms@hotmail.com. Tile- or wood-floored, high-ceilinged rooms, some en suite and relatively quiet for a seafront location, lovingly restored by proprietors Don (New Zealander) and Dina (Greek), who live on-site. Best is the penthouse "suite" with private terrace. ❷

Fedra Mihaïl Livanoú 13 ☎22710 41130, ☎22710 41128. Well-appointed *pension* in an old mansion, with stone arches in the downstairs winter bar; in summer the bar operates outside, so ask for a rear room to avoid nocturnal noise. ❹

Grecian Castle Bella Vista shore avenue, en route to airport ☎22710 44740, ⊛www.greciancastle .gr. Occupying the shell of an old factory, and popular with package tourists, this is Híos Town's top-rated (A-class) digs. Lovely grounds and a sea-view pool, but the smallish main-wing rooms, despite their marble floors, wood ceilings and bug screens, aren't worth the rates charged; the rear "villa" suites are far more pleasant. Std rooms ❻, villa suites ❽

🏃 **Kyma** East end of Evyenías Handhrí ☎22710 44500, @kyma@chi.forthnet .gr. En-suite hotel rooms in a Neoclassical mansion or a modern extension, with TV, huge terraces on the sea-facing side and Jacuzzi tubs in some rooms. Theo's splendid service and big

breakfasts really make the place. The old wing saw a critical moment in modern Greek history in September 1922, when Colonel Nikolaos Plastiras commandeered it as his HQ after the Greek defeat in Asia Minor, and announced the deposition of King Constantine I. B&B; Aug ❺, otherwise ❹

Villa Maro Roïdhou 15 ☎22710 27003. Modern *pension* tucked onto a tiny plaza just inland from the water; rear rooms unfortunately overlook the public toilets, but all are en suite, tile-floored and well equipped, plus there's a pleasant breakfast/ snack-bar on the ground floor. ❹

The Town

South and east of the main platía, officially Plastíra but known universally as Vounakíou, extends the marvellously lively tradesmen's **bazaar**, where you can find everything from parrots to cast-iron woodstoves. Opposite the Vounakíou **taxi rank**, the grandiosely titled "**Byzantine Museum**", occupying the old **Mecidiye Mosque** (closed for renovation), is little more than an archeological warehouse, with a preponderance of Jewish marble gravestones in the courtyard – plus a few Armenian, Genoese and Turkish ones – testifying to Híos' varied population in past centuries.

Until the 1881 earthquake, the Byzantine-Genoese **Kástro** stood completely intact; thereafter developers razed the seaward walls, filled in much of the moat to the south and sold off the real estate thus created along the north waterfront. The most dramatic entry to the citadel is via the **Porta Maggiora** behind the town hall. The top floor of a medieval mansion just inside is home to the **Giustiniani Museum** (Tues–Sun 8.30am–3pm; €2), with a satisfying collection of unusual icons and twelve fourteenth-century frescoes of Old Testament prophets rescued from Panayía Krína church. The old residential quarter inside the surviving castle walls, formerly the Muslim and Jewish neighbourhoods, is well worth a wander. Among the wood and plaster houses you'll find assorted Ottoman monuments in various states of decay: a Muslim cemetery, the minaretless Bayraklı mosque, three ruined *hamams* (Turkish baths) and several inscribed **fountains**, the most ornate of which – with four facets – stands outside opposite the central park.

Further afield, three other museums beckon. The **Maritime Museum** at Stefánou Tsoúri 20 (Mon–Sat 10am–1pm; free) consists principally of model ships and oil paintings of various craft, all rather overshadowed by the mansion containing them. In the foyer are enshrined the knife and glass-globe grenade of Admiral Kanaris, who partly avenged the 1822 massacre by ramming and sinking the Ottoman fleet's flagship. In the centre of town, the **Argenti Folklore Museum** (Mon–Thurs 8am–2pm, Fri 8am–2pm & 5–7.30pm, Sat 8am–12.30pm; €2), on the top floor of the Koráï Library at Koráï 2, features ponderous genealogical portraits of the endowing family, an adjoining wing of costumes and rural impedimenta, plus multiple replicas of Delacroix's *Massacre at Hios*, a painting which did much to arouse sympathy for the cause of Greek independence.

The **archeological museum** on Mihálon (June–Aug daily 8am–7pm; Sept–May Tues–Sun 8.30am–3pm; €3) is a wide-ranging and well-lit collection, arranged both thematically and chronologically from Neolithic to Roman times, demanding at least an hour or so of exploration. Highlights include limestone column bases from the Apollo temple at Faná in the shape of lions' claws;

numerous statuettes and reliefs of Cybele (this Asiatic goddess was especially honoured here); Archaic faïence miniatures from Emborió in the shape of a cat, a hawk and a flautist; terracottas from various eras of a dwarf riding a boar; and figurines (some with articulated limbs) of *hierodouloi* or sacred prostitutes, presumably from an Aphrodite shrine. Most famous of all is an inscribed edict of Alexander the Great from 322 BC, ordering local political changes and setting out relations between himself and the Hiots.

Eating

Eating out in Híos Town can be more pleasurable than the fast-food joints and multiple *barákia* on the waterfront (plus American-style pizza parlours inland) would suggest; it is also usually cheaper than on neighbouring Sámos or Lésvos.

O Hotzas Yeoryíou Kondhýli 3, cnr Stefánou Tsoúri. Oldest (and arguably the best) taverna in town, with chef Ioannis Linos, the fourth generation of his family, presiding. Menu varies seasonally, but expect a mix of vegetarian dishes (black-eyed peas, cauliflower, stuffed red peppers), and *lahanodolmádhes*, sausages, baby fish and *mydhopílafo* (rice and mussels) washed down by own-brand ouzo or retsina. Dinner only, capacious garden in summer; closed Sun.

Inomayerio Iakovos Ayíou Yeoryíou Frouríou 20, Kástro. Iakovos himself has sold up but his chef, now owner, continues to offer a good balance of well-executed fishy dishes, grilled titbits, cheese-based recipes and vegetables; local white bulk wine or ouzo. Atmospheric garden seating in a vine-cloaked ruin opposite, or inside Oct–May. Closed Sun, and no lunch Sept–June.

Kronos Filíppou Aryéndi 2, cnr Aplotariás. The island's best, and own-made ice cream, purveyed since 1929. Limited seating or takeaway; open noon–midnight.

Ta Mylarakia By three restored windmills in Tambákika district, on the road to Vrondádhos ☎22710 40412. A large, well-priced seafood selection, every kind of Hiot ouzo and limited

waterside seating make reservations advisable in summer. Dinner all year, lunch also Oct–April.

Paleo Petrino Egéou 80. Standard, no-nonsense ouzerí with such delights as *iliókafto* (sun-dried fish). In the cooler months the interior, with 1950s Greek record and film posters, is more pleasant than quayside seating where you often ingest car fumes with your food.

Tavernaki tou Tassou Stávrou Livanoú 8, Bella Vista district. Superb all-rounder with creative salads, better-than-average bean dishes, dolmádhes, snails, properly done chips, a strong line in seafood and good barrel wine. A bit pricier than usual, but Tassos' and Tsambika's cooking (with son Dhimitris at the grill) is worth it. Open lunch and supper most of the year, with seaview garden seating during warmer months and heated gazebo in winter.

Theodhosiou Ouzeri Neoríon 33. The oldest, least expensive ouzerí on the quay, occupying a domed, arcaded building (though they plan a move to new premises at Kondári in 2007). A fair amount of meat grills for this type of eatery, plus a long list of seafood standards like shrimp-and-onion fry-up. Generally, best avoid fried platters in favour of grilled or boiled ones. Dinner only; closed Sun.

Drinking, nightlife and entertainment

The 1400 or so students at the local technical schools and economics/business management faculties of the University of the Aegean help keep things lively, especially along the portion of the waterfront between the two "kinks" in Egéou. Shooting **pool** is a big thing in Híos Town; many bars have several tables.

Bowling Club East end of Egéou. The seven alleys (and to a lesser extent, five pool tables) are very popular with local youth. Open until at least midnight.

Cine Kipos In central park from early June to mid-Sept only. Quality/art-house first-run fare, two screenings nightly; watch for flyers around town. During winter, the action shifts to Cine

Diana, under the eponymous hotel (two screenings nightly).

To Loukoumi Alley off Aplotariás 27/c. Old warehouse refitted as a café (8am–2pm), ouzerí (8pm–2am) and occasional events centre. Well executed and worth checking out, but closes May–Sept (when a summer premises near the airport operates) & Sun.

Metropolis/Metropol Egéou. The longest-lived and most civilized of the music bars on this stretch of the front, always crowded from sunset until the small hours.

Omirio South side of the central park. Cultural centre and events hall with frequently changing exhibitions; foreign musicians often come here after Athens concerts to perform in the large auditorium.

Beaches near Híos Town

The locals swim at tiny pebble coves near Vrondádhos, north of Híos Town, or from the somewhat grubby town beach in Bella Vista district, but for most visitors the closest decent one is at **Karfás**, 7km south beyond the airport and served by frequent blue buses. Once there you can **rent cars** at MG (booth opposite the Sunset Hotel). Most large Hiot package hotels are planted here, to the considerable detriment of the 500-metre-long beach itself, sandy only at the south end. The main bright spot is a unique **pension**, ☕ *Markos' Place* (☎ 22710 31990 or 697 32 39 706, ⓦ www.marcos-place.gr; April–Nov; ➋), installed in the disestablished **monastery of Áyios Yeóryios and Áyios Pandelímon**, on the hillside south of the bay. Markos Kostalas, who leases the premises from Thymianá municipality, has created a uniquely peaceful, leafy environment much loved by special-activity groups. Guests are lodged in the former pilgrims' cells, with a kitchen available or superior breakfasts laid on by arrangement; individuals are more than welcome (there are several single "cells"), as are families (2 "tower" rooms sleep 4), though reservations are advisable and the minimum stay is four days.

Shoreline **restaurants** aren't brilliant, though *Karatzas* (near mid-beach) and *Giamos* (south end) are striving valiantly to regain credibility after bad patches; *Giamos* has the edge in food quality. *Oasis*, between these two on the sand, is a popular breakfast, juice, snack and drinks café-bar; musical *La Notte*, up on the slope near *Markos' Place*, acquits itself well for **nightlife** into the autumn. Generally, though, it's better to strike inland for eating opportunities. *Ouzeri To Apomero* (open daily all year), in hillside Spiládhia district west of the airport (bear off the Pyrgí road towards Áyios Theodhósios and follow the many luminous green signs) has terrace seating with an eyeful of the Çeşme peninsula and some unusual dishes such as Cretan sausages and battered artichoke hearts. Between Thymianá and Neohóri, ☕ *Fakiris Taverna* (open all year but weekends only in winter) offers home-marinated aubergine and artichokes, goat baked in tomato sauce and excellent wood-fired pizzas along with well-executed seafood and pork-based *bekrí mezé* in big portions. The easiest way to find it is to head south on the road to Kalimassiá and then turn west onto the Ayíou Trafonos road, just before Neohóri, and proceed about 1km.

Some 2km further along the coast from Karfás, **AYÍA ERMIÓNI** is not a beach but a fishing anchorage surrounded by a handful of tavernas (none stands out) and apartments to rent. The nearest proper beach is at **Mégas Limniónas**, a few hundred metres further, smaller than Karfás but more scenic where low cliffs provide a backdrop. Both Ayía Ermióni and Mégas Limniónas are served by extensions of blue-bus routes to either Karfás or Thymianá, the nearest inland village. The coast road loops up to Thymianá, from where you can (with your own transport only) continue 3km south towards Kalimassiá to the turning for **Ayía Fotiní**, a 600-metre pebble beach with exceptionally clean water. Cars are excluded from the shore area; the pedestrian esplanade is lined with various blocks of rooms, less monopolized than formerly by tour companies, plus there's car hire locally. A few **tavernas** cluster around the point where the side road meets the sea, but there's far better food, specifically fish, at **KATARRÁKTIS** (return to the Kalimassiá road), where *O Tsambos* is the best and least expensive of several contenders.

Southern Híos

Besides olive groves, the gently rolling countryside in the south of the island is also home to the **mastic bush** (*Pistacia lentisca*), found across much of Aegean Greece but only here producing an aromatic resin of any quality or quantity. For centuries it was used as a base for paints, cosmetics and the chewable jelly beans, which became a somewhat addictive staple in the Ottoman harems. Indeed, the interruption of the flow of mastic from Híos to Istanbul by the revolt of spring 1822 was one of the root causes of the brutal Ottoman reaction.

The wealth engendered by the mastic trade supported twenty *mastihohoriá* (mastic villages) from the time the Genoese set up a monopoly in the substance during the fourteenth and fifteenth centuries, but the end of imperial Turkey and the development of petroleum-based products knocked the bottom out of the mastic market. Now it's just a curiosity, to be chewed – try the sweetened Elma-brand gum – or drunk as a liqueur called *mastíha*. It has also had medicinal applications since ancient times, and high-end cosmetics, toothpaste and mouthwash are now purveyed, most notably at the Mastiha Shop on Egéou in Híos Town. These days, however, the *mastihohoriá* live mainly off their tangerines, apricots and olives.

The towns themselves, the only settlements on Híos spared by the Ottomans in 1822, are architecturally unique, laid out by the Genoese but retaining a distinct Middle Eastern feel. The basic plan consists of a rectangular warren of tall houses, with the outer row doubling as the town's perimeter fortification, and breached by a limited number of arched gateways.

The mastic villages

ARMÓLIA, 20km from town, is the smallest and least imposing of the mastic villages; its main virtue is its pottery industry. **PYRGÍ**, 5km further south, is the most colourful of these communities, its houses elaborately embossed with *xystá*, geometric patterns cut into whitewash to reveal a layer of black volcanic sand underneath; strings of sun-drying tomatoes add a further splash of colour in autumn. On the northeast corner of the central square the twelfth-century Byzantine church of **Áyii Apóstoli** (Tues–Thurs & Sat 10am–1pm), embellished with much later frescoes, is tucked under an arcade. Of late, vast numbers of postcard racks and boutiques have sprung up on every main thoroughfare, detracting somewhat from the atmosphere. In the medieval core you'll find a **bank** (with ATM), a **post office** and an array of cafés and *souvláki* stalls on the central platía. **OLÝMBI**, 7km further west along the bus route serving Armólia and Pyrgí, is one of the less visited mastic villages, but not devoid of interest. The characteristic tower-keep, which at Pyrgí stands half-inhabited away from the modernized main square, here looms bang in the middle of the platía, its ground floor occupied by the community *kafenío* on one side, and a taverna-bar on the other; however, the best **eating** here is found at *Ayioryitiko* by the Káto Pórta, where the menu can encompass game and mushrooms in the right season, otherwise well-executed standards like *melitzánes* imám and various *píttes*.

Sombre, monochrome **MESTÁ**, 4km west of Olýmbi, is considered the finest example of the genre; despite more snack-bars and trinket shops than strictly necessary on the outskirts, Mestá remains just the right side of twee as most people here still work the land. From its main square, dominated by the **church of the Taxiárhis** (the largest on the island), a bewildering maze of cool, shady lanes with anti-seismic buttressing and tunnels, leads off in all directions. Most streets end in blind alleys, except those leading to the six portals; the northeast

△ Street scene, Pyrgí, Híos

one still has its original iron gate. There are half-a-dozen **rooms** in restored traditional dwellings managed by Dhimitris Pipidhis (☎22710 76029; ❸), or apartments through Dhespina Karambela (☎22710 76065 or ask at *O Morias eis ta Mesta* taverna; ❹). Alternatively, three separate premises managed by Anna Floradhi's gift shop (☎ & ℱ22710 76455; ❸) are more modernized. Of the two **tavernas** sharing table-space on the main platía, *Mesaionas* is better value and has the more helpful proprietor (she also has rooms: ☎22710 76494; ❸).

The mastic coast – and the Sykiás Olýmbon cave

The closest good **beaches** to Mestá lie just east of its under used port, Liménas Mestón: **Dhídhyma** (4km away), a double cove with an islet protecting it; **Potámi**, with the namesake stream feeding it; and the least scenic **Ayía Iríni** (8km), which does have a reliable taverna. All of these little bays will catch surf and flotsam when the north wind is up.

From Olýmbi, a paved, six-kilometre road heads to the well-signed **cave of Sykiás Olýmbon** (Easter–Oct Tues–Sun 10am–8pm; admission in groups of 25 or less every 30min; €3), only opened to the public in 2003. For years it was just a small hole in the ground where villagers disposed of their dead animals, but from 1985 on speleologists explored it properly. The cave, with a constant temperature of 18°C, evolved in two phases between 150 million and 50 million years ago, and has a maximum depth of 57m (though tours only visit the top 30m or so). The stalagmite and stalactite formations, with fanciful names like Chinese Forest, Medusa and Organ Pipes, are among the most beautiful in the Mediterranean. Before or after your subterranean tour, you can continue another 1500m on dirt surface to the little cape-top monastery of **Ayía Dhýnami** and two sheltered coves adjacent for a swim: the nearer sandy, the remoter gravel and sand.

Pyrgí village is closest to the two major beach resorts in this corner of the island. The nearest, 6km distant, is **EMBORIÓS**, an almost landlocked harbour with four passable **tavernas**; *Porto Emborios* has the edge with almost year-round operation, fair prices, home-made desserts and seafood like *atherína*-and-onion fry-up or small wild sea bass. British-excavated **ancient Emboreios** on the hill to the northeast and well signposted on the road in, was rehabilitated as an "archeological park" in 2004 – and is closed at the moment for lack of funds; Currently more accessible is the cruciform **early Christian baptistry**, signposted in a field just in from the water; it's protected by a later, round structure (locked but you can see everything through the grating).

For swimming, follow the road to its end at an oversubscribed car park and the beach of **Mávros Yialós** (Mávra Vólia), then continue by flagstoned walkway over the headland to the more dramatic pebble strand (part nudist) of purple-grey volcanic stones, **Fóki**, twice as long and backed by impressive cliffs. If you want sand (and amenities) you'll have to go to **KÓMI**, 3km northeast, also accessible from Armólia via Kalamotí; there are just a few **tavernas** (most reliably open of these are *Bella Mare* and *Nostalgia*, both laying on sunbeds to patrons), café-bars and seasonal apartments behind the pedestrianized beachfront.

Central Híos

The portion of Híos extending west and southwest from Híos Town matches the south in terms of interesting monuments, and good roads make touring under your own power an easy matter. There are also several beaches on the far shore of the island which, though not necessarily the best on Híos, are fine for a dip at the middle or end of the day.

The Kámbos

The **Kámbos**, a vast fertile plain carpeted with citrus groves, extends southwest from Híos Town almost as far as the village of Halkió. The district was originally settled by the Genoese during the fourteenth century, and remained a preserve of the local aristocracy until 1822. Exploring by bicycle or motorbike may be less frustrating than going by car, since the web of narrow, poorly marked lanes sandwiched between high walls guarantees disorientation and frequent backtracking. Behind the walls you catch fleeting glimpses of ornate old mansions built from locally quarried sandstone; courtyards are paved in pebbles or alternating light and dark tiles, and most still contain a pergola-shaded irrigation pond filled by a *mánganos* or donkey-powered waterwheel, used before the age of electric pumps to draw water from wells up to 30m deep.

Many of the sumptuous three-storey dwellings, constructed in a hybrid Italo-Turco-Greek style, have languished derelict since 1881, but an increasing number are being converted for use as private estates or unique **accommodation**. The best and most consistently attended of these are *Mavrokordatiko* (☎22710 32900, ⓦ www.mavrokordatiko.com; B&B; ❺), about 1.5km south of the airport, with enormous heated, wood-panelled rooms, and *Arhondiko Perleas* (☎22710 32217; B&B; ❺), set in a huge citrus grove, with ample breakfasts including organic jams.

Not strictly speaking in Kámbos, but most easily reached from it en route to the *mastihohoriá*, is an outstanding rural Byzantine monument. The thirteenth-century **church of Panayía Krína**, isolated amidst orchards and woods, is well worth the challenge of negotiating a maze of paved but poorly marked lanes beyond Vavýli village, 9km from town. It's closed indefinitely for snail's-pace restoration, but a peek through the apse window will give you a fair idea of the intricately frescoed interior, sufficiently lit by a twelve-windowed drum. All of the late-medieval frescoes, as well as some Byzantine work underneath, have been removed, and are sometimes displayed in Híos Town's Giustiniani Museums (see p.908). The alternating brick and stonework of the exterior alone justifies the trip here, though architectural harmony is marred by the later addition of a clumsy lantern over the narthex, and the visibly unsound structure is kept from collapse by cable-binding at the roofline.

Néa Moní

Almost exactly in the middle of the island, the **monastery of Néa Moní** was founded by the Byzantine Emperor Constantine Monomahos ("The Dueller") IX in 1042 on the spot where a wonder-working icon had been discovered. It ranks among the most beautiful and important monuments on any of the Greek islands; the mosaics, together with those of Dháfni and Ósios Loukás on the mainland, are among the finest surviving art of their age in Greece, and the setting – high up in still partly forested mountains 15km west of the port – is no less memorable.

Once a powerful and independent community of six hundred monks, Néa Moní was pillaged in 1822 and most of its residents (including 3500 civilians sheltering here) put to the sword. Since then many of its outbuildings have languished in ruins, though a recent EU grant has prompted massive restoration work, with the exterior cocooned in scaffolding until further notice. The 1881 tremor caused comprehensive damage, while exactly a century later a forest fire threatened to engulf the place until the resident icon was paraded along the perimeter wall, miraculously repelling the flames. Today the monastery, with its giant refectory and vaulted water cisterns, is inhabited by just a couple of lay workers.

Bus excursions formerly provided by the KTEL have been suspended since the main focus of interest, the *katholikón*, is closed to the public until at least late 2007, whilst much-needed restoration proceeds; neither is it worth shelling out specially for a taxi at the moment, but do stop in briefly if touring under your own power.

Just inside the main gate (daily 8am–1pm & 4–8pm, afternoon hours 5–8pm in summer) stands a **chapel/ossuary** containing some of the bones of those who met their death here in 1822; axe-clefts in children's skulls attest to the savagery of the attackers. The **katholikón**, with the cupola resting on an octagonal drum, is of a design seen elsewhere only in Cyprus; the frescoes in the exonarthex are badly damaged by holes allegedly left by Turkish bullets, but the **mosaics** are another matter. The narthex contains portrayals of the various saints of Híos sandwiched between *Christ Washing the Disciples' Feet* and the *Betrayal*, in which Judas's kiss has unfortunately been obliterated, but Peter is clearly visible lopping off the ear of the high priest's servant. In the dome of the sanctuary, which once contained a complete life cycle of Christ, only the *Baptism*, part of the *Crucifixion*, the *Descent from the Cross*, the *Resurrection* and the evangelists Mark and John survived the earthquake.

The west coast

Some 5km west of Néa Moní sits **AVGÓNYMA**, a cluster of dwellings on a knoll overlooking the coast; the name means "Clutch of Eggs", an apt description when it's viewed from the ridge above. Since the 1980s, the place has been almost totally restored as a summer haven by descendants of the original villagers, though the permanent population is just seven. A returned Greek-American family runs a reasonable, simple-fare **taverna**, O Pyrgos (open all year), in an arcaded mansion on the main square. The classiest **accommodation** option here is *Spitakia*, a cluster of small restored houses for up to five people (☎22710 20513 or 22710 81200, ⊛www.spitakia.gr; ❹), though *O Pyrgos* restaurant also keeps more modernized units in the village (☎22710 42175; ❸).

A paved side road continues another 4km north to **ANÁVATOS**, whose empty, dun-coloured dwellings, soaring above pistachio orchards, are almost indistinguishable from the 300-metre-high bluff on which they're built. During the 1822 insurrection, some four hundred inhabitants and refugees threw themselves over this cliff rather than surrender to the besieging Ottomans, and it's still a preferred suicide leap. Anávatos can now only muster two permanent inhabitants, and given a lack of accommodation, one mediocre snack bar, plus an eerie, traumatized atmosphere, it's no place to be stranded at dusk.

West of Avgónyma, the main road descends 6km to the sea in well-graded loops. Turning right (north) at the junction leads first to the beach at **Elínda**, alluring from afar but rocky and murky up close; it's better to continue towards more secluded, mixed sand-and-gravel coves to either side of Metóhi – best of these are **Tigáni** and **Makriá Ámmos**, the latter nudist. **SIDHIROÚNDA**, the only village hereabouts (with a competent summer **taverna**), enjoys a spectacular hilltop setting overlooking the sea.

All along this coast, as far southwest as Liménas Mestón, are round **watchtowers** erected by the Genoese to look out for pirates – the second swimmable cove you reach after turning left from the junction bears the name **Kastélla** (officially Trahíli), again mixed sand and gravel. The first cove, more protected and popular, is **Xeropótamos**. A sparse weekday-only bus service resumes 9km south of the junction at **LITHÍ**, a friendly village perched on forested ledge overlooking the sea. There are tavernas and *kafenía* in the older, central core, but most visitors head 2km downhill to **Paralía Lithíou**, a popular weekend target of Hiot townies for the sake of its large but hard-packed, windswept beach. The better of two adjacent, pricey fish **tavernas** here is *Ta Tria Adherfia*.

Some 5km south of Lithí, the valley-bottom village of **VÉSSA** is an unsung gem, more open and less casbah-like than Mestá or Pyrgí, but still homogeneous.

Its honey-coloured buildings are arrayed in a vast grid punctuated by numerous belfries; there's a nameless *kafenío* installed on the ground floor of the tower-mansion on the main through road, while across the square *Kostas* (aka *Froso's*) does excellent *yíros*, *loukániko* and *souvláki*.

Northern Híos

Northern Híos never really recovered from the 1822 massacre, and between Pityós and Volissós the desolation left by 1980s fires will further dampen inquisitive spirits. Since the early 1900s the villages have been left all but deserted much of the year, which means correspondingly sparse bus services. About one-third of the former population lives in Híos Town, returning only during major festivals or to tend smallholdings; others, based in Athens or the US, visit their ancestral homes for just a few midsummer weeks.

The road to Kardhámyla

Blue urban buses run north from Híos Town up to **VRONDÁDHOS**, an elongated coastal suburb that's a favourite residence of the island's many seafarers. Homer is reputed to have lived and taught here, and in the terraced parkland just above the little fishing port and pebble beach you can visit his purported lectern, more probably an ancient altar of Cybele. Accordingly many of the buses heading out here are labelled DARJAKOPESQA, "the Teacher's Rock".

Some 14km out of town, the tiny bayside hamlet of **PANDOUKIÓS** can muster an excellent if pricey waterside **taverna**, the *Kourtesis*, where lobster can sometimes be had. But **LANGÁDHA**, 2.5km beyond, is probably the first point on the eastern coast road where you'd be tempted to stop, though there is no proper beach nearby. Set at the mouth of a deep valley, this attractive little harbour settlement looks across its bay to a pine grove, and beyond to Turkey. Night-time visitors come for the sustaining seafood at two adjacent **tavernas** on the quay: *Tou Kopelou*, better known as *Stelios'*, and second-choice *Paradhisos*.

Just beyond Langádha an important side road leads 5km up and inland to **PITYÓS**, an oasis in a mountain pass presided over by a round castle; people come here from some distance to **eat** at *Makellos* on the southwest edge of the village, a shrine of local cuisine (late June to early Sept daily lunch/dinner; rest of year Fri–Sun evenings only). Continuing 4km more brings you to a junction allowing quick access to the west of the island and the Volissós area (see opposite).

Kardhámyla and around

Most traffic proceeds to **ÁNO KARDHÁMYLA** and **KÁTO KARD-HÁMYLA**, the latter 37km out of the main town. Positioned at opposite edges of a fertile plain rimmed by mountains, they initially come as welcome relief from Homer's crags. Káto, better known as **MÁRMARO**, is larger – indeed, the island's second town – with a bank (no ATM), post office and filling station. However, there is little to attract a casual visitor other than some Neoclassical architecture; the port, mercilessly exposed to the *meltémi*, is strictly business-like, and there are few tourist facilities. A sterling exception is *Hotel Kardamyla* (☎22720 23353, ℻22720 23354; ❺ Aug, ❹ otherwise), co-managed with Híos Town's *Hotel Kyma*, offering spacious, fan-equipped **rooms** and a few suites. It has the bay's only pebble beach, and the in-house restaurant is a reliable source of lunch (July & Aug) if you're touring. Worthwhile independent **tavernas** include *Ouzeri Barba Yiannis* (run by Irini Tsirigou; all year), beside the port authority, or *Iy Vlyhadha* (summer only), facing the bay of the same name west over the headland.

For better swimming head west 5km to **Nagós**, a gravel-shore bay at the foot of an oasis, which is where the summertime bus line terminates. Lush greenery is nourished by active springs up at a bend in the road, enclosed in a sort of grotto overhung by tall cliffs. The place name is a corruption of *naos*, after a large Poseidon temple that once stood near the springs, but centuries of orchard-tending, antiquities-pilfering and organized excavations after 1912 mean that nothing remains visible. Down at the shore the swimming is good, if a bit chilly; there are two mediocre **tavernas** (there's a better one inland, by the spring) and a few **rooms** to rent. Your only chance of relative solitude in July or August lies 1km west at **Yióssonas**; this is a much longer beach, but less sheltered, rockier and with no facilities.

Volissós and around

VOLISSÓS, 42km from Híos Town by the most direct road (but just 44km by the much easier route via Avgónyma), was once the market town for a dozen remote hill villages beyond. Its old stone houses still curl appealingly beneath the crumbling hilltop Byzantine fort, whose towers were improved by the Genoese. Volissós can seem depressing at first, with the bulk of its 250 mostly elderly permanent inhabitants living in newer buildings around the main square, but opinions improve with longer acquaintance. This backwater ethos may not last; the upper quarters are in the grip of a restoration mania, most of it done in admirable taste, with ruins changing hands for stratospheric prices.

Grouped around the platía you'll find a **post office**, a **bank** ATM and three mediocre **tavernas**. A pair of filling stations operate 2.5km out of town, the only one hereabouts; if reliant on public transport, you should plan on overnighting since the bus only ventures out here on Sundays on a day-trip basis, plus two weekly workdays in the early afternoon (unless you care to travel at 4.30am). This should cause no dismay, since the area has the best beaches and some of the more interesting **accommodation** on Híos. The most reasonable and longest established of a few restoration projects are sixteen old houses, mostly in Pýrgos district, available through ⚲ *Volissos Travel* (☎22740 21413 or 693 69 75 470, ⓦwww.volissostravel.gr; May–Sept; ◐). Units usually accommodate two people – all have terraces, fully equipped kitchens, air conditioning and features such as tree trunks upholding sleeping lofts, reflecting proprietress Stella's past as a sculptor. She often has spring/autumn specials including a hire car.

LIMNIÁ (sometimes Limiá), the port of Volissós, lies 2km south though ferry/*kaïki* service from here to Psará is suspended. The most consistent **taverna** here is *O Zikos* (open all year) at the far end of the quay, with good grills and a superb house salad featuring sun-dried tomatoes, plus occasional seafood. At Limniá you're not far from the fabled beaches either. A 1.5-kilometre drive or walk southeast over the headland brings you to **Mánagros**, a seemingly endless sand-and-pebble beach, though a major resort project here is being debated. More intimate, sandy **Lefkáthia** lies just a ten-minute stroll along the cement drive threading over the headland north of the harbour; amenities are limited to a seasonal snack shack on the sand, and Ioannis Zorbas's apartments (☎22740 21436, Ⓕ22740 21720; ◐), beautifully set in a garden where the concrete track joins an asphalt road down from Volissós. This is bound for **Límnos** (not to be confused with Limniá), the next protected cove, 400m east of Lefkáthia, where *Taverna Iy Limnos* is the better of two tavernas, with fish grills and specials like *kokorás krasáto* (coq au vin), and the spruce *Latini Apartments* (☎22740 21461, ⓕ22740 21871; ❹) are graced with multiple stone terraces.

Ayía Markélla, 5km further northwest of Límnos, stars in many local postcards: it's a long, stunning beach fronting the **monastery** of Híos's patron saint (festival July 22), the latter not especially interesting or useful for outsiders, since its cells are reserved for Greek pilgrims. In an interesting variation on the expulsion of the money changers from the temple, only religious souvenirs are allowed to be sold in the holy precincts, while all manner of plastic junk is displayed just outside.

The dirt road past the monastery grounds is passable by any vehicle, with care, and emerges up on the paved road running high above the northwest coast. Turn left and proceed to the remote village of **ÁYIO GÁLA**, whose claim to fame is a **grotto-church** complex, built into a stream-lapped palisade at the bottom of the village. Signs ("Panayía Ayiogaloúsena") point to a lane crossing the water, but for access you'll need to find the key-keeper (ask at the central *kafenío*), and descend via a flight of stairs starting beside a eucalyptus tree. Of the two churches inside the cavern – whose nether depths are being developed as a tourist attraction, so admission will become more formalized – the larger one near the mouth of the grotto dates from the fifteenth century but seems newer owing to a 1993 external renovation. Inside, however, a fantastically intricate *témblon* vies for your attention with a tinier, older chapel, built entirely within the rear of the cavern. Its frescoes are badly smudged, except for a wonderfully mysterious and mournful Virgin, surely the saddest in Christendom, holding a knowing Child.

Satellite islands: Psará and Inoússes

There's a single settlement, with beaches and an isolated rural monastery, on both of Híos's satellite isles, but each is surprisingly different from the other, and of course from their large neighbour. **Inoússes**, the nearer and smaller islet, has a daily *kaïki* service from Híos Town in season; **Psará** has less regular services subject to weather conditions (in theory most days from Híos Town, plus a few weekly subsidized-line ferries), and is too remote to be done justice on a day-trip.

Psará

The birthplace of revolutionary war hero Admiral Kanaris, **Psará** devoted its merchant fleets – the third largest in 1820s Greece – to the cause of independence, and paid dearly for it. Vexed beyond endurance, the Turks landed overwhelming forces in 1824 to stamp out this nest of resistance. Perhaps 3000 of the 30,000 inhabitants escaped in small boats, which were rescued by a French fleet, but the majority retreated to a hilltop powder magazine and blew it (and themselves) up rather than surrender. The nationalist poet Dhionysios Solomos immortalized the incident in famous stanzas:

On the Black Ridge of Psará,
Glory walks alone.
She meditates on her heroes
And wears in her hair a wreath
Made from a few dry weeds
Left on the barren ground.

Today, it's a sad, stark place fully living up to its name ("the mottled things" in Greek), and never really recovered from the holocaust. The Turks burned whatever houses and vegetation the blast had missed, and the official population now barely exceeds four hundred. The only positive recent development was a 1980s revitalization project instigated by a French-Greek descendant of Kanaris and a Greek team. The port was improved, mains electricity and pure water provided, a secondary school opened, and cultural links between France and the island established, though this has not been reflected in increased tourist numbers.

Arrival can be something of an ordeal; the regular small ferry from Híos Town can take up to four hours to cover the 57 nautical miles of generally rough sea. A few times weekly, large ferries on the subsidized Lávrio–Sígri (Lésvos)–Límnos line appear at odd hours; there is currently no *kaïki* service from Límnia.

Since few buildings in the east-facing harbour community predate the twentieth century, it's a strange hotchpotch of ecclesiastical and secular architecture that greets the eye on disembarking. There's a distinctly southern feel, more like the Dodecanese or the Cyclades, and some peculiar churches, of which no two are alike in style.

For **staying overnight**, there's a choice between a handful of fairly basic rooms and three more professional outfits: *Psara Studios* (☎22740 61233; ❹) and *Apartments Restalia* (☎22740 61201, ℻22740 61000; ❹ Aug, ❷–❸ otherwise), both a bit stark but with balconies and kitchens, or the EOT *xenónas* (☎22740 61293; ❹) in a restored prison. A few **tavernas**, a **post office**, bakery and shop complete the list of amenities; there's no full-service bank.

Psará's **beaches** are decent, improving the further northeast you walk from the port. You quickly pass Káto Yialós, Katsoúni and Lazarétto with its off-putting power station, before reaching **Lákka** ("narrow ravine"), fifteen minutes along, apparently named after its grooved rock formations in which you may have to shelter – much of this coast is windswept, with a heavy swell offshore. **Límnos**, 25 minutes from the port along the coastal path, is big and attractive, but there's no reliable taverna here, or indeed at any of the beaches. The only other thing to do on Psará is to walk north across the island – the old track there has been paved – to the **monastery of the Kímisis (Assumption)**; uninhabited since the 1970s, this comes to life only in the first week of August, when its revered icon is carried in ceremonial procession to town and back on the eve of August 5.

Inoússes

Inoússes has a permanent population of about three hundred – less than half its prewar figure – and a very different history from Psará. For generations this medium-sized islet, first settled around 1750 by Hiot shepherds, has provided the Aegean with many of her wealthiest shipping families: various members of the Livanos, Lemos and Pateras clans (with every street or square named after the last-named family) were born here. This helps explain the large villas and visiting summer yachts in an otherwise sleepy Greek backwater – as well as a **maritime museum** (daily 10am–1pm; €1.50) near the quay, endowed by various shipping magnates. At the west end of the quay, the bigwigs have also funded a large nautical academy, which trains future members of the merchant navy.

On Sundays in season you can make an inexpensive **day-trip** to Inoússes from Híos with the locals' ferry *Inousses II*; on most other days of the week this arrives at 3pm, returning early the next morning. Otherwise, during the tourist season you must participate in the pricier excursions offered from Híos, with return tickets running more than double the cost of the regular ferry.

Two church-tipped islets, each privately owned, guard the unusually well-protected harbour; the **town** of Inoússes is surprisingly large, draped over hillsides enclosing a ravine. Despite a wealthy reputation, its appearance is unpretentious, the houses displaying a mix of vernacular and modest Neoclassical style. There is just one, fairly comfortable, **hotel**, the recently renovated *Thalassoporos* (☎22720 55475; ❹), on the main easterly hillside lane, but no licensed *dhomátia*. Aside from the restaurant in the hotel, **eating out** is similarly limited; the most reliable option is the simple *Taverna Pateronisso*, conspicuous at the base of the disembarkation jetty, though every season a few simple ouzerís off towards the nautical academy try their luck – the most durable of these is *O Glaros*. Café-bars such as *Naftikos Omilos*, *Karnayio* and (inland uphill) *Trigono* provide a semblance of **nightlife**. Otherwise, be prepared to patronize one of the three shops (one on the waterfront, two up the hill). Beside the museum you'll find a **post office** and a **bank**.

The rest of this tranquil island, at least the southern slope, is surprisingly green and well tended; there are no springs, so water comes from a mix of fresh and brackish wells, as well as a reservoir. The sea is extremely clean and calm on the sheltered southerly shore; among its beaches, choose from **Zepága**, **Biláli** or **Kástro**, respectively five, twenty and thirty minutes' walk west of the port. More secluded **Fourkeró** (Farkeró in dialect) lies 25 minutes east: first along a cement drive ending at a seaside chapel, then by path past pine groves and over a ridge. As on Psará, there are no reliable facilities at any of the beaches.

At the end of the westerly road stands the somewhat macabre convent of **Evangelismoú**, endowed by a branch of the Pateras family. Inside reposes the mummified body of the lately canonized daughter, Irini, whose prayers to die in place of her terminally ill father Panagos were answered early in the 1960s; he's entombed here also, having outlived Irini by some years. The abbess, presiding over about twenty nuns, is none other than the widowed Mrs Pateras; only women are admitted, and casual visits are not encouraged.

Lésvos (Mytilíni)

Lésvos, the third-largest Greek island after Crete and Évvia, is not only the birthplace of Sappho, but also of Aesop, Arion and – more recently – the Greek primitive artist Theophilos, the Nobel laureate poet Odysseus Elytis and the novelist Stratis Myrivilis. Despite these artistic associations, Lésvos may not at first strike the visitor as particularly beautiful or interesting; much of the landscape is rocky, volcanic terrain, dotted with thermal springs and varying between vast grain fields, salt pans or even near-desert. But there are also oak and pine forests as well as endless olive groves, some of these over five hundred years old. With its balmy climate and suggestive contours, the island tends to grow on you with prolonged acquaintance.

Lovers of medieval and Ottoman **architecture** certainly won't be disappointed. Castles survive at the main town of Mytilíni, at Mólyvos, Eressós, Sígri and near Ándissa; most of these date from the late fourteenth century, when Lésvos was given as a dowry to a Genoese prince of the Gattilusi clan following his marriage to the sister of one of the last Byzantine emperors. Apart from Crete and Évvia, Lésvos was the only Greek island where Turks settled significantly in rural villages (they usually stuck to the safety of towns), which explains the odd Ottoman bridge, box-like mosque or crumbling minaret often found in the middle of nowhere. Again unusually for the Aegean islands,

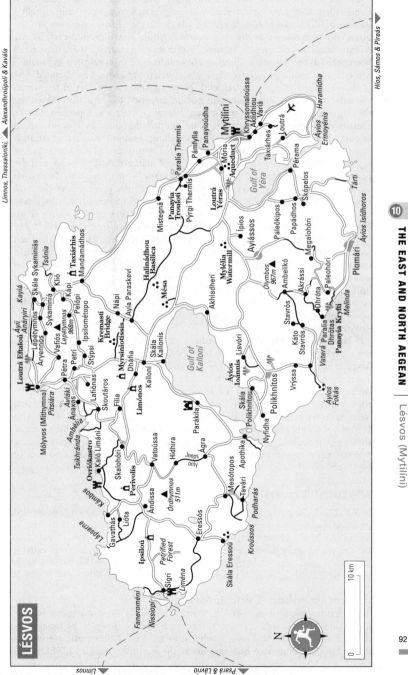

LÉSVOS

Limnos, Thessaloníki, ▲ Alexandhroúpoli & Kavála

Híos, Sámos & Pireás ▶

Psará & Lávrio ▶

Límnos ▶

Límnos

Mólyvos (Míthymna)
Pitsiára
Loutrá Eftaloú Áyii
Anáyiri
Lepétymnos
Árvennos
Tsónia
Kayiá
Skála Sykaminiás
Klió
Taxiárhis
Mandamádhos

Pétra
Pelópi
Kápi
Sykaminiá
Vafiós
Lepétymnos
968m
Ipsilométopo

Avláki
Ánaxos
Petrí
Krémasti
Bridge
Nápi
Ayía Paraskeví

Tsikhránda
Ambélia
Lafiónas
Stýpsi
Dháfia
Myrsiniótissa
Pérama

Orriókastro
Kaló Limáni
Skoútaros
Filia
Kalloní
Skála
Kallonís

Kémbos
Skalohóri
Limónos

Lápsarma
Gavathás
Lióta
Vatoússa
Hidhíra
Agra
Jeeps
only
Paráklia

Faneroméni
Nissiópi
Ándissa
Órdhymnos
511m
Mesótopos
Apothíka

Ipsiloú
Petrified
Forest
Eressós
Tavári
Podharás

Skála Eressoú
Sígri
Liména
Kr400ssós
Nyfídha

Mistegná
Panayía
Troulotí
Paralía Thermís
Pámfylla
Panayíoúdha
Mytilíni
Khryssomaloússa
Akidhíou
Variá
Móría
Aqueduct
Loutrá
Yéras
Taxiárhes
Loutrá
Áyios
Ermoyénis
Haramídha

Halinádhou
Basilica
Mésa
Pyrgí Thermís
Gulf of
Yéra
Skópelos
Papádhos
Megalohóri
Paleohóri
Tárti
Áyios Isídhoros

Myélia
Watermill
Ípios
Ayiássos
Paleókipos
Akrássi
Dhróta
Panayía Kryfti
Plomári
Melínda

Akhladherí
Ólymbos
967m
Ambelikó
Dhrótas
Vaterá Paralía
Dhrótas

Ayios
Ioánnis
Lisvóri
Stavrós
Káto
Stavrós
Vrýssa
Áyios
Fokás

Mésa
Gulf of
Kallóni
Skála
Polikhnítou
Polikhnítos

N

0   10 km

Ottoman reforms of the eighteenth century encouraged the emergence of a Greek Orthodox land- and industry-owning aristocracy, who built rambling mansions and tower-houses, a few of which survive. More common are the bourgeois townhouses of the worthies in Mytilíni town, erected early in the twentieth century to French Second Empire models; many of these have often been pressed into service as government buildings or even restored as hotels.

Social and economic idiosyncrasies persist: anyone who has attended one of the extended village *paniyíria*, with hours of music and tables in the streets groaning with food and drink, will not be surprised to learn that Lésvos has the highest alcoholism rate in Greece. Breeding livestock, especially horses, remains disproportionately important, and traffic jams caused by mounts instead of parked cars are not unheard of – signs reading "Forbidden to Tether Animals Here" are still common, as are herds of apparently unattended donkeys wandering about. Much of the acreage in olives is still inaccessible to vehicles, and the harvest can only be hauled out by those donkeys – who are duly loaded en masse onto the back of trucks to be transported to the point where the road fizzles out. Organic production has been embraced enthusiastically as a way of making Lésvos agricultural products more competitive – *Violoyikó Ktíma* (Organic Plot) or *Violoyikí Kaliéryia* (Organic Cultivation) signs abound.

Historically, the olive plantations, ouzo distilleries, animal husbandry and fishing industry supported those who chose not to emigrate, but with these enterprises relatively stagnant, tourism has made visible inroads. However, it still accounts for under ten percent of the local economy: there are few large hotels outside the capital, Skála Kalloní or Mólyvos. Visitor numbers have in fact dipped since 1996, the result of stalled plans to expand the airport, unrealistic hotel pricing and the dropping of the island from several tour operators' programmes.

Public **buses** tend to observe schedules for the benefit of villagers coming to town on errands, not day-tripping tourists. Carrying out such excursions from Mytilíni is next to impossible anyway, owing to the size of the island – about 70km by 45km at its widest points – and a lingering handful of appalling roads (most others have been improved, along with their signposting). Moreover, the topography is complicated by the two deeply indented gulfs of Kalloní and Yéra, with no bridges across their mouths, which means that going from A to B involves an obligatory change of bus at either Mytilíni, on the east shore, or the town of Kalloní, in the middle of the island. It's best to decide on a base and stay there for a few days, exploring its immediate surroundings on foot or by rented vehicle.

Mytilíni Town

MYTILÍNI, the port and capital, sprawls between and around two bays divided by a fortified promontory, and in Greek fashion often doubles as the name of the island. Many visitors are put off by the combination of urban bustle and (in the traditionally humbler northern districts) slight seediness, and contrive to leave as soon as possible; the town returns the compliment by being a fairly impractical and occasionally expensive place to base yourself.

Arrival, transport and information

The **airport** has a single ATM in arrivals as well as three car rental booths. There's no bus link, so a taxi for the 7km into Mytilíni Town is the usual shuttle method; Olympic Airways is southwest of the main harbour at Kavétsou 44. As on Híos, there are two **bus terminals**: the *iperastykó* (standard KTEL) buses

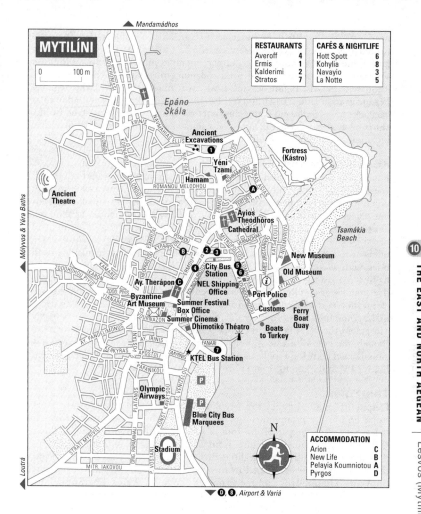

▲ *Mandamádhos*

MYTILÍNI

0   100 m

RESTAURANTS		CAFÉS & NIGHTLIFE	
Averoff	4	Hott Spott	6
Ermis	1	Kohylia	8
Kalderimi	2	Navayio	3
Stratos	7	La Notte	5

Epáno Skála

Ancient Excavations ❶

Yéni Tzamí

Hamam

Fortress (Kástro)

◀ *Mólyvos & Yéra Baths*

Ancient Theatre

Ayios Theodhóros Cathedral

Tsamákia Beach

New Museum

City Bus Station

Old Museum

Ay. Therápon

NEL Shipping Office

Port Police

Byzantine Art Museum

Summer Festival Box Office

Customs

Summer Cinema

Ferry Boat Quay

Dhimotikó Théatro

Boats to Turkey

◀ *Loutrá*

KTEL Bus Station ❼

Olympic Airways

Blue City Bus Marquees

Stadium

N

ACCOMMODATION	
Arion	C
New Life	B
Pelayia Koumniotou	A
Pyrgos	D

▼ ❶, ❽, *Airport & Variá*

leave from a small station near Platía Konstandinopóleos at the southern end of the harbour, while the *astykó* (blue bus) service departs from a marquee at the top of the harbour. If you're driving, use the enormous free public **car park** a few blocks south of the KTEL, or the oval plaza near the new archeological museum – there are no other easily available spaces in the centre. If you're intent on getting over to Ayvalık in Turkey, you've a choice of two boats (Jale or Mytilini); book through the agency at Koundouriótou 78 (☎22510 46668) or Dimakis Tours at Koundouriótou 73 (☎22510 27865). GA ferries is handled by Picolo Travel at no. 73a (☎22510 27000), while Saos Ferries and LANE are handled by Pan Tours at no. 87 (☎22510 46595). NEL Ferries has a dedicated agency at Koundouriótou 47 (☎22510 28480), though in fact nearly everyone sells their tickets.

    Car rental is best arranged through reputable major or local-chain franchises like Payless/Auto Moto at Koundouriótou 49 (☎22510 43555, ✉automoto@otenet. gr), Budget at no. 51 (☎22510 29600, ✉budget@lesvosholidays.com), Just at no. 53 (℡22510 43080), Hertz at no. 87 (℡22510 37355) or Best at no. 89 (℡22510 37337, ⓦwww.best-rentacar.com) – though it can be cheaper to rent at the resort of your choice. Other amenities include the **post office** on Vournázon, behind the central park, and numerous **banks** along Koundouriótou with ATMs. Before leaving town, you might visit the **EOT** regional headquarters at James Aristárhou 6 (Mon–Fri 8am–2.30pm) to get hold of their excellent town and island maps, plus other brochures, or the Newsstand **bookshop** on Kavétsou near Olympic for a limited selection of English literature, including a few Rough Guides.

Accommodation

Finding **accommodation** can be initially daunting: the waterfront hotels are noisy and exorbitantly priced. If you need to stay, it's preferable to hunt down better-value rooms in the backstreets, with supply usually exceeding demand. The friendly if basic rooms of Pelayia Koumniotou at Yeoryíou Tertséti 6 (℡22510 20643; ❷) are partly air-conditioned. *New Life* at the end of Olýmbou, a cul-de-sac off Ermoú (℡22510 42650 or 693 22 79 057; ❸), offers wood-floored, en-suite rooms in an old mansion, or similarly priced ones with wood or mosaic floor, but with bizarre modern murals in the halls, at co-managed *Arion* down the street at Aríonos 4. The most distinctive hotel is pricey *Pyrgos*, Eleftheríou Venizélou 49 (℡22510 25069, ⓦwww.pyrgoshotel.gr; ❼), a converted mansion with utterly over-the-top kitsch decor in the communal areas. However, the rooms – most with a balcony – are perfectly acceptable; the best ones are the three round units in the tower. If you've a car, though, the best local base is probably the ⚓ *Votsala* (℡22510 71231, ⓦwww.votsalahotel.com; ❹), a sophisticated beachfront hotel with well-tended gardens but no TV in the rooms, 13km north in Paralía Thermís.

The Town

Despite its logistical difficulties, Mytilíni offers enough to justify a few hours' stopover. On the promontory sits the Byzantine-Genoese-Ottoman **fortress** (May–Sept Tues–Sun 8.30am–7pm; Oct–April Tues–Sun 8.30am–2.30pm; €2), comprising ruined structures from all these eras and an Ottoman inscription above a Byzantine double-headed eagle at the south gate. Further inland, the town skyline is dominated in turn by the Germanic-Gothic belfry spire of **Áyios Theodhóros** and the mammary dome of **Áyios Therápon**, both expressions of the post-Baroque taste of the nineteenth-century Ottoman Greek bourgeoisie. They stand more or less at opposite ends of the bazaar, whose main street, Ermoú, links the town centre with the little-used north harbour of Epáno Skála. On its way there Ermoú passes several expensive and rather picked-over antique shops near the roofless, derelict **Yéni Tzamí** at the heart of the old Muslim quarter, just a few steps east of a superb Turkish **hamam**, restored to its former glory but now locked unless a special exhibit is being held. Between Ermoú and the castle lies a maze of atmospheric lanes lined with grandiose belle époque mansions and elderly vernacular houses, though most of the ornate townhouses are to be found in the southerly districts of Sourádha and Kióski, on the way to the airport.

Mytilíni's excellent **archeological collection** is housed in **two separate galleries** (May–Sept Tues–Sun 8am–7.30pm; Oct–April Tues–Sun 8.30am–3pm; €3), a few hundred metres apart. The newer, upper museum, at the base of 8-Noemvríou, is devoted to finds from wealthy Roman Mytilene, in particular three rooms of well-displayed mosaics from second/third-century AD villas – highlights are a crude but engaging scene of Orpheus charming all manner of beasts, and two fishermen surrounded by clearly recognizable (and edible) sea creatures. Earlier eras are represented in the older wing (same hours as Roman wing, same ticket admits), located in a former mansion just behind the ferry dock. The ground floor has Neolithic finds from Áyios Vartholoméos cave and Bronze Age Thermí, but the star, late-Classical exhibits upstairs include minutely detailed terracotta figurines: a pair of acrobats, two *kourotrophoi* figures (goddesses suckling infants, predecessors of all Byzantine Galaktotrofoússa icons), children playing with a ball or dogs, and Aphrodite riding a dolphin. A specially built annexe at the rear contains stone-cut inscriptions of various edicts and treaties, plus a Roman sculpture of a drunken satyr asleep on a wineskin.

There's also a worthwhile **Byzantine Art Museum** (Mon–Sat 9am–1pm; €2) just behind Áyios Therápon, containing various icons rescued from rural churches, plus a canvas of the Assumption by Theophilos (see p.overleaf).

Eating, drinking and nightlife

The obvious, if blatantly touristy, venue for a seafood blowout is the cluster of **tavernas** on the southerly quay known as Fanári; *Stratos* at the far end is marginally the best, and doesn't tout aggressively. For *mayireftá* (including early-morning *patsás* or tripe soup), look no further than the *Averoff* on the west quay, popular for lunch before an afternoon ferry departure. Finally, there are two traditional ouzerís at opposite ends of the bazaar. *Kalderimi* (closed Sun) occupies two premises around Thássou 2, with seating under the shade of vines; the fare is large-portioned if a bit plainly presented. For a bit less outlay (and with friendlier service), you might be better off at the *Ermis* (open daily), best of a few ouzerís up at Epáno Skála; a 1999 refit didn't much affect its century-old decor (panelled ceiling, giant mirrors, faded oil paintings), or its claimed two centuries of purveying titbits to a jolly, mixed crowd in the pleasant courtyard.

For **snacks and drinks**, *Navayio* at the head of the harbour is the acknowledged favourite, with an unbeatable combo **breakfast** for under a fiver. With an important university in residence, Mytilíni can offer decent **nightlife and entertainment**, especially along the northeast quay, which the trendy contingent has claimed as its own. Here, all in a row, you'll find *La Notte* (a late-night dance club) and the durable *Hott Spott*, interspersed with other bars which change yearly. Out by the airport, the *Kohilia* beach-club has live and DJ'd happenings in summer. Formal live events constitute the Lesviakó Kalokéri, staged in the castle or the waterfront Dhimotikó Théatro during July and August. The summer cinema Pallas is between the post office and the park on Vournázon; there's also a winter cinema, the Arion, near the KTEL station.

Around Mytilíni

Beyond the airport and Krátigos village, the paved road loops around to **Haramídha**, 14km from town and the closest decent (pebble) beach (the fee-entry town "beach" at Tsamákia is mediocre); the eastern bay has a few **tavernas**, best of these by some way being Grioules. The double cove at **Áyios Ermoyénis**, 3km west and more directly accessible from Mytilíni via Loutrá village, is more scenic and sandy, with a single taverna, but small and crowded at weekends. For other pleasant immersions near Mytilíni, make for **Loutrá Yéras**, 8km along the main road to Kallóni. These public baths (daily: June–Sept 8am–7pm; April–May & Oct 8am–6pm; Nov–March 9am–5pm; €2.50) are just the thing if you've spent a sleepless night on a ferry, with ornate spouts that feed 38°C water to marble-lined pools in vaulted chambers; there are separate facilities for men and women.

The Variá museums

The most rewarding single targets near Mytilíni are a pair of museums at **VARIÁ**, 5km south of town (hourly buses). The **Theophilos Museum** (May–Sept Tues–Sun 9am–2.30pm & 5–8pm; Oct & April 9am–1pm & 4–6pm; Nov–March 9am–2pm; €2 includes key-catalogue) honours the painter, born here in 1873, with four rooms of wonderful, little-known compositions specifically commissioned by his patron Thériade (see below) during the years leading up to Theophilos' death in 1934. A wealth of detail is evident in elegiac scenes of fishing, reaping, olive-picking and baking from the pastoral Lésvos which Theophilos obviously knew best; there are droll touches also, such as a cat slinking off with a fish in *The Fishmongers*. In classical scenes – Sappho and Alkaeos, a landscape series of Egypt, Asia Minor and the Holy Land, and episodes from wars historical and contemporary – Theophilos was on shakier ground. In *Abyssinians Hunting an Italian Horseman*, the subject has clearly been conflated with New World Indians chasing down a conquistador.

The adjacent, imposing **Thériade Museum** (Tues–Sun 9am–2pm & 5–8pm; €2) is the brainchild of another native son, Stratis Eleftheriades (1897–1983). Leaving the island at an early age for Paris, he Gallicized his name to Thériade and went on to become a renowned avant-garde art publisher, convincing some of the leading artists of the twentieth century to participate in his ventures. The displays consist of lithographs, engravings, wood-block prints and watercolours by the likes of Miró, Chagall, Picasso, Matisse, Le Corbusier, Léger, Rouault and Villon, either annotated by the painters themselves or commissioned as illustrations for the works of prominent poets and authors: an astonishing collection for a relatively remote Aegean island.

Southern Lésvos

The southernmost portion of the island is indented by two great inlets, the gulfs of **Kalloní** and **Yéra**, the first curving in a northeasterly direction, the latter northwesterly, creating a fan-shaped peninsula at the heart of which looms 967-metre Mount Ólymbos. Both shallow gulfs are almost landlocked by virtue of very narrow outlets to the open sea, which don't – and probably never will – have bridges spanning them. This is the most verdant and productive olive-oil territory on Lésvos, and the stacks of pressing-mills stab the skyline.

PÉRAMA is one of the larger places on the Gulf of Yéra, and has a regular **kaïki-ferry** service (no cars) linking it with Koundoroudhiá and blue city buses to/from Mytilíni on the far side. Amongst an oddly attractive townscape of disused olive-oil warehouses, Makis the pelican has been resident in the central square since 1980. A more likely reason to show up is to patronize one of the better **taverna-ouzerís** in the region: ✷ *Balouhanas* (all year; lunch and dinner), northernmost of a line of eateries on the front, with a wooden, cane-roofed balcony jutting out over the water. The name's a corruption of *balıkhane* or "fish-market" in Turkish, and seafood is a strong point, whether grilled or made into croquettes, as are regional starters like *giouzlemés* (cheese-stuffed fried crêpe) and own-made desserts.

Plomári and around

Due south of Mount Ólymbos, at the edge of the "fan", **PLOMÁRI** is the only sizeable coastal settlement hereabouts, and indeed the second-largest municipality on Lésvos. It presents an unlikely juxtaposition of scenic appeal and its famous ouzo industry, courtesy of several local distilleries. Despite a resounding lack of good beaches within walking distance, it's besieged in summer by

Scandinavian tourists, but you can usually find a **room** (they are prominently signposted) at the edge of the old, charmingly dilapidated town, or (better) 1km west in **Ammoudhélli** suburb, which has a small pea-gravel beach. Your best bet for an on-spec vacancy is the welcoming ☀ *Pension Lida* above the inland Platía Beniamín (☎ & ⓕ 22520 32507; ❷), a fine restoration inn occupying adjacent old mansions, with seaview balconies for most units. Rustling up a decent meal presents more difficulties; Ammoudhélli can offer *To Ammoudhelli*, perched unimprovably over the beach and under new management; skip the printed menu and ask for dishes of the day (*ambelofásola* – runner beans – and sardines in late summer) or *orektiká* like *tyrokafterí* and grilled octopus.

Áyios Isídhoros, 3km east, is where most tourists actually stay; pick of the **hotels** here, not completely overrun with package tours, is the *Pebble Beach* (☎ 22520 31651, ⓕ 22520 31566; ❹), with many of the large rooms overlooking a slightly reefy section of beach – though avoid those near the in-house bar if you wish to sleep. **Eating** out locally, the clear winner is *Taverna tou Panaï* (all year) at the rear of an olive grove just by the northerly "Áyios Isídhoros" town limits sign; here you'll find big, no-nonsense portions of salubrious meat, seafood and *mayireftá* dishes, and mostly Greeks in attendance.

Melínda, another 700-metre sand-and-shingle beach at the mouth of a canyon, lies 6km west of Plomári by paved road. Here there are several inexpensive **taverna-rooms** outfits, of which *Maria's* (☎ 22520 93239; ❶) is an endearingly ramshackle place with simple but reasonably priced food and lodging. *Melinda Studios* (☎ 22520 93282; ❷) near mid-beach presents a better standard (though no meals), as does *Melinda* (aka *Dhimitris Psaros*; ☎ 22520 93234; ❷) at the west end of the strand, with a more elaborate menu. Equally unspoilt (thanks to a formerly dreadful ten-kilometre side road in, now paved for 6km), **Tárti**, some 22km in total from Plomári, is a 300-metre-wide cove sown with three beachfront **tavernas** (sunbeds offered), plus **rooms** lining the final stretch of road (or behind the sand) should you want to stay.

The **bus** into Plomári travels via the attractive villages of Paleókipos and Skópelos (as well as Áyios Isídhoros); the road north from Plomári to Ayiássos has paving and public transport only as far as Megalohóri.

Ayiássos and Mylélia

AYIÁSSOS, nestled in a remote, wooded valley under the crest of Mount Ólymbos, is the most beautiful hill town on Lésvos, its narrow cobbled streets lined by ranks of tiled-roof houses. On the usual, northerly approach, there's no hint of the enormous village until you see huge knots of parked cars at the southern edge of town (where the bus leaves you after the 26-kilometre run from Mytilíni).

Don't be put off by endless ranks of kitsch wooden and ceramic souvenirs or carved "Byzantine" furniture, aimed mostly at Greeks, but continue past the central **church of the Panayía Vrefokratoússa**, originally built in the twelfth century to house an icon supposedly painted by the Evangelist Luke, to the **old bazaar**, with its *kafenía*, yoghurt shops and butchers' stalls. With such a venerable icon as a focus, the local August 15 *paniyíri* is one of the liveliest in Greece, let alone Lésvos. Ayiássos also takes Carnival very seriously; there's a club dedicated to organizing it, opposite the post office. The best **restaurants** are *Dhouladhelli*, on your left as you enter the village from the extreme south (bus stop) end, or the idiosyncratic nocturnal ouzerí *To Stavri*, at the extreme north end of the village in Stavrí district.

If you're headed for Ayiássos with your own transport, you might visit the **Mylélia water mill** (ⓦ www.mylelia.gr), whose inconspicuously signposted access track takes off 1km west of the turning for Ípios village. The name means "place of the mills", and there were once several hereabouts, powered by a spring, up-valley at Karíni. The last survivor (open daily 9am–6pm), restored to working order, has not been made twee in the least; the keeper will show you the mill race and paddle-wheel, as well as the flour making its spasmodic exit, after which you're free to buy gourmet pastas at the adjacent shop. Of late, Mylélia has branched out into cheeses, jams, salted fish, even cooking courses – and their products are sold at designated outlets in every Lésvos resort.

Vaterá, Skála Polikhnítou – and spas en route

A different bus route from Mytilíni leads to Vaterá beach via the inland villages of Polikhnítos and Vrýssa. **VRÝSSA** itself has a **natural history museum** (daily 9.30am–5pm; €1) dedicated to local paleontological finds – it's not exactly required viewing at present, but a new, more extensive gallery is planned. Until 20,000 years ago, Lésvos (like all other east Aegean islands) was joined to the Asian mainland, the gulf of Vaterá was a subtropical lake, and all manner of creatures flourished here, their fossilized bones constituting the star exhibits.

If you're after a hot bath, head for the small, vaulted **spa house** 1.5km east of **Polikhnítos**, well restored by an EU programme (daily: July & Aug 9am–1pm & 5–8pm, spring/autumn 9am–1pm & 4–6pm); there are separate, pink-tinted chambers for each sex. Alternatively, there are more **hot springs** at **Áyios Ioánnis**, signposted 3km below the village of Lisvóri; on the far side of the stream here are two pools housed in whitewashed, vaulted chambers – the left-hand one's nicer, and there's no gender segregation or dress code. These baths are under the energetic management of Lazaros (€2 fee when he's around), who also runs a **snack bar** and a few rooms adjacent.

VATERÁ, 9km south of Polikhnítos, is a huge, seven-kilometre-long sand beach, backed by vegetated hills; the sea here is delightfully calm and clean, the strand itself rated as one of the best in the islands. If you intend to stay here you'll probably want your own transport, as the closest well-stocked shops are 4km away at Vrýssa, and the bus appears only a few times daily. Development straggles for several kilometres to either side of the central T-junction, consisting mostly of seasonal villas and apartments for locals; at the west end of the strip is one of the very few consistently attended and professionally run hotels, the Greek- and American-owned *Vatera Beach* (T 22520 61212, W www .vaterabeach.gr; ❺ but ❹ for web bookings), whose rooms offer air conditioning and fridges. It also has a good attached restaurant with own-grown produce and shoreline tables from where you can gaze at the cape of **Áyios Fokás** 3km to the west, where only foundations remain of a temple of Dionysos and a super-imposed early Christian basilica. The little tamarisk-shaded anchorage here has an acceptable fish **taverna**, *Akrotiri/Angeleros*; it's usually better than most eateries east of the T-junction at Vaterá, but not so good as those at **SKÁLA POLIKHNÍTOU**, 4km northwest of Polikhnítos itself, where *T'Asteria*, *Iliova-silema* and *Akroyiali* can be recommended. Skála itself is pleasantly workaday, with only a short, narrow beach but one unusual accommodation option, "Soft Tourism" run by Lefteris and Erika (T 22520 42678; ❷). They generally host walking groups April to June and September, but welcome independent travellers during July and August.

East from Vaterá, a mostly paved road leads via Stavrós, and then Akrássi to either Ayiássos or Plomári within ninety minutes, making day-trips there feasible. When going north towards Kallóní, use the completely paved, fast short cut via the naval base and seashore hamlet at Akhladherí.

Western Lésvos

The main road west of Loutrá Yéras is surprisingly devoid of settlement, with little to stop for before Kalloní other than the traces of an ancient **Aphrodite temple** at **Mésa** (Méson), 1km north of the main road, and signposted just east of the Akhladherí turn-off. At the **site** (may be closed for excavations), just eleventh-century BC foundations and a few column stumps remain, plus the ruins of a fourteenth-century Genoese-built basilica wedged inside; it was once virtually on the sea, but a nearby stream has silted things up in the intervening millennia. All told, it's not worth a special trip, but certainly make the short detour if passing by with your own transport. With more time, you can turn northeast towards **Ayía Paraskeví** village, midway between two more important monuments from diverse eras: the Paleo-Christian **basilica of Halinádhou**, and the large **medieval bridge of Kremastí**.

KALLONÍ itself is an unembellished agricultural and market town more or less in the middle of the island, with various shops and services (including a **post office** and three **banks** with ATMs). Some 3km south lies **SKÁLA KALLONÍS**, a somewhat unlikely package resort backing a long but coarse-sand beach on the lake-like gulf. It's mainly distinguished as a bird-watching centre, attracting hundreds of twitchers for the March–May nesting season in the adjacent salt marshes. Pick of a half-dozen **hotels** is the human-scale bungalow complex *Malemi* (☎22530 22594, ✉malemi@otenet.gr; ⑤), with a variety of units from doubles to family suites, attractive grounds, tennis court and a large pool. **Tavernas** lining the quay with its fishing fleet are generally indistinguishable – though most offer the gulf's celebrated, plankton-fed sardines, best eaten fresh-grilled from August to October (though they're available salt-cured all year round).

Inland monasteries and villages

West of Kalloní, the road winds 4km uphill to the **monastery of Limónos**, founded in 1527 by the monk Ignatios, whose actual cell is maintained in the surviving medieval north wing. It's a huge, rambling complex, with just a handful of monks and lay workers to maintain three storeys of cells around a vast, plant-filled courtyard. The *katholikón*, with its ornate carved-wood ceiling and archways, is built in Asia Minor style and is traditionally off-limits to women; a sacred spring flows from below the south foundation wall. A former abbot established a **museum** (daily 9.30am–6.30pm, may close 3pm off-season; €1.50) in the west wing; only the ground-floor ecclesiastical collection is currently open, with the more interesting upstairs ethnographic gallery off-limits indefinitely. Content yourself with an overflow of farm implements stashed in a corner storeroom below, next to a chamber where giant *pithária* (urns) for grain and olive oil are embedded in the floor.

The main road beyond passes through **VATOÚSSA**, a beautiful landlocked settlement in the heart of Lésvos's westernmost land mass, with a **folk museum** in the ancestral mansion of Grigorios Gogos. Just beyond Vatoússa a paved turning leads 7km to the outskirts of **HÍDHIRA**, where the Methymneos Winery (daily July–Sept 30 9am–6pm, otherwise by appointment on ☎22530 51518; ⓦwww.methymneos.gr) has successfully revived the local ancient grape variety, decimated by phylloxera some decades ago. Because of the altitude (300m) and sulphur-rich soil (you're in the caldera of Órdhymnos volcano), their velvety, high-alcohol, oak-aged red can be produced organically. Proprietor Ioannis Lambrou gives a highly worthwhile twenty-minute tour of the state-of-the-art premises, in English.

Some 8km beyond Vatoússa, a short track leads down to the sixteenth-century **monastery of Perivolís** (daily 8am–1hr before sunset; donation, no photos), built in the midst of a riverside orchard (*perivóli*). Feeble electric light is available to view the narthex's fine if damp-damaged frescoes. In an apocalyptic panel worthy of Bosch (*The Earth and Sea Yield up their Dead*) the Whore of Babylon rides her chimera and assorted sea monsters disgorge their victims; just to the right, towards the main door, the Three Magi approach the Virgin enthroned with the Christ Child. On the north side you see a highly unusual iconography of *Abraham, the Virgin, and the Penitent Thief of Calvary in Paradise*, with the Four Rivers of Paradise gushing forth under their feet; just right are assembled the Hebrew kings of the Old Testament.

ÁNDISSA, 3km further on, nestles under the arid west's only substantial pine grove; at the western edge of the village a sign implores you to "Come Visit Our Square", not a bad idea for the sake of a handful of tavernas and *kafenía* sheltering under three sizeable plane trees. Directly below Ándissa a paved road leads 6km north to the fishing village of **GAVATHÁS**, with a shortish, partly protected beach (there's a bigger, surf-buffeted one at Kámbos just to the east) and a bare handful of places to eat and stay – among these *Pension Restaurant Paradise* (T22530 56376; ❷), serving good fish and locally grown vegetables.

Just west of Ándissa there's an important junction. Keeping straight leads you past the still-functioning **monastery of Ipsiloú**, founded in 1101 atop an outrider of the extinct volcano of Órdhymnos. The *katholikón*, tucked in one corner of a large, irregular courtyard, has a fine wood-lattice ceiling but had its frescoes repainted to detrimental effect in 1992; more intriguing are portions of Iznik tile stuck in the facade, and the handsome double gateway. One of a few monks will admit you to the upstairs **museum** (donation), whose exhibits encompass a fine collection of *epitáfios* (Good Friday) shrouds, ancient manuscripts, portable icons and – oddest of all – a *Deposition* painted in Renaissance style by a sixteenth-century Turk. Ipsiloú's patron saint is John the Theologian, a frequent dedication for monasteries overlooking apocalyptic landscapes like the surrounding parched, boulder-strewn hills.

Signposted just west is the paved, five-kilometre side road to the main concentration of Lésvos's rather overrated **petrified forest** (daily: June–Sept 8am–sunset, rest of year closes 3pm; €2), a fenced-in "reserve" which is toured along 3km of walkways. For once, contemporary Greek arsonists cannot be blamed for the state of the trees, created by the combined action of volcanic ash from Órdhymnos and hot springs some fifteen to twenty million years ago. The mostly horizontal sequoia trunks average 1m or less in length, save for a few poster-worthy exceptions; another more accessible (and free) cluster is found south of Sígri.

Sígri

SÍGRI, near the western tip of Lésvos, has an appropriately end-of-the-line feel; the bay here is guarded both by an Ottoman castle and the long island of Nissiopí, which protects the place somewhat from prevailing winds. Until the early 1990s it was an important NATO naval base; battleships have now been replaced by a few weekly ferries on the Lávrio–Psará–Áyios Efstrátios–Límnos line – ring the local agent (T22530 54430) for current details. The eighteenth-century **castle** (built atop the ruins of an earlier one) sports the reigning sultan's monogram over the entrance, something rarely seen outside Istanbul, and a token of the high regard in which this strategic port with a good water supply was held. The vaguely Turkish-looking **church of Ayía Triádha** is in fact a converted mosque, with a huge water cistern taking up the ground floor by the belfry; this supplied, among other things, the half-ruined *hamam* just south. At the top of town stands the worthwhile **Natural History Museum of the Lésvos Petrified Forest** (daily: May 15–Oct 15 8.30am–8pm, otherwise 8.30am–4.30pm; €2), which engagingly covers pan-Aegean geology with samples and maps (including, ominously, seismic patterns), as well as the expected quota of petrified logs and plant fossils from epochs when the surrounding hills were far more vegetated. Sígri itself presents an odd mix of vernacular and cement dwellings, while the town beach, south of the castle headland, is narrow and hemmed in by the road. There are much better beaches at **Faneroméni**, 3.5km north by coastal dirt track from the northern outskirts of town, plus at **Liména**, 2km south, just below the fifteen-kilometre dirt track to Eressós (passable with care in 35min); neither beach has any facilities.

Some **accommodation** is allotted to two British tour companies (Direct Greece and Sunvil), but on-spec vacancies might be found at *Nelly's Rooms and Apartments* (☎22530 54230; ❸), overlooking the castle. Among several **tavernas**, the best all-rounder, just inland, is Italian-run, ultra-hygienic ✹ *Una Faccia Una Razza* (April to mid-Oct), with lovely grilled garlicky vegetables, creative salads, pizza, pasta, grilled seafood and an Italian wine list. The *Australia*, a bit seaward, has the Greek standards and an enviable position under the tamarisks. For **nightlife**, look no further than durable *Notia* (June–Sept), with frequent live sessions.

Skála Eressoú

Most visitors to western Lésvos park themselves at the resort of **SKÁLA ERESSOÚ**, accessible via a southerly turning between Ándissa and Ipsiloú. The three-kilometre beach here rivals Vatera's in quality, and consequently the place ranks just behind Mólyvos, Pétra and Plomári for numbers of visitors, who form an uneasy mix of Brits, Germans, Scandinavians, Greek families, neo-hippies and lesbians. Behind stretches the largest and most attractive agricultural plain on Lésvos, a welcome green contrast to the volcanic ridges above.

There's not much to central Skála – just a roughly rectangular grid of perhaps five streets by twelve, angling up to the oldest cottages on the slope of **Vígla hill** at the east end of the beach. The waterfront pedestrian zone (officially Papanikolí) is divided by a café-lined round platía midway along, dominated by a bust of **Theophrastos**, the renowned botanist who hailed from ancient Eressós. This was not, as you might suppose, on the site of the modern inland village, but atop Vígla hill; some of the remaining citadel wall is still visible from a distance. On top, the ruins prove scanty, but it's worth the scramble up for the views – you can discern the ancient jetty submerged beyond the modern fishing anchorage.

Another famous reputed native of ancient Eressós was **Sappho** (ca. 615–562 BC), the ancient poetess and reputed lesbian. There are thus always considerable numbers of gay women here paying homage, particularly in the clothing-optional zone of the beach west of the river mouth, where a small community of terrapins lives. Ancient Eressós endured into the Byzantine era, the main legacy of which is the **basilica of Áyios Andhréas** behind the modern church, merely foundations and a fragmentary if restored floor mosaic; the **tomb** of the saint, an early bishop of Crete (not the patron of Scotland), huddles just beyond the basilica.

Skála has countless **rooms and apartments**, but ones near the sea fill early in the day and can be noisy; in peak season you should aim for something quiet and inland, overlooking a garden or fields. Since the start of the new millennium, most package companies have dropped the resort, usually citing a lack of commitment to "family values" – ie, the radical lesbian contingent was a bit hard for the other tourists to handle – so vacancies are now fairly easy to come by. Still, it's wise to entrust the search to Sappho Travel (T22530 52202 or 22530 52140, Wwww.sapphotravel.com). Joanna and her staff are switched-on and helpful, also serving as a car-rental station, ferry agent and air-ticket source; they are happy to place walk-ins in accommodation (❷–❹). Otherwise, there are just a handful of bona fide **hotels** in the village, and three of these – the remote *Antiopi* (T22530 53311, Wwww.antiopi.net; rooms ❶, studios ❸); the seafront *Sappho the Eressia* (T22530 53495, ESappho_sarani@hotmail.com; ❸) and *Maskot* (book through Sappho Travel; ❸), inland from the preceding – are run exclusively by and for lesbians. The straight alternative is the understandably popular seaview *Kyma* (T22530 53555, F22530 53556; ❹), at the east end of the front.

Most **tavernas**, with elevated wooden dining platforms, crowd the beach; in the wake of the tourism crash, they've been subjected to a harsh winnowing, with more closures or changeovers likely. The *Kyani Sardhini/Blue Sardine* at the far west end of the front is a creditable seafood ouzerí, while next to *Sappho the Eressia*, *Karavoyiannos* features local traditional recipes (at a price) and bulk wine from the local Methymneos winery; nearby *Soulatsos* is one of the more reliable grill-and-*mezédhes* outfits. In terms of **nightlife**, the gay-women contingent favours *Dhekati Mousa/Tenth Muse*, on the Theophrastos platía, or *Mylos* at the east end of the strip; *Parasol* and *Cooya Caribu* are straighter café-bars. There's also an open-air **cinema** (July to early Sept) in the centre. Skála has a **post office** near the church, as well as a **bank** ATM attached to Sappho Travel, and a small **Internet café**, *Cybersurf*, just east of *Dhekati Mousa*.

If you're returning to the main island crossroads at Kalloní, you can complete a loop from Eressós along the western shore of the Gulf of Kalloní via the hill villages of Mesótopos and Ágra; this route is entirely paved, and quicker than returning via Ándissa and Skalohóri. Just off this route there's an excellent beach at **Kroússos**, with a cult ⋇ **taverna** installed in an immobilized bus at the east end; here Kyra-Maria lays on home-style fare (snails, *dolmádhes*, beans, maybe sea urchin roe) a world away from resort platters, at attractive prices.

Northern Lésvos

The main road north of Kalloní winds up a piney ridge and then down the other side into attractive countryside stippled with poplars and blanketed by olive groves. Long before you can discern any other architectural detail, the cockscomb silhouette of **Mólyvos castle** indicates your approach to the oldest-established tourist spot on Lésvos.

Mólyvos (Míthymna)

MÓLYVOS (officially Míthymna), 61km from Mytilíni, is arguably the most beautiful village on Lésvos, with tiers of sturdy, red-tiled houses, some standing defensively with their rear walls to the sea, mounting the slopes between the picturesque harbour and the **Byzantine-Genoese castle** (Tues–Sun: summer 8am–7pm; winter 8am–2.30pm; €2), which provides interesting rambles around its perimeter walls and views of Turkey across the straits. Closer examination reveals a score of weathered Turkish fountains along flower-fragrant, cobbled alleyways, reflecting the fact that before 1923 Muslims constituted over a third of the local population and owned many of the finest dwellings. The **Komninaki Kralli** mansion, high up in the town, is particularly worth getting into (daily 9am–5pm; free); the lower floor houses a **"School of Fine Arts"**

△ View over Mólyvos harbour, Lésvos

(as the building is signposted), but the wall- and ceiling-murals on the upper storey (dated 1833) compare with those of the Vareltzídena mansion in Pétra (see p.935). A panel in the smallest room portrays some dervish musicians, while other murals depict stylized versions of Constantinople and Mytilíni Town; you can tell the men's and women's quarters apart by the wider recessed "throne" provided for the latter. Barely excavated **ancient Mithymna** to the northwest of the village is of specialist interest, though a necropolis has been unearthed next to the bus stop and main car park.

Modern dwellings and hotels have been banned from the municipal core, but this hasn't stopped a steady drain of all the authentic life from the upper bazaar; just one lonely tailor still plies his trade amongst souvenir shops vastly surplus to requirements. Once an exclusive resort, Mólyvos is now firmly middle of the road, with the usual silly T-shirts and other trinkets carpeting every vertical surface of a stage-set, albeit an attractive one, for package tourism.

The shingly **town beach** is mediocre, improving considerably as you head towards the sandy southern end of the bay, called **Pitsiára**, with its clothing-optional zone. Advertised **boat excursions** to remote bays seem a frank admission of this failing; there are also frequent daily bus shuttles in season, linking all points between Anaxos and Eftaloú.

Arrival and information

The municipal **tourist office** (summer Mon–Fri 9am–3pm & 5–9pm, Sat–Sun 10am–3pm; spring/autumn Mon–Fri 9am–3pm) by the **bus stop**, **taxi rank** and main **car park** at the southeast edge of town keeps lists of rented rooms, but no longer acts as a booking agency. Immediately adjacent you'll find three **bank** ATMs, plus numerous **motorbike and car rental** places, including Kosmos (☎22530 71710), Best (☎22530 72145) and Hertz (☎22530 72471), the latter two offering the ability to pick up here and drop off in Mytilíni or the airport. The main **post office** is near the top of the upper commercial street; Centraal, down near the harbour, is the principal **Internet** café.

Accommodation

The main sea-level thoroughfare of Mihaïl Goútou heads past the tourist office towards the harbour; just below it stand a number of bona fide **hotels** or **pensions** not completely taken over by packages. These include the *Hermes* on the beach (☎22530 71250; ❸), with variable, marble-floored rooms, and the *Molyvos* I next door (☎22530 71496, ⓕ22530 71640; ❹), with large balconied rooms, and breakfast served on the flagstoned terrace under the palms. For more comfort, you'll need to head 1km south of town to the ♣ *Delfinia* (☎22530 71315, ⓦwww.hoteldelfinia.com; open all year; ❺ rooms, ❼ bungalows), set in seventy acres of greenery, with friendly staff and direct access to Pitsiára beach.

Rooms are scattered along the lanes leading uphill from the upper market thoroughfare. Best of these are *Studios Voula* below the castle car park (☎22530 72017 or 694 52 41 994), which has studios (❸) and a restored four-person house (❺), both with knockout views. Families should consider the high-standard restored *Captain's House* offered by Theo and Melinda (☎22530 71241, ⓦwww.lesvosvacations.com), up by the Komninaki Kralli mansion; it sleeps up to six, and seasonal rates vary from €90 to €140 for the entire premises. The official **campsite**, *Camping Methymna* (late June–Sept), lies 2km northeast of town on the Eftaloú road.

Eating, drinking and nightlife

The sea-view **tavernas** on the lower market lane of 17-Noemvríou are all much of a muchness, where you pay primarily for the view; it's far better to head for the fishing port, where ♣ *The Captain's Table* (with unpainted chairs; supper only) combines the virtues of squirmingly fresh seafood, meat grills and vegetarian *mezédhes*, washed down by their very palatable, own-label wine. *Tò Khtapodhi*, in the old customs house by the port entrance, attracts a mostly Greek crowd and is best treated as an ouzerí with treats such as salt-cured sardines. *Babis*, at the town approaches with semi-rural seating, is the place to head for good grills and a few *mayireftá* of the day. For snacks, look no further than *Iy Agora* (*To Dhimotiko Kafenio*), just downhill from the converted mosque/conference centre, with a lovely wood interior, view balcony and an excellent ouzo-*mezés* combo for under €2.

Midsummer sees a short **festival of music and theatre** up in the castle, and there's also a well-regarded outdoor **cinema** (June–Sept) next to the taxi rank. **Nightlife** revolves around musical bars: most durable is youth-orientated, tropical-themed *Congas* (May–Sept) down by the shore, with DJ'd events and theme nights; *Opus 6*, just up from the harbour, hosts high-quality live Greek or Western music every evening, while *Molly's Bar* just opposite is the thirty-somethings' preferred hangout, with taped music at a conversational level and a cozy balcony.

Pétra and Ánaxos

Since there are political and practical limits to the expansion of Mólyvos, many package companies have shifted emphasis to **PÉTRA**, 5km due south. The place has sprawled untidily behind its broad sand beach and seafront square, but two attractive nuclei of old stone houses, some with Levantine-style balconies overhanging the street, remain. Pétra takes its name from the giant **rock monolith** located some distance inland and enhanced by the eighteenth-century **church of the Panayía Glykofiloússa**, reached via 114 rock-hewn steps. Other local attractions include the sixteenth-century **church of Áyios Nikólaos**, with three phases of well-preserved frescoes, and the intricately decorated **Vareltzídhena mansion** (Tues–Sun 8am–2.30pm; free), with naive wall paintings of courting couples and a stylized view of a naval engagement at Constantinople.

Most small **hotels** and studios are block-booked, so on-spec arrivals should contact the Women's Agricultural Tourism Cooperative on the south side of the seafront square (☎22530 41238, ✉womes@otenet.gr), which arranges rooms or studios (❷–❸) in a number of scattered premises. For more comfort, try the *Hotel Michaelia* behind the south waterfront (☎22530 41730, ✆22530 22067; ❹). The Women's Coop **restaurant**, under separate management, is excellent and inexpensive with both grills and *mayireftá* served at rooftop seating. Alternatives include *Symposio*, with good starters (though minus points for prefab chips; *Rigas* (evenings only) in the more inland settlement, a characterful ouzerí, the oldest in Pétra; and *Tsalikis Café* on the square for excellent own-made ice cream. You may prefer to head out of town – either to ⚓ *Taverna Petri* (all day May to mid-Oct) in **PETRÍ** village 3km inland, with superb home-recipe *mayireftá* and a view terrace, or to **Avláki**, 1.5km southwest en route to Ánaxos, where there's a competent, signposted taverna/ouzerí behind a tiny beach.

ÁNAXOS, 3km south of Pétra, is a higgledy-piggledy package resort fringing by far the cleanest beach and seawater in the area: 1km of sand well sown with sunbeds and a handful of tavernas. From anywhere along here you enjoy beautiful sunsets between and beyond three offshore islets.

Around Mount Lepétymnos

East of Mólyvos, the villages of 968-metre **Mount Lepétymnos**, marked by tufts of poplars, provide a day's rewarding exploration. The first stop, though not exactly up the hill, might be **Loutrá Eftaloú** thermal baths 5km along the road passing the campsite. Patronize the hot pool under the Ottoman-era domed structure, not the sterile modern tub-rooms (daily: Dec–April unrestricted access; May & Oct 9am–1pm & 3–7pm; June–Sept 10am–2pm & 4–8pm;

€3.50 for group pool). The spa is well looked after, with the water mixed up to a toasty 39–41°C, so you'll need to cool down regularly; outside stretches the long, good pebble beach of **Áyii Anáryiri**, broken up by little headlands, with the remotest two coves nudist. There's a single, fetchingly positioned **taverna** here, the *Khrysi Akti*, which also lets small but en-suite **rooms** (☎22530 71879; ❷), the former cells of the adjacent monastery.

Eftaloú itself has a considerable number of fancy hotels and bungalow complexes, the friendliest and best value (though tour-dominated like the others) being the *Eftalou* (☎22530 71584, ✉parmakel@otenet.gr; ❹), with a pool, well-tended garden and loyal repeat clientele. A highly recommendable **taverna**, within sight of the spa and open all year (except around Christmas), is ✴ *Iy Eftalou*, where the food (meat/fish grills) and tree-shaded setting are both splendid.

The main paved road around Lepétymnos first heads 5km east to **VAFIÓS**, with its clutch of three fairly comparable view **tavernas** (*Vafios, Ilias, Petrino*; avoid heavy, deep-fried dishes at all three), before curling north around the base of the mountain. The exquisite hill village of **SYKAMINIÁ** (**Sykamiá**) was the birthplace of the novelist Stratis Myrivilis; below the "Plaza of the Workers' First of May", with its two traditional *kafenía* and views north to Turkey, one of the imposing basalt-built houses is marked as his childhood home. A marked trail shortcuts the twisting road down to **SKÁLA SYKAMINIÁS**, easily the most picturesque fishing port on Lésvos. Myrivilis used it as the setting for his best-known work, *The Mermaid Madonna*, and the tiny rock-top chapel at the end of the jetty will be instantly recognizable to anyone who has read the book.

On a practical level, Skála has a few pensions, such as the central, partly air-con *Gorgona* (☎22530 55301; ❸), with a shaded breakfast terrace, and several **tavernas**. The most durable of these is *Iy Skamnia* (aka *Iy Mouria tou Myrivili*), with seating under the mulberry tree in which Myrivilis used to sleep on hot summer nights, though newer *Anemoessa* (closest to the chapel, open winter weekends also) has overtaken it quality-wise, with good stuffed squash blossoms complementing fresh seafood. The only local beach is the pebble-on-sand-base one of **Kayiá** 1.5km east, where at least one – sometimes two – tavernas operate each season.

Continuing east from upper Sykaminiá, you soon reach **KLIÓ**, whose single main street (marked "*kendrikí agorá*") leads down to a platía with a plane tree, fountain, *kafenía* and more views across to Turkey. The village is set attractively on a slope, down which a six-kilometre road, now half-paved, descends to **Tsónia** beach, 600m of beautiful pink volcanic sand.

South of Klió, the route forks at Kápi, from where you can complete a loop of the mountain by bearing west along a completely paved road. **PELÓPI** is the ancestral village of unsuccessful 1988 US presidential candidate Michael Dukakis (who finally visited the island in 2000), and the main street is now named after him. Garden-lush **IPSILOMÉTOPO**, 5km further along, is punctuated by a minaret (but no mosque) and hosts revels on July 17, the feast of Ayía Marína.

Mandamádhos and Taxiárhis monastery

The main highway south from Klió and Kápi leads back to the capital through **MANDAMÁDHOS**. This attractive inland village is famous for its pottery, including the Ali Baba-style *pithária* (olive-oil urns) seen throughout Lésvos, but more so for the "black" icon of the Archangel Michael, whose enormous **monastery of Taxiárhis** (daily: May–Sept 6am–9.30pm; Oct–April

6.30am–7pm), in a valley just northeast, is the focus of a thriving cult. The image – supposedly made from a mixture of mud and the blood of monks slaughtered in a massacre – is really more idol than icon, both in its lumpy three-dimensionality and in the methods of its veneration. First there was the custom of the coin-wish, whereby you pressed a coin to the Archangel's forehead – if it stuck, your wish would be granted. This practice (along with candle-lighting next to it) has long been forbidden, with supplicants referred to an alternative icon by the main entrance. It's further believed that while carrying out his errands on behalf of the faithful, the Archangel gets through more footwear than Imelda Marcos. Accordingly the icon used to be surrounded by piles of miniature, votive, gold and silver shoes. The ecclesiastical authorities, embarrassed by such "primitive" practices, removed them all in 1986, though since then several pairs of tin slippers, which can be filled with money and left in front of the icon, have reappeared.

Límnos

Límnos is a sizeable agricultural and military island whose remoteness and peculiar ferry schedules protected it until the 1990s from most trappings of the holiday trade. Conventional tourism was late in coming because the islanders made a reliable living off the visiting relatives of the numerous soldiers stationed here; most summer visitors are still Greek, particularly from Thessaloníki, though the locals are now used to numbers of Danes, Brits, Austrians and Italians flown in by ever-more-regular charter flights. Accommodation tends to be comfortable if overpriced, and **backpackers**

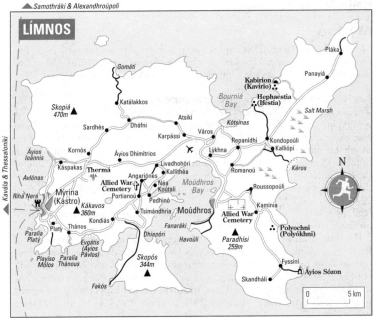

are explicitly **discouraged**. Bucolic Límnos has been getting positively trendy of late: there are upscale souvenir shops, village houses restored by mainlanders (and foreigners) as seasonal retreats, and some sort of noon-to-small-hours music bar during summer at nearly every beach.

The island has long been the focus of recurring disputes between the Greek and Turkish governments; Turkey has a perennial demand that Límnos be demilitarized, and Turkish aircraft regularly intrude Greek air space overhead, prompting immediate responses from the Greek Air Force squadron here. Límnos' **garrison** ran to 25,000 soldiers at the nadir of Greco-Turkish relations during the 1980s, though it is now down to about 6,000, and set to fall further when Greece abolishes conscription and most of the remaining army camps (but not the air base) close.

The bays of **Bourniá** and **Moúdhros**, the latter one of the largest natural harbours in the Aegean, divide Límnos almost in two. The west of the island is dramatically bare and hilly, with abundant basalt put to good use as street cobbles and house masonry. Like most volcanic islands, Límnos produces excellent wine – good dry whites, rosés and quality retsina – plus ouzo at Kondiás. The east is low-lying and speckled with marshes popular with duck-hunters, where it's not occupied by cattle, combine harvesters and vast corn fields.

Despite off-islander slander to that effect, Límnos is not flat, barren or treeless; much of the countryside consists of rolling hills, well vegetated except on their heights, and with substantial clumps of almond, jujube, myrtle, oak, poplar and mulberry trees. The island is, however, quite dry, with irrigation water pumped from deep wells, and a limited number of potable springs in the western half. Yet various streams bring sand to several long, **sandy beaches** around the coast, where it's easy to find a stretch to yourself. The bays shelve gently, making them ideal for children and quick to warm up in spring, with no cool currents except near the river mouths, and few of the jellyfish which used to pour out of the Dardanelles to plague bathers.

Mýrina

MÝRINA (aka Kástro), the capital and passenger port on the west coast, has the ethos of a provincial market town rather than of a resort. With about five thousand inhabitants, it's pleasantly low-key, if not especially picturesque.

Arrival, information and transport

The modern civilian **airport** lies 18km east of Mýrina, almost at the exact geographic centre of the island, sharing a runway with an enormous air-force base; there are three car rental booths, a bank ATM, a few taxis outside – and no shuttle bus into town. **Ferries** currently dock at the southern edge of Mýrina, in the shadow of the castle, though a new jetty is being built on the far side of the bay, under the hilltop church of Áyios Nikólaos, ready within the lifetime of this edition. There are separate **agencies** for the sailings of NEL boats (℡22540 22460), GA and LANE ferries (Pravlis Travel, ℡22540 24617) and Saos Ferries (℡22540 29571), as well as a rather glum, useless **tourist information** office on the harbour (Mon–Fri 8am–3pm).

The **bus station** is on Platía Eleftheríou Venizélou, at the north end of Kydhá. One look at the sparse schedules (only a single daily afternoon departure to most points, slightly more frequently to Kondiás and Moúdhros) will convince you of the need to rent a vehicle from one of many agencies clustered around the harbour area. **Cars**, **motorbikes** and **bicycles** can be rented from Limnos Car Rental (℡22540 23777, airport ℡694 54 95 104), Myrina

Rent a Car (☏22540 24476), Petrides Travel (☏22540 22039, airport ☏22540 92700) amd Holiday (☏22540 24347, airport 693 24 81 056); rates for bikes are only slightly above the island norm, but cars are expensive. A motorbike (most obviously from Moto Lemnos, ☏22540 25002) is generally enough to explore the coast and the interior of the closer villages, as there are few steep gradients but many perilously narrow streets, some controlled by traffic lights dictating alternating one-way passage. A new bypass road from Áyios Nikólaos port, probably ready by the time you read this, should relieve most of Mýrina's **traffic** bottlenecks; **parking**, however, will remain nightmarish, with spaces possible only at the outskirts.

All **banks**, most of them along Kydhá, have ATMs; the **post office** and Olympic airlines office are adjacent to each other on Garoufalídhou, with a **laundry** across the way by the *Hotel Paris*. There are **Internet** facilities at *NetPoint*, halfway along Kydhá, and at *Joy*, next to the post office.

Accommodation

Despite Límnos's steady gentrification, you may still be met off the boat with offers of a **room**; there are officially two dozen or so licensed establishments in Mýrina, with the northern districts of Rihá Nerá and Áyios Pandelímonas better bets for **studios**. Otherwise you'll find a pair of decent town **hotels** plus upmarket complexes at nearby beaches. In Romeïkós Yialós a few restored houses serve as small inns, though most are affected by evening noise from the seafront bars. There's **no official campsite**; Greek caravanners and campers have been banished from the north end of Platý beach, though a few tents still sprout furtively at Kéros (see p.943).

Apollo Pavilion On Frýnis ☏22540 23712, Ⓦwww.apollopavilion.com. Hidden away in a peaceful cul-de-sac about halfway along Garou-falídhou, this offers three-bed studios with air con, TV and mini-kitchen. Most units have balconies, with views of either the castle or the mountains. Open all year; the friendly owner's wine is excellent. ❹

Arhondiko Corner Sakhtoúri and Filellínon, Romeïkós Yialós ☏22540 29800, Ⓦwww.questinn .com. Límnos' first hotel in the nineteenth century, this 1851-built mansion was reopened in 2003 as three floors of medium-sized, wood-trimmed rooms with all mod cons. There's a pleasant ground-floor bar/breakfast lounge. ❺

Ifestos Ethnikís Andístasis 17, Andhróni district, inland from Rihá Nerá ☏22540 24960, Ⓕ22540 23623. Quiet, professionally run C-class hotel, with

pleasant common areas. Slightly small rooms have air con, fridges, balconies and again a mix of sea or hill views. ❹

Porto Myrina Avlónas beach, 1.5km north of Rihá Nerá ☏22540 24805, Ⓦwww.portomyrina.com. The island's best beachfront lodging, though its five-star rating is probably one too many. Standard rooms and free-standing bungalows surround an Artemis temple found during construction; vast common areas include tennis courts, a footie pitch, one of the largest (salt-water) pools in Greece, and summer watersports on the beach. Open May–Oct 15; standard rooms ❼, bungalows ❽.

Romeïkos Yialos Sakhtoúri 7 ☏22540 23787 or 22540 22197. Venerable pension in a Romeïkós Yialós mansion that's quieter than waterfront outfits; just eight good-sized if plain rooms, some with air con. ❸

The Town

Mýrina's main attraction is the Byzantine **castle** (unrestricted access), perched on a craggy headland between the ferry dock and Romeïkós Yialós, the town's chic beach-lined esplanade backed by ornate Neoclassical mansions. In a ruined state despite later additions by the Genoese and Ottomans, the fortress is flatteringly lit at night and warrants a climb at sunset for views over the town, the entire west coast and – in clear conditions – over to Mount Áthos, 35 nautical miles west (which can also be glimpsed from any suitable height east of town). Also worth exploring is the town's core neighbourhood of old stone houses dating from the Ottoman era. Few explicitly Turkish monuments have survived, though an unassuming **fountain** at the harbour end of the main drag, Kydhá, retains its calligraphic inscription and is still highly prized for its drinking water.

The town's shops and amenities are mostly to be found along Kydhá and its continuation Karatzá – which meanders north from the harbour to Romeïkós Yialós – or Garoufalídhou, its perpendicular offshoot, roughly halfway along. As town **beaches** go, Romeïkós Yialós and Néa Mádhitos (ex-Toúrkikos Yialós), its counterpart to the southeast of the harbour, are not at all bad; Rihá Nerá, the next bay north of Romeïkós Yialós, is even better, with watersports on offer.

The **archeological museum** (Tues–Sun 8.30am–3pm; €2) occupies a handsome Ottoman mansion right behind Romeïkós Yialós, not far from the site of partly excavated Bronze Age Myrina. Finds are assiduously labelled in Greek, Italian and English, and the entire premises are exemplary in terms of presentation – the obvious drawback being that the best items have been spirited away to Athens, leaving a collection that's essentially of specialist interest. The south ground-floor gallery is mainly devoted to pottery from Polychni (Polyókhni); the north wing contains more of the same, plus items from ancient Myrina; the upstairs galleries feature post-Bronze Age artefacts from Kabirion (Kavírio) and Hephaestia (Ifestía). The star upper-storey exhibits are votive lamps in the shape of sirens, found in an Archaic sanctuary at Hephaestia, much imitated in modern local jewellery. Rather less vicious than Homer's creatures, they are identified more invitingly as the "muses of the underworld, creatures of superhuman wisdom, incarnations of nostalgia for paradise". Another entire room is devoted to metalwork, of which the most impressive items are gold jewellery and bronze objects, both practical (cheese graters, door-knockers) and whimsical-naturalistic (a snail, a vulture).

Eating, drinking and nightlife

Seafood is excellent on Límnos owing to its proximity to the Dardanelles and seasonal fish migrations; for affordable waterside dining, 🌿 *To Limanaki* rates as best of several ouzerís around the little fishing harbour, with good portions and strong ouzo in bulk. About halfway along Kydhá, *O Platanos* serves traditional *mayireftá* to big crowds on an atmospheric little square under two plane trees. Not too surprisingly given the twee setting, most of the restaurants lining Romeïkós Yialós are pretty poor value; the tree-shaded tables of *Iy Tzitzifies* at Rihá Nerá are a far better option. Romeïkós Yialós is, however, where **nightlife** kicks off, with a sunset drink in the shadow of the castle; doyenne of the **café-bars** here is *Karagiozis* at no. 32 (by the bridge, 11am–late). Choices elsewhere in town are limited, for example to stunningly appointed *Alexandros* at the base of the jetty; the closest after-hours beach bars are *Kioski* (July–August) on the sand at Avlónas, and oriental-themed *Al Bazaar/Oasis* just inland by the old Avlónas river bridge. There's also the Maroula **cinema-theatre** on Garoufalídhou.

Western Límnos

Besides Mýrina's respectable town beaches, the closest good sand lies 3km north at Avlónas, with its aforementioned beach-bar, unspoilt except for the local power plant just inland. Just beyond, the road splits: the right-hand turning wends its way through **Káspakas**, its north-facing houses in neat tiers and a potable spring (but no taverna) on its handsome platía, before plunging down to **Áyios Ioánnis**, also reached directly by the newer bypass. There are a fair number of **rooms** to let here, plus a few **tavernas**, most distinctive the one (late June to late Aug) featuring seating in the shade of piled-up volcanic boulders, but the beach beyond is not the best – bearing the brunt of southwesterlies – and the whole area in fact resembles a vast building site.

More unusual immersions and meals are found a short distance east. The old Ottoman baths at **Thermá** have been restored and operate as a contemporary health spa, with all conceivable treatments laid on – or you can just have a hydromassage soak (daily 10am–2pm & 5–9pm; €6). Some 7km north of here, **SARDHÉS** is the highest village on the island, with a celebrated central **taverna**, ✻ *Man-Télla* (all year, lunch and dinner). Portions are large and the fare rich, so arrive hungry; in season you'll need to book for dinner (☎22540 61349) in the pleasant courtyard.

Beyond Sardhés, via the villages of Dháfni and Katálakkos, 5km below the latter, lies the spectacular, well-signposted **dune environment at Gomáti**, one of the largest such in Greece. There are two zones reached by separate dirt tracks: one at a river mouth, with a bird-rich marsh, and the other to the northwest. Despite the lack of facilities and exposure to the wind, they're a popular outing locally.

Platý to Paleó Pedhinó

PLATÝ, 2km southeast of Mýrina, has had its profile spoilt by the kind of modern villa construction that is blighting many Limnian villages, but it does have two nocturnally popular **tavernas**. Much the better of these is ✻ *O Sozos*, just off the main platía, where groups should reserve in season on ☎22540 25085. The menu has contracted since Sozos himself was killed in a freak accident, but his daughter carries on with huge, well-priced portions of grills, salads and a few *mayireftá* like dolmádhes, washed down by *tsípouro* and local bulk wine. The long sandy **beach**, 700m below, is popular, with non-motorized watersports available; except for the unsightly Mark Warner compound at the south end, the area still (just) remains rural, with sheep parading to and fro at dawn and dusk. The single **hotel**, low-rise *Plati Beach* (☎22540 23583; ❹), has an enviable position in the middle of the beach, but be sure to get an upperstorey room or attic suite. Nearby, *Grigoris* proves a reliable, popular beachside **taverna**, with fish in season. The highest standard of **studios** in the area, if not the whole island, is ✻ *Villa Afroditi* (☎22540 23141, ⓦwww.afroditivillasa .gr; mid-May to end Sept; B&B; ❺), with its spectacularly unmissable topiary specimens, a pleasant pool bar, weekly barbecue nights for guests, and one of the best buffet breakfasts in the islands.

THÁNOS, 2km further southeast, seems a bigger, more architecturally characterful version of Platý village, with Nikos Dhimou's high-standard mock-trad **bungalows** at the east edge (☎22540 25284; ❹). **Paralía Thánous**, 1.5km below the village, is perhaps the most scenic of the southwestern beaches, flanked by weird volcanic crags and with views on a clear afternoon to Áyios Efstrátios island. There's good-value **accommodation** at *Villa Thanos Beach* (☎22540 23496 or 697 37 10 543; ❸), with a lush front garden and sunset views, plus good food (if surly service) at *Yiannakaros* **taverna**; their beach bar and one other divide the (complimentary) sunbeds between them. Beyond Thános, the road curls over to the enormous beach at **Evgátis** (Áyios Pávlos), reckoned the island's best, with more igneous pinnacles for definition. Again, a pair of music bar/*kantínas* offer sunbeds, while a full-service taverna across the road has a few comfortable **rooms** (☎22540 51700; ❸).

Some 3km further along (11km from Mýrina), **KONDIÁS** is the island's third-largest settlement, cradled between two hills tufted with Límnos's biggest pine forest. Stone-built, often elaborate houses and a row of sail-less windmills combine with the setting to make Kondiás the most attractive inland village, a fact not lost on the Greeks and foreigners restoring fine old houses with varying degrees of taste. Short-term facilities are nonexistent, however; the closest **tavernas** are 2.5km away at **TSIMÁNDHRIA**, where *O Meraklis* (all year) on the central platía are roast-chicken specialists, or at **PALEÓ PEDHINÓ** 5km northeast, where *Petrino Horio* (dinner only, end June–Aug) offers fine meat and an enchanting setting (if shambolic service) on the flagstoned platía of this mostly abandoned village.

Eastern Límnos

The shores of **Moúdhros Bay**, glimpsed south of the trans-island road, are muddy and best avoided unless you're a clam-digger. The bay itself enjoyed considerable importance during World War I, culminating in the Ottoman surrender aboard the British warship HMS *Agamemnon* here on October 30, 1918. **MOÚDHROS**, the second-largest town on Límnos and the main cargo port, is a dreary place, with only a wonderfully kitsch, two-belfried church to recommend it. There are three **hotels** in Moúdhros, the best of which is the overpriced *Kyma* (☎22540 71333; ❹). Its more reasonable, but run-of-the-mill, **restaurant** is convenient for a lunch break if you're visiting the archeological sites and beaches of eastern Límnos. The closest decent beaches are at **Havoúli**, 4km south by dirt track, and recently cleaned-up **Fanaráki** 4km west, but both have somewhat muddy sand and don't really face open sea.

About 800m along the Roussopoúli road, you pass an **Allied military cemetery** (unlocked) maintained by the Commonwealth War Graves Commission; its neat lawns and rows of white headstones seem incongruous in such parched surroundings. In 1915, Moúdhros Bay was the principal staging area for the disastrous Gallipoli campaign. Of the roughly 36,000 Allied

△ Portianoú World War I Allied cemetery

dead, 887 – mainly battle casualties who died after having been evacuated to the base hospital at Moúdhros – are buried here, with 348 more at another signposted, immaculately maintained graveyard behind the hilltop church in Portianoú.

KALLIÓPI, 8km northeast of Moúdhros via Kondopoúli, has smart **rooms** (*Keros*, ☎22540 41059; ❹) at the start of the dirt road down to **Kéros** beach, the best in this part of the island but exposed and often dirty. A 1500-metre stretch of sand with dunes and a small pine grove, plus shallow water, it attracts a number of Greek tourists and foreigners with camper vans and windsurfers; a small *kantína* operates with sunbeds during July and August only.

On the other side of Kondopoúli, reached via Repanídhi village, the hard-packed beach of **Kótsinas** is set in the protected western limb of Bourniá Bay. The nearby anchorage (follow signs to "Kótsinas Fortress") offers a pair of **tavernas**, the better being *To Korali* by the water, reliably open all day, with a wide range of *mezédhes* and affordable fish. Up on a knoll overlooking the jetty, there's a corroded, sword-brandishing statue of Maroula, a Genoese-era heroine who delayed the Ottoman conquest by a few years, and a large **church of Zoödhóhou Piyís** (the Life-Giving Spring). This is nothing extraordinary, but beside it 63 steps lead down through an illuminated tunnel in the rock to the potable (if slightly mineral) spring in question, oozing into a cool, vaulted chamber.

Ancient sites

Indications of the most advanced Neolithic civilization in the Aegean have been unearthed at **Polyochni** (**Polyókhni**), 3km from the gully-hidden village of Kamínia (7km east of Moúdhros). The site occupies a bluff overlooking a long, narrow beach flanked by stream valleys. Since the 1930s, Italian excavations have uncovered five layers of settlement, the oldest from late in the fourth millennium BC, predating Troy on the Turkish coast opposite. The town met a sudden, violent end from war or earthquake in about 2100 BC. The **ruins** (Tues–Sun 9am–2pm; free) are well labelled but mostly of specialist interest, though the bouleuterion (assembly hall), a mansion and the landward fortifications are impressive enough. A small but well-presented museum behind the entrance kiosk helps bring the place to life.

Hephaestia and Kabirion, the other significant ancient sites on Límnos, are reached via the village of Kondopoúli; both sites are remote, and only reachable with your own transport. **Hephaestia** (present-day Ifestía; Tues–Sun 9am–3pm), 4.5km from Kondopoúli by rough, signposted track, has been re-excavated since 2001 and can now offer an admirably reconstructed theatre, overlooking its former harbour. **Kabirion**, also signposted as 'Kabeiroi' (modern Kavírion), on the opposite shore of Tigáni Bay and accessed by a paved road, remains more evocative. The **ruins** (Tues–Sun 9am–3pm; free) are those of a sanctuary connected with the cult of the Samothracian Kabiroi (see p.946), though the site here is probably older. Little survives other than the ground plan, but the setting is undeniably impressive. Eleven column stumps stake out a *stoa*, behind eight spots marked as column bases in the *telestirio* or shrine where the cult mysteries took place. A nearby sea grotto has been identified as the Homeric **Spiliá toú Filoktíti**, where the Trojan war hero Philoctetes was abandoned by his comrades-in-arms until his stinking, gangrenous leg had healed. Landward access to the cave is via steps leading down from the caretaker's shelter, though final access (from a little passage on the right as you face the sea) involves some wading.

Áyios Efstrátios (Aï Strátis)

Áyios Efstrátios is indisputably one of the quietest and loneliest islands in the Aegean. Historically, the only outsiders staying here were compelled to do so – it served as a place of exile for political prisoners under both the Metaxas regime of the 1930s and the various right-wing governments that followed the civil war. Before that, it was only permanently settled during the sixteenth century, and its land is still largely owned by three monasteries on Mount Áthos.

ÁYIOS EFSTRÁTIOS village – the only habitation on the island – must be one of the ugliest in Greece. Devastation caused by an earthquake in February 1968, which killed 22 and injured hundreds, was compounded by the reconstruction plan: the contract went to a company with junta connections, who prevented the survivors from returning to their old homes and used army bulldozers to raze even those structures – part of one of the more beautiful ports in these islands – that could have been repaired. From the hillside, some two dozen surviving houses of the old village overlook its replacement, whose grim rows of prefabs constitute a sad monument to the corruption of the junta years.

Architecture apart, Áyios Efstrátios still functions as a traditional fishing and farming community, with the prefabs set at the mouth of a wooded stream valley draining to the sandy harbour beach. Tourist amenities consist of just two basic **tavernas** (one operating July–Aug only), plus a total of four **pensions**. Best of these, in one of the surviving old houses, is the *Xenonas Aï-Stratis* (☎22540 93329; ❹); Andonis Paneras (☎22540 93209; ❸), Stavros Katakouzinos (☎22540 93362; ❸) and Apostolos Paneras (☎22540 93343; ❸) have more conventional **rooms** in the prefabs. These stiff prices for such an out-of-the-way place reflect Aï Strátis' increasing popularity with Greeks, and you may have to ring all four spots for a vacancy in season.

As you walk away from the village – there are few cars and no paved roads – things improve rapidly. The landscape, dry hills and valleys scattered with a surprising number of oak trees, is deserted apart from wild rabbits, sheep, an occasional shepherd, and some good **beaches**. **Alonítsi**, on the north coast – a ninety-minute walk from the village following a track up the north side of the valley – is a two-kilometre stretch of sand with rolling breakers and views across to Límnos.

South of the village, there's a series of grey-sand beaches, most with wells and drinkable water, although, with few real paths in this part of the island, getting to them can be something of a scramble. **Lidharió**, at the end of an attractive wooded valley, is the first worthwhile beach, but again it's a ninety-minute walk, unless you can persuade a fisherman to take you by boat.

Ferries on the Kavála/Alexandhroúpoli–Límnos–Lávrio line call at Áyios Efstrátios several times weekly much of the year; in summer a small Límnos-based ferry, the *Aiolis*, sails every weekday (Mon–Fri) at 3pm from Límnos, returning the next day at 6.30am. Despite harbour improvements, this is still a very exposed anchorage, and in bad weather you could end up stranded here far longer than you bargained for. If an indefinite stay does not appeal, it's best to visit from Límnos on a day-trip (offered once or twice weekly in season).

Samothráki (Samothrace)

Samothráki has one of the most dramatic profiles of all the Greek islands, second only to that of Thíra (Santorini): its dark mass of granite rises abruptly from the sea, culminating in the 1611-metre **Mount Fengári**. Seafarers have

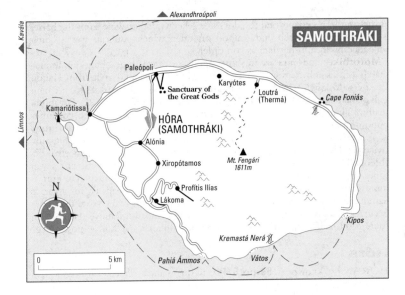

always been guided by its imposing outline, clearly visible from the mainland, and, in legend, its summit provided a vantage point for Poseidon to watch over the siege of Troy. Landing is very much subject to the vagaries of the notoriously unpredictable weather, but that did not deter pilgrims who, for hundreds of years in Antiquity, journeyed to the island to visit the **Sanctuary of the Great Gods** and were initiated into its mysteries. The sanctuary remains the main archeological attraction of the island which, too remote for most tourists, combines earthy simplicity with natural grandeur. The tourist season is relatively short-lived – essentially (late) July and August – but you will find some facilities open as early as Easter and one or two all year round.

Kamariótissa

All ferries and hydrofoils dock at the dull village of **KAMARIÓTISSA**, where you're unlikely to want to spend much time. That said, it could be your most convenient base, since some of Samothráki's best **hotels** lie along or just behind the tree-lined seafront and various **rooms** for rent, many of them more than acceptable, can be found in the maze of streets behind; owners often meet incoming vessels. As on most islands with a short season, accommodation can be pricey for what you get, and bargaining is not always productive, especially in midsummer. Along the shore, some way east of your point of arrival, is *Kyma* (T25510 41263; ❸), where rooms overlooking the pebbly beach can get noise from the string of little bars that constitutes Samothráki's main nightlife; avoid the hotel restaurant – the taverna (see below) is much better. Calmer, but somewhat pricier, is the *Niki Beach* (T25510 41561; ❹) beyond the far north end of the quay. Above, occupying a bluff and visible from out to sea, is the slightly impersonal *Aeolos* (T25510 41595, F25510 41810; ❺); with a large pool and quiet, spacious rooms, it's the island's most comfortable accommodation and offers good half-board deals out of season. Bars and cafés on the harbour front serve snacks and breakfasts, but the only commendable **taverna** is the *Limanaki*, at the southern end, beyond the docks: excellent Limniot wine from the barrel is perfect with the fish and seafood on offer, which you can watch being unloaded by local fishermen as you order.

Motorbikes and cars are in short supply, so it's worth grabbing one immediately on disembarkation – or even reserving a bike in advance from Hanou Brothers (℡25510 41511) or a car from Niki Tours (℡25510 41465), which sells plane tickets as well; also try Kyrkos car rental (℡697 43 71 122). For information about and tickets for **ferries and hydrofoils**, a converted container opposite the docks acts as offices. A fairly reliable timetable for island **buses** is also posted here; these travel up to eight times daily in season (but only twice weekly in deepest winter) along the north coast to Loutrá (Thermá) via Paleópoli, near the site of the Sanctuary, or Karyótes, or directly inland seven times daily to the largest village, Hóra. As with lodging, rented transport is more expensive than on most islands, but if you've the means go for a car, as Samothracian roads are often dangerously windswept for bikes. Note that there is currently only one fuel pump on the entire island, 1km above the port, en route to Hóra. Kamariótissa also has a **bank** with an ATM, but no post office.

Hóra

HÓRA, also known as **Samothráki**, is the island's capital. Far larger than implied by the portion visible from out at sea, it's an attractive town of Thracian-style stone houses, some whitewashed, clustered around a hollow in the western flanks of Mount Fengári. It is dominated by the Genoese Gateluzzi fort, of which little survives other than the gateway. Half an hour or so can be whiled away at the charming **folklore museum**, which is free, but the opening hours are erratic; it contains a motley collection of clothing, domestic items and miscellany.

Hóra has no reliable short-term accommodation, though asking for unadvertised rooms in the various *kafenía* along the winding commercial street can be productive. On the atmospheric, irregularly shaped platía, a couple of **tavernas**, *Iy Platia* and the more down-to-earth *To Kastro*, provide the best suppers on the island, with such delicacies as stuffed squid and *mýdhia saganáki* (mussels with cheese). There have been mutterings of moving the administrative capital down to Kamariótissa, but until further notice the island's **post office** is here.

The Sanctuary of the Great Gods

From Hóra it is 3km to the hamlet of Paleópoli (see opposite) and, in a stony but thickly wooded ravine between it and the plunging northwestern ridge of Mount Fengári, the remains of the **Sanctuary of the Great Gods**. Buses from Kamariótissa stop nearby, opposite a small car park on the seashore. From the late Bronze Age until the early Byzantine era, the mysteries and sacrifices of the cult of the Great Gods were performed on Samothráki, indeed in ancient Thracian dialect until the second century BC. The island was the spiritual focus of the northern Aegean, and its importance in the ancient world was comparable (although certainly secondary) to that of the Mysteries of Eleusis (see p.192).

The religion of the Great Gods revolved around a hierarchy of ancient Thracian fertility figures: the Great Mother Axieros, a subordinate male deity known as Kadmilos, and the potent and ominous twin demons the Kabiroi, originally the local heroes Dardanos and Aeton. When the Aeolian colonists arrived (traditionally ca. 700 BC) they simply syncretized the resident deities with their own – the Great Mother became Cybele, her consort Hermes and the Kabiroi were fused interchangeably with the *Dioskouroi* Castor and Pollux, patrons of seafarers. Around the nucleus of a sacred precinct the newcomers made the beginnings of what is now the sanctuary.

Despite their long observance, the mysteries of the cult were never explicitly recorded, since ancient writers feared incurring the wrath of the Kabiroi (who could reputedly brew up sudden, deadly storms), but it has been established that two levels of initiation were involved. Both ceremonies, in direct opposition to the elitism of Eleusis, were open to all, including women and slaves. The lower level of initiation, or *myesis*, may, as is speculated at Eleusis, have involved a ritual simulation of the life, death and rebirth cycle; in any case, it's known that it ended with joyous feasting, and it can be conjectured, since so many clay torches have been found, that it took place at night. The higher level of initiation, or *epopteia*, carried the unusual requirement of a moral standard (the connection of theology with morality, so strong in the later Judeo-Christian tradition, was rarely made by the early Greeks). This second level involved a full confession followed by absolution and baptism in bull's blood.

The only **accommodation** near the sanctuary is in the tiny hamlet of **PALEÓPOLI**, where the old and basic *Xenia Hotel* (T 25510 41166 or 25510 41230; ❹) offers a downmarket alternative to the smart but overpriced *Kastro Hotel* (T 25510 89400, W www.kastrohotel.gr; ❺), which comes with pool, restaurant and sea views; there are also some basic but en-suite rooms (❸) down on the seashore below the *kástro*.

The site

The **site** (Tues–Sun 8.30am–8.30pm, or dusk if earlier; €3 combined ticket with museum but no charge for site when museum is closed) is well labelled, simple to grasp and strongly evokes its proud past, while commanding views of the mountains and the sea. You might like to visit the **archeological museum** first (Tues–Sun 8.30am–3pm), and its exhibits spanning all eras of habitation, from the Archaic to the Byzantine, since it explains the significance of the

△ Sanctuary of the Great Gods, Samothráki

sanctuary. Highlights include a **frieze** of dancing girls from the propylon of the Temenos, entablatures from different buildings, and Roman votive offerings such as coloured glass vials from the necropolis of the ancient town east of the sanctuary. You can also see a reproduction of the exquisitely sculpted marble statue, the *Winged Victory of Samothrace*, which once stood breasting the wind at the prow of a marble ship in the Nymphaeum (see below). Discovered in 1863 by a French diplomat to the Sublime Porte, it was carried off to the Louvre, where it is a major draw, and the well-crafted copy was graciously donated to this museum a mere century later.

The **Anaktoron**, or hall of initiation for the first level of the mysteries, dates in its present form from Roman times. Its inner sanctum was marked by a warning stele, now in the museum, and at the southeast corner you can make out the **Priestly Quarters**, an antechamber where candidates for initiation donned white gowns. Next to it is the **Arsinoeion**, the largest circular ancient building known in Greece, used for libations and sacrifices. Within its rotunda are the fourth-century BC walls of a double precinct where a rock altar, the earliest preserved ruin on the site, has been uncovered. A little further south, on the same side of the path, you come to the **Temenos**, a rectangular area open to the sky where the feasting probably took place, and, edging its rear corner, the conspicuous **Hieron**, the site's most immediately impressive structure. Five columns and an architrave of the facade of this large Doric edifice, which hosted the higher level of initiation, have been re-erected; dating in part from the fourth century BC, it was heavily restored in Roman times. The stone steps have been replaced by modern blocks, but Roman benches for spectators remain *in situ*, along with the sacred stones where confession was heard. To the west of the path you can just discern the outline of the theatre, while just above it, tucked under the ridge, is the **Nymphaeum (Fountain) of Nike**, which the *Winged Victory* used to preside over. West of the theatre, occupying a high terrace, are remains of the main *stoa*; immediately north of this is an elaborate medieval fortification made entirely of antique material.

The north coast

With its running streams, giant plane trees and namesake hot springs, **LOUTRÁ** (aka **THERMÁ**), 6km east of Paleópoli, is a pleasant place to stay, although in late July and August it is packed, mainly with an incongruous mixture of foreign hippies and elderly Greeks, here to take the sulphurous waters. Far more appealing than the grim baths themselves, the low waterfalls and rock pools of **Gría Váthra** are signposted 1.5km up the paved side road leading east from the main Thermá access drive.

Loutrá is the prime base for the tough, six-hour climb up the 1611-metre **Mount Fengári** (known to the ancients as **Sáos**, a name found on some maps to this day), the highest peak in the Aegean islands; the path starts at the top of the village, beside a concrete water tank and a huge plane tree. Tell your accommodation proprietors that you're going, but no one else, as the police may try to stop you – army teams have been summoned on occasion to rescue ill-prepared climbers on what can be an unforgiving mountain. Fengári is Greek for "moon" and, according to legend, if you reach the top on the night of a full moon your wish will come true – most of those foolhardy enough to attempt this will just hope to get back down safely.

Loutrá is a rather dispersed place, with its winding dead-end streets, all ghostly quiet in winter, and its miniharbour – built as an alternative to

Kamariótissa, but never used. **Accommodation** includes the *Kaviros Hotel* (☎25510 98277; ❹), just east of the "centre", and, further downhill, 700m from the beach, the *Mariva Bungalows* (☎25510 98258; ❹). Of the tavernas, *Paradhisos* has the best setting, up under the trees, and charges accordingly. About halfway along the track to Gría Váthra, *Safki*, a summer-only café–bar, occupies the delightful old schoolhouse.

Beyond Loutrá and a ford, on the wooded coastline and reached by a road initially signposted "military camp", are two municipal **campsites**: the first, 1.5km from the village, although large, has no facilities except toilets, while the second, 3km from the village, is more expensive but has hot water, electricity, a small shop, restaurant and bar. The Loutrá bus sometimes goes to either site if you ask nicely.

Beaches on Samothráki's north shore are mostly clean but uniformly pebbly and exposed, but it's still worth continuing along the road east from Loutrá for the views and one or two minor sights. At **Cape Foniás** there's a ruined Gateluzzi watchtower and, 45 minutes' walk inland along the stream, there are **waterfalls** and cold pools much more impressive than those at Gría Váthra, though the signposted description of "canyon" is exaggerated. Some 15km from Loutrá along a fine corniche road is **Kípos beach**, a long strand facing the Turkish-held island of Gökçeada (Ímvros to the Greeks) and backed by open pasture and picturesque crags. The water is clean and there's a rock overhang for shelter at one end, a spring, shower and seasonal drinks *kantína*, but no food available.

The south coast

From the warmer south flank of the island, with its fertile farmland dotted with olive groves, there are fine views out to sea – as far as Gökçeada on a clear day. Up to three daily buses go from Kamariótissa via the sleepy village of Lákoma as far as **PROFÍTIS ILÍAS**, an attractive hill village with a number of good **tavernas** – the best being *Paradhisos*, with a wonderful terrace – but no accommodation to speak of, except for some basic **rooms** (❷). From Lákoma it is 8km east to aptly named **Pahiá Ámmos** ("coarse sand"), a long, clean beach with a taverna-rooms outfit (☎25510 94235; ❸) at the west end. The nearest (meagre) supplies are in Lákoma, but this doesn't deter big summer crowds who also arrive by excursion *kaïkia*. These continue east to **Vátos**, a secluded beach (naturism tolerated) also accessible by land, the **Kremastá Nerá** coastal waterfalls, and finally round to Kípos beach (see above).

Thássos

Just 12km from the mainland, **Thássos** has long been a popular resort island for northern Greeks, and since the early 1990s has also attracted a cosmopolitan variety of tourists, in particular from central and eastern Europe, plus plenty of Western Europeans on packages. They are all entertained by vast numbers of *bouzoúkia* (music halls) and tavernas that lay on music at weekends (and during the week in July and August), while nature lovers can find some areas of outstanding beauty, especially inland. Moreover, the island's traditional industries have managed to survive the onslaught of modernity. Thássos still makes a substantial living from the pure-white marble that constitutes two-thirds of the land mass, found only here and quarried at dozens of sites (legal and unlicensed)

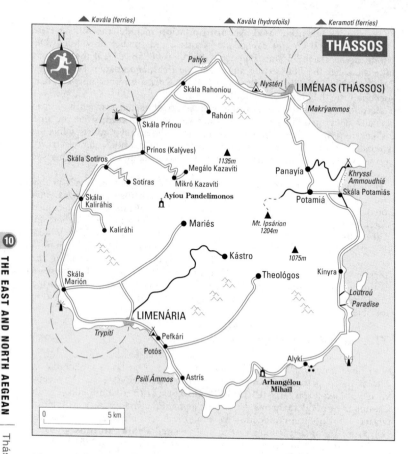

in the hills between Liménas and Panayía. Olives, honey, fruit and nuts (often sold candied) are also important products. The spirit *tsípouro*, rather than wine, is the main local tipple; pear extract, onions or spices like cinnamon and anise are added to home-made batches.

Inhabited since the Stone Age, Thássos was settled by Parians in the seventh century BC, attracted by gold deposits between modern Liménas and Kínyra. Buoyed by revenues from these, and from silver mines under Thassian control on the mainland opposite, the ancient city-state here became the seat of a medium-sized seafaring empire. Commercial acumen did not spell military invincibility, however; the Persians under Darius swept the Thassian fleets from the seas in 492 BC, and in 462 BC Athens permanently deprived Thássos of its autonomy after a three-year siege. The main port continued to thrive into Roman times, but lapsed into Byzantine and medieval obscurity.

Sadly, the salient fact of more recent history has been a series of devastating, deliberately set **fires** in the 1980s and 1990s. Only the northeastern quadrant of the island, plus the area around Astrís and Alykí, escaped, though the surviving forest is still home to numerous pine martens.

Thássos is just small enough to circumnavigate in one full day by rented motorbike or car. The KTEL will do the driving for you – albeit with little chance for stopping – some four times daily. **Car rental** is dominated by Potos Car Rental (℡25930 23969), with branches in all main resorts, or Rent-a-Car Thassos (℡25930 22535), also widely represented, as are most of the major international chains, such as Budget at Theayénous 2 in the capital, **Liménas** (℡25930 23050). Vigorous bargaining with the local one-off outfits is often productive of 35-percent discounts on official rates – particularly in early June or mid-September. On the other hand, don't bother showing up in Thássos much before or after these dates, as most facilities will be shut, and the weather can be dodgy in any case. Most hotels are closed between October and the end of April, so call ahead to check.

Liménas

Largely modern **LIMÉNAS** (also signposted as Limín or Thássos) is the island's capital, though not the only port. At first glance Liménas seems an unlikely resort, plagued as it is with surprisingly clogged vehicle traffic and often noisy bars, but it is partly redeemed by its picturesque fishing harbour and the substantial remains of the ancient city which appear above and below the streets.

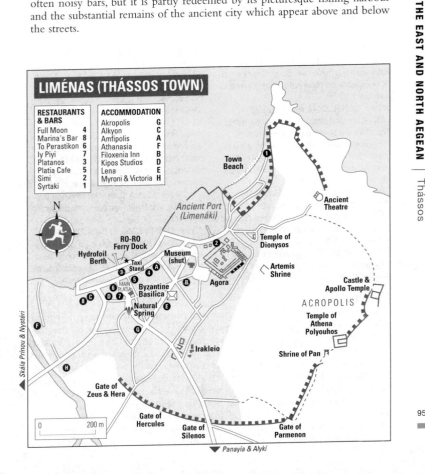

LIMÉNAS (THÁSSOS TOWN)

RESTAURANTS & BARS	
Full Moon	4
Marina's Bar	8
To Perastikon	6
Iy Piyi	7
Platanos	3
Platia Cafe	5
Simi	2
Syrtaki	1

ACCOMMODATION	
Akropolis	G
Alkyon	C
Amfipolis	A
Athanasia	F
Filoxenia Inn	B
Kipos Studios	D
Lena	E
Myroni & Victoria	H

Arrival, transport and information

Kavála-based ferries stop down the coast at Skála Prínou, with a KTEL bus always on hand to meet arrivals. Mountain and motorbikes can be rented from Billy's Bikes (℡25930 22490), Thomai Tsipou (℡25930 22815) or Babis (℡25930 22129). The KTEL office is on the front, virtually opposite the ferry mooring; the service is good, with several daily **buses** to Panayía and Skála Potamiás, Limenária via Potós, Theológos, Kínyra and Alykí. The **taxi** rank is just in front of the bus stop. Thassos Tours (℡25930 23250), at the east end of the waterfront, is the principal airline agent (the closest airport is Kavála's Alexander the Great, 14km from Keramotí on the mainland; see p.562). Several **banks** have ATMs.

Accommodation

Few **hotels** enjoy any tranquillity or decent views but there are some worthy finds; if none from the list below suits, there are also some relatively quiet rooms (❷–❸) just behind the town beach. Note that most of the town hotels are shut from October to early May. The closest **campsite** to town is at Nystéri cove, 2.5km west; the beach is reasonable, and its snack-bar has tables out on a lawn, but the site is small, basic and on hard ground.

As formal addresses are nonexistent, see the map opposite for the locations of the following listings.

Akropolis ℡25930 22488, ℻25930 22441. Occupying a fine traditional house with flagstone floors and a rear garden-bar, though it can get traffic noise; worth a try now that package companies don't use it. ❸

Alkyon ℡25930 22148, ℻25930 23662. Certainly the most pleasant of the harbour hotels; English tea and breakfast plus friendly, voluble management make it a home away from home for independent British travellers. Open most of the year; ask also about their cottage in Sotíras and beach villa at Astris. B&B ❸

Amfipolis ℡25930 23101, ℻25930 22110. Housed in a folly, this atmospheric hotel is the town's most exclusive accommodation outfit – and you pay dearly for the privilege of staying here; it also has a stylish drinks terrace. ❺

Athanasia ℡25930 23247. Giant and eccentrically furnished rooms with balconies; take the lane inland from behind the *Xenia Hotel* to reach it. Run by a friendly fisherman, this place takes the overflow from the *Alkyon.* ❷

Filoxenia Inn ℡25930 23331, ℻25930 22231. Quietly situated behind the archeological museum, this has immaculate rooms with fridges, designated breakfast areas and a garden with a small pool. ❺

Kipos Studios ℡25930 22469. In a quiet cul-de-sac next to *Iy Piyi* taverna, this has cool lower-ground-floor doubles (❸) and four-person galleried apartments of a fair standard (❹); a pool has been installed in the garden, ostensibly to make the premises attractive to package companies.

Lena ℡25930 23565. Good-value hotel near the post office, with English-speaking management; no packages. ❷

Myroni ℡25930 23256, ℻25930 22132. Excellent value, well run and allergic to package companies. It's co-managed with the more modest (no air con) *Victoria* (℡25930 23556; ❸) next door, with which it shares a common breakfast room. ❹

The Town

With its mineral wealth and safe harbour, **ancient Thassos** prospered from Classical to Roman times. The largest excavated area is the agora, a little way back from the fishing harbour. The site (free) is fenced but not always locked, and is most enjoyably seen towards dusk. Two Roman stoas are prominent, but you can also make out shops, monuments, passageways and sanctuaries from the remodelled Classical city. At the far end of the site (away from the sea) a fifth-century BC passageway leads through to an elaborate sanctuary of Artemis, a substantial stretch of Roman road and a few seats of the odeion. The nearby archeological museum is closed indefinitely for extensive expansion.

From a **temple of Dionysos** behind the fishing port, a path curls up to a **Hellenistic theatre**, fabulously positioned above a broad sweep of sea. It's currently open, but is a chaos of excavation, with summer-festival performances set to resume in the distant future. On the same corner of the headland as the theatre, you can still see the old-fashioned *kaïkia* being built, and gaze across to the uninhabited islet of Thassopoúla. It's possible to rent boats from the fishing harbour, self-skippered or not, to take you there and elsewhere.

From just before the theatre, the trail winds on the right up to the **acropolis**, where a Venetian-Byzantine-Genoese fort arose between the thirteenth and fifteenth centuries, constructed from recycled masonry of an Apollo temple, which stood here. You can continue, following the remains of a massive circuit of fifth-century walls to a high terrace supporting the foundations of the Athena Polyouhos (Athena Patroness of the City) temple, with Cyclopean walls. From the exit at the southern end of the temple, a short path leads to an artificial cavity in the rock outcrop which was a shrine of Pan, shown in faint relief playing his pipes. Following the path to the left around the summit brings you to a precipitous rock-hewn stairway with a metal handrail, which provided a discreet escape route to the Gate of Parmenon, the only gate in the fortifications to have retained its lintel; it name comes from an ancient inscription ("Parmenon Made Me") on a nearby wall slab. From here a track, then a paved lane, descend through the southerly neighbourhoods of the modern town, completing a satisfying one-hour circuit.

Eating, drinking and nightlife

Given the cheap-and-cheerful-package ethos, cuisine is not Liménas's strong point, and eateries are generally overpriced. The picturesque **tavernas** around the old harbour are predictably touristy – sophisticated *Simi* is marginally the best, and serves memorably good wine. Another good option is *Syrtaki*, at the far eastern end of the overly popular town beach. In the town centre, greasy fast food is all too abundant, though a dependable favourite for *mayireftá* is *Iy Piyi*, up at the south corner of the main square, next to the natural sunken spring of the name. *Platanos*, with a pleasant terrace opposite the ferry docks, is the place to head for breakfast, be it English style or ambrosia-like yoghurt and honey, and its coffee is highly drinkable. Finally, *To Perastikon*, at the northwest corner of the square near *Iy Piyi*, serves the best ice cream on the island. By contrast, there's plenty of choice in local **bars**: *Full Moon* near the *Hotel Amfipolis* is the main Anglophile watering-hole, and comes with a paperback-swap library. *Platia Cafe Bar*, on yet another corner of the basilica square, has good music, while *Marina's Bar* near the *Hotel Alkyon* is the best waterfront night spot, attracting a mainly Greek clientele.

Around the coast

Whether you plan to circumnavigate the island clockwise, or in the opposite direction, plan on a lunch stop at **Alykí**, roughly a third of the way along in the circuit described below, and the most photogenic spot along the coast.

Panayía, Potamiá and Mount Ipsárion

The first beach east of Liménas, **Makrýammos**, is a purpose-built, controlled-access compound for package tourists, so carry on to **PANAYÍA**, the attractive hillside village overlooking Potamiá Bay. It's a large, thriving place where life revolves around the central square with its large plane trees, fountain and slate-roofed houses. Top **accommodation** choice in both senses is the *Hotel Thassos Inn* (☎25930 61612, ℉25930 61027; ❹), up in the Tris Piyés district near the Kímisis church, with fine views over the rooftops. Down on the main road, beside the municipal car park, the newish, clean *Pension Stathmos* (℡ 25930 61666; ❸) is the quietest of several nearby, with stunning views out the back; there are also high-standard rooms (℡ 25930 61981; ❷) below the school basketball courts. There have been complaints about high-pressure touting tactics from the hotly competing tavernas on the square; for a more low-key approach, try *Iy Thea*, a view-terrace *psistariá* at the southeast edge of town en route to Potamiá.

POTAMIÁ, much lower down in the river valley, is far less prepossessing – with modern red tiles instead of slates on the roofs – and thus little visited, though it has a lively winter carnival. It also offers the **Polygnotos Vayis Museum** (Tues–Sat 9.30am–12.30pm, summer also 6–9pm, Sun 10am–1pm; free), devoted to the locally born sculptor; though Vayis emigrated to America when young, he bequeathed most of his works to the Greek state. Potamiá also marks the start of the preferred route up to the 1204-metre summit of **Mount Ipsárion**. Follow the bulldozer track to the big spring near the head of the valley extending west of the village (the last source of water), where you'll see the first red-painted arrows on trees. Beyond this point, cairns mark the correct turnings in a modern track system; forty minutes above the spring, take an older, wide track, which ends ten minutes later at a narrow ravine with a stream and the current trailhead. The path is steep, strenuous and unmaintained, and you'll be dependent on cairns and painted arrows. Go early in the day or season, and allow four hours up from Potamiá, and nearly as much for the descent.

Skála Potamiás and Khryssí Ammoudhiá

The onward road from Potamiá is lined with rooms for rent and apartment-type accommodation. A side road some 12km from Liménas takes you down to **SKÁLA POTAMIÁS**, at the southern end of the bay, where some fairly uninspired **tavernas** line the harbour front; a road off to the left brings you to sand dunes extending all the way to the far northern end of the bay. An honourable exception amongst the tavernas is *Flor International* (no sign), at the corner where the bus (hourly 7am–8pm to Liménas) turns around; the *Afrodite*, a short way along, is also acceptable for *mayireftá*. Worth a mention is *Eric's Bar* on the main road just outside the village, where one Stratos Papafilippou has made a career of his uncanny resemblance to footballer Eric Cantona; full English breakfast is available, you can watch Premiership matches on satellite TV and there is a heated outdoor swimming pool.

The best places to **stay** are either above the plane-shaded traffic turnaround area by the port, beyond the tavernas – where the *Hera* (℡ 25930 61467; ❷), just on the left looking inland, or the *Delfini* (℡ 25930 61275; ❷), 200m straight back, are peaceful but basic – or, if you're prepared to pay more, there's the *Miramare* (℡ 25930 77209; ❹), which has a swimming pool among well-manicured gardens, further up the same lane. Alternatively, head north along the shore towards the sandy beach, for **rooms** (❷–❸), to either side of the *Arion* (℡ 25930 61486; ❸) and *Anna* (℡ 25930 61070; ❷) hotels, which represent the best value hereabouts. The north end of this beach is called **Khryssí Ammoudhiá** ("golden sands"), an increasingly chaotic, built-up cluster of tavernas, hotels and a campsite; a direct road (plied by an infrequent bus service) spirals for 5km down from Panayía. Once there, you can choose between the self-catering *Villa Emerald* (℡ 25930 61979; ❹) or the *Golden Sand* (℡ 25930 61771 or 25930 61209; ❸), nearer the sands. The *Golden Beach* campsite (℡ 25930 61472) is the only official one on this side of the island.

Kínyra and Alykí

The dispersed hamlet of **KÍNYRA**, some 24km south of Limenás, marks the start of the burnt zone which overlooks it, though incipient greenery suggests that recovery is underway; it's endowed with a poor beach, a couple of grocery stores and several small hotels. Those not block-booked include *Villa Athina* (☎25930 41214; ❶) at the north end of things, whose top-floor rooms see the water over the olive trees, and the welcoming *Pension Marina* (☎25930 31384; ❶). *Yiorgos* and *Faros* are the best tavernas here. Kínyra is convenient for the superior **beaches** of Loutroú (1km south) and partly nudist Paradise (3km along) – officially called Makrýammos Kinýron – both of which can be reached down poorly signposted dirt tracks. The latter ranks as most scenic of all Thassian beaches, with still-forested cliffs inland, a namesake islet offshore beyond the extensive shallows and much cleaner water than at Khryssí Ammoudhiá. A couple of mediocre snack-bars behind the sand overcharge bathers.

The south-facing coast of Thássos has the balance of the island's best beaches. **ALYKÍ** hamlet, 35km from Limenás and just below the main road, faces a perfect double bay, which almost pinches off a headland. Uniquely, it retains its original whitewashed, slate-roofed architecture, since the presence of extensive antiquities here has led to a ban on any modern construction. Those ruins include an ancient temple to an unknown deity, and two exquisite early Christian basilicas out on the headland, with a few columns re-erected. The sand-and-pebble west bay gets oversubscribed in peak season, though you can always head off to the less crowded, rocky east cove, or snorkel in the crystal-clear waters off the marble formations on the headland's far side. Dominating the western inlet on the roadward side, well-established **taverna** *Glaros* serves fresh fish and has decent **rooms** (❸) to let. A lively bar and a row of water-edge tavernas also compete for your custom, with *To Limanaki/The Little Mole* winning, if only for its more varied menu – it also tends to open earlier in the year than the others. One kilometre further along the coast, at secluded **Kékes** beach among a pine grove, traditional taverna *Skidhia* also has **rooms** in plain but comfortable bungalows, with air-conditioning and en-suite bathrooms (☎25930 31528; ❸).

Arhangélou Mihaïl to Potós

Some 5km west of Alyki, the **convent of Arhangélou Mihaïl** (open reasonable daylight hours) clings spectacularly to a cliff on the seaward side of the road. Though founded in the twelfth century above the spot where a spring had gushed forth, the convent has been hideously renovated by the nuns, resident here since 1974. A dependency of Filothéou on Mount Athos (see p.554), its prize relic is a purported nail from the Crucifixion.

At the extreme south tip of Thássos, 9km further west, **ASTRÍS** (Astrídha) can muster two uninspiring medium-sized hotels, a few rooms and a good beach. Just 1km west is another better but crowded beach, Psilí Ámmos, with watersports on offer. A few kilometres further, **POTÓS** is the island's prime Germanophone package venue, its centre claustrophobically dense, with the few non-block-booked rooms overlooking cramped alleys. However, the kilometre-long beach is still unspoilt. For a less touristy place to eat, the **taverna** *Piatsa*, one of the cheaper and better places, is tucked away at the southern end of the seafront, in a semi-pedestrianized street; next door, *Michael's Place* has great ice cream and breakfasts. Along the harbour front a string of varyingly trendy **bars and cafés** offers viable alternatives. There are plenty of rental outlets for **cars**, scooters and mountain bikes, including the headquarters of Potos Rent a Car. **Pefkári**, with its manicured beach and namesake pine grove,

1km west, is essentially an annexe of Potós, with a few mid-range **accom-modation** options such as *Prasino Veloudho* (Ⓣ25930 52001, Ⓕ25930 51232; ❸) and the rather more upmarket *Thassos* (Ⓣ25930 51596, Ⓕ25930 51794; ❹). The **campsite**, *Pefkari* (Ⓣ25930 51190; June–Sept), with its attractive wooded location and clean facilities, is one of the best on Thássos.

Limenária and the west coast

LIMENÁRIA, the island's second town, was built to house German mining executives brought in by the Ottomans between 1890 and 1905. Their remaining mansions, scattered on the slopes above the harbour, lend some character, but despite attempts at embellishing the waterfront, it's not the most attractive place on Thássos, though it is handy for its **banks** and ATMs, **post office** and seasonal hydrofoil connections. The best **accommodation** is the Hotel George (Ⓣ25930 51413, Ⓕ25930 52530; ❹), with bright and modern rooms at the lower end of the main street leading down to the harbour front. At the east end of the quay, in some 1960s blocks, are a cluster of very basic hotels such as the *Sgouridis* (Ⓣ25930 51241; ❸). There are also plenty of **rooms** on offer (❷–❸). For eating and drinking, choose from among half-a-dozen each of bars and eateries along the front, of which *Mouragio* is the only one that comes close to having some charm.

The nearest good beach is **Trypití**, a couple of kilometres west – turn left into the pines at the start of a curve right. All development – mostly package villas – is well inland from the broad, 800-metre long strand, although there are umbrellas and sun loungers for rent. The cleft that the name refers to (literally "pierced" in Greek) is a slender tunnel through the headland at the west end of the beach, leading to a tiny three-boat anchorage.

Continuing clockwise from Limenária to Liménas, there's progressively less to stop off for as the western coast is the most exposed and scenically least impressive. The various *skáles* (harbours) such as Skála Kaliráhis and Skála Sotíros – originally the ports for namesake inland villages – are bleak, straggly and windy. **Skála Marión**, 13km from Limenária, is the exception that proves the rule: an attractive little bay, with fishing boats hauled up on the sandy foreshore, and the admittedly modern low-rise village arrayed in a U-shape all around. There are **rooms** available (❷–❸), a few tavernas and, most importantly, two fine beaches on either side. **Skála Prínou** has little to recommend it, other than ferry connections to Kavála. Buses are usually timed to coincide with the ferries, but if you want to stay, there are several hotels, numerous rooms, quayside tavernas and an EOT **campsite** (Ⓣ25930 71171; June–Sept) 1km south of the ferry dock. **Skála Rahoníou**, between here and Liménas, has more accommodation (including the *Perseus* campsite) and fish restaurants, as well as proximity to **Pahýs beach**, 9km short of Liménas, by far the best strand on the northwest coast. Narrow dirt tracks lead past various tavernas through surviving pines to the sand, partly shaded in the morning.

The interior

Few people get around to exploring inland Thássos – with the post-fire scrub still struggling to revive, it's not always rewarding – but there are several worthwhile excursions to or around the **hill villages**, besides the aforementioned trek up Mount Ipsárion from Potamiá (see p.954).

From Potós you can head 10km along a well-surfaced but poorly signposted road to **THEOLÓGOS**, founded in the sixteenth century by refugees from Constantinople and the island's capital under the Ottomans. Its houses, most with oversized chimneys and slate roofs, straggle in long tiers to either side of the main street, surrounded by generous kitchen gardens or walled courtyards. A stroll along the single high street, with its couple of *kafenía*, a soldiers' bar, sandalmaker and traditional bakery, is rewarding and quickly dispels the off-putting effect of vigorous advertising at the outskirts for "Greek Nights" at local tavernas. Two that eschew musical gimmicks and rely on their good fare are the long-running *Psistaria Lambiris*, at the entrance into town, and *Kleoniki/Tou Iatrou*, in the very centre, on the right-hand side past the bus stop and police station. They're at their best in the evening when the roasting spits, loaded with goat and suckling pig, start turning.

Despite its proximity as the crow flies, there's no straightforward way from Theológos to **KÁSTRO**, the most naturally protected of the anti-pirate redoubts; especially with a car, it's best to descend to Potós before heading up a rough, seventeen-kilometre dirt track from Limenária. Thirty ancient houses and a church surround a rocky pinnacle, fortified by the Byzantines and the Genoese, which has a sheer drop on three sides. Summer occupation by shep-herds is becoming the norm after total abandonment in the nineteenth century, when mining jobs at Limenária proved irresistible. There's only one *kafenío*, on the ground floor of the former school, one telephone therein, no mains elec-tricity and far more sheep than people.

From Skála Marión an unmarked but paved road (slipping under the main highway bridge to the north) proceeds 11km inland through gnarled old olive trees to well-preserved **MARIÉS** at the top of a wooded stream valley; of two tavernas here, the well-signed one to the right, *Bethel*, is preferable. From Skála Sotíros, a very steep road heads 3.5km up to **SOTÍRAS**, the only interior village with an unobstructed view of sunset over the Aegean and thus popular with foreigners, who've bought up about half of the houses for restoration. On the ridge opposite are exploratory shafts left by the miners, whose ruined lodge looms above the church. On the plane-shaded square below the old fountain, *O Platanos* taverna is congenially run by Maria and Manolis, who offer grills plus one *mayireftá* dish-of-the-day, good bulk wine and sometimes their potent, home-made *tsípouro*, but only in July and August.

From Prínos (Kalýves) on the coast road, you've a six-kilometre journey inland to the Kazavíti villages, shrouded in greenery that escaped the fires; they're (poorly) signposted and mapped officially as Megálo and Mikró Prínos but still universally known by their Ottoman name. **MIKRÓ KAZAVÍTI** marks the start of the track south for **MEGÁLO KAZAVÍTI**, where the magnificent platía, one of the prettiest spots on the whole island, is home to a couple of decent, normal-priced **tavernas**, while *Vassilis*, below in a beautifully restored house, is regarded as a cut above. Some 4km up from its *skála* (harbour), **RAHÓNI** is well set at the head of a denuded valley. The road up to the square has plenty of simple tavernas, such as *Iy Dhrosia*.

Travel details

Ferries

To simplify the lists that follow we've excluded several regular peripheral services on generally north-to-south routes. These are the weekly LANE sailing between Crete, Kárpathos, Rhodes, Kós, Kálymnos, Sámos, Híos, Lésvos, Límnos and Alexandhroúpoli (40hr for the full run, usually over the weekend), the Agoudimos sailing between Crete and Thessaloníki via Kárpathos, Rhodes, Kós, Kálymnos, Sámos and Thessaloníki (39hr for the full run); and the GA sailing linking Kavála with Límnos, Lésvos, Híos, Sámos and Ikaría (total journey time 26hr).

Áyios Efstrátios 4–5 weekly on Saos Ferries to Límnos, Kavála and Lávrio; 1–2 weekly on Saos to Psará, Sígri (Lésvos), Samothráki; 5 weekly by small local ferry to Límnos.

Foúrni 3 weekly to Sámos (northern ports) and Pireás, on GA; daily 7–7.30am except Sun on *Samos Sun* or *Samos Spirit* to Karlóvassi, returning 2pm; 4 weekly on *Samos Spirit* (7am) to Áyios Kírykos (Ikaría) and Vathý, returning 2.15pm.

Híos 11–14 weekly on NEL Lines to Pireás (10hr slow ferry, 5hr high-speed) and Lésvos (3hr 30min/1hr 30min); 3 weekly to Límnos on NEL, 1 weekly on Saos; 2 weekly to Sámos & Ikaría with Saos Ferries and/or *Panayía Psarianí*; 1 weekly to Sýros/Mýkonos & Lávrio on Saos Ferries. Daily 2pm *kaïki* to Inoússes except Sun morning, and Tues in off-season; 5–6 weekly on *Panayia Psariani* – usually at 3pm – from Híos Town to Psará (3hr 30min).

Ikaría At least daily from either Áyios Kírykos or Évdhilos to Sámos (both northern ports) and Pireás, on Hellenic Seaways or GA; 2 weekly to Foúrni from Áyios Kírykos on GA; 5–6 weekly to Mýkonos and Sýros from Áyios Kírykos on GA, 2 weekly to same from Évdhilos on Hellenic Seaways; 2 weekly to Náxos & Páros from Évdhilos on Hellenic Seaways; daily *kaïki* or small ferry from Áyios Kírykos to Foúrni, at either 2pm or 6pm; 3 weekly *kaïkia*, typically Mon, Wed & Fri mornings, from Manganítis to Áyios Kírykos.

Lésvos 11–14 weekly on NEL Lines from Mytilíni to Pireás (10–12hr direct, 13hr via Híos, 7hr high-speed; 10–12 weekly to Híos (3hr 30min, or 1hr 30min high-speed); 2 weekly on NEL from Mytilíni, 3 weekly on Saos Ferries from Sígri, to Límnos (5hr, 2hr 30min high-speed); 2 weekly to Thessaloníki on NEL (13hr, 6hr 30min high-speed); 1–2 weekly to Kavála on NEL (12hr); 1 weekly to Áyios Efstrátios, Samothráki and Alexandhroúpoli on Saos

from Sígri; 1 weekly to Mýkonos, Tínos, Sýros and Lávrio on Saos.

Límnos 3 weekly on NEL Lines to Lésvos (Mytilíni) & Híos, 3 weekly on Saos Ferries; 4–5 weekly to Áyios Efstrátios & Lávrio on Saos Ferries; 2–3 weekly to Sígri (Lésvos) and Samothráki on Saos Ferries; 4–5 weekly to Kavála on Saos, 1 weekly direct on NEL; 2 weekly direct to Thessaloníki on NEL; 2 weekly to Alexandhroúpoli on Saos; 3 weekly to Piraeus on NEL, 1 on Saos; 1 weekly to Sámos and Ikaría on Saos; 1–2 weekly to Kými (Évvia), Alónissos, Skópelos, Skiáthos and Vólos on Saos.

Sámos (Karlóvassi) As for Vathý, but no Agoudimos or LANE service.

Sámos (Pythagório) 4 weekly (Mon, Wed, Fri & Sun afternoon) with the *Nissos Kalymnos* to Agathónissi, Arkí, Lipsí, Pátmos, Léros and Kálymnos, with onward connections to all other Dodecanese (see p.877 for the full schedule).

Sámos (Vathý) 1–2 daily, on GA or Hellenic Seaways, to Ikaría (Áyios Kírykos or Évdhilos) and Pireás (11–14hr); 2 weekly to Páros & Náxos, on GA; 3 weekly to Foúrni on GA; 4–6 weekly to Mýkonos and Sýros on GA or Hellenic Seaways.

Samothráki 2–3 daily to Alexandhroúpoli (2hr 30min) in season, dropping to 5–6 weekly out of season. Also 2 weekly late spring & early autumn, up to 3 weekly in July & Aug, to Kavála (and thence other north Aegean islands). Also during July & Aug, 1 weekly (usually Fri) direct to Límnos.

Thássos At least 7 daily, in summer months only (1 daily Oct–May), between Kavála and Skála Prínou (1hr 15min; 8am–8pm, 6am–7pm to Kavála from the island); 10 daily all year round between Keramotí and Liménas (40min; 7am–10pm, 6am–8.30pm from Thássos).

Hydrofoils

Two companies, **Samos Flying Dolphins** and **Aegean Flying Dolphins**, operate out of Pythagório (Sámos). Full details of Aegean Flying Dolphins' Dodecanese service are given on p.878. The single craft of Sámos Flying Dolphins provides service to the east Aegean as follows: to Foúrni (3 weekly, 1hr–1hr 20min) and Ikaría, Áyios Kírykos (4 weekly, 1hr–1hr 25min).

Samothráki Served by hydrofoil from Alexandhroúpoli April–Nov 4–7 times weekly, usually at 8am (1hr); mid-June to mid-Sept 1–2 extra daily departures at 1 and/or 5pm. 2–4 times weekly the morning or early afternoon sailing may continue on to Límnos, but don't rely on this.

Thássos (Liménas) Service limited to summer: 8–15 times daily, 7am–9pm (6am–8pm from Thássos); in the high season there may also be 2–3 daily departures from Kavála to the west-coast resorts of Skála Kalirahón, Skála Marión and Limenária.

International ferries

Híos–Çeşme (Turkey) 2–13 boats weekly at 8.30am and/or 6.30pm, depending on season; Thurs evening (Turkish boat) & Sat morning (Greek boat) services tend to run year-round. Passenger fares on the Greek boat (*San Nicholas*, Sunrise Tours) or Turkish vessel (*Ertürk II*) are nominally about €40, including Greek taxes (no Turkish tax), but "special offers" of €30–35 are frequent; one way €25. Small cars €65–70 one way, €110 return, plus small Greek tax. Journey time 30min (*San Nicholas*) or 45min (*Ertürk II*).

Mytilíni (Lésvos)–Ayvalık (Turkey) Daily May–Oct; winter link unreliable. Two Mytilíni-based craft, the Turkish *Jalehan* and the Greek *Mytilinii*, depart Mytilíni 8–8.30am most days. Passenger rates €29 one way or round trip, all taxes inclusive. Small cars (each boat carries two) €60 one way, €90 return. Journey time 1hr 20min.

Vathý (Sámos)–Kuşadası (Turkey) 2 daily, early May to late Oct. Greek boat at 8am; afternoon (4.45pm) Turkish boats (usually 2 craft in season). Rates are €35–40 one way including taxes on both the Greek and Turkish sides (Turkish boat slightly cheaper),

€45 day return including taxes, €60 open return including taxes. The Turkish boats are not allowed to carry cars owing to deficient insurance; cars are only ferried on the Greek craft Fri, Sat & Sun (€50 one way, €100 return for a small car, plus €10 Turkish tax each way). Journey time 1hr 30min.

Flights

NB: All flights on Olympic Airlines/Aviation unless otherwise specified. Frequencies are for the period June–Sept.

Híos to: Athens (4–5 daily on Olympic, 2 daily on Aegean; 50min); Límnos (2 weekly, both via Lésvos; 1hr 35min); Rhodes (2 weekly, 1 via Sámos; 55min–1hr 45min); Thessaloníki (4 weekly, 2 via Lésvos/Límnos; 1hr 10min–2hr 45min).

Lésvos to: Athens (3–5 daily on Olympic, 3 daily on Aegean; 1hr); to Límnos (5 weekly; 40min); Rhodes (5 weekly, 3 via Híos/Sámos; 1hr 5min–1hr 40min); Sámos (2 weekly, 1 direct; 45min–1hr 30min); Thessaloníki (10 weekly, 5 via Límnos, on Olympic; 1 daily direct on Aegean; 1hr 10min–1hr 50min).

Límnos to: Athens (2–3 daily; 1hr); Lésvos (5 weekly; 35min); Rhodes (5 weekly; 2hr 5min–2hr 50min); Thessaloníki (6 weekly; 45min).

Sámos to: Athens (4–5 daily; 55min); Rhodes (2 weekly; 45min); Lésvos (2 weekly, 1 via Híos; 50min–1hr 30min); Límnos (2 weekly, via Lésvos/Híos; 1hr 35min–1hr 55min); Thessaloníki (2 weekly direct, 2 via intervening islands; 1hr 20min–3hr 45min).

The Sporades and Évvia

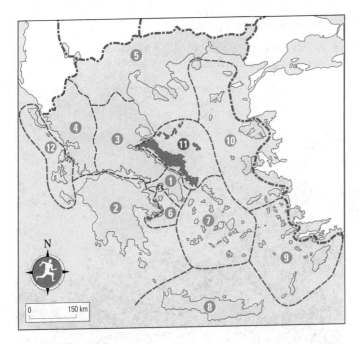

N

0   150 km

* **Lalária beach, Skiáthos** This
beautiful beach of smooth
white stones and turquoise
waters, backed by steep
cliffs and framed by a famous
natural arch, is only accessible by boat. **See p.967**

* **Skópelos and Glóssa**
Pristine facades, slate roofs,
bushy palms and luxuri-
ant bougainvillea make
these two of the prettiest
island towns in the whole of
Greece. **See p.970 & p.973**

* **Skýros** Goaty goings-on,
fancy furniture and painted

pottery – just some of the
attractions of one of the
least spoiled islands in the
Aegean. **See p.980**

* **Convent of Ayíou Nikoláou
Galatáki, Northern Évvia** A
convent decorated with vivid
sixteenth-century frescoes.
See p.993

* **Loutrá Edhipsoú** Belle
Époque splendours in
Greece's top spa town, and
an international music festival:
all to be found at the remoter
end of Greece's second
biggest island. **See p.994**

△ Skýros Town

The Sporades and Évvia

The **Sporades**, as their Greek name suggests, are a group of islands scattered like seeds in the Aegean, just off the central mainland, their mountainous terrain betraying their origin as extensions of Mount Pílio (see p.371). The three main northern islands are archetypal holiday islands, with fine beaches, transparent waters and lively nightlife – all are very crowded in July and August. **Skiáthos**, nearest to the mainland, is the busiest in the group as it boasts the best beaches and an airport, but **Skópelos**, an emerald isle of thick pine forests, is catching up fast. The quietest and most primitive of the three, **Alónissos**, farthest from the continent, falls within the National Marine Park, a destination more for nature lovers than night-owls.

Skýros, the remotest of the main Sporades, is located some way to the south-east. It retains more of its traditional culture than the others, though tourist development is now well under way. While the dramatically located main town remains a working village rather than a resort, its main street is not without its fast-food and souvenir shops, and a couple of popular beach resorts are situated nearby.

Between Skýros and the continent, the huge island of **Évvia** (classical "Euboea") runs for 150km alongside the mainland. One of the most attractive Greek islands, with a forested mountain spine and long stretches of rugged, largely undeveloped coast, it is explored by few foreign tourists. This is perhaps because it lacks any impressive ruins or real island feel owing to its size and proximity to the mainland. Even so, Athenians and other mainlanders visit the island in force and have erected holiday homes around a handful of seaside resorts.

The northern Sporades are well connected by **bus** and **ferry** with Athens (via Áyios Konstandínos or Vólos), and less often by boat from Thessaloníki; it's easy to island-hop between them. The only connection to Skýros is from Kými on Évvia via a car and passenger ferry. Évvia is linked to the mainland by a couple of bridges at its capital Halkídha, and by local ferries from half a dozen strategic points on the mainland. Only Skiáthos and Skýros have **airports**. Many people come to the Sporades to hike – the pines provide welcome shade. The best **maps** are those published for each island by Anavasi, widely available in Athens and on the islands themselves, for €5–6.

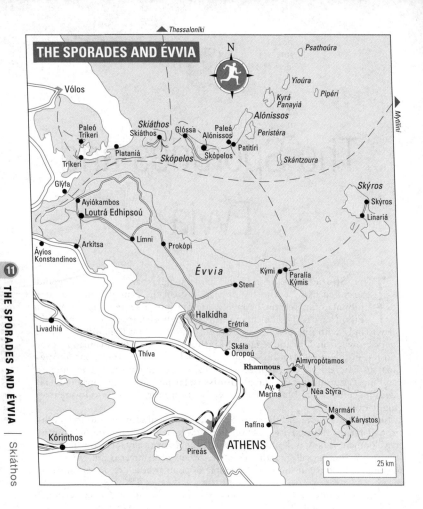

Skiáthos

An easy-on-the-eye green landscape, a couple of fine Orthodox monasteries and the labyrinthine streets of the main town are certainly attractions, but the real business of **Skiáthos** is **beaches**: the best, if most crowded, in the Sporades. Tourist literature claims that they number more than sixty, but that's still not enough to soak up the hordes of summer visitors. At the height of season, the island population of four thousand is outnumbered with up to fifty thousand visitors - only Corfu (Kérkyra), Mýkonos and Rhodes (Ródhos) are busier. Along the south and southeast coasts, the road serves an almost unbroken line of villas, hotels and restaurants, and although this doesn't take away the island's natural beauty, it does make it difficult to find anything particularly Greek about it. Nonetheless, you can escape the rush and bustle of the southern coastal strip by heading for the hills: **hiking** through most of northern Skiáthos will bring you to some refreshingly deserted vistas, while an all-terrain vehicle will also get you well off the beaten track. If you're planning to **camp**, bear in mind that pitching your tent outside official sites is strongly discouraged, since summer turns the dry pine-needles to tinder.

Skiáthos Town

SKIÁTHOS TOWN, the main town and port, clambers over two small promontories, dividing the picturesque fishing port from the workaday ferry dock and marina. The western side, with its cubist architecture, maze-like lanes and shady squares rewards aimless exploration while tourist development has scarred the east side of town and main drag Alexándhrou Papadhiamándi, where most services, tackier shops, "English" pubs and eateries are located. Conversely, some pockets of real charm are tucked into the alleys in the older, higher quarter – houses, gardens and flowers galore. As a result, and thanks to some good restaurants and nightclubs, Skiáthos can be fun in a crowded, boisterous sort of way.

Arrival and Information

Buses and taxis ply from the area around the **ferry harbour**. Buses run along the main south coast road to Koukounariés, at least hourly in summer (every fifteen minutes at peak times), the last bus returning at 1am; the stops are numbered one to twenty-five.

A large number of competing **rental outlets** in town, most on the front behind the ferry harbour, offer bicycles, motorbikes, cars and motorboats. For an honest and helpful approach, try the efficient Heliotropio (℡24270 22430, Ⓔheiio@skiathos.gr) opposite the ferry berth, also excellent for accommodation. The cheapest, smallest cars go for around €30 per day for one week's rental, while scooters go for between €15 and €20 per day depending on the

length of rental. Several travel agents also organize "round-the-island" mule trips (€20 a day).

Other than using the buses or the various rental outlets in town, you can also get your bearings on a **boat trip** around the island (€20 per person; 5–6hr; leaving 10am daily in high season). Longer excursions, taking in the National Marine Park (see p.979), cost around €30. You could also make a boat trip to the islet of **Tsougriá** (opposite Skiáthos Town), where there's a good beach and a taverna; boats leave from the fishing harbour beyond the Boúrtzi. Boats to the east coast of the island leave from the quay area in front of the bus station, while a bewildering array of tour boats moor at the fishing harbour.

Most other facilities are on Alexándhrou Papadhiamándi, including the **post office** and **banks** (several with **ATMs**); you can check **email** at Internet Zone, Evangelistrías 28.

Accommodation

Much of the island's **accommodation** is in Skiáthos Town. The few reasonably priced hotels or pensions are heavily booked in season, though you can usually find a room (❹–❺), albeit at a slightly more elevated price than on most islands. At other times, supply exceeds demand and you can find very cheap **rooms** with a little bargaining. There is a room-owners' association kiosk on the quay that opens for the best part of the day in high season, but at other times bookings can be made through several tourist agencies.

Good, small **hotels** include the jointly run *Bourtzi* (☎24270 22694, ⓦwww .hotelbourtzi.gr; ❺) on Moraïtou, and *Pothos* (☎24270 22694; ❺), on Evangelistrías, both immaculate with delightful gardens; the former has a swimming pool, the latter only a shady patio. You might also try the *Meltemi* (☎24270 22493; ❺), a pleasant hotel with well-maintained rooms some with balconies, on the waterfront, near the taxi rank. Nearby is the *Akti Hotel* (☎24270 22024, ⓕ24270 22430; ❺) another fine option whose top-floor penthouse, sleeping four, is a good deal if you can land it.

Of the island's three official **campsites**, the closest is that at Xánemos beach, 3km to the northeast of Skiáthos Town next to the airport runway. Apart from being within walking distance of town and close to the beach, there's little to recommend it.

The Town

There aren't many sights to speak of in Skiáthos, but the **Papadiamantis Museum** (Tues–Sun 9.30am–1.30pm & 5–8pm), housed in the nineteenth-century home of one of Greece's best-known writers, Alexandros Papadiamantis, is worth a look. The first floor of the two-storey building has been maintained as the writer's original house, while the ground floor operates as a bookshop-cum-exhibition-area featuring traditional artefacts from the island. The Galerie Varsakis **antique shop** (open usual shop hours), on Platía Trión Ierarhón just inland from the fishing port, has one of the best **folklore displays** in Greece, and many of the older items would do Athens' Benáki Museum (see p.143) proud; the proprietor neither expects, nor wants, to sell the more expensive of these, which include antique textiles, handicrafts and jewellery.

Eating and drinking

There is no shortage of places to **eat**, but nothing is keenly priced apart from the few burger/*yíros* joints, mostly along the main street and nearby. The best fish restaurants tend to be at the far end of the old harbour promenade – their prices reflect this.

1901 En Skiatho In a charming old stone building, close to Platía Trión Ierarhón, this reliable place offers up *bouzoúki*, guitar or jazz to accompany your good-value meal of impeccably prepared traditional Greek fare, accompanied by mellow wine from the barrel.

Alexandros Kapodistríou. This well-signposted taverna is a decent, preferred-by-locals joint with good bulk wine.

Calypso New harbour front. Surprisingly sophisticated Italian-influenced trattoria, serving specials such as black pasta with seafood and wine by the glass.

Dinos Papadhiamándi. One of the most convenient places for breakfast – offering the whole works.

Maria's Syngroú 6. Tucked away up in the back-streets, this is a place to sample excellent pizzas.

Mesogeia Above and to the west of Platía Trión Ierarhón. Of the more traditional and consequently cheaper places to eat, it has excellent moussaka and other home-cooked dishes.

The Windmill Well-signposted, high up overlooking the harbour, this is the decided favourite in the haute cuisine stakes with carefully crafted fish dishes, and commendable pasta and roast vegetables.

Nightlife

In addition to the ultra-trendy waterfront **bars** around the fishing port, with names like Slip Inn, Stay Cool, Bar Fly and Cassa Blanca - **nightlife** centres on the clubs on or near Polytekhníou. The outdoor **cinema**, Refresh Paradiso, on the ring road, shows new releases in their original language. Another source of entertainment is the little offshore Boúrtzi fortress, transformed into an outdoor **theatre** and home to occasional plays and musical performances during the summer.

Adagio Evangelistrías. A bar for those who prefer the softer tones of classical music.

Admiral Benbow Polytekhníou. This very Anglicized and rather small pub plays 1970s and 80s British pop hits to accompany draft cider and English ale.

Borzoi Polytekhníou. The oldest club on the island, playing an eclectic sampling of Latino, blues, rock and jazz.

Kentavros Near the Papadiamantis Museum, on Mitropolítou Ananíou. This long-established and much-loved bar plays jazz and blues.

Around the island

Stopping at two dozen halts along the way, the island bus shuttles between the main town and Koukounariés, a busy resort whose majestic sandy bay of clear, gradually deepening water is backed by acres of pines. Beaches are most people's destination for the day but, with your own transport or if you are prepared to hike, you can escape the crowds, explore the hinterland and visit a monastery or two.

The beaches

The beaches on the northeast coast aren't easily accessible unless you pay for an excursion kaïki: reaching them on foot requires extremely arduous treks. In any case, the prevailing summer meltémi wind blows from the north, so the beaches on the south coast are usually better protected, and you can easily reach a good number of them from the coast road, served by bus. Most of the popular ones have at least a drinks/snacks stall; those at Vromólimnos, Asélinos and Troúlos have proper tavernas.

The famed **Lalária** beach, featuring on all postcard-stands, is situated almost at the northernmost point of Skiáthos, and can be reached only by taxi-boats from the town. Covered in smooth white pebbles, with steep cliffs rising behind and an artistic natural arch, it's undeniably beautiful and the swimming is excellent, but beware the undertow. Nearby three natural grottoes – Skotiní, Galázia and Halkiní – are included in many of the "round-the-island" trips.

△ Beach on the Kalamáki peninsula, Skiáthos

A short way to the north of Skiáthos town, accessible by road, are the grey-ish sands of **Mégas Yialós**, one of the less crowded beaches, and **Xánemos**, a nudist beach, but both suffer from airport noise. As you head south, the beaches before the **Kalamáki peninsula** are no great shakes either, but on the promontory itself are the excellent **Tzaneriá** and **Vromólimnos**; Vromólimnos offers windsurfing and water-skiing and is now home to a pumping beach party scene replete with a bungee-jump crane. Overlooking Tzaneriá beach on the eastern side of the Kalamáki peninsula, the Dolphin Diving Centre (☎24270 22599) at the *Nostos* hotel offers **scuba diving**.

Just before Troúlos beach you can turn right up a paved road, which runs 3.5km north to **Megálos Asélinos**, an exposed sandy beach with a bar, reasonable taverna and a decent **campsite**, *Aselinos* (☎24270 49312; April–Oct). A daily bus and excursion boats call here, so it's crowded in season. The fork in the paved road leading to Panayías Kounístras convent (see below) continues to **Mikrós Asélinos**, just east of its larger neighbour and somewhat quieter.

The beaches at **KOUKOUNARIÉS**, the island's second biggest settlement, are excellent if you don't mind the crowds; wooden walkways traverse the sand to a series of *kantínas* selling drinks and light snacks. The approach road runs behind a small lake at the back of the pine trees, and features a string of **hotels**, **rooms** and **restaurants**, as well as a campsite, *Koukounaries* (☎24270 49250; May 15–Sept 15), which is fairly decent with standard facilities. Here, the *Strofilia Apartments* (☎24270 49251, ✉strophilia@n-skiathos.gr; ❻) are particularly nicely furnished. The prominent *Lake Hotel* (☎24270 49362; ❹), right opposite the lake itself, is also decent value. Jet-skis, motorboats, windsurfing and waterskiing are all available off the beach and there's horse-riding at the well-signposted Skiathos Riding Centre.

Signposted across the headland, "**Banana beach**" (officially known as Krasás), is one of the island's trendiest beaches with watersports, a couple of bars and tolerance of nude bathing; named for its crescent of yellow sand, it is divided by rocks into Big Banana and partly gay Small Banana. The turnoff from the coast road for neighbouring **Ayía Eléni** leads 1km to a more accessible, family-oriented beach with a drinks kiosk. Further north, **Mandhráki** and **Eliá** beaches have similar facilities, but are only accessible on foot or by scooter along dirt tracks.

The monasteries and Kástro

Founded at the end of the eighteenth century, the **monastery of Evangelistrías** (daily 8am–noon & 4–8pm) is exceptionally beautiful, even beyond the grandeur of isolation you find in all Greek monasteries. The Greek flag was raised here in 1807, and heroes of the War of Independence such as Kolokotronis pledged their oaths to fight for freedom here. From Skiáthos Town, you can reach Evangelistrías by motorized transport in less than ten minutes or on foot in just over an hour. From the centre, head 500m along the road towards the airport; where the asphalt veers to the right, take a prominently signposted paved side road that veers left; be careful to stick to this and not to wander off onto the dirt roads.

Beyond Evangelistrías, a mule track continues to the abandoned **Ayíou Haralámbou** monastery, from where it's possible to walk northwest to the ruined capital of Kástro (see below) along another dirt road; this takes about two hours. To reach Kástro from Skiáthos Town, it's quicker to take the direct paved road towards it on a motorbike, or take a *kaïki* ride round the island and get off at the beach below.

Continuing west from Evangelistrías, first on track, then on *kalderími*, you reach the paved, Kástro-bound road noted above; turn left, and after 200m or so bear right (west) onto the well-used, signposted dirt track heading towards the abandoned fifteenth-century monastery of **Theotókou Kekhreás**, three hours' walk from town. This is purported to be the oldest monastery on the island and has a colony of bats inside. It's a beautiful walk (or organized donkey-ride), and there are three pebbly beaches below, one with a welcoming stream-waterfall that provides a cool shower. Back on the paved road, you can continue on to the **Kástro** in about thirty minutes – a spectacular spot, built on a windswept headland. In the past, the entrance was only accessible by a drawbridge, which has been replaced by a flight of steps. The original settlement was built in the sixteenth century, when the people of the island moved here for security from pirate raids. It was abandoned three hundred years later in 1830, following independence from Turkey, when the population moved back to build the modern town on the site of ancient Skiáthos. The ruins are largely overgrown, and only four churches survive intact, the largest still retaining some original frescoes. From outside the gates, a path leads down the rocks to a good pebble **beach**; with a stream running down from the hills and a daytime café (with slightly overpriced food and drinks), it makes a good place to camp. For an apparently inaccessible spot, though, it does attract a surprising number of people. All the island excursion boats call here, and even when they've gone, there's little chance of having the ruins or beach to yourself.

Finally, the seventeenth-century **Panayías Kounístras** can be reached by taking the right fork along the paved road that runs north across the island from Tróulos to Asélinos beach. It's a very pretty little nunnery, with splendid icons hanging from a beautiful carved screen.

Skópelos

Painted a soothing green by its extensive pine-forests, **Skópelos** is bigger and more rugged than Skiáthos and almost as busy, but its concessions to tourism are lower key and in better taste. Although most of the larger beaches have sunbeds, umbrellas and some watersports, smaller, secluded coves do exist. Inland are prolific olive-groves, and orchards of plums (prunes are a local speciality), pears and almonds. **Skópelos (Hóra)** and **Glóssa**, the two main towns, are also among the prettiest in the Sporades, clambering uphill along paved steps, their houses distinguished by attractive wooden balconies and grey slate roofs.

A number of **nationalities** have occupied the island at various stages of its history, among them the Romans, Persians, Venetians, French and, of course, the Ottomans. The Ottoman pirate-admiral Barbarossa (Redbeard) – actually a Greek renegade from Lésvos – had the entire population of the island slaughtered in the sixteenth century. These days Greeks still manage to outnumber foreign visitors, thanks to the lack of an airport.

Skópelos, especially the pine-clad uplands of its western tract, is prime **walking** territory. Englishwoman and long-time Skópelos resident Heather Parsons runs guided **walking tours** (☎694 52 49 328, ⓦwww.skopelos-walks.com), some ending up at beaches and restaurants.

Skópelos town and around

SKÓPELOS Town (Hóra) slopes down a hill at one corner of a huge, almost circular bay: the tree-lined harbour front, a cascade of handsome mansions and an array of glistening white churches is revealed slowly as the boat rounds the final headland. Though more and more people seem to have discovered Skópelos town, the locals are making a tremendous effort to keep it from going the way of Skiáthos. So while the harbour area is practically wall-to-wall tavernas and cafés, the shops and eateries in the back alleys tend to be imaginative and tasteful, with wooden, hand-painted name signs. Spread below the ruins of a Venetian fortress or **kástro** is an enormous number of

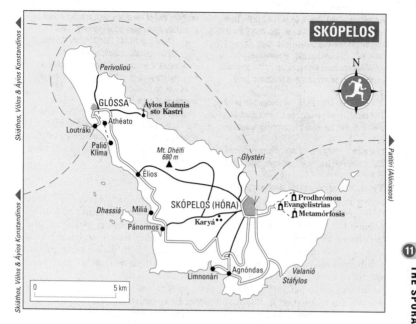

Perivolioú

GLÓSSA   Áyios Ioánnis
          sto Kastrí

Loutráki   Athéato

Palió
Klíma   Mt. Dhélfi
        680 m   Glystéri

Élios

Dhassiá   Miliá   SKÓPELOS (HÓRA)   Prodhrómou
                                    Evangelistrías
Pánormos   Karyá   Metamórfosis

Limnonári   Agnóndas   Valanió
                        Stáfylos

0   5 km

chapels and churches – 123 reputedly, though some are small enough to be mistaken for houses and most are locked except for their annual festival day.

Arrival and Information

The **ferry quay** is at the middle of a long promenade, lined with an array of boutiques, bars, stores and restaurants. Hydrofoil and ferry agencies are opposite the ferry quay; the **bus station** is 100m to the left of the port as you exit. Opposite the harbour entrance, a short road leads into a maze of lanes and signposts to the **post office**, and there are **banks** (with ATMs) about 50m from the ferry quay. You can access the **Internet** at a cybercafé opposite the Metro Club on Doulídhis.

From 7am to 10.30pm, **buses** (6–8 daily) ply the main paved road between Skópelos Town and Loutráki via Glóssa, stopping at the paths to all the main beaches and villages. Among the several **motorbike rental** outlets, friendly service can be had at Panos Wheels (℡24240 23696), near the start of the road towards Glóssa. If you prefer to explore from the sea, day-long **boat cruises** cost around €15 for a trip around the island, or to Alónissos and the National Marine Park (see p.979).

Accommodation

Unless you've booked through a tour operator, you're unlikely to find space in one of the larger, more expensive **hotels** with pools on the hill above the port, but there are dozens of **rooms** (❸–❹) for rent just behind the harbourside promenade or in the backstreets. These can be arranged through the Association of Room Owners office (daily 9am–noon & 6–8pm; ℡ & ℻24240 24567), on the seafront opposite the ferry dock. Madro Travel, by the northern quay (℡24240 22145), is also an excellent place to ask about accommodation, in addition to boat excursions and the like.

Adonis ℡24240 22231, ℗24240 23239. This brightly painted establishment, just above the mid-seafront, is fine though it can be noisy. ❺

Aperitton ℡24240 22256, ⓦwww.aperitton .gr. A modern hotel with pool, up on the ring road, combining contemporary and traditional local architecture. ❼

Dionysos ℡24240 23210, ⓔdionysos@otenet.gr. This first-rate, neo-rustic hotel, with a palm-fringed pool, is one of the more sophisticated lower-town options. ❻

Georgios L. ℡24240 22308, ⓔgeorgios-hotel @skopelos.net. This bland, old-style hotel at the

northern end of the promenade is a fair standby, especially if you have a car (parking). ❹

Mando ℡24240 23917. Easily the best of accommodation down at Stáfylos (see below); it is extremely friendly and quiet with neat studios set among bowling-green lawns, a short way up from its own rocky beach. ❺

Skopelos Village ℡24240 22517, ⓦwww .skopelosvillage.gr. Located some 500m around the bay from the docks, to the south side of Hóra, these smart bungalows and studios (mostly snapped up by package companies) are set among a green oasis. ❻

The Town and around

Sights include a poorly displayed **folklore museum** (daily 10am–2.30pm & 6–10pm; €2), featuring a motley collection of valuable nineteenth and early-twentieth-century embroidered cloths, traditional costumes, weaving and decorative artefacts; the highly informative illustrated panels explaining local customs and the religious calendar save the day. High-quality photography exhibitions are held at the **Photographic Centre** (summer: daily 10am–8pm; €1.50) at the eastern end of town.

Outside town, perched on the slopes opposite the quay, are two convents worth visiting for their seclusion and views: **Evangelistrías** (daily 8am–1pm & 4–7pm), which is within view of the town, and **Prodhrómou** (daily 8am–1pm & 5–8pm). Also on this promontory, the monastery of **Metamórfosis**, nestled among lush vegetation, was abandoned in 1980 but is now being restored by the monks and is open to visitors. Access is simplest via an old road behind the line of hotels along the bay to Evangelistrías (an hour's walk). From there it's an extra half-hour's scramble over mule tracks to Pródhromos (with signs to Metamórfosis en route), the remotest and most beautiful of the three. Ignore the new road that goes part way – it's longer, and misses most of the beauty of the walk.

Some 4km south of town, **Stáfylos** is the closest good beach, and is getting increasingly crowded even though rather small and rocky. The road between here and Hóra is lined with more and more places to stay, but these have neither the advantage of Hóra's nightlife and facilities nor Stáfylos' seafront. When Stáfylos beach gets too busy, head a short walk east along the coast to **Valanió**, where you've a better chance of escaping the crowds. Nudity is tolerated and, although the official campsite has long since closed, you shouldn't be hassled if you stay a night or two. There's spring water and a *kantína* here, too.

Eating and drinking

Skópelos Town offers a wide variety of **places to eat**, ranging from acceptable *souvlaki*-joints to truly excellent tavernas serving slightly different food at reasonable prices.

To Aktaion At the northern end of the promenade. One of the most reliable fish tavernas in town.

Anna's Tucked high up in the backstreets behind the port, but well-signposted, this taverna, with a terrace beneath a palm-tree, does Greek food with a slightly Gallic flavour; slow service.

Le Bistro Just behind the seafront near the docks. This sophisticated newcomer offers delicacies such

as hare in a red wine sauce, in addition to more conventional seafood pasta and the like; doubles up as a cocktail bar in the early evening.

La Frianderie Opposite the ferry quay. This delicatessen with a range of fresh baguettes, cakes and drinks, plus Greek pies and pastries, is perfect for a quick pre-ferry snack or breakfast.

Klimataria Near the Town Hall. Perhaps the most popular of all the traditional fish tavernas.

Nostos Towards the docks end of the seafront promenade, this taverna has exceptionally pleasant staff and large, delicious and reasonably priced portions of moussaka and the like.

Perivoli Up a narrow street from the square where you'll find the *Platanos* duo of *souvláki*-joints: an excellent, professionally run taverna in an exquisite garden, preparing good-value Greek food with a cordon bleu twist; wine by the glass.

O Platanos Not one but two *souvláki* places, just inland in the shade of the namesake plane-tree, competing for the distinction of having the best *yíros*; the one with blue chairs has a much wider menu.

Nightlife

Nightlife in Skópelos is increasing, but is more of the late-night-**bar** than the nightclub variety. If you want to head for something more like a **club**, try the enormous, masted, beached galleon, Karavi, reaching out over the harbour perimeter road on the south side. For news of music venues, look for signs around town with their opening days and times.

Anatoli Old rebétika hand Yiorgos Xintaris performs until late on weekends at this small ouzerí on top of the *kástro*.

Bambalo One of two live Greek music clubs up on the ring road.

Platanos Jazz Club A long-standing club on the north side of the harbour, still hanging on (just).

Rembetiki Istoria A popular joint on the ring road which, not surprisingly, features a programme of rebétika music.

Vengera Look out for this classy bar in a restored house in the backstreets; mellow ambience and good music.

Glóssa, Loutráki and around

Skopelos' sleepy second town, **GLÓSSA**, 25km from Hóra at the northern end of the island, seems much further away, and few visitors to the island even bother to explore the place. A fair-sized village of handsome houses, some Cycladic cubes, others Macedonian-style mansions with wooden balconies, it dangles down a steep hillside. Along its winding narrow streets, mostly car-free, you can unearth several *kafenía*, an excellent taverna and a few **rooms** to let, some of which are hot and musty, with erratic water pressure. An exception, *Kostas and Nina's Place* (☎24240 33686; ❸) has simple, clean rooms, some with a view; they also rent out studios longer term. Otherwise you could stay at the *Selinounda Apartments* (☎24240 33570; ❹) on the road down to Loutráki. The well-signposted central **taverna**, justly popular *To Agnandi*, serves excellent, innovative food – try the pork with prunes or the almond cake with elderflower syrup - and has a roof terrace with wonderful views.

Hydrofoils and some car ferries call at the diminutive port of **LOUTRÁKI** ("Glóssa" on ferry and hydrofoil schedules), 3km from Glóssa proper down a steep snaking road. It is little more than a narrow pebble beach with a couple of hotels and rooms for rent. If you need to stay over, you could try any of the **rooms** (❸) advertised just in from the seafront. Though most of the quayside **tavernas** don't offer value for money, there are exceptions: the *Orea Ellas* by the harbour is shaded by beautiful chestnut trees and sells a highly recommended, home-made retsina, while the *Flisvos*, on the far west side of the port, is a friendly place with decent pasta dishes.

Ninety minutes' walk up to the north coast from Glóssa will bring you to **Perivolioú beach**. The walk itself is worthwhile: near a stone cairn you will pass a **monastery** containing masses of human bones and skulls. There's also a huge hollow oak tree here, in the heart of which is a small tank of drinking water. The beach, when you get there, is nothing out of the ordinary, but there's pure spring water and a cave for shade.

East of Glóssa, a dirt road leads to the splendidly sited church of **Áyios Ioánnis stó Kastrí**, perched on the top of a rock high above a small sandy cove where you can swim. An unsightly house nearby has spoiled the isolation somewhat, but the walk from Glóssa (again, about ninety minutes) is beautiful and peaceful, with hawks and nightingales for company.

Around the rest of the island

West of Skópelos Town, various jeep tracks and old paths wind through olive and plum groves towards **Mount Dhélfi** and the Vathiá forest, or skirt the base of the mountain northeast to **Revýthi** hill with its fountains and churches, and the site of **Karyá**, with its sendoúkia (ancient rock-cut tombs, possibly early Christian). To the northwest of Skópelos Town, reached by boat trips, **Glystéri** is a small pebble beach with no shade, whose taverna is much frequented by locals on Sundays.

On the other side of the island, some 5km due south of Hóra is the tiny horseshoe-shaped harbour of **AGNÓNDAS**, where you'll find three fish tavernas and rooms to rent. *Pavlina Apartments* (⊕24240 23272, ⓔpavlinaskopelos@mail.gr; ❸), just back from the beach, have four high-ceilinged, self-contained and tasteful, wood-furnished apartments on offer. *Pavlos* is the best choice of the restaurants, on the waterfront; count on good, solid grills and fresh fish. Next up and reachable by a paved side road is **LIMNONÁRI**, 300m of fine sand set in a closed, rocky bay. The *Limnonári Beach Restaurant*, right on the beach, serves delicious spiral-shaped local *tyrópites* and rents **rooms** (⊕24240 23046; ❹). A little further around the bay, *Ouzeri O Thomas* is another decent option.

Further up Skópelos's southwest coast, **PÁNORMOS** is very much a full-blown, commercial resort, with rooms, tavernas, a campsite, yacht anchorage and watersports. The beach here is gravelly and shelves steeply, but there are small, secluded sandy bays close by. Of places to **stay**, the thirty-room *Panormos Beach Hotel* (⊕24240 22711, ⓦwww.panormosbeach-hotel.gr; ❻) has a beautiful garden and fine views, and is lovingly looked after; beyond it, the ⚓ *Adrina Beach* (⊕24240 23373, ⓦwww.adrina.gr; ❻), occupies ivy-clad buildings, with a large pool, its own taverna, fabulous views and relative isolation.

Slightly further on at **Miliá**, there's a tremendous, 1500m sweep of tiny pebbles beneath a bank of pines, facing the islet of Dhassiá. Though this used to be a fairly quiet and secluded getaway, a very popular party scene has developed here in recent years, with a beach bar attracting scores of hedonistic boys and girls bent on a good time.

Further north, **ÉLIOS**, 9km short of Glóssa, is a medium-sized, fairly new resort settled by residents of the earthquake-damaged villages above it; it has a pleasant beach. Beyond here, the renovated village of **Palió Klíma** marks the start of a beautiful forty-minute **trail** to Glóssa, via the empty hamlet of Áyii Anáryiri and the oldest village on the island, **Athéato** (aka Mahalás).

Alónissos

Thanks to its remoteness, the lack of an airport, the infrequency of ferry connections and a slightly negative reputation, **Alónissos** has tended to attract fewer casual foreign visitors than the other Sporades. Arid and ascetic in appearance – the once famed vineyards were wiped out by phylloxera in the 1950s – Alónissos is surrounded by some of the cleanest water in the Aegean, but is

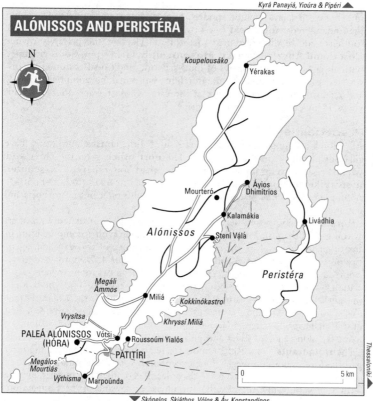

Thessaloníki ▶

▼ Skópelos, Skiáthos, Vólos & Áy. Konstandínos

lacking in photogenic sandy beaches. Nonetheless the number of middle-class Greek visitors has increased sharply in recent years and the island is now considered quite fashionable. Accordingly it can get very crowded from mid-July to the end of August.

Although its harsh, more rugged landscape makes it less congenial to **hiking** than neighbouring Skópelos, you might still consider joining one of the excellent **walking tours** run by Chris Browne (Ⓦ www.alonnisoswalks.co.uk), taking you to churches, beaches and around some of the minor islets nearby.

Patitíri

The island's port and de facto capital, **PATITÍRI**, occupies a pretty cove flanked by pine trees and ringed by busy bars, cafes and restaurants. It is a little soulless – the inhabitants of the old town (Hóra) were forced to move here after an earthquake in 1965 – but it has tried hard to rectify that by means of a paved waterfront and a general tidying up. It's easy, though, to pick up connections here for beaches and Hóra, and it has some good hotels to choose from. Sights include, halfway along the seafront, a huge **wine barrel** (patitíri) of the kind that gave the place its name; and the **Mom Information Centre** (daily 10am–5pm, sometimes open later in midsummer; free; Ⓦ www.mom.gr), on the first floor of a nearby building, whose

975

informative displays include models, photos, videos and slide shows about the endangered **monk seal** (see box). In a splendid stone building on the southern side of the cove, next to the hotel Haravyi, the privately owned **Costas and Angela Mavrikis Museum** (daily 11am–7pm; €3) is crammed with an eclectic set of displays of local artwork, traditional costumes, reconstructed island interiors, war memorabilia, wine-making equipment, piracy and seafaring in general; a drink at the café, whose terrace offers fabulous views, is included in the entrance price.

Practicalities

All Alónissos's important facilities are in Patitíri; **buses** and **taxis** have adjacent terminals on the waterfront. The **post office** is on the Hóra road, while kaïkia leave from the inner ferry quay. You can **rent a scooter, motorbike** or even a car at reasonable prices at I'm Bikes (℡24240 65010). A couple of the rental places on the waterfront also offer out motorboats and dinghies.

Rooms are easy to find here, and you'll probably be approached with offers as you get off the ferry or hydrofoil. If you need help with accommodation, or any other useful travel information, you have a choice of two excellent agencies on the harbour front: Albedo Travel (℡24240 65804, Ⓦwww.albedotravel .com) and Alonniso Travel (℡24240 66000). The local room-owners' association (℡ & Ⓕ24240 66188), on the waterfront, can also find you a room (mostly ❸) in Patitíri or nearby Vótsi. Other options include the *Ioulieta Pension* (℡24240 65463; ❸) and *Haravyi* (℡24240 65090, Ⓕ24240 65189; ❹). Best in the higher price range is *Liadromia* (℡24240 65521, Ⓔliadromia@alonissos .com; ❺), along a raised street above the port.

The **restaurants** along Patitíri's port are reasonably priced, but for the most part the food is nothing special. One exception is *Anaïs*, offering up a selection of ready-made *mayireftá* and grills to order. Recommended ouzerís include ☆*To Kamaki* (July and August only), two blocks up towards the post office from the waterfront, with an amazing selection of seafood *mezédhes*. Heading up to Hóra, you'll pass the family-run *Babis*; the food is good, with a special spin on local pies.

Nightlife is low-key, mostly confined to the seafront bars; for music there are *Enigma* (international) and *Rembetika*, on the road to the old town, for Greek music.

Paleá Alónissos

PALEÁ ALÓNISSOS (Hóra) was damaged by an earthquake in 1965 and virtually the entire population was transferred down to Patitíri, from where it can be reached by a fine but steep fifty-minute walk via a signposted traditional kalderími. Alternatively, there's a frequent bus service (10 min; €1) between the two in the mornings and evenings. Some houses are still derelict, but much of the village has been painstakingly restored, mainly by foreigners. Only a few local families continue to live here, which gives the village a rather odd and un-Greek atmosphere, but it is picturesque and the views make the trip worthwhile.

If you decide **to stay** up here, *Konstantina's Studios* (℡ & Ⓕ24240 66165; ❻) is a small, renovated building with eight studios and one apartment, all enjoying exceptionally good views, while the simple and clean *Fadasia House* (℡24240 65186; ❸) has its own little restaurant. As for **restaurants**, *Astrofengia*, at the entrance to the village, combines the cuisines of Greece

△ Windmill, Alónissos

and the Middle East, and the *Paraport*, up on the main square, offers excellent original fish dishes.

The rest of the island

The roads between Patitíri, Stení Vála and the northernmost point on the island are paved, and the dirt roads down to the beaches – with some exceptions – are in good condition: easier to deal with than the twisting, busy roads on Skiáthos and Skópelos. There's a very limited **bus service** along the Hóra–Patitíri–Stení Vála route, but *kaïkia* run half-hourly from Patitíri north to Khryssí Miliá, Kokkinókastro, Stení Vála, Kalamákia and Áyios Dhimítrios, and south around the coast to Marpoúnda, Výthisma and Megálos Mourtiás. *Kaïkia* also sail occasionally to Livádhia on Peristéra islet.

At Patitíri, there's decent swimming from the rocks around the promontory to the north; pick your way along a hewn-out path past the hotels. In

The Mediterranean monk seal

The **Mediterranean monk seal** (*Monachus monachus*) has the dubious distinction of being the European mammal most in danger of extinction – fewer than four hundred survive worldwide, the majority around the Portuguese Atlantic island (ironically) of Madeira. There are other populations along the coasts of Morocco, Algeria, Libya, Croatia and Cyprus. Small numbers survive in the Ionian and Aegean seas of Greece; the largest such community, of around thirty seals, lives and breeds around the deserted islands north of Alónissos.

Monk seals can travel up to 200km a day in search of food, but they usually return to the same places to rear their **pups**. They have one pup every two years, and the small population is very vulnerable to disturbance. Originally, the pups would have been reared in the open, but increasing disturbance by man has led to the seals retreating to isolated sea caves with partly submerged entrances, particularly around the coast of the remote islet of Pipéri.

Unfortunately, the seals compete with fishermen for limited stocks of fish and, in the overfished Aegean, often destroy nets full of fish. Until recently it was common for seals to be killed by fishermen. This occasionally still happens, but in an attempt to protect the seals, the seas around the northern Sporades have been declared a wildlife reserve, the **National Marine Park of Alónissos Northern Sporades**: fishing is restricted in the area north of Alónissos and prohibited within 5km of Pipéri. On Alónissos, the conservation effort and reserve have won a great deal of local support, mainly through the efforts of the **Hellenic Society for the Protection of the Monk Seal** (HSPMS), based at Stení Vála. The measures have been particularly popular with local fishermen, as tight restrictions on larger, industrial-scale fishing boats from other parts of Greece should help restore local stocks, and eventually benefit the fishermen financially.

Despite this, the government has made no serious efforts to enforce the restrictions, and boats from outside the area continue to fish around Pipéri. On a more positive note, the HSPMS, in collaboration with the Pieterburen Seal Creche in Holland, has reared several abandoned seal pups, all of which have been successfully released in the seas north of Alónissos.

For the moment, your chances of actually seeing a seal are remote, unless you plan to spend a few weeks on a boat in the area. It's not recommended that you visit Pipéri – officially prohibited in any case – or approach sea caves on other islands which might be used by seals, or try to persuade boat-owners to do so. If spotted, the seals should be treated with deference; they cannot tolerate human disturbance.

the populous south of the island, **MARPOÚNDA** features a large hotel and bungalow complex and a rather small beach. It's better to turn right before Marpoúnda towards **Megálos Mourtiás**, a pebble beach with several tavernas that's also linked by paved track to Paleá Alónissos, 200m above. The island's two best beaches are **Výthisma** and **Vrysítsa** – though the latter is sited a little too close to the island's rubbish dump for comfort, and is on the more exposed north coast. Výthisma, just before Megálos Mourtiás, is best reached by boat, the path here having been washed out. Further north, visible from Paleá Alónissos, Vrysítsa is tucked into its own finger-like inlet. There's a mill, sand and a taverna, but little else.

To the north, above the headlands, Patitíri merges into two adjoining settlements with reasonable beaches, **ROUSSOÚM YIALÓS** and **VÓTSI**. For better beaches, you'll have to get in a boat or on a bike. **Khryssí Miliá**, the first good beach north of Patitíri, has a taverna and pine trees behind the quite decent stretch of sand; there's a couple of new hotels on the hillside above, such as the upmarket *Milia Bay* (☎24240 66035, ✉milia-bay@forthnet.gr; ❼), and it can get crowded in summer. At **Kokkinókastro**, over the hill further north, excavations have revealed the site of ancient Ikos and evidence of the oldest known prehistoric habitation in the Aegean. There's nothing much to see, but it's a beautiful spot with a good red-pebble beach, and, in July and August, a daytime bar.

STENÍ VÁLA is a haven for the yachts and flotillas that comb the Sporades, and has almost become a proper village, with a shop or two, several houses, a bar, rooms and a handful of tavernas, one of which, the *Kyra Tasia* (offically the *Steni Vála*), stays open more or less throughout the year and is famous for its *tyrópitta*. The **Monk Seal Treatment and Rehabilitation Centre**, housed in a small hut on the beach, can provide information about the endangered mammal and insight into the work of the HSPMS (see box opposite). There's an unofficial campsite (☎24240 65258) in an olive grove by the harbour, a long pebble beach – Glýfa, where boats are repaired – and some stony beaches within reasonable walking distance in either direction.

KALAMÁKIA, farther to the north, also has a couple of tavernas and a few rooms, while further on still, at the point where the sealed road ends, **ÁYIOS DHIMÍTRIOS** is rapidly becoming the favourite "remote" beach amongst growing numbers of mainlanders. Backing a curving pebbly beach, the small settlement now has a snack-bar, beach taverna and even a card-phone. There's a good, signposted circular **walking trail** (2hr 30min) from here, that follows the coast for a while before heading up and back to Áyios Dhimítrios via the Kastanórema stream bed.

If you want real solitude you'll need to head north along the paved road that runs the length of the island, though there's nothing in the way of facilities past the turnoff to Steni Vála. At the northernmost point of Alónissos, the old shepherds' village of **YÉRAKAS** is a bit of a disappointment, with only a desultory, seldom-used jetty and a scrappy beach.

The National Marine Park of Alónissos – Northern Sporades

The **National Marine Park**, created in 1992, protects seals, cetaceans and other wildlife, including some rare seabirds, in an area that includes the whole of Alónissos, plus half a dozen tiny **islets** that speckle the Aegean to the north-east: Peristéra, Kyrá Panayiá, Yioúra, Psathoúra, Skántzoura and Pipéri. **Pipéri** lies within the core zone of the park – it is a seabird and monk-seal refuge, visitable only by scientists who've been granted permission from a ministry of the environment representative. Virtually none of the islets has any permanent population, or a ferry service, but Peristéra and Kyrá Panayiá can be visited by excursion *kaïki* (ask at the excursion-boat stands on the harbour in Patitíri), weather permitting. No boats are allowed to take you to the other, more remote islets, as they fall within the restricted zone of the park. Although it is possible to be left for a night or more on Peristéra and Kyrá Panayiá, be sure to bring more supplies than you need: if the weather worsens you'll be marooned until such time as small craft can reach you.

Peristéra, the closest islet to Alónissos, is graced with some sandy beaches and there is rarely anyone around, though some Alonissans cross for short periods to tend the olive groves, and in season there are regular evening "barbecue boats" from the main island. A few unofficial campers are tolerated, but there is only one spot, known locally as "Barbecue Bay", where campfires are allowed. Fertile **Kyrá Panayiá,** the next islet out, belongs to the Meyístis Lávras monastery of Mount Athos, and there are two monasteries here, one still inhabited. There's no other permanent population besides wild goats. Boats call at a beach on the south shore, one of many such sandy stretches and coves around the island. Nearby **Yioúra** boasts a stalactite cave reputed to be the previous abode of Polyphemus, the Cyclops who imprisoned Odysseus, but you won't be able to check its credentials as no one is allowed within 500m of the island; tiny, northernmost **Psathoúra** is dominated by its powerful modern lighthouse, the tallest in the Aegean; and roughly halfway between Alónissos and Skýros, green **Skántzoura**, hosts nothing more than a single empty monastery and a few seasonal shepherds.

Skýros

Despite its airport and natural beauty, the island of **Skýros** has stayed off the beaten track of Aegean tourism, perhaps thanks to a lack of major sites or

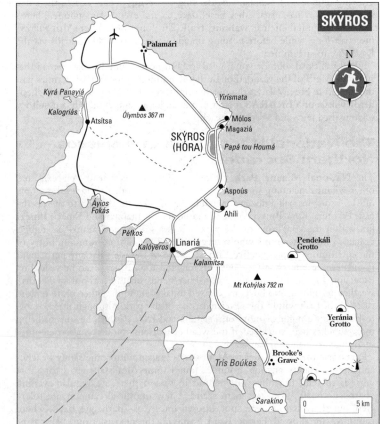

resorts, and its distance from Athens by the land-and-sea route. The popular theory that it was originally two islands seems doubtful, but certainly the character of its two parts is very different. The **north** has a green, gentle landscape and, away from main towns, retains much of its original pine forest, while the sparsely inhabited **south** is mountainous, rocky and barren; there are few trees and the landscape is more reminiscent of the Cyclades than the Sporades.

Compared with the other Sporades, Skýros isn't a great place for beaches. Most of those along the west coast attract a certain amount of seaborne rubbish and, although the scenery is sometimes spectacular, the swimming isn't that good. The beaches along the east coast are all close to Skýros Town, and the best option is probably to stay here rather than head for somewhere more isolated. At the north end of the island the beaches have been commandeered by a big air-force base, which otherwise keeps a low profile.

Considering it is not so far from Athens, Skýros was a very traditional and idiosyncratic island until fairly recently when it began to gain popularity among chic Athenians and foreign visitors, many of whom check into the "New Age" Skyros Centre, to "rethink the form and direction of their lives".

All this notwithstanding, Skýros still ranks as one of the most interesting places in the Aegean. It has a long tradition of painted **pottery** and ornate **wood-carving**, in particular the *salonáki skyrianó* (a handmade set of sitting-room furniture). A very few old men still wear the vaguely Cretan traditional costume of cap, vest, baggy trousers, leggings and *trohádhia* (Skyrian sandals), and some elderly women still wear the favoured yellow scarves and long embroidered skirts, but this is dying out. It's also worth sampling **lobster** in Skýros: it's a local (and expensive) speciality, often served flaked into pasta as *astakomakaronádha*.

Linariá

Ferries dock at the tiny port of **LINARIÁ**, a quiet, functional place on the island's west coast. Less active than Skýros Town, Linariá is certainly a pleasant spot to while away time waiting for the ferry.

△ Wild ponies, Skýros

A good paved road connects Linariá to Skýros town, 10km away, and then continues round past the airport to Atsítsa, where the Skyros Centre has its main branch; **buses** to Skýros Town, and to Magaziá on the coast below, leave regularly from the quay. Midway up the Linariá–Skýros town route, a paved side-road strikes off east to Ahíli and Kalamítsa. Most other roads are passable by scooter, though the hilly, windswept south does not always lend itself to two-wheeled explorations.

Kalamítsa beach, 7km east of Linariá, reached by a good coastal road, is a narrow strand of pebbles and clear water, but the 🍴 *Mouries* **taverna** between it and Linariá, shaded by the namesake row of mulberry trees, is worth a detour for its famed lamb, delicious wine and delightful setting. In high season, excursion *kaïkia* (€25 including lunch) offer trips from Linariá to the islet of **Sarakíno**, which has a fine beach, stopping at various south coast grottoes. See Monika at the port for details.

If you decide to **stay** (often convenient for catching the morning boat), there are two very reasonable options in Linariá: *King Lykomides* 🍴 (☎22220 93472, Ⓦ www.inskyros.gr/kinglykomides.htm; ❹), right next to the harbour, has a dozen or so spotless, air-conditioned, standard rooms with little balconies, TV and gleaming bathrooms, while behind and above it, at the start of the Kalamítsa road, the reliable *Linaria Bay Rooms* (☎22220 93274; ❹) has a mixture of rooms and traditional Skyrian studios. For **eating**, try the *Psariotis Ouzeri* or the *Filippeos* fish taverna, down at the harbour. The splendidly situated *Kavos Bar*, a short but steep walk up the main island road, welcomes the arrival of the ferry each evening with a rousing musical fanfare, and is open day and night for **drinks** and snacks; the views down to the village are superb.

Skýros Town

SKÝROS Town (Hóra), with its decidedly Cycladic architecture, sits on the landward side of a high rock that rises precipitously from the coast (according to legend, King Lykomedes pushed Theseus to his death from its summit). With its workaday atmosphere, the town doesn't feel like a resort, but away from the tattier outskirts it's decidedly picturesque. The older and more intriguing parts are higher up, climbing towards the **kástro**, a mainly Byzantine building erected on the site of the ancient **acropolis**. There are few traces of the acropolis, although remains of the classical city walls survive below on the seaward side of the rock. The kástro is open to visitors; to reach its upper parts you pass through a rather private-looking gateway into the monastery, then through an attractive shaded courtyard and up a whitewashed tunnel. There's little to see at the top, apart from a few churches in various states of ruin, but there are great views over the town and the island; the climb up takes you through the quieter, older part of town with its traditionally decorated houses. With their gleaming copper pots, porcelain plates and antique embroideries decorating the hearth, these dwellings are a matter of intense pride among the islanders, who are often found seated in their doorways on tiny carved chairs.

At the northern end of town is the striking and splendidly incongruous **memorial to Rupert Brooke,** the British poet adopted as the paragon of patriotic youth by Kitchener and later Churchill, despite his socialist and internationalist views. The monument is a bronze statue of "Immortal Poetry" whose nakedness caused a scandal among the townspeople when it was first erected. Brooke, who visited the south of the island very briefly in April 1915, died shortly afterwards of blood poisoning on a French hospital ship anchored offshore, and was buried in an olive grove above the bay of Tris Boúkes (see below). He became something of a local hero despite his limited acquaintance with the island.

Just below the Brooke statue, the **Archeological Museum** (Tues–Sun 8.30am–3pm; €2) has a modest collection of pottery and statues from excavations on the island, and a reconstruction of a traditional Skýros house interior. Nearby, in a nineteenth-century house built over one of the bastions of the ancient walls, the privately run **Faltaïts Museum** (daily 10am–noon & 5.30–8pm/6–9pm in summer; €2) is more interesting, with a collection of domestic items, costumes, embroidery, porcelain and rare books.

Practicalities

The **bus** from Linariá leaves you by the school, 200m below the main square; in season, schedules are guaranteed to meet the ferries, but otherwise services can be limited, and you might be better off getting a taxi. The **post office** and **banks** are both near the square. Skyros Travel (☎22220 91600), on the main street north of the square, can provide **information** or advice, and can find a room or hotel, plus **motorbike and car rental**; in high season it's a good idea to phone them in advance. You can access the **Internet** at Meroi on the main street.

You'll probably be met off the bus with offers of **rooms** (mostly ❸). If you'd like to stay in a traditional Skyrian house, those of Anna Stergiou (☎22220 91657) and Maria Mavroyiorgi (☎22220 91440) are clean and cosy (both ❸). A basic option is the *Elena* (☎22220 91738; ❸), near the main square, which has very cheap singles with shared bathrooms. There's a rather scruffy **campsite** nearer the beach, at the bottom of the steps below the archeological museum, with basic amenities. Alternatively, you could try the pleasant, *Nefeli Hotel & Skyriana Spitia* (☎22220 91964, ℉22220 92061; ❻) on the main road before the square offering rooms or traditionally designed studios.

The square and the main street running by it are the centre of village life, with a few noisy pubs and a wide choice of *kafenía*, tavernas and fast-food places, though only a few are outstanding places to **eat**. Top of the list is ⚡ *O Pappous ki Ego*, a very pleasant little ouzerí with a good range of *mezédhes* and quality Greek music on the stereo (and sometimes live); try the local speciality of kid in lemon sauce. *To Metopo*, just below the square, is another decent, reasonably priced ouzerí and is a little cheaper, while *Maryetis* up on the main street above the main square always draws queues for its solid grills, pasta and *mayireftá*. Near the Brooke statue (away from the bustling crowds) and a little more relaxed in style, *Anatolikos Anemos* dishes up Mediterranean and has good sea views from the patio.

The town's **nightlife** is mostly bar-based until very late, when the few clubs get going. The most popular **bars** are the trendy *Kalypso*, playing jazz and blues, as well as dance-oriented *Kata Lathos* and the rockier *Iroön*. Later on, *Iy Stasis* is one of the most popular places. The best **clubs** include the *Skyropoula*, on the coastal road, and, in town, *Mylos* and the *Stone Club*, while you can listen to live Greek music at *Tzivaeri*.

Magaziá and Mólos: the beaches

A direct path, as well as a longer paved road, lead down past the archeological museum towards the small coastal village of **MAGAZIÁ**, coming out by the official campsite. From Magaziá, an 800-metre-long sandy beach stretches to the adjacent village of **MÓLOS**; in recent years, though, a sprawl of new development between the road and the beach has more or less joined the two settlements together. With a villagey feel, Magaziá is still the livelier of the two and has the better selection of rooms; Mólos is more open and scattered, and has a good range of studios plus a more alluring stretch of **beach**, with umbrellas and loungers for hire; the buzzy *Juicy Beach Bar*, attracting a mainly Greek clientele, with its beach volleyball, is located halfway between the two.

The narrow road down to Magaziá beach holds a clutch of very similar **rooms** for rent; of these, the air-conditioned *Georgia Tsakami* (☎22220 91357; ❸), some twenty metres from the beach and opposite a handy car park, is as close as you'll get to the sand and sea. If it's full, try the *Perigiali* (☎22220 91889, ⓔperigiali@skyrosnet.gr; ❹) in Magaziá, a very pleasant mix of studios and air-conditioned rooms with phone, surrounding a large garden. Half-way between Magaziá and Mólos, *Pension Galini* (☎22220 91379; ❸) is a quiet and slightly more expensive choice, while the nearby *Motel Hara* (☎22220 91601; ❹) is another quiet option.

The beachfront **tavernas** often compare favourably with those in town: on the Magaziá side, *Stefanos* is reliable and popular, and overlooks the beach. At Mólos, try the *Kokalenia*, a restaurant in a garden and the ouzerí at *Balabani's Mill*, all at the end of the beach.

For quieter beaches, carry on past Mólos, or try the excellent and undeveloped unofficial nudist beach, **Papá toú Houmá**, directly below the *kástro*. The path down starts 150m beyond the *Skyropoula* disco, and isn't obvious from above. Further along the road south of here, the beaches are disappointing until **Aspoús**, which has a couple of tavernas and rooms to rent, as well as the smart *Ahillion* hotel (☎22220 93300, ⓕ22220 93303; ❺).

Around the rest of the island

In summer, buses visit the more popular beaches, but if you want to branch out on your own, rent a car or a scooter. Tracks and footpaths diverge from the main circular road, leading inward and seaward. Among the most interesting places to head for is **Palamári**, northwest of Hóra, the neglected site of an early Bronze Age settlement set above a fine but exposed beach.

Home to the Skyros Centre, **ATSÍTSA**, in the northwest corner of the island, is set in an attractive bay with pine trees down to the sea, and has a very good fish taverna (❦ *O Andonis*) and an increasing number of rooms. The rocky beach isn't great for swimming, but there are small sandy coves a short way to the north at **Kalogriás** and **Kyrá Panayiá**, with the seasonal taverna at Kalogriás, *O Yiorgos* being the only source of food here. For a taste of the island's wooded interior, you could hike following the dirt track from Skýros Town to Atsítsa; it takes three to four hours, and is too rough for a scooter.

Elsewhere in the coniferous northern half of the island, **Áyios Fokás** and **Péfkos** bays are easiest reached by a turning from the main road near Lineriá, though access from Atsítsa is via a reasonable dirt road. Áyios Fokás is home to *Kali Rooms* (☎693 70 90 848; ❸), an excellent, very well-run taverna where you can bed down for the night. In Péfkos, set in a beautiful pine-fringed bay, the best **rooms** option is *Barba Mitsos* (❸).

As for the barren southern half of the island, dominated by the great mountain of **Kohýlas**, exploring is best attempted only if you have a four-wheel-drive vehicle, as the tracks are poor away from the main west-coast road to the naval base at **Tris Boúkes** (where Rupert Brooke is buried). Do not ignore the signs prohibiting photography – this is a military zone.

Évvia (Euboea)

ÉVVIA, the second-largest Greek island (after Crete), seems more like an extension of the mainland to which it was once joined. At **Halkídha**, the gateway to the island, the curious old drawbridge link to the mainland has only a forty-metre channel to span, Évvia reputedly having been split from Attica and Thessaly by a blow from Poseidon's trident (earthquakes and subsidence being the more pedestrian explanations). Besides the newer suspension bridge bypassing Halkídha and also linking Évvia to the mainland, there are ferry crossings at no fewer than six points along its length, and the south of the island is far closer to Athens than it is to the northern part.

Nevertheless, Évvia *is* an island, in places a very beautiful one. But it has an idiosyncratic history and demography, and has largely been kept out of the mainstream of tourism. A marked **Albanian influence** in the south, and scattered Lombard and Venetian watchtowers across the island, lend a distinctive flavour. Indeed, Évvia was the longest-surviving south-mainland outpost of the Ottoman Turks, who had a keen appreciation of the island's wealth. The last **Ottoman garrison** was not evicted until 1833, hanging on in defiance of the peace settlement that awarded Évvia to the new Greek state. Substantial Turkish communities, renowned for their alleged brutality, remained in the northwest half of the island until 1923.

Economically, Évvia has always been prized. By Greek standards, it's exceptionally **fertile**, producing everything from grain, corn and cotton to kitchen vegetables and livestock. The classical name, Euboea, means "rich in cattle", but nowadays cows are few and far between; its kid and lamb, however, are highly rated, as is the local retsina. Greek tourists predominate, especially in the north around the spa of **Loutrá Edhipsoú**. In July and August, Évvia can seem merely a beach annexe for Athens and the mainland towns across the Evvian Gulf.

The rolling countryside of the **north** is the most conventionally scenic part of the island, with grain combines whirling on sloping hay meadows between olive groves and pine forest, echoing the beauty of the smaller Sporades. The **northeast coast** is rugged and largely inaccessible, its few sandy beaches surf-pounded and often plagued by flotsam and jetsam; the **southwest** is gentler and more sheltered, though much disfigured by industrial operations. The **centre** of

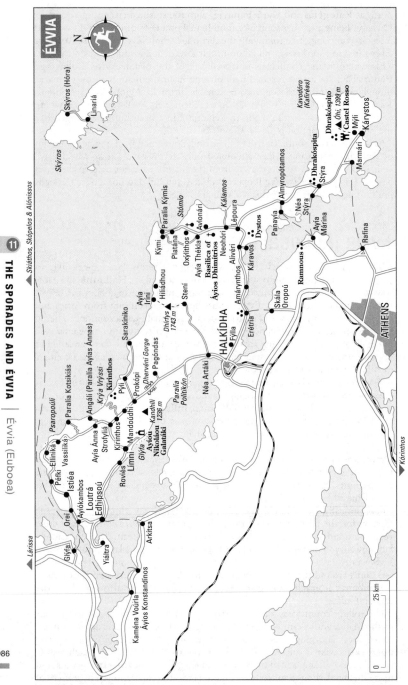

ÉVVIA

N

Skýros (Hóra)
Linariá

Skýros

◄ Skiáthos, Skópelos & Alónissos

Kavodóro (Kafiréas)
Dhrakóspito
Óhi, 1399 m
Castel Rosso
Dhrakóspita
Mýli
Kárystos
Marmári
Styra
Néa Styra
Rafína
Almyropótamos
Panayía
Áyia Marína
Lépoura
Kálamos
Néohóri
Dystos
Káravos
Avlonári
Oxýlithos
Stómio
Paralía Kými
Kými
Basilica of Áyios Dhimítrios
Áyia Thékla
Platána
Alivéri
Amárynthos
Skála Orópoú
Ramnous
Erétria
Fýlla
HALKÍDHA
Hiliádhou
Steni
Áyia Iríni
Dhírfys 1743 m

ATHENS

Sarakíniko
Pýli
Prokópi
Kirínthos
Pagóndas
Dhervéni Gorge

Paralía Politikón

Néa Artáki

Kandhíli 1236 m

Paralía Kotsikiás
Angáli (Paralía Ayías Ánnas)
Kirínthos
Kryá Vrýssi
Pseropoúli
Ayía Ánna
Strofyliá
Roviés
Mandoúdhi
Limni
Glyfá
Áyiou Nikoláou
Galatáki
Ellinká
Vassiliká
Péfki
Istiéa
Ayiókambos
Loutrá
Edhipsoú
Oreí
Glyfá
Yiáltra
Arkítsa
Kaména Voúrla
Áyios Konstandínos

◄ Lárissa

◄ Kórinthos

Kórinthos ►

25 km

0

the island, between Halkídha and the easterly port of Kými, is mountainous and dramatic, while the far **southeast** is mostly dry and very isolated.

Public transport consists of passable bus services along the main roads to Kárystos in the southeast, and Límni and Loutrá Edhipsoú in the northwest. Explorations are best conducted by rented car; any two-wheeler will make little impact on the relatively great distances involved.

Halkídha

The heavily industrialized island-capital of **HALKÍDHA** (the ancient Chalkis, an appellation still in use today) is the largest town on Évvia, with a population of over 50,000. A shipyard, rail-sidings and cement works do little to make it attractive, but things improve in the old Ottoman quarter, **Kástro**, south of Venizélou, in the area around the Turkish fortress on the mainland and along the waterfront promenade, Leofóros Voudhoúri, backed by tavernas and trendy café-bars. Hardly a trace remains of Halkídha's once-thriving Jewish community, whose presence here dates back around 2500 years.

The entrance to the *kástro* – on the right as you head inland from the old Euripos bridge – is marked by the handsome fifteenth-century **mosque**, nominally a museum of Byzantine artefacts, but permanently locked. Beyond lie the remains of Karababa (the seventeenth-century Ottoman fortress), an arcaded Turkish aqueduct and the unusual **basilica of Ayía Paraskeví** (shut except during services); its oddness is due to its conversion into a Gothic cathedral by the Crusaders in the fourteenth century. In the opposite direction, in the new town, an **archeological museum** at Venizélou 13 (Tues–Sun 8.30am–3pm; €2) has a good display of prehistoric, Hellenic and Roman finds from all over the island.

Halkídha's waterside overlooks the **Évripos** (Euripus), a narrow channel of sea, whose strange currents have baffled scientists for centuries. You can stand on the bridge that spans the narrowest point and watch the water swirling by like a river; every few hours the current changes and the "tide" reverses. Aristotle is said to have thrown himself into the waters in despair at his inability to understand what was happening, so if you're puzzled you're in good company; there is still no entirely satisfactory explanation.

Practicalities

Trains arrive on the mainland side of the channel, beneath the old fortress; given numerous, quick rail links with Athens, there's little reason to stay overnight. Should you want to, though, the basic *Kentrikon* hotel (☎22210 22375; ❹), at Angéli Govíou 5, is a far better deal than the huge waterfront establishments it backs onto. Most other services of interest lie within sight of the old Euripus bridge. The **bus station** is currently 400m from the bridge along Kótsou, then 50m right, but is due to move to the eastern edge of town by 2007; you should get a connection for any corner of the island as long as you show up by 2pm, later for Kými or Límni.

Halkídha is noted for its superior seafood and ouzerís; the waterfront **restaurants** are popular at weekends with Athenians but are not necessarily the best-value options. The exception is *Apanemo* (☎22210 22614), at the northern end of shoreline, in the Fanári district, just before the lighthouse, which has tables on the sand and is so popular that booking is recommended. Inland you might try *Ta Pende Fi* at Evvías 61, a classic fish taverna in a peaceful setting, or the more central, long-running *Tsaf* at Papanastasíou 3, off Platía Agorás, again strong on seafood titbits. *O Yiannis*, at Frízi 8, is an excellent, reasonably priced ouzerí serving up all manner of shellfish. For the truly impecunious or time-pressured, there's also a handful of acceptable grills serving adequate lunches in the immediate vicinity of the old bus station.

Halkídha to Kými

The coast road heading east out of Halkídha offers an exceptionally misleading introduction to the interior of Évvia. The sprawling industrial zone gives way to nondescript hamlets, succeeded between Erétria and Amárynthos by sequestered colonies of Athenian second homes, rather bleak beaches and large hotels frequented by British and German package-tour visitors.

The first town along the main road is modern **ERÉTRIA**, a dreary resort laid out on a grid plan; for most travellers its main asset is the ferry service across to Skála Oropoú in Attica. The site of **ancient Eretria** is more distinguished, though much of it lies under the town. A few scanty remains are dotted around the town centre, most conspicuously an **agora** and a **temple of Apollo**, but more interesting are the excavations in the northwest corner, behind the excellent small **museum** (Tues–Sun 8.30am–3pm; €2), run in collaboration with the Swiss School of Archeology. Here a **theatre** has been uncovered; steps from the orchestra descend to an underground vault used for sudden entrances and exits. Beyond the theatre are the ruins of a **gymnasium** and a **sanctuary**, while the museum guard will be happy to unlock the fourth-century-BC **House of Mosaics**, five minutes' walk from the museum. One of the more affordable and interesting hotels is the municipal tourist complex *Dreams Island* (℡22290 61224, Ⓦwww.dreams-island.gr; ⑤), on a tiny offshore islet linked by causeway to the end of the bay. The handy and central *Pension Diamando* (℡22290 62214; ③), right in the middle of the long waterfront promenade, is a less expensive option and a little more convenient for the busy nightlife.

Nine kilometres further east, **Amárynthos** is a smaller and more pleasant resort to stay in. Though the town boasts nothing of particular interest, the seafront square is picturesque and there is an ample selection of good eateries, such as *Stefanos* or *Thodoros*, two reliable fish tavernas on the waterfront, and *To Limanaki* 200m further west. Two good accommodation options are *Iliaktidhes Hotel Apartments* (℡22290 37605; ④), just off the main road, and the B-class *Stefania Hotel* (℡22290 38382, Ⓕ22290 38384; ⑤), 1km west of the centre right on the beach.

A way east, the enormous modern power plant and virtually intact medieval castle just before dreary **Alivéri** are incongruously juxtaposed, while more Frankish towers look down from nearby hills. The fishing harbour of **KÁRA-VOS** has several pleasant watering holes, among them the *Vlahos* taverna. Thereafter the scenery improves drastically as the road heads inland towards the junction village of **Lépoura** from where a road heads southeast towards Kárystos. As you continue north towards Kými, you will cross some of the most peaceful countryside in Greece. With your own vehicle you can detour east after 5km at Neohóri to the secluded beaches at **Kálamos** and **Korasídha**: the selection of places to stay at the former include the very pleasant *To Egeon* (℡22230 41865; ③), with a downstairs restaurant.

Twelve kilometres north of Lépoura, at Háni Avlonaríou, stands the Romanesque thirteenth- or fourteenth-century **basilica of Áyios Dhimítrios**, Évvia's largest and finest (ask for the key at the café next door). **AVLONÁRI** proper, 2km east, is dominated by a hill crowned by a huge Lombard (or Venetian) tower, rearing above the Neoclassical and vernacular houses that tier the lower slopes. There's a single taverna below the platía, but no accommodation. Avlonári was an archiepiscopal see from the sixth century onwards, and this part of Évvia is particularly well endowed with Byzantine chapels.

Just north of Háni Avlonaríou, you reach a fork in the road: the left fork is the inland road, taken by the bus, direct to Kými. On the way it leads past the hamlet of **Ayía Thékla**, where a small, shed-like **chapel** of that saint, probably slightly later than Áyios Dhimítrios, hides in a lush vale below the modern church. Inside, fresco fragments, depicting large-eyed faces, suggest what has been lost over time.

As for **KÝMI**, the upper part of town is built on a green ridge overlooking the sea, while Paralía Kýmis, the ferry port, is 4km below, via a winding road. All buses from Halkídha deposit you in the upper town, except for the one or two daily that connect with the ferry. In the lower reaches of the town, on the harbour-bound road, the **folklore museum** (daily 10am–1pm and 6–8.30pm; free) houses an improbably large collection of costumes, household and agricultural implements and old photos recording the doings of Kymians both locally and in the US, where there's a huge community. Among the emigrants was Dr George Papanikolaou, deviser of the "Pap" cervical smear test, and there's a statue honouring him up in the upper-town platía, where you might ask about **rooms** (⑤). Kými boasts some good **tavernas**, the best being *To Balkoni* on the main road towards the shore; it offers a superb view and the chance to sample the produce of the local vineyards.

The right fork north of Háni Avlonaríou is the coast road, taking you past **OXÝLITHOS**, home to the elaborate chapels of **Áyios Nikólaos** and **Ayía Ánna**, both at least a hundred years older than Áyios Dhimítrios. The road hits the coast at **Stómio,** an unappealing strand before the equally dreary seaside village of **PLATÁNA**. Press on to the functional port of **PARALÍA KÝMIS**, for ferry connections to Skýros; despite its name it has no real beach, and is not a particularly congenial place to be stuck overnight waiting for your boat (if you are, move up to Kými proper). The best **taverna** here is *Iy Skyros*, near the docks.

Southeast Évvia

So narrow that you can sometimes glimpse the sea on both sides, the spit of land southeast of Lépoura has a flavour very distinct from the rest of the island. Often bleak and windswept, it forms a geological unit with neighbouring Ándhros to the southeast, with shared slates and marble. Like Ándhros it was heavily settled by Albanian immigrants from the early fifteenth century onwards, and Arvanítika – a **medieval dialect** of Albanian – was until recently the first language of the remoter villages here. Even non-Arvanítika speakers often betray their ancestry by their startlingly fair colouring and aquiline features.

Immediately southeast of Lépoura, Lake Dhýstos is a shadow of its former self, having been mostly drained and reclaimed as farmland; some migratory birds do still frequent its shallow marshes, however. Atop the almost perfectly conical hill in the centre of its flat basin are the sparse fifth-century-BC ruins of **ancient Dystos** and a subsequent medieval citadel, though they're hard to explore because the surroundings are so swampy.

Beyond the Dhýstos plain, the main road continues along the mountainous spine of the island to Kárystos, at the southern end of the paved road and bus line. The nondescript village of **ALMYROPÓTAMOS** lies just off the main road, a couple of kilometres from its namesake port (aka **Panayía**) from where there is an infrequent ferry crossing to Ayía Marína.

If you have your own transport, it's worth stopping off at **STÝRA**, above which is a cluster of **dhrakóspita** ("dragon houses"), signposted at the north edge of the village and reached by track, then trail. So named because only mythological beings were thought capable of shifting into place their enormous masonry blocks, their origins and uses have yet to be definitively established. The most convincing theory suggests that they are sixth-century BC temples built by immigrants or slaves from Asia Minor working in the nearby marble and slate quarries.

The shore annexe of **NÉA STÝRA**, 5km down from the hill village, is a fairly standard package resort, worth knowing about only for its handy ferry connection to Ayía Marína. Much the same can be said for **MARMÁRI**, 19km south, except in this case the ferry link is with Rafína, and now serves as Kárystos's de facto ferry link too. Here there are a few decent places to eat; *Zafíris* has shaded tables right on the waterfront, while if you fancy a walk, head for *Tò Akriogiali*, at the far southern end of the waterfront on a platform over the water. Stýra and Marmári are linked by an impressive, high corniche road, known as the **Eagles' Road** (Dhrómos tón Aetón).

Kárystos and around

The new road between Marmári and **KÁRYSTOS** completes Évvia's "super-highway", allowing you to enjoy the nether reaches of the island as you cruise down to its last major settlement. Studded with modern buildings, at first sight Kárystos is a rather boring grid (courtesy of nineteenth-century Bavarian town-planners), which ends abruptly to east and west. However, King Otho liked the site so much that he contemplated transferring the Greek capital here, and there are still some graceful Neoclassical buildings dating from the mid-nineteenth century. Though you're unlikely to want to stay for more than a day or two, Kárystos does improve given prolonged acquaintance, with a superb (if often windy) beach to the west, the smaller, sandier **Psilí Ámmos** ten minutes' walk to the east and a lively, genuine working-port atmosphere. Only one plot of fenced-in foundations, in the central bazaar, bears out the town's ancient provenance, and the oldest obvious structure is the fourteenth-century Venetian **Boúrtzi** (locked except for occasional summer-evening art exhibitions) on the waterfront; this small tower is all that remains of once-extensive fortifications. Opposite the Boúrtzi inside the Cultural Centre, a small but interesting **archeological museum** (Tues–Sun 8.30am–3pm; €2) displays finds from the local area – mostly statues and temple carvings, plus a few smaller votive objects. In the evenings, the shore road is blocked by a gate to create an undisturbed promenade.

Practicalities

No passenger ferries serve the town directly: Marmári, 15km back up the road, acts as Kárystos's passenger port. Frequent **buses** link the two centres, arriving at the bus station, a few blocks inland from the waterfront next to the Town Hall on Kotsíka, the street leading directly up from the port. The station (T22240 26303) displays information on the extremely infrequent (once daily at best) departures to the remote villages of the Kavodóro (Kafiréas) cape to the east.

Finding affordable **accommodation** is not a big problem. The big *Galaxy* (T22240 22600; ❸) offers air-conditioned rooms on the west side of the waterfront, while in the park beyond the Boúrtzi the excellent ✴ *Karystion* (T22240 22391, Wwww.karystion.gr; B&B; ❹) is the best place to stay, with filling breakfasts and living up to its slogan, Relax and Hospitality, Leisure and Serenity.

Good choices for **eating out** include the *Kavo Doro*, a friendly and reasonable taverna one block west of the square on Párodos Sakhtoúri, serving *mayireftá*; *Ta Kalamia*, at the west end of the esplanade by the start of the beach, is a cheap, filling and popular lunchtime option, while 2km east of town at Aetós, the quiet *Tò Kýma* is an ideal spot for an evening meal or Sunday lunch by the sea. On Kotsíka are several reliable *psistariés*, serving the local lamb and goat for which Kárystos is renowned: *O Panourgias* or the *Karystaki* are two of the better ones.

Mount Óhi

The obvious excursion from Kárystos is inland towards **Mount Óhi** (1399m) Évvia's third highest peak. Some 3km straight inland, **MÝLI**, a fair-sized village around a spring-fed oasis, makes a good first stop with a few tavernas. The medieval castle of **Castel Rosso** beckons above, a twenty-minute climb up from the main church (longer in the frequent, howling gales). Inside, the castle is a total ruin, except for an Orthodox **chapel of Profítis Ilías** built over the Venetians' water cistern, but the sweeping views over the sea and the town make the trip worthwhile.

Behind, the ridges of Óhi are as lunar and inhospitable as the broad plain around Kárystos is fertile. From Mýli, it's a three-hour-plus hike up the largely bare slopes, mostly by a path cutting across the new road, strewn with unfinished granite columns, abandoned almost two thousand years ago. The path passes a little-used alpine club shelter (fed by spring water) and yet another *dhrakóspito*, even more impressive than the three smaller ones at Stýra; built of enormous schist slabs, seemingly sprouting from the mountain, it's popularly supposed to be haunted.

Northwest from Halkídha

Due north from Halkídha, the main road passes a few kilometres of flat farmland and salt marsh before reaching the bustling refugee settlement of Néa Artáki. Here a road served by buses from Halkídha leads up to **STENÍ**, a sprawling alpine village at the foot of Mount Dhírfys. The village has a couple of decent hotels, the *Dirfys* (℡22280 51217; ❸) and the *Steni* (℡22280 51221; ❸). On the main square, in addition to a café and grill, is *Iy Mouria*, a traditional taverna beneath its namesake mulberry tree. This is a fine area for hiking, most notably up the peaks of Dhírfys and Xirovoúni, and beyond to the isolated beach hamlets of Hiliádhou and Ayía Iríni, though you'll need a specialist hiking guide to find the routes (see "Books", p.1148).

Beyond Néa Artáki, the main road snakes and climbs steeply through forested hills and the **Dhervéni gorge**, gateway to Évvia's north. The large village of **PROKÓPI** lies beyond the narrows, in a valley defined by the rich and beautiful woods that make it famous. A counterpoint, in the village itself is the unprepossessing 1960s pilgrimage **church of St John the Russian**, which holds the saint's relics. The "Russian" was actually a Ukrainian soldier, captured by the Ottomans in the early eighteenth century and taken to Turkey, where he died. According to locals, his mummified body began to promote miracles, and the saint's relics were brought here by Orthodox Greeks from Cappadocian Prokópi (today Ürgüp) in the 1923 population exchange.

Evvian Prokópi is still referred to by the locals as **Akhmétaga**, the name of the old Turkish fiefdom here that was bought in 1832 by Edward Noel, an English nobleman, a Philhellene and Romantic, and relative of Lady Byron; a direct descendant of his, Philip Noel-Baker, was awarded the Nobel Peace Prize in 1959. Konaki, the main house of the Candili estate, dominating a bluff overlooking the village, is now home to Noel-Baker's namesake grandson, and operates partly as a hotel and creative course centre; comfortable en-suite accommodation (Ⓦwww.candili.gr; ❻), in the tastefully converted granaries and stables, can usually be booked for a minimum of a week and is intended for groups.

From Prokópi a road leads northeast to **Pýli**, on the coast, and then east to some unspoilt beaches on the way to **Cape Sarakíniko.** The main road, however, follows a shady, stream-fed glen for 8km to **MANDOÚDHI**: at the signposted beach of Paralía Mandoúdhi there's nothing more than abandoned magnesite quarries and crushing plants. The closest serviceable **beach** is at **Paralía Kírinthos**, better known as **KRÝA VRÝSSI** (take a right-hand turning off the main road at the tiny hamlet of **Kírinthos**, 3km beyond Mandoúdhi). At the coast, a river and an inlet bracket a small beach, with the headland south of the river supporting the extremely sparse remains of ancient **Kirinthos**. At the Dutch-run **hotel** Kirinthos (Ⓣ22270 23662; ❸), some of whose impeccable rooms enjoy sumptuous sea views, you can also learn crafts such as weaving, pottery and icon-painting.

At a fork at **Strofyliá**, 8km north of Mandoúdhi, a road heads west to Límni (see opposite). Yet another 8km north brings you to **AYÍA ÁNNA** (aka Ayiánna), where most travellers are interested in the prominently marked turn-off for **Angáli beach**, 5km east. Billed as the area's best, it's nothing more than a broad, long and dark swath of sand protected only at the northern end. For **accommodation**, the Agali Hotel (Ⓣ22270 97104, Ⓕ22270 97067; ❹) is a pretty congenial option, while for **eating**, Armata at the northern end is the only place with tables on the beach. Horseriding on the beach is a well-advertised and popular diversion.

Signs off the next stretch of the main road point to the scruffy, uninteresting beaches of Paralía Kotsikiás and Psaropoúli; **Elliniká**, the next signposted beach, lies just 800m below its namesake village inland - it's far smaller than Angáli or Psaropoúli, but is cleaner and certainly the most picturesque spot on this coast, with a church-capped islet offshore as a target to swim to. The approach driveway has a very limited number of facilities: a mini-market and a few **studios** for rent. Motel Egeo (Ⓣ22260 42262; ❹) is as good as any if you want to stay, while the O Paradisos taverna is the best of a fairly limited choice of eating options.

Beyond Elliniká, the road (and bus line) skirts the northern tip of Évvia to curl southwest towards **PÉFKI**, a seaside resort mobbed with Greeks in summer, which straggles for some 2km along a mediocre beach. The best **restaurants**, near the north end of this strip, include Ouzeri Ta Thalassina, Psitopolio O Thomas and O Lambros. **Accommodation** is the usual Evvian mix of self-catering units, and a few seaside hotels such as Galini (Ⓣ22260 41208, Ⓕ22260 41650; ❺) and Myrtia (Ⓣ22260 41202; ❺), both resolutely pitched at mainlanders; the campsite, Camping Pefki, 2km north of town behind the beach, is rather pricey and geared to people with caravans. Excursion **boats** and occasionally **hydrofoils** leave for Skiáthos, during summer months only.

The next resort, 14km southwest, past the major northern settlement of **ISTIÉA** (a dull place but important as the destination shown on many northern road signs), is **OREÍ**, is a low-key fishing village, whose west-facing **cafés** are great places to watch the sunset. In a glass case near the harbourside chapel is a fine Hellenistic statue of a bull, hauled up from the sea in 1965. Nearby **Néos Pýrgos** beach has a selection of **rooms** and restaurants.

Some 7km further along the coast, **AYIÓKAMBOS** is useful for its regular ferry connections to Glýfa on the mainland opposite, from where there are buses to Vólos. Ayiókambos is surprisingly pleasant considering its port function, with a patch of beach, two or three tavernas and a few rooms for rent. Buses from Halkídha continue to Loutrá Edhipsoú, 11km to the south.

Límni and Loutrá Edhipsoú

Low-key Límni, a largely Neoclassical, tile-roofed town, built from the wealth engendered by nineteenth-century shipping prowess, is the most appealing on the island, with serviceable beaches and a famous convent nearby. Farther up the coast, at the island's northwestern tip, Loutrá Edhipsoú has been famous for its spas since antiquity – its water supposedly cures everything from gallstones to depression. Each town is the terminus of bus routes from Halkídha, and both are also linked by bus along the scenic corniche road, via Roviés.

Límni

On the west coast, 19km from Strofyliá, **LÍMNI** is a delightful fishing town, whose small **folk art museum** (Mon–Sat 9am–1pm, Sun 10.30am–1pm; €2) featuring pottery, coins and sculpture fragments, plus local costumes, fabrics and furniture, is well worth a visit. **Buses** from Halkídha stop at the north side of the quay. The **post office** and **banks** are situated inland.

Downtown **rooms** and **hotels** are disappointing, but usually easily available outside August. An outstanding exception, on the main through-road into town from Strofyliá, from where it commands majestic sea and mountain views, is the delightfully welcoming ⚘ *Vateri* (☎22270 32493; ❺), with spacious rooms, traditional furnishings and copious breakfasts based on home-produced breads and preserves. Just over 2km northwest, on the Loutrá Edhipsoú road, is the gravel strand of **Kohýli**, with a basic but leafy **campsite** out on the cape, 500m beyond mid-beach. Other congenial places **to stay** hereabouts include *Dennis House* (☎22270 31787; ❺), down on the shore – the spacious rooms have balconies – and, on the main road, the more luxurious *Ostria* (☎22270 32247; B&B; ❺), with a pool; both are clearly signposted. Every summer the hamlet hosts an **international drama and music festival**, with regular performances mostly of classical music, in a purpose-built amphitheatre surrounded by ancient olive-trees.

Back in Límni itself, the best **place to eat** in terms of setting, menu and popularity is O *Platanos* (under the enormous quayside plane tree), with the adjacent *Avra* not far behind. Other local favourites include the newer *To Fyki*, also on the waterfront, and *Lambros*, 800m along the way to Katoúnia beach to the south of town.

Ayíou Nikoláou Galatáki

Around 7km south of Límni - under your own steam - is the **convent of Ayíou Nikoláou Galatáki**, superbly set on the wooded slopes of Mount Kandhíli, overlooking the north Evvian Gulf. To get there, veer up and left at the unsigned fork off the coast road; there's no formal scheme for visiting, but the gates are shut around sunset. Though much rebuilt since its original Byzantine foundation atop a Poseidon temple, the convent retains a thirteenth-century tower built to guard against pirates, and a crypt. One of a dozen or so nuns will show you **frescoes** in the katholikón, dating from the principal sixteenth-century renovation. Especially vivid, on the right of the narthex, is the Entry of the Righteous into Paradise: the righteous ascend a perilous ladder to be crowned by angels and received by Christ, while the wicked miss the rungs and fall into the maw of Leviathan.

Below Ayíou Nikoláou Galatáki are the pebble-and-sand beaches of **Glýfa**, arguably the best on this part of Évvia's southwest-facing coast. There are several in succession, leading up to the very base of Mount Kandhíli, some reachable by paths, the last few only by boat. The shore is remarkably clean, considering the number of summer campers who pitch tents here for weeks on end; a single roadside spring, 2km before the coast, is the only facility hereabouts.

Loutrá Edhipsoú

The coastal road north from Limni glides past **ROVIÉS**, famous for its olives and a medieval tower and with **rooms**, **hotels**, an excellent **campsite** and other services, if you decide **to stay**. It then brings you to the fishing port of **LOUTRÁ EDHIPSOÚ**, better known as one of Greece's most exclusive **spa** towns. Unlike the island's flagship hotel *Thermae Sylla*, the baths themselves are inexpensive (€2 for 20min) and quite an experience; you can always bathe for free at the public beach next to the hotel, where hot spa water gushes out freely into an artificial set of cascades. There are less-regimented **hot springs** at **Yiáltra**, 15km west around the head of Edhipsós bay, where the water boils up on the rocky beach, warming the shallows to comfortable bath temperature.

The vast number of **hotels**, some old and creaky, which service the summer influx means good deals can be had. On the seafront, the classy 1920s–vintage *Egli* (☎22260 22215, ⓕ22260 22886; ❹) is a good choice, albeit on the old-fashioned side, while the rather flashy *Lito* (☎22260 22081; ❻), up a quieter sidestreet at Ermoú 25, was refurbished in 2004. You can really push the boat out at the 1897-built ⚓ *Thermae Sylla* (☎22260 60100, ⓦwww.thermaesylla .gr; ❽), an elegant French-style monument atop what's claimed to be the best thermal spring in Greece; even if you're not a guest you can use the exclusive hotel spa for around €20. For **eating** there is an abundance of tavernas strung along the front; try the leafy restaurant of the *Egli* or the traditional *To Fagadhiko tou Barous*, which offers a wide selection of *mezédhes*.

A frequent **ferry** service links Loutrá Edhipsoú to Arkítsa on the mainland.

Travel details

Ferry services to the northern Sporades run out of Vólos and Áyios Konstandínos; an additional service links Thessaloníki with Iráklion via Skiáthos and a couple of the more popular Cyclades. Hydrofoils from Vólos and Áyios Konstandínos to the Sporades, and the jet ferry between Áyios Konstandínos and the Sporades, run reliably only between early June and mid-September. Hydrofoils are pricier than the ferries, but cut journey times virtually in half, while the jet ferry is noticeably faster than the car-carrying catamaran out of Vólos. The only ferry to Skýros is from Kými on Évvia. NB: Departure frequencies given are for the June-to-mid-Sept period, and may fall sharply at other times. For more details of all services and ferry company websites, visit ⓦwww.gtp.gr.

Skiáthos, Skópelos and Alónissos

Ferries

Skiáthos to: Iráklion (1–2 weekly); Thessaloníki (1–2 weekly); select Cyclades (1–2 weekly).
Vólos to: Skiáthos (2 daily; 2hr 30min); Skópelos (2 daily; 3hr 30min); Alónissos (1 daily; 4hr 20min). Also one weekly service to Límnos and Lésvos via Skiáthos and Skópelos.

Jet Ferry

Áyios Konstandínos to: Alónissos (4–6 weekly; 4hr); Skiáthos (1–2 daily; 3hr); Skópelos (1–2 daily; 3hr 30min).

Hydrofoils

Áyios Konstandínos to: Skiáthos, Glóssa, Skópelos and Alónissos (3 daily).
Vólos to: Skiáthos, Glóssa, Skópelos Town and Alónissos (4 daily).

Flights

Athens to: Skiáthos (mid-June to mid-Sept 1 daily, otherwise 3 weekly; 50min).

Skýros

Ferries

The car ferry from Kými takes 1hr 30min. Services are once or twice daily from mid-June to early Sept (around noon or late afternoon), and once daily (late afternoon) the rest of the year; there may be an additional boat on designated peak travel days in July and August – call ☎ 22220 22020 (Kými) or 22220 91790 (Skýros) for current information. There is a connecting bus service for the late-afternoon boat, from the Liossíon 260 terminal in Athens.

Évvia

Buses

Athens (Liossíon 260 terminal) to: Halkídha (every 30min 5.30am–9.30pm; 1hr 30min); Kými (5 daily; 3hr 15min).
Halkídha to: Kárystos (2 daily; 3hr); Kými (8 daily; 1hr 45min); Límni (5 daily; 1hr 30min); Loutrá Edhipsoú (4 daily; 3hr).

Trains

Athens (Laríssis station) to: Halkídha (20 daily; 1hr 30min).

Ferries

Arkítsa to: Loutrá Edhipsoú (at least hourly July–mid-Sept, every 1–2hr otherwise; 45min).

Ayía Marína to: Néa Stýra (12 daily; 45min); Almyropótamos/Panayía (4-5 weekly; 45min).
Glýfa to: Ayiókambos (12 daily summer, 4 daily winter; 30min).
Rafína to: Marmári (5 daily in summer, 4 in winter).
Skála Oropoú to: Erétria (March–Oct every 30min during the day, hourly in the evening; 30min).
NB: Connecting buses from Athens run to Rafína (every 30min; 1hr), Ayía Marína (5 daily; 1hr 15min) and Skála Oropoú (hourly; 1hr 30min), all from the Mavromatéon terminal, and to Arkítsa and Glýfa from the Liossíon 260 terminal.

The Ionian Islands

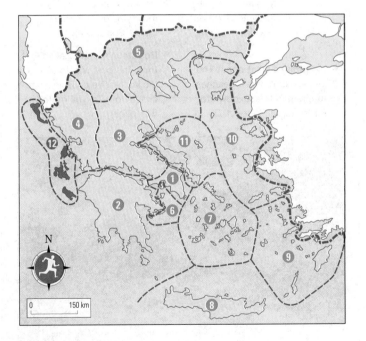

※ **Kérkyra (Corfu) Town** Venetian fortresses, beautiful churches, fine museums and appealing architecture. See p.1002

※ **Perouládhes, Corfu** Shaded till early afternoon and backed by sheer vertical cliffs, this beach is an excellent hangout. See p.1012

※ **Andípaxi** Some of the Ionian's best swimming and snorkelling is on offer at the exquisite beaches of Paxí's little sister. See p.1023

※ **Lefkádha's west coast** The archipelago's finest beaches run from Áï Nikítas down to Pórto Katsíki. See p.1029

※ **Melissáni Cave, Kefalloniá** See dappled sunlight on the water amid rock formations on a boat trip inside this once-enclosed underwater cave. See p.1034

※ **Mount Énos, Kefalloniá** The highest point in the Ionians has stunning vistas of sea and distant land. See p.1039

※ **Itháki's Homeric sites** Relive the myths on Odysseus's island. See p.1042

※ **Boat tour around Zákynthos** The best way to see the impressive coastline is to cruise from Zákynthos Town. See p.1047

△ Lefkádha's remote Yialós beach

The Ionian Islands

T he six Ionian islands, shepherding their satellites down the west coast of the mainland, float on the haze of the Ionian sea, their green, even lush, silhouettes coming as a shock to those more used to the stark outlines of the Aegean. The fertility of the land is a direct result of the heavy rains that sweep over the archipelago – and especially Corfu – from October to May, so if you visit at this time, come prepared.

The islands were the Homeric realm of Odysseus, centred on Ithaca, (modern Itháki) and here alone of all modern Greek territory (except for Lefkádha) the Ottomans never held sway. After the fall of Byzantium, possession passed to the **Venetians** and the islands became a keystone in Venice's maritime empire from 1386 until its collapse in 1797. Most of the population remained immune to the establishment of Italian as the official language and the arrival of Roman Catholicism, but Venetian influence remains evident in the architecture of the island capitals, despite damage from a series of earthquakes.

On Corfu, the Venetian legacy is mixed with that of the **British**, who imposed a military "protectorate" over the Ionian islands at the close of the Napoleonic Wars, before ceding the archipelago to Greece in 1864. There is, however, no question of the islanders' essential Greekness: the poet Dhionyssios Solomos, author of the national anthem, hailed from the Ionians, as did Nikos Mantzelos, who provided the music, and the first Greek president, Ioannis Kapodhistrias.

Today, **tourism** is the dominating influence, especially on **Corfu** (Kérkyra), which was one of the first Greek islands established on the package-holiday circuit, though the recent general downturn means it does not feel as swamped as in the past. Nevertheless, parts of its coastline are among the few stretches in Greece with development to match the Spanish *costas*. Yet the island is large enough to contain parts as beautiful as anywhere in the group. The southern half of **Zákynthos** (Zante) – which with Corfu has the Ionians' most over-subscribed beaches – has also gone down the same tourist path, but elsewhere the island's pace and scale of development is a lot less intense. Little **Paxí** lacks the water to support large-scale hotels and has limited facilities tucked into just three villages, meaning it gets totally packed in season, when connections to Corfu and the mainland peak. Perhaps the most rewarding trio for island-hopping are **Kefalloniá**, **Itháki** and **Lefkádha**. The latter is connected to the mainland by a causeway and iron bridge but still has quite a low-key straggle of tourist centres and only two major resorts, despite boasting some excellent beaches, strung along its stunning west coast. Kefalloniá offers a series of "real towns" and a life in large part independent of tourism, as well as a selection of worthwhile attractions. Finally Itháki, Odysseus's rugged capital, is protected from a tourist influx by an absence of sand. The Ionian islands' claims to

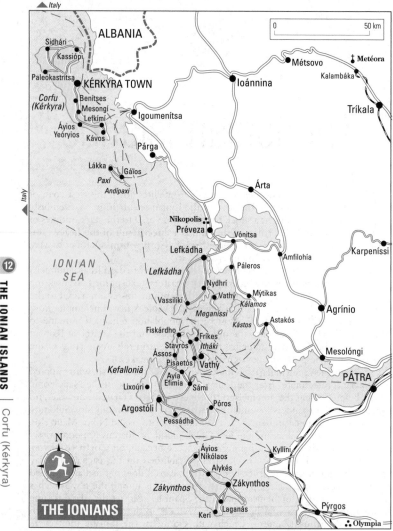

Homeric significance are manifested in the countless bars, restaurants and streets named after characters in the *Odyssey,* including the "nimble-witted" hero himself, Penelope, Nausicaa, Calypso and the Cyclops.

Corfu (Kérkyra)

Dangling between the heel of Italy and the west coast of mainland Greece, green, mountainous **Corfu (Kérkyra)** was one of the first Greek islands to attract mass tourism in the 1960s. Indiscriminate exploitation turned parts into eyesores, but much of the island still consists of olive groves, mountain or woodland. The majority of package holidays are based in the most developed resorts, but unspoiled terrain is often only a few minutes' walk away.

Corfu is thought to have been the model for Prospero and Miranda's place of exile in Shakespeare's *The Tempest*, and was certainly known to writers such

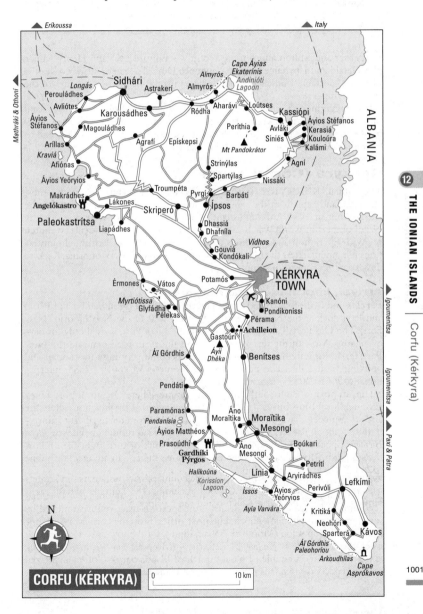

CORFU (KÉRKYRA)

0   10 km

The islands of **Kýthira** and **Andikýthira**, isolated at the foot of the Peloponnese, are historically part of the Ionian islands. However, at some 200km from the nearest other Ionians, and with no ferry connections to the northerly Ionians, they are most easily reached from **Yíthio** or **Neápoli** and are thus covered in Chapter Two.

Similarly, the island of **Kálamos**, Lefkádha's most distant satellite, is inaccessible from the Ionian group and covered therefore in Chapter Four.

as Spenser and Milton and – more recently – Edward Lear and Henry Miller, plus Gerald and Lawrence Durrell. Lawrence Durrell's *Prospero's Cell* evokes the island's "delectable landscape", still evident in some of the best beaches of the whole archipelago.

The staggering amount of accommodation (over 5000 places) on the island means that competition keeps prices down even in high season, at least in many resorts outside of Kérkyra Town. Prices at restaurants and in shops also tend to be a little lower than average for the Ionians.

Kérkyra (Corfu) Town

The capital, **KÉRKYRA (CORFU) TOWN**, has been one of the most elegant island capitals in the whole of Greece since it was spruced up for the EU summit in 1994. Although many of its finest buildings were destroyed by Nazi bombers in World War II, two massive forts, the sixteenth-century church of Áyios Spyrídhon and buildings dating from French and British administrations remain intact. As the island's major port of entry by ferry or plane, Kérkyra Town can get packed in summer.

Arrival, information and services

Ferries and hydrofoils to and from Italy, the mainland (Igoumenítsa and Pátra) and Paxí dock at the New Port (Néo Limáni) west of the Néo Froúrio (New Fort). The Old Port (Paleó Limáni), east of the New Port, is used only for day-excursions. Most of the ferry offices are on the main road opposite the New Port; ferries to Italy or south towards Pátra become very busy in summer and booking is advisable. The port authority (domestic ☎26610 32655, international ☎26610 30481) can advise on services.

The **airport** is 2km south of the city centre. There are no airport buses, although local **blue buses** #5 and #6 can be flagged at the junction where the airport approach drive meets the main road (500m from terminal). It's a thirty-minute walk on flat terrain into town (follow the road running beside the *Hotel Bretagne* opposite the junction for the shortest route or turn right then follow the sea road). **Taxis** charge at least €6 (but agree the fare in advance) or phone ☎26610 33811 for a radio cab.

The **tourist office** (Mon–Fri 8am–2pm; ☎26610 37520, ✉e.o.t.corfu@otenet .gr), housed temporarily inside the Customs Building at the New Port, has accommodation and transport details – the location may well have moved by summer 2006 so phone to check. The **post office** is on the corner of Alexándhras and Zafirópoulou (Mon–Fri 7.30am–8pm). Of the town's several Internet cafés, the best value is *X-plore*, N. Lefteriti 4 (Mon–Sat 9am–2pm & 6–11pm; €4.80 per hour), a couple of blocks north of Plyatía Saróko (often anglicized to San Rocco, though it is officially named Platía Yeoryíou Theotóki).

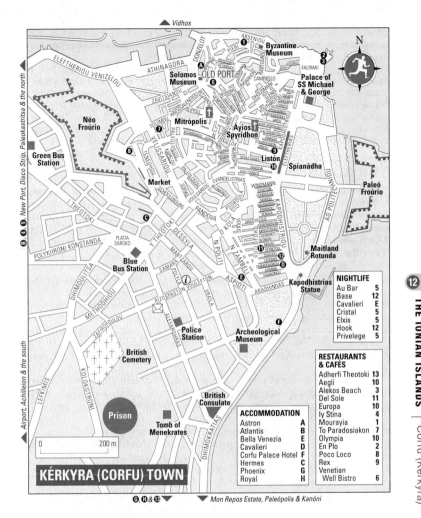

Vídhos

KÉRKYRA (CORFU) TOWN

Mon Repos Estate, Paleópolis & Kanóni

NIGHTLIFE

Au Bar	5
Base	12
Cavalieri	E
Cristal	5
Elxis	5
Hook	12
Privelege	5

RESTAURANTS & CAFÉS

Adherfi Theotoki	13
Aegli	10
Alekos Beach	3
Del Sole	11
Europa	10
Iy Stina	4
Mourayia	1
To Paradosiakon	7
Olympia	10
En Plo	2
Poco Loco	8
Rex	9
Venetian Well Bistro	6

ACCOMMODATION

Astron	A
Atlantis	B
Bella Venezia	E
Cavalieri	D
Corfu Palace Hotel	F
Hermes	C
Phoenix	G
Royal	H

Accommodation

Accommodation in Kérkyra Town is busy all year round, and not always the best value when compared to the rest of the island. Room owners sometimes meet mainland and international ferries, or you can try the Room Owners' Association, near the tourist office at D.Theotóki 2A (Mon–Fri 9am–1.30pm, plus summer Tues, Thurs & Fri 6–8pm; ☎26610 26133, @oitkcrf@otenet .gr). Budget travellers might best head straight for the nearest **campsite** at Dhassiá (see p.1008).

Astron Dónzelot 15 ☎26610 39505, @hotel_ astron@hol.gr. Tastefully renovated hotel in the Old Port. Good deals available outside the short peak season. All rooms with fan and optional air con. **④**

Atlantis Xenofóndos Stratigoú 48 ☎26610 35560, @atlanker@mail.otenet.gr. Large and spacious

air-con hotel in the New Port; its functional 1960s ambience rather lacks character. **④**

Bella Venezia Zambéli 4 ☎26610 46500, @wwwbellaveneziahotel.com. Smart, yellow Neoclassical building just behind the *Cavalieri*, with all the *Cavalieri*'s comforts, but cheaper. **⑥**

1003

Cavalieri Kapodhistríou 4 ☎ 26610 39041, ⓦ www .cavalieri-hotel.com. Smart and friendly, with all mod cons, great views and a roof bar open to the public. ⑥

Corfu Palace Hotel Leofóros Dhimokratías 2 ☎ 26610 39485, ⓦ www.corfupalace.com. Luxury hotel with pools, landscaped gardens and excellent rooms, each with a marble bath. The smartest place on the island. ⑧

Hermes Markorá 14 ☎ 26610 39268, ⓕ 26610 31747. An old favourite in a busy part of town. The cheapest rooms have shared bathrooms. Overlooks the noisy market. ③

Phoenix Khryssostómou Smýrnis 2, Garítsa ☎ 26610 42290, ⓕ 26610 42990. Small, stylish hotel between the airport and the seafront. Good value, B&B ③

Royal Kanni ☎ 26610 39915, ⓕ 26610 44690. Splendidly located on a hill 3km south of town and extremely good value. There's a pool and all rooms have balconies with bay views. ④

The Town

Kérkyra Town comprises a number of distinct areas. The **Historic Centre**, the area enclosed by the Old Port and the two forts, consists of several smaller districts: **Campiello**, the oldest, sits on the hill above the harbour; **Kofinéta** stretches towards the Spianádha (Esplanade); **Áyii Apóstoli** runs west of the Mitrópolis (orthodox cathedral); while tucked in beside the Néo Froúrio are **Ténedhos** and what remains of the old **Jewish quarter**. These districts form the core of the old town, and their tall, narrow alleys conceal some of Corfu's most beautiful architecture. **Mandoúki**, beyond the Old Port, is the commercial and dormitory area for the port, and is worth exploring as a living quarter of the city, away from the tourism racket. The town's **commercial area** lies inland from the Spianádha, roughly between Yeoryíou Theotóki, Alexándhras and Kapodhistríou streets, with the most shops and boutiques around Voulgaréos, Yeoryíou Theotóki and off Platía Saróko. Tucked below the southern ramparts of the Néo Froúrio is the old morning **market**, which sells fish and farm produce.

The most obvious sights are the forts, the **Paleó Froúrio** and **Néo Froúrio**, whose designations (*paleó* – "old", *néo* – "new") are a little misleading, since what you see of the older structure was begun by the Byzantines in the mid-twelfth century, just a hundred years before the Venetians began work on the newer citadel. They have both been damaged and modified by various occupiers and besiegers, the last contribution being the Neoclassical shrine of **St George**, built by the British in the middle of Paleó Froúrio during the 1840s. Looming above the Old Port, the Néo Froúrio (daily 9am–10pm, closes earlier off-season; €2) is the more interesting of the two architecturally. The entrance, at the back of the fort, gives onto cellars, dungeons and battlements, with excellent views over the town and bay; there's a small gallery and café at the summit. The Paleó Froúrio (Mon–Fri 8am–7pm, Sat & Sun 8.30am–3pm; €4) is not as well preserved and contains some incongruous modern structures, but has an interesting Byzantine museum just inside the gate, and even more stunning views from the central Land Tower. It also hosts daily son et lumière shows.

Just west of the Paleó Froúrio, the **Listón**, an arcaded street built during the French occupation by the architect of the Rue de Rivoli in Paris, and the green **Spianádha** (Esplanade) it overlooks, are the focus of town life. The cricket pitch, still in use at the northern end of the Spianádha, is another British legacy, while at the southern end the **Maitland Rotunda** was built to honour the first British High Commissioner of Corfu and the Ionian islands. The neighbouring statue of Ioannis Kapodhistrias celebrates the local hero and statesman (1776–1831) who led the diplomatic efforts for independence and was made Greece's first president in 1827. At the far northern end of the Listón, the nineteenth-century **Palace of SS Michael and George**, a solidly British edifice built as the residence of their High Commissioner (one of the last of whom was the future British prime minister William Gladstone), and later used as a palace by the Greek monarchy. The former state rooms house the **Asiatic Museum** (Tues–Sun 8am–3pm; €3) which is a must for aficionados of Oriental culture. Amassed by Corfiot diplomat Gregorios Manos (1850–1929) and others, it includes Noh theatre masks, woodcuts, wood and brass statuettes, samurai weapons and art works from Thailand, Korea and Tibet. The adjoining **Modern Art Gallery** (Tues–Sun 9am–5pm, special exhibitions 9am–1pm & 6–9pm; €1.50) holds a small collection of contemporary Greek art. It's an interesting diversion, as are the gardens and café-bar secreted behind the palace.

In a nearby backstreet off Arseníou, five minutes from the palace, is the museum dedicated to modern Greece's most famous nineteenth-century poet, **Dhionysios Solomos** (Mon–Sat 9.30am–2pm; €1). Born on Zákynthos, Solomos was author of the poem A*mnos stín Elefthería* (*Hymn to Liberty*), which was to become the Greek national anthem. He studied at Corfu's Ionian Academy, and lived in a house on this site for much of his life.

Up a short flight of steps on Arseníou, the **Byzantine Museum** (Tues–Sun 9am–3pm; €2) is housed in the restored church of the Panayía Andivouniótissa. It houses church frescoes and sculptures and sections of mosaic floors from the ancient site of Paleópolis, just south of Kérkyra Town. There are also some pre-Christian artefacts, and a collection of icons dating from the fifteenth to nineteenth centuries.

A block behind the Listón, down Spyrídhonos, is the sixteenth-century **church of Áyios Spyrídhon** (daily 8am–9pm), whose maroon-domed campanile dominates the town. Here you will find the silver-encrusted coffin of the island's patron saint, **Spyridhon** – Spyros in the diminutive – after whom seemingly half the male population is named. Four times a year (Palm Sunday and the following Sat, Aug 11 and the first Sun in Nov), to the accompaniment of much celebration and feasting, the relics are paraded through the streets of Kérkyra Town. Each of the days commemorates a miraculous deliverance of the island credited to the saint – twice from plague during the seventeenth century, from a famine of the sixteenth century and (a more blessed release than either of those for any Greek) from the Turks in the eighteenth century.

The next most important of the town's many churches, the **Mitrópolis** (orthodox cathedral), perched at the top of its own square opposite the Old Port, also houses the remains of a saint, in this case St Theodora, the ninth-century wife of Emperor Theophilos. The building dates from 1577 and the plain exterior conceals a splendid iconostasis, as well as some fine icons, including a fine sixteenth-century image of *Saint George Slaying the Dragon* by the Cretan artist Mihaïl Dhamaskinos, and three dark, atmospheric Italianate paintings.

Kérkyra Town's **Archeological Museum** (Tues–Sun 8.30am–3pm; €3), just south round the coast, is the best in the archipelago. The most impressive exhibit is a massive (17m) gorgon pediment excavated from the Doric temple of Artemis at Paleópolis, just south of Kérkyra Town; this dominates an entire room, the gorgon flanked by panthers and mythical battle scenes. The museum also has fragments of Neolithic weapons and cookware, and coins and pots from the period when the island was a colony of ancient Corinth.

Just south of Platía Saróko and signposted on the corner of Methodhíou and Kolokotróni, the well-maintained **British cemetery** features some elaborate civic and military memorials. It's a quiet green space away from the madness of Saróko and, in spring and early summer, it comes alive with dozens of species of orchids and other exotic blooms.

The outskirts

Each of the following sights on the outskirts of the city is easily seen in a morning or afternoon, and you can conceivably cover several in one day.

Around the bay from the Rotunda and Archeological Museum, tucked behind Mon Repos beach, the area centered around the **Mon Repos** estate (8am–7pm; free) contains the most accessible archeological remains on the island, collectively known as **Paleópolis**. Within the estate, thick woodland conceals two **Doric temples**, dedicated to Hera and Poseidon. The Neoclassical **Mon Repos villa**, built by British High Commissioner Frederic Adam in 1824 and handed over to Greece in 1864, is the birthplace of Britain's Prince Philip and has been converted into the **Paleópolis Museum** (daily 8.30am–7pm; €3). As well as various archeological finds from the vicinity, including some fine sculpture, it contains period furniture *in situ*, and temporary modern art exhibitions. Other remains worth a peek outside the confines of the estate include the **Early Christian Basilica** (Tues–Sun 8.30am–3pm; free) opposite the entrance, the **Temple of Artemis**, a few hundred metres west, and the eleventh-century church of **Áyii Iáson and Sosípater**, back towards the seafront on Náfsikas.

The most famous excursion from Kérkyra Town is to the islets of **Vlahérna** and **Pondikoníssi**, 2km south of town below the hill of Kanóni, named after the single cannon trained out to sea atop it. A dedicated bus (#2) leaves Platía Saróko every half-hour, or it's a pleasant walk of under an hour. Reached by a short causeway, the tiny white convent of Vlahérna is one of the most photographed images on Corfu. Pondikoníssi (Mouse Island) can be reached by a short boat trip from the dock at Vlahérna (€2.50 return). Tufted with greenery and the small chapel of Panayía Vlahernón, Vlahérna is identified in legend with a ship from Odysseus's fleet, petrified by Poseidon in revenge for the blinding of his son Polyphemus, the Homeric echoes somewhat marred by the thronging masses and low-flying aircraft from the nearby runway. A quieter destination is **Vídhos**, the wooded island visible from the Old Port, reached from there by an hourly shuttle *kaïki* (€1 return, last boat back 1.30am). It makes a particularly pleasant summer evening excursion, when there is live music at the municipal restaurant near the jetty.

Four kilometres further to the south, past the resort sprawl of Pérama, is a rather more bizarre attraction: the **Achilleion** (daily 8am–7pm; €6), a palace built in a (fortunately) unique blend of Teutonic and Neoclassical styles in 1890 by Elizabeth, Empress of Austria. Henry Miller considered it "the worst piece of gimcrackery" that he'd ever laid eyes on and thought it "would make an excellent museum for surrealistic art". The house is predictably grandiose, but the gardens are pleasant to walk around and afford splendid views in all directions.

Eating and drinking

Although there are the inevitable tourist traps, Kérkyra Town offers some excellent, quality restaurants. As well as those listed below, there are several decent *psarotavérnes* on the Garítsa seafront, though you need to be wary of the fish prices.

Adherfi Theotoki M. Athanassíou, Garítsa. By far the best of the several establishments tucked behind the seafront park, this popular family taverna serves excellent *mezédhes*, meat and good-value fish dishes.

Alekos Beach Faliráki jetty. Set in the tiny harbour below the palace, with great views, this place offers simple, mostly grilled meat and fish dishes at good prices.

Del Sole Guildford 17. The town's most authentic Italian food such as smoked salmon antipasti and seafood or meat spaghetti dishes at a little above taverna prices.

Iy Stina Xenofóndos Stratigoú 78, Mandoúki. Quaint traditional taverna one block back from the seafront, serving a fine range of *mezédhes* and main courses, including tasty meat from the oven.

Mourayia Arseníou 15–17. This unassuming, good-value ouzerí near the Byzantine Museum does a range of tasty *mezédhes*, including sausage and seafood such as mussels and shrimp in exquisite sauces. One of the best establishments in town, with views of passing ferries and Vídhos island.

To Paradosiakon Solomoú 20. Behind the Old Port, this friendly place serves good fresh food, especially home-style oven dishes such as *stifádho* and *kokkinistó*.

Poco Loco 1st Párodhos Solomoú 1, Spiliá. At the foot of the steps to the Néo Froúrio, this newly converted Tex-Mex restaurant serves a range of reasonably priced Mexican favourites and slightly pricier items like ostrich and kangaroo.

Rex Kapodhistríou 66 (the Listón). Pricey owing to its location, but some of the best food in the centre, especially the delicious oven food, mixing Greek with north European.

Venetian Well Bistro Platía Kremastí. A well-kept secret, tucked away in a tiny square a few alleys to the south of the cathedral, this is the nearest you're likely to get to Greek nouvelle cuisine, with large portions, and exotica such as Iraqi lamb and Albanian calves' livers in ouzo. Very expensive.

Cafés and Nightlife

Kérkyra Town has a plethora of **cafés**, most noticeably lining Listón, the main pedestrianized cruising street. None of these popular establishments is cheap, but among the more reasonable are the *Aegli*, *Europa* or *Olympia*, all guaranteed to be packed from morning till late at night. *En Plo* on Faliráki jetty, however, has an unbeatably brilliant and breezy setting and is much quieter, as is the leafy *Art Café*, behind the Palace of SS Michael and George.

Moving on from Corfu Town

Corfu's **bus** service radiates from the capital. There are **two** terminals: the islandwide green bus service is based on Avramíou (also for Athens and Thessaloníki), and the suburban blue bus system, which also serves nearby resorts such as Benítses and Dhassiá, is based in Platía Saróko. Islandwide services stop between 6 and 9pm, suburban ones at between 9 and 10.30pm. Printed English timetables are available for both and can be picked up at the tourist office or the respective terminals.

Frequent **ferries** run throughout the day from the New Port to Igoumenítsa on the mainland, as well as regular services to Pátra and several Italian ports. All the major lines have franchises on the seafront opposite the port: Agoudimos (℡26610 80030, ⊛www.agoudimos-lines.com), Anek (℡26610 24503, ⊛www.anek.gr), Fragline (℡26610 38089, ⊛www.fragline.gr), Minoan (℡26610 25000, ⊛www.minoan. gr), Superfast (℡26610 32467, ⊛www.superfast.com), Ventouris (℡26610 21212, ⊛www.ventouris.gr) and Snav (℡26610 36439, ⊛www.snav.it). Two companies now run **hydrofoil** services to Paxí: Ionian Lines, managed by the Petrakis agency (℡26610 25155, ⊛www.ionian-cruises.com), who also operate tours to Albania, Párga and other Ionian islands at much cheaper rates than the travel agents in the resorts; and Paxos Flying Dolphins through International Tours (℡26610 35808).

In late 2004 the much-fanfared **seaplane** service (⊛www.airsealines.com) to Paxí finally got off the ground. It now also flies to Ioánnina on the mainland and hopes to expand to other islands and even Brindisi in the near future. It actually takes off from Gouviá marina (see overleaf). For further details on all public transportation see "Travel details" p.1054.

Increasing numbers of visitors rent their own vehicles to get round the sizeable island. **Cars** can be rented from international agencies at the airport or in town; try Avis, Ethnikís Andístasis 42 (℡26610 24404, airport 26610 42007), behind the new port, Budget, Venizélou 22 (℡26610 28590; airport 26610 44017) or Hertz, Ethnikí Lefkímis (℡26610 38388, airport 26610 35547). Among local companies, Sunrise, Ethnikís Andístasis 14 (℡26610 44325) is reliable and many agents listed throughout the resorts offer competitive deals. **Motorbikes** and **scooters** can be rented from Easy Rider, Venizélou 4 (℡26610 43026) or Lazy Bone, Venizélou 52 (℡26610 40580) both in the New Port.

The hippest youth **bars** in town are the trio on Kapodhistríou adjacent to the *Cavalieri* hotel, of which *Hook* is the rockiest and *Base* offers a mixture of pop, rock and dance sounds. The rooftop bar at the *Cavalieri* itself is more middle-of-the-road musically but can be heaven at night.

Club action takes place at Corfu's self-proclaimed **disco** strip, a couple of kilometres north of town, past the New Port. This only revs up after midnight, when it becomes classic *kamáki* territory, although in summer many of its macho regulars forsake it for the resorts in order to hunt foreign females. The currently "in" joints are *Privelege*, a standard disco, *Au Bar*, a large indoor club which mixes in some Latin, *Elxis*, which boasts an impressive lightshow for its Euro/Greek sounds, and *Cristal*, whose DJs favour trance and ethnic.

Kérkyra Town's two **cinemas** – the winter Orfeus on the corner of Akadhimías and Aspióti and the open-air summer Phoenix down the side street opposite – both show mostly English-language films.

The northeast and the north coast

The **northeast**, at least beyond the immediate suburbs, is the most typically Greek part of Corfu – it's mountainous, with a rocky coastline chopped into pebbly bays and coves, above wonderfully clear seas. Green **buses** between Kérkyra Town and Kassiópi serve all resorts, along with some blue suburban buses as far as Dhassiá.

Kérkyra Town to Ípsos

The landscape just north of Kérkyra Town is an industrial wasteland, and things don't improve much at the first village you come to, **KONDÓKALI**, overrun by holiday developments. The old town consists of a short street with a number of bars and traditional *psistariés*, the best of which are *Gerekos* and *Takis*, an international restaurant, *Flags*, and the pricey *Lithari* fish taverna.

Neighbouring **GOUVIÁ** is home to Corfu's largest yachting marina. The village boasts a couple of small **hotels**, notably the *Hotel Popi Star* (☎26610 91500, ☎26610 91502; ❸) and great-value *Gouvia View* by the beach (☎26610 9167; ❷). For **rooms**, try Karoukas Travel (☎26610 91596, ✉karoukas@otenet .gr; ❸). There are a number of decent **restaurants**, including all-purpose tavernas *The Captain's* and *Gorgona*, the basic but excellent *Steki psistariá* and pizzerias such as *La Bonita*. The very narrow shingle **beach**, barely 5m wide in parts, shelves into sand; given the sea traffic, the water quality is doubtful.

Two kilometres beyond Gouviá the coastline begins to improve at **DHAF-NÍLA** and **DHASSIÁ**, set in adjacent wooded bays with pebbly beaches. The latter is much larger and contains nearly all the area's facilities, including a trio of **watersports** enterprises. It is also home to the most respected UK-qualified doctor on the island, Dr John Yannopapas (☎26610 97811), whose surgery is on the main road. Two luxury sister **hotels**, the *Dassia Chandris* and *Corfu Chandris* (both ☎26610 97100–3, ⓦwww.chandris.gr; ❼), dominate the resort, with extensive grounds, pools and beach facilities. Down at the beach the modest but friendly *Spiros Beach* (☎26610 93666; ❸) is the best bet, followed by the twin Dassia Beach/Dassia Margarita (☎26610 93224, ☎26610 93864; ❸). Independent **rooms** can be scarce, the most reliable source being Emka Travel (☎26610 93738, ⓦwww.emkatravel.com; ❷. Dhafníla does, however, have the best **campsite** on the island, *Dionysus Camping Village* (☎26610 91417, ⓦwww.dionysuscamping.com); tents are pitched under terraced olive trees. *Dionysus* also has simple bungalow huts, a pool, shop, bar and restaurant, while the friendly, multilingual owners offer a ten-percent discount to Rough Guide readers. Two of the best eateries in Dhassiá are *Andreas*, a pleasant fish taverna on the beach, and *Karydia*, a multi-cuisine restaurant on the main road.

ÍPSOS, 2km north of Dhassiá, can't really be recommended to anyone but hardened bar-hoppers. The thin pebble beach lies right beside the busy coast road and the resort is generally pretty tacky. Most **accommodation** is prebooked by package companies, although Pelais Travel (T26610 97564, Wwww.pelaistravel.com; ❸) can offer rooms. *Camping Ipsos Beach* (T26610 93246, F26610 93741) has a bar and restaurant, and offers standing tents. Ípsos is also home to one of the island's major **diving centres**, Waterhoppers (T26610 93867, Ediverclub@hotmail.com). **Eating** on the main drag is dominated by fast food, though a more traditional meal and a quieter setting can be found in the *Akrogiali psistariá* and *Asteria* taverna, both by the marina to the south of the strip, or you can get a decent curry at the *Viceroy*. The northern end is largely devoted to competing **bars** and **discos** such as *Monte Christo*, *B52* and *Shooters*.

North to Áyios Stéfanos

Ípsos has now engulfed the neighbouring hamlet of Pyrgí, which is the main point of access for the villages and routes leading up to **Mount Pandokrátor** from the south; the road, signposted Spartýlas, is 200km beyond the junction in Pyrgí. A popular base for walkers is the village of **STRINÝLAS**, 16km from Pyrgí. Accommodation is basic but easy to come by: the *Elm Tree* taverna, a long-time favourite with walkers, can direct you to rooms. In summer the main routes are busy, but there are quieter walks taking in the handsome Venetian village of Epískepsi, 5km northwest of Strinýlas – anyone interested in walking the Pandokrátor paths is advised to get the **map** of the mountain by island-based cartographer Stephan Jaskulowski or one of Hilary Whitton-Paipeti's walking books, available locally.

The coast road beyond Ípsos mounts the slopes of Pandokrátor towards **BARBÁTI**, 4km further on. Here you'll find the best beach on this coast, though its charm has been somewhat diminished recently by the construction of the gargantuan *Riviera Barbati* apartment complex. The beach is a favourite with families, and much **accommodation** is prebooked in advance. However, there are some rooms available on spec – try *Paradise* (T26630 91320, F26630 91479; ❸) or Helga Travel Agency (T26630 91547, Ehelga@otenet.gr; ❸), both up on the main road.

The mountainside becomes steeper and the road higher beyond Barbáti, and the population thins drastically. **NISSÁKI** is a sprawling roadside settlement rather than a village, with a number of coves, the first and last accessible by road, the rest only by track – the furthest dominated by the gigantic and rather soulless *Nissaki Beach Hotel* (T26630 91232, Wwww.nissakibeach.gr; ❺ half-board). There are a couple of shops and a bakery, and a few travel and **accommodation agencies**. The British-owned Falcon Travel (T26630 91318, Wwww .falcon-travel-corfu.com; ❸) rents out apartments above the first beach, a tiny, white-pebble cove with a trio of fine tavernas – try the quayside *Mitsos*. The *Nissaki Holiday Center* (T26630 91166, Wwww.nissakiholidays; ❷), up by the junction, may have some cheaper rooms.

Three pebbly coves no one visiting this coast should miss are Agní, not far past the *Nissaki Beach Hotel*, Kalámi and neighbouring Kouloúra: the first for its trio of fine tavernas, the second for its Durrell connection, the third for its exquisite bay. Crowds flock to **AGNÍ** for the fine eating – *Nikolas* is the oldest taverna and just pips *Toula* and *Agni* for quality; it also runs the peaceful *Nikolas Apartments* (T26630 91243, Wwww.kalamits.com; ❹). **KALÁMI** is on the way to being spoilt, but the village is still small and you can imagine how it would have looked in the year Lawrence Durrell spent here on the eve of World War II. The **White House**, where Durrell wrote *Prospero's Cell*, is now split in two: the ground floor is an excellent taverna; the upper floor is let through CV Travel (see Basics, p.31). Sunshine Travel (℡26630 91170, Ⓦwww.sunshineclub.gr) and Kalami Tourist Services (℡26630 91062, Ⓦwww.kalamits.com) both have a range of rooms (❷) on their books; see if one's going at *Villa Rita* (℡26630 91030; ❸). The **restaurant** at the White House is recommended, as are *Kalami Beach* and *Thomas' Place*, both above average tavernas on the beach. Two cocktail bars compete for the happy-hour trade.

The tiny harbour of **KOULOÚRA** has managed to keep its charm intact, set at the edge of an unspoilt bay with nothing to distract from the pine trees and *kaïkia*. The fine sole **taverna** here is one of the most idyllic settings for a meal in the whole of Corfu.

Around the coast to Aharávi

Two kilometres beyond Kouloúra, down a shady lane, the large pebble cove of **Kerasiá** shelters the family-run *Kerasia Taverna*. The most attractive resort on this stretch of coast, however, 3km down a lane from Siniés on the main road, is **ÁYIOS STÉFANOS** (officially Áyios Stéfanos Sinión to distinguish it from a namesake in northwestern Corfu). Most **accommodation** here is of the upmarket prebooked villa sort, and the village has yet to succumb to any serious development; the only independent rooms and apartments are managed by the *Kochili* taverna (℡26630 81522; ❸). For food, as well as the friendly *Kochili* itself, try the *Galini* and *Eucalyptus* **tavernas**; the latter, over by the village's small beach, is pricier but serves more adventurous fare such as pork with artichokes. The *Damianos* cocktail bar is the main spot to idle with a drink.

△ Kassiópi harbour and castle

A thirty-minute walk from the coastguard station above Áyios Stéfanos, along a newly surfaced road, stretches the beach of **Avláki**, a pebble bay that provides lively conditions for the **windsurfers** who visit the beach's windsurf club. There are two **tavernas**, the *Cavo Barbaro* and *Avlaki*, but the only accommodation is taken by upmarket package companies.

Further round the coast is **KASSIÓPI**, a fishing village that's been transformed into a major party resort. The Roman emperor Tiberius had a villa here, and the village's sixteenth-century Panayía Kassópitra church is said to stand on the site of a temple of Zeus once visited by Nero. Little evidence of Kassiópi's past survives, apart from an abandoned Angevin *kástro* on the headland – most visitors come for the nightlife and the five pebbly beaches. Most nonpackage **accommodation** in Kassiópi is rented through village agencies; the largest, Travel Corner (☎26630 81220, ⓦwww.kassiopi.com; ❷), with offices near the square and the harbour, is a good place to start. An independent alternative, the great-value *Kastro* restaurant-cum-pension (☎26630 81045, Ⓔkyrosai@hol.gr; ❷), overlooks the beach behind the castle, while *Panayiota Apartments* (☎26630 81063; ❸) offers bargain studios one block behind Kalamíones beach on the west side. The most popular **restaurants** are multi-cuisine tavernas, which supplement a traditional Greek diet with various international dishes, such as *Janis*, by the corner of Kalamíones beach. Other options include the *Porto* fish restaurant at the harbour and *Sze Chuan* Chinese on the main road.

At night, Kassiópi rocks to the cacophony of its music and video bars: the flashiest is the gleaming hi-tech *Eclipse*, which also shows DVDs, closely followed by the *Jasmine* and *Visions*, all within falling-over distance of the small town square. The *Passion Club* is the liveliest spot down at the otherwise laid-back harbour. The village is also home to one of the most reliable diving operations, Corfu Divers (☎26630 81218, ⓦwww.corfudivers.com), which is partly British-run. You can get online at Photonet (€4.5 per hr).

The coastline beyond Kassiópi is overgrown and marshy until you get to little-developed **Almyrós** beach, one of the longest on the island, with only a few apartment buildings and one huge new resort dotted sporadically behind it. For a peaceful stay you could try *Villa Maria* (☎26630 63359; ❸) and eat at *Avra*, a pleasant taverna further along the beach. The **Andinióti lagoon**, smaller than Korissíon in the south but still a haven for birds and twitchers, backs Cape Ayías Ekaterínis to the east, which marks the northern end of the Corfu Trail (see p.1019). The beach extends east all the way to **AHARÁVI**, whose wide stretch of the main coast road is vaguely reminiscent of an American Midwest truck stop. The village proper is tucked on the inland side of the road in a quiet crescent of old tavernas, bars and shops. Aharávi makes a quieter beach alternative to the southerly strands, and should also be considered by those seeking alternative routes up onto **Mount Pandokrátor**. Roads to small hamlets such as Áyios Martínos and Láfki continue onto the mountain, and even a stroll up from the back of Aharávi will find you on the upper slopes in under an hour.

Accommodation isn't always easy to find, but a good place to start is Castaway Travel (☎26630 63541, ⓦwww.corfucastaway.com). One independent hotel is *Dandolo* (☎26630 63557, Ⓔdandolo@otenet.gr; ❹), set in lush grounds towards the old village, though it is sometimes booked out to Italian groups in high season. Of the many **restaurants** on Aharávi's main drag the *Pump House* steak and pasta joint and *To Ellinikon psistariá*-taverna are the best. Meanwhile *Neraïda*, which specializes in meat dishes with mushroom or pepper sauces and trout salad, takes the prizes on the beach and the excellent *Theritas* taverna in the old village wins the authenticity award. The main drag's bar-restaurants tend to get quite rowdy at night, although the light and airy *Captain Aris* is a pleasant watering hole. For a quieter drink, head for, the friendly anonymous *kafenío* or the cosy *Hole in the Wall* pub, both in the old village.

Ródha, Sidhári and Avliótes

Continuing further west, **RÓDHA** has tipped over into overdevelopment, and can't be wholeheartedly recommended for those after a quiet time. Its central crossroads have all the charm of a service station, and the beach is rocky in parts and swampy to the west. "Old Ródha" is a small warren of alleys between the main road and the seafront, where you'll find the best **restaurants** and **bars**: the *Taverna Agra* is the oldest in Ródha and the best place for fish, while the sadly-named *Opa* and *New Port* are reasonable alternatives. For drinks, try *Crusoe's Pub* or *Maggie's Bar*, both with Sky Sports, or the trendier bar-club *Skouna*. If for some reason you decide **to stay**, the friendly seafront *Roda Inn* (☎26630 63358; ❸) has good value en-suite rooms. Both the Anglo-Greek HN Travel (☎26630 62249, ⓦwww.hntravel.gr; ❷), on the main drag, and Corfu Nostos Travel on the seafront (☎26630 64602, Ⓔe.kostaki@otenet.gr; ❷) rent rooms and handle car rental. The smart *Roda Beach Camping* (☎26630 93120) is a little way east of the resort, while even pleasanter *Karoussades Camping* (☎ & Ⓕ26630 31415) is to the west, towards Sidhári. Myron's good-rate motorbike rental (☎26630 63477) and Costas horse-riding (☎694 41 60 011; €15 for 2hr) are also based in Ródha. Several kilometres inland from Ródha, just east of Agrafí, the relatively undiscovered ⚔ *Angonari mezedhopolío* serves an excellent range of dishes and great barrelled wine in a relaxed garden with subtle live music.

The next notable resort, **SIDHÁRI**, is constantly expanding and totally dominated by British-package tourists; its small but pretty town square, with a bandstand set in a small garden, is lost in a welter of bars, shops and joints. The beach is sandy but not terribly clean, and many people tend to head just west to the curious coves, walled by wind-carved sandstone cliffs, around the vaunted Canal d'Amour. The biggest accommodation agency is run by young tycoon Philip Vlasseros, whose Vlasseros Travel (☎26630 95695, Ⓕ26630 95969) also handles car rental, horse-riding and excursions, including day-trips to the Dhiapóndia islands (see p.1019). Sidhári's **campsite**, *Dolphin Camping* (☎26630 31846), is over 1km inland from the junction at the western end of town. Most **restaurants** are pitched at those looking for a great night out rather than a quiet meal in a taverna. The pricey *Olympic* is the oldest taverna here; better value is to be found at *Sea Breeze* or at *Kavvadias*, on the eastern stretch of beach. Asian cuisine, such as the Indian food at *Kohenoor*, and cheap full-on English breakfasts are also readily available. There are no quiet bars in Sidhári, and several **nightclubs** vie for late custom, such as *IQ*, *Mojo* and *Caesar's*. Sidhári also has its own waterpark with free entry, a good place to keep the kids happy.

The Sidhári bus usually continues to **AVLIÓTES**, a handsome hill town with the odd kafenío and tavernas but few concessions to tourism. The town is note-worthy for two reasons: its accessibility to quiet **Perouládhes** in the very northwest and **Áyios Stéfanos** (see p.1014) to the southeast, both only a few kilometres away. Stunning **Longás beach**, bordered by vertical reddish layer-cake cliffs that make for shady mornings, lies below Perouládhes. You can stay 200m back from the beach at *Logas Beach Studios* (☎26630 95412, Ⓔgiorkou@mailbox.gr; ❸) or enjoy a splendid sunset dinner at the cliff-top *Panorama* taverna.

Paleokastrítsa and the northwest coast

The northwest conceals some of the island's most dramatic coastal scenery, the violent interior mountainscapes jutting out of the verdant countryside. The area's honeypot attraction is **Paleokastrítsa**, the single most picturesque resort on Corfu, which suffers from its popularity. Further north, the densely olive-clad hills conceal better, sandier beaches, such as **Áyios Yeóryios** and **Áyios Stéfanos**. Public **transport** all along the west coast is difficult: virtually all buses ply routes from Kérkyra Town to single destinations, and rarely link resorts.

Paleokastrítsa

PALEOKASTRÍTSA, a small village surrounded by dramatic hills and cliffs, has been identified as the Homeric city of Scheria, where Odysseus was washed ashore and escorted by Nausicaa to the palace of her father Alkinous, king of the Phaeacians. It's a stunning site, as you would expect, though one that's long been engulfed by tourism. The focal point of the village is the car park on the seafront, which backs onto the largest and least attractive of three **beaches**, home to sea taxis and *kaïkia*. The second beach, to the right and signed by flags for Mike's Ski Club, is stony with clear water, and the best of the three is a small unspoilt strand reached along the path by the *Astakos Taverna*. Protected by cliffs, it's undeveloped apart from the German-run Korfu-Diving Centre (T 26630 41604) at the end of the cove. From the first beach you can get a **boat trip** to some nearby seawater caves, known as the "blue grottoes" (€8 for a half-hour trip), which is worth taking for the spectacular coastal views. Boats also serve as a taxi service to three neighbouring beaches, Áyia Triánda, Palatákia and Alípa, which all have snack-bars.

On the rocky bluff above the village, the **Theotókou monastery** (7am–1pm & 3–8pm; free, donations welcome) is believed to have been established in the thirteenth century. There's also a museum, resplendent with icons, jewelled bibles and other impedimenta of Greek Orthodox ritual, though the highlight is the gardens, with spectacular coastal views. Paleokastrítsa's ruined castle, the **Angelókastro**, is around 6km up the coast; only approachable by path from the hamlet of Kríni, it has stunning, almost circular views of the surrounding sea and land. For a drink or snack with tremendous views on the way up, it's worth stopping at the execellent *O Boulis* taverna in Lákones or the *Bella Vista* or *Golden Fox* tavernas, between there and Makrádhes.

Accommodation is not too hard to find but sprawls a long way back from central Paleokastrítsa, often leaving quite a walk to the beach. A good **hotel** is the family-run *Odysseus* (T 26630 41209, W www.odysseushotel.gr; half-board ❹), on the road into town, while the nearby modern *Akrotiri Beach* (T 26630 41237, W www.akrotiri-beach.com; ❼) is upmarket but unpretentious. Along the first turning back from the centre on the north side of the main road, the friendly family-run *Villa Korina* (T 26630 44064; ❷) has great value **rooms**, as does the *Dolphin Snackbar* (T 26630 41035; ❷), further back above Alípa beach. Michalas tourist bureau (T 26630 41113, E michalastravel@ker.forthnet.gr) is another source, as well as offering all the usual services. *Paleokastritsa Camping* (T 26630 41204, F 26630 41104) is just off the main road, almost a half-hour walk from the centre.

There isn't a huge choice of **restaurants** in the centre of Paleokastrítsa. The *Astakos Taverna* and *Corner Grill* are two traditional places, while the seafront *Smurfs* has a good seafood menu despite the dreadful name. Also recommended is the very smart *Vrahos*, which offers pricey fish and some unusual dishes like artichokes. **Nightlife** hangouts include the restaurant-bars in the centre, and those straggling back up the hill, such as the relaxing *Petrino* bar. By the Lákones turning is Paleokastrítsa's one nightclub, *The Paleo Club*, a small disco-bar with a garden.

Áyios Yeóryios to Áyios Stéfanos

Like many of the west-coast resorts, **ÁYIOS YEÓRYIOS**, 6km north of Pale-okastrítsa, isn't actually based around a village, though it is sometimes referred to as Áyios Yeóryios Pagón after the inland village of Payí to avoid confusion with its southern namesake. The resort has developed in response to the popularity of the large sandy bay, and it's a major **windsurfing** centre, busy even in low season. Contrary to the general trend, more **accommodation** is now block-booked here than in the past but independent rooms are available at at bargain rates in the cute walled-garden complex of Kóstas Bardhís (☎26630 96219; ❶), towards the north end of the beach, and at the Arista supermarket (☎26630 96350; ❶) or *Studio Eleana* (☎ & ℻26630 96366; ❸), both behind the central section of beach. The *San George* campsite (☎26630 51759) is nearly 1km back from the beach towards Kavvadhádhes. *To Vrahos* at the northern end and *Spiros* halfway along are among the better restaurants, both serving Greek and international cuisine, while gaily-painted *Ostrako* is unbeatable for seafood in the far south. Nearby *Noa Noa* is one of the liveliest nightspots.

On the way north towards Áyios Stéfanos, the pleasant sandy beach of **Aríllas** has given rise to gradual development, including several **tavernas** – try *Kostas on the Beach* or the *Brouklis psistariá*, 200m back inland. Accommodation can be arranged through Arillas Travel (☎26630 51280, ⓦwww.arillastravel .gr; ❸), which is very friendly and has a couple of quality hotels on its books, or there is the smart *Akti Arilla* hotel (☎26630 51201, ⓔaktiaril@otenet.gr; ❹ half-board).

The northernmost of the west coast's resorts, **ÁYIOS STÉFANOS** is low-key, popular with families and a quiet base from which to explore the north-west and the Dhiapóndia islands, visible on the horizon. Day-trips to Mathráki, Othoní and Eríkoussa (see p.1020) run several times a week in season (€15–20 per person), as well as cheaper passenger services (€7–9 return) most days on the Aspiotis lines *kaïki*. Áyios Stéfanos's oldest **hotel**, the *Nafsika* (☎26630 51051, ⓦwww.nafsikahotel.com; ❸), has a large restaurant, a favourite with villagers, and gardens with a pool and bar. Also behind the main southern beach are the *Hotel San Stefano* (☎26630 51053, ℻26630 51202; ❸) and **rooms** at the *Sunset* taverna (☎26630 51185, ⓦwww.corfusunset.com; ❸), while the *Restaurant Evinos* (☎ & ℻26630 51766; ❸) has small apartments above the northern end of the village. For those on a budget, Peli and Maria's gift shop offers bargain **rooms** (☎26630 51424; ❷) and a number of travel agencies handle accommodation, among them San Stefanos (☎26630 51910, ⓦwww .san-stefano.gr; ❷) in the centre. Besides the above-mentioned establishments, good options for **eating** include the *Waves* and very reasonable *Mistral* tavernas above the beach, while *O Manthos* taverna serves Corfiot specialities such as *sofríto* and *pastitsádha*. For **nightlife**, lively *Magnet* and more laid-back *Sundowner* stand out among the handful of music bars.

Central and southern Corfu

Two natural features divide the centre and south of Corfu. The first is the **plain of Rópa**, whose fertile landscape backs on to some of the best beaches on this coast, such as delightful **Myrtiótissa**. Settlements and development stop a little to the south of Paleokastrítsa and only resume around **Érmones** and **Pélekas**

– a quick bus ride across the island from Kérkyra Town. Down to the south, a second dividing point is the **Korissíon lagoon**, the sandy plains and dunes that skirt this natural feature being great places for botanists and ornithologists. Beyond, a single road trails the interior, with sporadic side roads to resorts on either coast. The landscape here is flat, an undistinguished backdrop for a series of increasingly developed beaches and, in the far south, **Kávos**, Corfu's big youth resort.

Érmones to the Korissíon lagoon: the west coast

ÉRMONES, around 15km south of Paleokastrítsa by road, is one of the busiest resorts on the island, its lush green bay backed by the mountains above the Rópa River. The resort is dominated by the luxury *Ermones Beach* **hotel** (T 26610 94241, W www.sunmarotelermones.gr; ❽), which provides guests with obligatory full board and a funicular railway down to the beach. Of the two mid-range hotels on the other side of the river, the *Philoxenia* (T 26610 94091, W www.hotelphiloxenia.com; ❹) is better value, while cheaper rooms can be found at the *Pension Katerina* (T 26610 94615; ❷) and *Georgio's Villas* (T 26610 94950; ❷), further back on the hillside above the road that leads to the beach. Both the *Maria* and *Nafsica* **tavernas** above the beach provide good, filling *mezédhes* and main dishes. Just inland is the Corfu Golf and Country Club (T 26610 94220), the only golf club in the archipelago, and said to be one of the finest in the Mediterranean.

The nearby small village of **VÁTOS**, on the Glyfádha bus route from Kérkyra Town, has only a shop-cum-café and a quaint church, as all the other facilities are to be found on the main road 1km below. Here, the *Olympic Restaurant and Grill* (T 26610 94318; ❷) has rooms and apartments, as well as the only food, while the *Villa Frederiki* (T 26610 94003; ❸), opposite, consists of two large double studios. The Myrtiótissa turning is signposted just beyond the extremely handy, if basic, *Vatos Camping* (T 26610 94393), 500m further south.

Far preferable to the gravelly sand of Érmones, are the sandy beaches just south of the resort at Myrtiótissa and Glyfádha. In *Prospero's Cell*, Lawrence Durrell described **Myrtiótissa** as "perhaps the loveliest beach in the world"; it was for years a well-guarded secret but is now a firm favourite, especially with nudists, and gets so busy in summer that it supports three *kantínes*, meaning it's at its best well out of high season. Above the north end of beach is the tiny, whitewashed **Myrtiótissa monastery**, dedicated to Our Lady of the Myrtles. There are a few **rooms**, just off the approach road at the friendly *Myrtia* taverna (T 26610 94113, E sks_mirtia@hotmail.com; ❸), which serves tasty home-style cooking.

The sandy bay of **GLYFÁDHA**, walled in by cliffs, is dominated by the huge *Louis Grand* hotel (T 26610 94140, W www.louishotels.com; ❽), well overpriced despite including half-board. Far more reasonable **accommodation** is available at the extreme north end of the beach at two good adjacent tavernas; *Glyfada Beach* (T 26610 94258, F 26610 94257; ❷) and *Glyfada* (T 26610 94224; ❶), whose simple rooms are a real bargain. Nightlife centres on two music bars, the *Kikiriko* and *Aloha*, which pump out heavy-duty sounds all day, as the beach is popular with young Greek and Italian trendies.

PÉLEKAS, inland and 2km south of Glyfádha, has long been popular for its views – the **Kaiser's Throne** viewing tower, just above the town, was Wilhelm II's favourite spot on the island. As the only inland resort, there are some good **room** deals here, including the friendly *Pension Paradise* (T 26610 94530; ❷), on the way in from Vátos, the *Alexandros* pension (T 26610 94215, W www.alexandrospelekas .com; ❸) and *Thomas* (T 26610 94441; ❸), both on the way towards Kaiser's

Throne. Among the **tavernas**, *Alexandros*, *Pink Panther* and *Roula's Grill House*, the latter especially good for simple succulent meat, are all highly recommended. Colourful *Zanzibar* is a pleasant spot for a drink by the diminutive square, whose Odhiyítria church, renovated in 1884, is worth a peek.

Pélekas's sandy **beach** is reached down a short path. Here you'll find *Maria's Place*, an excellent family-run **taverna** with **rooms** (T 26610 94601; ❷), serving fish caught daily by the owner's husband. Sadly, the beach has been rather spoilt by the monstrous *Pelekas Beach* hotel that now looms over it.

Around 7km south of Pélekas, **AÏ GÓRDHIS** is one of the key play beaches on the island, largely because of the activities organized by the startling **Pink Palace** complex (T 26610 53103, W www.thepinkpalace.com), which dominates the resort. It has pools, games courts, Internet access (€3/hr), restaurants, a shop and a disco. Backpackers cram into communal rooms for up to ten (smaller rooms and singles are also available) for €18–26 a night, including breakfast and an evening buffet. Other accommodation is available on the beach, notably at *Michali's Place* taverna (T 26610 53041; ❸); the neighbouring *Alex in the Garden* **restaurant** is also a favourite.

Inland from the resort is the south's largest prominence, the humpback of **Áyii Dhéka** (576m), reached by path from the hamlet of Áno Garoúna; it is the island's second-largest mountain after Pandokrátor. The lower slopes are wooded, and it's possible to glimpse buzzards wheeling on thermals over the higher slopes. The monks at the tiny monastery just below the summit lovingly tend a bountiful orchard.

Around 5km south by road from Aï Górdhis, the fishing hamlet of **PENDÁTI** is still untouched by tourism. There is no accommodation here, but *Angela's* café and minimarket and the *Strofi* grill cater to villagers and the few tourists who wander in. Another 4km on, **PARAMÓNAS** has slowly evolved over the years but remains a low-key resort with some fine **accommodation** deals: at the beach, the *Sunset* taverna (T 26610 75149, F 26610 75686; ❷) and smart *Paramonas* hotel (T 26610 76595, W www.paramonas-hotel.com; ❹), just behind it, both offer panoramic sea views, while the *Areti Studios* (T 26610 75838; ❸), on the lane in from Pendáti, have a rural air.

The town of **ÁYIOS MATTHÉOS**, 3km inland, is still chiefly an agricultural centre, although a number of *kafenía* and tavernas offer a warm if slightly bemused welcome to passers-by: head for the *Mouria* snack-bar/grill, or the modern *Steki*, which can rustle up tasty *mezédhes*. On the other side of Mount Prasoúdhi, 2km by road, is the **Gardhíki Pýrgos**, the ruins of a thirteenth-century castle built in this unlikely lowland setting by the despots of Epirus. The road continues on to the northernmost tip of splendid and deserted **Halikoúna** beach on the sea edge of the **Korissíon lagoon**, which, if you don't have your own transport, is most easily reached by walking from the village of Línia (on the Kávos bus route) via **Íssos** beach; other, longer routes trail around the north end of the lagoon from Áno Mesongí and Khlomotianá. Over 5km long and 1km wide at its centre, Korissíon is home to turtles, tortoises, lizards and numerous indigenous and migratory birds. For one of the quietest stays on the island, try *Marin Christel Apartments* (T 26610 75947; ❸), just north of Halikoúna beach, or *Logara Apartments* (T 26610 76477; ❹), 500m inland. *Spiros* has the slightly better selection of the two tavernas on this stretch of road. The beach is an idyllic spot for rough camping but only a seasonal canteen operates in the immediate vicinity.

Benítses to Petrití: the east coast

South of Kérkyra Town, there's nothing to recommend before **BENÍTSES**, a once-notorious bonking-and-boozing resort, whose old town at the north end

Wild Greece

Read the holiday brochures and you might think Greece is all sunbed-packed beaches, luxury hotels and watersports. However, venture inland and the country reveals extraordinary wilderness landscapes ranging from cloud-grazing craggy peaks to bird-filled coastal wetlands. These wilderness areas are some of Europe's most dramatic and act as home to a range of wildlife – including populations of large carnivores such as bears and wolves that have survived despite persecution over many centuries.

Mount Taïyetos

Nowadays there are a number of categories of wildlife and habitat reserves, with varying degrees of protection. While reserves often have **restrictions** on the times and place of entry, much of Greece's wild country is still wide open to anyone prepared to make the effort to get there. Visitors to these areas – particularly the mountains – need to be well-prepared, competent and self-sufficient, as these are lands without the benefit of search and rescue. However, for those willing to make the effort, the rewards are unlimited.

Mountains and gorges

Today, at the start of the twenty-first century, Greece's mountain peaks are still resolutely remote; the rocky slopes, though often slashed and cicatrized by dirt roads, conceal places into which even an all-terrain vehicle would not venture. The **White Mountains** above Samaria and the **North Píndhos** of Víkos are genuine wildernesses; the first a waterless lunar desert of grey and white rocks over which lammergeier vultures fly, the latter a mixture of densely wooded valleys (home to many of Greece's largest mammals, as well golden jackals), abrupt escarpments, alpine meadows and scree-covered peaks. Different as they are, snow can lie on the high ground in both regions until well into July.

Hikers in the Samarian Gorge, Crete

At the base of these mountains, huge gorges cut the landscape, formed by the native karst limestone – a medley of high plateaux, limestone pavements, sinkholes, cave systems and subterranean streams – and frequent earthquake activity. Crete's famous **Samarian Gorge** is a stark geological masterclass and at 18km, one of Europe's longest ravines. The cliffs, partly due to their inaccessibility to grazing animals, are home to a number of rare plants, unique to Crete: perfectly adapted to this precarious habitat of severe drought and extreme temperatures, but unable to survive away from it. In the northeast of the mainland, the **Víkos Gorge** of the River Voïdhomátis is the equal of Samariá in majesty, but is softer and verdant with trees – including native 25m horse chestnut trees, spectacular when in flower.

The southern Peloponnese – and its climate – are divided into eastern and western halves by the great wall of the **Taïyetos**, a sixty-five-kilometre mountain range of limestone and dolomite flanked by fir-covered cliffs and deep ravines. The chain is capped by the great bare rock pyramid of Profítis Ilías; the considerable effort of reaching this summit is rewarded by extraordinary views. On the Sparta side, the steep gorges channel the snowmelt floodwaters and debris that maintain the fertility of the Evrótas plain below. On the Kalamáta side, the more elongated and elaborately winding

Vikos Gorge

valleys absorb much of the floods en route; the remainder runs into the sea. The mountains are home to twenty-three types of flower – including bellflowers, violets and an autumn snowdrop – found nowhere else, as well as several endemic butterflies.

Storks nesting (Mytilini Island)

Marshes and wetlands

Belying the popular image of a Greece with perpetual summer-holiday temperatures and a marked rainfall deficit, the mainland does have significant amounts of freshwater, particularly in the north. The deep and ancient **Prespá lakes** on the northwestern border constitute one of the largest bodies of water in the Balkans, with large breeding colonies of spoonbills and two species of pelican. Another significant northern wetland is the complex of brackish and **freshwater lakes** around Vistonídha and Pórto Lágos, near Xánthi. Here there is a large population of flamingoes, as well as rarities such as the pygmy cormorant and the globally endangered white-headed duck. Emblematic of a healthy aquatic environment are the **storks** that nest on nearby churches and telegraph poles, bringing up their young on the plentiful supply of marsh frogs.

The Mountain of the Gods

Further south, **Mount Olympus** is – at 2917m – the second-highest point in the entire Balkans, and its summit is the fabled home of the ancient Greek deities. It's extremely unusual in mainland Europe for its combination of height, isolation and proximity to the sea. The resultant ecosystem is home to over sixteen-hundred species of wild plant in just forty square kilometres – a similar number to that found in the entire United Kingdom; around thirty-two types of plant are confined to this mountain alone – the most famous being *Jankaea*, a small relative of the African violet. First climbed less than a century ago, Olympus's highest summits still demand respect from those who would enter into their dominion; the mountain and its swiftly changing weather continue to regularly claim the lives of hikers and climbers.

Voïdokiliá beach, Peloponnese

More accessibly, the Peloponnese's humid western coast also has some remarkable and stunningly beautiful **coastal wetlands**, including the salty, reed-fringed lagoons behind the fabulous perfect crescent of **Voïdokiliá beach**, which shelter migrating cranes and flamingoes and a small resident population of chameleons. Further north, near Kalogriá, are the sandy woods and multi-coloured **swamps** of Strofyliá where the aptly-named umbrella pines have their easternmost outpost, and rare birds such as collared pratincoles nest on muddy gravel.

Woodlands

Woodlands have, since ancient times, been under pressure as a source of fuel and building materials; however, in the northeastern corner of Greece, squeezed between the Bulgarian and Turkish borders, the **Dhadhiá Forest** reserve shelters fine virgin forest. Reaching towards the Rodhópi mountains, this is some of the best woodland in the country, sheltering a remarkable variety of **raptors** – hawks, eagles and particularly vultures.

On the gentle slopes of **Mount Ménalo**, in the dead centre of the Peloponnese, there are still – despite recent fire damage – forests of densely green and symmetrical fir trees. Usually visited during the skiing season when everything lies under deep snow and wildlife is dormant, this high altitude area is verdant in summer when the groves shelter a plethora of woodland flowers and **orchids**, interspersed with alpine meadows bright blue with larkspur.

Woodlands near the Meteora rocks, Thessaly

has long since reverted to a quiet bougainvillea-splashed Greek village. There are a couple of minor attractions, namely the modest ruins of a Roman bathhouse at the back of the village and the small but impressive **Shell Museum** (March–Oct daily 9am–7pm; €4). **Rooms** are plentiful, as visitor numbers have never returned to heyday levels: try the Best Travel (℡26610 72037, ℻26610 71036) and Achilles Tourist Centre (℡26610 72228, ✉kapsoandre@ker.otenet .gr) agencies (both ❷). Among **hotels** offering good deals, the central *Hotel Potamaki* (℡26610 71140, ⓦwww.potamakibeachhotel.gr; ❹), is a gigantic 1960s throwback, while the jointly run *Hotel Benitsa/Agis* (℡26610 39269; ❷) offer quiet rooms set back from the main road. Benítses has its fair share of decent **tavernas**, notably *La Mer de Corfu* and the Corfiot specialist *O Paxinos*, as well as the plush Italian *Avra*. Lively **bars** such as *Lacey's* and *Sunshine* are concentrated behind the crescent-shaped park that separates the old village from the coast road, while larger **nightclubs** like *Casanovas 2000* or *Stadium* are at the southern end of the main strip.

   MORAÏTIKA's main street is an ugly strip of bars, restaurants and shops, but its beach is the best between Kérkyra Town and Kávos. Confusingly, the biggest touristic landmark in the area, the *Messonghi Beach* **hotel** complex (℡26610 75830, ⓦwww.messonghibeach.gr; ❻), set in lush landscaped gardens and home to the Nautilus diving centre (daily 5–7pm; ℡26610 83295), actually lies just within the limits of Moraïtika, which is separated from neighbouring Mesongí by the Mesongís River. Other reasonable beachside **hotels** include the *Margarita Beach* (℡26610 75267, ⓦwww.corfu-hotel-margarita.com; ❹) and the plusher *Three Stars* (℡26610 75263, ℻26610 75862; ❹). Budget Ways Travel (℡26610 76768, ℻26610 76769; ❸) offers a range of accommodation and there are **rooms** between the main road and beach, such as those at the *Firefly* taverna (℡26610 75850; ❸). Much of the main drag is dominated by souvenir shops and minimarkets, as well as a range of **bars**, including the village's oldest, *Charlie's*, which opened in 1939, and the lively *Very Coco* nightclub. The *Rose Garden* **restaurant** is just off the main road and has a fair mix of vegetarian, Greek and international food, as does the beach restaurant *Kavouria*, where the seafood and special salads are excellent The village proper, **ÁNO MORAÏTIKA**, is signposted a few minutes' hike up the steep lanes inland, and is virtually unspoilt. Its tiny houses and alleys are practically drowning in bougainvillea, among which you'll find two **tavernas**: the *Village Taverna* and the *Bella Vista*, the latter of which has a basic menu but justifies its name with a lovely garden, sea views and breezes.

   Commencing barely a hundred metres on from the Moraïtika seafront, **MESONGÍ** continues this stretch of package-tour-oriented coast but is noticeably quieter and has a range of accommodation deals. Both the *Hotel Gemini* (℡26610 75221, ⓦgeminihotel.gr; ❺) and far better value, British-run *Pantheon Hall* (℡26610 75802, ⓦwww.corfu-summer.com; ❷) have pools and gardens, and en-suite rooms with balconies. Mesongí has a number of good **restaurants**: notably the *Memories* taverna, which specializes in Corfiot dishes and serves its own barrel wine, and the upmarket *Castello*. An alternative is to head for the beachside *Bacchus* and *Spanos* tavernas a short walk south on the road to Boúkari. Try the *Olive Tree Pub* bar for a relaxed drink.

   The quiet road from Mesongí to Boúkari follows the seashore for about 3km, often only a few feet above it. **BOÚKARI** itself comprises little more than a handful of tavernas, a shop and a few small, family-run hotels; the ⚓ *Boukari Beach*, 1km north of the tiny harbour, is the best of the **tavernas**, offering fresh fish and live lobster. The very friendly Vlahopoulos family who run the taverna also offer rooms and own two small hotels nearby, the fully renovated *Penelopi* and *Villa Alexandra* (☎26620 51269, Ⓦwww.boukaribeach.com; ❸). Boúkari is out of the way, but an idyllic little strip of unspoilt coast for anyone fleeing the crowds elsewhere on the island, and inland from here is the unspoiled wooded region around **Aryirádhes**, rarely visited by tourists and a perfect place for quiet walks.

Back on the coastline, the village of **PETRITÍ**, only created in the 1970s when geologists discovered the hill village of Korakádhes was sliding downhill, fronts onto a small but busy harbour. It is mercifully free of noise and commerce, with a beach of rock, mud and sand, set among low olive-covered hills. The *Pension Egrypos* (☎26620 51949, Ⓦwww.egrypos .gr; ❸) has **rooms** and a restaurant. At the harbour, three **tavernas** serve the trickle of sea traffic: the smart *Limnopoula* guarded by caged parrots, and the more basic but friendly *Dimitris* and *Stamatis*. Back from the village, near the hamlet of Vassilátika, is the elegant *Regina* **hotel**, with gardens and pool (☎26620 52132, Ⓦwww.reginahotel.de; ❹), mainly occupied by Germans. Barely 2km south of Petrit, the rocky coves of **Nótos** beach are little visited and conceal a wonderful and friendly place to stay in the shape of *Panorama Apartments* (☎26620 51707, Ⓦwww.panoramacorfu.gr; ❷), which also has a fine shady restaurant.

Southern Corfu

Across the island on the west coast, the beach at **ÁYIOS YEÓRYIOS** spreads as far south as Ayía Varvára, and north to encircle the edge of the Korissíon lagoon, around 12km of uninterrupted sand. The resort itself, however, is an unprepossessing seafront sprawl and tourism here has the most mercenary air of anywhere on the island. British package operators dominate the scene, with bars competing to present bingo, quizzes and video nights. The smart *Golden Sands* (☎26620 51225, Ⓦwww.corfugoldensands.com; ❸) has a pool, open-air restaurant and gardens, but the best **hotel** bargain is the smaller *Blue Sea* (☎26620 51624, Ⓦwww.bluesea-hotel.com; ❸); both are situated midway along the seafront road. The easiest place to look for good **rooms** is at Star Travel (☎26620 52800, Ⓦwww.startravel.com; ❷), further north. Most **restaurants** are predictably bland but you can eat well enough at the *Stamatis* and *Splendid* taverna/grill houses. **Nightlife** centres around music and pool bars like the *Gold Hart* and *Bluebell*, although laid-back *Amazona* cocktail bar and lively *Mad Mike's*, one of the few places off the seafront, have a better atmosphere.

A few minutes' walk north of Áyios Yeóryios, **Íssos** is a far better and quieter beach; the dunes north of Íssos towards the Korissíon lagoon are an unofficial nude bathing area. Facilities around Íssos are sparse: one **taverna**, the *Rousellis Grill*, a few hundred metres from the beach on the lane leading to Línia on the main road; the smart new yellow-and-maroon *Vicky's Apartments* (☎26620 53161; ❹), above a bend in the lane; and the *Friends* snack-bar in Línia itself. An English-run **windsurfing school** (Ⓦwww.mermanwindsurf.com) operates on the beach and can arrange all-in packages.

Anyone interested in how a Greek town works away from the bustle of tourism shouldn't miss **LEFKÍMI**, towards the island's southern tip. The second-largest settlement after Kérkyra Town, it's the administrative centre for the south of the island as well as the alternative ferry port to or from Igoumenítsa, with half a dozen daily crossings in summer. The town has some fine architecture, including several striking churches: **Áyii Anáryiri** with a huge double belfry, **Áyios Theódhoros**, on a mound above a small square, and **Áyios Arsénios**, with a vast orange dome that can be seen for miles.

There are some **rooms** at the *Cheeky Face* taverna (☎26620 22627; ❷), by the bridge over the canal that carries the Himáros River through the lower part of town, and the *Maria Madalena* apartments (☎26620 22386; ❷) further up. For **food** look no further than the home-cooking at the tiny *Maria estiatório*, on the opposite side of the canal to *Cheeky Face*. A few **bars** are tucked in corners of the upper town and see so few tourists that you are likely to receive a friendly welcome: *Hermes* has a leafy garden, while *Mersedes* and *Enigma* both play Greek and foreign sounds in their dimly lit interiors.

There are no ambiguities in **KÁVOS**, 6km south of Lefkími: either you like 24-hour drinking, clubbing, bungee-jumping, go-karts, video bars named after British sitcoms and chips with almost everything, or you should avoid the resort altogether. Kávos stretches over 2km of decent sandy beach, with watersports galore. This is very much Club 18–30 territory; if you want independent **accommodation**, try Pandis Travel (☎26620 61400, Ⓔncpandis@otenet.gr) or Island Holidays (☎26620 61357, Ⓔvvera@otenet.gr; both ❷). The nearest to genuine Greek **food** you'll find is at the *Two Brothers psistariá*, at the south end of town. Fast food and British-style Asian cuisine are much easier to come by. *Buzz* is the most happening **club**, with imported north European DJs, followed by *The Barn*, *42nd St* and *Sex*. Favourite **bars** include *Time*, *Truants*, *The Face*, *Black Duck* and *Bonkers*, and at night the main drag is one unbroken crowd of young revellers.

Beyond the limits of Kávos, where few visitors stray, a path leaving the road south to the hamlet of Sparterá heads through unspoilt countryside; after around thirty minutes of walking it reaches the cliffs of **Cape Asprókavos** and the crumbling **monastery of Arkoudhílas**. The cape looks out over the straits to Paxí, and down over deserted **Arkoudhílas** beach, which can be reached from Sparterá, a pleasant village 5km by road but only 3km by the signed path from Kávos; its *Fantasia* and *Paradise* tavernas are far more appealing and authentic than any in the resort. Even wilder is **Áï Górdhis Paleohoríou** beach, 3km further on from Sparterá, one of the least visited on the island and not to be confused with the eponymous beach further north; a municipal café provides the only refreshment. The Cape is also the southern starting point for the **Corfu Trail**, inaugurated in 2001, after years of planning by local walkers. Signposted by yellow waymarkers the trail meanders back and forth over 200km of varying terrain all the way to Cape Ayías Ekaterínis on the north coast and is designed to take at least ten days. Those interested should get a copy of Hilary Whitton Paipeti's *Walking the Corfu Trail* or check out Ⓦwww.travelling.gr/corfutrail for more details.

Corfu's satellite islands

Corfu's three inhabited satellite islands, **Eríkoussa**, **Othoní** and **Mathráki**, in the quintet of **Dhiapóndia islands**, are scattered up to 20km off the northwest coast. Some travel agencies in the northern resorts offer **day-trips** to Eríkoussa only, often with a barbecue thrown in – fine if you're happy to spend the day on the beach. A trip taking in all three islands from Sidhári or Áyios Stéfanos is excellent value: they are between thirty and sixty minutes apart by boat, and most trips allow you an hour on each (usually longer on sandy Eríkoussa).

Locals use day-trip boats between the islands, so it's possible to pay your way between them. There is also a **ferry** three times a week from Kérkyra Town, the *Alexandros II*, which brings cars and goods to the islands, but given that it has to sail halfway round Corfu first, it's the slowest way to proceed.

Mathráki

Hilly, densely forested and with a long empty beach, beautiful **Mathráki** has the fewest inhabitants of the three islands. Portéllo beach begins at the edge of the tiny harbour, **Plákes**, and extends south for 3km of fine, dark-red sand. A single road rises from the harbour into the interior and the scattered village of **KÁTO MATHRÁKI**, where just one friendly taverna-*kafenío*-shop overlooks the beach and Corfu. The views are magnificent, as is the sense of isolation. However, Mathráki is gradually gearing up towards visitors, and islanders Tassos Kassimis (☎26630 71700; ❷) and Khristos Aryiros (☎26630 71652; ❸) already rent **rooms** and **studios** on Portéllo beach. At Plákes the *Port Centre* restaurant specializes in freshly caught fish. The road continues to the village of **Áno Mathráki**, with its single, old-fashioned *kafenío* next to the church, but this is beyond walking distance on a day-visit.

Othoní

Eight kilometres northwest, **Othoní** is the largest, and at first sight the least inviting of Corfu's satellite islands. The island has a handful of places to stay and eat in its port, **ÁMMOS**, but the reception from islanders who aren't in the tourism trade is rather cool. Ámmos has two beaches, both pebbly, one on each side of the jetty. The village *kafenío*, *O Mikros*, serves as a very basic shop, and there's one smart **restaurant**, *La Locanda dei Sogni*, which also has **rooms** (☎26630 71640; ❸) – though these tend to be prebooked by Italian visitors. Two tavernas, *New York* and tiny *Lakis*, offer decent but fairly limited menus; the owner of the *New York* also offers rooms for rent (☎26630 71581; ❷). The number of beds on the island has greatly increased with the opening of the *Hotel Calypso* (☎26630 72162, ☞26630 71578; ❸), 200m east of the jetty. The island's interior is dramatic, and a road up out of the village leads through rocky, tree-covered hills to the central hamlet, **Horió**, after a thirty-minute walk. Horió, like other inland villages, is heavily depopulated – only about one hundred people still live on the island through the winter – but it's very attractive, and the architecture is completely traditional. On the north coast of the island **Fýki Bay**, accessible via a path from Dhamaskátika, has the longest stretch of sand but there are no facilities and you'll only have time to reach it if you spend at least a night.

Eríkoussa

Some 10km east of Othoní, **Eríkoussa** is the most popular destination for day-trippers. It's invariably hyped as a "desert island" trip, although this is a desert island with a medium-sized hotel, rooms, tavernas and a year-round community. In high season, it gets very busy: Eríkoussa has a large diaspora living in America and elsewhere who return to family homes in their droves in summer, so you may find your *yiásou* or *kaliméra* returned in a Brooklyn accent.

Eríkoussa has an excellent golden sandy beach right by the harbour, with great swimming, and quieter **Bragíni** beach, reached by a path across the wooded island interior. The island's cult following keeps its one **hotel**, the *Erikousa* (☎26630 71110; ☜www.hotelerikousa.gr; ❹), busy through the season; rooms are en suite with balconies and views. Simpler rooms next door are sometimes available from Theodora Kateni (☎26630 71821; ❶). If you're hoping to stay, phoning ahead is essential, as is taking anything you might not be able to buy – the only shop just sells basic groceries and provisions. The *Erikousa* also boasts the only bona fide **taverna**, serving great fish, meat and starters, although a couple of smaller snack-bars, such as the *Oasis*, can rustle up breakfast or simpler meals.

Paxí (Paxos) and Andípaxi

Verdant, hilly and still largely unspoilt, **Paxí (Paxos)** is the smallest of the main Ionian islands. Barely 12km by 4km, it has no sandy beaches, no historical sites, only three hotels and a serious water shortage, yet is so popular it is best avoided in high season. It's a particular favourite of yachting flotillas, whose spending habits have brought the island an upmarket reputation, making it just about the most expensive place to visit in the Ionian islands and lending it a rather cliquey air. Pockets of unauthorized camping, however, are tolerated in the absence of an official site. Most accommodation is block-booked by travel companies, though there are local tour operators whose holiday deals are often a fraction of the price. The capital, **Gáïos**, is quite cosmopolitan, with delis and boutiques, but northerly **Lákka** and tiny **Longós** are where hardcore Paxophiles head.

Gáïos and around

Most visitors arrive at the new port, 1km north of **GÁÏOS**, a pleasant town built around a small square on the seafront overlooking two islands, Áyios Nikólaos and Panayía. Given the shortage of rooms, it's advisable to phone ahead: try Gáïos Travel (℡26620 32033, ⓦwww.gaiostravel.com) or Bouas Tours (℡26620 32401, ⓦwww.bouastours.gr), both situated on the seafront (❸). Paxí's two most established seasonal **hotels** are both near Gáïos: the *Paxos Beach Hotel* (℡26620 32211, ⓦwww.paxosbeachhotel.gr; ❻ half-board) which has smart en-suite bungalows on a hillside above a pebbly beach 2km south of town, and the fairly luxurious *Paxos Club* (℡26620 32450, ⓦwww.paxosclub .gr; ❼), nearly 2km inland from Gáïos.

Gáïos boasts a number of decent **tavernas**, most of which are on the pricey side. The best of the bunch are *Dodo's*, set in a garden inland from the

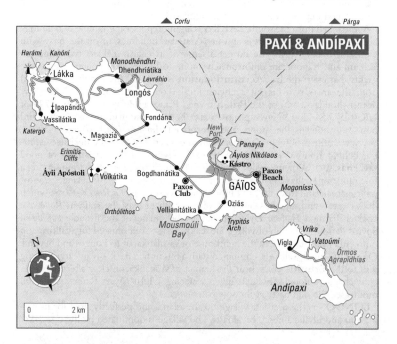

PAXÍ & ANDÍPAXI

Anemoyiannis statue, which has a full range of *mezédhes* and main courses; *Apangio*, most reasonable of the seafront establishments; and *Vassilis*, which has the best selection and prices of the trio to the left of the road up towards the bus stop. *The Cellar* at the top of the square is the best place for a tasty *souvláki*. *Gonia*, by the Párga *kaïki* mooring, is the last remaining traditional place for a coffee or drink. Trendier bars include *Remego* on the southern seafront and *Alter Ego* round the quay towards the new port. The *Phoenix* club, out by the new port, opens sporadically after midnight and has a terrace for sublunar fun, while the inland *Castello Music Club*, beyond the bus stop, is a more reliable summer disco.

Inland are some of the island's oldest settlements, such as Oziás and Vellianitátika, in prime walking country, but with few, if any, facilities. Noel Rochford's book, *Landscapes of Paxos*, lists dozens of walks, and cartographers Elizabeth and Ian Bleasdale's *Paxos Walking Map* is on sale in most travel agencies.

The **coast south** of Gáïos is punctuated by the odd shingly cove, none ideal for swimming, until matters improve towards the tip at **Mogoníssi** beach, which shares some of Andípaxi's sandier geology. There is an eponymous taverna and en route you can take a peek at Fiat supremo Agnelli's distinctive hillside mansion, turrets and all.

The north of the island

Paxí's one main road runs along the spine of the island, with a turning at the former capital **Magaziá**, leading down to the tiny port of Longós. The main road continues to Lákka, the island's funkiest resort, set in a breathtaking horseshoe bay. Buses ply the road between Gáïos and Lákka four or five times a day, most diverting to swing through Longós. The Gáïos–Lákka bus (30min) affords panoramic views, and the route is an excellent walk of under three hours (one way). A taxi between the two costs around €8.

Approached from the south, **LÁKKA** is an unprepossessing jumble of buildings, but once in its maze of alleys and neo-Venetian buildings, or on the quay with views of distant Corfu, you do get a sense of its charm. Lákka's two **beaches**, Harámi and Kanóni, are unfortunately prone to high-season pollution from the yachts that cram the bay. **Accommodation** is plentiful (except in high season) from the area's two biggest agencies: local Routsis (☎26620 31807, ⓦwww .routsis-holidays.com) or the British-owned Planos Holidays (☎26620 31744 or UK 01373 814200, ⓦwww.planos.co.uk), both on the seafront (❷). Paxí's third bona-fide hotel is the snooty and overpriced *Amfitriti Hotel* (☎26620 30011, ⓦwww.amfitriti-hotel.gr; ❼). Mercifully, the practise of low-key, freelance camping behind Kanóni has not been affected. There's an embarrassment of good **tavernas**, such as the friendly *Nionios* and neighbouring *Pounentes*, both serving a fine range of Hellenic favourites on the square, the secluded *Alexandros*, great for *gourounópoulo* and fresh fish, and more upmarket seafront *La Rosa di Paxos*, which does risottos and ravioli. There's a similar wealth of bars: the seafront *Romantica* cocktail bar and *Harbour Lights*, *Serano's* in the square, or the friendly *kafenío* of Spyros Petrou – the hub of village life. Lákka is also well situated for **walking**: up onto either promontory, to the lighthouse or Vassilátika, or to Longós and beyond. One of the finest walks – if combined with a bus or taxi back – is an early evening visit to the **Erimítis cliffs**, near the hamlet of Voïkátika: on clear afternoons, the cliffs change colour at twilight like a seafacing Uluru (Ayers Rock), while full moons see the odd party at the sole bar, *Sunset*.

LONGÓS is the prettiest village on the island, and perfectly sited for morning sun and idyllic alfresco breakfasts. The village is dominated by the upmarket villa crowd, making the Planos office here (☎26620 31530) the best place to look for accommodation. Longós has some of the island's best restaurants: the seafront *Vassilis*, which does terrific fish dishes and tasty starters, *Nassos*, also with a wide variety of fish and seafood, and *Iy Gonia*, a much simpler and cheaper *psistariá*. *Tò Taxidhi* on the quay is a nice spot for coffee or an early drink, while *Roxi Bar* and *Ores* pander to the night-owls.

Longós has a small, scruffy beach, with sulphur springs favoured by local grannies, but most people swim off **Levrehió** beach in the next bay south, which gets the occasional camper. Islanders are touchy about camping for fear of fires so it's politic to ask at the beach taverna if it's acceptable. Longós is at the bottom of a steep winding hill, making **walking** a chore, but the short circle around neighbouring **Dhendhriátika** provides spectacular views and allows access to the small but excellent **Monodhéndhri** beach, and the walk to **Fondána** and **Magaziá** can be done to coincide with a bus back.

Andípaxi

A mile south, Paxí's tiny sibling **Andípaxi** has scarcely any accommodation and no facilities beyond several beach tavernas open during the day in season. It is most easily reached by the frequent shuttle *kaïkia* from Gáïos (€6 return). The glass-bottomed boat (€15 return) also takes you to its sea stacks and caves, the most dramatic in the Ionians. Andípaxi's sandy, blue-water coves have been compared with the Caribbean, but you'll have to share them with *kaïkia* and sea taxis from all three villages, plus larger craft from Corfu and the mainland resorts.

Boats basically deposit you either at the sandy **Vríka** beach or the longer pebble beach of **Vatoúmi**. Vríka has a taverna at each end, of which *Spiros* (☎26620 31172) has great grilled and oven food and can arrange self-catering accommodation up in **Vígla**, the island's hilltop settlement, on a weekly basis.

△ Vatoúmi beach, Andípaxi

Vatoúmi also has two restaurants, the justifiably named *Bella Vista* restaurant, perched on a cliff high above the beach, and the newer *Vatoumi*, a little way back from the beach.

For a swim in quieter surroundings the trick is to head south, away from the pleasure-craft moorings, although path widening has made even the quieter bays more accessible. Paths also lead inland to connect the handful of homes and the southerly lighthouse, but there are no beaches of any size on Andípaxi's western coastline and thick thorny scrub makes it difficult to approach. In low season, there's also the risk of bad weather keeping pleasure craft in port and stranding you on the island.

Lefkádha (Lefkas)

Lefkádha is an oddity. Connected to the mainland by a long causeway through lagoons, it barely feels like an island, at least on the busier eastern side – and historically it isn't. It is separated from the mainland by a canal cut by Corinthian colonists in the seventh century BC, which has been re-dredged (after silting up) on various occasions since, and today is spanned by a thirty-metre, pontoon-swivel-bridge. Lefkádha was long an important strategic base, and approaching the causeway you pass a series of fortresses, climaxing in the fourteenth-century castle of **Santa Maura** – the Venetian name for the island. These defences were too close to the mainland to avoid an Ottoman tenure, which began in 1479, but the Venetians wrested back control a couple of centuries later. They were in turn overthrown by Napoleon in 1797 and then the British took over as Ionian protectors in 1810. It wasn't until 1864 that Lefkádha, like the rest of the Ionian archipelago, was reunited with Greece.

At first glance Lefkádha is not overwhelmingly attractive, although it is a substantial improvement on the mainland just opposite. The whiteness of its rock strata – *lefkás* has the same root as *lefkós*, "white" – is often brutally exposed by road cuts and quarries, and the highest ridge is bare except for ugly military and telecom installations. With the marshes and boggy inlets on the east coast, mosquitoes can be a midsummer problem. On the other hand, the island is a fertile place, supporting cypresses, olive groves and vineyards, particularly on the western slopes, and life in the mountain villages remains relatively untouched, with the older women still wearing traditional local dress – two skirts (one forming a bustle), a dark headscarf and a rigid bodice. The rugged west coast also boasts some of the finest beaches in the Ionians.

Lefkádha has been home to various literati, including two prominent Greek poets, Angelos Sikelianos and Aristotelis Valaoritis, and the British writer Lafcadio Hearn. Support for the arts continues in the form of a well-attended international **festival** of theatre and folk-dancing, now extended throughout the summer, with most events staged in the Santa Maura castle. On a smaller scale, frequent village celebrations accompanied by *bouzoúki* and clarinet ensure that the strong local wine flows well into the early hours.

Lefkádha remains relatively undeveloped, with just two major resorts: **Vassilikí**, in its vast bay in the south, claims to be Europe's biggest windsurf centre; **Nydhrí**, on the east coast, overlooks the island's picturesque archipelago, and is the launching point for the barely inhabited island of **Meganíssi**. The completion of the capital's superb **marina** in 2003, however, with a smart reception centre and ample mooring, refuelling and restocking facilities has increased the island's appeal to yachties.

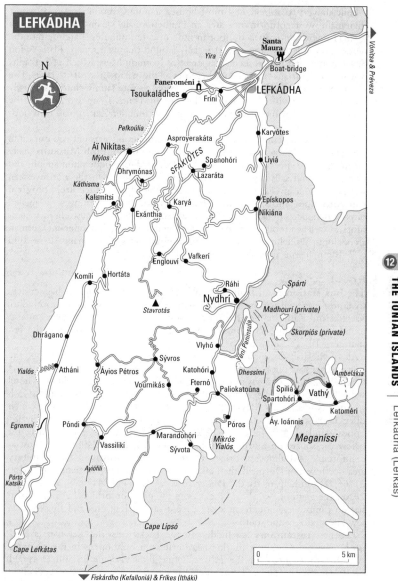

LEFKÁDHA

Santa
Maura
Yíra
Boat-bridge
Faneroméni
Tsoukaládhes
Fríni
LEFKÁDHA
▲ Vónitsa & Préveza

Pefkoúlia
Karyótes
Asproyerakáta
Áï Nikítas
Mýlos
Spanohóri
Liyiá
Dhrymónas
SFAKIÓTES
Lazaráta
Káthisma
Kalamítsi
Karyá
Epískopos
Exánthia
Nikiána

Vafkerí
Englouví
Ráhi
Spárti
Komíli
Hortáta
Nydhrí
Madhourí (private)
Stavrotás
Skorpiós (private)

Dhrágano
Vlyhó
Sývros
Katohóri
Dhessími
Ambelákia
Yialós
Athání
Áyios Pétros
Vournikás
Fternó
Paliokatoúna
Spiliá
Vathý
Egremní
Póndi
Spartohóri
Katoméri
Marandohóri
Póros
Áy. Ioánnis
Meganíssi
Vassilikí
Mikrós
Yialós
Sývota
Ayiófíli
Pórto
Katsíki
Cape Lipsó

Cape Lefkátas
0   5 km

▼ Fiskárdho (Kefalloniá) & Fríkes (Itháki)

Lefkádha Town and around

LEFKÁDHA TOWN sits at the island's northernmost tip, hard by the cause-way. Like other (southerly) capitals in the southern Ionian, it was hit by the earthquakes of 1948 and 1953, and the town was devastated, with the exception of a few **Italianate churches**. As a precaution against further quakes, little was rebuilt above two storeys, and most houses acquired second storeys of wood, giving the western dormitory area an unintentionally quaint look. The town is small – you can cross it on foot in little over ten minutes – and despite the destruction, still very attractive, especially around the main square, Platía Ayíou Spyridhónos, and the arcaded high street of Ioánnou Méla. Much of Lefkádha Town is pedestrian-only, mainly because of the narrowness of its lanes. The centre boasts over half a dozen richly decorated private family churches, usually locked and best visited around services. Many contain rare works from the Ionian School of painting, including work by its founder, Zakynthian Panayiotis Doxaras.

The folklore museum has been closed for a number of years but you can catch a glimpse of the old way of life at the quaint little **Phonograph Museum** (daily 10am–2pm & 7–midnight; free), which is dedicated to antique phonographs and bric-a-brac, and sells cassettes of rare traditional music. On the northwestern seafront a modern Cultural Centre houses the newly expanded **archeological museum** (Tues–Sun 8.30am–3pm; €2), which contains interesting, well-labelled displays on aspects of daily life, religious worship and funerary customs in ancient times, as well as a room on prehistory dedicated to the work of eminent German archeologist Wilhelm Dörpfeld. The **municipal art gallery** (daily 10am–1pm & 7–10pm; free) is now also housed in the same complex.

Practicalities

The **bus station** is on Dhimítri Golémi opposite the marina. It has services to almost every village on the island, with extensive daily schedules to Nydhrí, Vassilikí and Káthisma beaches on the west coast. Car and motorbike rental is useful for exploring; try EuroHire, Golémi 5 (℡26450 26776), near the bus station or I Love Santas (℡26450 25250) next to the *Ionian Star* hotel.

All of the half-dozen **hotels** are in busy areas and none is cheap, but the more expensive ones are glazed against the noise and heat. The *Ionian Star* (℡26450 24672, ⓦwww.ionianstar.gr; ❻), Panágou 2, is the plushest hotel with brand-new fittings and a pool. The best mid-range hotels are the stylish seafront *Nirikos*, Ayías Mávras (℡26450 24132, ⓦwww.nirikos.gr; ❺), which offers fairly spacious rooms, and the cosy but comfortable *Santa Maura*, Spyrid-hónos Viánda 2 (℡26450 21308, ⓕ26450 26253; ❹). The *Pension Pyrofani*, just below the square on Dörpfeld (℡26450 25844, ⓕ26450 24084; ❹), is just as comfortable and almost as pricey. There are simple **rooms** in the dormitory area northwest of Dörpfeld: the Lefkádha Room Owners Association (℡26450 21266; ❷) can help, or try the *Pinelopis Rooms* (℡26450 24175; ❷) at Pinelópis 20, off the seafront two short blocks from the pontoon bridge. Lefkádha Town has no campsite, although there are decent sites at Karyótes and Epískopos, a few kilometres to the south.

The best **restaurants** are hidden in the backstreets: the *Regantos* taverna, on Dhimárhou Venióti is the local favourite, but only opens in the evenings. At other times, head for the *Eftyhia*, a fine little *estiatório* just off Dörpfeld, or *Romantika* on Mitropóleos, which has nightly performances of Lefkadhan *kantádhes* (a hybrid of Cretan folk song and Italian opera ballad). Tasty meat, fish and *mezédhes* at very fair prices can be enjoyed at *Sto Molo*, on Golémi, although you have to contend with the traffic noise.

The most traditional place for a tipple is the *Cafe Karfakis*, on Ioánnou Méla, an old-style *kafenío* with splendid *mezédhes*. Of the **bars** in the main square, the *Cäsbäh* is the most popular and trendy haunts such as *Excess* and *Il Posto* line the seafront west of the bridge. The town's outdoor **cinema**, Eleni, on Faner-oménis, has two showings and programmes change daily.

Around Lefkádha Town

The town has a decent and lengthy shingle-and-sand beach west of the lagoon at **Yíra**, a thirty-minute walk from the centre. Roughly 4km long, the beach is often virtually deserted even in high season; there's a **taverna** at either end, and at the western end a couple of **bars** in the renovated windmills, as well as the trendy *Club Milos*. The beach's western extension, **Aïyánnis**, is growing in popularity and now has several restaurants, including *Tilegraphos* (T 26450 24881, W www.tilegraphos.gr; ❸), which also lets out some **rooms**.

The uninhabited **Faneroméni monastery** (daily 8am–2pm & 4–8pm; free) is reached by any of the west-coast buses, or by a steep hike on foot from town (45min) through the hamlet of Fríni. There's a small museum and chapel, and an ox's yoke and hammer, used when Nazi occupiers forbade the use of bells. There are wonderful views over the town and lagoon from the Fríni road.

The island's **interior**, best reached by bus or car from Lefkádha Town, offers imposing mountainscapes and excellent walking between villages only a few kilometres apart. **KARYÁ** is its centre, and offers the *Karia Village Hotel* (T 26450 41004; ❹), under renovation at the time of writing, and some rooms: try the Kakiousis family (T 26450 61136; ❷) or Haritini Vlahou (T 26450 41634; ❶). The leafy town square has a popular taverna, *Iy Klimataria*, just below it and two *psistariés* on it, *Ta Platania*, and the smarter *O Rousos*. Karyá is the centre of the island's lace and weaving industry, with a small but fascinating **folklore museum** set in a lacemaker's home (April–Oct daily 9am–9pm; €2.50). The historic and scenic villages of **Vafkerí** and **Englouví** are within striking distance, with the west-coast hamlets of **Dhrymónas** and **Exánthia** a hike over the hills.

The east coast to Vassilikí

Lefkádha's east coast is the most accessible and the most developed part of the island. Apart from the campsite at Karyótes, *Kariotes Beach* (T & F 26450 71103), there's little point stopping before the small fishing port of **LIYIÁ**, which has some rooms and the hotel *Konaki* (T 26450 71127, W www .hotelkonaki.gr; ❻), as well as some restaurants such as *O Xouras psarotavérna* and, as you head south, the inexpensive and excellent garden taverna *Iy Limni*, which features unique dishes such as *spartiátiko*, a delicious concoction of pork, peppers, mushroom, cheese, wine and cognac. Further on, beyond the *Episcopos Beach* campsite (T 26450 71388), lies **NIKIÁNA**, another fishing village where you'll find the hotel *Pegasos* (T 26450 71766, W www .hotelpegasos.gr; ❸), as well as the *Christina* pension (T 26450 25194; ❸). In addition, Nikiána has a selection of fine tavernas, notably *Pantazis psistariá*, which also has rooms to let (T 26450 71211; ❸), and *Lefko Akroyiali*, a good fish restaurant further south. Beaches here tend to be pebbly and small.

Most package travellers will find themselves in **NYDHRÍ**, the island's biggest resort by far, with ferry connections to Meganíssi and myriad **boat trips** around the nearby satellite islands. The German archeologist Wilhelm Dörpfeld believed Nydhrí, rather than Itháki, to be the site of Odysseus's capital, and did indeed find Bronze Age tombs on the plain nearby. His theory identifying ancient Ithaca with Lefkádha fell into disfavour after his death in 1940, although his obsessive attempts to give the island some status over its neighbour are honoured by a statue on Nydhrí's quay. Dörpfeld's tomb is tucked away at Ayía Kyriakí on the opposite side of the bay, near the house in which he once lived, visible just above the chapel and lighthouse on the far side of the water.

Nydhrí is an average resort, with some good pebble beaches and a lovely setting, but the centre is an ugly strip with heavy traffic. The best **place**

.y is the *Hotel Gorgona* (☎26450 95634, ⓕ26450 92268; ❸), set in .h garden away from the traffic a minute along the Ráhi road, which .ds to Nydhrí's very own **waterfall**, a 45-minute walk inland. Rooms are best arranged through any of the resort's many travel agencies – try Nidri Travel (☎26450 92514, ⓕ26450 92256; from ❷). The town's focus is the Aktí Aristotéli Onássi quay, where most of the rather ritzy **restaurants** and **bars** are found. Tourist traps like the *Barrel* taverna are rather pricey but reliable, whereas the *Titanic* on the beach is both quieter and better quality. The cheapest places to eat are predictably on the noisy main drag – try *Agrabeli* or *Ta Kalamia*. Nightlife centres around bars like *No Name* and *The Old Saloon*, and later on *Tropicana* or the *Sail Inn Club*, which claims to be open for 22 hours of the day.

Nydhrí sits at the mouth of a deep inlet stretching to the next village, somnolent **VLYHÓ**, with a few good tavernas and mooring for yachts. Over the Yéni peninsula across the inlet is the large **Dhessími Bay**, home to two campsites: *Santa Maura Camping* (☎26450 95007, ⓕ26450 26087) and *Dessimi Beach Camping* (☎26450 95374, ⓕ26450 95190), one at each end of the beach but often packed with outsized mobile homes. The *Pirofani* beach taverna in between them is excellent.

The coast road beyond Vlyhó turns inland and climbs the foothills of Mount Stavrotás, through the hamlets of Katohóri and Paliokatoúna to **Póros**, a quiet village with few facilities. Just south of here is the increasingly busy beach resort of **MIKRÓS YIALÓS**, more widely known as Póros beach. It boasts a handful of **tavernas**, a few rooms at *Oceanis Studios* (☎ & ⓕ26450 95095; ❸), plus the posh *Poros Beach Camping* (☎26450 95452, ⓦwww.porosbeach .com.gr), which has bungalows (❸), shops and a pool. For food, try the *Rouda Bay* taverna opposite the beach, which also has smart rooms (☎26450 95634, ⓔmanolitsis@otenet.gr; ❺).

A panoramic detour off the main road to quiet **Vournikás** and **Sývros** is recommended to walkers and drivers (the Lefkádha–Vassilikí bus also visits); both places have tavernas and some private rooms. It's around 14km to the next resort, the fjord-like inlet of **SÝVOTA**, 2km down a steep hill (bus twice daily). There's no beach except for a remote cove, but some fine tavernas, mostly specializing in fish: the *Palia Apothiki* is the most attractive and serves giant shrimps wrapped in bacon, but the *Delfinia* and *Ionion* also draw numerous customers. Just above the middle of the harbour there are **rooms** of varying sizes at *Sivota Apartments* (☎26450 31347, ⓕ26450 31151; ❸) or you can ask at any of the seafront supermarkets.

Beyond the Sývota turning, the mountain road dips down towards Kondárena, almost a suburb of **VASSILIKÍ**, the island's premier watersports resort. Winds in the huge bay draw vast numbers of windsurfers, with light morning breezes for learners and tough afternoon blasts for advanced surfers. Booking your **accommodation** ahead is advisable in high season: *Pension Hollidays* (☎26450 31011, ⓕ26450 31426; ❸), round the corner from the ferry dock, is a reasonable option with air conditioning and TV in all rooms. In the centre of town, the two main hotels are the classy *Vassiliki Bay Hotel* (☎26450 31077, ⓦwww.vassilikibay.gr; ❹) and the *Hotel Lefkatas* (☎26450 31801, ⓕ26450 31804; ❹), which operates in high season only. Rooms and apartments are available along the beach road to Póndi: try the smart and purpose-built *Billy's House* (☎26450 31418; ❸) or ask at the central Samba Tours (☎26450 31520, ⓦwww.sambatours.gr; ❸). The largest of the three beach windsurf centres, *Club Vassiliki*, offers all-in **windsurf tuition** and accommodation deals. Vassilikí's only **campsite**, the large *Camping Vassiliki*

Beach (☎26450 31308, 🖷26450 31458), is about 500m along the beach road; it has its own restaurant, bar and shop.

Vassilikí's pretty quayside is lined with **tavernas** and bars: the most popular eateries are *Penguins*, specializing in fish and seafood dishes like *marinara*, and *Alexander*, which has pizza as well as Greek cuisine. Quieter spots round the headland include the *Jasmine Garden* Chinese and the leafy *Apollo* taverna. The best place for a **drink** is *Livanakis kafenío* (next to the bakery), now modernized but still genuine and cheap.

The beach at Vassilikí is stony and poor, but improves 1km on at tiny **Póndi**; most non-windsurfers, however, use the daily *kaïki* trips to nearby Ayiófili or around Cape Lefkátas to the superior beaches at Pórto Katsíki and Egremní on the sandy west coast (see overleaf). There's a gradually increasing number of **places to stay** at Póndi, some with great views of the bay and plain behind. One fine spot is the terrace of the *Ponti Beach Hotel* (☎26450 31572, 🖷26450 31576; ❺), which is very popular with holidaying Greeks, and has a decent restaurant and bar. The *Nefeli* (☎26450 31378, 🄴clubnefeli@hotmail.com; ❹), right on the beach, is much better value though. The *Panorama* **taverna** serves delights such as garlic prawns and steak Diana.

The west coast

Tsoukaládhes, just 6km from Lefkádha Town, is developing a roadside tourism business, but better beaches lie a short distance to the southwest, so there's very little reason to stay here. Four kilometres on, the road plunges down to the sand-and-pebble **Pefkoúlia** beach, one of the longest on the island, with two tavernas towards the north end, one of which, *Pelagos*, has rooms (☎26450 97070, 🄴mypelagos@can.gr; ❹) and unofficial camping down at the other end, over 1km away. This part of the island suffered severe structural damage but mercifully no fatalities in the earthquake of summer 2003, which closed the main road, now protected by huge concrete and steel mesh barriers.

Jammed into a gorge between Pefkoúlia and the next beach, Mýlos, is **ÁÏ NIKÍTAS**, the prettiest resort on Lefkádha, a jumble of lanes and small wooden buildings. The back of the village is a dust-blown car park, which has completely taken over the former campsite, but this means that the village itself is now a pedestrian zone. The most attractive **accommodation** is in the ☪ *Pension Ostria* (☎26450 97483, 🖷26450 97300; ❹), a beautiful blue-and-white building above the village, decorated in a mix of beachcomber and ecclesiastical styles. The *Villa Milia* (☎26450 97475; ❷), by the junction offers better rates than most. Other options line the main drag or hide in the alleys running off it; the best bets are the small *Aphrodite* (☎26450 97372; ❸) and quieter *Olive Tree* (☎26450 97453, 🆆www.olivetreelefkada.com; ❹), which is also signposted from the main road. The best tavernas include the *Sapfo* fish taverna by the sea, the *T'Agnantio*, just above the main street, which serves excellent traditional cuisine, and *O Lefteris*, a good inexpensive restaurant on the main street. *Captain's Corner* near the beach is the liveliest drinking venue, while *En Plo* is a pleasant café-bar overlooking the sea.

Sea taxis (€2 one way) ply between Áï Nikítas and **Mýlos** beach, or it's a 45-minute walk (or bus ride) to the most popular beach on the coast, **Káthisma**, a shadeless kilometre of fine sand, which becomes nudist and a lot less crowded beyond the large jutting rocks halfway along – freelance camping still goes on at this end too. Of the two tavernas on the beach choose the barn-like *Kathisma* (☎26450 97050, 🆆www.kathisma.com; ❹), with smart apartments. The new *Club Copla* attracts the night-time crowd with house parties. Above the beach the upgraded *Sunset* has **rooms** (T26450 97488, Wwww.sunsetstudios.gr; ⑥), while the nearby *Hotel Sirius* (T26450 97025, Wwww.hotelsirios.gr; ⑤) also commands fine views. Beyond Káthisma, hairpin bends climb the flank of Mount Méga towards the small village of **KALAMÍTSI**, a much cheaper base for this area. Good-value **rooms** or apartments can be found at *Hotel Lenia* (T26450 99125; ❷), *Hermes* (T26450 99417; ❷), the smart *Blue and White House* (T26450 99413, Wwww.bluewhitehouse.com; ❸) and the newer *Pansion Nontas* (T26450 99451; ❸). There are also a few decent **tavernas**, including the *Paradeisos*, set in its own garden with fountain, the more basic *Ionio* and, just north of the village, the aptly titled *Panoramic View*. Three kilometres down a newly paved road is the village's quiet sandy beach.

South of Kalamítsi, past the hamlets of Hortáta, which boasts the excellent *Lygos* taverna with rooms (T26450 33395, Elola26@ch.gr; ❷), and Komíli, the landscape becomes almost primeval. At 38km from Lefkádha Town, **ATHÁNI** is the island's most remote spot to stay, with a couple of good tavernas which both have great-value rooms: the *Panorama* (T26450 33291, F26450 33476; ❷) and *O Alekos* (T26450 33484; ❷), the latter only open in high season. Three of the Ionian's choicest **beaches**, where azure and milky turquoise waves buffet strands enclosed by dramatic cliffs, are accessible from Atháni: the nearest, reached by a 4km paved road, is **Yialós**, followed by **Egremní**, down a steep incline unpaved for the last 2km; the former has the *Yialos* café-restaurant and a couple of *kantínes*, the latter just one *kantína*. Further south an asphalted road leads to the dramatic and popular twin beach of **Pórto Katsíki**, where there are several better-stocked *kantínes* on the cliff above.

Keeping to the main road for 14km from Atháni will bring you to barren **Cape Lefkátas**, which drops abruptly 75m into the sea. Byron's Childe Harold sailed past this point, and "saw the evening star above, Leucadia's far projecting rock of woe: And hail'd the last resort of fruitless love". The fruitless love is a reference to Sappho, who in accordance with the ancient legend that you could cure yourself of unrequited love by leaping into these waters, leapt – and died. In her honour the locals termed the place Kávos tis Kyrás ("lady's cape"), and her act was imitated by the lovelorn youths of Lefkádha for centuries afterwards. And not just by the love-lorn, for the act (known as *katapondismós*) was performed annually by scapegoats – always a criminal or a lunatic – selected by priests from the Apollo temple whose sparse ruins lie close by. Feathers and even live birds were attached to the victims to slow their descent and boats waiting below took the chosen one, dead or alive, away to some place where the evil banished with them could do no further harm. The rite continued into the Roman era, when it degenerated into little more than a fashionable stunt by decadent youth. These days, in a more controlled modern re-enactment, Greek hang-gliders hold a tournament from the cliffs every July.

Lefkádha's satellites

Lefkádha has four satellite islands clustered off its east coast, although only one, **Meganíssi**, the largest and most interesting, is accessible. **Skorpiós**, owned by the Onassis family, fields armed guards to deter visitors. **Madhourí**, owned by the family of poet Nanos Valaoritis, is private and similarly off-limits, while tiny **Spárti** is a large scrub-covered rock. Day-trips from Nydhrí skirt all three islands, and some stop to allow swimming in coves.

Meganíssi

Meganíssi, twenty minutes by frequent daily ferries from Nydhrí, is a large island with limited facilities but a magical, if bleak landscape. Ferries stop first at **Spiliá**, ten minutes by foot below **SPARTOHÓRI**, an immaculate village with whitewashed buildings and an abundance of bougainvillea. The locals – many returned émigrés from Australia – live from farming and fishing and are genuinely welcoming. You arrive at a jetty on a pebble beach with a few tavernas and a primitive but free (for a night or two only) campsite behind the excellent *Stars Taverna*. The village proper boasts three restaurants: a pizza place called the *Tropicana*, which can direct you to **rooms** (☎ 26450 51486; ②–③), as can the simple *Gakias* (☎ 26450 51050; ③); the trio is completed by the fine traditional taverna *Lakís*. Further west round the coast at Áyios Ioánnis there is a good beach with the *Il Paradiso* taverna and a makeshift campsite, a great spot to unwind in.

The attractive inland village of **KATOMÉRI** is an hour's walk through magnificent country. It has the island's one **hotel**, the *Meganissi*, a comfortable place with a restaurant and pool (☎ 26450 51240, Ⓕ 26450 51639; ④), and a few café-bars. Ten minutes' walk downhill is the main port of **VATHÝ**, with some accommodation such as *Different Studios* (☎ 26450 22170; ③) and several highly rated restaurants, notably the waterside taverna, *Porto Vathi*, which Lefkadans flock to on ferries for a Sunday fish lunch, and the *Rose Garden*. The *Twins Bar* by the ferry dock is a friendly spot for a drink. After the high-season madness of Nydhrí, Meganíssi's unspoilt landscape is a tonic, and it's easy to organize a **day-trip** from Nydhrí, getting off at Spiliá, walking via Spartohóri to Katoméri for lunch at the *Meganissi* or down at Vathý, from where you can catch the ferry back. Paths lead from Katoméri to remote beaches, including popular **Ambelákia**, but these aren't realistic on a day-trip.

Kefalloniá

KEFALLONIÁ is the largest of the Ionian islands – a place that has real towns as well as resorts. Like its neighbours, Kefalloniá was overrun by Italians and Germans in World War II; the "handover" after Italy's capitulation in 1943 led to the massacre of over five thousand Italian troops on the island by invading German forces, as chronicled by Louis de Bernières in his novel, *Captain Corelli's Mandolin*.

Until the late 1980s, the island paid scant regard to tourism; perhaps this was partly due to a feeling that Kefalloniá could not easily be marketed. Virtually all of its towns and villages were levelled in the 1953 earthquake, and these masterpieces of Venetian architecture had been the one touch of elegance in a severe, mountainous landscape. A more likely explanation, however, for the island's late emergence on the Greek tourist scene is the Kefallonians' legendary reputation for insular pride and stubbornness, plus a good measure of eccentricity.

There are definite attractions here, with some **beaches** as good as any in the Ionian islands, and a fine (if pricey) local wine, the dry white Robola. Mercifully, the anticipated "Corelli factor" did not lead to the island becoming either oversubscribed or over-expensive, despite some predictable theming. Moreover, the island seems able to soak up a lot of people without feeling at all crowded, and the magnificent scenery speaks for itself, the escarpments culminating in the 1632-metre bulk of **Mount Énos**, a national park.

For **airport** arrival see the Argostóli section on p.1037. Kefalloniá's **bus** system is basic but reliable, and with a little legwork it can be used to get you almost anywhere on the island. Key routes connect Argostóli with the main tourist centres of **Sámi**, **Fiskárdho**, **Skála** and **Póros**. There's a useful connection

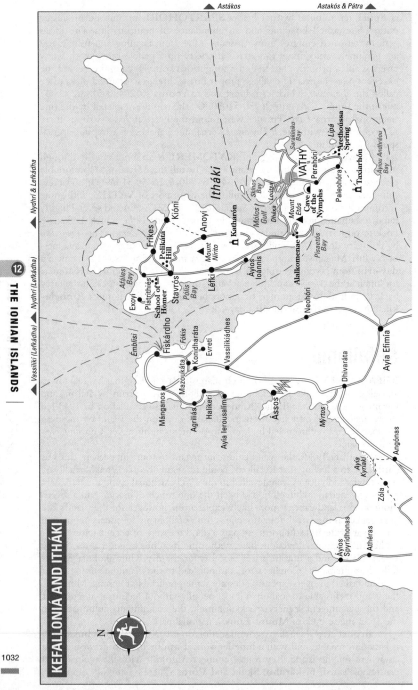

KEFALLONIÁ AND ITHÁKI

N

Ithaki

Lipá
Arethoússa
Spring
VATHÝ
Perahóri
Paleohóri
Taxiárhon
Sarakíniko
Bay
Áyiou Andhréou
Bay
Síkinos
Bay
Loútsa
Dhéxa
Cave of the
Nymphs
Mólos
Gulf
Mount
Etós
Anoyí
Katharón
Kióni
Fríkes
Pelikáta
Hill
Mount
Nírito
Pisaetós
Bay
Alalkomenae
Exoyí
Platríthiés
School of
Homer
Stavrós
Pólis
Bay
Afáles
Bay
Léfki
Áyios
Ioánnis
Neohóri
Émblisi
Fiskárdho
Fókis
Évreti
Konidharáta
Vassilikiádhes
Ayía Efimía
Mánganos
Mazoukáta
Halikéri
Agriliás
Ayía Ierousalím
Ássos
Mýrtos
Dhivaráta
Angónas
Ayía
Kyriakí
Zóla
Áyios
Spyridhónas
Athéras

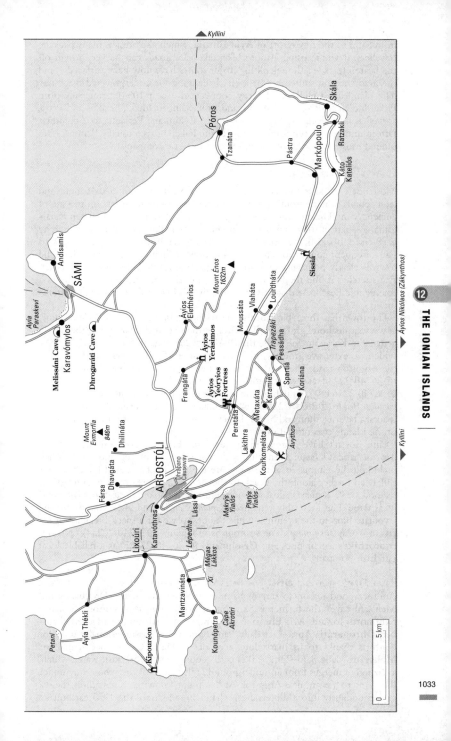

▲ *Kyllíni*

Skála
Ratzaklí
Markópoulo
Káto
Kateliós
Pástra
Tzanáta
Póros

Sissiá

Lourdháta
Viaháta
Moussáta

Andisamis
SÁMI

Ayía Paraskeví

Melissáni Cave
Karavómylos
Dhrogaráti Cave

Áyios
Elefthérios

Mount Énos 1632m ▲

Trapezáki
Pessádha
Spartiá
Koriána

Áyios Yerásimos
Áyios Yeóryios Fortress
Frangáta

Metaxáta
Keramiés

Peratáta
Lakíthra
Koutroméláta
Avythos

Mount Evmorfía ▲ *846m*
Dhilináta

Fársa
Dhavgáta

ARGOSTÓLI
Dhrápano Causeway

Lássi
Makrýs Yialós
Platýs Yialós

Katavóthres
Lixoúri
Lépedha

Mégas Lákkos
Xi
Mantzavináta

Petáni
Ayía Thékli
Kounópetra
Cape Akrotíri
Kipouréon

Ayios Nikólaos (Zákynthos) ▶

Kyllíni ▶

THE IONIAN ISLANDS 12

5 km
0

1033

from Sámi to the tiny resort of **Ayía Efimía**, which also attracts many package travellers. If you're using a motorbike, take care: roads can be very rough off the beaten track – although all the major routes have now been surfaced – and the gradients can sometimes be a bit challenging for underpowered machines. The island has a plethora of **ferry** connections (see p.1054), principally from Fiskárdho to Lefkádha and Itháki, and from Sámi to Itháki, Astakós and Pátra, as well as links from Argostóli and Póros to Kyllíni and Pessádha to Zákynthos. Direct sailings between Sámi and one of the Italian ports – usually Brindisi – are offered most years in peak season only, by just one company.

Sámi and around

Most boats dock at the large and functional port town of **SÁMI**, built and later rebuilt near the south end of the Itháki straits, more or less on the site of ancient Sami. This was the capital of the island in Homeric times, when Kefalloniá was part of Ithaca's maritime kingdom: today the administrative hierarchy is reversed, Itháki being considered the backwater. With the only ferry link to Pátra, frequent connections to Itháki and direct (albeit erratic) links to Italy, the town is clearly preparing itself for a burgeoning future. The long sandy beach that stretches round the bay is quite adequate; 2km beyond ancient Sami lies a fine pebble beach, **Andísamis**, with the lively *Andissa Club* providing refreshments.

The town has three big **hotels**: the friendly *Athina Beach* (℡26740 23067, ⓦwww.athinahotel.gr; ⑤), is the better of the two at the far end of the beach, actually in Karavómylos, while the *Pericles* (℡26740 22780, ⓕ26740 22787; ④), which has extensive grounds, two pools and sports facilities, lies over 1km along the Argostóli road. The best mid-range bet is the comfortable seafront *Kastro* (℡26740 22282, ⓦwww.kastrohotel.com; ④), followed by the *Melissani* (℡ & ⓕ26740 22464; ④), up behind the main dock. Sámi's **campsite**, *Camping Karavomilos Beach* (℡26740 22480, ⓔvalettas@hol.gr), has over 300 well-shaded spaces, a taverna, shop and bar, and opens onto the beach – it is by far the better of the island's two official sites.

Sámi doesn't have a great many **tavernas** beyond those on the seafront; *Mermaid* and *O Faros*, both with a decent selection of veg and meat dishes, including the famous local meat pie, are the best of the central bunch. Better still, head further along the beach to the *Akroyiali*, where you can sample fresh seafood, or *To Karnayio*, great for succulent home-cooked meat dishes and good local wine. The inevitably renamed *Captain Corelli's* and *Aqua Marina* are the favourite **bars** in the evenings, while the best place for a snack breakfast or ice cream is *Captain Jimmy's*. The seafront Sami Center (℡26740 22254) rents out **motorbikes** at fair rates and Gerolimatos (℡26740 23405) is a reliable local **car hire** company.

The Dhrogaráti and Melissáni caves

Another good reason to stay in Sámi is its proximity to the Drogharáti and Melissáni caves; the former is 5km out of town towards Argostóli, the latter 3km north towards Ayía Efimía. A very impressive stalagmite-bedecked chamber, **Dhrogaráti** (April–Oct daily 9am–8pm; €3.50) is occasionally used for concerts thanks to its marvellous acoustics – Maria Callas once sang here. **Melissáni** (daily 8am–7pm; €5) is partly submerged in brackish water, which, amazingly, emerges from an underground fault that leads the whole way under the island to a point near Argostóli. At that point, known as Katavóthres, the sea gushes endlessly into a subterranean channel – and, until the 1953 earthquake

△ Melissáni cave, Kefalloniá

disrupted it – the current was used to drive sea mills. That the water, now as then, still ends up in the cave has been shown with fluorescent tracer dye. The beautiful textures and shades created by the light pouring through the collapsed roof of the cave make it a must.

Ayía Efimía

AYÍA EFIMÍA, 9km north of Sámi, is a friendly little fishing harbour popular with package operators, yet with no major developments. Its two drawbacks are its beaches, or lack thereof – the largest, risibly named Paradise beach, is a pathetic 20m of shingle, although there are other coves to the south – and its poor transport connections (only two daily buses to Sámi and Fiskárdho). **Accommodation** here is good at two small, smart **hotels**: *Boulevard Pyllaros* (℡26740 61800, ℻26740 61801; ❻) and the better-value *Moustakis* (℡26740 61030, ℗www.moustakishotel.com; ❾); and there are also apartments offered by Yerasimos Raftopoulos (℡26740 61233, ℻26740 61216; ❷). The *Paradise Beach* **taverna**, furthest round the headland past the harbour, is the place for moderately priced island cuisine; the *Pergola* and *To Steki Tou Kalofaga* also both offer a wide range of island specialities and standard Greek dishes. Predictably, the café-bar where the film crew and actors used to hang out has been renamed *Captain Corelli's*, while the *Strawberry zaharoplastío* is the place for a filling breakfast. The town's nightclub is *Paranoia*, 700m out of town towards Fiskárdho. If you are making your own way between here and Sámi, the 🗽 *Ayía Paraskeví* taverna, at the tiny cove of the same name, is famous for its delicious spaghetti with mussel marinade and boasts a great setting.

Southeast Kefalloniá

Travel **southeast from Sámi** has been made a lot easier by the completion of the asphalt road to **Póros** and the consequent addition of a twice-daily bus route between the two. Continuing south, Póros is connected to **Skála** by another paved coastal road.

Póros

PÓROS was one of the island's earliest developed resorts, and definitely gives the impression of having seen better days. The town's small huddle of hotels and apartment blocks is almost unique on Kefalloniá, and not enhanced by a scruffy seafront and thin, pebbly beach.

Póros does, however, have a regular ferry link to **Kyllíni** on the Peloponnesian mainland, a viable alternative to the Sámi–Pátra route. Póros is actually made up of two bays: the first, where most tourists are based, and the actual harbour, a few minutes over the headland. There are plenty of rooms, apartments and a few **hotels**. The best deal is at the cosy *Santa Irina* (T 26740 72017, E maki@otenet. gr; B&B; ❷), by the crossroads inland, whose low rate includes breakfast, while the nearby *Odysseus Palace* (T 26740 72036, W www.odysseuspalace.com; ❺) often gives good discounts. Among **travel agents**, Poros Travel by the ferry dock (T 26740 72476, F 26740 72069) offers a range of accommodation, as well as services such as car rental and ferry bookings. The main seafront has the majority of the **restaurants** and **bars**. The *Fotis Family* taverna serves good food in a pleasant setting and the *Mythos* bar has Internet access.

The aforementioned road twists 12km around the rocky coastline from Póros to Skála at the southern extremity of the island. It's a lovely, isolated route, with scarcely a building on the way, save for a small chapel, 3km short of Skála, next to the ruins of a **Roman temple**.

Skála

In total contrast to Póros, the resort of **SKÁLA** is a low-rise development set among handsome pines above a few kilometres of good sandy beach. A **Roman villa** (daily 10am–2pm & 5am–8pm, longer hours in summer; free) and some mosaics were excavated here in the 1950s, near the site of the *Golden Beach Palace* rooms, and are open to the public.

A faithful return crowd keeps Skála busy until well after Póros has closed for the season, and **accommodation** can be hard to find. There are studios and apartments at *Dionysus Rooms* (T 26710 83283; ❷), a block south of the main street, or a range is available through Etam Travel Service (T 26710 83101, E etam-kef@otenet.gr; ❷). Of hotels, the cosy *Captain's Hotel* (T 26710 83389, W www.captainshouse.net; ❸), on the road parallel to the main street to the east, is comfortable and friendly, while he more upmarket *Tara Beach Hotel* (T 26710 83250, W www.tarabeach.gr; ❺) has rooms and individual bungalows in lush gardens on the edge of the beach. Skála boasts a number of **tavernas**: *Ta Pytharia* and the *Flamingo* are both good spots with a standard range of Greek and continental cuisine, while, on the beach, *Paspalis* serves fish and home-cooking and *Sunrise* offers pizza as well as Greek food. Drinkers head for *The Loft* cocktail **bar** and the beachside *Stavento* restaurant-bar, which plays the coolest sounds.

Skála to Lourdháta

Some of the finest sandy beaches on the island are just beyond Skála below the village of Ratzaklí, and around the growing micro-resort of **KÁTO KATELIÓS**, which already has a couple of hotels: the smart *Odyssia* (T 26710 81615, F 26710 81614; ❹) and the mostly German-occupied *Galini Resort* (T 26710 81582, W www.galini.de; ❹), which has good deals on **apartments** for four. There are also some rooms and apartments available through the *Lighthouse* taverna (T 26710 81355; ❸) or the local branch of CBR Travel (T 26710 22770, W www.cbr-rentacar.com; ❸). Of the half a dozen restaurants and cafés at the seafront, the *Blue Sea* taverna is renowned for the freshness and quality of its fish, the *Arbouro* offers a wide selection of dishes, while the *Cozy* bar is the prime drinking location. The coast around Káto Kateliós is also Kefalloniá's key breeding ground for the loggerhead **turtle** (see box, p.1051). Camping on the nearby beaches is therefore discouraged.

The inland village of **MARKÓPOULO**, claimed by some to be the birthplace of homophonous explorer Marco Polo, witnesses a bizarre snake-handling ritual every year on August 15, the **Assumption of the Virgin festival**. The church where this ritual is enacted stands on the site of an old convent. The story goes that when the convent was attacked by pirates, the nuns prayed to be transformed into snakes to avoid being taken prisoner. Their prayers were supposedly answered, and each year the "return" of a swarm of small, harmless snakes is meant to bring the villagers good luck. As Mother Nature is unlikely to keep to such a schedule, some discreet snake-breeding on the part of the village priests must be suspected.

The coastline is largely inaccessible until the village of **VLAHÁTA**, which has some rooms and restaurants, but there's little point in staying up here, when you can turn 2km down to **LOURDHÁTA**, which has a kilometre-long shingle beach, mixed with imported sand. *Adonis* (☎26710 31206; ❸) and *Ramona* (☎26710 31032; ❸) have **rooms** just outside the village on the approach road, while the smart new *Thomatos Apartments* (☎26710 31656, ✉critithomas@yahoo .com; ❹), behind the beach, comprise fully equipped kitchen-studios. Of the smattering of **tavernas**, the *Diamond,* on the tiny plane-shaded village square, does a good range of vegetarian items. Further up the hill is the smarter *Spiros* steak-and-grill house and, closer to Vlaháta, *Dionysus*, serving taverna standards; at the beach itself *Klimitis* is good for inexpensive fish. The beachside *Astrabar* is friendly and plays a good mix of English and Greek music into the wee hours. Another fine beach, reached by a turning from Moussáta, west of Vlaháta, is **Trapezáki**, an attractive strand with just one restaurant by the small jetty.

Argostóli and around

ARGOSTÓLI, Kefalloniá's capital, is a large and thriving town – virtually a city – with a marvellous site on a bay within a bay. The stone bridge, connecting the two sides of the inner bay, was initially constructed by the British in 1813. The bridge, known as Dhrépano owing to its sickle shape, was closed to traffic indefinitely in 2005, making it a much more pleasant walk than previously. The town was totally rebuilt after the 1953 earthquake, but has an enjoyable atmosphere that remains defiantly Greek, especially during the evening *vólta* around **Platía Valiánou** (formerly Platía Metaxá) – the nerve centre of town – and along the pedestrianized Lithóstrotou, which runs parallel to the seafront.

Arrival and information

Argostóli's modern **Kefalloniá airport** lies 7km south of town. There are no airport buses, and suburban bus services are so infrequent or remote from the terminal that a taxi (at an inflated flat rate of around €10) is the only dependable connection. Those arriving in Argostóli by bus from Sámi or elsewhere will wind up at the KTEL **bus station**, a minute from the Dhrépano causeway and ten minutes' walk south of the main square, Platía Valianoú. Argostóli's friendly **tourist office** (Mon–Fri 7.30am–2.30pm; ☎26710 22248, ☎26710 24466), on Andoníou Trítsi at the north end of the seafront, next to the port authority, has information about rooms, piles of brochures and trail guides, and can advise on transport, sites and all resorts around the island. The island-wide Sunbird agency

(℡26710 23723, ⓦwww.sunbird.gr) is a reliable outlet for car or motorbike rental. Excelixis (Mon–Sat 9am–2.30pm & 6–10pm; €4 per hour) at Minoös 3, behind the church on Lithóstrotou, has Internet facilities.

Accommodation

Hotels in Argostóli open all year and are mostly mid-range, the best value of these being the ⚑ *Ionian Plaza* (℡26710 25581, ⓦwww.ionianplaza.gr; ❺), right on the square. A good option in the opposite corner of the square is the *Mirabel* (℡26710 23454, ⓦwww.mirabel.gr; ❹); one of the best deals going, if you don't mind sharing a bathroom, is the friendly *Chara* (℡26710 22427; ❶), set in a lovely shady courtyard at the corner of Y.Vergóti and Dhevossétou near Dhrépano bridge. The newly upgraded *pension* attached to the *Tsima Cavo* cafeteria (℡26710 23941; ❸), opposite the Lixoúri ferry ramp, is good value, with TV in all the air-conditioned rooms. In a working town with a large permanent population, **private rooms** aren't too plentiful, but you can call the Room-Owners Association (℡26710 29109) to see what's on offer. A number of travel agencies also offer rooms, apartments and villas: try Ainos Travel (℡26710 22333, ⓦwww.ainostravel.gr; from ❷), opposite the Archeological Museum, or Myrtos at A. Trítsi 117 (℡26710 25895, ⓔmyrtostr@hol.gr; from ❸). The town's **campsite**, *Argostoli Camping* (℡26710 23487), lies 2km north of the centre, just beyond the Katovóthres sea mills; there's only an infrequent bus service in high season, so you'll probably have to walk and it's rather basic with limited shade.

The town

The **Korgialenio History and Folklore Museum** (Mon–Sat 9am–2pm; €3), on Ilía Zervoú behind the Municipal Theatre, has a rich collection of local religious and cultural artefacts, including photographs taken before and after the earthquake. Insight into how the island's nobility used to live can be gained from a visit to the **Focas-Cosmetatos Foundation** (Mon–Sat 9.20am–1pm, plus summer 7–10pm; €3), on Valiánou opposite the provincial government building. It contains elegant furniture and a collection of lithographs and paintings, including works by nineteenth-century British artists Joseph Cartwright and Edward Lear. The refurbished **Archeological Museum** (Tues–Sun 8.30am–3pm; €3), on nearby R.Vergóti, has a sizeable collection of pottery, jewellery, funerary relics and statuary from prehistoric, through Mycenaean to late Classical times. It is well laid out and labelled, rivalling Kérkyra Town's (see p.1005) as the best such museum in the Ionians. Island-inspired works by Peter Hemming, a resident British artist, are on display (and for sale) at **The Gallery** (Mon–Sat 10am–2pm & daily 6.30-10pm; free), behind the playground a few blocks north of the square.

Eating, drinking and nightlife

The *Tzivras estiatório* (only open until 5pm), opposite the seafront fruit market on Vandhórou, is one of the best places to try Kefallonian cuisine; the upmarket *Captain's Table* **taverna** just off the main square is worth a splurge for its live *kantádhes*, though they are just about as easily heard from the far more reasonable *Arhontiko* next door. Of the seafront eateries, the friendly ⚑ *Kiani Akti*, perfectly located beyond the Lixoúri ferry, has a great, high-quality selection of seafood and *mezédhes*, which can be enjoyed from the wooden deck that juts out above the water. For a change of diet, try *Kohenoor*, 50m towards the front from the square, which dishes up good, authentic Indian food.

Local posers hang out at the café-bars lining the square, while more discerning drinkers head for *Pub Old House*, a relaxed hangout next to The Gallery, or the more modern *Bodega* en route to it. *Bass*, by the museum, is the town's big late-night indoor club. The quayside bars, particularly the *Aristofanis kafenío* by the Dhrépano bridge, are quiet, cheap and have the best views.

South of Argostóli: beaches and Áyios Yeóryios

Many package travellers will find themselves staying in **LÁSSI**, a short bus ride or twenty-minute walk from town. Lássi sprawls unattractively along a busy main road and it cannot be recommended to the independent traveller. At least it has a couple of good sandy beaches, namely **Makrýs Yialós** and **Platýs Yialós**, although they're right under the airport flight path. Further on, **beaches** such as **Ávythos** are well worth seeking out, although if you're walking beyond **Kourkomeláta** there is a real, if occasional, risk of being attacked by farm dogs, particularly during the hunting season (Sept 25–Feb 28). There is very little accommodation in the region, and precious few shops or bars. **Pessádha** has a twice-daily ferry link with Zákynthos in summer, but little else, and be warned that the pathetic bus service from Argostóli is no good for connecting with the boats. You'll have to hitch or take an expensive taxi in most cases.

With a scooter, the best inland excursion is to **ÁYIOS YEÓRYIOS**, the medieval Venetian capital of the island. The old town here supported a population of 15,000 until its destruction by an earthquake in the seventeenth century: substantial ruins of its **castle** (summer Tues–Fri 8.30am–7pm, Sat & Sun 8.30am–3pm; rest of year Tues–Sun 8.30am–3pm; free), now reopened after extensive renovations, churches and houses can be visited on the hill above the modern village of Peratáta. Byron lived for a few months in the nearby village of Metaxáta and was impressed by the view from the summit in 1823; sadly, as at Mesolóngi, the house where he stayed no longer exists. The *Astraia* **café-bar** provides refreshments and great views from near the castle gates. Two kilometres south of Áyios Yeóryios is a fine collection of religious icons and frescoes kept in a restored church that was part of the nunnery of Áyios Andhréas.

Mount Énos

At 15km from a point halfway along the Argostóli–Sámi road, **Mount Énos** isn't really a walking option, but roads nearly reach the official 1632-metre summit. The mountain has been declared a national park, to protect the *Abies cephalonica* firs (named after the island), which clothe the slopes. There are absolutely no facilities on or up to the mountain, but the views from the highest point in the Ionian islands out over its neighbours and the mainland are wonderful. In low season, watch the weather, which can deteriorate with terrifying speed. Not far before the mountain turning, taking a detour towards Frangáta is doubly rewarded by the huge and lively **Áyios Yerásimos monastery** (daily 8am–1pm & 3–7pm), which hosts two of the island's most important festivals (Aug 15 and Oct 20); the most interesting feature is the double cave beneath the back of the sanctuary, where the saint meditated for lengthy periods. Right behind the monastery, the **Robola winery** (April–Oct daily 7am–8.30pm; Nov–March Mon–Fri 7am–3pm), which offers a free self-guided tour and generous wine-tasting.

Lixoúri and its peninsula

Half-hourly ferries (hourly in winter) ply between the capital and **LIXOÚRI** throughout the day until after midnight. The town was flattened by earthquakes, and hasn't risen much above two storeys since. It's a little drab, but has good restaurants, quiet hotels and is favoured by those who want to explore the eerie quake-scapes left in the south and the barren north of the peninsula. **Hotels** are not especially plentiful or cheap, but two comfortable air-conditioned options are the *La Cité* (☎26710 92701, ℱ26710 92702; ➍), four blocks back from the front, and a beach hotel just south of town, *Summery* (☎26710 91771, ⓦwww .hotelsummery.gr; ➎). Two agencies offer cheaper accommodation (from ➋) in town: A. D. Travel (☎26710 93142, ⓦwww.adtravel.gr) on the main road through town, and Perdikis Travel (☎ & ℱ26710 92503) on the quay. Among the tavernas, *Akrogiali* on the seafront is excellent and cheap, drawing admirers from all over the island. *Iy Avli*, on the block behind, serves a variety of dishes in a leafy garden, while *Adonis* is a good basic *psistariá* at the back of the square. *Overdose* is the trendy place to drink on the square, while the old seafront *kafenía* have also been replaced by youth-orientated cafés such as *LA Dreams*.

Lixoúri's nearest beach is **Lépedha**, a two-kilometre walk south. Like the **Xí** and **Mégas Lákkos** beaches (served by bus from Lixoúri and both with restaurants and accommodation), it has rich-red sand and is backed by low cliffs. Those with transport can also strike out for the monastery at **Kipouréon**, and north to the spectacular beach at **Petaní**. Here there are two restaurants, the better being the further of the two, *Xougras*, whose friendly Greek-American owner Dina directs those wishing to stay in these relaxing surroundings up the hill to the *Niforo* apartments (☎26710 97350), pending completion of her own rooms.

The west coast and the road north

The journey between Argostóli and Fiskárdho is the most spectacular ride in the archipelago. Leaving town, the road rises into the Evmorfía foothills, where you can detour a short way inland to visit the modest **Museum of Natural History** (daily 9am–1pm, Mon–Sat 6–8pm; €1.50) at **Dhavgáta**. Continuing to rise beyond Agónas, the coast road clings to near-sheer cliffs as it heads for Dhivaráta, which has a smattering of rooms, such as *Mina Studios* (☎26740 61716, ⓔmarkela1@hol.gr; ➌), a couple of restaurants, and is the stop for **Mýrtos** beach. It's a four-kilometre hike down the motorable road, with just one snack-bar on the beach, but from above or below this is the most dramatic beach in the Ionian islands – a splendid strip of pure-white sand and pebbles. Sadly, it's shadeless and gets mighty crowded in high season.

Six kilometres on is the turning for the atmospheric village of **ÁSSOS**, clinging to a small isthmus between the island and a huge hill crowned by a ruined fort. Accommodation is scarce – villagers invariably send you to the chic ⚐ Andhreas Rokos' rooms (☎26740 51523; ➋) on the approach road, which are extremely welcoming and great value, or you can opt for the posher *Kanakis Apartments* opposite (☎26740 51631, ℱ26740 51660; ➍). Ássos has a small pebble beach, and three tavernas, notably the *Nefeli* and the *Platanos Grill*, on a plane-shaded village square backed by mansions, mostly now restored after being ruined in the quake. It can get a little claustrophobic, but there's nowhere else quite like it in the Ionians.

Fiskárdho
FISKÁRDHO, on the northernmost tip of the island, sits on a bed of limestone that buffered it against the worst of the quakes. Two **lighthouses**, Venetian and Victorian, guard the bay, and the ruins on the headland are believed to be from a twelfth-century chapel begun by Norman invader Robert Guiscard, who gave the place its name. The nineteenth-century harbour frontage is intact, nowadays occupied by smart restaurants and chic boutiques. There is a new **Environmental and Nautical Museum** (summer daily 10am–7pm;

donations), housed in a renovated Neoclassical mansion on the hill behind the village. The volunteers who curate it conduct valuable ecological research and can also arrange **scuba diving** (T 26740 41182, W www.fnec.gr).

The island's premier resort, Fiskárdho remains busy through to the end of October, with **accommodation** at a premium. The cheapest rooms are those of Sotiria Tselenti (T 26740 41204, W www.fiskardo-ellis.gr; ❸), arranged through the bakery 50m back from the tiny square, and *Regina's* (T & F 26740 41125; ❸), which has its own café at the back of the village, next to the car park. A splendid if pricey option is the beautifully converted mansion *Archontiko* (T & F 26740 41342; ❻), above and behind a harbourfront mini-market. Pama Travel (T 26740 41033, W www.pamatravel.com; from ❸), on the seafront furthest away from the ferry quay, is another source of rooms and costlier apartments. There's a wealth of good but mostly expensive **restaurants**. Two to try on the seafront are the *Tassia,* which has a vast range of seafood (but check how much fish you are actually ordering), and the *Captain's Table,* serving succulent Greek and Kefallonian fare. On the square, *Alexis* serves pizzas and pastas, while *Lagonderia,* just round the corner, specializes in tasty oven food. *Irida's* and *Theodora's* are two of the most popular harbourside **bars**. The dance spot is *Kastro Club* up at the back of the village. There are two good pebble beaches – **Émblisi** 1km back out of town and **Fókis** just to the south – and a nature trail on the northern headland. Daily **ferries** connect Fiskárdho to Itháki and Lefkádha in season.

Itháki

Rugged **Itháki**, Odysseus's legendary homeland, has yielded no substantial archeological discoveries, but it fits Homer's description to perfection: "There are no tracks, nor grasslands . . . it is a rocky severe island, unsuited for horses, but not so wretched, despite its small size. It is good for goats." In Constantine Cavafy's splendid poem *Ithaca*, the island is symbolized as a journey to life:

When you set out on the voyage to Ithaca
Pray that your journey may be long
Full of adventures, full of knowledge.

Despite the romance of its name, and its proximity to Kefalloniá, very little tourist development has arrived to spoil the place. This is doubtless accounted for in part by a dearth of beaches, though the island is good walking country, with a handful of small fishing ports and inland villages. In the north, apart from the ubiquitous drone of scooters, the most common sounds are sheep bells jangling and cocks (a symbol of Odysseus) crowing.

Itháki's beaches are admittedly minor and mainly pebbly with sandy seabeds, but relatively clean and safe; the real attractions are the interior and sites from the **Odyssey**. Some package travellers will find themselves flying into Kefal-loniá and being bused to Fiskárdho (sit on the left for the bus ride of your life), for a short ferry crossing to **Fríkes** or the premier resort **Kióni**. Most visitors, however, will arrive at **Vathý**, the capital.

Vathý

Ferries from Pátra, Astakós and a minority of those from Kefalloniá land at the main port and capital of **VATHÝ**, a bay within a bay so deep that few realize the mountains out "at sea" are actually the north of the island. This snug town is compact, relatively traffic-free and boasts the most idyllic seafront setting of all the Ionian capitals. Like its southerly neighbours, it was heavily damaged by the 1953 earthquake, but some fine examples of pre-quake architecture remain here and in the northern port of **Kióni**. Vathý has a small **archeological museum** on Kalliníkou (Tues–Sun 8.30am–3pm; free), a short block back from the quay. Near the corner of the quay behind the Agricultural Bank, there is also the moderately interesting **Folklore & Cultural Museum** (summer Tues–Sat 10am–2pm & 5–9pm; €1). There are banks, a post office, police and a medical centre in town.

Vathý now has four **hotels**, the oldest of which is the refurbished and air-conditioned *Mentor* (T 26740 32433, W www.hotelmentor.gr; ⑥) in the south-east corner of the harbour. Further on round the bay are the posh *Omirikon* (T 26740 33598, F 26740 33596; ⑦), and, just beyond it, the much better-value ⚓ *Captain Yiannis* (T 26740 33419, F 26740 32849; ⑧), complete with tennis court and pool. The small *Odyssey* (T 26740 32268, F 26740 32668; ⑨) is perched on the hillside a short way up the road to Skínos beach. Room owners rarely meet boats so the best source of rooms, studios or villas is the town's two main quay-side travel agents, Polyctor Tours (T 26740 33120, E polyctor@ithakiholidays .gr) and Delas Tours (T 26740 32104, E delas@otenet.gr).

Even though it's tiny, Vathý has a wealth of **tavernas** and **bars**. Many locals head off south around the bay towards the friendly, family-run ⚓ *Paliocaravo* (aka *Gregory's*), popular for its lamb and fish and best of the three fine eateries in that direction. In town, the excellent *O Nikos*, just off the square, fills early, while *To Kohili* is by far the best of the half-dozen harbourside tavernas. The *Sirenes Ithaki Yacht Club* is upmarket with a nautical theme but, as usual, the town's ancient *kafenío* one street back from the front is the spot for a quiet and inexpensive tipple with the locals.

There are two reasonable pebble **beaches** within fifteen minutes' walk of Vathý: **Dhéxa**, over the hill above the ferry quay, and tiny **Loútsa**, opposite it around the bay. Better beaches at **Sarakíniko** and **Skínos** are an hour's trek along recently improved roads leaving the opposite side of the bay. In season, daily *kaïkia* ply between the quay and remote coves.

Odysseus sights

Three of the main **Odysseus** sights are just within walking distance of Vathý: the Arethoússa Spring, the Cave of the Nymphs and ancient Alalkomenae, although the last is best approached by **moped** or **taxi** (no more than €15 round-trip).

The Arethoússa Spring

The walk to the **Arethoússa Spring** – allegedly the place where Eumaeus, Odysseus's faithful swineherd, brought his pigs to drink – is a three-hour round trip along a track signposted next to the seafront telecoms office. The unspoilt but shadeless landscape and sea views are magnificent, but the walk crosses slippery inclines and might best be avoided if you're nervous of heights.

Near the top of the lane leading to the spring path, a signpost points up to what is said to have been the **Cave of Eumaeus**. The route to the spring continues for a few hundred metres, and then branches off onto a narrow footpath through gorse-covered steep cliffs. Parts of the final downhill track involve scrambling across rock fields (follow the splashes of green paint), and care should be taken around the small but vertiginous ravine that houses the

spring. The ravine sits below a crag known as **Kórax** (the raven), which matches Homer's description of the meeting between Odysseus and Eumaeus. In summer it's just a dribble of water. You have to return by the same route but you might have time to swim in a small cove a short scramble down from the spring.

The Cave of the Nymphs

The **Cave of the Nymphs** (Marmarospíli) is about 2.5km up a rough but navigable road signposted on the brow of the hill above Dhéxa beach. The cave is atmospheric, but it's underwhelming compared to the caverns of neighbouring Kefalloniá and, these days, is illuminated by coloured lights. The claim that this is the *Odyssey's* Cave of the Nymphs, where the returning Odysseus concealed the gifts given to him by King Alkinous, is enhanced by the proximity of Dhéxa beach, although there is some evidence that the "true" cave was just above the beach, and was unwittingly demolished during quarrying many years ago.

Alalkomenae and Pisaetós

Alalkomenae, Heinrich Schliemann's much-vaunted "Castle of Odysseus", is signposted on the Vathý–Pisaetós road, on the saddle between Dhéxa and Pisaetós, with views over both sides of the island. The actual site, however, some 300m uphill, is little more than foundations spread about in the gorse. Schliemann's excavations unearthed a Mycenaean burial chamber and domestic items such as vases, figurines and utensils (displayed in the archeological museum), but the ruins actually date from three centuries after Homer. In fact, the most likely contender for the site of Odysseus's castle is above the village of Stavrós (see below).

The road (though not buses) continues to the harbour of **Pisaetós**, about 2km below, with a large pebble beach that's good for swimming and popular with local rod-and-line fishermen. There is just one *kantína* here, serving those awaiting the regular ferries from Sámi on Kefalloniá.

Northern Itháki

The main road out of Vathý continues across the isthmus and takes a spectacular route to the northern half of Itháki, serving the villages of **Léfki**, **Stavrós**, **Fríkes** and **Kióni**. There is usually one daily **bus**, which is timed to take kids to school from the north to the capital at 7am, returning at 2pm; out of term the schedule is much more fluid. The north of Itháki is, however, excellent scooter country; the close proximity of the settlements, small coves and Homeric interest also make it good rambling terrain. Once a day a *kaïki* also visits the last two of those communities – a cheap and scenic ride used by locals and tourists alike to meet the mainline ferries in Vathý. As with the rest of Itháki there is only a limited amount of accommodation.

Stavrós and around

STAVRÓS, the second-largest town on the island, is a steep two kilometres above the nearest beach (Pólis Bay). It's a pleasant enough town nonetheless, with *kafenía* edging a small square dominated by a rather fierce statue of Odysseus. There is even a tiny **museum** (Tues–Sun 8.30am–3pm; free) off the road to Platrithriés, displaying local archeological finds. Stavrós's Homeric site is on the side of **Pelikáta Hill**, where remains of roads, walls and other structures have been suggested as the possible site of Odysseus's castle. Stavrós is useful as a base if both Fríkes and Kióni are full up, and is an obvious stopping-off point for exploring the northern hamlets and the road up to the medieval village of Anoyí (see below). Both Polyctor and Delas handle **accommodation** in Stavrós; the traditional *Petra* taverna (☎26740 31596; ❸) offers rooms, or there's the *Porto Thiaki pension* (☎26740 31245, ℱ26740 31638; ❸) above the pizzeria. The oldest and best **taverna** is *Fatouros*, and the *Margarita zaharoplastío* is a good place for a drink or to sample the local sweet *rovaní* (syrupy rice cakes).

A scenic mountain road leads 5km southeast from Stavrós to **ANOYÍ**, which translates roughly as "upper ground". Once the second-most important settlement on the island, it is almost deserted today. The centre of the village is dominated by a free-standing Venetian campanile, built to serve the (usually locked) church of the **Panayía**, which comes alive for the annual *paniyíri* on August 14, the eve of the Virgin's Assumption; at other times enquire at the *kafenío* about access to the church, the Byzantine frescoes of which have been heavily restored following centuries of earthquake damage. On the outskirts of the village are the foundations of a ruined **medieval prison**, and in the surrounding countryside are some extremely strange rock formations, the biggest being the eight-metre-high Iraklis (Hercules) rock, just east of the village. The **monastery of Katharón**, 3km further south along the road, has stunning views down over Vathý and the south of the island, and houses an icon of the *Panayía* discovered by peasants clearing scrubland in the area. The monastery celebrates its festival on September 8 with services, processions and music.

Two roads push north of Stavrós: one, to the right, heads 2km down to Fríkes, while the main road, to the left, loops below the hill village of **Exoyí**, and on to **Platrithiés**, where the new *Yefiri* taverna serves a wide range of tasty fare. Just off the start of the road up to Exoyí a signpost points about 1km along a rough track to the supposed **School of Homer**, where excavations still in progress have revealed extensive foundations, a well and ancient steps. The site is unfenced and well worth a detour for its views of **Afáles Bay** as much as the remains. On the outskirts of Platrithiés a track leads down to Afáles, the largest bay on the entire island, with an unspoiled and little-visited pebble-and-sand beach. The landscape around here, thickly forested in parts and dotted with vineyards, provides excellent walking.

Fríkes

At first sight, tiny **FRÍKES** doesn't appear to have much going for it. Wedged in a valley between two steep hills, it was only settled in the sixteenth century, and emigration in the nineteenth century almost emptied the place – as few as two hundred people live here today – but the protected harbour is a natural year-round port. Consequently, Fríkes stays open for tourism far later in the season than neighbouring Kióni, and has a better range of tavernas. There are no beaches in the village, but plenty of good, if small, pebble strands a short walk away towards Kióni. When the ferries and their cargoes have departed, Fríkes falls quiet and this is its real charm: a downbeat but cool place to lie low.

Fríkes's one **hotel** is the upmarket *Nostos* (☎26740 31644, ⓦwww .hotelnostos-ithaki.gr; ❺), which has a pool, or you can try the equally comfy *Aristotelis Apartments* (☎26740 31079, ⓦwww.aristotelis-ithaca.gr; ❸). The Gods souvenir shop (☎ & ℱ26740 31021; from ❷) can help find **rooms**, though in peak season chances are slim. Fríkes has a quartet of good seafront **tavernas**, all serving a decent mixture of Greek and international cuisine:

the *Symposium*, the *Rementzo*, the *Penelope* and *Ulysses*. Tucked in the corner of the harbour, *Café Bemenis* often springs into life late at night as the north's main meeting place for youngsters.

Kióni

KIÓNI sits at a dead end 5km southeast of Fríkes. On the same geological base as the northern tip of Kefalloniá, it avoided the very worst of the 1953 earthquakes, and so retains some fine examples of pre-twentieth-century architecture. It's an extremely pretty village, wrapped around a tiny harbour, and tourism here is dominated by British blue-chip travel companies and visiting yachts.

The bay has a small **beach**, 1km along its south side, a sand-and-pebble strand below a summer-only snack-bar. Better pebble beaches can be found within walking distance towards Fríkes. While the best **accommodation** has been snaffled by the Brits, some local businesses have rooms and apartments to let, among them *Captain's Apartments* (☎26740 31481, ℱ26740 31090; ❹), *Maroudas Apartments* (☎26740 31691, ℱ26740 31 753; ❸) and *Kioni Vacations* (☎26740 31668; ❸). A quieter option, just a short walk uphill on the main road in the hamlet of Ráhi, are the rooms and studios run by Captain Theofilos Karatzis and his family (☎26740 31679; ❸), which have panoramic views.

Kióni's **restaurants** are dotted around the picturesque harbour, but compare unfavourably with those in Fríkes; *Oasis* has a wide selection and is the best of the bunch, the *Avra* fish taverna and *Kioni* pizzeria are adequate, while the upmarket *Calypso* taverna has interesting dishes but is overpriced. Village facilities stretch to two well-stocked shops, a post office and a couple of bars and cafés, of which *Spavento* is the place for eclectic sounds.

Zákynthos (Zante)

Zákynthos, southernmost of the six core Ionian islands, is somewhat schizophrenically divided between underdevelopment and indiscriminate commercialization. Much of the island is still green and unspoilt, with only token pockets of tourism, and the main resorts seem to be reaching maximum growth without encroaching too much on the quieter parts.

The island has three distinct zones: the barren, mountainous northwest; the fertile central plain; and the eastern and southern resort-filled coasts. The biggest resort – rivalling the busiest on Corfu – is **Laganás**, on Laganás Bay in the south, a 24-hour party venue that doesn't give up from Easter until the last flight home in October. There are smaller, quieter resorts north and south of the capital, and the southerly Vassilikós peninsula has some of the best countryside and beaches, including exquisite **Yérakas**.

Although half-built apartment blocks and a few factories are spreading into the central plain, this is where the quieter island begins: farms and vineyards, ancient villages and the ruins of Venetian buildings levelled in the 1948 and 1953 earthquakes. The island still produces fine wines, such as the white Popolaro, as well as sugar-shock-inducing *mandoláto* nougat, whose honey-sweetened form is best. Zákynthos is also the birthplace of *kantádhes*, which can be heard in tavernas in Zákynthos Town and elsewhere. It also harbours one of the key breeding sites of the endangered **loggerhead sea turtle** at Laganás Bay. The loggerhead (see box, p.1051) is the subject of a continuing dispute between tourism businesses and environmentalists.

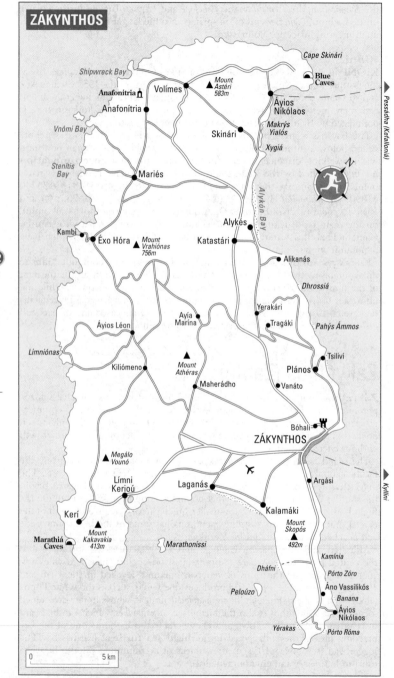

ZÁKYNTHOS

Cape Skinári

Shipwreck Bay

Blue Caves

Anafonítria

Volímes

Mount Astéri 583m

Áyios Nikólaos

Anafonítria

Makrýs Yialós

Vnómi Bay

Skinári

Xygiá

Stenítis Bay

Mariés

Alykón Bay

Kambí

Éxo Hóra

Mount Vrahiónas 756m

Alykés

Katastári

Alikanás

Dhrossiá

Yerakári

Ayía Marína

Tragáki

Pahýs Ámmos

Áyios Léon

Limniónas

Kilíomeno

Mount Athéras

Tsiliví

Plános

Maherádho

Vanáto

Bóhali

ZÁKYNTHOS

Megálo Vounó

Límni Kerioú

Laganás

Argási

Kerí

Kalamáki

Marathiá Caves

Mount Kakavakia 413m

Marathoníssi

Mount Skopós 492m

Kamínia

Dháfni

Pórto Zóro

Peloúzo

Áno Vassilikós

Banana

Áyios Nikólaos

Yérakas

Pórto Róma

N

Pessádha (Kefalloniá)

Kyllíni

0   5 km

Zákynthos town

The town, like the island, is known as both **ZÁKYNTHOS** and Zante. This former "Venice of the East" (*Zante, Fior di Levante*, "Flower of the Levant", in an Italian jingle), rebuilt on the old plan after the 1953 earthquake, has bravely tried to re-create some of its style, though reinforced concrete can only do so much.

Arrival and information

Zákynthos is a working town with limited concessions to tourism, although there are hotels and restaurants aplenty, and it's the only place to stay if you want to see the island by public transport. The **bus** station is one block back from the seafront, about halfway along it. On the front nearby, the **tourist police** have a fairly welcoming office (May–Oct daily 8am–10pm; ☎26950 24482) in the main police station, which can supply basic information and help people find accommodation.

Accommodation

The Room Owners Association (☎26950 49498) can be contacted for accommodation around town and all over the island. Of the central seafront **hotels**, the *Egli*, on Loútzi (☎26950 28317; ❹) is the best bet, tucked in beside the gargantuan eyesore of the *Strada Marina*. There are quieter hotels in the Repára district beyond Platía Solomoú: try either the *Plaza*, Kolokotróni 2 (☎26950 45733, ℱ26950 48909; ❸), or the classy and surprisingly inexpensive ⚓ *Palatino*, Kolokotróni 10 (☎26950 27780, ⓦwww.palatinohotel.gr; ❹), both near the municipal lido. Cheaper options at the back of town include the cosy *Haravyi pension*, Xanthopoúlou 4 (☎26950 23629; ❷), to the south.

The town

The town stretches beyond the length of the wide and busy harbour, its main section bookended by the grand **Platía Solomoú** at the north, and the church of **Áyios Dhionýsios** (daily 7am–1pm & 5–10pm), patron saint of the island, at the south. The church is well worth a visit for the dazzling giltwork and fine modern murals inside, and a new **museum**, which has some fine paintings and icons (daily 9am–1pm & 5–9pm; €2). The vestments of St Dhionysios are kept in the restored church of Áyios Nikólaos tou Mólou on Platía Solomoú. The **square** is named after the island's most famous son, the poet Dhionysios Solomos, the father of modernism in Greek literature, who was responsible for establishing demotic Greek (as opposed to the elitist *katharévousa* form) as a literary idiom. He is also the author of the lyrics to the national anthem, an excerpt from which adorns the statue of Liberty in the square. There's an impressive **museum** (daily 9am–2pm; €3) devoted to the life and work of **Solomos** and other Zakynthian luminaries in nearby Platía Ayíou Márkou. It

Boat trips from Zákynthos

At least ten pleasure craft offer **day-trips** around the island from the quay in Zákynthos Town for around €15. All take in sights such as the **Blue Caves** at Cape Skinári, and moor in **To Naváyio (Shipwreck Bay)** and the **Cape Kerí** caves. You might want to shop around for the trip with the most stops, as eight hours bobbing round the coast can become a bore. Check also that the operators actually take you into the caves.

△ Zákynthos's famed Shipwreck Bay

shares its collection with an eponymous museum on Corfu (see p.1005), where Solomos spent most of his life. Another local man of letters, who had a museum dedicated to him by the town council in 1998, is novelist and playwright **Grigorios Xenopoulos**. His eponymous **museum** (Mon–Fri 9am–2pm; free), which occupies the small house he inhabited in Gaïta street, not far from Áyios Dhionýsios church, displays a modest collection of manuscripts, books and photographs, as well as the house's original furniture.

Platía Solomoú is home to the town's **library**, which has a small collection of pre- and post-quake photography, and the massive **Byzantine Museum** (Tues–Sun 8am–2.30pm; €3), sometimes referred to as the Zákynthos Museum, most notable for its collection of artworks from the Ionian School, the region's post-Renaissance art movement, spearheaded by Zakynthian painter Panayiotis Doxaras. The movement was given impetus by Cretan refugees, unable to practise their art under Turkish rule. It also houses some secular painting and a fine model of the town before the earthquake.

Zákynthos's other main attraction is its massive **kástro**, brooding over the hamlet of Bóhali on its bluff above the town. The ruined Venetian fort (daily 8am–7.30pm in summer, 8am–2pm in winter; €1.50) has vestiges of dungeons, armouries and fortifications, plus stunning views in all directions. Its shady carpet of fallen pine needles makes it a great spot to relax or picnic. Below the *kástro* walls, **Bóhali** has a good though expensive taverna with panoramic views. The ugly new **amphitheatre** on the road up from town sometimes hosts concerts. Further towards the *kástro* the **Maritime Museum** (daily 9am–2pm & 6–9pm; €2.50) contains plenty of naval paraphernalia and presents an interesting chronological history of Hellenic seafaring.

Eating, drinking and nightlife

Most of the **restaurants** and bars on the seafront and Platía Ayíou Márkou are bedevilled by traffic, although the seafront *Psaropoula* does fine meat and fish, and the pricey but elegant *Komis*, across the quay from Áyios Dhionýsios, serves unusual seafood dishes and is far enough away from the bustle. First stop though, should be the friendly ⚲ *Arekia* beyond the lido, which offers a succulent range of dishes and the best nightly *kantádhes* to be heard anywhere. The *Green Boat*, further along, serves up quality fare in a romantic waterside setting. When the bored teens get off their bikes, they go **clubbing** to bars like *Base* on Ayíou Márkou, which plays anything from ethnic to trance, or the *Jazz Café*, on Tertséti which, despite the name, is actually a techno bar with DJs and a token cover charge.

The south and west

The busy southern end of the island comprises the **Vassilikós peninsula**, headed by the package resort of **Argási**, and the large sweep of **Laganás Bay**, whose resort of the same name is a major party destination. At the far southwest end of the bay, the landscape ascends into the mountains around **Kerí**, the first of a series of villages along the sparsely inhabited **west coast**.

Argási

The road heading southeast from Zákynthos passes through **ARGÁSI**, the busiest resort on this coast, but with a beach barely a few feet wide in parts. Although independent travellers would be better off basing themselves at one of the places further down, it could be used as a jumping-off point for the Vassilikós peninsula; there are rooms at the *Pension Vaso* (☎26950 44599; ❸) and *Soula* (☎26950 44864; ❸) just off the main road entering the village, and the seafront boasts some smart hotels, among them the *Locanda* (☎26950 45386, ☎26950 23769; ❹) and the *Iliessa Beach* (☎26950 27800, ⓦwww.iliessa.com; ❹). Beyond a few indigenous tavernas – try *Three Brothers* or *The Big Plate* restaurant – culture is mainly lowbrow with set-piece "Greek nights", one notable exception being the *Venetsiana*, which accompanies traditional food with nightly *kantádhes*. Argási is also home to some of the island's biggest and most popular discos on the town side, such as *Vivlos* and *Barrage*, and a host of cheap and cheerful bars in the village.

The Vassilikós peninsula

The peninsula that stretches southeast of Argási is one of the most attractive parts of the island, with a happy blend of development and natural beauty.

Various maps vaguely identify different inland spots as **Vassilikós** villages, but the real interest lies in the series of small beach resorts, mainly situated on the east coast. The first two are recently developed **Kamínia**, with the comfortable *Levantino* rooms (℡26950 35366, ⓦwww.levantino.gr; ❹), and the more established **Pórto Zóro**, a better strand with the good-value eponymous hotel (℡26950 35304, ⓦwww.portozorro.gr; ❸) and restaurant. The only real facilities away from the coast are to be found at the sprawling village of **Áno Vassilikós**, which serves the nearby beaches of **Iónio** and **Banana**. Among accommodation possibilities are the *Vassilikos Apartments* (℡26950 35280; ❸), on the main road, and *Angelika* (℡26950 35201; ❷), by the church just off it. Among the **tavernas**, on the main road, *O Adherfos tou Kosta* is well worth a try, as is the *Logos Rock Club*. Isolated **Áyios Nikólaos** has a good beach and lures day-trippers from Argási, Kalamáki and Laganás with a **free bus** service in season. Its expanding *Vasilikos Beach* (℡26950 35325, ⓦwww .hotelvasilikosbeach.gr; ❺) complex is the focal point of a fast-emerging hamlet with a few restaurants and rooms – the neat white *Christina's* (℡26950 39474; ❷) is one of the best deals on the island.

At the very tip of the peninsula is its star: **Yérakas**, a sublime crescent of golden sand. It's also a key loggerhead turtle breeding ground, and is therefore off-limits between dusk and dawn; the excellent open-air **Turtle Information Centre** (ⓦwww.earthseasky.org) provides interesting background on these and other sea creatures. Otherwise, there's little here beyond three tavernas back from the beach – try *To Triodi* – and some pleasant, if remote, cabin accommodation at *Liuba Apartments* (℡26950 35372; ❸). The beach does draw crowds, but the 6am bus out of Zákynthos Town should secure you a few hours of Yérakas to yourself. Compared with Yérakas, **Pórto Róma**, back on the east coast, is a disappointment, a small sand-and-pebble bay with a taverna and bar, some rooms on the approach road and occasional hardy campers, although there is a more genuinely Greek flavour to it. The only beach on the west coast of the peninsula really worth visiting, especially in the quieter months, is **Dháfni**; the road to it is now paved and there are a couple of tavernas, such as the fine *Mela Beach*.

Laganás and Kalamáki

The majority of the hundreds of thousands of people who visit Zákynthos each year find themselves in **LAGANÁS**. The nine-kilometre beach in the bay is good, if trampled, and there are entertainments from watersports to ballooning, and even an occasional funfair. Beachfront bars and restaurants stretch for well over a kilometre, the bars and restaurants on the main drag another kilometre inland. Some stay open around the clock; others just play music at deafening volume until dawn. The competing video and music bars can make Laganás at night resemble the set of *Bladerunner*, but that's how its predominantly English visitors like it. If this is your bag, there's no place better; if it isn't, flee. **Accommodation** is mostly block-booked by package companies. There's a basic campsite on the southern edge of town, where there are also quietish private rooms, or you can contact the Union of Room Owners (daily 8.30am–2pm & 5–8pm; ℡26950 51590). As for hotels, try the old-fashioned *Byzantio* (℡26950 51136; ❸), near the crossroads, *Pension Tasoula* (℡26950 51560; ❸), between the beach and the campsite, or the larger *Ionis* (℡26950 51141, ⓦwww.hotelionis.com; ❹), on the main drag towards the beach. *Dionysos*, halfway along the main drag, and *Zougras*, just before the river along the Kalamáki road, are among the more authentic **tavernas**, the latter hosting *kantádhes* most nights, and respectable Chinese and Indian food can be had at *Bee Garden* or *Taj Mahal* respectively. Favourite **bars** include *Kamikazi*, *Must*, *Potters Bar* and *Zeros* nightclub.

Neighbouring **KALAMÁKI** has a better beach than Laganás, and is altogether quieter, although it does suffer from some airport noise. There are several sizeable, mostly package-oriented hotels, but the upmarket *Crystal Beach* (☎26950 42788, Ⓦwww.crystalbeachhotel.info; ❻) keeps some rooms aside and the islandwide Spring Tours agency (☎26950 43795, Ⓦwww.springtours.gr; ❸) can also arrange accommodation. The two *Stanis* tavernas have extensive menus of Greek and international dishes, although the beachside version is geared more to lunches and its sibling more to evening meals. Alternatives include the standard *Afrodite* and *Merlis* tavernas or the *Guru* curry house. **Nightlife** centres around bars like the *Rose'n'Crown* and *Down Under* on the Laganás road, and the *Cave Club* or *Byzantio* discos on the hillside above the village, which play the usual mixture of foreign and Greek dance music.

Kerí

The village of **KERÍ** is hidden in a fold above the cliffs at the island's southernmost tip. The village retains a number of pre-quake, Venetian buildings, including the church of the **Panayía Kerioú**; the Virgin is said to have saved the island from marauding pirates by hiding it in a sea mist. A rough path leaving the southern end of the village leads 1km on to the lighthouse, with spectacular

---

Loggerhead turtles

The Ionian islands harbour the Mediterranean's main concentration of **loggerhead sea turtles**, a sensitive species which is, unfortunately, under direct threat from the tourist industry. Easily frightened by noise and lights, these creatures lay their eggs at night on sandy coves and are therefore uneasy cohabitants with rough campers and late-night discos. Each year, many turtles fall prey to motorboat injuries, nests are destroyed by bikes and the newly hatched young die, entangled in deckchairs and umbrellas left out at night.

The Greek government has passed laws designed to protect the loggerheads, including restrictions on camping at some beaches, but local economic interests tend to prefer a beach full of bodies to a sea full of turtles. On Laganás, nesting grounds are concentrated around the fourteen-kilometre bay, and Greek marine zoologists are in angry dispute with those involved in the tourist industry. Other important locations include the turtles' nesting ground just west of Skála on Kefaloniá, although numbers have dwindled to half their former strength, and now only about 800 remain. Ultimately, the turtles' best hope for survival may rest in their potential draw as a unique tourist attraction in their own right.

While capitalists and environmentalists are still at, well, loggerheads, the **World Wildlife Fund** has issued guidelines for visitors:

1. Don't use the beaches of Laganás and Yérakas between sunset and sunrise.
2. Don't stick umbrellas in the sand in the marked nesting zones.
3. Take your rubbish away with you – it can obstruct the turtles.
4. Don't use lights near the beach at night – they can disturb the turtles, sometimes with fatal consequences.
5. Don't take any vehicle onto the protected beaches.
6. Don't dig up turtle nests – it's illegal.
7. Don't pick up the hatchlings or carry them to the water, as it's vital to their development that they reach the sea on their own.
8. Don't use speedboats in Laganás Bay – a 9kph speed limit is in force for vessels in the bay.

views of the sea, rock arches and stacks and a taverna. The beach next to **Límni Kerioú** at the southwestern end of Laganás Bay has developed into a laid-back and picturesque resort and is home to the Turtle Beach Diving Centre (℡26950 48768, ⓦwww.diving-center-turtle-beach.com). **Rooms** can be found at the friendly *Pension Limni* (℡26950 48716, ⓦwww.pensionlimni.com; ❸) or through the local Room-Owners Association (℡ & 🄵26950 45105). For **food** there is the *Poseidon* overlooking the bay from the far end and the *Keri* restaurant, which has good daily specials.

Maherádho, Kilíómeno and Kambí

The bus system does not reach the wild western side of the island, but a rental car or sturdy motorbike will get you there. **MAHERÁDHO** boasts impressive pre-earthquake architecture set in beautiful arable uplands, surrounded by olive and fruit groves. The church of **Ayía Mávra** has an impressive free-standing campanile and, inside, a splendid carved iconostasis and icons. The town's major festival – one of the biggest on the island – is the saint's day, which falls on the first Sunday in June. The other notable church in town, that of the Panayía, commands breathtaking views over the central plain.

KILÍÓMENO is the best place to see surviving pre-earthquake domestic architecture, in the form of the island's traditional two-storey houses. The town was originally named after its church, **Áyios Nikólaos**, whose impressive campanile, begun over a hundred years ago, still lacks a capped roof. The *Alitzerini* taverna (usually supper only) still occupies a cave-like house that dates from 1630 and dishes up superb traditional food. The road from Kilíómeno passes through the nondescript village of Áyios Léon, from where two turnings lead through fertile land and down a newly-paved loop road to the impressive rocky coast at **Limniónas**, where there is a tiny bay and a taverna.

Further along the main road another turning leads to the tiny clifftop hamlet of **KAMBÍ**, popular with day-trippers, who come to catch the sunset over the sea; there are extraordinary views to be had of the 300-metre-high cliffs and western horizon from Kambí's three clifftop **tavernas**. The best of the three is named after the imposing concrete **cross** above the village, constructed in memory of islanders killed here during the 1940s, either by royalist soldiers or Nazis. The tiny village of **Mariés**, 5km to the north and set in a wooded green valley, has the only other coastal access on this side of Zákynthos, a seven-kilometre track leading down to the rocky inlet of **Stenítis Bay**, where there's a taverna and yacht dock, and another road to the uninspiring **Vrómi Bay**, from where speedboats run trips to Shipwreck Bay (see p.1047).

The north

A few kilometres north of the capital the contiguous resorts of **Tsiliví** and **Plános** are the touristic epicentre of this part of the island. Further north they give way to a series of tiny beaches, while picturesque villages punctuate the lush landscape inland. Beyond **Alykés**, as you approach the island's tip at **Cape Skinári**, the coast becomes more rugged, while the mountains inland hide the weaving centre of **Volímes**.

Tsiliví, Plános and around

North and inland from Zákynthos Town, the roads thread their way through luxuriantly fertile farmland, punctuated with tumulus-like hills. **Tsiliví**, 5km north of the capital, is the first beach resort here, and is in effect one with the hamlet of **PLÁNOS** and matches Argási for development. Unfortunately, this part of the coastline suffers from occasional oil pollution, with nothing but the winter storms to clear it. There's a good, basic **campsite**, *Zante Camping* (T 26950 61710), beyond Plános, and, for a prime package-tour location, a surprising variety of accommodation – try the beachside *Anetis Hotel* (T 26950 44590, F 26950 28758; ❸), which has air conditioning and TV in all rooms; *Gregory's* rooms (T 26950 61853; ❷); or contact Tsilivi Travel (T 26950 44194, E akis-125@otenet.gr; from ❷), on the inland road in from town. *The Olive Tree* taverna is the best of a touristy bunch, while the *Mandarin* Chinese is fairly authentic. Pubs such as *The Local* and *Red Lion* tend to be Brit-oriented.

The beaches further along this stretch of coast become progressively quieter and pleasanter, and they all have at least a smattering of accommodation and restaurants to choose from. Good choices include **Pahiá Ámmos**, with the *Pension Petra* (T 26950 61175; ❷) and *Porto Roulis* fish taverna. Also recommended is **Dhrossiá**, where you can find the *Avouris* (T 26950 61716; ❷) and *Drosia* apartments (T 26950 62256; ❸) and eat at another popular fish taverna, *Andreas*.

Alykés and its bay

Órmos Alykón, 12km north of Tsiliví, is a large sandy bay with lively surf and two of the area's largest resorts. The first, **ALIKANÁS**, is a small but expanding village, much of its accommodation being overseas villa rentals; the second, **ALYKÉS**, named after the spooky salt pans behind the village, has the best beach north of the capital. There are **rooms** near the beach, most easily found through the local branch of Spring Tours (T 26950 83035, W www.springtours.gr; from ❷), and a number of **hotels** set back from it, but with sea views – try the *Ionian Star* (T 26950 83416, W www.ionian-star.gr; ❸) or the *Montreal* (T 26950 83241, W www.montreal.gr; ❹), although the best deal is off the crossroads at the chaotic *Eros Piccadilly* (T 26950 83606, W www.erospiccadilly.com; ❷). There are many eating joints, among the best the *Vineleaf*, which has unusual items such as jalapeño peppers stuffed with cream, and more standard *Fantasia* and *Ponderosa* tavernas. Alykés is the last true resort on this coast, and the one where the bus service largely gives out. **Xygiá** beach, 4km north, has sulphur springs flowing into the sea – follow the smell – which provide the odd sensation of swimming in a mix of cool and warm water. The next small beach of **Makrýs Yialós**, which has a good taverna and makeshift campsite, also makes for an extremely pleasant break on a tour of the north.

Áyios Nikólaos, 6km on, is a small working port serving daily ferries to and from Pessádha on Kefalloniá. Few visitors **stay** here, which perhaps explains why it hosts one of the most exclusive establishments in the Ionian, the classy stone *Nobelos* apartments (T 26950 31131, W www.nobelos.gr; ❽), as well as the more modest *Panorama* (T 26950 31013, E panorama@altecnet.gr; ❸). Pre-ferry meals can be had at *La Storia* fish restaurant or *Orizodes* taverna. From here there are trips by **kaïki** (€8) to the extreme northern tip of the island, where the **Blue Caves** are some of the more realistically named of the many contenders in Greece. They're terrific for snorkelling, and when you go for a dip here your skin will appear bright blue. The road snakes onwards through a landscape of gorse bushes and dry-stone walls until it ends at the lighthouse of **Cape Skinári**. With only a taverna and a cafeteria, and a view of the mountainous expanse of Kefalloniá, it's a good spot for unofficial camping, or you could stay in the unique setting of a converted windmill rented out by *To Faros* taverna (T 26950 31132; ❺), whose friendly family also run the cheapest boat trips to the Blue Caves (€7; €15 combined with Shipwreck Bay).

Katastári, Ayía Marína and Volímes

The northern towns and villages are best explored with a car or sturdy motor-bike, although there are guided coach tours from the resorts and limited bus services. Two kilometres inland from Alykés, **KATASTÁRI** is the largest settlement after the capital. Precisely because it's not geared towards tourism, it's the best place to see Zakynthian life as it's lived away from the usual racket. Its most impressive edifice is the huge rectangular church of Iperáyia Theotókos, with a twin belfry and small new amphitheatre for festival performances. *To Kendro psistariá* does tasty grills at rock-bottom prices. A couple of kilometres south of Katastári, the tiny hamlet of **Pighadhákia** is the unlikely setting for the **Vertzagio Cultural Museum** (summer daily 9am–3pm & 5–7pm; €3), which houses an interesting array of agricultural and folk artefacts. There is also the diminuitive **Áyios Pandeléïmon** chapel, which has the unusual feature of a well, hidden beneath the altar. Just above it the *Kaki Rahi* taverna provides tasty local cuisine.

AYÍA MARÍNA, a few kilometres southwest of Katastári, has a church with an impressive Baroque altar screen, and a belfry that's being rebuilt from the remnants left after the 1953 earthquake. As in most Zákynthos churches, the bell tower stands detached, in Venetian fashion. Just above Ayía Marína is the *Parthenonas* taverna, rightly boasting one of the best views on the island. From here you can see the whole of the central plain from beyond Alykés in the north to Laganás Bay in the south.

VOLÍMES is the centre of the island's embroidery industry and numerous shops sell artefacts produced here. With your own transport, you could make it to the **Anafonítria monastery**, 3km south, thought to have been the cell of the island's patron saint, Dhionysios, whose festivals are celebrated on August 24 and December 17. A paved road leads on to the cliffs overlooking **Shipwreck Bay** (Naváyio), with hair-raising views down to the shipwreck (a cargo ship which ran aground in the Sixties), and a taverna to regain your composure in.

Travel details

Ferries

The following listings are based on summer schedules, which are often reduced drastically in winter; any services that stop altogether are marked as being summer only. Tourist craft and *kaïkia* are not included below.

Corfu:
Corfu Town to: Eríkoussa/Mathráki/Othoní (3 weekly; 2–4hr); Igoumenítsa (every 10–45min; 1hr 15min); Pátra (6–10 daily; 7–9hr).
Lefkími to: Igoumenítsa (6 daily; 40min).

Ithaka:
Fríkes to: Fiskárdho (Kefalloniá; 1 daily; 1hr); Nydhrí (Lefkádha; daily; 1hr 30min).
Pisaetós to: Sámi (Kefalloniá; 3 daily; 45min).

Vathý to: Astakós (1 daily; 2hr 30min); Pátra (2 daily; 3hr 30min); Sámi (Kefalloniá; 2 daily; 1hr).

Kefalloniá:
Argostóli to: Kyllíni (1 daily; 2hr 15min); Lixoúri (every 30min; 20min).
Fiskárdho to: Fríkes (Itháki; 1 daily; 1hr); Nydhrí (Lefkádha; 1 daily; 2hr 15min); Vassilikí (Lefkádha; 2 daily; 1hr).
Pessádha to: Áyios Nikólaos (Zákynthos; 2 daily May–Sept; 1hr 30min).
Póros to: Kyllíni (3–5 daily; 1hr 15min).
Sámi to: Astakós (1 daily; 2hr 30min); Corfu Town (2 weekly; 5hr); Pátra (1–2 daily; 3hr 30min); Pisaetós (Itháki; 3 daily; 40min); Vathý (Itháki; 1–2 daily; 1hr).

Lefkádha:
Nydhrí to: Fiskárdho (Kefalloniá; 1 daily; 2hr 15min); Fríkes (Itháki; 1 daily; 1hr 30min); Meganíssi (7 daily; 20min).
Vassilikí to: Fiskárdho (Kefalloniá; 2 daily; 1hr); Fríkes (Itháki; 1 daily; 2hr).

Paxí:
Gáïos to: Igoumenítsa (1–2 daily; 1hr).

Zákynthos:
Zákynthos Town to: Kyllíni (7 daily; 1hr 30min).
Áyios Nikólaos to: Pessádha (Kefalloniá; 2 daily May–Sept; 1hr 30min).

International Ferries

Corfu Town is a main stop on many of the ferry routes to Italy from Pátra and a stopover can be added for free with many companies. The frequency and journey time to the various Italian ports is: Ancona (1–2 daily; 14hr); Bari (2–3 daily; 11hr); Brindisi (3–5 daily; 4–9hr); and Venice (2–3 weekly; 25hr).

Hydrofoils

Corfu Town to: Gáïos (Paxí; 3–7 daily; 50min).
Gáïos to: Corfu Town (3–7 daily; 50min).

Buses

Corfu:
Corfu Town to: Athens (3 daily; 10–11hr); Thessaloníki (1 daily; 9–10hr).

Kefalloniá:
Argostóli to: Athens (4 daily; 7–8hr); Pátra (1 daily; 4–5hr).
Póros to: Athens (1 daily; 6–7hr).
Sámi to: Athens (2 daily; 6–7hr).

Lefkádha:
Lefkádha Town to: Athens (1 daily; 2hr 15min); Pátra (2 weekly; 3hr 30min); Préveza (4 daily; 30min); Thessaloníki (2 weekly; 10–11hr).

Zákynthos:
Zákynthos Town to: Athens (5–6 daily; 6hr); Pátra (4 daily; 3hr); Thessaloníki (3 weekly; 11–12hr).

Flights

All domestic flights listed below are on Olympic or Aegean except for the new seaplane service from Corfu to Paxí and Ioánnina. For international flights see "Basics" p.29.
Corfu to: Athens (4–8 daily; 1hr); Kefalloniá (1 weekly; 1hr 10min); Paxí (2–3 daily; 20min); Préveza (1 weekly; 25min); Ioánnina (10 weekly; 40min); Zákynthos (1 weekly; 1hr 55min).
Kefalloniá to: Athens (1–2 daily; 1hr); Corfu (1 weekly; 1hr 10min); Préveza (1 weekly; 25min); Zákynthos (1 weekly; 25min).
Zákynthos to: Athens (1–2 daily; 55min); Corfu (1 weekly; 1hr 55min); Kefalloniá (1 weekly; 25min); Préveza (1 weekly; 1hr 15min).

Contexts

Contexts

A History of Greece

The geographical position of Greece on the Mediterranean and at the crossroads of Europe, Asia and Africa has long presented it with unique opportunities and dangers. The Greeks are a people who have suffered calamities, yet they have also achieved the highest reaches of human accomplishment. In the areas of politics, philosophy, literature, science and art, Greece has influenced Western society more than any other nation in history. After four thousand years the Greek language continues to be spoken and remains as vigorous as ever, while the culture and the identity of the Greeks have been forged and tempered by a remarkable history. Now, as Greece enters the twenty-first century, there is much to learn about its present condition, and about our own, from understanding the Greek past.

Prehistoric Greece: to 2100 BC

Evidence of human habitation in Greece goes back half a million years, as demonstrated by the discovery in 1976 of the skeleton of a **Neanderthal** youth embedded in a stalagmite in the **Petralóna Cave**, 50km east of the northern city of Thessaloníki. Cooked animal remains were found amid debris in the floor of the cave at a level corresponding to **500,000 years ago**, which makes this the earliest known site of a man-made fire in Europe.

Only very much later, about **40,000 years ago**, did **Homo sapiens**, the anatomically modern form of man from which we are descended, make his first appearance in Greece after migrating out of Africa. Several sites occupied by Homo sapiens have been identified in **Epirus** in northwest Greece, where they used tools and weapons of bone, wood and stone to gather wild plants and hunt. Even between **20,000 and 16,000 years ago**, when the Ice Age was at its peak, **Stone Age man** continued to make a home in Greece, though it was only when the glaciers finally receded about **10,000 BC** that a considerably warmer climate set in, altering the Greek environment to something more like that of present times.

The Neolithic period

Agricultural communities first appeared in **Macedonia** around **6500 BC** and in **Thessaly** a thousand years later. But whether agriculture developed indigenously or was introduced to Greece by migrants from Asia Minor where animal husbandry and crop cultivation had already been practised for two thousand years cannot be determined conclusively from the archeological evidence. What is certain, however, is agriculture's revolutionary effect.

When leading their hunter-gatherer way of life, the Stone Age inhabitants of Greece had been almost entirely at the mercy of nature; but now for the first time they were able to produce their own food and assure themselves of a more ample and certain supply. They built mud brick houses which they stood on stone foundations as if announcing their intention to stay; they sowed seeds and reaped harvests season after season. Though still reliant on stone technology, this new farming culture was a significant break with the past, so that from 6500 BC a "new stone age" or **Neolithic Period** is said to have begun in Greece.

As the strong variety of flint needed for weapons and tools was rare in Greece, the mainlanders imported obsidian, the hard black glassy stone formed by rapidly cooling volcanic lava, found on the island of **Melos** (Mílos) in the southern Cyclades. This was the earliest **seaborne trade** known anywhere in the world and clearly involved a mastery of building and handling boats.

Cycladic culture and trade

In about **3000 BC** a new people settled in the **Cyclades**, probably from Asia Minor, bringing with them the latest metallurgical techniques. They continued the old trade in obsidian, but they also developed the **trade in tin** and were making prodigious voyages westwards as far as Spain by 2500 BC. The mining of **gold and silver** in the Cyclades may have dated from this period, too. Long before Crete or the Greek mainland, these new inhabitants of the islands became specialists in **jewellery-making**, **metalwork** and **stone-cutting**.

From the marble in which the Cyclades abound, they sculpted statuettes, most of which were female figures. Slender, spare and geometric, these **Cycladic sculptures** are startlingly modern in appearance, and have inspired admiration and imitation from such artists as Epstein, Brancusi, Modigliani and Henry Moore. Usually described as idols, the statuettes were probably used in worship, as well as in burials – where they were perhaps intended as spirit guides. They were exported widely, to Crete and mainland Greece. Indeed during the Early Bronze Age the Eastern Mediterranean witnessed a proliferation in the manufacture and trade of **ritual objects**, probably because ritual itself was becoming more elaborate as societies grew wealthier, more complex and hierarchical.

The beginnings of the Greek Bronze Age

In about 3000 BC, also from the Cyclades, bronze technology was introduced to the mainland, marking the beginning of the **Bronze Age** in Greece. By **2500 BC** the widespread use of bronze and the acquisition of metallurgical techniques had transformed farming and fighting throughout the Eastern Mediterranean and the Middle East.

This rapid spread of bronze technology was due to a well-established network of long-distance trade. Great **palace-cities** had grown up in the Middle East as the culmination of the agricultural revolution and the consequent increase in wealth and population; all political and economic activities were administered from the palace which stood at the centre of these cities, including the trade in precious materials such as gold from Egypt, lapis lazuli from Afghanistan and timber from Lebanon.

To these were added **tin**, which when mixed with copper, a soft metal, created bronze, a tough alloy in demand for tools and weapons. But whereas copper was available locally almost everywhere throughout the Middle East and Europe, tin was a different matter. In the East it could be obtained only in isolated pockets of the Caucasus, Persia and Afghanistan, while in the West sources were confined to Cornwall, Brittany, northwest Spain and northern Italy. The Aegean became an important trade route, accounting for the burst of development that now took place along the eastern coast of **central Greece** and the **Peloponnese**, and on the **Aegean islands** which linked the Greek mainland to Asia Minor and the Middle East.

It is uncertain what **language** was spoken at this time on the mainland and the islands, but one thing is clear: it was not yet Greek. Indeed, when **Greek-speaking people** did arrive on the mainland in about 2100 BC their destructive impact, evident at sites like Lerna, paralysed its development for five hundred years, while the large and secure island of **Crete** – which they did not invade or settle – flourished and dominated the Aegean.

The coming of the Greeks

The destruction of numerous mainland sites in about **2100 BC**, followed by the appearance of a new style of pottery, has suggested to archeologists the violent arrival of a **new people**. They domesticated the horse, they introduced the potter's wheel, and they possessed considerable metallurgical skills. These newcomers replaced the old religion centred on female fertility figures with **hilltop shrines** which, it is believed, were dedicated to the worship of male sky gods like Zeus. And they brought with them a new language, an early form of **Greek**, though they were also obliged to adopt existing native words for such things as olives, figs, vines, wheat and the sea, suggesting that these new migrants or invaders may have come from some distant inland steppes where they had been pastoral highlanders, not farmers, fishermen or sailors.

The shock of domination was followed by five hundred years of adjustment and intermingling. The population increased, new settlements grew up, and there were advances in metallurgy. Yet in comparison with the Cyclades and Crete, which the invaders had never reached, the Greek mainland seems to have been a backward region, its archeological record sparse and unimpressive. Only around **1600 BC**, and then under the influence of Crete, did progress on the mainland quicken – until within little over a hundred years **Crete** itself was conquered by the Greek-speaking mainlanders.

Minoan and Mycenaean civilizations: 2100–1100 BC

The history of the Aegean during the second millennium BC can be seen as a struggle between two cultures, the **Mycenaean culture** of the **Greek mainland** and the **Minoan culture** of **Crete**. Situated halfway between mainland Greece and Asia Minor, Crete was favourably placed to take advantage of the Bronze Age boom in trade, and by the beginning of the second millennium BC it was the dominant power in the Aegean. Its distinctive civilization, called Minoan (a modern term derived from the island's legendary king Minos), and its beneficial economic influence were felt throughout the islands and also on the mainland. The Greek-speaking mainland invaders were "Minoanised", gradually developing a culture known as Mycenaean (after Mycenae, a principal mainland Bronze Age site) which owed a lot to Crete.

Minoan Crete

A large and fertile island with good natural harbours, **Crete**'s coastal plains and highland pastures provided the islanders with an abundance of crops and livestock, producing a surplus in oil and wool that were exported. Among the Cretans' most impressive tools, quite literally at the cutting edge of the new technology, was a four-foot-long bronze saw which readily converted the island's forest-clad mountains into an ample source of **timber for ships**. Some of this timber was probably also exported, most likely to treeless Egypt.

The excellence of Cretan craftsmanship meant that its metalwork, jewellery and pottery were commonly exported to the mainland and beyond. **Kamares ware**, as Cretan pottery of this period is known, was especially valued for its harmony between shape and decoration, its emphatic colours and the boldness of its designs from nature; it has been found all along the Cretans' 1400-mile-long maritime trade route to the East – on the Aegean islands of Rhodes and Sámos, on the coast of Asia Minor at Miletus, and in Syria and Egypt.

On Crete itself, Minoan power was concentrated on three vast **palace complexes** – at **Knossos**, **Phaestos** and **Malia**, all in the central segment of the island. First built around 2000 BC, their similarity of plan and their lack of significant defences suggest that some form of confederacy had by now replaced any regional rivalries on the island, while Minoan sea power induced a sense of security against foreign invasion. Like the palaces of the Middle East, these were all centres of political, economic and religious activity, though Minoan forms of worship also involved communing with the gods of nature at shrines in caves and on mountain tops. Not that prosperity was confined to the palace centres; the numerous remains of villas of the Minoan gentry and of well-constructed villages shows that the wealth generated by the palaces was redistributed among a significant proportion of the island's population. Following an **earthquake** around 1700 BC the palaces at Knossos and Phaestos were rebuilt, and a more modest palace was constructed at **Zakros** on the east coast, this activity coinciding with an apparent centralization of power at Knossos, whose ruler installed a vassal at Phaestos and seems to have united the entire island into a single kingdom, giving rise to a **Minoan golden age**.

Mycenaean dominance

But suddenly around **1500 BC** the Mycenaeans gained control of the palace of Knossos and were soon in full possession of Crete. How this happened is unknown, but probably it marked the culmination of a growing rivalry

The Trojan War

For the Greeks, the story of the **Trojan War** was the central event in their early history, and in their minds Homer's *Iliad* was more than a poem of heroic deeds sung at noble courts but the epic of their first great national adventure.

Excavations in the late nineteenth century by Heinrich Schliemann in fact uncovered many Troys of several periods, but the layer known as **Troy VIIa** clearly suffered violent destruction in about 1220 BC. The Mycenaeans are the likeliest perpetrators, though the abduction of a Greek beauty called **Helen** would not have been the only reason they launched a thousand ships against the Trojans. Rather a significant part of Mycenaean prosperity depended on trade with the Eastern Mediterranean, where the increasingly unsettled conditions made it imperative that the Mycenaeans secure their lines of **trade and supply**. Troy commanded a strategic position overlooking the Hellespont, the narrow waterway (today called the Dardanelles) dividing Europe and Asia and linking the Aegean to the Black Sea, where it controlled important trade routes, especially those for tin.

The capture of Troy was the last great success of the Mycenaeans, and perhaps for that reason it was remembered long after in poetry and song, inspiring later generations of Greeks in their dreams of overseas expansion, culminating in the fourth century BC with **Alexander the Great** who carried with him a copy of the *Iliad* when he marched across Asia, founding Greek cities as he went, and stood with his army on the banks of the Indus River.

△ The so-called "Death mask of Agamemnon", unearthed at Mycenae by Heinrickh Schliemann

between the Mycenaeans and the Minoans for control of the Aegean trade, which perhaps coincided with the effects of a **volcanic explosion** on the island of Thera (Thíra/Santoríni) and its consequent **tsunami**.

Greek now became the language of administration at Knossos and at the other former Minoan palaces, as well as on the mainland – indeed this is the earliest moment that the existence of the Greek language can definitely be identified, as from this point the palace records on Crete are written in a new script known as **Linear B**, which when deciphered in 1953 was shown to be a form of Greek. Having wrested control of the Aegean trade from the Minoans, the **Mycenaeans** enjoyed dominance for another three hundred years, at the end of that period famously laying siege to and destroying yet another rival, the city of **Troy** in about 1220 BC: the events that form the basis of Homer's great poetic narrative, the **Iliad**.

Yet within a generation the Mycenaean world was overwhelmed by a vast **migration** of northerners from somewhere beyond the Black Sea. Probably victims of a catastrophic change in climate which brought drought and famine to their homelands, these **Sea Peoples**, as the ancients called them, swept down through Asia Minor and the Middle East and also crossed the Mediterranean to Libya and Egypt, disrupting trade routes and destroying empires as they went. In Greece, invading marauders, whether Sea Peoples or others taking advantage of the wider disruption, burned and looted the mainland Mycenaean palace sites, causing the administrative and economic systems to collapse. Fleeing the destruction and chaos at home, a first wave of Greeks settled in **Cyprus**.

With the palace-based Bronze Age economies destroyed, the humbler **village-based economies** which replaced them lacked the concentration of wealth and the technological means to make a mark in the world. Instead Greece was plunged into a Dark Age, and knowledge of the Minoan and Mycenaean civilizations slipped into dim and uncertain memory.

The Dark Age and Awakening: 1150–720 BC

Massive migrations and the disruption of trade routes during the late Bronze Age helped undermine the great empires of the Middle East and destroyed the palace organization of Mycenaean civilization, casting Greece into a **Dark Age** of poverty, depopulation and isolation from the world. With the loss of trade, Greece became entirely dependent on agriculture and could no longer support anyone who did not work directly on the land. Many towns and villages were abandoned, and by about 1000 BC the population, which was now entirely illiterate, had fallen by sixty percent to its lowest level in a thousand years. During the next two centuries almost nothing of note was produced in architecture or sculpture, where crudely worked wood was the standard material used for temples and statues, and the backwardness of the times was reflected in the dominant religious image of the **xoanon**, a figure roughly shaped with the minimum of detail from a tree trunk.

Yet the darkness did not extend everywhere. **Athens** was something of an exception to the poverty and isolation that characterized Dark Age Greece, and the reason was **seaborne trade**. Escaping the destruction that accompanied the fall of Mycenaean civilization, Athens maintained trading links abroad and became the route through which the **Iron Age** was introduced to mainland Greece with the importation of iron weapons, implements and technological know-how in about 1100 BC. In Athens too a new cultural beginning was made in the form of pottery painted in the **Geometric style**, a highly intricate and controlled design which would lie at the heart of later Greek architecture, sculpture and painting.

Emigration

At the nadir of Greece's fortunes, many among its desperate population crossed the Aegean. In about 1125 BC Greeks began **emigrating** to the **Dodecanese islands** in the eastern Aegean, others in Cilicia along the south coast of **Asia Minor**, while a further wave of Greeks settled in **Cyprus** which now became Greek-speaking. Later, around 1000 BC, Greeks began settling in large numbers along the western coast of Asia Minor, a remarkable migration which continued for two hundred years until the Aegean became culturally and politically a Greek lake. The desire to escape poverty was probably the cause, though until recently many authorities believed that this second migration was the consequence of an invasion of mainland Greece by a Greek-speaking people from the north called the **Dorians**, who as they pushed their way southwards towards the Peloponnese uprooted the local populations who then fled across the sea. But modern research has turned up no archeological evidence for a Dorian invasion of Greece, and it seems more likely that a pattern of dialects had developed in the broken and mountainous landscape of Greece and was exported in turn to Asia Minor by enterprising migrants.

The Greeks had been a great seafaring people in Mycenaean times, but when the sea lanes were cut by the Sea Peoples, four hundred years of disruption to trade followed. Even during the tenth and ninth centuries BC, after their great migration to Asia Minor, the Greeks inhabited a world of limited horizons, with little evidence that they sailed beyond the Aegean or the Gulf of Corinth. Rather it was the **Phoenicians**, sailing from Sidon and Tyre in present-day

Lebanon, who opened up the old sea trading routes again during the eighth century BC, re-establishing contact between the Middle East and the Aegean world. But soon the Greeks were following in their wake, their ships sailing into the Eastern Mediterranean, where they established a trading station at Al Mina at the mouth of the Orontes as the Mycenaeans had done long before at Ugarit.

The city-state

From 750 BC Greek civilization developed with remarkable rapidity; no other people achieved so much over the next few centuries. The institution most responsible for this extraordinary achievement was the **city-state** or **polis**, where political responsibility belonged to the citizen who nevertheless operated within a disciplined collective ideal. The city-state came into being at a time of rapidly growing populations, greater competition for land and resources, increasing productivity and wealth, expanding trade and more complex relationships with neighbouring states. By mobilising manpower and resources to meet these new conditions, the city-state was expected to protect its citizens, ensure their liberty and provide them with opportunities.

Life not lived in a city-state, the Greeks believed, was semi-barbarous, for it provided the centralized and coordinated **political life** essential for a happy and rational existence. The city-state was small, perhaps only a few square miles and not more than a few hundred, but it was independent in all its affairs. It

Homer and the Iliad and the Odyssey

The **Iliad** and the **Odyssey**, the oldest and greatest works in Greek literature, were the brilliant summation of a long poetic tradition spanning five hundred years or so which had been developed by nameless bards whose recitations were originally accompanied by music. Completed by 725 BC, they are far older than the *Pentateuch*, the first five books of the Old Testament (*Genesis, Exodus, Leviticus, Numbers, Deuteronomy*), which achieved their finished form only in about 400 BC. The admiration of the whole Greek world for the Homeric epics was unique, and their influence upon the subsequent development of Greek literature, art and culture in general cannot be overstated. Few works, and probably none which have not been used in worship, have had such a hold on a nation for so many centuries.

But from time to time the old argument flares up again: did the blind poet **Homer** write the *Iliad* and the *Odyssey*? The best answer came from Mark Twain who said, "The *Iliad* and the *Odyssey* were written by the blind poet Homer or by another blind poet of the same name". For in truth, apart from being the name to which authorship of the poems is ascribed, virtually nothing is known of Homer beyond the tradition that he was blind and was born into the eighth-century BC world of the Asian Greeks, perhaps at Smyrna or opposite on the island of Híos.

The *Iliad* is the story of a few days' action in the tenth and final year of the Trojan War which recalls in its tales of heroic exploits the golden age of the Mycenaeans. The *Odyssey* begins after the war and follows the adventures of Odysseus who takes ten years to return to his island home of Ithaca on the western side of Greece, his voyages showing the new Greek interest during the eighth century BC in the geography to the northeast around the Black Sea and to the west towards Italy and Sicily. Taken together, the epics recover the past and look forwards into the future, and in this they are an Ionian achievement, for it was in Asia Minor that Greek civilization first and most shiningly emerged from the Dark Age. But they are also a celebration of an emerging **panhellenic identity**, of a national adventure encompassing both shores of the Aegean and beyond.

was governed by law, which even if at first unwritten was a guarantee against arbitrary justice, while the intimacy and intensity of city life released a boundless and versatile energy in **literature**, **art** and **philosophy**, while not the least of its achievements was the widescale **Greek colonization** of the **Western Mediterranean** and **Black Sea** which began after 750 BC.

The city-state became the Greek ideal, and by the early seventh century BC it had spread throughout Greece itself and wherever Greeks established colonies overseas. The city-state was a peculiarly Western institution; nothing like it developed in the East either then or later. It put political responsibility in the hands of its citizens; it was the birthplace of **democracy** and of equality before the law.

The revival of commerce with the East restored Greece to prosperity and stimulated the development of the city-state, which would be the foundation of Greek society for nearly a thousand years. Trade also acted as a cultural stimulus. Contact with other peoples made the Greeks aware of what they shared among themselves, and led to the development of a **national sentiment**, notably expressed and fostered by the **panhellenic sanctuaries** which arose during the eighth century BC, of **Hera** and **Zeus** at **Olympia**, where the first **Olympic Games** were held in 776 BC, and of **Apollo** and **Artemis** at **Delos**, as well as the **oracles** of **Zeus** at **Dodona** and of **Apollo** at **Delphi**.

From the Phoenicians the Greeks obtained the basics of the **alphabet**, which they adapted to their own tongue and developed into a sophisticated tool for recording laws, composing literature and chronicling events. **Greek art**, under Eastern influence, saw the Geometric style gradually give way to depicting animals, mythical and real, and finally around 750 BC, for the first time in four hundred years, **human figures** were introduced to vase decorations, most strikingly in group scenes with a story to tell. This was at about the same time as **Homer** was composing his great narrative epics, the **Iliad** and the **Odyssey**, which served not only as witnesses to the glories of the past but reflected also the reawakening of the present.

Expansion and Renaissance: 720–491 BC

The revival of seafaring and commerce in the early centuries of the first millennium BC contributed to the rise of the city-state around 750 BC, which in turn had two dramatic results that were as swift and fundamental as any in human history. One was the Greeks' **colonization movement** throughout the Mediterranean; the other was **radical social and political change** at home.

Colonization

The Greeks began by founding **colonies** in the Western Mediterranean, especially in **Sicily** and **southern Italy** which became known as **Greater Greece**, and a century later, around 650 BC, they began establishing colonies round the shores of the **Black Sea**. By the fifth century BC Greeks seemed to sit upon the shores of the entire world, in Plato's words like "frogs around a pond". Sometimes these colonies were founded on uninhabited land, but otherwise the native inhabitants, usually still living in the Bronze Age, were driven inland.

In any case the colonies were always Greek settlements, not the imposition of Greek rule and ways on non-Greeks.

One cause of the colonization movement was competition between the Greeks and the Phoenicians over trade routes; but there was also competition among the Greek city-states themselves, with **Chalkis**, **Eretria** and **Corinth** the major Greek colonisers in the West, while the **Ionian Greeks**, prevented from expanding into the interior of Asia Minor by Phrygia and Lydia, were the chief colonisers around the Black Sea. When the Spartans needed more land, they conquered neighbouring Messenia in 710 BC, but generally land shortage, and also famine, drove Greeks overseas, notably the colonists from Thera (Thíra) who were sent to found Cyrene in North Africa and were forbidden to return on pain of death. Sometimes the colonizing motive was political, with the aristocracies that ruled Greek city-states during the eighth and seventh centuries BC encouraging emigration to alleviate discontent, just as there were those who were happy to make a new life elsewhere rather than endure discrimination by the aristocracy at home. Yet the colonies, for whatever reason they were founded, usually kept up close relations with their mother cities, while the new city-states of Greater Greece in particular made a major contribution to the literature, philosophy and art of the Hellenic world.

Democracy, tyranny and slavery

In the city-states, which would be the foundation of Greek society for nearly a thousand years, tension arose between the **aristocracy** and the **people**, the one group defending privilege, the other demanding justice. Ultimately wealth from trade undermined the aristocracy and in place of their oligarchic form of government gave rise to **democracy** instead. A new **urban population** developed as commerce became more important relative to agriculture, and this doubtless helped the democratic movement. Ironically, the transition to democracy was often effected by **tyrannies** which were established in many city-states of Greece and Asia Minor around the middle of the seventh century BC. Though tyrants were virtual dictators, they never claimed to rule by divine right, and in theory were always responsible to the public interest, fulfilling the role of professional public servant or statesman. Usually they won power as champions of the people and in some cases were even elected by them; they inaugurated programmes of public works both to give jobs to the poor and to beautify their cities; and like the Renaissance Medicis they were patrons of culture, entertaining poets and seeking out the most brilliant architects and artists to built and adorn the local temples. Their type is illustrated by **Pisistratos**, tyrant of Athens during the sixth century BC, who ensured Athenian prosperity by gaining control of the route into the Black Sea, who ordered that Homer's works be set down in their definitive form and performed regularly at the Panathenaic festival, and who encouraged the theatrical festivals of Dionysus where Greek drama would be born.

Yet at about the same time as they were founding city-states, and faced with a shortage of free men to support the development of trade and manufacturing, Greeks turned to **slavery**, which they organized on a commercial scale from about 700 BC onwards. Previously, household slaves, as found in Homer, were usually war captives; their numbers were not many, nor was Greek society dependent on them. But during the seventh century BC slavery became a widespread, organized and pernicious institution, involving the import of large numbers from Thrace, Asia Minor and the coasts of the Black Sea.

Egypt and Lydia

With the opening up of **Egypt** to Greek traders in about the middle of the seventh century BC, that country was to exercise a profound influence on the culture of Greece, particularly in the fields of stone architecture and sculpture. But immediately more crucial was **Lydia**, on which for better or for worse the Greeks of Asia Minor were largely dependent, prospering on the trade that passed between the two, but always fearing that if Lydia grew too powerful it would threaten the independence of the Greek coastal cities.

Yet the ultimate importance of Lydia was as a buffer between Greece and the great empires of the East; it kept Greece from coming into direct contact with the empire of **Assyria**, and for sixty years it served as a bulwark between the Greeks and the **Persian empire**. But when that barrier was swept away, the course was set for two centuries of conflict between the West and East.

Athens and the Golden Age: 490–431 BC

The **Athenian Acropolis** was inhabited at least as far back as 5000 BC. Men were attracted by its natural springs and the defence provided by its precipitous height. The Mycenaeans fortified it; tyrants later imposed their rule from it. The Acropolis has these associations of primitive succour and power. But with the fall of the Pisistratid dictatorship in 510 BC the Athenians reserved the Acropolis to the exclusive inhabitation of their gods. It was an act of respect to the **deities** but also a shrewd political move by a people bent on democracy. Without tyrants over them and with their gods provided for, down below the citizens could say that they themselves should be the measure of all things. In the century that followed Athens achieved its apotheosis and lived a golden age.

Athenian democracy

Democracy in Athens and its hinterland of Attica was not the mass democracy of today. In all, the population amounted to not more than 400,000 people, of whom about 80,000 were slaves, 160,000 resident foreigners, and another 160,000 free-born Athenians. Out of this last category came the **citizens**, those who could vote and be elected to office, their number amounting to no more than 45,000 adult men.

Yet if the powers of democracy were in the hands of the few, the energy, boldness and creative spirit that it released raised Athens to greatness. Throughout the **fifth century BC** the political, intellectual and artistic activity of the Greek world was centred on the city. In particular Athens was the patron of **drama**, both tragedy and comedy. Whereas the patrons of lyric poetry were tyrants and the aristocracy, drama was the art of a democratic people. Without being necessarily tragic in the modern sense, Greek tragedy, which is to say **Athenian tragedy**, always addressed the great issues of life and death and the relationship of man to the gods. And indeed the Athenians themselves seemed to be conscious of living out a high drama as they fought battles, argued policy, raised temples and wrote plays that have decided the course and sensibility of Western civilization.

A high proportion of the ancient sites that can still be seen in Greece today were built as **shrines and temples to the gods**. They include spectacular sites such as Delphi and the Acropolis in Athens, but also very many other sanctuaries, great and small, in marketplaces and by roadsides, in cities and on islands, on mountaintops and headlands – everywhere, in fact, because the gods themselves were everywhere.

There were many lesser and local gods such as the Nymphs and Pan, but the great gods known to all were the **twelve** who lived on **Mount Olympus**. Ten were already recognised by Homer in the eighth century BC: **Zeus**, the lord of the heavens and supreme power on Olympus; **Hera**, his wife and sister, and goddess of fertility; **Athena** the goddess of wisdom, patron of crafts and fearless warrior; **Apollo** the god of music, of prophecy and the arts; his sister **Artemis**, the virgin huntress and goddess of childbirth; **Poseidon**, the god of the sea and the forces of nature; the beautiful **Aphrodite**, goddess of love and desire; **Hermes**, the messenger who leads the souls of the dead to the underworld, but also the protector of the home and of the market; **Hephaestus**, the lame god of craftsmen and for a while the husband of Aphrodite; and **Ares**, the god of war, who in cuckolding Hephaestus was subdued by the goddess of love. In the fifth century BC these were joined by two deities who had something of a mystical quality of rebirth about them: **Demeter**, the goddess of crops and female fertility; and **Dionysus**, the god of wine and intoxication.

Though limited in number, the Olympian deities could be made to play an infinite number of roles in local cult calendars by the addition of epithets, so that Zeus became "Zeus of the city" or "Zeus of mountaintops", as well as "kindly" or "fulfilling" as place and occasion required. The gods had human form, and they were born and had sexual relations among themselves and humankind, but they never ate human food nor did they age or die. Yet it is notable that whereas the gods of most nations claim to have created the world, the Olympians made no such claim. The most they ever did was to conquer it and then enjoy its fruits, not so unlike mankind itself.

These were the deities, worshipped, feared and admired, who formed the basis for the ancient Greek religion until **paganism** was banned throughout the newly Christianized Roman Empire in AD 391.

The Persian Wars

The wars between Greece and Persia began with a revolt against Persian rule by Ionian Greeks in Asia Minor. They were given support by Athens and Eretria, who in 498 burnt the city of Sardis in Asia Minor. This act of insolence provided a pretext for **Darius**, the Persian king, to launch a punitive expedition against the Greeks. But the **Persians'** unexpected repulse at **Marathon** in 490 BC demanded that Darius hurl his full military might against Greece to ensure its subjection once and for all to the Persian Empire.

When Darius died in 486 BC the execution of this plan was left to **Xerxes** who in 483 BC began preparations that lasted two years and were on a fabulous scale. Bridges of boats were built across the Hellespont near Abydos, modern Çanakkale, for Persia's vast imperial army to parade into Europe, and a canal was cut through the peninsular finger now occupied by the Mount Athos monasteries so that the Persian fleet could avoid the danger of storms while rounding the headlands of the Halkidhikí. Though the Greek historian **Herodotus** claimed that there were one million eight hundred thousand soldiers in Xerxes' army, his figure is probably a tenfold exaggeration. Even so, it was a massive force, an army of forty-six nations under Xerxes' command, dressed and armed according to the ways of their native lands – Persians, Medes

For the Athenians, victory in the **Battle of Marathon** set the seal on their democracy and marked the beginning of a new self-confident era. And indeed, it was the most remarkable of victories.

Fearing that it would be fatal to attack the larger numbers of Persian infantry supported by cavalry and archers, the Athenian army kept to its position astride the mountain pass leading into the plain of Marathon and waited there for Spartan reinforcements. On the fifth day the Persians gave up hope of joining battle at Marathon and embarked their cavalry to advance on Athens by sea, sending their infantry forwards to cover the operation. With the Persian forces divided, **Miltiades** saw his opportunity, Spartan help or no, and sent his hoplites racing downhill to get quickly under the hail of Persian arrows and engage their infantry in close combat. The Athenian centre was kept weak while the wings were reinforced, so that when the Persians broke through the centre of the charging line, the momentum of the Greek wings soon engulfed them on either side and to the rear. The Persians panicked, fell into disorder, and were beaten into the marshes and the sea. Seven Phoenician ships were lost and 6400 Persians killed. The 192 Athenian dead were buried on the spot, among them Kallimachos, and covered by a mound which can still be seen today. An unrecorded number of Plataeans also died.

The remainder of the Persian force now sailed round Cape Sounion to land within sight of the Acropolis at Phaleron, but Miltiades had brought the army back to Athens by forced march and stood ready to meet the enemy for the second time that day. That astonishing burst of energy – 10,000 men marching 26 miles in full armour after fighting one battle to fight, if need be, another – overwhelmed the Persians' morale, and their expedition returned to Asia.

and Cissians; Hyrcanians, Assyrians and Bactrians; Sacae, Indians, Ethiopians, Sarangians and Sagartians; Caspians, Colchians and Thracians, and many more. In addition, Xerxes' fleet of probably eight hundred triremes was furnished by Phoenicians, Egyptians, Cypriots, Cilicians, Pamphylians, Lycians, Carians and subject Ionian Greeks, his ships carrying almost as many sailors as there were soldiers in his army.

Yet both at sea off **Salamis** in 480 BC and on land at **Plataea** the following year, the might of Asia was routed. It was the culmination of that great theme that gives shape to Herodotus's history, the ancient struggle between Europe and Asia which he traced back to the walls of Troy. But it was not at Plataea that Herodotus quite completed his account. Within a few days of that battle came another, near **Miletus**. Following the defeat of his fleet at Salamis, Xerxes had feared a renewed uprising in Ionia, and so leaving his army under the command of Mardonius (who would die at Plataea) he came to Sardis to take charge of his reserves. The Ionians had indeed sent to Greece for help, and now a Greek fleet sailed for **Mycale**, off Samos, where the battle was won when Xerxes' subject Ionians went over to their fellow Hellenes. Xerxes could do no more than return to Susa, his capital deep in Persia, leaving the entire Aegean free.

Though there would be occasional reversals, this sudden shift in the balance of power between East and West would endure, so far as most of Asia Minor was concerned, for the next one thousand five hundred years. Within one hundred and fifty years Alexander the Great would achieve in Asia what Xerxes had failed to achieve in Europe, and the Persian Empire would succumb to a Greek conqueror.

Themistocles

The greatest Athenian statesman, and architect of the victory over Persia, was **Themistocles**. Since the Ionian revolt he understood that a clash between Persia and Greece was inevitable, and he had the genius to recognise that Athens' security and potential lay in its command of the sea. His great achievement was advancing its naval policy in the face of scepticism and opposition. He began the work when he was archon in 493–492 BC by developing **Piraeus** (Pireás) as the harbour of Athens, in place of the open roadstead of Phaleron. He used the hostility of the island of Aegina (Égina) to convince Athenians of his policy, but always his eyes were on the more distant but far greater Persian danger.

When the Persians marched into Attica in the late summer of 480 BC, the oracle at Delphi told the Athenians to trust in their wooden wall, which many took to mean the wooden wall built round the citadel of the Athenian Acropolis, but Themistocles argued that the prophecy referred to the Athenian fleet. Determined to fight at sea, Themistocles warned his Peloponnesian allies against retreating to the Isthmus where they too had built a wall, threatening that if they did the entire citizenry of Athens would sail in their ships to make new homes in southern Italy, leaving the rest of Greece to its fate. On the eve of the Battle of Salamis, as the Persians stormed the walls of the Acropolis, slaughtering its defenders and burning down its temples, the taunt came back from the Peloponnesians that Athens had no city anyway. But Themistocles replied that so long as the Athenians had 200 ships they had a city and a country.

The Greek victory at Salamis cut the Persians' maritime lines of supply and contributed to their defeat at Plataea the following year. Athens and its allies, who now had command of the sea, carried the war across the Aegean, and by the end of 479 BC succeeded in freeing the Greek cities of Asia Minor and the Hellespont from Persian rule. For his pains the Athenians later drove Themistocles into exile. He died at Magnesia on the Maeander, upriver from Miletus, where by way of a pension he was made governor by the Persian king.

The Rise of the Athenian Empire: 478–431 BC

The chronology of the period after the Persian invasion is sketchy: Herodotus ends his history with the capture of Sestos, and Thucydides managed only a scant narrative leading up to his account of the Peloponnesian War. But in outline the trend is clear. The first consequence of the Greek victory against the Persians was not, as might have been expected, the aggrandisement of **Sparta**, the pre-eminent Greek military power, whose soldiers had obediently sacrificed themselves at Thermopylae and had won the final mainland battle at Plataea. Instead, after the repulse of Persia many Greek city-states round the Aegean voluntarily placed themselves under the leadership of Athens.

This confederation was named the **Delian League** – after the island of Delos, sacred to Apollo, at the centre of the Cyclades where the allies kept their treasury – and its first task was to protect the Greeks of Asia Minor against a vengeful Xerxes and to reduce Persia's forward posts. This was the opposite of the policy proposed by Sparta and supported by its Peloponnesian allies, which called for the abandonment of Greek homes across the Aegean and the resettlement of Asian Greeks on the lands of those who had submitted to the Persians in northern Greece.

This policy was in keeping with the attitude shown by Sparta throughout the Persian crisis. Then Sparta had shown no initiative and acted only at the last minute; its policy was provincial, protecting its position in the Peloponnese rather than pursuing the wider interests of Greece. This narrowness and conservatism followed through into the peace. Sparta lacked vision and adventure and experience of the sea; what could not be achieved by land was impossible, it believed. Also Sparta lacked the mercantile ethos; it could not prosper on the widening opportunities presented by the opening of the sea routes to trade. And so over the coming decades Sparta lost prestige to Athens, which Themistocles had established as a maritime power and whose imperial potential was realised under Pericles.

This was the **Athenian golden age**, and in so far as Athens was also "the school of Hellas", as the city's leader **Pericles** said, it was a golden age for all Greece. The fifty years following Salamis and Plataea witnessed an extraordinary flowering in architecture, sculpture, literature and philosophy; men recognised the historical importance of their experience and gave it realisation through the creative impulse. Just as **Herodotus**, the "father of history", made the contest between Europe and Asia the theme of his great work, so **Aeschylus**, who fought at Marathon, made Xerxes the tragic subject of his play *The Persians* and in the process brought the art of drama to life. Indeed in the intoxicating

Aeschylus and Sophocles: The development of Greek tragedy

Tragedy was invented in Athens late in the sixth century BC at a time when peasants were settling in the city but were still in touch with their country traditions. Among these traditions was the fertility ritual celebrating the life and death of Dionysus, the god of the vine, who shed his blood for mankind. Goats were sacrificed in the worship of Dionysus, and so the ritual, in which a chorus danced and sang, was called *trag-odia*, a goat-song. In about 520 BC the story moved away from the Dionysus cycle and an actor was introduced who came and went, changing costumes and playing different roles in a succession of episodes.

Aeschylus changed things greatly by introducing a second actor and increasing the amount of dialogue, while correspondingly reducing the size and role of the chorus, so that tragedy truly became drama, driven by exchanges of words and actions. Aeschylus had fought at Marathon and probably at Salamis too, perhaps explaining the urgency of his play, *The Persians*, the oldest surviving Greek tragedy. Aeschylus was a religious man who believed in the overwhelming power of the gods, but he makes clear that it is man himself, through the free choices he makes rather than as a creature of fate, who steps into the appalling conflicts of the tragic situation.

By tradition four plays were submitted to Athens' annual Dionysian festival, three of them tragedies, the fourth a satyr play providing comic relief, and here too Aeschylus made an innovation, making his three tragedies successive phases of one story – famously in the late work of his maturity, the *Oresteia*, a great drama of revenge and expiation turning on Agamemnon's return home from the Trojan War and his murder. By this time Aeschylus was using a third actor and also painted scenery, ideas taken from **Sophocles**, his younger rival.

Sophocles' innovation of a third actor made it possible to present plots of considerable complexity. He was a man of orthodox piety; he was not in rebellion against the world; but it is a world of inescapable consequences, in his *Oedipus Rex*, for example, where to be unseeing is not enough, or in the *Antigone* which presents the ultimate tragic conflict – between right and right.

The effect of the tragedies of Aeschylus and Sophocles was to leave their audiences with an enhanced sense of pity or of terror; the unspoken moral being "You are in this too", the cathartic experience leaving everyone stronger – as though Athens, democratic, confident and imperial, was preparing itself to meet the blows of destiny.

Athenian atmosphere it seemed that the warriors who turned back the Persian tide had fought in the same cause as Homer's heroes at the walls of Troy. In thanksgiving and celebration the temples upon the Acropolis which the Persians had destroyed were rebuilt, the city ennobling itself as it ennobled the houses of its gods – most notably, of course, with the building of the **Parthenon**.

Yet still Athens was just one among numerous city-states, each ready to come together during a common danger but reasserting its sovereignty as the foreign threat receded. This was illustrated by the ten-year struggle beginning in 461 BC between Athens and various **Peloponnesian states**, which was a warning of a yet greater war to come between Athens and Sparta itself. Perhaps 451 BC marks the fatal moment when Athens passed up the opportunity to create an institution more generous, and more inclusive, than the city-state. Instead Pericles supported the parochial and populist demand that **Athenian citizenship** should not be extended to its allies, thereby stoking up the flames of envy and foregoing the chance of creating a genuine and enduring Greek confederacy.

△ A bust of Pericles, Athens' great statesman, found near Tivoli, Italy

Pericles and his times

Pericles (c.495 BC–429 BC) announced himself on the public stage in 472 BC when he gave his backing to Themistocles by financing the chorus for the *Persians* by Aeschylus; he entered politics during the following decade as prosecutor of the conservative leader, Kimon. In 461 BC, he was elected to the position of *strategos* (general) – the most important elected position in Athens, for the ten strategoi proposed the legislation that was then voted on in the Assembly. Pericles possessed a brilliance in winning over audiences, so that in a society where the people was sovereign the reality was that he governed the state; with only two exceptions, he was annually re-elected *strategos* until his death in 429 BC.

Given the reactionary forces that had to be contended with at home, it is not surprising that after the death of Kimon, head of the conservative pro-Spartan party in Athens, Pericles concluded a **peace with Persia** in 449 BC, the better to turn his attention to **Sparta**, that bastion of reaction in Greece. Pericles believed that Athenian power was not only Greece's best defence against Persia but also the best hope for the unification of Greece under enlightened rule, for he also believed that culturally Athens was "the school of Hellas". The visible expression of this cultural excellence could be seen atop the Acropolis where Pericles was directly responsible for the construction of the Propylaea and the Parthenon, but it was true too in sculpture, painting, drama, poetry, history, teaching and philosophy, their achievement not only celebrated in Athens at the time of Pericles but since then and everywhere informing the values of mankind. Politically, as both Pericles and his enemies understood, the advance of democracy in Greece depended on the success of that Athenian imperialism which grew out of the Delian League.

But whatever the excellence of Athens, whatever the ideals of its power, the jealousies of the Peloponnesians were excited all the more, and it is a testimony to Pericles that he was able to avoid war with Sparta for as long as he did. Thucydides, the historian of the Peloponnesian War, greatly admired Pericles for his integrity and also for the restraint he exercised over Athenian democracy, which never descended into demagoguery under his rule.

The decline of the city-state: 431–338 BC

From about the time of the battle of Eurymedon in 468 BC, association with Athens through the **Delian League** ceased to be voluntary. Allegiances were enforced and contributions became tributes, so that when Sparta and its Peloponnesian allies declared war on Athens in 431 BC, they could claim that they were fighting to restore political independence to all those states, in Greece and across the Aegean, that the Athenians had "enslaved". At war's end, however, when Athens had been defeated, both those who had been subject to its empire as well as others who had been allies of Sparta discovered that a new and far more oppressive power had taken Athens' place: the very Spartans who had proclaimed themselves as liberators. More fundamentally, the **Peloponnesian War**, which had been fought to assert the sovereignty of city-states, in fact left them weaker and more vulnerable in the long term to outside forces, which in the end meant seeing Greece reduced to a province of the new Macedonian empire.

The writing of history began among the Greeks, first with **Herodotus**, then with Thucydides. But with Herodotus there is the feeling that he prefers telling a good story, that he still inhabits Homer's world of epic poetry, whereas with **Thucydides** the paramount concern is to analyse events. In that sense Thucydides is the first modern historian; wherever possible he seeks out primary sources, and his concern is always with objectivity, detail and chronology, for these are the elements of his historical analysis. Not that there is anything dry about Thucydides; the vividness and insight of his writing make reading him as powerful an experience as watching a Greek drama.

Thucydides began writing his history at the outset of the **Peloponnesian War** with the intention of giving an account of its whole duration, but for reasons unknown he abruptly stopped writing in the twentieth year, though he is thought to have survived the war by a few years, living until about 400 BC. He was born into a wealthy and conservative Athenian family in about 455 BC, though he himself was a democrat and an admirer of Pericles, and through his reconstruction of Pericles' speeches he presents the most eloquent expression of the Athenian cause. But when Thucydides was exiled from his city seven years into the war, this was the making of him as a historian, for as he himself said, "Associating with both sides, with the Peloponnesians quite as much as with the Athenians, because of my exile, I was thus enabled to watch quietly the course of events".

However much the statesmen and generals in his history rationalise war, Thucydides was himself a military man who understood war at first hand and knew that there was always the irrational element of chance. He also understood that the best chance for overcoming the hazards of chance came from courage and resourcefulness, from flexibility of mind and clarity of thought. Hence his concern for method in his research and analysis in his writing, for he intended his book to be useful to future generals in conducting war and to future statesmen in forming policy. For these reasons we have a better understanding of the Peloponnesian War than of any conflict in ancient times until Julius Caesar began writing his own first-hand accounts of his campaigns. And for these reasons too, Thucydides' history stands on a par with the greatest literature of ancient Greece.

C

The Peloponnesian War

The **Peloponnesian War** which began in **431 BC** was really a continuation of the conflict that broke out in 461 BC between Athens and its principal commercial rivals, Corinth and Aegina and their various allies in the Peloponnese. Sparta had at that time stood aside as its interests were not directly affected. But by 432 BC when Corinth again agitated for war, following the bruisings it had received over Corcyra (Corfu) and Potidea, the **Spartans** had become fearful of growing Athenian power. Behind this was their dread that Athens might one day loosen Sparta's hold over the Laconian and Messenian plains; yet they saw no contradiction in joining with their allies of the Peloponnesian League in going to war with the proclaimed aim of "liberating" Greece from the Athenian empire.

The Athenian empire was built on trade. **Piraeus** had grown enormously since the days of Themistocles so that it was now one of the great ports of the Mediterranean, its cosmopolitan population of alien residents controlling most of its manufacturing and mercantile activities. On the initiative of Pericles, the town of Piraeus had been rebuilt by Hippodamus, an architect of Miletus, its streets arranged in a rectangular grid system – the first such layout in Europe and the model for later Greek cities throughout the world. "The fruits of the whole earth flow in upon us", as Pericles said to his fellow Athenians, "so that we enjoy the goods of other countries as freely as of our own." And as well as goods, great wealth and human talent was drawn to Athens, so that Pericles could rightly proclaim that Athens was the centre of Greek culture.

That Athens was a great sea power with 300 triremes while the members of Sparta's **Peloponnesian League** were land powers without significant navies determined the nature of the war. When the Peloponnesians combined with their Boeotian allies they could put 30,000 hoplites into the field without calling on reserves. The Athenians had only half this number and would have to call up reserves to match it. Just as the strategy of Themistocles had been to fight the Persians by sea, so Pericles followed the same plan against Sparta and its allies, avoiding major battles against the superior land forces of the Peloponnesian League. Athens and Piraeus were protected by their walls, but the Peloponnesians and their Boeotian allies were allowed to invade Attica with impunity nearly every year, and there was constant warfare in Thrace. On the other hand the Peloponnesians lacked the seapower to carry the fighting into Asia Minor and the Aegean islands or to interfere with Athens' routes of trade, while the Athenians used their maritime superiority to launch attacks against the coasts of the Peloponnese, the Ionian islands and the mouth of the Gulf of Corinth in the hope that they would succeed in detaching members from the Peloponnesian League. As long as Athens remained in command of the sea, with its trade routes and its prosperity intact, it had every reason to expect that it could wear down its enemies' resolve.

Pericles' death in 329 BC was an early blow to the Athenian cause. **Kleon,** his successor, has received a critical press in the writings of Thucydides and the comic plays of Aristophanes for being an uncouth man of the people who too aggressively pursued the war. But if Pericles' empire was justified, then Kleon's policy of vigorous action was likewise justified, and he served Athens better than the ditherings of Nikias and the peace lobby. A peace party existed at Athens throughout the war, and the city insisted on giving it an audience, not only in political debate but on the stage, for example in the 415 BC production of Euripides' *Trojan Women*, performed on the eve of what proved to be the disastrous Sicilian expedition. By then Kleon was dead, and instead of operational responsibility for the Sicilian expedition being put in the hands of the ablest general, the Assembly divided the command and constantly interfered, so that a bold operation designed to win Sicily to the Athenian cause turned into a catastrophic debacle. The failure, as Thucydides observed, was political, not military, and the same can be said generally about Athens' conduct throughout the second half of the war, where the Assembly's failure to adopt a consistent position led to ultimate defeat.

City-state rivalries

The Peloponnesian War left **Sparta** the supreme power in Greece, but it took very little time for those whom the Spartans had "liberated" to realise that they had simply acquired a new and inferior master, one that entirely lacked the style, the ability and the intelligence of Athens. Nor was it forgotten that Sparta had gained its victory by bargaining away to Persia the freedom of the **Asia Minor Greeks**. Famous for their discipline and incorruptibility at home, the moment the Spartans found themselves in charge of an empire abroad they became avaricious and petty tyrants; they demanded tribute more brutally than Athens had done, and their allies never saw a penny of it.

Isolationist, old-fashioned, autocratic and terrified of overseas commitments, Sparta proved totally inept at playing the leading role in Greece.

Meanwhile Athens had lost its empire but not its trade, which was built on firm foundations, so that not only did Corinth fail in its demands to have its defeated rival razed to the ground, but it faced no less mercantile competition than before. Moreover during the first decade of the fourth century Athens was able to restore much of its naval power in the Aegean. To contain any challenge from Greece, whether from the Spartans or the Athenians, the **Persians** now played one off against the other while giving aid to each, so that for example in 393 BC, just eleven years after they were demolished, the Long Walls between Athens and Piraeus were rebuilt – with Persian money.

Adding to the intrigues between Persia, Athens and Sparta were a bewildering and unstable variety of alliances involving numerous other Greek states. The most important of these was **Thebes**, which had been an ally of Sparta during the Peloponnesian War but came round to the Athenian side, and then for a spectacular moment under its brilliant general **Epaminondas** became the greatest power in Greece. At the **battle of Leuctra** in **371 BC** the Thebans defeated the Spartan army and with it the myth of Spartan invincibility. The following year Epaminondas went further, and after marching through Laconia in a display of strength, he liberated Messenia on which the Spartan economy depended. Sparta suffered an immediate loss of wealth and power from which it never recovered, and its population went into permanent decline.

Almost the whole of Theban energy and power was bound up in the person of Epaminondas, and when he was killed in the **battle of Mantinea** in **362 BC**, Thebes relinquished its ambitions in the Peloponnese. For the first time in over a century Greece found itself free from the dictates of Persia or any overpowerful Greek state. Exhausted and impoverished by almost continuous war, it was an opportunity for Greece to peacefully unite. But along the way the political and moral significance of the city-state had eroded, and with the **rise of Macedonia** came the concept of an all-embracing kingship.

The Macedonian Empire and Hellenistic Greece: 348–146 BC

Despite its large size and population, **Macedonia** had played little role in early Greek affairs. Its weakness was due to the constitutional position of the king who was not assured the throne by primogeniture; rather a member of the royal family who asserted his right to the kingship was subject to approval by a vote of the nobility. Rivalries among potential heirs and fears of usurpation limited royal power. Moreover, the Greeks did not consider the Macedonians to be properly Greek, not in speech, culture or political system. They did not live in city-states, which Aristotle said was the mark of a civilised human being, rather they were a tribal people who were closer to the barbarians.

Philip II and the rise of Macedonia

But towards the middle of the fourth century, and in contrast to the exhaustion and lack of leadership among the Greek city-states, the power of Macedonia grew. This was due to the accession of **Philip II**, who strengthened royal authority by building up the army on the basis of personal loyalty to himself,

The Golden Age of Athens under Pericles, and the period of city-state rivalry after the Peloponnesian War, saw the **birth of Western philosophy** under the towering figures of Socrates, Plato and Aristotle.

Socrates (c.470–399 BC)

Socrates was born the son of an Athenian sculptor and for a time was a sculptor himself. He fought bravely for Athens as a hoplite in the Peloponnesian War, though long before it, in his twenties, he had turned to philosophy, which he practised in his own peculiar style. He promoted no philosophical position of his own but asserted, ceaselessly, the supremacy of reason. Often this was done in the streets of Athens, button-holing some self-regarding Athenian of the older generation, asking him questions, picking his answers to pieces, until he came up with a definition that held water or, more likely, the spluttering victim were reduced to a confession of his own ignorance in front of crowds of Socrates' mirthful young supporters.

By this "Socratic method" he asked for definitions of familiar concepts such as piety and justice; his technique was to argue people into exposing the ignorance that hid behind the bandying about of terms, even as he claimed a similar ignorance for himself. Indeed when the Delphic oracle proclaimed that no man was wiser than Socrates, he explained this by saying wisdom lies in knowing how little one really knows. Because he valued this question-and-answer process over settling on fixed conclusions, Socrates never wrote anything down. Yet his influence was pivotal; before his time philosophical inquiry concerned itself with speculations on how the natural world was formed and how it operates; afterwards it looked to the analysis of concepts and to ethics.

Socrates's method could be irritating, especially when he called into question conventional morality, and his friendships with people associated with oligarchy, like Alcibiades and Kritias, did not put him in good stead with a democratic Athens that had just lost an empire and a war. Probably many factors directed the city's anger, fear and frustration at Socrates, and Athenians wanted to see the back of him. The means used were to try him for impiety and corrupting the young, then to sentence him to death, but to give him the option of naming another penalty, probably expecting that he would choose exile. Instead Socrates answered that if he was to get what he deserved, he should be maintained for life at the public expense. At this the death penalty was confirmed, but even then it was not to be imposed for two months, with the tacit understanding that Socrates would escape. Instead Socrates argued that it was wrong for a citizen to disobey even an unjust law, and in the company of his friends he drank the cup of hemlock. "Such was the end", wrote Plato, who describes the scene in his *Phaedo*, "of our friend; of whom I may truly say, that of all the men of his time whom I have known, he was the wisest and justest and best."

Plato (c.427–c.347 BC)

As a young man, Plato painted, composed music and wrote a tragedy, as well as being a student of Socrates. He intended a career in politics, where his connections would have ensured success; his father could claim descent from the last king of Athens, his mother was descended from Solon, and the family had been close allies of Pericles. But Socrates' death made Plato decide that he could not serve a government that had committed such a crime, and instead his mission became to exalt the memory of his teacher. In Plato's writings, many of them dialogues, Socrates is frequently the leading participant, while at the Academy in Athens, which Plato founded, the Socratic question-and-answer method was the means of instruction.

Plato's philosophy is elusive; he never sets out a system of doctrines, nor does he tell us which of his ideas are most basic, nor rank them in a hierarchical order, nor show how they interrelate. Nevertheless, certain themes recur. He believed that men possess immortal souls separate from their mortal bodies. Also knowledge, he believed, was the recollection of what our souls already know, so that we do not gain knowledge from experience, rather by using our reasoning capacity to draw more closely to the realm of our souls. The true objects of knowledge are not the transient, material things of this world, for these are only reflections of a higher essence which Plato called Forms or Ideas. Forms are objects of pure thinking, cut off from our experience; but also Forms motivate us to grasp them, so that the reasoning part of us is drawn to Forms as a kind of mystic communion.

Plato's notion of a mystic union with a higher essence would play an important role in later religious thought. But more immediately his teachings at the Academy concerned themselves with logic, mathematics, astronomy and above all political science, for its purpose was to train a new ruling class. Prominent families sent him their sons to learn the arts of government, and Plato, an aristocrat born into a calamitous age marked by Athens' imperial defeat, responded by teaching that the best form of government was a constitutional monarchy, at its head a philosopher-king with that higher knowledge of Justice and the Good drawn from the realm of Forms. Though it was a utopian vision, Plato's political philosophy helped prepare the intellectual ground for the acceptance of an absolutist solution to the increasing uncertainties of fourth-century BC Greece.

Aristotle (384–322 BC)

Aristotle grew up in Pella, the capital of an increasingly powerful Macedonia, where his father had been appointed doctor to King Amyntas II; it is therefore not unlikely that Amyntas's son, the future Philip II, and Aristotle were boyhood friends. However, at the age of seventeen, Aristotle was sent to Plato's Academy at Athens to continue his education, and he remained there, first as a student, then as a teacher, a faithful follower of Plato's ideas. His independent philosophy matured later, during the years he spent, again at Pella, as tutor to Alexander the Great, and later still, after 335 BC, when he founded his own school, the Lyceum, in Athens.

Aristotle came to reject Plato's dualism. He did not believe that the soul was of a substance separate from the body, rather that it was an aspect of the body. Likewise with Plato's theory of Forms. Instead of Plato's inward looking view, Aristotle sought explanations of the physical world and of human society from the viewpoint of an outside observer. Essentially a scientist and a realist, he was bent on discovering the true rather than establishing the good, and he believed that sense perception was the only means of human knowledge. Following this vision, his output was vast and covered many fields of knowledge – logic, metaphysics, ethics, politics, rhetoric, art, poetry, physiology, anatomy, biology, zoology, physics, astronomy and psychology. Everything could be measured, analysed and described, and he was the first person to classify organisms into genera and species. He is probably the only person who has ever assimilated the whole body of existing knowledge on all subjects and brought it within a single focus.

The exactitude of Aristotle's writings does not make them easy reading, and Plato has always enjoyed a wider appeal owing to his literary skill. All the same, Aristotle's influence has been enormous on Western intellectual and scientific tradition.

not to tribe or locality. Philip was also determined to hellenise his country. Borrowing from Greek ways and institutions, he founded the city of **Pella** as his capital and lured teachers, artists and intellectuals to his court, among them **Aristotle** and **Euripides**. Philip was an admirer of Athens with which he sought an alliance that would make them joint-masters of the Greek world. But the Athenians opposed him, and he took matters into his own hands.

In **338 BC** Philip brought about the unity of the mainland Greeks, not by their voluntary adhesion that had been envisioned by Isocrates, the Athenian statesman, rather on the battlefield at **Chaironeia**. There, to the east of Delphi, the Theban and Athenian forces were defeated by one of the most formidable fighting units the world has ever seen, the **Macedonian phalanx**. Armed with the *sarissa*, an eighteen-foot pike tapering from butt to tip, its infantrymen were trained to move across a battlefield with all the discipline of a parade ground drill. Instead of relying on a headlong charge, its effectiveness lay in manipulating the enemy line, pinning it down here, advancing obliquely against it there, or by performing that most difficult of manoeuvres, a fighting withdrawal going suddenly over to a forceful and concentrated attack – its purpose always to open up a gap in the enemy line through which the cavalry could make its decisive strike.

Alexander's conquests

After Chaeronia, Philip summoned the Greek states to a meeting at Corinth where he announced his plans for a panhellenic conquest of the Persian Empire. But Philip was murdered two years later and to his son **Alexander** fell his father's plans for an **Asian campaign** – throughout which, it is said, he slept with a copy of the *Iliad* under his pillow.

In the East too there was an assassination, and in 335 BC the Persian throne passed to **Darius III**, namesake of the first and doomed to be the last king of his line. For by using essentially his father's tactics, Alexander would lead his army through a series of astonishing victories, usually against greater numbers, until he reached the heart of the Persian Empire. In May of **334 BC**, with thirty thousand foot soldiers and five thousand horse, Alexander crossed the Hellespont. By autumn all the Aegean coast of **Asia Minor** was his; twelve months later he stood on the banks of the Orontes river in **Syria**; in the winter of 332 BC **Egypt** hailed him as pharaoh; and by the spring of 330 BC the great Persian cities of **Babylon**, **Susa**, **Persepolis** and **Pasargadae** had fallen to him in rapid succession until, at **Ecbatana**, he found Darius in the dust, murdered by his own supporters. Alexander wrapped the corpse in his Macedonian cloak, and in turn he assumed the lordship of Asia.

Hellenistic Greece

No sooner had **Alexander** died at Babylon in 323 BC at the age of thirty-three that Athens led an alliance of Greeks in a **war of liberation** against Macedonian rule. But the Macedonians had built up a formidable navy which inflicted heavy losses on the Athenian fleet. Unable to lift the Macedonian blockade of Piraeus, Athens surrendered and a pro-Macedonian government was installed. The episode marked the end of Athens as a sea power and left it permanently weakened.

Greece was now irrevocably part of a new dominion, one that entirely altered the scale and orientation of the Greek world, for it had been Alexander's strategic vision to see the Mediterranean and the East as two halves of a greater whole. Opened up to Greek settlement and enterprise, and united by Greek learning, language and culture, if not always by a single power, this **Hellenistic Empire** meant an enormous increase in international trade, the creation of unprecedented prosperity, and the establishment of an **ecumene**, the notion of one world, no longer divided by the walls of city-states but a universal concept that was the common possession of all civilized peoples.

"To the strongest", was Alexander's deathbed reply when asked to whom he bequeathed his empire. Forty years of warfare between his leading generals gave rise to three dynasties, the **Antigonid** in Macedonia, which ruled over mainland Greece, the **Seleucid** which ultimately centred on Syria and Asia Minor, and the **Ptolemaic** in Egypt, which ruled from Alexandria, founded by Alexander himself, which in wealth and population, not to mention literature and science, soon outshone anything in Greece.

The emergence of Rome

In the Western Mediterranean, **Rome** was a rising power, its dominance there confirmed in 202 BC when at Zama in North Africa the Carthaginian army under Hannibal was defeated by the legions of Scipio Africanus. **Philip V** of Macedonia had earlier feared the growth of Roman power in the Adriatic and in 215 BC had agreed with Hannibal a treaty of mutual assistance. Now with Hannibal defeated, Rome's legions marched eastwards and at the battle of **Cynoscephalae** in Thessaly in 197 BC they attacked the flanks of the less manoeuvrable Macedonian phalanx and routed Philip's army.

Rome declared Greece liberated and granted autonomy to its **city-states** to order their own affairs. Its actions were marked by a genuine philhellene sentiment, and it was from this time that Rome took on the trappings of **Hellenistic culture**, in architecture, sculpture, literature, philosophy and much else. Continuing eastwards, the Romans first set foot on Asian soil in 190 BC; and as they followed in Alexander's footsteps, it was Rome's generals, and not the Greeks, who first called Alexander "the Great". But Rome's benevolence towards the Greeks ended when Macedonia recovered its former power and found anti-Roman sympathisers among the city-states in Greece. At **Pydna** in 167 the Roman legions again tore into the flanks of the Macedonian phalanx. Macedonia was reduced to a federation of smaller states, and tens of thousands of Greeks who had given it their support were sold into slavery while others were interned for decades without trial in Italy.

The harsh policy stoked up resentment among the Greeks which manifested itself in an **uprising of the Achaean League**, a confederation of city-states in the Peloponnese, which, led by Corinth, raised an army that in 146 BC overran central Greece before it was defeated by Roman legions called in from Italy and the recently annexed province of Macedonia. To guard against further disorder, Rome dissolved the league into its component city-states, turned the Peloponnese and central Greece into the **Roman province of Achaea**, and authorised the Roman governor of Macedonia to interfere whenever necessary to ensure the peace. For good measure they **razed Corinth** and sold off its inhabitants as a warning to any Greeks who might think of resisting Rome again.

Roman Greece: 146 BC–330 AD

With the crushing of the Achaean League in 146 BC, the history of Greece became part of **Roman history**. During the first century BC Rome was riven by a series of civil wars whose climactic battlefields were often in Greece, but Greece was only a bystander in the vaster struggle which determined the shape and mastery of the expanding Roman imperium.

In 49 BC the Roman Republic was in its dying days when **Julius Caesar** defeated his rival Pompey at **Pharsalus** in Thessaly; in 42 BC Caesar's assassins were beaten by **Mark Antony** and **Octavian** at **Philippi** in Macedonia; and in 31 BC **Antony** and his Ptolemaic ally **Cleopatra** were routed by **Octavian** in a sea battle off **Actium** in western Greece before committing suicide in Egypt the following year, Octavian marking the event by changing his name to Augustus and effectively inaugurating the **Roman Empire** – though an empire which in its eastern half continued to speak Greek.

By the first century AD Greece had become a **tourist destination** for well-to-do Romans (and a relatively comfortable place of exile for troublemakers). They went to Athens and Rhodes to study literature and philosophy, and all round the country to see the temples with their paintings and sculpture. They also visited the **Olympic Games** which were by now thoroughly professionalised. When the emperor **Nero** came to Greece in AD 67, he entered the Games as a contestant, the judges prudently declaring him the victor in every competition, even when, as in the case of the chariot race, he was thrown and failed to finish.

Under the Romans there was much **new building** in **Athens** and elsewhere, notably by the emperor Hadrian. The centre of the Athenian Agora, which had long ceased to serve the purposes of a democracy, was filled with an odeon, a covered theatre with seating for a thousand people, the gift of Augustus' general Agrippa. Nearby Hadrian built his public library; he loved Athens and stayed there in 125 and 129, completing the vast **Temple of Olympian Zeus** begun nearly six hundred years before by Pisistratos. **Herodes Atticus**, born into a wealthy Greek family and who served as tutor to the future Roman emperor and philosopher Marcus Aurelius, was a generous patron of the arts in Athens and in the 160s built the odeon that bears his name at the foot of the Acropolis which is still used for plays and concerts today.

Saint Paul and early Christianity

Greece had an early taste of **Christian teaching** when **Saint Paul** came to preach to Jews and Gentiles in 49–52 AD. In Athens he was brought before the Court of the Areopagus, a powerful body that exercised authority over religious affairs, and was asked to defend his talk of the death and resurrection of his foreign god, after which he was dismissed as one of the many cranks who frequented the city. Paul then spent eighteen months in **Corinth** where he made some converts, though as his subsequent Epistles to the Corinthians show, too often their idea of Christianity amounted to celebrating their salvation with carousing and fornication. In the last decades of the century, **Saint John the Divine**, who was proselytising at Ephesus on the coast of Asia Minor, was exiled by the Romans to Patmos where in a cave still shown to visitors today he is said to have written *Revelation*, the apocalyptic last book of the Bible.

Yet though the books of the New Testament were composed in Greek, they were the works of people in the Greek East, while Christianity seems to have made little headway among the inhabitants of Greece itself. Throughout all the **Roman persecutions** of the third and early fourth centuries, in 202 under Septimius Severus, in 249–50 under Decius, in 257 under Valerian and in 303 under Diocletian, in which hundreds of thousands died in Egypt, the Middle East and Asia Minor, there are few recorded martyrs in Greece – probably, it is thought, because there were few Greek Christians.

Barbarian incursions

During the mid-third century the **Heruli**, a tribe in southern Russia associated with the Goths, succeeded in passing through the Bosphorus and into the Aegean where they ravaged far and wide, plundering and burning **Athens** in 267. New city walls were built with the marble rubble from the wreckage, but their circumference was now so small that the ancient Agora, littered with ruins, was left outside, while what remained of the city huddled round the base of the Acropolis. It was a familiar scene throughout Greece, as prosperity declined and population fell, except in the north along the **Via Egnatia**, the Roman road passing through their province of Macedonia, linking ports on the Adriatic with Thessaloniki on the Aegean.

Byzantine and Medieval Greece: 330–1460 AD

That coalescence of Roman authority, Hellenistic culture and the transcendental spirit of the East that we now call the **Byzantine Empire** began in May 330 when the **emperor Constantine** declared that Nova Roma (as he called the city of Byzantium – known today as Istanbul) was the new capital of the Roman Empire. Founded on the banks of the Bosphorus by Greek colonists in the seventh century BC, Byzantium occupied the one supremely defensible and commanding point from where the entire trade between the Black Sea and the Mediterranean could be controlled. But it was only now, a thousand years later, that its full potential was realised. **Constantinople**, the city of Constantine, as it at once became popularly known, was perfectly positioned for the supreme strategic task confronting the empire: the defence of the Danube and the Euphrates frontiers. Moreover the new capital stood astride the flow of goods and culture emanating from the East, that part of the empire richest in economic resources, most densely populated and the home of fertile intellectual and religious activity.

The Christian empire

Constantine's other act with decisive consequences was to **legalise** – and to a considerable extent patronise – the **Christian church**. Here again Constantinople was important, for while Rome's pagan traditions could not yet be disturbed, the new capital was consciously conceived as a Christian city, and within the century Christianity was established as the religion of state, with its liturgies (still in use in the Greek Orthodox Church), the Creed and the New Testament all in Greek.

By allying himself with the Christians, Constantine won the support of the strongest single group in the Roman world. Though perhaps only one in seven of the empire's population were by then admitted Christians, persecution had if anything enhanced their sense of solidarity. Being well organized, their influence extended further than their numbers would suggest, and by preaching the equality and salvation of the individual soul, Christianity could appeal to everyone – men and women, rich and poor, freemen and slaves – while its satisfying synthesis with Greek philosophical thought made it attractive to many of the best intellects of the time. Combining in his person the supreme secular and spiritual authority, Constantine's successors became Christ's vice-regent on earth, while likewise the empire took on a sanctity and a mission that would give it the resilience to survive more than a thousand years to come.

In 391 the emperor **Theodosius I** issued an edict banning all expressions of **paganism** throughout the empire. In Greece the mysteries at Eleusis ceased to be celebrated the following year, and in 395 the Olympic Games were suppressed, their athletic nudity an offence to Christianity. Around this time too the Delphic oracle fell silent. The conversion of pagan buildings to Christian use began in the fifth century. Under an imperial law of 435 the Parthenon and the Erectheion on the Acropolis and the mausoleum of Galerius (the Rotunda) in Thessaloniki and other temples elsewhere were all converted to churches. But even this did not eradicate pagan teaching: in Athens philosophy and law continued to be taught at the Academy, founded by Plato in 385 BC, until prohibited by the emperor Justinian in 529.

Theodosius was the last ruler of a unified Roman Empire, which for much of the past century had seen distinct rulers of its **West and Eastern empires**, and at his death in **395** the split was made permanent, with his sons Honorus and Arcadius appointed Augustus of each respective territory. In 476 **Rome fell** to the barbarians and as the Dark Ages settled on Western Europe Byzantium inherited the sole mantle of the empire. Latin remained the official language of its administration, though after the reign of Justinian (527–565) the emperors joined the people in speaking and writing Greek. Nonetheless they and their people continued to call themselves *Romaioi*, that is Romans.

Plague and invasion

Thessaloníki, the second city of the Byzantine Empire, was relatively close to Constantinople, yet even so the journey by land or sea took five or six days. The rest of Greece was that much farther and, remote from the centre of administration and culture, Attica and the Peloponnese grew decidedly provincial. Conditions worsened sharply in the late sixth century when Greece was devastated by **plague**. In Athens after 580 life came almost to an end, as the remaining inhabitants withdrew to the Acropolis, while at Corinth the population removed itself entirely to the island of Aegina. Only Thessaloníki fully recovered.

Islam and the iconoclastic controversy

The advent of Islam in the mid-seventh century had its effect on Greece. Syria fell to the Arabs in 636 and Egypt in 642, and the loss of these Christian provinces was followed by an attack by an Arab fleet in 677 on Constantinople itself, and again in 717–718 when a combined Arab naval and land force beleaguered the city, while in 823 the Arabs occupied Crete.

The proximity and pressure of Islam helped fuel the great iconoclastic controversy that ignited passions and pervaded many aspects of daily life throughout the Byzantine Empire for over a century. In 730 the emperor Leo III, who was born on the Syrian frontier and earned the epithet "Saracen-minded", proscribed images in the Orthodox Church, claiming they amounted to idolatry. His strongest support came from the farmer-soldiers of Asia Minor, that is those closest to the lands recently conquered by the Muslims, while his opponents, the iconodules, who favoured icons, were found in the monasteries and in Greece. Indeed, it was the empress Irene, an Athenian, who briefly restored the images in 780, though they were again proscribed by imperial decree from 815 to 843, with the effect that almost no representational Byzantine art survives in Greece from before the ninth century.

Following the plague, Greece was invaded by two barbarian tribes, the **Slavs** and **Avars**, who attacked Thessaloníki in 597 and by 600 reached the Peloponnese. Numbering about a hundred thousand in all, the invaders settled throughout the country, and it was not until the tenth century that they were fully pacified by the emperors and converted to Christianity by the Orthodox Church and so assimilated into Greek society.

Meanwhile the **Bulgars** had taken advantage of Byzantine weakness to overrun much of northern Greece. But they were driven out by **Basil II** of the militaristic Macedonian dynasty who in 1018–19 destroyed the Bulgar empire, then celebrated his victory with a visit to Athens, the first in centuries by an emperor, and left magnificent gifts in the Church of the Theotokos Atheniotissa, as the Parthenon had become.

The Crusades

Compared to the Balkans, life in Asia Minor was far more stable and secure. Greeks had been settled on its Aegean shores since the early first millennium BC, and since Alexander's time Greek language and culture had extended eastwards beyond the headwaters of the Euphrates and Tigris rivers. But in 1071 the **Byzantine army** was destroyed at **Manzikert**, a fortress town on the eastern frontier, by the **Seljuk Turks** who went on to occupy almost the whole of Asia Minor.

The Byzantine emperor turned to the West for help to recover his territories from the Muslims, and in 1095 the Roman Catholic Pope replied by launching the **First Crusade**. Together, the Crusaders and the Byzantines won a series of victories over the Seljuks in Asia Minor, but the Byzantines, wary of possible Crusader designs on the empire itself, were content to see their Latin allies from the West advance alone on Jerusalem, which they captured in 1099.

A century later and the worst fears of the Byzantines were borne out when in 1204 the **Fourth Crusade** attacked **Constantinople** itself. Following the recapture of Jerusalem by Saladin, the crusade had embarked from Venice to

Plethon replants the seed of Hellas

The encroaching Ottoman threat led to a remarkable reassessment of Byzantine values. Though the Byzantines had never lost sight of their ancient heritage and throughout their history could as readily quote from Homer as from the Bible, now from the first half of the fourteenth century Byzantine intellectuals began to place their hope for regeneration in their classical heritage, in that unconquerable empire of past glory that lay beyond the military and spiritual trespass of the Catholic West and the Muslim East. Among these was **Plethon**, a native of Constantinople, who in the 1420s came to Mystra where he founded a Platonic Academy.

Convinced that Christianity offered no solutions, Plethon proposed instead the salvation of society through a return to the ideals of ancient Greece, supported by a revived Hellenic religion and an ethical system based on Neo-Platonic philosophy. He also supported a new terminology. Until now the word *Hellenes* had been used by the Byzantines to describe the pagan Greeks as opposed to the *Romaioi* of the Christianized Roman Empire. But with the empire reduced to little more than a few city-states, and with a rising admiration in the West for the ancient Greeks, Byzantine intellectuals dropped the word *Romaioi* and began to call themselves Hellenes. And indeed as things turned out, *Rum* became a distasteful appellation, the term applied to subject Greeks of the Ottoman Empire, while as Hellenes they would win independence for the modern state of Greece.

the East. But its purpose was perverted by the **Venetians**, whose aim was to gain the monopoly of the Levant trade from their Byzantine rivals. The Crusaders were indebted for their ships and victuals to the Venetians, who played upon their lust for plunder and their envy of the Greeks to divert them towards the imperial city. After seizing Constantinople and executing the emperor, they installed in his place one of their leaders, **Baldwin, Count of Flanders**, while his vassals shared out Greece in a bewildering patchwork of feudal holdings.

In outline, the Peloponnese went to a **Frank** who established himself **Prince of Achaia**; Attica and Boeotia fell to a Burgundian who styled himself **Duke of Athens**; the Lombards set up the **Kingdom of Thessaloníki**; and **Venice**, to ensure its control of the maritime trade, took many of the islands and the chief ports of the Peloponnese. Greeks held only the **Despotate of Epirus** in the northwest of the country, which together with **Nicaea** and **Trebizond** in Asia Minor became the last redoubts of Byzantium.

In 1261 the **Palaeologos dynasty** in Nicaea recovered Constantinople, and the following year the Byzantines made further advances, taking Mistra, Mani and Monemvasiá from which they gradually extended their authority. But a new Turkish dynasty, the **Ottomans**, emerged in the late-thirteenth century and by 1400 controlled Asia Minor and had conquered all of Byzantine Greece except Thessaloníki and the Peloponnese. In 1452 the Ottomans invaded the Peloponnese as a diversion to the main attack on **Constantinople**, which fell to **Sultan Mehmet II** on May 23, 1453.

The Byzantine empire was reduced to a few last enclaves. In 1456 the Ottomans captured **Athens** from the Venetians and turned the Parthenon church into a mosque, and in 1460 Mehmet entered Mistra and conquered the **Peloponnese**. The following year, **Trebizond** fell and the Byzantine empire was no more.

Greece under Turkish occupation: 1460–1821

After 1460 Western possessions in Greece amounted to **Rhodes** – which was held by the Knights of St John – and, under **Venetian rule**, the Peloponnesian ports of **Koróni, Methóni** and **Monemvasiá**, and the islands of **Évvia, Crete, Corfu, Aegina** and (later) **Cyprus**. Outside these areas Greeks lived under **Turkish domination**, the one exception being the **Mani** – the wild mountainous peninsula at the foot of the Peloponnese, where neither Westerner nor Turk dared venture and where the feuding population of Greeks enjoyed a primitive liberty. And the Ottomans continued to extend their power. In 1522 they drove the Knights of St John from Rhodes, and within two more decades they had captured all of the Venetian mainland colonies in Greece, leaving them in control of only Cyprus and Crete.

The nature of Ottoman rule

Sklavía – "slavery" – is the term the Greeks apply to the Turkish occupation, though in exchange for submitting to Muslim rule and paying tribute, the Greeks were free to pursue their religion and were left very much in charge of their own religious and civil affairs. In accordance with Islamic tradition, the

Ottoman sultan regarded his Orthodox Christian subjects as a nation (*millet*) of which the **Patriarch of Constantinople** was both the spiritual and temporal ruler. In effect the patriarch presided over a state within the state, exercising its entire civil and ecclesiastical administration.

The essence of the Turkish administration was **taxation**. The collection of these taxes was often farmed out to the leaders of the Greek communities, to local magistrates for example, who profited from the taxes they collected, enabling some to exercise a dominant role not only within their own region but in the Ottoman Empire at large.

The other important institution within Greece was the **Orthodox Church**. For all its apparent venality and despite the ignorance and bigotry of much of the clergy, the Church preserved the traditional faith, kept alive the written form of the Greek language, and was the focus of Greek nationalism. Also the Orthodox Church was wealthy and powerful; Greeks preferred to give their lands to the monasteries than have them occupied by the Turks, while the Muslims found it easier to allow the Church to act in a judicial capacity rather than have to invent a new administration. Thus Christians took their legal disputes to bishops to decide according to Roman law.

Turks sometimes formed a substantial minority of the population, while in other places there were no Turks at all. Generally the Ottomans controlled the towns and the plains but left the mountains almost entirely to the Greeks. These were controlled by **armatoli**, who were essentially Ottoman-sanctioned Christian militia, and by **klephts** – bandits who exacted contributions from the villages and preyed off Turks whenever they could. The armatoli and the klephts were the counterparts of each other. The *armatoli* were necessary to control the *klephts*, and the *klephts* provided many of the recruits for the *armatoli*. In unsettled times, when the *armatoli* became discontented, the numbers of *klephts* increased. As to the cities, Athens declined, while **Thessaloníki** became comparatively prosperous, particularly after the influx of a large number of **Jewish refugees from Spain** at the end of the fifteenth century. A cosmopolitan outpost, it

The devshirme

The *devshirme* was an institution of the Ottoman state: a slave levy imposed on the Christian populations living at peace within its borders. Every few years the sultan's commissioners were sent round the villages of Asia Minor and the Balkans where fathers of Christian families were obliged to present for inspection all their male children aged between eight and twenty. Only parents with one child were excepted. Otherwise the commissioners were free to choose, taking away those children, usually one in five, who seemed the fittest and most intelligent.

Denied access to the outside world and subjected to conditions of the strictest discipline, the boys underwent conversion to Islam and were given martial training and an education best suited to their aptitudes. Severed from their families, their homelands and their culture, they owed their fortune to the sultan and, though they were slaves, they could, on the basis of merit, rise to the highest military and official positions in the empire. The most talented, about one in ten, were taken into the sultan's service within the palace itself. The rest became *janissaries*: charging into battle at the critical moment, after the cavalry and the irregulars had done their work, their job was to seize the victory. The *devshirme* both enhanced the authority of the sultan against the hereditary claims of the Turkish aristocracy which in time was all but excluded from key positions, and accounted for much of the vitality of the early Ottoman state. It was a system that remained in operation until the early eighteenth century.

developed a very mixed population of Greeks, Slavs, Albanians, Vlachs, Armenians, Jews and Turks.

But in fact the term "**Turks**" needs to be qualified, in all these instances, for even before the capture of Constantinople the Ottoman Empire had long since ceased to be run by Turks, rather by Christian youths swept up in the *devshirme* (see box overleaf) who became Muslim converts loyal to the sultan. The ancestors of Mehmet II had so intermarried with Greeks and Serbs or had produced heirs from the women of the harem, Circassians, Georgians, Greeks, Albanians, Serbs and Italians, that Mehmet probably carried no more than one sixty-fourth part of Turkish blood in his veins. And so it was for others of the ruling class, which meant that being an Ottoman had almost nothing to do with ethnic or social origins but was rather to have become a Muslim, to be loyal to the sultan and to practice the complicated system of customs, behaviour and language understood as the Ottoman way. The heights of **Ottoman administration** and society became in fact the preserve of a non-Turkish meritocracy, a great many of whom were Greeks.

Ottoman conquests and the eclipse of Venice

Ottoman troops landed on **Cyprus** in **1570** and, despite the great walls built round Nicosia by the Venetians, the city was taken within the year and 30,000 of its inhabitants were slaughtered. Along with the introduction of Ottoman administration, a large number of Anatolian Turks were settled on Cyprus, the origin of the present minority Turkish population there.

News of Turkish brutality in Cyprus horrified Europe. Under the aegis of the Pope the **Holy League** was formed, Spain and Genoa joining Venice in assembling a fleet led by Don John of Austria, the bastard son of the Spanish king, its lofty aim not only to retake the island but in the spirit of a crusade to recapture all Christian lands that had been taken by the Ottomans. In the event, it was ineffectual to a fault, with no serious attempt made even to launch an expedition to relieve Cyprus. Yet out of it something new arose – the first stirrings of **Philhellenism**, a desire to liberate the Greeks whose ancient culture stood at the heart of Renaissance thought and education.

There was, too, the encouragement of a naval victory, when in 1571 Don John's fleet caught the Ottoman fleet off guard, at its winter quarters at **Lepanto** on the Gulf of Corinth in western Greece. Despite its much greater size, the Ottoman fleet was overwhelmingly defeated. Two hundred and sixty-six of its vessels were sunk or captured, fifty thousand of its sailors died and fifteen thousand Christian galley slaves were freed. Throughout Europe the news of the naval victory at Lepanto was received with extraordinary rejoicing; it was the first time that Europe had won a battle against the Ottomans, and its symbolic importance was profound.

Militarily and politically, however, the Ottomans remained dominant, and the following century **Venice** lost its last outpost in the Eastern Mediterranean, when **Crete** fell to the Ottomans in 1669 after a twenty-year siege. For the Cretans it meant the end of their Byzantine culture which had continued to flourish under Venetian protection since the fall of Constantinople in 1453. Numerous Greek writers, thinkers and painters left the island for the Christian West, mostly to Italy, though Domenico Theotokopoulos preceded them by almost a century, first studying painting in Venice, then by about 1577 settling in Spain where he became known as El Greco. Venice went into terminal decline after the loss of Crete; nothing of its empire was left but the **Ionian islands** which it kept until they were taken by Napoleon in 1797.

Greek nationalist stirrings

Meanwhile during the eighteenth century the islanders of **Ídhra** (Hydra), **Spétses** and **Psará** – most of them Christian Albanian settlers – built up a Greek merchant fleet which traded throughout the Mediterranean where thriving colonies of Greeks were established in many ports. Greek merchant families were also established in the sultan's provinces of **Moldavia** and **Wallachia**, the area of present-day Romania. The rulers of these provinces were exclusively Greeks, chosen by the sultan from wealthy **Phanariot families**, that is residents of the Phanar, the quarter along the Golden Horn in Constantinople and site of the Greek Orthodox Patriarchate which itself enjoyed considerable privileges and was an integral part of the administration of the Ottoman Empire.

These wealthier and more educated Greeks enjoyed greater opportunities for advancement within the Ottoman system than they ever had before, while the Greek peasantry, unlike the Muslim inhabitants of the empire, did not have to bear the burden of military service, nor did they any longer suffer from the *devshirme*, which had fallen out of use. Nevertheless the Greeks had their grievances against the Ottoman government, which mostly concerned the arbitrary, unjust and oppressive system of taxation. But among the Greek peasantry it was primarily their religion that opposed them to their Muslim neighbours – as much as one fifth of the population – and to their Ottoman overlords. Muslim leaders had long preached hatred of the infidel, a view reciprocated by the priests and bishops of the Orthodox Church.

The War of Independence: 1821–32

The **ideology behind the War of Independence** came from the Greeks of the diaspora, particularly those merchant colonies in France, Italy, Austria and Russia who had absorbed new European ideas of nationalism and revolution. Sometime around 1814 a number of such Greeks formed a secret society, the Friendly Society as it was called, **Philiki Etairia**. But their sophisticated political concepts went uncomprehended by the peasantry who assumed that the point of an uprising was the extermination of their religious adversaries. And so when war finally broke out in **spring 1821** almost the entire settled **Muslim population of Greece** – farmers, merchants and officials – was **slaughtered** within weeks by roaming bands of Greek peasants armed with swords, guns, scythes and clubs. They were often led by Orthodox priests, and some of the earliest Greek revolutionary flags portrayed a cross over a severed Turkish head.

The war

While the Greeks fought to rid themselves of the Ottomans, their further aims differed widely. Landowners assumed that their role was to lead and sought to retain and reinforce their traditional privileges; the peasantry saw the struggle as a means towards land redistribution; and Westernised Greeks were fighting for a modern nation-state. Remarkably, by the end of **1823** it seemed that the Greeks had won their independence. Twice the sultan had sent armies into Greece and twice they had met with defeat. Greek guerrilla leaders, above all **Theodoros**

Kolokotronis from the Peloponnese, had gained significant military victories early in the rebellion, which was joined by a thousand or so **European Philhellenes**, almost half of them German, though the most important was the English poet, **Lord Byron**.

But the situation was reversed in 1825 with the invasion of the Peloponnese by formidable Egyptian forces loyal to the sultan. Aid for the Greek struggle had thus far come neither from Orthodox Russia, nor from the Western powers of France and Britain, both wearied by the Napoleonic Wars and suspicious of a potentially anarchic new state. But the death of Lord Byron from a fever while training Greek forces at **Mesolóngi** in 1824 had galvanised European public opinion in the **cause of Greece**, so that when Mesolóngi fell to the Ottomans in 1826, Britain, France and Russia finally agreed to seek autonomy for certain parts of Greece, and they sent a combined fleet under Admiral Codrington to put pressure on the sultan's army in the Peloponnese and the Turkish-Egyptian fleet harboured in Navaríno Bay. Events took over, and an accidental naval battle at **Navaríno** in October 1827 resulted in the destruction of almost the entire Ottoman fleet. The following spring, Russia itself declared war on the Ottomans, and Sultan Mahmud II was forced to accept the existence of an autonomous Greece.

The deal

At a series of conferences from 1830 to 1832, **Greek independence** was confirmed by the Western powers, and borders were drawn in 1832. These included just 800,000 of the six million Greeks living within the Ottoman Empire, and territories, which were for the most part the poorest of the classical and Byzantine lands: **Attica**, the **Peloponnese** and the islands of the **Argo-Saronic**, the **Sporades** and the **Cyclades**. The rich agricultural belt of **Thessaly**, **Epirus** in the west and **Macedonia** in the north remained in Ottoman hands, as did the Dodecanese. Meanwhile after the Napoleonic wars the **Ionian islands** had passed to British control.

The emerging state: 1832–1939

Modern Greece began as a **republic**, and **Ioannis Kapodistrias**, its first president, concentrated his efforts on building a viable central authority and government in the face of diverse protagonists from the independence struggle. Almost inevitably he was assassinated – by two chieftains from the ever-disruptive Mani – and perhaps equally inevitably the "Great Powers" – Brtiain, France and Germany – stepped in. They created a **monarchy**, gave aid and set on the throne a Bavarian prince, Otho (Otto). By 1834, Greece also had a national, state-controlled **Orthodox Church** of its own, independent from the Patriarchate in Constantinople; however, at the same time, two-thirds of the monasteries and convents were closed down and their assets converted to funding secular public education.

Despite the granting of a constitution in 1844, **King Otho** proved an autocratic and insensitive ruler, bringing in fellow Germans to fill official posts and ignoring all claims by the landless peasantry for redistribution of the old estates. In 1862 he was forced from the country by a popular revolt, and the Europeans produced a new prince, this time from Denmark, whose accession was marked by Britain's decision to hand over the **Ionian islands** to Greece, at once increasing the kingdom's population by a fifth. During the reign of the new king, **George I** (1863–1913), the first roads and railways were built in Greece, land reform began in the Peloponnese, and the borders of Greece were extended.

The Great Idea and expansionist wars

From the very beginning, the motive force of Greek foreign policy was the **Megáli Idhéa** (Great Idea) of redeeming ethnically Greek populations outside the country and incorporating the old territories of Byzantium into the new kingdom. There was encouragement all around, as Ottoman control was suddenly under pressure across the Balkans. In 1875 there were revolts by Serbs and Montenegrins, followed by attacks by Russia on Anatolia and Bulgaria. These culminated in the creation of an independent Serbia-Montenegro and autonomous Bulgaria at the 1878 Treaty of Berlin while, as part of the same negotiations, Britain took over the administration of **Cyprus**.

In 1881, revolts broke out among the Greeks of **Crete**, **Thessaly** and **Epirus**, aided by guerrillas from Greece, Britain forced the Ottoman Empire to cede Thessaly and Arta to Greece, but Crete remained Ottoman, and when in 1897 Cretan Greeks set up an independent government and declared *enosis* (union) with Greece, the Ottomans responded by invading the mainland and came within days of reaching Athens. The Great Powers came to the rescue by warning off the Turks and placing Crete under an international protectorate. Only in 1913 did **Crete** unite with Greece.

It was from Crete, nonetheless, that the most distinguished modern Greek statesman emerged: **Eleftherios Venizelos**, having led a civilian campaign for his island's liberation, was elected as Greek prime minister in 1910. Two years later he organized an alliance of Balkan powers to fight the **Balkan Wars** (1912–13), campaigns that saw the Ottomans virtually driven from Europe, and the Bulgarian competition bested in the culmination of a bitter, four-decade campaign for the hearts and minds of the **Macedonian** population. With Greek borders extended to include the **northeast Aegean islands**, **northern Thessaly**, **central Epirus** and parts of **Macedonia**, the Megáli Idhéa was approaching reality. At the same time Venizelos proved himself a shrewd manipulator of domestic public opinion by revising the constitution and introducing a series of liberal social reforms.

Division, however, was to appear with the outbreak of the **First World War**. Venizelos urged Greek entry on the Allied side, seeing in the conflict possibilities for the liberation of Greeks in Thrace and Asia Minor, but the new king, **Constantine I**, who was married to a sister of the German Kaiser, imposed a policy of neutrality. Eventually Venizelos set up a revolutionary government in Thessaloníki, polarising the country into a state of **civil war** along Venezelist–Royalist lines, and in 1917 Greek troops entered the war to join the French, British and Serbians in the Macedonian campaign against Bulgaria and Germany. Upon the capitulation of Bulgaria and the Ottoman Empire, the Greeks occupied **Thrace** (both western and eastern), and Venizelos presented demands at Versailles for the predominantly Greek region of **Smyrna** on the Asia Minor coast to become part of the Greek state.

The Catastrophe and its aftermath

The demand for Smyrna triggered one of the most disastrous episodes in modern Greek history, the so-called **Katastrofí** (Catastrophe). Venizelos was authorized to move forces into Smyrna in 1919, but a new Turkish nationalist movement was taking power under Mustafa Kemal, or **Atatürk** as he came to be known. In 1920 Venizelos lost the elections and monarchist factions took over, at which the Allies withdrew their support for the venture. Nevertheless the monarchists ordered Greek forces to advance upon Ankara in an attempt to bring Atatürk to terms. The Greeks' **Anatolian campaign** ignominiously collapsed in summer 1922 when Turkish troops forced the Greeks back to the coast and a hurried evacuation from **Smyrna**. As the Greek army left Smyrna, the Turks moved in and **massacred** much of the **Armenian and Greek** population before burning most of the city to the ground.

For the Turks, this was the successful conclusion of what they call their War of Independence; already the First World War had cost the Ottoman sultan his empire, and in 1922 the sultan himself was deposed and the borders of modern Turkey, as they are today, were established by the **1923 Treaty of Lausanne**. The treaty also provided for the **exchange of religious minorities** in each country – in effect, the first large-scale regulated ethnic cleansing. Turkey was to accept 390,000 Muslims resident on Greek soil. Greece, mobilized almost continuously for the last decade and with a population of under five million, was faced with the resettlement of over **1,300,000 Christian refugees** from **Asia Minor.** Many of these had already read the writing on the wall after 1918 and arrived of their own accord – from Bulgaria and revolutionary Russia as well as Asia Minor; significant numbers were settled across Macedonia, western Thrace, Epirus and in Athens, as well as on Limnos, Lesvos, Hios, Samos, Evvia and Crete. The Megáli Idhéa had turned in upon itself.

The consequences of the Katastrofi were intense and far-reaching. The bulk of the agricultural estates of **Thessaly** were finally redistributed – completing a program begun in 1909 – both to Greek tenants and refugee farmers, and huge shanty towns grew into new quarters around **Athens**, **Pireás** and **Thessaloníki**, a spur to the country's then almost non-existent industry. Politically, reaction was even swifter. By September 1922, a group of Venízelist army officers under Colonel Nikolaos Plastiras assembled after the retreat from Smyrna, "invited" King Constantine to abdicate and executed six of his ministers held most responsible for the debacle. Democracy was nominally restored with the proclamation of a **republic**, but for much of the next decade changes in government were brought about by factions within the armed forces. Meanwhile, among the urban refugee population, unions were being formed and the **Greek Communist Party (KKE)** was established.

The End of Venizelos and the rise of Metaxas

Elections in 1928 **returned Venizelos to power**, but his freedom to manoeuvre was restricted by the Great Crash of the following year. He had borrowed heavily abroad and was unable to renegotiate loan terms in 1931. Late 1932 saw a local crash caused by Britain abandoning the gold standard, with Greek currency heavily devalued and Venizelos forced from office. His supporters under Plastiras tried forcibly to reinstate him in March 1933, but their coup was put down and Venizelos fled to Paris, where he died three years later.

In 1935 a plebiscite restored the king, **George II**, to the throne, and in the following year he appointed as prime minister **General John Metaxas**, who had opposed the Anatolian campaign. But Metaxas had little support in parliament, and when a series of KKE-organized strikes broke out, the king, ignoring attempts to form a broad liberal coalition, dissolved parliament without setting

△ Inhabitants of Smrna (now Izmir) escape by boat after the city is attacked by Turkish forces under Mustafa Kemal Atatürk, September 1922

a date for new elections. It was a blatantly unconstitutional move and opened the way for five years of ruthless and at times absurd **dictatorship**. Metaxas averted a general strike with military force and proceeded to set up a state based on fascist models of the era. Left-wing and trade-union opponents were imprisoned or forced into exile, a state youth movement and secret police were set up and rigid censorship, extending even to passages of Thucydides, was imposed. But it was at least a Greek dictatorship, and though Metaxas was sympathetic to fascist organizational methods and economics, he completely opposed German or Italian domination.

World War II and the Civil War: 1939–1950

Britain and France declared war on Germany in September 1939, but the most immediate threat to Greece was **Italy** which had invaded Albania in April. Even so, Metaxas hoped that Greece could remain neutral, and when the Italians torpedoed the Greek cruiser Elli in Tinos harbour on August 15, 1940, they failed to provoke a response. **Mussolini**, however, was determined to have a war with Greece, and after accusing the Greeks of violating the Albanian frontier, he delivered an ultimatum on October 28, 1940, to which Metaxas famously if apocryphally answered "**ohi**" (no), though in fact he said "This means war". Galvanized by the crisis, the Greeks not only drove the invading Italians out of Greece but managed to gain control over the long-coveted and predominantly Greek-populated area of northern Epirus in southern Albania. ("Ohi Day" is still celebrated as a national holiday.)

The Greek minorities

The principal Greek minorities – Vlachs, Sarakatsani, Jews, Turks, Slavophones, Catholics and gypsies – are little known, even within Greece. In addition to these traditional groups, recent immigration has introduced new minorities to Greece (see "Immigration" box on p.1104)

Vlachs

The Vlachs' homeland is in the remote Pindos mountains in northwestern Greece near the Albanian frontier, though their range of habitation extends well into the lower hills of western Macedonia. Traditionally they were transhumant shepherds, and they played a major role in Balkan mule-back haulage and running caravanserais where mule convoys halted. They are an ancient community who speak a Romance tongue, possibly acquired through service to the Romans as highway guards along the Via Egnatia which connected Thessaloníki with the Adriatic. Increasingly the Vlachs are abandoning their traditional annual migration with their flocks of sheep; the hardships are too many and the returns too small.

Sarakatsani

The Sarakatsani, celebrated in Patrick Leigh Fermor's *Roumeli* and J. K. Campbell's *Honour, Family and Patronage*, speak an archaic form of Greek. Until the 1940s they were true transhumants, moving between winter quarters well below the snowline and summer pastures in the Pindos mountains. A few still return each summer to the heights, where they pasture their sheep on land rented from the village councils.

Greek Jewry

The Jews of Greece are perhaps the oldest established Jewish community in Europe, dating back to the early Hellenistic period. These original Romaniots, as they are known, were joined in 1493 by Sephardim when Sultan Beyazit II invited Jews expelled from Spain and Portugal to settle in the Ottoman Empire. Thessaloníki in the late nineteenth and early twentieth centuries was one of the largest Jewish cities in the world. Jews made up roughly half the population, and dominated the sailing, shipping and chandlery trades, such that the harbour ceased operations on Saturday but functioned on Sunday. From 1913, however, with a rapid influx of Greek Orthodox into the conquered city, Thessaloníki began to lose its strong Hebraic character; the fire of 1917, emigration to Palestine, the arrival of fiercely nationalistic Greek Orthodox refugees from Anatolia after 1923 and finally the Nazi occupation brought this era to a close.

To make good Mussolini's floundering performance, Hitler determined to send his own troops into Greece, while the British rushed an expeditionary force across the Mediterranean from Egypt where they were already hard-pressed by the Germans. On April 6, 1941 the **Germans invaded**, but while rapidly advancing on Thessaloníki, they simultaneously drove on Belgrade, leading to the swift collapse of the ill-prepared Yugoslav army. Within days the German army was pouring through the Monastir Gap into central Greece, isolating the Greeks on the Albanian front while wheeling round the exposed western flank of the British holding the line along the Aliakmon River. Outmanoeuvered by the enemy's highly mechanized forces and at the mercy of the Luftwaffe's superiority in the air, resistance was soon broken. When the Germans occupied Crete towards the end of May, King George and his ministers fled to Egypt where they set up a government-in-exile in Cairo. Metaxas himself had died before the German invasion.

"Turks"

Greeks talk of "Turks" within Greece when in fact they mean the Muslim remnants of the Ottoman Empire who may have been Greek converts or Albanians and not necessarily ethnic Turks. Even after the 1881 and 1913 acquisitions of Thessaly, Epirus and Macedonia, Muslim villages continued to exist in these regions. Western Thrace was always home to large numbers of Muslims and remained so after the 1919–22 Asia Minor war when the Treaty of Lausanne (1923) confirmed their right to stay in return for a continued Greek Orthodox presence in Istanbul and nearby islands, a bargain the Greeks have honoured but the Turkish government has not. Today Muslims still make up a third of the population of Greek Thrace, where they grow most of the tobacco crop. Additionally there are the Turks of the Dodecanese. Many of the Turks who live in the old town of Rhodes have been there since the sixteenth century and will proudly tell you that they have every right to be considered native Rhodians. In Kos, Cretan Muslims settled both in the port town – where they remain economically active – and at Platani, which still has a mixed Greek Orthodox and Turkish population.

Slavophones

Despite a "voluntary" population exchange between Greece and Bulgaria in 1919, and the flight of many Slavophones abroad after 1948, there remain approximately 40,000 individuals in Greece whose mother tongue is some approximation of Macedonian. They dwell in a ribbon along the northern frontier where some Greeks nervously view them as a potential fifth column for a theoretically expansionist Former Yugoslav Republic of Macedonia (FYROM).

Catholics

The Catholics of the Cyclades, numbering no more than 12,000, are a legacy of Venetian settlement in the Aegean. In Athens there are at least 25,000 more Catholics of Cycladic descent, helping to support a dozen parishes in the city. Often Italianate last names (Dellaroka) or given names (Leonardhos, Frangiskos) distinguish them from their neighbours.

Gypsies

Gypsies – probably from Rajasthan on the Indian subcontinent – first came to the Balkans in about the eleventh century, and were soon well enough established to figure in Byzantine chronicles of the 1300s. The great majority are nominally Greek Orthodox and the rest are Muslim. Generally they offer themselves as transient seasonal labour or drive about Greece in outsize trucks selling cheap goods and agricultural produce.

Occupation and Resistance

The joint Italian-German-Bulgarian Axis **occupation of Greece** was among the bitterest experiences of the European war. Nearly half a million Greek civilians starved to death over the winter of 1941–42, as all available food was requisitioned, principally by the Germans, to feed the occupying armies. In addition, entire villages throughout the mainland, but especially on Crete, were burned at the least hint of resistance and nearly 130,000 civilians were slaughtered up to autumn 1944. In their northern sector, which included Thássos and Samothráki, the Bulgarians demolished ancient sites and churches to support any future bid to annex "Slavic" Macedonia. Meantime, the Germans supervised during the summer of 1944 the **deportation** to extermination camps of the entire **Jewish populations** of Kavála, Ioánnina and Thessaloníki.

No sooner had the Axis powers occupied Greece than a spontaneous resistance movement sprang up in the mountains. The National Popular Liberation Army, known by its initials **ELAS**, founded in September 1941, attracted a wide range of popular support because of its wholehearted commitment to fighting the occupation, and it quickly grew to become the most effective resistance organization. Working in tandem with ELAS was **EAM**, the National Liberation Front, which was founded in September, though with a programme that went beyond resistance and looked towards a radical postwar alteration of the structure of Greek society. Communists formed the leadership of both organizations, but opposition to the occupation and disenchantment with the pre-war political order meant that they won the support of many non-communists. By 1943 ELAS/EAM was in control of most areas of the country and working with the British SOE, Special Operations Executive against the occupiers.

But the Allies – Britain, the United States and the Soviet Union – already had their eyes on the shape of postwar Europe, and British prime minister **Winston Churchill** was determined that Greece should not fall into the communist sphere. Ignoring advice from British agents in Greece that ELAS/EAM were the only effective resistance group, and that the king and his government-in-exile had little support within the country, Churchill gave orders that only rightwing

Greek Jewry and World War II

Following the German invasion of Greece, Jews who lived in the Italian zone of occupation were initially no worse off than their fellow Greeks. But after Italy capitulated to the Allies in September 1943 and German troops took over from the Italian troops, the Jewish communities in Rhodes and Kos in the Dodecanese, as well as in Crete, Corfu, Vólos, Évvia and Zákynthos, were exposed to the full force of Nazi racial doctrine. The Germans applied their "final solution" in Greece during the spring and summer of 1944 with the deportation of virtually the entire Jewish population, about 80,000 in all, to extermination camps in Poland. Thessaloníki alone contained 57,000, the largest Jewish population of any Balkan city, and there were significant populations in all the Greek mainland towns and on many of the islands.

Greek Christians often went to extraordinary lengths to protect their persecuted countrymen. For example, when the Germans demanded the names of the Jews of Zákynthos prior to a roundup, Archbishop Khrysostomos and Mayor Loukas Karrer presented them with a roster of just two names – their own – and secretly oversaw the smuggling of all the island's 275 Jews to remote farms. Their audacious behaviour paid off, as every Zakynthian Jew survived the war. In Athens, the police chief and the archbishop arranged for false identity cards and baptismal certificates to be issued, which again saved large numbers of Jews. Others around the country were warned in good time of what fate the Germans had in store for them, and often took to the hills to join the partisans.

The paltry number of survivors returning from the death camps to Greece was insufficient to form the nucleus of a revival in most provincial towns, and moving to Athens – where about 3000 of today's 5000 Greek Jews live – or emigration to Israel was often a preferable alternative to living with ghosts. In Thessaloníki there are less than a thousand Sephardim, while Lárissa retains about three hundred Sephardim, many of them in the clothing trade. Small Romaniot communities of a hundred persons or less also continue to exist in Halkídha, Ioánnina, Corfu, Tríkala and Vólos. The Kos, Haniá and Rhodes congregations were effectively wiped out, and today only about thirty Jews – many of these from the mainland – live in Rhodes Town, where the Platia ton Evreon Martaron (Square of the Jewish Martyrs) commemorates over 1800 Jews of Kos and Rhodes deported and murdered by the Germans.

groups like **EDES**, the National Republican Greek Army, which opportunisti-cally swung its support to the monarchy, should receive British money, intelli-gence and arms. In August 1943 a resistance delegation came to Cairo to see the Greek king, George, asking for a postwar coalition government in which EAM would hold the ministries of the interior, justice and war, and asking that the king himself not return to Greece without popular consent expressed through a plebiscite. Backed by Churchill, King George flatly rejected their demands.

The EAM contingent returned to Greece divided, and a conflict broke out between those who favoured working peacefully to gain control of any govern-ment imposed after liberation, and the hard-line Stalinist ideologues, who forbade Popular-Front-type participation in any "bourgeois" regime. Armed conflict broke out between ELAS and EDES, with often ferocious actions pres-aging the civil war that was to come.

Liberation and Civil War

As the Germans began to withdraw from Greece in September 1944, most of the ELAS/EAM leadership agreed to join a British-sponsored interim govern-ment headed by the liberal anti-communist politician **George Papandreou** in which it held six ministerial portfolios. Also ELAS/EAM agreed to place its forces under the control of the new government, which effectively meant under General Robert Scobie, commander in chief of the British troops who landed in Greece that October. But many among the ELAS partisans felt that they were losing their chance to impose a communist government and refused to lay down their arms as General Scobie ordered them to do by December 10. On December 3 the police fired on an EAM demonstration in Athens, kill-ing at least sixteen, and the following day vicious **street fighting** broke out between members of the Greek Communist Party (KKE) and British troops which lasted throughout the month, until 11,000 people were killed and large parts of Athens destroyed. In the countryside ELAS rounded up its most influ-ential and wealthy opponents in the larger towns, and marched them out to rural areas in conditions that guaranteed their death.

After Papandreou resigned and the king agreed not to return without a plebi-scite, a **ceasefire** was signed on February 12, 1945, and a new British-backed government agreed to institute democratic reforms. Many of these were not implemented, however. The army, police and civil service remained in right-wing hands, and while collaborators were often allowed to retain their posi-tions, leftwing sympathisers, many of them merely Venizelist Republicans and not communists, were excluded. The elections of March 1946 were boycotted by the KKE, which handed victory to the parties of the right, and a **rigged plebiscite** followed which brought the king back to Greece. Rightwing gangs now roamed the towns and countryside with impunity, and by the summer of 1946 eighty thousand leftists who had been associated with ELAS had taken to the mountains.

By 1947 guerrilla activity had again reached the scale of a **full civil war**, with ELAS reorganized into the Democratic Army of Greece (**DSE**). In the interim, King George had died and been succeeded by his brother Paul, while the Americans had taken over the British role and began implementing the **Truman Doctrine**, the beginning of the Cold War against Soviet intimidation and expansion, which involved giving massive economic and military aid to an amenable Greek government. In the mountains American military advisors trained the initially woeful Greek army for campaigns against the DSE, and in the cities there were mass arrests, courtmartials and imprisonments. From their stronghold on the slopes of Mount Grámmos on the border of Greece and Albania, the partisans continued to fight a losing guerrilla struggle. At the beginning of 1948 Stalin withdrew Soviet support, and in the autumn of 1949, after Tito closed the Yugoslav border, denying the partisans the last means of outside supplies, the remnants of the DSE retreated into Albania and the KKE admitted defeat by proclaiming what it called a temporary suspension of the civil war.

Reconstruction and dictatorship: 1950–74

After a decade of war that had shattered much of Greece's infrastructure (it is said that not one bridge was left standing by 1948), and had killed twelve percent of the 1940 population, it was a demoralized, shattered country that emerged into the Western political orbit of the 1950s. Greece was perforce **American-dominated**, enlisted into the **Korean War** in 1950 and **NATO** the following year. In domestic politics, the US embassy – still giving the orders – foisted upon the Greeks a winner-takes-all **electoral system**, which was to ensure victory for the Right over the next twelve years. Overt leftist activity was banned (though a "cover" party for communists was soon founded), and many of those who were not herded into political "re-education" camps or dispatched by firing squads, legal or vigilante, went into exile throughout Eastern Europe, to return only after 1974. The 1950s also saw the wholesale **depopulation of remote villages** as migrants sought work in Australia, America and Western Europe, or the larger Greek cities.

Constantine Karamanlis and Cyprus

The American-backed right-wing **Greek Rally** party, led by **General Papagos**, won the first decisive post-civil-war elections in 1952. After the general's death, the party's leadership was taken over – and to an extent liberalised – by **Constantine Karamanlis**. Under his rule, stability of a kind was established and some economic advances registered, particularly after the revival of Greece's traditional German markets. Health and life expectancy improved dramatically as the age-old scourges of tuberculosis and malaria were finally confronted with American-supplied food and pesticides. Less commendable was Karamanlis's encouragement of the law of *andiparohí*, whereby owners of small refugee shanties or Neoclassical mansions alike could offer the site of their property to apartment-block developers in exchange for two flats (out of eight to ten) in the finished building. This effectively ripped the heart out of most Greek towns, and explains their baleful aesthetics a half-century on.

The main crisis in foreign policy throughout this period was **Cyprus**, where a long terrorist campaign was waged against the British by Greek Cypriots who demanded self-determination with a view to achieving *enosis* (union) with Greece. Turkey adamantly opposed *enosis* and said that if Britain left Cyprus it should revert to Turkish rule. In 1959 a compromise was reached which granted independence to the island and protection for its Turkish Cypriot minority but ruled out any union with Greece.

By 1961, unemployment, the Cyprus issue and the presence of US nuclear bases on Greek soil were changing the political climate, and when Karamanlis was again elected there was strong suspicion of intimidation and fraud carried out by rightwing elements and the army. After eighteen months of strikes and protest demonstrations, during which the leftwing deputy **Grigoris Lamb-rakis** was assassinated in Thessaloníki in May 1963 (an event which became the subject of the Costa-Gavras film *Z*), Karamanlis resigned and went into voluntary exile in Paris.

George Papandreou and the Colonels

New elections held in February 1964 gave the **Centre Union Party**, headed by **George Papandreou**, an outright majority and a mandate for social and economic reform. The new government was the first to be controlled from outside the right since 1935, and in his first act as prime minister, Papandreou sought to heal the wounds of the civil war by **releasing political prisoners** and allowing exiles to return. When King Paul died in March and his son came to the throne as **Constantine II**, it seemed as though a new era had begun.

But soon **Cyprus** was again taking centre stage. Intercommunal fighting between Turkish Cypriots who wanted partition and Greek Cypriots who wanted *enosis* broke out in 1963, and in 1964 it was only the intervention of the United States that dissuaded Turkey from invading the island. In the mood of military confrontation between Greece and Turkey – both of them NATO members – Papandreou questioned Greece's role in the Western alliance, to the alarm of the Americans and the Greek right.

The right was also opposed to Papandreou's economic policies which were having an inflationary effect, and it feared the growing power of the Left, fears that were bolstered in May 1965 when a plot by **Aspida** (Shield), a subversive group of left-wing army officers, was uncovered – and linked, it was claimed, with Papandreou's son Andreas, a minister in his father's government. More serious were indications of rightwing plots within the army against the government, and when Papandreou moved to purge the army of disloyal officers, the Right took this as an attack on their traditional domination of the armed forces. In July, when the king would not support the prime minister in his attempts to dismiss certain officers, Papandreou resigned in order to gain a fresh mandate at the polls, but the king would not order new elections, instead persuading members of the Centre Union to defect and organize a coalition government. Punctuated by strikes, resignations and mass demonstrations, the political situation in Greece became increasingly unstable over the next year and a half until new elections were eventually set for May 1967.

It was a foregone conclusion that George Papandreou's Centre Union Party would win the 1967 poll against the discredited coalition partners. But **King Constantine**, disturbed by the party's leftward shift, was said to have briefed senior generals for a coup. True or not, the king, like almost everyone else in Greece, was caught by surprise when a group of unknown **colonels** staged their own **coup** on April 21, 1967. In December the king staged a counter-coup against the colonels, but when it failed he went into exile.

The junta announced itself as the "**Revival of Greek Orthodoxy**" against corrupting Western influences, not least long hair and miniskirts, which hardly helped the tourist trade. All political activity was banned, independent trade unions were forbidden to recruit or meet, the press was so heavily censored that many papers stopped printing, and thousands of communists and others on the left were arrested, imprisoned and often tortured. Among these were both Papandreous, father and son, the composer Mikis Theodorakis and Amalia Fleming, the widow of the discoverer of penicillin Alexander Fleming.

Thousands were permanently maimed physically and psychologically in the junta's torture chambers. The world famous Greek actress Melina Mercouri was stripped of her citizenship in absentia, and thousands of prominent Greeks joined her in exile. Culturally, the colonels put an end to popular music (closing down most of the live *rebétika* clubs) and inflicted ludicrous censorship on literature and the theatre, including (as under Metaxas) a ban on the production of classical tragedies. Meantime, the TV and radio broadcast endless speeches by chief colonel **Papadopoulos** – rambling, illiterate texts that became a byword for bad grammar, obfuscation and Orwellian Newspeak. Convinced that he had acquired the job of ruling Greece for life, in 1973 Papadopoulos abolished the monarchy and declared Greece a republic with himself as president.

Restoration of democracy

The colonels lasted for seven years, and whatever initial support they may have met among Greeks, after the first two years they were opposed by the vast majority, including a great many on the right who were embarrassed by their oafishness. Opposition was voiced from the beginning by exiled Greeks in London, the United States and Western Europe, but only in 1973 did demonstrations break out openly in Greece – the colonels' secret police had done too thorough a job of infiltrating domestic resistance groups and terrifying everyone else into docility. On **November 17** the students of the **Athens Polytechnic** began an occupation of their buildings. The ruling clique sent armoured vehicles to storm the Polytechnic's gates and a still-undetermined number of students (estimates range from 34 to 300) were killed. Martial law was tightened and Colonel Papadopoulos was replaced by the even more noxious and reactionary **General Ioannides**, head of the secret police.

The end came within a year when the dictatorship embarked on a disastrous political adventure in **Cyprus**, essentially the last playing of the Megali Idhea card. By attempting to topple the Makarios government and **impose enosis** on the island, the junta provoked a **Turkish invasion** and occupation of forty per cent of Cypriot territory. The army finally mutinied and **Constantine Karamanlis** was invited to return from Paris to again take office.

Karamanlis swiftly negotiated a ceasefire in Cyprus, and in November 1974 he and his **Néa Dhimokratía** (New Democracy) party were rewarded by a sizeable majority in elections, with a centrist and socialist opposition. The latter was the Panhellenic Socialist Movement (PASOK), a new party led by **Andreas Papandreou**.

Europe and a new Greece: 1974 to the present

To Karamanlis's enduring credit his New Democracy party oversaw an effective and firm return to **democratic stability**, even legalizing the KKE (the Greek Communist Party) for the first time in its history. Karamanlis also held a **referendum on the monarchy**, in which seventy per cent of Greeks rejected the return of Constantine II. So a largely symbolic, German-style presidency was instituted instead, which Karamanlis himself occupied from 1980 to 1985, and again from 1990 to 1995.

PASOK comes to power

"Change" and "Out with the Right" were the slogans of the election campaign that swept the socialist party, **PASOK**, and its leader Andreas Papandreou to power on October 18, 1981. PASOK won 174 of the 300 parliamentary seats and the Communist KKE, though not a part of the new government, returned another 13 deputies. The manifesto of Greece's first socialist government was to devolve power to local authorities, nationalize heavy industry, improve the skeletal social services, purge bureaucratic inefficiency and malpractice, end bribery and corruption, and to follow an independent foreign policy after removing US bases and withdrawing from NATO and the European Community.

The new era started with a bang as long-overdue **social reforms** were enacted. Peasant women were granted pensions for the first time; wages were indexed to the cost of living; civil marriage was introduced, family and property law was reformed in favour of wives and mothers; demanding dowries was forbidden (though it still continues informally); and equal rights legislation was put on the statute book. In addition, ELAS was officially recognised and was permitted to take part in ceremonies commemorating the wartime resistance. This prompted fears that the military might again intervene, especially when Andreas Papandreou, imitating his father, briefly assumed the defence portfolio himself. But he went out of his way to soothe military susceptibilities, increasing their salaries, buying new weaponry and being fastidious in his attendance at military functions.

Economically, Papandreou promised a bonanza which he must have known, as an academically trained economist, was strictly fantasy. As a result he pleased nobody. He could not fairly be blamed for the inherited lack of investment, low productivity, deficiency in managerial and labour skills and other chronic problems besetting the Greek **economy**. But he certainly aggravated the situation by allowing his supporters to indulge in violently anti-capitalist rhetoric, which frightened off potential investors. At the same time Papandreou's government

△ Andreas Papandreou rouses the PASOK faithful, 1985

had to cope with the effects of **world recession**. Shipping, the country's main foreign-currency earner, was devastated. Remittances from émigré workers fell off as they became unemployed in their host countries, and tourism diminished. Unemployment rose, inflation hit 25 per cent and the national debt soared.

Under the slogan "Vote PASOK for Even Better Days", backed by a public spending spree intended to buy votes, and a shamelessly nationalistic "Greece-for-the-Greeks" foreign policy, Papandreou won a second term in June 1985. But by October, PASOK had imposed a two-year wage freeze and import restrictions, abolished the wage-indexing scheme and devalued the drachma by fifteen per cent. In the event it was the **European Community**, once Papandreou's bête noire, which rescued him from his follies with a huge two-part loan on condition that an austerity programme was maintained. Increasingly autocratic, Papandreou responded to criticism from the left by firing trade union leaders and expelling three hundred dissenting members of his own party. Fearing that only the presence of US bases in Greece guaranteed protection from Turkish aggression, Papandreou's demand for their removal was dropped. Nor with the European Community – soon to become the European Union – propping up Greece financially would Papandreou now bite the hand that feeds.

Despite Papandreou's many failings and about-turns, it seemed unlikely that PASOK would be toppled in the 1989 elections. But the collapse of Soviet rule in Eastern Europe was reflected by a shift away from the left in Greece, and then there was Papandreou's very public affair with an Olympic Airways hostess half his age and his humiliation of his wife and family, not to mention a whole raft of economic scandals. In consequence, PASOK lost power as a trio of inconclusive elections finally resulted in the New Democracy party winning a tiny majority, its leader **Constantine Mitsotakis** becoming prime minister.

On assuming power, Mitsotakis prescribed a course of austerity measures to revive the chronically ill economy. Little headway was made, though given the world recession that was hardly surprising. Greek inflation was still approaching twenty percent annually, and at nearly ten percent, unemployment remained stubbornly high. Other measures introduced by Mitsotakis included laws to combat strikes, but these were ineffectual, as breakdowns in public transport, electricity and rubbish collection all too frequently illustrated.

The Macedonian problem and return of PASOK

The last thing the increasingly unpopular Mitsotakis needed was a major foreign policy headache. But that was exactly what he got in 1991 when one of the breakaway republics of the **former Yugoslavia** named itself **Macedonia**. Greeks felt threatened because Macedonia was a name historically associated with northern Greece, and the fear was that this new and unstable country was laying claim to a part of Greek heritage and territory. Greek diplomacy and propaganda fought tooth and nail against anyone recognising the breakaway state, let alone its use of the name Macedonia, but Greece became increasingly isolated, and by 1993 the new country had gained official recognition from both the EU and the UN – albeit under the provisional title of the "**Former Yugoslav Republic of Macedonia**" (FYROM). Salt was then rubbed into Greek wounds when the FYROM started using the Star of Vergina, symbol of the ancient Macedonian kings, as a national symbol on its new flag, as well as having passages in its constitution referring to "unredeemed" Aegean territories.

The Macedonian problem effectively led to Mitsotakis' political demise, after the defection of a senior party figure, Andonis Samaras, and his creation of a new party, Politiki Anixi, based on the issue of Macedonia. When parliament reconvened in September to approve stringent new budget proposals, the government failed to muster sufficient support, and early elections were called for October 1993. On October 11 Papandreou romped to victory; and the youthful Miltiades Evert, ex-mayor of Athens, replaced Mitsotakis as head of the New Democracy party.

So a frail-looking **Andreas Papandreou**, now well into his seventies, became prime minister for the third time. He soon realized that he was not going to have nearly so easy a ride as in the 1980s, with the economy still in dire straits, and nor could PASOK claim to have won any diplomatic battles over Macedonia, despite a lot of tough posturing. The only concrete move was the imposition in October 1993 of a trade embargo on the FYROM, which merely landed the Greeks in trouble with the European Court of Justice – and succeeded in virtually shutting down the port of Thessaloniki. By contrast, alone among NATO members, Greece was conspicuous for its open support of **Serbia** in the wars wracking ex-Yugoslavia, ostentatiously supplying trucks to Belgrade via Bulgaria. In November, Greece lifted its embargo on the FYROM, opening the borders for tourism and trade in return for the former Yugoslav state suitably editing its constitution and removing the offending emblem from its flag. Relations, in fact, were instantly almost normalized, with only the name still a moot point.

Domestically, the emerging critical issue was the 76-year-old Papandreou's obstinate clinging to power despite obvious signs of dotage. Numerous senior members of PASOK became increasingly bold and vocal in their criticism, and in January 1996, after months in hospital intensive care, Papandreou finally resigned the premiership, which went to technocrat **Kostas Simitis**. On assuming office, Simitis vowed *not* to play to the gallery, saying: "Greece's intransigent nationalism is an expression of the wretchedness that exists in our society. It is the root cause of the problems we have had with our Balkan neighbours and our difficult relations with Europe." **Andreas Papandreou** died in June, "a common cheat", as Karamanlis called him in his tart memoirs, when it was discovered that he had accumulated a vast fortune beyond anything he could have earned legitimately as a public servant. But for the time being, Papandreou's death generated a wave of pro-PASOK sentiment which Simitis successfully exploited by quickly calling elections in September and gaining victory. Evert resigned as the New Democracy leader and was succeeded by Karamanlis's nephew Kostas.

Earthquake diplomacy and the Euro

September 1997 saw a timely boost to national morale with the awarding of the 2004 Olympic Games to Athens. Meanwhile, Kostas Simitis, who unlike Papandreou was genuinely pro-European, devoted himself to the unenviable task of getting the Greek economy in sufficiently good shape to meet the criteria for European **monetary union**. The fact that inflation stayed consistently down in single figures for the first time in decades was testament to his ability; indeed his nickname, among both foes and supporters, was "the accountant".

An unexpected and dramatic change in **Greece's relations with Turkey** came when a severe **earthquake** struck northern Athens on September 7, 1999, killing scores and rendering almost 100,000 homeless. It came less than a month after a devastating earthquake in northwest Turkey, and proved to be the spur for a thaw between the two historical rivals. Greeks donated massive amounts of blood and foodstuffs to the Turkish victims, and were the earliest foreign rescue teams on hand in Turkey; in turn they saw Turkish disaster-relief squads among the first on the scene in Athens. Soon afterwards, foreign minister George Papandreou (son of Andreas) announced that Greece had dropped its long-time opposition to EU financial aid to Turkey in the absence of a solution to the outstanding Cyprus and Aegean disputes, and further indicated that Greece would no longer oppose Turkish candidacy for accession to the EU.

With his handling of the Turkish detente and progress towards European monetary union the main campaign issues, Simitis called elections five months earlier than required, on April 9, 2000. In the event, PASOK squeaked into office for a third consecutive term by a single percentage point. But the crucial factor was voters' mistrust of new ND leader Kostas Karamanlis's manifest inexperience. Simitis capped his election victory by announcing Greece's official entry into the euro-currency zone on June 20, though it later turned out that the conditions were met only by his government falsifying its budget deficit data. Greece adopted **the euro** on January 1, 2002.

The year also saw a strange saga played out with the arrest of apparently the entire operational members of the terrorist group **Dhekaeftá Novemvríou**. This shadowy, leftist organization, named after the Polytechnic uprising against the Colonels, had been a thorn in Greece's security since 1974, killing twenty-four

Immigration – and the Albanian influx

Greece may continue to occupy the EU's economic cellar with Portugal, but it's still infinitely wealthier (and more stable) than many of its neighbours, and this has acted as a magnet for a permanent underclass of immigrants. Since 1990 they have arrived in numbers estimated at 800,000 to well over a million, a huge burden for a not especially rich country of just over ten million citizens. These days your waiter, hotel desk clerk or cleaning lady is most likely to be Albanian, Bulgarian or Romanian, to cite the three largest groups of arrivals. There are also significant communities of Pakistanis, Egyptians, Poles, Bangladeshis, Syrians, Filipinos, Ukrainians, Russians, Equatorial Africans, Kurds and Georgians, not to mention ethnic Greeks from the Caucasus – a striking change in what had hitherto been a homogeneous and parochial culture.

The Greek response to this has been decidedly mixed. The Albanians, making up roughly half the influx, are almost universally detested (except for the ethnic-Greek northern Epirots), and blamed for all manner of social ills. For the first time, crime – especially burglaries – is a significant issue. The newcomers have also prompted the first significant anti-immigration measures in a country whose population is more used to being on the other side of such laws – Greece is a member of the Schengen visa scheme and sees itself, as in past ages, as the first line of defence against the barbarian hordes from the East. The Aegean islands regularly receive boatloads of people from every country in Asia.

In June 2001, as an attempt to cope, legal residence was offered to the estimated half-million illegals who could demonstrate two years' presence in Greece, and pay a hefty amount for retroactive social security contributions. This and a subsequent amnesty legalized about 300,000 residents. Not that the other illegals are likely to be deported en masse, as they do the difficult, dirty and dangerous work that Greeks now disdain, especially farm labour, restaurant work and rubbish collection. From an employer's point of view, they are cheap – thirty to forty per cent less costly than native Greeks – and they are net contributors to the social welfare system, especially to pensions where Greece, like much of Europe, is seeing its population shrinking and aging. The Albanians in particular are also buoying up much of the banking system by their phenomenal saving habits and wiring of funds home.

Though there is much that is positive about immigration, it must also be said that it is having the effect of making Greece less identifiably Greek and of making the native Greeks themselves less welcoming and more self-absorbed than formerly.

industrialists, politicians and NATO military personnel, and bombing the property of foreign corporations in Athens and elsewhere. As with all the best police actions, their demise came through a stroke of luck, when a bomb exploded prematurely in the hands of an operative. After a nine-month trial, fifteen of the group's members received multiple life sentences.

Olympian hurdles and a new Karamanlis

In the October 2002 municipal and prefectural elections, New Democracy took substantial control. PASOK had now been in power nationally for nineteen out of the last twenty-three years, and sentiment was growing for a change. In February 2004 Simitis stood down as party leader, signalling his belief that one of his main reforms had been effected: an end to personality-based politics, and the completed evolution of an issue-based, centrist, technocratic party. That said, both parties had familiar dynastic names in charge, with **George Papandreou** taking over leadership of PASOK, and fighting an election against New Democracy, led by **Kostas Karamanlis**, nephew of Constantine.

New Democracy won comfortably and Karamanlis, who became prime minister, dedicated himself to negotiations over divided **Cyprus** in an attempt to get the entire island into the EU on May 1, 2004 (in the event the internationally recognized Republic of Cyprus did join, but without the Turkish-occupied north). He also took personal responsibility for ensuring completion of all preparations for the **2004 Olympic Games**. In a last-minute rush all facilities were ready in August, in time for the games in Athens, but the cost rose to three times the original estimates, and as a result of poor marketing, jacked-up hotel prices and fears of terrorism, tourism to Greece actually fell during the year and the Games turned in a deficit.

The after effects of Olympic spending, and Greece's joining the euro at too high a level after rigging its accounts, were felt in March 2005 when trade unions launched a wave of twenty-four hour strikes across the country in protest at high inflation and rising unemployment. In April the Greek parliament ratified the EU constitution, but it soon became a dead letter when it was rejected by referendums elsewhere. A further wave of **industrial action** followed in June over the government's plans for labour and pension reforms.

But there was at least some positive economic news, with **shipping** undergoing something of a boom; nearly a fifth of the world's merchant fleet is owned by Greek companies, and their fortunes have a significant impact on the country. And as the dust settled, the Olympics, for all their faults showed enduring benefits to **Greek infrastructure**, particularly in completion of the new **metro system** for Athens, which now speedily and cheaply connects a new airport with the city. These improvements should lay the foundation for the country's future development.

Archeology in Greece

U ntil the second half of the nineteenth century, archeology was a very hit-and-miss, treasure-hunting affair. The early students of antiquity went to Greece to draw and make plaster casts of the great master-pieces of Classical sculpture. Unfortunately, a number soon found it more convenient or more profitable to remove objects wholesale, and might be better described as looters than scholars or archeologists.

Early excavations

The **British Society of Dilettanti** was one of the earliest promoters of Greek culture, financing expeditions to draw and publish antiquities. Founded in the 1730s as a club for young aristocrats who had completed the Grand Tour and fancied themselves arbiters of taste, the society's main qualification for member-ship (according to most critics) was habitual drunkenness. Its leading spirit was **Sir Francis Dashwood**, a notorious rake who founded the infamous Hellfire Club. Nevertheless, the society was the first body organized to sponsor system-atic research into Greek antiquities, though it was initially most interested in Italy. Greece, then a backwater of the Ottoman Empire, was not a regular part of the Grand Tour and only the most intrepid adventurers undertook so hazardous a trip.

In the 1740s, two young artists, **James Stuart** and **Nicholas Revett**, formed a plan to produce a scholarly record of ancient Greek buildings. With the support of the society they spent three years in Greece, principally in and around Athens, drawing and measuring the antiquities. The first volume of *The Antiquities of Athens* appeared in 1762, becoming an instant success. The publication of their exquisite illustrations and the 1764 publication of **Johann Winckelmann**'s *History of Art*, in which the **Parthenon** and its sculptures were exalted as the eternal standard by which beauty should be measured, gave an enormous fillip to the study of Greek sculpture and architecture, which became the fashionable craze among the educated classes; many European Neoclassical town and country houses date from this period.

The Dilettanti financed a number of further expeditions to study Greek antiquities, including one to Asia Minor in 1812. The expedition was to be based in Smyrna, but while waiting in Athens for a ship to Turkey, the party employed themselves in excavations at **Eleusis**, where they uncovered the **Temple of Demeter**. It was the first archeological excavation made on behalf of the society, and one of the first in Greece. After extensive explorations in Asia Minor, the participants returned via Attica, where they excavated the **Temple of Nemesis** at **Rhamnous** and examined the **Temple of Poseidon** at **Soúnio**.

Several other antiquarians of the age were less interested in discoveries for their own sake. A French count, **Choiseul-Gouffier**, removed part of the **Parthenon frieze** in 1787 and his example prompted **Lord Elgin** to detach much of the rest in 1801. These were essentially acts of looting – "Bonaparte has not got such things from all his thefts in Italy", boasted Elgin – and their legality was suspect even at the time.

Other discoveries of the period were more ambiguous. In 1811, a party of English and German travellers, including the architect **C. R. Cockerell**, uncovered the **Temple of Aphaia** on **Égina** and shipped away the pediments.

They auctioned off the marbles for £6000 to Prince Ludwig of Bavaria, and, inspired by this success, returned to Greece for further finds. This time they struck it lucky with 23 slabs from the **Temple of Apollo Epikourios** at **Bassae**, for which the British Museum laid out a further £15,000. These were huge sums for the time and highly profitable exercises, but they were also pioneering archeology for the period. Besides, removing the finds was hardly surprising: Greece, after all, was not yet a state and had no public museum; antiquities discovered were sold by their finders – if they recognized their value.

The new nation

The Greek War of Independence (1821–28) and the establishment of a modern Greek nation changed all of this – and provided a major impetus to archeology. Nationhood brought an increased pride in Greece's Classical heritage, nowhere more so than in Athens, which succeeded Náfplio as the nation's capital in 1834 largely on the basis of its ancient monuments, especially those on the acropolis, and its glorious past.

As a result of the selection of Prince Otto of Bavaria as the first king of modern Greece in 1832, the **Germans**, whose education system laid great stress on Classical learning, were in the forefront of archeological activity. One of the dominant Teutonic figures during the early years of the new state was **Ludwig Ross**. Arriving in Greece as a student in 1832, he was on hand to show the new king around the antiquities of Athens when Otto was considering making the town his capital. Ross was appointed deputy keeper of antiquities to the court, and in 1834 began supervising the excavation and restoration of the **Acropolis**. The work of dismantling the accretion of Byzantine, Frankish and Turkish fortifications began the following year. The graceful **Temple of Athena Nike**, which had furnished many of the blocks for the fortifications, was rebuilt, and Ross's architect, Leo von Klenze, began the **reconstruction of the Parthenon**.

The Greeks themselves had begun to focus on their ancient past when the first stirrings of the independence movement were felt. In 1813 the **Philomuse Society** was formed, which aimed to uncover and collect antiquities, publish books and assist students and foreign philhellenes. In 1829 an orphanage on the island of Égina, built by Kapodistrias, the first president of Greece, became the first **Greek archeological museum**.

In 1837 the **Greek Archeological Society** was founded "for the discovery, recovery and restoration of antiquities in Greece". Its moving spirit was **Kyriakos Pittakis**, a remarkable figure who during the War of Independence had used his knowledge of ancient literature to discover the Klepsydra spring on the Acropolis – solving the problem of lack of water during the Turkish siege. In the first four years of its existence, the Archeological Society sponsored excavations in Athens at the **Theatre of Dionysos**, the **Tower of the Winds**, the **Propylaia** and the **Erechtheion**. Pittakis also played a major role in the attempt to convince Greeks of the importance of their heritage; antiquities were still being looted or burned for lime.

The great Germans: Curtius and Schliemann

Although King Otto was deposed in 1862 in favour of a Danish prince, Germans remained in the forefront of Greek archeology in the 1870s. Two men dominated the scene: Heinrich Schliemann and Ernst Curtius.

Ernst Curtius was a traditional Classical scholar. He had come to Athens originally as tutor to King Otto's family and in 1874 returned to Greece to secure permission for conducting the excavations at **Olympia**, one of the richest of Greek sanctuaries and site of the most famous of the ancient pan-Hellenic games. The reigning Kaiser Wilhelm I intended that the excavation would proclaim to the world the cultural and intellectual pre-eminence of his empire. Curtius took steps to set up a **German Archeological Institute** in Athens and negotiated the **Olympia Convention**, under the terms of which the Germans were to pay for and have total control of the dig; all finds were to remain in Greece, though the excavators could make copies and casts; and all finds were to be published simultaneously in Greek and German.

This was an enormously important agreement, which almost certainly prevented the treasure of Olympia and Mycenae following that of Troy to a German museum. But other Europeans were still in very acquisitive mode: **French consuls**, for example, had been instructed to purchase any "available" local antiquities in Greece and Asia Minor, and had picked up the Louvre's great treasures, the **Venus de Milo** and **Winged Victory of Samothrace**, in 1820 and 1863 respectively.

At **Olympia**, digging began in 1875 on a site buried beneath river mud, silt and sand. Only one corner of the **Temple of Zeus** was initially visible, but within months the excavators had turned up statues from the east pediment. Over forty magnificent sculptures, as well as terracottas, statue bases and a rich collection of bronzes, were uncovered, together with more than four hundred inscriptions. The laying bare of this huge complex was a triumph for official German archeology.

While Curtius was digging at Olympia, a man who represented everything that was anathema to orthodox Classical scholarship was standing archeology on its head. **Heinrich Schliemann**'s beginnings were not auspicious for one who aspired to hunt for ancient cities. The son of a drunken German pastor, he left school at fourteen and spent the next five years as a grocer's assistant. En route to seeking his fortune in Venezuela, he was left for dead on the Dutch coast after a shipwreck; later, working as a book-keeper in Amsterdam, he began to study languages. His phenomenal memory enabled him to master four by the age of 21. Following a six-week study of Russian, Schliemann was sent to St Petersburg as a trading agent and had amassed a fortune by the time he was 30. In 1851 he visited California, opened a bank during the Gold Rush and made another fortune.

His financial position secure for life, Schliemann was almost ready to tackle his life's ambition – the **search for Troy** and the vindication of his lifelong belief in the truth of Homer's tales of prehistoric cities and heroes. By this time he spoke no fewer than seventeen languages, and had excavated on the island of **Ithaca**, writing a book, which earned him a doctorate from the University of Rostock.

Although most of the archeological establishment, led by Curtius, was unremittingly hostile to the millionaire amateur, Schliemann sunk his first trench at the hill called Hisarlik, in northwest Turkey, in 1870; excavation proper began in 1871. In his haste to find Homer's city of Priam and Hector, and to convince the world of his success, Schliemann dug a huge trench straight through the mound, destroying a mass of important evidence, but he was able nevertheless to identify nine cities, superimposed in layers. In May 1873 he discovered the so-called **Treasure of Priam**, a stash of gold and precious jewellery and vessels. It convinced many that the German had indeed found **Troy**, although others contended that Schliemann, desperate for academic recognition, assembled it from other sources. The finds disappeared from Berlin at the end of World War II, but in 1994 archeologists discovered that artefacts held by some museums in Russia originated in Troy; most of these are currently on display in the Pushkin Museum in Moscow, with a few items also in the Hermitage collection in St Petersburg. The Germans have requested their return but as the Russian government has since linked this matter to the vexed question of reparations for the damage done to their land and property by the German army, it seems that they are destined to remain in Russia for the foreseeable future.

Three years later Schliemann turned his attentions to **Mycenae**, again inspired by Homer, and once more following a hunch. Alone among contemporary scholars, he sought and found the legendary graves of Mycenaean kings inside the existing Cyclopean wall of the citadel rather than outside it, unearthing in the process the magnificent treasures that today form the basis of the **Bronze Age collection** in the National Archeological Museum in Athens.

He dug again at Troy in 1882, assisted by a young architect, **Wilhelm Dörpfeld**, who was destined to become one of the great archeologists of the following century (though his claim that Lefkádha was ancient Ithaca never found popular acceptance). In 1884 Schliemann returned to Greece to excavate another famous prehistoric citadel, this time at **Tiryns**.

Almost single-handedly, and in the face of continuing academic obstruction, Schliemann had revolutionized archeology and pushed back the knowledge of Greek history and civilization a thousand years. Although some of his results have been shown to have been deliberately falsified in the sacrifice of truth to beauty, his achievement remains enormous.

The last two decades of the nineteenth century saw the discovery of other important Classical sites. Excavation began at **Epidaurus** in 1881 under the Greek archeologist **Panayotis Kavvadias**, who made it his life's work. Meanwhile at **Delphi**, the **French**, after gaining permission to transfer the inhabitants of the village to a new site and demolishing the now-vacant village, began digging at the **sanctuary of Apollo**. Their excavations proved fruitful and continued nonstop from 1892 to 1903, revealing the extensive site visible today; work on the site has gone on sporadically ever since.

Evans and Knossos

The beginning of the twentieth century saw the domination of Greek archeology by an Englishman, **Sir Arthur Evans**. An egotistical maverick like Schliemann, he too was independently wealthy, with a brilliantly successful career behind him when he started his great work and recovered another millennium for Greek history. Evans excavated what he called the "Palace of Minos" at **Knossos** on **Crete**, discovering one of the oldest and most sophisticated of Mediterranean societies, which he christened Minoan.

The son of a distinguished antiquarian and collector, Evans read history at Oxford, failed to get a fellowship and began to travel. His chief interest was in the Balkans, where he was special correspondent for the *Manchester Guardian* during the 1877 uprising in Bosnia. He took enormous risks in the war-torn country, filing brilliant dispatches and still finding time for exploration and excavation. In 1884, at the age of 33, Evans was appointed curator of the Ashmolean Museum in Oxford. He travelled whenever he could, and it was in 1893, while in Athens, that his attention was drawn to Crete. Evans, though very short-sighted, had almost microscopic close vision. In a vendor's stall he came upon some small drilled stones with tiny engravings in a hitherto unknown script; he was told they came from Crete. He had seen Schliemann's finds from

Mycenae and had been fascinated by this prehistoric culture. Crete, the crossroads of the Mediterranean, seemed a good place to look for more.

Evans visited Crete in 1894 and headed for the legendary site of Knossos, which had earlier attracted the attention of Schliemann (who had been unable to agree a price with the Turkish owners of the land) and where a Cretan, appropriately called Minos, had already done some impromptu digging, revealing massive walls and a storeroom filled with jars. Evans succeeded in buying the site and in March 1900 began excavations. Within a few days, evidence of a great complex building was revealed, along with artefacts which indicated an astonishing cultural sophistication. The huge team of diggers unearthed elegant courtyards and verandahs, colourful wall-paintings, pottery, jewellery and sealstones – the wealth of a civilization which dominated the eastern Mediterranean 3500 years ago.

Evans continued to excavate at Knossos for the next thirty years, during which time he established, on the basis of changes in the pottery styles, the **system of dating** that remains in use today for classifying **Greek prehistory**: Early, Middle and Late Minoan (Mycenaean on the mainland). He published his account of the excavation in a massive six-volume work, *The Palace of Minos*, between 1921 and 1936. Like Schliemann, Evans attracted criticism and controversy for his methods – most notably his decision to speculatively reconstruct parts of the palace in concrete – and for many of his interpretations of what he found. Nevertheless, his discoveries and his dedication put him near to the pinnacle of Greek archeology.

△ Sir Arthur Evans holding a Cretan sculpture of a bull's head at an exhibition of relics from Knossos

Into the twentieth century: the foreign institutes

In 1924 Evans gave to the **British School at Athens** the site of **Knossos** along with his on-site residence, the Villa Ariadne, and all other lands within his possession on Crete (it was only in 1952 that Knossos became the property of the Greek State). At the time the British School was one of several foreign archeological institutes in Greece; founded in 1886, it had been preceded by the **French School**, the **German Institute** and the **American School**.

Greek archeology owes much to the work and relative wealth of these foreign schools and others that would follow. They have been responsible for the excavation of many of the most famous sites in Greece: the **Heraion** on **Sámos** (German); the sacred island of **Delos** (French); sites on **Kós** and in southern **Crete** (Italian); **Corinth**, **Samothráki** and the **Athenian Agora** (American), to name but a few. Life as a resident foreigner in Greece at the beginning of the twentieth century was not for the weak-spirited – one unfortunate member of the American School was shot and killed by bandits while on a trip to visit sites in the Peloponnese – but there were compensations in unlimited access to antiquities in an unspoilt countryside.

The years between the two World Wars saw an expansion of excavation and scholarship, most markedly concerning the prehistoric civilizations. Having been shown by Schliemann and Evans what to look for, a new generation of archeologists was uncovering numerous **prehistoric sites** on the mainland and Crete, and its members were spending proportionately more time studying and interpreting their finds. Digs in the 1920s and 1930s had much smaller labour forces (there were just 55 workmen under Wace at Mycenae, as compared with hundreds in the early days of Schliemann's or Evans's excavations) and they were supervised by higher numbers of trained archeologists. Though perhaps not as spectacular as their predecessors, these scholars would prove just as pioneering as they established the history and clarified the chronology of the newly discovered civilizations.

One of the giants of this generation was **Alan Wace** who, while director of the British School at Athens from 1913 to 1923, conducted excavations at **Mycenae** and established a chronological sequence from the nine great *tholos* tombs on the site. This led Wace to propose a new chronology for prehistoric Greece, which put him in direct conflict with Arthur Evans. Evans believed that the mainland citadels had been ruled by Cretan overlords, whereas Wace was convinced of an independent Mycenaean cultural and political development. Evans was by now a powerful member of the British School's managing committee, and his published attacks on Wace's claims, combined with the younger archeologist's less than tactful reactions to Evans's dominating personality, resulted in the abrupt halt of the British excavations at Mycenae in 1923 and the no less sudden termination of Wace's job. Wace returned to Mycenae in 1950, nine years after Evans's death, and found examples of the "Minoan" **Linear B script**, which British architect **Michael Ventris** deciphered in 1952 as the earliest Greek language. This meant that the Mycenaean Greeks had conquered the Minoans in approximately 1450 BC, which vindicated Wace.

Classical archeology was not forgotten in the flush of excitement over the Mycenaeans and Minoans. The period between the wars saw the continuation of excavation at most established sites, and many new discoveries, among them the sanctuary of **Asklepios** and its elegant Roman buildings on **Kós**, excavated by the Italians from 1935 to 1943, and the Classical Greek city of **Olynthos**, in northern Greece, which was dug by the American School from 1928 to 1934. After the wholesale removal of houses and apartment blocks that had occupied the site, the American School also began excavations in the **Athenian Agora**, the ancient marketplace, in 1931, culminating in the complete restoration of the **Stoa of Attalos**.

The advent of **World War II** and the invasion of Greece first by the Italians and then the Germans called a halt to most archeological work, although the Germans set to work again at **Olympia**, supposedly owing to Hitler's personal interest. A few Allied-nation archeologists also remained in Greece, principal among them **Gorham Stevens** and **Eugene Vanderpool**, of the American School, both of whom did charitable work. Back in America and Britain, meanwhile, archeologists were in demand for the intelligence arm of the war effort, both for their intimate knowledge of the Greek terrain and their linguistic abilities, which proved invaluable in decoding enemy messages.

More recent excavations

Archeological work was greatly restricted in the years after World War II, and in the shadow of the Greek civil war. A few monuments and museums were restored and reopened but it was not until 1948 that excavations were resumed with a Greek clearance of the **Sanctuary of Artemis** at **Brauron** in Attica. In 1952 the American School resumed its activities with a dig at the Neolithic and Bronze Age site of **Lerna** in the Peloponnese, and **Carl Blegen** cleared **Nestor's Palace** at **Pylos** in Messenia. Greek archeologists began work at the Macedonian site of **Pella**, the capital of ancient Macedonia, and at the **Nekromanteion of Ephyra** in Epirus.

These and many other excavations – including renewed work on the major sites – were relatively minor operations in comparison to earlier digs. This reflected a modified approach to archeology, which laid less stress on discoveries and more on **documentation**. Instead of digging large tracts of a site, archeologists concentrated on small sections, establishing chronologies through meticulous analysis of data. Which is not to say that there were no spectacular finds. At **Mycenae**, in 1951, a second circle of graves was unearthed; at Pireás, a burst sewer in 1959 revealed four superb Classical bronzes; and a dig at the **Kerameikos** cemetery site in Athens in 1966 found four thousand potsherds used as ballots for ostracism. Important work has also been undertaken on restorations – in particular the **theatres** at the **Athens Acropolis**, **Dodona** and **Epidaurus**, which are used in summer festivals.

A number of postwar excavation were as exciting as any in the past. In 1961 the fourth great **Minoan palace** (following the unearthing of Knossos, Phaestos and Malia) was uncovered by torrential rains at the extreme eastern tip of the island of Crete at **Káto Zákros** and cleared by Cretan archeologist **Nikolaos Platon**. Its harbour is now thought to have been the Minoans' main gateway port to and from Southwest Asia and Africa, and many of the artefacts discovered in the palace storerooms – bronze ingots from Cyprus, elephants' tusks from Syria, stone vases from Egypt – seem to confirm this. Greek teams have found more Minoan palaces at **Arhánes**, **Haniá**, **Galatás** and **Petrás**, and a new generation of scholars believe that these were ceremonial buildings and not the seats of dynastic authority, as Evans proposed. American excavations at **Kommós**, in southern Crete, have uncovered another gateway site, like Káto Zakrós, of the Minoan and Mycenaean periods.

At **Akrotíri** on the island of **Thíra** (Santoríni), **Spyros Marinatos** revealed, in 1967, a Minoan-era site that had been buried by volcanic explosion in either 1650 or 1550 BC – the jury is still deliberating that one. Its buildings were two or three storeys high, and superbly frescoed. Marinatos was later tragically killed while at work on the site when he fell off a wall, and is now buried there.

A decade later came an even more dramatic find at **Vergina – ancient Aegae** – in northern Greece, the early capital of the Macedonian kingdom, which later became its necropolis. Here, **Manolis Andronikos** found a series of royal tombs dating from the fourth century BC. Unusually, these had escaped plundering by ancient grave robbers and contained an astonishing hoard of exquisite gold treasures. Piecing together clues – the haste of the tomb's construction, an ivory effigy head, gilded leg armour – Andronikos showed this to have been the **tomb of Philip II** of Macedon, father of Alexander the Great. Subsequent forensic examination of the body's remains supported historical accounts of Philip's limp and blindness. It was an astonishing and highly emotive find, as the artefacts and frescoed walls showed the sophistication and Hellenism of ancient Macedonian culture. With the background of an emerging, self-styled Slavo-Macedonian state on Greece's northern border, archeology had come head-to-head with politics.

At the beginning of this century the various foreign schools, recently joined by the Australian, Austrian, Belgian, Canadian, Danish, Dutch, Finnish, Georgian, Irish, Norwegian, Spanish, Swedish and Swiss, along with Greek universities and the 25 *ephorates*, or inspectorates, of Prehistoric and Classical Antiquities are still at work in the field, although the emphasis today is equally concerned with the task of **conserving and protecting** what has been revealed as well as unearthing new finds. All too often newly discovered sites have been inadequately fenced off or protected, and a combination of the elements, greedy developers and malicious trespassers – sometimes all three – have caused much damage and deterioration.

The American School continues its work on the **Athenian Agora** and also in excavating **Roman Corinth** and a number of sites in Crete's Mirabello region. The British School maintains its interest in **Knossos**; the **Spartan Acropolis**, **Lefkandí** in Évvia (where **Hugh Sackett**'s team discovered an important Iron Age town and Heroon); and at **Paleókastro** in eastern Crete, the site of the ancient **Diktaion** – the sacred precinct of Cretan Zeus – where a superb Minoan gold and ivory *kouros* was found recently. In Crete too, the French School is carrying out further excavations in the town surrounding the Minoan palace at **Mália**; they are also continuing restoration work in the **Sanctuary of Apollo** on the island of **Delos**.

Meanwhile, and in the footsteps of Curtius, the German Institute continues its long-standing association with excavations at **Olympia** and the **Kerameikos** cemetery in Athens and is still at work on the **Heraion**, the mammoth sanctuary dedicated to the goddess Hera, on the island of **Sámos**. The Italian School is based mainly in Crete where, among other sites, the impressive forum of the island's Roman capital at **Gortys** is being revealed. Italian archeologists have also been busy at the important site of **Polyochni** on **Límnos**.

Since World War II Greek archeologists have also played a leading role and the Greek Archeological Society is involved in excavation and conservation work in all parts of Greece including **Marathon**, **Epidaurus** and **Dodona** as well as at **Akrotíri**, where more of the remarkable Minoan era site with paintings and multistoried buildings is slowly and spectacularly being excavated and protected.

Wild Greece

F or anyone who has first seen Greece at the height of summer with its brown parched hillsides and desert-like ambience, the richness of the wildlife – in particular the flora – may come as a surprise. As winter warms into spring, the countryside (and urban waste ground) transforms itself from green to a mosaic of coloured flowers, which attract a plethora of insect life, followed by birds. Isolated areas, whether true islands or remote mountains such as Olympus, have had many thousands of years to develop their own individual species. Overall, Greece has around six thousand species of native flowering plants, nearly four times that of Britain but in the same land area. Many are unique to Greece, and make up about one-third of Europe's endemic plants.

Despite an often negative attitude to wildlife, Greece was probably the first place in the world where it was an object of study. **Theophrastos** (372–287 BC) from Lésvos was the first recorded botanist and a systematic collector of general information on plants, while his contemporary, **Aristotle**, studied the animal world. And during the first century AD the distinguished physician **Dioscorides** compiled a herbal study that remained a standard work for over a thousand years.

Some background

In early antiquity Greece was thickly forested: pines and oak grew in coastal regions, giving way to fir or black pine in the hills and lower mountains. But this **native woodland** contracted rapidly as human activities expanded. By Classical times, the pattern was set of forest clearance, followed by agriculture, abandonment to scrub and then a resumption of cultivation or grazing. Huge quantities of timber were consumed for ships and construction work and in the production of charcoal for pottery and smelted metal. Small patches of virgin woodland remain, mostly in the north and northeast, but even these are threatened by loggers and arsonists.

Greek **farming** often lacks the rigid efficiency of north European agriculture. Many peasant farmers still cultivate patches of land, and even city-dwellers travel at weekends to collect food plants from the countryside. Wild greens under the generic term *hórta* are gathered and cooked like spinach. The young shoots of capers, and the fruit of wild figs, carobs, plums, strawberry trees, cherries and sweet chestnuts are harvested. Emergent snails and mushrooms are collected after wet weather. The more resilient forms of wildlife can coexist with these uses, but for many Greeks only those species that have practical uses are regarded as having any value. Nowadays, access to heavier earth-moving machinery means a farmer can sweep away an ancient meadow full of orchids in an easy morning's work – often to produce a field that is used for forage for a year or two and then abandoned to coarse thistles. Increasingly, the pale scars of dirt tracks crisscross mountainsides, allowing short-termist agricultural destruction of previously undisturbed upland habitats.

During the 1950s the official policy of draining **wetlands**, for conversion to agriculture, meant important areas were lost to wildlife completely. Those lakes, lagoons and deltas that remain are, in theory, now protected for their fragile biodiversity and their environmental and scientific value – but industrial and sewage pollution, disturbance and misuse are unchecked. Visit, for example, the Peloponnese's **Yiálova lagoon** reserve – one of Greece's most stunningly beautiful wetlands – to understand the problems of many protected areas. Four-wheel-drive vehicles and noisy motorbikes race through dunes destroying the surface stability and decimating the nesting chameleons; military aircraft practice low-flying over flamingo flocks; rows of illegally overnighting camper vans disfigure the beaches; and locals drive here to dump unwanted televisions and fridges. On Lésvos, the **Kallóní salt-pans**, once beloved by rare birds and birdwatchers, are being poisoned by sewage. In the mainland interior, increasing demand for power brings huge **hydroelectric schemes** to remote rivers and gorges with little chance for opposition to be heard. Even the **Orthodox Church**, whose lands once provided wildlife with a refuge from hunters, is now capitalizing on their value for major tourist developments, with the development of mass **tourism and golf courses** around the monastery of Toploú in eastern Crete, already one of Greece's most water-deficient areas. In the north, the forests of sacred **Mount Áthos** are being surrendered to commercial logging. On the bright side, the **Kárla marsh-lake** near Vólos is being allowed to partially refill again, to the delight of migratory birds.

Since the 1970s, tourist developments have ribboned along **coastlines**, sweeping away both agricultural plots and wildlife havens. These expanding resorts increase local employment, attracting inland workers to the coast; the generation that would have been shepherds on remote hillsides now works in tourist bars and tavernas. Consequently, the pressure of domestic **animal grazing** has been significantly reduced, allowing the regeneration of tree seedlings; Crete, for example, has more woodland now than at any time in the last five centuries. However, **forest fires** remain a threat everywhere. Since 1980, fires have destroyed much of the tree cover in Thássos, southern Rhodes, Kárpathos, Híos, Sámos and parts of the Peloponnese; the trees may well regenerate eventually, but by then the complex shade-dependent ecology is irrecoverably lost.

Flowers

Whereas in temperate northern Europe plants flower from spring until autumn, the arid summers of Greece confine the main **flowering period** to the spring, a narrow climatic window when days are bright, temperatures not too high and the groundwater supply still adequate. **Spring** starts in the southeast, in Rhodes, in early March, and travelling progressively westwards and northwards. Rhodes, Kárpathos and eastern Crete are at their best in March, western Crete in early April, the Peloponnese and eastern Aegean later April, and the Ionian islands in early May, though a cold dry winter can cause several weeks' delay. In the high mountains the floral spring arrives in the chronological summer, with the alpine zones of Crete in full flower in June, and mainland mountain blooms emerging in July.

The delicate flowers of early spring – orchids, fritillaries, anemones, cyclamen, tulips and small bulbs – are replaced as the season progresses by more robust shrubs, tall perennials and abundant annuals, but many of these close down completely for the fierce **summer**. A few tough plants, like thyme and savory, continue to flower through the heat, acting as magnets for butterflies.

Once the worst heat is over, and the first **autumn** showers arrive, so does a second "spring", on a much smaller scale but welcome after the brown drabness of summer. Squills, cyclamen, crocus and other small bulbs all come into bloom, while seeds start to germinate for the following year's crop of annuals. By the new year, early-spring bulbs and orchids are flowering in the south.

Seashore

Plants on the **beach** grow in a difficult environment: fresh water is scarce, salt is in excess, and dehydrating winds are often very strong. Feathery **tamarisk** trees are adept at surviving this habitat, and consequently often planted to provide shade; they "sweat" away surplus saltwater from their foliage.

Sand dunes in the southern and eastern islands support decreasing numbers of the low gnarled trees of prickly **juniper**. These provide shelter for colourful small plants, while the sandy depressions behind the dunes – where they have not been illegally ploughed for short-term forage crops – are home to a variety of plants. Open stretches of beach sand usually have fewer plants, particularly in resort areas where the bulldozed "spring cleaning" of the beach removes both the winter's rubbish and all the local flora.

Watercourses

Large areas of **freshwater** are naturally scarce, particularly in the warmer south. Many watercourses dry up completely in the summer, and dry river-beds are often simply flood channels; consequently, there are few true aquatic plants. However, species that survive periodic drying-out can flourish, such as the giant reed or **calamus**, a bamboo-like grass reaching up to 8m in height and often cut for use as canes. It frequently grows in company with the shrubby, pink- or white-flowered and highly poisonous **oleander**.

Cultivated land

Arable fields can be rich with colourful weeds: scarlet poppies, blue bugloss, yellow or white daisies, wild peas and gladioli. Small, unploughed **meadows** may be equally colourful, with slower-growing plants such as orchids in extraordinary quantities. In the absence of herbicides, olive groves have an extensive underflora. In the presence of herbicides there is usually a yellow spring carpet of the introduced, weedkiller-resistant Oxalis, now occurring in sufficient quantity to show up in satellite photographs.

Lower hillsides

The rocky earth on some hillsides makes cultivation difficult and impractical; agriculture is often abandoned and areas regenerate to a rich mixture of shrubs and perennials – known as **garigue**. With time, some wet winters, and in the absence of grazing, a few shrubs will develop into small trees, intermixed with tough climbers, forming much denser **maquis** vegetation. The colour yellow often predominates in early spring, followed by the blues, pinks and purples of bee-pollinated plants. An abundance of the pink and white of Cistus rockroses is usually indicative of an earlier fire, since they are primary recolonizers.

A third vegetation type is **phrygana** – smaller, frequently aromatic or spiny shrubs, often with a narrow strip of bare ground between each hedgehog-like bush. Many aromatic herbs such as lavender, rosemary, savory, sage and thyme are native to these areas, intermixed with other less tasty plants such as the toxic euphorbias and the spiny burnet or wire-netting bush.

Nearly 190 species of **orchid** are believed to occur in Greece; their complexity blurs species' boundaries, keeping botanists in a state of taxonomic flux. In particular, the bee and spider orchids have adapted themselves, through subtleties of lip colour and false scents, to seduce small male wasps. Mistaking the flowers for a potential mate, these insects unintentionally assist the plant's pollination. Other orchids mimic the colours and scents of nectar-producing plants, to lure bees. Though all species are officially protected, many are still picked.

Mountains and gorges

The **higher mountains** of Greece have winter snow cover, and cooler weather for much of the year. The **limestone peaks** of the mainland, and of islands such as Corfu, Kefalloniá, Crete, Rhodes, Sámos and Thássos, hold rich collections of attractive **rock plants**, flowers whose nearest relatives may be from the Balkan Alps or the Turkish mountains. **Gorges** are another spectacular habitat, particularly rich in Crete; inaccessible cliffs act as refuges for plants that cannot survive the grazing or more extreme climates of open areas. Many of Greece's endemic plants are confined to cliffs, gorges or mountains.

Much of the surviving **original woodland** covers mountain areas. In the south, it includes cypress: native to the south and east Aegean, but, in its columnar form, planted everywhere with a Mediterranean climate. The cooler shade of woodland provides a haven for plants which cannot survive full exposure to the Greek summer, including peonies and numerous ferns.

With altitude, the forest thins out to scattered individual conifers and kermes oak, before finally reaching a limit at around 1500–2000m on the mainland – much lower on the islands. Above this treeline are **summer meadows**, and then bare rock. If not severely grazed, these habitats are home to many gnarled, low-growing, often splendidly floriferous plants.

Birds

Migratory species which winter in East Africa move north, through the eastern Mediterranean, from around **mid-March to mid-May**. Some stop in Greece to breed; others move on into the rest of Europe. The southern islands are the first landfall after a long sea-crossing, and smaller birds recuperate briefly before moving on. Larger birds such as storks and ibis often fly very high, and binoculars are needed to spot them as they pass over. In autumn, birds return, but usually in more scattered numbers. Although some are shot, such as quail and turtle dove, there is not the wholesale slaughter that occurs in some other Mediterranean countries.

Swallows and martins constantly swoop through the air to catch insects, as do the larger and noisier swifts. Warblers are numerous; other small insect-eaters include stonechats, fly-catchers and woodchat shrikes. At **night**, the tiny Scops owl has a very distinct, repeated single-note call, like the sonar beep of a submarine; the equally diminutive little owl, with a weird repertoire of cries, may be visible by day in ruined buildings. Near wooded streams, the most evocative nocturnal bird is the nightingale, most audible in the May mating season.

Larger raptors occur in remoter areas, preferring mountain gorges and cliffs. Buzzards are the most abundant, and often mistaken by over-optimistic birdwatchers for the rarer, shyer eagles. Griffon vultures, however, are quite unmistakable, soaring on broad, straight-edged wings, whereas the lammergeier is a state-of-the-art flying machine with narrow, swept wings, seen over mountain tops by the lucky few; the remaining nine or ten pairs in Crete are now the Balkan's largest breeding population. Also in the mountains are ravens, and smaller, colourful birds such as alpine choughs, common choughs, black and white wheatears, wallcreepers and the blue rock thrush.

In **lowland areas**, hoopoes are a startling combination of pink, black and white, obvious when they fly, and the only natural predator of processionary caterpillars, a major pest of pine forests. The shy golden oriole has an attractive song but is adept at hiding its brilliant colours among the olive trees. Multicoloured flocks of elegant bee-eaters fill the air with their soft calls as they hunt insects. Brightest of all is the kingfisher, often seen sea-fishing.

In areas of **wetland** that remain undrained and undisturbed, such as salt-marshes, coastal lagoons, estuaries and freshwater ponds, osprey, egrets, ibis, spoonbills, storks, pelicans and many waders can be seen feeding. Flamingos sometimes occur, as lone individuals or small flocks, particularly in eastern Aegean salt pans between December and May.

Mammals

Greece's small **mammal** population ranges from rodents and shrews to hedgehogs, hares and squirrels (including the dark-red Persian squirrel on Lésvos). Medium-sized mammals include badgers, foxes and the persecuted golden jackal, but the commonest is the ferret-like stone (or beech) marten, named for its habit of decorating stones with its droppings to mark territory.

In the mainland mountains, mostly in the north, are found the shy chamois and wild boar, with even shyer predators like lynx, wolves and brown bear. Occasionally seen running wild in Crete's White Mountains, but more often as a zoo attraction, is an endemic ibex, known to hunters as the *agrími* or *krí-krí*. Formerly in danger of extinction, a colony of them was established on the offshore islet of Dhía, where they thrived, exterminating the rare local flora.

Reptiles and amphibians

Reptiles flourish in the hot dry summers of Greece, the commonest being **lizards**. Most of these are small, agile and wary, rarely staying around for closer inspection. They're usually brown to grey, subtly spotted, striped or tessellated, though in adult males the undersides are sometimes brilliant orange, green or blue. The more robust green lizards, with long whip-like tails, can be 50cm or more in length, but are equally shy and fast-moving unless distracted by territorial disputes.

Nocturnal **geckos** are large-eyed, short-tailed lizards. Their spreading toes have claws and ingenious adhesive pads, allowing them to cross house walls and ceilings in their search for insects, including mosquitoes. Groups will lie in wait near bright lights that attract their prey; small ones living indoors have very pale, translucent skins. Despite local unpopularity – one Greek name, *miaró*, means "defiler" after their outsized faeces – they should be left alone. The rare chameleon is a slow-moving, swivel-eyed inhabitant of eastern Crete, Yiálova and some eastern Aegean islands including Sámos. Essentially green, it has the ability to adjust its colouration to match the surroundings.

Once collected for the pet trade, **tortoises** can be found on much of the mainland, and some islands, though not Crete. Usually their noisy progress through hillside vegetation is the first signal of their presence, as they spend their often long lives grazing the vegetation. Closely related **terrapins** are more streamlined, freshwater tortoises which love to bask on waterside mud by streams or ponds. Shy and nervous omnivorous scavengers, usually only seen as they disappear underwater, their numbers have recently declined steeply on many islands.

Sea turtles occur mostly in the Ionian Sea, but also in the Aegean. Least rare are the loggerhead turtles (*Caretta caretta*), nesting on Zákynthos, Kefalloniá, the Peloponnese, and occasionally in Crete. Their nesting grounds are disappearing under tourist resorts, although they are a protected endangered species (see the box on p.1051).

Snakes are abundant in Greece and many islands; most are shy and non-venomous. Several species, including the Ottoman and nose-horned vipers, do have a poisonous bite, though they are not usually aggressive; they are adder-like and often have a very distinct, dark zigzag stripe down the back. Snakes are only likely to bite if a hand is put in the crevice of a wall or a rock-face where

Flora and fauna field guides

In case of difficulty obtaining titles listed below from conventional booksellers, try Summerfield Books (☎017683/41577; ⊛www.summerfieldbooks.com).

Flowers
Hellmut Baumann *Greek Wild Flowers and Plant Lore in Ancient Greece*. Crammed with fascinating ethnobotany, plus good colour photographs.

Marjorie Blamey and Christopher Grey-Wilson *Mediterranean Wild Flowers*. Comprehensive field guide, with coloured drawings; reasonably up to date.

Lance Chilton *Plant Check-lists*. Small booklets which also include birds, reptiles and butterflies, for a number of Greek islands and resorts. Available direct: ☎ & ⓕ 01485/532710, ⊛www.marengowalks.com.

Pierre Delforge *Orchids of Britain and Europe*. A comprehensive guide, with recent taxonomy, though beware small inaccuracies in the translation.

John Fielding and Nicholas Turland *Flowers of Crete* (2005). Large volume with 1900 colour photos of the Cretan flora, much of which is also widespread in Greece.

Oleg Polunin *Flowers of Greece and the Balkans*. Classic, older field guide, with colour photographs and line drawings; good on regional geology, climate and habitats.

Kit Tan and Gregoris Iatrou *Endemic Plants of Greece – The Peloponnese*. The first of three large volumes planned to cover the entire Greek flora; detailed text and drawings.

Birds
Richard Brooks *Birding on the Greek Island of Lesvos*. Superb guide with colour photos which includes a list of birdwatching sites, with detailed maps, plus an annotated species-by-species bird list. Contact the author directly at ⓔemail@richard-brooks.co.uk.

Stephanie Coghlan *A Birdwatching Guide to Crete* (1996). Another excellent island guide.

George Handrinos and T. Akriotis *Birds of Greece* (1997). A comprehensive guide that includes island birdlife.

Lars Jonsson *Birds of Europe with North Africa and the Middle East*. The ornithologist's choice for the best coverage of Greek birds, with excellent descriptions and illustrations.

Mammals
Corbet and Ovenden *Collins Guide to the Mammals of Europe*. The best field guide on its subject.

Reptiles
Arnold, Burton and Ovenden *Collins Guide to the Reptiles and Amphibians of Britain and Europe*. A useful guide, though it excludes the Dodecanese and east Aegean islands.

Jiri Cihar *Amphibians and Reptiles* (o/p). Selective coverage, but includes most endemic species of the Dodecanese and east Aegean isles.

Insects
Michael Chinery *Collins Guide to the Insects of Britain and Western Europe*. Although Greece is outside the geographical scope of the guide, it will provide generic identifications for many insects seen.

Lionel Higgins and Norman Riley *A Field Guide to the Butterflies of Britain and Europe*. A thorough and detailed field guide that illustrates nearly all species seen in Greece.

Marine life
B. Luther and K. Fiedler *A Field Guide to the Mediterranean* (o/p). Very thorough; includes most Greek shallow-water species.

one of them is resting, or if they are molested. Unfortunately, the locals in some areas attempt to kill any snake they see, thereby greatly increase the probability of their being bitten. Leave them alone, and they will do the same for you (but if bitten, see the advice on p.44). Most snakes are not only completely harmless to humans, but beneficial since they reduce populations of rats and mice. There are also three species of legless lizards, including glass lizards: equally harmless, but killed when mistaken for snakes.

Frogs and toads are the most obvious amphibians throughout much of Greece, particularly during the spring breeding season. The green toad has a cricket-like trill. Frogs prefer the wettest places, and the robust marsh frog revels in artificial water-storage ponds, whose concrete sides magnify their croaking impressively. Tree frogs are tiny, emerald green jewels, with huge, strident voices at night, sometimes to be found in quantity on the leaves of waterside oleanders. Orange-on-black fire salamanders may be found promenading in mountain woodlands after rain.

Insects

Greece teems with insects: some pester, like flies and mosquitoes, but most are harmless to humans.

Grasshoppers and **crickets** swarm through open areas in summer, with larger species that are carnivorous and can bite if handled. Larger still are greybrown locusts, flying noisily before crash-landing into shrubs. The high-pitched, endlessly repeated chirp of house crickets can drive one to distraction, as can the summer whirring of cicadas on the trunks of trees.

From spring to autumn, Greece is full of **butterflies**. Swallowtail species are named for the drawn-out corners of the hind-wings, in shades of cream and yellow, with black and blue markings. The unrelated, robust, brown-and-orange pasha is Europe's largest butterfly. In autumn black-and-orange African monarchs may appear, sometimes in large quantities.

Some Greek **hawkmoths** are equally spectacular, and their large caterpillars can be recognized by their tail horn. The hummingbird hawkmoth, like its namesake, hovers at flowers to feed, supported by a blur of fast-moving wings. Tiger moths, with black-and-white forewings and startling bright orange hindwings, are the "butterflies" occurring in huge quantity in sheltered sites of islands such as Rhodes and Páros.

Other insects include the camouflaged **praying mantis**, holding their powerful forelegs in a position of supplication until another insect comes within reach. The females are notorious for eating the males during mating. Ant-lion adults resemble an ineffectually fluttery dragonfly, but their young are huge-jawed and build pits in the sand to trap ants. Hemispherical scarab beetles collect balls of dung and push them around with their back legs. Cockroaches of varying species live in buildings, particularly hotels, restaurants and bakeries, attracted by warmth and food scraps.

Corfu and the Epirot mainland opposite are famous for their extraordinary **fireflies**, which flutter in quantities across meadows and marshes on May nights, speckling the darkness with bursts of cold light to attract partners; look carefully in nearby hedges, and you may spot the less flashy, more sedentary glow-worm. Other **non-vertebrates** of interest include the land crabs, which are found in the south and east of Greece. They need freshwater to breed, but cause surprise when seen crawling across remote hillsides. There are plenty of genuine marine creatures, particularly in shallow seawater sheltered by rocks – sea cucumbers, sea butterflies, octopus, starfish and sea urchins.

Greek Popular Music

Music is ubiquitous in modern Greek culture; even the most indifferent visitor will be aware of it in ferries, tavernas and other public spaces. Like so many aspects of Greece, it is an amalgam of "native" and Anatolian styles, with occasional contributions from points further west, and it survives alongside and often in preference to Western-style pop. In fact, Western music made little impression in Greece until the 1950s, when disputes arose between adherents of indigenous styles and those spurning ethnic roots in favour of jazz, rock or symphonic idioms – a reflection of the broader modernizing-versus-traditionalism debates which preoccupied the country.

Many older songs in Eastern-flavoured minor scales (or more correctly, modes) have direct antecedents in the forms and styles of both **Byzantine religious chant** and the popular music of the **Ottoman Empire**, though more nationalist-minded musicologists claim their original descent from the now-lost melodies of ancient Greece. Almost all native Greek instruments are near-duplicates of ones used throughout the Islamic world, though it's an open question as to whether the Byzantines, Arabs or Persians first constructed particular instruments. To this broadly Middle Eastern base Slavs, Albanians and Italians have added their share, resulting in an extraordinarily varied repertoire.

Regional Folk Music

The best opportunities for hearing live Greek folk music are the numerous summer **paniyíria** (saints' day festivals) or more tourist-oriented **cultural programmes**, when musicians based in Athens or city clubs during winter tour the islands and villages. All too often, alas, traditional instrumentation is replaced by rock instruments, with excess reverb and pick-ups tacked on to string instruments not meant for amplification. However, a number of high-quality revival groups are attempting to recapture the musicianship of the old-timers, which have been well archived on CD in recent years.

Island music

The arc of southern Aegean islands comprising **Crete**, **Kássos**, **Kárpathos** and **Hálki** is one of the most promising areas in Greece to hear live music. The dominant instrument here is the **lýra**, a lap-fiddle directly related to the Turkish *kemençe*. It is played not on the shoulder but balanced on the thigh, with – in the Dodecanese – a loose bow which can touch all three of the gut strings (the middle being a drone) simultaneously, making double chords possible. The contemporary **Cretan lýra** is larger, tuned lower (like a Western violin), played with a much tauter bow, and lacks a drone string. Among outstanding Cretan players are the brothers **Nikos** and **Andonis Xylouris**.

Usually, the *lýra* is backed up by a **laoúto**, which is related to the Turkish/Arab *oud* but more closely resembles a mandolin, with a long fretted neck and four sets of double strings. Usually restricted to percussive chords, these are rarely used to lead or solo, but a virtuoso player will enter a true dialogue with the *lýra*, using well-chosen rhythms and melodic phrases in chime-like tones; poor ones rely more on rhythm.

In parts of the southern and eastern Aegean, most notably **Kálymnos** and northern **Kárpathos**, you also find a simple, **droneless bagpipe** with a double chanter – the **askómandoura** or *tsamboúna*. On most islands, though, this instrument is seen as fit for carnival noise only – played in conjunction with a two-headed, shoulder-strung drum called the *toumbáki*. It seems, sadly, on the way out: Crete, Náxos, Sámos, Ikaría and Tínos each have just one elderly player apiece, with no younger disciples. And much the same goes for the **sandoúri**, or hammer dulcimer – which, if you know Kazantzakis's classic novel, or its film, *Zorba the Greek*, you may recall was played by his Cretan hero. The instrument, which today tends to have a supporting role (at best), was introduced to the islands in the 1920s by Asia Minor refugees.

On most Aegean islands, particularly in the **Cyclades**, the *lýra* is replaced by a more familiar-looking **violí**, essentially a Western violin. Accompaniment was provided until recently by *laoúto* or *sandoúri*, though these days you're most likely to be confronted by a bass guitar and rock drums. Among the better fiddle players, **Stathis Koukoularis** (from Náxos) and younger **Nikos Ikonomidhes** (Skhinoússa/Híos) or **Kyriakos Gouvendas**, are well worth seeking out. Unlike on Crete, where you often catch the best music in special clubs or *kéndra*, Aegean island performances tend to be public, community-based shows, in village squares or monastery courtyards.

Island folk songs – **nisiótika** – feature melodies which, like much folk music the world over, rely heavily on the pentatonic scale. Lyrics, especially on the smaller islands, touch on the perils of the sea, exile and (in a society where long separations and arranged marriages were the norm) thwarted love. The prolific and decidedly uneven **Konitopoulos** clan from Náxos has become virtually synonymous with nisiótika, but older stars like **Anna and Emilia Hatzidhaki**, **Effi Sarri** and **Anna Karabesini** – all from the Dodecanese archipelago – offer a warmer, more innocent delivery.

Lésvos occupies a special place in terms of island music; before the turbulent decade of 1912–22, its "mainland" was Asia Minor rather than Greece, its urban poles Smyrna and Constantinople rather than Athens. As a consequence, its music is far more varied and sophisticated than the Aegean norm, having absorbed melodies and instrumentation from the various groups who lived in neighbouring Anatolia; it is the only island with a vital **brass-band** tradition, and nearly every Greek dance rhythm is represented in local music.

By way of complete contrast, the **Ionian islands** (except for Lefkádha) alone of all modern Greek territory never saw Turkish occupation and have a predominantly Western musical tradition. Their indigenous song-form is Italian both in name – **kantádhes** – and in its instrumentation (guitar and mandolin) and vocalization (major scales, choral delivery); it's most often heard these days on Lefkádha, Kefaloniá and Zákynthos.

Mainland music

In the **Peloponnese** and **central/western Greece**, many of the folk songs – known as **dhimotiká tragoúdhia** – hark back to the years of Ottoman occupation and the War of Independence; others, in a lighter tone, refer to aspects of pastoral life (sheep, elopements, fetching water from the well). Their essential instrument is the **klaríno** (clarinet), which reached Greece during the 1830s, introduced either by Gypsies or by King Otto's Bavarian entourage. Backing was traditionally provided by a *koumpanía* consisting of *kithára* (guitar), *laoúto*, *laoutokythára* (a hybrid in stringing and tuning) and *violí*, with *toumberléki* (lap drum) or *défi* (tambourine) for rhythm.

Many mainland tunes are **dances**, divided by rhythm into such categories as *kalamatianó* (a line dance), *tsámiko*, *hasaposérviko* or *syrtó*, the quintessential circle dance of Greece. Those that aren't danceable include the slow, stately *kléftiko*, similar to the *rizítiko* of Crete, both of which relate, baldly or in metaphor, incidents or attitudes from the years of the Ottomans and the fight for freedom. Stalwart vocalists to look for on old recordings include **Yiorgos Papasidheris** and **Yioryia Mittaki**, the latter actually of Arvanitic (Albanian-speaking) origin, as well as **Tassia Verra**, **Sofia Kollitiri**, **Stathis Kavouras** and **Takis Karnavas** from the 1960s to the 1980s. Among instrumentalists, the violinist **Yiorgos Koros** and clarinetist **Vassilis Saleas** are especially remarkable.

The folk music of **Epirus (Ípiros)** exhibits strong connections with that of northern Epirus (now in neighbouring Albania) and the Former Yugoslav Republic of Macedonia, particularly in the **polyphonic pieces** sung by both men and women. The repertoire tends to fall into three categories, also found further south: *mirolóyia* or laments (the instrumental counterpart is called a *skáros*); drinking songs or *tís távlas*; and various danceable melodies as noted above, common to the entire mainland and many islands also. Most notable of the Epirot **clarinettists** are the late **Vassilis Soukas** and **Tassos Halkias**, and the younger (unrelated) **Petros-Loukas Halkias** – all good examples of the (mostly) **Gypsy** or Gypsy-descent musicians who dominate instrumental music on the mainland.

Macedonia and Thrace in the north remained Ottoman territory until early in the twentieth century, with a bewilderingly mixed population, so music here can still sound more generically Balkan. Meriting a special mention are the **brass bands**, introduced in the nineteenth century by Ottoman military musicians, peculiar to western Macedonia. Owing to the huge influx of Anatolian refugees after 1923, these regions have been a treasure-trove for collectors and ethnomusicologists seeking to document the old music of Asia Minor. Noteworthy singers – both still alive and active – include **Xanthippi Karathanassi** and **Khronis Aïdhonidhis**.

Among Thracian instruments, the **kaváli** (end-blown pastoral flute) is identical to the Turkish and Bulgarian article, as is the local drone bagpipe or **gáïda**, made like its island counterpart from a goat-skin. The **zournás**, a screechy, double-reed oboe similar to the Islamic world's *shenai*, is much in evidence at weddings or festivals, together with the deep-toned *daoúli* drum, as a typically Gypsy ensemble. Other percussion instruments like the *daïrés* or tambourine and the *darboúka*, the local version of the *toumberléki*, provide sharply demarcated dance rhythms such as the *zonarádhikos*. The *klaríno* is present here as well, as are two types of *lýras*, but perhaps the most characteristic melodic instrument of Thrace is the **oúti** (*oud*), whose popularity received a boost after refugee players arrived. **Nikos Saragoudas** is its acknowledged living master.

Rebétika

Rebétika began as the music of the Greek urban dispossessed – petty criminals, bar-girls, refugees, drug-users, defiers of social norms in general. It existed in some form in **Greece**, **Smyrna** and **Constantinople** since at least the beginning of the twentieth century – probably a few decades earlier. But it is as hard to define as jazz or blues, with which spurious comparisons are often made. Although *rebétika* shares marked similarities in spirit with these genres, there's none whatsoever in its musical form. That said, the themes of the earlier songs – illicit or frustrated love, drug addiction, police oppression, disease and death; and their tone – resignation to the singer's lot, coupled with defiance of authority – will be familiar to old time blues fans.

Even the word "*rebétika*" is of uncertain derivation, most likely from *harabati*, an old Turkish word meaning, variously, "a shanty town", "a privileged drunkard" and "unconventionally dressed bohemian" – all aspects of early *rebétika* culture. Accordingly, searches for its beginnings must be conducted in the Asia Minor of the last years of the Ottoman empire as well as in Greece proper.

Origins: café-aman

Most people equate traditional Greek music with the **bouzoúki**, a long-necked, fretted, three-stringed lute derived, like the Turkish *saz*, from the Byzantine *tambourás*. Early in the twentieth century, however, only a few Greek mainland musicians used it. At the same time, across the Aegean in Smyrna and Constantinople, musical cafés, owned and staffed almost entirely by Greeks, Jews, Armenians, Slavs and even a few Gypsies, had become popular. They featured groups comprising a violinist, a *sandoúri* player and a (usually female) vocalist, who might also jingle castanets and dance. The metrically free, improvisational songstyle became known as **café–aman** or **amanés**, after the frequent repetition of the exclamation *aman aman* (Turkish for "alas, alas"), used both for its sense and to fill time while the performers searched for more articulate lyrics.

Despite sparse instrumentation, the *amanés* was an elegant, riveting style requiring considerable skill, harking back to similar vocalization in central Asia. Among its greatest practitioners were **Andonis "Dalgas" Dhiamandidhis**,

so nicknamed (Dalgas means "Wave") for the undulations in his voice; **Roza Eskenazi**, a Greek Jew who grew up in Constantinople, whose voice inimitably combined innocence and sensuality; her contemporary rival **Rita Abatzi**, from Smyrna, with a huskier, more textured tone; **Marika Papagika**, from the island of Kós, who emigrated to America where she made her career; **Agapios Tomboulis**, a *tambur* and *oud* player of Armenian background; and **Dhimitris "Salonikiyé" Semsis**, a master fiddler from northern Macedonia who in the course of his career travelled across the Mediterranean. This spectrum of origins of these performers gives a good idea of the cosmopolitan influences in the years immediately preceding the emergence of "real" *rebétika*.

△ *Bouzoúki* player, Athens

The 1919–22 Greco-Turkish war and the resulting **1923 exchange of populations** were key events in the history of *rebétika*, resulting in the influx to Greece of over a million Asia Minor Greeks, many of whom settled in shanty towns around Athens, Pireás and Thessaloníki. The *café-aman* musicians, like most of the refugees, were far more sophisticated than the Greeks of the host country; many were highly educated, could read and compose music and had even been unionised in the towns of Asia Minor. Such men included the Smyrniots **Vangelis Papazoglou**, a noted songwriter, and **Panayiotis Toundas**, another composer who later ran Columbia Records.

But less lucky refugees lived on the periphery of the new society: most had lost all they had in the hasty evacuation, and many, from inland Anatolia, initially spoke only Turkish. In their misery they sought relief in another Ottoman institution, the **tekés** or hashish den, whose habitués were known as *dervíses* (dervishes). This apparent burlesque of the Islamic mystical tradition was in fact not so flippant as it appears; the Turkish word *harabati*, noted above, is in turn derived from the Arabo-Persian *kharabat*, the Sufi musician's quarter in Afghan or Persian towns, "the place you go to be destroyed (and reborn)" by partaking in the rituals.

The tekédhes and Pireás-style rebétika

In the *tekédhes* of Pireás, Athens and Thessaloníki, a few men would sit around a charcoal brazier, toking from a *nargilés* (hookah) filled with hashish. One of them might improvise a tune on the *baglamás* or the *bouzoúki* and begin to sing. The words would be heavily laced with insiders' argot incorporating Turkish and Venetian words (plus a few Arabic or Albanian ones). As the *taxími* (long, studied introduction) was completed, one of the smokers might rise and begin to dance a **zeïbékiko**, named after the Zeybeks, a warrior caste of western Anatolia. Following an unusual metre (9/8), this would be a slow, intense, introverted performance, danced not for the benefit of others but for himself.

By the early 1930s, various key (male) musicians had emerged from the *tekés* culture. Foremost among them was a Pireás-based quartet: the beguiling-voiced **Stratos Payioumtzis**; composer and lyricist **Anestis Delias** (aka **Artemis**), who succumbed to hard drugs and died in the street of an overdose in 1943; *baglamá*-player Yiorgos Tsoros, better known as **Batis**, an indifferent musician but another excellent composer; and **Markos Vamvakaris**, a Catholic from Sýros who became the linchpin of the group. After a tough childhood, he'd stowed away aged fifteen on a boat for Pireás; within six months of arrival, he had taught himself *bouzoúki* as a way out of a particularly grim job in a slaughterhouse, and was soon playing with the other three. Though an indisputable master instrumentalist, he initially considered that his voice, ruined perhaps from too much hash-smoking, was no good for singing. But he soon bowed to the encouragement of record label Columbia, and his gravelly, unmistakable style set the standard for male *rebétic* vocals until the 1940s. His only close peer as an instrumentalist and composer was **Ioannis Papaïoannou**, with whom he played steadily from 1936 to 1939.

Songs about getting stoned – known as *mastoúriaka* or *hasiklídhika* – were a natural outgrowth of the *tekédhes*. One of the most famous, composed by Batis and first recorded in the mid-1930s with Stratos singing, commemorated the quartet's exploits:

On the sly I went out in a boat
And arrived at the Dhrákou Cave
Where I saw three men stoned on hash

Stretched out on the sand.
It was Batis, and Artemis,
And Stratos the Lazy.
Hey you, Strato! Yeah you, Strato!
Fix us a terrific nargilé,
So old Batis can have a smoke...

Subsequent decades saw such lyrics bowdlerized, for reasons set forth below; the most commonly heard version of this song, from the 1950s, substitutes "Play us a fine bit of *bouzoúki*" for "Fix us a fine *nargilé*", and so forth.

Persecution

This "Golden Age" of *rebétika* – as indeed it was, despite the unhappy lives of many performers, and necessarily limited audience – was short lived. The association of the music with a drug-laced underworld would prove its undoing. After the imposition of the puritanical **Metaxas dictatorship** in 1936, musicians with uncompromising lyrics and lifestyles were blackballed by the recording industry; anti-hashish laws were systematically enforced, and police harassment of the *tekédhes* was stepped up. In Athens, even possession of a *bouzoúki* or *baglamás* became a criminal offence – thus frequent lyrics about instruments being hidden under coats or smashed by the cops – and several big names did time in jail. Others went to Thessaloníki, where the police chief Vassilis Mouskoundis was a big fan of the music and allowed its practitioners to smoke in private.

For a while, such persecution – and the official encouragement of tangos and frothy Italianate love songs (which always had a much wider audience) – failed to dim the enthusiasm of the *mánges* ("wide boys") who frequented the hash dens. Police beatings or prison terms were taken in stride; time behind bars could be used, as it always had been around the Aegean, to make *skaptó* (dugout) instruments. A *baglamás* could easily be fashioned from a gourd cut in half or even a tortoise shell (the sound box), a piece of wood (the neck), catgut (frets) and wire for strings, and the result would be small enough to hide from the guards. **Jail songs** were composed and became popular in the underworld. The lyrics below, with some literal translation from the 1930s argot, are from a typical, much-recorded song, "Iy Lahanádhes" ("The Pickpockets," or literally "The Cabbage-Dealers") by Vangelis Papazoglou:

Down in Lemonádhika there was a ruckus
They caught two pickpockets who acted innocent
They took 'em to the slammer in handcuffs
They'll get a beating if they don't cough up the loot.
Don't beat us, Mr. Copper, you know very well
This is our job, and don't expect a cut.
We "eat cabbages" and pinch "slippers" so we can
Have a regular rest in jail.
Death don't scare us, it's only hunger we mind,
That's why we nick "cabbage" and get along fine.

The unfortunate *rebétes* incurred disapproval from the puritanical Left as well as the puritanical Right; the growing **Communist Party** of the 1930s considered the music and its habitués hopelessly decadent and politically unevolved. When Vamvakaris was about to join the leftist resistance army ELAS in 1943, he was admonished not to sing his own material; the Left preferred

andártika (Soviet-style revolutionary anthems), although **Sotiria Bellou**, a *rebétissa* (female rebetic musician) and active communist whose career began late in the 1940s, was a conspicuous exception. Despite this, *rebétika* was strangely popular amongst the rank-and-file on both sides of the 1946–49 civil war – perhaps the only taste uniting a fatally polarized country.

Rebétika goes mainstream, declines, then revives

Bellou was one of several important female vocalists to accompany **Vassilis Tsitsanis**, the most significant composer and *bouzoúki* player to emerge after Vamvakaris; the others were **Marika Ninou**, an Armenian refugee from the Caucasus, and **Ioanna Yiorgakopoulou**, the latter also a composer in her own right. From Tríkala in Thessaly, Tsitsanis abandoned law studies to cut his first record in 1936 for Odeon, directed by rebetic composer **Spyros Peristeris**. The war interrupted his – and everyone else's – recording career by closing the studios from late 1940 until late 1945, a period which Tsitsanis spent more comfortably than many, running a musical taverna in Thessaloníki.

When World War II, and the civil war that followed, ended, a huge backlog of songs composed during the interim finally went onto vinyl. The traumatic decade between 1939 and 1949 had erased any lingering fashion for *mastoúriaka*; the Greek public of the 1950s instead craved softer **Neapolitan melodies**, words about love and new heroes. Tsitsanis was happy to oblige on all three counts, and for the first time *rebétika* enjoyed something like a mass following. But his love lyrics were anything but insipid; the demoralization of the war years led him also to compose darker works, most famous of these "Synnefias-meni Kyriaki":

Cloudy Sunday, you seem like my heart
Which is always overcast, Christ and Holy Virgin!
You're a day like the one I lost my joy.
Cloudy Sunday, you make my heart bleed.
When I see you rainy, I can't rest easy for a moment;
You blacken my life and I sigh deeply.

Although Tsitsanis performed almost up to his death in 1984 – his funeral in Athens was attended by nearly a quarter of a million people – 1953 effectively marked the end of the original *rebétic* style. In that year, **Manolis Hiotis** added a **fourth string** to the **bouzoúki**, allowing it to be tuned tonally rather than modally; electrical amplification to reach larger audiences, maudlin lyrics and over-orchestration were not long in following. Performances in huge, barnlike clubs, also called *bouzoúkia*, became debased and vulgarized. Virtuoso *bouzoúki* players like **Hiotis**, **Yiorgos Mitsakis** and **Yiorgos Zambetas**, assisted by large-chested female vocalists of little distinction, became immensely rich – the so-called *arhondorebétes*. The clubs themselves were clip-joints where Athenians paid large sums to break plates and watch dancing whose flashy steps and gyrations were a travesty of the simple dignity and precise, synchronized footwork of the old-time *zeïbékiko*.

Ironically, the original *rebétika* material was rescued from oblivion by the **colonels' junta** of 1967–74. Along with dozens of other features of Greek culture, most *rebétika* verses were banned. The younger generation coming of age under the dictatorship took a closer look at the forbidden fruit and derived solace, and deeper meanings, from the nominally apolitical lyrics. When the junta fell in 1974 – even a little before – there was an outpouring of reissued recordings of the old masters.

Over the next decade or so live *rebétika* also enjoyed a revival, beginning with a reunion of old-timers in 1973, and continuing with a clandestine 1978 club near the old Fix brewery in Athens, whose street cred was validated when it was raided and closed by the police. These smoky attempts to recapture pre-war atmosphere, and eventually larger venues, saw performances by revival groups such as the Athens-based **Ta Pedhia apo tin Patra**, **Iy Rebetiki Kompania** and **Iy Opisthodhromiki Kompania**, and from Thessaloníki, **Hondronakos, Maryo** and **Agathonas Iakovidhis** with his **Rebetika Synkrotima Thessalonikis**. Both of the latter are still performing, Agathonas in a new quartet, **Rebetiki Tetras**, with Glykeria, Babis Goles and Babis Tsertos.

A feature film by Kostas Ferris, **Rembetiko** (1983), based loosely on the life of Marika Ninou, attempted to trace the music from Asia Minor of the 1920s to Greece of the 1950s, and garnered worldwide acclaim. Today, however, the *rebétika* fashion has long since peaked in Greece, and hardly any clubs and bands remain from the dozens which existed between 1978 and 1986. Interestingly, *rebétika* has garnered a new lease of life overseas, with a keen following and revival groups in such unlikely countries as Sweden, but the music is now effectively retro and historic.

The éntekhno revolution

The "Westernization" of *rebétika* that had begun with Tsitsanis and been completed by the *arhondorebétes* paved the way for the **éntekhno music** which emerged during the late 1950s. *Éntekhno*, literally "artistic" or "sophisticated", meant an orchestral genre where folk or *rebetic* instruments and melodies would be interwoven into a much larger symphonic fabric, but with a still recognizably Greek sound.

Its first and most famous exponents were **Manos Hatzidhakis** and **Mikis Theodhorakis**, both classically trained musicians and admirers of *rebétika*. Already in 1948, Hatzidhakis had defended *rebétika* in a lecture, suggesting that Greek composers be inspired by it, rather than bow to the prevailing prejudices against it. At a time when most Greek tunes imitated Western light popular music, he had transcribed *rebétika* for piano and orchestra, keeping only the spirit and nostalgic mood of the original. Theodhorakis, a disciple of Tsitsanis, included *zeïbékika* on his earliest albums, with Grigoris Bithikotsis or Stelios Kazantzidhis on vocals and Manolis Hiotis as *bouzoúki* soloist.

The *éntekhno* of Theodhorakis and Hatzidhakis combined not only *rebetic* and Byzantine influences with orchestral arrangements, but also successfully used the country's rich **poetic tradition**. Among Theodhorakis's first albums was his 1958 *Epitafios/Epifaneia*, settings of poems by **Yiannis Ritsos** and **George Seferis** respectively, and its successor, *To Axion Esti*, a Byzantine-flavoured oratorio incorporating verses by Nobel laureate **Odysseas Elytis**. Hatzidhakis countered with *Matomenos Gamos*, a version of Garcia Lorca's *Blood Wedding* translated by poet-lyricist **Nikos Gatsos**, and also tried his hand at rendering Elytis in song. These early works changed Greek perceptions of *bouzoúki*-based music, popularized Greek poetry for a mass audience and elevated lyricists such as Gatsos and **Manos Eleftheriou** to the status of bards.

The down-side of increased sophistication was an inevitable distancing from indigenous roots, in particular the modal scale which had served Greece so well since antiquity. And with its catchy tunes, *éntekhno* fell prey to the demands of the local film industry – writing a soundtrack became an obligatory rite of passage for composers – and at its worst degenerated to muzak cover versions. Hatzidhakis composed **soundtracks** for various movies starring Melina

Mercouri, most notably *Never on Sunday* (1960); Theodhorakis' international reputation subsequently became distorted by his overplayed and over-covered 1965 soundtrack for *Zorba the Greek*. Soon after this he shunned Byzantine/ folk/*rebétic* influence completely in favour of quasi-classical, overtly political symphonic works and film soundtracks dictated by his communist affiliation. Hatzidhakis (who died in 1994) mostly steered clear of political statements; instead he launched, during the 1980s, his own record label, Seirios, to provide a forum for non-mainstream musicians.

Theodhorakis and Hatzidhakis paved the way for less classicizing and more folk-leaning successors such as **Stavros Xarhakos**, most famous for his soundtracks to the films *Ta Kokkina Fanaria* (The Red Lanterns) and *Rembetiko*; Xarkhakos's contemporary **Yiannis Markopoulos** also paid his soundtrack dues (*Who Pays the Ferryman*, 1978) but is arguably the most consistently Greek-sounding of these four composers to emerge from the 1960s. His best work dates from the early-to-mid-1970s – the Indian summer of *éntekhno*.

Laïká: son of rebétika

Diametrically opposed to *éntekhno* was the authentic **laïká** ("popular") music of the 1950s and 1960s, its gritty, tough style a direct heir to *rebétika*, undiluted by Western influences. *Laïká* used not only *zeïbékiko* and *hasápiko* time signatures but also the *tsiftetéli*, another Asia Minor rhythm mistakenly known as belly-dance music overseas. Once again, "debased" oriental influences dominated Greek pop, much to the chagrin of those who objected to the apolitical, decadent, escapist song content.

The most notable *laïká* performer was **Stelios Kazantzidhis** (1931–2001), whose volcanic, mournful style was never equalled. His work, often in duets with **Marinella** and **Yiota Lidhia**, immortalized the joys and sorrows of the Greek working class which emerged from the 1940s faced with a choice of life under restrictive regimes, or emigration. "Stellaras" (as he was nicknamed) inspired fanatical devotion in his fans over a fifty-year career: truck-drivers emblazoned their cabs with a single word, "Yparho" (the name of his biggest hit). On the day he died seemingly every CD player in the land played Kazantzidhis songs in tribute, and his funeral in Elefsína was thronged by thousands.

Top *laïká* star of the next generation has indubitably been **Yiorgos (George) Dalaras**, a musical phenomenon in Greece since he made his 1968 vinyl debut with composer Manos Loïzos. Born in 1952, the son of a *rebétika* musician, Dalaras has featured on well over a hundred recordings, spanning all Greek genres, the works of Theodhorakis, Hatzidhakis and Markopoulos, and collaborations with the flamenco guitarist Paco de Lucia and American blues star Al Di Meola. Dalaras has also been a staunch supporter (through benefit concerts) of progressive causes, enough to forgive him his recent symphonic efforts.

Amongst notable *laïká* composers and lyricists, **Apostolos Kaldharas** was the most prolific during the 1950s and 1960s; he gave singer **Yiannis Parios** his start, and introduced *laïká* star **Haris Alexiou** with his landmark 1972 album *Mikra Asia*. **Khristos Nikolopoulos** was a *bouzoúki* virtuoso who emerged during the 1970s as a composer for Kazanthzídhis, and subsequently went on to mega-selling co-efforts with Dalaras and Alexiou. **Akis Panou** (1934–99) was less prolific and commercially successful – taking time out to be a painter and copper-engraver – but he too produced noteworthy albums with Dalaras, Bithikotsis and Stratos Dhionysiou as well as Kazantzidhis.

Although *laïká* and *éntekhno* represented opposite poles, these extremes sometimes met, with *éntekhno* composers – especially Markopoulos – often hiring *laïká* singers for dates, or trying their hand at writing in *laïká* style. These syntheses became increasingly rare as Greek record labels tried to marginalize *laïká* – a trend accelerated under the junta, and a disaster for many types of music. Not only was the greater portion of *laïká* banned from the radio as being too "oriental" and "defeatist", but folk music – already disparaged as old-fashioned by a generation coming of age with The Beatles – fell into more disrepute through its use for propaganda purposes. In these conditions, only *elafrolaïká* (literally "light popular songs") and *éntekhno*, with its minority audience and potential for coded messages within oblique lyrics, flourished. But the stage was set for the emergence of singer-songwriters – many of them from Thessaloníki – and groups of folk-rockers, who together arrested the decline of Greek music.

Singer-songwriters and folk-rock

The first significant musician to break out of the *bouzoúki* mould was Thessalonian **Dhionysis Savvopoulos**, who burst on the scene in 1966 with a maniacal, rasping voice and angst-ridden lyrics, his persona rounded out by shoulder-length hair and outsized glasses. Initially linked with the short-lived **néo kýma** movement – a blend of watered-down *éntekhno* and French *chanson* performed in Athenian *boîtes* soon closed by the colonels – Savvopoulos's work soon became impossible to pigeonhole: perhaps equal parts twisted northern Greek folk, Bob Dylan and Frank Zappa at his jazziest. Though briefly detained and tortured, he resumed performing, and became something of a touchstone for the generation coming of age under the junta.

Out of Savvopoulos's **"Balkan rock"** experiments sprang a short-lived movement whose artists alternated electric versions of traditional songs with original material. The most significant of these were folk "updater" **Mariza Koch**, the Gypsy protest guitarist-singer **Kostas Hatzis**, **Nikos Portokaloglu** at the head of folk-rock group **Fatme**, and folk/*éntekhno* performer **Arletta**, all of whom are still active to various degrees.

Despite a modest discography, it's difficult to overestimate Savvopoulos's effect on younger artists. Credit (or blame) for much Greek rock and fusion can be laid at his door; during his brief tenure as head of Lyra records, and later as an independent producer, Savvopoulos gave breaks to numerous younger artists, many of them also from northern Greece. Among his spiritual heirs were **Nikos Xydhakis** and **Manolis Rasoulis**, whose landmark 1978 pressing, *Iy Ekdhikisi tis Yiftias* (The Revenge of Gypsydom) actually embodied the backlash of *laïká* culture (*laïká*, in Greek, means "common" or "low-class" as well as "popular") against the pretentiousness of 1960s and 1970s *éntekhno* and other "politically correct" music. Its spirited, defiant lyrics – with Nikos Papazoglou on most vocals – and *tsiftetéli* rhythms were both homage to and send-up of the music beloved by Greek truck-drivers, Gypsy or otherwise.

Real **Gypsies** have been disproportionately important in *laïká*, both as performers and composers, though many go to considerable length to conceal the fact; however, for every assimilated personality there are others, such as **Eleni Vitali**, **Makis Khristodhoulopoulos** and **Vassilis Païteris** who make no bones about their identity.

Contemporary roots: the 1980s to the present

After an equally successful 1979 reprise (*Ta Dhithen*) with much the same personnel, **Xydhakis** and **Papazoglou** went on to pursue successful independent careers, Xydhakis in a notably orientalized style reflecting perhaps his Egyptian childhood. His most successful venture in this vein was the 1987 *Konda sti Dhoxa mia Stigmi* with rising star **Eleftheria Arvanitaki** guesting on vocals. Arvanitaki, who began her career on a Savvopoulos album, and next with the *rebétika* revival group Opisthodhromiki Kompania, went on to try her hand at various genres, and by the millennium was Greece's hottest vocalist, drawing World Music as well as Greek audiences. A Thessalonian like Savvopoulous, Nikos Papazoglou is a more varied, though less prolific, song-writer than Xydhakis; his material, also based on *laïká* and folk, often has a harder electric-rock edge, though he can match Xydhakis for introspection and orientalism. Other performers emerging from the "Salonica Scene" after 1981 included **Himerini Kolymvites** led by Aryiris Bakirtzis, Papazoglou disciple **Sokratis Malamas** and his frequent collaborator Melina Kana.

Back in Athens, Westernizing trends took longer to relax their grip, under the aegis of composers such as classically trained **Thanos Mikroutsikos**, briefly Minister of Culture after Melina Mercouri's death, who despite his high-brow leanings has worked with Alexiou, Dalaras and top vocalist **Dhimitra Galani**. Lyricist **Lina Nikolakopoulou** also made a splash with a number of thought-ful, if somewhat slick, albums stretching into the 1990s, exploring the bounda-ries between rock, jazz-cabaret and *éntekhno*.

An offshoot of *éntekhno* since the mid-1970s involved combining folk and Byzantine traditions. Notable in this was musicologist and arranger **Khris-todhoulos Halaris** with his riveting *Dhrossoulites* – featuring Dhimitra Galani with Khrysanthos, a high-voiced male singer of Pontic descent, and with lyrics by Nikos Gatsos – and his version of the medieval Cretan epic *Erotokritos*, show-casing Nikos Xylouris and Tania Tsanaklidou.

Ottoman rather than Byzantine Constantinople was the inspiration for **Bosphorus/Vosporos**, a group co-ordinated in Istanbul from 1986 to 1992 by Nikiforos Metaxas to explore Ottoman classical, devotional and popular music. Since then the group, briefly rebaptized as **Fanari tis Anatolis**, has handled a variety of Greek folk material with Anatolian songs or mystical Alevî ballads. Most recently they've joined forces with **Mode Plagal**, since 1995 Greece's most accomplished funky deconstructors of folk material.

English-born but Irish by background, **Ross Daly** frequently appears live in Athens clubs or tours abroad. He plays a dozen traditional Greek instruments and has absorbed influences not only from Crete, where he was long resident, but from throughout the Near East. Alone or with a group, he offers strikingly contemporary interpretations of traditional pieces, as well as original improvisa-tional compositions. Two other exports from Crete were mandolinist **Loudho-vikos ton Anoyeion**, originally one of Hatzidhakis's late-1980s finds at Seirios, and the six-member, all-acoustic group **Haïnidhes**. To foreign ears either can seem more accessible than orthodox, scholarly revivalists such as octagenarian **Domna Samiou**, who ranks as the foremost living collector and interpreter of Greek folk material; since the 1960s, she has also nurtured a generation-plus of young traditional musicians.

A range of other, less durable groups have attempted to explore eastern influ-ences on Greek music with varying success. Often this eclecticism has gone too far, with bells, sitar, ney and synthesizer resulting in a bland, New Agey sound not identifiably Greek. Individuals who have managed to avoid this trap include innovative young clarinettist **Manos Achalinotopoulos**; *oud* player **Haig Yagdjian**; the group **Notios Ikhos**, led by Ahilleas Persidhis; singer **Savina Yiannatou**; and the **Greeks-and-Indians** fusion concerts and recordings coordinated by the visionary **Alexandhros Karsiotis**.

Discography

The following CDs are among the best available for each of the genres detailed in our Greek music article: ✗ denotes a particular recommendation. Unless another country is specified, all are Greece-based labels. For listings of good Greek record stores, see the Athens shopping section (p.181). Online, you'll find some of our choices at Amazon, but rather more at the London-based specialist Trehantiri (⊕ www.trehantiri.com), which operates a worldwide mail order service. In Greece, look out also for the monthly music magazine *Dhifono* (⊕ www.difono.gr), which includes a covermount CD of Greek roots-oriented music with each issue.

Folk

Compilations

✗ **Lesvos Aiolis** *Tragoudhia ke Hori tis Lesvou/Songs & Dances of Lesvos* (University Press of Crete, 2 CDs). Two decades' (1974–96) of field recordings of the last traditional music on the island, supervised by musicologist Nikos Dhionysopoulos. The quality and uniqueness of the instrumental pieces, and lavishly illustrated booklet, merit the expense.

Seryiani sta Nisia Mas, vol 1 (MBI). Excellent retrospective of various *nisiótika* hits and artists, mostly from the 1950s; the easiest way to hear the vintage starsRebé. A highlight is Emilia Hatzidhaki's rendering of "Bratsera".

Thalassa Thymisou/Sea of Memories: Tragoudhia ke Skopi apo tis Inousses (Navtiko Mousio Inousson-En Khordais). Superb result of Thessalonian musicologists' "field trip" school to Inoússes, a small islet near Híos; a mix of live sessions in Inoussan tavernas and studio recordings.

Artists

Khronis Aïdhonidhis ✗ *TAïdhonia tis Anatolis: Songs of Thrace and Asia Minor* (Minos). This flawlessly produced 1990 session features the top singer of material from Thrace and western Asia Minor, plus an orchestra directed by Ross Daly, and guest Yiorgos Dalaras.

Petro-Loukas Halkias ✗ *Petro-Loukas Chalkias and Kompania* (World Network, Germany). Halkias is in top form here, as are his *kompanía* (group) of *laoúto*, *violí*, guitar and percussion. Meaty *oud* solos and fiddle-licks realize the true sense of the *kompanía*: tight coordination, yet clearly articulated instrumental voices.

Xanthippi Karathanasi *Tragoudhia ke Skopi tis Makedhonias/Songs and Tunes of Macedonia* (University Press of Crete). A native of Halkidhikí, Karathanasi is a foremost interpreter of northern material – and her sidemen are so good they almost steal the show.

Andonis Xylouris (Psarandonis) *Palio Krasi In'iy Skepsi Mou* (Musurgia Graeca) and *Idheon Antron* (Musurgia Graeca). Psarandonis has an idiosyncratically spare and percussive *lyra* style, but there is no doubting his musical integrity on these varied collections, with unusual instruments well integrated into a densely textured whole. And on *Idheon Antron* daughter Niki does a gorgeous rendition of "Meraklidhiko Pouli".

Nikos Xylouris ✗ *Itane mia Fora* (2 CDs, EMI). A thorough selection of Xylouris' best 1970s work, with Yiannis Markopoulos and others, that should give you some idea why he is still worshipped nearly three decades after his tragically early death.

Rebétika

Compilations

The Greek Archives Series (FM Records). This luxuriously packaged series has skeletal English notes but they are all well chosen selections. From the first, twelve-volume series, go for no. 1 (*Rembetiko Song in America 1920–1940*); no. 6 (*Women of the Rembetiko Song*); no. 7 (*Unknown Recordings from Smyrna 1922–1940*); no. 8 (*Armenians, Jews, Turks & Gipsies*) and no. 9 (*Constantinople in Old Recordings*). From the second series, *Anthology of Rebetiko Songs 1933–1940*, *Anthology of Smyrnean Songs 1920–1933* and *Songs of the Sea* are wonderful.

Greek Orientale: Smyrneic-Rembetic Songs and Dances (Arhoolie-Polylyric, US). Superb collection spanning 1911 to 1937, with Roza, Rita, Marika Papagika and Dhimitris Semsis.

Rembetika: Songs of the Greek Underground 1925–1947 (Trikont, Germany). This crammed-full, 2-CD set makes an excellent starter collection, with classics such as Papaïoannou's "Pende Ellines ston Adhi" and Kaldaras' "Nykhtose Horis Fengari".

Rough Guide to Rebetika (World Music Network, UK). The best single introduction to the genre, with performers from its earliest recorded days to current revivalists.

Artists

Agathonas (Iakovidhis) *Tou Teke keh Tis Tavernas* (Eros). A varied and intimate outing of 1930s material, with a top violinist; *Tis Yerakinas Yios* (Eros, Greece) is typical of his group Rebetiki Tetras, with mostly 1950s material and a more commercial-club sound.

Roza Eskenazi: Rembetissa (Rounder, US/Direct, UK). Ace renditions of standards and rare gems with her usual sidemen, Semsis, Tomboulis, and Lambros on *kanonáki*.

Marika Ninou *Stou Tzimi tou Hondrou/At Jimmy the Fat's* (Venus-Tzina). Poor sound quality as it was a clandestine recording, but still a classic, and one of the few documents of a live rebetic evening. Ninou performs with Tsitsanis at their habitual club in 1955.

Rebetiki Kompania *Pos Tha Perasi Iy Vradhia* (Lyra-Zodiac) Under lead singers/instrumentalists Dhimitris Kondoyiannis and Manolis Dhimitrianakis, this is the easiest found offering from a group which spearheaded the late-1970s *rebétika* revival.

Vangelis Papazoglou 1897–1943 (Lyra). Compositions from the 1920s and 1930s, sung by top stars of the era, including Stellakis Perpiniadhis, Roza Eskenazi, Kostas Roukounas and Rita Abatzi. Marred by poor sound quality, but several versions of his classic "Iy Lahanadhes".

Vassilis Tsitsanis *Vassilis Tsitsanis 1936–1946* (Rounder, US/Direct, UK). Mostly male singers, but includes several rare (for him) *mastoúriaka*.) *Ta Klidhia* (EMI Regal) – look for the double keys (*klidhiá*) on the cover – pairs him with such mid-1960s stars as Grigoris Bithikotsis, Panos Gavalas, Poly Panou and Manolis Hiotis.

Markos Vamvakaris *Bouzoúki Pioneer 1932–1940* (Rounder, US/Direct, UK). Excellent sound quality, good notes and unusual material make this a first choice.

Stavros Xarhakos *Rembetiko* (CBS). Soundtrack to the namesake film, and virtually the only "original" *rebétika* composed in the last fifty years; lyrics by Nikos Gatsos.

Éntekhno

Manos Hatzidhakis *Matomenos Gamos: Paramythi horis Onoma*

(Columbia). Nikos Gatsos lyrics, with Lakis Pappas singing. *O Megalos Erotikos* (Lyra MBI) has lyrics based on Greek poetry from Sappho to Elytis.

Yannis Markopoulos 🎿 *Rizitika* (Minos EMI). "La Chante Profunde de Crète" – the French subtitle – says it all: stirring anthems like "Pote Tha Kamei Xasteria", which launched Xylouris' *éntekhno* career. *Thiteia* (Minos EMI), with lyrics by Manos Eleftheriou and enduring hits like "Malamatenia Logia" is also a sentimental favourite.

Mikis Theodhorakis 🎿 *Epitafios/ Epifaneia* (EMI/HMV) with Bithikotsis and Hiotis, and *To Axion Esti* (EMI/HMV) with Manos Katrakis, are among his most influential, reputation-justifying works, out in white-boxed remasters of the original sessions.

🎿 **Stavros Xarhakos/Nikos Xylouris** *Sylloyi* (Minos EMI). More lyrics by Nikos Gatsos, Xylouris's crystalline voice and orchestra (including funky electric guitar licks) conducted by Khristodhoulos Halaris made this 1973 recording a landmark; the wistful "Itane mia Fora" is particularly loved and still ubiquitously heard.

Laïka

Haris Alexiou 🎿 *Ta Tragoudhia tis Haroulas* (Minos EMI). From a huge discography, start with this album, with lyrics by Manolis Rasoulis and Manos Loïzos, which secured her position as the queen of 1980s *laïká*. *Ta Tsilika* (Minos EMI) has her *rebétika* interpretations. *Yirizondas ton Kosmo* (Mercury), is a more recent live *éntekhno/*pop disc.

Eleftheria Arvanitaki *Ta Kormia ke ta Mahairia* (Polydor). Best-selling, introspective venture with music by Ara Dinkjian and lyrics by Mihala Ganas; 🎿 *Tragoudhia yia tous Mines*

(Polygram) is more upbeat and *laïká*-based. In *Ektos Programmatos* (Mercury) Eleftheria returns to Greek roots in lively sessions at Athens and Thessaloníki clubs.

Yiorgos Dalaras *Latin* (Minos EMI). A 1987 team-up with Al Di Meola, Glykeria, Alkistis Protopsalti and others, plus Latin rhythms and instrumentalists, resulted in nearly half a million copies sold. *A Portrait: George Dalaras* (EMI, UK) is a "best-of" sampler spanning his career up to the late 1990s.

Glykeria (Kotsoula) *Me ti Glykeria stin Omorfi Nhykhta* (Lyra MBI). Live recording showcases this versatile *laïká* singer and *rebétika/nisiótika* revivalist active from the 1980s on.

Apostolos Kaldharas *Mikra Asia* (Minos EMI) marked Haris Alexiou's 1972 vinyl debut and helped spark the *rebétika* revival.

Stelios Kazantzidhis *Iy Zoi Mou Oli* (2 CD, Minos EMI). A retrospective of all the classic hits that made him a national monument.

Singer-Songwriters

🎿 **Himerini Kolymvites (Lyra).** First and best of their CDs, with surreal lyrics plus rich, drunken melodies.

Sokratis Malamas 🎿 *Ena* (Lyra MBI). A 2000 release that embodies his mature, confident style, with just voice and guitar.

Lina Nikolakopoulou and Stamatis Kraounakis *Kykloforo ke Oploforo* (Polydor). First and best of their collaborations, featuring Alkistis Protopsalti. Protopsalti and Nikolakopoulou later linked up with Goran Bregovic for the rootsily Balkan *Paradekhtika*, featuring Ferus Mustafov on clarinet.

Nikos Papazoglou 🎿 *Synerga* (Lyra MBI). A gentle, mystical album, rather in the mould of Xydhakis, rather than his rock material.

Manolis Rasoulis & Petros Voyiopoulos *Valkanizater* (Eros). Rollicking and accessible acoustic soundtrack to the hit 1995 film, with vocals by Eleni Vitali, Glykeria and Paskhalis Terzis, among others.

Dhionysis Savvopoulos 🏃 *Trapezakia Exo* (Lyra MBI). The best outing from the man who set off the folk-rock movement.

🏃 **Nena Venetsanou** This female singer has a deep, earthy voice lending itself to a number of genres. *Ikones* (Musrugia Greca) reworks everything from Hatzidhakis to *nisiótika* to chanson; *Zeïbekika* (MBI) is a suprisingly successful recasting of this rebetic style as "profane prayers", performed in French chapels.

Nikos Xydhakis, Thodhoros Gonis, Eleftheria Arvanitaki 🏃 *Konda sti Dhoxa mia Stigmi* (Lyra MBI). One of the best recordings of the late 1980s, with haunting Xydhakis arrangements and compositions.

🏃 **Nikos Xydhakis, Nikos Papazoglou, Manolis Rasoulis** *Iy Ekdhikisi tis Yiftias* (Lyra MBI). Ground-breaking 1978 outing, still much listened to in Greece; its equally good follow-up *Ta Dhithen* (Lyra MBI) contained the single "Iy Manges Dhen Yparhoun Pia", covered later by Haris Alexiou.

Folk Revival and Fusion

Bosphorus (Fanari tis Anatolis) 🏃*Beyond the Bosphorus* (Hitch-Hyke Records). Since 1994, Bosphorus have been alternating vocals in Greek and Turkish, while retaining previous instrumental virtuosity. This album is a tour de force, with guests Mode Plagal working the same transformation on Constantinopolitan melodies as they had done previously on Greek ones.

Ross Daly *Selected Works* (Oriente, Germany). A representative compilation from his many albums. *Mitos* (World Network, Germany) captures 1991 concert recordings.

Haïnidhes 🏃 *Haïnidhes* (MBI) and *Kosmos ki Oneiro ine Ena* (MBI) are their first two, and arguably best, albums, with folk-influenced original compositions taking precedence over old standards.

Loudhovikos Ton Anoyion 🏃 *O Erotas stin Kriti ine Melangolikos* (Seirios) helped resurrect the Cretan mandolin from its rhythm-backing ghetto; *Pyli tis Ammou* (Mylos) exemplifies his evolution in a larger group, with Malamas, Papazoglou and Venetsanou as guests.

Mode Plagal *Mode Plagal II* (Lyra MBI). The best of their four solo albums; folk tunes meet funky guitar and saxophone licks à la Coltrane and Miles.

Savina Yiannatou *Anixi sti Saloniki/Spring in Salonika* (Musurgia Graeca). Settings of Ladino Sephardic songs, with crisp backing from Kostas Vomvolos' orchestra; Savina's voice (and trademark vibrato) can take some getting used to, though.

Greeks & Indians (6-vol set on Saraswati label): This series (vols 1 & 5 🏃 are highlights) sees top performers of Greek regional music – including Petro-Loukas Halkias, Ross Daly, Nikos and Yiasemi Saragoudhas, Sokaratis Sinopoulos and Yiorgos Koros – joining forces with some of the best North Indian musicians around.

Books

H ere is a selection of the most interesting, most informative and most enjoyable books about Greece, or books by Greeks, including a scattering of modern Greek fiction and ancient classics. The ones we like best are marked with the ✪ symbol. Titles currently out of print are indicated as "o/p", while "UP" designates University Press.

Most of our recommended books are readily available online. Amazon is an obvious first stop, and for out of print, or secondhand books, sites such as ⓦwww.abebooks.com or ⓦwww.bookfinder.com. Better still, try the specialist Greek bookshops Hellenic Bookservice (91 Fortress Rd, London NW5 1AG; T 020/7267 9499; Wwww.hellenicbookservice.com), or Zeno's (57a Nether St, London N12 7NP; T 020/8446 1985, ⓦwww .thegreekbookshop.com). Athens also has some good bookshops (see p.181).

Travel/Impressions

✪ **Kevin Andrews** *The Flight of Ikaros* (o/p but easy to find). An intense, compelling account of an educated, sensitive archeologist wandering the backcountry during the civil war. Half a century on, it is still one of the best books on Greece as it was before "development".

James Theodore Bent *Aegean Islands: The Cyclades*, or *Life Among the Insular Greeks* (Tecla, UK). Originally published in 1881, this remains the most authoritative account of Greek island customs and folklore, and a highly readable chronicle of a year's Aegean travel.

Gillian Bouras *A Foreign Wife*; *A Fair Exchange*; *Aphrodite and the Others* (all o/p). This series of books by a woman who married a Greek-Australian and moved to the Peloponese in 1980, are absorbing reads, full of insights into Greek rural life and the migrant experience in both directions.

Gerald Durrell *My Family and Other Animals* (Penguin, UK). Funny and entrancing anecdotes of Durrell's childhood on Corfu during the 1930s, where his very odd family

settled, and where he developed a passion for the island's fauna – toads, tortoises, scorpions – while elder brother Lawrence entertained Henry Miller and others. Durrell wrote two further books about the time, which have been collected, with *My Family*, as *The Corfu Trilogy* (Penguin, UK).

Lawrence Durrell *Prospero's Cell* and *Reflections on a Marine Venus* (Faber & Faber, UK). The former is the elder Durrell's Corfu book, from his time there with Gerald and the family as World War II loomed. *Marine Venus* recounts his 1945–47 experiences of Rhodes and other Dodecanese islands.

✪ **Patrick Leigh Fermor** *Roumeli and Mani* (John Murray, UK). Sir Patrick – he was knighted in 2004 for his writing and contribution to British-Greek relations – is an aficionado of rural Greece's vanishing minorities and disappearing customs. These two volumes, written in the late 1950s and early 1960s respectively, are true classics: scholarly travelogues interspersed with strange and hilarious yarns. They remain among the best books on any aspect of modern Greece.

Peter France *A Place of Healing for the Soul: Patmos* (Grove Press, US). A former BBC documentary maker, France settled on Patmos with his Greek Orthodox wife, and slowly moved to adopt her faith. As such, this is more spiritual than travel journey, but the daily life of a Greek island is nicely observed, too.

Eleni Gage *North of Ithaka* (Bantam, UK/St Martin's Press, US). Eleni is the daughter of Nicholas Gage – and the namesake and granddaughter of the Eleni, whose murder he famously set out to avenge (see p.1142). A journalist in New York, like her father, she set out to spend a year in her grandmother's old village in Epirus in 2002, rebuilding the family house and roots. Her account is open, moving and impressive.

Yorgos Ioannou *Refugee Capital* (Kedros, Greece). Brilliant essays on the city by this native of Thessaloníki, ranging through its political powerlessness, the deportation of the Jews, and the grip of the Orthodox church, to praise of its flowering shade trees, and gay cruising at its old cinemas.

Sheelagh Kanneli *Earth and Water: A Marriage in Kalamata* (Efstathiadhis, Greece). Fine account of a foreign woman integrating successfully into provincial Greek society in the 1960s. Rich in period detail of pre-earthquake Kalamáta.

Edward Lear *The Corfu Years* and *The Cretan Journal* (Denise Harvey, Greece); *Journals of a Landscape Painter in Greece and Albania* (o/p). Highly entertaining –and beautifully illustrated – journals from the 1840s and 1850s by the landscape painter and author of *The Book of Nonsense*.

Peter Levi *The Hill of Kronos* (o/p). Beautifully observed landscape, monuments, personalities and politics as the poet and classical scholar Levi describes his first journeys to Greece in the 1960s, and becomes drawn into resistance to the colonels' junta.

Sidney Loch *Athos, The Holy Mountain* (Molho, Greece). Resident in the tower at Ouranópoli, the port to Mount Áthos, from 1924 to 1954, Loch recounts the legends surrounding the various monasteries, as gleaned from his years of walking around the monks' republic.

Willard Manus *This Way to Paradise: Dancing on the Tables* (Lycabettus Press, Greece). American expatriate's memoir of nearly four decades in Líndhos, Rhodes, beginning long before its descent into mass-tourist tattiness. Wonderful period detail, including hippie/bohemian excesses and often hilarious cameos from the likes of S.J. Perelman, Germaine Greer and Martha Gellhorn.

Henry Miller *The Colossus of Maroussi* (W.W. Norton). Corfu, Crete, Athens and the soul of Greece in 1939, with Miller, completely in his element, at his most inspired. Funny, sensual and transporting.

James Pettifer *The Greeks: The Land and People Since the War* (Penguin, UK). Useful, if patchy, introduction to contemporary Greece – and its recent past (it was last updated in 2000). Pettifer charts the state of the nation's politics, family life, religion and tourism.

Dilys Powell *An Affair of the Heart* and *The Villa Ariadne* (Efstathiadis, Greece). These accounts of Greece from the 1930s to the 1950s have aged well. Powell accompanied archeologist husband Humfry Payne on a dig of the sanctuary at Perahóra, Korinthía, and forged a lifelong bond with the villagers there, described in *An Affair*. After his sudden death in 1936, she travelled across the country from Epirus to Crete, which she describes in *The Villa Ariadne*.

C

Tim Salmon *The Unwritten Places* (Lycabettus Press, Greece). Salmon has spent half his life in Greece and here describes his love affair with the mountains, and the Vlach communities of the Píndhos, in particular. The heart of the book is a journey on foot following the last clan and their flocks on the autumn migration (*dhiáva*) to the flatlands.

Leon Sciaky *Farewell to Salonica* (Paul Dry Books, US). Belle Époque memoir of boyhood in a middle class Sephardic Jewish home, before his family's 1915 emigration to the US. The Sciakys had close links with Bulgarian Kilkís peasants – and the author is far more sympathetic to Bulgaria than to the new Greek Orthodox regime, which took over control of the cosmopolitan city, and its Jewish community, in 1912.

Terence Spencer *Fair Greece, Sad Relic: Literary Philhellenism from Shakespeare to Byron* (Denise Harvey, Greece). A compelling account of how travellers and poets steeped in the classics – culminating in Byron – fueled European support for the 1821 Revolution, despite misgivings about the Greeks themselves.

Tom Stone *The Summer of My Greek Taverna.* (Simon & Schuster, US). An enjoyable cautionary tale for those entertaining fantasies of a new life in the Aegean sun. Moving to Pátmos in the early 1980s, Stone, a rather trusting American, tries to mix friendship and business at the beach, running a taverna.

Richard Stoneman, ed *A Literary Companion to Travel in Greece* (Getty Trust, US). Ancient and medieval authors, plus Grand Tourists – an excellent selection that really does make a good travel companion.

🏃 **Patricia Storace** *Dinner with Persephone* (Granta Books, UK/Vintage, US). A New York

poet, resident for a year in Athens (with forays to the provinces) puts the country's mid-1990s psyche on the couch, while avoiding predatory males. Storace has a sly humour, a fine style, and an interesting take on Greece's "imprisonment" in its imagined past.

🏃 **Sofka Zinovieff** *Eurydice Street* (Granta Books, UK). An anthropologist and journalist by training, Zinovieff first came to Greece in the early 1980s, then returned in 2001 with her diplomat husband and two daughters to live in Athens. With sharp observations on everything from nationalism to leisure, this is probably the best single account of life in today's urban Greece.

Photo books

Yann Arthus-Bertrand *Greece from the Air* (Thames & Hudson, UK). Greece gets the aerial treatment from Arthus-Bertrand – and it looks great, from the Parthenon to the most remote islands and ancient sites.

🏃 **Chris Hellier** *Monasteries of Greece* (o/p). Magnificently photographed survey of the surviving, active monasteries and treasures, with insightful accompanying essays.

🏃 **Constantine Manos** *A Greek Portfolio* (W.W. Norton, US). The fruits of a gifted Greek-American photographer's three-year odyssey in the early 1960s through a country on the edge of modernization, still essentially unchanged from the 1930s. The quality and insight you'd expect from a member of the Magnum co-operative, in elegiac black-and-white photos.

Mark Ottaway and Hugh Palmer *The Most Beautiful Villages of Greece* (Thames & Hudson, UK). Greece at its most seductive, charted in 285 mainland and island images.

Clay Perry *Vanishing Greece* (Parkway, UK/Newsstand, Greece).

Well-captioned photos depict the threatened landscapes and relict ways of life in rural Greece.

🏃 **Suzanne Slesin et al** *Greek Style*. (Thames & Hudson, UK).

This has been in print for nearly twenty years: and rightly so: its images get beyond designer homes, ranging widely through village houses, monasteries, summer villas, and so on.

History and Art

General

Timothy Boatswain and Colin Nicolson *A Traveller's History of Greece* (Weidenfeld & Nicholson, UK/Interlink, US). A well-written overview of the important Greek periods and personalities, from earliest times to the present (last updated in 2003).

Ancient History

This is just a small selection of what is a vast literature on every aspect of Ancient Greek history and culture.

General

William R. Biers *Archeology of Greece: An Introduction* (Cornell UP, US). A good survey of the subject, published in 1987.

🏃 **John Boardman** *Greek Art* (Thames & Hudson, UK). This is a classic study, in the *World of Art* series, first published in 1964. Or for more detailed treatment, there are three period volumes: *The Archaic Period, The Classical Period, The Late Classical Period*.

Early Greece

🏃 **A.R. Burn** *History of Greece* (Penguin, UK). **Paul Cartledge** *Cambridge Illustrated History of Ancient Greece* (Cambridge UP). These are the two the best general introductions to ancient Greece. Take your

pick between brief paperback, or large illustrated tome.

🏃 **Walter Burkert** *Greek Religion: Archaic and Classical*. Superb overview of deities and their attributes and antecedents, rites, the protocol of sacrifice and the symbolism of major festivals; especially good on relating Greek worship to its predecessors in the Middle East.

Mary Lefkowitz *Greek Gods, Human Lives: What We Can Learn from Myths* (Yale UP). Rather than being frivolous, immoral or irrelevant, ancient religion and its myths, in their bleak indifference of the gods to human suffering, are shown as being more "grown up" than the later creeds of salvation and comfort.

🏃 **M.I. Finley** *The World of Odysseus* (New York Review of Books, US). Reprint of a 1954 warhorse, pioneering in its investigation of the historicity of the events and society related by Homer. Breezily readable and stimulating.

Reynold Higgins *Minoan and Mycenaean Art* (Thames & Hudson, UK). A clear, well-illustrated roundup of the culture of Mycenae, Crete and the Cyclades, again in the *World of Art* series.

Oswyn Murray *Early Greece* (Fontana, UK/Harvard UP, US). The Greek story from the Mycenaeans and Minoans through to the beginning of the Classical period.

Robin Osborne *Greece in the Making 1200–479 BC* (Routledge, UK). Well-illustrated paperback on the rise of the city-state.

Colin Renfrew *The Cycladic Spirit* (Thames & Hudson, UK). A fine study, illustrated with the core of the Goulandris Collection in Athens, and convincing on the meaning and purpose of Cycladic artefacts.

Classical

Mary Beard *The Parthenon* (Profile, UK). A compelling reassessment of the building, both in terms of its real purpose and the possible meaning of its various relief sculptures, in light of the discoveries made during the ongoing reconstruction work.

Paul Cartledge *The Spartans: The World of the Warrior-Heroes of Ancient Greece* (Vintage, US). A modern reassessment of this much maligned city-state, secretive and a source of speculation from outside even in its own time.

James Davidson *Courtesans and Fishcakes (Fontana, UK).* An absorbing book on the politics, class characteristics and etiquette of consumption and consummation – with wine, women, boys and seafood – in Classical Athens.

The classics

Many of the classics make excellent companion reading for a trip around Greece – especially the historians Thucydides and Herodotus. Reading Homer's *Odyssey* when you're resigning yourself to the vagaries of island ferries puts your own plight into perspective. Here are a few choices for beginners: most of them are published in a range of paperback editions, from Penguin Classics, Oxford University Press, University of Chicago Press, Routledge, Duckworth and others. Where there is an outstanding edition, it is noted.

Mary Beard and John Henderson *The Classics: A Very Short Introduction* (Oxford UP, UK). Exactly as it promises: an excellent overview.

Herodotus *The Histories*. Revered as the father of narrative history – and anthropology – this fifth-century-BC Anatolian writer chronicled both the causes and campaigns of the Persian Wars, as well as the contemporary, assorted tribes and nations inhabiting Asia Minor.

Homer *The Iliad and The Odyssey*. The first concerns itself, semi-factually, with the late Bronze Age war of the Achaeans against Troy in Asia Minor; the second recounts the hero Odysseus's long journey home, via seemingly every corner of the Mediterranean. The best modern prose translations are by Martin Hammond (Penguin), and in verse Richmond Lattimore (Chicago UP). For a vibrant and very loose verse *Iliad*, try also Christopher Logue's version, published as *War Music* (Faber & Faber).

Ovid *The Metamorphoses* (trans A.D. Melville). Collected by a first-century-AD Roman poet, this remains one of the most accessible renditions of the more piquant Greek myths, involving transformations as divine blessing or curse.

Pausanias *The Guide to Greece*. This was essentially the first-ever guidebook – intended for Roman pilgrims to the holy sites of the central mainland and Peloponnese. Invaluable for later archeologists in assessing damage or change to temples over the intervening centuries, or (in some cases) locating them at all. The Penguin edition, annotated by Peter Levi, has notes on modern identifications of sites.

Thucydides *History of the Peloponnesian War*. Bleak month-by-month account of the conflict, by a cashiered Athenian officer whose affiliation and dim view of human nature didn't usually obscure his objectivity.

Xenophon *The History of My Times*. Thucydides' account of the Peloponnesian War stops in 411 BC; this eyewitness account continues events until 362 BC.

J.K. Davies *Democracy and Classical Greece* (Fontana, UK/Harvard UP, US). Established, accessible account of the Classical period and its political developments.

Simon Hornblower *The Greek World 479–323 BC* (Routledge, UK). An erudite survey of ancient Greece at its zenith, from the end of the Persian Wars to the death of Alexander.

Roger Ling *Classical Greece* (Phaidon, UK). A survey of the greatest period of Greek civilization, from the 5th to the 1st century BC, taking in the arts, military and political history, and surveying archeology on the period.

Hellenistic

Paul Cartledge *Alexander the Great: The Hunt for a New Past* (Overlook Press, US). An evocative, meticulous and accessible biography, that stints on neither the emperor's brutality nor his achievement.

Robin Lane Fox *Alexander the Great* (Penguin, UK). An absorbing study, which mixes historical scholarship with imaginative psychological detail.

R.R.R. Smith *Hellenistic Sculpture* (Thames & Hudson, UK). A modern reappraisal of the art of Greece under Alexander and his successors.

F.W. Walbank *The Hellenistic World* (Fontana, UK/Harvard UP, US). Greece under the sway of the Macedonian and Roman empires.

Byzantine and Medieval Greece

General

Nicholas Cheetham *Medieval Greece* (o/p). A general survey of the period and its infinite convolutions in Greece, with Frankish, Catalan, Venetian, Byzantine and Ottoman struggles for power.

Byzantine history and art

John Beckwith *Early Christian and Byzantine Art* (Yale UP, US/UK). Wide-ranging illustrated study placing Byzantine art within a wider context.

John Julius Norwich *Byzantium: The Early Centuries; Byzantium: the Apogee* and *Byzantium: The Decline* (Penguin, UK/US). Perhaps the main surprise for first-time travellers to Greece is the fascination of Byzantine monuments, above all at Mystra. This is an astonishingly detailed yet readable trilogy of the empire that produced them. There is also an excellent, one-volume abridged version, *A Short History of Byzantium* (Penguin, UK/US).

Steven Runciman *Byzantine Style and Civilization* (o/p). An out of print Penguin, well worth tracking down for a survey of the empire's art, culture and monuments.

Steven Runciman *The Fall of Constantinople, 1453* (Cambridge UP, UK). A superb narrative of perhaps the key event of the Middle Ages, and its repercussions throughout Europe and the Islamic world.

Archbishop Kallistos (Timothy Ware) *The Orthodox Church* (Penguin, UK). A good introduction to what is still the established religion of Greece, by the UK's Orthodox archbishop. Part One describes the history of Orthodoxy, Part Two its currently held beliefs.

Modern Greece

General

Richard Clogg *A Concise History of Greece* (Cambridge UP, UK). This is the single volume Greek history you need to read: a remarkably clear and well-illustrated account, from the decline of Byzantium to 2000, with the emphasis on recent decades.

🏃 **John S. Koliopoulos and Thanos M. Veremis** *Greece: The Modern Sequel, from 1831 to the Present* (C. Hurst, UK/New York UP, US). A thematic rather than chronological study that pokes into corners rarely illuminated by conventional histories, with some tart opinions and debunkings; especially good on Macedonian issues, brigandage and the Communists, on which Koliopoulos is an expert. Best read after you've digested Clogg.

Mark Mazower *Salonica, City of Ghosts: Christians, Muslims and Jews* (HarperPerennial, UK/Knopf, US). A vivid history of the multi-ethnic port, one of the most cosmopolitan cities of Europe under Ottoman rule, and its sad history, assailed by the exchange of Muslim and Christian populations, and then the Nazis' removal of the Jewish community.

C.M. Woodhouse *Modern Greece: A Short History* (Faber & Faber, UK). Woodhouse, long a Conservative MP, was a key figure in liaisons with the Greek Resistance during World War II. Writing from a more right-wing perspective than Clogg, his account – from the foundation of Constantinople to 1990 – is briefer and drier, but scrupulous with facts.

The War of Independence and Unification

David Brewer *The Flame of Freedom: The Greek War of Independence 1821–1833* (Overlook Press, US). Published in 2001, this was the first account for some decades of the War of Independence. Its narrative is strong on the background of Ottoman Greece, as well as the progress of the war.

🏃 **Michael Llewellyn Smith** *Ionian Vision: Greece in Asia Minor, 1919–22* (C. Hurst & Co, UK). The subject is the disastrous Anatolian campaign, which led to the exchange of populations between Greece and Turkey. Llewellyn-Smith's account evinces considerable sympathy for the post-1920 royalist government pursuing an unwanted, inherited, unwinnable war.

World War II, Civil War, and its aftermath

🏃 **David H. Close** *The Origins of the Greek Civil War* (Longman, UK). Excellent, readable and impressively even-handed study that focuses on the social conditions in 1920s and 1930s Greece that made the country so ripe for conflict.

🏃 **Mark Mazower** *Inside Hitler's Greece: The Experience of Occupation 1941–44.* A fascinating, exceptionally well illustrated account of how the demoralization of the country and incompetence of conventional politicians led to the rise of ELAS and the onset of civil war.

🏃 **C.M. Woodhouse** *The Struggle for Greece, 1941–49.* A masterly, well-illustrated account of this crucial decade, exploring all of the so-called "three rounds" of resistance and rebellion, and how Greece emerged without a communist government.

Wartime accounts

There have been many accounts of World War II in Greece, and the Civil War, written by Greeks and British involved. These include:

Nicholas Gage *Eleni* (Ballantine, US/Harvill Press, UK). Controversial account by a Greek-born *New York Times* correspondent who returns to Epirus to avenge the death of his mother, condemned by an ELAS tribunal in 1948. The descriptions of village life, then and now, are superbly evocative. But the book has its agenda and its political "history" is at best selective.

Iakovos Kambanellis *Mauthausen* (Kedros, Greece). Kambanellis was active in the Resistance, caught by the Germans, and sent to Mauthausen, a concentration camp for politicians or partisans who opposed the Nazis' rise to power. Harrowing atrocities in flashback there are aplenty, but the main thrust of the book is post-liberation, describing how the idealist inmates are slowly disillusioned as they see that the "New World Order" will be scarcely different from the old. The basis of a play, and a Theodhorakis oratorio of the same name.

Eddie Myers *Greek Entanglement* (o/p). The inside story of the Gorgopotamos viaduct sabotage operation by the British brigadier who led it, and lots else about co-ordinating the resistance from 1942 to 1944. Myers comes across as under no illusions as to the qualities of the various Greeks he had to deal with.

Adrian Seligman *War in the Islands.* Collected oral histories of a little-known Allied unit: a flotilla of *kaïkia* organized to raid the Axis-held Aegean islands. Boy's Own stuff, with service-jargon-laced prose, but lots of fine period photos and detail.

Michael Ward *Greek Assignments: SOE 1943–UNSCOB 1948* (Lycabettus Press, Greece). The author, British consul in Thessaloníki from 1971 to 1983, parachuted into the Píndhos as a guerrilla and walked the width of the country; most revealing is how the Germans controlled only the towns, leaving the countryside to the Resistance. He married a Greek and later returned to observe the civil war.

Ethnography

Juliet du Boulay *Portrait of a Greek Mountain Village* (Denise Harvey, Greece). An account of the village of Ambéli, on Évvia, during the 1960s. The habits and customs of an all-but-vanished way of life are evoked in an absorbing narrative.

John K. Campbell *Honour, Family and Patronage* (Oxford UP, UK). Early 1960s study of a Sarakatsáni community on Mount Gamíla in the Píndhos, with much wider applicability to rural Greece.

Richard Clogg, ed. *The Greek Minorities* (C. Hurst, UK). Collection of articles on all the various Greek ethnic and religious minorities, current to the mid-1990s – despite its age, error-free and authoritative.

Rae Dalven *The Jews of Ioannina* (Lycabettus Press, Greece). The history and culture of the thriving pre-Holocaust community, related by a poet and translator of Cavafy, herself an Epirot Jew.

Loring Danforth and Alexander Tsiaras *The Death Rituals of Rural Greece* (Princeton UP, US). Many visitors and foreign residents find Greek funeral customs – the wailing, the open-casket vigils, the disinterment of the bones after five years – the most disturbing aspect of the culture; this book helps make sense of it all.

Renée Hirschon *Heirs of the Greek Catastrophe: the Social Life of Asia Minor Refugees in Piraeus* (Berghahn Books, US/Clarendon Press, UK). A classic 1981 study that shows how this community in Kokkinia maintained a separate identity three generations after 1923. It's inevitably nostalgic, as increasing wealth has largely dissolved the community, but helps you understand why Athens is so higgledy-piggledy.

Gail Holst-Warhaft *Road to Rembétika: Songs of Love, Sorrow and Hashish* (Denise Harvey, Greece). The most intriguing Greek urban musical style of the past century, evocatively traced by a Cornell University professor and long-term observer of the Greek music scene.

Anastasia Karakasidou *Fields of Wheat, Hills of Blood* (Chicago UP, US). Excellent and controversial work establishing how Macedonia only became "Greek" politically and ethnically in the early twentieth century, by means of a deliberate and official Hellenization process. Sensationally declined for initial publication by Cambridge – its editorial board resigned in protest – after threats from ultra-nationalists both in Greece and in the diaspora.

John Cuthbert Lawson *Modern Greek Folklore and Ancient Greek Religion: A Study in Survivals* (RA Kessinger, US). Fascinating: the study is exactly as the title states, and still applicable a century after first publication.

Fiction

Greek Writers

Maro Douka *Fool's Gold* (Kedros, Greece). An upper-class young woman's involvement, and subsequent disillusionment, with the clandestine resistance to the junta.

Apostolos Doxiades *Uncle Petros and the Goldbach Conjecture*. (Faber & Faber, UK). One of the best novels, in any language, of the past decade. Its central characters, Uncle Petros and his (narrator) nephew, are mathematicians and the story inspires a real excitement for the subject, even for non-initiates.

Eugenia Fakinou *The Seventh Garment* (Serpents Tail, UK). Greek history from the War of Independence to the colonels' junta is told through the life stories (interspersed in counterpoint) of three generations of women.

Oriana Falacci *A Man* (o/p). Gripping tale of the junta years, relating the author's involvement with Alekos Panagoulis, the army officer who attempted to assassinate Colonel Papadopoulos in 1968. Issued ostensibly as a "novel" in response to threats by those who were implicated in Panagoulis's own murder in 1975.

Andreas Franghias *The Courtyard* (Kedros, Athens). This well-observed but relentlessly depressing tale follows the struggling (and just plain scheming) inhabitants of a working-class Athens shanty town during the early 1950s.

Rhea Galanaki *Eleni, or Nobody* (Northwestern UP, US). Fine novelization of the life of Eleni Altamura, Greece's first, mid-nineteenth-century woman painter, who lived in Italy for some years disguised as a man.

Panos Karnezis *Little Infamies* and *The Maze* (Vintage, UK/Farrar, Straus and Giroux, US). Karnezis is the big new name in Greek fiction – and these two books have had deserved success. The author grew up in Greece, but is now resident in London, and writes in English. However, his concerns and subject matter is utterly Greek. *Little Infamies* is a collection of short stories set in his native Peloponnese in the late 1950s and early 1960s: cleverly constructed, with a rather pleasing love of old fashioned twists. *The Maze* is a darker-shaded, more ambitious novel concerning the Asia Minor Catastrophe of 1923, and thus an interesting counterpoint to Louis de Bernières' novel (below).

Nikos Kazantzakis *Zorba the Greek; The Last Temptation of Christ; Christ Recrucified / The Greek Passion; Freedom or Death / Captain Michalis; The Fratricides; Report to Greco* (Faber & Faber, UK/Touchstone, US). Whether in intricate Greek or somehow not-quite-adequate English, Kazantzakis can be hard going, yet the power of his writing shines through. *Zorba the Greek* is a dark, nihilistic work, worlds away from the two-dimensional characters of the film. By contrast, the movie version of *The Last Temptation of Christ* provoked riots amongst Orthodox fanatics in Athens in 1989. *Christ Recrucified* (*The Greek Passion* in the US) resets the Easter drama against the backdrop of Christian/Muslim relations, while *Freedom or Death* (aka *Captain Michalis*) chronicles the rebellions of nineteenth-century Crete. *The Fratricides* portrays a family riven by the civil war. *Report to Greco* – perhaps the most accessible of his works – is an autobiographical exploration of the novelist's Greekness.

Artemis Leontis (ed) *Greece: A Traveller's Literary Companion*. A nice idea, brilliantly executed: various regions of the country as portrayed in (very) short fiction or essays by modern Greek writers.

Kostas Mourselas *Red Dyed Hair* (Kedros, Greece). A modern picaresque epic – imagine *Zorba* crossed with *Last Exit to Brooklyn* – of a particularly dysfunctional Pireás *paréa* (the group you hang out with from youth till middle age). At its centre stands anti-hero Emmanuel Retsinas, mad, bad and dangerous to know. A particularly good translation of a Greek original which became a popular TV series.

Stratis Myrivilis *Life in the Tomb* (Quartet, UK). A harrowing and unorthodox war memoir, based on the author's experience on the Macedonian front in 1917–18, well translated by Peter Bien.

Alexandros Papadiamantis *Tales from a Greek Island* (Johns Hopkins UP, US). Papadiamantis is sometimes compared to Hardy and Maupassant. He lived and wrote on and about the island of Skiathos: quasi-mythic tales of generally grim fate. His novel, *The Murderess* (o/p), has also been translated (by Peter Levi).

Nick Papandreou *Father Dancing / A Crowded Heart* (Penguin, UK/Picador, US). A novel by the late Andreas's younger son that's actually thinly-veiled autobiography, in which Papandreou Senior, not too surprisingly, comes across as a gasbag and petty domestic tyrant.

Dido Sotiriou *Farewell Anatolia* (Kedros, Greece). A perennial favourite since its initial appearance in 1962, this epic chronicles the traumatic end of Greek life in Asia Minor, from World War I to the catastrophe of 1922, as narrated by a fictionalized version of the author's father.

Stratis Tsirkas *Drifting Cities* (Kedros, Greece). Set by turns in the Jerusalem, Cairo and Alexandria of World War II, this unflinchingly honest and humane epic of a Greek army hero secretly working for the Leftist resistance got the author expelled from the Communist Party.

Vassilis Vassilikos *Z* (o/p). A novel based closely enough on events – the 1963 political assassination of Gregoris Lambrakis in Thessaloníki – to be banned under the colonels' junta, and brilliantly filmed by Costa-Gavras in 1968.

Alki Zei *Achilles' Fiancée* (Kedros, Greece). An often moving portrait of the friendships and intrigues amongst

The Greek myths and legends are fantastic terrain for kids, perfect holiday reading in their original location. And with Terry Deary's "Horrible History" series, the whole of ancient Greek history is an open book.

Ingri and Edgar Parin D'Aulaires *D'Aulaires' Book of Greek Myth* (Doubleday, US). A rather more serious, traditional treatment. Enjoyable nonetheless.

Terry Deary *Gruesome Greeks* and *Greek Legends* (Scholastic, UK/US). Even decently read adults will find themselves delving into these very funny, brilliantly conceived books for a refresher on Ancient Greek history and myths and legends. here's a sample from the script for the Trojan War: *Achilles* "Give the girl back, you daft old bat". Irresistible.

Anthony Horowitz *Myths and Legends* (Kingfisher, UK/US). Greece supplies only half of this book, but the storytelling by Horowitz (*Stormbreaker*, etc) is top class.

Caroline Lawrence *The Roman Mysteries series* (Orion, UK). This is a great series of Roman-era mystery books for 8–11-year-olds, featuring a group of kids, and full of authentic details. The fifth and sixth books, *The Colossus of Rhodes* and *Fugitive from Corinth* transport the action to Greece.

Mary Renault *The King Must Die; The Last of the Wine; The Masks of Apollo; The Praise Singer* (Arrow, UK/Vintage, US). Mary Renault's imaginative reconstructions are more than the teen reading they're often taken for, with impeccable research and tight writing. But they are great for kids, nonetheless. The quartet above retell, respectively, the myth of Theseus, the life of a pupil of Socrates, that of a fourth-century-BC actor and the fortunes of poet Simonides at the court of Samian tyrant Polykrates. The life of Alexander the Great is told in *Fire from Heaven*, *The Persian Boy* and *Funeral Games*, available separately or as *The Alexander Trilogy*.

Francesca Simon *Helping Hercules* (Orion, UK). If your kid(s) are into *Horrid Henry*, then make a bee-line for this clever retelling of Greek myths by the same author, who has a kid called Susan sort out the not-so-heoric heroes.

a collection of communist exiles floating between Athens, Rome, Moscow, Paris and Tashkent in the years between the civil war and the colonels' junta. Largely autobiographical, it captures the flavour of the illusions, nostalgia and endemic party-line schisms.

Greece in foreign fiction

Louis de Bernières *Captain Corelli's Mandolin* (Vintage, UK/US). Set on Kefalloniá during the World War II occupation and aftermath, this accomplished 1994 tragi-comedy quickly acquired cult, then word-of-mouth bestseller status in the UK and US. But in Greece it was a scandal, after Greek Left intellectuals and surviving Italian partisans woke up to its virulent portrayal of ELAS. It seems the novel was closely based on the experiences of one Amos Pampaloni, an artillery captain on Kefalloniá in 1942–44 who later joined ELAS, and who accused De Bernières of distorting the roles of both Italians and ELAS on the island. The Greek translation was suitably abridged to avoid causing offence, and the movie, watered down to a pallid love story as a condition for filming on the island, sank without trace after a few weeks in 2001. All of which said, the first two parts of the novel are spellbinding.

John Fowles *The Magus* (Vintage, UK/Laurel, US). Fowles' biggest and best novel: a tale of mystery and manipulation – plus Greek island life – inspired by his stay on Spétses as a teacher during the 1950s.

Olivia Manning *The Balkan Trilogy, Volume 3: Friends and Heroes*. A wonderfully observed and moving tale, in which Guy and Harriet Pringle escape from Bucharest to Athens, in the last months before the invasion of 1941.

Steven Pressfield *The Virtues of War: A Novel of Alexander the Great* (Doubleday, US). The emperor tells his warrior's tale to his brother-in-law, Itanes. And he does it well, for Pressfield informs his drama with impressive scholarship.

Evelyn Waugh *Officers and Gentleman* (Penguin, UK/Back Bay, US). This second volume of Waugh's brilliant, acerbic wartime trilogy includes an account of the Battle of Crete and subsequent evacuation.

Greek poetry

With two twentieth century Nobel laureates – George Seferis and Odysseus Elytis – modern Greece has an intense and dynamic poetic tradition. Translations of all of the following are excellent.

Anthologies

Peter Bien, Peter Constantine, Edmund Keeley, Karen Van Dyck, eds *A Century of Greek Poetry, 1900–2000* (Cosmos, US). Well produced bilingual volume, with some lesser-known surprises along with the big names.

Nanos Valaoritis and Thanasis Maskaleris, eds *An Anthology of Modern Greek Poetry* (Talisman House, UK). English-only text, but excellent biographical info on the poets and good renditions by two native Greek speakers.

Individual poets

C.P. Cavafy *Collected Poems* (Harcourt Brace, US). The complete works, translated by Rae Dalven, of perhaps the most accessible modern Greek poet, resident for most of his life in Alexandria.

Odysseus Elytis *Collected Poems* (Johns Hopkins UP, US); *The Axion Esti* (Anvil Press, UK). The *Collected Poems* includes virtually everything except *The Axion Esti*, which was cited for his Nobel Prize.

Yannis Kondos *Absurd Athlete* (Arc, UK). One of the best of the latest generation of poets, well translated in a bilingual edition by David Connolloy.

Yannis Ritsos *Repetitions, Testimonies, Parentheses* (Princeton UP, US). A fine volume of Greece's foremost Leftist poet, including work from 1946 to 1975.

George Seferis *Collected Poems, 1924–1955* (Princeton UP, US). Virtually the complete works of the Nobel laureate, with Greek and English verses on facing pages.

Food and wine

Rosemary Barron *Flavours of Greece* (Grub Street, UK). The leading Greek cookbook – among many contenders – by an internationally recognized authority. Contains over 250 recipes.

Andrew Dalby *Siren Feasts: A History of Food and Gastronomy in Greece* (Routledge, UK). This analysis of ancient texts demonstrates just how little Greek cuisine has changed in three millennia; also excellent on the introduction and etymology of common vegetables and herbs.

Konstantinos Lazarakis *The Wines of Greece* (Mitchell Beazley, UK). An excellent, up-to-date overview of what's happening in Greece's eleven recognized wine-producing regions.

Nikos Stavroulakis *Cookbook of the Jews of Greece* (Lycabettus Press, Athens; Cadmus Press, US). Tasty if often fiddly recipes interspersed with their relation to the Jewish liturgical year, plus potted histories of the communities which produced them.

Specific guides

Some specialist guides that you might want to complement this one. See also the Wildlife guides detailed on p.1119.

Archeology

A.R. and Mary Burn *The Living Past of Greece: A Time Traveller's Tour of Historic and Prehistoric Places* (Harper Perennial, UK). This wide-ranging guide covers sites from Minoan through to Byzantine and Frankish, with good clear plans and lively text.

Paul Hetherington *Byzantine and Medieval Greece: Churches, Castles and Art of the Mainland and Peloponnese* (Diane Publishing, UK). A gazetteer of all major mainland sites – readable, authoritative and with useful plans. For the islands see his more recent *The Greek Islands: Guide to Byzantine and Medieval Buildings and their Art* (Quiller, UK), equally good and with more illustrations, though there are some peculiar omissions of worthy monuments.

Hiking

Lance Chilton Various walking-pamphlets (Marengo Publications, UK). Small but thorough guides to the best walks at various mainland and island charter resorts, accompanied by three-colour maps. Available online at ⑩www.marengowalks.com.

Marc Dubin *Trekking in Greece* (o/p). Though many sections are showing their 1988–92 age (and the depredations of bulldozers), this out-of-print Lonely Planet volume is still a useful walkers' guide, expanding on the hikes covered in this book.

Tim Salmon *The Mountains of Greece: A Walker's Guide* (Cicerone, UK). The emphasis in this practical walkers' handbook, updated in 2006, is more specifically on the mainland mountains. Its core is a superb traverse, roughly following the E4 trail along the Píndhos crest, from Delphi to Albania. Beware that some of the estimated walking times are impossibly fast.

Loraine Wilson *The White Mountains of Crete* (Cicerone, UK). Nearly sixty walks and treks, from easy to gruelling, by the doyenne of foreign trekking guides in Crete; implicitly trustworthy directions and prudent warnings.

Sailing

Rod Heikell *Greek Waters Pilot* (Imray, Laurie, Norie & Wilson, UK). This has taken over from H.M. Denham's *Aegean* guide as standard reference for Greek waters. It is updated to 2004.

Regional guides

Rough Guides publishes regional Greek guides to: The Ionian Islands, The Dodecanese and East Aegean Islands; Crete; Corfu; and Athens. In addition, you might want to check out these...

Peter Greenhalgh and Edward Eliopoulos *Deep Into Mani* (o/p). A former member of the wartime Resistance revisits the Máni forty years after first hiding there, and 25 years after Patrick Leigh Fermor's work, in the company of a British scholar. The result is a superb guide

– with very exact directions – and excellent armchair reading.

Oliver Rackham and Jennifer Moody *The Making of the Cretan Landscape* (Manchester UP, UK). It's hard to classify this hugely impressive academic press product written for the casual visitor. It takes in geology, natural history, agricultural practices, place names, architecture and demography, all arranged by topic.

Nikos Stavroulakis *Jewish Sites and Synagogues of Greece* (Talos Press, Greece). A lavishly illustrated alphabetical gazetteer of all Jewish monuments in Greece, with town plans and histories of the communities that created them. A few have been demolished since publication, however.

Lycabettus Press Guides (Athens, Greece). This series takes in many of the more popular islands and certain mainland highlights; most, despite decade-long intervals between revisions, pay their way both in interest and usefulness – in particular those on Páros, Kós, Pátmos, Náfplio, Ídhra and the travels of Saint Paul.

Language

Language

Greek

So many Greeks have lived or worked abroad in North America, Australia and, to a much lesser extent, Britain, that you will find someone who speaks **English** in the tiniest island village. Add to that the thousands attending language schools or working in the tourist industry – English is the lingua franca of most resorts, with German second – and it is easy to see how so many visitors come back having learned only half a dozen restaurant words.

You can certainly get by this way, but it isn't very satisfying, and the willingness and ability to say even a few words will transform your status from that of dumb *tourístas* to the more honourable one of *xénos/xéni*, a word which can mean foreigner, traveller and guest all rolled into one.

Learning basic Greek

Greek is not an easy language for English-speakers – translators' unions in the UK rate it as harder than German, slightly less complex than Russian – but it is a very beautiful one, and even a brief acquaintance will give you some idea of the debt owed to it by Western European languages. Greek **grammar** is predictably complicated; **nouns** are divided into three genders, all with different case endings in the singular and in the plural, and all adjectives and articles have to agree with these in gender, number and case. To simplify life for beginners, all adjectives are arbitrarily cited in the neuter form in the boxed lists on following pages. **Verbs** are even more complex; they come in two conjugations, in both active and passive voices, with passively constructed verbs often having transitive sense. As a novice, the best thing is simply to say what you know the way you know it, and dispense with the niceties.

Teach-yourself Greek courses

Breakthrough Greek (Pan Macmillan; book and 4 cassettes). Excellent, basic teach-yourself course; no Greek lettering, but good for classicists who need to unlearn bad habits.

Greek Language and People (BBC Publications, UK; book and 2 cassettes available). More limited in scope but good for acquiring the essentials, and the confidence to try them.

Anne Farmakides *A Manual of Modern Greek* (Yale UP; McGill UP; 3 vols). If you have the discipline and motivation, this is one of the best for learning proper, grammatical Greek; indeed, mastery of just the first volume will get you a long way.

Hara Garoufalia *Teach Yourself Holiday Greek* (Hodder & Stoughton, UK; book and cassette available). Unlike many quickie courses, this provides a good grammatical foundation, but you'll need a dictionary to supplement the scanty vocabulary lists.

David Hoton et al *Greek: A Comprehensive Grammar of the Modern Language* (Routledge). A bit technical in terminology, so not for rank beginners, but it covers just about every conceivable construction.

Aristarhos Matsukas *Teach Yourself Greek* (McGraw Hill; book and two cassettes). A complete course, touching on idiomatic expressions too.

Niki Watts *Greek in Three Months* (Hugo, Dorling Kindersley; book and 4 cassettes). Delivers as promised; equals or exceeds *Breakthrough Greek*.

Phrasebooks and dictionaries

Greek, a Rough Guide Phrasebook Up-to-date and accurate pocket phrasebook, full of phrases that you'll actually need. The English–Greek section is sensibly transliterated, though the Greek–English part requires basic mastery of the Greek alphabet. Feature boxes fill you in on cultural know-how.

The Oxford Dictionary of Modern Greek. A bit bulky in its wide format, but generally considered the best Greek–English, English–Greek paperback dictionary.

Collins Pocket Greek Dictionary. Very nearly as complete as the Oxford and probably better value for money. The inexpensive *Collins Gem Greek Dictionary* (UK only) is palm-sized but exactly the same in contents – the best day-pack choice.

Oxford Greek–English, English–Greek Learner's Dictionary. If you're planning a prolonged stay, this pricey, hardbound, two-volume set is unbeatable for usage and vocabulary. There's also a more portable one-volume *Learner's Pocket Dictionary*, and the even smaller *Oxford Greek Mini Dictionary*.

Katharévoussa, dhimotikí and dialects

Greek may seem complicated enough in itself, but problems are multiplied when you consider that since the early 1800s there has been an ongoing dispute between two versions of the language: **katharévoussa** and **dhimotikí**.

When Greece first achieved independence in the nineteenth century, its people were almost universally illiterate, and the language they spoke – *dhimotikí*, "demotic" or "popular" Greek – had undergone enormous change since the days of the Byzantine empire and Classical times. The vocabulary had assimilated countless borrowings from the languages of the various invaders and conquerors, such as the Turks, Venetians and Slavs, and the grammar had been considerably streamlined since ancient times.

The finance and inspiration for the new Greek state, as well as some of its early leaders, came largely from the diaspora – Greek families who had been living in the sophisticated cities of central and eastern Europe, in Constantinople or in Russia. With their European-Enlightenment notions about the grandeur of Greece's past, and lofty conception of Hellenism, they set about obliterating the memory of subjugation to foreigners in every possible field. And what better way to start than by purging the language of foreign accretions and reviving its Classical purity?

They accordingly created what was in effect a new form of the language, *katharévoussa* (literally "cleansed" Greek). The complexities of Classical grammar and syntax were largely reinstated, and Classical words, long out of use, were reintroduced. To the country's great detriment, *katharévoussa* became the language of the schools and the prestigious professions, government, business, the law, newspapers and academia. Everyone aspiring to membership in the elite strove to master it, and to speak it – even though there was no consensus on how many of the words should be pronounced.

The *katharévoussa/dhimotikí* debate remained a highly contentious issue until the early 1980s. Most writers – from Solomos and Makriyiannis in the nineteenth century to Seferis, Kazantzakis and Ritsos in the twentieth – have championed the demotic, or some approximation of it, in their literature, with advocacy of demoticism became increasingly linked to left-wing politics during the twentieth century. Meanwhile, crackpot right-wing governments forcibly (re)instated *katharévoussa* at every opportunity. Most recently, the **colonels' junta** (1967–74) reversed a decision of the previous government to use *dhimotikí* as the medium of instruction in schools, bringing back *katharévoussa*, even on sweet wrappers, as part of their ragbag of notions about racial purity and heroic ages.

Dhimiotikí returned once more after the fall of the colonels and now seems here to stay. Perhaps the final blow to the classicizers was the official decision, in 1981, to do away with breath marks (which in fact no longer signified anything) and abolish the three different stress accents in favour of a **single accute accent** (though there are still plenty of pre-1981 road-signs displaying the older system). *Dhimotikí* is used in schools, on radio and TV, and after a fashion in newspapers (with the exception of the extreme right-wing *Estia*). The only institutions which refuse to bring themselves up to date are the church and the legal professions – so beware rental contracts and official documents.

This is not to suggest that there is now any less confusion. The Metaxas dictatorship of the 1930s, elaborating on attempts at the same by previous regimes, changed scores of village names from Slavic, Turkish or Albanian words to Greek ones – often reviving the name of the nearest ancient site – and these official **place names** still hold sway on most road signs and maps – even though the local people may use the *dhimotikí* or non-Greek form. Thus you will see "Plomárion" or "Spétsai" written, while everyone actually says "Plomári" or "Spétses"; Pándhrossos on Sámos, and Ayía Paraskeví in Epirus, are still preferably known by locals as Arvanítes and Kerásovo respectively.

Dialects and minority languages

If the lack of any standardized Greek were not enough, Greece still offers considerable linguistic diversity, both in its regional dialects and minority languages. Ancient **dialects** survive in many remote areas, and some of them are quite incomprehensible to outsiders. The dialect of Sfákia in Crete is one such; Tsakónika (spoken in the east-central Peloponnese) is another, while the dialect of the Sarakatsáni shepherds is said to be the oldest, a direct descendant of the language of the Dorian settlers.

The language of the Sarakatsáni's traditional rivals, the **Vlachs**, on the other hand, is not Greek at all, but derived from early Latin, with strong affinities to Romanian. In the regions bordering the FYROM and southwestern Bulgaria, you can still hear **Slavic Macedonian** spoken, while small numbers of Sephardic Jews in the north and on Rhodes speak **Ladino**, a medieval form of Spanish. Until a few decades ago **Arvanítika** – a dialect of medieval Albanian – was the first language of many villages of inland Attica, southern Évvia, northern Ándhros, and much of the Argo-Saronic area; lately the clock has been turned back, so to speak, as throngs of Albanian immigrants circulate in Athens and other parts of the country. In Thrace there is also a substantial **Turkish-speaking** population, as well as some speakers of **Pomak** (a relative of Bulgarian with a large Greco-Turkish vocabulary), while Gypsies across the country speak Romany.

The Greek alphabet: transliteration and accentuation

On top of the usual difficulties of learning a new language, Greek presents the additional problem of an entirely separate **alphabet**. Despite initial appearances, this is in practice fairly easily mastered – a skill that will help enormously if you are going to get around independently (see the alphabet box below). In addition, certain combinations of letters have unexpected results. This book's transliteration system should help you make intelligible noises, but you have to remember that the correct **stress** (marked throughout the book with an acute accent or sometimes dieresis) is crucial. With the right sounds but the wrong stress people will either fail to understand you, or else understand something quite different from what you intended – there are numerous pairs of words with the same spelling and phonemes, distinguished only by their stress.

The **dieresis** is used in Greek over the second of two adjacent vowels to change the pronunciation that you would expect from the table below; often in this book it can function as the primary stress. In the word *kaïki* (caique), the presence of the dieresis changes the pronunciation from "cake-key" to "ka-ee-key" and additionally the middle "i" carries the primary stress. In the word *païdhákia* (lamb chops), the dieresis again changes the sound of the first syllable from "pay" to "pah-ee", but in this case the primary stress is on the third syllable. It is also, uniquely among Greek accents, used on capital letters in signs and personal-name spellings in Greece, and we have followed this practice on our maps.

Set out below is the Greek alphabet, the system of transliteration used in this book and a brief aid to pronunciation.

Greek	Transliteration	Pronounced
Α, α	a	a as in father
Β, β	v	v as in vet
Γ, γ	y/g	y as in yes except before consonants or a, o or ou when it's a breathy g, approximately as in gap
Δ, δ	dh	th as in then
Ε, ε	e	e as in get
Ζ, ζ	z	z sound
Η, η	i	i as in ski
Θ, θ	th	th as in theme
Ι, ι	i	i as in ski
Κ, κ	k	k sound
Λ, λ	l	l sound
Μ, μ	m	m sound
Ν, ν	n	n sound
Ξ, ξ	x	x sound, never z
Ο, ο	o	o as in toad
Π, π	p	p sound
Π, σ	r	r sound
Σ, σ, ς	s	s sound, except z before m or g; single sigma has the same phonic value as double sigma

Τ, τ	t	t sound
Υ, υ	y	y as in barely
Φ, φ	f	f sound
Χ, χ	h before vowels, kh before consonants	harsh h sound, like ch in loch
Ψ, ψ	ps	ps as in lips
Ω, ω	o	o as in toad, indistinguishable from o

Combinations and diphthongs

ΑΙ, αι	e	e as in hey
ΑΥ, αυ	av/af	av or af depending on following consonant
ΕΙ, ει	i	long i, exactly like i or h
ΕΥ, ευ	ev/ef	ev or ef, depending on following consonant
ΟΙ, οι	i	long i, exactly like i or h
ΟΥ, ου	ou	ou as in tourist
ΓΓ, γγ	ng	ng as in angle; always medial
ΝΓ, νγ	g/ng	g as in goat at the beginning of a word, ng in the middle
ΜΠ, μπ	b/mb	b at the beginning of a word, mb in the middle
ΝΤ, ντ	d/nd	d at the beginning of a word, nd in the middle
ΤΣ, τσ	ts	ts as in hits
ΤΖ, τζ	tz	dg as in judge, j as in jam in some dialects

Greek words and phrases

Essentials

Né	Yes		Méra	Day
Málista	Certainly		Níkhta	Night
Óhi	No		Tó proï	In the morning
Parakaló	Please		Tó apóyevma	In the afternoon
Endáxi	OK, agreed		Tó vrádhi	In the evening
Efharistó (polý)	Thank you (very much)		Edhó	Here
(Dhén) Katalavéno	I (don't) understand		Ekí	There
Miláte angliká?	Do you speak English?		Aftó	This one
Signómi	Sorry/excuse me		Ekíno	That one
Símera	Today		Kaló	Good
Ávrio	Tomorrow		Kakó	Bad
Khthés	Yesterday		Megálo	Big
Tóra	Now		Mikró	Small
Argótera	Later		Perisótero	More
Anikhtó	Open		Ligótero	Less
Klistó	Closed		Lígo	A little

Polý	A lot	Horís	Without
Ftinó	Cheap	Grígora	Quickly
Akrivó	Expensive	Sigá	Slowly
Zestó	Hot	Kýrios/Kyría	Mr/Mrs
Krýo	Cold	Dhespinís	Miss
Mazí (mé)	With (together)		

Other needs

Trógo/píno	To eat/drink	Trápeza	Bank
Foúrnos	Bakery	Leftá/Khrímata	Money
Farmakío	Pharmacy	Toualéta	Toilet
Tahydhromío	Post office	Astynomía	Police
Gramatósima	Stamps	Yiatrós	Doctor
Venzinádhiko	Petrol station	Nosokomío	Hospital

Requests and questions

To ask a question, it's simplest, though hardly elegant, to start with *parakaló*, then name the thing you want in an interrogative tone.

L

LANGUAGE | Greek words and phrases

Parakaló, o foúrnos?	Where is the bakery?	Póso?	How much?
Parakaló, ó dhrómos yiá . . . ?	Can you show me the road to . . . ?	Póte?	When?
		Yiatí?	Why?
Parakaló, éna dhomátio yiá dhýo átoma	We'd like a room for two	Tí óra . . . ?	At what time . . . ?
		Tí íne/Pió íne . . . ?	What is/Which is . . . ?
Parakaló, éna kiló portokália?	May I have a kilo of oranges?	Póso káni?	How much (does it cost)?
Poú?	Where?	Tí óra aníyi?	What time does it open?
Pós?	How?		
Póssi, pósses or póssa?	How many?	Tí óra klíni?	What time does it close?

Talking to people

Greek makes the distinction between the informal (*essý*) and formal (*essís*) second person, as French does with "tu" and "vous". Young people, older people and country people often use *essý* even with total strangers, though if you greet someone familiarly and they respond formally, it's best to adopt their usage as the conversation continues, to avoid offence. By far the most common greeting, on meeting and parting, is *yiá sou/ yiá sas* literally "health to you". Incidentally, as across most of the Mediterranean, the approaching party utters the first greeting, not those seated at sidewalk *kafenío* tables or doorsteps – thus the silent staring as you enter a village.

Hérete	Hello	Adío	Goodbye
Kalí méra	Good morning	Tí kánis/Tí kánete?	How are you?
Kalí spéra	Good evening	Kalá íme	I'm fine
Kalí níkhta	Good night	Ké essís?	And you?

Pós se léne?	What's your name?	Dhén xéro	I don't know
Mé léne ...	My name is ...	Thá sé dhó ávrio	See you tomorrow
Parakaló, na	Speak slower, please	Kalí andhámosi	See you soon
milísate pió sigá		Páme	Let's go
Pós léyete avtó stá	How do you say it	Parakaló, ná mé	Please help me
Elliniká?	in Greek?	voithíste	

Greek's Greek

There are numerous words and phrases which you will hear constantly, even if you don't have the chance to use them. These are a few of the most common.

Éla!	Come (literally) but also Speak to me! You don't say! etc.	Po-po-po!	Expression of dismay or concern, like French "O là là!"
Oríste!	Literally, Indicate!; in effect, What can I do for you?	Pedhí moú	My boy/girl, sonny, friend, etc.
Embrós!/Léyete!	Standard phone responses	Maláka(s)	Literally "wanker", but often used (don't try it!) as an informal term of address.
Tí néa?	What's new?		
Tí yínete?	What's going on (here)?	Sigá sigá	Take your time, slow down
Étsi k'étsi	So-so	Kaló taxídhi	Bon voyage
Ópa!	Whoops! Watch it!		

Accommodation

Xenodhohío	Hotel	Zestó neró	hot water
Xenón(as)	Inn	Krýo neró	Cold water
Xenónas neótitos	Youth hostel	Klimatismós	Air conditioning
Éna dhomátio ...	A room ...	Anamistíra	Fan
yiá éna/dhýo/ tría átoma	for one/two/three people	Boró ná tó dhó?	Can I see it?
yiá mía/dhýo/ trís vradhiés	for one/two/three nights	Boroúme na váloume tí skiní edhó?	Can we camp here?
mé dhipló kreváti	with a double bed	Kámping/Kataskínosi	Campsite
mé doús	with a shower	Skiní	Tent

On the move

Aeropláno	Aeroplane	Dhelfíni	Hydrofoil
Leoforío, púlman	Bus, coach	Tréno	Train
Aftokínito, amáxi	Car	Sidhirodhromikós stathmós	Train station
Mihanáki, papáki	Motorbike, scooter	Podhílato	Bicycle
Taxí	Taxi	Otostóp	Hitching
Plío/vapóri/karávi	ship	Mé tá pódhia	On foot
Tahyplóö, katamarán	high-speed, boat Catamaran	Monopáti	Trail

Praktorío leoforíon, KTEL	Bus station	Kondá	Near
Stássi	Bus stop	Makriá	Far
Limáni	Harbour	Aristerá	Left
Ti óra févyi?	What time does it leave?	Dhexiá	Right
		Katefthía, isia	Straight ahead
Ti óra ftháni?	What time does it arrive?	Éna isitírio yiá . . .	A ticket to . . .
		Éna isitírio mé epistrofí	A return ticket
Póssa hiliómetra?	How many kilometres?	Paralía	Beach
Pósses óres?	How many hours?	Spiliá	Cave
Poú pás?	Where are you going?	Kéndro	Centre (of town)
Páo stó . . .	I'm going to . . .	Eklissía	Church
Thélo ná katévo stó . . .	I want to get off at . . .	Thálassa	Sea
O dhrómos yiá . . .	The road to . . .	Horió	Village

Numbers

énas/éna/mía	1	triánda	30
dhýo	2	saránda	40
trís/tría	3	peninda	50
tésseres/téssera	4	exínda	60
pénde	5	evdhomínda	70
éxi	6	ogdhónda	80
eftá	7	enenínda	90
okhtó	8	ekató	100
ennéa (or more slangy, enyá)	9	ekatón penínda	150
dhéka	10	dhiakóssies/ dhiakóssia	200
éndheka	11	pendakóssies/ pendakóssia	500
dhódheka	12		
dhekatrís	13	hílies/hília	1000
dhekatésseres	14	dhío hiliádhes	2000
íkossi	20	éna ekatomírio	1,000,000
íkossi éna (all compounds written separately thus)	21	próto	first
		dhéftero	second
		tríto	third

Days of the week and the time

Kyriakí	Sunday	Mía iy óra/dhío iy óra/trís iy óra	One/two/three o'clock
Dheftéra	Monday		
Tríti	Tuesday	Tésseres pará íkossi	Twenty minutes to four
Tetárti	Wednesday	Eftá ké pénde	Five minutes past seven
Pémpti	Thursday	Éndheka ké misí	Half past eleven
Paraskeví	Friday	Sé misí óra	In half an hour
Sávato	Saturday	S'éna tétarto	In a quarter-hour
Ti óra íne?	What time is it?	Sé dhío óres	In two hours

Months and seasonal terms

NB: You may see *katharévoussa*, or hybrid, forms of the months written on schedules or street signs; these are the spoken demotic forms.

Yennáris	January	Septémvris	September
Fleváris	February	Októvrios	October
Mártis	March	Noémvris	November
Aprílis	April	Dhekémvris	December
Maïos	May	Therinó dhromolóyio	Summer schedule
Ioúnios	June		
Ioúlios	July	Himerinó dhromolóyio	Winter schedule
Ávgoustos	August		

A food and drink glossary

Basics

Aláti	Salt
Avgá	Eggs
(Horís) ládhi	(Without) oil
Hortofágos	Vegetarian
Katálogos, menoú	Menu
Kréas	Meat
Lahaniká	Vegetables
O logariasmós	The bill
Méli	Honey
Neró	Water
Psári(a)	Fish
Psomí....	Bread...
Olikís	Wholemeal
Sikalísio	Rye
Kalambokísio	Corn
Thalassiná	Seafood
Tyrí	Cheese
Yiaoúrti	Yoghurt
Záhari	Sugar

Cooking terms

Akhnistó	Steamed
Frikasé	Stew, either lamb, goat or pork, made with celery
Iliókafto	Sun-dried
Kondosoúvli	Any spit-roasted beast, whole or in chunks
Kourkoúti	Egg-and-flour batter
Makaronádha	Any spaghetti/pasta-based dish
Pastó	Marinated in salt
Psitó	Roasted
Saganáki	Cheese-based red sauce; also any fried cheese
Skáras	Grilled
Sti soúvla	Spit-roasted
Stó foúrno	Baked
Tiganitó	Pan-fried
Tís óras	Grilled/fried to order
Yakhní	Stewed in oil and tomato sauce
Yemistá	Stuffed (squid, vegetables, etc)

Soups and starters

Avgolémono	Egg and lemon soup
Bouréki, bourekákia	Courgette/zucchini, potato and cheese pie
Dolmádhes, yaprákia	Vine leaves stuffed with rice
Fasoládha	Bean soup
Fáva	Purée of yellow peas, served with onion and lemon
Féta psití	Baked feta cheese slabs with chili
Galotýri	Curdled creamy dip
Hortópitta	Turnover or pie stuffed with wild greens
Kápari	Pickled caper leaves

Kopanistí, khtypití	Pungent, fermented cheese purée
Krítamo	Rock samphire
Lahanodolmádhes	Stuffed cabbage leaves
Mavromátika	Black-eyed peas
Melitzanosaláta	Aubergine/eggplant dip
Piperiá florínes	Marinated red sweet Macedonian peppers
Plevrótous	Oyster mushrooms
Rengosaláta	Herring salad
Revythokeftédhes	Chickpea (garbanzo) patties
Skordhaliá	Garlic dip
Soúpa	Soup
Taramosaláta	Cod roe paté
Trahanádhes	Crushed wheat and milk soup, sweet or savoury
Tyrokafterí	Cheese dip with chilli, different from kopanistí
Tzatzíki	Yoghurt and cucumber dip
Tzirosaláta	Cured mackerel dip

Vegetables

Ambelofásola	Crimp-pod runner beans
Angináres	Artichokes
Angoúri	Cucumber
Ánitho	Dill
Bámies	Okra, ladies' fingers
Briám, tourloú	Ratatouille of zucchini, potatoes, onions, tomato
Domátes	Tomatoes
Fakés	Lentils
Fasolákia	French (green) beans
Fasóles	Small white beans
Horiátiki (saláta)	Greek salad (with olives, feta etc)
Hórta	Greens (usually wild), steamed
Kolokythákia	Courgette/zucchini
Koukiá	Broad fava beans
Maroúli	Lettuce
Melitzánes imám	Aubergine/eggplant slices baked with onion, garlic and copious olive oil
Patátes	Potatoes
Piperiés	Peppers
Pligoúri, pinigoúri	Bulgur wheat
Radhíkia	Wild chicory – a common hórta
Rókka	Rocket, arrugula
Rýzi/Piláfi	Rice (usually with sáltsa – sauce)
Saláta	Salad
Spanáki	Spinach
Vlíta	Notchweed – another common hórta
Yígandes	White haricot beans

Fish and seafood

Ahini	Sea urchins
Astakós	Aegean lobster
Atherína	Sand smelt
Bakaliáros	Cod or hake, usually latter
Barbóuni	Red mullet
Fangrí	Common bream
Foúskes	Uovo de mare (Italian), violet (French); no English equivalent for this invertebrate.
Galéos	Dogfish, hound shark, tope
Garídhes	Shrimp, prawns
Gávros	Mild anchovy
Glóssa	Sole
Gónos, Gonákia	Any hatchling fish
Gópa	Bogue
Kalamarákia	Baby squid
Kalamária	Squid
Karavídhes	Crayfish
Kefalás	Axillary bream
Koliós	Chub mackerel
Koutsomoúra	Goatfish (small red mullet)
Kydhónia	Warty Venus
Lakérdha	Light-fleshed bonito, marinated
Marídhes	Picarel
Melanoúri	Saddled bream
Ménoula	Sprat

Mýdhia	Mussels
Okhtapódhi	Octopus
Pandelís	Corvina; also called sykiós
Petalídhes	Limpets
Platý	Skate, ray
Sardhélles	Sardines
Sargós	White bream
Seláhi	Skate, ray
Skáros	Parrotfish
Skathári	Black bream
Skoumbrí	Atlantic mackerel
Soupiá	Cuttlefish
Spiníalo or spinóalo	Marinated foúskes
Synagrídha	Dentex
Tsipoúra	Gilt-head bream
Xifías	Swordfish
Yermanós	Leatherback
Yialisterés	Smooth Venus; common ouzerí shellfish

Meat and meat-based dishes

Arní	Lamb
Bekrí mezé	Pork chunks in red sauce
Biftéki	Hamburger
Brizóla	Pork or beef chop
Hirinó	Pork
Keftédhes	Meatballs
Kokorétsi	Liver/offal roulade, spit-roasted
Kopsídha	(Lamb) shoulder chops
Kotópoulo	Chicken
Kounélli	Rabbit
Loukánika	Spicy course-ground sausages
Moskhári	Veal
Moussakás	Aubergine, potato and lamb-mince casserole with béchamel topping
Païdhákia	Rib chops, lamb or goat
Papoutsákia	Stuffed aubergine/ eggplant "shoes" like moussakás without bechamel

Pastítsio	Macaroni "pie" baked with minced meat
Pastourmás	Cured, highly spiced meat; traditionally camel, nowadays beef
Patsás	Tripe soup
Psaronéfri	Pork tenderloin medallions
Salingária	Garden snails
Soutzoukákia	Minced meat rissoles/ beef patties
Spetzofáï	Sausage and pepper red-sauce stew
Stifádho	Meat stew with tomato and boiling onions
Sykóti	Liver
Tiganiá	Pork chunks fried with onions
Tziyéro sarmás	Lamb's liver in cabbage leaves
Yiouvétsi	Baked clay casserole of meat and kritharáki (short pasta)

Sweets and dessert

Baklavás	Honey and nut pastry
Bougátsa	Salt or sweet cream pie served warm with sugar and cinammon
Galaktobóureko	Custard pie
Halvás	Sweetmeat of sesame
Karydhópita	Walnut cake
Kréma	Custard
Loukoumádhes	Dough fritters in honey syrup and sesame seeds
Pagotó	Ice cream
Pastélli	Sesame and honey bar
Ravaní	Spongecake, lightly syruped
Ryzógalo	Rice pudding
Smigdhalísios halvás	Semolina-based halva

Fruits

Akhládhia	Big pears

Aktinídha	Kiwis
Fistíkia	Pistachio nuts
Fráoules	Strawberries
Himoniátiko	Autumn (cassava) melon
Karpoúzi	Watermelon
Kerásia	Cherries
Krystália	Miniature pears
Kydhóni	Quince
Lemónia	Lemons
Míla	Apples
Pepóni	Melon
Portokália	Oranges
Rodhákino	Peach
Sýka	Figs
Stafýlia	Grapes
Yiarmádhes	Autumn peaches

Cheese

Ayeladhinó	Cow's-milk cheese
Féta	Salty-creamy white cheese
Graviéra	Gruyère-type hard cheese

Katsikísio	Goat cheese
Kasséri	Medium-sharp cheese
Myzíthra	Sweet cream cheese
Próvio	Sheep cheese

Drinks

Alisfakiá	Island sage tea
Boukáli	Bottle
Býra	Beer
Gála	Milk
Galakakáo	Chocolate milk
Kafés	Coffee
Krasí	Wine
áspro	white
kokkinélli/rozé	rosé
kókkino/mávro	red
Limonádha	Lemonade
Metalikó neró	Mineral water
Portokaládha	Orangeade
Potíri	Glass
Stinyássas!	Cheers!
Tsáï	Tea
Tsáï vounoú	"Mountain" (mainland sage) tea

L

LANGUAGE | Greek words and phrases

A glossary of words and terms

Acropolis Ancient, fortified hilltop.

Agora Market and meeting place of an ancient Greek city; also the "high street" of a modern village (*agorá* in modern Greek).

Amphora Tall, narrow-necked jar for oil or wine.

Áno Upper; common prefix element of village names.

Apse Curved recess at the east end of a church nave.

Archaic period Late Iron Age period, from around 750 BC to the start of the Classical period in the fifth century BC.

Architrave Horizontal masonry atop temple columns; same as **entablature.**

Arhondikó A lordly stone mansion, as in Kastoriá or Pílio, often restored as boutique accommodation.

Astykó (Intra) city, municipal, local; adjective applied to phone calls and bus services.

Áyios/Ayía/Áyii Saint or holy (m/f/plural). Common place-name prefix (abbreviated Ag or Ay), often spelled **Agios** or **Aghios** .

Basilica Colonnaded, "hall-" or "barn-" type church adapted from Roman models, most common in northern Greece.

Bema Rostrum for oratory (and later the chancel) of a church.

Bouleuterion Auditorium for meetings of an ancient town's deliberative council.

Capital The flared top, often ornamented, of a column.

Cavea Seating curve of an ancient theatre.

Cella Sacred room of a temple, housing the cult image.

Classical period Essentially from the end of the Persian Wars in the fifth century BC until the unification of Greece under Philip II of Macedon (338 BC).

Conch Concave semi-dome surmounting a church apse, often frescoed.

Corinthian Decorative columns, festooned with acanthus florettes; a temple built in this order.

Dhimarhío Town hall.

Dhomátia Rooms for rent in purpose-built blocks or (seldomly these days) private houses.

Dorian Northern civilization that displaced and succeeded the Mycenaeans and Minoans through most of Greece around 1100 BC.

Doric Minimalist, unadorned columns, dating from the Dorian period; a temple built in this order.

Drum Cylindrical or faceted vertical section, usually pierced by an even number of narrow windows, upholding a church cupola.

Entablature The horizontal linking structure atop the columns of an ancient temple.

Eparhía Greek Orthodox diocese, also a subdivision of a modern province, analogous to a county.

Exedra Display niche for statuary.

Exonarthex The outer vestibule or entrance hall of a church, when a true **narthex** is present.

Forum Market and meeting place of a Roman-era city.

Frieze Band of sculptures around a temple. Doric friezes consist of various tableaux of figures (**Metopes**) interspersed with grooved panels (**triglyphs**); Ionic ones have continuous bands of figures.

Froúrio Medieval citadel; nowadays, can mean a modern military headquarters.

Garsoniéra/es Studio villa/s, self-catering apartment/s.

Geometric period Post-Mycenaean Iron Age era named for the style of its pottery; begins in the early eleventh century BC with the arrival of Dorian peoples. By the eighth century BC, with the development of representational styles, it becomes known as the **Archaic period** .

Hellenistic period The last and most unified "Greek empire", created in the wake of Alexander the Great's Macedonian empire and finally collapsing with the fall of Corinth to the Romans in 146 BC.

Heroön Shrine or sanctuary, usually of a demigod or mortal; war memorials in modern Greece.

Hóra Main town of an island or region; literally it means "the place". An island *hóra* is often known by the same name as the island.

Ierón Literally, "sacred" – the space between the altar screen and the apse of a church, reserved for priestly activities.

Ikonostási Screen between the nave of a church and the altar, supporting at least three icons.

Ionic Elaborate, decorative development of the older **Doric** order; Ionic temple columns are slimmer, with deeper "fluted" edges, spiral-shaped capitals and ornamental bases.

Iperastykó Long-distance – as in phone calls and bus services.

Kafenío Coffee house or café; in a small village the centre of communal life.

Kaïki (plural **kaïkia**) Caique, or medium-sized boat, traditionally wooden and used for transporting cargo and passengers; now refers mainly to island excursion boats.

Kalderími A cobbled mule-track or footpath.

Kámbos Fertile agricultural plain, usually near a river mouth.

Kantína Shack, caravan or even a disused bus on the beach, serving drinks and perhaps sandwiches or quick snacks.

Kástro Any fortified hill, but most often the oldest, highest, walled-in part of an island *hóra*, intended to protect civilians.

Katholikón Central chapel of a monastery.

Káto Lower; common prefix element of village names.

Kendrikí platía Central square.

Kouros Nude Archaic statue of an idealized young man, usually portrayed with one foot slightly forward of the other.

Megaron Principal hall or throne room of a Mycenaean palace.

Meltémi North wind that blows across the Aegean in summer, starting softly from near the mainland and hitting the Cyclades, the Dodecanese and Crete full on.

Metope See Frieze.

Minoan Crete's great Bronze Age civilization, which dominated the Aegean from about 2500 to 1400 BC.

Moní Formal term for a monastery or convent.

Moreas Medieval term for the Peloponnese; the outline of the peninsula was likened to the leaf of a mulberry tree, *mouriá* in Greek.

Mycenaean Mainland civilization centred on Mycenae and the Argolid from about 1700 to 1100 BC.

Naos The inner sanctum of an ancient temple; also, any Orthodox Christian shrine.

Narthex Western vestibule of a church, reserved for catechumens and the unbaptized; typically frescoed with scenes of the Last Judgement.

Neolithic Earliest era of settlement in Greece; characterized by the use of stone tools and weapons together with basic agriculture. Divided arbitrarily into Early (ca. 6000 BC), Middle (ca. 5000 BC) and Late (ca. 3000 BC).

Néos, Néa, Néo "New" – a common prefix to a town or village name.

Nomós Modern Greek province – there are more than fifty of them. Village bus services are organized according to their borders.

Odeion Small theatre, used for musical performances, minor dramatic productions or councils.

Orchestra Circular area in a theatre where the chorus would sing and dance.

Palaestra Gymnasium for athletics and wrestling practice.

Paleós, Paleá, Paleó "Old" – again a common prefix in town and village names.

Panayía Virgin Mary.

Pandokrátor Literally "The Almighty"; generally refers to the stern portrayal of Christ in Majesty frescoed or in mosaic in the dome of many Byzantine churches.

Paniyíri Festival or feast – the local celebration of a holy day.

Paralía Beach, or seafront promenade.

Pediment Triangular, sculpted gable below the roof of a temple.

Pendentive Any of four triangular sections of vaulting with concave sides, positioned at a corner of a rectangular space to support a circular or polygonal dome; in churches, often adorned with frescoes of the four Evangelists.

Períptero Street kiosk.

Peristereónes Pigeon towers, in the Cyclades.

Peristyle Gallery of columns around a temple or other building.

Pinakothíki Picture gallery, ancient or modern.

Pithos (plural **pithoi**) Large ceramic jar for storing oil, grain, etc. Very common in Minoan palaces and used in almost identical form in modern Greek homes.

Platía Square, plaza.

Polygonal masonry Wall-building technique of the Classical and Hellenistic period, which used unmortared, closely joined stones; often called "Lesvian polygonal" after the island where the method supposedly originated. The much-(ab)used term **Cyclopean** refers only to Mycenean/Bronze Age mainland sites such as Tiryns and Mycenae itself.

Propylaion Monumental columned gateway of an ancient building; often used in the plural, **propylaia**.

Pýrgos Tower or bastion; also tower-mansions found in the Máni or on Lésvos.

Skála The port of an inland island settlement, nowadays often larger and more important than its namesake, but always younger since built after the disappearance of piracy.

Squinch Small concavity across a corner of a columnless interior space, which supports a superstructure such as a dome.

Stele Upright stone slab or column, usually inscribed with an edict; also an ancient tombstone, with a relief scene.

Stoa Colonnaded walkway in Classical-era marketplace.

Távli Backgammon; a favourite café pastime, especially among the young. There are two more difficult local variations (*févga* and *plakotó*) in addition to the standard international game (*pórtes*).

Témblon Wooden altar screen of an Orthodox church, usually ornately carved and painted and studded with icons; more or less interchangeable with **ikonostási**.

Temenos Sacred precinct, often used to refer to the sanctuary itself.

Theatral area Open area found in most of the Minoan palaces with seat-like steps around. Probably a type of theatre or ritual area.

Tholos Conical or beehive-shaped building, eg a Mycenaean tomb.

Triglyph See **Frieze**.

Tympanum The recessed space, flat or carved in relief, inside a pediment.

Votsalotó Mosaic of coloured pebbles, found in church or house courtyards of the Dodecanese and Spétses.

Acronyms

ANEK Anónymi Navtiliakí Etería Krítis (Shipping Co of Crete, Ltd), which runs most ferries between Pireás and Crete, plus many to Italy.

EAM National Liberation Front, the political force behind ELAS.

ELAS Popular Liberation Army, the main Resistance group during World War II and the basis of the Communist army during the civil war.

ELTA Postal service.

EOS Greek Mountaineering Federation, based in Athens.

EOT Ellinikós Organismós Tourismoú, National Tourist Organization.

FYROM Former Yugoslav Republic of Macedonia.

KKE Communist Party, unreconstructed.

KTEL National syndicate of bus companies. The term also refers to individual bus stations.

LANE Lasithiakí Anónymi Navtiliakí Etería (Lasithian Shipping Company Ltd), based in eastern Crete.

ND Conservative (Néa Dhimokratía) party.

NEL Navtiliakí Etería Lésvou (Lesvian Shipping Co).

OA Standard abbreviation and international airline code for Olympic Airlines.

OSE Railway corporation.

OTE Telephone company.

PASOK Socialist party (Pan-Hellenic Socialist Movement).

SEO Greek Mountaineering Club, based in Thessaloníki.

Travel store

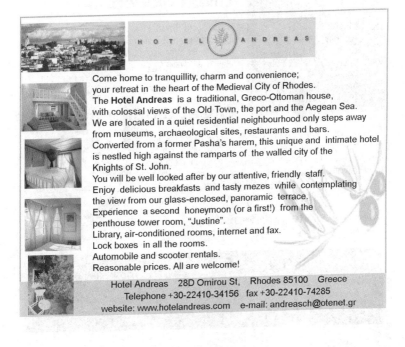

TRAVEL

& MORE

Visit us online
www.roughguides.com
Information on over 25,000 destinations around the world

- **Read** Rough Guides' trusted travel info

- **Share** journals, photos and travel advice with other readers

- Get exclusive Rough Guide **discounts** and travel deals

- Earn membership points every time you contribute to the

  Rough Guide community and get free books, flights and trips

- Browse thousands of **CD reviews** and artists in our music area

ONLINE

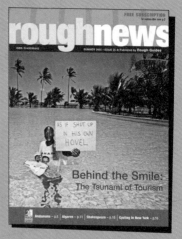

NOTES

Small print and

Index

A Rough Guide to Rough Guides

Published in 1982, the first Rough Guide – to Greece – was a student scheme that became a publishing phenomenon. Mark Ellingham, a recent graduate in English from Bristol University, had been travelling in Greece the previous summer and couldn't find the right guidebook. With a small group of friends he wrote his own guide, combining a highly contemporary, journalistic style with a thoroughly practical approach to travellers' needs.

The immediate success of the book spawned a series that rapidly covered dozens of destinations. And, in addition to impecunious backpackers, Rough Guides soon acquired a much broader and older readership that relished the guides' wit and inquisitiveness as much as their enthusiastic, critical approach and value-for-money ethos.

These days, Rough Guides include recommendations from shoestring to luxury and cover more than 200 destinations around the globe, including almost every country in the Americas and Europe, more than half of Africa and most of Asia and Australasia. Our ever-growing team of authors and photographers is spread all over the world, particularly in Europe, the USA and Australia.

In the early 1990s, Rough Guides branched out of travel, with the publication of Rough Guides to World Music, Classical Music and the Internet. All three have become benchmark titles in their fields, spearheading the publication of a wide range of books under the Rough Guide name.

Including the travel series, Rough Guides now number more than 350 titles, covering: phrasebooks, waterproof maps, music guides from Opera to Heavy Metal, reference works as diverse as Conspiracy Theories and Shakespeare, and popular culture books from iPods to Poker. Rough Guides also produce a series of more than 120 World Music CDs in partnership with World Music Network.

Visit www.roughguides.com to see our latest publications.

Rough Guide travel images are available for commercial licensing at www.roughguidespictures.com

Rough Guide credits

Text editors: Sarah Eno and Alice Park
Layout: Umesh Aggarwal, Pradeep Thapliyal and Diana Jarvis
Cartography: Ed Wright
Picture editor: Mark Thomas
Production: Katherine Owers
Proofreaders: Janet McCann, David Paul and Madhu Mohapatra
Cover design: Chloë Roberts
Editorial: London Kate Berens, Claire Saunders, Geoff Howard, Ruth Blackmore, Polly Thomas, Richard Lim, Clifton Wilkinson, Alison Murchie, Karoline Densley, Andy Turner, Keith Drew, Edward Aves, Nikki Birrell, Helen Marsden, Lucy White, Joe Staines, Duncan Clark, Peter Buckley, Matthew Milton, Tracy Hopkins, Ruth Tidball; **New York** Andrew Rosenberg, Richard Koss, Steven Horak, AnneLise Sorensen, Amy Hegarty, Hunter Slaton, April Isaacs, Sean Mahoney
Design & Pictures: London Simon Bracken, Dan May, Jj Luck, Harriet Mills; **Delhi** Ajay Verma, Amit Verma, Ankur Guha, Jessica Subramanian
Production: Sophie Hewat, Aimee Hampson

Cartography: London Maxine Repath, Katie Lloyd-Jones; **Delhi** Manish Chandra, Rajesh Chhibber, Jai Prakash Mishra, Ashutosh Bharti, Rajesh Mishra, Animesh Pathak, Jasbir Sandhu, Karobi Gogoi, Amod Singh
Online: New York Jennifer Gold, Suzanne Welles, Kristin Mingrone; **Delhi** Manik Chauhan, Narender Kumar, Shekhar Jha, Lalit K. Sharma, Rakesh Kumar, Chhandita Chakravarty
Marketing & Publicity: London Richard Trillo, Niki Hanmer, David Wearn, Demelza Dallow, Louise Maher, Jess Carter; **New York** Geoff Colquitt, Megan Kennedy, Katy Ball
Delhi Reem Khokhar
Custom publishing and foreign rights: Philippa Hopkins
Manager India: Punita Singh
Series editor: Mark Ellingham
Reference Director: Andrew Lockett
PA to Managing and Publishing Directors: Megan McIntyre
Publishing Director: Martin Dunford
Managing Director: Kevin Fitzgerald

Publishing information

This eleventh edition published May 2006 by
Rough Guides Ltd,
80 Strand, London WC2R 0RL, UK
345 Hudson St, 4th Floor,
New York, NY 10014, USA
14 Local Shopping Centre, Panchsheel Park,
New Delhi 110017, India
Distributed by the Penguin Group
Penguin Books Ltd,
80 Strand, London WC2R 0RL, UK
Penguin Putnam, Inc.
375 Hudson Street, NY 10014, USA
Penguin Group (Australia)
250 Camberwell Road, Camberwell,
Victoria 3124, Australia
Penguin Books Canada Ltd,
10 Alcorn Avenue, Toronto, Ontario,
M4V 1E4, Canada
Penguin Group (New Zealand)
Cnr Rosedale and Airborne roads
Albany, Auckland, New Zealand
Cover concept by Peter Dyer.

Typeset in Bembo and Helvetica to an original design by Henry Iles.

Printed and bound in China.

1208pp includes index.

A catalogue record for this book is available from the British Library.

ISBN 13: 978-1-84353-611-6
ISBN 10: 1-84353-611-0

SMALL PRINT

Help us update

We've gone to a lot of effort to ensure that the eleventh edition of **The Rough Guide to Greece** is accurate and up to date. However, things change – places get "discovered", opening hours are notoriously fickle, restaurants and rooms raise prices or lower standards. If you feel we've got it wrong or left something out, we'd like to know, and if you can remember the address, the price, the time, the phone number, so much the better.

We'll credit all contributions, and send a copy of the next edition (or any other Rough Guide if you prefer) for the best letters. Everyone who writes to us and isn't already a subscriber will receive a copy of our full-colour thrice-yearly newsletter.

Please mark letters: **"Rough Guide Greece Update"** and send to: Rough Guides, 80 Strand, London WC2R 0RL, or Rough Guides, 4th Floor, 345 Hudson St, New York, NY 10014. Or send an email to **mail@roughguides.com**

Have your questions answered and tell others about your trip at
www.roughguides.atinfopop.com

Acknowledgements

Andrew Benson wishes to thank Elias and Dimitris in Athens for their hospitality, Denise for a marvellous evening on Evvia, the Noel-Bakers for a great time, and everyone at the Imaret for their goodwill and impeccable taste; thanks also to Sarah and Geoff, plus all the team back in London, for their confidence, patience and quest for perfection.

Lance Chilton thanks wife Hilary; Chris and Dave Windell in Pyrgiótika; Nick Turland in St Louis; Katerina and Yiannis Katranis in Spárti; Dimitris Papandropoulos of the Láppa Information Centre; Dimitris Pollalis in Arhángelos; the staff at the Byzantion in Monemvasiá; Babis Doufexis and Nicola Dyas of Doufexis Travel in Stoúpa; Nikos Kourtidis and Graham Pond of First Choice in Stoúpa.

Marc Dubin thanks: the Papalexis family in Galaxídhi, the Sakellaris brothers in Náfpaktos, Jill Sleeman in Moúressi, the Boutos family in Karytsá, Anthoula Gouri in Tsepelovo, Kostas and Marianthi Pappas in Ioánnina, Thanassis and Toula Nakas in Metéora, Theo and Melinda Kosmetos in Mólyvos, Markos Kostalas, Theodhore and Güher Spordhilis, and Stella Tsakiri, on Híos, Alexis, Ippokratis and Dionysia Zikas on Kós, David, Lisa, Iain and Lynn on Tílos, Kim Sjögren and his staff at Triton, Constance Rivemale, Efi and Spyros Dedes, Gerald Brisch, Patrick and Anna on Rhodes, Roger Jinkinson, Mihalis, and the Yializis family on Kárpathos, Nikos, Wendy, Adriana and Nicholas on Sými, Andonis and Themelina Andonoglou on Kálymnos, Elina Skoutari on Pátmos, Rena Paradhisi on Lipsí, the managements of the hotels Porphyris (Níssyros), Australia (Astypálea), Crithoni's Paradise (Léros) and Magda's Apartments (Párga) for their support, Panayiotis and Aphrodite Papasotiriou on Límnos, Dudley der Partogh at Sunvil, and Carol Coulter at Skycars, for travel facilities, and last but not least to the Zdravets for sharing travels to various corners of Greece.

Nick Edwards would like to thank everybody who helped him on the last tour, especially Maria of the Hotel Gorgona in Nydhrí, Panayiotis of the Hara in Argostoli and Kostas of the Boukari Beach. Also thanks to Andronikos of the Kyani Akti in Argostóli and Kostas of the Angonari near Ágrafi for fine feasts. Once more gratitude goes to Mariana, Petros, Orestes and Orfeas for excellent hospitality in Horepískopi. Cheers to Peter Hemming for the Lixouri tour and yiasas to Pam and all at Pub Old House. And here's to the old friends who joined in at various stages: Ann, Steve, Carol & Simon and Gordon. Finally, a huge hug to Maria for minding the homestead.

Mark Ellingham would like to thank Michael Haag (History), George Pissalides (Music) and Sandy MacGillivray (Archeology) for their contributions to the Contexts section of the book; and Sarah Eno, Alice Park and Geoff Howard for their excellent editorial work, overhauling this new edition of the guide.

John Fisher thanks Miranda Rashidian, Kate Donnelly, Nick Edwards and the examination crew, Dimitris Koutoulas and Leonidas Tsagaris; to everyone at Rough Guides especially Sally, Sarah and Ed for a great job on the maps; and as ever to A and the two Js for love and support.

Geoff Garvey would like to thank Nikos Karellis editor of *Stigmes* magazine, Iráklion, for sharing his encyclopedic knowledge of all things Cretan; a grateful "efharisto pára poli" also goes to Manolis Sergentakis in Kastélli Kissámou, Irene Michaelakis in Haniá, Yiannis & Katerina Hatzidakis in Sitía, Heracles Papadakis in Spili, Lambros Papoutsakis in Thrónos, Froso Bora in Réthymnon, and last but by no means least to the indomitable Stelios Manousakas of Aryiroúpolis (long may his avocados flourish).

Readers' letters

Thanks to all those readers of the tenth edition who took the trouble to write in with their amendments and additions. Apologies for any misspellings or omissions.

Roger Alsop, Horacio Amarilho, Zaynab Ayub, Thijs Backus, Neil Bailey, Julie Barrie, Tony Birkett, Mario Bottaro, Terence Brace, Sarah Callan, Carlomaria Cairoli, Richard Ciecierski, Martin Coppen, Nuala Crotty, Terence Cuff, Janet Davidson, Barbara Dorf, John Engel, Francesco, Marco Gandini, Stuart Gates, Margaret Gorrie and Barry Williamson, Amanda Gray and Adam Knight, Margaret Green, Averil Harrison and John Sessions, Gordon D. Hillhouse, Steve Hounslow, Jens Erik Jørgensen, Zane Katsikis, Mike Leggett, Mike Lippman and Laura Gross, Gina and Duncan Langford, Henry Long, Rebecca Macky, Bob Mark, Richard Marks, Debbie Marshall, Andy McCosh, Phil Meade, Daniel Mills, Roger Moorhouse, Michael O'Flaherty, Sue Quinn, Susan Raphael Ben Rees, Julie Reeves, Yizhar Regev, Yoram Regev, Mabel Richmond, Peter Riley, Alan Rooks, Paul Schollmeier, Nic Shannon, Pieter Steine, Pieter Steinz, David Tricker, Peter "Pav" Verity, Jeffrey Walter, Peter Watson, Graham Whitehouse, Rachel Williams, Don Wilson, Nick Wurr, Duncan K. Young.

Photo credits

All photos © Rough Guides except the following:

Title page
Mountain village, Crete © Peter M Wilson/Axiom

Full page
Roussánou Monastery, Metéora © Peter M Wilson/Axiom

Introduction
Church bell, Santoríni © Neil Emmerson/Getty Images
Parthenon, Athens © Naki Kouyioumtzis/Axiom
Olive grove © Images Etc Ltd/Alamy
Eye amulet © Helene Rogers/Trip
Church overlooking the sea, Kefalloniá © Peter Adams/Getty Images
Greengrocer's shop, Corfu © Steve Outram/Getty Images
Períptero © Jean Pierre Amet/Corbis

Things not to miss
01 Samos landscape © Bob Turner/Alamy
02 Metéora © Marc Dubin
03 Loggerhead Turtle © David Boag/Alamy
04 Ósios Loukás mosaics © Marc Dubin
05 Ídhra © Jose Fuste Raga/Corbis
06 Zagóri, Víkos gorge © Marc Dubin
08 Lion Gate © Marc Dubin
09 Mount Pílio © Marc Dubin
10 Mani Tower © Luck White/Axiom
11 Volcano floor, Níssyros © Doug Houghton
12 Knossos palace, Crete © Roger Wood/Corbis
13 Windsurfing off Acrocorinth © Jack Moscrop/Axiom
14 Temple of Poseidon © Marc Dubin
15 Fortifications of Acrocorinth © Marc Dubin
16 Ayíou Monastery © Tim Thompson/Corbis
17 Samaria Gorge © Alberto Arzoz/Axiom
18 Trekking on Mount Olympus © Marc Dubin
19 Monemvasiá © Joseph Becker/Alamy
21 Préspa Lakes © Andrew Benson
22 Lindos acropolis, Rhodes © Marc Dubin
23 Haniá old town © Peter M Wilson/Axiom

24 The Tholos, Delphi © David Norton Photography/Alamy
26 Herodes Atticus Theatre © Michael Nicholson/Corbis
27 Koróni town © Marc Dubin
28 View over Firá © Walter Bibikow/Getty Images
29 Mystra © Marc Dubin
30 Váï Beach © Rob Rayworth/Alamy
31 Harbour, Sými © Mark Azzavedo
32 Náfplio © Petr Svarc /Alamy
33 The Acropolis © Antonio M. Rosario/Getty Images
34 Osióu Grigoriou Monastery © Oliviero Olivieri/Getty Images

Colour insert: Greek Cuisine
Pátmos village square tavernas © Simeon Huber/Getty Images
Olive mill © Thorsten Eckert/Alamy
Goats cheese © FoodPix/Jupiter Images
Vineyard in Macedonia © aliki image library/Alamy
Moussaka © Profimedia.CZ s.r.o./Alamy
Ouzo Distillery © IML Image Group/Alamy

Colour insert: Orthodox Greece
Whitewashed church, Santoríni © Hugh Sitton/Getty Images
Easter procession, Corfu © IML Image Group/Alamy
Monk reading scripture on boat, Mount Áthos © James P Blair/Getty Images
Fountain illustration, Crete © Religious Stock One/Alamy
Holy Flame procession © Barry Lewis/Alamy
Icon of Ayía Katerina (St Katherine), Crete © J Marshall, Tribaleye Images/Alamy

Colour insert: Wild Greece
Horseshoe orchid, Mani © Bob Gibbons/Alamy
Mount Taïyetos © Charlie Waite/Getty Images
Walking in the Samarian Gorge © Karsten Wrobel/Alamy

SMALL PRINT

Víkos Gorge © Wilmar Photography.com/Alamy

Storks nesting in a chimney © Teery Harris Just Greece Photo Library/Alamy

Voïdokiliá Bay and Lagoon © Konrad Wothe/ imagebroker/Alamy

Metéora rocks and woodland © Sotirios Milionis/ Alamy

Black and white pictures

p.134 Shopping in Pláka © Naki Kouyioumtzis/ Axiom

p.149 Bronze statue, Cycladic Art Museum © Yiorgos Karahalis/Corbis

p.155 Boats at Piréas port © Naki Kouyioumtzis/ Axiom

p.171 Man selling bouzoukis © Terry Harris Just Greece Photo Library/Alamy

p.191 Eleusis Fragmentary columns © Roger Wood/Corbis

p.196 The Palaestra at Olympia © Marc Dubin

p.214 The Treasury of Atreus © Lance Chilton

p.220 Port Náfplio © Petr Bonek/Alamy

p.234 Panayia tis Elonis monastery © Lance Chilton

p.241 View of Simos Beach © IML Images Group/Alamy

p.259 Vathia village the Mani Peninsula © Sean Burke/Alamy

p.273 The Pantanassa Convent © Sean Burke/ Alamy

p.284 Dimitsana an Arcadia © R. Hackenberg/ Corbis

p.295 Fortress Methony © Rainer Hackenberg/ Alamy

p.313 Patras reserve © IML Images Group/Alamy

p.320 The Rio-Andirio bridge © Marc Dubin

p.328 Ósios Loukás mosaic © Marc Dublin

p.340 The Tholos, Delphi © Peter Wilson

p.351 Glaxidhi © Marc Dubin

p.362 Megálo Horió and Mount Kaliakoudha © Marc Dubin

p.372 Taverna tables at Vyzitsa, Pílio © Marc Dubin

p.392 George Schwarz Mansion, Ambelákia © Marc Dubin

p.404 Roussánou convent, Metéora © Marc Dubin

p.414 Ancient Kassopi © Marc Dubin

p.427 Island in Ioánnina Lake © Ioannis Semitsoglou/Alamy

p.440 Bridge over the Víkakis Ravine © Marc Dubin

p.457 Váltos beach, Párga © Marc Dubin

p.469 Panayía Parigorítissa in Arta © IML Images Group/Alamy

p.480 Préspa Lakes © Andrew Benson

p.494 The Rotonda, Thessaloníki © IML Image Group/Alamy

p.504 Café, Thessaloníki © Dexter Hodges /Axiom

p.512 Mount Olympus © John Heseltine/Corbis

p.524 Nymféo Village © Ioannis Semitsoglou/Alamy

p.538 Village church, Áfytos © Elmtree Images/ Alamy

p.553 Fresco, Hilandharíou Monastery © Dj. Nenad Pavlovic/Diomedia/Alamy

p.574 Pelicans, on the Evros delta © FLPA/Alamy

p.580 Ídhra Town © Marc Dubin

p.593 Póros Town © David Ball/Corbis

p.603 Ayía Paraskeví bay, Spétses © IML Image Group Ltd/Alamy

p.606 Church of Ekatondapliani, Parikía, Páros © Marc Dubin

p.628 Roman amphitheatre and Mílos Bay © Robert Harding Picture Library/Alamy

p.638 Dove house, Tínos © Peter M Wilson/Alamy

p.665 Ayios Nikólaos, Ermoúpoli © Terry Harris Just Greece Photo Library/Alamy

p.662 Fishermen in Náoussa, Páros © Yuri Lev/Alamy

p.682 Monastery of Hozoviotíssas, Amorgós © Marc Dubin

p.695 Firá, Santoríni © IML Image Group/Alamy

p.708 Minoan fresco, Knossos © Bob Turner/Alamy

p.729 Matala Beach, Crete © Alberto Arzoz/Axiom

p.741 Ayíos Nikolaos © Peter M Wilson/Alamy

p.764 Hánia harbour and Mosque of the Janissaries © Peter M Wilson/Alamy

p.774 Samaria Gorge © Peter M Wilson/Alamy

p.784 Hora © Marc Dubin

p.795 Hiking near Ólymbos, northern Kárpathos © Robert Harding Picture Library/Alamy

p.803 Buttressed lanes, Rhodes Old Town © Simon Bracken/Alamy

p.817 Emborió quayside, Hálki © David Trevor/ Alamy

p.834 Langadhaki district, Mandhráki, Níssyros © Stefan Auth/Alamy

p.845 Ancient agora, Kos © Jon Arnold Images/ Alamy

p.857 Sponge-seller, Pothia, Kálymnos © IML Image Group/Alamy

p.870 Fresco outside the monastery of Ayíou Ioannou Theologou, patmos © Terry Harris Just Greece Photo Library/Alamy

p.880 Myrina harbour, Límnos © IML Image Group Ltd/Alamy

p.884 Samos landscape © Bob Turner/Alamy

p.903 View from Foúrni toward Thýmena and Ikaría © IML Image Group/Alamy

p.933 View over Mólyvos harbour, Lésvos © Alan Novelli/Alamy

p.942 Portianou World War I Allied cemetery © Marc Dubin

p.946 Sanctuary of the Great Gods, Samothráki © Ioannis Semitsoglou/Alamy

p.962 Skýros Town © Terry Harris Just Greece Photo Library/Alamy

p.968 Beach on the Kalamáki peninsula, Skiáthos © Adrian Muttitt/Alamy

p.981 Wild ponies, Skýros © Terry Harris Just Greece Photo Library

p.1035 Melissáni cave, Kefalloniá © IML Image Group/Alamy

p.1063 Mask of Agamemnon © Archivo Iconografico S.A. Corbis

p.1073 Bust of Pericles © Time Life Pictures/ Getty Images

p.1093 Inhabitants of Smyrna escaping by boat whilst under attack from Turkish forces © Tropical Press Agency/Getty Images

p.1101 Andreas Papandreou speaking at campaign rally in the Olympic Stadium © David Rubinger/Getty Images

p.1110 English archeologist Sir Arthur John Evans holding a Cretan sculpture of a bull's head © David Savill/Getty Images

p. 1124 Makrigiani bouzouki player © David Sanger Photography/Alamy

Index

Map entries are in colour.

INDEX

O

1203

W

X

Y

Z

INDEX